AMERICAN
ELECTRICIANS'
HANDBOOK

OTHER McGRAW-HILL HANDBOOKS OF INTEREST

AMERICAN INSTITUTE OF PHYSICS · American Institute of Physics Handbook

BAUMEISTER AND MARKS · Standard Handbook for Mechanical Engineers

BEEMAN · Industrial Power Systems Handbook

BLATZ · Radiation Hygiene Handbook

BRADY · Materials Handbook

BURINGTON AND MAY · Handbook of Probability and Statistics with Tables

COCKRELL · Industrial Electronics Handbook

CONDON AND ODISHAW · Handbook of Physics

COOMBS · Printed Circuits Handbook

ETHERINGTON · Nuclear Engineering Handbook

FINK AND CARROLL · Standard Handbook for Electrical Engineers

GRUENBERG · Handbook of Telemetry and Remote Control

HAMSHER · Communication System Engineering Handbook

HARPER · Handbook of Electronic Packaging

HENNEY · Radio Engineering Handbook

HENNEY AND WALSH · Electronic Components Handbook

HUNTER · Handbook of Semiconductor Electronics

HUSKEY AND KORN · Computer Handbook

IRESON · Reliability Handbook

JASIK · Antenna Engineering Handbook

JURAN · Quality Control Handbook

KLERER AND KORN · Digital Computer User's Handbook

KOELLE · Handbook of Astronautical Engineering

KORN AND KORN · Mathematical Handbook for Scientists and Engineers

KURTZ · The Lineman's and Cableman's Handbook

LANDEE, DAVIS, AND ALBRECHT · Electronic Designers' Handbook

MACHOL · System Engineering Handbook

MARKUS · Electronics and Nucleonics Dictionary

MARKUS · Handbook of Electronic Control Circuits

MARKUS AND ZELUFF · Handbook of Industrial and Electronic Circuits

PERRY · Engineering Manual

SHEA · Amplifier Handbook

SKOLNIK · Radar Handbook

SMEATON · Motor Application and Maintenance Handbook

STETKA · NFPA Handbook of the National Electrical Code

TERMAN · Radio Engineers' Handbook

TRUXAL · Control Engineers' Handbook

AMERICAN ELECTRICIANS' HANDBOOK

A Reference Book for the Practical Electrical Man

TERRELL CROFT *Editor*, 1913 to 1921
CLIFFORD C. CARR *Editor*, 1932 to 1961

JOHN H. WATT *Editor*

Electrical Field Engineer
National Fire Protection Association

Ninth Edition

McGRAW-HILL BOOK COMPANY

New York   St. Louis   San Francisco   Düsseldorf   Johannesburg
Kuala Lumpur   London   Mexico   Montreal   New Delhi
Panama   Rio de Janeiro   Singapore   Sydney   Toronto

AMERICAN ELECTRICIANS' HANDBOOK

ISBN 07-013929-6

12 13 14 15 16 17   KPKP   7 9 8 7 6

PREFACE TO THE NINTH EDITION

In the preparation of this latest edition of what has long been a classic reference work, the present editor has tried to continue the tradition of practicality, helpfulness, and dependability established by his predecessors. The entire text has been carefully revised and updated in accordance with the advancement of the art, the latest good practice, and the 1968 edition of the National Electrical Code. Many new subjects, including illustrations, have been added.

Some of the more outstanding advances are new types of insulated conductors (such as THWN–THHN, XHHW, TFFN–TFN, and FEP–FEPB); wiring systems (such as cablebus, rigid nonmetallic conduit, continuous rigid cable supports, and aluminum-sheathed cable); and the latest developments in wiring devices, overcurrent devices, lighting equipment and lamps, equipment insulation and sound ratings, electric space heating and solid-state devices.

Every effort has been made to continue the original purpose of the Handbook, which is to provide a compilation of data and information on the various types of electric equipment and materials, presented without advanced mathematics, and arranged so as to be a helpful guide to the selection, installation, operation, and maintenance of the equipment.

The editor wishes to express his sincere appreciation to the many associations and companies and their representatives who have supplied illustrations and data. The revision of this book would have been impossible without this assistance. Special appreciation is extended to Robert J. Lawrie, Associate Editor, *Electrical Construction and Maintenance;* Berlon C. Cooper, fellow member, IES; and Sy Coopersmith, R. L. Faber and Associates, Inc., for their major contributions in the subjects of electronics and solid-state devices, lighting systems and equipment, and electric comfort conditioning. I appreciate the assistance given by my wife, Lois, in preparing manuscripts, proofreading, and handling the endless details that made this book possible.

John H. Watt

v

CONTENTS

Division 10 ELECTRIC LIGHTING

Division 11 WIRING AND DESIGN TABLES

DIVISION ONE

Fundamentals

USEFUL TABLES

1. Natural Trigonometric Functions

Angle (θ or lag angle), deg	Sine (or reactive factor)	Cosine (or power factor)	Tangent	Cotangent	Secant	Cosecant	Angle (θ or lag angle), deg
0	0.00000	1.00000	0.00000	Infinite	1.0000	Infinite	180
1	0.01774	0.99985	0.01745	57.290	1.0001	57.299	179
2	0 03490	0.99939	0.03492	28.636	1.0006	28.654	178
3	0.05234	0.99863	0.05241	19.081	1.0014	19.107	177
4	0.06976	0.99756	0.06993	14.301	1.0024	14.335	176
5	0 08715	0.99619	0.08749	11.430	1.0038	11.474	175
6	0.10453	0.99452	0.10510	9.5144	1.0055	9.5668	174
7	0 12187	0.99255	0.12278	8.1443	1.0075	8.2055	173
8	0.13917	0.99027	0.14054	7.1154	1.0098	7.1853	172
9	0.15643	0.98769	0.15838	6.3137	1.0125	6.3924	171
10	0.17365	0.98481	0.17633	5.6713	1.0154	5.7588	170
11	0.19081	0.98163	0.19438	5.1445	1.0187	5.2408	169
12	0.20791	0.97815	0.21256	4.7046	1.0223	4.8097	168
13	0.22495	0.97437	0.23087	4.3315	1.0263	4.4454	167
14	0.24192	0.97029	0.24933	4.0108	1.0306	4.1336	166
15	0.25882	0.96592	0.26795	3.7320	1.0353	3.8637	165
16	0.27564	0.96126	0.28674	3.4874	1.0403	3.6279	164
17	0.29237	0.95630	0.30573	3.2708	1.0457	3.4203	163
18	0.30902	0.95106	0.32492	3.0777	1.0515	3.2361	162
19	0.32557	0.94552	0.34433	2.9042	1.0576	3.0715	161
20	0.34203	0.93969	0.36397	2.7475	1.0642	2.9238	160
21	0.35837	0.93358	0.38386	2.6051	1.0711	2.7904	159
22	0.37461	0.92718	0.40403	2.4751	1.0785	2.6695	158
23	0.39073	0.92050	0.42447	2.3558	1.0864	2.5593	157
24	0.40674	0.91354	0.44523	2.2460	1.0946	2.4586	156
25	0.42262	0.90631	0.46631	2 1445	1.1034	2.3662	155
26	0.43837	0.89879	0.48773	2.0503	1.1126	2.2812	154
27	0.45399	0.89101	0.50952	1.9626	1.1223	2.2027	153
28	0.46947	0.88295	0.53171	1.8807	1.1326	2.1300	152
29	0.48481	0.87462	0.55431	1.8040	1.1433	2.0627	151
30	0 50000	0.86603	0.57735	1.7320	1.1547	2.0000	150
31	0.51504	0.85717	0.60086	1.6643	1.1666	1.9416	149
32	0.52992	0.84805	0.62487	1.6003	1.1792	1.8871	148
33	0.54464	0.83867	0.64941	1.5399	1.1924	1.8361	147
34	0.55919	0.82904	0.67451	1.4826	1.2062	1.7883	146
35	0.57358	0.81915	0.70021	1.4281	1.2208	1.7434	145
36	0.58778	0.80902	0.72654	1.3764	1.2361	1.7013	144
37	0.60181	0.79863	0.75355	1.3270	1.2521	1.6616	143
38	0.61566	0.78801	0.78128	1.2799	1.2690	1.6243	142
39	0.62932	0.77715	0.80978	1.2349	1.2867	1.5890	141
40	0.64279	0.76604	0.83910	1.1917	1.3054	1.5557	140
41	0.65606	0.75741	0.86929	1.1504	1.3250	1.5242	139
42	0.66913	0.74314	0.90040	1.1106	1.3456	1.4945	138
43	0 68200	0.73135	0.93251	1.0724	1.3673	1.4663	137
44	0.69466	0.71934	0.96569	1.0355	1.3902	1.4395	136
45	0.70711	0.70711	1.0000	1.0000	1.4142	1.4142	135

Natural Trigonometric Functions (*Continued*)

Angle (θ or lag angle), deg	Sine (or reactive factor)	Cosine (or power factor)	Tangent	Cotangent	Secant	Cosecant	Angle (θ or lag angle), deg
46	0.71934	0.69466	1.0355	0.96569	1.4395	1.3902	134
47	0.73135	0.68200	1.0724	0.93251	1.4663	1.3673	133
48	0.74314	0.66913	1.1106	0.90040	1.4945	1.3456	132
49	0.75471	0.65606	1.1504	0.86929	1.5242	1.3250	131
50	0.76604	0.64279	1.1917	0.83910	1.5557	1.3054	130
51	0.77715	0.62932	1.2349	0.80978	1.5890	1.2867	129
52	0.78801	0.61566	1.2799	0.78128	1.6243	1.2690	128
53	0.79863	0.60181	1.3270	0.75355	1.6616	1.2521	127
54	0.80902	0.58778	1.3764	0.72654	1.7013	1.2361	126
55	0.81915	0.57358	1.4281	0.70021	1.7434	1.2208	125
56	0.82904	0.55919	1.4826	0.67451	1.7883	1.2062	124
57	0.83867	0.54464	1.5399	0.64941	1.8361	1.1922	123
58	0.84805	0.52992	1.6003	0.62487	1.8871	1.1792	122
59	0.85717	0.51504	1.6643	0.60086	1.9416	1.1666	121
60	0.86603	0.50000	1.7320	0.57735	2.0000	1.1547	120
61	0.87462	0.48481	1.8040	0.55431	2.0627	1.1433	119
62	0.88295	0.46947	1.8807	0.53171	2.1300	1.1326	118
63	0.89101	0.45399	1.9626	0.50952	2.2027	1.1223	117
64	0.89879	0.43837	2.0503	0.48773	2.2812	1.1126	116
65	0.90631	0.42262	2.1445	0.46631	2.3662	1.1034	115
66	0.91354	0.40674	2.2460	0.44523	2.4586	1.0946	114
67	0.92050	0.39073	2.3558	0.42447	2.5593	1.0864	113
68	0.92718	0.37461	2.4751	0.40403	2.6695	1.0785	112
69	0.93358	0.35837	2.6051	0.38386	2.7904	1.0711	111
70	0.93969	0.34202	2.7475	0.36397	2.9238	1.0642	110
71	0.94552	0.32557	2.9042	0.34433	3.0715	1.0576	109
72	0.95106	0.30902	3.0777	0.32492	3.2361	1.0515	108
73	0.95630	0.29237	3.2708	0.30573	3.4203	1.0457	107
74	0.96126	0.27564	3.4874	0.28647	3.6279	1.0403	106
75	0.96592	0.25882	3.7320	0.26795	3.8637	1.0353	105
76	0.97029	0.24192	4.0108	0.24933	4.1336	1.0306	104
77	0.97437	0.22495	4.3315	0.23087	4.4454	1.0263	103
78	0.97815	0.20791	4.7046	0.21256	4.8097	1.0223	102
79	0.98163	0.19081	5.1445	0.19438	5.2408	1.0187	101
80	0.98481	0.17365	5.6713	0.17633	5.7588	1.0154	100
81	0.98769	0.15643	6.3137	0.15838	6.3924	1.0125	99
82	0.99027	0.13917	7.1154	0.14054	7.1853	1.0098	98
83	0.99255	0.12187	8.1443	0.12278	8.2055	1.0075	97
84	0.99452	0.10453	9.5144	0.10510	9.5668	1.0055	96
85	0.99619	0.08715	11.430	0.08749	11.474	1.0038	95
86	0.99756	0.06976	14.301	0.06993	14.335	1.0024	94
87	0.99863	0.05234	19.081	0.05241	19.107	1.0014	93
88	0.99939	0.03490	28.634	0.03492	28.654	1.0006	92
89	0.99985	0.01745	57.290	0.01745	57.299	1.0001	91
90	1.00000	0.00000	Infinite	0.00000	Infinite	1.0000	90

2. Fractions of Inch Reduced to Decimal Equivalents

Halves	4ths	8ths	16ths	32ds	64ths	Decimal equivalents	Halves	4ths	8ths	16ths	32ds	64ths	Decimal equivalents
...	...	...	...	...	1/64	0.015625	...	...	...	...	...	33/64	0.515625
...	...	...	...	1/32	...	0.03125	...	...	...	...	17/32	...	0.53125
...	...	...	...	...	3/64	0.046875	...	...	...	...	...	35/64	0.546875
...	...	...	1/16	...	...	0.0625	...	...	...	9/16	...	...	0.5625
...	...	...	...	...	5/64	0.078125	...	...	...	...	...	37/64	0.578125
...	...	...	...	3/32	...	0.09375	...	...	...	...	19/32	...	0.59375
...	...	...	...	...	7/64	0.109375	...	...	...	...	...	39/64	0.609375
...	...	1/8	...	...	...	0.125	...	...	5/8	...	...	...	0.625
...	...	...	...	...	9/64	0.140625	...	...	...	...	...	41/64	0.640625
...	...	...	...	5/32	...	0.15625	...	...	...	...	21/32	...	0.65625
...	...	...	...	...	11/64	0.171875	...	...	...	...	...	43/64	0.671875
...	...	...	3/16	...	...	0.1875	...	...	...	11/16	...	...	0.6875
...	...	...	...	...	13/64	0.203125	...	...	...	...	...	45/64	0.703125
...	...	...	...	7/32	...	0.21875	...	...	...	...	23/32	...	0.71875
...	...	...	...	...	15/64	0.234375	...	...	...	...	...	47/64	0.734375
...	1/4	...	...	...	...	0.25	...	3/4	...	...	...	...	0.75
...	...	...	...	...	17/64	0.265625	...	...	...	...	...	49/64	0.765625
...	...	...	...	9/32	...	0.28125	...	...	...	...	25/32	...	0.78125
...	...	...	...	...	19/64	0.296875	...	...	...	...	...	51/64	0.796875
...	...	...	5/16	...	...	0.3125	...	...	...	13/16	...	...	0.8125
...	...	...	...	...	21/64	0.328125	...	...	...	...	...	53/64	0.828125
...	...	...	...	11/32	...	0.34375	...	...	...	...	27/32	...	0.84375
...	...	...	...	...	23/64	0.359375	...	...	...	...	...	55/64	0.859375
...	...	3/8	...	...	...	0.375	...	...	7/8	...	...	...	0.875
...	...	...	...	...	25/64	0.390625	...	...	...	...	...	57/64	0.890625
...	...	...	...	13/32	...	0.40625	...	...	...	...	29/32	...	0.90625
...	...	...	...	...	27/64	0.421875	...	...	...	...	...	59/64	0.921875
...	...	...	7/16	...	...	0.4375	...	...	...	15/16	...	...	0.9375
...	...	...	...	...	29/64	0.453125	...	...	...	...	...	61/64	0.953125
...	...	...	...	15/32	...	0.46875	...	...	...	...	31/32	...	0.96875
...	...	...	...	...	31/64	0.484375	...	...	...	...	...	63/64	0.984375
1/2	...	...	...	...	...	0.5							

3. In figuring discounts on electrical equipment, it is often necessary to apply primary and secondary discounts. By using the values in Table **4,** time and labor may be conserved. To find net price, multiply the list or gross price by the multiplier from the table which corresponds to the discounts.

Example. The discount on iron conduit may be quoted as 25 and 10 with 2 per cent for cash in 10 days. To obtain the actual cost, 25 per cent would be deducted from the list price, then 10 per cent from that result, and finally 2 per cent from the second result. Assuming that the list price of ½-in. conduit is $12 per 100 ft, its actual price with the 25, 10, and 2 per cent discounts would be:

$$\$12 \quad \text{minus } 0.25 \times \$12 \quad = \$12 \quad - \$3 \quad = \$9$$
$$\$9.00 \text{ minus } 0.10 \times \quad \$9.00 = \quad \$9.00 - \$0.90 = \$8.10$$
$$\$8.10 \text{ minus } 0.02 \times \quad \$8.10 = \quad \$8.10 - \$0.16 = \$7.94$$

Therefore, the net cost of the conduit would be $7.94 per 100 ft. Now by using the multiplier (from Table 4) corresponding to a primary discount of 25 per cent and secondary discounts of 10 and 2 per cent, which is 0.661,

$$\$12.00 \times 0.661 = \$7.94$$

This is the same result as that obtained by using the longer method.

4. Table for Figuring Total Discount Multiplier by Combining Primary and Secondary Discounts

Primary discount, per cent	Secondary discounts						
	2 %	5 %	10 %	15 %	5 and 2 %	10 and 2 %	10 and 5 %
	Multiplier						
0	0.980	0.950	0.900	0.850	0.931	0.882	0.855
5	0.931	0.902	0.855	0.807	0.884	0.838	0.812
10	0.882	0.855	0.810	0.765	0.838	0.794	0.769
11	0.872	0.845	0.801	0.756	0.829	0.785	0.761
12	0.862	0.836	0.792	0.748	0.819	0.776	0.752
13	0.853	0.826	0.783	0.740	0.810	0.767	0.744
14	0.843	0.817	0.774	0.731	0.801	0 758	0.735
15	0.833	0.807	0.765	0.722	0.791	0.750	0.727
16	0.823	0.798	0.756	0.714	0.782	0.741	0.718
17	0.813	0.788	0.747	0.705	0.773	0.732	0.710
18	0.803	0.779	0.738	0.697	0.763	0.723	0.701
19	0.794	0.770	0.729	0.688	0.754	0.714	0.692
20	0.784	0.760	0.720	0.680	0.745	0.705	0.684
25	0.735	0.712	0.675	0.638	0.698	0.661	0.641
30	0.686	0.665	0.630	0.595	0.652	0.617	0.598
35	0.637	0.617	0.585	0.552	0.605	0.573	0.556
40	0.588	0.570	0.540	0.510	0.559	0.529	0.513
45	0.539	0.522	0.495	0.468	0.512	0.485	0.470
50	0.490	0.475	0.450	0.425	0.465	0.441	0.428
55	0.441	0.427	0.405	0.382	0.419	0.397	0.385
60	0.392	0.380	0.360	0.340	0.372	0.353	0.342
65	0.343	0.333	0.315	0.298	0.326	0.309	0.299
70	0.294	0.285	0.270	0.255	0.279	0.265	0.256

5. Multipliers for Computing Selling Prices Which Will Afford a Given Percentage Profit

Percentage profit desired	To obtain selling price, multiply actual cost (invoice cost + freight) by the following value		Percentage profit desired	To obtain selling price, multiply actual cost (invoice cost + freight) by the following value	
	When percentage profit is based on cost	When percentage profit is based on selling price		When percentage profit is based on cost	When percentage profit is based on selling price
5	1.05	1.053	36	1.36	1.563
6	1.06	1.064	37	1.37	1.588
7	1.07	1.075	38	1.38	1.613
8	1.08	1.087	39	1.39	1.640
9	1.09	1.100	40	1.40	1.667
10	1.10	1.111	41	1.41	1.695
11	1.11	1.124	42	1.42	1.725
12	1.12	1.136	43	1.43	1.754
13	1.13	1.149	45	1.45	1.818
14	1.14	1.163	46	1.46	1.852
15	1.15	1.176	47	1.47	1.887
16	1.16	1.190	48	1.48	1.923
17	1.17	1.204	49	1.49	1.961
18	1.18	1.220	50	1.50	2.000
19	1.19	1.235	52	1.52	2.084
20	1.20	1.250	54	1.54	2.174
21	1.21	1.267	56	1.56	2.272
22	1.22	1.283	58	1.58	2.381
23	1.23	1.299	60	1.60	2.500
24	1.24	1.316	62	1.62	2.631
25	1.25	1.334	64	1.64	2.778
26	1.26	1.352	66	1.66	2.941
27	1.27	1.370	68	1.68	3.126
28	1.28	1.390	70	1.70	3.333
29	1.29	1.409	72	1.72	3.572
30	1.30	1.429	74	1.74	3.847
31	1.31	1.450	76	1.76	4.168
32	1.32	1.471	78	1.78	4.545
33	1.33	1.493	80	1.80	5.000
34	1.34	1.516	90	1.90	10.000
35	1.35	1.539	100	2.00	Infinity

6. Table Showing Percentage Net Profit

Percentage markup above cost	Percentage overhead							
	10 %	12 %	14 %	16 %	18 %	20 %	22 %	24 %
	Percentage net profit based on selling price for a given percentage overhead based on gross sales							
10	−0.90	−2.90	−4.90	−6.90	−8.90	−10.90	−12.90	−14.90
15	3.05	1.05	−0.95	−2.95	−4.95	−6.95	−8.95	−10.95
20	6.67	4.67	2.67	0.67	−1.33	−3.33	−5.33	−7.33
25	10.00	8.00	6.00	4.00	2.00	0.00	−2.00	−4.00
30	13.08	11.08	9.08	7.08	5.08	3.08	1.08	−0.92
33⅓	15.00	13.00	11.00	9.00	7.00	5.00	3.00	1.00
35	15.93	13.93	11.93	9.93	7.93	5.93	3.93	1.93
40	18.57	16.57	14.57	12.57	10.57	8.57	6.57	4.57
45	21.00	19.00	17.00	15.00	13.00	11.00	9.00	7.00
50	23.33	21.33	19.33	17.33	15.33	13.33	11.33	9.33
55	25.50	23.50	21.50	19.50	17.50	15.50	13.50	11.50
60	27.50	25.50	23.50	21.50	19.50	17.50	15.50	13.50
65	29.40	27.40	25.40	23.40	21.40	19 40	17.40	15.40
70	31.18	29.18	27.18	25.18	23.18	21.18	19.18	17.18
75	32.85	30.85	28.85	26.85	24.85	22.85	20.85	18.85
80	34.45	32.45	30.45	28.45	26.45	24.45	22.45	20.45
85	35.95	33.95	31.95	29.95	27.95	25.95	23.95	21.95
90	37.37	35.37	33.37	31.37	29.37	27.37	25.37	23.37
95	38.72	36.72	34.72	32.72	30.72	28.72	26.72	24.72
100	40.00	38.00	36.00	34.00	32.00	30.00	28.00	26.00

NOTE. Minus (−) values indicate a net loss.

7. Net Profits. In figuring the net profit of doing business, Table **6** will be found to be very useful. The table may be used in three ways as explained below.

To Determine the Percentage of Net Profit on Sales That One Is Making. Locate, at the top of one of the vertical columns, your percentage overhead — your "cost of doing business" in percentage of gross sales. Locate, at the extreme left of one of the horizontal columns, your percentage markup. The value at the intersection of these two columns will be the percentage profit which you are making.

Example. If your cost of doing business is 18 per cent of your gross sales and you mark your goods at 35 per cent above cost, your net profit is then 7.93 per cent of gross sales, obtained by carrying down from the column headed 18 per cent and across from the 35 per cent markup.

To Determine What Percentage Overhead Cost of Doing Business Would Yield a Certain Net Profit for a Given Markup Percentage. Locate in the extreme left-hand column the percentage that the selling price is marked above the cost price. Trace horizontally across from this value until the percentage net profit desired is located. At the top of the column in which the desired net profit is located will be found the percentage overhead cost of doing business that will allow this profit to be made.

Example. If the markup is 45 per cent and the profit desired is 15 per cent, an overhead cost of doing business of 16 per cent can be allowed, obtained by carrying across from the 45 per cent markup to the 15 per cent profit and finding that this column is headed by 16 per cent overhead.

To Determine What Percentage Should Be Added to the Cost of Goods in Order to Make a Certain Percentage Net Profit on Sales. Select the vertical column which shows the percentage cost of doing business at its top. Trace down the column until the desired percentage profit is found; from this value trace horizontally to the extreme left-hand column, in which will be found the markup percentage—the percentage to be added to the cost to afford the desired profit.

Example. It is desired to make a 12 per cent net profit when the cost of doing business is 20 per cent of the gross sales. Select the vertical column with 20 per cent at its top. Trace down the column to locate the net profit desired of 12 per cent. This will be part way between 11.00 and 13.33. Carrying across to the left from these values gives a required markup between 45 and 50, or approximately 47 per cent.

For values which do not appear in the table, approximate results can be obtained by estimation from the closest values in the table. If more accurate results are desired for these intermediate values, the following formulas may be used:

$$P = 100 - h - \frac{10,000}{100 + m} \tag{1}$$

or

$$m = \frac{100(P + h)}{100 - (P + h)} \tag{2}$$

or

$$h = 100 - P - \frac{10,000}{100 + m} \tag{3}$$

where m = percentage markup based on cost of goods; h = percentage overhead based on gross sales; P = percentage net profit based on selling price.

If you sell your goods at the retail list prices set by the manufacturers, you can use the table by converting the trade discount which you receive to an equivalent percentage markup, according to the following table:

Manufacturer's discount	Equivalent percentage markup	Manufacturer's discount	Equivalent percentage markup
10	11	35	54
15	17½	40	66⅔
20	25	45	81¾
25	33⅓	50	100
30	43		

Intermediate values may be calculated from the following formula:

$$m = \frac{100Q}{100 - Q} \tag{4}$$

where m = percentage markup based on cost of goods and Q = manufacturer's discount.

CONVERSION FACTORS

("Standard Handbook for Electrical Engineers")

These factors were calculated with a double-length slide rule and checked with those given by Carl Hering in his "Conversion Tables."

8. Length

1 mil = 0.0254 mm = 0.001 in.
1 mm = 39.37 mils = 0.03937 in.
1 cm = 0.3937 in. = 0.0328 ft.
1 in. = 25.4 mm = 0.083 ft = 0.0278 yd = 2.54 cm.
1 ft = 304.8 mm = 12 in. = 0.333 yd = 0.305 m.
1 yd = 91.44 cm = 36 in. = 3 ft = 0.914 m.
1 m = 39.37 in. = 3.28 ft = 1.094 yd.
1 km = 3,281 ft = 1,094 yd = 0.6213 mile.
1 mile = 5,280 ft = 1,760 yd = 1,609 m = 1.609 km.

9. Surface

1 cir mil = 0.7854 sq mil = 0.0005067 sq mm = 0.0000007854 sq in.
1 sq mil = 1.273 cir mil = 0.000645 sq mm = 0.000001 sq in.
1 sq mm = 1,973 cir mil = 1,550 sq mil = 0.00155 sq in.
1 sq cm = 197,300 cir mil = 0.155 sq in. = 0.00108 sq ft.
1 sq in. = 1,273,240 cir mil = 6.451 sq cm = 0.0069 sq ft.
1 sq ft = 929.03 sq cm = 144 sq in. = 0.1111 sq yd = 0.0929 sq m.
1 sq yd = 1,296 sq in. = 9 sq ft = 0.8361 sq m are = 0.000207 acre.
1 sq m = 1,550 sq in. = 10.7 sq ft = 1.195 sq yd = 0.000247 acre.
1 acre = 43,560 sq ft = 4,840 sq yd = 4,047 sq m = 0.4047 hectare = 0.004047 sq km = 0.001562 sq mile.
1 sq mile = 27,880,000 sq ft = 3,098,000 sq yd = 2,590,000 sq m = 640 acres = 2.59 sq km.

10. Volume

1 cir mil-ft = 0.0000094248 cu in.
1 cu cm = 0.061 cu in. = 0.0021 pt (liq) = 0.0018 pt (dry).
1 cu in. = 16.39 cu cm = 0.0346 pt (liq) = 0.0298 pt (dry) = 0.0173 qt (liq) = 0.0148 qt (dry) = 0.0164 l or cu dm = 0.0036 gal = 0.0005787 cu ft.
1 pt (liq) = 473.18 cu cm = 28.87 cu in.
1 pt (dry) = 550.6 cu cm = 33.60 cu in.
1 qt (liq) = 946.36 cu cm = 57.75 cu in. = 8 gills (liq) = 2 pt (liq) = 0.94636 l or cu dm = 0.25 gal.
1 l = 1,000 cu cm = 61.023 cu in. = 2,1133 pt (liq) = 1.8162 pt (dry) = 0.908 qt (dry) = 0.2642 gal (liq) = 0.03531 cu ft.
1 qt (dry) = 1,101 cu cm = 67.20 cu in. = 2 pt (dry) = 0.03889 cu ft.
1 gal = 3,785 cu cm = 231 cu in. = 32 gills = 8 pt = 4 qt (liq) = 3.785 l = 0.1337 cu ft = 0.004951 cu yd.
1 cu ft = 28,317 cu cm = 1,728 cu in. = 59.84 pt (liq) = 51.43 pt (dry) = 29.92 qt (liq) = 28.32 l = 25.71 qt (dry) = 7.48 gal = 0.03704 cu yd = 0.02832 cu m or stere.
1 cu yd = 46,656 cu in. = 27 cu ft = 0.7646 cu m or stere.
1 cu m = 61,023 cu in. = 1,001 l = 35.31 cu ft = 1.308 cu yd.

11. Weight

1 mg = 0.01543 gr = 0.001 g.
1 gr = 64.80 mg = 0.002286 oz (av).
1 g = 15.43 gr = 0.03527 oz (av) = 0.002205 lb.
1 oz (av) = 437.5 gr = 28.35 g = 16 drams (av) = 0.0625 lb.
1 lb = 7,000 gr = 453.6 g = 256 drams = 16 oz = 0.4536 kg.
1 kg = 15,432 gr = 35.27 oz = 2.205 lb.
1 ton (short) = 2,000 lb = 907.2 kg = 0.8928 ton (long).
1 ton (long) = 2,240 lb = 1.12 tons (short) = 1.016 tons (metric).

12. Energy

Torque units should be distinguished from energy units: Thus, foot-pound and kilogram-meter for energy, and pound-foot and meter-kilogram for torque (see Sec. **67** for further information on torque).

1 ft-lb = 13.560,000 ergs = 1.356 joules = 0.3239 g-cal = 0.1383 kg-m = 0.001285 Btu = 0.0003766 watt-hr = 0.0000005051 hp-hr.
1 kg-m = 98,060,000 ergs = 9.806 joules = 7.233 ft-lb = 2.34 g-cal = 0.009296 Btu = 0.002724 watt-hr = 0.000003704 hp-hr (metric).
1 Btu = 1,055 joules = 778.1 ft-lb = 252 g-cal = 107.6 kg-m = 0.5555 lb-centigrade heat unit = 0.2930 whr = 0.252 kg-cal = 0.0003984 hp-hr (metric) = 0.0003930 hp-hr.
1 whr = 3,600 joules = 2,655.4 ft-lb = 860 g-cal = 367.1 kg-m = 3.413 Btu = 0.001341 hp-hr.
1 hp-hr = 2,684,000 joules = 1,980,000 ft-lb = 273,700 kg-cm = 745.6 whr.
1 kwhr = 2,655,000 ft-lb = 367,100 kg-m = 1.36 hp-hr (metric) = 1.34 hp-hr.

13. Power

1 g-cm per sec = 0.00009806 watt.
1 ft-lb per min = 0.02260 watt = 0.00003072 hp (metric) = 0.00000303 hp.
1 watt = 44.26 ft-lb per min = 6.119 kg-m per min = 0.001341 hp.
1 hp = 33,000 ft-lb per min = 745.6 watts = 550 ft-lb per sec = 76.04 kg-m per sec = 1.01387 hp (metric).
1 kw = 44,256.7 ft-lb per min = 101.979 kg-m per sec = 1.3597 hp (metric) = 1.341 hp = 1,000 watts.

14. Resistivity

1 ohm per cir mil-ft = 0.7854 ohm per sq mil-ft = 0.001662 ohm per sq mm-m = 0.0000001657 ohm per cu cm = 0.00000006524 ohm per cu in.
1 ohm per sq mil-ft = 1.273 ohms per cir mil-ft = 0.002117 ohm per sq mm-m = 0.0000002116 ohm per cu cm = 0.00000008335 ohm per cu in.
1 ohm per cu in. = 15,280,000 ohms per cir mil-ft = 12,000,000 ohms per sq mil-ft = 25,400 ohms per sq mm-m = 2.54 ohms per cu cm.

15. Current Density

1 amp per sq in. = 0.7854 amp per cir mil = 0.155 amp per sq cm = 1,273,000 cir mils per amp = 0.000001 amp per sq mil.
1 amp per sq cm = 6.45 amp per sq in. = 197,000 cir mils per amp.
1,000 cir mils per amp = 1,273 amp per sq in.
1,000 sq mils per amp = 1,000 amp per sq in.

16. Centigrade and Fahrenheit Thermometer Scales

Deg C	Deg F	Deg C	Deg F	Deg C	Deg F	Deg C	Deg F	Deg C	Deg F
0	32.	21	69.8	41	105.8	61	141.8	81	177.8
1	33.8	22	71.6	42	107.6	62	143.6	82	179.6
2	35.6	23	73.4	43	109.4	63	145.4	83	181.4
3	37.4	24	75.2	44	111.2	64	147.2	84	183.2
4	39.2	25	77.	45	113.	65	149.	85	185.
5	41.	26	78.8	46	114.8	66	150.8	86	186.8
6	42.8	27	80.6	47	116.6	67	152.6	87	188.6
7	44.6	28	82.4	48	118.4	68	154.4	88	190.4
8	46.4	29	84.2	49	120.2	69	156.2	89	192.2
9	48.2	30	86.	50	122.	70	158.	90	194.
10	50.	31	87.8	51	123.8	71	159.8	91	195.8
11	51.8	32	39.6	52	125.6	72	161.6	92	197.6
12	53.6	33	91.4	53	127.4	73	163.4	93	199.4
13	55.4	34	93.2	54	129.2	74	165.2	94	201.2
14	57.2	35	95.	55	131.	75	167.	95	203.
15	59.	36	96.8	56	132.8	76	168.8	96	204.8
16	60.8	37	98.6	57	134.6	77	170.6	97	206.6
17	62.6	38	100.4	58	136.4	78	172.4	98	208.4
18	64.4	39	102.2	59	138.2	79	174.2	99	210.2
19	66.2	40	104.	60	140.	80	176.	100	212.
20	68.								

For values not appearing in the table use the following formulas:

$$\text{Temp } °C = \tfrac{5}{9} \times (\text{temp } °F - 32) \tag{5}$$
$$\text{Temp } °F = (\tfrac{9}{5} \times \text{temp } °C) + 32 \tag{6}$$

17. Greek Alphabet
(Anaconda Wire & Cable Co.)

Greek letter	Greek name	English equivalent
A α	Alpha	a
B β	Beta	b
Γ γ	Gamma	g
Δ δ	Delta	d
E ε	Epsilon	e
Z ζ	Zeta	z
H η	Eta	é
Θ θ	Theta	th
I ι	Iota	i
K κ	Kappa	k
Λ λ	Lambda	l
M μ	Mu	m
N ν	Nu	n
Ξ ξ	Xi	x
O ο	Omicron	ŏ
Π π	Pi	p
P ρ	Rho	r
Σ σ	Sigma	s
T τ	Tau	t
Υ υ	Upsilon	u
Φ φ	Phi	ph
X χ	Chi	ch
Ψ ψ	Psi	ps
Ω ω	Omega	ō

GRAPHICAL ELECTRICAL SYMBOLS

18. Standard graphical symbols for electrical diagrams were approved by the American Standards Association on Mar. 29, 1954. The complete list of the standardized symbols is given in the American Standards Association publication "Graphical Symbols for Electrical Diagrams," No. Y32.2 — 1954. A selected group of these symbols for use in one-line electrical diagrams is given in Secs. **19** and **20** through the courtesy of the Rome Cable Corporation.

19. Graphical Symbols for One-line Electrical Diagrams
From American Standard (ASA) Y32.2 − 1954, sponsored by AIEE and ASME.

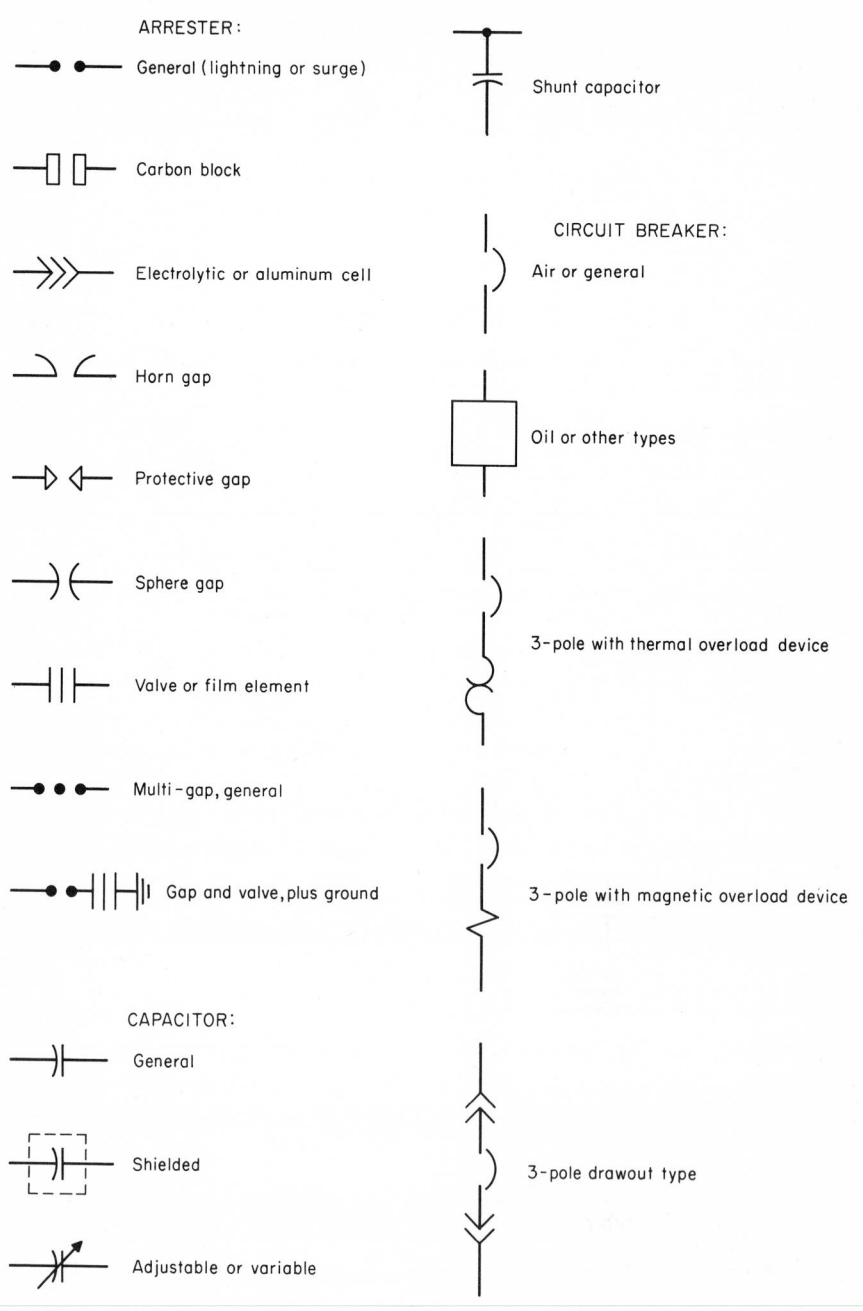

ARRESTER:

General (lightning or surge)

Carbon block

Electrolytic or aluminum cell

Horn gap

Protective gap

Sphere gap

Valve or film element

Multi-gap, general

Gap and valve, plus ground

CAPACITOR:

General

Shielded

Adjustable or variable

Shunt capacitor

CIRCUIT BREAKER:

Air or general

Oil or other types

3-pole with thermal overload device

3-pole with magnetic overload device

3-pole drawout type

Graphical Symbols (*Continued*)

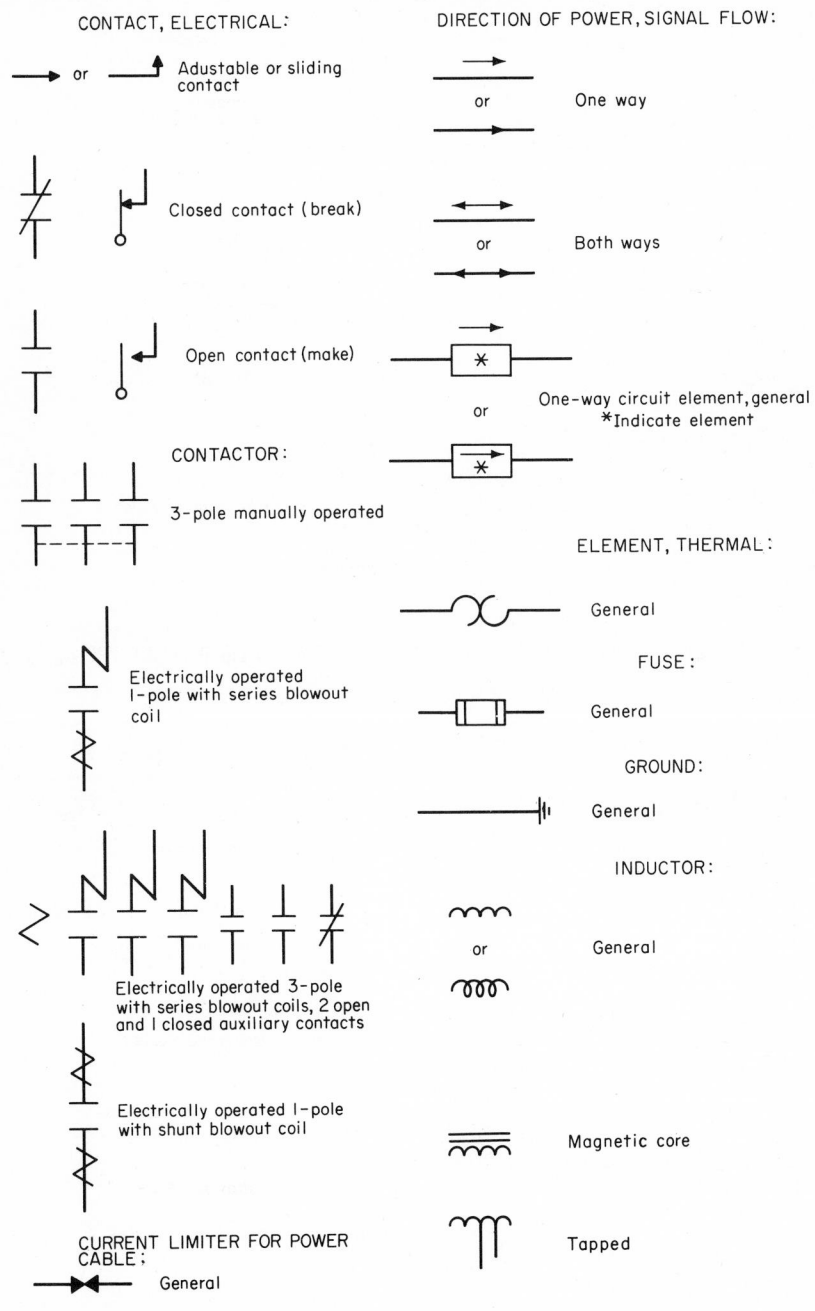

CONTACT, ELECTRICAL:

or — Adustable or sliding contact

Closed contact (break)

Open contact (make)

CONTACTOR:

3-pole manually operated

Electrically operated I-pole with series blowout coil

Electrically operated 3-pole with series blowout coils, 2 open and I closed auxiliary contacts

Electrically operated I-pole with shunt blowout coil

CURRENT LIMITER FOR POWER CABLE:

General

DIRECTION OF POWER, SIGNAL FLOW:

or — One way

or — Both ways

or — One-way circuit element, general
*Indicate element

ELEMENT, THERMAL:

General

FUSE:

General

GROUND:

General

INDUCTOR:

or — General

Magnetic core

Tapped

Graphical Symbols (*Continued*)

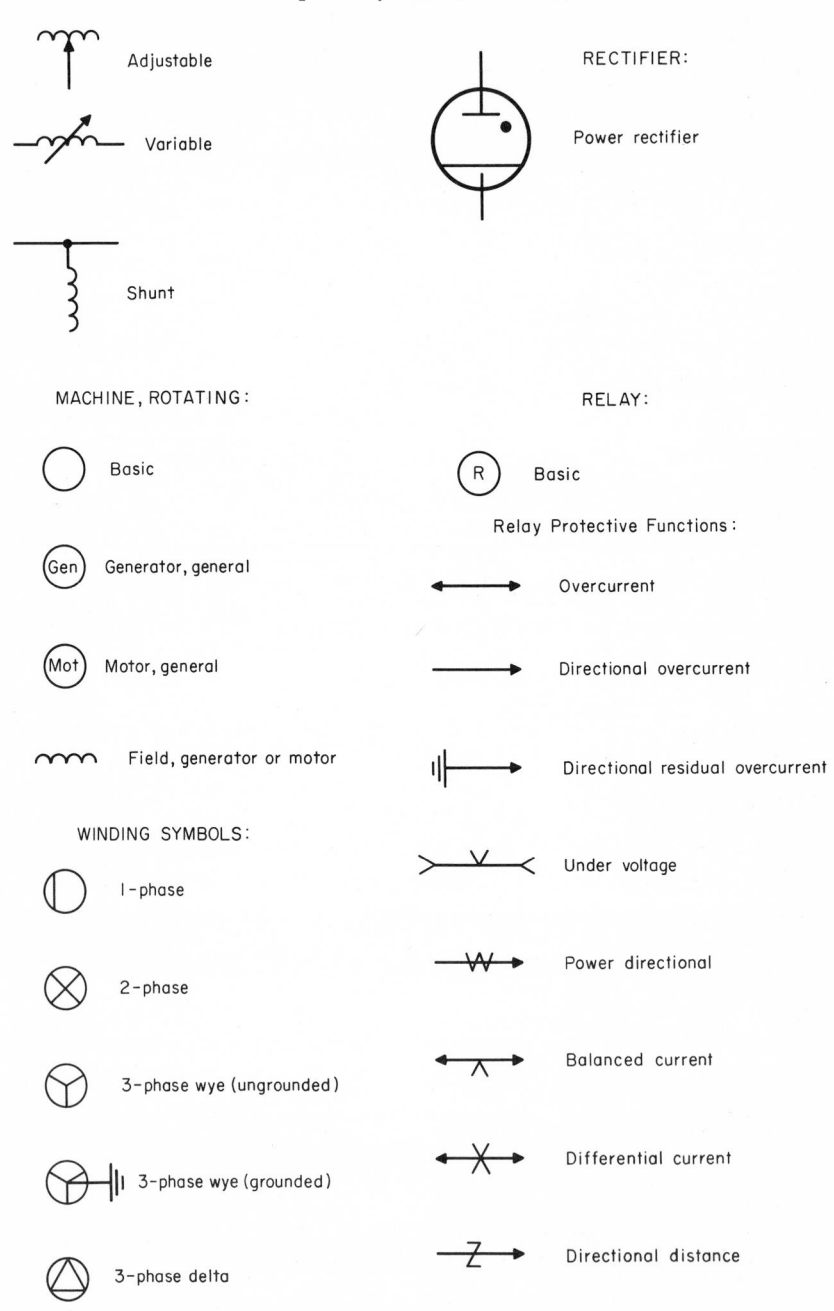

Adjustable

Variable

Shunt

RECTIFIER:

Power rectifier

MACHINE, ROTATING:

Basic

Gen   Generator, general

Mot   Motor, general

Field, generator or motor

WINDING SYMBOLS:

1-phase

2-phase

3-phase wye (ungrounded)

3-phase wye (grounded)

3-phase delta

RELAY:

R   Basic

Relay Protective Functions:

Overcurrent

Directional overcurrent

Directional residual overcurrent

Under voltage

Power directional

Balanced current

Differential current

Directional distance

Graphical Symbols (*Continued*)

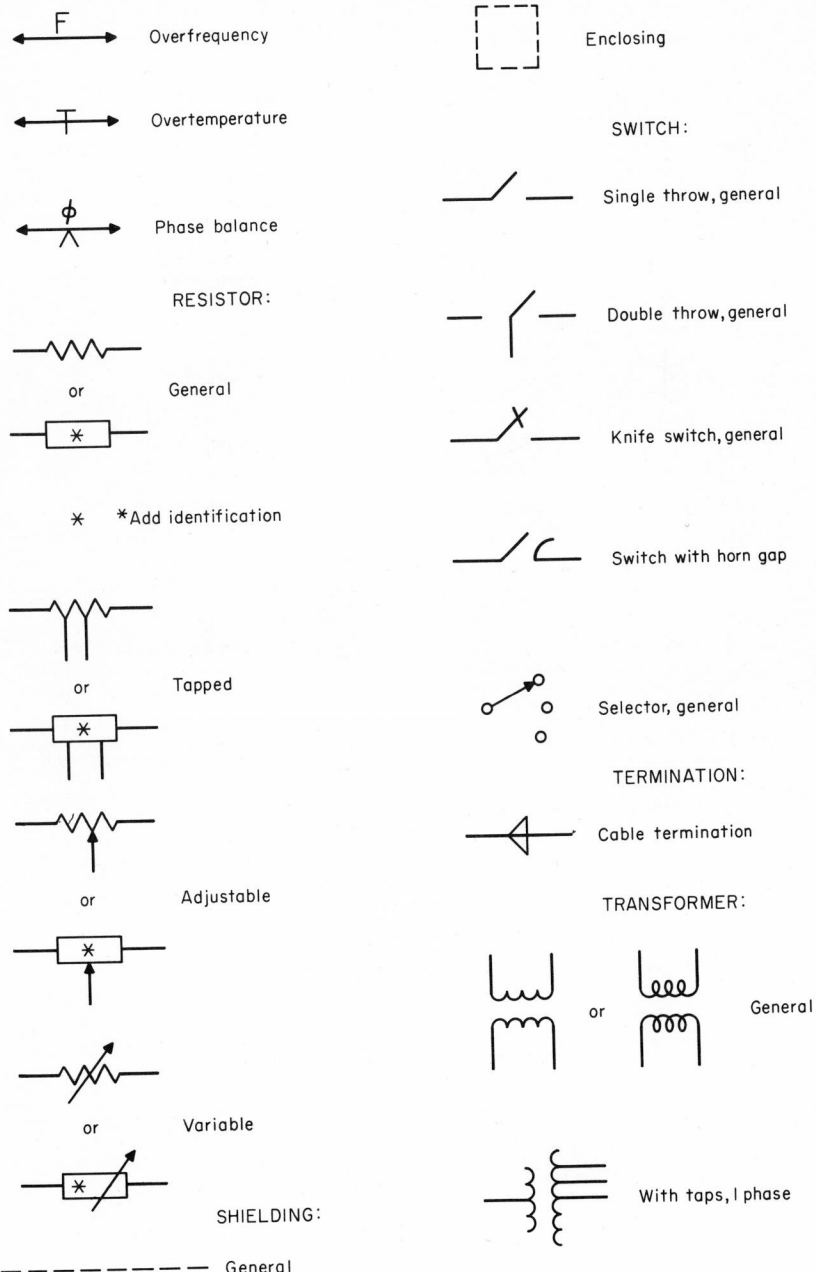

F — Overfrequency

— Overtemperature

φ — Phase balance

RESISTOR:

or — General

＊ — *Add identification

or — Tapped

or — Adjustable

or — Variable

SHIELDING:

— — — — — — — General

Enclosing

SWITCH:

— Single throw, general

— Double throw, general

— Knife switch, general

— Switch with horn gap

— Selector, general

TERMINATION:

— Cable termination

TRANSFORMER:

or — General

— With taps, 1 phase

Graphical Symbols (*Continued*)

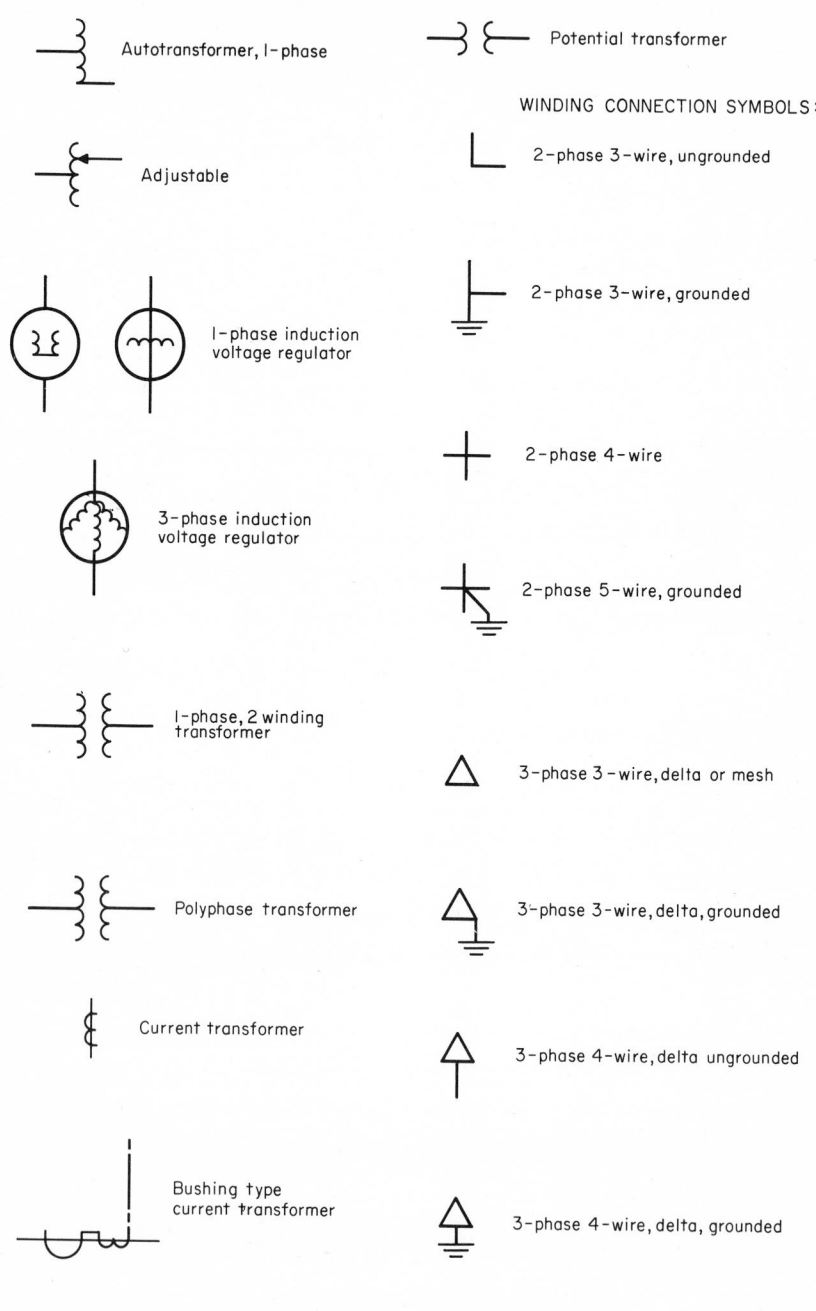

Autotransformer, I-phase

Adjustable

I-phase induction voltage regulator

3-phase induction voltage regulator

I-phase, 2 winding transformer

Polyphase transformer

Current transformer

Bushing type current transformer

Potential transformer

WINDING CONNECTION SYMBOLS:

2-phase 3-wire, ungrounded

2-phase 3-wire, grounded

2-phase 4-wire

2-phase 5-wire, grounded

3-phase 3-wire, delta or mesh

3-phase 3-wire, delta, grounded

3-phase 4-wire, delta ungrounded

3-phase 4-wire, delta, grounded

Graphical Symbols (*Continued*)

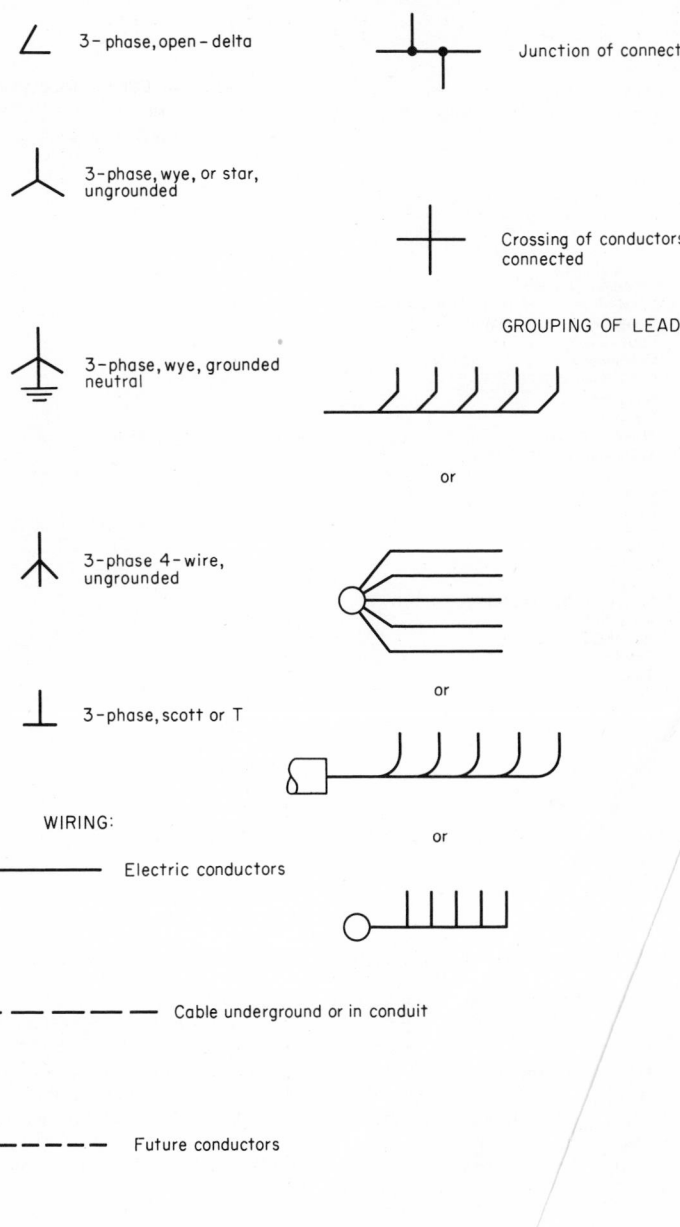

∠ 3–phase, open–delta

Junction of connected paths

⅄ 3–phase, wye, or star, ungrounded

Crossing of conductors not connected

GROUPING OF LEADS

3–phase, wye, grounded neutral

or

3–phase 4–wire, ungrounded

or

3–phase, scott or T

WIRING:

—————— Electric conductors

or

— — — — — Cable underground or in conduit

— — — — — Future conductors

——●—— Spliced conductors or change of type or size

20. Graphical Symbols for Meters or Instruments
From American Standard (ASA) Y32.2 – 1954

Note – The asterisk is not a part of the symbol. Always replace the asterisk by one of the following letter combinations, depending on the function of the meter or instrument, unless some other identification is provided in the circle and explained on the diagram.

A	Ammeter
AH	Ampere-hour meter
CMA	Contact-making (or breaking) ammeter
CMC	Contact-making (or breaking) clock
CMV	Contact-making (or breaking) volt-meter
CRO	Oscilloscope or cathode-ray oscillograph
D	Demand meter
DB	DB (decibel) meter
DBM	DBM (decibels referred to 1 milliwatt) meter
DTR	Demand-totalizing relay
F	Frequency meter
G	Galvanometer
GD	Ground detector
I	Indicating
M	Integrating
μA or UA	Microammeter
MA	Milliammeter
N	Noise meter
OHM	Ohmmeter
OP	Oil pressure
OSCG	Oscillograph, string
PH	Phase meter
PI	Position indicator
PF	Power-factor meter
RD	Recording demand meter
REC	Recording
RF	Reactive-factor meter
S	Synchroscope
TLM	Telemeter
T	Temperature meter
TT	Total time
VH	Varhour meter
V	Voltmeter
VA	Volt-ammeter
VAR	Varmeter
VI	Volume indicator
VOM	Volt-ohm meter
VU	Standard volume indicator
W	Wattmeter
'H	Watthour meter

See Note.

PRINCIPLES OF ELECTRICITY AND MAGNETISM – UNITS

agnets and Magnetism. Any body which has the ability to attract iron or steel a magnet. The attractive ability of such a body is called magnetism. Certain m of iron ore sometimes possess the property when they are taken from the illu natural specimens will attract and hold iron filings and are called natural are c oadstones. The attraction for the filings will be greatest at two ends as from it Fig. 1B. The two ends that have the greatest attraction for the iron filings until the poles of the magnet. If a natural magnet were suspended by a string ing north that it were free to turn, it would be found that the magnet would turn pointing sou ugh its poles is lying north and south. The end or pole which is point- It is possible the north pole of the magnet, and the other end or pole, which is to magnetize a lled the south pole. the property of m tain means discussed in Sec. 24 to produce artificial magnets, i.e., permanent. Tempo iron or steel that did not originally in its natural state possess ism. Artificial magnets are of two types: (1) temporary and (2) magnets are those which will hold their magnetism only as

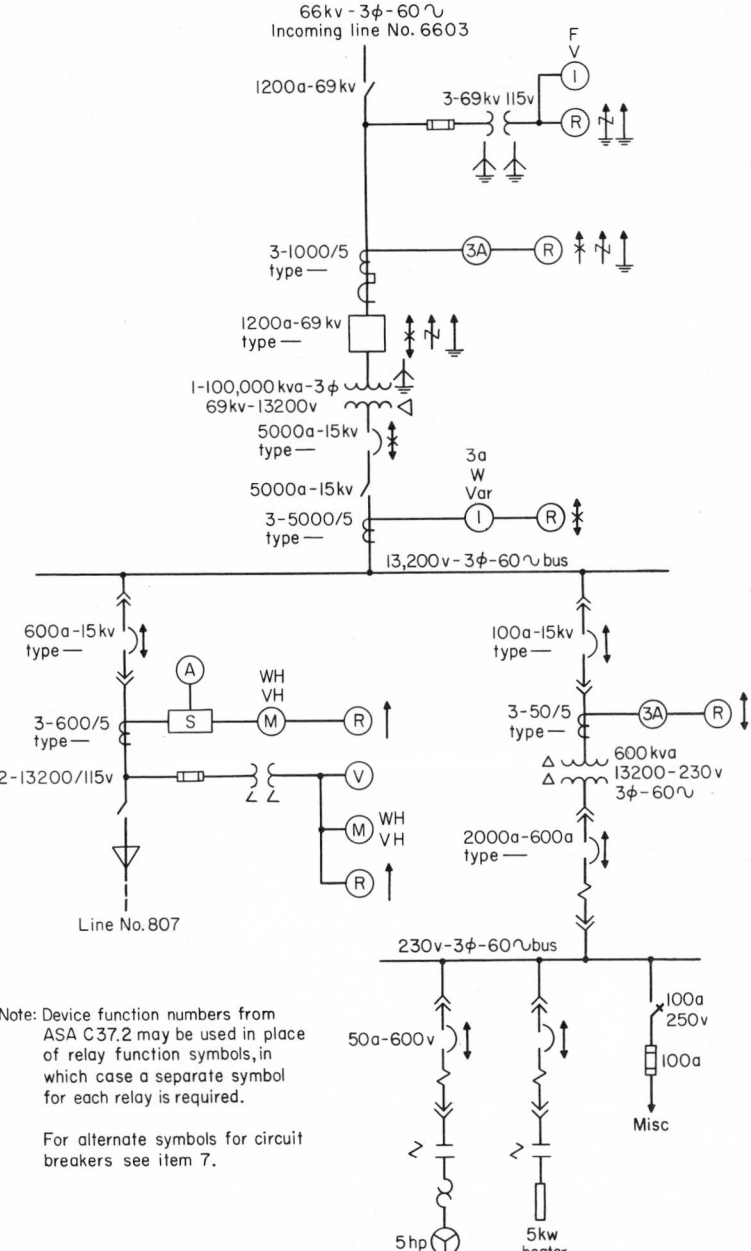

FIG. 1A *Typical single-line diagram for power equipment. (USA Standards Institute.)*

long as the magnetizing force is maintained. **Permanent magnets** are those which will hold their magnetism after the magnetizing force has been removed and continue to be magnets for a long period of time unless they are demagnetized by some means such as by being jarred or heated.

Any material that can be magnetized or that is attracted by a magnet is called a magnetic material.

FIG. 1B   *Loadstone with iron filings.*

22. Magnetic Field. The region around a magnet has peculiar properties that exist only as long as the magnet is present. This property of the region around a magnet is that there will be a force exerted upon any piece of magnetic material if it is placed in the space in proximity to the magnet. This property or condition of the space around a magnet is called a magnetic field. If a magnet is covered with a sheet of paper sprinkled with iron filings, the filings will arrange themselves in definite curves extending from pole to pole, as shown in Fig. 2. The direction taken by the filings shows the direction of the magnetic field, i.e., the direction of the force exerted upon a magnetic material if placed in the region around the magnet. The presence of this property (magnetic field) in the space around a magnet can be demonstrated by means of a compass needle. A compass needle is a small, light magnet suspended so that it can turn freely. If a compass needle is placed in the region around a magnet, it will turn into a definite position, thereby demonstrating that there is a force acting upon a magnetic material placed in the region around a magnet. The magnitude or strength of the magnetic field, i.e., the magnitude of the force exerted upon a magnetic material in the space around a magnet, will be different at different points. The field will be strongest at the poles.

The direction of a magnetic field at any point is the direction in which a force is exerted upon the north pole of a compass needle if placed at that point in the field. It will be the direction in which the north pole end of the axis of the compass needle points.

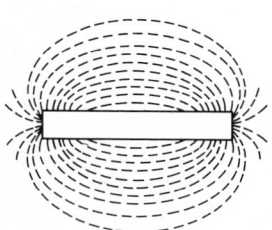

FIG. 2   *Arrangement of iron filings around a magnet.*

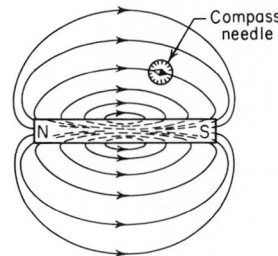

FIG. 3   *Lines of magnetic flux around a bar magnet.*

23. Magnetic Flux. The magnetic field of a magnet may be depicted by curved lines from the north to the south pole as shown in Fig. 3. Arrows placed on the lines, which are picturing the condition in the space, indicate the direction of the force that would be exerted upon the north pole of a compass needle at that point. The density with which the lines are drawn represent the magnitude of the field, i.e., the magnitude of the force that would be exerted upon a magnetic material placed at that point in the field. These lines, which picture the condition in the space around a magnet, are called lines of magnetic flux or simply magnetic flux.

24. Methods of Producing Artificial Magnets. A magnetic material can be magnetized to a certain degree by stroking it with a permanent magnet or by placing it in the field of another magnet. Either of these means will normally produce only relatively weak magnets. The general method of magnetizing a material or of producing a magnetic field is by means of passing an electric current through a coil of wire (see Secs. **85** and **86**).

25. The electron theory states that all matter is made of electricity. Matter is anything which has weight and occupies space according to the laws of physics. All matter is made up of molecules, of which there are millions of different kinds. Molecules are made up of atoms, of which there are a limited number. That is, there are only around 100 elements now known. All atoms are believed to be composed of electrons, which are minute particles of negative electricity which are, normally, held in place in each atom by a positively charged, electrical something which has been named the nucleus.

NOTE. The electrons thus interlocked in the atoms are, it is believed, constantly revolving at great speeds in orbits around the positive nuclei. In this, they may be thought of as resembling the eight satellites which rotate about the planet Saturn. In a normal atom the amount of negative electricity of the electrons is exactly neutralized by an equal amount of opposite or positive electricity of the nucleus. Thus a normal atom exhibits no external sign of electrification.

26. The different kinds of atoms (the atoms of the different elements) differ only in the number of and the arrangement of the electrons and in the magnitude of the positive nuclei which compose them. The lighter elements have few electrons; the heavier elements many. A normal atom of any given element always has the same number of electrons and a positive nucleus of the same magnitude.

Examples. An atom of hydrogen, the lightest element, it is believed, consists of one electron and a corresponding positive nucleus. An atom of uranium, the heaviest element, has probably 92 electrons and a corresponding greater positive nucleus.

27. Thus everything about us, all matter, is composed of electricity. The electrons can, under certain circumstances, be forced from the atoms. The positive nuclei, except under very special conditions (disruption of the atom), cannot be moved from the atom. Electrical phenomena occur when some of this electricity (electrons) is moved or when the electrical balance which normally obtains within the atoms is disturbed.

28. Electrons are exceedingly small. It is estimated that each has a diameter of about a thirteen million millionth of an inch $\left(\dfrac{1}{12,700,000,000,000} \text{ in.}\right)$. An electron weighs about one thirty billion billion billionth of an ounce

$$\left(\frac{1}{31,500,000,000,000,000,000,000,000,000} \text{ oz}\right)$$

or about an eighteen hundredth ($1/1845$) as much as does an atom of hydrogen.

29. Electricity cannot be generated. It is evident that there is in the universe a certain definite amount of electricity. Electricity can neither be created nor destroyed. It can, however, be forced to move and thus transmit power or produce electrical phenomena. Electrical energy (not electricity) can be generated (i.e., produced, from energy of some other form) by forcing electrons to move in certain paths.

30. An emf (electromotive force) is the force or pressure – measured in **volts** – which makes electrons move or tends to do so. Thus, if an emf is impressed across the two ends of a wire, it will force the electrons of the atoms which compose the wire to move from atom to atom, in the direction of the emf, along through the wire, assuming, of course, that a closed conducting path is provided. A lightning flash is merely a movement of electrons between the atoms of the atmosphere caused by an emf or voltage existing between the clouds and the earth.

31. An electric current – measured in **amperes** – consists of a movement or flow of electricity. Thus the thing which we call an electric current is merely a shifting of electricity. An electric current could consist of the motion of only negative electricity, of the motion of only positive electricity, or of the motion in opposite directions of both negative and positive electricity. The effects of the current would be the same in all cases. In most cases current consists of a motion of electrons, negative electricity.

32. Electric currents may be divided into two general classes: (1) direct currents, (2) alternating currents.

33. A direct current is one which flows always in the same direction.

34. An alternating current is one the direction of which is reversed at regular intervals.

35. Further classifications of direct currents are (1) continuous currents, which are steady, nonpulsating, direct currents; (2) constant currents, which continue to flow for a considerable time in the same direction and with unvarying intensity; (3) pulsating currents, which are regularly varying continuous currents.

36. The coulomb is the name which has been given to the unit of quantity of electricity. It is somewhat analogous to our unit of quantity of water — the gallon. A coulomb of electricity, so calculations show, comprises approximately six million million million electrons. However, it is **rate of flow,** which is measured in amperes, that is of importance to the electrician rather than the total quantity of electricity which flows. Hence, the unit coulomb is almost never directly used in practical work.

37. The ampere is the name which has been given to the practical unit of rate of flow of electricity, and it is analogous to "gallons per minute" in hydraulics. The ampere represents a rate of flow of 1 coulomb per second. That is, it is equivalent to a flow of six million million million electrons per second. It has been internationally agreed (recommended by the Chicago International Electrical Congress of 1893 and legalized by act of Congress 1894) that the ampere shall be defined as "that unvarying current, which, when passed through a solution of nitrate of silver in water in accordance with standard specifications, deposits silver at the rate of one thousand one hundred and eighteen millionths (0.001118) of a gram per second."

The ampere, also, is that unvarying current which when passed through two straight parallel conductors of infinite length and negligible cross section, located at a distance of 1 meter from each other in vacuum, will produce a force between the conductors of 2×10^{-7} newton per meter of length.

NOTE. The flow of water in a pipe is measured by the quantity of water which flows through it in a second, as 1 gal per sec, 8 gal per sec, etc. Similarly, the flow of electricity in a circuit is measured by the amount of electricity that flows through it in a second, as: 1 coulomb per second.

Examples. If 2 coulombs flow in a second, then the average rate of flow is 2 coulombs per second and the average current is 2 amp. If 20 coulombs flow per second, then the current is 20 amp, etc.

Examples. The current flowing in an ordinary 40-watt incandescent Mazda lamp is about ⅓ amp. Series street-lighting lamps require from 6.6 to 20 amp. The current in a telegraph wire is approximately 0.04 amp.

38. Resistance, R or r, is the name which has been given to that opposition which is offered by the internal structure of the different materials of the earth to the movement of electricity through them, i.e., to the maintenance of an electric current in them. This opposition results in electrical energy being converted into heat in accordance with the formula $W = I^2R$, where W = watts; I = intensity of current expressed in amperes; and R = ohms of resistance.

The electrons of some materials, the metals for example, can be moved from atom to atom within the material with relative ease, i.e., by the application of a small emf. All materials offer some opposition to the maintenance of a current through them, and there is no material in which some current cannot be produced, although it may be very minute.

39. Conductors is the name given to those materials through which it is relatively easy to maintain an electric current.

40. Insulators is the name given to those materials through which it is very difficult to produce an electric current. Some examples of good insulating materials are glass, mica, and porcelain.

41. A resistor is an object having resistance; specifically, a resistor is a conductor inserted in a circuit to introduce resistance. A rheostat is a resistor so arranged that its effective resistance can be varied.

42. The ohm is the name which has been given to the practical unit of electrical resistance. A resistance of 1 ohm is that opposition which will result in electrical energy being converted into heat at the rate of 1 watt per ampere of effective current. In any circuit the rate at which electrical energy is converted into heat is given by the formula $W = I^2R$ of Sec. 38.

It has been agreed that the International Ohm shall be represented by the resistance offered to an unvarying electric current by a column of mercury, at the temperature of

0°C, which has a mass of 14.4521 grams, a constant cross section, and a length of 106.3 cm.

43. Impedance, Z or z, is the name which has been given to the total opposition of a circuit or part of a circuit to the passage of an electric current through it, caused by the combined effects of the characteristics of the circuit of resistance, inductance, and capacitance. Impedance is measured in ohms.

44. Self-inductance is the phenomenon whereby an emf is induced in a circuit by a change of current in the circuit itself. This emf is always in such a direction that it opposes the change of current which produces it.

Whenever current passes through a conductor, it tends to set up a magnetic field around the conductor. If the current through the conductor changes, the flux produced by it will change. The change in the flux will produce a voltage in the conductor. This voltage is the voltage of self-induction. Since inductance has an effect only when the current in the conductor is changing, inductance will have no effect on a closed d-c circuit but will have an effect in a-c circuits where the current is always changing from instant to instant.

45. Inductance L is defined as the property of a circuit that causes a voltage to be induced in the circuit by a change of current in the circuit. The henry is the unit of inductance. A circuit has an inductance of 1 henry when, if the current is changed at the rate of 1 amp per sec, 1 volt will be induced in the circuit.

46. Inductive reactance x_L is the name given to the opposition to the flow of changing current due to inductance. It is measured in ohms the same as resistance.

47. Capacitance C is the phenomenon whereby a circuit stores electrical energy. Whenever two conducting materials are separated by an insulating material, they have this ability of storing electrical energy. Such an arrangement of materials (two conductors separated by an insulator) is called a capacitor or condenser. If a source of d-c voltage is connected between the two conducting materials of a capacitor, a current will flow for a certain length of time. The initial current will be relatively large but will rapidly diminish to zero. A certain amount of electrical energy will then be stored in the capacitor. If the source of voltage is removed and the conductors of the capacitor are connected to the two ends of a resistor, a current will then flow from the capacitor through the resistor for a certain length of time. The initial current will be relatively large but will rapidly diminish to zero. The direction of the current will be opposite to the direction of the current when the capacitor was being charged by the d-c source. When the current reaches zero, the capacitor will have dissipated the energy which was stored in it as heat energy in the resistor. The capacitor will then be said to be discharged.

The two conducting materials, often called the plates of the capacitor, will be electrically charged when electrical energy is stored in the capacitor. One plate will have an excess of positive electricity and therefore will be positively charged with a certain number of coulombs of excess positive electricity. The other plate will have an excess of negative electricity and therefore will be negatively charged with an equal number of coulombs of excess negative electricity. When in this state the capacitor is said to be charged. When a capacitor is charged, a voltage will be present between the two conductors, plates, of the capacitor.

When a capacitor is in a discharged state, no electrical energy is stored in it, and there will be no potential difference, no voltage, between its plates. Each plate will contain just as much positive as negative electricity, and neither plate will have any electric charge.

From the above discussion it is seen that a capacitor has a sustained current only as long as the voltage is changing. A capacitor connected to a d-c supply will not have a sustained current. In an a-c circuit, the voltage is continually changing from instant to instant. Therefore, when a capacitor is connected to an a-c supply, an alternating current continues to flow. The current is first in one direction, charging the capacitor, and then in the opposite direction, discharging the capacitor.

48. The farad is the unit of capacitance. It is designated by the symbol C. A circuit or capacitor will have a capacitance of 1 farad if, when the voltage across it is increased 1 volt, its stored electricity is increased by 1 coulomb. Another definition for a capacitance of 1 farad, which results in the same effect, is given below. A circuit or capacitor will have a capacitance of 1 farad when, if the voltage impressed upon it is changed at the rate of 1 volt per sec, 1 amp of charging current flows.

49. Capacitive reactance X_C is the name given to the opposition to the flow of alternating current due to capacity. It is measured in ohms the same as resistance and inductive reactance.

50. The ohm is the unit in which all opposition to the maintenance of an electric current is measured. A circuit or part of a circuit has an opposition of 1 ohm when an emf of 1 volt will produce an effective current of 1 ampere. In any circuit or part of a circuit the current is equal to the emf in volts divided by the total opposition in ohms. Thus,

$$I = \frac{E}{Z} \qquad E = IZ \qquad Z = \frac{E}{I} \qquad (7)$$

Although all opposition to electric current is measured in ohms, the nature of the two types, resistive opposition and reactive opposition, are quite different. Resistance results in loss of electric energy from the circuit. Reactance results in the interchange of energy between electromagnetic fields and the circuit. It does not result in loss of energy from the circuit. Inductive reactance results in the interchange of energy between a magnetic field and a circuit. Capacitive reactance results in the interchange of energy between an electric field and a circuit. Current passing through any type of opposition results in loss of voltage, voltage drop.

51. The volt is the unit of emf, i.e., it is the unit whereby the tendency to establish and maintain electric currents may be measured. The ampere and the ohm having been arbitrarily defined as previously stated, the volt may now be readily defined:

By international agreement it has been decided that 1 volt shall be taken as that emf which will establish a current of 1 amp through a resistance of 1 ohm.

52. Admittance, Y or y, is the name given to the quantity which is the reciprocal of impedance. It expresses the ease with which an emf can produce a current in an electric circuit. It is measured in a unit called the mho. A circuit or part of a circuit has an admittance of 1 mho when an emf of 1 volt will produce an effective current of 1 ampere. In any circuit or part of a circuit the current is equal to the emf in volts multiplied by the total admittance in mhos. Thus,

$$I = EY \qquad E = \frac{I}{Y} \qquad Y = \frac{I}{E} \qquad (8)$$

53. Conductance, G or g, is the component of the admittance which results in loss of power from the circuit in the form of heat. It is measured in mhos. For a d-c circuit conductance becomes the reciprocal of the resistance.

54. Susceptance, B or b, is the component of the admittance which results in no loss of power from the circuit. It is measured in mhos. It does not exist for a d-c circuit.

55. Conductivity. The relative ease with which an electric current can be passed through a material is called its percentage conductivity. The conductivity of pure annealed copper is taken as the base of reference, so that pure annealed copper is said to have 100 per cent conductivity. Copper of 100 per cent conductivity has a resistance of 10.371 ohms per cir mil-ft at 20°C. The resistance per circular mil-foot of any material can be found, if its percentage conductivity is known, by dividing 10.371 by the percentage conductivity of the material.

56. Work is the overcoming of mechanical resistance through a certain distance. Work is measured by the product of the mechanical resistance times the space through which it is overcome. Work is measured by the product of the moving force times the distance through which the force acts in overcoming the resistance. Work is, therefore, measured in foot-pounds (ft-lb).

Example. What work is done if a weight of 6 lb is lifted through a distance of 8 ft?
Solution. Work = ft × lb = 8 × 6 = 48 ft-lb.

Example. If 20 gal of water is pumped to a vertical height of 32 ft, what work has been done?
Solution. A gallon of water weighs 8 lb. Therefore

$$\text{Work} = \text{ft} \times \text{lb} = 32 \times (20 \times 8) = 5{,}120 \text{ ft-lb}$$

Example. If the piston in a steam engine travels 1½ ft during a certain interval, and the total pressure on the piston is 40,000 lb, what work is done during the interval?

Solution. Work = ft × lb = 1.5 × 40,000 = 60,000 ft-lb.

57. Energy is capacity for doing work. Any body or medium which is of itself capable of doing work is said to possess energy. A coiled clock spring possesses energy because, in unwinding, it can do work. A moving projectile possesses energy because it can overcome the resistance offered by the air, by armor plate, etc., and thus do work. A charged storage battery possesses energy because it can furnish electric energy to operate a motor. Energy can be expressed in foot-pounds.

58. Power is the time rate of doing work. The faster work is done, the greater the power that will be required to do it. For example, if a 10-hp motor can raise a loaded elevator a certain distance in 2 min, a 20-hp motor will (approximately) be required to raise it the same distance in 1 min.

59. The horsepower is the unit of power and is about equal to the power of a strong horse to do work for a short interval. Numerically hp is 33,000 ft-lb per min = 550 ft-lb per sec = 1,980,000 ft-lb per hr. Expressed as a formula,

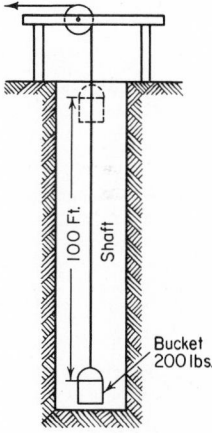

FIG. 4   *Bucket in shaft.*

$$\text{Hp} = \frac{L \times W}{33,000 \times t} = \frac{\text{ft-lb per min}}{33,000} \qquad (9)$$

where hp = horsepower; L = distance in feet through which W is raised or overcome; W = weight in pounds of the thing lifted or the push or pull in pounds of the force overcome; and t is the time in minutes required to move or overcome the weight W through the distance L.

Example. What horsepower is required in raising the load and bucket weighing 200 lb shown in Fig. 4 from the bottom to the top of the shaft, a distance of 100 ft, in 2 min?

Solution. Substitute in the formula:

$$\text{Hp} = \frac{L \times W}{33,000 \times t} = \frac{100 \times 200}{33,000 \times 2} = 0.3 \text{ hp}$$

Example. What average horsepower is required while moving the box loaded with stone, Fig. 5, from A to B, 650 ft, in 3 min? It takes a horizontal pull of 150 to move the box.

Solution. Substitute in the formula:

$$\text{Hp} = \frac{L \times W}{33,000 \times t} = \frac{650 \times 150}{33,000 \times 3} = 0.98 \text{ hp}$$

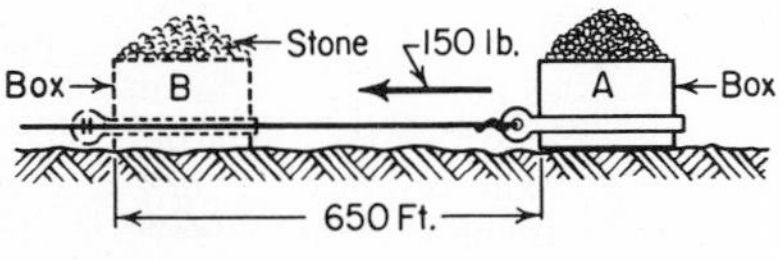

FIG. 5   *Moving loaded box.*

60. Electric power is the rate of doing electrical work. The unit is the watt or kilowatt. A kilowatt is 1,000 watts. Work is being done at the rate of 1 watt when a constant current of 1 amp is maintained through a resistance by an emf of 1 volt.

61. Energy of one sort may be transformed into energy of another sort. Heat energy in coal may be transformed (with a certain loss), with a boiler, a steam engine, and a generator, into electrical energy. The energy possessed by a stream of falling water may be transformed, with a water wheel and generator, into electrical energy. There is a definite numerical relation between different sorts of energy. Thus 1 Btu (the unit of heat energy) = 778 ft-lb. In electrical units, energy is expressed in watthours or kilowatthours.

62. A kilowatthour represents the energy expended if work is done for 1 hr at the rate of 1 kw.

63. A horsepower-hour represents the energy expended if work is done for 1 hr at the rate of 1 hp. One horsepower-hour therefore equals 60 × 33,000 = 1,980,000 ft-lb.

64. To Reduce Horsepower to Watts and Kilowatts and Vice Versa. One horsepower equals 746 watts; therefore

$$Hp = \frac{watts}{746} = watts \times 0.00134$$

$$Watts = hp \times 746 \qquad (10)$$

$$Hp = \frac{kw}{0.746} = kw \times 1.34$$

$$Kw = hp \times 0.746 \qquad (11)$$

Example. Watts = 2,460; hp = ?
Solution. Substitute in formula:

$$Hp = \frac{watts}{746} = 2,460 \div 746 = 3.3 \text{ hp}$$

Example. A motor takes 30 kw. How many horsepower is it taking?
Solution. Substitute in the formula:

$$Hp = \frac{kw}{0.746} = 30 \div 0.746 = 40.24 \text{ hp}$$

Or instead, using the other formula:

$$Hp = kw \times 1.34 = 30 \times 1.34 = 40.2 \text{ hp}$$

65. Efficiency is the name given to the ratio of output to input. No machine gives out as much useful energy or power as is put into it. There are some losses in even the most perfectly constructed machines.

$$Efficiency = \frac{output}{input} \qquad (12)$$

Although efficiency is basically a decimal quantity and is so used in making calculations, nevertheless it is usually expressed as a percentage. Percentage efficiency is equal to the decimal expression of efficiency multiplied by 100. An efficiency of 0.80 expressed as a decimal is an efficiency of 80 per cent expressed in percentage.

Basically efficiency deals with energy. However, when the rate of energy conversion is constant, the values of output and input in terms of power may be used in dealing with efficiency.

$$Input = \frac{output}{efficiency} \qquad (13)$$

and $$Output = input \times efficiency \qquad (14)$$

When the formulas are used, output and input must be expressed in the same units and efficiency as a decimal.

66. Output is the useful energy or power delivered by a machine, and **input** is the energy or power supplied to a machine.

Example. If 45 kw is supplied to a motor and its output is found to be 54.2 hp, what is its efficiency?
Solution. Since 1 hp = 0.746 kw, 54.2 hp = 54.2 × 0.75 = 40.6 kw. Then, substituting in the formula,

$$Efficiency = \frac{output}{input} = \frac{40.6}{45} = 0.90 = 90 \text{ per cent}$$

67. Torque is the measure of the tendency of a body to rotate. It is the measure of a turning or twisting effort and is usually expressed in pound-feet or in pounds force at a given radius. Torque is expressed as the product of the force tending to produce rotation times the distance from the center of rotation to the point of application of the force. Thus in Fig. 6 there is a torque of 50 × 1 = 50 lb-ft tending to turn the windlass due to the weight attached to the rope. In the motor of Fig. 7 the group of conductors under the north pole produces a combined force of 10 lb. The torque produced by this group of conductors will be $10 \times \frac{9}{12} = 7.5$ lb-ft. The group of conductors under the

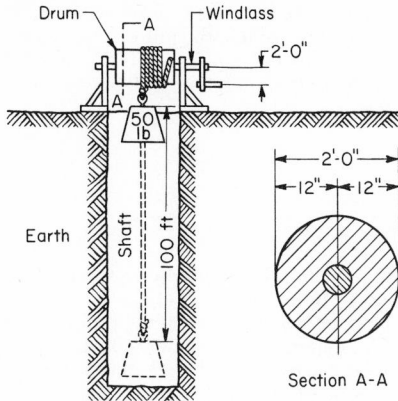

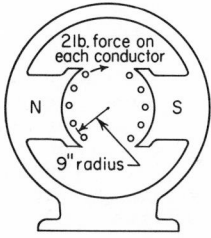

FIG. 6 *Example of work and torque.*

FIG. 7 *Torque produced by the force on the conductors of a motor.*

south pole will similarly produce $10 \times \frac{9}{12} = 7.5$ lb-ft. Both of these torques tend to produce rotation in the same direction. Therefore, the total torque produced by the motor will be $7.5 + 7.5 = 15$ lb-ft.

Torque exists even if there is no motion. Thus, in Fig. 6 the torque exerted by the weight is 50 lb-ft as long as the weight is supported, whether the drum is moving or standing still. In the motor of Fig. 7 a torque of 15 lb-ft is exerted upon the armature tending to produce rotation, whether the motor is revolving or standing still. If there is no rotation, no work can be done, yet there is torque tending to produce rotation.

68. Relation between Horsepower and Torque.

$$\text{Hp} = \frac{6.28 \times \text{rpm} \times T}{33,000} \tag{15}$$

or

$$T = \frac{33,000 \text{ hp}}{6.28 \times \text{rpm}} \tag{16}$$

where $T = $ torque in lb-ft.

Example. What is the torque of a 10-hp motor if delivering full load at 1,150 rpm?

$$T = \frac{33,000 \times 10}{6.28 \times 1,150} = 45.7 \text{ lb-ft}$$

69. Torque and Force Relations in Mechanisms. In any mechanism such as the windlass of Fig. 6 or a motor belted or geared to a load, if the losses are neglected so that the efficiency is 100 per cent, the power output will be equal to the power input. For such a perfect mechanism the following relations will hold true:

$$T_1 \times \text{rpm}_1 = T_2 \times \text{rpm}_2 \tag{17}$$

or

$$\frac{T_1}{T_2} = \frac{\text{rpm}_2}{\text{rpm}_1}$$

where $T_1 = $ torque at point 1 in the mechanism; $\text{rpm}_1 = $ rpm at point 1 in the mechanism; $T_2 = $ torque at point 2 in the mechanism; and $\text{rpm}_2 = $ rpm at point 2 in the mechanism.

In the windlass of Fig. 6 the rpm for all points in the mechanism are the same. Therefore the torque at any point is equal to the torque at any other point. The torque that must be exerted at the handle of the windlass in order to raise the weight at a uniform rate of speed would have to be equal to the torque exerted by the weight. This is neglecting the weight of the rope and the friction. The force that must be exerted on the handle will be $\frac{50}{2} = 25$ lb.

The motor of Fig. 7 is equipped with a pulley on the shaft for driving a belt. The pulley has a diameter of 6 in. The force exerted upon the belt (the tension of the belt) would be determined in the following manner: Since the rpm of the pulley is the same as the rpm of the motor armature, the torque produced by the conductors is the same as the torque exerted by the pulley. The force on the belt is therefore 15/0.5 = 30 lb.

70. Emfs may be produced in the following ways:
1. Electromagnetic induction.
2. Thermal action.
3. Chemical action.
4. Changing electric fields.
5. Contact between unlike substances.
6. Vibration or heating of crystals.

71. Emfs may be produced by electromagnetic induction in the following three ways:
1. By moving a conductor across a magnetic field. If the conductor of Fig. 8 is moved up or down so as to cut the lines of flux of the magnetic field between the poles of the magnet, an emf will be generated between the two ends of the conductor. This is the method employed for the production of voltage in d-c generators (see Sec. **74**).

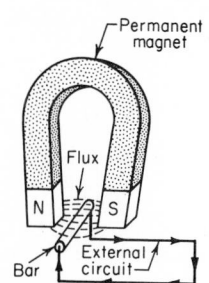

FIG. 8   *Emf generated by magnetic flux.*

2. By moving a magnetic field across a conductor. If in Fig. 8 the conductor is held stationary and the magnet is moved up or down so that the lines of flux of the magnetic field between the poles of the magnet will cut the conductor, an emf will be generated between the two ends of the conductor. This is the method employed for the production of voltage in most a-c generators (see Sec. **144**).

3. By changing the strength of the magnetic field linked with a conductor. If in Fig. 9 an alternating electric current is passed through winding A, this current will set up a magnetic field through the iron ring. This magnetic field will be continually changing in strength, owing to the changing magnitude of the current. There will therefore be a continual change in the magnetic flux linked with winding B. This change in the magnetic flux linked with B will generate a voltage between the two ends of winding B. It is this phenomenon that makes possible the operation of transformers (see the division on Transformers).

Wherever large quantities of electrical energy are required, the necessary emf is produced by one of the means of electromagnetic induction.

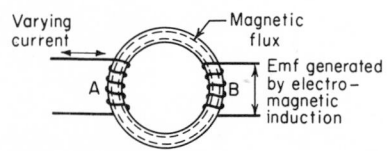

FIG. 9   *Method of producing an emf by electromagnetic induction.*

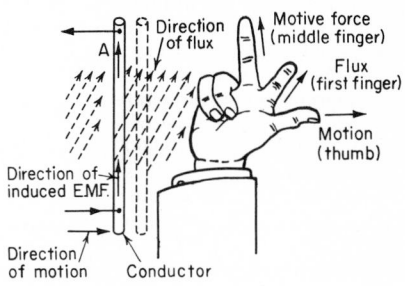

FIG. 10   *Application of right-hand rule.*

72. A Hand Rule to Determine the Direction of an Induced Emf (see Fig. 10). Use the **right hand.** Extend the thumb in the direction of the motion, or of the equivalent motion, of the conductor and extend the forefinger in the direction of the magnetic flux. Then the middle finger will point in the direction of the induced emf. (Magnetic flux flows from the north (N) to the south (S) pole outside a magnet; from south to north inside the magnet.) This rule can be remembered by associating the sounds of the following word groups: thumb—motion, forefinger—force, and middle finger—motive force. This is also known as Fleming's rule.

73. A-C Generator (Alternator). A very simple elementary a-c generator is shown in Fig. 11. As the conductors are revolved through the magnetic field, a voltage will be produced in each conductor. Considering the series circuit formed by the two conductors, the voltages produced by the two conductors will act to send current through the circuit in the same direction. The total voltage between the terminals of the ma-

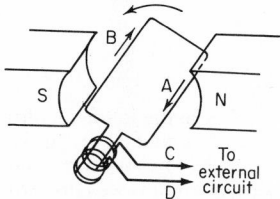

FIG. 11 *Elementary a-c generator.*

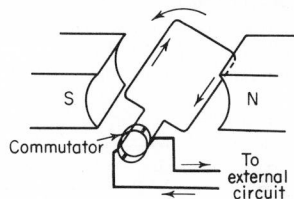

FIG. 12 *Elementary d-c generator.*

chine will be the summation of the voltages produced by the two conductors at that instant. As long as conductor A is under the north pole and conductor B is under the south pole, there will be a terminal voltage which will send current through the external circuit from C to D. When the conductors are midway between poles, they will not be cutting any flux and no voltage will be produced. As conductor A moves under the south pole and conductor B under the north pole, the conductors will again be cutting flux and there will again be voltages produced in the conductors. The direction of these voltages will, however, be just opposite to the direction of the voltages when A was under the north pole and B under the south pole. The terminal voltage of the machine is therefore periodically reversing in direction, and the machine is an a-c generator.

74. A d-c generator (dynamo) is shown in Fig. 12. The production of voltage in the conductors is exactly the same as for the elementary a-c generator of Sec. **73.** As the conductors revolve, an alternating voltage is produced in them. In order that the terminal voltage can always act upon the external load in the same direction, some device must be inserted between the conductors and the terminals. This device must reverse the connections of the conductors to the external circuit at the instant when the voltage of the conductors is zero and changing in direction. Such a device is called a commutator.

75. The magnitude of the voltage produced by electromagnetic induction depends upon the rate at which the lines of flux are cut by the conductor. Whenever 100,000,000 lines of flux are cut per second, 1 volt is produced. The voltage produced is therefore equal to the number of lines of flux cut per second divided by 100,000,000.

76. Emfs are produced by thermal action in the following ways:

1. **Seebeck Effect.** In a closed circuit consisting of two different metals, an emf will be produced if the two junctions between the different metals are kept at different temperatures (see Fig. 13). Thermocouples function through this phenomenon. The magnitude of the emf produced will depend upon the material of the

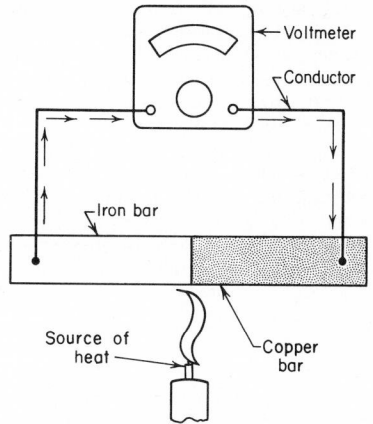

FIG. 13 *Emf generated by heat.*

metals and the difference in temperature between the hot junction and the cold ends. Only very small voltages can be produced in this way, so that the method is not applicable where electrical energy of any quantity is required. However, this method is of great practical value for application in temperature measurements.

2. **Peltier Effect.** When current passes through the junction between two different metals, energy conversion takes place between energy in heat form and energy in electric form. The action is reversible, and the direction of energy conversion depends upon the direction in which the current passes across the junction. This phenomenon is entirely different and distinct from the conversion of electric energy into heat caused by the passage of a current through the resistance of the junction of the two materials.

3. **Thomson Effect.** When the temperature along a metallic conductor varies in magnitude, a very small emf is produced.

77. Emfs Produced by Chemical Action. Certain combinations of chemicals will generate emfs. For instance, if a piece of zinc (Fig. 14) and a piece of carbon are immersed in a solution of sal ammoniac, there will be an emf produced between the zinc and the carbon. Such a combination is called a battery. If the key in Fig. 14 is closed, an electric current will flow and the bell will ring. The voltage of dry cells and storage batteries is produced in this way by chemical action.

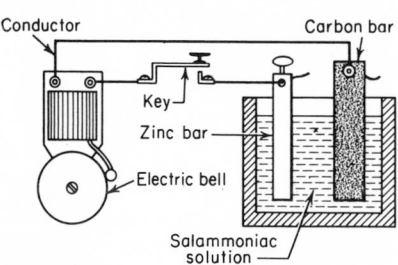

FIG. 14   *Emf generated by chemical action.*

78. Emfs Produced by Electric Fields. Whenever there is a voltage between two conductors, there are certain conditions produced in the space around and between the conductors. This condition in the surrounding space is called an electric field. A discussion and explanation of this phenomenon are outside the scope of this book. However, emfs produced by changes in this electric field are of great practical importance, since these changes induce changing voltages in neighboring conductors. Voltages are produced by this means in telephone lines from neighboring electric power lines and may cause serious interference with communication over the telephone lines.

79. Contact Emf. When any two different materials are brought into contact with each other, a very small emf is produced. However, voltages of considerable magnitude may be produced by this phenomenon by the rapid rubbing together of different materials. The rubbing results in rapid change of the contact points between the two materials and thus in an accumulation of the small individual contact emfs into a voltage of considerable magnitude. Practical illustrations of voltages produced by this means are voltages on belts produced by the motion of the belt over the pulleys between automobile bodies and the ground produced by the revolution of the rubber tires over the road. These voltages often are called frictional voltages.

80. Emfs Produced by Crystals. Certain crystals, such as quartz and rochelle salt crystals, have the property of producing very small emfs between opposite faces of the crystals when the crystals are subjected to a pressure. Certain crystals, such as tourmaline, when heated produce a very small emf between opposite faces. Although emfs produced by these means are of very small magnitude, still they are of great practical value in microphones and instruments for the measurement of vibrations in machinery.

81. Emf, which is measured in volts, causes electricity to flow. A higher voltage is required to force a given current of electricity through a small wire than through a large one. If the voltage impressed on a circuit is increased the current will be correspondingly increased (see Fig. 15).

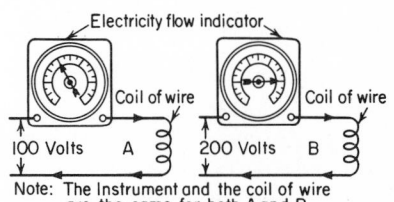

FIG. 15   *Illustrating the effect of increasing voltage.*

82. The distinction between amperes and volts should be clearly understood. The amperes represent the rate of electricity flow (see Secs. **31** and **37**) through a circuit, while the volts represent the tendency causing the flow. There may be a tendency (voltage) and yet no current. If the path of electricity is blocked by an open switch (Fig. 16), there will be no current of electricity, though the tendency to produce (voltage) may be high. With a given voltage a greater current of electricity will flow through a large wire than through a small one.

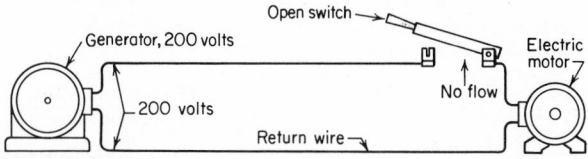

FIG. 16 *Electricity flow blocked by an open switch.*

83. Direction of Electric Current. Although in most cases current consists of the actual motion of negative electricity in a certain direction, the conventional direction of a current is the direction in which positive electricity would move in order to result in the same effects as are produced by the actual motion of electricity. The direction of current, therefore, as it is usually considered, is in the opposite direction to the motion of the electrons.

84. Symbols for indicating the direction of an emf or currents into or out of the end of a conductor are shown in Fig. 17.

85. Effects of an Electric Current. The two principal effects of an electric current are (1) heating effect and (2) magnetic effect.

Whenever an electric current passes through a material, there is a heating effect due to the current. This effect is indicated by the increase in temperature of the material. A certain portion of the electrical energy that is put into the circuit is transformed into heat energy owing to the opposition offered to the flow of current by the resistance of the material. This loss of electrical energy (transferred to

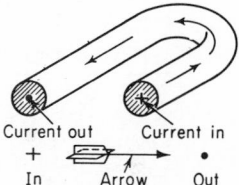

FIG. 17 *Symbols indicating direction of current flow.*

heat energy) is associated with a drop in voltage. This drop in voltage is produced by the amount of voltage that is required to force the current through the resistance. This heating effect with its associated drop of voltage and temperature rise of the material always takes place any time a current is passed through a circuit. These are also known as I^2R (watts) or IR (drop losses).

There is an association between electricity and magnetism because a magnetic field can be produced by an electric current. In fact, whenever an electric current is passed through a conductor, the electric current tends to set up a magnetic field around the conductor. The presence of this field can be demonstrated by holding a compass near a wire that is carrying a current (Fig. 23). The compass needle will be deflected in a definite direction with the direction of current flow.

86. Magnetic Effect of Electric Current. The magnetic lines of flux (magnetic field) that are produced by a current passing through a straight wire can be determined by passing the wire through a sheet of paper upon which iron filings are sprinkled as illustrated in Fig. 18. The direction of the lines of flux will be in concentric circles around the axis of the conductor. The field will be strongest close to the conductor.

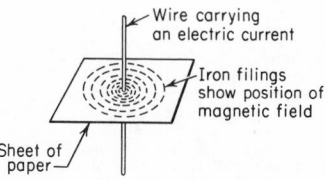

FIG. 18 *Magnetic field around a conductor.*

If the current is passed through a coil of wire wound around a piece of iron, as in Fig. 19, it will be found that the iron is magnetized in a definite direction. Such a magnet is called an electromagnet. This is the method always employed for producing strong magnets or setting up strong magnetic fields. A coil of wire carrying current will act like a magnet and will produce a magnetic north pole at one end and a magnetic south pole at the other (see Fig. 20). The direction of the magnetic field produced will be from the north pole end around through the space outside of the coil to the south pole end and thence back through the interior of the coil to the north pole end.

87. Hand Rule for Direction of Magnetic Field about a Straight Wire (see Fig. 21). If a wire through which electricity is flowing is so grasped with the **right hand** that the thumb points in the direction of electricity flow, the fingers will point in the direction of the magnetic field and vice versa.

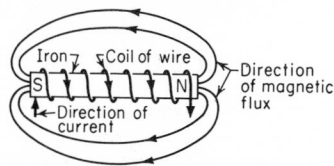

FIG. 19 *Elementary electromagnet.*

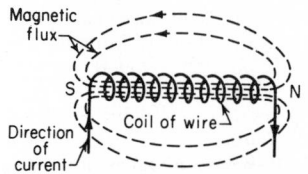

FIG. 20 *Magnetic field from current flowing through a coil of wire.*

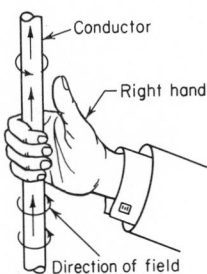

FIG. 21 *Hand rule for direction of field.*

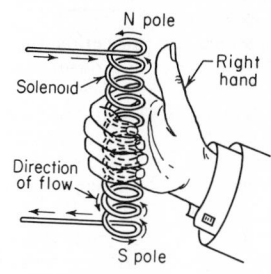

FIG. 22 *Hand rule for determining polarity of a solenoid.*

88. Hand Rule for Polarity of a Solenoid or Electromagnet (see Fig. 22). If a solenoid or an electromagnet is so grasped with the **right hand** that the fingers point in the direction of the current, the thumb will point in the direction of the magnetic field through the solenoid, i.e., toward the north pole of the solenoid.

89. Rule for Determining Direction of Current Flow with a Compass (see Fig. 23). If a compass is placed under a conductor in which electricity is flowing from south to north, the north end of the needle will be deflected to the west. If the compass is placed over the conductor, the north end of the compass will be deflected to the east. If the direction of current flow in the conductor is reversed, the direction of deflection of the needle will be reversed correspondingly.

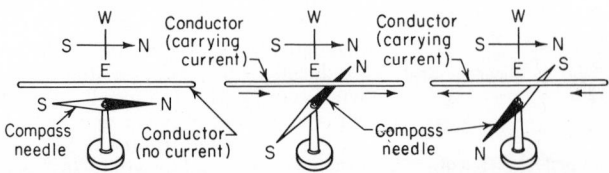

FIG. 23 *Performance of a compass needle near a conductor.*

90. The resistances of different materials vary greatly. Some, such as the metals, conduct electricity very readily and hence are called conductors. Others such as wood or slate are, at least when moist, partial conductors. Still others, such as glass, porcelain, and paraffin, are called insulators because they are practically nonconducting. No material is a perfect conductor and no material is a perfect insulator (see Sec. **38**).

The resistance of a conductor depends not only upon the material of the conductor but also upon the dimensions of the conductor and the distribution of the current throughout the cross section of the conductor. The resistance of a given conductor will have its minimum value when the current is uniformly distributed throughout the cross section of the conductor. Uniform current distribution exists in the conductors of most d-c circuits. In the conductors of a-c circuits the current never is exactly uniformly distributed. The resistance of a circuit to alternating current is always somewhat greater than it is to direct current (refer to Sec. **122**). The amount that the a-c resistance is greater than the d-c value depends upon several factors.

Unless otherwise stated, values of resistance should be taken as the resistance for uniform distribution of the current. They are the values to use for d-c circuits.

The resistance of materials also depends upon the temperature of the material.

91. A circular mil is the area of a circle $\frac{1}{1000}$ in. in diameter. A mil is $\frac{1}{1000}$ of an inch (see Fig. 24). The areas of electric conductors are usually measured in circular mils. Since the area of any figure varies as the square of its similar dimensions, the area of any

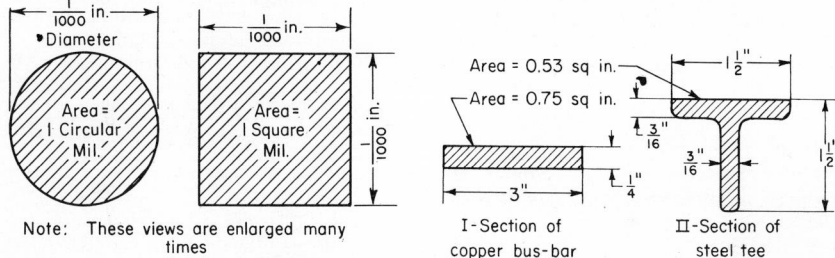

FIG. 24   *Circular mil and square mil.*   FIG. 25   *Conductor sections.*

circle can be expressed in circular mils by squaring its diameter expressed in thousandths. Thus, since $\frac{3}{8} = \frac{375}{1000} = 0.375$, the area of a circle $\frac{3}{8}$ in. in diameter would be $375 \times 375 = 140{,}625$ cir mils. The area of a circle 0.005 in. in diameter would be $5 \times 5 = 25$ cir mils.

92. A square mil is the area of a square having sides $\frac{1}{1000}$ in. long (see Fig. 24). Areas of rectangular conductors are sometimes measured in square mils. Areas in square mils are obtained by multiplying together the length and breadth of the rectangle expressed in thousandths of an inch. Thus, the area of a rectangle $\frac{1}{2}$ in. wide and 2 in. long would be $500 \times 2{,}000 = 1{,}000{,}000$ sq mils. In actual area, a circular mil is about $\frac{8}{10}$ as great as a square mil.

93. To reduce square mils or square inches to circular mils, or the reverse, apply one of the following formulas.

$$\text{Sq mils} = \text{cir mils} \times 0.7854 \tag{18}$$

$$\text{Cir mils} = \frac{\text{sq mils}}{0.7854} \tag{19}$$

$$\text{Cir mils} = \frac{\text{sq in.}}{0.0000007854} \tag{20}$$

$$\text{Sq in.} = \text{cir mils} \times 0.0000007854 \tag{21}$$

Example. The sectional area of the bus bar, in Fig. 25, I, is, in circular mils:

Cir mils $= (\text{sq in.})/(0.0000007854) = (3 \times \frac{1}{4}) \div 0.0000007854$

$$= 0.75 \div 0.0000007854 = 955{,}000 \text{ cir mils}$$

Example. The sectional area of the steel *T*, shown in Fig. 25, II, in circular mils is:

Cir mils $= \text{sq in.} \div 0.0000007854 = 0.53 \div 0.0000007854 = 674{,}800 \text{ cir mils}$

94. The circular mil-foot (cir mil-ft) is the unit conductor. A wire having a sectional area of 1 cir mil and a length of 1 ft is a circular mil-foot of conductor. The resistance of a circular mil-foot of a metal is sometimes called its **specific resistance** or its **resistivity.** The resistance of a circular mil-foot of copper under different conditions is given in Fig. 26. Resistances for other metals and alloys are given in Table **99**.

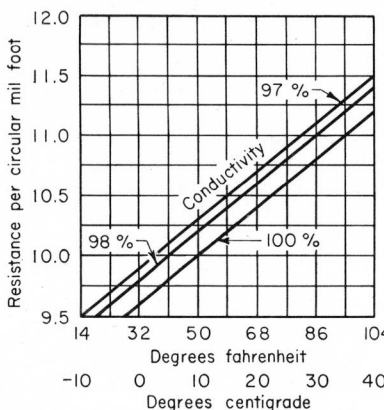

FIG. 26 *Curves showing resistance per circular mil–foot of pure copper at various temperatures and conductivities.*

95. To compute the resistance of a conductor of any common metal or alloy use the value given for the resistance of a circular mil-foot of the material in Table **99** in the following formula:

$$R = \frac{p \times l}{\text{cir mils}} \quad \text{or} \quad \frac{p \times l}{d^2} \qquad (22)$$

where R = resistance of the conductor in ohms; p = resistance of a cir mil-ft of the material composing the conductor, from Table **99**; l = length of conductor in feet; d = diameter in mils; and d^2 = diameter in mils squared or, what is the same thing, the area of the conductor in circular mils.

The other forms of the formula are

$$p = \frac{d^2 \times R}{l} \qquad l = \frac{d^2 \times R}{p} \qquad d = \sqrt{\frac{p \times l}{R}}$$

$$(23)$$

Example. Taking from Table **99** the resistance of a circular mil-foot of copper at 23°C (75°F) as 10.5 ohms, what is the resistance of 500 ft of copper wire 0.021 in. in diameter?

Solution. Substituting in the formula:

$$R = \frac{pl}{d^2} = \frac{10.5 \times 500}{21 \times 21} = \frac{5,250}{441} = 11.9 \text{ ohms}$$

96. An approximate rule for computing the resistance of round copper wire, in ohms per thousand feet, is: Divide 10,500 by the size of the wire in circular mils. This rule should be used only for rough estimating computations.

Example. Thus, for a 4/0 wire (211,600 cir mils), the resistance is approximately $R = 10,500/211,600 = 0.05$ ohm per 1,000 ft.

97. The resistance of conductors that are not circular in section can be computed by first getting their areas in square inches and then reducing this square-inch value to circular mils as given in Sec. **93**. Then proceed with the formula in the preceding paragraph.

98. Change of Resistance with Change of Temperature. The resistance of all pure metals increases as they become hot. The resistance of certain alloys is not affected by the temperature. The resistance of a few materials, carbon for instance, decreases as their temperature increases. The proportion that resistance changes per degree rise in temperature is called the temperature coefficient of resistance (see Table **99** for values). Unless otherwise stated the temperature coefficient is positive; i.e., the resistance increases with increase of temperature. For all pure metals, the coefficient is practically the same and is 0.004 for temperatures in degrees centigrade and 0.0023 for temperatures in degrees Fahrenheit.

99. Approximate Specific Resistances and Temperature Coefficients of Metals and Alloys
("Electrical Engineer's Handbook," International Textbook Company)

Metal	Resistance of 1 cir mil-ft in ohms p		Average temperature coefficient per degree C between 0 and 100°C a	Average temperature coefficient per degree F between 32 and 212°F a	Percentage conductivity	Relative resistance
	0°C or 32°F	23.8°C or 75°F				
Silver, pure annealed..............	8.831	9.674	0.004000	0.002220	108.60	0.925
Copper, pure annealed.............	9.390	10.351	0.004280	0.002380	102.10	0.980
Copper, annealed.................	9.590	10.505	0.004020	0.002230	100.00	1.000
Copper, hard-drawn...............	9.810	10.745	0.004020	0.002230	97.80	1.022
Gold (99.9 per cent pure).........	13.216	14.404	0.003770	0.002090	72.55	1.378
Aluminum (99.5 per cent pure)......	15.219	16.758	0.004230	0.002350	63.00	1.587
(Commercial—97.5 per cent pure)...	16.031	17.699	0.004350	0.002420	59.80	1.672
Zinc (very pure).................	34.595	37.957	0.004060	0.002260	27.72	3.608
Iron (approx. pure)..............	54.529	62.643	0.006250	0.003470	17.50	5.714
Iron E.B.B. iron wire............	58.702	65.190	0.004630	0.002570	16.20	6.173
Platinum (pure).................	65.670	71.418	0.003669	0.002038	14.60	6.845
Iron, B.B. iron wire.............	68.680	76.270	0.004630	0.002570	13.50	7.407
Nickel.........................	74.128	85.138	0.006220	0.003460	12.94	7.726
Tin (pure).....................	78.489	86.748	0.004400	0.002450	12.22	8.184
Steel (wire)...................	81.179	90.150	0.004630	0.002570	11.60	8.621
Substance						
Brass..........................	43.310	......	....	....	22.15	4.515
Phosphor bronze.................	51.005	......	0.000640	0.000356	18.80	5.316
Aluminum bronze.................	73.989	......	0.001000	0.000556	12.96	7.714
German silver (Cu 50, Zn 35, Ni 15)......	127.800	......	0.000400	0.000220	7.50	17.300
Platinoid [Cu, 59, Zn 25.5, Ni 14, W (tungsten) 55]...	251.030	......	0.000310	0.000172	3.82	26.180
Manganin (Cu 84, Ni 4, Mn 12)......	280.790	......	0.000000	....	3.41	29.330
Constantan (Cu 58, Ni 41, Mn 1).....	{300.77 / 312.80}	......	±0.000010	0.000005	{3.19 / 3.07}	{31.35 / 32.57}
Gray cast iron.................	684.000	......	....	....		

100. To find the resistance of a conductor at any ordinary temperature, use this formula:

$$R_h = R_c + [a \times R_c(T_h - T_c)] \qquad \text{or} \qquad T_h - T_c = \frac{R_h - R_c}{a \times R_c} \qquad (24)$$

where R_h = resistance, in ohms, hot; R_c = resistance, in ohms, cold; T_h = temperature of conductor hot, in degrees; T_c = temperature of conductor cold, in degrees; and a = the temperature coefficient of the material of the conductor from Table **99**. (This is an approximate method, but it is sufficiently accurate for all ordinary work.)

Example. The resistance of 1 cir mil-ft of annealed copper is 9.59 ohms at 32°F. What will its resistance be at 75°F?

Solution. From Table **99** the coefficient is 0.00223. Now substitute:

$$R_h = R_c + [a \times R_c(T_h - T_c)] = 9.59 + [0.00223 \times 9.59(75 - 32)]$$
$$= 9.59 + [0.00223 \times 9.59 \times 43] = 9.59 + 0.92 = 10.51 \text{ ohms, at } 75°F$$

101. The temperature rise in a conductor can be determined with the formula of Sec. 100 by measuring hot and cold resistance. The expression $T_h - T_c$ is the difference between the hot and cold temperature and is therefore the temperature rise or fall.

Example. The resistance of a set of copper coils measured 20 ohms at a room temperature of 20°C. After carrying current for some time the resistance measured 20.78 ohms. What was the temperature rise in the coil?

Solution. The temperature coefficient of copper per degree centigrade is, from Table **99**, 0.004. Substitute in the formula:

$$T_h - T_c = \frac{R_h - R_c}{aR_c} = (20.78 - 20.0) \div (0.004 \times 20) = 0.78 \div 0.08 = 9.75°C$$

Therefore the average temperature rise in the coil was 9¾°C.

102. Contact resistance is the resistance at the point of contact of two conductors. When current flows, heat is always developed at such a point. The greater the clamping pressure between the conductors in contact and the greater the area of contact, the less the contact resistance will be. The nature of the surfaces in contact must also be considered. Smooth surfaces have less contact resistance than do rough surfaces. Contacts should always be so designed that, for a given current, the area of contact will be large enough to prevent the contact resistance from being so great as to cause excessive heating. Table **103** indicates safe values.

103. Safe Current Densities for Electrical Contacts and for Cross Sections

Kind of contact or cross section	Material	Current density	
		Amp per sq in.	Sq mils per amp
Sliding contact (brushes)	Copper brush	150– 175	5,700– 6,700
	Brass gauze brush	100– 125	8,000–10,000
	Carbon brush	30– 40	25,000–33,300
Spring contact (switch blades)	Copper on copper	60– 80	12,500–16,700
	Composition on copper	50– 60	16,700–20,000
	Brass on brass	40– 50	20,000–25,000
Screwed contact	Copper to copper	150– 200	5,000– 6,700
	Composition to copper	125– 150	6,700– 8,000
	Composition to composition	100– 125	8,000–10,000
Clamped contact	Copper to copper	100– 125	8,000–10,000
	Composition to copper	75– 100	10,000–13,000
	Composition to composition	70– 90	11,000–14,000
Fitted contact (taper plugs)	Copper to copper	125– 175	5,700– 8,000
	Composition to copper	100– 125	8,000–10,000
	Composition to composition	75– 100	10,000–13,000
Fitted and screwed contact	Copper to copper	200– 250	4,000– 5,000
	Composition to copper	175– 200	5,000– 5,700
	Composition to composition	150– 175	5,700– 6,700
Cross section	Copper wire	1,200–2,000	500– 800
	Copper wire cable	1,000–1,600	600– 1,000
	Copper rod	800–1,200	800– 1,200
	Composition casting	500– 700	1,400– 2,000
	Brass casting	300– 400	2,500– 3,300
	Brass rod	575– 750	1,300– 1,700

104. Ohm's Law. From the preceding sections it is evident that a voltage is required to force a current through a circuit against the resistance caused by the material of the conductor. The relation between current, resistance, and voltage is known as Ohm's law. It is merely a restatement, as applied to electric circuits, of the general law which governs all physical phenomena, i.e., the result produced is directly proportional to the effort or cause and inversely proportional to the opposition. For the phenomenon dealing with current passing through resistance, the emf is the cause, the current is the result or effect, and the resistance is the opposition. Thus,

$$I = \frac{E}{R} = \left(\text{amperes} = \frac{\text{volts}}{\text{ohms}}\right) \qquad \text{(amperes)} \quad (25)$$

$$R = \frac{E}{I} = \left(\text{ohms} = \frac{\text{volts}}{\text{amperes}}\right) \qquad \text{(ohms)} \quad (26)$$

$$E = I \times R = \text{volts} = (\text{amperes} \times \text{ohms}) \qquad \text{(volts)} \quad (27)$$

where I = the effective current, in amperes, which flows through the resistance in the circuit or in the portion of the circuit under consideration; R = the resistance in ohms of the circuit or the portion of the circuit under consideration; and E = the effective emf in volts required to force the current through the resistance of the circuit or the portion of the circuit under consideration.

105. Application of Ohm's Law. Great care must be exercised in the use of Ohm's law. The voltage given by Eq. (27) may or may not be the voltage that must be impressed on the circuit in order to force the given current through the circuit. When the circuit contains only resistance, then the voltage given by Ohm's law is the voltage impressed on the circuit. Ohm's law holds true for all circuits both direct and alternating, but the voltage obtained by its use is only the voltage required to overcome the resistance of the circuit. Ohm's law cannot be used for a complete motor circuit in order to determine the resistance of the circuit.

106. Use Ohm's law for:

1. Determination of the voltage required to provide a given current through only a resistance.

2. Determination of the current which would be produced by a given voltage impressed upon only a resistance.

3. Determination of the voltage drop caused by a current passing through a resistance.

4. Calculations of complete d-c circuits which do not contain any emf other than the impressed voltage.

5. Any circuit or portion of a circuit which consists only of resistance.

107. Do not use Ohm's law for:

1. A-c circuits in general.

2. Complete motor circuits.

3. Complete circuits containing any emf other than the impressed voltage.

Refer to Secs. **131** and **132** for calculation of a-c circuits.

108. Examples of the application of Ohm's law.

Example. What will be the current in the d-c circuit of Fig. 27?

Solution. An entire circuit is shown. It is composed of a dynamo, line wires, and a resistance coil. The emf developed by the dynamo (do not confuse this with the emf impressed by the

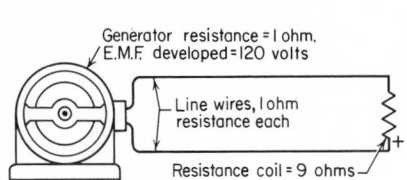

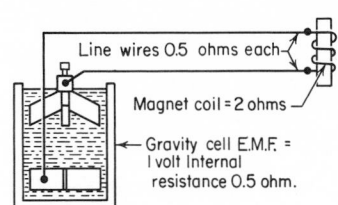

FIG. 27   *An entire dynamo circuit.*   FIG. 28   *An entire battery circuit.*

dynamo on the line) is 120 volts. The resistance of the entire circuit is the sum of the resistances of dynamo, line wires, and resistance coil. Substituting in the formula:

$$I = \frac{E}{R} = \frac{120}{1+1+9+1} = \frac{120}{12} = 10 \text{ amp}$$

Example. What current will flow in the circuit of Fig. 28?

Solution. This again is an entire circuit. Substituting in the formula:

$$I = \frac{E}{R} = \frac{1}{0.5 + 0.5 + 2 + 0.5} = \frac{1}{3.5} = 0.28 \text{ amp}$$

Note that the internal resistance of the battery must be considered.

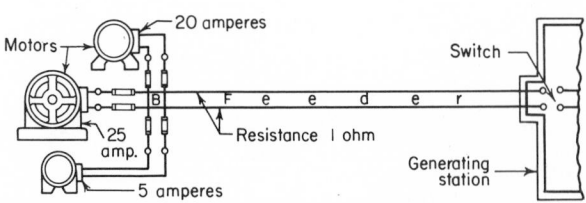

FIG. 29   *Feeder to motors.*

Example. With 10 amp flowing, what will be the voltage drop in the line wires in Fig. 29?

Solution. Each has a resistance of 1.0 ohm; hence

$$E = I \times R = 10 \times 2 = 20 \text{ volts}$$

Example. What is the resistance of the incandescent lamp of Fig. 30A? It is tapped to a 120-volt circuit, and the ammeter reads 0.5 amp. The branch wires are so short that their resistance can be neglected.

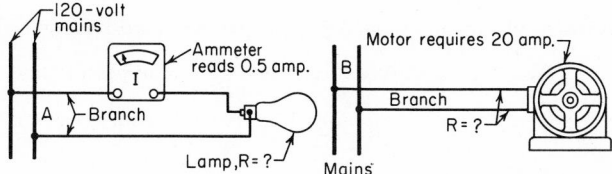

FIG. 30 *Portions of circuits.*

Solution. Substitute in the formula:

$$R = \frac{E}{I} = \frac{120}{0.5} = 240 \text{ ohms}$$

Example. The d-c motor of Fig. 30B takes 20 amp, and the drop in voltage in the branch wires should not exceed 5 volts. What is the greatest resistance that can be permitted in the branch conductors?

Solution. Substitute in the formula:

$$R = \frac{E}{I} = \frac{5}{20} = 0.25 \text{ ohm}$$

This (0.25 ohm) is the resistance of both wires. Each would have a resistance of 0.125 ohm.

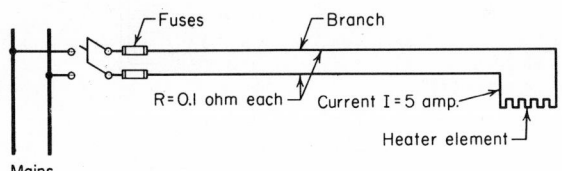

FIG. 31 *Portion of a circuit.*

Example. The electric heater (Fig. 31) takes 5 amp. The resistance of each branch wire is 0.1 ohm. What will be the drop in volts in each branch wire?

Solution. Substitute in the formula:

$$E = I \times R = 5 \times 0.1 = 0.5 \text{ volt}$$

In both branch wires or in the branch circuit the volts lost would be $2 \times 0.5 = 1$ volt.

Example. Three d-c motors (Fig. 29) taking respectively 20, 25, and 5 amp (these values were stamped on the name plates of the motors) are located at the end of a feeder having a resistance of 1.0 ohm on each side. What will be the volts drop in the feeder?

Solution. Substitute in the formula:

$$E = R \times I = (1 + 1) \times (20 + 25 + 5) = 2 \times 50 = 100 \text{ volts}$$

109. D-C Circuits. In constant-current d-c circuits there is only one characteristic of the circuit that affects the value of the current, i.e., the resistance offered by the material of which the circuit is made. Therefore, Ohm's law applies to complete d-c circuits or any portions of the circuit which do not contain any emf other than the impressed voltage. For a motor circuit, therefore, Ohm's law will apply only to the line conductor portion of the circuit. Ohm's law will give the voltage required to overcome the resistance of the line conductors, the voltage drop of the circuit. The total impressed voltage will be equal to the summation of the voltage at the motor terminals plus the *IR* voltage of the line conductors. The voltage impressed on the motor will be equal to the impressed line voltage minus the *IR* voltage drop in the line conductors.

110. Power in d-c circuits is equal to the product of volts and amperes. Expressing this as a formula

$$W = I \times E \qquad I = \frac{W}{E} \qquad E = \frac{W}{I} \tag{28}$$

and also in circuits where all the energy is converted into heat energy

$$W = I^2 \times R \qquad W = \frac{E^2}{R} \qquad I = \sqrt{\frac{W}{R}} \qquad E = \sqrt{R \times W} \tag{29}$$

$$R = \frac{E^2}{W} \qquad R = \frac{W}{I^2} \tag{30}$$

where I = current in amperes; E = voltage or emf in volts; R = resistance in ohms; and W = power in watts.

111. In applying the above equations be careful that the values of current, voltage, and resistance used in any one problem all apply to the same circuit or to the same portion of a circuit.

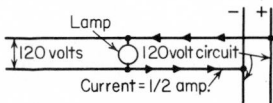

FIG. 32 *Incandescent lamp branch circuit.*

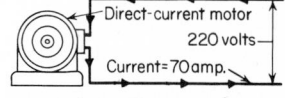

FIG. 33 *Electric motor.*

Example. How many watts are consumed by the incandescent lamp in Fig. 32?
Solution. Substitute in the formula:

$$W = I \times E = \tfrac{1}{2} \times 120 = 60 \text{ watts}$$

Example. How many watts are taken by the motor of Fig. 33? How many kilowatts? How many horsepower?
Solution. Substitute in the formula:

$$W = I \times E = 70 \times 220 = 15{,}400 \text{ watts}$$

$$kw = \frac{watts}{1{,}000} = \frac{15{,}400}{1{,}000} = 15.4 \text{ kw}$$

$$hp = \frac{watts}{746} = \frac{15{,}400}{746} = 20.6 \text{ hp}$$

Example. In the feeder of Fig. 34, what amount of power will be lost in the line wires to the motor?
Solution. Substitute in the formula:

$$W = I^2 \times R = (40 \times 40) \times (0.3 + 0.3) = 1{,}600 \times 0.6 = 960 \text{ watts}$$

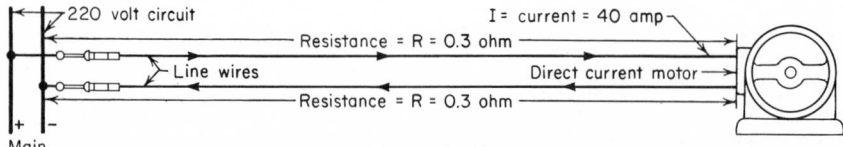

FIG. 34 *Feeder.*

112. Wave Form of Alternating Currents and Voltages. An alternating current or voltage is one which is reversed at regular intervals. The curve formed by plotting the instantaneous values of the voltage or current against time is called the wave form of the voltage or current. It is best to have the value of an alternating current or voltage vary with time according to what is known as the sine law. The instantaneous values of an alternating current varying according to this law are shown in Fig. 35. A voltage or current which varies in this manner is called a sinusoidal voltage or cur-

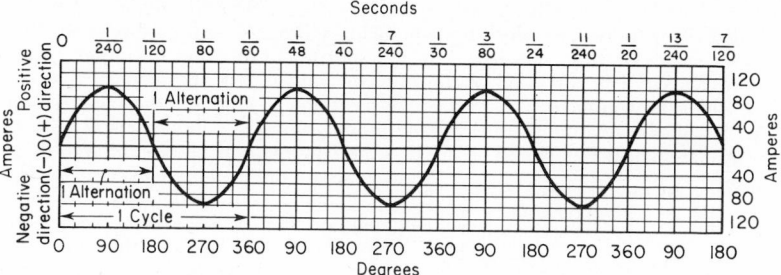

FIG. 35 *Graph of a 60-cycle alternating current having a maximum value of 100 amp.*

rent. Most modern a-c generators produce a voltage which is very nearly sinusoidal and are generally so considered. The current in some a-c circuits will be very nearly sinusoidal and in others may differ considerably from the sine law. In most cases, however, for practical work both alternating voltages and currents can be considered as following the sine law. For cases where it is not satisfactory to do this, the calculations become quite complicated, and a discussion of them is outside the scope of this book.

113. A cycle is a complete set of values through which an *alternating current* (see previous Sec. **34** for explanation of "Alternating Current") repeatedly passes (see Fig. 35). The expression "60 cycles per second" means that the current referred to makes 60 complete cycles in a second. It therefore requires ¹⁄₆₀ sec to complete 1 cycle. See Fig. 35. With a 25-cycle current, ¹⁄₂₅ sec is required to complete 1 cycle. See Fig. 36. The newly adopted term for cycles is **hertz** (Hz).

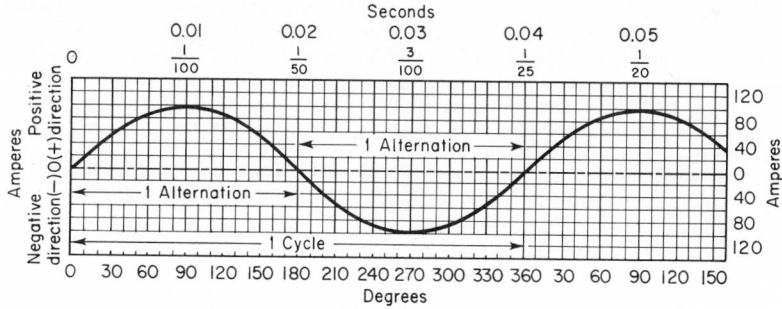

FIG. 36 *Curve of a 25-cycle alternating current.*

114. The frequency of an alternating current is the number of cycles completed in 1 sec. A frequency of 60 cycles is practically standard for lighting and power installations. Most electric power companies generate, transmit, and distribute their power at this frequency. For railroad electrification, 25 cycles is sometimes employed. If 25 cycles is used for lighting, there will be flickering of the lamps. Some of the older stations in this country still generate at 50 cycles. In Europe 50 cycles has commonly been used for light and power and 16²⁄₃ cycles for railroad electrification.

115. Electrical Degrees. The instantaneous values of an a-c voltage can be studied from Fig. 37, which shows an elementary four-pole generator and the wave form of voltage for one complete revolution of the conductor. When the conductor is in the position marked *A*, halfway between adjacent poles, it will not be cutting any flux and therefore there will be no voltage induced in the conductor. As the conductor moves from this position, it will start to cut flux and will cut flux at a greater and greater rate until the conductor is in the position *B*. At this point, flux will be cut at the maximum rate, and the voltage produced will be maximum. As the conductor moves from position B to position C, it will cut flux at a decreasing rate, until, when position C is reached (halfway between poles), the conductor will not be cutting flux at all. As the conductor moves on from position C, it will start to cut flux, but the direction of the flux is reversed. The direction of the induced voltage will therefore reverse at the instant when the conductor passes through position C. Pursuing the same reasoning for the rest of the revolution, the voltage produced in the conductor will follow the wave form shown in Fig. 37. The arc that the conductor must pass through in order

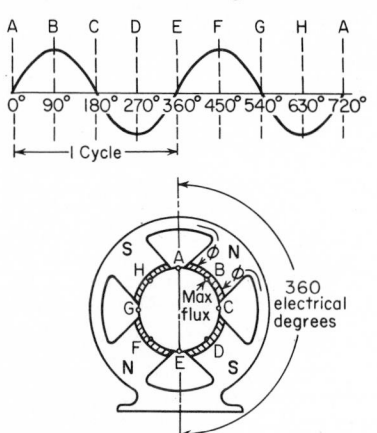

FIG. 37 *Elementary a-c generator, illustrating electrical degrees and wave form.*

to generate one complete cycle of voltage is called 360 electrical degrees. In any a-c generator there are therefore 360 electrical degrees in the arc between the center line of one pole and the center line of the next pole of the same polarity. The number of electrical degrees in one complete revolution for any generator is equal to 360 times the number of pairs of poles for which the machine is wound. One electrical degree is equal to 1 (pair of poles) part of a mechanical degree.

If the elementary generator of Fig. 37 was producing a 60-cycle voltage, the conductor would have to make 1,800 rpm. This would mean that the conductor makes 1 revolution in $^{60}/_{1800}$ or $^{1}/_{30}$ sec. Since the voltage goes through 2 cycles in 1 revolution (see Fig. 37), it takes $^{1}/_{60}$ sec for 1 cycle. This means that in $^{1}/_{60}$ sec the conductor moves from position A to position E.

Refer to Fig. 37 and take A position as zero instant of time and as zero electrical degrees. When the conductor has moved from position A to B, it will have passed through $^{360}/_4$ or 90 electrical degrees, and the elapsed time will be $1/(4 \times 60)$ or $^{1}/_{240}$ sec. Electrical degrees and time are therefore proportional. Therefore instead of the instantaneous values of the voltage being plotted against time, they can be plotted against electrical degrees. These two methods of plotting such curves are shown in Figs. 35 and 36.

116. The word phase, which is used in a-c terminology, refers basically to time. When two alternating currents are in phase, they reach their corresponding zero, maximum, and intermediate values at exactly the same instants. Two in-phase a-c quantities are shown in Fig. 38. If currents or voltages are not in phase, they reach corresponding values at different instants of time, as shown in Fig. 39. Since electrical degrees are proportional to time, it is standard practice to state the out-of-phase relation of two quantities in electrical degrees. In specifying the phase relation of two quantities, it is necessary to state whether it is a leading or lagging relationship. For example, referring to Fig. 39, it is not complete to state that quantity A is 45 degrees out of phase with B. The correct statement is either "A leads B by 45 degrees," or "B lags A by 45 degrees." The number of degrees that two quantities are out of phase

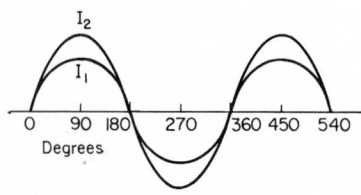

FIG. 38 *Two alternating currents in phase.*

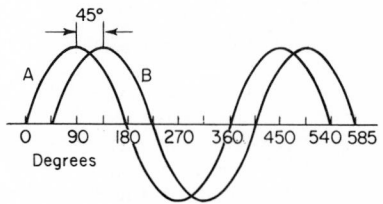

FIG. 39 *Two alternating currents out of phase.*

is the number of electrical degrees that must elapse in the time between the occurrence of a certain instantaneous value of one quantity and the occurrence of the corresponding instantaneous value of the other quantity. For example, referring to Fig. 39, quantity B does not reach its maximum positive value until 45 degrees after quantity A has reached its maximum positive value. Quantity B, therefore, lags quantity A by 45 degrees. The number of electrical degrees that two quantities are out of phase is called the phase angle.

117. A three-phase current consists of three different alternating currents out of phase 120 degrees with each other. A **two-phase current** consists of two different alternating currents out of phase 90 deg with each other.

118. The maximum value of an alternating current or voltage is the greatest value that it attains. This is an instantaneous value (see Fig. 40).

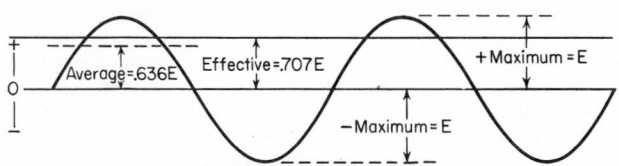

FIG. 40   *Alternating emf values.*

119. The so-called average value of an alternating current or voltage is the average of the instantaneous values for ½ cycle. Average values are not of much value to the practical man.

120. Effective values of alternating current and voltage are the ones ordinarily referred to when speaking of alternating quantities. Alternating voltages and currents are constantly changing in value, within a certain range, from instant to instant even if the load is constant. It is not practicable to deal with or indicate with instruments these constantly changing values. The effective value of an alternating current or voltage is the value of a direct current or voltage that will have the same heating effect. A sinusoidal alternating current which has a maximum value of 14.14 amp will have the same heating effect as a 10-amp direct current. The effective value of the alternating current is therefore 10 amp. The practical man deals almost exclusively with effective values. Alternating-current measuring instruments indicate effective values. The relation between effective and maximum values for sinusoidal quantities is given below and illustrated in Fig. 40. Effective value is also referred to as rms value (root mean square).

$$\text{Effective value} = 0.707 \times \text{maximum value} \tag{31}$$

$$\text{Maximum value} = \frac{\text{effective value}}{0.707} \tag{32}$$

Example. What is the effective voltage of a circuit that has a maximum voltage of 156?
Solution. Substitute in the formula:

$$\text{Effective value} = 0.707 \times \text{maximum value} = 0.707 \times 156 = 110 \text{ volts}$$

Example. If a voltmeter on an a-c circuit reads 2,200, what is the maximum instantaneous voltage?
Solution. Substitute in the formula:

$$\text{Maximum value} = \frac{\text{effective value}}{0.707} = \frac{2,200}{0.707} = 3,110 \text{ volts}$$

121. Characteristics of A-C Circuits. All three of the circuit characteristics, resistance, inductance, and capacitance, may affect the value of the current in an a-c circuit.

122. Resistance of A-C Circuits. As mentioned in Sec. **90** the resistance of a circuit to alternating current may be considerably different from its resistance to direct current. This increase in the resistance may be due to two factors. One of these factors takes place inside the conductors. It is called skin effect and is discussed in the following sections. The other factor is due to the proximity of magnetic and electrical conducting material to the circuit. The varying magnetic field produced by the alternating current results in electric and magnetic power losses in these neighboring materials. These power losses must be supplied by the power delivered to the electric circuit and therefore result in increasing the effective resistance of the circuit over what it was for direct current. Refer to Sec. **157** for examples of effective resistance to an alternating current.

123. Skin Effect. When an alternating current flows through a conductor, there is an inductive action whereby the current in the conductor is forced toward its surface. The current density is greater at the surface than at the center, and under certain conditions there may be practically no current flowing along the axis of the conductor. Although skin effect and self-induction both originate from the same magnetic field, they are not otherwise related. Since it increases voltage drop and energy loss, skin effect amounts to an increase in resistance and is so considered. Table **63** of Div. 11 gives values by which d-c resistances of conductors must be multiplied to obtain their resistances to alternating currents. Nonconducting cores are sometimes placed in the centers of large cables for alternating currents so that all the metal will be effectively used (see Div. 2 for such conductors).

124. Skin effect in conductors of magnetic materials is much greater than in those of nonmagnetic materials owing to the stronger magnetic field that a given current will set up in a magnetic metal.

125. The effect of inductance in an a-c circuit is that it produces opposition to the flow of the current and tends to make the current lag behind the voltage in time or phase. If a pure inductive circuit (one with only inductance, no resistance) could be built, the current would lag 90 degrees, or 1/4 cycle, behind the voltage. In actual circuits containing both resistance and inductance, the current will lag some angle between 0 and 90 degrees behind the voltage. The angle of lag will depend upon the relative value of the resistance and inductance.

126. The opposition to alternating current which is produced by inductance is called inductive reactance (see Sec. **46**). For a sinusoidal current the value of the inductive reactance is

$$X_L = 2\pi f L \tag{33}$$

where X_L = inductive reactance in ohms; f = frequency in cycles per second; and L = inductance in henrys.

127. The angle of lag of a current in an inductive circuit can be calculated from the following equation:

$$\text{Tangent of angle of lag} = \frac{X_L}{R} \tag{34}$$

where X_L = inductive reactance in ohms and R = a-c resistance (not d-c resistance). Also see method of Sec. **133**.

128. The effect of capacitance in an a-c circuit is that it produces opposition to the flow of the current and tends to make the current lead the voltage. For a pure capacitive circuit (one with only capacitance, no resistance) the current would lead the voltage by 90 degrees or 1/4 cycle. For a circuit with both resistance and capacitance, the current will lead the voltage by some angle between 0 and 90 degrees, depending upon the relative value of the resistance and the capacitance.

129. The opposition to alternating current which is produced by capacitance is called capacitive reactance (see Sec. **49**). For a circuit with sinusoidal relations the value of the capacitive reactance is

$$X_C = \frac{1}{2\pi f c} \tag{35}$$

where X_C = capacitive reactance in ohms; f = frequency in cycles per second; and c = capacity in farads.

130. The angle of lead of a current in a capacitive circuit can be calculated from the following equation:

$$\text{Tangent of angle of lead} = \frac{X_C}{R} \tag{36}$$

where X_C = capacitive reactance in ohms and R = a-c resistance (not d-c resistance). Also see method of Sec. **133.**

131. Impedance is the name given to the total opposition to the flow of alternating current. It is the combined opposition of resistance, inductive reactance, and capacitive reactance. Impedance is measured in ohms and is expressed by the symbol Z. The impedance of a series circuit may be calculated by the following formulas:

For a circuit containing resistance, inductance, and capacitance

$$Z = \sqrt{R^2 + (X_L - X_C)^2} \tag{37}$$

For a circuit containing resistance and inductance

$$Z = \sqrt{R^2 + X_L{}^2} \tag{38}$$

For a circuit containing resistance and capacitance

$$Z = \sqrt{R^2 + X_C{}^2} \tag{39}$$

For a circuit containing only resistance

$$Z = R \tag{40}$$

For a circuit containing only inductance

$$Z = X_L \tag{41}$$

For a circuit containing only capacitance

$$Z = X_C \tag{42}$$

where Z = impedance in ohms; X_L = inductive reactance in ohms; and X_C = capacitive reactance in ohms.

132. Relations between voltage, current, and impedance are

$$E = IZ \tag{43}$$

$$I = \frac{E}{Z} \tag{44}$$

$$Z = \frac{E}{I} \tag{45}$$

where E = voltage impressed on circuit in volts; I = current in amperes; and Z = impedance in ohms.

The above equations apply to complete a-c circuits or any portions of the circuit which do not contain any emf other than the impressed voltage. For a motor circuit, therefore, they will apply only to the line conductor portion of the circuit. They will give the voltage required to overcome line impedance, the IZ voltage of the circuit.

It is noticed that Ohm's law (Sec. **105**) can be used for a complete a-c circuit only when the circuit contains only resistance.

133. The phase angle of a circuit containing only resistance, inductance, and capacitance can be found from the following formula:

$$\text{Cosine of phase angle} = \frac{R}{Z} \tag{46}$$

where Z = impedance in ohms and R = resistance in ohms.

134. Power in A-C Circuits. The power of an a-c circuit is very seldom equal to the direct product of the volts and amperes. In order to calculate the power of a single-phase a-c circuit, the product of the volts and amperes must be multiplied by a certain factor called the power factor (see Sec. **136**).

135. Apparent power is the term applied to the product of voltage and current in an a-c circuit. It is expressed in volt-amperes (va) or in kilovolt-amperes (kva) or megavolt-amperes (mva).

136. Power factor is the ratio of the true power or watts to the apparent power or volt-amperes. The power factor is expressed as a decimal or in percentage. Thus power factors of 0.8 or of 80 per cent are the same. In giving the power factor of a circuit, it should be stated whether it is leading or lagging. The current is always taken with respect to the voltage. A power factor of 0.75 lagging means that the current lags the voltage. The power factor may have a value anywhere between 0 and 1.0 but can never be greater than 1.0.

Example. In Fig. 41, which shows a single-phase circuit, the ammeter I reads 10 amp and the voltmeter E, 220 volts. The apparent power is the product of volts and amperes or $IE = 10 \times 220 =$

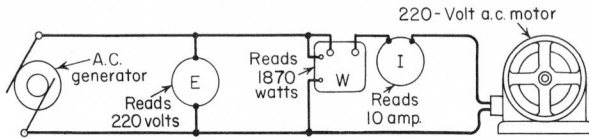

FIG. 41 *Example of power factor.*

2,200 volt-amperes. But the wattmeter W reads 1,870 watts. A wattmeter always indicates real or true power. Therefore the power factor (for a single-phase circuit) is

$$\text{Power factor} = \frac{\text{true watts}}{\text{apparent power}} = \frac{1,870}{2,200} = 0.85 \text{ or } 85 \text{ per cent}$$

137. The cosine of the angle of lag or lead is equal to the power factor. Cosines for different angles can be found in trigonometric tables in handbooks (see Sec. **1**). The symbol θ, a Greek letter, pronounced theta, is often used to designate the angle of lag or lead; hence power factor is sometimes referred to as cos θ (cosine theta). This means the cosine of the angle θ.

138. The power factor in a noninductive circuit, one containing resistance only, is always 1, or 100 per cent; i.e., the product of volts and amperes in such a circuit gives true power.

139. The power factor in a circuit containing inductance or capacitance may be anything between 0 and 1 (0 and 100 per cent), depending on the amount of inductance or capacitance in the circuit.

140. Typical power factors of various kinds of central-station loads are as follows:
INCANDESCENT LIGHTING. 1.0.
INCANDESCENT LIGHTING WITH SMALL STEPDOWN TRANSFORMERS. 0.95 to 0.98.
INCANDESCENT STREET-LIGHTING SERIES CIRCUITS. 0.6 to 0.8.
SODIUM-VAPOR STREET LIGHTING, PARALLEL CIRCUITS. 0.8 to 0.85.
SODIUM-VAPOR STREET LIGHTING, SERIES CIRCUITS. 0.5 to 0.7.
FLUORESCENT LIGHTING. Depends on type of auxiliary used, 0.5 to 0.95.
MERCURY-VAPOR LIGHTING. Depends on type of auxiliary used, 0.5 to 0.95.
SINGLE-PHASE INDUCTION MOTORS, SQUIRREL-CAGE ROTOR. $\frac{1}{20}$ to 1 hp, power factor, 0.55 to 0.75, average 0.68 at rated load; 1 to 10 hp, power factor, 0.75 to 0.86, average 0.82 at rated load.
POLYPHASE INDUCTION MOTORS, SQUIRREL-CAGE ROTOR. 1 to 10 hp, power factor, 0.75 to 0.91, average 0.85 at rated load; 10 to 50 hp, power factor, 0.85 to 0.92, average 0.89 at rated load.
POLYPHASE INDUCTION MOTORS, PHASE-WOUND ROTORS. 5 to 20 hp, power factor, 0.80 to 0.89, average 0.86 at rated load; 20 to 100 hp, power factor, 0.82 to 0.90, average 0.87 at rated load.
INDUCTION MOTOR LOADS IN GENERAL. Power factor from 0.60 to 0.85, depending on whether motors are carrying their rated loads.
ROTARY CONVERTERS, COMPOUND WOUND. Power factor at full load can be adjusted to practically 100 per cent. At light loads it will be lagging and at overloads slightly leading.
ROTARY CONVERTERS, SHUNT WOUND. The power factor can be adjusted to any desired value and will be fairly constant at all loads with the same field rheostat adjustment. Rotary converters, however, should not be operated below 0.95 power factor leading or lagging at full load or overload.
SMALL HEATING APPARATUS. This load has the same characteristics as an incandescent-lighting load. The power factor of the load unit is practically unity, but the distributing transformers will lower it to some extent.

ARC FURNACES.   Power factor 0.80 to 0.90.

INDUCTION FURANCES.   Power factor 0.60 to 0.70.

ELECTRIC-WELDING TRANSFORMERS.   Power factor 0.50 to 0.70.

SYNCHRONOUS MOTORS.   Adjustment between 0.80 power factor leading to unity power factor.   (1) Operating power factors above 0.95 will be obtained only when practically all the load is synchronous motors or converters which can be operated at practically unity power factor.   (2) Power factors of 0.90 to 0.95 can be safely predicted only when the load is entirely incandescent lighting or heating or if a large non-inductive load, such as synchronous motors or converters, is used with a smaller pro-portion of inductive motor load.   (3) For the average central-station load, consisting of lighting and motor service, a power factor of 0.80 should be assumed.   (4) A power factor of 0.70 should be assumed for a plant having a large proportion of induction motors, fluorescent lighting, electric furnaces, or electric welding load.

141. Kilowatts and Kilovolt-amperes (General Electric Company).   The term kilo-watt (kw) indicates the measure of power which is all available for work.   Kilovolt-amperes (kva) indicate the measure of apparent electrical power made up of two com-ponents, an energy component and a wattless or induction component.   Kilowatts indicate real power and kilovolt-amperes apparent power.   They are identical only when current and voltage are in phase, i.e., when the power factor is 1.   Ammeters and voltmeters indicate total effective current and voltage regardless of the power factor, while a wattmeter indicates the effective product of the instantaneous values of emf and current.   A wattmeter, then, indicates real power.

Standard guarantees on a-c generators are made on the basis of loads at 80 per cent power factor.   However, it must not be inferred that a given generator will deliver its rated power output at all power factors.   The generator rating in kilowatts will be reduced in proportion to the power factor and probably in a greater ratio if the power factor is very low.   The method of rating a-c generators by kilovolt-amperes instead of by kilowatts is now in general use.

In discussing an a-c load, it is well to state it in terms of kilowatts, power factor, and kilovolt-amperes, thus: 200 kw, 80 per cent power factor (250 kva).   This shows that the current in the circuit corresponds to 250 kva and heats the generator and conduc-tors to that extent but that only 200 kw is available for doing work.   An illustration of the distinction between kilowatts and kilovolt-amperes is given in Fig. 42.

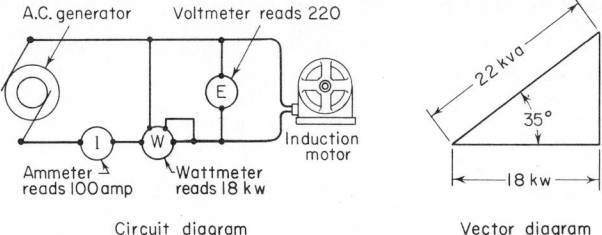

FIG. 42   *Illustrating the distinction between kilowatts and kilovolt-amperes.*

142. Effects of Low Power Factor.   It is sometimes considered that the wattless com-ponent of a current at low power factor is circulated without an increase of mechan-ical input over that necessary for actual power requirements.   This is inaccurate because internal work or losses due to this extra current are produced and must be sup-plied by the prime mover.   Since these extra losses manifest themselves in heat, the capacity of the machine is reduced.   Also wattless components of current heat the line conductors, just as do energy components, and cause losses in them.   The loss in any conductor is always (see Sec. **38**)

$$W = I^2R \qquad (47)$$

where W = the loss in watts; I = the current in amperes in the conductor; and R =

the resistance in ohms. It requires much larger equipment and conductors to deliver a certain amount of power at a low power factor than at a power factor close to unity.

143. Correction of Low Power Factor. In industrial plants, excessively low power factor is usually due to underloaded induction motors because the power factor of motors is much less at partial loads than at full load. Where motors are underloaded new motors of smaller capacity should be substituted (see Induction Motors, Index). Power factor can be corrected (1) by installing synchronous motors (see Index) which, when overexcited, have the property of neutralizing the wattless or reactive components of currents or (2) by connecting static capacitors across the line.

144. A single-phase alternating emf will be induced in an armature coil which (S_1 and F_1, Fig. 43) has its sides set, in a generator frame, the same distance apart as are a north and a south magnet which are forced to sweep continuously past the coil sides at a uniform speed. The distance between a north and a south pole is always called 180 electrical degrees. The distance between a north and the next north pole is called 360 electrical degrees. In any given generator, the circumferential distance is the same between any two adjacent north and south poles.

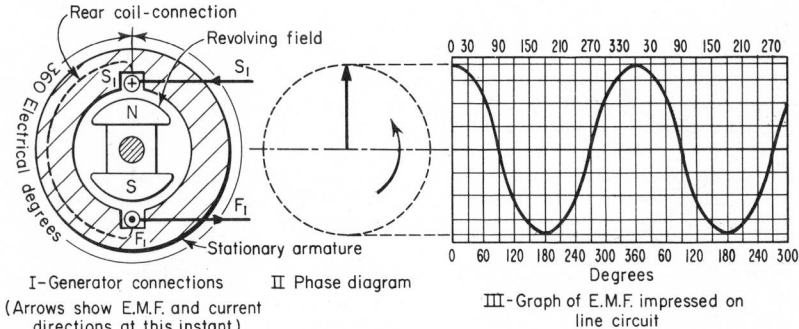

I–Generator connections   II Phase diagram
(Arrows show E.M.F. and current
directions at this instant)

III–Graph of E.M.F. impressed on
line circuit

FIG. 43   *Elementary two-pole single-phase a-c generator.*

145. In actual a-c single-phase generators, there are a number of pairs of north and south poles arranged on a revolving-field structure. There is a corresponding number of coils arranged around the frame, each having its sides set approximately 180 electrical degrees apart. Then, the coils are connected in series so that their emfs will be additive. The combination of their emfs is the voltage which is impressed by the generator on the circuit. Some small revolving-armature a-c generators have rotating armatures and stationary fields, but their principle is the same as that of the revolving-field machines.

146. For a single-phase circuit the relations between kilowatt and kilovolt-amperes are

$$\text{Kilovolt-amperes} = \frac{\text{volts} \times \text{amperes}}{1,000} \quad \text{or} \quad \text{Kva} = \frac{E \times I}{1,000} \tag{48}$$

$$\text{Kw} = \text{kva} \times \text{power factor} \quad \text{Kva} = \frac{\text{kw}}{\text{power factor}} \tag{49}$$

$$\text{Power factor} = \frac{\text{kw}}{\text{kva}} \tag{50}$$

For an example see Fig. 42.

147. For a single-phase circuit, the following equations show the relations between power, current, voltage, and power factor.

$$I = \frac{W}{E \times \text{pf}} \quad E = \frac{W}{I \times \text{pf}} \quad W = E \times I \times \text{pf} \quad \text{pf} = \frac{W}{E \times I} \tag{51}$$

where I = current in amperes; W = power in watts; E = voltage between lines; and pf = power factor.

Examples. Figures 42 and 44 show examples of application of the above equations. The product of volts and amperes (EI) is called volt-amperes; see above paragraph.

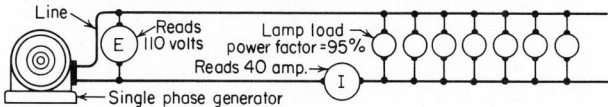

FIG. 44 *A power-factor problem.*

Example. In the circuit of Fig. 44, what is the actual load in watts? In kilowatts? Current = 40 amp, voltage at load = 110, power factor of load = 95 per cent.

Solution. Substitute in the formula:

$$W = E \times I \times \text{pf} = 110 \times 40 \times 0.95 = 4{,}180 \text{ watts}$$

$$\text{Kw} = \frac{\text{watts}}{1{,}000} = \frac{4{,}180}{1{,}000} = 4.18 \text{ kw}$$

148. A two-phase current consists of two currents that differ in phase by 90 degrees (see curves of Fig. 45). If two sets of coils are arranged on an armature (Fig. 45) so that their "starts" S_1 and S_2 are 90 electrical degrees apart, then the emf in one set

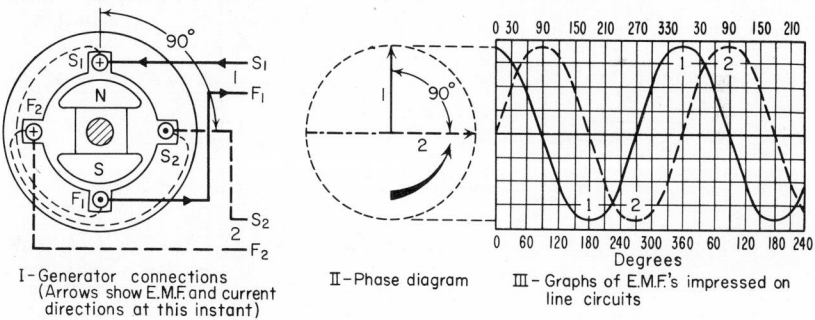

I — Generator connections
(Arrows show E.M.F. and current directions at this instant)

II — Phase diagram

III — Graphs of E.M.F.'s impressed on line circuits

FIG. 45 *Two-pole two-phase a-c generator illustrating elementary principles.*

will attain its maximum value 90 degrees later than that in the other. The emf will force two-phase currents through an external circuit. Instead of being on the same armature, each of the sets of coils might be on different armatures which are so mechanically connected together as to preserve the 90-degree phase relation (see Div. 7 on Motors and Generators for information on practical machines).

149. Coil Connections for Two-phase Windings. Figure 46 shows three methods of connecting two-phase generator coils.

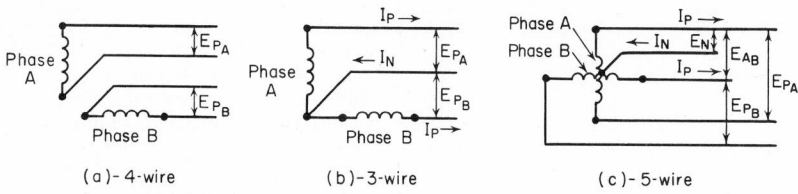

(a) - 4-wire   (b) - 3-wire   (c) - 5-wire

FIG. 46 *Connections for two-phase generator windings.*

150. Relations of Voltage, Current, and Power That Apply to Balanced Two-phase Circuits.

$$I_p = \frac{W}{2E_p \times \mathrm{pf}} \qquad E = \frac{W}{2I_p \times \mathrm{pf}} \qquad W = 2E_p \times I_p \times \mathrm{pf} \qquad \mathrm{Pf} = \frac{W}{2E_p \times I_p} \qquad (52)$$

$$\text{Kilovolt-amperes} = \frac{2E_p \times I_p}{1{,}000} \qquad \text{or} \qquad \text{Kva} = \frac{\mathrm{kw}}{\mathrm{pf}} \qquad (53)$$

$$\text{Kw} = \text{kva} \times \mathrm{pf} \qquad (54)$$

$$\text{Pf} = \frac{\mathrm{kw}}{\mathrm{kva}} \qquad (55)$$

where I_p = phase current in amperes as designated in Fig. 46; E_p = phase voltage as designated in Fig. 46; W = power in watts; and pf = power factor.

151. Application of the Two-phase System. Many years ago certain engineers advocated two-phase generators and distributing systems in preference to three-phase. It was then believed by them that unbalanced load on the phases would have less adverse effect on the performance of the two-phase equipment. Experience has proved that the three-phase system is preferable to and more economical than the two-phase for both transmission and distribution. It is seldom that two-phase equipment is now purchased except for additions to existing two-phase installations. See Sec. **23** of Div. 3 for relative weights of copper for different systems.

152. A three-phase current consists of three alternating currents that differ in phase by 120 degrees, as indicated in Fig. 47. If three coils are arranged with their "starts," S_1, S_2, and S_3, 120 degrees apart on an armature (Fig. 47) and connected each to an external circuit, a single-phase alternating emf will be impressed by each coil on its own external circuit when the field is rotated at uniform speed. The emfs will differ in

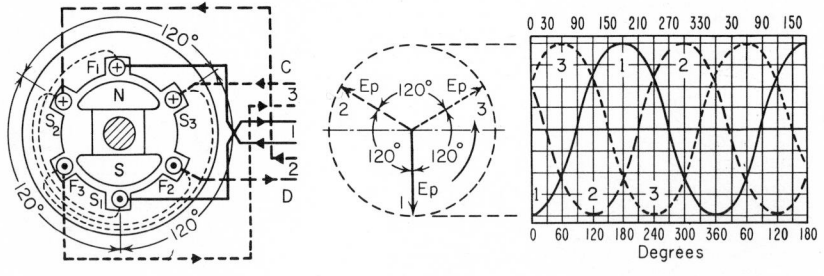

I – Generator connections   II – Phase diagram   III – Graphs of E.M.F.'s impressed on line circuits

FIG. 47   *Two-pole three-phase alternator ensures 120 degrees phase difference between emfs in line wires.*

phase by 120 degrees and therefore will constitute a three-phase system. The currents in the circuits will be 120 degrees out of phase with each other. Three single-phase generators, if mechanically coupled together so as to maintain a 120-degree phase relation, would produce a three-phase system. Practical three-phase generators usually have more than two poles and consequently have more coils than indicated in Fig. 47. Most alternating-current generators have revolving fields and stationary armatures.

153. Phase Connections. Figure 48 shows four methods of connecting the phases of a three-phase generator (or other apparatus) and the external circuits for each. Method I, although it would work, is seldom used for economic reasons hereinafter given. It shows the elementary three-phase circuit and illustrates the principle. Each of the three phases would carry a current differing in phase by 120 degrees from the currents in the other two. One common return N, as shown at II, can be substituted for the three return wires of I. Now with a balanced load, i.e., one loading each of the phases equally, this return wire would carry no current; hence it may be omitted (star or Y **connection** of III). In IV is shown the delta connection.

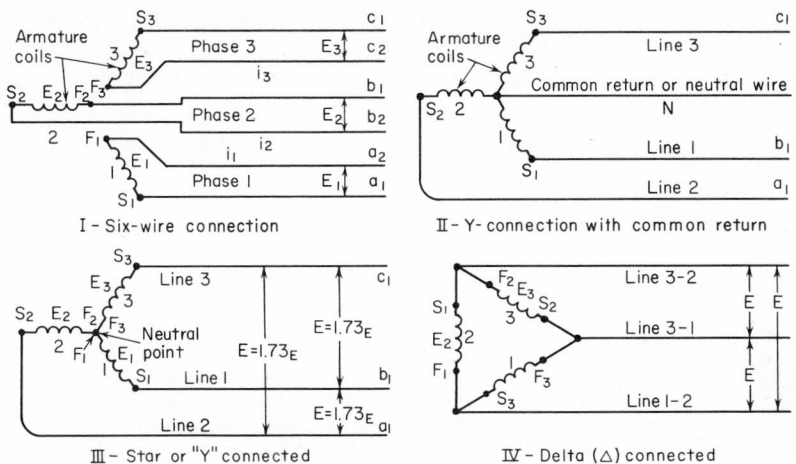

FIG. 48   *Connections for three-phase-generator windings.*

154. The voltage and current relations in a star or Y-connected three-phase circuit are indicated in Fig. 49. The armature coils of the generator shown in Fig. 49 are 120 electrical degrees apart (Fig. 47). These emfs will combine as shown in the phase diagram (Fig. 49) to produce the voltage E between line wires. The resultant voltage de-

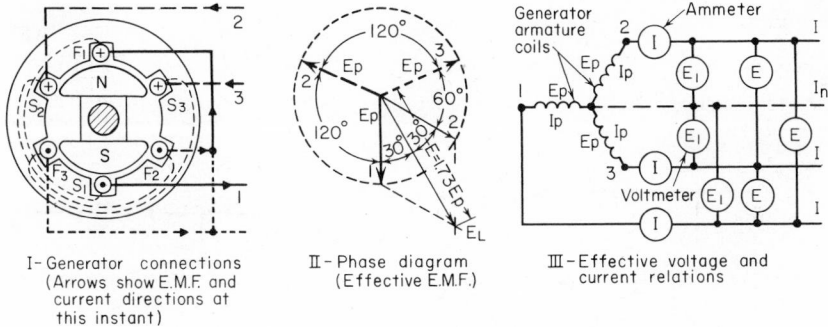

FIG. 49   *Star or Y-connected three-phase generator and diagrams.*

veloped by any two of the coils is then equal to $\sqrt{3}$ or 1.73 times the voltage developed in one coil. The following formulas show the relation of voltage and current in the circuit. (All are effective values and balance is assumed. See Fig. 49.)

$$I = I_p \tag{56}$$

$$E = E_p \times \sqrt{3} = E_p \times 1.73 \tag{57}$$

$$E_p = \frac{E}{\sqrt{3}} = \frac{E}{1.73} = E \times 0.577 \qquad \text{or approx. } E_p = 0.58E \tag{58}$$

$$I_N = 0 = \sqrt{(I_p1)^2 + (I_p2)^2 + (I_p3)^2 - (I_p1 \cdot I_p2) - (I_p2 \cdot I_p3) - (I_p3 \cdot I_p1)} \tag{59}$$

where I = amperes per phase in the line; I_p = amperes per phase in each coil; E = volts between phase wires on the line; E_p = volts across each group of armature coils connected across each phase; and E_1 = volts between phase wires and neutral. The coils in Fig. 49, III, may represent the phase windings of a three-phase generator or transformer, or each coil may represent a transformer or other device, three of which are Y-connected on a three-phase line.

Example. What will be the voltage across line wires of the three-phase circuit for the 120-volt Y-connected lamps in Fig. 50?

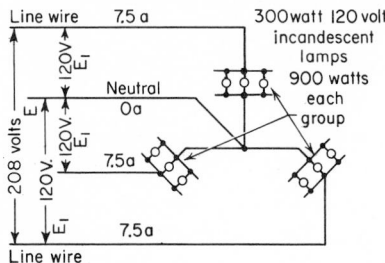

FIG. 50   *Incandescent lamp groups connected in star or Y.*

Solution. Substitute in the formula:

$$E = E_p \sqrt{3} = 120 \times 1.73 = 208 \text{ volts}$$

155. Relations for a delta-(Δ) connected three-phase circuit are shown in Fig. 51. When armature coils of a generator (see I) are connected as indicated, the voltages generated in them are 120 degrees apart. It would appear that the current might flow around through the coils and not into the external circuit, but it is evident from the phase diagram II that the sum of the effective voltages 1 and 3 generated by two of the coils is equal and opposite to that of the third. Hence, instead of tending to force current around internally, the voltages tend to force current out into the line. The following formulas indicate the relations of the voltages and currents. (All are effective values, and the circuit is assumed to be balanced. See Fig. 51.)

$$I_L = I_p \times \sqrt{3} = I_p \times 1.73 \tag{60}$$

$$I_p = \frac{I_L}{\sqrt{3}} = I_L \times 0.577 \qquad \text{or approx. } I_p = I_L \times 0.58 \tag{61}$$

$$E = E_p \tag{62}$$

where the symbols have the same meanings as in Fig. 51, III.

NOTE. Each coil (Fig. 51) may represent the phase windings of a three-phase transformer or generator or each coil may represent a transformer or other device, three of which are Δ-connected on a three-phase line.

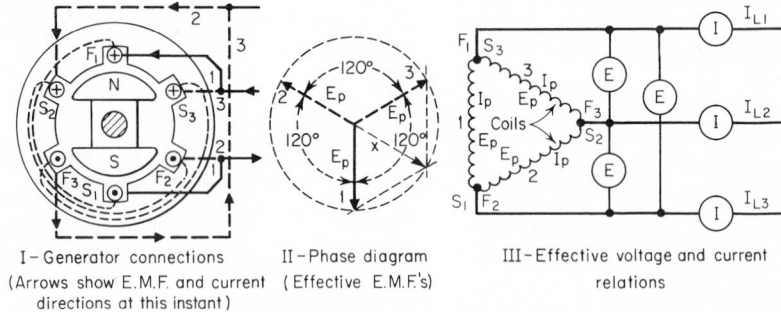

I – Generator connections   (Arrows show E.M.F. and current directions at this instant)

II – Phase diagram   (Effective E.M.F.'s)

III – Effective voltage and current relations

FIG. 51   *Delta (Δ)-connected three-phase generator and circuit.*

Example. If each of the coils of the generator in Fig. 51 can carry 100 amp, what value of current may be drawn from the line wires leading from the machine?

Solution. Substitute in the formula:

$$I_L = I_p \times \sqrt{3} = 100 \times 1.73 = 173 \text{ amp}$$

156. Relations of voltage, current, and power that apply to any balanced three-wire three-phase circuit either delta- or Y-connected. Refer to Fig. 52 for a key to the letters that appear in the following formulas. For a unity power factor load

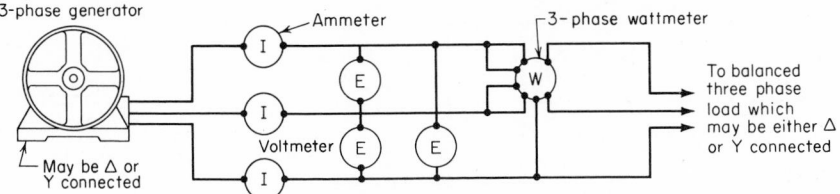

FIG. 52   *Relations for any (Δ- or Y-connected) three-phase circuit.*

$$I = \frac{W}{E \times \sqrt{3}} = \frac{0.577 \times W}{E} \quad \text{or approx.} = \frac{0.58 \times W}{E} \tag{63}$$

$$E = \frac{W}{I \times \sqrt{3}} = \frac{0.577 \times W}{I} \quad \text{or approx.} = \frac{0.58 \times W}{I} \tag{64}$$

$$W = E \times I \times \sqrt{3} = 1.73 \times E \times I \tag{65}$$

For any load

$$\text{Pf} = \frac{W}{1.73 \times I \times E} = \frac{0.577 \times W}{I \times E} \quad \text{or approx.} = \frac{0.58 \times W}{I \times E} \tag{66}$$

$$E = \frac{W}{\text{pf} \times 1.73 \times I} = \frac{0.577 \times W}{\text{pf} \times I} \quad \text{or approx.} = \frac{0.58 \times W}{\text{pf} \times I} \tag{67}$$

$$I = \frac{W}{\text{pf} \times 1.73 \times E} = \frac{0.577 \times W}{\text{pf} \times E} \quad \text{or approx.} = \frac{0.58 \times W}{\text{pf} \times E} \tag{68}$$

$$W = 1.73 \times E \times I \times \text{pf} \tag{69}$$

$$VA = 1.73 \times E \times I \tag{70}$$

where I = line current, in each of the three wires, in amperes; W = the power transmitted by all three wires in watts; E = voltage across lines; pf = the power factor of the circuit.

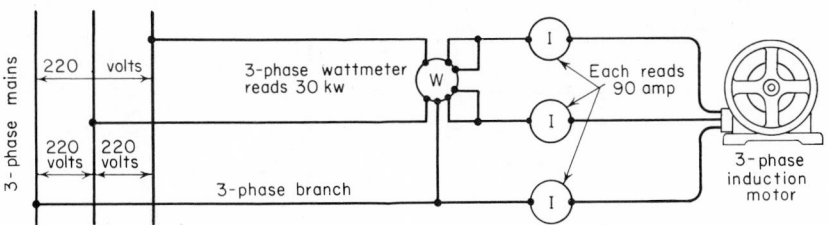

FIG. 53   *Motor on a three-phase circuit.*

Example.   What is the power factor in the 220-volt circuit to the motor in Fig. 53?   The three ammeters each indicate 90 amp, and the three-phase wattmeter indicates 30 kw (30,000 watts).
Solution.   Substitute in the formula:

$$\text{Pf} = \frac{0.577 \times W}{I \times E} = 0.577 \times \frac{30,000}{90 \times 220} = \frac{17,310}{19,800} = 0.88 = 88 \text{ per cent power factor}$$

Example.   The power factor on the feeder of Fig. 54 is known to be 70 per cent.   The current in each line is 80 amp, and the voltage across each phase is 220.   What actual power is being delivered to the panel?
Solution.   Substitute in the formula:

$$W = 1.73 \times E \times I \times \text{pf} = 1.73 \times 220 \times 80 \times 0.70 = 21,313.6 \text{ watts}$$

$$\text{Kw} = \frac{\text{watts}}{1,000} = \frac{21,313.6}{1,000} = 21.3 \text{ kw}$$

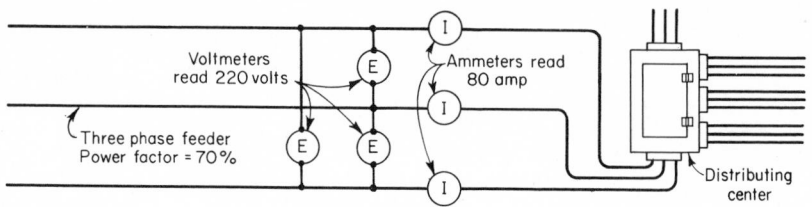

FIG. 54   *Load on a three-phase circuit.*

Examples. Figure 55 shows some numerical examples of voltage and current relations in a three-phase circuit. Note that when a group of three devices or coils is connected in delta, as in the motor, each device or coil has line voltage impressed on it and must be designed for that voltage. The current in the line will be 1.73 times the current through the coil. When Y-connected, as on the low-voltage side of the transformers, each of the three coils need only be designed for 1/1.73 or 0.577 times the line voltage, and the line current will be the same as the current through each coil. Single-phase loads may be supplied either from line to neutral as with the 120-volt lamps or from two lines as with the 208-volt heater.

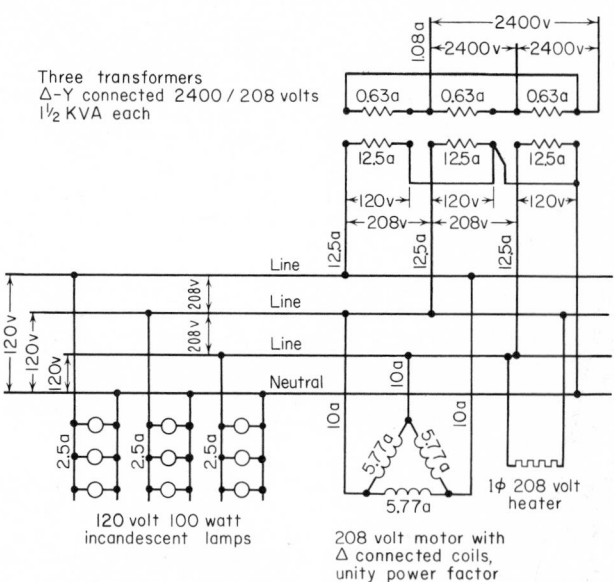

FIG. 55   *Examples of current and voltage relations in three-phase circuits.*

157. The power loss in any circuit traversed by an alternating or a direct current is

$$W = I^2 \times R \qquad \text{or} \qquad I = \sqrt{\frac{W}{R}} \qquad \text{or} \qquad R = \frac{W}{I^2} \tag{71}$$

where W = the **power** lost in heat in the circuit in watts; I = effective current in amperes in the conductor; and R = resistance of conductor in ohms. This rule is perfectly general and applies to all d-c circuits and all a-c circuits of ordinary voltages and frequencies. The watts **power** loss W reappears as heat **power** and heats the conductors. Watts loss is commonly called I^2R loss.

Example. What is the **power** loss in the incandescent lamp in Fig. 56?
Solution. Substitute in the formula:

$$W = I^2 \times R = (2.2 \times 2.2)98 = 4.84 \times 98 = 474 \text{ watts}$$

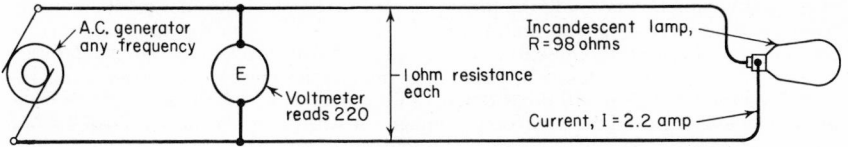

FIG. 56   *Resistance in an a-c circuit.*

Example. What is the **power** loss in the inductive winding of Fig. 57 with an alternating current of 3 amp?

Solution. Substitute in the formula:

$$W = I^2 \times R = (3 \times 3)7 = 9 \times 7 = 63 \text{ watts}$$

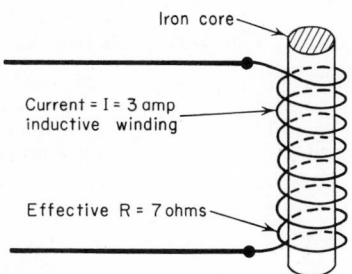

FIG. 57   *Effective resistance in an inductive a-c circuit.*

NOTE.   In the circuit of Fig. 57 the resistance of the coil to direct current is only 5 ohms. The increase in resistance to alternating current over its d-c value is due to the power losses produced in the iron core (refer to Sec. **122**).

158. Approximate Sparking Distances, in Air, for Various Mean Effective Voltages between Sharp Needle Points.   Sine-wave-form Voltage
(Locke Insulator Company)

Voltage	Distance		Voltage	Distance	
	In.	Cm		In.	Cm
1,000	0.06	0.152	20,000	1.00	2.54
2,000	0.13	0.33	25,000	1.30	3.3
3,000	0.16	0.41	30,000	1.63	4.1
4,000	0.22	0.56	35,000	2.00	5.1
5,000	0.23	0.57	40,000	2.45	6.2
10,000	0.47	1.19	50,000	3.55	9.0
15,000	0.73	1.84	100,000	9.60	24.4

NOTE.   Above 100,000 volts, the gap between needle points is approximately 1 in. per 10,000 volts. Using infinitely sharp needle points up to at least 10,000 volts, a graph of the voltage and the corresponding sparking distance would probably result in a straight line passing through the origin.   (H. W. Fisher, *Trans. Int. Elect. Cong.*, vol. II, p. 294, 1904.)

159. Dielectric Strength.   When there is an emf between two conductors that are separated by an insulating material, there are electrical forces exerted upon the electrons in the atoms of the insulating material.   These electric forces are trying to pull the electrons out of the atoms.   If these forces succeed in pulling the electrons out of the atoms, the material ceases to be an insulator and becomes a conductor.   When this occurs, it would be said that the insulation had broken down.   When the voltage between the conductors is small, the forces exerted in the atoms are not great enough to pull the electrons out of the atoms. As the voltage between the conductors is increased, the forces on the electrons are increased. If the voltage continues to be increased, the forces will eventually become great enough to pull the electrons out of the atoms and the insulation will break down. The voltage at which the material ceases to be an insulator is called the breakdown voltage. Any insulating material can be broken down and cease to be an insulator if the voltage impressed across it is raised high enough. The breakdown voltage of any material depends upon the thickness, condition of the surface, and homogeneity of the material. The breakdown voltage does not increase directly with the thickness of the material; a piece of material 2 in. thick will break down at a voltage less than twice the breakdown voltage of a piece 1 in. thick. Any irregularities or sharp points on the surface will lower the breakdown voltage.

It is the above considerations that govern the thickness of insulation required on conductors, the spacing of bare conductors, distance between live parts and ground, etc.

MEASURING, TESTING, AND INSTRUMENTS

160. The magneto test set is one of the most valuable testing instruments to the practical man because of its simplicity and the fact that it is always ready for service. Figure 58 shows the circuit and Fig. 59 a perspective view of a testing magneto. The apparatus consists of a small hand-operated a-c generator in series with a polarized

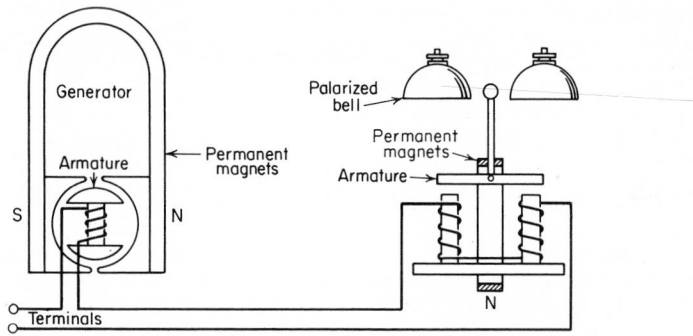

FIG. 58 *Circuits of testing magneto.*

electric bell. Alternating current will ring bells of this type. If the external circuit connected to the terminals of the magneto is closed and the crank of the generator is turned, current will flow and the bell will ring.

The resistance through which magnetos will ring is determined by their design. An ordinary magneto will ring through possibly 20,000 to 40,000 ohms. Electrostatic capacity effects must be considered when testing with a magneto. When long circuits are tested, such as telephone lines or circuits that are carried in cable for a considerable distance, the bell of the magneto may ring, owing to capacity, apparently indicating a short circuit, whereas the circuit may be perfectly clear or open. Circuits associated with iron, such as field coils of generators, may have considerable inductance. With highly inductive circuits under test, the magneto may "ring open," i.e., the bell may not ring at all, even though the inductive circuit connected to it be actually closed. In ordinary interior-wiring work the effects of capacity and inductance are usually negligible, and the true condition of the circuit will be indicated by the performance of the magneto bell.

161. A telephone receiver in combination with one or two dry cells constitutes an excellent equipment for certain tests. A "head"-telephone receiver (Fig. 60) is usually preferable to those of the watchcase types, because it is held on the head by the metal strap, allowing the unrestricted use of both hands. Metal testing clips are soldered to the flexible testing cords. The telephone receiver is extremely sensitive and will give a weak "click" even when the current to it passes through an exceedingly high re-sistance. In using, one clip is gripped on one conductor of the circuit to be tested and the other clip is tapped against the other conductor. Prolonged connection should be avoided because it will "run down" the battery. A vigorous click of the receiver in-dicates a closed circuit, while a weak click or none at all indicates an open circuit. After practice it is possible to determine approxi-mately the resistance of the circuit under test by the intensity of the receiver click. When the battery and receiver test set are connected to a circuit having some electrostatic capacity, the receiver will give a vigorous click when the clips are first touched to the circuit termi-nals, even though the circuit be open. With successive touchings the click will diminish in intensity if the circuit is open but will not diminish appreciably if the circuit is closed.

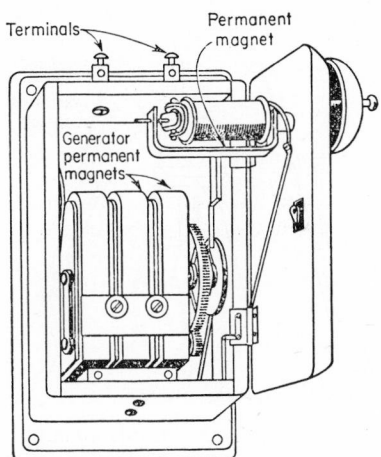

FIG. 59 *Assembly of testing magneto.*

162. The advantages of the telephone re-ceiver over the magneto for work of certain classes are: (1) The receiver and battery outfit costs little. (2) The outfit can be made so compact that it can be carried in the pocket. (3) In making insulation tests with a magneto the circuit may "ring clear," i.e., the bell will not ring, apparently indicating high insula-tion resistance, whereas the circuit may not be clear, but instead the magneto may be out of order or its local circuit open. The indication is negative. With the tele-phone receiver a slight click is produced even when testing through the highest re-sistances. The absence of a click usually signifies an open in the testing apparatus it-self. Thus the telephone receiver indication is positive.

163. A telegraph sounder is sometimes used for testing. It is connected in the same way as the telephone receiver of Fig. 60 and is adaptable for rough work. When the circuit under test is closed and the flexible-cord clips are touched to the circuit con-ductors, the sounder clicks. Where the circuit is open there is no click. One feature of the sounder method is that the click is audible at a considerable distance from the instrument.

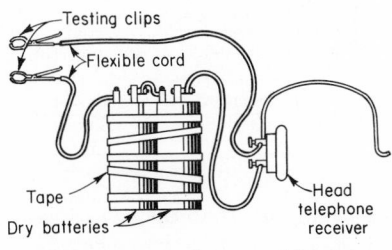

FIG. 60 *Head-telephone and dry-battery testing set.*

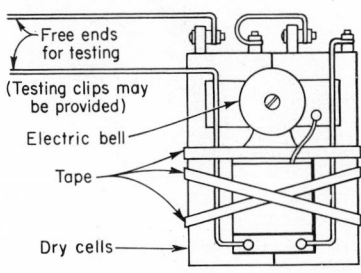

FIG. 61 *Electric-bell testing outfit.*

164. An electric-bell outfit for testing is shown in Fig. 61. When the free ends for testing are touched to a closed circuit of not too high resistance the bell rings. Where the circuit is open the bell will not ring. Flexible cord can be used for the testing con-ductors of the outfit, and testing clips can be provided as in Fig. 60.

165. A test lamp (Fig. 62), consisting merely of a weatherproof rubber-insulated socket into which is screwed an incandescent lamp of the highest voltage rating of the circuits involved, is very convenient for rough tests on interior-lighting and motor-wiring systems. Porcelain sockets are undesirable because they are so readily broken. Brass sockets should not be used because they may fall across conductors and thereby cause short circuits. Testing clips may be soldered to the ends of the leads which are molded in the socket. Some uses of the testing lamp are given in a following paragraph, and it is very convenient for testing for defective fuses.

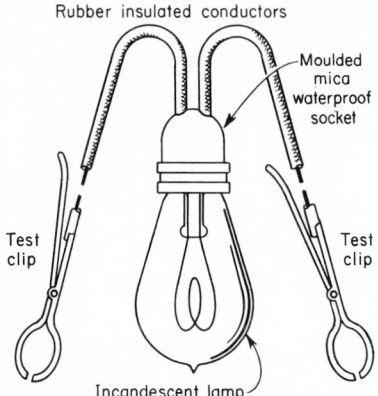

FIG. 62 *A practical test-lamp outfit.*

166. A very convenient and inexpensive test outfit consists of a pointer which moves along a scale inside an insulated case (Fig. 63). It indicates whether the circuit is alternating or direct current by vibrating on alternating current, the frequency of vibrations showing whether it is 25 or 60 cycles. It indicates the range of voltage of the circuit up to 550 a-c or 600 d-c. The sharp points on the end of the lead wires can be used to pierce insulation for checking insulated leads without destroying the insulation.

167. Neon-glow lamp testers provide a very convenient and compact device for determining if a circuit is live, for determining polarity of d-c circuits, and for determining if a circuit is alternating or direct current. A neon tester for low-voltage work is illustrated in Fig. 64. It consists of a very small neon lamp in series with a 200,000-ohm protective resistance enclosed in a molded case. This tester is satisfactory for use on circuits of from 90 volts d-c or 60 volts a-c to 500 volts a-c or d-c. With the test tips connected to a circuit, the presence of voltage within the above limits will be indicated by the glowing of the neon lamp. If both electrodes in the bulb glow the voltage of the circuit is alternating. On direct current,

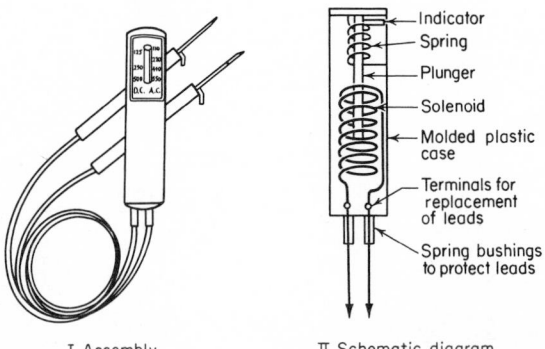

I Assembly   II Schematic diagram

FIG. 63   *Voltage tester, 110 to 600 volts. (Square D. Company.)*

only one electrode, the one connected to the negative side of the circuit, will glow. With experience the voltage of the line can be approximately determined by the intensity of the glow. In testing a circuit it is best first to touch only one side of the line with one test tip, keeping the other test tip free. A glow with this connection will indicate the presence of high voltage. The tester indicated is well constructed for safety. The molded case has a voltage breakdown value of 25,000 volts, and the leads are insulated for 5,000 volts and provided with insulated test prods.

Glow-tube testers are available for testing for the presence of voltage on high-voltage circuits. In testing high-voltage circuits by this means, no direct connection is made to the circuit. The end of the tester which contains the glow tube is simply held in proximity to the circuit. The changing electrostatic field will ionize the gas inside the tube and cause it to glow. These testers or statiscopes as they are called will indicate the presence of potential in a-c circuits, pulsating d-c circuits, X-ray equipment circuits, static from belting, high-frequency circuits, condenser discharges, and automobile ignition. On a-c circuits they will give positive indication on 2,000 volts and up. Materials which will act as shields to the electrostatic field, such as lead on underground conductors, metal cabinets, and grounded framework, must not be between the tester and the conductors of the circuit being tested. A pocket type of statiscope is shown in Fig. 65*b*. They are also made in types especially adapted for the testing of overhead lines and station equipment (Fig. 65*a*).

168. A neon lamp tester and fuse puller is shown in Fig. 66. It is made of transparent plastic with the fuse puller jaws at one end and two hinged prongs at the other end. The test prongs are of proper size for testing plugs and baseboard receptacles. By using the tester with a screw plug, lamp sockets can be tested without danger of short circuits or of burning out a regular bulb. The hinged prongs can be folded back against the inside of the legs for testing with the regular points. Portable test leads are available. They are sturdily constructed with a plug on one end for engaging the hinged prongs of the tester and with a rubber-insulated clamp and test prod on the other ends of the leads. The leads are 2 ft long and provide a 4-ft spread for test purposes.

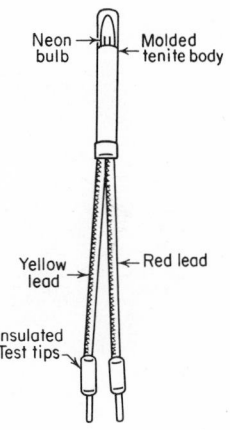

FIG. 64 *Neon glow-lamp tester. (Littlefuse, Inc.)*

169. Instruments for general-circuit and other industrial testing purposes are shown in Fig. 67. They are applicable for measurements on either d-c or a-c circuits. Only one instrument is required for measurements of voltage, current, and resistance.

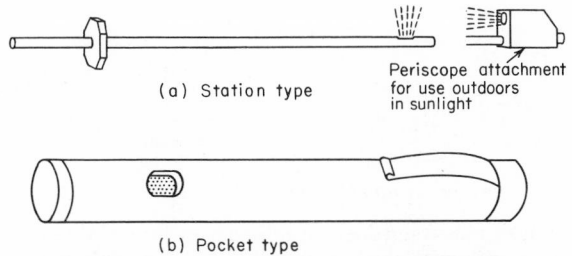

(a) Station type

Periscope attachment for use outdoors in sunlight

(b) Pocket type

FIG. 65 *Statiscopes. (Minerallac Electric Co.)*

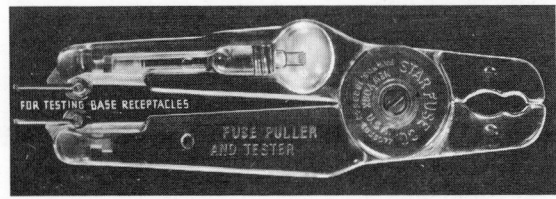

FIG. 66 *Neon-lamp fuse puller and tester. (Martindale Electric Co.)*

170. Rules for Use of Ammeter and Voltmeter (*Timbie,* "Elements of Electricity"). Place ammeter in series, always using a short-circuiting switch, where possible, as shown in Fig. 68, to prevent injury to the instrument. Place voltmeter in shunt (Fig. 68). Put the + side of the instrument on the + side of the line. Figure 68 shows the

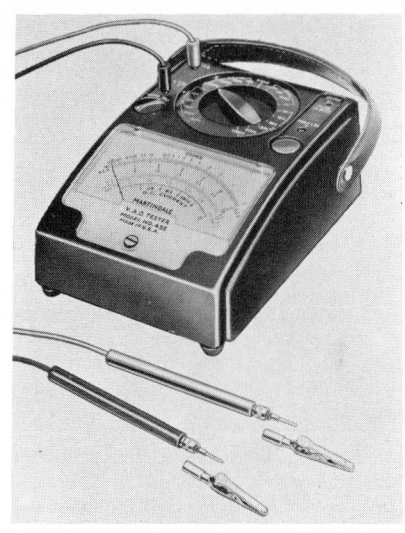

FIG. 67A   *Industrial   circuit   tester.*
(Weston Instruments.)

FIG. 67B   *V.A.O.   tester.   (Martindale*
Electric Co.)

correct use of an ammeter and a voltmeter to measure the current and the voltage supplied to the motor.   The short-circuiting switch S must be opened before the ammeter is read.   All the current that enters the motor must then flow through the ammeter and be indicated.   The ammeter is of very low resistance (about 0.001 or 0.002 ohm) and does not appreciably cut down the flow of current.   The voltmeter is of very high re-

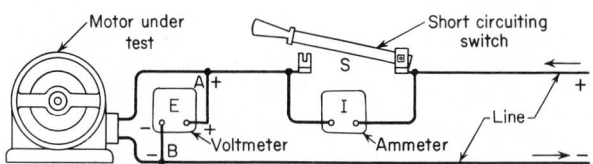

FIG. 68   *Ammeter and voltmeter connections.*

sistance (about 15,000 ohms) and does not allow any appreciable current to flow through it.   Yet enough goes through the voltmeter to cause it to indicate the voltage across the terminal AB of the motor.   Suppose the voltage across the motor to be 110; what would happen if an ammeter of 0.002-ohm resistance were by mistake placed across AB?   (Remember Ohm's law is always in operation.)

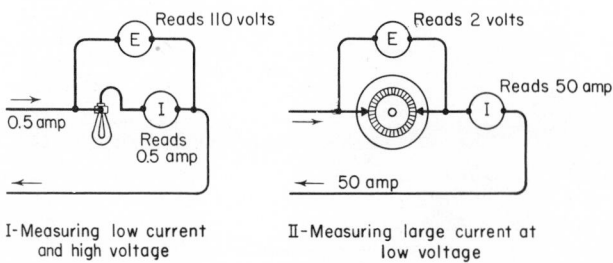

I–Measuring low current
and high voltage

II–Measuring large current at
low voltage

FIG. 69   *Correct methods of connecting instruments.*

171. All ammeters and voltmeters (except electrostatic) consume power when in use and introduce some error (Timbie, "Elements of Electricity"). For minimum error (see Fig. 69, I) when measuring a low current and high voltage, the voltmeter should be placed around both the ammeter and the apparatus under test.

When measuring the power consumed by a piece of apparatus through which a large current at low voltage is flowing, the voltmeter should be placed immediately across the piece of apparatus under test and should not include the ammeter (Fig. 69, II).

172. A method of measuring current with a voltmeter is shown in Fig. 70. If a resistor of known resistance is connected in series in a circuit and the voltage across the resistor measured with a voltmeter, the current can be determined by Ohm's law, thus:

Example (Fig. 70). If the drop around a 0.4-ohm resistance in series in a circuit is 20 volts, what is the current in the circuit?

Solution. Substitute in the Ohm's law formula:

$$I = \frac{E}{R} = \frac{20}{0.4} = 50 \text{ amp}$$

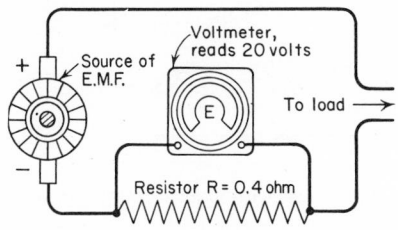

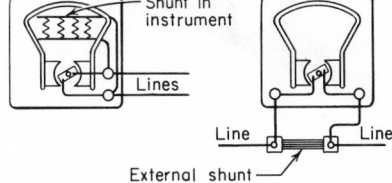

FIG. 70   *Current measurement with volt-meter.*

FIG. 71   *Millivoltmeters and shunts.*

173. A millivoltmeter is generally used for making measurements like that of Sec. **172.** A millivoltmeter reads in thousandths of volts, so that a resistor of small resistance can be used. Ammeters, particularly those for large currents, are often millivoltmeters calibrated in amperes which are connected around a resistor, in series with the circuit (Fig. 71). The resistor is sometimes in the instrument case and is sometimes inserted in the bus bars of a switchboard (see Fig. 71). Such resistors are called **shunts** and when furnished by instrument makers are carefully calibrated.

174. "Tong-Test" ammeters provide a very useful and convenient test instrument. In many instances when it is desired to measure the current flowing in a cable or other conductor, it is inconvenient, even if it is permissible to break the circuit, to insert an ammeter. The "Tong-Test" ammeter instantly measures alternating or direct current without opening or interrupting the circuit. Merely encircle the conductor with the tongs as illustrated in Fig. 72. As soon as the jaws close, a clear accurate reading is instantly registered on the scale.

Accurate readings can be taken on a-c frequencies from 25 to 400 cycles, as well as on direct current.

FIG. 72   *Application of "Tong-Test" ammeter. (Martindale Electric Co.)*

Readings can be made on either bare or insulated conductors. The jaws of the tongs are insulated, and the bakelite handle and shield protect the operator from shock. The Tong-Test meter is operated entirely by the magnetic field set up by the current, and it cannot be burned out, as it has no electrical wiring.

The tongs are opened by a moderate pressure of one finger on the trigger and are self-closing, requiring only one hand.

When d-c measurements are made, the jaws should be opened and closed immediately before the reading is taken in order to reduce the error caused by hysteresis if the current is rising or falling. If the current is steady, the error can be minimized by reversing the tongs and taking the average of the two readings.

175. Resistances can be measured with a voltmeter as indicated in Fig. 73. This method is satisfactory for the measurement of resistances whose values range from a few to a few hundred ohms. A resistor of known resistance, a source of direct current,

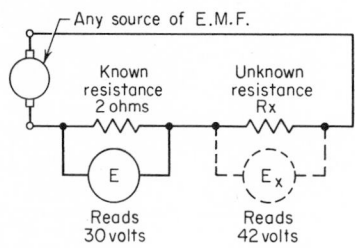

FIG. 73   *Resistance measurement.*

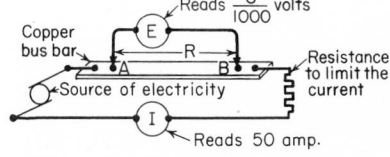

FIG. 74   *Measurement of very low resistance.*

and one voltmeter are required. The same constant current flows through both the known and the unknown resistance. The voltmeter reading E is taken and then the reading E_x. The voltage drops will be proportional to the resistances or

$$\frac{R}{E} = \frac{R_x}{E_x} \quad \text{or} \quad R_x = \frac{E_x \times R}{E} \tag{72}$$

Example. Substituting the values from Fig. 72 in the formula,

$$R_x = \frac{E_x \times R}{E} = \frac{42 \times 2}{30} = \frac{84}{30} = 2.8 \text{ ohms}$$

176. Very small resistances can be measured, as indicated in Fig. 74, with an ammeter and a millivoltmeter. This method is generally satisfactory for resistances having a value of less than 1 ohm and is convenient for measuring the resistance of bus bars, joints between conductors, switch contacts, brush-contact resistance, and other low resistances. As large a current as is feasible should be used. This is another application of Ohm's law.

Example. What is the resistance of the portion of the bus bar between A and B, Fig. 74? *Solution.* Substitute in Ohm's law formula:

$$R = \frac{E}{I} = \frac{0.008}{50} = 0.00016 \text{ ohm}$$

In the application of Ohm's law as given here, the current through the voltmeter is neglected. Since the resistance of the voltmeter is generally large compared with the resistance to be measured, the error involved by neglecting the voltmeter current is generally negligible.

177. Insulation resistance is frequently measured as suggested in Fig. 75. A voltmeter of known resistance, preferably of high resistance, and a source of emf (batteries or a generator) are required. First the voltage of the emf source is taken as shown at I or II. The apparatus is then arranged as shown at III to measure the resistance from each side of the circuit to ground. At IV or V are shown the connections for measuring the resistance between conductors. If E = voltage of source; E_1 = reading of voltmeter

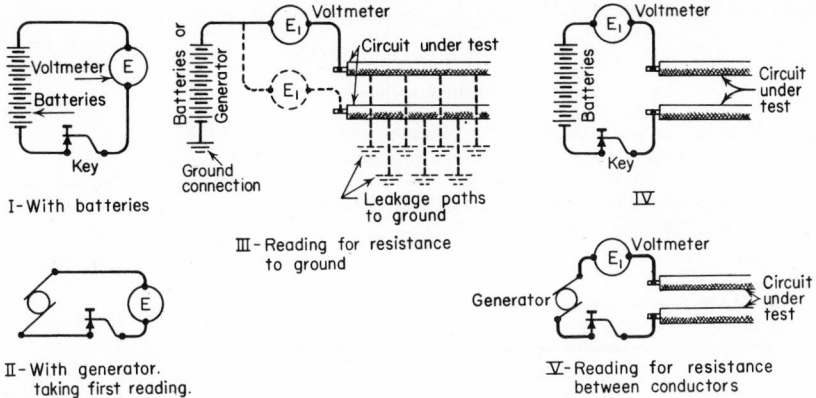

FIG. 75 *Measuring insulating resistance.*

when connected in series with insulation resistance to be measured; R_v = resistance, in ohms, of voltmeter; and R_x = insulation resistance sought, the following formula is used (see Fig. 75):

$$R_x = R_v \left(\frac{E}{E_1} - 1 \right) \tag{73}$$

Example. In a certain test (Fig. 76) where a 110-volt generator was used as a source of emf and a voltmeter having a resistance of 15,000 ohms was used to read voltages, the readings indicated in

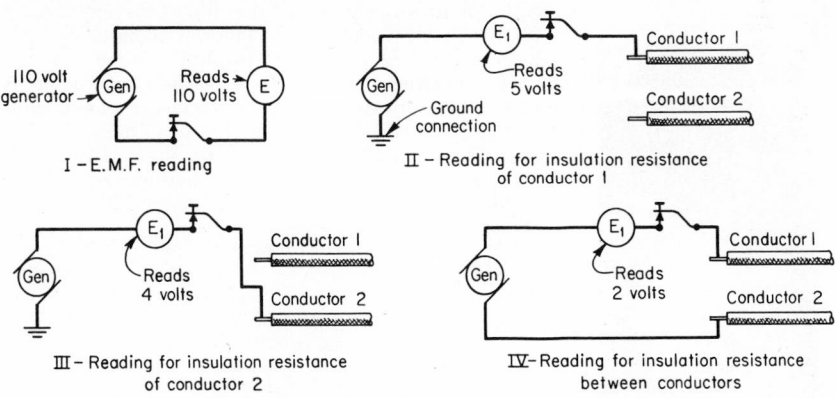

FIG. 76 *Example of insulation-resistance measurement.*

Fig. 76 were obtained. What was the insulation resistance to ground of each side of the circuit and what was the insulation resistance between circuits?

Solution. For the resistance of conductor 1 (see Fig. 76) substitute in the formula:

$$R_x = R_v \left(\frac{E}{E_1} - 1 \right) = 15,000 \left(\frac{110}{5} - 1 \right) = 15,000(22 - 1) = 15,000 \times 21$$

$$= 315,000 \text{ ohms} = \text{insulation resistance of conductor 1 to ground}$$

For the resistance of conductor 2 (see Fig. 76, III):

$$R_x = R_v \left(\frac{E}{E_1} - 1 \right) = 15,000 \left(\frac{110}{4} - 1 \right) = 15,000(27.5 - 1) = 15,000 \times 26.5$$

$$= 397,500 \text{ ohms} = \text{insulation resistance of conductor 2 to ground}$$

For the insulation resistance between conductors:

$$R_x = R_v \left(\frac{E}{E_1} - 1\right) = 15{,}000\left(\frac{110}{2} - 1\right) = 15{,}000(55 - 1) = 15{,}000 \times 54$$

$$= 810{,}000 \text{ ohms} = \text{insulation resistance between conductors 1 and 2}$$

178. The insulation resistance of a generator can be determined with a voltmeter of known resistance which is successively connected and read in positions I and II (Fig. 77). The formula of Sec. **177** is used. The external circuit connected to the generator should be cut off while the measurements are being taken so that its insulation resistance will not affect the readings.

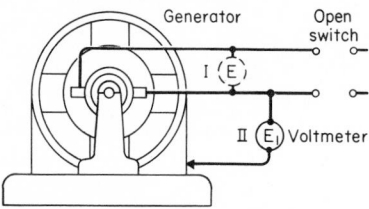

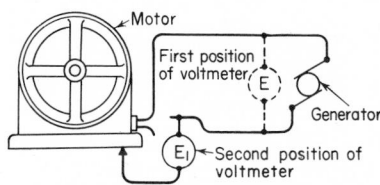

FIG. 77 *Measuring insulation resistance of a generator.*

FIG. 78 *Measuring insulation resistance of a motor.*

179. The insulation resistance of a motor can be measured with a voltmeter as suggested in Fig. 78. The formula of Sec. 78. **177** is used. Unless the external circuit has high insulation resistance, its resistance will affect the result.

180. The ohmmeter is an instrument to measure resistance directly. The one illustrated in Fig. 79 has an accuracy of 2 per cent. It is especially advantageous for work in the field, since its small size allows the meter to be carried in one's pocket. The meter is operated by a No. 2 dry cell, which is mounted inside the meter case.

181. A Megger (Fig. 80) is an instrument frequently used to measure high resistance. It consists of a magneto which is turned by a crank on the side of the case. The scale is calibrated directly in ohms. The resistance to be measured is connected across two terminals. The crank is turned at a moderate speed (about 120 rpm) until the pointer reaches a steady deflection.

182. Power, in d-c or unity-power-factor single-phase a-c electric circuits, can be measured with a voltmeter and an ammeter. For two-wire circuits the power in watts, in accordance with Ohm's law, equals the product of volts times amperes; thus

$$W = I \times E \qquad (74)$$

where W = the power in watts; I = the current in amperes; and E = the emf in volts.

FIG. 79 *Ohmmeter.*
(Weston Instruments.)

Example. See Sec. **111** for examples of power problems. Although no instruments are shown in these, the principles are the same as if instruments were used.

Example. In Fig. 81, I, the power taken by the motor is, substituting in the formula,

$$W = I \times E = 40 \times 220 = 8{,}800 \text{ watts}$$

or in kilowatts = 8,800/1,000 = 8.8 kw.

Example. In Fig. 81, II, the power taken by the lamps is

$$W = I \times E = 3 \times 110 = 330 \text{ watts}$$

or in kilowatts 330/1,000 = 0.33 kw.

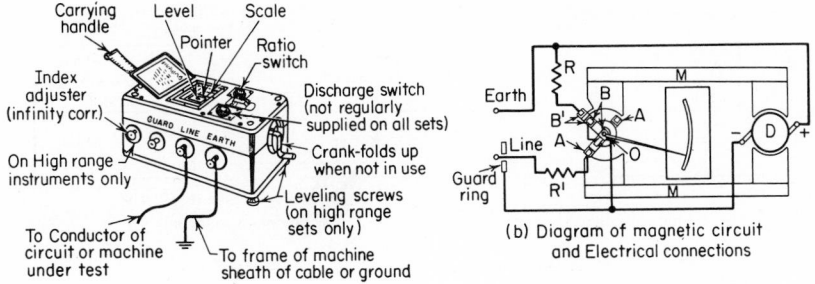

(a) Instrument showing connection
of circuit to be tested

(b) Diagram of magnetic circuit
and Electrical connections

FIG. 80 *Megger. (James G. Biddle Co.)*

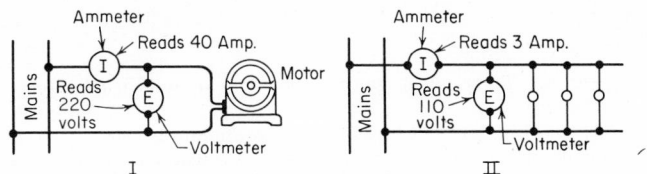

FIG. 81 *Power measurements.*

183. Power in single-phase a-c circuits must be measured with a wattmeter unless the power factor is unity. A wattmeter can also be employed for measuring the power of a d-c circuit. A wattmeter has two internal coils, namely, a voltage coil and a current coil. The voltage coil is connected across the circuit in which the power is to be measured, and the current coil is connected in series with the circuit. The wattmeter gives a direct indication of the power of the circuit. Two methods of connecting a wattmeter for measuring the power of a d-c or of a single-phase a-c circuit are shown in Figs. 41 and 42. In Fig. 41 the voltage coil is connected between the generator and the current coil of the wattmeter, while in Fig. 42 the voltage coil is connected between the load and the current coil of the wattmeter. The connection of Fig. 41 should be used for loads of small current and that of Fig. 42 for loads of large current.

184. Power in a two-phase system can be measured with two single-phase wattmeters connected as shown in Fig. 82. Each phase is treated as a separate circuit. One wattmeter reads the power of one phase, and the other the power of the second phase. The total power is the arithmetical sum of the two wattmeter readings, i.e.,

$$\text{Total power} = W_1 + W_2 \qquad (75)$$

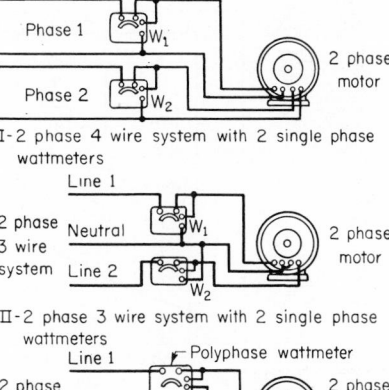

I-2 phase 4 wire system with 2 single phase
wattmeters

II-2 phase 3 wire system with 2 single phase
wattmeters

III-2 phase 3 wire system with a poly phase
wattmeter

FIG. 82 *Measurement of power in two-phase systems.*

A polyphase wattmeter, connected as shown in Fig. 82, III, can be used for the measurement of the power of a two-phase system.

185. Power in three-phase circuits can be measured with wattmeters by several dif-

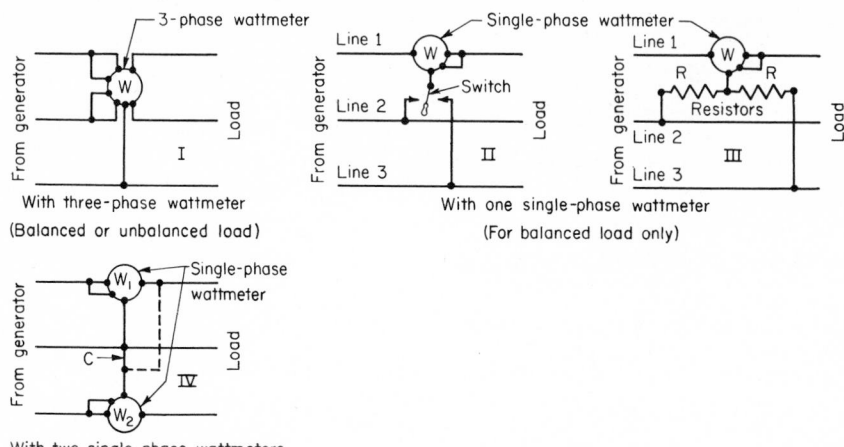

FIG. 83 *Three-phase power measurements with wattmeters.*

ferent methods (see Fig. 83). At I a polyphase wattmeter is shown. An instrument of this type automatically adds the portions of power consumed in each phase and indicates their sum. Instruments made by different manufacturers are arranged differently and must be connected accordingly. Directions accompany each instrument. Diagrams II and III show how the power can be measured, in a balanced circuit, with one wattmeter. One potential lead is connected to the line in which the wattmeter is inserted, and the other potential lead is connected successively to the other two lines. The total power in II is equal to the sum or difference of the two readings. If resistors

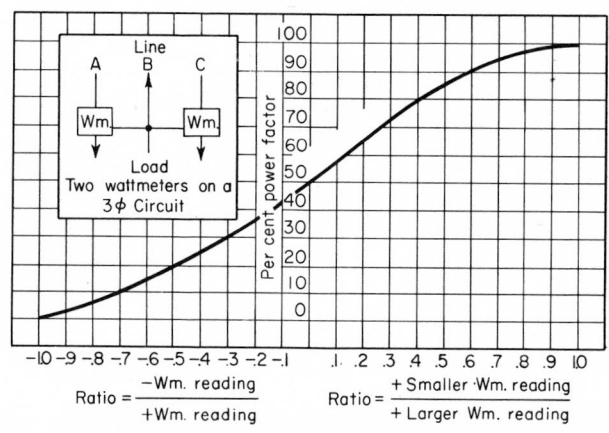

$$\text{Ratio} = \frac{-\text{Wm. reading}}{+\text{Wm. reading}} \qquad \text{Ratio} = \frac{+\text{Smaller Wm. reading}}{+\text{Larger Wm. reading}}$$

Directions

Case I: -Both readings positive- Divide smaller by larger reading. Find this ratio on right side of center line above. Follow up the ordinate at this point to its intersection with curve. Opposite this on center line find corresponding per cent power factor (above 50 per cent)

Case II: -One reading negative- Divide negative by positive reading. Find this ratio on left side of center line above. Follow up the ordinate at this point to its intersection with curve. Opposite this on center line find corresponding per cent power factor (below 50 per cent)

FIG. 84 *Power-factor curve.*

are used as indicated in III, the power can be ascertained without any shifting of leads. The wattmeter reading of III multiplied by 3 will be the true power in a balanced circuit. The resistance of each of the resistors R and R must be equal to the resistance of the potential or voltage coil of the wattmeter.

With two wattmeters (as in Fig. 83, IV) the total power is equal to the sum or difference of the two wattmeter readings. If the power factor is greater than 0.50, the total power is the arithmetical sum of the readings. If it is lower than 0.50, one of the readings is negative and the power is their arithmetical difference. To ascertain whether one of the wattmeters is reading negative, temporarily transfer the connection of one of the potential wires (for example c in IV, as shown by the dotted line) from the middle wire to the outside wire. If its wattmeter reverses, one of the instruments, that of the lesser indication, is reading negatively. The nature of the load usually enables one to judge roughly what the power factor is. With incandescent lamps and fully loaded motors the power factor will be high, but with under- and lightly loaded motors is is likely to be low. See Sec. **187** for method of determining the **power factor** of three-phase circuits **with wattmeters.**

186. The power factor of a circuit can be determined from readings of voltmeters, ammeters, and wattmeters by use of the formulas of Secs. **146, 147, 150,** and **156.** The power factors of circuits can also be determined by instruments called power-factor meters, which when properly connected in a circuit read the power factor directly.

187. The method of determining three-phase power factor with wattmeters was well described by C. E. Howell in *Electrical World.* It is necessary to know the power factor in order to connect watthour meters correctly where the wiring is concealed. An abstract follows:

Figure 84 shows the power-factor curve for two single-phase meters on a polyphase circuit. It also gives a diagram of connections and instructions as to how to use the curve. The figure should be self-explanatory.

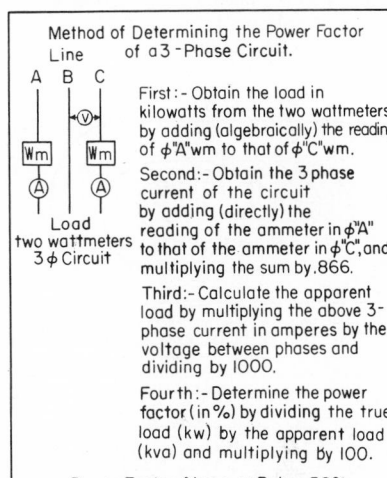

Method of Determining the Power Factor of a 3-Phase Circuit.

First:- Obtain the load in kilowatts from the two wattmeters by adding (algebraically) the reading of ϕ"A"wm to that of ϕ"C"wm.

Second:- Obtain the 3 phase current of the circuit by adding (directly) the reading of the ammeter in ϕ"A" to that of the ammeter in ϕ"C", and multiplying the sum by .866.

Third:- Calculate the apparent load by multiplying the above 3-phase current in amperes by the voltage between phases and dividing by 1000.

Fourth:- Determine the power factor (in %) by dividing the true load (kw) by the apparent load (kva) and multiplying by 100.

Power Factor Above or Below 50%

If induction motor load, throw off all load and run motors "light". The power factor will be below 50% and one wattmeter, or element of a polyphase meter, should read negatively. Now load up circuit to within 20% of total capacity. The single phase wattmeter, or elements which read negatively on light load should now read positively but not as high as meter or element, which gave a positive reading on light load. If the meters, or elements, are connected properly, they should fulfill the above conditions.

FIG. 85 *Chart of instructions for power-factor test.*

tory. Figure 85 gives, first, a method of checking results obtained by employing the curve given in Fig. 84 and a diagram of the connections for obtaining data for the check. The second part of Fig. 85 gives a method of determining the correct connections for two single-phase meters or one polyphase meter on a three-phase circuit. If this part of Fig. 85 is followed, errors in meter connections on three-phase circuits due to the power factor being near 50 per cent should be minimum.

To illustrate the use of the above instructions: A 100-hp three-phase 440-volt induction motor was operating on 30 per cent full load or 30 hp (29.8 kw) at 60 per cent power factor (afterward determined) when an order "came through" to place a polyphase watthour meter on the installation. Immediately after the meter had been connected the following question was asked: "Should the light element add to or subtract from the heavy element; i.e., is the power factor above or below 50 per cent?" As the meter leads were encased in pipe, they could not be traced; therefore the instructions in the second figure pertaining to this point were applied. The connected load of the motor having been thrown off, it was found that one element of the meter gave a negative reading. Sufficient load was then put on to bring the motor to about 80 per cent of its full-load rating. Each element of the meter (taken separately) now read positively, but the element which on no load gave a negative reading on 80 per cent load read lower than the heavy element. The meter had been correctly connected when installed. Later both methods given above to determine the power factor of a three-phase circuit were applied, and both gave approximately 60 per cent power factor (at 30 per cent load).

188. To read correctly the consumption indicated on the dials of a recording watt-hour meter (sometimes, but erroneously, called a recording wattmeter) these directions should be followed (Rules and Regulations of the Commonwealth Edison Co., Chicago; see Fig. 86 for examples):

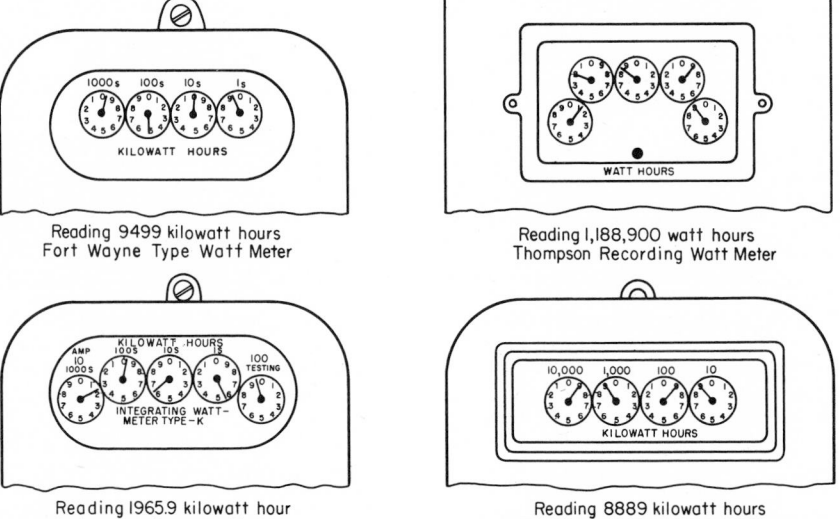

FIG. 86 *Examples of watthour meter readings.*

The pointer on the right-hand dial of a five-dial meter registers $\frac{1}{10}$ kwhr or 100 watt-hr for each division of the dial. A complete revolution of the hand on this dial will move the hand of the second dial one division and register 1 kwhr or 1,000 watt-hr. A complete revolution of the hand of the second dial will move the third hand 1 division and register 10 kwhr or 10,000 whr and so on.

Accordingly, read the hands from left to right and add two ciphers to the reading of the lowest dial to obtain the reading of the meter in watt-hours. Where there are four dials on the meter, the pointer on the right-hand dial registers 1 kwhr or 1,000 whr for each division of the dial, and it is necessary to add three ciphers to the reading on the lowest dial to obtain the reading in watthours, or the meter reads directly in kilowatt-hours.

Hands should always be read as indicating the figure which they have last passed, and not the one to which they are nearest. Thus, if a hand is very close to a figure, whether it has passed this figure or not must be determined from the next lower dial. If the hand of the lower dial has just completed a revolution, the hand of the higher dial has passed the figure, but if the hand of the lower dial has not completed a revolution, the hand of the higher dial has not yet reached the figure, even though it may appear to have done so.

When one pointer is on 9, special care must be taken that the pointer on the next higher dial is not read too high, as it will appear to have reached the next number but will not have done so until the hand at 9 has come to zero.

The hands on adjacent dials revolve in opposite directions. Therefore a reading should always be checked after being written down, as it is easy to mistake the direction of the rotation.

To determine the consumption for a given time, subtract the reading at the beginning of the period from the reading at the end. Always observe if a constant is marked at the bottom of the dial plate. If so, the difference of the readings must be multiplied by this constant to obtain the consumption.

189. The Wheatstone bridge is an instrument for measuring medium and high resistances. It is not suitable for measuring resistances of less than 1 ohm. An elementary diagram is shown in Fig. 87. R_1, R_2, and R are adjustable resistances, R_x is the unknown resistance, and G is a delicate galvanometer. A battery supplies emf. It can be shown that if, when both keys are pressed, the galvanometer shows no deflection, then

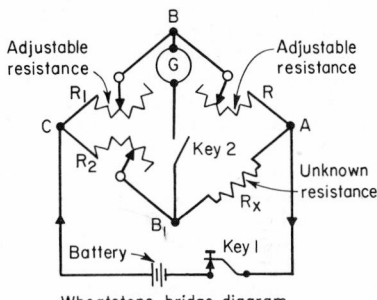

FIG. 87 *Elementary diagram of the Wheatstone bridge.*

$$\frac{R_1}{R} = \frac{R_2}{R_x} \qquad \text{or} \qquad R_x = \left(\frac{R_2}{R_1}\right) R \tag{76}$$

Example. If $R_2 = 100$ ohms, $R_1 = 10$ ohms, and $R = 672$ ohms, what is the value of the unknown resistance?

Solution. Substitute in the formula:

$$R_x = \left(\frac{R_2}{R_1}\right) R = \left(\frac{100}{10}\right) 672 = 10 \times 672 = 6{,}720 \text{ ohms}$$

The unknown resistance is 6,720 ohms.

In commercial bridges, the adjustable resistances R_2 and R_1 are usually so arranged that the ratio R_2/R_1 will be a fraction like $\frac{1}{10}$ or $\frac{1}{100}$ or a number like 10 or 100 so that R_x can be obtained readily by dividing or multiplying R by an easily handled number. R_1 and R_2 are sometimes called the ratio arms, and R is called the rheostat arm. For most accurate results the resistances R, R_1, and R_2 should be as nearly as possible equal to R_x.

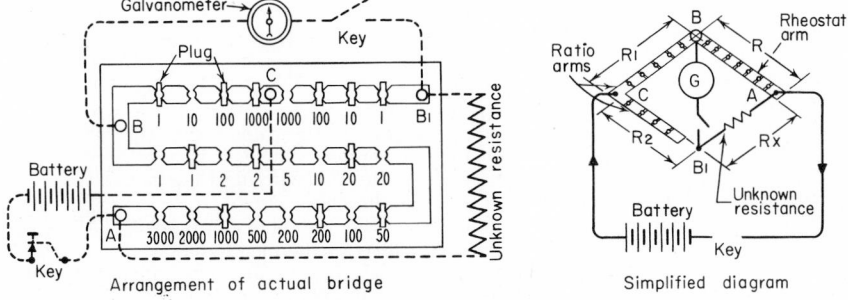

FIG. 88 *Post-office pattern of Wheatstone bridge.*

190. A diagram of a commercial bridge of the post-office pattern is shown in Fig. 88. Its principle is similar to that of Fig. 87. Brass plugs are used to vary the resistance in arms R, R_1, and R_2. When a plug is inserted in the opening between two resistance coils, it shunts out the coil. When this bridge is used, the ratio R_2/R_1 is arranged by the operator, depending upon the relative value of R_x as compared with R. Then R is adjusted until a balance is obtained. When R_x is greater than R, the ratio must be 10,

100 or 1,000, and when R_x is smaller than R, the ratio must be 0.1 or 0.01 or 0.001. If $R_1 = R_2$ the value of R_x equals R.

191. Directions for Using a Wheatstone Bridge. (1) Insert the unknown resistance. (2) Make a mental estimation of the probable value of the unknown resistance. If it is not greater than the total resistance in the arm R or smaller than that of any one coil in R, R_1 and R_2 can be made equal by taking plugs from the proper holes. (3) Take a plug from a coil, in R, of about the estimated resistance of R_x and press the keys. Note the deflection of the needle, whether it is to the right or left. Now unplug a coil in R of about twice the resistance of the first one unplugged. If the needle now deflects in the opposite direction, the value of R_x lies between these two values. If the deflection is in the same direction, the unplugged resistance in R is too great, and a value of about one-half that originally selected should be tried. Systematically narrow down the limits until the best possible balance is obtained. (4) Usually it is impossible to secure an exact balance. When this is the case, proceed as indicated in the following example: Assume that the coil of smallest resistance in the R arm is of 0.1 ohm. With this added, the galvanometer deflects two divisions to the right. The deflection without is three divisions to the left. Therefore a difference of 0.1 ohm makes a difference of five scale divisions. The resistance that would give no deflection is $\frac{3}{5} \times 0.1 = 0.06$ ohm. (5) Be careful not to allow the metal parts of the bridge plugs to become wet or greasy from the hands. (6) Use a twisting motion when inserting the plugs. Put them in firmly but do not use enough force to twist off the insulating handles. (7) When closing the keys, close the battery first, and in opening the keys, open the galvanometer key first.

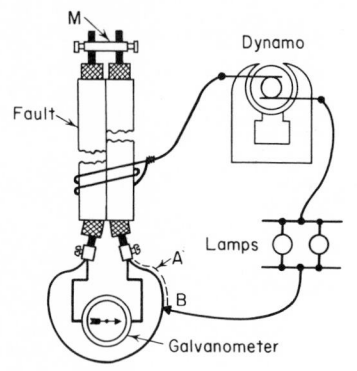

FIG. 89   *Locating a fault in a cable.*

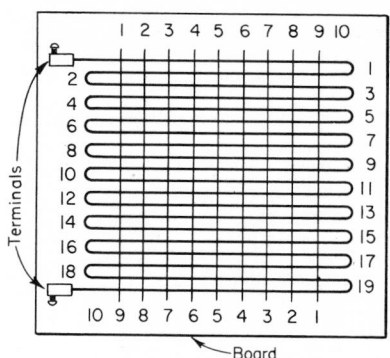

FIG. 90   *Homemade wire bridge.*

192. Locating Faults in a Cable (Standard Underground Cable Co.). Figure 89 shows a simple method, using a dynamo, a galvanometer, and 10 or 15 ft of bare wire. This method is applicable only when both conductors of the cable are of the same size. After making the connections shown, it is only necessary to move the stylus along the bare wire until the galvanometer is not deflected in either direction.

Let A = the length of the wire between the balance point B and the faulty conductor, C = the total length of the wire, and L = the total length of the cable circuit = twice the length of the cable. Then distance to the fault = $(A \times L)/C$.

Figure 90 shows a simple form of wire bridge which can be used for tests of this kind. The length A can be read directly, and the value of C is 200. A telephone receiver can be used in place of the galvanometer.

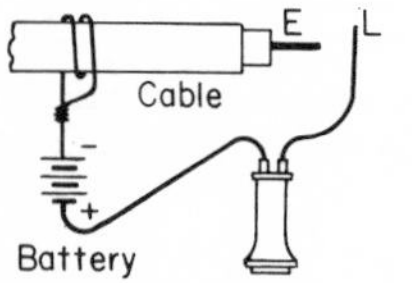

FIG. 91   *Test for insulation resistance.*

193. Testing Cable Insulation with a Telephone Receiver and Battery (Standard Underground Cable Co.). An extremely simple way to determine whether or not the insulation resistance of any particular wire is high is as follows: A telephone receiver and battery are connected as shown in Fig. 91. One side of the battery is attached to the lead sheath of the cable or to ground, and the other side to a telephone receiver. A rubber-insulated wire is attached to the other side of the telephone. To test, press the telephone receiver to the ear and touch the wire L to the conductor E; a click will always be heard the first time. After keeping both wires in contact for several seconds, break and make the connection once more; if no sound is heard at the instant of reconnection, the wire is not faulty. With intervals of time between break and make of 1 sec with a battery of 1 volt it can be assumed that no click indicates at least a resistance of 50 megohms. When more battery is used, this number is increased about in proportion to the number of cells. Care must be taken that sounds in the telephone due to induction are not misconstrued for those produced by leaks.

194. Grounds on series lighting circuits frequently reveal their locations automatically. If there are two good grounds on the circuit, the lamps connected in the line between the grounds will not burn because the grounds will shunt them out. For example, in Fig. 92 with a good ground at 1 and 11, lamps 2 to 10 would be shunted out. Sometimes there may be two grounds on a circuit, but they may not be "good" enough to shunt out the lamps. (This paragraph and those that follow on testing series circuits are from *Electrical World.*)

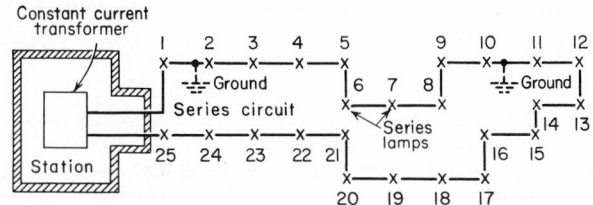

FIG. 92 *Effect of two grounds on a series circuit.*

The presence of but one ground on a circuit, irrespective of how "good" it is, will not reveal itself automatically, and the proper operation of the circuit will not be affected by one ground. However, where there is one ground, it constitutes a serious menace to the lives of the station operators and trouble men. Furthermore, another ground may occur at any time that may cause the shunting out of lamps or possibly a fire or destruction of equipment. Hence, it is very desirable to maintain the circuits entirely clear of grounds. It is the practice in all well-maintained stations to test each series circuit for grounds, some time during every afternoon, and if a ground is discovered, a trouble man is sent out to locate and clear it before the circuit is thrown into service for the night.

195. The usual method of testing dead series circuits for grounds is to disconnect the circuit from all station apparatus and then to connect one terminal of a magneto test set to the circuit and the other to ground. If the bell rings vigorously when the crank is turned, the circuit is grounded. If it does not, the circuit is clear. If the circuit is very long or in cable for a considerable portion of its length, the bell may ring a little even if the circuit is clear of grounds.

196. The method of locating a ground on a dead series circuit is illustrated in Fig. 93. Disconnect all station apparatus and temporarily ground one side of the circuit as at B (Fig. 93). Proceed out along the line and connect some testing instrument (a magneto

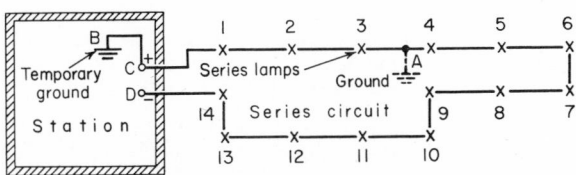

FIG. 93 *Locating a ground on a dead series circuit.*

test set is most frequently used) in series with the circuit at some point. If, when the crank is turned, the magneto bell rings, indicating a closed circuit, the tester is between the station ground and the ground on the circuit. If the magneto rings open, the tester is between the circuit ground and the ungrounded station end of the circuit. If in Fig. 93 the test is inserted at lamp 1, 2, or 3, the magneto should ring closed, while if inserted at any of the other lamps it should ring open.

197. In locating either a ground or an open on a series circuit, unless the tester has an idea as to the location of the trouble, he should proceed first to the middle point of the circuit and there make his first test. This first test will indicate on which side of the middle point the trouble is. He should then proceed to the middle point of the half of the circuit that shows trouble and there make another test. This will localize the trouble to one quarter of the circuit. This "halving" of the sections of the circuit should be continued until the trouble is finally found.

If there is more than one ground on a series circuit, the trouble is tedious to locate. If the tests made at different points on the circuit are confusing, indicating the existence of several grounds, the best procedure is to open the circuit into several distinct sections and then test each one as a unit, following the methods described in preceding paragraphs.

198. A ground on a series circuit can sometimes be located with the current from the transformer, by placing a temporary ground on the circuit at the station. For example, if in Fig. 93 a temporary ground is connected to terminal B and the device that supplies the operating current to the circuit is connected to terminals C and D and normal operating current thrown out on the circuit, lamps 1, 2, and 3 will not burn, indicating that the ground is between lamps 3 and 4. The use of this method is attended by some fire risk; hence, the method should be used with caution.

199. A method of locating a ground on a series circuit with a lamp bank is suggested in Fig. 94. A bank of 110-volt incandescent lamps, each of the same wattage, is connected in series as indicated, and one end of the bank is permanently grounded. There should be a sufficient number of lamps in the bank so that the sum of the voltages of all of the lamps is at least equal to the voltage impressed on the series circuit by the transformer. For instance, if the voltage impressed on the series circuit is 6,600, there should be at least sixty 110-volt incandescent lamps in the bank $(6{,}600 \div 110 = 60)$.

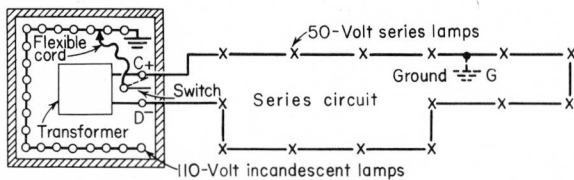

FIG. 94   *Locating a ground on a "live" series circuit with an incandescent lamp bank.*

In locating a ground, the flexible cord which is connected to the center point of the double-throw switch is successively placed on different points on the conductor that connects the incandescent lamps in series, the switch being thrown to one or the other of the circuit terminals C or D. Move the flexible cord along until the incandescent lamps in the bank, between the point of connection of the cord and the permanent ground, burn at about full brilliancy. When this condition obtains, the voltage impressed across the lamps that are burning fully brilliant is approximately equal to the voltage impressed on the portion of the circuit (to which the switch connects) between the station and the ground. The voltage required across each lamp of the outside circuit being known, the number of lamps between the station and the ground can be readily computed, and thereby the ground is located.

Great care must be exercised in using this method. Practically all series lighting circuits operate at very high voltage. Hence, when the flexible cord is being moved along the lamp bank, the transformer should be entirely disconnected. If it is not, voltage dangerous to life is present.

Example. Consider Fig. 94. There is a ground on the circuit. It is found that two of the incandescent lamps of the bank burn at full brilliancy between the flexible-cord connector and the lamp-bank ground. Since 110-volt lamps are used in the bank the voltage across these two is 220. This means that the voltage on the circuit between points C and G is about 220. Since the series lamps each require about 50 volts, there must be $220 \div 50 = 4.4$, or in round numbers, 4 series lamps between C and the ground G. After making a test with the switch point on C, it should be thrown over to D, and a check test made from the other end of the circuit. The method of figuring is the same in each case.

200. To locate an "open" on a series circuit, ground one end of the circuit at the station as in Fig. 93. Then make tests at different points out on the circuit with the magneto connected in between line and ground. As long as the magneto bell indicates a closed circuit, the open is on the line side of the tester. When the magneto indicates an open circuit, the open is toward the station from the tester.

201. The testing out of a concealed wiring system for proper connections is illustrated in Fig. 95. It is assumed that the wires are installed and that the locations of their runs are concealed by the plastering. Only the ends of the conductors are visible at the outlets. It is necessary to identify the conductor ends at each outlet. These

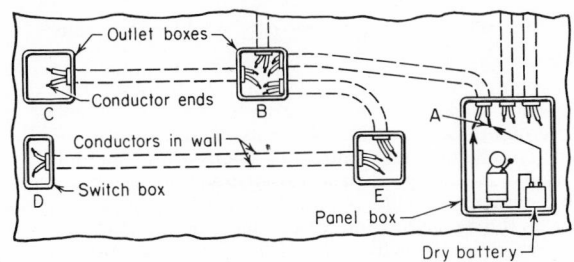

FIG. 95 *Testing out wiring for proper connections.*

tests are usually made with an electric-bell outfit (Fig. 61) because the sound of the bell will indicate a closed circuit to the wireman in a distant room. Hence, one man can test out such a system. In testing out, first skin the ends of all of the conductors and see that none is in contact with any other or with the outlet box. Next, select a pair of conductors (A, Fig. 95), preferably the pair that serves the group, and connect the bell outfit to the ends of the pair as shown. Then proceed to the outlet (B, Fig. 95) at which the pair of conductors should terminate and successively touch together the ends of all the wires that terminate in that box until a pair is discovered whose ends touched together ring the bell. This identifies one pair. Tag this pair so that it can be readily found again and repeat the process on some other pair. Continue this until all of the conductors are identified. (These paragraphs on practical electrical tests are from *Electrical Engineering.*)

202. The method of testing out the connections for three-way switches is shown in Fig. 96. When finally connected, the circuits should be as shown at I. It is assumed that the conductors are in place and concealed within walls or ceilings and that only the ends are visible at the outlets, as at Fig. 96, II. First, identify the feed conductors and bend back their ends at the outlet box as at A_3. Next, twist together, temporarily, the bared ends of any two of the conductors at each of the switch outlets as at A_3 and C_3. The conductors having their ends thus twisted together will be the switch conductors. Now, at the lamp outlet, or outlets, identify the short-circuited switch conductors as directed in a preceding paragraph and connect and solder these switch conductors together as at B_3. Connect the remaining conductor ends at the lamp outlets to the lamps, B_4, connect one of the feed conductors to the center point of the three-way switch (A_4), and connect the other feed conductor to the lamp wire. The switch conductors are connected to the two points of the switch. At C_4 the same procedure is followed.

203. In testing out a new wiring installation for faults each branch circuit, main, and feeder should be treated individually. It is usually impracticable to test an installa-

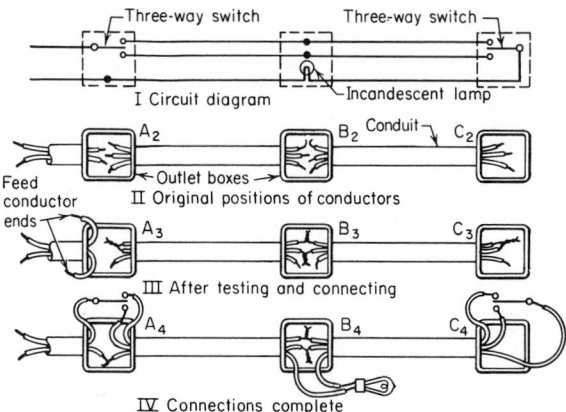

FIG. 96   *Testing out three-way switch connections.*

tion as a unit, as open switches and loose connections in cutouts may render such a test worthless. If a test is made from the cutout on the two conductors of each individual circuit, the above-mentioned possible elements of uncertainty are eliminated. Test each side of each circuit separately unless the lamps are in position.

204. Open circuits in multiple wiring installations are usually readily located. If the lamps are in position and lighting voltage available, it can be impressed on the circuit. The lamps on the generator side of the "open" will then burn while those on the far side will not, which localizes the open. Where lighting voltage is not available, all the lamps can be taken out of the sockets, and each of the sides of the circuit can be grounded at the cutout. Then a telephone-and-battery, a bell-and-battery, or a magneto test set can be connected temporarily and successively between one line and ground and between the other line and ground at each outlet on the branch. When the test set indicates an open circuit, the "open" is between the tester and the ground made at the cutout.

205. The test for short circuits on a multiple system is made by temporarily connecting a test set across the terminals of each branch circuit at the cutout. If there is a short circuit on the lines under test, its presence will be immediately evident by the indication of a closed circuit.

206. The test for continuity of multiple wiring circuits is made by temporarily connecting a test set across the terminals of each branch cutout and successively short-circuiting, one at a time, the sockets of the branch with a screw driver, a nail, or other metal object. The test set will then indicate whether the wiring of the circuit is open or closed. Where lighting voltage is available and plug cutouts are used, a lamp can be screwed into one socket of the cutout and a plug fuse into the other. Then the tester can proceed from socket to socket and short-circuit each. Where circuit to the socket is continuous, the lamp will light when the socket is short-circuited.

207. The test for grounds on a multiple wiring installation is made by temporarily connecting between line and ground a test set of one of the types previously described. If the test set indicates a closed circuit, the line being tested is grounded.

208. The testing of three-wire circuits to identify the neutral is effected as suggested in Fig. 97. Where the neutral is grounded, a test lamp can be successively connected between each of the three conductors and ground (Fig. 97, I). When the ungrounded side of the lamp is touched to the neutral wire, it will not burn, but when touched to either of the outside wires, it will burn. A method that can be used with either a grounded or an ungrounded neutral is illustrated in Fig. 97, II. Connect the two test lamps in series successively between one of the line wires and the other two. When connected across the two outer wires, both lamps will burn at full voltage, but when connected between one of the outer wires and neutral, they will burn at only half voltage.

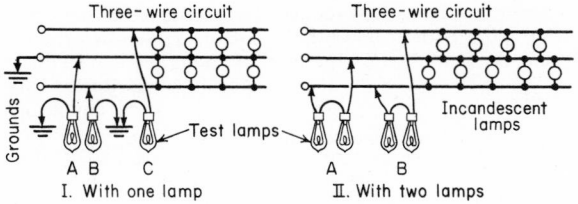

FIG. 97 *Locating neutral wire with test lamp.*

209. To determine the polarity of d-c circuits hold the two conductors in a glass vessel of water as in Fig. 98. It may be necessary to pour a little common salt or acid into the water to render it conducting. Pure water is a poor conductor. Bubbles will form only on the negative conductor, indicating the presence of current and the polarity of the circuit. Be careful not to touch the conductor ends together and cause a short circuit (see also Fig. 99, and neon testers, Sec. **167**).

210. The direction of current flow in a d-c circuit can be determined with a compass as described in Sec. **89**.

211. Ground detectors are desirable on ungrounded systems in order that when an accidental ground occurs, it can be remedied before a second ground on

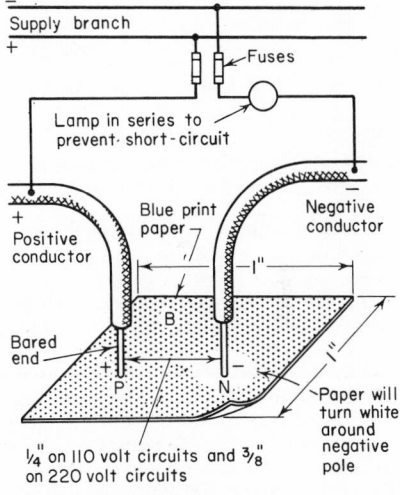

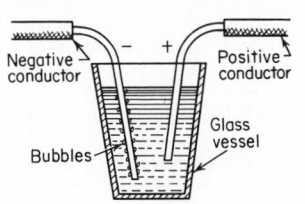

FIG. 98 *Determination of polarity with conductor ends in water.*

FIG. 99 *Blueprint paper used for testing polarity.*

another wire causes a short circuit. Control circuits especially should be suitably equipped with ground detectors, as a double ground may cause the closing or tripping of circuits carrying load, with serious consequences.

212. Ground Detectors for Two-wire D-C Circuits. Figure 100 shows a very good and simple detector for any two-wire low-voltage system. The lamps for the detector should each be of the same wattage and voltage—the voltage being about the same as that of the regular lamps in the plant—and two lamps should be selected which, when connected in series, burn with equal brilliancy. Although somewhat greater sensitiveness can be obtained with low-wattage lamps, such as 25-watt, for example, it is believed in general to be better to use lamps of the same wattage as those throughout the plant, as then a burned-out or broken detector lamp can be immediately replaced by a good lamp from the regular stock, thus avoiding the necessity of keeping on hand a few spare special lamps.

The detector lamps, being two in series across the proper voltage for one lamp, burn only dimly. If, however, a ground occurs on any circuit, as at *a*, the current from the positive bus bar through lamp 1 divides on reaching *b*, instead of all going through lamp 2, as it did when there was no ground. Part now goes down the ground wire and through the ground to *a*, as indicated by the broken line, and thence through the wires to the negative bus bar. This reduces the resistance from b to the negative bus bar, and therefore more current flows through lamp 1 than before, while less current flows through lamp 2. Lamp 1 consequently brightens and lamp 2 dims. If the ground had occurred at c instead of a, lamp 2 would have brightened and lamp 1 would have dimmed.

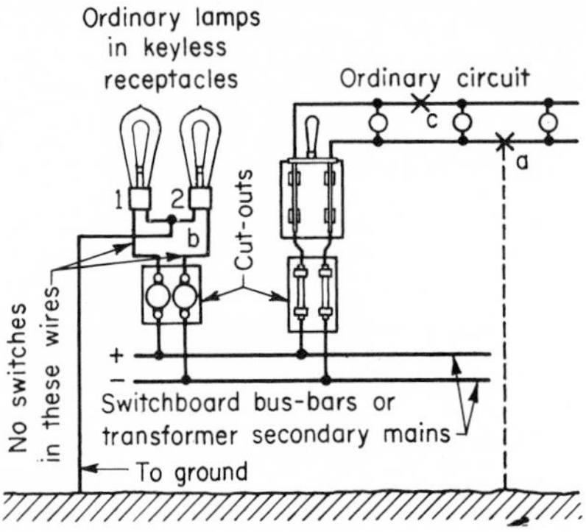

Attention is called to the following points, which are frequently neglected in this form of detector:

1. The lamp receptacles should be keyless, and there should be no switches of any kind in any of the connecting wires, so that the detector will always be in operation. In order to be of the greatest value, the indications must be given instantly when a ground occurs. The observer should not have to wait until the engineer or electrician remembers to close a switch.

2. The wires should be protected by small fuses where they connect to the bus bars. If these fuses are omitted, a short circuit across these wires would either burn up the wires or blow the main generator fuses.

FIG. 100   *Two-lamp ground detector.*

3. The lamps should be placed very close together, within 1 or 2 in. of each other if possible. The farther apart they are, the harder it is to detect any slight difference in brilliancy between them.

4. The ground wire should be carefully clamped to a pipe which is thoroughly connected to the ground, or some other equally good ground connection should be provided.

213. On d-c control circuits, a telegraph-type relay, which will sound an alarm, is preferable to the lamps, since sufficient current can flow through the lamps as a result of double grounds to operate some relays and cause circuit breakers to operate.

214. An ordinary voltmeter can be used as an intermittent ground detector on d-c circuits of any voltage, as shown in Fig. 101. The voltmeter ordinarily used to indicate the voltage on the system can, of course, be used for this purpose, the voltmeter switch shown in the cut being arranged to give the different desired connections.

If, for example, the system shown in Fig. 101 were of about 100 volts, the voltmeter would register 100 when the levers of the switch were on the inside contact points as shown. If, now, the right-hand lever were moved to the outside contact point as shown dotted and there were a ground on the system, as at a, current would pass from the positive bus bar through the circuit to a, thence through the ground to the ground wire, and through the voltmeter to the negative bus bar, causing the voltmeter to read something below 100, unless the ground at a were practically a perfect connection. In that case the voltmeter reading would be 100. If the positive side of the system were entirely free from grounds, the voltmeter reading would be 0.

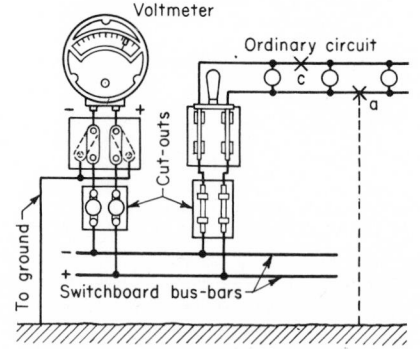

FIG. 101   *Voltmeter ground detector.*

Assume that under these conditions the voltmeter reads 50 and that the resistance of the voltmeter itself is 20,000 ohms. Since with no external resistance, when the voltmeter is connected directly to the bus bars, it reads 100, while now it reads 50, the total resistance under the new conditions must be 40,000 ohms. The resistance of the ground at a is $40,000 - 20,000 = 20,000$ ohms.

If the voltmeter had read only 20 the total resistance would have been $^{100}/_{20} \times 20{,}000 =$ 100,000, and the resistance of the ground $100{,}000 - 20{,}000 = 80{,}000$ ohms.

215. Ground Detectors for Ordinary Low-voltage Three-phase A-C Circuits. A lamp detector connected as in Fig. 102 can be used. The indication is the same as that with the lamp detectors described above. Thus, when a ground comes on one wire, the lamp attached to that wire dims and the other two brighten.

For ordinary two-phase (or quarter-phase) systems, where the phases are entirely insulated from each other, the two-lamp detector can be used, one detector on each phase. There are, however, in this class of wiring several complicated systems, to all of which the lamp detector principle is applicable, although the exact method of connections differs in each case, so that no general rule can be given.

216. Electrostatic ground detectors are used for high-voltage ungrounded a-c systems. This

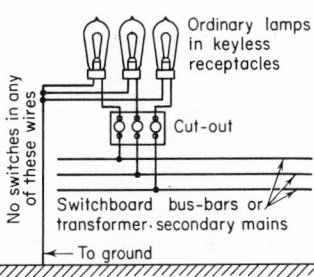

FIG. 102 *Three-phase lamp detector.*

instrument for use on three-phase circuits consists of a semispherical vane flexibly supported (Fig. 103). Around the circumference of the vane are three stationary curved plates, each being connected through a capacitor to one of the three phase lines. The operation is due to the electrostatic field created between the plates. The vane is grounded, and a ground on any line removes the charge between the plate connected to that line and the ground. This causes the vane to move toward the other two plates against the action of a spring. Thus the vane being off center indicates a ground. The capacitors (Fig. 103) insulate the instrument from the high voltage of the line. A single-phase electrostatic ground detector is shown in Fig. 104.

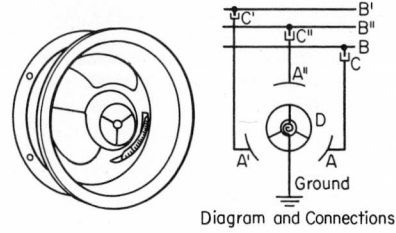

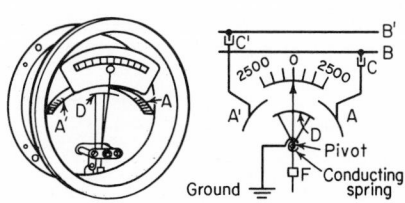

FIG. 103 *Three-phase electrostatic ground detector. (Westinghouse Electric Corp.)*

FIG. 104 *Single-phase electrostatic ground detector. (Westinghouse Electric Corp.)*

217. A triplex voltmeter, which is an instrument containing three voltmeter movements with short scales (Fig. 105), can also be used on a-c systems. Each voltmeter is connected between one line and ground. With no grounds all voltmeters should read zero, but a ground on one line will cause the other two meters to read. The magnitude of the reading will depend on the resistance of the meter and the resistance of the ground, a good ground being indicated by full line-voltage reading.

218. Test to Determine Horsepower of an Electric Motor. Applying the principles, outlined elsewhere in this division, to a motor under test for output, the power delivered being measured with a prony brake (Fig. 106) may be taken as an example.

Example. The torque is 10 lb at 3-ft radius, or 30 lb-ft, or 30 lb at 1-ft radius. Since the motor pulley is turning at the rate of 1,000 rpm, a point on its circumference travels $2\pi r R = 2 \times 3.14 \times 1 \times$ 1,000 = 6,280 ft per min. At its circumference the pulley is overcoming a resistance of 30 lb. Therefore it is doing work at the rate of $30 \times 6{,}280 = 188{,}400$ ft-lb per min. Since, when work is done at the rate of 33,000 ft-lb per min, a horsepower is developed, the motor is delivering 188,400 ÷

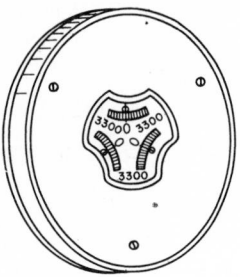

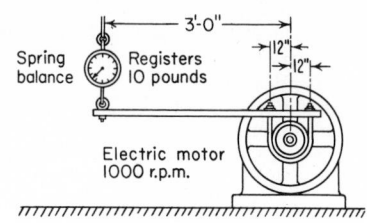

FIG. 105 *Electrostatic ground detector (triplex voltmeter type). (General Electric Co.)*

FIG. 106 *Horsepower determination with a prony brake.*

33,000 = 5.7 hp. It should be noted that, though the torque at the circumference of the motor pulley was considered in the example, it is not necessary to take the torque at that point. The torque may be taken at any point if the radius to that point is used instead of the radius of the pulley. The formula for determining the horsepower output of a motor under test with a prony brake is

$$Hp = 2 \times \pi TS \div 33,000$$

where $\pi = 3.1416$; T = torque in pound-feet; and S is the speed of the motor in rpm. Substituting the values from the above example in this formula,

$$Hp = 2 \times 3.14 \times 30 \times 1,000 \div 33,000 = 5.7 \text{ hp}$$

This is the same result secured by the former and longer method. In metric units, work is expressed in kilogram-meters, so, conversely, torque should be expressed in meter-kilograms or in kilograms at a given radius in meters.

219. The testing of motors and generators for faults is treated in Div. 7 on Motors and Generators.

DIVISION TWO

Properties and Splicing of Conductors

ELECTRICAL CONDUCTING WIRES AND CABLES

1. Electrical conducting wires and cables are available in a great variety of different types and forms of construction. To cover this one subject completely would require a large volume. The aim of the author has been, therefore, to include in this division sufficient general information with respect to the materials employed, method of construction, and types available so that it will enable a person to select intelligently the proper cable for a given application. At the end of the section, more detailed tabular information is included for the types of cables that the average worker will use most frequently.

2. Electric Wire and Cable Terminology

Wire. A slender rod or filament of drawn metal. (The definition restricts the term to what would ordinarily be understood by the term "solid wire." In the definition, the word "slender" is used in the sense that the length is great in comparison with the diameter. If a wire is covered with insulation, it is properly called an insulated wire, although primarily the term "wire" refers to the metal; nevertheless when the context shows that the wire is insulated, the term "wire" will be understood to include the insulation.)

Conductor. A wire or combination of wires not insulated from one another, suitable for carrying a single electric current. (The term "conductor" is not to include a combination of conductors insulated from one another, which would be suitable for carrying several different electric currents. Rolled conductors, such as bus bars, are, of course, conductors but are not considered under the terminology here given.)

Stranded Conductor. A conductor composed of a group of wires or any combination of groups of wires. (The wires in a stranded conductor are usually twisted or braided together.)

Cable. (1) A stranded conductor (single-conductor cable), or (2) a combination of conductors insulated from one another (multiple-conductor cable).

The component conductors of the second kind of cable may be either solid or stranded, and this kind of cable may or may not have a common insulating covering. The first kind of cable is a single conductor, while the second kind is a group of several conductors. The term "cable" is applied by some manufacturers to a solid wire heavily insulated and lead-covered; this usage arises from the manner of the insulation, but such a conductor is not included under this definition of "cable." The term "cable" is a general one, and in practice it is usually applied only to the larger sizes. A small cable is called a stranded wire or a cord, both of which are defined below. Cables may be bare or insulated, and the latter may be armored with lead or with steel wires or bands.

Strand. One of the wires or groups of wires of any stranded conductor.

Stranded Wire. A group of small wires, used as a single wire. (A wire has been defined as a slender rod or filament of drawn metal. If such a filament is subdivided into several smaller filaments or strands and is used as a single wire, it is called stranded wire. There is no sharp dividing line of size between a stranded wire and a cable. If used as a wire, for example in winding inductance coils or magnets, it is called a stranded wire and not a cable. If it is substantially insulated, it is called a cord, defined below.)

Cord. A small cable, very flexible and substantially insulated to withstand wear. (There is no sharp dividing line in respect to size between a cord and a cable and likewise no sharp dividing line in respect to the character of insulation between a cord and a stranded wire. Usually the insulation of a cord contains rubber.)

Concentric Strand. A strand composed of a central core surrounded by one or more layers of helically laid wires or groups of wires.

Concentric-lay Conductor. A conductor composed of a central core surrounded by one or more layers of helically laid wires. (Ordinarily known as concentric strand conductor. In the most common type, all the wires are of the same size and the central core is a single wire.)

Concentric-lay Cable. A multiple-conductor cable composed of a central core surrounded by one or more layers of helically laid insulated conductors.

Rope-lay Cable. A cable composed of a central core surrounded by one or more layers of helically laid groups of wires. (This cable differs from a concentric-lay conductor in that the main strands are themselves stranded and all wires are of the same size.)

Multiple-conductor Cable. A combination of two or more conductors insulated from one another. (Specific cables are called "3-conductor cable" or "19-conductor cable," etc.)

Multiple-conductor Concentric Cable. A cable composed of an insulated central conductor with one or more tubular stranded conductors laid over it concentrically and insulated from one another. (This kind of cable usually has two or three conductors.)

N-conductor Cable. A combination of N conductors insulated from one another. (It is not intended that the name as here given be actually used. One would instead speak of a 3-conductor cable, a 12-conductor cable, etc. In referring to the general case, one may speak of a multiple-conductor cable, as in the definition for "cable" above.)

N-conductor Concentric Cable. A cable composed of an insulated central conducting core with tubular stranded conductors laid over it concentrically and separated by layers of insulation. (Usually only 2-conductor or 3-conductor. Such conductors are used in carrying alternating currents. The remark on the expression "N-conductor" given for the preceding definition applies here also.)

Duplex Cable. A cable composed of two insulated single-conductor cables twisted together with or without a common covering.

Twin Cable. A cable composed of two insulated conductors laid parallel and either attached to each other by the insulation or bound together with a common covering.

Twin Wire. A cable composed of two small insulated conductors laid parallel, having a common covering.

Twisted Pair. A cable composed of two small insulated conductors twisted together without a common covering.

Triplex Cable. A cable composed of three insulated single-conductor cables twisted together.

Sector Cable. A multiconductor cable in which the cross section of each conductor is approximately the sector of a circle.

Shielded-type Cable. A cable in which each insulated conductor is enclosed in a conducting envelope so constructed that substantially every point on the surface of the insulation is at ground potential or at some predetermined potential with respect to ground under normal operating conditions.

Shielded-conductor Cable. A cable in which the insulated conductor or conductors is/are enclosed in a conducting envelope or envelopes, so constructed that substantially every point on the surface of the insulation is at ground potential or at some predetermined potential with respect to ground.

Composite Conductor. A composite conductor consists of two or more strands of different metals, such as aluminum and steel or copper and steel, assembled and operated in parallel.

Round Conductor. Either a solid or stranded conductor of which the cross section is substantially circular.

Cable Filler. Cable filler is the material used in multiple-conductor cables to occupy the spaces formed by the assembly of the insulated conductors, thus forming a core of the desired shape.

Cable Sheath. Cable sheath is the protective covering applied to cable.

Insulation of a Cable. The insulation of a cable is that part which is relied upon to insulate the conductor from other conductors or conducting parts or from ground.

Insulation Resistance of an Insulated Conductor. The insulation resistance of an insulated conductor is the resistance offered by its insulation to an impressed direct voltage, tending to produce a leakage of current through the same.

Lead-covered Cable (Lead-sheathed Cable). A lead-covered cable is a cable provided with a sheath of lead for the purpose of excluding moisture and affording mechanical protection.

Serving of a Cable. Serving of a cable is a wrapping applied over the core of a cable before the cable is leaded or over the lead if the cable is armored.

NOTE: Materials commonly used for serving are jute, cotton, duck tape.

Resistive Conductor. A resistive conductor is a conductor used primarily because it possesses the property of high electric resistance.

3. Wire Sizes. The size of wire is usually expressed according to some wire gage. The different sizes are referred to by gage numbers. Unfortunately several different systems of gages have been originated by different manufacturers for their products. However, it has become standard practice in the United States to employ the American wire gage (AWG), also known as the Brown and Sharpe (B & S), for the designation of copper and aluminum wire and cable used in the electrical industry. The names, abbreviations, and uses of the most important gages used for the measurement of wires and sheet-metal plates are given in Sec. **4.** A numerical comparison of these gages is given in Table **84.** It will be observed that in most cases the larger the gage number, the smaller the size of the wire.

4. Names, Abbreviations, and Uses of the Principal Wire and Sheet-metal Gages

Col. No. in Table 84	Names and abbreviations		Ordinarily used for measuring
	Usual	Others	
1.	American wire gage (AWG)	Brown and Sharpe (B&S)	Copper, aluminum, and other nonferrous wires, rods, and plates. Wall thickness of tubes
2.	Steel wire gage (SWG)	Roebling, American Steel and Wire, Washburn & Moen, National G. W. Prentiss	Iron and steel wire. Wire nails. Brass and iron escutcheon pins
3.	Birmingham wire gage (BWG)	Stubs Iron Wire Gage, Iron Wire Gage	Galvanized iron and steel wire. Iron rivets, copper rivets. Thickness of wall of nonferrous seamless tubing
4.	Stubs steel wire gage	. . . .	Drill rod
5.	British standard wire gage (SWG)	Imperial Standard Wire Gage, Standard Wire Gage, English Legal Standard	Legal standard wire gage for Canada and Great Britain. Used sometimes by American telephone and telegraph companies for bare copper line wire
6.	Steel music wire gage (MWG)	Hammacher, Schlemmer, Felten & Guilleaume	Steel music wire
7.	Manufacturers Standard Gage (MSG)	. . . .	Legal standard for iron and steel plate. Monel metal. Galvanized sheets
8.	American Zinc	. . . .	Sheet zinc
9.	Birmingham gage (BG)	. . . .	Legal standard for iron and steel sheets in Canada and England

5. How to Remember the AWG or B & S Wire-gage Table (Westinghouse Diary). A wire that is three sizes larger than another wire has half the resistance, twice the weight, and twice the area. A wire that is ten sizes larger than another wire has one-tenth the resistance, ten times the weight, and ten times the area. Number 10 wire is 0.10 in. in diameter (more precisely 0.102); it has an area of 10,000 cir mils (more precisely 10,380); it has a resistance of 1 ohm per 1,000 ft at 20°C (68°F), and weighs 32 lb (more precisely 31.4 lb) per 1,000 ft.

The weight of 1,000 ft of No. 5 wire is 100 lb. The relative values of resistance (for decreasing sizes) and of weight and area (for increasing sizes) for consecutive sizes are 0.50, 0.63, 0.80, 1.00, 1.25, 1.60, 2.00. The relative values of the diameters of *alternate* sizes of wire are 0.50, 0.63, 0.80, 1.00, 1.25, 1.60, 2.00. To find resistance, drop one cipher from the number of circular mils; the result is the number of feet per ohm.   To find weight, drop four ciphers from the number of circular mils and multiply by the weight of No. 10 wire.

6. Wire measuring gages (Figs. 1 and 2) are made of steel plate.   With the kind shown in Fig. 1 the wire being measured is inserted in the slots in the periphery until a slot is found in which the wire just fits.   Its gage number is indicated opposite the slot.   A measuring gage like that of Fig. 1 indicates the numbers of one gage or system

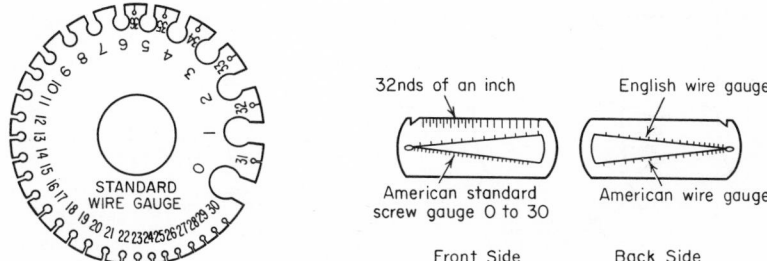

FIG. 1   *Standard wire gage (greatly reduced).*

FIG. 2   *Angular wire gage (greatly reduced).*

only.   A gage like that of Fig. 2 indicates the numbers of four gages but has the disadvantage that, to use it, the end of the wire must be available to push through the slot. The wire is pushed as far toward the small end of the slot as it will go, and its gage number will be indicated opposite the point where the wire stops.   The gage of Fig. 2 is arranged to indicate gage numbers for the American screw gage, English wire gage, and American wire gage, and one scale is divided into thirty-seconds of an inch.

7. A micrometer is frequently used for determining the size of a given wire or cable. It provides an accurate means of measuring the diameter of the wire or cable to thousandths of an inch and estimating to ten-thousandths.   After the diameter is determined, the corresponding gage size may be ascertained by referring to a wire table. The wire to be measured is placed between the thumbscrew and the anvil (Fig. 3), and

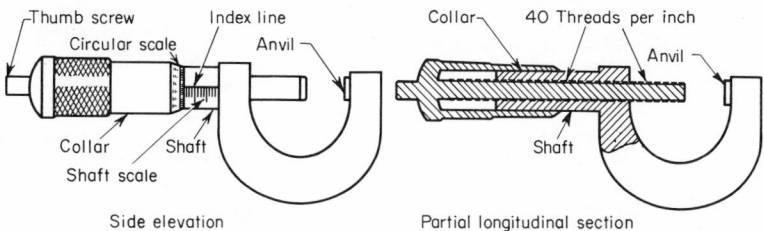

FIG. 3   *A micrometer caliper.*

the screw turned until the wire is lightly held between the screw and the anvil.   The screw has 40 threads to the inch, so that one complete turn of the screw in a left-hand direction will open the micrometer $\frac{1}{40}$ of an inch.   On the edge of the collar is a circular scale divided into 25 divisions; hence, when the screw is turned through one of these divisions, the micrometer will open $\frac{1}{25} \times \frac{1}{40}$ in. = $\frac{1}{1000}$ in.   The shaft on which the collar turns is marked into tenths of an inch, and each $\frac{1}{10}$ is subdivided into four parts.   Each of these parts must be equal to $\frac{1}{10}$ in. by $\frac{1}{4} = \frac{1}{40}$ in. = 0.025 in.   Therefore a complete rotation of the collar or 25 of its divisions will equal one division of the shaft, or 0.025 in.

8. To read a micrometer (see Fig. 4 and the paragraph above) note the number on the circular scale nearest the index line. This indicates the number of thousandths. Note the number of small divisions uncovered on the shaft scale. Each one of these small divisions indicates 0.025 in. ($^{25}/_{1000}$). Add together the number of thousandths indicated on the circular scale and 0.025 × the number of small divisions wholly uncovered on the shaft scale. The sum will be the distance that the jaws are apart.

Examples are shown in Fig. 4.

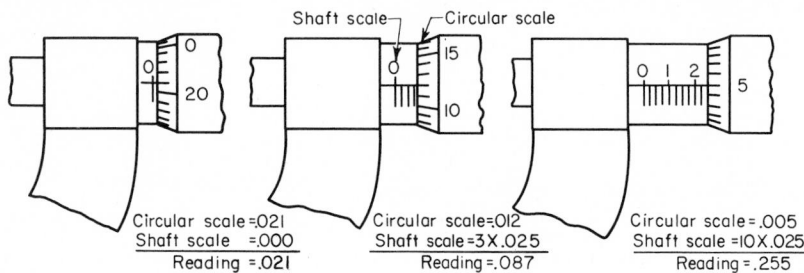

FIG. 4   *A micrometer caliper.*

9. Classification of Wires or Cables.   Electrical conducting wires and cables may be classified in several different ways depending upon the particular factor of consideration as follows:

1. According to degree of covering of wire or cable.
2. According to material and make-up of electrical conductor.
3. According to number of conductors in cable.
4. If insulated, according to insulation employed.
5. According to protective covering.
6. According to service.

10. Classification According to Degree of Covering.   Probably the broadest classification of electrical wires and cables is according to the degree of covering employed, as follows:

1. Bare.
2. Covered but not insulated.
3. Insulated and covered.

In many cases **bare** conductors without any covering over the metallic conductors are employed for electrical circuits. The conductors are supported on insulators so spaced, depending upon the voltage of the circuit, that the length of the air space between the conductors will provide sufficient insulation. Bare conductors are employed for the majority of overhead transmission lines. They are also used for certain overhead telephone and telegraph circuits. The National Electrical Code by special permission will allow bare conductors for feeder circuits not exceeding 600 volts provided they are installed in a chase, channel, or shaft of noncombustible material in a building of fire-resistant construction.

There is a definite distinction between the meaning of the words **covered** and **insulated** as applied in electrical cable terminology. **Insulated** wires and cables consist of an electrical conductor covered with some form of electrical insulation with or without an outer protective covering. With **covered** wires the conductor is protected against mechanical injury by some form of covering applied directly over the conductor. This covering, however, does not provide insulation of the wet conductor to any great extent and often even becomes a fair conductor itself when moist. The covering cannot, therefore, be relied upon to afford consistently any insulation beyond that of the air spacing between the conductors.

Weatherproof wires may be divided into two general classes: (1) those with fibrous coverings and (2) those with homogeneous coverings (Sec. **12**).

11. Weatherproof covered wire with fibrous coverings is available in two types.

Both types are designated as U R C and are manufactured according to specifications recommended by the Utilities Research Commission. The two types are distinguished by at least one manufacturer as O. K.-U R C and Peerless U R C. The O. K. is the more common type. The wire is covered with two or three weatherproof cotton braids applied directly over the conductor. The braids are saturated with a black asphaltic compound. The outside surface of the outer braid is coated with mica flake to provide a smooth surface free of tackiness. The Peerless type is a better-grade covering and in addition to its longer life characteristics provides some degree of over-all electrical insulation to the conductor. The construction consists of a compacted pad of unspun cotton wrapped helically directly around the conductor and filled with asphalt. This provides a homogeneous wall of insulation without the usual braid interstices encountered in ordinary weatherproof covered wire. The asphalt-impregnated cotton pad is covered with a standard outer weatherproof braid. Peerless wire is made in two types which are designated as double and triple braid. Actually there is only one braid in both types, but the combination of the cotton pad of different thicknesses, respectively, and the braid gives a covering which is equivalent in thickness to the regular double- or triple-braid O. K. wires. Weatherproof covered wire is available with the conductor material consisting of copper, solid copperweld, solid bronze, composite copper-copperweld, all aluminum, or steel-reinforced aluminum.

12. Weatherproof covered wire with homogeneous covering is available in two types: (1) neoprene type, and (2) polyethylene type.

The neoprene type has a homogeneous covering which consists of a tough and durable vulcanized neoprene compound. This type has the following advantageous characteristics:

Highly weather-resistant.

Not brittle under extreme low temperatures. Will not migrate under abnormally high temperatures.

A homogeneous covering preventing normal moisture ingress to conductor, thus permitting maximum continuity of service under storm conditions.

Tough, with excellent resistance to mechanical abuse.

Light in weight, smooth surface, with adhesion to the conductor. Can be handled and installed without special precautions.

The polyethylene type has a homogeneous, seamless, thermoplastic covering which is applied by extrusion. Its more important characteristics may be summarized as follows:

Excellent resistance to weathering, being both weather- and sun-resistant.

Good physical strength.

Good abrasion resistance.

Inherently tight on the conductor.

Wide temperature range, $-94°F$ ($-70°C$) to $176°F$ ($80°C$).

Light in weight.

13. Material and Make-up of Electrical Conductors. The conductor may consist of a single solid wire or a stranded cable made up of several individual bare wires twisted together. Stranded conductors are more flexible than a single solid wire. The flexibility of the cable increases with the number of strands and also depends upon the manner of arranging the individual strands in the make-up of the conductor. Solid wires are used for conductors of the smaller sizes, and stranded cables for the larger sizes. In the intermediate sizes both solid and stranded conductors are available.

Electrical conducting cables are made of copper, aluminum, steel, bronze, or a combination of either copper or aluminum with steel. Copper is the material most commonly employed, owing to its high conductivity. Practically all insulated wires and cables employ copper or aluminum conductors. Aluminum or steel wires and cables are frequently found to be more economical for certain classes of aerial construction. All-steel conductors are employed for telephone and telegraph work and certain rural distribution lines with light load densities. Steel-copper conductors are employed for long-span river crossings of power lines and for certain rural distribution lines.

A classification of electrical conductors with respect to standard materials and make-ups available is given below:

A. Copper.
1. Solid.
 a. Round.
 b. Grooved.
 c. Figure eight.
 d. Figure nine.
 e. Square or rectangular.
2. Standard concentric stranded.
 a. Class AA.
 b. Class A.
 c. Class B.
 d. Class C.
 e. Class D.
3. Standard rope stranded.
 a. Class G.
 b. Class H.
4. Bunched stranded.
5. Bunched and rope stranded.
 a. Class J.
 b. Class K.
 c. Class L.
 d. Class M.
 e. Class O.
 f. Class P.
 g. Class Q.

6. Annular concentric stranded.
7. Special stranded.
8. Compack stranded.
 a. Round.
 b. Sector.
 c. Segmental.
9. Hollow-core stranded.
10. Tubular segmental (Type HH).
B. Iron or steel.
1. Solid.
2. Stranded.
C. Copper-steel.
1. Copperweld.
 a. Solid.
 b. Stranded.
2. Copperweld and copper.
3. Copper and steel stranded.
D. Aluminum:
1. Solid.
2. Stranded.
E. Aluminum and steel.   (ACSR.)
F. Bronze.

Refer to Table **85** for illustrations and applications of different make-ups. Refer to Table **86** for guide to applications of conductor materials.

14. Copper wire is made in three grades of hardness known as hard-drawn, medium hard-drawn, and soft or annealed. Hard-drawn wire has the greatest tensile strength and the least amount of elongation under stress and is the stiffest and hardest to bend and work. Soft-drawn or annealed wire has the lowest tensile strength and the greatest elongation under stress and is very pliable and easily bent. Medium hard-drawn wire has characteristics intermediate between those of hard-drawn and soft-drawn wire. The conductivity of copper wires decreases slightly as the degree of hardness increases. However, there is relatively little difference in the conductivity of the different grades.

Hard-drawn wire is used for long-span transmission lines, trolley contact wires, telephone wires, and other applications where it is desirable to have the highest possible tensile strength.

Medium hard-drawn wire is employed for such applications as short-span distribution circuits and trolley feeders, where slightly lower tensile strength is satisfactory and greater pliability is desired.

Soft-drawn or annealed copper is used for all covered or insulated copper conductors except weatherproof covered cables. Wires with this covering are available in all the three grades of hardness of copper. Bare or weatherproof covered soft wire is used only for short spans.

Copper wire used for rubber-insulated cable must be **tinned** by coating with pure tin in order to protect the copper against chemical action caused by contact with the rubber.

15. Make-up of Copper Conductors. Copper conductors are manufactured in various forms of make-up as listed in Sec. **13**, depending upon their size and application. An understanding of the construction of the different make-ups and their applications can be gained from Table **85**. The employment of solid or stranded conductors and the class of stranding used depend upon the degree of flexibility desired. Tables **89** to **100** give information on the standard strandings. For very flexible cables for special applications, special strandings are employed. There is no fixed standard for these special strandings, practice varying with different manufacturers. Data for bare copper conductors of the different standard make-ups are given in Tables **88** to **100.**

16. Iron or Steel Electrical Conductors. All-steel conductors for power circuits are made from special low-resistance high-strength steel stock. They are available in both solid and three-strand construction. Each wire is protected by a heavy galvanized coating of zinc. Since the economical field of application of all-steel conductors is only for light electrical loads, these conductors are manufactured in only three standard sizes (see Table **102**). The stranded conductors are used in preference to the solid wires for longer span construction, owing to their inherent damping capacity which reduces the amplitude of their vibration in strong lateral winds.

Commercial galvanized iron wire for telephone and telegraph circuits has been made for many years in three types designated as Extra Best Best (EBB), Best Best (BB), and steel (see Table **101**). These designations are somewhat misleading. They were adopted many years ago and refer to the electrical conductivity of the different grades. All three types are made from high-grade materials, and the same standard of galvanizing.

Extra Best Best wire has the best conductivity but the lowest tensile strength. Its weight per mile-ohm is from 4,700 to 5,000 lb. It is uniform in quality, pure, tough, and pliable. It is largely used by commercial telegraph companies, in railway telegraph service, for tie wires, and for signal bonding.

Best Best wire has a lower value of conductivity but greater tensile strength. Its weight per mile-ohm is from 5,600 to 6,000 lb. This grade is very largely used by telephone companies.

Steel is a stiff wire of high tensile strength and low conductivity. It is very difficult to work but is used on short lines that must be erected at low cost, where conductivity is of little importance. Its weight per mile-ohm is 6,500 to 7,000 lb.

Additional types have been developed more recently. These newer types along with their special characteristics are given in Table **101**.

17. Copper-Steel Conductors. Electrical conductors consisting of a combination of copper and steel are frequently employed for certain types of circuits (see Sec. **13** and Tables **86** and **110**). Three general types of construction are listed in Sec. **13** and are illustrated in Table **85**.

Copperweld wire is composed of a steel core with a copper covering thoroughly welded thereto by a molten welding process. This process produces a permanent bond between the two metals which prevents any electrogalvanic action and which will withstand hot rolling, cold drawing, forging, bending, twisting, or sudden temperature changes. This wire is made in three grades: 30 per cent conductivity, extra high strength; 30 per cent conductivity, high strength; and 40 per cent conductivity, high strength (see Table **109**). Solid conductors are made in sizes from No. 12 to No. 4/0 AWG (see Table **111**). Concentric stranded cables are available in sizes with outside diameters from 0.174 to 0.910 in. (see Table **113**). Weatherproof covered copperweld solid wire is made in sizes from No. 12 to No. 2 AWG. Rubber-insulated twisted pair cables in size Nos. 14 and 17 are made for telephone, telegraph, and signal work. Single-conductor rubber-insulated wire may be obtained in any size. Rubber-insulated parallel drop wire is made in one size only, No. 17 AWG.

Composite cables **(copperweld and copper)** consisting of a combination of certain strands of copper wire with a number of strands of copperweld wire are often found to be economical for aerial circuits requiring more than average tensile strength combined with liberal conductance (see Table **112** for data).

Copper and steel cables consist of a combination of copper and steel wires stranded together. In the design of the cable the strands of the different materials are not intended to serve in any dual capacity. The conductivity of the cable is determined by the sectional area of the copper strands. The size of the cable is designated according to its total sectional area of copper, not according to the total sectional area of the whole cable. For instance, a cable designated as No. 4, consisting of two copper strands and one steel, has a total sectional area of 62,610 cir mils and a sectional area of copper of 41,740. The area of the copper, 41,740 cir mils, corresponds to the area of a No. 4 wire. The cable is, therefore, designated as a No. 4 cable, although its total sectional area of copper and steel is between that of a No. 3 and that of a No. 2 wire.

These copper and steel cables are available in sizes from No. 2 to No. 12. All sizes except Nos. 10 and 12 consist of two plain hard-drawn copper wires and one extra-galvanized steel wire. Wire cables of size Nos. 10 and 12 consist of one galvanized hard-drawn copper wire and two extra-galvanized steel wires (see Table **122**).

18. Aluminum and aluminum steel-reinforced conductors are often found to be economical for transmission and rural distribution circuits. Commercial hard-drawn aluminum wire has a conductivity at 20°C of 60.97 per cent or a resistance of 17.010 ohms per cir mil-ft. Its weight is 0.000000915 (or 91.5×10^{-8}) lb per cir mil-ft. An all-aluminum wire for equal conductivity must have a diameter 126 per cent and an area 160 per cent of that of a copper wire (see Table **114** for comparative values). All-aluminum conductors are available in bare, weatherproof-covered, rubber-insulated, and thermoplastic-insulated constructions. Aluminum steel-reinforced conductors, owing to their high tensile strength, are frequently used for long spans and for high-capacity lines requiring heavy conductors. They consist of a concentric stranded aluminum cable with a reinforcing steel core. Except in the smaller sizes the steel core is made up of several steel strands. Aluminum steel-reinforced conductors are available either bare or weatherproof-covered (refer to Tables **120** and **121** for data).

19. Number of Conductors. Bare or covered (not insulated) cables must, of course, always be single-conductor. Insulated cables are manufactured with one, two, three, and in some cases more conductors per cable. The choice between single- or multiple-conductor cable is affected by so many factors, which vary with the particular installation, that only some general suggestions can be made here. The selection will be influenced by the practical field conditions and facilities of installation, cost of cable and enclosure, physical dimensions of cable and of available enclosure, electrical load requirements, and the voltage and type of power supply system. Multiconductor cables usually result in lower cable cost, smaller voltage drop, and more economical utilization of duct space. On the other hand, single-conductor cables are more flexible and are easier to splice and install. For underground transmission and primary distribution applications, single-conductor cable is generally used when the voltage is above 35 kv or when the load is 50,000 kva or more. For all other underground transmission and primary distribution applications, both single conductor and multiconductor are employed. In the past the use of multiconductor cable was most common, but at present the practice of using single-conductor cable for this field is rapidly growing. Single-conductor cable is generally preferred for secondary distribution because of the ease in making taps. For interior building wiring, single-conductor cable is most commonly employed in raceway systems.

20. Cable Assembly. In the application of electrical conducting wires and cables, it is essential to have a general knowledge of the materials employed in their manufacture and also of the manner of assembling the component parts in the manufacture of the finished cable. In the simple case of a bare wire the assembly is, of course, very simple, consisting only of the solid or stranded wire of the conductor. For insulated cables and especially for multiconductor ones the use of many materials and different forms of assembly is involved. The different component parts for the more common of insulated cables in the order that the parts are employed in the manufacture of the cable are as follows:

A. Single-conductor cables.
    1. Conductor.
    2. Insulation.
    3. Protective covering.
B. Multiconductor cables.
    1. Without shielding or belting (no insulation around group of conductors).
       a. Conductor.
       b. Conductor insulation.
       c. Conductor covering.
       d. Fillers.
       e. Protective covering.

    2. Belted type (insulation around group of conductors).
       a. Conductor.
       b. Conductor insulation.
       c. Conductor covering.
       d. Fillers.
       e. Belt insulation.
       f. Protective covering.
    3. Shielded type.
       a. Conductor.
       b. Conductor insulation.
       c. Conductor shield.
       d. Fillers.
       e. Binder tape.
       f. Protective covering.

21. Electrical shielding is often necessary on power cable in order to confine the dielectric field to the inside of the cable insulation so as to prevent damage from corona or ionization. The shield usually consists of a thin (3 mils) conducting tape of copper or aluminum applied over the insulation of each conductor. The shielding tape sometimes is perforated to reduce power losses due to eddy currents set up in the shield. Sometimes a semiconducting tape consisting of specially treated fibrous tapes or braids is used. These semiconducting tapes are frequently employed for the shielding of aerial cable, since, owing to their adhering more closely to the insulation, they tend to prevent corona.

22. Fillers are used in the manufacture of most multiconductor cables. Their purpose is to fill up the spaces between the conductors in order to produce a solid round structure for the complete cable. The materials commonly employed for these fillers are saturated jute, asbestos-base calk, rubber, and, in some cases, cotton.

23. Binder tapes are used in the construction of many multiconductor cables in order to bind the conductors, shields, and fillers together in proper form during the additions of the protective covering. The more common types of binder tapes employed are rubber-filled cloth tape, combinations of cotton cloth and rubber compounds, steel, and bronze.

24. Insulation of Electrical Conductors. Except for aerial construction, interior exposed wiring on insulators, and special cases of interior-wiring feeder circuits, it is necessary to cover electrical conductors with some form of electrical insulation. An ideal insulating material for this purpose should have the following characteristics:

1. Long life.
2. Long-time high dielectric strength.
3. Resistance to corona and ionization.
4. Resistance to high temperature.

5. Mechnical flexibility.
6. Resistance to moisture.
7. Low dielectric loss.

It is impossible to find any one material that is best when all these essential characteristics are considered. For instance, impregnated paper has the highest electrical breakdown strength coupled with longest life of all the materials employed for the insulation of conductors. On the other hand, it is not moisture resistant, is not so flexible as some other materials, and will not withstand such high temperature as asbestos. Several different types of insulation are therefore employed. For each particular application the insulation should be selected whose over-all characteristics best meet the conditions of service for that particular case. Section 31 of Div. 9 gives a classification of the different types of insulation with respect to temperature.

25. Rubber Insulation. At the present time rubber is the word used with respect to insulation to designate insulations consisting of compounds of natural rubber and/or synthetic rubber, combined with such other ingredients as vulcanizing agents, antioxidants, fillers, softeners, and pigments. These natural-rubber and synthetic rubberlike compounds are used more than any other material for the insulation of electrical conductors. They have the desirable characteristics of moisture-resisting qualities, ease of handling and termination, and extreme flexibility. On the other hand, they will not withstand such high temperatures or voltage without deterioration as will some of the other types of insulation. The different ingredients of the compound are combined by the process of vulcanization into a single homogeneous material.

A large number of different rubber compounds are available which have different characteristics, depending upon the service conditions for which they have been developed. It is feasible to include here only those which are in most common use. For applications which require special characteristics the experts of the cable manufactures should be consulted for advice with respect to the best available compound.

In general the character of the physical and electrical properties of the compound increases with the rubber content. However, rubber alone would not provide a suitable insulation. The proper choosing and proportioning of the other ingredients are important factors in obtaining the desired characteristics.

Code-grade rubber compound is the standard National Electrical Code rubber compound which complies with the minimum requirements for rubber insulation as specified by the Underwriters' Laboratories. It is designated as **Type R** insulation and represents the minimum standard of quality for a rubber insulation. It must meet certain requirements of the Underwriters' Laboratories with respect to elasticity, recovery from strain, tensile strength, and resistance to deterioration caused by age or temperature. Type R wire is no longer manufactured.

Heat-resisting rubber compounds have been developed which will withstand considerably higher temperatures than the Code-grade rubber compound. Such compounds meeting the Underwriters' Laboratories specifications are designated as **Type RH** and **Type RHH** insulation.

Moisture-resistant rubber compounds are available for installations where the wire will be subjected to wet conditions. These compounds are called moisture-resistant and submarine compounds. Those meeting the Underwriters' Laboratories specifications for interior wiring installation in wet locations are designated as **Type RW** insulation. However, this wire is no longer manufactured.

Moisture- and heat-resistant compounds are available which combine the temperature- and moisture-resistance characteristics of the **Type RH** and the **Type RW** insulations. These compounds are recognized by the Underwriters' Laboratories designation of **Type RHW**, which is approved for use in wet or dry locations at a maximum conductor temperature of 75°C.

A very high grade compound consisting of 90 per cent unmilled grainless rubber is called latex rubber and is designated as **Type RUH** and **Type RUW**. The **Type RUH** is approved for use in dry locations at a maximum conductor temperature of 75°C. The **Type RUW** is approved for use in wet locations at a maximum conductor temperature of 60°C.

Type SA wire, which is called silicone-asbestos wire, is insulated with a silicone rubber compound. The outer covering of this type of wire must consist of heavy glass, asbestos-glass, or asbestos braiding impregnated with a heat-, flame-, and moisture-resistant compound.

Many wire and cable manufacturers have a rubber compound for use on general power cables which is of a higher quality than required by the Underwriters' Laboratories specifications. These especially high grade rubber compounds are designated by the individual manufacturer's trade name. Several other nonstandardized compounds, designated by the individual manufacturer's trade name, are available to meet special conditions of service, such as resistance to chemicals, ozone, and corona.

A low-voltage compound called **neoprene,** although not a rubber compound, is recognized by the Underwriters' Laboratories as an approved insulation for **Type RHW** building wire without additional covering over the insulation. It is also widely used in many applications where its superior mechanical properties are needed, such as for self-supporting secondaries for services and service-drop cables, overhead line wires, and motor and appliance lead wires.

26. Thermoplastic Insulation. Thermoplastic compounds have been developed for insulations of electrical wires. Those meeting the specifications of the Underwriters' Laboratories are designated as **Type T, TW, THW, THWN, THHN, TA, TBS, MTW,** or **THW-MTW. Type T** insulation is suitable only for dry locations, and **Type TW, THW,** or **THWN** is moisture-resistant and can be used in wet locations. **Type THW** or **THWN** is both moisture- and heat-resistant and is approved for use in wet or dry locations at a maximum conductor temperature of 75°C. **Type TBS** is thermoplastic insulation with a flame-retardant fibrous outer braid, and it is acceptable only for switchboard wiring. **Type TA** is a combination thermoplastic and asbestos insulation for switchboard wiring only. **Type THWN** is a moisture- and heat-resistant insulation approved for wet and dry locations at a maximum conductor temperature of 75°C. It has an outer nylon jacket. **Type THHN** is similar to **THWN,** except that it is not moisture-resistant, and may be used only in dry locations at a maximum conductor temperature of 90°C. **Type MTW** is moisture-, heat-, and oil-resistant and is restricted to use in machine-tool wiring at a maximum conductor temperature of 60°C in wet locations and 90°C in dry locations. **Type THW-MTW** is approved in wet or dry locations at an insulation rating of 75°C. It has a 90°C rating at 1,000 volts when it is used within electric discharge lighting equipment.

27. Thermosetting Insulation. Three high-quality wires are **Types XHHW, FEP,** and **FEPB. Type XHHW** is a moisture- and heat-resistant, cross-linked, thermosetting polyethylene with an insulating rating of 75°C in wet locations and 90°C in dry locations. **Types FEP** and **FEPB** have heat-resistant, fluorinated ethylene-propylene insulation and are suitable for use in dry locations at a maximum conductor temperature of 90°C and 200°C for special applications.

28. Mineral Insulation. The objective in developing this insulation was to provide a wiring material which would be as noncombustible as possible and thus eliminate the hazards of fire resulting from faults or overloads. This insulation consists of highly compressed magnesium oxide and is designated as **Type MI** cable. The outer metallic sheath is copper. A complete description of this cable is given in Sec. **53** and Div. 9.

29. Paper Insulation. Impregnated-paper insulation provides the highest electrical breakdown strength, greatest reliability, and longest life of any of the materials employed for the electrical insulation of conductors. It will safely withstand higher operating temperatures than either rubber or varnished-cambric insulations. On the other hand it is not moisture-resistant and must always be protected by a covering which will protect the insulation from moisture, such as a lead sheath. Paper-insulated cables are not so flexible and easy to handle as varnished-cambric or rubber-insulated cables and require greater care and time for the making of splices. Paper-insulated cables are available in the following types:

1. Solid-type insulation.
2. Low-pressure gas-filled.
3. Medium-pressure gas-filled.
4. Low-pressure oil-filled.
5. High-pressure oil-filled (pipe enclosed).
6. High-pressure gas-filled (pipe enclosed).
7. High-pressure gas-filled (self-contained).

The **solid-type** insulation is composed of layers of paper tapes applied helically over the conductor and impregnated with mineral oil (sometimes mixed with resin when so specified). A tightly fitting lead sheath is extruded over the assembled conductors and impregnated insulation. The oil must be heavy enough to prevent bleeding when the cable is cut for splicing and terminations but at the same time must remain semifluid at the lowest operating temperatures. For cables installed as vertical risers, on steep grades, or under high operating temperatures, a heavier oil, designated as nonmigrating compound, is sometimes employed in order to prevent the migration of the oil from the high to the low points of the cable. The ordinary solid-type impregnated-paper insulation will give off inflammable and explosive gases when exposed to extremely high temperatures. It is common practice to clear cable failures on low-voltage network cables by leaving the power on and burning the fault clear. In order to reduce the possibility of damage to ducts and manhole structures from consequent explosions, special nonflammable, nonexplosive compounds are sometimes used for the impregnation of the paper insulation.

Low-pressure gas-filled cable, operating under nitrogen gas pressure of 10 to 15 lb per sq in., is manufactured and impregnated in the same manner as "solid-type" cable but prior to leading is drained in a nitrogen atmosphere at a temperature somewhat above the maximum allowable operating temperature. In order to give the gas free access to the insulated conductors, longitudinal gas feed channels are placed in the filler interstices of the three-conductor construction and flutes or other type of channel under the sheath of the single-conductor construction. In the three-conductor construction, two of the three gas feed channels are obtained either by omission of filler material from the interstice or by use of an open helical coil made from steel strip. The third channel is a solid-wall metal tube filled with dry nitrogen gas and sealed off at each end before treatment of the cable length. The end of this solid-wall metal channel is opened at each joint location and ensures positive control of the pressure over the entire cable length by furnishing a bypass path for the gas at low points or dips in the cable run where "slugs" of surplus compound may gradually collect in service in the open-wall channels.

Cable operating records indicate that a majority of service failures are attributable to damage to lead sheaths arising from a variety of causes, leaks in joint wipes, terminals, or other accessories. An important advantage of low-pressure gas-filled cable, in common with low-pressure oil-filled cable, is that service failures from these causes are practically eliminated because a positive internal pressure is maintained continuously within the sheath, the entrance of moisture is prevented, and operation can continue until it is convenient to make repairs.

Medium-pressure gas-filled cables operate under a nitrogen pressure of about 49 lb per sq in. They are constructed in a manner similar to the low-pressure gas-filled cables, except that, in order to permit the use of the increased gas pressure, a reinforced lead sheath is employed.

In **low-pressure oil-filled cables** the paper is impregnated with a relatively thin liquid oil which is fluid at all operating temperatures. The cable is so constructed that channels are provided for longitudinal flow of the oil, and oil reservoirs are provided at suitable points in the cable installation. A positive pressure of moderate magnitude is thus maintained on the oil at all times, which prevents the formation of voids in the insulation due to changing temperature, stretching, or deformation of the lead sheath. When the cable is heated by load, the oil expands and flows lengthwise of the cable through the channels of the cable into the joints and out into the reservoirs. When the cable cools and the oil in the cable contracts, oil is forced back through the channels of the cable from the oil reservoirs. Any damage to the lead sheath will allow the entrance of moisture into a solid-type insulated cable. With oil-filled cable, unless the damage is too severe, the positive internal oil pressure will prevent the entrance of moisture, so that, although there will be some loss of oil, operation can continue until it is convenient to make repairs.

High-pressure oil-filled (pipe enclosed) cables are insulated and impregnated in the same manner as single-conductor solid-type cable. The necessary number of single-conductor cables are then pulled into a welded steel line pipe which is protected by a high-grade corrosion-protective covering. The enclosing pipe is then filled with oil, which is maintained under constant high pressure. The oil pressure of approximately 200 lb per sq in. prevents the formation of voids in the insulation and is maintained by means of oil pumps located at one or more points on the line.

To provide protection against moisture entrance during shipment, the cable may be shipped with a temporary lead sheath or on a special weathertight reel without a lead covering. In the former case a thin temporary lead sheath is extruded over the skid wires and is stripped from the cable during the pulling operation. When the cable is shipped without a temporary lead sheath, the weathertight reel is of construction with all seams carefully welded. The outer layer of cable is covered by a "blanket" of material having a very low rate of moisture absorption and diffusion. The edges of the "blanket" are tightly sealed to the inside surface of the reel flange by means of a moisture-repellent plastic adhesive and sealing compound. Joints between external mechanical protection, such as lags, sheet-metal layers, etc., and the steel rim of the reel flange are sealed in a similar manner. Each reel is also equipped with a pocket containing a desiccant, and prior to shipment the reel interior is flushed carefully with dry nitrogen gas.

High-pressure gas-filled cable (pipe enclosed) is similar to the high-pressure oil-filled type in that the insulated conductors comprising the circuit are installed in a metal pipe but differs from the latter in that nitrogen gas at a pressure of approximately 200 lb per sq in. is employed as a pressure medium in place of oil.

In the mass-impregnated type, the paper tape is applied to the conductor and the cable is impregnated in the same manner as solid type. Shipment is carried out in the same manner as that for high-pressure oil-filled cables, described above, i.e., either with a temporary lead sheath or on a weathertight reel without a lead covering.

High-pressure gas-filled (self-contained) cables use a lead sheath reinforced with metallic tapes as the pressure-retaining member in place of the steel pipe. In these cables, the permanent lead sheath and the associated reinforcement and protective coverings are applied to the cable prior to shipment from the factory.

A special grade of untreated paper is sometimes employed for insulating magnet wires. It is applied to the conductor in ribbon form as a helix with approximately one-third to one-half lap. This makes a low-cost insulation of constant thickness and slightly higher dielectric strength than that provided by cotton yarn, but it is less sturdy.

30. Varnished-cambric insulation has characteristics which are, in almost every respect, midway between those of rubber and paper. It is more flexible than paper but not so flexible as rubber except for large insulated cables. It is reasonably moisture-resisting, so that it does not always have to be covered with a lead sheath, but it cannot be operated without such protective covering if continuously immersed or if in continuously moist surroundings. With respect to dielectric strength, allowable temperature, and resistance to ionization and corona it is better than rubber but not so good as impregnated paper. Varnished cambric is not affected by ordinary oils and greases and will withstand hard service.

The term varnished cambric is misleading, since the cotton-fabric base of the insulation is not cambric. The correct designation should be varnished cloth, but because of long-established custom it is designated as varnished-cambric insulation. Varnished-cambric-insulated cable consists of conductors which are helically wrapped with cotton tape which has been previously filled and coated on both sides with insulating varnish. During the wrapping process a heavy nonhardening mineral compound is applied between the tapings to act as a lubricant when the cable is bent and, also, to fill up all spaces so as to prevent ionization and possible capillary absorption of moisture.

31. Asbestos provides a truly heat-resisting insulation which is suitable for use at temperatures beyond the limits allowable for other standard forms of cable insulation. However, it is satisfactory only for low-voltage installations (not more than 8,000 volts), since it cannot be applied to the conductors in a manner to give high-dielectric-strength characteristics to the cable insulation. Asbestos-insulated cables for power work are made in two types of construction: all asbestos or felted asbestos and asbestos-varnished cambric.

All-asbestos or **felted-asbestos** insulated cable is made by covering the conductor with a wall of felted-asbestos fibers. In some insulations the asbestos is saturated with flame- and heat-resisting compound or flame-, heat-, and moisture-resisting compound.

Asbestos–varnished-cambric cable is insulated with a wall of impregnated asbestos combined with a wall of varnished cloth tapes applied in a series of helical wraps. The different standard types with the Underwriters designations are as follows:

TYPE A.   Nonimpregnated asbestos without an asbestos braid.

TYPE AA.   Nonimpregnated asbestos with outer asbestos braid.

TYPE AI.   Impregnated asbestos insulation without asbestos braid.

TYPE AIA.   Impregnated asbestos insulation with outer asbestos braid.

TYPE AVA.   Asbestos–varnished-cambric insulation with outer asbestos braid.

TYPE AVL.   Asbestos–varnished-cambric insulation with an outer asbestos braid covered with a lead sheath.

TYPE AVB.   Asbestos–varnished-cambric insulation with outer flame-retardant cotton braid.

TYPE SA.   Silicone rubber insulated with outer heavy glass, asbestos-glass, or asbestos braid. (See Sec. **25.**)

Asbestos coverings are used for magnet wire which must operate at high temperatures. It is bonded to the conductor by means of a coat of bonding insulating varnish. The asbestos covering is generally coated with insulating varnish or some compound in order to retard the penetration of moisture into the insulation and to increase the dielectric strength, thermal conductivity, and abrasion resistance.

32. Cotton yarn is often employed for the insulation of magnet wire. The wire is covered with one or more wraps of helically wrapped unbleached cotton yarn. When more than one wrap is employed, each wrap is applied in the reverse direction to that of the next inner wrap. The untreated cotton is neither heat-resisting nor impervious to moisture. It is not fully considered to be an insulation, and coils wound with it should be treated or impregnated with an insulating compound by an approved process. The cotton yarn acts as a mechanical separator holding the conductors apart and providing a medium for the absorption and retention of the impregnating material. Cotton yarn is also used as a protective covering for enamel-insulated magnet wire.

33. Enamel is widely used as an insulation for magnet wire. It has excellent resistance to moisture, heat, and oil and possesses high dielectric strength. Enamel wire consists of a comparatively thin even coating of high-grade organic insulating enamel applied directly to the bare wire. It is made in various types as given in Sec. **81.**

34. Silk yarn is employed in the same manner as cotton yarn (Sec. **32**) for the insulation of magnet wire. Silk coverings have better dielectric characteristics, give a neater appearance, and are mechanically stronger than cotton. Otherwise, all the statements in Sec. **32** respecting cotton-yarn insulations apply to silk.

Cellulose-acetate (artificial silk) tape or yarn is being used in many applications for the insulation of magnet wire as a substitute for or in combination with natural silk. Artificial silk has somewhat better electrical characteristics and gives a more uniform thickness of insulation. Its strength and abrasion resistance are not so good as those of natural silk.

35. Fibrous glass yarn has been developed for the insulation of conductors. Up to the present time it has been employed only for the insulation of dynamo windings and magnet wire for classes of service requiring operation at high temperatures. The conductors are wound with one or more wraps of alkali-free fibrous-glass yarn.

36. Protective Coverings. Most insulated conductors have the insulation protected from wear and deterioration due to surrounding conditions by some form of covering applied to the cable over the insulation. Protective coverings are also used on some noninsulated cables such as the weatherproof wire used for distribution purposes (see Covered Wires, Secs. **10** and **11**). The materials most commonly used for these protective coverings are listed in Sec. **37**. There is no one covering that will fulfill all the protective functions that are required for all classes of installations. Each one has its own particular advantages and limitations and consequently proper field of application. In many cases a combination of two or more of the different types of coverings is required in order to provide the necessary protection to the conductor and its insulation.

37. Protective Covering Materials and Finishes

I. Nonmetallic.
  A. According to material of covering.
    1. Fibrous braids.
      a. Cotton.
        (1) Light.
        (2) Standard.
        (3) Heavy.
        (4) Glazed cotton.
      b. Seine twine or hawser cord.
      c. Hemp.
      d. Paper and cotton.
      e. Jute.
      f. Asbestos.
      g. Silk.
      h. Rayon.
      i. Fibrous glass.
    2. Tapes.
      a. Rubber-filled cloth tape.
      b. Combination of cotton cloth and rubber compounds.
    3. Woven covers (loom).
    4. Unspun felted cottom.

    5. Rubber jackets.
    6. Synthetic jackets.
    7. Thermoplastic jackets.
    8. Jute and asphalt.
  B. According to saturant.
    1. Asphalt.
    2. Paint.
    3. Varnish.
  C. According to finish.
    1. Stearin pitch and mica flake.
    2. Paint.
    3. Wax.
    4. Lacquer.
    5. Varnish.
II. Metallic.
  A. Pure lead sheath.
  B. Reinforced lead sheath.
  C. Alloy-lead sheath.
  D. Flat-band armor.
  E. Interlocked armor.
  F. Wire armor.
  G. Basket-weave armor.

38. Fibrous braids are used extensively for protective coverings of cables. These braids are woven over the insulation of the cable so as to form a continuous covering without joints. The braid is generally saturated (Sec. **44**) with some compound in order to give resistance to some class of exposure such as moisture, flame, acid, etc. The outside braid is given one of the finishes described in Sec. **44** depending upon the application of the cable.

The most common braid is one woven from **light, standard,** or **heavy cotton yarn.** These coverings are designated, respectively, as IPCEA Classes A, B, and C. IPCEA are the initials of the Insulated Power Cable Engineers Association. The cotton can be furnished in a variety of colors for identification following an established color code in the industry.

Glazed cotton braid is composed of light cotton yarn treated with a sizing material before fabrication.

Seine-twine or **hawser-cord braid** is composed of cable-laid, hard-twisted cotton yarn, braided to form a heavy durable covering which will withstand more rough usage than a braid made from common cotton yarn.

Hemp braid is woven from strong, durable, long-fibered hemp yarn which will withstand even rougher usage than seine-twine braid.

Paper and cotton braid is composed of paper twine interwoven with cotton threads.

Jute braid is woven from yarn composed of twisted jute fibers.

Asbestos braid is closely woven from long-fibered chrysotile asbestos yarn.

Silk and rayon braids are manufactured in the same manner as glazed cotton braid from real or artificial silk yarn.

Fibrous-glass braid is woven from fine, flexible glass threads and forms a covering resistant to flame, acids, alkalies, and oils.

39. Fibrous-tape coverings are frequently used as a part of the protective covering of cables. With tape coverings the material employed is fabricated into a tape before application to the cable, while with braid coverings the yarn is woven into a fabric during its application to the cable. In applying tape coverings the tape is wrapped helically around the cable, generally with a certain amount of overlapping of adjacent turns. The more common types of fibrous tapes employed in cable manufacture are listed in Sec. **37.** Except for the duck tape, tape coverings are never used for the outer covering of a cable. They are employed for the covering directly over the insulation of individual conductors and for the inner covering over the assembled conductors of a multiconductor cable. They are frequently used under the sheath of a lead-sheathed cable. Duck tape made of heavy canvas webbing presaturated with asphalt compound is frequently used over a lead-sheathed cable for protection against corrosion and mechanical injury.

40. Woven covers commonly called **loom** are used for applications requiring exceptional abrasive-resisting qualities. These covers are composed of thick, heavy, long-fibered cotton yarn woven on the cable in a circular loom like that used for fire hose. (It is not a braid.) Although braid coverings are also woven, they are not designated as such.

41. Unspun felted cotton is manufactured into a solid felted covering for cables for some special classes of service.

42. Several types of rubber and synthetic jacket coverings are available for the protection of insulated cable. There does not seem to be any standardization of these types of coverings. The different manufacturers have their own special compounds designated by their individual trade names. These compounds differ from the rubber compounds used for the insulation of cable in the fact that they have been perfected not for their insulating qualities but for resistance to abrasion, moisture, oil, gasoline, acids, earth solutions, alkalies, etc. Of course, no one jacket compound will provide protection against all the above exposures, as each one has its particular qualifications and limitations.

A nonrubber compound which has some very excellent characteristics for a jacket material is called neoprene.

Thermoplastic compounds are becoming more and more popular as jacket materials. Although no one material is perfect in all respects for jacket-covering use, many of the necessary characteristics for jacket coverings are possessed by thermoplastic compounds.

43. Jute and asphalt coverings are commonly used as a cushion between the cable insulation and a metallic armor. Frequently it is also employed as a corrosion-resisting covering over lead sheath or metallic armor. It consists of asphalt-impregnated jute yarn served helically around the cable or of alternate layers of asphalt-impregnated jute yarn serving and asphalt weatherproofing compound.

44. Saturants and Finishes for Fibrous Coverings. Fibrous braids used for covering cables are thoroughly saturated and the outer surface is finished in order to provide protection against moisture, flame, weathering, or oil, etc. The common materials employed for saturating the braids are listed under B of Sec. **37,** and the common materials employed for finishing the outer surface under C of Sec. **37.**

45. A pure lead sheath of uniform thickness tightly applied over the insulated cable by the extrusion process is practically the standard covering for cable for use in underground ducts and other wet locations. Where the cable will be exposed to special forms of corrosion, electrolytic action, or mechanical strain, one of the other coverings is used in combination with the lead sheath as a protective covering over the sheath.

46. A reinforced lead sheath is employed for mechanical strength when internal cable hydrostatic pressures exceed 15 lb per sq in. This construction consists of a double lead sheath. Around the inner sheath is wrapped a tape of hard-drawn copper, bronze, or other elastic metal, preferably nonmagnetic in character. This thin tape imparts considerable additional strength and elasticity to the sheath. However, it must be protected against wear and corrosion. For this reason a second lead sheath is applied over the tape. Such a finish is recommended for internal pressures up to 30 lb per sq in. It is commonly used on oil-filled cable near the bottom of severe grades or on solid cable at the base of vertical risers and at the bottom of extreme grades where pressure can accumulate.

47. An alloy-lead sheath is employed where additional mechanical strength and resistance to crystallization of the sheath are required. The most common alloy is one containing 2 per cent tin. Sometimes an antimony lead alloy is used. An alloy sheath is more resistant to gouging and abrasion during or after installation than a pure lead one.

48. Flat-band armor usually consists of two steel tapes applied on the outside of the cable in such a way that the openings between successive turns of the inner tape are covered by the outer tape. Usually these tapes are applied over a jute bedding introduced between them and the lead sheath or cable insulation, and they are frequently finished with an over-all layer of asphalted jute as a protection against corrosion. Ordinarily, plain steel tapes are recommended. Where corrosion conditions are apt to be severe, galvanized steel or nonferrous materials should be used.

49. Interlocked armor consists of a single strip of interlocking metal tape so applied over the insulation of the cable that the cable is always protected throughout its length. The interlocking construction prevents adjacent tapes from being squeezed together during installation or in service, with the consequent damage to the edges of the tapes, which sometimes occurs with flat-band steel armor, and, in addition, it eliminates gaps or open spaces as there is no break in the continuity of the interlocking strip. The shape of the armor is such that its physical strength against mechanical injury to the cable is superior to that of flat-band armor. The rounded surface of the armor tends to deflect blows from shovels or picks and also offers an additional buffer effect to blows that tend to pierce the armor, thereby minimizing damage to the lead sheath and insulation over which it is applied.

For rubber- or varnished-cambric-insulated cables used for interior work the armor is generally applied over a jute bedding which is introduced between the armor and the cable insulation.

For underground installation a lead sheath under the jute bedding of armor is required for paper cables, varnished-cambric cables, or 20 or 25 per cent Code-rubber cables.

An over-all asphalt-jute finish is sometimes used as an additional protection against corrosion, particularly if the cable is to be buried in the earth.

A thermoplastic jacket is often applied over the armor, particularly where corrosive conditions exist, such as in chemical plants, paper and steel mills, and similar industries.

Galvanized steel is the standard material for armor employed in interior building wiring. For other power applications plain-steel armor is standard and suitable for most installations although galvanized armor will give a longer life. Nonmagnetic materials may be furnished for the larger single-conductor cables. Aluminum, copper, or bronze is frequently used where corrosion conditions are apt to be severe.

50. Wire armor consists of a layer of round metal wires wound helically and concentrically about the cable. The standard type employs galvanized-steel wires, but, if desired, wire armor constructed of nonferrous materials can be obtained. Wire armor is recommended where extreme tensile strength and greatest mechanical protection are necessary. Galvanized-steel construction is stronger than nonferrous. Usually a layer of asphalt-treated jute is introduced between the armor and the sheath to prevent mechanical damage and to minimize electrolytic action. Galvanized armor can be used where corrosion would damage the iron, and further protection in the form of an overall asphalt-jute finish is not uncommon.

51. Basket-weave armor is used where light weight and compactness are important. It consists of a braid of metal wire woven directly over the cable as an outer covering. Galvanized-steel, bronze, copper, or aluminum wire is used for the braid, depending upon the service for which the cable is intended. This armor finish is used largely for shipboard wiring.

52. General-purpose power cables for underground ducts and interior wiring are available with rubber-, thermoplastic-, varnished-cambric-, paper-, or asbestos-insulated copper or aluminum conductors. The particular type of any one of these insulations may be any of the types previously listed, depending upon the requirement of the service.

Class B stranding is the adopted standard for copper conductors of these cables, but any one of the more flexible standard concentric or rope strandings is available. In addition, varnished-cambric- and paper-insulated copper conductor cable may be obtained with the following construction:

Construction	Available for
Compack round....................	Single conductor from No. 1 to 1,000,000. Multiconductor from No. 1 to 1,000,000. (Generally employed only for No. 1)
Compack sector....................	Multiconductor No. 1/0 and larger
Annular concentric	Single conductor, 750,000 to 5,000,000 cir mils
Compack segmental..............	Single conductor, 1,000,000 to 4,000,000 cir mils
Hollow-core stranded............	Single conductor, oil-filled paper cables, No. 2/0 to 2,000,000 cir mils

General-purpose power cables are normally constructed in single- and three-conductor cables for all types of insulations mentioned. Rubber-insulated wires are also regularly made in two-conductor construction. Four-conductor cables are not standard construction but can be obtained.

One common type of protective covering consists of a rubber-filled cloth tape and an outer cotton braid treated with moisture-resisting, flame-resistant, or moisture- and flame-resistant compounds. Another common protective covering is a neoprene jacket. For applications where the cable will be subjected to rough usage the outer braid should be made of seine twine, hawser cord, or hemp. Where high flame resistance is required, asbestos braid should be used for the protective covering. For underground duct installation and interior wiring in wet locations, suitable types should be used. Where protection against corrosion, electrolysis, or damage due to accidental short-circuiting of open-circuited sheaths is required, the lead sheath is protected by an outer covering of duck tape, reinforced rubber, or jute and asphalt. For cable subjected to special exposures such as acids, alkalies, gasolines, etc., a suitable rubber or synthetic sheath should be employed (see Sec. **42**). Thermoplastic and latex-insulated wires do not require an outer protective covering. Interlocked metal armor is advantageous as the outer covering for many installations, both indoor and outdoor.

The covered (not insulated) wires described in Sec. **10** would be included under the classification of general-purpose power cables.

General-purpose power cables with insulation and covering meeting the minimum requirements of the National Electrical Code are frequently called building wires and cables. The Code designation letters for these cables according to the type of insulation employed are given in Div. 9. In addition to these type letters, the Code also uses the following suffix letters:

1. No suffix letter indicates a single insulated conductor.

2. Suffix letter *D* indicates a twin wire with two insulated conductors laid parallel under an outer fibrous covering.

3. Suffix letter *M* indicates an assembly of two or more insulated conductors twisted together under a common outer fibrous covering.

4. Suffix letter *L* indicates an outer covering of lead.

If no number follows the designating letters of a cable, it indicates that the cable is for use at not more than 600 volts. Cables for use at higher voltages are so designated by adding the following numerical suffixes to the letter designations.

Numerical suffix	Maximum permissible voltage	Numerical suffix	Maximum permissible voltage
10	1,000	40	4,000
20	2,000	50	5,000
30	3,000		

The maximum voltages referred to in the table above are the operating voltages between phases of single- and two-phase systems and three-phase systems with grounded or ungrounded neutral.

The maximum voltages referred to in the table above are the operating voltages between phases of single- and two-phase systems and three-phase systems with grounded or ungrounded neutral.

53. MI (mineral-insulated) cable was developed to meet the needs for a noncombustible, high heat- and water-resistant cable. As described by the National Electrical Code "MI cable (see Fig. 5) is a cable in which one or more electrical conductors are insulated with a highly compressed refractory mineral insulation and enclosed in a liquidtight and gastight metallic tube sheathing." It is available in single-conductor construction in sizes from No. 16 to No. 4/0, in two- and three-conductor construction in sizes from No. 16 to No. 4, in four-conductor construction in sizes from No. 16 to No. 6, and in seven-conductor construction in sizes from No. 16 to No. 10.

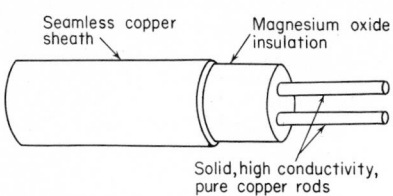

Seamless copper sheath

Magnesium oxide insulation

Solid, high conductivity, pure copper rods

FIG. 5　*MI cable construction (General Cable Corp.)*

The cable is fabricated in the following manner: Magnesium oxide in powder form is molded into cylinders under great pressure, approximately 2 in. in diameter and length, with as many holes through the body of the cylinder as there are conductors in the cable. After molding, the magnesium oxide cylinders are completely dehydrated in electric furnaces. The cylinders are then placed inside a seamless uncoated copper tube whose inside diameter is slightly larger than the diameter of the molded cylinders. Solid uncoated high-conductivity copper rods are then inserted in the holes in the magnesium oxide cylinders. After the ends of the filled copper tube are sealed, it goes through a series of drawing and annealing operations. In the drawing process the compressive forces reduce the magnesium oxide cylinders to powder form and produce a dense homogeneous mass of magnesium oxide which transmits the compressive forces to the conductor rods. This drawing produces, in effect, the equivalent of a solid homogeneous rod with all members, copper tube, copper rods, and magnesium oxide, maintaining the same relative position one to the other while being proportionately reduced in diameter and cross section, and increased in length. (Each component maintains its original proportionate size and relative position throughout the remainder of the process until the desired finished sheath diameter is reached.) The assembly is annealed at intervals during the drawing process to eliminate the effect of work-hardening on the metal, and the finished cable is supplied fully annealed.

Recently, a departure from the fabrication method just described has been adopted for some constructions. In this method the same starter tube stands vertically while the starter conductors are inserted and jigged into position. Then dried magnesium oxide powder is introduced into the tube and tamped to the desired density. After completion of this vertical filling operation, a drawing and annealing sequence is employed as with the horizontal, plug-type filled cable assembly.

54. Nonmetallic-sheathed building cable is employed for the economical wiring of residences, farm buildings, small stores, etc. It consists of a two-, three-, or four-conductor, rubber- or thermoplastic-insulated cable. When desired, a bare copper ground wire is incorporated in the cable assembly. The ground wire is laid in the interstices between the circuit conductors under the outer braid. Nonmetallic-sheathed cable is manufactured under several different trade names. The over-all dimensions will differ somewhat with different manufacturers. Type designations are **NM** and **NMC.**

55. Metal-clad building cable consists of rubber- or thermoplastic-insulated copper wire protected by a flexible galvanized-steel armor. It is manufactured with or without a lead sheath under the armor for protection against excessive dampness. The nonleaded type is regularly available in one-, two-, three-, and four-conductor assemblies in sizes from No. 14 to No. 2, and also in size No. 1 for single conductor only. The leaded type is standard in two- and three-conductor assemblies in sizes from No. 14 to No. 6 and also in size No. 4 for three conductors only. Individual conductors are finished in different colors for identification of any conductor in installation. In installing these cables a short fiber bushing (see Div. 9) is inserted between the conductors and the steel armor wherever the cable is cut. For this reason the cables are frequently called armored bushed cables **(ABC).** The National Electrical Code designation is **AC** for the nonleaded type and **ACL** for the leaded type. They are also commonly called **BX** and **BXL.** Larger sizes (No. 4 and over) are called **Type MC.**

Armored ground wire consists of a bare copper conductor with a flexible steel armor covering applied directly over the wire.

56. Aluminum-sheathed Cable. This cable is designated as **Type ALS.** It is a factory-assembled cable consisting of one or more insulated conductors enclosed in an impervious, continuous, closely fitting tube of aluminum. **Type ALS** cable may be used for both exposed and concealed work, in dry and wet locations. Refer to Div. 9 for a complete description of this cable.

57. Cablebus. This is an approved assembly of insulated conductors mounted in spaced relationship in a ventilated metal-protective supporting structure, including fittings and conductor terminations. **Cablebus,** usually assembled at the installation site from components furnished or specified by the manufacturer, may be used at any voltage or current for which the spaced conductors are rated. Components of this wiring system are described in Div. 9.

58. Annunciator or dampproof office wire is used for low-tension signaling circuits in residences and low-cost installations. Annunciator wire consists of a solid copper conductor covered with two servings of soft cotton saturated with paraffin. Dampproof office wire consists of a solid copper conductor covered with a weatherproof cotton wrap and an outer combination colored cotton braid.

59. Service Cables. Special multiconductor cables have been developed to meet the requirements for connecting the pole line of the street distribution system with the service-entrance equipment on the consumer's premises. The following terminology derived from their application is used for service cables:

1. SERVICE-DROP CABLES. Overhead service conductors between pole and building.

2. SERVICE-ENTRANCE CABLES. Service conductors which extend along the exterior and enter buildings to the meter, switch, or service equipment.

3. COMBINATION SERVICE-DROP AND SERVICE-ENTRANCE CABLES. Service conductors continuing without break from the pole to the meter, switch, or service equipment.

4. UNDERGROUND SERVICE-ENTRANCE CABLES. Service conductors installed in conduit or directly in the earth and entering the building to the meter, switch, or service equipment.

Service cable is made in three different types designated by the Underwriters' Laboratories as follows:

1. TYPE SD. Service-drop cable.

2. TYPE SE. Service-entrance cable.

3. TYPE USE. Underground service-entrance cable.

Information on the application of the different types is given in Div. 9.

Type SD cable is available in three types: (1) braid-covered type, (2) neutral-messenger type, and (3) tamper-resisting type. In the braid-covered type, the cable assembly is covered with an over-all outer cotton braid. The neutral-messenger type consists of one, two, or three insulated conductors twisted around a bare neutral-messenger conductor which is used for supporting the cable. The tamper-resisting type consists of two insulated conductors concentrically overwrapped with a bare stranded neutral conductor. This construction makes diversion of current difficult and practically impossible without leaving evidence.

Type USE service-entrance cable is similar in general construction to general power cables for direct burial in the earth.

Service cables are either rubber- or thermoplastic-insulated.

Service cables are available in two- and three-conductor assemblies.

60. Aerial Cables. Bare, weatherproof (weather-resisting) covered, and rubber-insulated tree wire are all used for overhead pole-line power circuits. Bare wire is used for most power-transmission circuits. See Sec. **13** and Table **86** for conductor materials employed and their field of application. Weatherproof (heat-resisting) covered wire is the general standard for distribution and low-voltage transmission circuits. Tree wire is used in distribution circuits where heavy tree growth would make the use of weatherproof wire unsuitable. Tree wire consists of a rubber-insulated copper wire protected with an abrasion-resisting covering.

The application of multiconductor aerial power cables is continually increasing. For messenger-type construction, general-purpose power cable with an alloy-lead sheath is commonly employed. In order to minimize weight of extremely large cables, it is generally advisable to eliminate the lead sheath. For such installations two types of cable construction have proved satisfactory. One type consists of either paper- or varnished-cambric-insulated cable supplied with a rubber hose jacket and an over-all band or interlocked armor of either steel or bronze. The other construction has utilized rubber- or varnished-cambric-insulated shielded cable and an over-all seine twine or hawser braid saturated with a moisture-resisting compound. A layer of rubberized tape or presaturated duck tape is interposed between the over-all shielding band and the outer braid. The rubber insulation should be a corona-resisting compound except for the lower voltages.

Most of the new installations of multiconductor aerial power cables are of the preassembled self-supporting type. These cables consist of one or more (usually three) rubber-insulated conductors bound to a suitable messenger cable by means of a flat metallic strip applied with open-lay helical wrap. In some cables each insulated conductor is covered by a neoprene jacket. In others the insulation of each conductor is covered with a tough abrasion- and corrosion-resistant aluminum-bronze shielding tape. In a third type of construction each insulated conductor is shielded by means of a tinned-copper tape and then covered with a neoprene jacket.

61. Power cables for direct burial in the earth without ducts are available in both metallic and nonmetallic armored types. Cables of different manufacturers are fairly common in general construction but differ in details of assembly and manufacture.

The metallic types consist of a lead-sheathed general-purpose power cable protected with a jute and asphalt covering or a combination covering of a flat or interlocking tape armor together with jute and asphalt. Rubber is generally used for the insulation, but paper or varnished cambric may be employed if desired. They are available in one-, two-, and three-conductor assemblies. These metallic types are commonly called parkway cables.

The nonmetallic types consist of rubber-insulated conductors protected with some form of nonmetallic covering that will provide a moisture seal, resistance to corrosion, and sufficient mechanical strength. One type of armor assembly consists of a combination of layers of asbestos-base calk coatings, asbestos braid filled with asbestos-base calk, and treated fibrous tape, all enclosed in a presaturated heavy duck tape. The outer surface is finished with pitch and mica flake. A common armor assembly is the jute and asphalt covering described in Sec. **43**. Rubber and synthetic jackets are also employed for the protective covering of nonmetallic cables for direct burial in the earth. The jackets are frequently enclosed in a saturated duck tape or sisal braid. All the nonmetallic types mentioned are available in one-, two-, and three-conductor assemblies. Some two-conductor cables are made with one central insulated conductor and one noninsulated conductor concentrically stranded over the insulation of the inner conductor.

Thermoplastic-insulated single-conductor and multiple-conductor Type UF cables are also availabe for use up to and including 600 volts.

62. Network cables were developed primarily for underground duct installation for low-voltage secondary network service. They are single-conductor nonmetallic-sheathed cables suitable for circuits operating at not more than 600 volts. These cables are insulated with a special rubber compound covered with a neoprene jacket. Braid-covered or lead-sheathed network cables are also available.

63. Series street-lighting cables differ from other power cables in the thickness of the insulation employed on the wires. They are rubber, varnished cambric or thermoplastic insulated single-conductor cables. They are available in shielded or unshielded types. Rubber-insulated cables can be obtained with an outer neoprene jacket or with lead sheath. The lead-sheathed cables can be obtained with additional coverings of jute or jute and double flat steel-tape armor with jute overall for conditions of use requiring the added protection. Varnished-cambric-insulated cables are always lead-sheathed and may be supplied with any of the additional coverings mentioned above for rubber-insulated leaded cable.

64. Ornamental-pole and bracket cable is a two-conductor, rubber-insulated cable specially designed for great flexibility and small over-all diameter. It is used for the interior wiring of ornamental lighting poles fed by underground cable and for the exterior wiring of pole-type bracket or mast-arm street-lighting fixtures. For voltages not exceeding 4,000, twin-type cable construction is employed, consisting of two rubber-insulated, single-cotton-braid-covered conductors laid parallel and enclosed in over-all tape and weatherproof braid. For voltages greater than 4,000, belted construction is employed. This assembly consists of two rubber-insulated and single-cotton-braid-covered conductors laid parallel and enclosed in a close-fitting belt of insulating compound. The belt insulation is covered with a tape and weatherproof braid. Another assembly for belted cable consists of two thermoplastic-insulated conductors laid parallel and enclosed in a close-fitting belt of plastic which serves as both insulation and a jacket.

65. Borehole or mine-shaft cables are specially designed to withstand the mechanical strains to which long lengths of vertically suspended cable are subjected. Both rubber and varnished cambric are employed for the insulation of these cables. The rubber-insulated ones are made both with and without a lead sheath, while the varnished-cambric cables are always lead-sheathed. The cable is protected with a steel-tape or steel-wire armor. Steel-tape armor should not be used unless supports can be provided at intervals not exceeding 50 ft. When the cable must be supported entirely from the top, wire armor must be used. The armor should be designed to support the entire cable weight with a factor of safety of at least 5 and based on a tensile strength of 70,000 lb per sq in. The wire armor should be served with bands of steel wire to provide a suitable bond. Conductor-supported cables, instead of the above-described armor-supported ones, are sometimes used for this class of service. The rubber-insulated conductors are protected with a strong loom covering and installed in metallic borehole casings or conduit. Medium hard-drawn copper is used for the conductors, which entirely support the cable through conductor clamps and strain insulators.

Cables similar to the steel-armor borehole cables are employed for the vertical risers of tall buildings. For nonleaded construction a factor of safety of at least 7 should be used in designing the wire armor, while for leaded construction the minimum factor of safety should be 4.

66. Submarine cables for installation under water in rivers, lakes, harbors, etc., are rubber-insulated power cables protected with a wire armor. The more common types of coverings employed are jute and wire armor; jute, wire armor, and jute; lead, jute, and wire armor; and lead, jute, wire armor, and jute. It is best to consider each submarine installation as a separate engineering problem and obtain the recommendations of the cable experts of reliable cable manufacturers.

67. Control cables consist of an assembly of several small conductors for carrying the relatively small currents for remote control of motors, circuit breakers, or other power equipment; for relay and metering circuits; for traffic-light control systems; etc. The standard assemblies vary from one conductor per cable to 37 conductors per cable. The size of the conductors ranges from No. 14 to No. 9. For most installations a 30 per cent rubber compound is used for the insulation of the conductors, although varnished cambric and thermoplastic are also employed. For installations where the temperature is higher than normal, either a heat-resisting rubber compound or felted asbestos should be employed, the choice depending upon the temperature of the surroundings. Each individual conductor is covered with a color-coded cotton braid for protection of the insulation and identification of circuits. The conductors are assembled with jute fillers and bound together with a rubber-faced or asbestos binder tape.

For rubber-insulated cables the outer covering may be a standard cotton weatherproof braid with a black weatherproof wax finish, a lead sheath, a neoprene jacket, a metallic or nonmetallic armor for direct burial in the earth as described for power cable in Sec. 61 of this division, or a braid or jute bedding protected by interlocking steel-tape armor. With the rubber-jacket construction, the binder tape is eliminated. For asbestos-insulated cables the outer covering is an asbestos braid saturated with flame-, heat-, and moisture-resisting compound. For thermoplastic-insulated cables the outer covering is a thermoplastic jacket.

68. Traffic-control, fire-alarm, and signal cables are specially designed to meet the conditions encountered in these municipal signal systems. Both rubber- and thermoplastic-insulated cables are used. For the rubber-insulated cables various outer coverings are employed, depending upon the installation conditions. These coverings include heavy cotton braid, plain lead sheath, protected lead sheath, and neoprene jacket. For thermoplastic-insulated cables the outer covering is a thermoplastic or similar type of jacket.

69. Special cables for electric transportation equipment are manufactured in order to meet the particular requirements of this class of service with respect to flexibility and resistance to vibration. The conductors are rubber-insulated. The cable covering usually consists of cotton braid or a rubber jacket.

70. Cables for gas-tube sign and oil-burner ignition systems should be of a type approved by the Underwriters' Laboratories for this service.

The Underwriters' kilovolt designations for cables for this service are GTO-5, GTO-10, and GTO-15. In each case the numeral indicates the cable rating in kilovolts. Approved cables made by different manufacturers differ in details of construction. At one time these cables were rubber-insulated. Today most of them are thermoplastic-insulated with an outer thermoplastic jacket.

71. X-ray cables are designed to meet the special conditions encountered in the power-supply circuits to high-voltage X-ray tubes and similar equipment. As made by one manufacturer, they consist of a core made up of two rubber-insulated wires and two uninsulated wires. A semiconducting rubber compound is extruded over these conductors. This coating is covered with a layer of rubber insulation. Another semiconducting coating is applied over this insulation, and it, in turn, is covered with a close-covering annealed-copper shielding braid. The outer covering may be either cotton braid or a neoprene jacket.

72. Drive-in-theater cables are designed for direct installation in the earth under outdoor motion-picture-theater lots to serve for sound-distribution networks from the projection booth to speaker posts installed adjacent to the designated automobile parking stations. Two types of cable are available for this service: (1) two-conductor rubber-insulated cable with an outer neoprene jacket and (2) a two-conductor cable with a uni-insulation and jacket of thermoplastic compound.

73. Portable power cables are designed for circuits supplying power to portable power equipment such as electric shovels, dredgers, air compressors, welders, etc. The individual conductors are generally insulated with a 40 per cent rubber compound. Cables of this type for voltages not exceeding 600 volts may be obtained with the following protective coverings: heavy cotton braid, seine-twine braid, loom sheath, rubber jacket, or jute and wire armor. These coverings are listed in the order of increasing resistance to wear. Only rubber jackets or jute-and-wire-armor coverings are employed for cables for voltages exceeding 600 volts. These high-voltage cables may be obtained in the following types:

Type	Covering	Ground wires	Shielding	Max voltage recommended
W	Rubber jacket	Without	None	2,500
G	Rubber jacket	With	None	5,000
SH-A	Rubber jacket	Without	On each conductor	
SH-B	Rubber jacket	Without	Over cabled conductor	
SH-C	Rubber jacket	With	Over cabled conductor	6,000
SH-D	Rubber jacket or jute and wire armor	With	On each conductor	
			No standard, consult manufacturers	

The conductors of portable power cables are made especially flexible by the use of Class G or H stranding (see Table **92**), or, for special applications requiring even greater flexibility, special stranding may be employed. Single-conductor cables are regularly available in sizes from No. 8 to 700,000 cir mils. Two-, three-, and four-conductor cables are standard in sizes from No. 8 to No. 4/0.

74. Fixture wire is used for the wiring of electrical fixtures. There are 22 approved types, which are listed and described in Table **75**. Those wires with a single **F** in their designation may be either solid or stranded. Those with **FF** must be made of wire with especially flexible stranding.

Flexible cords of Types CFPO, CFPD, AFC, AFSJ, AFS, and AFPD are multi-conductor cords of CF and AF type of construction and may be employed for the wiring of fixtures. Rubber-covered flexible cords are also used for the wiring of fixtures.

75. Fixture Wire

Trade name	Type letter	Insulation	Thickness of insulation	Outer covering
Rubber-covered fixture wire, solid or 7-strand	RF-1	Code rubber	18...$\frac{1}{64}$ in.	Nonmetallic covering
	RF-2	Code rubber	18-16.....................................$\frac{2}{64}$ in.	Nonmetallic covering
		Latex rubber	18-16....................................18 mils	
Rubber-covered fixture wire, flexible stranding	FF-1	Code rubber	18...$\frac{1}{64}$ in.	Nonmetallic covering
	FF-2	Code rubber	18-16.....................................$\frac{2}{64}$ in.	Nonmetallic covering
		Latex rubber	18-16....................................18 mils	
Heat-resistant rubber-covered fixture wire, solid or 7-strand	RFH-1	Heat-resistant rubber	18...$\frac{1}{64}$ in.	Nonmetallic covering
	RFH-2	Heat-resistant rubber	18-16.....................................$\frac{2}{64}$ in.	Nonmetallic covering
		Heat-resistant latex rubber	18-16....................................18 mils	
Heat-resistant rubber-covered fixture wire, flexible stranding	FFH-1	Heat-resistant rubber	18...$\frac{1}{64}$ in.	Nonmetallic covering
	FFH-2	Heat-resistant rubber	18-16.....................................$\frac{2}{64}$ in.	Nonmetallic covering
		Heat-resistant latex rubber	18-16....................................18 mils	
Thermoplastic-covered fixture wire, solid or stranded	TF	Thermoplastic	18-16.....................................$\frac{2}{64}$ in.	None
Thermoplastic-covered fixture wire, flexible stranding	TFF	Thermoplastic	18-16.....................................$\frac{2}{64}$ in.	None

Fixture Wire (Continued)

Trade name	Type letter	Insulation	Thickness of insulation	Outer covering
Heat-resistant thermo-plastic-covered fixture wire, solid or stranded	TFN	Thermoplastic	18-16.....................................15 mils	Nylon-jacketed
Heat-resistant thermo-plastic-covered fixture wire, flexible stranded	TFFN	Thermoplastic	18-16.....................................15 mils	Nylon-jacketed
Cotton-covered, heat-resistant fixture wire	CF	Impregnated cotton	18-14 ....$^2/_{64}$ in.	None
Asbestos-covered heat-resistant fixture wire	AF	Impregnated asbestos	18-14 ....$^2/_{64}$ in.	None
Silicone-insulated fixture wire, solid or 7-strand	SF-1	Silicone rubber	18...$^1/_{64}$ in.	Nonmetallic covering
	SF-2	Silicone rubber	18-14 ....$^1/_{32}$ in.	Nonmetallic covering
Silicone-insulated fixture wire, flexible stranding	SFF-1	Silicone rubber	18...$^1/_{64}$ in.	Nonmetallic covering
	SFF-2	Silicone rubber	18-14 ....$^1/_{32}$ in.	Nonmetallic covering
Fluorinated ethylene propylene fixture wire, solid or 7-strand	PF	Fluorinated ethylene propylene	18-14................................20 mils	None
	PGF		18-14...................................14 mils	Glass braid
Fluorinated ethylene propylene fixture wire, flexible stranding	PFF	Fluorinated ethylene propylene	18-14................................20 mils	None
	PGFF		18-14...................................14 mils	Glass braid

76. Flexible cord is the name applied to wires used for connecting portable appliances, small tools, or machinery to the receptacles of the wiring installation or for the wiring of the portable device itself. Flexible cords also are used in the wiring of pendant fixtures from the outlet box to the fixture. Table **126** lists the different types of approved flexible cords with their uses as allowed by the National Electrical Code rules.

77. Radio and TV Wires. Special types of wires have been developed to meet the special needs of the radio and TV industry. They include antenna, lead-in, coil-lead, hookup, and transmission-line wires and microphone cable.

78. Automotive and aircraft wires and cables are specially designed to meet the special requirements of these two classes of service. They include high-tension ignition cables, primary wires for low-voltage service, and starter cables.

79. The telephone industry requires the use of special types of wires and cables. The multiconductor cables for main distribution circuits are dry-paper-insulated, lead-covered. A lead-antimony sheath is generally employed for aerial and underground installation in conduit or ducts. For direct burial in the earth and for some aerial work the lead sheath is protected with jute and steel-tape armor. Specially designed steel-wire-armored cables are used for submarine installation. It is common practice to terminate these paper-insulated cables by splicing to them a short length of textile-insulated lead-covered cable. A common type of this textile-insulated cable employs two layers of silk and one layer of cotton insulation on each conductor with the cable protected with a pure lead sheath. Rubber-insulated two-conductor cables protected with a weatherproof braid are used for service drops from pole to house. Hard-drawn copper, bronze, and copperweld conductors are used for these cables.

For circuits exposed to severe moisture and requiring from 2 to 12 conductors, rubber-insulated lead-covered cables are frequently used.

For interior wiring of individual telephone circuits, twisted-pair rubber-insulated cotton-braid-covered cables are employed. There is a trend toward the use of thermoplastic-insulated conductors with thermoplastic or similar outer sheaths for interior work and direct burial in earth.

80. Cables for shipboard use should be designed for the special requirements and severe service encountered in installations on board ship. Such cables are generally made in accordance with IEEE specifications, which are approved by the IPCEA.

81. Magnet wire is the name applied to single-conductor insulated wires manufactured for the purpose of winding coils for electrical circuits. Round magnet wire is made of soft annealed solid copper wire in sizes from No. 46 to No. 4/0. Square- and rectangular-cross-section magnet wires are also available. Insulations which are used for magnet wire include baked films (enamel), cotton, silk, nylon yarn, paper, asbestos, fibrous glass, Dacron-glass, or combinations of these materials. The temperature rating of magnet wires depends upon the insulation employed and is based upon the temperature limits stated in Publication No. 1 of the Institute of Electrical and Electronic Engineers (refer to Div. 7, Sec. **128**). All magnet wire made by a reliable manufacturer will meet certain specifications with respect to physical and electrical characteristics that have been standardized by the National Electrical Manufacturers' Association.

Enamel Coatings:

CONVENTIONAL ENAMEL (generally referred to merely as enamel). A baked-film insulation of an oleo-resinous varnish having good moisture resistance and dielectric properties. Used widely in magnet wire coils of all types. 105°C—Class A insulation.

FORMVAR ENAMEL. A baked-film insulation from a varnish based on vinyl acetal resin. Has excellent resistance to heat, abrasion, and solvents, combined with exceptional flexibility and adherence. 105°C—Class A insulation.

SELF-BONDING FORMVAR. A baked-film insulation consisting of Formvar over which is applied a thermoplastic overcoat. When formed into coils and baked or otherwise suitably heat-treated, the turns of wire, because of the thermoplastic overcoat, become bonded together, thus facilitating fabrication of self-supporting coil assemblies. 105°C —Class A insulation.

NYLON ENAMEL. A baked-film insulation from a varnish based on polyamide resin which solders readily (self-fluxing) unless it is overbaked. Excellent winding qualities. Not so good as Formvar in electrical properties and moisture resistance. 105°C—Class A insulation.

FORMVAR AND NYLON ENAMEL. A baked-film insulation consisting of Formvar over which is applied a coat of nylon enamel. Combines advantages of good winding properties of the outer nylon enamel coating with the better electrical properties and moisture resistance of the underlying Formvar enamel coating. 105°C—Class A insulation.

ENAMEL G. A baked-film insulation from a varnish based on polyurethane resin. Solders readily (self-fluxing). Good winding and moisture-resistance qualities. Good electrical properties even at high frequencies. Well suited for electronic and communication applications. 120°C—between Class A and Class B insulation.

ENAMEL CLASS B. A baked-film insulation from a varnish based on polyester resin such as isonel or comparable materials. Handling properties comparable to Formvar except for somewhat poorer heat shock test. Although stable up to 150°C, it is generally used as Class B (130°C) insulation.

Coverings:

COTTON. Unbleached fine long-staple cotton yarn applied with proper techniques to provide a firm, even layer winding. Rated as 90°C Class O insulation when used alone. When impregnated or immersed in liquid dielectric it is rated as 105°C Class A insulation.

NYLON YARN. High-quality nylon tram supplied as an alternate to silk covering. When used alone it is rated as 90°C Class O insulation.

SILK. Best grade of tram silk is particularly suitable for low-loss radio-frequency coils where interturn and interlayer capacitances must be kept to a minimum. When used alone it is rated as 80°C Class O insulation.

PAPER. One hundred per cent manila rope stock or equivalent grade in tape thicknesses of 0.85 to 3.0 mils. When used alone, rated 90°C Class O insulation. When impregnated or immersed in liquid dielectric it is rated as 105°C Class A insulation.

FIBROUS GLASS. Pure, alkali-free, continuous-filament glass yarn is wrapped, saturated, and bonded to the conductor with high-grade insulating varnishes or compounds so applied as to yield a smooth, uniform, homogeneous insulating covering. When impregnated with conventional varnish it is rated as 130°C Class B insulation. When treated with silicone varnish it is rated as 180°C Class H insulation.

DACRON-GLASS. A combination insulation consisting of glass and Dacron fibers. Much better abrasion resistance, insulation adhesion, and flexibility than all-glass insulation. When impregnated with standard varnish it is rated as 130°C Class B insulation. Rating when treated with silicone varnish is not yet established.

82. In the selection of the proper type of magnet wire for any application the following factors should be considered:

1. Utilization of winding space.
2. Resistance to abrasion.
3. Cost.
4. Insulating qualities.
5. Appearance.
6. Operating temperatures.

83. Method of Determining the Approximate Diameter of Any Cable. When the approximate over-all diameter of a wire or cable not listed in conventional tables is desired, it may be determined by means of one of the following formulas. Results obtained from these formulas will as a rule give minimum outside diameters. In order to allow for manufacturing tolerances, add 50 mils to the outside diameters as obtained from the formulas to obtain approximate maximum diameters.

For single-conductor cables:

$$OD = d + 2T + 2t_c \tag{1}$$

For multiconductor nonshielded or belted cables:

$$OD = K(d + 2T + 2t_c) + 2t_o \tag{2}$$

For multiconductor belted cable:

$$OD = K(d + 2T) + 2t_B + 2t_o \tag{3}$$

For multiconductor shielded cable:

$$OD = K(d + 2T + 0.032) + 0.020 + 2t_o \tag{4}$$

where OD = outside diameter in inches; d = diameter of bare round conductor in inches; T = thickness of conductor insulation in inches; t_c = thickness of covering over insulation of individual conductors in inches; t_B = thickness of belt insulation in inches; t_o = thickness of over-all protective covering in inches; and K = value from following table:

Conductor	Value of K
Two conductor, round	2.00
Two conductor, flat, max diam	2.00
Two conductor, flat, min diam	1.00
Three conductor, round	2.16
Three conductor, ordinary sector	1.95
Three conductor, compack sector	1.90
Four conductor, round	2.41
Four conductor, ordinary sector	2.20
Four conductor, compack sector	2.15

For any conductor or cable with a known outside diameter, the outside cross-sectional area may be determined by:

$$CSA \text{ (sq in.)} = d^2 \times 0.7854 \tag{5}$$

where d = outside diameter in inches.

84. Comparison of Wire and Sheet-metal Gage Diameters or Thicknesses in Inches

Gage No.	(1) American wire gage (AWG)[a]	(2) Steel wire gage	(3) Birmingham iron wire gage (Stubs)	(4) Stubs steel wire gage	(5) (British) standard wire gage	(6) Steel music wire gage	(7) U.S. standard[b]	(8) American zinc	(9) Birmingham
15/0	......	......	.....	.....	......	......	......	.....	1.0000
14/0	......	......	.....	.....	......	......	......	.....	0.9583
13/0	......	......	.....	.....	......	......	......	.....	0.9167
12/0	......	......	.....	.....	......	......	......	.....	0.8750
11/0	......	......	.....	.....	......	......	......	.....	0.8333
10/0	......	......	.....	.....	......	......	......	.....	0.7917
9/0	......	......	.....	.....	......	......	......	.....	0.7500
8/0	......	......	.....	.....	......	......	......	.....	0.7083
7/0	......	0.4900	.....	.....	0.5000	......	0.5000	.....	0.6666
6/0	......	0.4615	.....	.....	0.4640	......	0.4687	.....	0.6250
5/0	......	0.4305	.....	.....	0.4320	.....	0.4375	.....	0.5883
4/0	0.4600	0.3938	0.454	.....	0.4000	......	0.4062	.....	0.5416
3/0	0.4100	0.3625	0.425	.....	0.3720	......	0.3750	.....	0.5000
2/0	0.3650	0.3310	0.380	.....	0.3480	0.0087	0.3437	.....	0.4452
1/0	0.3250	0.3065	0.340	.....	0.3240	0.0039	0.3125	.....	0.3964
1	0.2890	0.2830	0.300	0.227	0.3000	0.0098	0.2812	0.002	0.3532
2	0.2580	0.2625	0.284	0.219	0.2760	0.0106	0.2656	0.004	0.3147
3	0.2290	0.2437	0.259	0.212	0.2520	0.0114	0.2500	0.006	0.2804
4	0.2040	0.2253	0.238	0.207	0.2320	0.0122	0.2344	0.008	0.2500
5	0.1820	0.2070	0.220	0.204	0.2120	0.0138	0.2187	0.010	0.2225
6	0.1620	0.1920	0.203	0.201	0.1920	0.0157	0.2035	0.012	0.1981
7	0.1440	0.1770	0.180	0.199	0.1760	0.0177	0.1875	0.014	0 1764
8	0.1280	0.1620	0.165	0.197	0.1600	0.0197	0.1719	0.016	0.1570
9	0.1140	0.1483	0.148	0.194	0.1440	0.0216	0.1562	0.018	0.1398
10	0.1020	0.1350	0.134	0.191	0.1280	0 0236	0.1406	0.020	0.1250
11	0.0910	0.1205	0.120	0.188	0.1160	0.0260	0.1250	0.024	0.1113
12	0.0810	0.1055	0.109	0.185	0.1040	0.0283	0.1094	0.028	0.0991
13	0.0720	0.0915	0.095	0.182	0.0920	0.0305	0.0937	0.032	0.0882
14	0.0640	0.0800	0.083	0.180	0.0800	0.0323	0.0821	0.036	0.0785
15	0.0570	0.0720	0.072	0.178	0.0720	0.0342	0.0703	0.040	0.0699
16	0.0510	0.0625	0.065	0.175	0.0640	0.0362	0.0625	0.045	0.0625
17	0.0450	0.0540	0.058	0.172	0.0560	0.0382	0.0562	0.050	0.0556
18	0.0400	0.0475	0.049	0.168	0.0480	0.0400	0.0500	0.055	0.0495
19	0.0360	0.0410	0.042	0.164	0.0400	0.0420	0.0437	0.060	0.0440
20	0.0320	0.0348	0.035	0.161	0.0360	0.0440	0.0375	0.070	0.0392
21	0.0285	0.0317	0.032	0.157	0.0320	0.0460	0.0344	0.080	0.0349
22	0.0253	0.0286	0.028	0.155	0.0280	0.0480	0.0312	0.090	0.0312
23	0.0226	0.0258	0.025	0.153	0.0240	0.0510	0.0281	0.100	0.0278
24	0.0210	0.0230	0.022	0.151	0.0220	0.0550	0.0250	0.125	0.0247
25	0.0179	0.0204	0.020	0.148	0.0200	0.0590	0.0219	0.250	0.0220
26	0.0159	0.0181	0.018	0.146	0.0180	0.0630	0.0187	0.375	0.0196
27	0.0142	0.0173	0.016	0.143	0.0164	0.0670	0.0172	0.500	0.0175
28	0.0126	0.0162	0.014	0.139	0.0148	0.0710	0.0156	1.000	0.0156
29	0.0113	0.0150	0.013	0.134	0.0136	0.0740	0.0141	.....	0.0139
30	0.0100	0.0140	0.012	0.127	0.0124	0.0780	0.0125	.....	0.0123
31	0.0089	0.0132	0.010	0.120	0.0116	0.0820	0.0109	.....	0.0110
32	0.0080	0.0128	0.009	0.115	0.0108	0.0860	0.0101	.....	0.0098
33	0.0071	0.0118	0.008	0.112	0.0100	......	0.0094	.....	0.0087
34	0.0063	0.0104	0.007	0.110	0.0092	......	0.0086	.....	0.0077
35	0.0056	0.0095	0.005	0.108	0.0084	......	0.0078	.....	0.0069

Comparison of Wire and Sheet-metal Gage Diameters or Thicknesses in Inches (*Continued*)

Gage No.	(1) American wire gage (AWG)[a]	(2) Steel wire gage	(3) Birmingham iron wire gage (Stubs)	(4) Stubs steel wire gage	(5) (British) standard wire gage	(6) Steel music wire gage	(7) U.S. standard[b]	(8) American zinc	(9) Birmingham
36	0.0050	0.0090	0.004	0.106	0.0076	......	0.0070	.....	0.0061
37	0.0045	0.0085	.....	0.103	0.0068	......	0.0066	.....	0.0054
38	0.0040	0.0080	.....	0.101	0.0060	......	0.0062	.....	0.0048
39	0.0035	0.0075	.....	0.099	0.0052	......	......	.....	0.0043
40	0.0031	0.0070	.....	0.097	0.0048	......	......	.....	0.0039
41	......	0.0066	.....	0.095	0.0044	......	......	.....	0.0034
42	......	0.0062	.....	0.092	0.0040	......	......	.....	0.0031
43	......	0.0060	.....	0.088	0.0036	......	......	.....	0.0027
44	......	0.0058	.....	0.085	0.0032	......	......	.....	0.0024
45	......	0.0055	.....	0.081	0.0028	......	......	.....	0.00215
46	......	0.0052	.....	0.079	0.0024	......	......	.....	0.0019
47	......	0.0050	.....	0.077	0.0020	......	......	.....	0.0017
48	......	0.0048	.....	0.075	0.0016	......	......	.....	0.0015
49	......	0.0046	.....	0.072	0.0012	......	......	.....	0.00135
50	......	0.0044	.....	0.069	0.0010	......	......	.....	0.0012
51	......	....	.....	.....	....	......	......	.....	0.0011
52	......	....	.....	.....	....	......	......	.....	0.00095

[a] The American wire gage sizes have been rounded off to about the usual limits of commercial accuracy.

[b] Now known as Manufacturers Standard Gage (MSG).

85. Make-ups of Electrical Conductors

Type	Illustration	Application
Copper		
Solid, round..............		Bare wire in sizes Nos. 4/0 to 45. Covered, non-insulated in sizes Nos. 4/0 to 14. Insulated in sizes Nos. 6 to 14 for power work. Insulated in sizes Nos. 1/0 to 46 for magnet wire
Solid, grooved.............		Trolley contact wire sizes 350,000 cir mils to No. 1/0
Solid, figure eight...........		Trolley contact wire sizes 350,000 cir mils to No. 1/0
Solid, figure nine............		Trolley contact wire size 400,000 cir mils
Solid, square...............		Magnet wire and windings for electrical equipment
Solid, rectangular..........		Magnet wire, windings for electrical equipment, bus bars
Solid, channels.............		Bus bars
Solid, angle................		Bus bars
Solid, tubes................		Bus bars
Standard, concentric-stranded.		Bare, covered, and insulated in sizes 5,000,000 cir mils to No. 20
Standard, rope stranded.......		Rubber-sheathed cords and cables in sizes 5,000,000 cir mils to No. 8

Make-ups of Electrical Conductors (*Continued*)

Type	Illustration	Application
Copper		
Bunched stranded...........		Flexible cords and fixture wire in sizes Nos. 10 to 22
Annular concentric-stranded with rope core..............		Varnished-cambric-insulated and solid-type paper-insulated single-conductor cables in sizes 5,000,000 to 750,000 cir mils
Compack-stranded, round.....		Varnished-cambric-insulated and solid-type paper-insulated cables in sizes 1,000,000 cir mils to No. 1 single conductor and size No. 1 for multiconductor
Compack-stranded, sector.....		Multiconductor paper-insulated cables both solid and oil-filled types in sizes 1,000,000 cir mils to No. 1/0
Compack-stranded, segmental.		Varnished-cambric-insulated and solid-type paper-insulated single-conductor cables in sizes 4,000,000 to 1,000,000 cir mils
Hollow-core, stranded........		Oil-filled paper-insulated single-conductor cables in sizes 2,000,000 cir mils to No. 2/0
Tubular-segmental, Type HH.		High-voltage long-distance transmission
Iron or Steel		
Solid, round................		Bare in sizes Nos. 4, 6, and 8 for power work. Bare in sizes Nos. 4 to 14 for telephone and telegraph work
Three-strand................		Bare in sizes Nos. 4, 6, and 8
Copperweld		
Solid, round................		Bare in sizes Nos. 4/0 to 12. Weatherproof covered in sizes Nos. 2 to 12. Rubber-insulated, single conductors in size Nos. 4/0 to 12 and two conductors in sizes Nos. 14 and 17
Concentric-stranded.........		Bare or rubber-covered, single conductor in diameters from 0.910 to 0.174 in.

Make-ups of Electrical Conductors (*Continued*)

Type	Illustration	Application
Copperweld and Copper		
Stranded..................		Bare in various combinations of strands in cable sizes from 586,800 cir mils to No. 8.—Weatherproof covered in sizes Nos. 2 to 8
Copper and Steel		
Three-strand...............		Bare in sizes Nos. 2 to 12
All Aluminum		
Stranded..................		Bare or weatherproof covered in sizes 1,590,000 cir mils to No. 4
Aluminum and Steel (ACSR)		
Annular aluminum, stranded with steel core............		Bare in sizes 1,590,000 cir mils to No. 4 Weatherproof covered in sizes Nos. 4/0 to 8
Bronze		
Solid, round...............		Bare or weatherproof covered in sizes Nos. 4 to 14

86. Application Guide for Electrical Conductor Materials

Application			Copper, soft drawn	Copper, medium hard drawn	Copper, hard drawn	Copperweld	Copperweld and copper	Copper and steel stranded	All aluminum	Aluminum and steel ACSR	Steel or iron	Bronze
Bare transmission and distribution wires	Heavy and medium loads	Short and medium spans		✓	✓					✓	✓	
		Long spans			✓		✓				✓	
	Light loads	Short and medium spans		✓	✓					✓	✓	
		Long spans			✓	✓		✓		✓	✓	
Covered noninsulated transmission and distribution wires	Heavy loads	Short and medium spans	✓	✓						✓		
		Long spans		✓						✓		
	Light loads	Short and medium spans	✓	✓						✓		
		Long spans			✓	✓	✓			✓		✓
Insulated cables			✓							✓		
Telephone and telegraph lines, ground wires					✓	✓					✓	
Signal circuits					✓	✓						
Trolley contact wires					✓							✓
Trolley feeders				✓								

87. Factors for Determining Diameter of Concentric-stranded Copper Cables[a]

Number of strands	3	7	12	19	37	61	91	127 and over
Factor	1.244	1.134	1.199	1.147	1.151	1.152	1.153	1.154

[a] To determine approximate diameter of bare concentric-stranded copper cables, multiply diameter of solid wire of same cross-sectional area by the proper factor from above table.

88. Solid Bare Copper Conductors
(Anaconda Wire and Cable Co.)

Size, AWG	Wire diam, in.	Cross sectional area		Weight		Hard-drawn wire		Medium hard-drawn wire		Soft or annealed wire	
		Cir mils	Sq in.	Per 1,000 ft, lb	Per mile, lb	Min breaking strength, lb[a]	Max resistance per 1,000 ft at 20°C, ohms[b]	Min breaking strength, lb[a]	Max resistance per 1,000 ft at 20°C, ohms[b]	Max breaking strength, lb[a]	Max resistance per 1,000 ft at 20°C, ohms[b]
4/0	0.4600	211,600	0.1662	640.5	3,382	8,143	0.05045	6,980	0.05019	5,983	0.04993
3/0	0.4096	167,800	0.1318	507.9	2,682	6,722	0.06361	5,667	0.06329	4,745	0.06296
2/0	0.3648	133,100	0.1045	402.8	2,127	5,519	0.08021	4,599	0.07980	3,763	0.07939
1/0	0.3249	105,500	0.08289	319.5	1,687	4,517	0.1011	3,730	0.1006	2,984	0.1001
1	0.2893	83,690	0.06573	253.5	1,338	3,688	0.1287	3,024	0.1282	2,432	0.1262
2	0.2576	66,370	0.05213	200.9	1,061	3,003	0.1625	2,450	0.1617	1,929	0.1592
3	0.2294	52,630	0.04134	159.3	841.2	2,439	0.2049	1,984	0.2038	1,530	0.2007
4	0.2043	41,740	0.03278	126.4	667.1	1,970	0.2584	1,584	0.2570	1,213	0.2531
5	0.1819	33,100	0.02600	100.2	529.1	1,591	0.3258	1,264	0.3241	961.9	0.3192
6	0.1620	26,250	0.02062	79.46	419.6	1,280	0.4108	1,010	0.4087	762.9	0.4025
7	0.1443	20,820	0.01635	63.02	332.7	1,030	0.5181	806.6	0.5154	605.0	0.5075
8	0.1285	16,510	0.01297	49.97	263.9	826.0	0.6533	643.9	0.6499	479.8	0.6400
9	0.1144	13,090	0.01028	39.63	209.3	661.2	0.8238	514.2	0.8195	380.5	0.8070
10	0.1019	10,380	0.008155	31.43	165.9	529.2	1.039	401.4	1.033	314.0	1.018
11	0.09074	8,234	0.006467	24.92	131.6	422.9	1.310	327.6	1.303	249.0	1.283
12	0.08081	6,530	0.005129	19.77	104.4	337.0	1.652	261.6	1.643	197.5	1.618
13	0.07196	5,178	0.004067	15.68	82.77	268.0	2.083	208.8	2.072	156.6	2.040
14	0.06408	4,107	0.003225	12.43	65.64	213.5	2.626	166.6	2.613	124.2	2.573
15	0.05707	3,257	0.002558	9.858	52.05	169.8	3.312	133.0	3.295	98.48	3.244
16	0.05082	2,583	0.002028	7.818	41.28	135.1	4.176	106.2	4.154	78.10	4.091
17	0.04526	2,048	0.001609	6.200	32.74	107.5	5.266	84.71	5.239	61.93	5.158
18	0.04030	1,624	0.001276	4.917	25.96	85.47	6.640	67.61	6.606	49.12	6.505
19	0.03589	1,288	0.001012	3.899	20.59	67.99	8.373	53.95	8.330	38.95	8.202
20	0.03196	1,022	0.0008023	3.092	16.33	54.08	10.56	43.05	10.50	30.89	10.34
21	0.02846	810.1	0.0006363	2.452	12.95	43.07	13.31	34.36	13.24	24.50	13.04
22	0.02535	642.5	0.0005046	1.945	10.27	34.26	16.79	27.41	16.70	19.43	16.45
23	0.02257	509.5	0.0004001	1.542	8.143	27.25	21.17	21.87	21.06	15.14	20.74
24	0.02010	404.0	0.0003173	1.233	6.458	21.67	26.69	17.45	26.56	12.69	26.15
25	0.01790	320.4	0.0002517	0.9699	5.121	17.26	33.66	13.92	33.49	10.07	32.97

Solid Bare Copper Conductors (Continued)

Size, AWG	Wire diam, in.	Cross sectional area		Weight		Hard-drawn wire		Medium hard-drawn wire		Soft or annealed wire	
		Cir mils	Sq in.	Per 1,000 ft, lb	Per mile, lb	Min breaking strength, lb[a]	Max resistance per 1,000 ft at 20°C, ohms[b]	Min breaking strength, lb[a]	Max resistance per 1,000 ft at 20°C, ohms[b]	Max breaking strength, lb[a]	Max resistance per 1,000 ft at 20°C, ohms[b]
26	0.01594	254.1	0.0001996	0.7692	4.061	13.73	42.44	11.11	42.23	7.983	41.58
27	0.01420	201.5	0.0001583	0.6100	3.221	10.92	53.52	8.863	53.25	6.331	52.43
28	0.01264	159.8	0.0001255	0.4837	2.554	8.698	67.49	7.070	67.14	5.021	66.11
29	0.01126	126.7	0.00009954	0.3836	2.026	6.918	85.10	5.640	84.66	3.981	83.37
30	0.01003	100.5	0.00007894	0.3042	1.606	5.502	107.3	4.499	106.8	3.157	105.1
31	0.008928	79.70	0.00006260	0.2413	1.274	4.376	135.3	3.589	134.6	2.504	132.6
32	0.007950	63.21	0.00004964	0.1913	1.010	3.485	170.6	2.862	169.8	1.986	167.2
33	0.007080	50.13	0.00003937	0.1517	0.8011	2.772	215.2	2.283	214.1	1.575	210.8
34	0.006305	39.75	0.00003122	0.1203	0.6353	2.204	271.3	1.821	269.9	1.249	265.8
35	0.005615	31.52	0.0002476	0.09542	0.5038	1.755	342.1	1.452	340.4	0.9904	335.2
36	0.005000	25.00	0.00001963	0.07567	0.3996	1.396	431.4	1.158	429.2	0.7854	422.6
37	0.004453	19.83	0.00001557	0.06001	0.3169	1.110	544.0	0.9238	541.2	0.6228	532.9
38	0.003965	15.72	0.00001235	0.04759	0.2513	0.8829	686.0	0.7367	682.4	0.4939	672.0
39	0.003531	12.47	0.000009793	0.03774	0.1993	0.7031	865.0	0.5876	860.5	0.3917	847.4
40	0.003145	9.888	0.000007766	0.02993	0.1580	0.5592	1,091	0.4685	1,085	0.3106	1,069
41	0.002800	7.842	0.000006159	0.02374	0.1253	0.4434	1,375	0.3716	1,368	0.2464	1,347
42	0.002494	6.219	0.000004884	0.01882	0.09939	0.3517	1,734	0.2947	1,725	0.1954	1,699
43	0.002221	4.932	0.000003873	0.01493	0.07882	0.2789	2,187	0.2337	2,176	0.1549	2,142
44	0.001978	3.911	0.000003072	0.01184	0.06251	0.2212	2,758	0.1853	2,743	0.1229	2,702
1 Mil	0.001000	1.000	0.000000785	0.003027	0.01598	0.05655	10,790	0.04738	10,730	0.03142	10,570

[a] The breaking strengths are based on ASTM specification requirements, using minimum values for hard- and medium hard-drawn wire, and maximum values for soft wire.

[b] The resistance values in this table are trade maximums and are higher than the average values for commercial wire. The following values for the conductivity of copper were used:

ASTM Requirements

	Conductivity, IACS % at 20°C	Resistivity, lb per mile-ohm at 20°C
Hard-drawn, 0.325 in. and larger................	97.16	900.77
Hard-drawn, 0.324 in. and smaller................	96.16	910.15
Medium hard-drawn, 0.325 in. and larger.........	97.66	896.15
Medium hard-drawn, 0.324 in. and smaller........	96.66	905.44
Soft or annealed................................	98.16	891.58

89. Stranded Bare Copper Conductors
(Anaconda Wire and Cable Co.)

Size				Weight[b]		Hard-drawn, min breaking strength, lb[c]	Medium hard-drawn, min breaking strength, lb[c]	Soft-drawn, max breaking strength, lb[c]
Cir mils	AWG	Strand-ing, class[a]	Cable diam., in.	Per 1,000 ft, lb	Per mile, lb			
5,000,000	...	B	2.581	15,890	83,910	219,500	173,200	145,300
5,000,000	...	A	2.580	15,890	83,910	216,300	171,800	145,300
4,500,000	...	B	2.448	14,300	75,520	200,400	156,900	130,800
4,500,000	...	A	2.448	14,300	75,520	197,200	154,600	130,800
4,000,000	...	B	2.309	12,590	66,490	178,100	139,500	116,200
4,000,000	...	A	2.307	12,590	66,490	175,600	138,500	116,200
3,500,000	...	B	2.159	11,020	58,180	155,900	122,000	101,700
3,500,000	...	A	2.158	11,020	58,180	153,400	120,200	101,700
3,000,000	...	B	1.998	9,353	49,390	134,400	104,600	87,180
3,000,000	...	A	1.998	9,353	49,390	131,700	103,900	87,180
2,500,000	...	B	1.824	7,794	41,150	111,300	87,179	72,650
2,500,000	...	A	1.823	7,794	41,150	109,600	85,800	72,650
2,000,000	...	B	1.632	6,175	32,600	90,050	70,210	58,120
2,000,000	...	A	1.630	6,175	32,600	87,790	69,270	58,120
1,750,000	...	B	1.526	5,403	28,530	78,800	61,430	50,850
1,750,000	...	A	1.526	5,403	28,530	77,930	61,020	50,850
1,500,000	...	B	1.412	4,631	24,450	67,540	52,650	43,590
1,500,000	...	A	1.411	4,631	24,450	65,840	51,950	43,590
1,250,000	...	B	1.289	3,859	20,380	56,280	43,880	36,320
1,250,000	...	A	1.288	3,859	20,380	55,670	43,590	36,320
1,000,000	...	B, A	1.152	3,088	16,300	45,030	35,100	29,060
1,000,000	...	AA	1.151	3,088	16,300	43,830	34,350	29,060
900,000	...	B, A	1.094	2,779	14,670	40,520	31,590	26,150
900,000	...	AA	1.092	2,779	14,670	39,510	31,170	26,150
800,000	...	B, A	1.031	2,470	13,040	36,360	28,270	23,250
800,000	...	AA	1.029	2,470	13,040	35,120	27,710	23,250
750,000	...	B, A	0.998	2,316	12,230	34,090	26,510	21,790
750,000	...	AA	0.997	2,316	12,230	33,400	26,150	21,790
700,000	...	B, A	0.964	2,161	11,410	31,820	24,740	20,340
700,000	...	AA	0.963	2,161	11,410	31,170	24,410	20,340
600,000	...	B	0.893	1,853	9,781	27,530	21,350	18,140
600,000	...	A, AA	0.891	1,853	9,781	27,020	21,060	17,440
500,000	...	B, A	0.813	1,544	8,151	22,510	17,550	14,530
500,000	...	AA	0.811	1,544	8,151	21,950	17,320	14,530
450,000	...	B, A	0.772	1,389	7,336	20,450	15,900	13,080
450,000	...	AA	0.770	1,389	7,336	19,750	15,590	13,080
400,000	...	B	0.728	1,235	6,521	18,320	14,140	11,620
400,000	...	A, AA	0.726	1,235	6,521	17,560	13,850	11,620
350,000	...	B	0.681	1,081	5,706	16,000	12,450	10,580
350,000	...	A	0.679	1,081	5,706	15,590	12,200	10,170
350,000	...	AA	0.710	1,081	5,706	15,140	12,020	10,170
300,000	...	B	0.630	926.3	4,891	13,870	10,740	9,071
300,000	...	A	0.629	926.3	4,891	13,510	10,530	8,718
300,000	...	AA	0.657	926.3	4,891	13,170	10,390	8,718
250,000	...	B	0.575	771.9	4,076	11,560	8,952	7,559
250,000	...	A	0.574	771.9	4,076	11,360	8,836	7,265
250,000	...	AA	0.600	771.9	4,076	11,130	8,717	7,265
211,600	4/0	B	0.528	653.3	3,450	9,617	7,479	6,149
211,600	4/0	A, AA	0.552	653.3	3,450	9,483	7,378	6,149
211,600	4/0	A, AA[d]	0.522	653.3	3,450	9,154	7,269	6,149

Stranded Bare Copper Conductors (*Continued*)

Size				Weight[b]		Hard-drawn, min breaking strength, lb[c]	Medium hard-drawn, min breaking strength, lb[c]	Soft-drawn, max breaking strength, lb[c]
Cir mils	AWG	Stranding, class[a]	Cable diam., in.	Per 1,000 ft, lb	Per mile, lb			
167,800	3/0	B	0.470	518.1	2,736	7,698	5,970	5,074
167,800	3/0	A, AA	0.492	518.1	2,736	7,556	5,890	4,876
167,800	3/0	A, AA[d]	0.464	518.1	2,736	7,366	5,812	4,876
133,100	2/0	B	0.419	410.9	2,170	6,153	4,766	4,025
133,100	2/0	......	0.437	410.9	2,170	6,049	4,704	3,868
133,100	2/0	A, AA	0.414	410.9	2,170	5,927	4,641	3,868
105,500	1/0	B	0.373	325.7	1,720	4,899	3,803	3,190
105,500	1/0	......	0.390	325.7	1,720	4,840	3,753	3,190
105,500	1/0	A, AA	0.368	325.7	1,720	4,750	3,703	3,066
83,690	1	B	0.332	258.4	1,364	3,898	3,037	2,531
83,690	1	A	0.328	258.4	1,364	3,804	2,958	2,432
83,690	1	AA	0.360	255.9	1,351	3,620	2,875	2,432
66,370	2	B, A	0.292	204.9	1,082	3,045	2,361	2,007
66,370	2	AA	0.320	202.9	1,071	2,913	2,299	1,929
52,630	3	B, A	0.260	162.5	858.0	2,433	1,885	1,591
52,630	3	AA	0.285	160.9	849.6	2,359	1,835	1,529
41,740	4	B, A	0.232	128.9	680.5	1,938	1,505	1,262
41,740	4	AA	0.254	127.6	673.8	1,879	1,465	1,213
33,100	5	B	0.206	102.2	539.6	1,542	1,201	1,001
26,250	6	B	0.184	81.05	427.9	1,228	958.6	793.7
20,820	7	B	0.164	64.28	339.4	977.2	765.3	629.6
16,510	8	B	0.146	50.98	269.1	777.2	610.7	499.2
13,090	9	B	0.130	40.42	213.4	618.1	487.3	395.8
10,380	10	B	0.116	32.05	169.2	491.6	388.9	313.9
6,530	12	B	0.0915	20.16	106.5	311.1	247.7	197.5
4,107	14	B	0.0726	12.68	66.95	197.1	157.7	124.2
2,583	16	B	0.0576	7.975	42.11	124.7	100.4	81.15
1,624	18	B	0.0456	5.014	26.47	78.98	63.89	51.02
1,022	20	B	0.0363	3.155	16.66	50.06	40.69	32.11

[a] Class of stranding in accordance with ASTM Specification B 8-35T.
[b] Weight increased 2 per cent to allow for cabling, except as follows:

Cir Mils	Per Cent
5,000,000 and 4,500,000	5
4,000,000 and 3,500,000	4
3,000,000 and 2,500,000	3

[c] The breaking strengths are based on ASTM specification requirements, using minimum values for hard- and medium hard-drawn cable, and maximum values for soft cable.
[d] Optional construction, see Table 90.

90. Stranding Data for Copper Conductors — Concentric Stranded, USA Standards

Size		Class AA			Class A			Class B		
AWG	Cir mils	Number of strands	Diam of individual strands, mils	Approx over-all diam, in.	Number of strands	Diam of individual strands, mils	Approx over-all diam, in.	Number of strands	Diam of individual strands, mils	Approx over-all diam, in.
	5,000,000	...	.....	.....	169	172.0	2.580	217	151.8	2.581
	4,500,000	...	.....	.....	169	163.2	2.448	217	144.0	2.448
	4,000,000	...	.....	.....	169	153.8	2.307	217	135.8	2.309
	3,500,000	...	.....	.....	127	166.0	2.158	169	143.8	2.159
	3,000,000	...	.....	.....	127	153.7	1.998	169	133.2	1.998
	2,500,000	...	.....	.....	91	165.7	1.823	127	140.3	1.824
	2,000,000	...	.....	.....	91	148.2	1.630	127	125.5	1.631
	1,900,000	...	.....	.....	91	144.5	.....	127	122.3	
	1,800,000	...	.....	.....	91	140.6	.....	127	119.1	
	1,750,000	...	.....	.....	91	138.7	1.526	127	117.4	1.526
	1,700,000	...	.....	.....	91	136.7	.....	127	115.7	
	1,600,000	...	.....	.....	91	132.6	.....	127	112.2	
	1,500,000	...	.....	.....	61	156.8	1.411	91	128.4	1.412
	1,400,000	...	.....	.....	61	151.5	.....	91	124.0	
	1,300,000	...	.....	.....	61	146.0	.....	91	119.5	
	1,250,000	...	.....	.....	61	143.1	1.288	91	117.2	1.289
	1,200,000	...	.....	.....	61	140.3	.....	91	114.8	
	1,100,000	...	.....	.....	61	134.3	.....	91	109.9	
	1,000,000	37	164.4	1.151	61	128.0	1.152	61	128.0	1.152
	900,000	37	156.0	1.092	61	121.5	1.094	61	121.5	1.094
	800,000	37	147.0	1.029	61	114.5	1.031	61	114.5	1.031
	750,000	37	142.4	0.997	61	110.9	0.998	61	110.9	0.998
	700,000	37	137.5	0.963	61	107.1	0.964	61	107.1	0.964
	650,000	37	132.5	.....	61	103.2	.....	61	103.2	
	600,000	37	127.3	0.891	37	127.3	0.891	61[c]	99.2	0.893
	550,000	37	121.9	.....	37	121.9	.....	61[d]	95.0	
	500,000	19	162.2	0.811	37	116.2	0.814	37	116.2	0.814
	450,000	19	153.9	0.770	37	110.3	0.772	37	110.3	0.772
	400,000	19	145.1	0.726	19	145.1	0.726	37	104.0	0.728
	350,000	12	170.7	0.710	19	135.7	0.679	37	97.3	0.681
	300,000	12	158.1	0.657	19	125.7	0.629	37	90.0	0.630
	250,000	12	144.3	0.600	19	114.7	0.574	37	82.2	0.575
4/0	211,600	7[a]	173.9	0.522	7[a]	173.9	0.522	19	105.5·	0.528
3/0	167,800	7[b]	154.8	0.464	7[b]	154.8	0.464	19	94.0	0.470
2/0	133,100	7	137.9	0.414	7	137.9	0.414	19	83.7	0.418
1/0	105,500	7	122.8	0.368	7	122.8	0.368	19	74.5	0.373
1	83,690	3	167.0	0.360	7	109.3	0.328	19	66.4	0.332
2	66,370	3	148.7	0.320	7	97.4	0.292	7	97.4	0.292
3	52,630	3	132.5	0.285	7	86.7	0.260	7	86.7	0.260
4	41,740	3	118.0	0.254	7	77.2	0.232	7	77.2	0.232
5	33,100	...	.....	.....	....	.....	.....	7	68.8	0.206
6	26,250	...	.....	.....	....	.....	.....	7	61.2	0.184
7	20,820	...	.....	.....	....	.....	.....	7	54.5	0.164
8	16,510	...	.....	.....	....	.....	.....	7	48.6	0.146
9	13,090	...	.....	.....	....	.....	.....	7	43.2	0.130
10	10,380	...	.....	.....	....	.....	.....	7	38.5	0.116
12	6,530	...	.....	.....	....	.....	.....	7	30.5	0.0915
14	4,107	...	.....	.....	....	.....	.....	7	24.2	0.0726
16	2,583	...	.....	.....	....	.....	.....	7	19.2	0.0576
18	1,624	...	.....	.....	....	.....	.....	7	15.2	0.0456
20	1,022	...	.....	.....	....	.....	.....	7	12.1	0.0363

[a] Optional construction for No. 4/0 AWG size in Class AA and Class A is 12 wires of 132.8 mils diameter.
[b] Optional construction for No. 3/0 AWG size in Class AA and Class A is 12 wires of 118.3 mils diameter.
[c] Optional construction for 600,000 CM size in Class B is 37 wires of 127.3 mils diameter.
[d] Optional construction for 550,000 CM size in Class B is 37 wires of 121.9 mils diameter.
The above data are approximate and subject to normal manufacturing tolerances.

91. Stranding Data for Copper Conductors — Concentric Stranded, USA Standards

Size		Class C			Class D		
AWG	Cir mils	Number of strands	Diam of individual strands, mils	Approx over-all diam, in.	Number of strands	Diam of individual strands, mils	Approx over-all diam, in.
	5,000,000	271	135.8	2.580	271	135.8	2.580
	4,500,000	271	128.9	2.448	271	128.9	2.448
	4,000,000	271	121.5	2.307	271	121.5	2.307
	3,500,000	217	127.0	2.158	271	113.6	2.158
	3,000,000	217	117.6	1.998	271	105.2	1.998
	2,500,000	169	121.6	1.824	217	107.3	1.824
	2,000,000	169	108.8	1.631	217	96.0	1.631
	1,900,000	169	106.0	.....	217	93.6	
	1,800,000	169	103.2	.....	217	91.1	
	1,750,000	169	101.8	1.526	217	89.8	1.526
	1,700,000	169	100.3	.....	217	88.5	
	1,600,000	169	97.3	.....	217	85.9	
	1,500,000	127	108.7	1.414	169	94.2	1.414
	1,400,000	127	105.0	.....	169	91.0	
	1,300,000	127	101.2	.....	169	87.7	
	1,250,000	127	99.2	1.290	169	86.0	1.290
	1,200,000	127	97.2	.....	169	84.3	
	1,100,000	127	93.1	.....	169	80.7	
	1,000,000	91	104.8	1.153	127	88.7	1.154
	900,000	91	99.4	1.095	127	84.2	1.096
	800,000	91	93.8	1.032	127	79.4	1.032
	750,000	91	90.8	0.999	127	76.8	1.000
	700,000	91	87.7	0.965	127	74.2	0.966
	650,000	91	84.5	.....	127	71.5	
	600,000	91	81.2	0.893	127	68.7	0.894
	550,000	91	77.7	.....	127	65.8	
	500,000	61	90.5	0.815	91	74.1	0.817
	450,000	61	85.9	0.773	91	70.3	0.774
	400,000	61	81.0	0.730	91	66.3	0.731
	350,000	61	75.7	0.683	91	62.0	0.684
	300,000	61	70.1	0.632	91	57.4	0.633
	250,000	61	64.0	0.577	91	52.4	0.578
4/0	211,600	37	75.6	0.529	61	58.9	0.530
3/0	167,800	37	67.3	0.471	61	52.4	0.471
2/0	133,100	37	60.0	0.419	61	46.7	0.419
1/0	105,500	37	53.4	0.376	61	41.6	0.376
1	83,690	37	47.6	0.333	61	37.0	0.333
2	66,370	19	59.1	0.295	37	42.4	0.296
3	52,630	19	52.6	0.261	37	37.7	0.262
4	41,740	19	46.9	0.230	37	33.6	0.231
5	33,100	19	41.7	0.209	37	29.9	0.210
6	26,250	19	37.2	0.186	37	26.6	0.186
7	20,820	19	33.1	0.166	37	23.7	0.166
8	16,510	19	29.5	0.147	37	21.1	0.148
9	13,090	19	26.2	0.131	37	18.8	0.132
10	10,380	19	23.4	0.107	37	16.7	0.117
12	6,530	19	18.5	0.093	37	13.3	0.093
14	4,107	19	14.7	0.074	37	10.5	0.074
16	2,583	19	11.7	0.058			
18	1,624	19	9.2	0.046			
20	1,022	19	7.3	0.037			

The above data are approximate and subject to normal manufacturing tolerances.

92. Stranding Data for Copper Conductors — Rope Stranded; IPCEA Standards

Size, cir mils or AWG	Flexible stranding (Class G)				Extra-flexible stranding (Class H)				Approx over-all diam, in.	Weight per 1,000 ft, net lb
	Total number of strands	Diam of individual strands, mils	Number of ropes	Number of strands each rope	Total number of strands	Diam of individual strands, mils	Number of ropes	Number of strands each rope		
5,000,000	1,159	65.7	61	19	1,729	53.8	91	19	2.959	16,200
4,500,000	1,159	62.3	61	19	1,729	51.0	91	19	2.805	14,600
4,000,000	1,159	58.7	61	19	1,729	48.1	91	19	2.646	13,000
3,500,000	1,159	55.0	61	19	1,729	45.0	91	19	2.475	11,400
3,000,000	1,159	50.9	61	19	1,729	41.7	91	19	2.294	9,470
2,500,000	703	59.6	37	19	1,159	46.4	61	19	2.088	8,000
2,000,000	703	53.3	37	19	1,159	41.5	61	19	1.868	6,470
1,900,000	703	52.0	37	19	1,159	40.5	61	19	1.823	6,160
1,800,000	703	50.6	37	19	1,159	39.4	61	19	1.773	5,830
1,750,000	703	49.9	37	19	1,159	38.9	61	19	1.751	5,680
1,700,000	703	49.2	37	19	1,159	38.3	61	19	1.724	5,510
1,600,000	703	47.7	37	19	1,159	37.2	61	19	1.674	5,200
1,500,000	427	59.3	61	7	703	46.2	37	19	1.617	4,860
1,400,000	427	57.3	61	7	703	44.6	37	19	1.561	4,530
1,300,000	427	55.2	61	7	703	43.0	37	19	1.505	4,210
1,250,000	427	54.1	61	7	703	42.2	37	19	1.477	4,060
1,200,000	427	53.0	61	7	703	41.3	37	19	1.446	3,890
1,100,000	427	50.8	61	7	703	39.6	37	19	1.386	3,570
1,000,000	427	48.4	61	7	703	37.7	37	19	1.320	3,240
900,000	427	45.9	61	7	703	35.8	37	19	1.253	2,920
800,000	427	43.3	61	7	703	33.7	37	19	1.180	2,590
750,000	427	41.9	61	7	703	32.7	37	19	1.145	2,440
700,000	427	40.5	61	7	703	31.6	36	19	1.106	2,270
650,000	427	39.0	61	7	703	30.4	37	19	1.064	2,110
600,000	427	37.5	61	7	703	29.2	37	19	1.022	1,940
550,000	427	35.9	61	7	703	28.0	37	19	0.980	1,790
500,000	259	43.9	37	7	427	34.2	61	7	0.923	1,610
450,000	259	41.7	37	7	427	32.5	61	7	0.878	1,460
400,000	259	39.3	37	7	427	30.6	61	7	0.826	1,290
350,000	259	36.8	37	7	427	28.6	61	7	0.773	1,130
300,000	259	34.0	37	7	427	26.5	61	7	0.716	969
250,000	259	31.1	37	7	427	24.2	61	7	0.653	808
4/0	133	39.9	19	7	259	28.6	37	7	0.602	686
3/0	133	35.5	19	7	259	25.5	37	7	0.536	540
2/0	133	31.6	19	7	259	22.7	37	7	0.477	428
1/0	133	28.2	19	7	259	20.2	37	7	0.424	339
1	133	25.1	19	7	259	18.0	37	7	0.378	269
2	49	36.8	7	7	133	22.3	19	7	0.336	213
3	49	32.8	7	7	133	19.9	19	7	0.299	168
4	49	29.2	7	7	133	17.7	19	7	0.266	133
5	49	26.0	7	7	133	15.8	19	7	0.237	106
6	49	23.1	7	7	133	14.0	19	7	0.210	83
8	49	18.4	7	7	133	11.1	19	7	0.167	52

AWG size for individual strands are permissible, provided their area is not more than 2 per cent below required area. Sizes Nos. 2, 3/0, and 4/0 AWG can be supplied in alternate combinations as follows:

Wire size	No. 2 AWG	No. 3/0 AWG	No. 4/0 AWG
Total number of strands.....................	259	427	427
Diameter individual strands (mils)............	16.0	19.8	22.3
Number of ropes............................	37	61	61
Number of strands each rope.................	7	7	7

Flexible stranded conductors Nos. 10 to 22 AWG are normally supplied in bunched-stranded form; refer to Tables 94 and 95.

Conforms to all requirements of IPCEA Project 46.

The above data are approximate and subject to normal manufacturing tolerances.

93. Stranding Data for Copper Conductors – Bunch and Rope Stranded; from IPCEA and ASTM Standards

Size, AWG or cir mils	Class K				Class M			
	All wires No. 30 AWG				All wires No. 34 AWG			
	Nominal No. of wires	Suggested construction	Approx over-all diam, in.	Approx weight, lb per 1,000 ft	Nominal No. of wires	Suggested construction	Approx over-all diam, in.	Approx weight, lb per 1,000 ft
20	10	1 × 10	0.038	3.2	26	1 × 26	0.038	3.2
18	16	1 × 16	0.048	5.0	41	1 × 41	0.048	5.0
16	26	1 × 26	0.060	8.0	65	1 × 65	0.060	8.0
14	41	1 × 41	0.078	12.8	104	1 × 104	0.078	12.8
12	65	1 × 65	0.101	20.3	168	7 × 24	0.101	21.0
10	104	1 × 104	0.126	32.5	259	7 × 37	0.126	32.5
9	133	7 × 19	0.150	42	336	7 × 48	0.146	42
8	168	7 × 24	0.157	53	420	7 × 60	0.162	53
7	210	7 × 30	0.179	66	532	19 × 28	0.196	67
6	266	7 × 38	0.210	84	665	19 × 35	0.215	84
5	336	7 × 48	0.235	106	836	19 × 44	0.240	105
4	420	7 × 60	0.272	132	1,064	19 × 56	0.269	134
3	532	19 × 28	0.304	169	1,323	7 × 7 × 27	0.305	169
2	665	19 × 35	0.338	211	1,666	7 × 7 × 34	0.337	212
1	836	19 × 44	0.397	266	2,107	7 × 7 × 43	0.376	268
1/0	1,064	19 × 56	0.451	338	2,646	7 × 7 × 54	0.423	337
2/0	1,323	7 × 7 × 27	0.470	425	3,325	19 × 7 × 25	0.508	427
3/0	1,666	7 × 7 × 34	0.533	535	4,256	19 × 7 × 32	0.576	547
4/0	2,107	7 × 7 × 43	0.627	676	5,320	19 × 7 × 40	0.645	684
250,000	2,499	7 × 7 × 51	0.682	802	6,384	19 × 7 × 48	0.713	821
300,000	2,989	7 × 7 × 61	0.768	960	7,581	19 × 7 × 57	0.768	975
350,000	3,458	19 × 7 × 26	0.809	1,120	8,806	37 × 7 × 34	0.825	1,130
400,000	3,990	19 × 7 × 30	0.878	1,290	10,101	37 × 7 × 39	0.901	1,300
450,000	4,522	19 × 7 × 34	0.933	1,465	11,396	37 × 7 × 44	0.940	1,465
500,000	5,054	19 × 7 × 38	0.988	1,635	12,691	37 × 7 × 49	0.997	1,630
550,000	5,453	19 × 7 × 41	1 056	1,765	13,664	61 × 7 × 32	1.035	1,755
600,000	5,985	19 × 7 × 45	1.125	1,940	14,945	61 × 7 × 35	1.084	1,920
650,000	6,517	19 × 7 × 49	1.166	2,110	16,226	61 × 7 × 38	1.133	2,085
700,000	6,916	19 × 7 × 52	1.207	2,240	17,507	61 × 7 × 41	1.183	2,250
750,000	7,581	19 × 7 × 57	1.276	2,455	18,788	61 × 7 × 44	1.207	2,415
800,000	7,980	19 × 7 × 60	1 305	2,585	20,069	61 × 7 × 47	1.256	2,580
900,000	9,065	37 × 7 × 35	1.323	2,935	22,631	61 × 7 × 53	1.331	2,910
1,000,000	10,101	37 × 7 × 39	1.419	3,270	25,193	61 × 7 × 59	1.404	3,240

94. Stranding Data for Copper Conductors — Bunched-stranded Ropes; IPCEA Standards

Nominal size, cir mils or AWG	Class J Min number of No. 30 AWG strands	Class L Min number No. 34 AWG strands	Approx OD, in.	Nominal size, AWG	Class J Min number of No. 30 AWG strands	Class L Min number No. 34 AWG strands	Approx OD, in.
1,000,000	9,951	......	1.52	1	836	2,109	0.44
900,000	8,956	......	1.43	2	661	1,672	0.39
800,000	7,961	......	1.35	3	524	1,326	0.36
750,000	7,463	......	1.31	4	410	1,052	0.31
700,000	6,966	......	1.28	5	330	832	0.27
650,000	6,468	......	1.25	6	262	661	0.22
600,000	5,971	......	1.21	7	208	524	0.20
550,000	5,473	......	1.17	8	165	416	0.17
500,000	4,976	12,579	1.08	9	131	330	0.16
450,000	4,478	11,321	1.00	10	104	262	0.12
400,000	3,981	10,063	0.96	12	65	165	0.10
350,000	3,483	8,806	0.90	14	41	104	0.08
300,000	2,986	7,557	0.82	16	26	65	0.06
250,000	2,488	6,297	0.78	18	16	41	0.05
4/0	2,106	5,330	0.73	20	10	26	0.04
3/0	1,670	4,227	0.61				
2/0	1,325	3,353	0.55				
1/0	1,050	2,658	0.49				

95. Stranding Data for Copper Conductors, Bunched Stranded — IPCEA Special Strandings

Nominal size, AWG	Class P Fixture wire, commercial Number strands	Size strand, AWG	Class Q 10,000-cycle heater cord Number strands	Size strand, AWG	Class R Special fixture wire, portable cords, etc. Number strands	Size strand, AWG	Class S Type S cord Number strands	Size strand, AWG	Class T Oscillating fan cord Number strands	Size strand, AWG
10	65	28	...	...	165	32	104	30		
12	41	28	...	...	104	32	84	31		
14	26	28	...	...	65	32	84	33		
16	16	28	104	36	41	32	65	34		
18	10	28	65	36	26	32	41	34	165	40
20	7	28	41	36	16 ·	32	26	34	104	40

96. Recommended Stranding Practice for Copper Conductors

Type of Stranding	Recommended Uses
Class AA	For bare cable
Class A	For weather-resistant (weatherproof), slow-burning, and slow-burning weather-resistant cables, and for bare cable where greater flexibility than is afforded by Class AA is required
Class B	For cable insulated with various materials such as rubber, paper, varnished cloth, etc., and for the cables indicated under Class A where greater flexibility is required
Class C and Class K	For cable where greater flexibility is required than is provided by Class B cable
Class G	For all rubber-sheathed cords and cables for normal use
Class H	For all rubber-sheathed cords and cables where extreme flexibility is required, such as for use on take-up reels, over sheaves, etc.
Class J	For use in fixture wire, portable cords, etc.
Class L	For use in welding cable, heater cord, Type SJ cord
Class P	For commercial fixture wire
Class Q	For 10,000-cycle heater cord
Class R	For special fixture wire, portable cords, etc.
Class S	For Type S cord
Class T	For oscillating-fan cord
Bunched stranded	For extremely flexible conductors of sizes from No. 10 to No. 22

97. Annular, Concentric-stranded, Rope-core Conductors — IPCEA Standard
(General Cable Corp.)

Nominal size, cir mils	Actual area, cir mils	Approx. rope core size, in.	Number of strands	Diam individual strands, in.	Max over-all diam, in.	Weight per 1,000 ft	
						Copper only, net lb	Copper and core, net lb
750,000	741,735	0.375	54	0.1172	1.108	2,312	2,362
800,000	800,865	0.468	65	0.1110	1.164	2,497	2,575
900,000	906,565	0.500	66	0.1172	1.234	2,826	2,905
1,000,000	1,023,766	0.563	65	0.1255	1.346	3,192	3,304
1,250,000	1,260,020	0.750	80	0.1255	1.533	3,928	4,127
1,500,000	1,512,024	1.000	96	0.1255	1.783	4,714	5,068
1,750,000	1,753,083	1.125	107	0.1280	1.923	5,466	5,914
2,000,000	1,978,387	1.3125	120	0.1284	2.114	6,168	6,778
2,500,000	2,488,320	1.500	120	0.1440	2.394	7,758	8,555
3,000,000	3,044,304	1.625	116	0.1620	2.627	9,492	10,427
3,500,000	3,595,428	2.000	137	0.1620	3.007	11,319	12,735
4,000,000	4,015,332	2.250	153	0.1620	3.262	12,641	14,433
4,500,000	4,408,992	2.500	168	0.1620	3.517	14,013	16,226
5,000,000	4,960,116	2.875	189	0.1620	3.897	15,765	18,691

The following tolerances are included in over-all diameters:

Nominal Size, M Cir Mils	Tolerance, In.
750–3,000	0.030
3,001–3,500	0.035
3,501–4,000	0.040
4,001–4,500	0.045
4,501–5,000	0.050

The following allowances for stranding are included in the metallic weight:

Nominal Size, M Cir Mils	Tolerance, Per Cent
750–3,000	3
3,001–4,000	4
4,001–5,000	5

98. Compack-stranded Conductors — Segmental

(General Cable Corp.)

Size, cir mils	Number of strands	Approx over-all diam, in.	Size, cir mils	Number of strands	Approx over-all diam, in.
1,000,000	148	1.152	2,500,000	244	1.825
1,250,000	148	1.288	3,000,000	364	2.000
1,500,000	148	1.412	3,500,000	364	2.159
1,750,000	244	1.526	4,000,000	364	2.308
2,000,000	244	1.631			

99. Compack-stranded Conductors — Round and Sector

(General Cable Corp.)

Size, AWG or cir mils	Round		120-degree sector		90-degree sector	
	Number of strands	Over-all diam, in.	V-gage depth,[a] in.	Number of strands	V-gage depth,[a] in.	Number of strands
1	19	0.299				
1/0	19	0.336	0.288	19	0.340	19
2/0	19	0.376	0.323	19	0.382	19
3/0	19	0.423	0.364	37		
4/0	19	0.475	0.417 (L) / 0.410 (H)	37 / 37	0.482	37
250,000	37	0.520	0.455 (L) / 0.477 (H)	37 / 37	0.525	37
300,000	37	0.570	0.497 (L) / 0.490 (H)	37 / 37	0.572	37
350,000	37	0.616	0.539 (L) / 0.532 (H)	37 / 37	0.620	37
400,000	37	0.659	0.572 (L) / 0.566 (H)	37 / 37		
500,000	37	0.736	0.642 (L) / 0.635 (H)	61 / 61	0.740	61
600,000	61	0.813	0.700 (L) / 0.690 (H)	61 / 61		
700,000	61	0.877	0.754 (L) / 0.742 (H)	91 / 91		
750,000	61	0.908	0.780 (L) / 0.767 (H)	91 / 91		
800,000	61	0.938	0.795[b]	91		
1,000,000	61	1.060	0.900[b]	91		

The above data are approximate and subject to normal manufacturing tolerances.

L and H indicate V-gage depths of the bare conductor for "light" walls (up to and including $1\frac{3}{64}$ in.) and "heavy" walls ($1\frac{5}{64}$ in. and over), respectively. The shape of the sector and, therefore, the V-gage depth in the larger sizes depend on whether a light or heavy wall of insulation is to be applied.

[a] V-gage depth is the distance from the center point of the exterior arc of the bare sector to the point where the lines of the sides of the conductor if prolonged would intersect. For rough calculation purposes, V-gage depth in inches can be taken as 90 per cent of the square root of the nominal area of the conductor expressed in circular inches.

[b] Representative values; exact values depend on insulation thickness to be used and will be furnished on request.

100. Hollow-core Stranded Conductors
(General Cable Corp.)

Size, AWG or cir mils	Over-all conductor diam, in.		Size, AWG or cir mils	Over-all conductor diam, in.	
	ID of spring core = 0.500 in.	ID of spring core = 0.690 in.		ID of spring core = 0.500 in.	ID of spring core = 0.690 in.
2/0	0.736	. . . . .	700,000	1.151	1.256
3/0	0.768	0.924	750,000	1.180	1.286
4/0	0.807	0.956	800,000	1.212	1 309
250,000	0.837	0.983	850,000	1.242	1.341
300,000	0.880	1.017	900,000	1.261	1.365
350,000	0.917	1.049	1,000,000	1.310	1.416
400,000	0.953	1.082	1,250,000	1.434	1.524
450,000	0.989	1.112	1,500,000	1.547	1.635
500,000	1.028	1.145	1,750,000	1.650	1.730
600,000	1.084	1.201	2,000,000	1.760	1.833
650,000	1.121	1.228			

The above data are approximate and subject to normal manufacturing tolerances.

101. Iron or Steel Telephone and Telegraph Wire
(American Steel and Wire Co.)

Size, BWG	Diam, in.	Approx weight, lb		Approx breaking strength, lb			Resistance per mile (International Ohms) at 68°F		
		Per 1,000 ft	Per mile	EBB	BB	Steel	EBB	BB	Steel
4	0.238	153	811	2,028	2,271	2,433	5.98	7.15	8.32
6	0.203	112	590	1,475	1,652	1,770	8.22	9.83	11.44
8	0.165	74	390	975	1,092	1,170	12.43	14.87	17.31
9	0.148	60	314	785	879	942	15.44	18.47	21.50
10	0.134	49	258	645	722	774	18.79	22.48	26.16
11	0.120	39	206	515	577	618	23.54	28.16	32.77
12	0.109	32	170	425	476	510	28.52	34.12	39.71
14	0.083	19	99	247	277	297	48.98	58.59	68.18

Amertel-85 Wire

Size, BWG	Nominal diam, in.	Approx weight per mile, lb	Approx coil length, miles	Min breaking strength, lb	Resistance per mile, ohms
9	0.148	314	½	1462	18.47
10	0.134	258	½	1199	22.48
12	0.109	170	½	793	34.12
14	0.083	99	½	460	58.59

Amertel-135 Wire

Size, BWG............................	No. 12
Nominal diameter, in....................	0.109
Minimum breaking strength, lb...........	1213
Resistance per mile, ohms...............	38.23
Approximate weight per mile, lb..........	170
Approximate weight per coil, lb...........	150
Approximate length per coil, ft...........	4,659

Amertel-195 Wire

Size, BWG................................	No. 12
Nominal diameter, in........................	0.109
Minimum breaking strength, lb................	1800
Resistance per mile (Ohms)....................	38.8
Approximate weight per mile, lb...............	170
Approximate weight per coil, lb................	160
Minimum weight per coil, lb, approx..........	144
Maximum weight per coil, lb, approx..........	176
Approximate length per coil, ft.................	4,970
Minimum length per coil, ft, approx..........	4,470
Maximum length per coil, ft, approx..........	5,470

102. All-steel Conductors

(American Steel and Wire Co.)

Type	Size and diameter			Area		Approx weight		Breaking strength, lb
	Size, BWG	Number and diameter of wires	Diam of conductor, in.	Cir mils	Sq in.	Lb per 1,000 ft	Lb per mile	
S	4	1	0.238	56,644	0.0445	153	808	5,560
S	6	1	0.203	41,209	0.0324	112	591	4,270
S	8	1	0.165	27,225	0.0214	74	391	2,820
S-3	4	3/0.138	0.297	57,132	0.0448	156	823	5,560
S-3	6	3/0.117	0.252	41,067	0.0322	112	591	4,270
S-3	8	3/0.096	0.207	27,648	0.0217	75	396	2,820

Modulus: Type S, 29,000,000; Type S-3, 25,000,000.
Coefficient of expansion: 0.0000066.

103. Trolley Wire—Copper and Bronze
(Anaconda Wire and Cable Co.)

Nominal size AWG or MCM	Cross-sectional area Nominal MCM	Actual MCM	Sq in.	Weight Lb per 1,000 ft	Lb per mile	Min conductivity, % IACS[a]	D-c resistance or volts drop per amp at 20°C (68°F) Ohms or volts per 1,000 ft	Ohms or volts per mile	Min tensile strength, lb per sq in.	Min breaking load, lb	Elongation in 10 in., %
Round 97.16% Conductivity Hard-drawn Copper											

Round 97.16% Conductivity Hard-drawn Copper

Nom. size	Nom. MCM	Actual MCM	Sq in.	Lb per 1,000 ft	Lb per mile	% IACS	Ohms/1,000 ft	Ohms/mile	Tensile	Breaking load	Elong. %
1/0	105.6	105.6	0.0829	319.5	1,687	97.16	0.1011	0.5339	54,500	4,518	2.40
2/0	133.1	133.1	0.1045	402.8	2,127	97.16	0.08021	0.4235	52,800	5,519	2.80
3/0	167.8	167.8	0.1318	507.8	2,681	97.16	0.06362	0.3359	51,000	6,720	3.25
4/0	211.6	211.6	0.1662	640.5	3,382	97.16	0.05045	0.2664	49,000	8,143	3.75
300	300.0	300.0	0.2356	908.0	4,794	97.16	0.03558	0.1879	46,400	10,930	4.50

Grooved 97.16% Conductivity Hard-drawn Copper

Nom. size	Nom. MCM	Actual MCM	Sq in.	Lb per 1,000 ft	Lb per mile	% IACS	Ohms/1,000 ft	Ohms/mile	Tensile	Breaking load	Elong. %
2/0	133.1	137.9	0.1083	417.6	2,205	97.16	0.07741	0.4087	50,200	5,437	2.80
3/0	167.8	167.3	0.1314	506.4	2,674	97.16	0.06380	0.3369	48,500	6,373	3.25
4/0	211.6	212.0	0.1665	641.9	3,389	97.16	0.05035	0.2659	46,600	7,759	3.75
300	300.0	299.8	0.2355	907.6	4,792	97.16	0.03560	0.1880	44,200	10,410	4.50
350	350.0	351.2	0.2758	1,063.0	5,612	97.16	0.03040	0.1605	42,800	11,800	4.50

Figure-8 97.16% Conductivity Hard-drawn Copper

Nom. size	Nom. MCM	Actual MCM	Sq in.	Lb per 1,000 ft	Lb per mile	% IACS	Ohms/1,000 ft	Ohms/mile	Tensile	Breaking load	Elong. %
1/0	105.6	105.6	0.0829	319.5	1,687	97.16	0.1011	0.5340	51,800	4,294	2.40
2/0	133.1	133.1	0.1045	402.8	2,127	97.16	0.08021	0.4325	50,200	5,246	2.80
3/0	167.8	167.8	0.1318	508.0	2,682	97.16	0.06361	0.3359	48,500	6,392	3.25
4/0	211.6	211.6	0.1662	640.5	3,382	97.16	0.05044	0.2663	46,600	7,745	3.75
350	350.0	350.1	0.2750	1,060.0	5,597	97.16	0.03049	0.1610	42,800	11,770	4.50

Figure-9 Deep-section 97.16% Conductivity Hard-drawn Copper

Nom. size	Nom. MCM	Actual MCM	Sq in.	Lb per 1,000 ft	Lb per mile	% IACS	Ohms/1,000 ft	Ohms/mile	Tensile	Breaking load	Elong. %
350	350.0	348.9	0.2740	1,056.0	5,576	97.16	0.03060	0.1616	42,800	11,730	4.50
400	400.0	397.2	0.3120	1,202.0	6,347	97.16	0.02687	0.1419	41,300	12,890	4.50

Round 85% Conductivity Hitenso A Bronze

Nom. size	Nom. MCM	Actual MCM	Sq in.	Lb per 1,000 ft	Lb per mile	% IACS	Ohms/1,000 ft	Ohms/mile	Tensile	Breaking load	Elong. %
1/0	105.6	105.6	0.0829	319.5	1,687	85	0.1156	0.6105	68,000	5,638	2.40
2/0	133.1	133.1	0.1045	402.8	2,127	85	0.09172	0.4843	66,000	6,898	2.75
3/0	167.8	167.8	0.1318	507.8	2,681	85	0.07275	0.3841	64,000	8,433	3.25
4/0	211.6	211.6	0.1662	640.5	3,382	85	0.05768	0.3046	61,500	10,220	3.75
300	300.0	300.0	0.2356	908.0	4,794	85	0.04069	0.2148	58,300	13,740	4.50

Grooved 85% Conductivity Hitenso A bronze

Nom. size	Nom. MCM	Actual MCM	Sq in.	Lb per 1,000 ft	Lb per mile	% IACS	Ohms/1,000 ft	Ohms/mile	Tensile	Breaking load	Elong. %
2/0	133.1	137.9	0.1083	417.6	2,205	85	0.08849	0.4672	66,000	7,148	2.25
3/0	167.8	167.3	0.1314	506.4	2,674	85	0.07293	0.3851	64,000	8,410	2.75
4/0	211.6	212.0	0.1665	641.9	3,389	85	0.05756	0.3039	61,500	10,240	3.25
300	300.0	299.8	0.2355	907.6	4,792	85	0.04069	0.2149	58,300	13,730	4.00
350	350.0	351.2	0.2758	1,063.0	5,612	85	0.03475	0.1835	57,000	15,720	4.00

Trolley Wire—Copper and Bronze (Continued)

Nominal size AWG or MCM	Cross-sectional area			Weight		Min conductivity, % IACS[a]	D-c resistance or volts drop per amp at 20°C (68°F)		Min tensile strength, lb per sq in.	Min breaking load, lb	Elongation in 10 in., %
	Nominal MCM	Actual MCM	Sq in.	Lb per 1,000 ft	Lb per mile		Ohms or volts per 1,000 ft	Ohms or volts per mile			
Round ASTM Alloy 80 Hitenso BB Bronze											
1/0	105.6	105.6	0.0829	319.5	1,687	80	0.1228	0.6485	72,000	5,969	2.40
2/0	133.1	133.1	0.1045	402.8	2,127	80	0.09742	0.5144	69,000	7,212	2.75
3/0	167.8	167.8	0.1318	507.8	2,681	80	0.07727	0.4080	67,000	8,828	3.25
4/0	211.6	211.6	0.1662	640.5	3,382	80	0.06127	0.3235	65,000	10,800	3.75
300	300.0	300.0	0.2356	908.0	4,794	80	0.04322	0.2282	61,500	14,490	4.50
Grooved ASTM Alloy 80 Hitenso BB Bronze											
2/0	133.1	137.9	0.1083	417.6	2,205	80	0.09402	0.4964	69,000	7,473	2.25
3/0	167.8	167.3	0.1314	506.4	2,674	80	0.07749	0.4091	67,000	8,804	2.75
4/0	211.6	212.0	0.1665	641.9	3,389	80	0.06115	0.3229	65,000	10,820	3.25
300	300.0	299.8	0.2355	907.6	4,792	80	0.04324	0.2283	61,500	14,480	4.00
350	350.0	351.2	0.2758	1,063.0	5,612	80	0.03692	0.1949	59,500	16,410	4.00
Figure-9 Deep-section ASTM Alloy 80 Hitenso BB Bronze											
335	335.0	336.4	0.2642	1,020.0	5,386	80	0.03854	0.2035	56,800	15,010	4.00
Round ASTM Alloy 65 Trolley Bronze "65"											
1/0	105.6	105.6	0.0829	319.5	1,687	65	0.1511	0.7978	68,000	5,638	2.40
2/0	133.1	133.1	0.1045	402.8	2,127	65	0.1199	0.6329	65,000	6,794	2.75
3/0	167.8	167.8	0.1318	507.8	2,681	65	0.09507	0.4791	63,000	8,301	3.25
4/0	211.6	211.6	0.1662	640.5	3,382	65	0.07538	0.3980	61,000	10,140	3.75
300	300.0	300.0	0.2356	908.0	4,794	65	0.05317	0.2808	57,800	13,620	4.50
Grooved ASTM Alloy 65 Trolley Bronze "65"											
2/0	133.1	137.9	0.1083	417.6	2,205	65	0.1157	0.6110	65,000	7,040	2.25
3/0	167.8	167.3	0.1314	506.4	2,674	65	0.09537	0.5036	63,000	8,278	2.75
4/0	211.6	212.0	0.1665	641.9	3,389	65	0.07526	0.3974	61,000	10,160	3.25
300	300.0	299.8	0.2355	907.6	4,792	65	0.05321	0.2810	57,800	13,610	4.00
350	350.0	351.2	0.2758	1,063.0	5,612	65	0.04544	0.2399	56,200	15,500	4.00
Figure-9 Deep-section ASTM Alloy 65 Trolley Bronze "65"											
335	335.0	336.4	0.2642	1,020.0	5,386	65	0.04742	0.2504	54,000	14,270	4.00
Round ASTM Alloy 55 Hitenso C Bronze											
1/0	105.6	105.6	0.0829	319.5	1,687	55	0.1786	0.9431	76,000	6,301	2.40
2/0	133.1	133.1	0.1045	402.8	2,127	55	0.1417	0.7480	73,000	7,630	2.75
3/0	167.8	167.8	0.1318	507.8	2,681	55	0.1124	0.5934	71,000	9,356	3.25
4/0	211.6	211.6	0.1662	640.5	3,382	55	0.08910	0.4705	69,000	11,470	3.75
300	300.0	300.0	0.2356	908.0	4,700	55	0.06285	0.3319	64,800	15,270	4.50

Trolley Wire — Copper and Bronze (*Continued*)

Nominal size	Cross-sectional area			Weight		Min conductivity, % IACS[a]	D-c resistance or volts drop per amp at 20°C (68°F)		Min tensile strength, lb per sq in.	Min breaking load, lb	Elongation in 10 in., %
	Nominal	Actual									
AWG or MCM	MCM	MCM	Sq in.	Lb per 1,000 ft	Lb per mile		Ohms or volts per 1,000 ft	Ohms or volts per mile			

Grooved ASTM Alloy 55 Hitenso C Bronze

2/0	133.1	137.9	0.1083	417.6	2,205	55	0.1368	0.7220	73,000	7,906	2.25
3/0	167.8	167.3	0.1314	506.4	2,674	55	0.1127	0.5951	71,000	9,329	2.75
4/0	211.6	212.0	0.1665	641.9	3,389	55	0.08895	0.4697	69,000	11,490	3.25
300	300.0	299.8	0.2355	907.6	4,792	55	0.06289	0.3320	64,800	15,260	4.00
350	350.0	351.2	0.2758	1,063.0	5,612	55	0.05370	0.2835	62,500	17,240	4.00

Figure-9 Deep-section ASTM Alloy 55 Hitenso C Bronze

335	335.0	336.4	0.2642	1,020.0	5,386	55	0.05605	0.2959	61,500	16,250	4.00

Round ASTM Alloy 40 Electric Bronze

1/0	105.6	105.6	0.0829	319.5	1,687	40	0.2456	1.297	76,000	6,301	2.40
2/0	133.1	133.1	0.1045	402.8	2,127	40	0.1948	1.029	73,000	7,630	2.75
3/0	167.8	167.8	0.1318	507.8	2,681	40	0.1545	0.8160	71,000	9,356	3.25
4/0	211.6	211.6	0.1662	640.5	3,382	40	0.1225	0.6470	69,000	11,470	3.75
300	300.0	300.0	0.2356	908.0	4,700	40	0.08644	0.4564	64,800	15,270	4.50

Grooved ASTM Alloy 40 Electric Bronze

2/0	133.1	137.9	0.1083	417.6	2,205	40	0.1880	0.9928	73,000	7,906	2.25
3/0	167.8	167.3	0.1314	506.4	2,674	40	0.1550	0.8183	71,000	9,329	2.75
4/0	211.6	212.0	0.1665	641.9	3,389	40	0.1223	0.6458	69,000	11,490	3.25
300	300.0	299.8	0.2355	907.6	4,792	40	0.08647	0.4566	64,800	15,260	4.00
350	350.0	351.2	0.2758	1,063.0	5,612	40	0.07384	0.3899	62,500	17,240	4.00

Figure-9 Deep-section ASTM Alloy 40 Electric Bronze

335	335.0	336.4	0.2642	1,020.0	5,386	40	0.07708	0.4070	61,500	16,250	4.00

a These are minimum values of conductivity and usually are exceeded.
These data are approximate and subject to normal manufacturing tolerances.

104. Flat Bus-bar Copper

Size, in.	Weight, lb per ft	Area cir mils	Area sq in.
1⁄16 × ½	0.12	39,470	0.031
1⁄16 × ¾	0.18	59,842	0.047
1⁄16 × ⅞	0.21	68,755	0.055
1⁄16 × 1	0.24	80,213	0.063
1⁄16 × 1¼	0.30	99,312	0.078
1⁄16 × 1½	0.36	119,684	0.094
⅛ × ¾	0.36	119,684	0.094
⅛ × 1	0.48	159,154	0.125
⅛ × 1¼	0.60	198,624	0.156
⅛ × 1½	0.72	239,368	0.188
⅛ × 2	0.96	318,308	0.250
⅛ × 2½	1.20	398,523	0.313
⅛ × 3	1.44	477,463	0.375
⅛ × 3½	1.68	557,677	0.438
⅛ × 4	1.92	636,618	0.500
⅛ × 5	2.40	795,772	0.625
³⁄₁₆ × 1	0.72	239,368	0.188
³⁄₁₆ × 1¼	0.90	298,402	0.234
³⁄₁₆ × 1½	1.085	358,098	0.281
³⁄₁₆ × 1¾	1.266	417,780	0.328
³⁄₁₆ × 2	1.44	477,993	0.375
³⁄₁₆ × 2¼	1.62	537,140	0.422
³⁄₁₆ × 2½	1.81	596,829	0.469
³⁄₁₆ × 2¾	1.99	656,512	0.516
³⁄₁₆ × 3	2.17	716,196	0.563
³⁄₁₆ × 4	2.88	954,928	0.750
³⁄₁₆ × 5	3.62	1,193,659	0.938
³⁄₁₆ × 6	4.34	1,432,390	1.125
¼ × 1	0.96	318,308	0.250
¼ × 1½	1.44	477,463	0.375
¼ × 2	1.93	636,618	0.500
¼ × 2½	2.41	795,772	0.625
¼ × 3	2.89	954,928	0.750
¼ × 3½	3.38	1,114,082	0.875
¼ × 4	3.86	1,273,236	1.00
¼ × 4½	4.34	1,313,024	1.13
¼ × 5	4.82	1,591,545	1.25
¼ × 6	5.78	1,909,857	1.50
¼ × 7	6.76	2,228,164	1.75
¼ × 8	7.72	2,546,473	2.00
⅜ × 1½	2.17	716,196	0.563
⅜ × 2	2.89	954,928	0.750
⅜ × 2½	3.61	1,193,659	0.938
⅜ × 3	4.34	1,432,390	1.13
⅜ × 3½	5.06	1,671,123	1.31
⅜ × 4	5.79	1,909,854	1.50
⅜ × 4½	6.51	2,148,586	1.69
⅜ × 5	7.23	2,387,318	1.88
⅜ × 6	8.68	2,864,781	2.25
⅜ × 8	11.57	3,819,708	3.00
⅜ × 10	14.47	5,774,636	3.75
½ × 3	5.79	1,909,857	1.50
½ × 3½	6.75	2,228,164	1.75
½ × 4	7.72	2,546,472	2.00
½ × 4½	8.68	2,864,780	2.25
½ × 5	9.64	3,183,090	2.50
½ × 5½	10.61	3,501,398	2.75
½ × 6	11.58	3,819,708	3.00
½ × 7	12.50	4,456,328	3.50
½ × 8	15.43	5,092,944	4.00
½ × 9	17.36	5,729,560	4.50
½ × 10	19.29	6,366,180	5.00

105. Round Copper Rod

Diameter		Approx weight, lb per ft	Cir mils, approx	Cross section, sq in. approx
In.	Decimal equivalent			
⅛	0.125	0.047	15,600	0.01227
5⁄32	0.1562	0.077	24,400	0.01917
3⁄16	0.1875	0.106	35,000	0.02761
¼	0.250	0.189	62,500	0.04909
5⁄16	0.3125	0.296	97,800	0.07670
⅜	0.375	0.426	140,000	0.11045
7⁄16	0.4375	0.580	191,800	0.15033
½	0.500	0.757	250,000	0.19635
9⁄16	0.5625	0.959	316,000	0.24850
⅝	0.625	1.184	390,000	0.30680
¾	0.750	1.70	562,500	0.44179
⅞	0.875	2.32	765,000	0.60132
15⁄16	0.9375	2.68	880,000	0.69029
1	1.000	3.03	1,000,000	0.78540
1⅛	1.125	3.83	1,270,000	0.99402
1¼	1.250	4.73	1,560,000	1.2272
1⅜	1.375	5.73	1,900,000	1.4849
1½	1.500	6.82	2,250,000	1.7671
1⅝	1.625	8.04	2,650,000	2.0739
1 11⁄16	1.6875	8.68	2,850,000	2.2365
1¾	1.750	9.28	3,070,000	2.4053
1⅞	1.875	10.72	3,500,000	2.7612
2	2.000	12.12	4,000,000	3.1416
2½	2.500	19.05	6,250,000	4.9087
3	3.000	27.44	9,000,000	7.0686
3½	3.500	37.23	12,250,000	9.6211

106. Copper Tubing—Standard Iron-pipe Size

Size, in.	Approx OD	OD	ID	Wall thickness	Weight, lb per ft	Area, cir mils	Area, sq in.
⅛	13⁄32	0.405	0.281	0.062	0.259	85,064	0.066
¼	35⁄64	0.540	0.375	0.082	0.459	150,000	0.117
⅜	11⁄16	0.675	0.484	0.095	0.644	221,369	0.173
½	27⁄32	0.840	0.625	0.107	0.958	314,975	0.246
¾	1 1⁄16	1.050	0.822	0.114	1.298	426,816	0.335
1	1 5⁄16	1.315	1.062	0.126	1.829	601,381	0.470
1¼	1 43⁄64	1.660	1.368	0.146	2.689	884,176	0.694
1½	1 29⁄32	1.900	1.600	0.150	3.193	1,050,000	0.824
2	2⅜	2.375	2.062	0.156	4.224	1,388,781	1.087
2½	2⅞	2.875	2.500	0.187	6.130	2,015,625	1.579
3	3½	3.500	3.062	0.219	8.741	2,874,156	2.257
3½	4	4.000	3.500	0.250	11.41	3,750,000	2.945
4	4½	4.500	4.000	0.250	12.93	4,250,000	3.337

107. Copper Tubing—Extra-heavy Iron-pipe Size

Size, in.	Approx OD	OD	ID	Wall thickness	Weight, lb per ft	Area, cir mils	Area, sq in.
1/8	13/32	0.405	0.205	0.100	0.371	122,000	0.095
1/4	35/64	0.540	0.294	0.123	0.624	205,164	0.161
3/8	11/16	0.675	0.421	0.127	0.847	278,384	0.218
1/2	27/32	0.840	0.542	0.149	0.253	411,836	0.323
3/4	1 1/16	1.050	0.736	0.157	1.706	560,804	0.440
1	1 5/16	1.315	0.951	0.182	2.509	824,849	0.647
1 1/4	1 43/64	1.660	1.272	0.194	3.460	1,137,616	0.893
1 1/2	1 29/32	1.900	1.494	0.203	4.191	1,377,858	1.082
2	2 3/8	2.375	1.933	0.221	5.791	1,904,140	1.495
2 1/2	2 7/8	2.875	2.315	0.280	8.839	2,906,500	2.282
3	3 1/2	3.500	2.892	0.304	11.82	3,886,320	3.052
3 1/2	4	4.000	3.358	0.321	14.37	4,723,820	3.710
4	4 1/2	4.500	3.818	0.341	17.25	5,672,860	4.455

108. Copper Tubing—Double Extra-heavy Iron-pipe Size

Size, in.	Approx OD	OD	ID	Wall thickness	Weight lb per ft	Area, cir mils	Area, sq in.
1/2	27/32	0.840	0.252	0.294	1.945	642,096	0.504
3/4	1 1/16	1.050	0.434	0.308	2.768	914,144	0.718
1	1 5/16	1.315	0.599	0.358	4.152	1,370,449	1.076
1 1/4	1 43/64	1.660	0.896	0.382	5.916	1,952,784	1.534
1 1/2	1 29/32	1.900	1.100	0.400	7.271	2,410,000	1.885
2	2 3/8	2.375	1.503	0.436	10.246	3,381,620	2.656
2 1/2	2 7/8	2.875	1.771	0.552	15.541	5,130,300	4.028
3	3 1/2	3.500	2.300	0.600	21.087	6,960,000	5.466
3 1/2	4	4.000	2.728	0.636	25.930	8,568,000	6.721
4	4 1/2	4.500	3.152	0.674	31.253	10,314,080	8.101

109. General Characteristics of Copperweld Wire

Grade	Conductivity, %	Density	Weight per cir mil per 1,000 ft, lb	Tensile strength per sq in., 0.162-in. wire, lb	Normal resistivity per cir mil-ft, at 68°F, ohms
Extra high strength.......	30	8.15	0.002775	157,000	34.57
High strength............	30	8.15	0.002775	130,000	34.57
High strength............	40	8.15	0.002775	118,000	25.928

Modulus of elasticity (conventional):

Solid wire.................................. 24,000,000 lb per sq in.

Stranded cable........................... 23,000,000 lb per sq in.

Coefficient of linear expansion per degree Fahrenheit: 0.0000072.

Thirty per cent conductivity is not recommended in sizes finer than No. 10 AWG. Finer sizes are supplied in 40 per cent conductivity only.

110. Application Guide for Copperweld Products

Companies and uses

Product	Power companies	Railroad	Electric railway	Telephone and telegraph	Municipal	Construction mill, etc.
Bare wire	Telephone and signal lines / Overhead ground wire / Grounding wire / Lightly loaded lines / Tie wires, mousing wire / Light guys / Remote-control lines / Counterpoise wire	Signal, telegraph, and telephone lines / Control circuits / Overhead ground wire / Grounding wire / Bond wires, tie wires / CTC circuits	Telephone and signal lines / Overhead ground / Light span wire / Light guys	Line wires / Guys / Antenna wire	Police and fire-alarm circuits	Telephone lines / Grounding wire / Crane trolley / Pipe-insulation wrapping wire
Copperweld-copper[a]	Copperweld-copper cables of numerous combinations for long spans, rural distribution and transmission conductors	Copperweld-copper / Catenary messenger / Feeder cables for electrification	Copperweld-copper / Catenary messenger / Feeder cables			Copperweld-copper Cables for long spans
Weatherproof and plastic-jacketed wire	Telephone and signal lines / Remote control	Signal lines, control circuits, tie wires / CTC circuits	Telephone and signal lines	Tree wire / Grounding wire / Line wire	Signal and alarm circuits / Tie wires	Signal and alarm circuits
Rubber- and neoprene-covered wire	Drop wires for telephone and signal lines	Drop wires for telephone signal lines	Drop wires for telephone lines	Drop wires and block wire	Alarm circuits / Drop wires	Telephone and signal lines / Drop wires
Strand 3, 7, 19 wire etc.	Guy and messenger / Overhead ground wires / long spans / stack guys	Rail bonds / Guy and messenger / Overhead ground wire / Long spans / Pull-offs for electrifications	Span wire / Guy wire / Catenary messenger / Pull-offs / Overhead ground	Guy and messenger / Long spans	Guy and messenger / Long spans	Guy and messenger / Overhead ground / Stack guys / Long spans
Ground rods and clamps	For all electrical grounding installations, where good earth connections are required					
Anchor rods	For all types of anchors and anchoring installations					
Cable rings and lashing wire	Use with copperweld messenger strand for all types of aerial cable installations					
Fencing and barbed wire	Wherever high strength, nonrusting property protection is required. Available in many forms of fencing made from copperweld wire					
Staples, nails	Grounding wire molding, Insulator pins, etc.	Grounding wire, insulator pins, trunking, bond wires to ties, etc., Conduit	Grounding wire, insulator pins, etc.	Grounding wire, insulator pins, conduit, etc.	Grounding wire, conduit, etc.	Roofs and building
Wall ties						Cavity walls

a Copperweld is used by mines, forestries, and game preserves for telephone and signal lines and grounding; by broadcasting stations and individuals for radio antennas, leadins, grounding, etc.; in the home for clothes lines and in the construction industry for building and roofing nails and wall ties for masonry cavity wall construction.

111. Solid Copperweld Conductors

Size, AWG	Diam, in.	Area		Weight		Tensile strength, nominal			Breaking strength		
		Cir mils	Sq in.	Per 1,000 ft, lb	Per mile, lb	30 % extra high strength, lb per sq in.	30 % high strength, lb per sq in.	40 % high strength, lb per sq in.	30 % extra high strength, lb	30 % high strength, lb	40 % high strength, lb
4/0	0.460	211,600	0.1662	587	3,100	. . . . .	90,000	80,000	. . . . .	14,960	13,290
3/0	0.410	168,100	0.1320	466	2,460	. . . . .	90,000	80,000	. . . . .	11,880	10,560
2/0	0.365	133,225	0.1046	370	1,954	. . . . .	90,000	80,000	. . . . .	9,410	8,370
1/0	0.325	105,625	0.08296	293	1,547	. . . . .	94,000	82,000	. . . . .	7,800	6,800
1	0.289	83,520	0.06560	232	1,225	. . . . .	102,000	90,000	. . . . .	6,690	5,900
2	0.258	66,565	0.05228	185	977	123,000	109,000	97,000	6,430	5,700	5,070
3	0.229	52,440	0.04119	146	771	133,500	115,000	103,000	5,490	4,740	4,240
4	0.204	41,615	0.03269	116	612	142,500	125,000	108,000	4,660	3,920	3,530
5	0.182	33,125	0.02602	91.9	485	150,500	125,000	113,000	3,910	3,250	2,940
6	0.162	26,245	0.02061	72.8	384	157,000	130,000	118,000	3,240	2,680	2,430
7	0.144	20,735	0.01629	57.5	304	164,000	135,000	123,000	2,670	2,200	2,000
8	0.128	16,385	0.01287	45.5	240	170,000	140,000	128,000	2,190	1,800	1,650
9	0.114	12,995	0.01021	36.1	191	. . . . .	145,000	133,000	. . . . .	1,480	1,360
10	0.102	10,404	0.00817	28.9	153	. . . . .	150,000	138,000	. . . . .	1,230	1,130
11	0.091	8,281	0.00650	23.0	121	. . . . .	. . . . .	138,000	. . . . .	. . . . .	900
12	0.081	6,561	0.00515	18.2	96	. . . . .	. . . . .	138,000	. . . . .	. . . . .	710

112. Composite Copper-Copperweld Bare Conductors
(Anaconda Wire and Cable Co.)

Hard-drawn copper equivalent area AWG or MCM[a]	Type	Diameter, in.	Number and diameter of EHS 30% conductivity copperweld wires, in.	Number and diameter of hard-drawn copper wires, in.	Actual area Cir mils	Actual area Sq in.	Min ultimate strength, lb	Weight Lb per 1,000 ft	Weight Lb per mile	D-c resistance at 20°C (68°F) Ohms per 1,000 ft
350	E	0.788	7 × .1576	12 × .1576	471,900	0.3706	32,420	1,403	7,409	0.03143
350	EK	0.735	4 × .1470	15 × .1470	410,600	0.3225	23,850	1,238	6,536	0.03143
350	V	0.754	3 × .1751	9 × .1893	414,500	0.3255	23,480	1,246	6,578	0.03143
300	E	0.729	7 × .1459	12 × .1459	404,400	0.3177	27,770	1,203	6,351	0.03667
300	EK	0.680	4 × .1361	15 × .1361	351,900	0.2764	20,960	1,061	5,602	0.03667
300	V	0.698	3 × .1621	9 × .1752	355,100	0.2789	20,730	1,068	5,639	0.03667
250	E	0.666	7 × .1332	12 × .1332	337,100	0.2648	23,920	1,002	5,292	0.04400
250	EK	0.621	4 × .1242	15 × .1242	293,100	0.2302	17,840	884.2	4,669	0.04400
250	V	0.637	3 × .1480	9 × .1600	296,100	0.2326	17,420	889.9	4,699	0.04400
4/0	E	0.613	7 × .1225	12 × .1225	285,100	0.2239	20,730	848.3	4,479	0.05199
4/0	G	0.583	2 × .1944	5 × .1944	264,500	0.2078	15,640	789.4	4,168	0.05199
4/0	EK	0.571	4 × .1143	15 × .1143	248,200	0.1950	15,370	748.4	3,951	0.05199
4/0	V	0.586	3 × .1361	9 × .1472	250,600	0.1968	15,000	753.2	3,977	0.05199
4/0	F	0.550	1 × .1833	6 × .1833	235,200	0.1847	12,290	710.2	3,750	0.05199
3/0	E	0.545	7 × .1091	12 × .1091	226,200	0.1776	16,800	672.7	3,552	0.06556
3/0	J	0.555	3 × .1851	4 × .1851	239,800	0.1884	16,170	706.7	3,732	0.06556
3/0	G	0.519	2 × .1731	5 × .1731	209,700	0.1647	12,860	626.0	3,305	0.06556
3/0	EK	0.509	4 × .1018	15 × .1018	196,900	0.1546	12,370	593.5	3,134	0.06556
3/0	V	0.522	3 × .1212	9 × .1311	198,800	0.1561	12,200	597.3	3,154	0.06556
3/0	F	0.490	1 × .1632	6 × .1632	186,400	0.1464	9,980	563.2	2,974	0.06556
2/0	K	0.534	4 × .1780	3 × .1780	221,800	0.1742	17,600	645.9	3,411	0.08265
2/0	J	0.494	3 × .1648	4 × .1648	190,100	0.1493	13,430	560.6	2,960	0.08265
2/0	G	0.463	2 × .1542	5 × .1542	166,400	0.1307	10,510	496.6	2,622	0.08265
2/0	V	0.465	3 × .1080	9 × .1167	157,600	0.1237	9,846	473.8	2,502	0.08265
2/0	F	0.436	1 × .1454	6 × .1454	148,000	0.1162	8,094	446.8	2,359	0.08265
1/0	K	0.475	4 × .1585	3 × .1585	175,900	0.1381	14,490	512.0	2,703	0.1043
1/0	J	0.440	3 × .1467	4 × .1467	150,600	0.1184	10,970	444.3	2,346	0.1043
1/0	G	0.412	2 × .1373	5 × .1373	132,000	0.1036	8,563	393.6	2,078	0.1043
1/0	F	0.388	1 × .1294	6 × .1294	117,200	0.09206	6,536	354.1	1,870	0.1043
1	N	0.464	5 × .1546	2 × .1546	167,300	0.1314	15,410	481.3	2,541	0.1315
1	K	0.423	4 × .1412	3 × .1412	139,600	0.1096	11,900	406.2	2,144	0.1315
1	J	0.392	3 × .1307	4 × .1307	119,600	0.09392	9,000	352.5	1,861	0.1315
1	G	0.367	2 × .1222	5 × .1222	104,500	0.08210	6,956	312.2	1,649	0.1315
1	F	0.346	1 × .1153	6 × .1153	93,060	0.07309	5,266	280.9	1,483	0.1315
2	P	0.462	6 × .1540	1 × .1540	166,000	0.1304	16,870	471.1	2,487	0.1658
2	N	0.413	5 × .1377	2 × .1377	132,700	0.1042	12,680	381.7	2,015	0.1658
2	K	0.377	4 × .1257	3 × .1257	110,600	0.08687	9,730	322.1	1,701	0.1658
2	J	0.349	3 × .1164	4 × .1164	94,840	0.07449	7,322	279.5	1,476	0.1658
2	A	0.366	1 × .1699	2 × .1699	86,600	0.06801	5,876	256.8	1,356	0.1658
2	G	0.327	2 × .1089	5 × .1089	83,010	0.06520	5,626	247.6	1,307	0.1658
2	F	0.308	1 × .1026	6 × .1026	73,690	0.05787	4,233	222.8	1,176	0.1658
3	P	0.411	6 × .1371	1 × .1371	131,600	0.1033	13,910	373.6	1,973	0.2090
3	N	0.368	5 × .1226	2 × .1226	105,200	0.08264	10,390	302.7	1,598	0.2090
3	K	0.336	4 × .1120	3 × .1120	87,810	0.06896	7,910	255.5	1,349	0.2090
3	J	0.311	3 × .1036	4 × .1036	75,130	0.05901	5,955	221.7	1,171	0.2090
3	A	0.326	1 × .1513	2 × .1513	68,680	0.05394	4,810	203.6	1,075	0.2090
4	P	0.366	6 × .1221	1 × .1221	104,400	0.08196	11,420	296.3	1,564	0.2636
4	N	0.328	5 × .1092	2 × .1092	83,470	0.06556	8,460	240.0	1,267	0.2636
4	D	0.348	2 × .1615	1 × .1615	78,250	0.06145	7,340	225.5	1,191	0.2636
4	A	0.290	1 × .1347	2 × .1347	54,430	0.4275	3,938	161.5	852	0.2636

Composite Copper-Copperweld Bare Conductors (*Continued*)

Hard-drawn copper equivalent area AWG or MCM[a]	Type	Diameter, in.	Number and diameter of EHS 30% conductivity copperweld wires, in.	Number and diameter of hard-drawn copper wires, in.	Actual area Cir mils	Actual area Sq in.	Min ultimate strength, lb	Weight Lb per 1,000 ft	Weight Lb per mile	D-c resistance at 20°C (68°F) Ohms per 1,000 ft
5	P	0.326	6 × .1087	1 × .1087	82,710	0.06496	9,311	234.9	1,240	0.3291
5	D	0.310	2 × .1438	1 × .1438	62,040	0.04872	6,035	178.9	944.4	0.3291
5	A	0.258	1 × .1200	2 × .1200	43,200	0.03393	3,193	128.1	676.3	0.3291
6	D	0.276	2 × .1281	1 × .1281	49,230	0.03866	4,942	141.8	748.9	0.4150
6	A	0.230	1 × .1068	2 × .1068	34.220	0.02688	2,585	101.6	536.3	0.4150
6	C	0.225	1 × .1046[b]	2 × .1046	32,820	0.02578	2,143	97.34	514.0	0.4150
7	D	0.246	2 × .1141	1 × .1141	39,060	0.03067	4,022	112.5	594.0	0.5232
7	A	0.223	1 × .1266	2 × .08949	32,040	0.02517	2,754	93.66	494.6	0.5232
8	D	0.219	2 × .1016	1 × .1016	30,970	0.02432	3,256	89.21	471.0	0.6598
8	A	0.199	1 × .1127	2 × .07969	25,400	0.01995	2,233	74.27	392.2	0.6598
8	C	0.179	1 × .0808[b]	2 × .08336	20,430	0.01604	1,362	60.67	320.3	0.6598
9½	D	0.174	2 × .0808[b]	1 × .0808	19,590	0.01539	1,743	56.46	298.1	0.9170

[a] Hard-drawn copper cable, 97.5 per cent conductivity, IACS, having the same d-c resistance as that of the composite cable after allowing for increases in resistance due to stranding based on Table II, ASTM B229-52. Manufactured in accordance with ASTM Specification B229-52.

[b] High-strength copperweld, 40 per cent conductivity.

These data are approximate and subject to normal manufacturing tolerances.

113. Stranded Copperweld Conductors

Nominal diam, in., number of strands, and size, AWG	Diam, in.	Area Cir mils	Area Sq in.	Weight Per 1,000 ft, lb	Weight Per mile, lb	Breaking strength 30% extra high strength, lb	Breaking strength 30% high strength, lb	Breaking strength 40% high strength, lb
⅞ (19 No. 5)	0.910	629,375	0.4944	1,770	9,346	66,860	55,570	50,270
13/16 (19 No. 6)	0.810	498,655	0.3916	1,403	7,408	55,400	45,880	41,550
23/32 (19 No. 7)	0.720	393,695	0.3095	1,108	5,850	45,660	37,620	34,200
21/32 (19 No. 8)	0.640	311,315	0.2445	877	4,630	37,450	30,780	28,210
9/16 (19 No. 9)	0.570	246,905	0.1940	696	3,675	30,610	25,300	23,250
⅝ (7 No. 4)	0.612	291,305	0.2288	820	4,330	29,360	24,700	22,240
9/16 (7 No. 5)	0.546	231,875	0.1821	650	3,432	24,630	20,480	18,500
½ (7 No. 6)	0.486	183,715	0.1443	515	2,720	20,410	16,880	15,300
7/16 (7 No. 7)	0.432	145,145	0.1140	407	2,149	16,820	13,860	12,600
⅜ (7 No. 8)	0.384	114,695	0.0901	322	1,700	13,800	11,340	10,390
11/32 (7 No. 9)	0.342	90,965	0.0715	255	1,346	11,280	9,320	8,570
5/16 (7 No. 10)	0.306	72,828	0.0572	204	1,077	9,200	7,750	7,120
3 No. 6	0.349	78,735	0.0618	220	1,162	8,260	6,830	6,200
3 No. 7	0.310	62,205	0.0489	174	919	6,800	5,610	5,100
3 No. 8	0.276	49,155	0.0386	138	729	5,580	4,590	4,210
3 No. 9	0.246	38,985	0.0306	109	576	4,560	3,770	3,470
3 No. 10	0.220	31,212	0.0245	87	460	3,720	3,140	2,880
3 No. 11	0.196	24,843	0.0195	69.6	367	......	......	2,480
3 No. 12	0.175	19,683	0.01545	55.0	290	......	......	2,040

To determine copper equivalent of copperweld conductor, multiply circular-mil area by percentage conductivity expressed as a decimal.

114. Comparative Characteristics of Aluminum and Copper Wire

Characteristic	Commercial hard-drawn aluminum wire	Commercial hard-drawn copper wire	Standard annealed copper wire
Conductivity	60.97 % of IACS	97 % of IACS	100 % of IACS
Resistance per circular mil-foot	17.010 ohms	10.692 ohms	10.371 ohms
Temperature coefficient of resistance	0.403 % per °C	0.393 % per °C	0.393 % per °C

IACS stands for the International Annealed Copper Standard, which is the internationally accepted value for the resistivity of annealed copper of 100 per cent conductivity. This value is 10.371 ohms per mil-ft at 20°C and was adopted by the International Electro-Technical Committee (IEC) in 1913.

115. Bare Solid All-aluminum Hard-drawn Wire
(ASTM Standard B230-55T)

Size, AWG	Diameter, in.	Area Cir mils	Area Sq in.	Hard-drawn copper equivalent size, AWG	Net weight, lb per 1,000 ft	Breaking strength, lb	Average tensile strength, lb per sq in.	Nominal d-c resistance, ohms per 1,000 ft 68°F (20°C)
8	0.1285	16,510	0.01297	10	15.20	324.2	25,000	1.030
7	0.1443	20,820	0.01635	9	19.16	400.7	24,500	0.8165
6	0.1620	26,240	0.02061	8	24.15	494.7	24,000	0.6478
5	0.1819	33,090	0.02599	7	30.45	623.7	24,000	0.5138
4	0.2043	41,740	0.03278	6	38.41	786.8	24,000	0.4073
3	0.2294	52,620	0.04133	5	48.43	971.3	23,500	0.3231
2	0.2576	66,360	0.05212	4	61.07	1225	23,500	0.2562

116. Construction Requirements of Concentric-lay-stranded Hard-drawn Aluminum Conductors
(ASTM)

| Conductor size | | Hard-drawn copper equivalent | | Stranding | | | | | | | | | |
| | | | | Class AA | | Class A | | Class B | | Class C | | Class D | |
Cir mils	AWG	Cir mils	AWG	Number of wires	Diameter of wire, mils	Number of wires	Diameter of wire, mils	Number of wires	Diameter of wire, mils	Number of wires	Diameter of wire, mils	Number of wires	Diameter of wire, mils
4 000 000...	....	2 520 000	....	...	.....	169	153.8	217	135.8	271	121.5	271	121.5
3 500 000...	....	2 200 000	....	...	.....	127	166.0	169	143.9	217	127.0	271	113.6
3 000 000...	....	1 890 000	....	...	.....	127	153.7	169	133.2	217	117.6	271	105.2
2 500 000...	....	1 570 000	....	...	.....	91	165.7	127	140.3	169	121.6	217	107.3
2 000 000...	....	1 260 000	....	...	.....	91	148.2	127	125.5	169	108.8	217	96.0
1 900 000...	....	1 195 000	....	...	.....	91	144.5	127	122.3	169	106.0	217	93.6
1 800 000...	....	1 132 000	....	...	.....	91	140.6	127	119.1	169	103.2	217	91.1
1 750 000...	....	1 101 000	....	61	169.4	91	138.7	127	117.4	169	101.8	217	89.8
1 700 000..	....	1 069 000	.....	61	166.9	91	136.7	127	115.7	169	100.3	217	88.5
1 600 000ª..	....	1 006 000	....	61	162.0	91	132.6	127	112.2	169	97.3	217	85.9
1 500 000...	....	943 000	....	61	156.8	61	156.8	91	128.4	127	108.7	169	94.2
1 400 000...	....	880 000	....	61	151.5	61	151.5	91	124.0	127	105.0	169	91.0
1 300 000...	....	818 000	....	61	146.0	61	146.0	91	119.5	127	101.2	169	87.7
1 250 000ª..	....	786 000	....	61	143.1	61	143.1	91	117.2	127	99.2	169	86.0
1 200 000...	....	755 000	....	61	140.3	61	140.3	91	114.8	127	97.2	169	84.3
1 100 000...	....	692 000	....	61	134.3	61	134.3	91	109.9	127	93.1	169	80.7
1 000 000ᵇ..	....	629 000	....	37	164.4	61	128.0	61	128.0	91	104.8	127	88.7
900 000...	....	566 000	....	37	156.0	61	121.5	61	121.5	91	99.4	127	84.2
800 000ª..	....	503 000	....	37	147.0	61	114.5	61	114.5	91	93.8	127	79.4
750 000...	....	472 000	....	37	142.4	61	110.9	61	110.9	91	90.8	127	76.8
700 000...	....	440 000	....	37	137.5	61	107.1	61	107.1	91	87.7	127	74.2
650 000...	....	409 000	....	37	132.5	61	103.2	61	103.2	91	84.5	127	71.5
636 000...	....	400 000	....	37	131.1	37	131.1	...	.....	...	.....	...	.....
600 000...	....	377 000	....	37	127.3	37	127.3	61	99.2	91	81.2	127	68.7
550 000...	....	346 000	....	37	121.9	37	121.9	61	95.0	91	77.7	127	65.8
500 000...	....	314 000	....	19	162.2	37	116.2	37	116.2	61	90.5	91	74.1
477 000...	....	300 000	....	19	158.4	37	113.5	...	.....	...	.....	...	.....
450 000...	....	283 000	....	19	153.9	37	110.3	37	110.3	61	85.9	91	70.3
400 000ª..	....	252 000	....	19	145.1	19	145.1	37	104.0	61	81.0	91	66.3
350 000...	....	220 000	....	12	170.8	19	135.7	37	97.3	61	75.7	91	62.0
336 400...	....	....	0000	12	167.4	19	133.1	...	.....	...	.....	...	.....
300 000...	....	188 700	....	12	158.1	19	125.7	37	90.0	61	70.1	91	57.4
266 800...	....	....	000	12	149.1	19	118.5	...	.....	...	.....	...	.....
250 000...	....	157 200	....	12	144.3	19	114.7	37	82.2	61	64.0	91	52.4
211 600...	0000	....	00	7	173.9	7	173.9	19	105.5	37	75.6	61	58.9
167 800...	000	....	0	7	154.8	7	154.8	19	94.0	37	67.3	61	52.4
133 100...	00	....	1	7	137.9	7	137.9	19	83.7	37	60.0	61	46.7
105 600...	0	....	2	7	122.8	7	122.8	19	74.5	37	53.4	61	41.6
83 690...	1	....	3	7	109.3	7	109.3	19	66.4	37	47.6	61	37.0
66 360...	2	....	4	7	97.4	7	97.4	7	97.4	19	59.1	37	42.4
52 620...	3	....	5	...	.....	7	86.7	7	86.7	19	52.6	37	37.7
41 740...	4	....	6	...	.....	7	77.2	7	77.2	19	46.9	37	33.6
33 090...	5	....	7	...	.....	7	68.8	7	68.8	19	41.7	37	29.9

117. Stranded Aluminum Conductor, Bare — Classes AA, and A^a (Hard-drawn EC-H19)

(Aluminum Co. of America)

Conductor size		Copper equivalent based on equal d-c resistance, Cu 97 % Al 61 %	Stranding		Cable diam, in.	D-c resistance at 20°C, ohms per 1,000 ft (61 %)	Ultimate strength, lb	Weight per 1,000 ft, lb
Cir mils or AWG	Square inches		Class	Number and diam of wires, in.				
6	0.0206	8	A	7 × 0.0612	0.184	0.6606	528	24.6
4	0.0328	6	A	7 × 0.0772	0.232	0.4155	826	39.2
3	0.0413	5	A	7 × 0.0867	0.260	0.3295	1,022	49.4
2	0.0521	4	AA, A	7 × 0.0974	0.292	0.2613	1,266	62.3
1	0.0657	3	AA, A	7 × 0.1094	0.328	0.2072	1,537	78.5
1/0	0.0829	2	AA, A	7 × 0.1228	0.368	0.1643	1,865	99.1
2/0	0.1045	1	AA, A	7 × 0.1379	0.414	0.1303	2,350	124.9
3/0	0.1318	1/0	AA, A	7 × 0.1548	0.464	0.1033	2,845	157.5
4/0	0.1662	2/0	AA, A	7 × 0.1739	0.522	0.08195	3,590	198.6
266,800	0.2095	3/0	. . . . .	7 × 0.1953	0.586	0.06500	4,525	250.4
266,800	0.2095	3/0	A	19 × 0.1185	0.593	0.06500	4,800	250.4
336,400	0.2642	4/0	AA, A	19 × 0.1331	0.666	0.05155	5,940	315.8
397,500	0.3122	250,000	AA, A	19 × 0.1447	0.724	0.04363	6,880	372.5
477,000	0.3746	300,000	AA	19 × 0.1585	0.793	0.03636	8,090	447.8
477,000	0.3746	300,000	A	37 × 0.1135	0.795	0.03636	8,600	447.8
556,500	0.4371	350,000	. . . . .	19 × 0.1711	0.856	0.03116	9,440	522.4
556,500	0.4371	350,000	AA, A	37 × 0.1226	0.858	0.03116	9,830	522.4
636,000	0.4995	400,000	AA, A	37 × 0.1311	0.918	0.02727	11,240	597.0
715,500	0.5620	450,000	AA	37 × 0.1391	0.974	0.02424	12,640	671.6
715,500	0.5620	450,000	A	61 × 0.1083	0.975	0.02424	13,150	671.6
795,000	0.6244	500,000	AA	37 × 0.1466	1.026	0.02181	13,770	746.3
795,000	0.6244	500,000	A	61 × 0.1142	1.028	0.02181	14,330	746.3
874,500	0.6868	550,000	AA	37 × 0.1538	1.077	0.01983	14,830	820.9
874,500	0.6868	550,000	A	61 × 0.1198	1.078	0.01983	15,760	820.9
954,000	0.7493	600,000	AA	37 × 0.1606	1.124	0.01818	16,180	895.5
954,000	0.7493	600,000	A	61 × 0.1251	1.126	0.01818	16,860	895.5
1,033,500	0.8117	650,000	AA	37 × 0.1672	1.170	0.01678	17,530	970.1
1,033,500	0.8117	650,000	A	61 × 0.1302	1.172	0.01678	18,260	970.1
1,113,000	0.8741	700,000	AA, A	61 × 0.1351	1.216	0.01558	19,660	1,045
1,192,500	0.9366	750,000	AA, A	61 × 0.1398	1.258	0.01454	21,000	1,119
1,272,000	0.999	800,000	AA, A	61 × 0.1444	1.330	0.01363	22,000	1,193
1,351,500	1.062	850,000	AA, A	61 × 0.1489	1.340	0.01283	23,400	1,269
1,431,000	1.124	900,000	AA, A	61 × 0.1532	1.379	0.01212	24,300	1,343
1,510,500	1.186	950,000	AA, A	61 × 0.1574	1.417	0.01148	25,600	1,418
1,590,000	1.249	1,000,000	AA	61 × 0.1615	1.454	0.01091	27,000	1,493
1,590,000	1.249	1,000,000	A	91 × 0.1322	1.454	0.01091	28,100	1,493

^{a} Class AA stranding is usually specified for bare conductors used on overhead lines. Class A stranding is usually specified for conductors to be covered with weather-resistant (weatherproof) materials and for bare conductors where greater flexibility than afforded by Class AA is required.

118. Stranded Aluminum Conductor, Bare—Class B[a]

Hard-drawn (EC-H19)—Three-quarter Hard (EC-H26)—
Intermediate Temper (EC-H24)
(Aluminum Co. of America)

Conductor size Cir mils or AWG	Sq in.	Copper equivalent based upon equal d-c resistance, Cu 97 % Al 61 %	Stranding, number and diam of wires, in.	Cable diam, in.	D-c resist- ance at 20°C, ohms per 1,000 ft (61 %)	Ultimate strength, lb, EC-H19	Min ultimate strength, lb, EC-H26	Min ultimate strength, lb, EC-H24	Weight per 1,000 ft, lb
6	0.0206	8	7 × 0.0612	0.184	0.6606	528	316	280	24.6
4	0.0328	6	7 × 0.0772	0.232	0.4155	826	500	440	39.2
3	0.0413	5	7 × 0.0867	0.260	0.3295	1,022	630	560	49.4
2	0.0521	4	7 × 0.0974	0.292	0.2613	1,266	800	700	62.3
1	0.0657	3	19 × 0.0664	0.332	0.2072	1,685	1,000	890	78.5
1/0	0.0829	2	19 × 0.0745	0.373	0.1643	2,090	1,270	1,120	99.1
2/0	0.1045	1	19 × 0.0837	0.419	0.1303	2,586	1,600	1,410	124.9
3/0	0.1318	1/0	19 × 0.0940	0.470	0.1033	3,200	2,015	1,780	157.5
4/0	0.1662	2/0	19 × 0.1055	0.528	0.08195	3,890	2,540	2,240	198.6
250,000	0.1964	157,300	37 × 0.0822	0.575	0.06937	4,860	3,000	2,650	234.7
300,000	0.2356	188,800	37 × 0.0900	0.629	0.05781	5,830	3,600	3,180	281.6
350,000	0.2749	220,200	37 × 0.097	0.681	0.04955	6,680	4,200	3,710	328.6
400,000	0.3142	251,500	37 × 0.1040	0.728	0.04336	7,350	4,800	4,240	375.5
450,000	0.3534	283,000	37 × 0.1103	0.772	0.03854	8,110	5,400	4,770	422.4
500,000	0.3927	314,500	37 × 0.1162	0.813	0.03468	9,010	6,000	5,300	469.4
550,000	0.4320	346,000	61 × 0.0950	0.855	0.03153	10,490	6,610	5,830	516.3
600,000	0.4712	377,000	61 × 0.0992	0.893	0.02890	11,450	7,210	6,360	563.2
650,000	0.5105	409,000	61 × 0.1032	0.929	0.02668	11,940	7,810	6,890	610.2
700,000	0.5498	440,000	61 × 0.1071	0.964	0.02477	12,860	8,410	7,420	657.1
750,000	0.5890	472,000	61 × 0.1109	0.998	0.02312	13,510	9,010	7,950	704.0
800,000	0.6283	503,000	61 × 0.1145	1.031	0.02168	14,410	9,610	8,480	751.0
900,000	0.7069	566,000	61 × 0.1215	1.094	0.01927	15,900	10,810	9,540	844.8
1,000,000	0.7854	629,000	61 × 0.1280	1.152	0.01734	17,670	12,020	10,600	938.7
1,100,000	0.8639	692,000	91 × 0.1099	1.209	0.01576	20,210	13,220	11,660	1,033
1,200,000	0.9425	755,000	91 × 0.1148	1.263	0.01445	21,630	14,420	12,720	1,126
1,250,000	0.9818	786,000	91 × 0.1172	1.289	0.01387	22,530	15,020	13,250	1,173
1,300,000	1.021	818,000	91 × 0.1195	1.315	0.01334	23,430	15,620	13,780	1,220
1,400,000	1.100	880,000	91 × 0.1240	1.364	0.01239	24,750	16,830	14,850	1,314
1,500,000	1.178	943,000	91 × 0.1284	1.412	0.01156	26,500	18,020	15,900	1.408
1,600,000	1.257	1,006,000	127 × 0.1122	1.459	0.01084	28,840	19,230	16,970	1,502
1,700,000	1.335	1,069,000	127 × 0.1157	1.504	0.01020	30,630	20,400	18,020	1,596
1,750,000	1.374	1,101,000	127 × 0.1174	1.526	0.00991	31,530	21,000	18,550	1.643
1,800,000	1.414	1,132,000	127 × 0.1191	1.548	0.00963	32,450	21,600	19,090	1,690
1,900,000	1.492	1,195,000	127 × 0.1223	1.590	0.00913	33,570	22,800	20,100	1,784
2,000,000	1.571	1,258,000	127 × 0.1255	1.632	0.00867	35,340	24,000	21,200	1,877
2,500,000	1.964	1,570,000	127 × 0.1403	1.824	0.00694	43,300	30,000	26,500	2,370
3,000,000	2.356	1,890,000	169 × 0.1332	1.998	0.00578	53,010	36,000	31,800	2,844
3,500,000	2.749	2,200,000	169 × 0.1439	2.158	0.00495	60,610	40,500	37,100	3,350

[a] Class B stranding is usually specified for conductors to be insulated with various materials such as rubber, paper, varnished cloth, etc.

119. Stranded Aluminum Conductor, Bare — Class C[a]

Hard-drawn (EC-H19)—Three-quarter Hard (EC-H26)—
Intermediate Temper (EC-H24)
(Aluminum Co. of America)

Conductor size		Copper equivalent based upon equal d-c resistance, Cu 97% Al 61%	Stranding, number and diam of wires, in.	Cable diam, in.	D-c resistance at 20°C, ohms per 1,000 ft (61%)	Ultimate strength, lb, EC-H19	Min ultimate strength, lb, EC-H26	Min ultimate strength, lb, EC-H24	Weight per 1,000 ft, lb
Cir mils or AWG	Sq in.								
2	0.0521	4	19 × 0.0591	0.296	0.2613	1,360	800	705	62.3
2/0	0.1045	1	37 × 0.0600	0.420	0.1303	2,725	1,600	1,410	124.9
3/0	0.1318	1/0	37 × 0.0673	0.471	0.1033	3,380	2,015	1,780	157.5
4/0	0.1662	2/0	37 × 0.0756	0.529	0.08195	4,190	2,540	2,240	198.6
250,000	0.1964	157,300	61 × 0.0640	0.576	0.06937	5,040	3,000	2,650	234.7
300,000	0.2356	188,800	61 × 0.0701	0.631	0.05781	5,940	3,600	3,180	281.6
350,000	0.2749	220,200	61 × 0.0757	0.681	0.04955	6,930	4,200	3,710	328.6
400,000	0.3142	251,500	61 × 0.0810	0.729	0.04336	7,780	4,800	4,240	375.5
450,000	0.3534	283,000	61 × 0.0859	0.773	0.03854	8,750	5,400	4,770	422.4
500,000	0.3927	314,500	61 × 0.0905	0.815	0.03468	9,540	6,000	5,300	469.4
550,000	0.4320	346,000	91 × 0.0777	0.855	0.03153	10,880	6,600	5,830	516.3
600,000	0.4712	377,000	91 × 0.0812	0.893	0.02890	11,660	7,200	6,360	563.2
650,000	0.5105	409,000	91 × 0.0845	0.930	0.02668	12,630	7,800	6,890	610.2
700,000	0.5498	440,000	91 × 0.0877	0.964	0.02477	13,600	8,400	7,420	657.1
750,000	0.5890	472,000	91 × 0.0908	0.999	0.02312	14,310	9,000	7,950	704.0
800,000	0.6283	503,000	91 × 0.0938	1.032	0.02168	15,270	9,600	8,480	751.0
900,000	0.7069	566,000	91 × 0.0994	1.093	0.01927	17,180	10,800	9,540	844.8
1,000,000	0.7854	629,000	91 × 0.1048	1.153	0.01734	18,380	12,000	10,600	938.7
1,100,000	0.8639	692,000	127 × 0.0931	1.210	0.01576	21,000	13,200	11,660	1,033
1,200,000	0.9425	755,000	127 × 0.0972	1.264	0.01445	22,900	14,400	12,720	1,126
1,250,000	0.9818	786,000	127 × 0.0992	1.290	0.01387	23,900	15,000	13,250	1,173
1,300,000	1.021	818,000	127 × 0.1012	1.316	0.01334	23,900	15,600	13,780	1.220
1,400,000	1.100	880,000	127 × 0.1050	1.365	0.01239	25,700	16,800	14,850	1,314
1,500,000	1.178	943,000	127 × 0.1087	1.413	0.01156	27,600	18,000	15,900	1,408
1,600,000	1.257	1,006,000	169 × 0.0973	1.460	0.01084	30,500	19,200	16,970	1,502
1,700,000	1.335	1,069,000	169 × 0.1003	1.505	0.01020	31,200	20,400	18,020	1,596
1,750,000	1.374	1,101,000	169 × 0.1018	1.527	0.00991	32,100	21,000	18,550	1,643
1,800,000	1.414	1,132,000	169 × 0.1032	1.548	0.00963	33,100	21,600	19,090	1,690
1,900,000	1.492	1,195,000	169 × 0.1060	1.590	0.00913	34,900	22,800	20,100	1,784
2,000,000	1.571	1,258,000	169 × 0.1088	1.632	0.00867	36,800	24,000	21,200	1,877
2,500,000	1.964	1,570,000	169 × 0.1216	1.824	0.00694	44,200	30,000	26,500	2,346

[a] Class C stranding is specified for conductors where greater flexibility than provided by Class B is required.

120. Aluminum Conductor, Steel-reinforced (ACSR) Bare

(Aluminum Co. of America)

ACSR Cross section — Aluminum Cir mils or AWG	Aluminum Sq in.	Total Sq in.	Copper equivalent based upon equal d-c resistance Cu 97% Al 61%	Stranding Aluminum	Stranding Steel	Diameter Complete cable	Diameter Steel core	D-c resistance at 20°C ohms per 1,000 ft (61%)	Ultimate strength, lb [a]	Weight per 1,000 ft Total	Al	Steel	Weight per mile Total	Al	Steel	% total wt Al	Steel
6	0.0206	0.0240	8	6 × 0.0661	1 × 0.0661	0.198	0.0661	0.6573	1,170	36.1	24.5	11.6	190	129	61	67.9	32.1
5	0.0260	0.0303	7	6 × 0.0743	1 × 0.0743	0.223	0.0743	0.5213	1,460	45.5	30.9	14.6	240	163	77	67.9	32.1
4	0.0328	0.0383	6	6 × 0.0834	1 × 0.0834	0.250	0.0834	0.4134	1,830	57.4	39.0	18.4	303	206	97	67.9	32.1
4	0.0328	0.0411	6	7 × 0.0772	1 × 0.1029	0.257	0.1029	0.4134	2,288	67.1	39.0	28.1	354	206	148	58.1	41.9
3	0.0413	0.0482	5	6 × 0.0937	1 × 0.0937	0.281	0.0937	0.3279	2,250	72.4	49.2	23.2	382	260	122	67.9	32.1
2	0.0521	0.0608	4	6 × 0.1052	1 × 0.1052	0.316	0.1052	0.2600	2,790	91.3	62.0	29.3	482	327	155	67.9	32.1
2	0.0521	0.0653	4	7 × 0.0974	1 × 0.1299	0.325	0.1299	0.2600	3,525	106.7	62.0	44.7	563	327	236	58.1	41.9
1	0.0657	0.0767	3	6 × 0.1182	1 × 0.1182	0.355	0.1182	0.2062	3,480	115.2	78.2	37.0	608	413	195	67.9	32.1
1/0	0.0829	0.0967	2	6 × 0.1327	1 × 0.1327	0.398	0.1327	0.1635	4,280	145.2	98.6	46.6	767	521	246	67.9	32.1
2/0	0.1045	0.1219	1	6 × 0.1490	1 × 0.1490	0.447	0.1490	0.1297	5,345	183.1	124.3	58.8	967	656	311	67.9	32.1
3/0	0.1318	0.1538	1/0	6 × 0.1672	1 × 0.1672	0.502	0.1672	0.1028	6,675	230.9	156.8	74.1	1,219	828	391	67.9	32.1
4/0	0.1662	0.1939	2/0	6 × 0.1878	1 × 0.1878	0.563	0.1878	0.08155	8,420	291.1	197.7	93.4	1,537	1,044	493	67.9	32.1
266,800	0.2095	0.2211	3/0	18 × 0.1217	1 × 0.1217	0.609	0.1217	0.06500	7,100	289.7	250.4	39.3	1,530	1,322	208	86.45	13.55
266,800	0.2095	0.2367	3/0	6 × 0.2109	7 × 0.0703	0.633	0.2109	0.06500	9,645	343.3	250.4	91.9	1,812	1,322	485	73.2	26.8
266,800	0.2095	0.2436	3/0	26 × 0.1013	7 × 0.0788	0.642	0.2364	0.06531	11,250	367.3	251.7	115.6	1,939	1,329	610	68.6	31.4
300,000	0.2356	0.2740	188,700	26 × 0.1074	7 × 0.0835	0.680	0.2505	0.05809	12,650	412.9	283.0	129.9	2,180	1,494	686	68.6	31.4
336,400	0.2642	0.2789	4/0	18 × 0.1367	1 × 0.1367	0.684	0.1367	0.05155	8,950	365.3	315.8	49.5	1,929	1,668	261	86.45	13.55
336,400	0.2642	0.3072	4/0	26 × 0.1138	7 × 0.0885	0.721	0.2655	0.05181	14,050	463.0	317.3	145.7	2,444	1,675	769	68.6	31.4
336,400	0.2642	0.3259	4/0	30 × 0.1059	7 × 0.1059	0.741	0.3177	0.05193	17,040	527.1	318.1	209.0	2,783	1,679	1,104	60.35	39.65
397,500	0.3122	0.3295	250,000	18 × 0.1486	1 × 0.1486	0.743	0.1486	0.04363	10,400	431.0	372.5	58.5	2,276	1,967	309	86.45	13.55
397,500	0.3122	0.3630	250,000	26 × 0.1236	7 × 0.0961	0.783	0.2883	0.04384	16,190	547.2	375.0	172.2	2,889	1,980	909	68.6	31.4
397,500	0.3122	0.3850	250,000	30 × 0.1151	7 × 0.1151	0.806	0.3453	0.04395	19,980	622.8	375.9	246.9	3,288	1,984	1,304	60.35	39.65
477,000	0.3746	0.3954	300,000	18 × 0.1628	1 × 0.1628	0.814	0.1628	0.03636	12,300	518.0	447.8	70.2	2,735	2,364	371	86.45	13.55
477,000	0.3746	0.4231	300,000	24 × 0.1410	7 × 0.0940	0.846	0.2820	0.03653	17,200	614.5	450.0	164.5	3,243	2,376	867	73.25	26.75

Al circ mils	Cu eq circ mils	Al stranding	Steel stranding	(A)	(B)	(C)	(D)	(E)	(F)	(G)	(H)	(I)	(J)	(K)	(L)	(M)	dia A	dia B
477,000	300,000	26 X 0.1355	7 X 0.1355	0.1054	0.3162	0.858	0.03653	19,430	656.6	450.0	206.6	3,467	2,376	1,091	68.6	31.4	0.3746	0.4356
477,000	300,000	30 X 0.1261	7 X 0.1261	0.1261	0.3783	0.883	0.03662	23,300	747.3	451.0	296.3	3,945	2,381	1,406	60.35	39.65	0.3746	0.4620
556,500	350,000	18 X 0.1758	1 X 0.1758	0.1758	0.1758	0.879	0.03116	14,300	604	522	82	3,189	2,756	433	86.45	13.55	0.4371	0.4614
556,500	350,000	24 X 0.1523	7 X 0.1015	0.1015	0.3045	0.914	0.03132	19,850	717	525	192	3,785	2,772	1,013	73.25	26.75	0.4371	0.4938
556,500	350,000	26 X 0.1463	7 X 0.1463	0.1138	0.341	0.927	0.03132	22,400	766	525	241	4,044	2,772	1,272	68.6	31.4	0.4371	0.5083
556,500	350,000	30 X 0.1362	7 X 0.1362	0.1362	0.409	0.953	0.03139	27,100	872	526	346	4,604	2,777	1,827	60.35	39.65	0.4371	0.5391
605,000	380,500	24 X 0.1588	7 X 0.1059	0.1059	0.318	0.953	0.02880	21,500	779	571	208	4,113	3,015	1,098	73.25	26.75	0.4752	0.5368
605,000	380,500	26 X 0.1525	7 X 0.1186	0.1186	0.356	0.966	0.02880	24,100	833	571	262	4,398	3,015	1,383	68.6	31.4	0.4752	0.5526
605,000	380,500	30 X 0.1420	19 X 0.0852	0.0852	0.426	0.994	0.02888	30,000	939	572	367	4,958	3,020	1,938	60.9	39.1	0.4752	0.5835
636,000	400,000	24 X 0.1628	7 X 0.1085	0.1085	0.326	0.977	0.02740	22,600	819	600	219	4,324	3,168	1,156	73.25	26.75	0.4995	0.5643
636,000	400,000	26 X 0.1564	7 X 0.1216	0.1216	0.365	0.990	0.02740	25,000	875	600	275	4,620	3,168	1,452	68.6	31.4	0.4995	0.5809
636,000	400,000	30 X 0.1456	19 X 0.0874	0.0874	0.437	1.019	0.02747	31,500	988	601	387	5,216	3,173	2,043	60.9	39.1	0.4995	0.6134
666,600	419,000	24 X 0.1667	7 X 0.1111	0.1111	0.333	1.000	0.02614	23,700	859	629	230	4,530	3,321	1,209	73.25	26.75	0.5235	0.5914
715,500	450,000	54 X 0.1151	7 X 0.1151	0.1151	0.345	1.036	0.02436	26,300	921	675	246	4,863	3,564	1,299	73.25	26.75	0.5620	0.6348
715,500	450,000	26 X 0.1659	7 X 0.1290	0.1290	0.387	1.051	0.02436	28,100	985	675	310	5,201	3,564	1,637	68.6	31.4	0.5620	0.6535
715,500	450,000	30 X 0.1544	19 X 0.0926	0.0926	0.463	1.081	0.02441	34,600	1,111	676	435	5,866	3,569	2,297	60.9	39.1	0.5620	0.6901
795,000	500,000	45 X 0.1329	7 X 0.1329	0.0886	0.266	1.063	0.02192	22,900	896	750	146	4,731	3,960	771	83.7	16.3	0.6244	0.6676
795,000	500,000	54 X 0.1214	7 X 0.1214	0.1214	0.364	1.093	0.02192	28,500	1,024	750	274	5,407	3,960	1,447	73.25	26.75	0.6244	0.7053
795,000	500,000	26 X 0.1749	7 X 0.1360	0.1360	0.408	1.108	0.02192	31,200	1,094	750	344	5,776	3,960	1,816	68.6	31.4	0.6244	0.7261
795,000	500,000	30 X 0.1628	19 X 0.0977	0.0977	0.489	1.140	0.02197	38,400	1,235	752	483	6,521	3,971	2,550	60.9	39.1	0.6244	0.7668
874,500	550,000	54 X 0.1273	7 X 0.1273	0.1273	0.382	1.146	0.01993	31,400	1,126	825	301	5,945	4,356	1,589	73.25	26.75	0.6868	0.7759
900,000	566,000	54 X 0.1291	7 X 0.1291	0.1291	0.387	1.162	0.01936	32,300	1,159	849	310	6,120	4,483	1,637	73.25	26.75	0.7069	0.7985
954,000	600,000	45 X 0.1456	7 X 0.0971	0.0971	0.291	1.165	0.01827	26,900	1,075	900	175	5,676	4,752	924	83.7	16.3	0.7493	0.8011
954,000	600,000	54 X 0.1329	7 X 0.1329	0.1329	0.399	1.196	0.01827	34,200	1,229	900	329	6,489	4,752	1,737	73.25	26.75	0.7493	0.8464
1,033,500	650,000	45 X 0.1516	7 X 0.1516	0.1011	0.303	1.213	0.01686	28,900	1,165	975	190	6,151	5,148	1,003	83.7	16.3	0.8117	0.8678
1,033,500	650,000	54 X 0.1384	7 X 0.1384	0.1384	0.415	1.246	0.01686	37,100	1,331	975	356	7,028	5,148	1,880	73.25	26.75	0.8117	0.9169
1,113,000	700,000	45 X 0.1573	7 X 0.1573	0.1049	0.315	1.259	0.01573	30,900	1,260	1,055	205	6,653	5,571	1,082	83.8	16.2	0.8741	0.9346
1,113,000	700,000	54 X 0.1436	19 X 0.0862	0.0862	0.431	1.293	0.01573	40,200	1,431	1,055	376	7,556	5,571	1,985	73.7	26.3	0.8741	0.9849
1,192,500	750,000	45 X 0.1628	7 X 0.1628	0.0185	0.326	1.302	0.01469	33,200	1,349	1,130	219	7,122	5,966	1,156	83.8	16.2	0.9366	1.001
1,192,500	750,000	54 X 0.1486	19 X 0.0892	0.0892	0.446	1.333	0.01469	43,100	1,533	1,130	403	8,094	5,966	2,128	73.7	26.3	0.9366	1.0552
1,272,000	800,000	45 X 0.1681	7 X 0.1121	0.1121	0.336	1.345	0.01377	35,400	1,440	1,206	234	7,603	6,368	1,235	83.8	16.2	0.9990	1.068
1,272,000	800,000	54 X 0.1535	19 X 0.0921	0.0921	0.461	1.382	0.01377	44,800	1,635	1,206	429	8,633	6,368	2,265	73.7	26.3	0.9990	1.1256
1,351,500	850,000	45 X 0.1733	7 X 0.1733	0.1151	0.347	1.386	0.01298	37,600	1,529	1,281	248	8,073	6,674	1,309	83.8	16.2	1.062	1.135
1,351,500	850,000	54 X 0.1582	19 X 0.0949	0.0949	0.475	1.424	0.01298	47,600	1,737	1,281	456	9,172	6,674	2,408	73.7	26.3	1.0615	1.1959
1,431,000	900,000	45 X 0.1783	19 X 0.1189	0.1189	0.357	1.427	0.01224	39,800	1,620	1,357	263	8,554	7,165	1,389	83.8	16.2	1.124	1.202
1,431,000	900,000	54 X 0.1628	19 X 0.0977	0.0977	0.489	1.465	0.01224	50,400	1,840	1,357	483	9,715	7,165	2,550	73.7	26.3	1.124	1.2663

a Based on standard-weight zinc-coated steel core wire.

Aluminum Conductor, Steel-reinforced (ACSR) Bare (*Continued*)

ACSR Cross section			Copper equivalent based upon equal d-c resistance Cu 97% Al 61%	Stranding, number and diameter of strands, in.		Diameter, in.		D-c resistance at 20°C ohms per 1,000 ft (61%)	Ultimate strength, lb[a]	Weight, lb						% of total weight	
Aluminum		Total		Aluminum	Steel	Complete cable	Steel core			Per 1,000 ft			Per mile			Al	Steel
Cir mils or AWG	Sq in.	Sq in.								Total	Al	Steel	Total	Al	Steel		
1,510,500	1.186	1.268	950,000	45 × 0.1832	7 × 0.1221	1.466	0.366	0.01159	41,600	1,709	1,432	277	9,024	7,561	1,463	83.8	16.2
1,510,500	1.186	1.3366	950,000	54 × 0.1675	19 × 0.1004	1.506	0.502	0.01159	53,200	1,942	1,432	510	10,254	7,561	2,693	73.7	26.3
1,590,000	1.249	1.335	1,000,000	45 × 0.1878	7 × 0.1252	1.502	0.376	0.01101	43,800	1,799	1,507	292	9,499	7,957	1,542	83.8	16.2
1,590,000	1.249	1.4076	1,000,000	54 × 0.1716	19 × 0.1030	1.545	0.515	0.01101	56,000	2,044	1,507	537	10,792	7,957	2,835	73.7	26.3
1,780,000	1.398	1.512	1,119,000	84 × 0.1456	19 × 0.0874	1.602	0.437	0.00984	53,600	2,074	1,687	387	10,950	8,907	2,043	81.3	18.7
80,000	0.0628	0.0847	50,310	8 × 0.1000	1 × 0.1000	0.367	0.1670	0.2168	5,200	149.0	75.1	73.9	787	397	390	50.4	49.6
101,800	0.0800	0.1266	64,160	12 × 0.0921	7 × 0.0921	0.461	0.2763	0.1712	9,860	254.1	96.0	158.1	1,342	507	835	37.8	62.2
110,800	0.0870	0.1378	69,700	12 × 0.0961	7 × 0.0961	0.481	0.2883	0.1573	10,730	276.6	104.5	172.1	1,460	552	908	37.8	62.2
134,600	0.1057	0.1674	84,600	12 × 0.1059	7 × 0.1059	0.530	0.3177	0.1295	12,920	336.0	127.0	209.0	1,774	671	1,103	37.8	62.2
159,000	0.1249	0.1977	100,000	12 × 0.1151	7 × 0.1151	0.576	0.3453	0.1096	15,200	396.8	150.0	246.8	2,095	792	1,303	37.8	62.2
176,900	0.1359	0.2200	111,200	12 × 0.1214	7 × 0.1214	0.607	0.3642	0.09851	16,440	441.5	166.9	274.6	2,331	881	1,450	37.8	62.2
190,800	0.1499	0.2373	120,000	12 × 0.1261	7 × 0.1261	0.631	0.3783	0.09134	17,730	476.3	180.0	296.3	2,515	950	1,565	37.8	62.2
211,300	0.1660	0.2628	132,900	12 × 0.1327	7 × 0.1327	0.663	0.3981	0.08248	19,640	527.5	199.3	328.2	2,785	1,052	1,733	37.8	62.2
203,200	0.1596	0.3020	127,800	16 × 0.1127	19 × 0.0977	0.714	0.4885	0.08576	27,500	676.7	191.7	485.0	3,573	1,012	2,561	28.3	71.7

NOTES:

1. An amount not exceeding 10 per cent of the total weight of any one order may be shipped in random lengths, but no piece shorter than 50 per cent of the standard length will be shipped. No random length will be wound on the same reel with a standard length, and all reels will be marked showing number of pieces, length of piece.

2. The actual weight of cable will be held within a tolerance of plus or minus 2 per cent of the weights listed. Invoicing will be based on actual weight.

3. Shipments to each destination will be made to the nearest package specified on each item ordered.

121. Aluminum Conductor, Steel-reinforced (ACSR) Bare

With Class B and Class C Zinc-coated Steel Core (B261-55T)
(Aluminum Co. of America)

Size, cir mils or AWG	ACSR		Ultimate strength, lb			% reduction in strength	
	Stranding, number and diameter of strands, in.		Standard-weight coating	Class B coating	Class C coating	Class B coating	Class C coating
	Aluminum	Steel					
6	6 × 0.0661	1 × 0.0661	1,170	1,170	1,150	0.0	2.0
5	6 × 0.0743	1 × 0.0743	1,460	1,460	1,440	0.0	1.4
4	6 × 0.0834	1 × 0.0834	1,830	1,830	1,800	0.0	1.6
4	7 × 0.0772	1 × 0.1029	2,288	2,245	2,205	1.9	3.6
3	6 × 0.0937	1 × 0.0937	2,250	2,220	2,180	1.3	3.1
2	6 × 0.1052	1 × 0.1052	2,790	2,745	2,705	1.6	3.0
2	7 × 0.0974	1 × 0.1299	3,525	3,385	3,255	4.0	7.7
1	6 × 0.1182	1 × 0.1182	3,480	3,430	3,370	1.4	3.2
1/0	6 × 0.1327	1 × 0.1327	4,280	4,140	4,000	3.3	6.5
2/0	6 × 0.1490	1 × 0.1490	5,345	4,910	4,820	8.1	9.8
3/0	6 × 0.1672	1 × 0.1672	6,675	6,135	6,020	8.1	9.8
4/0	6 × 0.1878	1 × 0.1878	8,420	7,730	7,590	8.2	9.8
266,800	18 × 0.1217	1 × 0.1217	7,100	6,985	6,870	1.6	3.2
266,800	6 × 0.2109	7 × 0.0703	9,645	9,645	9,410	0.0	2.4
266,800	26 × 0.1013	7 × 0.0788	11,250	11,250	11,075	0.0	1.6
300,000	26 × 0.1074	7 × 0.083	12,650	12,650	12,460	0.0	1.5
336,400	18 × 0.1367	1 × 0.1367	8,950	8,810	8,660	1.6	3.2
336,400	26 × 0.1138	7 × 0.0885	14,050	14,050	13,830	0.0	1.6
336,400	30 × 0.1059	7 × 0.1059	17,040	16,740	16,430	1.8	3.6
397,500	18 × 0.1486	1 × 0.1486	10,400	10,050	9,960	3.4	4.2
397,500	26 × 0.1236	7 × 0.0961	16,190	15,930	15,680	1.6	3.2
397,500	30 × 0.1151	7 × 0.1151	19,980	19,600	19,240	1.9	3.7
477,000	18 × 0.1628	1 × 0.1628	12,300	11,800	11,700	4.1	4.9
477,000	24 × 0.1410	7 × 0.0940	17,200	16,940	16,700	1.5	2.9
477,000	26 × 0.1355	7 × 0.1054	19,430	19,130	18,820	1.5	3.1
477,000	30 × 0.1261	7 × 0.1261	23,300	22,500	21,600	3.4	7.3
556,500	18 × 0.1758	1 × 0.1758	14,300	13,770	13,650	3.7	4.5
556,500	24 × 0.1523	7 × 0.1015	19,850	19,560	19,280	1.5	2.9
556,500	26 × 0.1463	7 × 0.1138	22,400	22,100	21,700	1.3	3.1
556,500	30 × 0.1362	7 × 0.1362	27,200	26,200	25,200	3.7	7.4
605,000	24 × 0.1588	7 × 0.1059	21,500	21,250	20,950	1.2	2.6
605,000	26 × 0.1525	7 × 0.1186	24,100	23,800	23,400	1.2	2.9
605,000	30 × 0.1420	19 × 0.0852	30,000	30,000	29,500	0.0	1.7
636,000	24 × 0.1628	7 × 0.1085	22,600	22,400	22,000	0.9	2.7
636,000	26 × 0.1564	7 × 0.1216	25,000	24,200	23,400	3.2	6.4
636,000	30 × 0.1456	19 × 0.0874	31,500	31,500	31,000	0.0	1.6
666,600	24 × 0.1667	7 × 0.1111	23,700	23,400	23,100	1.3	2.5
715,500	54 × 0.1151	7 × 0.1151	26,300	26,000	25,600	1.1	2.7
715,500	26 × 0.1659	7 × 0.1290	28,100	27,200	26,300	3.2	6.4
715,500	30 × 0.1544	19 × 0.0926	34,600	34,000	33,300	1.7	3.8
795,000	45 × 0.1329	7 × 0.0886	22,900	22,900	22,700	0.0	0.9
795,000	54 × 0.1214	7 × 0.1214	28,500	27,700	26,900	2.8	5.6
795,000	26 × 0.1749	7 × 0.1360	31,200	30,200	29,200	3.2	6.4
795,000	30 × 0.1628	19 × 0.0977	38,400	37,700	37,000	1.8	3.6

Aluminum Conductor, Steel-reinforced (ACSR) Bare (*Continued*)

Size, cir mils or AWG	ACSR Stranding, number and diameter of strands, in. Aluminum	ACSR Stranding, number and diameter of strands, in. Steel	Ultimate strength, lb Standard-weight coating	Ultimate strength, lb Class B coating	Ultimate strength, lb Class C coating	% reduction in strength Class B coating	% reduction in strength Class C coating
874,500	54 × 0.1273	7 × 0.1273	31,400	30,500	29,600	2.9	5.7
900,000	54 × 0.1291	7 × 0.1291	32,300	31,400	30,500	2.8	5.6
954,000	45 × 0.1456	7 × 0.0971	26,900	26,600	26,400	1.1	1.9
954,000	54 × 0.1329	7 × 0.1329	34,200	33,300	32,300	2.6	5.6
1,033,500	45 × 0.1516	7 × 0.1011	28,900	28,600	28,300	1.0	2.1
1,033,500	54 × 0.1384	7 × 0.1384	37,100	36,100	35,000	2.7	5.7
1,113,000	45 × 0.1573	7 × 0.1049	30,900	30,600	30,300	1.0	2.0
1,113,000	54 × 0.1436	19 × 0.0862	40,200	40,200	40,100	0.0	0.3
1,192,500	45 × 0.1628	7 × 0.1121	33,200	32,800	32,500	1.2	2.1
1,192,500	54 × 0.1486	19 × 0.0892	43,100	43,100	43,000	0.0	0.2
1,272,000	45 × 0.1681	7 × 0.1121	35,400	35,000	34,700	1.1	2.0
1,272,000	54 × 0.1535	19 × 0.0921	44,800	44,200	43,600	1.3	2.7
1,351,500	45 × 0.1733	7 × 0.1151	37,600	37,200	36,800	1.1	2.1
1,351,500	54 × 0.1582	19 × 0.0949	47,600	47,000	46,300	1.3	2.7
1,431,000	45 × 0.1783	7 × 0.1189	39,800	39,400	39,000	1.0	2.0
1,431,000	54 × 0.1628	19 × 0.0977	50,400	49,800	49,000	1.2	2.8
1,510,500	45 × 0.1832	7 × 0.1221	41,600	40,700	39,900	2.2	4.1
1,510,500	54 × 0.1675	19 × 0.1004	53,200	52,500	51,800	1.3	2.6
1,590,000	45 × 0.1878	7 × 0.1252	43,800	42,700	41,800	2.5	4.6
1,590,000	54 × 0.1716	19 × 0.1030	56,000	55,300	54,500	1.3	2.7
80,000	8 × 0.1000	1 × 0.1670	5,200	4,655	4,550	10.5	12.5
101,800	12 × 0.0921	7 × 0.0921	9,860	9,615	9,385	2.5	4.8
110,800	12 × 0.0961	7 × 0.0961	10,730	10,480	10,220	2.3	4.8
134,600	12 × 0.1059	7 × 0.1059	12,920	12,620	12,310	2.3	4.7
159,000	12 × 0.1151	7 × 0.1151	15,200	14,850	14,480	2.3	4.7
176,900	12 × 0.1214	7 × 0.1214	16,440	15,640	14,830	4.9	9.8
190,800	12 × 0.1261	7 × 0.1261	17,730	16,860	16,000	4.9	9.8
211,300	12 × 0.1327	7 × 0.1327	19,640	18,700	17,700	4.8	10.0
203,200	16 × 0.1127	19 × 0.0977	27,500	26,800	26,100	2.5	5.1

122. Copper-Steel Conductors
(American Steel and Wire Co.)

Size, SCP or SCG	Equivalent to hard-drawn copper Size, AWG	Equivalent to hard-drawn copper Cir mils	Approx diam, in. Strand	Approx diam, in. Each wire	Modulus of elasticity	Min. breaking strength, lb	Approx weight, lb Per 1,000 ft	Approx weight, lb Per mile	Total cross-sectional area Cir mils	Total cross-sectional area Sq in.
2	2	66,370	0.392	0.182	19,800,000	6,378	291	1,536	99,372	0.0781
4	4	41,740	0.310	0.144	19,800,000	4,486	182	961	62,208	0.0489
6	6	26,250	0.248	0.115	19,800,000	3,060	116	613	39,675	0.0312
8	8	16,510	0.196	0.091	20,500,000	2,112	73	385	24,843	0.0195
10[a]	10	10,380	0.220	0.1019	21,700,000	3,853	88	464	31,140	0.0244
12[a]	12	6,530	0.172	0.0808	21,700,000	2,426	55	290	19,590	0.0154

Coefficient of linear expansion:
Sizes 2 to 8—0.0000082 per °F; sizes 10 to 12—0.0000075 per °F.
[a] Made up of one copper and two steel.

123. Conductor Insulations
(National Electrical Code)

Trade name	Type letter	Insulation	Thickness of insulation	Outer covering
Heat-resistant	RH RHH	Heat-resistant rubber	14–12 [a] .... $\frac{2}{64}$ in. 10 .... $\frac{3}{64}$ 8–2 .... $\frac{4}{64}$ 1–4/0 .... $\frac{5}{64}$ 213–500 .... $\frac{6}{64}$ 501–1000 .... $\frac{7}{64}$ 1001–2000 .... $\frac{8}{64}$	Moisture-resistant flame-retardant non-metallic covering [b]
Moisture- and heat-resistant	RHW	Moisture- and heat-resistant rubber	14–10 .... $\frac{3}{64}$ in. 8–2 .... $\frac{4}{64}$ 1–4/0 .... $\frac{5}{64}$ 213–500 .... $\frac{6}{64}$ 501–1000 .... $\frac{7}{64}$ 1001–2000 .... $\frac{8}{64}$	Moisture-resistant flame-retardant non-metallic covering [b]
Heat-resistant latex rubber	RUH	90% unmilled grainless rubber	14–10 .... 18 mils 8–2 25	Moisture-resistant flame-retardant non-metallic covering
Moisture-resistant latex rubber	RUW	90% unmilled grainless rubber	14–10 .... 18 mils 8–2 25	Moisture-resistant flame-retardant non-metallic covering
Thermoplastic	T	Flame-retardant thermoplastic compound	14–10 .... $\frac{2}{64}$ in. 8 .... $\frac{3}{64}$ 6–2 .... $\frac{4}{64}$ 1–4/0 .... $\frac{5}{64}$ 213–500 .... $\frac{6}{64}$ 501–1000 .... $\frac{7}{64}$ 1001–2000 .... $\frac{8}{64}$	None
Moisture-resistant thermoplastic	TW	Flame-retardant moisture-resistant thermoplastic	14–10 .... $\frac{2}{64}$ in. 8 .... $\frac{3}{64}$ 6–2 .... $\frac{4}{64}$ 1–4/0 .... $\frac{5}{64}$ 213–500 .... $\frac{6}{64}$ 501–1000 .... $\frac{7}{64}$ 1001–2000 .... $\frac{8}{64}$	None
Heat-resistant thermoplastic	THHN	Flame-retardant heat-resistant thermoplastic	14–12 .... 15 mils 10 .... 20 8–6 .... 30 4–2 .... 40 1–4/0 .... 50 250–500 MCM 60	Nylon jacket
Moisture- and heat-resistant thermoplastic	THW	Flame-retardant, moisture- and heat-resistant thermoplastic	14–10 .... $\frac{3}{64}$ in. 8–2 .... $\frac{4}{64}$ 1–4/0 .... $\frac{5}{64}$ 213–500 .... $\frac{6}{64}$ 501–1000 .... $\frac{7}{64}$ 1001–2000 .... $\frac{8}{64}$	None
Moisture- and heat-resistant thermoplastic	THWN	Flame-retardant moisture- and heat-resistant thermoplastic	14–12 .... 15 mils 10 .... 20 8–6 .... 30 4–2 .... 40 1–4/0 .... 50 250–500 MCM 60	Nylon jacket
Moisture- and heat-resistant cross-linked thermosetting polyethylene	XHHW	Flame-retardant cross-linked polyethylene	14–10 .... 30 mils 8–2 .... 45 1–4/0 .... 55 213–500 .... 65 501–1000 .... 80 1001–2000 95	None

[a] For 14–12 sizes RHH shall be $\frac{3}{64}$-in.-thickness insulation. For insulated aluminum conductors, the minimum size is No. 12 AWG.

[b] Outer covering is not required over rubber insulations which have been specifically approved for the purpose.

Conductor Insulations (*Continued*)

Trade name	Type letter	Insulation	Thickness of insulation		Outer covering

Trade name	Type letter	Insulation	Thickness of insulation	Outer covering
Moisture-, heat- and oil-resistant thermoplastic	MTW	Flame-retardant, moisture-, heat-, and oil-resistant thermoplastic	$\begin{array}{ll} & A & B \\ 22\text{--}12 \ldots\ldots\ldots\ldots {}^2/_{64} & 15 \\ 10 \ldots\ldots\ldots\ldots {}^2/_{64} & 20 \\ 8 \ldots\ldots\ldots\ldots {}^3/_{64} & 30 \\ 6 \ldots\ldots\ldots\ldots {}^4/_{64} & 30 \\ 4\text{--}2 \ldots\ldots\ldots\ldots {}^4/_{64} & 40 \\ 1\text{--}4/0 \ldots\ldots\ldots\ldots {}^5/_{64} & 50 \\ 213\text{--}500 \text{ MCM} \ldots\ldots {}^6/_{64} & 60 \\ 501\text{--}1000 \text{ MCM} \ldots\ldots {}^7/_{64} & 70 \end{array}$	(A) None (B) Nylon jacket
Moisture-, heat-, and oil-resistant thermoplastic	THW– MTW	Flame-retardant, moisture-, heat-, and oil-resistant thermoplastic	$14\text{--}10 \ldots\ldots\ldots {}^3/_{64}$ in. $8\text{--}2 \ldots\ldots\ldots {}^4/_{64}$ $1\text{--}4/0 \ldots\ldots\ldots {}^5/_{64}$ $213\text{--}500 \ldots\ldots\ldots {}^6/_{64}$ $501\text{--}1000 \ldots\ldots\ldots {}^7/_{64}$ $1001\text{--}2000 \ldots\ldots\ldots {}^8/_{64}$	None
Thermoplastic and asbestos	TA	Thermoplastic and asbestos	$\begin{array}{ll} & C \quad D \\ 14\text{--}8 \ldots\ldots 20 \quad 20 \\ 6\text{--}2 \ldots\ldots 30 \quad 25 \\ 1\text{--}4/0 \ldots\ldots 40 \quad 30 \end{array}$	Flame-retardant non-metallic covering
Thermoplastic and fibrous braid	TBS	Thermoplastic	$14\text{--}10 \ldots\ldots\ldots {}^2/_{64}$ in. $8 \ldots\ldots\ldots {}^3/_{64}$ $6\text{--}2 \ldots\ldots\ldots {}^4/_{64}$ $1\text{--}4/0 \ldots\ldots\ldots {}^5/_{64}$	Flame-retardant non-metallic covering
Synthetic heat-resistant	SIS	Heat-resistant rubber	$14\text{--}10 \ldots\ldots\ldots {}^2/_{64}$ in. $8 \ldots\ldots\ldots {}^3/_{64}$ $6\text{--}2 \ldots\ldots\ldots {}^4/_{64}$ $1\text{--}4/0 \ldots\ldots\ldots {}^5/_{64}$	None
Mineral-insulated metal-sheathed	MI	Magnesium oxide	$16\text{--}4 \ldots\ldots\ldots 50$ mils $3\text{--}250 \text{ MCM} \ldots\ldots 55$	Copper
Silicone–asbestos	SA	Silicone rubber	$14\text{--}10 \ldots\ldots\ldots {}^3/_{64}$ in. $8\text{--}2 \ldots\ldots\ldots {}^4/_{64}$ $1\text{--}4/0 \ldots\ldots\ldots {}^5/_{64}$ $213\text{--}500 \ldots\ldots\ldots {}^6/_{64}$ $501\text{--}1000 \ldots\ldots\ldots {}^7/_{64}$ $1001\text{--}2000 \ldots\ldots\ldots {}^8/_{64}$	Asbestos or glass
Fluorinated ethylene propylene	FEP	Fluorinated ethylene propylene	$14\text{--}10 \ldots\ldots\ldots 20$ mils $8\text{--}2 \ldots\ldots\ldots 30$	None
	FEPB	Fluorinated ethylene propylene	$14\text{--}8 \ldots\ldots\ldots 14$ mils	Glass braid
			$6\text{--}2 \ldots\ldots\ldots 14$ mils	Asbestos braid
Varnished cambric	V	Varnished cambric	$14\text{--}8 \ldots\ldots\ldots {}^3/_{64}$ in. $6\text{--}2 \ldots\ldots\ldots {}^4/_{64}$ $1\text{--}4/0 \ldots\ldots\ldots {}^5/_{64}$ $213\text{--}500 \ldots\ldots\ldots {}^6/_{64}$ $500\text{--}1000 \ldots\ldots\ldots {}^7/_{64}$ $1001\text{--}2000 \ldots\ldots\ldots {}^8/_{64}$	Nonmetallic covering or lead sheath

For insulated aluminum conductors, the minimum size is No. 12 AWG.
Dimensions are in mils, unless inches are specified.
A   Inches.
B   Mils.
C   Thermoplastic.
D   Asbestos.

Conductor Insulations (*Continued*)

Trade name	Type letter	Insulation	Thickness of insulation	Outer covering
Asbestos and varnished cambric	AVA and AVL	Impregnated asbestos and varnished cambric	E F G H 14–8 *c* .... – 30 20 25 14–8 .... 10 30 15 25 6–2 .... 15 30 20 25 1–4/0 .... 20 30 30 30 213–500 .... 25 40 40 40 501–1000 .... 30 40 40 40 1001–2000 .... 30 50 50 50	AVA — asbestos braid or glass AVL — lead sheath
Asbestos and varnished cambric	AVB	Impregnated asbestos and varnished cambric	F D 18–8 .... 30 20 6–2 .... 40 30 1–4/0 .... 40 40 D F I 14–8 .... 10 30 15 6–2 .... 15 30 20 1–4/0 .... 20 30 30 213–500 .... 25 40 40 501–1000 .... 30 40 40 1001–2000 .... 30 50 50	Flame-retardant cotton braid (switchboard wiring) Flame-retardant cotton braid
Asbestos	A	Asbestos	14 .... 30 mils 12–8 40	Without asbestos braid
Asbestos	AA	Asbestos	14 .... 30 mils 12–8 .... 30 6–2 .... 40 1–4/0 60	With asbestos braid or glass
Asbestos	AI	Impregnated asbestos	14 .... 30 mils 12–8 40	Without asbestos braid
Asbestos	AIA	Impregnated asbestos	J K 14 .... 30 30 12–8 .... 30 40 6–2 .... 40 60 1–4/0 .... 60 75 213–500 .... 90 501–1000 105	With asbestos braid or glass
Paper		Paper		Lead sheath

For insulated aluminum conductors, the minimum size is No. 12 AWG.
Dimensions are in mils, unless inches are specified.
E   First asbestos.
F   Varnished cambric.
G   AVA — second asbestos.
H   AVL — second asbestos.
I   Second asbestos.
J   Solid.
K   Stranded.
c Solid only.

124. Insulation Thickness—Over 600 Volts
(National Electrical Code)

The thickness of insulation for conductors for use at over 600 volts shall conform to the following:

Thickness of Rubber Insulation for Rubber-covered Wires and Cables, in 64ths of an Inch

Conductor size, AWG or MCM	Classification				
	RH 10	RH 20	RHW 30 [a]	RHW 40 [a]	RHW 50 [a]
14–12	4	5			
10–9 [b]	4	5	7	9	10
6–2	5	6	8	9	10
1–4/0	6	7	8	9	10
213–500	7	8	9	10	11
501–1000	8	9	9	10	11
1001–2000	9	9	10	11	12

Thickness of Varnished-cambric Insulation for Single-conductor Cables, in 64ths of an Inch

Conductor size, AWG or MCM	For voltages not exceeding				
	1,000	2,000	3,000	4,000	5,000
14	4				
12	4	5			
10	4	5	6		
8–2	4	5	6	7	9
1–4/0	5	6	6	7	9
213–500	6	6	7	8	10
501–1000	7	7	7	8	10
1001–2000	8	8	8	9	10

Thickness of Varnished-cambric Insulation for Multiple-conductor Cable, in 64ths of an Inch

Conductor size, AWG or MCM	For voltages not exceeding									
	1,000		2,000		3,000		4,000		5,000	
	C [c]	B	C	B	C	B	C	B	C	B
14	4	0								
12	4	0	5	0						
10	4	0	5	0	5	2				
9–2	4	0	5	0	5	2	6	3	6	4
1–4/0	5	0	6	0	6	2	6	3	6	4
213–500	6	0	6	0	6	2	6	3	7	4
501–1000	6	2	6	2	6	3	6	4	7	4
1001–2000	7	2	7	2	7	3	7	4	7	5

Thickness of Asbestos and Varnished-cambric Insulation for Single-conductor Cable, Types AVA, AVB, and AVL, in Mils

Conductor size, AWG or MCM	1st wall asbestos	Varnished cambric					2d wall asbestos
	For voltages not exceeding						
	1,000–5,000	1,000	2,000	3,000	4,000	5,000	1,000–5,000
14–2	15	45	60	80	100	120	25
1–4/0	20	45	60	80	100	120	30
213–500	25	45	60	80	100	120	40
501–1000	30	45	60	80	100	120	40
1001–2000	30	55	75	95	115	140	50

[a] Shall be of approved ozone-resistant type for operation at voltages over 2,000.
[b] No. 8 AWG is the minimum conductor size for 5,000 volts operation.
[c] The thickness given in columns headed C are for the insulation on the individual conductors. Those given in the columns headed B are for the thickness of the over-all belt of insulation.

125. Data for MI Cable
(General Cable Corp.)

Cable section	Conductor size, AWG	Outside diam, mils Cable	Outside diam, mils Conductor	Approx weight, lb per 1,000 ft	Nominal coil length, ft	Cables	Reference Nos. end seal	Threaded gland[a]	Equivalent conduit size (NPT glands)	Single isolated cables	Grouped cables[b]
One-conductor											
	16	0.215	0.051	77	1950	215/1	215/1	215	3⁄8	25	20
	14	0.230	0.064	89	1650	230/1	230/1	230	3⁄8	30[c]	25[c]
	12	0.246	0.081	104	1500	246/1	246/1	246	3⁄8	40[c]	30[c]
	10	0.277	0.102	133	1075	277/1	277/1	277	3⁄8	55[c]	40[c]
	8	0.309	0.128	170	900	309/1	309/1	309	1⁄2	70[c]	50[c]
	6	0.340	0.162	217	750	340/1	340/1	340	1⁄2	100[c]	70[c]
	4	0.402	0.204	305	510	402/1	402/1	402	1⁄2	135[c]	90[c]
	3	0.434	0.229	361	430	434/1	434/1	434	3⁄4	155[c]	105[c]
	2	0.465	0.258	425	360	465/1	465/1	465	3⁄4	180[c]	120[c]
	1	0.496	0.289	498	335	496/1	496/1	496	3⁄4	210[c]	140[c]
	1/0	0.543	0.325	603	285	543/1	543/1	543	3⁄4	245[c]	155[c]
	2/0	0.590	0.365	726	230	590/1	590/1	590	1	285[c]	185[c]
	3/0	0.637	0.410	869	205	637/1	637/1	637	1	330[c]	210[c]
	4/0	0.699	0.460	1060	175	699/1	699/1	699	1	385[c]	235[c]
Two-conductor											
	16	0.340	0.051	166	720	340/2	340/2	340	1⁄2	20	
	14	0.371	0.064	199	620	371/2	371/2	371	1⁄2	25[c]	
	12	0.402	0.081	237	500	402/2	402/2	402	1⁄2	30[c]	
	10	0.449	0.102	300	415	449/2	449/2	449	3⁄4	40[c]	
	8	0.512	0.128	395	305	512/2	512/2	512	3⁄4	50[c]	
	6	0.590	0.162	534	230	590/2	590/2	590	1	70[c]	
	4	0.684	0.204	734	170	684/2	684/2	684	1	90[c]	
Three-conductor											
	16	0.355	0.051	184	675	355/3	355/3	355	1⁄2	20	
	14	0.387	0.064	222	525	387/3	387/3	387	1⁄2	25[c]	
	12	0.434	0.081	283	420	434/3	434/3	434	3⁄4	30[c]	
	10	0.480	0.102	356	355	480/3	480/3	480	3⁄4	40[c]	
	8	0.543	0.128	470	280	543/3	543/3	543	3⁄4	50[c]	
	6	0.621	0.162	636	210	621/3	621/3	621	1	70[c]	
	4	0.730	0.204	901	150	730/3	730/3	730	1	90[c]	
Four-conductor											
	16	0.387	0.051	217	555	387/4	387/4	387	1⁄2	16	
	14	0.418	0.064	260	490	418/4	418/4	418	3⁄4	20[c]	
	12	0.465	0.081	329	350	465/4	465/4	465	3⁄4	24[c]	
	10	0.527	0.102	432	290	527/4	527/4	527	3⁄4	32[c]	
	8	0.590	0.128	566	225	590/4	590/4	590	1	40[c]	
	6	0.684	0.162	785	170	684/4	684/4	684	1	56[c]	
Seven-conductor											
	16	0.449	0.051	294	500	449/7	449/7	449	3⁄4	13	
	14	0.496	0.064	368	410	496/7	496/7	496	3⁄4	17.5[c]	
	12	0.543	0.081	461	325	543/7	543/7	543	3⁄4	21[c]	
	10	0.621	0.102	622	250	621/7	621/7	621	1	28[c]	

[a] This number appears on all metal terminal components.
[b] Not more than three cables per group.
[c] National Electrical Code.
The above data are approximate and subject to normal manufacturing tolerances.

126. Flexible Cords
(National Electrical Code)

Trade name	Type letter	Size AWG	No. of conductors	Insulation	Braid on each conductor	Outer covering	Use		
Parallel tinsel cord	TP^a	27	2	Rubber	None	Rubber	Attached to an appliance	Damp places	Not hard usage
	TPT^a	27	2	Thermoplastic	None	Thermoplastic	Attached to an appliance	Damp places	Not hard usage
Jacketed tinsel cord	TS^a	27	2 or 3	Rubber	None	Rubber	Attached to an appliance	Damp places	Not hard usage
	TST^a	27	2 or 3	Thermoplastic	None	Thermoplastic	Attached to an appliance	Damp places	Not hard usage
Asbestos-covered heat-resistant cord	AFC	18–10	2 or 3	Impregnated asbestos	Cotton or rayon	None	Pendant	Dry places	Not hard usage
	AFPD		2 / 2 or 3		None	Cotton, rayon, or saturated asbestos			
Cotton-covered heat-resistant cord	CFPD	18–10	2 or 3 / 2 or 3	Impregnated cotton	Cotton or rayon / None	None / Cotton or rayon	Pendant	Dry places	Not hard usage
Parallel cord	PO–1^b	18	2	Rubber	Cotton	Cotton or rayon	Pendant or portable	Dry places	Not hard usage
	PO–2	18–16							
	PO	18–10							
All-rubber parallel cord	SP–1	18	2	Rubber	None	Rubber	Pendant or portable	Damp places	Not hard usage
	SP–2^c	18–16							
	SP–3^c	18–12		Rubber	None	Rubber	Refrigerators or room air conditioners	Damp places	Not hard usage
All-plastic parallel cord	SPT–1	18	2	Thermoplastic	None	Thermoplastic	Pendant or portable	Damp places	Not hard usage
	SP–2^c	18–16							

							Refrigerators or room air conditioners		
All-plastic parallel cord	SPT-3c	18-10	2	Thermoplastic	None	Thermoplastic		Damp places	Not hard usage
Lamp cord	C	18-10	2 or more	Rubber	Cotton	None	Pendant or portable	Dry places	Not hard usage
Twisted portable cord	PD	18-10	2 or more	Rubber	Cotton	Cotton or rayon	Pendant or portable	Dry places	Not hard usage
Vacuum cleaner cord	SV, SVO	18	2	Rubber	None	Rubber	Pendant or portable	Damp places	Not hard usage
	SVT	18-17				Thermoplastic			
	SVTOc	18		Thermoplastic or rubber					
Heat-resistant vacuum cleaner cord	SVHT	18-17	2	Thermoplastic	None	Thermoplastic	Pendant or portable	Damp places	Not hard usage
Junior hard-service cord	SJ	18-16	2, 3, or 4	Rubber	None	Rubber	Pendant or portable	Damp places	Hard usage
	SJO					Oil-resistant compound			
	SJT SJTO			Thermoplastic or rubber		Thermoplastic			
Hard-service cord	Sa	18-2	2 or more	Rubber	None	Rubber	Pendant or portable	Damp places	Extra-hard usage
	SOy			Thermoplastic or rubber		Oil-resistant compound			
	STv					Thermoplastic			
	STO					Oil-resistant thermoplastic			
Rubber-jacketed heat-resistant cord	AFSJ	18-16	2 or 3	Impregnated asbestos	None	Rubber	Portable	Damp places	Portable heaters
	AFS	18-16-14							
Heater cord	HC	18-12	2, 3, or 4	Rubber and asbestos	Cotton	None	Portable	Dry places	Portable heaters
	HPD	18-12	2, 3, or 4	Rubber with asbestos or all neoprene	None	Cotton or rayon			

See Notes 1 and 2 on page 2-77.

Flexible Cords (*Continued*)

Trade name	Type letter	Size AWG	No. of conductors	Insulation	Braid on each conductor	Outer covering	Use		
Rubber-jacketed heater cord	HSJ	18-16	2, 3, or 4	Rubber with asbestos or all neoprene	None	Cotton and rubber	Portable	Damp places	Portable heaters
Jacketed heater cord	HSJO	18-16	2, 3, or 4	Rubber with asbestos or all neoprene	None	Cotton and oil-resistant compound	Portable	Damp places	Portable heaters
	HS	14-12				Cotton and rubber or neoprene			
	HSO	14-12				Cotton and oil-resistant compound			
Parallel heater cord	HPN[c]	18-12	2	Thermosetting	None	Thermosetting	Portable	Damp places	Not hard usage
Heat- and moisture-resistant cord	AVPO	18-10	2	Asbestos and varnished cambric	None	Asbestos, flame-retardant moisture-resistant	Pendant or portable	Damp places	Not hard usage
	AVPD		2 or 3						
Range, drier cable	SRD	10-4	3 or 4	Rubber	None	Rubber or neoprene	Portable	Damp places	Ranges, driers
	SRDT	10-4	3 or 4	Thermoplastic	None	Thermoplastic	Portable	Damp places	Ranges, driers
Data processing cable	DPT	30-min.	2 or more	Thermoplastic	None	Thermoplastic	Data processing systems	Dry places	Power and signal circuits
Elevator cable	E[e]	18-14	2 or more	Rubber	Cotton	Three cotton, outer one flame-retardant and moisture-resistant[f]	Elevator lighting and control	Nonhazardous locations	
	EO[e]					One cotton and a neoprene jacket[f]	Elevator lighting and control	Hazardous locations	
Elevator cable	EN[e]	18-14	2 or more	Rubber	Flexible nylon jacket	Three cotton, outer one flame-retardant and moisture-resistant[f]	Elevator lighting and control	Nonhazardous locations	
						One cotton and a neoprene or thermoplastic jacket		Hazardous locations	
	ET[e]			Thermoplastic	Rayon	Three cotton, outer one flame-retardant and moisture-resistant		Nonhazardous locations	
	ETP			Thermoplastic	Rayon	Thermoplastic		Hazardous locations	

See Notes 1 and 2 on page 2-77.

NOTES TO TABLE 126:

1. Except for Types PO-1, PO-2, PO, SP-1, SP-2, SPT-1, SPT-2, TP, TPT, and AVPO, individual conductors are twisted together.

2. The individual conductors of all cords except those of heat-resistant cords (Types AFC, AFPD, AFS, AFSJ, AVPO, AVPD, and CFPD) shall have a rubber or thermoplastic insulation, except that the grounding conductor, where used, shall be in accordance with paragraph 400-14(*b*) of the National Electrical Code. A rubber compound shall be vulcanized except for heater cords (Types HC, HPD, and HSJ).

a Types TP, TPT, TS, and TST are suitable for use in lengths not exceeding 8 ft when attached directly, or by means of a special type of plug, to a portable appliance rated at 50 watts or less and of such nature that extreme flexibility of the cord is essential.

b Type PO-1 is for use only with portable lamps, portable radio receiving appliances, portable clocks, and similar appliances which are not liable to be moved frequently and where appearance is a consideration.

c A third conductor in these cables is for grounding purposes only.

d Types S, SO, and ST are suitable for use on theater stages, in garages, and elsewhere where flexible cords are permitted by this Code.

e Traveling cables for operating, control, and signal circuits may have one or more nonmetallic fillers or may have a supporting filler of stranded steel wires having its own protective braid or cover. Cables exceeding 100 ft in length shall have steel supporting fillers, except in locations subject to excessive moisture or corrosive vapors or gases. Where steel supporting fillers are used, they shall run straight through the center of the cable assembly and shall not be cabled with the copper strands of any conductor.

Types E, EO, and EN cables may incorporate in the construction No. 20 gage conductors formed as a pair and covered with suitable metallic shielding for telephone circuits. The insulation of the conductors may be rubber or thermoplastic of thickness specified for Type E and EO cables. The shield shall have its own protective covering. This component may be incorporated in any layer of the cable assembly, and shall not run straight through the center.

f Rubber-filled or varnished-cambric tapes may be substituted for the inner braids.

127. Types and Symbols of Magnet Wires
(General Cable Corp.)

Type	Symbol	Conductor covering or coating		
		First	Second	Third
Coatings:				
Single and heavy enamel........	E, E2	Enamel		
Single and heavy Formvar......	R, R2	Formvar		
Triple Formvar...............	R3	Formvar		
Quadruple Formvar............	R4	Formvar		
Single and heavy Formeze (Type O and Type I or A)..........	RB, RB-2	Formvar	Bonding material	
Triple Formeze (Type II or B)..	RB-3	Formvar	Bonding material	
Quadruple Formeze (Type III or C).......................	RB-4	Formvar	Bonding material	
Single and heavy Formlon.......	RY, RY-2	Formvar	Nylon enamel	
Single and heavy nylon enamel..	Y, Y2	Nylon enamel		
Single and heavy enamel G......	U, U2	Enamel G		
Triple enamel G..............	U3	Enamel G		
Single and heavy Class B enamel.	K, K2	Class B enamel		
Single, heavy, and triple Lecton..	L, L2, L3	Lecton		
Coverings:				
Single and double cotton........	C, C2	Cotton	Cotton (double only)	
Single and double glass bonded..	GB, G2B or GHB, G2HB	Glass (varnish)	Glass (varnish) (double only)	
Single and double dacron-glass...	DG, DG2	Dacron-glass	Dacron-glass (double only)	
Double nylon yarn............	N2	Nylon yarn	Nylon yarn	
Double silk..................	S2	Silk	Silk	
Single and double paper........	P, P2	Paper	Paper (double only)	
Single and double Quinterra-Mylar	QM, QM-2 or QMQ, QMQ-2	Quinterra-Mylar	Quinterra-Mylar (double only)	
Combination insulations:				
Single and heavy enamel single cotton....................	EC, E2C	Enamel	Cotton	
Single and heavy enamel double cotton....................	EC2, E2C2	Enamel	Cotton	Cotton
Single and heavy enamel single glass bonded...............	EGB, E2GB	Enamel	Glass (varnish)	
Single and heavy enamel double glass bonded	EG2B, E2G2B	Enamel	Glass	Glass (varnish)
Single and heavy enamel single paper bonded..............	EPB, E2PB	Enamel	Paper	
Single and heavy enamel double paper.....................	EP2, E2P2	Enamel	Paper	Paper
Enamel nylon yarn............	EN	Enamel	Nylon yarn	
Enamel silk..................	ES	Enamel	Silk	
Single and heavy Formvar single cotton....................	RC, R2C	Formvar	Cotton	
Single and heavy Formvar double cotton....................	RC2, R2C2	Formvar	Cotton	Cotton
Single and heavy Formvar single glass bonded...............	RGB, R2GB	Formvar	Glass (varnish)	
Single and heavy Formvar double glass bonded	RG2B, R2G2B	Formvar	Glass	Glass (varnish)
Single and heavy nylon enamel single cotton.................	YC, Y2C	Nylon enamel	Cotton	
Single and heavy nylon enamel double cotton................	YC2, Y2C2	Nylon enamel	Cotton	Cotton
Single paper single cotton.......	PC	Paper	Cotton	
Double paper single cotton......	P2C	Paper	Paper	Cotton

128. Data for Round Copper Magnet Wire
(General Cable Corp.)

Insulated conductors, max over-all diam, in.

Size, AWG	Area, cir mils	Single enamel (E)	Heavy enamel (E2)	Single — Formvar (R) Formeze (RB) Formlon (RY) Nylon (Y) Enamel G(U)[a] Class B Enamel (K)[b] Lecton (L)[c]	Heavy — Formvar (R2) Formeze (RB-2) Formlon (RY-2) Nylon (Y2) Enamel G(U2)[a] Class B Enamel (K2)[b] Lecton (L2)[c]	Enamel single cotton (EC)	Enamel bonded paper (EPB)	Enamel single silk (ES) Enamel single nylon (EN)	Enamel single glass (EGB)	Single — Glass (GB)(GHB) Dacron-glass (Da)	Double — Glass (G2B)(G2HB) Dacron-glass (Da 2)	Double cotton (C2)
4/0	211,600	.....	.....	.....	.....	.....	.....	.....	.....	.....	.....	0.4806
3/0	167,800	.....	.....	.....	.....	.....	.....	.....	.....	0.4207	0.4247	0.4297
2/0	133,100	.....	.....	.....	.....	.....	.....	.....	.....	0.3754	0.3794	0.3844
1/0	105,600	.....	.....	.....	.....	.....	.....	.....	.....	0.3351	0.3391	0.3441
1	83,690	.....	.....	.....	.....	.....	.....	.....	.....	0.2992	0.3032	0.3082
2	66,360	.....	.....	.....	.....	.....	.....	.....	.....	0.2672	0.2712	0.2762
3	52,620	.....	.....	.....	.....	.....	.....	.....	.....	0.2387	0.2427	0.2477
4	41,740	.....	.....	0.2092	0.2114	.....	.....	.....	.....	0.2133	0.2173	0.2223
5	33,090	.....	.....	0.1866	0.1886	.....	.....	.....	.....	0.1907	0.1947	0.1997
6	26,240	.....	.....	0.1663	0.1682	.....	.....	.....	.....	0.1706	0.1746	0.1776
7	20,820	.....	.....	0.1484	0.1501	.....	.....	.....	.....	0.1527	0.1567	0.1597
8	16,510	0.1324	0.1342	0.1324	0.1342	0.1404	0.1374	.....	0.1394	0.1368	0.1408	0.1438
9	13,090	0.1181	0.1198	0.1181	0.1198	0.1251	0.1231	.....	0.1251	0.1225	0.1265	0.1275
10	10,380	0.1054	0.1071	0.1054	0.1071	0.1114	0.1104	.....	0.1114	0.1089	0.1119	0.1139
11	8,230	0.0941	0.0957	0.0941	0.0957	0.0996	0.0981	.....	0.1001	0.0976	0.1006	0.1011
12	6,530	0.0840	0.0855	0.0840	0.0855	0.0895	0.0880	.....	0.0900	0.0876	0.0906	0.0911
13	5,180	0.0750	0.0765	0.0750	0.0765	0.0805	0.0790	.....	0.0810	0.0787	0.0817	0.0822
14	4,110	0.0670	0.0684	0.0670	0.0684	0.0725	0.0710	.....	0.0730	0.0707	0.0737	0.0742
15	3,260	0.0599	0.0613	0.0599	0.0613	0.0654	0.0639	0.0619	0.0659	0.0637	0.0667	0.0672
16	2,580	0.0534	0.0548	0.0534	0.0548	0.0589	0.0574	0.0554	0.0594	0.0573	0.0603	0.0608
17	2,050	0.0478	0.0492	0.0478	0.0492	0.0533	0.0518	0.0498	0.0538	0.0518	0.0548	0.0553
18	1,620	0.0426	0.0440	0.0426	0.0440	0.0481	0.0466	0.0446	0.0486	0.0467	0.0497	0.0502
19	1,290	0.0382	0.0395	0.0382	0.0395	0.0437	0.0422	0.0402	0.0442	0.0423	0.0453	0.0458
20	1,020	0.0341	0.0353	0.0341	0.0353	0.0396	0.0381	0.0361	0.0401	0.0383	0.0413	0.0418

Data for Round Copper Magnet Wire (Continued)

Insulated conductors, max over-all diam, in.

Size, AWG	Area, cir mils	Single enamel (E)	Heavy enamel (E2)	Single — Formvar (R) Formeze (RB) Formlon (RY) Nylon (Y) Enamel G (U2)ᵃ Class B Enamel (K2)ᵇ Lecton (L)ᶜ	Heavy — Formvar (R2) Formeze (RB-2) Formlon (RY-2) Nylon (Y2) Enamel G (U2)ᵃ Class B Enamel (K2)ᵇ Lecton (L2)ᶜ	Enamel single cotton (EC)	Enamel bonded paper (EPB)	Enamel single silk (ES) Enamel single nylon (EN)	Enamel single glass (EGB)	Single — Glass (GB) (GHB) Dacron-glass (Dɑ)	Double — Glass (G2B) (G2HB) Dacron-glass (Dɑ 2)	Double cotton (C2)
21	812	0.0306	0.0317	0.0306	0.0317	0.0361	0.0346	0.0326	0.0366	0.0348	0.0378	0.0383
22	640	0.0273	0.0284	0.0273	0.0284	0.0323	0.0313	0.0293	0.0333	0.0316	0.0346	0.0346
23	511	0.0244	0.0255	0.0244	0.0255	0.0294	0.0284	0.0264	0.0304	0.0288	0.0318	0.0318
24	404	0.0218	0.0229	0.0218	0.0229	0.0268	0.0258	0.0238	0.0258	0.0243	0.0263	0.0293
25	320	0.0195	0.0206	0.0195	0.0206	0.0240	0.0225	0.0215	0.0235	0.0221	0.0241	0.0266
26	253	0.0174	0.0185	0.0174	0.0185	0.0219	0.0204	0.0194	0.0214	0.0201	0.0221	0.0246
27	202	0.0156	0.0165	0.0156	0.0165	0.0201	0.0186	0.0176	0.0196	0.0183	0.0203	0.0228
28	159	0.0139	0.0148	0.0139	0.0148	0.0184	0.0169	0.0159	0.0179	0.0167	0.0187	0.0212
29	128	0.0126	0.0134	0.0126	0.0134	0.0171	0.0156	0.0146				0.0199
30	100	0.0112	0.0120	0.0112	0.0120	0.0157	0.0142	0.0132				0.0186
31	79.2	0.0099	0.0107	0.0100	0.0108	0.0144	0.0129	0.0119				0.0175
32	64.0	0.0090	0.0097	0.0091	0.0098	0.0135		0.0110				0.0166
33	50.4	0.0080	0.0087	0.0081	0.0088	0.0125		0.0100				0.0157
34	39.7	0.0071	0.0077	0.0072	0.0078	0.0116		0.0091				0.0149
35	31.4	0.0063	0.0069	0.0064	0.0070	0.0108		0.0083				0.0142
36	25.0	0.0057	0.0062	0.0058	0.0063	0.0100		0.0077				0.0131
37	20.2	0.0051	0.0056	0.0052	0.0057	0.0094		0.0071				0.0126
38	16.0	0.0046	0.0050	0.0047	0.0051	0.0089		0.0066				0.0121
39	12.2	0.0040	0.0044	0.0041	0.0045	0.0083		0.0060				0.0116
40	9.61	0.0036	0.0039	0.0037	0.0040	0.0079		0.0056				0.0112
41	7.84	0.0032	0.0035	0.0033	0.0036							
42	6.25	0.0029	0.0031	0.0030	0.0032							
43	4.84	0.0025	0.0028	0.0026	0.0029							
44	4.00	0.0023	0.0026	0.0024	0.0027							

The above data are approximate and subject to normal manufacturing tolerances. ᵃ Single and heavy enamel G (symbols U and U2) available in sizes 10 to 44 AWG inclusive. ᵇ Single and heavy Class B enamel (symbols K and K2) available in sizes 10 to 44 AWG inclusive. ᶜ Single and heavy Lecton (symbols L and L2) available in sizes 14 to 24 AWG inclusive.

129. Properties of Metals and Alloys for Resistance Wires
(Driver-Harris Co.)

Material	Specific resistance at 20°C (68°F)		Temperature coefficient of resistance		Coefficient of linear expansion		Specific heat, g.-cal	Thermal conductivity, watts per cm °C	Approx melting point, °C	Tensile strength at 20°C per sq in.		Specific gravity	Weight, lb per cu in.
	Microhm per cu cm	Ohms per cir mil-ft	Temp coeff	Diff in temp, °C	Coeff of exp	Diff in temp, °C				Max	Min		
Driver-Harris alloys:													
Ohmax	167	1000	−0.00035	20–500	0.0000156	20–1000			1,500	200,000	125,000	6.80	0.246
Radiohm	133	800	0.0007	20–500	0.0000155	20–1000	0.107	0.136	1,350	175,000	90,000	7.30	0.263
Nichrome	112	675	0.00017	20–100	0.000017	20–1000	0.104	0.149	1,400	175,000	95,000	8.247	0.2979
Nichrome V	108	650	0.00013	20–100	0.000017	20–1000	0.110	0.130	1,380	200,000	100,000	8.412	0.3039
525 Alloy	100	600	0.000125	20–500	0.0000151	20–500	0.109	0.136	1,388	150,000	70,000	7.99	0.288
Nirex	98.1	590	0.00088	20–500	0.0000161	20–750	0.114	0.135	1,480	175,000	80,000	8.55	0.3089
Comet	95	570			0.000015	20–500		0.110	1,480	160,000	75,000	8.15	0.294
Nilvar	80.5	484			0.000001	20–100	0.123		1,425	150,000	70,000	8.08	0.292
D-H-Nirosta	73	438	0.00094	20–500	0.00002	20–1000	0.117	0.200	1,399	300,000	100,000	7.93	0.286
42 Alloy	66.5	400	0.0012	20–500	0.0000053	20–400			1,425	150,000	70,000	8.12	0.293
52 Alloy	43.2	260	0.0029	20–500	0.0000095	20–450			1,425	150,000	70,000	8.247	0.2979
Advance	49	294	0.0002	20–100	0.0000149	20–100	0.094	0.218	1,210	135,000	60,000	8.9	0.321
Manganin	48.2	290	±0.000015	15–35	0.0000187	15–35			1,020	90,000	40,000	8.192	0.296
Lucero	48.2	290	±		0.0000125	20–100	0.127	0.250	1,350	150,000	70,000	8.19	0.296
Filmetal D	41.5	250	0.0010	20–250	0.0000143	20–500			1,450	175,000	95,000	8.590	0.3103
Midohm	30	180	0.00179	20–400	0.0000175	20–500			1,100	100,000	50,000	8.9	0.321
R-63 Alloy	25	150	0.0027	20–100	0.0000152	20–500	0.126	0.385	1,425	175,000	70,000	8.72	0.315
Hytemco	20	120	0.0045	20–250	0.000015	20–1000	0.125	0.289	1,425	150,000	70,000	8.46	0.305
Magno	20	120	0.0036	20–100	0.0000143	20–500	0.127	0.271	1,435	135,000	60,000	8.750	0.316
Manganese nickel	14	85	0.0045	20–100	0.0000146	20–500	0.129	0.272	1,435	135,000	60,000	8.813	0.3184
Pure nickel	10	60	0.0050	0–100	0.000015	20–500	0.130	0.615	1,450	135,000	60,000	8.9	0.321
Lohm	10	60	0.00071	20–100	0.000018	20–500			1,100	100,000	50,000	8.9	0.321
High brass	8.3	50	0.0016	0–100				1.29	905	125,000	55,000	8.53	0.308
Low brass	7.0	40	0.0071	0–100				1.55	960	85,000	43,000	8.6	0.310
Com. bronze	4.2	25	0.0020	0–100				2.11	1,015	75,000	37,000	8.7	0.314
Pure metals:													
Platinum	10.610	63.80	0.00398		0.0000089	0–20	0.0275	0.695	1,755			21.45	0.7750
Iron	9.780	58.82	0.00726		0.0000117	0–20	0.109	0.619	1,535			7.86	0.2840
Zinc	5.916	35.58	0.00347		0.0000033	0–20	0.0931	1.13	419.4			7.14	0.2579
Molybdenum	5.632	33.87	0.00479		0.000005	0–20	0.0647	1.46	2,620			10.2	0.3685
Tungsten	5.523	33.22	0.00524		0.000004	0–20	0.0336	1.60	3,370			19.3	0.6973
Aluminum	2.670	16.06	0.00446		0.000024	0–20	0.2089	2.03	660			2.7	0.0975
Gold	2.350	14.13	0.00365		0.0000142	0–20	0.0316	2.96	1,063			19.3	0.6973
Copper	1.724	10.37	0.00393		0.0000166	0–20	0.0951	3.88	1,083			8.92	0.3223
Silver	1.622	9.755	0.00361		0.0000189	0–20	0.0559	4.19	960			10.5	0.3793

130. Electrical resistance wire is wire that has the characteristic of high resistance to the flow of electric current. It is this higher-resistance characteristic which distinguishes resistance wire from conducting wire. The material used for conducting wires should have as low a resistance as possible. Electrical resistance wire is used for the wiring of rheostats, resistors, heaters, furnaces, electric ranges, etc. Metal alloys are used for the manufacture of resistance wires. The more common alloys employed are nickel-chromium, nickel-copper, nickel-chromium-iron, nickel-iron, and manganese-nickel. In Table **129** are listed the properties of metals and alloys manufactured by the Driver-Harris Co. for resistance wire. Although the table gives the trade names for the one company, it will be found to be fairly representative for the alloys of the other manufacturers.

CABLE JOINTS AND TERMINAL CONNECTIONS

131. Cable joints and connections are an essential part of any electric circuit. It is of utmost importance that they be properly made, since any system is only as strong as its weakest link. The basic requirements of any joint or connection are that it shall be both mechanically and electrically as strong as the cable with which it is used. High-quality workmanship and materials must be employed so that permanently good electrical contact and insulation (if required) will be ensured. The more common satisfactory methods of making joints and connections in electric cables are discussed in the following sections.

132. Joints and Connections for Insulated Cables. There are two methods of making joints or connections for insulated cables: by means of soldered connections and by means of solderless connection devices (see Sec. **206**). Soldered connections were the old accepted standard, but in the past few years solderless splicing devices and connectors have gained wide favor for low-voltage work. The use of such devices materially reduces the amount of time required for the making of splices and terminal lug connections. Moreover, if the device is of good design, in addition to the mechanical strength of the connection being fully as great as that of a good soldered connection, the solderless connection has the advantage that the electrical contact will not fail under short circuits or continuous overloads due to the melting of solder.

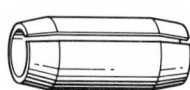

FIG. 6   *Split copper cable connecting sleeve.*

Soldered joints may be made by means of soldered splices (see Secs. **139** to **159**) or by a copper sleeve (see Fig. 6 and Secs. **160** to **162**) thoroughly sweated to the cable.

133. Insulation of Joints. Every joint in insulated cable must be covered with insulation equivalent in insulating properties to that on the cable itself. Soldered joints in rubber-insulated cables are insulated with rubber tape. The rubber employed is a self-vulcanizing rubber tape often referred to as splicing gum. Different rubber tapes are available made from different types of rubber compound. One type is made from normal-aging compound and may be used for cables insulated with Code, intermediate, ASTM 30 per cent Class AO, or performance rubber compounds. A better grade of tape having better aging, heat-resisting, and moisture-resisting properties was developed for performite-compound-insulated cables. It may be used for high-grade joints in any type of rubber-insulated cables. For insulating joints in cables insulated with an oil-base compound (corona and ozone resisting) a corona-resisting tape made from an oil-base compound should be used.

Soldered joints in thermoplastic-insulated wires and cables should be insulated with pressure-sensitive thermoplastic-adhesive tape.

Soldered joints in varnished-cambric- and paper-insulated cables are insulated with varnished-cambric tape.

Joints made with solderless connectors may be insulated as described above for soldered joints, or an insulating cover may be employed.

Refer to Secs. **163** and **164** for more detailed instructions for application of insulating tapes.

134. Protection of Joints. Some form of protection should be supplied over the insulating tape of a joint. For all types of braided cables the joint is protected by applying two layers of friction tape over the insulated joint. Friction tape is made of closely woven cotton fabric treated on both sides with a rubber compound of adhesive character.

Joints in thermoplastic-jacketed cable are protected with pressure-sensitive thermoplastic tape to the same thickness as the cable jacket. Joints in rubber-insulated neoprene-jacketed cable are protected with neoprene tape applied to the same thickness as the cable jacket. These joints are further protected by a covering of anhydrous tape painted with cable paint.

135. Completed Joints. Cross-sectional views of typical completed joints are shown in Figs. 7, 8, 32 to 35, and 40 to 46.

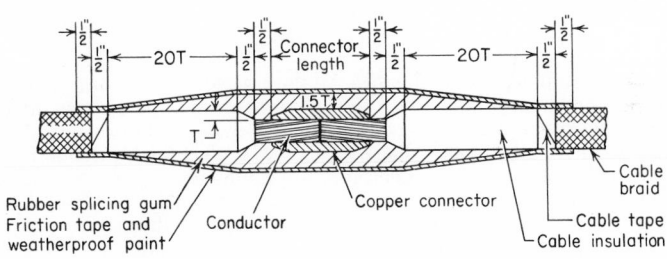

FIG. 7 *Joint in rubber-insulated, braided cable.*

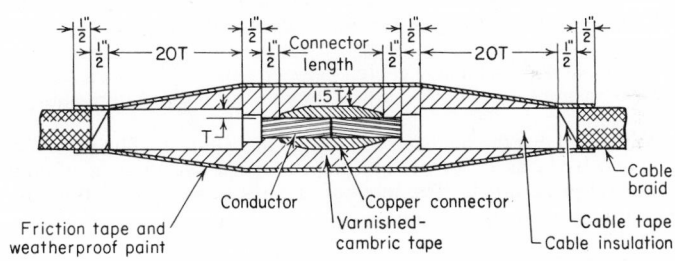

FIG. 8 *Joint in varnished-cambric-insulated braided cable.*

136. Removing Protective Covering. For braided cable strip back the protective covering a sufficient distance from the ends of the cables to be jointed. Trim the edges with a sharp knife, taking great care not to cut the insulation or leave loose ends to get under taping.

For lead-sheathed cable proceed as follows (Rome Cable Corp.):

The length of lead sheath to be removed from single-conductor cables is determined by the creepage distance required for the operating voltage. For multiple-conductor cable the axial length required for offsetting the conductors is the determining factor. The length of sheath to remove from each cable end is approximately 1½ in. less than one-half the total length of the lead sleeve indicated.

Cut halfway through the lead sheath all around at the location determined, and cut the sheath lengthwise to the end. Remove this section of sheath by grasping with pliers and tearing off. This will leave the remaining sheath ends slightly belled.

If belted cable, remove belt, insulation, and fillers to within 1 in. of the end of the lead sheath.

If single-conductor shielded cable, remove shielding to within approximately ¼ in. of the end of the lead sheath. If multiple-conductor cable, remove binder tape and fillers to the end of the lead sheath; remove the shielding tape as far as possible into the crotch.

If the cable is neoprene-jacketed, remove the jacket, underlying tapes, and shielding, if any. Use care not to damage the factory insulation on the cable.

137. Removing Insulation from Rubber- or Thermoplastic-insulated Cables. Completely remove the insulation for a distance sufficient for making the joint. Cover the bared conductor with a few turns of friction tape so that the conductor will not be nicked. Pencil down the conductor insulation for a distance of ½ in. (see Figs. 7 and 9). This penciling should be smooth and even and can be done best with a sharp knife,

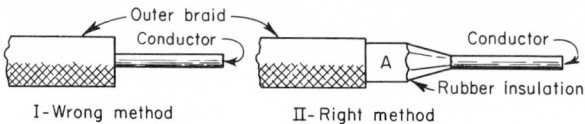

I–Wrong method   II–Right method

FIG. 9 *Methods of "skinning" wire.*

being careful not to injure the conductor. All the exposed conductor insulation should then be made smooth with fine emery cloth in order to provide a good surface for the application of the splicing gum. Wrap the tapered ends of the insulation tightly with dry cotton tape, and tie the tape in place. This is to protect the insulation from scorching while the connector is being soldered to the conductors.

138. Removing Insulation from Paper- or Varnished-cambric-insulated Cable (General Electric Co.). The cable insulation should be removed in steps as indicated in Fig. 10. For paper-insulated cable, the steps should be made by tearing the paper tapes. A convenient way to do this is to hold a loop of fine steel wire (about 0.015 in. in diameter) in place around the insulation at each step in turn, beginning with the step farthest away from the end of the cable, and tear the tapes at the wire. A weight of about 1½ lb attached to each end of the wire will hold the loop in place while tearing the tape.

For varnished-cambric-insulated cable, the steps should be made by cutting the cloth tapes, exercising care to avoid cutting through tapes that will remain on the conductor.

It is recommended that the first step adjacent to the conductor be, in each case, about ¹⁄₃₂ in. in height by ½ in. in length and that the remaining steps be of equal height and spaced about ¾ in. apart. The number of steps in any case will be the same as that shown in the illustration, but the height of the steps will vary with the thickness of the insulation on the conductor.

The number of tapes to be removed for any given step must be determined by counting the total number of tape layers and measuring the thickness of each. The total insulation usually comprises either paper tapes varying in thickness from 0.004 to 0.008 in. or varnished-cambric tapes about 0.012 in. in thickness.

Cotton yarn should be bound into the stepped corners of the insulation and into the corners between insulation and conductor parts (Fig. 10). When doing this the following procedure should be observed: Wash the exposed surfaces of stepped insulation and all metal conductor parts with high-quality Transil oil at a temperature of about 110°C in order to remove all impurities. Dip the roll of cotton yarn in clean Transil oil at a temperature of 110°C to remove possible moisture. Then wind the yarn in all the stepped corners of the insulation, the corners between the conductor and the insulation, and the corners between the conductor and the connector. In passing from one step of insulation to the next, bind down the tape ends with a turn of yarn. Exces-

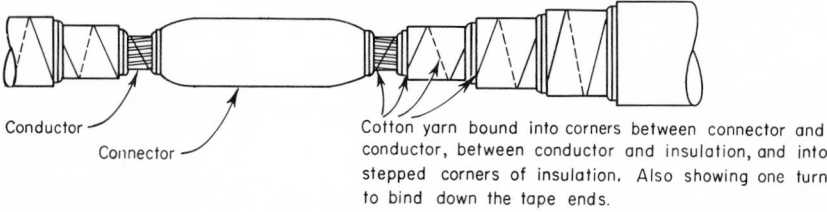

Conductor
Connector

Cotton yarn bound into corners between connector and conductor, between conductor and insulation, and into stepped corners of insulation. Also showing one turn to bind down the tape ends.

FIG. 10 *Method of stepping and binding insulation.*

sive yarn should be avoided; that is, one turn in the lower steps and two in the higher steps should be sufficient.

139. Cleaning Wire Ends. The bare wire ends should be scraped bright with the back of a knife blade or rubbed clean with sandpaper or emery cloth to ensure that the solder will adhere readily.

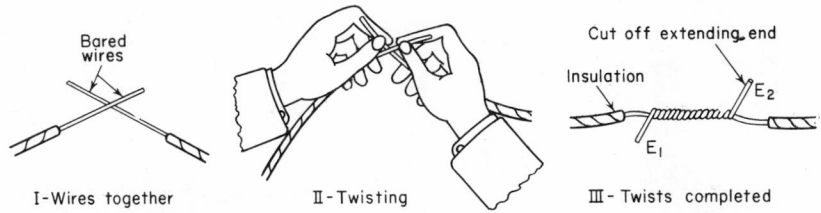

FIG. 11 *Method of forming joints in wires No. 18 and smaller.*

140. When splicing wires of No. 18 Brown and Sharpe gage or smaller (Fig. 11), the insulation, which is usually of paraffined cotton, is removed for a distance of about 2 in. from each wire end. Then, I, the wires should be crossed and held firmly between the thumb and fingers. Next, they should be twisted together, II, into the splice as shown at III. The projecting ends E_1 and E_2 are snipped off with the plier cutters and the whole joint is squeezed into compact form between the jaws of the pliers.

141. The Western Union joint (Fig. 12) is used more frequently than any other. It is used in interior wiring in joining two lengths of wire to extend the conductors from outlet to outlet. In outside wiring, it is used extensively. The joint is made (Fig. 12) by crossing the bared ends as shown at II and forming in them a long twist or neck (III) on either side of which five short turns should be formed as in III and IV. The pliers are employed in making a joint of this type in wires of No. 8 American wire gage and smaller. For larger wires, both the pliers and connectors should be used. For No. 14 wires about a 3-in. length of insulation should be removed from each wire end; for No. 6 wire about 8 in. Care should be exercised to ensure that the free ends in the completed joint are squeezed down flush with the outer short turns so that sharp corners will not cut through the tape.

142. The rat-tailed joint (Fig. 13) is often employed in connecting lighting-fixture leads, but the joints illustrated in Figs. 14 and 15 are, usually, preferable for this purpose. It is used principally in joining conductors in outlet boxes. It is satisfactory if no longitudinal strain is impressed on it. A longitudinal strain is apt to untwist the joint.

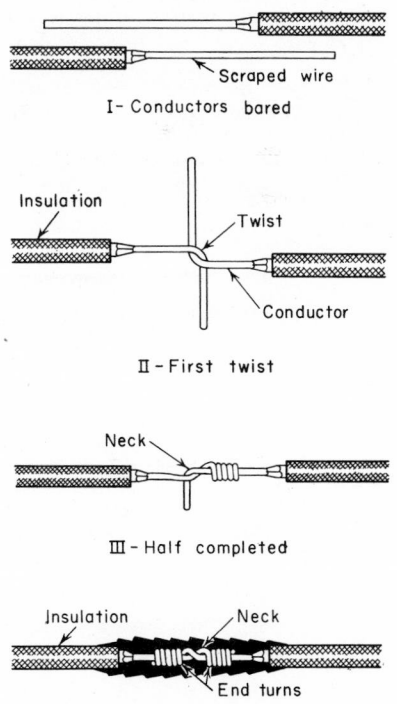

FIG. 12 *Method of preparing wires for Western Union joint.*

143. The end fixture splice (Fig. 14) is used when a fixture wire, usually No. 18 Brown and Sharpe gage, is to be joined to a terminating branch conductor, which is most frequently of No. 14 gage.   The larger wire is bared for about 2 in. and the fixture wire for about 3 in.   Then a 2-in. length of the fixture wire is wrapped around the bared No. 14 wire.   Next, the end of the larger wire is bent back over the joint and the remaining portion of the fixture wire is wound about it.

144. The back-turn splice (Fig. 15) is sometimes employed instead of the fixture splice shown in Fig. 14 or instead of the rat-tailed joint of Fig. 13. This joint (Fig. 15) will withstand considerable longitudinal strain.

145. The Britannia joint (Fig. 16) is used frequently in interior

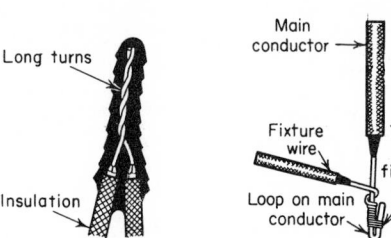

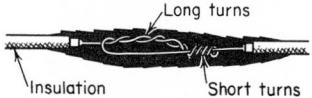

FIG. 13 *Rat-tailed joint.*   FIG.   14   *End   fixture*   FIG. 15 *Back-turn splice.*
                                        splice.

wiring where solid wires larger than No. 8 are to be spliced.   The wire ends are bared and scraped for a distance of about 4 or 5 in.   Then, the extreme end of each is bent almost to a right angle with the axis of the wire.   Next, a piece of bared and scraped No. 18 wire about 5 or 6 ft long is doubled on itself.   Now, the large wires are held in the position which they are to occupy in the finished splice, with a pair of connectors or pliers, and the middle point of the doubled wrapping wire is placed over the center of the two large wires.   Then, one bight of the wrapping wire is served around the two large wires from the center to one end of the joint and a few finishing turns are wound on the single wire.   The other bight of the wrapping wire is then wound around the other portion of the joint in like manner.

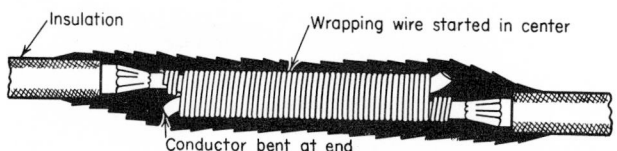

FIG. 16 *Britannia joint.*

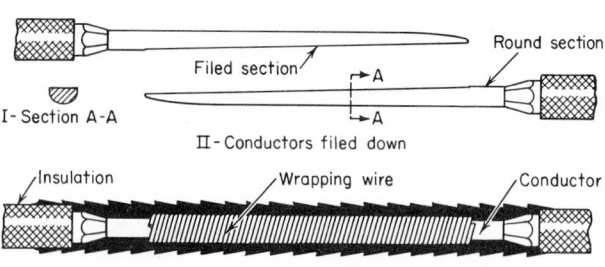

FIG. 17 *Scarf joint.*

146. The scarf joint (Fig. 17) is utilized only for joining solid wires when the over-all diameter of the joint must not exceed the diameter of the wire.   The end of each wire is filed to a wedge shape as shown at I.   The two are laid together, and a No. 18 duplex binding wire is wound around them.   The binding wire is started in the center and is wound to each end in the same manner as above described for the Britannia joint. A few end turns of the binding wire should extend along the round unmutilated portion of each large wire so that the filed-down pieces will not shift prior to soldering.

147. The ordinary tap joint (Fig. 18) is the one which is usually made in splicing a tap conductor to a through conductor. It is made by wrapping the tap wire around the main wire. Joints of this type should, preferably, be wrapped as shown in Fig. 19 with long turns from *A* to *B*. Solder should not be applied to the joint at *A.* If wrapped as in Fig. 18 or if wrapped as in Fig. 19, and if solder is applied at location *A* of the joint, it is inflexible. Hence, the tap conductor is liable to be broken off if subjected to vibration.

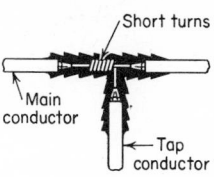

FIG. 18 *Ordinary tap joint.*

148. The knotted tap joint (Fig. 20), though it is seldom used in practice, has the advantage that the tap wire cannot untwist from the main wire. It is made by bending the tap wire end into a U shape, hooking it over the main wire, bending it over itself, and then bending the remaining bight into short turns around the main wire.

149. Cross joints (Figs. 21 and 22) may be used where it is necessary to splice a branch wire, which extends each way from the main conductor, to the main conductor. The plain cross joint (Fig. 21) is made by wrapping two ordinary taps (Fig. 18) onto the main conductor. One tap is wound from right to left and the other from left to right.

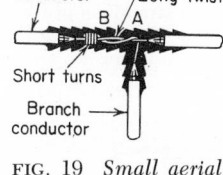

FIG. 19 *Small aerial.*

150. The duplex cross joint (Fig. 22) is made by wrapping both tap wires in parallel on the main wire in the same direction.

151. The wrapped tap joint (Fig. 23) is used in interior wiring for wires of No. 6 gage and larger. It is seldom employed in outside construction. It is made by bending the bared end of the tap wire into an L shape, holding it along the side of and against the main wire, and binding the two together as in the Britannia joint.

152. Through joints in stranded conductors or cables (Figs. 24 and 25) may be of either of the two types illustrated. The single-wrapped joint of Fig. 24 is used most frequently because of the difficulty encountered in making a multiple-wrapped (Fig. 25) splice.

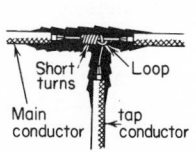

FIG. 20 *Knotted tap joint.*

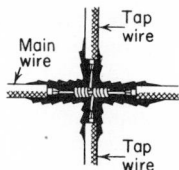

FIG. 21 *Plain cross joint.*

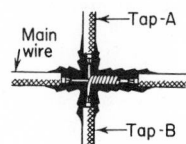

FIG. 22 *Duplex cross joint.*

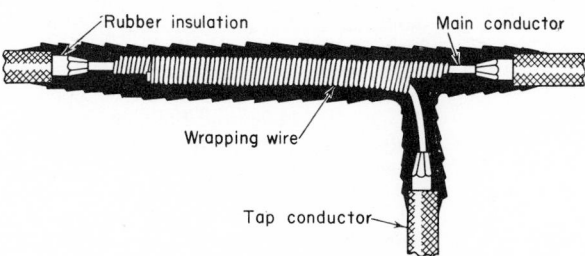

FIG. 23 *The wrapped tap joint.*

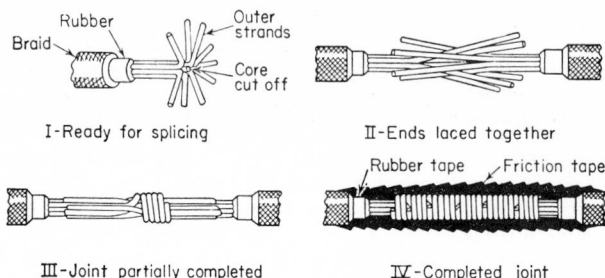

I–Ready for splicing   II–Ends laced together

III–Joint partially completed   IV–Completed joint

FIG. 24   *Single-wrap cable splice.*

153. The single-wrapped cable splice (Fig. 24) is made as follows: First, "skin" the ends of the two cables which are to be spliced. The end of a No. 6 cable should be skinned for a distance of about 6 in.; 1/0, 8 in.; 4/0, 11 in.; 500,000 cir mils, 16 in. Spread out the wires composing the cable as shown at I and pull each straight and cut away the core or a few of the inner wires so that the splice will not be bulky. Clean each wire with sandpaper. Force the wires back to nearly their normal positions. Lace together the two ends as shown at II so that the end of each strand comes between two ends from the other cable. Wrap each free end (III) around the main conductor and wrap similarly each strand of each conductor in their order going around the joint. Wrap each end around as many times as it will go. Each strand should be cut off where it meets the next strand to be wrapped, as indicated at IV. The joint is, preferably, soldered by pouring, with a ladle, molten solder through and over it. Tape servings around the joint, to the thickness of the insulation on the original wire, complete the splice.

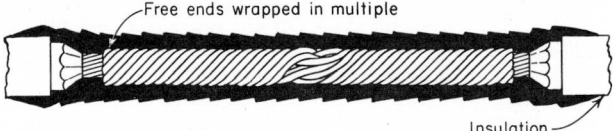

FIG. 25   *Multiple-wrap cable splice.*

154. The multiple-wrapped cable splice (Fig. 25) is made in exactly the same manner as is that of Fig. 24 except that the free ends are wrapped "all together" in multiple instead of separately.

155. The multiple-wrapped cable tap is shown in Figs. 26 and 27. After the component wires have been cleaned, the strands of the tap cable are equally divided into two portions and bent so that the portions form the legs of a V. The apex of the V (Fig. 26) is held against the main cable. All the wires in one portion are wound from left to right around the main conductor in multiple. The wires of the other portion are similarly wound in the other direction. The core wire, and possibly some of the inside wires, should be cut away before the wires are cleaned so that the splice will not be bulky.

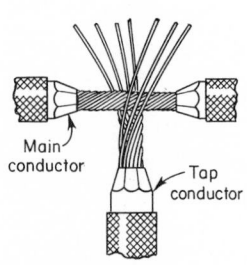

FIG. 26   *"Fanning" of tap cables.*

156. The split cable tap (Fig. 28) is made in practically the same way as is the multiple-wrapped cable tap of Fig. 27, with this exception: First, an opening is made in the center of the bared portion of the main cable by forcing a screw driver through between its strands. Then the bared end of the tap cable is pushed through this hole. Finally the end strands of the tap cable are "made up" around the main cable as in Fig. 28.

157. Soldering Splices in Small Wires. Joints made by the splicing of small wires (smaller than No. 8) may be soldered with either an alcohol torch (Fig. 29) or a soldering

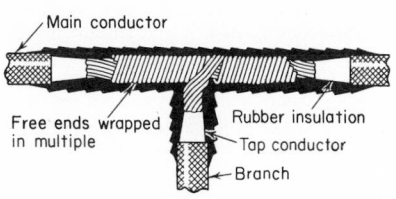

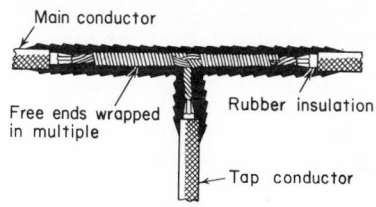

FIG. 27   *Multiple-wrap cable tap.*   FIG. 28   *Split-cable tap.*

copper. Wherever it is feasible, a soldering copper should be used. In soldering a joint with a torch, unless great care is taken, the insulation and covering of the conductors are liable to be ignited. This burning will injure the adjacent insulation and cause a thick smoke which blackens any object on which it deposits.

158. In using a soldering copper, heat it in the flame of a blowtorch. To solder the joint, the hot tool is placed under and in close contact with the joint. After the joint has become sufficiently hot to melt solder, wire solder is held against and is fed into the turns of the joint. After the solder has flowed over the entire surface of the joint, the iron is removed and the joint is shaken to throw off surplus solder. With this method there is neither ignition of insulation nor sooty smoke. The soldering copper can be used in confined spaces where the use of a torch would be impossible. Wires to be

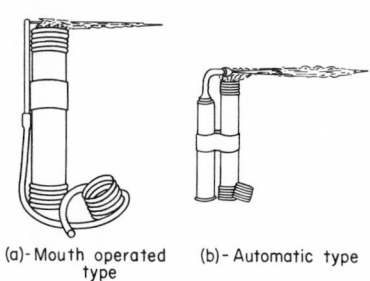

(a)-Mouth operated type   (b)-Automatic type

FIG. 29   *Alcohol torches.*

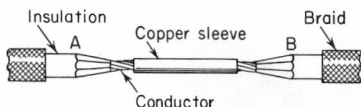

FIG. 30   *Splicing rubber-insulated conductor with copper sleeve.*

soldered must always first be scraped clean and bright. Any of the commercial soldering pastes or compounds can be used as a flux.

159. Soldering Splices in Medium-sized and Large Wires. In soldering splices in stranded wires, a plumber's fire pot may be effectively used for heating the solder. The molten solder is dipped from the pot with a ladle and poured over the splice through and around the joint until the joint becomes thoroughly hot so that the solder runs freely through the strands of the splice and thoroughly permeates the joint. Where possible the joint may be held over the plumber's fire pot during the soldering operations so that the molten solder will drain back into the pot. Where this is not possible, a second ladle should be held under the joint to catch the solder. After the joint has been uniformly heated and appears to be tinned over its entire surface, a piece of wet waste can be held on it to cool it quickly. After cooling, any sharp projections should be smoothed off with a file and fine emery cloth.

160. Soldering Joints with Split-copper Connecting Sleeves. The connector (Fig. 6) is the split or slotted cylindrical piece that joins the two conductors. If necessary, this connector may be pried open at the slot to permit placing it over the conductors, but usually it will be possible to separate the conductors a sufficient amount to permit slipping the connector over one conductor, then joining the conductors, and sliding the connector in place across both conductors so that the assembly of Fig. 30 is produced. See that the connector is closed in maximum contact with the conductor, that it is placed concentrically on the conductors with the slot in position to receive the solder, and that the conductors are moved together, axially, until their ends butt centrally within the connector.

Before assembling the cables and connector, as described above, clean and tin the connector and conductor ends. After assembly, solder each connector solidly to its conductor by pouring hot solder over and into the connector, catching the excess solder in a second ladle held under the joint. The intermittent application of soldering flux will expedite soldering. When the spaces between the conductor strands and the connector are filled to overflowing with solder, fill the slot completely. Permit the solder to cool partially, and, immediately prior to hardening, remove all burrs and superfluous solder by wiping with a piece of clean white tape looped around the connector and conductors. After cooling, any sharp projections should be smoothed off with a file and fine emery cloth.

161. Split Copper Sleeves for Standard Concentric Round Stranded Copper Conductors

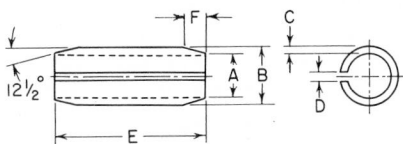

FIG. 31 *Split copper sleeve.*

(Rome Cable Corp.)

Dimensions in Inches

Conductor size, AWG or MCM	Inside diam A	Outside diam B	Wall thickness C	Slot width D	Over-all length E	Length bevel F
8	0.151	0.201	0.025	0.030	1.5	
7	0.169	0.225	0.028	0.030	1.5	
6	0.189	0.251	0.031	0.030	1.5	
5	0.211	0.281	0.035	0.030	1.5	
4	0.237	0.315	0.039	0.030	2.0	
3	0.265	0.353	0.044	0.030	2.0	
2	0.297	0.395	0.049	0.030	2.0	
1	0.337	0.449	0.056	0.070	2.0	0.077
1/0	0.378	0.504	0.063	0.070	2.0	0.109
2/0	0.423	0.565	0.071	0.070	2.0	0.145
3/0	0.475	0.635	0.080	0.070	2.0	0.185
4/0	0.533	0.713	0.090	0.070	2.5	0.231
250	0.581	0.778	0.098	0.120	2.5	0.267
300	0.635	0.849	0.107	0.120	2.5	0.307
350	0.690	0.920	0.115	0.120	2.5	0.343
400	0.740	0.986	0.123	0.120	3.0	0.379
450	0.784	1.046	0.131	0.120	3.0	0.415
500	0.826	1.102	0.138	0.120	3.0	0.447
550	0.868	1.154	0.143	0.175	3.0	0.470
600	0.906	1.206	0.150	0.175	3.5	0.501
650	0.948	1.260	0.156	0.175	3.5	0.528
700	0.983	1.307	0.162	0.175	3.5	0.556
750	1.018	1.356	0.169	0.175	3.5	0.587
800	1.052	1.400	0.174	0.175	4.0	0.610
850	1.083	1.441	0.179	0.220	4.0	0.632
900	1.115	1.483	0.184	0.220	4.0	0.655
950	1.145	1.525	0.190	0.220	4.0	0.682
1000	1.175	1.565	0.195	0.220	4.5	0.704
1250	1.320	1.754	0.217	0.220	4.5	0.804
1500	1.440	1.912	0.236	0.280	5.0	0.889
1750	1.560	2.074	0.257	0.280	5.5	0.984
2000	1.664	2.214	0.275	0.280	6.0	1.065
2500	1.855	2.455	0.300	0.280	6.5	1.178
3000	2.033	2.683	0.325	0.300	7.5	1.178

162. A soldering flux removes or prevents the formation of an oxide during the operation of soldering, so that the solder will flow readily and unite firmly the members to be joined. For copper wires the following solution of zinc chloride is recommended by the Underwriters and is good: saturated solution of zinc chloride, 5 parts; alcohol, 4 parts; glycerine, 1 part. Solutions made with acids should be avoided, as there is usually more or less corrosion in joints made with them. The commercial soldering pastes and sticks give good satisfaction in cleaning joints which are to be soldered.

163. Insulation of Joints in Rubber-insulated Cable. Remove the cotton tape that was wrapped around the tapered ends of the insulation. Clean the rubber insulation with a cloth dampened with high-test gasoline and allow it to dry. The surface over which the splicing tape is to be applied should then be covered with rubber cement, and the solvent allowed to evaporate until it is quite tacky. The rubber splicing tape should then be placed over the joint. Each layer should be applied smoothly and under tension so that there will be no air spaces between the layers. In putting on the first layer, start near the middle of the joint instead of at the end. The diameter of the completed insulated joint should be greater than the over-all diameter of the original cable, including the insulation. When a standard split-copper connector is used, the thickness of applied insulation over the maximum diameter of the connector should be at least 50 per cent greater than the thickness of the insulation on the original cable as indicated in Fig. 7. Most splicing tapes are self-vulcanizing, and therefore it is not necessary to vulcanize the joint later.

164. Insulation of Joints in Varnished-cambric- or Paper-insulated Cables. Varnished-cambric tape of various widths is used for insulating these joints. One-half-inch tape is used in the spaces between the cable insulation and the connector end; $3/4$-in. tape is used to continue the insulating to the original level of the cable insulation. One-inch tape is used to complete the insulation of the joint or, in the case of joints for three-conductor belted-type cables, the over-all of the crotch; 1-in. tape is also used either for spacing reinforced conductors or for binding together reinforced conductors in the case of joints for 5-kv belted-type cables.

Before applying the tape, flush all exposed surfaces of the insulation and intervening conductor parts with high-quality Transil oil at 110°C in order to remove all impurities. Also, during the application of the tape, all surfaces on which the tape is applied and each layer of tape during wrapping should be flushed with a heavy oil compound applied at a temperature of about 20°C with a brush that has been cleaned in high-quality Transil oil at a temperature of approximately 110°C. Tape of $1/2$- or $3/4$-in. width should be applied by drawing it tightly in half-lap wrappings; 1-in. tape should be applied in butt wrappings.

The applied tape insulation should be built up until the thickness of insulation over the maximum diameter of the connector or splice is 50 per cent greater than the thickness of the insulation on the original conductor (see Fig. 8).

165. Applying Lead Sleeve to Lead-sheathed Cable (Rome Cable Corp.). The lead sleeve is slid in place and the ends beaten down with a wood tool to fit snugly the lead sheath of the cable. Scrape the wiping surfaces clean and apply stearine flux. Apply paper pasters to limit the length of the wipes. Make the wiped joints by pouring molten solder on the joint. As the solder cools and becomes plastic, work the solder by wiping with a cloth.

Cut and raise V notches in the lead sleeve for filling and venting. Fill the lead sleeve with insulating compound, heated to recommended temperature and poured into the sleeve through a funnel. The joint is completed by binding the V notch flaps back in place and sealing them with 50-50 solder.

166. Cable Joints. The following instructions in Secs. **167** to **170** for the splicing of cables are reproduced here through the courtesy of the Rome Cable Corp.

167. Straight Splice for Single-conductor Unshielded Cables (Fig. 32)

    A. RUBBER-INSULATED NEOPRENE-JACKETED CABLE:

    1. Form the two cables to be joined into their final position, allowing the ends to overlap. Mark the center line of the joint on both cables, and cut off at this point so that the cables butt squarely together.

    2. Strip the factory-applied jacket, insulation, and underlying tape, if any, from both cables for a distance equal to one-half the length of connector plus $1/4$ in.

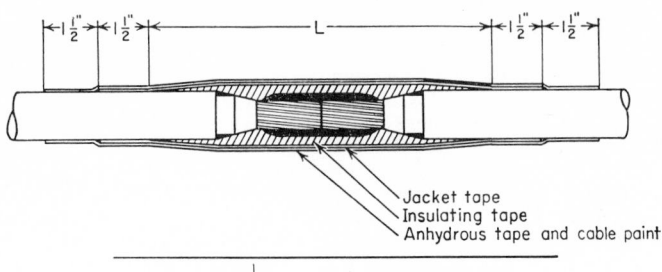

Conductor size, AWG or MCM	Length of L, in.		
	600 volts	3,000 volts	5,000 volts
8–4/0	6.5	7.5	8.5
250–500	7.5	8.5	9.5
600–1,000	8.5	9.5	10.5

FIG. 32 *Straight splice for single-conductor unshielded cable.* (*Rome Cable Corp.*)

3. Apply compression or solder-type split tinned connector.

4. Pencil the jacketed insulation for a distance of four times the over-all thickness of jacket and insulation. Apply special cement to the connector, exposed portions of the conductor, the pencils, and the adjacent jacket, allowing the cement to become tacky before proceeding with the joint.

5. Insulate with ozone-resistant rubber splicing tape applied one-half lap to a thickness over the connector of $1\frac{1}{2}$ times the factory-applied insulation and tapering off over the jacket to a point of $\frac{1}{2}L$ from the center.

6. Cover the hand-applied insulation and adjacent jacket for a distance of $1\frac{1}{2}$ in. with special cement, allowing it to become tacky. Apply neoprene tape over the entire joint to the same thickness as the factory-applied jacket and extending $1\frac{1}{2}$ in. beyond the end of the insulating tape.

7. Serve the entire joint with anhydrous tape extending this serving $1\frac{1}{2}$ in. beyond the end of the hand-applied jacket tape.

8. Paint the entire joint with cable paint.

B. RUBBER-INSULATED THERMOPLASTIC-JACKETED CABLE:

Follow the procedure given in A, substituting the following for step 6:

6. Apply pressure-sensitive thermoplastic tape over the entire joint to the same thickness as the factory-applied jacket and extending $1\frac{1}{2}$ in. beyond the end of the insulating tape.

C. THERMOPLASTIC-INSULATED THERMOPLASTIC-JACKETED CABLE:

1–2. Follow steps 1 and 2 as in A.

3. Clean the conductors, and apply a compression-type connector with hydraulic press and dies.

4. Pencil the jacketed insulation for a distance of six times the over-all thickness of jacket and insulation.

5. Insulate with polyethylene-base splicing tape applied one-half lap to a thickness over the connector of two times the factory-applied insulation and tapering off over the jacket to a point $\frac{1}{2}L$ from the center.

6. Apply pressure-sensitive thermoplastic tape over the entire joint to the same thickness as the factory-applied jacket and extending $1\frac{1}{2}$ in. beyond the jacket end.

7. Complete as in steps 7 and 8 of A.

168. Straight Splice for Single-conductor Shielded Cables (Fig. 33)

A. RUBBER-INSULATED NEOPRENE-JACKETED CABLE:

1. Form the two cables to be joined into their final position, allowing the ends to overlap. Mark the center line of the joint on both cables, and cut off at this point so that the cables butt squarely together.

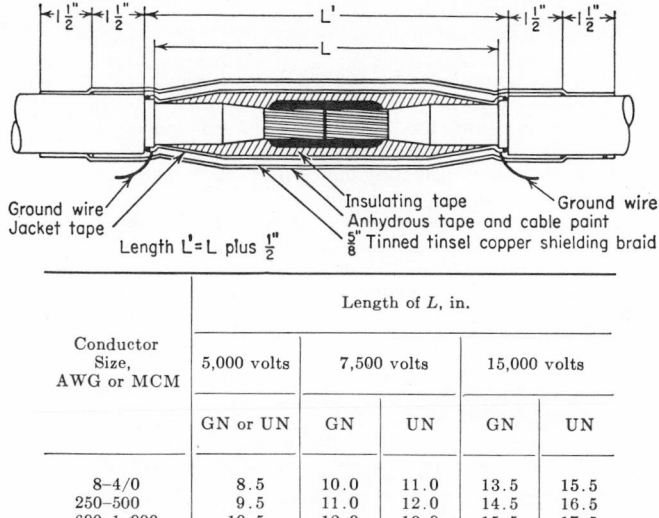

FIG. 33   *Straight splice for single-conductor shielded cable.   (Rome Cable Corp.)*

Conductor Size, AWG or MCM	Length of L, in.				
	5,000 volts	7,500 volts		15,000 volts	
	GN or UN	GN	UN	GN	UN
8–4/0	8.5	10.0	11.0	13.5	15.5
250–500	9.5	11.0	12.0	14.5	16.5
600–1,000	10.5	12.0	13.0	15.5	17.5

2. Remove the jacket and underlying tapes, if any, down to the factory-applied shielding from both cables for a distance equal to $\frac{1}{2}L$. Remove the factory-applied shielding and underlying tape, if any, to within $\frac{1}{4}$ in. of the end of the jacket or for a distance of $\frac{1}{2}L$.

3. Strip the factory-applied insulation and underlying tape, if any, from both cables for a distance equal to one-half the length of connector plus $\frac{1}{4}$ in.

4. Apply compression or solder-type split tinned connector.

5. Pencil the factory-applied insulation for a distance equal to four times its thickness. Apply special cement to the connector, exposed portions of conductor, the pencils, and the adjacent insulation, allowing the cement to become tacky before proceeding with the joint.

6. Insulate with ozone-resistant rubber splicing tape applied one-half lap to a thickness over the connector of $1\frac{1}{2}$ times the factory-applied insulation on the cable and tapering off over the cable insulation up to the end of the factory-applied shielding.

7. Cover the hand-applied insulating tape with $\frac{5}{8}$-in. tinned tinsel copper shielding braid, applied butt edge on the cylindrical portion and one-half lap on the tapered portions. Solder to the factory-applied shielding at both ends, and also apply a light line of solder along the tapered portions to prevent slippage. Use care to do this soldering quickly so as not to damage the shielding braid or insulation. Attach securely and solder the ground wires to the factory-applied shielding at each end of the joint.

8. Cover the shielding braid and the adjacent jacket for a distance of $1\frac{1}{2}$ in. with special cement, allowing it to become tacky. Apply neoprene tape over the entire joint to the same thickness as the factory-applied jacket and extending $1\frac{1}{2}$ in. beyond the jacket end.

9. Serve the entire joint with anhydrous tape, extending this serving $1\frac{1}{2}$ in. beyond the end of the hand-applied jacket tape.

10. Paint the entire joint with cable paint.

11. Connect the cable shielding tape ground wires to ground.

B. RUBBER-INSULATED THERMOPLASTIC-JACKETED CABLE:

Follow procedure given in A, substituting the following for step 8:

8. Apply pressure-sensitive thermoplastic tape over the entire joint to the same thickness as the factory-applied jacket and extending $1\frac{1}{2}$ in. beyond the jacket end.

C. THERMOPLASTIC-INSULATED THERMOPLASTIC-JACKETED CABLE:

1. Follow steps 1, 2, and 3 as in A.

4. Clean the conductors and apply a compression-type connector with hydraulic press and dies.

5. Pencil the factory-applied insulation for a distance equal to six times its thickness.

6. Insulate with polyethylene-base splicing tape applied one-half lap to a thickness over the connector of two times the factory-applied insulation and tapering off over the cable insulation up to the end of the factory-applied shielding.

7. Cover the hand-applied insulating tape with ⅝-in. tinned tinsel copper shielding braid applied as in step 7 of A.

8. Apply pressure-sensitive thermoplastic tape over the entire joint to the same thickness as the factory-applied jacket and extending 1½ in. beyond the jacket end.

9. Complete as in steps 9, 10, and 11 of A.

169. Straight Splice for Three-conductor Unshielded Cable (Fig. 34)

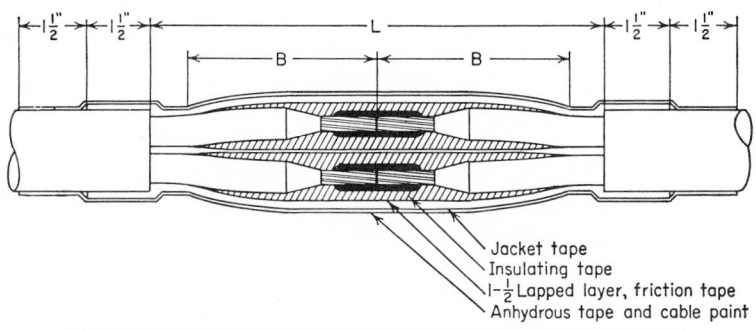

Jacket tape
Insulating tape
1-½ Lapped layer, friction tape
Anhydrous tape and cable paint

Conductor Size AWG or MCM	Length of L and B, in.					
	600 volts		3,000 volts		5,000 volts	
	L	B	L	B	L	B
8–1	8.0	3.25	9.0	3.50	10.0	4.00
1/0–4/0	9.5	3.75	10.5	4.00	11.5	4.50
250–500	12.0	4.75	13.0	5.00	14.0	5.50
600–1,000	15.0	6.00	16.0	6.25	17.0	6.75

FIG. 34   *Straight splice for three-conductor unshielded cable.   (Rome Cable Corp.)*

A. RUBBER-INSULATED NEOPRENE-JACKETED CABLE:

1. Form the two cables to be joined into their final position, allowing the ends to overlap. Mark the center line of the joint on both cables and cut off at this point so that the cables butt squarely together.

2. Remove the jacket and underlying tape, if any, from both cables for a distance equal to ½L. Remove the fillers and cut at the ends of the jacket. Bind the conductors of each cable tightly together with a piece of dry cotton tape applied at the end of the jacket. This is to prevent breaking the jacket when spreading the conductors. Spread the conductors radically, and form them into their final position, taking care not to spread them any more than is necessary for insulating. Strip the factory-applied insulation and underlying tape, if any, on each conductor for a distance equal to one-half the length of the connector plus ¼ in.

3. Apply compression or solder-type split tinned connector.

4. Pencil the factory-applied insulation on each conductor for a distance equal to four times the thickness of the factory-applied insulation. Cover the connectors, the exposed portions of the conductors, the pencils, and the adjacent insulation with special cement, allowing it to become tacky before proceeding with the joint.

5. Insulate with ozone-resistant rubber splicing tape applied one-half lap to a thickness over the connector of 1½ times the factory-applied insulation on each conductor, tapering off over the insulated conductor to a point B from the center.

6. Apply a one-half lapped layer of friction tape over each insulated conductor, extending it as far as possible into the crotches. Squeeze the conductors together by hand, and bind them in place with a serving of friction tape.

7. Cover the entire joint and adjacent jacket for a distance of 1½ in. with special cement, allowing it to become tacky. Apply neoprene tape over the entire joint to the same thickness as the factory-applied jacket and extending 1½ in. beyond the jacket end.

8. Serve the entire joint with anhydrous tape, extending this serving 1½ in. beyond the end of the hand-applied jacket tape.

9. Paint the entire joint with cable paint.

B. Rubber-insulated Thermoplastic-jacketed Cable:

Follow the procedure given in A, substituting the following for step 7.

7. Apply pressure-sensitive thermoplastic tape over the entire joint to the same thickness as the factory-applied jacket and extending 1½ in. beyond the jacket end.

C. Thermoplastic-insulated Thermoplastic-jacketed Cable:

1–2. Follow steps 1 and 2 as in A.

3. Clean the conductors, and apply a compression-type connector with hydraulic press and dies.

4. Pencil the factory-applied insulation on each conductor for a distance equal to six times its thickness.

5. Insulate with polyethylene-base splicing tape applied one-half lap to a thickness over the connector of two times the factory-applied insulation over each conductor, tapering off over the insulated conductor to a point B from the center.

6. Apply a one-half lapped layer of friction tape over each insulated conductor, extending it as far as possible into the crotches. Squeeze the conductors together by hand, and bind them in place with a serving of friction tape.

7. Apply pressure-sensitive thermoplastic tape over the entire joint to the same thickness as the factory-applied jacket and extending 1½ in. beyond its end.

8. Complete as in steps 8 and 9 of A.

170. Straight Splice for Three-conductor Shielded Cable (Fig. 35)

A. Rubber-insulated Neoprene-jacketed Cable:

1. Form the two cables to be joined into their final position, allowing the ends to overlap. Mark the center line on both cables, and cut off at this point so that the cables butt squarely together.

2. Remove the jacket and underlying tape, if any, from both cables for a distance equal to ½L. Remove the fillers and cut at the ends of the jacket. Bind the conductors of each cable tightly together with a piece of dry cotton tape applied at the end of the jacket. This is to prevent breaking the jacket when spreading the conductors. Spread the conductors radially, and form them into their final position, taking care not to spread them any more than is necessary for insulating. Secure the shielding on each conductor at a point about ¼ in. greater than B from the center of the joint, and strip the shielding and underlying tape, if any, from the point to the end. Strip the factory-applied insulation and underlying tape, if any, on each conductor for a distance equal to one-half the length of the connector plus ¼ in.

3. Apply compression or solder-type split tinned connector.

4. Pencil the factory-applied insulation on each conductor for a distance equal to four times the thickness of the factory-applied insulation. Cover the connectors, the exposed portion of the conductors, the pencils, and the adjacent insulation with special cement, allowing it to become tacky before proceeding with the joint.

5. Insulate with ozone-resistant rubber splicing tape applied one-half lap to a thickness over the connector of 1½ times the factory-applied insulation on each conductor, tapering off over the insulated conductor to a point B from the center.

6. Cover the hand-applied insulating tape with ⅝-in. tinned tinsel copper shielding braid, applied butt edge on the cylindrical portion and one-half lap on the tapered portions. Solder to the factory-applied shielding at both ends, and also apply a light line of solder along the tapered portions to prevent slippage. Use care to do this

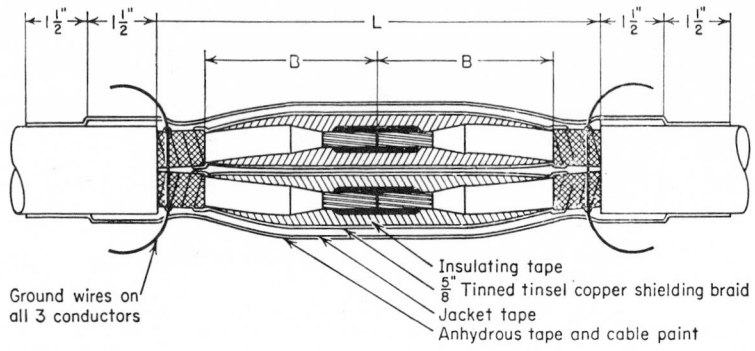

Conductor size, AWG or MCM	Length of L and B, in.									
	5,000 volts		7,500 volts GN		7,500 volts UN		15,000 volts GN		15,000 volts UN	
	L	B	L	B	L	B	L	B	L	B
8–1	10.5	4.25	11.5	5.00	12.5	5.50	15.0	6.75	17.5	7.75
1/0–4/0	12.0	4.50	13.0	5.25	14.0	5.75	16.0	7.00	18.5	8.00
250–500	14.0	4.75	15.0	5.50	16.0	6.00	18.0	7.25	20.5	8.25
600–1,000	17.0	5.75	18.0	6.50	19.0	7.00	21.0	8.25	23.5	9.25

FIG. 35 *Straight splice for three-conductor shielded cable. (Rome Cable Corp.)*

soldering quickly so as not to damage the shielding braid or insulation. Attach securely and solder ground wires to the factory-applied shielding on all three conductors at both ends of the joint. Squeeze the conductors together by hand, and bind them in place with a serving of friction tape.

7. Cover the entire joint and adjacent jacket for a distance of 1½ in. with special cement, allowing it to become tacky. Apply neoprene tape over the entire joint to the same thickness as the factory-applied jacket and extending 1½ in. beyond the jacket end.

8. Serve the entire joint with anhydrous tape, extending this serving 1½ in. beyond the end of the hand-applied jacket tape.

9. Paint the entire joint with cable paint.

10. Connect the cable shielding tape ground wire to ground.

B. RUBBER-INSULATED THERMOPLASTIC-JACKETED CABLE:

Follow the procedure given in A above, substituting the following for step 7.

7. Apply pressure-sensitive thermoplastic tape over the entire joint to the same thickness as the factory-applied jacket and extending 1½ in. beyond the jacket end.

C. THERMOPLASTIC-INSULATED THERMOPLASTIC-JACKETED CABLE:

1–2. Follow steps 1 and 2 as in A.

3. Clean the conductors and apply a compression-type connector with hydraulic press and dies.

4. Pencil the factory-applied insulation on each conductor for a distance equal to six times its thickness.

5. Insulate with polyethylene-base splicing tape applied one-half lap to a thickness over the connector of two times the factory-applied insulation over each conductor, tapering off over the insulated conductor to a point B from the center.

6. Cover the hand-applied insulating tape with ⅝-in. tinned tinsel copper shielding braid applied as in step 6 of A.

7. Apply pressure-sensitive thermoplastic tape over the entire joint to the same thickness as the factory-applied jacket and extending 1½ in. beyond the jacket end.

8. Complete as in steps 8, 9, and 10 of A.

171. Terminating Power Cables. The following instructions in Secs. **171** to **179** for terminating power cables are reproduced here through the courtesy of the Rome Cable Corp.

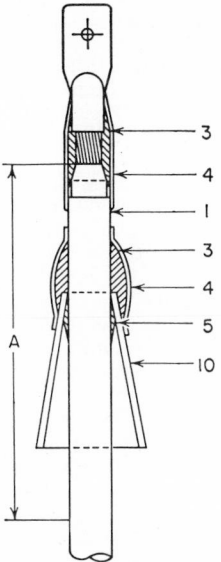

A - Minimum length to
     grounded surface
I - Jacket
3 - Insulating tape
4 - Anhydrous tape —
    cable paint
5 - Friction tape
I0 - Rain shield

Conductor size, AWG or MCM	Length of A, in.		
	600 volts	300 volts	5,000 volts
8–1,000	5	7	10

FIG. 36 *Outdoor termination for single-conductor unshielded cable. (Rome Cable Corp.)*

General Instructions: This discussion covers outdoor and indoor terminations for single- and three-conductor unshielded and shielded, rubber- or thermoplastic-insulated cables with neoprene or thermoplastic jackets.

Although outdoor terminations are included for 7,500 and 15,000 volts, grounded and ungrounded neutral, porcelain potheads are recommended for permanent installations.

In general, cables fall into three classifications: unshielded, leaded, and shielded. Unshielded cables are simply terminated by applying the conductor terminal lug and forming a watertight seal, providing sufficient flashover distance to the nearest ground.

When a leaded or shielded cable is to be terminated, the grounded sheath or shielding must be removed from the cable end to provide sufficient flashover distance. Also, the electric field at the end of the grounded shield is concentrated owing to the divergence of the flux lines toward the thin edge of the shielding and must be relieved, since the high potential gradients may lead to eventual cable failure in this area.

This concentration of electrical stress is relieved by adding a "stress-relief cone" to the exposed insulation surface of the cable, which consists of a double cone of additional insulation with the metallic shielding extended up to the middle of the double cone.

Stress-relief cones are recommended for all shielded cables and for 12 kv and higher single-conductor lead-covered cables. (Belling out the lead sheath is usually sufficient for lower-voltage lead-covered cables.)

On rubber-insulated cables, ozone-resistant rubber splicing tape is used as the cone insulation and tinned copper tinsel braid for the cone shielding. On thermoplastic-insulated cables, a polyethylene-base splicing tape is used.

In building the cone, start at the unshielded end and wrap the insulating tape down to the edge of the cable shielding. Continue wrapping back and forth to build up the double cone of proper dimensions. Starting at the middle of the cone, apply the copper tinsel braid to the lower half, making sure that the upper edge is smooth and even. The copper tinsel braid is then tucked under and soldered to the lead sheath or wrapped over and soldered to the cable shielding.

172. Outdoor Termination for Single-conductor Unshielded Cable (Fig. 36).

RUBBER- OR THERMOPLASTIC-INSULATED NEOPRENE- OR THERMOPLASTIC-JACKETED CABLE:

1. Remove the jacket, factory-applied insulation, and underlying tape, if any, for a distance from the end of the cable equal to the depth of the hole in the lug plus ½ in. for cable sizes up to 4/0 AWG and 1 in. for larger cables.

2. Apply a shoulder of friction tape to support the rainshield, when required. This support should be so located that when the rubber rainshield is seated on the support, the bottom will be about 3 in. from any grounded surface and the distance *A* as given in the tables. Put rainshield in place, and apply ozone-resistant rubber splicing tape to form a watertight seal.

3. Apply a compression or solder-type lug on the conductor. A compression-type lug must be used on thermoplastic-insulated cables. Pencil the factory-applied insulation and jacket for a distance equal to four times the over-all thickness of insulation and jacket. Apply ozone-resistant rubber splicing tape to form a watertight seal.

4. Apply two one-half lapped layers of anhydrous tape over the tape seals at the lug and upper end of the rainshield. Paint the anhydrous tape with cable paint.

173. Indoor Termination for Single-conductor Unshielded Cable. Follow the procedure given in Sec. **172**, eliminating the rainshield and using the following table for dimension *A*, which would be the minimum length to grounded surface.

Conductor size, AWG or MCM	Length of *A*, in.		
	600 volts	3,000 volts	5,000 volts
8–1,000	3	5	8

174. Outdoor Termination for Single-conductor Shielded Cable (Fig. 37).

A. RUBBER-INSULATED NEOPRENE- OR THERMOPLASTIC-JACKETED CABLE:

1. Remove the jacket, factory-applied shielding, insulation, and underlying tapes, if any, for a distance from the end of the cable equal to the depth of the hole in the lug plus ½ in. for cable sizes up to 4/0 AWG and 1 in. for larger cables.

2. Remove all outer coverings down to the factory-applied shielding for a distance *A* from the end of the factory-applied insulation. Remove the factory-applied shielding and underlying tape to within ¼ in. of the jacket.

3. The factory-applied shielding must be terminated in a stress cone. Form a stress cone of the proper dimensions, using ozone-resistant rubber splicing tape. Shield the stress cone with ⅝-in. tinned tinsel copper shielding braid, terminating the shielding

at the point of maximum diameter with a binder of fine copper wire. Solder the braid to the end of the factory-applied shielding and attach the ground wire. Complete the stress cone with a serving of two one-half lapped layers of anhydrous tape extending up over the end of the jacket.

4. Seal the rainshield and complete the termination as in steps 2, 3, and 4 of Sec. **172.**

B. THERMOPLASTIC-INSULATED THERMOPLASTIC-JACKETED CABLE:

Same as A except apply a compression-type lug with hydraulic press and dies. If unpigmented polyethylene-insulated cable is being terminated, it should be covered with two layers of black pressure-sensitive thermoplastic tape applied one-half lap for the distance A prior to application of stress cone and rainshield after removal of shielding tapes.

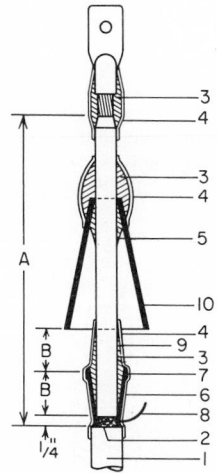

A- Minimum length	6- Tinsel shielding braid
B- Stress cone length	7- Binding wire
I - Jacket	8- Ground wire
2- Cable shielding	9- Stress cone – thickness, same as cable insulation
3 - Insulating tape	
4- Anhydrous tape – cable paint	10- Rain shield
5- Friction tape	

Conductor size, AWG or MCM	Length of A and B, in.					
	5,000 volts		7,500 volts		15,000 volts	
	A	B	A	B	A	B
8–1,000	14	2	17	2.5	24	3.5

FIG. 37 *Outdoor termination for single-conductor shielded cable.* (*Rome Cable Corp.*)

175. Indoor Termination for Single-conductor Shielded Cable. Follow the procedure given in Sec. **174,** eliminating the rainshield and using the following table for dimensions A and B.

Conductor size, AWG or MCM	Length of A and B, in.					
	5,000 volts		7,500 volts		15,000 volts	
	A	B	A	B	A	B
8–1,000	10	2	13	2.5	20	3.5

176. Outdoor Termination for Three-conductor Unshielded Cable (Fig. 38)

A. RUBBER-INSULATED NEOPRENE- OR THERMOPLASTIC-JACKETED CABLE:

1. Remove the jacket and underlying tape, if any, for the distance A as measured from the center conductor of the termination. (NOTE: Allowance must be made for forming the outer conductors into position.) Remove the fillers and cut at the end of the jacket. Bind the conductors tightly together with a piece of dry cotton tape applied at the end of the jacket before the conductors are spread apart. Spread the conductors radially, and form them into their final position, taking care not to spread them any

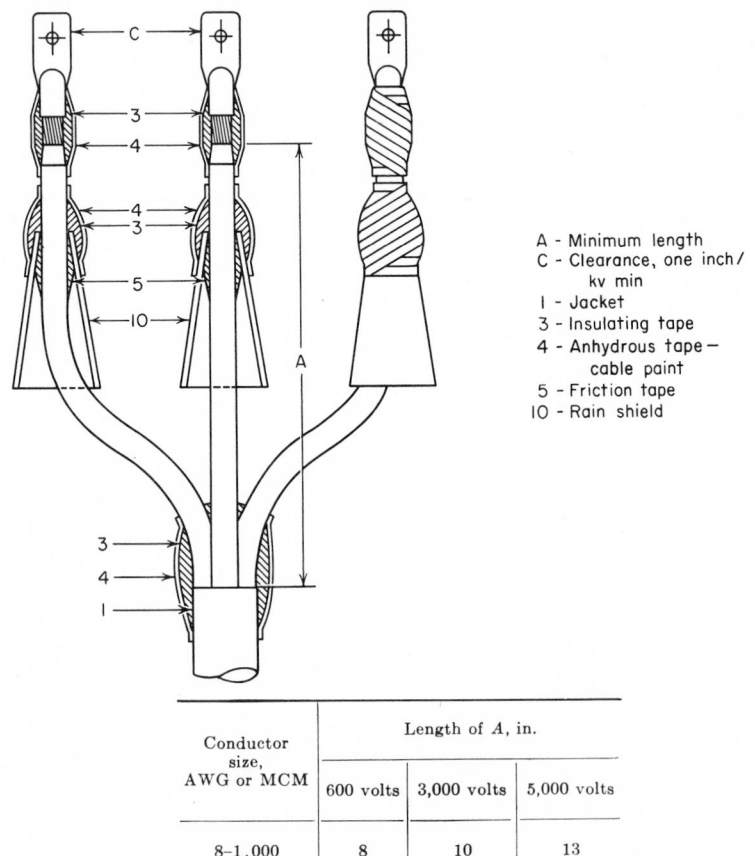

A - Minimum length
C - Clearance, one inch/kv min
I - Jacket
3 - Insulating tape
4 - Anhydrous tape — cable paint
5 - Friction tape
10 - Rain shield

Conductor size, AWG or MCM	Length of A, in.		
	600 volts	3,000 volts	5,000 volts
8–1,000	8	10	13

FIG. 38   *Outdoor termination for three-conductor unshielded cable.* (*Rome Cable Corp.*)

more than necessary to permit applying the rainshields and allowing sufficient clearance (1 in. per kv) between lugs. Bare the end of each conductor for a length equal to the depth of the hole in the lug plus ½ in. for cable sizes up to 4/0 AWG and 1 in. for larger cables.

2. Terminate each conductor as described in steps 2, 3, and 4 of Sec. **172.**

3. Form a watertight seal with ozone-resistant rubber splicing tape at the end of the jacket. Apply two one-half lapped layers of anhydrous tape over the tape seal, and paint with cable paint.

B. THERMOPLASTIC-INSULATED THERMOPLASTIC-JACKETED CABLE:

Same as A except apply a compression-type lug with hydraulic press and dies. If unpigmented polyethylene-insulated cable is being terminated, it should be covered with two layers of black pressure-sensitive thermoplastic tape applied one-half lap for the distance A prior to application of stress cone and rainshield.

177. Indoor Termination for Three-conductor Unshielded Cable. Follow the procedure given in Sec. **176,** eliminating the rainshield and using the following table for dimension A.

Conductor size, AWG or MCM	Length of A, in.		
	600 volts	3,000 volts	5,000 volts
8–1,000	8	10	12

178. Outdoor Termination for Three-conductor Shielded Cable (Fig. 39).

A. RUBBER-INSULATED NEOPRENE- OR THERMOPLASTIC-JACKETED CABLE:

1. Remove the jacket and underlying tape, if any, for the distance A as measured for the center conductor of the termination. (NOTE: Allowance must be made for forming the outer conductors into position.) Remove the fillers and cut at the end of the jacket. Bind the conductors tightly together with a piece of dry cotton tape applied at the end of the jacket before the conductors are spread apart. Spread the conductors radially, and form them into their final position, taking care not to spread them any more than necessary to permit applying the rainshields and allowing sufficient clearance (1 in. per kv) between lugs. Bare the end of each conductor for a length equal to the depth of the hole in the lug plus ½ in. for cable sizes up to 4/0 AWG and 1 in. for larger cables.

2. Terminate each conductor as described in steps 2, 3, and 4 of Sec. **174.** (NOTE: Remove shielding and underlying tapes to within 6 in. of the jacket.)

3. Form a watertight seal with ozone-resistant rubber splicing tape at the end of the jacket. Apply two one-half lapped layers of anhydrous tape over the tape seal and paint with cable paint.

B. THERMOPLASTIC-INSULATED THERMOPLASTIC-JACKETED CABLE:

Same as A except apply a compression-type lug with hydraulic press and dies. If unpigmented polyethylene-insulated cable is being terminated, it should be covered with two layers of black pressure-sensitive thermoplastic tape applied one-half lap for the distance A prior to application of stress cone and rainshield.

179. Indoor Termination for Three-conductor Shielded Cable. Follow the procedure given in Sec. **178,** eliminating the rainshield and using the following table for dimensions A and B.

Conductor size, AWG or MCM	Length of A and B, in.			
	5,000 volts		7,500 volts	
	A	B	A	B
8–1,000	16	2	19	2.5

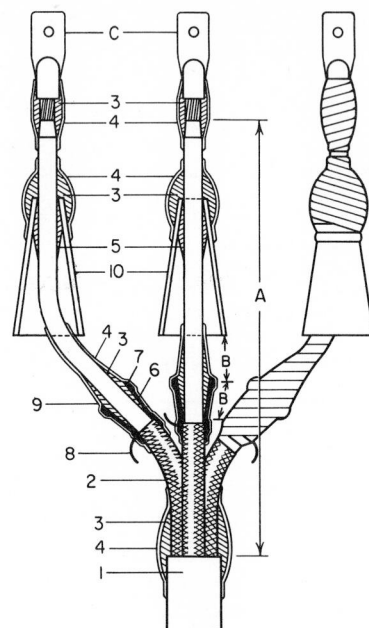

A - Minimum length

B - Stress cone length

C - Clearance, one inch/kv min.

1 - Jacket

2 - Cable shielding

3 - Insulating tape

4 - Anhydrous tape - cable paint

5 - Friction tape

6 - Tinsel shielding braid

7 - Binding wire

8 - Ground wire

9 - Stress cone - thickness, same
    as cable insulation

10 - Rain shield

	Length of *A* and *B*, in.			
Conductor, size, AWG or MCM	5,000 volts		7,500 volts	
	A	*B*	*A*	*B*
8–1,000	20	2	22	2.5

FIG. 39 *Outdoor termination for three-conductor shielded cable.   (Rome Cable Corp.)*

180. Arc-proofing (Rome Cable Corp.).   Underground systems require arc-proofing where primary cables or a combination of primary and secondary cables are contained in a manhole.   If a primary cable fails, even though fast cutoff devices are used, fire protection is necessary to prevent damaging the adjacent cables.

Procedure. 1. Make up splices when required, and form cables into their final position in close triangular configuration, binding them together with a 12-in. serving of ⅛-in. tarred marlin twine.

2. Apply a butted layer of heavy 3-in.-wide wetted asbestos tape on the exposed bound-together cables, tying the starting and finishing ends of each roll with tarred marlin twine.   Wrap a second layer of wetted asbestos tape so that the butted joints will occur midway between the butted joints of the first layer, tying the starting and finishing ends with tarred marlin twine.

3. On unshielded cables, a helical wrap of No. 6 AWG solid copper wire should be applied over the asbestos tape with a 2-in. lay in opposite direction to the lay of the asbestos tapes.   The starting and finishing ends should have three close-wrapped turns with sufficient overlength for connecting to ground.

4. Apply a ⅜-in. layer of asbestos cement over the wet asbestos tape extending into the duct mouths.

5. Ground the ends of the No. 6 AWG copper drain wire.

181. Portable-cable Joints. The following instructions in Secs. **182** to **195** for making joints in all-rubber portable cables have been reproduced here through the courtesy of the General Electric Co.

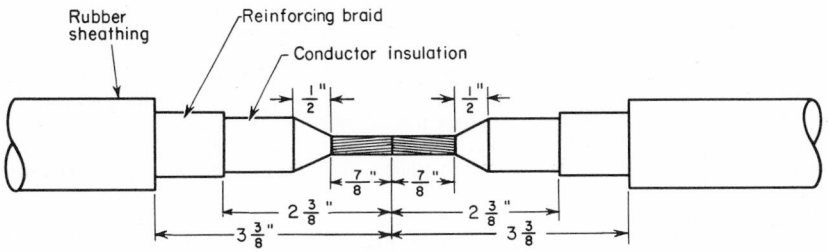

(a) - Rubber sheathing, reinforcing braid, and conductor insulation removed, and conductor insulation penciled

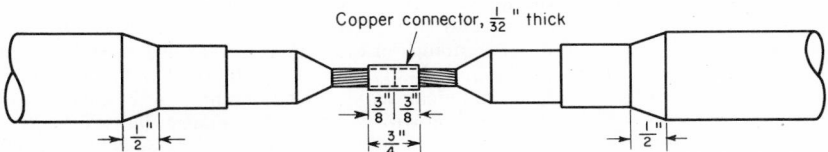

(b)-Copper connector assembled and rubber sheathing penciled

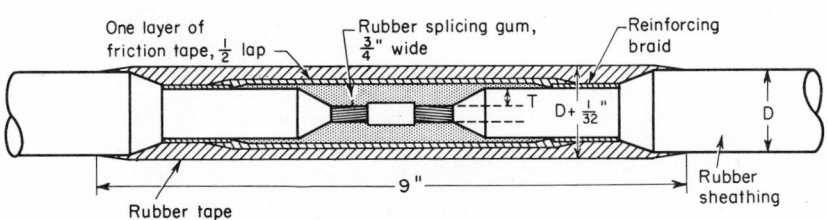

(c) - Splice completed with splicing gum, friction tape, and rubber tape applied. The joint should now be vulcanized

TABLE OF DIMENSIONS

Conductor size, AWG	Thickness of insulation, T, in.	Over-all diam of cable, D, in.	Conductor size, AWG	Thickness of insulation, T, in.	Over-all diam of cable, D, in.
8	$\frac{3}{64}$	0.44	3	$\frac{3}{64}$	0.64
6	$\frac{3}{64}$	0.50	2	$\frac{3}{64}$	0.67
5	$\frac{3}{64}$	0.53	1	$\frac{5}{64}$	0.73
4	$\frac{3}{64}$	0.58	0	$\frac{5}{64}$	0.82

FIG. 40 *Single-conductor soldered joint in all-rubber portable cable.* (*General Cable Co.*)

182. A typical single-conductor portable-cable joint is shown in Fig. 40, and the directions to be observed in making this kind of joint are as follows, with reference to that figure:

1. Bring the cables in position for splicing, with their ends overlapping a little, and cut the cable ends off squarely.

2. Remove $3\frac{3}{8}$ in. of rubber sheathing from the end of each cable. Remove the reinforcing braid for a distance of $2\frac{3}{8}$ in., and remove the conductor insulation for a distance of $\frac{7}{8}$ in.

3. Pencil down the conductor insulation for a distance of $\frac{1}{2}$ in. This penciling should be smooth and even and can be done best with a sharp knife, taking care not to injure the conductor. All the exposed conductor insulation should then be made smooth with fine emery cloth in order to provide a good surface for the application of the splicing gum, which is to be done later.

4. Wrap the tapered ends of the insulation tightly with dry cotton tape and tie the tape in place. This is to protect the insulation from scorching while the connector is being soldered to the conductors.

5. Assemble the connector in place over the conductor joint. The connector should be made of soft-drawn copper strap, $\frac{3}{4}$ in. wide and $\frac{1}{32}$ in. thick and long enough to wrap around the conductor without overlapping. Apply a coating of nonacid soldering flux over the surface of the conductor and then slide the connector over the conductor; let the connector slot come at the top and place it so that the two conductors butt at the center of the connector. Pinch the connector with pliers so that it closes into maximum contact with the conductor. Solder the conductor fast to the connector by pouring hot solder over the joint until it is thoroughly heated and the solder runs freely through the slot and into the strands of the cable. Solder that collects on the bottom of the connector should be brought to the top to fill the slot. Before the solder sets, wipe the connector smooth and clean with a piece of cloth. After cooling, any sharp projections should be smoothed off with a file and fine emery cloth.

6. Remove the cotton tape that was wrapped around the tapered ends of the insulation. Clean the rubber insulation with a cloth dampened with high-test gasoline, and allow it to dry. Then apply a coating of rubber cement over the entire surface on which the splicing gum is to be applied, and allow the solvent to evaporate before applying any tape.

7. Apply the splicing gum and build it up over the rubber insulation to a diameter of about $\frac{1}{16}$ in. larger than the rubber insulation on the cable, as shown in Fig. 40.

8. Apply one layer of friction tape half-lapped over the splicing gum and over the ends of the reinforcing braid, as shown in Fig. 40.

9. Pencil the rubber sheathing as shown and clean the tapered surface and the outside surface of the cable for a distance of at least $\frac{3}{4}$ in. at each end with fine emery cloth and high-test gasoline, and allow to dry.

10. Cover the entire surface of the joint with a coating of rubber cement. Be sure to cover all the surface over which the final wrapping is to be applied.

11. After the solvent has evaporated, apply the rubber tape in half-lapping; build it up to a diameter of about $\frac{1}{16}$ in. greater than the diameter of the cable, and let it extend over the surface of the rubber sheathing as indicated in Fig. 40, so that the over-all length of the joint will be 9 in.

12. The joint should now be vulcanized in a suitable mold. The inside diameter of the mold should be about the same as the diameter of the cable. If a steam vulcanizer is used, a steam pressure of about 30 lb should be applied for 15 to 30 min, depending on the size of the mold and the joint that is being vulcanized.

13. To complete the process, cover the joint with black wax and wipe it smooth.

183. Typical examples of multiconductor portable-cable joints are shown in Figs. 41 and 42. In each case, sufficient rubber sheathing and fillers are removed from the cable ends to permit staggering the individual splices as shown in Fig. 43, in order to obtain a flexible joint of approximately the same outside diameter as the cable. The individual conductors are spliced in the same way as described for single-conductor cable. The individual joints and the ends of the rubber-filled tape, if present, are bound with one layer of friction tape, half-lapped, as shown in the illustrations.

In order to maintain the over-all length of the joint within a given dimension it is necessary that the first splice be at a certain minimum distance from the end of the rubber sheathing. This dimension is given in the data accompanying the illustrations. The distance between the individual splices is approximately 3 in.

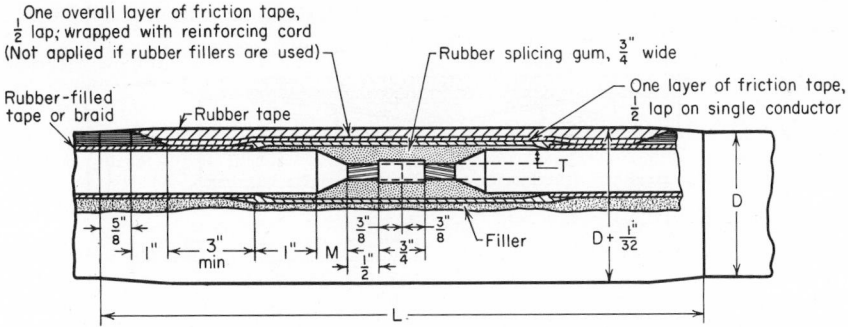

FIG. 41 *Joint for multiconductor Type W and Type G portable cable and two-conductor flat cable. (General Electric Co.)*

In splicing Type G cable, exercise care to avoid damaging the ground wires. These wires should be bent out of the way until the individual conductors are insulated.

In splicing Type SH, Class A cable, each of the single conductors must be completely shielded; i.e., the copper-mesh shielding must be carried across the joint and soldered. This is shown in Fig. 42. The cable-shielding braid is removed ½ in. farther than the rubber-filled tape on each end of each conductor. The remaining braid is then opened and turned back ½ in., taking care not to loosen the braid farther than this point; such loosening is prevented by applying and soldering at this point three or four turns of tightly drawn 0.0126-in. tinned-copper wire. The ¾- by 0.015-in. flat copper braid is then applied half-lapped over the unshielded portion of the insulation. The ½ in. of cable-shielding braid, which was just turned back, is drawn over the ¾-in.-wide shielding braid, and the two shields are bound together by continuing the tightly drawn butt wraps of 0.0126-in. tinned-copper wire for a total distance of ⅞ in. The wire should then be soldered to the braid, using a nonacid soldering flux; this is necessary because there must be a positive electric contact across the joint. In applying the shield, be sure that no gaps or openings are left, since the opening in the shielding of one conductor might lead to corona.

Bring the single conductors together with approximately the same twist as the rest of the cable.

In the case of Type G cable, the ground wires should now be cut to their proper length. They should be connected in the same manner as the cable conductors, and all sharp projections removed. The bare wire must be wrapped with friction tape, half-lapped. The ground wire should then be placed in the interstices.

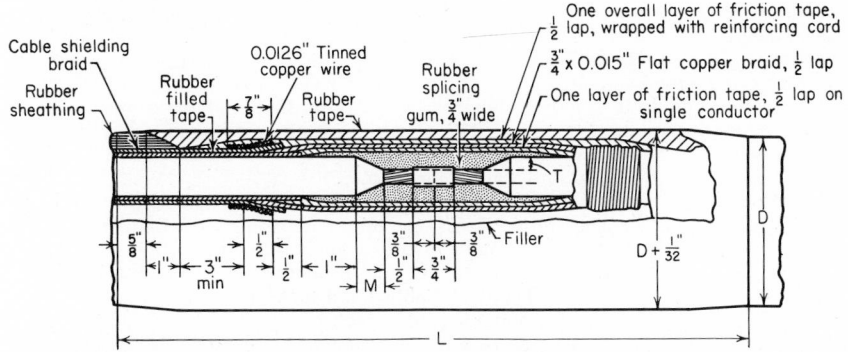

FIG. 42 *Joint for Type SH, Class A portable cable. (General Electric Co.)*

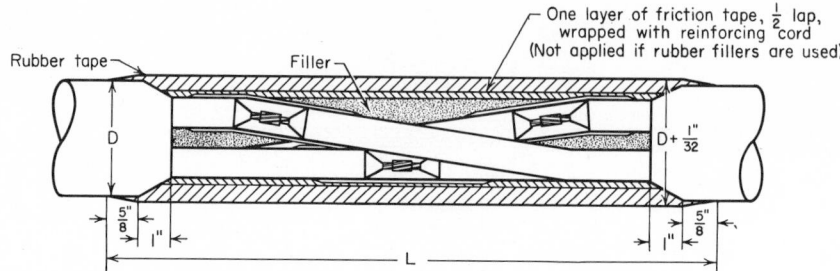

FIG. 43 *Joint for 600-volt three-conductor portable Type W cable, showing the staggering of individual splices. (General Electric Co.)*

In joining the shields of Type SH, Classes B, C, and D cable, follow in general the same instructions as given for Type SH, Class A, and in joining the ground wires of Type SH, Classes C and D cable, follow the instructions for Type G cable.

Returning to the instructions for all types, the interstices are then filled and the cable made its proper shape by means of a suitable filler. The type of filler used depends on the make-up of the cable being spliced. If rubber filler is used in the cable, rubber filler should be used in the joint. If jute fillers are used in the cable, jute fillers should be used in the joint.

Rubber filler is applied by placing a coating of rubber cement over the entire surface of the individual conductors and filler space and, when the solvent has evaporated, laying strips of splicing tape longitudinally in the interstices until they are filled completely.

When jute fillers are used, the individual conductors, the jute fillers, and the ground wires, if any, should be covered completely with one layer of half-lapped friction tape. The surface of the friction tape should then be wrapped with reinforcing cord. Apply the cord in tightly drawn wraps spaced ½ in. apart, having a pitch of approximately 2 in. The joint should be wrapped first with the pitch in one direction and then with the pitch in the opposite direction, thereby obtaining the equivalent of a reinforcing braid. Tie the cord firmly at both ends.

The rubber sheathing should then be tapered and cleaned as described for single-conductor cable. All the surface that is to be covered with splicing gum should be covered with a coating of rubber cement. When the solvent has evaporated, wrap the surface with splicing tape to the diameter shown in the illustrations.

The joint is now ready to be vulcanized. The same vulcanizing process is used for both shielded and nonshielded cables. Preheat the vulcanizer before inserting the joint and vulcanize according to instructions furnished with the particular vulcanizing equipment. If a steam vulcanizer is used, a steam pressure of about 30 lb should be applied for 30 to 60 min, depending on the size of the mold and the joint that is being vulcanized. It is sometimes necessary to apply a dressing of thin paper to the mold to prevent sticking of the rubber. After vulcanizing, the joint should be covered with black wax and wiped smooth (see the instructions for vulcanizing).

Where the voltage is 2,500 or above, a feeder cable that contains provision for a ground connection should be used. The power-line end must be grounded to a suitable permanent ground, and the end at the apparatus must be grounded securely through a bolted connection to the apparatus frame.

Included in this instruction is one method for making the conductor splice. Other methods can be used successfully. Most operating companies have their own ideas as to how these joints should be made. One suggestion is added: that the copper splice be made as smooth as possible and as close to the original diameter as practical.

184. Nonsoldered Joints (for Types of Cable Used in Mines). These instructions apply to those types of all-rubber portable cable which are widely used in coal and other mines on such equipment as gathering reel locomotives, cutters, loaders, and drills. The types covered are single-conductor, two-conductor flat (with the conductors side by side), and two-conductor concentric (with an inner and outer conductor).

Dimensions, in Inches, of Multiconductor Cable Joints
(See Figs. 41, 42, and 43)
Type W, 600 volts, 2-, 3-, and 4-conductor

Conductor size, AWG	T	2-conductor			3-conductor			4-conductor		
		D	L	M	D	L	M	D	L	M
8	$\frac{3}{64}$	0.75			0.78			0.84		
6	$\frac{4}{64}$	0.91			0.95			1.03		
4	$\frac{4}{64}$	1.06			1.12			1.27		
3	$\frac{4}{64}$	1.12	18	$\frac{1}{2}$	1.19	21	$\frac{1}{2}$	1.36	24	$\frac{1}{2}$
2	$\frac{4}{64}$	1.19			1.31			1.42		
1	$\frac{4}{64}$	1.41			1.50			1.62		
0	$\frac{5}{64}$	1.55			1.62			1.84		

Type W, 2,500 and 3,500 volts, 3- and 4-conductor

Conductor size, AWG	T	2,500 volts						T	3,500 volts					
		3-conductor			4-conductor				3-conductor			4-conductor		
		D	L	M	D	L	M		D	L	M	D	L	M
8	$\frac{6}{64}$	1.18			1.28			$\frac{8}{64}$						
6	$\frac{6}{64}$	1.30			1.41				1.50			1.61		
4	$\frac{6}{64}$	1.47			1.58				1.62			1.77		
3	$\frac{6}{64}$	1.53	22	$\frac{1}{2}$	1.66	25	$\frac{1}{2}$		1.70	23	$\frac{3}{4}$	1.84	26	$\frac{3}{4}$
2	$\frac{6}{64}$	1.59			1.76				1.77			1.91		
1	$\frac{7}{64}$	1.80			1.95				1.88			2.03		
0	$\frac{7}{64}$	1.91			2.06				1.97			2.14		

Type G, 2,500, 3,500, and 5,000 volts, 3-conductor

Conductor size, AWG	2,500 volts				3,500 volts				5,000 volts			
	T	D	L	M	T	D	L	M	T	D	L	M
8	$\frac{6}{64}$	1.19										
6	$\frac{6}{64}$	1.30			$\frac{8}{64}$	1.50			$\frac{19}{64}$	1.66		
4	$\frac{6}{64}$	1.47			$\frac{8}{64}$	1.63			$\frac{19}{64}$	1.80		
3	$\frac{6}{64}$	1.53	22	$\frac{1}{2}$	$\frac{8}{64}$	1.70	23	$\frac{3}{4}$	$\frac{19}{64}$	1.86	24	1
2	$\frac{6}{64}$	1.59			$\frac{8}{64}$	1.77			$\frac{19}{64}$	1.94		
1	$\frac{7}{64}$	1.80			$\frac{8}{64}$	1.87			$\frac{19}{64}$	2.03		
0	$\frac{7}{64}$	1.90			$\frac{8}{64}$	1.97			$\frac{19}{64}$	2.14		

Type SH, 2,500, 3,500, and 5,000 volts, 3-conductor

Conductor size, AWG	2,500 volts				3,500 volts				5,000 volts			
	T	D	L	M	T	D	L	M	T	D	L	M
8	$\frac{19}{64}$	1.66										
6		1.77				1.86				2.00		
4		1.94				2.09				2.20		
3		2.04	24	$\frac{1}{2}$	$\frac{11}{64}$	2.14	25	$\frac{3}{4}$	$\frac{13}{64}$	2.24	26	1
2		2.06				2.21				2.33		
1		2.23				2.34				2.44		
0		2.33				2.43				2.53		

Two-conductor, flat, 600 volts

Conductor size, AWG	2-conductor			
	T	D	L	M
8	$\frac{3}{64}$	0.60 × 0.81		
6	$\frac{4}{64}$	0.75 × 0.98		
4	$\frac{4}{64}$	0.84 × 1.09		
3	$\frac{4}{64}$	0.88 × 1.16	18	$\frac{1}{2}$
2	$\frac{4}{64}$	0.88 × 1.29		
1	$\frac{5}{64}$	1.13 × 1.43		

This method of jointing eliminates solder, and, although it is thus particularly applicable to work that has to be done in a mine where the explosive hazard is high, it can, of course, be used for any (600 volts and below) job where the omission of solder seems to be justified or desirable. This type of connector is useful for emergency repairs, because it is simply and easily installed.

185. Nonsoldered Joint for Single-conductor Portable Cable (refer to Fig. 44)

1. Remove the outer jacket and insulation for a distance of approximately 5 in. from each cable end.

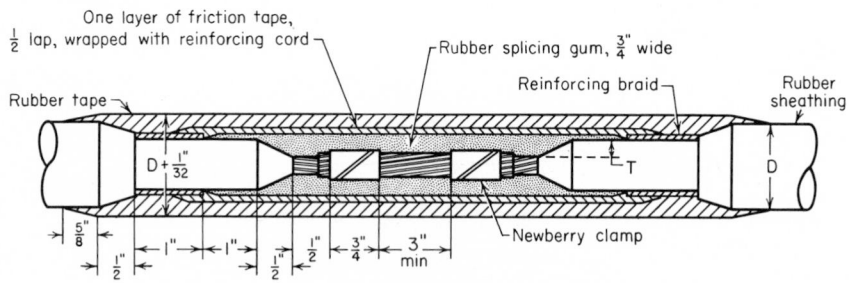

FIG. 44   *Nonsoldered single-conductor cable joint.* (*General Electric Co.*)

2. Overlap the two conductor ends, as shown in the drawing, and install two Newberry clamps at the ends of the conductors.

3. Taper the insulation on each side of the joint, leaving ½ in. of bare conductor between the end of the taper and the edge of the connector.

4. Remove the outer jacket and reinforcing braid to the final dimensions.

5. Thoroughly clean the surface to which splicing gum is to be applied and cover with a coating of rubber cement. Allow the solvent to evaporate.

6. Apply splicing gum to the dimensions as shown in Fig. 44.

7. Cover the splicing gum with one layer of friction tape, half-lapped and finally wrapped with reinforcing cord.

8. Taper the ends of the outer rubber jacket and clean the entire surface of the joint.

9. Apply a coating of rubber cement over the entire joint. When the solvent has evaporated, apply the outer jacket with wrappings of splicing gum.

10. Vulcanize the joint.

186. Nonsoldered Joint for Two-conductor (Flat) Portable Cable (refer to Fig. 45)

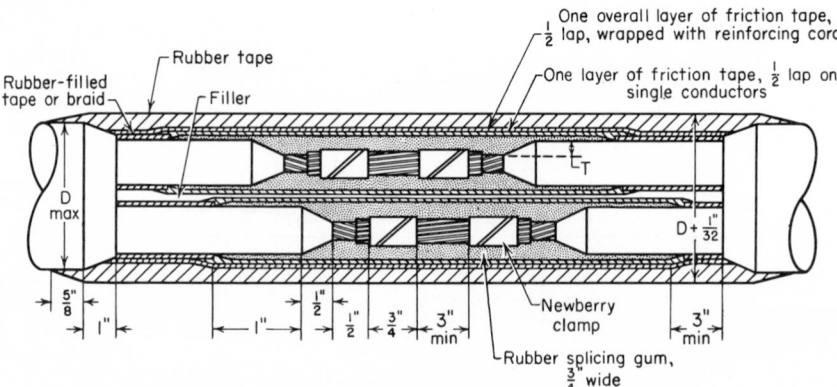

FIG. 45   *Nonsoldered two-conductor (flat) cable joint.* (*General Electric Co.*)

1. Remove the outer jacket to the dimensions shown in the drawing, making an allowance for approximately a 5-in. overlap of the conductors.

2. When the cable is supplied with jute fillers, these fillers should be laid back over the cable and reassembled later.

3. Remove sufficient insulation from each of the four cable ends to allow installation of the connectors.

4. The conductors are then connected by overlapping the two ends as shown in the drawing, and a Newberry clamp is installed at each of the conductor ends. This clamp has been used very successfully around mines for a number of years.

5. Remove the outer tape or braid to the dimensions shown.

6. Taper the conductor insulation on each side of the connectors as shown in the drawings.

7. Thoroughly clean the surface over which splicing gum is applied, and apply a coating of rubber cement. After the solvent has evaporated, wrap splicing gum to a diameter slightly greater than that on the original cable.

8. Cover each insulated conductor with a layer of friction tape half-lapped.

9. If the original cable is supplied with jute or rope fillers, they should be replaced in the interstices of the joint. If rubber fillers were used in the original cable, they should be replaced by rubber fillers (see standard instructions for splicing portable cables in Sec. **183).**

10. After the fillers have been applied, cover the insulated conductors and fillers with a layer of friction tape half-lapped and wrap with reinforcing cord (see the instructions for the splicing of standard portable cables).

11. Taper the ends of the over-all jacket, thoroughly clean the entire surface which is to be covered by rubber tape, and apply a coat of rubber cement.

12. After the solvent has evaporated, apply the outer jacket with wrappings of rubber tape to the dimensions that are shown on the drawing.

13. Vulcanize the joint.

187. Nonsoldered Joint for Two-conductor (Concentric) Portable Cable (refer to Fig. 46). 1. Remove the outer jacket to the distance shown on the drawing, allowing for the overlapping of the conductors. Note that more jacket must be removed from the left-hand end of the joint than from the right-hand end. This is necessary to make room for connecting the outer conductor later.

2. Bend back the outer conductor strands as shown in the drawing. Do not bend the strands to too short a radius, since, if the wires become kinked, it will be difficult to replace them later.

3. Remove sufficient insulation from each of the inner conductor ends.

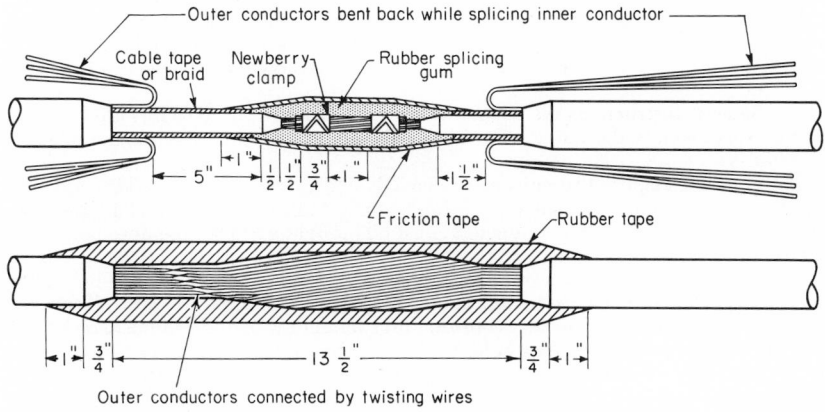

FIG. 46 *Nonsoldered two-conductor (concentric) cable joint.* (*General Electric Co.*)

4. Overlap the conductors and apply a Newberry clamp at each end. These clamps have been used for years in the mining field with satisfactory results.

5. Taper the insulation on each side of the conductor joint and remove approximately 1 in. of the cable tape or braid, starting at the maximum diameter of the taper.

6. Thoroughly clean the surface over which the splicing gum is to be applied and cover it with a layer of rubber cement.

7. After the solvent has evaporated, apply splicing gum to the dimensions as shown in Fig. 46. The diameter of the joint insulation should be slightly greater than the diameter of the original cable.

8. Wrap the insulation just applied with one layer of friction tape half-lapped.

9. The outer conductor should now be placed back over the joint. The strands should be laid back carefully, approaching as near as possible the original lay of the cable strands.

10. The conductor ends are connected together by twisting the several strands together with a pair of pliers. The excess copper is cut off and the ends bent parallel to the axis of the cable. Note that these strands are connected together at the long end of the joint where the diameter is smaller than it is directly over the inner conductor splice.

11. Thoroughly clean the entire surface to be covered with tape, and apply a coat of rubber cement.

12. After the cement solvent has evaporated, apply the outer jacket, using wrappings of splicing tape.

13. Vulcanize the joint.

188. Vulcanizers are easy to operate and can be used very successfully with little experience. These instructions should enable anyone to operate the average steam vulcanizer without any trouble. Steam vulcanizers are generally shipped without water in the jacket. The user should make sure the water is placed in the unit to the proper level before the vulcanizer is used.

Most units are equipped with a relief or safety valve. This valve is set to "pop" at a given pressure. This valve can be adjusted by removing the top and tightening the screw to increase pressure or loosening the screw to lower the pressure. The pressure control can be set to open at from 30 to 65 lb pressure and to close at from 25 to 60 lb. This control can generally be adjusted by tightening or loosening the control-spring tension in the same way as the relief valve is adjusted.

The heaters should always be covered with water to prevent their burning out. If there is no escaping of steam anywhere, a filling of water should last a considerable time, even when used daily. The water should normally be checked about once a week. The vulcanizer should be placed in a practically level position while the current is connected; otherwise the water may drain away from the immersion heaters.

Most steam vulcanizers are operated with electric heating units, but any form of heat can be used, provided it can be carefully controlled so that a constant heat is applied to the joint to be vulcanized. Gas furnaces and blowtorches have been successfully used.

189. General Instructions for Operation of Vulcanizers. Three factors are essential for the successful vulcanizing of rubber-jacketed cables: time, termperature, and cleanliness.

190. The time required to vulcanize rubber is approximately 20 min; however, this does not mean that any vulcanizing job can be done in this time. First of all, the mass of rubber, cable, and copper conductors must be brought up to temperature before the cure begins.

The outer rubber that comes in direct contact with the mold begins to cure before the inner mass, but the work must be left in the vulcanizer long enough to cure all the rubber. Therefore, the time will vary considerably, depending on the volume to be heated and the temperature of the work before it is put into the vulcanizer. For instance, in the wintertime a cable brought into the shop or repaired outdoors will require more time than if vulcanized in the hot summertime. Also, a large cable will require more time than a small one. With these factors in mind, it is readily seen that, owing to varying conditions, a definite time schedule cannot be set forth.

It will be found that in most cases the time will be between 30 and 45 min, although there are sometimes conditions that require 1 hr or even more and others that require only 20 min.

The exact length of time for curing is not known. In the first place, there is no positive schedule to follow. After a few jobs are done, the time can be estimated. It is best to leave the first few jobs in slightly longer than might seem necessary to be sure of a full cure. Then reduce the time as you gain experience. An approximate schedule for a novice is as follows:

Cable Size, In.	Time, Min
$3/4$ and smaller	20
$3/4$–$1\frac{1}{4}$	25
$1\frac{1}{4}$–$1\frac{3}{4}$	30
$1\frac{3}{4}$–$2\frac{1}{4}$	35
$2\frac{1}{4}$–3	40
3 –$3\frac{1}{2}$	50

This schedule is an estimate for complete splices. When only small patches are made, the time will be somewhat less, as the small volume of rubber and the adjacent old rubber are quickly brought up to temperature and may be cured before the mass of cable is fully heated.

Care must be taken not to undercure a joint, because undercured rubber deforms easily and therefore makes a poor joint from the abrasion standpoint. A simple method of determining an undercure is to cut in two a piece of the surplus fin, and if the fin will stick together where it was cut, the joint was undercured. Because the fin is thin, it will always cure first. Therefore, the fin might be overcured, but the joint itself might still be undercured.

This indication does not necessarily mean an unsatisfactory job but is simply mentioned as an aid to the operator.

191. Temperature for Vulcanizing. The controls on the vulcanizers are set to open at from 30 to 65 lb steam pressure and close at from 25 to 60 lb. This range under ordinary conditions provides a sufficiently accurate temperature for curing the rubber.

About the only condition that might require any change would be subzero weather during which the vulcanizer itself is exposed. In such cases the radiation is so severe that it may be necessary to increase the pressure by adjusting the control. Since cables are usually repaired indoors, however, extremely cold weather is seldom a factor.

192. Cleanliness in Vulcanizing. The important reason for vulcanizing electric-cable splices is to make them watertight and give them added strength. Obviously, it is necessary for the applied rubber to mold into a solid mass and, furthermore, stick to the old cable jacket.

One of the chief aids in obtaining these results is keeping the work clean. Oil or grease is known to be detrimental to rubber, and dust or dirt on the surface of the rubber being applied is likely to prevent its molding together. When new rubber is applied to the old cable jacket, it must be absolutely clean to obtain adhesion.

193. How to Patch a Jacket. The amount of work to be done depends on the extent of the injury. For instance, a small cut can in many cases be patched simply, whereas a severe injury may require the removal of the portion of jacket that is injured and replacing this portion with new rubber. In any case, thoroughly inspect the conductor insulation at the injury to be sure it is not also injured. If it is, the jacket should be removed for a sufficient length to repair properly the conductor insulation. It may be necessary to make a complete splice.

To vulcanize new rubber to old rubber, it is necessary to roughen the old rubber and scrape or grind off any old scale or coating at the place where the new rubber is expected to stick. The old rubber should also be prepared for 1 in. around the injured spot.

When the jacket must be removed, it will be found easier to clean and roughen the cable for about 2 in. each way beyond the portion to be removed before cutting it out.

There are two kinds of rubber used in the repair of electric cables: jacket rubber and insulating rubber.

The insulating rubber is used only for conductor insulation. The jacket rubber is used for all outside work.

When new rubber is applied to the old, proceed as follows:

1. Clean and roughen old rubber as described previously.

2. With naphtha or benzol, thoroughly clean the areas where the rubber is to be applied and allow them to dry.

3. Brush rubber cement over the surfaces to which the new rubber is expected to stick, as well as an inch or so beyond. Allow the solvent to evaporate.

4. Apply new rubber, which is supplied in tape form. If the rubber is wrapped tightly and evenly, all air is excluded, and the new rubber does not have to be built up much larger than the mold. Only a little experience is necessary to demonstrate how much rubber to apply.

5. The repair is now ready to vulcanize. Naturally a suitable mold must be on hand. Molds are made in several types and sizes to fit the particular joint in question.

The proper mold should be hot when ready to use. Swab or brush sparingly an application of mold dressing in the mold before putting in the job.

Shut mold to within $1/8$ in. of being closed, depending on size of cable, and allow to set for about 5 min to permit the rubber to soften; then close mold. When this procedure is followed, there is a better chance of filling out low places due to unevenness in wrapping. Furthermore, when a complete splice is made, there may be a distortion of core assembly if full pressure is applied before the rubber is allowed to soften.

6. After curing, remove from mold, cut off surplus fins, apply wax, and the job is finished. The joint should be allowed to cool somewhat before it is removed from the mold.

194. Temporary Vulcanizing Equipment. Frequently it is necessary to vulcanize a cable joint in the field, and no equipment is available. To take care of this condition, temporary vulcanizing equipment can be constructed.

An open-top vat of suitable size should be obtained. This vat should be large enough to allow the entire joint to be submerged in the heated liquid of the vat when the spliced cable is placed directly over the vat, allowing the cable joint to dip into the vat.

Paraffin is generally used in the vat for the vulcanizing medium, but any wax with a high enough boiling point could be used. In no case should oil be used.

After the joint has been constructed in the usual manner, it should be placed in a suitable mold. There are a number of different molds that can be easily constructed.

1. Split a piece of pipe which has approximately the same inside diameter as the completed splice. The two pieces of pipe should be held tightly on the joint by wrappings of wire or metal tape or standard "U" clamps.

2. In a metal block, drill a hole approximately the same diameter as the splice. Split the block in half, and place it over the joint. The two halves of the block should be held tightly together by means of bolts or acceptable clamps.

If it is possible, the molds should be heated up to about 275°F before they are placed over the joint. The inside of molds should also be coated with an approved mold dressing to obtain the best and most workmanlike finished splice.

195. The procedure to follow in vulcanizing a joint with the equipment of Sec. 194 is as follows:

1. Make up the joint in the usual manner.

2. Preheat the molds if possible up to 275°F, coat them with a mold dressing, and clamp them over the joint.

3. In the meantime, the paraffin in the vat should be heated and held to from 275 to 300°F by satisfactory heating equipment. Blowtorches or gas furnaces can be used for this purpose, or any available heating equipment which will hold these temperatures satisfactorily.

4. Place the joint in the heated paraffin, bearing in mind that the entire joint and mold are submerged in the liquid.

5. Hold the joint in this medium for a period of time depending on the size of joint involved and the thickness of rubber to be vulcanized, holding the temperature of the paraffin as nearly constant as possible. The approximate time required to vulcanize the joint is listed in the steam-vulcanizer instructions. The exact time for curing a splice can best be obtained by experience with the particular equipment used.

6. When the splice is cured, it should be removed from the vat and allowed to cool for a time before removing the mold.

It is natural that perfect results cannot be obtained with this temporary equipment, but a number of splices have been vulcanized by this method and all have operated satisfactorily when properly made.

The mold dressing generally used is a saturated solution of soap chips.

196. Terminal connections of conductors should be made by means of solder lugs or solderless connectors, except that No. 8 or smaller conductors may be connected to binding posts by means of clamps or screws, provided the terminal plates of the binding parts have upturned lugs. The upturned plates are necessary so that the wires will not be forced out of place as the screw or nut is tightened.

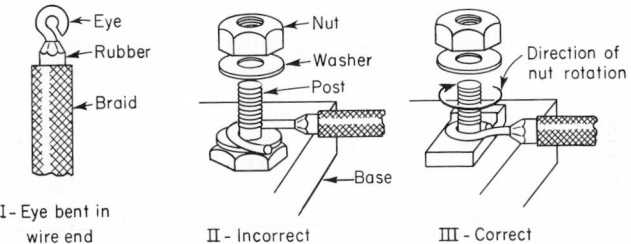

FIG. 47   *Showing how a wire should be "made up" on a binding post.*

197. The correct method of "making up" a lead wire around a binding post is shown in Fig. 47. First, an eye, of such internal diameter that it will slip over the post, is bent with the pliers in the bared-and-cleaned end of the lead wire, as illustrated at I. Then the eye is dropped down over the post (III) in such a position that rotation of the bolt or nut in tightening will tend to wrap the eye end around the post rather than to unwrap it. That is, the eye should wrap around the post in a right-handed direction, in the same direction as that in which the nut rotates while being turned on. If the eye is laid on left-handed as at II, it will unwrap and open while the nut is being turned tightly down on it.

198. When soldering wires in terminal lugs, if many lugs are to be soldered, a convenient and time-saving method of making the connections is to melt a pot of solder over a plumber's furnace, heat the lug in the solder, pour the solder in the hole in the lug, and then plunge the bared end of the conductor into it, as shown in Fig. 48. The insides of the holes of many commercial lugs are "tinned" so the solder adheres to them readily. The bared end of the conductor should also first be tinned. This may be done as follows: The end of the wire is carefully scraped with a knife or with a piece of fine sandpaper (the sandpaper is best because it cannot nick the wire) and then smeared with soldering flux and thrust into the solder pot. If a soldering stick is used, the wire must be heated in the solder before the stick compound will melt and adhere. It requires but a short time to tin the wire end in the pot.

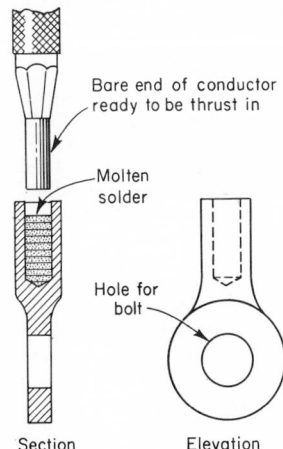

FIG. 48   *Soldering wire in lug.*

NOTE. Immediately after the tinned end is pushed into the hole in the lug, the lug should be soused with a piece of wet waste to cool it rapidly. Scrape or file off any shreds or globules of solder that adhere to the exposed surfaces of the lug and brighten it with fine sandpaper if necessary.

199. In "skinning" a wire end which is to be soldered into a lug, the insulation should be cut back just far enough so that it will abut against the shoulder of the lug, as suggested in Fig. 49, I. The appearance is very unsightly and indicates careless work if there is a gap between the shoulder and the insulation, as at II. If, because of some mishap, there results a connection which has the appearance of II, a partial correction can be made by filling the gap with servings of tape, as shown at III. The tape of the standard ¾-in. width should be torn into strips about ¼ in. wide before applying.

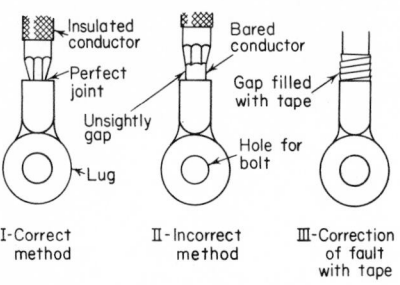

I-Correct method
II-Incorrect method
III-Correction of fault with tape

FIG. 49 *Finished connections.*

200. Only enough molten solder should be poured into the hole in the lug to fill it almost to the brim when the conductor is in position. If too much is poured in, it will be squeezed out by the wire and will flow over the lug. It must then be removed at a sacrifice of time.

201. To ensure proper adhesion between wire, solder, and lug the temperature of all three must be above the melting point of solder when they are brought together in soldering. If this condition is not fulfilled, only a good friction fit of all three parts will result. Such a friction fit does not afford a good electrical connection. To secure maximum mechanical strength and electrical conductivity, it is absolutely essential that the solder be maintained at the melting point until it has thoroughly permeated the interstices of the conductor.

202. The wire terminal and lug should be held in the molten solder until they acquire the temperature of the solder. To prevent adhesion of solder to the outside of the lug a light oil or possibly soft soap should be applied to its outer surfaces. Be careful to see that no oil is permitted to reach the inside of the lug. It will be found advisable, when holding the bared ends of heavy conductors in the solder pot, to wrap the insulation with a rag previously wrung out in cold water to prevent, in so far as is possible, the melting of the insulating compound and the consequent smearing of the terminal. Any such smearing will not impair the effectiveness of the joint if it is properly made, though it will detract from the appearance of the finished job.

203. Another method of soldering wires in lugs is to heat the lug with a blowtorch flame. When the lug is sufficiently hot, wire solder is fed into the hole. The solder melts and the bared conductor end is then thrust into it, as above described. However, the use of a blowtorch in this way should be avoided if possible, as it blackens the exposed surfaces of the lug. A cleaning with fine sandpaper is then necessary, and it requires considerable time.

204. Some suggestions for handling blowtorches are: Only the very best grade of gasoline should be used, and it must be clean and kept in a clean can; otherwise the burner will become clogged. Never try to fill a torch from a big can. A pint or quart receptacle should be used for this purpose. If this is done, the torch can be held in one hand and filled with the other without danger of overfilling or spilling. The torch should be a little more than two-thirds full, so that there will be room for sufficient air to prevent the necessity of frequent repumping to maintain the pressure. See that the filler plug is closed tight to prevent the escape of air from tank. The fiber washer under the plug must be replaced when worn out. Common washing soap rubbed into thread and joints will stop leaks. The pump should be in good working order; a few drops of lubricating oil well rubbed in will soften the pump washer. Do not turn the needle valve too tight, as there is danger of enlarging the orifice of the burner. See that the burner is sufficiently heated when starting. One filling of the drip cup is generally sufficient if the flame is shielded from draft while heating the burner; if it is not, fill the cup again and light the gasoline as before. A long or yellow flame or raw gasoline shooting from the burner shows that the burner is not hot enough to properly generate gas. When a gasoline torch is used as much as 90 per cent of its heat may be dissipated, without doing any work whatever. When performing most blowtorch operations, a great part of this heat may be readily saved by making a shield of sheet iron or asbestos to direct the heat to the object to be heated.

205. Wire Connectors. The selection of proper wire connectors for various sizes, combinations, and types of conductors is an extremely important factor in a sound electrical installation.

Wire connectors are generally classified as either thermal or pressure types.

Thermal connectors include those in which heat is applied to form soldered, brazed, or welded joints and terminals. Soldered joints and lugs for copper conductors have been used for many years and, except for service wire and ground connections, are still permitted. However, soldering is rarely used in modern installations because of the greater dependability and installation ease of present-day solderless pressure connectors. And although it is possible to solder aluminum conductors, this is not recommended unless the installer is fully familiar with the special techniques involved. On the other hand, welded aluminum connections in circular-mil sizes are very satisfactory and provide the best possible joint for aluminum conductors. At the same time, this process is generally restricted to the types of installations in which the cost of the necessary equipment and skilled labor can be justified.

Grounding grids or bussing are widely used on large construction jobs, and grounding connections must be permanent in the interests of safety. For joining bare copper conductors together or to reinforcing rods, ground rods, or steel surfaces, a mold-type welding process is highly recommended. This process consists of a mold and starting and mixing powder. After conductors, sleeves, and/or lugs are placed in the mold a flint gun is used to ignite the starting powder. This forms a liquid copper, which fuses conductors into a solid mass and welds a permanent electrical connection. Offered by several manufacturers, the mold-type welding process can be performed easily without special training.

206. Solderless Connectors. A solderless pressure connector is a device which establishes the connection between two or more conductors or between one or more conductors and a terminal by means of mechanical pressure and without the use of solder. This broad definition includes the bulk of solderless connectors and terminal lugs.

207. Screw-on Pigtail Connectors. The common screw-on pigtail connector (see Fig. 50) consists of an insulated cap made of plastic, Bakelite, porcelain, or nylon and an internal threaded core with or without a metallic coil spring. Such connectors require no hand tools and are simply twisted onto appropriate combinations of bared conductors. Connector types consisting of metallic spring coils (copper-coated or steel) are listed by Underwriters' Laboratories as pressure cable connectors, which means that they can be used for connecting branch-circuit conductors No. 14 and larger according to listed sizes and combinations; and in certain instances, these connectors can also be used as fixture-splicing connectors in which case they will be dual-listed by Underwriters.

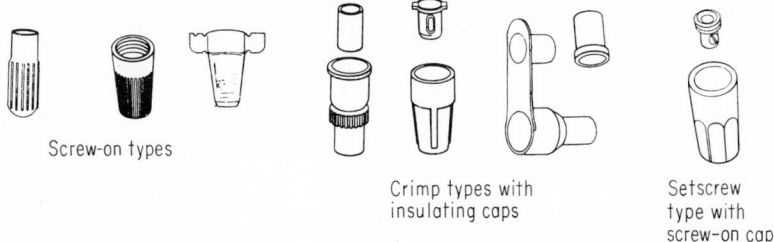

Screw-on types

Crimp types with
insulating caps

Setscrew
type with
screw-on cap

FIG. 50 *Typical solderless pigtail connectors.* (*Electrical Construction and Maintenance.*)

Connectors without metallic coil springs are regarded as fixture-type splicing connectors for joining fixture wires or branch-circuit wires to fixture wires in a combination of sizes from No. 18 to No. 10 within the listed capacities of the connector. They are not acceptable for general use in branch-circuit wiring.

Most of the screw-on connectors are designed for copper-to-copper wire connections. An exception is the type with a coated-steel coil spring, which is suitable for aluminum-to-aluminum wire connections as well as copper-to-aluminum connections. However, no pressure connector, including the screw-on type, is approved or recommended for splicing aluminum and copper conductors together where the two different metals are in direct physical contact with each other in **wet locations.**

With screw-on-type connectors, solid conductors are inserted parallel into the connector. Then the connector is twisted, thus forming a locking action on the conductors and providing a dependable connection. Stranded wires in the smaller sizes are twisted together before the connector is installed. And in all cases, proper size connectors should be selected to accommodate the size and combination of conductors involved in each splice.

Maximum voltage ratings for screw-on connectors are 600 volts (or 1,000 volts inside a fixture or sign), although some types cannot be used on circuits of over 300 volts. Also, temperature ratings will vary according to the type of insulating cap. Data for voltage and temperature ratings of the various connectors can be obtained from the individual manufacturer's catalog.

208. Bolted-type pressure connectors include those for making pigtail, straight, tee, or terminal connections. Such connectors depend on the applied force of bolts or screws to produce the clamping and contact pressures between conductors and the connector. Figure 51 shows typical examples.

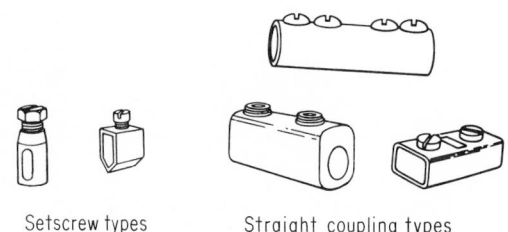

Setscrew types   Straight coupling types

FIG. 51 *Typical coupling-type solderless pressure connectors.* (*Electrical Construction and Maintenance.*)

For making pigtail connections in wire combinations up to No. 10, set-screw connectors with separate insulated caps, which thread onto the connectors after securing the wires, are readily available. These connectors are used in branch-circuit wiring, fixture hanging, and equipment hookups. The only tool required is a screwdriver, and the connectors can be reused. As such, they are especially recommended in installations where wiring connections will be changed frequently. Various set-screw connectors with thread-on insulated caps are suitable as pressure wire connectors and/or fixture-splicing connectors according to individual manufacturer's listings (see Fig. 50).

Other types of bolted connectors are available for practically any desired wire combinations, sizes, or arrangements. Such connectors are constructed of copper, bronze, or alloys of similar metals for use with copper conductors. Connectors for joining aluminum wires together are constructed of aluminum, tin-plated silicon bronze or tin-plated copper alloy materials.

Where copper conductors will be connected to aluminum conductors, connectors should be selected which are designed for this purpose, and which provide bimetal or tinned spacers in other than dry locations. The bimetal or tinned spacers permit separation of aluminum and copper conductors, thus preventing the possibility of galvanic corrosion. Careful compliance with manufacturers' recommendations as to cleaning aluminum conductors, applying connector aids, and properly positioning the aluminum and copper conductors will provide a satisfactory joint.

209. Run and Tap Connectors. Many forms of bolted connectors, such as shown in Fig. 52, are designed for making branch connections from main conductors. In such instances, minimum and maximum wire sizes are listed for both main and branch (tap) ranges. Such ranges in wire sizes are listed for each connector, and for satisfactory connections should be carefully observed. Split-bolt, clamp-type, gutter-tap, and parallel cable-tap connectors are a few of the common types used for splicing branch conductors to main conductors. Except for the parallel cable-tap type, these con-

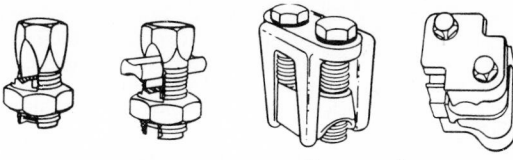

Split-bolt types   Clamp-on types

FIG. 52 *Typical run and tap solderless pressure connectors. (Electrical Construction and Maintenance.)*

nectors must be taped after the wires have been connected. Some parallel cable-tap connectors feature a two-piece molded-plastic cover that fits over the connector and covers uninsulated parts. This eliminates the time required for taping, and makes it possible to remove the connector quickly if this is a factor to be considered.

210. Bolted-type Lugs. Wires are fastened to bolted-type lugs by one or more bolts, depending on design and ampere ratings. Two- to four-barrel lugs are used to terminate multiple conductors.

211. Terminal Blocks. Where numerous connections are necessary, as in complex control circuitry, consideration should be given to the use of terminal blocks and terminal block kits made available by a number of manufacturers. Such assemblies contain bolted-type terminal blocks. The terminal blocks can be obtained in fully assembled or individual blocks, and the terminals are available for a wide range of wire sizes. With these units, connections can be made quickly, and all terminals can be readily identified, thus simplifying trouble-shooting or later changes in circuitry. And the terminal blocks can be installed in standard pull boxes or auxiliary gutters.

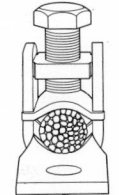

212. Compression-type connectors and lugs include those in which hand, pneumatic, or hydraulic tools indent or crimp tube-like sleeves which hold one or more conductors. The crimping action changes the size and shape of the connector; and a properly crimped joint deforms the conductor strands enough to provide good electrical conductivity and mechanical strength. With the smaller sizes of solid wires, some indenter splice caps require that the wires be twisted together before being placed in the cap and crimped, whereas others are intended to be inserted parallel. This will vary with the type of indentations, and the

FIG. 53 *Solderless connectors of pressure-washer type. (National Electric Div. of H. K. Porter Co., Inc.)*

manufacturer's recommendations on the correct method of making the splice should be followed. See Figs. 50 and 55.

One of the disadvantages of indenter or crimp connectors is that special tools are required to make the joint. However, this can be justified by the assurance of a dependable joint and low cost of connectors.

 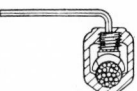  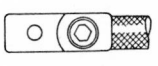

(a)-Nat. Elec. Prod. Corp.   (b)-Thomas and Betts Co.   (c)-Thomas and Betts Co.   (d)-Trumbull Elec. Mfg. Co.

FIG. 54 *Solderless lugs of pressure-washer type.*

213. Connector Designations and Markings. Connectors are designed for either copper or aluminum conductors, or both. Connectors with no markings are generally suitable for copper conductors only. Where a connector bears the marking AL, it is designed solely for the connection of aluminum conductors. And connectors marked CU–AL are for use with either copper or aluminum conductors.

Straight coupling connectors marked CU-AL are ideal where aluminum conductors are run to equipment with terminals designed for copper conductors. In such cases, a short piece of copper wire extends from the equipment terminals to one side of the straight coupling connector; and the aluminum conductor is connected to the opposite side. On the other hand, terminals in many new meter sockets, switches, and panel boards are designed for connection to either copper or aluminum wires. If this is the case, a statement to that effect will appear on the inside of the enclosure, and no markings will be found on the terminals.

Crimp – type lugs

FIG. 55 *Typical compression connectors, crimp or indenter types. (Electrical Construction and Maintenance.)*

214. Splice Kits for Circuits over 600 Volts. For electrical connections in circuits rated above 600 volts, proper insulation is as important as providing the actual continuity of the current path. Splices and terminals must be made carefully in full conformity with instructions of connector manufacturers.

Several manufacturers feature splicing kits for making high-voltage splices. These kits will vary according to the circuit voltage and type of cable (interlocked armor, neoprene-jacketed with or without shielding, or lead-covered) for the particular conductor insulations.

A common high-voltage connecting device is the pothead, which is used to connect cables to equipment or to other circuits. A pothead is a sealed terminal which provides connection to the conductor in the cable, provides moisture-proofing for the conductor's insulation, and seals in cable-impregnating oil. Stress cones are also available in kit forms.

215. Splices in bare copper aerial conductors may be made by means of a soldered splice as shown in Fig. 56, by means of a solderless splicing sleeve as shown in Fig. 57, or by means of a rolled or drawn copper connector as shown in Figs. 58 and 59. A soldered splice should be mechanically and electrically secure before solder is applied. There should be at least five turns in the neck of a splice to ensure that the unsoldered splice will be as strong as the wire of which it is made. All splices in wires which carry electricity should be soldered in the neck. It is not always necessary to solder the end turns.

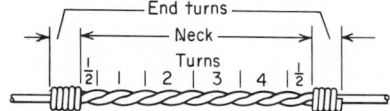

FIG. 56 *Bare-copper-line-wire splice.*

Joints made with seamless solderless splicing sleeves (Fig. 57) are generally considered to be more reliable than soldered joints. The sleeves are made of high-con-

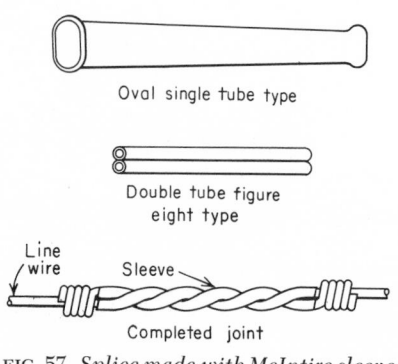

Oval single tube type

Double tube figure eight type

Line wire · Sleeve

Completed joint

FIG. 57 *Splice made with McIntire sleeve.*

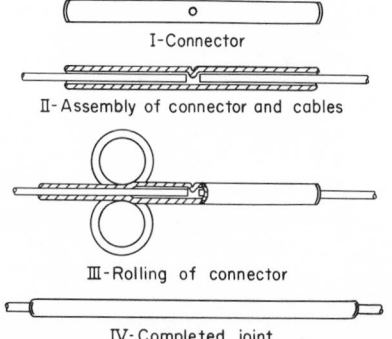

I-Connector

II-Assembly of connector and cables

III-Rolling of connector

IV-Completed joint

FIG. 58 *Rolled seamless connector for bare copper wire. (Anaconda Wire and Cable Co.)*

ductivity copper and may be of the double-tube figure-eight type or of the oval single-tube type. These sleeves are sometimes called McIntire sleeves. In making a splice, the sleeve should be twisted with long-handled tongs for 3½ or 4 turns in a direction so that the helix of the twisted sleeve will be in the opposite direction to the lay of the strand.

A splice of the highest grade is undoubtedly made with a rolled or drawn seamless connector. The drawn connector will produce a splice of the lowest resistance and highest tensile strength. The rolled seamless connector consists of a piece of seamless copper tubing with an inside lacquered surface. Embedded in the lacquer are hard carbon particles that lock both ways on the conductor and in the connector as the connector is rolled on the wire. The connector is rolled on with a simple tool, which exerts heavy pressure, fitting the wire so tightly that internal corrosion is prevented, and therefore the ohmic resistance of the splice remains constant. Rolling the connector works the metal so that it is hardened and lengthened to give a long, sure grip on the wire.

Figure 58 illustrates the connector, assembly of joint, method of rolling, and finished joint. The rolling tool employed is shown in Fig. 59.

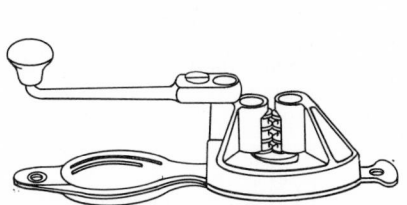

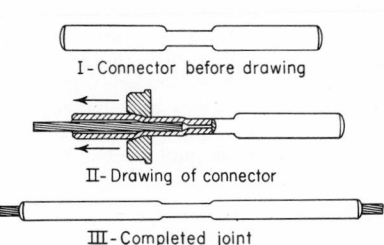

I - Connector before drawing

II - Drawing of connector

III - Completed joint

FIG. 59 *Rolling tool for applying rolled seamless connectors. (Anaconda Wire and Cable Co.)*

FIG. 60 *Drawn seamless copper connector for bare copper wire. (Anaconda Wire and Cable Co.)*

Drawn seamless connectors consist of a short piece of seamless copper tubing with its center reduced for a short distance to a diameter slightly less than that of the die to be used in making the splice. The conductors to be joined are inserted the full length of the opening in each end of the connector. The connector is made large enough to fit easily over the conductor ends. The connector is compressed radially over the conductor by means of a split die started at the reduced portion of the connector and drawn over each end in turn. Figure 60 illustrates the connector, assembly of joint, method of drawing, and finished joint.

216. Splices in covered aerial conductors are made in the same manner as for bare aerial conductors of the same material. The splice may be covered simply with friction tape as shown in Fig. 61, but it is preferable to apply rubber tape covered with two layers of friction tape as shown in Fig. 62.

217. Splices in steel, or copper and steel, stranded cables are generally made with seamless solderless splicing sleeves in the same manner as described in Sec. **215** for bare copper wires. Steel sleeves are used for all-steel wires, and either copper or steel sleeves for the combination cables.

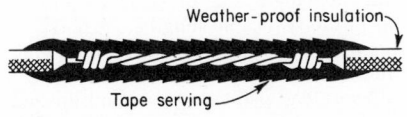

Weather-proof insulation

Tape serving

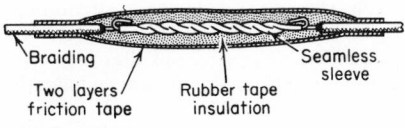

Braiding

Two layers friction tape

Rubber tape insulation

Seamless sleeve

FIG. 61 *Western Union splice insulated with tape.*

FIG. 62 *Splice in covered conductor.*

218. Splices in copperweld, or copperweld and copper, cables are made in the same manner as for bare copper wires discussed in Sec. **215.** Two sleeves should be used for making each splice in extra-high-strength cable.

219. Splices in all-aluminum cable, or aluminum cable, steel-reinforced, are made by means of twisted solderless oval sleeves or solderless compression sleeves. The former joints are made with oval single-tube sleeves of seamless aluminum similar to the copper sleeves used for splicing copper wires as shown in Fig. 57. For all-aluminum cables, one sleeve is sufficient for each joint. For aluminum cable, steel-reinforced,

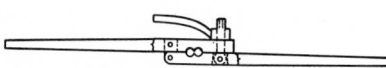

FIG. 63 *Twisting wrench for applying aluminum twisting sleeves. (Aluminum Co. of America.)*

two sleeves should be used for each joint, except for Nos. 8 and 7 cables, where one sleeve is sufficient. Two twisting wrenches (Fig. 63) are employed for twisting the sleeve and cable into the finished joint. The wrenches should be rotated in a clockwise direction when facing the mouth of the sleeve. Before making the joint be sure that the inside of the sleeves and the ends of the cable are perfectly clean and free from dirt and grease. The following methods of making the joints are recommended by the Aluminum Co. of America.

1. For aluminum cable, steel-reinforced (ACSR), sizes 4/0 to 1/0, give each sleeve 4½ complete twists distributed as shown in Fig. 64. This requires setting one wrench at the inner end of each sleeve and setting the other wrench three times progressing toward the outer end of each sleeve. Make these in the order shown in the illustration. At the ends of the joint the wrench should not be less than ¼ in. from the end of the sleeve.

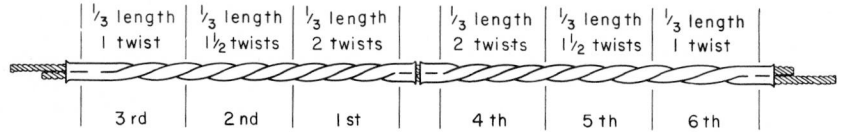

FIG. 64 *Joint for ACSR cable sizes 4/0 to 1/0. (Aluminum Co. of America.)*

2. For aluminum cable, steel-reinforced (ACSR), sizes 1 to 6, give each sleeve four complete uniform twists as shown in Fig. 65. This requires one setting of the twisting wrenches at the ends of each sleeve. The wrenches should not be less than ¼ in. from the end of the sleeve.

3. For twisting joints consisting of a single sleeve, as used on all-aluminum cables and sizes 7 and 8 ACSR, give the middle third as many complete twists as it will stand (from 2 to 3½ depending upon the size of cable and length of sleeve). Then give each end third length one complete twist.

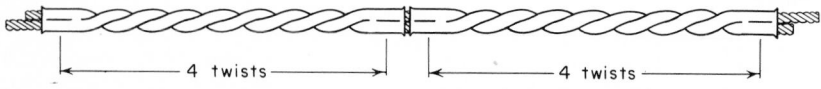

FIG. 65 *Joint for ACSR cable sizes 1 to 6. (Aluminum Co. of America.)*

220. Compression joints on all-aluminum cable are made by compressing a seamless aluminum sleeve (Fig. 66) over the butted ends of the two cable lengths. A portable hydraulic compressor and dies are required for making these joints. The following method of making a joint is recommended by the Aluminum Co. of America.

1. Impregnate the cable ends thoroughly with red-lead paint (red lead and linseed oil) by dipping them in a bucket of paint a little deeper than one-half the length of the joint.

2. Slip the cable ends into the joint, taking care that they meet exactly at the middle.

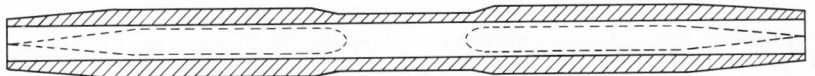

FIG. 66   *Seamless aluminum sleeve for compression joint in all-aluminum cables.* (*Aluminum Co. of America.*)

3. Compress the joint, starting at the center and working. toward the ends, allowing dies always to overlap previous position.

For old or blackened cable, each strand should be scraped or sand-papered clean. The bore of the joint is large enough to make it easy to insert the end of the cable after the strands have been opened up, cleaned, and rearranged.

In making a repair joint between a piece of new cable and a piece of old cable, the most convenient method is first to run the end of the old cable clear through the joint, then open up and clean the end of each strand for a distance equal to one-half the length of the joint. Replace the strands, impregnate with red-lead paint, and pull the cable back until the end is exactly in the middle of the joint. Then insert the new cable at the outer end of the joint after first removing grease from the strands and impregnating with red-lead paint.

221. Compression joints for most aluminum cable, steel-reinforced, consist as illustrated in Fig. 67 of a steel compression sleeve (item 1) on the steel core and an aluminum compression sleeve (item 2) on the complete cable. The over-all compression sleeve is fitted with two holes through which a heavy red-lead filler is injected. The holes are sealed with aluminum plugs (item 3). The following method of making a joint is recommended by the Aluminum Co. of America.

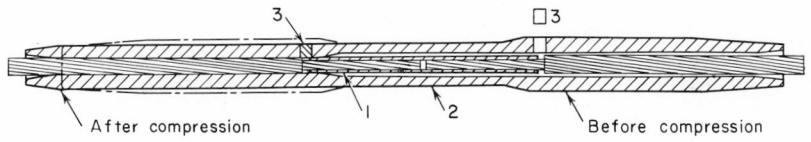

FIG. 67   *Compression joint for ACSR cable.* (*Aluminum Co. of America.*)

1. Before applying the joint see that its bore and the ends of cable to be jointed are free from grease and dirt, i.e., thoroughly clean.

2. Slip the aluminum compression joint over one cable end and back out of the way along the cable.

3. Using a hack saw, cut off the aluminum strands, exposing the steel core for a distance of a little more than half the length of the steel compression joint. Use care not to nick the steel core with the saw. Before doing this, serve the cable with wire just back of the cut.

4. Insert the steel core into the steel compression joint, bringing the ends exactly to the center.

5. Compress the steel compression joint, beginning at the center and working out toward the ends, allowing dies always to overlap the previous position.

6. Remove serving from the cable and slip the aluminum compression joint up over the steel compression joint. Center the aluminum joint by sighting the ends of the steel joint through the filler holes in the aluminum joint.

7. Using a calking gun (¼-in. round nozzle, maximum), inject heavy red lead (approximately 93 per cent red lead, 7 per cent linseed oil by weight) through both holes provided in the aluminum joint until the space between the aluminum joint and the steel joint is completely filled. This can be observed through the filling holes.

8. Insert the aluminum plugs in the filler holes and hammer them firmly in place. They will be completely locked during compression.

9. Compress the aluminum compression joint, starting at the center and working toward the ends, allowing dies always to overlap the previous position.

Some types of aluminum cable, steel-reinforced, have such a large percentage of steel that the steel compression sleeve of the above joint has a larger diameter than the complete cable. This necessitates the use of the joint shown in Fig. 68. One end of the over-all aluminum sleeve is counterbored so that this end of the aluminum sleeve can be slipped over the steel sleeve. The space between the counterbore and the cable is filled with a third aluminum sleeve (item 4). The procedure in making such a joint is in general the same as previously described. It is self-evident, however, that the

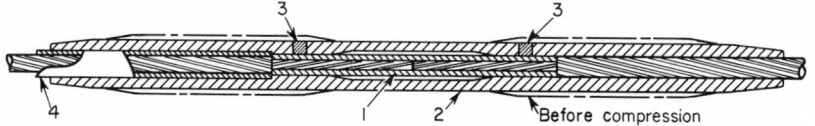

FIG. 68 *Compression joint for ACSR cable with large steel core. (Aluminum Co. of America.)*

aluminum joint (item 2) must be slipped over the cable with that end which has the smaller bore first, and also the sleeve (item 3) must be slipped on the other end of the cable — both before the steel joint (item 1) is applied. After the steel joint is applied and before the aluminum joint is slipped into place, the sleeve is slipped along until flush with the ends of the aluminum strands. Otherwise the procedure is the same as previously described for making compression joints in aluminum cable, steel-reinforced.

DIVISION THREE

Circuits and Circuit Calculations

TYPES OF CIRCUITS

1. A series circuit is one in which all components are connected in tandem as in Figs. 1 and 2. The current at every point of a series circuit is the same. Series circuits find their most important commercial application in series street lighting. They are seldom if ever used in this country for the transmission of power.

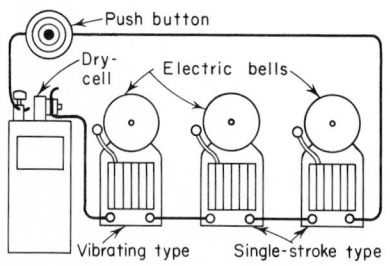

FIG. 1 *Series electric-bell circuit.*

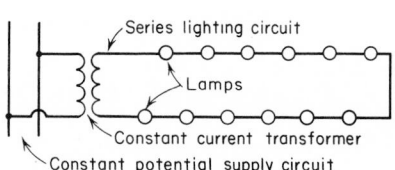

FIG. 2 *Series street-lighting circuit.*

2. Multiple, parallel, or shunt circuits are those in which the components are so arranged that the current divides between them (Figs. 3 and 4). Commercially, the distinction between multiple and series circuits is that in series lighting circuits the current is maintained constant and the generated emf varies with the load whereas with multiple circuits the current through the generator varies with the load and the generator emf is maintained practically constant.

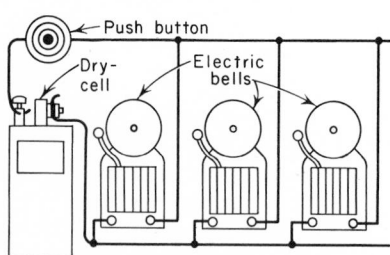

FIG. 3 *Electric bells in parallel.*

3. Adding receivers in parallel on multiple circuits is really equivalent to increasing the cross section of the imaginary conductor formed by all the receivers in parallel between the + and the − sides of the circuit.

4. The distribution of current in a multiple circuit is shown in Fig. 5. Motors, heating devices, or other equipment requiring electricity for their operation could be substituted for the incandescent lamps if the proper current values were substituted for those shown. Note that the current in the main conductors decreases toward the end of the run and that the current supplied by

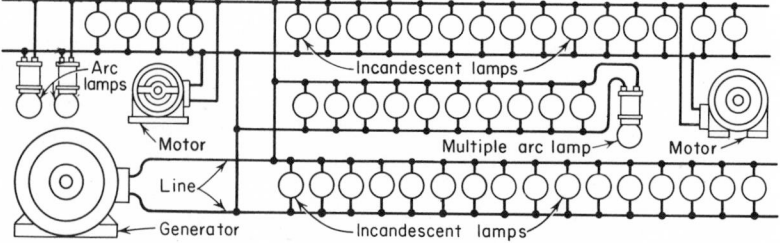

FIG. 4 *A multiple circuit for light and power.*

3–2

the source—the generator—is equal to the sum of the currents required by all the components. The voltage at the end of the run is less than that at the generator.

5. A multiple-series or parallel-series circuit consists of a number of minor circuits in series with each other and with several of these series circuits then connected in parallel, as shown in Figs. 6 and 7.

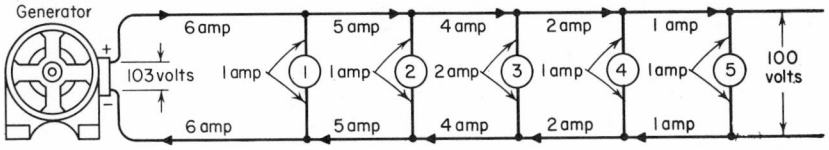

FIG. 5 *Multiple-circuit currents.*

Incandescent lamps and motors used in railway work are sometimes arranged in this way. For example, on a railway car operating from a 600-volt third rail, the 120-volt lamps are connected 5 in series (see Fig. 6). The motors on railway cars which operate from a 3,000-volt d-c overhead trolley wire are usually connected 2 in series so that the voltage per motor will be only 1,500 volts (see Fig. 7).

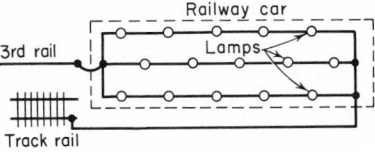

FIG. 6 *Multiple-series circuit supplying lamps on a railway car.*

6. A series-multiple or series-parallel circuit is one wherein a number of minor circuits are first connected in parallel and then several of the parallel-connected minor circuits are connected in series across a source of emf as in Fig. 8. This method of connection is seldom used. (There appears to be a difference of opinion as to what constitutes a series-multiple and what a multiple-series circuit. The definitions of Secs. **5** and **6** are in accordance with the practice of the General Electric and Westinghouse companies.)

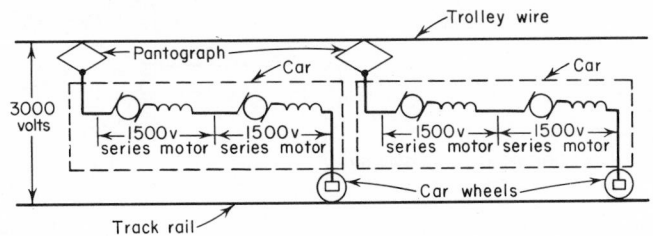

FIG. 7 *Multiple-series circuit supplying motors on railway cars.*

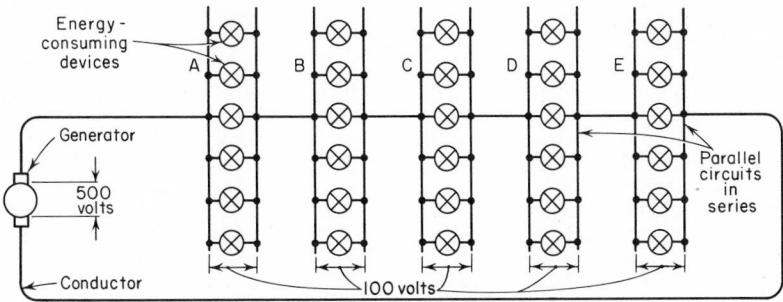

FIG. 8 *A series-parallel or series-multiple circuit.*

7. A divided circuit (Fig. 9) is really one form of multiple or parallel circuit. The distinction between the two sorts appears to be that, as ordinarily used, the term "divided" refers to an isolated group of a few conductors in parallel rather than to a group of a large number of conductors in parallel.

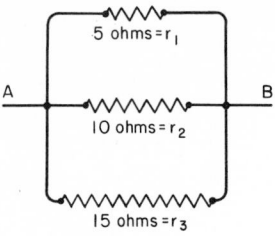

FIG. 9   *A divided circuit.*

8. The joint resistance of a number of conductors in parallel can be computed with the following formula. There should be as many terms in the denominator of the formula as there are conductors in parallel.

$$R = \cfrac{1}{\cfrac{1}{r_1} + \cfrac{1}{r_2} + \cfrac{1}{r_3} + \cfrac{1}{r_4}}, \text{ etc.} \tag{1}$$

Example. What is the joint resistance of the conductors in the divided circuit shown in Fig. 9? In other words, what is the resistance from A to B?

Solution. Substitute in the formula:

$$R = \cfrac{1}{\cfrac{1}{r_1} + \cfrac{1}{r_2} + \cfrac{1}{r_3}} = \cfrac{1}{\cfrac{1}{5} + \cfrac{1}{10} + \cfrac{1}{15}} = \cfrac{1}{\cfrac{6}{30} + \cfrac{3}{30} + \cfrac{2}{30}} = \cfrac{1}{\cfrac{11}{30}} = 1 \times \frac{30}{11} = 2.73 \text{ ohms}$$

9. Multiple circuits are employed for the distribution of electrical energy for all lighting and power work with the exception of street lighting, where series circuits frequently are used.

10. The complete electric system from the generating plant to the particular piece of equipment utilizing the electrical energy for heating, lighting, power, etc., may be divided into three main parts. These are the transmission system, the distribution system, and the interior wiring in the building where the energy is utilized. Two simple complete electric systems illustrating the component parts are shown in Figs. 10 and 11.

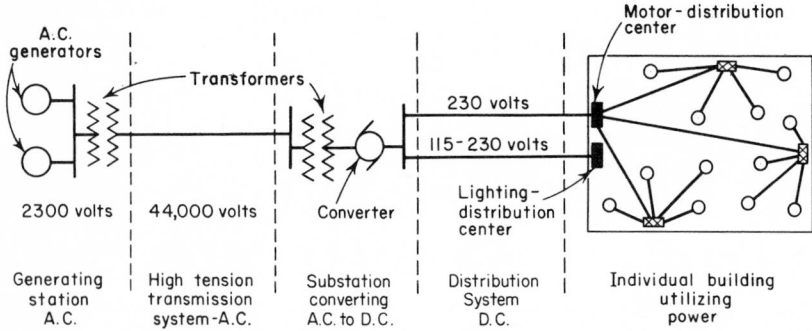

FIG. 10   *Simple complete electric system, generating and transmitting alternating current, distributing direct current.*

All wires of a circuit are represented for simplicity by a single line. Voltages commonly used for the different parts of the system are indicated on the figures. In the system shown in Fig. 10 the electricity is generated as alternating current at 2,300 volts. At the generating station it is stepped up to 44,000 volts and transmitted at this voltage over the transmission system to the substation. In the substation the energy is converted by means of a rotary converter to direct current. From the substation the energy is distributed over two distribution systems to the different buildings. One of these distribution systems is two-wire, 230-volt direct current for the motor load, and the other is three-wire, 115- to 230-volt direct current supplying the energy for lighting. In the system of Fig. 11 the energy is generated, transmitted, and distributed as alternating current throughout. This is more common.

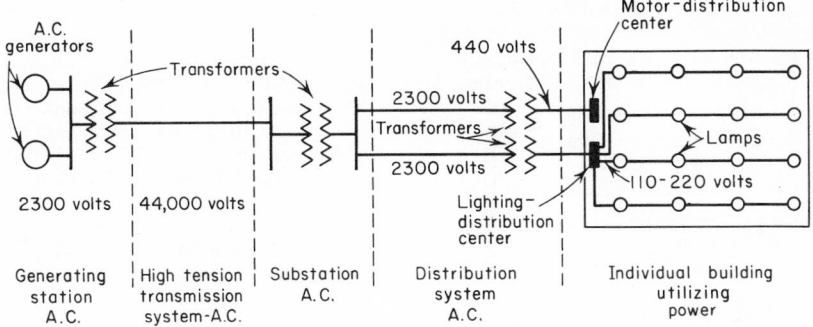

FIG. 11 *Simple complete electric system, generating, transmitting, and distributing alternating current.*

11. A feeder (or feeder circuit) (Figs. 12 and 13) is a set of conductors in a distributing system extending from the original source of energy in the installation to a distributing center and having no other circuits connected to it between the source and the center. The source may be a generating station or a substation or, in the case of building or house wiring, a connection to the service conductors from the street (see Figs. 12 and 13).

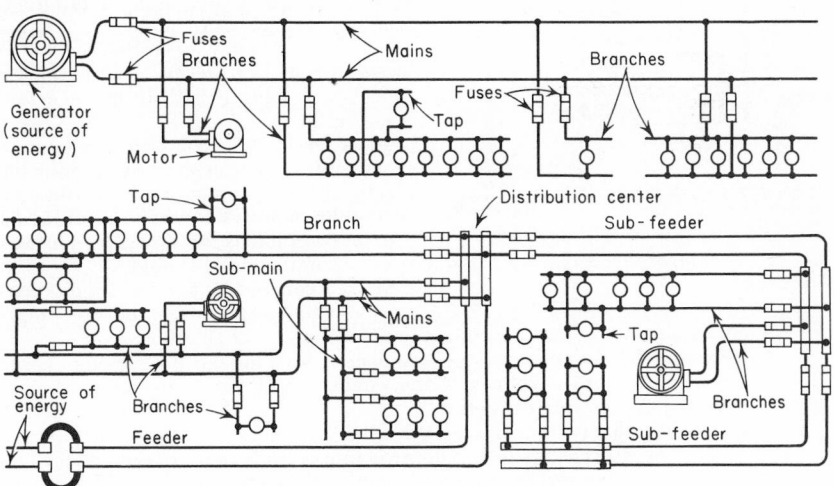

FIG. 12 *Diagram illustrating circuit nomenclature.*

12. A subfeeder is an extension, fed through a cutout, of a feeder or of another subfeeder, from one distributing center to another and having no other circuit connected to it between the two distributing centers.

13. A main (Figs. 12 and 13) is any supply circuit to which other energy-consuming circuits (submains, branches, or services) are connected through automatic cutouts (fuses or circuit breakers) at different points along its length and which is of the same size wire for its entire length and which has no cutouts in series with it for its entire length. Where a main is supplied by a feeder, the main is frequently of smaller wire than the feeder which serves it. An energy-utilizing device is never connected directly to a main, a cutout always being interposed between the device and the main.

14. A submain (Fig. 12) is a subsidiary main, fed through a cutout from a main or from another submain, to which branch circuits or services are connected through cutouts. A submain is usually of smaller wire than the main or other submain which serves it.

15. A branch or branch circuit (Fig. 12) is a set of conductors feeding, through an automatic cutout (from a distribution center, main, or submain) to which one or more energy-consuming devices are connected directly, i.e., without the interposition of additional cutouts. The only cutout associated with a branch is the one through which the branch is fed at the main, submain, or distribution center.

16. A tap or tap circuit (Fig. 12) is a circuit which serves a single energy-utilizing device and is connected directly to a branch without the interposition of a cutout.

17. A distributing or distribution center in an electrical-energy distribution system is the location at which a feeder, subfeeder, or main connects to a number of subordinate circuits which it serves. The switches and automatic cutouts for the control and protection of the subcircuits are, usually, grouped at the distributing center. In interior-wiring parlance, a distributing center is often an arrangement or group of fittings whereby two or more minor circuits are connected at a common location to another larger circuit. A panel board or a group of porcelain cutouts is a distribution center (see Fig. 12).

18. A service is the conductors and equipment for delivering electric energy from the electrical supply system to the wiring system of the premises served.

A service cable is the service conductors made up in the form of cable.

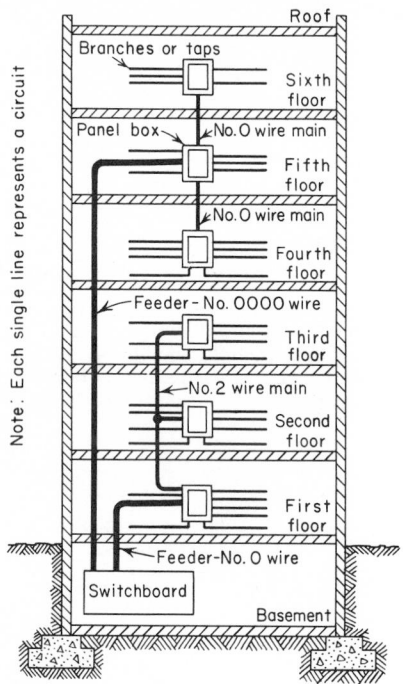

FIG. 13 *Examples of feeders, mains, and branches.*

Service conductors are the supply conductors which extend from the street main or from transformers to the service equipment of the premises supplied.

A service drop is the overhead service conductors from the last pole or other aerial support to and including the splices, if any, connecting to the service-entrance conductors at the building or other structure.

A service lateral is that portion of underground service conductors between the street main, including any risers at a pole or other structure or from transformers, and the first point of connection to the service-entrance conductors in a terminal box inside or outside the building wall. Where there is no terminal box, or meter or other enclosure with adequate space, the point of connection shall be considered to be the point of entrance of the service conductors into the building.

Service-entrance Conductors, Overhead System. The service conductors between the terminals of the service equipment and a point usually outside the building, clear of building walls, where joined by tap or splice to the service drop.

Service-entrance Conductors, Underground System. The service conductors between the terminals of the service equipment and the point of connection to the service lateral.

Where service equipment is located outside the building walls, there may be no service-entrance conductors or they may be entirely outside the building.

Service Equipment. The necessary equipment, usually consisting of circuit-breaker or switch and fuses and their accessories located near point of entrance of supply conductors to a building and intended to constitute the main control and means of cutoff for the supply to that building.

ELECTRICAL SYSTEMS

19. Electrical Systems. There are several systems that can be used for distributing electrical energy over the various arrangements of circuits previously described. They are as follows:

1. Direct-current two-wire (Fig. 14).
2. Direct-current three-wire (Fig. 15).
3. Single-phase two-wire (Fig. 14).
4. Single-phase three-wire (Fig. 15).
5. Two-phase four-wire (Fig. 17).
6. Two-phase three-wire (Fig. 18).
7. Two-phase five-wire (Fig. 19).
8. Three-phase three-wire (Fig. 20).
9. Three-phase four-wire (Fig. 21).

It is generally not good practice to supply lamps and motors from the same circuit (unless the motors are small, fractional-horsepower sizes) for the following reasons:

1. When motors are started, the large starting current causes a voltage drop on the feeder, which will make the lights grow dim or blink.

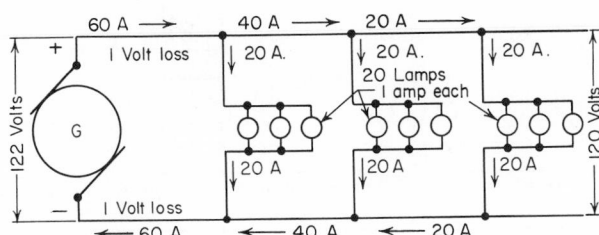

FIG. 14 *Two-wire system (direct current or single phase).*

2. Overloads and short circuits are more common on motor circuits and should not be the cause of putting the lights out.

3. Lamps for satisfactory service must operate within closer voltage limits than motors, and therefore the circuits must be designed for less voltage drop than is allowable on motor circuits.

4. Frequently it is more economical to operate motors on a higher voltage than that of the lighting circuit.

In installations where bus way wiring is employed, it is often very satisfactory to have a common motor and lighting bus for the feeders and mains. These systems if properly planned with generous allowance in the size of the buses will overcome the above criticisms of the common system and provide a very economical installation.

In the illustrations of the various systems, motors and lamps are shown connected to the same circuits simply to indicate the manner in which the different loads would be connected to that type of circuit. The reader is cautioned against forming the impression that they should be connected to the same circuit except in special cases. Considering any one of the illustrations, if one were dealing with a motor circuit, the lamps should be eliminated from the figure or, vice versa, if dealing with a lighting circuit, the motors should be eliminated.

20. The three-wire d-c or single-phase a-c system is used because it saves copper (see Figs. 15 and 22). Incandescent lamps for 110 to 120 volts are more economical than those for higher or lower voltages. A system of any consequence operating at 110 volts would require very large conductors to maintain the line drop within reasonable limits. With the three-wire system, a low voltage, say 110, is impressed on the receivers while one twice as great, say 220, is used for distribution. Since the weight of conductors for a given power loss varies inversely as the square of the voltage, it is evident that a considerable saving is possible with the three-wire system. In this country the three-wire system is of most importance as applied to 110/220-volt lighting systems.

21. The principle of the three-wire d-c or single-phase a-c system is illustrated in Fig. 22. Incandescent lamps for 110 volts could be connected two in series across 220

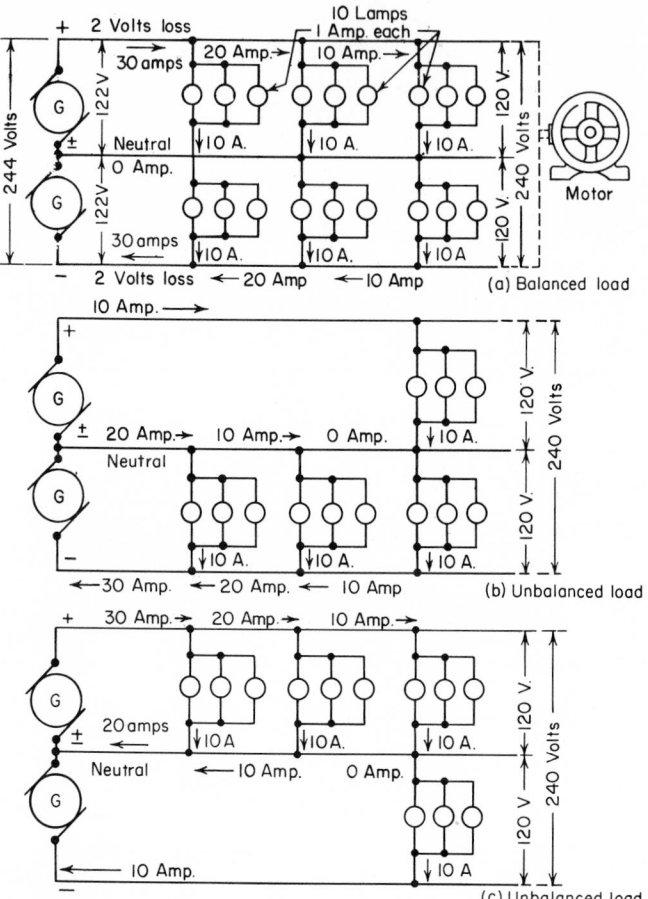

FIG. 15   *Three-wire system (direct current or single phase).*

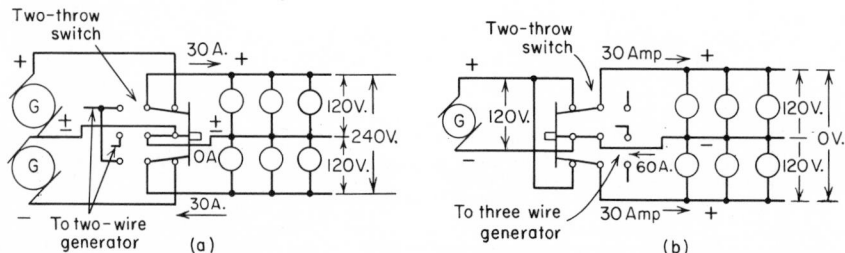

FIG. 16   *Three-wire convertible system (direct current or single phase). (a) Connections when operating three-wire. (b) Connections when operating two-wire. It is important, in the case of arc lamps and Cooper-Hewitt lamps, that they all be connected on the side of the circuit which does not reverse polarity when operating two-wire.*

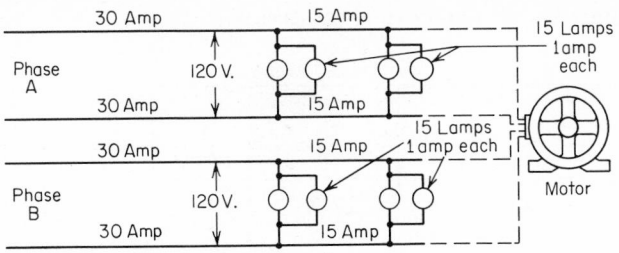

FIG. 17 *Two-phase four-wire system.*

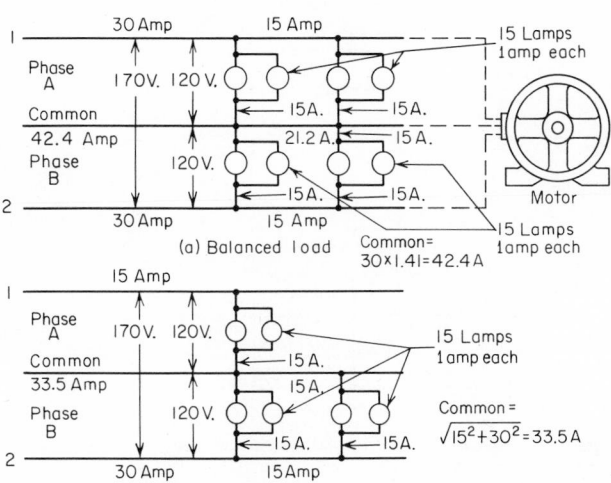

FIG. 18 *Two-phase three-wire system.*

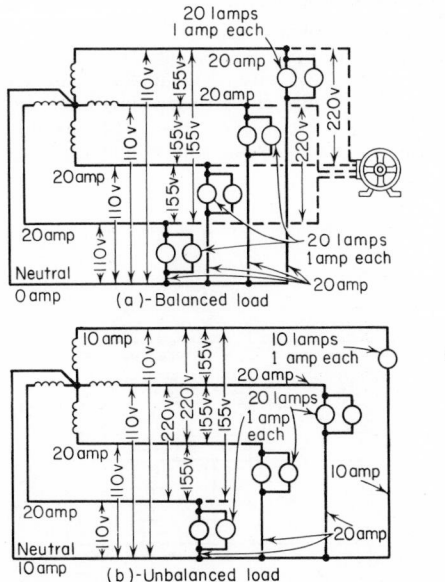

FIG. 19 *Two-phase five-wire system.*

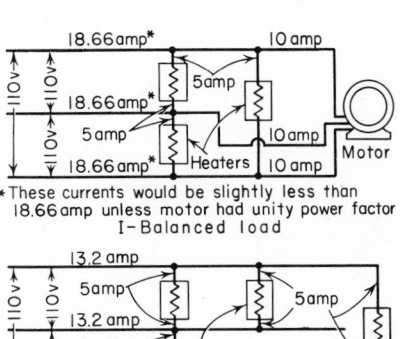

FIG. 20 *Three-phase three-wire system.*

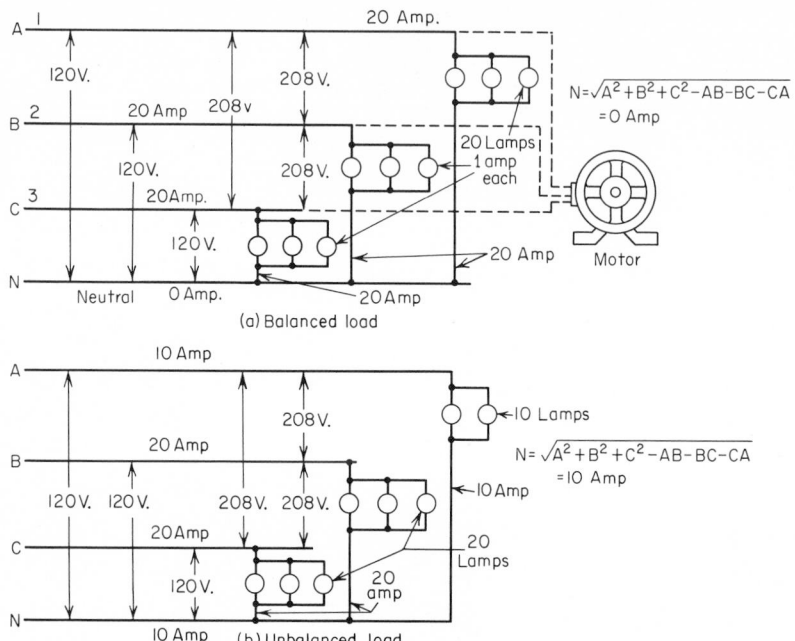

FIG. 21   *Three-phase four-wire wye system.*

volts as shown at I, and, although each lamp would operate at 110 volts, the energy to the group would be transmitted at 220 volts and the outside conductor could, with equal loss, be one-fourth the size that would be necessary if the energy was transmitted at 110 volts.   This arrangement (Fig. 22, I), although it would operate, is not commercially feasible because each lamp of each pair of lamps in series must be of the same size, and if one lamp goes out, its partner is also extinguished.   These disadvantages might be partially corrected by running a third wire as at Fig. 22, II.   Then one lamp might be turned off and the others would burn and a single lamp might be added to either side of the system between the third wire and either of the outside wires.   But unless the total resistance of all the lamps connected to one side was

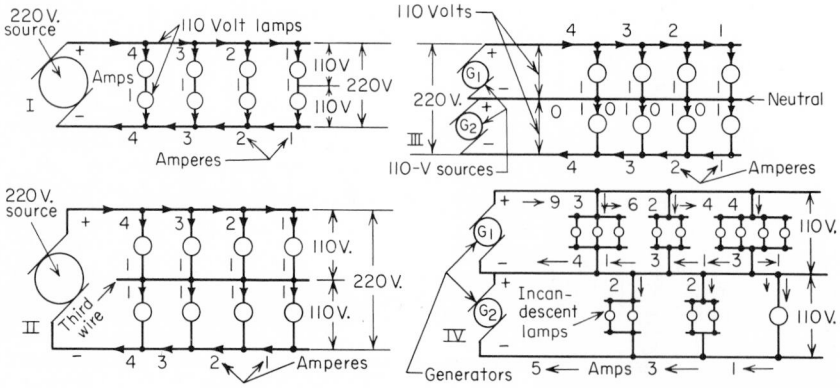

FIG. 22   *Elements of the three-wire system.*

practically equal to that of all the lamps connected to the other side, the voltage across one side would be higher than that across the other. On the high side the lamps would burn bright and on the low side dim. Obviously, it is not feasible in practice to arrange or "balance" the sides so that they will have the same resistance. Hence some other method must be used in practicable three-wire systems whereby the electricity will be transmitted at, say, 220 volts, and the pressure across the lamps will be, say, 110 volts.

22. Commercial three-wire d-c or single-phase a-c systems consist (Fig. 22, III and IV) of two outer conductors, having (for lighting installations) a pressure of 220 volts impressed across them and a neutral wire so connected to sources of voltage that the pressure between it and either of the outside wires is 110 volts. In Fig. 22, III, generators are the sources of voltage. The neutral wire joins at the point where the generators are connected together. When the system is perfectly balanced, the neutral wire carries no current and the system is in effect a 220-volt system. Perfect balance seldom obtains in practice. When the balance is not perfect, the neutral wire conveys a current equal to the difference between the current taken by one side and that taken by the other side. Note from Fig. 22, IV, that the current in different parts of the neutral wire may be different and that it is not necessarily in the same direction in all parts of the neutral wire. Each incandescent lamp in Fig. 22, IV, is assumed to take 1 amp, and the small figures indicate the currents in different parts of the circuit.

23. Comparisons of Systems. The relative weights of copper required for the different systems are given in Fig. 23. The weight of the copper required for the conductors of a two-wire d-c circuit is assumed for convenience to be 100 per cent. The values given in the column headed "Relative weights of copper in percentage based on voltage drop" are true for direct current, assuming for all systems equal voltages on the lamps or other receivers, equal amounts of power transmitted, equal voltage drops, and balanced loads. For a-c circuits the values are true for circuits where the effect of inductance is negligible. For a-c circuits where the effect of inductance is not negligible, the amount of copper to produce the same voltage drop would be somewhat larger than the values shown in the table. The values given in the last column are based on the assumption that the carrying capacity of a wire is directly proportional to its cross-sectional area. Since the larger the wire, the smaller is the allowable carrying capacity per unit of cross-sectional area, the percentages for systems of more than two wires would be somewhat less than shown. The actual saving in dollars gained by one of the systems that employs more than two wires will not be so great as that indicated in the table, owing to the fact that the total cost for a single large wire is less than for two small wires containing the same total amount of copper.

24. Application of Alternating Current and of Direct Current. Alternating-current systems have become almost universally standard in the United States for the transmission, distribution, and utilization of electrical energy. This is true because of the flexibility of a-c systems in economically stepping up or down the voltage without the use of rotating equipment. Some vestiges of old Edison d-c systems still exist both for city distribution and in old office buildings served by isolated plants.

When special characteristics of the load, such as electroplating or adjustable-speed motors, make the utilization of direct current either necessary or advisable, the alternating current can be converted to direct current by means of motor-generator sets, rectifiers, or in special cases converters.

System	Connections	Voltage relations	Relative weights of copper in percentage based on voltage drop	Relative weights of copper in percentage based on carrying capacity
Two-wire, d-c or single-phase	Fig. 14	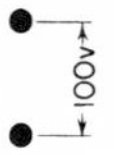 100v	100	100
Three-wire, d-c or single-phase	Fig. 15	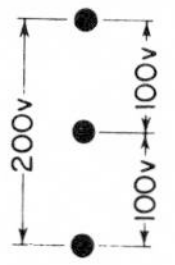 200v 100v 100v	With neutral same size as outside conductors 37.5 — With neutral 0.70 the size of the outside conductors 34	With neutral same size as outside conductors 75 — With neutral 0.70 the size of the outside conductors 67.5
Three-wire, convertible, d-c or single-phase	Fig. 16	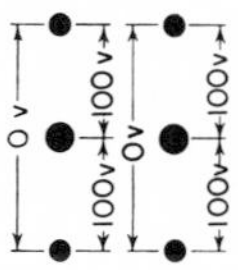 100v 100v 100v 100v	Neutral double size of outside conductors 100	Neutral double size of outside conductors 100
Two-phase, four-wire	Fig. 17	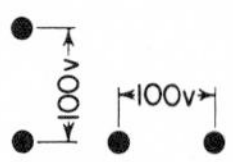 100v ⊢100v⊣	100	100
Two-phase, three-wire	Fig. 18	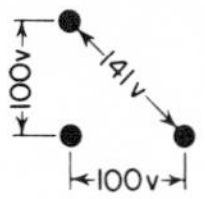 100v 141v ⊢100v⊣	Common 1.41 times as large as outside conductors 73	Common 1.41 times as large as outside conductors 85
Two-phase, five-wire	Fig. 19	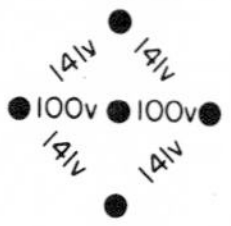 141v 141v 100v 100v 141v 141v	With common 1.41 times as large as outside conductors 34 — With common same size as outside conductors 31.3	With common 1.41 times as large as outside conductors 67 — With common same size as outside conductors 62.5
Three-phase, three-wire delta	Fig. 20	 100v 100v 100v	75	87
Three-phase, four-wire wye	Fig. 21	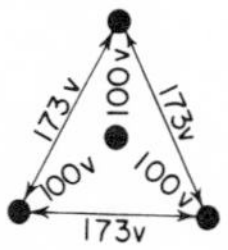 173v 100v 173v 100v 100v 173v	With neutral same size as outside conductors 33.3 — With neutral 0.70 as large as outside conductors 31	With neutral same size as outside conductors 67 — With neutral 0.70 as large as outside conductors 62

FIG. 23 *Copper economics of different electric systems.*

25. Standard D-C Voltages and Their Applications

Voltages		Application
Generators and energy-delivering apparatus	Motors and energy-utilization apparatus	
125[a]	115	Used for multiple-circuit lighting. Usually obtained from a 115/230-volt, three-wire system
125[a]–250[a] 575–600[a]	{ 110 –220 115[a]–230[a] 550[a] }	Direct-current motors
600[a]	. . . .	Urban and interurban electric railways
1,200 1,500	. . . . }	Interurban railways
3,000	. . . .	Trunk-line railways

[a] Electric Power Club standard voltage ratings.

26. Standard A-C Voltages and Their Applications

Voltage		Application
Generators and energy-delivering apparatus	Motors and energy-utilization apparatus	
120/208	110 110 single-phase motors 110–120 lamps and appliances	Single-phase, used for small motors, lighting, and appliances, usually obtained from a 120/240-volt, three-wire, single-phase system or a three-phase, four-wire system
240 480 600	220 440 550	Usually three-phase three-wire, used for distribution for power for polyphase motors up to possibly 50 to 60 hp sizes. 220 volts used occasionally for lamps and heaters. 265/460 volt, four-wire, three-phase system is often used (265 volts for fluorescent lamps and 460 volts for supplying motors)
2,400	2,200	Single phase for primary distribution in residential districts; three-phase, three-wire for polyphase motors greater than about 60 or 100 hp, feeders for large industrial plants
2,400/4,160	2,300/4,000	For three-phase four-wire distribution in moderately heavily loaded districts
6,900 11,500 13,800 18,000	6,600 11,000 13,200	Highest voltages for which generators or motors can, ordinarily, be effectively designed. Distribution systems for large cities; for power transmission over distances of a few miles. For high-voltage distribution feeders in industrial plants and large office buildings
22,000 33,000 44,000 66,000 88,000 110,000 132,000	The voltages higher than 13,200 are used for transmission only and not for generation or utilization.	For power transmission overhead and underground, for distances up to about 125 miles, selection being roughly on the basis of 1,000 volts per mile of transmission distance
154,000 220,000 275,000	. . . .	For long-distance power transmission over aerial lines

NOTE. The voltages up to 13,800 have been standardized by the United States of America Standards Institute, the National Electrical Manufacturers' Association, and the Institute of Electrical and Electronic Engineers. The voltages from 22,000 to 154,000 were standardized by the National Electric Light Association and are in common use by power companies. The 220,000- and 275,000-volt systems have been used on a few transmission lines.

27. Selection of a Frequency.   There are two frequencies now standard in this country: 25 and 60 cycles. A frequency of 50 cycles has been used considerably in Europe and in some installations in this country. All other things being equal, 25 cycles would seem at first sight preferable because there is less inductive effect with it than with a higher frequency. It therefore follows that the inherent voltage regulation of a 25-cycle system is better than that of a 60-cycle system and also that the 25-cycle system is a trifle more efficient. For transmission distances of less than a few miles neither of these factors is of much consequence one way or the other. Alternating current at 25 cycles is not particularly well adapted for electric lighting because a flickering due to the filament cooling down every half cycle while the current is at a low value is very noticeable and causes eyestrain. At 60 cycles the time of low current values is so short that no flickering is noticeable.

Many years ago, 25 cycles was considered necessary for the satisfactory operation of rotary converters, so most d-c electric traction systems have used a 25-cycle transmission system. All d-c railroad electrifications have also used 25 cycles because of the higher power factor and better commutation of the 25-cycle series motors. Again, it is not economically feasible to build large slow-speed motors for main drives in steel mills and cement plants at 60 cycles, so these types of plants have often adopted 25 cycles. Transformers and most other apparatus, except the motors indicated, are cheaper for 60 cycles, and the time for delivery is shorter.

Since 60 cycles is best for most installations, it has become practically the standard frequency in this country, and probably over 95 per cent of the equipment sold here is for 60 cycles. Most of the 50-cycle installations have been or are being changed over to 60 cycles.

Higher frequencies than the standard 60-cycle distribution frequency are sometimes used for special applications, such as operation of high-speed motors and fluorescent lamps (refer to Divs. 7 and 10). These higher application frequencies are obtained from the 60-cycle supply by means of conversion equipment.

28. Table Showing Effect of Increased Voltage and Decreased Voltage on Generators, Lines, Transformers, Meters, Lamps, and Motors. Sometimes it is necessary or desirable to adopt, for some existing installation, a voltage either higher or lower than that which has been in use. The table indicates the general effects of such a change. The voltage impressed on incandescent lamps should be something between 110 and 120. In new installations, it is well to adopt a high lamp voltage, say about 120. The operating voltage of an old installation may be gradually increased sometimes as much as 10 volts, without adverse results. (*Electrical World.*)

Effect of Increased Voltage on	Effect of Decreased Voltage on
Generators: Increase in excitation. Will the exciter voltage be sufficient to produce the required excitation at full load or at partial load of low power factor? Will the fields overheat at the increased excitation required? Increase in core loss. Will the iron overheat? Decrease in armature copper loss for same kilovolt-ampere output. Will this offset the additional field and core loss?	Generators: Decrease in excitation. Is the resistance of the field rheostat sufficient to maintain the lower voltage at no load? Decrease in core loss. Increase in armature copper loss for the same kilovolt-ampere output. Will this be offset by the reduction in field and core losses?
Lines: Increase in transmission radius for the same kva output.	Lines: Decrease in transmission radius for the same kva output.
Transformers: For the same kva output, increase in core losses, decrease in copper losses, somewhat lower all-day efficiency.	Transformers: For the same kva output, decrease in core losses, increase in copper losses, somewhat higher all-day efficiency.
Meters: Effect negligible.	Meters: Effect negligible.
Lamps: No effect after the new voltage lamps are installed.	Lamps: No effect after the new voltage lamps are installed.
Motors: Reduced slip. Increased torque. Increased efficiency. Decreased power factor of induction motors.	Motors: Increased slip. Decreased torque. Decreased efficiency. Increased power factor of induction motors.

29. Common Distribution Systems (Electrical Systems Design). The basic classification of distribution systems is according to voltage level used to carry the power either directly to the branch circuits or to load center transformers or substations at which feeders to branch circuits originate. The following are the most common types of distribution systems based on voltage:

1. 120/240-VOLT THREE-WIRE SINGLE-PHASE COMBINATION LIGHT AND POWER DISTRIBUTION to lighting and appliance branch-circuit panel boards and to power panels (Fig. 24). This type of system is restricted to applications where the total load is small and is primarily lighting. Stores, small schools, and other small commercial occupancies use this system. In most cases of small commercial buildings, the use of

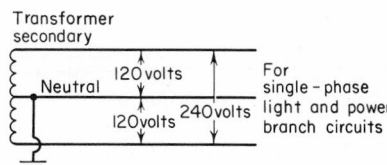

FIG. 24 *Single-phase three-wire distribution system.*

208Y/120-volt three-phase distribution offers greater economy due to higher operating efficiency of three-phase circuits. In those cases where 120/240-volt distribution is used as the basic distribution, the service to the premises is made at that voltage. Of course, 120/240-volt distribution is frequently an effective and economical system for lighting-subfeeder distribution in electrical systems which use a higher-voltage basic distribution system with load-center step-down to utilization voltages for local and incidental lighting and receptacle circuits.

2. 208Y/120-VOLT THREE-PHASE FOUR-WIRE DISTRIBUTION (Fig. 25a) is the most common type of system used in commercial buildings, in some institutional occupancies, and in some industrial shops with limited electrical loads. This system offers substantial economy over the 120/240-volt system in the amount of copper conductor required to carry a given amount of power to a load. It is a combination light- and power-distribution system, providing 120 volts phase-to-neutral for lighting and single-phase loads and 208 volts phase-to-phase for single- or three-phase motor or other power loads. This distribution system is used as the basic distribution in those occupancies in which the service to the building is of the same voltage. It is also the most common subdistribution system for lighting and receptacle circuits in those occupancies using higher-voltage distribution to load centers.

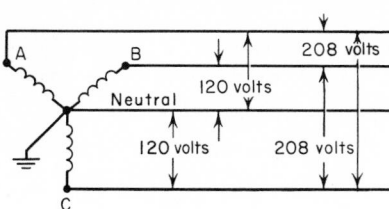

For three-phase power circuits and single-phase light and power branch circuit

(a)- Three-phase, 4 wire wye (or star) with grounded neutral rated 120/208 volts

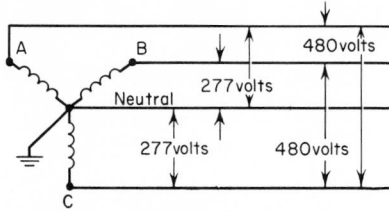

For three-phase power circuits and lighting circuits using 227 volt ballasts.

120 volt lighting and receptacle loads are fed from this system through single-phase transformers rated 480/120-240 volts or three phase transformers rated 480/120-208 volts

(b)-Three phase, 4-wire wye (or star) with grounded neutral rated 480Y/277 or 460Y/265, depending upon voltage spread under local conditions

FIG. 25   *Three-phase wye distribution systems.*

3. 240-VOLT THREE-PHASE THREE-WIRE DISTRIBUTION (Fig. 26) is a common system for power loads in commercial and industrial buildings. In such cases, service to the premises is made at 240 volts, three-phase. Feeders carry the power to panel boards or wireways supplying branch circuits for

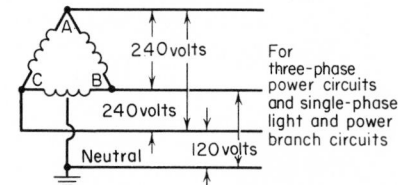

For three-phase power circuits and single-phase light and power branch circuits

FIG. 26   *Three-phase delta distribution system.*

motor loads. Lighting loads are usually handled by a separate single-phase service to the building. This system offers economic application where the power load is large compared with the lighting load. In some 240-volt, three-phase three-wire systems, a grounded center tap on one of the phases is used as a neutral to provide 120 volts for lighting and receptacle circuits.

4. 480-VOLT THREE-PHASE THREE-WIRE DISTRIBUTION is commonly used in commercial and industrial buildings with substantial motor loads. Service to the building can be made at this voltage, and the 480-volt feeders carried to motor loads and to step-down transformers for lighting and receptacle circuits. In many cases, 480-volt feeders will be derived from load-center substations within the building and carried to motor loads or power panels.

5. 480Y/277-VOLT THREE-PHASE FOUR-WIRE DISTRIBUTION (Fig. 25*b*) has become an important system for use in commercial buildings and industrial buildings. In office and other commercial buildings, the 480-volt, three-phase, four-wire feeders are carried to each floor where 480 volts, three-phase, is tapped to a power panel or to motors; general area fluorescent lighting using 277-volt ballasts is connected between each phase leg and the neutral; and 208Y/120-volt, three-phase, four-wire circuits are derived from step-down transformers for local lighting, appliance, and receptacle circuits. Application of this system offers economic advantage over a 208Y/120-volt system when less than about half of the load devices require 120- or 208-volt power. Where the 480Y system can be used, it will cost less than the 208Y/120-volt system owing to copper savings through the use of smaller sizes of conductors and lower cost of system elements due to lower current capacities. If the required amount of 120- or 280-volt power is over half of the total load in a building, the cost of the step-down transformers to supply these circuits will offset the savings in the 480-volt circuiting. The 480Y system is more advantageous in high-rise or other large-area buildings than in small buildings.

6. 2,400-VOLT THREE-PHASE DISTRIBUTION is an industrial-type system used to feed heavy motor loads directly and motor and lighting loads through load-center substations and lighting transformers.

7. 4,160/2,400-VOLT THREE-PHASE FOUR-WIRE DISTRIBUTION with a grounded neutral is a more common industrial system than the above 2,400 volt, delta-connected system. This system is widely used to supply load-center substations in which the voltage is stepped down to 480 to feed motors and lighting transformers for 120/240- and/or 208Y/120-volt circuits. It can also be used in distribution to substations stepping down the voltage directly to 208Y/120.

8. 4,800-VOLT THREE-PHASE DISTRIBUTION is a delta-connected industrial system for feeding 480-volt substations supplying motors and lighting transformers.

9. 7,200-VOLT THREE-PHASE DISTRIBUTION is another industrial system used with substations for stepping down voltage to lower levels for power and lighting.

10. 13.2Y/7.2-KV (or 13.8-KV) THREE-PHASE FOUR-WIRE DISTRIBUTION is a modern, widely used distribution system for large industrial plants. Power at this voltage is delivered to substations which step down the voltage to 480 for motor loads and which supply 480/120/240- or 480/208Y/120-volt transformers for lighting. Or 480Y/277-volt substations can be used to supply motor loads, and 277-volt fluorescent or mercury-vapor lighting for office and industrial areas. Lighting transformers are then used to supply 120-volt circuits for lighting and convenience receptacles.

The voltage values given for these distribution systems are, of course, subject to the usual variation or spreads due to distance of transmission and distribution, local conditions of utility supply, and settings of transformer taps. In addition to the distribution voltages given, other systems may operate at 6.6, 8.3, 11, and 12 kv. Of the high-voltage (over 600 volts) distribution systems, 4,160 and 13,200 volts are the most common and represent good design selection and economy of application for most cases. In many areas, delta-connected supplies have been changed to four-wire Y systems with consequent increase in power-handling capacity as a result of increased phase-to-phase voltage. The trend today is toward the use of the 13-kv systems over other high-voltage distribution systems for large industrial plants. To a limited extent, high-voltage distribution finds application in large commercial buildings. The most recent trend in distribution in office and other multifloor commercial buildings is to distribution at 480Y/277 volts, three-phase, four-wire with grounded neutral.

CIRCUIT CALCULATIONS

30. There are five factors that should be considered in determining the size of wire for the distribution of electricity. A wire should be of such size that (1) the current will not heat it to a temperature that would ruin the insulation or cause a fire, (2) it will have sufficient mechanical strength so that it will not be broken under the ordinary strains to which it is reasonable to assume that it will be subjected, (3) it will not be so large as to exceed the limitations required for its economical installation, (4) it will carry the electricity to the point where it will be used without an excessive drop or loss of voltage, and (5) the cost of energy lost—the I^2R loss—due to the voltage overcoming the resistance will not be excessive (refer to Sec. **82**). A conductor may satisfy any one of the five conditions and not satisfy the four others.

31. Safe current-carrying capacity should always be considered in designing circuits. When current passes through a conductor, some of the electrical energy is converted into heat energy, the amount of energy thus converted being equal to I^2R (see Div. 1). This heat energy raises the temperature of the conductor and its insulation and covering above that of the surrounding medium and is dissipated into the atmosphere through thermal conduction of the metal of the conductor, conductor insulation and covering, and surrounding materials (such as conduit, ducts, earth, etc.) and through convection of the surrounding air over these materials. It is not good practice to operate bare conductors at a temperature in excess of from 70 to 80°C, since trouble is apt to occur at joints and connections when they are operated at higher temperatures. A curve for determining current capacities of bare copper conductors is given in Sec. **15** of Div. 11. For covered and insulated cables the maximum allowable temperature of the conductor is limited by the maximum temperature that will not be harmful to the insulating and covering materials. Refer to Div. 2 for maximum safe temperatures for different types of insulation. The allowable safe current-carrying capacity of an insulated conductor will therefore depend upon the type of conductor insulation and covering, the conditions of installation (whether in conduit, exposed to air, or buried in earth, and the number of conductors grouped in close proximity to each other), and the temperature of the surrounding atmosphere or earth (ambient temperature). A curve for determining the carrying capacity of weatherproof copper conductors when installed outside buildings is given in Sec. **16** of Div. 11. Curves for aluminum cable, steel-reinforced, are given in Sec. **23** of Div. 11, and a table for parkway cables buried directly in the ground is given in Sec. **24** of Div. 11. It would require more space than is available in this book to include the necessary tables for allowable carrying capacities of cables installed in underground duct systems. Complete tables can be obtained from the various cable manufacturers or from the Insulated Power Cable Engineers Association.

The maximum allowable safe current-carrying capacities of wires for interior wiring are definitely specified by the National Electrical Code (see Tables **17** to **21** of Div. 11). The maximum current that a wire will have to carry should never exceed the allowable safe carrying capacity for the size of wire, type of insulation employed on the wire, and method of installation as given in these tables, except in the case of motor circuits. Motors draw a current at the instant of starting that is much greater than the normal full-load running current. Owing to the fact that this large starting current lasts for only a short time, the Code does not require that the carrying capacity of the wires for motor circuits be as great as the starting current. For branch circuits supplying continuous-duty motors the size of the wire must be sufficient to carry at least 125 per cent of the full-load rated current of the motor. The wires of branch circuits supplying motors in classes of service having short-time duty must have carrying capacities as large as the average load currents required by the motors. In the majority of cases, the average load currents required by motors of this class will not exceed the percentages of the full-load rated currents given in Table **12** of Div. 11. The wires between the slip rings of wound-rotor induction motors and the secondary controller must have a carrying capacity of at least 125 per cent of the full-load secondary current of the motor. The wires between the secondary controller and the resistors must have a carrying capacity that is not less than the percentages of the full-load secondary currents given in Table **13** of Div. 11. The size of wire for motor feeders or mains must be sufficient to carry at least the maximum-demand running current of the motors supplied by the circuit. The method of computing the maximum-demand running current is given in Sec. **54**.

The ampacities which are listed in Tables **18** to **21** of Div. 11 are based upon room temperatures of 30°C. If the room will have a temperature greater than this, the ampacities listed in the table should be multiplied by the proper correction factor as given in Note 15 of Sec. **17**, Div. 11.

32. Mechanical Strength of Wires. Wires should be of sufficient size so that their mechanical strength will be great enough to withstand the strains of installation and of the service to which they will be subjected. For general overhead distribution mains, no wire of soft-drawn copper smaller than No. 6 should be used. If medium- or hard-drawn copper is used, no wire smaller than No. 8 should be employed. For overhead outside wiring on private premises, no wire smaller than No. 10 should be used for spans up to 50 ft and no wire smaller than No. 8 for longer spans. Service drops from an overhead distribution main to the service-entrance conductors must not be smaller than No. 10 if of soft-drawn copper or smaller than No. 12 if of medium- or hard-drawn copper. The service-entrance conductors to a building shall not be smaller than No. 6 except that:

1. For installations consisting of not more than two two-wire branch circuits they shall not be smaller than No. 8.

2. By special permission due to limitations of supply source or load requirements they shall not be smaller than No. 8.

3. For installations to supply only limited loads of a single branch circuit, such as small polyphase power, controlled water heaters, and the like, they shall not be smaller than the conductors of the branch circuit and in no case smaller than No. 12.

Single-family residences with an initial load of 10 kw or more than five two-wire branch circuits must have a 100-amp service.

In the interior wiring of buildings no wire smaller than No. 14 can be used except for the following special cases:

1. For fixture wiring and flexible cords Nos. 16 and 18 can be used. Also, tinsel cords or cords having equivalent characteristics of smaller size may be approved for use with specific appliances.

2. Number 18 wire can be used for stationary motors, rated 1 hp or less, for the conductors between the motor and an approved terminal enclosure.

3. For elevator, dumbwaiter, and escalator wiring, except for conductors which form an integral part of control equipment, the minimum allowable size of conductors is as follows:

    a. Traveling Cables.

      (1) For lighting circuits: No. 14, except that No. 20 or larger conductors may be used in parallel provided the carrying capacity is equivalent to at least that of No. 14 wire.

      (2) Operating control and signal circuits: No. 20.

    b. Other Wiring. All operating control and signal circuits: No. 20.

4. In the wiring for cranes and hoists No. 16 wire may be used for some circuits under certain conditions (see Div. 9).

5. For machine-tool wiring the following exceptions are allowed:

    a. Conductors to moving parts: Copper conductors for control purposes to continuously moving parts may be No. 16 where all such conductors are insulated for the maximum voltage of any conductor in the cable or tubing.

    b. Conductors to electronic and precision devices: Copper conductors to electronic and precision devices may be No. 20, except that where pulled into raceways they shall not be smaller than No. 18.

6. For remote-control, low-energy, low-voltage power and signal circuits Nos. 18 and 16 gage conductors may be used provided they are installed in a raceway or a cable approved for the purpose or in approved flexible cords. (Class 1 circuits.) The National Electrical Code gives detailed rules for these cases.

33. There are certain limitations in the size of wires that it is feasible to employ in order to satisfy construction and installation requirements. For convenience in installation, it is seldom advisable to use larger than 3-in. conduit. When all the wires of a circuit are run in the same conduit, this limits the size of the conductors to 500,000 cir mils. If only one wire were run in a conduit, the size of wire could be considerably larger. It is seldom wise or convenient to install conductors of larger size than 1,000,000 cir mils. A 2½-in. conduit is about as large as can usually be installed between floors and ceilings. In such cases, therefore, the size of wire is limited to 300,000 cir mils if two or three wires are placed in the same conduit. For open wiring, wires larger than 1,000,000 cir mils are cumbersome to handle.

34. Percentage line drop or voltage loss can be figured as either a percentage of the

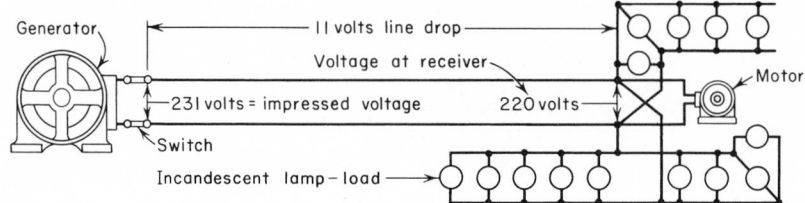

FIG. 27 *Illustrating percentage line drop.*

voltage required at the receiver or as a percentage of the voltage impressed by the generator or other energy source on the line. For instance, in Fig. 27, the voltage impressed on the receivers—lamps and motor—is 220. The line loss is 11 volts; hence the pressure impressed on the line = 220 + 11 = 231 volts. The voltage loss as a percentage of the voltage at the receiver = 11/220 = 0.05 = 5 per cent. The voltage loss as a percentage of the voltage impressed on the line is 11/231 = 0.048 = 4.8 per cent. In practical work the percentage loss or drop is usually taken as a percentage of the voltage required at the receivers, because this is the most convenient and direct method. In this book the term percentage drop refers to a percentage of the voltage required at the receivers unless otherwise noted.

35. Allowable Voltage Drops. The conductors of an interior wiring system should be of sufficient size so that the voltage drop from the point of service entrance to the equipment utilizing the energy, such as lamps or motors, is not excessive. If the voltage drop is too great, the operating conditions will not be satisfactory, owing to one or more of the following causes:

1. Shortened life of lamps caused by overvoltage under light load conditions.
2. Unsatisfactory illumination under maximum load conditions.
3. Unsatisfactory motor speed, torque, or temperature.

No definite standards have been adopted for the maximum allowable voltage drop. The National Electrical Code recommends that the voltage drop from the point of service entrance to the final distribution point should not be greater than 3 per cent for power, lighting, or heating loads.

For **lighting loads** the voltage drop from the point of service entrance to any lamp should not exceed 5 per cent. If it is possible without employing excessively large conductors, it is good practice to keep this total voltage drop within 3 per cent. The voltage drop in any branch lighting circuit or in any lighting feeder should not be greater than 2 per cent.

For **power loads** the voltage drop from the point of service entrance to any motor or heating unit should not exceed 5 per cent. The distribution of this voltage drop among the different parts of the system will depend upon the layout of the wiring installation. For systems operating at 208 volts or higher, it is generally good practice to limit the voltage drop in branch circuits to 1 per cent and in feeders to 4 per cent. Only in exceptional cases should the voltage drop in a motor branch circuit exceed 2 per cent.

Values of voltage drop that will be in accordance with good practice for different systems are given in Sec. **54** of Div. 11.

36. Allowance for Growth in Planning Circuits. In installing the wiring for electric-power and lighting installations, the demands that may be placed upon the system in the future should be carefully considered. It requires a relatively small additional expense, when installing a system, to put in wires somewhat larger than are required by the present lighting equipment. On the other hand, if the wires installed are of just sufficient size to accommodate the present load and it is necessary to increase the load at some future date, the cost of removing the old installation and installing a new one is considerable.

Standards of illumination have been continually increasing, and it is reasonable to assume from the trend of practice that the general level of illuminating intensities employed will be still further increased. Both employees and employers are appreciating more and more the benefits to be gained from high intensities of illumination.

It is, therefore, good practice to limit the initial loading of branch lighting circuits to 50 per cent of their maximum allowable load. Such limitation of the initial loading will allow the load on branch lighting circuits in most commercial and industrial installations to be increased to 160 per cent of their initial loading. It would appear that the loading could be increased to 200 per cent of the initial loading. This is not true, since the National Electrical Code requires that the total load connected to branch lighting and appliance branch circuits shall not exceed 80 per cent of their rating where in normal operation the load will continue for 3 hr or more, such as in store lighting and similar loads. In the following sections dealing with the calculation of the loads on lighting and appliance circuits, the term future load means the load that would be placed on the circuit if it were loaded to 80 per cent of its rating.

The layout and equipment in industrial and commercial buildings are continuously being changed. These changes frequently involve increased load requirements. Therefore, there are no definite rules that can be laid down for the proper allowance that should be made for growth, since the conditions vary so widely for different installations. Each installation requires careful study with respect to probable future load requirements. The actual connected loads on the circuit should be increased a sufficient amount so that the size of circuit will be ample to accommodate whatever loads it is estimated may be connected to the circuit in the future. For good general practice, it is recommended that the allowance for growth be at least 50 per cent of the initial load.

37. Calculation of Load in Amperes on Two-wire Branch Lighting and/or Appliance Circuits. The actual load in amperes on a two-wire branch lighting circuit is equal to the sum of the watt ratings of the individual loads connected to the circuit divided by the voltage of the circuit. Each heavy-duty lampholder outlet for lighting other than general illumination should be figured at 5 amp. Each plug receptacle outlet connected to the circuit should be figured at at least 1.5 amp per outlet. If the load to be connected to a plug outlet is known to be more than 1.5 amp, its load should be considered as the actual known wattage that it will supply.

For show-window lighting a load of not less than 200 watts for each linear foot of show window, measured horizontally along its base, may be allowed in lieu of the 1.5 amp per outlet. Where fixed multioutlet assemblies are supplied by the circuit, each 5 ft or fraction thereof of each separate and continuous length of the assembly should be considered as a load of 1.5 amp, except in locations where a number of appliances are likely to be used simultaneously. In that case each 1 ft or fraction thereof should be considered as a load of 1.5 amp. In computing the load of lighting units that employ ballasts, transformers, or autotransformers, such as fluorescent lighting units, the load must be based on the volt-ampere load or current of the complete unit and not simply the wattage of the lamp. Refer to Sec. **125** of Div. 10 for information on these loads. For incandescent lighting units the volt-ampere loads will be the same as the rated watts of the lamps. For branch lighting circuits it is sufficiently accurate to assume that the total volt-ampere load is equal to the direct numerical summation of the individual volt-ampere loads. This is also true for the summation of lighting loads in terms of amperes.

As stated in Sec. **36,** the future load on branch lighting and appliance circuits in commercial and industrial installations is taken as 80 per cent of the rating of the branch circuit.

The standard sizes of lamps are given in Table **1** of Div. 11 with more complete data in Div. 10.

Example. A two-wire, 110-volt, 20-amp branch lighting circuit supplies five 200-watt incandescent lamps. Determine the actual connected and probable future load.

Solution. Present connected load $= \dfrac{5 \times 200}{110} = 9.1$ amp

Future load $= 0.80 \times 20 = 16$ amp

Example. A two-wire 110-volt 20-amp branch lighting circuit supplies four 150-watt and three 200-watt incandescent lamps. Determine the actual connected and probable future load.

Solution. Present connected load $= \dfrac{(4 \times 150) + (3 \times 200)}{110} = 10.9$ amp

Future load $= 0.80 \times 20 = 16$ amp

38. Calculation of Load in Amperes on Three-wire Branch Lighting and/or Appliance Circuits. The actual and future loads in amperes on either side of a three-wire branch lighting circuit can be computed in the same manner as for two-wire circuits in Sec. **37**, the voltage between the neutral and either outside wire and the loads connected between the neutral and the one outside wire under consideration being used.

Example. A three-wire, 110/220-volt, 15-amp branch lighting circuit supplies the loads in the following diagram. Determine the actual connected and probable future loads.

Solution. Present connected load 1 to $N = \dfrac{4 \times 200}{110} = 7.3$ amp

Present connected load 2 to $N = \dfrac{5 \times 150}{110} = 6.8$ amp

Future load 1 to $N = \dfrac{0.80 \times 15}{110} = 12$ amp

Future load 2 to $N = \dfrac{0.80 \times 15}{110} = 12$ amp

39. Calculation of Load in Amperes on Branch Electric-range Circuits. For electric ranges and other cooking appliances of 1¾-kw rating or less, the load on the branch circuit is equal to the ratings of the appliances. For ranges or cooking appliances of ratings greater than 1¾ kw, the watt load on the branch can be computed in accordance with Table **2** of Div. 11.

For two-wire branches, the load in amperes is equal to the watt load, as determined above, divided by the voltage of the circuit. For three-wire branches, the load in amperes on each outside wire of the circuit is equal to the watt load, as determined above, divided by the voltage between outside wires. The load in amperes on the neutral wire can be taken as 70 per cent of the load on an outside wire.

40. Calculation of Lighting and Appliance Load on Two-wire D-C or Single-phase Distribution Panels. The actual connected load is equal to the sum of the actual connected loads of all the branch circuits fed from the panel. Each appliance circuit in the panel should be figured at at least 10 amp for a circuit rated 15 amp and at least 15 amp for a circuit rated 20 amp. The future load on the panel is figured in the same manner as the actual load, the future loads of the branch circuits being used instead of the actual loads and each appliance or spare circuit being figured at at least 15 amp. If an appliance circuit is of a type allowing more than 15 amp, the circuit should be figured at its maximum allowable amperage as given in Div. 9.

Example. Determine the actual connected and probable future loads on a two-wire, 110-volt lighting panel supplying the following circuits:

Circuit number and rating	Present load, amp	Future load, amp
1–15 amp lighting	10	12
2–15 amp lighting	7	12
3–20 amp lighting	9	16
4–15 amp appliance	10	15
5–15 amp lighting	8	12
6–20 amp appliance	15	20
7–15 amp spare		15
8–15 amp spare		15
	59	117

Solution. Present connected load on panel = 59 amp
Probable future load = 117 amp

41. Calculation of Lighting and Appliance Load on Three-wire D-C or Single-phase Distribution Panels. The actual connected load on each side of the panel is computed in the same manner as for two-wire panels in Sec. **40,** using the voltage between the neutral and one outside wire and making separate calculations for each line wire. If the circuits have been well laid out, there should not be much difference between the loads on the two sides of the panel.

Example. A three-wire 110/220-volt lighting panel supplies the following circuits. All branch circuits are two-wire, 110 volts. Determine the actual connected and the probable future loads. All circuits are rated 15 amp.

Branch circuits between wire 1 and neutral			Branch circuits between wire 2 and neutral		
Circuit	Present load, amp	Future load, amp	Circuit	Present load, amp	Future load, amp
1	7	12	1	8	12
2	8	12	2	7	12
3	8	12	3	8	12
4	7	12	4 (plug)	10	15
5 (plug)	10	15	5 (spare)		15
6 (spare)		15	6 (spare)		15
	40	78		33	81

Solution. The present connected load would be taken as 40 amp. The future load would be taken as 81 amp.

42. Calculation of Lighting and Appliance Load on Two-phase Three-wire Distribution Panels. The loads for the two-line wires are computed as in Sec. **41.** The actual and future loads on the common wire of the panel are taken as equal to 1.41 times the actual and future loads, respectively, of the more heavily loaded side of the panel.

Example. A three-wire two-phase 110-volt lighting panel supplies the same circuits on the two sides of the panel as given in the example under the three-wire single-phase panel. Determine the actual connected and probable future loads.
Solution. The actual connected load on each outside wire of the panel would be taken as 40 amp. The future load on each outside wire of the panel would be taken as 81 amp.
The actual connected load on the neutral would be 1.41 × 40 = 56.4 amp.
The future load on the neutral would be 1.41 × 81 = 114.2 amp.

43. Calculation of Lighting and Appliance Load on Four-wire Three-phase Distribution Panels. The actual connected load on any one bus except the neutral bus is computed as in Sec. **41.** The load on each of the four buses usually is taken as being equal to that of the most heavily loaded outside bus.

44. Fundamentals of Load Calculations on Mains and Feeders. In some cases the carrying capacity of feeders or mains need not be so great as the total ampere load of all the equipment supplied by the circuit. This is due to the fact that all the apparatus may not be operating at the same time or, if operating, may not all be taking full-load current from the line at the same time. A demand factor is employed in order to determine the maximum current that it is estimated the circuit will ever be required to carry. A demand factor is the ratio between the maximum current that the circuit will ever have to carry and the total load connected to the circuit. The maximum-demand current of a circuit, therefore, is equal to the total connected load times the proper demand factor (see Table **4,** Div. 11, for lighting demand factors; Table **6,** Div. 11, for maximum-demand factors for motor circuits; Table **2,** Div. 11, for demand factors for household electric ranges, wall-mounted ovens, counter-mounted cooking units, and other household cooking appliances; and Table **3,** Div. 11, for demand factors for household electric clothes driers). Where four or more fixed appliances, in addition to electric ranges, air-conditioning equipment, or space heating equipment, are connected to the same feeder or main in a single or multifamily dwelling, a demand factor of 75 per cent may be applied to the fixed-appliance load, not including the electric ranges. The computed load of a feeder supplying fixed electrical space heating equipment shall be the total connected load on all branch circuits, except that where reduced loading of the conductors results from units operating on duty cycle, intermittently, or from all units not operating at one time, the authority enforcing this code may grant permission for feeder conductors to be of a capacity less than 100 per cent provided the conductors are of sufficient capacity for this load.

45. Calculation of Load on Two-wire D-C or Single-phase A-C Lighting and Appliance Feeders or Mains. The ampere or watt load is equal to the sum of the maximum-demand lighting and portable-appliance load, the maximum-demand fixed-appliance load, and the maximum-demand electric-range load. The present or future maximum-demand lighting and portable-appliance load is equal to the sum of the actual or future lighting and portable-appliance loads fed from the circuit times the proper demand factor as determined from Table **4**, Div. **11**. The maximum-demand fixed-appliance load is figured in accordance with Sec. **44**. The maximum-demand electric-range load is figured in accordance with Table **2**, Div. **11**.

In single-family dwellings, in individual apartments of multifamily dwellings having provisions for cooking by tenants, and in each hotel suite having a serving pantry, a feeder load of not less than 1,500 watts for each two-wire 20-amp branch circuit shall be included for small appliances (portable appliances supplied from receptacles of 15 to 20 amp rating) in pantry and breakfast room, dining room, family room, kitchen, and laundry. This is a National Electrical Code requirement.

Example. An apartment in a multifamily dwelling has a total floor area of 700 sq ft. It is not equipped with an electric range. Determine the maximum-demand present load for a two-wire 115-volt feeder supplying the apartment.

Solution

General lighting load from Table **4**, Div. 11, $= 700 \times 3 = 2{,}100$ watts
Small appliance load, two circuits, each at 1,500 watts $= 3{,}000$ watts
$$\text{Total computed load} = 5{,}100 \text{ watts}$$

Application of demand factor:

$$3{,}000 \text{ watts at } 100\% = 3{,}000 \text{ watts}$$
$$2{,}100 \text{ watts at } 35\% = \underline{735} \text{ watts}$$
$$\text{Maximum-demand load} = 3{,}735 \text{ watts}$$

$$\text{Maximum-demand current} = \frac{3{,}735}{115} = 32.5 \text{ amp}$$

46. Calculation of Load on Three-wire D-C or Single-phase A-C Lighting and Appliance Feeders or Mains. The load on either outside wire is equal to the sum of the maximum-demand lighting and portable-appliance load, the maximum-demand fixed-appliance load, the maximum-demand electric-range load, and the maximum-demand household electric-clothes-drier load fed from that wire. The present or future maximum-demand lighting and portable-appliance load is equal to the sum of the actual or future lighting and portable-appliance loads of all the panels fed from that wire times the proper demand factor as determined from Table **4**, Div. 11. The maximum-demand fixed-appliance load is equal to the sum of all the fixed-appliance load fed from that wire times the proper demand factor as given in Sec. **44**. The maximum-demand current for the electric-range load is equal to the maximum-demand watt range load as determined in accordance with Table **2**, Div. 11, divided by the voltage between outside wires of the circuit. Refer to Sec. **45** for required allowance for small appliances in dwelling occupancies. The maximum-demand current for the household electric-clothes-drier load is equal to the maximum-demand watt clothes-drier load as determined in accordance with Table **3**, Div. 11, divided by the voltage between outside wires of the circuit. In adding branch-circuit loads for space heating and air cooling in dwelling occupancies, the smaller of the two loads may be omitted from the total where it is unlikely that both of the loads will be served simultaneously. The air-cooling (air-conditioning) load is a motor load. Therefore for the calculation of load on circuits of this character refer to Secs. **53, 54,** and **55.**

The load on the neutral wire is the maximum unbalance of the load on the two sides of the system. The maximum unbalanced load is the sum of the maximum-demand lighting and portable-appliance load, the maximum-demand fixed-appliance load, and the maximum-demand electric-range load for the more heavily loaded side of the circuit. The maximum-demand household electric-range load is considered as 70 per cent of the electric-range load on the outside conductors as determined from Table 2 of Div. 11. If the maximum unbalanced load for the neutral as determined from the above procedure is more than 200 amp, then a further demand factor of 70 per cent can be applied to that portion of the unbalanced load in excess of 200 amp. There shall be no reduction of the neutral capacity for that portion of the load which consists of electric discharge lighting.

The National Electrical Code allows the following optional method of calculation of load for a one-family residence or apartment unit. For each dwelling unit served by a 115/230-volt, three-wire, 100-amp or larger service where the total load is supplied by one feeder or one set of service-entrance conductors, the following percentages may be used in lieu of the method of determining feeder (and service) loads detailed previously in this section.

Optional Calculation for One-family Residence or Apartment Unit

Load, kw or kva	Per Cent of Load
Air conditioning and cooling including heat pump compressors	100
Central electrical space heating	100
Less than four separately controlled electrical space heating units	100
First 10 kw of all other load	100
Remainder of other load	40

All other load shall include 1,500 watts for each 20-amp appliance outlet circuit; lighting and portable appliances at 3 watts per sq ft; all fixed appliances (including four or more separately controlled space heating units, ranges, wall-mounted ovens, and counter-mounted cooking units) at nameplate rated load (kva for motors and other low-power-factor loads).

The following example is given in the National Electrical Code for explanation of the optional method of load calculation for a one-family dwelling.

Example. The dwelling has a floor area of 1,500 sq ft exclusive of unoccupied cellar, unfinished attic, and open porches. It has a 12-kw range, a 2.5-kw water heater, a 1.2-kw dishwasher, 9 kw of electric space heating installed in five rooms, a 4.5-kw clothes drier, and a 6-amp 230-volt room air-conditioning unit.

Solution. The air conditioner is $6 \times 230 \div 1,000 = 1.38$ kw. This is less than the connected load of 9 kw of space heating; therefore the air-conditioner load need not be included in the service calculation.

1,500 sq ft at 3 watts	4.5 kw
Two 20-amp appliance outlet circuits at 1,500 watts each	3.0 kw
Laundry circuit	1.5 kw
Range (at nameplate rating)	12.0 kw
Water heater	2.5 kw
Dishwasher	1.2 kw
Space heating	9.0 kw
Clothes drier	4.5 kw
	38.2 kw

First 10 kw at 100% = 10.00 kw
Remainder at 40% (28.2 kw × 0.4) = 11.28 kw
Calculated load for service size = 21.28 kw = 21,280 watts
21,280 ÷ 230 = 92.5 amp

Therefore this dwelling may be served by a 100-amp service.

47. Calculation of Load on Four-wire Two-phase Lighting and Appliance Feeders or Mains. The ampere loads on either phase can be computed as in Sec. **45,** considering each phase as a separate single-phase circuit.

48. Calculation of Load on Three-wire Two-phase Lighting and Appliance Feeders or Mains. For the two-line wires proceed as in Sec. **46.**

The load on the neutral wire will be 1.41 times the load for the neutral as determined in accordance with the procedure of Sec. **46.** If the load on the neutral as determined in this manner is more than 200 amp, no further demand factor can be applied to that portion of the load for this type of system.

Example. Determine the present and future loads for a three-wire two-phase feeder in an industrial building of 9,000 sq ft supplying the following loads:

	Panels connected between wire 1 and common wire			Panels connected between wire 2 and common wire	
Panel	Present load, amp	Future load, amp	Panel	Present load, amp	Future load, amp
A	50.8	65.2	A	47.8	61.3
B	43.7	55.6	B	52.7	67.9
C	41.4	54.7	C	36.8	45.9
	135.9	175.5		137.3	175.1

Solution. From Table **4,** Div. 11, the demand factor is 1.0.
Present load on wire 1 = 135.9 × 1.0 = 135.9 amp.
Future load on wire 1 = 175.5 × 1.0 = 175.5 amp.
Present load on wire 2 = 137.3 × 1.0 = 137.3 amp.
Future load on wire 2 = 175.1 × 1.0 = 175.1 amp.
Present load on common wire = 137.3 × 1.41 = 193.6 amp.
Future load on common wire 175.5 × 1.41 = 248 amp.

49. Calculation of Load on Five-wire Two-phase Lighting and Appliance Feeders or Mains. For the four line wires proceed as for the line wires in Sec. **46.**
The following example shows how to compute the maximum demand for the four-line conductors and the common neutral of a typical five-wire, two-phase system:

Example. The actual connected loads on the four outside wires of a five-wire, two-phase lighting feeder are 100.5, 97.8, 95.4, and 100.0 amp. The feeder is supplying the load in a factory building. Determine the present load for the neutral wire.
Solution. From Table **4,** Div. 11, the demand factor is 1.0. The load on the neutral = (100.5 × 1.0)1.41 = 142 amp.

50. Calculation of Load on Four-wire Three-phase Lighting and Appliance Feeders or Mains. The ampere load on any outside wire is computed as in Sec. **46,** except for the calculation of the maximum-demand current for the electric-range load. The maximum-demand current for the range load should be determined from the following formula:

$$\text{Maximum-demand range current} = \frac{\begin{pmatrix}\text{watt load as determined from Table }\textbf{2}\text{, Div.}\\ \text{11, for twice the number of ranges con-}\\ \text{nected between any two outside wires}\end{pmatrix}}{\begin{pmatrix}2 \times \text{(voltage between an outside wire and}\\ \text{neutral)}\end{pmatrix}} \quad (2)$$

For the ampere load of the neutral wire, proceed as for the neutral in Sec. **46.**

Example. Thirty ranges rated at 12 kw each are supplied by a three-phase, four-wire, 120/208-volt feeder, 10 ranges on each phase. Determine the maximum-demand current for each outside wire.
Solution. As there are 20 ranges connected to each ungrounded conductor, the load should be calculated on the basis of 20 ranges (or in case of unbalance, twice the maximum number between any two-phase wires) since diversity applies only to the number of ranges connected to adjacent phases and not to the total.
The current in any one conductor will be one-half the total watt load of two adjacent phases divided by the line-to-neutral voltage. In this case, 20 ranges, from Table **2,** Div. 11, will have a total watt load of 35,000 watts for two phases; therefore, the current in the feeder conductor would be

$$17,500 \div 120 = 146 \text{ amp}$$

51. Determining Size of Lighting and Appliance Distribution Panel Buses. The required ampere capacity of the buses in lighting and appliance distribution panels can be calculated in the same manner as given in the preceding sections for the calculation of the ampere loads on feeders and mains.

52. Minimum Allowable Load to Use for Any Lighting Feeder or Main. The National Electrical Code specifies definite rules for computing the minimum loads for a given area. Feeders or mains must be of sufficient size to carry safely at least the amperes required by these rules regardless of the actual connected load. The areas employed in applying the rules should be gross floor areas as determined from the outside dimensions of the building and the number of floors. Floor areas of open porches, garages in connection with dwelling occupancies, and unfinished and unused spaces in dwellings, unless adapted for future use, need not be included.

The minimum allowable watt load for the feeder or main supplying power to any area for lighting and appliances must be equal to the sum of the minimum allowable general-lighting load, the portable-appliance load, the fixed-appliance load (other than ranges), fixed electrical space-heating equipment load, and the electric-range load. The minimum allowable general-lighting load is equal to the area times the minimum allowable watts per square foot for that type of area times the proper demand factor. The minimum allowable watts per square foot and the allowable demand factors for different types of areas are given in Table 5 of Div. 11. The portable-appliance load requirements are given in Table 5 of Div. 11. Where in normal operation the load on the installation will continue for three hours or more, such as in store lighting, the minimum allowable load, as determined above, must be increased by 25 per cent. The fixed-appliance load is equal to the summation of the watt rating of the actual fixed appliances installed in the area, where the number of such appliances is four or less. For electric ranges and other cooking appliances of 1¾ kw rating or less, a load equal to the summation of the watt ratings of the ranges or appliances installed must be included. For electric ranges and other cooking appliances rated more than 1¾ kw, the minimum allowable load can be computed from Table 2 of Div. 11. Where a number of ranges are supplied by a three-phase, four-wire feeder, the minimum allowable watt load should be computed from the following formula:

$$\text{Minimum allowable range watt load} = 3 \times \frac{\begin{array}{c}\text{watt load as determined from Table}\\ \text{2 of Div. 11 for twice the number of}\\ \text{ranges connected between any two}\\ \text{outside wires}\end{array}}{2} \qquad (3)$$

The minimum allowable load for motor circuits is identical with the values obtained from the instructions of Secs. **53** and **54.**

The minimum allowable load for circuits supplying both motors and other loads is equal to the motor load plus the minimum allowable load of other types. After the minimum allowable watt load has been determined, the corresponding ampere load can be determined from the following formulas and instructions, depending upon the type of electric system employed:

$$I = \frac{\text{minimum allowable watts}}{KE} \qquad (4)$$

where $K = 1$ for two-wire d-c or two-wire single-phase a-c.
   $= 1.73$ for three-wire three-phase a-c.
   $= 2$ for three-wire d-c; three-wire single-phase a-c; three-wire two-phase a-c; or four-wire two-phase a-c.
   $= 3$ for four-wire three-phase a-c.
   $= 4$ for five-wire two-phase a-c.
 $E =$ voltage between outside wire and neutral if the system has a neutral; otherwise the voltage between any two line wires.
and $I =$ current in any line wire except the neutral.

Neutral for three-wire d-c; three-wire single-phase a-c; or four-wire three-phase: Follow instructions given in Sec. **46.**

Neutral for three-wire or five-wire two-phase: Follow instructions given in Secs. **48** and **49.**

Example. Determine the minimum allowable loading of a feeder supplying a multifamily dwelling having an area of 30,800 sq ft with 44 apartments. No electric-range load.

Solution. From Table **5**, Div. 11, 3.0 watts must be allowed for each square foot plus 3,000 watts for appliances for each apartment. The demand factor from Table **5** of Div. 11 is 1.0 for the first 3,000 watts, 0.35 for the next 117,000 watts, and 0.25 for all load in excess of 120,000 watts.

Lighting load $= 3 \times 30,800$	$= 92,400$
Appliance load $= 44 \times 3,000$	$= 132,000$
Total load based on area	$= 224,400$ watts

Minimum allowable watt load $= 3,000 + (117,000 \times 0.35)$
$$+ (224,400 - 120,000)0.25 = 70,050 \text{ watts}$$

For a two-wire 115-volt single-phase or d-c system:
$$I = \frac{70,050}{115} = 609.1 \text{ amp}$$

For a three-wire 115/230-volt single-phase or d-c system:
$$I \text{ (outside wires)} = \frac{70,050}{2 \times 115} = 304.6 \text{ amp}$$
$$I \text{ (neutral)} = 200 + (104.6 \times 0.70) = 273.2 \text{ amp}$$

For a four-wire 115-volt two-phase system:
$$I = \frac{70,050}{2 \times 115} = 304.6 \text{ amp}$$

For a three-wire 115-volt two-phase system:
$$I \text{ (outside wires)} = \frac{70,050}{2 \times 115} = 304.6 \text{ amp}$$
$$1.41 \times 304.6 = 429.5 \text{ amp}$$
$$I \text{ (common wire)} = 429.5 \text{ amp}$$

For a five-wire 115/230-volt two-phase system:
$$I \text{ (outside wires)} = \frac{70,050}{4 \times 115} = 152.3 \text{ amp}$$
$$I \text{ (neutral)} = 1.41 \times 152.3 = 214.7 \text{ amp}$$

For a four-wire 208Y/120-volt three-phase system:
$$I \text{ (outside wires)} = \frac{70,050}{3 \times 120} = 194.6 \text{ amp}$$
$$I \text{ (neutral)} = I \text{ (outside wire)} = 121 \text{ amp}$$

Example. Determine the minimum allowable loading for a three-wire 115/230-volt feeder supplying an apartment house having a total floor area of 32,000 sq ft with 40 apartments. One-half of the apartments are equipped with electric ranges of 10 kw each.

Solution. From Table **5**, Div. 11, 3 watts must be allowed for each square foot plus 3,000 watts for appliances for each apartment. The demand factor for the lighting and appliance load from Table **5** of Div. 11 is 1.0 for the first 3,000 watts, 0.35 for the next 117,000 watts, and 0.25 for all load in excess of 120,000 watts. From Table **2** of Div. 11, the maximum demand for the range load is 35 kw.

Lighting load $= 3 \times 32,000$	$= 96,000$
Appliance load $= 40 \times 3,000$	$= 120,000$
Total lighting and appliance load	$= 216,000$ watts

Minimum allowable lighting and appliance load $= 3,000$
$$+ (117,000 \times 0.35) + (216,000 - 120,000)0.25 = 67,950 \text{ watts}$$

Range load	$= 35,000$ watts
Total minimum allowable watt load	$= 102,950$ watts

$$I \text{ (outside wires)} = \frac{102,950}{2 \times 115} = 447.6 \text{ amp}$$

Neutral feeder:

Lighting and small-appliance load = 67,950 watts
Range load, 35,000 watts at 70%   = 24,500 watts
Computed load (neutral)   = 92,450 watts

$$92,450 \div 230 = 402 \text{ amp}$$

Further demand factor:

200 amp at 100% = 200   amp
202 amp at 70% = 141.4 amp
Maximum-demand neutral wire = 341.4 amp

Example. Determine the minimum allowable, general lighting load for a feeder supplying an office building having an area of 100,000 sq ft.

Solution. From Table **5**, Div. 11, 5 watts must be allowed per square foot. From Table **5**, Div. 11, the demand factor is 1.0.

$$\text{Watt load based on area} = 100,000 \times 5 = 500,000 \text{ watts}$$

For a four-wire 120/208-volt three-phase system:

$$I \text{ (outside wires)} = \frac{500,000}{3 \times 120} = 1,389 \text{ amp}$$

$$I \text{ (neutral)} = 200 + (1,389 - 200)0.70$$
$$= 1,032 \text{ amp}$$

53. Calculation of Load on Motor Branch Circuits. For continuous-duty motors the load on the branch circuit feeding a single motor is taken as 125 per cent of the full-load rated current of the motor. The load on a branch circuit supplying a motor in a class of service having short-time duty depends upon the character of the loading. In the majority of cases the load need not be greater than the percentages of the full-load rated currents given in Table **12** of Div. 11. The average full-load rated currents of the different types and sizes of motors are given in Tables **7** to **10** of Div. 11.

The load on conductors connecting the secondary of a wound-rotor, polyphase induction motor to its controller is taken as 125 per cent of the full-load secondary current of the motor for continuous-duty motors and not less than the percentages given in Table **12** of Div. 11 of the full-load secondary current for short-time-duty motors. The loads on the conductors connecting the controller with the secondary resistors must be taken at not less than the proper percentage, as given in Table **13** of Div. 11, of the full-load secondary current. The value of the full-load secondary current, if not marked on the nameplate of the motor, should be obtained from the manufacturer of the motor, since its value will depend upon the design of the motor. For preliminary studies the secondary current may be taken equal to the motor full-load line current for values of full-load current up to about 20 amp. For larger motors the secondary current is usually less than the full-load line current. For a motor with a full-load line current of about 50 to 70 amp, the secondary current is about two-thirds of that value; for a full-load line current of about 80 to 120 amp, the secondary current is about one-half of that value; for a full-load line current of about 150 to 250 amp, the secondary current is about one-third the full-load line value.

54. Calculation of Load on Motor Feeders and Mains. Two values of load should be computed for motor feeders or mains: one the maximum-demand starting current and the other the maximum-demand running current. The maximum-demand running current can be used in determining the size of wire required to carry the current safely. Although this meets the requirements of the National Electrical Code, many authorities consider it better practice to use the maximum-demand starting current in determining the size of wire according to carrying capacity, since then the circuit can be protected against both straight overload and short circuit. When the maximum-demand running current is used for determining the size of wire according to carrying capacity, the circuit can be protected only against short circuit or very heavy overloads and not against overloads of moderate severity. The maximum-demand running current is used for computing the voltage drop of the circuit. The maximum-demand starting current is employed in determining the proper size of protective equipment for the circuit. Values of the average starting currents of motors are given in Tables **39, 40,** and **41** of Div. 11.

The National Electrical Manufacturers' Association (NEMA) adopted in 1940 a standard of identifying code letters that must be marked by the manufacturers on motor nameplates to indicate the motor kilovolt-ampere input with locked rotor. These code letters with their classification are given in Table **39** of Div. 11. At the time of this writing, the code letters have not been classified with respect to the types of motors to which each will normally apply. In determining the starting current to employ for circuit calculations, use values from Table **40** of Div. 11 if the motor nameplate is marked with the NEMA identifying code letter; otherwise, use values from Table **41** of Div. 11.

In many installations where the number of motors is greater than five, all the motors would not be running at full load at the same time. It is general practice, therefore, on such feeders or mains to use a maximum-demand factor so that the estimated maximum-demand current is less than the sum of the full-load rated currents of all the motors fed from the circuit. Values of maximum-demand factors that have been found satisfactory for ordinary installations are given in Table **6** of Div. 11. It should be remembered, in applying these demand factors, that they are average values satisfactory for ordinary installations. Before they are used, a careful study of the operating conditions of the plant should be made in order to determine whether the conditions of instantaneous loading of the motors will come within the average conditions or there are some special requirements that will submit the feeders to a greater loading than will be taken care of by these factors.

Permission for the use of a demand factor must be obtained from the authority enforcing the Code. Some authorities recommend that no demand factor be used in determining the size of circuit to install so that the additional current capacity, thus allowed in the circuit, will give some spare capacity for growth. Refer to Sec. **36** for further discussion on allowance for growth.

The following formulas give the methods of computing the maximum-demand starting and running currents for motor feeders and mains:

$$\begin{pmatrix} \text{Starting} \\ \text{current} \end{pmatrix} = \begin{pmatrix} \text{starting current} \\ \text{of largest motor} \end{pmatrix} + \left[\begin{pmatrix} \text{demand} \\ \text{factor} \end{pmatrix} \times \begin{pmatrix} \text{sum of full-load rated cur-} \\ \text{rents of all the motors except} \\ \text{the largest} \end{pmatrix} \right] \quad (5)$$

$$\begin{pmatrix} \text{Running} \\ \text{current} \end{pmatrix} = \begin{pmatrix} 1.25 \times \text{full-load} \\ \text{current of larg-} \\ \text{est motor} \end{pmatrix} + \left[\begin{pmatrix} \text{demand} \\ \text{factor} \end{pmatrix} \times \begin{pmatrix} \text{sum of full-load rated cur-} \\ \text{rents of all motors except} \\ \text{largest} \end{pmatrix} \right] \quad (6)$$

Where a number of motors of equal horsepower rating are the largest in the group supplied by the circuit, one of these motors should be taken as the largest motor for the calculation of the load on the circuit.

Where two or more motors must be started at the same time, it will generally be necessary to increase the load on the circuit above the values obtained from Eqs. (5) and (6).

Example. Determine the load on a 220-volt feeder supplying two 10-hp and two 15-hp motors. All the motors are three-phase, squirrel-cage induction, normal-starting-current type started at reduced voltage.

Solution. From Table **10** of Div. 11, the full-load current of a 10-hp 220-volt squirrel-cage induction three-phase motor is 28 amp, and the full-load current of a 15-hp motor is 42 amp. The starting current of a 15-hp squirrel-cage induction motor started at reduced voltage from Table **41** of Div. 11 is 200 per cent of the full-load current.

$$\begin{aligned} \text{Maximum-demand starting current} &= (2.00 \times 42) + 42 + (2 \times 28) \\ &= 84 + 42 + 56 \\ &= 182 \text{ amp} \end{aligned}$$

$$\begin{aligned} \text{Maximum-demand running current} &= (1.25 \times 42) + 42 + (2 \times 28) \\ &= 150 \text{ amp} \end{aligned}$$

Example. Determine the load on a 440-volt feeder supplying three 5-hp motors, two 10-hp motors, and three 15-hp motors. All the motors are of the low-starting-current, squirrel-cage type, three-phase.

Solution. From Table **10** of Div. 11 the full-load current of a 5-hp three-phase low-starting-current squirrel-cage motor is 7.6 amp; of a 10-hp motor, 14 amp; and of a 15-hp motor, 21 amp. From Table **6** of Div. 11 the maximum-demand factor is 0.75. Permission has been obtained for the use of this factor.

$$\text{Maximum-demand starting current} = (2.5 \times 21) + 0.75[(3 \times 7.6) + (2 \times 14) + (2 \times 21)]$$
$$= 52.5 + 0.75(22.8 + 28 + 42)$$
$$= 122 \text{ amp}$$

$$\text{Maximum-demand running current} = (1.25 \times 21) + 0.75[(3 \times 7.6) + (2 \times 14) + (2 + 21)]$$
$$= 26.25 + 0.75(22.8 + 28 + 42)$$
$$= 95 \text{ amp}$$

Example. Determine the load on a 230-volt d-c feeder supplying three 3-hp motors, five 5-hp motors, and one 20-hp motor.

Solution. From Table **7** of Div. 11 the full-load current of a 3-hp 230-volt d-c motor is 12.2 amp; of a 5-hp motor, 20 amp; of a 20-hp motor, 72 amp. The starting current of a d-c motor from Table **41** of Div. 11 is 150 per cent of its full-load current. From Table **6** of Div. 11 the maximum-demand factor for nine motors is 0.75. Permission has been obtained for the use of this factor.

$$\text{Maximum-demand starting current} = (1.50 \times 72) + 0.75[(3 \times 12.2) + (5 \times 20)]$$
$$= 108 + 0.75(36.4 + 100)$$
$$= 108 + 102 = 210 \text{ amp}$$

$$\text{Maximum-demand running current} = (1.25 \times 72) + 0.75[(3 \times 12.2) + (5 \times 20)]$$
$$= 90 + 0.75(36.4 + 100)$$
$$= 90 + (0.75 \times 136.4)$$
$$= 90 + 102 = 192 \text{ amp}$$

55. Load on Combined Motor and Lighting Circuits. In cases where both motors and lamps are fed from the same circuit, proceed as follows in determining the total load of the circuit:

1. Determine the lighting and appliance load.
2. Determine the motor load.
3. Total load is equal to the sum of the lighting and motor loads.

56. General Considerations in Computing Voltage Drop. When calculations are made for the voltage drop in a circuit, the future current (Sec. **36**) should be used for lighting and appliance circuits, the maximum running current with allowance for growth (Secs. **36** and **54**) for motor feeders or mains, and the full-load current for motor branch circuits.

The resistance employed in the calculations should be the value corresponding to the operating temperature of the conductors. The following rules with respect to the values of operating temperatures to employ in voltage-drop calculations represent good practice for wires loaded between 50 and 100 per cent of their allowable carrying capacity.

1. Use 50 to 60°C for wires insulated with Code or moisture-resistant rubber compounds, synthetic rubberlike compounds, or thermoplastic compounds. Types RUW, T, and TW wires.

2. Use 70°C for wires insulated with heat-resistant rubber compound, varnished cambric, paper, thermoplastic and asbestos, slow-burning or weatherproof compounds. Types RH, RHH, RHW, RUH, THW, THWN, and MI.

3. Use 100°C for all wires not included in 1 and 2 above. For wires loaded less than 50 per cent of their allowable carrying capacity the temperature should be reduced from 15 to 20° below the above values. The resistance of copper wire varies somewhat with the method of drawing the wire. As a general rule the voltage drop of a circuit will depend upon several variables, the value of which cannot possibly be determined accurately. It is not practical, therefore, to spend too much time in accurately determining the value of the resistance of the wires. An average value of 98 per cent conductivity for copper wires is generally satisfactory. Copper of 98 per cent conductivity has a resistivity of approximately 10.6 ohms per cir mil-ft at 20°C, 11.2 ohms at 30°, 11.6 at 40°, 11.8 at 50°, 12.3 at 60°, and 12.7 at 70°. Tables of resistance of wires are given in Div. 11.

The length of the circuit should be taken as the distance along the circuit from the supply end to the load center. Where a load is distributed along the circuit, the total current does not flow the complete length of the circuit. Therefore, if the actual length of the circuit were used in computing the voltage drop, the drop determined would be greater than the drop that would actually occur. The load center of a circuit is that point in the circuit where, if the load were concentrated at that point, the drop would be the same as the voltage drop to the farthest load in the actual circuit.

57. The load center of a circuit can be determined in the following manner: Multiply each load by its distance from the supply end of the circuit. Add these products for all the loads fed from the circuit and divide this sum by the sum of the individual

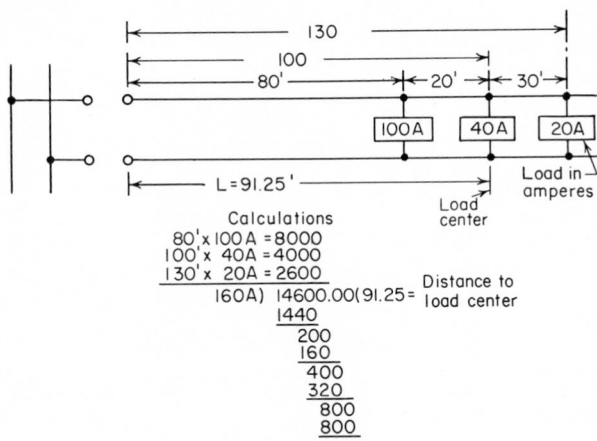

FIG. 28   *Method of computing location of load center.*

loads. The result thus obtained is the distance from the supply end of the circuit to the load center. It is this length that should be employed in computing the voltage drop of the circuit (see solution of example in Fig. 28).

The load center of a group of receivers symmetrically arranged (Fig. 29) and all of the same output will be in the middle of the group. Always take the distance along the circuit as *L*, Fig. 29.

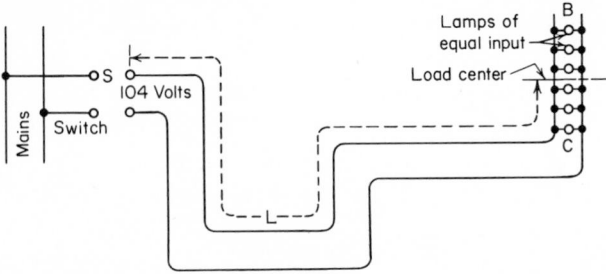

FIG. 29   *Illustrating location of load center.*

58. Calculation of Voltage Drop in D-C Two-wire Circuits by Means of Formula. The voltage drop can be calculated by means of either Eq. (7) or (8), and the size of wire to produce a given voltage drop can be calculated by Eq. (9).

$$V = 2R \times L \times I \tag{7}$$

where V = drop in volts in the circuit; R = resistance of wire in ohms per foot (values of resistance for copper or aluminum conductors can be obtained from Table **64** of Div.

11); I = current in amperes; and L = length one way of circuit in feet, or

$$V = \frac{2K \times L \times I}{\text{cir mils}} \tag{8}$$

where V = drop in volts in the circuit; K = resistivity of material of conductor in ohms per circular mil-foot (values of K for copper conductors can be obtained from Sec. 56; sufficient accuracy will be obtained for most cases by using the following more approximate values: 12 for circuits loaded between 50 and 100 per cent of their allowable carrying capacity and 11 for circuits loaded less than 50 per cent of their allowable carrying capacity); I = current in amperes; L = length one way of circuit in feet; cir mils = area of conductor in circular mils. K = 18 for aluminum conductors.

$$\text{Cir mils} = \frac{2K \times I \times L}{V} \tag{9}$$

59. Determination of Voltage Drop in D-C Two-wire Circuits by Means of Chart. A graph for computing the voltage drop in circuits (Sec. 55 of Div. 11) was originally proposed by R. W. Stovel and N. A. Carle in *The Electric Journal* for June, 1908. It is based on a resistivity of 10.7 ohms per circular mil-foot of copper wire. The chart will, therefore, give satisfactory results for circuits loaded less than 50 per cent of their allowable carrying capacity. For most circuits which are loaded to between 50 and 100 per cent of their allowable carrying capacity, the voltage drop obtained from the chart should be increased by 10 per cent. The length of the circuit that should be employed in using the chart is the distance from the supply end to the load center. The voltage drop as read from the chart is the total drop in both wires. In order to determine the voltage drop of a circuit from the chart, proceed as follows:

1. Start on the lower left-hand scale with the current for the circuit.
2. Follow this point vertically upward to the diagonal line for the size of wire of the circuit.
3. From this intersection proceed horizontally to the right to the diagonal line representing the length of the circuit one way.
4. At this intersection drop vertically to the voltage-drop scale.
5. The reading on the voltage-drop scale will be the drop in volts in both wires of the circuit for lightly loaded circuits as discussed above.
6. For normally loaded circuits the voltage drop will be equal to 1.1 times the value read from the chart.

Example. What will be the voltage drop of the motor feeder for the last problem of Sec. 54 if the length of circuit is 150 ft and a No. 4/0 Type RH wire is employed?

Solution. The maximum-demand running current of 195 amp should be used in determining voltage drop. From Table 67 of Div. 11 a No. 4/0 wire has 211,600 cir mils and from Table 19 of Div. 11 has a carrying capacity of 230 amp.

Using the formula

$$V \times \frac{24 \times I \times L}{\text{cir mils}} = \frac{24 \times 195 \times 150}{211,600} = 3.32 \text{ volts drop}$$

Using the chart: Start at the bottom of the chart on the left-hand side at 195 amp and follow this point vertically upward until it intersects the diagonal line marked No. 0000. From this intersection proceed horizontally to the right until the diagonal line marked 150 is reached. At this intersection drop vertically downward to the voltage-drop scale, and read 3.0 volts. Since the wire is loaded to more than 50 per cent of its capacity, the voltage drop equals 3.0 × 1.1 = 3.3 volts.

60. Determination of Voltage Drop in D-C Three-wire Circuits. Either the formulas of Sec. 58 or the chart of Sec. 55, Div. 11, can be used for determining the voltage drop of d-c three-wire circuits. In either case the current used should be that of the more heavily loaded outside wire and the size of conductor that of the outside conductors. The drop thus obtained from either the formula or the chart will be the drop between the outside wires. What is desired is the drop across each receiver or the drop between an outside wire and the neutral wire. The approximate voltage drop to each receiver will be one-half of the value determined from either the formula or the chart. This value will be correct for a balanced load. When the load is unbalanced, the current in the neutral wire will cause an additional voltage drop which will not have the same effect on the two sides of the circuit. Since in a well-laid-out system the load will be nearly balanced, the method given is satisfactory for most cases.

Example. Determine the voltage drop on a three-wire lighting feeder 100 ft long. The actual load on one side is 147 amp, and on the other side 158 amp. The future load on one side is 170 amp, and on the other side 175 amp. A No. 4/0 Type T wire is used for the outside copper conductors.

Solution. The future load on the more heavily loaded side should be used in determining voltage drop. A No. 4/0 Type T wire from Table **67**, Div. **11**, has 211,600 cir mils, and from Table **19**, Div. **11**, a carrying capacity of 195 amp.

Using the formula

$$V = \frac{24 \times I \times L}{\text{cir mils}} = \frac{24 \times 175 \times 100}{211,600} = 1.98 \text{ volts}$$

Using the chart: Start at the bottom of the chart on the left-hand side at 175 amp and follow this point vertically upward until it intersects the diagonal line marked No. 0000. From this intersection follow horizontally to the right until the diagonal line marked 100 is reached. At this intersection drop vertically downward to the voltage-drop scale, and read 1.8 volts drop. The voltage drop will be equal to $1.8 \times 1.1 = 1.98$.

The drop across each receiver is one-half of the drop determined by the formula or chart. The drop across each receiver is, therefore, 0.99 volt determined from either the formula or chart.

61. The voltage drop in a-c circuits is affected by several factors that have no effect in d-c circuits. These factors are (1) power factor of the load, (2) inductance of the circuit, (3) capacity of the circuit, and (4) increased resistance of the circuit to alternating current.

As discussed in Div. 1, when alternating current flows in a circuit, the resistance is increased, owing to skin effect. This increase in resistance for most circuits is so small that it need not be considered. Unless the size of the conductor is greater than 750,000 cir mils for 25-cycle circuits or 300,000 cir mils for 60-cycle circuits, skin effect can be neglected and the resistance of the wire taken the same as for direct current. When skin effect must be considered in copper conductors, its effect can be allowed for by multiplying the d-c resistance of the wire by the proper factor from Table **65**, **68**, or **69** of Div. **11**. The a-c resistances for all-steel, copper-steel, and aluminum cable, steel-reinforced, can be determined directly from Tables **70** to **75** in Div. **11**.

As discussed in Div. 1 the phenomenon of inductance causes a voltage to be induced in an a-c circuit which opposes the flow of current in the circuit. Inductance, therefore, offers opposition to the flow of alternating current in a circuit. This opposition is called the inductive reactance of the circuit and is represented by the symbol X_L. The value of the inductive reactance of a circuit depends upon the size of the wire, the distance between the wires of the circuit, the frequency of the current flowing in the circuit, the material of the conductor, and the presence of any magnetic material in proximity to the circuit. The voltage drop due to inductance produced in a circuit is equal to the current times the inductive reactance. For small-sized conductors the effect of inductance is so small that it can be neglected (see Sec. **56** of Div. **11**).

The two conductors of any circuit with the insulation between them produce a capacitor. They therefore introduce capacity into the circuit. The effect of capacity in an a-c circuit is to offer opposition to the flow of current. This opposition is called capacity reactance and is denoted by the symbol X_c. The voltage drop in a circuit due to capacity is equal to the current times the capacity reactance. The effect of capacity upon the voltage drop of the circuit is so small except for high-voltage, long-distance transmission lines that it is neglected.

The total voltage drop in an a-c circuit due to the resistance and reactance is affected by the power factor of the load connected to the circuit.

62. Summary of Factors That Must Be Considered in Calculating Drop for A-C Circuits. Skin effect can usually be neglected unless the size of wires is greater than 300,000 cir mils for 60-cycle circuits or 750,000 cir mils for 25-cycle circuits.

The effect of capacity can be neglected except for long-distance transmission lines.

The effect of inductance can be neglected unless the size of wire exceeds the values given in Table **56** of Div. 11.

63. Line or circuit reactance can be reduced in three ways. One of these is to diminish the distance between wires. The extent to which this can be carried is limited, in the case of a pole line, to the least distance at which the wires are safe from swinging together in the middle of a span. In inside wiring (knob or tube work), it is limited by the spacings required by the National Electrical Code. In conduit work, nothing can be done about reducing the distance between wires. Another way of reducing the reactance is by increasing the size of the conductors, but it is not possible to secure much reduction by this method unless the size is increased an excessive amount. The third way of reducing reactance is to divide the load into a greater number of circuits. Voltage drop in lines due to inductive reactance is best diminished (Mershon) by subdividing the copper or by bringing the conductors closer together. It is little affected by changing the size of conductor.

64. Determining Power Factors of Feeders or Mains. Although the values of power factors obtained by the following method are approximate, they are accurate enough for most circuit calculations. To determine the power factor of a circuit supplying several motors proceed as follows:

1. Multiply the horsepower of each motor by its power factor at 75 per cent of rated load.

2. Add these products for all the motors fed from the line.

3. The approximate power factor of the circuit will equal the sum obtained in (2) divided by the total horsepower connected to the circuit.

Approximate power factors of different types of loads are given in Table **58** of Div. 11.

Example. Determine the power factor for a feeder supplying two 5-hp motors, five 10-hp motors, and one 50-hp motor.
Solution

$$\text{Hp of motor} \times \text{power factor} = \text{product of hp and pf}$$
(From Table **58**, Div. 11)

5	×	0.83	=	4.15
5	×	0.83	=	4.15
10	×	0.86	=	8.6
10	×	0.86	=	8.6
10	×	0.86	=	8.6
10	×	0.86	=	8.6
10	×	0.86	=	8.6
50	×	0.89	=	44.5
110 total connected hp				95.8

$$\text{Approximate power factor of circuit} = \frac{\text{sum of products of hp and pf}}{\text{total connected hp}}$$

$$= \frac{95.8}{110} = 87.1$$

65. Calculation of Voltage Drop in Two-wire Single-phase Circuits When Effect of Inductance Can Be Neglected. These circuits can be calculated in the same way as d-c circuits, by means of either the formulas of Sec. **58** or the chart of Sec. **55** of Div. 11.

66. Calculation of Voltage Drop in Three-wire Single-phase Circuits When Effect of Inductance Can Be Neglected. Circuits of this type can be calculated in exactly the same manner as three-wire, d-c circuits (see Sec. **60**).

67. Calculation of Voltage Drop in Four-wire Two-phase Circuits When Effect of Inductance Can Be Neglected. A four-wire, two-phase circuit can be considered as two separate single-phase circuits, and the voltage drop computed in the same manner as given for two-wire, d-c circuits in either Sec. **58** or Sec. **59**.

68. Calculation of Voltage Drop in Three-wire Two-phase Circuits When Effect of Inductance Can Be Neglected. The voltage drop in the common wire of three-wire, two-phase systems somewhat unbalances the voltages of the two phases, and therefore, the voltage drop of the two phases is not the same. An exact method of the calculation of the voltage drop of these circuits is too complicated for the scope of this book. The following method will give the approximate voltage drop on the phase having the greater voltage drop. It is accurate enough for most interior-wiring calculations. Proceed as follows:

1. Determine the voltage drop in one outside wire. It will be equal to one-half of the voltage drop determined by means of either the formulas of Sec. 58 or the chart of Sec. 55 in Div. 11.

2. Determine the voltage drop in the common wire. This will be equal to one-half of the voltage drop determined by means of either the formulas of Sec. 58 or the chart of Sec. 55 in Div. 11, the size of wire and current for the common wire being used.

3. The total voltage drop is taken as equal to the drop in one outside wire plus 0.8 times the voltage drop in the common wire.

Example. Determine the voltage drop of a three-wire two-phase 60-cycle lighting feeder which is 200 ft long and installed in conduit. The current in each outside wire is 130 amp. A No. 2/0 wire is used for the outside wires, and a No. 4/0 for the common wire. All wires are Type T.

Solution. Since the largest wire used is No. 4/0 from Table 56 of Div. 11 the effect of inductance can be neglected. From Table 67 of Div. 11 a No. 2/0 wire has 133,100 cir mils, and a No. 4/0 wire 211,600 cir mils. From Table 19 of Div. 11 all wires are loaded to more than 50 per cent of their carrying capacity.

$$\text{Drop in two outside wires} = \frac{24 \times I \times L}{\text{cir mils}} = \frac{24 \times 130 \times 200}{133,100} = 4.7 \text{ volts}$$

$$\text{Drop in one outside wire} = \frac{4.7}{2} = 2.35 \text{ volts}$$

$$\text{Current in common wire} = 1.41 \times 130 = 183.5 \text{ amp}$$

$$\text{Drop in common wire} = \frac{24 \times I \times L}{2 \times \text{cir mils}} = \frac{24 \times 183.5 \times 200}{2 \times 211,600} = 2.08 \text{ volts}$$

$$\text{Total voltage drop} = 2.35 + (0.8 \times 2.08) = 2.35 + 1.66$$

$$= 4.01 \text{ volts drop}$$

69. Calculation of Voltage Drop in Five-wire Two-phase Circuits When Effect of Inductance Can Be Neglected. In a well-laid-out system the load will be very nearly balanced under normal conditions. Therefore, there would be practically no current in the neutral wire. For lighting loads supplied by this system the lamps are connected between the neutral wire and the respective outside wires. The drop to any lamp therefore would be equal to the drop in one outside wire. The drop in one outside wire will be equal to one-half of the drop determined by either the formulas of Sec. 58 or the chart of Sec. 55 of Div. 11. The drop to motors fed by this system would be equal to the drop in two outside wires and, therefore, to the drop determined by either the formula or the chart.

70. Calculation of Voltage Drop in Three-wire Three-phase Circuits When Effect of Inductance Can Be Neglected. The voltage drop in these circuits will be equal to 0.866 times the voltage drop of a two-wire d-c circuit carrying the same current as the three-phase circuit. This drop may be determined from either the formulas of Sec. 58 or the chart of Sec. 55 of Div. 11.

Example. Determine the voltage drop of a three-wire three-phase 60-cycle motor feeder which is 150 ft long. Three No. 2 Type T wires are installed in conduit. The current is 85 amp.

Solution. Since the size of wire is No. 2 from Table 56 of Div. 11 the effect of inductance can be neglected. From Table 67 of Div. 11 a No. 2 wire has 66,370 cir mils, and from Table 19 of Div. 11 a carrying capacity of 95 amp.

$$\text{Drop in a two-wire d-c circuit carrying 85 amp over a No. 2 wire} = \frac{24 \times I \times L}{\text{cir mils}}$$

$$= \frac{24 \times 85 \times 150}{66,370} = 4.61 \text{ volts}$$

Therefore   Drop of the three-phase system $= 0.866 \times 4.61$

$$= 4.0 \text{ volts}$$

71. Calculation of Voltage Drop in Four-wire Three-phase Circuits When Effect of Inductance Can Be Neglected. In a well-laid-out system the load will be very nearly balanced under normal load conditions. Therefore, there will be practically no current in the neutral wire. For lighting loads supplied by this system the lamps are connected between the neutral wire and the respective outside wires. The drop to any lamp, therefore, is equal to the drop in one outside wire. The drop in one outside wire will be equal to one-half of the drop determined by either the formulas of Sec. **64** or the chart of Sec. **55** of Div. 11. The drop to motors fed by this system is the drop between any two outside wires. This drop is equal to 0.866 times the voltage drop of a two-wire d-c system carrying the same current as the three-phase system. (Use either the formulas of Sec. **58** or the chart of Sec. **55** of Div. 11 for determining the d-c drop.)

72. Calculation of Circuits When Effect of Inductance Cannot Be Neglected. Two methods are given in the following paragraphs for calculating the voltage drop of circuits when the effect of inductance is so great that it cannot be neglected (see Sec. **56** of Div. 11 for rules indicating when inductance must be considered). In one of these methods the voltage drop in the actual a-c circuit is calculated by multiplying the drop of a d-c circuit by a factor called the drop factor. This drop factor is the ratio between the actual drop and the drop that would occur if there were no inductance. The drop factor is affected by the size of wire, spacing of the wires of the circuit, the frequency of the current, and the power factor of the load. Values of drop factors for various conditions in which concentric stranded copper conductors are used are given in Table **61** of Div. 11.

The other method given for computing the voltage drop of circuits when the effect of inductance cannot be neglected makes use of a diagram called the Mershon diagram (Fig. 30).

Under ordinary conditions of use both of these methods will give results of about the same degree of accuracy. If the Mershon diagram is used carefully, it will give the more accurate results of the two. But since in the calculation of most circuits several factors are based on assumption, the greater accuracy of the Mershon diagram is of questionable value. The drop-factor method is certainly accurate enough for the calculation of all interior-wiring circuits, and the author believes that it is the more easily applied method of

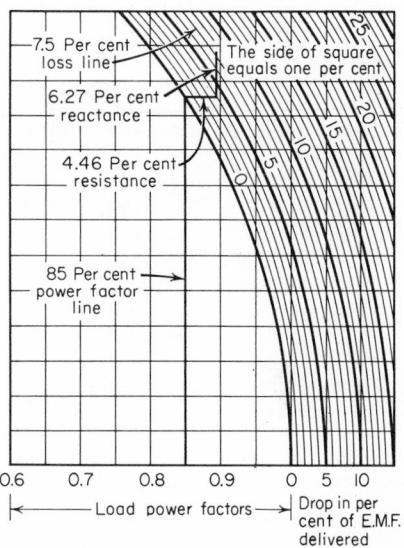

FIG. 30 *Illustrating the application of the Mershon Diagram for computing a single-phase circuit. The side of each small square equals 1 per cent; percentage resistance is measured horizontally and percentage reactance vertically.*

the two. For circuits employing some type of conductor material or construction other than stranded copper, the Mershon diagram will have to be used, since no data are given for drop factors for conductors of other types.

73. Drop-factor Method of Calculating Voltage Drop When Effect of Inductance Cannot Be Neglected. Proceed as follows:

1. Determine from either Sec. **58** or **59** the voltage drop of a two-wire d-c system carrying the same current and using the same size wire.

2. Determine the ratio of reactance to resistance for the size of wire, spacing of wires, and frequency of the circuit considered (see Table **59** or **60** of Div. 11).

3. Determine power factor of circuit (see Sec. **64** and Table **58** of Div. 11).

4. Determine the drop factor for the circuit corresponding to the determined ratio of reactance to resistance and power factor of the circuit from Table **61** of Div. 11.

5. The voltage drop of the circuit then is determined as follows, depending upon the electric system:

For two-wire single-phase systems:

$$\text{Voltage drop} = \text{drop factor} \times \text{d-c voltage drop} \tag{10}$$

For three-wire single-phase systems:

$$\text{Voltage drop between outside wires} = \text{drop factor} \times \text{d-c voltage drop} \tag{11}$$

Voltage drop between outside wire and neutral (lamps)

$$= \tfrac{1}{2}(\text{drop factor} \times \text{d-c voltage drop}) \tag{12}$$

For four-wire two-phase systems, each phase is considered as a separate two-wire single-phase system.

$$\text{Voltage drop} = \text{drop factor} \times \text{d-c voltage drop} \tag{13}$$

For three-wire system tapped from four-wire three-phase system:

$$\text{Voltage drop} = 0.75(\text{drop factor} \times \text{d-c voltage drop}) \tag{14}$$

For three-wire two-phase systems two d-c drops must first be determined: one for a two-wire d-c circuit carrying the same current and with the same size wire as the outside conductors of the two-phase system, and the other for a two-wire d-c circuit carrying the same current and with the same size wire as the common wire of the two-phase system. Then

$$\substack{\text{Voltage drop of two-}\\ \text{phase three-wire system}} = \left[\frac{\left(\substack{\text{drop}\\ \text{factor}}\right) \times \left(\substack{\text{d-c voltage drop for current}\\ \text{and size of outside wire}}\right)}{2} \right]$$
$$+ \left[0.8 \times \frac{\left(\substack{\text{drop}\\ \text{factor}}\right) \times \left(\substack{\text{d-c voltage drop for current and}\\ \text{size of wire of common wire}}\right)}{2} \right] \tag{15}$$

For five-wire, two-phase systems:

$$\text{Voltage drop for lamps} = \frac{\text{drop factor} \times \text{d-c voltage drop}}{2} \tag{16}$$

$$\text{Voltage drop for motors} = \text{drop factor} \times \text{d-c voltage drop} \tag{17}$$

For three-wire, three-phase systems:

$$\text{Voltage drop} = 0.866 \times \text{drop factor} \times \text{d-c voltage drop} \tag{18}$$

For four-wire, three-phase systems:

$$\text{Voltage drop for lamps} = \frac{\text{drop factor} \times \text{d-c voltage drop}}{2} \tag{19}$$

$$\text{Voltage drop for motors} = 0.866 \times \text{drop factor} \times \text{d-c voltage drop} \tag{20}$$

Example. Determine the voltage drop of a two-wire single-phase 60-cycle motor circuit carrying a current of 250 amp for a distance of 150 ft. A 300,000-cir-mil Type RH wire is used, installed in conduit. The power factor of the circuit is 80 per cent.

Solution. From Table **56** of Div. 11, since the size of wire is 300,000 cir mils, the effect of inductance cannot be neglected. The carrying capacity from Table **19** of Div. 11 is 285 amp.

The drop of a two-wire d-c circuit carrying 250 amp over a 300,000-cir-mil wire for 150 ft $= \dfrac{24 \times I \times L}{\text{cir mils}} = \dfrac{24 \times 250 \times 150}{300,000} = 3.0$ volts.

From Table **59** of Div. 11 the ratio of reactance to resistance for a 300,000-cir-mil wire installed in conduit on a 60-cycle system is 1.01.

From Table **61** of Div. 11 the drop factor for a ratio of reactance to resistance of 1.01 and a power factor of 80 per cent is 1.40.

Voltage drop of the actual circuit = drop factor $\times$ d-c drop = $1.40 \times 3.0 = 4.2$ volts.

Example. Determine the voltage drop of the above circuit, if it were a three-wire single-phase one.

Solution. The voltage drop between outside wires would be equal to the drop factor times the drop of a two-wire d-c system carrying the same current = $1.40 \times 3.0 = 4.2$ volts.

Voltage drop across lamps if connected to the circuit would be the drop between an outside wire and the neutral $= \dfrac{1.40 \times 3.0}{2} = 2.1$ volts.

Example. Determine the voltage drop of the above circuit if it were three-wire tapped from a four-wire three-phase system.

Solution. Voltage drop across lamps = 0.75 × 1.4 × 3.0 = 3.15 volts.

Example. Determine the voltage drop of the preceding circuit, if it were a four-wire two-phase system.

Solution. Voltage drop = drop factor × d-c drop

$$= 1.40 \times 3.0 = 4.2 \text{ volts}$$

Example. Determine the voltage drop of the preceding circuit, if it were a three-wire two-phase one. The 250 amp is the current in the outside wires.

Solution. The current in the common wire = 1.41 × 250 = 352 amp. Use a 500,000-cir-mil wire for the common.

The voltage drop for a two-wire d-c system carrying 250 amp over a 300,000-cir-mil wire for 150 ft $= \dfrac{24 \times I \times L}{300,000} = \dfrac{24 \times 250 \times 150}{300,000} = 3.0$ volts.

The voltage drop for a two-wire d-c circuit carrying 352 amp for 150 ft over a 500,000-cir-mil wire $= \dfrac{24 \times I \times L}{500,000} = \dfrac{24 \times 352 \times 150}{500,000} = 2.54$ volts.

From preceding problems the drop factor for the outside conductors = 1.40.

From Table 59 of Div. 11 the ratio of reactance to resistance for a 500,000-cir-mil wire installed in conduit on a 60-cycle system is 1.75.

From Table 61 of Div. 11 the drop factor for a ratio of reactance to resistance of 1.75 and a power factor of 80 per cent is 1.88.

$$\text{Voltage drop of actual circuit} = \frac{\left(\begin{smallmatrix}\text{drop}\\\text{factor}\end{smallmatrix}\right) \times \left(\begin{smallmatrix}\text{d-c voltage drop}\\\text{for current and}\\\text{size of wire of}\\\text{outside wires}\end{smallmatrix}\right)}{2} + 0.8 \times \frac{\left(\begin{smallmatrix}\text{drop}\\\text{factor}\end{smallmatrix}\right) \times \left(\begin{smallmatrix}\text{d-c voltage drop}\\\text{for current and}\\\text{size of wire of}\\\text{common wire}\end{smallmatrix}\right)}{2}$$

$$= \frac{1.40 \times 3.0}{2} + \frac{0.8 \times 1.88 \times 2.54}{2} = 2.1 + 1.91$$

$$= 4.01 \text{ volts}$$

Example. Determine the voltage drop of the preceding circuit, if it were a five-wire, two-phase system.

Solution. Voltage drop for motors = drop factor × d-c voltage drop

$$= 1.40 \times 3.0 = 4.2 \text{ volts}$$

If there were any lamps connected to the circuit, the voltage drop across each lamp

$$= \frac{\text{drop factor} \times \text{d-c voltage drop}}{2}$$

$$= \frac{1.40 \times 3.0}{2} = 2.1 \text{ volts}$$

Example. Determine the voltage drop of the preceding circuit, if it were a three-wire, three-phase system.

Solution. Voltage drop = 0.866 × drop factor × d-c voltage drop
$$= 0.866 \times 1.40 \times 3.0 = 3.64 \text{ volts}$$

Example. Determine the voltage drop of the preceding circuit, if it were a four-wire, three-phase system.

Solution. Voltage drop for motors = 0.866 × drop factor × d-c voltage drop
$$= 0.866 \times 1.40 \times 3.0 = 3.64 \text{ volts}$$

If there were any lamps connected to the circuit the voltage drop across each lamp

$$= \frac{\text{drop factor} \times \text{d-c voltage drop}}{2}$$

$$= \frac{1.40 \times 3.0}{2} = 2.1 \text{ volts}$$

74. Calculation of Voltage Drop of Two-wire Single-phase Circuits by Mershon Diagram When Effect of Inductance Cannot Be Neglected. Proceed as follows:

1. Determine the a-c resistance of the total length of wire. This will be equal to the resistance per foot of wire of the size and material employed multiplied by two times

the length of circuit one way in feet. Care should be exercised in taking values of resistance from the tables to observe in what units the resistance is given. Some values are given in ohms per 1,000 ft, and others in ohms per mile. For copper conductors use Table **63, 65, 68,** or **69** of Div. 11. The a-c resistance will be equal to the d-c resistance at the working temperature of the wire times the skin-effect correction factor. For all-steel conductors use Table **70** of Div. 11; for copper-steel, Tables **71** to **74** of Div. 11; and for aluminum cable, steel-reinforced, Table **75** of Div. 11. These three tables give the values of a-c resistance directly. In using Table **75,** it is first necessary to determine the amperes per square inch for the cable employed. The area in square inches will be equal to the area in circular mils times 0.7854 divided by 1,000,000.

2. Determine the resistance volts drop. This will be equal to the resistance of the total length of wire as determined in step 1 multiplied by the current.

3. Determine the inductive reactance of the total length of wire. This will be equal to the reactance per foot of wire for the size, material, and spacing of wires multiplied by two times the length of circuit one way in feet. Care should be exercised in taking values of reactance from the tables to observe in what units the reactance is given. Some values are given in ohms per 1,000 ft, and others in ohms per mile. For copper conductors use Secs. **77** to **81** of Div. 11. If a cable has a metallic armor of magnetic material or other magnetic binder, the correction factors of Table **63** of Div. 11 should be applied to the reactance values in Secs. **77** to **81** of Div. 11. For all-steel conductors use Table **82** of Div. 11; for copper-steel, Table **83** of Div. 11; for copperweld, Table **84** of Div. 11; and for aluminum cable, steel-reinforced, Table **85** or **86** of Div. 11. In using Table **85** or **86** the amperes per square inch must be determined in order to select the proper column.

4. Determine the reactance volts drop. This will be equal to the reactance of the total length of wire as determined in step 3 multiplied by the current.

5. Find what percentage the resistance volts drop is of the voltage delivered at the end of the line.

6. Find what percentage the reactance volts drop is of the voltage delivered at the end of the line.

7. Determine the power factor of the circuit (see Sec. **64,** and Table **58** of Div. 11).

8. On the Mershon diagram (Fig. 30) start at the point where the vertical line corresponding to the power factor of the circuit intersects the smallest circle.

9. From this point lay off horizontally to the right the percentage of resistance volts drop. From the point thus obtained lay off vertically upward the percentage of reactance volts drop.

10. The circle upon which the last point obtained falls will give the voltage drop in percentage of the voltage at the end of the line.

Example. Determine the voltage drop of a 60-cycle 110-volt circuit carrying 200 amp a distance of 222 ft. The power factor of the circuit is 85 per cent. The wires are No. 4/0, Type T, spaced 6 in. apart.

Solution. From Sec. **56** the temperature of the conductors would be taken as 50°C, since Type T wire is used and it will be loaded to more than 50 per cent of its allowable carrying capacity. From Table **63** of Div. 11, the skin-effect correction factor is 1.00, so that the resistance per 1,000 ft will be the same as for direct current at 50°C. From the table this is 0.0552.

$$\text{Resistance volts drop} = \frac{0.0552}{1,000} \times 2 \times 222 \times 200 = 4.91 \text{ volts}$$

$$\text{Percentage resistance volts drop} = \frac{4.91}{110} \times 100 = 4.46 \text{ per cent}$$

From the curves of Sec. **78** of Div. 11 a circuit of No. 4/0 wire, 1,000 ft long on a 60-cycle system with the wires spaced 6 in. apart, has a reactance of 0.0775 ohm.

$$\text{Reactance volts drop} = \frac{0.0775}{1,000} \times 2 \times 222 \times 200 = 6.89 \text{ volts}$$

$$\text{Percentage reactance volts drop} = \frac{6.89}{110} \times 100 = 6.27 \text{ per cent}$$

Applying the Mershon diagram to this problem as shown in Fig. 30 the total drop in percentage of the 110 volts at the end of the line is 7.5 per cent.

$$\text{Total volts drop} = \frac{110 \times 7.5}{100} = 8.25 \text{ volts}$$

75. Calculation of Voltage Drop by Mershon Diagram for Any Circuit When Effect of Inductance Cannot Be Neglected.   First determine, as outlined in Sec. **74,** the voltage drop for a two-wire single-phase circuit of the same size wire carrying the same current as the actual circuit.   Then, proceed as follows for the particular system involved:

Three-wire single-phase:

$$\text{Voltage drop between outside wires} = \text{drop as read from diagram} \quad (21)$$

Voltage drop between outside wire and neutral (lamps) =

$$\frac{\text{drop as read from diagram}}{2} \quad (22)$$

Three-wire tapped from three-phase four-wire:

Voltage drop between outside wire and neutral (lamps) =

$$0.75(\text{drop as read from diagram}) \quad (23)$$

Four-wire two-phase systems: Each phase is considered as a separate two-wire single-phase system.

Three-wire two-phase systems: Determine two drops from the diagram, one for a circuit with size of wire and current of outside wires of two-phase system, and the other for a circuit with size of wire and current of common wire.

Then

$$\text{Voltage drop} = \left(\frac{\begin{array}{c}\text{drop for circuit with}\\\text{size of wire and current}\\\text{of outside wires}\end{array}}{2}\right) + 0.8 \times \left(\frac{\begin{array}{c}\text{drop for circuit with}\\\text{size of wire and current}\\\text{of common wire}\end{array}}{2}\right) \quad (24)$$

Five-wire two-phase systems:

$$\text{Voltage drop for lamps} = \frac{\text{drop from diagram}}{2} \quad (25)$$

$$\text{Voltage drop for motors} = \text{drop as read from diagram} \quad (26)$$

Three-wire three-phase systems:

$$\text{Voltage drop} = 0.866 \times \text{drop as read from diagram} \quad (27)$$

Four-wire three-phase systems:

$$\text{Voltage drop for lamps} = \frac{\text{drop from diagram}}{2} \quad (28)$$

$$\text{Voltage drop for motor} = 0.866 \times \text{drop as read from diagram} \quad (29)$$

Example.   Determine the voltage drop for the circuit of the example in Sec. **74** for the different systems.

Solution.   Referring to the problem in Sec. **74,** the voltage drop of the circuit for a two-wire single-phase system is 8.25 volts.

For a three-wire single-phase system:

$$\text{Voltage drop for motors} = \text{drop as read from diagram}$$
$$= 8.25 \text{ volts}$$

$$\text{Voltage drop for lamps} = \frac{\text{drop as read from diagram}}{2} = \frac{8.25}{2} = 4.13$$

For a four-wire two-phase system:

$$\text{Voltage drop} = \text{drop as read from diagram} = 8.25 \text{ volts}$$

For a three-wire two-phase system:

Use must be made of the Mershon diagram to determine another voltage drop.   The drop obtained in Sec. **74** is for a two-wire single-phase circuit carrying the same current as the outside wires of the three-wire two-phase circuit, and with the same size wire as the outside wires.   Another voltage drop for a two-wire single-phase circuit carrying the same current as the common wire of the three-wire two-phase circuit, and with the size of wire of the common, must be determined.

$$\text{Current in common wire} = 1.41 \times 200 = 282 \text{ amp}$$

Assume that a 400,000-cir-mil wire is used for common wire (as large a size would not be required by carrying capacity).

From Table **63** of Div. 11 a circuit of 400,000-cir-mil wire, 1,000 ft long on a 60-cycle system, will have a resistance of 0.0292 ohm per 1,000 ft if operated at 50°C.

$$\text{Resistance volts drop} = \frac{0.0292}{1,000} \times 2 \times 222 \times 282$$

$$= 3.66 \text{ volts}$$

$$\text{Percentage resistance volts drop} = \frac{3.66}{110} \times 100 = 3.32 \text{ per cent}$$

From the curves of Sec. **78** of Div. 11 a circuit of 400,000-cir-mil wire, 1,000 ft long on a 60-cycle system, with the wires spaced 6 in. apart, will have a reactance of 0.071 ohms per 1,000 ft.

$$\text{Reactance volts drop} = \frac{0.071}{1,000} \times 2 \times 222 \times 282$$

$$= 8.88 \text{ volts}$$

$$\text{Percentage reactance volts drop} = \frac{8.88}{110} \times 100 = 8.07 \text{ per cent}$$

If the Mershon diagram is applied, a two-wire single-phase circuit of 85 per cent pf carrying 282 amp over 400,000-cir-mil wires spaced 6 in. apart will give a 7.3 per cent volts drop, or $\frac{7.3 \times 110}{100} =$ 8.03 volts.

$$\text{Voltage drop for three-wire two-phase circuit} = \frac{8.25}{2} + \left(0.8 \times \frac{8.03}{2} \right)$$

$$= 4.13 + 3.21$$
$$= 7.34$$

For a five-wire two-phase system:

$$\text{Voltage drop for lamps} = \frac{\text{drop from diagram}}{2} = \frac{8.25}{2} = 4.13$$

$$\text{Voltage drop for motors} = \text{drop as read from diagram}$$
$$= 8.25 \text{ volts}$$

For a three-wire three-phase system:

$$\text{Voltage drop} = 0.866 \times \text{drop as read from diagram}$$
$$= 0.866 \times 8.25 = 7.15 \text{ volts}$$

For a four-wire three-phase system:

$$\text{Voltage drop for lamps} = \frac{\text{drop from diagram}}{2} = \frac{8.25}{2}$$

$$= 4.13 \text{ volts}$$
$$\text{Voltage drop for motors} = 0.866 \times \text{drop as read from diagram}$$
$$= 0.866 \times 8.25 = 7.15 \text{ volts}$$

76. How to Proceed in Determining the Proper Size of Wire for a Circuit
1. Determine the ampere load on the circuit.

For branch lighting and appliance circuits refer to Secs. **36** to **38**.

For two-wire d-c or single-phase a-c lighting and appliance mains or feeders refer to Secs. **40, 44,** and **45.**

For three-wire d-c or single-phase a-c lighting and appliance mains or feeders refer to Secs. **41, 44,** and **46.**

For four-wire two-phase lighting and appliance mains or feeders refer to Secs. **44** and **47.**

For three-wire and two-phase lighting and appliance mains or feeders refer to Secs. **42, 44,** and **48.**

For five-wire two-phase lighting and appliance mains or feeders refer to Secs. **44** and **49.**

For four-wire three-phase lighting and appliance mains or feeders refer to Secs. **43, 44,** and **50.**

For circuits supplying electric ranges refer to Secs. **39** and **45.**

For branch motor circuit refer to Sec. **53.**

For motor feeders or mains refer to Sec. **54.**

2. For branch lighting or appliance circuits refer to Div. 9 and determine if outlets and equipment supplied by circuit meet the National Electrical Code requirements.

3. For lighting feeders or mains determine the minimum allowable load (refer to Sec. **52**).

4. Select from Secs. **17** to **21** of Div. 11 the size of wire that will carry safely the current with the type of insulation employed on the wires (see also Secs. **30** and **31**).

For 15-amp branch lighting circuits, although No. 14 wire will safely carry the current, it is best not to use smaller than No. 12 wire. If the length of the branch lighting circuit to the load center is over 75 ft, wire at least as large as No. 10 should be used.

A branch circuit supplying an electric range of 8¾ kw or more rating must not be smaller than No. 8 except for the neutral conductor, which must not be smaller than No. 10.

For lighting feeders or mains use the estimated future load current unless it is less than the minimum allowable load, when the minimum allowable load should be used.

For continuous-duty branch motor circuits use 125 per cent of the full-load rated current of the motor.

For branch motor circuits supplying short-time-duty motors, use the proper percentage of the rated current as given in Table **12** of Div. 11.

For motor feeders or main use the maximum-demand running current with allowance for growth.

For the determination of the required carrying capacity of the neutral wire refer as follows:

For three-wire d-c or single-phase systems refer to Sec. **46.**

For three-wire two-phase systems refer to Sec. **48.**

For five-wire two-phase systems refer to Sec. **49.**

For four-wire three-phase systems refer to Sec. **46.**

The neutral conductor of a three-wire circuit supplying a household electric range, a wall-mounted oven, or a counter-mounted cooking unit with a maximum demand of 8¾ kw or more is allowed to have a carrying capacity of only 70 per cent of the outside wires, provided that the neutral is not smaller than No. 10.

5. Determine if the size of wire required according to carrying capacity is sufficient for mechanical strength (refer to Sec. **32**).

Be sure that the size of wire required according to carrying capacity is not too large for satisfactory installation (refer to Sec. **33**).

6. Find the distance to the load center of the circuit (refer to Sec. **57**).

7. Decide what voltage drop is allowable in the circuit (refer to Sec. **35**, and Table **54** of Div. 11).

8. Determine what will be the voltage drop in the circuit using the size of wire required according to carrying capacity.

If the circuit is an a-c one, before calculating the voltage drop, determine from Sec. **62** and Sec. **56** of Div. 11 whether or not the effects of inductance and skin effect can be neglected.

For branch lighting circuits use the future-load current, unless the maximum allowable load for the type of branch circuit as given in Div. 9 is less than this value. In that case, use the maximum allowable load.

For lighting feeders or mains use the future-load current unless it is smaller than the minimum allowable load, when the minimum allowable load should be used.

For branch motor circuits use the full-load current of the motor.

For motor feeders or mains use the maximum-demand running current with proper allowance for growth.

For the length of the circuit use the distance from the source of supply to the load center, measured along the circuit.

For method of calculating voltage drop refer to the following sections:

3–44   CIRCUITS AND CIRCUIT CALCULATIONS

9. If the voltage drop determined in step 8 is greater than the allowable amount, take the next larger conductor and determine the voltage drop it will give. Proceed in this way until the conductors are large enough to keep the voltage drop within the required amount. For a-c circuits, this would sometimes require too great an increase in the size of the conductors. In such cases it is best to replan the system so as to divide the load among a greater number of circuits. For systems employing a common or neutral wire, when the size of wire must be increased in order to keep the voltage drop within the allowable amount, it is best to increase the size of the neutral in the same proportion as the outside wires are increased.

Example. Determine the proper size of wire to use for a two-wire single-phase 15-amp 60-cycle 115-volt branch lighting circuit supplying six 150-watt lamps. The length of the circuit to the load center is 50 ft. The wires are to be installed in conduit and have rubber insulation.
Solution
$$\text{Actual connected load} = \frac{6 \times 150}{115} = 7.8 \text{ amp}$$
$$\text{Future load (Sec. } \mathbf{37}) = 0.80 \times 15 = 12 \text{ amp}$$

The future load of 12 amp will be used in selecting the size of wire according to both carrying capacity and voltage drop.
From item 4 of this section at least a No. 14 wire is required by the code but it is best to use not smaller than No. 12 wire.
From Table **54** of Div. 11 a voltage drop of 2.3 volts would be allowable.
Determine the voltage drop (Sec. **58** or **59**) for a No. 12 wire carrying 12 amp 50 ft.
$$\text{Voltage drop with No. 12 wire} = \frac{24 \times 12 \times 50}{6,530} = 2.21 \text{ volts}$$

Since this drop is less than the allowable amount, two No. 12 wires should be used.

Example. A two-wire 15-amp single-phase 60-cycle 115-volt branch lighting circuit supplies seven 150-watt lamps. The length of the circuit to the load center is 100 ft. The wires are to be installed in conduit and to be rubber-insulated. Determine the proper size of wire to use.
Solution.
$$\text{Actual connected load} = \frac{7 \times 150}{115} = 9.13 \text{ amp}$$
$$\text{Future load} = 0.80 \times 15 = 12 \text{ amp}$$

The future load of 12 amp will be used in selecting the size of wire according to both carrying capacity and voltage drop.
From item 4 of this section at least a No. 14 wire is required, but it will be best to use not smaller than No. 10 wire when the circuit is over 100 ft long.
From Table **54** of Div. 11 a voltage drop of 2.3 volts would be allowable.
From Table **56** of Div. 11 the effect of inductance can be neglected for a lighting circuit using No. 10 wire on a 60-cycle system.
$$\text{Voltage drop with No. 10 wire} = \frac{24 \times 12 \times 100}{10,380} = 2.77 \text{ volts}$$

Since this voltage drop is greater than the allowable amount, take the next larger size of wire, No. 8, and check for voltage drop.
$$\text{Voltage drop with No. 8 wire} = \frac{24 \times 12 \times 100}{16,510} = 1.74 \text{ volts}$$

Since this voltage drop is less than the allowable amount, two No. 8 wires should be used.

Example. Determine the proper size of wire for the three-wire 115/230-volt d-c main of the first example under Sec. **46.** The length of the circuit is 125 ft. The wires are to be thermoplastic-covered, Type T, and installed in conduit. The installation has only a main and branch circuits, no feeder.

Solution. From Sec. **46,**

Present load on more heavily loaded outside wire = 145 amp
Future load on more heavily loaded outside wire = 242 amp
From Sec. **52** and Table **5** of Div. 11 minimum allowable load = 5.0 × 10,000 × 1.0
= 50,000 watts

$$\text{Minimum allowable current in outside conductor} = \frac{50,000}{2 \times 115} = 217.4 \text{ amp}$$

Since the future load is greater than the minimum allowable load, the future load on the more heavily loaded side of 242 amp will be used in determining the size of wire according to both carrying capacity and voltage drop.

From Table **19** of Div. 11 a 350,000-cir-mil wire is required for the outside conductors in order to carry 242 amp.

Since the future load on the neutral is 229.4 amp, then from Table **19** of Div. 11, a 300,000-cir-mil wire is required to carry 229.4 amp.

From Table **54** of Div. 11 a voltage drop of 2.3 volts is allowable on the lamps.

$$\text{Voltage drop across lamps (Sec. 60)} = \frac{1}{2} \times \frac{24 \times 242 \times 125}{350,000} = 1.04 \text{ volts}$$

Since this voltage drop is less than the allowable amount, the circuit should have outside wires of 350,000 cir mils and a neutral of 300,000 cir mils.

Example. Determine the proper size of wire to use for a branch motor circuit supplying a 10-hp 440-volt three-phase squirrel-cage induction motor on continuous duty. The motor is of the normal-starting-current normal-torque type started with reduced voltage. It is a 60-cycle system. The length of the circuit is 50 ft. The wires are to be thermoplastic-covered, Type T, installed in conduit.

Solution. From Table **10** of Div. 11 the full-load current = 14 amp.

125 per cent of the full-load current = 14 × 1.25 = 17.5 amp

From Table **19** of Div. 11 a No. 12 wire is required to carry 17.5 amp.
From Table **54** of Div. 11, 4.4 volts drop is allowable.
From Table **56** of Div. 11 the effect of inductance can be neglected for a 60-cycle motor circuit using No. 12 wire.

The voltage drop on a two-wire d-c circuit carrying 14 amp (full-load current) over a No. 12 wire for 50 ft $= \dfrac{24 \times 14 \times 50}{6,530} = 2.58$ volts.

$$\text{Voltage drop of actual circuit} = 0.866 \times 2.58 = 2.24 \text{ volts}$$

Since this drop is less than the allowable amount, three No. 12 wires should be used.

Example. Determine the proper size of wire to use for a branch motor circuit supplying a series-wound d-c motor on a 30-min rating varying duty. The motor is a 15-hp 230-volt machine. The length of the circuit is 100 ft. The wires are Type RH and installed in conduit.

Solution. From Table **7** of Div. 11 the full-load current is 55 amp.

Since it is a short-time-duty service, referring to Table **12** of Div. 11, use 150 per cent of the full-load current in determining size of wire according to carrying capacity.

From Table **19** of Div. 11 a No. 4 wire is required to carry (1.50 × 55) = 83 amp when Type RH wire is used.

From Sec. **54** of Div. 11, 4.4 volts drop is allowable.
In determining voltage drop use full-load current.

$$\text{Voltage drop} = \frac{24 \times 55 \times 100}{41,740} = 3.16 \text{ volts}$$

Since this drop is less than the allowable amount, two No. 4 wires would be used.

Example. Determine the proper size of wire to use for a three-wire, three-phase, 440-volt, 60-cycle feeder supplying five 10-hp motors, six 15-hp motors, and two 50-hp motors. All the motors are of the normal-torque, normal-starting-current, squirrel-cage type, started with reduced voltage. It is a 60-cycle circuit, 200 ft long. The wires are installed open with a regular flat spacing of 6 in. Type RHH insulation is employed on the wires. Permission to use a demand factor of 0.6 has been obtained from the officials enforcing the Code.

Solution. From Table **10** of Div. 11 the full-load current of a 10-hp motor of this type is 14 amp; of a 15-hp motor, 21 amp; and of a 50-hp motor, 65 amp.

Using the formula of Sec. **54,**

Starting current of 50-hp motor (Sec. **41** of Div. 11) $= 2.0 \times 65 = 130$ amp

Maximum-demand starting current of feeder

$$= [(5 \times 14) + (6 \times 21) + (1 \times 65)] \times 0.6 + 130 = (261 \times 0.6) + 130 = 286 \text{ amp}$$

Maximum-demand running current of feeder

$$= [(5 \times 14) + (6 \times 21) + (1 \times 65)]0.6 + (65 \times 1.25) = (261 \times 0.6) + 81 = 238 \text{ amp}$$

From Table **18** of Div. 11 a No. 1/0 wire is required to carry 238 amp (maximum-demand running current) if Type RHH (90°C) insulation is employed.

From Sec. **54** of Div. 11, 17.6 volts drop is allowable.

Effective spacing of the wires (Sec. **57,** Div. 11) $= 1.26 \times 6 = 7.56$

From Sec. **56** of Div. 11 the effect of inductance cannot be neglected.

Determine the voltage drop according to the method given in Sec. **73** using the maximum-demand running current.

Voltage drop of a two-wire d-c circuit carrying 238 amp 200 ft over No. 1/0 wire $= (24 \times 238 \times 200)/105,560 = 10.8$ volts.

Ratio of reactance to resistance for No. 1/0 wires spaced 8 in. apart on a 60-cycle circuit (Table **59** of Div. 11) $= 0.9$.

Power factor of circuit (Sec. **64** and Table **58, Div. 11**):

$$
\begin{array}{r}
5 \times 10 \times 0.86 = 43.0 \\
6 \times 15 \times 0.86 = 77.4 \\
2 \times 50 \times 0.89 = \underline{89.0} \\
209.4
\end{array}
$$

$$\text{pf} = \frac{209.4}{240} = 87.5$$

Drop factor of circuit from Table **61** of Div. 11 for a ratio of reactance to resistance of 0.9 and a power factor of 0.875 = 1.34.

Voltage drop of circuit $= 0.866 \times 1.34 \times 10.8 = 12.3$ volts.

Since this drop is less than the allowable amount use three No. 1/0 wires.

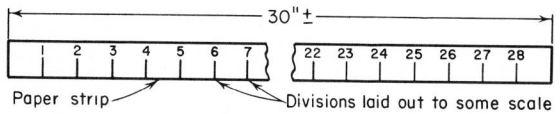

FIG. 31 *Paper scale for measuring circuit lengths.*

77. In determining circuit lengths from drawings or blueprints a long piece of tough paper divided (see Fig. 31) into the same measure as the drawing can be effectively used in scaling distances. Always allow for rises or drops for wall outlets. The rotometer (Fig. 32) is a convenient tool for scaling distances. The little wheel is run over the course of the circuit. The pointer indicates feet directly for drawings of certain scales. For other scales the dial reading must be multiplied by a constant to obtain actual lengths.

78. Indicating Loads on Diagrams. In computing the ampere loads on circuits, if drawings are available, it is good practice to note the amperes of the loads on the drawings alongside the circuits. It is good practice to indicate both the present and the estimated future loads, one colored pencil being used for the present load and another color for the future loads.

79. Use of Tables in Circuit Calculations. If tables that will give the values of loads, voltage drops, etc., are laid out when circuit calculations are made, much time can be saved in checking over the size of circuits or in making changes in the system. A typical table is given in Sec. **80.**

80. Branch Lighting Circuits

Panel	Branch circuit	Present load, amp	Future load, amp	Size wire according to carrying capacity	Length, ft	Volts drop	Size wire to use	Remarks
A	1	10.0	12	No. 14	50	3.50	No. 10	No. 10 used to keep drop to 1.39
.....	2	7.8	12	No. 14	25	1.75	No. 14	
.....	3	9.1	12	No. 14	30	2.10	No. 12	To keep voltage drop down
.....	4	8.0	12	No. 14	20	1.40	No. 14	
B	etc.		48					

81. The question of energy loss in a circuit should not be slighted in circuit calculations. It is well known that, in overcoming resistance, electrical energy is wasted, and as it costs money to develop or buy electrical energy, it is evident that in any commercial system such waste must be kept to a minimum. This can be done by decreasing the resistance of the conductors or, what amounts to the same thing, increasing the size of the conductors. Inasmuch as this is also an expensive matter, care must be exercised that the additional sum added to the expenditure in copper (and conduit if used) is not so excessive as to more than counterbalance the cost of the energy continually saved.

82. Conductor economy in interior wiring installations should always be considered as a matter subordinate to the National Electrical Code and permissible-voltage-drop requirements. Obviously, any conductor selected for a specific installation must fulfill the requirements of mechanical strength, ample carrying capacity, and permissible voltage drop. Frequently one of these three considerations will definitely determine the size of the conductor; however, a calculation may show that the resistance or I^2R (power) loss is excessive. Then it may be desirable to use a larger size of conductor than would otherwise be necessary.

83. Annual charges may be considered, in connection with the economical selection of a conductor size, as being made up of two items: (1) **resistance-loss charges** and (2) **investment charges.** Resistance-loss charges depend upon the resistance, the current, and the unit cost of energy and can be decreased by an increase of conductor size. This, however, calls for a greater investment with correspondingly larger investment charges. A conductor should, for maximum economy, be selected of such a size that the total annual charge will be a minimum. In Fig. 33 the effect of a variation of conductor size on resistance-loss charge, investment charge, and total annual charge is shown graphically for wires not installed in raceways. The interest charges on the conductor increase directly with its cross-sectional area (curve A, Fig. 33). If the wires were

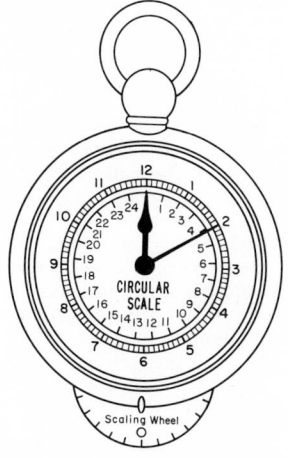

FIG. 32 *A rotometer.*

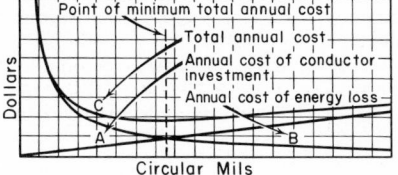

FIG. 33 *Graph illustrating Kelvin's law.*

installed in conduit, the cost of the conduit and fittings should be added to the conductor cost. The resistance-loss charges decrease inversely as the cross-sectional area of the conductor (curve *B*, Fig. 33). The total annual charge (curve *C*, Fig. 33), the sum of curves *A* and *B*, is at its minimum value directly over the point where curves *A* and *B* intersect. That is, the conductor size which will have the least total annual cost is that one for which the annual interest charge equals the annual resistance-loss charge. This proposition has been demonstrated mathematically by Lord Kelvin.

84. Kelvin's law was deduced in 1881 by Sir William Thomson (Lord Kelvin). The original law was modified into the following more exact form by Gilbert Kapp. "The most economical area of conductor is that for which the annual cost of energy wasted is equal to the interest on that portion of the capital outlay which can be considered proportional to the weight of copper used." On the basis of the above law it can be shown that

$$\text{Cir mils} = 55{,}867 \times I \times \sqrt{\frac{C_e}{C_c \times A}} \, ^* \tag{30}$$

where cir mils = area, in circular mils, of the most economical conductor; I = the mean annual current; C_e = cost of energy per kilowatthour, in dollars; C_c = cost of copper, in dollars, per pound installed; and A = annual charge, in percentage, of the cost of the conductor. This can ordinarily be assumed to be about 10 per cent. Note that the length of the circuit is not a factor in the equation. The above equation is best adapted to the solution of cases where the conductors are not insulated. The method of the following paragraph should always be used to check it.

85. Method of Determining Economical Conductor Size. The method involves the preparation of a table, as shown below, showing energy cost and interest cost of an arbitrarily chosen length of conductor for a number of sizes of conductor. The cost per unit length of conductors (preferably 1,000 ft or 305 m) can be obtained from the manufacturers' wire lists. For conduit installations the corresponding cost of conduit and fittings should be added to the cost of conductors. The cost of energy lost can be computed from the equations of Sec. **86** or from Sec. **87**. By use of a comparative table, as shown below, costs are effectively shown and a decision can be speedily reached. This method can be used as a check upon Kelvin's-law equation. In the table, the least total annual cost is $15.69. Hence a 4/0 conductor is, for this case, the one of maximum economy.

Size of rubber-covered conductor	No. 3/0 wire	No. 4/0 wire	250,000– cir-mil wire	300,000– cir-mil wire
Cost of 400 ft of conductor.............................	$100.00	$120.00	$160.00	$200.00
Annual charges on above cost at 10 per cent..................	$ 10.00	$ 12.00	$ 16.00	$ 20.00
Cost of energy lost in conductor at 2 cts per kwhr..........	$ 5.94	$ 3.69	$ 2.64	$ 2.27
Total annual cost of conductor..................	$ 15.94	$ 15.69	$ 18.64	$ 22.27

86. Cost of Energy Lost. Taking 12 ohms as the resistance of a circular mil-foot of commercial copper wire at 50°C, the power loss in any conductor can be found thus:

$$P = \frac{12 \times I^2 \times L}{\text{cir mils}} \tag{31}$$

where P = power lost in the conductor in watts; I = the mean annual current in amperes in the conductor; L = length of the conductor in feet; and circular mils = area of the conductor in circular mils.

The cost of energy lost can be computed from the following formula:

$$\text{Cost of energy lost per year in dollars} = \frac{N \times P \times 8{,}760 \times R}{1{,}000 \times 100} \tag{32}$$

---

* For derivation see "The Electrical Engineer's Pocketbook" (International Textbook Company). See also "Transmission of Electrical Energy," by A. V. Abbot; "Electric Power Transmission," by Dr. Louis Bell; and "Overhead Electric Power Transmission," by Alfred E. Still.

where N = number of conductors; P = power loss in one conductor; and R = cost of electric energy in cents per kilowatthour. In the formula, the 8,760 is the number of hours in a year, the 1,000 is the factor to change watts to kilowatts, and the 100 changes cents to dollars.

87. Cost of Energy Lost for 500 Hr of Operation with Cost of Electrical Energy at 2 Cts per Kilowatthour

Wire size, AWG	Length of run, ft	Load, amp													
		6	10	15	20	25	30	35	40	50	60	70	80	90	100
14	50	$0.10	$0.26	$0.60											
	100	0.19	0.52	1.20											
	200	0.38	1.04	2.40											
	300	0.57	1.06	3.60											
12	50	0.06	0.16	0.36	$0.64										
	100	0.12	0.32	0.72	1.28										
	200	0.24	0.64	1.44	2.56										
	300	0.36	0.96	2.16	3.84										
10	50	0.04	0.10	0.22	0.40	$0.62	$0.90								
	100	0.08	0.20	0.45	0.80	1.24	1.80								
	200	0.16	0.40	0.90	1.60	2.48	3.60								
	300	0.24	0.60	1.35	2.40	3.72	5.40								
8	50	0.03	0.06	0.15	0.25	0.40	0.60	$0.77	$1.06						
	100	0.05	0.12	0.30	0.50	0.80	1.20	1.54	2.12						
	200	0.09	0.24	0.60	1.00	1.60	2.40	3.08	4.24						
	300	0.14	0.36	0.90	1.50	2.40	3.60	4.62	6.36						
6	50	0.02	0.04	0.09	0.16	0.25	0.36	0.49	0.64	$1.00	$1.44				
	100	0.03	0.08	0.18	0.32	0.50	0.72	0.98	1.28	2.00	2.88				
	200	0.06	0.16	0.36	0.64	1.00	1.44	1.76	2.56	4.00	5.76				
	300	0.09	0.24	0.54	0.96	1.50	2.16	2.64	3.84	6.00	8.64				
4	50	0.01	0.03	0.06	0.08	0.15	0.22	0.32	0.40	0.62	0.90	$1.22	$1.60		
	100	0.02	0.05	0.12	0.16	0.30	0.44	0.64	0.80	1.24	1.80	2.44	3.20		
	200	0.04	0.10	0.24	0.32	0.60	0.88	1.28	1.60	2.48	3.60	4.88	6.40		
	300	0.05	0.15	0.36	0.48	0.90	1.32	1.92	2.40	3.72	5.40	7.32	9.60		
2	50	.....	0.02	0.04	0.06	0.10	0.13	0.18	0.24	0.40	0.60	0.77	1.00	$1.26	$1.60
	100	0.01	0.03	0.07	0.12	0.20	0.25	0.36	0.48	0.80	1.20	1.54	2.00	2.52	3.20
	200	0.02	0.06	0.14	0.24	0.40	0.50	0.72	0.56	1.60	2.40	3.08	4.00	5.04	6.40
	300	0.04	0.10	0.21	0.36	0.60	0.75	1.08	1.44	2.40	3.60	4.62	6.00	7.56	9.60

$$\text{Cost of energy lost per year in dollars} = \frac{H \times R \times K}{500 \times 2} \qquad (33)$$

where H = hours of operation of circuit per year; R = cost of electrical energy in cents per kilowatthour; K = dollars as obtained from table for size of wire, current, and length of run. The table and formula can be used for d-c or single-phase a-c circuits. If the load on a three-wire d-c or single-phase a-c circuit is nearly balanced, the formula will give satisfactory results if the current is taken as the current in the more heavily loaded wire.

88. Factors for Determining the Mean Annual Current. To ascertain the mean annual current for substitution in the Kelvin's-law equation (30) or in Eq. (31) of Sec. **86** multiply the maximum current by the ratio applying to the conditions under consideration, which is given in the column headed "Factor" in the following table. The table is calculated on a basis 24 hr × 365 days = 8,670 hr per year.

Example. If a maximum current of 1,000 amp (I) flows ¾ of the time or 6,570 hr per year and a current of 750 amp (¾I) flows ¼ of the time or 2,190 hr per year the factor 0.944 would be used.

That is, $0.944 \times 1{,}000$ amp $= 944$ amp $=$ mean annual current for substitution in Kelvin's-law equation.

Proportion of maximum current I carried				Factor
$\frac{1}{4}I$	$\frac{1}{2}I$	$\frac{3}{4}I$	I	
0	0	0	1	1.000
0	0	$\frac{1}{4}$	$\frac{3}{4}$	0.944
0	$\frac{1}{4}$	0	$\frac{3}{4}$	0.901
0	0	$\frac{1}{2}$	$\frac{1}{2}$	0.844
0	0	0	$\frac{3}{4}$	0.866
$\frac{1}{4}$	0	0	$\frac{3}{4}$	0.875
0	$\frac{1}{4}$	$\frac{1}{4}$	$\frac{1}{2}$	0.838
0	0	$\frac{3}{4}$	$\frac{1}{4}$	0.820
$\frac{1}{4}$	0	$\frac{1}{4}$	$\frac{1}{2}$	0.810
0	$\frac{1}{2}$	0	$\frac{1}{2}$	0.790
0	$\frac{1}{4}$	$\frac{1}{2}$	$\frac{1}{4}$	0.771
$\frac{1}{4}$	$\frac{1}{4}$	0	$\frac{1}{2}$	0.760
$\frac{1}{4}$	0	$\frac{1}{2}$	$\frac{1}{4}$	0.744
$\frac{1}{2}$	0	0	$\frac{1}{2}$	0.729
0	$\frac{1}{2}$	$\frac{1}{4}$	$\frac{1}{4}$	0.718
0	0	0	$\frac{1}{2}$	0.707
$\frac{1}{4}$	$\frac{1}{4}$	$\frac{1}{4}$	$\frac{1}{4}$	0.685
0	$\frac{3}{4}$	0	$\frac{1}{4}$	0.661
$\frac{1}{2}$	0	$\frac{1}{4}$	$\frac{1}{4}$	0.650
$\frac{1}{4}$	$\frac{1}{2}$	0	$\frac{1}{4}$	0.611
$\frac{1}{2}$	$\frac{1}{4}$	0	$\frac{1}{4}$	0.586
$\frac{3}{4}$	0	0	$\frac{1}{4}$	0.545
0	0	0	$\frac{1}{4}$	0.500

Proportion of time current is carried

DIVISION FOUR

General Electrical Equipment and Batteries

INTRODUCTION

1. Introduction. In this division the miscellaneous equipment, materials, and devices which are employed for electrical installations are discussed. Certain items which are used for specific types of installations have not been included in this division, but explanation of these devices or materials will be found in Div. 8 on Outdoor Distribution or in Div. 9 on Interior Wiring. Since there is so much material to cover for generators, motors, and transformers, a separate division (Div. 7) has been devoted to generators and motors and another (Div. 5) to transformers.

The aim in the preparation of Div. 4 has been to present the different types of equipment, materials, and devices which are available, with sufficient explanation of their characteristics, installation, and maintenance so that proper equipment can be intelligently selected, installed, and maintained in good condition for satisfactory service. Much useful information that is not ordinarily readily available at short notice has been included.

SWITCHES

2. A switch is a device for making, breaking, or changing connections in an electric circuit under the conditions of load for which it is rated. It is not designed for interruption of a circuit under short-circuit conditions. Refer to Sec. **59** for discussion of difference between circuit breakers and switches.

3. Switches may be classified in several different ways as follows:

I. According to number of poles.
   A. Single pole.
   B. Two or double pole.
   C. Three or triple pole.
      1. Standard.
      2. Solid neutral.
   D. Four pole — standard.
   E. Four pole — solid neutral.
   F. Five pole — standard.
   G. Five pole — solid neutral.
II. According to number of closed positions.
   A. Single throw.
   B. Double throw.
III. According to type of contact.
   A. Knife blade.
   B. Butt contact.
      1. Single line.
      2. Multiple line.
      3. Surface.
   C. Mercury.
IV. According to number of breaks.
   A. Single break.
   B. Double break.
V. According to method of insulation.
   A. Air break.
   B. Oil immersed.
VI. According to method of operation.
   A. Operating force.
      1. Manual.
      2. Magnetic.

      3. Motor or solenoid.
   B. Mechanism.
      1. Lever.
      2. Dial.
      3. Drum.
      4. Snap.
         a. Tumbler.
         b. Rotary.
         c. Push button.
VII. According to speed of operation.
   A. Quick break.
   B. Quick make.
   C. Slow break.
   D. Quick break.
VIII. According to enclosure.
   A. Open.
   B. Enclosed.
      1. General purpose.
      2. Driptight.
      3. Weather resisting.
      4. Watertight.
      5. Dusttight.
      6. Submersible.
      7. Hazardous locations.
      8. Bureau of Mines.
IX. According to protection provided to circuits or apparatus.
X. According to type of service.
   A. Power switches.
      1. General purpose.
         a. Open.

b. Safety.
2. Disconnecting.
3. Motor circuit.
4. Motor starting.
5. Field switches.
6. Service entrance.
7. Bolted pressure contact.
B. Wiring switches.
   1. According to method of instal-
      lation.
      a. Flush mounting.
         (1) Standard.
         (2) Interchangeable.
         (3) Combination.
      b. Surface.
      c. Pendant.
      d. Through cord.
      e. Door.

f. Canopy.
g. Appliance.
h. Special exposures.
2. According to function.
   a. General purpose.
      (1) Single pole.
      (2) Double pole.
   b. Three way.
   c. Four way.
   d. Three or four pole.
   e. Multiple circuit or elec-
        trolier.
   f. Momentary contact.
   g. Heater.
   h. Dimmer.
C. Control switches.
D. Instrument switches.
E. Miscellaneous types.

4. A pole of a switch is that part of a switch which is used for the making or breaking of a connection and which is electrically insulated from other contact-making or -breaking parts. A single-pole switch will make or break the connections in only one conductor or leg of a circuit; a two-pole switch in two legs, etc. Schematic diagrams illustrating the meaning of number of poles are shown in Fig. 1.

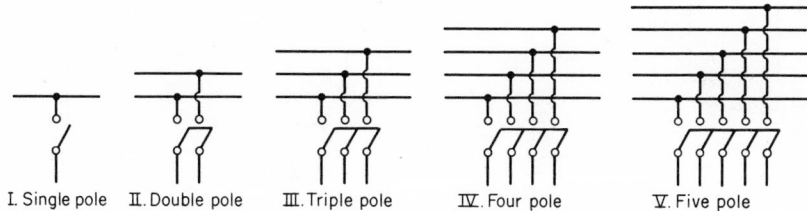

I. Single pole   II. Double pole   III. Triple pole   IV. Four pole   V. Five pole

FIG. 1 *Illustrating meaning of poles.*

For some installations in systems having a grounded neutral wire, it is always desirable to break the neutral connection as the circuit passes through a switch. For these cases, a regular switch with a number of poles one less than the number of conductors of the circuit can be used. The neutral conductor is then carried directly to a neutral bar in the switch. Another installation can be made by the use of what is called a solid-neutral switch (Fig. 2). The number of switch blades or contacts for a solid-neutral switch is one less than the number of conductors of the circuit, but a neutral strap is located between two of the switch blades or contacts for carrying the neutral leg solidly through the switch without breaking the circuit of the neutral conductor. A switch designated as a three-pole, solid-neutral switch will accommodate a three-conductor circuit and provides two switched poles and one solid-neutral strap. A solid-neutral switch is shown in Fig. 2, II. Figure 15 shows a three-pole switching-neutral fused switch, which satisfies National Electrical Code requirements.

5. A single-throw switch (Fig. 3, I) is one which will make a closed circuit only when the switch is thrown in one position. A **double-throw switch** (Fig. 3, II) will make a closed circuit when thrown in either of two positions. Special **multiple-throw switches** can be made to meet the requirements of special conditions which require that the switch make a closed circuit when thrown in more than two positions. Some examples of multiple-throw switches are the dial and drum switches employed for control and instrument work.

6. Switch Contacts. In the construction of switches, different methods are employed for making contact between the movable and stationary parts of the poles.

Knife-blade switches consist of some form of movable copper blade which makes contact by being forced between forked contact jaws as illustrated in Fig. 4.

The manner of constructing the contact members of **butt-contact** switches varies widely with different manufacturers.   In all cases, however, the contact is formed by pressing the movable member against the stationary contact.   (The two contacts are butted together when closed.)   The two members are so constructed that there will be a stiff spring action between them in order to ensure a good contact when in the closed position.   The contact formed between the two members may be of the **single-line, multiple-line,** or **surface** type. **Single-line** contact is obtained by making the surface of the contacting members in a curved form so that, when closed, the members are in contact only along a single line instead of over the entire surface.   With **multiple-line** contacts the two members are not in contact over their entire surfaces but contact is made along several lines.   The multiple lines of contact are obtained by making the movable member of laminated (brush) or cylindrical construction.   In butt-contact switches of the **surface** type, the contact members when in the closed

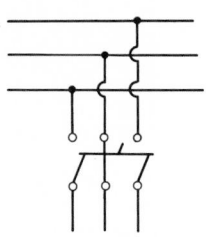

I Schematic diagram of three-
pole solid-neutral switch

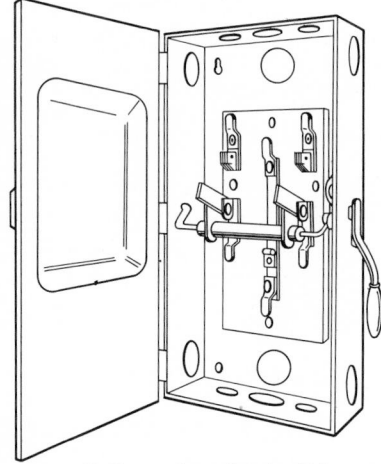

Ⅱ Three pole, unfused switch

FIG. 2   *Solid-neutral switch and connections.*

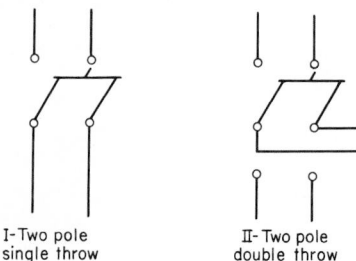

I- Two pole
single throw

Ⅱ- Two pole
double throw

FIG. 3   *Illustrating single- and double-throw switches.*

position are butted together so that they are in contact over as much of the entire surface as possible.   The disadvantage of the surface type of contact is that it is very difficult to obtain a good contact over the entire surface.   Typical butt-contact constructions are illustrated in Fig. 5.

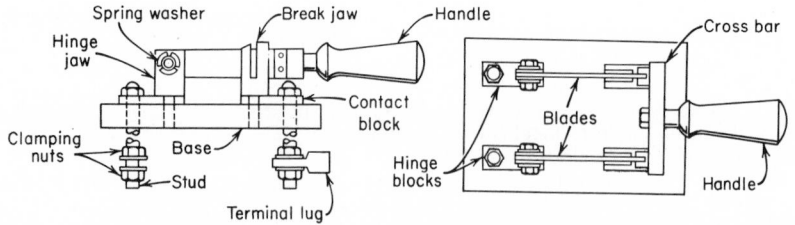

FIG. 4   *Names of knife-blade switch parts.*

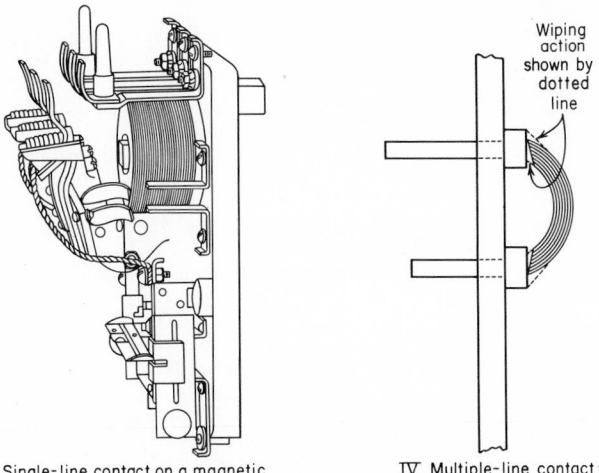

I. Single-line contact on a magnetic switch (single break).

IV. Multiple-line contact with double break.

Wiping action shown by dotted line

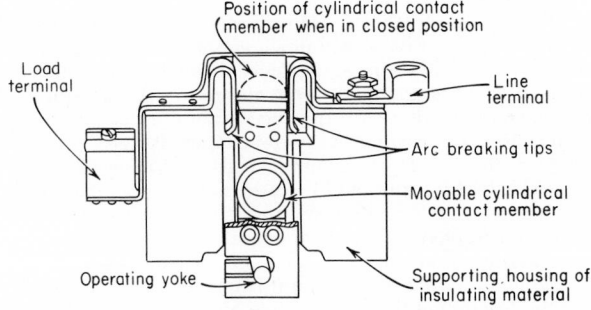

Position of cylindrical contact member when in closed position

Load terminal

Line terminal

Arc breaking tips

Movable cylindrical contact member

Operating yoke

Supporting housing of insulating material

II. Single-line contact with double break (switch in open position).

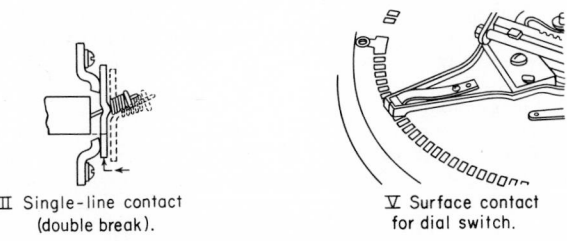

III. Single-line contact (double break).

V. Surface contact for dial switch.

FIG. 5   *Butt-contact constructions.*

One of the essential functions of any switch is to maintain a good low-resistance contact when in the closed position. If the contact is poor, there will be considerable resistance at this point. The high contact resistance will result in overheating of the switch and possible opening of the circuit due to functioning of circuit-overload protective devices. Switches are generally constructed so that the contacts will be closed under pressure with a sliding or rolling action in order to maintain clean, low-resistance contacts. The contact surfaces are frequently silver plated in order to prevent oxidation and reduce contact resistance.

7. Mercury contact switches are used sometimes for low-capacity circuits in control and branch circuit wiring. They consist of a glass tube containing mercury and two stationary contact members located in opposite ends of the tube. The tube is mounted in a supporting case so that the position of the axis of the tube can be changed by means of an operating handle. When the handle is in the "off" position, the axis of the tube is tilted so that the mercury is at one end of the tube and makes contact with only one of the stationary contacts. When the handle is thrown to the closed position, it rotates the tube, causing the mercury to move in the tube in a manner that closes the circuit from the stationary contact at one end of the tube through the mercury to the stationary contact at the other end of the tube. Refer to Secs. **30** and **31** for further information on wiring switches for interior-wiring work.

8. Both knife-blade and butt-contact switches are made in single- and double-break types. A single-break type of switch, in opening, breaks each pole of the circuit at only one point. A double-break type of switch, in opening, breaks each pole of the circuit at two points. Breaking the circuit in two places doubles the quenching effect of the switch in suppressing the arc. This reduction in the arcing at the contacts prolongs the life of the contacts by reducing the formation of destructive beads and pitted areas.

9. Insulation of Switches. The great majority of switches are designed to interrupt the circuit in the surrounding air. The live parts must be spaced sufficiently far apart so that the air space between them will have sufficient insulating ability for the voltage which exists between the adjacent parts. Oil switches (Fig. 6) have the contact parts immersed in oil so that the circuit is interrupted under oil.

10. Switches can be operated by hand (Fig. 7), by electromagnets (Fig. 8), by motors (Fig. 8), or by means of solenoids (Fig. 8). Most power switches are operated by means of simple lever action (Fig. 4) or by means of a lever attached to the switch through a toggle mechanism. Dial switches consist of a movable contact, mounted on a rotatable arm, and several fixed contacts arranged in circular form. As the arm is rotated, the movable contact makes connection with the successive fixed contacts, one at a time. This type of switch is used for instrument; control; storage-battery, end-cell; and transformer tap-changing switches. Drum switches consist of a set of contact segments mounted on a central movable drum and a set of stationary contact fingers (Fig. 9). Drum switches are employed for motor starting, control, and instrument switches.

Magnetic switches consist of switch contacts operated by means of an electromagnet. They are used extensively as the switching element for motor controllers. They also find application in general wiring work when it is desired to control a circuit at some point remote from the location of the switch. See Secs. **36** and **37**.

Snap switches are small-capacity switches in which the circuit is made or broken with a quick motion independent of the speed of operation of the switch by the operator. In the rotary type of snap switch (Fig. 10), the switch blades are given a rotary motion by means of the handle or button through a spring-and-cam mechanism. The blades of a push-button switch (Fig. 11) are operated by a rocking action imparted to them by means of the push button through a spring-and-cam mechanism. The tumbler or toggle switch (Fig. 12) is operated in a manner similar to the push-button switch except that the blades are actuated by means of a lever instead of a button.

11. Speed of Operation of Switches. With an ordinary manual switch the speed of closing or of opening a switch is dependent upon the operator. Where current conditions are such that an arc may be drawn, attachments should be provided which make it impossible to open the switch slowly and thus draw a dangerous arc. Many switches are provided with quick-make features as well as quick-break. A quick-break attachment for an open knife switch is shown in Fig. 13. When the switch is opened, the auxiliary blade is held in the switch jaws by friction until after the main blade has been withdrawn. Withdrawal of the main blade increases the spring tension so that it suddenly jerks the auxiliary blade out of the jaws and quickly breaks the circuit. In switches of the enclosed safety type, the operating handle is frequently connected through linkages and a spring so that after the handle has been moved a certain distance, the spring quickly completes the closing or opening action, giving the switch quick-break or -make features.

12. Enclosure of Switches. Switches may be classified as open or enclosed, depending upon whether their current-carrying parts are exposed or enclosed in a protecting

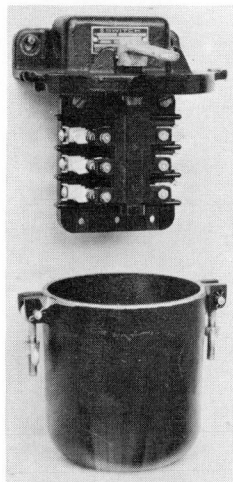 

I. *Small-capacity three-pole double throw. (General Electric Co.)*

II. *Switchboard type. (General Electric Co.)*

 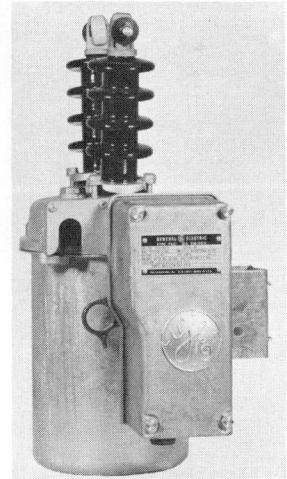

III. *Medium-voltage industrial type. (Westinghouse Electric Corp.)*

IV. *High-voltage industrial type. (General Electric Co.)*

FIG. 6   *Oil switches.*

box or casing. All switches should be of the enclosed type (externally operated) unless they are mounted on switchboards or panel boards. Even in these cases it is generally better practice to use switchboards and panel boards of the dead-front-construction type. In no case should open switches be employed where they may be operated by unqualified persons.

Switches can be obtained with enclosures to meet the requirements of different

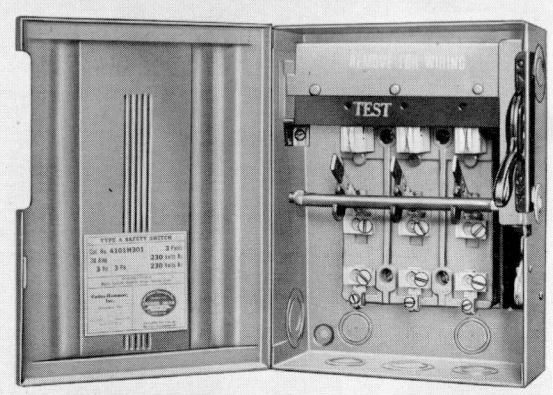

I. *Lever and operating-arm mechanism. (Cutler-Hammer Inc.)*

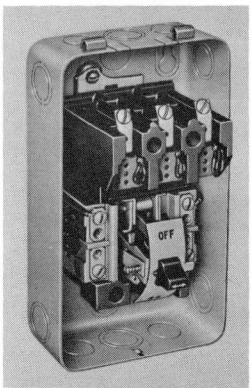
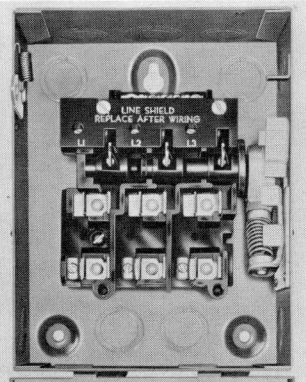

II. *Lever   and   toggle mechanism. (Westinghouse Electric Corp.)*   III. *Rotary motion operated by lever outside box. (General Electric Co.)*

FIG. 7   *Operating mechanisms for manual switches.*

classes of exposures. The standard NEMA types of nonventilated switch enclosures are as follows:

TYPE 1. GENERAL-PURPOSE. A general-purpose enclosure is intended primarily to prevent accidental contact with the enclosed apparatus. It is suitable for general-purpose applications indoors where it is not exposed to unusual service conditions.

TYPE 3R. RAINTIGHT. A raintight enclosure is intended primarily to meet the requirements for raintight apparatus. It will also meet the requirements for driptight, splashproof, and moisture-resistant. It is suitable for general applications outdoors where sleetproof construction is not required.

TYPE 4. WATERTIGHT. A watertight enclosure is designed to exclude water applied in the form of a hose stream. It is suitable where the apparatus may be subjected to a stream of water during cleaning operations and the like. It will also meet the requirements for driptight, splashproof, and moisture-resistant.

TYPE 7. CLASS I HAZARDOUS LOCATIONS, GROUPS A, B, C, OR D—AIR BREAK. These are enclosures for use in the Class I hazardous locations described in the NE Code.

I. *Electromagnetic-operated switch.* (*Cutler-Hammer Inc.*)

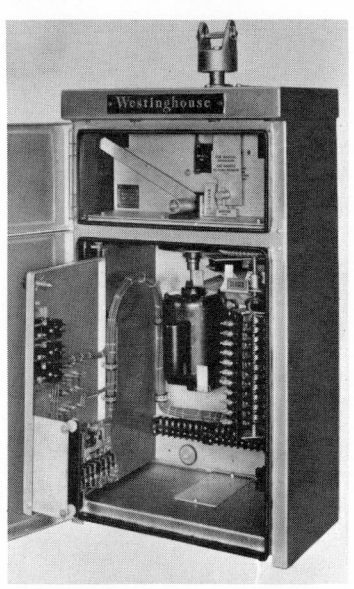

II. *Solenoid-operating mechanism.* (*Westinghouse Electric Corp.*)

III. *Motor-operating mechanism.* (*Westinghouse Electric Corp.*)

FIG. 8 *Electrically operated switches.*

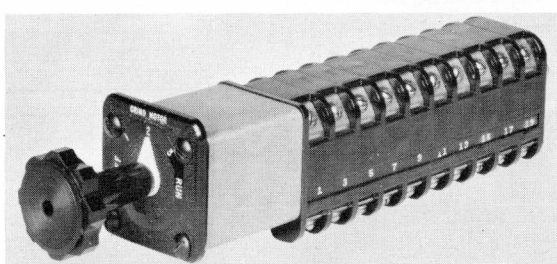

FIG. 9 *Drum-type control switch.* (*General Electric Co.*)

TYPE 9. CLASS II HAZARDOUS LOCATIONS, GROUPS E, F, OR G. These are for use in the Class II hazardous locations as described in the NE Code.

It should be noted that these NEMA switch enclosures are based on a 1958 standard. At this writing consideration is being given to update these enclosure classifications to be the same as or similar to the NEMA enclosures listed in Sec. **253**, Div. 7.

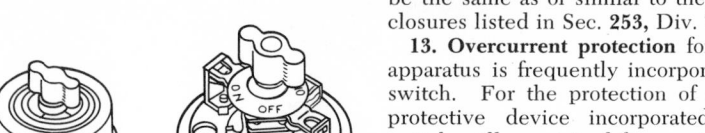

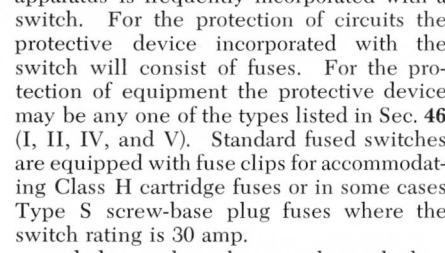

FIG. 10   *Rotary snap switch—surface-mounting type.*

13. Overcurrent protection for circuits or apparatus is frequently incorporated with a switch. For the protection of circuits the protective device incorporated with the switch will consist of fuses. For the protection of equipment the protective device may be any one of the types listed in Sec. **46** (I, II, IV, and V). Standard fused switches are equipped with fuse clips for accommodating Class H cartridge fuses or in some cases Type S screw-base plug fuses where the switch rating is 30 amp.

Fused switches used on systems with a grounded neutral may have one less pole than the number of conductors of the circuit, or a solid-neutral or switching-neutral switch may be employed. In the first case, the neutral leg is not carried through the switch, but the neutral conductor is simply carried through the switch box in the space around

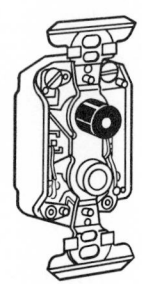

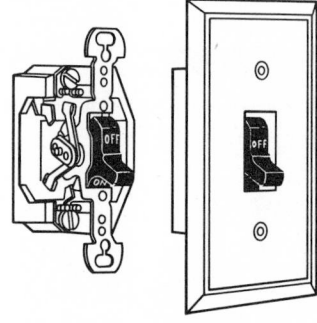

FIG. 11   *Push-button   switch—flush-mounting type, old style.*

FIG. 12   *Toggle or tumbler switch—flush-mounting a-c, d-c type.*

the switch. A solid-neutral switch (Fig. 14) has one less blade or contact than the number of conductors of the circuit, with a neutral strap located in the space between two of the switch blades or contacts for carrying the neutral leg solidly through the switch without breaking the circuit of the neutral conductor. No fuse is located in the neutral leg. A switching-neutral switch (Fig. 15) has a blade or contact for each conductor of the circuit. The blade or contact for the neutral conductor is connected by means of a copper strap to its terminal without any fuse clips. Such a switch opens the neutral conductor leg and all other circuit conductors when the switch is opened and satisfies National Electrical Code rules.

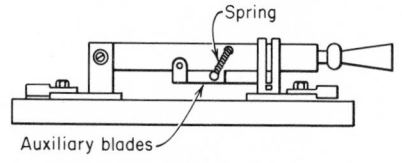

FIG. 13   *A quick-break switch.*

14. General-purpose   or   general-use power switches are switches intended for use in general distribution and branch circuits. They are rated in amperes and are capable of interrupting their rated current at their rated voltage. They may be of the open or enclosed externally operated type. The enclosed switches are generally referred to as safety switches.

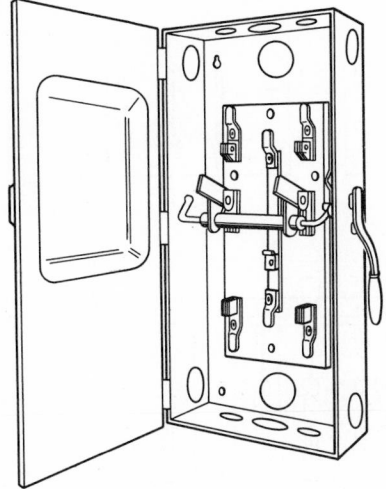

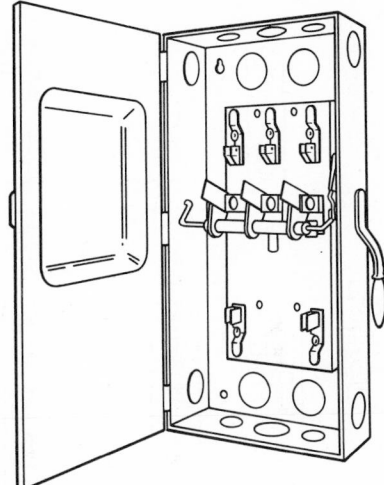

FIG. 14   *Three-pole solid-neutral fused switch.*

FIG. 15   *Three-pole switching-neutral fused switch.*

General-purpose or general-use switches are NEMA designated as Type HD, ND, or LD switches, depending upon the severity of service for which they are designed. **Type HD** (heavy duty) switches are the most ruggedly constructed switches of the three types and are designed for the heaviest duty service with respect to both frequency of operation and current capacity for handling heavy overloads. **Type ND** (normal duty) switches are of lighter construction than Type HD and are designed for service conditions where frequent operation is not required and where overload conditions are not severe. **Type LD** (light duty) switches are of light construction and are designed primarily for entrance service and general-purpose use where load is light and operation very infrequent.

15. Open switches are switches constructed with their current-carrying parts exposed. Most open switches are of the plain lever knife-blade type. Knife-blade switches in very heavy current-carrying capacities are hard to operate owing to the large rubbing contact surfaces required. For this reason open switches of very large capacity are usually of the brush-butt-contact type (Fig. 5, IV).

Most open-lever-type knife-blade switches are of the single-break type and are made in a variety of different forms. They can be obtained in single-, double-, triple-, and four-pole types, for either front or rear connection (see Figs. 16 and 17). They may be of the fused or unfused type and either single or double throw.

Open switches are used principally for mounting on live-front switchboards.

16. The names of knife-switch parts are given in Fig. 4. The contact between the break jaws and the blade should be carefully inspected, as it is at this point that knife switches are most apt to give trouble by overheating. The contact between the hinge jaws and the blade seldom limits the capacity of a switch, because it is under pressure from the hinge bolt and the spring washers. The capacity of a switch is determined by its temperature rise.

About 1,000 amp per sq in. of copper section and 50 to 75 amp per sq in. of sliding contact surface are usually allowed in designing switches.

A switch that will carry, possibly, 1,000 amp with a 20°C temperature rise, will carry possibly 2,000 amp with about a 60°C rise. The radiation of heat from the switch increases more rapidly than does the rise in temperature, and as the heat generated varies as the square of the current, it is evident that the temperature rise will be somewhat less than proportional to the square of the current.

With a given current, a switch will break about double the voltage with alternating

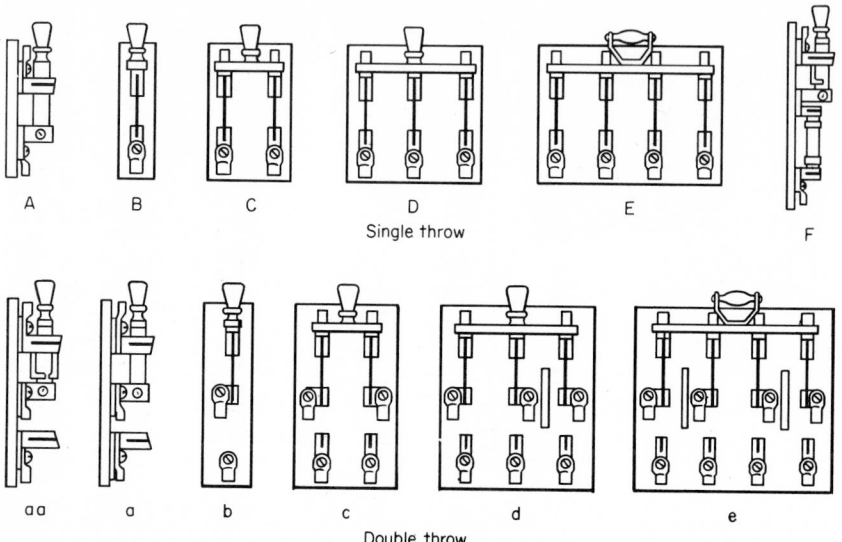

FIG. 16　*Front-connected knife-blade switches.* (*Electric System Handbook*)

current as with direct current. This is due to the fact that an alternating current decreases to a zero value during each cycle. The Code recognizes this and specifies that the spacings for 250 volts d-c are also approved for 500 volts a-c.

The voltage drop from contact block to hinge block of a good switch should not exceed about 12 millivolts with full-load current.

17. Safety switches consist of a switch mounted inside a sheet-metal or cast-iron box and operated from outside the box by means of a handle connected to the switch mechanism. Various types are available with contacts of either the single- or double-break type employing either knife-blade or butt-contact construction. The operating handle may be located on the side of the switch box, in the center of the front cover, or in the front side of the box (see Fig. 18).

Safety switches of certain types are so arranged that their doors cannot be opened when the switch is closed. Others possess this feature and the additional one that, when the switch and door are open, absolutely no live metal parts are exposed.

Safety switches are made in two-, three-, four-, and five-pole assemblies either fused or unfused and in single- or double-throw types. The three-, four-, and five-pole

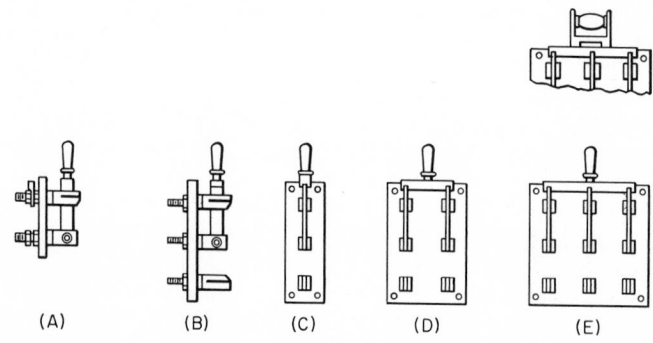

FIG. 17　*Rear-connected knife-blade switches.* (*Electric System Handbook*)

 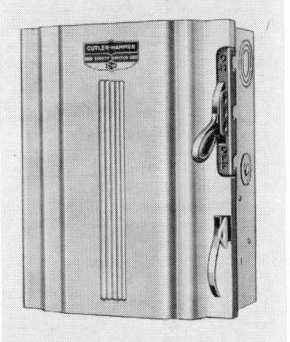

I. *Handle located in middle. (General Electric Co.)*   II. *Handle located on side. (General Electric Co.)*   III. *Handle located in front side. (Cutler-Hammer Inc.)*

FIG. 18   *Safety switches showing different types of operating-handle arrangement.*

switches may be of the standard, solid-neutral, or switching-neutral type. Safety switches are made in HD, ND, and LD types of construction. They can be obtained with or without quick-break mechanism. Many switches are constructed so as to give quick-make action in the closing of the switch as well as the quick-break action in opening. Typical constructions for Class HD knife-blade-type safety switches are shown in Figs. 19 and 20. Butt-contact design (Fig. 21) generally results in a more compact construction with smaller over-all dimensions. A very compact type of rotary knife-blade switch (Fig. 22) is made, however, in 30- to 100-amp sizes.

18. To make a contact between switch blade and jaws, considerable skill is required. After a switch is assembled, the jaws are first bent into correct position either by hand or by driving a block of wood against the distorted portion with a hammer. Then they are "ground in" with Vaseline and fine (FF) pumice. Often the "fit" of a switch is reasonably good at the start, and merely working the blade in and out of the jaws by hand will grind them in. Before the grinding process is started, the portion of the blade that wipes the jaws should be daubed with the Vaseline-and-pumice compound. The abrasive not only "grinds in the fit" but wears off the lacquer, which, if it remained, might be the cause of a bad contact. The surplus compound should be removed with a rag.

19. A test for good blade contact can be made by trying to insert a "feeler," which is a leaf of very thin steel, mica, or paper, between the jaws and blade at the corners and sides. About 0.001 to 0.004 in. is about the right thickness for a feeler. An excellent feeler can be made by hammering down to a knife-edge the edges of a strip of very thin metal possibly 4 in. long and ¾ in. wide. If the feeler slips in at any point, it is evident that the fit is poor at that point and the contact bad. Proper forming of the jaw will correct the difficulty. There have been cases where switches have been made to carry, without excessive temperature rise, currents 50 per cent greater than their normal ratings, by merely carefully fitting their jaws to their blades.

20. The standard sizes of general-purpose power switches are listed in Table **43,** Div. 11.

21. High-capacity Switches. There are three basic types of fused high-capacity, load-break switches in ratings from 800 to 6,000 amp (a-c). These switches are shown in Fig. 24.

1. Bolted-pressure-contact switches contain a pressure mechanism which firmly "bolts" the blades to the contacts when the switch handle is moved to the closed position. Auxiliary springs maintain an initial pressure during opening and closing of the blades to prevent arcing and pitting of the main contacts. Class L fuses are bolted to fuse terminals.

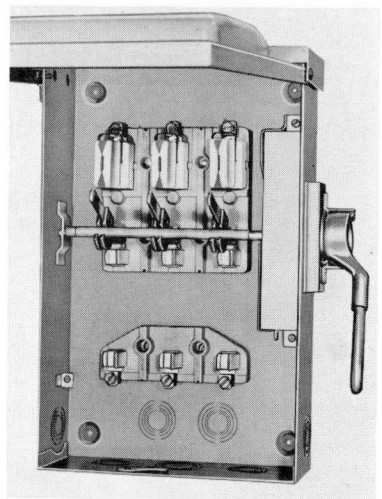

FIG. 19 *Fusible safety switch in rain-tight enclosure. (Cutler-Hammer, Inc.)*

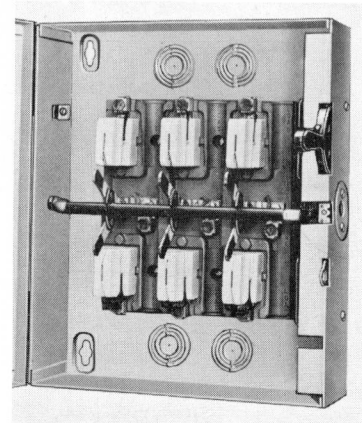

FIG. 20 *Non-fusible, double-throw safety switch. (Cutler-Hammer, Inc.)*

FIG. 21 *Fusible safety switch in cast-iron enclosure. (General Electric Co.)*

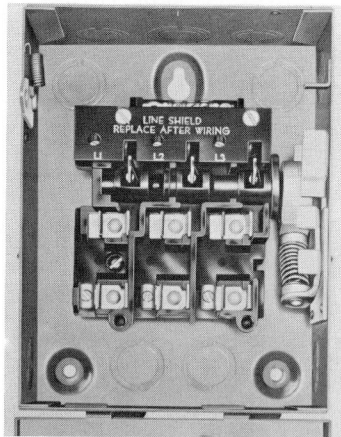

FIG. 22 *Rotor-blade safety switch. (General Electric Co.)*

2. Circuit-breaker-type switches are actually circuit breakers with the overload trips removed, and bolt-on Class L, current-limiting fuses are used as the overcurrent protection.

3. Fused circuit breakers include all the mechanical features of conventional large-capacity circuit breakers, and, in addition, have replaceable Class L fuses which function to increase the fault-current interrupting ability. They are intended to be used in the same manner as other circuit breakers and are mounted in enclosures with hinged doors or covers over the accessible fuses. They are rated at 600 volts or less.

Fused circuit breakers are classified in two categories: Classes 1 and 2.

a. Class 1 fused circuit breakers meet all the performance requirements of large branch-circuit and service circuit breakers. The Class L fuses function only to extend

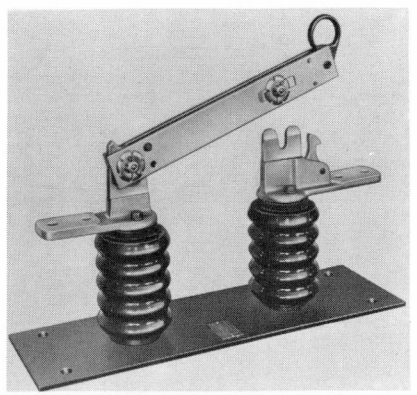 

I. *Nonfusible type.* *(Westinghouse Elec-*   II. *Fused type.* *(General Electric Co.)*
tric Corp.)

FIG. 23   *Open-type knife-blade disconnecting switches.*

the fault-current interrupting rating beyond the short-circuit test requirement applicable.

b. Class 2 fused circuit breakers use fuses so coordinated that they function at currents below those specified in short-circuit test requirements. Except for this feature of short-circuit operation, Class 2 fused circuit breakers meet all requirements applicable to large branch-circuit and service circuit breakers, and, in addition, are required to clear circuits up to and including 25 times their ampere rating, and circuits of 1,000 amp or less regardless of ampere rating, without causing operation of any fuses which are a part of the device. Class 2 devices are limited to constructions which are designed to accommodate and coordinate with Class L fuses.

All the high-capacity switches described in Sec. **21** use Class L current-limiting fuses with interrupting current (IC) ratings of 100,000 or 200,000 amp rms, and they are designed for a-c circuits. Typical switch ratings are 240, 480, 500, or 600 volts. Since the National Electrical Code prohibits the use of fuses in parallel, one of these switch types will be required where fuse ratings larger than 600 amp are required for a given service or circuit.

All these high-capacity switches incorporate a manual means of disconnection. In addition, shunt-trip coils can be provided to permit electrical operation of the switch. With an electrically operated switch ground-fault interrupters can be added to open the

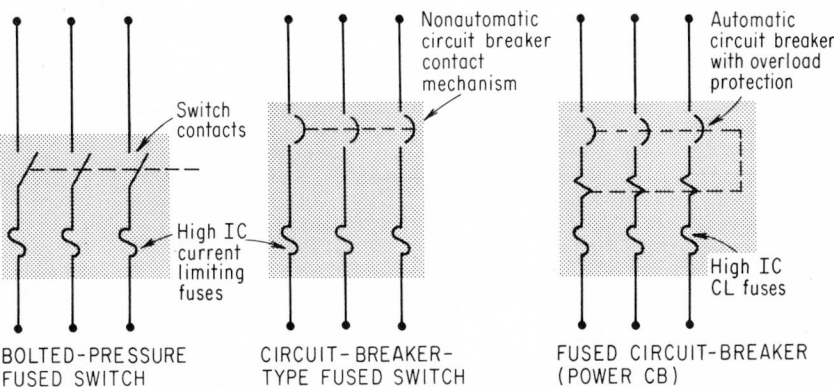

FIG. 24   *High-capacity switches (800 to 6,000 amp).*

main circuit in the event of line-to-ground faults. Such devices are described in Sec. 71 and shown in Fig. 101.

22. Isolating switches are intended simply for isolating circuits from their source of power. They are not intended to be used for interrupting the current of the circuit and are to be operated only when the circuit has been opened by some other means. The principal application of these switches is for isolating equipment or parts of an electric circuit for inspection or repair. They are commonly used on circuits rated at more than 600 volts. They are made in a great variety of open knife-blade types to meet different requirements of both indoor and outdoor service. Since they are generally located out of arm's reach, they are provided with an eye on the free end of the blade for operation with a hook rod. Typical switches of this type are shown in Fig. 23. Enclosed safety industrial disconnecting switches are shown in Figs. 25 and 26.

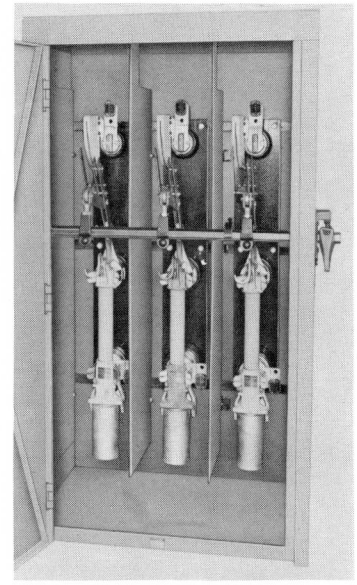

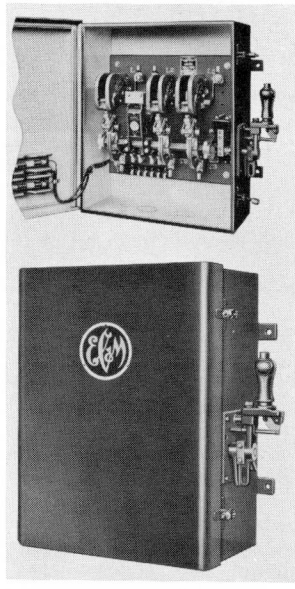

FIG. 25 *Safety-enclosed fusible discon-*
necting switch. (General Electric Co.)

FIG. 26 *Manual-magnetic safety discon-*
necting switch (Square D Company).

23. Motor-circuit switches are used for the interruption of current in motor circuits. They are rated in horsepower and must be capable of interrupting at their rated voltage the maximum operating overload current of a motor of the same horsepower as the switch rating. The maximum operating overload current is taken as six times the rated full-load motor current for a-c motors and four times the rated full-load motor current for d-c motors. Motor circuit switches are of the same construction as the general-purpose safety switches discussed in Sec. 17. See Table **45,** Div. 11, for horsepower ratings of fused switches. The switch is rated in amperes for general use and is given a horsepower rating for motor-circuit application.

24. Motor-starting switches are employed for the starting of motors which may be started directly across-the-line. Standard motor-circuit switches may be used for this purpose, but it is generally better practice to employ a switch designed specifically for starting duty. They are made in manual and magnetic types. These motor-starting switches generally are provided with some form of motor-overload protective device. For a discussion of motor-starting switches refer to across-the-line starting equipment in Div. 7. When the control of a d-c motor is mounted on a switchboard, a multiple-contact, open knife switch (Fig. 27) is frequently employed for cutting out the starting resistance. These switches may be provided with a ratchet device on the hand lever so that the switch cannot be moved too rapidly from step to step.

25. Field switches are used for the interruption of the field current of generators and synchronous motors. These switches (Fig. 28) are provided with an auxiliary contact, an extra blade attached to one of the main blades, and auxiliary quick-break blades attached to each main blade. In operating the switch for disconnecting the field from its source, the auxiliary quick-break blades do not break contact with their jaws until after the short auxiliary blade has made contact with the extra jaws. Thus the field circuit is shorted through the discharge resistance before the circuit is disconnected from its source. Since the field circuit is highly inductive, if the circuit were suddenly broken, a high induced voltage would be produced which might puncture the insulation of the field coils. The field switch of Fig. 28 is for mounting on the front of the switchboard or panel. A preferable arrangement is to employ a switch mounted on the rear of the board as shown in Fig. 29. Electrically operated field switches can be obtained which allow the field switch to be mounted near its machine, while its operation is controlled from the switchboard.

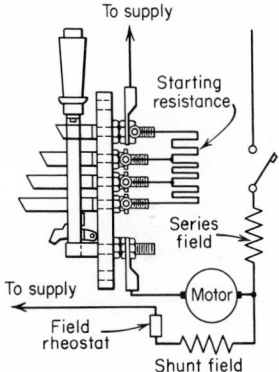

FIG. 27   *Multiple-contact open knife-blade switch for motor starting. (Electric System Handbook.)*

26. Service or Entrance Switches. The service equipment to a building consists of the necessary circuit breaker or switch and fuses and their accessories, which are located near the point of entrance of the supply conductors. It constitutes the main control and means of cutoff for the supply to that building. In large industrial plants comprising several buildings, the service equipment for each building will generally consist simply of a fused safety switch or an industrial circuit breaker. For single buildings supplied directly from the utility's lines, the service equipment must include a switch, fuses, and a meter or a circuit breaker and a meter. The meter is furnished by the utility, but the rest of the equipment must generally be supplied by the

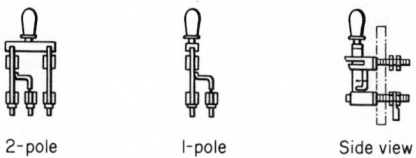

2-pole   I-pole   Side view

I. *Field switch for mounting on the front of a switchboard.*

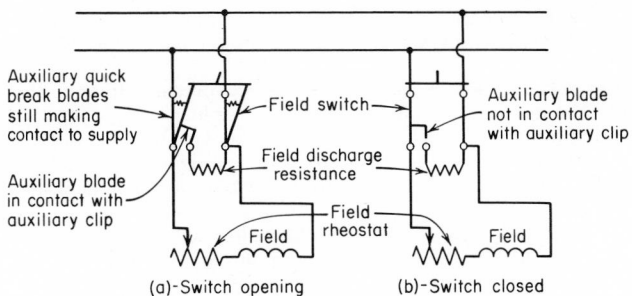

(a)-Switch opening   (b)-Switch closed

II. *Schematic diagram showing functioning of a switch.*

FIG. 28   *Field switch.*

consumer. Service or entrance switches are ones specifically designed to meet these entrance conditions so that the meter and fused switch can be mounted in a convenient, neat, and compact manner. One end of many switch boxes is provided with knockouts or hubs for conduit connection (Fig. 32). This allows the box to be connected by means of conduit to a separate meter trough either for a single meter or for several meters as shown in Fig. 30. Combination units consisting of the switching member and a meter socket, Fig. 33, are available in different types of design.

27. Service or entrance switches are made in a great variety of types in order to meet the desired sequence between meter, switch, and fuses (refer to Div. 9) and the other requirements of individual utility companies. It has been impossible to introduce any standardization into the types of service switch owing to the divergence of opinion among the utility representatives. Some of these switches simply include the entrance switching device (Figs. 30, 31, and 32) and overload protection for the service. Others have in addition a switching device and overload protection for an electric-range circuit. Still others combine the service-entrance equipment with overload protection for branch circuits and frequently are called load and service centers (Figs. 34 and 35). Types are available which include test links

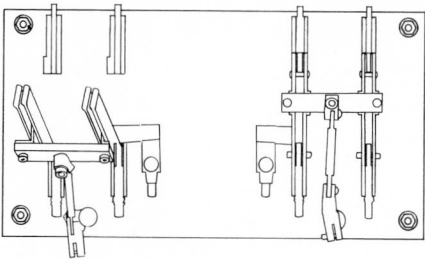

I. *Switch open at left, closed at right.*

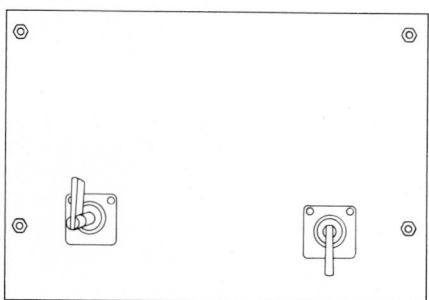

II. *Operating handles.*

FIG. 29 *Field switch for mounting on the rear of a switchboard with front-operating handle.*

mounted on the main switch base so that the utility can test the meters without disconnecting the load and interrupting the customer's service. In some types the main fuses are accessible to the customer, while in others they may be sealed by the power company so that they are not accessible to the customer.

Service switches may be divided broadly into three types, depending upon the type of main switching device: fuse-puller switches (Figs. 31, 34, and 35), circuit breakers (Figs. 32 and 33), and the standard type of safety switch (Fig. 30). When the main switching device is a circuit breaker, the equipment generally is of the load-center type with each branch provided with a circuit breaker. This type has the advantage that it provides a means of switching as well as overload protection for each branch. The other types of load center provide only overload protection for the branches with no means of switching.

28. The latest development in service-entrance equipment is the detachable, socket type of meter. The meter is provided with prongs that fit into clips or jaws provided in a meter-mounting trough. Some of these troughs are wired on the job, and others are factory-wired by the manufacturer. They are made in indoor and outdoor weatherproof types. Examples of troughs and installations of this type are shown in Figs. 33, 36, and 37.

29. Service switches are available in raintight enclosures so that the service-entrance equipment can be located on the outside of the building. Typical equipment is shown in Figs. 32, 33, and 34.

30. Wiring switches, as designated in this book, include all the relatively small switches that are employed in interior wiring installations for the control of branch circuits and individual lamps or appliances. Except for mercury switches, the switch-

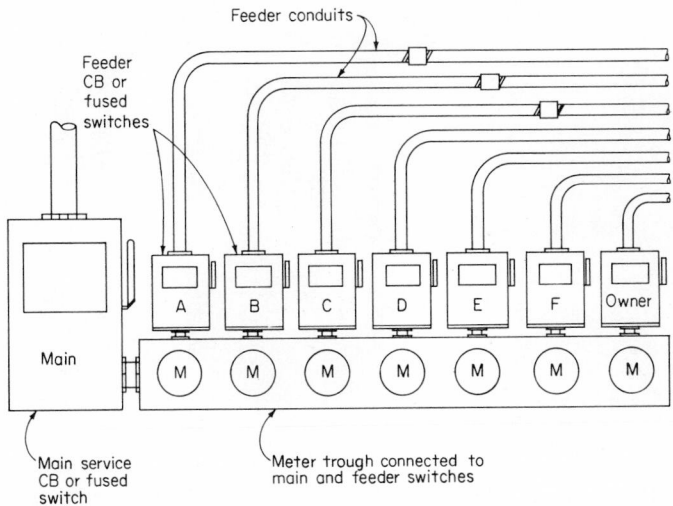

FIG. 30   *Installation of service switches connected with conduit to separate meter trough.*

ing mechanism consists of a snap action operated by one of the methods given in Sec. **10.** Wiring switches are made in many types in order to meet the requirements for different conditions of mounting.

The **flush** a-c, d-c switch (Figs. 38 and 39) consists of a switch mechanism mounted in a porcelain or composition molded case with the complete unit designed to be mounted inside a switch box, outlet box, or conduit fitting so that the operating handle or button is the only portion of the switch which extends beyond the cover of the box or conduit fitting. The contacts may be of the knife-blade or mercury type (Sec. **7**). Those with knife blades are available with toggle (tumbler), push-button, or locking types of operating mechanisms. Mercury switches are almost completely silent in operation, making practically no noise on the make or break. They are used in installations where the click of a switch might prove disturbing, such as in hospitals, nurseries, etc., and they are rated as a-c snap switches as well as a-c, d-c types. Locking switches do not

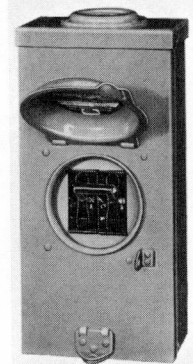

I. *Indoor type.*   II. *Raintight type.*

FIG. 31   *Fuse-puller type of service switch.* (*Murray Mfg. Corp.*)

FIG. 32   *Circuit-breaker type of service switches.* (*Murray Mfg. Corp.*)

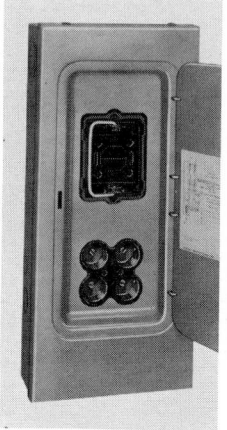

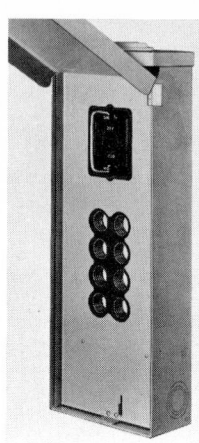

I. *Indoor type.*   II. *Raintight type.*

FIG. 33 *Raintight combination meter socket and circuit-breaker type of service switch. (Murray Mfg. Corp.)*

FIG. 34 *Combination fuse-puller service switch and load center. (Murray Mfg. Corp.)*

have a protruding operating handle but are operated by a key inserted in a slot in the face of the switch mounting.

Flush-mounted switches may be classified into subtypes depending upon the physical size and mounting of the switch. The **standard line** of switches (Figs. 38 and 39) is made with more generous proportions and is the most rugged of the two types. It should be used for heavy-duty installations and where frequent operation is required. The overall dimensions range from 1 to 2 in. in depth, $1\frac{7}{16}$ to 2 in. in width, and from

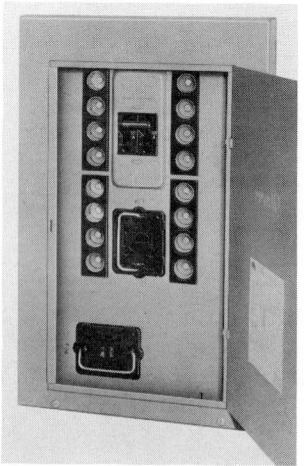

FIG. 35 *Combination circuit-breaker-type service switch and load center. Load center includes two fuse-puller switches. (Murray Mfg. Corp.)*

FIG. 36 *Raintight socket meter trough for a single meter. (Murray Mfg. Corp.)*

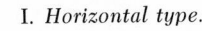

I. *Horizontal type.*   II. *Vertical type.*

FIG. 37   *Multiple-socket meter troughs. (Murray Mfg. Corp.)*

$2\frac{3}{8}$ to $3\frac{3}{16}$ in. in length. Most of these switches are supplied with two sets of supporting screw holes, spaced from center to center $3\frac{9}{32}$ and $2\frac{3}{8}$ in., respectively. They are made in sizes up to 30 amp capacity. Switches of standard-line dimensions are made in regular tumbler, push-button, locking, and mercury types.

The **a-c** snap switches (Fig. 40) represent a major development in the wiring device field. These switches are quiet in operation and have a long life because of silver-alloy butt contacts. Unlike a-c, d-c switches the a-c snap switch can be used up to its full ampere rating for incandescent lamp and fluorescent lamp loads and any other resistive or inductive loads except motors. Motor loads are limited to 80 per cent of the a-c switch rating.

Although the a-c snap switch is limited to a-c circuits, it is obvious that such switches can be used on the majority of installations because a-c supplies represent over 98 per cent of the systems in the United States. Ratings of a-c snap switches are 15 or 20 amp at 120 or 120/277 volts. These switches are widely used for local control of 277-volt fluorescent luminaires, which are supplied by 480Y/277-volt branch circuits.

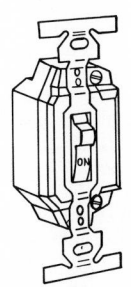
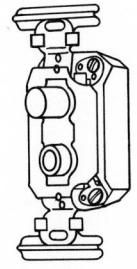
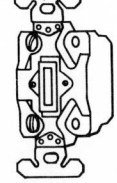

I-Tumbler type with
porcelain body

II-Tumbler type with
composition body

III-Push button type
with porcelain body

I-Switch

II-Key for
operation of
switch

FIG. 38   *Standard line of flush a-c, d-c snap switches.*
(Pass & Seymour, Inc.)

FIG. 39   *Locking type of tumbler flush switch, standard line construction.*

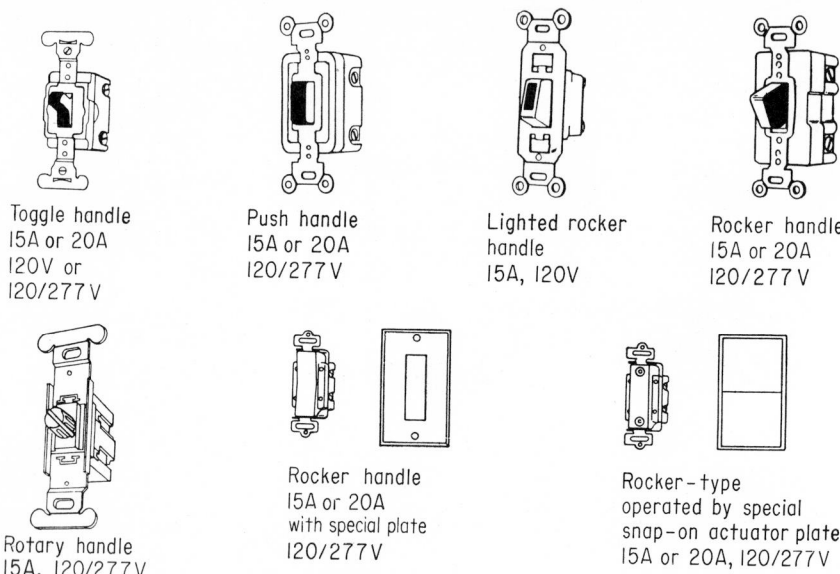

Toggle handle
15A or 20A
120V or
120/277V

Push handle
15A or 20A
120/277V

Lighted rocker
handle
15A, 120V

Rocker handle
15A or 20A
120/277V

Rotary handle
15A, 120/277V

Rocker handle
15A or 20A
with special plate
120/277V

Rocker-type
operated by special
snap-on actuator plate
15A or 20A, 120/277V

FIG. 40   *Typical types and ratings of modern a-c snap switches.*

As shown in Fig. 40, a-c snap switches are available in a wide variety of shapes and styles to blend with modern decor. The switches are available in single-pole, double-pole, three-way, four-way, and momentary-contact types. Also lighted (to indicate an "off" position) or pilot-light (to indicate an "on" position) operating handles are available in these switches. Terminals are either screw-type or pressure-locking push-in types. Only the screw terminals are suitable for connection of aluminum conductors. See Sec. **3** of Div. 9 for definitions of various types of snap switches.

The modern **dimmer** snap switch is an electronic device which provides full-range dimming of incandescent lamps from "off" to full brightness. These devices are rated from 600 to 1,000 watts and are wired in the same manner as standard single-pole switches. A description of this switch is given in Sec. **110** of Div. 6. Similar devices are available for use with special rapid-start ballasts for dimming fluorescent lamps.

The **interchangeable line** of switches (Figs. 41 and 42) is constructed in a much more compact manner with less generous proportions. As many as three of these switches can be installed in the same space required for a single standard-line switch. The largest size switch made in this line is 20 amp. Three switches or a combination of three units of switches, receptacles, and pilot lights can be assembled on a single supporting strap yoke and mounted in a single gang outlet box or switch box (see Figs. 41 and 42).

Surface switches (Figs. 43 and 44) are designed for mounting on the surface of a wall, ceiling, or box so that all or practically all the switch body extends beyond the surface upon which it is mounted. The contacts are of the knife-blade type operated by tumbler or rotary action. A line of outlet fittings for surface mounting is available for use with exposed nonmetallic-sheathed-cable wiring (refer to Sec. **203,** Div. 9).

Pendant switches (Fig. 45) are used for the control of lamps or other devices which are mounted overhead out of reach from persons standing on the floor. They are supported at the end of a pendant two-conductor cord.

Through-cord switches (Fig. 46) are designed to be inserted in a portable cord for control of the cord circuit.

Door switches (Fig. 47) are for the purpose of controlling circuits through the opening and closing of doors. They are mounted in boxes located in the doorjamb. Two types are available, one constructed so that the switch is closed when the door is open and the other so that the switch is closed when the door is closed.

Canopy switches (Fig. 48) are small compact switches for mounting in the canopies of lighting fixtures for the control of the lamps directly at the fixture. They can be obtained in pull-chain or toggle-switch types.

Appliance switches are made in a variety of types for mounting in the appliance enclosure.

Rotary surface switches can be obtained mounted in special enclosures to meet the conditions of special exposures such as weather, water, or explosive atmospheres.

31. Wiring switches are available in different types in order to perform different functions in the wiring system. The regular switches designated simply as **single pole** or **double pole** are for the general-purpose use of opening and closing circuits for control of lamps or other devices from a single point. The single-pole switches (Fig. 49, I and II) break the circuit of only one side of the line, while the double-pole switch (Fig. 49, III) breaks the circuit of both sides.

Three-way switches are used where it is desired to control lights from two different points, such as a hall light to be controlled from the lower hall and the upper hall. The lights can be turned on or off from either position. Three-way switches when properly connected (see Sec. **32**) break the circuit of only one side of the line; they do not isolate the circuit from the supply. The method of controlling a lamp from two positions with two three-way switches is shown in Fig. 50.

Four-way switches in conjunction with two three-way switches are used where it is desired to control lights from three or more different points. Two three-way switches are required with as many four-way switches connected between the two three-way ones as there are points of control in excess of two. Thus to control lights from four different points requires two three-way switches with two four-way switches connected between them. The method of control from three different locations is shown in Fig. 51. Four-way switches when properly connected break the circuit of only one side of the line.

Momentary-contact switches are used where it is desired to close or open a circuit for only a short length of time. The switch is provided with a

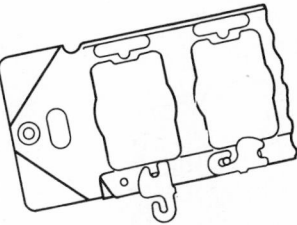

I-Open cam

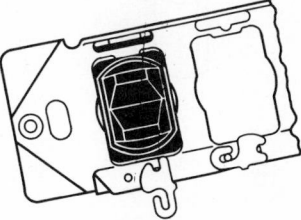

2-Insert device

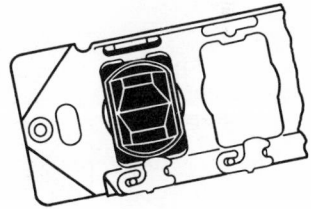

3-Close cam

FIG. 41   *Method of assembling units and strap.* (*Pass & Seymour, Inc.*)

spring so that it will return to its original position as soon as the handle or button is released. They are available in standard-line tumbler and push-button types of flush switches and in push-button surface types.

Heater switches are designed for the control of circuits for electric ranges and electric heating devices. They are made in single- and double-pole types for control of single, double, or triple heats.

32. Caution should be exercised in connecting three-way and four-way switches, since it is possible to connect these switches with both sides of the circuit connected to each switch. This is an improper connection which should never be used. The switch is not designed for this purpose and in case of failure of the switch mechanism a short circuit may result. The acceptable methods of connections are shown in Fig. 58. Refer to Sec. **40** for additional information on connection of these switches.

33. Rating of snap switches for general wiring installation must be in accordance with the requirements of the National Electrical Code. For this purpose the Code classifies loads into three types: (1) noninductive loads other than tungsten-filament lamps, (2) tungsten-filament lamps, and (3) inductive loads.

Snap switches for controlling noninductive loads other than tungsten-filament lamps are required merely to have an ampere rating at least equal to the ampere rating of the loads which they control. The only common example of a noninductive load other than tungsten-filament lamps is that of electrically heated appliances.

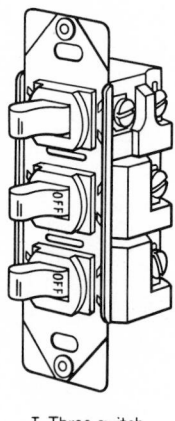
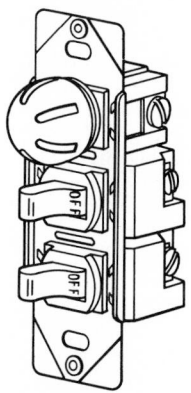
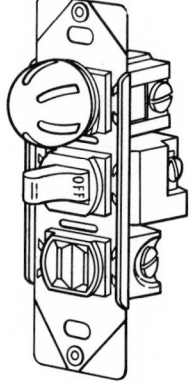

I Three switch assembly

II Two switches assembled with one pilot or night light

III One switch, receptacle, and light assembly

FIG. 42 *Typical assemblies of interchangeable wiring devices.* (*Pass & Seymour, Inc.*)

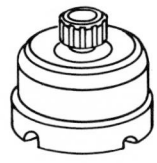

I-Tumbler type   II-Rotary type

FIG. 43 *Surface-wiring switches.* (*Pass & Seymour, Inc.*)

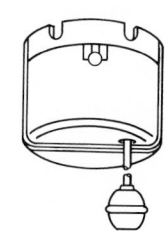

FIG. 44 *Ceiling types of pull rotary switches.*

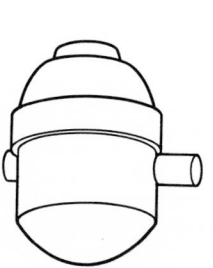
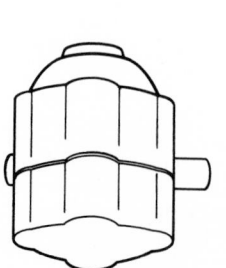
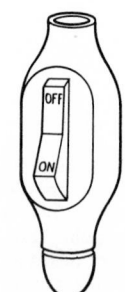

I Brass shell   II Porcelain shell   III Bakelite shell

FIG. 45 *Pendant switches.* (*I, II, General Electric Co.; III, Pass & Seymour, Inc.*)

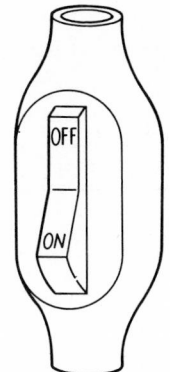
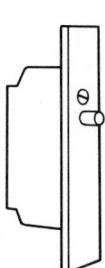

FIG. 46 *Through-cord switch.* *(Pass &*   FIG. 47 *Door switch.* *(General Electric*
Seymour, Inc.)   *Co.)*

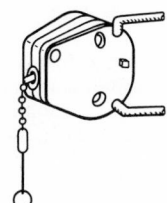
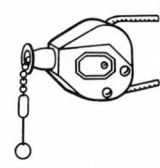

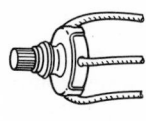

FIG. 48 *Various types of canopy switches.* *(General Electric Co.)*

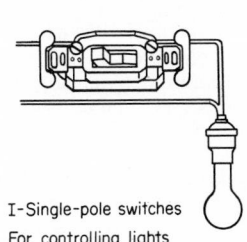
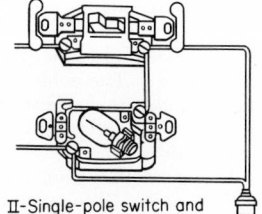
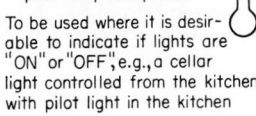
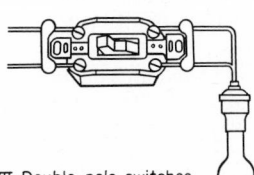

I–Single-pole switches

For controlling lights
from one point-breaking
one side of line

II–Single-pole switch and
pilot lamp receptacle

To be used where it is desirable to indicate if lights are
"ON" or "OFF", e.g., a cellar
light controlled from the kitchen
with pilot light in the kitchen

III–Double-pole switches

For controlling lights from
one point-breaking both
sides of line

FIG. 49 *Connections and functions of single- and double-pole switches.*

Snap switches for the control of loads consisting of only tungsten-filament lamps or
of tungsten-filament lamps combined with any other noninductive load should be T
rated, or on a-c circuits a-c snap switches are suitable. If all the three following conditions are fulfilled a T rated or a-c switch is not required.

1. If switches are used in branch-circuit wiring systems in private homes, in rooms in
multiple-occupancy dwellings used only as living quarters by tenants, in private
hospital or hotel rooms, or in similar locations but not in public rooms or places of
assembly.

2. Only when such a switch controls permanently connected fixtures or lighting

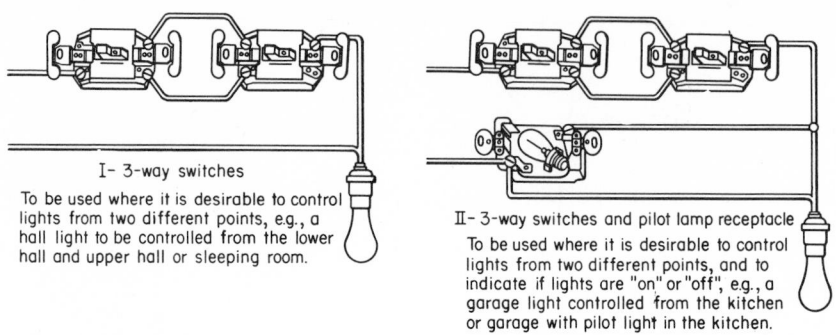

I- 3-way switches

To be used where it is desirable to control lights from two different points, e.g., a hall light to be controlled from the lower hall and upper hall or sleeping room.

II- 3-way switches and pilot lamp receptacle

To be used where it is desirable to control lights from two different points, and to indicate if lights are "on" or "off", e.g., a garage light controlled from the kitchen or garage with pilot light in the kitchen.

FIG. 50 *Connections and functions of three-way switches.*

outlets in one room only or in one continuous hallway where the lighting fixtures may be located at different levels or on porches or in attics or basements not used for assembly purposes.

3. When the switch is rated at not less than 10 amp, 125 volts; 5 amp, 250 volts; or for the 4-way types, 5 amp, 125 volts; 2 amp, 250 volts.

The T rating of an a-c, d-c switch is its ability to control satisfactorily a tungsten-filament lamp load of that rating. The peculiar current characteristic of a tungsten-filament lamp over other types of circuit loading is that the resistance of the tungsten filament to the passage of current is extremely low when the lamp filament is cold. Thus, when the circuit is closed, there is a heavy inrush current at first. As the temperature of the lamp filament increases, the current decreases and very soon reaches its normal value. Therefore, switches used with these loads must be capable of satisfactorily handling the inrush current, which will be considerably greater than the normal hot operating current of the circuit.

A-c, d-c snap switches for controlling inductive loads must have an ampere rating twice the ampere rating of the load unless they are approved as part of an assembly or for the purpose employed. On alternating-current circuits, general-use alternating-current snap switches may be used to control inductive loads other than motors not exceeding the ampere rating of the switch. The common types of inductive loads encountered in general wiring installations are fluorescent lamps and mercury-vapor lamps. Switches used on signs and outline lighting must conform with the Code requirements given in Art. 600 of the Code.

34. Control switches are used for controlling from a switchboard the operation of electrically operated equipment such as switches, circuit breakers, rheostats, prime-mover governors, etc. They are generally of the drum or rotary type. Two representative control switches are shown in Figs. 52 and 53. Pilot lamps are generally used in connection with control switches in order to indicate to the operator the position of the controlled equipment.

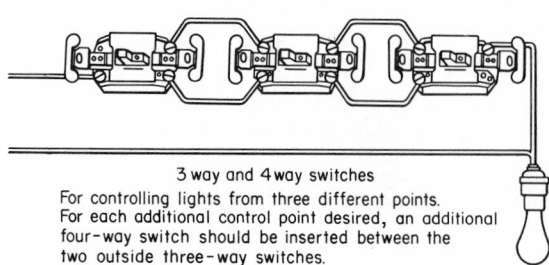

3 way and 4 way switches

For controlling lights from three different points. For each additional control point desired, an additional four-way switch should be inserted between the two outside three-way switches.

FIG. 51 *Connections and functions of three-way and four-way switches.*

FIG. 52   *Rotary type of control switch with cover removed. (Westinghouse Electric Corp.)*

35. Instrument switches are employed for changing the connections of meters from one circuit to another. The most common type is of rotary construction as shown in Fig. 54. The plug-and-receptacle type of switch is also employed for connecting a common voltmeter, ammeter, or synchroscope to various circuits. One plug is used for each set of common receptacles so that it is impossible to make cross connections. Examples of plug-and-receptacle equipment are shown in Figs. 55 and 56.

36. Low-voltage relay control systems are widely used in installations which require multiple switch control of outlets. To a large degree such systems replace conventional three-way and four-way switch control, particularly where a large number of multiple switch locations are required in a given installation. Figure 57 shows three basic types of low-voltage relay switching systems. The system shown in Fig. 57, 1, operates on a 24-volt system, and the switching relay, located at the controlled outlet, contains an "on–off" latching-type double coil wired to one or more

FIG. 53   *Control switch. (General Electric Co.)*

single-pole, double-throw, momentary-contact switches. Pressing to the "on" position of any switch operates the "on" coil and closes the single-pole contact which completes the circuit to the connected load. After releasing the "on" button the current does not flow through the coil, but the single-pole "line" contacts remain in the closed position because they are mechanically latched. Pressing to the "off" position of any of the paralleled switches energizes the "off" coil in the relay and the single-pole line

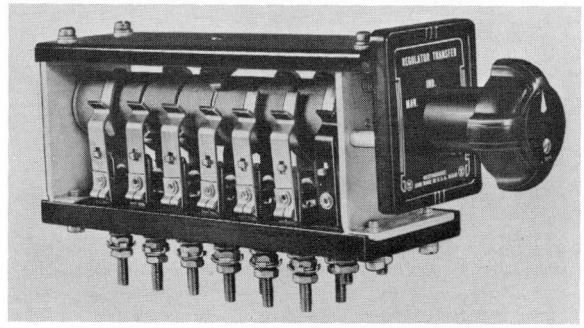

FIG. 54   *Rotary type of instrument switch with cover removed. (Westinghouse Electric Corp.)*

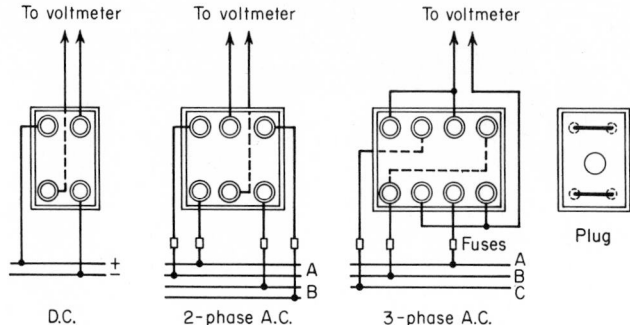

FIG. 55   *Voltmeter receptacles and plug.*   (*Electric System Handbook.*)

contacts are opened, disconnecting the load, and the contacts remain mechanically latched in the open position until the "on" switch position is operated again.

In Fig. 57, 2, a two-wire latching relay is operated at 12 or 24 volts by one or more single-pole, single-throw, momentary-contact switches (placed in parallel). Thus, every time a momentary-contact switch is actuated, the relay either closes or opens the circuit and latches in either position like a pull-chain-type fixture.

The system shown in Fig. 57, 3, uses a compact transformer relay in a single unit and is located at each controlled outlet. This unit operates on a thermal principle and trips the single-pole 115-volt contacts into the "on" or "off" position according to the operation of the single-pole, double-throw, momentary-contact switches. Although this transformer-relay system is no longer manufactured, it is described so that the reader will understand the principle of operation because numerous systems of this type are still in existence.

The system in Fig. 57, 1, is the most popular low-voltage relay system and is available from several manufacturers. This system lends itself to a "master" and "submaster" control so that many circuits can be operated at once through a motorized master unit. Special relays and switches are also available to provide pilot-light indication at switches to show when the controlled load is in the "on" position. In most cases the relay is located at the outlet to which the controlled load is connected.

The system in Fig. 57, 2, is available from only one manufacturer. Generally, the relays are in a large centrally located junction box or panel, and the 115-volt circuits extend from this central point to each controlled outlet. This system can also be converted to a master system, and pilot-light indicators are also available.

Full details, diagrams, and suggested layouts are available from manufacturers of

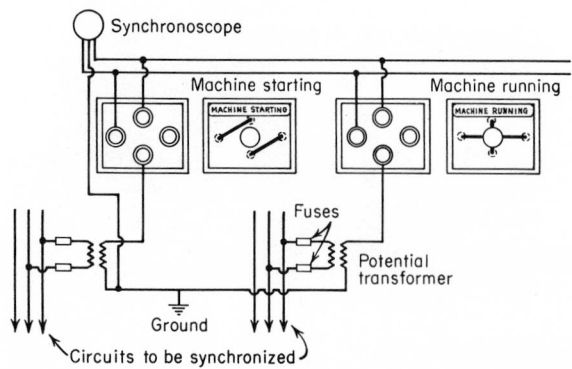

FIG. 56   *Synchronizing plugs and receptacles.*   (*Electric System Handbook.*)

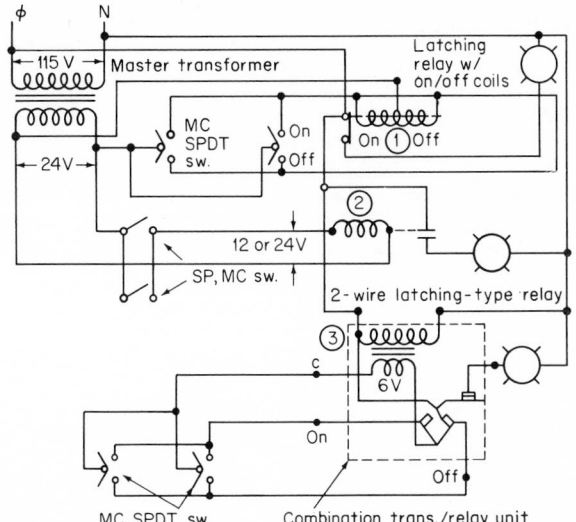

FIG. 57   *Three types of low-voltage relay-switching systems.*

these systems in the form of wiring handbooks. Switch ratings are 10 to 15 amp at 120 or 277 volts.

37. Magnetic switches in ratings up to several hundred amperes are available in either magnetically held or mechanically held types. Voltage ratings are 600 volts or less.

A magnetically operated switch is an "on–off" switch in which the opening and closing operations are effected by energizing an electromagnetic mechanism. Such switches or contactors are used to provide automatic and/or remote switching of feeders, branch circuits, and individual loads.

The basic switch is operated by energizing its coil to close the contacts, and it is held in the closed position by maintaining current through the coil.

A variation of the magnetically held contactor is the mechanically held contactor, in which the operating coil is "momentarily" energized to close the contacts and momentarily energized to open the contacts. Because of the definite switch action—with mechanically maintained open and closed positions—such a magnetic contactor is commonly distinguished from the magnetically held type by calling it a "remote switch"—a mechanical switch which can be operated by means of a control circuit to a remote switch.

A remote switch permits operation of the contact assembly from one or more distant control stations. In such applications the switch is placed in the circuit which it is to control. This may be in the middle of a split-bus panel board where the switch controls one section of bus. It may be adjacent to a panel, where the switch controls a branch circuit or feeder from the panel. Or it may be placed upon a column, where it switches lighting circuits for a given area. Then in each case, control conductors are run in cable or conduit from the switch enclosure to one or more control points at which pilot devices provide for operation of the remote switch. The pilot devices may be push buttons, toggle switches, or an automatic device, such as a time switch.

A basic contactor application for a full panel control might involve locating the contractor at widely spaced lighting panel boards supplying outdoor lighting with all the control circuits brought to pilot switches at a common point of control. For control of individual circuits supplying lighting loads, contactors may be located near the panel board or near the load.

38. Various miscellaneous types of switches are available for special applications. Knife-blade switches of reduced dimensions are available for low-voltage circuits such as telephone, signaling, and battery circuits.

INSTALLATION OF SWITCHES

39. A switch or circuit breaker must not be installed so that it will disconnect a grounded conductor of a circuit unless the switching mechanism simultaneously disconnects all wires of the circuit or is so arranged that the grounded conductor cannot be disconnected until the ungrounded conductor or conductors have first been disconnected.

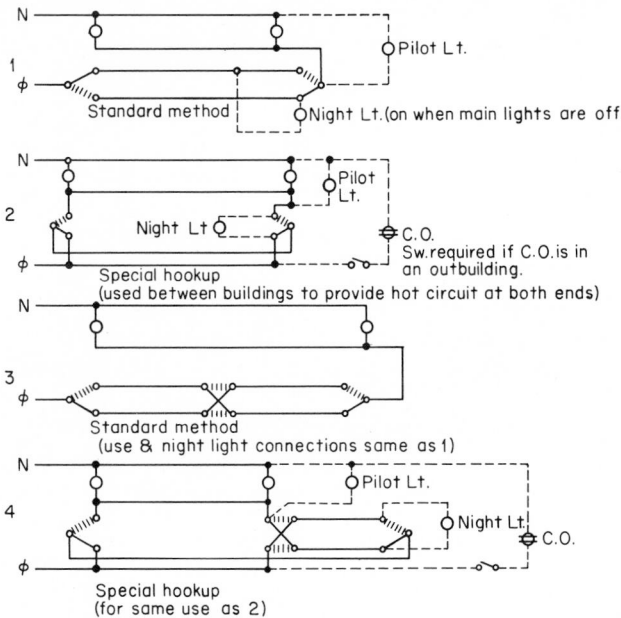

FIG. 58 *Standard and special hookups with three- and four-way switches and connections of night (neon) lights and pilot lights.*

40. Three-way and four-way switches are in reality single-pole switches and therefore must be installed so that all switching is done only in the ungrounded conductor. When the wiring for these switches is enclosed in a metal enclosure, the wiring must

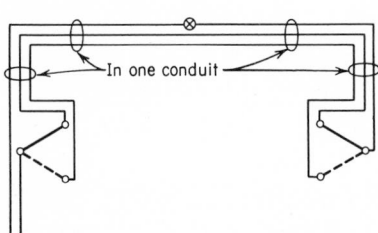

FIG. 59 *Illustrating how wires of opposite polarity must be enclosed in same conduit in the wiring of three-way switches.*

be so installed that at every point the same enclosure includes wires of both polarities. Standard and special methods of wiring such switches are illustrated in Figs. 58 and 59. Refer to Secs. **31** and **32** for additional information on three- and four-way switches.

41. Position of Mounting. Single-throw knife switches should be so mounted that gravity will tend to open and not to close them (Figs. 60 and 61). Double-throw switches can be mounted so that the throw is either vertical or horizontal. If mounted with the throw vertical, the switch must be provided with a locking device which will hold the blades in the open position when so set.

42. In connecting knife switches in a circuit the switch should be wired so that the blades will be dead when the switch is open (Figs. 62 and 63).

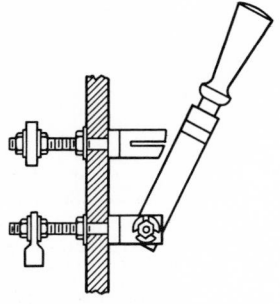

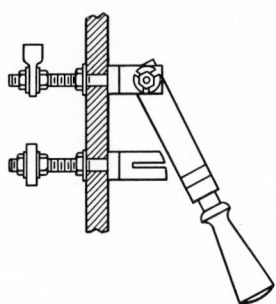

FIG. 60 *A single-throw switch mounted vertically so that gravity will not tend to close it. (NFPA Handbook of the National Electrical Code.)*

FIG. 61 *Wrong method of mounting a single-throw switch. In this position gravity tends to close the switch.*

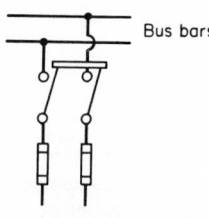

Proper method
Switch blades dead when
Switch is open

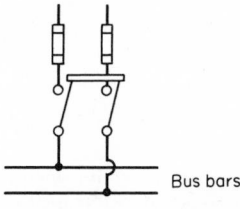

Switch blades alive when
switch is open. This connection
should be avoided

FIG. 62 *Approved method of connecting a knife switch. (NFPA Handbook of the National Electrical Code.)*

FIG. 63. *Unapproved method of connecting a knife switch. (NFPA Handbook of the National Electrical Code.)*

A fused switch should always be wired so that the fuses will be dead when the switch is open.

PROTECTIVE DEVICES

43. Various forms of protective devices are employed for protecting electrical circuits and equipment from injury under abnormal conditions. These devices may be classified as follows according to the type of protection which they provide.
1. Overload protection.
2. Underload protection.
3. Undervoltage protection.
4. Overvoltage protection.
5. Reverse-current or power protection.
6. Reverse phase rotation.
7. Lightning and surge protection.
8. Ground-fault protection.

44. Relays and Releases. Protection for the various types of abnormal conditions is in many cases provided by means of relays or release devices which actuate the opening of circuit breakers or switches. If protection is afforded by means of a simple release device, the abnormal condition causes the functioning of the release device, which acts directly upon a holding catch of the switch or breaker mechanism. With relay protection the abnormal condition causes the functioning of the relay, which opens or closes an auxiliary electric circuit, which in turn trips the switch or breaker mechanism.

Release devices may be of the thermal or magnetic types. Thermal releases can be employed only for overload protection. Their operation depends upon the deflection of a bimetallic element as it is heated by the current of the circuit. Magnetic releases consist of a solenoid acting upon an iron plunger or armature. For current protection the coil of the solenoid is connected in series with the circuit, while for voltage protection the coil is connected across the circuit which is to be protected.

Relays may be of the thermal, magnetic, or induction types. The principles of operation of the thermal and magnetic types are the same as those for releases of the same type. Induction relays operate upon the same general principle as induction motors and, therefore, are applicable only to a-c systems.

45. Time Characteristics. Relays and release devices may be classified according to the time that will elapse between the occurrence of the abnormal condition and the opening of the circuit. There are three general types: the instantaneous or high speed, the definite time, and the inverse time. In the instantaneous type, time delay is purposely omitted from its action so that the circuit is opened almost instantaneously upon the occurrence of the abnormal condition for which the release or relay is set. A definite time relay or release is purposely so designed that there is a definite time delay in its action. The abnormal condition must exist for a definite time before the device will function to open the circuit. The length of time of the disturbance required to cause the device to function is independent of the magnitude of the disturbance. An inverse-time relay or release is purposely so designed that there is a time delay in its action. The length of time of the disturbance required to cause the device to function is dependent upon the magnitude of the disturbance. The greater the magnitude of the disturbance, the quicker will the device function to open the circuit. All thermal relays and releases, owing to the principle of their construction, provide inverse-time protection.

46. Overload protective devices are used in order to protect wires, wiring fittings and devices, and apparatus against excessive currents. The several types of overload protective devices may be divided into the following groups:

Means of Protection	For Protection of
I. Fuses:	
A. Low-voltage fuses:	
1. Ordinary plug fuses	Branch incandescent lighting and heating appliance circuits
2. Dual-element plug fuses	Any type of branch circuit and for small motors
a. Standard screw-base type	
b. Type S	
3. Ordinary one-time cartridge fuses	Mains or feeders where faults occur very infrequently
4. Time-delay renewable cartridge fuses	Mains or feeders where faults occur frequently
5. Dual-element cartridge fuses	Majority of mains or feeders, motor or appliance branch circuits, and overload on motors
6. Silver-sand fuses:	
a. High-interrupting type	Mains and feeders where high-interrupting capacity is necessary
b. Current-limiting type	Mains and feeders where magnitude of fault current must be limited
B. High-voltage fuses	
II. Thermal cutouts	Motors
III. Circuit breakers actuated by:	
A. Thermal overload release device	Circuits
B. Thermal relay	Circuits
C. Magnetic release device	Circuits and apparatus
D. Magnetic relay	Circuits and apparatus
E. Combined thermal and magnetic release	Circuits and apparatus
F. Induction relays	Circuits and apparatus
IV. Manual switches actuated by thermal releases	Motors
V. Magnetic switches actuated by:	
A. Thermal relays	Motors
B. Magnetic relays	Motors
IV. Ground-fault interrupters	Circuits, persons, and apparatus

With fuses and thermal cutouts the circuit is opened, in case of overload, inside the device itself. These two overload protective devices must be capable, therefore, of interrupting the line current and of extinguishing the arc that is thus formed. Relays or overload release devices themselves do not interrupt the line current of the circuit which they are protecting. An overload release device, when operated by a current greater than that for which it is set, trips the holding catch of the switch mechanism and thus allows the switch mechanism to open. The current is interrupted by the switch mechanism and not by the overload release device. An overload relay, instead of acting directly upon the holding catch of the switch mechanism, opens an auxiliary circuit. This auxiliary circuit may be the operating coil of a magnetic switch or the shunt trip coil of a circuit breaker. As with the overload release devices, the relay does not interrupt the main-line current itself. The main circuit is opened by the contacts of the switch mechanism.

47. Fuses and circuit breakers are used for the overload protection of both circuits and apparatus. Thermal cutouts, thermal overload release devices, and thermal relays are used for the protection of motors against overloads. They should not be used for the protection of circuits unless they are specifically designed and approved for that purpose. Thermal overload protective devices have admirable characteristics for the protection of motors against overloads, but they should not be relied upon for protection against short circuits unless they are specifically designed and approved for that purpose. Unless so designed in the case of a short circuit there is danger of the excessive current destroying the thermal element before it has actuated the switch mechanism, with the consequent failure of opening the circuit. Circuit breakers actuated by thermal overload release devices and designed for protection against short circuit have been developed and are widely used for the protection of circuits of small and medium current-carrying capacity. When thermal overload protective devices are employed for the protection of motors, fuses of the proper rating or circuit breakers with the proper setting should always be located at some point back in the line ahead of the thermal protective device.

47A. Short-circuit Calculations. When considering the use of circuit breakers and fuses the amount of short-circuit current available at the **line terminals** of such devices must be known so that an overcurrent device with the proper interrupting capacity (IC) rating can be selected.

Ordinary plug fuses and Class H cartridge fuse, in general, are tested for short circuits not exceeding 10,000 amp. Most common-type small-frame-size, molded-case circuit breakers have IC ratings of 5,000 amp. Larger breakers have IC ratings of 10,000, 15,000, 25,000, and up to 100,000 amp, according to types and voltage ratings. The IC ratings for high-interrupting-capacity and/or current-limiting fuses are shown in Fig. 65.

Under normal conditions a circuit draws current according to the load impedance and applied voltage. When a solid short circuit occurs, there will be an abnormally high flow of fault current until the overcurrent device opens. If the short-circuit current is higher than the interrupting rating of the affected overcurrent device, the device may be completely destroyed and may cause considerable damage to other equipment.

There is no easy method of calculating available short circuits at various points of a given installation because there are numerous factors and terms that must be clearly understood before such calculations can be made accurately. To explain these factors would require a complete book. However, an excellent series of articles titled "Protecting against Short Circuits," by H. W. Reichenstein, can be purchased from *Electrical Construction and Maintenance*, McGraw-Hill, Inc. These articles provide a clear description of all the elements involved in understanding short-circuit problems, rating of overcurrent devices, applying proper calculations, and definitions of short-circuit terminologies.

A conservative rule-of-thumb formula which can be used to determine the short-circuit current at the load terminals of a supply transformer would be:

$I_{sc} = 100\%/\%Z_t \times I_s$, where I_{sc} = maximum secondary short-circuit current based on transformer impedance and assuming a primary source of *infinite capacity*; $\%Z_t$ = transformer impedance; and I_s = full-load secondary current.

Example. Assume a 75-kva transformer with a 5 per cent impedance and a 120/240-volt secondary. The full-load secondary current $I_s = 75{,}000/240 = 312$ amp; then $I_{sc} = 100\%/5\% \times 312 = 6{,}240$ amp. Thus, the maximum short-circuit current is **20 times** the full-load secondary current for this transformer. If the transformer impedance was 2½ per cent, the short-circuit current would be 40 times the full-load secondary current, or 12,480 amp. Thus, the transformer impedance is a major factor in determining the maximum secondary short-circuit current. Equally important is the available primary current, which is almost always less than what would be considered as an "infinite" capacity. For a given transformer, the lower the available primary current, the lower the secondary short-circuit current, which identifies the previously described formula as quite conservative.

Another major point is that the maximum secondary short-circuit current determined by the previous formula is applicable directly at the secondary terminals of the transformer. The short-circuit current will be reduced at all downstream points according to the line impedance of the secondary supply conductors. As a result, a fairly long run of conductors from a pole transformer to the service switch would appreciably reduce the maximum short-circuit current available at this point from that shown in the previous example.

It should also be emphasized that certain equipment, such as motors or capacitors, in operation at the time a fault occurs, will **add** current to the fault and **increase** the short-circuit current.

This brief discussion should indicate the many complexities of short-circuit calculations, and, therefore, a complete discussion in this Handbook would be impractical.

48. Diameters of Wires of Various Materials That Will Be Fused by a Current of a Given Strength
(Knox, "Electric Light Wiring"; derived from tables of W. H. Preece)

Current, amp	Copper Diam, in.	Copper Nearest B&S gage	Aluminum Diam, in.	Aluminum Nearest B&S gage	German silver Diam, in.	German silver Nearest B&S gage	Iron Diam, in.	Iron Nearest B&S gage
1	0.0021	43	0.0026	41	0.0033	39	0.0047	37
2	0.0034	39	0.0041	38	0.0053	35	0.0074	33
3	0.0044	37	0.0054	35	0.0069	33	0.0097	30
4	0.0053	35	0.0065	34	0.0084	31	0.0117	29
5	0.0062	34	0.0076	32	0.0097	30	0.0136	27
10	0.0098	30	0.0120	28	0.0154	26	0.0216	24
15	0.0129	28	0.0158	26	0.0202	24	0.0283	21
20	0.0156	26	0.0191	24	0.0245	22	0.0343	19
25	0.0181	25	0.0222	23	0.0284	21	0.0398	18
30	0.0205	24	0.0250	22	0.0320	20	0.0450	17
35	0.0227	23	0.0277	21	0.0356	19	0.0498	16
40	0.0248	22	0.0303	20	0.0388	18	0.0545	15
45	0.0268	21	0.0328	20	0.0420	18	0.0589	15
50	0.0288	21	0.0352	19	0.0450	17	0.0632	14
60	0.0325	20	0.0397	18	0.0509	16	0.0714	13
70	0.0360	19	0.0440	17	0.0564	15	0.0791	12
80	0.0394	18	0.0481	16	0.0616	14	0.0864	12
90	0.0426	18	0.0520	16	0.0667	14	0.0935	11
100	0.0457	17	0.0558	15	0.0715	13	0.1003	10
120	0.0516	16	0.0630	14	0.0808	12	0.1113	9
140	0.0572	15	0.0698	14	0.0895	11	0.1255	8
160	0.0625	14	0.0763	13	0.0978	10	0.1372	7
180	0.0676	14	0.0826	12	0.1058	10	0.1484	7
200	0.0725	13	0.0886	11	0.1135	9	0.1592	6
225	0.0784	12	0.0958	10	0.1228	8	0.1722	5
250	0.0841	12	0.1028	10	0.1317	8	0.1848	5
275	0.0897	11	0.1095	9	0.1404	7	0.1969	4
300	0.0950	11	0.1161	9	0.1487	7	0.2086	4

49. Low-voltage enclosed fuses (600-volt or less) may be classified as follows:

A. Type of enclosure and contact construction.
    1. Plug.
    2. Cartridge.
        a. Ferrule contact – Class G, H, J, or K.
        b. Knife blade – Class H, J, K, or L.
B. Renewability.
    1. One-time.
    2. Renewable.
C. Time overload must exist for fuse to blow.
    1. Ordinary type – very little time delay.
    2. Time delay.

The basic features of the different types of enclosures and contact construction are shown in Figs. 64 and 65. Plug fuses are made in sizes up to and including 30 amp. Class G, H, J, and K cartridge fuses with ferrule contacts are made in sizes up to and including 60 amp. Class H, J, and K cartridge fuses with knife-blade contacts are made in sizes from 70 up to and including 600 amp. Above 600 amp, Class L current-limiting fuses are available in ratings up to 6,000 amp.

One-time fuses cannot be used after they have once blown from the occurrence of a fault. Renewable fuses are designed so that the fusible element can be replaced, after it has blown, by a new element. Thus the fuse cases can be used over and over and, thereby, reduce the fuse expense in services where the blowing of fuses is frequent and short-circuit currents are less than 10,000 amp.

A certain lapse of time exists for all fuses between the occurrence of an overload and the opening of the circuit by rupture of the fusible element. For the ordinary type (the original one-time fuse) this lapse of time is very short. The ordinary plug fuse, for example, opens the circuit in approximately 3 sec at 200 per cent load. The time lapse required for a fuse to blow can be controlled through proper design. According to the standards of the Underwriters' Laboratories any fuse which has an opening time of greater than 12 sec at 200 per cent load is characterized as a time-delay (often termed time-lag) fuse. Such fuses are marked with the letter "D."

Low-voltage fuses rated 600 amp or less are of standard ratings and dimensions as established by the National Electrical Code and the Underwriters' Laboratories. The standard dimensions for Class H cartridge fuses are given in Sec. 51. The dimensions for fuses rated above 600 amp are under consideration by the standardizing boards but have not yet been established.

Fuses are made in several types as listed previously. Certain types are definitely limited in their application, some can be used for nearly any application, and others are designed for special applications where their characteristics are required in order that proper protection may be realized and system coordination maintained.

50. The Underwriters' Standards on fuses require that all fuses must meet the following requirements:

1. The Standard on fuses requires that the fuses be of certain dimensions within specified tolerances and requires the fuses to meet the following tests:

2. Must withstand heavy short circuits. Failure to do this would result in a very great fire hazard, as such failure would mean that the fuse would explode or belch fire.

3. Must operate at a reasonably low temperature. Failure to do this would make a hazard of the fuse.

4. Must carry rated current. Failure to do so would result in premature burnout, causing unnecessary expense and annoyance. All fuses are required to carry a 10 per cent overload indefinitely when tested in the open. When fuses are installed in enclosures, as is usually the case, they carry less current. Hence the 10 per cent overload requirement so as to be sure they will carry rated current in actual practice.

5. Must blow promptly at an overload. Failure to do this would result in repair bills amounting to many times the cost of the fuse. The requirements are that fuses blow at a 35 per cent overload when tested in the open so that they will blow at a 25 per cent overload when installed in an enclosure, as they usually are. The blowing time permitted on 0- to 60-amp fuses is 1 hr and on larger fuses 2 hr.

51. Dimensions of Underwriters' Laboratories Listed Cartridge-enclosed Class H Fuses

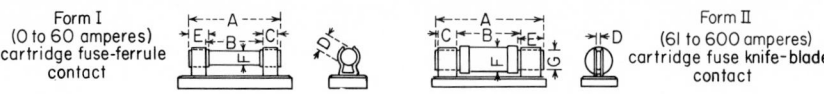

FIG. 64 *Class H standard fuses and holders.*

Voltage	Rated capacity, amp.	A	B	C	D	E	G
		Length over terminals, in.	Distance between contact clips, in.	Width of contact clips, in.	Diam of ferrules or thickness of terminal blades, in.	Min length of ferrules or of terminal blades outside of tube, in.	Width of terminal blades, in.
0–250 (Form I)	{ 0–30	2	1	$\frac{1}{2}$	$\frac{9}{16}$	$\frac{1}{2}$	
	31–60	3	$1\frac{3}{4}$	$\frac{5}{8}$	$1\frac{3}{16}$	$\frac{5}{8}$	
(Form II)	61–100	$5\frac{7}{8}$	4	$\frac{7}{8}$	$\frac{1}{8}$	1	$\frac{3}{4}$
	101–200	$7\frac{1}{8}$	$4\frac{1}{2}$	$1\frac{1}{4}$	$\frac{3}{16}$	$1\frac{3}{8}$	$1\frac{1}{8}$
	201–400	$8\frac{5}{8}$	5	$1\frac{3}{4}$	$\frac{1}{4}$	$1\frac{7}{8}$	$1\frac{5}{8}$
	401–600	$10\frac{3}{8}$	6	$2\frac{1}{8}$	$\frac{1}{4}$	$2\frac{1}{4}$	2
251–600 (Form I)	{ 0–30	5	4	$\frac{1}{2}$	$1\frac{3}{16}$	$\frac{1}{2}$	
	31–60	$5\frac{1}{2}$	$4\frac{1}{4}$	$\frac{5}{8}$	$1\frac{1}{16}$	$\frac{5}{8}$	
(Form II)	61–100	$7\frac{7}{8}$	6	$\frac{7}{8}$	$\frac{1}{8}$	1	$\frac{3}{4}$
	101–200	$9\frac{5}{8}$	7	$1\frac{1}{4}$	$\frac{3}{16}$	$1\frac{3}{8}$	$1\frac{1}{8}$
	201–400	$11\frac{5}{8}$	8	$1\frac{3}{4}$	$\frac{1}{4}$	$1\frac{7}{8}$	$1\frac{5}{8}$
	401–600	$13\frac{3}{8}$	9	$2\frac{1}{8}$	$\frac{1}{4}$	$2\frac{1}{4}$	2

52. Cartridge Fuse Types. Cartridge fuses come in a wide range of types, sizes, and ratings. Various classes are designated by NEMA Standards and Underwriters Laboratories' Standards. In broad terms, these fuses are classified as one-time; renewable; dual-element; current-limiting; or high-interrupting-capacity.

Present NEMA and UL Standards indicate that standard (so-called National Electrical Code type) cartridge fuses of generally one-time or renewable types are designated as Class H. Such fuses are generally classified at an interrupting capacity rating of 10,000 amp. Refer to **Sec. 51** for dimensions at 250- or 600-volt ratings.

Cartridge fuse classifications, based on existing UL requirements at IC ratings above 10,000 rms symmetrical amperes, are Class J, L, G, or K. These fuses are high-interrupting-capacity or current-limiting types. They are shown in Fig. 65. The term "high-interrupting-capacity fuse" indicates a fuse-interrupting rating at some value above 10,000 to about 200,000 rms symmetrical amperes, depending upon the particular fuse. A "current-limiting fuse" is a fuse which safely interrupts all available currents within its interrupting rating and limits the peak let-through current I_p and the total amperes squared seconds I^2t to a specified degree. UL states that "current-limiting" indicates that a fuse, when tested on a circuit capable of delivering a specific short-circuit current (rms amperes symmetrical) at rated voltage, will start to melt within 90 electrical degrees and will clear the circuit within 180 electrical degrees ($\frac{1}{2}$ cycle).

1. CLASS J AND L FUSES. Both the Class J and Class L fuses are current-limiting, high-interrupting-capacity types. The interrupting ratings are 100,000 or 200,000 rms symmetrical amperes, and the designated rating is marked on the label of each Class J or L fuse.

Class J fuse dimensions are different from those for standard Class H cartridge fuses of the same voltage rating and ampere classification. As such, they will require special fuseholders that will not accept non-current-limiting fuses. This arrangement complies with the last sentence of Section 240-23(*b*) of the National Electrical Code, which reads: "Fuseholders for current-limiting fuses shall not permit insertion of fuses which are not current limiting."

Class J fuses of 60 amp or less are ferrule types; and from 61 to 600 amp, they have slots in the fuse blades to permit bolted or knife-blade connections to fuseholders.

Class L fuses are divided into several different amperage classifications; and fuse-blade mounting holes, the number of which varies according to fuse sizes, permit bolted connection to fuseholders.

UL standards list specific dimensions for Class J fuses and recommend specific dimensions for Class L fuses. And both Class J and Class L fuses, covered in these UL rules, closely parallel the existing NEMA Standard (FU-1-1963), "Low-Voltage Cartridge Fuses," which includes construction and test recommendations for Class J and Class L fuses.

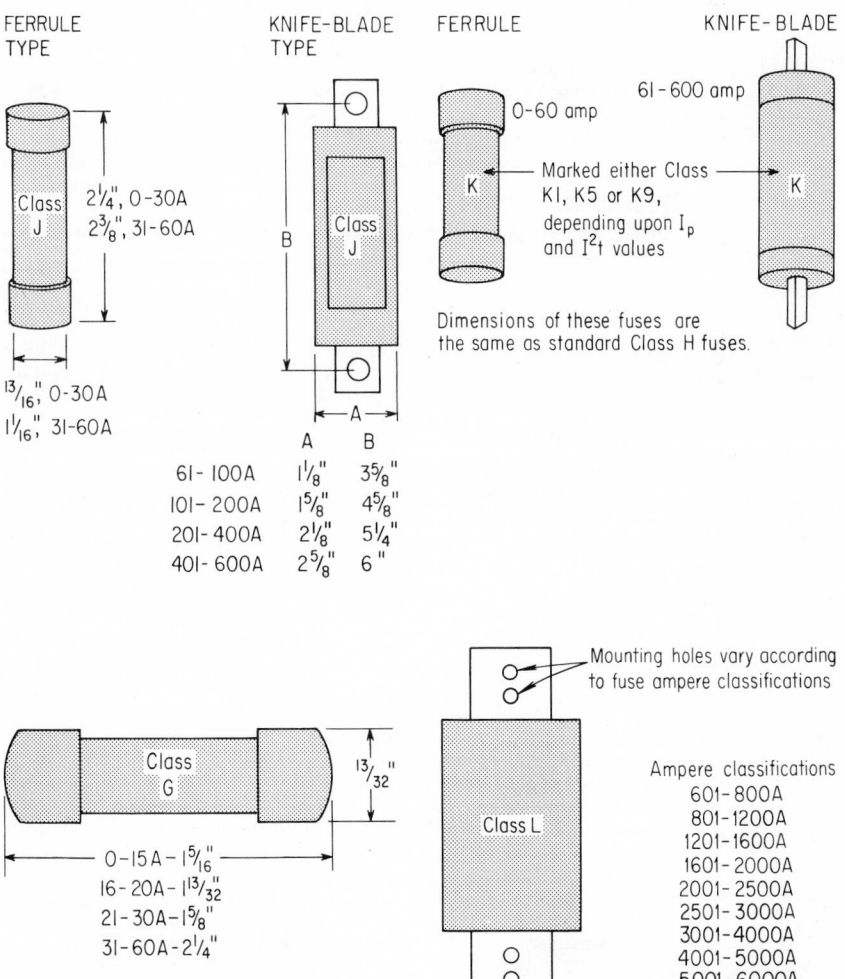

FIG. 65 *Ampere classifications of Class G, H, K, J, and L high-interrupting-capacity or current-limiting cartridge fuses.*

2. CLASS G FUSES. Any 300-volt cartridge fuse intended to be used on circuits exceeding 10,000 rms symmetrical amperes has been given a designation by UL as Class G. These 300-volt cartridge fuses successfully passed UL-supervised tests at 100,000 rms symmetrical amperes. Figure 65 shows the dimension of these fuses.

3. CLASS K FUSES have interrupting ratings from 50,000 to 200,000 rms symmetrical amperes at various peak let-through currents I_p and maximum let-through energy conditions I^2t. Initially these fuses have been divided into three groups: K1, K5, and K9. These groups indicate the degree of I^2t and I_p values. Class K1 fuses provide more current limitation than K5 or K9 fuses. UL can verify proposed available current ratings of switches or motor starters, based on the use of a specific K-type fuse (K1, K5, etc.).

All presently UL-listed Class K fuses have the same dimensions as conventional Class H 250-volt or 600-volt, 0 to 600-amp fuses (Fig. 64). Because of this interchangeable feature, Class K fuses are not labeled "Current-Limiting" even though the I_p and I^2t values of K1 fuses compare closely with those for Class J fuses. However, consideration is being given to provide "rejection" features for Class K fuseholders and fuses so that Class H fuses cannot be substituted.

53. The ordinary one-time cartridge fuse (Fig. 66) is the oldest type of cartridge fuse in common use today. It consists of a tube of vulcanized fiber, paper, or some similar material within which the fuse is mounted. The fuse terminals are connected to contact pieces at the ends of the tube. An insulating, porous powder resembling chalk surrounds the fuse and fills or nearly fills the tube. When the fuse blows, the powdered material quenches the arc. The ordinary type of cartridge fuse is available in ratings from 1 up to and including 600 amp and for use on circuits with maximum voltages of 250 or 600 volts, respectively. These fuses have

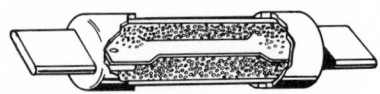

FIG. 66   *Ordinary one-time fuse. (Bussmann Mfg. Div. of McGraw-Edison Co.)*

very little time delay, and their use, therefore, is limited to short-circuit protection on circuits in which faults occur infrequently. This is known as a Class H fuse and usually has an interrupting-capacity rating of 10,000 amp in UL listings.

53A. Renewable cartridge fuses (Figs. 67 to 69) are designed so that the fusible element can be readily replaced when blown by a new element. They are available in ratings from 3 up to and including 600 amp and for use on circuits with maximum voltages of 250 or 600 volts, respectively. Most renewable cartridge fuses are of the time-delay type. The time delay is accomplished through special link construction employing the combination of parts with heavy cross-sectional area with parts having very reduced cross-sectional area. As an example, consider the super-lag fuse shown in Fig. 69. In this super-lag fuse, heavy lag plates are attached to the center of the link. The principal blowing parts of the fuse are near the terminals. The heavy lag plates keep the center of the link relatively cool. An extra reduced section is provided in the center of these lag plates so that they do not increase the current-carrying capacity of the link too much. As a result the lag plates serve only to help the terminals conduct away and temporarily store some of the heat generated in the weak spots so that it takes a longer time to get the weak spots heated sufficiently to blow. Thus a time lag is obtained far in excess of other types of fuses.

On light overloads the center weak spot of the super-lag link will sometimes burn out. This is because the rise in temperature of the entire strip is so gradual that the

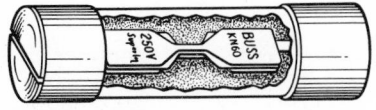

FIG. 67   *Ferrule-contact time-lag, renewable cartridge fuse. (Bussmann Mfg. Div. of McGraw-Edison Co.)*

FIG. 68   *Knife-blade contact time-delay, renewable cartridge fuse. (Economy Fuse Div. of Federal Pacific Electric Co.)*

heavy metal terminals of the fuse can conduct the heat away from the end weak spots fast enough to keep them relatively cool. Whether or not the two end weak spots or the center weak spot of the bus super-lag fuse blows first, it makes no difference in regard to the superior time lag that is obtained through the use of the lag plates.

When a short circuit occurs, the two end weak spots melt instantaneously, and because of the well-known fact that two arcs in series cannot maintain themselves as long as a single arc on the same voltage, much less metal is vaporized.

The thick lag plates also serve to reduce the amount of metal vaporized. First, their cooling effect at ordinary overloads makes it possible to reduce the amount of metal in the weak spots. Second, the thick lag plates in the center of the link serve to keep cooler the entire mass of metal in the center, and therefore the arc that follows the short circuit cannot so

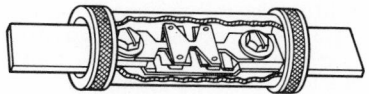

FIG. 69 *Cutaway view of time-lag fuse of the renewable type. (Super-lag fuse of the Bussmann Mfg. Div. of McGraw-Edison Co.)*

readily melt this center section. As a consequence of this, less metal is vaporized on short-circuit blows than on any other type of fuse. This means that less pressure is created in the fuse and therefore the danger of a fuse rupturing or exploding or belching fire on short circuits is considerably reduced.

The time-delay renewable fuse is used to take advantage of lower replacement costs for the protection of mains and feeders in which faults occur frequently.

54. Dual-element Class K cartridge fuses combine a thermal element for protection against overloads up to approximately 800 per cent of their rating and a fuse link element for protection against heavier overloads and short shorts. They are available in ratings of $\frac{1}{10}$ up to and including 600 amp and for use on circuits with maximum voltages of 250 or 600 volts, respectively.

A typical dual-element fuse is shown in Fig. 70. It consists of two copper links *A* and *C* located in the two end sections of the container and a heavy copper center

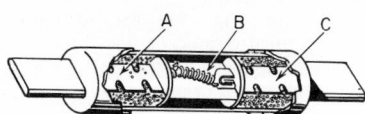

FIG. 70 *Nonrenewable dual-element cartridge fuse. (Fusetron of the Bussmann Mfg. Div. of McGraw-Edison Co.)*

strap *B*. The center strap *B* is held in position by a soldered connection to a spring. The soldered connection of the spring acts as the thermal element, while the copper links in the end sections provide the short-circuit element. Moderate overloads will not blow the short-circuit fuse element but will open the circuit through the action of the thermal element. The center strap *B* is heated by the light overloads. When *B* is heated up to the melting point of the solder, the spring is released and the thermal-cutout portion opens. The heat coil and center strap are quite heavy, so that it takes considerable time to raise the temperature of the strap sufficiently to melt the solder. This feature together with the time required to melt the solder gives the fuse its time-lag characteristics. On heavy overloads the fuse link blows immediately, before the thermal-cutout portion has time to function.

Dual-element fuses provide highly desirable protection for the majority of circuits, including mains, feeders, lighting and appliance branch circuits, as well as motor branch circuits and the overload protection of the motor itself. Their long time lag prevents useless shutdowns caused by ordinary fuses or breakers opening on motor-starting currents or other harmless overloads. They will hold even if all motors on a circuit start at one time — yet they protect against short circuit with all the speed of an ordinary fuse.

Dual-element fuses have a lower resistance than any ordinary fuse. Hence switches and panel boards will operate at a much cooler temperature with dual-element fuses than with ordinary fuses. This prevents damage and wipes out needless blowing of fuses so often caused by excessive heating.

Dual-element fuses also give a new kind of protection to switches and panel boards — thermal protection. The thermal cutout in a dual-element fuse will open whenever its temperature reaches approximately 280°F. Thus if poor contact heat develops from any cause, the dual-element fuse cuts off the current before damaging temperatures can be reached.

On motor installations dual-element fuses are particularly advantageous. On normal installations, due to their *long time-lag,* a size about 100 to 125 per cent of ampere rating of motor can be installed in disconnect switch or branch-circuit panel. When so used dual-element fuses give motor-running protection as safe and dependable as furnished by the most expensive devices made.

Double protection can be given to motors already protected by other thermal devices simply by replacing the fuses used for short-circuit protection with dual-element fuses of motor-running protection size. Then if such other devices fail for any reason, the dual-element fuses will open to protect against any dangerous overload or single phasing condition.

On new installations, dual-element fuses permit use of proper size switches and panels instead of oversize. With ordinary fuses, switches and panels must be oversize because fuses much larger than the operating load must be used to hold the starting current. But dual-element fuses hold starting currents; therefore proper size switches and panels to fit the load can be installed. This often solves the problem of finding space for the switch or panel and generally saves money as well.

On present installations, by replacing oversize fuses with dual-element fuses, switches or panels can be loaded near to their capacity. A larger motor or additional motors can often be installed without the trouble of changing the switch or panel.

Refer to Table **45,** Div. 11, for increased horsepower ratings of fused switches when time-delay fuses are used as the branch-circuit protection for motors.

55. Small-dimension fuses are available for the protection of instruments and other special apparatus. Fuses for instrument protection generally are enclosed in clear glass containing tubes.

56. Fuse accessories are available which are advantageous in the use of fuses for special applications.

Clip-clamps (Fig. 71) are available which will ensure good contact between the fuse terminals of cartridge fuses and the fuse clips.

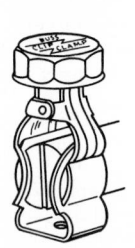

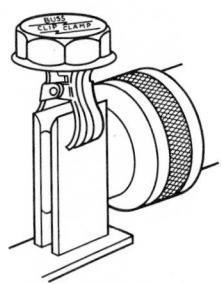

(a) Clip-Clamp in place on 0 to 60 amp fuse clip.

(b) Clip-Clamp in place on 70 to 600 amp fuse clip.

FIG. 71 *Clip-clamps for cartridge fuses. (Bussmann Mfg. Div. of McGraw-Edison Co.)*

60 to 30 amp
250 volt

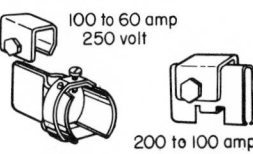

100 to 60 amp
250 volt

200 to 100 amp
250 & 600 volt

FIG. 72 *Fuse reducers. (Bussmann Mfg. Div. of McGraw-Edison Co.)*

Fuse reducers (Fig. 72) make it possible to use cartridge fuses of a smaller size than that for which the fuse clips are intended. They are available for the following reductions:

For 250-volt Fuses, Amp	For 600-volt Fuses, Amp
60- 30	60- 30
100- 30	100- 30
100- 60	100- 60
200- 60	200- 60
200-100	200-100
400-200	400-200
600-400	600-400

57. Plug fuses are available in three types (refer to Fig. 73): (*a*) the ordinary type, (*b*) the time-delay type with standard screw base, and (*c*) the Type S (tamper-resisting) type. All plug fuses are of the one-time type. The standard sizes are 15, 20, 25, and

(a) Ordinary   (b) Time-delay   (c) Type S
type   type

FIG. 73 *Types of plug fuses. (Bussmann Mfg. Div. of McGraw-Edison Co.)*

30 amp. Other sizes of 1, 2, 3, 5, 6, 8, and 10 amp are also regularly available. Fuses of 15-amp capacity or less are provided with a hexagonal window, and those of greater capacity with a round window. Plug fuses should be used only in circuits not exceeding 125 volts or circuits of a system having a grounded neutral and no conductor at more than 150 volts to ground. Plug fuses installed in residences should be of the time-delay type on circuits of 20 amp or less.

The ordinary plug fuse (Fig. 74) consists of a wire or strip of fusible alloy mounted in a porcelain container. The container is fitted with a screw base corresponding to the standard medium lamp-base dimensions and threads. The top of the container is transparent to make the fuse link visible. Since the ordinary plug fuse has very little time delay (opens in approximately 3 sec at 200 per cent load), it is subject to blowing on harmless transient overloads. This practically limits the satisfactory use of the ordinary plug fuse to incandescent-lighting or heating-appliance circuits.

Plug fuses of the time-delay type are available in both the Edison-base type (Fig. 75) and the Type S (tamper-resisting type) (Fig. 76). Edison-base plug fuses are approved only as a replacement item in existing installations where there has been no evidence of overfusing or tampering.

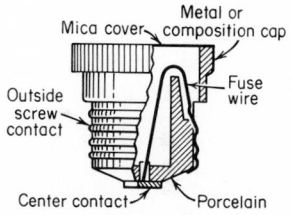

FIG. 74 *Edison-base type of plug fuse.*

A dual-element, time-delay type of standard screw-base plug fuse is shown in Figs. 77 and 78. This fuse consists of a fuse link to which a thermal cutout is added. The internal construction of the screw-base type is shown in Fig. 77. An overload causes the thermal cutout to heat up, and if the overload is continued long enough, the solder in the thermal cutout softens and permits the spring to pull out the end of the fuse link, thus opening the circuit. Because it takes some time to melt solder, even with a heavy current, the thermal cutout cannot open quickly, and the fuse link is heavy enough so it will not open quickly on motor-starting currents. Hence the time-lag fuse will not

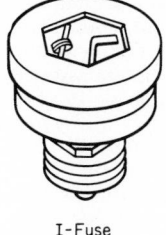
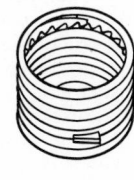

I-Fuse   II-Adapter

FIG. 75 *Time-lag fuse with Edison screw base. (Buss Fusetron of the Bussmann Div. of McGraw-Edison Co.)*

FIG. 76 *Time-lag fuse with tamperproof Type S screw base. (Buss Fustat of the Bussmann Mfg. Div. of McGraw-Edison Co.)*

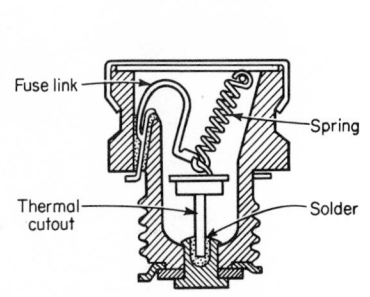

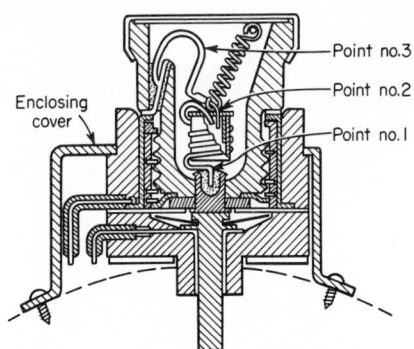

FIG. 77 *Construction of time-lag fuse of screw-base type.* (*Bussmann Mfg. Div. of McGraw-Edison Co.*)

FIG. 78 *Time-lag fuse for protection of small motors.* (*Bussmann Mfg. Div. of McGraw-Edison Co.*)

open on motor-starting currents that last only a short while. When a short circuit or an overload of approximately 800 per cent occurs, the fuse link opens in exactly the same manner as an ordinary fuse.

A time-lag fuse designed especially for the protection of small motors is shown in Fig. 78. It is intended to be mounted directly on the motor. When the receptacle is properly installed, the heat from the motor windings is conducted to the thermal cutout in the time-lag fuse at point 1. Should the windings reach a prohibitive temperature, with just a normal amount of current flowing, the time-lag fuse will open at point 1, and the motor will be shut down. The opening of the time-lag fuse under these conditions is primarily due to the heat of the motor windings rather than to the current flowing through the fuse. Thus the motor is automatically protected against an excessive rise of the ambient temperature or failure of air circulation or any other condition causing excessive heating of the motor without a corresponding rise in the flow of current. If on the other hand the flow of current is so high that the insulation in the motor will be injured or destroyed before the mass of the motor is heated sufficiently to operate the time-lag fuse as mentioned above, the thermal cutout is heated by the excessive flow of current through the heat coil and opens at point 2. The flow of current is stopped no matter how cold the exterior of the motor may be. If the motor does not properly come up to speed, owing to low voltage, tight belt, dry bearings, or any other cause, the time-lag fuse will open at point 1 or 2. If the motor should be stalled, the excessive flow of current would cause the time-lag fuse to open at point 2. If a short or ground should occur, the excessive current would cause the fuse to open in the fuse link, point 3. However, this method generally has been replaced with thermal devices similar to those described in Sec. **66.**

The tamper-resisting type of plug fuse (Fig. 76) is known as the Type S fuse. It is identical with the standard screw-base type of time-delay plug fuse except for the construction of the base. The Type S fuse has a different size base which is screwed into an adapter. The complete assembly is then screwed into a regular Edison-base fuseholder. Adapters are made in sizes from 1 to 30 amp. The 15-amp adapter will take fuses of any size from 7 to 15 amp. The 20-amp adapter will take only a 20-amp fuse, and the 30-amp adapter will accommodate a 20-, 25-, or 30-amp fuse. Type S fuses make safe protection remain safe, since (1) once the correct adapter has been installed, an oversize fuse cannot be inserted and (2) bridging and tampering are practically impossible. They give the best fuse protection for ordinary lighting, appliance, and small motor branch circuits, and they are required when plug fuses are to be used as overcurrent protection in new installations.

58. High-voltage Fuses. Fuses for circuits having a voltage greater than 600 are specially constructed so that they will be safe for the interruption of current under these voltages. Two types for protection of power circuits are shown in Figs. 79 and 80. The

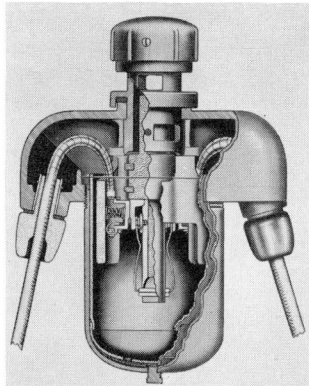 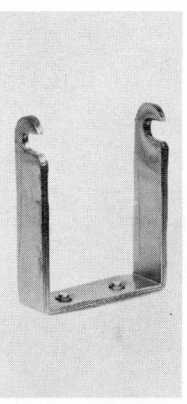

I. *Cutaway view of assembly.*   II. *Fuse   link   of*
cutout.

FIG. 79   *D & W oil fuse cutout.   (General Electric Co.)*

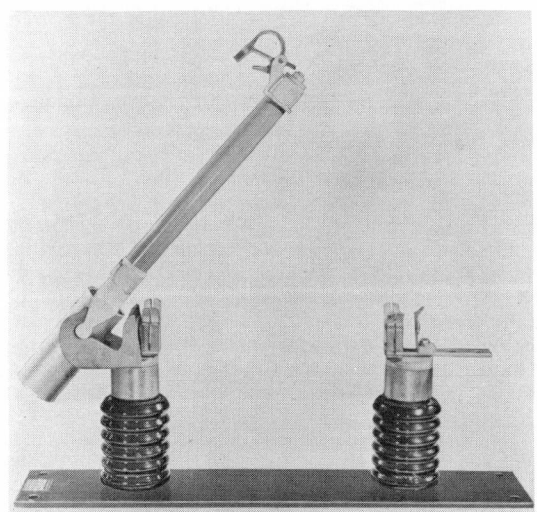

I. *BA "De-ion" fuse.*

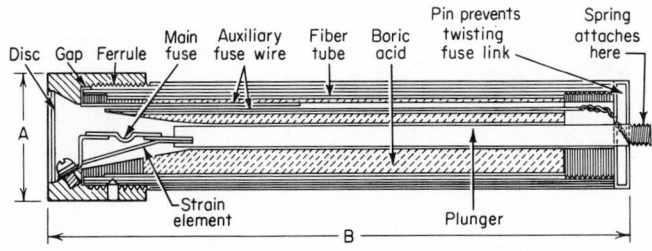

II. *Cross-section view of BA "De-ion" power-fuse refill showing construction details.*

FIG. 80   *High-voltage power fuse of the boric acid type.   (Westinghouse Electric Corp.)*

fuse of Fig. 79 is of the oil-fuse cutout type. The fuse link shown at II has a section of fusible alloy at the bottom. The entire link except the top laminated-metal terminals is enclosed in flat tubing of insulating material. The link is mounted in a casing and immersed in oil. The fuse of Fig. 80 consists of a tube lined with boric acid, which provides a source of deionization for extinguishing the arc. A high-voltage fuse for protecting a potential transformer is shown in Fig. 81.

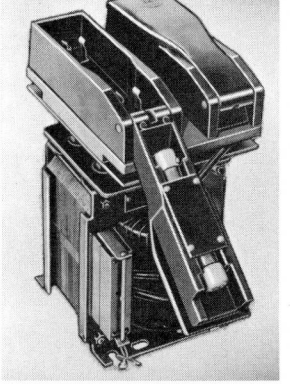

59. A circuit breaker is a switching device which is designed to open a current-carrying circuit under abnormal current conditions without injury to itself. It is adjusted to interrupt the current upon the occurrence of an overload of definite amount. It must be capable of interrupting short-circuit currents. The distinction between circuit breakers and switches is in their current-interrupting abilities. A switch is not designed for the interruption of short-circuit currents, while a circuit breaker is.

The actuation of a circuit breaker upon the occurrence of an overload can be performed by means of thermal releases or relays, magnetic releases or relays, combination thermal and magnetic releases, or induction relays. The thermal devices will have inverse-time characteristics. The magnetic and induction devices may be designed for instantaneous-, inverse-, or definite-time action. Release devices are generally employed for manually operated breakers, and relays for electrically operated ones.

FIG. 81 *High-voltage fuse mounted on potential transformer. (Westinghouse Electric Corp.)*

The basic principles of operation of the three types of circuit breakers (thermal, thermal-magnetic, and magnetic) are illustrated in the following discussion and in Fig. 86.

A thermal circuit breaker responds only to temperature change in the control element. The principle of operation of a breaker actuated by a bimetallic thermal-release element is shown in Fig. 82. This element is made of two strips of different metals, bonded together. The lengths of these strips increase with temperature—but not equally—so that the composite element bends more and more as its temperature rises. Current flows through the bimetallic element itself and generates heat. The greater the current, the higher the temperature of the element. The mechanism is adjusted so that the bimetallic element bends just enough to open the contacts as a specified current.

A thermal-magnetic breaker responds to normal overloads in exactly the same man-

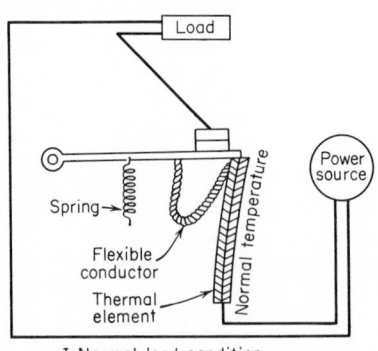
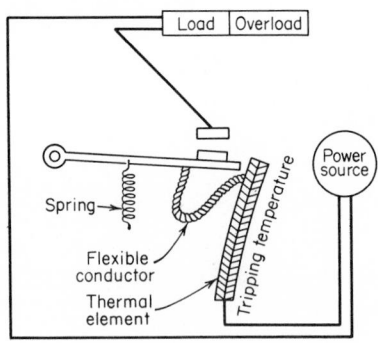

FIG. 82 *Principle of thermal breaker.*

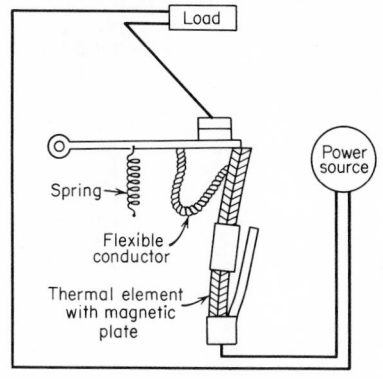
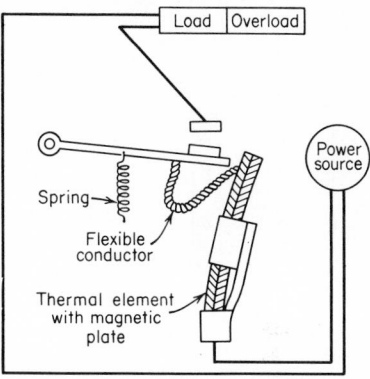

I Normal load condition   II Overload

FIG. 83 *Principle of thermal-magnetic breaker.*

ner as the thermal breaker through the temperature change in the control element. However, under heavy overloads or short circuits magnetic action takes over and gives instantaneous response by the breaker. The principle of operation of a thermal-magnetic breaker actuated by a thermal-magnetic release element is shown in Fig. 83. This element consists of a thermal, bimetallic element to which a magnet-plate element has been added. Below heavy short circuits, the magnetic force produced by the magnetic-plate element is so slight that it is not a factor in the operation of the release and only the heating up of the bimetallic element operates the release. On a heavy short circuit the magnet-plate element produces so much force that it actuates the release immediately without waiting for the bimetallic element.

A fully magnetic circuit breaker responds to changes in *current* only if they are sufficient to attract an armature by *magnetic* force. The current rating of a fully magnetic breaker is determined by the number of turns and wire size of the magnet coil. The principle of operation of a fully magnetic breaker actuated by a magnetic release is shown in Fig. 84.

Within the magnet coil, a hermetically sealed, nonmagnetic tube contains a movable iron core immersed in silicone fluid. A compression spring normally holds the iron core at the end of the tube, away from the pole face. If the current through the coil is sufficient to draw the movable core into the coil and toward the pole face, the consequent reduction in length of the air gap will produce a greater magnetic pull on the armature and cause attraction.

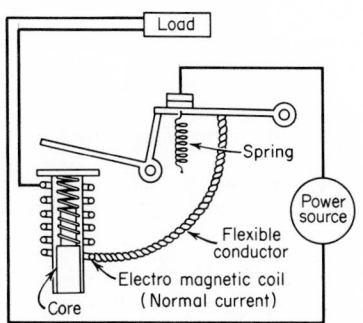

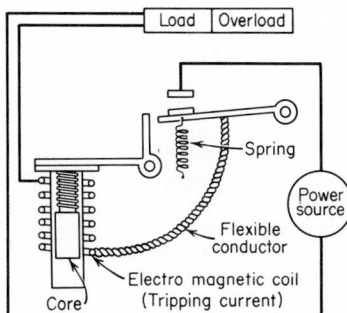

I Normal load condition   II Overload

FIG. 84 *Principle of magnetic breaker.*

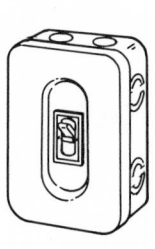
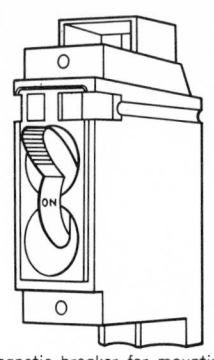
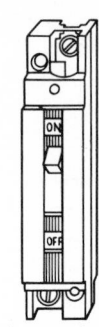

I Magnetic breaker mounted
in outlet box
(Heinemann Elec. Co.)

II Magnetic breaker for mounting
in outlet box or conduit fitting
(Heinemann Elec. Co.)

III Thermal magnetic breaker
for panelboard mounting
(Westinghouse Elec. & Mfg. Co.)

FIG. 85 *Small circuit breakers for branch circuits.*

At loads up to and including rated current of the breaker, neither core nor armature moves and nothing happens. At slight overloads the force of the spring is overcome and the core moves slowly toward the armature, which is then attracted and opens the contacts. The greater the overload, the faster the core moves through the retarding fluid to open the contacts.

At short-circuit overloads—ten times rating and above—the magnetomotive force is sufficient to overcome the reluctance of the magnetic circuit at any core position, assuring instantaneous short-circuit tripping.

The terms **primary** and **secondary** or **auxiliary circuit breakers** are sometimes employed. So-called secondary or auxiliary circuit breakers are in reality not circuit breakers at all, since they are not capable of satisfactorily interrupting short-circuit currents. Actually they are manual motor-starting switches provided with protection against overload by means of thermal overload releases. The only real circuit breakers are those classed as primary breakers.

Circuit breakers are available to meet the requirements of all classes of service from a small breaker for 15-amp branch circuits (Fig. 85) to the very large units for controlling large amounts of power. Those used for the protection of branch circuits must be so designed that it is difficult to alter the setting of the current trip point or to change the time required for the operation of the breaker. Breakers may be of the air-break type (Figs. 85, 86, and 88) or of the oil-immersed type (Fig. 87). The air circuit breakers may be of open construction for switchboard mounting or of the safety enclosed type for either panel-board mounting (Fig. 85, III) or individual mounting (Figs. 85, I and II; and 88).

60. Current-limiting Fused Circuit Breakers. The current-limiting fused circuit breakers consist simply of the combination of a circuit breaker and a current-limiting fuse in one compact device. The schematic diagram of such a combination is shown in Fig. 89. The circuit breaker of the combination functions to open the circuit upon the occurrence of a low-magnitude fault while the current-limiting fuse takes care of high-magnitude faults and through its fast action limits the value of the fault current (see Sec. 21 also).

61. Current-limiting Circuit Breakers. The General Electric Co. has developed a truly current-limiting circuit breaker—one which does not require the use of a current-limiting fuse as described in Sec. 60. Figure 90 illustrates how one pole of a current-limiting circuit breaker operates electrically. The operating mechanism is entirely mechanical and is electrically isolated from the conducting elements. The three tripping elements of a three-pole circuit breaker are in series (only one pole is shown in Fig. 90).

Overloads and short circuits below 3,000 amp are interrupted by the conventional thermal and adjustable magnetic elements, respectively.

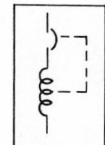

FULLY MAGNETIC CB

Time-delay and instantaneous elements are unaffected by ambient temperature—will trip only on overcurrent, the same at low or high temperature.

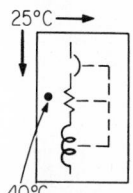

UNCOMPENSATED THERMAL–MAGNETIC CB

CB calibrated at 25°C in open air. Used in any enclosure, in an ambient of 25°C around enclosure, CB will be at 40°C and will have to be derated in its current-trip rating.

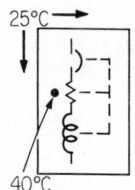

ENCLOSURE COMPENSATED THERMAL–MAGNETIC CB

When installed in 25°C ambient, CB in enclosure is at 40°C, but was calibrated at that temperature. No derating needed.

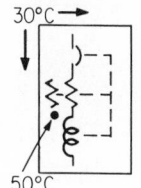

AMBIENT COMPENSATED THERMAL–MAGNETIC CB

Built-in compensator makes CB insensitive to temperatures up to 50°C at the CB in enclosure. Elevated ambients do not require derating.

FIG. 86 *Temperature consideration for molded-case circuit breakers.*

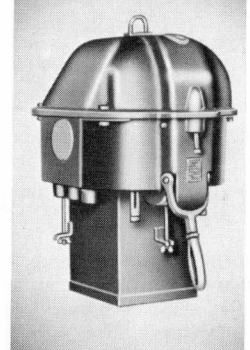

I. *Switchboard mounting type.*   II. *Industrial type.*
FIG. 87 *Oil circuit breakers. (Westinghouse Electric Corp.)*

I. *Small-capacity breaker.* (*Heinemann Electric Co.*)

II. *Medium-capacity breaker.* (*Heinemann Electric Co.*)

III. *Medium-capacity breaker.* (*I-T-E Circuit Breaker Co.*)

IV. *Medium-capacity breaker.* (*I-T-E Circuit Breaker Co.*)

V. *Large- or medium-capacity breaker.* (*General Electric Co.*)

VI. *Large- or medium-capacity breaker.* (*I-T-E Circuit Breaker Co.*)

FIG. 88   *Safety enclosed air circuit breakers.*

The current-limiting circuit breaker is similar in appearance to and modular compatible with FJ-frame molded-case circuit breakers except for its 17-in. height. The extended height accommodates the novel switching and muffling features which give the circuit breaker its special operating characteristics. It is presently marketed in the 100-amp frame size with ratings of 15 to 100 amp. According to published technical data it will interrupt a 100,000-amp, 600-volt three-phase short circuit, capable of producing 230,000 peak instantaneous amperes, in 1.84 msec and will limit the current to 36,000 peak instantaneous amperes, and let-through energy to 0.6×10^6 amp²-sec.

62. Class CTL Devices. Class CTL (circuit-limiting) devices are insert-type circuit breakers (or insert-type fusible assemblies) intended to be used with lighting and appliance branch-circuit panel boards in accordance with National Electrical Code rules.

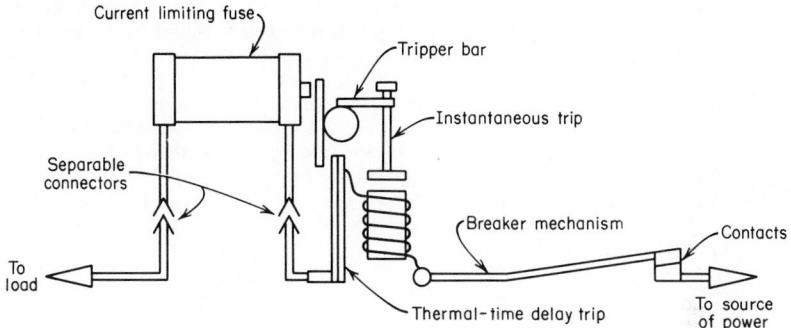

FIG. 89   *Schematic drawing of fused circuit breaker.   (I-T-E Imperial Corp.)*

Class CTL devices take the place of the familiar Class NI devices that had been used in panel boards since 1960. Whereas the Class NI concept featured "noninterchangeability," Class CTL stresses "circuit limitation"—an entirely different approach.

The first steps were taken in the 1965 National Electrical Code when section 240-25(g), pertaining to NI circuit breakers, was deleted. At the same time, two code rules (sections 384-15 and 384-16) were revised to achieve better overcurrent protection for panel boards in a more practical and workable fashion.

Section 384-15 permits 42 overcurrent devices **exclusive** of those provided for in the mains. The second paragraph of section 384-15 states: "A lighting and appliance branch-circuit panel board shall be provided with physical means to prevent the installation of more overcurrent devices than that number for which the panel board was designed, rated, and approved." Hence, the new concept of limiting the number of branch-circuit overcurrent devices to replace the old idea of noninterchangeability (NI) gave birth to Class CTL devices.

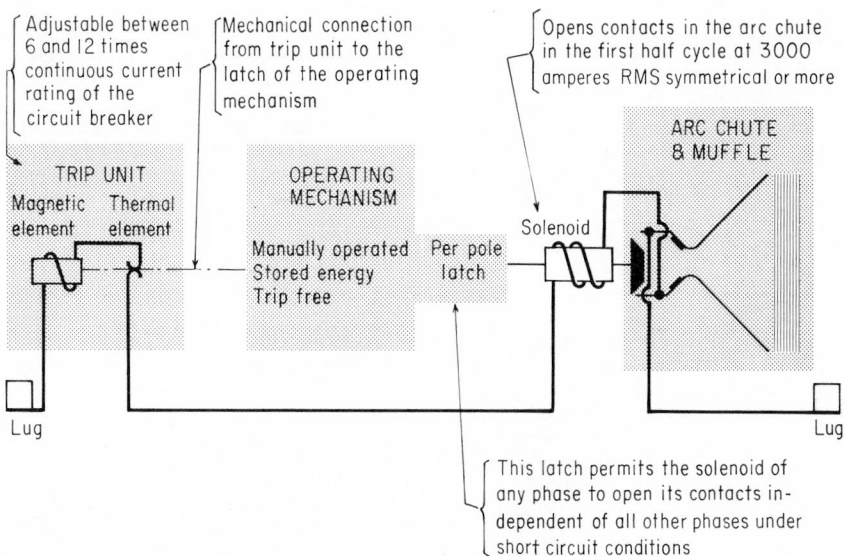

FIG. 90   *Schematic diagram of a typical pole of a three-pole current-limiting circuit breaker.   (General Electric Co.)*

Another significant part of the new concept is section 384-16(a), which requires, in general (there are two exceptions), that "each lighting and appliance branch-circuit panel board shall be individually protected on the supply side by more than two main circuit breakers or two sets of fuses having a combined rating not greater than that of the panel board." Also, section 384-16(c) states that except where an assembly, including the overcurrent device, is approved for continuous duty at 100 per cent of its rating, the total load on any overcurrent device in a panel board shall not exceed 80 per cent of its rating where in normal operation the load will continue for 3 hr or more.

Class CTL marking became mandatory on all UL-listed lighting and appliance panels and units after July 1, 1967. Class NI devices may still have UL listings only as replacements for **existing** NI equipment.

In computing the maximum number of CTL devices in a given panel board, the total rating per bus-bar pole is generally based on 10 amp for each CTL overcurrent device. Figure 91 provides an example of the CTL concept.

Basic device (smallest *dimensional* size CTL device which can be attached to panelboard busbars)

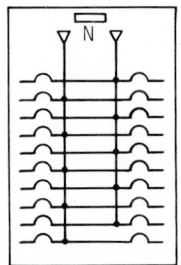

100-amp 120/240-volt lighting and appliance branch-circuit panelboard designed for ten BASIC DEVICES per pole.

FIG. 91 *Class CTL insert-type overcurrent devices and panel assemblies limit the number of circuits in lighting panel boards.*

Because each lighting and appliance branch-circuit panel board must have individual main protection, either in the panel or in another enclosure, and this main protection cannot exceed the panel board rating, the panel board will not be overloaded regardless of the size of branch-circuit overcurrent devices that may be inserted.

Another important feature of the Class CTL system is a practical approach to previous difficulties with the so-called half-size, full-size, and duplex-type circuit breakers. In the NI system half-size or duplex-type circuit breakers could often replace a full-size circuit breaker on the basis of "two poles for one." This led to doubling the number of branch-circuit overcurrent devices, and in many cases resulted in overcrowded (with wiring) and overheated panel boards.

With CTL units this problem is solved by figuring the panel rating on the basis of half-size circuit breakers if a particular panel or part of a panel will permit the insertion of such units.

63. Magnetic switches provided with overload protection by means of thermal or magnetic relays are commonly used for the overload protection of motors. These switches are discussed in Div. 7.

64. Manual switches provided with overload protection by means of thermal releases are commonly used for the combined purpose of motor starters and motor overload protection. They are discussed in Div. 7.

65. Thermal relays are made in several different forms, depending upon the ideas of the manufacturer. They provide inverse-time overload protection. The greater the overload, the shorter the length of time required for the relay to function. Two designs of thermal overload relays, which are used on a-c magnetic motor starters, are shown in Fig. 92. In both of these relays the overload protection is obtained by a bimetallic snap-action disk. These relays provide reliable precision protection. An understand-

I   II

FIG. 92   *Thermal overload relays.   (Westinghouse Electric Corp.)*

ing of the manner in which these relays function can be obtained from the following explanation coupled with a study of Fig. 93.   The bimetallic disk consists of two dissimilar metals laminated together and pressed into a concave disk.   When heated to a predetermined temperature by the heater element adjacent to the disk, the more rapid expansion of one metal increases disk tension until it suddenly snaps to its convex position, opening the contacts and stopping the motor.   When the disk cools it snaps back to its original position.   These disks retain their precise action and accurate calibration.

Thermal relays are extensively used in connection with magnetic switches for the overload protection of motors.   They are not generally employed with circuit breakers.

66. Thermal overload release devices operate on the same general principle as thermal relays.   The essential difference is that the thermal element of the release device in expanding acts directly upon the holding catch of the switch or circuit breaker while the relay opens an auxiliary circuit which trips the switch.   The relays are used on magnetic switches, and the release devices on manually operated switches and circuit breakers.

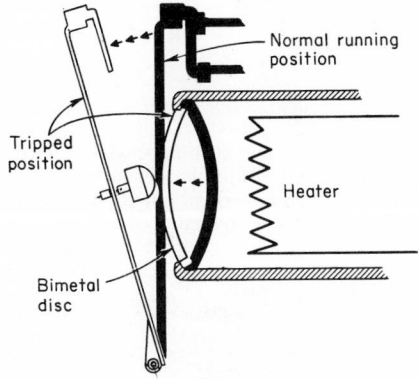

FIG.   93   *Snap-action   bimetallic-disk thermal overload relay.   (Westinghouse Electric Corp.)*

The operation of one type of thermal overload release is shown in Fig. 94.   The type of release illustrated is used on some manual a-c motor starters.   Overload pro-

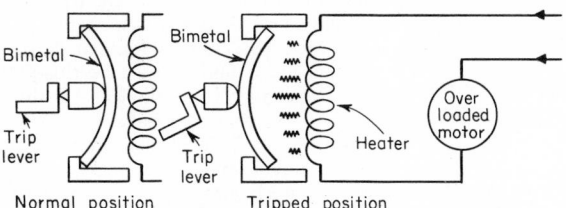

Normal position   Tripped position

FIG. 94   *Snap-action bimetallic-disk overload release.   (Westinghouse Electric Corp.)*

tection is provided by a snap-action bimetallic disk similar in design to those used in thermal overload relays as described in Sec. **65**. When a motor reaches the point of dangerous overload, the resultant increase in heat causes the bimetallic disk to snap instantly from a concave to a convex position. This movement is transferred to the starter trip lever which causes the contacts to open and disengages the motor from the line. When the disk cools, it snaps back to its original position.

67. Magnetic relays and magnetic overload release devices consist of a solenoid acting upon an iron plunger or armature (Fig. 95). The coil of the solenoid is connected in series with the circuit to be protected or frequently in a-c circuits to the secondary of a current transformer which has its primary connected in series with the

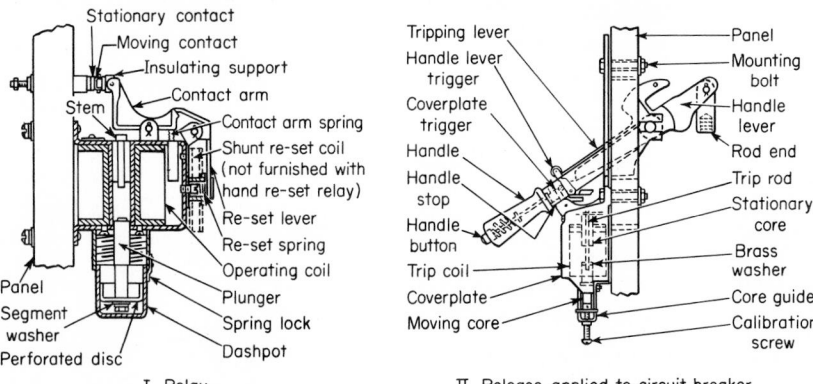

I Relay   II Release applied to circuit breaker

FIG. 95 *Magnetic overload relay and release. (Westinghouse Electric Corp.)*

main circuit. The current at which the relay will function can be regulated by adjusting the height of the plunger or the position of the movable armature. Instantaneous-type relays and overload release devices function instantaneously upon the occurrence of an overload of any value of current above that for which the device is set.

FIG. 96 *Magnetic inverse-time overload relay. (Allen-Bradley Co.)*

By the attachment of an air bellows or an oil dashpot to the plunger the device can be given inverse- or definite-time characteristics. With the inverse-time type, the time that an overload must exist, before the device functions, is inversely proportional to the severity of the overload. A slight overload must continue for a considerable time before the device will function, while a heavy overload will cause the device to function almost instantaneously. With the definite-time type, the device does not function until the overload has persisted for a certain definite length of time, depending upon the setting of the device. The elapsed time between the occurrence of the overload and the functioning of the device does not depend upon the severity of the overload. The essential difference between a magnetic relay and a magnetic overload release device is the same as for thermal relays and thermal overload release devices. The overload release device acts directly upon the catch of the switch mechanism, while a relay acts upon an auxiliary circuit which in turn trips the switch mechanism.

Magnetic relays are used in conjunction with circuit breakers and magnetic switches for overload protection. Magnetic overload release devices are employed in conjunction with circuit breakers only.

An inverse-time magnetic overload relay, which is used with magnetic contactors in motor controllers, is shown in Fig. 96.

A modified type of magnetic overload release, called a hydraulic-magnetic release, is used on some circuit breakers. A breaker equipped with this type of release is shown in Fig. 97. The hydraulic-magnetic tripping element of this circuit breaker is simply a solenoid coil wound around a hermetically sealed nonmagnetic cylinder containing a spring-loaded movable iron core and a silicone fluid. When a current up to and including the rated current is passing through the coil, the iron core stays at the end of the cylinder opposite the tripping armature, as shown in Fig. 98, I.

When the current reaches an overload point, the stronger magnetic flux created pulls the iron core upward into the armature end of the cylinder, causing a still stronger magnetic field. See Fig. 98, II. The silicone fluid controls the speed of travel and thus creates the inverse time delay.

When the iron core reaches the opposite end of the cylinder, the magnetic field has increased in intensity to a point to attract the armature. In turn, the armature releases

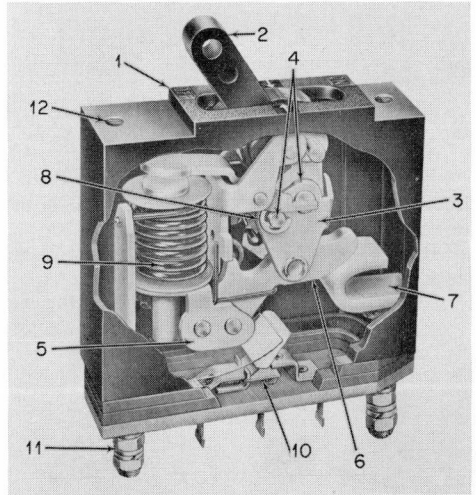

1. Moldarta case.
2. Handle indication. Operational positions of handle are clearly marked "on" and "off." After a fault clearance, service is restarted by turning handle back to "on" position.
3. Trip-free toggle mechanism.
4. Free bearing surfaces. These are of dissimilar metals to prevent sticking and bearing wear.
5. Corrosion resistance. All nonhardened ferrous parts are cadmium plated with a chromate dip which provides maximum resistance to corrosion.
6. Self-cleaning contact. Moving on a sliding pivot point, contact arm causes wiping motion of contacts every time they are opened or closed. This action assures low contact resistance and long contact life.
7. High-speed arc blowout. When circuit is broken, coil-formed stationary contact creates a magnetic field forcing arc into arcing chamber. Arcing takes place on special surfaces, not on those contact surfaces used for normal contact.
8. Accurate protection.
9. Hydraulic-magnetic trip unit.
10. Auxiliary switch. A single-pole, double-throw auxiliary switch is available as optional feature when required. These contacts are mechanically actuated by toggle mechanism, but are electrically isolated from breaker circuit. Auxiliary switches are rated 5 amp, 125 volts a-c; 1 amp, 50 volts d-c noninductive.
11. Rear-connected terminals.
12. Threaded inserts. To ensure simplicity of mounting, threaded brass inserts are provided to prevent stripping during installation.

FIG. 97 *Hydraulic-magnetic circuit breaker.* (*Westinghouse Electric Corp.*)

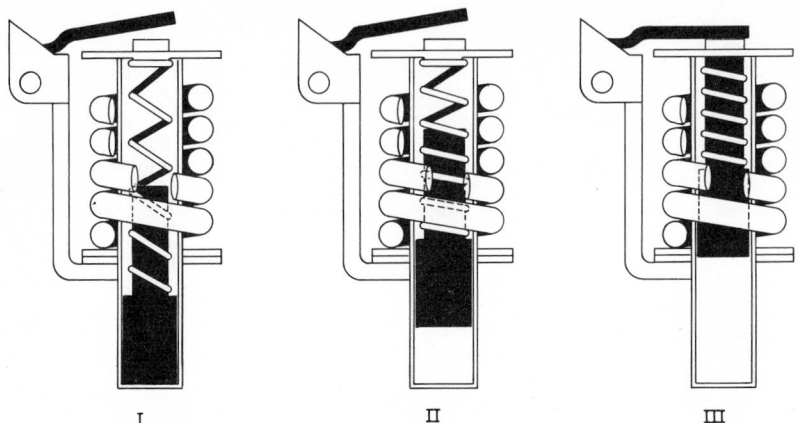

I   II   III

FIG. 98 *Hydraulic-magnetic overload release.* (*Westinghouse Electric Corp.*)

the tripping mechanism and the circuit breaker opens the circuit. See Fig. 98, III. On short circuits, the magnetic flux produced in the coil alone is strong enough to attract the armature, regardless of core position, and the circuit interruption is instantaneous.

68. A combined thermal and magnetic overload release is used on some circuit breakers. A breaker with this combined release is shown in Fig. 99. The inverse-time element of the thermal release provides overload protection for overloads of ordinary magnitude without causing circuit interruption on harmless overloads. The magnetic instantaneous trip provides for split-second tripping on short circuit.

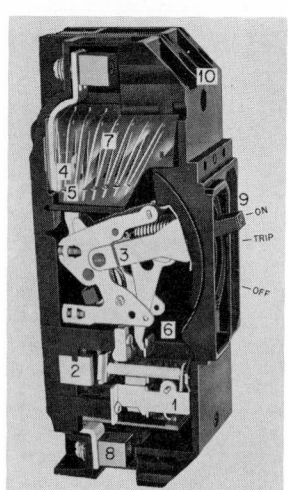

1. Thermal time-delay trip.
2. Magnetic instantaneous trip.
3. Over-center toggle mechanism.
4. Silver-alloy contacts.
5. High contact pressure.
6. Common tripper bar.
7. Arc chute.
8. Solderless pressure wire connectors.
9. Three-position handle. Indicates "on," "automatically tripped," or "off."
10. Totally enclosed case.

FIG. 99 *Combined thermal and magnetic-trip circuit breaker.* (*I-T-E Imperial Corp.*)

69. Induction-type overload relays are seldom used for ordinary interior-wiring work. They are widely used by central-station companies for protection of circuits and apparatus. A detailed discussion of these relays is outside the scope of this book. Induction relays operate upon the general principle of induction motors and, therefore, are applicable only to a-c systems. They can be obtained with instantaneous-, inverse-, or definite-time characteristics.

69A. Comparison of the Time Characteristics of Overload Protective Devices. Typical time-current characteristics of the different overload protective devices are illustrated in Fig. 100. The curve shown for thermal and magnetic devices is typical. All such devices will have a characteristic of the form shown, although different devices, depending upon design, will vary from that shown in time of opening of circuit for the various overloads. Time-lag fuses have characteristics similar to that shown for the thermal and magnetic devices. The curve labeled "fuse" is for the ordinary type of fuse, not for time-lag ones. It will be noticed that fuses of the regular type have a considerable time-delay characteristic. They will not blow immediately on an overload unless the overload is approximately 200 per cent or greater than the rating of the fuse. Fuses will carry indefinitely a current of 80 per cent of their rating. The inverse-time overload protective devices of the thermal, magnetic, and time-lag fuse types have a greater time-delay characteristic than regular fuses and will, therefore, allow much greater overloads for a short period without interrupting the circuit. These inverse-time characteristics make these overload protective devices ideal for

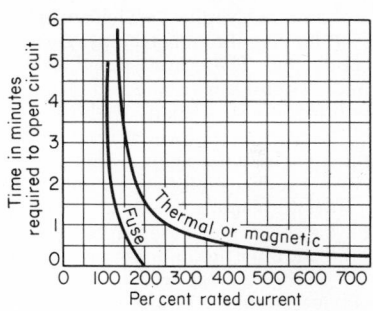

FIG. 100 *Time-current characteristics of overload protective devices.*

the overload protection of motors. They will allow the heavy starting current to pass but will protect the motor against sustained overloads that would be harmful to it. They will also permit the motor to operate with intermittent peak overloads of short duration. If ordinary fuses are used for the overload protection of induction motors, the fuses must be shorted during the starting period, for a fuse of proper rating to protect the motor would not allow the starting current to pass. Although ordinary fuses will permit a motor to operate with moderate intermittent peak overloads, they are not nearly so flexible in this respect as the thermal and magnetic protective devices. Devices with the inverse-time characteristics are also advantageous for protection of circuits, since they will prevent interruption of the circuit due to short overloads, which, although of high magnitude, would be harmless to the circuit.

70. Protection other than overload protection can be provided by means of release devices or relays employed in connection with circuit breakers or magnetic switches.

Undervoltage protection may be provided by means of relays or releases actuating hand-operated circuit breakers, or magnetic switches. On magnetic switches, undervoltage protection is generally provided through the operating coil of the switch. When the voltage drops below a certain value, the current of the operating coil is so reduced that it will no longer hold the switch in the closed position.

Underload, overvoltage, or reverse-current, power, or phase-rotation protection can be provided by means of relays employed in connection with circuit breakers or magnetic switches.

71. Ground-fault Interrupters. Another form of overcurrent protection is the ground-fault interrupter. Other types of overcurrent protection do not provide reliable protection from line-to-ground faults because of widely varying ground-path impedances, including the arc itself in arcing ground faults. As a result, conventional overcurrent devices may see the arcing ground fault only as a "load current." And the continuation of the arcing ground fault will eventually cause a fire or damage equipment.

The basic principle of a ground-fault interrupter is to sense current leakage to ground and then cause an interconnected overcurrent device to trip open the faulted circuit. Two basic types of ground-fault interrupters are shown in Fig. 101. In the first type (Fig. 101, 1) the interrupter is designed for *life protection,* which means that it must cause the circuit to open at very low magnitudes of current (about 5 ma). The heart of such an interrupter is a toroidal coil through which all circuit conductors pass. The interrupter senses any unbalance in the circuit, which would be a leakage to ground on one of the circuit conductors (but not on the other). After detecting this unbalance a differential transformer and solid-state circuitry supply sufficient current to operate a coil of a special circuit breaker, and the circuit is opened within milliseconds after the ground fault occurs. This type of ground-fault interrupter is widely used with 120-volt electrical circuits supplying swimming-pool equipment and any other applications where protection from line-to-ground shock hazards is deemed necessary.

The second type of ground-fault interrupter is designed for *equipment protection.* Figure 101, 2, shows the basic function of this system. With this type of interrupter an electrically operated main or feeder switch or circuit breaker is operated through current and time-delay relays, which are energized when a current transformer detects a ground fault flowing through a jumper from the metal enclosure to the insulated circuit neutral conductor. These units are adjustable so that the value of ground-fault current flowing in the circuit can be selected for a given installation before the switch or circuit breaker will trip open. Usually such interrupter devices are set at specific current ratings to allow downstream overcurrent devices to open when grounds occur on the load side of them. Thus, the main switch or circuit breaker opens only when downstream over-current devices fail to open under ground-fault conditions.

Several manufacturers can provide both types of ground-fault interrupters described in this section, and these interrupters are highly recommended as a means of optimum protection for life and property.

Recently a large and prominent industrial corporation installed a system of low-voltage ground-fault protection in their research and development laboratories to protect against shock.

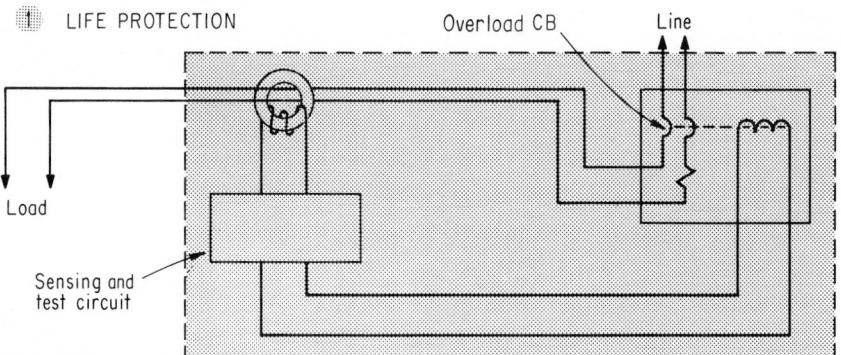

Interrupter senses unbalance in circuit when hot wire becomes grounded. Then a semiconductor differential CB causes circuit to open. Unit opens in less than 25/1000 th of a second when a leakage of 5 ma or more occurs

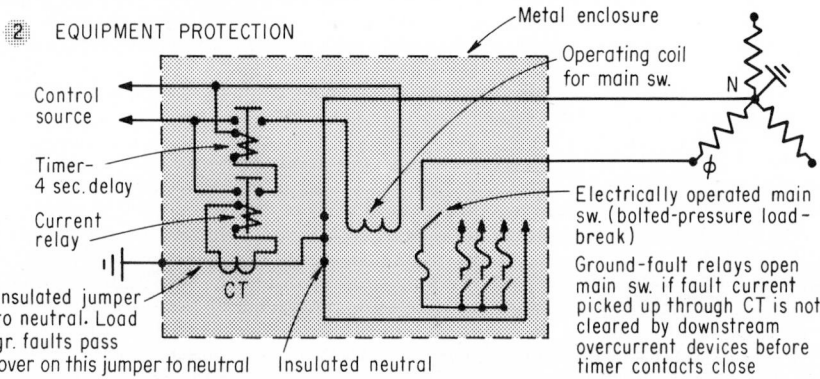

FIG. 101 *Two classifications of ground-fault circuit interrupters.*

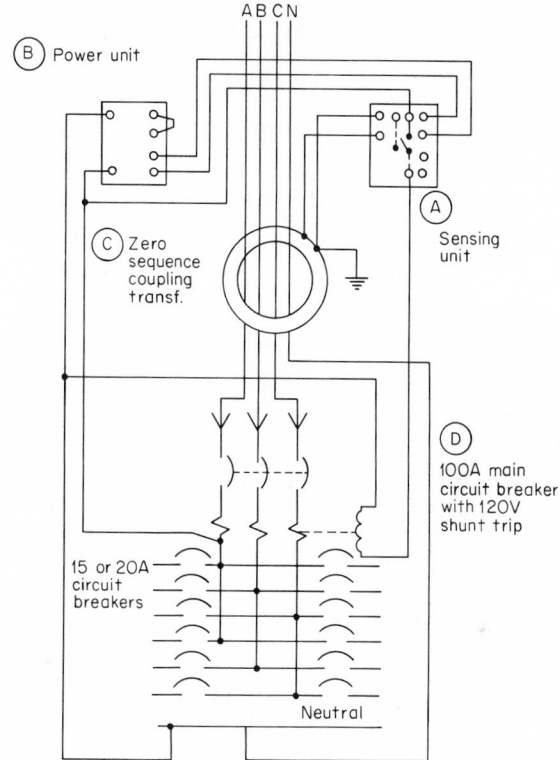

A B C N

B Power unit

C Zero
sequence
coupling
transf.

A

Sensing
unit

D

100A main
circuit breaker
with 120V
shunt trip

15 or 20A
circuit
breakers

Neutral

FIG. 101A   *Ground-fault interrupter in panel-board enclosure.* (*Federal Pacific Electric Corp.*)

The system encompasses all lab receptacles in which portable equipment of either 110 or 220 volts may be applied. The ground-fault equipment is mounted in a lighting panel enclosure which is only slightly larger than the standard size. The arrangement is shown in Fig. 101A.

The ground-fault system consists of five basic units: (A) ground relay, (B) power unit, (C) zero-sequence-coupling transformer, (D) 100-amp main circuit breaker with a 120-volt shunt-trip device mounted in the same enclosure. It functions as follows:

All incoming (three-phase and neutral) conductors pass through the window of the zero-sequence-coupling transformer. The secondary of this transformer is connected to the ground relay. The power unit provides d-c control voltage to the sensing element of the relay and the main breaker shunt trip for tripping from a 120 volt a-c source.

Under normal conditions, the load current flowing in the cables creates a magnetic flux in the zero-sequence-coupling transformer that characteristically balances exactly, thereby canceling the flux. No signal is produced. When insulation fails or when a **person becomes a line-to-ground conductor,** leakage current reaches a predetermined level anywhere on the downstream side of the zero-sequence-coupling transformer. This produces a signal to the trigger element, which, in effect, closes the circuit to the shunt trip instantly, thereby tripping the main circuit breaker and isolating the fault.

72. Lightning Protection. High voltages may be electrostatically induced in outdoor electric lines during lightning storms. These voltages produce traveling surges of high voltage which travel along the lines and into electrical equipment, whether it be located outdoors or inside buildings. The high induced voltages would puncture the insulation of equipment and be dangerous to life. Lightning arresters are used to limit these voltages to a safe value and provide a path to ground for the dissipation of the energy of the surge. In order to provide this protection satisfactorily, lightning arresters must fulfill the following functions:

1. They must not allow the passage of current to ground so long as the voltage is normal.

2. When the voltage rises to a definite amount above normal, they must provide a path to ground for dissipation of the surge energy without further rise in voltage of the circuit.

3. As soon as the voltage has been reduced below the setting of the arrester, it must stop the flow of current to ground and reseal itself so as to insulate the conductor from ground.

4. They must not be injured by the discharge and must be capable of automatically repeating their action as frequently as is required.

Lightning arresters should be provided on all overhead systems. For the small consumer who purchases his power from a public utility, this protection is supplied by the utility on its distribution circuits. For a large consumer it may be advantageous to install lightning arresters located between the public-utility lines and the consumer's substation. All communication circuits entering a building must be provided with a protector which will give protection against abnormal voltage to ground caused not only by lightning but by accidental contact between communication circuits and power circuits. This protection is usually provided by the communication company which is supplying the service. All signal circuits which are run outdoors for any part of their length or which are installed so that there is any possibility of accidental contact between the signal circuit and power conductors must be provided with a protector.

Radio equipment is required by the National Electrical Code to be protected against lightning as follows:

Receiving Stations. Each conductor of a leadin from an outdoor antenna shall be provided with a lightning arrester approved for the purpose, except that where the leadin conductors are enclosed in a continuous metallic shield, the lightning arrester may be installed to protect the shield or may be omitted where the shield is permanently and effectively grounded. Lightning arresters shall be located outside the building or inside the building between the point of entrance of the leadin and the radio set or transformers and as near as practicable to the entrance of the conductors into the building. The lightning arrester shall not be located near combustible material or in a hazardous location.

Grounding conductors shall be not smaller than No. 10 copper or No. 8 aluminum or No. 17 copper-clad steel or bronze.

73. Lightning arresters are made in many different forms. A discussion of the construction, application, and installation of the various types is outside the scope of this book. Typical types for power work are illustrated in Fig. 102, and types for signal and communication work in Fig. 103.

Lightning arresters can be installed indoors or outdoors. When located indoors they must be located well away from other equipment, passageways, and combustible material or parts of the building, and if they contain oil, they must be enclosed in vaults of construction similar to that required for oil-filled transformers (see Div. 5). If arresters which contain oil are located outdoors, provision must be made to drain away any accumulation of oil. This may be done by properly constructed ditches and drains, or the oil may be absorbed and danger of spreading removed by paving the yard with cinders or other absorbent material to a depth of several inches.

An arrester must not be located in a hazardous location (see Div. 9). When lightning arresters are used, an arrester should be installed for each ungrounded circuit wire. The National Electrical Code requires that the connections between an arrester and a line wire or bus and between the arrester and ground shall be of copper wire or cable or the equivalent. Except for secondary services these connections shall not be smaller than No. 6. The connections shall be made as short and as straight as practicable, avoiding as far as possible all bends and runs, especially sharp bends.

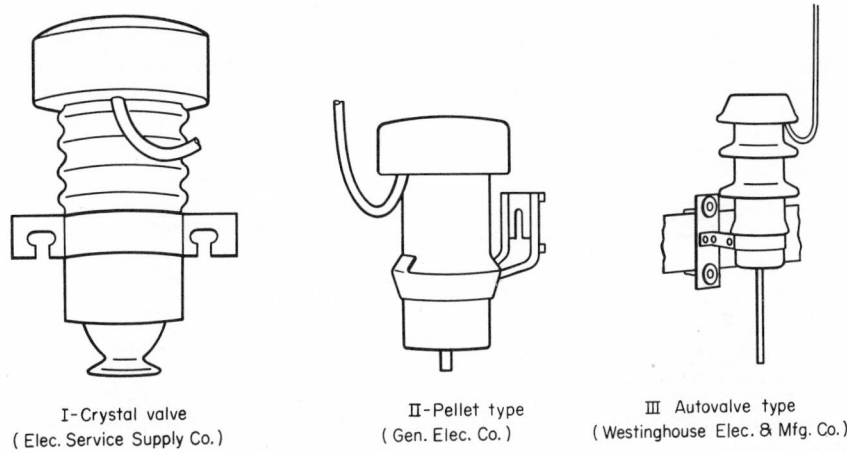

I-Crystal valve
(Elec. Service Supply Co.)

II-Pellet type
(Gen. Elec. Co.)

III Autovalve type
(Westinghouse Elec. & Mfg. Co.)

FIG. 102 *Lightning arresters of the power type.*

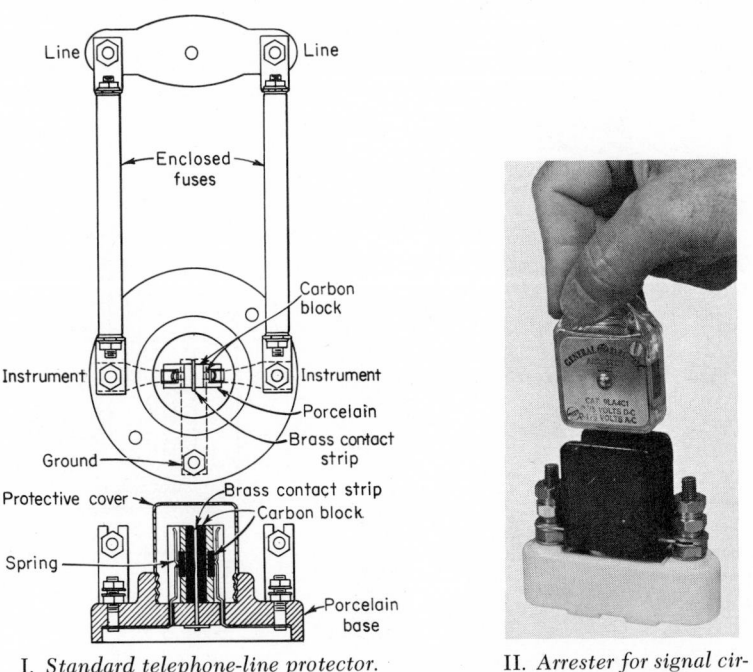

I. *Standard telephone-line protector.*

II. *Arrester for signal circuits.* (*General Electric Co.*)

FIG. 103 *Lightning arresters of the low-voltage type.*

Proper grounding of lightning arresters is of utmost importance. Refer to Div. 9 for discussion of grounding rules and practice.

74. Surge protective equipment is used in connection with lightning arresters and in large power systems for limiting the value of short-circuit current. They consist of coils of wire connected in series with the circuit for the purpose of introducing inductance. Those used with lightning arresters are called choke coils (Fig. 104). The inductance of the coil tends to shunt the high-frequency lightning surge away from the apparatus and through the arrester to ground. Those used for limiting short-circuit currents are called reactors. A typical construction of a reactor is shown in Fig. 105.

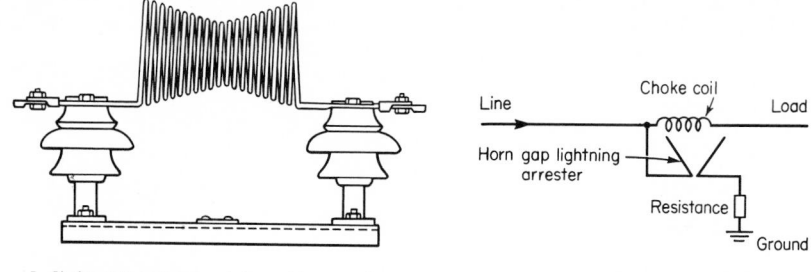

I Choke coil and support for outdoor service

II Circuit diagram showing location of choke coil

FIG. 104   *Choke coil for use with lightning arrester. (Electric System Handbook.)*

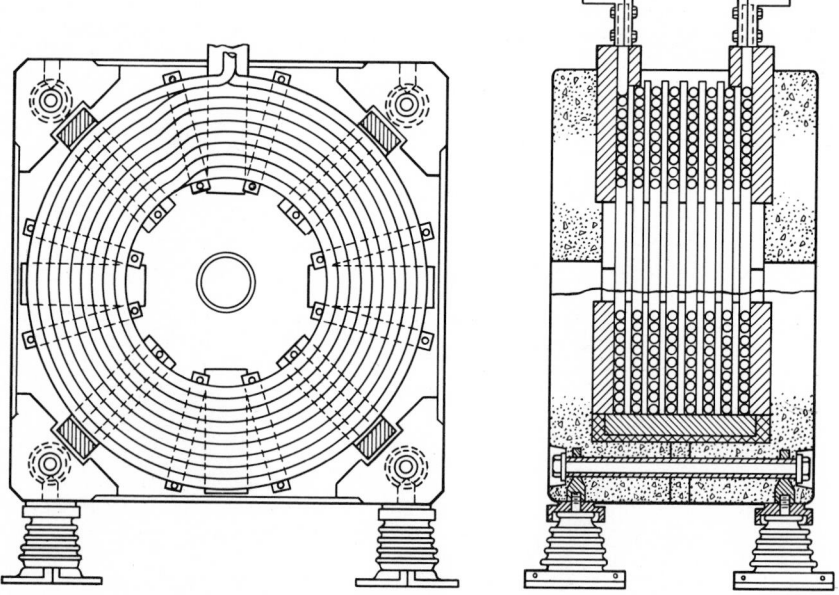

FIG. 105   *Current-limiting reactor, series-wound with single insulated cable—horizontal axis. (Electric System Handbook.)*

SWITCHBOARDS – SWITCHGEAR

75. A switchboard as defined in the National Electrical Code is a large single panel, frame, or assembly of panels on which are mounted, on the face or back or both, switches, overcurrent and other protective devices, buses, and, usually, instruments. Switchboards are generally accessible from the rear as well as from the front and are not intended to be installed in cabinets.

76. The types of switchboards with respect to basic features of construction are as follows:

1. Live-front vertical panels.
2. Dead-front boards.
3. Safety enclosed boards (metal-clad).

Live-front switchboards (Fig. 106) have the current-carrying parts of switching equipment mounted on the exposed face or front of the panels. They are not as a rule employed in new boards where the voltage exceeds 600 volts.

Large-capacity equipment with resultant increases in weight make enclosed metal-clad switchboards more desirable from a structural and safety point of view. Where high short-circuit currents are available it is much safer to confine short circuits to metal-clad equipment for the protection of personnel and buildings.

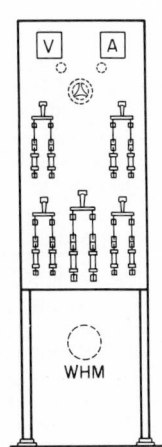

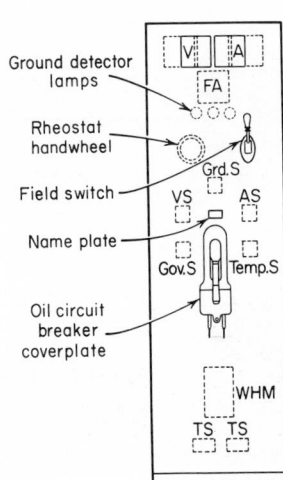

FIG. 106 *Live-front switchboard panel.*   FIG. 107 *Dead-front switchboard panel.*

On existing live-front switchboards, obsolete equipment and panels can be replaced with more modern components. In drilling new holes in slate or marble a standard steel twist drill may be used if the "heel" of the drill is ground off. This provides the drill with a sharper angle. Slate panels are drilled dry, whereas marble panels must be drilled with the use of water. It is best, however, to use modern masonry drills when drilling such panels.

Avoid excessive pressure when drilling through panels. Abandoned holes can be filled with cement or plaster.

Dead-front switchboards (Fig. 107) are the more modern type and are employed for systems of all voltages. With this type no live parts are mounted on the front of the board.

Safety enclosed boards are used for most new installations. Common terms used for designation of equipment of this type are metal-enclosed switchgear and metal-clad switchgear. Most of these safety enclosed boards are of the unit or sectional type. They consist of a combination of the desired number and type of standardized unit sections. Each section is a standard factory-assembled combination of a formed steel panel and apparatus mounted on a steel framework.

Safety enclosed switchgear of the truck- or draw-out type (Figs. 108 and 109) consists of a steel enclosure mounted on an angle-iron framework. All apparatus which requires attention or inspection is mounted on a truck or draw-out structure. The equipment for each circuit is mounted on either a separate truck, which can be easily rolled out from the rest of the structure, or a metal structure supported on guides so that it can easily be slid in and out from the enclosure (Fig. 109).

77. Safety enclosed switchgear may be classified with respect to purpose of application as follows:

1. General medium- or high-voltage switchgear.
2. Primary unit substations.
3. Rectifier unit substations.
4. Secondary unit substations or power centers.
5. General low-voltage switchgear.
6. Low-voltage distribution switchboards.
7. Motor-control center switchboards.

Medium-voltage switchgear (Fig. 110) provides for the required control and metering equipment for generators, transformer supply circuits, feeders, large motors, etc., for systems with voltage up to 15,000 volts. A large variety of standardized units is available.

Primary unit substations of the metal-clad type (Figs. 111 and 112) consist of one or more transformers mechanically and electrically connected to and coordinated with one or more feeder or motor-control sections. A variety of combinations is available in both outdoor and indoor construction.

Rectifier unit substations provide the transforming, rectifying, switching, metering, and control equipment necessary for the conversion of three-phase a-c power at any of the conventional voltages to direct current.

Secondary unit substations (Fig. 113) permit the distribution of power in industrial plants or other large buildings at the higher, more economical voltages and the transformation of the power to the desired utilization voltage at points near the load. They usually consist of three basic types of components: high-voltage (incoming) section, transformer section, and the low-voltage (outgoing) sections.

General low-voltage switchgear (Figs. 114 and 115) provides for the required control and metering equipment for generators, incoming circuits from transformers, feeders, large motors, etc., for systems with voltage not greater than 600 volts. A large variety of standardized units is available.

FIG. 108 *Draw-out type of safety enclosed circuit-breaker switchboard. (I-T-E Imperial Corp.)*

Low-voltage distribution switchboards may be of the so-called building type or of the multipurpose type. The building type is specifically designed for the control of low-voltage distribution circuits (600 volts and below) in offices, hospitals, and commercial types of buildings. A circuit-breaker type is shown in Fig. 116, and a fusible switch type in Fig. 117. Multipurpose distribution switchboards are for general use in commercial or industrial applications. Typical assemblies are shown in Fig. 118, which also indicates the major features of a well-designed modern switchboard.

In general, low-voltage distribution switchboards fall into three distinct NEMA classifications encompassing specific structural features, equipment arrangement, and electrical characteristics, which are noted as follows. Common to all classes are total metal enclosure (except bottom), top or bottom gutter, and vertical selections electrically connected.

1. Class I. Maximum current limited to 2,000 amp; group-mounted branches; wall-supported; front accessibility only for line and load connections; flush back.

I. *Cranking out a draw-out type of circuit breaker.*   II. *Circuit breaker completely withdrawn.*

FIG. 109   *Operation of draw-out type of circuit-breaker switchboard.* (*I-T-E Imperial Corp.*)

2. CLASS II.   No maximum current requirement; group-mounted branches; branches front-accessible only; main bus rear-accessible; self-supported.

3. CLASS III.   No maximum current requirement; individually mounted branches; branches and mains rear-accessible; self-supported.

Motor control centers (Fig. 119) provide a compact centralized location for full-voltage motor control equipment.   Each compartment contains a magnetic starter with a circuit breaker or fused switch.

FIG. 110   *Medium-voltage metal-clad switchgear.* (*Westinghouse Electric Corp.*)

FIG. 111 *Outdoor primary unit substation.* (*General Electric Co.*)

FIG. 112 *Outdoor metal-clad switchgear.* (*Westinghouse Electric Corp.*)

78. Materials employed for the panels of switchboards are slate, marble, ebony-asbestos, and steel. At one time slate was the material principally used for switch-board panels, but it has been almost entirely replaced by ebony-asbestos for live-front boards and steel for dead-front and safety enclosed ones. Marble is used sometimes

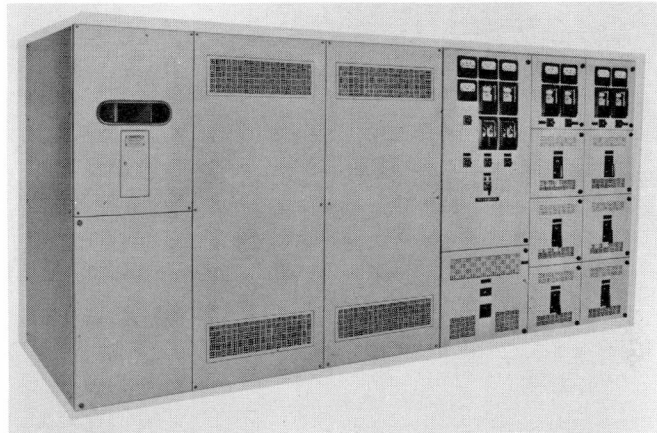

FIG. 113 *Secondary unit-power center.* (*Westinghouse Electric Corp.*)

on live-front boards for its higher insulation qualities over slate but more often for its better appearance.

The supporting frame for panels may be of angle iron or pipe.

79. Location of Switchboards. Switchboards of the safety enclosed type may be placed in any nonhazardous location without any restrictions. Switchboards with any exposed live parts must be located in permanently dry locations and only where they will be under competent supervision and accessible only to qualified persons. The rear of a switchboard may be made accessible only to qualified persons by a metal grill-work enclosure, entrance to which is by means of a locked door. Switchboards should be located so as to reduce to a minimum the probability of communicating fire to adjacent easily ignitible material. A clearance of at least 3 ft must be left between the top of a board and a nonfireproof ceiling unless an adequate fireproof shield is provided be-

FIG. 114 *General-purpose low-voltage switchgear assembly.* (*Westinghouse Electric Corp.*)

FIG. 115 *Typical low-voltage distribution switchgear assembly.* (*I-T-E Imperial Corp.*)

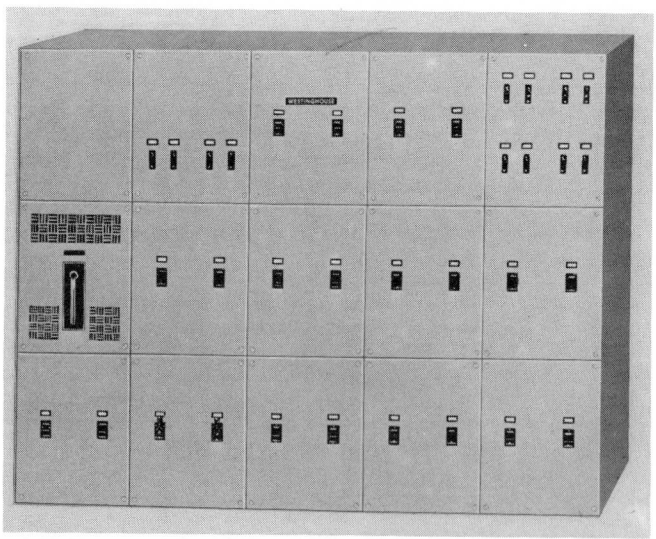

FIG. 116 *Building-type distribution switchboard.* (*Westinghouse Electric Corp.*)

tween the board and the ceiling. Refer to section 110-16 of the National Electrical Code for required clearances around switchboards and control centers.

80. Spacings Required by the National Electrical Code. Except at switches and circuit breakers, at least the following distance between bare metal parts, bus bars, etc., shall be maintained:

	Opposite polarity when mounted on the same surface, in.	Opposite polarity when held free in air, in.	Live parts to ground, in.[a]
Not over 125 volts........	¾	½	½
Not over 250 volts........	1¼	¾	½
Not over 600 volts........	2	1	1

[a] For spacing between live parts and doors of cabinets, see subparagraph a of section 373-11(a) of the Code.

It should be noted that the above distances are the minumum allowable, and it is recommended that greater distances be adopted wherever the conditions will permit.

At switches, enclosed fuses, etc., parts of the same polarity may be placed as close together as convenience in handling will allow unless close proximity causes excessive heating.

FIG. 117 *Power-control-center switchboard.* (*General Electric Co.*)

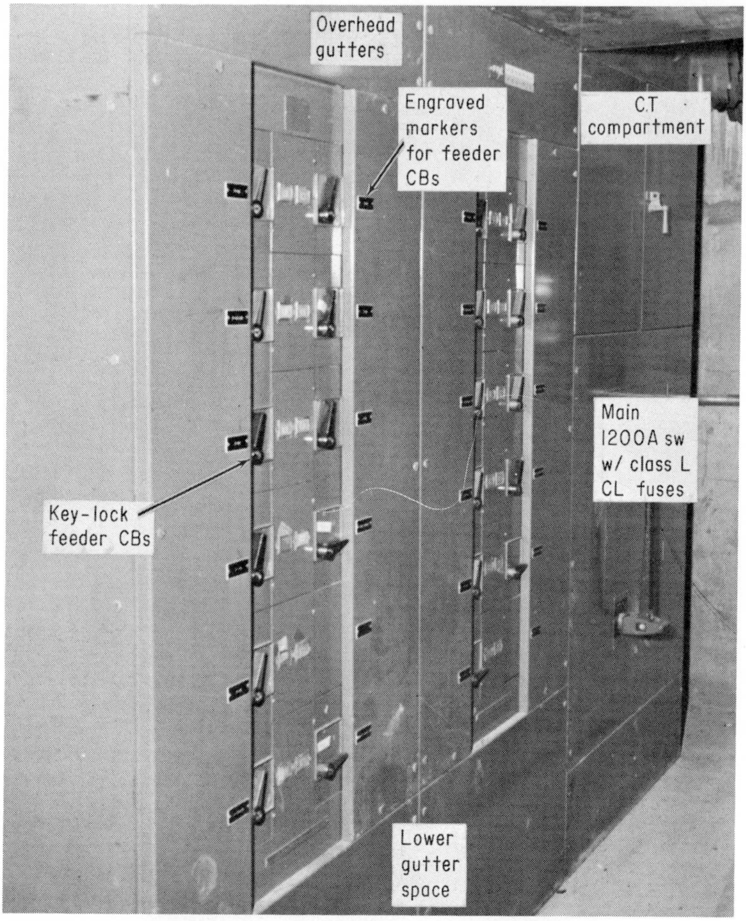

Overhead gutters

Engraved markers for feeder CBs

C.T compartment

Key-lock feeder CBs

Main 1200A sw w/ class L CL fuses

Lower gutter space

FIG. 118 *Major features of a modern switchboard.*

FIG. 119 *Motor-control center switchboard.* (*Square D Company.*)

81. Bus-bar Spacings, Minimum Distance between Parts of Opposite Polarity and Minimum Distance between Live Parts and Ground for Different Voltages

(Electrical Engineer's Equipment Co.)

Voltage	Distance between centers of buses, in.		Minimum distance between opposite live parts, in.		Minimum distance between live parts and ground, in.	
	A	*B*	*A*	*B*	*A*	*B*
250	1½–	2½	1 – 2		¾– 1½	
600	2 –	3	1½– 2½		1 – 2	
1,100	4 –	5	2½– 3½		1½– 2½	
2,300	5 –	6½	2¾– 4		2 – 2¾	
4,000	6 –	7½	3 – 4½		2¼– 3	
6,600	7 –	8	3½– 4½		2½– 3	
7,500	8 –	9	4 – 4½		2¾– 3¼	
9,000	9 – 10		4¼– 4½		3 – 3½	
11,000	9 – 11		4½– 4¾		3¼– 3¾	
13,200	9 – 12		4¾– 5		3½– 4¼	
15,000	9 – 14		5 – 5½		3¾– 4½	
16,500	10 – 14		5½– 6		4½– 5	
18,000	11 – 14		6 – 7		5 – 6	
22,000	12 – 15		7½– 9		6 – 7	
26,000	14 – 16		10 –12		8 – 9	
35,000	18 – 22		12 –15		10 –12	
45,000	22 – 27		16 –18		13½–15	
56,000	28 – 31		17½–19		16 –17½	
66,000	34 – 38		22 –24		18½–23	
75,000	36 – 42		26 –30		25 –27½	
90,000	46 – 54		32 –35		27 –29	
104,000	54 – 60		34½–39		28½–32	
110,000	60 – 72		38 –41		33 –36	
122,000	66 – 78		42 –47		35½–39	
134,000	74 – 84		48½–56		39 –41	
148,000	82 – 96		59 –67		45 –50	
160,000	88 –104		70 –84		53 –62	

NOTE. The distances given in the *A* columns are based on a safety factor of 3.5 between live parts of opposite polarity and safety factor of 3 between live parts and ground. *B* column shows good practice for the larger plants. Tubular buses should be used on all buses above 22,000 volts. Bus support porcelains should have a wet test of two times voltage used.

PANEL BOARDS

82. A panel board as defined by the National Electrical Code is a single panel or a group of panel units designed for assembly in the form of a single panel, including buses and with or without switches and/or automatic overcurrent protective devices for the control of light, heat, or power circuits of small individual as well as aggregate capacity, designed to be placed in a cabinet or cutout box placed in or against a wall or partition and accessible only from the front. Panel boards provide a compact and convenient method of grouping circuit switching and protective devices at some common point.

Panel boards may be of either the flush or surface type (Fig. 120). The flush type is used with concealed wiring installations and has the advantage of not taking up space in the room by extending beyond the surface of the wall. Surface-type boxes are used for installations employing

I-Surface mounting type   II-Flush mounting type

FIG. 120 *Panel boxes.*

exposed wiring. The boxes are generally constructed of sheet steel, which must be not less than No. 16 U.S. standard gage in thickness. The steel must be galvanized or covered with some other protective coating to prevent corrosion.

Gutters are provided around the panel boards in cabinets in order to allow sufficient space for wiring (Figs. 120 and 121). The Code requires that all cabinets which contain connections to more than eight conductors shall be provided with back or side wiring spaces. These wiring spaces must be separated from the panel board or other devices in the cabinet by partitions so that the wiring spaces will be separate closed compartments, unless all wires are led from the cabinet at points directly opposite their terminal connections to the panel board. The minimum width of gutters required where vertical conductors are deflected upon entering or leaving cabinets is given as follows:

Minimum Bending Space in Inches

AWG or circular-mil size of wire	Wires per terminal				
	1	2	3	4	5
14–8	Not specified				
6	1–½				
4–3	2				
2	2½				
1	3				
0–00	3½				
000–0000	4	6	8		
250 MCM	4½	6	8	10	
300–350 MCM	5	8	10	12	
400–500 MCM	6	8	10	12	14
600–700 MCM	8	10	12	14	16
750–900 MCM	8				
1,000–1,250 MCM	10				
1,500–2,000 MCM	12				

NOTE: The distance shall be measured in a straight line from the end of the lug or wire connector (in the direction that the wire leaves the terminal) to the wall or barrier.

A panel board consists of a set of copper or plated-aluminum bus bars, called mains, from which provision is made for tapping off several circuits through overload protective devices and/or switching mechanisms. The provisions for taps generally are built up from unit sections assembled to form the complete board. This plan allows the manufacturers to build a few standard types of unit sections which can be assembled in a great variety of combinations in order to meet the varying requirements of different installations. This results in economy of manufacture and in the greatest flexibility of possible combinations to meet all requirements. Typical panel-board construction is illustrated in Fig. 121. This figure shows several types of unit sections in the same panel board to illustrate the flexibility of assembly. Other, similar panel boards are designed for plug-in or bolt-on circuit breakers or fuse assemblies.

All panel boards have ampere ratings and such ratings are shown on the nameplate of each panel board, along with the voltage rating. The panel-board ampere rating is the ampacity of the bus bars to which the branch overcurrent units are connected.

Main circuit breakers, fused pull-outs, or fused switches can be provided in a panel board. A panel board without integral main overcurrent protection is called "mains only," which means that the panel has only main lugs. Such a panel board is shown in Fig. 123.

If a panel board supplies wiring installed by nonmetallic methods, or any other system which will include equipment grounding conductors in a raceway or cable, a grounding terminal bar must be installed to terminate all such grounding wires. The grounding terminal bar must be bonded to the cabinet. It can be bonded to the **neutral** bar of a panel board only in cases where the panel is used as service equipment.

To provide a high degree of selectivity and flexibility most panel boards today are designed for insert-type fusible or circuit breaker assemblies. These assemblies are plugged into or bolted onto "receiver" panel interior bus bars. With such an arrangement the installer or designer can select the proper size of overcurrent devices for circuits or feeders. Overcurrent device assemblies are available in single-, two-, and three-pole units.

In selecting a panel board for any installation it is good design to provide enough space so that additional overcurrent devices may be inserted at a later date.

It is also wise to use surface-mounted panel boards in areas where surface-type wiring is acceptable. This will enable new raceways or cables to be added with less difficulty.

1. Galvanized sheet-steel box.
2. Panel adjusting screws.
3. Galvanized channel irons.
4. Removable frame barrier separating wiring gutter from panel board, simplifying panel adjustments.
5. Molded Bakelite end section covering main lugs or neutral bar.
6. "Plug fuse only" unit section.
7. Branch-circuit terminal screws.
8. Single-fusing snap-switch, plug-fuse type of unit section.
9. Molded Bakelite section plates.
10. Double-fusing, two-pole snap-switch, plug-fuse type of unit section.
11. Index numbers for identification of circuits.
12. Single-fusing snap-switch, cartridge-fuse type of unit section.
13. Wiring gutter.
14. Double-fusing, two-pole snap-switch, cartridge-fuse type of unit section.
15. Snap switches *entirely* removable from front, each enclosed with an individual Bakelite cover.
16. Standard knockout arrangement, usually satisfactory for most installations.

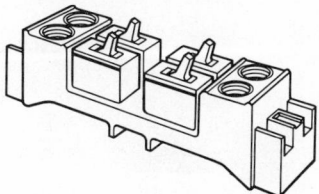

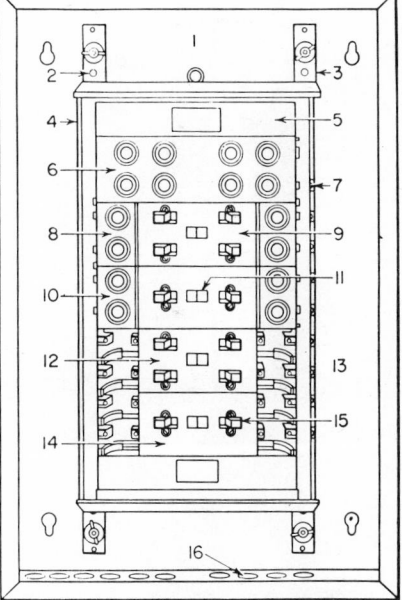

I. Unit section of tumbler switches and fuse-plug holders

II. Panel-board assembly, illustrating flexibility of construction

FIG. 121 *Typical panel-board construction. (General Electric Co.)*

Where installations require concealed wiring, spare conduits should be stubbed to accessible areas, such as above the lift-out-type ceiling panel construction in common use today.

Every panel board should include a circuit legend with a neatly typed and accurate description of the circuits supplied by each overcurrent device. Circuit identification is a National Electrical Code requirement, and is extremely useful when troubleshooting, repairs, or additional wiring are required.

Many panel boards and attached overcurrent devices contain terminals which are suitable for both copper and aluminum wire terminations. In such cases a CU/AL marking will appear in the panel board and/or on the overcurrent assemblies. Where there is no marking as to what type of conductor material may be attached to terminals, it can be assumed that only copper conductors are suitable. In such cases aluminum wire can still be used by splicing a short length of copper wire to the aluminum connector with a suitable connector, especially in the case of branch-circuit connections.

83. Lighting and Appliance Branch-circuit Panel Boards. In solving all installation problems with panel boards the first consideration is to determine whether the panel board will be considered as a lighting and appliance branch-circuit type. The reason for this is that National Electrical Code rules are much stricter for lighting and appliance branch-circuit panel boards than other types.

The National Electrical Code defines a lighting and appliance branch-circuit panel board as one having *more than* 10 per cent of its overcurrent devices rated 30 amp or less, for which neutral connections are provided. For example, if any panel board with less than ten overcurrent devices contains **one** overcurrent device rated at 30 amp for which neutral connections are provided, it would be considered as a lighting and appliance branch-circuit panel board ($1 \div 9 = 11\%$).

In another example, panel boards that supply loads without any neutral connections are not considered as lighting and appliance branch-circuit types whether or not the overcurrent devices are 30 amp or less.

When it is determined that a panel board is a lighting and appliance branch-circuit type the following National Electrical Code rules apply.

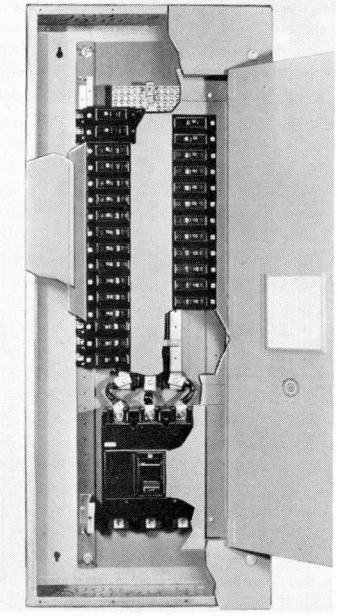

FIG. 122 *Circuit-breaker type of lighting panel board with main breaker. (General Electric Co.)*

FIG. 123 *A 480Y/277-volt circuit-breaker lighting panel board without integral main overcurrent protection. (General Electric Co.)*

1. Individual protection is required on the supply side, consisting of not more than two main circuit breakers or sets of fuses having a combined rating not greater than that of the panel board. This main protection may be contained within the panel board (as shown in Fig. 122) or in a separate enclosure ahead of it. There are two exceptions to this code rule.

a. Individual protection is not required when the panel-board feeder has overcurrent protection not greater than that of the panel board.

Example. Two 400-amp panel boards can be connected to the same feeder if the feeder *overcurrent device* is rated or set at 400 amp or less.

b. Individual protection is not required where such panel boards are used as service equipment in supplying an individual residential occupancy and where any bus supplying 15- or 20-amp circuits is protected on the supply side by an overcurrent device.

Example. A split-bus panel board where the line section contains three to six circuit breakers or fuses, none of which are rated 20 amp or less. In such an arrangement one of the main overcurrent devices supplies the second part of the panel, which contains 15- or 20-amp branch-circuit devices. The other main overcurrent devices (over 20 amp) supply feeders or major appliances such as cooking equipment, clothes driers, water heaters, or space conditioning equipment (refer to Fig. 124).

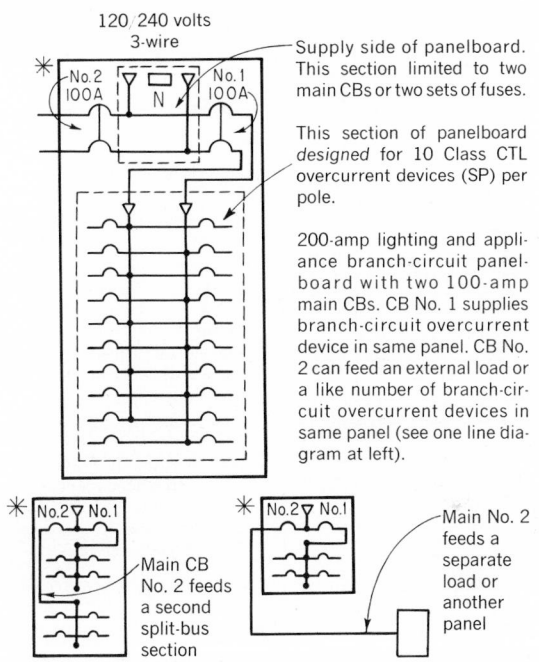

120/240 volts
3-wire

Supply side of panelboard. This section limited to two main CBs or two sets of fuses.

This section of panelboard *designed* for 10 Class CTL overcurrent devices (SP) per pole.

200-amp lighting and appliance branch-circuit panelboard with two 100-amp main CBs. CB No. 1 supplies branch-circuit overcurrent device in same panel. CB No. 2 can feed an external load or a like number of branch-circuit overcurrent devices in same panel (see one line diagram at left).

Main CB No. 2 feeds a second split-bus section

Main No. 2 feeds a separate load or another panel

FIG. 124 *Typical arrangements of split-bus lighting panel board which has two main circuit breakers and Class CTL branch breakers.*

2. A lighting and appliance branch-circuit panel board is limited to not over 42 overcurrent devices (excluding the main overcurrent devices) in any one cabinet or cutout box (refer to Fig. 125). In enumerating such devices a single-pole circuit breaker is counted as one overcurrent device; a two-pole circuit breaker as two overcurrent devices; and a three-pole circuit breaker as three overcurrent devices.

In addition to this, such panel boards shall be provided with a physical means to prevent the installation of more overcurrent devices than that number for which the panel board was designed, rated, and approved. This rule concerns a circuit-limitation concept and the use of Class CTL overcurrent devices, which are discussed in Sec. **62** and shown in Figs. 91 and 126.

The lighting panel board shown in Fig. 122 is a circuit-breaker type with a main 200-amp circuit breaker and 32 20-amp single-pole breakers. This panel is used for a four-wire three-phase grounded-neutral system. The main breaker is three-pole.

Other National Electrical Code provisions which apply to **all** types of panel boards are:

1. Panel boards equipped with snap switches, as shown in Fig. 121, shall have overcurrent protection not in excess of 200 amp. Circuit breakers are not considered as snap switches.

2. Panel boards having switches on the load side of any type of fuses shall not be installed except for use as service equipment. In Fig. 121 the snap switch is on the "line" side of the plug fuses and satisfies this code rule.

3. The total load on any overcurrent device located in a panel board shall not exceed 80 per cent of its rating where in normal operation the load will be continuous (3 hr or more), unless the assembly including the overcurrent device is approved for continuous duty at 100 per cent of its rating.

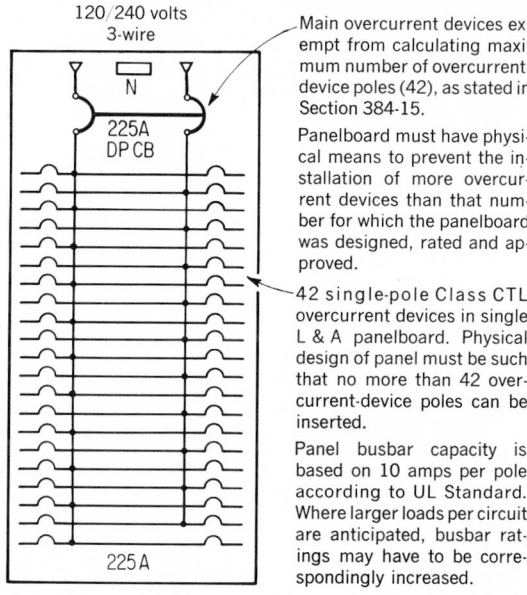

Main overcurrent devices exempt from calculating maximum number of overcurrent-device poles (42), as stated in Section 384-15.

Panelboard must have physical means to prevent the installation of more overcurrent devices than that number for which the panelboard was designed, rated and approved.

42 single-pole Class CTL overcurrent devices in single L & A panelboard. Physical design of panel must be such that no more than 42 overcurrent-device poles can be inserted.

Panel busbar capacity is based on 10 amps per pole according to UL Standard. Where larger loads per circuit are anticipated, busbar ratings may have to be correspondingly increased.

FIG. 125   *Typical arrangement which shows National Electrical Code rules for lighting panel boards.*

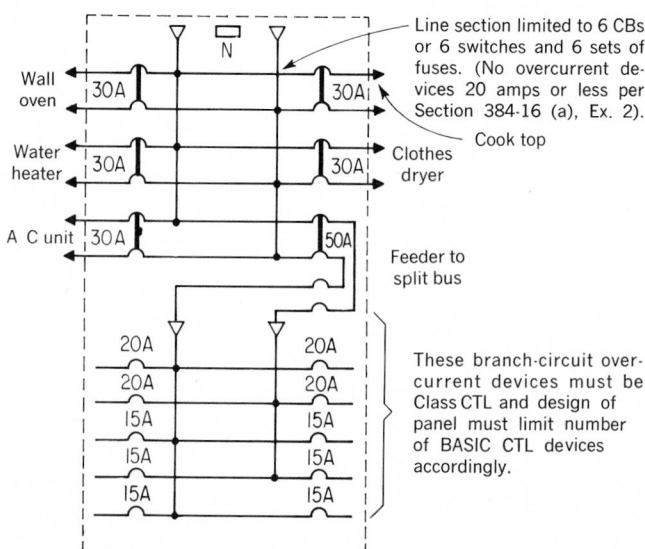

Line section limited to 6 CBs or 6 switches and 6 sets of fuses. (No overcurrent devices 20 amps or less per Section 384-16 (a), Ex. 2).

These branch-circuit overcurrent devices must be Class CTL and design of panel must limit number of BASIC CTL devices accordingly.

FIG. 126   *Suitable arrangement for a 200-amp lighting panel board used as service equipment for an individual residential occupancy.*

84. Service-equipment Panel Boards. For loads up to 800 amp, panel boards are available which contain six or fewer main fused switches, fused pullouts, or circuit breakers. These panels constitute service equipment and frequently contain split buses which supply branch-circuit or feeder overcurrent devices installed in the same enclosure (see Figs. 124 and 126).

85. Feeder distribution panels generally contain circuit overcurrent devices rated at more than 30 amp to protect **subfeeders** that extend to smaller branch-circuit panel boards.

86. Power distribution panels are similar to the feeder distribution type; have bus bars normally rated up to 1,200 amp at 600 volts or less; contain control and overcurrent devices sized to match connected motor or other power circuit loads. Generally, the devices are three-phase (see Figs. 127, 128, and 129).

FIG. 127 *Circuit-breaker type of power-distribution panel board. (General Electric Co.)*

FIG. 128 *Power panel board with fused-switch units. (Square D Company.)*

Special panel boards containing relays and contactors can be obtained and installed where remote control of specific equipment is specified. A thorough knowledge of all available types of panel boards facilitates selection and installation of the proper unit.

87. Panels with Delta Circuit Breakers. In many smaller installations there is a need of **one** three-phase branch circuit, and for such applications a panel board is used with what is called a "delta circuit breaker." This three-pole breaker is constructed so that two of its line poles are plugged in or bolted onto the two ungrounded bus bars of a conventional 120/240-volt three-wire panel board. Then the panel board is supplied by a 120/240-volt four-wire three-phase delta supply, which provides 120/240 volts with a grounded neutral for three-wire or two-wire single-phase loads. The third or "high leg" of the delta supply is connected directly to a line terminal of the three-pole delta

FIG. 129   *Converti-fuse power panel board; fuse-puller switching units.* (*General Electric Co.*)

breaker, and this provides a three-phase supply for a single branch circuit or feeder; hence the name "delta circuit breaker."

With the delta breaker application it is very important that the proper arrangement of branch and main overcurrent devices is followed, particularly where a panel contains a main **two-pole** circuit breaker as the overcurrent protection of the two ungrounded bus bars in the panel. Several panel boards are listed by Underwriters' Laboratories for use with or without a two-pole main circuit breaker or delta breaker. Instructions in the panel board clearly indicate that in no case where the two-pole main breaker is installed can the delta breaker be connected to the panel bus bars. This is to avoid dangerous feedbacks if only the main two-pole circuit breaker is opened and the delta breaker remains closed. Figure 130 shows suitable arrangements of these multiple-purpose panel boards. In Fig. 130a the two-pole main breaker supplies only single- or two-pole branch breakers. The delta breaker must not be used. In Fig. 130b the two-pole main breaker in the panel board has been eliminated, and the panel is protected by a main three-pole common-trip circuit breaker located in a separate enclosure. Then the delta breaker is connected as shown in the drawing. It should be emphasized that the main three-pole circuit breaker must be a common-trip type. Never use any other type of main protection (such as fuses or individual-pole-trip breakers) for this application because if only one pole opens, there is a chance for feedbacks or unbalanced voltage, which can create a shock hazard or damage equipment.

Figure 131 shows a panel board which contains six main circuit breakers, one of which is a three-pole delta breaker. This is a suitable arrangement. The various references in the drawing are to National Electrical Code rules.

The arrangement in Fig. 132 shows an ideal arrangement where the supply is four-wire delta. In this example a three-pole circuit breaker or fused switch supplies the three-phase load while a separate two-pole main supplies the 120/240-volt single-phase load. There is no hazard in this arrangement. Although a **single** main three-pole circuit breaker can supply a panel, as shown in Fig. 130a, this is often inconvenient because it is difficult to obtain a three-pole breaker with one smaller overcurrent unit. Thus, the arrangement in Fig. 132 is highly desirable, and either circuit breakers or fused switches can be used. However, never use a fused switch as a **single main** disconnect for a four-wire delta supply because the opening of only one fuse can provide dangerous feedbacks or unbalanced voltages, depending on how circuits are connected and on the circuit parameters when a fuse opens.

88. Location and Installation. All panel boards should be located as near as possible to the loads that they supply and control. Mounting heights should be such that the dis-

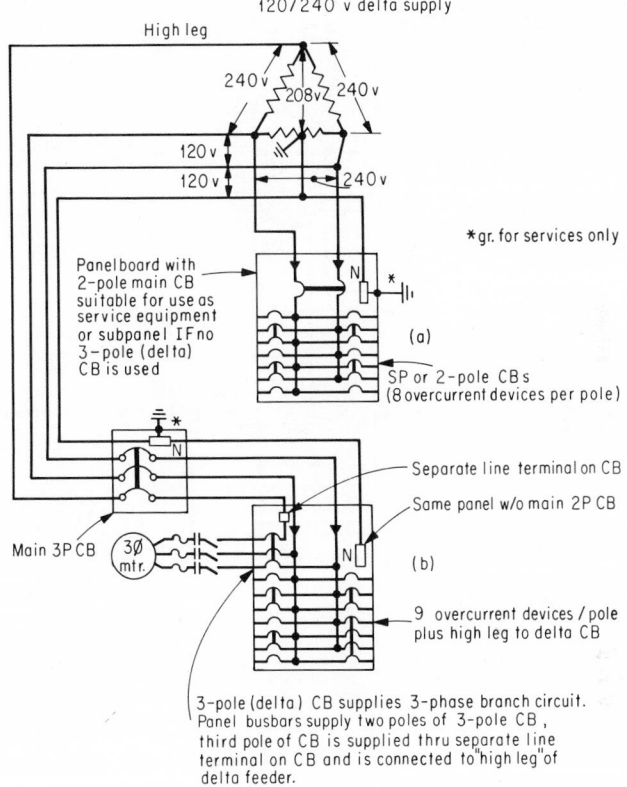

120/240 v delta supply

High leg

240 v   208v   240 v

120 v

120 v   240 v

*gr. for services only

Panelboard with
2-pole main CB
suitable for use as
service equipment
or subpanel IF no
3-pole (delta)
CB is used

N   *

(a)

SP or 2-pole CBs
(8 overcurrent devices per pole)

Separate line terminal on CB

Same panel w/o main 2P CB

Main 3P CB   3Ø
mtr.   N   (b)

9 overcurrent devices / pole
plus high leg to delta CB

3-pole (delta) CB supplies 3-phase branch circuit.
Panel busbars supply two poles of 3-pole CB,
third pole of CB is supplied thru separate line
terminal on CB and is connected to "high leg" of
delta feeder.

Where panelboard busbars contain more
than 6 CBs per ungrounded pole.

FIG. 130 *Acceptable arrangements for panel boards with or without delta circuit breakers.*

tance from the floor or working level to the top of the uppermost overcurrent device is
not more than 7 ft, and the distance from the lowest overcurrent device to the floor is
not less than 6 in.

Panels to be installed in wet or damp locations, in dust-laden areas, outdoors, or in
any hazardous area must be of the type approved for use in such locations.

If qualified persons only are to have access to panel boards, install panel trims with
locking-type catches on the doors.

There are several precautions that can simplify panel-board installation, improve
workmanship, and produce a neater job. Among them are:

1. Coordinate panel-board cabinet installation with the raceway system, and maintain proper alignment.

2. Align floor-slab conduit stub-ups with openings in the bottom of the cabinets.
Maintain alignment during a concrete pour by using interlocking conduit spacer caps
or a wood or metal template. This is exceptionally important when the cabinet is to be
surface-mounted.

3. Cabinet knockouts should be properly sized and spaced to match feeder and
branch-circuit raceway layouts. Most often the standard prestamped single and/or
multiple-concentric cabinet knockouts are used. On some installations, however, it is
best to order blank enclosures and cut the required knockouts at the job site.

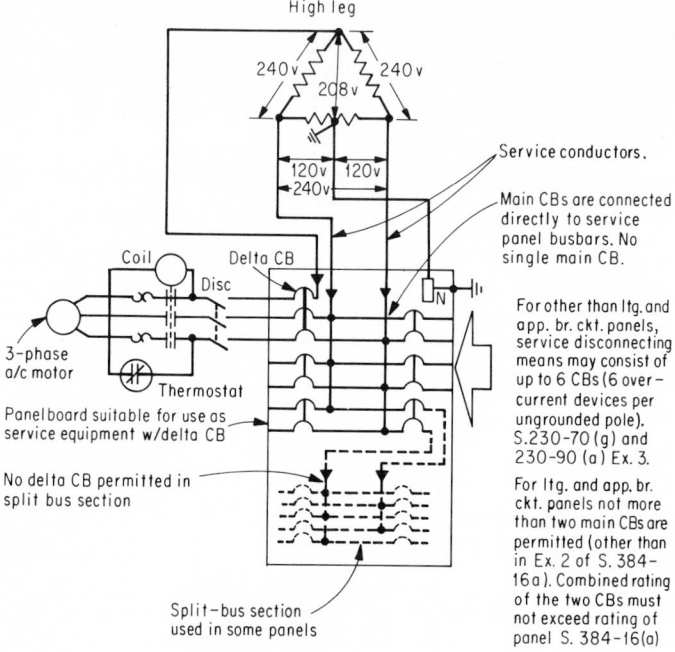

FIG. 131 *Panel board with five two-pole breakers and one three-pole delta breaker used as service equipment. National Electrical Code rules are noted.*

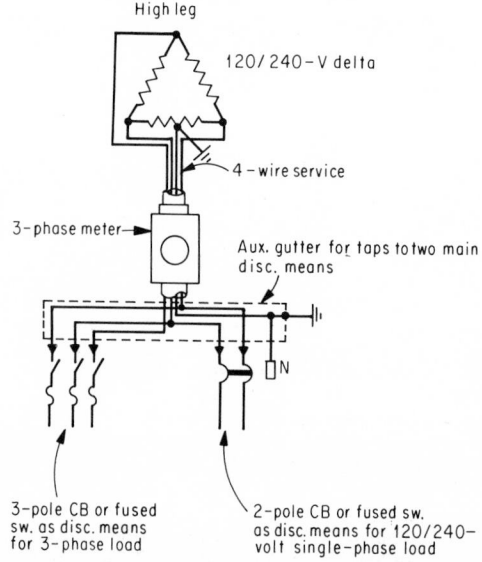

FIG. 132 *An effective way of separating single- and three-phase loads of four-wire delta supplies.*

4. Where cabinets are to be installed flush in a wall, provide temporary anchoring facilities to securely position the cabinet until the wall is constructed. Enclosures supported only by conduit attachments often are knocked out of alignment.

5. Surface-mounted panel-board enclosures should be securely fastened to the wall or other structural surface. In the case of large, heavy panel boards, the addition of supplementary pedestals or "legs" (structural steel or pipe sections with floor flanges) will increase rigidity and help distribute the weight.

6. Where a number of panel-board enclosures are to be mounted side by side, the addition of a suitably sized auxiliary gutter, wiring trough, or pull box in between, above, or below the grouped cabinets will facilitate cable pulling and circuit installation. In many cases, it will eliminate the need for oversize cabinets to accommodate the required conductors. Section 373-8 of the National Electrical Code definitely prohibits the use of enclosures for switches and overcurrent devices (and this includes panel-board cabinets) as a feed-through or splicing gutter for conductors unless the enclosure has been designed to provide adequate space for this.

GENERAL WIRING MATERIALS AND DEVICES

89. Insulators of various types are employed for interior-wiring work where the conductors are not installed in raceways. The more common types may be classified as knobs, cleats, tubes, crane insulators, and rack insulators. The accompanying sections and illustrations give data on many standard types. Insulators for outdoor and underground installations are discussed in Div. 8.

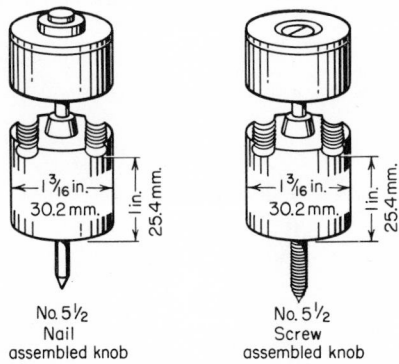

No. 5½
Nail
assembled knob

No. 5½
Screw
assembled knob

FIG. 133 *Assembled wiring knobs for No. 12 to No. 14 wire.*

Split knobs are shown in Figs. 133 and 134. Those of Fig. 133 are factory-assembled with a supporting nail or screw. Various standard types of solid knob insulators are shown in Fig. 135. Standard types of rack insulators are shown in Fig. 136. Standard wire cleats are shown in Figs. 137 and 138. Crane insulators are shown in Fig. 139. All these insulators are made of porcelain.

90. Wire Table for Single-wire Cleats [a]
(Knox Porcelain Corp.)

AWG or Circular Mil Size of Wire Received	Catalog Numbers
14–8	1
6–4	1½–2
1/0–2/0	2½
2/0–4/0	3
4/0–300 MCM	3½
300–500 MCM	4

[a] See Fig. 138.

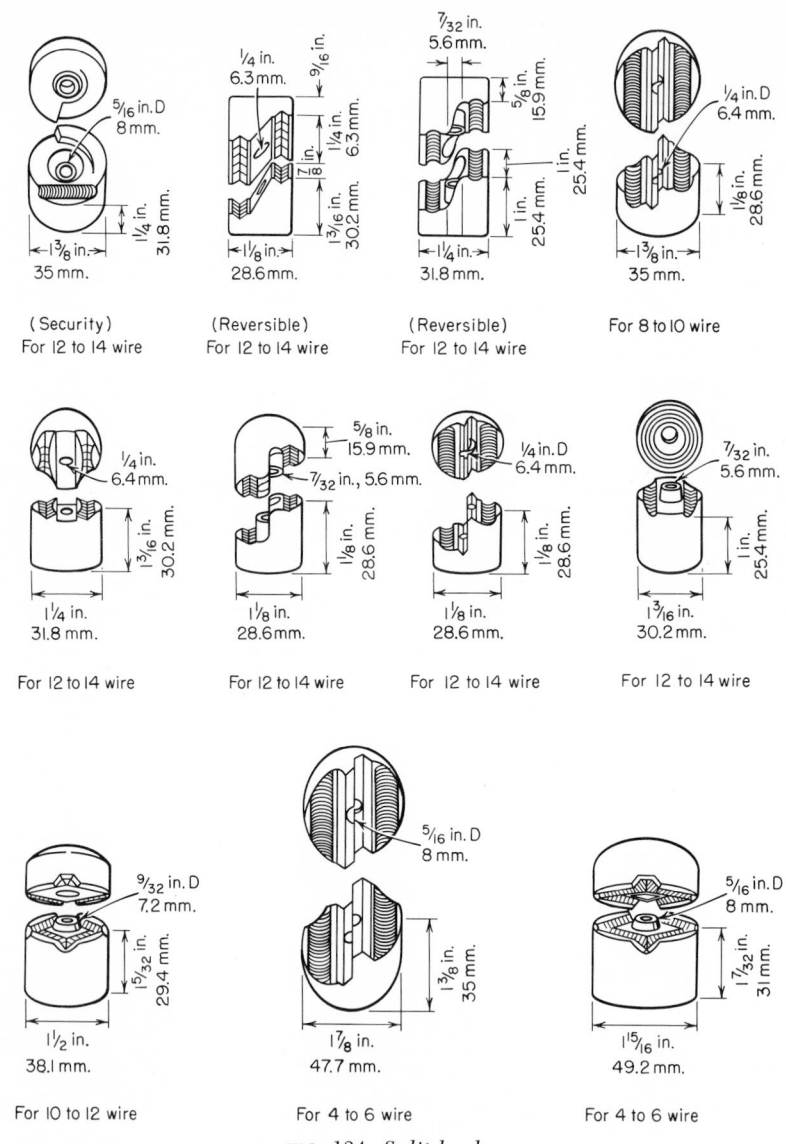

FIG. 134 *Split knobs.*

91. Use of Screws or Nails with Split Knobs. Nails hold better than screws in certain woods. The breaking of knobs at the time of putting them up with screws is not the only source of trouble, for the binding tension applied often acts to crack the knob a considerable time after it has been put in place. It is an objectionable practice of many wiremen in putting up knobs with screws to drive the screws in nearly all the way with a hammer, giving them only a couple of turns with a screwdriver to tighten them. The principal argument in favor of the use of the nail is the great saving of the wiremen's time that results as compared with that required for putting in screws. The insulating value of either construction is practically the same.

92. Insulated racks are often convenient for supporting cables in open wiring installations. They consist (Fig. 140) of porcelain insulators mounted in an iron base and clamped together with an iron top for d-c work and a brass top for a-c work. They are made in assemblies for one, two, three, and four cables and can be supplied with insulator openings of inside diameters ranging from $3/16$ to 3 in. The diameters vary by $1/16$ in. from $3/16$- to $5/8$-in. sizes and by $1/8$ in. from $5/8$- to 3-in. sizes.

93. Universal insulator supports (Fig. 141) are malleable-iron clamps fitted with cup-pointed, core-hardened, steel setscrews for securing porcelain and glass insulators to exposed steel framework.

94. Porcelain tubes are made in three types: standard solid tube, split tube, and floor tube. The standard lengths, as indicated by the L dimension in Fig. 142, are $1/2$, 1, $1\frac{1}{2}$, 2, $2\frac{1}{2}$, 3, 4, 5, 6, 8, 10, 12, 14, 16, 18, 20, 22, and 24 in. The diameters are given in Sec. **95**.

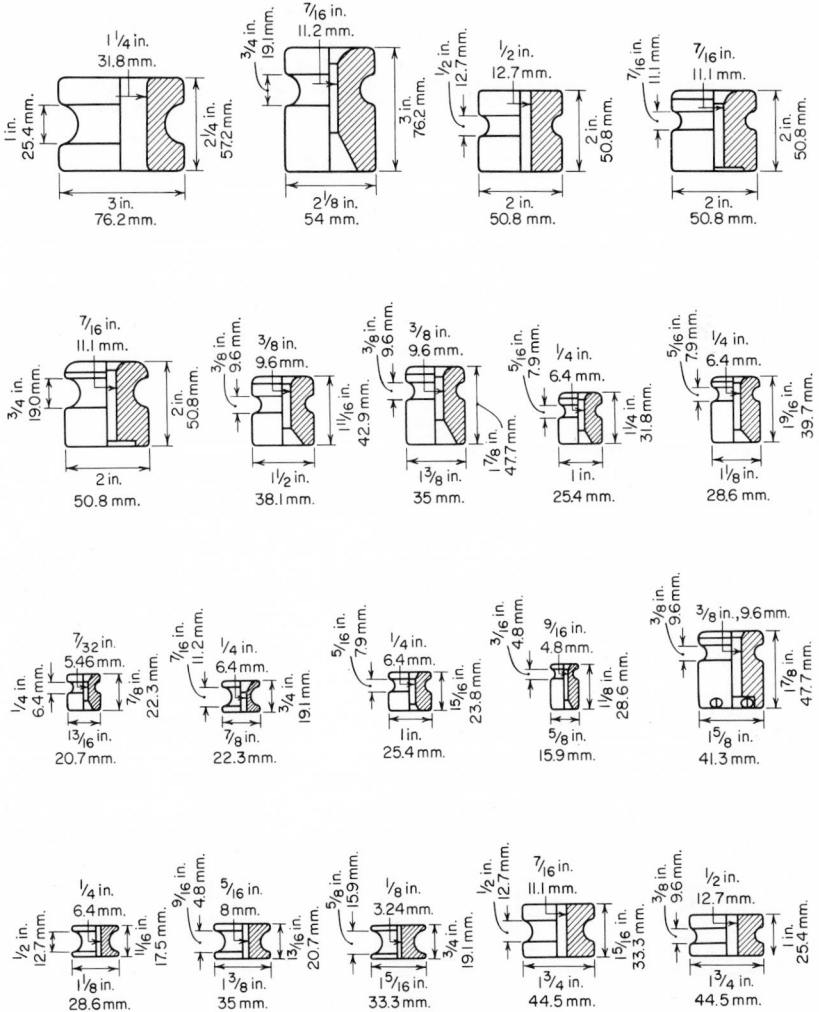

FIG. 135 *Various standard types of solid knob insulators.*

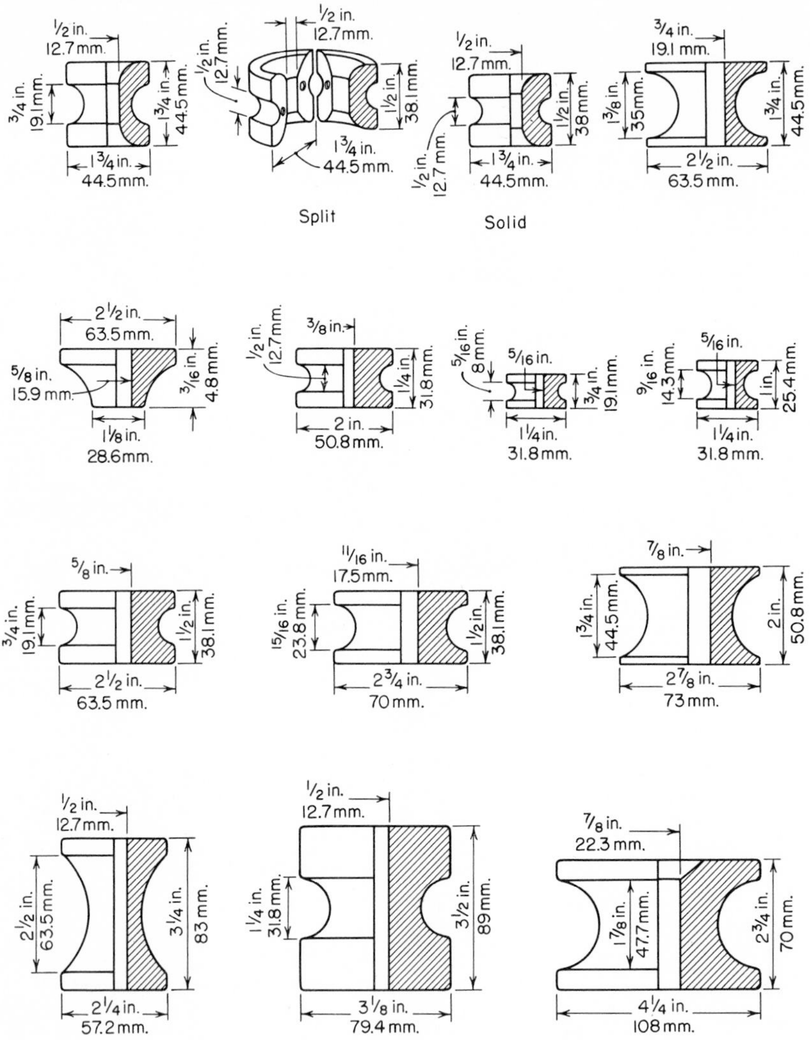

Split

Solid

FIG. 136 *Various standard types of rack insulators.*

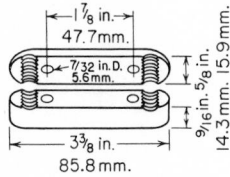

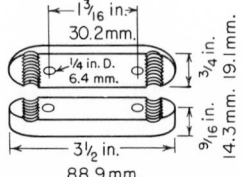

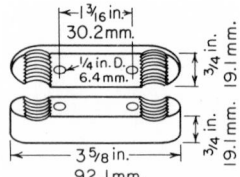

FIG. 137 *Two-wire cleats.*

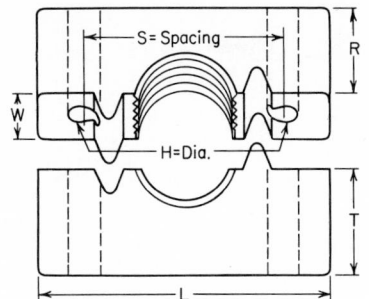

FIG. 138 *Single-wire cleats (See Sec. 90).*

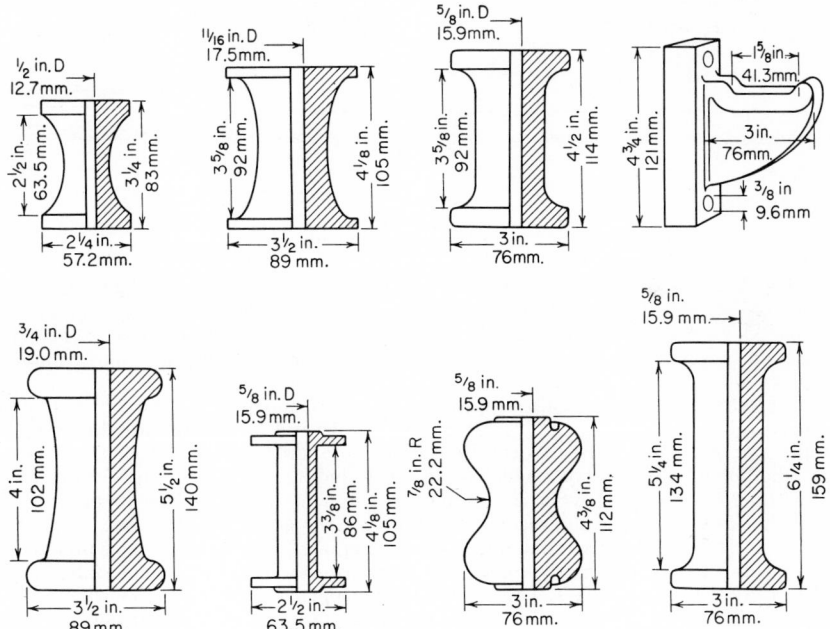

FIG. 139 *Crane insulators.*

95. Tube Diameters

Diameters	Tube size (see Sec. 94)													
	$\frac{5}{16}$	$\frac{3}{8}$	$\frac{1}{2}$	$\frac{5}{8}$	$\frac{3}{4}$	1	$1\frac{1}{4}$	$1\frac{1}{2}$	$1\frac{3}{4}$	2	$2\frac{1}{4}$	$2\frac{1}{2}$	$2\frac{3}{4}$	3
Outside diam, in........	$\frac{9}{16}$	$1\frac{1}{16}$	$1\frac{3}{16}$	$1\frac{5}{16}$	$1\frac{3}{16}$	$1\frac{7}{16}$	$1\frac{13}{16}$	$2\frac{3}{16}$	$2\frac{9}{16}$	$2\frac{15}{16}$	$3\frac{5}{16}$	$3\frac{11}{16}$	$4\frac{1}{4}$	$4\frac{1}{2}$
Outside diam, mm.......	14.3	17.5	20.6	23.8	30.2	36.5	46.1	55.6	65.1	74.6	84.1	93.7	108	114
Inside diam, in.........	$\frac{5}{16}$	$\frac{3}{8}$	$\frac{1}{2}$	$\frac{5}{8}$	$\frac{3}{4}$	1	$1\frac{1}{4}$	$1\frac{1}{2}$	$1\frac{3}{4}$	2	$2\frac{1}{4}$	$2\frac{1}{2}$	$2\frac{3}{4}$	3
Inside diam, mm........	7.9	9.5	12.7	15.9	19.1	25.4	31.7	38.1	44.5	50.8	57.1	63.5	69.8	76.2

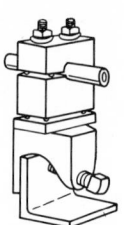

FIG. 140 *Insulated cable rack.* (*Westinghouse Electric Corp.*)

I- Showing No. 502 support with No. 3½ insulator. Support is tapped standard for No. 24-16 thread machine screw.

II- Showing No. 502 support with attachment for type A No.2 B.&D.cleat Support is tapped standard for No.24-16 thread machine screw.

FIG. 141 *Universal insulator supports.* (*Steel City Div. of Midland-Ross Corp.*)

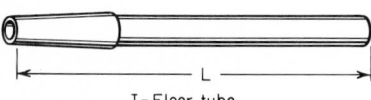

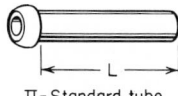

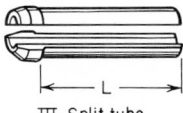

I- Floor tube   II- Standard tube   III- Split tube

FIG. 142 *Porcelain insulating tubes.*

96. Receptacles and caps or plugs are wiring devices for the purpose of providing a convenient means of attaching cord-and-plug-connected appliances or equipment.

Such devices are available in a wide variety of voltage (600 volts or less) and ampere (10 to 400 amp) ratings. The two broad classifications are grounding and nongrounding types.

The National Electrical Code requires all 15- and 20-amp receptacles to be grounding types, and the nongrounding-type receptacles shown in Fig. 143 can only be used for replacement purposes. Because millions of nongrounding-type receptacles have been installed before the Code rule which required grounding types, it was obvious that nongrounding types would have to continue to be manufactured for replacement purposes. Also, because many existing receptacle outlets are not grounded, the Code states that grounding-type receptacles shall not replace nongrounding-type receptacles unless the receptacle outlets are properly grounded. The reason for this is to prevent a false sense of security that would exist if a grounding-type receptacle were attached to an existing outlet with no ground connection to the grounding terminal of the receptacle.

Another significant development concerning receptacles is a National Electrical Code rule which states: **"Grounding-type** receptacles shall be installed only on circuits of the **voltage class and current** for which they have been approved." Figures 144 and 145 list the various receptacles and caps for general-purpose, nonlocking and locking types.

The nonlocking-type plug and receptacle configurations shown in Fig. 144 include both grounding and nongrounding types. Current ratings are 15 to 60 amp and voltage ratings range from 125 to 600 volts and two-pole, two-wire to four-pole, five-wire.

Figure 145 shows the receptacle and plug configurations for locking types, in ratings of 15, 20, and 30 amp at 125 to 600 volts, two-pole, two-wire to four-pole, five-wire.

Figures 144 and 145 are the configurations adopted by the National Electrical Manufacturers' Association (NEMA), and these configurations satisfy the National Electrical Code rule which calls for specific voltage and current ratings for all grounding-type receptacles. Also, these configurations are designed so that lower-voltage-rated receptacle caps cannot be inserted into receptacles supplied at higher voltages. This plan also achieves a high degree of standardization so that manufacturers of cord-and-plug-equipped apparatus can provide standard plug caps for such equipment and be reasonably assured that installers will provide a matching receptacle for a given current and voltage class.

Another significant advantage of these NEMA configurations is the wide selectivity of receptacles to allow different configurations on the same installation where several different voltages, classes of current (a-c or d-c), or different frequencies are used. In such cases, maintenance personnel usually install plug caps to match specific receptacle configurations.

97. Single- or Double-wipe Contacts and Terminal Connections. In many smaller ratings, such as 15 amp, 125 volts, receptacles are available with single-wipe or double-wipe contacts to receive plug caps. The single-wipe contact is in contact on only one side of the blade of an inserted plug cap. The other side of the plug cap blade is wedged against a non-current-carrying part of the receptacle. With double-wipe contacts **both sides** of a plug cap blade are in contact with the receiving part of the receptacle when inserted, and this ensures better contact. Better-grade receptacles have double-wipe contacts, and they should be used whenever possible to avoid early failures or loose connections when plug caps are inserted frequently.

In general, smaller receptacles (15 or 20 amp) use binding screws, recessed pressure-locking terminals, or a combination of both as a means of connecting supply wires. With binding screws, supply wires are skinned and wrapped around the screw in a **clockwise** direction. Since the screw is tightened in a clockwise position, this ensures a secure connection. Never fasten a wire around a binding screw in a counterclockwise direction because a poor connection will result when the binding screw is tightened.

The pressure-locking terminals are recessed inside of the receptacles. The sup-

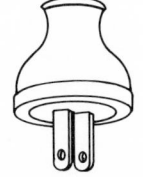 

I – Single receptacle   II – Double (duplex)
   regular type   receptacle, regular
        type

(a)   Receptacles

I – Rubber or   II – Cord clamp
composition type   type with
with parallel blades   parallel blades

(b) Plugs

FIG. 143 *Nongrounding-type receptacles and plugs, 125 volt, 15 amp. (Pass & Seymour, Inc.)*

ply wires are simply skinned about ½ in. and are then pushed through a hole (usually in the rear of the receptacle) into the pressure-locking contact. As the wire is inserted, the spring-held contact separates, and when the wire is pushed all the way in, it is firmly gripped.

Some receptacles contain binding screws and pressure-locking terminals so that an installer can select either method of connection. Another reason is that such receptacles can be used with either copper or aluminum wire. Since spring-contact pressure-locking terminals are not suitable for aluminum wire connections, the binding-screw method can be used. It should be noted that binding screws are considered acceptable for fastening aluminum wires (No. 12 or No. 10 solid), regardless of the material used for the binding screw and back plate. Such screws and plates are usually brass, copper, steel-plated, or unplated.

Receptacles 30 amp or larger generally have **set-screw** terminals, and in such cases the terminals will be marked CU/AL if suitable for the connection of aluminum conductors. If there is no such marking, it can be assumed that only copper wire connections are permitted.

98. Split-bus Receptacles. In the 125-volt 15- or 20-amp sizes, parallel-blade-type duplex receptacles are available with break-off jumpers or links so that one or both sides of the receptacles can be separated to avoid feed-through connections. With such receptacles it is common practice to break the connection on only the side of the receptacle that contains the screw connections for the ungrounded circuit conductors.

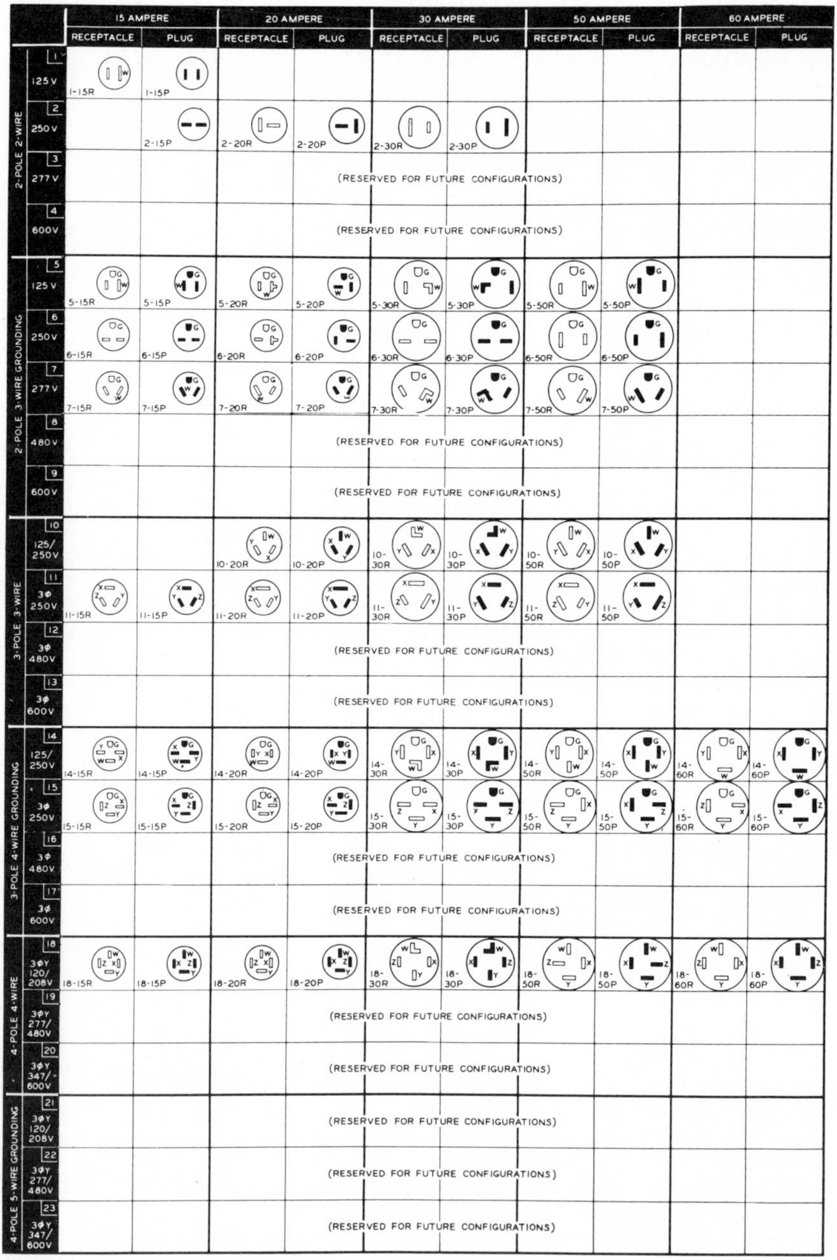

FIG. 144 *NEMA configurations for general-purpose nonlocking plugs and receptacles.* (*National Electrical Manufacturers' Association.*)

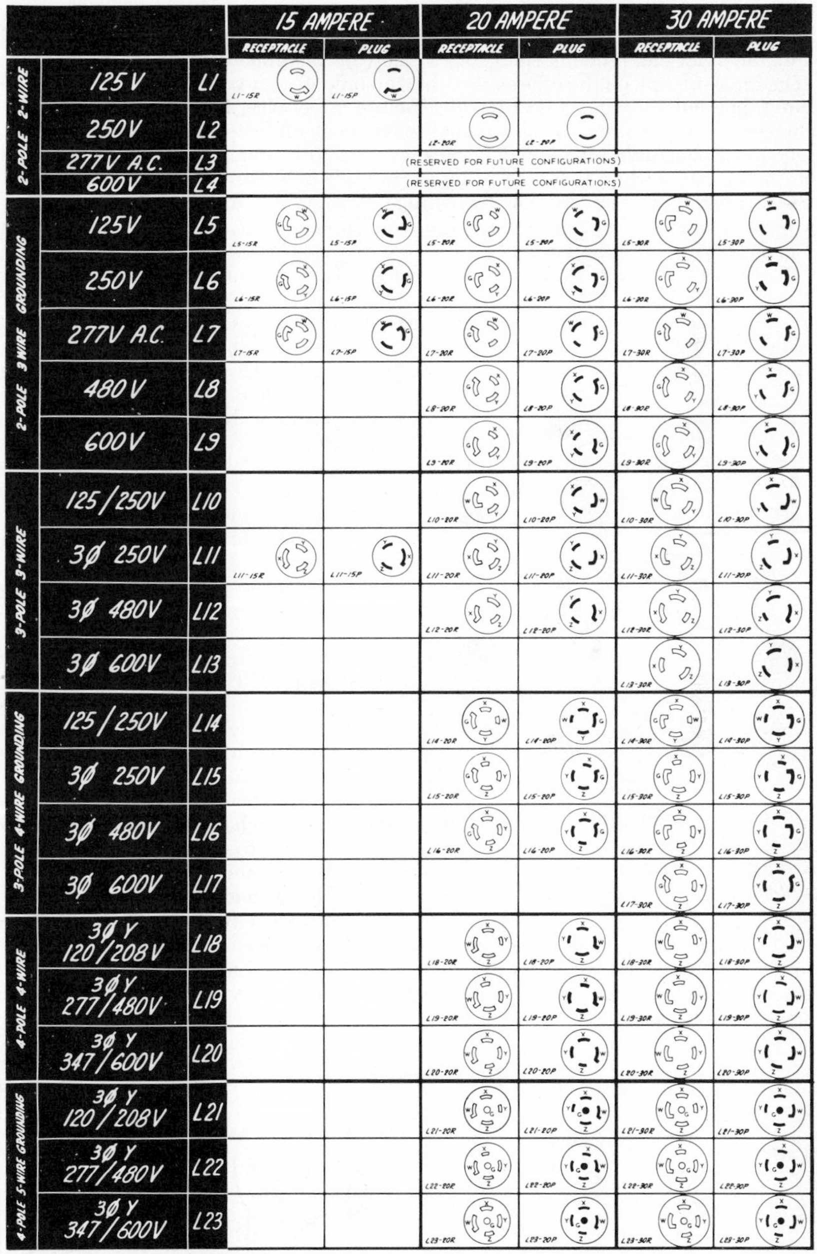

			15 AMPERE		20 AMPERE		30 AMPERE	
			RECEPTACLE	PLUG	RECEPTACLE	PLUG	RECEPTACLE	PLUG
2-POLE 2-WIRE	125 V	L1	L1-15R	L1-15P				
	250 V	L2			L2-20R	L2-20P		
	277 V A.C.	L3			(RESERVED FOR FUTURE CONFIGURATIONS)			
	600 V	L4			(RESERVED FOR FUTURE CONFIGURATIONS)			
2-POLE 3 WIRE GROUNDING	125 V	L5	L5-15R	L5-15P	L5-20R	L5-20P	L5-30R	L5-30P
	250 V	L6	L6-15R	L6-15P	L6-20R	L6-20P	L6-20R	L6-30P
	277 V A.C.	L7	L7-15R	L7-15P	L7-20R	L7-20P	L7-30R	L7-30P
	480 V	L8			L8-20R	L8-20P	L8-30R	L8-30P
	600 V	L9			L9-20R	L9-20P	L9-30R	L9-30P
3-POLE 3-WIRE	125/250V	L10			L10-20R	L10-20P	L10-30R	L10-30P
	3Ø 250V	L11	L11-15R	L11-15P	L11-20R	L11-20P	L11-30R	L11-30P
	3Ø 480V	L12			L12-20R	L12-20P	L12-30R	L12-30P
	3Ø 600V	L13					L13-30R	L13-30P
3-POLE 4-WIRE GROUNDING	125/250V	L14			L14-20R	L14-20P	L14-30R	L14-30P
	3Ø 250V	L15			L15-20R	L15-20P	L15-30R	L15-30P
	3Ø 480V	L16			L16-20R	L16-20P	L16-30R	L16-30P
	3Ø 600V	L17					L17-30R	L17-30P
4-POLE 4-WIRE	3Ø Y 120/208V	L18			L18-20R	L18-20P	L18-30R	L18-30P
	3Ø Y 277/480V	L19			L19-20R	L19-20P	L19-30R	L19-30P
	3Ø Y 347/600V	L20			L20-20R	L20-20P	L20-30R	L20-30P
4-POLE 5-WIRE GROUNDING	3Ø Y 120/208V	L21			L21-20R	L21-20P	L21-30R	L21-30P
	3Ø Y 277/480V	L22			L22-20R	L22-20P	L22-30R	L22-30P
	3Ø Y 347/600V	L23			L23-20R	L23-20P	L23-30R	L23-30P

FIG. 145 NEMA *configurations for locking-type plugs and receptacles.* (*National Electrical Manufacturers' Association.*)

With this connection separated, each half of the duplex receptacle can be connected to a different circuit or switch, or one-half of the receptacle can be controlled by a switch while the other half remains energized at 120 volts continuously.

The break-off link on the other side is broken only when two separate circuits are required, particularly when these circuits are **not** three-wire, 120/240 volts. Some receptacles with pressure-locking terminals have break-off features also.

99. Interchangeable Line. Receptacles for use in the interchangeable line are available in 15- and 20-amp two-pole two-wire and two-pole, three-wire. One such type rated at 15-amp 125-volt two-pole two-wire is shown in Fig. 42, along with other interchangeable devices. For new installations such a receptacle would have to be a two-pole, **three-wire** grounding type.

100. Special Four-pole Five-wire Receptacles. Harvey Hubbell, Inc., has developed a line of five-wire receptacles and caps, rated at 30 amp, 250 volts a-c, d-c, or 600 volts a-c, which retain the advantages of locking-type receptacles. These receptacles are available in eight noninterchangeable center-pin and slot configurations as illustrated

FIG. 146 *Noninterchangeable center-pin and slot configurations permit use of eight differently rated circuits. (Harvey Hubbell, Inc.)*

in Fig. 146. This permits a user to designate one configuration for one voltage, amperage, and/or frequency; a different configuration for a different voltage, amperage, and/or frequency; and so on. Such a system prevents the connection of equipment into the wrong source of power.

101. Heavy-duty Industrial Receptacles. Figure 147 shows typical heavy-duty industrial receptacles which are available in ratings up to 400 amp at 600 volts a-c. The receptacles shown in Fig. 147 are five-pole four-wire and are rated at 60 amp, 250 volts d-c, 600 volts a-c. One receptacle contains a spring door which closes the plug opening when the receptacle cap is removed, and the other receptacle has a threaded cover which is screwed in place when the receptacle is not in use. Such covers are recommended in many industrial applications to prevent the entry of water, dirt, or dust.

102. Range and Clothes Drier Receptacles. Figure 148 shows three-pole flush-and surface-mounted range receptacles rated at 250 volts a-c, 50 amp. This crow-foot configuration is commonly used for connecting cord-and-plug-equipped 115/230-volt household electric ranges in which the neutral conductor is used to ground the frame of

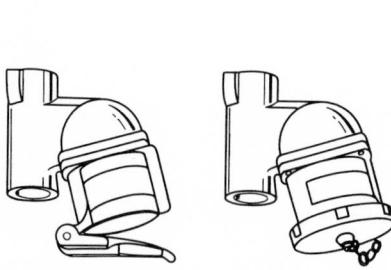

FIG. 147 *Heavy-duty industrial receptacles. (Crouse Hinds Co.)*

a- Receptacle

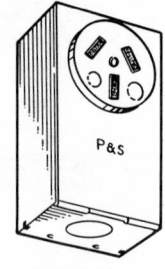

b- Outlet box mounting

FIG. 148 *50-amp range outlet. (Pass & Seymour, Inc.)*

the range. A similar receptacle, rated at 30 amp, is used for the connection of cord-and-plug-equipped electric clothes driers of 5.5 kw or less at 115/230 or 120/208 volts. The major difference is that the neutral pole is an L shape.

103. Special receptacle housings are available for receptacles installed outdoors, in hazardous locations, or for other applications where receptacles must be protected from weather elements, contaminants, or hazardous concentrations of flammable gases, liquids, or dust.

104. A box must be installed at each outlet, switch, or junction point for all wiring installations except for exposed wiring on insulators or of cable. An outlet is any point in a wiring system where current is taken for supplying fixtures, lamps, heaters, or any other current-consuming equipment. The boxes must be constructed of metal except for open wiring on insulators, concealed knob and tube work, or other nonmetallic wiring methods. In these installations boxes made of insulating material can be used (see Div. 9). Boxes used in interior wiring work may be classified as outlet, utility, sectional switch, and floor boxes. Utility boxes are designed principally for exposed wiring. Conduit fittings (see Div. 9) are used at the outlets for many exposed-conduit wiring installations. Sectionalized device boxes are used in concealed wiring when not embedded in masonry structure. Floor boxes are used for making outlets in floors from conduit wiring systems. Boxes are made of No. 10 to 14 gage sheet steel. The surfaces are galvanized. Galvanized boxes will resist corrosion and preserve the electrical conductivity of the raceway system. The different types of boxes are illustrated in Sec. **113** with the dimensions in which they are most commonly available.

105. Box accessories consist of support brackets or ears, studs, cable clamps, and covers. Many boxes are equipped with some form of mounting bracket or with mounting ears. Some of the types of supporting brackets which are available are shown in Table **111**. Standard mounting ears for the support of device boxes are shown in Table **117** along with other methods of supporting sectional device boxes. Many boxes are provided with fixture studs for the support of a fixture which receives its electrical supply through the outlet box. Many boxes are equipped with clamps for attaching armored cable or nonmetallic-sheathed cable to the box. Different types of clamps are shown in Table **112**.

106. Covers for outlet boxes are made in a variety of types. Some of the types available are shown in Table **114**.

107. Outlet boxes are made in round, square, octagonal, and oblong shapes. Round boxes should never be used where a conduit must enter the box through the side, as it is difficult to make a good connection with a lock nut or bushing on a rounded surface.

The **round** and **octagonal** boxes are used for ceiling outlets in all types of concealed wiring installed in buildings of all types of construction. The octagonal boxes are also used for wall-bracket lighting outlets. Both round and octagonal boxes are made with various combinations of knockouts in sides and bottom and with built-in clamps for armored cable or nonmetallic-sheathed cable. They can be obtained with built-in $3/8$- or $1/2$-in. fixture studs or with holes for mounting a separate fixture stud. Various types of covers are available for these boxes as shown in Sec. **114**. Some are of the flat type, while others have the central portion of the cover raised so that additional interior space is made available in the box. Octagonal boxes constructed especially for concrete work have the bottom or back plate, as it is called, detachable from the sides. The back plate and sides are provided with conduit knockouts. The back plate may be provided with $3/8$- or $1/2$-in. built-in fixture studs or with holes for mounting a separate fixture stud.

Square and **oblong** boxes are used principally for side-wall outlets in conduit wiring when embedded in masonry or installed in brick or tile walls. Sometimes they also are used with conduit wiring in other types of building construction. The square boxes are used sometimes for ceiling outlets. The oblong boxes frequently are called gang boxes and are used where more internal space is required than is provided by the square boxes. The term **gang** refers to the number of standard-line wiring devices which the box will accommodate. A three-gang box will accommodate three standard wiring devices mounted side by side. They are made with various combinations of knockouts in sides and bottom. The square boxes may be provided with $3/8$- or $1/2$-in. built-in fixture studs or with holes for mounting separate fixture studs. Various types of covers are available for the square boxes as shown in Sec. **114**. Covers are available with openings and supporting lugs for the accommodation of flush wiring devices. The opening is then covered with a standard flush plate. The portion of the box cover around the central opening is raised so that the box is set back a slight amount in the wall and the cover brings the surface of the wiring device flush with the wall surface. The box and the box cover are plastered over a sufficient amount so that the remaining opening will be completely covered with the flush plate. Covers are available with the central portion raised different amounts in order to accommodate different thicknesses of plaster. The covers for the oblong boxes are always of the type just described. When the square boxes are used in exposed wiring, a flush plate would not give a neat appearance, so that an outlet box cover is used which covers the entire opening of the box. Openings in the cover accommodate switch handles or receptacles.

108. Utility boxes are designed for use in exposed-conduit wiring installations in order to provide a neat-appearing job. They are provided with knockouts in bottom and sides. Data on covers are given in Sec. **114.**

109. Sectional device boxes are employed in concealed wiring installations which are not embedded in masonry. They are constructed with removable sides so that any number of boxes can be ganged side by side in order to provide compactly for several wiring devices at one location. No covers are required, since they are designed to accommodate the standard flush wiring devices with standard flush plates. They are made in types with conduit knockouts and with clamps for armored cable, nonmetallic-sheathed cable, and loom. Most boxes are 3 in. long and 2 in. wide.

110. Extension rings (Fig. 149) are available for octagonal and square boxes in order to increase the depth of the box. The standard depths in which they are available for the different boxes are given in Sec. **113.**

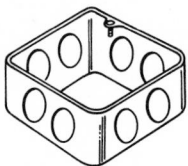

I - For square box

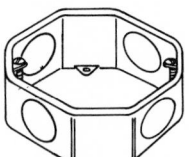

II - For octagonal box

FIG. 149 *Outlet-box extension rings.*

111. Bracket Identification [a]

Bracket designation		Description and application
B		For mounting on the face of stud. Can be offset from studding to clear door frame or snugged up against studding as desired
F		A sturdy, simple flat bracket for easy side mounting. Exceptionally rigid and easy to install. Hugs close to studding
A		Angle bracket snugs against both face and side of studding. When nails are driven both ways, it becomes the strongest mounting available. Stands up under the strain of marking box openings in dry wall
O		Side-mount bracket mounts on face and side of studding. Locating lugs engage face of studding for normal plaster thickness. Lugs are easily removed so box can be mounted on side of studding in various positions to accommodate all wall thicknesses
D		The D bracket is an integral part of the box, affording great strength and rigidity. These boxes are extremely versatile—easily adapted for $\frac{3}{8}$, $\frac{1}{2}$ and $\frac{5}{8}$-in. wall thickness. Wall thickness is marked on box
E		Face-mounting bracket on end of device box for horizontal mounting of switches or receptacles
T		Exceptionally strong **twin** mounting bracket for oversize 4- by 2-in. device boxes. Can be nailed from front or side or both. Box stands out from stud for door frame clearance

[a] Courtesy of General Electric Co.

112. Clamp Identification [a]

Clamp designation		For use with	Description and application
C		BX armored cable	For outlet and bar hanger boxes. Two-way entrance design permits cable to enter through side or back of box. Well suited for ceiling work
K		Nonmetallic and BX armored cable	For outlet boxes and device boxes. Provides visual inspection of antishort bushings. Holds bushings tightly against armor stop
D		Nonmetallic cable	For outlet boxes and device boxes. Two-way entrance design permits cable to enter through side or back of box. Compresses when tightened; grips cables firmly
L		Nonmetallic cable	For outlet boxes and device boxes. Compresses when tightened; grips cable firmly. Particularly adaptable for side-entry installations
No. 9		Nonmetallic cable or loom	For ceiling pan installations
No. 10		Nonmetallic cable	For ceiling pan installations. Tapped for outside clamp screw. Compresses when tightened; grips cable firmly
No. 12		BX armored cable	For shallow pans. Tapped hole for outside clamp screw
BD		Nonmetallic cable	For beveled-corner device boxes. Holds cable with even pressure

[a] Courtesy of General Electric Co.

113. Data on Wiring Boxes

(Courtesy of General Electric Co.)

	Sketch No.	Depth, in.	Accessories			Knockouts			
						Sides		Bottom	
			Stud	Ears	Clamps	Conduit	Cable 21/32 in.	Conduit	Cable 21/32 in.
3¼-in. Octagon Boxes									
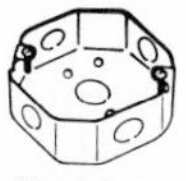	1	1½	. . .	. . .	. . .	Four ½″	. . .	One ½″	
Sketch 1		1½	. . .	. . .	. . .	Four ¾″	. . .	One ½″	
3¼-in. Extension Rings									
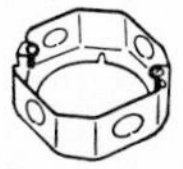	2	1½	. . .	. . .	. . .	Four ½″			
Sketch 2		1½	. . .	. . .	. . .	Four ¾″			
3½-in. Octagon Boxes									
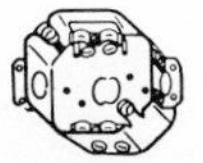		1½	. . .	. . .	2-C	Two ½″	4	One ½″	4
		1½	. . .	. . .	2-L	Two ½″	4	One ½″	4
Sketch 3	3	1½	. . .	Yes	2-L	Two ½″	4	One ½″	4

Data on Wiring Boxes (*Continued*)

4-in. Octagon Boxes

	Sketch No.	Depth, in.	Accessories				Knockouts			
							Sides		Bottom	
			Brkt.	Stud	Ears	Clamps	Conduit	Cable $2\frac{1}{32}$ in.	Conduit	Cable $2\frac{1}{32}$ in.
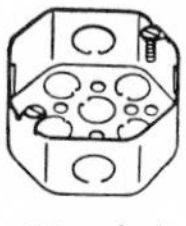	4	1½	...	...	...	...	Four ½″	...	Five ½″	
		1½	...	...	...	...	Four ¾″	...	Three ½″ Two ¾″	
Sketch 4		1½	...	...	...	...	Two ½″ Two ¾″	...	Three ½″ Two ¾″	
	5	1½	...	...	...	2-C	Two ½″	4	One ½″	4
		1½	...	...	Yes	2-C	Two ½″	4	One ½″	4
		1½	...	Yes	...	2-C	Two ½″	4	....	4
Sketch 5		1½	...	...	...	2-L	Two ½″	4	One ½″	4
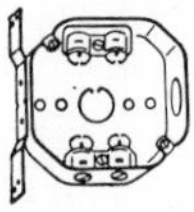	6	1½	F	No	No	2-L	Two ½″	4	One ½″	4
		1½	...	Yes	...	2-D	Two ½″	4	....	4
		1½	...	Yes	Yes	2-D	Two ½″	4	....	4
	7	1½	...	...	...	2-D	Two ½″	4	One ½″	4
Sketch 6		1½	...	...	Yes	2-D	Two ½″	4	One ½″	4
	8	1½	...	...	...	2-K	Two ½″	4	One ½″	4
		1½	...	Yes	...	2-K	Two ½″	4	....	4
		2⅛	...	...	...	...	Four ½″	...	Five ½″	
Sketch 7		2⅛	...	...	...	...	Four ¾″	...	Three ½″ Two ¾″	
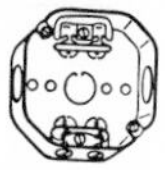		2⅛	...	...	...	...	Four 1″	...	Three ½″ Two ¾″	
Sketch 8		2⅛	...	...	...	...	Two ½″ Two ¾″	...	Three ½″ Two ¾″	
4-in. Octagon Extension Rings										
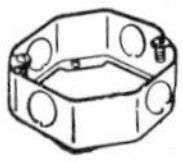	9	1½	...	...	...	...	Four ½″			
		1½	...	...	...	...	Four ¾″			
Sketch 9		1½	...	...	...	...	Two ½″ Two ¾″			
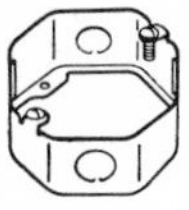	10	2⅛	...	...	...	...	Four ½″			
		2⅛	...	...	...	...	Four ¾″			
		2⅛	...	...	...	...	Four 1″			
Sketch 10		2⅛	...	...	...	...	Two ½″ Two ¾″			

Data on Wiring Boxes (*Continued*)

4-in. Square Boxes

	Sketch No.	Depth, in.	Clamps	Brkt.	Sides Conduit	Sides Cable $2\frac{1}{32}$ in.	Bottom Conduit	Bottom Cable $2\frac{1}{32}$ in.
 Sketch 11		1¼	...	...	Twelve ½″	...	Five ½″	
		1¼	...	B	Twelve ½″	...	Five ½″	
	11	1½	...	...	Twelve ½″	...	Five ½″	
		1½	...	...	Eight ¾″	...	Three ½″ Two ¾″	
		1½	...	...	Eight ½″ Four ¾″	...	Three ½″ Two ¾″	
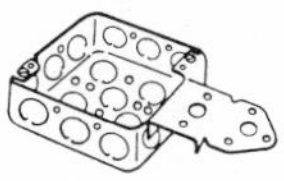 Sketch 12	12	1½	...	B	Twelve ½″	...	Five ½″	
		1½	...	B	Six ¾″	...	Three ½″ Two ¾″	
		1½	...	B	Six ½″ Three ¾″	...	Three ½″ Two ¾″	
		1½	...	A	Nine ½″	...	Five ½″	
		1½	...	F	Nine ½″	...	Five ½″	
		1½	...	O	Nine ½″	...	Five ½″	
		1½	...	O	Six ¾″	...	Three ½″ Two ¾″	
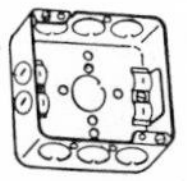 Sketch 13		1½	...	...	Twelve ½″			
		1½	2-C	...	Six ½″	4	One ½″	4
		1½	2-C	B	Six ½″	4	One ½″	4
		1½	2-C	F	Three ½″	4	One ½″	4
	13	1½	2-C	O	Three ½″	4	One ½″	4
		1½	2-L	...	Six ½″	4	One ½″	4
		1½	2-L	B	Six ½″	4	One ½″	4
		1½	2-D	...	Six ½″	4	One ½″	4
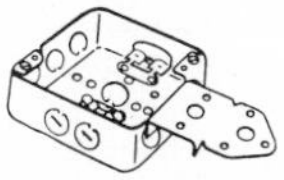 Sketch 14		1½	2-D	A	Three ½″	4	One ½″	4
		1½	2-D	B	Six ½″	4	One ½″	4
		1½	2-D	F	Three ½″	4	One ½″	4
		1½	2-K	...	Six ½″	4	One ½″	4
	14	1½	2-K	B	Six ½″	4	One ½″	4
	15	2⅛	...	...	Twelve ½″	...	Five ½″	
		2⅛	...	...	Eight ¾″	...	Three ½″ Two ¾″	
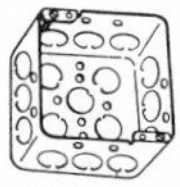		2⅛	...	...	Eight 1″	...	Three ½″ Two ¾″	
		2⅛	...	...	Four 1¼″	...	Three ½″ Two ¾″	
Sketch 15		2⅛	...	...	Eight ½″ Four ¾″	...	Three ½″ Two ¾″	

4-in. Square Extension Rings

	Sketch No.	Depth, in.	Clamps	Brkt.	Sides Conduit			
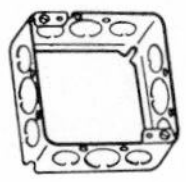 Sketch 16		1½	...	...	Twelve ½″			
		1½	...	...	Eight ¾″			
	16	1½	...	...	Eight ½″ Four ¾″			
		2⅛	...	...	Twelve ½″			
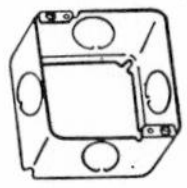		2⅛	...	...	Eight ¾″			
	17	2⅛	...	...	Eight 1″			
		2⅛	...	...	Four 1¼″			
Sketch 17		2⅛	...	...	Eight ½″ Four ¾″			

Data on Wiring Boxes (*Continued*)

$4\frac{11}{16}$-in. Square Boxes

	Sketch No.	Depth, in.	Knockouts	
			Sides	Bottom
	18	$1\frac{1}{2}$	Twelve $\frac{1}{2}''$	Three $\frac{1}{2}''$, two $\frac{3}{4}''$
		$1\frac{1}{2}$	Eight $\frac{3}{4}''$	Three $\frac{1}{2}''$, two $\frac{3}{4}''$
		$1\frac{1}{2}$	Eight $\frac{1}{2}''$, four $\frac{3}{4}''$	Three $\frac{1}{2}''$, two $\frac{3}{4}''$
Sketch 18	19	$2\frac{1}{8}$	Twelve $\frac{1}{2}''$	Three $\frac{1}{2}''$, two $\frac{3}{4}''$
		$2\frac{1}{8}$	Eight $\frac{3}{4}''$	Three $\frac{1}{2}''$, two $\frac{3}{4}''$
		$2\frac{1}{8}$	Eight $1''$	Three $\frac{1}{2}''$, two $\frac{3}{4}''$
		$2\frac{1}{8}$	Four $1\frac{1}{4}''$	Three $\frac{1}{2}''$, two $\frac{3}{4}''$
		$2\frac{1}{8}$	Eight $\frac{1}{2}''$, four $\frac{3}{4}''$	Three $\frac{1}{2}''$, two $\frac{3}{4}''$
Sketch 19				

$4\frac{11}{16}$-in. Square Extension Rings

	Sketch No.	Depth, in.	Sides	
	20	$1\frac{1}{2}$	Twelve $\frac{1}{2}''$	
		$1\frac{1}{2}$	Eight $\frac{3}{4}''$	
		$1\frac{1}{2}$	Eight $\frac{1}{2}''$, four $\frac{3}{4}''$	
		$2\frac{1}{8}$	Twelve $\frac{1}{2}''$	
Sketch 20		$2\frac{1}{8}$	Eight $\frac{3}{4}''$	
		$2\frac{1}{8}$	Eight $1''$	
	21	$2\frac{1}{8}$	Four $1\frac{1}{4}''$	
		$2\frac{1}{8}$	Eight $\frac{1}{2}''$, four $\frac{3}{4}''$	
Sketch 21				

$3\frac{1}{2}$-in. Round—$\frac{1}{2}$-in. Deep

	Sketch No.	Accessories			Knockouts	
		Studs	Ears	Clamps	Conduit	Loam or cable $2\frac{1}{32}$ in.
Sketch 22	22	No	Yes	Two No. 9	Three $\frac{1}{2}''$	4

$3\frac{1}{2}$-in. Round—$\frac{3}{4}$-in. Deep

	Sketch No.	Studs	Ears	Clamps	Conduit	Loam or cable $2\frac{1}{32}$ in.
	23	Yes	Yes	Two No. 10	....	4
		No	Yes	Two No. 10	One $1\frac{1}{2}''$	4
Sketch 23						
		Yes	Yes	Two No. 12	....	4
	24	No	Yes	Two No. 12	One $\frac{1}{2}''$	4
Sketch 24						

4-in. Round—$\frac{1}{2}$-in. Deep

	Sketch No.	Studs	Ears	Clamps	Conduit	Loam or cable $2\frac{1}{32}$ in.
Sketch 25	25	No	Yes	No	Five $\frac{1}{2}''$	1

Data on Wiring Boxes (*Continued*)

3-in. Long by 2-in. Wide Device Boxes

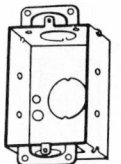 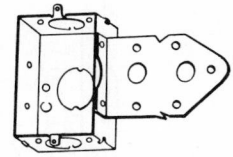 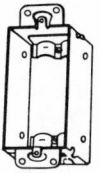 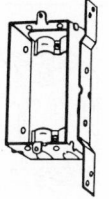 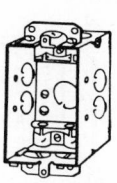

Sketch 26	Sketch 27	Sketch 28	Sketch 29	Sketch 30

Sketch No.	Depth, in.	Accessories			Knockouts					
					Each end		Each side		Bottom	
		Brkt.	Clamps	Ears	Conduit	Cable $2\frac{1}{32}$ in.	Conduit	Cable $2\frac{1}{32}$ in.	Conduit	Cable $2\frac{1}{32}$ in.
26	$1\frac{1}{2}$	No	No	Yes	One $\frac{1}{2}''$	....	......	.....	One $\frac{1}{2}''$	
	$1\frac{1}{2}$	F	No	No	One $\frac{1}{2}''$	....	......	.....	One $\frac{1}{2}''$	
27	$1\frac{1}{2}$	B	No	No	One $\frac{1}{2}''$	....	......	.....	One $\frac{1}{2}''$	
	$1\frac{1}{2}$	No	1-L	Yes	One $\frac{1}{2}''$	Corner K.O.'s for N-M cable 1 end				
28	$1\frac{1}{2}$	No	2-L	Yes	......	Corner K.O.'s for N-M cable				
29	$1\frac{1}{2}$	F	2-L	No	......	Corner K.O.'s for N-M cable				
	$1\frac{1}{2}$	B	2-L	No	......	Corner K.O.'s for N-M cable				
	2	No	No	No	One $\frac{1}{2}''$	....	Two $\frac{1}{2}''$	.....	One $\frac{1}{2}''$	
	2	No	No	Yes	One $\frac{1}{2}''$	....	Two $\frac{1}{2}''$	.....	One $\frac{1}{2}''$	
	2	F	No	No	One $\frac{1}{2}''$	....	Two $\frac{1}{2}''$	.....	One $\frac{1}{2}''$	
	2	A	No	No	One $\frac{1}{2}''$	....	Two $\frac{1}{2}''$ in 1 side	.....	One $\frac{1}{2}''$	
30	2	B	No	No	One $\frac{1}{2}''$	....	Two $\frac{1}{2}''$		One $\frac{1}{2}''$	
	2	No	2-K	Yes	......	2	......	2	One $\frac{1}{2}''$	
	2	No	2-L	Yes	......	2	......	2	One $\frac{1}{2}''$	

Data on Wiring Boxes (*Continued*)

3-in. Long by 2-in. Wide Device Boxes (*Continued*)

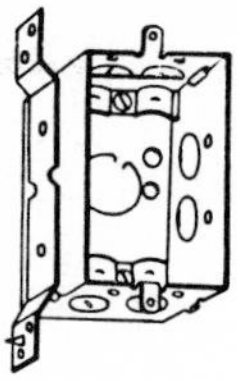

Sketch 31

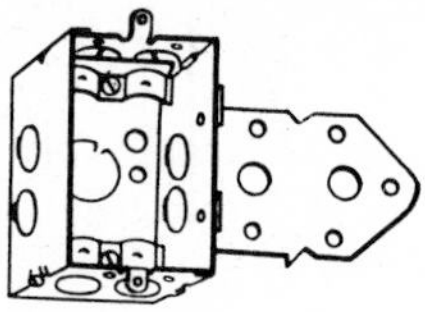

Sketch 32

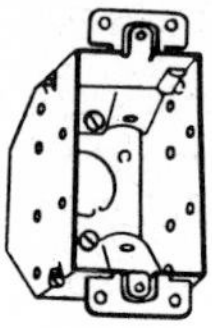

Sketch 33

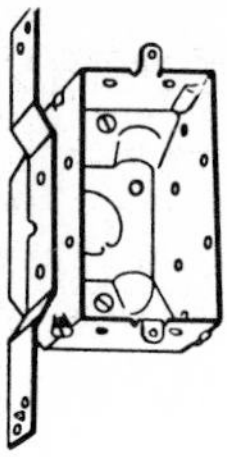

Sketch 34

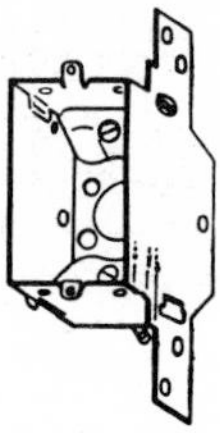

Sketch 35

Sketch No.	Depth, in.	Accessories			Knockouts					
					Each end		Each side		Bottom	
		Brkt.	Clamps	Ears	Conduit	Cable $^{21}/_{32}$ in.	Conduit	Cable $^{21}/_{32}$ in.	Conduit	Cable $^{21}/_{32}$ in.
	2	F	2-K	No	......	2	......	2 in 1 side	One ½″	
31	2	F	2-L	No	......	2	......	2 in 1 side	One ½″	
	2	A	2-K	No	......	2	......	2 in 1 side	One ½″	
	2	A	2-L	No	......	2	......	2 in 1 side	One ½″	
	2	B	2-K	No	......	2	......	2	One ½″	
32	2	B	2-L	No	......	2	......	2	One ½″	
	2¼	No	2-BD	Yes	......	Ea. bevel corner 2	......	.....	One ½″	
	2¼[a]	No	No	No	......	Ea. bevel corner 2	......	.....	One ½″	
	2¼	No	No	Yes	......	Ea. bevel corner 2				
	2¼[a]	No	2-BD	No	......	Ea. bevel corner 2	......	.....	One ½″	
33	2¼	No	2-BD	Yes (single screw)	......	Ea. bevel corner 2	......	.....	One ½″	
	2¼	D	No	No	......	Ea. bevel corner 2	......	.....	One ½″	
34	2¼	F	2-BD	No	......	Ea. bevel corner 2	......	.....	One ½″	
35	2¼	D	2-BD	No	......	Ea. bevel corner 2	......	.....	One ½″	
	2¼	A	2-BD	No	......	Ea. bevel corner 2	......	.....	One ½″	

[a] Leveling bumps and straight through nail holes.

Data on Wiring Boxes (*Continued*)
3-in. Long by 2-in. Wide Device Boxes (*Continued*)

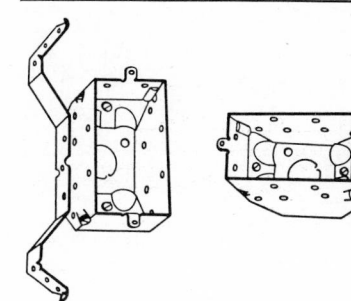
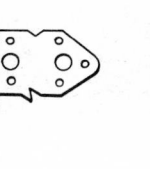
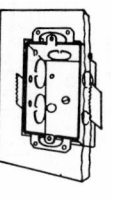

Sketch 36   Sketch 37   Sketch 38   Sketch 39

Sketch No.	Depth, in.	Accessories			Knockouts					
					Each end		Each side		Bottom	
		Brkt.	Clamps	Ears	Conduit	Cable $2\frac{1}{32}$ in.	Conduit	Cable $2\frac{1}{32}$ in.	Conduit	Cable $2\frac{1}{32}$ in.
36	$2\frac{1}{4}$	O	2-BD	No	......	Ea. bevel corner 2	......	.....	One $\frac{1}{2}''$	
	$2\frac{1}{4}$	B	2-BD	No	......	Ea. bevel corner 2	......	.....	One $\frac{1}{2}''$	
37	$2\frac{1}{4}$	E	2-BD	No	......	Ea. bevel corner 2	......	.....	One $\frac{1}{2}''$	
	$2\frac{1}{2}$	No	No	No	One $\frac{1}{2}''$	....	Two $\frac{1}{2}''$	.....	One $\frac{1}{2}''$	
	$2\frac{1}{2}$	No	No	Yes	One $\frac{1}{2}''$	....	Two $\frac{1}{2}''$	.....	One $\frac{1}{2}''$	
	$2\frac{1}{2}$	F	No	No	One $\frac{1}{2}''$	....	Two $\frac{1}{2}''$ in 1 side	.....	One $\frac{1}{2}''$	
	$2\frac{1}{2}$	A	No	No	One $\frac{1}{2}''$	....	Two $\frac{1}{2}''$ in 1 side	.....	One $\frac{1}{2}''$	
	$2\frac{1}{2}$	B	No	No	One $\frac{1}{2}''$	....	Two $\frac{1}{2}''$	.....	One $\frac{1}{2}''$	
	$2\frac{1}{2}$	O	No	No	One $\frac{1}{2}''$	....	Two $\frac{1}{2}''$ in 1 side	.....	One $\frac{1}{2}''$	
	$2\frac{1}{2}$	E	No	No	One $\frac{1}{2}''$	....	Two $\frac{1}{2}''$	.....	One $\frac{1}{2}''$	
38	$2\frac{1}{2}$	SP970	No	Yes	One $\frac{1}{2}''$	....	Two $\frac{1}{2}''$		One $\frac{1}{2}''$	
	$2\frac{1}{2}$ a	No	2-K	No	......	2	......	2	One $\frac{1}{2}''$	
	$2\frac{1}{2}$ a	No	2-L	No	......	2	......	2	One $\frac{1}{2}''$	
	$2\frac{1}{2}$	No	2-K	Yes	......	2	......	2	One $\frac{1}{2}''$	
39	$2\frac{1}{2}$	No	2-L	Yes	......	2	......	2	One $\frac{1}{2}''$	
	$2\frac{1}{2}$	F	2-K	No	......	2	......	2 in 1 side	One $\frac{1}{2}''$	
	$2\frac{1}{2}$	F	2-L	No	......	2	......	2 in 1 side	One $\frac{1}{2}''$	

a Leveling bumps and straight through nail holes.

Data on Wiring Boxes (*Continued*)

3-in. Long by 2-in. Wide Device Boxes (*Continued*)

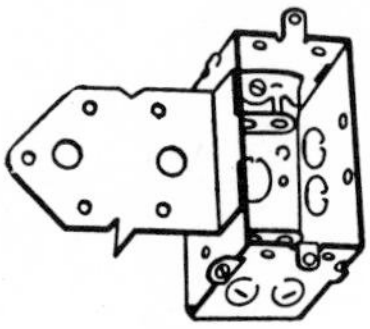

Sketch 40

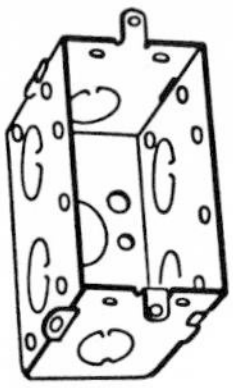

Sketch 41

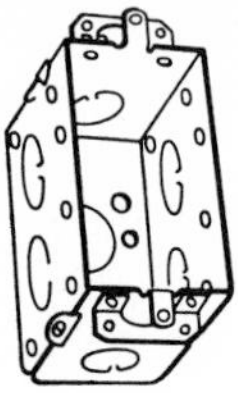

Sketch 42

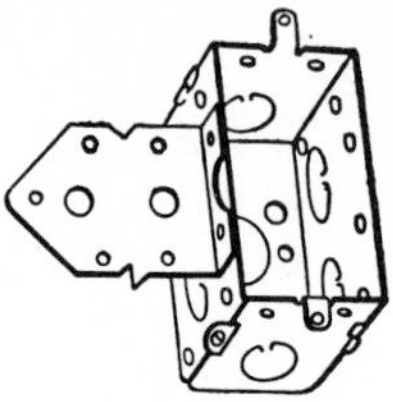

Sketch 43

Sketch No.	Depth, in.	Accessories			Knockouts					
					Each end		Each side		Bottom	
		Brkt.	Clamps	Ears	Conduit	Cable 21/32 in.	Conduit	Cable 21/32 in.	Conduit	Cable 21/32 in.
	2½	A	2-K	No	......	2	......	2 in 1 side	One ½″	
	2½	A	2-L	No	......	2	......	2 in 1 side	One ½″	
40	2½	B	2-K	No	......	2	......	2	One ½″	
	2½	B	2-L	No	......	2	......	2	One ½″	
	2½	O	2-K	No	......	2	......	2 in 1 side	One ½″	
	2½	O	2-L	No	......	2	......	2 in 1 side	One ½″	
	2½	E	2-K	No	......	2	......	2	One ½″	
	2½	E	2-L	No	......	2	......	2	One ½″	
	2½[a]	No	2-D	No	......	2	......	2	One ½″	4
	2½	No	2-D	Yes	......	2	......	2	One ½″	4
	2½	O	2-D	No	......	2	......	2 in 1 side	One ½″	4
41	2¾	No	No	No	One ½″	....	Two ½″	.....	One ½″	
	2¾	No	No	No	One ¾″	....	Two ½″	.....	One ½″	
42	2¾	No	No	Yes	One ½″	....	Two ½″	.....	One ½″	
	2¾	No	No	Yes	One ¾″	....	Two ½″	.....	One ½″	
	2¾	A	No	No	One ¾″	....	Two ½″ in 1 side	.....	One ½″	
43	2¾	B	No	No	One ½″	....	Two ½″	.....	One ½″	
	2¾	O	No	No	One ¾″	....	Two ½″ in 1 side	.....	One ½″	

[a] Leveling bumps and straight through nail holes.

Data on Wiring Boxes (*Continued*)

3-in. Long by 2-in. Wide Device Boxes (*Continued*)

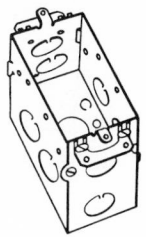

Sketch 44

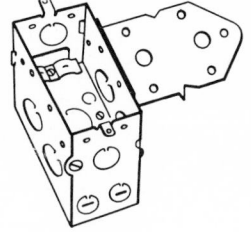

Sketch 45

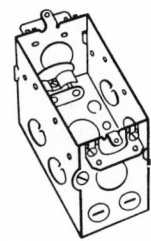

Sketch 46

Sketch No.	Depth, in.	Accessories			Knockouts					
		Brkt.	Clamps	Ears	Each end		Each side		Bottom	
					Conduit	Cable $2\frac{1}{32}$ in.	Conduit	Cable $2\frac{1}{32}$ in.	Conduit	Cable $2\frac{1}{32}$ in.
44	$3\frac{1}{2}$	No	No	Yes	Two $\frac{1}{2}''$	....	Two $\frac{1}{2}''$	.....	One $\frac{1}{2}''$	
	$3\frac{1}{2}$	No	No	Yes	One $\frac{3}{4}''$	....	Two $\frac{3}{4}''$	.....	One $\frac{1}{2}''$	
	$3\frac{1}{2}$	B	2-K	No	One $\frac{1}{2}''$	2	Two $\frac{1}{2}''$	.....	One $\frac{1}{2}''$	
45	$3\frac{1}{2}$	B	2-L	No	One $\frac{1}{2}''$	2	Two $\frac{1}{2}''$	.....	One $\frac{1}{2}''$	
46	$3\frac{1}{2}$	No	2-K	Yes	One $\frac{1}{2}''$	2	Two $\frac{1}{2}''$	.....	One $\frac{1}{2}''$	
	$3\frac{1}{2}$	No	2-L	Yes	One $\frac{1}{2}''$	2	Two $\frac{1}{2}''$	.....	One $\frac{1}{2}''$	

4-in. Long by 2-in. Wide Device Boxes

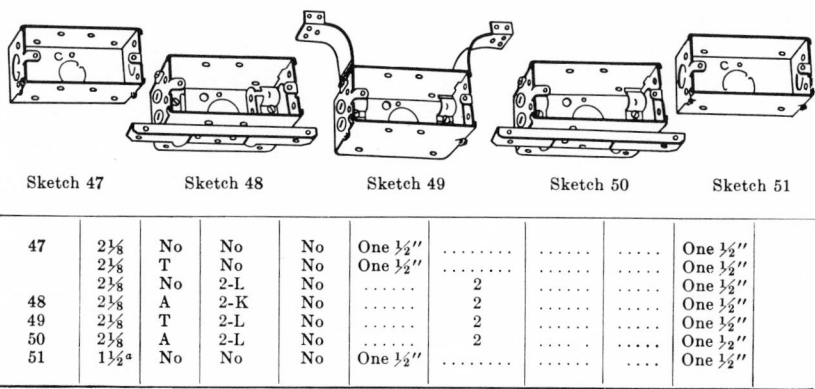

Sketch 47   Sketch 48   Sketch 49   Sketch 50   Sketch 51

47	$2\frac{1}{8}$	No	No	No	One $\frac{1}{2}''$	....	......	.....	One $\frac{1}{2}''$	
	$2\frac{1}{8}$	T	No	No	One $\frac{1}{2}''$	....	......	.....	One $\frac{1}{2}''$	
	$2\frac{1}{8}$	No	2-L	No	......	2	......	.....	One $\frac{1}{2}''$	
48	$2\frac{1}{8}$	A	2-K	No	......	2	......	.....	One $\frac{1}{2}''$	
49	$2\frac{1}{8}$	T	2-L	No	......	2	......	.....	One $\frac{1}{2}''$	
50	$2\frac{1}{8}$	A	2-L	No	......	2	.... .	.....	One $\frac{1}{2}''$	
51	$1\frac{1}{2}$[a]	No	No	No	One $\frac{1}{2}''$	....	......	....	One $\frac{1}{2}''$	

[a] Straight through nail holes.

Data on Wiring Boxes (*Continued*)

Utility Boxes
$3\frac{3}{4}$ by $1\frac{1}{2}$ by $1\frac{1}{2}$ In.

Sketch	Sketch No.	Bracket	Knockouts		
			Each end	Each side	Bottom
Sketch 52	52	None	One $\frac{1}{2}''$	Three $\frac{1}{2}''$	Three $\frac{1}{2}''$

4 by $2\frac{1}{8}$ by $1\frac{1}{2}$ In.

	53	None	One $\frac{1}{2}''$	Three $\frac{1}{2}''$	Three $\frac{1}{2}''$
Sketch 53		B	One $\frac{1}{2}''$	Three $\frac{1}{2}''$ one side	Three $\frac{1}{2}''$
Sketch 54	54	None	One $\frac{1}{2}''$	Three $\frac{1}{2}''$	

4 by $2\frac{1}{8}$ by $1\frac{7}{8}$ In.

		None	One $\frac{1}{2}''$	Three $\frac{1}{2}''$	Three $\frac{1}{2}''$
Sketch 55		A	One $\frac{1}{2}''$	Three $\frac{1}{2}''$ one side	Three $\frac{1}{2}''$
	55	F	One $\frac{1}{2}''$	Three $\frac{1}{2}''$ one side	Three $\frac{1}{2}''$
Sketch 56	56	None	One $\frac{3}{4}''$	Two $\frac{3}{4}''$	Two $\frac{3}{4}''$

4 by $2\frac{1}{8}$ by $2\frac{1}{8}$ In.

		None	One $\frac{1}{2}''$	Three $\frac{1}{2}''$	Three $\frac{1}{2}''$
	57	A	One $\frac{1}{2}''$	Three $\frac{1}{2}''$ one side	Three $\frac{1}{2}''$
	58	B	One $\frac{1}{2}''$	Three $\frac{1}{2}''$ one side	Three $\frac{1}{2}''$
Sketch 57		F	One $\frac{1}{2}''$	Three $\frac{1}{2}''$ one side	Three $\frac{1}{2}''$
		None	One $\frac{3}{4}''$	Two $\frac{3}{4}''$	Two $\frac{3}{4}''$
		B	One $\frac{3}{4}''$	Two $\frac{3}{4}''$ one side	Two $\frac{3}{4}''$
Sketch 58		O	One $\frac{3}{4}''$	Two $\frac{3}{4}''$ one side	Two $\frac{3}{4}''$

Data on Wiring Boxes (*Continued*)

Standard Gang Boxes 1⅝ In. Deep., 4½ In. Wide

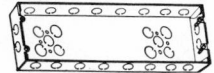

Knockouts						No. of gangs	Length outside, in.
Sides		Ends		Bottoms			
½ in.	¾ in.	½ in.	¾ in.	½ in.	¾ in.		
8	...	4	...	3	2	2	6¹³⁄₁₆
...	8	...	4	3	2	2	6¹³⁄₁₆
4	4	2	2	3	2	2	6¹³⁄₁₆
10	...	4	...	6	4	3	8⅝
...	10	...	4	6	4	3	8⅝
6	4	2	2	6	4	3	8⅝
12	...	4	...	6	4	4	10½
...	12	...	4	6	4	4	10½
6	6	2	2	6	4	4	10½
14	...	4	...	6	4	5	12¼
...	14	...	4	6	4	5	12¼
8	6	2	2	6	4	5	12¼
16	...	4	...	6	4	6	14¹⁄₁₆
...	16	...	4	6	4	6	14¹⁄₁₆
8	8	2	2	6	4	6	14¹⁄₁₆
18	...	4	...	6	4	7	15¹⁵⁄₁₆
...	18	...	4	6	4	7	15¹⁵⁄₁₆
10	8	2	2	6	4	7	15¹⁵⁄₁₆
20	...	4	...	6	4	8	17⅝
...	20	...	4	6	4	8	17⅝
10	10	2	2	6	4	8	17⅝
22	...	4	...	6	4	9	19½
...	22	...	4	6	4	9	19½
12	10	2	2	6	4	9	19½

3-gang box will take both 3 and 4 gang covers.   4-gang box will take both 4 and 5 gang covers. 5-gang box will take both 5 and 6 gang covers.   6-gang box will take both 6 and 7 gang covers.   7-gang box will take both 7 and 8 gang covers.   8-gang box will take both 8 and 9 gang covers.   9 gang box will take both 9 and 10 gang covers.

Concrete Boxes			Concrete Box Plates

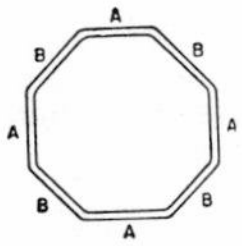

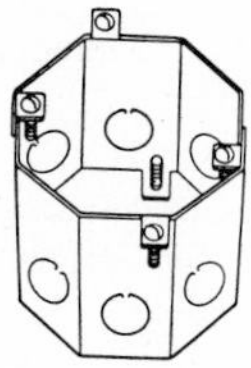

	Depth, in.	Knockouts	
		A, in.	B, in.
	2	½	¾
	2½	½	¾
	3	½	¾
	3	¾	1
	3½	½	¾
	3½	¾	1
	4	½	¾
	4	¾	1
	5	½	¾
	6	½	¾

Three ½″ K.O., two ¾″ K.O., no stud

Two ½″ K.O., two ¾″ K.O., ⅜″ stud

114. Box Covers

Illustration	Description
For 3¼-in. Round and Octagonal Boxes	
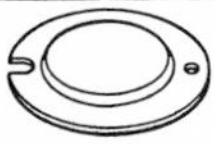	Raised, closed; ⅜ in. deep
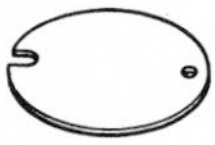	Flat, closed
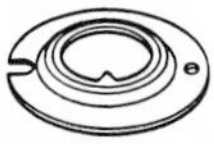	Raised, with 1²¹⁄₃₂-in. keyed opening for Federal sign receptacle. ⅜ in. deep
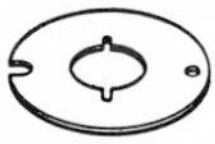	Flat, with 1⁹⁄₁₆-in. opening and screw holes on 1¾-in. centers for Benjamin sign receptacle
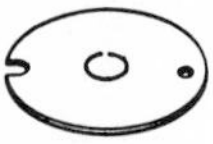	Flat, with ½-in. knockout in center
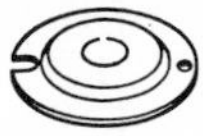	Raised, with ½-in. knockout in center; ⅜-in. deep
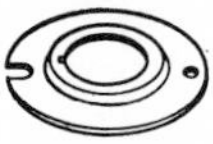	Raised, with 1½-in. opening for sign receptacles notched for protruding lug on porcelain; ⅜ in. deep
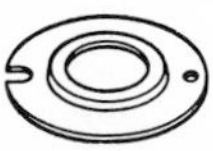	Raised, with 1½-in. diameter opening and bent tongue to fit notches in new standard sign receptacles; ⅜ in. deep
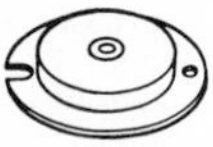	Raised, with ²⁷⁄₆₄-in. metal eyelet for drop cord; ⅜ in. deep
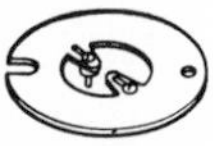	Flat, with slots for surface devices; opening 1¹⁵⁄₁₆ in., screw centers ¹⁵⁄₁₆ in. to 1¹³⁄₁₆ in.
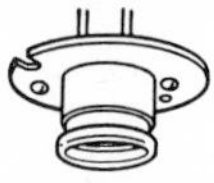	Cover with pigtail receptacle
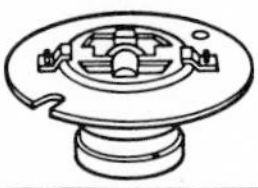	Cover with terminal receptacle
For 3½-in. Round and Octagonal Boxes	
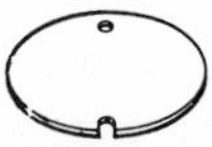	Flat, closed
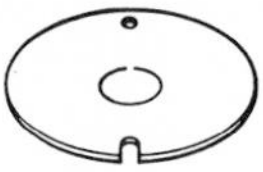	Flat with ½-in. knockout in center
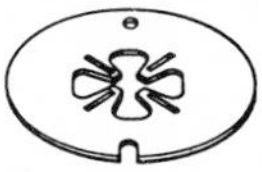	Flat with slots for surface devices
	Raised, closed; ⅝ in. deep
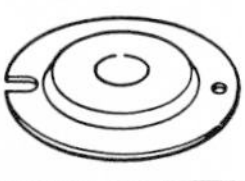	Raised with ½-in. knockout in center, ⅝ in. deep
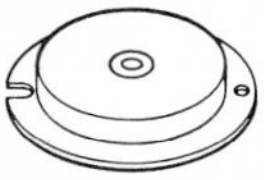	Raised with ⅜-in. eyelet; ⅝ in. deep
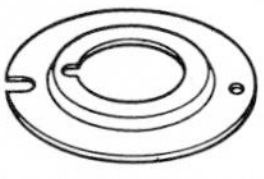	Raised with 1½-in. grooved opening; ⅝ in. deep
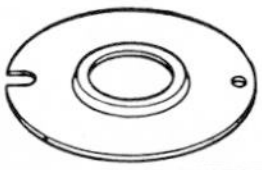	Raised with plain 1½-in. opening; ⅝ in. deep
For 4-in. Round and Octagonal Boxes	
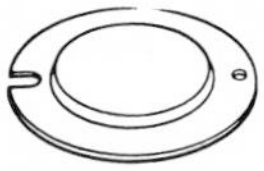	Raised, closed, ⅝ in. deep
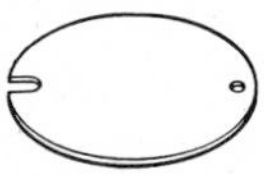	Flat, closed
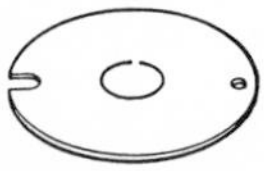	Flat, with ½-in. knockout in center
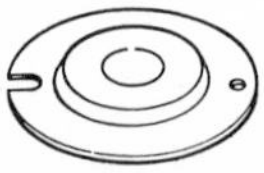	Raised, with ½-in. knockout in center; ⅝ in. deep
	Raised, with 2¾-in. opening; ⅝ in. deep

Box Covers *(Continued)*

Illustration	Description
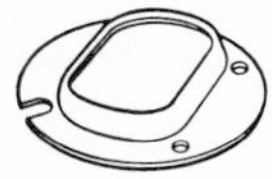	Raised, $\frac{5}{8}$ in. high, for one flush device; also suitable for bracket outlet
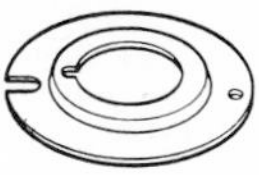	Raised, $\frac{5}{8}$ in. high with $1\frac{1}{2}$ in. diameter opening for sign receptacles notched for protruding lug on porcelain
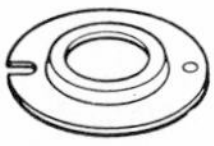	Raised $\frac{5}{8}$-in., with $1\frac{1}{2}$-in. diameter opening and bent tongue to fit notches in new standard sign receptacles
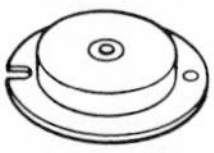	Raised $\frac{5}{8}$ in., with $\frac{27}{64}$-in. metal eyelet for drop cord
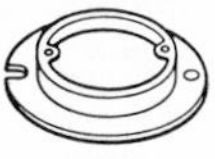	Raised $\frac{5}{8}$ in., $2\frac{3}{4}$ in. opening, $1\frac{1}{16}$ in. deep lugs tapped 8-32 on $2\frac{3}{4}$-in. centers
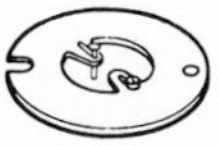	Flat, with slots for surface devices; opening $1\frac{15}{16}$ in., screw centers $1\frac{5}{16}$ to $1\frac{13}{16}$ in.; two $\frac{7}{8}$-in. × 6-32 screws
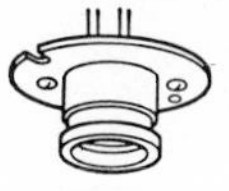	Cover with pigtail receptacle
	Cover with terminal receptacle
For 4-in. Square Boxes	
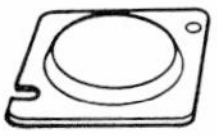	Raised, closed, $\frac{5}{8}$ in. deep
	Flat closed cover
	Flat with $\frac{1}{2}$-in. knockout in center
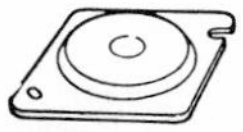	Raised, $\frac{5}{8}$ in. deep with $\frac{1}{2}$-in. knockout in center
	Raised with $2\frac{3}{4}$-in. opening; $\frac{5}{8}$ in. deep

Illustration	Description
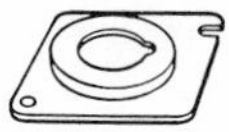	Raised with $1\frac{1}{2}$-in. opening for sign receptacles, notched for protruding lug on porcelain; $\frac{5}{8}$ in. deep
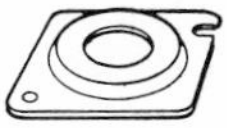	Raised with $1\frac{1}{2}$-in. opening and bent tongue to fit notches in new standard sign receptacle; $\frac{5}{8}$ in. deep
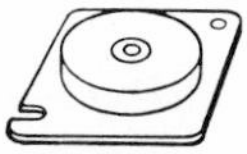	Raised with $\frac{27}{64}$-in. metal eyelet for drop cord; $\frac{5}{8}$ in. deep
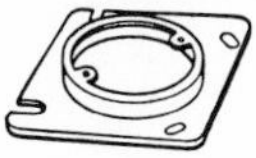	Raised with $2\frac{3}{4}$-in. opening, $\frac{5}{8}$ in. deep; lugs tapped 8-32 on $2\frac{3}{4}$-in. centers
	Flat, with slots for surface devices, opening $1\frac{15}{16}$ in., screw centers $1\frac{5}{16}$ and $1\frac{13}{16}$ in.
For 4-in. Square Boxes to Accommodate Flush Wiring Devices with Flush Plate Covers	
	Raised $\frac{1}{4}$ in. for one-gang plate
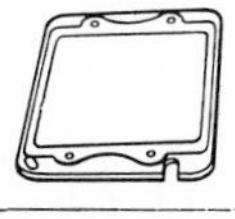	Raised $\frac{1}{4}$ in. for two-gang plate
	Raised $\frac{1}{2}$ in. for one-gang plate
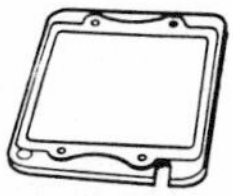	Raised $\frac{1}{2}$ in. for two-gang plate
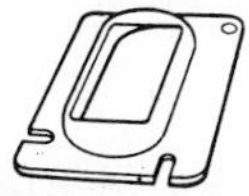	Raised $\frac{3}{4}$ in. for one-gang plate
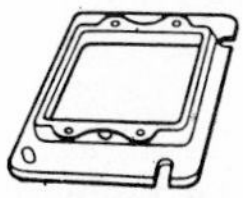	Raised $\frac{3}{4}$ in. for two-gang plate
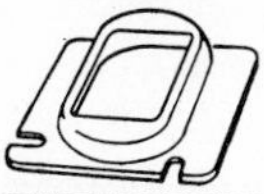	Raised 1 in. for one-gang plate

Box Covers (Continued)

Illustration	Description	Illustration	Description
	Raised 1 in. for two-gang plate		Raised ½ in.; for one push-button switch and one single flush receptacle
	Raised 1¼ in. for one-gang plate		Raised ½ in.; for one square-handle toggle switch and one single flush receptacle
	Raised 1¼ in. for two-gang plate		Raised ½ in.; for one push-button switch and one duplex receptacle
For 4-in. Square Boxes for Accommodating Flush Wiring Devices in Exposed Wiring			Raised ½-in.; for one square-handle toggle switch and one duplex receptacle
	Raised ½ in.; for one push-button switch	**For 4¹¹⁄₁₆-in. Square Boxes**	
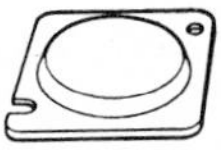	Raised ½ in.; for one square-handle toggle switch		Raised, closed; ⅝ in. deep
	Raised ½ in.; for one single flush receptacle		Flat, closed
	Raised ½ in.; for one duplex receptacle		Flat with ½-in. knockout in center
	Raised ½ in.; for two push-button switches		Raised, with ½-in. knockout in center; ⅝ in. deep
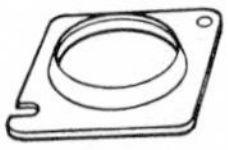	Raised ½ in.; for two square-handle toggle switches		Raised, with 2¾-in. opening; ⅝ in. deep
	Raised ½ in.; for two single flush receptacles		Raised, with 2⁷⁄₆₄-in. metal eyelet for drop cord; ⅝ in. deep
	Raised ½ in.; for two duplex receptacles		Raised, with 2¾-in. opening, ⅝-in. deep; lugs tapped 8-32 on 2¾-in. centers

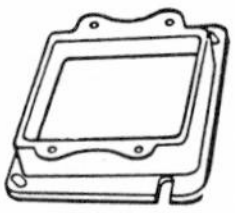

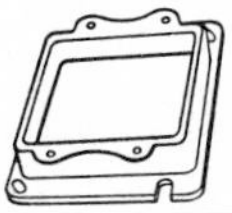

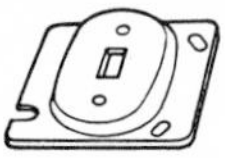

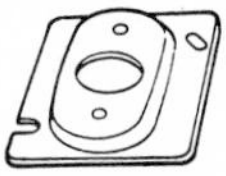

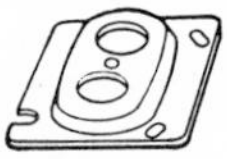

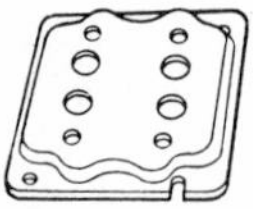

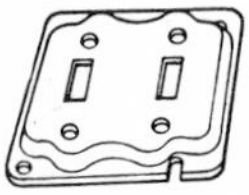

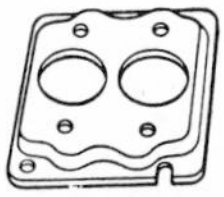

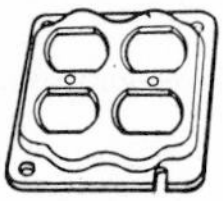

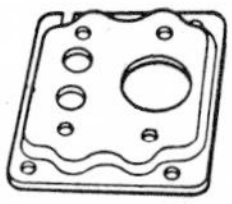

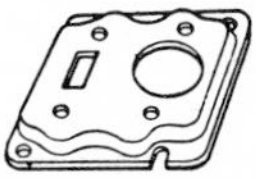

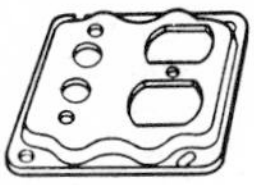

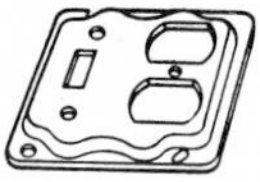

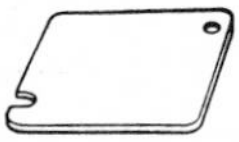

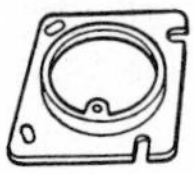

Box Covers (*Continued*)

Illustration	Description	Illustration	Description
For 4¹¹⁄₁₆-in. Square Boxes for Accommodating Flush Wiring Devices and Flush Plate Covers		For Utility Boxes	
	Raised ¾ in. for one-gang plate		Blank
	Raised 1 in. for one-gang plate		For single push-button switch
	Raised 1¼ in. for one-gang plate		For standard duplex receptacle
	Raised ¾ in. for two-gang plate		For standard square-handle toggle switch
For Oblong Gang Boxes for Accommodating Flush Wiring Devices and Flush Plate Covers			For single T-slot and Edison-base receptacle
	Available for two-, three-, four-, five-, six-, seven-, eight-, and nine-gang flush plates		Cover with knockouts for inter-changeable devices

115. Nonmetallic Boxes. The material used in the construction of nonmetallic boxes is porcelain, polyvinyl chloride (PVC), or Bakelite. Except for surface-type wiring with nonmetallic-sheathed cable, porcelain boxes are not used because they are easily broken.

Polyvinyl chloride (PVC) boxes are widely used with rigid nonmetallic conduits, and the boxes are shaped similar to the more common metal types. Refer to Div. 9 for uses of these boxes with nonmetallic conduits.

When nonmetallic-sheathed cable or knob-and-tube wiring is used for concealed work, the most popular and desirable nonmetallic boxes are fiber-reinforced Bakelite types. These boxes are very rugged and are available in many popular sizes. Figure 150 shows photos of a ceiling outlet and a device box. In Fig. 150a the Bakelite box contains an integral mounting bracket and nails. This 3½-in.-round, 2-in.-deep box has the equivalent internal cubic inch capacity of a 4 × 1½ in. metal octagonal box. Also the box can be quickly secured to wood members.

The Bakelite deep box in Fig. 150b is 3 in. deep and has the equivalent internal cubic inch capacity of a 3½ × 2 × 3 in. metal device box.

Both boxes shown in Fig. 150 have no cable clamps. As a result, this permits one more wire in the box in determining the maximum number according to section 370-6(a) of the National Electrical Code. Without cable clamps nonmetallic sheathed cables must be supported within 8 in. of nonmetallic boxes. Another important advantage is that no grounding connection is required to the box as with metallic boxes. When nonmetallic cables, which contain grounding wires, enter nonmetallic boxes, they are spliced together with an approved solderless pigtail connector. If a grounding-type receptacle is attached to a nonmetallic box, the pigtail connection should include a short lead for connection to the grounding terminal on the receptacle.

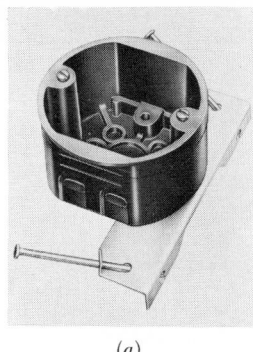 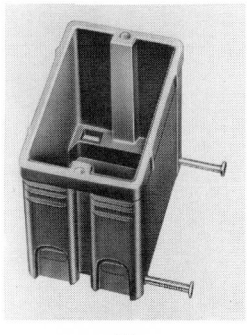

(a)   (b)

FIG. 150   *Typical nonmetallic boxes constructed of Bakelite with reinforced fibers.* (*Union Insulating Co.*)

If a metallic switch plate is to be attached to a flush switch, switches are available with a grounding terminal. Then the grounding conductor of the supply cable is connected to this terminal, and the metal frame of the switch is grounded, which, in turn, will ground the attached metal switch plate. Such switches should be used if the switch attached to a nonmetallic box is located within 5 ft horizontally or 8 ft vertically of a grounded object (water pipes, concrete floors, etc.).

116. Flush plates are covers which are used with flush wiring devices in concealed wiring installations in order to produce a neat covering of the outlet. They are supported by screws turning into tapped holes in mounting ears or straps on sectional boxes or on covers for square or oblong boxes as described in Sec. **114.** Holes in the plates accommodate the handles of flush switches or plugs for flush receptacles. They are made in single-, two-, and three-gang sizes with various types and combinations of openings to meet almost any combination of flush wiring devices. Flush plates made of Bakelite, brass, enameled metal, or stainless steel can be obtained. The standard finish for brass plates is brush brass. Plates can be obtained with almost any special finish in order to meet the requirements of any interior. Some of these special finishes are listed below:

FLUSH PLATE FINISHES

Aluminum (spray).	Bronze, polished.	Gilt, rich.
Barff, Bauer lacquer.	statuary (light).	Gun metal.
Black lacquer.	Brown lacquer (imita-	Ivory enamel.
Brass, sand blast,	tion Bakelite).	Nickel, dull.
antique.	Cadmium, brushed.	polished.
sand blast, brush.	polished.	Silver, butler's
Flemish.	Chromium, dull.	(brushed).
lemon.	polished.	oxidized.
oxidized.	Copper, antique.	polished.
polished.	brush.	satin.
Bronze antique.	mottled.	Verde-antique lacquer.
brush.	oxidized.	White enamel.
Japanese (dark).	polished.	Various colors.
		Wood grain.

Flush plates are made for the standard and interchangeable lines of wiring devices. Typical plates are shown in Figs. 151 and 151A. Some manufacturers offer engraved plates to identify standard or special equipment.

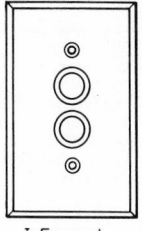
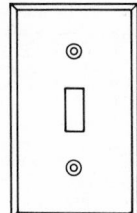
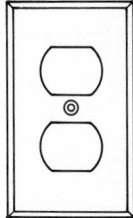
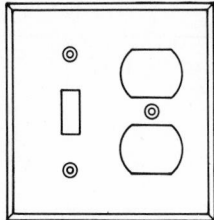

I-For push-
button switch

II-For tumbler
switch

III-For double
receptacle

IV-Two-gang for
tumbler switch and
double receptacle

FIG. 151 *Flush plates for standard-line wiring devices.*

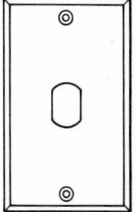
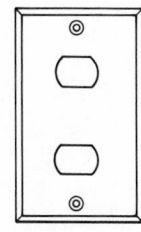

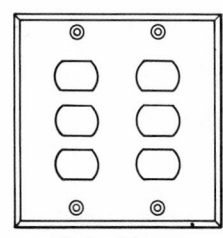

I -Single-gang
for one device

II-Single-gang
for two devices

III-Single-gang
for three devices

IV-Double-gang
for six devices

FIG. 151A *Flush plates for interchangeable-line wiring devices.*

117. Types of Mounting Features for Sectional Boxes

Name	Illustration	Description
Standard mounting ears		Box equipped with two ears, one secured to each end of box with two 8-32 large fillister-head screws. Ears adjustable and reversible. Set of extra holes (not tapped) in each side for changing position of ears to sides if desired (8-32 tap required)
Rectangular mounting bracket without lath support		For plaster or wallboard jobs, with holes for gripping plaster and with aligning-cleat prongs and four nail holes. Bracket is perfectly flat so it does not interfere with wallboard. Bracket is welded to box
Extended mounting ears	Ears on ends for vertical mounting in plaster with lath support.	For mounting in plaster or baseboard. Each ear fastened to box with two 8-32 fillister-head screws. Can be located on sides or ends. Tapped mounting holes supplied regularly only on ends. Aligning cleat prongs and adequate nail holes for rigid fastening
Box supports and lath holders		For mounting in plaster walls. Supports available in lengths of 16½, 18½, 20½, 22½, 24½, and 26½ in.
Rectangular mounting bracket with lath support		Same as item 2 with lath supports welded to box for wood-lath or wallboard jobs. Back lip of support projects beyond front lip providing adequate support behind wall board and still retaining channel for supporting end of wood lath front and back
Extended mounting ears	Ears on sides for horizontal mounting in baseboards. Ears on sides for horizontal mounting in plaster. Ears on ends for vertical mounting in plaster without lath support.	For mounting in plaster or baseboard. Each ear fastened to box with two 8-32 fillister-head screws. Can be located on sides or ends. Tapped mounting holes supplied regularly only on ends. Aligning cleat prongs and adequate nail holes for rigid fastening

118. Depth of Outlet Boxes. The National Electrical Code specifies that outlet boxes must have an internal depth of at least 1½ in. for concealed work except that, where the installation of such a box is impracticable, a box of not less than ½ in. internal depth may be used. Outlet boxes with conduits entering the side should be 2⅛ in. deep for installation in lath and plaster. Boxes 1½ in. deep will generally be satisfactory for brickwork. The shallow boxes of ½- or ¾-in. depth are sometimes used on terra-cotta ceilings with the box set on the surface of the tile and embedded in the plaster. The conduits are brought into the back of the box.

119. Metal straps for supporting outlet boxes can be obtained in various types with or without attached fixture studs. Several representative types are described below.

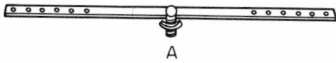

A

For shallow boxes in new work or for holding boxes to concrete forms. With boxes of a depth of ½ in., where bar is nailed to joists or studding, edge of box will be flush with ordinary plaster. Will fit any box having ½-in. knockout. Made in 18- and 24-in. lengths.

B

For boxes 1½ in. deep without switch covers or plaster rings; offset brings box edge flush with plaster. Will fit any box having ½-in. knockout. Length of bar 19½ in. Offset 1¹⁄₁₆ in. deep.

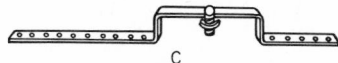

C

For boxes 1½ in. deep with switch covers or plaster rings; offset brings covers ⅝ in. high, flush with plaster. Will fit any box having ½-in. knockout. Length of bar 19½ in. Offset 1¹¹⁄₁₆ in. deep.

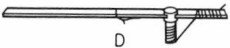

D

For mounting shallow boxes or plates in buildings already plastered. Make a small hole about 1½ in. in diameter; push bar all the way into hole, long end first as shown in cut; hold stud in one hand and pull wire with the other until bar is centered across hole. Will fit any box having ½-in. knockout. Length of bar 12 in.

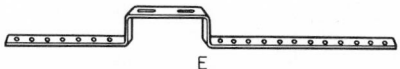

E

For boxes 1½ in. deep with covers and integral studs, or without studs. Offset has slots for stove bolts to hold box and is right depth to bring ⅝-in. covers flush with plaster. Length of bar 21 in. Offset 1¹¹⁄₁₆ in. deep.

120. Wallboard Hanger (General Electric Co.). Instructions for supporting a switch box with a special wallboard hanger are given below and illustrated in Fig. 152.

For installing switch boxes in old work where plaster, wallboard, plasterboard, or similar construction is present:

1. Cut hole exact size of switch box.
2. Assemble switch box and hanger. Only partially tighten bolt.
3. Push assembly into wall hole until the sides of the hanger spring free on inside wall.
4. Tighten by screwing bolt on inside of box.

Inside and outside pressure against the wall give box a rigid installation.

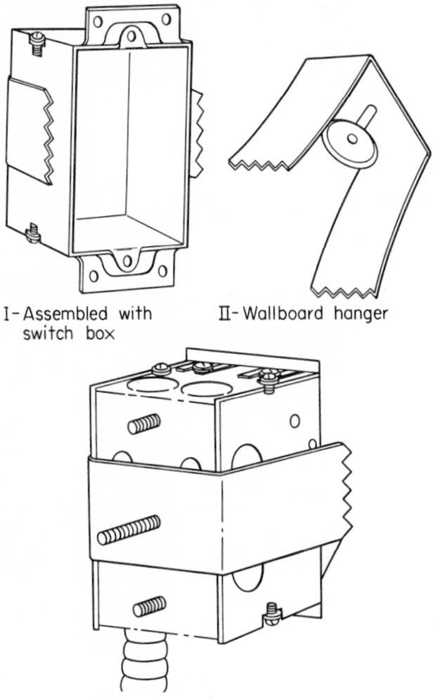

Metal cap

Blank plug

Floor plate

Gasket

Receptacle

Adjusting ring provides $3/4$" vertical adjustment

Threaded steel cover

Box body with adjusting screws (made in sheet steel or threaded cast–iron assemblies)

I–Assembled with switch box

II–Wallboard hanger

III– Rear view, installed

FIG. 152 *Wallboard switch hanger.* *(General Electric Co.)*

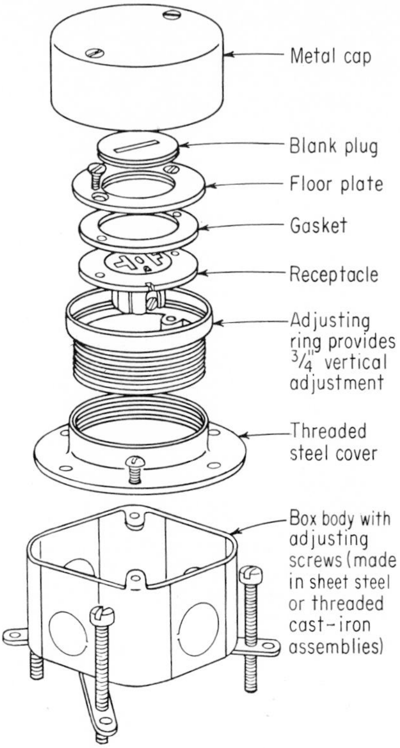

FIG. 153 *Adjustable floor box with flush grounding-type receptacle.* *(Steel City Div. of Midland-Ross Corp.)*

121. Floor boxes (Fig. 153) are made in adjustable and nonadjustable types for providing outlets from concealed conduits embedded in floors. The adjustable ones allow the top to be adjusted in height and angle to suit the floor conditions. They may be obtained in single- and multiple-outlet units.

122. Door boxes (Fig. 154) are for the installation of door switches in the jamb of the door. They are made in different types in order to accommodate the different types of door switches.

123. Pull boxes are described in Div. 9.

124. Lamp holders consist of an assembly for supporting lamps, comprising the lamp socket, protective and insulating covering, and means for attachment to some form of support. The term socket is sometimes incorrectly used in place of lamp holder. Each lamp holder must have a lamp socket, but the socket is only the part of the lamp holder which engages with the base or terminal of the lamp. Lamp holders are

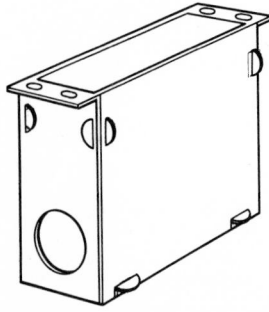

FIG. 154 *One type of door box.*

made in a great variety of types in order to fulfill the requirements of all classes of installations and types of lamp bases.

125. Brass-shell-type interchangeable lamp holders are the old standard type for incandescent lamps. They consist of two fundamental parts, a body (Fig. 155, III)

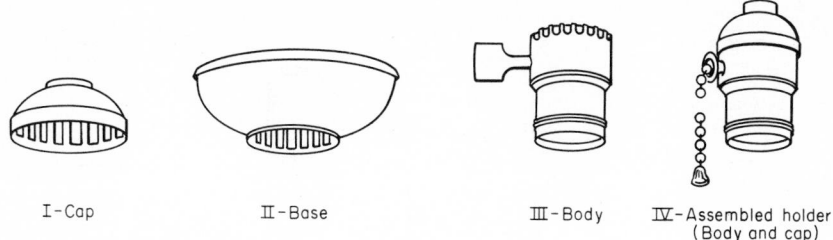

I–Cap   II–Base   III–Body   IV–Assembled holder
                                                        (Body and cap)

FIG. 155   *Fluted-catch interchangeable lamp holders.   (General Electric Co.)*

and a cap (Fig. 155, I) or base (Fig. 155, II). The two parts are held together by means of a fluted catch which allows them to be easily separated or assembled. Any cap or base can be used with any body. The body consists of the socket mounted on a porcelain or composition support and encased in an outside brass shell. The socket is insulated from the shell by means of a fiber casing. When the porcelain or composition portion of the body simply forms a support and assembly for the socket and electric circuit connecting screws, it is known as a keyless body. If the body contains a small switch for turning the lamp on or off, it may be of the key, pull-chain, or push type (Fig. 156). Caps are made with standard inside pipe thread for connection to $1/8$-, $1/4$-, $3/8$-, or $1/2$-in. pipe or with $3/8$-in. male thread. Caps are also constructed with porcelain- or composition-bushed holes or with cord-lamp grip for pendant support on a drop cord. The cord holes are 0.406 in. in diameter, and the cord grips will accommodate cords from 0.375 to 0.5000 in. in diameter. Bases are available for mounting directly on outlet boxes and for exposed wiring either of the cleat-mounting or concealed-base type.

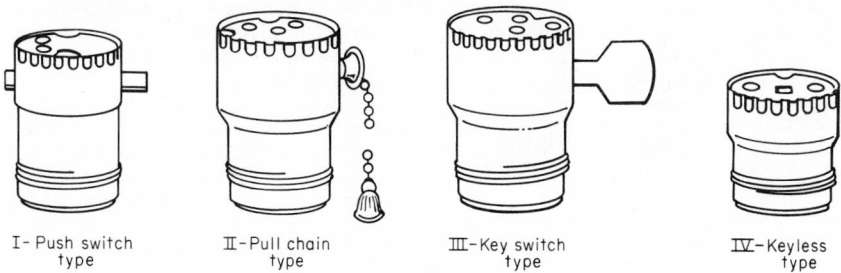

I– Push switch   II–Pull chain   III–Key switch   IV–Keyless
     type   type   type   type

FIG. 156   *Types of fluted-catch lamp-holder bodies.   (Pass & Seymour, Inc.)*

126. Threaded-catch interchangeable lamp holders for incandescent lamps (Fig. 157) are a newer development. They consist of a body fastened by means of a threaded ring to a cap or base. The bodies, caps, and bases may have outer brass shells or may be made of composition. The same types of bodies, caps, and bases are made as for the fluted-catch ones of Sec. 125. The line is interchangeable in that any cap or base will fit any body.

127. The porcelain snap-catch interchangeable line of lamp holders for incandescent lamps (Fig. 158) is used in installations subjected to moisture, acid fumes, or other corroding influences. The bodies are fitted with two bayonet hooks which engage two flexible phosphor-bronze contacts in the cap or base. The two parts are thus securely locked together when assembled but permit easy disassembly without affecting the wiring. The bayonet hooks and bronze contact catches provide the electrical connection between cap and body as well as supplying the means of mechanically supporting the body from the cap. The same general types of caps, bases, and bodies are included in this line as for the fluted-catch line. A porcelain line for the same type of applications is made with the cap and body fastened together by means of two screws.

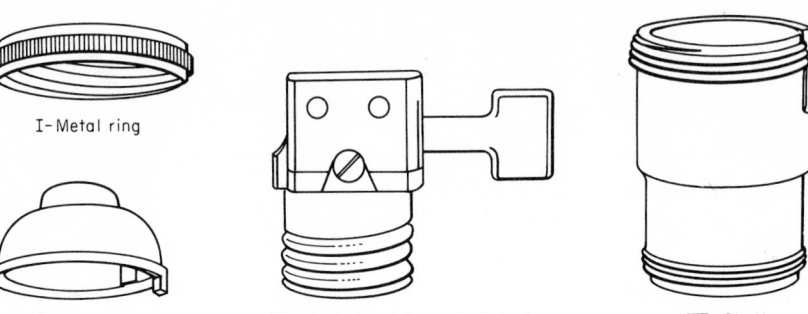

I-Metal ring

II-Cap   III-Socket and key switch body   IV-Shell

FIG. 157 *Threaded-catch interchangeable lamp holders. The threaded metal ring (I), knurled to provide a grip, holds the cap and shell together. The cap (II) cannot pull loose from the shell, and no amount of vibration will loosen the threaded ring when properly assembled. A lug in the cap fits in the shell slot, preventing rotation between cap and shell. After the cap has been fitted to the shell, the flange on the threaded ring fits over the flange on the cap, and the ring is securely threaded to the shell. (General Electric Co.)*

128. Noninterchängeable lamp holders are made in a great variety of types to meet the requirements for lamp holders for show-window, show-case, cove, trough, or reflector lighting; candelabra or intermediate-base lamps; lumiline or fluorescent lamps; mounting on outlet boxes; mounting in fixture canopies; lamp outlets in exposed wiring on insulators; and sign lighting, etc. Most of these holders are made of porcelain, but plastic materials are used to a limited extent. A few of the more common types are shown in Fig. 159.

Phosphor bronze contact catches   Bayonet hooks

I Assembled holder of key switch type   II Cap   III Push switch body

FIG. 158 *Porcelain snap-catch interchangeable lamp holders. (General Electric Co.)*

129. Holders are available for surface mounting for use primarily in installations wired with nonmetallic-sheathed cable (Figs. 160 and 161). For dry locations these holders have cases of all-plastic construction. Holders for excessively moist or dusty locations have porcelain bases and plastic tops. Both types are made in keyless and pull-chain constructions.

130. Weatherproof lamp holders (Fig. 162) with one-piece porcelain, composition, or rubber cases are made with sealed-in leads for wet locations.

131. Shade Holders. Many lamp holders have the body supplied with threads or grooves for engaging shade holders. Shade holders are made with openings of 2¼,

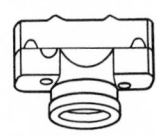

I A plastic body lampholder for outlet box mounting. Porcelain holders of same type more commonly used.   II Screw ring porcelain lampholder for mounting in fixture canopies   III Porcelain lampholder for surface mounting   IV Porcelain lampholder for surface mounting in cleat wiring installation

FIG. 159 *A few types of interchangeable lamp holders.*

FIG. 160 *All-plastic lamp holders for use with nonmetallic sheathed cable. (Pass & Seymour, Inc.)*

FIG. 161 *Porcelain-base lamp holders for use with nonmetallic-sheathed cable. (Pass & Seymour, Inc.)*

3¼, and 4 in. diameter for accommodating shades. Shades may be held to the shade holder with a wire spring or by means of screws (Fig. 163).

132. Insulating socket bushings must be used where a cord enters a socket to protect it against abrasion and grounding against the shell. The most popular bushings are of hard rubber or of a compound resembling it. Patented bushings which automatically grip the cord by a wedging action can be purchased.

Most lamp holders of the pendant type are fitted with an approved bushing constructed as an integral part of the lampholder cap.

133. Rosettes are devices for supporting and connecting to the circuit the cord and sockets of flexible drop cords. They are made in different types for open wiring and for attaching to outlet boxes or moldings.

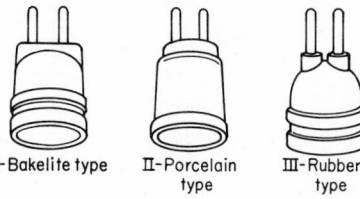

I-Bakelite type   II-Porcelain type   III-Rubber type

FIG. 162 *Weatherproof lamp holders. (General Electric Co.)*

Rosettes similar to the one shown in Fig. 164 are used for open wiring work, and ones similar to that of Fig. 165 for attachment to outlet boxes. The drop cord passes through the hole in the center and is attached to connections inside the body of the rosette. The connections should be relieved of any strain by making a knot in the wires just inside

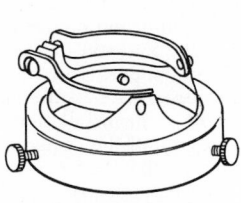 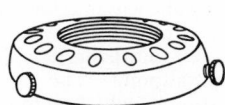 

I-Clamp type for lampholders with grooves

II-Threaded type for lampholders with threads. Supporting screws for shade

III-Threaded type with wire spring support for shade

FIG. 163 *Shade holders. (Pass & Seymour, Inc.)*

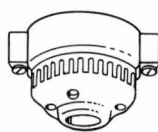 

FIG. 164 *Cleat-base rosette for open wiring.*

FIG. 165 *Rosette for attachment to outlet box.*

the rosette body. Fused rosettes were at one time employed, but they are no longer allowed by the National Electrical Code rules.

An all-plastic rosette for use with nonmetallic-sheathed cable is shown in Fig. 166.

134. Lamp holders for fluorescent lamps are available in various types to meet all the usual conditions of installation. Combination lamp holders and starter sockets also are available. Typical constructions are shown in Fig. 167.

POWER CAPACITORS

135. Power capacitors are capacitors with relatively large values of capacity which are used on power-distribution systems or

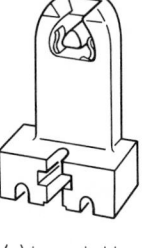
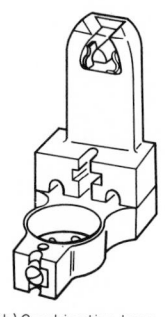

(a) Lamp holder

(b) Combination lamp holder and starter socket

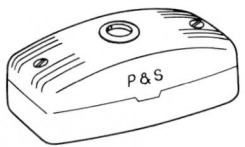

FIG. 166 *All-plastic rosette for use with nonmetallic-sheathed cable. (Pass & Seymour Inc.)*

FIG. 167 *Lamp holders for fluorescent lamps. (Harvey Hubbell, Inc.)*

in industrial plants for improving the power factor. Since many power companies include low-power-factor penalties, kilovolt-ampere demand rates, or power-factor bonuses in their rate schedules, it is often economical for industrial consumers to install capacitors for power-factor improvement. These capacitors are connected across the line and neutralize the effect of lagging power-factor loads, thus reducing the current for a given kilowatt load. The amount of reactive kilovolt-amperes of capacitors required to raise the power factor to any given value can easily be determined from the chart of Fig. 168.

The best point to connect capacitors to the circuit depends upon cost considerations. Relatively small capacitor units, A in Fig. 169, can be connected at the individual loads, or the total capacitor kilovolt-amperes can be grouped at one point and connected to the main bus. Both of these methods are shown schematically in Fig. 169. Greater power-factor corrective effect for a given total capacitor kilovolt-ampere will result with the capacitors located directly at each individual load, since the current is thereby reduced all the way from the load to the source. The first cost of an installation of individual capacitors will be greater, however, than that for one unit of the same total kilovolt-amperes located at a central point. The greater saving in operating expense due to individual capacitors must be weighed against their increased first cost.

136. A complete capacitor bank is made up of the necessary standard units to give the desired kilovolt-amperes, connected in parallel with each other. Each unit consists of one or more cells enclosed in a hermetically sealed steel box (Fig. 170). The cells are aluminum-foil, paper-insulated capacitors impregnated with insulating oil or a nonflammable insulating medium. A nonflammable insulating medium is generally used, such as the General Electric Company's Pyranol or Westinghouse Electric Corporation's Inerteen. Standard units can be obtained with the cells internally connected for single-, two-, or three-phase operation. The units may be of enclosed- or rack-type construction. The enclosed construction is made primarily for individual motor applications (Fig. 174). It consists of a dusttight steel conduit box (Fig. 171) mounted on top of the hermetically sealed capacitor. The conduit box contains the terminals, discharge resistor, and fuses if desired (see Fig. 175). Rack-type banks consist of the required number of hermetically sealed capacitors with exposed terminals, supported on a steel rack. The complete structure may be provided with enclosing screens,

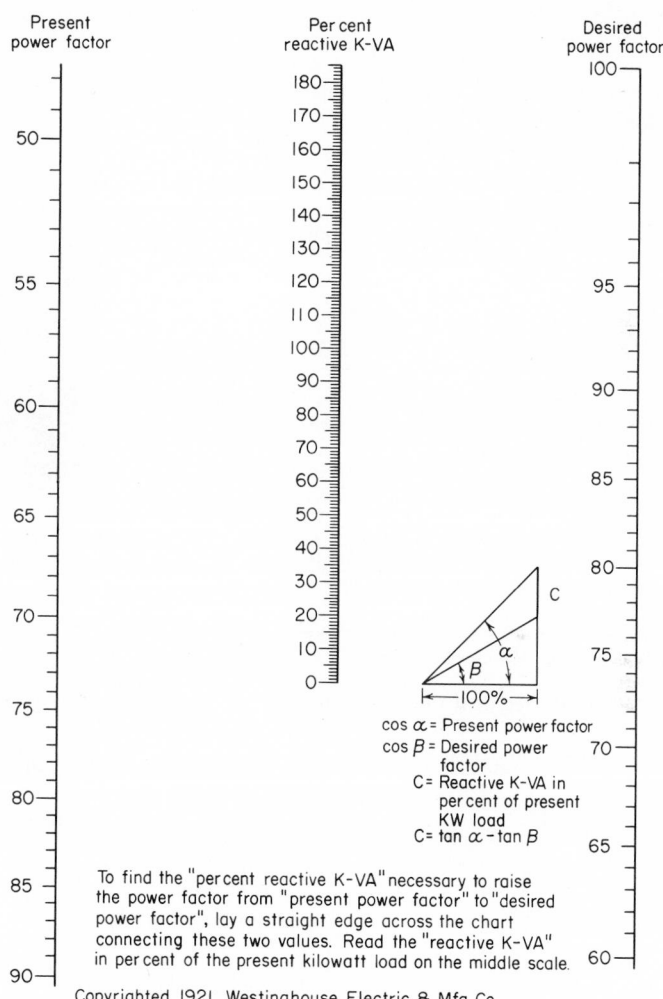

Present power factor

Per cent reactive K-VA

Desired power factor

cos α = Present power factor
cos β = Desired power factor
C = Reactive K-VA in per cent of present KW load
C = tan α – tan β

To find the "percent reactive K-VA" necessary to raise the power factor from "present power factor" to "desired power factor", lay a straight edge across the chart connecting these two values. Read the "reactive K-VA" in percent of the present kilowatt load on the middle scale.

Copyrighted 1921. Westinghouse Electric & Mfg. Co.

FIG. 168 *Chart for use in determining the percentage of reactive kva required to raise the power factor to a desired value.*

dusttight steel enclosing cases, or a steel enclosing cabinet for outdoor installation. Each capacitor unit of the bank is individually fused, and the entire bank is provided with discharge resistors or coils inside the enclosure (see Fig. 176). Typical assemblies for wall and ceiling mounting are shown in Figs. 172 and 173.

137. Drainage of Stored Charge. When capacitors are disconnected from the supply, they are generally in a charged state. Considerable energy is stored in the capacitor under this condition, and there is a voltage present between its terminals. If the capacitor were left in this charged state, a person servicing the equipment might receive a dangerous shock or the equipment might be damaged by an accidental short circuit. Therefore, all capacitors must be provided with a means of draining the stored charge (see Figs. 175 and 176). The National Electrical Code requires that the drainage equipment shall be so designed that it will discharge the capacitor to 50 volts or less within 1 min after the capacitor is disconnected from the source of supply in capacitors rated 600 volts or less and in 5 min in capacitors rated more than 600 volts. The discharge equipment may consist of resistors or inductive coils which are permanently connected to the terminals of the capacitor bank. If the discharge circuit is not permanently connected to the terminals of the capacitor bank, automatic means must be provided for connecting the capacitor to the discharge circuit on removal of supply voltage. When capacitors are connected directly to other equipment without switch or overcurrent device interposed, no discharge equipment is required, since the charge will drain off rapidly through the windings of the equipment (Fig. 174).

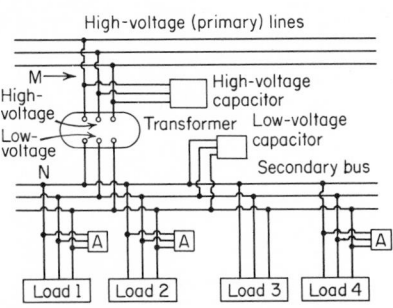

FIG. 169 *Location of capacitors on electric system. (General Electric Co.)*

FIG. 170 *Three-phase capacitor unit enclosed in a hermetically sealed steel box. (Westinghouse Electric Corp.)*

138. The National Electrical Code rules for size of conductors, overcurrent protection, and disconnecting means are given below:

1. CAPACITOR RATING. The total kvar rating of capacitors which are connected on the load side of a motor controller shall not exceed the value required to raise the no-load power factor of the motor to unity. (Capacitors of this maximum rating will usually result in a full-load power factor of 95 to 98 per cent. The maximum capacitor ratings permitted for use with NEMA-type three-phase 60-cycle Classification B motors are given in Table 11 of Div. 11.)

2. CAPACITOR CIRCUITS. Capacitor circuits shall conform to the following:

a. Conductor Ratings. The current-carrying capacity of capacitor circuit conductors shall be not less than 135 per cent of the rated current of the capacitor. The current-carrying capacity of conductors which connect a capacitor to the terminals of a motor or to motor circuit conductors shall be not less than one-third the carrying capacity of the motor circuit conductors but not less than 135 per cent of the rated current of the capacitor.

b. Overcurrent Protection. (1) An overcurrent device shall be provided in each ungrounded conductor.

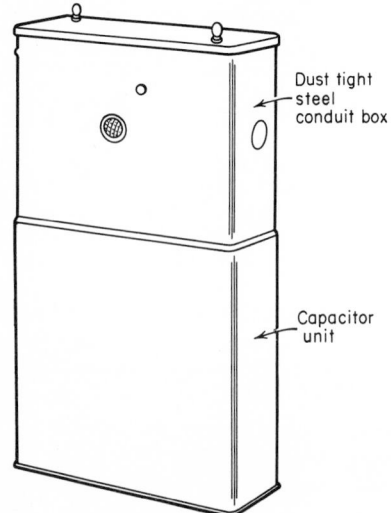

FIG. 171 *Enclosed capacitor unit.*

Exception: A separate overcurrent device is not required on the load side of a motor-running overcurrent device.

I. *Single-capacitor unit.* II. *Four-capacitor unit.*

FIG. 172 *Typical wall-mounting bracket capacitor assemblies. (Westinghouse Electric Corp.)*

FIG. 173 *Typical small rack capacitor bank for wall or ceiling mounting. (Westinghouse Electric Corp.)*

(2) The rating or setting of the overcurrent device shall be as low as practicable.

c. *Disconnecting Means.*

(1) A disconnecting means shall be provided in each ungrounded conductor.

Exception: A separate disconnecting means is not required for a capacitor connected on the load side of a motor overcurrent device.

(2) The disconnecting device need not open all ungrounded conductors simultaneously.

(3) The disconnecting device may be used for disconnecting the capacitor from the line as a regular operating procedure.

(4) The continuous current carrying capacity of the disconnecting device shall be not less than 135 per cent of the rated current of the capacitor.

3. RATING OR SETTING OF THE MOTOR OVERCURRENT DEVICE. Where a motor installation includes a capacitor connected on the load side of the motor-running overcurrent device and the overcurrent device used can be adjusted, the rating or setting

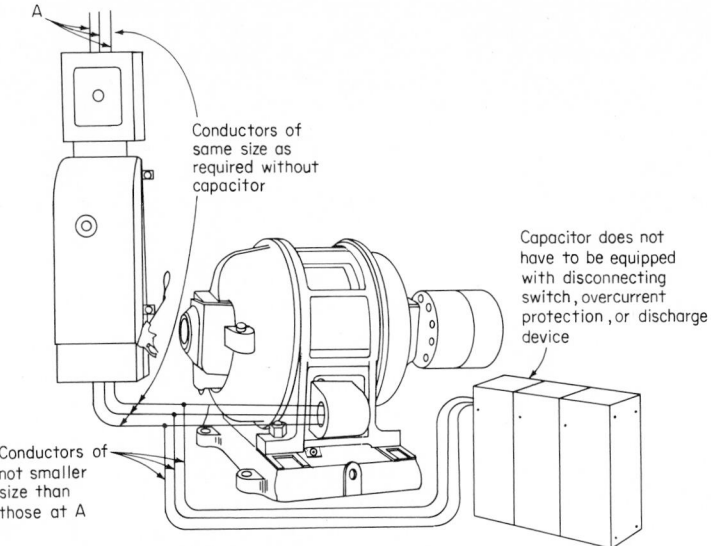

FIG. 174 *Schematic diagram of connections when an enclosed capacitor is installed at motor terminals. (General Electric Co.)*

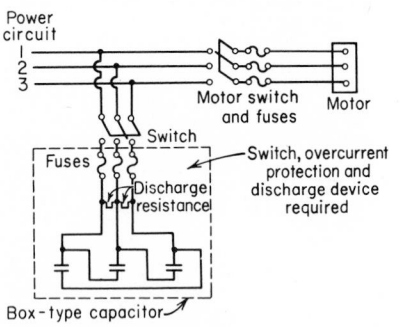

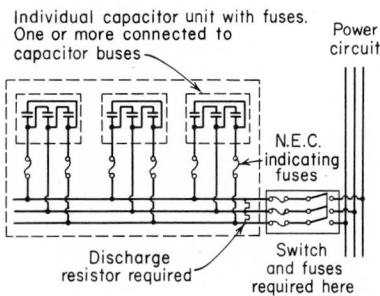

FIG. 175 *Connection diagram of enclosed capacitor unit, with fuses, installed on line side of motor switch.*

FIG. 176 *Connection diagram of rack-type three-phase 230-, 460-, or 575- volt capacitor installed on power circuit.*

of the motor overcurrent device shall be determined in accordance with Sec. **430** of Div. 7 except that, instead of using the full-load rated current of the motor as provided in that section, a lower value corresponding with the improved power factor of the motor circuit shall be used. Section **437** of Div. 7 applies with respect to the rating of the motor circuit conductors.

4. GROUNDING. Capacitor cases shall be grounded in accordance with Div. 9.

5. GUARDING. All live parts of capacitors which are connected to circuits of more than 600 volts between conductors and are accessible to unqualified persons shall be enclosed or isolated. For isolation by elevation, see Sec. **34** of Div. 11.

6. MARKING. Each capacitor shall be provided with a nameplate giving the maker's name, rated voltage, frequency, kvar or amperes, number of phases, and, if filled with a combustible liquid, the amount of liquid in gallons. When filled with a nonflammable

liquid, the nameplate shall so state. The nameplate shall indicate whether or not a capacitor unit has a discharge device inside the case.

139. Capacitors which are constructed with a liquid which will not burn can be located at any convenient location provided that they are not exposed to mechanical injury. If exposed to combustible dust or flyings or if located in vicinity of easily ignitible material, they must be enclosed in dusttight metal enclosures. Capacitors constructed with a liquid which will burn must be installed in vaults unless each container does not contain more than 3 gal of liquid. Vaults when required should be constructed so as to meet the same requirements as for transformers (see Div. 5).

BATTERIES—GENERAL

140. An electric battery is a device for producing an emf by chemical means. When such a source of emf is connected to a closed electric circuit, chemical energy is transformed into electrical energy. An emf will be produced by chemical means whenever two dissimilar solid conductors are immersed in a conducting liquid. The solid conductors are called electrodes, and the conducting liquid is called the electrolyte. Such a combination of chemicals resulting in the production of an emf is called a voltaic cell. A battery may consist of a single cell or a combination of cells. The voltage of a cell depends upon the material of the electrodes and the electrolyte and is independent of the dimensions of the cell. The current and power capacity of a cell are, however, directly dependent upon the dimensions of the cell and the weight of active material in the electrodes. Although there are an infinite number of different combinations of electrodes and electrolytes which will produce a voltaic cell, there are only a limited number of combinations which are practicable.

141. Classifications of Batteries. For practical purposes, batteries may be classified as primary and secondary. A **primary battery** is used only for discharge (conversion of chemical energy into electrical energy). As such a battery is discharged, the material of one of the electrodes goes into solution in the electrolyte. The electrode is thus consumed, and the character of the electrolyte altered so that with primary batteries it is necessary to renew from time to time both the electrode which goes into solution and the electrolyte. A **secondary battery** is alternately discharged and charged. As a battery discharges, the electrodes and electrolyte undergo chemical changes. After a secondary battery has been discharged, the electrodes and electrolyte can be restored to their original charged condition by passing a current through the battery in the reverse direction from that of discharge. In charging a battery, electrical energy is transformed into chemical energy. **Secondary batteries** are generally called **storage batteries.**

142. The internal resistance of batteries is the resistance offered to the flow of current inside the battery due to its electrodes and electrolyte. Owing to this internal resistance, the voltage at the terminals of a battery is less when it is discharging than when it is on open circuit. The internal resistance of a battery will change with the condition of discharge. As the battery discharges, the internal resistance increases, so that the terminal voltage decreases as the battery discharges. The terminal voltage of a battery is thus dependent upon the rate of discharge and the length of discharge. The voltage of a battery will decrease rather slowly as the battery discharges until nearly all the active material of the electrode has gone into solution. The battery is then discharged, and the voltage will drop rapidly to a very low value with any further attempt to discharge.

PRIMARY BATTERIES

143. The standard Daniell's cell is a primary cell which has an emf which is practically 1 volt when delivering a constant current. There are many forms of Daniell's cell, each of which is particularly adapted to certain service but all having very nearly the same emf (1.07+ volts). The emf is not changed appreciably by the degree of concentration of the solutions, by the temperature, by the resistance, or by the purity of the zinc or copper, etc. In short, it makes a very good rough-and-ready standard.

A very good model is that used by the British Post Office. The jar is made with two compartments: one containing a porous cup immersed in water, in which are placed a copper plate and crystals of copper sulfate, the other containing a zinc plate and a 50 per cent saturated solution of zinc sulfate. The zinc plate is fastened so as to be just clear of the solution, and a pencil of zinc is placed in the bottom. When in use, the porous cup is placed in the second compartment, thus raising the level of the zinc solution so as to immerse the zinc. Under working conditions the emf is about 1.07 volts; when new it is about 1.079 volts.

144. The gravity-type primary cell, which is used in telegraph work, is suitable for closed-circuit work but should not be used for applications where it is apt to stand for a long time on open circuit.

145. In setting up the gravity cell, place the copper electrode (−) in the bottom of the jar and pour in about 3 lb of copper sulfate crystals. Next place the zinc electrode (+) and fill with water to cover the zinc; to the water add a tablespoonful of sulfuric acid. Cover the electrolyte with a layer of pure mineral oil, which should be free from naphtha or acid and have a flash point about 400°F. If the oil is not used, the creeping can be stopped by dipping the edge of the jar in hot paraffin. When the cell is thus set up it should be short-circuited for a day or two to form zinc sulfate which will protect the zinc electrode; this preliminary run also reduces the internal resistance. The temperature of the cells should be kept above 70°F, since the resistance increases rapidly with a decrease in temperature.

The internal resistance of the gravity cell is ordinarily from 2 to 3 ohms. A blue color in the bottom of the cell denotes a good condition, but a brown color shows that the zinc is deteriorating. When renewing the copper sulfate it is best to empty the cell and set it up with a completely new electrolyte. The blue line, which marks the boundary between the copper sulfate and the zinc sulfate, should stand about halfway between the electrodes. If it comes too close to the zinc, some of the copper sulfate can be siphoned out, or the cell can be short-circuited so as to produce more zinc sulfate. If the blue line goes too low, some water and crystals of copper sulfate should be added.

146. The Fuller cell is well adapted to telephone work or any intermittent work. It can stand on open circuit for several months at a time without any appreciable deterioration.

147. The Fuller cell is set up as follows: Mix the electrolyte by adding 6 oz of potassium bichromate and 17 oz of sulfuric acid to 56 oz of soft water; pour this mixture into a suitable glass jar. Into a suitable porous cup put 1 teaspoonful of mercury and 2 teaspoonfuls of salt; place the cup and a zinc electrode in the glass jar and fill to within 2 in. of the top with soft water. Put on the cover, insert a carbon electrode, and the cell is ready for use.

The color of the solution is orange when in working order. The resistance varies from 0.5 to 4 ohms depending upon the condition and dimensions of the porous cup and upon the concentration of the solution.

148. The Lalande cell, frequently called the caustic soda cell, is suitable for either open- or closed-circuit work. The mechanical construction of this cell is especially good. The positive pole is a plate of compressed oxide of copper, the surfaces of which are reduced to metallic copper to improve the conductivity. This form of plate also acts as a depolarizer. The negative pole is of pure zinc amalgamated throughout by adding mercury when the casting is made. The electrolyte is a solution of caustic soda. The top of the solution is covered with a heavy mineral oil to prevent the solution from evaporating.

The emf of all types and sizes of caustic soda cell initially is approximately 0.90 volt per cell. The voltage on closed circuit will depend upon the rate of discharge and the size of cell. The larger sizes having lower internal resistance will, of course, have a higher voltage for a given rate of discharge than the smaller cells under similar conditions. For ordinary purposes, however, it is safe to figure a mean effective voltage of approximately 0.67 volt per cell at normal temperature.

149. Primary batteries are manufactured by the Primary Battery Division of Thomas A. Edison Industries in three types: the renewable carbon type, the nonrenewable Carbonaire battery, and the renewable copper-oxide type.

These batteries are an ideal power supply for many low-voltage d-c services where the utmost freedom from power interruptions is extremely important. Their inherent operating advantages make them particularly desirable for the following applications in which batteries are generally used either for direct operation or as an emergency standby power supply:

Navigation aids (river, channel, pier and obstruction lights)

Alarm systems (municipal, police and fire alarm installations; fire and burglar alarms in factories, schools, office buildings, banks, public institutions and private properties)

Annunciator systems

Electric fences

Elevator signals

Farm radios

Laboratory services and apparatus (industrial, school, and scientific)

Mine-signal and communication systems

Railway signal and communication service

Telegraph service (local sounder and main line circuits)

Telephone service (operation of transmitters on magneto switchboards; intercommunicating systems; interrupters or pole changers)

Time-clock systems (program, self-winding, etc., in schools, factories and public buildings)

These primary batteries offer the following advantages:

1. They provide a self-contained power supply requiring no charging as do storage cells. They can be applied anywhere, whether or not commercial power is accessible, and are therefore particularly ideal for operating isolated installations.

2. They consistently deliver rated ampere-hour capacity at satisfactory operating voltage in continuous or intermittent service.

3. They require little attention or maintenance other than occasional inspection from the time they are placed in service until they are exhausted.

4. They eliminate the cost of providing and maintaining battery-charging facilities.

5. They are easy to install without experienced help. Transporting batteries to and from a charging station is unnecessary.

6. In the renewable-type cells, there are accurate visual indicator panels which warn of approaching and complete exhaustion of rated capacity. This feature makes it possible to see and make sure that ample battery capacity is always available—a decided advantage in preventing service failures due to exhausted batteries.

150. The Edison carbon cell is a renewable, wet primary battery. It is depolarized by oxygen extracted from the air which reaches the depolarizing area through a porous carbon electrode. In this respect it differs from the copper-oxide cell, where a fixed supply of depolarizing oxygen is stored in the copper-oxide plates.

Edison carbon cells are manufactured in three types: the A-500 (Fig. 177), which has a 500 ampere-hour capacity; the A-1000 (Fig. 178), with 1,000 ampere-hour capacity; and the RE-1000 (Fig. 179), with 1,000 ampere-hour capacity. These cells will fit standard AAR battery jars of the sizes and shapes indicated in the table below. Special porcelain covers with air vents are required for all cells.

Type of cell	Jar shape	Ampere-hour capacity	Over-all dimensions of cell, in.
A-501	Round	500	$6\frac{3}{4}$ diam × $12\frac{3}{4}$
A-502	Rectangular	500	$5\frac{3}{4}$ × $6\frac{3}{4}$ × $12\frac{1}{4}$
A-504	Barrel	500	$7\frac{1}{16}$ diam × $11\frac{5}{8}$
A-505	Round	500	$7\frac{3}{16}$ diam × 12
A-1001	Round	1,000	$8\frac{3}{16}$ diam × $14\frac{5}{8}$
A-1002	Rectangular	1,000	$6\frac{5}{8}$ × $8\frac{5}{8}$ × $14\frac{3}{4}$
RE-1001	Round-501	1,000	$6\frac{3}{4}$ diam × $12\frac{3}{4}$
RE-1004	Barrel-504	1,000	$7\frac{1}{16}$ diam × $11\frac{5}{8}$
RE-1005	Round-505	1,000	$7\frac{3}{16}$ diam × 12

FIG. 177 *Complete Edison carbon cell. Type A-500.* (*Thomas A. Edison Industries Div. of McGraw-Edison Co.*)

FIG. 178 *Complete Edison carbon cell, Type A-1000.* (*Thomas A. Edison Industries Div. of McGraw-Edison Co.*)

These carbon cells are provided with visual indications to warn of approaching exhaustion of cell capacity. These indications occur in two indicator panels (see Fig. 180) which are molded into the outside surface of each zinc plate. The panels gradually perforate as the capacity of the cell is consumed. When they are completely eaten away, the cell is ready for renewal. An entire battery set should be renewed when the *majority* of the indicator panels are completely eaten out.

A complete Edison carbon cell consists of the following:

One assembled element of two zinc plates and one carbon block, with insulated negative terminal wire and positive terminal suspension bolt.

One or two cans of caustic potash which, when mixed with water, forms the electrolyte.[1]

[1] The Types A-500 and RE-1000 take only one can of caustic potash. The Type A-1000 comes with *two* cans of caustic potash, and the entire contents of *both* cans are required in setting up a cell.

One can of regenerative material, for Type RE-1000 batteries only, which is placed in the bottom of the jar of Type RE-1000 cells after the solution is mixed.

One jar of heat-resisting glass.

One porcelain cover with air vents.

One bottle of special battery oil.

One hexagonal nut for attaching element to cover.

Two wing nuts with washers.

FIG. 179   *Complete Edison carbon cell, Type RE-1000.   (Thomas A. Edison Industries Div. of McGraw-Edison Co.)*

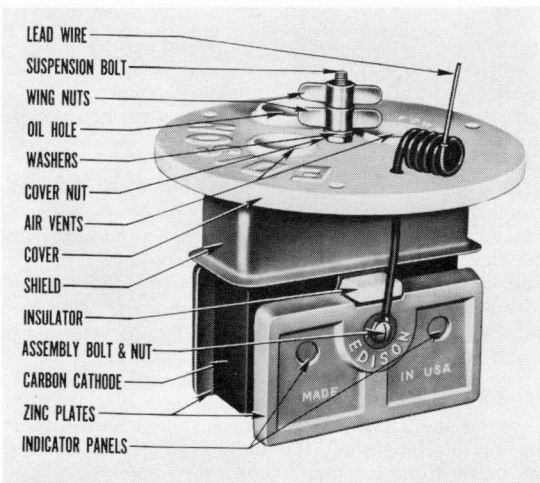

FIG. 180   *Assembled element and cover for Edison carbon cell.   (Thomas A. Edison Industries Div. of McGraw-Edison Co.)*

The jar, oil, nut, and washers are the same as furnished with Edison copper-oxide cells. The permanent parts of the cell are the jar, cover, nuts, and washers. These are used indefinitely.

An exhausted Edison carbon cell can be readily restored to full capacity by renewing only the active materials. Material for renewing one cell consists of (1) assembled element; (2) one or two cans of caustic potash (one can for Type A-500, one can for Type RE-1000, and two cans for Type A-1000); (3) bottle of battery oil; and (4) one can of regenerative material for Type RE-1000. These items are sold in complete units known as Renewals.

Type RE-1000 cells differ from Type A-500 and Type A-1000 cells through the addition of a can of regenerative material. The addition of this regenerative material doubles the ampere-hour capacity of the cell.

The average closed-circuit voltage of Edison carbon cells varies somewhat with the current rate and temperature, the value normally falling in the region of 1.10 to 1.30 volts. Recommended maximum continuous discharge rates are as follows:

Solution temperature	Maximum discharge-amperes[a]		
	A-500	A-1000	RE-1000
75° F.	1.10	1.50	1.50
25° F.	1.00	1.20	1.20

[a] To cut-off voltage of 1.0 volt.

The average current consumption for RE-1000 cells should not exceed 6 amp-hr per 24 hr. In case of emergency, this maximum rate may be sustained for a much longer period; however, to get maximum life, the average discharge should not exceed 6 amp-hr per day over the life of the battery.

In general, intermittent currents higher than 1.10 amp for the A-500 and 1.50 amp for the A-1000 may be sustained for only relatively short periods. The allowable duration of such discharges may range from seconds to periods of many minutes, depending upon the actual rate of current, the frequency characteristic of the discharge, the temperature, the state of exhaustion of the battery, and the minimum voltage that is required.

In any installation, the following precautions should be observed:

1. The carbon cell gives best results where plenty of fresh air is available. When battery housings are provided, a slight amount of ventilation is always necessary to let in air and to dissipate dampness. Most forms of battery housing meet this requirement and do not need special ventilation.

2. Charging may be harmful to Edison carbon cells. Where these cells are floated across a rectifier, adjustment of rectifier output should always be made so the battery does not receive a charge.

3. It is not recommended that Edison carbon cells be used in any installation where the battery service life is expected to exceed two years.

151. The Edison Carbonaire battery is a nonrenewable primary battery of the air-depolarized, add-water type, sealed in a single, molded, hard rubber case. The battery is shipped dry and is made ready for use merely by adding a small quantity of water.

The add-water construction has a distinct advantage in that the battery is kept inert and free from internal deterioration during storage.

During its service life, the Carbonaire requires no maintenance other than infrequent inspections of the solution height and the addition of a small amount of water if the solution has fallen below the recommended operating level.

There are no visual indications of exhaustion in the Carbonaire and its service life must be calculated on the basis of the known current consumption of the connected apparatus.

I. *Type 2-S-J-1 Carbonaire.* II. *Type 3-S-J-1 Carbonaire battery.*   III. *Type Y.*

FIG. 181   *Edison Carbonaire batteries.* (*Thomas A. Edison Industries Div. of McGraw-Edison Co.*)

Carbonaire batteries (Fig. 181) are manufactured in four types: the 2-S-J-1, the 3-S-J-1, the 2-M-J-1, and the Type Y.

The technical details and nominal service ratings for these batteries are given in the table below. They may be applied to many services where a large ampere-hour reserve of dependable, low-voltage current is needed and where their simplicity of handling, setting up, and maintenance may be used to good advantage.

Characteristics	2-S-J-1	2-M-J-1	3-S-J-1	Y
Over-all dimensions, in.				
Length..........................	$8\frac{5}{16}$	$8\frac{5}{16}$	12	$8\frac{1}{4}$
Width...........................	$7\frac{3}{8}$	$7\frac{3}{8}$	$7\frac{3}{8}$	$8\frac{1}{4}$
Height..........................	$9\frac{1}{2}$	$9\frac{1}{2}$	$9\frac{1}{2}$	$13\frac{1}{2}$
Shipping weight, lb..............	24	24	35	$33\frac{1}{2}$
Service weight, lb...............	$29\frac{1}{4}$	$29\frac{1}{4}$	45	$40\frac{1}{2}$
Nominal capacity, amp-hrs........	1000	2000	1000	2500
Nominal voltage.................	2.4–2.5	1.2–1.25	3.6–3.75	1.2–1.25
Nominal current, amp............	0.25	0.50	0.25	1.00

When the battery is filled, it will get warm and then cool off, which causes the solution to rise a little and then to recede. This is normal and no more water need be added on this account.

There is no advantage in maintaining the solution level at any exact point during the battery life except that, if it falls below 2 in. from the top of the filler, the level should be brought up to $1\frac{1}{2}$ in. by adding water. The top of the battery, especially the central carbons, should be kept clean and dry.

If the battery is used out-of-doors, it should be protected in a well-ventilated housing. Where temperatures are extreme, the housing should be partially sunk in the ground, but constructed of material not permeable to dampness. Ventilation provides air for the battery to breathe and dissipates dampness.

Under adverse climatic conditions, there may be a minor wetness, or salt formation, around the battery top. This may be wiped off.

In connection with battery housings, it should be noted that, since the Carbonaire requires oxygen for its operation, it should never be installed in completely airtight or watertight housings.

The batteries may be stored for any reasonable length of time and they will remain inert and free from internal deterioration. This is because they are shipped dry with the openings sealed at the factory.

151A. An Edison copper-oxide cell is a device for the direct transformation of chemical energy into electrical energy. It consists of at least one copper-oxide and two zinc plates in a solution of caustic soda (sodium hydroxide).

In operation, electricity is produced by the chemical processes of oxidation and reduction. The copper-oxide (positive) plate loses oxygen and is thereby reduced to pure copper. The zinc plates (negative) gain oxygen to form zinc oxide, which is immediately dissolved in the electrolyte. This dissolving action is one of the important functions of the electrolyte. The only part of the chemical reaction that can be seen is the gradual disappearance of the zinc plate.

The pattern of this chemical process is always the same. It follows very definite and unchangeable natural laws.

During the discharge, the consumption of zinc is uniform, provided the solution is properly stirred. This is the reason it is practical to have visual indications of approaching exhaustion by constructing, in the outside zinc plates, areas which are thinner than the rest of the plate.

There are three distinct types of Edison copper-oxide primary cells, each type being designated by a prefixed letter as follows: The prefix S indicates cells for light duty application; M for medium duty; and HA for heavy duty applications. A group of typical copper-oxide cells is shown in Fig. 182.

A complete cell consists of (1) unit assembly of zinc and copper-oxide plates; (2) can of caustic soda; (3) jar of heat-resisting glass; (4) porcelain cover; (5) bottle of special battery oil; (6) nuts and washers for attaching element to cover and making connections to positive terminal. A complete cell is shown in Fig. 183 and the details of a cell assembly in Fig. 183A.

An exhausted Edison copper-oxide battery can be readily restored to full capacity by renewing only the active materials. Material for renewing one cell consists of (1) assembled element; (2) can of caustic soda; (3) bottle of battery oil. These items are sold in complete units known as Renewals. The jar, cover, nuts, and washers of each cell are permanent parts. As a result, the cost of renewing cells is only about 50 per cent of their original cost. It is very important, when renewing cells, that renewals of the correct type and capacity be used.

One of the regular maintenance procedures is to inspect visually the indicator panels to ascertain when the cells are approaching exhaustion. These panels are located in the depressed areas, at the bottom of the outside zincs in each Edison copper-oxide cell. The state of exhaustion of a cell is determined by the perforations which occur in these panels.

There are two distinct types of indicator panels used in Edison copper-oxide cells:

1. For all S- and M-type cells a two-panel indicator is provided in which each panel is of the same size and thickness. First perforations (Fig. 184A, I) occur in both panels when about 85 per cent of the cell capacity has been withdrawn, and continue gradually

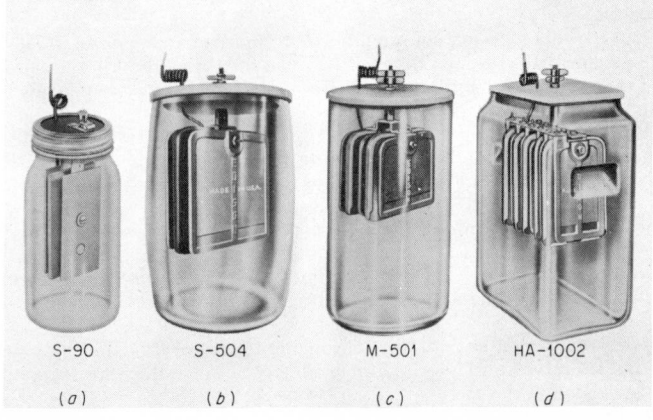

S-90	S-504	M-501	HA-1002
(a)	(b)	(c)	(d)

FIG. 182 *Group of typical Edison copper-oxide cells.* (*Thomas A. Edison Industries Div. of McGraw-Edison Co.*)

(Fig. 184*A*, II) until the panels are entirely open (Fig. 184*A*, III). The cell has then delivered its full rated capacity and is ready for renewal.

2. For all HA-type cells each panel in this two-panel indicator is of the same size but of different thickness in order to provide a progressive indication of exhaustion. Perforation starts in the left-hand panel. When this panel is completely eaten away (Fig. 184*B*, I), the cell has delivered 75 per cent of its rated capacity. The right-hand panel then continues to perforate, and the entire perforation of both panels (Fig. 184*B*, II) indicates that the cell has delivered rated capacity.

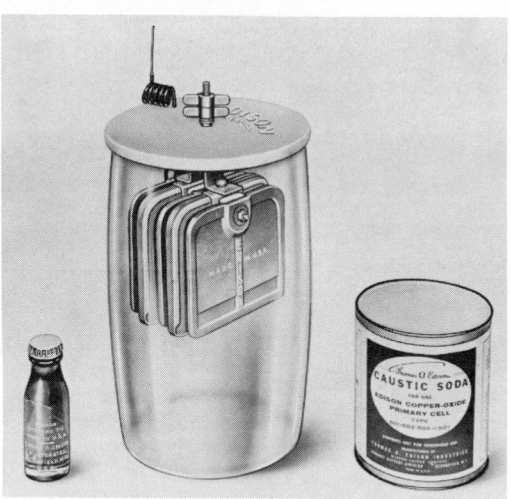

FIG. 183 *Complete Edison copper-oxide cell, Type M-504. (Thomas A. Edison Industries Div. of McGraw-Edison Co.)*

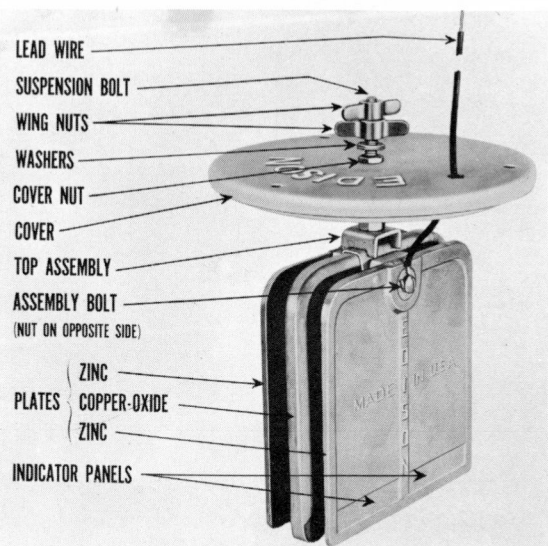

FIG. 183A *Assembled copper-oxide cell and cover. (Thomas A. Edison Industries Div. of McGraw-Edison Co.)*

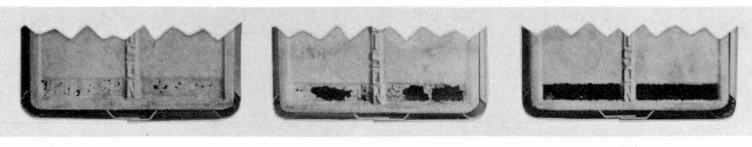

I   II   III

FIG. 184A   *Exhaustion indicator panels for Types S and M Edison copper-oxide cells.* (*Thomas A. Edison Industries Div. of McGraw-Edison Co.*)

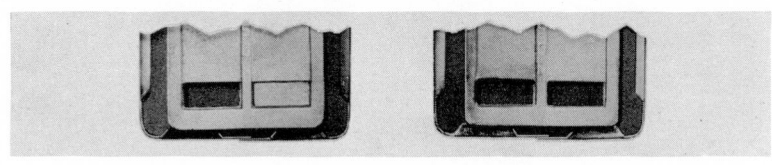

I   II

FIG. 184B   *Exhaustion indicator panels for Type HA Edison copper-oxide cells.* (*Thomas A. Edison Industries Div. of McGraw-Edison Co.*)

An entire battery should be renewed when the majority of all panels of the S- and M-type cells and the majority of the right-hand panels of the HA-type cells show complete perforation.   The battery as a whole has then delivered its rated capacity.

As a safety factor, all Edison copper-oxide cells are designed to deliver approximately 10 per cent more than rated capacity after panels have become perforated.

151B. Cell Data Table

Type No.	Amp-hr capacity	Jar data		Approx. wt of cell made up, lb	Over all dimensions of cell, in.	Recommended services
		Shape	Reference number			
S-90	90	Round	Type 90	3¾	3¾ diam × 7¾	Telephone transmitter and ringing circuits. Switch lock circuits.
S-252	250	Rectangular	9-B-J-13	11¾	3⅜ × 5⅞ × 12	
S-501	500	Round	9-B-J-2	21	6¾ diam × 12¾	Straight and a-c primary systems for: Track circuits. Semaphore signals (motor, hold-clear, line and electric lighting circuits). Locking circuits at interlocking plants. Crossing bells. Indication lamps on track diagrams. Slide fences. Dispatcher's telephone circuits. Searchlight signals (low wattage lamps and control circuits).
S-502	500	Rectangular	9-B-J-5	21¾	5¾ × 6¾ × 12¼	
S-504	500	Barrel	9-B-J-1	21½	7 diam × 11⅝	
S-505	500	Round	9-B-J-11	24	7 3/16 diam × 11 11/16	
M-501	500	Round	9-B-J-2	21	6¾ diam × 12¾	Straight and a-c primary systems for: Track circuits. Semaphore signals (motor, hold-clear, line and electric lighting circuits). Color light and Searchlight signals (low wattage lamps and control circuits). Low voltage switch machines.
M-502	500	Rectangular	9-B-J-5	21¾	5¾ × 6¾ × 12¼	
M-504	500	Barrel	9-B-J-1	21½	7 diam × 11⅝	
M-505	500	Round	9-B-J-11	24	7 3/16 diam × 11 11/16	
M-1001	1,000	Round	9-B-J-4	38¼	8⅛ diam × 14⅝	
M-1002	1,000	Rectangular	50006	39	6½ × 8¼ × 14¾	
HA-501	500	Round	9-B-J-2	23½	6¾ diam × 12¾	Straight and a-c primary systems for: all types of light signals (lamp and control circuits). Highway crossing signals. Low voltage switch machines. Low voltage mains at interlocking plants.
HA-502	500	Rectangular	9-B-J-5	24¼	5¾ × 6¾ × 12¼	
HA-504	500	Barrel	9-B-J-1	24	7 diam × 11⅝	
HA-505	500	Round	9-B-J-11	26½	7 3/16 diam × 11 11/16	
HA-901	500	Round	9-B-J-4	37	8⅛ diam × 14⅝	
HA-902	500	Rectangular	50006	37¾	6½ × 8¼ × 14¾	
HA-1001	1,000	Round	9-B-J-4	39⅛	8⅛ diam × 14⅝	
HA-1002	1,000	Rectangular	50006	39⅞	6½ × 8¼ × 14¾	
HA-1302	1,000	Rectangular	50023	54	6¾ × 8½ × 17¾	

151C. Service Current Ratings

Type no.	Amp-hr capacity	Maximum recommended service discharge, amperes			
		Signal cases	Battery boxes	Deep wells	Heated buildings
S-90	90		*a*	*a*	0.65
S-252	250		*a*	*a*	1.00
S-501, S-502, S-504, S-505	500		1.00	1.40	2.00
M-501, M-502, M-504, M-505	500		1.30	1.70	2.20
M-1001, M-1002	1000		2.50	3.10	4.00
HA-501, HA-502, HA-504, HA-505	500		3.60	5.00	6.70
HA-901, HA-902	500	2.60	6.40	8.10	12.20
HA-1001, HA-1002	1000		4.50	7.00	9.50
HA-1302	1000	2.00	8.00	12.00	19.20

Table **151C** covers discharge ratings for intermittent service. For continuous service the ratings would run from 50 to 80 per cent of those shown in the table, depending upon temperature.

151D. Selection of Cells. With the aid of Fig. 185, the proper type and number of Edison copper-oxide primary cells can be readily determined for a wide range of low-voltage d-c power requirements where the batteries will be installed in housings normally heated during cold weather. Only the following information is necessary to use the chart:

1. Maximum current in amperes required by the apparatus the cells are to operate. Selection of cells should always be based on highest current rate, whether continuous or intermittent.

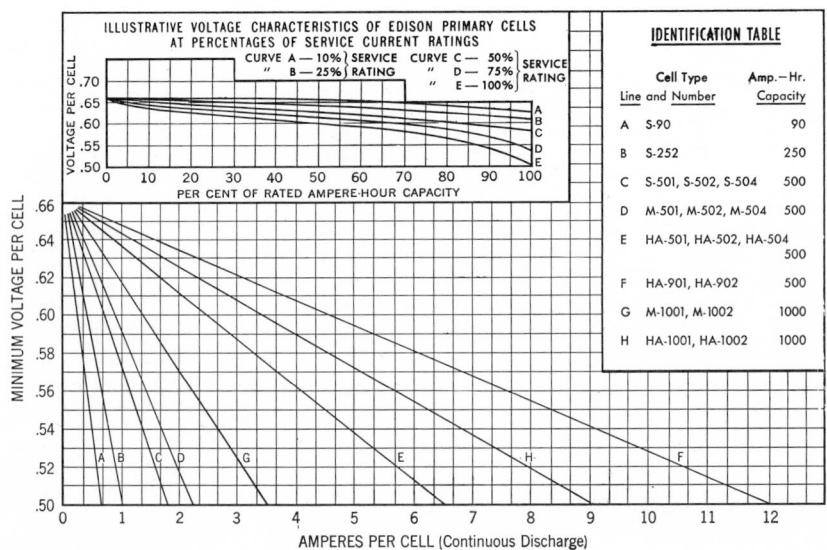

FIG. 185 *Characteristics of Edison copper-oxide cells. (Thomas A. Edison Industries Div. of McGraw-Edison Co.)*

2. Minimum ampere-hour battery capacity desired. 90, 250, 500, and 1,000 amp-hr capacities are standard for Edison cells.

3. Minimum voltage required at the battery. Allowance should be made for voltage drop between battery and apparatus due to resistance of line, contacts, etc.

Along the bottom of the chart, locate the point which corresponds to the maximum current required (1). From this point, follow a vertical line up to its intersection with the first sloping line on which is found a cell having an ampere-hour capacity nearest to that desired (2). The cell designated on this line will most economically deliver the maximum current needed.

From the point where the vertical and sloping lines intersect, follow a horizontal line to the left side of the chart to find the voltage of the cell. This point on the voltage scale shows minimum voltage at which cell will deliver its rated ampere-hour capacity at the maximum current which it will be called upon to furnish to connected apparatus.

To determine the proper number of cells of the type selected which should be used in series, divide the minimum cell voltage into the minimum battery voltage (3) required to operate the apparatus satisfactorily.

For applications where cells will be subject to low temperatures for extended periods, detailed conditions and requirements should be submitted to the manufacturer for recommendations. This same procedure should also be followed when cells are desired for intermittent service where maximum discharge will be of only a few seconds duration.

152. The Leclanché cell is adapted only to intermittent work such as bells, telephones, etc. It is cheap and easy to maintain.

153. The Leclanché cell is set up as follows: Put 3 or 4 oz of sal ammoniac in the jar; pour about one-third full of water and stir until the sal ammoniac is all dissolved; place the carbon electrode in the porous cup and pack manganese dioxide and crumbled carbon around it; then insert the porous cup and the zinc electrode into the jar, and the cell is ready for use.

Practically the only attendance consists in renewing the evaporated water. The zinc is replaced when worn out. When it becomes necessary to add sal ammoniac, the solution should be thrown out and a new one made. If the porous cell becomes clogged, soaking in warm water will improve it.

The resistance depends upon the dimensions of the electrodes, the state of the porous cup, and the condition of the cell. Under proper working conditions and with a carbon electrode having about 8 sq in. of surface, the resistance will be about 1.5 ohms.

154. The modern dry cell is a modification of the Leclanché cell. The chief difference is that only sufficient water is added to its electrolyte to moisten an absorbent lining of pulpboard, blotting paper, cheesecloth, or starch paste. This lining separates the positive and negative poles. The negative pole, which also serves as a container, is usually a hollow sheet-zinc cylinder, 6 in. high and $2\frac{1}{2}$ in. in diameter. The bottom of this cylinder is also, usually, made of zinc. A majority of the dry cells made in the United States are, probably, of these dimensions. The positive pole is a carbon rod which may be either smooth cylindrical or fluted. The absorbent layer above mentioned is placed next to the zinc and is saturated with a solution of sal ammoniac and zinc chloride. The space between this lining and the carbon electrode is filled with a mixture of granulated carbon and manganese dioxide, the latter being the depolarizer. The top of each cell is usually sealed with a pitch compound. When exhausted, the cell is thrown away. Frequently the life can be extended by punching a hole in the top and pouring in water.

Although dry cells are made in several different sizes, the two most commonly used sizes are the No. 6 and the standard flashlight battery. The No. 6 cell is $2\frac{1}{2}$ in. in diameter and 6 in. high. The standard flashlight cell is $1\frac{1}{4}$ in. in diameter and $2\frac{1}{4}$ in. high. The capacity of the usual No. 6 cell is about 30 amp-hr, and that of the flashlight cell is about 3 amp-hr. Heavy-duty cells of both types are available with capacities up to 50 and 5 amp-hr, respectively.

STORAGE BATTERIES—GENERAL

155. A storage battery is a device which can be used repeatedly for storing energy at one time in the form of chemical energy for use at another time in the form of electrical energy. It consists of two kinds of plates bearing the necessary electrochemically active materials immersed in a proper solution. The solution is called the electrolyte. Charging a battery consists of connecting the two terminals to a d-c supply of proper polarity for a sufficient length of time. Electrical energy is delivered by the d-c supply to the battery, in which it produces certain chemical reactions so that the energy is converted into chemical energy. If a charged battery has its two terminals connected through a closed external electric circuit, the active materials of the plate will react chemically with the electrolyte, producing a flow of current in the circuit. This conversion of chemical energy into electrical energy is called discharging the battery. Charging is the process of putting energy into the battery (delivering energy to the battery), while discharging is the process of taking energy from the battery (battery delivering energy to external electric circuit).

156. Storage cell is the name given to the fundamental unit of any storage battery. It consists of one positive plate or a group of positive plates electrically connected together, one negative plate or a group of negative plates electrically connected together, separators, electrolyte, and a suitable container. A storage battery may consist of a single cell or a group of cells electrically interconnected.

157. Types of Storage Batteries. Storage batteries may be classified in two ways as follows:

1. According to fundamental type of service for which it is suitable.
    a. Stationary.
    b. Portable.
2. According to fundamental materials of construction.
    a. Lead-acid.
    b. Nickel-iron-alkaline.
    c. Nickel-cadmium.

Stationary batteries are those designed for service in a permanent location.

Portable batteries are those designed for service requiring the transportation of the batteries during service.

158. Storage-battery Terminology. Most of the following definitions of terms are taken from the standards of the Institute of Electrical and Electronic Engineers.

Active Materials. Materials of plates reacting chemically to produce electrical energy during the discharge. The active materials of storage cells are restored to their original composition, in the charged condition, by oxidation or reduction processes produced by the charging current.

Grid. A metallic framework for conducting the electric current and supporting the active material.[1]

Positive Plate. The grid and active material from which the current flows to the external circuit when the battery is discharging.

Negative Plate. The grid and active material to which the current flows from the external circuit when the battery is discharging.

Electrolyte. An aqueous solution of sulfuric acid used in lead cells and of certain hydroxides used in nickel-iron-alkaline cells.

Separator. A device for preventing metallic contact between the plates of opposite polarity within the cell.

Group. Assembly of a set of plates of the same polarity for one cell.

Element. The positive and negative groups with separators assembled for a cell.

Couple. The element of a cell containing two plates, one positive and one negative. This term is also applied to a positive and negative plate connected together as one unit for installation in adjacent cells.

---

[1] In certain types of batteries the active material is enclosed in containers which are held in place by the grid.

Jar. The container for the element and electrolyte of a cell. Specifically a jar for lead-acid cells is usually of hard-rubber composition or glass, but for nickel-iron-alkaline cells it is a nickel-plated steel container frequently referred to as a "can."

Tank. A lead container, supported by wood, for the element and electrolyte of a cell. This is restricted to some relatively large types of cells.

Case. A container for several cells. Specifically wood cases are containers for cells in individual jars; rubber or composition cases are provided with compartments for the cells.

Tray. A support or container for one or more cells.

Terminal Posts. The points of the cell or battery to which the external circuit is connected.

End Cells. The cells of a battery which may be cut in or out of the circuit for the purpose of adjusting the battery voltage.

Pilot Cell. A selected cell whose temperature, voltage, and specific gravity of electrolyte are assumed to indicate the condition of the entire battery.

Ampere-hour Capacity. The number of ampere-hours which can be delivered by a cell or battery under specified conditions as to temperature, rate of discharge, and final voltage.

Energy Density. The watthours per pound (wh/lb) of battery weight.

Power Density. The watts per pound (w/lb) of battery weight.

Watthour Capacity. The number of watthours which can be delivered by a cell or battery under specified conditions as to temperature, rate of discharge, and final voltage.

Time Rate. The rate in amperes at which a battery will be fully discharged in a specified time, under specified conditions of temperature and final voltage, as, for example, the 8-hr rate or the 20-min rate.

Open-circuit Voltage. The voltage of a cell or battery at its terminals when no current is flowing. For the purpose of measurement, the small current required for the operation of a voltmeter is usually negligible.

Closed-circuit Voltage. The voltage at the terminals of a cell or battery when current is flowing.

Average Voltage. The average value of the voltage during the period of charge or discharge. It is conveniently obtained from the time integral of the voltage curve.

Initial Voltage. The voltage of a cell or battery at the beginning of a charge or discharge. It is usually taken after the current has been flowing for a sufficient period of time for the rate of change of voltage to become practically constant.

Final Voltage. The prescribed voltage upon reaching which the discharge is considered complete. The final voltage is usually chosen so that the useful capacity of the cell is realized. Final voltages vary with the type of battery, the rate of the discharge, temperature, and the service in which the battery is used.

Polarity. An electrical condition determining the direction in which current tends to flow. By common usage the discharge current is said to flow from the positive or peroxide plate through the external circuit. In a nickel-iron-alkaline battery the positive plate is that containing nickel peroxide.

Charge. The conversion of electrical energy into chemical energy within the cell or battery. This consists of the restoration of the active materials by passing a unidirectional current through the cell or battery in the opposite direction to that of the discharge. A cell or battery which is said to be "charged" is understood to be fully charged.

Charging Rate. The current expressed in amperes at which a battery is charged.

Constant-current Charge. A charge in which the current is maintained at constant value. For some types of lead batteries this may involve two rates called the starting and the finishing rates.

Constant-voltage Charge. A charge in which the voltage at the terminals of the battery is held at a constant value. A modified constant-voltage system is usually one in which the voltage of the charging circuit is held substantially constant but in which a fixed resistance is inserted in the battery circuit producing a rising voltage characteristic at the battery terminals as the charge progresses. This term is also applied to other methods for producing automatically a similar characteristic.

Boost Charge. A partial charge, usually at a high rate for a short period.

Equalizing Charge. An extended charge given to a battery to ensure the complete restoration of the active materials in all the plates of all the cells.

Trickle Charge. A continuous charge at low rate approximately equal to the internal losses and suitable to maintain the battery in a fully charged condition. This term is also applied to very low rates of charge suitable not only for compensating for internal losses but for restoring intermittent discharges of small amount delivered from time to time to the load circuit.

Finishing Rate. The rate of charge expressed in amperes to which the charging current for some types of lead batteries is reduced near the end of charge to prevent excessive gassing and temperature rise.

Discharge. The conversion of the chemical energy of the battery into electrical energy.

Reversal. Change in normal polarity of a storage cell.

Local Action or Self-discharge. The internal loss of charge which goes on continuously within a cell regardless of connections to an external circuit.

Floating. A method of operation in which a constant voltage is applied to the battery terminals sufficient to maintain an approximately constant state of charge.

Specific Gravity of Electrolyte. The electrolyte of lead-acid batteries increases in concentration to a fixed maximum value during charge and decreases during discharge. The concentration is usually expressed as the specific gravity of the solution. This variation of specific gravity of the solution affords an approximate indication of the state of charge.

The specific gravity of the electrolyte in nickel-iron-alkaline batteries does not change appreciably during charge or discharge and therefore does not indicate the state of charge. The specific gravities, however, are indication of the electrochemical usefulness of the electrolyte.

Gassing. The evolution of oxygen or hydrogen or both.

Efficiency. The ratio of the output of a cell or battery to the input required to restore the initial state of charge under specified conditions of temperature, current rate, and final voltage.

Ampere-Hour Efficiency (Electrochemical Efficiency). The ratio of the ampere-hours output to the ampere-hours of the recharge.

Volt Efficiency. The ratio of the average voltage during the discharge to the average voltage during the recharge.

Watthour Efficiency (Energy Efficiency). The ratio of the watthours output to the watthours of the recharge.

General. Batteries are usually rated in terms of the number of ampere-hours which they are capable of delivering when fully charged and under specified conditions as to temperature, rate of discharge, and final voltage. For different classes of service, different time rates (see definition of time rate) are frequently used. For comparing the capacities of batteries of different size but of the same general design, it is customary to use the same time rate, and a comparison based on the different lengths of time they will discharge at the same rate is not recommended, as it is misleading.

Misrating. A battery which fails to deliver its rated capacity on the third successive measured cycle of charge and discharge under specified current rates, temperature of electrolyte, specific gravity, and final voltage shall be considered to be improperly rated.

LEAD-ACID STORAGE BATTERIES

159. Lead-Acid Batteries.[1] In the charged condition the active materials consist of lead peroxide on the positive plate and sponge lead on the negative plate. The electrolyte is a mixture of sulfuric acid and water. The strength of the electrolyte is measured in terms of specific gravity, which is the ratio of the weight of a given volume of electrolyte to an equal volume of water. Concentrated sulfuric acid has a specific gravity of about 1.830; water has a specific gravity of 1.000. The acid and water are mixed in a proportion to give the specific gravity desired. For example, an acid manu-

---

[1] A large portion of the following information in this section on lead-acid batteries has been taken from the literature of the Electric Storage Battery Co.

facturer to supply electrolyte of 1.210 gravity will mix roughly about 1 part of concentrated acid to 4 parts of water.

In a fully charged battery all the active material of the positive plates is lead peroxide and that of the negative plates is pure sponge lead. In a fully charged battery all the acid is in the electrolyte and the specific gravity is at its maximum value. The active material of both the positive and negative plates is porous, so that it has absorption qualities similar to a sponge, and the pores are therefore filled with some of the battery solution. As the battery discharges, the acid, which is in the pores of the plates, separates from the electrolyte, forming a chemical combination with the active material, changing it to lead sulfate. As the discharge continues, additional acid is drawn or diffused from the electrolyte into the pores of the plates and further sulfate is formed. It can be readily understood that, as this process continues, the specific gravity of the electrolyte will gradually decrease, because the proportion of acid is decreasing. On charge the reverse action takes place: the acid in the sulfated active material is driven out and back into the electrolyte. This return of the acid to the electrolyte increases the specific gravity, so that it will continue to rise until all the acid is driven out of the plates and back into the electrolyte. After all the acid is driven back into the electrolyte, further charging will not raise the specific gravity any higher, as all the acid in the cells is in the electrolyte, and the battery is said to be fully charged. The material of the positives is again lead peroxide and that of the negatives is spongy lead; the specific gravity is maximum.

Practically speaking, on discharge the plates absorb acid, and the specific gravity of the electrolyte decreases. On the charge the plates return the absorbed acid to the electrolyte and the specific gravity increases. Figure 186, showing a cell charged, discharging, discharged, and charging, illustrates clearly the chemical action which takes place on charge and discharge:

When a cell is fully charged [Fig. 186(1) of the diagram], the negative plate is lead sponge, Pb; the positive plate is lead peroxide, PbO_2; and the specific gravity of the electrolyte (sulfuric acid, H_2SO_4, and water, H_2O) is at its maximum. Chemical energy is stored in the cell in this condition.

When a cell is put on discharge [Fig. 186(2)], the H_2SO_4 of the acid is divided into H_2 and SO_4. The H_2 passes in the direction of the current to the positive plates and combines with some of the oxygen of the lead peroxide and forms H_2O; the SO_4 combines with the liberated Pb of the positive plate to form lead sulfate. The SO_4 also forms lead sulfate at the negative or lead sponge (Pb) plate. As the discharge progresses, both plates finally contain considerable lead sulfate, $PbSO_4$ [see Fig. 186(3)]. The water formed has diluted the acid, lowering the specific gravity of the electrolyte. When the plates are entirely sulfated, current will cease, since the plates are then identical, and any active electric cell requires two dissimilar plates in electrolyte. In common practice, however, the discharge is always stopped before the plates have become entirely reduced to lead sulfate.

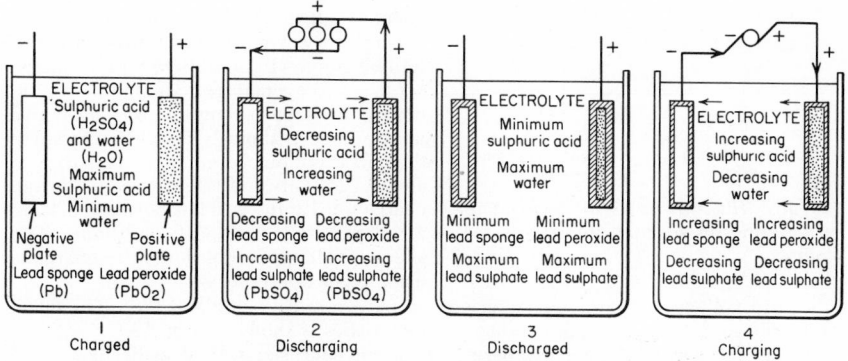

FIG. 186 *Chemical action in a cell on cycle of discharge and charge.*

During charge [Fig. 186(4)], the lead sulfate, $PbSO_4$, on the positive plate is converted into lead peroxide, PbO_2, while the lead sulfate on the negative plate is converted into sponge lead, Pb, and the electrolyte gradually becomes stronger as the SO_4 from the plates combines with hydrogen from the water to form acid, H_2SO_4, until no more sulfate remains and all the acid has been returned to the electrolyte. It will then be of the same strength as before the discharge, and the same acid will be ready to be used over again during the next discharge.

160. Change in Electrolyte during Charge and Discharge. During discharge, as stated in Sec. **159**, some of the acid leaves the electrolyte and combines with the plates. During charge, the acid which has been absorbed by the plates is driven back into the electrolyte. When all the acid has been driven back into the electrolyte, the battery is fully charged.

When all the acid has been driven into the electrolyte, the electrolyte is stronger than when some of the acid is in the plates. This strength is measured in terms of specific gravity. The specific gravity of the electrolyte, therefore, changes as the battery charges or discharges. It falls on discharge and rises on charge. It is, then, an excellent indication of the state of charge of a battery, being greatest when the cell is fully charged and least when discharged.

The difference between the full charge and discharge values of the gravity depends upon the type of cell under consideration. For example, for the type of cell in use in starting work in automobiles, the full-charge gravity in temperate climates is 1.280, discharged 1.150.

The specific gravity of the electrolyte is readily determined by means of a float called a hydrometer. With a high specific gravity, the hydrometer or float does not sink so far in the electrolyte as it does when the specific gravity is low (see Fig. 187).

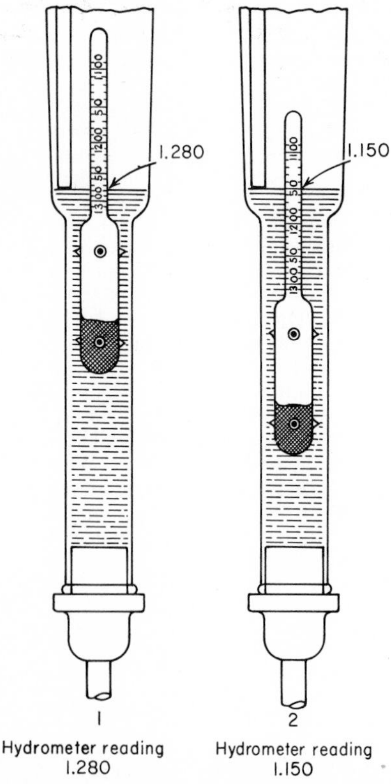

161. Voltage Characteristics. The voltage of each cell is approximately 2 volts on an open circuit but is higher than this when the battery is being charged and lower when being discharged. The nominal voltage of a battery is, therefore, the number of cells multiplied by two.

The voltage at any time on discharge or charge depends upon several factors, such as the current rate, the state of charge or discharge, and the temperature. No general averages to cover all conditions can therefore be given. In usual 6- to 8-hr discharge service, the average cell voltage (Sec. **158**) during discharge is roughly 1.95 volts with a final voltage of about 1.75 volts. As soon as the cell is put on charge, its voltage rises to about 2.15 volts and then increases during charge until at the end it is between 2.4 and 2.7, depending upon local conditions. The average voltage during the entire charge is usually considered to be 2.33 volts.

I

Hydrometer reading
1.280

2

Hydrometer reading
1.150

FIG. 187 *Illustrating use of hydrometer in determining specific gravity of electrolyte.*

Typical voltage-discharge characteristics are given in Figs. 188 and 189. The effect of the discharge rate upon the voltage characteristics is shown in Fig. 190.

162. High discharge rates (amperes) are often confused with overdischarge (too many ampere-hours taken out). A lead-acid battery of the type sold under the trade names Exide, Chloride, and Ironclad can be discharged, without injury to the plates, at

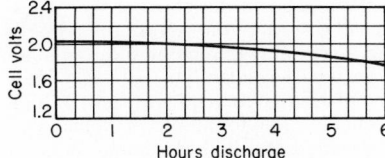

FIG. 188 *Type MVM Exide-Ironclad discharge characteristics at the 6-hr rate. (Electric Storage Battery Co.)*

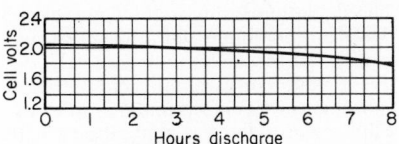

FIG. 189 *Type MVM Exide-Ironclad discharge characteristics at the 8-hr rate. (Electric Storage Battery Co.)*

any rate of current that it will deliver. The maximum permissible rate of discharge is limited only by the current-carrying ability of the wiring, motor, or other apparatus to which the battery is connected or by the current-carrying ability of the cell terminals and connectors and not by the plates themselves.

163. Rating of Lead-Acid Batteries. All batteries are given a normal − ampere-hour − capacity rating based on a certain time rate of discharge under specified conditions of temperatures and final voltage. For example, a certain battery may have an 8-hr rating of 1,000 amp-hr discharging to 1.75 volts per cell at a temperature of 77°F.

The ampere-hour capacity of a battery depends upon the amount of available active material in the plates that can be reached by the electrolyte, the amount of sulfuric acid in the electrolyte, the rate of discharge, and the allowable safe limit of discharge. To produce an ampere-hour of electricity on discharge requires the combination of a certain amount of sponge lead (negative active material) and a certain amount of peroxide of lead (positive active material) with a certain amount of sulfuric acid from the electrolyte. The allowable rating therefore de-

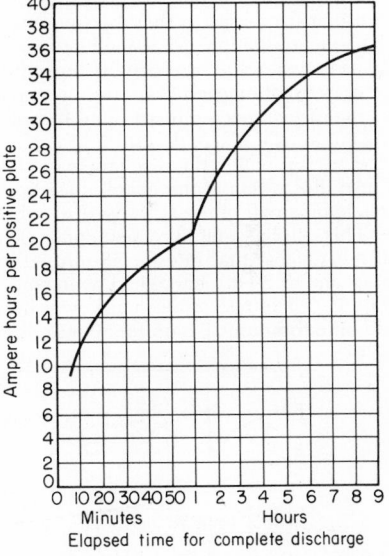

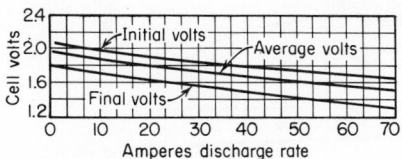

FIG. 190 *Type MVM Exide-Ironclad initial, average, and final volts at various discharge rates. (Electric Storage Battery Co.)*

FIG. 191 *Curve illustrating effect of discharge rate upon available ampere-hour capacity of lead-acid storage batteries. (Electric Storage Battery Co.)*

pends upon the construction of the plates and the number of plates that are constructed in parallel on each side of the battery.

164. Effect of Discharge Rates on Discharge Capacity of Lead-Acid Batteries. The useful ampere-hour capacity of a storage battery depends on the rate of discharge and is greater for a long low rate or intermittent rate than for a short high rate. Any particular battery is given a so-called normal rate. This so-called normal rate is not the capacity obtainable under all conditions. Each different rate of discharge governs the available capacity that can be obtained from the battery.

When a battery is discharged continuously at a constant rate, its available ampere-hour capacity is a function of the rate of discharge, the available capacity being lower at the higher rates, as is shown in Fig. 191. The reduction in available capacity of high-rate continuous discharge is due to depletion of the acid in the pores of the plates. The depletion is due to the fact that at high rates of discharge the acid in the pores of the plates combines with the active material and is withdrawn from the solution more rapidly than it can be replenished by diffusion from the free electrolyte in the cell. It is this limitation of available acid in the pores of the plates that limits the capacity at high continuous rates of discharge, rather than any limitation due to the plates themselves. This explains the fact that, after a battery is exhausted at a high discharge rate, the balance of its normal capacity can be obtained by continuing the discharge at lower rates or by allowing the battery to recuperate while standing on open circuit for a time and then continuing the high-rate discharge. For this reason also, as stated in Sec. **162,** it is impossible to damage the plates by overdischarge at high rates, as the voltage of the battery will drop below a usable value before the active material in the plates is discharged to the danger point.

Figure 191 shows the available capacity per positive plate of an Exide-Ironclad battery when discharged continuously, in varying lengths of time.

If a battery is discharged intermittently, it is evident that during periods of rest between discharges diffusion will continue, thus renewing the strength of acid in the pores of plates and increasing the available capacity corresponding to the discharge rate. The rate of diffusion depends on the difference in strength of the acid in the pores and that outside the plates, and if this difference is great, the diffusion is rapid at first but decreases as they become more nearly equal. It follows from this reasoning that the reduction in available capacity due to high rates of discharge largely disappears when the discharge is intermittent.

If the total elapsed time during which discharges are made is greater than 6 hr, and if the discharges are distributed throughout that time so that there is time for this diffusion to take place, the full 6-hr capacity of the battery will be available regardless of the rates at which the discharges are taken.

An illustration of the effect of acid diffusion is given in Fig. 192, which shows a test made on a cell of the type used in submarine boats by the U.S. government.

This cell has a rated capacity of 3,000 amp for 1 hr. The curve shows it to have been discharged at that rate for 58 min, at which time it was practically exhausted at that rate, and if the discharge had been continued at that rate, the voltage would have fallen rapidly. The rate of discharge was, however, reduced to 1,350 amp and continued for 45 min, then to 910 amp for 30 min, then to 525 amp for 1 hr and 20 min, and finally to

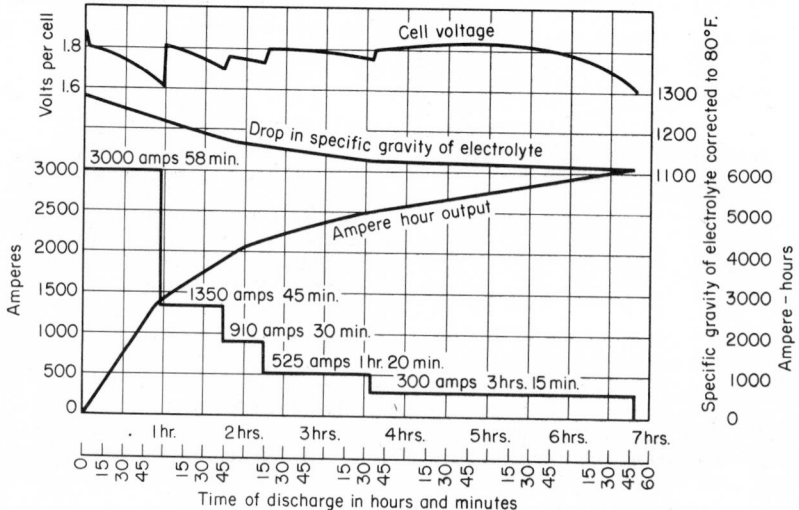

FIG. 192 *Curves showing effect of acid diffusion in lead-acid storage batteries on intermittent discharge. (Electric Storage Battery Co.)*

300 amp for 3 hr and 15 min. At each reduction in the rate of discharge the rate of acid absorption by the plates was reduced, thus allowing diffusion to strengthen the acid in the pores of the plate and so allowing the discharge to be continued. In each case the voltage at the lower discharge rate was higher than the voltage at the preceding higher rate. During the 300-amp discharge it will be noted that the voltage continued to rise for over an hour after the start at that rate, showing that the acid from the free electrolyte was entering the pores of the plates faster than it was being absorbed.

The curve showing ampere-hour output shows that 6,000 amp-hr was delivered by the cell and that, after the battery had been exhausted at the high rate of discharge, as much more energy was still available at lower rates.

165. Discharge Limits of Lead-Acid Batteries. In an emergency, little if any permanent harm will result if the battery is discharged to the full amount that it will give, provided that it is promptly recharged.

It has already been pointed out that the drop in specific gravity of electrolyte should not exceed a certain definite value, which varies according to the type of cell and will be furnished on application to the manufacturer.

The danger of harm from overdischarge may be illustrated by a comparison between the active material of the plates and the action which goes on when some of the electrolyte is allowed to act on copper wiring terminals of a battery. It is noticeable that a comparatively large amount of copper sulfate is formed when only a small quantity of the metal is eaten away by the acid. In the same manner, when the acid combines with the lead in the active material, the resulting lead sulfate occupies more space than the active material from which it is formed. The active material of all battery plates is porous, and this expansion of the sulfated material is accommodated by reduction in the size of pores in the active material. All battery plates are designed to accommodate a certain amount of this expansion of the active material during sulfation, and in batteries of the type under consideration this is limited to the amount represented by a certain specific-gravity reading.

Further discharge, even if it can be obtained at a satisfactory voltage, results in an excessive expansion, which so closes the pores in the active material that it becomes increasingly difficult to recharge the battery properly after an excessive discharge, and unless a proper recharge is given, the battery is likely to deteriorate.

166. Charging and Charging Rates for Lead-Acid Batteries. A battery must, of course, be charged with direct current, and the current must be connected to the battery so that it will go through it in the proper direction. The positive pole of the charging source must be connected to the positive terminal of the battery, and the negative of the charging source to the negative of the battery.

While a battery is being charged, the amount of sulfate in the plates decreases, and the ability of the plate to give up the acid becomes reduced; in other words, during the early part of a charge the plates can give up the acid at a rapid rate, as there is a large amount of sulfate available. Therefore a battery that is considerably discharged can be charged at a high rate, but as the charge approaches completion, currents at high rate cannot be utilized, and if high rates are maintained, only a portion of the current is used to withdraw acid from the plates, and the balance of the current acts to decompose the water in the electrolyte into oxygen and hydrogen, which are given off in the form of gas. Gassing of the battery, therefore, at any time shows whether or not the charging rate is too high. Consequently, when the cells are gassing on charge the rate of charge should be reduced so as not to waste the current. Furthermore, the action of the bubbles of gas escaping from the pores of the plates and in "boiling" to the top of the electrolyte has a tendency to wash and wear the active material away from the plates, particularly the positive.

It is a well-known fact that batteries wear out. This wear shows itself to the eye principally in the positive plate, the active material of which softens with use, and were it not for this unavoidable fact, the life of batteries would be very much longer than at present. As the active material of the plate softens with use, there is a tendency for the softened material on the surface of the plate to fall to the bottom of the jar in the form of sediment. The action of the gas in escaping from the pores of the plates and the little whirlpools created in the electrolyte when the bubbles of gas boil to the surface hasten this shedding of material and shorten the life of the battery.

Excessive gassing, therefore, should be avoided if the best life of the battery is to be obtained. A small amount of gassing at low rates and for a short time, at the completion of a charge, is not objectionable, but violent gassing having the appearance of boiling should be avoided.

167. Charging Methods for Lead-Acid Batteries. In practice, charging methods vary with the type of service. For example, in propelling electric vehicles, the battery is discharged over a period of time and then recharged. The rate in amperes to use for recharge depends upon the time available and type of cell. The lower the rate of charge, the longer will be the time required. The shorter the time available, the higher the rate must be to recharge, provided the rate is not higher than recommended for the type of cell. In any event, the rate must always be low at the end of charge when gassing begins. This is known as the finish charge rate.

Batteries charged by this cycle method of discharge and charge can have their charging equipment arranged and designed to provide a taper charge rate automatically and inherently, i.e., high at the start of charge, when a high rate can be utilized, and low at the end of charge when gassing begins. In addition, the equipment can be arranged to stop the charge at the proper time, and all without any manual attention whatever.

Batteries used in starting, lighting, and ignition work on automobiles equipped with a generator for charging are charged whenever the engine is running at ordinary speeds. At very low speeds or when the engine is not running, the battery supplies current for lights, ignition, and cranking. In automobile service, the rate must be sufficient to keep the battery charged and yet not overcharge it.

Batteries used for reserve emergency, stand-by, or voltage regulation are kept fully charged by a trickle current or floating charge. A constant voltage of appropriate value impressed across the battery terminals is sufficient for proper charging.

Regardless of the charging method, the rate in amperes must not cause excessive gassing, neither should the cell temperature rise above 110°F.

168. Equalizing Charge for Lead-Acid Batteries. Wherever practicable, batteries are given an equalizing charge at regular intervals, for example, weekly for batteries used in propelling vehicles and other services in which the battery is discharged considerably and then recharged, monthly in floating service.

In cycle service an equalizing charge is a continuation of the regular charge at a low rate. In floating service the equalizing charge is obtained by raising the voltage across the battery to increase the current into the battery. The equalizing charge continues until all cells gas freely and until it is certain by taking voltage and gravity readings that *all* cells are fully charged.

As has already been pointed out, the object of charging is to withdraw all acid from the plates. In practice, the regular charges in cycle service are not always given long enough to withdraw all the acid completely from the plates. In fact, this is not necessary, provided the acid is completely withdrawn regularly by giving an equalizing charge. If this is not done and some sulfate is allowed to remain in the plates for a considerable time, it will gradually increase, the pores of the plate will become clogged, and the battery loses capacity and deteriorates in such a way that it becomes increasingly difficult to restore it to its normal condition. To carry frequent (such as daily) regular charges to the full extent would involve an unnecessary amount of charging and gassing which is not desirable.

A battery is not fully charged until all the acid is driven out of the plates by charging. To charge a battery fully, do not try to charge to a fixed or definite gravity, but charge until the specific gravity or voltage stops rising.

169. Effect of Temperatures upon Lead-Acid Batteries. The cell temperature should not exceed 110°F. The effect of high temperature is primarily to shorten the life of the wood separators which are installed between the positive and negative plates of some types of cells.

There is always a tendency for wood in contact with sulfuric acid to become carbonized. This tendency is greatly increased at temperatures above 110°F. If a battery is operated regularly under such conditions, it will probably be necessary to renew the wood separators before the battery itself is worn out.

In the materials used in any commercial storage battery, some impurities are also present which cause very slight action in the cell, even when it is not in active operation. At high temperatures, these internal losses are increased, as is evidenced by the fact that a battery placed in storage will not lose its charge seriously over a period of, say, 6 months if kept in a cool place. If kept in a temperature around 100°F, it will lose much more of its charge in, say, 3 months.

Low temperature temporarily decreases both the discharge voltage and the ampere-hour capacity which can be taken out of the battery. The battery acts as if it were numbed by the cold and unable to make the same effort as at normal temperature. The

FIG. 193 *Automobile type of lead-acid storage battery.* *(Electric Storage Battery Co.)*

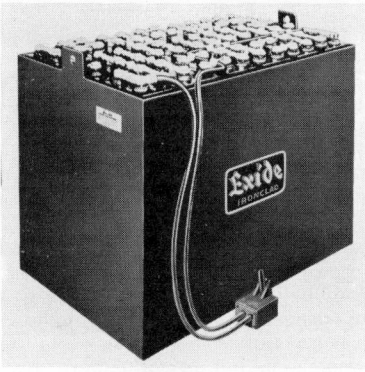

FIG. 194 *Ironclad type of lead-acid storage battery.* *(Electric Storage Battery Co.)*

effect of cold is only temporary, the battery returning to its normal state upon its return to normal temperature even without charge. There is no danger of the electrolyte freezing in a fully charged cell, but it is likely to occur in an overdischarged battery or in one that has had the water added without subsequent charging.

170. Types of Lead-Acid Storage Batteries. Lead-acid storage batteries may be roughly divided into three groups depending upon the class of service for which they are intended. Those for automobile starting, lighting, and ignition work consist of cells assembled in a single hard-rubber container (Fig. 193). Those for electric-vehicle applications consist of iron-clad-type cells assembled in a suitable container (Fig. 194). Those for stationary service consist of cells enclosed in glass jars (Fig. 195).

171. Lead-acid batteries are easily kept in good condition for a long time of trouble-free service if the following maintenance instructions are observed:

1. Keep battery clean outside (Sec. **172**).
2. Add water at regular intervals (Secs. **173** and **174**).
3. Maintain battery in a healthy state of charge (Secs. **176** and **177**).
4. Keep written records (Sec. **178**).

172. Cleanliness. 1. Keep the battery, its connections, and surrounding parts clean and dry by wiping with a dry rag, but do not remove the grease from the seal nuts. Keep the vent plugs in place and tight, and make sure their gas-escape holes are open. If electrolyte is spilled or if any

FIG. 195 *Lead-acid storage battery in enclosing glass jar.* *(Electric Storage Battery Co.)*

parts are damp with acid, apply a solution of ammonia or of baking soda (in the proportions of 1 lb of soda to 1 gal of water), then rinse with water and dry; do not allow solution to get into cells. If this treatment is given two or three times a year and the battery kept clean between times by regular washings with water or blowing off with an air jet, the life and service of the battery in general and trays or supports in particular will be increased considerably. Before hosing battery without removing it from compartment, consult equipment manufacturer for permission. When washing high-voltage batteries, open the connections at several places to avoid possible shocks.

2. If the terminals or connections show any tendency to corrode, scrape the corroded surface clean, wash it with soda solution or with ammonia solution, rinse with water, and coat it thinly with Vaseline or No-Ox-Id grease. No corrosion will occur unless electrolyte is spilled and allowed to remain.

3. Soda solution or ammonia will neutralize the effect of acid on clothing, cement, etc.

173. Adding Water. 1. During operation, water must be regularly added to each cell. Do not allow the surface of the electrolyte to get below the level specified by the manufacturer. Keep it above this point by removing the vent plugs regularly from all the cells and adding sufficient approved water to each cell as often as necessary. Do not fill so high that electrolyte will be lost through the vent plugs, eventually resulting in ruined cells. Less harm will result in allowing the level to get a little low than in adding water too high. After filling, be sure to replace and securely tighten the plugs. The intervals at which water must be added depend largely on the operating schedule, but it should not be necessary to add water more often than once a week; otherwise the battery is being given too much charge.

2. In cold weather the time to add water is just before a charge, so that gassing (bubbling of the electrolyte resulting from charging) will ensure thorough mixing and any danger of the water freezing be avoided.

3. Electrolyte loses some of its water by the charging of the battery and some by evaporation, but its acid is never lost in this manner; therefore, it will not be necessary to add new electrolyte unless some should get outside the cell through carelessness or by adding too much water so that the container is too full.

4. Nothing but water is required to be added to storage batteries. Never add any special powders, solutions, or jellies. A great many special powder solutions or jellies are injurious, having a corrosive or rotting action on the battery plates, reducing the voltage and capacity of the cells.

5. All the cells in the battery should take the same amount of water. If one cell takes more than the others, examine it for leakage.

6. Keep a written record of the amount of water added from time to time.

174. Kind of Water. 1. The quality of water to add is distilled (not merely boiled) or other approved water. By approved water is meant that of which the battery manufacturer has analyzed a sample and found safe for his batteries. The local source of water is usually suitable, but before using it the battery manufacturer should be consulted. Most companies will do this without charge for users of their batteries. Transportation charges should be prepaid, and the sample marked for identification.

2. If water is drawn from a tap or spigot, it should be allowed to run a few moments before it is used, to remove pipe accumulations. Water should not be transported or stored in any metallic vessel except lead. Glass, earthenware, rubber, plastic, or wooden receptacles that have not been used for any other purpose are satisfactory.

175. Discharge Limits. 1. In an emergency, little if any permanent harm will result if the battery is discharged to the full amount that it will give, provided that it is promptly and fully recharged.

2. If an ampere-hour meter is in use, the discharge should be stopped and the battery promptly recharged before or upon reaching its capacity limit in ampere-hours, as given by the manufacturers. The ampere-hour meter will run slow if the discharge is at high rates or if the meter is not calibrated at proper intervals and will then show less discharge than the battery actually gives. This fact should not be overlooked.

3. The specific gravity of the electrolyte falls on discharge and is therefore an indication of the amount of discharge. The difference between the full-charge and discharge values of the gravity depends on the type of cell. The manufacturer of the battery should be consulted for the proper values for any particular cell.

176. Hydrometer Readings—Specific Gravity. 1. If the specific-gravity or hydrometer reading is known, one can tell if the battery is fully charged or the amount it is discharged. With all cells connected in series, the gravity reading of one cell, known as a pilot cell, will indicate the state of discharge or charge of the whole battery.

2. The specific gravity is easily determined by allowing a hydrometer to float in the electrolyte. When the specific gravity is high, the hydrometer will not sink so far into the electrolyte as when the specific gravity is low (see Fig. 187).

3. To take a reading, insert the nozzle of the hydrometer syringe (Fig. 196) into the cell, squeeze the bulb and then slowly release it, drawing up just enough electrolyte from the cell to float the hydrometer freely. With the syringe held vertically, the reading on the stem of the hydrometer at the surface of the liquid is the gravity reading of the electrolyte. After testing, always return the electrolyte to the cell from which it was taken.

4. Both temperature and level of electrolyte affect the specific gravity reading somewhat, and it is therefore desirable to record the temperature and level of the electrolyte at the same time its gravity reading is taken. A gravity reading should not be taken immediately after adding water, as the reading will give a false indication of the specific gravity. Allow a day or so for the water to mix with the electrolyte by gassing (bubbling) of the electrolyte resulting from charging or floating the battery.

5. After every fifty-odd gravity readings of a pilot cell, a different cell should be used as a pilot in order to avoid lowering of its gravity due to possible loss of a small amount of electrolyte each time the gravity is read.

6. Hydrometer syringes are available for mounting through the vent plug of a pilot cell (Fig. 197). Since they are continuously in place, no dripping is experienced and the pilot cell need not be changed after every fifty-odd readings.

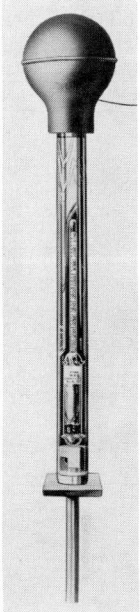
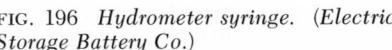
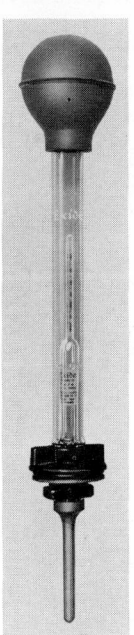

FIG. 196 *Hydrometer syringe. (Electric Storage Battery Co.)*

FIG. 197 *Vent-plug hydrometer syringe. (Electric Storage Battery Co.)*

177. Full-charge Specific Gravity. 1. The proper specific gravity of the electrolyte with the cells fully charged and with the electrolyte at the proper level, as specified by the maker, will vary somewhat with different types of batteries. The manufacturer should be consulted for the proper value.

2. The specific gravity of a new battery is adjusted at the factory and will not require adjusting during the life of the battery unless electrolyte is actually lost out of the bat-

tery. If, however, electrolyte is lost, it should be replaced with electrolyte of about the same specific gravity as in the surrounding cells.

3. The full-charge specific gravity will decrease in value as the battery ages. No definite value can be given, but this decrease is very small, not over a few points per year at the most. This change is mentioned so that it will be understood.

4. Before adjusting low gravity, first make sure charging will not raise gravity. To do this, continue an equalizing charge until the specific gravity shows no rise and then for 3 hr more. Never make a gravity adjustment on a cell which does not gas on charge.

5. To adjust low gravity, first have ready sulfuric acid of specific gravity between 1.265 and 1.300, sufficiently pure for storage-battery use. Add this instead of water when restoring level until the gravity at the end of an equalizing charge is normal. Then stop adding acid and return to the use of water. A quicker method, but one requiring more work and acid, is to withdraw some of the low-gravity electrolyte from the cell and at once replace it with this new electrolyte. Do not allow a cell to stand partly empty. The amount to withdraw will have to be determined by trial, as it depends upon the gravities of both the old and new electrolyte. Charge until all cells have been gassing for 1 hr. Then, if the gravity is not normal, repeat adjustment until it is.

6. To adjust high gravity, remove some of the electrolyte and replace with water until the gravity at the end of an equalizing charge is normal.

178. Readings — Written Records. 1. To facilitate following the operation of the battery, it is advisable to record the specific gravity and voltage of each cell at intervals. The relative state of charge should be the same each time readings for record are taken — for instance, on a manually cycled battery, at the end of a charge; on a floated battery, 10 to 15 min after starting the monthly equalizing charge.

2. Cell voltage readings should be taken while the charging current is being maintained and not after it is reduced or interrupted. During these readings the battery voltage or the charging current into the battery should be kept constant. Cell gravities should be taken 10 or 15 min after charge is completed and not while cells are gassing heavily.

3. The individual cell voltages, read to the hundredth of a volt, should be recorded once a month, in which case three or four times a year will be sufficient for recording the cell gravities. Otherwise cell gravities should be recorded monthly.

4. Review the monthly cell readings and compare with those for the previous month promptly. Plotting the readings saves time in reviewing and comparing. Prompt action upon indication of trouble may save time and expense later (see Sec. **179**).

179. Trouble. 1. The chief indications of trouble in a cell are:
Falling off in gravity or voltage relative to the rest of the cells.
Lack of gassing on equalizing charge.

2. If a battery seems to be in trouble, the first thing to do is to give it an equalizing charge (Sec. **168**). Then take a gravity reading of each cell. If all the cells gas evenly on the equalizing charge and the gravity of them all goes above a certain value as specified by the manufacturer, then all the battery needed was the charge. Before making an adjustment, determine whether the jar is cracked by adding water to the proper height and allowing cell or jar to stand several hours, noting whether level falls. If a jar is cracked, change it. Never make a gravity adjustment on a cell which does not gas. If a cell will not gas on the equalizing charging, investigate for impurities or inspect it for short circuits. For the latter, remove the elements from the jar and examine the separators carefully to make sure that none is broken or damaged, thus causing a short circuit. Also examine plates to see that they are in good condition and note the height of sediment in the bottom of the jar. Remove any collection of "moss" on the top or edges of the plates. Handle elements very carefully, so that plates will not be broken from the straps. Replace damaged separators.

180. Impurities. Impurities in the electrolyte will cause a cell to work irregularly. Should it be known that any impurity has got into a cell, it should be removed at once. In case removal is delayed and any considerable amount of foreign matter becomes dissolved in the electrolyte, this solution should be replaced with new immediately, thoroughly flushing the cell with water before putting in the new electrolyte. If in doubt as to whether the electrolyte contains impurities, a sample should be submitted for test.

181. Sediment. The sediment which collects underneath the plates need cause no alarm unless it deposits too rapidly, in which case there is something wrong with the way the battery is operated. In a new battery there is always a thin layer at the start. As the battery wears, the sediment becomes higher, but for batteries which are floated, the plates usually wear out before the sediment space is filled.

182. Putting Battery into Storage. 1. If the use of the battery is to be temporarily discontinued, give it a charge until all the cells gas and add water to the cells during this charge so that the gassing will ensure thorough mixing and prevent its freezing in cold weather. Add enough water to raise the level of the electrolyte to the proper level. After the charge is completed, remove all fuses to prevent the use of the battery during the idle period. Make sure all vent plugs are in place.

2. At certain periods the battery should be reconnected, water added, and the battery charged. These periods are every 2 months in climates averaging 70 to 80°F and every 6 months in climates averaging 40°F.

183. Putting Battery into Commission Again. Add water, if needed, and give a charge until the gravity of the electrolyte has ceased·rising over a period of 3 hr.

NICKEL-IRON-ALKALINE BATTERIES

184. The Edison storage battery is the result of an effort to avoid many of the disadvantages of the lead–sulfuric acid combination and is a radical departure therefrom in every detail of construction. The positive plate consists of hollow, perforated, sheet-steel tubes filled with alternate layers of nickel hydrate and metallic nickel. The hydrate is the active material and the metal, which is made in the form of microscopically thin flakes, is added to provide good conductivity between the walls of the tube and the remotest active material. The negative plate is made up of perforated, flat, sheet-steel boxes or pockets loaded with iron oxide and a small amount of mercury oxide, the latter also for the sake of conductivity. The grids which support these tubes and pockets are punchings of sheet steel. The cell terminals and container are likewise of steel, and all metallic parts are heavily nickel-plated. The electrolyte is a 21 per cent solution of caustic potash containing also a small amount of lithium hydrate. All separators and insulating parts are made of rubber. The details of construction are shown in Fig. 198.

The current used in charging causes an oxidation of the positive plate and a reduction of the negative, and these operations on discharge are reversed. The electrolyte acts merely as a medium and does not enter into combination with any of the active material as it does in the acid battery. Its specific gravity remains practically constant throughout the complete cycle of charge and discharge. The charge and discharge curves are shown in Fig. 199.

The chief characteristics of the battery are ruggedness, due to its solid, steel construction; low weight, due to its stronger and lighter supporting metal; long life, due to the complete reversibility of the chemical reactions and the absence of shedding active material; and low cost of maintenance, due to its freedom from the diseases, such as sulfation, so commonly met with in storage-battery practice and from the necessity of internal cleaning and plate renewals. The arguments against it are high first cost and high internal resistance. The importance of these must, of course, be weighed with the advantages and the resultant considered in each proposed installation. The battery has attained its chief prominence in vehicle propulsion, but its characteristics also recommend it for many other purposes.

185. Voltage Characteristics. The voltage of each cell is approximately 1.5 volts on open circuit, but is higher than this when the battery is being charged and lower when being discharged. The voltage at any time depends upon state of charge or discharge, the temperature, and the density of the electrolyte. The average discharge voltage is approximately 1.2 volts per cell. Typical voltage charge and discharge curves are shown in Fig. 199. Cells are generally discharged until the voltage drops from 1.0 to 0.9 volt per cell. Further discharge is generally not satisfactory, since the voltage drops very rapidly if the discharge is continued past this point. The maximum voltage during charge will be between 1.80 and 1.90 volts per cell. The voltage for any degree of discharge is affected slightly by the rate of discharge, as shown in Fig. 200.

186. Rating of Nickel-Iron-Alkaline Batteries. All batteries are given a normal ampere-hour capacity rating based on a certain rate of discharge to a final voltage of 1.0

volt per cell.   Some current ratings are based on a 5-hr continuous discharge rate, and others on a 3⅓-hr continuous rate.

The ampere-hour capacity for discharging continuously at a constant rate to a final voltage of 1.0 volt per cell will be affected by the rate of discharge (Fig. 200).   The higher the rate of discharge, the lower is the capacity of the battery.   The effect upon the capacity will not be so great, however, as it is for lead-acid batteries.   After a high rate of discharge, the balance of the normal capacity of the battery can be obtained by

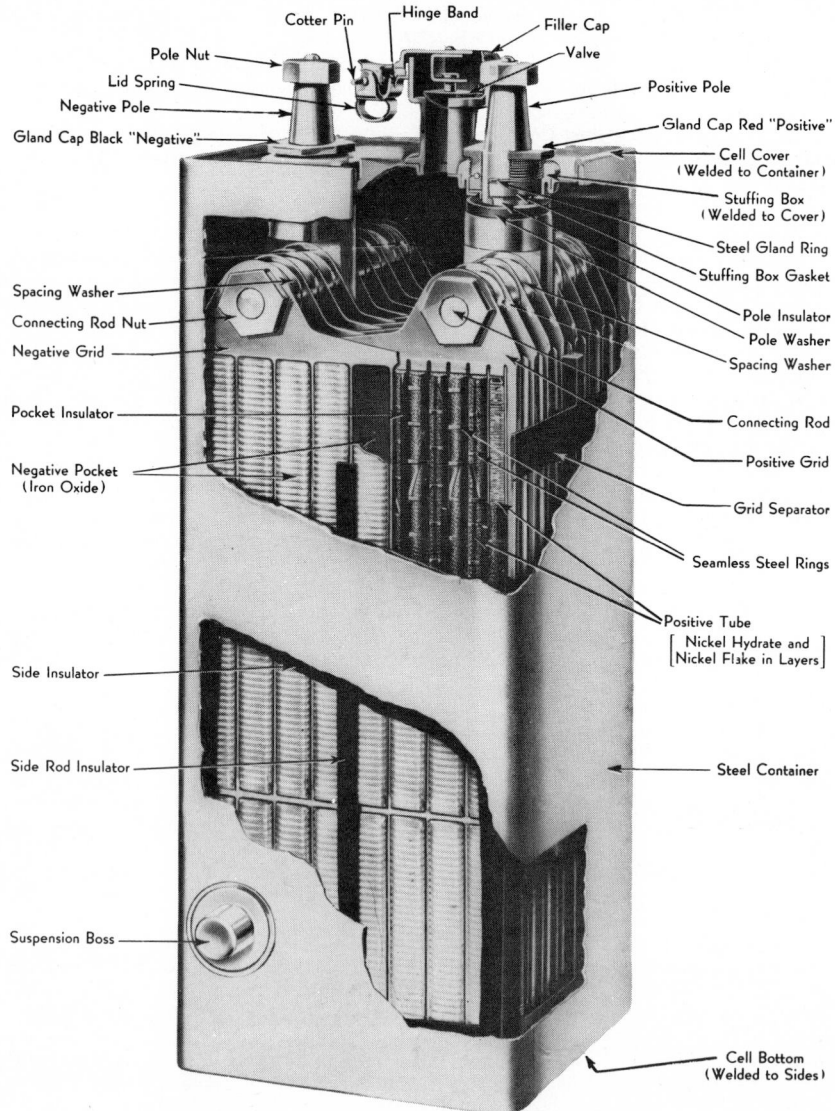

FIG. 198   *Edison nickel-iron-alkaline storage cell with container cut away to show construction detail.   (Electric Storage Battery Co.)*

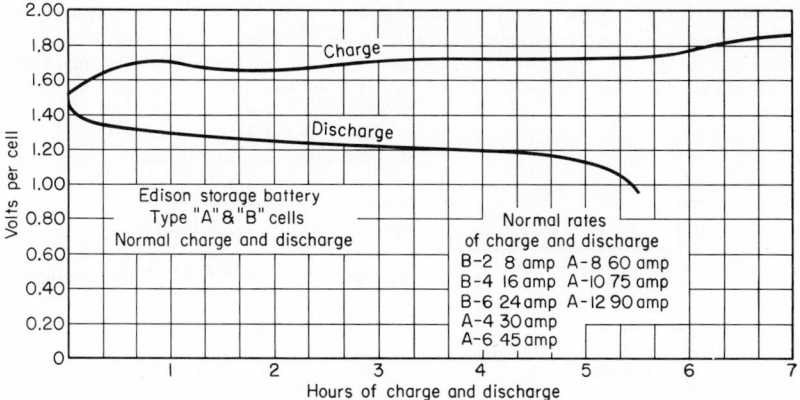

FIG. 199 *Charge and discharge curves of Edison battery.*

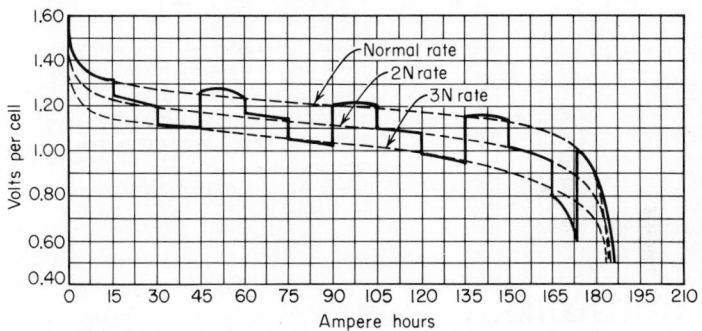

FIG. 200 *Discharging at high rates: a 4-cell battery, normal rate 30 amp, discharged successfully at 30, 60, and 90 amp, with comparison of continuous discharge at each of these rates.* (*Electric Storage Battery Co.*)

continuing the discharge at a lower rate. If the battery is discharged intermittently, the normal capacity can be obtained unless the total elapsed time of discharge is excessively short. These batteries are very rugged and withstand very severe service. They are not harmed by occasional short-circuit discharges.

187. Charging. The best method of charging Edison batteries is by the average-constant-current method. The battery is connected in series with an adjustable resistance to a constant-potential, d-c supply, as shown in Fig. 201. The positive terminal of the battery should be connected to the positive terminal of the supply. The maximum voltage available at the batteries should be at least 1.85 times the number of cells in series. Throughout the charging period the rheostat should be periodically adjusted so that the average current will be maintained at its normal rated value. At each adjustment the current should be set a few amperes above the rated value so that by the time the next adjustment is made the current will not have dropped much below normal. The battery should be charged until a maximum voltage has been reached and maintained for 30 min. If an ampere-hour meter is used with the battery in charge and discharge, satisfactory charge is generally obtained by charging the battery at its rated current until the ampere-hours of charge is 125 per cent of the ampere-hours of discharge. The condition of charge cannot be judged by means of specific-gravity readings. Automatic equipment for the control of the current during charge is being used to a greater extent.

Before starting to charge, see that the solution is at the proper level. If the solution is low, bring it to the proper level by adding pure distilled water as instructed under watering. If the battery is in a compartment, open the covers before starting a charge. If necessary, and if full capacity is not required, a battery can be taken off charge at any time and used.

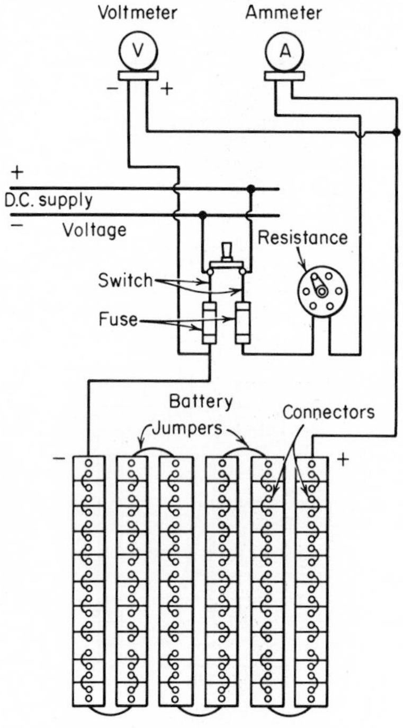

FIG. 201 *Showing correct connections for charging a battery at constant current through a variable resistor. (Electric Storage Battery Co.)*

188. Effect of Temperature. Do not charge in a hot place or allow the temperature of the solution to exceed 115°F on charge. High temperatures during charge or discharge will shorten the life of any kind of battery. Better efficiency is obtained if cells are charged at a temperature of 80 to 90°F. If the temperature of the solution exceeds 115°F while charging, allow the cells to cool before continuing the charge.

189. Charging at High Rates. In an emergency, when time for a normal charge is not available, charging can be done at any higher rates than normal, provided there is no frothing and the temperature does not rise above 115°F.

190. Charging at Low Rates. Where the discharge requirements are such that a low constant rate is used or where there is an intermittent rate of such value that for a given time period a low average rate will be had, then a charge rate of less than normal can be used, provided that this charge rate is approximately 120 per cent of the constant or average discharge rate. The term low discharge rate is to be construed to mean a constant or average rate of less than 80 per cent of normal.

When charging at low rates it must be thoroughly understood that the required ampere-hour input must be put in and that, therefore, the time periods of charge must be correspondingly increased over that necessary to fully charge a cell at normal rate.

191. Boosting Charge. An Edison battery can be boosted, i.e., given a supplementary charge, at high rates during brief periods of idleness, thereby materially adding to the available capacity. The principal limiting feature is that the temperature of the solution in the cells nearest the center or the warmest part of the battery does not exceed 115°F. A battery can be boosted whether it is entirely discharged or only partially discharged. The object of the boost is to supplement the remaining charge so that additional work can be done without waiting for regular charge.

The following table gives figures that can be used under average conditions, but values that will not cause excessive heating must be determined in each case by experience:

5 min at five times normal
15 min at four times normal
30 min at three times normal
60 min at two times normal

Frothing at the filler opening is an indication that the boosting has been carried too far (if the solution is at the proper height), and the boosting should be discontinued at once.

192. Overcharging is to be interpreted as charging a battery at the normal rate for periods in excess of the specified Hours Normal Charge. For A, B, C, and N Types, 12 hr is considered an overcharge when the previous discharge has been taken only to an average of approximately 0.5 volt per cell, and 15 hr is considered an overcharge when the previous discharge has been taken to zero voltage and short-circuited. For G and L Types these overcharge periods are, respectively, 8 and 10 hr.

Overcharging in conjunction with proper discharges is used to compensate for either lack of work of battery or change of solution. In those cases where batteries have become sluggish owing to lack of work, such as where batteries are seldom totally discharged in regular service, the battery should be periodically completely discharged to zero at normal rate and then short-circuited for 1 or 2 hr. Follow with a regular overcharge.

With new Edison batteries better capacities will result if they are given plenty of work. It is, therefore, advisable to give new batteries additional work every 2 weeks for the first 2 months and every 2 months thereafter for 6 months. This should consist of a complete discharge to zero at normal rate with a short circuit of at least 2 hr followed by an overcharge.

When an Edison battery does not give satisfactory capacity on discharge at rates several times normal, it is considered sluggish. This sluggishness or low capacity may result from persistent low-rate discharging, frequent low-rate charging, long stands, seldom discharging completely, or weak solution. With the exception of the last named the primary cause is lack of work. Edison batteries thrive on work; therefore, the proper procedure is to discharge the battery completely at normal rate to zero and then short-circuit it for 2 hr. Follow this by a overcharge. If the condition is rather pronounced, the cycle should be repeated. In the worst cases results can usually be obtained by several repetitions of the above. Ordinarily, this method will restore underworked batteries.

Completely discharge batteries before starting overcharges. Test for height of solution and bring the solution to the proper height. Tests of solution height should be made before and after the battery is completely discharged at normal rate, followed by a short circuit of at least 2 hr and then an overcharge.

193. Data for Nickel-Iron-Alkaline Batteries
(Electric Storage Battery Co.)

Cell type	Rating[a]		Weight,[b] lb per cell	
	Ampere-hour capacity	Normal rate, amp	Standard	High type
N2	11¼	2¼	1.94	
L20	12½	3¾	1.88	
L30	18¾	5⅝	2.64	
L40	25	7½	3.24	
B1, B1 *H*[c]	18¾	3¾	5.3	6.7
B2, B2 *H*[c]	37½	7½	6.0	7.2
B4, B4 *H*[c]	75	15	9.5	10.9
B6, B6 *H*[c]	112½	22½	13.0	15.2
A4, A4 *H*[c]	150	30	16.5	19.3
A5, A5 *H*[c]	188	37½	19.6	22.5
A6, A6 *H*[c]	225	45	22.4	25.5
A7, A7 *H*[c]	263	52½	25.8	28.6
A8, A8 *H*[c]	300	60	31.2	35.9
A10, A10 *H*[c]	375	75	38.1	43.8
A12, A12 *H*[c]	450	90	47.3	53.5
A14, A14 *H*[c]	525	105	56.6	60.8
A16, A16 *H*[c]	600	120	62.9	68.0
A20 *H*[c]	750	150	.....	84.8
A24 *H*[c]	900	180	.....	102.5
G4, G4 *H*[c]	100	30	12.5	19.0
G6, G6 *H*[c]	150	45	17.5	21.1
G7, G7 *H*[c]	175	52½	20.8	23.0
G9, G9 *H*[c]	225	67½	24.0	27.5
G11, G11 *H*	275	82½	30.4	36.2
G14, G14 *H*	350	105	37.2	44.5
G18, G18 *H*	450	135	52.4	56.8
G22 *H*[c]	550	165	.....	70.0
C4	225	45	24.3	
C5	281	56¼	29.3	
C6	338	67½	34.4	
C7	394	78¾	39.8	
C8	450	90	45.5	
C10	563	112½	61.3	
C12	675	135	71.0	
D6	450	90	45.6	
D8	600	120	60.0	
D10	750	150	77.3	
D12	900	180	91.6	

[a] Ratings are on basis of 5-hr rate for A, B, C, and N Type cells and 3⅓-hr rate for G and L Type, with average of 1.2 volts per cell and final of 1.0 volt per cell.

[b] Weights are for completely assembled cells, including trays, connectors, etc.

[c] The letter *H* indicates high-type cells; these cells have the same characteristics as the standard-type cells but are built higher so as to hold more electrolyte and are used in installations where frequent flushing is not convenient.

194. Maintenance of Nickel-Iron-Alkaline Batteries. The attention required by this battery is of the simplest character. It is chiefly important that the electrolyte be replenished from time to time with distilled water so that the plates will be entirely immersed and the outside of the cells be kept clean and dry, for, if this is not done, leakage of current will occur with consequent corrosion of containers by electrolysis. Perhaps once or twice during the total useful life of the cell, the electrolyte may need renewal.

195. Cleaning. The cells, trays, and battery compartment must be kept dry, and care must be taken that dirt and other foreign substances do not collect at the bottom or between the cells.

Dirt and dampness are likely to cause current leakage, which may result in serious injury to the cells.

Where protection of cell tops from moisture is required, they should be given a light coat of Rosin or Liquid Esbaline, this material being applied to the cover of the cell and sparingly to the outside of the filling aperture, care being taken not to get any great quantity on the lid hinge. Esbaline can be applied best with a small paintbrush, care being taken not to get any on the inside of lugs or on cell poles.

Rosin Esbaline must be applied warmed to approximately 170 to 190°F and thinned to good paint consistency with benzine, etc.

A wet steam jet or even an air blast will be found most satisfactory for cleaning but must not be used on cells while they are in the compartments. It has been found that a pressure of 70 lb with a 1-in. rubber steam hose about 10 ft long into which has been inserted a piece of iron pipe about 12 in. long with an orifice ⅛ in. in diameter will give wet steam with a velocity to clean the battery satisfactorily. (This orifice can be made by plugging one end of an iron pipe and drilling out with a ⅛-in. drill.) When removing encrustations from the tops of cells, do not allow them to fall between or into the cells. Before reassembling, make sure that all poles, connectors, and jumper lugs are clean. Also cells, trays, and compartments must be dry before the battery is replaced.

Occasionally, cells and trays after being cleaned should be recoated with Esbalite, an alkaliproof insulating paint put up by the Electric Storage Battery Co.

The cells should be thoroughly cleaned of all grease, dirt, dried salts, and paint blisters or flakes and be perfectly free from all moisture. Painting may be done with a brush or, if the quantity is large, by dipping.

When cleaning and recoating with any cell coating, be careful not to allow any of the materials to get into the cells.

196. Water or Flushing. Do not allow the level of the solution to drop below the tops of the plates. Never fill higher than the proper level. If filled too high, solution will be forced out during charge.

For replenishing solution in Edison cells during operation use only pure distilled water or water which has been tested and approved by the Electric Storage Battery Co. Although pure distilled water is recommended for use in storage batteries generally, there are certain points in the country where the local water supply is of such purity that it can be satisfactorily used. It is extremely important that no other water than pure distilled water be used unless it has received the approval of the Electric Storage Battery Co., after test at the factory's laboratories. The use of impure water will result in a slow poisoning of the electrolyte by an accumulation of impurities, the effect of which may not appear within a few months but will ultimately become apparent within the course of several years.

When solution has been spilled, use standard refill solution, which has a specific gravity of approximately 1.215 at 60°F.

Battery compartments and trays must be kept dry and clean at all times, so take care, when filling cells, not to spill water over and around the cells and not to exceed specified height.

Test for height of solution before placing battery on charge. Do not test for solution height while battery is charging; the gassing during charge creates a false level.

A reasonably heavy-walled glass tube about 8 in. long and of not less than ³/₁₆ in. inside diameter with ends cut straight and fused enough to round the edges can be used as illustrated in Fig. 202 to find level of electrolyte above plate tops. A short length of tightly fitting rubber tube forced over one end and projecting about ⅛ in. will prove a very good finger grip. Insert the tube until the tops of the plates are touched; close the upper end with the finger and withdraw the tube. The height of the liquid in the tube should be as specified by the manufacturer.

197. Specific Gravity of Nickel-Iron-Alkaline Batteries. The density or specific-gravity reading of the electrolyte of an Edison cell has no value in determining the state of charge or discharge, as the specific gravity does not change during the charging or discharging of the cell to any marked extent. The small changes ordinarily observed are due either to large changes in temperature or to loss of water from the electrolyte by evaporation or electrolysis in operating the cell. Therefore it is not necessary to take frequent readings to determine the specific gravity. The only time it is necessary to obtain specific-gravity reading is to determine when a change of electrolyte would be advantageous. When making these readings, certain fundamental conditions must be observed. A suitable hydrometer must be obtained and used in accordance with the rules laid down in Sec. **176** on hydrometer readings. The glass container must be clean and must not contain acid or other impurities, as these tend to give lower readings than the true specific gravity.

Do not take specific-gravity reading when the cell is charging, as the bubbles of gas contained in the electrolyte will cause a lower reading than the true one. Readings taken when the temperature of the electrolyte is either very high or very low will give results that will vary with the temperature. The specific gravities quoted in this section are for 60°F. Temperatures very much higher than this will give lower gravity readings, while temperatures very much lower than this will give higher readings.

Specific-gravity readings taken immediately after watering the cell are of no value, as the water has had no chance to be thoroughly mixed with the electrolyte and the resulting readings will be low. The specific gravity should be taken when the electrolyte is at the proper height after a complete charge. It is best to allow the cells to stand for a short period after the completion of the charge to allow free bubbles of gas to dissipate before taking readings. Corrections for temperature should be made by adding 0.0025 for each 10° above 60°F to the observed reading or subtracting 0.0025 for every 10° below 60°F.

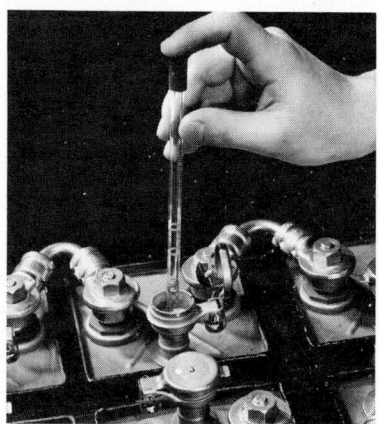

FIG. 202 *Quick method of determining height of solution. (Electric Storage Battery Co.)*

After taking a specific-gravity reading, return the solution to the same cell from which it was taken. Otherwise the gravity of the solution in the cell to which it is added will be increased and the gravity of the solution in the cell from which it was taken will be decreased owing to the addition of water being made necessary.

The potash electrolyte in Edison cells has a normal specific gravity of approximately 1.200 at 60°F when at the normal level and thoroughly mixed by charging and when a sample is taken at least 1/2 hr after charge to allow for dissipation of gas.

198. Solution Renewal. Throughout the total useful life of the cell the electrolyte gradually weakens and may need renewal once or twice, depending on the severity of service, and in some cases, where maintenance and operation have been poor or where contamination has been allowed by the use of impure water, etc., a third time might be necessary.

The low-limit specific gravity beyond which it is inadvisable to run an electrolyte is 1.160. Operation at lower specific gravity than 1.160 should not be allowed, since such operation will produce sluggishness, loss of capacity, and rapid breakdown on severe service. Should the specific gravity be above 1.160 and at the same time sluggishness and loss of capacity be evident, do not immediately renew the electrolyte until it is found that an electrolyte sample sent to the factory shows a prohibitive accumulation of impurities and until the following treatment fails to produce marked improvement:

1. Discharge at normal rate to zero voltage. (When the current can no longer be kept up, either reverse the battery on the line with sufficient resistance in series or connect in series with another more nearly charged battery; then continue the discharge.) It is of prime importance that the rate be kept at normal throughout.

2. Short-circuit the battery in groups of not more than about five cells each for at least 2 hr.

3. Charge at normal rate for 15 hr for A, B, C, and N Types and 10 hr for G and L Types.

4. Discharge at normal rate to approximately 1.0 to 0.9 volt per cell.

5. Charge at normal rate for 7 hr for A, B, C, and N Types and 4¾ hr for G and L Types.

6. Discharge at normal rate to approximately 1.0 to 0.9 volt per cell.

If the cells do not respond noticeably to this treatment, there is probably very marked contamination of the electrolyte, and the result of the analysis of a representative sample sent to the manufacturer's factory in accordance with instructions will show this. Therefore, regardless of the specific gravity, the electrolyte should be replaced as follows:

1. When previous electrolyte has reached approximately the low limit of 1.160, the new solution should be Standard Renewal.

2. When previous electrolyte is 1.190, or above, the new solution should be Standard Refill.

It is always advisable, in case the battery exhibits trouble of any sort, to communicate all details to the manufacturer or his representative, so that immediate advice may be obtained.

Do not use any other solution than Edison Electrolyte. Do not pour out old solution until you have received new and are ready to use it. Never allow cells to stand empty. State type and number of cells when ordering Edison Electrolyte for renewal.

When ready to renew solution, first completely discharge the battery at normal rate to zero and short-circuit for 2 hr or more. This is to protect the elements. Then empty cells completely. It is not necessary to shake or rinse cells, and under no circumstances should cells be filled with water.

Immediately after emptying each cell pour in new solution. Do not allow to stand empty. Fill to exactly the proper height. For this purpose use a clean glass or enamelware funnel. A plain iron funnel can be used if it has no soldered seams, but do not by any means use one of tinned or galvanized iron. A clean rubber tube can be used to siphon the solution directly from the container to the cell. If the tube is new, it should be thoroughly soaked in electrolyte for a couple of hours or filled with electrolyte and allowed to stand a couple of hours in such a position as to retain the solution. This is to remove thoroughly any impurities on the rubber. Fill to exactly the proper height, for if cells are filled too full when renewing the solution and allowed to remain that way, the specific gravity of the electrolyte will be too high when the level of the solution returns to proper height. This condition may lead to serious results and can easily be avoided by reasonable care.

Do not attempt to put in all solution received, as an excess is allowed to make up for any loss due to spilling. It may be necessary to add some more electrolyte after cells have stood a little time, as some electrolyte may be absorbed by the plates.

The specific gravity of the Edison Electrolyte for renewal as shipped is about 1.250, but this will quickly fall to normal when put into a battery, owing to mixture with the old, weak solution remaining in the plates.

Do not attempt to use the Electric Filler for refilling cells. It was not designed for this purpose and will not work.

When the new electrolyte is in and the battery is again connected for service, give it an overcharge at the normal rate as outlined under Sec. **192**, Overcharging.

199. Cautions in Operation of Nickel-Iron-Alkaline Batteries. 1. Never put lead battery acid into an Edison battery or use utensils that have been used with acid; you may ruin the battery.

2. Never bring a lighted match or other open flame near a battery.

3. Never lay a tool or any piece of metal on a battery.

4. Always keep the filler caps closed except when necessary to have them open for filling.

5. Keep batteries clean and dry externally.

6. Edison electrolyte is injurious to the skin or clothing and must be handled carefully. Solution spilled on the person should be immediately washed away with plenty of water.

200. Laying Up Nickel-Iron-Alkaline Batteries. If the battery is to be laid up for any length of time, be sure that the plates are covered to the proper height by solution or electrolyte. The battery should be stored in a dry place. Do not leave it in a damp place, as damage to the containers may result from electrolysis. Never let the battery stand unfilled.

Edison batteries are easy to lay up. Merely discharge to zero voltage and short-circuit. They can be left standing idle indefinitely in this condition without injury.

New Edison cells have received sufficient cycles of charge and discharge before shipment to give considerable capacity above rated. However, Edison cells will increase still further in capacity if thoroughly worked in. Therefore it is best, if new cells are to stand for some time before being put into commission, to discharge them to zero at normal rate and short-circuit at least 6 hr.

When putting the battery back into commission, go over each cell and see that all poles and connections are in good condition as for a new cell. See that the plates are properly covered with electrolyte and then charged as here instructed: First, if not already discharged, discharge cells to zero at normal rate and short-circuit. Follow this by an overcharge at normal rate and then discharge at normal rate. Then charge at normal rate for normal hours of charge. If the battery shows signs of sluggishness, repeat the overcharge and carry the discharge down to zero until cells are fully active; then give regular charge.

NICKEL-CADMIUM BATTERIES

201. Nickel-Cadmium batteries are a relatively new addition in the United States to the storage-battery family. These batteries consist of an interleaved assembly of positive and negative plates (Fig. 203).

Cell containers are made of nickel-plated steel. Active materials, nickel hydroxide (positive) and cadmium oxide (negative), are encased in finely perforated steel pockets.

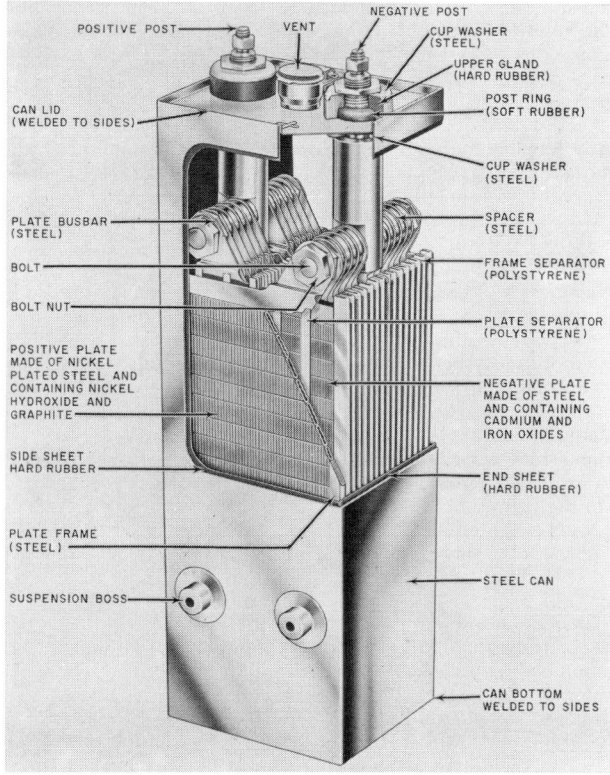

FIG. 203 *Cutaway view of a nickel-cadmium battery. (Nicad Div. of Gould-National Batteries, Inc.)*

Plates consist of rows of pockets crimped together and locked into steel frames under many tons of pressure.

Positive and negative plates are welded or bolted to heavy steel bus bars. Plate groups are interleaved and are separated by thin plastic rods.

The alkaline electrolyte is a solution of potassium hydroxide.

The active materials are converted on charging and discharging in accordance with the chemical reaction which may be written as follows:

$$2Ni(OH)_3 + Cd \rightleftharpoons 2Ni(OH)_2 + Cd(OH)_2$$

On discharge of the battery the reaction proceeds in the forward direction, while on charge the reaction is reversed. The system stores chemical energy when the battery is charged, and this chemical energy is converted back to electrical energy on discharge. Reversibility of this reaction under extreme environmental conditions is one of the outstanding properties of the nickel-cadmium electrochemical system.

During charge or discharge of a nickel-cadmium cell there is practically no change in the specific gravity of the electrolyte. The sole function of the electrolyte is to act as a conductor for the transfer of hydroxide ions from one electrode to the other depending on whether the cell is being charged or discharged.

202. Data for Nickel-Cadmium Batteries
(Nicad Division of Gould-National Batteries, Inc.)

Cell type No.	Amp-hr capacity at 8-hr rate	Width of tray, in. over all	Height of tray, in. over all	Length of tray containing, in. over all				Weight per cell, lb	
				2 cells	3 cells	4 cells	5 cells	Net	Ship.
EBZ17	80	6	16	13¼	20⅛	25½	32¼	21.0	24.0
EBZ19	90	6½	16	13¼	20⅛	25½	32¼	23.2	26.3
EBZ22	105	7¼	16	13¼	20⅛	25½	32¼	26.5	30.7
EBZ25	120	8	16	13¼	20⅛	25½	32¼	29.7	33.5
EBZ28	135	8¾	16	13¼	20⅛	25½	32¼	32.8	37.4
EBZ31	150	9½	16	13¼	20⅛	25½	32¼	36.1	41.7
ERX23	165	7½	18	15¼	23⅛	29⅝	37¼	36.1	41.7
ERX25	180	8	18	15¼	23⅛	29⅝	37¼	38.7	45.6
ERX27	195	8½	18	15¼	23⅛	29⅝	37¼	41.3	49.2
ERX29	210	9	18	15¼	23⅛	29⅝	37¼	43.8	52.1
ERX33	240	10	18	15¼	23⅛	29⅝	37¼	49.0	57.8
ERX37	270	11	18	15¼	23⅛	29⅝	37¼	54.0	63.8

203. Characteristics:
Nominal Voltage per Cell. 1.2 volts (a 6-volt battery consists of 5 cells).
Temperature Range. −60 to +200°F.
Maximum Discharge Current. Up to 25 times rated ampere-hour capacity.
Capacity at −60°F. Up to 90 per cent at low rates.
Internal resistance very low. 0.001 ohm for 10-amp-hr type cell.
Full Charge. By constant potential in 1 hr at 1.55 volts per cell.
Full Charge. By constant potential in 6 hr at 1.43 volts per cell.
Charge, Trickle. 1.35 volts per cell to maintain a charged battery.
Gassing Discharge. None.
Gassing Charge. Virtually none below 1.47 volts per cell.
Vibration Resistance. Excellent.
Shock. 80G.
Altitude. Pressure-release valve opens 25 lb per sq in. above ambient.
Cycle Life. No known limit.
Storage Life. No known limit in any state of charge.
Charge Retention. Up to 70 per cent after one year at room temperature.
Orientation. Any position on discharge.

204. Advantages of nickel-cadmium batteries as stated by Nicad Division of Gould-National Batteries, Inc.

High Surge Currents. Good voltage maintenance under extremely high current discharge conditions.

Constant-voltage Source. Close voltage regulation during discharge (see Figs. 204 and 205).

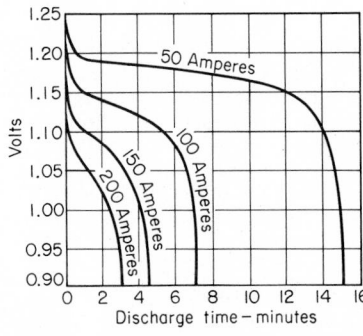

FIG. 204 *Typical discharge characteristics for a high-rate nickel-cadmium cell. (Nicad Div. of Gould-National Batteries, Inc.)*

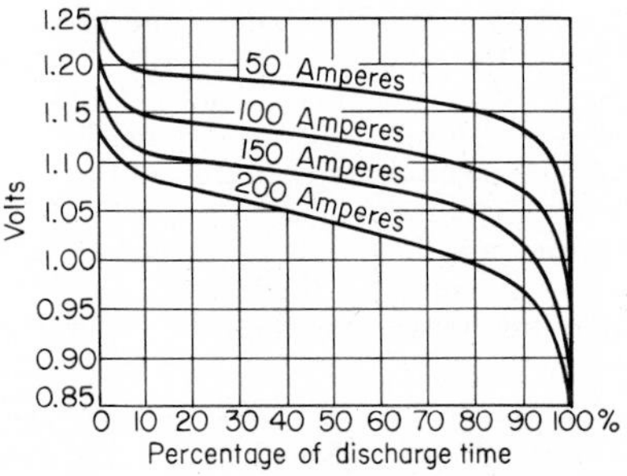

FIG. 205 *Discharge-voltage characteristics of nickel-cadmium cell. (Nicad Div. of Gould-National Batteries, Inc.)*

Rapid-charge Acceptance. Can be completely recharged at high rates without damage.

Long Life. Designed to give exceptionally long life under cycle and float service.

Extreme-temperature Operation. Normal and high rate discharge and charge is possible at temperatures from −40 to +165°F.

Excellent Charge Retention. Charged cells filled with electrolyte will retain approximately 70 per cent of their charge after one year of idle storage at normal temperature.

Storageability. Can be laid up in any state of charge for long periods without attention or fear of deterioration.

Discharges in Any Position. Can be discharged in any position.

Easy Maintenance. Negligible loss of water during service. Records of specific gravity are not necessary.

Vibration- and Shock-resistant. Capable of withstanding up to 50G shock and severe vibration.

Alkaline Electrolyte. The potassium hydroxide electrolyte does not give off corrosive fumes on charge or discharge.

Pressure-sealed. The smaller cells are normally provided with pressure-sensitive sealed vents.

Economical. Low cost per year due to long life span. Very low maintenance costs. Low-cost high-rate performance.

Small and Lightweight. Nicad sintered plate batteries are smaller and lighter than conventional batteries under high-current-drain conditions.

205. Installation and Care of Nickel-Cadmium Batteries. The following instructions for the installation and care of nickel-cadmium batteries are those recommended by the Nicad Division of the Gould-National Batteries, Inc.

206. Important Precautions

1. Maintain the battery compartment, cells, and trays in a clean and dry condition. Dirt and moisture will cause self-discharge, corrosion, and eventual leakage of cell containers.

2. Check the electrolyte level *before* adding distilled water. Maintain correct

electrolyte level, but do not add water in excess of the recommended maximum level. Do not spill water or electrolyte on the cells or trays.

3. The electrolyte is an alkaline solution of caustic potash—*not* sulfuric acid as used in lead batteries.

4. Sulfuric acid or traces thereof will rapidly ruin the Nicad battery by corroding its steel plates and cell containers. Therefore, use only the hydrometer and level test tube furnished with the battery.

5. Do not discharge at normal rates below 1.10 volts per cell. Repeated over-discharges will damage the battery.

6. Always keep the vent caps closed, except when checking the electrolyte or adding water.

7. Never examine the cells with an open flame. Keep tools and other metal objects away from the battery.

8. Apply boric acid solution if electrolyte is splashed on person or clothing.

207. Installing the Battery. Place the battery in a clean, dry room located so that it can be easily inspected and watered. On mobile equipment such as vehicles or ships it must be securely tied down.

Avoid placing the battery in a hot location (above 125°F or 52°C) or where it will be exposed to corrosive gases or fumes.

It is not good practice to install Nicad batteries and lead-acid batteries in the same room unless there is ample ventilation to carry away fumes from the lead-acid batteries.

All battery rooms and compartments must have good ventilation and drainage and at the same time keep out cinders, road dirt, soot, dust, rain, snow, and sea water.

Accumulations of dirt and moisture on cell tops and particularly between the cells will cause corrosion and leakage of cell containers.

Holes or gratings which permit ready entry of dust, water, etc., must be closed up. However, four small drainage holes (maximum diameter of holes $\frac{1}{4}$ in.) should be provided in the bottom, one at each corner of the compartment.

Compartments which have previously housed lead-acid batteries must be washed out, neutralized with ammonia or washing soda solution, allowed to dry thoroughly, and then painted with Nicadvar asphalt paint. Wood liners must be removed and replaced by new ones. Ample space should be provided above the battery for inserting the electrolyte level test tube and the hydrometer into the cells.

If the battery is to be serviced through the top of a compartment, allow a minimum clearance of 2 in. (50 mm) between the top of the battery and the underside of the access cover.

If the battery is to be serviced from the side, the clearance between the battery and the ceiling of the compartment should be at least 8 in. (200 mm).

Small stationary batteries can be placed directly on a clean, dry floor or on a suitable wall shelf. Large batteries should be placed on racks.

Check the electrolyte level and the specific gravity and be sure that the battery is thoroughly clean and dry before placing it in position.

Nothing should be placed or allowed to lodge in the open spaces between or underneath the cells. These air gaps serve as electrical insulation between the cells and are an essential part of the design of the battery. For this reason they must be maintained open, clean, and unobstructed at all times.

Variation of specific gravity may be found between individual cells. A maximum variation of plus or minus 0.005 point is permissible. For example, if normal specific gravity called for is 1.210, a minimum of 1.205 and a maximum of 1.215 specific gravity is satisfactory.

The cell containers must not be grounded, and the bottoms of the cells must not be allowed to rest on any object. Battery trays should never be stacked directly on top of one another, nor should water or spilled electrolyte be allowed to accumulate under the battery.

All cables leading to the battery posts should be fitted with nickel-plated cable lugs. Do not use bare copper cable lugs or connectors. After connecting cable lugs to battery, cover lugs with Nicad petroleum jelly No. 32982.

All wiring to the battery should be properly spaced and firmly secured to prevent any chance of a short circuit.

Wires or cables should never be allowed to rest on top of the cells.

Never connect a device or instrument to the battery that might cause an unnecessary constant drain, however small, as it will ultimately discharge the battery when left standing on open circuit. Voltmeters, for instance, should be connected to the battery only by means of a normally open push-button switch.

If either side of a high-voltage battery is grounded, it will expose personnel and battery to hazardous conditions. The shock hazard to personnel is obvious. In such cases additional high-resistance grounds in any part of the circuit will cause trouble and possibly a serious short circuit. For example, an inductive surge from breaker operations can cause a slight ground to become larger and rapidly discharge the battery. When checking battery voltage, also take readings between each terminal of the battery and ground for possible leakage, as ground indicator lights may not show slight grounds.

Most storage batteries consist of a single series of cells of the same type and ampere-hour capacity. Where the battery consists of more than one tray, be sure that the negative end terminal of each tray is connected to the positive end terminal of the following tray. Cells wrongly connected will receive a reverse charge and will be damaged if the condition is allowed to continue.

On completing the installation make sure that no loose objects such as screws or tools have been accidentally left in the battery compartment.

Check and tighten all cell post nuts, as loose electrical connections will heat up and can cause sparking.

Verify that every person who is going to take care of the battery has a copy of these instructions. Further copies can be obtained free of charge.

Mount the instruction card accompanying the battery in a conspicuous position for future reference.

208. Charging. The positive terminal post of every cell is identified by a plus mark on the cell container. When charging, always connect the positive terminal of the battery to the positive lead from the charger. Only direct current can be used for charging storage batteries. If only alternating current is available, a rectifier or a motor generator is necessary to convert the alternating into direct current. Information concerning various types of charging equipment is available from manufacturers.

When a battery is first placed in service, the charging rate may vary some before it is stabilized. During the first week or two the adjustment should be checked every few days. A reasonable amount of overcharging, particularly at low- or trickle-charge rates, has a beneficial effect on Nicad batteries. When in doubt at any time as to the state of charge it is advisable to overcharge rather than to undercharge.

Variations in line voltage due to local conditions can be large enough to throw charge voltages off normal. A normal setting during the day may rise to a point of overcharge and excessive charging at night and on week ends. If such a condition exists, it is desirable to install a constant-voltage transformer ahead of the charger.

The open-circuit voltage is the voltage of a storage battery when standing idle, i.e., when it is neither on charge nor on discharge. All types of storage batteries standing idle for a period of time have an open-circuit voltage independent of the state of charge. It, therefore, cannot be used to indicate the state of charge of a battery.

The open-circuit voltage of a Nicad cell is approximately 1.30 volts. Nicad batteries possess the characteristic common to all storage batteries that their voltage rises throughout the charge. Hence when the battery voltage ceases to rise and the charge current remains steady, it is an indication that the battery is fully charged. The voltage of a fully charged battery, still on charge, will depend upon the magnitude of the charge current; the heavier the current, the higher the battery voltage.

The accuracy of voltmeters and ammeters is of considerable importance. Temperature changes and even slight vibration can change their adjustment. Good storage-battery maintenance requires that meters, particularly panel-mounted ones, be checked periodically to an accuracy of $1/2$ of 1 per cent.

Several methods of charging batteries are described below.

209. Charging Engine-starting Batteries. The generator voltage regulator should be set so as to hold the battery voltage between 1.45 and 1.50 times the number of cells in the battery. Readings should be taken at the battery terminal posts with the voltage regulator at proper working temperature, with its cover in place, and only after the battery voltage has ceased to rise.

If the engine is started infrequently, as in emergency standby services, or if the engine is operated only for very short periods at a time (insufficient to keep the battery in a fully charged condition), it is recommended that the battery be maintained on constant trickle charge, preferably from a dry disk or plate, metallic rectifier, at a voltage equal to 1.40 to 1.45 times the number of cells in the battery. At the above charge voltage the battery may require watering as often as every 6 to 9 months.

210. Trickle Charging or Floating. Fully charged batteries floated across the line should be maintained at a voltage equal to 1.40 times the number of cells in the battery. Where the discharges, although momentary, are relatively heavy and frequent, the voltage should be raised to 1.45 times the number of cells in the battery in order to ensure that the total input will exceed the total output over a period of time. Otherwise, the battery will become slowly discharged and require so-called equalization or overcharges from time to time to bring it back to a fully charged condition.

The recommended battery voltages will hold the individual cell voltages below 1.47 volts. Above 1.47 volts the cells will begin to gas and hence consume water. Variations in voltage up to a maximum of 0.05 volt between the individual cells of a battery on float should be disregarded, as they are of no importance. One of the most valuable features of the Nicad battery is that its floating voltage is not critical, provided, of course, that it is high enough to compensate for the loads imposed on the battery from time to time. Floating at above 1.47 volts per cell will not harm the battery, but its water consumption will be considerably increased, requiring additional attention.

Trickle charging is actually a preservation charge and should be used only to keep a charged battery in a fully charged condition. It cannot be used as a substitute for normal charging of a discharged battery. Trickle chargers should be equipped with a variable resistance and a voltmeter of suitable range and accuracy. Information on suitable equipment for trickle and high-rate charging of Nicad batteries will be furnished by the manufacturer upon request.

211. Constant-current Charging. This method consists of charging at a constant current, not for a definite length of time or to a definite end voltage, but until the battery voltage ceases to rise, indicating that the battery is fully charged.

The length of time required to charge the battery by this method depends on the magnitude of the charge current and the state of charge of the battery at the time it is put on charge.

It is usual to insert a variable resistance of suitable size between the d-c line and the battery and to reduce the resistance from time to time by hand, during the charge, so as to hold the charge current reasonably constant.

A d-c line voltage of 1.40 times the number of cells in the battery is necessary at the beginning of the charge and 1.85 times the number of cells in the battery at the end of the charge. In theory, practically any rate of charge can be employed, provided that the electrolyte temperature, which is the limiting factor, is not allowed to exceed 145°F (63°C).

Too high a charge current, however, particularly if the electrolyte is above the maximum permissible level, may cause the electrolyte to be forced out of the cell vents.

When charged by the constant-current method at the normal (7-hr) charge rate, Nicad batteries will commence to gas after about 4½ hr, i.e., when the battery voltage has risen to about 1.47 volts per cell. Therefore, if a period of more than 7 hr between discharges is available, it is desirable to charge at a lower rate than normal. This will reduce gassing and consequently the amount of water required by the battery. For example, a 100-amp-hr battery has a "normal" charge rate of 20 amp (for 7 hr) but may conveniently be charged at 14 amp for 10 hr or 10 amp for 14 hr. The specific gravity of the electrolyte remains practically constant during charge and discharge; therefore, specific gravity readings are not necessary.

212. Ascertaining State of Charge. Open-circuit voltage readings (no current passing into or being delivered by the battery) *cannot* be used as indication of the state of charge of any storage battery.

The density of the electrolyte of the Nicad battery does not change appreciably on charge or discharge, and specific-gravity measurements, therefore, do *not* indicate its state of charge at any time.

To determine the state of charge of a partially charged battery it becomes necessary to take simultaneous current and voltage readings. There are several ways of doing this, and for services where it is necessary to determine the state of charge frequently, a satisfactory method can generally be worked out.

For certain applications involving heavy rate discharges of short duration, such as switch tripping, it has been found advantageous to install a voltmeter and a fixed resistance near the battery to provide an artificial load equal in value to the normal load. Voltage readings obtained while the battery is connected momentarily to the artificial load indicate the ability of the battery to carry the normal load.

Information regarding methods and equipment can be obtained from manufacturers of nickel-cadmium batteries.

213. Discharging. Heavy discharges (such as engine starting) will not damage the Nicad battery. Do not, however, discharge the battery below 1.10 volts per cell at from 3- to 10-hr rates or below 1.20 volts per cell at lower current rates. Overdischarging at low rates regularly continued below these end voltages will damage the battery and is an indication that the battery is too small for its work.

214. Maintenance. Keep the cells and trays clean and dry externally at all times. Moisture and dirt allowed to accumulate on top of and particularly between the cells will permit stray intercell currents, resulting in corrosion through electrolysis of the cell containers. For this reason any water or electrolyte spilled on the cells or the trays must be wiped off. Use compressed air or, better still, low-pressure steam to clean cells and trays. Do not allow dirt to enter the vents when cleaning cells. After cleaning, regrease the cell tops and connectors with Nicad petroleum jelly No. 32982 to protect the metal.

Batteries that are charged at high rates may gas heavily toward the end of charge, giving off minute quantities of potassium hydroxide. This combines with carbon dioxide in the air, forming potassium carbonate which deposits as a noncorrosive, inert white powder on the cell tops and connectors. Potassium carbonate is electrically conductive when damp and if allowed to build up can cause current leakage and possibly discharge the battery. Any accumulation should be removed with a brush or damp cloth.

Keep all vent caps closed to prevent air from entering the cells. Open caps only to check the electrolyte. Caps must be closed when the battery is charging.

Always check and service only one cell at a time.

Never place or drop any metal articles, such as post nuts, cable lugs, or tools, on or between the cells. These will cause heavy short circuits which may damage the cell containers.

Never permit sparks, open flame, or lighted cigarettes near a storage battery. All storage batteries when gassing give off a highly explosive mixture of hydrogen and oxygen. A nonmetallic flashlight is desirable for battery inspection. Keep all connections tight.

Use only spirit thermometers when taking temperature readings. Ordinary mercury thermometers may break. Mercury running into the cell between its plates will cause sparking and explosions.

Always keep the plates covered with electrolyte. Serious damage can be caused by exposing the tops of the plates to the air. If electrolyte has been spilled accidentally from the battery, proceed as described in Sec. **217.**

215. Damage from Impurities. Impurities of all kinds must be kept out of the cells, as they have a harmful effect and can eventually ruin the battery.

Even a trace of sulfuric acid can ruin a Nicad battery by attacking and corroding its steel plates and cell containers. To prevent contamination never use any tools or utensils such as hydrometers, funnels, rubber hoses, battery fillers, etc., which have been used at any time for servicing lead-acid batteries.

Any vegetable oil or grease accidentally introduced into the cells will cause them to froth on charge.

216. Electrolyte. The electrolyte (the "solution") in Nicad batteries is alkaline and consists of specially purified caustic potash (KOH, potassium hydroxide) dissolved in distilled water. The specific gravity of the electrolyte does not change with the state of charge but remains practically constant on charge and discharge.

The use of other than Nicad electrolyte can damage the battery. Ordinary commercial grades of caustic potash should never be used as they are not sufficiently pure.

Nicad Refill or Renewal Electrolyte of proper specific gravity is available in non-returnable containers holding 5, 10, 15, 20, and 130 lb. Use an enamelware or glass pitcher and funnel for filling cells with electrolyte or water. Earthenware, hard rubber, and plastic utensils are also suitable.

Refill Electrolyte is used to replace electrolyte accidentally lost in transit or otherwise, while Renewal Electrolyte is used when changing the electrolyte, as described in Sec. **220.**

If electrolyte should be lost by accident from any of the cells, replace the lost quantity with Refill Electrolyte. If Refill Electrolyte is not available, take the battery out of service and add enough water to cover the plates (so as to prevent damage to the plates by exposing them to the air) and procure Renewal Electrolyte. Upon its arrival empty out all the old electrolyte and fill the cells with Renewal Electrolyte. Charge the battery and check that the specific gravity is correct and uniform in all the cells before putting the battery back into service.

217. Method of Adjusting Electrolyte Specific Gravity. Cells having lost their electrolyte in shipping or by accident should be immediately filled to the proper level with Nicad Refill Electrolyte, and no adjustment of electrolyte specific gravity will be needed. If, however, they have been filled with water pending the arrival of Refill Electrolyte, the following electrolyte adjustment treatment will be necessary:

Dump the weak electrolyte-water mixture from the cells and fill with Refill Electrolyte. Cells which have lost electrolyte in varying amounts need adjustment of electrolyte specific gravity. Adjustment should be made during charge and toward the end of the charge when the cells are gassing freely.

If electrolyte is too strong, add distilled water. If electrolyte is too weak, add special 1.400-specific-gravity electrolyte supplied by Nicad on request. Three adjustments may have to be made before the normal specific-gravity reading is obtained. Allow 30 min between each adjustment during charge.

The amount of distilled water or special 1.400-specific-gravity electrolyte required can be found only by trial. For example, one cell may only need half a syringe full in order to bring the electrolyte to normal specific gravity. Yet another cell may need several syringes full depending on the size of the cell and the strength of the electrolyte in the cell.

Each time electrolyte is withdrawn from a cell during this adjustment, it should be replaced with an equal amount of special electrolyte or water to maintain correct electrolyte level above the plate tops.

Once adjusted to the correct specific gravity at maximum level, the cell will only need distilled water in order to keep the electrolyte at maximum level.

The above-described method of adjusting the electrolyte specific gravity may seem slow and cumbersome but is necessary to assure good performance and to maintain the capacity of the cells.

The electrolyte will readily absorb carbon dioxide from the air to form potassium carbonate, which has the effect of temporarily lowering the capacity of the battery. Electrolyte must therefore be stored in airtight containers. Cell vent caps should be kept closed at all times except when adding water or checking the electrolyte, and this should always be done as quickly as possible, opening only one vent cap at a time.

When handling electrolyte wear goggles and rubber gloves; avoid splashes. The electrolyte is injurious to skin and clothing and must therefore always be handled carefully. Particularly guard the eyes! A generous quantity of concentrated boric acid solution (5 oz of boric acid powder to each quart of water) should be kept handy in a bottle or open bowl for neutralizing any accidental splashes on person or clothing. Use an eye cup for eye injuries.

Boric acid powder will dissolve in warm water within 1 hr. With cold water allow 24 hr. Do not use the boric acid solution on cells or trays.

218. Checking the Electrolyte. Storage batteries normally lose water through natural evaporation and particularly when gassing freely on charge. While there are no corrosive or obnoxious gases given off by Nicad batteries, traces of the potassium hydroxide are lost with the gas, resulting in a gradual lowering of the specific gravity of the electrolyte over the years.

The level of the electrolyte as well as its specific gravity must therefore be checked periodically, as serious damage will be done to the plates if the electrolyte level falls below the top of the plates or the specific gravity is less than the minimum value stated on the wall card.

The electrolyte level is determined by inserting the 3/16-in. (5-mm) bore plastic tube, shipped with the battery through the vent until it rests on top of the plates, then placing the finger tightly over the end and withdrawing the tube for inspection. Be sure to return the electrolyte in the tube to the cell from which it was withdrawn.

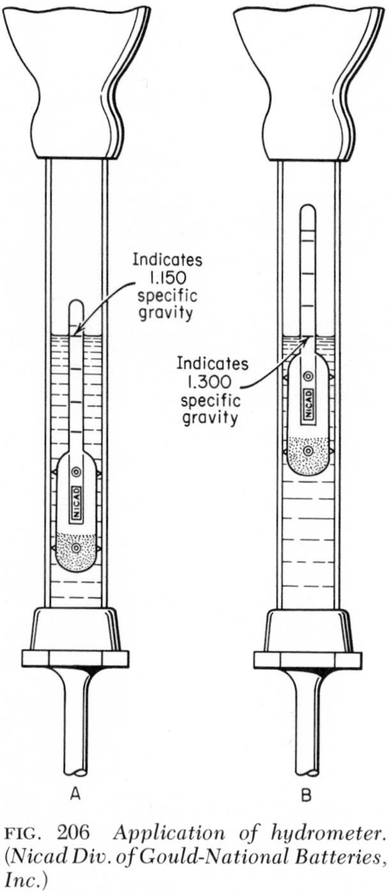

A hydrometer (Fig. 206) is used to check the specific gravity of the electrolyte, which should be within the range specified on the wall card. The illustrations show the positions of the float in electrolyte which is too weak (Fig. 206A) and too strong (Fig. 206B).

Use only a Nicad hydrometer to take specific-gravity readings. First rest the tip of the nozzle firmly on top of the plates in the cell; then squeeze and release the bulb. This method will prevent Celoil (see Sec. 221) from being drawn up into the barrel. Draw up sufficient solution to permit the float to move freely, and then tap the glass barrel of the hydrometer gently with the finger to prevent the float from giving a false reading by sticking to the barrel wall.

The maximum level of the electrolyte is halfway between the tops of the plates and inside the cell covers (do not include vent height). At this level and down to the minimum level of 1/2 in. (12 mm) above the plate tops, the specific gravity of the electrolyte should be within the range specified on the wall card. These figures apply to normal temperatures. When extreme temperatures prevail and the observed hydrometer readings are outside these limits, it will be necessary to apply temperature- and electrolyte-volume-correction factors as described below.

In order to arrive at the true specific gravity of the electrolyte at 72°F (22°C) (the temperature used as a base for purposes of calculation) observe and make a record of:

Indicates 1.150 specific gravity

Indicates 1.300 specific gravity

A   B

FIG. 206   *Application of hydrometer.* *(Nicad Div. of Gould-National Batteries, Inc.)*

1. The electrolyte specific gravity.
2. The electrolyte temperature.
3. The electrolyte level above the plates.

If the electrolyte temperature is above 72°F, add to the specific gravity reading 0.001 for every 4° above 72°F.

If the temperature is below 72°F, subtract 0.001 from the specific gravity reading for every 4° below 72°F.

For every 1/4 in. of electrolyte above the top of the plates add 0.005 to the specific-gravity reading.

The following examples show typical calculations:

Example 1. Hydrometer reads 1.190. Electrolyte temperature is 96°F; add 0.001 × (96 − 72) ÷ 4 = 0.006. Specific gravity, corrected for temperature (only), is 1.196. Electrolyte level is 1¾ in.; add 0.005 × 1¾ ÷ ¼ = 0.035. Specific gravity, corrected for both temperature and volume, is 1.231.

Example 2. Hydrometer reads 1.190. Electrolyte temperature is 40°F; subtract 0.001 × (72 − 40) ÷ 4 = 0.008. Specific gravity, corrected for temperature (only), is 1.182. Electrolyte level is ¾ in.; add 0.005 × ¾ ÷ ¼ = 0.015. Specific gravity, corrected for both temperature and volume, is 1.197.

A Nicad spirit thermometer part No. 91791 is necessary in order to apply proper temperature-correction factors to the hydrometer readings.

Gas bubbles in samples of electrolyte withdrawn from cells which are gassing must be allowed to disappear; otherwise false readings will be obtained.

Specific-gravity readings should not be taken on cells to which water or special 1.400-specific-gravity electrolyte has just been added, but deferred until they have had time to mix properly with the electrolyte during charge.

Always return the sample of electrolyte to the cell from which it was taken. After use wash out the hydrometer thoroughly with water to remove all traces of electrolyte, as any electrolyte allowed to remain in the hydrometer will absorb carbon dioxide from the air to form a thin coating on the float, which will cause false readings.

219. Adding Water. Always check the electrolyte level before adding any water to the cells. For maximum permissible level of the electrolyte refer to Sec. **218** or the wall card packed with the battery. Do not overfill.

Nicad batteries use very little water, particularly when they are on float or trickle charge. Batteries on float at a voltage equal to 1.40 times the number of cells in the battery will usually be found to require watering less than once a year.

If the cells are overfilled, the electrolyte will be forced out of the vents on charge and saturate the trays, causing electrolysis between the cells, corrosion of the cell containers, and troublesome grounds in the electrical circuit. Overfilling will also dilute the electrolyte to such an extent that the specific gravity will become too weak and the plates will be damaged.

Maintain the proper electrolyte level by the periodic addition of distilled water; do not add electrolyte. Do not use so-called "distilled water for storage batteries," as it generally contains small amounts of sulfuric acid through being stored in carboys having contained sulfuric acid intended for use in lead batteries.

Some drinking water may be usable, but it is always advisable to forward the manufacturer a laboratory analysis or a sample of the water to be used. Transportation should be prepaid. The minimum quantity of water to be sent is 2 qt and the minimum quantity of electrolyte is 1 qt for proper analysis. Ship in thoroughly cleaned glass or plastic bottles. Tag for easy identification. Do not send by mail. Send by Railway Express. Label electrolyte "Corrosive Liquid."

Although the quantity of any impurities introduced into the battery each time the battery is watered may be insignificant, the cumulative destructive effect over a number of years will be considerable. Distilled water is so inexpensive and in most cases so easily procured that its use is easily justified in terms of battery life. Stills for producing distilled water at very low cost are available from a number of reliable manufacturers. Store distilled water in clean, airtight glass or plastic bottles or jars.

220. Change of Electrolyte. Batteries which are charged at high rates for long periods and hence gas freely, with consequent loss of water and potassium hydroxide, may require change of electrolyte. Nicad batteries seldom if ever require change of electrolyte. However, it is desirable to check the specific gravity about once a year. When the specific gravity of the electrolyte, at a height of ½ in. (12 mm) above the tops of the plates, has fallen to the minimum specified, further operation of the battery will cause a rapid reduction in its life. At this point the battery should be discharged at the 7-hr discharge rate to a voltage of 0.5 to 0.8 volt per cell and have its electrolyte changed.

Remove the cells from their trays, and working on only one tray at a time, turn them upside down and empty out the electrolyte. Do not rinse the cells with water or electrolyte. Do not allow the cells to stand empty more than 30 min, as exposure of the plates to the air will damage the capacity. Fill immediately to the maximum height, i.e., halfway between the tops of the plates and inside the cell covers, with Renewal Electrolyte. The Renewal Electrolyte should, of course, always be procured in advance and be available before starting to empty the cells.

Avoid splashes. Protect the eyes! Wear goggles and rubber gloves.

While the above operations are performed, the trays or cells should not be stacked on top of one another nor should the cell posts be allowed to touch anything except insulation. Any chance of short-circuiting the cells should be avoided. The trays should be examined for damage, and any broken parts replaced. Note that the trays are so designed that there is a clear space between the cells and the surface on which the trays rest.

After being thoroughly cleaned, preferably by steam or compressed air, the cells and the trays should be allowed to dry thoroughly and then painted or, preferably, dipped in Nicadvar, a specially prepared corrosion-resisting asphalt-base paint. After the battery has been reassembled, it should be given a 14-hr charge at the 7-hr charge rate before being put back into service.

221. Celoil. Nicad batteries normally contain a ¼-in. (6-mm) layer of Celoil floating on top of the electrolyte, which retards the natural evaporation of water from the electrolyte.

Celoil is a pure, acid-free, and nonsaponifying oil specially prepared for use in Nicad cells. Do not use anything but Nicad Celoil.

222. Laying Up. When a Nicad battery is to be laid up for a few months, make sure that the specific gravity of the electrolyte is within the specified range and that the level is at least ½ in. (12 mm) above the tops of the plates.

Nicad batteries can be taken out of service in any state of charge and left idle for years without deterioration.

Remove all the intertray connectors to break any stray currents and store the battery in a cool place free from dust and moisture.

Regrease the cell tops to protect the metals with Nicad petroleum jelly No. 32982.

If the battery has been stored for some time, give it a freshening charge before placing back in service. Charge battery for 7 hr at normal rate or for 14 hr at half normal rate.

223. Returning Cells to Factory. If a cell or battery appears to be abnormal in any respect or if an accident has occurred, it may be necessary to return it to the factory for test and repair.

Before a cell or battery is returned, a complete description of the unusual condition should be reported to the service department. If in the opinion of the company the return is indicated, full shipping instructions will be sent with return material authorization.

Return shipments cannot be accepted without the company's authorization.

In case a cell has to be returned to the factory, it should be discharged at the 7-hr rate to 0.5 to 0.8 volt. The electrolyte must be left in the cell.

Tighten the post nuts and drive a tapered rubber or wooden plug of suitable size into the vent hole. Turn the cell upside down. Leave it standing in this position for 1 hr and then check that no electrolyte has leaked out.

Pack the cell, surrounded by a large quantity of liquid-absorbing material, such as sawdust, in a suitable container and ship prepaid in accordance with instructions which will be furnished by Nicad.

INSTALLATION OF STORAGE BATTERIES

224. In installing storage batteries, follow the rules of the National Electrical Code, which are given below.

225. Scope. The provisions of this section shall apply to all stationary installations of storage batteries using acid or alkali as the electrolyte and consisting of a number of cells connected in series with a nominal voltage in excess of 16 volts.

226. Definition of Nominal Voltage. The nominal battery voltage shall be calculated on the basis of 2.0 volts per cell for the lead-acid type and 1.2 volts per cell for the alkali type.

227. Wiring and Apparatus Supplied from Batteries. Wiring, appliances, and apparatus supplied from storage batteries shall be subject to the requirements of the Code applying to wiring, appliances, and apparatus operating at the same voltage, except as otherwise provided for communication systems in Art. 800 of the National Electrical Code.

228. Insulation of Batteries of Not over 250 Volts. The provisions of this section shall apply to storage batteries having the cells so connected as to operate at a nominal battery voltage not exceeding 250 volts.

1. LEAD-ACID BATTERIES. Cells in lead-lined wood tanks, where the number of cells in series does not exceed 25, shall be supported individually on glass or glazed-porcelain insulators. If the number of the cells in series exceeds 25, the cells shall be supported individually on oil insulators (see Fig. 207).

2. ALKALI-TYPE BATTERIES. Cells of the alkali type in jars made of conducting material shall be installed in trays of nonconducting material (Fig. 208), with not over 20 cells in a series circuit in any one such tray, or the cells may be supported singly or in groups on porcelain or other suitable insulators.

3. UNSEALED JARS. Cells in unsealed jars made of nonconductive material shall be assembled in trays of glass or supported on glass or glazed-porcelain insulators or, if installed on a rack, shall be supported singly or in groups on glass or other suitable insulators (see Fig. 209).

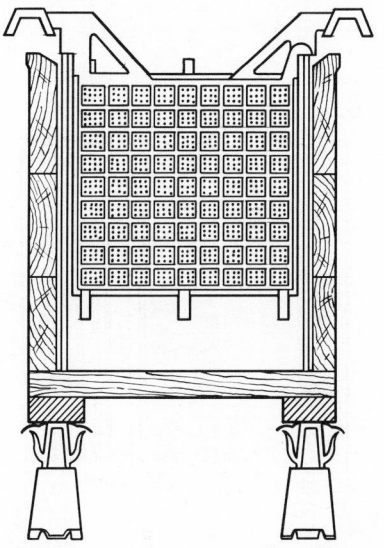

FIG. 207 *A cell in a lead-lined wood tank, supported on oil insulators.*

4. SEALED RUBBER JARS. Cells in sealed rubber or composition containers shall require no additional insulating support if the total nominal voltage of all cells in series does not exceed 150 volts. If the total voltage exceeds 150 volts, batteries shall

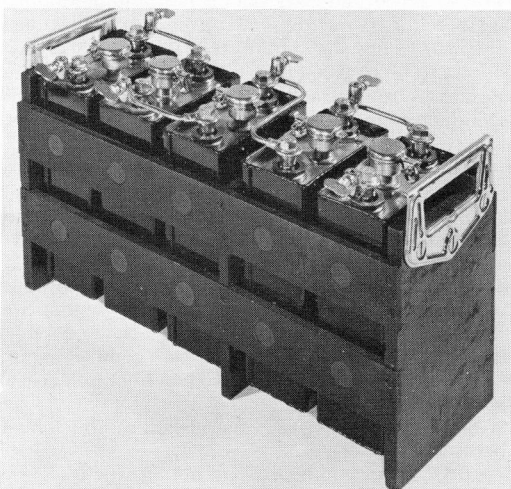

FIG. 208 *Alkali-type battery with cells mounted in an insulating tray. (Electric Storage Battery Co.)*

be sectionalized into groups of 150 volts or less and each group shall have the individual cells installed in trays or on racks.   If trays or racks are required for this type of cell, such trays or racks shall be supported on glass or glazed-porcelain insulators or oil-type insulators.

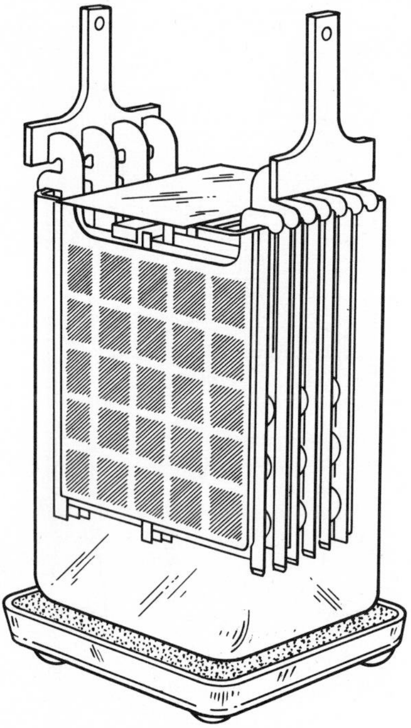

5. SEALED GLASS OR PLASTIC JARS. Cells in sealed glass jars or in sealed jars of approved heat-resistant plastic, with or without wood trays, require no additional insulation.

229. Insulation of Batteries of over 250 Volts. The provisions of Sec. 228 shall apply to storage batteries having the cells so connected as to operate at a nominal voltage exceeding 250 volts, and in addition, the provisions of this section shall also apply to such batteries.

1. Cells shall be installed in groups having a total nominal voltage of not over 250 volts, in trays or on racks supported on oil insulators.   However, if each individual cell or subgroup in the tray or rack is supported on oil insulators, no additional insulation for the group need be provided.   Also, cells of not over 10 amp-hr capacity in sealed glass jars may be grouped in trays, the total nominal voltage of all cells in such a group not to exceed 250 volts and each such tray to be supported on glass or glazed-porcelain insulators, the trays being mounted on racks supported on oil insulators with a total nominal voltage of not over 500 volts for all cells in series on each such insulated rack.

Maximum protection is secured by sectionalizing high-voltage batteries into cell groups insulated from each other.

FIG. 209 *A cell in an unsealed glass jar, mounted on a sand tray.*

230. Racks and Trays. Racks and trays shall conform to the following:

1. RACKS. Racks, as required in this section, refer to frames designed to support cells or trays (see Fig. 210).   They shall be substantial and made of any of the following:

a. Wood, so treated as to be resistant to deteriorating action by the electrolyte.

b. Metal, so treated as to be resistant to deteriorating action by the electrolyte and provided with nonconducting members directly supporting the cells or with suitable insulating material on conducting members.

c. Other similar suitable construction.

2. *Trays.* Trays refer to frames such as crates or shallow boxes usually of wood or other nonconducting material, so constructed or treated as to be resistant to deteriorating action by the electrolyte (see Fig. 211).

231. Battery Rooms. Battery rooms shall conform to the following:

1. USE. Separate battery rooms or enclosures shall be required only for batteries in unsealed jars and tanks where the aggregate capacity at the 8-hr discharge rate exceeds 5 kwhr.

2. WIRING METHOD. In storage-battery rooms, bare conductors, open wiring, Type MI cable, Type ALS cable, or conductors in rigid conduit or electrical metallic tubing shall be used as the wiring method.

3. VARNISHED-CAMBRIC CONDUCTORS. Varnished-cambric-covered conductors, Type V, shall not be used.

4. BARE CONDUCTORS. Bare conductors shall not be taped.

5. RACEWAY. Rigid metal conduit or electrical metallic tubing, if used, shall be of corrosion-resistant material or shall be suitably protected from corrosion.

FIG. 210   *Installation of lead-acid batteries in sealed glass jars mounted on a three-tier rack.* (*Electric Storage Battery Co.*)

6. TERMINALS.   If metal raceway or other metallic covering is used in the battery room, at least 12 in. of the conductor at the end connected to a cell terminal shall be free from the raceway or metallic covering and shall be bushed by a substantial glazed insulating bushing.   The end of the raceway shall be sealed tightly to resist the entrance of electrolyte by spray or by creepage.   Sealing compound, rubber insulating tape, or other suitable material shall be used for this purpose.

7. VENTILATION.   Provision shall be made for sufficient diffusion and ventilation of the gases from the battery to prevent the accumulation of an explosive mixture in the battery room.

232. Danger from Gas with Storage Batteries.   The hydrogen and oxygen given off from the battery during charge, when unmixed with a large amount of air, form a combination that will explode violently if ignited by an open flame or an electric spark.   If the battery is in a compartment, open or ventilate compartment while the battery is being charged in order that these gases may become mixed with air.   Do not bring exposed flame, match, cigar, etc., near the battery when charging or shortly after.

FIG. 211   *Lead-acid battery of cells in sealed glass jars mounted in a supporting tray.* (*Electric Storage Battery Co.*)

GENERAL CONSTRUCTION MATERIALS

233. Wire nails are formed from wire of the same diameter as the shank of the nail is to be.   The wire from which nails are made, hence the nail diameters, are measured by the steel-wire gage (see Table **84**, Div. 2), which is the same as the Washburn & Moen gage and is used by practically all nail manufacturers, though it is sometimes given a different name.

The size of nails is designated by the "penny" system. The penny system of designating nails originated in England. Two explanations are offered as to how this curious designation came about. One is that the sixpenny, fourpenny, tenpenny, etc., nails derived their names from the fact that 100 cost sixpence, fourpence, etc. The other explanation, which is more probable, is that 1,000 tenpenny nails, for instance, weighed 10 lb. The ancient as well as modern abbreviation for penny is "d," which is the first letter of the Roman coin denarius; the same abbreviation in early history was used for the English pound in weight. At any rate, the penny has persisted as a term in the nail industry.

Ordinary nails are made of steel wire with a natural bright-steel finish. The following special coatings, finishes, and heat treatments can be obtained at some additional cost:

Galvanized (hot process).	Brass plated.	Blued.
Galvanized (electro).	Cadmium plated.	Annealed.
Cement coated (regular).	Nickel plated.	Oil-quench hardened.
Cement coated (clear).	Chromium plated.	Japanned.
Coppered.	Painted.	Parkerized.
Tinned.	Acid etched.	

Nails made of copper, aluminum, brass, or stainless-steel wire are also available.

Nails are made in several different forms to meet the requirements of different applications. The more common types with dimensional data are given in the following sections.

234. Dimensions of Common Nails and Brads
(American Steel & Wire Co.)

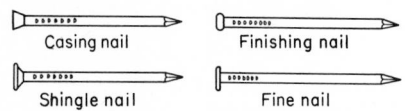

FIG. 212 *Casing, finishing, shingle, and fine nails.*

Size	Length, in.	Steel-wire gage	Approx no. per lb	Diam in decimals, in.	Approx diam, in.	Nearest B&S gage
2d	1	15	876	0.0720	$\frac{5}{64}$	13
3d	$1\frac{1}{4}$	14	568	0.0800	$\frac{5}{64}$	12
4d	$1\frac{1}{2}$	$12\frac{1}{2}$	316	0.0985	$\frac{7}{64}$	10
5d	$1\frac{3}{4}$	$12\frac{1}{2}$	271	0.0985	$\frac{7}{64}$	10
6d	2	$11\frac{1}{2}$	181	0.1130	$\frac{7}{64}$	9
7d	$2\frac{1}{4}$	$11\frac{1}{2}$	161	0.1130	$\frac{7}{64}$	9
8d	$2\frac{1}{2}$	$10\frac{1}{4}$	106	0.1314	$\frac{1}{8}$	8
9d	$2\frac{3}{4}$	$10\frac{1}{4}$	96	0.1314	$\frac{1}{8}$	8
10d	3	9	69	0.1483	$\frac{9}{64}$	7
12d	$3\frac{1}{4}$	9	63	0.1483	$\frac{9}{64}$	7
16d	$3\frac{1}{2}$	8	49	0.1620	$\frac{5}{32}$	6
20d	4	6	31	0.1920	$\frac{3}{16}$	6
30d	$4\frac{1}{2}$	5	24	0.2070	$1\frac{3}{64}$	4
40d	5	4	18	0.2253	$\frac{7}{32}$	3
50d	$5\frac{1}{2}$	3	14	0.2437	$\frac{1}{4}$	2
60d	6	2	11	0.2625	$1\frac{7}{64}$	2

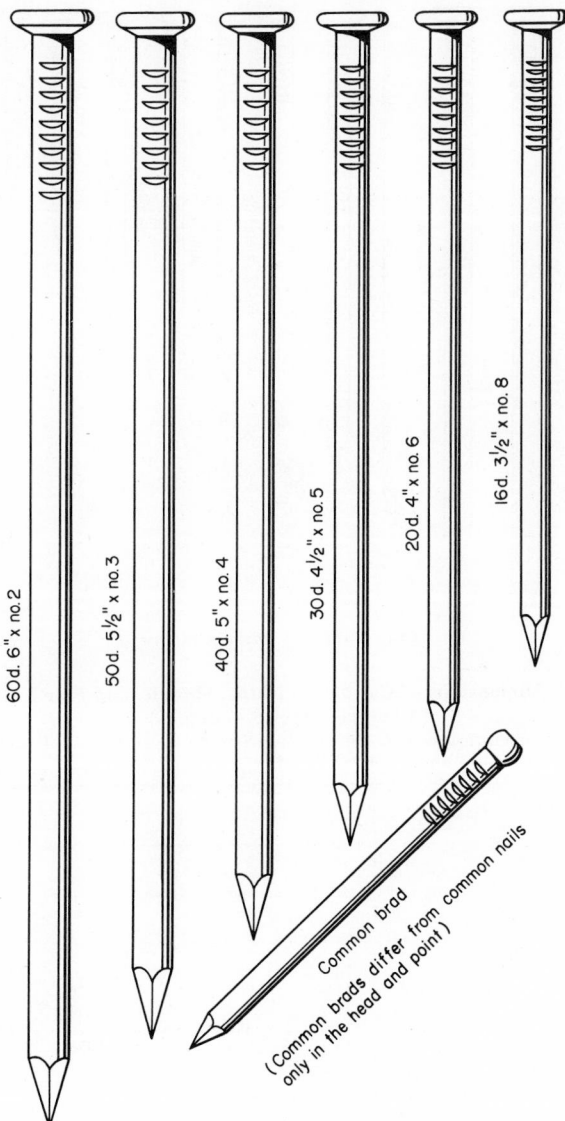

FIG. 213 *Common nails. (Actual size).*

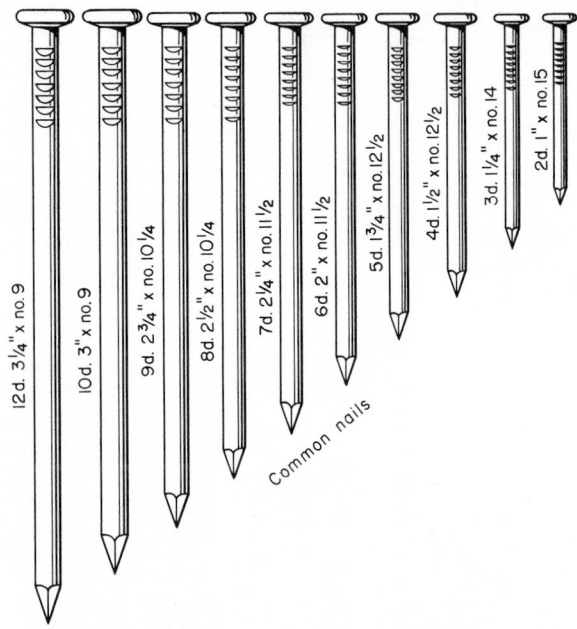

FIG. 214 *Common nails (continued).*

235. Dimensions of Casing, Finishing, Shingle, and Fine Nails
(American Steel & Wire Co.)

Nail diameters are measured by the steel-wire gage. See Div. 2, Table **84.** Equivalent B & S gage numbers and fractional-inch equivalents are given in Fig. 212.

Size	Length, in.	Casing Gage	Casing Approx no. per lb	Finishing Gage	Finishing Approx no. per lb	Shingle Gage	Shingle Approx no. per lb	Fine Gage	Fine Approx no. per lb
2d	1	15½	1,010	16½	1,351	....	...	16½	1,351
3d	1¼	14½	635	15½	807	13	429	15[b]	778
3½d	1⅜	....	.....	....	.....	12½	345		
4d	1½	14	473	15	584	12	274	14	473
5d	1¾	14	406	15	500	12	235		
6d	2	12½	236	13	309	12	204		
7d	2¼	12½	210	13	238	11	139		
8d	2½	11½	145	12½	189	11	125		
9d	2¾	11½	132	12½	172	11	114		
10d	3	10½	94	11½	121	10	83		
12d	3¼	10½	87	11½	113				
16d	3½	10	71	11	90				
20d	4	9	52	10	62				
30d	4½	9	46						
40d	5	8	35						
2d[a]	1	....	.....	....	.....	....	...	17	1,560
3d[a]	1⅛	....	.....	....	.....	....	...	16	1,015

[a] These sizes are called Extra Fine.
[b] This nail is only 1⅛ in. long.

236. Dimensions of Wood Screws. Roundheaded wood screws do not measure full length but are from 1/16 to 3/16 in. short. For example, a No. 4 by 1/2-in. roundheaded wood screw measures about 7/16 in. long under the head, and a No. 20 by 2-in. screw measures about 1 7/8 in. under the head.

237. Wood Screws. Diameters are measured by the American Screw Co.'s gage, and range in size from No. 0 to No. 30. They range in length from 1/4 to 6 in. The increase in length is by eighths of an inch up to 1 in., then by quarters of an inch up to 3 in., and by half inches up to 5 in. Manufacturers' standards vary, but generally the threaded portion is approximately seven-tenths of the total length. There is no standard number of threads per inch for the products of all manufacturers. The gage and diameter refer to the unthreaded portion of the screw. They are available in three types of head (Fig. 215): flat, round, and oval. The oval head (see illustration for machine screws, Fig. 216)

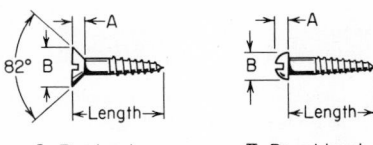

I - Flat head   II - Round head

FIG. 215 *Wood screws.*

Screw gage No.	Diam, in. In decimals	Diam, in. In fractions	Diam, in. Nearest B&S gage	Flat head A	Flat head B	Round head A	Round head B	Round head Counterbore for head	Clearance drill No.	Clearance drill Diam, in.	Greatest length obtainable, in.
0	0.05784	1/16 −	15	1/16	7/64+	....	....	....	.....	......	3/8
1	0.07100	5/64 −	14	1/16	9/64 −	....	....	....	....	......	1/2
2	0.08416	5/64 +	12	1/16	5/32+	1/16	13/64	7/32	44	0.086	7/8
3	0.09732	3/32+	11	1/16	3/16	5/64	13/64	....	....	......	1 1/2
4	0.11048	7/64+	9	1/16	7/32 −	5/64	13/64	7/32	33	0.113	1 1/2
5	0.12364	1/8 −	8	1/16	15/64+	3/32	15/64	....	....	......	2 1/2
6	0.13680	9/64 −	7	5/64	17/64+	3/32	1/4	17/64	28	0.1415	3
7	0.14996	5/32 −	7	3/32	19/64 −	7/64	9/32	....	....	......	3
8	0.16312	5/32+	6	7/64	5/16+	7/64	19/64	5/16	18	0.1695	4
9	0.17628	11/64+	5	7/64	11/32+	1/8	21/64	....	....	......	4
10	0.18944	3/16+	5	7/64	3/8 −	1/8	11/32	23/64	10	0.1935	4
11	0.20260	13/64 −	4	1/8	25/64+	9/64	3/8	....	....	......	4
12	0.21576	7/32+	4	1/8	27/64	5/32	25/64	13/32	7/32	0.2188	6
13	0.22892	15/64 −	3	1/8	29/64	5/32	27/64	....	....	......	6
14	0.24208	1/4 −	3	9/64	15/32+	5/32	29/64	29/64	1/4	0.250	6
15	0.25524	1/4 +	2	9/64	1/2	11/64	29/64	....	....	......	6
16	0.26840	17/64+	2	5/32	17/32 −	11/64	31/64	....	....	......	6
17	0.28156	9/32	1	5/32	35/64+	11/64	1/2	....	....	......	6
18	0.29472	19/64 −	1	11/64	37/64	3/16	17/32	35/64	....	0.302	6
19	0.30788	5/16 −	0	3/16	39/64 −	....	17/32	....	....	......	6
20	0.32104	21/64 −	0	13/64	5/8 +	13/64	9/16	37/64	....	0.323	6
21	0.33420	21/64+	0	13/64	21/32	13/64	19/32	....	....	......	6
22	0.34736	11/32+	0	13/64	11/16 −	7/32	5/8	....	....	......	6
23	0.36052	23/64+	2/0	7/32	45/64+	7/32	41/64	....	....	......	6
24	0.37368	3/8 −	2/0	7/32	47/64	15/64	21/32	43/64	....	0.377	6
25	0.38684	25/64 −	3/0	7/32	49/64	15/64	11/16	....	....	......	6
26	0.40000	13/32 −	3/0	15/64	25/32+	1/4	45/64	....	....	......	6
27	0.41316	13/32+	3/0	15/64	13/16	1/4	23/32	....	....	......	6
28	0.42632	27/64+	3/0	1/4	27/32	1/4	47/64	....	....	......	6
29	0.43948	7/16+	4/0	1/4	55/64+	17/64	3/4	....	....	......	6
30	0.45264	29/64	4/0	17/64	57/64	9/32	25/32	....	....	......	6

Note (vertical, in Counterbore column): Depth of hole = height of head A

is used for especially high-grade work such as cabinet work, which must present a very neat appearance.

The ordinary materials used for making wood screws are steel and brass. The flat-headed screws are regularly available in steel, with a natural bright finish or gal-vanized, and in brass. The roundheaded screws are made of steel, with a blued or nickel-plated finish, and of brass. The oval-headed screws are regularly made of brass with a nickel-plated finish.

238. Machine Screws. Diameters are designated by the American Screw Co.'s gage and range in size from No. 2 to No. 34. They range in length from 1/8 to 4 in. The increase in length is by sixteenths of an inch up to 1 in., by eighths of an inch up to 2 in., and by quarters of an inch up to 4 in. The threaded portion extends over either all or nearly all the total length. Machine screws are designated by their gage number and

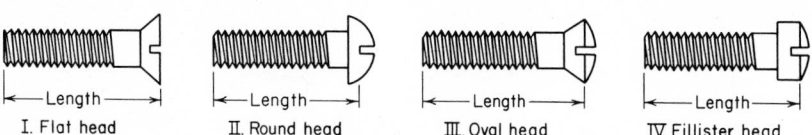

|—— Length ——→| |—— Length ——→| |—— Length ——→| |—— Length ——→|

I. Flat head   II. Round head   III. Oval head   IV. Fillister head

FIG. 216   *Machine screws.*

number of threads per inch. A No. 10-24 screw has a diameter corresponding to size No. 10 of the American screw gage and has 24 threads per inch. The gage number refers to the diameter over the thread. They are available with heads of four different types: flat, round, oval, and fillister (Fig. 216). The length of flatheaded screws is measured over-all, the length of roundheaded ones includes about one-half of the head, the length of oval-headed screws includes the countersinks, and the length of fillister-headed ones is measured from the rim of the head.

Standard machine screws are made of iron, aluminum, plastic, nylon, or brass. The iron screws may be provided with any one of the following finishes: natural bright, blued, nickel, brass or silver plated, silver or copper oxidized, various bronzes, japanned, lacquered, coppered, tinned, galvanized, bower barffed, or gun metal.

239. Data for Machine Screws

Screw gage No.	Diam, in.	Standard threads per in.	Screw gage No.	Diam, in.	Standard threads per in.
2	0.08416	48, 56, or 64	12	0.21576	20 or 24
3	0.09732	48 or 56	14	0.24208	18, 20, or 24
4	0.11048		16	0.26840	
5	0.12364	} 32, 36, or 40	18	0.29472	} 16, 18, or 20
6	0.13680	30, 32, or 36	20	0.32104	16 or 18
7	0.14996	30 or 32	24	0.37368	14, 16, or 18
8	0.16312	30, 32, or 36	30	0.45264	14 or 16
9	0.17628		34	0.50528	13
10	0.18944	} 24, 30, or 32			

240. Machine Bolts and Nuts. Machine bolts are designated by the diameter of the shank of the bolt. They range in length from 1½ to 30 in. The increase in length is by half inches up to 8 in. and by inches up to 30 in. Bolts are regularly furnished with one nut. The standard number of threads per inch for the bolts and nuts are as follows:

Diam..	1/4	5/16	3/8	7/16	1/2	9/16	5/8	11/16	3/4	7/8	1
No. of threads per in............................	28	24	24	20	20	18	18	16	16	14	14

Bolts are made with either square or hexagonal heads and may be furnished with nuts of the corresponding shape. They are made of iron and may be finished with a natural black or galvanized coating.

241. Dimensions and Strengths of Machine Bolts and Nuts

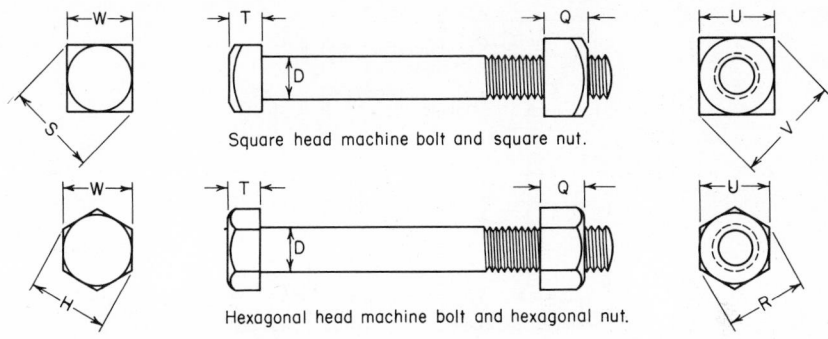

Square head machine bolt and square nut.

Hexagonal head machine bolt and hexagonal nut.

FIG. 217 *Machine bolts and nuts.*

D	T	W	S	H	Q	U	R	V	Safe tensile strength of bolt at root of thread at 6,000 lb per sq in.	Safe shearing strength at 7,500 lb per sq in.	
										Full bolt	Root of thread
1/4	3/16	3/8	17/32	7/16	3/16	7/16	1/2	5/8	160	370	200
5/16	15/64	15/32	21/32	35/64	1/4	17/32	5/8	3/4	270	575	340
3/8	9/32	9/16	51/64	21/32	5/16	5/8	47/64	57/64	410	830	510
7/16	21/64	21/32	15/16	3/4	3/8	23/32	27/32	1 5/64	560	1,130	700
1/2	3/8	3/4	1 1/16	27/32	7/16	13/16	61/64	1 5/32	760	1,470	940
5/8	15/32	15/16	1 21/64	1 5/64	9/16	1	1 5/32	1 27/64	1,210	2,300	1,510
3/4	19/32	1 1/8	1 19/32	1 9/64	11/16	1 3/16	1 3/8	1 43/64	1,810	3,310	2,260
7/8	21/32	1 5/16	1 55/64	1 1/2	13/16	1 3/8	1 19/32	1 61/64	2,520	4,510	3,140
1	3/4	1 1/2	1 1/2	1 47/64	1 5/16	1 9/16	1 13/16	2 7/32	3,300	5,890	4,130
1 1/8	27/32	1 11/16	2 25/64	1 13/32	1 1/8	1 13/16	2 3/32	2 9/16	4,160	7,450	5,200
1 1/4	15/16	1 7/8	2 21/32	2 5/32	2 1/4	1 1/4	2 3/16	2 17/32	5,350	9,200	6,670
1 3/8	1 1/32	2 1/16	2 59/64	2 25/64	1 3/8	2 3/16	2 17/32	3 3/32	6,340	11,130	7,900
1 1/2	1 1/8	2 1/4	3 3/16	2 19/32	1 1/2	2 3/8	2 47/64	3 3/8	7,770	13,250	9,700
1 5/8	1 7/32	2 7/16	3 3/4	2 13/16	1 5/8	2 9/16	2 13/16	3 5/8	9,090	15,550	11,360
1 3/4	1 5/16	2 5/8	3 23/32	3 1/32	1 3/4	2 3/4	3 3/16	3 57/64	10,470	18,000	13,080
1 7/8	1 13/32	2 13/16	3 63/64	3 1/4	1 7/8	2 15/16	2 25/64	4 5/32	12,300	20,700	15,370
2	1 1/2	3	4 1/4	3 15/32	2	3 1/8	3 5/8	4 27/64	13,800	23,560	17,250

242. Data on carriage bolts are given in Div. 8.

243. Toggle bolts, which are used for fastening raceways and electrical devices to hollow tile or plaster-on-metal-lath surfaces, are of two general types. The screw type (Fig. 218) is the most frequently used but has the disadvantage that if it is ever necessary to remove the screw entirely, the toggle is lost within the wall. Where the object fastened must be removed and replaced, a nut-type toggle bolt (Figs. 219 and 220) can be used. When the type of Fig. 219 is used, it is usually necessary, after the device is in place, to cut off the part of the bolt that extends so as to give a neat appearance. The so-called plumbers' toggle bolt (Fig. 220) has a removable, hexagonal cap so that the device can be inserted in the wall before the object to be fastened is slipped over the bolt. Then, on putting the cap in place, the whole bolt is backed into the wall, hiding the surplus thread from view. Cone-headed toggles (Fig. 221) are used principally for the erection of metal raceway and have the advantage that the toggle head will readily pass through the hole in the raceway backing. A spring-in type of toggle bolt is shown in Fig. 222. The wings are tempered spring steel having a cam action against the

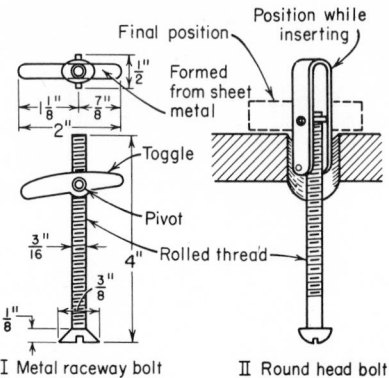

FIG. 218 *Screw-type toggle bolts.*

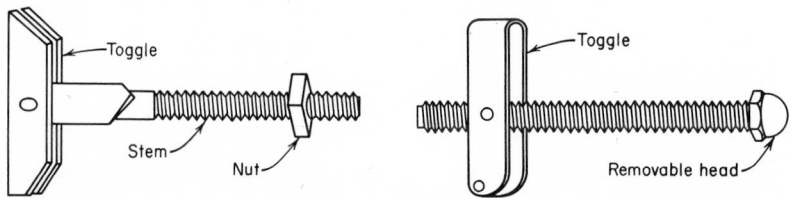

FIG. 219 *Nut-type toggle bolt.*   FIG. 220 *Plumbers' toggle bolt.*

saddle which throws them to the open position. Toggle bolts are made in several diameters and lengths.

244. Lag screws are discussed in Div. 8.

245. Expansion sleeves, shields, and bolts are used for attaching equipment and devices to stonelike materials such as concrete, brick, tile, etc. They are made in a variety of types and consist of a lead sleeve or malleable-iron expansion shield which is inserted in a hole cut in the masonry. The equipment to be supported is attached to the sleeve or shield by means of a wood, machine, or lag screw, depending upon the design of the sleeve or shield. As the screw is turned into the sleeve or shield, it expands the body of the sleeve or shield against the sides of the hole in the masonry so that it grips the masonry with considerable holding power. These devices are called by various trade names such as expansive anchors, expansion sleeves, expansion screws, or expansion bolts and anchors. Data and illustrations of some common types are given in the following sections.

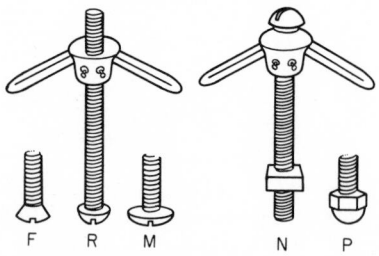

F — with flat-head screw
R — with round-head screw
M — mushroom head, furnished in ⅛-in. diameter only
N — reverse R or F screw and add nut on any size
P — plumbers' toggle; reverse R or F screw and add cap nut on any size

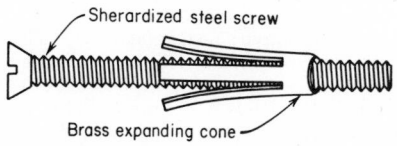

FIG. 221 *Toggle bolt for metal raceway.*

FIG. 222. *Spring-in toggle bolt.*

246. Diamond Multisize Screw Anchors. These are designed to accommodate in one anchor several diameters of wood screws. The purpose is to reduce the number of anchors required to accommodate all sizes of screws. They are made in several lengths covering the majority of uses and are put up in boxes of 100.

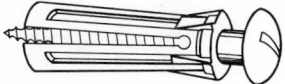

FIG. 223

For wood screws, No.	Length, in.	Size of drill, in.	Weight, lb per 100
6– 8	¾	¼	1
6– 8	1½	¼	1¾
10–14	¾	⁵⁄₁₆	1½
10–14	1	⁵⁄₁₆	2
10–14	1½	⁵⁄₁₆	2¾
16–18	1	⅜	3
16–18	1½	⅜	4¼
20–24	1¾	⁷⁄₁₆	5¼

247. Diamond Calking Anchors for Use with Machine Screws

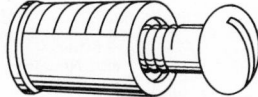

FIG. 224

Diam of bolt or screw	Hole size, in.		Suggested safe load, lb	Weight, lb per 100
	Diam	Depth		
6–32	¼	⅜	80	1
8–32	⁵⁄₁₆	½	90	1½
10–24	⅜	⅝	175	2
12–24	⁷⁄₁₆	¾	320	3½
¼–20	½	⅞	400	4½
⁵⁄₁₆	⅝	1	480	11
⅜	¾	1¼	720	16
⁷⁄₁₆	⅞	1½	950	24
½	⅞	1½	1,000	24
⅝	1	2	1,250	41

Calking anchors are put up in standard packages of 100 for sizes No. 10-24 and smaller, and in packages of 50 for sizes No. 12-24 and larger. One calking tool is in each box. All suggested safe loads are based on ideal conditions.

248. Ackerman-Johnson Expansive Screw Anchors

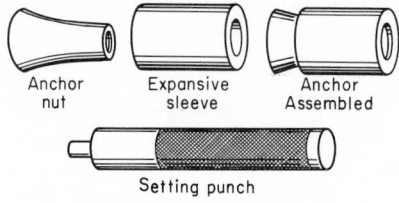

| Anchor | Expansive | Anchor |
| nut | sleeve | Assembled |

Setting punch

FIG. 225

The Ackerman-Johnson expansive screw anchor consists of a hard, biconoidal, internally threaded nut, within a lead-composition expansive sleeve. It is used for attaching fixtures or wiring to any stonelike material such as concrete, brick, tile, etc.

Method of Installing Anchor. When installed, the sleeve is driven farther toward the base of the tapered nut, being thereby expanded and swaged tightly against the sides of the hole, giving perfect holding contact throughout the length and circumference of the anchor.

To determine the anchor size best suited for the work, first select the screw or bolt to be preferred and then anchors of corresponding size number; for example, for work demanding No. 10-24 screws, specify No. 10-24 anchor; if $3/8$-in. bolts are required, use No. $3/8$-in. anchor.

A setting punch is included with every package of 50 or 100 anchors.

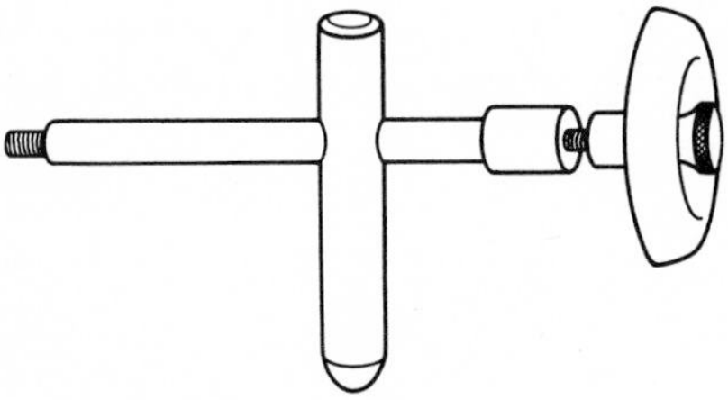

FIG. 226 *Hammerless setting tool.*

Anchor size No.	Minimum dimensions of holes required, in.		Shipping weight, lb per 1,000
	Diam	Depth	
6–32	$1/4$	$3/8$	$7 1/2$
8–32	$5/16$	$1/2$	15
10–24	$3/8$	$5/8$	$22 1/2$
12–24	$7/16$	$3/4$	34
$1/4$–20	$1/2$	$7/8$	$50 1/2$
$5/16$–18	$5/8$	1	95
$3/8$–16	$3/4$	$1 1/4$	162
$7/16$–14	$7/8$	$1 1/2$	221
$1/2$–13	$7/8$	$1 1/2$	231
$5/8$–11	$1 1/8$	2	512

Hammerless Setting Tool. Anchors are set perfectly, in tile or other thin materials in which the hole extends through or has a weak bottom, by means of the hammerless setting tool (see Fig. 226).

The stud is screwed into the anchor, which is then inserted in position; turning the wheel moves the threaded stud rearward, thus drawing the anchor nut into its ductile sleeve, expanding the latter to any degree required for safe anchorage. The tool is furnished in sizes to use with the following sizes of anchor: 8-32, 10-24, 12-24, and $1/4$-20.

249. Diamond Lag-screw Shield

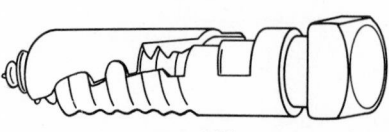

FIG. 227

Diam screw, in.	Outside diam and drill required, in.	Standard package	Long standard pattern		Short standard pattern	
			Length shield, in.	Shipping weight, lb	Length shield, in.	Shipping weight, lb
1/4	1/2	100	1 1/2	4 1/2	1	3
5/16	1/2	100	1 3/4	5	1 1/4	3
3/8	5/8	100	2 1/4	10	1 3/4	7 1/2
1/2	3/4	100	3	16	2	10
5/8	7/8	100	3 1/2	21		
3/4	1	50	3 1/2	24		

The lag-screw shield is made of malleable iron in two wedge-shaped halves. The outer wedge slides forward when the screw is turned, creating a powerful expansion. The shield is galvanized by Diamond hot-dip process.

250. Interlocking Keystone Expansion Shields (for use with machine bolts or machine screws)

Diam, in.	Length, in.	Outside diam and drill required, in.	Weight, lb per 100	Diam, in.	Length, in.	Outside diam and drill required, in.	Weight, lb per 100

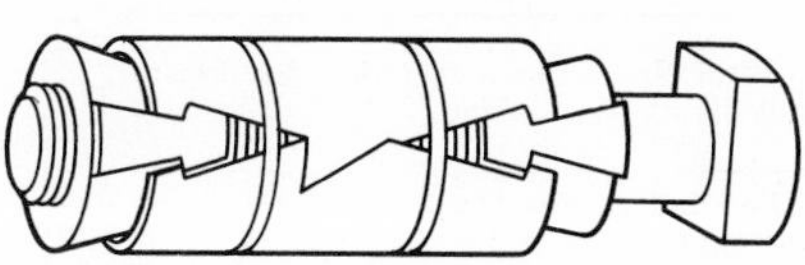

FIG. 228 *Double.*   FIG. 229 *Single.*

Diam, in.	Length, in.	Outside diam and drill required, in.	Weight, lb per 100	Diam, in.	Length, in.	Outside diam and drill required, in.	Weight, lb per 100
1/4	1 1/2	1/2	6	1/2	1 5/16	1/2	6
5/16	1 3/4	9/16	7	5/16	1 1/2	9/16	6
3/8	2	11/16	11	3/8	1 5/8	11/16	10
7/16	2 1/2	7/8	16	1/2	1 7/8	7/8	16
1/2	2 1/2	7/8	20	5/8	2	1	20
5/8	2 7/8	1	29	3/4	2 3/4	1 3/16	46
3/4	3 1/4	1 1/8	52				
7/8	4	1 1/2	88				
1	4 1/4	1 5/8	114				
1 1/4	6	2 1/8	300				
1 1/2	7 1/2	2 1/2	450				

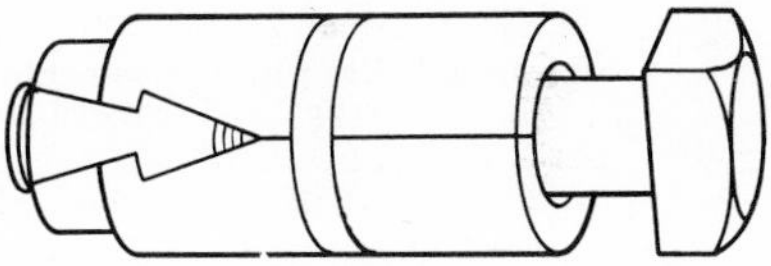

251. Rawlplugs (Fig. 230) are made from stiffened strands of jute fiber. The fiber strands are compressed together by a patented process. Once in place, a Rawlplug can never crumble or pulp. It is unaffected by moisture or change in temperature.

The screw entering the Rawlplug automatically threads it, which permits removal and replacement of the screw as often as desired without stripping the threads so formed. The screw cannot be withdrawn by direct or indirect pull.

Rawlplugs require only a small hole. This makes installation easy and assures a neat job. The Rawlplug is invisible when in position, as the diameter of the hole and Rawlplug is smaller than the head of the screw, giving the screw the appearance of being screwed into the masonry itself.

Owing to the composition, Rawlplugs resist and absorb shocks. They cannot work loose, slip, sheer, or lose their viselike grip. When properly inserted the Rawlplug

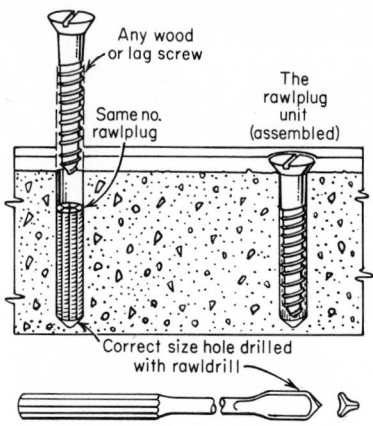

FIG. 230　*Installation of Rawlplugs.*

should develop the entire strength of the screw or of the surrounding material, such as concrete, brick, stone, slate, marble, plaster, glass, hard rubber, gypsum block, wallboard, terra cotta, composition walls and floors, wood, and metal.

They are made in the sizes listed below in lengths of $\frac{5}{8}$, $\frac{3}{4}$, 1, $1\frac{1}{4}$, $1\frac{1}{2}$, 2, $2\frac{1}{2}$, 3, and $3\frac{1}{2}$ in.

Rawlplug No.	Use with screw No.	Diam drill required, in.	Rawldrill No. (not diam)	Use with tool holder No.	Size twist drill, in.
Rawlplug, Rawldrill, and Tool-holder Size Data					
6	5–6	$\frac{5}{32}$	6	14	$\frac{5}{32}$
8	7–8	$\frac{11}{64}$	8	14	No. 15
10	9–10	$\frac{3}{16}$	10	14	No. 10
12	11–12	$\frac{1}{4}$	12	14	$\frac{1}{4}$
14	14ᵃ	$\frac{9}{32}$	14	14	$\frac{9}{32}$
16	16ᵃ	$\frac{5}{16}$	16	20	$\frac{5}{16}$
20	20ᵇ	$\frac{3}{8}$	20	20	$\frac{3}{8}$
Lag-screw Sizesᶜ					
$\frac{3}{8}$	$\frac{3}{8}$	$\frac{7}{16}$			
$\frac{7}{16}$	$\frac{7}{16}$	$\frac{1}{2}$			
$\frac{1}{2}$	$\frac{1}{2}$	$\frac{5}{8}$			
$\frac{5}{8}$	$\frac{5}{8}$	$\frac{3}{4}$			

ᵃ Or $\frac{1}{4}$-in. lag screw.
ᵇ Or $\frac{5}{16}$-in. lag screw.
ᶜ For $\frac{1}{4}$-in. lag screw use No. 14 or No. 16 Rawlplug.　For $\frac{5}{16}$-in. lag screw use No. 20.

252. Rawl-drives (Fig. 231) consist of a high-grade, heat-treated steel pin with a flat head and split expanded central portion, which, when driven in, grips the side of the hole with a spring action.　They are easily and quickly installed, since they drive like a nail into a drilled hole no larger than the diameter of the pin itself.　They are for use only in solid masonry of brick, concrete, or stone.　They should not be used in soft or brittle materials, such as plaster, wood, composition wood, glass, tile, etc.　The manufacturer specifies that they have the following holding powers:

Holding Power of Rawl-drives

Size Rawl-drive, in.	Average direct pull, lb	
	1-2-4 concrete	Common brick
$3/16 \times 1\frac{1}{4}$	1,285	634
$1/4 \times 1\frac{1}{2}$	2,050	1,183
$5/16 \times 1\frac{1}{2}$	3,500	1,833
$3/8 \times 2$	5,010	2,150
$1/2 \times 3$	6,015	3,700

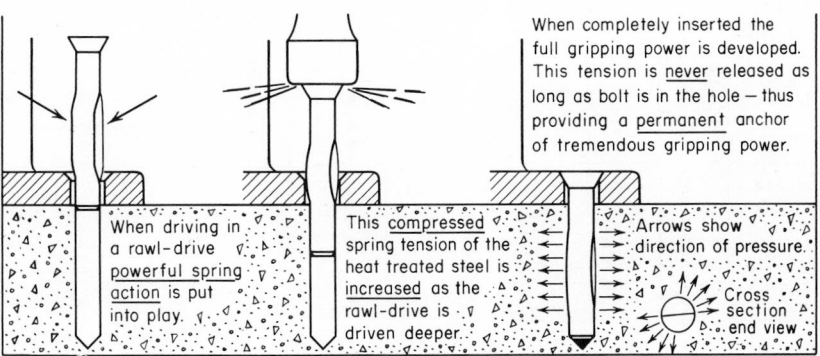

When completely inserted the full gripping power is developed. This tension is _never_ released as long as bolt is in the hole — thus providing a _permanent_ anchor of tremendous gripping power.

When driving in a rawl-drive powerful spring action is put into play.

This _compressed_ spring tension of the heat treated steel is _increased_ as the rawl-drive is driven deeper.

Arrows show direction of pressure.

Cross section end view

FIG. 231 *Illustration of principle of Rawl-drive.*

253. Data for Rawl-drives

Diam of bolt and drill, in.	Length of bolt, in.	Use Rawldrill No. or size	Packed[a] in boxes of	Approx weight, lb per 100 bolts
$3/16$	1	No. 10	100	$1\frac{3}{4}$
$3/16$	$1\frac{1}{4}$	No. 10	100	2
$1/4$	$1\frac{1}{4}$	No. 12	100	3
$1/4$	$1\frac{1}{2}$	No. 12	100	$3\frac{1}{2}$
$1/4$	2	No. 12	100	4
$5/16$	$1\frac{1}{2}$	No. 16	50	6
$5/16$	$1\frac{1}{2}$	No. 16	50	7
$3/8$	2	No. 20	25	10
$3/8$	$2\frac{1}{2}$	No. 20	25	12
$3/8$	3	No. 20	25	13
$3/8$	$3\frac{1}{2}$	No. 20	25	15
$1/2$	3	$1/2$ in.	25	25
$1/2$	$3\frac{1}{2}$	$1/2$ in.	25	28
$1/2$	4	$1/2$ in.	25	30

[a] A standard package consists of four boxes of the same size, length and type.

254. Anchor Selection Chart by Type of Material
(The Rawlplug Co., Inc.)

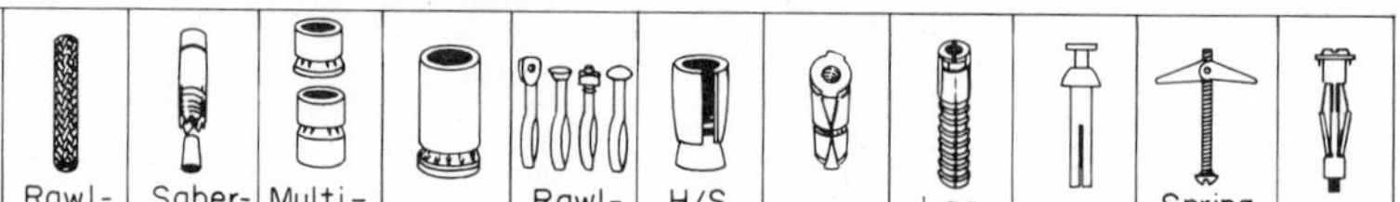

	Rawl-plug	Saber-tooth	Multi-calk	Calk-in	Rawl-drive	H/S drop-in	Double	Lag shield	Nailin	Spring-wing	Rawly
Brick		●	●	●	●	●		●	●		
Concrete		●	●	●	●	●	●	●	●		
Concrete block						●			●	●	●
Cinder block						●				●	●
Stone	Use in any masonry material	●	●	●	●	●	●		●		
Marble		●		●		●			●		
Building tile						●				●	●
Ceramic tile						●				●	●
Terrazzo		●		●		●			●		
Terra cotta						●				●	●
Plaster										●	●
Dry wall										●	●
Slate						●					●
Stucco											
Glass											

255. Powder-actuated Tools. A highly efficient method of attaching fasteners or materials to concrete or steel is the powder-actuated tool and fastening system. This integrated system (Fig. 232) permits fastening without drilling in one time-saving operation. It consists of a tool, a powder charge, and a fastener; and it fastens wood and steel to concrete of any compressive strength and to structural steel up to 1 in. thick. A line of more than 100 drive pins, eyepins, and threaded studs meets the requirements for most jobs.

There are several major manufacturers of powder-actuated tool systems, and it is suggested that users be fully familiar with these tools and fastening materials. These manufacturers provide guidebooks on how to use the systems efficiently and safely. In some states and local areas mechanics who use powder-actuated tools are required to be certified or licensed to indicate that they completely understand the use or proper applications of these systems.

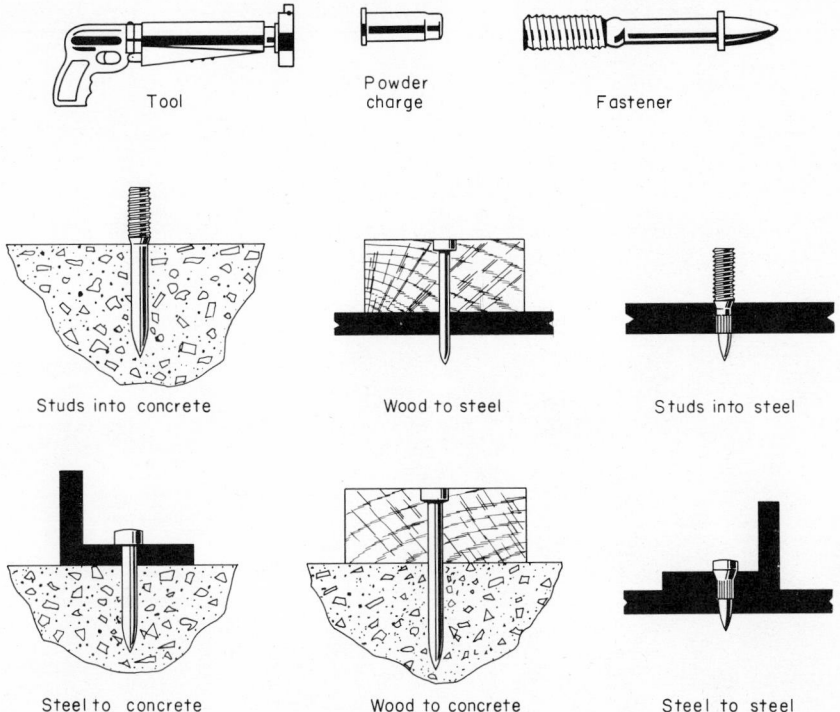

Tool

Powder
charge

Fastener

Studs into concrete

Wood to steel

Studs into steel

Steel to concrete

Wood to concrete

Steel to steel

FIG. 232 *A basic powder-actuated tool system.*   (*Ramset, Winchester-Western Div. of Olin Mathieson Chemical Corp.*)

DIVISION FIVE

Transformers

CONSTRUCTION, TYPES, AND CHARACTERISTICS

1. A transformer is an apparatus for converting electrical power in an a-c system at one voltage or current into electrical power at some other voltage or current without the use of rotating parts.

2. A constant-potential transformer (Fig. 1) consists essentially of three parts: the primary coil which carries the alternating current from the supply lines, the core of magnetic material in which is produced an alternating magnetic flux, and the secondary coil in which is generated an emf by the change of magnetism in the core which it surrounds. Sometimes the transformer may have only one winding, which will serve the dual purpose of primary and secondary coils.

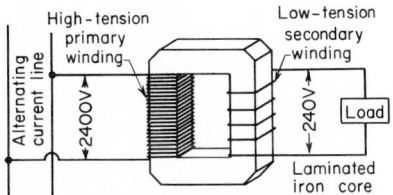

FIG. 1 *The elementary transformer.*

The high-tension winding is composed of many turns of relatively fine copper wire, well insulated to withstand the voltage impressed on it. The low-tension winding is composed of relatively few turns of heavy copper wire capable of carrying considerable current at a low voltage.

3. Transformer Terminology. The **primary winding** is the winding of the transformer which is connected to the source of power. It may be either the high- or the low-voltage winding, depending upon the application of the transformer.

The **secondary winding** is the winding of the transformer which delivers power to the load. It may be either the high- or the low-voltage winding, depending upon the application of the transformer.

The **core** is the magnetic circuit upon which the windings are wound.

The **high-tension winding** is the one which is rated for the higher voltage.

FIG. 2 *Assembly of transformer-core laminations.* (*Wagner Electric Corp.*)

FIG. 3 *Transformer assembly.* *(Wagner Electric Corp.)*

The **low-tension winding** is the one which is rated for the lower voltage.

A **step-up transformer** is a constant-potential transformer so connected that the delivered voltage is greater than the supplied voltage.

A **step-down transformer** is one so connected that the delivered voltage is less than that supplied; the actual transformer may be the same in one case as in the other, the terms step-up and step-down relating merely to the application of the apparatus.

4. Transformer Cores. Until recently all transformer cores were made up of stacks of sheet-steel punchings firmly clamped together. One method of assembly and clamping of the sheets is shown in Figs. 2 and 3. Sometimes the laminations are coated with a thin varnish in order to reduce eddy-current losses. When the laminations are not coated with varnish, a sheet of insulating paper is inserted between laminations at regular intervals.

A new type of core construction consists of a continuous strip of silicon steel which is wound in a tight spiral around the insulated coils and firmly held by spot welding at the end. The core and windings of such a transformer are shown in Fig. 4. This type of construction reduces the cost of manufacture and reduces the power loss in the core due to eddy currents.

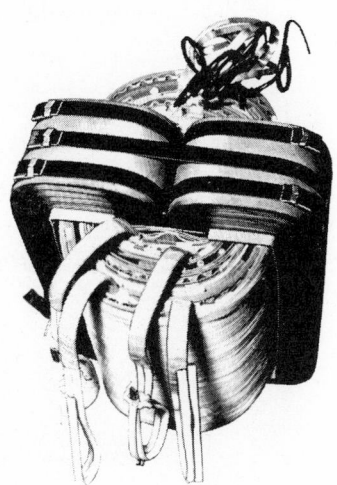

FIG. 4 *Assembled core and coils for wound-core distribution transformer. (Marcus Transformer Co.)*

5. Classification of Transformers

1. According to method of cooling.
   a. Self-air-cooled (dry type).
   b. Air-blast-cooled (dry type).
   c. Liquid-immersed, self-cooled.
   d. Oil-immersed, combination self-cooled and air-blast.
   e. Oil-immersed, water-cooled.
   f. Oil-immersed, forced-oil-cooled.
   g. Oil-immersed, combination self-cooled and water-cooled.
2. According to insulation between windings.
   a. Windings insulated from each other.
   b. Autotransformers.
3. According to number of phases.
   a. Single-phase.
   b. Polyphase.
4. According to method of mounting.
   a. Pole and platform.
   b. Subway.
   c. Vault.
   d. Special.
5. According to purpose.
   a. Constant potential.
   b. Varying potential.
   c. Current.
   d. Constant current.
6. According to service.
   a. Large power.
   b. Distribution.
   c. Small power.
   d. Sign lighting.
   e. Control and signaling.
   f. Gaseous-discharge lamp transformers.
   g. Bell ringing.
   h. Instrument.
   i. Constant current.
   j. Series transformers for street lighting.

6. Cooling of Transformers.   A certain amount of the electrical energy delivered to a transformer is transformed into heat energy due to the resistance of its windings and to the hysteresis and eddy currents in the iron core.   Means must be provided for removing this heat energy from the transformer and dissipating it into the surrounding air. If this is not done in a satisfactory manner, the transformer would operate at an excessively high temperature, which would destroy or harm the insulation of the transformer. The different methods of cooling employed are listed in Sec. **5** and described below.

In **self-air-cooled** transformers (Fig. 5) the windings are simply surrounded by air at atmospheric pressure.   The heat is removed by natural convection of the surrounding air and by radiation from the different parts of the transformer structure.   Air cooling

 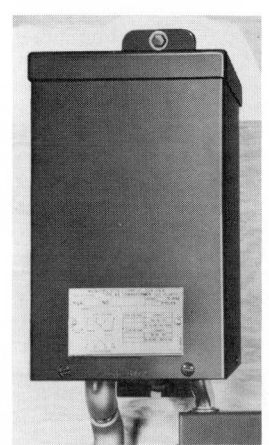

I. *With louver in cover to aid circulation of air around element.*   II. *With solid metal casing.*

FIG. 5   *Dry-type transformers.   (Wagner Electric Corp.)*

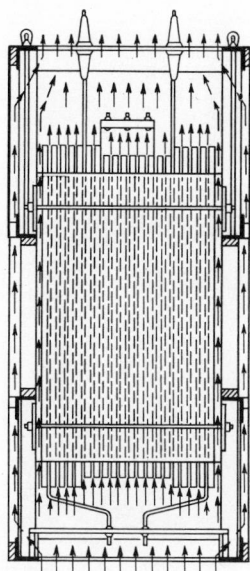

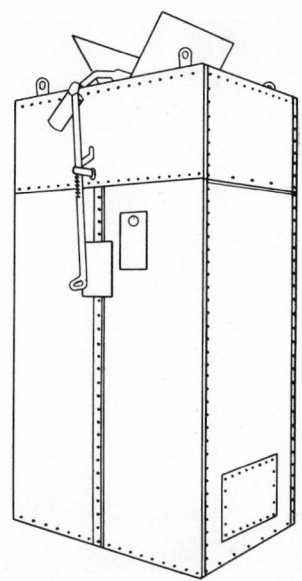

FIG. 6 *Longitudinal section of air-blast transformer, showing direction of air currents.*

FIG. 7 *Exterior view of 1,330-kva air-blast transformer, showing the sheet-steel casing.*

has long been employed for transformers of very small capacity. The development of satisfactory coil insulation materials, such as porcelain, mica, glass, and asbestos, which will withstand higher temperatures than the more common insulating materials, has made possible the application of air cooling to transformers of large capacity. Except in the smaller sizes, the sheet-metal enclosure is provided with louvers or gratings to allow free circulation of the air over and through the windings. Self-air-cooled trans-formers are commonly called dry-type trans-formers. The present-day use of self-air-cooled transformers has been extended to units of at least 3,000 kva capacity at 15,000 volts.

In **air-blast-cooled** transformers (Figs. 6 and 7) the core and windings are enclosed in a metal enclosure through which air is circulated by means of a blower. This method has been used for large power transformers in ratings up to 15,000 kva with voltages not exceeding 35,000.

In **liquid-immersed, self-cooled trans-formers,** the core and windings are immersed in some insulating liquid and enclosed in a metal tank. The liquid, in addition to providing some of the required insulation between the windings, carries the heat from the core and windings to the surface of the tank. The heat is then removed into the surrounding

FIG. 8 *Small distribution transformer with smooth tank. (Moloney Electric Co.)*

atmosphere by natural convection of the surrounding air and by radiation from the tank. In the smaller sizes the tanks have a smooth surface (Fig. 8). In larger sizes tanks are corrugated or finned (Fig. 9) or have external tubes (Fig. 10), and in very large units the tanks must be supplied with external radiators (Fig. 11), through which the oil circulates

FIG. 9 *Medium-sized transformer with corrugated tank. (Moloney Electric Co.)*

FIG. 10 *Tubular-type tank as used on medium-sized power transformers. (Moloney Electric Co.)*

FIG. 11 *Large self-cooled transformer with radiators. (Moloney Electric Co.)*

by natural convection due to differences in temperature in the liquid. This method can be employed for units of any size or voltage rating, although large-capacity units become rather expensive and bulky. The common liquid employed is an insulating oil. Nonflammable and nonexplosive liquids have been developed for use as a cooling and insulating medium for electrical equipment. These liquids are used in transformers where their nonflammable and nonexplosive qualities warrant their additional expense. The use of such a liquid is particularly advantageous for transformers installed in buildings, since the transformer can then be installed in general areas without the use of a fireproof vault enclosure. Transformers insulated with such a liquid are designated as askarel-insulated transformers.

Large oil-immersed transformers are frequently cooled by means of a combination of **self-cooling** and **air blast** (Fig. 12). The construction of the transformer is in general the same as for those which are oil-immersed and self-cooled, with the addition of a motor-driven blower or blowers mounted integrally with the transformer tank. The blowers provide a forced circulation of air up through the radiators in order to supplement the natural convection air currents. The blower motors are generally automatically controlled by means of a thermostat. When the oil temperature reaches a certain value, the thermostat closes the motor circuit. After the temperature has been reduced to a definite value, the thermostat opens the motor circuit, shutting off the fans.

Oil-immersed water-cooled transformers (Fig. 13) are sometimes employed for large units. Where a plentiful supply of cooling water is available at small cost, they may prove more economical than the self-cooled types. In these transformers a coil of copper or brass pipe is installed near the top of the transformer enclosing tank. Water is circulated through this coil and carries the heat away from the hot oil as it rises in the tank.

In some cases of very large oil-immersed units, a combination of **self- and water-cooling** is employed.

7. The oil used in transformers ("Standard Handbook for Electrical Engineers") performs two important functions. It serves to insulate the various coils from each other and from the core, and it conducts the heat from the coils and core to some cooler surfaces, where it is either dissipated in the surrounding air or transferred to some cooling medium. It is evident that the oil should be free from any conducting material, it should be sufficiently thin to circulate rapidly when subjected to differences of temperature at different places, and it should not be ignitible until its temperature is raised to a very high value. Although numerous kinds of oils have been tried in transformers, at the present time mineral oil is used almost exclusively. This oil is obtained by fractional distillation of petroleum unmixed with any other substances and without subsequent chemical treatment. A good grade of transformer oil should show very little evaporation at 100°C, and it should not give off gases at such a rate as to produce an explosive mixture with the surrounding air at a temperature below 180°C. It should not contain moisture, acid, alkali, or sulfur compounds.

It has been shown by Mr. C. E. Skinner that the deteriorating effect of moisture on the insulating qualities of an oil is very marked; moisture to the extent of 0.06 per cent reduces the dielectric strength of the oil to about 50 per cent of the value when it is free from moisture, but there is very little further decrease in the dielectric strength with an increase in the amount of moisture in the oil.

Dry oil will stand an emf of 25,000 volts between two 0.5-in. knobs separated 0.15 in. The presence of moisture can be detected by thrusting a red-hot nail in the oil; if the oil "crackles," water is present. Moisture can be removed by raising the temperature slightly above the boiling point of water, but the time consumed (several days) is excessive. The oil is subsequently passed through a dry-sand filter to remove any traces of lime or other foreign materials.

8. The insulating value of the oil, in oil-immersed transformers ("Standard Handbook"), is depended on very largely to help insulate the transformer; this is done by providing liberal oil ducts between coils and between groups of coils, in addition to the solid insulation. The oil ducts thus serve the double purpose of insulating and cooling the windings.

Since the oil is a very important part of the insulation, every effort is made in modern transformers to preserve both its insulating and cooling qualities. Oxidation and

I

II

FIG. 12   *Large oil-immersed transformers equipped with radiators and blowers for cooling by combination of self-cooling and air blast.   (Moloney Electric Co.)*

FIG. 13   *Large water-cooled transformer.*   (*Moloney Electric Co.*)

moisture are the chief causes of deterioration.   Oil takes into solution about 15 per cent by volume of whatever gas is in contact with it.   In the open-type transformer, oil rapidly darkens, owing to the effects of oxygen in solution in the oil and the oxygen in contact with the top surface of the hot oil.

1. EXPANSION TANK (OR CONSERVATOR).   One of the first devices used to reduce oxidation was the expansion tank (or conservator), which consisted of a small tank mounted above and connected with the main tank by means of a constricted connection so that the small tank could act as a reservoir to take up the expansion and contraction of the oil due to temperature changes and reduce the oil surface exposed to air.

2. THE INERTAIRE TRANSFORMER has the space above the oil in the tank filled with a cushion of inert gas which is mostly nitrogen.   The nitrogen atmosphere is initially blown in from a cylinder of compressed nitrogen and is thereafter maintained by passing the in-breathing air through materials which remove the moisture and the oxygen, permitting dry nitrogen to pass into the case.   A breathing regulator, which consists of a mercury U tube with unequal legs, allows in-breathing of nitrogen when the pressure in the case is only slightly below atmospheric but prevents out-breathing unless the pressure in the case becomes 5 lb per sq in. higher than atmospheric pressure.   The elimination of oxygen from within the transformer case eliminates the oxidation of the oil and prevents fire and secondary explosion within the case.

9. **Insulation between Windings.**   The great majority of transformers are constructed with two or more windings which are electrically insulated from each other.   In some cases a single winding is employed, parts of the winding functioning both as primary and secondary.   These transformers are called autotransformers.   They are frequently used when the voltage ratio is small.   Autotransformers should never be used for high-voltage ratios, as the low-voltage winding is not insulated from the high-voltage one, so

that in case of trouble it would be dangerous to both life and equipment. Refer to Sec. 32 for further discussion.

10. Transformer Insulation. The type of insulation used in dry-type transformer design and construction has a definite bearing on the size and operating temperature of the unit. Currently there are four classes of insulation being used, each having a separate NEMA specification and temperature limit. A look at these will facilitate selection of the proper unit to meet prescribed installation and operating conditions.

1. CLASS A TRANSFORMERS, when properly applied and loaded in an ambient not over 40°C, will operate at not more than a 55°C temperature rise on the winding. These units can be used as control-type transformers where higher temperatures might affect other temperature-sensitive devices in the enclosure, or as distribution transformers in areas (textile mills, saw mills, etc.) where combustible flyings might be present in the surrounding atmosphere.

2. CLASS B TRANSFORMERS have a higher temperature insulating system and are physically smaller and about half the weight of Class A units of corresponding rated capacities. When properly loaded to rated kva and installed in an ambient not over 40°C, Class B units will operate at a maximum 80°C rise on the winding. For years, dry-type distribution transformers have been of the Class B type.

3. CLASS F TRANSFORMERS also have a high-temperature insulating system and, when properly loaded and applied in an ambient not over 40°C, will operate at no more than 115°C rise on the winding. These units are smaller in size than similarly rated Class B units and currently are available from a number of manufacturers in ratings of 25 kva and lower, both single- and three-phase design. One manufacturer designs in-wall, flush-mounted dry-type transformers as Class F units.

4. CLASS H TRANSFORMERS are insulated with a high-temperature system of glass, silicone, and asbestos components, and are probably the most compact units available. When properly loaded and applied in an ambient not over 40°C, Class H transformers will operate at a maximum 150°C rise on the winding. This class of insulation is used primarily in designs where the core and coil are completely enclosed in a ventilated housing. Generally, this covers units with ratings of 30 kva and larger. Some experts recommend that the hottest spot on the metal enclosure be limited to a maximum rise of 40°C above a 40°C ambient.

It should be noted that Class B insulation is being replaced with Class F or H insulation in transformers of recent design.

Another significant factor which concerns all dry-type transformers is that they should never be overloaded. The way to avoid this is to size the primary or secondary overcurrent device as close as possible to the full-load primary or secondary current for other than motor loads. If close overcurrent protection has not been provided, loads should be checked periodically. Overloading a transformer causes excessive temperature, which, in turn, produces overheating. This results in rapid deterioration of the insulation and will cause complete failure of the transformer coils.

11. Transformers are built in both single- and polyphase units. A polyphase transformer consists of separate, insulated electric windings for the different phases, wound upon a single core structure, certain portions of which are common to the different phases.

THREE-PHASE TRANSFORMERS ("Standard Handbook"). Although there are numerous possible arrangements of the coils and cores in constructing a polyphase transformer, yet it can be stated that a polyphase transformer generally consists of several one-phase transformers with separate electric circuits but having certain magnetic circuits in common. A three-phase transformer is illustrated in Fig. 14, together with the component one-phase transformer. It will be observed that a three-phase transformer requires three times as much copper as the one-phase component transformer but less than three times as much iron. Thus in comparison with three individual transformers the three-phase unit is somewhat lighter and more efficient. Each component transformer operates as though the others were not present, the flux of one transformer combining with that of an adjacent transformer to produce a resultant flux exactly equal to that of each one alone. Figure 15 shows the interior of a Westinghouse three-phase transformer.

12. Application of Three-phase Transformers (A. D. Fishel). For central stations of medium size, three-phase transformers are rarely superior to single phase except where the large sizes can be applied, in which case the transformers are normally installed in substations or central stations. The chief reason for this is the nonflexibility of a three-phase transformer. It is usually purchased for a particular size and type of load, and if that load should be changed, the transformer, representing a comparatively heavy investment, remains on the hands of the central station, whereas a single-phase transformer of one-third the size could usually be adapted for some other service.

This feature becomes of less importance as the central station increases its size, and

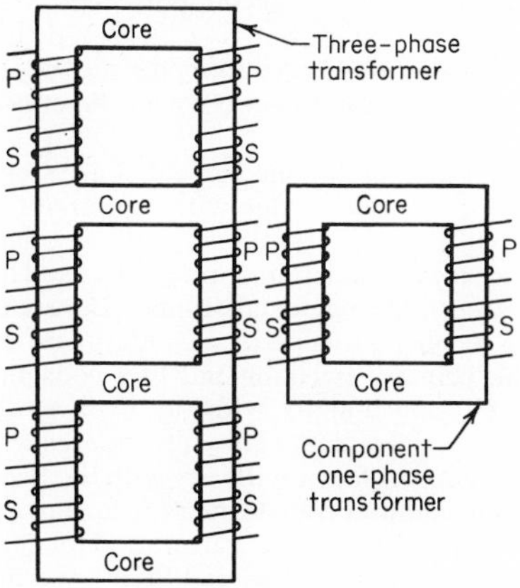

FIG. 14 *Three-phase core-type trans-former.*

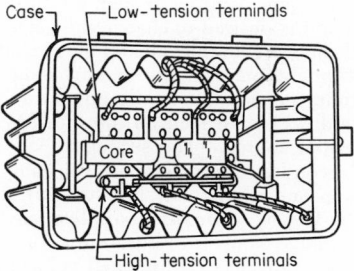

FIG. 15 *Interior view of a three-phase transformer.*

three-phase transformers for purely power service are now being used by a considerable number of the large central stations of this country. The three-phase transformer costs less to install, and the connections are simpler, points that are of importance in connection with outdoor installations. The fact that a failure of a three-phase transformer would interrupt service more than the failure of one single-phase transformer in a bank of three is of little importance because of the comparatively few failures of modern transformers. On the other hand, especially for 2,200-volt service, the single-phase transformer has been carried to a high degree of perfection and is manufactured in much larger quantities, so that better performance is usual and, in some cases, initial cost is lower. Three-phase distribution transformers are used extensively in underground city network service on account of the smaller space required by them in the manhole, their higher efficiency, and their lower initial cost. For overhead service for pole or platform mounting, three single-phase units are more common on account of the ease of handling and mounting the smaller-sized units.

13. Methods of Mounting. Transformers are constructed with different types of metal enclosing structures in order to meet the requirements of different conditions of installation. One type of enclosure (Figs. 8 and 19) is designed **for mounting on poles,** either directly or with hanger irons, for use in overhead distribution work. Another type of enclosure, called the **platform type** (Figs. 10, 11, and 12), is suitable for installations where the transformer stands upon its own base. It can be mounted on any flat horizontal surface having sufficient mechanical strength, such as a floor or a platform between poles. **Subway transformers** have watertight tanks which are designed primarily for underground installations where the transformer may be completely submerged in water. **Vault transformers** also have watertight enclosures so that they will not be injured by total submersion, but they are not designed to operate satisfactorily under such conditions. The vault transformers are intended for operation in underground vaults where dampness is prevalent and where occasional submersion might occur but where the transformer would not be required to operate for any considerable length of time while submerged. Small transformers for power and special application as listed in Sec. 5 (6c to 6j) are designed with special types of mounting in order to meet the requirements of installation for these types of service.

14. Purpose of Transformers.   Transformers can be classified as given in Sec. 5 (5) according to the purpose of transformation for which they are employed.

The function of a **constant-potential** transformer is to change the voltage of a system. It is designed to operate with its primary connected across a constant-potential supply and to provide a secondary voltage which is substantially constant from no load to full load. It is the ordinary common type of transformer. The currents of both primary and secondary vary with the load supplied by the transformer. A **varying-potential** transformer is also intended for changing the voltage of a system but is so designed that when operated with its primary connected to a constant-potential supply the secondary voltage will vary widely with the load. Such transformers are necessary for the operation of many gaseous-discharge lamps.

A **current** transformer is one which is designed for changing the current of a system. The primary winding of such a transformer is connected in series with the circuit of which it is desired to change the current. The voltage of both primary and secondary will change with the value of the current of the system. Such transformers are used for instrument transformers and in some series street-lighting installations. **Constant-current** transformers are designed for supplying a constant value of secondary current regardless of the load on the transformer. The primary is connected to a constant-potential source. The secondary voltage varies proportionally with the load, while the secondary current remains constant. The primary current and kilovolt-amperes will be constant for all loads, but the kilowatt input and power factor will vary with the load.

15. The most important application of constant-potential transformers is for raising the voltage of an electric transmission circuit so that energy can be transmitted for considerable distances with small voltage drop and small energy loss and then lowering the voltage for safe usage by motors, lights, and appliances.

16. The Theory of Operation of the Constant-potential Transformer (see Fig. 1). It has been shown in Div. 1 that turns of wire wound on an iron core have self-induction. When an alternating voltage is applied to such turns, a current flows through them that generates a countervoltage or emf that opposes the applied voltage. From formulas, the transformer designer can compute just how many turns are necessary for a transformer of a given size so that it will generate a countervoltage equal to the applied voltage. So, in designing the primary winding of the transformer of Fig. 1, the designer would select such a number of turns for the primary winding that the countervoltage generated by it would be nearly 2,400 volts. Hence, when the primary winding is connected to a 2,400-volt circuit, it generates a countervoltage of practically 2,400 and no appreciable current flows. A small current, the exciting current, just enough to magnetize the core, does flow, but it is so small that it can be disregarded in this discussion.

Since the primary and secondary windings are on the same core, the magnetic flux generated by the magnetizing or exciting current flowing in the primary winding also cuts the turns of the secondary winding and generates an emf in them. This emf will be, in accordance with a well-known law, opposite in direction to that impressed on the primary. If the secondary circuit is open, no current can flow in it, but if it is closed, a certain current, proportional to the impedance of the secondary circuit, will flow. This current, because of the direction of the emf generated in the secondary, will be in such a direction that the magnetic flux produced in the core by it will oppose the flux due to the primary winding. It will therefore decrease the effective or resultant flux in the core by a small amount which will decrease the counter-emf of the primary winding and permit more current to flow into the primary winding. As noted elsewhere, the ratio of the number of turns in the primary winding to the number of turns in the secondary winding determines the ratio of the primary to the secondary voltage.

If the voltage impressed on the transformer is maintained constant, the voltage of the secondary will be nearly constant also. When more current flows in the secondary, there will be a corresponding increase in primary current. As the load on a transformer increases, the impressed voltage remaining constant, there is actually a slight drop from the no-load voltage of the secondary, due to certain inherent characteristics of the transformer, but in a properly designed device this drop will be very small. Although the construction and elementary theory of the transformer are very simple, a theoretical explanation of all the phenomena involved in its operation is very complicated. Only the principal features have been described. Some minor, though very important, considerations that would complicate the explanation have not been treated.

17. Transformer Ratios. The voltage ratio of a constant-potential transformer, i.e., the ratio of primary to secondary voltage, depends primarily upon the ratio of the primary to the secondary turns. The voltage ratio will vary slightly with amount and power factor of the load. For general work the voltage ratio can be taken equal to the turn ratio of the windings.

The current ratio of a constant-potential transformer will be approximately equal to the inverse ratio of the turns in the two windings. For example, for transforming or "stepping down" from 2,400 to 120 volts the ratio of the turns in the windings will be 20:1. The currents in the primary and the secondary windings will be, very closely, inversely proportional to the ratio of the primary and secondary voltages, because, disregarding the small losses of transformation, the power put into a transformer will equal the power delivered by it. For example, considering a transformer with windings having a ratio of 20:1, if its secondary winding delivers 100 amp at 50 volts, the input to its primary winding must receive almost exactly 5 amp at 1,000 volts. The input and output are each (practically) equal, and each would equal (almost exactly) 5,000 watts.

18. The regulation of a transformer is the change in secondary voltage from no load to full load. It is generally expressed as a percentage of the full-load secondary voltage:

$$\text{Per cent regulation} = \frac{\text{no-load secondary voltage} - \text{full-load secondary voltage}}{\text{full-load secondary voltage}} \times 100 \quad (1)$$

The regulation depends upon the design of the transformer and the power factor of the load. Although with a noninductive load such as incandescent lamps the regulation of transformers is within about 3 per cent, with an inductive load the drop in potential between no load and full load increases to possibly about 5 per cent. If the motor load is large and fluctuating and close lamp regulation is important, it is desirable to use separate transformers for the motors.

19. The efficiency of a transformer is, as with any other device, the ratio of the output to input or, in other words, the ratio of the output to the output plus the losses. As a formula it can be expressed thus:

$$\text{Efficiency} = \frac{\text{output}}{\text{input}} = \frac{\text{output}}{\text{output} + \text{copper loss} + \text{iron loss}} \quad (2)$$

Average efficiencies of transformers are given in Sec. **43** to **57**.

20. The copper loss of a transformer is determined by the resistances of the high-tension and low-tension windings and of the leads. It is equal to the sum of the watts of I^2R losses in these components at the load for which it is desired to compute the efficiency.

21. The iron loss of a transformer is equal to the sum of the losses in the iron core. These losses consist of eddy- or Foucault-current losses and hysteresis losses. Eddy-current losses are due to currents generated by the alternating flux circulating within each lamination composing the core, and they are minimized by using thin laminations and by insulating adjacent laminations with insulating varnish. Hysteresis losses are due to the power required to reverse the magnetism of the iron core at each alternation and are determined by the amount and the grade of iron used for the laminations for the core.

22. Transformer Ratings. Transformers are rated at their kilovolt-ampere (kva) outputs. If the load to be supplied by a transformer is at 100 per cent power factor (pf), the kilowatt (kw) output will be the same as the kilovolt-ampere output. If the load has a lesser power factor, the kilowatt output will be less than the kilovolt-ampere output proportionally as the load power factor is less than 100 per cent.

Example. A transformer having a full-load rating of 100 kva will safely carry 100 kw if the 100 kw is at 100 per cent pf, 90 kw at 90 per cent pf, or 80 kw at 80 per cent pf.

Transformers are generally rated on the kilovolt-ampere load which the transformer can safely carry continuously without exceeding a temperature rise of 55°C for Class A insulation or 80°C for Class B insulation when maintaining rated secondary voltage at rated frequency and when operating with an ambient temperature of 40°C. (Ambient temperature is the temperature of the surrounding atmosphere.) The actual temperature of any part of the transformer is the sum of the temperature rise of that part plus the ambient temperature.   See Sec. **10** for an explanation of transformer insulation classifications.

The usual service conditions under which a transformer should be able to carry its rated load are:

1. At rated secondary voltage or not in excess of 105 per cent of rated value.

2. At rated frequency.

3. Temperature of the surrounding cooling air at no time exceeding 40°C and average temperature of the surrounding cooling air during any 24-hr period not exceeding 30°C.

4. Altitude not in excess of 3,300 ft.

5. If water-cooled the temperature of the cooling water does not exceed 30°C and the average temperature of the cooling water during any 24-hr period does not exceed 25°C.

Guide for Loading Oil-Immersed Distribution and Power Transformers

23. The following sections on guidance for loading of transformers are excerpts from the United States of America Standard Institute's publication Appendix 057.92. This publication is not a part of the USA Standard but is, as stated, a guide for the use of transformers.

The actual output which a transformer can deliver at any time in service without undue deterioration of the insulation may be more or less than the rated output, depending upon the ambient temperature and other attendant operating conditions.

24. Loading on Basis of Test Temperature Rise. For each degree centigrade in excess of 2° that the test temperature rise is below the standard temperature rise specified in the standard, the transformer load may be increased above rated kilovolt-amperes by the percentages shown in column 3 of the following table. Making use of this factor gives the kilovolt-amperes that the transformer can deliver with 55°C temperature rise. The leeway of 2° is to provide for a negative tolerance in the measurement of temperature rise.

Loading on Basis of Ambient Temperature

Type of cooling	Per cent of rated kva	
	Decrease load for higher temperature	Increase load for lower temperature
Self-cooled......	1.5	1.0
Water-cooled.............	1.5	1.0
Forced-air-cooled..........	1.0	0.75
Forced-oil-cooled..........	1.0	0.75

Some transformers are designed to have the difference between hottest-spot and average copper temperatures greater than the nominal allowance of 10°C. This will result in a temperature rise for average copper of less than 55°C, but the hottest-spot copper temperature rise may be at the limiting value of 65°C. Such transformers should not be loaded above rating as outlined under this heading. The manufacturer should be consulted to give information as to design of hottest-spot allowances.

25. Loading on Basis of Ambient Temperature. For each degree centigrade that the average temperature of the cooling medium is above or below 30°C for air or 25°C for water, a transformer can be loaded for any period of time below or above its kilovolt-ampere rating as specified in the table of Sec. **24**. Average temperature should be for periods of time not exceeding 24 hr with maximum temperatures not more than 10°C greater than average temperatures for air and 5°C for water. On the basis used in this guide for calculating loss of life, life expectancy will be approximately the same as if it had been operated at rated kilovolt-amperes and standard ambient temperatures over that period.

The use of transformers in cooling air above 50°C or below 0°C or with cooling water above 35°C is not covered by the table of Sec. 24 and should be taken up with the manufacturer.

26. Loading on Basis of Load Factor. When the load factor for a period of time not exceeding 24 hr is below 100 per cent, the maximum loading of a transformer during that period may be increased above rated kilovolt-amperes by the percentages shown in the following table for each per cent that the load factor is below 100 per cent. On the basis used in this guide for calculating loss of life, life expectancy will be approximately the same as if it had been operated at rated kilovolt-amperes during that period.

Loading on Basis of Load Factor

Type of cooling	Increase in per cent of rated kva	Maximum per cent increase[a]
Self-cooled...................	0.5	25
Water-cooled..............	0.5	25
Forced-air-cooled...........	0.4	20
Forced-oil-cooled...........	0.4	20

[a] Corresponds to 50 per cent load factor.

27. Loading on Basis of Short-time Loads above Rating. When short-time loads above rating occur not more than once in any 24-hr period, the maximum loading of a transformer during that period can be increased conservatively above rated kilovolt-amperes, as given in Table 28. On the basis used in this guide for calculating loss of life, life expectancy will be approximately the same as if it had been operated at rated kilovolt-amperes during that period.

28. Daily Overloads to Give Normal Life Expectancy

Time, hr	Times rated kilovolt-amperes								
	Self-cooled and water-cooled transformers			Forced-air-cooled transformers rated 133% or less of self-cooled rating			Forced-air-cooled transformers rated more than 133% of self-cooled rating and all forced-oil-cooled		
Initial load, %[a]	90	70	50	90	70	50	90	70	50
½	1.59	1.77	1.89	1.45	1.58	1.68	1.36	1.47	1.50
1	1.40	1.54	1.60	1.31	1.38	1.50	1.24	1.31	1.34
2	1.24	1.33	1.37	1.19	1.23	1.26	1.14	1.18	1.21
4	1.12	1.17	1.19	1.11	1.13	1.15	1.09	1.10	1.10
8	1.06	1.08	1.08	1.06	1.07	1.07	1.05	1.06	1.06

[a] Percentages fix the load which is assumed to exist before the short-time load is applied. Use either average load for 2 hr previous to load above rating or average load for 24 hr (less overload period), whichever is greater.

Ambient temperature assumed for this table is 30°C for air and 25°C for water.

As the loads may be applied once every 24 hr, and as there is some evidence that the rate of insulation deterioration at about 100°C doubles with less than 8°C increase in insulation temperature, the values have been based on 4 rather than on 8°C.

29. Effect of Various Factors Existing at One Time. When two or more of the following factors affecting loading for normal life expectancy exist at one time, the effects are cumulative and the increase in loads due to each can be added to secure the maximum suggested load (each increase must be based on rated kilovolt-amperes):

1. Loading on basis of test temperature rise.

2. Loading on basis of ambient temperature.

3. Either loading on basis of load factor or loading on basis of short-time overloads. Do not use both.

30. Capacities of Transformers for Induction Motors
(General Electric Co.)

Size of motor, hp	Kva per transformer		
	Two single-phase transformers	Three single-phase transformers	One three-phase transformer
1	0.6	0.6	
2	1.5	1.0	2.0
3	2.0	1.5	3.0
5	3.0	2.0	5.0
7½	4.0	3.0	7.5
10	5.0	4.0	10.0
15	7.5	5.0	15.0
20	10.0	7.5	20.0
30	15.0	10.0	30.0
50	25.0	15.0	50.0
75	40.0	25.0	75.0
100	50.0	30.0	100.0

31. Capacities of Transformers for Operating Motors (General Electric Co.). For the larger motors the capacity of the transformers in kilovolt-amperes should equal the output of the motor in horsepower. Thus a 50-hp motor requires 50 kva in transformers. Small motors should be supplied with a somewhat larger transformer capacity, especially if, as is desirable, they are expected to run most of the time near full load or even at slight overload. Transformers of less capacity than those noted in Table **30** should not be used even when a motor is to be run at only partial load.

32. The Autotransformer ("Standard Handbook"). The most efficient and effective method of operating a stationary transformer (when the ratio of transformation is not too large) is as an autotransformer, i.e., with certain portions of the windings used simultaneously as the primary and the secondary circuit. The electrical circuits of a one-phase autotransformer (sometimes called a compensator or a balance coil) are indicated in Fig. 16. The autotransformer has only one coil, a certain portion of which is used for both the high-tension and the low-tension winding. The number of turns of this coil is the same as would be required if it were used exclusively for the high-tension winding and a separate additional coil were used for the low-tension winding. Moreover, when the ratio of transformation is 2:1 or 1:2, the amount of copper in the one coil is exactly the same whether it is used as an autotransformer or as a high-tension coil of a two-coil transformer of the same rating. Not only is less copper required for an autotransformer than for a two-coil transformer, but less iron is needed to surround the copper.

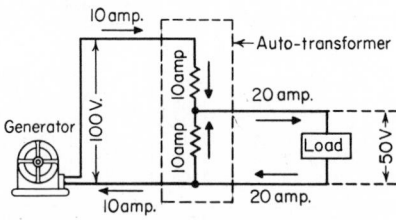

FIG. 16   *Electric circuits of a 1-kva single-phase autotransformer.*

Referring again to Fig. 16, it is to be noted that the one-coil transformer is designed for 10 amp throughout and for a total emf of 100 volts. The voltage per turn is uniform throughout, so that to obtain 50 volts it is necessary merely to select any two points on the continuous winding such that one-half of the total number of turns is included between them. The load current of 20 amp (required for 1,000 watts at 50 volts) is op-

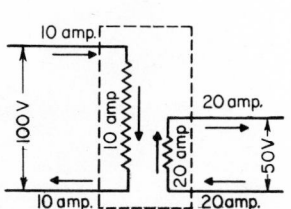

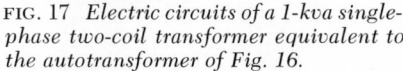

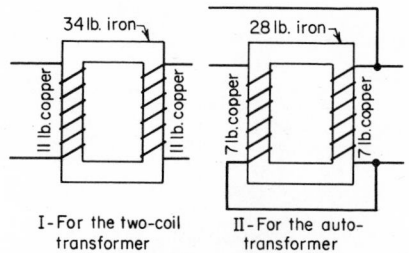

I-For the two-coil transformer   II-For the auto-transformer

FIG. 17 *Electric circuits of a 1-kva single-phase two-coil transformer equivalent to the autotransformer of Fig. 16.*

FIG. 18 *Comparison of constructive material required for a two-coil transformer and for an autotransformer.*

posed by the superposed 10 amp of primary current, so that even in this section of the coil the resultant current is only 10 amp.

If an ordinary two-coil transformer had been used, the circuits would have been as noted in Fig. 17, while the required constructive material would have been approximately as indicated in Fig. 18, I. With respect to its constructive material, a 1-kw 2:1 ratio autotransformer is the equivalent of a 1:1 ratio 0.5-kw two-coil transformer as shown in Fig. 18, II. The latter transformer requires about 14 lb of copper and 28 lb of iron as compared with about 22 lb of copper and 34 lb of iron for the transformer of Fig. 18, I. Moreover, the losses of the autotransformer are correspondingly less than those of a two-coil transformer. Refer to Sec. **117** for limitations in the allowable use of autotransformers.

33. Constant-potential transformers for the transformation of a large amount of power, more than 500 kva, are called power transformers. Transformers for general constant-potential power transformation, whose rating is 500 kva or less, are called distribution transformers. All the methods of cooling are employed for power transformers. The choice depends upon which will result in the best over-all economy including first cost, operating expense, and space occupied. Distribution transformers generally are liquid-immersed, self-cooled. Power and distribution transformers are normally of the standard type with the windings insulated from each other, although those with autotransformer construction can be obtained for special applications where the voltage ratio is small. Power transformers are always of the platform type. Distribution transformers are made with tanks for pole and platform mounting and with tanks of the subway and vault types. The tanks of the platform type of transformers of 50-kva capacity and smaller are equipped with lugs or brackets (Fig. 19) for direct pole mounting or for the attachment of hanger irons for crossarm pole mounting.

34. Network transformers are distribution transformers specially constructed and equipped with attached auxiliaries such as junction boxes and switches for disconnecting and grounding the high-voltage cable in order to meet the requirements of transformers for supplying low-voltage networks.

35. Self-protected distribution transformers are equipped with lightning and overload protective equipment built integrally with the transformers. They are made in two types: completely self-protecting (CSP), i.e., having both overload and lightning protection, and with only surge protection (SP). The connections of the lightning protective equipment can be made in different ways in order to satisfy any desired grounding practice. A sectional view of such a CSP transformer is shown in Fig. 20.

36. Voltage Taps. It is frequently desirable on transformers to obtain a voltage ratio which is slightly different from the standard ratio obtained with the complete winding. Most transformers are provided with two 5 per cent taps on the high-voltage winding for this purpose. The taps are for reduced voltage and allow the rated secondary voltage to be obtained when the supply voltage is below the rated value. Many transformers are equipped with a ratio adjuster (Fig. 21). The ratio adjuster provides a means of changing taps on the transformer by simply turning an operating handle without having to take down and remake connections. The diagram of connections of a ratio

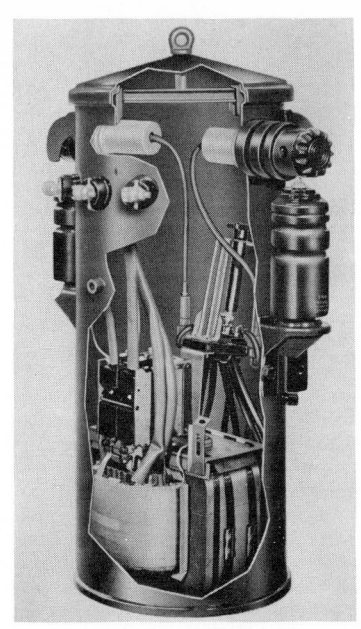

FIG. 19 *Distribution transformer for pole mounting. (Marcus Transformer Co.)*

FIG. 20 *Sectional view of CSP transformer. (Westinghouse Electric Corp.)*

adjuster is shown in Fig. 22. The transformer of the illustration is provided with two primary coils instead of one, as would be the more general practice. The transformer should be disconnected from the line before the taps are changed with the ratio adjuster, as the device is not intended for operation under load.

The standard taps for distribution transformers are given in Secs. **38** and **39**. A rated-kilovolt-ampere tap is a tap through which the transformer can deliver its rated kilovolt-ampere output without exceeding its rated temperature rise. A reduced-kilovolt-am-

Ratio adjuster

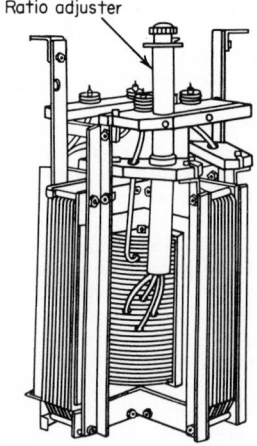

FIG. 21. *Core and coils for a 6,600 volt-distribution transformer showing ratio adjuster. (General Electric Co.)*

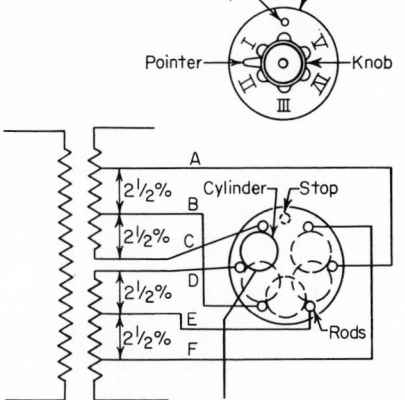

Position	Connecting	% of Winding
I	C to D	100
II	B to D	97.5
III	B to E	95
IV	A to E	92.5
V	A to F	90

FIG. 22 *Diagram of ratio adjuster connections to transformer with four 2½ per cent taps.* (*General Electric Co.*)

pere tap is a tap through which the transformer can deliver only a kilovolt-ampere output less than its rated value without exceeding its rated temperature rise.

Large power transformers frequently are equipped with load-ratio control equipment by means of which the connections to taps of the transformer can be changed under load.

37. Preferred Ratings of Transformers
Kva Ratings

Single-phase				Three-phase			
3	100	2,500	20,000	9	300	5,000	37,500
5	167	3,333	25,000	15	500	7,500	50,000
10	250	5,000	33,333	30	750	10,000	60,000
15	333	6,667		45	1,000	12,000	75,000
25	500	8,333		75	1,500	15,000	100,000
37½	833	10,000		112½	2,000	20,000	
50	1,250	12,500		150	2,500	25,000	
75	1,667	16,667		225	3,750	33,333	

38. Standard Ratings for Single-phase Transformers
(United States of America Standards Institute)

Preferred nominal system voltage	Transformer high-voltage — Rating (9)	BIL, kv	Taps — Above	Taps — Below	120/240 (2)	240/480 (2)	240 × 480 (3)	600	2,400 or 4,800	2,520 or 5,040	6,900	7,200 or 7,560 or 7,980
480	480(8)	30	None	2–5%	3–100							
600	600(8)	30	None	2–5%	3–100							
2,400 or 2,400/4,160Y	2,400	60	None 2–2½%	4–2½% 2–2½%	10–167 — — — 250–500	10–100 — — —	— — 167 250–500	25 50 100 167 333–500				
2,400/4,160Y	4,160	75	None 2–2½%	4–2½% 2–2½%	3–100	10–100						
4,800 or 4,800/8,320Y	4,800	75	None 2–2½%	None 2–2½%	3–167 — — — 250–500	10–100 — — —	— — 167 250–500	25 50 100 167 333–500				
2,400 or 2,400/4,160Y or 4,800 or 4,800/8,320Y	2,400 × 4,800	75	None	None	3–100							

Standard kva ratings for low-voltage ratings of (1)

Nominal system voltage	Rated voltage	BIL	Taps			kVA ratings (stacked values as printed)
7,200 or 7,200/12,470Y	7,200	95	None	None	2-2½%	3-50 · 3-167 · 10-100 · — · — · 167 · 250-500 · — · 25 · 50 · 100 · 167 · 333-500 · 50 · 100 · 167-500 · 333-500
7,200/12,470Y	12,470GrdY/7,200 (4)	95	None	None	4-2½%	3-25 · 3-50 · 10-100 · — · — · 167 · 250-500 · — · 25 · 50 · 100 · 167 · 333-500
7,620/13,200Y	7,620	95	None	2-2½%	2-2½%	3-167 · 3-25 · 3-50 · 167 · 250-500 · 25 · 50 · 100 · 167 · 333-500
7,620/13,200Y	13,200GrdY/7,620 (4)	95	None	2-2½%		3-5 · 3-5 · 3-25 · 3-50 · 250-500 · 167 · 250-500
12,000	12,000	95	None	4-2½%	2-2½%	5-167 · 10-100 · 167 · 250-500 · 25 · 50 · 100 · 167 · 333-500 · 50 · 100 · 167-500 · 333-500
13,200	13,200	95	None	2-2½%		37½-167 · 250-500 · — · 167 · 250-500 · — · 167 · 333-500 · 167-500 · 333-500

NOTE. Numbers in parentheses appear at end of table.

Standard Ratings for Single-phase Transformers (*Continued*)

Preferred nominal system voltage	Transformer high-voltage Rating (9)	BIL, kv	Taps Above	Taps Below	Standard kva ratings for low-voltage ratings of (1) 120/240 (2)	240/480 (2)	240 × 480 (3)	600	2,400 or 4,800	2,520 or 5,040	6,900	7,200 or 7,560 or 7,980
14,400	13,800	95	14,400/14,100	13,500/13,200	167 250–500 —	— — —	167 250–500 —	167 333–500 —	167–500	333–500		
13,200 or 14,400	14,400(5)	95	None	13,800/13,200 12,870/12,540(6)	10–100	10–100	— —	25 50 100	50 100			
23,000	22,900	150	24,100/23,500	22,300/21,700	25 100	25 50 100	— 167 333–500 —	100 167 333–500 —	100–167 333–500	— 333–500	— 333–500	167 333–500
34,500	34,400	200	36,200/35,300	33,500/32,600	25 100	25 50 100	167 333–500 —	167 333–500 —	167 333–500	— 333–500	— 333–500	167 333–500
46,000	43,800	250	46,200/45,000	42,600/41,400	50 100	50 100	167 333–500 —	167 333–500 —	167 333–500	— 333–500	— 333–500	167 333–500
69,000	67,000	350	70,600/68,800	65,200/63,400	100 — —	100 — —	167 333–500 —	167 333–500 —	167 333–500	333–500	— 333–500	167 333–500

(1) Standard kva ratings are: 3, 5, 10, 15, 25, 37½, 50, 75, 100, 167, 250, 333, 500. Kilovolt-ampere ratings separated by a dash (—) indicate that all intervening standard ratings are included. Groupings by kva ratings are as given in original USASI publication.

(2) Low-voltage rating of 120/240 or 240/480 volts is suitable for series, multiple, or three-wire service.

(3) Low-voltage rating 240 × 480 volts or high-voltage rating 2,400 × 4,800 volts is suitable for series or multiple service but not for three-wire service.
(4) One high-voltage bushing only.
(5) Transformers in this class are designed to cover in one rating the general voltage range 13,000–15,000 volts.
(6) The lowest voltage shall be reduced kva rating. All others shall be at rated kva.
(7) Suitable only when system ground conditions permit the use of 18-kv arresters.
(8) Not equipped with tap changers.
(9) Transformers of the following ratings will also be available:

Transformer high-voltage rating	Basic impulse level	High-voltage taps		Standard kva ratings for low-voltage ratings of (1)		
		Above	Below	120/240(2)	240/480(2)	240 × 480(3)
16,340	95	17,200/16,770	15,910/15,480	5-25 50 100	10-100 — —	167 333–500
24,940GrdY/14,400(4) (7)	125	None	13,800/13,200 12,870/12,540(6)	3-25 3-50		
14,400/24,940GrdY(7)	125	None	13,800/13,200 12,870/12,540(6)	3-50	10-50	

39. Standard Ratings for Three-phase Transformers
(United States of America Standards Institute)

Preferred nominal system voltage	Transformer high voltage		Taps		Standard kva ratings for low-voltage ratings of:[a,c]					
	Rating[c]	Basic impulse level (BIL), kv	Above	Below	208Y/120	240[b] or 480	240 × 480[b]	240 × 480	2,400 or 4,160Y / 2,400 or 4,800	12,470Y/7,200 or 13,200Y/7,620
2,400	2,400	45	None	None	9-75	9-45	75			
			None	4-2½%	112½-150 / 225-500		112½-150 / —	225-500		
	4,160Y/2,400	60	2-2½%	2-2½%	— / —	— / —				
			None	None	9-75	9-45	75			
2,400/4,160Y	4,160Y	60	None	4-2½%	112½-150 / 225-500		112½-150 / —			
			2-2½%	2-2½%				225-500		
	4,160	60	1-5%	1-5%		9-45	75			
			None	2-5%	9-75					
			None	4-2½%	112½-150 / 225-500					
4,800	4,800	60	None	None	9-75	9-45	75			
			2-2½%	2-2½%	150 / 300-500		150 / —	300-500		
	8,320Y/4,800	75	None	None	9-75	9-45	150			
			None	4-2½%	150 / 300-500					

Table rotated 90° on the page. Reconstructed in reading orientation:

4,800/8,320Y	8,320Y	75	None / 2-2½%	None / 2-2½%	—	9-45 / — / —	75 / 150 / —	300-500	
7,200	7,200	75	None / None / 1-5% / 2-2½%	None / None / 2-5% / 4-2½%	9-75 / 112½-150 / 225-500	9-45	75 / 112½-150 / —	225-500	
12,000	12,000	95	None / None / 1-5% / 2-2½%	None / None / 2-5% / 4-2½%	15-75 / 112½-150 / 225-500	15-45 / — / —	75 / 112½-150 / —	— / 225-500 / —	150 / 300-500
7,200/12,470Y	12,470Y/7,200	95	None / None	None / None	15-75 / 112½-150 / 225-500	15-45			
	12,470Y	95	1-5% / 2-2½%	1-5% / 2-2½%	—	15-45 / — / —	75 / 112½-150 / —	225-500	
7,620/13,200Y	13,200Y/7,620	95	1-5% / 2-2½%	1-5% / 2-2½%	15-75 / 112½-150 / 225-500				
	13,200Y	95	1-5% / 2-2½%	1-5% / 2-2½%	—	15-45 / — / —	75 / 112½-150 / —	225-500	

Note. Footnotes appear at end of table.

Standard Ratings for Three-phase Transformers (*Continued*)

Preferred nominal system voltage	Transformer high voltage				Standard kva ratings for low-voltage ratings of:[a,c]					
	Rating[c]	Basic impulse level (BIL), kv	Taps Above	Taps Below	208Y/120	240[b] or 480	240 × 480[b]	240 × 480	2,400 or 4,160Y / 2,400 or 4,800	12,470Y/7,200 or 13,200Y/7,620
13,200	13,200	95	None	4–2½%	112½–150	—	112½–150	—	150	
			2–2½%	2–2½%	225–500	—	—	225–500	300–500	
14,400	13,800	95	14,400	13,200	15–75	15–45	75	—	150	
			14,400/14,100	13,500/13,200	112½–150 225–500	—	112½–150	225–500	300–500	
23,000	22,900	150	24,100/23,500	22,300/21,700	—	—	—	150 300–500	150 300–500	150 300–500
34,500	34,400	200	36,200/35,300	33,500/32,600	—	—	—	300–500	300–500	300–500
46,000	43,800	250	46,200/45,000	42,600/41,400	—	—	—	300–500	300–500	300–500
69,000	67,000	350	70,600/68,800	65,200/63,400	—	—	—	500	500	500

[a] Standard kva ratings are 9, 15, 30, 45, 75, 112½, 150, 225, 300, 500. Kilovolt-ampere ratings separated by a dash (—) indicate that all intervening ratings are included.

[b] A 120-volt reduced kva tap is provided.

[c] All transformers are delta-connected unless otherwise specified.

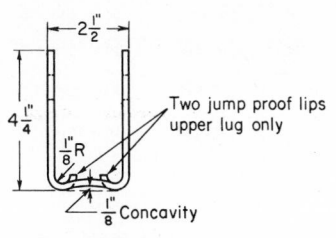

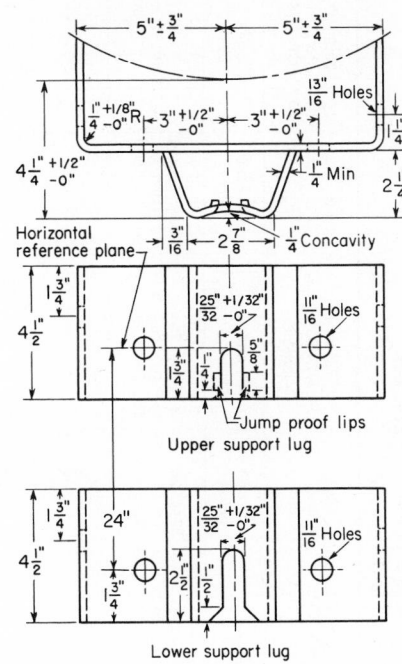

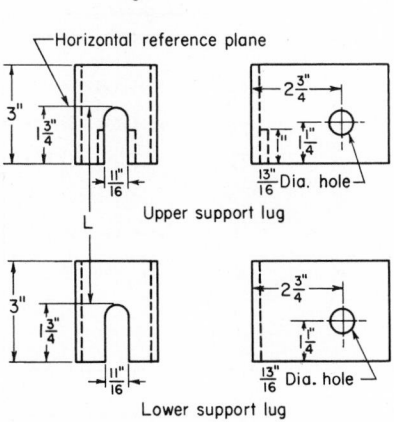

Upper support lug

Lower support lug

Upper support lug

Lower support lug

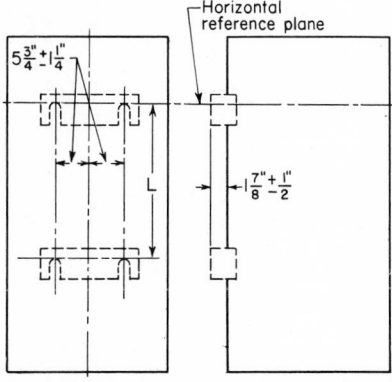

NOTES:

1. Both support lugs No. 10 gage USS (minimum) steel.

2. May be flanged for welding to tank.

3. External side surfaces to be flat and parallel.

4. Jumpproof lips omitted on lower lug.

5. Support lugs are spaced at 3/4 in. less than spacing of pole bolts for ease in mounting.

6. Tolerance for bolt-slot dimensions shall be ±1/64 in. Tolerance for all other dimensions shall be ±1/16 in.

7. Support lugs to be used with 5/8-in. pole bolts.

8. For L dimension, see USASI Table 12-27.001a and b.

FIG. 23   *Transformer support lug A.*
(USA Standards Institute.)

NOTES:

1. Support lugs attached to transformer and intended for bolting to adapter plates for direct pole mounting or to conventional crossarm hangers.

2. Slots or holes shall be suitable for 5/8-in. bolts.

3. Support-lug faces are to be in one plane.

4. For L dimension see USASI Table 12-27.001a and b.

5. The dimensions shown must be maintained to obtain a standard mounting and are not intended to show details of construction.

NOTES:

1. Support lugs may be flanged for welding to tank.

2. Jumpproof lips omitted on lower support lug.

3. Tolerance, except where indicated otherwise, shall be ±1/16 in.

4. Support lugs to be used with 3/4-in. pole bolts.

FIG. 24   *Transformer support lug B.*
(USA Standards Institute.)

FIG. 25   *Transformer support lug C.*
(USA Standards Institute.)

40. Standard Accessory Equipment for Single-phase Transformers
(United States of America Standards Institute)

High-voltage, kv	12.47GrdY/7.2 13.2 GrdY/7.62 24.94 GrdY/14.4	12.47GrdY/7.2 13.2 GrdY/7.62 24.94 GrdY/14.4		5 and below				7.2 to 15 14.4/24.94 GrdY/16.34				22.9 to 67			Above 600			
Low-voltage, volts	120/240	120/240		600 and below				5,000 and below			600 and below	600 and below			7.2 to 15	22.9 to 67	22.9 to 67	7.2 to 67
Kva	3 to 25	3 to 25	37½ to 50	3 to 25	37½ to 50	75 to 100	167	3 to 25	37½ to 50	75 to 100	167	25, 50, 100	167	250 to 500	167	100	167	250 to 500
Support lug, Type (see Figs. 23, 24, 25)	A	A	B	A	B	B	C	A	B	B	C	B	B	B	C	B	B	B
Combination oil-drain plug and sampling device							X	X	X	X	X	X	X	X	X			X
Combination oil drain, filter-press connection, and sampling valve	X															X	X	X
Liquid-level marking			X		X	X		X	X	X	X	X	X	X	X	X	X	X
Magnetic liquid-level gage														X				X
Dial-type thermometer													X	X				X
Upper filter-press connection												X			X			
Upper filter-press valve	X	X	X	X	X	X	X	X	X	X	X	X	X	X	X	X	X	X
Tap changer, internal operation																		
Tap changer, external operation																	X	
Pressure-vacuum gage provision		X	X	X	X	X	X	X	X	X	X	X	X	X	X	X	X	X
Jacking provision	X	X	X	X	X	X	X	X	X	X	X	X	X	X	X	X	X	X
Rolling provision	X	X	X	X	X	X	X	X	X	X	X	X	X	X	X	X	X	X
Handhole in cover	X	X	X	X	X	X	X	X	X	X	X	X	X	X	X	X	X	X
Lifting lugs		X	X	X	X	X	X	X	X	X	X	X	X	X	X	X	X	X
Tank grounding provision	X	X	X	X	X	X	X	X	X	X	X	X	X	X	X	X	X	X
Tank grounding connector	X	X	X	X	X	X	X	X	X	X	X	X	X	X	X	X	X	X
Low-voltage grounding connection	X	X	X	X	X	X	X	X	X	X	X	X	X	X	X	X	X	X
Low-voltage grounding provision		X	X	X	X	X	X	X	X	X	X	X	X	X	X	X	X	X
High-voltage bushing terminals	X	X	X	X	X	X	X	X	X	X	X	X	X	X	X	X	X	X
Low-voltage bushing terminals	X	X	X	X	X	X	X	X	X	X	X	X	X	X	X	X	X	X
Low-voltage bushing arrangement	X	X	X	X	X	X	X	X	X	X	X	X	X	X	X	X	X	X
Nameplate location	A	A	A	A	A	A	A	A	A	A	A	B	B	B	A	B	B	B
Nameplate extension	A	A	A	A	A	A	A	A	A	A	A			B	A	B	B	B
Nameplate, type	A	A	A	A	A	A	A	A	A	A	A	B	B	B	A	B	B	B
Stenciled rating	X	X	X	X	X	X	X	X	X	X	X				X			

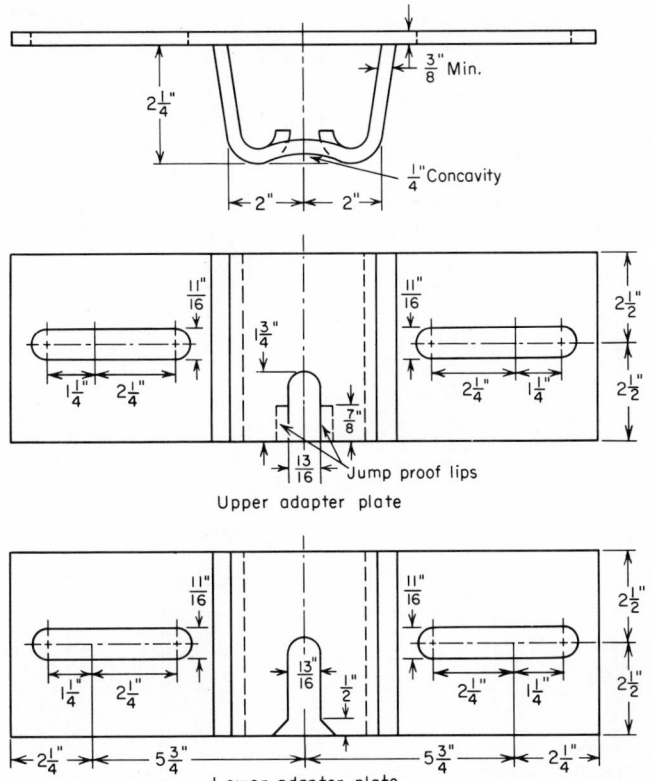

NOTES:

1. Upper and lower adapter plates are identical, except that bolt slot is ¾ in. longer and jump-proof lips are omitted on lower plate and bottom of bolt slot is chamfered.

2. Use ⅝-in. bolts to bolt adapter plates to transformer support lugs. Use ¾-in. bolts to bolt adapter plates to pole.

3. For ease of inserting pole bolts in adapter-plate slots and for tolerance in boring pole-bolt holes, the distance between the tops of bolt slots is ¾ in. less than bolt spacing, and lower edges of slots are chamfered on lower adapter plate.

4. Tolerances, except where indicated otherwise, shall be ±¹⁄₁₆ in., except that adapter-plate bolt slot tolerances shall be ±¹⁄₆₄ in.

5. Adapter plates, nuts, and bolts shall be hot-dip-galvanized.

6. For use with 75-112½ kva three phase, 15 kv and below.

FIG. 26 *Type C adapter plates for direct pole mounting of transformers.* (*USA Standards Institute.*)

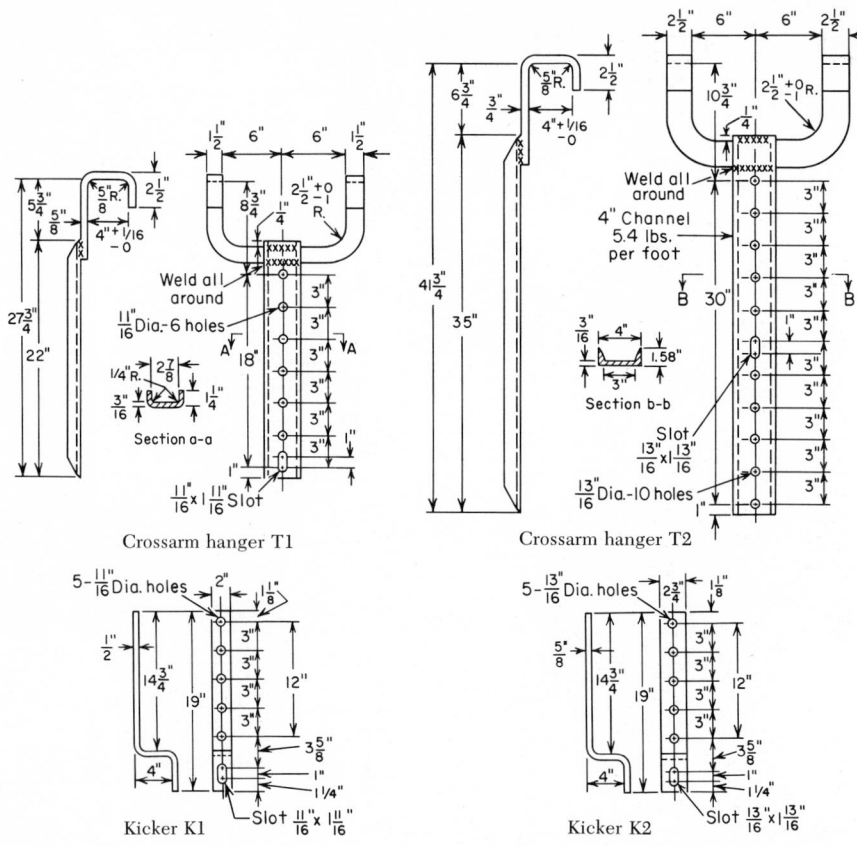

Crossarm hanger T1

Crossarm hanger T2

Kicker K1

Kicker K2

Hanger crossarm size	Kicker size	Number of ⅝-in. bolts and nuts		Number of ¾-in. bolts and nuts		kva range of use for HV 15 kv and below (4)	
		Hanger	Kicker	Hanger	Kicker	Single phase	Three phase
T1	K1	2	1	....	...	3–25	9
T2 (1)	K2	2 (2)	...	2 (3)	1	37½–50	15–45

(1) Both sizes of bolts are included.
(2) For use on 15 kva, three phase.
(3) For use on 37½–50 kva, single phase, and 30–45 kva, three phase.
(4) Including 24.94GrdY/14.4 kv, 14.4/24.94GrdY kv, 16.34 kv.
NOTE:
Tolerances, except where indicated otherwise, shall be ±1/16 in., except that bolt hole and slot tolerances shall be ±1/64 in.
All bolts and nuts to be square-headed NC threads.
⅝-in. bolts, 1¾ in. long, and threaded within 3/16 in. or less of bolt head.
¾-in. bolts, 2¼ in. long, and threaded within 3/8 in. or less of bolt head.
All T-crossarm hangers, kickers, nuts, and bolts shall be hot-dip-galvanized.

FIG. 27 *T-crossarm hangers and kickers for mounting of transformers. (USA Standards Institute.)*

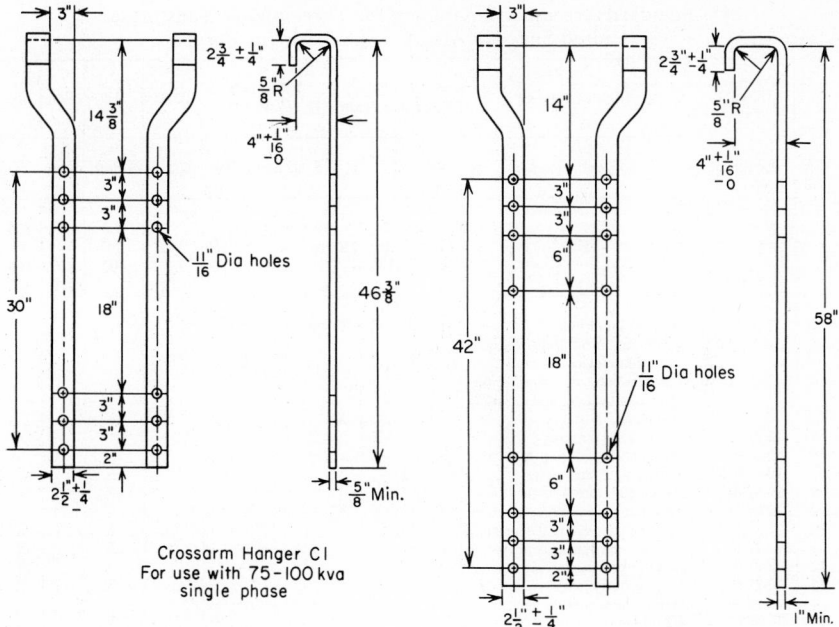

Crossarm Hanger C1
For use with 75-100 kva
single phase

Crossarm Hanger C3
For use with 75-150 kva three phase
and 167 kva single phase

NOTES:

1. Crossarm hangers shall be hot-dip-galvanized.

2. C1- and C3-crossarm hangers each to be equipped with four square-head bolts and square nuts having NC threads as follows:

C1—⅝-in. bolts, 2 in. long, threaded to within ³⁄₁₆ in. or less of bolt head.

C3—⅝-in. bolts, 2½ in. long, threaded to within ⅜ in. or less of bolt head.

3. Tolerances, except where indicated otherwise, shall be ±¹⁄₁₆ in. except that bolt hole and slot tolerance shall be ±¹⁄₆₄ in.

FIG. 28   *Crossarm hangers. (USA Standards Institute.)*

41. Standard Accessory Equipment for Three-phase Transformers
(United States of America Standards Institute)

Item No.	Paragraph reference	High-voltage, kv → Low-voltage, volts → Kva	4.8 and below 8.32Y and below / 600 and below: 9 to 15	30 to 45	75 to 112½	150	7.2 to 13.8 12.47Y to 13.2Y / 5,000 and below: 9 to 15	30 to 45	75 to 112½	150	22.9 / 600 and below: 150	All / 600 and below: 225 to 500	22.9 / Above 600: 150	All / Above 600: 300 to 500
1	12-27.950	Support lug, type	A	B	C	C	A	B	C	C				
3	12-27.661	Combination oil-drain plug and sampling device		X	X			X	X					
4	12-27.662	Combination oil drain, filter-press connection, and sampling valve				X				X	X	X	X	X
5	12-27.621	Liquid-level marking	X	X	X	X	X	X	X	X				
6	12-27.622	Magnetic liquid-level gage									X	X	X	X
7	12-27.630	Dial-type thermometer									X	X		X
8	12-27.663	Upper filter-press connection									X	X	X	X
9	12-27.611	Tap changer, internal operation	X	X	X	X	X	X	X	X				
10	12-27.612	Tap changer, external operation									X	X	X	X
11	12-27.650	Pressure-vacuum gage provision										X		X
12	12-27.671	Jacking provision										X		X
13	12-27.672	Rolling provision										X		X
14	12-27.932	Handhole in cover				X	X	X	X	X				
15	12-27.933	Handhole in cover									X	X	X	X
16	12-27.673	Lifting lugs	X	X	X	X	X	X	X	X	X	X	X	X
17	12-27.991	Tank grounding provision	X	X	X	X	X	X	X	X				
18	12-27.992	Tank grounding provision									X	X	X	X
21	12-27.995	Low-voltage grounding provision	X	X	X	X	X	X	X	X				
22	12-27.114	High-voltage bushing terminals	X	X	X	X	X	X	X	X	X	X	X	X
23	12-27.115	Low-voltage bushing terminals	X	X	X	X	X	X	X	X	X	X	X	X
24	12-27.152	Low-voltage bushing arrangement	X	X	X	X	X	X	X	X	X	X	X	X
25	12-27.751.1	Nameplate location	X	X			X	X						
26	12-27.751.2	Nameplate location			X	X			X	X				
27	12-27.751.3	Nameplate location									X	X	X	X
29	12-27.755	Nameplate extension	X	X	X	X	X	X	X	X				
30	12-27.752	Nameplate, type	A	A	A	A	A	A	A	A	B	B	B	B
31	12-27.762	Stenciled rating	X	X	X	X	X	X	X	X				

NOTE. Paragraph references (col. 2) are to USASI publication.

42. Average data for distribution transformers are given in Secs. **43** to **57**. The tables will give approximate information for transformers with ratings on the low-voltage side of 120/240, 240/480, 600, or 2,400 volts.

43. Performance of 60-cycle Single-phase Oil-filled Distribution Transformers
Standard Voltages of 600 or 2,400 Volts on High-voltage Side

Kva	No load loss	Total loss at 75°C	Efficiencies at 75°C				Regulation at 75°C		% impedance at 75°C
			Full	¾	½	¼	100 % pf	80 % pf	
1½	20	66	95.8	96.1	95.9	94.2	3.1	3.6	3.6
3	27	98	96.9	97.1	97.1	96.0	2.4	2.6	2.5
5	41	134	97.4	97.6	97.5	96.4	1.9	2.6	2.5
7½	55	184	97.6	97.8	97.7	96.8	1.8	2.3	2.3
10	59	241	97.7	97.9	97.9	97.3	1.9	2.3	2.3
15	80	333	97.8	98.0	98.1	97.5	1.7	2.2	2.2
25	120	496	98.1	98.3	98.3	97.7	1.6	2.7	2.9
37½	154	649	98.3	98.5	98.5	98.1	1.4	2.6	2.8
50	190	795	98.4	98.6	98.6	98.2	1.3	2.3	2.5
75	288	1,194	98.4	98 6	98.6	98.1	1.3	3.1	3.6
100	357	1,553	98.5	98.6	98.7	98.2	1.3	3.2	3.8
150	550	2,292	98.5	98.7	98.7	98.3	1.3	3.8	4.8
200	800	2,905	98.6	98.7	98.7	98.2	1.2	3.7	4.8
250	1,115	3,815	98.5	98.6	98.6	98.0	1.2	3.7	4.8
333	1,310	4,665	98.6	98.7	98.7	98.2	1.2	3.7	4.8
500	1,675	6,325	98.8	98.9	98.9	98.5	1.1	3.6	4.8

44. Performance of 60-cycle Single-phase Oil-filled Distribution Transformers
Standard Voltages of 7,200 Volts on High-voltage Side

Kva	No load loss	Total loss at 75°C	Efficiencies at 75°C				Regulation at 75°C		% impedance at 75°C
			Full	¾	½	¼	100 % pf	80 % pf	
1½	22	65	95.9	96.1	95.8	93.8	2.9	2.9	3.0
3	32	106	96.6	96.9	96.7	95.4	2.6	3.1	3.0
5	51	164	96.8	97.1	96.9	95.6	2.3	2.5	2.6
7½	59	229	97.0	97.3	97.3	96.4	2.3	3.0	3.0
10	71	288	97.2	97.5	97.6	96.8	2.3	3.0	3.0
15	97	364	97.6	97.9	97.9	97.1	1.9	3.1	3.3
25	144	544	97.9	98.1	98.1	97.4	1.7	3.1	3.4
37½	208	725	98.1	98.3	98.2	97.5	1.5	2.9	3.2
50	270	940	98.2	98.3	98.3	97.6	1.4	3.1	3.6
75	370	1,310	98.3	98.4	98.4	97.8	1.4	4.0	5.1
100	470	1,700	98.3	98.5	98.4	97.8	1.4	3.8	4.8
150	725	2,425	98.4	98.5	98.5	97.8	1.3	3.9	5.0
200	915	3,180	98.4	98.6	98.5	97.9	1.3	3.9	5.0
250	1,115	3,815	98.5	98.6	98.6	98.0	1.3	3.9	5.0
333	1,310	4,665	98.6	98.7	98.7	98.2	1.2	3.8	5.0
500	1,675	6,325	98.8	98.9	98.9	98.5	1.1	3.8	5.0

45. Performance of 60-cycle Single-phase Oil-filled Distribution Transformers
Standard Voltage of 13,200 Volts on High-voltage Side

Kva	No load loss	Total loss at 75°C	Efficiencies at 75°C				Regulation at 75°C		% impedance at 75°C
			Full	¾	½	¼	100% pf	80% pf	
2½	44	113	95.7	95.8	95.3	92.8	2.7	3.1	3.1
5	58	180	96.5	96.8	96.6	95.0	2.5	2.9	2.9
10	92	288	97.2	97.4	97.2	96.0	2.0	2.8	2.8
15	122	396	97.4	97.6	97.5	96.4	1.9	2.9	3.0
25	170	550	97.9	98.0	97.9	97.0	1.6	3.0	3.3
37½	230	748	98.1	98.2	98.1	97.3	1.5	3.0	3.3
50	300	958	98.1	98.3	98.2	97.4	1.4	2.9	3.2
75	415	1,375	98.2	98.3	98.3	97.5	1.4	4.0	5.0
100	530	1,755	98.3	98.4	98.3	97.6	1.4	4.0	5.1
150	750	2,520	98.3	98.5	98.4	97.8	1.3	3.9	5.0
200	950	3,240	98.4	98.5	98.5	97.9	1.3	3.9	5.0
250	1,115	3,815	98.5	98.6	98.6	98.0	1.3	3.9	5.0
333	1,310	4,665	98.6	98.7	98.7	98.2	1.2	3.8	5.0
500	1,675	6,325	98.8	98.9	98.9	98.5	1.1	3.8	5.0

46. Performance of 60-cycle Single-phase Oil-filled Distribution Transformers
Standard Voltage of 22,000 Volts on High-voltage Side

Kva	No load loss	Total loss at 75°C	Efficiencies at 75°C				Regulation at 75°C		% impedance at 75°C
			Full	¾	½	¼	100% pf	80% pf	
10	135	420	96.0	96.2	96.0	94.2	3.0	4.9	5.2
15	175	530	96.6	96.8	96.6	95.0	2.5	4.7	5.2
25	230	740	97.1	97.3	97.2	96.0	2.2	4.6	5.2
37½	300	985	97.4	97.6	97.5	96.4	2.0	4.5	5.2
50	375	1,225	97.6	97.8	97.7	96.7	1.9	4.4	5.2
75	500	1,630	97.9	98.0	98.0	97.0	1.7	4.2	5.2
100	610	1,995	98.1	98.2	98.1	97.3	1.7	4.2	5.2
150	825	2,715	98.2	98.3	98.3	97.5	1.4	4.1	5.2
200	1,015	3,430	98.3	98.4	98.4	97.7	1.4	4.1	5.2
250	1,200	3,930	98.5	98.6	98.5	97.8	1.3	4.0	5.2
333	1,450	4,810	98.6	98.7	98.6	98.0	1.2	4.0	5.2
500	1,950	6,570	98.8	98.8	98.8	98.2	1.1	3.9	5.2

47. Performance of 60-cycle Single-phase Oil-filled Distribution Transformers
Standard Voltage of 44,000 Volts on High-voltage Side

Kva	No load loss	Total loss at 75°C	Efficiencies at 75°C				Regulation at 75°C		% impedance at 75°C
			Full	¾	½	¼	100 % pf	80 % pf	
25	310	858	96.7	96.8	96.5	94.8	2.4	5.0	5.7
37½	400	1,122	97.1	97.2	97.0	95.5	2.1	4.8	5.7
50	490	1,370	97.3	97.4	97.2	95.8	2.0	4.8	5.7
75	630	1,810	97.6	97.7	97.6	96.4	1.8	4.6	5.7
100	770	2,225	97.8	97.9	97.8	96.7	1.7	4.6	5.7
150	1,010	3,003	98.0	98.1	98.0	97.1	1.5	4.5	5.7
200	1,230	3,743	98.2	98.3	98.2	97.3	1.5	4.4	5.7
250	1,420	4,405	98.3	98.4	98.3	97.5	1.4	4.4	5.7
333	1,695	5,395	98.4	98.5	98.5	97.7	1.3	4.4	5.7
500	2,200	7,030	98.6	98.7	98.7	98.0	1.2	4.3	5.7

48. Performance of 60-cycle Single-phase Oil-filled Distribution Transformers
Standard Voltage of 66,000 Volts on High-voltage Side

Kva	No load loss	Total loss at 75°C	Efficiencies at 75°C				Regulation at 75°C		% impedance at 75°C
			Full	¾	½	¼	100 % pf	80 % pf	
50	640	1,515	97.1	97.1	96.7	94.7	2.0	5.3	6.5
75	820	1,950	97.5	97.5	97.1	95.5	1.8	5.1	6.5
100	970	2,385	97.7	97.7	97.4	95.9	1.7	5.1	6.5
150	1,220	3,160	97.9	98.0	97.8	96.5	1.5	5.0	6.5
200	1,440	3,900	98.1	98.1	98.0	96.9	1.5	4.9	6.5
250	1,630	4,615	98.2	98.3	98.1	97.2	1.4	4.9	6.5
333	1,875	5,635	98.3	98.4	98.3	97.5	1.4	4.9	6.5
500	2,400	7,380	98.5	98.6	98.6	97.9	1.3	4.8	6.5

49. Performance of 60-cycle Three-phase Oil-filled Distribution Transformers
Standard Voltage of 2,400 Volts on High-voltage Side

Kva	No load loss	Total loss at 75°C	Efficiencies at 75°C				Regulation at 75°C		% impedance at 75°C
			Full	¾	½	¼	100 % pf	80 % pf	
10	90	345	96.7	97.0	97.0	96.0	2.6	3.4	3.4
15	113	443	97.1	97.4	97.5	96.5	2.3	3.3	3.4
25	162	650	97.5	97.7	97.8	97.0	2.0	3.3	3.4
37½	214	890	97.7	97.9	98.0	97.3	1.9	3.9	4.3
50	275	1,117	97.8	98.0	98.1	97.4	1.9	4.2	4.9
75	370	1,525	98.0	98.2	98.2	97.7	1.7	3.8	4.4
100	455	1,860	98.2	98.4	98.4	97.9	1.5	3.8	4.6
150	590	2,445	98.4	98.6	98.6	98.1	1.4	3.4	4.1
200	785	3,093	98.5	98.6	98.6	98.2	1.3	3.4	4.2
300	1,100	4,350	98.6	98.7	98.7	98.3	1.2	3.7	4.8
450	1,550	6,125	98.4	98.8	98.8	98.6	1.2	3.7	4.8

50. Performance of 60-cycle Three-phase Oil-filled Distribution Transformers
Standard Voltage of 4,800 Volts on High-voltage Side

Kva	No load loss	Total loss at 75°C	Efficiencies at 75°C				Regulation at 75°C		% impedance at 75°C
			Full	¾	½	¼	100% pf	80% pf	
10	94	354	96.6	96.9	96.9	95.8	2.7	3.7	3.7
15	120	465	97.0	97.3	97.3	96.3	2.4	3.7	3.8
25	170	685	97.3	97.6	97.7	96.9	2.2	3.4	3.5
37½	225	935	97.6	97.8	97.9	97.2	2.0	3.7	4.0
50	275	1,165	97.7	98.0	98.0	97.4	1.9	3.6	4.0
75	370	1,585	97.9	98.2	98.2	97.7	1.8	3.5	4.0
100	455	1,955	98.1	98.3	98.3	97.8	1.6	3.5	4.0
150	615	2,615	98.3	98.5	98.5	98.0	1.4	3.4	4.0
200	785	3,275	98.4	98.6	98.6	98.1	1.4	3.4	4.0
300	1,100	4,350	98.6	98.7	98.7	98.3	1.2	3.7	4.8
450	1,550	6,125	98.7	98.8	98.8	98.4	1.2	3.7	4.8

51. Performance of 60-cycle Three-phase Oil-filled Distribution Transformers
Standard Voltage of 7,200 Volts on High-voltage Side

Kva	No load loss	Total loss at 75°C	Efficiencies at 75°C				Regulation at 75°C		% impedance at 75°C
			Full	¾	½	¼	100% pf	80% pf	
10	100	385	96.3	96.7	96.7	95.5	2.9	2.9	3.0
15	132	512	96.7	97.0	97.0	96.0	2.6	3.3	3.3
25	190	735	97.2	97.4	97.5	96.5	2.3	3.4	3.5
37½	260	1,000	97.4	97.7	97.7	96.9	2.1	3.4	3.5
50	315	1,205	97.7	97.9	97.9	97.1	1.9	3.1	3.2
75	440	1,650	97.8	98.0	98.0	97.3	1.7	3.1	3.4
100	560	2,050	98.0	98.2	98.1	97.4	1.6	3 4	3.9
150	730	2,760	98.2	98.4	98.4	97.8	1.5	3.5	4.2
200	850	3,370	98.4	98.5	98.5	98.0	1.4	3.5	4.2
300	1,150	4,470	98.5	98.7	98.7	98.2	1.3	3 9	5.0
450	1,600	6,300	98.6	98.8	98.8	98.3	1.2	3.9	5.0

52. Performance of 60-cycle Three-phase Oil-filled Distribution Transformers
Standard Voltage of 12,000 Volts on High-voltage Side

Kva	No load loss	Total loss at 75°C	Efficiencies at 75°C				Regulation at 75°C		% impedance at 75°C
			Full	¾	½	¼	100 % pf	80 % pf	
10	110	410	95.1	96.4	96.4	95.1	3.1	4.7	4.8
15	145	545	96.5	96.8	96.8	95.7	2.8	4.7	5.0
25	207	775	97.0	97.3	97.3	96.2	2.4	3.7	4.0
37½	275	1,035	97.3	97.6	97.6	96.7	2.2	3.7	4.0
50	345	1,275	97.5	97.7	97.7	96.9	2.0	3.9	4.3
75	475	1,745	97.7	97.9	97.9	97.1	1.9	3.9	4.6
100	600	2,160	97.9	98.1	98.1	97.3	1.8	4.6	5.7
150	765	2,895	98.1	98.3	98.3	97.6	1.5	3.7	4.4
200	890	3,540	98.3	98.4	98.4	97.9	1.4	3.6	4.4
300	1,225	4,795	98.4	98.6	98.6	98.1	1.4	3.9	5.0
450	1,650	6,690	98.5	98.7	98.7	98.3	1.3	3.9	5.0

53. Performance of 60-cycle Three-phase Oil-filled Distribution Transformers
Standard Voltage of 13,200 Volts on High-voltage Side

Kva	No load loss	Total loss at 75°C	Efficiencies at 75°C				Regulation at 75°C		% impedance at 75°C
			Full	¾	½	¼	100 % pf	80 % pf	
15	165	565	96.4	96.7	96.6	95.2	2.8	4.6	4.8
25	230	800	96.9	97.2	97.1	96.0	2.4	3.6	3.6
37½	305	1,065	97.3	97.5	97.4	96.4	2.2	4.1	4.5
50	375	1,305	97.5	97.7	97.6	96.6	2.0	4.0	4.5
75	515	1,785	97.7	97.9	97.8	96.9	1.8	3.2	3.5
100	630	2,190	97.9	98.0	98.0	97.2	1.7	4.5	5.5
150	790	2,920	98.1	98.3	98.2	97.6	1.6	3.8	4.5
200	930	3,580	98.3	98.4	98.4	97.8	1.5	3.7	4.5
300	1,225	4,795	98.4	98.6	98.6	98.1	1.4	3.9	5.0
450	1,650	6,690	98.5	98.7	98.7	98.3	1.3	3.9	5.0

54. Performance of 60-cycle Three-phase Oil-filled Distribution Transformers
Standard Voltage of 22,000 Volts on High-voltage Side

Kva	No load loss	Total loss at 75°C	Efficiencies at 75°C				Regulation at 75°C		% impedance at 75°C
			Full	¾	½	¼	100 % pf	80 % pf	
37½	330	1,250	96.8	97.1	97.1	96.1	2.6	4.8	5.2
50	385	1,510	97.1	97.4	97.4	96.5	2.4	4.7	5.2
75	525	1,945	97.4	97.7	97.7	96.8	2.1	4.5	5.2
100	640	2,365	97.7	97.9	97.9	97.1	1.9	4.4	5.2
150	800	3,085	98.0	98.2	98.2	97.6	1.7	4.3	5.2
200	985	3,815	98.1	98.3	98.3	97.7	1.6	4.2	5.2
300	1,355	5,320	98.3	98.4	98.5	97.9	1.5	4.2	5.2
450	1,850	7,100	98.4	98.6	98.6	98.1	1.3	4.1	5.2

55. Performance of 60-cycle Three-phase Oil-filled Distribution Transformers
Standard Voltage of 44,000 Volts on High-voltage Side

Kva	No load loss	Total loss at 75°C	Efficiencies at 75°C				Regulation at 75°C		% impedance at 75°C
			Full	¾	½	¼	100 % pf	80 % pf	
75	675	2,230	97.1	97.3	97.2	96.0	2.3	4.9	5.7
100	840	2,635	97.4	97.6	97.5	96.3	2.0	4.7	5.7
150	1,100	3,485	97.7	97.9	97.8	96.8	1.8	4.6	5.7
200	1,350	4,290	97.9	98.0	98.0	97.0	1.7	4.6	5.7
300	1,765	5,830	98.1	98.2	98.2	97.4	1.6	4.5	5.7
450	2,340	7,865	98.3	98.4	98.4	97.7	1.4	4.4	5.7

56. Performance of 60-cycle Three-phase Oil-filled Distribution Transformers
Standard Voltage of 66,000 Volts on High-voltage Side

Kva	No load loss	Total loss at 75°C	Efficiencies at 75°C				Regulation at 75°C		% impedance a. 75°C
			Full	¾	½	¼	100 % pf	80 % pf	
150	1,450	3,970	97.4	97.5	97.3	95.9	1.9	5.2	6.5
200	1,700	4,800	97.7	97.8	97.6	96.4	1.8	5.2	6.5
300	2,200	6,340	97.9	98.0	97.9	96.8	1.6	5.0	6.5
450	2,850	8,420	98.2	98.3	98.1	97.2	1.5	4.9	6.5

57. Performance of 60-cycle Single-phase Air-cooled Transformers
Standard Voltage of 2,400 Volts on High-voltage Side

Kva	No load loss	Total loss at 75°C	Efficiencies at 75°C				Regulation at 75°C		% impedance at 75°C
			Full	¾	½	¼	100 % pf	80 % pf	
150	755	2,265	98.51	98.60	98.51	97.78	1.2	3.8	5.0
200	925	2,890	98.58	98.66	98.60	97.95	1.1	3.8	5.0
250	1,080	3,495	98.62	98.72	98.67	98.07	1.1	3.8	5.0
333	1,325	4,460	98.68	98.78	98.75	98.20	1.1	3.6	5.0
500	1,760	6,315	98.75	98.86	98.85	98.39	1.1	3.7	5.0

58. Small power transformers (Figs. 5 and 29) are constant-potential, self-air-cooled transformers for industrial purposes. The windings are completely enclosed in metal casings. They are available in single- and three-phase construction of conventional or autotransformer types with cases designed for open or conduit wiring. Single-phase units are available in sizes up to 50 kva, while three-phase units are made as large as 150 kva. Primary voltage ratings range from 125 to 2,400. Standard secondary voltages are 115/230 or 230/460.

FIG. 29 *Small power transformers, self-air-cooled. (General Electric Co.)*

FIG. 30 *Replacement-type domestic oil-burner ignition transformers. (General Electric Co.)*

59. Small power transformers are available for taking power from motor disconnecting switches for localized lighting at the machine. Types are available for operating 115-, 64-, 32-, or 6-volt lamps from 115-, 230-, 460-, or 575-volt power circuits. Standard sizes are 75, 150, 225, and 300 watts. Another type of small power transformer is the one designed for domestic oil-burner ignition (see Fig. 30).

60. Sign-lighting transformers are single-phase, constant-potential, self-air-cooled transformers for stepping down from 115 or 230 volts to the proper voltage for low-voltage incandescent lamps in signs. They are made in sizes up to 5 kva with the windings completely enclosed in metal casings.

61. Control and signal transformers are constant-potential, self-air-cooled transformers for the purpose of supplying the proper voltage for control circuits of electrically operated switches or other equipment and for signal circuits. They may be of the open type with no protective casing over the windings or of the enclosed type with a metal casing over the windings. Some of the available mounting types are shown in Figs. 31 and 32.

62. Transformers for many gaseous-discharge lamps must be of the varying-voltage type. These transformers are designed so that the secondary voltage drops rapidly with load. This voltage characteristic is accomplished by means of a three-winding transformer with magnetic leakage paths between the primary and each secondary, as shown in Fig. 33. As the load increases, the leakage flux of the primary produces a greater voltage drop in the primary winding, thereby reducing the secondary voltage. Some of these transformers are equipped with a capacitor mounted inside the same enclosing case for power-factor improvement. The transformers are of the self-air-cooled type. Various mounting types for luminous-tube work are shown in Fig. 34.

I. *Open type with flexible terminal leads.*

II. *Open type with lug terminals.*

III. *Semienclosed type.*

IV. *Enclosed type with terminal cover removed.*

FIG. 31 *Typical control transformers. (Westinghouse Electric Corp.)*

FIG. 32 *Control transformer. (General Electric Co.)*

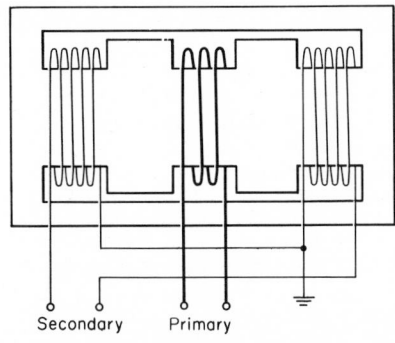

Secondary   Primary

FIG. 33 *Cross section of a typical neon-sign transformer, showing windings and leakage paths in magnetic circuit.*

63. Bell-ringing transformers are especially designed small-capacity constant-potential transformers for applications such as the operation of doorbells, buzzers, door openers, and annunciators. They are self-air-cooled units enclosed in metal cases. They can be obtained for primary voltages of 120 or 240 with a single secondary voltage of 10 or with three secondary voltages of 6, 12, and 18.

FIG. 34 *Luminous-tube transformers rated 3,000 to 15,000 volts, 30 to 120 ma, showing low- and high-voltage terminals. (General Electric Co.)*

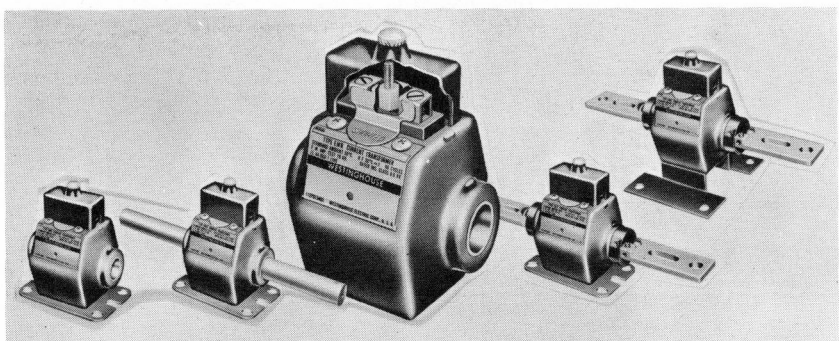

FIG. 35 *Typical current instrument transformers. (Westinghouse Electric Corp.)*

64. Instrument transformers are employed for the purpose of stepping down the voltage or current of a circuit for the operation of instruments, such as ammeters, voltmeters, wattmeters, etc., and relays for various protective purposes. It would be practically impossible to build delicate devices such as instruments and relays so that they would have satisfactory insulation for high voltages. Frequently such devices while energized must be accessible to operators, so that it is necessary to have the devices insulated from the high-voltage circuit. Instrument transformers are of two types: potential and current. They are made in various types depending upon the voltage of the circuits, requirements of installations, and accuracy required. Instrument transformers will always introduce a certain amount of error into the readings obtained on instruments supplied by them. The transformers are not rated on a thermal basis of the load which they can safely carry, but upon an accuracy basis. The volt-ampere rating is the load which the transformer will carry without exceeding the specified accuracy limit. If accuracy can be sacrificed, the transformers can be used for loads considerably above their rated values. Instrument transformers are made in indoor, outdoor, and portable types for test purposes. Potential transformers have a normal secondary voltage of 120 volts. Current transformers have a normal secondary current of 5 amp. Typical instrument transformers are shown in Figs. 35 and 36.

65. The current transformer ("Standard Handbook"), considered electrically and omitting any reference to the change in its design to accomplish its specific duty, differs from the shunt or potential transformer merely in the method of use. The latter transformer is ordinarily supplied with a constant impressed voltage, the load being changed by varying the impedance (load) of the total secondary circuit, while the total impedance of the secondary circuit of the former transformer is normally held constant, and the change in load is due to a simultaneous change in the primary current and emf. In the potential transformer the actual ratio of the primary to the secondary current is of minor importance, while every effort is made to design the apparatus so that the ratio of the secondary power to the primary power is as nearly unity as possible. In the design of a series transformer no thought whatsoever is

 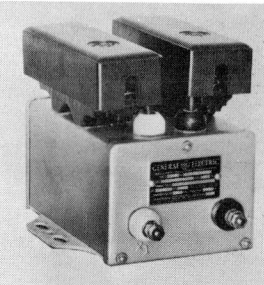 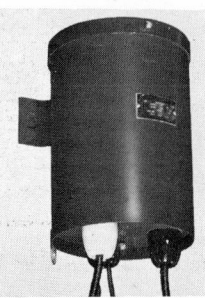

I. *Relatively low volt-age, unfused; dry, in-door type.*

II. *Relatively low voltage, fused; dry, indoor type.*

III. *Relatively low voltage, unfused; dry, outdoor type.*

IV. *Medium and high voltage, fused; oil-filled, indoor type.*

V. *Medium and high voltage, fused; oil-filled, both indoor and outdoor type.*

FIG. 36 *Typical potential transformers.* (*General Electric Co.*)

given to the ratio of the primary and secondary watts, but attention is concentrated on the endeavor to obtain a definite ratio of secondary to primary amperes.

The electric and magnetic circuits of a current transformer can conveniently be

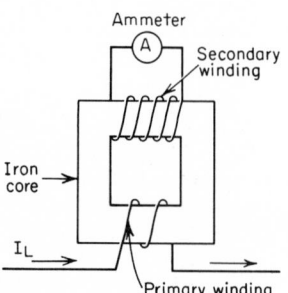

FIG. 37 *Elementary series transformer.*

represented by the diagram shown in Fig. 37, where it is used for reducing the line current to a value suitable for measurement by a low-reading ammeter, which can be thoroughly insulated from the main circuit. Neglecting the small transformer loss, the current through the ammeter A is, since the ratio of turns $M = 2:5$, equal to two-fifths the line current I_L.

66. Application of the Current Instrument Transformer. When an alternating current is so large that to connect measuring or operating instruments directly in the circuit would be impracticable, or when the voltage is so high that to do so would be unsafe, the current transformer provides a means of reproducing the effect of the primary current on a scale suited to the instrument and of insulating the instrument from the main circuit. It is a special development of the transformer principle in which a constant ratio of primary to secondary current is the important consideration instead of the usual constant ratio of primary to secondary voltage.

Current transformers are used with a-c ammeters, wattmeters, power-factor meters, watthour meters, compensators, protective and regulating relays, and the trip coils of circuit breakers. It is a standard practice in this country to design current transformers (regardless of their capacity or ratios of transformation) to supply a rated secondary current of 5 amp.

Example. A 600-amp current transformer has a ratio of 120:1; i.e., when a current of 600 amp flows in the primary circuit, 600 ÷ 120 = 5 amp will flow in the secondary circuit.

Measuring instruments for use with these transformers are so designed and are provided with scales such that they give a normal scale deflection when 5 amp flows through them.

67. It is unsafe to open the secondary circuit of a current transformer when there is any current in the primary. When the secondary circuit is closed, the current in this circuit creates an mmf which is in opposition to the mmf of the primary current, and the core flux is thereby limited to the value necessary to generate in the secondary coil an emf sufficient to produce therein a current only slightly less than the primary current in magnetizing effect. When the secondary is open, there is no opposing mmf for limiting the core flux, which may reach a high value. Thus even a small value of primary current produces an excessive value of core flux and a correspondingly large secondary emf. The secondary voltage under these conditions reaches a value which may both damage the insulation and prove dangerous to life. Absolutely no harm can come from short-circuiting the secondary terminals of the current transformer, and this method is used when it is necessary to insert or disconnect instruments in the secondary circuit.

68. The Constant-current Transformer ("Standard Handbook"). The operation of low-voltage lamps in parallel on a constant-potential system necessitates a prohibitive expenditure for conducting material when the area to be lighted is extensive and the lamps are widely separated. For such service it is the common practice to operate the lamps, which are connected in series, with a constant current. The constant-current transformer is a special form of transformer which converts alternating current at a constant potential to a constant (alternating) current with a voltage varying with the load. It consists of a primary coil upon which the constant voltage is impressed, a secondary coil (or coils) movable with respect to the primary, and a core of low magnetic reluctance. It depends for its regulation upon the magnetic leakage between the primary and secondary coils.

Consider first the primary coil; with the constant emf impressed upon this coil the total magnetism within the coil will be practically constant under all conditions. The emf generated in the secondary will depend upon the strength of the field which it surrounds. In all types of stationary transformers the secondary current is opposite in general time direction to the primary, so that there is not only a repulsive thrust between the two coils but also a considerable tendency for the magnetic lines from the primary to be forced out into space without penetrating the secondary. In the ordinary constant-potential transformer the repelling action between the two currents is prevented from producing motion of the coils by the rigid mechanical construction, while the proximity of the primary and secondary coils limits the magnetic leakage.

In the constant-current transformer, however, the repelling action is utilized to adjust the relative positions of the primary and secondary coils; when the coils are widely separated, the paths for the leakage lines are increased and the lines which the secondary surrounds are fewer than when the coils are quite close together. The counterweights mechanically attached to the movable coil (or coils) are so arranged that when the desired current exists in the secondary coil (independent of its position along the core), the weights are just balanced. An increase in the current increases the repulsion and causes the coils to separate. With any current less than normal, the repelling force diminishes and the primary and secondary coils approach each other, thereby restoring the current to normal. The primary can be wound for any reasonable potential (say as high as 10,000 volts), while the secondary can be wound for the voltage required for operating the number of lamps in the circuit—from 15 to 200 or more lamps.

69. Mechanical Construction of the Constant-current Transformer. The magnetic circuit of a constant-current transformer is usually of the "shell" type, the three limbs being placed vertically. In small sizes (Fig. 38) one of the coils is arranged in a fixed position while the other is movable. In some of the larger sizes there are two fixed primary coils and two movable secondary coils, while in others both the primary and secondary coils are movable. In any event the gravitational action on the movable coil or the gravitational action of one movable coil against another to which it is mechanically interconnected is counterbalanced accurately with an excess or deficiency just equal to the repulsive thrust of the primary and secondary coils at the desired load current. By the use of cam mechanisms for the counterweights or of eccentrically placed extra weights, the excess force of the counterweights can be arranged to be equal to the variable repulsive thrust corresponding to a constant value of current in the coils at all positions of the movable coils. In fact, the transformer can be adjusted to regulate for a current of constant value at all loads or for one which either increases or decreases with increase of loads, while both the real value of the load current and its rate of change with the variation in load can be adjusted at will. In order to prevent any "hunting" action of the movable coils each transformer is sometimes equipped with a dashpot (see Fig. 38).

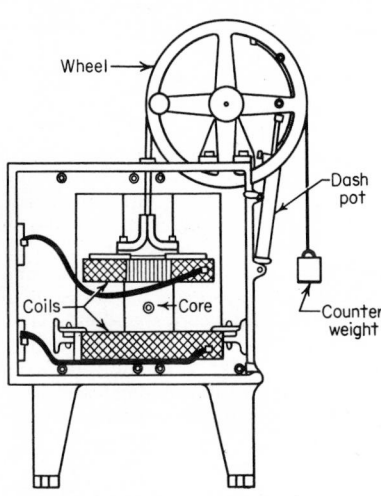

Wheel

Dash pot

Coils

Core

Counter weight

FIG. 38 *Constant-current transformer.*

70. Commercial constant-current transformers are built for natural air cooling or for immersion in oil. Oil has proved an excellent medium for insulation, cooling, and lubrication. This type of transformer is extensively used for series street-lighting service with either gaseous-discharge or incandescent lamps. The efficiency of a constant-current transformer is high, being about 96 per cent at full load for a 100-lamp transformer. The power factor, which depends upon the magnetic leakage, is low at all loads; it reaches from 75 to 80 per cent at full load and decreases therefrom in almost direct proportion to the decrease in load.

Constant-current transformers are made in outdoor-pole-mounting, subway-mounting, and indoor-station types. A primary voltage of 2,400 is standard. The secondary current may be 6.6 or 20 amp. The standard ratings are 5, 10, 15, 20, 25, 30, 35, 40, 50, 60, and 70 kva.

71. Series transformers are for use with series incandescent street lamps for operation of lamps at a different value of current from that of the main series circuit or for isolation of a lamp of the same current value as the main circuit from the main circuit, which operates at a high voltage. The principle of operation is the same as for instrument current transformers. The primary is connected in series with the main series circuit. The lamp or lamps are connected to the secondary. These transformers are made in single-lamp types for operating one 6.6-, 15-, or 20-amp series lamp from a 6.6-amp main circuit; in two-lamp series type for operating two 6.6-, 15-, or 20-amp series lamps connected in series to the secondary; in two-lamp multiple type for operating two 6.6-, 15-, or 20-amp series lamps connected to two separate secondaries; in group series type for operating a group of 6.6-amp series lamps connected in series to the secondary; and in single-lamp type for operating a single 115-volt lamp from a series 6.6-amp main circuit. The group series type is made in ratings of 0.25, 0.5, 1.0, 2, 3, 4, 5, 7.5, and 9.0 kva. The single-lamp type for 115-volt lamp is made in sizes to accommodate one lamp of any watt size from 40 to 1,000 watts. They are made in types for vault or subway mounting, for mounting in bases of ornamental lighting poles, and for pole mounting (Figs. 39 and 40).

72. The induction regulator (Fig. 41) is a special type of transformer, built like an induction motor with a coil-wound secondary, which is used for varying the voltage delivered to a synchronous converter or a-c feeder system. In comparison with a variable-ratio transformer it possesses the advantage of being operated without opening the circuit and without short-circuiting any transformer coil. The primary of the induction regulator is subjected to the constant voltage of the supply system, the delivered voltage obtained from the secondary winding being varied by rotating the primary structure through a certain number of degrees with reference to the secondary structure. The primary structure is normally stationary, although it is movable either automatically or by hand for the purpose of varying the secondary voltage.

73. The step-by-step potential regulator is merely a stationary transformer provided with a large number of secondary taps and equipped with a switching mechanism for joining any desired pair of these taps to the delivery circuit, according to the emf required. A diagram of the circuits of a regulator of this type is shown in Fig. 42. In

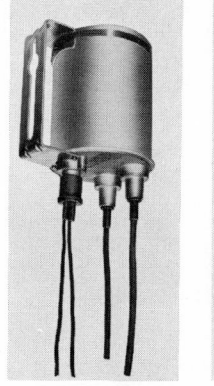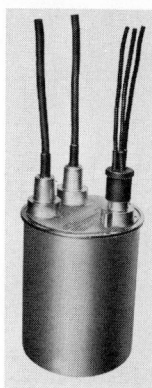

I. *Aerial type.*   II. *Pole-base type.*

FIG. 39 *Series transformers for supplying a single lamp from series street-lighting circuits. (General Electric Co.)*

comparison with the induction type of regulator the step-by-step type is less noisy in operation, requires less magnetizing current, and is more rapid in action. However, it provides only a limited number of voltage steps and may give trouble from arcing at the switch contacts.

CONNECTIONS – POLARITY

74. Polarity of Transformers (Line Material Co.). The polarity of a transformer is simply an indication of direction of flow of current from a terminal at any one instant. The idea is quite similar to the polarity marking on a battery.

I. *Small.*   II. *Medium.*   III. *Large.*

FIG. 40 *Series transformers for operation of a group of lamps from series street-lighting circuits. (General Electric Co.)*

As you face the high-voltage side of a transformer, the high-voltage terminal on your right is always marked H_1 and the other high-voltage terminal is marked H_2. This is an established standard.

By definition, the polarity is additive if when you connect the adjacent high-voltage and low-voltage terminals (Fig. 43a) and excite the transformer, a voltmeter between the other two adjacent terminals reads the sum of the high-voltage and low-voltage winding voltages. For additive polarity, the low-voltage terminal on your right when facing the low-voltage side should then be marked X_1 and the other low-voltage terminal X_2.

For subtractive polarity, the voltmeter in Fig. 43b reads the difference between the two winding voltages. In other words, the voltages subtract. In the case of subtractive polarity, the low-voltage terminal on your left when facing the low-voltage side is marked X_1.

In making transformer connections, particularly bank connections, polarity of individual transformers must be checked. In making such connections it is necessary

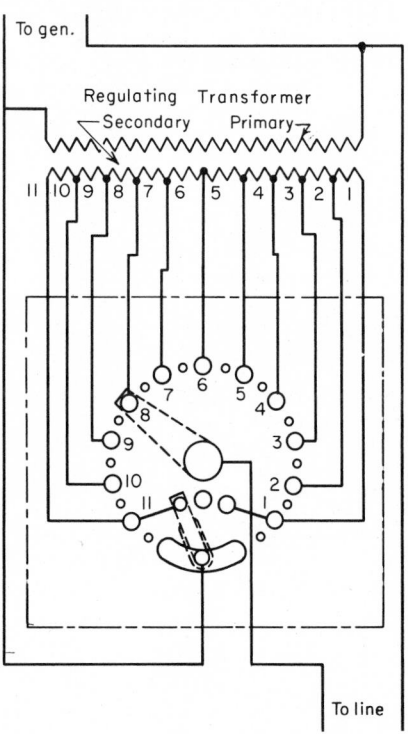

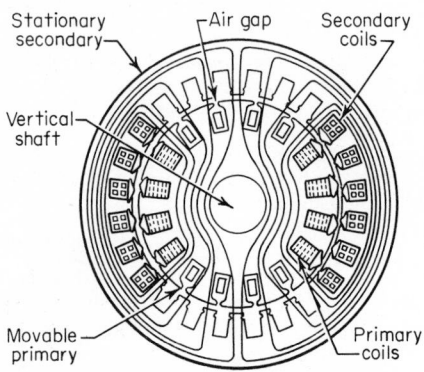

FIG. 41   *Section through a single-phase induction-type potential regulator.*

FIG. 42   *Single-phase step-by-step-type potential regulator.*

to remember that all H_1 terminals are of the same polarity and all X_1 terminals are of the same polarity. Thus, if you were connecting two single-phase transformers in parallel, you should connect the two H_1 terminals together, then the two H_2 terminals together, the two X_1 terminals together, and the two X_2 terminals together. By follow-

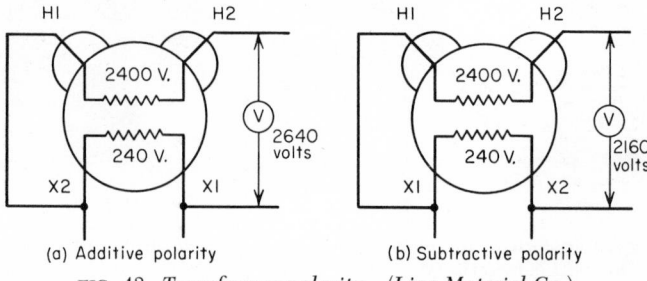

FIG. 43   *Transformer polarity.   (Line Material Co.)*

ing this procedure, you can satisfactorily parallel transformers regardless of whether they are both of the same polarity or one is additive and one is subtractive polarity.

75. Tests for Polarity of Single-phase Transformers. Where a standard transformer of known correct polarity and of the same ratio and voltage as the transformer to be tested is available, the following simple method can be used: Connect together (Fig. 44, I) the high-tension and the low-tension leads as if for parallel operation, inserting a fuse in one of the secondary leads. If both transformers are of the same polarity, no

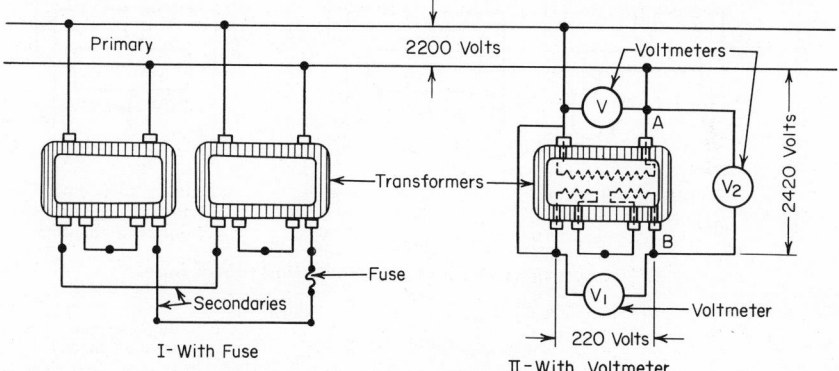

FIG. 44 *Testing transformers for polarity.*

current will flow in the low-tension windings and the fuse will not blow. If the transformers are of opposite polarities, the low-tension windings will short-circuit each other and the fuse will blow. The fuse should be sufficiently small so that there can be no possibility of injuring the transformers.

A method of testing for polarity of single-phase transformers with a voltmeter is shown in Fig. 44, II. Connect the transformer as shown. Make, successively, voltmeter readings V, V_1, and V_2. If the transformer has what is called additive polarity, $V + V_1$ will equal V_2. If the transformer has what is called subtractive polarity, V_2 will equal $V - V_1$. For example, in Fig. 44, II, the transformer has additive polarity, and the primary line voltage V (2,200 volts) plus the secondary transformer voltage V_1 (220 volts) equals the voltage between A and B, or 2,420 volts. With subtractive polarity the voltmeter V_2 would read (2,200 − 220) 1,980 volts.

SINGLE-PHASE CONNECTIONS

76. Connections for standard distribution transformers are shown in Figs. 45 and 46. Distribution transformers of medium and small capacity are almost invariably arranged with two secondary coils, which can be connected in series or parallel with each other so that the same transformer can be used to supply either of two different secondary voltages or a three-wire system. In transformers of the 120/240-volt type, their secondary windings can be so connected as to deliver 120 or 240 volts or for a 120/240-volt three-wire circuit. The connections of the secondary coils are made, either by splicing the secondary leads or with connectors, outside the transformer case. Some transformers are constructed with two primary coils as shown in Fig. 45. If the necessary primary-coil connections are made, they can be used on primary circuits of either of two voltages. Standard practice with respect to number of coils and voltage ratings is given in Secs. **38** and **39**.

77. Transformer connections for three-wire secondary service are shown in Figs. 45, 46, and 47. In the arrangement Figs. 45 and 46, one transformer only is used. Its secondary windings are connected in series, and a tap is made to the point of connection between the two windings, providing 240 volts between the two outside wires and 120 volts on each of the side circuits. The transformer should have a capacity

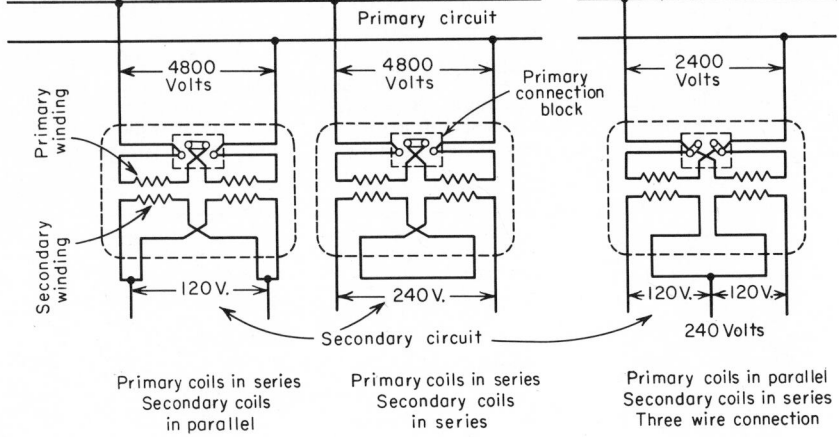

FIG. 45 *Connections of standard distributing transformers.*

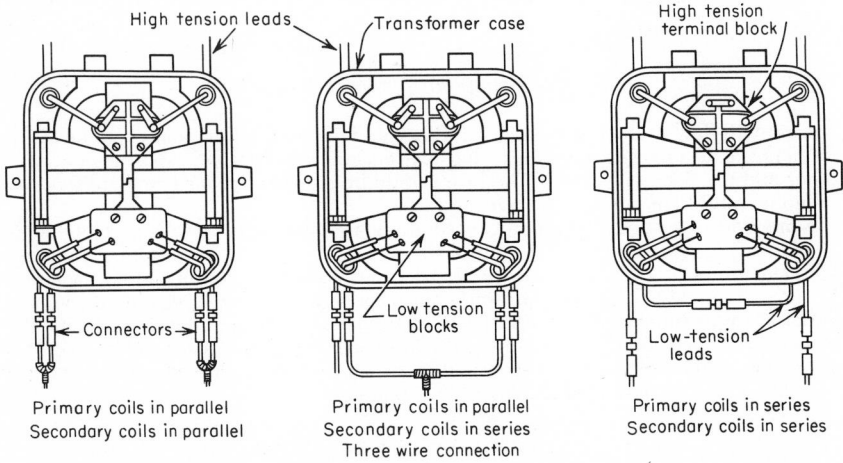

FIG. 46 *Method of interconnecting transformer secondaries with connectors.*

equal to the load to be supplied, and the three-wire circuits should be carefully balanced. If the three-wire circuits are decidedly unbalanced, the transformer should have a capacity equal to twice the load on the most heavily loaded of the two side circuits.

In Fig. 47, two transformers are shown connected to serve a three-wire circuit. The three-wire load should be balanced as nearly as possible, and where it is very nearly balanced, each transformer should have a capacity equal to one-half of the total load. If the load is badly unbalanced, each transformer should have a capacity equal to the load on its side of the circuit. See discussion of Parallel Operation.

TWO-PHASE CONNECTIONS

78. Transformers connected to four-wire two-phase circuits are shown in Fig. 48. As a rule, two-phase primary lines are four-wire as shown, and to such a four-wire line the transformers are connected to each of the side circuits, as if each side circuit were

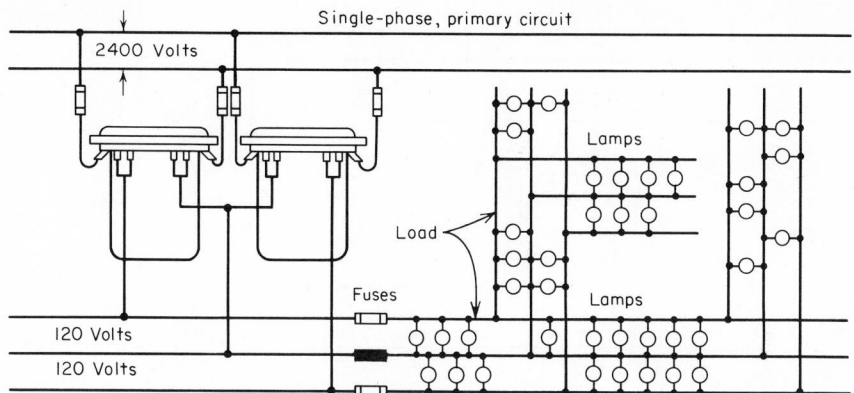

FIG. 47 *Two transformers serving a three-wire circuit.*

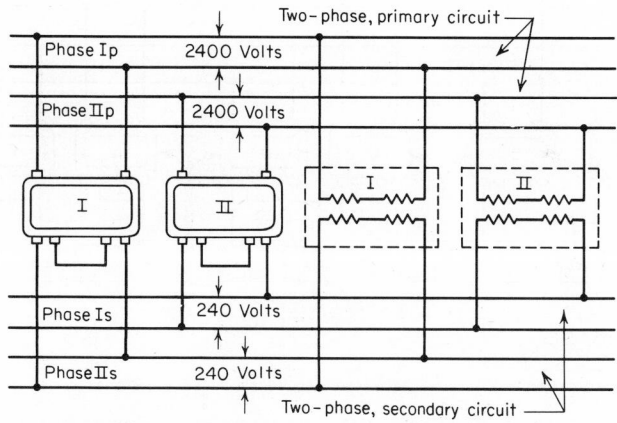

FIG. 48 *Transformers with two-phase to two-phase four-wire connection.*

a single-phase circuit not having any connection with the other. The total load should be so divided between the phases that the loads on each will be equal as nearly as possible. Each transformer should be designed for line voltage and will carry line current. Each transformer should have a kilovolt-ampere capacity equal to one-half of the kilovolt-ampere load that is served by the two transformers.

79. Transformers connected to three-wire two-phase circuits are shown in Fig. 49. The current in the center line wire *AA* for balanced load is 1.41 times the current in either of the outer wires. Each transformer has line voltage impressed on it and carries one-half the total load. A General Electric Co. publication comments thus: "Considerable unbalancing of voltage at the end of a transmission line or cable is experienced with the three-wire, two-phase system owing to the mutual induction between phases. Where the power factor is low, a still worse regulation is obtained, making satisfactory operation difficult. Very few systems now operate on this plan, and practically all of them could be improved by the use of some other system."

80. Mixed connections are sometimes made with two-phase transformers as shown in Fig. 50. With improper connections such as those shown, difficulty will be experienced in the operation of motors and they may not run at all.

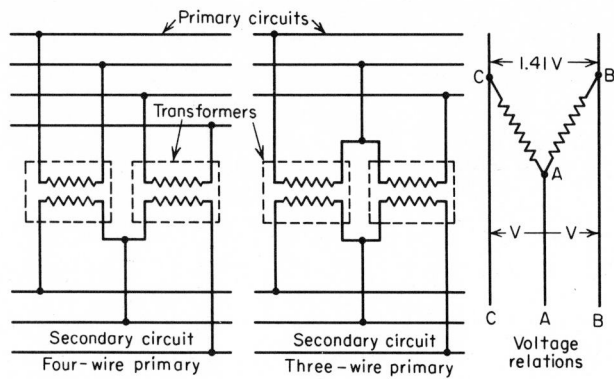

FIG. 49   *Connections for transformers on three-wire two-phase circuits.*

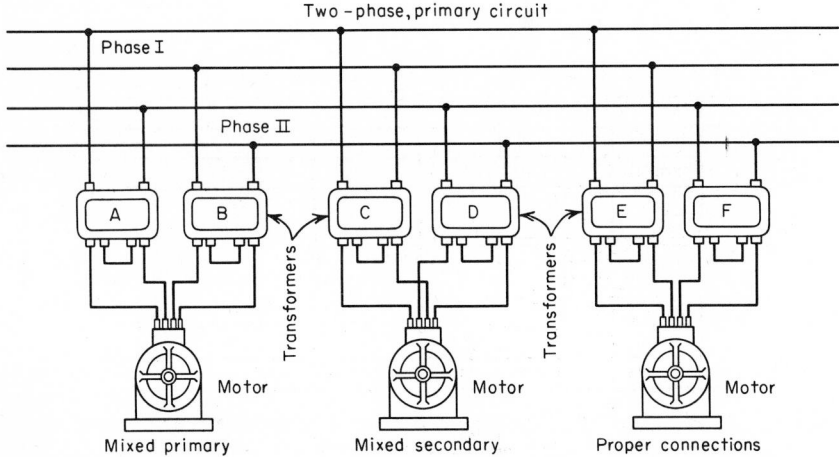

FIG. 50   *Correct and incorrect connections for transformers serving two-phase motors.*

THREE-PHASE CONNECTIONS

81. Comparison of one three-phase transformer as against a group of single-phase transformers ("Standard Handbook") that can be employed for obtaining the same service has been summed up by J. S. Peck as follows: Advantages of three-phase transformer: (1) lower cost, (2) higher efficiency, (3) less floor space and less weight, (4) simplification in outside wiring, and (5) reduced transportation charges and reduced cost of installation. The disadvantages of the three-phase transformer are (1) greater cost of spare units, (2) greater derangement of service in the event of breakdown, (3) greater cost of repair, (4) reduced capacity obtainable in self-cooling units, and (5) greater difficulties in bringing out taps for a large number of voltages. It is considered that the three-phase transformer has certain real and positive advantages over the one-phase type, while its disadvantages are chiefly those which result in the event of breakdown—an abnormal condition which occurs at rarer and rarer intervals as the art of transformer design and manufacture advances.

82. Connections of transformers for the transformation of three-phase power are given in Figs. 51 to 58 inclusive. In all these figures the polarity of the transformer units is additive. If the transformers had subtractive polarity, the interconnections between transformers would be made in exactly the same manner as shown in the figures insofar as terminal marking is concerned. The interconnections for subtractive polarity would be different with respect to the relative location of terminals. The connections shown in these figures result in standard angular displacements.

Much of the material in the following sections has been taken from a publication of the Line Material Company.

83. Transformers with both primary and secondary coils delta-(Δ)connected are shown in Fig. 51*a*. All three of the transformers are connected in series in a closed circuit, and each line wire is connected to the connection between two of the trans-

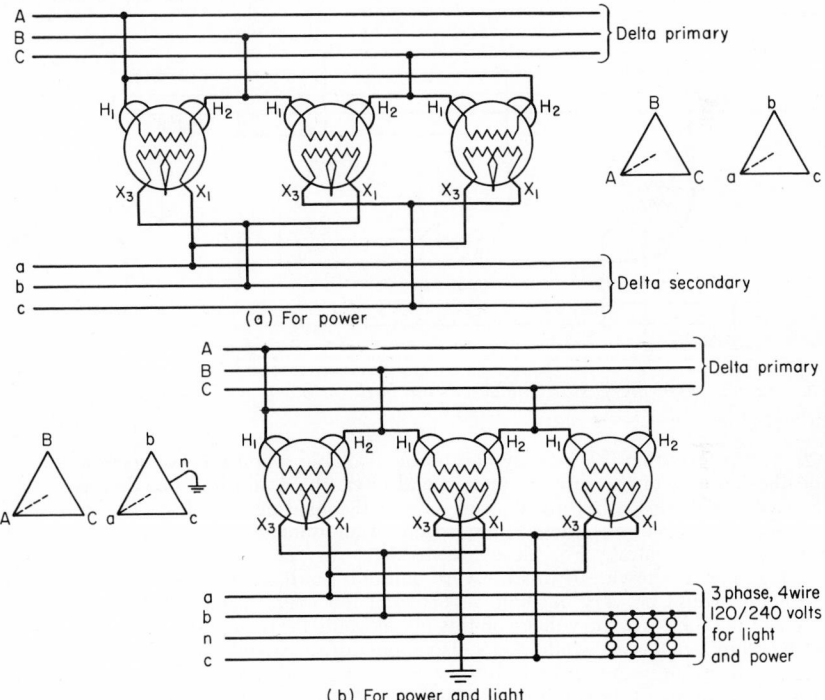

FIG. 51 *Transformers delta-connected on both primary and secondary.*

formers. The voltage imposed on either the primary or secondary of the transformer is the primary or secondary line voltage, respectively. The current in either winding = line current ÷ $\sqrt{3}$, or line current × 0.58. The kilovolt-ampere capacity of each transformer should be equal to one-third the total kilovolt-amperes of the load to be served. The total kilovolt-ampere load transmitted by a balanced three-phase line = $1.73IE$ (where I is the line current in each line wire and E is the voltage between wires). Therefore, the kilovolt-ampere capacity of each transformer should be $1.73IE \div 3 = 0.58IE$. This type of three-phase transformation has been the one most commonly used in the past. The ungrounded primary system will continue to supply power even though one of the lines is grounded owing to a fault. If one of the transformers in the bank should fail, secondary power can be supplied from the two remaining units by changing to the open delta connection. Thus this type of connection is ideal from the standpoint of service continuity.

When light and power are to be supplied from the same bank of transformers, the mid-tap of the secondary of one of the transformers is grounded and connected to the fourth wire of the three-phase secondary system as shown in Fig. 51*b*. The lighting load is then divided between the two hot wires of this same transformer, the grounded wire being common to both branches.

84. Transformers with both primary and secondary coils, star-connected, from a three-wire primary circuit are shown in Fig. 52. The current in each transformer winding is the same as the line current, and the voltage imposed on each winding = line voltage ÷ $\sqrt{3}$ = line voltage × 0.58. The kilovolt-ampere capacity of each transformer should be equal to one-third the total kilovolt-amperes of the load to be served. The total kilovolt-ampere load transmitted by a balanced three-phase line = 1.73IE (where I is the line current in each line wire and E is the voltage between wires). Therefore, the kilovolt-ampere capacity of each transformer should be 1.73IE ÷ 3 = 0.58IE.

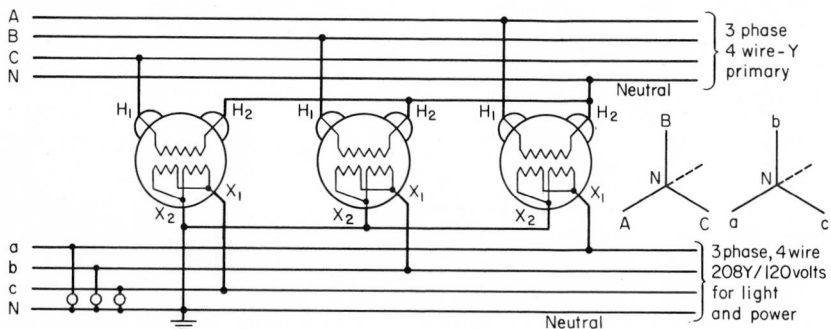

FIG. 52   *Transformers star-connected on both primary and secondary (four-wire primary circuit).*

It is necessary that the primary neutral be available when this connection is used, and the neutrals of the primary system and of the bank are tied together as shown. If the three-phase load is unbalanced, part of the load current flows in the primary neutral. Also the third-harmonic component of the transformer exciting current flows in the primary neutral. For these reasons, it is very necessary that the neutrals be tied together as shown. If this tie were omitted, the line to neutral voltages on the secondary would be very unstable. That is, if the load on one phase were heavier than on the other two, the voltage on this phase would drop excessively and the voltage on the other two phases would rise. Also, large third-harmonic voltages would appear between lines and neutral, both in the transformers and in the secondary system, in addition to the 60-cycle component of voltage. This means that for a given value of rms voltage, the peak voltage would be much higher than for a pure 60-cycle voltage. This overstresses the insulation both in the transformers and in all apparatus connected to the secondaries.

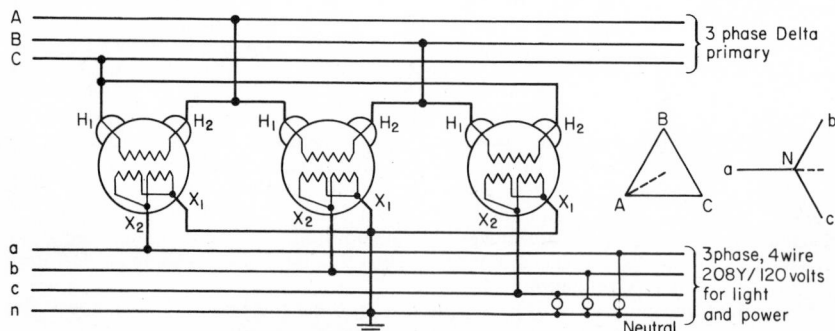

FIG. 53   *Transformers delta-connected primary and star-connected secondary.*

85. Transformers delta-connected to the primary circuit and star-connected to the secondary circuit are shown in Fig. 53. Any group of transformers can have either their primary or secondary coils connected in either star or delta. With the primary delta-connected and the secondary star-connected as shown, the secondary voltage will be 1.73 times what it would be if it were delta-connected. The neutral of the secondary three-phase system is grounded. The single-phase loads are connected between the different phase wires and neutral while the three-phase power loads are connected to the three-phase wires. Thus, 120 volts is supplied to the lighting loads and 208 volts to the power load. Advantages of this type of bank are the fact that the single-phase load can be balanced on the three phases in each bank by itself and the fact that the secondaries of different banks can be tied together.

86. Transformers star-connected primary and delta-connected secondary are shown in Fig. 54. This is the reverse of the grouping described in Sec. **85,** and the secondary voltage will be but 0.58 times as great as if both secondary and primary were star-connected.

The present tendency in utilities is to replace the 2,400 delta system with the 2,400/4,160Y-volt three-phase four-wire system. This change in effect raises the distribution voltage from 2,400 to 4,160 volts without any major changes in connected equipment. The same transformers that were previously connected between lines on the 2,400-volt delta system are now connected between lines and neutral on the new 2,400/4,160Y-volt system. Three-phase banks that had previously been connected delta-delta are now connected Y-delta as shown.

When service for both light and power is to be supplied, the Y-delta bank takes the form shown in Fig. 54*b.*

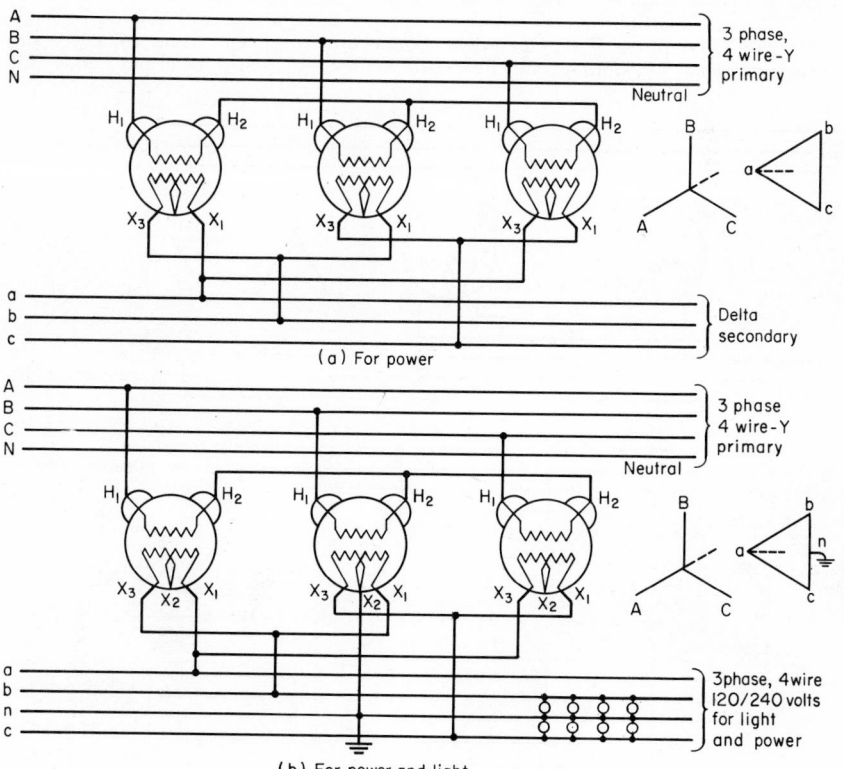

(a) For power

(b) For power and light

FIG. 54   *Transformers star-connected primary and delta-connected secondary.*

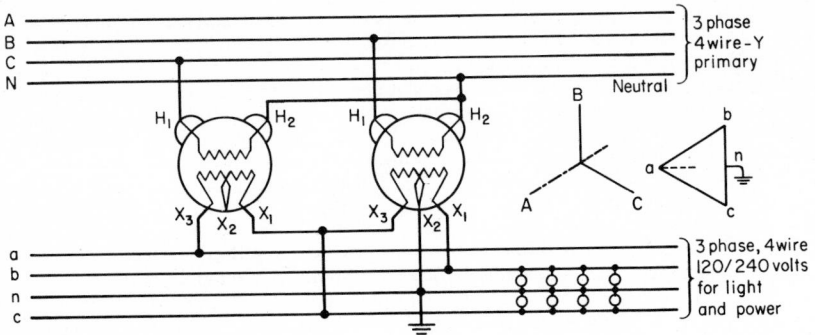

FIG. 55 *Y-delta connection with one unit missing.*

If one unit of a Y-delta bank goes bad, service can be maintained by means of the connection of Fig. 55. In the regular Y-delta bank with three units, the neutral of the primaries of the transformers is not ordinarily tied in with the neutral of the primary system. In fact, this bank can be used even when the primary neutral is not available. In the bank with two units, however, it is necessary to connect to the neutral as shown. The main disadvantage of this hookup is the fact that full-load current flows in the neutral even though the three-phase load may be balanced. In addition to maintaining service in an emergency, this type of bank is satisfactory where the main part of the load is lighting and the three-phase load is small.

87. The Three-phase V or Open-delta Connection (Fig. 56). Line voltage is impressed on each transformer, and line current flows in each transformer coil. This

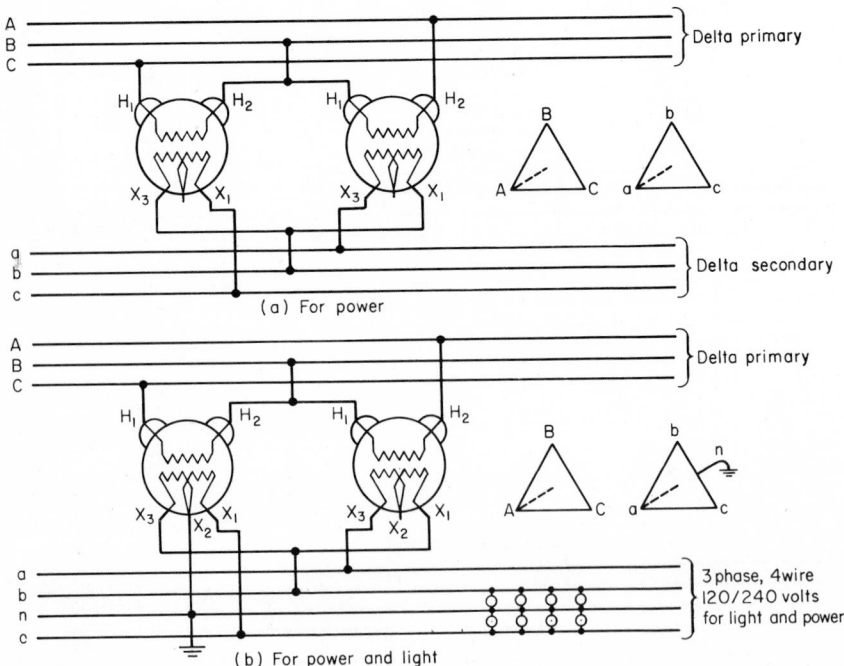

FIG. 56 *Three-phase V or open-delta connection of two transformers.*

method is considerably used for motors but has the objection that if one of the transformers becomes inoperative, the three-phase circuit served will be fed by but one transformer and hence will be inoperative.

The combined capacity of two transformers (Gear and Williams) connected by this method and serving a given load should be 15.5 per cent greater than the combined capacity of three transformers delta- or star-connected and serving the same load. For instance if three 5-kva transformers (total capacity 15 kva) are required for a certain installation and they are replaced by two 7½-kva transformers (total capacity 15 kva), the two transformers will be overloaded by 15.5 per cent at a full load of 15 kw at 100 per cent pf.

For example, assume that in a three-transformer installation the current in the secondary line is 17.3 amp. This imposes a load of 10 amp on the transformer secondary coils. At 200 volts this is 2 kw per transformer, or 6 kw in all. If two 3-kw transformers are put in to replace the three 2-kw units, the capacity of the secondary coils would be 15 amp. But, as above noted, with the open-delta connection the current in the secondary coil is the same as the current in the line, and the 15-amp winding must carry 17.3 amp or 15.5 per cent overload.

In the grouping of Fig. 56, to reverse the direction of a motor served by the group, interchange any two of the primary phase wires or reverse any two of the secondary wires.

In some cases two transformers for open-delta grouping of proper aggregate capacity to serve a given load will be cheaper than three transformers for star or delta grouping to serve the same load, but this is not always the case.

The open-delta connection can be used in an emergency in case one of the transformers in a delta-delta bank fails. This type of bank is also used to supply power to a three-phase load which is temporarily light but which is expected to grow. When the load increases to a point where the two transformers in the bank are overloaded, an increase in capacity of 1.732 times can be obtained by adding another unit of the same size and using the delta-delta connection.

When the secondary circuits are to supply both light and power, the open-delta bank takes the form shown in Fig. 56b. In addition to the applications listed above for the open-delta bank for power, this type of bank is used where there is a large single-phase load and only a small three-phase load. In this case, the two transformers would be of different kva sizes, the one across which the lighting load is connected being the larger.

88. Disadvantages of the V or Open-delta Connection ("Standard Handbook"). For normal operation not only must each of the V-connected transformers be larger than each of the delta-connected transformers, but the two transformers must have a combined rating 15.5 per cent greater than the three transformers. This fact taken alone does not represent a disadvantage of the V-connection, because the two larger transformers are exactly equal in constructive material and operating efficiency to the three smaller transformers. The real objection to the V-connection for serious work resides in the tendency for the local impedance of the transformers to produce an enormous unbalance of the secondary voltages and of the primary currents. In spite of this disadvantage (which is really of little consequence in 2,200-volt primary distribution work) many V-connected groupings are in satisfactory operation.

89. Comparison between the Delta, the Star, and the Open-delta Methods of Connection ("Standard Handbook"). The choice between the methods would be governed largely by the service requirements. When the three transformers are delta-connected, one can be removed without interrupting the performance of the circuit—the two remaining transformers, in a manner, acting in series to carry the load of the missing transformer. The desire to obtain immunity from a shutdown due to the disabling of one transformer has led to the extensive use of the delta connection of transformers, especially on the low-potential delivery side. It is to be noted that in case one transformer is crippled, the other two will be subjected to greatly increased losses.

Thus, if three delta-connected transformers be equally loaded until each carries 100 amp, there will be 173 amp in each external circuit wire. If one transformer be now removed and 173 amp continues to be supplied to each external circuit wire, each of the remaining transformers must carry 173 amp, since it is now in series with an external circuit. Therefore, each transformer must now show three times as much copper loss as when all three transformers were active, or the total copper loss is now increased to a value of six relative to its former value of three. An open-delta installation is made frequently where considerable future increase in load is expected. The increase can be accommodated by adding the third transformer to the bank at a later date and thus increasing the capacity of the load that can be carried by about 75 per cent.

A change from delta to Y in the secondary circuit alters the ratio of the transmission emf to the receiver emf from 1 to $\sqrt{3}$. On account of this fact, when the emf of the transmission circuit is so high that the successful insulation of transformer coils becomes of constructive and pecuniary importance, the three-phase line sides of the transformers are connected in "star" and the neutral is grounded. The windings of most transformers operating on systems of 100,000 volts or more are star-connected.

See also Sec. 88 regarding properties of an open-delta connected group.

90. Comparative Cost of Transformers for Different Grouping for Three-phase Service. The following table shows the costs in 1930 of the single-phase transformers, of proper capacities for either a delta or an open-delta grouping and of a three-phase transformer to serve a 75-kva installation. The relative costs will be the same for the present date.

Method of connection or grouping	Number of transformers required	Capacity of each transformer, kva	Aggregate capacity	Cost per transformer	Aggregate cost
Delta (Δ)......................	3	25	75	$317	$951
Open delta (V)ᵃ................	2	50	100	522	1,044
Three-phase transformer..........	1	75	75	950	950

ᵃ The theoretical aggregate capacity of two single-phase transformers for open-delta grouping for a 75-kva three-phase load would be (see Sec. 87): $75 \times 1.15 = 86.3$ kva or $86.3 \div 2 = 43.2$ kva per transformer. The nearest commercial capacity to 43.2 kva is 50 kva, which gives an aggregate capacity of 100 kva.

91. Nonstandard Angular Displacement. All the transformer connections shown in Figs. 51 to 56 inclusive are made so as to give the standard angular displacement or vector relation between the primary and secondary voltage systems as defined by the different standards publications including the USASI. These standard angular displacements are 0° for delta-delta or Y-Y connected banks and 30° for delta-Y or Y-delta banks.

Angular displacement becomes important when two or more three-phase banks are interconnected into the same secondary system or when three-phase banks are paralleled. In such cases it is necessary that all of the three-phase banks have the same displacement.

If subtractive polarity transformers are used in the connections illustrated in Figs. 51 to 56, it is found that the secondary connections are much simplified from that shown for the additive polarity units. The additive polarity connections for standard angular displacement are somewhat complicated, particularly in cases with a delta-connected secondary, by the crossed secondary interconnections between units.

For this reason simplified bank connections are sometimes used with additive polarity units which give nonstandard angular displacement between the primary and secondary systems. The diagrams of Figs. 57 and 58 cover these simplified bank connections for three additive polarity units for the more common three-phase connections with the delta-connected secondary.

SPECIAL TRANSFORMER CONNECTIONS

92. Transformers connected for transforming from three-phase to two-phase or the reverse are illustrated in Fig. 59, which shows what is known as the Scott connection. The transformers required are special, and each has a lead brought out from the middle point of the high-tension winding, and a special voltage tap is arranged giving 86.6 per cent of the high-tension winding. Usually two transformers just alike are purchased

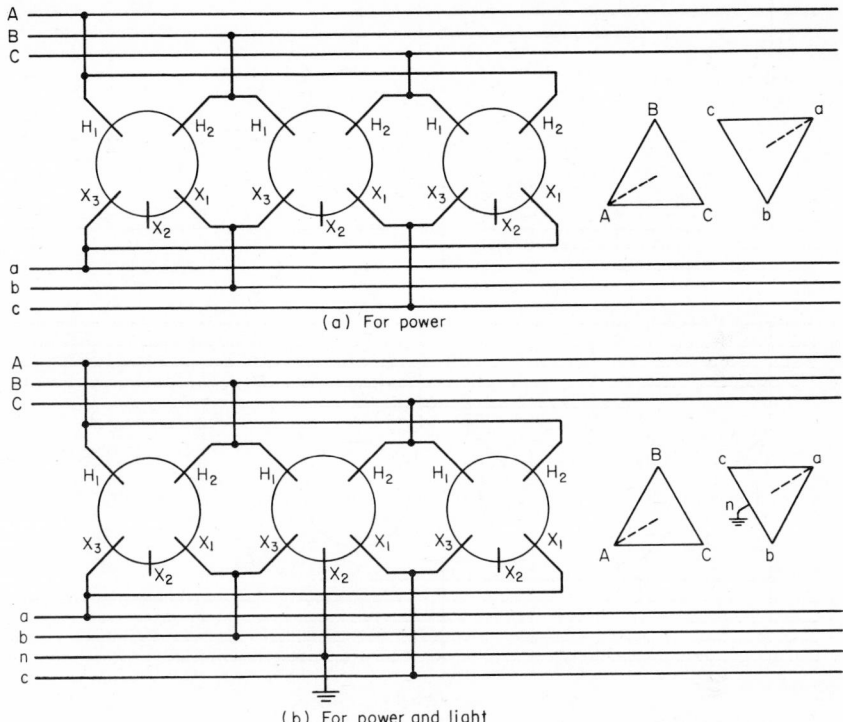

(a) For power

(b) For power and light

FIG. 57 *Delta-delta connections with nonstandard angular displacements.*

so that they will be interchangeable. These special transformers can be purchased from any of the large manufacturers. Those shown are Westinghouse transformers. Two standard single-phase transformers for such service should have an aggregate kilovolt-ampere rating 15½ per cent greater than their group or nominal rating.

93. Explanation of the Transformation from Three-phase to Two-phase ("Standard Handbook"). Assume the simple case of a total power of 30,000 watts, 1.0 pf, at 100 volts, three-phase, to be transformed (without loss) to 30,000 watts, 100 volts, two-phase (see Fig. 60). Assuming that the load is balanced on the two-phase side, there will be 15,000 watts per phase, or 150 amp at 100 volts. Since the three-phase power is represented as $\sqrt{3}\,IE = 30{,}000$, where I is the current per line wire and E is the emf between line wires, I must equal 173.2 amp, because E has been taken as 100 volts.

As shown in Fig. 60, the three-phase coils of one transformer must be designed for 100 volts and 173.2 amp while the three-phase coils of the other transformer must be designed for 86.6 volts and 173.2 amp. The current through the coil CD divides equally. A part (86.6 amp) goes through DA and an equal part (86.6 amp) passes differentially through DB; thus the mmf of these two currents has a resultant of zero, and it has no effect upon the core flux so far as transformer T' is concerned. The coil ADB carries a total value of current of 173.2 amp throughout all its turns, but the current in one half is 60 time degrees out of phase with that in the other half. That is to say, the 173.2 amp in one half is made up of a load current of 150 amp, in leading time quadrature with which is 86.6 amp, while that in the other half is made up of a load current of 150 amp, in lagging time quadrature with which is a superposed current of 86.6 amp. The magnetizing effect of the 173.2 amp is, therefore, 150 amp, and the current in the two-phase side of transformer T' is 150 amp. In the T transformer the mmf of 173.2 amp in 86.6 per cent turns is just equal to that of 150 amp in

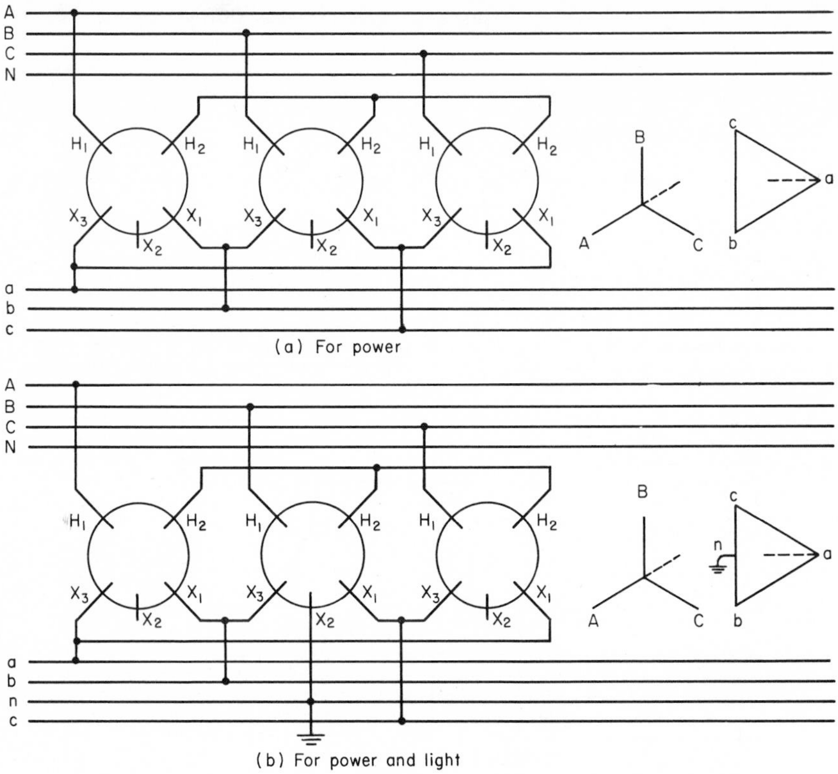

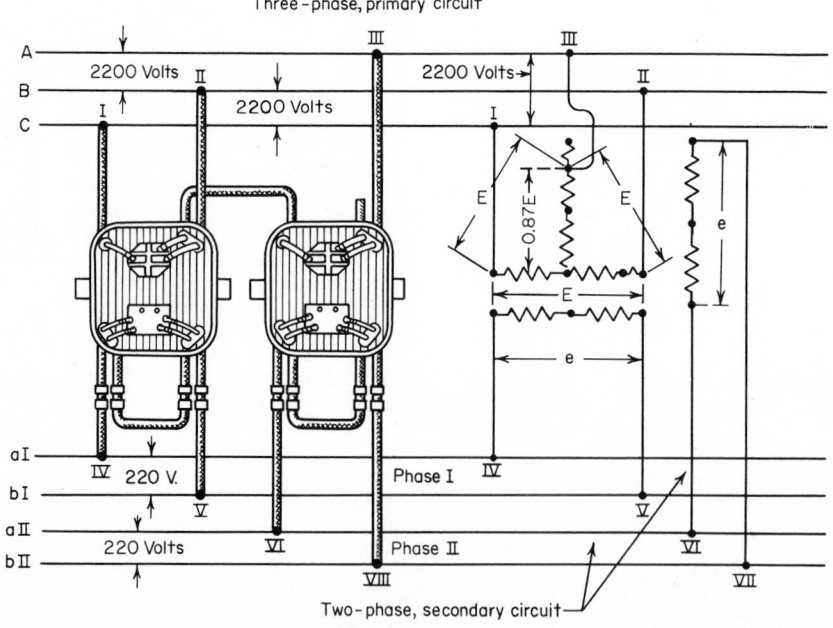

(a) For power

(b) For power and light

FIG. 58 *Y-delta connections with nonstandard angular displacements.*

Three-phase, primary circuit

aI — IV 220 V. Phase I IV
bI — V
aII — VI
bII — 220 Volts VI Phase II VIII

Two-phase, secondary circuit

FIG. 59 *Transformers connected for three-phase to two-phase transformation.*

100 per cent turns; these two currents are directly in time-phase opposition, and the apparatus operates in all respects like a one-phase transformer. The phase relations and the relative values of the several components of currents are shown in the vector diagram of Fig. 60.

94. Kilovolt-ampere Ratings of Transformers for Scott Connection (Three-phase to Two-phase) for Serving a Given Horsepower Load. The following table gives the ratings recommended by the Westinghouse Electric & Manufacturing Co. for transformers serving squirrel-cage induction motors and indicates the efficiency of the installation. The temperature guarantee with performances as shown is a 50°C rise.

Hp of motor	Number of transformers	Kva capacity of each transformer	Total kva load imposed on the group of two transformers when motor is operating at full load	Efficiency of bank of transformers with full load on motor
½	2	½	0.75	92.8
1	2	½	1.35	94.5
2	2	1	2.40	95.2
3	2	1½	3.4	95.9
5	2	2½	5.5	96.4
7½	2	4	8.1	97.0
10	2	5	10.7	97.2
15	2	7½	15.7	97.4
20	2	10	20.9	97.6
30	2	15	31.5	97.8
40	2	20	42.0	98.0
50	2	25	51.0	98.0
75	2	37½	77.0	98.3

$$\text{Kva on each transformer} = \frac{\text{hp} \times 0.746 \times 0.59}{(\text{eff} \times \text{pf of motor})}$$

$$\text{Efficiency} = \frac{\text{kw on transformer}}{\text{kw transformer loss} + \text{kw on transformer}}$$

95. T-connected Transformers for Transforming from Three-phase to Three-phase ("Standard Handbook"). A method of employing two transformers in three-phase transformation which practically overcomes the disadvantages of the V connection and possesses considerable merit is found in the T connection. As indicated in Fig. 61, one transformer is connected across between two of the line wires while the other is joined between the third line wire and the middle point of the first transformer. The current in the primary coil of each transformer is the same in value as that in the primary coil of the other, and the secondary currents in the two transformers are likewise equal in value. The voltage impressed across one transformer is only 86.6 per cent of that across the other, so that, if each transformer is designed especially for its work, one will have a rating of EI and the other a rating of $0.866EI$, where I is the current in each line wire and E is the emf between lines. The combined rating will therefore

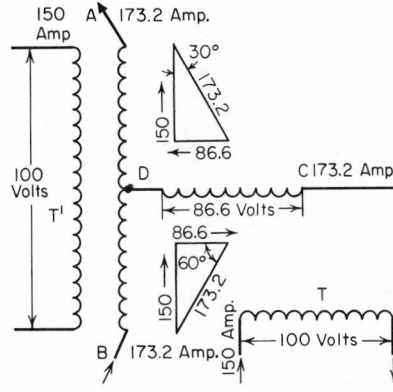

FIG. 60 *Three-phase to two-phase transformation.*

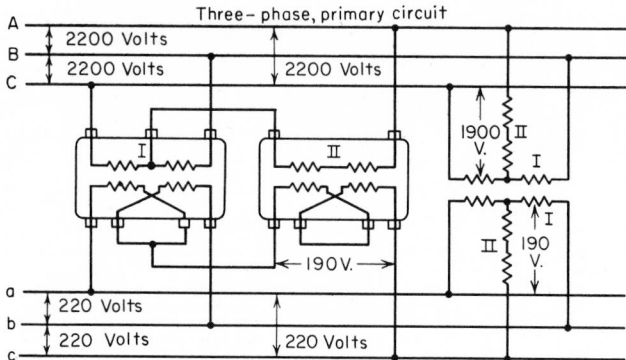

FIG. 61   *Transformers, T-connected for three-phase transformation.*

be 1.866 as compared with 1.732*EI* for three one-phase transformers connected either Δ or Y, or with 2.0*EI* for two V-connected transformers.

96. Requisites for Transformers for T Connection.   The two transformers should possess the same ratio of primary to secondary turns, and a tap should be brought out from the central point of one of the transformers.   It is not essential that the former transformer be designed for exactly 86.6 per cent of the voltage of the latter; the normal voltage of one can be 90 per cent of the other without producing detrimental results. Moreover, transformers designed for the same normal emf and intended for V connection can be T-connected with considerable improvement in service.

97. In comparing the T connection with the Δ or the Y connection ("Standard Handbook"), it is to be noted that each connection accomplishes the transformation without sensible distortion of phase relations.   The T connection allows the neutral point to be reached equally as well as does the Y connection.   The Δ connection, however, is the only one capable of transforming in emergencies with one disabled transformer. With reference to its ability to maintain balanced phase relations, the T connection is much better than the V connection.

The aggregate kilovolt-ampere rating of two T-connected transformers should be 15½ per cent greater than the nominal kilovolt-ampere rating of the group.

98. Booster Transformers ("Electric Central Station Distributing Systems," Gear and Williams, Van Nostrand Co.).   Ordinary distributing transformers applied as illustrated (Fig. 62) are used where it is necessary to raise, by a fixed percentage, the voltage delivered by a line, as is necessary when transformer ratios do not give quite the right voltage or when line drop is excessive.   A booster raises the voltage of any primary circuit in which it may be inserted by the amount of the secondary voltage of the booster (see Fig. 62).

Examples.   On a long single-phase 2,080-volt lighting branch so heavily loaded that the pressure drops more than the amount for which the normal regulation of the feeder will compensate, a 110-volt transformer inserted in the line as a booster will raise the pressure of the primary branch on the load side of the booster by 110 volts.   This raises the secondary pressure 5.5 per cent on all the transformers beyond the booster.

With 440-volt service supplied by star-connected 230-volt transformers, a 10 per cent booster in each phase raises the normal pressure of 230/400 volts to 253/440 volts.

The connections for a simple booster are shown in Fig. 62, I, the line pressure being raised from 2,080 to 2,184 volts, or 5 per cent.   The connection at II is that for an augmented booster in which the line pressure is raised from 2,080 to 2,190 volts, because the primary of the booster is connected across the line on the far side and the booster is boosted as well as the line.   This gives an increase of 5.5 per cent in the line pressure.

Figure 62, III, shows a 10 per cent simple booster and IV an augmented 11.1 per cent booster.

The transformers shown in Fig. 62 have a 10:1 or 20:1 ratio, and the percentages shown apply only to transformers of this ratio.   If boosters having a ratio of 2,080 to 115/230 are used, the percentages are increased by about 10 per cent.   Figure 62, I, would then become 5.5 per cent; II, 6.05 per cent; III, 11.1 per cent; and IV, 12.2 per cent.

99. The proper connection of the secondary for a booster or bucking transformer must usually be determined by trial for a transformer of any given type, but once it has been determined, the same connection can be used for any transformer of the same type. The connections shown in Figs. 62 and 63 are correct for transformers of

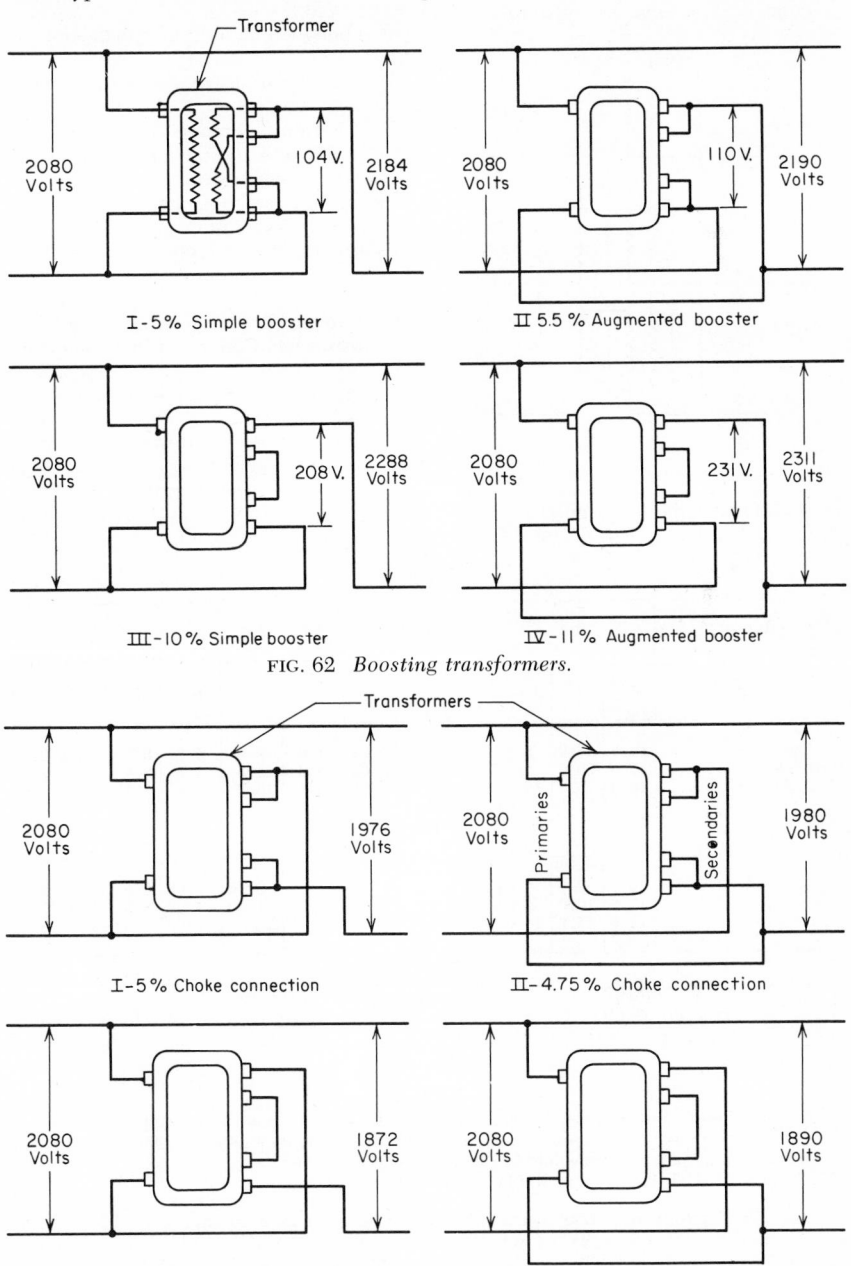

FIG. 62 *Boosting transformers.*

FIG. 63 *Bucking (choking) transformers.*

the principal makers. Boost and buck transformers are also widely used in circuits of 600 volts and less. See Sec. **109.**

100. Boosters are connected in a two-phase circuit in a manner similar to that shown in Fig. 62 for a single-phase circuit. In three-wire two-phase feeders the boosters (secondary windings) are cut into the outer wires, and the primary windings are connected between the middle and the outside wires.

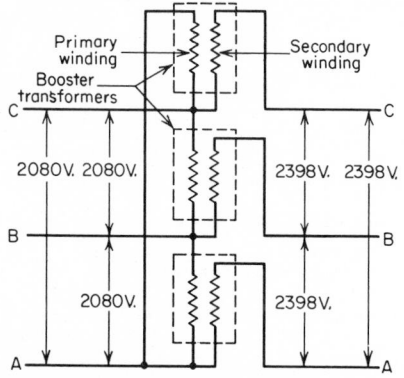

101. Booster transformers in three-phase circuits are connected as shown in Fig. 64 ("Electric Central Station Distributing Systems"). The insertion in any phase wire of the booster voltage affects two phases. The boosting and bucking effects, with transformers of various ratios, with the boosting transformers used in one, two, or three phases, are expressed in percentage of the primary voltage in the table of Sec. **102.**

102. Voltage Boosting and Bucking Effect of Transformers Connected in Three-phase Circuits ("Electric Central Station Distributing Systems"). Values in the body of the tables are the percentages that the voltages will be increased or decreased, respectively, by the insertion of booster or bucking transformers, of different ratios, in one,

FIG. 64 *Booster transformers in a three-wire, three-phase circuit.*

two, or three of the phase wires. Transformers are connected for boosting as shown in Fig. 64. The letters *AB*, *BC*, and *CA* refer to the three phases of Fig. 64.

Boosting

Ratios	10:1			20:1			9:1			18:1		
Booster in	*AB*	*BC*	*CA*	*AB*	*BC*	*CA*	*AB*	*BC*	*CA*	*AB*	*BC*	*CA*
A phase............	10.0	10.0	5.3	5.00	0.00	2.65	11.0	0.0	5.8	5.5	0.00	2.9
A and *B*............	15.3	10.0	5.3	7.65	5.00	2.65	16.8	5.5	5.8	8.4	2.75	2.9
A, *B*, and *C*........	15.3	15.3	15.3	7.65	7.65	7.65	16.8	16.8	16.8	8.4	8.40	8.4

Bucking

	10:1			20:1			9:1			18:1		
A phase............	10.0	0.0	4.6	5.0	0.0	2.3	11.00	0.00	5.06	5.5	0.00	2.53
A and *B*............	14.6	10.0	4.6	7.3	5.0	2.3	16.06	11.00	5.06	8.3	5.50	2.53
A, *B*, and *C*........	14.6	14.6	14.6	7.3	7.3	7.3	16.06	16.06	16.08	8.03	8.03	8.03

103. Bucking Transformers ("Electric Central Station Distributing Systems"). When the secondary is connected in reverse order the transformer becomes a "choke," reducing the line pressure instead of raising it.

Examples. A 5 per cent choke connection is shown in Fig. 63, I, a 4.75 per cent choke in II, a 10 per cent choke in III, and a 9.1 per cent choke in IV.

The transformers shown in Fig. 63 have a ratio of 10:1 or 20:1, and the percentages shown are only for transformers of that ratio. If bucking transformers having a ratio of 2,080 to 115/230 are used, the choking percentages would be changed to the following values: Fig. 63, I, 5.5 per cent; II, 5.24 per cent; III, 11 per cent; and IV, 10 per cent.

104. The capacity of a transformer that is to be used as a booster (Fig. 65) will be determined by (1) the current I which will flow in the a-c line and (2) the voltage E by which the emf on the line will be "boosted." If, for example, the current in the line is 20 amp and it is desired to raise the voltage (Fig. 65) by 110 volts, then required

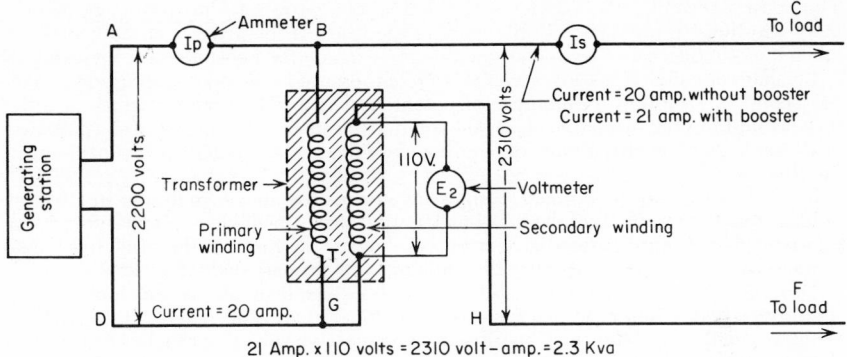

FIG. 65 *Example in computing capacity required for a booster transformer.*

capacity of the boosting transformer = 20 amp × 110 volts = 2,200 va = 2.2 kva. Hence, for these conditions it would be necessary to use at I a standard 2½-kva transformer. The secondary coils of this transformer would be connected in multiple so that they would develop 110 volts.

If it is desired to boost the voltage by 220 volts, then 20 amp × 220 volts = 4,400 va = 4.4 kva. Hence, theoretically a 4.4-kva transformer would be required. Note that in any case the secondary winding of the boosting transformer must be capable of carrying the primary line current (20 amp, in Fig. 65). Furthermore, the secondary coils of the boosting transformer must be so designed and connected that they will produce at their terminals the voltage by which it is desired to "boost" the emf which is impressed on the line by the generator in the station.

105. As a practical proposition it is usually desirable to select for the "boost" voltage one of the voltages for which the secondaries of distributing transformers are regularly designed or for which they can be connected. That is, the boosting voltage should, ordinarily, be either 110, 220, or 440. If a boosting voltage other than one of these standard voltages is necessary, it will then probably be necessary to obtain a specially designed transformer or to obtain a transformer which has taps on the secondary coils.

106. In every case the line current will be increased somewhat by the boosting transformer. If the load remains constant, the increase in that portion of the circuit *HFCB* (Fig. 65) will be in the ratio by which the voltage impressed on this portion of the circuit has been boosted. For example, if the current in the a-c line *HFCB* of Fig. 65 was 20 amp before the boosting transformer was inserted, the current after its insertion would be computed in this way:

$$\frac{I_2}{I_1} = \frac{E_2}{E_1} \tag{3}$$

$$I_2 = \frac{E_2 \times I_1}{E_1} \quad \text{amp} \tag{4}$$

where I_1 = the line current, in amperes, before inserting the booster transformer; E_1 = emf, in volts, across *BH* (Fig. 65) before inserting the booster transformer; I_2 = current, in amperes, in *HFCB* after the booster is inserted; and E_2 = emf, in volts, across *BH* after the booster is inserted.

Example. Substituting the values from Fig. 65 in Eq. (4), the current in *HFCB* after inserting the booster = $I_2 = (E_2 \times I_1) \div E_1 = (2,310 \times 20) \div 2,200 = 21$ amp. After inserting the booster, the current I_p in *ABCD* will be 21 amp + the current carried by the primary winding. The value of 20 amp in Sec. **104** is not strictly correct, but this relatively small difference will not appreciably affect the kilovolt-ampere rating of the booster transformer which would be used.

107. There are certain precautions that should be observed in the installation of boosters ("Electric Central Station Distributing Systems") to protect them from injury.

The booster secondary is in series with the line, and current is drawn through its primary windings in proportion to the load on the line. If the primary of the booster is opened while the secondary is carrying the line current, the booster acts as a choke coil in the main circuit. This causes a large drop of pressure in the booster, imposing upon its secondary windings a difference of potential of two to five times normal. Under these conditions the insulation of a 2,000-volt transformer can be subjected to a pressure of 10,000 to 20,000 volts or more depending upon the load carried by the main circuit at the time.

If a fuse is used in the primary, its blowing creates the above condition, and the arc holds across the terminals of the fuse block until it burns itself clear. It has often been observed that where boosters have been "protected" by fuses in this way, the transformer has burned out shortly after the blowing of its primary fuses if not at the time.

Also, in using ordinary static transformers as boosters, it should be remembered that the service is different from that for which the transformer is designed. If this feature is neglected, the insulation may be subjected to excessive voltages or dielectric stresses, thus causing breakdown. The standard distributing transformer is designed to withstand a pressure of about 10,000 volts between the high-voltage coils and the case, while the low-voltage coils (the 220-volt coils) are designed to withstand a test pressure of 4,000 volts between coils, core, and case for a period of 1 min.

When a 2,200–110/220-volt transformer is used as a booster, the low-voltage coils are subjected to a continuous pressure of about 2,300 volts above ground. This sustained voltage will, if the case is grounded, be likely to destroy the insulation of the low-voltage coils. Therefore the transformer case should, if feasible, be insulated from the ground, although this may involve life hazard. When the transformer is installed on a pole, the insulation is automatically provided, since the pole acts as the insulating medium.

108. Booster Cutout (Gear and Williams). In connecting or disconnecting a booster the main line should be opened before putting it in or out. If service on the line cannot be interrupted, or if it is desired to switch the booster in or out at certain times, it can be done with a series arc cutout as in Fig. 66. The operation of the cutout simultaneously opens the primary and short-circuits the secondary of the booster. The switch must be of a type having a positive action so that arcing will not damage its contacts at the moment when the secondary is short-circuited. The arc cutout must have sufficient carrying capacity to carry the main-line current when the booster is shunted out, and standard series cutouts should not be used where the line current is likely to exceed 20 to 25 amp.

When the augmented booster is used, the terminals of the primary winding of the transformer which goes to the cutout should be connected to the terminal of the cutout which is shown as not being in use in Fig. 66.

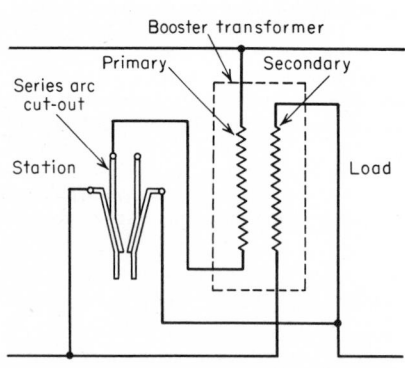

FIG. 66   *Series arc cutout for a booster.*

109. Boost-Buck Transformers in Low-voltage Circuits. For circuits of 600 volts or less, the most common application for a boost-buck transformer is boosting 208 to 230 or 240 volts and vice versa for industrial and commercial air-conditioning systems, boosting 110 to 120 volts, and 240 to 277 volts for lighting systems, and voltage correction for heating systems and all types of induction motors.

In such cases a buck-boost transformer raises or lowers a supply line voltage up to ±20 per cent. A typical transformer has two primary (input) windings, both rated at either 120 or 240 volts, and two secondary (output) windings, both rated at 12, 16, or 24 volts. With this arrangement the primary and secondary windings can be connected together so that the electrical characteristics are changed from those of an "insulating transformer" to a "boosting or bucking" autotransformer.

Connections are quite similar to those shown in Figs. 62 and 63, and complete literature on boost and buck transformers can be obtained from Acme Electric Corp.

CONNECTIONS FOR THREE-PHASE TRANSFORMERS

110. Methods of Connecting the Windings of Three-phase Transformers ("Standard Handbook"). The windings of each component transformer are connected to the external circuits just as though this component were a one-phase unit; i.e., the primaries can be connected either Y or delta. More-over the relative advantages of the Y connection and the delta connection are quite the same with one three-phase transformer as with three one-phase transformers. The delta connection is advantageous in some cases in that if the windings of one phase become damaged by short circuiting, grounding, or any other defect, it is possible to operate with the other phase windings V-connected.

111. In operating a damaged three-phase transformer on two coils it is necessary to separate the damaged transformer windings electrically from the other coils, as indicated in Fig. 67. The high-potential winding of the damaged phase should be short-circuited upon itself, and the corresponding low-potential winding should also be short-circuited upon itself. The winding thus short-circuited will choke down the flux passing through the portion of the core surrounded by the windings

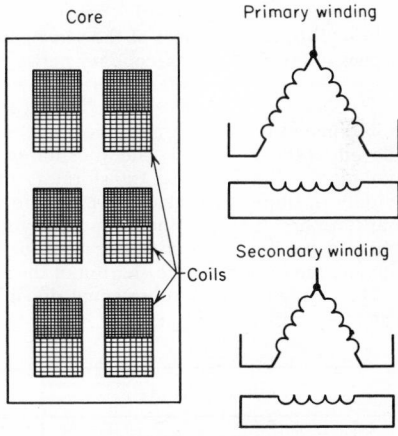

FIG. 67 *Operating a damaged three-phase transformer.*

without producing in any portion of the winding a current greater than a small fraction of the current which would normally exist in such portion at full load.

PARALLEL OPERATION

112. Parallel Operation of Transformers. Transformers will operate satisfactorily in parallel (Fig. 68), i.e., with their high- and low-tension windings respectively connected directly to the same circuits provided that they have (1) the same ratio of trans-

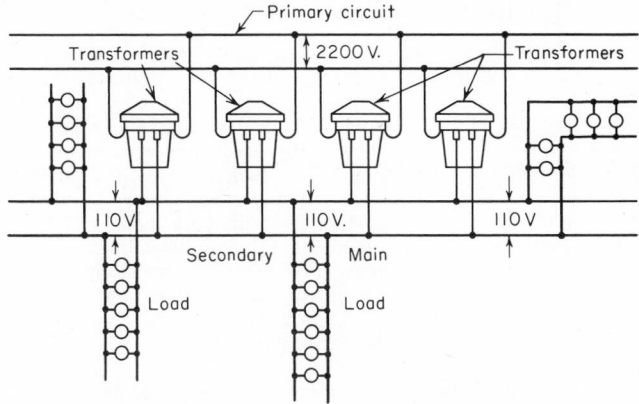

FIG. 68 *Transformers banked or operating in parallel.*

formation, (2) the same voltage ratings, and (3) approximately the same regulation. If the low-tension voltages are different, the transformer having the highest voltages will circulate current to those of lower voltage and cause a continuous loss. If transformers connected in parallel do not have the same regulation, they will not share the total load in proportion to their ratings. The greater share of the load will be taken by the transformer having the best regulation.

In connecting large transformers in parallel, especially when one of the windings is for a comparatively low voltage, it is necessary that the resistance of the joints and interconnecting leads does not vary materially for the different transformers, or it will cause an unequal division of load.

113. With transformers of the same general voltage and capacity characteristics connected in multiple in a secondary network ("Distributing Transformers," A. D. Fishel) little trouble will be encountered, as the impedance of the line between two transformers on separate poles spaced about 100 or 200 ft apart will normally neutralize any difference in the transformer impedances. When transformers operated in multiple are placed on the same pole, the question of equal sharing of the load may be of some importance. The standard transformers of reliable manufacturers do not differ very widely in impedance characteristics, however, and it is usually practicable to operate transformers of the various standard types in parallel. Often the commercial desirability of paralleling transformers of different sizes will overbalance the undesirability of some inequality in the sharing of the load which might result.

114. A method of forcing equal division of load between transformers having considerably different impedance characteristics ("Distributing Transformers," A. D. Fishel) is shown in Fig. 69. Standard 2,200-volt distributing transformers are usually provided with arrangements for the series-parallel connecting of both the high-tension and the low-tension windings, and therefore the connections shown can be used. As the high-tension windings are in series, the currents in the primary windings will be the same; hence the transformers will be equally loaded.

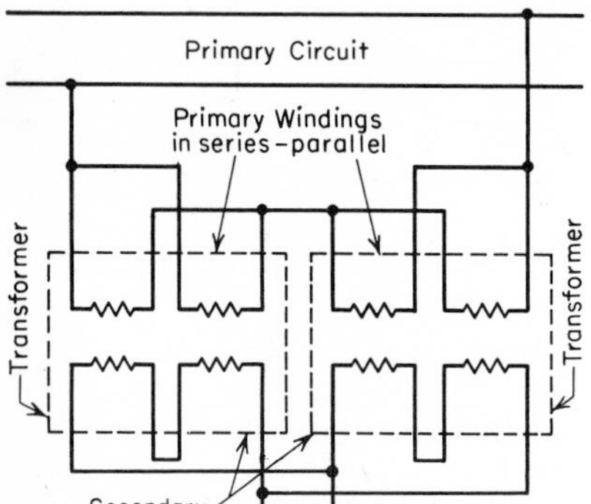

FIG. 69 *Connection for forcing parallel operation of transformers which have different impedance characteristics.*

115. Some three-phase transformers can be paralleled and some cannot (W. M. McConahey, *Electric Journal*). A transformer having its coils connected in delta on both high-tension and low-tension sides cannot be made to parallel with one connected either in delta on the high-tension and star on the low-tension or in star on the high-tension and in delta on the low-tension side. However, a transformer connected in delta on the high-tension and in star on the low-tension side can be made to parallel with transformers (having their coils joined in accordance with certain schemes) connected in star on the high-tension side and in delta on the low-tension side. Some three-phase transformers cannot be made to parallel (without changing the internal connection arrangement of their coils) with others using the same type of connections for the two windings. For example, a transformer connected delta to delta may have its coils so interconnected that it will not parallel with another transformer connected delta to delta. By changing the internal connections between the coils, however, it will be possible to bring out the terminals in such a way that parallel operation can be obtained.

116. How to Determine Whether or Not Three-phase Transformers Will Operate in Parallel. If the transformers are available, connect them as indicated in Fig. 70, leaving two leads on one of the transformers unjoined. Test with a voltmeter across the unjoined leads. If there is no voltage between E and e or between F and f of transformer 2, the polarities of the transformers are the same, the connections can be completed, and the transformers put in service.

If a voltage difference is found between E and e or between F and f or between both, the polarities of the transformers are not the same. Then connect transformer lead A successively to mains 1, 2, and 3 and at each connection test with the voltmeter between e and f and the legs of the main to which lead A is not connected. If with any trial connection the voltmeter readings between f and e and either of the two legs is found to be zero, the transformer will operate with leads f and e connected to those two legs. If no system of connections can be found that will satisfy this condition, the transformer will not operate in parallel without changes in its internal connections, and it may be that it will not operate in parallel at all (see Sec. 115).

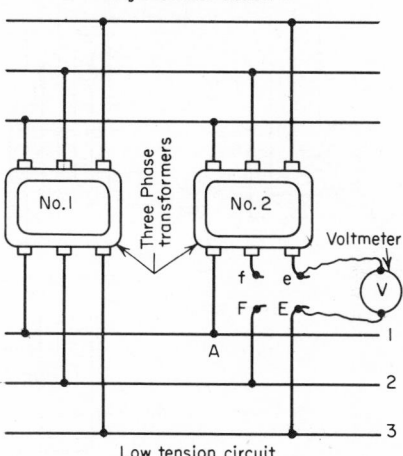

FIG. 70 *Testing three-phase transformers for parallel operation.*

CONNECTIONS AND APPLICATIONS OF AUTOTRANSFORMERS

117. Use of Autotransformers. The National Electrical Code allows the use of autotransformers for supplying interior wiring systems under certain conditions.

A branch circuit may be supplied through an autotransformer only if the system supplied has an identified grounded conductor which is solidly connected to a similar identified grounded conductor of the system supplying the autotransformer.

Autotransformers may be used as part of the ballast for lighting units. In these applications an autotransformer which raises the voltage to more than 300 volts shall be supplied only by a grounded system.

Autotransformers may be used as starting compensators for a-c motors. The compensator supplies a reduced voltage to the motor circuit while the machine is accelerating from rest. Ordinarily each autotransformer used for this purpose is provided with several taps so that a number of low voltages can be obtained.

118. A starting compensator arrangement for a two-phase induction motor ("Standard Handbook") is shown in Fig. 71. There are two transformers, the two separate phase lines being connected to the ends of the separate autotransformer windings. During the starting period the motor is connected between two of the ends and two intermediate taps. Figure 72 shows a starting compensator arrangement for a three-phase induction motor. The three autotransformer windings are Y-connected, and low-voltage points are permanently selected along each leg of the Y. It is not necessary to employ three autotransformers for starting a three-phase motor; two V-connected autotransformers are quite satisfactory for this purpose. Figure 73 shows two V-connected autotransformers for starting a three-phase induction motor and operating it at four different voltages.

119. The coils of a three-phase transformer can be connected for operation as an autotransformer equally as well as can those of a one-phase transformer. The interconnections would ordinarily be by the Y method, although the delta method or a combination of the Y and delta methods may be used. Figure 74 represents a Y connection for autotransformer operation.

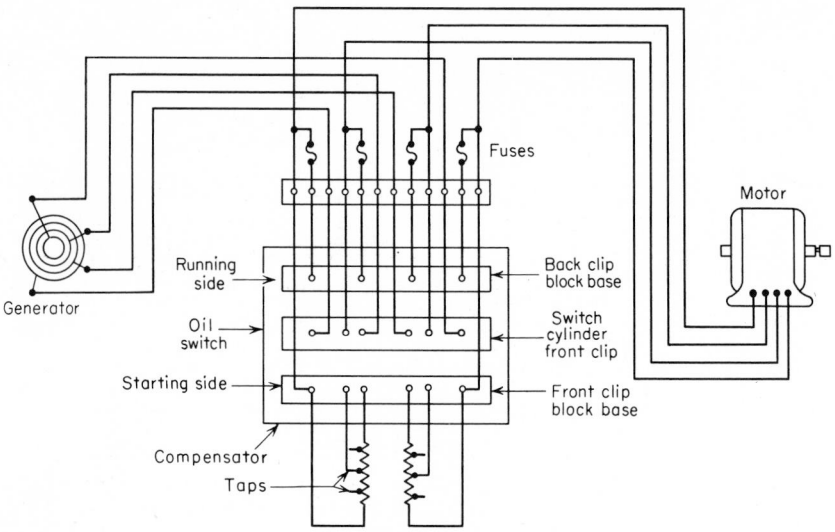

FIG. 71   *Two-phase starting compensator.*

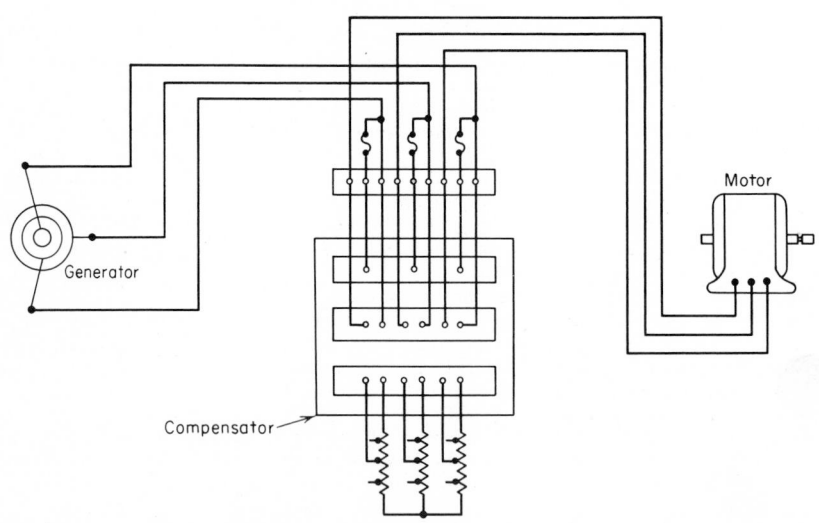

FIG. 72   *Three-phase starting compensator.*

INSTALLATION, CARE, AND OPERATION

120. The successful operation of transformers (Allis-Chalmers Manufacturing Co.) is dependent upon proper installation and operation as much as upon proper design and manufacture.   Although a transformer requires less care than almost any other type of electrical apparatus, neglect of certain fundamental requirements may lead to serious trouble, if not loss of the transformer.

121. The following sections (122 to 141) give the requirements of the National Electrical Code for the installation of transformers.   These rules have been taken directly

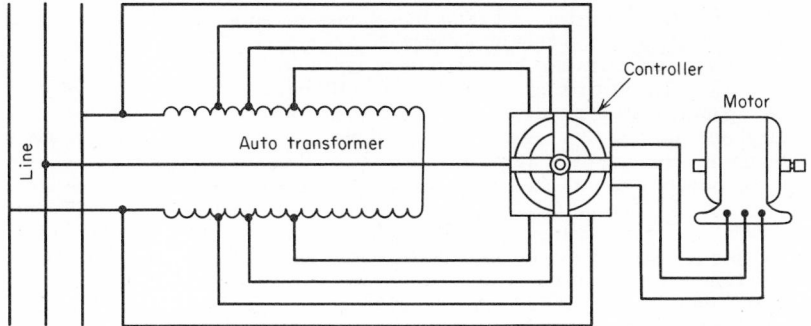

FIG. 73   *An autotransformer three-phase starting compensator.*

from the Code with only some slight rewording and change of section numbers. Where additional material has been added, it is indicated by being printed in italics.

122. Application.   This article applies to the installation of all transformers except (1) current transformers, (2) dry-type transformers which constitute a component part of other apparatus and which conform to the requirements for such apparatus, (3) transformers which are an integral part of an X-ray or high frequency apparatus, (4) transformers used with Class 1 low-voltage power circuits or Class 2 remote-control low-energy power and signal circuits which shall conform to art. 725 of the Code, (5) transformers for sign and outline lighting which shall conform to art. 600 of the Code, and (6) transformers for electric discharge lighting which shall conform to art. 410 of the Code.

This article of the Code applies to the installation of transformers in hazardous locations except as modified by art. 500 of the Code.

123. Location.   Transformers and transformer vaults shall be readily accessible to qualified personnel for inspection and maintenance.   The location of oil-insulated transformers and transformer vaults is covered in Secs. **132, 133,** and **134;** dry-type transformers in Sec. **130;** and askarel-insulated in Sec. **131.**

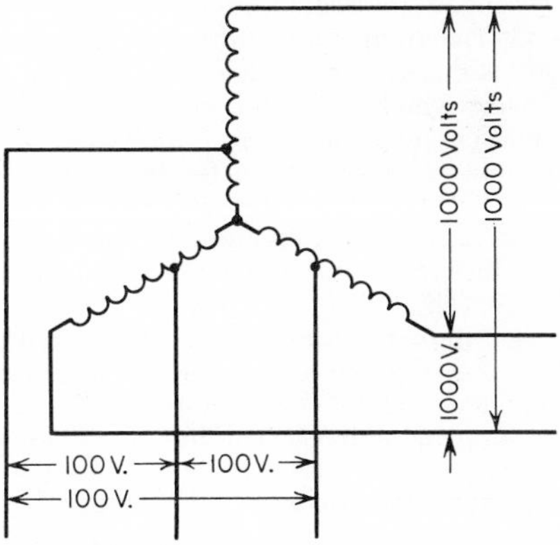

124. Overcurrent Protection.   Overcurrent protection shall conform to the following.   As used in this section, the word "transformer" means a transformer or a polyphase bank of two or three single-phase transformers operating as a unit.

FIG. 74   *Y-connected three-phase auto-transformer.*

A. PRIMARY SIDE.   Each transformer shall be protected by an individual overcurrent device in the primary connection, rated or set at not more than 250 per cent of the rated primary current of the transformer, except that an individual overcurrent device is not required if the primary circuit overcurrent device provides the protection specified in this paragraph and except as provided in paragraph B of this section.

B. PRIMARY AND SECONDARY SIDE.   A transformer having an overcurrent device in the secondary connection, rated or set at not more than 250 per cent of the rated secondary current of the transformer, or a transformer equipped with a coordinated thermal overload protection by the manufacturer is not required to have an individual overcurrent device in the primary connection, provided that the primary feeder overcurrent device is rated or set to open at a current value not more than six times the rated current of the transformers for transformers having not more than 6 per cent impedance and not more than four times rated current of the transformer for transformers having more than 6 but not more than 10 per cent impedance.

C. POTENTIAL (VOLTAGE) TRANSFORMERS. Potential transformers should have primary fuses. The fuse rating should not exceed 10 amp for circuits of 600 volts or less, and 3 amp for circuits of more than 600 volts. A resistor should be connected in series with high-tension fuses if necessary to limit the possible short-circuit current to a value within the interrupting capacity of the fuse.

125. Secondary Ties. As used in this section, the word "transformer" means a transformer or a bank of transformers operating as a unit. A secondary tie is a circuit operating at 600 volts or less between phases which connects two power sources or power-supply points, such as the secondaries of two transformers. The tie may consist of one or more conductors per phase.

A. TIE CIRCUITS. Tie circuits shall be provided at each end with overcurrent protection *according to the current-carrying capacity of the conductors,* except under the conditions described in subparagraphs A-1 and A-2 of this section, in which cases the overcurrent protection may be in accordance with subparagraph A-3 of this section.

1. *Loads at Transformer Supply Points Only.* If all loads are connected at the transformer supply points at each end of the tie and overcurrent protection is not provided, the rated current-carrying capacity of the tie shall be not less than 67 per cent of the rated secondary current of the largest transformer connected to the secondary tie system.

2. *Loads Connected between Transformer Supply Points.* If a load is connected to the tie at any point between transformer supply points and overcurrent protection is not provided, the rated current-carrying capacity of the tie shall be not less than 100 per cent of the rated secondary current of the largest transformer connected to the secondary tie system, except as otherwise provided in subparagraph A-4.

3. *Tie-circuit Protection.* Under the conditions described in subparagraphs A-1 and A-2 of this section, both ends of each tie conductor shall be equipped with a protective device which will open at a predetermined temperature of the tie conductor under short-circuit conditions. This protection shall consist of one of the following: (1) a fusible-link cable connector, terminal, or lug, commonly known as a limiter, each being of a size corresponding with that of the conductor and of approved construction and characteristics, according to the operating voltage and the type of insulation on the tie conductors, or (2) automatic circuit breakers actuated by devices having comparable current-time characteristics.

4. *Interconnection of Phase Conductors between Transformer Supply Points.* If the tie consists of more than one conductor per phase, the conductors of each phase shall be interconnected in order to establish a load supply point, and the protection specified in subparagraph A-3 shall be provided in each tie conductor at this point, except as follows:

Loads can be connected to the individual conductors of a multiple-conductor tie without interconnecting the conductors of each phase and without the protection specified in subparagraph A-3 at load connection points, provided: the tie conductors of each phase have a combined capacity not less than 133 per cent of the rated secondary current of the largest transformer connected to the secondary tie system; the total load of such taps does not exceed the rated secondary current of the largest transformer; the loads are equally divided on each phase and on the individual conductors of each phase as far as practicable.

5. *Tie-circuit Control.* If the operating voltage exceeds 150 volts to ground, secondary ties provided with limiters shall have a switch at each end which when open will de-energize the associated tie conductors and limiters. The current rating of the switch shall be not less than the rated current of the conductors connected to the switch. It shall be capable of opening its rated current, and it shall be constructed so that it will not open under the magnetic forces resulting from short-circuit current.

B. OVERCURRENT PROTECTION FOR SECONDARY CIRCUITS. When secondary ties are used an overcurrent device rated or set at not more than 250 per cent of the rated secondary current of the transformers shall be provided in the secondary connections of each transformer, and in addition an automatic circuit breaker actuated by a reverse-current relay set to open the circuit at not more than the rated secondary current of the transformer shall be provided in the secondary connection of each transformer.

126. Parallel Operation. Transformers can be operated in parallel and switched as a unit if the overcurrent protection for each transformer meets the requirements of Sec. **124.**

127. Guarding. Transformers shall be guarded as follows:

A. MECHANICAL PROTECTION. Appropriate provisions shall be made to minimize the possibility of damage to transformers from external causes if the transformers are located where they are exposed to physical damage.

B. CASE OR ENCLOSURE. Dry-type transformers shall be provided with a noncombustible moisture-resistant case or enclosure which will provide reasonable protection against the accidental insertion of foreign objects.

C. EXPOSED LIVE PARTS. The transformer installation shall conform with the Code provisions for Guarding of Live Parts.

D. VOLTAGE WARNING. The operating voltage of exposed live parts of transformer installations shall be indicated by signs or visible markings on the equipment or structures.

128. Grounding. Exposed non-current-carrying metal parts of transformer installations including fences, guards, etc., shall be grounded where required under the conditions and in the manner prescribed by the Code for electrical equipment and other exposed metal parts.

129. Marking. Each transformer shall be provided with a name plate giving the name of the manufacturer; rated kilovolt-amperes, frequency, primary and secondary voltage, and the amount and kind of insulating liquid, if any, if the transformer rating exceeds 25 kva. Where Class B insulation is used in the construction of dry-type transformers of more than 100 kva, the name plate shall indicate the temperature rise for this insulation system.

PROVISIONS FOR DIFFERENT TYPES OF TRANSFORMERS

130. Dry-type Transformers Installed Indoors. Transformers rated 112½ kva or less shall have a separation of at least 12 in. from combustible material unless separated therefrom by a fire-resistant heat-insulating barrier or unless of a rating not exceeding 600 volts and completely enclosed except for ventilating openings.

Transformers of more than 112½-kva rating shall be installed in a transformer room of fire-resistant construction unless they are constructed with Class B (80°C rise) insulation, or Class H (150°C rise) insulation, and are separated from combustible material not less than 6 ft horizontally and 12 ft vertically or are separated therefrom by a fire-resistant heat-insulating barrier.

Transformers rated more than 35,000 volts shall be installed in a vault.

131. Askarel-insulated Transformers Installed Indoors. Askarel-insulated transformers rated in excess of 25 kva shall be furnished with a pressure-relief vent. If installed in a poorly ventilated place, they shall be furnished with a means for absorbing any gases generated by arcing inside the case, or the pressure-relief vent shall be connected to a chimney or flue which will carry such gases outside the building. Askarel-insulated transformers rated more than 35,000 volts shall be installed in a vault.

132. Oil-insulated Transformers Installed Indoors. Oil-insulated transformers shall be installed in a vault constructed as specified in this article except as follows:

A. NOT OVER 112½-KVA TOTAL CAPACITY. The provisions for transformer vaults specified in this article apply except that the vault may be constructed of reinforced concrete not less than 4 in. thick.

B. NOT OVER 600 VOLTS. A vault is not required, provided suitable arrangements are made where necessary to prevent a transformer oil fire from igniting other materials and the total transformer capacity in one location does not exceed 10 kva in a section of the building classified as combustible or 75 kva in a section classified as fire-resistant.

C. ELECTRIC FURNACE TRANSFORMERS of a total rating not exceeding 75 kva may be installed without a vault in a building or room of fire-resistant construction if arrangements necessary to prevent a transformer oil fire from spreading to other combustible material are provided.

D. DETACHED BUILDINGS. Transformers may be installed in a building that does not conform with the Code provisions for transformer vaults provided that neither the building nor its contents presents a fire hazard to any other building or property and that the building is used only in supplying electric service and the interior is accessible only to qualified persons.

133. Oil-insulated Transformers Installed Outdoors. Combustible material, combustible buildings and parts of buildings, fire escapes, door and window openings shall be safeguarded from fires originating in oil-insulated transformers installed on, attached to, or adjacent to a building or combustible material. Space separations, fire resistant barriers, automatic water spray systems, and enclosures which confine the oil of a ruptured transformer are recognized safeguards. One or more of these safeguards shall be applied according to the degree of hazard involved in cases when the transformer installation presents a fire hazard. Oil enclosures may consist of fire-resistant dikes, curbed areas or basins, or trenches filled with coarse crushed stone. Oil enclosures shall be provided with trapped drains where the exposure and quantity of oil involved are such that removal of oil is important.

PROVISIONS FOR TRANSFORMER VAULTS

134. Location. Whenever practicable, vaults shall be located where they can be ventilated to the outside air without using flues or ducts.

135. Walls, Roof, and Floor. The walls and roofs of vaults shall be constructed of reinforced concrete, brick, load-bearing tile, concrete block, or other fire-resistive constructions which have adequate structural strength for the conditions, and a minimum fire resistance of 2½ hr according to ASTM Standard E119-67, Fire Tests of Building Construction and Materials (NFPA No. 251). The floors of vaults in contact with the earth shall be of concrete not less than 4 in. thick, but when the vault is constructed with a vacant space or other stories below it, the floor shall have adequate structural strength for the load imposed thereon and a minimum fire resistance of 2½ hr.

136. Doorways. Vault doorways shall be protected as follows:

A. TYPE OF DOOR. Each doorway leading into a building shall be provided with a tight-fitting door of a type approved for openings in Class A situations as defined in the NFPA Standard for the Installation of Fire Doors and Windows, No. 80 (National Fire Codes, Vol. 4). The authority enforcing this Code may require such a door for an exterior wall opening or on each side of an interior wall opening where conditions warrant.

B. SILLS. A door sill or curb of sufficient height to confine within the vault the oil from the largest transformer shall be provided, and in no case shall the height be less than 4 in.

C. LOCKS. Entrance doors shall be equipped with locks, and doors shall be kept locked, access being allowed only to qualified persons. Locks and latches shall be so arranged that the door may be readily and quickly opened from the inside.

137. Ventilation. The ventilation shall be adequate to prevent a transformer temperature in excess of the values prescribed in USAS C 57.1200-1965.

138. Ventilation Openings. When required by Sec. **137**, openings for ventilation shall be provided in accordance with the following:

A. LOCATION. Ventilation openings shall be located as far away as possible from doors, windows, fire excapes, and combustible material.

B. ARRANGEMENT. Vaults ventilated by natural circulation of air may have roughly half the total area of openings required for ventilation in one or more openings near the floor and the remainder in one or more openings in the roof or in the side walls near the roof, or all the area required for ventilation may be provided in one or more openings in or near the roof.

C. SIZE. In vaults ventilated to an outdoor area without using ducts or flues, the combined net area of all ventilating openings after deducting the area occupied by screens, gratings, or louvers shall be not less than 3 sq in. per kva of transformer capacity in service except that the net area shall be not less than 1 sq ft for any capacity under 50 kva.

D. COVERING. Ventilation openings shall be covered with durable gratings, screens, or louvers, according to the treatment required in order to avoid unsafe conditions.

E. DAMPERS. If automatic dampers are used in the ventilation openings of vaults containing oil-insulated transformers, the actuating device should be made to function at a temperature resulting from fire and not at a temperature which might prevail as a result of an overheated transformer or bank of transformers. Automatic dampers should be so designed and constructed as to minimize the possibility of accidental closing.

F. DUCTS. Ventilating ducts shall be constructed of fire-resistant material.

139. Drainage. Where practicable, vaults containing more than 100-kva transformer capacity shall be provided with a drain or other means which will carry off any accumulation of oil or water that may collect in the vault unless local conditions make this impracticable. The floor shall be pitched to the drain when provided.

140. Water Pipes and Accessories. Any pipe or duct systems foreign to the electrical installation should not enter or pass through a transformer vault. If the presence of such foreign systems cannot be avoided, appurtenances thereto which require maintenance at regular intervals shall not be located inside the vault. Arrangements shall be made if necessary to avoid possible trouble from condensation, leaks, and breaks in such foreign systems. Piping or other facilities provided for fire protection or for water-cooled transformers are not deemed to be foreign to the electrical installation.

141. Storage in Vaults. Materials shall not be stored in transformer vaults.

142. The following instructions (Secs. **143** to **166**) for procedure in installing, caring for, and operating transformers have been taken from National Electrical Manufacturers' Association Publication 37–46 and from Transformer Installation Book 5019A of the Allis-Chalmers Manufacturing Co. Except as noted the authority is the NEMA publication.

143. Location. Accessibility, ventilation, and ease of inspection should be given careful consideration in locating transformers.

Water-cooled transformers depend almost entirely upon the flow of water through the cooling coils for carrying away heat, so that the temperature of the surrounding air has little effect upon that of the transformers. For this reason air circulation is of minor importance, and water-cooled transformers can be located in any convenient place without regard to ventilation.

144. Self-cooled (dry-type) transformers depend upon surrounding air for carrying away their heat. For this reason care must be taken to provide adequate ventilation. For indoor installation the room in which the transformers are placed must be well ventilated so that heated air can escape readily and be replaced by cool air from outside. Inlet openings should be near floor level and distributed to be most effective. The outlet or outlets should be as high above the apparatus as construction of building will permit. The number and size of air outlets required will depend on their distance above the transformer and on the efficiency and load cycle of the apparatus. In general, about 20 sq ft of outlet opening or openings should be provided for each 1,000 kva of transformer capacity. Air inlets should be provided with the same total area as the outlets. If the transformer will be required to operate for considerable periods at continuous full load, the areas of the inlet and outlet openings should be increased to about 60 sq ft per 1,000 kva of transformer capacity.

145. Storage. When a transformer can be set up immediately in its permanent location and filled with oil, it is advisable to do so, even though it will not be put into service for some time. If this is not convenient, it should be stored in a dry place having no rapid or radical temperature changes and, if possible, filled with dry transformer oil. The transformer should not be stored or operated in the presence of corrosive gases such as chlorine, etc. If an indoor transformer is stored outdoors, it should be thoroughly covered to keep out rain.

146. Handling. When lifting a transformer, the lifting cables must be held apart by a spreader to avoid bending the lifting studs or other parts of the structure.

Where a transformer cannot be handled by a crane, it may be skidded or moved on rollers, but care must be taken not to damage the base or tip the transformer over. A transformer should never be lifted or moved by placing jacks or tackle under the drain valve, cooling-coil outlets, radiator connections, or other attachments. When rollers are used under large transformers, skids must be used to distribute the stress over the base.

When working about a transformer, particular care must be taken in handling all tools and other loose articles, since anything metallic dropped among the windings and allowed to remain there may cause a breakdown.

147. Inspection Preliminary to Installation. Transformers are in first-class operating condition when shipped by the manufacturer; i.e., they have been thoroughly tested for defects and are perfectly dry.

When received, examination should be made before removing from cars, and if any injury is evident or any indication of rough handling is visible, railroad claim should be filed at once and the manufacturer should be notified.

Moisture may condense on any metal if the metal is colder than the air, and if present, it lowers the dielectric strength and may cause a failure of the transformer. Therefore, if transformers or oil drums are brought into a room warmer than they are, they should be allowed to stand before opening until there is no condensation on the outside and they are thoroughly dry.

Before installation, each individual transformer should be thoroughly examined for indications of moisture and inspected for breakage, injury, or displacement of parts during shipment. In addition, all accessible nuts, bolts, and studs should be tightened if necessary. Before being placed in service, transformers having a plurality of voltage connections should be carefully checked to ensure that they are connected for operation at the required voltage and on the proper tap.

It is standard practice to ship transformers connected for their maximum voltage.

If transformers are water-cooled, the cooling coils should be tested for leaks at a pressure of 80 to 100 lb per sq in. Water, oil, or preferably air may be used in the coil for obtaining the pressure. The coil must be outside the tank, i.e., away from the winding insulation, if water is used for the pressure test. When pressure is obtained, the supply should be disconnected, and after 1 hr it should be determined whether any fall in pressure is due to a leak in the coil or to a leak in the fittings at the ends of the coil.

148. Transformers Shipped Filled with Oil. Each transformer shipped filled with oil should be inspected to see whether there is any condition indicating the entrance of moisture during shipment.

If the transformer is received in damaged condition, so that water or other foreign material has had a chance to enter the tank, the transformer should be emptied of oil and treated as though not shipped in oil, and in no case may drying be omitted.

In all cases samples of oil should be taken from the bottom and tested. The dielectric strength of the oil when shipped is at least 22 kv between 1-in. disks spaced 0.1 in. apart. A new transformer should not be put into service with oil which tests below this value.

149. Transformers Shipped Assembled without Oil. Each transformer shipped assembled but not filled with oil should be carefully inspected for damage in shipment. A thorough inspection can be made only by removing core and coils from the tank. All dirt should be wiped off and parts examined for breakage or other injuries. All conductors and terminals should be examined to check their proper condition and position. The coil and core clamps should be tightened if necessary.

The tank should be inspected and, if necessary, cleaned.

When a transformer is shipped assembled but not filled with oil, moisture may be absorbed during transportation. For this reason it is good practice to dry out all such transformers, especially transformers above 7,500 volts, before putting them into service.

150. Transformers Shipped Disassembled. Only very large transformers are shipped in this way, and special instructions covering features incident to this method of shipping are supplied by the manufacturer. These instructions should be carefully followed.

151. Drying Core and Coils. There are a number of approved methods of drying out transformer core and coils, any one of which will be satisfactory if carefully performed. However, too much stress cannot be laid upon the fact that, if carelessly or improperly performed, great damage may result to the transformer insulation through overheating.

The methods in use may be broadly divided into two classes:

1. Drying with the core and coils in the tank with oil.

2. Drying with the oil removed. The core and coils may or may not be removed from the tank.

152. Drying with Oil in Tank. Under the first class, the moisture is driven off by sending current through the winding while immersed in oil, with the top of the tank open to the air or with some other arrangement made for adequate ventilation. The current necessary for this class can be secured by the short-circuit method.

This method consists in heating the windings and oil up to a high temperature for a limited time under short circuit with a partial load on the windings, the high oil temperature being obtained by blanketing the tank (or reducing the flow of water for water-cooled transformers).

When a transformer is short-circuited in this manner, only a fraction of the normal voltage should be applied to one winding. When this method is used, the load current and maximum top-oil temperature should be in accordance with the following tabulation.

During the drying run, ventilation additional to that ordinarily provided should be maintained by slightly raising the manhole cover and protecting the opening from the weather. With good ventilation, the moisture, as it is driven off in the form of vapor, will escape to the outside atmosphere, and no condensation of moisture will take place on the underside of the cover or elsewhere, provided these parts are lagged with heat-insulating material to prevent condensation of moisture within.

The following table shows the short-circuit current in percentage of full-load current which can be used for this method of drying transformers, with the corresponding maximum allowable top-oil temperature in degrees centigrade. Less than 5 per cent of normal voltage will usually be required to circulate the current in the windings.

Self-cooled transformers	Water-cooled transformers	Maximum top-oil temperatures, °C
Short-circuit amp in percentage of full load		
50	50	85
75	60	80
85	75	75

These temperature limits and loads must be strictly adhered to in order to obtain the desired results without danger to the transformers.

It should be noted that the higher allowable temperatures go with the smaller loads; i.e., more blanketing or less water will be required for the smaller loads than for the higher, in order to bring the oil temperature up to the point shown in the table.

When to Discontinue Drying. Drying should be continued until oil from the top and bottom of the tank tests 22 kv or higher for seven consecutive tests taken 4 hr apart with the oil maintained at maximum temperature for the load held and without filtering. The testing of the oil for dielectric strength should be made between parallel 1-in.-diameter disks, spaced 1/10 in. apart. All ventilating openings should then be closed, the transformer kept at the same temperature for another 24 hr without filtering the oil, and as before the oil should be tested at 4-hr intervals. A decrease in the dielectric strength of the oil indicates that moisture is still passing from the transformer into the oil, and drying should be continued. The temperature of the oil samples when tested should preferably be at room temperature and not in excess of 40°C.

Unless constant or increasing dielectric strength as shown by these tests indicates that drying is completed, the ventilators should be opened, the oil filtered, and the drying process continued.

After the short-circuit run is discontinued, the transformer should be operated for 24 hr at approximately two-thirds voltage and at the same high temperature, similar tests of oil samples should be made, and the oil filtered if necessary. After satisfactory two-thirds-voltage test, full voltage should be applied for 24 hr and the same tests repeated. Water-cooled transformers may require some water to hold the top-oil temperature within the 85°C limit during this test.

153. Drying with Oil Removed. Typical of the second class, i.e., drying with the oil removed, are the three following methods:

1. By internal heat.
2. By external heat.
3. By internal and external heat.

1. BY INTERNAL HEAT. For this method alternating current is required. The transformer should be placed in its tank without the oil and with the cover left off to allow free circulation of air. Either winding can be short-circuited, and sufficient voltage should be impressed across the other winding to circulate enough current through the coils to maintain the temperature at from 75 to 80°C. About one-fifth of normal full rated current is generally sufficient to do this. The impressed voltage necessary to circulate this current varies within wide limits among different transformers but will generally be approximately one-half of 1 per cent to 1½ per cent of normal voltage, at normal frequency.

The end terminals of the winding must be used, not taps, so that current will circulate through the total winding. The amount of current can be controlled by a rheostat in series with the exciting winding. Proper precaution should be taken to protect the operator from dangerous voltage.

This method of drying out is superficial and slow and should be used only with small transformers and then only when local conditions prohibit the use of one of the other methods.

2. BY EXTERNAL HEAT. The transformer should be placed in a box with holes in the top and near the bottom to allow air circulation. The clearance between the sides of the transformer and the box should be small so that most of the heated air will pass up through the ventilating ducts among the coils and not around the sides. The heat should be applied at the bottom of the box. With some types of transformers it is better to distribute the heat evenly around the lower coils.

The best way to obtain the heat is from grid resistors, using either alternating or direct current. The temperature limits of ingoing air are 85 to 90°C. The transformer must be carefully protected against direct radiation from the heaters. Care must also be taken to see that there is no inflammable material near the heaters, and to this end it is advisable to line the wooden box completely with asbestos. Also, when forced air is used, suitable baffles should be placed between heater and inlet to the transformer enclosure.

Instead of the heater being placed inside the box containing the transformer, it can be placed outside, the heat being carried into the bottom of the box through a suitable pipe. Where this plan is followed, the heat may be generated by the direct combustion of gas, coal, or wood, provided that none of the products of combustion are allowed to enter the box containing the transformer. Heating by combustion is not advocated except when electric current is not available.

This method, although effective, requires a much longer time than method 3.

3. BY INTERNAL AND EXTERNAL HEAT. This is a combination of methods 1 and 2. The transformer should be placed in a box and external heat applied as in 2, and current circulated through the windings as in 1. The current should, of course, be considerably less than when no external heat is applied.

This method is used occasionally where direct current only is available, a certain amount of current being passed through the high-voltage winding only, as the cross-sectional area of the low-voltage conductor is generally too large for it to be heated with an economical amount of direct current. The use of direct current for drying out is not recommended except where alternating current cannot be obtained. When this method of drying is used, the temperature should be measured by the increase-in-resistance method.

Method 3 requires technically skilled supervision.

Time Required for Drying. There is no definite length of time for drying. Up to three weeks may be required, depending upon the condition of the transformer, the size, the voltage, and the method of drying used.

Insulation Resistance. The measurement or determination of insulation resistance is of value in determining the course of drying only when the transformer is without oil. If the initial insulation resistance is measured at ordinary temperatures, it may be high although the insulation is not dry, but as the transformer is heated up, it will drop rapidly.

As the drying proceeds at a constant temperature, the insulation resistance will generally increase gradually until toward the end of the drying period, when the increase will become more rapid. Sometimes the resistance will rise and fall through a short range one or more times before reaching a steady high point. This is caused by moisture in the interior parts of the insulation working its way out through the outer portions which were dried at first.

As the temperature varies, the insulation resistance also varies greatly; therefore the temperature should be kept nearly constant, and the resistance measurements should all be taken at as nearly the same temperature as possible. The insulation resistance in megohms varies inversely with the temperature, and, for a 10°C change of temperature, the megohms change by a ratio of 2:1. Measurements should be taken every 2 hr during the drying period.

Resistance Curve. A curve of the insulation-resistance measurements should be plotted with time as abscissa and resistance as ordinate. By observation, the knee of the curve (i.e., the point where the insulation resistance begins to increase more rapidly) can be determined, and the run should continue until the resistance is constant for 12 hr.

The Allis-Chalmers Manufacturing Co. further recommends that the insulation resistance should be as great as or greater than that given by the following formula and that the megohm resistance should be taken with all windings grounded except the one being tested.

Megohms at 85°C in air or at 40°C in oil are equal to

$$\frac{kv \times 30}{\sqrt{kva/cycles}}$$

where kv = kilovolts of winding involved and kva = kilovolt-amperes of transformer per phase.

The megohms vary inversely with the temperature, and for a 10°C change of temperature the megohms change in the ratio of 2:1. For example,

$$
\begin{aligned}
\text{Megohms at } 85°C &= 300 \\
\text{Megohms at } 75°C &= 600 \\
\text{Megohms at } 65°C &= 1{,}200 \\
\text{Megohms at } 55°C &= 2{,}400
\end{aligned}
$$

154. Precautions to Be Observed in Drying without Oil. As the drying temperature approaches the point where fibrous materials deteriorate, great care must be taken to see that there are no points where the temperature exceeds 85°C. Several thermometers should be used, and they should be placed well in among the coils near the top and screened from air currents. Ventilating ducts offer particularly good places in which to place some of the thermometers. As the temperature rises rapidly at first, the thermometers must be read at intervals of about ½ hr. In order to keep the transformer at a constant temperature for insulation-resistance measurements, one thermometer should be placed where it can be read without removing it or changing its position. The other thermometers should be shifted about until the hottest points are found and should remain at these points throughout the drying period. Wherever possible, the temperature should be checked by the increase-in-resistance method.

155. Caution in Drying Out. It is well to have a chemical fire extinguisher or a supply of sand at hand for use in case of necessity.

It is not safe to attempt the drying out of transformers without giving them constant attention.

156. Sampling and Testing of Oil. The sample container should be a large-mouthed glass bottle. All bottles should be cleaned and dried with gasoline before being used. A cork stopper should be used.

The sample for dielectric tests should be at least 16 oz; if other tests are to be made, 1 qt (32 oz).

Test samples should be taken only after the oil has settled for some time, varying from 8 hr for a barrel to several days for a large transformer. Cold oil is much slower in settling and may hardly settle at all. Oil samples from the transformer should be taken from the oil-sampling valve at the bottom of the tank. Oil samples from a barrel should be taken from the bottom of the drum. A brass or glass "thief" can be conveniently used for this purpose. The same method should be used for cleaning the "thief" as is used for cleaning the container.

When samples of oil are drawn from the bottom of the transformer or large tank, sufficient oil must first be drawn off to make sure that the sample will be comprised of oil from the bottom of the container and not from the oil stored in the sampling pipe. A glass receptacle is desirable so that, if water is present, it can be readily observed. If water is found, an investigation of the cause should be made and a remedy applied. If water is not present in sufficient quantity to settle out, the oil may still contain considerable moisture in a suspended state. It should, therefore, be tested for dielectric strength.

For testing oil for dielectric strength, some standard device for oil testing should be used. The standard oil-testing spark gap has disk terminals 1 in. in diameter spaced 0.1 in. apart. The testing cup should be cleaned thoroughly, to remove any particles of cotton fiber, and rinsed out with a portion of the oil to be tested.

The spark-gap receptacle should be filled with oil, both oil and spark gap being at room temperature or approximately 25°C. After filling the receptacle, allow ½ to 1 min for air bubbles to escape before applying voltage.

The rate of increase in voltage should be about 3,000 volts per sec. Five breakdowns should be made on each filling, and then the receptacle emptied and refilled with fresh oil from the original sample. The average voltage of 15 tests (5 tests on each of three fillings) is usually taken as the dielectric strength of the oil. It is recommended that the test be continued until the mean of the averages of at least three fillings is consistent.

The dielectric strength of oil when shipped is at least 22 kv tested in the standard gap. If the dielectric strength of the oil in a transformer in service tests at less than 17,500 volts, it should be filtered. New oil of less than the standard dielectric strength should not be put in a transformer.

157. Drying Oil and Filling Transformer. In removing moisture from transformer oil, it is preferable to filter from one tank and discharge into another, although if necessary it may be drawn from the bottom of a tank and discharged at the top. When there is much water in the oil, it should be allowed to settle and then be drawn off and treated separately.

Before the transformer is filled with oil, all accessories, such as valves, gages, thermometers, plugs, etc., must be fitted to the transformer and made oiltight. The threads should be filled in accordance with instructions from the manufacturer before putting them in place. The transformers must be thoroughly cleaned.

Metal hose must be used for filling instead of rubber hose, because oil dissolves the sulfur found in rubber and may cause trouble if the sulfur attacks the copper.

The oil used should be clean, dry oil of the grade recommended by the manufacturer.

The use of a filter press is recommended, and if one is not available, some precaution should be taken to strain the oil before putting it in the transformer.

After filling the transformer, the oil should be allowed to settle at least 12 hr, and then samples taken from the bottom should again be tested before voltage is applied to the transformer.

It is very important that the surfaces of the oil when cold (25°C) be at the oil level indicated by the mark on the oil gage. When the transformer is not in service, the oil level must never be allowed to fall to a point where it does not show in the gage. When it is necessary to replenish the oil, care must be taken to see that no moisture finds its way into the tank. As the oil heats up with the transformer under load, it will expand and rise to a higher level.

158. Putting into Service. When the voltage is first applied to the transformer, it should, if possible, be brought up slowly to its full value so that any wrong connection or other trouble can be discovered before damage results. After full voltage has been applied successfully, the transformer should preferably be operated in that way for a short period without load. It should be kept under observation during this time and also during the first few hours that it delivers load. After 4 or 5 days' service it is advisable to test the oil again for moisture.

If the transformer is water-cooled the main water valve should be opened as soon as the oil temperature reaches 45°C. If there are two or more sets of cooling coils in parallel, the valves of all sections should be adjusted for equal rates of flow. This can be estimated by feeling the weight of the discharge streams from the different sections. It can be determined best, however, by noting the difference in temperature between ingoing and outgoing water from each section. A careful measure should be taken of the total amount of water flowing through all sections, and the total rate of flow should be adjusted to a value not less than that specified.

159. Care. The idea that a transformer in service needs no attention may lead to serious results. Careful inspection is essential, and the directions given in this section should be followed.

In spite of all precautions, moisture may be absorbed by the transformer if it is of the open type, and during the first few days of operation it is well to inspect the inside of the manhole cover for moisture. If sufficient moisture has condensed to drip from the cover, the transformer should be taken out of service and dried. The oil should be tested and dried if necessary.

Closed-type transformers should have their oil tested at top and bottom after the first few days of operation to make sure that no moisture is being given off from the transformer into the oil.

Samples of oil from all transformers should be drawn and tested at least once every 6 months or according to the manufacturer's recommendations.

During the first month of service of transformers having a potential of 40,000 volts or over, samples of oil should be drawn each week from the bottom of the tank and tested. If at any time the oil should test below 17,500 volts, it should be filtered.

Closed-type transformers when properly dried out and installed will need thorough inspection only infrequently, i.e., only when there are specific indications of trouble. Other types of transformers should be taken out of service periodically for a thorough inspection. The inside of the cover and the tank above the oil should be regularly inspected to see that they are clean, dry, and free from moisture and that the thermometer bulb is clean. If an appreciable amount of dirt or sediment is found inside the case, it is best to untank the transformer and remove the oil from the tank. The transformer and the tank should then be cleaned thoroughly and the oil filtered and tested. In cleaning, only dry cloths or waste should be used. Care should be taken to see that all nuts are tight and that all parts are in their proper places. If the transformer is water-cooled, the cooling coils should be cleaned thoroughly. The transformer and the oil should be replaced in the tank, and when the cover is put on, all cracks and openings should be closed tightly.

In the case of water-cooled transformers the rate of flow should be checked from time to time, and if it is found to have diminished, the cause should be looked for and remedied. The most frequent cause of clogging of cooling coils is the presence of air in the water, resulting in the formation of a scaly oxide.

160. Removing Scale from Cooling Coils. Scale and sediment can be removed from a cooling coil without removing the coil from the tank. Both inlet and outlet pipes should be disconnected from the water system and temporarily piped to a point a number of feet away from the transformer, where the coil can be filled and emptied safely. Especial care must be taken to prevent any acid, dirt, or water from getting into the transformer.

All the water should be blown or siphoned from the cooling coils, which should then be filled with a solution of hydrochloric (muriatic) acid—specific gravity, 1.10. (Equal parts of commercially pure concentrated hydrochloric acid and water will give this specific gravity.)

It may be found necessary to force this solution into the cooling coils. When this is done, one end of the coil should be partially restricted, so that the solution will not be wasted when the coil is full. After the solution has stood in the coil about 1 hr, the coil should be flushed out thoroughly with clean water. If all the scale is not removed the first time, the operation should be repeated until the coil is clean, using new solution each time. The number of times it is necessary to repeat the process will depend on the condition of the coil, though ordinarily one or two fillings will be sufficient.

As the chemical action which takes place may be very violent and may often force acid, sediment, etc., from both ends of the coil, it is well to leave both ends partially open to prevent abnormal pressure.

161. Idle Cooling Coils. When a water-cooled transformer is idle and exposed to freezing temperatures, the water must be blown out of the cooling coil. In addition to blowing out the water, the cooling coils should be dried by forcing heated air through them. If it is not convenient to do this, the coil should be filled with transformer oil.

162. Stopping Oil Leaks (Allis-Chalmers Manufacturing Co.). Oil leaks at gasketed joints can often be stopped by tightening the bolts, but if this is not effective, new gaskets must be installed. Special cork is available for this purpose. An adhesive such as shellac, Bakelite varnish, or other suitable material should be used.

Oil leaks at welds can be stopped by peening, soldering, or welding. Peening is often effective for small stains, and soldering alone or a combination of peening and soldering will usually be effective with larger leaks. For this purpose a hard solder having a high melting point (about 365°F) can be used.

Leaks which cannot be stopped by any of these methods must be welded. When transformer tanks are welded with the core and coils in place, the oil should not be removed.

163. Operation (General). An artificially cooled transformer should not be run continuously, even at no load, without the cooling medium. Therefore, it is essential to maintain a proper circulation in the cooling system.

If the water circulation in a water-cooled transformer is stopped for any reason, the load should be immediately reduced as much as possible and close watch kept of the temperature of the transformer. When the oil at the top of the tank reaches 80°C, the transformer must be cut out of service at once. This temperature should be recognized as an absolute limit and must not be exceeded. It should be held only during an emergency period of short duration.

Nearly all cooling water will in time cause scale or sediment to form in the cooling coil. The time required to clog up the cooling coils depends on the nature and amount of foreign matter in the water. The clogging materially decreases the efficiency of the coil and is indicated by a high oil temperature and a decreased flow of water, load condition and water pressure remaining the same.

164. Temperature. Thermometers should be read daily or more often. If, at rated load or less, the oil temperature reaches 80°C for an oil-immersed, self-cooled transformer or an oil-immersed, forced-air-cooled transformer or 65°C for an oil-immersed, water-cooled transformer, it is advisable to check operating conditions.

Oil-immersed, self-cooled transformers or oil-immersed, forced-air-cooled transformers should not be operated for long periods of time at oil temperatures in excess of 80°C on account of increased rate of deterioration of the insulations. The oil temperature in these transformers should not be allowed to exceed 90°C even for short periods of time.

If the oil temperature in oil-immersed, water-cooled transformers should exceed 65°C at rated load or less, the cooling coils need cleaning, an insufficient amount of cooling water is being used, or the temperature of the cooling water is higher than 25°C. The oil temperature in oil-immersed, water-cooled transformers should not be allowed to exceed 75°C even for short periods of time. A lower oil temperature is recommended for oil-immersed, water-cooled transformers on account of the greater difference between the temperatures of the windings and of the oil than in oil-immersed, self-cooled transformers.

Regardless of oil temperatures as indicated by thermometers, transformers should not be operated continuously at overloads in excess of 1 per cent for each degree that the ambient is below 30°C for air and 25°C for water. In no case should the overload exceed 30 per cent for self-cooled transformers and 25 per cent for water-cooled transformers unless stipulated by the specification or contract. During overloads the transformer should be watched with special care.

Moisture may get into an open-type transformer owing to the fact that as oil is heated and cooled, it expands and contracts, causing air to be expelled from and drawn into the transformer. If the air which enters the transformer is at the same time cooled by contact with the cover to below its dew point, moisture will condense.

It is therefore good practice to operate transformers at several degrees above air temperatures at all times. This will largely prevent condensation.

165. Recommendations Relative to Pole-mounted Transformers. Pole Mounting. Convenient lugs or eyebolts are provided on the side of the case to which the rope lifting the transformer may be attached. It will be found convenient to fasten the hanger irons to the case before the transformer is raised to the crossarm. The transformer can then be raised up to and slightly above the crossarm, and the hooks on the hanger irons can then be made to engage the crossarm by lowering the transformer.

Pole-mounted transformers may be filled with oil either before or after mounting, as desired. It is sometimes necessary to add oil a short time after the transformer has been installed, owing to the fact that the insulation will absorb a certain amount of oil. It may be found necessary to replenish the oil from time to time during actual operation in order that the normal oil level be kept constant. When the transformer oil is replenished, care should be taken that no moisture finds its way inside the case.

Replacing the Cover. Great care should be exercised in putting on the cover. If the gasket is not properly in place or the cover not securely bolted to the case, moisture in the form of snow or rain may be driven into the transformer tank.

It is very important that the surface of the oil when cold (25°C) be at the oil level indicated on the inside of the tank or on the oil gage.

The following practice is recommended for the care of pole-mounted distribution transformers in service:

1. The oil level should be inspected once every year, and enough oil added to bring the level up to the mark inside the tank or on the oil gage.

2. Periodically the condition of the oil should be inspected, and if necessary the oil should be removed and replaced with good clean oil.

3. A periodic check of the load should be made to make sure a transformer is not being overloaded.

166. Care and operation of transformers immersed in nonflammable, nonexplosive liquids are, in general, the same as for those which are oil-immersed. The liquid may be dehydrated and filtered by means of special equipment designed for the purpose. Regular oil-filtering equipment cannot be used. The same great care with respect to moisture must be taken with these transformers as with the regular types. The transformer cover should not be taken off in a manhole.

Precaution should be taken in handling the liquid, as it has an irritating effect upon the skin, more so to some persons than others. Especially the eyes, nose, and lips are affected when coming in contact with the liquid, and safety precautions must be observed when handling it.

When handling the liquid or working on a transformer filled with the liquid, an application of castor oil is recommended for the eyes and castor oil or cold cream for the nose and lips. In case the liquid comes in contact with the skin, the part should be thoroughly washed and cleaned.

A person should be careful about looking down into the transformer case, as the liquid gives off a gas at 80°C which causes irritation to eyelids, nostrils, and lips. When working around one of these transformers the hands should be coated with grease and the eyes, nose, and lips protected as advised above.

THE NOISE PROBLEM

167. Transformer Noise. Transformers create noise when energized. Actually, the noise is a characteristic hum that is generated by vibrations in the laminated core structure. This hum has a fundamental frequency about twice that of the applied frequency. Its relative loudness to the ear is a function of transformer design and construction characteristics, the ambient noise level of the area where it is located, and the manner in which it is installed. In some applications, such as factories, transformer noise is "masked" by the higher level of surrounding noise, and it poses no problem. In low-noise-level or quiet areas (hospitals, schools, libraries, apartment buildings, office interiors, churches, etc.) transformer hum can be quite objectionable and cause serious concern. In fact, this has become such an application problem that manufacturers improved transformer design and construction, so that they now provide low-noise-level standard units and give them a definite sound rating in decibels.

168. Selection. The decibel (db), a unit of measure of sound level, has become a key factor in the selection and installation of transformers in areas where noise considerations are important. The following table of average ambient noise levels in common installation areas is the starting point:

Area	Average Sound Level, decibels
Average home	30–45
Retail store	45–55
Office area (without machines)	45–70
Office area (with machines)	50–75
Average factory	75–95

To facilitate comparison, transformer manufacturers publish the sound-level ratings (in decibels) of their units as determined by prescribed standard test procedures.

169. Typical ratings are listed in the following table:

Transformer Rating, kva	Average Sound Level, decibels
0– 9	40
10– 50	45
51–150	50
151–300	55
301–500	60

The tables in Secs. **168** and **169** comprise a handy reference when audible noise considerations are a factor in transformer applications. It is a simple matter of comparing transformer noise with ambient noise. Knowing the average ambient sound level of the installation area, one can select a transformer with the proper sound rating (from the table or manufacturer's data). A basic selection rule is to choose a transformer with a decibel rating lower than the average decibel level of the area in question. Otherwise, the installed results might be disappointing.

One point must be kept in mind. The sound level of a specific transformer, measured and recorded under established test conditions at the factory, may be quite different after the unit is installed. Because of location, mechanical, and/or acoustical conditions, and mounting methods, the audible sound level may be considerably higher. The ultimate objective must be to keep the "job-installed noise level" of the unit below the area ambient noise level.

170. Carefully check the sound-level ratings of standard transformers, particularly where applications are to be made in areas of medium and low ambient levels. Where ambient noise will be considerably higher than the transformer decibel ratings in the table in Sec. **169,** there should be no problem. Where the spread between transformer and ambient noise is not so great, careful attention must be given to installation. Often, the combination of a sufficiently quiet standard unit and recognized noise-attenuating mounting methods will resolve the problem. However, where audible noise in specific areas is especially critical, it may be necessary to order special quiet-type transformers from the factory.

171. Noise Attenuation. The manner in which a transformer is located and installed has a definite bearing on the over-all audible noise level in the area. If the unit is mounted in such a way that the noise vibrations are transmitted to a large vibrating surface—such as sheet metal or wood—the sound can be amplified to a higher level than the unit's decibel rating. Similar amplification occurs when the unit is located in the corner of a room or close to large reflecting surfaces which act like a megaphone and give the transformer hum an acoustical level boost. In some cases of poor mounting, a special quiet-type transformer can produce a louder sound output than that of a carefully mounted standard transformer.

Some experts claim that improper location and installation can increase transformer sound levels from 10 to 20 db. Such a condition might easily become intolerable because a three-decibel increase in sound level reportedly has the effect of almost doubling the sound volume as detected by the human ear.

172. There are a number of basic installation precautions and mounting techniques which, if carefully noted and followed, will minimize the audible sound level of energized transformers. Some of the major considerations are:

1. PROPER LOCATION is the first consideration in a low-sound-level installation. To keep within, or below, prescribed area decibel limits:

a. Keep the transformer as far away as possible from the area in which its noise would be most objectionable.

b. Avoid mounting the unit in a room corner up near the ceiling. Three-sided corners act as megaphones and amplify the sound.

c. Avoid installations in narrow halls and corridors or in corners of stairwells. The transformer sound reflected from the walls can become additive to the primary sound of the transformer and cause additional decibel buildup.

d. Where feasible, experimental temporary operation and positioning of a free-standing transformer in a room or area will quickly indicate the best location and orientation of the unit.

e. Where necessary, cover the walls of the transformer room with acoustical dampening material—fiber glass, acoustical tile, or similar absorbent materials—to reduce propagation of transformer noise from the room to any adjacent areas. It should be noted, however, that such material has a major effect on the high harmonics of transformer noise but little, if any, effect on the fundamental hum. Although there are special sound insulating materials available for the 120-cycle frequency range, their present form and cost make them impractical for the above application.

2. TRANSFORMER MOUNTING methods play an important role in control and reduction of the audible sound coming from the unit. The prime objective is to "isolate" the noise—that is, prevent its mechanical transmission to the supporting structure and connected raceway system. This can be accomplished with one or a combination of the following installation techniques:

a. Use solid mounting when the transformer can be secured to a heavy, solid mass which cannot vibrate audibly. Such would be reinforced concrete—floor or wall.

b. For installation on a structural frame, wall, ceiling, or column, use the flexible-mounting technique, employing special vibration isolating pads called "flexible mounts" or vibration dampeners. There must be no solid metal contact between the transformer and supporting surface; otherwise the vibration of the pads would be "short-circuited." These external pads are furnished and installed by the installer. Internal vibration dampeners between the core-coil assembly and enclosure are or can be furnished by the manufacturer.

c. Use flexible connections between the raceway system and the transformer enclosure to prevent transmission of noise vibrations from the enclosure to the raceway system, panels, and other mechanical parts. Flexible metal conduit and liquidtight flexible metal conduit are frequently used for these relatively short coupling sections.

POLE AND PLATFORM MOUNTING

173. Mounting Distributing Transformers. Units of the smaller capacities are supported either directly on the poles or on crossarms in accordance with instructions furnished by their manufacturers. Refer to Sec. **40** and Figs. 23 to 28 for details of transformer mounting lugs, adapter plates, crossarm hangers, etc.

With some of the newer transformer designs single transformers up to 167 kva can be mounted satisfactorily directly on a pole (Fig. 75). Three 50-kva transformers of the proper design can be safely supported from the crossarm on a single pole (Fig. 76). In crossarm mounting of transformers Gear and Williams recommend that, for transformers of capacities larger than 20 kva, double crossarms should be used at the top, as the top arms carry most of the weight. "Where the installation consists of three

15-kva or larger transformers it is advisable to use a larger sized crossarm than the standard. An arm having a cross section of 4 by 5½ in. has been found ample for installations aggregating 90 to 100 kva."

FIG. 75 A 167-kva transformer mounted directly on a pole. (Line Material Industries.)

"Where a large amount of power is needed which requires a number of 50-kva units which cannot be conveniently installed inside the building, they can be safely and conveniently installed on a platform between two or more poles as shown in Fig. 77." A platform for supporting three 50-kva units can be built by bolting in gains, between two poles, two 3- by 10-in. planks and nailing to them a floor of 2-in. plank. Three 167-kva transformers are shown in Fig. 78 mounted on a two-pole structure for supplying power to a building.

174. Methods of Crossarm and Platform Mounting of Transformers. The methods of mounting transformers described and illustrated in the following paragraphs were taken from a "Report of the Committee on Overhead Line Construction" of the Pennsylvania Electric Association. The practices outlined were those followed by the Allegheny County Light Co. The methods provide ample clearances for linemen climbing the poles and assure that the wiring will remain in place and not give trouble from short circuits. Platforms are recommended for supporting the larger transformers because of the accessibility for repairs or replacements that they provide.

175. Crossarm Method of Mounting Single Transformers of from 1- to 4-kva Capacity. The transformer should be supported by the iron hangers furnished by the manufacturer and hung at the central point on the crossarm and not out on the arm away from the pole. At the bottom of the hanger a section of an arm, not longer than the diameter of the pole, should be fastened to the pole with two lag bolts. The transformer can be hung on the bottom arm, if one is in place and supports lines, provided this arm is in the second gain or a lower one. The primary mains feeding the transformer should be on an upper arm.

FIG. 76 Three 50-kva transformers supported from crossarms on a single pole. (Line Material Industries.)

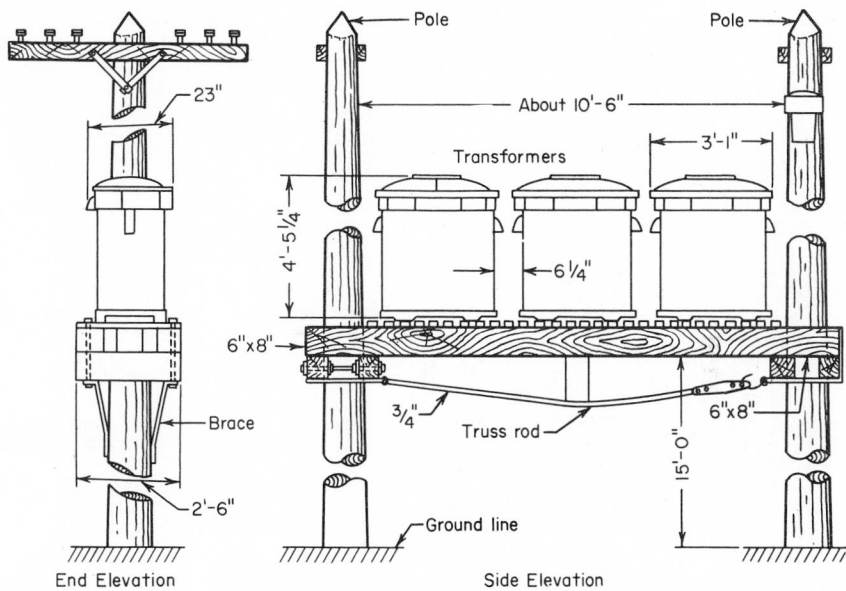

FIG. 77 *Platform for large transformers.*

In installations where the transformers are more than 4 ft below the arm supporting the primary mains, it is advisable to mount Western Union pins horizontally in the line arms. On these pins the primary wires can be tied to maintain them rigid. Iron pins should also be mounted in the transformer arm to take the stress imposed on the primary conductors by the fuse terminal screws.

176. Method of Mounting Transformers of from 5- to 10-kva Capacity (Fig. 79). The same rules should be followed as outlined in the preceding paragraph with the following additions: The transformers, on account of their increased weight and dimensions, should not be hung on a line arm. A specially placed arm should be used

FIG. 78 *Three 167-kva transformers supported from a two-pole structure.* (*Line Material Industries.*)

underneath existing arms and other apparatus. In addition to using the regular hangers which accompany transformers, a pair of iron braces 24 by 2 by ¼ in. should be placed between the transformer lugs and the hanger with the hanger bolts passing through one of the holes in the braces. These braces are to be run in an upward direction and fastened to the pole with a standard through bolt (see Fig. 79). If the arm weakens or entirely rots away, these two braces are of sufficient strength to support the transformer and permit crossarm replacement.

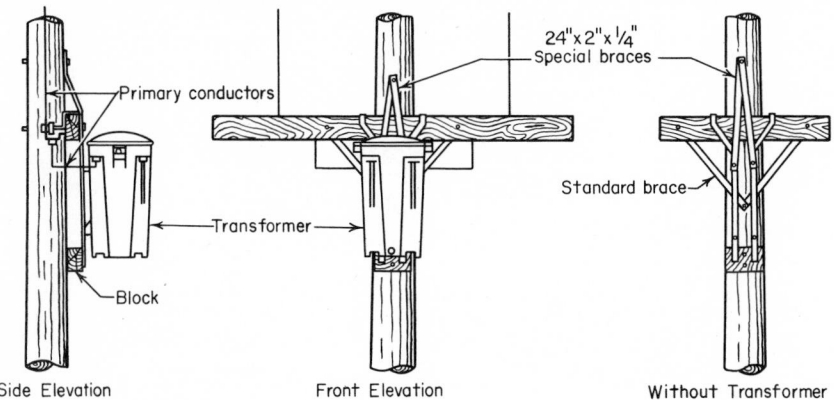

Side Elevation   Front Elevation   Without Transformer

FIG. 79   *Method of supporting a 5- to 10-kva transformer.*

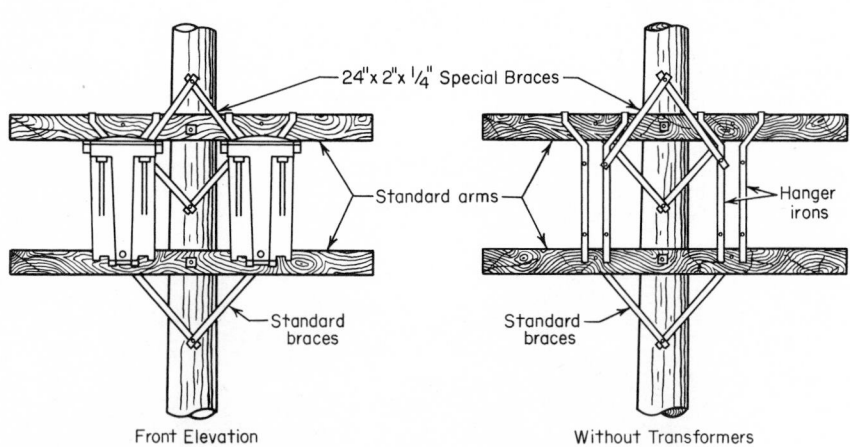

Front Elevation   Without Transformers

FIG. 80   *Method of supporting two 5-kva or two 10-kva transformers.*

177. Method of Mounting Two 5-kva or Two 10-kva Transformers (Fig. 80). Construction similar to that described above should be used except that a standard arm should be placed at the bottom on which the hanger irons can rest. Also only one special brace (24 by 2 by ¼ in.) per transformer should be placed between the lug and hanger iron next to the pole.

178. Method of Mounting Three 5-kva Transformers (Fig. 81). The construction should be similar to that outlined in the preceding paragraphs, except that the special braces supporting the outside transformers are 33 in. between centers of holes. It is also advisable to place an additional crossarm on the rear side of the pole. This arm braces the front arm and provides a place where fuse blocks can be mounted.

179. Method of Mounting Three 10-kva Transformers (Figs. 82 and 83). The con-

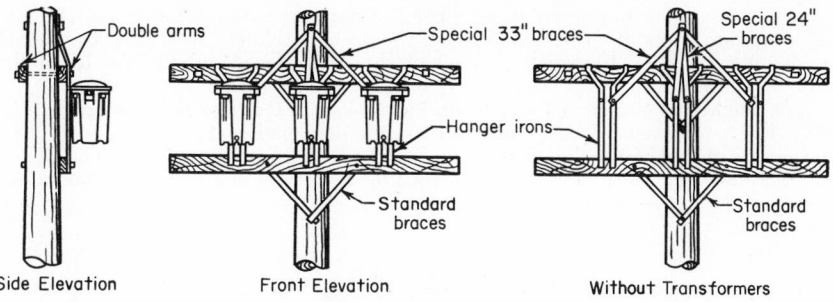

FIG. 81 *Method of supporting three 5-kva transformers.*

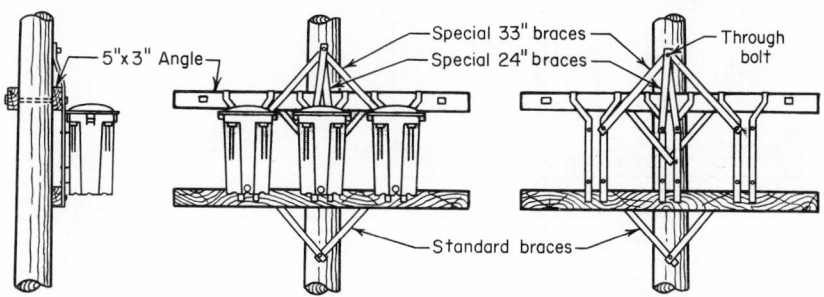

FIG. 82 *Method of supporting three 10-kva transformers.*

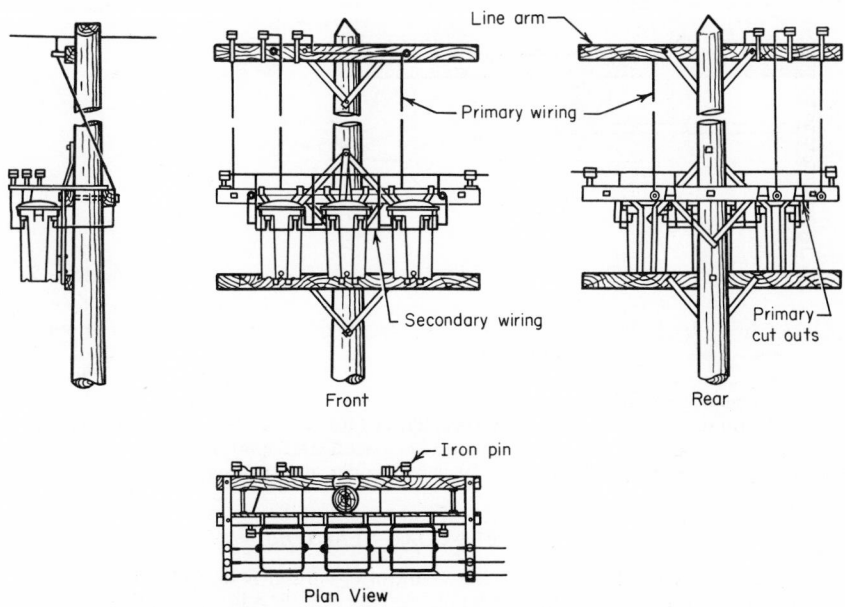

FIG. 83 *Wiring for three 5-kva or for three 10-kva transformers.*

struction is similar to that for three 5-kva transformers with the following addition: The top arm supporting the transformers should be reinforced over its entire length with a piece of 5- by 3-in. angle iron, which should be placed with the 3-in. leg on the top of the arm.

180. Method of Mounting Two 20-kva, Two 30-kva, or One 50-kva Transformer (Fig. 84). For transformers of these capacities a single-pole platform is recommended. The beams for the platform should be 4-in. by 6-lb channel iron 8 ft long. The braces used are a single piece of angle iron 3 by 3 by ⅜ in. bent in a V shape. Pine or oak

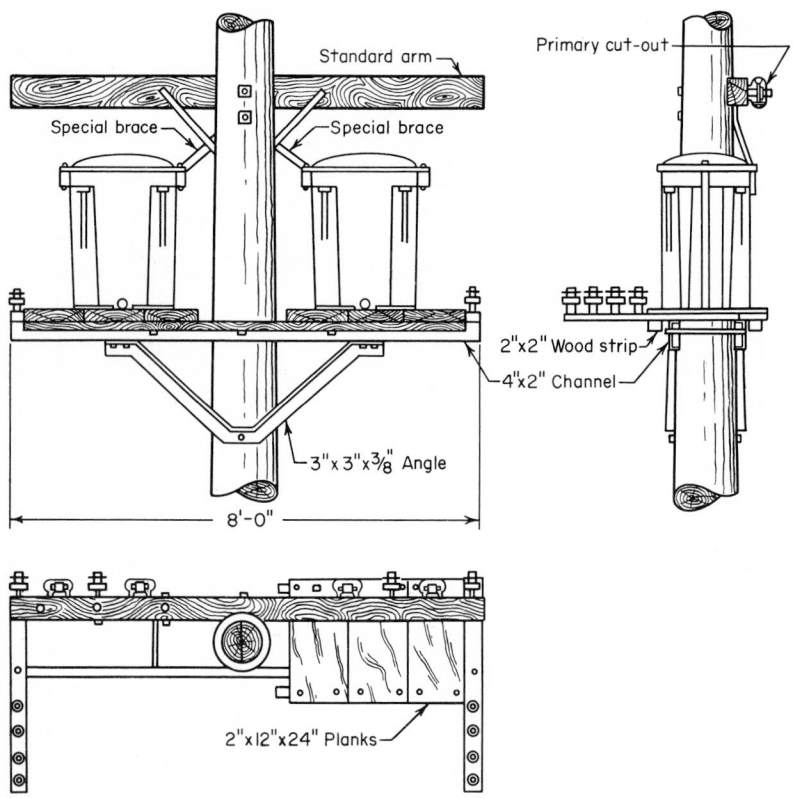

FIG. 84   *Single-pole platform for two 20-kva, two 30-kva, or one 50-kva transformer.*

planks 2 by 12 by 24 in. are to be laid across the channel irons for the transformers to rest upon. The wooden platform is to be held together by a 2- by 2-in. strip of wood running on the outside of the channel iron, to which the planks are secured by 4-in. wood screws or 20-penny nails.

181. Method of Mounting Three 20-kva, Three 30-kva, Two 50-kva, or Three 50-kva Transformers (Fig. 85). The poles should be spaced 10 ft apart on centers. The main channel irons are 6 in. by 10 lb by 10 ft 6 in. over all. Braces are of 3-in. by 4-lb channel.

SATURABLE-CORE REACTOR

182. Saturable-core Reactor. In many control circuits it is desirable to be able to control the value of the inductive reactance. This can often be accomplished advantageously by means of a device called a saturable-core reactor. A saturable-core

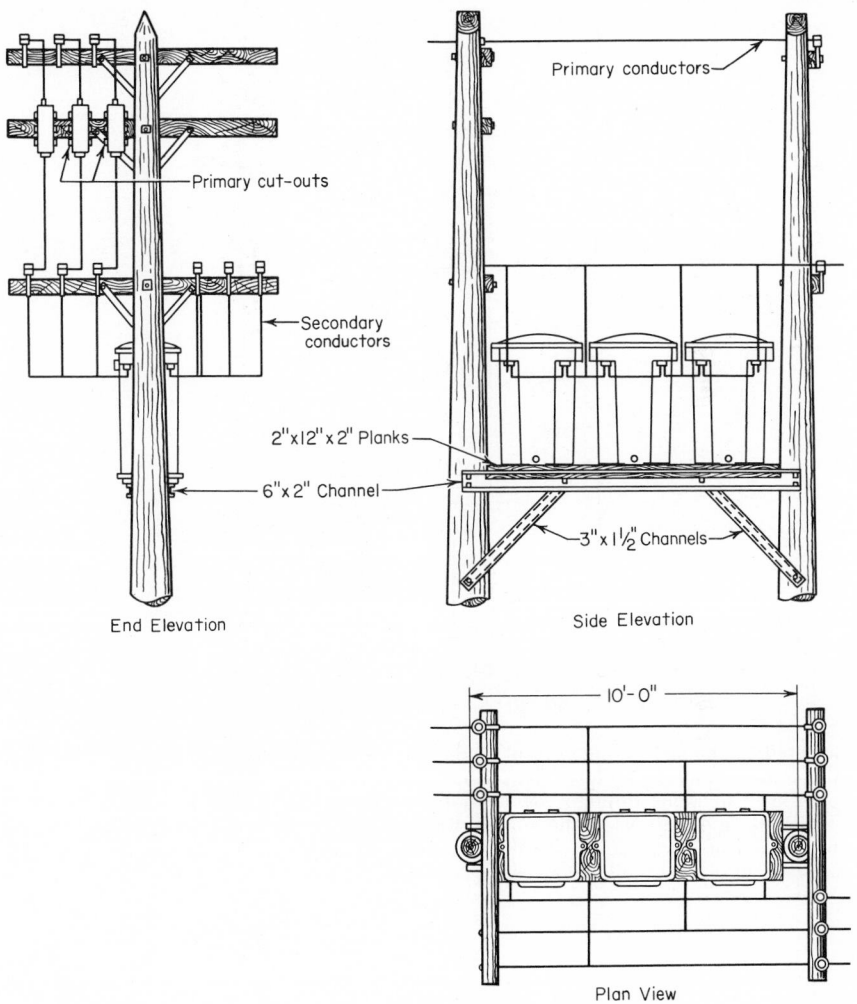

End Elevation   Side Elevation

Plan View

FIG. 85 *Double-pole platform for three 20-kva, three 30-kva, two 50-kva, or three 50-kva transformers.*

reactor consists of a magnetic core associated with d-c and a-c windings. A common form of construction is shown in Fig. 86. When there is no current in the d-c winding, the inductive reactance of the a-c winding will be high, since there will be a high rate of change of flux with current. If sufficient direct current is passed through the d-c winding to saturate the magnetic core, then the changing current in the a-c winding will produce only very small changes in the flux of the core and the inductive reactance of the a-c winding will be very small. If the current of the d-c winding is adjusted, the inductive reactance of the a-c winding can be varied smoothly from practically zero to its maximum value. It might appear that a saturable-core reactor could be constructed with one a-c and one d-c winding on a common core. This simple construction would not be satisfactory, since the variations of the flux produced by the alternating flux would induce large voltages of changing magnitude in the d-c winding. To be satisfactory, the reactor must be so constructed that the flux linked with the d-c winding is not

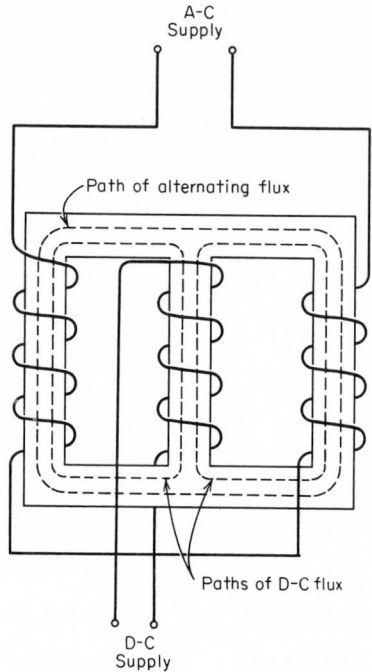

A-C
Supply

Path of alternating flux

Paths of D-C flux

D-C
Supply

FIG. 86   *Saturable-core reactor.*

affected by the alternating current in the a-c winding.   This can be accomplished by
the construction of Fig. 86.   The currents in the two a-c coils tend to produce flux in
opposite directions through the central core on which the d-c winding is wound.
Therefore, the currents in the a-c windings neutralize each other with respect to the
production of flux linking with the d-c winding.   Refer to Sec. **140** of Div. 7 for an
application of a saturable-core reactor in a control circuit.

DIVISION SIX

Electronic and Solid-state Devices and Circuits

FUNDAMENTALS OF ELECTRONICS

1. Electronics, as defined by the Institute of Electrical and Electronic Engineers, is that branch of science and technology which relates to the conduction of electricity through gases or in vacuum.

The reader should study Div. 1 before proceeding with this division on electronics and solid-state devices.

Electricity exists in two forms called positive and negative electricity, respectively. Positive electricity is that form of electricity which is associated with the nuclei of the atoms of all matter, and negative electricity is that form of electricity which is associated with the very minute particles of matter called electrons. In its normal state an atom of matter contains just as much positive electricity as negative electricity. Except under very unusual conditions, no electricity can be removed from the positive nucleus of an atom, and therefore, no positive electricity can be transferred from one atom to another or from one material to another. Electrons, however, can be removed or added to an atom and, after having been separated from an atom, can be transferred from one material or medium to another.

An atom, molecule, or piece of material that possesses more electricity of one kind than the other is said to be electrically charged. It is positively charged if some of the normal electrons have been removed from it, so that it contains more positive electricity than negative electricity. It is negatively charged if electrons have been added to it, so that it contains more negative electricity than positive electricity.

In matter in its solid form, the electrons are not absolutely bound to the nuclei of the atoms. Some electrons will break away from their atoms, move about in heterogeneous directions in the space between atoms, and eventually combine with other atoms. These electrons, which are relatively free of atoms, are called free electrons. It is the controlled motion of these free electrons which constitutes electric current in solid materials. Some materials possess a large number of free electrons, and current is therefore relatively easily produced through these materials. These materials are called conductors. Other materials possess only a very limited number of free electrons, and current is therefore very hard to produce through them. These materials are called insulating materials.

In any piece of solid material there are internal forces that tend to hold the free electrons inside the material. It is relatively easy to overcome these restraining forces at the boundary between two solid conducting materials. However, it is relatively hard to produce the emission of electrons from a conducting body through the boundary of the body into an insulating solid material, into a gas, or into a highly evacuated space.

Electronic devices (tubes) function principally through the conduction of free electrons through gas or in vacuum. The functioning of these devices, therefore, involves

1. The production of free electrons in an evacuated or gas-filled space (emission).

2. The production of motion of these free electrons through the evacuated or gas-filled space (production of current through the space).

3. The control of the motion of these free electrons through the space (control of the current through the space).

2. Electron Emission. The free electrons, which must be maintained inside an electron tube, are produced by emitting electrons from a conducting electrode into the highly evacuated or gas-filled space. The principal methods by which this emission is produced are

1. Thermionic emission.
2. Electric-field emission.
3. Photoelectric emission.
4. Secondary emission.

Thermionic emission is produced by heating a metal to a high enough temperature so that free electrons in the metal will be given sufficient energy to break through the surface of the metal and to be emitted into the space surrounding the metal. Only those metals are satisfactory for use as thermionic emitters which will produce liberal emission of electrons at temperatures well below the melting point of the metal. The principal materials used are tungsten, thoriated tungsten, and oxide-coated tungsten or platinum. The common coatings are oxides of barium and strontium.

Electric-field Emission. When voltage is impressed between two separated conductors, forces tending to remove electrons will be exerted upon the electrons in the conductor that is connected to the negative terminal of the supply. If the voltage is sufficient, electrons will be emitted from the surface of that conductor into the surrounding space. Solid metallic emitters, similar to those used as thermionic emitters, and pools of mercury are the principal materials used for electric-field emission.

Photoelectric Emission. When light falls upon an object, some of the radiant energy of the light is imparted to the body. In some substances sufficient energy is imparted by light to electrons in the substance so that electrons are emitted into the surrounding space. The light-sensitive substance, employed for photoelectric emitters, depends upon the particular wave lengths of light to which it is desired to have the emitter respond. Cesium oxide, potassium, and sodium are common light-sensitive materials employed for photoelectric emission.

Secondary Emission. The energy required to release electrons from a conducting surface can be provided by bombarding the surface with electrons or ions (electrically charged particles of matter) of sufficiently high kinetic-energy content. A bombarding electron at high speed may produce the liberation of up to 10 electrons. In a few specialized types of tubes, secondary emission is employed as the primary or contributory cause of emission, but in most cases it is to be avoided, since secondary emission may result in decreasing the useful purpose of the tube or in damage to the electrodes.

3. Conduction in Vacuo. A perfect or complete vacuum is perfectly void space, i.e., space containing absolutely nothing. It is impossible for man to produce a perfect vacuum. Our so-called vacuums are very highly evacuated space, i.e., space that contains only a very minute amount of matter in the gaseous form.

Consider the conditions of Fig. 1, in which two cold electrodes of conducting material A and B are enclosed in a highly evacuated chamber. Since the envelope cannot be completely evacuated and will contain a minute amount of gas, a very, very small number of free electrons will be present inside the chamber. With a moderate voltage of the polarity shown impressed between electrodes A and B, a very, very minute current would flow for an infinitesimal lapse of time. This current would consist of the motion to the electrode B of the few free electrons present in the evacuated chamber, and the current would cease as soon as all the free electrons present had been moved to electrode B. No current except this very, very minute initial current could exist

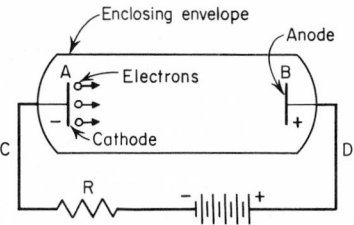

FIG. 1 *Conduction in vacuum.*

unless electrons were emitted into the chamber. If electrode B were caused to be an emitter of electrons, no current would exist through the chamber, since the voltage is of such polarity that it would immediately drive the emitted electrons back into electrode B. However, if electrode A were caused to be an emitter, the voltage would exert a force upon the emitted electrons, moving them through the chamber to electrode B. As long as electrode A continued to give emission, there would be current in the circuit. This current would consist of motion of electrons from the positive terminal of the voltage source, through the source to the negative terminal, through resistor R and conductor C to the negative electrode A, through the boundary of A into the chamber (emission of electrons from electrode A into the chamber), through the space of the evacuated chamber to electrode B, and through conductor D back to the positive terminal of the source. Either electrode A or B can be caused to be an emitter by thermionic, photo-emissive, or electric-field means. To cause either A or B to become an emitter by electric-field means would require a high voltage.

The magnitude of the current through a vacuum will be determined by (1) the rate of emission of electrons, (2) the voltage impressed between electrodes A and B, (3) the distance from electrode A to electrode B, and (4) the shape of the electrodes. As compared with other circuits, the current through a vacuum will be relatively small. In conduction through matter, both positive and negative electricity are present in the material. In conduction through a vacuum, only negative electricity is present in the vacuum. This presence in the space of only negative electricity (called space charge) results in forces that oppose the motion of the negative electrons away from the emitter. It is this opposition of the space charge to motion of electrons away from the emitter which limits the current per unit of impressed voltage to relatively low values. The voltage drop from electrode A to electrode B will increase with increased current because of greater space-charge effect. For a given rate of emission, the current will increase as the impressed voltage is increased until the electrons are moved across the vacuum space as fast as they are emitted. Any further increase in impressed voltage cannot increase the current.

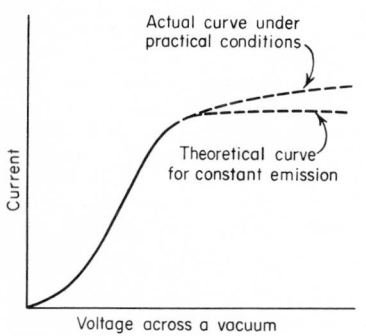

FIG. 2 *Typical current–voltage characteristics for conduction in vacuum.*

However, in the operation of a vacuum-tube circuit, it is impossible to hold the emission constant. As the voltage from A to B is increased, the emission is increased very slightly. A typical current-voltage characteristic of vacuum conduction is shown in Fig. 2. The shape of the lower portion of the curve will depend upon the shape and location of the electrodes.

4. Electronic Direction of Current. In the discussion of the current in Sec. **3**, it will be noted that the motion of the electrons constituting the current is opposite to the direction in which current is commonly considered to be. The early experimenters assumed current to consist of the motion of positive electricity, and that assumption is the basis for our present-day common terminology with respect to direction of current. We now know that, in most cases, current actually consists of the motion of negative electricity (electrons). However, since the effects produced by motion of negative electricity in one direction are the same as those produced by the motion of positive electricity in the opposite direction, no harm is done by considering the current to consist of equivalent motion of positive electricity. The conventional or common direction of current is the direction in which positive electricity would move in order to produce the same effects as those produced by the actual motion of negative electricity in the circuit. The conventional direction of current is always assumed unless otherwise stated. When the actual direction of motion of electrons is considered, it is called the electronic current.

5. Conduction in Gases. Since highly evacuated space is not a perfect vacuum, the enclosure does contain a minute amount of gas. This minute amount of gas, however, is so small that it plays no appreciable part in conduction through the highly evacuated space. If an appreciable amount of gas is present in an enclosure, it will alter the conduction characteristics, so that they differ to a marked degree from those present in highly evacuated space. The conduction conditions in gas will depend upon the pressure and the method of emission. The following discussion of gaseous conduction is for relatively low pressures, such as those which are employed in electron tubes.

Consider, first, the conditions of Fig. 3 in which two electrodes C and D are enclosed in a gas-filled chamber. Electrode C is constructed to produce liberal emission when it is heated to the proper temperature by current from the voltage source A. Electrode D will not produce emission unless an excessive voltage is impressed across the two electrodes. When a small voltage B of the polarity shown is impressed across the electrodes, the electrons emitted by C will be moved through the gas to the positive electrode D. Since the gas of itself will contain some free electrons in addition to those emitted by electrode C, the amount of current through the enclosure will be somewhat greater than it was when the chamber was highly evacuated, and the current-voltage characteristic will have a different shape, as shown in Fig. 4 from point 0 to 1. The conventional direction of current will be from electrode D through the gas of the enclosure to electrode C. If electrode C were made of positive polarity with respect to D, the electrons emitted by C would be driven back into the emitting electrode C and no current would pass through the gas. With D of positive polarity, the electrons in moving through the gas-filled space will be impeded in their motion by collisions with atoms of the gas. Some of the energy imparted to the moving electrons by the source of voltage will be transformed by these collisions into heat energy. As the voltage across electrodes C and D is increased, the electrons will be accelerated more rapidly in their motion toward the positive electrode D and therefore will possess more energy when they collide with an atom of the gas. When the voltage has been raised to a certain value, point 1 in Fig. 4, an electron will possess enough energy on collision with an atom so that an electron will be knocked off from the atom, and the atom will be left with a positive charge. This liberation of electrons and production of positively charged atoms is called ionization of the gas. These liberated electrons and positively charged atoms will provide a liberal number of

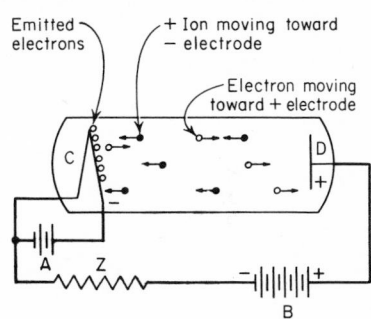

FIG. 3   *Conduction in a low-pressure gas.*

current carriers throughout the whole enclosure, and the gas will become a good conductor of electricity. This increased conductivity of the gas will allow the current to increase suddenly when point 1 in Fig. 4 is reached, and the voltage required to maintain the conduction will drop to the value corresponding with point 2. The current after condition 2 has been reached will consist of combined motion of negative electrons toward the positive electrode and of positively charged ions toward the negative electrode. Because of the presence of both negative electrons and positively charged ions throughout the space, there will be practically no net space charge inside the enclosure. In conduction in vacuum, the current was limited by space charge, and greater current required greater voltage drop across the electrodes to produce it. After ionization in gaseous conduction, the current will be independent of the voltage for a considerable range, as from point 2 upward in Fig. 4. Throughout this range the voltage drop between the electrodes will be constant regardless of the value of the current. The voltage to produce ionization (the voltage for point 1 in Fig. 4) is a few volts greater than the voltage required to maintain ionization (the voltage for point 2 in Fig. 4). The original production of the ionization is called the breakdown of the gas. With thermionic emission, if the current is allowed to reach too high a value, the bombardment of the emitter by the positively charged atoms will destroy the emitting surface of the emitter. An external impedance z must therefore be inserted in series with the circuit so as to limit the current to a safe value. Gas-filled tubes with thermionic emitters are operated on the points of the curve from point 2 upward to the safe value of current for the particular tube.

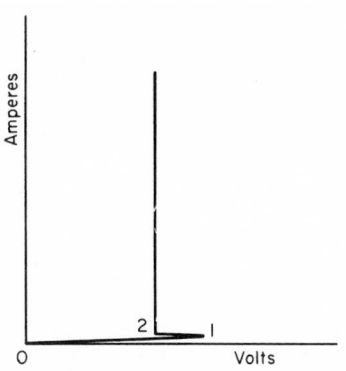

FIG. 4   *Plate current–plate voltage characteristic of a gas-filled tube with liberal emission.*

If the lower portion of the gaseous-conduction characteristic for liberal emission conditions is redrawn to an expanded scale, it will appear as shown in Fig. 5. If the emission produced by electrode C is reduced, the conduction characteristic will be as shown in curve 2 of Fig. 5. Reducing the emission will raise the voltage required to break down the gas and will reduce the magnitude of the current for the portion of the conduction characteristic from 0 to 1. The amount of emission produced by photoelectric means is limited, and gas-filled phototubes are operated on the lower portion of the conduction characteristic from 0 to 1.

If the two electrodes C and D are operated cold, so that neither electrode is heated by external means, as shown in Fig. 5, no current of any appreciable magnitude will exist through the gas for small values of impressed voltage. Actually a very, very minute current of approximately $1/100$ μa will pass from electrode D to C. This minute current will be maintained by a minute amount of emission from electrode C. The emission is undoubtedly caused by field emission. This minute current is shown in curve 3 of Fig. 5. If the voltage across C and D is increased above the value for point 1 on curve 3, the gas will be broken down and emission will be increased. The emission after point 1 is reached will be caused by all four of the methods described in Sec. 2. The same action of ionization and conduction will take place as described for the conditions when electrode C was a thermionic emitter. However, the voltage required to produce breakdown with cold electrodes will be much greater than for hot operation of electrode C. After breakdown of the gas with cold electrodes, the voltage across the electrodes will drop a much greater amount than for the hot-electrode operation. Over the current range from 2 to 3 of curve 3, the current will be independent of the voltage, and the voltage drop between the electrodes will be constant regardless of the value of the current.

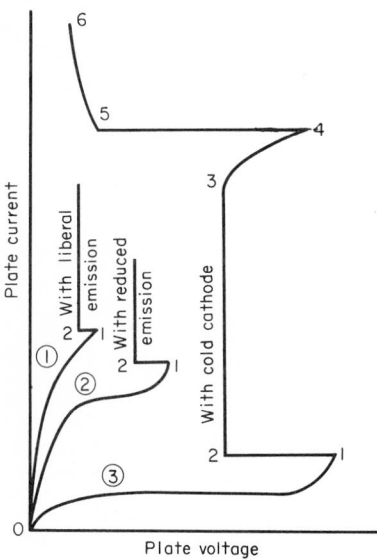

FIG. 5 *Plate current–plate voltage characteristic for gas-filled tubes.*

The constant voltage required to maintain conduction will be much greater throughout this range than for hot-electrode C operation. This is because a large portion of the voltage will be required to produce the necessary emission by electric-field emission. The magnitude of the current from 2 to 3 for cold-electrode operation will be limited to a relatively small value, because only limited emission can be produced from the cold electrode. However, if the current is allowed to increase above the value for point 3 on curve 3, the voltage drop from electrode C to D will increase as the current increases, as shown from point 3 to 4. The electrodes will be heated by the discharge to a much higher temperature, and liberal emission will take place when point 4 is reached. When the conditions of point 4 are reached, an arc will be produced between the electrodes, and the voltage required to maintain the arc will be very much less than the voltage required to start the arc, and even less than the voltage required throughout range 2 to 3. The conduction characteristic after the arc has been started from point 5 on will be unstable; i.e., the voltage drop across the electrodes will decrease with increase of the current. So-called cold-cathode tubes operate on the portion of the conduction characteristic from point 2 to 3. Mercury-pool tubes operate in the arc range of the conduction characteristic from point 5 upward.

ELECTRON-TUBE ESSENTIALS AND CLASSIFICATION

6. An electron tube is a device for the purpose of producing, maintaining, and controlling an electric current through a highly evacuated or gas-filled chamber. From the discussion of the preceding sections, any electron tube must have the following essential construction:

1. An enclosing envelope with the enclosed chamber either highly evacuated or containing gas or vapor at low pressure.
2. A conducting element (electrode) fulfilling the following conditions:
   a. Located inside the envelope with a conducting connection to the exterior of the chamber.
   b. So constructed and operated that the electrode will emit electrons into the enclosure.
3. A second conducting element (electrode) fulfilling the following conditions:
   a. Located inside the envelope and separated and insulated from the emitting electrode.
   b. Having a conducting connection to the exterior of the chamber.
   c. So constructed and operated that it will collect electrons emitted by the emitting electrode after they have passed across the enclosure.

The two electrodes listed above are the absolutely essential electrodes required for any electron tube and are designated as the main electrodes. The main electrode that is designed for the emission of electrons is called the **cathode.** The main electrode that is designed for the collection of electrons after they have passed through the space of the tube is called the **anode** or **plate.**

In addition to the absolutely essential main electrodes, an electron tube may have other conducting elements (electrodes) for the purpose of controlling the current between the two main electrodes. These additional electrodes are called **grids.** Each **grid** must be so constructed that

1. It is located inside the envelope.
2. It is separated and insulated from all other electrodes.
3. It is connected by means of a conducting connection to the exterior of the tube.
4. It is so constructed and located as to fulfill the particular desired control function.

7. Requirements for Tube Conduction. Conduction (the existence of current) can take place in an electron tube only when the following conditions are fulfilled:

1. The cathode is emitting.
2. The anode or plate is at positive potential with respect to the cathode.

8. Rectifier Action of Electron Tubes. Electron tubes are not the only electronic devices. Several types of lamps (see Div. 10) depend for their operation upon conduction through gas, and these lamps are therefore electronic devices. The lamps, however, are not constructed for the primary purpose of producing, maintaining, and controlling current through the enclosure. Current through the space is essential for their operation, but the primary purpose of the device is to produce light. The gaseous-discharge lamps consequently are not electron tubes as defined in Sec. **6.**

If the emitting electrode in an electronic device becomes positive with respect to the other electrode, the voltage between the electrodes will exert a force tending to drive the electrons back into the emitting electrode, and there can be no current through the enclosure. Electron tubes, with the exception of some cold-cathode tubes, are so constructed that, when the tube is operating properly, only one of the main electrodes will function as a cathode (an emitter of electrons). Therefore, under normal operating conditions, all electron tubes possess rectifying characteristics, i.e., will allow the passage of current in only one direction. The conventional direction of this current is from anode or plate to cathode, and the electronic direction of this current is from cathode to anode. Most electronic lamps (gaseous-discharge lamps), on the other hand, are so constructed that either electrode may become an emitter and function as a cathode while at the same time the other electrode will function as the anode. Most electronic lamps do not possess rectifying characteristics and will allow the passage of alternating current.

If the voltage impressed across the main electrodes of any electron tube is raised to a sufficient value, either electrode may function as a cathode. Too high a voltage across an electron tube will therefore destroy its rectifying characteristics, and it will then pass alternating current. Electron tubes should never be operated at voltages above their rated value.

9. Classification of Electron Tubes.   Electron tubes may be classified as follows:

A. According to material of enclosing envelope.
    1. Glass.
    2. Metal.
B. According to type of cathode.
    1. Thermionic.
        a. Directly heated.
        b. Indirectly heated.
    2. Mercury-pool.
    3. Cold-cathode.
    4. Photoemissive.
C. According to medium enclosed by envelope.
    1. Vacuum (highly evacuated).
    2. Gas-filled.
D. According to electrodes.
    1. Diode (having simply a cathode and an anode).
    2. Triode (having a cathode, an anode, and one grid).
    3. Tetrode (having a cathode, an anode, and two grids).
    4. Pentode (having a cathode, an anode, and three grids).
    5. Multianode (multipurpose).

10. The enclosing envelope may be formed from either glass or metal.   The main advantage of the glass tube is that observation can be made, especially in connection with maintenance, of whether the filament wire is hot or whether ionization of the gas is taking place.   The metal tube is less fragile, can be designed smaller in size because it is a better radiator of heat, and forms a natural shield against stray fields.

11. Types of Cathodes.   The different types of cathodes used in electron tubes are listed in Sec. **9.**   The cathode must be so constructed and operated that it will function as an efficient emitter of electrons.

Thermionic cathodes or hot cathodes are solid metal cathodes which in the operation of the tube are heated by a current and produce emission by thermionic means, as described in Sec. **2.**   The necessary heating of the cathode can be obtained by the passage of current through the cathode itself (*directly heated cathode*), or an electric heater coil distinct from the cathode can be employed for supplying the necessary heat to the cathode (*indirectly heated cathode*).   In either case, the heating current is separate from the current passing from anode to cathode and requires an independent circuit for its production.   Both the above types of cathode construction are employed in commercial tubes.   Typical cathode constructions are shown in Figs. 6 and 7.   The directly heated cathode is simpler in construction, but the indirectly heated cathode can be

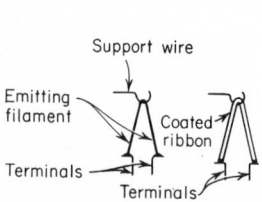

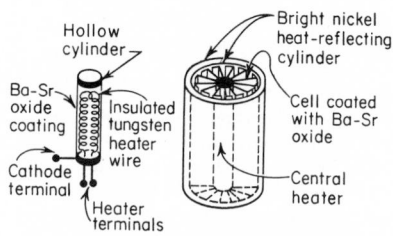

FIG. 6   *Directly   heated filament cathodes.*

FIG. 7   *Indirectly heated cathodes.*

constructed to give higher efficiency of emission per watt of heating power employed. The indirectly heated cathode has the advantage that the emitting surface of the cathode can be isolated electrically from the heating circuit.   The heating circuit can therefore be supplied with alternating current without the disadvantage of having the variations of the voltage in the cathode-heating circuit affect the main current from anode to cathode.

A pool of mercury is employed for the cathode in certain types of gas-filled tubes. Of course, it cannot be used for a high-vacuum tube. The mercury-pool cathode does not require any cathode-heating current, since the emission is produced by the forces exerted by the cathode-anode voltage upon the electrons in the surface of the mercury pool (electric-field emission; see Sec. **2**). No separate cathode-heating circuit is required. The mercury-pool cathode is advantageous for tubes that must handle large amounts of power, since its normal current-carrying possibilities and its overload-current possibilities are inherently high.

Cold cathodes, as the term is used, are composed of a simple metallic electrode that is not heated by any cathode-heating current. Emission during operation is produced by a very complex phenomenon consisting of a combination of all four of the methods of emission described in Sec. **2**. This type of cathode produces a very limited amount of emission and is therefore satisfactory only for special types of tubes where very low current capacity is required.

With cold cathodes, no auxiliary means, such as heating of the cathode or incident light on the cathode, are employed to produce emission. Emission is originated by the voltage impressed across the main electrodes (see Sec. **5**).

Photoemissive cathodes are constructed of photoemissive surfaces, as described in Sec. **2**. When the light-sensitive surface of the cathode is energized by impinging light of the proper wave length, electrons are emitted. No cathode-heating circuit is required, since the power required for emission is obtained from the impinging light. This type of cathode is used in phototubes.

12. Medium Enclosed by Envelope. Electron tubes are of two types, depending upon the medium enclosed by the envelope of the tube. The so-called **vacuum tubes** have the enclosure of the tube evacuated to as high a degree as is practically possible. The other types of tubes contain gas or vapor at a low pressure and are called **gas-filled tubes.** Mercury vapor is employed in a majority of the gas-filled tubes, but inert gases such as argon, neon, and helium are also used.

Vacuum tubes are constructed with either thermionic or photoemissive cathodes, depending upon the purpose of the tube. Common practice is to use the designation vacuum tube principally for the thermionic type of vacuum tube. **Gas-filled tubes** are constructed with thermionic, mercury-pool, photoemissive, or cold cathodes, depending upon the purpose, rating, and characteristics required.

13. Number of Electrodes. Tubes are classified as in Sec. **9** in accordance with the number of electrodes with which the tube is constructed. The simplest type of tube is the **diode,** which has only two main electrodes, the cathode (emitter) and the anode or plate (the collector). In order to control the anode-cathode current or to alter the operating characteristics, many tubes are constructed with additional electrodes. All electrodes in addition to the cathode and anode are called **grids.** The grid that is used to control the anode-cathode current is called the **control grid,** and the additional grids are called **screen** and **suppressor grids.** The number of grids possessed by tubes of the various electrode designations are given in Sec. **9**. Grids are made of conducting material and usually are constructed in the form of a fine mesh screen, a spiral of wire wound on supporting members, or a perforated cylinder.

14. Multianode tubes are made that are combinations of diodes, diodes with triodes, and diodes with pentodes. They consist of a common cathode and the different sets of anodes or anodes and grids in a single envelope. Each anode or each anode and its associated grids function independently of the other anodes, just as if separate tubes were employed. The common cathode supplies the emission for the various anodes. These multianode tubes are multipurpose tubes, and their advantages are economy and convenience. A multianode tube simply takes the place of as many individual tubes with single anodes as there are anodes in the multianode tube.

15. Table of Tube Symbols. The symbols employed in wiring diagrams to represent t. ＿ different types of tubes and their electrodes are shown in Fig. 8.

THERMIONIC VACUUM TUBES

16. Diode thermionic vacuum tubes are constructed with both directly and indirectly heated cathodes. Fundamental circuit diagrams are shown in Fig. 9. Unless the im-

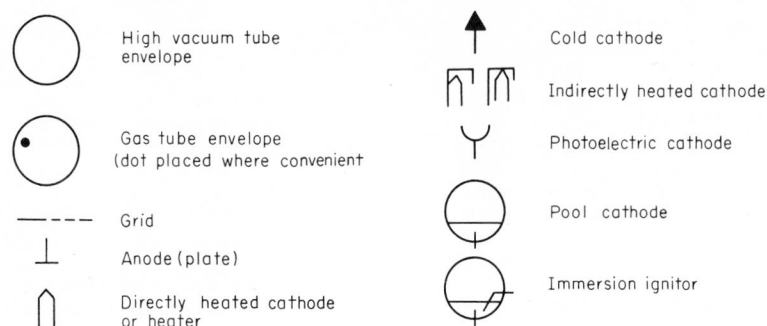

FIG. 8 *Standard symbols for electron-tube diagrams. (Institute of Electrical and Electronic Engineers.)*

pressed voltage is excessive, the tube will allow the passage of current in only one direction, from anode to cathode if conventional direction is considered or from cathode to anode if electronic current direction is considered. The operation of the tube requires two sources of voltage, one for the heating of the cathode and one for the main cathode-anode circuit. The cathode-heating circuit frequently is called simply the cathode circuit and is also designated as the **A** circuit. The cathode-anode circuit frequently is called simply the anode or plate circuit and is commonly designated as the **B** circuit. When the cathode is heated to emission temperature, the tube conducts according to the fundamental vacuum conduction principles of Sec. 3. The anode-current, anode-voltage characteristic will depend upon the temperature of the cathode. Typical characteristics are shown in Fig. 10. As shown by the figures, for the lower values of voltage, the anode current is practically independent of the cathode temperature, provided that the temperature of the cathode is high enough to give reasonable emission. In the lower portion of the curves, the current is limited by space charge (see Sec. 3). As the anode voltage is increased, a point will be reached, for each temperature of the cathode, at which the electrons are pulled across the anode practically as fast as they are emitted. Any further increase in the anode-to-cathode voltage will not materially increase the anode current. In the upper portions of the curves, the current is limited by emission. The voltage drop from cathode to anode varies with the current and the design of the tube and is of relatively high magnitude.

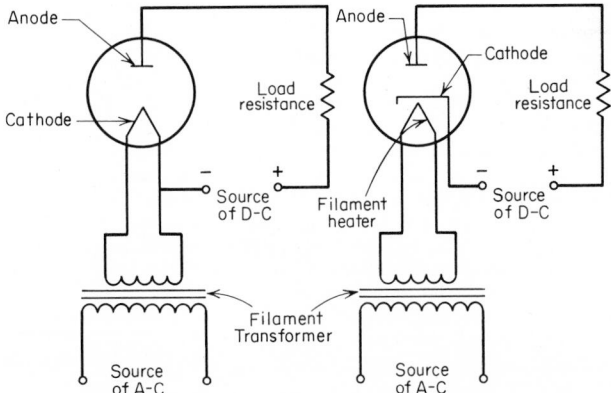

I. With directly heated cathode   II With indirectly heated cathode

FIG. 9 *Circuit diagrams for diode vacuum tube.*

17. Triode thermionic vacuum tubes employ either a directly heated or an indirectly heated cathode. As its name signifies, it has three electrodes: the cathode, the anode, and a control grid. The control grid is located between the cathode and the anode and provides a means for controlling or varying the cathode-anode current without changing the cathode-to-anode voltage. The tube should be operated with rated cathode-heating current so that copious emission will be produced. If the grid is made positive with respect to the cathode, the voltage from cathode to grid will aid the motion of the emitted electrons away from the cathode. Some of these electrons will pass to the grid structure and produce current in the grid circuit. The majority of the electrons, however, will pass through the openings in the grid structure and continue on to the anode under the influence of the higher anode positive potential. A positive grid voltage will therefore increase the anode current for a given anode voltage. On the other hand, if the grid is made negative with respect to the cathode, this voltage from cathode to grid will oppose the motion of the emitted electrons away from the cathode. A negative grid voltage will, therefore, reduce the anode current for a given anode voltage. With a negative grid, the electrons will be repelled from the grid structure and there will be no grid current. It is usually not advisable to have grid current, so that the tube is generally operated with a negative grid voltage.

A fundamental circuit diagram is shown in Fig. 11. The operation of the tube requires three circuits: the cathode circuit, the anode circuit, and the circuit from cathode to grid. The cathode-grid circuit, generally, is called simply the grid circuit and is designated as the **C** circuit.

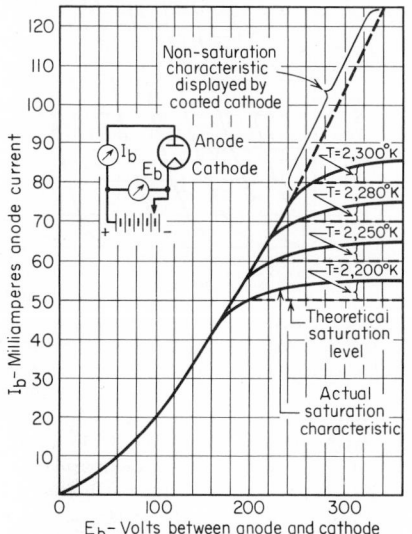

FIG. 10 *Anode current-voltage characteristics for a diode vacuum tube.*

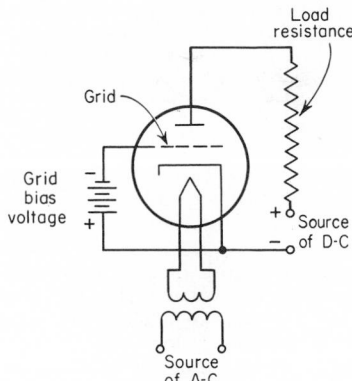

FIG. 11 *Circuit diagram for a triode vacuum tube.*

Typical characteristics of a triode tube are shown in Figs. 12 and 13. It will be observed from these characteristics that, when the grid is negative, the tube does not always conduct. For a given value of negative-grid voltage, a certain anode voltage is required before there is any anode current. For a given anode voltage, there will be no current until the negative-grid voltage has been reduced to a certain value. These points are called the cutoff points. The effect of the grid on the operation of the tube can be seen from a study of Figs. 12 and 13. It will be observed that the anode current can be completely stopped or varied from zero to the maximum allowable value simply through variation of the control-grid voltage. From a study of Figs. 12 and 13, it is seen that a given change of grid voltage will produce a greater change in the anode current than will be produced by the same amount of change in the anode voltage. The grid voltage is more effective in controlling the anode current than is the anode voltage. This is an important characteristic of the triode vacuum tube.

The cathode-anode voltage drop varies with the current, the grid voltage, and the design of the tube. This voltage drop is of relatively high magnitude. Unless excessive voltage is impressed in the cathode-anode circuit, the tube will pass current in only one direction.

18. Sources of Grid Voltage. In the operation of a triode vacuum tube, it generally is desired to control the anode current by a voltage that originates in some circuit external to the tube circuits. This voltage is called the **signal** voltage or simply the **signal.** The signal voltage may be a direct or an alternating voltage. The desired conditions generally cannot be met by having the entire grid voltage supplied by the signal. Usually the grid circuit is supplied by a constant potential connected in series with the signal voltage. The signal voltage varies the operation of the tube around an operating point established by

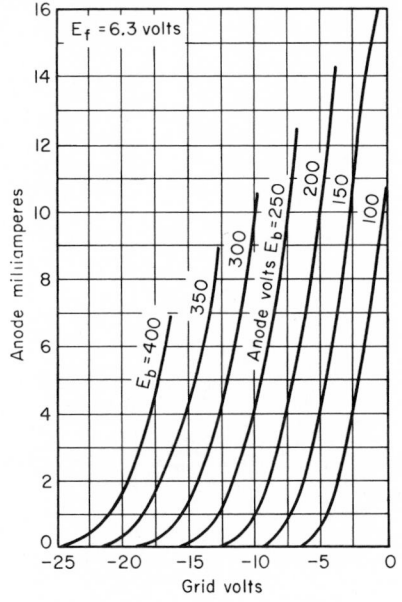

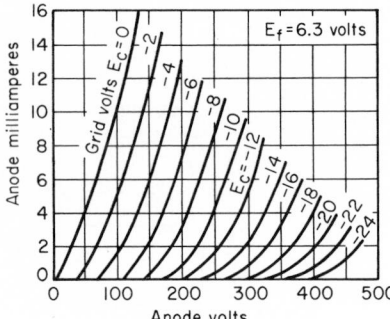

FIG. 12 *Anode current–voltage characteristic curves for a 6J5 triode vacuum tube. (RCA Mfg. Co.)*

FIG. 13 *Anode current–grid voltage characteristic curves for a 6J5 triode vacuum tube. (RCA Mfg. Co.)*

the constant grid voltage. The constant grid voltage is called the grid-bias voltage or simply the bias voltage. The grid-bias voltage may be obtained from an outside source of emf, or it may be obtained from a grid bias resistor, connected in series with the cathode so that the resistor will be common to both the cathode-anode and the cathode-grid circuits, as shown in Fig. 14. The anode current, in passing through the resistor, produces a voltage drop in such a manner that point A in Fig. 14 is made negative with respect to the cathode by the amount of this drop. The voltage drop of the resistor thus acts as a grid bias for the control grid. Since it is desirable to hold the grid bias at as constant a value as possible, it is necessary to connect a bypassing capacitor across the grid-bias resistor. The capacitor will tend to bypass variations in the anode current around the resistor so that the current through the resistor will stay practically constant.

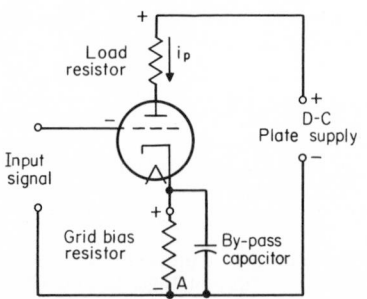

FIG. 14 *Vacuum-tube circuit showing use of grid-bias resistor to produce the negative grid supply voltage.*

19. The voltage and current of the plate circuit of a thermionic vacuum tube are usually variable but can be resolved into a steady d-c component and a sine wave varying a-c component. The a-c component of the current is in phase with the a-c component of the voltage. This circuit exhibits the qualities of a resistance, and certain calculations can be made in accordance with Ohm's law. Since the current is usually not proportional to the voltage, the resistance is variable in nature, and that fact must be taken into account. The opposition of the tube to the d-c component of voltage is called the **d-c plate resistance.** The opposition to the a-c component is called the **dynamic plate resistance,** or since this value is much more commonly used than the d-c one, it is shortened to just **plate resistance.**

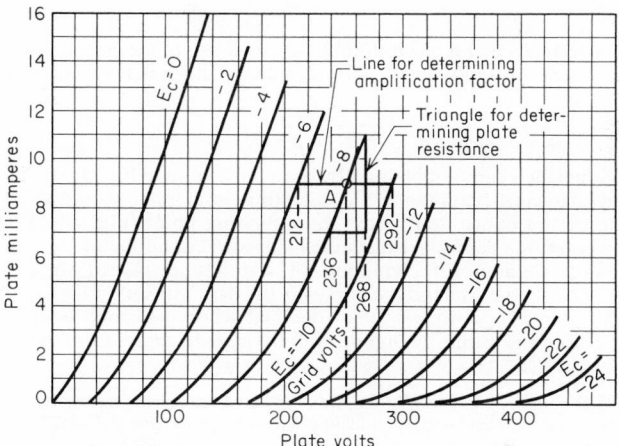

FIG. 15 *Plate current–voltage characteristic curves for a 6J5 triode showing graphical methods for obtaining amplification factor and plate resistance.*

20. The d-c plate resistance is obtained by dividing the voltage represented by any point on the plate voltage–plate current characteristic by the corresponding current expressed in amperes (Fig. 15). In making circuit calculations for an amplifier tube, the d-c plate resistance should be computed for the operating point.

$$r_{p_{dc}} = \frac{e_p}{i_p} \tag{1}$$

The voltage is the average value of the plate voltage, and the current is the average value of the plate current.

Example. With reference to a 6J5 tube, from available tables of tube-characteristic data, the suggested operating point is for a grid voltage of −8 and a plate current of 9 ma. Referring to Fig. 15, these data apply to operating point A corresponding to a plate voltage of 252 volts.

$$r_{p_{dc}} = \frac{252}{0.009} = 28,000 \text{ ohms}$$

21. The plate resistance (dynamic plate resistance) is obtained by drawing a tangent to the plate voltage–plate current characteristic curve at the operating point and constructing a right triangle with the tangent as the hypotenuse (Fig. 15). The change in voltage represented by the length of the base of the triangle expressed in volts divided by the change in plate current represented by the length of the vertical side of the triangle expressed in amperes will be the plate resistance.

$$r_p = \frac{e_{p_2} - e_{p_1}}{i_{p_2} - i_{p_1}} \tag{2}$$

The plate resistance is thus a measure of the opposition to a change in plate current which will be produced by a change in plate voltage. The plate resistance will be constant for all operating points for which the tangent to the curve makes the same angle with the horizontal. This will occur over quite a wide range of operating points as long as they are not taken too close to the sharply curving portion of the characteristic curves.

Example. Referring to Fig. 15 and using the triangle with the hypotenuse drawn through points *A*,

$$r_p = \frac{268 - 236}{0.011 - 0.007} = \frac{32}{0.004} = 8,000 \text{ ohms}$$

This value checks fairly closely with the value of 7,700 given for tube 6J5 in tables of tube-characteristic data.

22. Transconductance of a vacuum tube is a measure of the change in plate current caused by a change in grid voltage, with the plate voltage being held constant.

$$g_m = \frac{i_{p_2} - i_{p_1}}{e_{g_2} - e_{g_1}} \tag{3}$$

The transconductance can be obtained by drawing a vertical line on the plate voltage–plate current characteristic graph at the operating point and extending this line to the characteristic curves above and below the operating point (Fig. 22). The length of the line between these characteristic curves measured in milliamperes and changed to amperes is the numerator of the equation. The difference in grid voltage represented by the titles of the two characteristic curves is the denominator of the equation. Since the transconductance is always a small decimal when measured in mhos, it is customary to multiply the value by one million in order to express the transconductance in micromhos.

Example. With reference to a 6SK7 tube, from tables of tube-characteristic data, the suggested operating point is 9.2 ma plate current and 250 plate volts. Referring to Fig. 22, these data apply to operating point *B*.

$$g_m = \frac{(0.0122 - 0.0067)1,000,000}{-1.5 - (-4.5)} = \frac{0.0055 \times 1,000,000}{3} = 1,830 \text{ micromhos}$$

This value checks fairly closely with the value of 2,000 given for g_m for tube 6SK7 in tables of tube-characteristic data.

23. The amplification **factor** of a tube gives a measure of the relatively greater effect of a change in **grid** voltage on the plate current of a vacuum tube compared with a change of **plate** voltage.

$$\mu = \frac{e_{p_2} - e_{p_1}}{e_{g_2} - e_{g_1}} \tag{4}$$

The amplification factor can be obtained by drawing a horizontal line on the plate voltage–plate current characteristic graph at the operating point (Fig. 15). Take two points on this line, preferably at the intersection with the curves or at an easily estimated fraction between them. The difference in plate voltage represented on the plate-voltage scale between these two points is the numerator of the equation. The difference in grid voltage represented by these two points, interpolated between the curves if required, is the denominator of the equation.

Example. Referring to the horizontal line through point *A* in Fig. 15, running from $e_g = -6$ to $e_g = -10$.

$$\mu = \frac{292 - 212}{-10 - (-6)} = \frac{80}{-4} = -20$$

This checks exactly with the value of 20 given for the 6J5 tube in tables of tube-characteristic data. The minus sign merely indicates that the grid voltage is changed in a direction opposite to that of the plate voltage.

The relationship among amplification factor, plate resistance, and transconductance is given by Eq. (5).

$$\mu = r_p \times g_m \tag{5}$$

This can be proved as an identity as follows, by substituting for each of the terms its equal from the previous equations:

$$\frac{e_{p_2} - e_{p_1}}{e_{g_2} - e_{g_1}} = \frac{e_{p_2} - e_{p_1}}{i_{p_2} - i_{p_1}} \times \frac{i_{p_2} - i_{p_1}}{e_{g_2} - e_{g_1}} \tag{6}$$

The difference in plate currents will cancel out, leaving both sides of the equation equal.

24. The values for amplification factor, plate resistance, and transconductance for vacuum tubes for the usual operating points can be obtained from tables of tube-characteristic data. The tube manuals published by the manufacturing companies and carried in stock by radio supply stores give these curves for most tubes.

25. Tetrode thermionic vacuum tubes are frequently called **screen-grid tubes.** They are constructed with four electrodes: the cathode, the anode, and two grid electrodes. The circuits and arrangement of the grids are shown in Fig. 16. The grid located close to the cathode is a control grid and functions in the same manner to control the anode current as does the control grid of the triode tube. The second grid, or screen grid, as it is called, is located between the control grid and the anode. The screen grid is operated at a positive potential with respect to the cathode, somewhat lower in value than the anode potential with respect to the cathode. The addition of the screen grid alters the characteristics of the tube in two ways: (1) It reduces the capacitance of the capacitor formed by the control grid and anode, and (2) it tends to shield the anode from the cathode and thereby makes the anode less effective in attracting electrons from the cathode. These two effects make it possible to design tetrodes with much higher amplification factors μ than is possible with triodes.

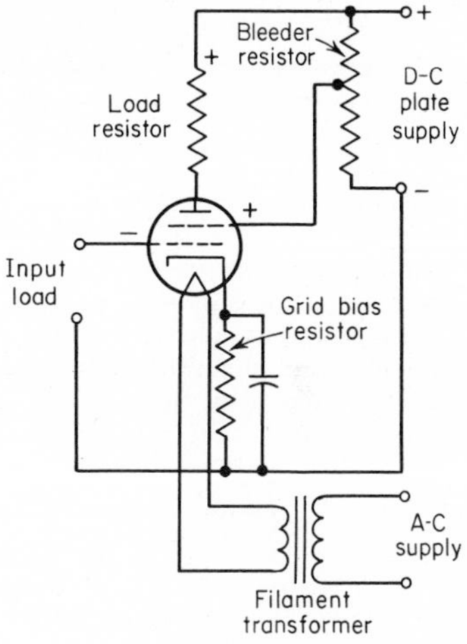

The operation of a tetrode involves four circuits: the cathode circuit, the anode circuit, the control-grid circuit, and the screen-grid circuit.

Typical characteristics for a tetrode are shown in Fig. 17. The tube should always be operated with an anode voltage that will cause operation on a portion of the curve to the right of the vertical line A in Fig. 17. Operation in the lower regions of the curves is unstable. The cathode-

FIG. 16 *Circuit for a vacuum screen-grid tube.*

anode voltage drop varies with the current, the grid-control voltage, the screen-grid voltage, and the design of the tube. This voltage drop is of relatively high magnitude. The amplification factor, plate resistance, and mutual conductance of tetrodes have the same significance and are determined in the same manner as for triodes.

26. The pentode thermionic vacuum tube has three grids in addition to the main electrodes of cathode and anode. These grids are called, respectively, the control grid, the screen grid, and the suppressor grid. A fundamental circuit diagram is shown in Fig. 18. The operation of the tube involves five circuits: the cathode circuit, the anode circuit, the control-grid circuit, the screen-grid circuit, and the suppressor-grid circuit. The suppressor grid usually does not require a separate source of voltage, since it is generally connected directly to the cathode and therefore operates at the same potential as the cathode.

The control grid is located close to the cathode and performs the same function of controlling the anode current as in the triode and tetrode tubes. The suppressor grid is located close to the anode and is connected externally to the tube and directly to the cathode. The negative potential, with respect to the anode, of the suppressor grid repels any electrons that are liberated from the anode by secondary emission and drives them back to the anode. This suppression of the anode secondary emission

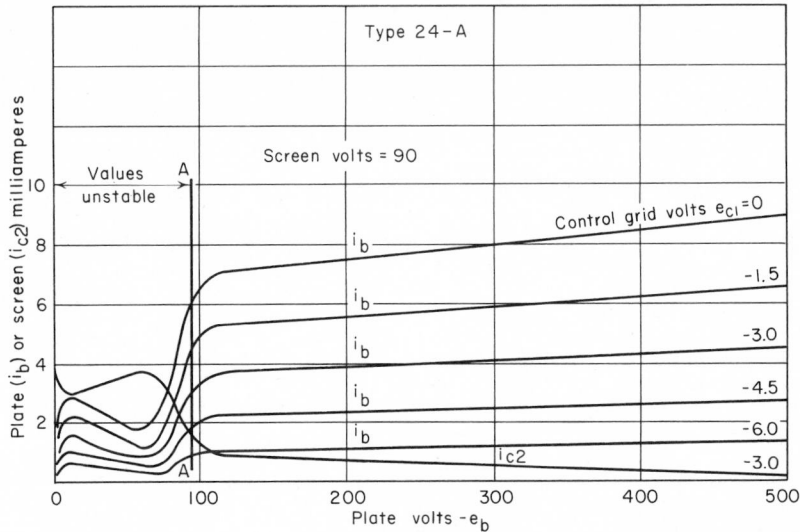

FIG. 17   *Plate current-voltage characteristic curves for a screen-grid tube.*

eliminates one of the limitations of the tetrode tube. In the tetrode tube, electrons, liberated at the anode by secondary emission, caused by bombardment of the anode by the electrons coming from the cathode, are attracted to the screen grid. The resulting current of electrons from anode to screen grid reduces the effective anode current. The screen grid of the pentode tube is located between the control and suppressor grids and performs the same functions as in the tetrode tube. It is energized by a voltage positive with respect to the cathode but of smaller magnitude than the anode voltage.

Typical characteristics for a pentode are shown in Fig. 19. The cathode-anode voltage drop varies with the anode current, the grid-control voltage, the screen-grid voltage, and the design of the tube. This voltage drop is of relatively high magnitude. The amplification factor; the anode, or plate, resistance; and the conductance of pentodes have the same significance and are determined in the same manner as for triodes.

27. X-ray Tubes. The first electronic device to be put to practical use was the X-ray tube. In the intervening years, it has been perfected and improved to a marked degree. The present-day X-ray tube is actually a special thermionic vacuum diode with a tungsten cathode and an anode of very rugged construction so that it can withstand the heavy electron bombardment to which it is subjected. The tube is constructed to operate with a very high cathode-to-anode potential, varying for different tubes from 10,000 to 1,000,000 volts. Because of the high cathode-to-anode potential, the electrons emitted by the cathode are rapidly accelerated in their motion toward the anode. When the electrons strike the anode, they have reached a velocity approaching that of light and consequently have acquired a high kinetic-energy level. This energy is sufficient to

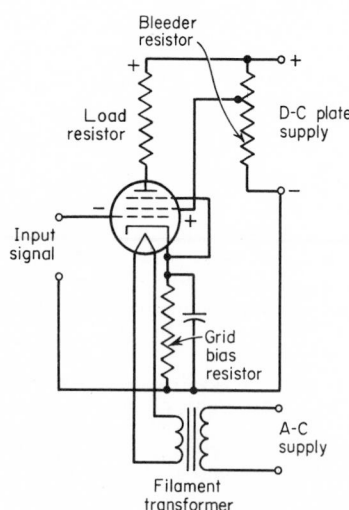

FIG. 18   *Circuit for a pentode vacuum tube.*

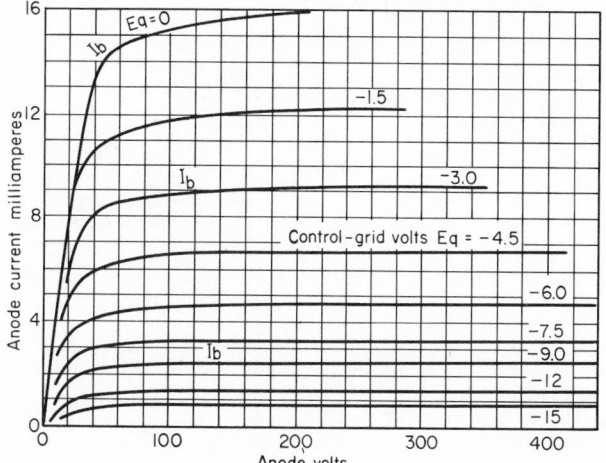

FIG. 19   *Anode current-voltage characteristic curves for a 6SK7 pentode vacuum tube.* (RCA Mfg. Co.)

cause the electrons to penetrate into the atoms of the material of which the target of the anode is constructed. The penetration of the high-energy-level electrons into the target atoms produces an energy transition. This energy transition results in the emanation of electromagnetic waves of very high frequency and corresponding short wave length. These very high frequency electromagnetic waves are called X rays and have the ability to penetrate several inches into any material they strike. Their penetrating power increases as the cathode-to-anode voltage of the producing tube is increased. The X-ray tube has been used for a long time for medical and scientific purposes. More recently it has been applied to industrial applications such as analysis of metal structure, examination of finished products, revealing of internal flaws in castings, and detecting the presence of foreign materials in packaged goods.

28. Equivalent Circuits for Vacuum Thermionic Tubes. The output or load of a vacuum thermionic tube is located in the cathode-anode circuit. The great majority of practical calculations, therefore, are for the cathode-anode circuit. The resistance characteristics of this circuit were discussed in Secs. **19** to **21.** Any voltage in the control-grid circuit affects the cathode-anode current. In so far as its effect on the cathode-anode circuit is concerned, a voltage in the control-grid circuit can be replaced by a voltage directly in series with the cathode-anode circuit. From Sec. **23** it is seen that this equivalent voltage in the cathode-anode circuit will have a value equal to the actual control-grid voltage times the amplification factor μ of the tube. For calculation purposes, therefore, the actual cathode-anode circuit can be replaced by the equivalent circuit of Fig. 20. In the majority of calculations, it is desired to determine the effect of the signal voltage on the load element of the anode circuit. In these cases, the d-c component of voltage and current can be neglected and only the varying or dynamic ones considered. For calculations of the dynamic characteristics of the cathode-anode circuit, the equivalent circuit of Fig. 21 is employed. In determining the values of the characteristics of the equivalent dynamic circuit, the following rules must be observed:

1. The amplification factor, employed to determine the equivalent anode-circuit voltage, must be the amplification factor of the tube for the grid bias voltage, the voltages of the other grids, and the cathode-anode voltage employed in the actual circuit. The cathode-anode voltage used to determine the amplification factor will not be the anode-circuit supply voltage but will be the anode-circuit supply voltage minus the voltage drop in the load.

2. The cathode-to-anode resistance of the tube must be the dynamic anode resist-

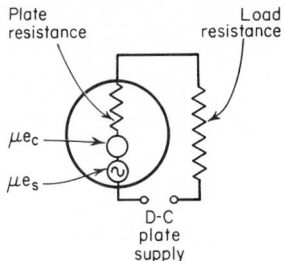

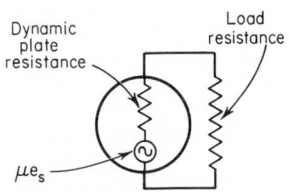

FIG. 20 ·*Equivalent circuit for an amplifier tube.*

FIG. 21 *Dynamic equivalent circuit for an amplifier tube.*

ance for the grid bias voltage, the voltages of the other grids, and the cathode-anode voltage employed. The d-c or ordinary resistance of the anode must not be used in the equivalent dynamic circuit.

29. The load line is a line that can be drawn on the plate voltage–plate current graph to study the operation of a vacuum tube as an amplifier. In using the tube as an amplifier, a load impedance r_L is connected in series with the plate, across the plate supply voltage E_B. The plate voltage e_p under any operating condition is then expressed by Eq. (7).

$$e_p = E_B - i_b r_L \tag{7}$$

This means that the plate voltage is less than the supply voltage by the amount of voltage drop in the load. When the load is a resistance, as it is in the majority of cases, values of e_p and i_b that satisfy Eq. (7) plot as a straight line. The most convenient way to draw this line (Fig. 22) is to obtain two points, one by letting $i_p = 0$ and solving for the corresponding value of e_p, the other by letting $e_p = 0$ and solving for the corresponding value of i_b. Then draw the straight line between them. In doing this, E_B and r_L must be known, having been previously selected or assumed if this is just a study. Any point on the load line is a possible operating condition, provided that the grid voltage is made the correct value.

Example. Referring to Fig. 22 and using $E_B = 525$ volts and $r_L = 30,000$, for $i_b = 0$, $e_p = E_B = 525$ volts; for $e_p = 0$, $i_p = E_B/r_L = 525/30,000 = 0.0175$ amp. These points are located at the points where the load line crosses the respective axes.

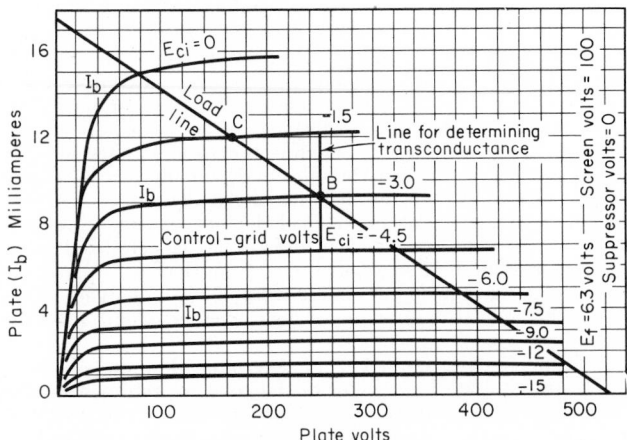

FIG. 22 *Plate current-voltage characteristic curves for a 6SK7 pentode showing a load line.*

The load line can be used to determine the operating conditions of the tube under any signal input. Referring to the data of the above example and to Fig. 22, if a signal of +1.5 volts is impressed on the grid in series with a −3.0 volt bias, the net grid voltage will be −3.0 + 1.5 = −1.5 volts. The intersection of the load line with the −1.5 characteristic curve at point C indicates that the plate current will then be 12 ma and the plate voltage will be 162 volts.

30. Thermionic vacuum tubes are rated in filament voltage and current, average value of plate current, average value of plate voltage, and, in the case of amplifier tubes, power output and amplification factor. In selecting a tube, it is important to see that the filament voltage is one that will be available from the power transformer. The standard ratings are 2.5, 6.3, 12, 50, and 117 volts. If the filaments of all the tubes in a chassis are to be in parallel, they must have the same voltage. If they are to be in series, they must be rated for the same current and the sum of their voltage ratings must equal the supply voltage. If the tube is to operate a relay, the plate current must be of a value that will be suitable for the relay coil. If the tube is to operate a speaker, the power output must check with the speaker rating. The direct current available from the power supply must be higher than the plate voltage recommended in order that the tube will have the correct plate voltage after allowing for the IZ drop in the load. The amplification factor should be large enough for the purpose for which the tube is to be used. It should be especially large for the first or second stage of an amplifier.

THERMIONIC GAS-FILLED TUBES

31. Diode thermionic gas-filled tubes are used infrequently in modern application because solid-state or metallic rectifiers have supplanted them in most instances. Some of these tubes, known as **phanotrons** or **tungar** or **rectigon tubes,** are still in use as rectifiers for small applications, such as for battery chargers.

32. Triode thermionic gas-filled tubes are known as **thyratrons.** Their construction is similar to that of phanotron tubes with the addition of a control-grid electrode (Fig. 23). The phanotron tubes pass only a very small current until the anode potential is high enough to break down and ionize the gas. After ionization, the current increases suddenly to a much higher value. It is often desirable to control the breakdown of the gas without changing the cathode-anode potential. This control of the breakdown of the gas can be obtained in the triode tube by means of the control grid, which is located between the cathode and the anode. When the grid is negative with respect to the cathode, force will be exerted by this grid voltage, tending to impede the acceleration of the electrons as they are emitted from the cathode. This opposition will require a higher cathode-anode voltage to produce breakdown of the gas and start normal conduction through the tube. With a definite anode voltage, if the grid is supplied with the proper voltage, breakdown of the gas and normal conduction will be prevented. If the grid is made positive, force will be exerted by this grid voltage tending to aid the acceleration of the electrons as they are emitted from the cathode, and a positive grid will therefore aid the anode voltage in breaking down the gas and producing normal conduction. In this type, unless the grid is made positive with respect to the cathode, the anode voltage will be unable to produce breakdown of the gas. Typical grid-control starting characteristics or breakdown characteristics are shown in Figs. 24 and 25. Some thyratrons are designed for control of breakdown through positive-grid control voltage, and others are designed for control of breakdown through negative-grid control voltage.

Operation of a thyratron requires three circuits, as shown in Fig. 26: the cathode-heating circuit, the cathode-anode circuit, and the control-grid circuit. The same precautions must be observed in the operation of thyratrons as are necessary for the operation of phanotron tubes. A resistor should be connected in series with the grid to limit grid current. When voltage is applied from cathode to anode and the cathode is heated to emission temperature, there will be no conduction of any appreciable magnitude through the tube until the cathode-anode voltage has been raised to the voltage that is required to break down the gas with the particular grid-control voltage that is applied to the grid. As stated previously, the value of the anode-cathode voltage

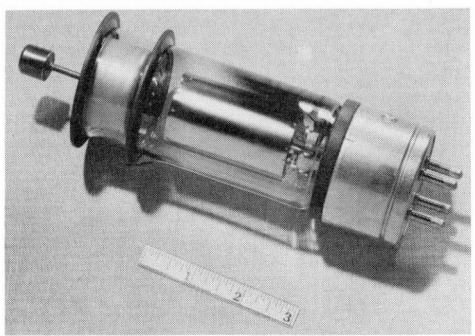

I. Metal glass construction.

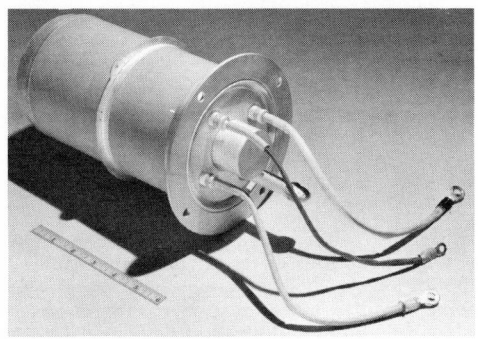

II. Metal ceramic construction.

FIG. 23   *Thyratron gas-filled tubes.   (General Electric Co.)*

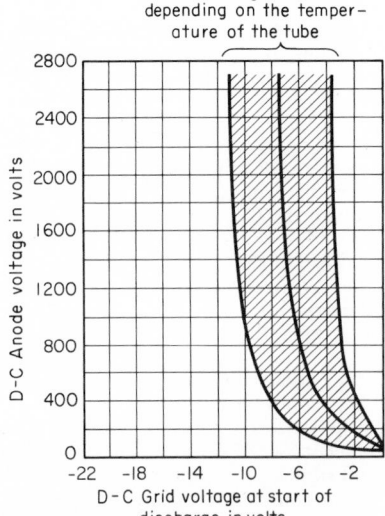

FIG. 24   *Negative breakdown characteristics for an FG-17 thyratron. (General Electric Co.)*

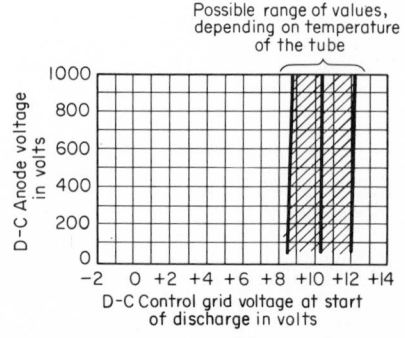

FIG. 25   *Positive breakdown characteristics for an FG-33 thyratron. (General Electric Co.)*

required to produce breakdown will be controlled by the value and polarity of the grid-control voltage. When the applied cathode-anode voltage is above breakdown, the gas will be ionized and the tube will pass current until the cathode-anode voltage is lowered to a value below the voltage drop of the tube. The grid voltage has no control over the anode current once the gas has broken down and conduction has started. Unless excessive reverse voltage is applied from cathode to anode, the tube will conduct in only one direction and will have rectifying characteristics.

The voltage drop from cathode to anode is relatively low and is practically independent of the current for inert-gas tubes and also is practically independent of the current for mercury-vapor tubes, provided that the operating temperature of the tube is held constant. The voltage-drop characteristics are practically the same as for phanotron tubes. As with phanotron tubes, because of the relatively low and constant voltage drop, it is always necessary to have sufficient impedance inserted in series with the anode circuit so as to limit the anode current to a safe value.

In the triode vacuum tube, the magnitude of the anode current is controlled by the magnitude and polarity of the control-grid voltage. This is not true in the thyratron tube. The grid in the gas tube will control the starting of conduction in the tube but has no control over the instantaneous anode current once ionization of the gas has been initiated and conduction has started. This lack of control by the grid over the magnitude of the instantaneous anode current is caused by the following action: As soon as the tube conducts,

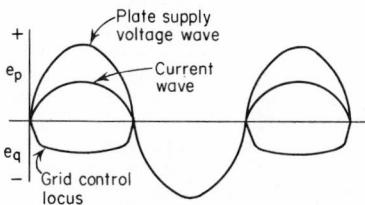

I - With small negative grid voltage

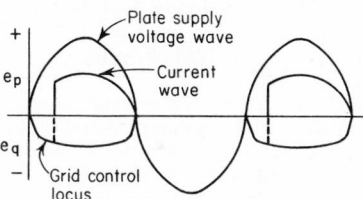

II - With medium negative grid voltage

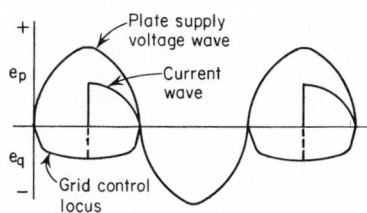

III- With larger negative grid voltage

FIG. 27 *Wave diagrams showing the principle of control of the average current with a thyratron tube employing d-c amplitude control of grid voltage.*

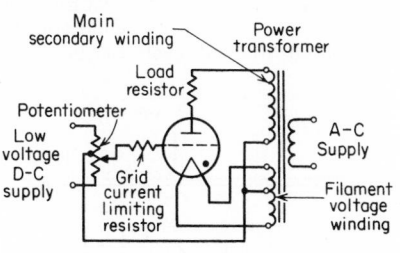

FIG. 26 *Circuit for a thyratron gas-filled tube.*

charged ions are attracted to the grid and form a sheath of charged ions around the grid structure. This sheath of ions, which will be of polarity opposite to that of the grid structure, shields the grid from the rest of the tube and renders the grid inactive with respect to the cathode-anode circuit.

Although the grid has no control over the magnitude of the instantaneous anode current, when a-c voltage is applied to the anode circuit, the *average* anode current can be controlled by controlling the period of conduction during each positive half cycle. With zero grid potential, anode current will start as soon as the anode voltage reaches a positive value equal to the breakdown voltage of the gas. Current will continue to flow until the voltage across the tube drops below the voltage drop of the tube. During the half cycle when the anode is negative, no current will flow because of the rectifying characteristic of the tube. If the grid is made somewhat negative, the anode current will not start until the anode voltage has reached a higher positive

value than that which started conduction with zero grid voltage. The tube will therefore conduct for a smaller portion of the positive half cycle. The average value of
the anode current will thereby be reduced. The fundamentals of the control of the
average anode current under a-c operation are shown in Fig. 27. Further discussion
of this control is given in Sec. **33**.

33. Control of Thyratrons. Circuits for controlling the breakdown, or firing, as it
is often called, of thyratron tubes may be divided into two general classes: (1) trigger
or amplitude control circuits and (2) phase-shift control circuits. With direct voltage
applied to the cathode-anode circuit, only amplitude control can be applied. With
alternating voltage applied to the cathode-anode circuit, either one of the methods can
be used. When direct voltage is applied to the cathode-anode circuit, the tube will
break down whenever the grid voltage is made more positive (less negative) than is
required to prevent breakdown and then will continue to pass current no matter what
is done to the grid voltage. In order to stop conduction and reduce the anode current
to zero, either the anode voltage must be reduced to practically zero or the anode circuit
must be opened by some switching means. When alternating voltage is applied to the
cathode-anode circuit, the grid will regain control every time the anode voltage becomes negative, since this will stop conduction in the anode circuit and require breakdown of the tube during each positive half cycle. The average current delivered to
the load by a thyratron tube operated on alternating current can be controlled by controlling the time during which current flows in each cycle. With trigger control, the
period of conduction of the tube can be gradually controlled from conduction throughout practically all of each positive half cycle to conduction throughout practically one-
half of each positive half cycle, but no control of conduction can be obtained throughout
the last half of each positive half cycle. Conduction can be entirely prevented, of
course, by a sufficiently negative grid. With phase-shift control, the period of conduction can be gradually controlled from conduction throughout practically all of each
positive half cycle down to the zero conduction period. Trigger control may employ
either direct or alternating voltage for the supply to the grid circuit. Phase-shift control requires an alternating voltage for the supply to the grid circuit.

The fundamentals of phase-shift control can be understood from a study of Fig. 28.
In part I of the figure, a grid-control locus curve is plotted for a given a-c anode voltage. The values for plotting this curve are obtained by taking instantaneous values
of the anode voltage and determining from the breakdown characteristic of the tube
the grid voltage that will just allow breakdown for each value of the anode voltage.
From the curves of I, the breakdown point in each positive half cycle can be deter-

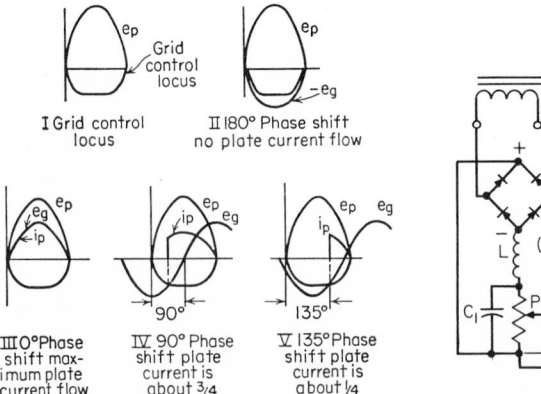

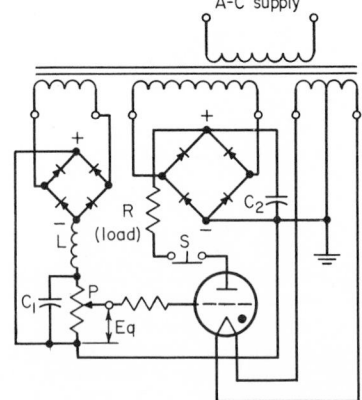

FIG. 28 *Wave diagrams showing phase-shift control of the average current of a thyratron tube.*

FIG. 29 *Control circuit for a thyratron tube with d-c anode voltage and d-c amplitude control.*

mined for any alternating voltage impressed on the grid.   In part II of the figure, an alternating voltage which is 180 deg out of phase with the anode voltage is impressed on the grid.   Since at all instants of time throughout the positive half cycle of the anode voltage the grid voltage is more negative than the critical grid voltage, the tube will be prevented from breaking down at any time.   Conduction in the anode circuit will be entirely prevented, and the anode current will be zero.   In part III of the figure, an alternating voltage which is in phase with the anode voltage is impressed on the grid.   Under these conditions, the tube will break down as soon as the anode voltage reaches a positive value equal to the breakdown voltage of the gas of the tube. This phase relationship of the grid voltage will give maximum length of conduction, and the tube will conduct throughout practically all of the positive half cycle of the anode voltage.   In part IV of the figure, the grid voltage is adjusted so that it lags the anode voltage.   The tube will break down at the instant that the grid-voltage curve crosses the grid-control locus curve, with the grid voltage decreasing in negative magnitude.   The tube will then conduct for only a portion of the positive half cycle of the anode voltage, and the average value of the anode current will be something less than the maximum amount obtained for conditions of part III of the figure.   In part V of the figure, the grid voltage is made to lag the anode voltage by a greater amount than for the conditions of part IV of the figure.   The tube then will not break down until a later point in the positive half cycle of the anode voltage than for part IV, and the average value of the anode current will be less than it was for IV.   As the angle of lag of the grid voltage is increased toward 180 degrees, the breakdown point will come later and later in the positive half cycle of the anode voltage, and the average anode current will be reduced until it reaches zero when the grid voltage is nearly 180 degrees lagging.   Thus, with phase-shift control, the conduction period of the tube can be controlled from conduction throughout practically all of the positive half cycle of the anode voltage to zero conduction, and the average value of the anode current can be gradually controlled from its maximum possible value down to zero.

A control circuit for operation of a thyratron with direct anode voltage is shown in Fig. 29.   The complete circuit is operated from an a-c supply with direct current supplied to the grid and anode circuits by means of bridge-connected contact rectifiers. The grid supply is filtered by means of the L-type inductance-capacitance filter (see Sec. **49**).   The anode supply is filtered by the capacitance filter C_2.   The grid voltage can be adjusted in magnitude by the potentiometer P.   When switch S is open, no conduction can take place, and the anode current is zero.   With switch S closed, the tube will fire or be prevented from firing, depending upon the setting of the potentiometer P.

A d-c trigger or amplitude-control circuit for operation of a thyratron with a-c anode voltage is shown in Fig. 30.   The variable direct grid-control voltage is obtained through the potentiometer P, which is energized from a bridge-connected contact rectifier.   The capacitor acts as a filter to smooth out the ripple in the d-c supply to the potentiometer.   Other means of obtaining the variable direct voltage for the grid circuit are a phototube supplied from a bridge-type rectifier, a grid-controlled amplifier tube, the voltage drop across a resistor, and the armature voltage of a small d-c generator. An a-c trigger-control circuit is shown in Fig. 31.

Three of the numerous circuits for producing phase-shift control are shown in Figs. 32, 33, and 34.   In the circuit of Fig. 32, phase shift of the grid voltage is obtained from a bridge circuit employing a variable resistor and a capacitor.   When the resistance R is zero, the grid voltage E_g is in phase with the anode voltage E_b.   As the value of the resistance R is increased, the grid voltage is made more lagging with respect to the anode voltage, and the average anode current of the thyratron is consequently decreased.   In the circuit of Fig. 33, phase shift of the grid voltage is obtained by means of a bridge circuit employing an inductive reactor and a variable resistor.   When the resistance R is zero, the grid voltage is 180 degrees out of phase with the anode voltage.   As the value of the resistance R is increased, the grid voltage is made less lagging with respect to the anode voltage and the average anode current of the thyratron is increased.   In an RL bridge circuit, the control of the amount of phase shift is often obtained by means of a fixed resistance in one arm of the bridge and a variable inductive reactance in the other arm.   A convenient means of varying the inductive reactance is

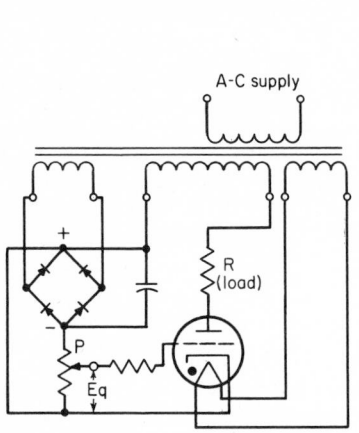

FIG. 30 *Control circuit for a thyratron tube with a-c anode voltage and d-c amplitude control.*

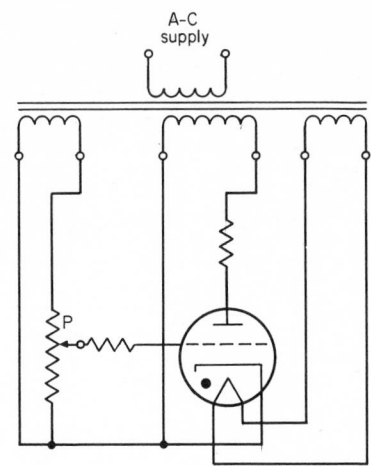

FIG. 31 *Control circuit for a thyratron tube with a-c anode voltage and a-c trigger control.*

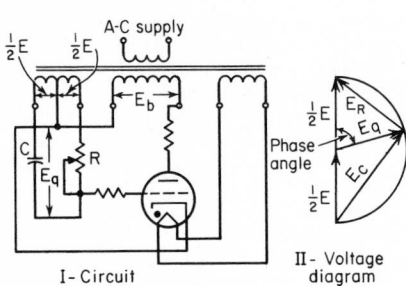

FIG. 32 *Control circuit for a thyratron tube using phase-shift control obtained from a variable resistance-capacitance bridge.*

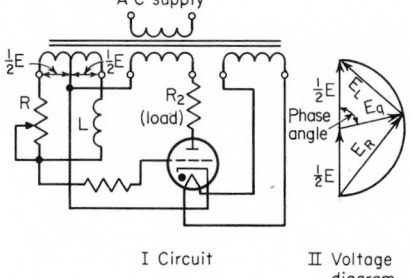

FIG. 33 *Control circuit for a thyratron tube using phase-shift control obtained from a variable resistance-inductance bridge.*

by means of a saturable-core reactor. Refer to Sec. **182** of Div. 5 for an explanation of a saturable-core reactor and to Sec. **140** of Div. 7 for an application of a phase-shift circuit employing a saturable-core reactor.

It is often desirable to control the phase shift through electronic means. One method of obtaining electronic phase-shift control is by varying the resistance of a phase-shift bridge circuit by means of a triode vacuum tube, as shown in Fig. 34. The anode circuit of the triode vacuum tube is in parallel with the resistance arm of the bridge R, C. As the grid voltage of the vacuum tube is made more positive, the resistance of the anode circuit of the tube is decreased. This decreases the total resistance of the resistance arm of the bridge and makes the grid voltage of the thyratron less lagging with respect to the anode voltage of the thyratron. The average current of the thyratron is thus increased.

A phase-shift control circuit employing a synchro for obtaining the phase shift of the grid voltage is shown in Fig. 35. If a synchro is energized from a three-phase supply, the phase relationship of the voltage induced in any one winding on the other element may be controlled by the setting of the position of the rotor of the synchro. Any phase

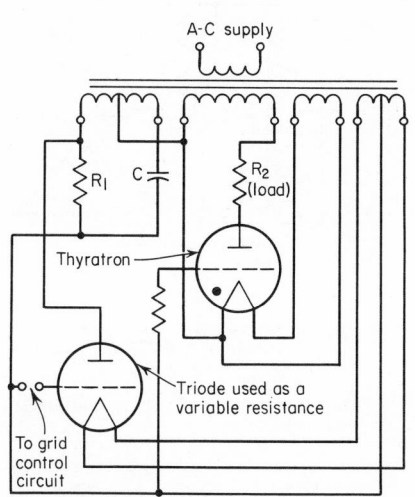

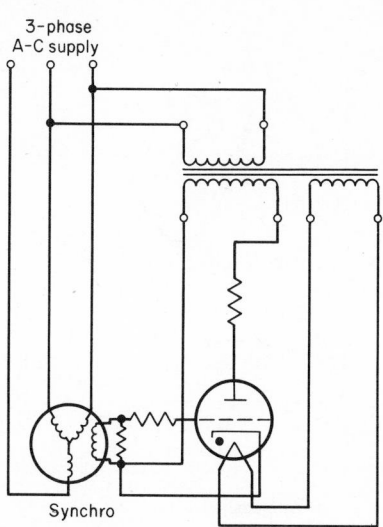

FIG. 34 *Control circuit for a thyratron tube using phase-shift control obtained from an amplifier-capacitor bridge.*

FIG. 35 *Control circuit for a thyratron tube using phase-shift control obtained from a synchro.*

relationship from in phase to 180 deg out of phase and back to in phase can be obtained.

Phase-shift control can also be obtained by means of an adjustable d-c grid-control voltage combined with an a-c voltage having a fixed phase shift. A circuit for this type of control is shown in Fig. 36. The phase-shift bridge supplying the a-c grid voltage usually is designed to make the a-c grid voltage lag the anode voltage by 90 degrees. When the d-c grid-control voltage is zero, the tube will fire slightly before the anode voltage reaches its maximum positive value, as shown in part I of Fig. 37.

When a positive d-c grid-control voltage is applied, the instant of breakdown of the tube will occur earlier in the positive half cycle of the anode voltage, as shown in part II of Fig. 37. With positive d-c grid-control voltage, the conduction period can be gradually adjusted from one-half of the positive half cycle to nearly the complete positive half cycle. When a negative d-c grid-control voltage is applied, the instant of breakdown of the tube is retarded, as shown in part III of Fig. 37. With negative d-c grid-control voltage, the conduction period can be gradually adjusted from one-half of the positive half cycle down to zero conduction. Thus, with this type of phase-shift control, the conduction period can be gradually adjusted from conduction throughout practically all of the positive half cycle down to zero conduction.

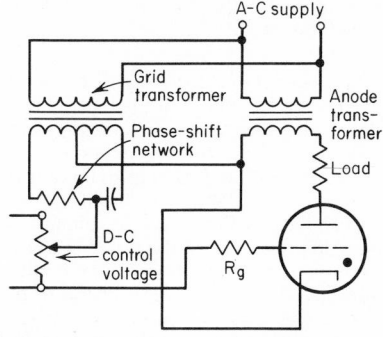

FIG. 36 *Thyratron controlled by fixed grid-voltage phase shift and adjustable d-c grid voltage.*

Another method of obtaining phase-shift control is by energizing the grid circuit by the secondaries of three transformers, as shown in Fig. 38. Transformer 1 is a peaking transformer. A peaking transformer is one designed so that its primary current will magnetize the core to saturation throughout the major portion of time. The relations of impressed voltage, primary current, and flux are shown in Fig. 39. With

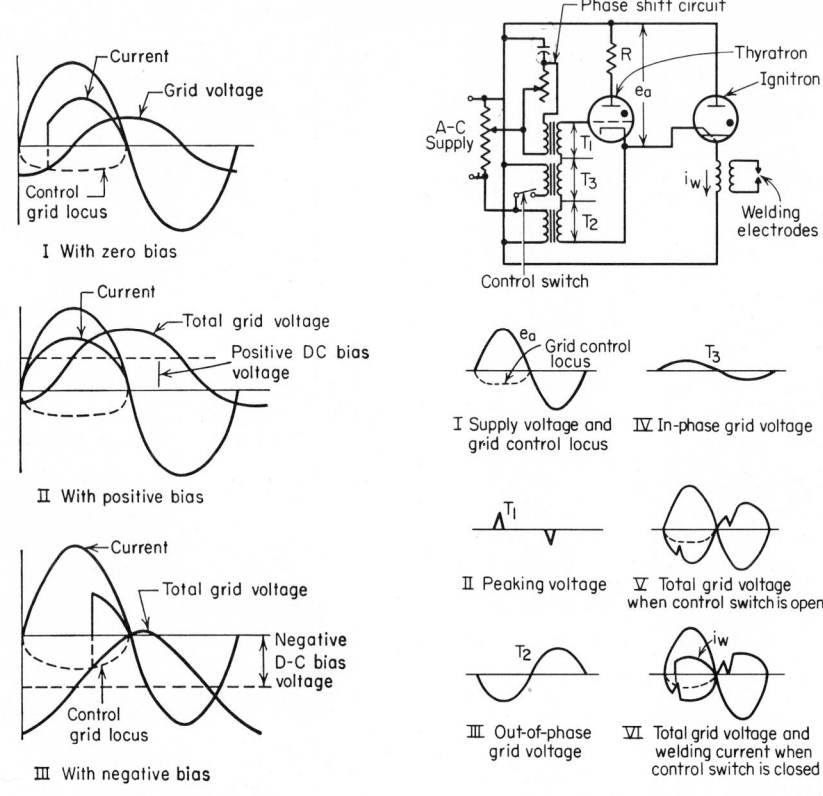

FIG. 37 *Wave diagrams showing thyra-tron control with fixed phase shift and adjustable bias.*

FIG. 38 *Control of welding circuit with a peaking transformer.*

such a transformer, there will be no change in the flux of the transformer except for the short intervals when the current and therefore the flux reverse in direction. During these short intervals, the flux will change rapidly and induce a sharp peak of voltage in the secondary winding, as shown in Fig. 39. The voltage relations of the grid circuit for phase-shift control employing a peaking transformer are shown in Fig. 38. Transformer 3 is connected so that its secondary voltage in the grid circuit is 180 degrees out of phase with the anode voltage. Its voltage is of sufficient magnitude to prevent the peaked voltage of the peaking transformer from firing the thyratron. Transformer 2 is connected so that its secondary voltage in the grid circuit is in phase with the anode voltage. When the circuit of transformer 2 is closed, the in-phase voltage of its secondary will raise the peaks of voltage to a value sufficient to fire the thyratron. The thyratron must be a positive-grid-controlled tube. The location of the peaks of voltage with respect to the cycle of anode voltage can be controlled through the phase-shift bridge, which supplies the primary of the peaking transformer. Thus the conduction period of the thyratron can be gradually controlled through the location of the voltage peaks from zero to conduction throughout practically all of the positive half cycle of anode voltage.

34. The tetrode thermionic gas-filled tube is generally called a **shield-grid thyra-tron.** It is similar in construction to the triode gas-filled tube with the addition of a second grid called the shield grid. The shield grid consists of a metallic envelope surrounding the cathode except for a hole at the top of the shield. This hole in the shield grid is in line with the control grid and the anode. The shield grid usually is held at cathode potential and serves to conserve the heat of the cathode, to shield the cathode from stray charges on the walls of the tube, to protect the control grid from contamination by active material evaporated from the cathode, and to protect the control grid from radiant heat radiated from the cathode. The general characteristics, operation, and control of the shield-grid thyratron are the same as for the triode thyratron.

35.   Thyratron tubes are specifically rated in cathode voltage and current, average value of plate current, peak value of plate current, peak forward voltage, and peak inverse voltage. The cathode voltage and current must be such that they are readily obtainable from the filament transformer.   The cathode voltage should be maintained within ±5 per cent of the rated value.   Large tubes usually are used with individual filament transformers; small ones with the filaments in parallel across one transformer.   The rated average value of plate current must be at least as large as the d-c output from the rectifier divided by the number of tubes in the rectifier. The rated peak value of current must be at least as great as the peak of the current output wave and must not be exceeded. The peak forward voltage is the highest voltage at which the grid can safely maintain control of the conduction.   The peak inverse voltage is the maximum negative voltage to which the plate should be subjected.   The greatest value of peak inverse voltage will occur in the case of full-wave single-phase rectification. In such a circuit, the peak inverse voltage will be $2\sqrt{2}$ times the value of the a-c voltage between a line terminal and the mid-point of the plate-circuit transformer.

MERCURY-POOL TUBES

36.   Diode mercury-pool tubes are probably the oldest form of electron tube. They have been known for years as **mercury-arc rectifiers.**   The mercury-arc rectifier consists of an enclosing envelope of glass or metal containing a pool of mercury at the bottom of the chamber.   The mercury pool forms the cathode of the tube.   One or more anodes made of iron or graphite

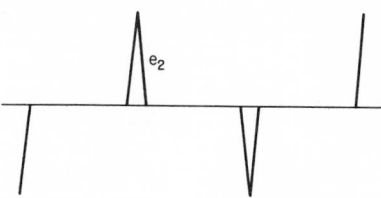

I Circuit

II Supply voltage

III Transformer primary Current and flux

IV Transformer secondary voltage

FIG. 39 *Generation of a peaking voltage pip with a saturated-core transformer.*

are supported by the enclosing structure at a proper distance above the surface of the pool. The present-day use of the mercury-arc rectifier tubes is principally in the larger sizes, which use a steel tank for the enclosure. A cross section of one of these large mercury-arc rectifiers is shown in Fig. 40. The low pressure required in the tube is maintained by means of a motor-driven vacuum pump. In order to start the rectifier, an auxiliary anode is required for striking an arc and producing mercury vapor from the surface of the mercury pool. In Fig. 40, the starting anode is raised or lowered by

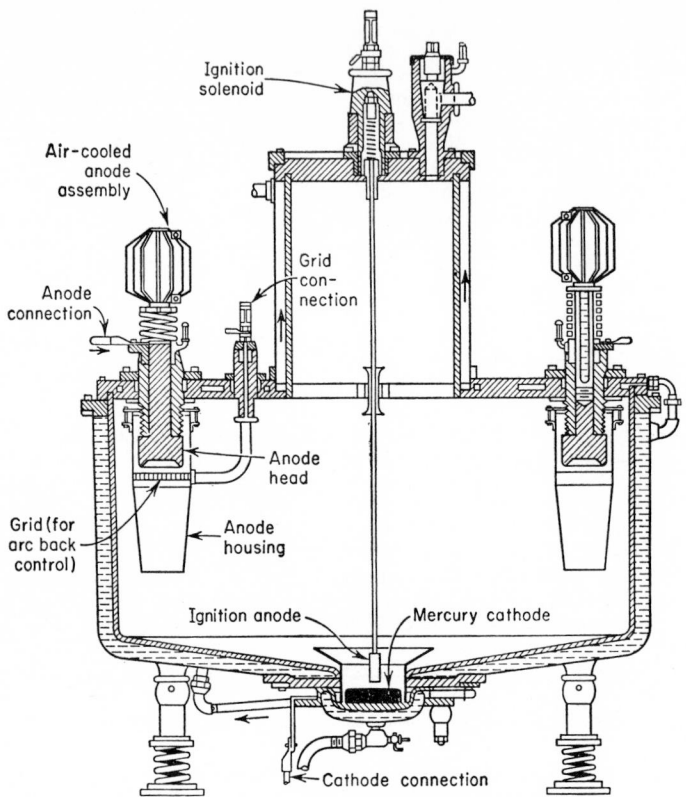

FIG. 40   *Tank-type mercury-arc rectifier.*

means of a solenoid. In starting the rectifier, the starting anode is lowered into the mercury pool and then withdrawn. As the starting anode is withdrawn from the mercury pool, an arc is formed which ionizes the mercury and fills the tube with ionized mercury vapor. Gaseous conduction will then take place from the mercury pool to the main anode or anodes. Conduction will be self-sustaining as long as the current does not drop to zero and an anode is maintained at positive potential with respect to the mercury-pool cathode. In polyphase rectifiers under normal operating conditions, conduction will shift from the anode of one phase before that anode has ceased to conduct to the anode of another phase. In this manner, the current is never allowed to drop to zero, and conduction is maintained until the circuit is broken by some switching means.

In the rectifier of Fig. 40, the solenoid, which operates the starting anode, is automatically controlled so that, if the arc is extinguished during operation because of some abnormal condition, the starting anode will automatically be lowered into the mercury pool and then withdrawn, striking an arc and restarting the rectifier. In single-phase rectifiers, an auxiliary keep-alive circuit is often provided. The keep-alive circuit requires that the tube be provided with an auxiliary set of anodes connected to a supply voltage in series with an inductance. The inductance load of the keep-alive circuit makes the current lag behind the voltage, and conduction is thereby maintained to one anode until conduction has started to the other auxiliary anode. The keep-alive circuit maintains ionized mercury vapor in the tube so that, if current to the main anodes is interrupted, conduction to the main anodes will be automatically reestablished as soon as any main anode becomes positive with respect to the cathode.

Small single-phase rectifiers are generally provided with an auxiliary starting anode mounted close to the mercury pool and continuously connected to a voltage supply whenever the tube is operating. An auxiliary automatically controlled mechanism tilts the tube for starting of the rectifier. As the tube tilts, mercury bridges the gap between the mercury pool and the starting anode. As the tube comes back to normal position, an arc is formed as the mercury recedes from the starting anode, mercury vapor is formed, and the keep-alive or main anodes become conducting.

The anode current of diode-mercury-pool tubes cannot be controlled by the tube. The voltage drop from cathode to anode is of relatively low value from 12 to 30 volts. The voltage drop is practically independent of the magnitude of the anode current. Unless excessive voltage is applied to the tube, the tube will allow the passage of current in only one direction between the cathode and any one anode. These tubes therefore have rectifier characteristics.

37. Triode mercury-pool tubes are known as **ignitrons.** They overcome the no-control-of-anode-current disadvantage of the diode mercury-pool rectifier tubes. Control of the point in the positive half cycle when current starts and therefore control of the average anode current is obtained by means of a control electrode called the ignitor. The essential elements of the construction of an ignitron tube are shown in Fig. 41. The cathode of the tube is provided by a pool of mercury at the bottom of the enclosing envelope. A single anode is mounted above the mercury pool. The ignitor (the control electrode) is made of high-resistance refractory material and has a conelike tip. The ignitor electrode is so mounted that its conelike tip is immersed in the mercury pool. Surface tension produces a very small separation between the tip of the ignitor and the mercury pool. When sufficient voltage is applied between the mercury pool and the ignitor, arcing occurs from the surface of the mercury pool across the small separation to the tip of the ignitor. This arc produces ionized mercury vapor throughout the enclosure of the tube. Gaseous conduction will then start from the mercury pool to the anode whenever the anode is positive with respect to the mercury-pool cathode. Conduction to the anode will continue until the voltage applied from cathode to anode drops below the voltage drop from cathode to anode.

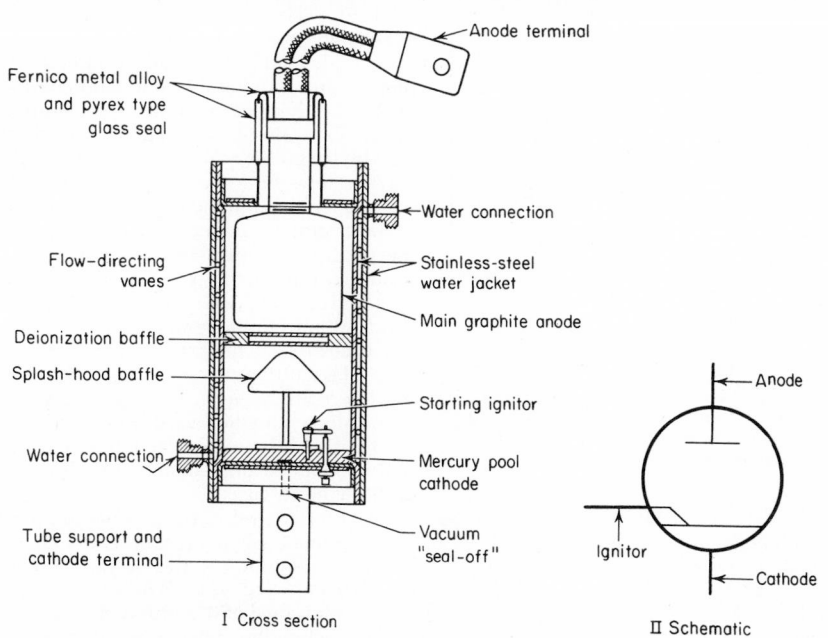

I Cross section   II Schematic

FIG. 41 *Ignitron tube.* (*General Electric Co.*)

If the ignitor circuit is continually energized or is energized at the start of each positive cycle of the anode voltage, current will flow in the cathode-anode circuit during practically all of each positive half cycle. If the time is controlled in the positive half cycle of anode voltage at which the ignitor circuit is energized, the portion of the positive half cycle during which anode conduction takes place can be controlled. Thus the average anode current of the ignitron tube can be controlled in a manner similar to that of a thyratron tube (see Sec. **33**).

The ignitor of the ignitron tube, like the grid of the thyratron tube, has control of only the starting of conduction and has no control over the magnitude of the anode current once conduction is started and the anode is maintained positive with respect to the cathode. Like the thyratron tube, however, the ignitron tube can control the average anode current when alternating voltage is applied to the cathode-anode circuit. The characteristic of the ignitron differs from that of the thyratron in that the ignitron will not start until forced to do so by energizing the ignitor circuit whereas the thyratron remains nonconducting only so long as it is prevented from starting by application of the proper potential to the control grid. The voltage drop of ignitron tubes is very nearly the same as for diode-mercury-vapor tubes and is practically independent of the magnitude of the anode current. Unless excessive voltage is applied from cathode to anode, ignitron tubes will allow the passage of current in only one direction.

38. Control of Ignitrons. The ignition potential for the ignitor circuit generally is secured from a diode or triode thermionic gas-filled tube or the combined use of both of these types of tubes. When no control of the conduction period is desired, the ignitor circuit is supplied by a diode tube. When the time of the conduction period must be controlled, the ignitor circuit is supplied by a triode or a circuit employing both a diode and a triode. Two general types of ignition circuits are employed. In one type, the ignition current passes through the load of the ignitron. These ignition circuits are known as load-current ignition circuits. In the other type, the power for ignition is obtained from a circuit separate from the load. These ignition circuits are known as separately excited ignition circuits.

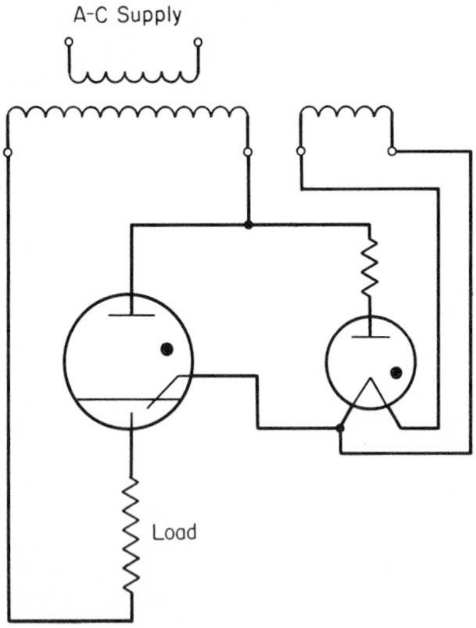

A simple load-current ignition circuit employing no control of the conduction period of the ignitron and using a diode ignition tube is shown in Fig. 42. When the anode of the diode ignition tube becomes positive, current flows from the positive terminal of the supply, through the diode ignition tube to the ignitor, through the load, and back to the negative terminal of the supply. The anode current of the ignitron is thus initiated, and current passes through the ignitron and load until the potential across the ignitron tube drops to the extinction point of the arc. The ignition process is repeated each positive half cycle. The ignition tube should have a higher arc drop than that of the ignitron tube so that the ignitor current will be stopped immediately after ignition of the ignitron takes place.

A-C Supply

Load

FIG. 42 *Circuit of an ignitron tube controlled by a gas-filled diode.* (*Load-current ignition.*)

A load-current ignition circuit that can be used for control of the conduction time of the ignitron is shown in Fig. 43. A triode thermionic gas-filled tube is employed for the control of the ignitron. Grid-bias voltage is supplied to the control tube by means of a contact rectifier with a capacitor filter (see Sec. **49**). When the control tube breaks down, current passes from the positive terminal of the supply through the control tube to the ignitor, through the load, and back to the negative terminal of the supply. As in the circuit of Fig. 42, the control tube should have a higher arc drop than

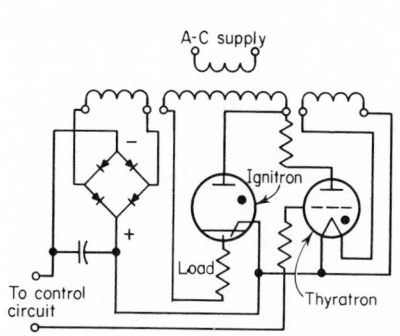

FIG. 43 *Circuit for an ignitron tube controlled by a thyratron. (Load-current ignition.)*

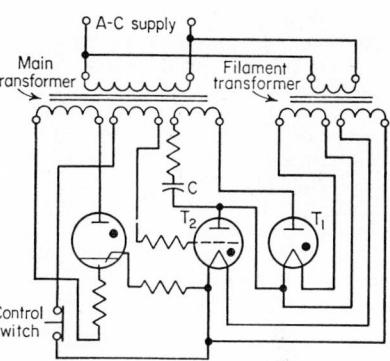

FIG. 44 *Circuit for an ignitron tube controlled by a capacitor discharge. (Separately excited ignition.)*

that of the ignitron. Control of the conduction time of the ignitron is obtained by controlling the point in the positive half cycle at which the control tube breaks down. Any of the methods described in Sec. **33** can be employed for this breakdown control.

A separately excited ignition circuit is shown in Fig. 44. This circuit employs two control tubes, a diode and a triode. During the half cycle when the anode of the ignitron is negative, the capacitor C is charged through the transformer and diode tube T_1. During the half cycle when the anode of the ignitron is positive, the polarity of the charged capacitor C is such that the capacitor cannot discharge through the diode tube T_1 but it is of the polarity so that it is possible for it to discharge through the circuit formed by the thyratron T_2 and the ignitor of the ignitron. The point in the cycle when the capacitor discharges through this circuit depends upon the point at which the triode tube T_2 breaks down. The breakdown point of tube T_2 will depend upon the grid-bias voltage and the grid-control voltage used for tube T_2. In Fig. 44, tube T_2 is biased with an alternating voltage obtained from the transformer at the top of the figure. The grid-control voltage is applied across the input terminals and could be obtained from some form of phase-shift circuit. When tube T_2 breaks down, the capacitor discharges through tube T_2 and the ignitor and thus initiates conduction through the ignitron tube and load.

39. Mercury-pool tubes are rated in average value of anode current, peak value of anode current, peak forward voltage, and peak inverse voltage. The ratings have the same meaning as explained in Sec. **35.**

COLD-CATHODE GAS-FILLED TUBES

40. Cold-cathode Gas-filled Tubes. In cold-cathode gas-filled tubes the cathode consists of a simple solid metallic electrode, which may or may not be coated to lower the required emission energy. The tube is generally filled with some inert gas at low pressure. When sufficient voltage is applied between the two main electrodes, the gas will be ionized and emission will be produced at one of the electrodes for maintaining the conduction. The emission of electrons from a cold cathode is a complex phenomenon and in most cases probably is a combination of all four of the causes of emission explained in Sec. **2.** The principal cause of emission in most cases undoubtedly is electric-field emission. The voltage from cathode to anode required to produce conduction with cold-cathode tubes is therefore much greater than is required with hot cathodes or mercury-pool cathodes. The amount of emission is also limited with cold-cathode tubes, and the anode current of cold-cathode tubes is therefore limited to small values. In cold-cathode tubes, the two main electrodes may have identical construction so that either electrode can function as either cathode or anode, depending upon the polarity of the impressed voltage. A tube with this construction will pass current in either direction and will not have rectifying characteristics. If the two main electrodes have different construction, so that it is much more difficult to produce emission from one of the electrodes than from the other, then only one of the electrodes will function as an emitter unless excessive voltage is applied to the tube. Tubes with this electrode construction, under normal operating conditions, will pass current in only one direction and will, therefore, possess rectifying characteristics. Cold-cathode tubes require appreciably more voltage to break down the gas and start conduction than is required to maintain conduction after it has been started. The cathode-anode voltage drop during conduction depends upon the type of gas and pressure employed in the tube and in some cases upon the temperature of the gas. The voltage drop is practically independent of the magnitude of the current. It is always necessary to have an impedance connected in series with the anode circuit in order to control the magnitude of the anode current and to limit the current to a safe value.

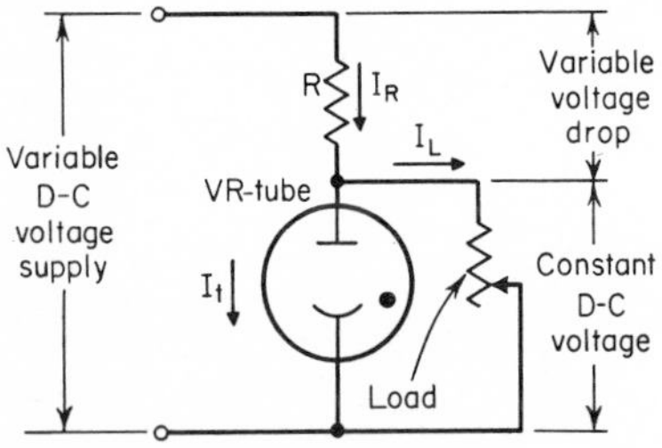

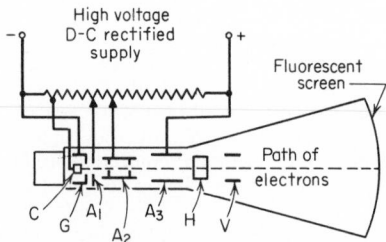

FIG. 45   *Voltage-regulating circuit employing a VR tube.*

The voltage drop will be much greater in the cold-cathode tube than in hot-cathode or mercury-pool-cathode tubes.

Diode tubes of the cold-cathode type are used as voltage-regulating devices in many electronic circuits for the purpose of providing a practically constant voltage source. When the tube is connected in series with a resistance to a source of voltage, a practically constant voltage can be obtained across the tube for the operation of some other circuit, as shown in Fig. 45.

Triode tubes of the cold-cathode type are used for control purposes in low-current applications where the cathode-heating power required for hot-cathode tubes would be detrimental or inconvenient. The control grid of a triode cold-cathode tube will function in the same manner as the control grid in a triode hot-cathode tube (the thyratron). The control grid of the cold-cathode tube will, therefore, have the ability to control the start of anode current but will have no control over the magnitude of the anode current once conduction has been started.

CATHODE-RAY TUBES

41. The cathode-ray tube is a special type of thermionic tube which produces a beam of electrons directed against a luminescent screen or target. It employs a glass envelope which usually is highly evacuated. Certain types of these tubes contain an inert gas at low pressure. The essential construction, functioning, and operation of a cathode-ray tube can be understood by study of Fig. 46. The construction consists of an indirectly heated cathode C; a control grid G for controlling the number of electrons in the beam; an anode A_1 to accelerate the electrons; an anode A_2 to focus the beam of electrons and further accelerate them; a high-voltage anode A_3 for further acceleration of the electrons; two sets of deflecting plates H and V for deflection of the beam

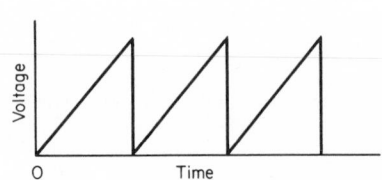

FIG. 46   *Arrangement of electrodes in a cathode-ray tube.*

FIG. 47   *Linear sweep voltage.*

in horizontal and vertical directions, respectively; and a luminescent screen consisting of a luminescent coating on the inner surface of the bulb. A certain number of the electrons emitted by the cathode, as controlled by the grid G, are highly accelerated and directed in a narrow beam by means of the small apertures in grid G and anodes A_1 and A_2 toward the screen. When no voltage is applied to either of the sets of deflecting plates H and V, the beam of electrons, when properly adjusted, will strike the screen at its center point and produce a luminous spot at that point. The direction of the beam and consequently the location of the luminous spot produced on the screen can be controlled by the application of voltages between the horizontal plates and between the vertical plates.

The cathode-ray tube, when combined with power supply and control circuits to form the instrument known as a cathode-ray oscilloscope, is a versatile measuring and testing instrument. The practical applications of the cathode-ray oscilloscope are growing continually.

The cathode-ray oscilloscope is provided with a control circuit, which will impress a voltage between the horizontal deflecting plates that will vary directly with respect to time. The wave form of such a voltage is shown in Fig. 47. The circuit is so constructed and controlled that this voltage between the horizontal plates will cause the spot on the screen to sweep across the screen horizontally at a uniform velocity. For this reason such control circuits are called sweep circuits. With the sweep circuit operating, if a varying voltage is applied between the vertical deflecting plates V, the spot will trace a luminous pattern on the screen. By proper adjustment of the frequency of the sweep circuit, a periodically varying voltage impressed on the vertical plates will produce a trace on the screen that will appear stationary and will show the wave form of the voltage.

PHOTOTUBES

42. Phototubes are photoemissive electron tubes. All phototubes are constructed as diodes. The cathode generally is constructed of sheet metal bent into semicircular form so as to give appreciable exposure to the incident lighting source. The inner surface of the cathode is coated with a light-sensitive emitting material (see Sec. **11**). The anode consists of a wire located approximately along the axis of the cathode. When light falls upon the coated cathode, electrons are emitted. The amount of emission will depend upon the wave length of the incident light, the material of the coating, and the amount of light falling upon the coating. When the anode is made positive with respect to the cathode and incident light is producing emission, conduction will take place from cathode to anode. Conduction in phototubes depends upon the anode being positive, and they therefore possess rectifying characteristics. Phototubes are made in both vacuum and gas-filled types.

In the vacuum type of phototube, the anode current for a given illumination of the cathode rises rapidly with increasing anode voltage until the electrons are pulled across to the anode as fast as they are emitted. Any further increase in the anode voltage produces little effect upon the anode current. Typical anode-current versus anode-voltage characteristics are shown in Fig. 48. Provided that the tube is operated with an anode voltage above the saturation point, the anode current is practically proportional to the amount of light falling on the coated cathode. Typical anode-current versus incident-light-flux characteristics are shown in Fig. 49.

In the gas-filled type of phototube, the anode current for a given illumination of the cathode increases continually as the anode voltage is increased. For low voltages, the current rises rapidly until the electrons are pulled across to the anode nearly as fast as they are emitted. Further increase in voltage at first increases the anode current only slightly. Up to this point on the characteristic the gas has not been materially ionized. As the voltage is still further increased, the gas is ionized, and the current increases rapidly with increase in voltage. Typical anode-current versus anode-voltage characteristics are shown in Fig. 50. For a definite anode voltage, the anode current increases with the amount of light falling upon the cathode, but the current is not proportional to the amount of incident light. In recent years, phototubes have been replaced by light-sensitive semiconductors.

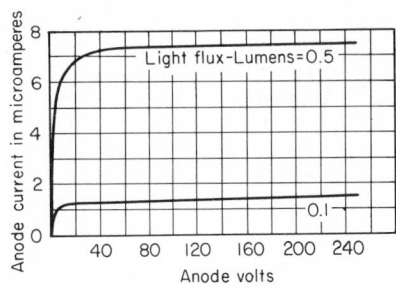

FIG. 48 *Plate current-voltage character-istic curves of an RCA type 925 vacuum phototube. (RCA Mfg. Co.)*

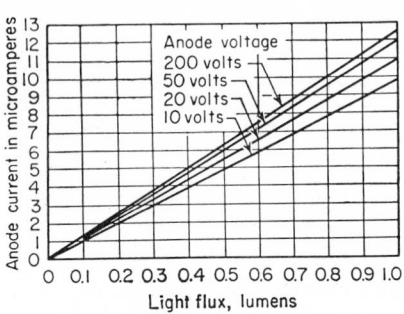

FIG. 49 *Plate current–light flux charac-teristic curves of a type PJ-22 vacuum phototube. (General Electric Co.)*

43. Photoconductive cells are photosensitive devices. They are not phototubes, and although they generally are classed as such, they are not strictly electronic devices. Although they may be enclosed in an evacuated space, their functioning does not depend upon conduction in a vacuum or in a gas. Photoconductive cells function through the effect of light upon the electrical resistance of certain materials. Some 15 or more natural minerals have been found that possess this photoconductive property. Selenium, however, is one material possessing this characteristic and it has been used to an appreciable extent for the construction of photoconductive cells. Typical construction of a selenium cell is shown in Fig. 51. A thin layer of platinum or gold is supported between two glass plates. A thin line is scratched through this conducting layer of platinum or gold, and the line is filled with selenium. The electric path through the cell is from terminal 1 through side A of the layer of platinum or gold to the line of selenium, through the selenium to side B of the platinum or gold, and through side B of the layer of platinum or gold to terminal 2.

Selenium is a semiconductor, i.e., neither a good conductor nor a good insulator. When it is illuminated, its resistance decreases so that it becomes a better conductor. Thus, in the selenium cell, as the light falling on the cell increases, the resistance from terminal 1 to terminal 2 decreases, and the current through the cell for a definite impressed voltage will increase. The increase in current caused by illumination is not directly proportional to the increase in light falling on the cell. Selenium cells have only a very limited field of application.

44. Photovoltaic cells are photosensitive devices but, like photoconductive cells, are

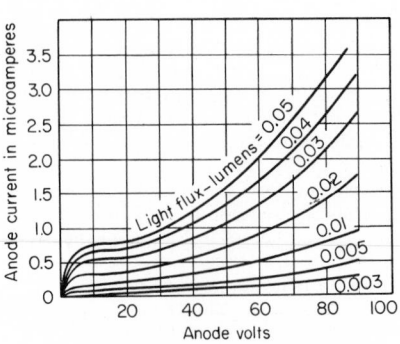

FIG. 50 *Plate current–voltage character-istic curves of an RCA type 920 gas-filled phototube. (RCA Mfg. Co.)*

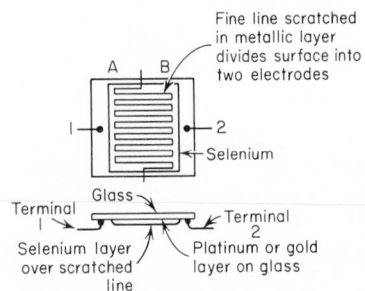

FIG. 51 *Selenium photoconductive cell.*

not phototubes nor are they strictly electronic devices. Photovoltaic cells function by virtue of the ability of certain types of barrier layers between two substances to produce an emf from one of the substances to the other when the barrier layer is illuminated. Two barrier layers that have been used in commercial photovoltaic cells are cuprous oxide and selenium. When the barrier layer is illuminated, a small voltage is produced between the two terminals of the cell. The magnitude of the voltage produced will increase with the amount of illumination of the sensitive barrier layer. A cuprous oxide cell is manufactured by the Westinghouse Electric Corp. and is known as the Photox cell. It consists of a layer of cuprous oxide between a copper disk and a thin transparent metallic film. A commercial selenium cell is the Weston Photronic cell. It consists of a thin layer of selenium on an iron disk. Photovoltaic cells are used widely for illumination measurements.

FUNCTIONS OF ELECTRON TUBES

45. Functions of Electron Tubes. The principal functions that electron tubes are capable of performing are
1. Rectification.
2. Amplification.
3. Relay.
4. Switch.
5. Oscillator.
6. Modulation.
7. Detection.

46. Electron Tubes as Rectifiers. As discussed in Sec. **8,** most electron tubes possess a rectifying characteristic, allowing, unless excessive voltage is applied, the passage of current through the tube in only one direction. The purpose of using the tube may not be to perform this rectifying function. The tube is called a rectifier only when it is used primarily to perform the function of rectification. Tubes are used extensively as rectifiers for the production of direct current from an a-c supply. They are applicable over the complete rectification field, from applications requiring the rectification of only very small amounts of power to those requiring the conversion of the largest amounts of power. Vacuum tubes are employed for rectification of power at high voltages and of low current values. Thermionic gas-filled tubes are used in low- and medium-voltage circuits having current capacities up to about 100 amp. Mercury-pool gas-filled tubes are used in low- and medium-voltage circuits requiring medium and high current capacities. Diode tubes are used for applications where it is not necessary for the tube to control the initiating of the current or the average value of the current. Triode tubes are employed where it is advantageous to have either the initiating of the current or the average value of the current controlled by the tube. Electronic rectifiers can be used for supplying direct current from either single-phase or polyphase sources.

47. Diode Rectifier Circuits. The simplest electronic rectifier circuit is the single-phase half-wave rectifier shown in Fig. 52. In this type of rectifier, the a-c power supply has a high ratio of peak load to average load, since it is delivering power only half the time. The single-phase full-wave rectifier circuit, shown in Fig. 53, overcomes this difficulty. During one half cycle the current path is from the transformer to the anode of one tube shown in the figure, through the tube to the load, and back to the center point of the transformer. During the other half of the cycle, the current passes from the transformer to the anode of the other tube, through the tube to the load, and back to the center point of the transformer. With this circuit, each half of the transformer winding is used only half of the time. Another type of full-wave rectifier circuit is known as the bridge type of rectifier. It employs four tubes connected as shown in Fig. 54. The bridge rectifier circuit utilizes all of the transformer winding continuously and gives a low ratio of peak power to average power. On the other hand, the bridge rectifier requires four tubes against two for the other type of full-wave rectifier.

Some diode tubes of the thermionic vacuum, thermionic gas-filled, and mercury-pool tubes are made with two anodes and a common cathode in the same enclosing envelope. These tubes are used for single-phase full-wave rectification and are con-

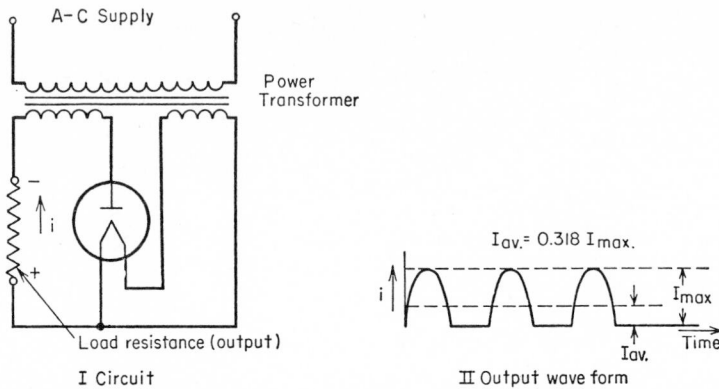

FIG. 52 *Single-phase half-wave rectifier.*

nected as shown in Fig. 55. Applications of such tubes are shown in the circuits of Figs. 59 to 63.

For large amounts of power, the rectifier supply is generally taken from all three phases of a three-phase source. Three-phase rectifier circuits are shown in Figs. 56 to 58.

48. Triode Rectifier Circuits. In the diode rectifier circuits of Sec. **47,** the amount of power delivered to a given load depends entirely on the supply voltage. Also the initiating of current depends entirely on the closure of the power supply and load circuits. Often it is advantageous to have either or both the initiation of current and the amount of power controlled by other means. This control is possible through the use of triode tubes and the control of the anode current by means of the control grid. Triode rectifiers are called controlled rectifiers. Vacuum tubes can be employed for controlled rectifiers, but the greater economy through lower voltage drop and the higher current capacities of gas-filled tubes eliminates the vacuum tubes for these applications except for high voltage or very low current applications. With the triode gas-filled rectifiers, the amount of power delivered to the load is controlled by the portion of the time during each cycle that current is allowed to pass through the tube to the load, as discussed in Sec. **33** for thyratron tubes and in Sec. **38** for ignitron tubes. The connections for the anode-load circuits of triode rectifiers are the same as for diodes, as given in Sec. **47.**

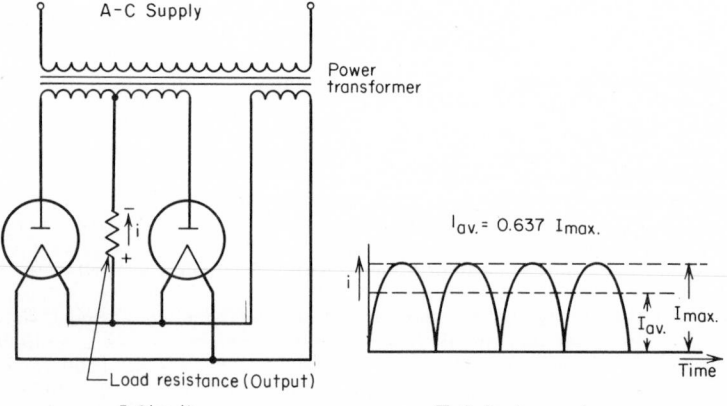

FIG. 53 *Single-phase full-wave rectifier.*

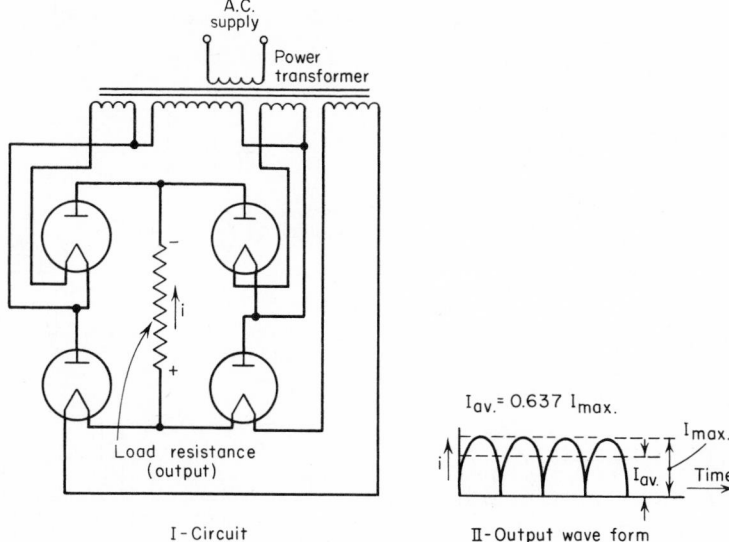

FIG. 54 *Single-phase bridge-type rectifier.*

To the anode-load circuits of these figures must be added the grid-control circuit for each tube. The fundamentals of these grid-control circuits are given in Secs. **33** and **38**.

49. Filters. The d-c output voltage and current of all the rectifier circuits discussed in Secs. **47** and **48** will not be of constant magnitude but will vary considerably. It is seen that the variation of the d-c output voltage is greatest for the half-wave single-phase rectifiers and that the amount of variation is decreased as the number of phases is increased. The variation in the output voltage is called a ripple. If the rectifier is supplying power to an inductive load, the inductance of the load will reduce the amount of ripple present in the current. In many cases, especially with single-phase rectifiers, a more constant d-c output voltage is required than can be obtained from the basic rectifier circuit. In order to produce this reduction of the ripples in the rectifier output and make the load current more constant, additional circuit elements are inserted between the output terminals of the rectifier and the load. The combinations of circuit elements employed for this purpose are called filters. They filter out the ripple in the d-c output

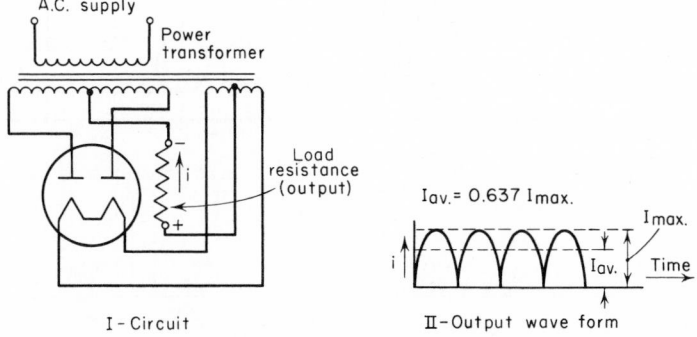

FIG. 55 *Single-phase full-wave rectifier, using a single full-wave rectifier tube.*

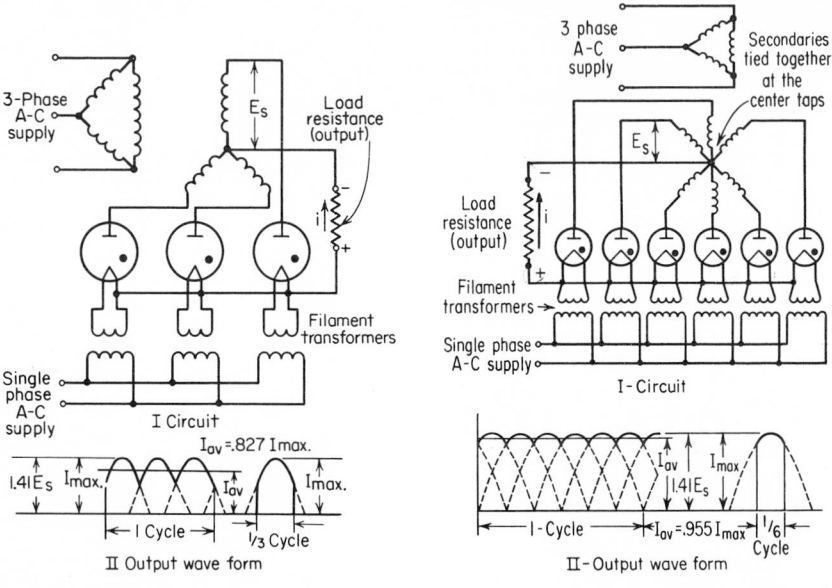

FIG. 56   *Three-phase half-wave three-tube rectifier.*

FIG. 57   *Three-phase full-wave six-tube rectifier.*

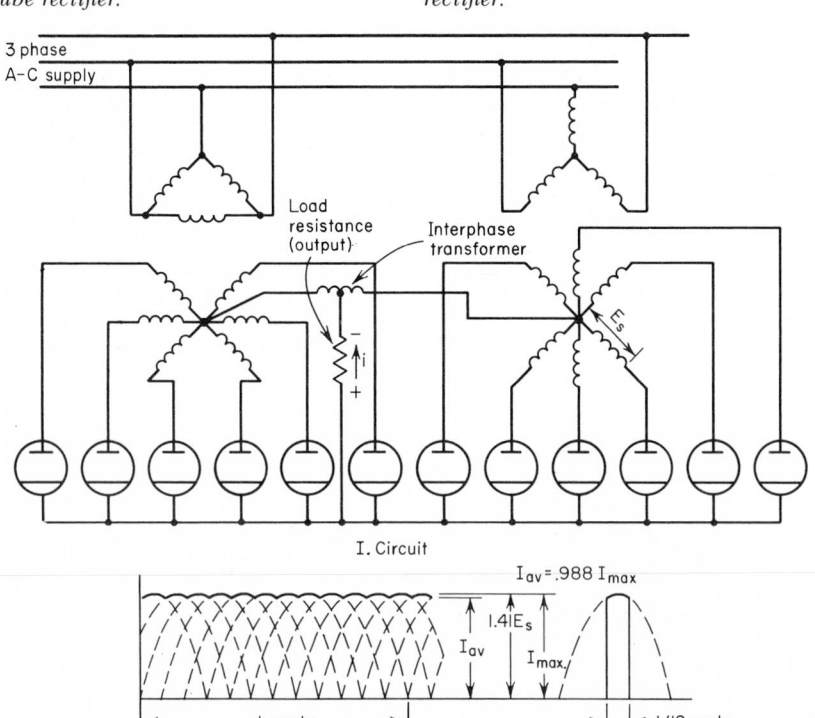

FIG. 58   *Three-phase 12-tube rectifier.*

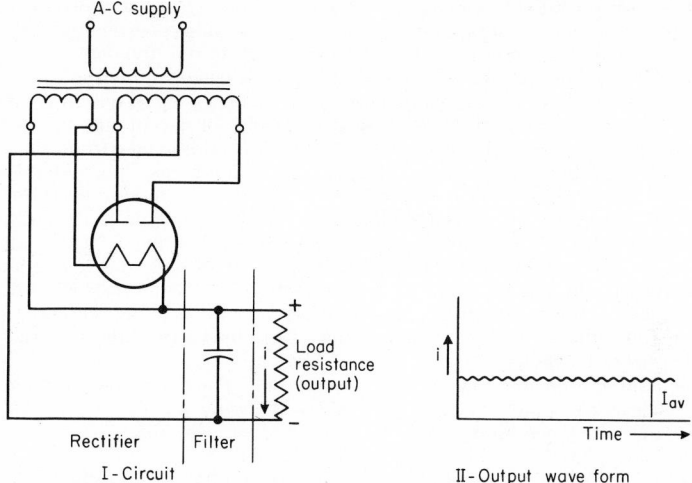

FIG. 59 *Full-wave rectifier tube with capacitor filter.*

delivered to the load so that the voltage and current of the load are more nearly of constant magnitude. It is not possible to eliminate the variations completely, and the degree to which the ripple is removed depends upon the complexity of the filter circuit employed.

The simplest form of filter for a rectifier consists either of a capacitor connected across the output terminals of the rectifier or of an inductance connected in series with the output of the rectifier. Such simple filters are shown in Figs. 59 and 60. The capacitor will offer relatively small opposition to the passage of current produced by the ripple components of the voltage but will offer practically infinite opposition to the passage of current produced by the constant portion of the voltage. The variations in the rectifier output voltage will therefore produce an alternating current through the capacitor, and this alternating current, in passing through the rectifier and its supply, will produce an alternating voltage drop. The capacitor does not cause any d-c component of current to flow through the rectifier, and there is therefore no d-c voltage drop in the rectifier because of the filtering capacitor. Thus some of the ripple voltage of the rectifier is consumed in the rectifier itself because of the alternating current drawn from it by the filtering capacitor. The voltage at the output terminals of the filtering capacitor therefore does not contain as much ripple as would be present without the filtering capacitor. The capacitor also helps to remove the ripple through an additional smoothing action.

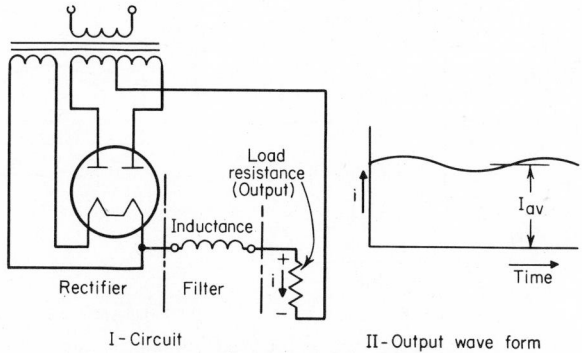

FIG. 60 *Full-wave rectifier with inductance filter.*

Since all the ripple cannot be removed by the previously explained filtering action, the output voltage will contain some ripple. Therefore, the output current will not be constant. As the output current tends to drop because of drop in the output voltage, the capacitor will discharge to the load, helping the rectifier to supply the load current. This relief of some of the load from the rectifier will tend to keep its output voltage from dropping. As the output current tends to rise because of rise in output voltage, the capacitor at the same time will be charging and pulling additional current through the rectifier. This additional current caused by the capacitor, as the voltage tends to rise, will produce greater voltage drop in the rectifier and thereby tend to keep the output voltage of the rectifier and capacitor filter from rising. The capacitor filter will also tend to hold the current through the rectifier more nearly constant as load changes and thereby to hold the output voltage more nearly constant with varying load conditions. The capacitor acts as a storage tank to aid the rectifier. At some instants of time, the capacitor is taking power from the rectifier and the capacitor is being charged. At other instants of time, the capacitor is discharging to the load and aiding the rectifier to supply the power to the load.

Consider the simple inductance filter of Fig. 60. The inductance filter element will, of course, have some resistance in addition to its inductance. When the supply voltage to the inductance filter is varying, as it will be in a rectifier circuit, the current will vary. The d-c component of the current supplied by the rectifier will produce a voltage drop in the filter element of a magnitude depending only on the resistance of the filter. The a-c, or ripple, component of the current will produce a voltage drop in the filter element depending upon both the resistance and the inductive reactance of the filter. Since the filter is designed so that its reactance is much greater than its resistance, the alternating voltage drop in the filter will be much greater than the direct voltage drop. A large portion of the ripple voltage will be consumed as voltage drop in the filter, and the voltage at the output terminals of the filter will be more constant than the output voltage of the rectifier.

Better filtering action of the supply voltage than can be obtained by either the simple capacitor or the inductance filter can be secured by proper combinations of parallel capacitors and series inductances. Common combinations employed for power-supply filters are shown in Figs. 61 and 62. As many sections of L or pi filters connected in series can be employed as are warranted by the degree of smoothness required in the wave form of the output voltage. In some cases where only moderate filtering is required, a pi type of filter using resistance instead of inductance is employed. Such a filter will not produce as good a smoothing action of the voltage wave form but will cost less than one employing inductance.

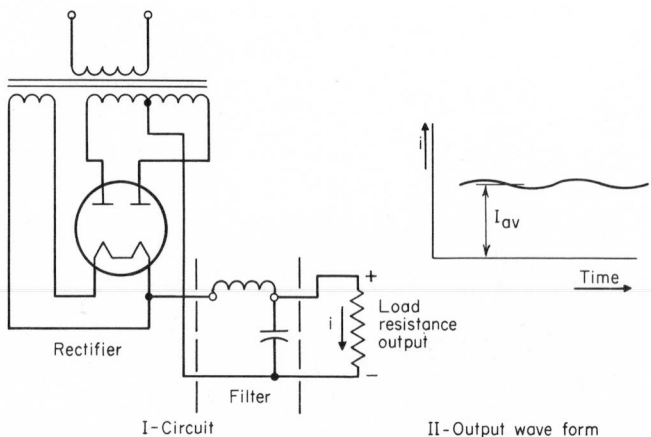

FIG. 61 *Full-wave rectifier with inverted-L inductive input filter.*

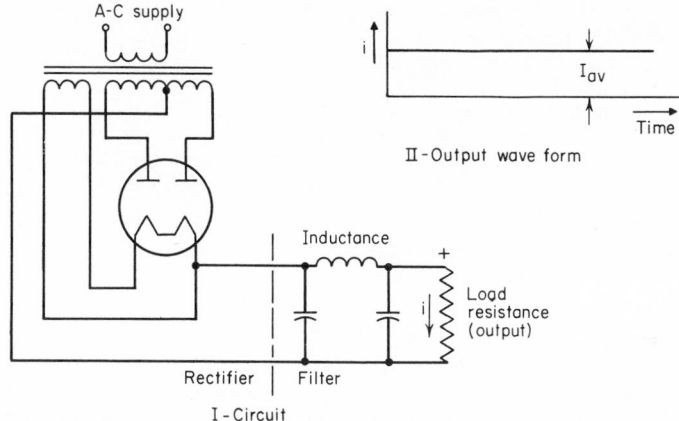

FIG. 62 *Full-wave rectifier tube with pi capacitance input filter.*

Capacitors are used as filtering devices in many electronic circuits for purposes other than that of removing the ripple in a rectified supply voltage. The other principal filtering applications are as **bypassing** and **blocking capacitors.** One application of a bypass capacitor is to eliminate as far as possible the variation in a supply voltage caused by a varying load. A capacitor connected across a supply, as previously discussed, will tend to charge and discharge as the load varies. The capacitor acts as a storage tank to hold the current drawn from the supply more nearly constant and thereby to keep the voltage output of the supply more nearly constant. The capacitor across the supply can be considered as a bypass around the supply for varying components of current. Another application of capacitors as a bypass is for the bypassing of a-c components or variations of the current around some particular part of a circuit. If a capacitor is connected in parallel with a particular portion of a circuit, the capacitor will offer a path of low impedance to alternating or varying components of the current but will offer practically infinite opposition to the direct component of the current. Such a bypassing capacitor will, therefore, result in practically all of the direct component of the current passing through the original part of the circuit and in practically all of the alternating or varying components passing through the bypassing capacitor. The current through the original part of the circuit will be practically constant in magnitude irrespective of the variations in the current in the other parts of the circuit. A bypass capacitor is sometimes called a **decoupling capacitor,** since it tends to prevent the passing on of the variations in certain parts of a circuit to other parts.

Blocking capacitors are capacitors that are used for the purpose of blocking the passage of direct components of current. A capacitor in any path of a circuit will offer practically infinite opposition to the passage of direct current through that path but will offer little opposition to the passage of alternating current. Thus a capacitor will block the passage of direct current through any path in series with the capacitor. Blocking capacitors are used principally when it is desired to have the variations of one circuit passed on or coupled to another circuit and where it is also necessary to prevent the passing on of the direct component of current in the first circuit to the second, or coupled, circuit. Blocking capacitors are sometimes called coupling capacitors. Refer to Sec. **53** for an application of a blocking, or coupling, capacitor.

50. Voltage Dividers. The power supply for many electronic circuits requires several voltages. If the demands of the different parts require voltages or currents of widely different magnitudes, it may be necessary or best to provide separate supplies for each part. Often, however, different parts of the circuit require voltages of somewhat different magnitude, and the current demands are either small or of magnitudes that do not differ from each other too widely. These requirements are generally best fulfilled by means of a voltage divider supplied from one common voltage source. A voltage divider consists of series resistances or a single tapped resistor connected to a source of voltage. By the proper design of these resistors, the required fraction of the total source voltage can be obtained for the different parts of the circuit. When the current requirements are intermittent or varying, a bypass capacitor is connected across the part of the divider so affected, in order, as explained in Sec. **49,** to hold the voltage more constant. Where the voltage must be held more nearly constant than can be obtained with this arrangement, the practically constant voltage characteristic of diode gas-filled tubes is employed for maintaining constant voltage. Such a diode will hold the voltage across a section at practically constant value. Refer to Sec. **40.**

51. Power Supplies for Electronic Circuits. Several different supply voltages are necessary for the operation of most electronic circuits. For example, the operation of a pentode tube requires one supply voltage for the cathode-anode circuit, another for the heating of the cathode, another for the bias of the control grid, and still another for the screen-grid circuit. When the circuit employs several tubes, the number of required supply voltages may be still further increased, even though a common supply voltage may be used for some of the circuits. Some of the supply voltages required may need to be alternating, and others may need to be direct. Alternating voltage is employed, generally, for the heater circuits of indirectly heated thermionic cathodes. In a tube employed for rectification, the cathode-anode voltage supply is, of course, always alternating. The grid and anode voltages, in probably the majority of cases, need to be direct voltages. In many of the fundamental electronic circuits so far shown, batteries have been indicated as the source of direct voltage. This was done because the purpose of the figures was to show fundamental principles and it was desired to keep the figures as simple and clear as possible. Although batteries are used in some special cases, they would be too expensive in first cost and renewal and too bulky to be satisfactory for use in most industrial electronic circuits. The necessary direct voltages, therefore, are usually obtained from an a-c source through the proper combination of transformers, tubes acting as rectifiers, filters, and voltage dividers. Contact rectifiers are sometimes used as the rectifying device in place of a rectifying tube. The grid-bias voltage for vacuum thermionic tubes is obtained generally from a grid-bias resistor, as explained in Sec. **18.** The fundamental principles and connections of power supplies for electronic circuits can be studied in Fig. 63, which shows the power supply for a two-stage amplifier.

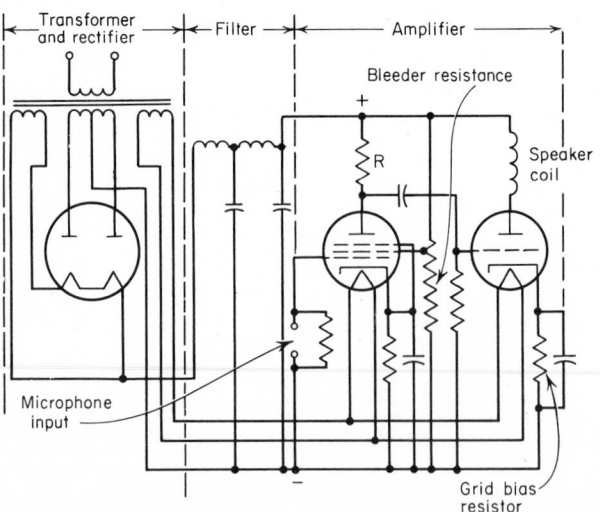

FIG. 63 *Filtered power supply connected to a two-stage audio amplifier.*

52. Electron Tubes as Amplifiers. One of the functions for which vacuum thermionic tubes are so useful is that of amplification. Amplification is the process of taking a relatively weak voltage impulse or signal and having it produce or control another voltage of much greater magnitude or power output ability. The controlled voltage or power should vary either directly or approximately directly with the signal voltage. The effect of the signal voltage is increased or amplified. A device that performs the function of amplification is called an amplifier. Because of the ability of small voltages in the control-grid circuit of vacuum thermionic tubes to produce much greater changes of voltage in the anode circuit, vacuum thermionic tubes having one or more grids are widely used as amplifiers to amplify the effect of weak potentials. By this means a very weak voltage impulse can produce much larger voltage changes in a circuit capable of delivering considerable power. If the purpose of the amplifier is simply to amplify the voltage, it is called a voltage amplifier. If the purpose of the amplifier is to produce a voltage with much greater power ability, it is called a power amplifier. The initiating voltage impulse is commonly called the signal. In addition to their extended use in radio and other communication circuits, electron-tube amplifiers are used in numerous industrial applications. True amplifier action can be obtained only with vacuum tubes. With triode gas-filled tubes, small signal voltages can be used to initiate or control large amounts of power, but this action is really relay or switch action and not strictly amplification.

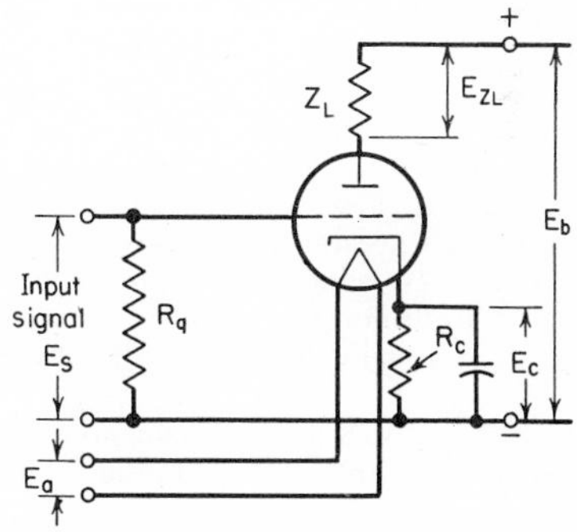

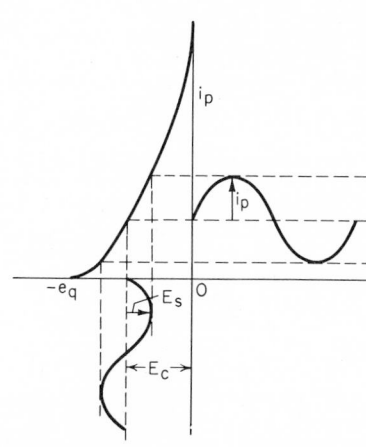

FIG. 64 *Single-stage amplifier showing voltages involved.*

The fundamental amplifier action of a vacuum tube can be explained with the aid of Figs. 64 to 66. The signal voltage is impressed across the resistance R_g, which is connected in series with the bias voltage E_c in the grid-cathode circuit of the tube. When the input, or signal, voltage is zero, the

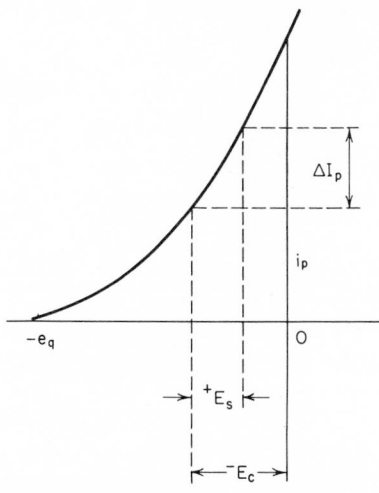

FIG. 65 *Grid voltage–plate current characteristic curve showing the effect of a positive signal voltage increasing the plate current.*

FIG. 66 *Dynamic grid voltage–plate current characteristic curves with input signal, output load, and grid-bias voltages indicated.*

anode current will be constant with a value corresponding to that given by the tube characteristic for a grid voltage of E_c. If a constant signal voltage of magnitude E_s is applied to R_g in such a manner that the grid of the tube is made less negative (more positive) with respect to the cathode, the anode current will increase by the amount ΔI_p shown in Fig. 65. This increase in plate current will increase the output voltage across the load impedance Z_L, and the increase in this output voltage will be several times the value of the input, or signal, voltage impressed on the grid circuit. If the signal voltage is an alternating voltage, the variations of the cathode-grid potential produced thereby will result in variations of the anode current, as shown in Fig. 66. These variations of the plate current will produce variations of the output voltage across the load impedance Z_L, and the variations in the output voltage will be much greater than the variations in the signal voltage. The load of the tube Z_L may be the final output device, which is to be controlled by the signal voltage, or the output voltage from Z_L may be impressed upon another tube for additional amplification or performance of other functions before the action of the signal reaches the final output device. If the output voltage is transmitted to another tube, voltage amplification is being employed; i.e., the useful output is a voltage E_{ZL} that varies with the signal voltage but with much greater magnitude of variation. If the load Z_L constitutes the final output device to be controlled by the signal voltage, then the tube is being employed as a power amplifier; i.e., the useful output is the power of Z_L. The power of Z_L will vary with the signal voltage but will possess much greater power than that of the input signal in R_g. Thus a signal possessing very little power can be amplified to control much greater amounts of power, capable of operating electromagnetic devices.

If the amplifier tube is operated on a straight portion of anode-current versus grid-voltage curve of the tube, the variations of the anode current will be in direct proportion to variations in the signal voltage. The point on the characteristic at which the tube operates is controlled by the value of the grid-bias voltage E_c employed.

An electronic amplifier employing only one tube is called a single-stage amplifier. One with two tubes operated in cascade, i.e., one tube feeding into the next, is called a two-stage amplifier, etc.

53. Amplifier Coupling. Where one stage of amplification is sufficient, the amplifier circuit is relatively simple. When more than one stage of amplification is necessary, the variations produced in the anode circuit of one tube must be coupled in a satisfactory manner to the grid circuit of the next following tube. The two most commonly employed methods of amplifier coupling are resistance-capacitance coupling and transformer coupling.

A resistance-capacitance-coupled two-stage amplifier is shown in Fig. 67. With this type of coupling, a common voltage supply can be employed for the plate circuits of all the tubes. The signal voltage impressed across Z_{g_1} varies the grid voltage of the first tube, which in turn produces amplified variations in the anode current of the first tube. As the anode current of the first tube varies, the potential from point a to point b will vary. From a study of the circuit it is seen that the circuit consisting of the coupling or blocking capacitor C and resistor R_{g_2} is in parallel with the circuit from a through the impedance Z_{L_1} and d-c supply to point b. Any constant voltage from a to b will not affect the circuit through C and R_{g_2} since the coupling capacitor C will block the passage of direct current. Any variations in the voltage from a to b, however, will affect the circuit through C and R_{g_2} and will produce variations in the voltage across R_{g_2}. The amplified variations in the anode current of the first tube will therefore set up corresponding variations in the voltage across R_{g_2}. But R_{g_2} is in the grid-control circuit of the second tube. The amplified variations of the signal voltage are therefore transmitted to the control grid of the second tube, which in turn will produce amplified variations of its anode current through Z_{L_2}. The impedance Z_{L_1} is generally a resistance, but an inductance can be employed.

A transformer-coupled two-stage amplifier is shown in Fig. 68. The amplified variations in the anode circuit of the first tube result in the production of voltage variations across the primary of the coupling transformer which are reproduced in increased magnitude in the secondary of the coupling transformer. Since the secondary is in the grid-control circuit of the second tube, the variations of the signal voltage are passed on in amplified form to the grid of the second tube. The second tube in turn will pro-

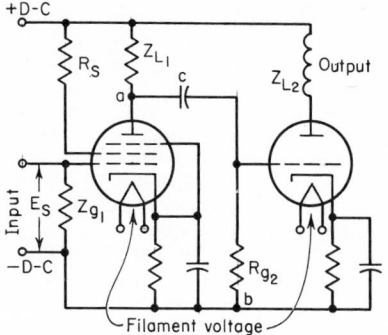
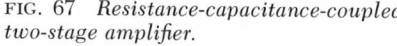

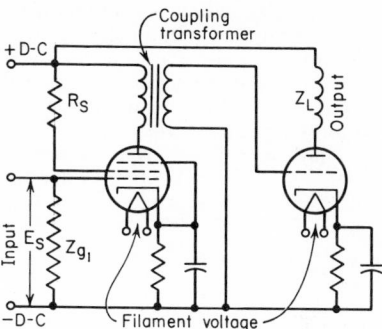

FIG. 67 *Resistance-capacitance-coupled two-stage amplifier.*

FIG. 68 *Transformer-coupled two-stage amplifier.*

duce amplified variations of its anode current through Z_L. Transformer-coupled amplifiers produce a greater over-all amplification than do capacitance-coupled ones when the same tubes are employed. On the other hand, the transformer-coupled amplifier is more expensive to build and does not give such faithful reproduction of the input-signal variations.

54. Push-Pull Amplifiers. The final stage of a power amplifier generally functions in what is called push-pull. The push-pull amplifier connection, shown in Fig. 69, provides greater power output with less distortion of the signal than can be obtained with the final stage employing only one tube. The push-pull stage of an amplifier is transformer-coupled to the anode circuit of the preceding stage. With respect to the grid circuits of the two tubes, the signal voltage on tube 1 will be positive when the signal voltage on tube 2 is negative, and similarly, the signal voltage on tube 1 will be negative when the signal voltage on tube 2 is positive. Thus the alternating current in *ab* will be 180 degrees out of phase with the current *cb*. But the two primaries *ab* and *cb* of the coupling transformer are so wound on the transformer core that, when the currents *ab* and *cb* are 180 degrees out of phase with each other, they will aid each other in producing flux in the transformer. The two tubes therefore work together to produce variations in the secondary of the output transformer in accordance with the variations of the signal voltage E_g.

55. Electron Tubes as Relays. Refer to Sec. **251** of Div. 7 for a definition of a relay. Any electron tube can perform the function of a relay. The only function a phototube can perform is that of a light-sensitive relay. Variations of light incident upon the cathode produce variations in the current of the phototube, and this current controls the operation of some other device. Diode tubes of the other types, although capable of performing relay function, do not lend themselves to so varied a field of relay application as do triodes. Variations in the voltage applied to the diode circuit will produce variations in the current of the circuit which can be used to control some other device. The fundamental circuit for a diode functioning as a relay is shown in Fig. 70.

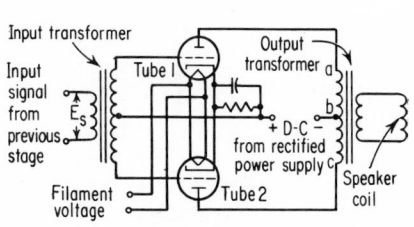

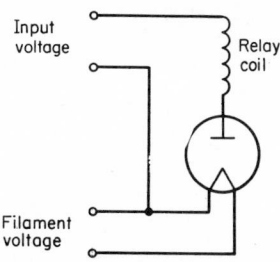

FIG. 69 *Push-pull amplifier stage.*

FIG. 70 *Diode functioning as a relay.*

An example of a diode gas-filled tube used for its relay function is the diode control tube in the ignitor circuit of the ignitron of Fig. 42. The diode operates through variations of the supply voltage to control the operation of the other device, the ignitron.

Any grid-controlled tube is admirably suited for fulfilling the function of a relay. Variations in the grid circuit produce variations in the anode circuit, which in turn may control some other device. Any tube in an electronic amplifier is, in fact, functioning as a relay, since variations in the grid circuit of the tube affect the operation of the next tube or of whatever device is connected in the anode circuit of the tube. However, if the primary purpose of the tube is to increase the magnitude of a signal, the function of the tube would be classified as amplification rather than relay function. Although every amplifier is really a relay, its primary function is not the relaying of the signal but the amplification of the signal. Tubes are often used in relay circuits in conjunction with electromagnetic relays. The signal is impressed on the grid of the tube, and the operating coil of the electromagnetic relay is connected in the anode circuit of the tube, as shown in Fig. 71. The signal voltage is amplified through the tube so that there will be sufficient power to operate the electromagnetic relay. If the tube is used in this manner simply because the signal voltage is not sufficiently great or does not have power enough to operate the electromagnetic relay directly, the function of the tube is not primarily relay function but is really amplification. The fundamental circuits for triode tubes functioning as relays are shown in Figs. 72 and 73. The input or initiating device of the relay may consist of some signal voltage, as in Fig. 72, or it may be a mechanically controlled contact, as in Fig. 73.

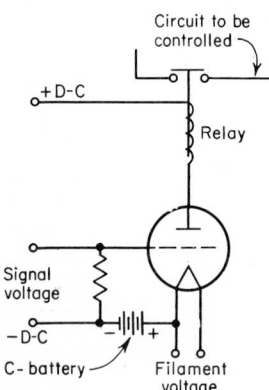

FIG. 71 *Triode functioning as a relay.*

Electron tubes are very advantageous as relays for applications where the initiating of the functioning of the relay is produced by a delicate mechanically controlled contact device. If the delicate contacts are connected directly in series with the operating coil of an electromagnetic relay, the sparking at the contact points will in time oxidize the contact surfaces. This oxidation will eventually increase the resistance in the coil circuit so that the relay will not operate. If a triode vacuum tube is used, as shown in Fig. 73, the initiating contacts carry a current so small that no arcing will occur. An electronic relay of this type can also be employed when the control contacts must work in an explosive atmosphere.

56. Light-sensitive Relays. Phototubes find a wide field of application in light-sensitive relays. Generally, the power output of a phototube is not sufficient to operate

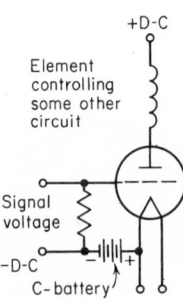

FIG. 72 *Circuit for controlling current through a load using a triode as a relay.*

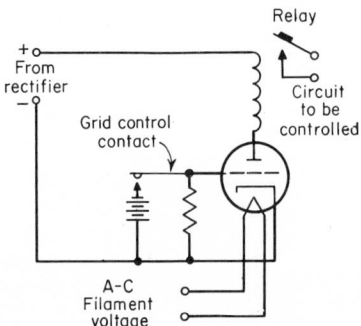

FIG. 73 *Grid-contact relay circuit.*

the controlled device, such as a magnetic contactor or switch, directly. Photoelectric relays therefore generally employ an amplifying tube in conjunction with the phototube and an electromagnetic contactor or relay. The principles of operation of light-sensitive relays, employing phototubes and one stage of amplification, are shown in Figs. 74 and 75. The circuit of Fig. 74 functions to close the relay when sufficient light falls on the phototube cathode, whereas the circuit of Fig. 75 functions to close the relay upon decrease in the light incident upon the phototube. In the circuit of Fig. 74,

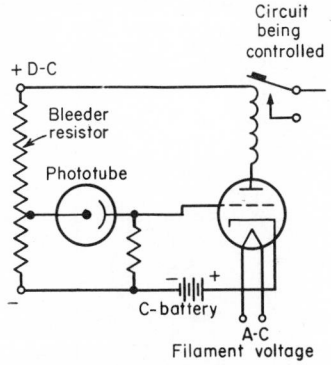

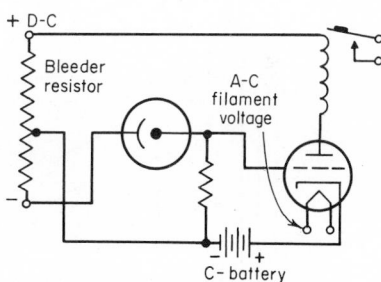

FIG. 74 *Positive phototube-controlled relay circuit.*

FIG. 75 *Negative phototube-controlled relay circuit.*

when light falls on the cathode of the phototube, current is produced from the battery through the phototube and coupling resistor. The current in the coupling resistor makes the grid of the triode vacuum tube more positive (less negative) and thereby increases the anode current of the tube. If this increase in the anode current is sufficient, the electromagnetic relay will close. In the circuit of Fig. 75, the electromagnetic relay is closed by the anode current of the triode vacuum tube when there is no light on the phototube. Light on the cathode of the phototube producing current through the coupling resistor makes the grid of the triode vacuum tube more negative and thereby reduces the anode current of the triode. The electromagnetic relay will open when the light is sufficient to reduce the anode current of the triode vacuum tube to a point that will not hold the relay closed.

The circuits of actual commercial photoelectric relays are more complicated than those of Figs. 74 and 75 because of the necessary additional tubes, resistors, and capacitors required for producing the voltage supplies for the phototube and amplifier tube. The panel wiring diagram of a fairly simple commercial phototube relay is shown in Fig. 76. Figure 77 shows the circuit diagram of this relay with the parts rearranged so that the diagram is simplified and it is easier to study the purpose and functioning of the different parts.

57. Electronic Timers. An important application of the relay function of tubes is in electric time-delay relays. These relays are often called electronic timers. Electronic timers provide time delay by controlling the conduction of an electron tube in accordance with the time required for the charging or discharging of a capacitor. The principles of an electronic timer are illustrated by the circuit of Fig. 78. This is a basic electronic time-delay circuit which is adapted to many time-control problems. When the operating switch is open, the capacitor C_1 is charged by the a-c supply voltage through the rectifier characteristics of the thyratron grid circuit. There will be no conduction in the anode circuit of the thyratron, since the cathode is connected through resistor R_8 to the same side of the line as the anode. When the operating switch is closed, the cathode of the thyratron is connected directly to the opposite side of the line from the anode. The tube will not conduct, however, until the capacitor C_1 has discharged to a certain level through resistor R_4. After a certain time delay depending upon the

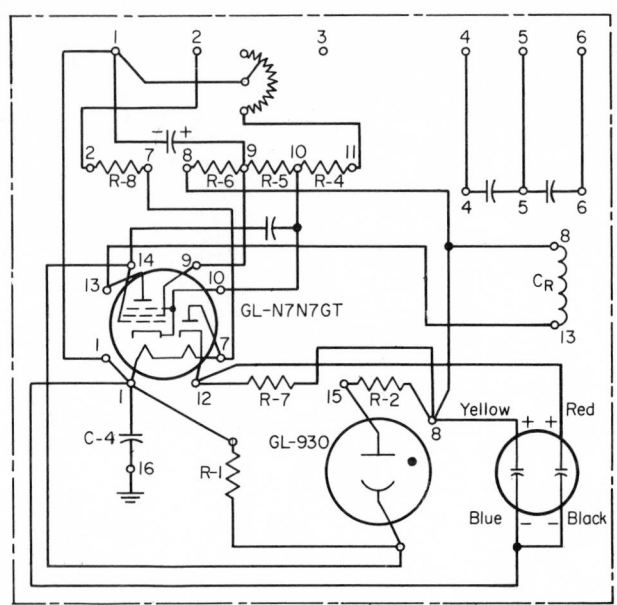

FIG. 76 *Panel wiring diagram for a photoelectric relay. (Bottom view.)*

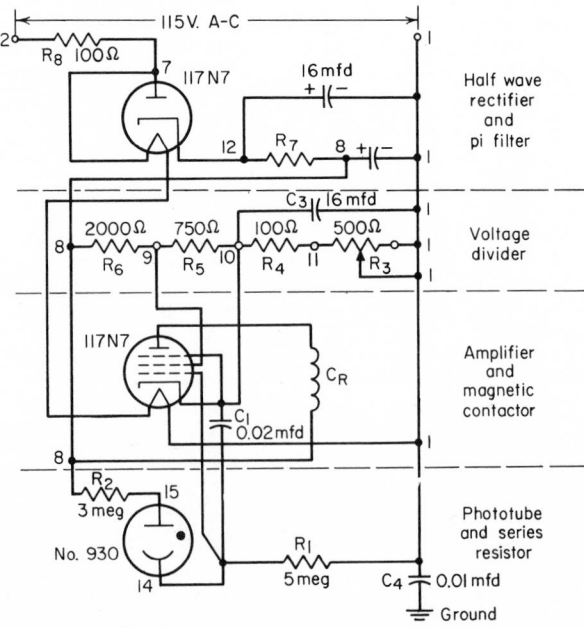

FIG. 77 *Schematic circuit of the panel diagram of Fig. 76.*

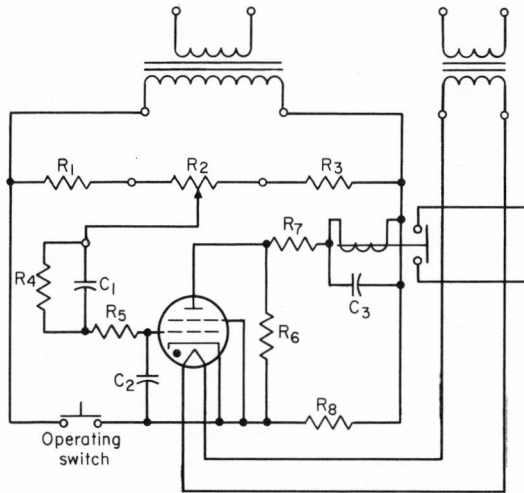

FIG. 78 *Electronic timer circuit.*

setting of R_2 and the time discharge characteristic of the C_1R_4 circuit, the thyratron conducts and operates the relay.

58. Electron Tubes as Switches or Contactors. Compared with other forms of switches or contactors, tubes have the advantage of not requiring the physical breaking of the connections of the circuit, do not require contacts or moving parts in the main circuit, and require only small consumption of control power. If the operation of the electronic switch is controlled by some other electron tube, then the electronic switch has the further advantage of quick response action and flexibility in circuit design and adjustment.

The reader may have some difficulty in distinguishing between switch and relay action. An electric switch is a device that functions to start or stop conduction in a circuit through the functioning of some auxiliary circuit. In a magnetic contactor or switch, the function is to open or close the contacts of the device through the action of the operating coil of the device. In the electronic switch, the function is to stop or start conduction in a circuit connected in series with the anode circuit of the tube. This switching action is produced through the action of the (auxiliary) grid circuit of the tube. A relay within itself does produce switch action, but it does not directly function as a switch in the main circuit to be controlled. The relay is an intermediate device that functions to cause the operation of some other device but does not itself open or close the main circuit that is to be controlled. A study of Fig. 79, which shows the function of an electromagnetic relay and a magnetic switch, should help in clarifying the distinction between a relay and a switch.

Any grid-controlled vacuum tube can be used to function as a switch or contactor for a d-c circuit.

A circuit for a triode vacuum tube employed as a switch is shown in Fig. 80. When the control contact in the grid circuit is closed, the tube will be biased to cutoff and no current will flow in the main circuit. When the control contact is open, there will be zero bias voltage and the main circuit will pass current. Although the circuit of Fig. 80 probably has little or no practical importance in itself, it will aid in obtaining an understanding of the functioning of an electron tube as a switch.

In any ignitron-tube rectifier circuit, the tube will function as a switch in the main circuit. When the ignitor circuit is closed, the main circuit will be conducting; and, when the ignitor circuit is open, no current will flow in the main circuit.

Tubes are seldom used in d-c circuits for the primary function of a switch, but, when tubes are used as rectifiers, the switch function of the tube can often be employed advantageously.

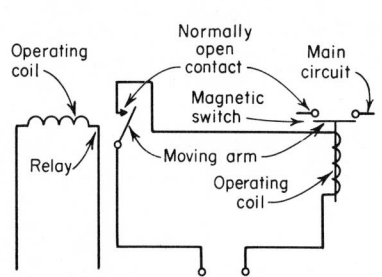
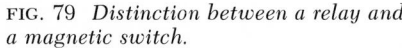

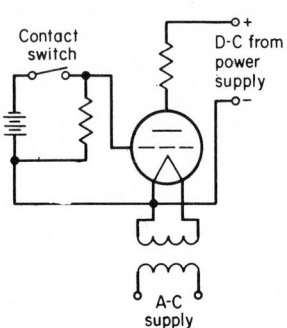

FIG. 79 *Distinction between a relay and a magnetic switch.*

FIG. 80 *Electronic switch.*

An electronic switch for an a-c circuit can be constructed by connecting two thyratron or ignitron tubes in inverse parallel in series with a circuit. Inverse-parallel connection of tubes is formed by connecting the tubes in parallel with the cathode of each tube connected to the anode of the other tube. The operation of the electronic a-c switch requires the use of contact rectifiers or of two diode tubes functioning as relays to control conduction of the main tubes. If thyratrons are used for the main tubes, they must be of the type that requires a positive grid for conduction to take place when the voltage of the main circuit is impressed on the cathode-anode circuit. The relay tubes may be vacuum or gas-filled depending upon the current requirements of the relay tubes. Typical circuits for electronic a-c switches or contactors are shown in Figs. 81 to 84. In all these switches, when the contact switch is open, the grid or ignitor circuits will be open. There will therefore be no conduction in the main switch tubes, and the main circuit will be "open"; i.e., there will be no current in the main circuit. When the contact switch is closed, the diode-controlled switches of Figs. 81 and 82 will function as follows: When point 1 is at positive polarity, current will pass from point 1 to 2, through diode D to point 10, through the contact switch to point 8, to point 7, and through the grid or ignitor circuit to point 3, to point 4, and through the load and back to the other side of the line at point 6. This will fire tube A, and current will then pass in the main circuit from point 1 through tube A to point 3, from point 3 to point 4, through the load, and back to the negative side of the line at point 6. This will be the conduction path for the half cycle when point 1 is of positive polarity. When point 6 is at positive polarity, current will pass from point 6, through the load to point 4, to point 3 and through diode

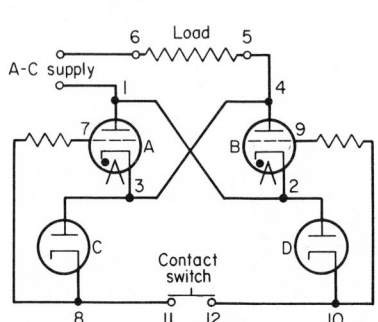

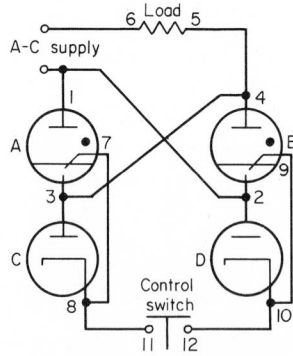

FIG. 81 *Thyratron tubes in inverse parallel controlled by diode rectifiers.*

FIG. 82 *Ignitron tubes in inverse parallel controlled by diode rectifiers.*

C to point 8, through the contact switch to point 10, to point 9 through the grid or ignitor circuit to point 2, and back to the other side of the line at point 1. This will fire tube B, and current will pass in the main circuit from point 6 through the load to point 4, through tube B to point 2, and back to the other side of the line at point 1. This will be the conduction path for the half cycle when point 6 is of positive polarity. Thus, when the control switch is closed, the electronic switch, composed of tubes A and B, allows current to pass in the main circuit during both the positive and negative half cycles, and when the control switch is open, no current is allowed to pass in the main circuit.

The contact-rectifier-controlled switches of Figs. 83 and 84 operate in the following manner: When the contact switch is closed and point 1 of the line is at positive polarity, current will pass from point 1 to point 2, through the contact rectifier F to point 10, through the contact switch to point 8, through the contact rectifier C to point 7, through the grid or ignitor circuit of tube A to point 3, to point 4, through the load, and back to the other side of the line at point 6. This will fire tube A, and current will pass through the main circuit from point 1 through tube A to point 3, to point 4, through the load, and back to the other side of the line at point 6. When the contact switch is closed and point 6 of the supply is at positive polarity, current will pass from point 6 through the load to point 4, to point 3, through the contact rectifier D to point 8, through the contact switch to point 10, through the contact rectifier E to point 9, through the grid or ignitor circuit of tube B to point 2, and back to the other side of the line at point 1. This will fire tube B, and current will pass in the main circuit from point 6, through the load to point 4, through tube B to point 2, and back to the other side of the line at point 1.

An electronic switch for a-c circuits can be used for the control of the current of the circuit in addition to its plain switch function. This feature is the great advantage of the electronic switch. The electronic switch is often used in a-c circuits when it is desired to control the average value of the current within close limits or to control the time of conduction in the circuit. The principal application of the a-c electronic switch is in the control of resistance welding circuits. With the a-c electronic switch, the current of the circuit can be controlled by using thyratron tubes as the relay tubes in the ignitor circuits for the control of the firing of the ignitor switch tubes. Through grid control of the thyratrons, the period of conduction throughout the positive half cycle of each ignitor tube can be controlled. The circuit for such an electronic switch would be the same as shown in Figs. 81 and 82, with the addition of the grids and the grid-control circuits for the relay tubes. Refer to Sec. **33** for typical grid-control circuits. Another method for the control of the current with an electronic a-c switch is to remove the contact switch of Figs. 81 to 84 and connect the terminals 11 and 12 to an external control circuit, such as an electronic timer. Through an external control circuit and an electronic timer, not only may the average current of the main circuit be controlled but also accurate timing of the conduction period may be obtained. This is the method so often employed for the control of electric resistance welding.

Another electronic contactor that gives partial switching action and will provide a method of controlling the average value of the current is shown in Fig. 85. When the thyratron tubes are not passing current, there will be no current in the secondary of the series impedance transformer. This transformer is then operating with an open circuit

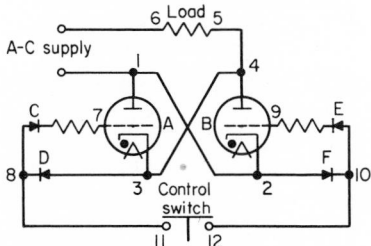

FIG. 83 *Thyratron tubes in inverse parallel controlled by contact rectifiers.*

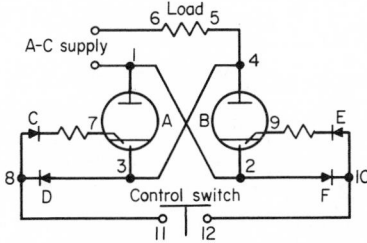

FIG. 84 *Ignitron tubes in inverse parallel controlled by contact rectifiers.*

secondary, and the primary of the transformer will introduce a high impedance into the main circuit. This is the "off" condition of the switch. This electronic switch has the disadvantage that the current in the circuit is not completely stopped in the "off" condition of the switch. However, the current is reduced to a very low value, which is satisfactory for certain applications, as in some welding circuits. When the thyratrons are conducting, they will practically short-circuit the secondary of the series impedance transformer and thereby reduce the impedance introduced by the primary

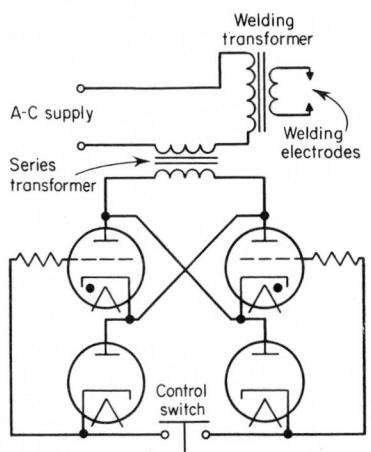

in the main circuit to a very low value. If the conduction periods of the thyratrons are controlled, the average value of the impedance introduced into the main circuit can be controlled. By this means, the contactor can control the average value of the current of the main circuit.

59. Electron Tubes as Oscillators. In the electrical sense of the word, oscillation is the periodic changing of a voltage or a current. An oscillator is a device for the production of an alternating voltage by means of setting up oscillations in a circuit that is energized from a d-c source. Oscillators are used as the generating means for alternating voltages of frequencies higher than those which can economically be produced by alternators. An important application of grid-controlled vacuum tubes is as the activating device to produce the necessary oscillations in oscillator circuits.

FIG. 85 *Circuit for welding control using series transformer and thyratron tubes.*

The amplifying effect of the control grid makes it possible to produce oscillations with a vacuum tube. The oscillations are produced by bleeding off a small amount of energy from the anode circuit and feeding this energy back to the grid circuit in proper amount and phase relation. The frequency of the oscillations can be controlled by a resonant circuit located in the grid circuit, in the anode circuit, or in both the grid and anode circuits. A resonant circuit is one containing both inductance and capacitance and in which the effects of inductance and capacitance just neutralize each other. The frequency of oscillations produced by an oscillator is controlled by adjusting the relative values of the inductance and capacitance of the resonant circuit. Fundamental oscillator circuits are shown in Figs. 86 to 89. In many practical oscillator circuits, one resonant circuit, or tuned circuit as it is often called, frequently is used to serve in both the grid and anode circuits, as shown in Fig. 88.

Vacuum-tube oscillators, in addition to their wide application in communication work, are used in industrial control circuits and are the main source of high-frequency voltage employed for high-frequency industrial heating (see Sec. **66**).

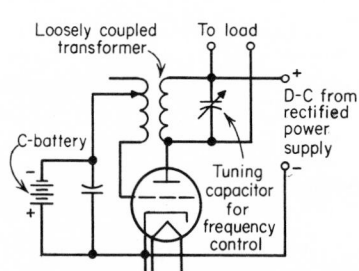

FIG. 86 *Tuned anode circuit oscillator.*

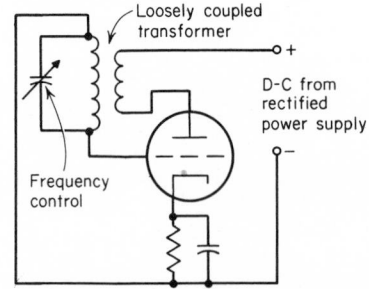

FIG. 87 *Tuned grid circuit oscillator.*

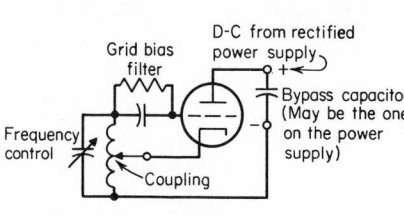

FIG. 88 *Hartley oscillator.*

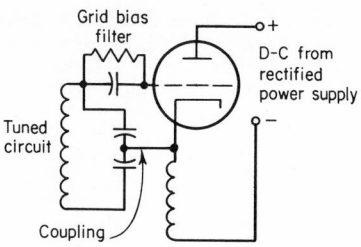

FIG. 89 *Colpitts oscillator.*

60. Electron Tubes as Modulators and Detectors. The application of electron tubes for the function of modulation and detection is confined entirely to communication work. A discussion of these functions is outside the scope of this book.

ELECTRONIC CIRCUITS AND APPLICATIONS

61. Electronic circuits and applications are so numerous and varied that it is impossible in the space available in this book to do more than give some helpful suggestions in the method of procedure for analyzing any particular circuit, the general fields of application, and explanation of the circuits for some typical examples.

62. Method of Analyzing Electronic Circuits. In the application of electron tubes to industry, the complete electronic circuit consists of a combination and elaboration of the basic circuits already discussed, in many cases with the addition of special refinements. Understanding these circuits directly from the actual wiring of the device or from the usual wiring diagram is difficult. However, with the aid of the following procedure, analyzing the functioning of the devices and their operation should not be too difficult.

A. Make a wiring diagram from the connections of the device if such a diagram is not already available.
B. Study the wiring diagram, and determine the primary function of the different tubes such as power-supply rectifier, amplifier, relay switch, or oscillator.
C. Study the wiring diagram, and determine if possible the purpose of the different circuit elements such as resistance, inductance, and capacitance. As a help in this determination, a summary of the more common purposes for which the different elements are employed follows:
  1. Resistance elements.
     a. Voltage divider sections.
     b. Grid-bias resistor.
     c. Screen-grid resistor.
     d. Series resistor in grid circuits for limitation of grid current.
     e. Series resistor in phototube circuits.
     f. Coupling resistor.
     g. Resistance arm of phase-shift circuit.
  2. Capacitance elements.
     a. Filtering element for filtering of voltage from rectified power supply.
     b. Filtering element across voltage supply to a varying load.
     c. Bypass capacitor across portion of circuit to maintain constant current in portion bypassed.
     d. Coupling and blocking capacitor for coupling variations of one circuit to another while at the same time blocking transfer of direct current.
     e. Capacitor arm of phase-shift circuit.
  3. Inductance elements.
     a. Filtering elements for filtering of voltage from rectified power supply.
     b. Inductance arm of phase-shift circuit.

D. Redraw the circuit segregating the parts according to their respective functions. Arrange the diagram so as to show in the simplest manner the purpose of each part and the over-all functioning of the circuit.

E. Study the simplified diagram of *D*, and determine the method and sequence of operation.

In the study of the wiring diagram, all the tubes employed should first be determined. The general type of each tube will be indicated by the symbol by which it is represented in the wiring diagram. Then the function for which each tube is employed should be discovered, followed by the determination of the general function of the circuit elements. In planning the general arrangement of the simplified circuit diagram, one good procedure is to start at the top of the diagram with the power supply, followed by power-supply transformers, cathode-heating circuits, rectifier for power supply to anodes and grids, power-supply filter, voltage divider, and then the anode and grid circuits of the individual tubes. The circuits of the different tubes should be segregated from each other and arranged in as logical an order as is possible in accordance with the sequence of operation. Before the circuit is redrawn, an estimate of the space that will be required should be made and then a sheet of paper about twice the size estimated should be used. The general tendency is to underestimate the space required; consequently, as the drawing progresses, it becomes necessary to crowd the different parts. Crowding of the diagram often results in errors and always hampers the study and understanding of the circuit. When the sheet has been selected, the space for the sections should be indicated and the tubes located in their respective sections. Then the connections from the original wiring diagram should be transferred to the new simplified one. In doing this, care should be taken to lay out the diagram so that it will be as open, clear, and with as few crossing connections as possible. Generally it will be advisable to redraw the diagram after the first attempt in order to get desired results of clarity and simplicity of arrangement. A study of Figs. 76 and 77 will help in understanding the method of procedure. The original wiring diagram of the device is shown in Fig. 76 and the corresponding rearranged diagram in Fig. 77.

63. Applications of Electron Tubes and Circuits. Some of the more important industrial applications of electron tubes and circuits are

1. Rectifiers. Refer to Secs. **46, 47, 48,** and **51.**
2. Motor-speed regulators. Refer to Secs. **136** and **158** of Div. 7.
3. Automatic electric-drive control. Refer to Sec. **140** of Div. 7.
4. Register regulators. Refer to Sec. **64.**
5. Resistance-welding control. Refer to Sec. **65.**
6. High-frequency heating. Refer to Sec. **66.**
7. Light-sensitive control devices. Refer to Sec. **67.**
8. X-ray equipment. Refer to Sec. **27.**
9. Voltage regulators. Refer to Sec. **68.**

64. Register regulators are devices for the automatic position control of processes performed upon moving webs, such as paper, cloth, and sheet metal. The web material to be processed is wound on rolls and fed through the processing machines. Some of the processes in which it is necessary to control the position of the material automatically are cutting, printing, slitting, trimming, and rewinding. Register regulators may be divided into two types, forward-position regulation and lateral, or side-position, control.

The general purpose of the forward register control is to control the process of cutting or printing of the material so that the operation is performed at the proper position on the sheet of material as it is fed through the machine. Spots are previously printed on the material, or holes are punched in it to designate the proper position of the operation on the web. These spots or holes are scanned by a phototube. The phototube controls an electronic circuit so as to synchronize the position of the material with the operation of cutting or printing. Many different circuits and arrangements of equipment have been employed for this synchronization. A discussion of them is beyond the scope of this book.

Side register control keeps the lateral position of the material in a given relation to the processing machine. In this control, a phototube scanning head observes the position of the edge of the moving web or a printed line on the web and produces a signal voltage whenever the lateral position deviates from the correct location. This voltage is indicative of the direction and the amount of deviation of the web from the desired position. The signal from the scanning head is amplified by an electronic amplifier and is used to control either contactors or the correcting motor directly or to excite the field of a control generator. The elements of a side register control are shown in Fig. 90. The correcting motor, when started by a signal from the phototube scanning head, will function to shift the web until the material has been brought back to the correct position, when the phototube scanner will no longer be energized.

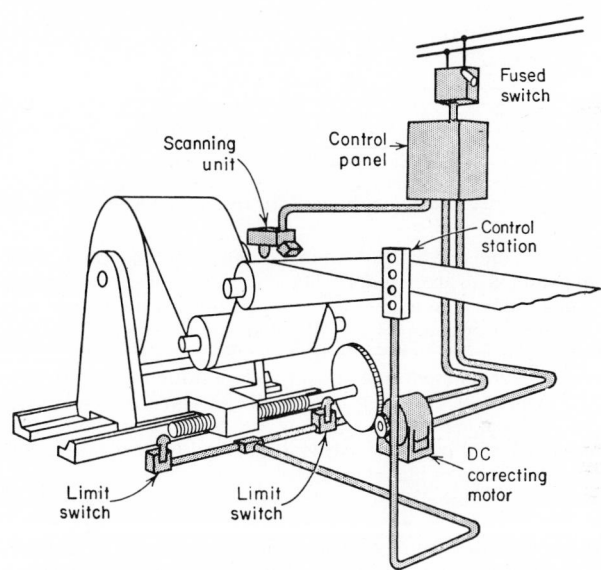

FIG. 90 *Arrangement of equipment for side register control.*

65. Resistance-welding Control. To join two metals by the resistance-welding method, the two parts to be welded are clamped together under pressure and a definite value of current is then passed through the junction of the two parts for a specified length of time (see Fig. 91). If the heat generated as a result of the I^2R losses is great enough and the duration of the current is long enough, the metal reaches the fusion temperature at the interface of the parts. To make consistently good welds, it is necessary to have control over the current density in the metal, the length of time the current is applied, and the resistance at the interface of the metals relative to the contact resistance between the electrodes and the metals. The basic equipment for resistance welding is shown in Fig. 92.

If the surfaces of the metal and the electrodes are clean (which is usually the case), the question of the resistance of the metal is reduced to determining ways to keep a constant, adequate pressure on the work. If the pressure is kept constant, the resistance effects caused by changes in pressure are constant.

One way commonly used to apply pressure to the work by the electrodes is illustrated in Fig. 92. In this system, the work is placed be-

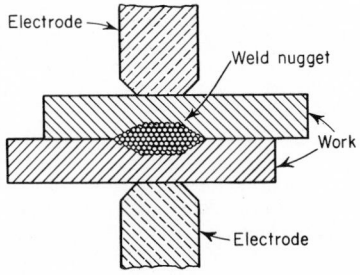

FIG. 91 *Cross section of a typical weld.*

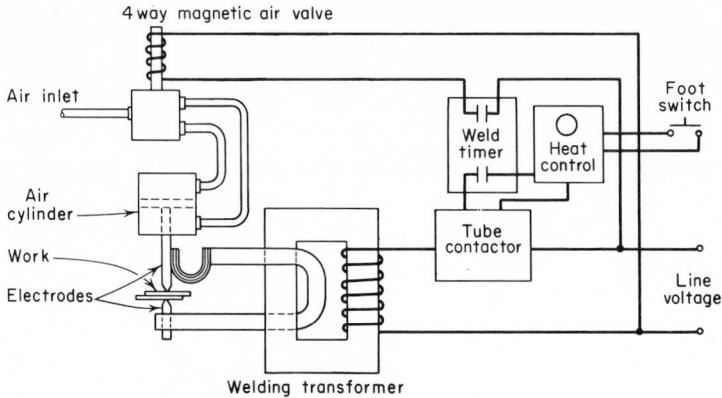

FIG. 92   *Basic equipment for resistance welding.*

tween the electrodes, one of which is stationary. The other electrode is rigidly fastened to the movable piston in an air cylinder. The upper and lower chambers of the cylinder are connected to a four-way solenoid air valve. If the solenoid valve is energized, air is released from the lower chamber and directed into the upper chamber. The piston moves downward, and the upper electrode touches the work and builds up a pressure on it. The pressure developed depends on the controlled air pressure and the electrode diameter. When it is desired to release the pressure, the electric solenoid valve is de-energized by breaking the contact in series with the solenoid. This causes the valve to assume its normal position. Air is discharged from the upper chamber of the cylinder and enters the lower chamber.

The current density and the length of time current is applied usually are controlled by electronic means. The necessary equipment consists of an electronic contactor (refer to Sec. 58), controlled through a heat-control unit and a weld timer. The heat-control unit controls the average value of the welding current throughout the duration of the welding time, and the weld timer controls the length of time current is applied. A complete circuit for a resistance welder is shown in Fig. 93.

The heat-control unit is an electronic contactor, consisting of two shield-grid thyratrons (tubes T_{U_1} and T_{U_2}) connected in inverse parallel in series with the ignition circuit of the main ignitron contactor. The point of firing of the ignitrons is thus controlled by the heat-control electronic contactor. The portion of each cycle that the heat-control contactor is closed will thus govern the average welding current. The conduction period of the thyratrons of the heat-control contactor is adjusted by an RL phase-shift circuit, as shown in Fig. 93.

The phase-shifting apparatus employed in the heat-control unit consists of a reactor L_1 and resistor R_3 in series across the terminals of the power-supply transformer. The heat-control potentiometer is connected between the mid-tap of the resistors, and one of the taps between 0.20 and 0.80 of the reactor. Voltages across the reactor and across the resistors are 90 degrees out of phase with one another. The voltage taken between any point on the reactor or the resistors and the mid-tap of the transformer secondary lags line voltage. The reactor is calibrated so that the voltage between tap 0.30, for example, and connection 14 lags the line voltage by an angle corresponding to a 30 per cent power-factor angle. This is the significance of the reactor tap markings; i.e., they are power-factor markings. Voltage between the resistor mid-tap and the center tap of the transformer secondary lags line voltage by 135 degrees.

Heat-control potentiometer P_1 is connected between that reactor tap marked by the power factor of the welding machine and the resistor mid-tap. Output voltage of the heat-control circuit is taken from P_1 to the transformer secondary mid-point. Hence, when the slider of the heat-control potentiometer is moved from left to right, the ignition point is retarded from that delivering maximum full-wave welding current to a point 135 degrees lagging the line voltage. Effective welding current, regardless of machine power factor, is correspondingly lowered.

The two grid transformers serve two purposes: (1) They reverse the phase of the voltage delivered to the grid of one tube with respect to that delivered to the other tube, since the anode-cathode voltages of these tubes are also 180 degrees apart, and (2) they insulate the grid circuits of these tubes, since the filaments are connected to opposite line-voltage terminals.

The function of potentiometer P_2 is to compensate for any variation in positive and negative currents that flow through the welding transformer. If the currents are the

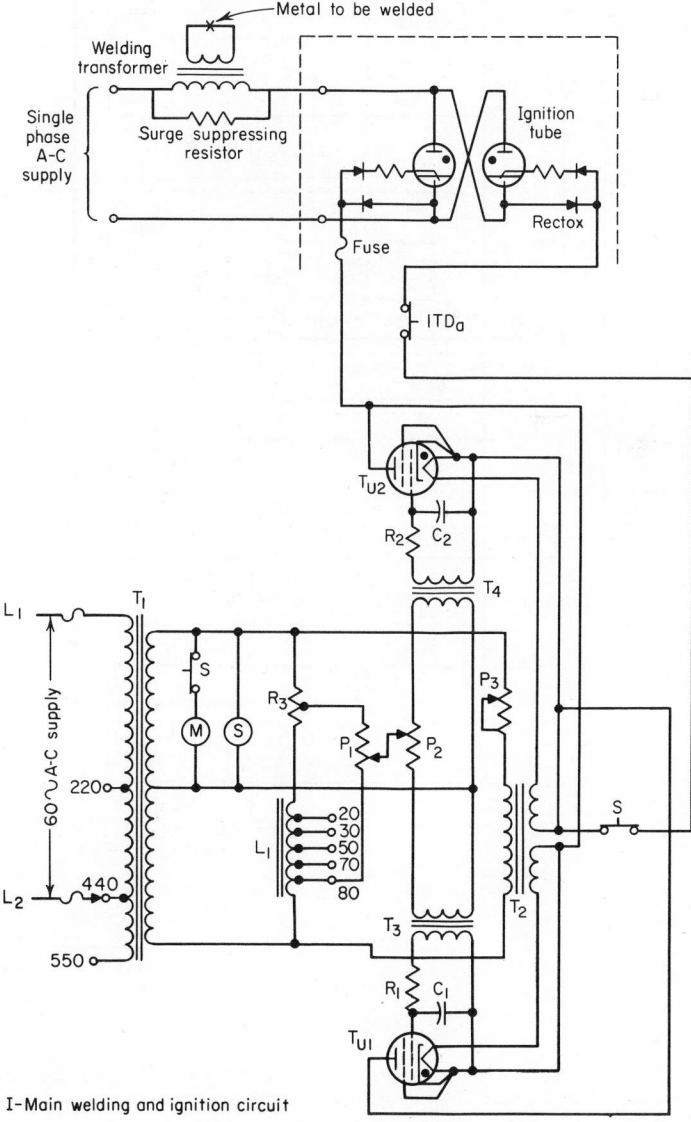

I-Main welding and ignition circuit

FIG. 93 *Part I. Weld-O-Tral. (Westinghouse Electric Corp.)*

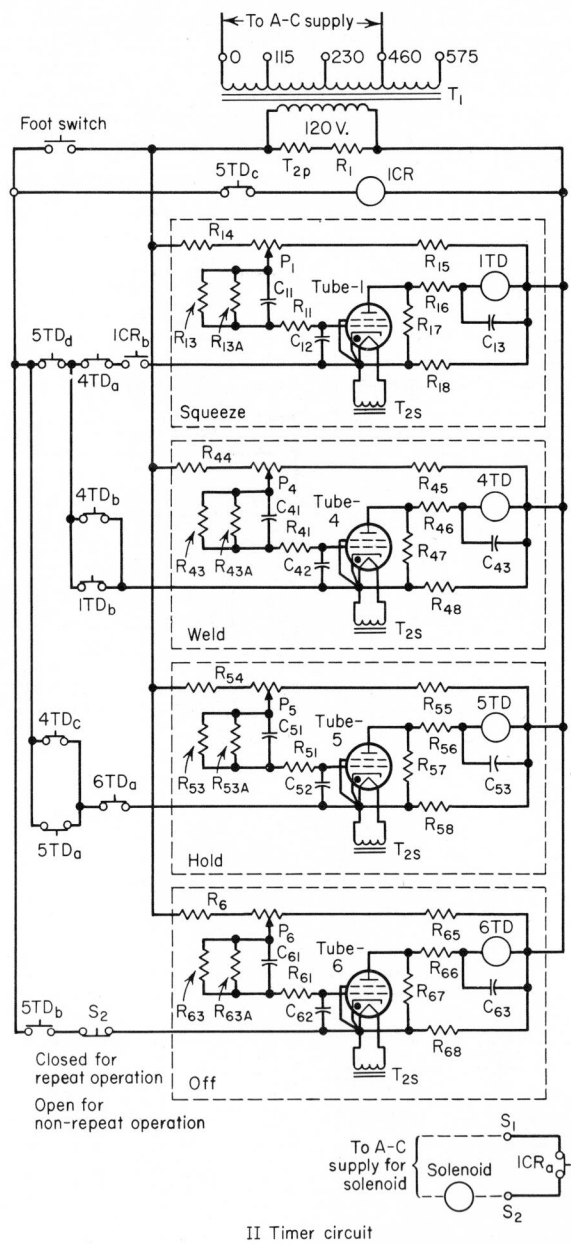

FIG. 93 *Part II. Weld-O-Tral. (Westinghouse Electric Corp.)*

same, the slider on P_2 is at the mid-point. If the positive and negative current loops are unequal, the slider is moved to delay the firing of one heat-control thyratron and advance the firing of the other.

Potentiometer P_3 is in the primary circuit of the transformer supplying filament power for the thyratron tubes. By means of it, the voltage applied to the tube filaments can be held constant with a supply-voltage fluctuation of as much as from 85 to 110 per cent of the nominal value.

The weld timer consists of four identical electronic timers. The principle of operation of each timer is the same as for the timer discussed in Sec. 57. Such a timer is used to control automatically a four-operation welding cycle consisting of squeeze, weld, hold, and off periods.

When the initiating foot switch is closed, a contact closes in the circuit of the solenoid and causes welding-machine electrodes to close on the work and apply pressure to the metal to be welded. After a preadjusted interval, a second contact energizes the ignition circuit of the main ignition contactor. This allows current to flow through the primary of the welding transformer. After another interval, the contactor in the ignition circuit opens and weld current ceases. A third time interval follows the cessation of welding current, at the end of which the contactor in the solenoid circuit opens, and the electrodes of the welding machine separate. At the same time, a set of contacts opens and prevents operation of the solenoid until a fourth period of time has elapsed, following which the entire cycle is repeated. This process is repeated as long as the foot switch is closed.

P_1 controls the length of the squeeze period, P_4 the length of the weld period, P_5 the length of the hold period, and P_6 the length of the off period.

If the foot switch is closed, $1CR$ becomes energized and contacts $1CRa$ and $1CRb$ close. Contact $1CRa$ operates the welding-machine solenoid; $1CRb$ allows the grid capacitor C_{11} of tube 1 to discharge. After C_{11} has discharged sufficiently, tube 1 fires. This energizes $1TD$ and causes its contacts $1TDa$ and $1TDb$ to close. Contact $1TDa$ is in the ignition circuit of the ignitrons of the main contactor. Welding current then flows under the control of the heat-control unit, as previously explained.

$1TDb$ allows the grid capacitor C_{41} of tube 4 to discharge. After C_{41} has discharged sufficiently, tube 4 fires and energizes $4TD$.

At this point, $4TDa$ opens. Since these contacts are in series with $1TD$, $1TD$ drops out and causes $1TDa$ to open and interrupt the welding current. At the same time, $4TDb$ and $4TDc$ close. Contact $4TDb$ is a lock-in contact and has no effect on the sequence; $4TDc$ allows C_{51} to discharge.

After C_{51} has lost sufficient charge, tube 5 fires. This energizes $5TD$, causing $5TDa$ and $5TDb$ to close and $5TDc$ to de-energize $1CR$, which in turn causes the solenoid to separate the electrodes of the welding machine. $5TDd$ opens the circuit of $4TD$. $5TDa$ is a lock-in contact and initiates no other circuit. $5TDb$, however, allows C_{61} to discharge.

When C_{61} has lost sufficient charge, tube 6 fires and energizes $6TD$. This opens $6TDa$, which de-energizes $5TD$. When the contacts of the $5TD$ relay return to their normal position, the circuit is the same as at the start, and the whole cycle is repeated as long as the foot switch is kept closed, provided that switch S_2 is closed. Switch S_2 is the repeat switch, and when it is open, it removes the circuit associated with tube 6 from the welding circuit. This means that the repetition of the welding cycle is not automatic. When switch S_2 is open, the welding cycle is repeated only after the operator releases the foot switch for a period sufficient in length to allow capacitors C_{11}, C_{41}, and C_{51} to charge and then closes the foot switch again.

66. High-frequency heating is the heating of materials through the heat generated in them by an electric source of power of high frequency. High-frequency heating is of two types: induction heating and dielectric heating. Induction heating is employed for the heating of metals or other conducting materials. Dielectric heating is employed for the heating of poor conducting materials such as plastics and plywood.

In induction heating, the conducting material to be heated is placed inside a coil which is usually called the inductor coil. The coil is connected to a high-frequency source of voltage capable of delivering the required power. The high-frequency magnetic field produced by the high-frequency current in the inductor coil will induce voltages of the same high frequency in the material enclosed by the coil (refer to Secs. **71** and **122** of Div. 1). These voltages will produce high-frequency currents in the material to be heated. Because of skin effect (see Sec. **123** of Div. 1), these induced currents will be crowded out toward the surface of the material. The depth of the current-carrying layer will decrease as the frequency increases. Thus it is possible, by the proper choice of frequency, to control the depth to which an object is heated.

In dielectric heating, the poor conducting mass is placed between two electrodes which are connected, respectively, to the two terminals of a high-frequency source of voltage. The electrodes and the material to be heated will constitute a capacitor, and an alternating electric field will be set up in the material between the two electrodes.

This alternating field, passing uniformly through the work, displaces or stresses the molecules of the material, first in one direction and then in the other, as the polarity of the field is reversed. Friction occurs because of this molecular motion in the work and generates heat uniformly throughout the mass. Such molecular friction and the resulting heat generation are proportional to the field reversals per second, and consequently, the higher the frequency, the faster the heating. Because of heat radiation from the surface, however, the center may be hotter than the outer layers. Suitable measures can be taken to correct this condition when it occurs.

Oscillators are used as the source of the high-frequency power required for induction and dielectric heating (refer to Sec. **59**).

67. Light-sensitive control devices have a broad field of application. The light-sensitive feature can be obtained by means of a phototube or semiconductors (Sec. **100**). Since the output of most phototubes is too low to operate sturdy electromagnetic devices, it is often necessary to amplify the output of the phototube with an electronic amplifier of one or more stages. Refer to Sec. **56** for a discussion of light-sensitive relays. The complete circuit of a light-sensitive device may involve other tubes and circuit elements, depending upon the function to be performed. General-purpose light-sensitive relays and light sources for their operation are available which are adaptable to many conditions and can be used as the base unit in building up a complete control system. Some of the more common light-sensitive control devices are:

Limit switches.
Automatic door openers and closers.
Counting of objects on a conveyor.
Elevator-floor leveling.
Elevator-door safety control.
Automatic control of artificial lighting.
Louver controllers.
Sorting, grading, and matching.

A circuit for automatic control of artificial lighting is shown in Fig. 94. When switch S is open, relay 1 is open, and its back contacts at 6 and 2 are closed, as shown in the figure. Contactor C is also open, as is the circuit to the lamps. When switch S is closed, current will flow from point 1 to 2, to 6 through the heating element of the thermal relay to point 3, through operating coil C of contactor C, through resistance R_1, and back to the other side of the line at point 7. However, the current through the operating coil of contactor C will not be sufficient to operate contactor C because of the resistance of the heating coil of the thermal relay. Contactor C, therefore, cannot close for a certain length of time. Closing of switch S also energizes the grid and anode circuits of tube B. The anode current of tube B depends upon the grid voltage of the tube. The grid voltage is a combination of the grid-bias voltage and the drop in resistor R_2 caused by the current of the phototube. The circuit is so connected that the drop in resistor R_2 decreases the negative grid voltage of tube B. Thus, as illumination on the phototube increases, the anode current of tube B increases. The grid-bias voltage of tube B is adjusted through potentiometer P_1 when contacts C_1 are open and through both potentiometers P_1 and P_2 when contacts C_1 are closed. Contacts C_1 are open when contactor C is closed and the lights are on. Contacts C_1 are closed when contactor C is open and the lights are off. Therefore, the grid-bias voltage of tube B is controlled through potentiometer P_1 when the lights are on and through both potentiometers P_1 and P_2 when the lights are off. When switch S is closed, if the illumination on the phototube is sufficient, the anode current of tube B will be strong enough to operate relay 1. Relay 1 in closing will close its contacts at 8 and open its back contacts at 6. Opening of the contacts at 6 will open the circuit from 1 through the operating coil C. Thus, if, upon the closing of switch S, the illumination of daylight is sufficient, depending upon the settings of P_1 and P_2, contactor C will not operate and the lights will remain off.

On the other hand, if, when switch S is closed, the illumination of the phototube is not sufficient to cause relay 1 to operate, then the thermal relay will operate after a short lapse of time and close its contacts T_1. Closing of contacts T_1 will short the heating element of the thermal relay, and the current through operating coil C will then be sufficient to operate contactor C. Contactor C in closing will close its contacts C_2 and C_3 and will open its contacts C_1. The circuit to the lamps is now closed, and the lamps will be lighted. The closing of contacts C_2 will short the thermal relay out of the circuit of the operating coil C of contactor C. Contactor C will be held closed as long as the illumination on the phototube is not sufficient to operate relay 1. Also the thermal relay will cool and reset itself.

When the light intensity on the phototube caused by daylight and the artificial lighting increases sufficiently, the anode current of tube B will be increased enough to cause relay 1 to operate. Closing of relay 1 will close its contacts at 8 and open its back contacts at 2. The heating element of the thermal relay is now connected in parallel with the operating coil C of contactor C. The heating element will eventually operate the thermal relay, closing its contacts T_1. Closing of contacts T_1 shorts the operating coil C of contactor C. Contactor C is no longer energized, and contacts C_2 and C_3 therefore open, while contacts C_1 close. Closing of C_1 alters the bias on the grid of tube B. The setting of P_2 should be such that the light intensity which caused the lights to be turned off will hold relay 1 closed, so that it will take the desired reduction of light intensity to reduce the anode current of tube B sufficiently so that it will no longer hold relay 1 closed. After contactor C opens, there is no longer current through either operating coil C or the heating element of the thermal relay as long as relay 1 stays closed. The thermal relay therefore resets itself. After the lights have been turned off, should the light intensity on the phototube decrease momentarily to a value so that relay 1 opens, current will pass from point 1 to 2, to 6 through the heater element of the thermal relay to 3, through operating coil C to 4, through resistor R_1 to 5, and back to the other side of the line at 7. The current through operating coil C will not be great

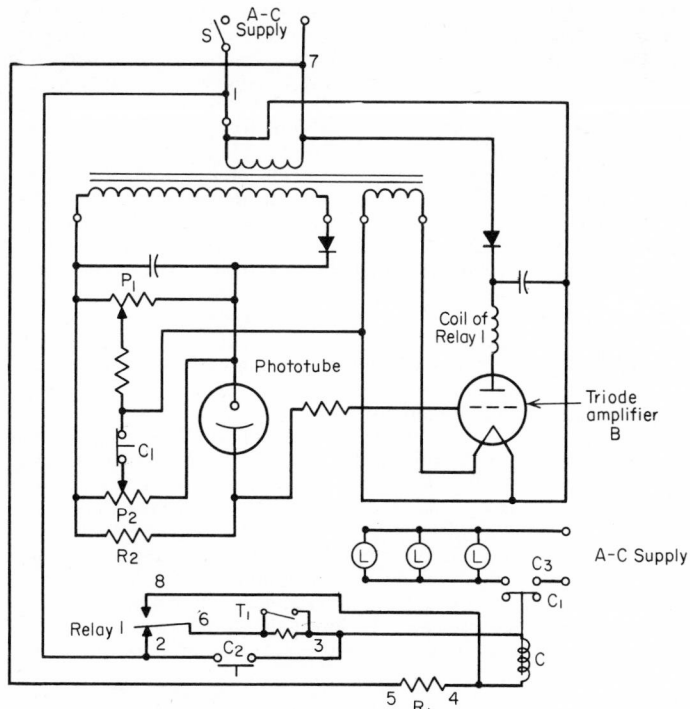

FIG. 94 *Circuit for phototube control of a lighting circuit.*

enough, however, to operate contactor C because of the resistance of the heating element of the thermal relay. Therefore, a momentary reduction of light intensity will not turn the lights on. If the reduction in light intensity persists, the thermal relay will function and close its contacts T_1. Closing of contacts T_1 will short the heating element of the thermal relay, and the current through operating coil C will be sufficient to close contactor C and turn the lights on.

68. Voltage Regulators. Several different electronic circuits have been devised for automatically holding the output voltage of generators at a constant value. Such voltage-regulator circuits have been employed with both d-c and a-c generators. Since the average electrical worker will seldom come in contact with these electronic voltage regulators, a discussion of the circuits is not warranted in this book.

FUNDAMENTALS OF SOLID-STATE DEVICES

69. Introduction to Semiconductors. In 1948 Bell Telephone Laboratories announced the development of the first transistor. This event ushered in the modern age of semiconductors, which are often called *solid-state* devices or *static* components. Since that time many hundreds of solid-state devices have been developed and placed into practical application. These components, such as Zener diodes, thyristors (commonly known as silicon-controlled rectifiers or SCRs), transistors, varistors, thermistors, and others are used frequently in a wide variety of electrical equipment and systems. Typical applications include amplifiers, light dimmers, motor speed controls, voltage regulators, temperature controls, switching, timing, and detection devices.

The chief advantages of solid-state devices are that they are highly reliable and compact and consume little power. Thus, electrical equipment and systems utilizing solid-state components are inherently dependable and small in size, require smaller power supplies, and are extremely efficient. Disadvantages of solid-state devices are their sensitivity to heat and overvoltages. Excessive heat and high-voltage surges can damage semiconductors. However, modern circuit design techniques, recent developments in semiconductor materials, and improved manufacturing methods have minimized these disadvantages. In addition, solid-state devices that will safely handle hundreds of amperes at high voltages are now available.

Comparison of a semiconductor to an electron tube is inevitable, because, for practically all functions performed by an electron tube, there is a solid-state device to take its place. Although solid-state devices have achieved remarkable success in recent years, they have not completely replaced vacuum tubes. For certain applications, vacuum tubes are still better suited, particularly where power requirements are high.

Unlike the vacuum tube, which is constructed with its parts (anode, cathode, etc.) separated by a vacuum or gas, the comparable parts of a solid-state component are in physical contact with one another. The primary purpose of these parts, in both the vacuum tube and the solid-state device, is to control the flow of electric current. In semiconductors, this control is provided by combining various treated materials, such as silicon and germanium, which have properties that will permit various amounts of current flow in predetermined directions.

In considering vacuum tubes and related circuits, the fundamental concept of movement of free electrons within the tube and associated circuits is essential to a comprehensive understanding of electronic theory. In studying solid-state devices, however, consideration of current flow as movement of free electrons *plus movement of holes* simplifies understanding of solid-state theory.

70. Atoms. A review of the structure of the atom is essential to a clear understanding of semiconductor operation. Atoms consist of protons, electrons, and neutrons. It is convenient to visualize the structure of an atom as consisting of a nucleus surrounded with orbiting rings of electrons. But it should be noted that such an atomic structure is purely symbolic. However, this representation is considered sufficiently accurate to explain *behavior* of atoms.

The nucleus of an atom is made up of protons and neutrons. Electrons circle the nucleus in definite orbits or shells. In theory, this configuration results because the typical atom is *electrically neutral*. Protons carry a positive charge which is equal to a negative charge carried by each electron. And, as their name implies, neutrons are electrically neutral. However, the existence of neutrons explains the differences in mass in various atoms. Other than noting that neutrons are included in atomic structure, further consideration of them serves no useful purpose in the study of semiconductors.

71. Valence Electrons. Atoms of various elements are distinguished from one another by the number of protons and neutrons in the nucleus and by the number and arrangement of electrons in orbit around the nucleus. Electrons in the inner orbits of the more complicated atoms are tightly fixed in position. These electrons are extremely difficult to displace. Electrons in the outermost ring of an atom are much more loosely bonded in place and are more easily dislodged. These electrons are called valence electrons. Figure 95 shows representations of typical atoms. Note that the silicon atom has four valence electrons.

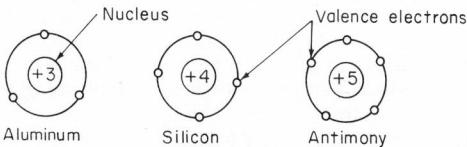

FIG. 95 *Representations of typical atoms.*

When a valence electron has been dislodged from orbit, it is called a *free electron*. In semiconductors, free electrons serve as current carriers which create electron flow. Examples of forces available that will dislodge valence electrons include heat, light, and applied voltage.

In some atoms, valence electrons are tightly bound to their nucleus. These are atoms of a classification of elements called *insulators*. The primary characteristic of an insulator is that free electrons are not readily available. Hence, electron flow is difficult to create and sustain.

On the other hand, the atoms of silver, aluminum, copper, and similar metals have valence electrons that are comparatively easy to release. These elements are called *conductors*.

In elements such as silicon and germanium, the bonding of valence electrons is intermediate. Such elements are called **semiconductors.**

72. Covalent Bonding. In typical semiconductor material, nearby atoms share valence electrons in an arrangement called covalent bonding. This additional bonding of valence electrons in their orbital position tends to stabilize the semiconductor material, which, in this structure, is in a crystalline state. As a result, the material exhibits the characteristics of an insulator.

The atomic structure of a silicon crystal is represented (in two dimensions only) in Fig. 96. Actually, a crystal of pure silicon will contain millions of such atoms—each joined to four other atoms by sharing outer-

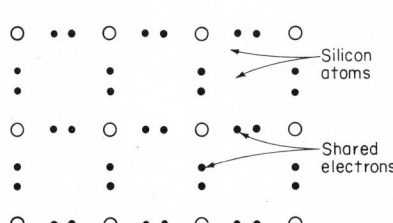

FIG. 96 *Atomic structure of silicon crystal.*

orbit electrons. The valence electrons of adjacent atoms in the crystal cross one another. Thus, the nucleus of neighboring atoms will act on the valence electrons, helping to keep them in place. And there are additional forces within the atomic structure that tend to keep these electrons in their respective orbits. As a result, free electrons are not readily available to serve as current carriers. This comparative scarcity of free electrons is characteristic of an insulator. Therefore, in order to serve as a practical semiconductor, typical semiconductor materials, such as germanium or silicon, must be altered by the addition of an "impurity."

73. Doping. The process of adding an impurity to germanium or silicon materials is called doping. This process results in the creation of a semiconductor material because the valence bonding of the crystal is disturbed and the material gains the ability to conduct current.

Only a minute amount of impurity is required—approximately one part in a million—to alter the current-carrying characteristics of the crystal. For example, a trace of impurity can produce, in a diode, 100,000,000,000 (10^{11}) free electrons for rectifying purposes. Impurities that may be added include elements such as arsenic, phosphorus, or antimony with five valence electrons each; or aluminum, boron, or indium with three valence electrons each.

74. Donor Impurities. Note in Fig. 95 that a silicon atom has four valence electrons as do germanium and certain other elements. Also, observe in Fig. 96 how these atoms share these valence electrons. However, when a trace of an element such as arsenic, which has five valence electrons, is fused to silicon, the "electron balance" of the crystal is disturbed. The arsenic atom upon being blended in with silicon atoms tends to behave like its neighbors. Four of the five valence electrons of the arsenic atom form a valence bond with electrons of the silicon atoms. The fifth electron cannot find any such convenient attachment and therefore is free to serve as a current carrier. Impurities such as arsenic which have five valence electrons are called donor impurities because they donate free electrons to the crystal.

75. Acceptor Impurities. A second impurity that disturbs the electron balance of the silicon crystal is the type that has three valence electrons, such as aluminum. When aluminum is fused to a silicon crystal, the aluminum atom forms a valence electron bond with its neighboring silicon atoms, as shown in Fig. 97. To do this the aluminum atom must take an electron from a neighboring silicon atom. The place where this electron originally was located is now empty and is called a *hole*. It should be noted that the hole will have a positive charge equal to the negative charge that left that location.

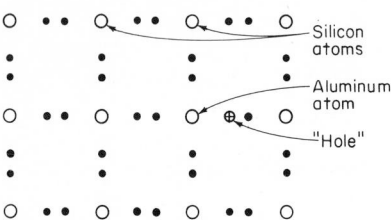

FIG. 97 *Silicon crystal with aluminum "impurity" added shows electron imbalance and creation of a "hole."*

76. p and n Materials. The type of impurity used determines the type of semiconductor material created. Donor-type impurities, which donate electrons, produce n-type semiconductors. The material is called n-type because current is carried primarily by electrons, which have a negative charge. Conversely, acceptor-type impurities, which accept electrons and result in the formation of holes, produce p-type semiconductors. The material is called p-type because current is carried primarily by holes, which have a positive charge.

77. Flow of Holes. Normally, current flow through tubes, wires, or other components is considered to be by electrons, which are negatively charged particles. This is also true, in general, of current flow in n-type semiconductor material. However, in p-type material, current flow is considered to be by holes, which have a positive charge.

It was pointed out that p-type material is created when an acceptor impurity is added to a semiconductor material. An atom of an acceptor impurity has but three valence electrons and takes an electron from an adjacent semiconductor atom, thus leaving a

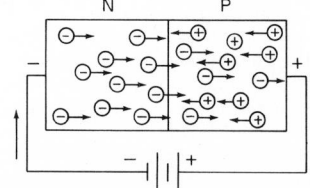

FIG. 98 *Forward bias of an n-p junction.*

hole in the covalent bond. Then, when a voltage is applied across the p-type semiconductor crystal, the holes will move toward the negative terminal of the applied voltage (Fig. 98). This action occurs because the hole created by the doping process is filled by an adjacent electron which travels toward the positive terminal of the applied voltage. And each electron, in turn, jumps into an adjacent hole, leaving behind another hole. The result is that of current flow by holes.

It should be noted that for circuits external to the semiconductor this flow of holes has the same effect as the flow of electrons, except that it is in the opposite direction. Thus, in studying the application of semiconductors, it is not necessary in most instances to consider the flow of holes, unless certain action within the semiconductor must be also considered.

78. Current Carriers. In *n*-type semiconductor material, the free electrons are termed *majority carriers*. A small quantity of holes are also available to carry current. These are called *minority carriers*. Similarly, holes are the majority carriers in *p*-type material, whereas electrons are considered to be the minority carriers. Familiarity with these terms should aid in understanding the operation of semiconductor diodes, transistors, and other solid-state devices.

SOLID-STATE DIODES

79. Crystal Diodes. When an *n*-type crystal and a *p*-type crystal are fused together, a diode is formed. Such a diode will pass current in one direction but not in the other; thus it performs as a rectifier.

The fusion process forms a *p-n* junction, which permits electrons in the *n*-type material and holes in the *p*-type material to cross the junction. After they cross the junction, they combine with each other and cancel each other out. The effect of this action is that fewer electrons now exist in the *n*-type material and fewer holes exist in the *p*-type material. Because of this, a positive charge is created in the *n*-type material and a negative charge in the *p*-type material.

As a result, a very small potential is created at the junction. Although this charge is small, it produces a *potential hill* or barrier to current carriers at the junction. To obtain current flow across this barrier, an outside source of energy must be applied in the proper direction.

80. Forward Bias. If a battery is connected so that the applied voltage decreases the potential hill, the carriers are forced across the junction, and current flows as shown in Fig. 98.

81. Reverse Bias. When a battery is connected so that it aids the potential hill at the *p-n* junction, the carriers are drawn away from the junction, and only a tiny current can flow. This small current is caused by minority carriers, which are always present in semiconductor materials.

82. Rectification. From the foregoing, it can be seen that if voltage is applied first in one direction, then in the other (which is what happens when an alternating voltage is applied), current will flow easily in one direction, but only a minute amount will flow in the other direction. The small current in the reverse direction (by minority carriers) is known as leakage current.

83. Zener Diode. If an increasing voltage is applied to a silicon diode in reverse bias, a voltage level is reached where the diode will break down. At this point, the current will increase very rapidly and is limited only by the resistance in series with the diode (Fig. 99).

The specific voltage at which the diode breaks down or conducts is called its Zener voltage. This breakdown does not damage the diode, because the diode recovers when the reverse voltage is removed. This unusual ability to conduct in the blocking direction at a specified voltage has proved to be very useful in many applications.

It is important to note that the amount of current flow is practically independent of applied voltage. Silicon diodes which are specially designed to operate at specific voltages over a wide current range are called Zener diodes. Typical applications are voltage regulators, clippers, clamps, protective elements, and fast-acting solid-state switches.

84. Tunnel Diode. The tunnel diode is a versatile semiconductor device with unusual characteristics. For example, electric charges travel through the tunnel diode at extremely high speeds (approaching the speed of light). This is much faster than speeds that occur in ordinary diodes and transistors. As a result, the tunnel diode can be effectively applied in circuits which operate at high frequencies (10,000 Mc). The tunnel diode can operate at temperatures up to approximately 700°F, whereas standard diodes cease to operate at about 400°F. In addition, the tunnel diode has a negative-

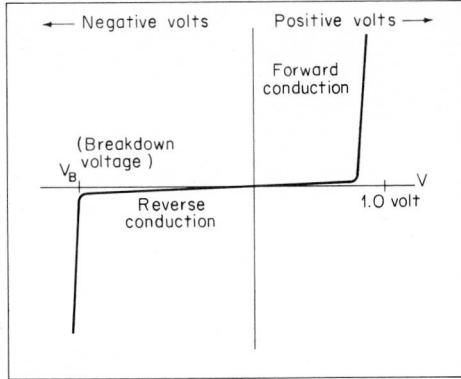

FIG. 99 *Typical characteristics of a silicon Zener diode.*

resistance characteristic, which allows it to be used as an amplifier or oscillator, or as a fast-operating switching device. In many applications, it has replaced the transistor.

The negative-resistance feature of the tunnel diode is illustrated by the unusual curve shown in Fig. 100. Note that as voltage is increased from zero, current increases normally to point A. As positive voltage is increased further, the current decreases instead of increasing further, as would be normally expected. Note how rapidly the current drops practically to zero. Also, when the applied voltage continues to increase, the current resumes its increase corresponding to the voltage. Because the diode current will decrease as voltage is increased between points A and B, the diode is said to have a negative-resistance characteristic.

Another important feature of the tunnel diode is that it can be made extremely small. Several hundred tunnel diodes could be packed into a thimble.

85. High-power Diode. Diodes that are used in high-current circuits must be able to withstand a relatively large temperature rise. These semiconductors are known as silicon cells, or silicon diode rectifiers. A typical high-power silicon cell (Fig. 101) consists of a disk of silicon with minute traces of impurity added. This silicon disk is placed between an aluminum plate and high-temperature solder. Then, the sandwich is assembled to the base stud and anode flexible lead. Next the rectify-

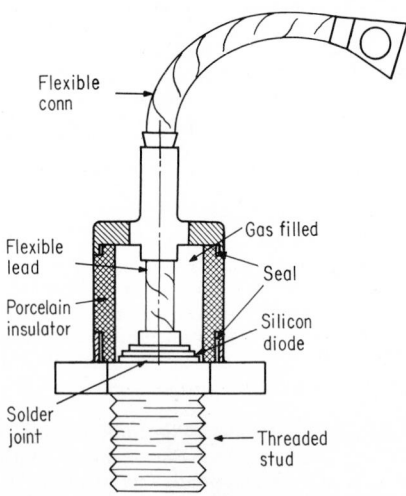

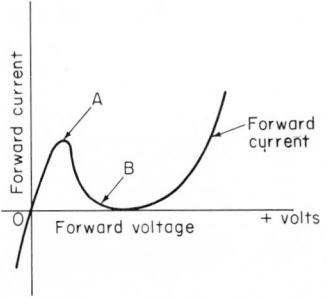

FIG. 100 *Negative-resistance curve of a tunnel diode.*

FIG. 101 *Construction of a high-power silicon diode. (Westinghouse Electric Corp.)*

ing junction is formed by fusing the sandwich at a very high temperature. Finally, the unit is sealed to prevent contamination.

An effective method of removing heat from the silicon cell is to transfer it to a larger, cooler body or "sink" (Fig. 102). This is achieved by intimate contact between the stud and the heat sink. When current levels are exceptionally high, silicon cells may be mounted on water-cooled bus bars, which serve the dual purpose of conductor and heat sink.

A single silicon cell of the stud-mount configuration can handle currents up to about 400 amp. Peak-inverse voltage ratings for silicon cells in this current range extend to approximately 700 volts. Silicon cells are often connected in series-parallel which enables the combination to carry very high currents at high voltages.

OPERATION OF THYRISTORS

86. Thyristors (SCRs). The thyristor, which has become the preferred name for the SCR (silicon-controlled rectifier), is a solid-state switch with the following main characteristics: (1) it can operate at high voltages and can carry high currents; (2) it can operate at high speeds (millionth of a second); (3) very little drive current is required for operation; (4) it is small in size and light in weight; (5) with no moving parts it offers long life, low maintenance, and high reliability.

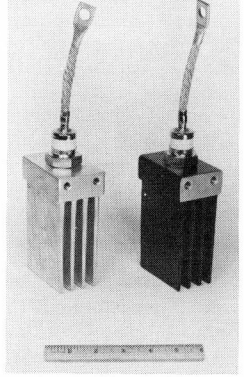

FIG. 102 *Typical silicon diodes mounted on heat sinks. (Westinghouse Electric Corp.)*

These features have made the thyristor an extremely popular solid-state device, and it is found in many types of solid-state apparatus. In many applications, it is replacing thyratrons, relays, contactors, switches, vacuum tubes, and other basic devices. Typical apparatuses that utilize the thyristor include motor speed controls, light dimmers, power switches, frequency converters, inverters, and temperature controls.

In application, the thyristor controls large blocks of power as commanded by a very low-level signal. In this function it is an amplifier. Also, the thyristor can switch heavy current, function as a rectifier, or when proper circuiting is provided, operate in a-c circuits to allow the flow of alternating current.

Physically, the thyristor is similar to the ordinary silicon diode except that it has a third lead (gate). Figure 103*b* shows the internal configuration of a thyristor. Four sections of semiconductor are combined in the order, *n, p, n, p,* as shown. In normal operation, this arrangement results in two forward-biased junctions and one reverse-biased junction. Regardless of the polarity of the voltage, current cannot flow because there is always at least one reverse-biased junction.

However, if a small amount of current is injected into the gate lead, the thyristor starts forward conduction because current is forced to flow through one of the forward junctions. This initiates the energy required to "fire" full forward conduction. Flow of forward current is limited only by the resistance of the external circuit. Removal of the

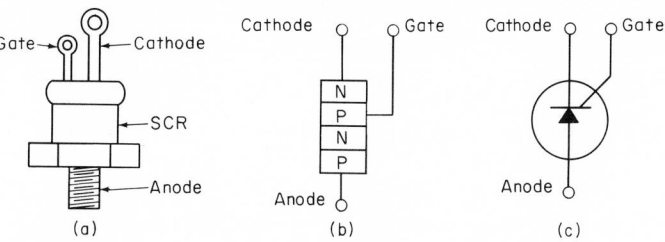

FIG. 103 *Construction of thyristors (silicon-controlled rectifiers).*

gate signal (current) does not take the thyristor out of the conducting state. It can be "turned off" by interrupting the forward current, or removing the anode voltage, or reversing the forward current by applying negative voltage to the anode.

87. Thyristor Switching Speed. The manner in which the thyristor is taken out of conduction has a definite effect on its switching speed. And its ability to switch quickly is one of the significant features of the thyristor. As an example, it can be turned on in 1 to 4 μsec. When a thyristor is conducting and a reverse voltage is placed on its anode, it can regain its blocking state in about 25 to 50 μsec. However, if the anode current is interrupted without a negative voltage being applied to the anode, the "turn-off" time can be up to 100 μsec.

Because it is capable of switching within microseconds, the thyristor can be "triggered" or "fired" into conduction at any point in a positive half cycle of an applied voltage wave. This method of control, which is termed phase control, is often used to obtain precise control of thyristor operation. The operating principles of phase control are discussed in Sec. **33,** which describes how phase control is applied to control "firing" of thyratron tubes. Phase control of SCRs is discussed in Secs. **107** and **111.**

TRANSISTORS

88. Transistors. A transistor is an assembly of three sections of semiconductor materials, arranged so that one type of transistor material is sandwiched between two sections of another type. Transistors perform many functions formerly accomplished by vacuum tubes, such as amplifiers, oscillators, or switching devices. The transistor most commonly used is called a junction transistor. Two general types are available— an n-p-n or p-n-p type. Arrangements of materials of typical junction transistors are shown in Fig. 104. Sections are termed emitter, base, and collector as shown. Metallic leads are attached, one to each section, for connection to external circuits.

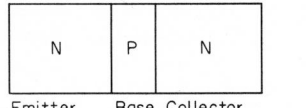 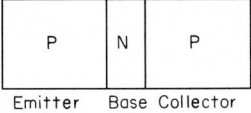

FIG. 104 *Arrangement of semiconductor materials of two major types of transistors.*

In most applications, transistors offer many advantages over vacuum tubes. They are significantly smaller and save space. They require no heater or filament power, operate at low voltages, consume little power, and have inherent reliability and long life. For these reasons as well as others they are used frequently in a variety of industrial control applications.

89. Transistor Operation. The circuit shown in Fig. 105 illustrates basic operation of an n-p-n junction transistor. Note that all sections of the transistor are labeled and that the base, which is p-type material, is sandwiched between the emitter and the col-

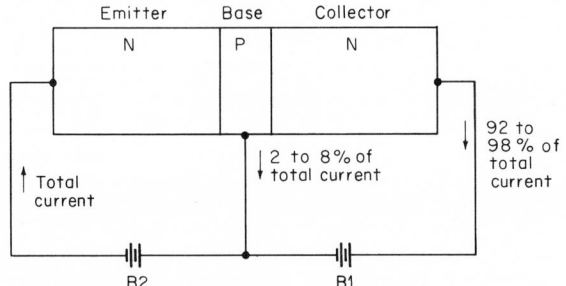

FIG. 105 *Basic operation of an n-p-n junction transistor.*

lector. Physically, the base is considerably smaller than either the emitter or the collector.

Battery $B1$, is connected so that the n-p junction between the emitter and the bases is forward-biased. As a result, current will flow from the negative side of the battery, through the emitter, the emitter-base junction, and the base, and back to the positive side of the battery $B1$.

At first observation, current flow through the p-n base-collector junction would seem unlikely because battery $B2$ applies a reverse bias between the base and the collector. It is important to note, however, that the base, which is p-type material, has comparatively few holes available because of its small size. This means that electrons coming from the emitter find comparatively few holes with which they can recombine. Also, battery $B2$, which is usually much larger than battery $B1$ and is in series with battery $B1$, creates a strong potential field which attracts practically all free electrons entering the base. These free electrons flow on through the collector and to the positive terminal of battery $B2$. Practically all electrons that enter the emitter continue on through the base and collector. Only a very small percentage (2 to 8 per cent) of the total available electrons return through the base to battery $B1$. It is important to note that the *voltage between the emitter and the base controls the amount of electron flow in the collector circuit.* Operation of a p-n-p transistor is similar except that the majority carriers are holes rather than electrons. Also, battery polarities must be reversed.

90. Base Control. The forward bias of the emitter-base junction supplies energy to current carriers on each side of the junction, allowing current flow across the junction. As more carriers cross the emitter-base junction, more carriers are available for collector current. It is significant that an increase of collector voltage does not change the availability of current carriers. Therefore, collector current remains fairly constant as collector voltage varies. This makes it evident that collector current is controlled by the voltage across the emitter and base.

91. Amplification. Amplification, often termed *gain*, is a measure of the difference between the transistor input of voltage, current, or power and its output. A small change of input voltage (emitter to base) causes a small change in base current. Because of the close relationship between base current and collector current, a corresponding change occurs in the collector current. Thus, a change in the small base current has resulted in a corresponding change in the larger collector current. This is *current amplification.*

When collector current is directed through a comparatively large load resistor connected in the collector circuit, the resulting IR drop will be relative to the input voltage. This is *voltage amplification.* It should be pointed out that although a transistor may have a current gain of less than one, it still may amplify as a result of current flowing through a large load resistor. Voltage gains of over 100 are common.

92. Physical Construction of Transistors. Most junction transistors are formed by heating and fusing pellets of the selected impurity on both sides of a crystal. For example, boron pellets fused into an n-type crystal result in a p-n-p "sandwich" of two sections of p-type material separated by a small section of n-type material. Then, the fused semiconductor crystal is shaped and polished, leads are attached, and the assembly is sealed into a protective case.

Transistors constructed in this manner are termed fused-junction or alloy-junction transistors. Another type of construction requires that impurities be added to the molten germanium crystal as it solidifies. If impurities are added in the proper amounts and at proper predetermined intervals, the junction transistor can be "grown" according to specifications. This type of transistor is called a grown junction transistor (see Fig. 106).

The transistor case offers adequate mechanical protection and is opaque to exclude light which can affect operation of the transistor. Various compounds are used to seal out moisture, dirt, or other contaminants. In general, modern transistors can withstand shock, vibrations, and temperature variations without damage. However, extreme temperature variations can cause unreliable operation of transistors.

It is important to note that transistors which serve in "power applications" (those that must carry comparatively high currents) are furnished with large metal cases that promote good heat transfer. Cases of "power transistors" may be made of copper, aluminum, or other good heat-conducting metal to aid removal of heat from the transistor. To promote additional heat removal, a power transistor may be mounted on a "heat sink." A heat sink is a large-area metal body that accepts and radiates heat from the transistor. The heat sink can be the metal chassis or a mass of metal furnished with radiating fins to aid dissipation of heat.

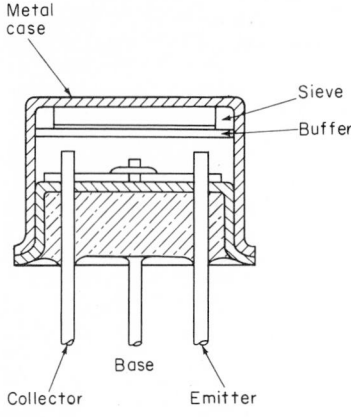

FIG. 106 *Construction of a grown junction transistor.*

93. Leads and Terminals. Most transistors in general use have leads that can be identified by one of the arrangements shown in Fig. 107. In 1 the collector terminal *C* is connected to the case, while the emitter and base terminals, which extend from the bottom of the case, are marked *E* and *B*, respectively. In 2 the collector is spaced away from the other leads. In 3 a red dot is sometimes marked on the case to identify the collector lead. Basing diagrams are available to identify leads of unusual arrangement.

94. Symbols. In circuit diagrams, a transistor generally is represented by one of the symbols shown in Fig. 108 and is designated by the letter *Q*. Additional symbols commonly used in the study of transistors are as follows:

V_{CB}	Collector-to-base voltage, d-c
V_{CE}	Collector-to-emitter voltage, d-c
V_{BE}	Base-to-emitter voltage, d-c
V_{CC}	Collector-circuit supply voltage, d-c
I_C	Collector current, average, d-c
i_c	Collector current, instantaneous
E_g	Generator or source voltage
P_D	Collector power dissipation
μ	Current amplification factor
I_E	Emitter current, average, d-c
i_e	Emitter current, instantaneous
I_B	Base current, average, d-c
i_b	Base current, instantaneous

In application, the transistor is usually connected in any one of three different configurations: common base, common emitter, and common collector (Fig. 109).

95. Common-base Connection. A transistor connected in this manner will have a very low (30 to 100 ohms) input impedance; output impedance is very high (from 100K ohms to 1 megohm). In addition, currents flowing in the input circuits and output circuits are approximately equal (current amplification is less than 1); voltage amplification ranges from 100 to 200; power gain is medium, and phase inversion does not occur.

96. Common-emitter Connection. This circuit offers medium input impedance (approximately 1,000 ohms) as well as a medium output impedance. Current gain is

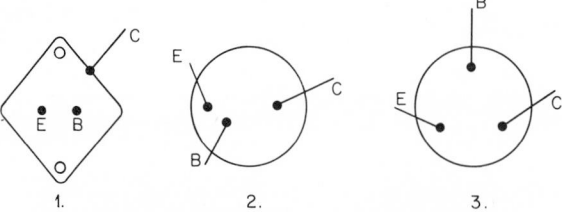

FIG. 107 *Standard transistor terminal markings.*

medium (20 to 100), while voltage gain is high (up to 600). Power gain is high and a 180-degree phase inversion from input to output takes place.

97. Common-collector Connection. This circuit is sometimes called an emitter follower because it resembles and has some of the characteristics of its electron tube counterpart, the cathode follower. A transistor connected in this configuration will have a high input impedance (10 K ohms to 1 megohm) and low output impedance (30 to 300 ohms). It offers a medium current gain but has a voltage gain of less than one. Power is low. This circuit is often used to obtain circuit impedance matching.

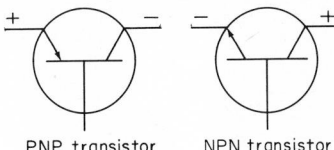

PNP transistor   NPN transistor

98. Characteristic Curves. Transistors have families of characteristic curves similar to those of electron tubes. These curves, which are often referred to as the static characteristics of the transistor, provide a great deal of information

FIG. 108 *Transistor symbols used in circuit diagrams.*

concerning the operation of the transistor at various applied voltages. Typical collector curves for a common-emitter circuit are shown in Fig. 110. The family is composed of a series of curves that show collector current and collector voltage at various base currents. For the common-emitter circuit, the base currents are expressed in microamperes.

Transistor operating values can be predicted by reference to characteristic curves. For example, as collector voltage V_c is varied, while base current I_b is held constant, collector current I_c varies only slightly. On the other hand, it is important to note that increases in base current cause much larger increases in collector current. As an example, read up the 5-volt line to the 20-μa curve. By reading across to the left, we note

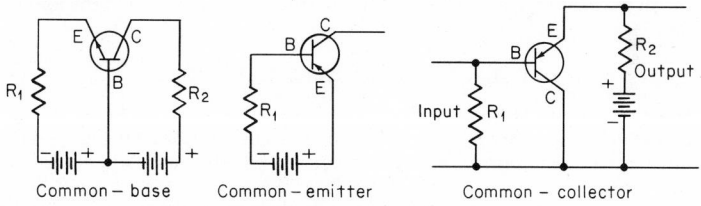

FIG. 109 *Basic transistor circuits.*

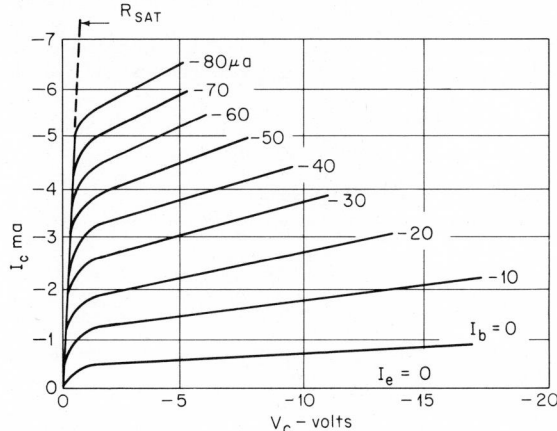

FIG. 110 *Typical collector characteristic curves for transistor connected in common-emitter circuit.*

that collector current will be 2.25 ma. At a base current I_b of 30 μa, the collector current will be 3 ma. Therefore, a 10-μa change in base current will cause a 750-μa (0.75-ma) change in collector current.

99. Special Transistors. In addition to the junction transistor, there are many other types of transistors in use, each of which serves a specific function. For example, the

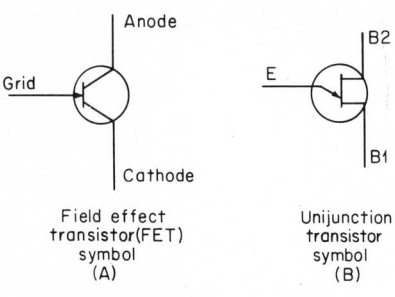

Field effect
transistor(FET)
symbol
(A)

Unijunction
transistor
symbol
(B)

FIG. 111 *Special transistors.*

field-effect transistor (FET) is used wherever a need exists for an extremely high input impedance. Input impedance as high as 200 megohms can be obtained with properly designed circuitry. Sometimes called the "stepping-stone from tube circuits to transistor circuits," the FET exhibits many characteristics of vacuum tubes. As such, its leads retain terminology applied to elements of vacuum tubes (Fig. 111A).

Another special transistor frequently encountered in solid-state industrial control circuits is the unijunction transistor. This device, shown schematically in Fig. 111B, is a three-terminal semiconductor consisting of an *n*-type silicon bar with connections at both ends and a layer of *p*-type material on the side of the bar. The silicon bar behaves as a resistance voltage divider. The emitter junction is connected to its center. The area between the emitter and base 1 will act as a variable resistance. Normally its resistance is about 20 per cent higher than that of the area between the emitter and base 2; however, when current flows from the emitter, the resistance of the *E-B*1 area drops to a very low value. This characteristic, in combination with proper resistance and capacitance elements, is useful in the application of a relaxation oscillator for control of SCRs.

USEFUL SOLID-STATE DEVICES

100. Other Solid-state Devices. There are many other semiconductor devices serving a wide variety of special applications. One very useful device is the *thermistor*. It is a resistor with a variable-resistance characteristic which changes in accordance with applied or surrounding temperature. Therefore, thermistors are often applied as temperature sensors to protect circuits or equipment from exposure to dangerous temperatures. In one particularly successful application, the thermistor provides overtemperature protection for motor windings. Because the typical thermistor is as small as a dime, it can be easily installed in equipment.

Another solid-state device that is particularly useful in industrial control equipment is the *triac*. This three-terminal device is a semiconductor a-c switch, which is triggered

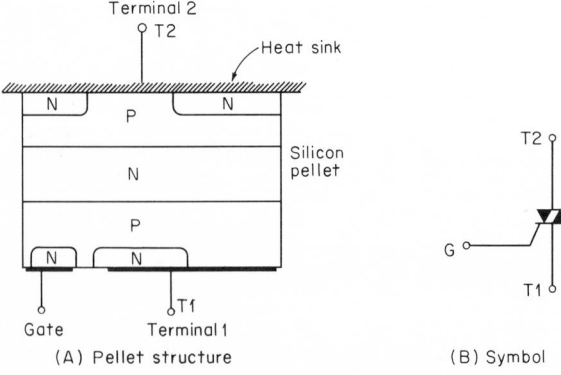

(A) Pellet structure   (B) Symbol

FIG. 112 *Arrangement of a triac.*

into conduction in a manner similar to that of a thyristor (SCR). The main difference between a triac and a thyristor is that the triac can conduct in opposite directions in accordance with the signal applied to the gate. The thyristor conducts in one direction only. Because the triac conducts in two directions, its terminals are identified simply as $T1$, $T2$, and gate (Fig. 112). Terminal $T1$ is normally used as a reference for measurement of voltage, current, or other circuit parameters. The main advantage offered by the triac is greatly simplified circuit arrangements, as compared with SCR circuits, to accomplish control functions.

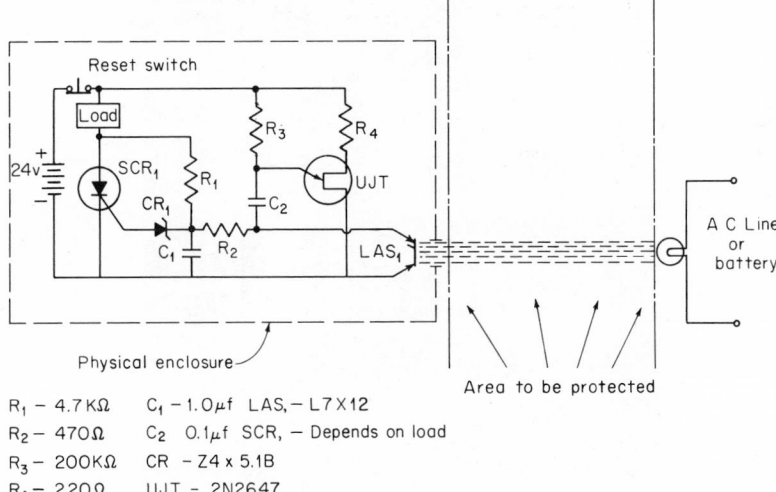

R_1 – 4.7 KΩ	C_1 – 1.0 μf LAS, – L7 X 12
R_2 – 470 Ω	C_2 0.1 μf SCR, – Depends on load
R_3 – 200 KΩ	CR – Z4 x 5.1B
R_4 – 220 Ω	UJT – 2N2647

FIG. 113   *Solid-state alarm system with a light-activated switch (LAS).   (General Electric Co.)*

The light-activated switch (LAS) is another useful solid-state device. The LAS is a two-lead (it does not have a gate lead) SCR-type device which is triggered into conduction by light, both visible and infrared. A typical circuit using an LAS in combination with a unijunction transistor and an SCR is shown in Fig. 113. In this circuit, interruption of the light beam initiates operation of the UJT relaxation oscillator, which fires the SCR, which, in turn, activates the load (alarm circuit or interlock).

OPERATION OF SOLID-STATE CIRCUITS AND EQUIPMENT

101. Silicon Rectifiers. Modern silicon rectifiers are the most effective and economical apparatus for d-c power conversion in numerous applications. For general-purpose applications, such as 250-volt industrial d-c power sources, silicon rectifiers are freestanding units in sizes from 3 to 300 kw. Larger units, up to about 20,000 kw, usually are supplied as d-c substations complete with protective devices, rectifier transformer, rectifier section, and d-c distribution switchgear (see Fig. 114).

Comparatively simple rectifiers are often used in control circuits to provide limited d-c power and to supply power to d-c apparatus such as small battery chargers, magnets, or plating systems.

For low-voltage high-current electrochemical applications, large silicon rectifiers may range in size up to about 50,000 kw.

In recent years, silicon rectifiers have practically replaced motor-generator sets, rotary converters, and mercury-arc rectifiers; and in many instances direct substitution is possible. Reasons for the popularity of silicon rectifiers are many, and they include higher efficiency, medium costs, lower installation costs, higher reliability, and longer life.

FIG. 114   *Silicon rectifier with silicon cells (arrow) mounted on side of transformer housing to save space (side panels removed).   (I-T-E Imperial Corp.)*

The basic silicon rectifier consists of banks of silicon diodes connected in series-parallel bridge arrangements.   Other essential components include diode protective devices and alarm circuits, cooling means, current-balancing devices, and voltage regulation equipment.

102. Silicon Rectifier Circuits.   Basic rectifier circuits are described in detail in Secs. **47, 48,** and **106.**   Silicon rectifier circuits are similar.   A circuit commonly used with silicon rectifiers is the six-phase double-way bridge, shown in Fig. 115.   A typical leg of the bridge, which is shown in an enlarged view, incorporates parallel diodes, fuses, and a resistance-capacitance (RC) network.   This series resistor and capacitor, connected across each leg of the bridge circuit, limits transient voltage spikes to safe levels.   Special selenium rectifiers and other protective devices are also used to protect silicon diodes against surges.

Diodes in parallel permit higher current-carrying capacity because total current will divide between the parallel legs.   If an overload occurs in any leg, the diode fuse will open, and an indicator lamp will signal that a silicon diode leg is out of service.   Normally, full-load current may continue to flow even with one failed diode in each leg of a bridge because of safety factors incorporated into the design.   However, good maintenance practice calls for replacement of the diode or fuse at the earliest opportunity.

103. Current Balancing.   Because silicon diodes have a low forward resistance, a difference in individual diode circuit resistance can permit large unbalance currents to flow in parallel circuits.   To provide an equal share of the total current, a preferred method uses magnetic cores and balancing reactors.   With this technique, the bus

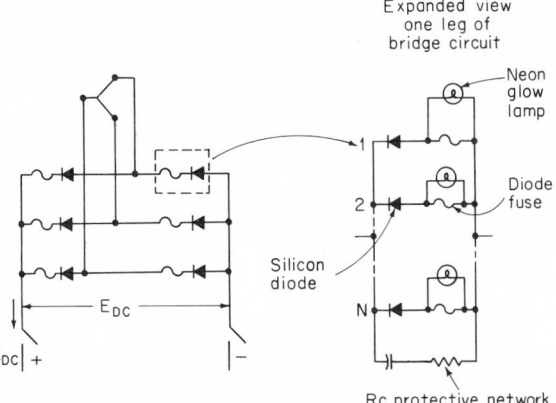

FIG. 115   *Six-phase double-way bridge is often used in conjunction with silicon rectifiers.* (*Westinghouse Electric Corp.*)

connecting the diodes is arranged in relation to the magnetic cores so that if one diode should attempt to carry more than its share, an opposing voltage is induced in its connecting lead until current balance is restored.

104. Cooling Methods. Although the forward resistance of a silicon cell is quite low, current flow generates I^2R heat losses which must be removed to maintain a safe junction temperature. To remove diode heat losses, several methods are employed. These include air cooling, water cooling, and techniques using heat exchangers. Essential to the effective operation of all these cooling systems is a heat sink. This may be a metal plate, an equipment chassis, a block of metal with fins to help dissipate heat quickly, or a large mass of metal that will conduct heat away from the silicon cell mounted on the heat sink.

Normally air-cooled silicon rectifiers operate at about 40°C maximum air temperature (operating plus ambient). Filtered air is forced through the rectifier cubicle and through the silicon-cell heat-sink cooling fins by a fan. Overtemperature devices operate an alarm circuit if temperatures exceed present limits. Typical recommended values for proper cooling are 1,500 cfm of air for a 1,000-kw silicon rectifier.

Water-cooling methods include a direct-cooling technique in which silicon cells are mounted directly on water-cooled bus bars. Water circulating in the bus bars removes heat. Another system employs an air-to-water heat exchanger in the rectifier enclosure.

105. Selenium Rectifiers. These devices are constructed of layers of selenium, which is a semiconductor, sandwiched between metal plates. Smaller rectifier stacks, sized about 2 by 2 by 2 in., are sometimes used to provide small d-c power supplies in electronic equipment, television sets, radios, etc. Larger units are packaged in cabinets with meters, required controls, and the like to provide d-c power for battery charging or welding. In recent years silicon rectifiers have been replacing selenium units for many applications. However, one application in which the selenium rectifier is popularly used is as surge protection for silicon rectifier cells. In this application the selenium cells are specially processed and are often called voltage surge suppressors. Normally, units are connected in parallel with the protected device to provide a shunt discharge path for transient overvoltages. An unusual feature of selenium rectifiers is their ability to heal or reseal ruptures caused by overvoltages within their rating.

A cross section of a selenium cell is shown in Fig. 116. Construction of a rectifier stack is shown in Fig. 117.

Another common type of rectifier is the copper oxide rectifier. This type is similar to the selenium rectifier except that the conducting-blocking material is cuprous oxide.

This material, like selenium, permits conduction easily in one direction while offering high resistance in the reverse direction.

106. Rectifier Circuits.   There are various methods by which rectifiers can be connected into a circuit, and the selection will depend a great deal on the particular application.   Several circuits commonly used in rectifying applications are illustrated.

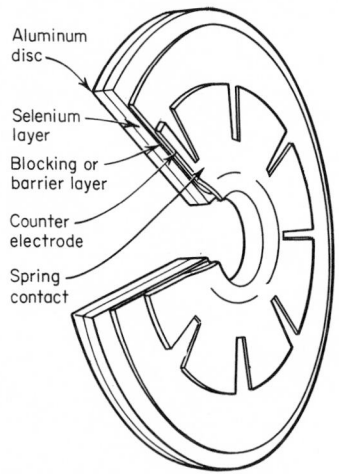

The simplest type of rectifier consists of an a-c power supply with a rectifier connected in series with the load as shown in Fig. 118.   This gives an intermittent pulsating power supply with the conducting period equal to one-half the cycle.   The actual calculation of the a-c and d-c voltage will depend on the particular rectifier characteristic.   The theoretical values using a perfect rectifier will give E_{DC} equal to $0.45E_{AC}$.   The a-c component, or effective heating value of the rectifier current, is equal to 1.57 times the direct current.

If two half-wave circuits were combined, the result would be a full-wave type of rectifier, as illustrated in Fig. 119.   This circuit is quite often used where low voltages are required.   The transformer construction will require a mid-tap.   The output is full-wave with the voltage reaching zero twice each cycle.   The theoretical a-c ripple in the output is 48 per cent. E_{DC} load voltage is equal to $0.9E_{AC}$, which is the a-c voltage measured across one-half the transformer secondary winding.

FIG. 116   *Cross section of selenium rectifier cell.*   (*General Electric Co.*)

By far the most common single-phase rectifier circuit is the full-wave bridge connection shown in Fig. 120.   This will give the same wave shape as that shown in Fig. 119, but it has the advantage that a mid-tapped transformer is not required.   In this circuit the a-c power will flow for one-half cycle through one leg, *B*, of the bridge, then on through the load and back through the other leg, *D*, to the other side of the a-c power supply.   During the other half cycle, the other two legs of the bridge circuit, *A* and *C*, will be conducting power.   The value of the d-c voltage across the load E_{DC} is equal to $0.9E_{AC}$.   The theoretical ripple is the same as for the full-wave mid-tapped circuit and is 48 per cent.

The single-phase power supply is normally used for smaller power demands where economy of construction is important.

It is customary to use a three-phase power supply where higher power outputs are required and efficiency of operation is important.   Several three-phase circuits are used, but only the most common ones are illustrated here.   Figure 121 represents a

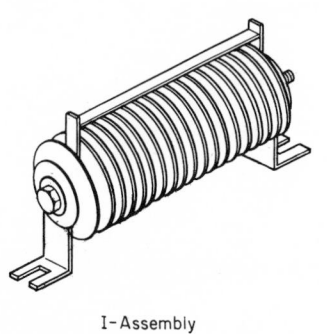

I–Assembly

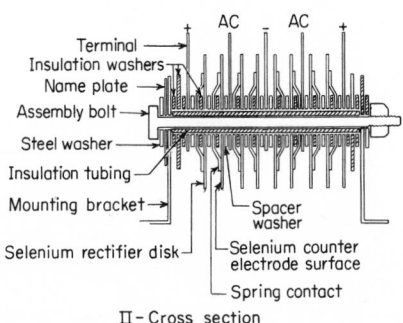

II – Cross section

FIG. 117   *Selenium rectifier stack.*   (*General Electric Co.*)

three-phase full-wave circuit with an interphase transformer connecting the two sets of secondary circuits.

If the interphase transformer is omitted, then the rectifier circuit becomes the standard six-phase connection. The conduction period with this interphase transformer omitted is one-sixth of a cycle, and, with the interphase transformer included in the circuit, the conduction period can be increased to one-third of a cycle. By use of the interphase transformer it is possible to increase the current rating of the rectifier output. With the interphase transformer, the d-c voltage output is equal to $1.17E_{AC}$.

Without the interphase transformer, the E_{DC} is equal to $1.35E_{AC}$. Here again these values are based on a perfect rectifier without any resistance, and it is, of course, necessary to apply empirical design data in order to obtain the correct voltage value. The ripple in the d-c output is approximately 4 per cent.

The conventional three-phase circuit used in the majority of rectifier applications, shown in Fig. 122, is the three-phase full-wave bridge. This is economical and requires only three secondaries in comparison with the six secondaries required on the full-wave circuit (Fig. 121). The d-c voltage output E_{DC} is equal to $2.34E_{AC}$. The conduction period is one-third of a cycle but still gives the typical six-phase ripple in the output with a theoretical magnitude of 4 per cent.

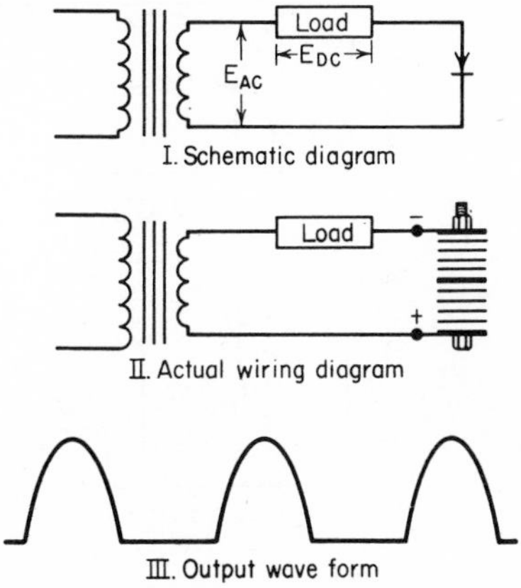

FIG. 118 *Single-phase half-wave rectifier. (General Electric Co.)*

107. Plug-in Motor Speed Control. A particularly useful device which utilizes thyristors (silicon-controlled rectifiers) is a plug-in speed control for portable tools and small appliances. Typical loads include drills, saws, sanders, lathes, fans, food mixers, or blenders, as long as these devices employ universal motors. The circuit diagram for the speed control is shown in Fig. 123.

Desired speed of the universal motor is selected by the setting of the movable arm on potentiometer R_2. During the positive half-cycle of input voltage, a fraction of the

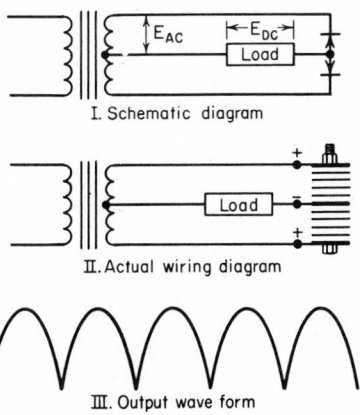

FIG. 119 *Single-phase full-wave rectifier. (General Electric Co.)*

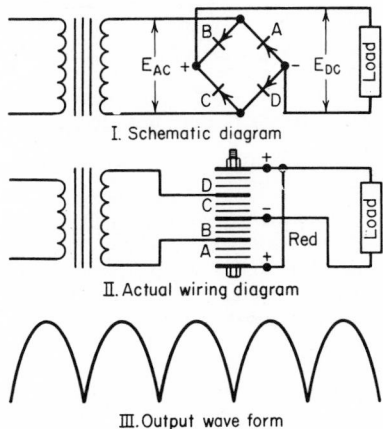

FIG. 120 *Full-wave bridge rectifier. (General Electric Co.)*

supply voltage is compared with the motor counter-emf at R_2. When R_2 voltage is stronger than the motor emf, the current flows through CR_1 and into the gate of the thyristor (SCR). This "fires" the SCR, permitting the remainder of that positive half-cycle of supply voltage to be applied to the motor. When the work load on the motor increases, the speed of the motor will tend to decrease. When this happens, the motor emf will decrease. Thus, the voltage at R_2 causes current to flow into the gate circuit of the SCR earlier in the cycle. As a result, the SCR is fired earlier in the cycle, and a higher voltage is supplied to the motor in an effort to maintain the preset speed.

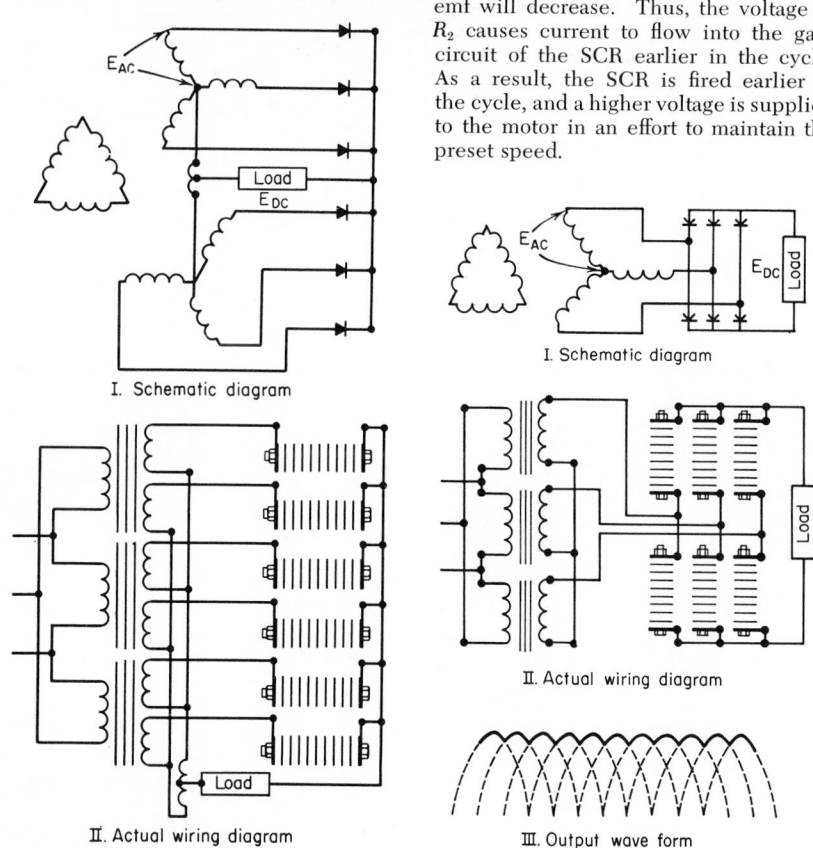

I. Schematic diagram

I. Schematic diagram

II. Actual wiring diagram

II. Actual wiring diagram

III. Output wave form

FIG. 121 *Three-phase full-wave (dou-ble-Y) rectifier. (General Electric Co.)*

FIG. 122 *Three-phase full-wave bridge rectifier. (General Electric Co.)*

Diode CR_1 prevents excessive reverse voltage from being applied to the gate. CR_2 prevents circulating currents from the motor from "free wheeling" in the SCR gate circuit. R_3 is adjusted to obtain the minimum motor speed at which stable operation is obtained. R_4 and C_1 shunt commutator noise around the gate of the SCR, thus improving the stability of operation. Normal operation at maximum speed can be obtained by closing the "full-speed" switch. This shunts out the SCR circuitry.

108. Temperature Control. A basic thyristor temperature control circuit is shown in Fig. 124. The temperature sensor, which is usually a thermistor or thermocouple, senses and reacts to temperature changes. For example, as temperature drops, the sensor causes the trigger circuit to fire the SCR earlier in the applied a-c cycle. Because of this phase control, more power is delivered to the load and temperature rises. If the controlled temperature rises, the sensor causes the SCR to be fired later in the cycle so that less power is delivered to the electric heater. Often the temperature-sensing circuit is a bridge circuit with the thermistor in one leg of the bridge, a fixed

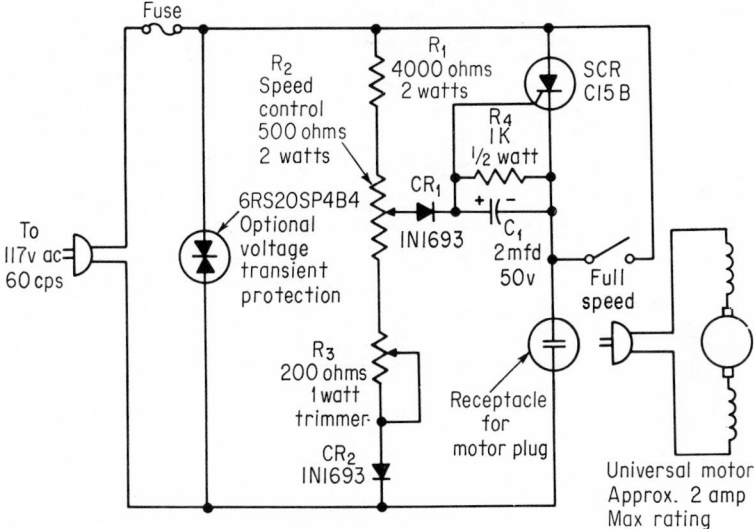

FIG. 123   *Solid-state motor speed control.   (General Electric Co.)*

resistor in each of two legs, and an adjustable resistor in the remaining leg.   A voltage source across the center of the bridge remains in check as long as the bridge is balanced. When the temperature varies, the resistance of the thermistor changes, causing an unbalance in the bridge.   Thus an output voltage is applied to the gate of the SCR, causing either an earlier firing of the SCR to obtain a temperature rise or a later firing to effect a temperature decrease.

109. Thyratron Replacement.   In many applications, a thyristor package can be used to perform functions formerly accomplished by the thyratron.   Packaged SCR circuits for direct (plug-in) replacement of thyratrons are available and offer a variety of significant advantages (see Fig. 125).   They are highly reliable, and if properly applied, they

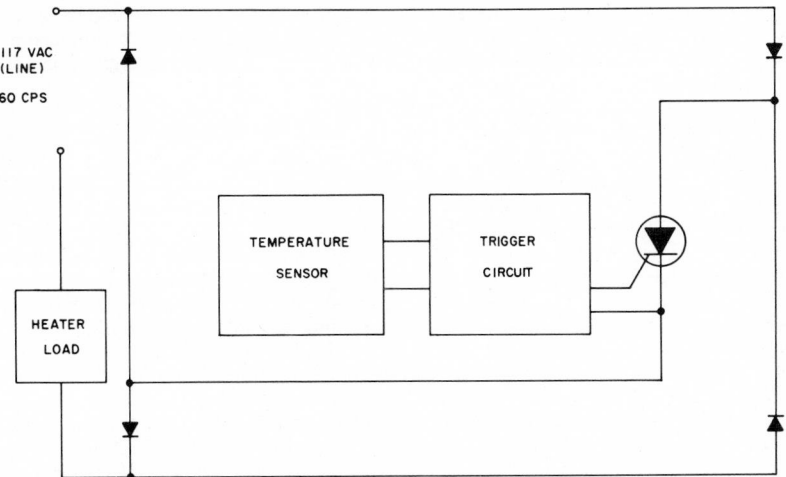

FIG. 124   *Thyristor temperature control.   (General Electric Co.)*

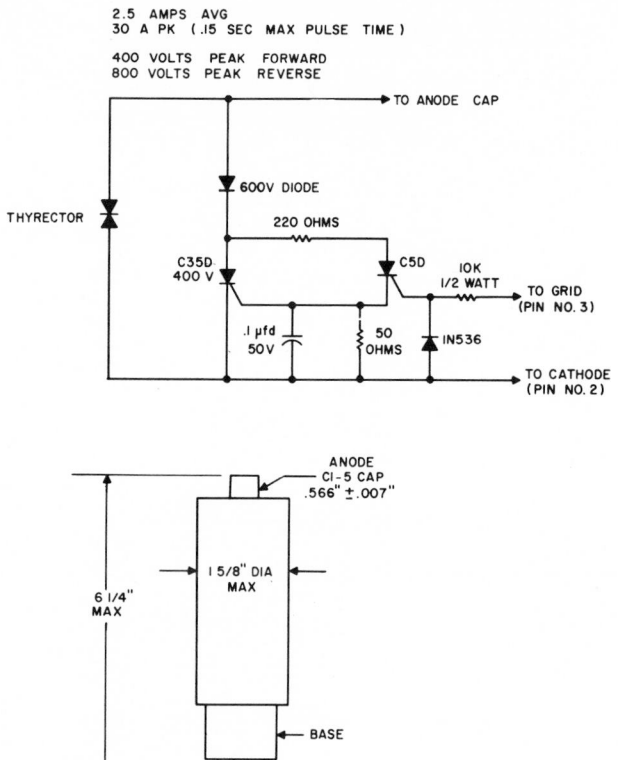

FIG. 125   *Solid-state replacement for thyratron.*   (*General Electric Co.*)

will last indefinitely because silicon-controlled rectifiers have no moving parts and no failure mechanism. They offer instantaneous operation and cooler operation because they do not require a filament or heater current. In addition, the thyristor replacement package has an inherent low forward voltage drop, which results in higher efficiency and cooler operation.

110. Light Dimmers. Popular solid-state light dimmer switches provide a variable voltage output to 120-volt incandescent lamps. Such dimmers are available in ratings up to 1,000 watts. Typical switches permit a continuous dimming range from full "off" to full "on," and a push-type knob allows "on-off" control at any setting on the dimmer. The dimmer switch has only two line leads and is connected into a circuit the same as a standard single-pole switch.

The first models of these small dimmer switches contained SCRs and other complex components, but later engineering developments have simplified the circuitry to a trigger diode, biswitch diode, fixed capacitors and resistors, and a potentiometer (variable resistor). An internal wiring diagram of a modern solid-state dimmer switch is shown in Fig. 126. This dimmer will control incandescent lamps up to a total of 600 watts. Capacitors $C1$ and $C2$ provide a filter circuit to prevent radio or intercom interference.

The heart of the dimmer shown in Fig. 126 is the silicon trigger diode $D1$ and silicon biswitch diode $D2$. These diodes conduct current in two directions (full wave), which means that they conduct both halves of a sine wave. But significantly they do not

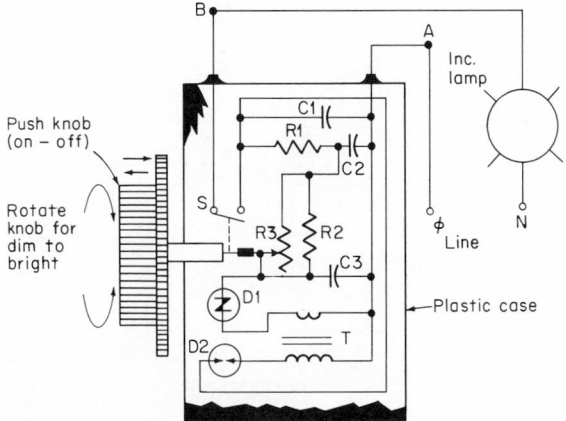

FIG. 126   *Solid-state light dimmer switch and circuit (side view).*

conduct until a "trigger" voltage is applied to them.   The actual point at which the trigger voltage is applied during each half cycle will determine lamp brightness.

If the trigger voltage is applied *after* the beginning of each half cycle, the lamp will be fully bright because the entire sine wave is utilized.   On the other hand, if the trigger voltage is not applied until near the end of each half cycle, the lamp will glow dimly because limited power is delivered to it.

The trigger diode $D1$ does not conduct in either direction until nearly 40 peak-to-peak volts is applied to it.

The biswitch diode $D2$ also conducts current in two directions but not before 200 peak-to-peak volts is applied to it.   As a result, $D1$ triggers or controls a large current flow in $D2$.

When 60-cycle alternating current is connected to the circuit (points A and B), capacitor $C3$ starts to charge at the beginning of the first half of the cycle through resistor $R1$ and the potentiometer (variable resistor) $R3$.   Thus $C3$, $R1$, and $R3$ form a time-constant circuit, and depending on the $R3$ setting, $C3$ will be quickly or slowly charged.

When the resistance in $R3$ is low, $C3$ will charge to about 40 volts just after the start of a cycle of input voltage, and $D1$ will not conduct until near the end of each half of a cycle.   Accordingly, $R3$ settings determine the time it takes for the voltage at the junction of $R3$ and $C3$ to reach the firing point of $D1$.

As $C3$ is charged to around 40 volts, $D1$ conducts and discharges $C3$, which, in turn, sends a current pulse to the primary winding of the transformer T.   This increases the current pulse to about 200 volts and applies it to $D2$, which is in series with the line and the lamp.   Because the switching voltage of $D2$ is exceeded, it conducts.   Thus it follows that the lamp will glow in proportion to how much of the sine wave is utilized. Since both diodes $D1$ and $D2$ conduct in two directions they function the same way on both the positive and negative halves of the sine wave, and this permits "full-wave" control from full "off" to full "on."

Similar solid-state dimmers are used for rapid-start fluorescent lamps, but these are special units designed for use with special ballasts.

111. D-C Adjustable Speed Drives.   Many industrial motor-speed-control applications require d-c motor drives because d-c systems offer the advantages of stepless speed control.   Modern speed controls for d-c motors are of solid-state design.   They offer many advantages over other types.   For example, they are compact and light in weight.   Also, they provide a high degree of control accuracy, and are extremely dependable because they have no moving parts or tubes to burn out or cause drifting.

Figure 127 shows a typical control panel which incorporates solid-state devices for

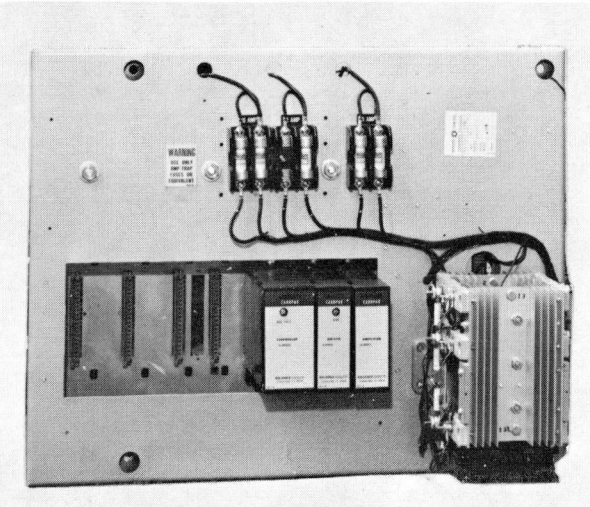

FIG. 127   *Main panel of d-c adjustable-speed drive.   (Reliance Electric Co.)*

control of d-c motors.   Rated at 230 volts input, the panel controls d-c motors ranging in size from 5 to 125 hp.   Continuously variable motor speed is obtained by controlling motor armature voltage and current.   Additional features include acceleration rate control, maximum armature current, and *IR* drop compensation.

Major components of a typical control system are three plug-in printed-circuit cards, silicon rectifiers and thyristors (SCRs) mounted on heat sinks.   The three plug-in cards contain the basic circuits which control output voltage and current.   These basic circuits are shown by block diagram in Fig. 128.

The setting of the speed pot (potentiometer) permits the proper voltage signal to be applied to the controller circuit.   And the armature voltage and current feedback signals are also applied.   These signals are compared to a bias or reference signal, and the resultant voltage is applied to the driver circuit.   The driver circuit sets the firing time of pulses for phase control of the thyristors, which are connected in a bridge circuit.   A three-stage amplifier circuit amplifies and peaks the pulses and applies them to the gates of thyristors.   The amount of time that the thyristors are gated (voltage pulse applied to gate) determines the bridge output voltage and the motor speed.

The output bridge section will consist of silicon diodes, thyristors (SCRs), fuses, and protective circuitry.   The circuit is shown schematically in Fig. 129.   Arrows indicate electron flow (reverse of conventional current flow) through output bridge and motor armature.   Electrons flow in on 81 down through 1SCR if a gate pulse is present, up through the motor armature, down through 2SR and out on 82.   A similar path can be traced for any chosen polarity.

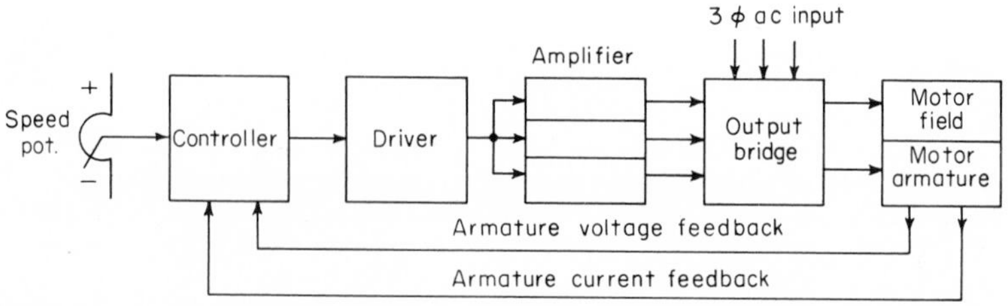

FIG. 128   *Block diagram of basic operation of d-c adjustable-speed drive.*

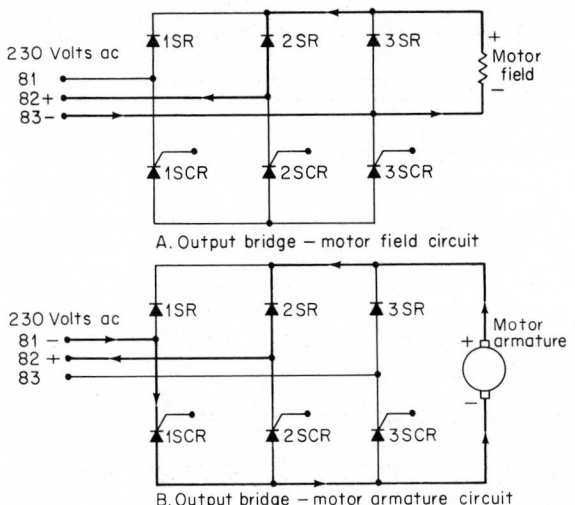

FIG. 129 *Output bridge circuits for motor field and armature circuits.*

Current flow and resulting motor armature voltage depends on when the gates of the thyristors receive a pulse or are fired. For example, if the three thyristors are each fired 120 deg late in the cycle, the output of the bridge will be comparatively low because the thyristors conduct for only a short time (from 120 to 180 deg). If the thyristors are pulsed at, say, 90 deg, the output will be higher because the thyristors will conduct for a longer time (from 90 to 180 deg). Maximum voltage output to the motor armature occurs at 55 deg, which is the earliest point at which the thyristors can be fired.

Firing of the thyristors is controlled by the driver circuit, which provides phase control through transistor-saturable-reactor-peaking transformer circuitry. The input signal from the controller circuit controls operation of a transistor that supervises operation of saturable reactors in each phase. The saturable reactors present a high impedance until they are saturated; then their impedance drops significantly. The saturation of the reactors regulates operation of transistors connected in series with a peaking transformer. This transformer provides a sharp rise in its secondary voltage which is delayed according to the saturation of the saturable reactors.

112. Static Inverters. A static inverter is an apparatus that changes d-c power to a-c power, using all semiconductor components connected in appropriate circuitry. A major application is in UPS (uninterruptible power source) systems. UPS systems essentially are emergency standby power systems, which instantaneously supply power to critical loads when normal power fails. Other important uses are as high-quality power supplies for computers, data processing, or critical control systems and as frequency converters for high-frequency lighting or adjustable-frequency variable-speed motor drives.

Significant features include precise control of voltage, frequency and response time, high reliability, minimum maintenance, light weight, and easy installation. Units range in size up to 300 kva single-phase or three-phase, and operate at efficiencies from 65 to 85 per cent.

Basic operation of a simplified inverter circuit is shown in Fig. 130. Major components are a battery power supply, thyristors, and an output transformer. Related components such as transistors or saturable reactors which control firing of the thyristors, diodes, chokes, commutating capacitors (capacitors which facilitate "turn-off" of the thyristors), and protective devices are not shown, in order to simplify the explanation.

When a firing pulse is applied to the gate of the thyristor SCR1, current will flow from

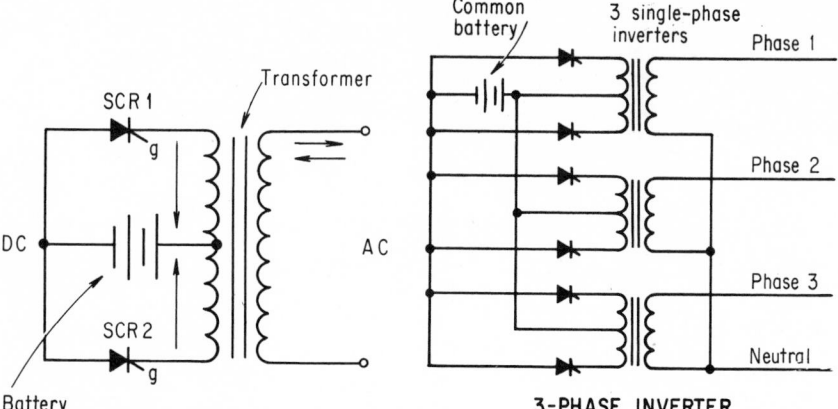

FIG. 130 *Simplified static inverter circuit.* (*Electric Storage Battery Co.*)

FIG. 131   *Basic three-phase static inverter circuit.* (*Electric Storage Battery Co.*)

the negative terminal of the battery through the thyristor and the transformer winding as indicated. If the firing pulse and a commutating voltage are synchronized to line frequency (60 cycles) SCR1 will permit current flow for $1/120$ second. Then SCR1 turns "off," while SCR2 turns "on," and current will flow in the opposite direction through the transformer for $1/120$ second. The result is an a-c flow in the secondary winding of the transformer at 60 cycles.

This basic operation is applicable whether the inverter is a single-phase unit or a three-phase unit, such as shown schematically in Fig. 131. Note that the battery and related control circuits are common to all three inverters in the three-phase unit.

113. Adjustable-frequency Variable-speed Motor Drives. Adjustable-frequency drive systems provide accurate speed control of a-c motors. Because the speed of a-c induction motors and synchronous motors is directly related to the frequency of the applied power source, it follows that adjustment of the applied frequency will cause motor speed to vary.

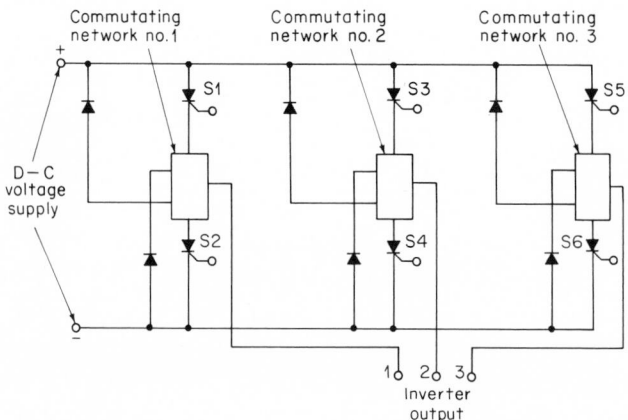

FIG. 132   *Simplified three-phase adjustable-frequency adjustable-speed induction motor drive.*

Several methods are used to obtain adjustable frequency. One common method uses equipment that incorporates a static rectifier with a static inverter and appropriate control circuits. The rectifier converts incoming 60-cycle a-c power to direct current. This d-c supply is then inverted to an adjustable output frequency.

Figure 132 shows a simplified three-phase inverter circuit in which the thyristors act as power switching devices to generate a-c output power. A master oscillator governs the frequency of operation. Output frequency can be adjusted by adjusting the setting of a control potentiometer. This "pot" selects the desired oscillation frequency and, in turn, sets the frequency of firing of the thyristors. Commutating circuits, which apply reverse voltage to the thyristors at the proper time, are required to turn off conducting thyristors in the proper sequence.

114. Static Frequency Converters. Some equipment will operate more efficiently on frequencies higher than 60 cycles. Typical examples are high-speed tools, certain aircraft systems, and high-frequency fluorescent lighting equipment. Also, high frequencies, ranging between 300 and 10,000 cycles, are used in induction heating applications.

Modern high-frequency lighting systems use power at 3,000 cycles. Systems using higher frequencies presently are under consideration. Although lamp operation is more efficient with high-frequency systems, these systems have not been widely accepted because over-all costs are higher than for conventional 60-cycle units. Present design trends are to lower initial costs.

Static-inverter units, which convert 60-cycle power to 3,000 cycles, are available in ratings up to 400 kva at voltages up to 600 volts. These units are very similar to the inverters described in Sec. **113** for adjustable-frequency variable-speed drives. Both types of inverters use thyristors, diodes, and firing and commutating circuits. The main difference is that the static frequency converter requires less complicated circuitry because a constant (rather than adjustable) frequency is required.

115. Solid-state Switches. The versatility of thyristors (SCRs) as switching devices has been known for many years, and they have been used as such *within* a variety of solid-state apparatuses. However, their application as direct-acting switches has been slow because standard mechanical switches serve most switching needs at economical costs. But when special features are required, the solid-state switch, which is made up of series-parallel circuits of thyristors, is the best choice.

As an example, the solid-state or "static" switch is often used where speed of operation is required. A common application is in UPS (uninterruptible power systems) where the load is so critical that a power failure of even a few cycles is intolerable. Mechanical switches are not able to transfer power fast enough (typical transfer time is about 10 cycles). A static switch can transfer the load to the standby power source in about ¼ cycle.

The solid-state switch also serves as a high-current, high-voltage circuit breaker. The prototype circuit breaker consists of 18 static switches connected in series-parallel

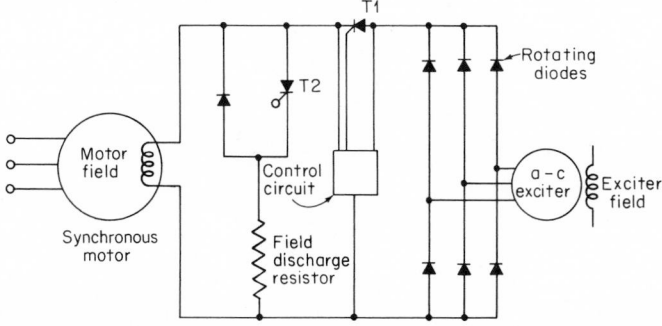

FIG. 133 *Circuit arrangement for a typical brushless synchronous motor.* (*Electric Machinery Mfg. Co.*)

circuits to handle 10,000 amp at 2,700 volts. The breaker, which has a peak interrupting capacity of 220,000 amp, protects high-power circuits in a giant induction melting process at a large steel mill.

116. Brushless Rotating Machines. Silicon diodes and thyristors mounted on the rotating shafts of a-c generators or synchronous motors simplify operation of these machines. Rotating diodes rectify generated alternating current from an exciter mounted on the machine shaft to provide direct current for the machine d-c field (both the a-c generator and the synchronous motor require d-c on field windings). In the synchronous motor, thyristors provide required control.

Figure 133 shows a basic circuit for a typical brushless synchronous motor. The stator of the motor and the stator of the exciter are supplied with a-c power. The field of the synchronous motor, the armature of the exciter, and the solid-state components are mounted on a common shaft. The rotating diodes (silicon rectifiers) rectify the exciter voltage to provide direct current for the motor field. *T1* functions as a contactor to apply and remove field power. *T2* also serves as a contactor to control the field discharge circuit. The control circuit, which consists of transistors, diodes, and other solid-state components, controls firing of thyristors.

DIVISION SEVEN

Generators and Motors

PRINCIPLES, CHARACTERISTICS, AND MANAGEMENT OF
D-C GENERATORS (DYNAMOS)

1. Direct-current generators impress on the line a direct or continuous emf—one that is always in the same direction. Commercial d-c generators have commutators and can thereby be distinguished from a-c generators. The function of the commutator and the elementary ideas of generation of emf and commutation are discussed in Div. 1. Additional information in regard to commutation as applied to d-c motors, which is in general true for d-c generators, is given hereinafter.

2. Excitation of Generator Fields. To generate an emf, conductors must cut a magnetic field which in commercial machines must be relatively strong. A permanent magnet can be used for producing such a field in a generator of small output, such as a telephone magneto or the magneto of a megger, but for generators for light and power the field is produced by electromagnets, which may be excited by the machine itself or "separately excited" from another source.

Self-excited machines may be of the series, shunt, or compound type depending upon the manner of connecting the field winding to the armature. In the series type of machine, the field winding (the winding which produces the magnetic field) is connected in series with the armature winding. In the shunt type, the field winding is connected in parallel, shunt, with the armature winding. Compound machines have two field windings on each pole. One of these windings is connected in series with the armature winding, and the other is connected in parallel or shunt with the armature winding.

3. Armature windings of d-c machines may be of the lap or wave type. The difference in the two types is in the manner of connecting the armature coils to the commutator. A coil is the portion of the armature winding between successive connections to the commutator. In the lap type of winding (see Fig. 1) the two ends of a coil are connected to adjacent commutator segments. In the wave type of winding (see Fig. 2) the two ends of a coil are connected to commutator segments that are displaced from each other approximately 360 electrical degrees.

The type of armature winding employed affects the voltage and current capacity of the machine but has no effect upon the power capacity. This is due to the fact that the number of parallel paths between armature terminals is affected by the type of winding. For a wave-wound machine there are always two paths in parallel in the armature winding between armature terminals. For a lap-wound machine there are as many parallel paths in the armature winding as there are pairs of poles on the machine. For the same number and size of armature conductors a machine when wave connected would generate a voltage that would be equal to the voltage generated

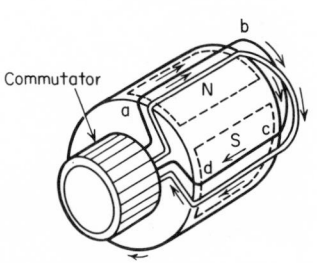

FIG. 1 *Two coils of a four-pole lap-wound armature.*

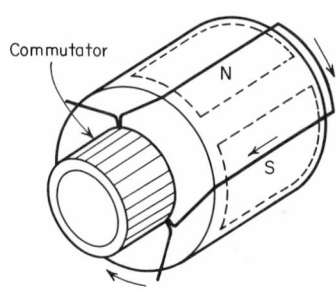

FIG. 2 *Coil on a four-pole wave-wound armature.*

when lap connected times the number of pairs of poles. But the current capacity would be decreased in the same proportion that the voltage was increased. The current capacity when wave connected is therefore equal to the capacity when lap connected divided by the number of pairs of poles.

4. The value of the voltage generated by a d-c machine depends upon the armature winding, the speed, and the field current. For a given machine therefore, the voltage generated can be controlled through adjusting either the speed or the field current. Since generators are usually operated at constant speed, the voltage must be controlled by means of adjustment of the field current.

5. Separately excited d-c generators are used for electroplating and for other electrolytic work where it is essential that the polarity of a machine be not reversed. Self-excited machines may change their polarities. The essential diagrams are shown in Fig. 3. The fields can be excited from any d-c constant-potential source, such as a storage battery or from a rectifier connected to an a-c supply.

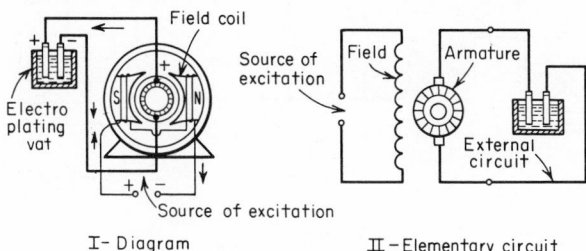

I– Diagram   II –Elementary circuit

FIG. 3   *Separately excited generator.*

The field magnets can be wound for any voltage because they have no electric connection with the armature. With a constant field excitation, the voltage will drop slightly from no load to full load because of armature drop and armature reaction.

Separate excitation is advantageous when the voltage generated by the machine is not suitable for field excitation. This is true for especially low- or high-voltage machines.

6. Series-wound generators have their armature winding, field coils, and external circuit connected in series with each other so that the same current flows through all parts of the circuit (see Fig. 4). If a series generator is operated at no load (external circuit open), there will be no current through the field coils, and the only magnetic flux present in the machine will be that due to the residual magnetism which has been retained by the poles from previous operation. Therefore, the no-load voltage of a series generator will be only a few volts produced by cutting the residual flux. If the external circuit is closed and the current increased, the voltage will increase with the increase in current until the magnetic circuit becomes saturated. With any further increases of load the voltage will decrease.

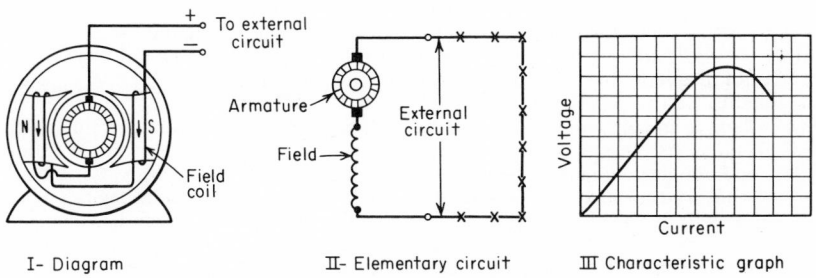

I- Diagram   II- Elementary circuit   III Characteristic graph

FIG. 4   *Series generator.*

Series generators are used sometimes in street-railway service. They are connected in series with long trolley feeders supplying sections of the system distant from the supply point, in order to boost the voltage. However, power rectifiers have replaced d-c generators for most installations of this type.

7. The shunt-wound generator is shown diagrammatically in Fig. 5, I, II. A small part of the total current, the exciting current, is shunted through the fields. The exciting current varies from possibly 5 per cent of the total current in small machines to 1 per cent in large ones. The exciting current is determined by the voltage at the brushes and the resistance of the field winding. Residual magnetism in the field cores permits a shunt generator to "build up." This small amount of magnetism that is retained in the field cores induces a voltage in the armature (Timbie, "Elements of

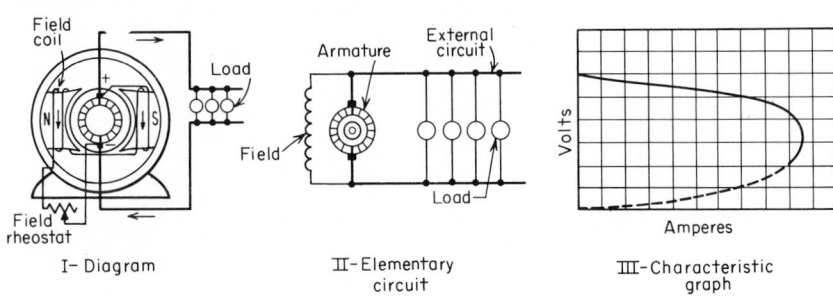

I- Diagram   II-Elementary circuit   III-Characteristic graph

FIG. 5 *Shunt generator.*

Electricity"). This voltage sends a slight current through the field coils, which increases the magnetization. Thus, the induced voltage in the armature is increased. This in turn increases the current in the fields, which still further increases the magnetization, and so on, until the normal voltage of the machine is reached and conditions are stable. This "building up" action is the same for any self-excited generator and often requires 20 to 30 sec.

If a shunt generator (Timbie) runs at constant speed, as more and more current is drawn from the generator, the voltage across the brushes falls slightly. This fall is due to the fact that it requires more and more of the generated voltage to force this increasing current through the windings of the armature; i.e., the armature IR drop increases. This leaves a smaller part of the total emf for brush emf, and then, when the brush voltage falls, there is a slight decrease in the field current, which is determined by the brush voltage. This and armature reactions cause the total emf to drop a little, which still further lowers the brush potential. These causes combine to gradually lower the voltage, especially at heavy overloads. The curve in Fig. 5, III, shows these characteristics. For small loads the curve is nearly horizontal, but at heavy overloads it shows a decided drop. The point where the voltage of a commercial machine drops off rapidly is beyond the operating range and is of importance only for short-circuit conditions.

The voltage of a shunt machine can be kept fairly constant by providing extra resistance in the field circuit (see Fig. 6), which may be cut out as the brush potential falls. This will allow more current to flow through the field coils and increase the number of magnetic lines set up in the magnetic circuit. If the speed is kept constant, the armature conductors cut through the stronger magnetic field at the same speed and thus induce a greater emf and restore the brush potential to its former value. This resistance can be cut out either automatically or by hand (see Rheostat in the Index).

A shunt-wound generator gives a fairly constant voltage, even with varying loads, and can be used for any system which incorporates constant-potential loads. These generators will operate well in parallel, because the voltage of the machines decreases as the load increases. Shunt generators running in parallel will "divide the load" well between themselves if the machines have similar characteristics.

The necessary change in connections when reversing the direction of rotation of a

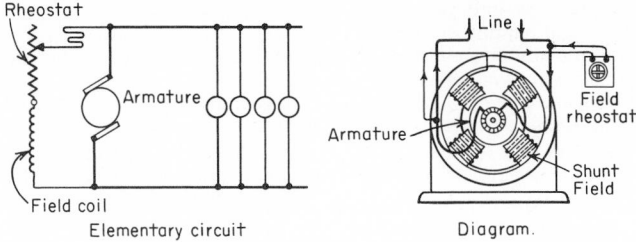

FIG. 6 *Shunt-wound generator with rheostat.*

shunt-wound machine is indicated in Fig. 7. Rotation is **clockwise** when, facing the commutator end of a machine, the rotation is in the direction of the hands of a clock. **Counterclockwise** rotation is the reverse. It is necessary, when changing the direction of rotation, not to reverse the direction of current through the field windings. If it is reversed the magnetism developed by the windings on starting will oppose the residual magnetism and the machine will not "build up."

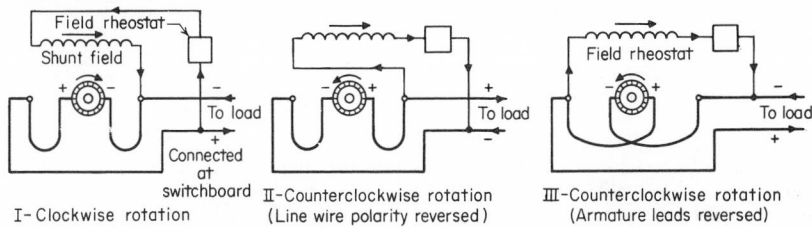

FIG. 7 *Changing rotation direction of shunt machine.*

8. Parallel Operation of Shunt Generators. As suggested in Sec. **7,** shunt-wound generators will in general operate very well in parallel and will divide the load well if the machines have similar characteristics. If the machines do not have similar characteristics, one machine will take more than its share of the load and may tend to drive the other as a motor. When it is running as a motor, its direction of rotation will be the same as when it was generating; hence the operator must watch the ammeters closely for an indication of this trouble. Shunt generators are now seldom installed. Figure 8 shows the connections for shunt generators that are to be operated in parallel.

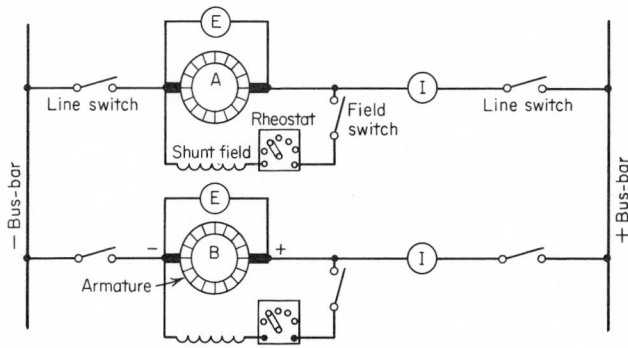

FIG. 8 *Connections for shunt generators for parallel operation.*

9. The compound-wound generator is shown diagrammatically in Fig. 9, I. If a series winding is added in a proper manner to a shunt generator (Fig. 5), the two windings will tend to maintain a constant voltage as the load increases. The magnetization due to the series windings increases as the line current increases, thus tending to increase the generated voltage. The drop of voltage at the brushes that occurs in a shunt generator can thus be compensated for.

It is necessary that the series winding be connected in such a manner that its current will aid that of the shunt-field winding in producing magnetic flux. With this proper

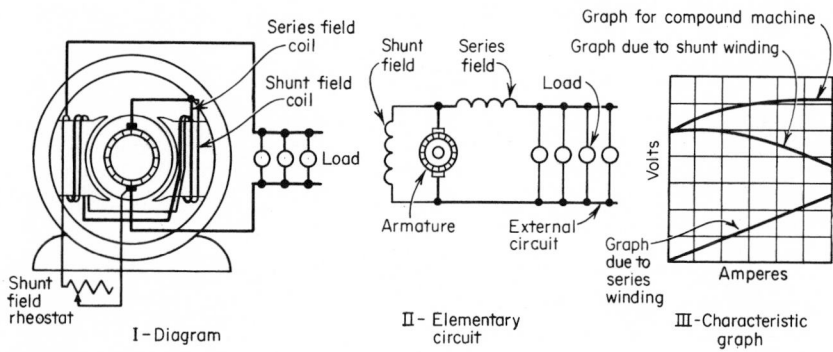

FIG. 9 *Compound generator.*

connection, the machine is said to be cumulatively connected. If the series field is connected in the reverse manner so that the series field tends to produce flux in the opposite direction to that produced by the shunt field, the machine is said to be differentially connected. The differential connection of compound machines is used in some very special cases.

10. A flat-compounded generator is one having its series coils so proportioned that the voltage remains practically constant at all loads from 0 to 1¼ full load.

11. An overcompounded generator has its series windings so proportioned that its full-load voltage is greater than its no-load voltage. Overcompounding is necessary where it is desirable to maintain a practically constant voltage at some point out on the line distant from the generator. It compensates for line drop. The characteristic curve (Fig. 9, III) indicates how the terminal voltage of a compound-wound machine is due to the action of both shunt and series windings. Generators are usually overcompounded, so that the full-load voltage is from 5 to 10 per cent greater than the no-load voltage.

Although compound-wound generators are usually provided with a field rheostat, it is not intended for regulating voltage as the rheostat of a shunt-wound machine is. It is provided to permit initial adjustment of voltage and to compensate for changes of the resistance of the shunt winding caused by heating. With a compound-wound generator, the voltage having been once adjusted, the series coils automatically strengthen the magnetic field as the load increases. For d-c power work, compound-wound generators are used almost universally where rectifiers are not used.

11A. An undercompounded generator is one with a relatively weak series-field winding, so that the voltage decreases with increased load.

12. If a compound-wound generator is short-circuited, the field strength due to the series windings will be greatly increased but the field due to the shunt winding will lose its strength. For the instant or so that the shunt magnetization is diminishing, a heavy current will flow. If the shunt magnetization is a considerable proportion of the total magnetization the current will decrease after the heavy rush and little harm will be done if the armature has successfully withstood the heavy rush. However, if the series magnetization is quite strong in proportion to the shunt, their combined effect may so magnetize the fields that the armature will be burned out.

13. A short-shunt compound-wound generator has its shunt field connected directly across the brushes (see Fig. 9, II). Generators are usually connected in this way because it tends to maintain the shunt-field current more nearly constant on variable loads, as the drop in the series winding does not directly affect the voltage on the shunt field with this arrangement.

14. A long-shunt generator has its shunt-field winding connected across the terminals of the generator (see Fig. 10).

15. Nearly all commercial d-c generators have more than two poles. A two-pole machine is a bipolar machine; one having more than two poles is a multipolar machine. Figure 11 shows the connections for a four-pole compound-wound machine.

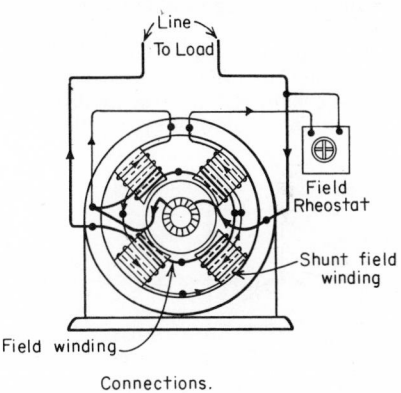

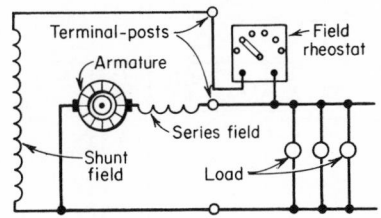

FIG. 10 *Long-shunt compound-wound generator.*

FIG. 11 *Diagram for four-pole compound-wound generator.*

Diagrams for machines having more poles would be similar. In multipolar machines there is usually one set of brushes for each pair of poles, but with wave-wound armatures, such as are used for railway motors, one set of brushes may suffice for a multipolar machine. The connections of different makes of machines vary in detail, and the manufacturers will always furnish complete diagrams, so no attempt will be made to give them here. The directions of the field windings on generator frames are given in Fig. 12. The directions of the windings on machines having more than four poles are similar in general to those of the four-pole machines.

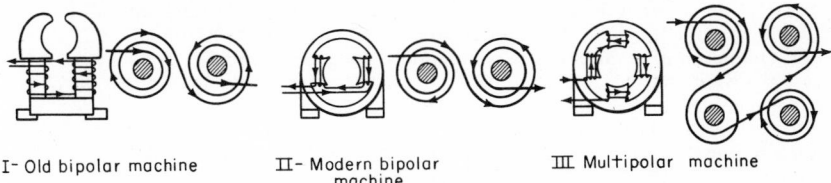

I- Old bipolar machine   II- Modern bipolar machine   III Multipolar machine

FIG. 12 *Direction of field windings on generator frames.*

16. A series shunt for a compound generator consists of a low-resistance connection across the terminals of the series field (see Figs. 13 and 14) by means of which the compounding effect of the series winding can be regulated by shunting more or less of the armature current around the series coils. The shunting resistance may be in the form of grids, on large machines, or of ribbon resistors. In the latter case it is usually insulated and folded into small compass.

17. Parallel operation of compound-wound generators is readily effected if the machines are of the same make and voltage or are designed with similar electrical characteristics (Westinghouse Electric Corp.). The only change that is usually required is the addition of an equalizer connection between machines. If the generators have different compounding ratios, it may be necessary to readjust the series-field shunts to obtain uniform conditions.

18. An equalizer, or equalizer connection, connects two or more generators operating in parallel at a point where the armature and series-field leads join (see Fig. 13), thus connecting the armatures in multiple and the series coils in multiple, in order that the load will divide between the generators in proportion to their capacities. The arrangement of connections to a switchboard (Westinghouse Electric Corp.) is illustrated in Fig. 14. Consider, for example, two overcompound-wound machines operating in parallel without an equalizer. If, for some reason, there is a light increase in the speed of one machine, it would take more than its share of load. The increased current flowing through its series field would strengthen the magnetism, raise the voltage, and cause the machine to carry a still greater amount until it carried the entire

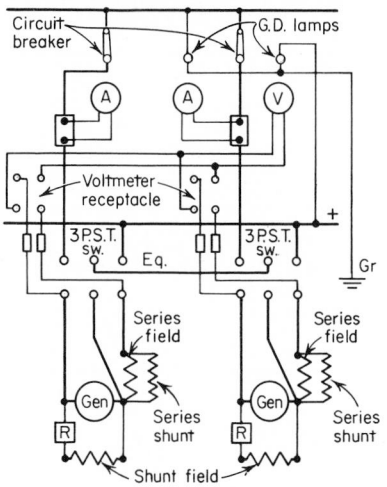

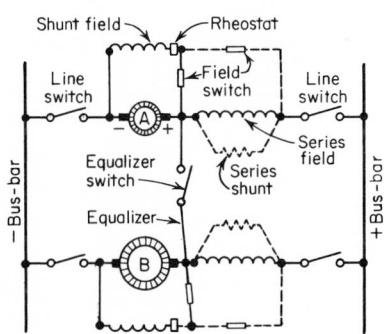

FIG. 13 *Elementary connections for parallel operation of compound-wound generators.*

FIG. 14 *Diagram of connections of two compound-wound generators to switchboard.*

load. Where equalizers are used, the current flowing through each series coil is inversely proportional to the resistance of the series coil circuit and is independent of the load on any machine; consequently, an increase of voltage on one machine builds up the voltage of the other at the same time, so that the first machine cannot take all the load but will continue to share it in proper proportion with the other generators.

19. Operation of a shunt and a compound dynamo in parallel is not successful because the compound machine will take more than its share of the load unless the shunt-machine field rheostat is adjusted at each change in load.

20. Connecting Leads for Compound Generators. See that all the cables for machines of equal capacity that lead from the series fields of the various machines to the bus bars are of equal resistance. This means that if the machines are at different distances from the switchboard, different sizes of wire should be used or resistance should be inserted in the low-resistance leads.

With generators of small capacity the equalizer is usually carried to the switchboard, as suggested in Figs. 14 and 15, but with larger ones it is carried under the floor directly between the machines (Fig. 16). The positive and the equalizer switch of each machine may be mounted side by side on a pedestal near the generator (Fig. 16). The difference in potential between the two switches is only that due to the small drop in the series coil. The positive bus bar is carried along under the floor near the machines. This permits leads of minimum length. Leads of equal lengths should be used for generators of equal capacities. If the capacities are unequal (see Sec. **24**), it may be necessary to loop the leads (see Fig. 16).

21. Ammeters and circuit breakers for compound generators should, as in Fig. 14, always be inserted in the lead not containing the compound winding. If the ammeters are put in the compound-winding lead, the current indications will be inaccurate be-

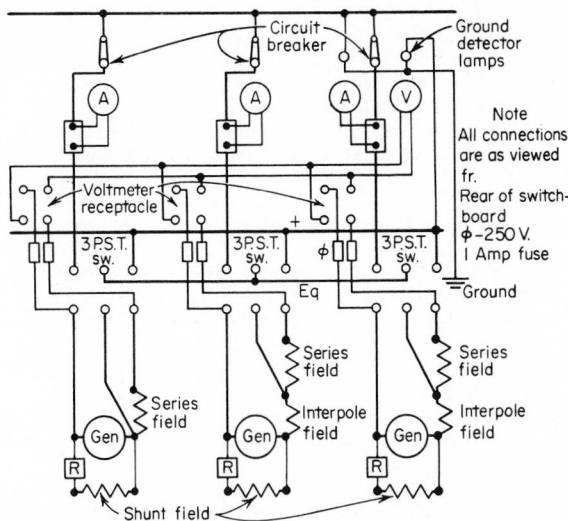

FIG. 15 *Diagram of connections of two d-c commutating-pole generators in parallel with one generator without commutating poles.*

cause current from this side of the machine can flow through either the equalizer or the compound-winding lead.

22. To Start a Shunt- or Compound-wound Generator. (1) See that there is enough oil in the bearings, that the oil rings are working, and that all field resistance is cut in. (2) Start the prime mover slowly and permit it to come up to speed. See that the oil rings are working. (3) When machine is up to normal speed, cut out field resistance until voltage of the machine is normal or equal to or a trifle above that on the bus bars.

(4) Throw on the load. If three separate switches are used, as in Fig. 13, close the equalizer switch first, the series coil line switch second, and the other line switch third. If a three-pole switch is used, as in Fig. 14, all three poles are, of course, closed at the same time. (5) Watch the voltmeter and ammeter and adjust the field rheostat until the machine takes its share of the load. A machine generating the higher voltage will take more than its share of the load, and if its voltage is too high, it will run the other as a motor.

23. To Shut Down a Shunt- or Compound-wound Generator Operating in Parallel with Others. (1) Reduce the load on the machine as much as possible by cutting resistance into the shunt-field circuit with the field rheostat. (2) Throw off the load by opening the circuit breaker if one is used;

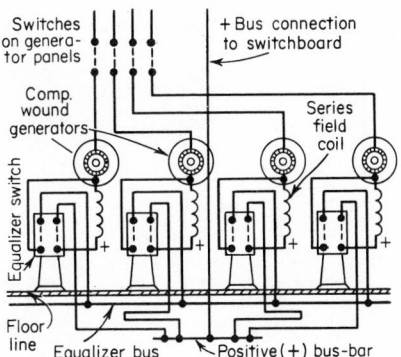

FIG. 16 *Equalizer carried directly between machines.*

otherwise open the main generator switches. (3) Shut down the driving machine. (4) Wipe off all oil and dirt, clean the machine, and put it in good order for the next run. Turn all resistance in the field rheostat. Open the main switch.

24. To Adjust the Division of Load between Two Compound-wound Generators. First adjust the series shunts of both machines so that, as nearly as possible, the voltages of both will be the same at one-fourth, one-half, three-fourths, and full load. Then connect the machines in parallel, as suggested in Fig. 13, for trial. If, upon loading, one machine takes more than its share of the load (amperes), increase the resistance of the path through its series-field coil path until the load divides between the machines proportionally to their capacities. Only a small increase in resistance is usually needed. The increase can be provided by inserting a longer conductor between the generator and the bus bar, or iron or german-silver washers can be inserted under a connection lug. Inasmuch as (when machines are connected in parallel) adjustment of the series-coil shunt affects both machines, nothing can be accomplished through making such adjustment.

25. Commutating-pole D-C Generators. Generators which do not have commutating poles (Westinghouse Electric Corp.) and which operate under severe overloads and over a wide speed range are apt to spark under the brushes at the extreme overloads and at the higher speeds. This is because the field due to the armature current distorts the main field to such an extent that the coils being commutated under the brush are no longer in a magnetic field of the proper direction and strength. To overcome this, commutating poles are placed between the main poles (see Fig. 17). These commutating poles introduce a magnetic field of such direction and strength as to maintain the magnetic field, at the point where the coils are commutated, at the proper strength for good commutation. Commutating poles are sometimes called interpoles. "Commutating poles" is a preferable term.

The winding on the commutating poles is connected in series with the armature so that the strength of the corrective field increases and decreases with the load. The adjustment and operation of commutating-pole generators are not materially different from those of noncommutating-pole machines.

When the brush position of a commutating-pole machine has once been properly fixed, no shifting is afterward required or should be made, and most commutating-pole generators are shipped without any shifting device. An arrangement for securely clamping the brush-holder rings to the field frame is provided.

In commutating-pole apparatus, accurate adjustment of the brush position is necessary. The correct brush position is on the no-load neutral point, which is located by

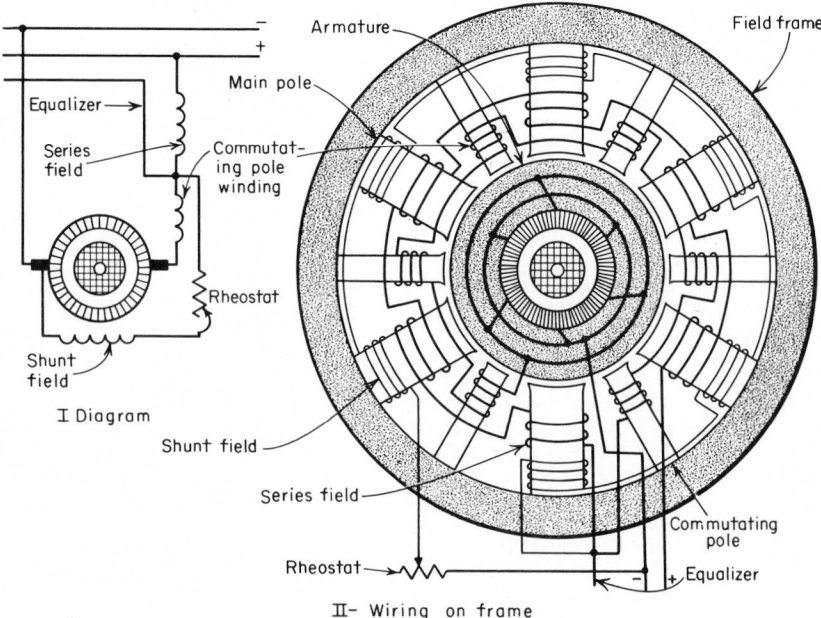

FIG. 17   *Diagram of compound-wound commutating-pole (interpole) machine.*

the manufacturer. A template is furnished with each machine, or some other provision is made whereby the brush location can be determined in the field. If the brushes are given a backward lead on a commutating-pole generator, the machine will overcompound and will not commutate properly. With a forward lead of the brushes, a generator will undercompound and will not commutate properly.

26. The object in using the commutating pole is to produce within the armature coil under commutation an emf of the proper value and direction to reverse the current in the coil while it is yet under the brush—a result that is essential to perfect commutation. The variation in the flux distribution in the air gap of a commercial d-c machine of the ordinary shunt-wound type, at no load and under full load, is shown in Fig. 18. Consider now the value and position of the flux in the coil under the brush when the machine is operating at full load. The motion of the armature through this flux causes the generation within the coil of an emf, and the sign of this emf is such as to tend to cause the current in the coil to continue in the direction which it had before the coil reached the brush, and hence it opposes the desired reversal of the current before the coil leaves the brush.

There is an additional detrimental influence which tends to retard the rapid reversal of the current even when all other influences are absent. This latter influence is due to the local magnetizing effect of the current in the coil under the brush. On account of this the lines of force which surround the conductor change in value with the fluctuations of the current as it tends to be reversed. This generates in the coil an emf which opposes the change in the value of the current. This reactive emf is in the same direction as that due to the cutting of the flux by the coil under the brush and is likewise proportional to the speed.

It will be apparent that even were the field distortion completely neutralized, the detrimental reactive emf would yet remain. The improved and practically perfect commutation of the commutating-pole machine is due to the fact that the flux, which is locally superposed upon the main field, not only counterbalances the undesirable main flux cut by the coil under the brush but causes to be generated within the coil an emf sufficient to equal and oppose the reactive emf just referred to. This effect will be appreciated from a study of Fig. 19, which represents the distorted flux of the motor of the usual design, as shown in Fig. 18, and indicates the results to be expected when the flux due to the auxiliary or commutating pole is given the relatively proper value.

It is worthy of note that this desirable effect is the more pronounced the weaker the main field; that the commutation voltage, if correct for a low speed, is correct for a high speed; that with increase of load-current and main-field distortion there is a proportional increase of countermagnetizing field produced in the coil under the brush, up to the point of magnetic saturation of the auxiliary pole; and that sparkless operation is ensured for all operating ranges of both speed and load.

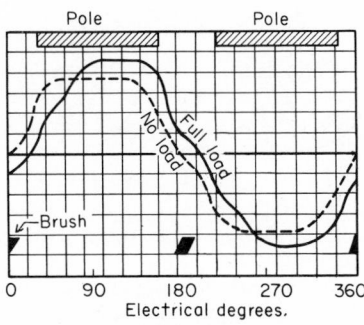

FIG. 18 *Distribution of magnetic flux at no load and at full load, without commutating poles.*

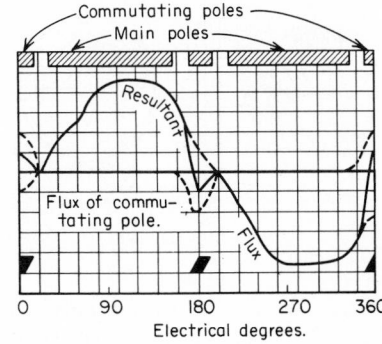

FIG. 19 *Distribution of magnetic flux at full load, with and without commutating poles.*

27. The action of the magnetic flux in a commutating-pole generator is illustrated in Fig. 20. The direction of the main field flux is shown by the dashed line. The direction of the armature magnetization is shown by the dotted lines. The direction of the flux in the commutating pole is shown by the full line. It is evident that the commutating-pole flux is in a direction opposite to that of the armature flux, and as the commutating-pole coil is more powerful at the commutating point in its magnetizing action than the armature coils, the flux of the armature coils is neutralized. With a less powerful magnetizing force from the commutating pole than from the armature at the commutating point, the armature would overpower the commutating pole and reverse the direction of the flux, which would result in a bad commutating condition.

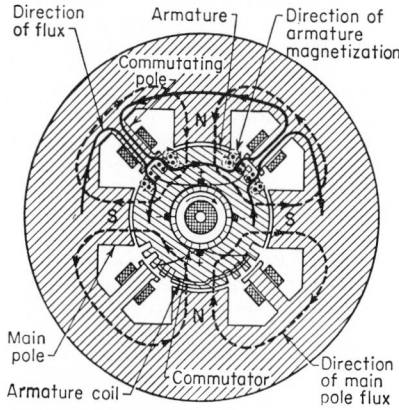

FIG. 20 *Distribution of flux in a commutating-pole generator.*

28. To Determine the Neutral Point of a Motor or Generator (Fig. 21). Two copper-wire contact points, or contactors, C are inserted in an insulating block and are allowed to extend through it about $\frac{1}{16}$ in. The distance between the centers of the points should be equal to the width of one commutator bar. The contactors are connected to a millivoltmeter V, which should, preferably, be of the differential type. Place both points on the commutator while the machine is being rotated with the brushes lifted from the commutator and the shunt field is being excited. While shifting the points around the periphery of the commutator, hold the block so that an imaginary line connecting the two contact points will be perpendicular to the axis of the commutator.

If a differential voltmeter is used, its needle will indicate either to the right or to the left of the zero point until the contacts are exactly over the neutral position; then the voltmeter will read zero. The brushes can now be shifted so that an imaginary line, parallel to the axis of the commutator and bisecting the bearing surface of the brush, will coincide with a point equidistant between the two contact points.

29. To Determine the Proper Polarity of the Commutating Poles. For a motor: proceeding from pole to pole around the frame in the direction of armature rotation, each commutating pole should have the same polarity as the main pole which just precedes it (Fig. 22, I). For a **generator:** proceeding from pole to pole around the

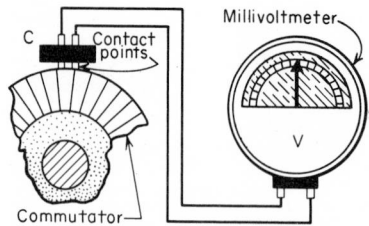

FIG. 21 *Connections for determination of the neutral point.*

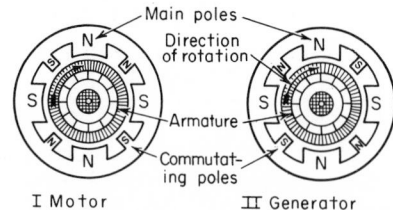

FIG. 22 *Diagram showing polarity of commutating poles (clockwise rotation).*

frame, in the direction of armature rotation, each commutating pole should have a polarity opposite to that of the main pole which just precedes it (Fig. 22, II).

30. Commutating-pole machines will run in parallel with each other and with non-commutating-pole machines, provided correct connections are made. See illustrations. The series-field windings on commutating-pole machines are usually less powerful than on noncommutating-pole machines, and particular attention should, therefore, be paid to getting the proper drop in accordance with instructions of Sec. **24.** A connection diagram is shown in Fig. 15.

30A. Compensating Field Windings. The commutating poles of a d-c motor or generator do not neutralize the effect of the armature current upon the flux of the machine. They simply produce a local flux at the commutating location of the armature conductors. For machines that must operate under very severe conditions of overload and speed range, it is necessary for satisfactory operation that means be provided to neutralize the tendency of the armature current to distort and change the flux of the machine. This neutralization is produced by means of an additional winding called a compensating field winding. A compensating field winding consists of coils embedded in slots in the pole faces of the machine, as shown in Figs. 22A and 22B. The compensating winding is connected in series with the armature in such a manner that the current through the individual conductors of the compensating field winding will be opposite to the direction of the corresponding armature conductors, as shown in Fig. 22A.

31. Three-wire d-c generators are ordinary d-c generators with the modifications

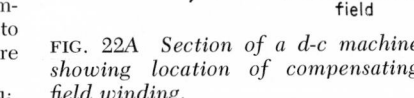

FIG. 22A *Section of a d-c machine showing location of compensating field winding.*

and additions described below. They are usually wound for 125/250-volt, three-wire circuits. In the case of commercial three-wire generators (Westinghouse Electric Corp.), four equidistant taps are made in the armature winding and each pair of taps diametrically opposite each other is connected together through a balance coil. These balance coils may be external (Fig. 23) or wound within the armature. The middle points of the two balance coils (see Index) are connected together, and this junction constitutes the neutral point to which the third or neutral wire of the system is connected. A constant voltage is maintained between the neutral and outside wires which, within narrow limits, is one-half the generator voltage. The generator shaft is

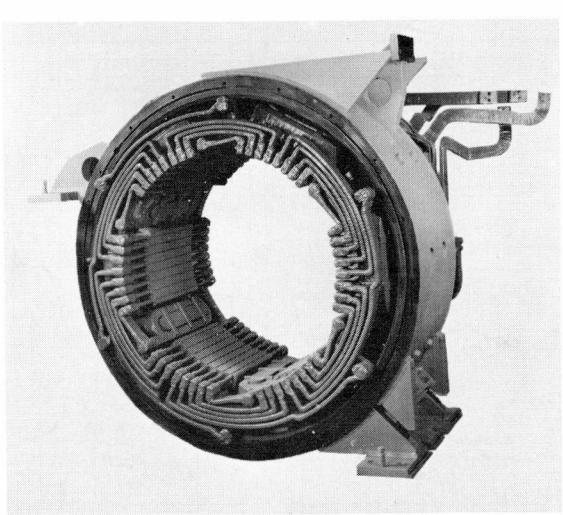

FIG. 22B *Frame and field structure of a d-c motor showing compensating windings in the faces of the main poles. (Westinghouse Electric Corp.)*

extended at the commutator end for the collector rings. Four collector brushes and brush holders are used in addition to the regular d-c brushes and brush holders.

32. The series coils of compound-wound three-wire generators are divided into halves (see Fig. 23), one of which is connected to the positive and one to the negative side. This is done to obtain compounding on either side of the system when operating on an unbalanced load. To understand this, consider a generator with the series field in the negative side only and with most of the load on the positive side of the system. The current flows from the positive brush through the load and back along the neutral wire without passing through the series field. The generator is then operating as an ordinary shunt machine. If most of the load is on the negative side, the current flows out the neutral wire and back through the series fields, boosting the voltage the maximum amount. Such operation is evidently not satisfactory, and so the divided series fields are provided.

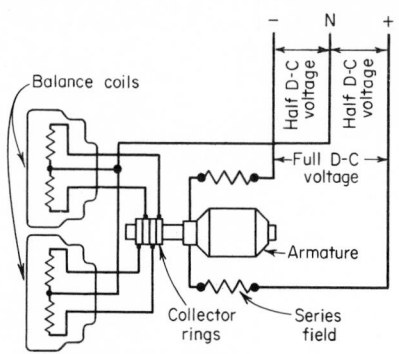

FIG. 23 *Diagram showing connections for three-wire generator.*

33. Switchboard Connections for Three-wire Generators. Figure 24 is a diagrammatical representation of the switchboard connections for two three-wire generators operated in multiple (Westinghouse publication). Two ammeters indicate the unbalanced load. The positive lead and equalizer are controlled by a double-pole circuit breaker; the negative lead and equalizer likewise. Note that both the positive

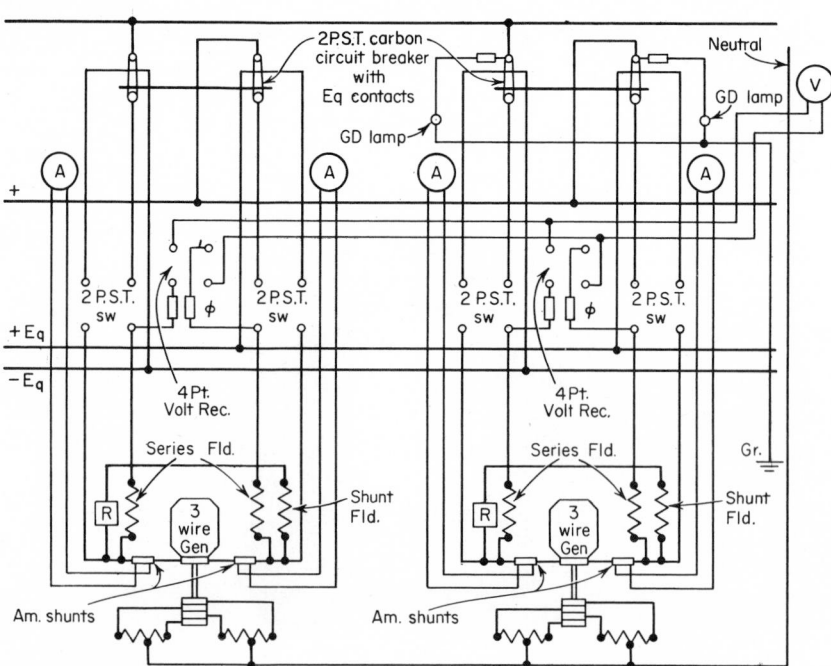

FIG. 24 *Diagram of connections of two three-wire d-c generators operating in parallel, 125–250 volts.*

and negative equalizer connections as well as both the positive and negative leads are run to the circuit breakers in addition to the main switches on the switchboard. It is necessary that this be done in all cases. Otherwise, when two or more machines are running in multiple and the breaker comes out, opening the main circuit to one of them but not breaking its equalizer leads, its ammeter is left connected to the equalizer bus bars and current is fed into it from the other machines through the equalizer leads, either driving it as a motor or destroying the armature winding (see also Figs. 25 and 26).

34. As there are two series fields, two equalizer buses are required when several three-wire machines are installed (see Fig. 24) and are to be operated in parallel. The two equalizers serve to distribute the load equally between the machines and to prevent cross currents due to differences in voltage on the different generators. Because of the equalizer connections, two small terminal boards are supplied, one for each side of the generator. Arrangement is also made for ammeter shunts on the terminal boards.

An ammeter shunt is mounted directly on each of the contact boards of the machine. The total current output of the machine can thereby be read at the switchboard. As the shunts are at the machine, there is no chance for current to leak across between generator switchboard leads without causing a reading on the ammeters. Two ammeters must be provided for reading the current in the outside wires. It is important that the current be measured on both sides of the system, for with an ammeter in one side of the system only, it is possible for a large unmeasured current to flow in the other side with disastrous results.

35. Wires connecting the balance coils to a three-wire generator must be short and of low resistance. Any considerable resistance in these will affect the voltage regulation. The unbalanced current flows along these connections; consequently, if they have much resistance, the resulting drop in voltage reduces the voltage on the heavily loaded side.

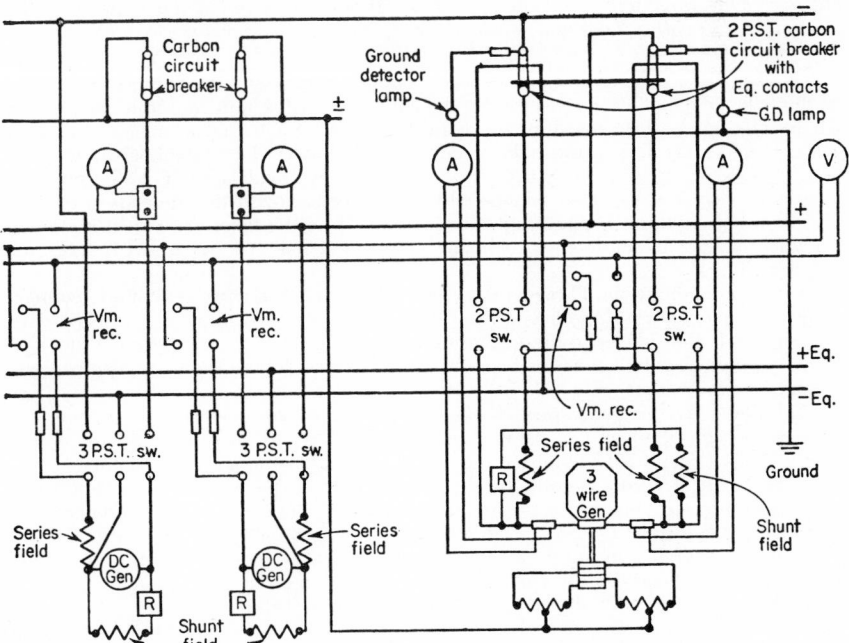

FIG. 25 *One three-wire d-c generator, 125/250 volts, in parallel with two two-wire generators, 125 volts. Diagram of connections.*

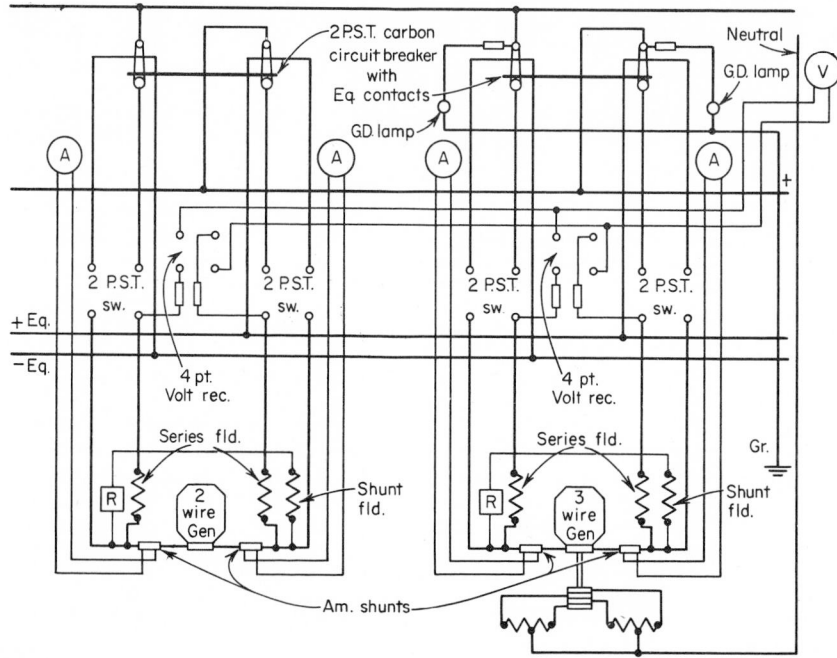

FIG. 26   *One three-wire d-c generator, 125/250 volts, in parallel with one two-wire generator, 250 volts.   Diagram of connections.*

Switches are ordinarily not placed in the circuits connecting the four collector rings to the balance coils.   When necessary, the coils can be disconnected from the generator by raising the brushes from the collector rings.   Switching arrangements often make it necessary to run the balance-coil connections to the switchboard and back, requiring heavy leads to keep the drop low, or if heavy leads are not used, then poor regulation may result.   The balance coils are so constructed that there is very little likelihood of anything happening to them that will not be taken care of by the main circuit breakers.   Complete switchboard connection diagrams are given in Figs. 24, 25, and 26.

36. Commutating-pole Three-wire Generators.   On three-wire generators, connections are so made that one-half of the commutating-pole winding is in the positive side and the other half is in the negative side.   This ensures proper action of the commutating pole at unbalanced load (see Figs. 24, 25, and 26 and the text accompanying them).

37. Three-wire d-c generators can be operated in parallel (Westinghouse publication) with each other and in parallel with other machines on the three-wire system (see Figs. 24, 25, and 26).   When a three-wire, 250-volt generator is operated in multiple with two-wire, 125-volt generators, the series fields of the two two-wire generators must be connected, one in the positive side and one in the negative side of the system, and an equalizer must be run to each machine.   Similarly, when a three-wire, 250-volt generator is operated in multiple with a 250-volt, two-wire generator, the series field of the 250-volt, two-wire generator must be divided and one-half connected to each outside wire.   The method of doing this is to disconnect the connectors between the series-field coils and reconnect these coils so that all the *N* pole fields will be in series on one side of the three-wire system and all the *S* pole fields in series on the other side of the system.

38. Testing for Polarity.   When a machine that is to operate in parallel with others is connected to the bus bars for the first time, it should be tested for polarity. The + lead of the machine should connect to the + bus bar and the − lead to the − bus bar (Fig. 27, I). The machine to be tested should be brought up to normal voltage but not connected to the bars. The test can be made with two lamps (Fig. 27, II), each lamp of the voltage of the circuit. Each is temporarily connected between a machine terminal and bus terminal of the main switch. If the lamps do not burn, the polarity of the new machine is correct, but if they burn brightly, its polarity is incorrect and should be reversed. A voltmeter can be used (Fig. 27, III). A temporary connection is made across one pair of outside terminals, and the voltmeter is connected across the other pair. No deflec-

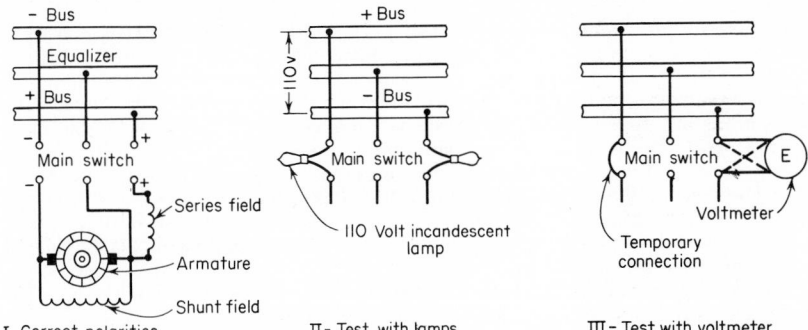

FIG. 27   *Tests for polarity.*

tion or a small deflection indicates correct polarity. (Test with voltmeter leads one way and then reverse them, as indicated by the dotted lines.) A full-scale deflection indicates incorrect polarity. Use a voltmeter having a voltage range equal to twice the voltage on the bus bars.

39. Third-brush generators were often used on automobiles for providing the necessary electric power for the charging of the storage battery and operation of lights. If an ordinary generator were employed for this purpose, the voltage would vary over a wide range as the speed of the car changed. The voltage would vary nearly proportionally to the speed. This, of course, would not be satisfactory either for the proper charging of the battery or for operation of the car lights. The third-brush generator is a special shunt generator with the field winding connected between one of the main brushes and the auxiliary or third brush (see Fig. 28). As the speed of the automobile

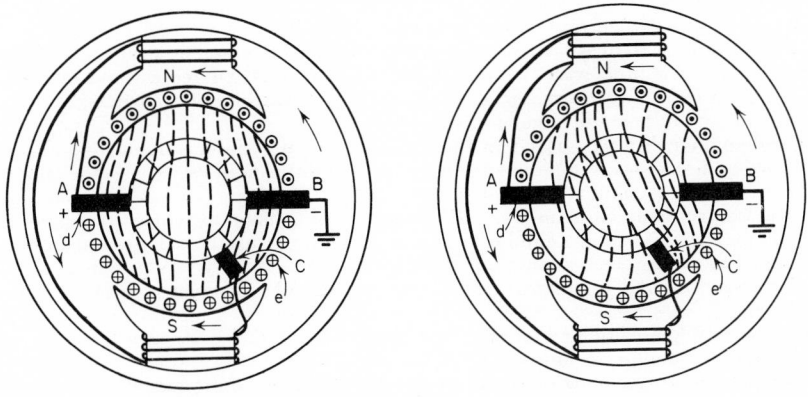

FIG. 28   *Third-brush generator.* (*From Dawes, "Electrical Engineering—Direct Currents."*)

increases, thereby increasing the speed of the generator, the voltage tends to increase. This increase in voltage increases the current delivered by the generator. But the increase in current so changes the magnetic-flux distribution in the machine that the voltage between the third brush and main brush A is reduced. This reduces the field current and therefore flux of the machine and tends to bring the main voltage between brushes A and C back to its former value. This action does not maintain absolutely constant voltage for different speeds, but the voltage is held within certain limits so that an excessive voltage is not developed at high speeds which would overcharge the battery and shorten the life of the lamps. It should be noted that present-day automobiles use an a-c generator (alternator) with rectifier diodes to provide 12-volt d-c supply.

40. Diverter-pole generators are a special type of d-c generator (developed by the Electric Products Co.) that have particular advantages for the charging of batteries by the floating method of charge. The machine is constructed with additional pole pieces (the diverter poles) located midway between the main poles in the same manner as commutating poles. Each main pole is connected by a magnetic bridge to one diverter pole. The windings of the main poles are connected in shunt with the armature winding, and the windings of the diverter poles in series with the armature winding. The construction, connections, and load-voltage characteristics for such a generator are shown in Fig. 29. These generators will produce an almost constant terminal voltage from no load to 110 per cent of rated load. Above 110 per cent of rated load the voltage drops very rapidly.

At no load, a part of the magnetic flux resulting from the shunt coil on the main pole piece is diverted and does not pass through the armature.

As the load increases, the series winding on the diverter pole rediverts this flux to the armature and provides a commutating field.

If the shunt and series windings are properly proportioned, the flux in the armature varies with the load so as to compensate for the IR drop in the generator and for speed changes of the driving motor.

A flat voltage curve is obtained, since the necessary magnetic changes produced by the series winding take place only in the diverter pole, the flux from the main pole remaining constant. The flux densities in the diverter pole are kept low, so that the magnetic changes which occur in this part of the magnetic circuit take place on the straight portion of the magnetization curve, thus eliminating most of the curvature from the voltage characteristic.

By correct adjustment of the diverter-pole winding by means of an adjustable shunt, a very straight flat curve is obtained with only a very slight rise on approaching zero load.

At some value of the load current the ampere-turns on the diverter pole will equal those on the main pole, and at this time, the magnetic flux leaking across the bridge to the diverter pole is all rediverted across the air gap; hence there is no further leakage flux for an increased current to redivert to the armature.

When the load is increased beyond this point, the increased ampere-turns on the diverter pole combine with the armature cross-magnetizing force to send magnetic flux in the reverse direction across the leakage bridge, which tends to demagnetize the main pole and reduce the generator voltage.

Good commutation is assured, as the diverter pole provides a commutating field of the correct direction for improving commutation, and this field varies with the current output just as in a commutating-pole generator.

41A. Control generators are specially designed d-c generators which are employed for the precise automatic control of d-c motors. They are used for performing a wide variety of functions, such as:

1. Controlling and regulating speed, voltage, current, or power accurately over a wide range.

2. Controlling tension and torque to maintain product uniformity in winding, drawing, and other similar operations.

3. Speeding up acceleration or deceleration to increase the production of high-inertia machines, etc.

I. *Frame and field-winding construction.*

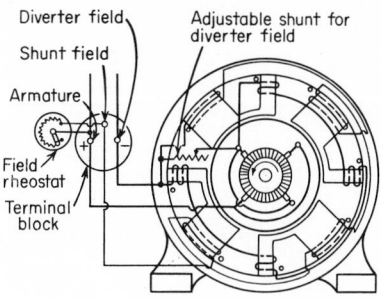

II. *Diagram of connections.*

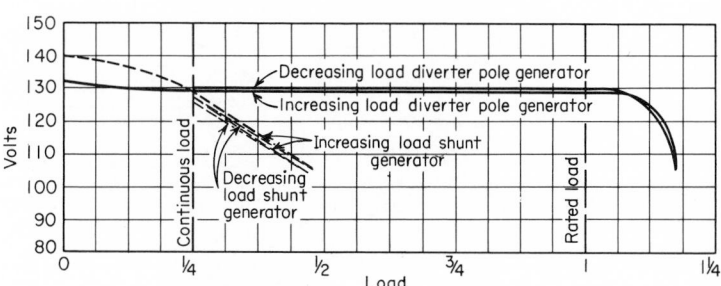

III. *Load-voltage characteristics.*

FIG. 29   *Diverter-pole generator. (Electric Products Co.)*

Small motors can be supplied directly with power from the control generator. In the majority of applications, however, the capacity of the control generator is not sufficient to supply the motor directly, and the control generator energizes the field of a main generator which supplies the motor with power. A control generator must possess the characteristics of moderately fast response and low power consumption from the activating control circuit. The application of control generators for motor control is discussed in more detail in Sec. **141.**

41B. The amplidyne is a control generator manufactured by the General Electric Co. The construction of the amplidyne, as shown in Fig. 30A, differs from the conventional d-c generator in the following ways:

1. Separately excited field windings (up to four individual windings) with only a small number of ampere-turns in each winding. The field windings are called control fields or control windings.

2. Brushes (A and B in Fig. 30A) located in the conventional neutral position are short-circuited on each other.

3. Pole structure split in two.

4. Addition of a second set of brushes (C and D in Fig. 30A) located 90 electrical degrees from the conventional neutral position. These brushes are the load brushes of the machine and are connected to the output terminals of the machine.

5. A compensating field winding wound around the pole structure of the machine instead of being located in slots on the face of the poles. The compensating field winding is connected in series with the load brush circuit.

The amplidyne functions in the following manner: When a control-field winding or windings are energized, a magnetic flux will be produced in paths G and H of Fig. 30A. The rotation of the armature through this flux will generate voltage in the armature conductors. However, because of the small number of ampere-turns in the control-field windings, the voltage generated from brush B to brush A will produce only a reasonable value of current in the short-circuited armature. The direction of this short-circuited armature current will be as shown by the designations inside the conductors

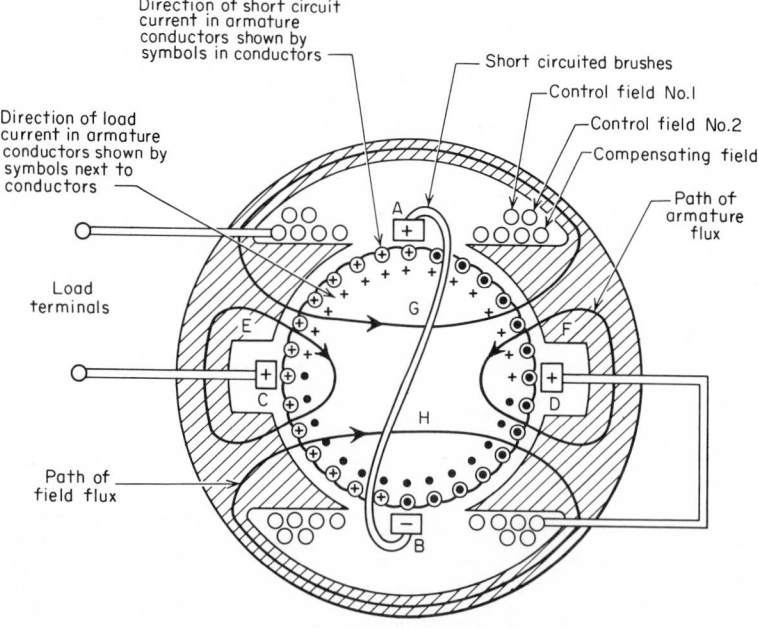

FIG. 30A   *Cross section of amplidyne generator.*

in Fig. 30A. The short-circuited armature current will produce magnetic flux in the paths E and F. Voltages will be induced in the armature conductors by this flux E and F. These conductor voltages will produce no net voltage from brush B to A, since the voltages in conductors from B to C and B to D will just neutralize the voltages produced in the conductors from C to A and D to A, respectively. A voltage will be produced, however, from brush C to brush D. Since brushes C and D are connected to the terminals of the machine, an output voltage will be produced whenever a control-field winding is energized. When brushes C and D are connected to an external load circuit, current will flow through the armature conductors because of the load current, in the directions designated in Fig. 30A by the markings alongside each conductor. The actual current through each individual armature conductor will be the combination of the armature short-circuit current in paths B to A and the armature load current in paths C to D. The load current in the armature should not materially affect the flux of the machine. Therefore, a compensating field winding is connected in series with the load. This winding is so located and designed that its ampere-turns will practically neutralize the ampere-turns produced by the armature load current. The functioning of the machine is summarized as follows:

1. Excitation of a control-field winding produces flux G and H.
2. Flux G and H produces no net voltage between brushes C and D but does produce net voltage in armature paths BCA and BDA.
3. Voltage in paths BCA and BDA produces current in armature because of short circuit AB.
4. Short-circuit current in armature produces flux E and F.
5. Flux E and F produces no net voltage between brushes A and B but does produce net voltage between brushes C and D. This is the load or output voltage of the machine.
6. Voltage CD produces load current in armature and external circuit.
7. Ampere-turns (flux-producing tendency) of load armature current are neutralized by ampere-turns of compensating field winding.

Thus the control-field current controls the short-circuit armature current, which in turn controls the output voltage. Since the control-field winding is designed with very small watt capacity, a very small change of input power to a control-field winding will produce a large change in output power.

The symbolic representation of an amplidyne generator as used in wiring diagrams is shown in Fig. 30B.

41C. The Rototrol is the trade name of the control generator that is made by the Westinghouse Electric Corp. The Rototrol is essentially a small d-c generator that is similar in electrical and mechanical construction to a standard d-c generator of equal size, except that the Rototrol is provided with a number of field windings. The voltage output of the machine depends entirely upon the control of and the interaction of these field windings. The Rototrol is provided with a self-energizing field winding and two or more control-field windings (see Fig. 30C). The self-energizing field wind-

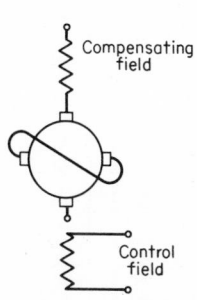

FIG. 30B *Basic symbol for amplidyne.*

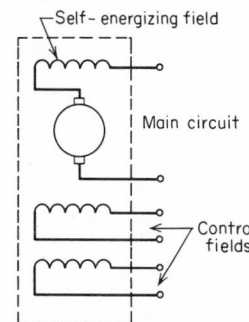

FIG. 30C *Basic symbol for Rototrol.*

ing is generally connected in series with the Rototrol armature and furnishes the necessary excitation for the normal operation of the machine. All the other field windings are called control-field windings. The control-field windings are used to measure and compare standard and actual values representative of the quantity to be regulated. One of the control-field windings is called a pattern-field winding, and the others are called pilot-field windings. The pattern field is the control field, which is separately excited from an independent source and is used as a calibration, or standard of comparison. The pilot fields are the remainder of the control-field windings, which measure directly or indirectly the quantity to be regulated.

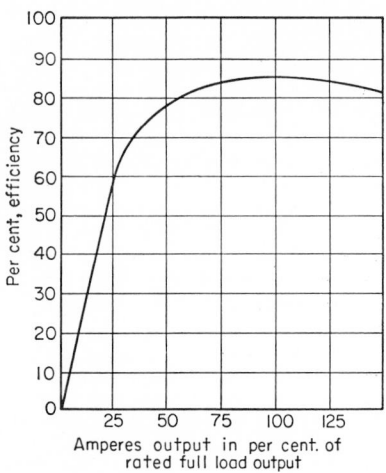

FIG. 31 *Efficiency graph of a 10-kw compound-wound d-c generator.*

42. **The efficiency of a d-c generator** increases with the load up to a certain point. Figure 31 indicates typical efficiency performances. Large-capacity machines have higher full-load efficiencies than small ones. Generators should be selected of such capacity that they will, insofar as possible, operate at loads in the neighborhood of their normal ratings.

43. Approximate Data on Standard Compound-wound D-C Commutating-pole Generators

The efficiency of a generator depends on its design, and, to a certain extent, on its speed and voltage. Average values are given in the following table that are fairly representative of modern practice.

Capacity, kw	Output current, amp			Efficiency, per cent		
	125 volts	250 volts	500 volts	½ load	¾ load	Full load
5	40	20	10	77.0	81.0	82.5
10	80	40	20	82.0	85.0	86.0
15	120	60	30	82.5	86.5	86.5
20	160	80	40	84.0	86.5	87.5
25	200	100	50	85.0	88.0	89.0
35	280	140	70	87.0	89.0	89.5
50	400	200	100	88.0	89.5	90.5
60	480	240	120	88.5	90.5	91.0
75	600	300	150	88.5	90.5	91.0
90	720	360	180	88.5	90.5	91.0
100	800	400	200	89.0	90.5	91.0
125	1,000	500	250	90.5	91.0	91.0
150	1,200	600	300	90.5	91.3	91.5
200	1,600	800	400	91.0	91.5	92.0
300	2,400	1,200	600	91.3	91.8	92.0
400	3,200	1,600	800	91.8	92.3	92.5
500	4,000	2,000	1,000	91.8	92.2	92.5
750	6,000	3,000	1,500	92.0	92.3	92.5
1,000	8,000	4,000	2,000	92.5	93.0	93.5

44. Rating of D-C Generators. The standard methods of rating generators are as follows:

Continuous Rating. A generator given a continuous power-output rating will carry its rated load continuously in an ambient temperature of 40°C without exceeding a specified rise in temperature. Generators rated on a 40°C rise basis will carry 115 per cent of their rated load continuously without injury to themselves, provided that the service conditions are normal. The factor of 1.15 is known as a service factor.

Nominal Rating. A generator given a nominal power-output rating will carry 50 per cent overload for a period of 2 hr without injury to itself.

Continuous with 2-hr 25 Per Cent Overload Rating. A generator rated on this basis in addition to carrying its rated power load continuously will carry 25 per cent overload for a period of 2 hr without injury to itself.

45. Brushes, Their Adjustment and Care (Westinghouse Instruction Book). The position of the brushes on a d-c generator should be on or near the no-load neutral point of the commutator. This neutral point on most standard, noncommutating-pole generators is in line with the center of the pole, and the brushes should be set a little in advance of this neutral point. The brushes of noncommutating-pole generators should be given a slight "forward lead" in the direction of rotation of the armature. Motor brushes should be set somewhat back of the neutral point, the "backward lead" in this case being approximately equal to the forward lead on generators. The exact position in either case is that which gives the best commutation at normal voltage for all loads. In no case should the brushes be set far enough from the neutral point to cause dangerous sparking at no load. For commutating-pole machines it is essential that the brushes be located at the neutral point.

The ends of all brushes should be fitted to the commutator so that they make good contact over their entire bearing faces. This can be most easily accomplished after the brush holders have been adjusted and the brushes inserted as follows: Lift a set of brushes sufficiently to permit a sheet of sandpaper to be inserted. Draw the sandpaper in one direction only, preferably in the direction of rotation, under the brushes (Fig. 32), being careful to keep the ends of the paper as close to the commutator surface as possible and thus avoid rounding the edges of the brushes, each set of brushes being similarly treated in turn. Start with coarse and finish with fine sandpaper. With copper-plated brushes, bevel their edges slightly so that the copper will not touch the commutator.

46. Operating Instructions. Do not lubricate the commutator with oil; a piece of muslin moistened with Vaseline can be used to clean and lubricate the commutator.

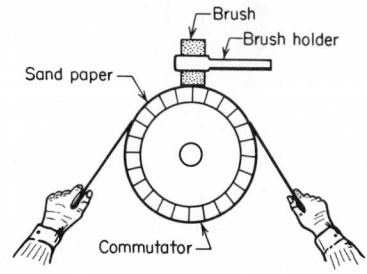

FIG. 32 *Sandpapering brushes.*

Emery is a conductor and should not be used in fitting brushes or cleaning the commutator; use sandpaper or sandstone (Sec. **77**) and do not use it on the commutator too frequently.

Do not use greater brush tension than necessary; tension greater than 2 lb per sq in. is seldom required. When replacing brushes, use the quality and size originally supplied with the machine and fit them to the commutator with sandpaper before use (Sec. **45**). Do not open generator-field circuits quickly; open the switch slowly, permitting the arc to extinguish gradually, which should take about 5 sec.

47. Direct-current Generator and Motor Defects

(From *Machinery*, by special permission)

	Fault		No.	Correction
Sparking at the brushes	Faults of	Brushes		
		Not set diametrically opposite	1	A. Should have been set properly at first, by counting bars, or by measurement on the commutator B. Can be done if necessary while running; move rocker until brush on one side sparks least, then adjust other brushes so they do not spark
		Not set at neutral points	2	Move rocker back and forth slowly until sparking stops
		Not properly trimmed	3	A. Brushes should be properly trimmed before starting. If there are two or more brushes one may be removed and retrimmed B. Clean with alcohol or ether, then grind and reset carefully (see 1, 4, 38)
		Not in line	4	Adjust each brush until bearing is on line and square on commutator bar, bearing evenly the whole width (see 12 A)
		Not in good contact	5	A. Clean commutator of oil and grit. See that brushes touch B. Adjust tension screws and springs to secure light, firm and even contact (see 38 B)
	Commutator	Rough; worn in grooves or ridges; out of round	6 7	A. Grind with fine sandpaper on curved block, and polish with crocus cloth. Never use emery in any form B. If too bad to grind down turn off true in a lathe or preferably in its own bearings, with a light tool and rest, a light cut; running slowly NOTE.—Armature should have $\frac{1}{16}$ to $\frac{1}{8}$-in. end motion when running, to wear commutator evenly and smoothly (see 31)
		High bars	8	Set "high bar" down carefully with mallet or block of wood, then clamp end nuts tightly, or file, grind, or turn true. A high bar may cause singing (see line 38)
		Low bars	9	Grind or turn commutator true to the surface of the low bars
	Armature	Weak magnetic field	10	A. Broken circuit } in field coils { repair if external B. Short circuit } { rewind if internal C. Machine not properly wound, or without proper amount of iron—no remedy but to rebuild it
		Short-circuited coils	11	A. Remove copper dust, solder, or other metallic contact between commutator bars B. See that clamping rings are perfectly free, and insulated from commutator bars; no copper dust, carbonized oil, etc., to cause an electrical leak C. Test for cross connection or short circuit, and if such is found rewind armature to correct D. See that brush holders are perfectly insulated. No copper dust, carbon dust, oil or dust, to cause an electrical leak (see 1, 2, 60)
Armature faults		Broken coils	12	A. Bridge the break temporarily by staggering the brushes until machine can be shut down (to save bad sparking) and then repair B. Shut down machine if possible, and repair loose or broken connection to commutator bar C. If coil is broken inside, rewinding is the only sure remedy. May be temporarily repaired by connecting to next coil, across mica D. Solder commutator lugs together, or put in a "jumper," and cut out, and leave open the broken coil. Be careful not to short-circuit a good coil in doing this (see 11)
		Cross connections	13	Cross connections may have same effect as short circuit, treat as such (see 11) Each coil should test complete without cross and no ground

Fault	Machine	Cause	No.	Remedy
Excessive current in armature / Sparking at the brushes	Generator	Excessive load	14	A. Reduce number of lamps and load
		Ground and leak from short circuit on line		B. Test out, locate, and repair
		Dead short circuit on line		C. NOTE. Dead short circuit will or should blow safety fuse. Shut down, locate fault, and repair before starting again and put in a new fuse
	Motor	Excessive voltage		D. Use proper current only and with proper rheostat, controller, and switch
		Excessive amperes on constant-current circuit		E. See that controller, etc., are suitable with ample resistance
		Friction		F. See that there is no undue friction or mechanical resistance anywhere (see 3 B and 35, 36)
		Too great load on pulley		G. Reduce load on motor to its rated capacity or less
Heating of parts	Armature	Overloaded	15	Overload. Too many amperes, lights, or too much power being taken from machine (see 11, 12, 13, 14)
		Short circuit	16	Short-circuited, generally dirt, etc., at commutator bars (see 11, 12, 13, 14)
		Broken circuit	17	Broken circuit often caused by a loose or broken band (see 11, 12, 13, 14)
		Cross connection	18	Cross connection. Often caused by a loose coil abrading on another coil or core (see 11, 12, 13, 14)
		Moisture in coils	19	Dry out by gentle heat. May be done by sending a small current through, or causing machine to generate a small current itself, by running slowly
		Eddy currents in core	20	Iron of armature hotter than coils after a run. Faulty construction. Core should be made of finely laminated insulated sheets. No remedy but to rebuild
		Friction	21	Hot boxes or journals may affect armature (see 23, 33)
	Field coils	Excessive current — Shunt	22	A. Decrease voltage at terminals by reducing speed. Increase field resistance by winding on more wire, or finer wire or putting resistance in series with fields
		Excessive current — Series		B. Decrease current through fields by shunt, removing some of field winding or rewind with coarser wire
				NOTE. Excessive current may be from a short circuit or from moisture in coils causing a leakage (see 10, 24)
		Eddy currents	23	Pole pieces hotter than coils after short run, due to faulty construction, or fluctuating current; if latter, regulate, and steady current
		Moisture in coils	24	Coils show less than normal resistance, may cause short circuit or body contact to iron of dynamo. Dry out as in 19 (see also 22, note)

Direct-current Generator and Motor Defects (Continued)

Category	Defect	No.	Remedy
Heating of parts — Bearings	Not sufficient or poor oil	25	A. See that plenty of good mineral oil, filtered clean and free from grit, feeds but be careful that it does not get on commutator or brush holder (see 11) B. Cylinder oil or vaseline can be used if necessary to complete run, mixed with sulfur or white lead, or hydrate of potash. Then clean up and put in good order
	Dirt or grit in bearings	26	A. Wash out grit with oil while running, then clean up and put in order. Be careful about flooding commutator and brush holder B. Remove caps and clean and polish journals and bearings perfectly, then replace. See that all parts are free and lubricate well C. When shut down, if hot, remove bearings and let them cool naturally; then clean, scrape and polish, and assemble; see that all parts are free, and lubricate well
	Rough journals or bearings	27	Smooth and polish in a lathe, removing all burrs, scratches, tool marks, etc., and rebabbitt old boxes and fit new ones
	Journals too tight in bearings; bent shaft	28 29	Slacken cap bolts, put in liners, and retighten till run is over, then scrape, ream, etc., as may be needed or bend or turn true in lathe or grinder. Possibly a new box or shaft will be needed
	Bearings out of line	30	Loosen bearing bolts, line up and block, until armature is in center of pole pieces, ream out dowel and bolt-holes and secure in new position
	End pressure of pulley hub or shaft collars	31	A. See that foundation is level and armature has free end motion B. If there is no end motion, file or turn ends of boxes or shoulders on shaft to provide end motion C. Then line up shaft and belt, so that there is no end thrust on shaft, but so that the armature plays freely endways when running
	Belt too tight	32	A. Reduce load so that belt may be loosened and yet not slip. Avoid vertical belts if possible B. Choose larger pulleys, wider and longer belts with slack side on top. Vibrating and flapping belts cause winking lamps
Noises	Armature out of center of pole pieces	33	A. Bearings may be worn out and need replacing, throwing armature out of center (see 36) B. Center armature in polar space, and adjust bearings to suit (see 30) C. File out polar space to give equal space all round D. Spring pole away from armature; this may be difficult or impossible in large machines
	Armature or pulley out of balance	34	Faulty construction, armature and pulley should have been balanced when made. May be helped by balancing on knife-edges now
	Armature strikes or rubs pole pieces	35	A. Bend or press down any projecting wires, and secure with tie bands B. File out pole pieces where armature strikes (see 30, 33)
	Collars or shoulders on shaft strike or rub box	36	Bearings may be loose or worn out. Perhaps new bearings are needed (see 30, 31)

			Remedy	No.
Noises	Loose bolt connection or screws		See that all bolts and screws are tight, and examine daily to keep them so	37
	Brushes sing or hiss		A. Apply stearic acid (adamantine) candle, vaseline, or cylinder oil to commutator and wipe off; only a trace should be applied B. Move brushes in and out of holder to get a firm smooth, gentle pressure, free from hum or buzz (see 3, 6, 7, 8, 9, 31)	38
	Flapping of belt		Use an endless belt if possible; if a laced belt must be used, have square ends neatly laced	39
	Slipping of belt from overload		Tighten belt or reduce load (see 32)	40
	Humming of armature lugs or teeth		A. Slope end of pole piece so that armature does not pass edges all at once B. Decrease magnetism of field, or increase magnetic capacity of tooth	41
Speed — Runs too fast	Engine fails to regulate with varying load		Adjust governor of engine to regulate properly, from no load to full load, or get a better engine	42
	Series motor, too much current, and runs away		A. Series motor on constant current: (1) put in a shunt and regulate to proper current; (2) use regulator or governor to control magnetism of field for varying load B. Series motor on constant potential: (1) insert resistance and reduce current; (2) use a proper regulator or controlling switch; (3) change to automatic speed-regulating motor	43
Runs too fast	Shunt motor	Field rheostat not properly set	A. Adjust field rheostat to control motor	44
		Not proper current	B. Use current of proper voltage and no other, with a proper rheostat	
		Motor not properly proportioned	C. Get a better motor, one properly designed for the work	
Runs too slow	45, Engine fails to regulate. 46, Overload. 47, Short-circuit in armature. 48, Striking or rubbing of armature. 49, Friction. 50, Weak magnetic field		45, same as 42; 46 see 14 A; 47, short circuit in armature (see 11); 48 rubbing armature (see 35); 49, friction (see 3 B); 50, weak magnetic field (see 10)	45 to 50
Motor — Stop or fail to start	Great overload (see 14 F and G)		Open switch and find and repair trouble. Keep switch open and rheostat "off" to see if everything is right	51
	Excessive friction (see 25, 33, 35)		Shunt motor on constant-potential circuit, fuse may blow or armature burn out	52
	Circuit open	Fuse melted or switch open Broken wire or connection Brushes not in contact Current fails or is shut off at station	A. Find and repair trouble after opening switch, then put in fuse (see 14 C) B. Open switch, find and repair trouble (see 12) C. Open switch and adjust (see 5) D. Open switch and return starting-box lever to off position, wait for current	53
	Short circuit of field Short circuit of armature Short circuit of switch		Test for and repair if possible. Examine insulation of binding posts and brush holders. Poor insulation, dirt, oil, and copper, or carbon dust often result in a short circuit	54 56
	Runs backward. Wrong connections		Connect correctly as per diagram; if no diagram is at hand, reverse connections to brushes or others until direction of rotation is satisfactory	57

Direct-current Generator and Motor Defects (*Continued*)

Dynamo or generator			
Reversed residual magnetism	Reversed current through field coils	A. Use current from another machine or a battery through field in proper direction to correct fault. Test polarity with a compass	58
	Reversed connections	B. If connections or winding are not known, try one way and test; if not correct reverse connections, try again and test	
	Earth's magnetism	C. Connect as per diagram for desired rotation, see that connections to shunt and series coils are properly made (see 57)	
	Proximity of another dynamo		
	Brushes not in right position (see 1, 2, 3)	D. Shift brushes until they operate better (see 1, 2, 3)	
Too weak residual magnetism		Same as 58 A	59
Short circuit in machine		See 11, 54, 56	60
Short circuit in external circuit		A lamp socket, etc., may be short-circuited or grounded, and prevent building up shunt or compound machines. Find and remedy before closing switch (see 54, 56)	61
Field coils opposed to each other		Reverse connections of one of field coils and test. Find polarity with compass; if necessary try 58 A, C, D. If necessary reverse connections and recharge in opposite directions	62
Open circuit	Broken wire	A. Search out and repair (see 12)	63
	Faulty connections	B. Search out and repair (see 37)	
	Brushes not in contact	C. Search out and repair (see 5)	
	Safety fuses melted or broken	D. Search out and repair (see 53 A)	
	Switch open	E. Search out and repair (see 53 D)	
	External circuit open	F. Search out and repair with dynamo switch open until repairs are completed	
Too great load on dynamo		Reduce load to pilot lamp on shunt and incandescent machines; after voltage is obtained close switches in succession slowly, and regulate voltage (see 14 A and 65)	64
Too great resistance in field rheostat		Bring up to voltage gradually with rheostat, and watch pilot lamp; regulate carefully	65

48. When starting, a generator may fail to excite itself (Westinghouse Instruction Book). This may occur even when the generator operated perfectly during the preceding run. It will generally be found that this trouble is caused by a loose connection or break in the field circuit, by poor contact at the brushes due to a dirty commutator or perhaps to a loss of residual magnetism, or by incorrect position of brushes. Examine all connections; try a temporarily increased pressure on the brushes; look for a broken or burned-out resistance coil in the rheostat. An open circuit in the field winding can sometimes be traced with the aid of a magneto bell, but this is not an infallible test, as some magnetos will not ring through a circuit of such high resistance and reactance even though it is intact. If no open circuit is found in the rheostat or in the field winding, the trouble is probably in the armature. But if it is found that nothing is wrong with the connections or the winding, it may be necessary to excite the field from another generator or some other outside source.

Calling the generator we desire to excite "1" and the other machine from which current is to be taken "2," this procedure should be followed. Open all switches and remove all brushes from generator 1; connect the positive brush holder of generator 1 with the positive brush holder of generator 2; also connect the negative holders of the machines together (it is desirable to complete the circuit through a switch having a fuse of about 5 amp capacity in series). Close the switch. Where the generator in trouble connects to bus bars fed by other generators, the same result can be effected by insulating the brushes of the machine in trouble from their commutator and closing the main switch (see Fig. 33A). If the shunt winding of generator 1 is all right, its field will show considerable magnetism. If possible reduce the voltage of generator 2 before opening the exciting circuit; then

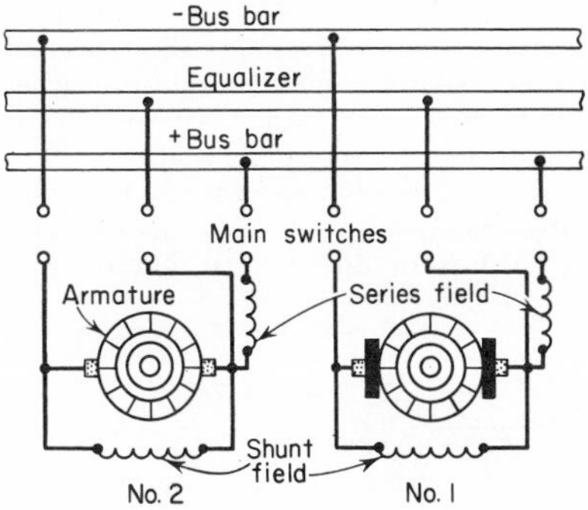

FIG. 33A *Exciting generator.*

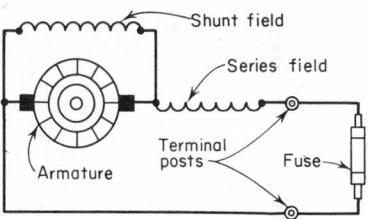

FIG. 33B *Another method of exciting a generator.*

break the connections. If this cannot be done, throw in all the rheostat resistance of generator 1; then open the switch very slowly, lengthening out the arc which will be formed until it breaks.

A simple means for getting a compound-wound machine to pick up is to short-circuit it through a fuse having approximately the current capacity of the generator (see Fig. 33B). If sufficient current to melt this fuse is not generated, it is evident that there is something wrong with the armature, either a short circuit or an open circuit. If, however, the fuse has blown, make one more attempt to get the machine to excite itself. If it does not pick up, it is evident that something is wrong with the shunt winding or connections.

If a new machine refuses to excite and the connections seem to be all right, reverse the connections of the shunt field; i.e., connect the wire which leads from the positive brush to the negative brush and the wire which leads from the negative brush to the positive brush. If this change of connections does no good, change back and locate the fault as previously suggested.

49. The proper connections for a shunt motor are as shown in Fig. 34. The field *B* is connected as shown, so that when the switch *D* is closed, it becomes excited before the armature circuit through the switch *E* is closed. Thus when the motor armature

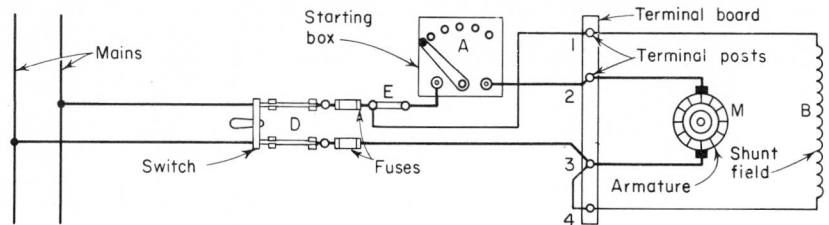

FIG. 34   *Control apparatus connections for a shunt motor.*

has current admitted to it through switch E and starting resistance box A, the field is already on and the full torque of the motor is obtained.   The torque of a motor is equal to the product of a constant, the flux per pole, the ampere-turns on the armature, and the number of poles.   Hence, if the full field is not on the motor at starting, full torque will not be obtained.

50. If a motor will not start when the starting box is operated and when current is flowing in the armature, an investigation should be made to see if field flux is present, which can be done by holding a piece of iron, such as a key, against the pole piece. If the flux exists, the key will be drawn strongly against the pole piece; if there is no flux, there will be practically no attraction.

51. Reversed Field-spool Connection.   There may be cases where the manufacturer has shipped a motor with one or more field spools reversed.   If such is the case, no torque or, perhaps, very weak torque will be noticed.   Under such conditions a trial with an iron key will indicate the presence of field magnetism, yet the weakness or total absence of torque will be present, and a trial of polarity should be made.

52. Running in the Wrong Direction.   Sometimes a motor when set up and started will run in the wrong direction.   The only change necessary is to reverse the field connection.   Thus Fig. 35, I, shows the connection for one direction of rotation and

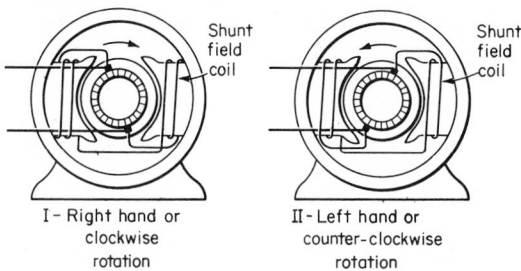

I – Right hand or
clockwise
rotation

II – Left hand or
counter-clockwise
rotation

FIG. 35   *Connections for shunt-wound motors.*

Fig. 35, II, that for the other.   Note that in Fig. 35, I, the brushes are shifted backward against the direction of rotation.   For the opposite rotation, a backward lead, as shown in Fig. 35, II, must be chosen.

53. Testing Polarity of Field.   This can be done in two ways: first, by using a compass, bringing it near the various poles and noting the direction of the deflection of the needle.   Since in all motors the poles alternate in magnetic polarity, in one pole the magnetism coming out and in the next going in, it follows that a certain end of a compass needle will point toward one pole and away from the next when conditions are normal.   If, however, two adjacent poles show similar magnetism, the trouble is located, and the offending spool should be reversed.   This should be done "end for end," not by turning the axis.   The latter operation does not change the direction of magnetism, while the former does.   Direction of magnetism is determined by the following rule:

"Looking at the face of an electromagnet (such as the field spool of a motor), a pole will be north if the current is flowing around it in a direction opposite to the motion of the hands of a watch" (Fig. 36) and south if in the same direction as the motion of the hands of a watch (see also the rules outlined in Div. 1).

Another method of determining whether the magnetism of the poles is correct is to use two ordinary nails, their lengths depending upon the distance between pole tips. The point of one nail should touch one pole tip, the point of the other nail the other pole tip, and the heads of nails should touch each other.

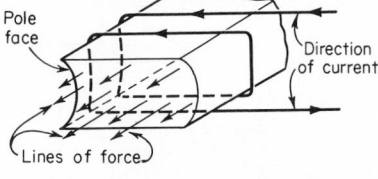

FIG. 36 *Direction of magnetism and current about a pole.*

When the current flows around the field spools, the polarity between any poles is properly related if the nails placed as suggested stick together by the magnetism. If there is no tendency to stick, the polarity of the two poles is alike and therefore wrong.

54. Open Field Circuit. If, on closing the field switch, no magnetism is obtained by trial with an iron key, as suggested above, there is an open circuit within one of the spools or in the wires leading to these spools. The open circuit can be located by shunting out one spool at a time and allowing current to flow through the rest until the defective spool is discovered. On a two-pole motor try first one spool and then the other. For a very short time, say, 10 min, double voltage can be carried on a spool. On a motor having four or more poles, three spools can always be left in circuit during the open-circuit investigations.

55. A method of locating an open-circuited field coil is illustrated in Fig. 37A. Connect one terminal of the voltmeter to one side of the field-coil circuit, and with the bared end of a wire or a contactor, successively touch the junctions of the field-coil leads around the frame. When the open coil is bridged, the voltmeter will show a full

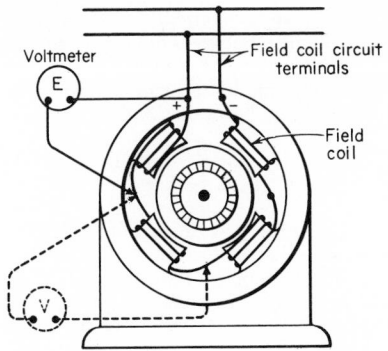

FIG. 37A *Locating field-coil troubles.*

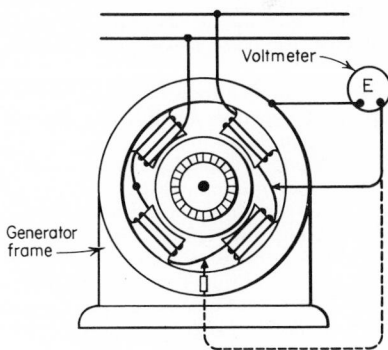

FIG. 37B *Locating grounded coil.*

deflection. Another way follows: Connect the field-coil circuit terminals to a source of voltage. Connect the voltmeter successively across each coil as indicated by the dotted lines in Fig. 37A. There will be no deflection on the voltmeter until the open coil is bridged, when the full voltage of the circuit will be indicated.

56. A grounded field coil can be located (Fig. 37B) by connecting a source of voltage to the machine terminals, having first raised the brushes from the commutator, if it is a d-c machine. Connect one terminal of the voltmeter to the frame and the other to a lead with a bared end. Tap exposed parts of the field circuit with the bared end of the lead. The voltmeter deflection will be least near the grounded coil.

57. Heating of Field Coils (Westinghouse Instruction Book). Heating of field coils may develop from any of the following causes: (1) too low speed, (2) too high voltage,

(3) too great forward or backward lead of brushes, (4) partial short circuit of one coil, and (5) overload.

58. Direct-current armatures can be tested for the common troubles with the arrangement of Fig. 38. Terminals b and c are clamped to the commutator at points displaced 180 electrical degrees from each other and connected with a source of steady current through an adjustable resistance and an ammeter. For a two-pole machine the terminals b and c will be located at opposite sides of the commutator. The terminals of a low-reading voltmeter (a galvanometer can often be used) are connected to two bare metal points, which are separated, by a distance equal to the width of one commutator segment plus the width of one mica strip, by an insulating block j. In use, the current is adjusted to produce a convenient deflection of the voltmeter when each of the points rests on an adjacent bar. The points are moved around the commutator and bridged across the insulation between every two bars. If the voltmeter deflection is the same for every pair of bars, it indicates that there is no trouble in the armature.

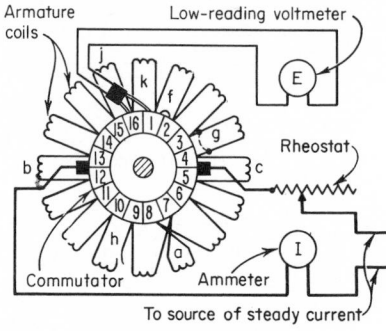

FIG. 38   *Method of testing an armature.*

59. Sparking Due to Open Armature Circuit. A cause of a sparking commutator is an open circuit in the winding, either in the armature body or, more often, where the lead from the armature winding is soldered to the commutator. In the latter case resoldering is a ready remedy. If, however, the location of the point of open circuit cannot be found, the bars can be bridged over on the commutator itself by fastening with solder, or otherwise, a strip of copper around the segments which indicate the break.

The indication of this trouble is very apparent, for, if an open circuit exists, the long heavy spark which accompanies it soon eats away the mica between the two segments which are on each side of the break. This shows positively where to bridge over. An open circuit also shows itself, when the machine is running, by the viciousness of the spark. It is unlike any other kind of commutator sparking, being heavy, long, and destructive in its action.

60. A poor connection between a bar and coil leads will cause a considerable deflection of the voltmeter (Fig. 38) when one of the points rests on the bar in trouble and the other rests on either of the adjacent bars.

61. An open-circuited coil, as h, Fig. 38, will prevent the flow of current through its half of the armature. There will be no deflection on that half of the armature until the "open" is bridged. Then the voltage of the testing circuit will be indicated.

62. Tests for Open Armature Circuits. Another method (Fig. 39A) is to apply to the commutator, at two opposite points, a low voltage, say from a battery or a dynamo with its voltage kept low. Place an ammeter in circuit and clean the surface of the commutator so that it is bright and smooth.

The terminal ends leading the current into and out of the commutator should be small, so that each rests only on a single segment (Fig. 39A). Note the ammeter reading and rotate the armature slowly. At the point where the open circuit exists, the ammeter needle will go to zero if the leads to the commutator bar have become entirely open-circuited. This is because the segment is attached to the winding through the commutator leads.

If the armature does not show the above symptoms, try connecting a low-reading voltmeter or a galvanometer to two adjacent segments while the current is passing through the armature as described from some external low-voltage source (Fig. 39B). Note the deflection. Pass from segment to segment in this manner, recording the drop between the successive pairs of bars. This drop, if the current is held constant from the external source, should be the same between each pair of adjacent segments. If any pair shows a higher drop than the others near it, a higher-resistance connection

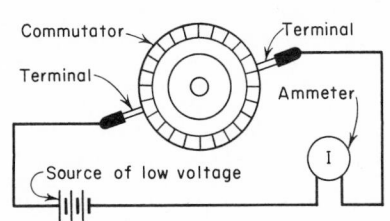
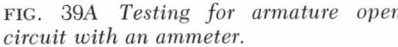

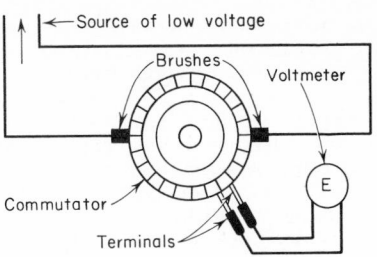

FIG. 39A *Testing for armature open circuit with an ammeter.*

FIG. 39B *Testing for armature open circuit with a voltmeter.*

exists there, perhaps causing sparking and biting of commutator insulation, to a less degree, to be sure, than with an actual open circuit, but enough, perhaps, to cause the trouble requiring the investigation.

63. The test for armature short circuits can be made as indicated in Fig. 39B. It is called a bar-to-bar test. It is most valuable in locating faults in armatures. It is the method to use if a short circuit from one segment to another is suspected. When the section in which the short circuit or partial short circuit exists comes under the contacts, a low or perhaps no deflection is shown on the galvanometer or voltmeter, thus locating the defective place. Such short circuits, if they occur when running, owing to defective insulation, burn out the coil short-circuited. When the coil passes through the active field in front of the pole piece, an immense current is induced in it, causing a destruction of the insulation. When this occurs, the coil should be open-circuited and bridged over, as suggested in a preceding paragraph, until a new coil can be inserted.

64. If two bars or a coil is short-circuited as at *f* or *g*, Fig. 38, respectively, there will be little or no voltmeter deflection when the two bars connecting to the "short circuit" are bridged by the points.

65. A grounded armature coil can be detected in the same manner as indicated in Fig. 39A for a field coil. Impress a low voltage on the terminals clamped to the commutator. Ground one side of the voltmeter on the shaft or spider, and touch a lead connected to the other side to all the bars in succession. The minimum deflection will obtain when the bars connecting to the grounded coil are touched.

66. Crossed coil leads as at *a* (Fig. 38) are indicated by a twice normal deflection when the points bridge the bars 6 and 7 to which the crossed coils should rightly connect. The crossing of the coil leads connects two coils in series between the adjacent commutator segments and, hence, causes twice normal drop.

67. Reversed Armature Coil. Instead of the armature winding progressing uniformly around from bar to bar of the commutator, there may at some point be a coil connected in backward. Such a reversed coil often causes bad sparking. One way to locate such a trouble is to pass a current through the armature at opposite points on the commutator. Then with a compass explore around the armature the direction of magnetism from slot to slot. If a coil is reversed when the compass comes before it, the needle will reverse, giving a very definite indication of the improperly connected coil.

68. Heating of Armature (Westinghouse Instruction Book). Excessive heating of the armature may develop from any of the following causes: (1) too great a load, (2) a partial short circuit of two coils heating the two particular coils affected, and (3) short circuits or grounds on armature or commutator.

69. Hot Armature Coils. Sometimes when a new machine is started, local heating occurs in the armature, following the exact shape of the armature coil. This may be because, in receiving its final turning off, the commutator bars were bridged with copper from one segment to another by the action of the turning tool. An examination of the commutator surface will reveal this bridging. When it is removed, satisfactory operation will ensue if the trouble has not gone too far and seriously injured the insulation of the coil.

70. Care of Commutators. They should be kept smooth by the occasional use of No. 00 sandpaper. A small quantity of Vaseline should be used as a lubricant. The lubricant should be applied to high-voltage generators by aid of a piece of cloth attached to the end of a dry stick. If the commutator gets "out of true," it should be turned down (refer to Sec. **77**). Inspect the commutator surface carefully to see that the copper has not been burned over from segment to segment in the mica, and remove by a scraper any particles of copper which may be found embedded in the mica. Keep oil away from the mica end rings of the commutator, as oily mica will soon burn out and ground the machine.

71. Process of Commutation and Correction of Glowing and Pitting. The path of the current is as shown in Fig. 40. A is the carbon brush; C, C', C'' are the commutator segments; B, B', B'' are the windings of the armature. At the position shown, coil B is short-circuited by the carbon, the current passing into the face of the brush and out again as shown by the dotted line. This local current may be many times larger than the normal flow of current and is the one that causes pitting.

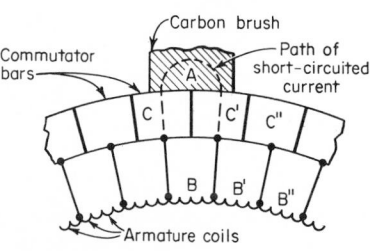

FIG. 40 *Armature coil short-circuited when commutating.*

With perfect commutation, with no sparking or glowing, there should be created in the short-circuited coil under the brush, by means of the flux from that pole tip away from which the armature is revolving, an emf. This should be just large enough to reverse the current within the short-circuited coil and to render it equal to the current in the winding proper. Since on one side of the brush the current is in one direction and on the other side in the other direction, the act of commutation beneath the brush is to reverse this current and bring it up to the correct amount in the opposite direction.

With copper brushes this reversal of current must be very accurately effected. With carbon brushes there is a much smaller tendency to spark; hence they will stand a certain inexactness of commutation adjustment. Experiments indicate that the carbon can resist as much as 3 volts creating current in the wrong direction and still not spark or glow. This is the property that has caused the use of carbon brushes instead of copper on most apparatus. When, however, this potential, induced in the wrong direction, rises above 3 volts during the passage of the armature coil underneath the brush, trouble from sparking and glowing occurs.

This is the reason that, in a motor, the brushes are pulled backward as far as possible at no load, so that the coil short-circuited by the brush can enter the fringe of flux from the pole tip, thus creating the proper reversal of current during the time the coil is passing under the brush. Since adjacent poles are opposite in polarity, only one can provide the proper flux direction for this reversal. In a motor it is always the pole behind the brush, and thus the brush requires a backward lead. In a generator it is the pole ahead of the brush in the direction of rotation. Hence generators require a forward lead.

If the motor gives trouble from glowing and pitting, the cause is probably this induced current, and the remedy is, first, to see that the lead of the brushes brings them in the most satisfactory position. If no change of lead or brush position can be found which will eliminate the trouble, the width of the brush must be changed. The wider the brush, the longer the coil suffers short circuit, as described. Conversely, the narrower the brush, the sooner the current must be reversed. There is, therefore, a width of brush which best satisfies both conditions.

Usually, however, where glowing occurs, the cause is too wide a brush, and often serious trouble from this cause can be entirely eliminated by varying the width of the brush perhaps only ⅛ in.

72. Sparking Due to Rough Commutator. First, the commutator surface may not be perfectly smooth after receiving its last turnoff. The work may have been poorly done by the manufacturer, with the result that the commutator surface, instead of being left smooth, is somewhat rough. The result of this, especially with high-speed commutators, is that the brush does not make first-class contact with the commutator surface. It may chatter with attending noise, and thus with many motors (especially those of high voltage) the operation will be attended with sparking. As a result, the commutator surface, instead of becoming bright and smooth with time, becomes rough and dull or raw in appearance. Under these conditions the brushes do not make good contact, and hence, the heat generated even under proper commutator conditions, owing to the resistance of brush contact, is multiplied several times, with consequent increase of temperature of the commutator. In addition, the friction of brush contact (which should give a coefficient of 0.2) is, with a rough commutator, much higher than it should be, which tends to increase the temperature.

73. Heating of commutator (Westinghouse Instruction Book) may develop from any of the following causes: (1) overload, (2) sparking at the brushes, (3) too high brush pressure, and (4) lack of lubrication on commutator.

74. Hot Commutator. All this trouble (Sec. 72) is cumulative. The result is that finally the temperature will rise to a point where the solder in the commutator will melt, perhaps short-circuiting or open-circuiting the winding. A commutator will stand very slight sparking, but where it is noticeable and where it is continued for long periods of time, trouble is apt to result. Where the load is usually very light on a motor, and where full load or overload are infrequent, a smoothing of the commutator occurs during the light-load period, which averts trouble. This is the reason that certain railway motors, which sometimes show sparking under their normal hour-rating load, give satisfaction as to commutation. The coasting of the car smooths up the imperceptible damage done by the sparking during the heavy load.

75. Loose Commutator Segments. A further and more serious cause of sparking and commutator trouble is due to the fact that the commutator may not be "settled" when shipped by the manufacturer. A commutator is made of many parts (Fig. 41) insulated one from another and all bound together by mechanical clamping arrangements. The segments themselves are held by a clamp ring on each end, which must be insulated from them and should hold each segment individually from any movement relative to another.

Since the clamp must touch and hold down all segments, a failure to do so in any case results in a loose bar, which moves relatively to the next bar and causes roughness and thus sparking, with all its attendant accumulative troubles.

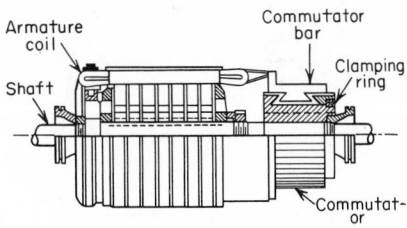

FIG. 41   *Section of d-c motor armature.*

The roughness of commutators due to poor turning or to poor design is shown uniformly over all the surface of the commutator on which brushes rest. A roughness due to a high or loose bar is shown by local trouble near the bad bar and its corresponding bars around the commutator. The jump of the brush occurs at the high bar and is the cause of the sparking (see also Secs. 76 and 78).

76. Blackening of the Commutator. Sparking due to a loose or high bar causes a local blackening instead of a uniform blackening, which occurs in case of poor design or poor commutator surface resulting from poor turning. Also, if the speed of the commutator is low enough, there will be a spark at the time the bad segment passes the brush. At ordinary speeds, or where there are several loose bars, the sparking in appearance will not be different from that due to poor design or poor turning. In such a case an examination of the commutator surface must be made to identify the cause.

It must be remembered that the slightest movement of a bar, especially with the higher voltage and high-commutator-speed machines, may cause the trouble. A splendidly designed motor may show very poor operation, owing to a commutator fault.

77. Grinding Commutators (Westinghouse Electric Corp.). When a commutator has to be resurfaced, this should always be done with a grinding rig, whether it is to be ground concentric or in order to remove high bars or flat spots. A hand stone should never be used on a commutator to obtain a true surface, because it simply follows the irregularities in the surface and in some cases may even exaggerate them. The grinding rig consists of an abrasive stone set up similarly to a lathe tool in a rigging or carriage which may be moved back and forth in an axial direction and may be equipped with a radial feed. It should be supported very rigidly so that the stone is subjected to a very minimum of vibration. In large d-c equipment, such a rigging can be mounted on a brush arm by removing the brush holders on that arm. In some cases, it may even be desirable to brace the brush-holder bracket arm while grinding, to obtain maximum rigidity. It is also possible by removing the brush rigging to support the grinder on parallels supported from the bedplate.

Grinding should be done when the machine is running in its own bearings and at rated speed in the case of a constant-speed machine. If grinding is done at low speed, any slight unbalance will cause the commutator to run eccentric at rated speed.

Great care must be exercised to prevent copper and stone dust from entering the windings. The grinding rig should be equipped with a vacuum-cleaner arrangement, fitted over the stone to catch all dust. If a suction system is not available, the necks of the commutator and the front end windings should be protected by pasting heavy paper over them or by covering with a cloth hood properly applied.

A simple, effective and inexpensive device for collecting dust during the grinding of commutators and collectors is illustrated in Fig. 42 and can be made from three small

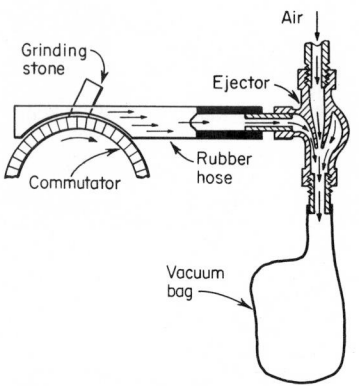

pieces of equipment, namely, (1) a 4-ft length of 1½-in. rubber hose, (2) a vacuum bag from a household vacuum cleaner, and (3) a small ejector which can either be purchased or improvised from a 1½-in. Y pipe fitting.

At one end of the rubber hose cut away, in the form of a long arc, the bottom and about half of the side walls to fit the radius of the commutator or ring to be ground. Cut a hole in the hose in the middle of the remaining arc portion to fit the grinding stone. Fit the hose to the stone and commutator or ring so as to form an enclosure or "shoe" around the grinding surface to collect the dust. Attach the other end of the hose to the intake of the ejector. Attach the vacuum bag to the exhaust of the ejector. Use compressed air from a shop air line to produce the suction.

FIG. 42 *Method of commutator grinding, showing dust collector. (Westinghouse Electric Corp.)*

The stones used in grinding commutators might be classed as rough, medium, and fine. The rough stone has a grit of about 80 mesh and is used only where a very large amount of copper is to be removed. It should be used very seldom, because, if sufficient copper is to be removed to warrant its use, it would be better to take a cut off the surface in a lathe. The medium stone has a grit of about 120 mesh and is used for the bulk of the grinding work, the fine stone being used only to obtain a fine finish. The fine stone should have a grit of about 200 mesh.

After grinding, all commutator slots should be cleaned out thoroughly and the edges of the bars beveled. This beveling accomplishes two things. It removes the burrs caused by the stone dragging copper over the slots and eliminates the sharp edge at the entering side of the bar under a brush. The bevel on the bars is done with a special beveling tool and should be about 1/32 in. chamfer at 45 deg, for medium thickness of bars. For thinner or wider bars, the beveling can be changed accordingly.

Practically all up-to-date machines have undercut mica. This undercutting should be kept 1/16 in. deep ± 1/64 in. If it is apparent that enough copper is going to be removed by grinding so that the undercutting will be shallow, the commutator should be re-undercut before grinding. This is done by means of a small circular high-speed saw about 0.003 in. thicker than the nominal thickness of the mica. In undercutting, great care must be taken to see that a thin sliver of mica is not left against one side of the slot. Sometimes this sliver must be removed by scraping by hand.

After grinding, undercutting the mica, and beveling the edges of the bars, the commutator surface should be polished, while operating at rated speed. Aloxite or sandpaper should first be used (never emery cloth or paper) as this will remove the burrs due to beveling. After a very fine grade of sandpaper is used, a high polish can be obtained by burnishing the commutator with dense felt or canvas. A further improvement of the surface can even be secured if a small amount of light oil is applied to the canvas during the polishing.

78. Loose Commutator Clamp Rings. First, draw the clamps of the commutator down firm, so that when the commutator is at normal temperature, the clamping rings cannot be screwed down farther without excessive effort. This is necessary so that all the bars may have a direct pressure from the clamp, rendering impossible any movement up or down. Second, after having drawn the clamps down, smooth off the surface of the commutator.

To get the clamps down firm, run the motor; if roughness appears, shut down at a convenient time, and, while hot, tighten the clamping rings. If it is found that the tightening bolts can be screwed up somewhat, the machine should again be put in service for at least 4 hr. At the end of this time shut it down again and make another trial on the tightening bolts. Now, if no more can be taken up on the tightening bolts, the commutator should be surfaced, either by turning with a tool or by grinding. If the clamps are down tight and the surface of the commutator has been properly smoothed, there will be no further trouble.

79. The Slotting of Commutators (Alan Bennett, *American Machinist*, Sept. 26, 1912). There seems to be a prevalent idea that slotting should cure all commutator troubles, irrespective of their causes. This is not true, but slotting is a cure for certain specific troubles. Where the peripheral speed of the commutator is so slow that the dirt which may collect in the slots between commutator bars will not be thrown out by centrifugal force, slotting may aggravate rather than correct commutation difficulties (see Sec. **83**).

80. The principal reason for slotting commutators is to relieve the commutators of high mica, i.e., mica that projects above the surface. High mica is generally due to one of two causes: Either the mica is too hard and does not wear down at an equal rate with the copper, or the commutator does not hold the mica securely between the segments, allowing it to work out by the combined action of centrifugal force and the heating and cooling of the commutator.

It is evident that a commutator with a surface made irregular by projecting mica rotating at high speed under a brush must impart to the brush a vibratory action and thus impair the close contact that should exist between brush and commutator. The result is that sparking takes place more or less violently, depending on the condition of the commutator surface and the rate of speed.

This condition generally manifests itself after the machine has been running for some time and in many cases will account for the development of sparking which did not occur at the time of installation. Often a case of this kind is aggravated by increasing the brush tension, causing a still faster rate of wear of copper over mica, with an attendant increased heating of the commutator.

81. What Is Accomplished by Slotting. A harder brush can at times be used, with the idea of grinding off the mica and thus bringing it down to the commutator surface. Instead of the trouble being cured, the commutator will, in the majority of cases, assume the raw appearance of being freshly sandpapered, instead of the glossy surface it should have, and both brush and commutator will wear rapidly.

This condition can be restored to normal and the commutator kept to a true surface by slotting, after which, with proper care and the use of proper brushes, commutator troubles will generally cease, provided the electrical design of the machine is not at fault. Even then there are cases that may be benefited to a certain extent by slotting, by reason of the good brush contact obtained. The majority of cases that show improvement are the ones in which the trouble is not inherent in the design of the machine but is due to mechanical causes.

With a slotted commutator it is possible to use a brush of fine grain and soft texture, inasmuch as there is not the same tendency to wear away the brush as with an unslotted commutator. The commutator will then take on the much-desired polish that is generally not possible with the harder brush. The life of both brush and commutator will be increased, and friction and the consequent heating will be reduced. These advantages will effect a saving that will more than offset the cost of slotting.

82. Various Methods of Slotting. There is a variety of slotting devices on the market (Figs. 43 to 47). Some operate with the armature swung between the centers of a lathe; others use a special tool in a shaper, with the armature secured to its bed. Still others are used by hand with the armature resting on blocks. In all cases the full width of the mica should be removed and the resulting slot carefully cleaned from burrs and rough edges. It is not necessary that the slotting be carried deeply in the commutator. One-sixteenth inch is generally considered sufficient (see also Sec. 77).

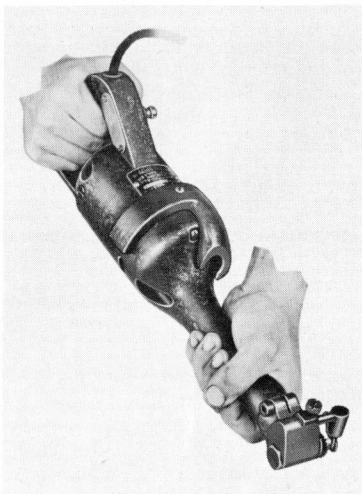

FIG. 43 *Hand-type mica miller. (The Martindale Electric Co.)*

83. A slotted commutator should have proper and frequent care, as there is a chance of small particles of copper being dragged across from bar to bar, and for dirt, oil, and carbon dust to accumulate in the slots and short-circuit the commutator.

84. High Mica in Commutators. Some motors, under certain conditions, roughen up their commutators after a short term of service, although there seems to be no excessive sparking under or at the edges of the brushes. This may occur even though the commutator has been well "settled." The commutator acts as if the mica used between bars to insulate the various segments, one from another, had protruded upward, causing roughness and excessive sparking.

Actual raising of the mica is a very rare occurrence, and if it occurs, it does so at certain spots and is easily and positively identified. An actual uniform protruding of mica all over a commutator, as described, is practically an unknown phenomenon. What actually does occur is an eating away of the copper surface of the commutator, leaving the high mica between the bars. A good machine will not spark enough to cause this condition. A poor machine will.

The phenomenon is easily identified, as the commutator surface looks raw all over instead of smooth and bright with a good brown gloss. If allowed to continue, a general roughness appears, accompanied by sparking, until finally the sparking and heating will increase so much that the machine may flash over from brush to brush, blowing the fuses or opening the circuit breakers. The trouble is aggravated if the motor operates continuously under heavy load. If there are periods of light load, the commutator has an opportunity to be smoothed down by the brushes. This condition is appreciated by

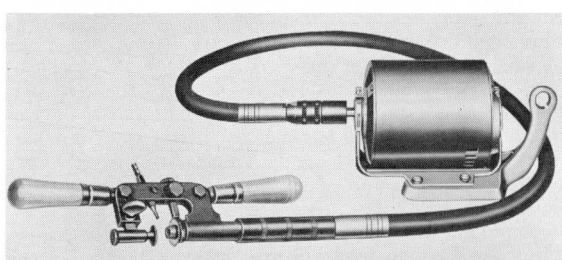

FIG. 44 *Suspension-type flexible-shaft undercutter. (The Martindale Electric Co.)*

FIG. 45 *Flexible-shaft undercutter in use on large generator. (The Martindale Electric Co.)*

railway motor designers. A railway motor coasts a considerable portion of the time. Thus the commutator is smoothed, neutralizing the roughening occurring under load.

85. To Remedy a Roughened High-mica Commutator. (1) Use it on work where the load is somewhat intermittent, (2) replace it altogether, or (3) slot the commutator. Then, as there are no longer two different materials to wear down or to be worn away by sparking, an unequal surface will not result. The mica need be cut down only 1/16 in., and a narrow, sharp chisel will do the work satisfactorily. No trouble will result from short circuiting in this case, since centrifugal force keeps the slots clean. Some manufacturers ship machines with slotted commutators.

86. Brush Troubles. When there is an excessive drop in speed from no load to full load, the position of the brushes on the commutator (Sec. **45**) should first be investigated. No brush position that causes sparking should be chosen. The following sections outline brush troubles and their remedies.

87. Sparking of the brushes may be due to one of the following causes (Westinghouse Instruction Book; see also Dynamo-defects Table): (1) The machine may be overloaded. (2) The brushes may not be set exactly at the point of commutation—a position can always be found where there is no perceptible sparking, and at this point the brushes should be set and secured. (3) The brushes may be wedged in the holders. (4) The brushes may not be fitted to the circumference of the commutator. (5) The brushes may not bear on the commutator with sufficient pressure. (6) The brushes may be burned on the ends. (7) The commutator may be rough; if so, it should be smoothed off. (8) A commutator bar may be loose or may project above the others. (9) The commutator may be dirty, oily, or worn out. (10) The carbon in the brushes may be unsuitable. (11) The brushes may not be equally spaced around the periphery of the commutator. (12) Some brushes may have extra pressure and may be taking more than their share of the current. (13) Mica may be high. (14) The brushes may be vibrating. (15) Brush toes may not be in line.

These are the more common causes, but sparking may be due to an open circuit or loose connection in the armature. This trouble is indicated by a bright spark which appears to pass completely around the commutator and can be recognized by the scarring of the commutator at the point of open circuit. If a lead from the armature winding to the commutator becomes loose or broken, it will draw a bright spark as the break passes the brush position. This trouble can be readily located, as the insulation on each side of the disconnected bar will be more or less pitted. The commutator should run smoothly and true, with a dark, glossy surface.

88. Glowing and Pitting of Carbon Brushes. This may be due to either of two causes: poor design or a wrong position of the brushes on the commutator. The error of design

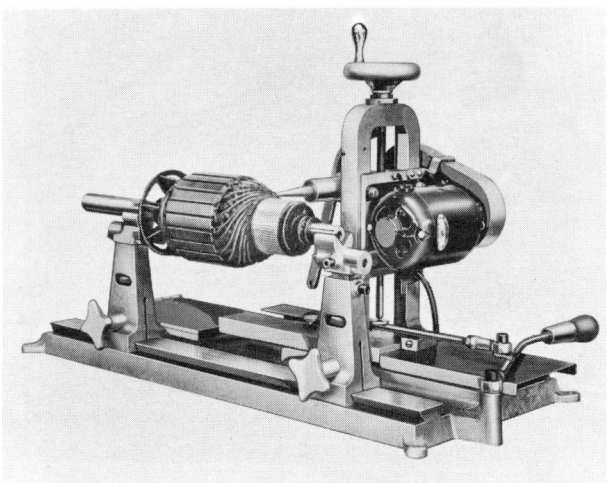

I. *Undercutting horizontal commutator.*

II. *Undercutting vertical commutator.*

FIG. 46 *Bench-type undercutter. (The Martindale Electric Co.)*

may be only in the choice of width of carbon brush used. The pitting is due to glowing. If the glowing is at the edge of the carbon it is plainly visible and easily located. It may, however, occur underneath the carbon, so that only with difficulty can it be seen. Such glowing pits the carbon face by heat disintegration. With some machines three-fourths of the brush face may be eaten away and the pits may be, perhaps, 1/4 to 1/2 in. deep when discovered. A usual (incorrect) decision is that the current per square inch of contact is too great, the calculation being made by dividing the *line amperes* by *the square-inch cross section of either the positive or the negative brushes.* If this calculation gives a value under 45 or 50, it is certain that the cause of the trouble has not been judged correctly.

The real cause of the glowing is, to be sure, excessive current through the carbon, but this is not the line current if the calculation, as stated, shows a brush-face density be-

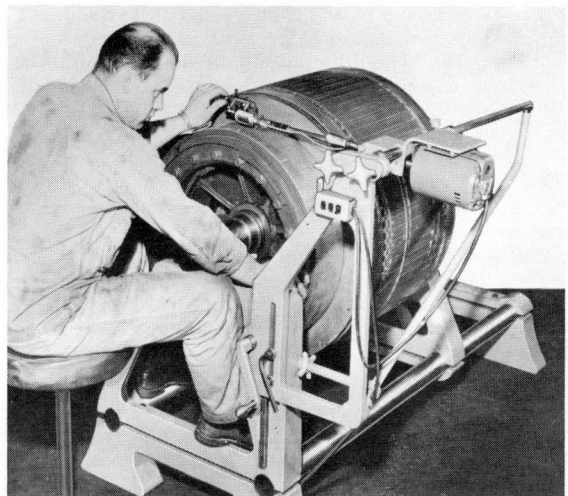

FIG. 47   *Shop-type undercutter. (The Martindale Electric Co.)*

low 50 amp per sq in.   It is a local current caused by the short circuiting of two or more segments of the commutator by the brush resting upon them.   The usual overlap of a carbon brush is about two segments, and while these two segments are under the brush, the armature coils connected to them are short-circuited.   If the design of the machine is such that the coil so short-circuited encloses stray flux from the pole tip, this flux will create in the short-circuited coil a current perhaps many times larger than the brush is capable of carrying, with the result that the glowing and pitting occurs.

89. Chattering of brushes is sometimes experienced on d-c machines.   Chattering under certain conditions may become so prominent as not only to be of annoyance but also actually to break the carbons.   An examination of the commutator will reveal no roughness, the surface being, perhaps, perfectly smooth and bright.   This trouble occurs principally with the type of brush holder which has a box guide for the carbon.   The spring which forces the brush into contact rests on top of the carbon, which has fairly free play in the box guide.   Chattering usually occurs with high-speed commutators, running at 4,000 to 5,000 ft per min peripheral speed.

Such brush holders are necessary on commutators which, like those on engine-driven machines, may run out of true on account of the shaft play in the bearings caused by the reciprocating motion of the engine.   The clamped type of holder is usually free from bad chattering but rocks on a commutator that runs out, causing poor contact and perhaps sparking.

Lubricating the commutator causes the chattering to disappear immediately, but there is no commutator compound which gives a lubricating effect lasting over possibly ½ hr.   Thus it is not practical to lubricate often enough to prevent the chattering.   There will be no chattering if the angle of the brush with the radial line, passing through the center of the carbon and the center of the commutator, is less than 10 deg and if the carbon trails on the commutator instead of leads.   Figure 48 shows the correct setting which will stop all serious chattering, together with two incorrect settings which may give trouble.

90. Low Speed.   The fault may be in the winding of the armature or field, in which case a remedy is difficult.   Considerable

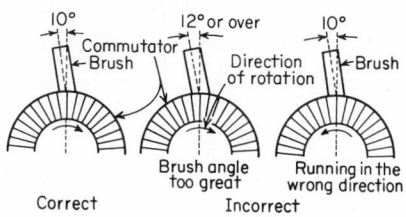

FIG. 48   *Methods of setting brushes.*

range of speed can be obtained by the choice of brush position on the commutator. For many motors a speed variation of 15 per cent can be obtained, without sparking, by brush shift. Therefore, if the discrepancy of speed is within this amount, the brushes should be moved to counteract it. A backward shift of brush gives increased speed, and a forward shift decreased speed. At any brush position, however, there must be practically no sparking. A first-class motor should run at full load within 4 per cent (up or down) of the nameplate speed if the voltage is as specified on the name plate. The speed at no load should not be more than 5 per cent higher than this; also the speed at full load, hot, should not be over 5 per cent greater than the speed at full load, cold.

91. Bearing Troubles of D-C Motors and Generators. See Troubles of A-C Motors and Generators, Sec. **236.**

92. Sporadic motor sparking has been known to occur on account of irregular short circuits on the line which were caused by the wind blowing the line wires together.

PRINCIPLES, CHARACTERISTICS, AND MANAGEMENT OF A-C GENERATORS (ALTERNATORS)

93. Types of A-C Generators. The different types of a-c generators (alternators), classified according to the method of producing the voltage, are listed below:

1. Synchronous alternators.
   a. Revolving field.
   b. Revolving armature.
2. Induction alternators.
   a. Stator winding is source of voltage.
   b. Rotor winding is source of voltage.
3. Inductor alternators.

94. Synchronous a-c generators are discussed in an elementary way in Secs. **73, 115, 144, 145, 148,** and **152** of Div. 1. These generators may be constructed with either the armature or the field structure as the revolving member. Small generators up to 50 kw are commonly made with the revolving-armature construction. Practically all other synchronous alternators employ the revolving-field construction. The required magnetic field is produced by d-c electromagnets, which are excited by a small d-c generator or exciter. The fundamental construction and connections for a revolving-field alternator are shown in Fig. 49.

95. The emf in a synchronous alternator is generated as suggested in Fig. 50. As each field coil, *D* for instance, sweeps past the armature coils, the lines of flux from the field coil cut the armature coils. As coil *D* passes from *A* to *C*, an alternating emf represented by the curve *ABC* will be generated in the armature. It should be under-

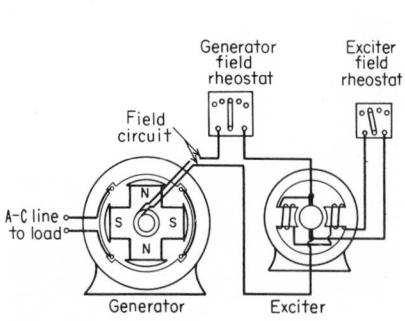

FIG. 49 *Elementary diagram of a-c generator and exciter.*

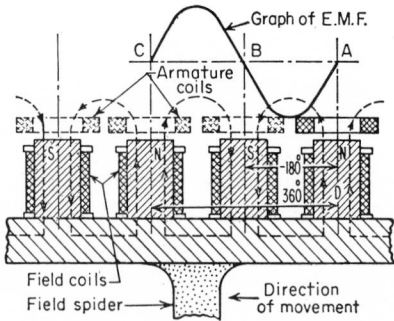

FIG. 50 *Armature and field structure developed.*

stood that in commercial alternators the armature coils are set in slots and differently arranged from that shown in Fig. 50, which only illustrates a principle.

The value of the voltage generated by a given synchronous alternator depends upon the speed and direct field current. Since the speed must be held constant in order to maintain the proper frequency, the voltage must be controlled by adjustment of the field current.

96. The speed and number of poles of an alternator determine the frequency which it generates.

$$f = \frac{p \times \text{rpm}}{120} \quad \text{or} \quad p = \frac{120f}{\text{rpm}} \quad \text{or} \quad \text{rpm} = \frac{120f}{p} \tag{1}$$

where $f =$ frequency in cycles per second, rpm = revolutions per minute of rotor, and $p =$ the number of field poles.

Example. What is the frequency of a two-pole alternator running at 3,600 rpm?
Solution. Substitute in the formula

$$f = \frac{p \times \text{rpm}}{120} = \frac{2 \times 3,600}{120} = \frac{7,200}{120} = 60 \text{ cycles per sec}$$

Example. How many poles has a 25-cycle alternator running to 500 rpm?
Solution. Substitute in the formula

$$p = \frac{120f}{\text{rpm}} = \frac{120 \times 25}{500} = \frac{3,000}{500} = 6 \text{ poles}$$

97. Synchronous Speeds—A-C Generators and Motors

Application to Generators. The table shows the speeds at which the rotor of an alternator which has a given number of field poles must turn to generate voltage at given frequencies.

Application to Motors. The table indicates the synchronous speed of the rotary magnetic field of an induction motor having a given number of poles and taking current at a given frequency.

The table also shows the speeds of synchronous motors having a given number of field poles and taking currents at given frequencies.

Number of poles	RPM when frequency is											
	25	30	33⅓	40	50	60	66⅔	80	100	120	125	133⅓
2	1,500	1,800	2,000	2,400	3,000	3,600	4,000	4,800	6,000	7,200	7,500	8,000
4	750	900	1,000	1,200	1,500	1,800	2,000	2,400	3,000	3,600	3,750	4,000
6	500	600	667	800	1,000	1,200	1,333	1,600	2,000	2,400	2,500	2,667
8	375	450	500	600	750	900	1,000	1,200	1,500	1,800	1,875	2,000
10	300	360	400	480	600	720	800	960	1,200	1,440	1,500	1,600
12	250	300	333	400	500	600	667	800	1,000	1,200	1,250	1,333
14	214	257	286	343	428	514	571	686	857	1,029	1,071	1,143
16	188	225	250	300	375	450	500	600	750	900	938	1,000
18	167	200	222	267	333	400	444	533	667	800	833	889
20	150	180	200	240	300	360	400	480	600	720	750	800
22	136	164	182	217	273	327	364	436	545	655	682	720
24	125	150	167	200	250	300	333	400	500	600	625	667
26	115	138	154	185	231	280	308	370	461	554	577	615
28	107	128	143	171	214	257	286	343	429	514	536	571
30	100	120	133	160	200	240	267	320	400	480	500	533
32	94	113	125	150	188	225	250	300	375	450	487	500
36	83	100	111	133	166	200	222	266	333	400	417	444
44	79	82	91	109	136	164	182	218	273	327	341	363
48	63	75	83	100	125	150	167	200	250	300	312	333
54	56	66	74	90	111	133	148	178	222	266	278	296
60	50	60	67	80	100	120	133	160	200	240	250	266
68	44	53	59	71	88	106	118	141	176	212	221	235
72	42	50	55	67	83	100	111	133	166	200	208	222
96	31	38	42	50	64	75	82	100	125	150	156	167
100	30	36	40	48	60	72	80	96	120	120	150	160

98. Single-phase Alternators. The circumferential distance from the center line of one pole to the center line of the next pole of the same polarity constitutes 360 electrical degrees. See Fig. 50 which shows how a single-phase emf is generated. Figure 49 is a diagrammatic illustration of a single-phase alternator, and Fig. 51 shows, diagrammatically, two different kinds of single-phase windings. Single-phase alternators are seldom made now, except for emergency or standby power.

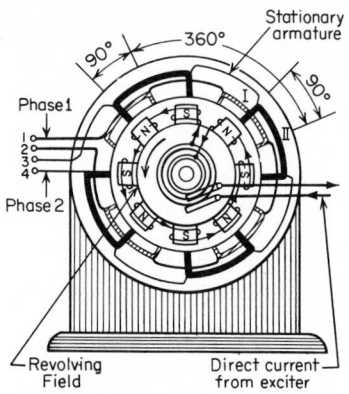

99. Two-phase Alternator. In a generator of the type indicated in Fig. 52, the centers of the

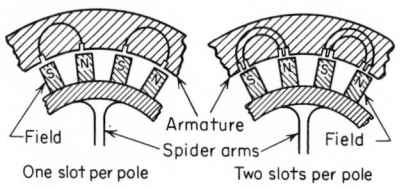

FIG. 51   *Single-phase armature windings.*

FIG. 52   *Diagram for two-phase alternator.*

two component coils I and II are situated 90 electrical degrees apart, and the single-phase emfs generated in coils I and II by the passage of the field system past them differ in phase by 90 degrees. This property has given rise to the term quarter-phase for this type of machine, but it is more frequently called a two-phase machine. The emf in coil I is zero when that in coil II is a maximum, and vice versa. The curves of emf in coils I and II can be plotted as indicated in Fig. 53. Figure 54 shows two methods of connecting the armature windings of two-phase alternators. The armature coils can be arranged in one or more slots per pole per phase, as diagrammatically suggested in Fig. 55. In commercial machines the windings are almost always arranged in more than one slot per pole. (See Div. 1 for further information in regard to two-phase currents.)

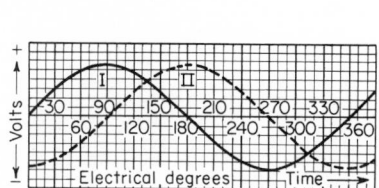

FIG. 53   *Graphs of two-phase current.*

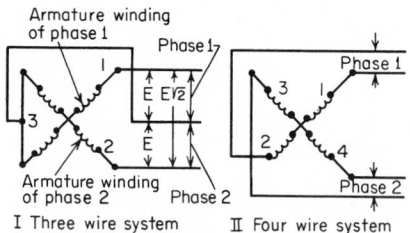

FIG. 54   *Methods of connecting two-phase generator armature windings.*

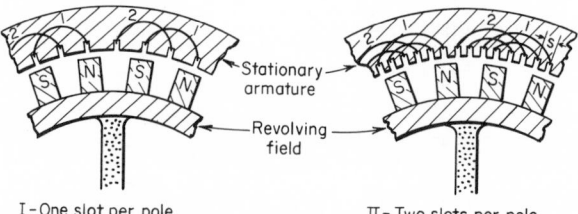

FIG. 55   *Two-phase armature windings.*

100. Three-phase alternator coils are arranged as illustrated in Fig. 58, and the curves of instantaneous emf are displaced from one another by 120 electrical degrees as indicated in Fig. 57. These curves also represent the emfs for the winding shown diagrammatically by coils I, II, and III in Fig. 56. Here three coils are distributed (60 electrical degrees apart) over a pole pitch, and the phase displacement between the emfs is 60 degrees. However, if in connecting the coils the middle coil is connected in the reverse

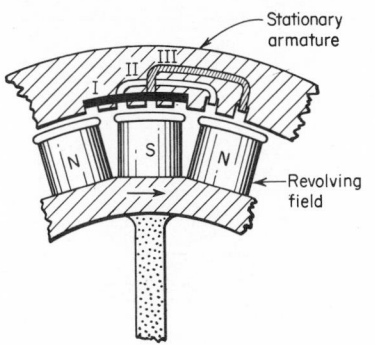

FIG. 56 *Six-phase grouping.*

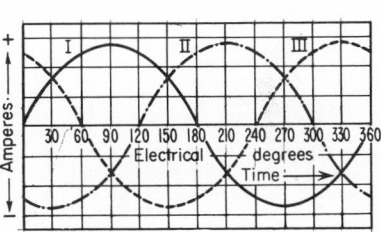

FIG. 57 *Graphs of three-phase currents.*

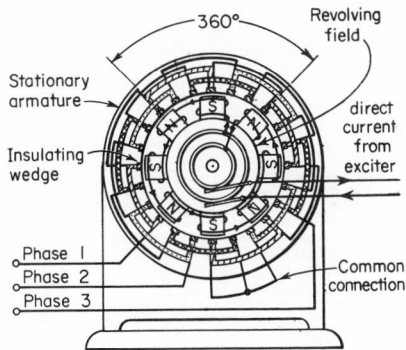

FIG. 58 *Diagram for three-phase Y-connected alternator.*

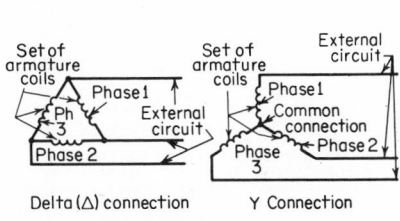

FIG. 59 *Methods of connecting three-phase armature coils.*

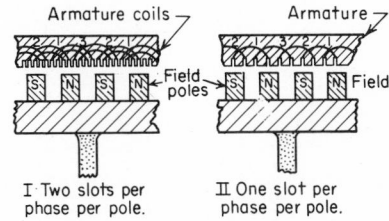

FIG. 60 *Three-phase armature windings.*

sense from the other two, the result will be three voltages 120 electrical degrees apart, as shown in Fig. 57.

The two methods of connecting three-phase armature windings are shown in Fig. 59. These methods are discussed in more detail in Div. 1. Armature windings can be arranged in one or more slots per pole per phase (Fig. 60). The Y method of connection is almost always used for three-phase generators.

101. Approximate Performance Values of A-C Generators
208Y/120, 240, 480Y/277, 480, 600, and 2,400 volts; three-phase

It should be understood that values will vary somewhat with speed and other conditions. Those given are general and approximate only and do not apply to any particular manufacturer's line.

A slow-speed machine is assumed to be one turning at from 100 to 200 rpm; a medium-speed machine, one turning at from 200 to 300 rpm; and a high-speed machine, one turning at from 300 to 1,200 rpm. In the table, S indicates slow speed, M medium speed, and H high speed.

Output, kva		Current				Efficiency			Exciter capacity required
		Three-phase							
		208Y/120, 240 volts	480Y/277, 480 volts	600 volts	2,400 volts	½ load	¾ load	Full load	
50	S M H	120.3	60.1	48.0	12.0	85.5[a] 86.6	88.0[a] 89.8	89.0[a] 90.8	7.0 2.0
75	S M H	180.4	90.2	72.2	18.0	88.0[a] 87.1	90.0[a] 89.7	91.3[a] 90.8	8.0 3.0
100	S M H	240.6	120.3	96.2	24.1	89.0[a] 87.7	91.0[a] 90.2	92.0[a] 91.3	9.0 3.0
125	S M H	301.0	150.0	120.0	30.1	91.0[a] 90.1	92.0[a] 91.7	92.5[a] 92.7	9.0 5.0
150	S M H	360.8	180.4	144.3	36.1	90.5[a] 91.0 90.2	91.7[a] 92.0[a] 91.8	92.2[a] 93.0[a] 92.8	14.0 9.0 4.5
200	S M H	481.1	241.6	192.4	48.1	90.7[a] 91.0 90.1	92.3[a] 93.0[a] 92.7	93.4[a] 93.5[a] 93.5	12.0 11.0 6.0
300	S M H	723.0	362.0	289.0	72.0	91.0[a] 92.0[a] 89.2	93.0[a] 93.5[a] 92.1	93.5[a] 94.2[a] 93.2	20.0 15.0 12.0
400	S M H	962.0	481.0	385.0	96.2	92.0[a] 92.0[a] 90.2	93.0[a] 94.0[a] 92.3	94.0[a] 94.5[a] 93.8	23.0 14.0 12.0
500	S M H	1,203.0	602.0	481.0	120.0	92.5[a] 91.8 90.8	94.0[a] 93.5 93.5	94.5[a] 94.4 94.5	23.0 16.0 13.0
600	S M H	1,450.0	722.0	578.0	144.0	92.5[a] 92.4 90.0	94.0[a] 94.1 92.4	94.5[a] 94.8 93.8	28.0 22.0 20.0
700	S M H	1,690.0	841.0	673.0	168.0	93.0[a] 91.8 90.0	94.0[a] 94.1 92.5	94.6[a] 95.0 94.0	35.0 24.0 20.0
800	S M H	1,930.0	977.0	773.0	193.0	92.8[a] 92.1 91.5	94.5[a] 94.0 93.0	95.3[a] 95.0 94.0	32.0 23.0 17.0
1,000	S M H	2,406.0	1,203.0	962.0	241.0	93.0[a] 92.3 92.5	94.0[a] 94.2 94.0	94.8[a] 95.0 94.6	35.0 29.0 25.0
1,250	S M H	3,000.0	1,500.0	1,200.0	300.0	93.5[a] 92.5 92.0	94.5[a] 94.6 94.2	95.7[a] 95.5 95.3	38.0 30.0 26.0
1,500	S M H	3,640.0	1,804.0	1,443.0	361.0	93.6[a] 92.2 93.0	94.7[a] 94.4 95.1	95.4[a] 95.5 95.9	42.0 38.0 22.0
2,000	S M H	4,850.0	2,420.0	1,924.0	481.0	94.0[a] 92.6 92.3	95.0[a] 94.8 94.7	95.8[a] 95.8 95.7	50.0 42.0 38.0

[a] Engine-type machines: efficiencies do not include friction of bearings.

102. Exciters for a-c generators are compound-wound d-c generators, flat-compounded and rated at 125 volts for the smaller sizes of generators and at 250 volts for the larger sizes. The systems of excitation which are in general use are:

1. Individual exciter for each generator unit.
   a. Direct-connected to the alternator shaft.
   b. Belt-connected to the alternator shaft.
   c. Brushless type with integral rectifiers.
2. Exciter-bus system supplied by one of the following combinations:
   a. Induction-motor-driven exciters and steam-driven exciters.
   b. Induction-motor-driven exciters and hydraulic-turbine-driven exciters.
   c. Built-in rectifiers, solid state.

The individual exciter unit (Fig. 61) has the advantage of rapid response at time of system short circuits or rapid fluctuations in load. It also has a high efficiency due to being driven by the highly efficient prime mover of the generator and due to eliminating the loss in a generator field rheostat, since the generator voltage is controlled through variation of the field current of the exciter. The direct connection to the generator shaft is used for 1,200-, 1,800-, and 3,600-rpm alternators. The belt connection is ordinarily used for slower speed alternators so that a cheaper, higher speed exciter (usually 1,800 rpm) can be used.

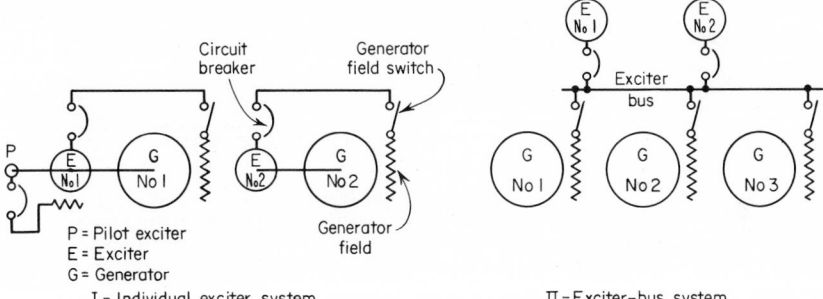

FIG. 61 *Systems of excitation for a-c generators.*

The exciter-bus system (Fig. 61) has the advantages of not crippling the alternator because of trouble with the exciter and of keeping closer voltage regulation in cases where the prime mover driving the alternator is subject to speed variations. With this system at least two of the exciters should be steam or hydraulic driven so as to ensure being able to start the plant up after a shutdown.

Since failure of the excitation power will of necessity produce a failure of the a-c generation and possible shutdown of the station, it follows that the exciter system should be made as reliable as possible. With the exciter-bus system there should be at least one or two spare exciter units. In some plants, for extreme reliability a storage battery is floated on the exciter bus to ensure continuity of the d-c excitation. Induction motors should be used for driving the exciters, because they can be started rapidly and will not fall out of step during voltage fluctuations caused by short circuits on the system.

Frequently with the individual-exciter system, pilot exciters are used to supply the field of the main exciter. This adds to the rapidity of response to voltage fluctuations.

103. Synchronizing. Two or more a-c generators will not operate satisfactorily in parallel unless (1) their voltages, as registered by a voltmeter, are the same; (2) their frequencies are the same; (3) their voltages are in phase. If the machines are not in phase, even if their indicated voltages and their frequencies are the same, the voltage of one will, at given instants, be different from that of the other and there will be an interchange of current between the machines. When two or more generators all satisfy the three above requirements, they are in synchronism. Synchronizing is the operation of getting machines into synchronism. Incandescent lamps or instruments are, as described in other paragraphs, used for indicating when machines are in synchronism.

104. Synchronizing a Single-phase Circuit with Lamps. The elementary principle involved in determining synchronism is indicated in Fig. 62. If the voltage and frequency of generators A and B are the same and the machines are in phase, point a will be at the same potential at every instant as will point a'. Hence the lamps between a and a' will not light so long as the three conditions are satisfied. So long as the conditions are not satisfied there will be a fluctuating cross current from a to a' and a constant fluctuating of the brilliancy of the incandescent lamps. When the lamps become dark and remain so, the generators are in synchronism and may be thrown together. Had the

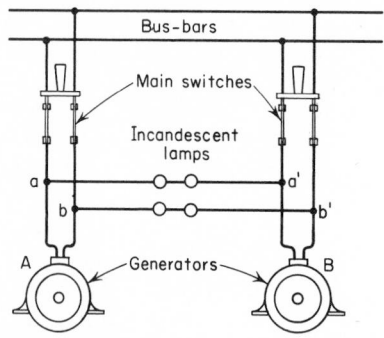

FIG. 62 *Circuits for synchronizing with lamps.*

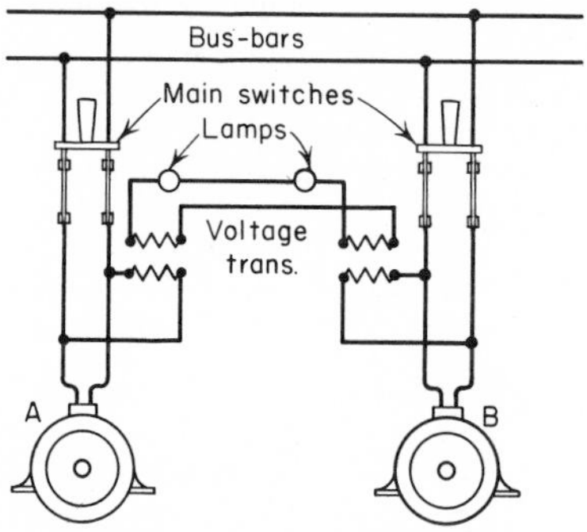

FIG. 63 *Circuits for synchronizing high-voltage circuits with lamps.*

connection at a' been made to the b' generator lead, the lamps would be bright when the generators were in synchronism, but for reasons outlined in another paragraph the connection shown, which provides the dark-lamp method of synchronizing, is preferred. The same conditions occur in the b—b' set of lamps as in the a—a' set. A voltmeter of proper rating can be substituted for the lamps.

Where the voltage generated is so high that it is not desirable to connect a sufficient number of lamps in series for it, a single lamp fed through voltage transformers can be used for synchronizing, as suggested in Fig. 63.

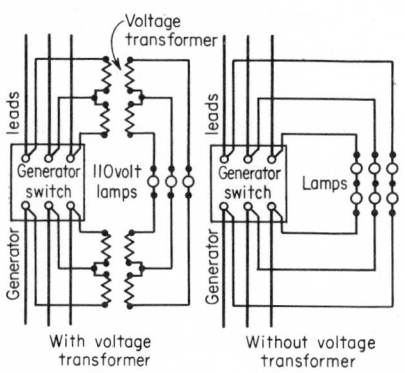

FIG. 64 *Connections for phasing-out three-phase circuits.*

105. Phasing-out Three-phase Circuits. Before connecting the leads, from a polyphase generator that is to operate in parallel with others, to the generator switch, the circuits must be "phased-out"; i.e., the leads must be so arranged that each lead from the generator will, when the generator switch is thrown, connect to the corresponding lead of the other generator. If this is not arranged, there may be considerable damage done, owing to an interchange of current when the two machines are in parallel. After once phasing-out it is necessary to synchronize but one phase of the machine with the corresponding phase of the other machine.

Connections for phasing-out three-phase circuits are shown in Fig. 64. If voltage transformers are not used, the sum of the voltages of the lamps in each line should be approximately the same as the voltage of the circuits. On 440-volt circuits, two 220-volt or four 110-volt lamps should be used in each phasing-out lead.

To phase-out, run the two machines at about synchronous speed. If the lamps do not all become bright and dark together, interchange any two of the main leads on one side of the switch, leaving the lamps connected to the same switch terminals, after which the lamps should all fluctuate together, which indicates that the connections are correct. The machines are in phase when all the lamps are dark.

106. The synchronizing connections for three-phase generators are shown in Fig. 65. A synchronizing plug can be used instead of the single-pole synchronizing switch shown. The illustration indicates the connections used where machines are to be synchronized to a bus. Where only two machines are to be synchronized, the connections are the same as shown in Fig. 65, except that the bus transformer and the corresponding lamp are omitted and one plug is required instead of two.

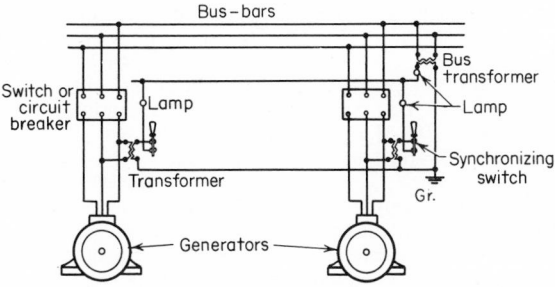

FIG. 65   *Connections for synchronizing three-phase circuits where transformers are required.*

107. Synchronizing Dark or Light. Synchronizing dark appears to be the preferable method. All the connections shown are for "synchronizing dark." When the lamps are "dark," the machines are in phase, and it is necessary to close the switch when the pulsation is the slowest obtainable or ceases altogether, i.e., at or just before the middle of the longest dark period.

Should a filament break, the synchronizing lamps would remain dark and thus apparently indicate synchronism and possibly cause an accident. Therefore it is considered desirable by some to reverse the synchronizing circuit connections and thereby synchronize "light." Synchronizing light eliminates the danger due to the breaking of a filament but has the disadvantage that the time of greatest brilliancy is difficult of determination. The "light" period is relatively long compared with the dark period, so that synchronizing light is usually considered the more difficult, and were it not that with the "synchronizing-light" method the danger due to filament breakage is eliminated, the method would never be used.

The probability of a filament breaking just at the time of approaching synchronism and when the machines are not in phase is remote. If it occurs at any other time in the operation, it will be noticed. As a protection against accidents due to breakage, two synchronizing lamps should always be placed in multiple.

108. The number of lamps to use in a group to indicate synchronism is determined by the voltage of the generators. With high-voltage circuits it is not feasible to use a sufficient number of lamps, so a transformer is employed that has a secondary voltage of 110 volts. See the diagrams. The greatest voltage impressed on the lamps is double that of one generator or the secondary voltage of one transformer. Thus the maximum voltage on the lamps where two 220-volt generators are being synchronized is 440 volts. The dark period can be shortened by impressing a voltage higher than their normal on the lamps. For two 220-volt machines, for example, three 110-volt lamps might be used, but the life of the lamps would be greatly reduced.

109. A synchroscope (see Fig. 66) is an instrument that indicates the difference in phase and frequency between two alternators. It shows whether the machine to be synchronized is running fast or slow. The pointer rotates clockwise if the machine is running fast and counterclockwise if it is running slow. When the pointer remains stationary pointing upward, the machines are in synchronism. It is quite common to use two synchronizing lamps in addition to a synchroscope, so that one system is a check against the failure of the other. Should the lamps remain dark for any greater length of time than a few seconds, the operator should look for trouble in either the lamps or the connections. After the main switches have been thrown, thus connecting the machines in parallel, the machines will hold themselves in synchronism.

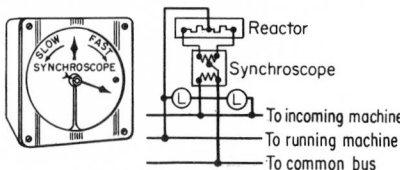

FIG. 66   *Synchroscope and wiring diagram.*

110. Although for successful parallel operation it is not necessary that a-c generators be of the same type, output, and speed, it is universally conceded that the question of wave shape is important, since, if the waves are of different shapes, cross currents will always be present. Similar wave shapes are more readily obtained with machines of similar type. Satisfactory parallel operation, the previously mentioned conditions being fulfilled, consists in obtaining:

1. Correct division of the load among the machines.
2. Freedom from hunting.

111. Division of Load. Machines with similar characteristics tend to divide the common load proportionally to the ratings of the machines. Such a proportional load division may be disturbed if the steam supply to the engines is defective or variable from any cause. The steam supply is regulated by the engine governors, and defects in one or more of these governors will give rise to poor load division. It is essential that the governors of all the engines shall have similar speed-regulation characteristics so that a sudden change in the load shall cause the same amount of regulation on each engine. Correct load division is therefore essentially a problem for the engine governors.

Varying the voltage of an alternator running in parallel with others by adjusting its field rheostat will not vary the load on it as with a d-c generator. To increase the energy delivered by an alternator it is necessary that the prime mover be caused to do more work. An engine should be given more steam or a water wheel more water.

112. Adjustment of Field Current. When the rheostats of two alternators running in parallel at normal speed are not adjusted to give a proper excitation, a cross current will flow between the armatures. The intensity of this current depends only upon the difference in the field currents and the impedances of the armature windings. It may vary over a wide range, from a minimum of zero when both field currents are normal to more than full-load current when they differ greatly. The effect of this cross current is to increase the temperature of the armatures and, consequently, to decrease the allowable useful output of the generators. It is important that the rheostats be so adjusted as to reduce it to a minimum. This cross current registers on the ammeters of both generators and usually increases both readings. The sum of the ammeter readings will be minimum when the idle or cross current is zero.

In general, the proper field current for a machine running in parallel with others is that which it would have if running alone and delivering its load at the same voltage. In order to determine the proper position of the rheostats it is necessary to make trial adjustments after the alternators are paralleled until that position is found at which the sum of the ammeter readings is minimum.

To illustrate this method let us consider two similar alternators A and B (Fig. 67) operating in parallel. When the generator field rheostats of both are properly adjusted, no cross currents will flow through the armatures, and the main ammeters will show equal readings if each machine is receiving the same amount of power from its prime mover. If the rheostat of A is partly cut in so as to reduce its field current, a cross current lagging in B and leading in A will flow between the armatures, the effect of which will be to strengthen A's magnetization and weaken B's until they are approximately equal. The resultant emf of the system will thereby be lowered.

On the other hand, if the rheostat of B is partly cut out so as to increase its field current, a cross current leading in A and lagging in B will flow between the armatures, strengthening A's magnetization and weakening B's magnetization until they are again

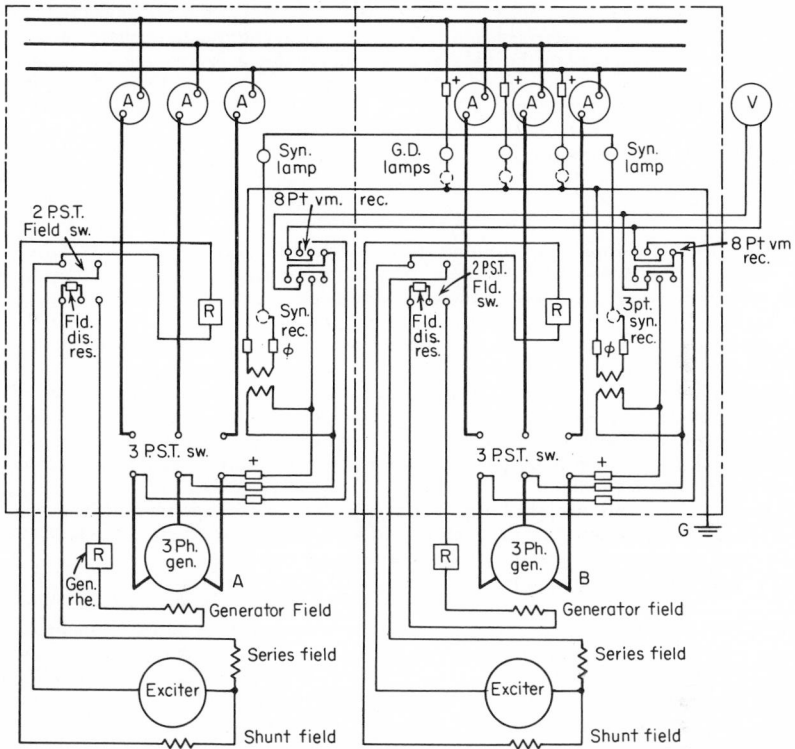

FIG. 67   *Two three-phase alternators of similar characteristics operating in parallel.*

equal. The resultant emf of the system will thereby be raised. A cross current of the same character is therefore produced by decreasing one field current or increasing the other; i.e., in both cases it will lead in the first machine and lag in the second. The emf of the system will, however, be decreased in one case and increased in the other.

It is obvious that by simultaneously adjusting the two rheostats the strength of the cross current can be varied considerably and the emf of the system maintained constant.

For the first trial adjustment, cut in *A*'s rheostat several notches and cut out *B*'s the same amount so as not to vary the emf of the system. If this reduces the sum of the main ammeter readings, continue the adjustment in the same direction until the result is minimum. After this point is reached, a further adjustment of the rheostat in either direction will increase the ammeter readings. If the first adjustment increases the sum of the ammeter readings, it is being made in the wrong direction, in which case move the rheostats back to the original positions and then cut out *A*'s rheostat and cut in *B*'s. If both adjustments increase the sum of the ammeter readings, the original positions of the rheostats are the proper ones.

In making these adjustments of the rheostats it may be found difficult to locate the exact points at which the cross current is minimum, as it may be possible to move the rheostats over a considerable range when near the correct positions without materially changing the ammeter readings. When the adjustment is carried this far, it is close enough for practical operation. If the generators are provided with power-factor meters, the same result can be obtained by adjusting the field currents until all the power-factor meters read the same, at the same time maintaining the voltage constant.

113. To Start a Single Alternator. (1) See that there is plenty of oil in the bearings, that the oil rings are free to turn, and that all switches are open. (2) Start exciter and adjust for normal voltage. Start generator slowly. See that the oil rings are turning. (3) Permit the machine to reach normal speed. Turn the generator field rheostat so that all its resistance is in the field circuit. Close the field switch. (4) Adjust the rheostat of the exciter for the normal exciting voltage. Slowly increase the alternator voltage to normal by cutting out the resistance of the field rheostat. (5) Close the main switch.

114. To Start an Alternator to Run in Parallel with Others. (1) Bring the exciter and generator to speed as described in the above paragraph. Adjust the exciter voltage and close the field switch, the generator field resistance being all in. (2) Adjust the generator field resistance so that the generator voltage will be the same as the bus-bar voltage. (3) Synchronize, as outlined in one of the preceding paragraphs. Close the main switch. (4) Adjust the field rheostat until cross currents are a minimum (see Sec. **112**) and adjust the governors of the prime movers so that the load will be properly distributed between the operating units in proportion to their capacities. (5) Adjust the governor of the machine which is to take the most load so that it will admit more steam.

115. To Cut Out a Generator Which Is Running in Parallel with Others (Westinghouse Instruction Book). (1) Preferably cut down the driving power until it is just sufficient to run the generator at no load. This will reduce the load on the generator. (2) Adjust the resistance in the field circuit until the armature current is at a minimum. (3) Open the main switch.

Caution. The field circuit of a generator which is to be disconnected from the bus bars must not be opened before the main switch has been opened, for if the field circuit is opened first, a heavy current will flow between the armatures.

116. Induction generators have the same construction as induction motors (see Sec. **144**). A revolving magnetic field is produced by the stator currents in exactly the same manner as in an induction motor (see Sec. **145**). Induction generators are made in two types as listed in Sec. **93**. The type in which the stator winding is the source of voltage is used for producing voltages of ordinary power frequencies, such as 25, 50, or 60 cycles. The type in which the rotor winding is the source of voltage is used for producing voltages of higher frequencies than ordinary power frequencies, such as 90, 100, 175, 180, or 400 cycles. These higher frequencies are often required for the operation of high-speed portable tools and machines and 400-cycle lighting.

Induction generators, in which the stator windings are the source of voltage, have their stator windings connected to the electric system which is to receive the power and their rotor windings short-circuited as shown in Fig. 68. The machine cannot function as a generator until a revolving magnetic field is produced in the machine. The current which produces the rotating magnetic field must therefore be supplied to the stator winding from a source external to the machine. Therefore, an induction generator of this type must be operated in parallel with a synchronous generator. Such an induction generator is, in effect, an induction motor which is driven at a speed above the speed of its rotating magnetic field.

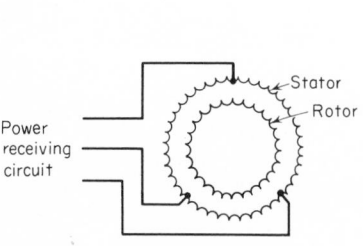

FIG. 68   *Induction generator connections.*

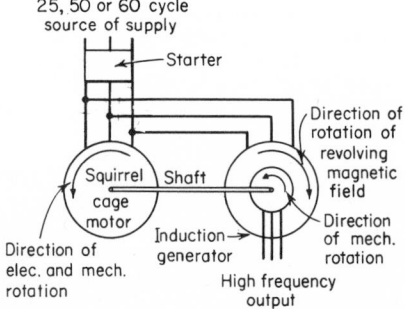

FIG. 69   *Schematic diagram of induction frequency-changer set.*

Suppose an induction motor which has a slip of 5 per cent at full load when operating as a motor is driven at a speed 5 per cent greater than the speed of the rotating magnetic field. The flux cut by the rotor conductors will be practically the same as when it was operating as a motor. But the direction of motion of the conductors relative to the flux will be reversed. Hence the machine will become a generator and deliver power to the line approximately equal to its full-load motor rating. The frequency of the current supplied by an induction generator will always be the same as that of the synchronous generator with which it is in parallel. The induction generator tends to supply a leading current, just as does a condenser. The power factor at which it operates is determined by the slip and the design and is not dependent upon the load.

Induction generators in which the rotor is the source of voltage are used for the generators in motor-generator frequency-changer sets. The stator windings are connected to 25-, 50-, or 60-cycle main power supply, and the rotor supplies the power to the higher-frequency circuits as shown in Fig. 69. If a 60-cycle current is passed into the primary winding of a standard wound-rotor motor and the motor is operated at synchronous or no-load speed, there is practically no voltage generated in the secondary. If, however, the rotor is held stationary, a 60-cycle voltage can be obtained from the secondary. If the rotor is revolved in the opposite direction to that in which it would revolve as a motor, a voltage of a frequency higher than 60 cycles is generated. The high frequency depends upon the speed and number of poles in the generator and can be calculated from the following formula:

$$\text{High frequency} = \frac{\text{poles} \times \text{rpm}}{120} + \text{line frequency} \qquad (2)$$

The voltage delivered by the induction frequency changer depends upon the design of the primary and secondary windings, the speed of the set, and the applied primary voltage.

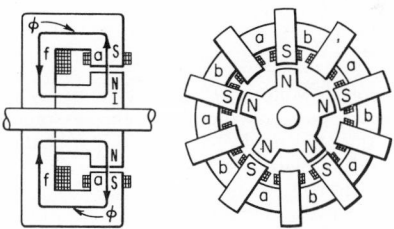

FIG. 70 *An inductor alternator. This type of construction has been used for relatively small alternators employed in radio transmission and gives as high as 200,000 cycles per sec. (From Sanderson.)*

117. Inductor alternators are employed for the production of voltages of frequencies between 500 and 10,000 cycles for supplying the power to induction furnaces for the melting and heating of steel and alloys. The rotating element carries no electrical windings but consists simply of a toothed steel member (Fig. 70). The stationary member supports two sets of windings: the field windings and the armature coils. As the toothed member revolves, it varies the reluctance of the magnetic paths and thereby varies the flux produced by the current in the field windings. The flux also links with the armature coils, and its variation induces a voltage in these coils.

PRINCIPLES, CHARACTERISTICS, AND MANAGEMENT OF ELECTRIC MOTORS

118. Types of Electric Motors. Electric motors are manufactured in a number of different types. They may be divided into three main groups, depending upon the type of electric system that they are designed to operate from: d-c, single-phase a-c, and polyphase a-c. There are several types of motors in each one of these groups, constructed so that they produce different starting and running characteristics. The principal types of electric motors are given in the following list:

Direct current.
   Shunt-wound.
   Series-wound.
   Compound-wound.
Polyphase alternating current.
   Induction.
      Squirrel cage.
         Normal torque, normal starting current.
         Normal torque, low starting current.
         High torque, low starting current.
         Low torque, low starting current.
         High-resistance rotor.
         Automatic start.
         Multispeed.
      Wound rotor.
      Commutator, brush-shifting.
   Synchronous.
      Standard type.
      Special-purpose.
Single-phase alternating current.
   Repulsion.
   Induction.
      Shading-pole starting.
      Inductively split-phase starting.
      Capacitor type.
      Repulsion start, induction run.
   Repulsion induction.
   Series.

119. Speed Classification of Motors. Each electric motor possesses a certain inherent speed characteristic by means of which it can be classified in one of several groups. The following classification of speed characteristics is that adopted by the National Electrical Manufacturers' Association (NEMA).

1. A CONSTANT-SPEED MOTOR is one whose speed is practically constant from no load to full load. Motors in this class may have an absolutely constant speed regardless of the load, or the speed may vary a few per cent from no load to full load.

2. AN ADJUSTABLE-SPEED MOTOR is one in which the speed can be varied gradually over a considerable range but, when once adjusted, remains practically constant regardless of the load. The base speed of these motors is taken as the lowest rated speed obtained at rated load with rated impressed voltage and rated temperature conditions.

3. A MULTISPEED MOTOR is one which can be operated at any one of several definite speeds but, when once adjusted, remains practically constant regardless of the load. It differs from the adjustable-speed motor in that the multispeed motor can be operated at only certain definite speeds without any gradual adjustment of the speed between these definite speeds.

4. A VARYING-SPEED MOTOR is one whose speed varies with the load, generally decreasing as the load increases.

5. AN ADJUSTABLE VARYING-SPEED MOTOR is one in which the speed can be varied gradually over a considerable range but in which the speed, when once adjusted for a given load, will vary in considerable degree with change in the load.

120. Service Classification of Motors. Electric motors are classified into two groups depending upon the type of service they are designed for. **General-purpose motors** are those motors designed for general use without restriction to a particular application. They are designed to meet certain specifications as standardized by the National Electrical Manufacturers' Association. A **definite-purpose motor** is one which is designed in standard ratings and with standard operating characteristics for use under service conditions other than usual or for use on a particular type of application.   A **special-purpose motor** is one with special operating characteristics or special mechanical construction or both which is designed for a particular application and which does not meet the definition of a general-purpose or a definite-purpose motor.

121. Brake motors are motors equipped with electrically controlled brakes as an integral part of the motor assembly.   The brake motor manufactured by one company consists of one or more rotating steel disks splined on a pinion on the motor shaft, with stationary friction linings on each side of each disk.   A helical spring in the center applies pressure to provide the required braking, and either two, three, or four magnets, depending on the rating of the brake, supply force to compress the spring and release the brake while the motor is running.

When power is applied to the motor, the brake is immediately energized, since the brake leads are connected directly to the motor leads in the conduit box.   The current energizes the magnets, and they pull the armature plate toward the end plate.   This removes the pressure on the revolving disks and allows them to move freely between the friction linings, releasing the brake.

Since the rotating disks are separated from the friction surfaces at all times except during actual braking, the motor delivers full rated horsepower at the output shaft.

When the motor is disconnected from the power supply, the magnets are immediately de-energized, and the spring pushes the armature plate away from the adjustable plate, toward the motor.   This applies braking pressure on the surfaces between the revolving disks and the friction linings, bringing the motor to a quick smooth stop.   This inherent smooth action, free from hammer blow, keeps stresses at the minimum in the brake and in belts, cables, gears, or chains through which the motor drives.

122. Gear motors are motors equipped with a built-in reduction gear as an integral part of the motor assembly.   The motor itself is generally an 1,800-rpm machine.   Output-shaft speeds between 2 and 1,550 rpm are available.   These motors can be obtained equipped with almost any type of general-purpose, polyphase induction; single-phase; or d-c motor.

Loads of the same horsepower and speed rating will require different gear sizes depending upon the type of load.   Therefore, time of operation and frequency and severity of shock must be determined in order to select the proper gear motor for a specific application.   To assist the engineer in his selection, AGMA has defined three classes of service, according to the degree to which all of these variables are present.   The classes of service are:

CLASS I.   Steady loads not exceeding the normal rating of the motor on 8-hr-per-day service, or moderate shock loads where service is intermittent.

CLASS II.   Steady loads not exceeding the normal rating of the motor on 24-hr-per-day service or moderate shock loads running 8 hr per day.

CLASS III.   Moderate shock loads on 24-hr-per-day service or heavy shock loads running 8 hr per day.

Classes of service for a great number of applications are given in Sec. **123.**

123. Application Classification.   Typical Gear-motor Applications Grouped According to Normal Character of Load
(General Electric Co.)

Application	Load classification	Gear-motor class	
		8–10 hr per day	24 hr per day
Agitators:			
Pure liquids	Uniform	I	II
Liquids and solids	Moderate shock	II	II
Liquids—variable density	Moderate shock	II	II
Blowers:			
Centrifugal	Uniform	I	II
Lobe	Moderate shock	II	II
Vane	Uniform	I	II
Brewing and distilling:			
Bottling machinery	Uniform	I	II
Brew kettles—continuous duty	Uniform	—	II
Cookers—continuous duty	Uniform	—	II
Mash tube—continuous duty	Uniform	—	II
Scale hopper—frequent starts	Moderate shock	II	II
Can-filling machines	Uniform	I	II
Cane knives	Moderate shock	II	II
Car dumpers	Heavy shock	III	—
Car pullers	Moderate shock	II	—
Clarifiers	Uniform	I	II
Classifiers	Moderate shock	II	II
Clay-working machinery:			
Brick press	Heavy shock	III	III
Briquette machine	Heavy shock	III	III
Clay-working machinery	Moderate shock	II	II
Pug mill	Moderate shock	II	II
Compressors:			
Centrifugal	Uniform	I	II
Lobe	Moderate shock	II	II
Reciprocating:[a]			
Multicylinder	Moderate shock	II	II
Single Cylinder	Heavy shock	III	III
Conveyors—uniformly loaded or fed:			
Apron	Uniform	I	II
Assembly	Uniform	I	II
Belt	Uniform	I	II
Bucket	Uniform	I	II
Chain	Uniform	I	II
Flight	Uniform	I	II
Oven	Uniform	I	II
Screw	Uniform	I	II
Conveyors—heavy duty not uniformly fed:			
Apron	Moderate shock	II	II
Assembly	Moderate shock	II	II
Belt	Moderate shock	II	II
Bucket	Moderate shock	II	II
Chain	Moderate shock	II	II
Flight	Moderate shock	II	II

For footnote references see end of table.

Application Classification. Typical Gear-motor Applications Grouped According to Normal Character of Load (*Continued*)

Application	Load classification	Gear-motor class 8–10 hr per day	Gear-motor class 24 hr per day
Live roll[b]		b	b
Oven	Moderate shock	II	II
Reciprocating	Heavy shock	III	III
Screw	Moderate shock	II	II
Shaker	Heavy shock	III	III
Cranes and hoists:			
Main hoists:			
Heavy duty	Heavy shock	III	III
Medium duty	Moderate shock	II	II
Reversing	Moderate shock	II	II
Skip hoists	Moderate shock	II	II
Travel motion	Moderate shock	II	II
Trolley motion	Moderate shock	II	II
Crushers:			
Ore	Heavy shock	III	III
Stone	Heavy shock	III	III
Dredges:			
Cable reels	Moderate shock	II	
Conveyors	Moderate shock	II	II
Cutter head drives	Heavy shock	III	III
Jig drives	Heavy shock	III	III
Maneuvering winches	Moderate shock	II	
Pumps	Moderate shock	II	II
Screen drive	Heavy shock	III	III
Stackers	Moderate shock	II	II
Utility winches	Moderate shock	II	
Elevators:			
Bucket—uniform load	Uniform	I	II
Bucket—heavy load	Moderate shock	II	II
Bucket—continuous	Uniform	I	II
Centrifugal discharge	Uniform	I	II
Escalators		I	I
Freight		II	II
Gravity discharge	Uniform	I	II
Man lifts			
Passenger[b]		b	b
Service-hand lift		III	
Fans:			
Centrifugal	Uniform	I	II
Cooling Towers:			
Induced draft		II	II
Forced draft[b]		b	b
Induced draft	Moderate shock	II	II
Large (mine, etc.)	Moderate shock	II	II
Large industrial	Uniform	I	II
Light (small diameter)	Uniform	I	II
Feeders:			
Apron	Moderate	II	II
Belt	Moderate	II	II
Disk	Uniform	I	II
Reciprocating	Heavy shock	III	III
Screw	Moderate shock	II	II
Food industry:			
Beet slicer	Moderate shock	II	II
Cereal cooker	Uniform	I	II

For footnote references see end of table.

Application Classification. Typical Gear-motor Applications Grouped According to Normal Character of Load (*Continued*)

Application	Load classification	Gear-motor class	
		8–10 hr per day	24 hr per day
Dough mixer	Moderate shock	II	II
Meat grinders	Moderate shock	II	II
Generators (not welding)	Uniform	I	II
Hammer mills	Heavy shock	III	III
Laundry washers, reversing	Moderate shock	II	II
Laundry tumblers	Moderate shock	II	II
Line shafts:			
Driving processing equipment	Moderate shock	II	II
Other line shafts	Uniform	I	II
Machine tools:			
Bending roll	....	—	II
Notching press—belt driven	Uniform	I	II
Plate planer	Heavy shock	III	III
Punch press—gear driven	Heavy shock	III	III
Tapping machines	....	—	III
Other Machine Tools:			
Main drives	Moderate shock	II	II
Auxiliary drives	Uniform	I	II
Metal mills:			
Draw bench—carriage	....	III	III
Draw bench—main drive	Uniform	II	III
Forming machines	Heavy shock	III	III
Pinch dryer and scrubber rolls, reversing[b]	....	[b]	[b]
Slitters[a]	Moderate shock	II	II
Table conveyors:			
Nonreversing	Moderate shock	II	II
Reversing[a]			
Wire drawing and flattening machine	Moderate shock	II	II
Wire winding machine	....	—	II
Mills, rotary type:			
Ball[a]	Moderate shock	II	II
Cement kilns[a]	....	—	II
Driers and coolers	Moderate shock	II	II
Kilns	Moderate shock	II	II
Pebble[a]	Moderate shock	II	II
Rod	Heavy shock	III	III
Tumbling barrels	Heavy shock	III	III
Mixers:			
Concrete mixers, continuous	Moderate shock	II	II
Concrete mixers, intermittent	Moderate shock	I	
Constant density	Uniform	I	II
Variable density	Moderate shock	II	II
Oil industry:			
Chillers	Moderate shock	II	II
Oil-well pumping[b]	....	[b]	[b]
Paraffin filter press	Moderate shock	II	II
Rotary kilns	Moderate shock	II	II
Paper mills:			
Agitators (mixers)	Moderate shock	II	II
Barker auxiliaries, hydraulic	....	—	III
Barker, mechanical	....	—	III
Barking drum	Moderate shock	II	II
Beater and pulper	Moderate shock	—	II
Bleacher	Uniform	I	II

For footnote references see end of table.

Application Classification. Typical Gear-motor Applications Grouped According to Normal Character of Load (*Continued*)

Application	Load classification	8–10 hr per day	24 hr per day
		Gear-motor class	
Calenders*a*...	Moderate shock	—	II
Calenders—super..	Heavy shock	—	III
Converting machines, except cutters and platers............	....	—	II
Conveyors..	Uniform	—	II
Couch..	Moderate shock	—	II
Cutters, platers...	....	—	III
Cylinders..	Moderate shock	—	II
Driers*a*...	Moderate shock	—	II
Felt stretcher...	Moderate shock	—	II
Felt whipper..	....	—	III
Jordans..	Heavy shock	—	III
Log haul...	....	—	III
Presses*a*..	Uniform	—	II
Pulp machines..	....	—	II
Reel...	....	—	II
Stock chests*a*..	Moderate shock	—	II
Suction roll*a*..	Uniform	—	II
Washers and thickeners..................................	....	—	II
Winders..	Uniform	—	II
Printing presses...	Uniform	I	II
Pullers:			
Barge haul...	....	II	III
Pumps:			
Centrifugal...	Uniform	I	II
Proportioning*a*...	Moderate shock	II	II
Reciprocating:			
Single acting, 3 or more cylinders........................	Moderate shock	II	II
Double acting, 2 or more cylinders.......................	Moderate shock	II	II
Single acting, 1 or 2 cylinders*b*.........................	....	*b*	*b*
Double acting, single cylinder*b*..........................	....	*b*	*b*
Rotary:			
Gear type..	Uniform	I	II
Lobe, vane...	Uniform	I	II
Rubber industry:			
Mixer..	Heavy shock	III	III
Rubber calendar*a*.......................................	Moderate shock	II	II
Rubber mill (2 or more)*a*................................	Moderate shock	II	II
Sheeter*a*..	Moderate shock	II	II
Tire-building machines...................................	....	II	II
Tire and tube press openers..............................	....	I	I
Tubers and strainers.....................................	Moderate shock	II	II
Sewage-disposal equipment:			
Bar screens...	Uniform	I	II
Chemical feeders..	Uniform	I	II
Collectors, circuline or straightline......................	Uniform	I	II
Dewatering screws.......................................	Moderate shock	II	II
Grit collectors..	Uniform	I	II
Scum breakers..	Moderate shock	II	II
Slow or rapid mixers.....................................	Moderate shock	II	II
Sludge collectors..	Uniform	I	II
Thickeners...	Moderate shock	II	II
Vacuum filters..	Moderate shock	II	II
Screens:			
Air washing...	Uniform	I	II
Rotary—stone or gravel..................................	Moderate shock	II	II
Traveling water intake...................................	Uniform	I	II

For footnote references see end of table.

**Application Classification. Typical Gear-motor Applications Grouped
According to Normal Character of Load** (*Continued*)

Application	Load classification	Gear-motor class	
		8–10 hr per day	24 hr per day
Slab pushers...	Moderate shock	II	II
Steering gear..	Moderate shock	II	II
Stokers...	Uniform	I	II
Textile industry:			
Batchers...	Moderate shock	II	II
Calenders..	Moderate shock	II	II
Card machines*..	Moderate shock	II	II
Cloth finishing machines (Washers, pads, tenters, driers, calenders, etc)...	Moderate shock	II	II
Dry cans...	Moderate shock	II	II
Dyeing machinery.....................................	Moderate shock	II	II
Looms..	Moderate shock	II	II
Mangles..	Moderate shock	II	II
Nappers..	Moderate shock	II	II
Range drives...	....	b	b
Soapers..	Moderate shock	II	II
Spinners...	Moderate shock	II	II
Tenter frames..	Moderate shock	II	II
Winders (other than batchers)........................	Moderate shock	II	II
Yarn preparatory machines (cards, spinners, slashers, etc.)....	Moderate shock	II	II
Windlass..	Moderate shock	II	II

ᵃ Classes listed are minimum, and normal conditions are assumed. In view of varying load conditions, it is suggested that these applications be carefully reviewed before final selection is made.
ᵇ Refer to Company.

124. Direction of Mounting of Motors. The standard type of motor is designed to be mounted with its shaft horizontal. Motors can be obtained, however, for mounting with their shafts vertical, but they are more expensive and require more careful attention.

125. Bearings for motors may be of the sleeve or ball-bearing type. Ball-bearing construction is of two types: (1) ball bearings with provision for in-service lubrication and (2) prelubricated ball bearings which require no service lubrication. Ball bearings generally are used for the smaller motors (up to 30 hp). The type to use is largely one of individual preference, since both types when properly designed and maintained will give satisfactory service. Most manufacturers are prepared to furnish from regular stock either with sleeve or ball bearings any type of motor up to 200 hp except some totally enclosed motors.

For especially quiet operation, sleeve bearings are preferable.

The application of grease-packed ball bearings is especially advantageous under the following conditions:

1. When the motor frame does not remain in a stationary position after installation.
2. Where the motor is located in an inaccessible place.
3. For many totally enclosed motor applications.
4. For motors with their shafts mounted vertically.
5. For high speeds.
6. For heavy thrust loads.

The cost of ball-bearing-equipped motors is slightly more than for sleeve-bearing motors.

126. Types of Motor Enclosure. The different types of electric motors can be obtained with constructions which give different degrees of enclosure and protection to the operating parts and windings. The different standard types as explained and defined by the National Electrical Manufacturers' Association are as follows:

OPEN

General-purpose. Ventilating openings permit passage of external cooling air over and around the windings of the machine.

Dripproof. Ventilating openings are so constructed that successful operation is not interfered with when drops of liquid or solid particles strike or enter the enclosure at any angle from 0 to 15 deg downward from the vertical.

Splashproof. Ventilating openings are so constructed that successful operation is not interfered with when drops of liquid or solid particles strike or enter the enclosure at any angle not greater than 100 deg downward from the vertical.

Guarded. Openings giving direct access to live or rotating parts (except smooth shafts) are limited as to size by the design of the structural parts or by screens, grills, expanded metal, etc., to prevent accidental contact with such parts.

Semiguarded. Part of the ventilating openings, usually in the top half, are guarded as in a "guarded machine," but others are left open.

Dripproof fully guarded. A dripproof machine with ventilating openings as in a "guarded machine."

Externally ventilated. A machine that is ventilated by means of a separate motor-driven blower mounted on machine enclosure. Mechanical protection may be as defined above.

Pipe-ventilated. Openings for admission of ventilating air are so arranged that inlet ducts or pipes can be connected to them.

Weather-protected. Type I: Ventilation passages are so designed as to minimize the entrance of rain, snow and airborne particles to the electrical parts. Type II: Ventilating passages at intake and discharge are so arranged that high-velocity air and airborne particles blown into the machine by storms or high winds can be discharged without entering the internal ventilating passages leading directly to the electric parts.

Encapsulated windings. An a-c squirrel-cage machine having random windings filled with an insulating resin which also forms a protective coating.

Sealed windings. An a-c squirrel-cage machine making use of form wound coils and having an insulation system which, through the use of materials, processes, or a combination of materials and processes, results in a sealing of the windings and connections against contaminants.

TOTALLY ENCLOSED

Nonventilated. Enclosure prevents free exchange of air between inside and outside of case, but not airtight.

Fan-cooled. Equipped for exterior cooling by means of a fan or fans, integral with machine, but external to the enclosing parts.

Fan-cooled guarded. All openings giving direct access to fan are limited in size by design of structural parts or by screens, grills, expanded metal, etc., to prevent accidental contact with fan.

Explosion-proof. Designed and built to withstand an explosion of gas or vapor within it and to prevent ignition of gas or vapor surrounding machine by sparks, flashes, or explosions which may occur within machine casing.

Dust-ignition-proof. Designed and built to exclude ignitible amounts of dust or amounts affecting performance or rating to prevent ignition of exterior dust on or in vicinity of enclosure.

Pipe-ventilated. Openings so arranged that inlet and outlet ducts or pipes may be connected to them for the admission and discharge of ventilating air.

Water-cooled. Cooled by circulating water; the water or water conductors come in direct contact with the machine parts.

Water-air-cooled. Cooled by circulating air which in turn is cooled by circulating water.

Air-to-air-cooled. Cooled by circulating internal air through heat exchanger which, in turn, is cooled by circulating external air.

See NEMA Standards MG1-1.25.26,27 for additional details.

127. Torques of Motors. The *starting or static torque* (locked-rotor torque) of a motor is the turning effort exerted by the motor at standstill at the instant that the motor is connected to the line. It is the turning effort that will be exerted in starting a load from rest.

The *pull-up torque* of a motor is the minimum turning effort developed by the motor during the period of acceleration from rest to full speed.

The *breakdown torque* of a motor is the maximum turning effort that the motor will develop when running without a sudden drop in the speed and stalling of the motor.

The *pull-in torque* of a synchronous motor is the maximum turning effort that the motor will exert to pull its connected inertia load into synchronism.

The *nominal pull-in torque* of a synchronous motor is the turning effort which the motor will exert when operating as an induction motor at 95 per cent of synchronous speed.

The *pull-out torque* of a synchronous motor is the maximum sustained turning effort which the motor will exert at synchronous speed for 1 min.

The *rated torque* of a motor is the turning effort exerted by the motor when delivering its rated horsepower load at rated speed.

The *maximum torque* of a motor is the maximum turning effort that the motor can exert. In some motors this maximum torque is developed under standstill conditions and in others at some definite speed.

All the above torque conditions are dependent upon rated impressed voltage and, also, for a-c motors are dependent upon rated frequency.

128. The rating of an electric motor includes the service classification (Sec. **120**), voltage, full-load current, speed, number of phases and frequency if alternating current, and full-load horsepower.

The horsepower rating that is stamped on the motor nameplate by its manufacturer is the horsepower load which the motor will carry without injury to any part of the motor.

In any motor a certain amount of the input energy is lost in the machine. This energy is dissipated in the form of heat, which raises the temperature of the motor. As the load on a motor is increased, the losses increase, and therefore the temperatures of the different parts of the machine increase with the load. If too great a load is put on the motor, the motor will become excessively hot, with probable injury to the insulation of the windings.

The different types of insulation employed in the construction of motors, together with their maximum safe operating temperatures, are given in the following list.

BASIC MOTOR INSULATION CLASSES

Class A. Materials or combinations of materials such as cotton, silk, and paper when suitably impregnated or coated, or when immersed in a dielectric liquid such as oil. Other materials or combinations of materials may be included in this class if by experience or accepted tests the total system can be shown to be capable of operation at **105°C.**

Class B. Materials or combinations of materials such as mica, glass fiber, asbestos, etc., with suitable bonding substances. Other materials or combinations of materials, not necessarily inorganic, may be included in this class if by experience or accepted tests the total system can be shown to be capable of operation at **130°C.**

Class F. Materials or combinations of materials such as mica, glass fiber, asbestos, etc., with suitable bonding substances. Other materials or combinations of materials, not necessarily inorganic, may be included in this class if by experience or accepted tests the total system can be shown to be capable of operation at **155°C.**

Class H. Materials or combinations of materials such as silicone elastomer, mica, glass fiber, asbestos, etc., with suitable bonding substances such as appropriate silicone resins. Other materials or combinations of materials may be included in this class if by experience or accepted tests the total system can be shown to be capable of operation at **180°C.**

New NEMA standards, arising from a 1964 motor rerate program, omit motor temperature **rise** from the nameplate. Instead, maximum allowable **ambient** temperature is shown. So far, however, this change is generally applicable only to motors in

NEMA frame 445 and below. Large motor nameplates continue to follow the former practice of showing rise rather than ambient.

In general, maximum ambient temperature is 40°C for any motor unless that motor is specifically designed for a different figure, in which case the correct ambient should be stamped elsewhere on the nameplate.

General-purpose open-type motors are usually rated for continuous operation in a 40°C ambient temperature under normal service conditions. These conditions include, in addition to the 40°C ambient temperature, operation at an altitude no greater than 3,300 ft above sea level; applied voltage within 10 per cent of rated value; system frequency within 5 per cent of rated value; combined variation of both voltage and frequency within 10 per cent of rated values; unobstructed or unhampered ventilation; and proper mounting and mechanical connection to the driven load. Motors may be provided with various classes of insulation as shown in the motor insulation list in this section.

129. Starting Currents of Motors. In stating the starting current taken by a motor, it should be specified just what current is meant, as starting currents are given in several different ways. In some cases the starting current pulled from the line is not the same as the current flowing into the motor itself at the instant of starting. If the rotating member of a motor is held stationary (locked rotor) and voltage is applied to the machine, a certain current would be indicated. This current is the first inrush current that will occur at starting. If the starting current is measured with a well-damped ammeter under actual starting conditions (rotor free to revolve), the current indicated on the ammeter will be less than the first inrush current. This is true owing to the fact that the ammeter does not have a chance to indicate the peak current before the motor has started to revolve and the current has decreased somewhat. It is standard practice to take the free-rotor value of starting currents as 75 per cent of the locked-rotor values.

The **locked-rotor current of a motor** is the current taken directly by the motor with the revolving part held stationary.

The **locked-rotor current of a motor and its starter** is the current taken from the line with the revolving part held stationary.

The **free-rotor current of a motor** is the maximum current taken directly by the motor during the starting period as indicated by a well-damped ammeter.

The **free-rotor current of a motor and its starter** is the maximum current drawn from the line during the starting period as indicated by a well-damped ammeter.

The **average starting current** of a motor is the average value of the starting current that must be considered in selecting fuses or circuit breakers. Fuses with a rating equal to the average starting current of a motor will allow the starting of the motor without rupturing the fuses. Owing to the time-lag characteristic of fuses, the peak value of the starting current will not rupture fuses of a rating considerably less than the peak value of the starting current.

130. Permissible Motor-starting Currents. The operating conditions of an electric power system are affected by the currents taken by motors under starting conditions. Excessive power fluctuations will cause large changes in the voltage of the system and excessive voltage drops under the peak current conditions. These power and voltage fluctuations may result in unsatisfactory operating conditions for one or more of the following reasons:

1. Actuation of undervoltage protective or release devices on motor controllers, causing shutdown of motors.

2. Stalling of induction motors that are operating close to full load or slightly over full load.

3. Objectionable dips in light output of lamps and flickering of lamps.

4. In the case of small private generating plants, danger of overloading of generators.

Each electric power company has definite rules with respect to permissible starting currents for motors supplied from its system. At the present time, there is no standardization of these rules, each power company having its own set of rules. Some of these rules limit the starting current on a basis of allowable percentage of full-load current of the motor. With one of the newer rules, which is called the increment method, the maximum starting current of any motor must not be greater than a certain number of amperes per kilowatt of maximum-demand load of the customer.

131. The speed regulation of a motor is the percentage drop in speed between no load and full load based on the full-load speed.

$$\text{Per cent speed regulation} = \frac{\text{no-load speed} - \text{full-load speed}}{\text{full-load speed}} \times 100 \qquad (3)$$

DIRECT-CURRENT MOTORS

132. Direct-current Motors. All d-c motors must receive their excitation from some outside source of supply. Therefore, they are always separately excited. The interconnection of the field and armature windings can be made, however, in one of the three different ways employed for self-excited d-c generators. A d-c motor may be designed, therefore, to operate with its field connected in parallel or in series with its armature, producing, respectively, a shunt or series motor. If the machine is provided with two field windings, one connected shunt and the other series, it is a compound motor. The speed of a shunt motor connected directly to the line is nearly constant from no load to full load, while the speed of a series motor drops off rapidly as the load is increased. If a series motor were operated at no load with normal voltage, it would attain a dangerous speed, so high in most cases that it would throw itself apart by centrifugal force. A series motor should never be operated at no load unless there is sufficient external resistance connected in series with the motor to limit its speed to a safe value. For this reason a belt drive should never be used with a series motor.

Standard compound motors are designed to operate with the shunt and series fields connected so as to aid each other (cumulative). They therefore have operating characteristics that are a compromise between those of the shunt and series motors. Their speed drops off considerably as the load is increased, but not nearly so much as with the series motor. The compound motor will not run away under no load. The amount of change of speed from no load to full load depends upon the strength of the series field. The stronger the series field is, the greater the change in speed from no load to full load. Special compound motors with their field windings connected so as to buck each other (differential) are used sometimes for special applications. If the series field is of just the proper strength, a differential compound motor will operate at a more constant speed than a shunt motor, but it tends to be unstable under overload conditions.

Many shunt motors have a weak series-field winding in addition to the shunt-field winding. The series-field winding is connected cumulative and consists of only a very few turns. The purpose of the series-field winding is to counteract partially the effect of the armature current upon the speed of the motor. The armature current tends to reduce the strength of the magnetic field of the motor. Therefore, as the load on the motor is increased, the decrease in the strength of the field may cause a rise in the speed. A motor with a rising-speed characteristic is unstable. A few series-field turns will sufficiently counteract the demagnetizing effect of the armature current and stabilize the speed characteristic of the motor. These motors, although actually cumulative compound motors with a very weak series field, are called stabilized shunt motors.

Typical characteristics are shown in Figs. 71, 72, and 73 for shunt, series, and compound motors.

The speed regulation of standard d-c motors which meet NEMA requirements will not exceed the following values.

	Constant speed, %	Adjustable speed, %
Shunt wound:		
To 1½ hp..........	12	25
2–5 hp.............	12	22
Above 5 hp........	10	15
Compound wound:		
All ratings.........	25	

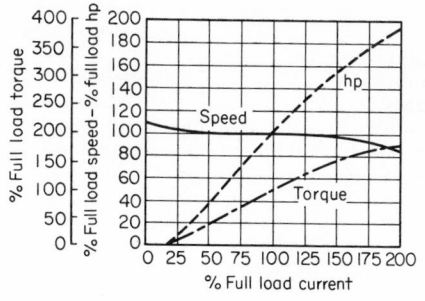

FIG. 71 *Typical characteristics for a shunt motor.*

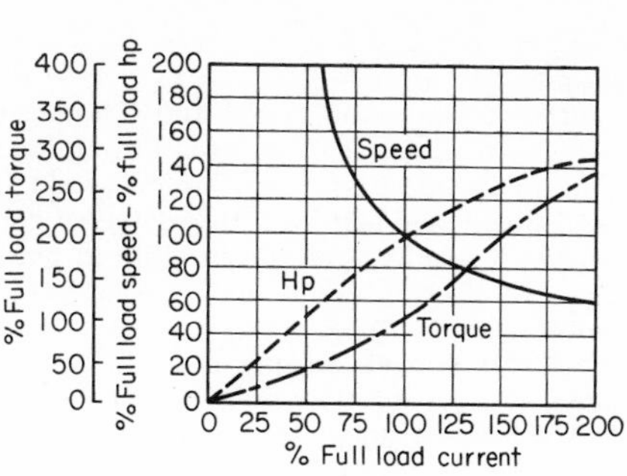

FIG. 72 *Typical characteristics for a series motor.*

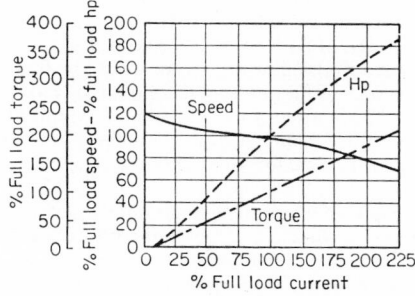

FIG. 73 *Typical characteristics for a compound motor.*

133. Torque Characteristics of D-C Motors. The torque developed by any one of the three types of d-c motors, either at starting or while running, depends upon the product of the magnetic flux and the armature current. Since in a shunt motor the flux is nearly constant at all times, the torque varies nearly directly with the value of the armature current. In a series motor the armature current flows directly through the field winding, so that the flux is not constant but varies almost directly with the value of the armature current. The torque of a series motor, therefore, varies approximately as the square of the armature current. Doubling the armature current will make the torque four times as great. The cumulative compound motor has a torque characteristic that is a compromise between that of the series motor and that of the shunt motor. The torque will increase faster than the increase in armature current but not so fast as the square of the armature current. In just what way the torque varies with the armature current for a cumulative compound motor depends upon the relative strength of the series and shunt fields. The curves of Fig. 74 indicate the relation between torque and armature current for the different types of d-c motors.

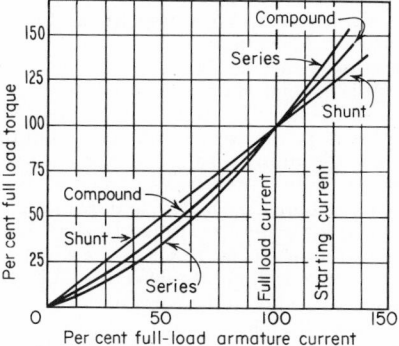

FIG. 74 *Torque characteristics for d-c motors.*

The maximum value of starting torque that it is satisfactorily possible for any d-c motor to produce is limited only by the commutating conditions. This usually limits the current to approximately 200 per cent of full-load current for a shunt motor and

250 per cent of full-load current for a series or compound motor. The corresponding torques are approximately 200 per cent of full-load torque for a shunt motor, 300 per cent for a compound motor, and 400 per cent for a series motor.

There is no value of pull-out torque for a d-c motor. If the load on a d-c motor was continually increased, the motor would gradually slow down as the load increased until finally the load would become so great that the motor would gradually stop. Of course, it would never be feasible in practice to overload the machine to such extent that it would stop, and long before such a load was reached the fuses in the circuit would blow.

134. Method of Starting D-C Motors (E C & M Division of Square D Co.). A d-c motor of any capacity, when its armature is at rest, will offer a very low resistance to the flow of current, and an excessive and perhaps destructive current would flow through it if it were connected directly across the supply mains while at rest. Consider a motor adapted to a normal full-load current of 100 amp and having a resistance of 0.25 ohm; if this motor were connected across a 250-volt circuit, a current of 1,000 amp would flow through its armature; in other words, it would be overloaded 900 per cent, with consequent danger to its windings and also to the driven machine. For the same motor, with a rheostat having a resistance of 2.25 ohms inserted in the motor circuit, at the time of starting, the total resistance to the flow of current would be the resistance of the motor (0.25 ohm) plus the resistance of the rheostat (2.25 ohms), or a total of 2.5 ohms. Under these conditions exactly full-load current, or 100 amp, would flow through the motor, and neither the motor nor the driven machine would be overstrained in starting. This indicates the necessity of a rheostat for limiting the flow of current in starting the motor from rest.

An electric motor is simply an inverted generator or dynamo. Consequently when its armature begins to revolve, a voltage is generated within its windings just as a voltage is generated in the windings of a generator when driven by a prime mover. This voltage generated within the moving armature of a motor opposes the voltage of the circuit from which the motor is supplied and hence is known as a counter-emf. The net voltage tending to force current through the armature of a motor when the motor is running is, therefore, the line voltage minus the counter-emf.

For the motor above cited, when the armature reaches such a speed that a voltage of 125 is generated within its windings, the effective voltage will be 250 minus 125, or 125 volts, and, therefore, the resistance of the rheostat may be reduced to 1 ohm without the full-load current of the motor being exceeded. As the armature further increases its speed, the resistance of the rheostat may be further reduced until, when the motor has almost reached full speed, all the rheostat may be cut out and the counter-emf generated by the motor will almost equal the voltage supplied by the line, so that an excessive current cannot flow through the armature.

It is general practice to provide a rheostat for starting a d-c electric motor, except for small fractional-horsepower motors of ¼ hp or smaller. In special cases, when the motor is started very infrequently and the starting load is light, larger motors can be started by throwing them directly across the line. Motors as large as 5 hp have been successfully started in this way, but the manufacturer should be consulted whenever one contemplates starting a motor larger than 1 hp by this method. The resistor providing the starting resistance is divided into sections and is so arranged that the entire length or maximum resistance of the rheostat is in circuit with the motor at the instant of starting and that the effective length of the resistance conductor, and hence its resistance, can be reduced as the motor comes up to speed.

In cutting out the resistance of a starting rheostat care must be used not to cut it out too rapidly. If the resistance is cut out more rapidly than the armature can speed up, a sufficient counter-emf will not be generated to oppose the flow of current properly and the current will be excessive.

The standard starting rheostat, when thrown into the first position, limits the armature current to about 150 per cent of the full-load current. This current will produce a starting torque of about 150 per cent of full-load torque for a shunt motor, of about 175 per cent for a standard cumulative compound motor, and of about 225 per cent for a series machine. If greater starting torque is required, it can be obtained by advancing the starter to the second or third point. The allowable starting torque that can be obtained in this way is limited by commutating conditions to about 200 per cent of full-load torque for a shunt motor, to 300 per cent for a compound motor, and to 400 per cent for a series motor. The currents corresponding to these maximum allowable torques are approximately 200 per cent of full-load current for a shunt motor, 250 per cent of full-load current for a cumulative compound motor, and 250 per cent of full-load current for a series motor.

135. Speed Control of D-C Motors. The speed of d-c motors for a given load can be controlled by the following methods:

1. Armature control.
  a. Variable resistance in series with armature.
  b. Variable-voltage generator supplying armature (Ward-Leonard system).
  c. Variable voltage supplied to armature by controlled electronic rectifier.
  d. Resistance shunted across armature.
2. Field control.
  a. Shunt-field rheostat.
  b. Variable-voltage generator supplying shunt field.
  c. Variable voltage supplied to shunt field by controlled electronic rectifier.
  d. Resistance shunted across series field.
3. Combination of armature and field control.

136. Armature Speed Control. Any d-c motor may have its speed reduced below normal by armature control. With this method, the speed is controlled by varying the voltage impressed upon the armature, while the voltage of the field is held constant. For a constant torque load, the speed will vary in approximate proportion to the voltage impressed on the armature. The allowable horsepower output will decrease proportionally to the decrease in speed.

Armature speed control can be obtained by inserting an external variable resistance in series with the armature circuit. The location of such a resistance for the different types of d-c motors is shown in Fig. 74A. This method is easy to apply and requires only simple and relatively inexpensive equipment, and gradual control of the speed down to practically zero speed can be obtained. Series armature resistance control, however, has the following objections:

1. BULK OF RHEOSTAT. This may not be very objectionable if only a few motors are so controlled. but for a number the extra space becomes a factor, and in many cases it is difficult to find sufficient room near the motor.

2. INEFFICIENCY OF THE SYSTEM. The same amount of power is supplied at all speeds, but at low speeds only a small part of it is converted into useful work, the balance being wasted in the rheostat as heat.

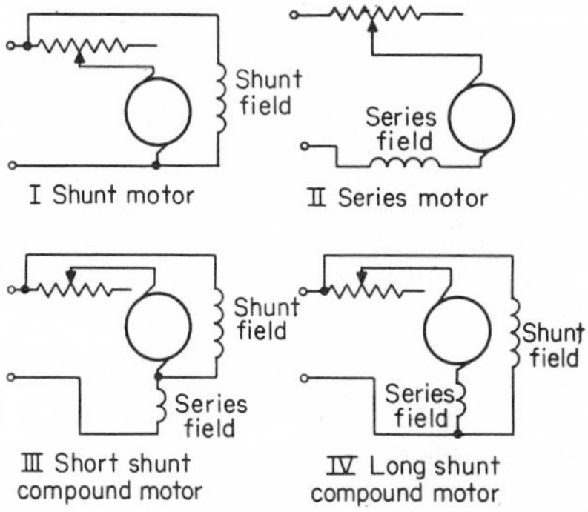

3. POOR SPEED REGULATION WITH

FIG. 74A *Speed control with armature resistance.*

VARYING LOADS. Since the impressed voltage at the armature terminals is equal to the line voltage minus the resistance drop in the rheostat $(V_t = V - I_a R_x)$, any change in the current drawn by the motor produces a change in the terminal voltage, the counter-emf, and therefore the speed.

Armature series resistance control is the type of speed control most commonly employed for series motors. Series motors requiring speed control are used chiefly for intermittent duty, and the total loss of energy in the control resistance is therefore not so great as it would be for continuous duty. Generally, armature series resistance control is not employed for shunt and compound motors unless a wider speed range is desired than can be obtained satisfactorily by means of field control or unless very low speeds are required.

Armature speed control obtained by a variable-voltage generator (Ward-Leonard system) requires an individual motor-generator set for each motor whose speed is to be controlled. Although this method is applicable to any type of d-c motor, it is most commonly used with shunt or compound motors. A schematic diagram is given in Fig. 75.

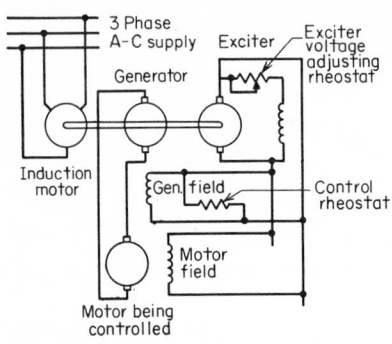

FIG. 75 *Ward-Leonard system of speed control.*

The Ward-Leonard system gives very close control of the speed over a wide range but has the disadvantage of requiring three full-sized machines for each motor drive. For automatic drive control with d-c motors, a variation of the Ward-Leonard system can be used, employing control generators (see Secs. 41A to 41C and Sec. 141).

The variable voltage for armature control can be obtained from a controlled electronic rectifier (see Sec. 48 of Div. 6). For very small fractional-horsepower motors, triode vacuum tubes can be employed for the rectification. The average voltage input to the motor armature is controlled by variation of the grid voltage of the tubes. Varying the grid voltage will vary the anode-to-cathode voltage drop of the tube and thereby vary the voltage impressed on the motor armature. For motors of any appreciable size, a vacuum-tube rectifier would be inefficient, since the power consumed by the tubes of the rectifier would be proportional to the reduction in speed obtained. Also the current-carrying capacities of vacuum tubes would be sufficient only for very small motors. For small and medium-sized motors, thyratron tubes would be used, and ignitron tubes would be used for medium- and large-sized motors. With both thyratron and ignitron rectifiers, the average voltage input to the motor armature would be controlled by controlling the period of conduction of the tubes (see Secs. 33 and 38 of Div. 6). A circuit for electronic speed control of a shunt motor is shown in Fig. 76. Electronic armature speed control gives close control of the speed over a wide range. Electronic control of d-c motor speed can be adapted for automatic drive control (see Sec. 140).

Resistance shunted across the armature is useful for controlling the speed of d-c motors to very low values at light loads. It is used only in conjunction with series armature-resistance control. Connections for this method are shown in Fig. 77.

137. Field Speed Control. The speed of d-c motors can be controlled by varying the field current of the motor while the armature voltage is held constant. Reducing the field current will reduce the flux and consequently increase the speed of the motor. Field control gives close control of the speed over a limited range. The speed of any shunt motor can be increased approximately 25 per cent above normal by field control. Where greater speed range than this is required, a shunt motor designed for adjustable-speed service should be used. A speed range of 4 : 1 is the practical limit for field control with an adjustable-speed shunt motor. The simplest method of obtaining field speed control for shunt or compound motors is by means of a field rheostat connected in series with the shunt field. The proper location of a field rheostat in motor circuits is shown in Fig. 78. This method is the one most commonly used for speed control of shunt and compound motors. It is very easy to apply, requires simple and inexpensive equipment that occupies only a very small space, does not consume any appreciable amount of power in the control equipment, and gives good speed regulation with varying loads.

Field control of shunt or compound motors can be obtained by energizing the shunt field from a variable-voltage generator. This method requires an individual motor-generator set for each motor to be controlled and has no advantage over the simple field rheostat method except for automatic drive control of small motors requiring only limited speed range. When this method is employed in automatic drive control, the shunt field of the motor is excited by a control generator (see Secs. 41A to 41C).

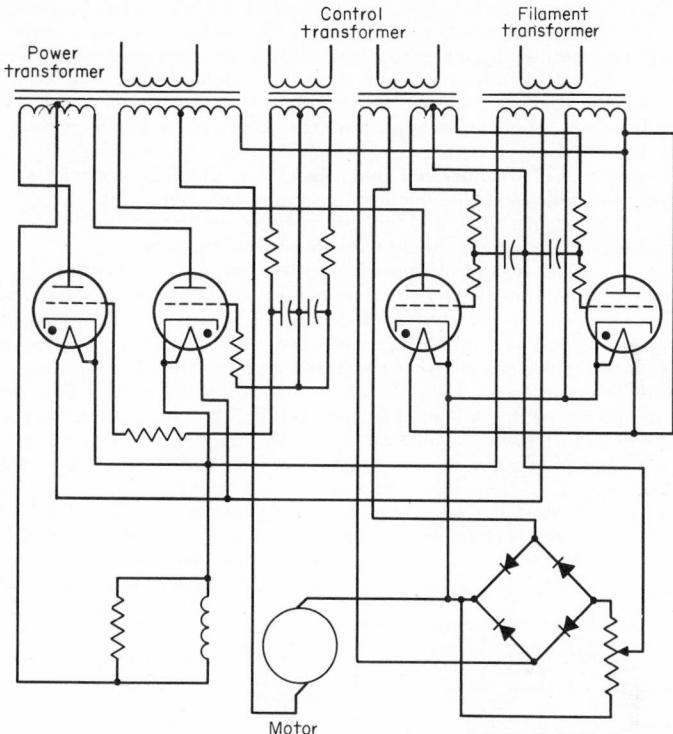

FIG. 76　*Electronic control of speed of a d-c motor.*

Field control of shunt and compound motors is sometimes obtained by supplying the shunt field from a controlled electronic rectifier. The fundamental principles and connections of the controlled rectifier are the same as those discussed for the rectifiers employed for electronic armature control. Electronic field control generally is employed only in combination with electronic armature control, where very wide speed range is required.

Field control of series motors is obtained by shunting a resistance across the series field. If a resistance or rheostat is placed in parallel with the field of a series-wound motor, the speed will be increased instead of decreased at a given load. This is known as shunting the field of the motor. This shunt would not be applied until the motor

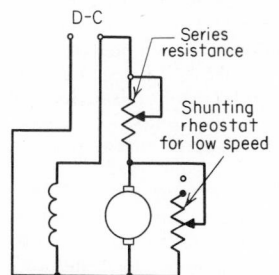

FIG. 77　*Speed control using shunt across armature.*

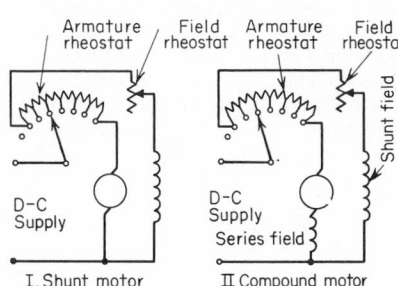

FIG. 78　*Control of speed with field rheostat.*

has been brought up to normal full speed by cutting out the starting resistance. With a "shunted field" a motor drives a load at a speed higher than normal and therefore requires a correspondingly increased current. With a shunted field more current is required to produce a given torque. The allowable torque at speeds above normal is, therefore, less than the rated full-load torque. With this type of speed control the motor is practically a constant-horsepower machine, the allowable rating being practically the same for all speeds.

138. Combination of armature and field control is employed where wide speed range is required. The following combinations are frequently employed:

1. Armature resistance combined with shunt-field rheostat.

2. Ward-Leonard system combined with shunt-field rheostat.

3. Electronic armature control combined with electronic field control.

A common combination which is used for controlling the speed of standard constant-speed motors is to employ armature control for reducing the speed to 50 per cent below normal and to use field control for increasing the speed 25 per cent above normal.

139. Automatic drive control (servo systems) is the automatic control of a motor to meet specified requirements of the driven equipment or material. A few of the more common requirements that are automatically fulfilled by automatic drive control are:

1. Production of uniform acceleration and deceleration.

2. Maintenance of constant speed regardless of load and control of speed over wide speed range.

3. Production of constant torque over wide speed range.

The essential elements of an electric-drive control system are shown in the block diagram of Fig. 79. An electric-drive control system must have the ability (1) to pick up a signal whenever there is a deviation from the required performance of a driven machine or process, (2) to convert this variation signal into a proportional electrical signal, (3) to compare this electrical signal with the desired standard, (4) to have the deviation from the standard activate a correction in the electrical input to the drive motor, and (5) to provide antihunting characteristics.

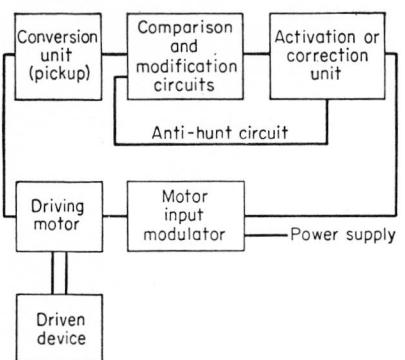

FIG. 79 *Block diagram of elements for automatic drive control.*

Requirements (1) and (2) above are fulfilled by the conversion element (pickup) of Fig. 79. The conversion element may take a variety of forms. It may be a pilot generator coupled to the drive motor or driven machine, which will pick up any variation in speed and translate this speed variation into a proportional voltage variation. It may be a resistor in series with the armature of the drive motor. The voltage across such a resistor will act as a pickup for any variation in the current delivered to the motor. Such a pickup can be used for constant torque control of a motor. Phototubes are used in many cases as the pickup device. A phototube circuit will pick up and convert into a voltage any deviation from the proper position of a machine tool or of a driven object. The pickup device may be a set of synchros, which will pick up and convert into a signal voltage any deviation from a desired angular position (see Sec. **177**).

Requirement (3) of the control system is fulfilled by the comparison circuit of Fig. 79. For example, consider the conditions for automatic speed control of a motor. The voltage of the conversion element (a pilot generator) is connected in series with a standard voltage, and any variation in the voltage of the pilot generator results in a variation of current in the comparison circuit. This variation in current will be controlled in magnitude and direction by the variation in the voltage of the pilot generator. The output of the comparison circuit may not be great enough to produce the proper functioning of the activation circuit. In these cases, a modification circuit, which will consist of an electronic amplifying circuit, must be employed. Often it is desired that the controlled machine be influenced by some other factor or factors in addition to the main controlling function. Such requirements are fulfilled by means of modification circuits.

Requirement (4) of the control system is fulfilled by the activation circuit of Fig. 79. The output of the comparison and modification circuit must be connected to an activation circuit, which will control the input circuit to the drive motor in such a manner as to correct the deviation of the driven device. For example, the output of the comparison circuit may act upon the grid-control circuit of a thyratron rectifier and in this manner control the input to the drive motor.

Requirement (5) of the control system is fulfilled through coupling or feedback circuits between comparison and activation circuits. The purpose of these antihunt circuits is to prevent overshooting of the correction and to prevent serious oscillations about the desired controlled condition. Although these antihunt circuits are in many cases essential, a discussion of them is beyond the scope of this book.

Since most types of a-c motors do not lend themselves to convenient control of their performance characteristics, d-c motors usually are employed where drive control is desired. In the majority of drive-control applications, the requirements are met through the use of d-c motors controlled by electronic or electrodynamic control systems. In both these control systems, the d-c motor performance is controlled through (1) control of input to the motor armature, (2) control of input to the motor field, or (3) combination control of input to the motor armature and field. In the electronic control systems, the motor input is adjusted by means of controlled vacuum, thyratron, or ignitron rectifiers. In the electrodynamic control systems, the motor input is adjusted by means of control generators (see Sec. **41A**). In many cases, electronic and electrodynamic control systems are competitive methods. In the electrodynamic control systems, electron tubes often are employed as a part of the system for amplifying or other modification purposes.

140. In electronic control of d-c motors, either the armature or field or both are supplied through electronic rectifiers. The output of the rectifiers is automatically controlled in accordance with the requirements of the driven machine or process. A simplified diagram of a circuit for constant-speed control obtained through armature control of the motor is shown in Fig. 80. A circuit employing field control would be similar, with the location of the field and armature simply interchanged. When both

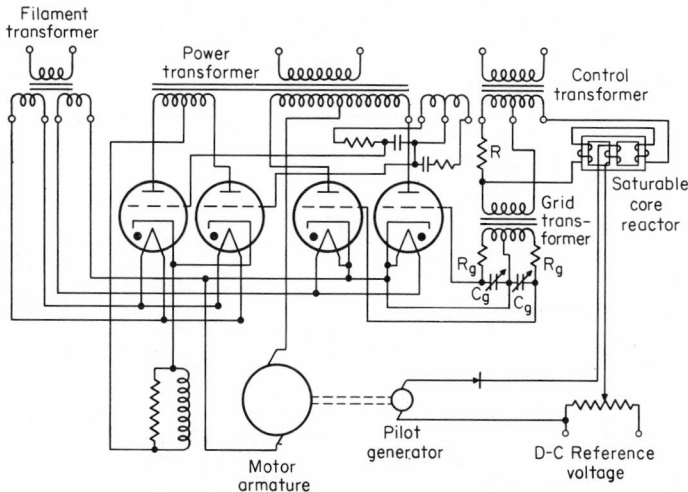

FIG. 80 *Automatic-drive electronic speed control.*

field and armature control are employed, for wide speed range, the armature and field supply circuits are essentially duplicates of each other. The automatic control feature for holding constant speed would be applied to only one of the supply circuits.

In the circuit of Fig. 80, the conversion element, or pickup, is the pilot generator, which is coupled to the d-c motor. The voltage of the pilot generator, which is proportional to the speed of the motor, is impressed upon the comparison circuit in such a manner as to oppose the reference voltage. The activation or correction circuit consists of an RL phase-shift grid-control circuit of the thyratrons. Variation of the phase shift is obtained by varying the reactance of the saturable-core reactor. The rectifier in the comparison circuit is for the purpose of blocking induced a-c voltages from the comparison circuit. The resistances R_g prevent excessive grid currents, and the capacitors C_g tend to absorb voltage surges in the grid circuits which would prevent satisfactory operation of the thyratrons.

The circuit of Fig. 80 functions in the following manner to hold the speed of the motor constant: The resistor R is adjusted to the proper value for the desired constant speed. If the speed of the motor rises above the value corresponding to the setting of R, the greater opposing voltage of the pilot generator will reduce the direct current through the center leg of the saturable reactor and thereby shift the phase of the thyratron grid voltages in such a manner as to reduce the conduction period of the thyratrons. Thus the input to the motor is reduced, and the speed of the motor is reduced until equilibrium conditions are reestablished. The equilibrium condition is the constant speed for which resistor R is set. In a similar manner, if the speed of the motor tends to drop below the constant speed, the circuit will function to increase the input to the motor armature and thereby restore equilibrium conditions. The circuit of Fig. 80 is simplified in order to bring out the fundamental principles. Actual circuits employed would be more complicated. Stable operation would require the addition of antihunt circuits and, in some cases, also filter circuits to smooth out the ripples in the rectified current supplied to the motor. The power supply, generally, would be taken from a three-phase system, and a three-phase thyratron rectifier would be used instead of the single-phase full-wave rectifier shown.

141. Automatic electrodynamic drive control is frequently called a **servo system.** In electrodynamic control of d-c motors, the input to the motor is automatically controlled in accordance with the requirements of the load by means of a control generator. Small motors may be directly supplied with power from the control generator. When the capacity of the control generator is not sufficient to supply the motor directly, the control generator energizes the field of a main generator and thus controls the input to the motor. Electrodynamic control circuits for constant-speed control of a d-c motor are shown in Figs. 81 and 82. The circuit of Fig. 81 employs an amplidyne control gen-

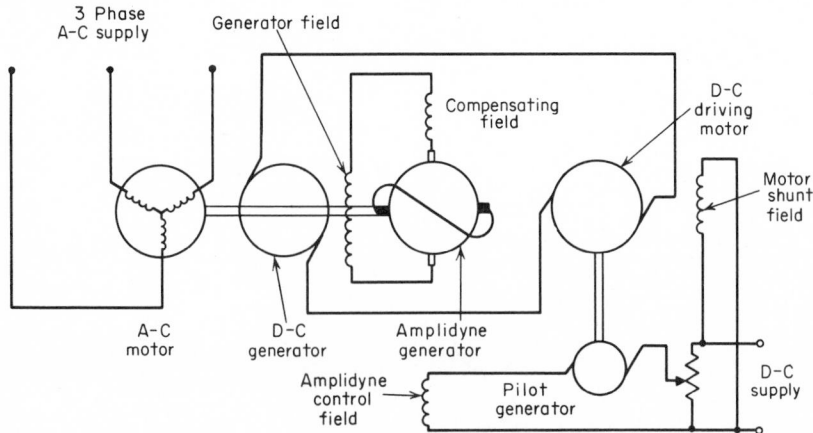

FIG. 81   *Speed control using amplidyne generator.*

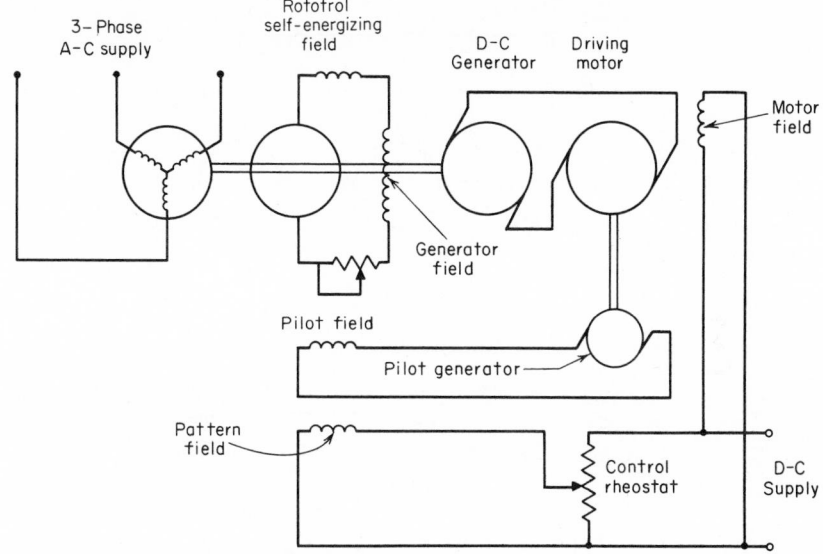

FIG. 82   *Speed control using Rototrol.*

erator, and that of Fig. 82 a Rototrol control generator. When a sufficient speed range can be obtained by field control, the control generator may control the input to the field of the motor instead of the input to the armature, as is shown in the figures. In the circuits of both Fig. 81 and Fig. 82 the conversion element, or pick up, is the pilot generator, which is coupled to the main d-c drive motor. In the circuit of Fig. 81, the voltage of the pilot generator is impressed upon the comparison circuit in such a manner as to oppose the reference voltage. In the circuit of Fig. 82, the voltage of the pilot generator energizes the pilot field of the Rototrol. The comparison circuit of Fig. 82 consists of the combination of the pilot- and pattern-field circuits. In the circuits of both figures, the activation circuit is the armature circuit of the control generator. When the signal voltage from the pilot generator is not sufficient to actuate the field circuit of the control generator directly, an electronic amplifier is inserted between the pickup circuit and the field of the control generator. In both the circuits shown in the figures, the circuit is adjusted for the desired speed by means of the adjusting rheostat.

In the amplidyne control circuit of Fig. 81, if the speed of the motor rises above the value corresponding to the setting of the adjusting rheostat, the greater opposing voltage of the pilot generator weakens the field of the amplidyne. This will lower the voltage output of the amplidyne and thereby weaken the field of the main generator. The voltage output of the main generator is thus reduced. Therefore, the input and consequently the speed of the motor are reduced until the speed has been brought back to the value determined by the setting of the adjusting rheostat.

In the Rototrol circuit of Fig. 82, if the speed of the motor rises above the value corresponding to the setting of the adjusting rheostat, the strength of the pilot field of the Rototrol is increased. Since the pilot field opposes the constant pattern field, the field flux of the Rototrol will be reduced. This will lower the voltage of the Rototrol and thereby weaken the field of the main generator. The voltage output of the main generator is thus reduced. Therefore, the input and consequently the speed of the motor are reduced until the speed has been brought back to the value determined by the setting of the adjusting rheostat.

Circuits for constant-current control of a d-c motor by means of electrodynamic control systems are shown in Figs. 83 and 84. The pickup element consists of a resistor in series with the motor armature circuit. Any deviation in the armature current will re-

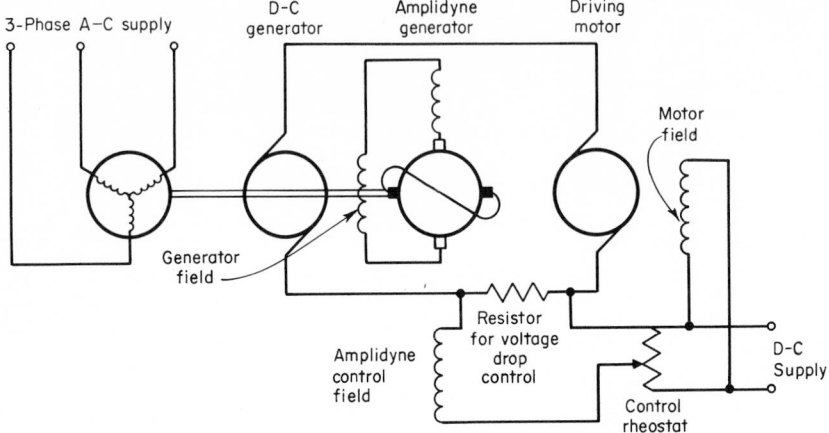

FIG. 83   *Constant-current control using amplidyne generator.*

sult in a proportionate change in voltage across this resistor.   The voltage across the resistor activates the comparison circuit in the same manner discussed for the constant-speed controls.

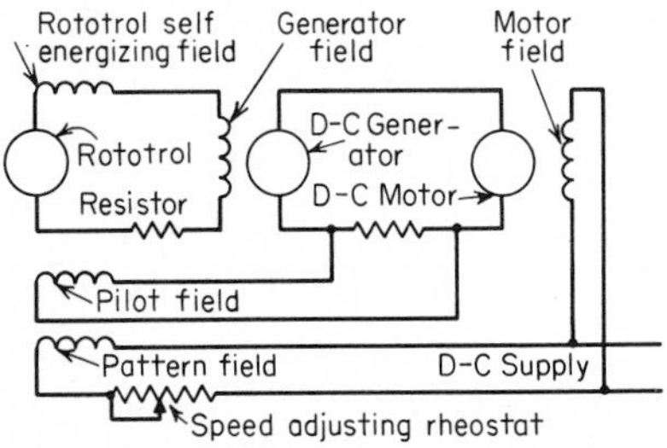

142. Position Control.   It is often desirable to have a control system that functions to control the position of a driven object or rotating machine.   The position of a driven object may be indicated by a phototube scanning the driven object.   The angular position of a rotating machine may be indicated by the error voltage of a synchro circuit (see Sec. **177**).   The phototube or synchro pickup and conversion element can actuate either an electronic or an electrodynamic control system so as to control the process or driven machine in accordance with the position desired.

FIG. 84   *Constant-current control using Rototrol control generator.*

143. Approximate Efficiencies of D-C Motors — Continuous Rated, 40°C Rise

Hp	Percentage efficiency			Hp	Percentage efficiency		
	One-half load	Three-fourths load	Full load		One-half load	Three-fourths load	Full load
½	62.0	65.0	68.0	20	82.0	85.0	86.5
¾	65.0	70.0	72.0	25	83.0	86.0	87.0
1	70.0	73.0	75.0	30	84.0	87.0	88.0
1½	72.0	76.0	78.0	40	85.0	87.5	88.5
2	72.0	77.5	81.0	50	85.5	88.0	89.5
3	72.0	77.0	79.0	60	85.5	88.0	90.0
5	77.0	81.0	81.5	75	86.0	89.0	90.5
7½	79.0	82.0	83.5	100	86.0	89.0	90.5
10	81.0	83.0	85.0	125	86.0	89.0	90.5
15	81.5	84.5	86.0	150	87.0	90.0	91.0
				200	89.0	91.5	92.0

ALTERNATING-CURRENT MOTORS

144. General Construction of Polyphase Induction Motors. Polyphase induction motors have two windings, one on the stationary part of the machine or stator and one mounted on the revolving part or rotor. The stator winding is embedded in slots in the inner surface of the frame of the machine and is similar to the armature winding of a revolving-field type of a-c generator. The rotor winding may be one of two types: squirrel cage or wound rotor. In a **squirrel-cage** machine the rotor winding consists simply of copper or aluminum bars embedded in slots in the iron core of the rotor and connected together at each end by means of a copper or aluminum ring. The rotor winding thus forms a complete closed circuit in itself. The rotor winding of the **wound-rotor** machine is similar to the armature winding of a revolving-armature type of a-c generator. The free ends of the winding are brought out to slip rings. The rotor circuit is not closed until the slip rings are connected either directly together or through some resistances external to the machine.

145. Principle of Operation of the Induction Motor. The induction motor differs from other types of motors in the fact that there is no electrical connection from the rotor winding to any source of electrical energy. The necessary voltage and current in the rotor circuit are produced by induction from the stator winding. The operation of the induction motor depends upon the production of a revolving magnetic field. The stator winding of a simple two-phase induction motor connected to a simple two-phase alternator is shown in Fig. 85.

Windings of the types shown in the illustration are not used in commercial machines, but the general theory involved is the same as with commercial windings. The revolving field (see illustration) of the generator, in turning in the direction shown by the arrow, generates a two-phase current, which is transmitted to the motor. The current in conductors of one phase magnetizes poles A and B, and that in the other phase the poles C and D. The winding is so arranged that a current entering at A will produce a south pole at A and a north pole at B. At the instant shown at I, the motor poles A and B are magnetized while poles C and D are not, because it is a property of a two-phase circuit that, when the current in one of the phases is at a maximum value, the current in the other phase is at a zero value. Hence, at this instant a magnetic field will be set up in the machine in a vertical direction, with a north pole at B and a south pole at A.

At another later instant, represented at II, the currents in both of the phases are equal and in the same direction. The motor poles will be magnetized as shown. The currents in changing from their values in I to their values in II have moved the magnetic field through an angle of 45 deg toward the right. At the instant illustrated at III, because of the properties of two-phase currents there is no current in the phase of the conductors which are wound on poles A and B, but the current in the phase of the conductors which magnetize poles C and D is at maximum. Hence, the magnetic field produced in the machine at instant III is in a horizontal direction with a south pole at C and a north pole at D. The magnetic field has been moved around another 45 deg. Similar action occurs during successive instants, and the magnetic field is caused to rotate continually in the same direction within the motor frame as long as the two-phase

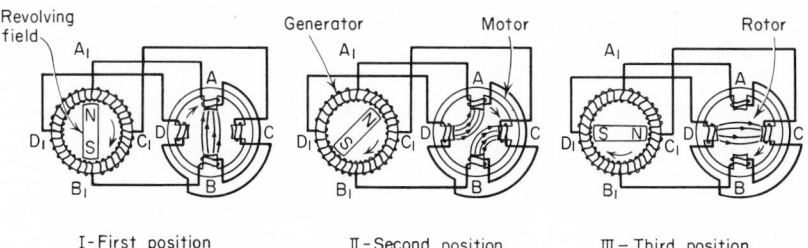

I–First position   II–Second position   III–Third position

FIG. 85 *Illustrating the principle of the induction motor.*

current is applied to the stator terminals. Thus, when the stator winding of a polyphase motor is connected to a source of polyphase power, a revolving field is produced inside the machine.

If a closed electric circuit such as the rotor winding of an induction motor is inserted in the machine, the revolving magnetic field will cut across the conductors of this winding and in that way produce a voltage in them. This voltage acting upon the closed rotor circuit will send a current through the different conductors of the rotor winding. The rotor conductors then will be carrying a current and lying in a magnetic field. Such a condition will produce a force upon the conductors of the rotor winding, tending to turn them in the same direction as that in which the magnetic field is revolving.

If the rotor winding was revolved at the same rate of speed as that at which the magnetic field revolves, there would be no relative motion between the field and the conductors of the rotor winding. Since there would be no relative motion, there would be no cutting of the magnetic field across the conductors and therefore no voltage or current produced in the rotor winding. If there is no current in the rotor winding, there can be no torque produced, tending to keep the machine revolving. As the machine slows down, however, the magnetic field will revolve at a higher speed than the rotor, producing a relative motion between the magnetic field and the conductors of the rotor winding. This relative motion produces a cutting of the conductors by the flux, with the resultant voltage and current necessary to develop a turning effort upon the rotor. The operation of an induction motor depends upon a difference in speed between the revolving magnetic field and the actual speed of the machine or rotor. This difference in speed is called the slip of the motor. The rotor is said to slip a certain number of revolutions behind the revolving magnetic field. The greater the load on an induction motor, the more the rotor must slip behind the revolving magnetic field in order to produce a greater cutting of the flux by the rotor conductors, with the resulting greater current in the rotor and greater turning effort to carry the greater load. Even at no load an induction motor cannot revolve as fast as the magnetic field revolves, since enough torque must be developed to overcome the friction and other losses in the motor.

146. Synchronous speed of an induction motor is the speed at which its magnetic field revolves. It depends upon the number of poles for which the stator is wound and the frequency of the supply voltage.

$$\text{Synchronous speed} = \frac{120f}{P} \tag{4}$$

where f = frequency of supply, P = the number of poles per phase for which the stator is wound, and synchronous speed is in revolutions per minute.

147. The slip of an induction motor is the ratio of the difference between the rotating magnetic-field speed (rpm or angular velocity) and the actual rotor speed to the rotating magnetic-field speed. The speed of the rotating magnetic field is equivalent to the synchronous speed of the machine (see table of synchronous speeds elsewhere in this section) which is determined by the frequency of the current and the number of poles of the machine (Sec. **146**). Then

$$\text{Slip in rpm} = \text{synchronous speed} - \text{actual speed} \tag{5}$$

$$\text{Per cent slip} = \frac{\text{synchronous speed} - \text{actual speed}}{\text{synchronous speed}} \times 100 \tag{5a}$$

When there is no load on a motor the slip is very small; i.e., the rotor speed is practically equal to the synchronous speed. Slip varies with the design of a motor and may vary from 4.0 to 8.5 per cent at full load in motors of from 1 to 75 hp of ordinary design.

Example. What is the slip at full load of a four-pole 60-cycle induction motor which has a full-load speed of 1,700 rpm?

Solution. From Table **97** or Sec. **146** the speed of the rotating field or the synchronous speed of a four-pole 60-cycle motor is 1,800 rpm. Then, substituting in the above formula,

$$\text{Per cent slip} = \frac{\text{synchronous speed} - \text{actual speed}}{\text{synchronous speed}} \times 100 = \frac{1,800 - 1,700}{1,800} \times 100$$

$$= \frac{100}{1,800} \times 100 = 5.5 \text{ per cent}$$

Therefore the slip is 5.5 per cent. The voltage of the motor and whether it is single-phase, two-phase, or three-phase are not factors in the problem.

148. The Breakdown Torque of an Induction Motor. Most induction motors will "break down" at some certain torque if they are overloaded. The "breakdown" limit—the maximum running torque that can be developed—is that point at which further increase in load will cause the motor speed to decrease rapidly and then to stop. This point is usually at between two and four times the full-load rated torque, depending on the design and the capacity of the motor. In a few cases there is no breakdown torque, the maximum torque occurring at standstill. Under these conditions there will be no sudden decrease in the speed as the load is increased. The speed will gradually decrease as load is increased until standstill is reached.

149. General Operating Characteristics of Induction Motors. The following rules, though somewhat approximate, are accurate enough for practical use under the normal range of operation of an induction motor from no load to 150 per cent of rated load.

The slip of an induction motor varies directly with the load. Doubling of the load will double the slip.

For any given load the slip varies directly with the resistance of the rotor circuit. If the resistance of the rotor circuit is doubled, the slip for the same load will be twice its original value.

For any load the slip varies inversely as the square of the voltage impressed on the stator winding. If the voltage is reduced to one-half of its normal value, the slip is increased to four times its normal value for any load.

The torque developed by an induction motor varies directly with the slip.

The torque developed at any particular slip varies inversely with the resistance of the rotor circuit.

The torque for any particular slip varies directly as the square of the voltage impressed on the stator.

The maximum torque is not affected by the resistance of the rotor circuit. A large value of resistance for the rotor circuit simply makes the maximum torque occur at a high slip.

The maximum torque varies directly with the square of the voltage impressed on the stator circuit.

150. Starting Characteristics of Induction Motors. The starting torque varies directly with the square of the voltage impressed on the stator. If three-fourths of normal voltage is impressed at starting, the starting torque will be equal to only nine-sixteenths of the torque developed with normal voltage impressed at starting.

The value of the starting torque of an induction motor also depends upon the value of the resistance of the rotor circuit. As the resistance of the rotor circuit is increased, the starting torque is increased until the resistance of the rotor circuit is of just the right value to make the maximum torque occur at starting. If the resistance of the rotor circuit is still further increased, the starting torque will be decreased. Thus, there is a certain value of rotor resistance that will produce maximum starting torque, either a greater or smaller value of rotor resistance than this amount producing less starting torque (see Fig. 88).

The current taken at starting by an induction motor depends upon the voltage impressed on the stator and the resistance of the rotor circuit. For a fixed rotor resistance the starting current varies directly with the impressed voltage. For a particular impressed voltage, increasing the resistance of the rotor circuit decreases the value of the starting current.

151. Characteristic Curves of the Induction Motor. The curves of Fig. 86 are fairly typical of the average normal-torque, normal-starting-current, commercial induction motor. It will be noted that the normal rating of the motor is taken at such a point that both the power factor and the efficiency are the highest possible. The motor could be so designed that either the power factor or the efficiency, but not both, could be higher than shown at normal load, but the design of an induction motor is a compromise between the leading factors resulting in the best efficiency and power factor obtainable with suitable overload and starting characteristics.

The characteristics of a polyphase induction motor running single-phase are shown

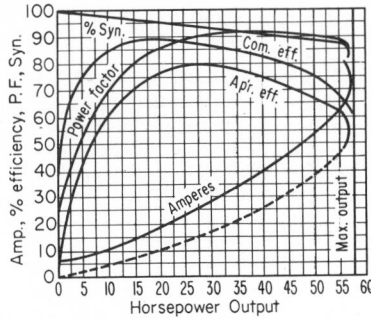

FIG. 86 *Typical performance graphs of a 20-hp three-phase induction motor.*

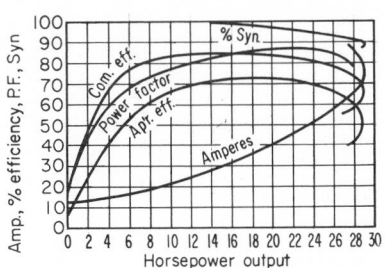

FIG. 87 *Performance graphs of the motor shown in Fig. 86 when running single-phase.*

in Fig. 87. In Fig. 89 is shown the speed-torque characteristic of a polyphase induction motor running single-phase. It will be noted that the starting torque when operated single-phase is zero. A polyphase induction motor will not start when connected to a single-phase supply. If it is once started, however, it will operate from a single-phase supply and carry approximately half rated load without overheating.

152. The torque curves of an induction motor with a wound rotor, from rest to synchronism, running both three-phase and single-phase with external resistance and without external resistance, are shown in Fig. 88. The curves are plotted with torque in foot-pounds at 1 ft radius. Curve *A* shows the torque from rest to synchronism without resistance in the rotor circuit. If the proper value of resistance is inserted, curve *B* is obtained, and the starting torque is 440 ft-lb against 170 ft-lb without resistance. Curve *C* indicates the torque where too much resistance is used in the rotor. Curve *E* illustrates the torque for single phase, which is zero at starting. A wound-rotor induction motor starts as shown on curve *B* until it reaches the point *F*, when the resistance is cut out and the motor adjusts itself to its operating position at *G*. Thus, if the torque required of the motor for which the curve is shown is greater than 440 ft-lb, shown at *H*, the motor will break down and come to rest. With the resistance in the rotor, a starting torque of 440 ft-lb is available, but this load cannot be brought up to normal speed. The motor can bring only the torque represented by the point *F*, in other words 290 ft-lb, up to normal speed.

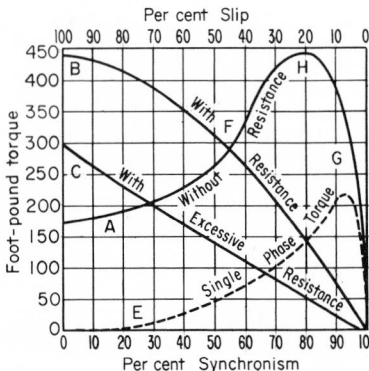

FIG. 88 *Torque graphs of a 30-hp induction motor.*

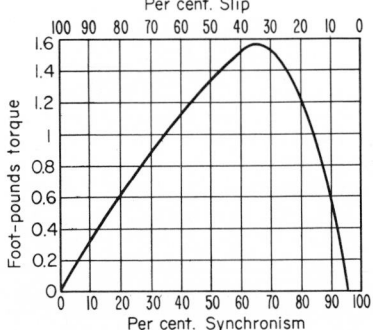

FIG. 89 *Torque graph of a 1-hp three-phase induction motor running single-phase.*

In Fig. 88 it will be noted that the torque of a three-phase motor rises to a maximum and then drops, reaching zero at synchronism. This means that an induction motor never runs at synchronous speed.

153. Speed Control of Induction Motors. It is possible to control the speed of an induction motor by any one of the following methods:

1. Changing impressed voltage.
2. Changing number of poles for which the machine is wound.
3. Changing the frequency of the supply.
4. Changing the resistance of the rotor circuit.
5. Introducing a foreign voltage into the secondary circuit.
6. Operating two or more motors connected in cascade.

154. Reducing the impressed voltage will increase the slip of an induction motor proportionally to the square of the voltage. At the same time, however, the breakdown torque of the motor is also reduced as the square of the voltage, so that there is danger of the motor stalling under load. For this reason, changing the impressed voltage is employed for the speed control of induction motors only in emergencies or other special cases.

155. Speed Control of Induction Motors by Changing the Number of Poles. The actual speed of an induction motor depends upon the speed of the revolving magnetic field produced by the stator winding (synchronous speed). The synchronous speed of an induction motor is inversely proportional to the number of poles for which the stator winding is wound. Thus, on a 60-cycle circuit a two-pole induction motor has a synchronous speed of 3,600 rpm; a four-pole motor, 1,800 rpm; an eight-pole motor, 900 rpm; etc. It is, therefore, possible to alter the speed of an induction motor by changing the number of its poles.

This can be accomplished by using two or more separate primary windings, each having a different number of poles, or by using a single winding which can be connected so as to form different numbers of poles. This method is, of course, not applicable to the ordinary type of induction motor but requires a motor with a number of leads brought out from the primary winding (see Multispeed motors, Sec. 171). Gradual speed control cannot be obtained by this method. Only a certain number of definite speeds, four at the most, can be obtained.

156. Speed Control of a Polyphase Motor by Adjusting the Frequency of the Primary Current. Since the synchronous speed of an induction motor is equal to the alternations per minute of the supply circuit divided by the number of poles in each phase circuit, a change in speed can be effected by changing the frequency of the supply circuit.

Figure 90 shows the speed-torque and other curves of a 60-cycle motor when operated at 60, 30, 15, and 6 cycles, or at 100, 50, 25, and 10 per cent of the normal frequency. The speed-torque curves corresponding to the above frequencies are a, b, c, and d. The current curves are A, B, C, and D. This figure shows that for the rated torque T the current is practically constant for all speeds, but the emf varies with the frequency. Consequently, the apparent power supplied, represented by the product of the current by emf, varies with the speed of the motor and is practically proportionate to the power developed.

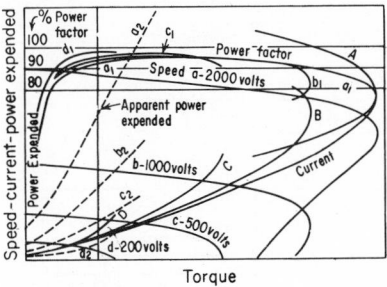

FIG. 90 *Performance graphs of a polyphase induction motor with different applied frequencies and different applied voltages.*

In a few cases, where only one motor is operated, the generator speed can be varied. If the generator is driven by a water wheel, its speed can be varied over a wide range and the motor speed will also vary. If the generator field is held at practically constant strength, then the motor speed can be varied from zero to a maximum at constant torque with a practically constant current.

Controlling the speed of an induction motor by changing the frequency of the supply requires a separate generator for each motor. This method is, therefore, not feasible for ordinary speed-control applications. It is sometimes employed in special cases for the control of large units requiring very fine speed control.

157. Speed Control of Induction Motors by Adjusting the Resistance of the Secondary Circuit. Inserting resistance in series with the rotor of an induction motor will decrease the speed of the motor. The amount of decrease in speed produced will depend upon the load on the motor. It is not possible to produce much change in speed by this method at light loads. This method of speed control is, of course, applicable only to wound-rotor motors. Speed control by adjusting the resistance of the rotor circuit has two drawbacks. After the speed has been adjusted for any load, the speed does not remain constant with change in load. With external resistance in series with the rotor, the motor has a varying speed characteristic. Considerable power is wasted in the external resistance required for changing the speed. The amount of power wasted depends upon the value of the external resistance. The efficiency of the motor is thus decreased approximately proportionally to the reduction in speed.

Speed control by means of adjustable secondary resistance is, however, very useful where constant speeds are not essential, for example, in operating cranes, hoists, elevators, and dredges and also for service in which the torque remains constant at each speed, as in driving fans, blowers, and centrifugal pumps. In service where reduced speeds are required only occasionally and where speed variation is not objectionable, this method of control can also be used to good advantage. On account of energy loss in the resistors, the efficiency is reduced when operating at reduced speeds, this reduction being greatest at the slowest speeds. The circuits are essentially the same as for starting by varying resistance in the rotor circuit, as shown in Fig. 174. The rotor usually has a Y-connected winding to which is connected, in series in each phase, an external resistance (Fig. 174). If the adjustable arm is moved, the amount of resistance in series in each phase can be varied from a maximum to zero and the speed varied gradually from the highest speed to the lowest.

158. Speed Control of Induction Motors by Introduction of a Foreign Voltage into the Secondary Circuit. If a foreign voltage is introduced into the secondary circuit of an induction motor, it will alter the speed of the motor. If this foreign voltage acts in a direction opposite to that of the voltage induced in the secondary circuit, the speed of the motor will be reduced. If the foreign voltage acts in the same direction as the voltage induced in the secondary circuit, the speed of the motor will be increased. With this method of speed control it is possible to obtain speeds both above and below the synchronous speed of the motor. Speed control by the introduction of a foreign voltage into the secondary circuit has two advantages. No power is wasted in resistance, and the speed is practically constant for all loads with the same value of foreign voltage introduced.

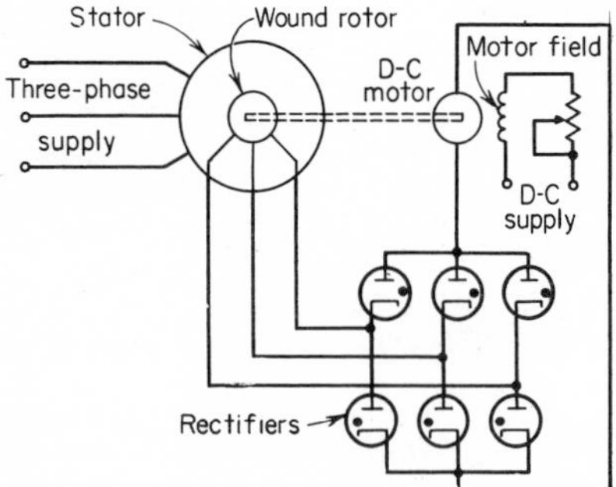

The brush-shifting type of polyphase induction motors, as explained in Sec. **176,** employs the foreign-voltage method of speed control. Where the operating characteristics of these motors are applicable, these motors provide a very efficient means of obtaining adjustable speed for a-c installations.

An electronic method of foreign-voltage speed control has been employed and is feasible for medium-sized and small motors. The diagram of the circuit for such a method is shown in Fig. 91. The armature of a d-c motor is connected through a three-phase full-wave ignitron or thyratron rectifier to the rotor slip rings of the induction motor. This connection introduces the counter-emf of the d-c motor into the rotor circuit of the induction motor. The value of the counter-emf of the d-c motor is adjusted by adjustment of the field rheostat of the d-c motor. The speed of the induction motor

FIG. 91 *Control of wound-rotor induction motor using electronic means.*

is, therefore, controlled through adjustment of the field rheostat of the d-c motor. The d-c motor may be mechanically coupled to the induction motor so that it helps to drive the load, or the d-c motor may drive an a-c generator so that the greater portion of the power taken by the d-c motor is returned to the a-c supply system.

There are other methods of obtaining speed control by the foreign-voltage method, but all of them require the use of additional revolving machines besides the motor itself. Their use is not feasible for ordinary applications. They are employed in special cases for the speed control of large motors.

159. Speed control of polyphase motors by operating two or more motors connected in cascade offers, under some conditions of service, the most convenient and economical method of speed variation. In this arrangement all the rotors are mounted on one shaft, or the several shafts are rigidly connected. The primary of the first motor is connected to the line; its secondary, which must be of the phase-wound, slip-ring type, is connected to the primary of the second motor. The secondary of the last motor can be of either the squirrel-cage or the phase-wound type. In practice more than two motors are rarely used. The arrangement is shown in Fig. 92.

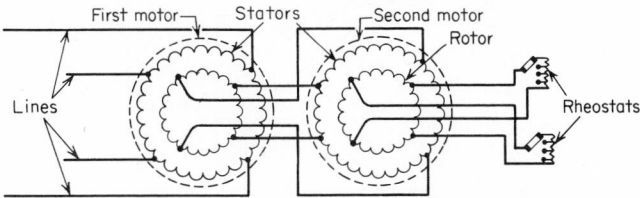

FIG. 92 *Two polyphase motors connected in cascade.*

Speed changes are obtained by varying the connections of the motors, the following combinations being possible with two motors: each motor can be operated separately at its normal speed with its primary connected to the line, the other motor running idle; the motors can be connected in cascade so that the rotors tend to start in the same direction (direct concatenation); or the motors can be connected so that the rotors tend to start in opposite directions (differential concatenation). If the first motor has 12 poles and the second 4, the following synchronous speeds can be obtained on a 25-cycle circuit:

1. Motor II (four poles) running single, 750 rpm.
2. Motors in differential concatenation (equivalent of 8 poles), 375 rpm.
3. Motor I (12 poles) running single, 250 rpm.
4. Motors in direct concatenation (equivalent of 16 poles), 187.5 rpm.

By the use of adjustable resistance in the secondary circuits, changes from one speed to the next can be made with uniform gradations.

A great number of speed combinations are possible by the use of this method; the control is simple and safe, as few leads are required and main circuits are not opened for most of the speeds. The rotors can be made with smaller diameters than is possible with other multispeed motors; hence the flywheel effect is reduced to a minimum. In general, a cascade set is applicable where speed changes must be frequently made with high horsepower output and primary voltage and where the speed ratios are other than 1:2.

160. Application of the Methods of Speed Control of Induction Motors. From the discussion in the preceding sections it is apparent that the ordinary squirrel-cage induction motor is not suitable for common adjustable-speed application. When a few definite speeds will be satisfactory, the multispeed motor can be employed. In special cases, squirrel-cage motors which have their speed controlled by a change in the frequency of the supply may be advisable. Therefore, when speed control is required on polyphase a-c systems, the wound-rotor motor with variable external resistance in the rotor circuit, or the brush-shifting type, must be employed, except for special applications.

161. Classification of Squirrel-cage Induction Motors. Integral-horsepower poly-phase squirrel-cage induction motors are classified by the NEMA standards into five design types as follows:

A Design A motor is a squirrel-cage motor designed to withstand full-voltage starting and developing locked-rotor torque as shown in Sec. **163,** breakdown torque as shown in Sec. **164,** with locked-rotor current higher than the values shown in Sec. **162** and having a slip at rated load of less than 5 per cent.[1]

A Design B motor is a squirrel-cage motor designed to withstand full-voltage start-ing, developing locked-rotor and breakdown torques adequate for general application as specified in Secs. **163** and **164,** drawing locked-rotor current not to exceed the values shown in Sec. **162** and having a slip at rated load of less than 5 per cent.[1]

A Design C motor is a squirrel-cage motor designed to withstand full-voltage start-ing, developing locked-rotor torque for special high-torque application up to the values shown in Sec. **163,** breakdown torque up to the values shown in Sec. **164,** with locked-rotor current not to exceed the values shown in Sec. **162** and having a slip at rated load of less than 5 per cent.

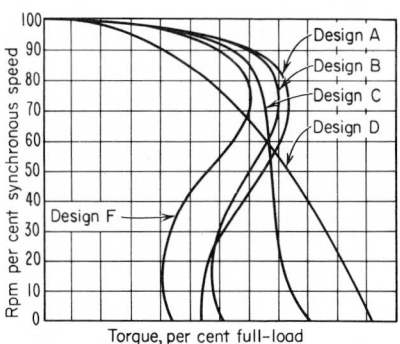

FIG. 93   *Typical speed-torque characteristics for squirrel-cage induction motors.* (*Westinghouse Electric Corp.*)

A Design D motor is a squirrel-cage motor designed to withstand full-voltage start-ing, developing high locked-rotor torque as shown in Sec. **163,** with locked-rotor current not greater than shown in Sec. **162** and having a slip at rated load of 5 per cent or more.

A Design F motor is a squirrel-cage motor designed to withstand full-voltage start-ing, developing low locked-rotor torque as shown in Sec. **163,** with locked-rotor current not to exceed the values shown in Sec. **162** and having a slip at rated load of less than 5 per cent.

Typical speed-torque curves for the five design types are given in Fig. 93.

[1] Motors with 10 and more poles may have slip slightly greater than 5 per cent.

162. Locked-rotor Current for Three-phase Integral-horsepower Squirrel-cage Induction Motors
(NEMA Standard)

The locked-rotor current of single-speed, three-phase, constant-speed induction motors, when measured with rated voltage and frequency impressed and with rotor locked, shall not exceed the following:

Three-phase, 60-cycle Motors at 220 Volts [a]

Hp	Locked-rotor current, amperes[a]	Design letters
1/2	20	B, D
3/4	25	B, D
1	30	B, D
1 1/2	40	B, D
2	50	B, D
3	64	B, C, D
5	92	B, C, D
7 1/2	127	B, C, D
10	162	B, C, D
15	232	B, C, D
20	290	B, C, D
25	365	B, C, D
30	435	B, C, D
40	580	B, C, D
50	725	B, C, D
60	870	B, C, D
75	1,085	B, C, D
100	1,450	B, C, D
125	1,815	B, C, D
150	2,170	B, C, D
200	2,900	B, C
250	3,650	B
300	4,400	B
350	5,100	B
400	5,800	B
450	6,500	B
500	7,250	B

[a] Locked-rotor current of motors designed for voltages other than 220 volts shall be inversely proportional to the voltages, except for motors rated at 230 volts.

163. Locked-rotor Torque of Single-speed Polyphase Squirrel-cage Integral-horse-power Motors with Continuous Ratings
(NEMA Standard)

1. The locked-rotor torque of Designs A and B, 60- and 50-cycle, single-speed, polyphase squirrel-cage motors, with rated voltage and frequency applied, shall be in accordance with the following values, which are expressed in percentage of full-load torque and represent the upper limit of the range of application for these motors. For applications involving higher torque requirements, see the locked-rotor torque values for Design C and D motors.

Hp	Synchronous speeds						
	60 cycles	3,600	1,800	1,200	900	720	600	514
	50 cycles	3,000	1,500	1,000	750	600	500	428
1/2		...	...	...	140	140	115	110
3/4		...	...	175	135	135	115	110
1		...	275	170	135	135	115	110
1 1/2		175	250	165	130	130	115	110
2		170	235	160	130	125	115	110
3		160	215	155	130	125	115	110
5		150	185	150	130	125	115	110
7 1/2		140	175	150	125	120	115	110
10		135	165	150	125	120	115	110
15		130	160	140	125	120	115	110
20		130	150	135	125	120	115	110
25		130	150	135	125	120	115	110
30		130	140	135	125	120	115	110
40		125	140	135	125	120	115	110
50		120	140	135	125	120	115	110
60		120	140	135	125	120	115	110
75		105	140	135	125	120	115	110
100		105	125	125	125	120	115	110
125		100	110	125	120	115	115	110
150		100	110	120	120	115	115	...
200		100	100	120	120	115	...	...

2. The locked-rotor torque of Design C, 60- and 50-cycle, single-speed, polyphase squirrel-cage motors, with rated voltage and frequency applied, shall be in accordance with the following values, which are expressed in percentage of full-load torque and which represent the upper limit of the range of application for these motors:

Hp	Synchronous speeds		
	60 cycles	1,800	1,200	900
	50 cycles	1,500	1,000	750
1/2				
3/4				
1				
1 1/2				
2				
3		...	250	225
5		250	250	225
7 1/2		250	225	200
10		250	225	200
15		225	200	200
20		200	200	200
25 to 200		200	200	200

3. The locked-rotor torque of Design D, 60- and 50-cycle, four-, six- and eight-pole, single-speed, polyphase squirrel-cage motors, with rated voltage and frequency applied, shall be 275 per cent, expressed in percentage of full-load torque, which represents the upper limit of application for these motors.

4. The locked-rotor torque of Design F, 60- and 50-cycle, four- and six-pole, single-speed, polyphase squirrel-cage motors, rated 30 hp and larger, with rated voltage and frequency applied, shall be 125 per cent, expressed in percentage of full-load torque, which represents the upper limit of application for these motors.

164. Breakdown Torque of Single-speed Polyphase Squirrel-cage Integral-horsepower Motors with Continuous Ratings, Designs B and C
(NEMA Standard)

The breakdown torque of Designs B and C, 60- and 50-cycle, single-speed, polyphase squirrel-cage motors, with rated voltage and frequency applied, shall be in accordance with the following values, which are expressed in percentage of full-load torque and which represent the upper limit of the range of application for these motors. For Design A, values are in excess of those for Design B.

Hp	Synchronous speed, rpm (60 and 50 cycles)	Breakdown torque per cent of full-load torque	
		Design B	Design C
½	900–750	225	
	Lower than 750	200	
¾	1,200–1,000	275	
	900–750	220	
	Lower than 750	200	
1	1,800–1,500	300	
	1,200–1,000	265	
	900–750	215	
	Lower than 750	200	
1½	3,600–3,000	250	
	1,800–1,500	280	
	1,200–1,000	250	
	900–750	210	
	Lower than 750	200	
2	3,600–3,000	240	
	1,800–1,500	270	
	1,200–1,000	240	
	900–750	210	
	Lower than 750	200	
3	3,600–3,000	230	
	1,800–1,500	250	
	1,200–1,000	230	225
	900–750	225	200
	Lower than 750	200	
5	3,600–3,000	215	
	1,800–1,500	225	200
	1,200–1,000	215	200
	900–750	205	200
	Lower than 750	200	
7½	3,600–3,000	200	
	1,800–1,500	215	190
	1,200–1,000	205	190
	900–750	200	190
	Lower than 750	200	
10	3,600–3,000	200	
	1,800–1,500	200	190
	1,200–1,000	200	190
	900–750	200	190
	Lower than 750	200	
15–300	All speeds	200	190

165. The Design A (normal-torque, normal-starting-current) motor is the old standard type of squirrel-cage induction motor. It is a constant-speed machine with a slip of from 2 to 5 per cent at full load. It is not adapted for speed-control service. The starting torques with rated voltage applied are at least as great as given in Sec. **163.**

The locked-rotor starting currents with rated voltage applied vary from 500 to 1,000 per cent of full-load current, the smaller values being for motors with the larger number of poles.

The full-voltage starting currents of motors of 5 hp and smaller will be within the limitations of most power companies, so they are generally started directly across the line. Motors of larger size than 5 hp will have full-voltage starting currents that will not be within the limitations of some power companies and in such cases are started with reduced voltage.

The breakdown torques are from 200 to 250 per cent of full-load torque.

166. The Design B (normal-torque, low-starting-current) squirrel-cage motor is so designed that its rotor has a high reactance and resistance at start but nearly normal reactance and resistance under running conditions. This enables this type of motor to produce approximately the same starting torque for a given voltage as the normal-torque, normal-starting-current motor but with a much smaller value of starting current.

The running performance will be very nearly but not quite so good as that of the normal-torque, normal-starting-current type, the efficiency, power factor, and breakdown torque being slightly less and the speed regulation slightly larger. The breakdown torques will be at least as great as given in Sec. **164.** The locked-rotor starting current with rated voltage applied will be not greater than given in Sec. **162.** The full-voltage starting currents of motors of 30 hp and smaller will be within the limitations of most power companies, so they are generally started directly across the line. Motors of larger size than 30 hp will have full-voltage starting currents that will not be within the limitations of many power companies and therefore frequently must be started with reduced voltage.

167. Design C (high-torque, low-starting-current) squirrel-cage induction motors are usually constructed with two squirrel-cage windings on the rotor, located one above the other in the rotor slots. During the starting period most of the current is carried by the top winding, which has a high resistance. This enables the motor to produce a larger starting torque with about the same value of starting current as the normal-torque, low-starting-current type of motor. After the motor has come up to speed, the two windings are equally effective in carrying the rotor current, and its operating characteristics are similar to those of the normal-torque, low-starting-current type of motor.

The locked-rotor starting currents with rated voltage applied will be not greater than given in Sec. **162.** The full-voltage starting current of motors of 30 hp and smaller will be within the limitations of most power companies, so that they are generally started directly across the line. Motors of larger size than 30 hp will have full-voltage starting currents that will not be within the limitations of many power companies and therefore frequently must be started with reduced voltage. The starting torques with rated voltage impressed will be at least as great as given in Sec. **163, part 2.** The breakdown torques will be at least as great as given in Sec. **164.**

168. The Design D (high-resistance-rotor type) squirrel-cage motor, owing to the high resistance of its rotor winding, produces a high starting torque with a low value of starting current.

These are made in two general types, which may be classified as medium slip and high slip. The medium-slip motors have full-load slips from 7 to 11 per cent, while the high-slip machines have full-load slips from 12 to 17 per cent. The medium-slip motors are suitable for driving punch presses, shears, bulldozers, and other heavy-inertia machinery which operates under heavy, fluctuating-load conditions and which is either provided with flywheels or has flywheel effect. These motors have full-voltage starting torques of at least 275 per cent of full-load torque and full-voltage starting currents which will be not greater than given in Sec. **162.** The maximum torque of the motor occurs at standstill, so that there is no noticeable breakdown torque. The full-voltage starting currents are within the limitations of most power companies. Reduced-voltage starting would not as a rule be satisfactory, owing to the nature of their application.

The high-slip motors are designed for meeting the requirements of elevator drive and small cranes and hoists. These motors have full-voltage starting torques of at least 275 per cent of full-load torque and full-voltage starting currents which will be not greater than given in Sec. **162.** Their full-voltage starting currents will meet the limitations of practically all power companies. Like the medium-slip motors they have no breakdown torque. Owing to the nature of their application, reduced-voltage starting would not be satisfactory.

169. Design F (low-torque, low-starting-current) squirrel-cage motors are made by some manufacturers in sizes 30 hp and larger. Above 30 hp the full-voltage starting current of the normal-torque, low-starting-current type of motor exceeds the limitations of many power companies. By designing a motor for a lower starting torque, however, it is possible to build motors of larger size that will meet these starting-current limitations. The full-voltage starting torque of these motors will be at least 125 per cent of full-load torque. The full-voltage starting currents will vary from 350 to 550 per cent of the full-load current. The breakdown torques will be at least 135 per cent of full-load torque. The full-voltage starting currents of these motors will be within the limitations of most power companies. They would not be used if reduced-voltage starting were required. This motor should be used only for drives which are started with light loads, such as motor generator sets, fans, and centrifugal pumps.

170. Automatic-start induction motors are so arranged that they start with a high-resistance rotor and, after coming up to speed, are automatically changed to have a low-resistance rotor. At start approximately one-third of the rotor copper is in service.

They are made in two types. In one type the machine is of generally normal construction but with two rotor windings, one of high resistance and the other of low resistance. At standstill the low-resistance rotor winding is open-circuited so that only the high-resistance winding is in service. As the motor speeds up, a centrifugal device short-circuits the low-resistance winding so that both windings are in service.

In the other type of motor the primary winding is located on the rotor. There are two secondary windings located on the stator, one of high resistance and the other of low resistance. The functioning of the two windings is controlled by magnetic switches so that there is no centrifugal device. The low-resistance winding is of the wound type, and the high-resistance one is a squirrel-cage winding. In starting, a magnetic contactor connects the primary to the line, with the low-resistance winding open-circuited. After a certain lapse of time, a second contactor closes, short-circuiting the low-resistance winding.

These automatic-start motors are started on full voltage and have starting torques from 225 to 250 per cent of full-load torque, with starting currents from 350 to 375 per cent of full-load current. Their breakdown torques vary from 200 to 250 per cent of full-load torque, and they have pull-in torques of from 150 to 200 per cent of full-load torque. They are suitable for high-starting-torque duty where the starting periods are not too frequent or of too long duration, such as compressors and air-conditioning-equipment service. They can be used in many places where the power company will not allow the starting currents drawn by the high-torque, low-starting-current motors when thrown directly across the line.

171. Multispeed induction motors are squirrel-cage induction motors constructed so that the number of poles for which the stator is wound can be altered. Since the speed of an induction motor depends upon the number of poles for which the stator is wound, changing the number of poles will alter the speed of the motor. The change in the number of poles is produced either by means of entirely separate windings or by changing the interconnections of the different parts of a single winding. In either case the necessary leads are brought out from the stator winding to a drum controller through which the necessary change in connections is made. A gradual speed control is not possible with the multispeed motor. Motors of this type which can be operated at two, three, or four different speeds can be obtained. Four different speeds is the maximum number for which it is feasible to construct multispeed induction motors. To design and construct a machine for more than four speeds would require too many complications in the wiring.

Multispeed induction motors have a practically constant speed from no load to full load for each one of their rated speed connections.

Multispeed induction motors are available in all the following types:
1. Normal torque, normal starting current.
2. Normal torque, low starting current.
3. High torque, low starting current.
4. Low torque, low starting current.

5. High resistance, medium or high slip.

Multispeed induction motors may be designed and rated for constant-torque service, constant-horsepower service, or varying-torque, varying-horsepower service. The allowable rating of the constant-torque motors varies directly with the speed. The constant-horsepower motors have the same rated horsepower for all speeds. With the varying-torque, varying-horsepower motors the full-load rated torque varies directly with the speed. The horsepower rating of these machines, therefore, varies as the square of the speed.

172. Average Efficiencies and Power Factors for Polyphase Squirrel-cage Induction Motors

Hp	Efficiency			Power factor		
	One-half load	Three-fourths load	Full load	One-half load	Three-fourths load	Full load
½	60.0	67.0	69.0	45	56	65
¾	64.0	68.0	69.0	48	58	65
1	75.0	77.0	76.0	57	69	76
1½	75.0	77.0	78.0	64	76	81
2	77.0	80.0	81.0	68	79	84
3	80.0	82.0	81.0	70	80	84
5	80.0	82.0	82.0	76	83	86
7½	83.0	85.0	85.0	77	84	87
10	83.0	85.0	85.0	77	86	88
15	84.0	86.0	88.0	81	85	87
20	87.0	88.0	87.0	82	86	87
25	87.0	88.0	87.5	82	86	87
30	87.5	88.5	88.0	83	86.5	87
40	87.5	89.0	89.5	84	87	88
50	87.5	89.0	89.5	84	87	88
60	88.0	89.5	89.0	84	87	88
75	88.5	89.5	89.5	84	87	88
100	89.0	90.0	90.5	84	88	88
125	90.0	90.5	91.0	84	88	89
150	90.0	91.5	92.0	84	88	89
200	90.0	91.5	92.0	85	89	90
250	91.0	92.5	93.0	84	89	90
300	92.0	93.5	94.0	84	89	90

173. Wound-rotor induction motors, when operated with no external resistance in the rotor circuit and with the slip rings short-circuited, have operating characteristics similar to those of the normal-torque, normal-starting-current, squirrel-cage machine. If external resistance is inserted in the rotor circuit, the speed of the motor can be controlled. With load on the motor the speed can be controlled over a wide range. At no load and with light loads on the motor, it is possible to obtain only slight changes in the speed. When the speed is adjusted for any particular load, the speed does not stay constant as the load varies but decreases considerably as the load increases. The amount that the speed drops off from no load to full load depends upon the amount of external resistance in the rotor circuit; the greater the resistance, the greater the speed change. The characteristics of the wound-rotor motor operating with external resistance in the rotor circuit are similar to those for a d-c motor with armature control. Considerable energy is lost in the external resistance, the efficiency of the motor being reduced approximately in proportion to the reduction in speed produced. Wound-rotor motors are started by throwing the stator directly across the line with external resistance in the rotor circuit. The value of the starting torque developed and the corresponding starting current depends upon the amount of external resistance in the rotor circuit (see Secs. **150** and **152**). The breakdown torque of a wound-rotor motor will be at least as large as given in Sec. **175**. With the proper amount of external resistance in the rotor to produce maximum torque at standstill the starting current will be from 250 to 300 per cent of the full-load current. The maximum value of the starting torque will be from 200 to 275 per cent of full-load torque.

Wound-rotor motors with speed control are constant-torque machines, the horsepower decreasing in proportion to the decrease in speed.

174. Average Efficiencies and Power Factors for Polyphase Wound-rotor Induction Motors (with Rotor Short-circuited)

Hp	Efficiency			Power factor		
	One-half load	Three-fourths load	Full load	One-half load	Three-fourths load	Full load
2	71.0	75.0	75.5	40	52	60
3	75.0	78.0	79.0	50	68	70
5	78.0	80.0	80.5	60	75	77
7½	78.5	81.0	81.5	65	75	78
10	80.0	82.0	82.5	65	75	79
15	80.0	82.0	82.5	65	75	79
20	84.0	85.5	86.0	70	76.5	81
25	86.0	88.0	88.0	70	77	81
30	86.0	88.0	88.0	72	78	82
40	86.0	88.0	88.0	72	78	82
50	86.0	88.0	88.0	78	84	86
60	86.5	88.5	88.5	79	85	88
75	88.0	88.0	88.8	82	87	89

175. Breakdown Torque of Polyphase Wound-rotor Integral-horsepower Motors with Continuous Ratings
(NEMA Standard)

The breakdown torques of 60- and 50-cycle polyphase wound-rotor motors, with rated voltage and frequency applied, shall be in accordance with the following values which are expressed in per cent of full-load torque and which represent the upper limit of the range of application for these motors:

Hp	Breakdown torque, per cent of full-load torque		
	Speed, rpm		
	1,800	1,200	900
1	. . .	. . .	250
1½	. . .	. . .	250
2	275	275	250
3	275	275	250
5	275	275	250
7½	275	250	225
10	275	250	225
15	250	225	225
20–200, incl.	225	225	225

176. In the commutator brush-shifting type of polyphase induction motor the relative location of the two windings is reversed from that of the ordinary induction motor. The primary winding, the winding that is connected to the supply, is located on the rotor. The secondary winding is placed in the stator slots. In addition to the primary winding, the rotor carries a second winding which is connected to a commutator in the same manner as in a d-c motor. The two ends of each phase of the secondary winding (the stationary winding) are connected to two brushes bearing upon the commutator. The arrangement and connection of the windings are indicated in Fig. 93A. The position of the two brushes of each phase can be shifted by means of a handwheel. When the handwheel is adjusted so that the brushes of each phase are on the same commutator segment, the secondary winding is short-circuited and the motor operates like a squirrel-cage machine. As the brushes are moved apart, a section of the ad-

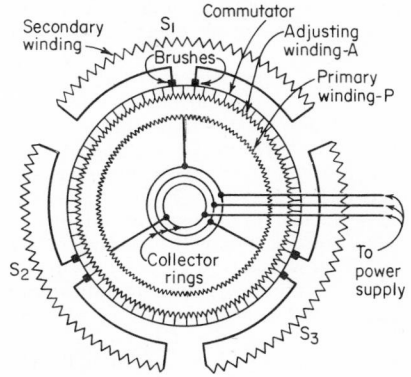

FIG. 93A *Diagram of commutator type of polyphase induction motor. (General Electric Co.)*

justing winding is placed in series with the secondary winding. This impresses upon the secondary an additional voltage to the one induced in it by the revolving magnetic field. If the brushes are moved in one direction, the voltage impressed by the adjusting winding will oppose the normal induced voltage. Such a shift of the brushes will, therefore, reduce the speed of the machine. A shifting of the brushes in the opposite direction causes the voltage from the adjusting winding to aid the normal induced voltage in the secondary and thus increases the speed of the motor. These machines are designed to give a speed range of 3:1. The highest speed is approximately 40 per cent above synchronous speed, and the lowest speed is approximately 60 per cent below synchronous speed. The decrease in speed from no load to full load is from 5 to 10 per cent at the high speeds, and from 15 to 25 per cent at the low speeds. Very low creeping speeds can be obtained by inserting resistance in the rotor circuit.

These brush-shifting motors are rated on a constant-torque basis, so that the horse-power rating decreases with the speed. The breakdown torque at low speeds is from 140 to 250 per cent of full-load torque. The breakdown torque increases somewhat with the speed, so that at the high speed it is from 300 to 400 per cent of normal torque.

These motors are started by connecting the primary directly to the line with the brushes in the low-speed position. In this way they will develop a starting torque of from 140 to 150 per cent of full-load torque with a starting current of from 125 to 175 per cent of full-load current for the maximum horsepower rating. In some special cases, resistance is connected in series with the secondary for starting.

177. Synchros are special a-c motors employed for:

1. Remote indication of position, such as indicating the position of generator rheostats, water-wheel governors, water-reservoir levels, gates or valves, and turntables.

2. Remote signaling systems, such as signaling from switchboard to generator room, steel-mill furnace to blower room, and marine signals between engine room and bridge.

3. Automatic or remote position control, such as system frequency, synchronizing of incoming generators, water-wheel governors, gates or valves, color screens on lights in theaters, and motor drives (see Sec. **142**).

4. Operation of two machines so as to maintain a definite time-position relation or a definite speed relation, such as lift bridges, hoists, kiln drives, elevators, unit printing presses, and conveyors.

Synchros are known by various trade names such as Selsyn, Synchrotie, Autosyn, and Telegon. Units are available in single-phase and three-phase types. The polyphase units conform in appearance and general characteristics to a three-phase wound-rotor induction motor. The single-phase units have a three-phase wound secondary and a single-phase primary. Some single-phase units are constructed with the primary located on the stationary member of the machine and others with the primary on the movable member. Depending upon the torque developed by the machine, synchros are classified as indicating synchros or power synchros. Power synchros are always of three-phase construction. Most of the indicating synchros are constructed single-phase. The indicating synchros are manufactured in a general-purpose type and a high-accuracy type. The general-purpose type will indicate angular position within an accuracy of plus or minus 5 deg, and the high-accuracy type provides an accuracy of indication within plus or minus 1 deg.

A synchro system requires the use of at least two synchro machines. The connections for two single-phase units are shown in Fig. 94 and those for two three-phase units in Fig. 95. With both the single-phase and the polyphase units, if the rotors of the two machines are in corresponding positions, the voltages of the two secondaries at each instant of time will be equal in magnitude and opposite in direction. Therefore, no current will flow in the rotor circuits, no torque will be developed in either machine, and the machines will be in equilibrium. When the two rotors are not in corresponding positions, the voltages of the two secondaries will not neutralize each other and a current will be produced in the two secondaries. This current will produce torque in the machines, which will act upon the rotors, tending to move them into corresponding positions.

In signaling or indicating applications, the synchro located at the sending end is called the transmitter and the synchro at the receiving end is called the receiver. If desired, a number of receivers can be connected in parallel to a single transmitter. The torque exerted upon each receiver will be reduced from that available when only

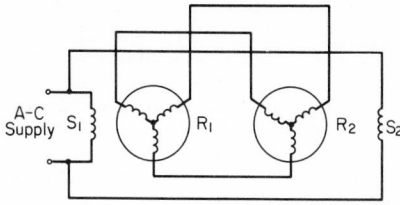
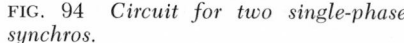

FIG. 94 *Circuit for two single-phase synchros.*

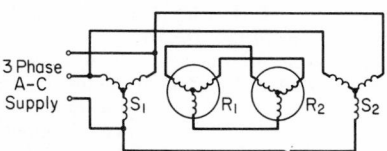

FIG. 95 *Circuit for two three-phase synchros.*

one receiver is used. The torque can be calculated from the following formula:

$$T_r = T_1 \times \frac{2}{N+1} \tag{5b}$$

where T_r is the torque available at each receiver, T_1 is the torque available if only one receiver is used, and N is the number of receivers.

When it is desired to have the position taken by the receiver differ from that of the transmitter, a three-phase synchro is introduced between the transmitter and the receiver. This intermediate synchro is called a differential synchro. With such a system, the receiver will take up a position that will be either the sum or the difference of the angles applied to the transmitter and the differential. Conversely, if two synchros are connected through a differential synchro and each is turned through an angle, the differential synchro will indicate the difference between the two angles.

The fundamental synchro circuit generally used for control purposes is shown in Fig. 96. When the positions of the rotors coincide, a maximum voltage will be induced in stator S_2. When the rotors are displaced 90 electrical degrees from each other, no resultant voltage will be produced between the terminals of S_2. This is true, since the axis of the winding S_2 will be located 90 electrical degrees from the axis of the field produced in machine 2. The system is adjusted so that, when the desired condition exists, the rotors will be 90 electrical degrees displaced from each other. This is the equilibrium position. The circuit there-

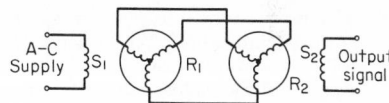

FIG. 96 *Fundamental synchro control circuit for production of an error voltage.*

fore functions to produce an error voltage in the stator of machine 2 whenever there is a displacement of the shafts from the equilibrium position. The relative polarity of the error voltage depends upon the direction of the displacement. The error voltage can be employed to instigate the functioning of other devices, which will operate to correct the condition causing the displacement. These correction devices will function until the synchros are brought into the equilibrium position, when absence of voltage in S_2 will stop their functioning. Refer to Sec. **142** for application of synchros in position drive control.

178. Synchronous Motors. The general construction of a synchronous motor is the same as that of synchronous a-c generators with the addition of an auxiliary winding similar to either the squirrel-cage or wound-rotor winding of an induction motor embedded in the pole faces. The purpose of the auxiliary winding is to produce starting torque so that the motor will be self-starting. A synchronous motor will not develop starting torque through synchronous-motor action. A synchronous motor is started without d-c field excitation by induction-motor action through its auxiliary winding. As the motor comes up to speed and d-c excitation voltage is applied to its field winding, a pull-in torque is developed, tending to pull the motor into step. If the inertia of the load is not too great, this pull-in torque will accelerate the motor to synchronous speed, and it will continue to operate as a synchronous motor. As long as the motor runs at synchronous speed, the auxiliary winding will be inactive, since there will be no voltage produced in the auxiliary winding under this condition. If the motor should instantaneously tend to run at a speed slightly greater or less than synchronous, a voltage is produced in the auxiliary winding, producing a flow of current. This current will produce a torque which will act to bring the motor back to synchronous speed. The auxiliary winding, therefore, in addition to providing a means of making the motor self-starting provides a dampening effect tending to eliminate instantaneous fluctuations of the speed.

A synchronous motor has two very important characteristics. It operates at constant speed, and its power factor is under the control of the operator. If the average speed of a synchronous motor deviates from synchronism, the motor pulls out of step and ceases to function as a synchronous motor. Unlike an induction motor the power factor is not a fixed value dependent upon the design and load. The power factor is dependent upon the value of the direct field current and can be adjusted by the operator to a leading, unity, or lagging power-factor value. For any particular load a certain field current will make the motor operate at unity power factor. This value of field current is called normal excitation. A field current less than normal excitation will produce a lagging power factor, and a field current more than normal will produce a leading power factor.

179. A synchronous motor can be used to correct low power factor of the system that feeds it in addition to driving a mechanical load provided it has sufficient capacity.

This characteristic is often of considerable importance. It is well known that the power factor of the induction motor, even under full-load conditions, is seldom greater than 95 per cent, and it often falls as low as 50 or 60 per cent at light load. The result is that an a-c generator driving a considerable number of induction motors ordinarily operates at a comparatively low power factor. If this alternator is loaded to its full kilowatt capacity at such a low power factor, overheating will result.

If the alternator is not loaded beyond its normal current capacity, it operates at a low energy load but with the same heating losses as at full load on account of the reduced power factor. The advantage of the synchronous motor on such a system is that by proper adjustment of its field current it can be made to draw from the line a current which is leading with respect to the voltage and which will neutralize the lagging current taken by the induction motors. The current in the a-c generator can thereby be brought into phase with the voltage, and the generator will operate under its normal conditions. When used in this manner as a compensator for lagging current, the synchronous motor must be of larger size than required by its power output on account of the excess current which it draws from the line.

A synchronous condenser is a synchronous motor that operates to correct power factor only and does not pull any mechanical load.

180. Classification of Synchronous Motors.

1. According to power-factor rating.
   a. 1.0 (unity) power factor.
   b. 0.8 (leading) power factor.
2. According to speed.
   a. High speed.
   b. Low speed.
3. According to service.
   a. General-purpose.
   b. Special-purpose.

The horsepower ratings of synchronous motors are based on unity or 0.8-pf operation. A unity power-factor motor is designed to carry its rated horsepower load when operating at unity power factor. An 0.8-pf motor is designed to carry its rated horsepower load when operating at 0.8 pf leading. Either a unity- or an 0.8-pf-rated motor can be operated at power factors below their rated amount provided so that the horsepower output is reduced below the rated value a sufficient amount so that the machine will not be overheated.

Synchronous motors are divided into two groups according to the value of their rated speed. Motors with speeds of 500 rpm or greater are called high-speed motors, and those with speeds below 500 rpm are classed as low-speed motors.

181. General-purpose synchronous motors are rated on a 40°C temperature-rise basis with a service factor of 1.15 (see Sec. **128**). When started with full voltage, these motors will have starting kva inrushes of from 550 to 700 per cent of the motor's normal kva rating. Normal torque values for these motors are given in Sec. **183.** The pull-in torques as given in Sec. **183** are based on the standardized normal Wk^2 of load as given in Sec. **185.**

182. Operation at Other than Rated Power Factors (NEMA Standard). 1. For an 0.8-pf motor which is to operate at 1.0 pf with normal 0.8-pf armature current and with field excitation reduced to correspond to that armature current at 1.0 pf, multiply the rated horsepower and torque values of the 0.8-pf motor by the following constants to obtain the horsepower at 1.0 pf and the torques in terms of the 1.0-pf horsepower rating:

Horsepower............................ 1.25
Locked-rotor torque................ 0.8
Pull-in torque 0.8
Pull-out torque....................... 0.7

For example, consider a 1,000-hp 0.8-pf motor which has a locked-rotor torque of 100 per cent, a pull-in torque of 100 per cent, and a pull-out torque of 200 per cent and which is to be operated at 1.0 pf. In accordance with the foregoing, this motor could be operated at 1,250 hp, 1.0 pf, 80 per cent locked-rotor torque (based upon 1,250 hp), 80 per cent pull-in torque (based upon 1,250 hp), and a pull-out torque of 140 per cent (based upon 1,250 hp).

2. For a 1.0-pf motor which is to operate at 0.8 pf with normal 1.0-pf field excitation and the armature current reduced to correspond to that excitation, multiply the rated horsepower and torque values of the 1.0-pf motor by the following constants to obtain the horsepower at 0.8 pf and the torques in terms of the 0.8-pf horsepower rating:

Horsepower............................ 0.35
Locked-rotor torque................ 2.85
Pull-in torque 2.85
Pull-out torque....................... 2.85

For example, consider a 1,000-hp 1.0-pf motor which has a locked-rotor torque of 100 per cent, a pull-in torque of 100 per cent, and a pull-out torque of 200 per cent and which is to be operated at 0.8 pf. In accordance with the foregoing, this motor could be operated at 350 hp, 0.8 pf, 285 per cent locked-rotor torque (based upon 350 hp), 285 per cent pull-in torque (based upon 350 hp), and a pull-out torque of 570 per cent (based upon 350 hp).

183. National Electrical Manufacturers' Association Minimum-torque Values for Synchronous Motors

Horsepower and rated power factor	No. of poles	Speed, rpm	Torques with rated voltage applied, percentage of rated full-load torque		
			Starting	Pull-in (based on normal external load WR^2)	Pull-out[a]
General Purpose					
1.0 pf to and including 200 hp	4	1,800	110	110	150
	6–14	1,200–514	110	110	175
0.8 pf to and including 150 hp	4	1,800	125	125	200
	6–14	1,200–514	125	125	250
Large High Speed					
1.0 pf:					
250 to 500 hp..........................	4–14	1,800–514	110	110	150
600 hp and larger......................	4–14	1,800–514	85	85	150
0.8 pf:					
200 to 500 hp..........................	4–14	1,800–514	125	125	200
600 hp and larger......................	4–14	1,800–514	100	100	200
Low Speed—Engine Type					
1.0 pf, all sizes..........................	16 and more	450 and below	40	40	150
0.8 pf, all sizes..........................	16 and more	450 and below	40	40	200

[a] With normal excitation.

184. Effect of Load Wk^2. The inertia of the load (load Wk^2) is very important in the selection and operation of synchronous motors. The load inertia that a synchronous motor can accelerate is limited by the thermal capacity of its amortisseur winding. Smaller synchronous motors can accelerate relatively higher load Wk^2 than the larger motors. The NEMA standards for the load Wk^2 which can be accelerated by standard synchronous motors are given in Sec. **185**.

185. Normal Wk^2 of Load
(NEMA Standard)

1. The pull-in torque of high-speed synchronous motors shall be based on loads having values of Wk^2 as follows:

Normal Wk^2 of Load (Exclusive of Motor Wk^2)

Hp	Speed, rpm					
	1,800	1,200	900	720	600	514
20	3.75	8.1				
25	4.63	10.5				
30	5.75	13	23.1			
40	8	18.1	32.1	50.2		
50	10.4	23.5	41.7	65.2	93.8	
60	12.9	28.9	51.3	80.2	115.5	
75	16.6	37.5	66.5	104	150	
100	23.1	52.2	92.6	145	209	284
125	29.9	67.2	119.5	186.5	268.5	366.5
150	36.9	83	147.5	230	331	452.5
200	51	115	205	320	460	627.5
250	66	149	264	412.5	594	810
300	82	184	327	512	736	1,005
350	98	220	391	612	880	1,200
400	113.5	255	455	711	1,024	1,388
450	129	290	516	807	1,165	1,586
500	147.5	330	587	920	1,325	1,800
600	181	408	725	1,130	1,625	2,225
700	217	487	865	1,350	1,950	2,650
800	253	568	1,010	1,575	2,275	3,100
900	289	650	1,160	1,813	2,600	3,550
1,000	328	738	1,312	2,050	2,950	4,025
1,250	422	950	1,686	2,640	3,800	5,175
1,500	522	1,172	2,090	3,265	4,700	6,400
1,750	622	1,400	2,490	3,890	5,590	7,625
2,000	725	1,625	2,890	4,525	6,512	8,875
2,250	832	1,875	3,325	5,200	7,500	10,250
2,500	935	2,100	3,725	5,840	8,400	11,450
3,000	1,160	2,610	4,650	7,250	10,470	14,250
3,500	1,375	3,100	5,525	8,625	12,450	17,000
4,000	1,612	3,630	6,440	10,060	14,500	19,750
4,500	1,840	4,130	7,350	11,500	16,550	22,500
5,000	2,090	4,680	8,325	13,000	18,750	25,500

Normal Wk² of Load (*Continued*)

2. The following are values of normal Wk^2 of load for various sizes of low-speed, 60-cycle synchronous motors:

Poles	40	36	32	30	28	26	24	22	20	18	16
Speed, rpm											
Hp	180	200	225	240	257	277	300	327	360	400	450
20	365	295	230	205	180	155	130	110	90	75	60
25	470	380	300	265	230	200	170	140	115	95	75
30	580	470	370	325	285	245	210	175	145	115	95
40	805	655	515	455	395	340	290	245	210	165	130
50	1,040	845	665	585	510	440	375	315	260	210	165
60	1,280	1,040	820	720	630	540	460	390	320	260	205
75	1,660	1,350	1,060	935	815	700	600	505	415	335	265
100	2,310	1,870	1,480	1,300	1,130	975	830	700	580	470	370
125	2,980	2,420	1,910	1,680	1,460	1,260	1,070	905	745	605	475
150	3,680	2,980	2,360	2,070	1,810	1,550	1,330	1,115	920	745	590
175	4,400	3,560	2,810	2,470	2,160	1,860	1,580	1,330	1,100	890	705
200	5,130	4,150	3,280	2,880	2,520	2,160	1,850	1,550	1,280	1,040	820
225	5,870	4,750	3,760	3,300	2,880	2,480	2,110	1,780	1,470	1,190	940
250	6,620	5,360	4,240	3,730	3,250	2,800	2,380	2,010	1,660	1,340	1,060
300	8,180	6,630	5,240	4,600	4,010	3,450	2,940	2,480	2,050	1,660	1,310
350	9,760	7,900	6,240	5,490	4,790	4,120	3,520	2,960	2,440	1,975	1,560
400	11,400	9,220	7,360	6,400	5,580	4,800	4,100	3,450	2,850	2,300	1,820
450	13,000	10,550	8,350	7,330	6,390	5,500	4,690	3,950	3,260	2,640	2,080
500	14,700	11,900	9,400	8,250	7,200	6,200	5,290	4,450	3,670	2,970	2,350
600	18,100	14,700	11,600	10,200	8,890	7,650	6,530	5,490	4,540	3,670	2,900
700	21,600	17,500	13,850	12,200	10,600	9,140	7,790	6,560	5,410	4,380	3,460
800	25,200	20,400	16,150	14,200	12,400	10,650	9,090	7,650	6,310	5,110	4,040
900	28,900	23,400	18,500	16,250	14,200	12,200	10,400	8,760	7,240	5,850	4,620
1,000	32,600	26,400	20,800	18,300	16,000	13,800	11,750	9,890	8,160	6,610	5,220
1,250	42,100	34,200	27,000	23,700	20,700	17,800	15,200	12,800	10,560	8,550	6,750
1,500	52,000	42,100	33,200	29,200	25,500	22,000	18,700	15,730	13,000	10,500	8,310
1,750	62,100	50,400	39,700	35,000	30,500	26,200	22,400	18,800	15,500	12,600	9,940
2,000	72,400	58,600	46,300	40,700	35,500	30,600	26,100	21,950	18,100	14,670	11,600
2,250	83,000	67,700	53,100	46,600	40,700	35,000	29,900	25,200	20,800	16,800	13,300
2,500	93,500	75,700	59,800	52,600	45,900	39,500	33,600	28,300	23,400	18,900	15,000
3,000	115,000	93,500	73,900	65,000	56,600	48,700	41,600	35,000	28,900	23,400	18,500
3,500	138,000	112,000	88,200	77,500	67,500	58,200	49,600	41,800	34,500	27,900	22,100
4,000	161,000	130,000	102,500	90,400	78,800	67,900	57,800	48,600	40,200	32,500	25,700
4,500	184,000	149,000	118,000	103,400	90,100	77,600	66,100	55,600	46,000	37,200	29,400
5,000	208,000	168,000	133,000	117,000	102,000	87,800	74,800	63,000	52,000	42,100	33,200

Normal Wk^2 of **Load** (*Continued*)

Poles	90	84	80	76	72	66	60	56	52	48	44
Speed, rpm	80	86	90	95	100	109	120	128	138	150	164
Hp											
20											440
25											565
30											700
40											970
50											1,250
60											1,550
75											2,000
100	11,700	10,110	9,250	8,290	7,480	6,300	5,200	4,560	3,930	3,320	2,780
125	15,100	13,090	11,900	10,700	9,660	8,140	6,710	5,900	5,080	4,300	3,600
150	18,600	16,100	14,700	13,200	11,900	10,000	8,290	7,280	6,260	5,300	4,440
175	22,200	19,250	17,600	15,800	14,200	12,000	9,890	8,690	7,480	6,330	5,300
200	25,900	22,450	20,500	18,400	16,600	14,000	11,500	10,130	8,730	7,390	6,170
225	29,700	25,700	23,500	21,100	19,000	16,000	13,200	11,600	10,000	8,450	7,070
250	33,500	29,000	26,500	23,800	21,500	18,100	14,900	13,100	11,300	9,540	7,980
300	41,400	35,800	32,700	29,400	26,500	22,300	18,400	16,200	13,900	11,800	9,850
350	49,400	42,700	39,000	35,000	31,000	26,600	22,000	19,300	16,600	14,000	11,800
400	57,500	49,900	45,500	40,800	36,900	31,500	25,600	22,500	19,400	16,400	13,800
450	65,900	57,000	52,100	46,700	42,200	35,500	29,300	25,800	22,200	18,800	15,700
500	74,200	64,200	58,600	52,600	47,500	40,400	33,000	29,000	25,000	21,100	17,700
600	91,600	79,400	72,500	65,000	58,700	49,400	40,700	35,800	30,800	26,100	21,800
700	109,500	94,800	86,500	77,600	70,100	59,000	48,700	42,800	36,800	31,200	26,100
800	128,000	110,600	101,000	90,700	81,900	68,800	56,800	49,900	42,900	36,400	30,400
900	146,000	126,600	116,000	103,700	93,700	78,700	65,000	57,100	49,100	41,600	34,800
1,000	165,000	143,000	130,000	117,000	106,000	88,000	73,400	64,500	55,500	47,000	39,300
1,250	214,000	185,000	169,000	151,400	137,000	115,000	95,000	83,500	71,700	60,700	50,900
1,500	263,000	227,500	208,000	186,000	168,000	142,000	117,000	103,000	88,400	74,800	62,600
1,750	314,000	272,000	249,000	223,000	201,000	169,000	140,000	123,000	106,000	89,500	74,800
2,000	366,000	317,000	290,000	260,000	234,000	197,000	163,000	143,000	123,000	104,000	87,300
2,250	420,000	363,000	332,000	298,000	268,000	226,000	187,000	164,000	141,000	119,000	100,000
2,500	473,000	410,000	374,000	336,000	303,000	255,000	210,000	185,000	159,000	135,000	113,000
3,000	584,000	505,000	462,000	415,000	374,000	315,000	260,000	228,000	197,000	166,000	139,000
3,500	698,000	604,000	552,000	495,000	446,000	376,000	310,000	272,000	235,000	199,000	166,000
4,000	812,000	704,000	642,000	576,000	520,000	438,000	361,000	317,000	273,000	230,000	193,000
4,000	930,000	805,000	735,000	660,000	595,000	501,000	414,000	364,000	313,000	265,000	221,000
5,000	1,050,000	910,000	831,000	745,000	673,000	566,000	467,000	411,000	354,000	299,000	250,000

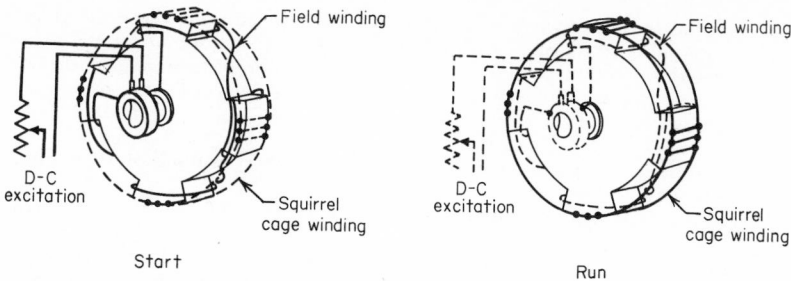

Start   Run

Conventional Design. Start: motors start like standard induction motors—by means of squirrel-cage windings embedded in the pole faces. *Run:* the motor comes up to speed and after a predetermined "definite time," the d-c field excitation is applied. This causes the motor to shift from induction to synchronous operation.

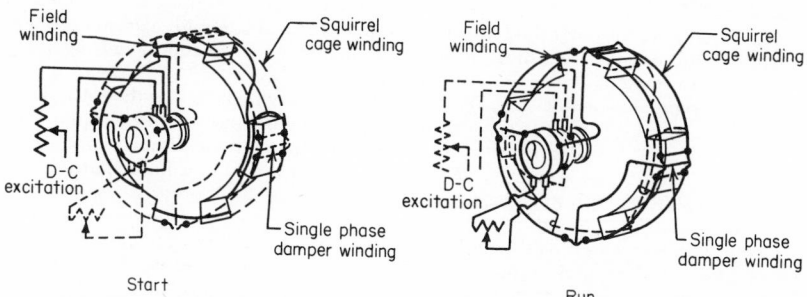

Start   Run

High Torque—Low Starting Kva. Start: motor gets high torques at start with low kva inrush, by a standard squirrel-cage winding plus a separate series winding on the pole faces connected to an external resistor. *Run:* the motor comes up to speed and after a predetermined "definite time," the d-c field excitation is applied. This causes the motor to shift from induction to synchronous operation.

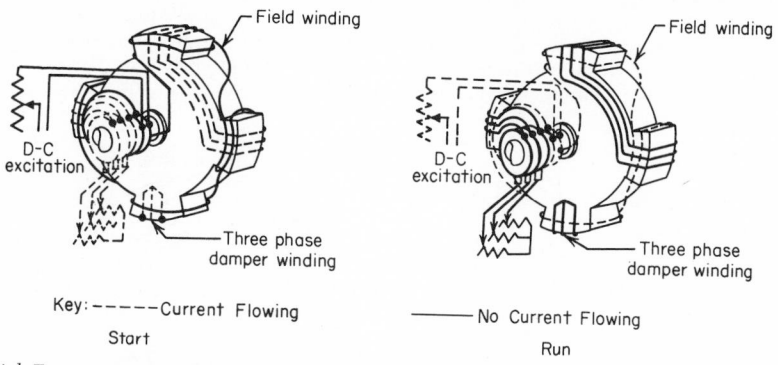

Key: – – – –Current Flowing   ————No Current Flowing
Start   Run

High Torque—Starting Kva 50 Per Cent or Less of Normal. Start: motor starts like any ordinary three-phase wound-rotor motor. The external resistor makes possible variable high torque together with extremely low starting kva. *Run:* the motor comes up to speed and after a predetermined "definite time," the d-c field excitation is applied. This causes the motor to shift from induction to synchronous operation.

FIG. 97 *Types of auxiliary windings for synchronous motors. (Westinghouse Electric Corp.)*

186. Special-purpose Synchronous Motors. For applications where the character-istics of general-purpose motors do not fit the operating requirements, the manufac-turer fits the design of the auxiliary windings and motor proportions to meet the qualifi-cations of the specific applications. These custom-made motors are made with the following types of auxiliary windings:

1. Conventional squirrel-cage winding.
2. Conventional squirrel-cage winding plus single-phase wound-rotor winding.
3. Three-phase wound-rotor winding.

The fundamental connections and functioning of the different types of auxiliary windings are illustrated in Fig. 97.

By means of proper design of a conventional squirrel-cage winding the torque charac-teristics can be varied over the limits given in Sec. **183**. Where higher starting torques with low starting kva are required, a wound-rotor auxiliary winding is employed (see Fig. 97). For applications requiring a fairly high starting torque with fairly low start-ing-inrush kva, a single-phase wound-rotor winding is added in addition to the conven-tional squirrel cage. For applications requiring exceptionally high starting torques with low starting kva, a three-phase wound-rotor winding is employed. Motors with a wound-rotor auxiliary winding are started under full voltage with external resistance inserted in the auxiliary winding in the same manner as that used in starting wound-rotor induction motors.

187. The repulsion motor (Fig. 98) has an armature which is like that of a d-c ma-chine. It is provided with two brushes E_1 and E_2, which are inclined to the axis of the stator winding. These brushes are connected by a low-resistance conductor D, which short-circuits the armature. A machine of this type has a high starting torque with a small starting current and a rapidly decreasing speed with increasing load, being similar in this respect to a d-c series motor. The power factor of the repulsion motor increases with the speed, and near synchronous speed it attains a value much higher than is generally obtained in induction motors. These motors are used principally for constant-torque applications such as printing-press drives, fans, and blowers. The direction of rotation of a repulsion motor can be reversed by shifting the brushes to the reverse side of the neutral.

188. The compensated repulsion motor (Fig. 99) is similar to the repulsion motor, except that it has a compensating winding and two compensating brushes C_1 and C_2, which the repulsion motor does not have. The compensating winding is wound on the stator. The compensating brushes are connected in series with the compensating winding. These motors have a starting torque equal to about $2\frac{1}{2}$ to 3 times full-load torque with approximately twice full-load current. Owing to the corrective action of the compensating winding, the power factor is very high at all loads. However, the efficiency of this machine is lower than that of the induction motor. Single-phase

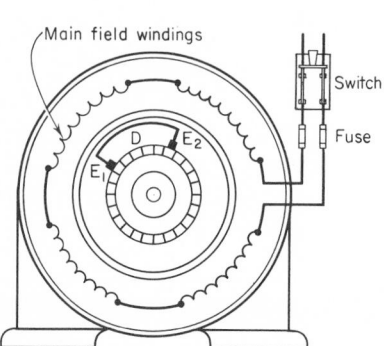

FIG. 98 *Diagram of repulsion motor.*

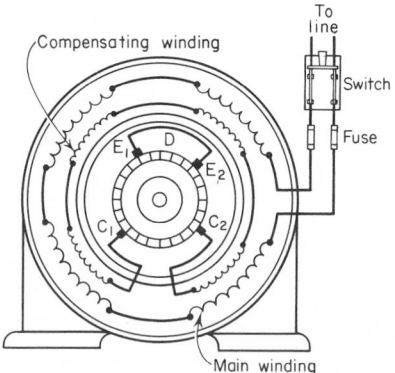

FIG. 99 *Diagram of compensated repul-sion motor.*

motors of this type are well adapted for loads involving heavy starting torque and sudden overloads.

189. Brush-shifting Type of Single-phase Motor. The brush-shifting, single-phase repulsion motor, as manufactured by the General Electric Co., is a compensated repulsion motor. It is an adjustable varying-speed type of motor. The adjustment of speed is obtained by shifting the position of the brushes on the rotor. The speed may be controlled directly at the motor by means of a brush-shifting handle attached to the brush rigging. If it is desired to control the speed from some point remote from the motor, the brush-shifting handle can be connected to a pedestal or foot controller by means of a rocker-shaft assembly (bracket, rocker shaft, and levers). These motors can be obtained in $1/4$- to 3-hp sizes for either reversing or nonreversing service. The motor is reversed by simply shifting the brushes in the opposite direction from the neutral point. The brush-shifting motor is a constant-torque motor. The rated horsepower is the allowable horsepower for the highest speed. As the speed is reduced, the allowable horsepower is reduced in proportion. A speed reduction of 3:1 is possible when operating against a constant torque of 75 per cent of the rated value. If operating against 100 per cent normal torque, a speed reduction of 4:1 can be obtained. The no-load speed is approximately 60 per cent above synchronous speed. At no load or with light loads very little speed reduction is possible. The starting torque of these motors with full voltage varies from 150 to 300 per cent of full-load rated torque for four-pole machines and from 125 to 250 per cent for six-pole motors, depending upon the brush position.

The breakdown torque is more than 400 per cent of full-load rated torque when the brushes are in the maximum-speed position. As the brushes are shifted for the lower speeds, the breakdown torque decreases. These motors are generally started with full voltage.

190. A single-phase induction motor, when its rotor is not revolving, has no starting torque. After the rotor commences revolving, there is a certain interaction of magnetic fields whereby there is exerted a continuous turning effort. Single-phase induction motors are provided, therefore, with some auxiliary means for making them self-starting. Single-phase induction motors can be divided into the following groups, depending upon the method employed for starting:

1. Shading coil.
2. Inductively split phase.
3. Condenser split-phase or capacitor motor.
4. Repulsion start induction run.
5. Repulsion induction.

191. Shading-coil Single-phase Induction Motors. Some fractional-horsepower motors, principally those used on small ventilating fans, are made self-starting by means of the shading-coil method. The stator winding of these motors is not distributed around the frame, as in most induction motors, but is wound on projecting pole pieces, as in d-c machines. In addition to the main stator winding a short-circuited coil, or shading coil, as it is called, is placed around only a portion of the pole piece (Fig. 100). This shading coil makes the flux in the portion of the pole piece surrounded by it lag behind the flux in the other portion of the pole. The shifting of the flux thus produced will develop sufficient torque to start small motors under very light

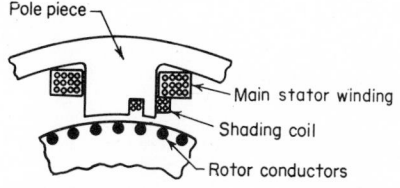

FIG. 100 *Construction of shading-coil motor.*

load conditions. These motors are made in sizes of from $1/250$ to $1/40$ hp and are used for driving small fans.

192. The inductively split-phase single-phase induction motor is provided with an auxiliary starting winding, in addition to the main stator winding. This winding is located in stator slots so that it is displaced 90 electrical degrees from the main stator winding, as shown in Fig. 101. If two currents sufficiently out of phase with each

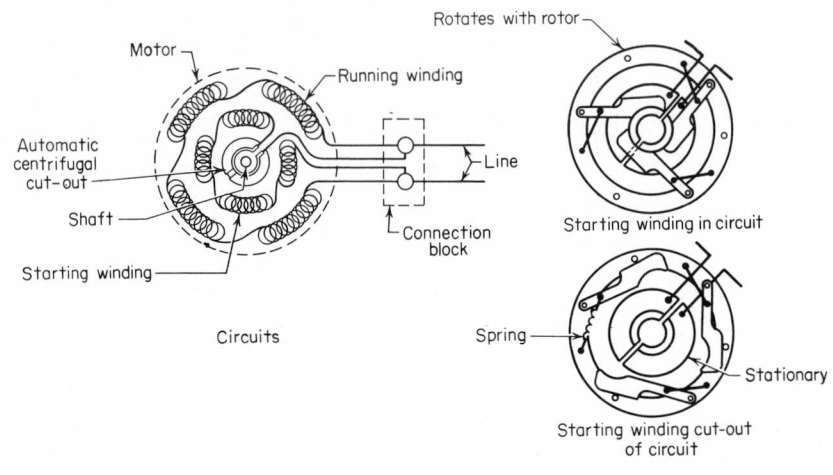

FIG. 101   *Single-phase motor diagram.*

other are passed through the main and auxiliary windings, conditions similar to those existing in a two-phase induction motor will be produced.   The necessary two currents, which are from 30 to 45 degrees out of phase with each other, are obtained from the single-phase supply by constructing one of the circuits with a relatively high inductance and the other with a relatively high resistance.   The main or running winding is normally of high inductance at the time of starting.   The auxiliary winding is wound with finer wire, making it have higher resistance than the main winding.   The running winding remains in the circuit at all times of operation, while the starting winding remains in the circuit only until the motor has reached 50 to 80 per cent of synchronous speed.   When the speed is reached at which the starting winding should be cut out, an automatic centrifugal switch (see illustration) operates and opens the "starting" circuit.   This type of single-phase induction motor thus starts as a two-phase machine until the starting winding is cut out, when it continues to operate, by virtue of the running winding only, as a single-phase motor.

These motors are constant-speed machines, not adapted for any speed control. They are made in sizes up to $\frac{1}{3}$ hp and in two types, the general-purpose type and the high-torque type.   The general-purpose type of motor has the following characteristics: full-voltage starting torque 75 to 175 per cent of full-load torque, full-voltage starting current within National Electrical Manufacturers' Association specifications of Sec. **200,** breakdown torque 175 to 225 per cent of full-load torque, and pull-up torque 75 to 200 per cent of full-load torque.   They are suitable for full-voltage starting on any power system.

The high-torque type of motor has the following characteristics: full-voltage starting torque 150 to 275 per cent of full-load torque, full-voltage starting current approximately 850 per cent of full-load current, breakdown torque 225 to 350 per cent of full-load torque, pull-up torque 225 to 325 per cent of full-load torque.   The full-voltage starting currents exceed the NEMA specifications of Sec. **200** and may not be permissible for some installations.

193. Capacitor motors are single-phase induction motors which have two stator windings displaced 90 electrical degrees from each other just the same as the inductively split-phase motor.   Therefore they have starting torque developed by two-phase action.   In the capacitor motor the necessary phase displacement between the currents of the two stator windings is produced by placing a capacitor in series with the auxiliary winding.   By this means the phase displacement can be made more nearly 90 degrees, which results in better starting torque with lower starting current than can be obtained with the inductively split-phase-started motor. Capacitor motors are available in the following types:

1. Capacitor start, induction run.
2. Capacitor start, capacitor run
    a. Two-value capacitor (high torque).
    b. Single-value capacitor (low torque).
3. Multispeed, capacitor start, capacitor run.

Capacitor motors have the advantages of quiet operation, high power factors, and reduction in radio interference.

194. The capacitor-start, induction-run motor starts by two-phase action. After the motor has reached approximately 75 per cent of full-load speed, a centrifugal switch opens the auxiliary circuit, and the motor continues to run as an ordinary single-phase induction motor. A diagram for a motor of this type is shown in Fig. 102. These motors develop starting torques of 275 to 400 per cent of rated full-load torque. The breakdown torque is from 200 to 300 per cent of rated full-load torque. Their starting currents are sufficiently low so that they are started with full voltage. Motors of this type are made in sizes of from 1/8 to 3/4 hp.

195. Capacitor-start, capacitor-run single-phase induction motors utilize both of the stator windings at all times. The motor secures its power from a single-phase supply but really operates when both starting and running as a two-phase motor. For the **two-value capacitor motor** a larger value of capacity is used during the starting period than is employed for running conditions. The larger capacity for starting can

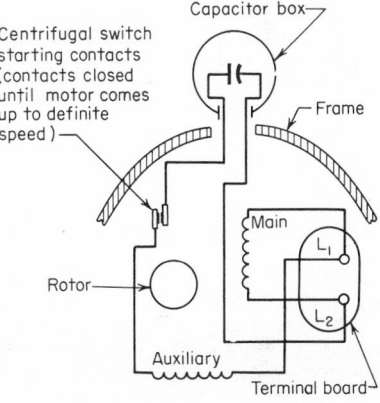

FIG. 102 *Connection diagram of capacitor-start induction-run motor. (Wagner Electric Corp.)*

be obtained by means of an additional capacitor (Figs. 103 and 104) or through changing the connections to an autotransformer which supplies the power to a single capacitor (Fig. 105). For small motors the change in the connections between starting and running is performed by means of a centrifugal switch (Fig. 103), while for larger motors a definite time relay is employed (Fig. 104). The two-value capacitor motor produces a high starting torque of 275 to 450 per cent of rated full-load torque with starting currents that are in most cases sufficiently low so that they can be started with full voltage. The breakdown torques will be from 200 to 300 per cent of rated full-load torque. These motors are available in sizes of from 1/8 to 10 hp.

The **single-value capacitor-start, capacitor-run** motor utilizes a single value of capacity that is the same for both starting and running (Fig. 106). There is no change in connections between the starting and running condition. These motors have low starting torques of a value between 40 to 60 per cent of rated full-load torque. The breakdown torques will be from 150 to 200 per cent of rated full-load torque. The starting current will generally be sufficiently low for full-voltage starting. These motors are made in sizes of from 1/8 to 10 hp.

The principal advantage of the capacitor-start, capacitor-run motors over the capacitor-start, induction-run motors is that they operate at a higher power factor.

196. Multispeed capacitor motors are single-value capacitor-start, capacitor-run motors equipped with a selector switch and autotransformer for supplying different voltages to the main winding. They are suitable only for special classes of services, since the breakdown torque is reduced in proportion to the square of the voltage impressed on the main winding. It is possible to provide the motor with a centrifugal

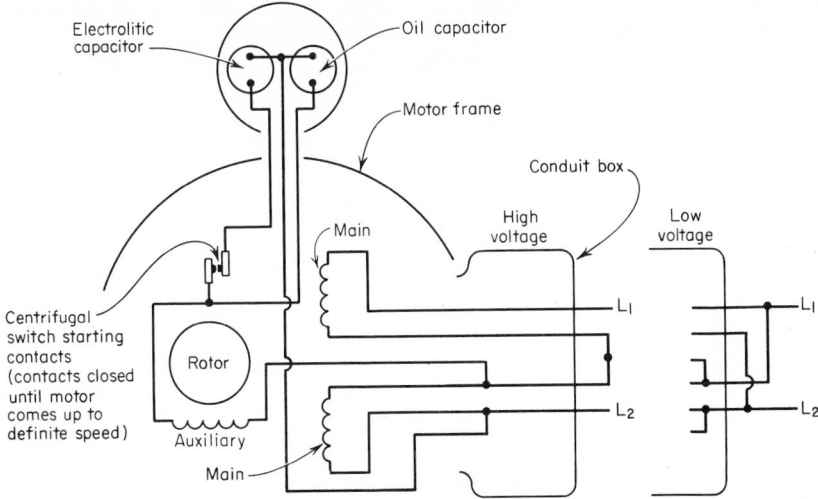

FIG. 103 *Connection diagram for two-value capacitor motor (capacitor-start, capacitor-run) with centrifugal switch. (Wagner Electric Corp.)*

switch so that when properly connected it is impossible to start the motor except with full voltage impressed upon the main winding.

197. Repulsion-start, Induction-run Single-phase Motors. Single-phase induction motors which are started by repulsion-motor action are constructed similarly to the straight-repulsion motor with the addition of a centrifugal device which shorts the commutator segments after the motor has come up to speed. The motor starts as a repulsion motor, but after it has come up to the required speed so that the commutator segments are short-circuited, it operates as a straight-induction motor. These motors are constant-speed machines not capable of speed control. The starting torques of different motors vary from 300 to 500 per cent of the full-load torque. The breakdown torque is at least 175 per cent of the full-load torque. The starting currents of these motors vary from 200 to 350 per cent of full-load current, so generally they can be started directly across the line. When it is necessary or desirable to limit the starting current to smaller values, a re-

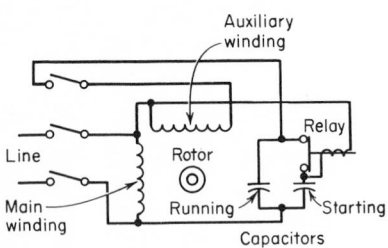

FIG. 104 *Connection diagram for two-value capacitor motor (capacitor-start, capacitor-run) with acceleration relay. (General Electric Co.)*

sistance type of starter is employed. They are made in sizes of from ⅛ to 15 hp.

198. The repulsion-induction motor has two rotor windings. One of these windings is an ordinary induction rotor winding, and the other is a repulsion winding connected to a commutator with short-circuited brushes. There is frequently a compensating winding on the stator connected to brushes bearing on the commutator, as discussed in Sec. **188.** This motor starts by repulsion-motor action. Since there is no short-circuiting device, after the machine has come up to speed, both the repulsion and the induction windings are active. Under running conditions the motor functions as a combined induction and repulsion motor. The starting torque with rated voltage impressed for different sizes and speeds varies from 225 to 300 per cent of the full-load torque. There is no definite breakdown point, the maximum torque occurring at stand-

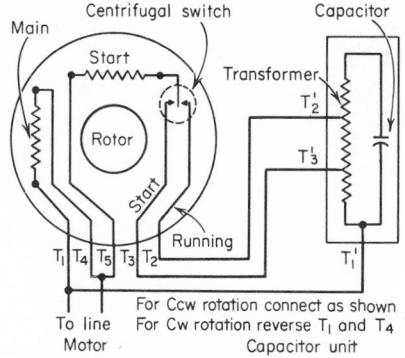

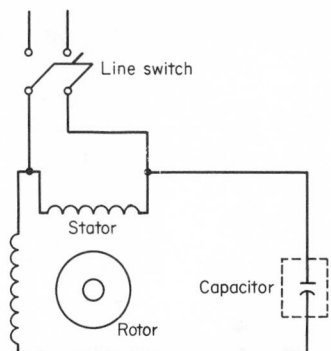

FIG. 105 *Diagram for a high-starting torque capacitor motor. (General Electric Co.)*

FIG. 106 *Diagram for a low-starting torque capacitor motor. (General Electric Co.)*

still. The starting currents of these motors, when thrown directly across the line, are within the requirements of most power companies. When it is desired to limit the starting currents to smaller values, a resistance type of starter is employed. The repulsion-induction motor is a constant-speed machine with a speed variation from no load to full load of about 6 per cent. Its speed cannot be adjusted. They are made in sizes of from ½ to 10 hp.

199. The single-phase series or "universal" motor (Fig. 107) comprises an armature of the d-c type connected in series with the field. It will operate successfully on either a-c or d-c circuits. The single-phase series motor finds its widest application in the fractional-horsepower services such as those for fans, appliance motors, and electric tools. These machines have approximately the same speed-torque characteristics as the d-c series machines. In the larger capacities, single-phase series motors are

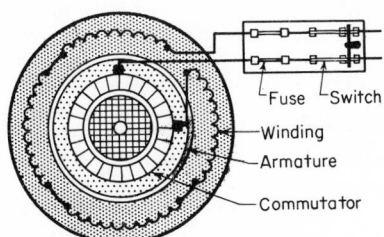

FIG. 107 *Diagram of a series or universal motor.*

equipped with compensating windings which compensate for the armature reaction. The compensating winding is placed in the pole face and must be so connected that at any instant the current will flow in the same direction in all the conductors under any one pole. The compensating winding can be connected in series with the armature. When so connected, it is called a conductively compensated winding. The compensating winding can be short-circuited on itself. When thus arranged, it receives its current by induction, and the machine is said to be inductively compensated.

200. Fractional-horsepower Single-phase Motors. The NEMA standardization rules specify that the minimum locked-rotor torque of single-phase, general-purpose, fractional-horsepower motors, with rated voltage and frequency applied, shall be not less than the following:

Hp	Minimum locked-rotor torque, oz-ft					
	60-cycle speed, rpm			50-cycle speed, rpm		
	3,600 3,450	1,800 1,725	1,200 1,140	3,000 2,850	1,500 1,425	1,000 950
⅛	...	24	32	...	29	39
⅙	15	33	43	18	39	51
¼	21	46	59	25	55	70
⅓	26	57	73	31	69	88
½	37	85	100	44	102	120
¾	50	119	...	60	143	
1	61	...	...	73		

The NEMA standards also specify that the locked-rotor current of 60-cycle single-phase general-purpose fractional-horsepower motors shall not exceed the values given in the following table for Design N motors.

Two-, Four-, Six- and Eight-pole 60-cycle Motors, Single-phase

Hp	Locked-rotor currents, amp Speeds 900 to 3,600 rpm, inclusive. Design N motors	
	115 volts	230 volts
⅙ and smaller	20	12
¼	23	15
⅓	31	18
½	45	25
¾	61	35

201. Single-phase integral-horsepower motors are classified by NEMA into two design types, Design L and Design M. The distinction between the two types is made on the basis of the value of the locked-rotor current of the motor. The NEMA standards specify that the locked-rotor current of single-phase, 60-cycle, Design L and M motors of all types, when measured with rated voltage and frequency impressed and with the rotor locked, shall not exceed the following values:

Hp	Locked-rotor current, amp		
	Design L motors		Design M motors, 230 volts
	115 volts	230 volts	
1	70	35	
1½	...	50	40
2	...	65	50
3	...	90	70
5	...	135	100
7½	...	200	150
10	...	260	200
15	...	390	300
20	...	520	400

In accordance with NEMA standards the locked-rotor torque of single-phase 60-cycle general-purpose integral-horsepower motors, with rated voltage and frequency applied, shall be not less than the following:

Hp	Minimum locked-rotor torque, lb-ft		
	Rpm		
	3,600	1,800	1,200
3/4	...	...	8.0
1	...	9.0	10.5
1½	4.5	12.0	13.0
2	5.5	16.0	16.0
3	7.5	22.0	23.0
5	11.0	33.0	
7½	16.0	45.0	

202. Methods of Reversing Motors. In the following paragraphs instructions are given for reversing the different types of motors.

Direct-current Shunt or Series Motors. Interchange the connections of either the field or the armature winding. Reversing the line leads will not change the direction of rotation. If the motor is not equipped with commutating poles, the brushes should be shifted to the same position on the opposite side of the neutral axis.

Direct-current Compound Motors.

METHOD 1. Interchange the connections of the two armature leads.

METHOD 2. Interchange the connections of the two shunt-field leads and also interchange the connections of the two series-field leads. Interchanging the connections of just the two shunt-field leads will change the direction of rotation, but the motor would then operate as a differential compound motor instead of cumulative. If the motor is not equipped with commutating poles, the brushes should be shifted to the same position on the opposite side of the neutral axis.

Any Four-wire Two-phase Induction Motor. Interchange the connections to the line of the two leads of either phase.

Any Three-wire Two-phase Induction Motor. Interchange the connections to the line of the two outside wires.

Any Three-phase Induction Motor. Interchange the connections to the line of any two leads. In reversing the commutator type of polyphase induction motor the brush-shifting mechanism must be adjusted to the proper position for the reversed rotation in addition to reversing the connections of two of the line leads.

Synchronous Motors. Ordinary synchronous motors are reversed in the same manner as induction motors.

Single-phase Induction, Shading-pole Starting. The direction of rotation cannot be reversed except in special cases. If the pole pieces of the machine can be removed, then the direction of rotation can be reversed by revolving the pole pieces 180 deg on their own axes. This will place the shading coils on the opposite sides of the pole pieces. Some special motors are built with shading coils on both sides of the pole pieces. With these machines, each shading-coil circuit must be provided with a switch. The direction of rotation depends on which shading-coil circuit is closed.

Single-phase Induction, Inductively Split-phase Starting. Interchange the connections of either the main or the auxiliary winding.

Single-phase Capacitor Motor. Interchange the connections of either the main or the auxiliary winding.

Single-phase Induction, Started by Repulsion Action. Shift the brushes to the same position on the opposite side of the neutral axis.

Single-phase Repulsion Motor. Shift the brushes to the same position on the opposite side of the neutral axis.

Single-phase Series Motor. Reversed in the same manner as d-c series motors.

202A. Electric-motor Braking. Braking of electric motors can be performed by (1) friction braking, (2) plugging, (3) dynamic braking, or (4) regenerative braking.

Friction braking of electric motors consists of retarding the motor speed or of completely stopping the motor by means of a solenoid-operated friction brake of the shoe or disk type.

Plugging is the method of retarding the motor speed and completely stopping the motor or of reversing the motor by the application of electric power in the reverse direction so that the motor develops torque in the opposite direction to the direction of rotation. Plugging will quickly bring a motor and its driven load to a stop. If the reverse power is not removed when the motor comes to a stop, the motor will reverse and accelerate in the opposite direction.

Dynamic braking is the method of retarding the motor speed or of completely stopping the motor through making the motor act as a generator with a resistance load.

Regenerative braking is the method of retarding the motor speed by making the motor, functioning as a generator, feed its generated power back into the supply line. Regenerative braking will not stop the motor. It is effective only for braking of overhauling loads. Overhauling loads are those which attain a speed greater than that of the motor speed-load characteristic and under which, therefore, the load tends to drive the motor.

203. Plugging of Motors. To employ plugging retardation of electric motors, a reversing switch or contactor must be provided in the control equipment. In order to stop or retard the speed of the motor by plugging, the connections to the power supply are simply reversed in the proper manner so that the motor develops torque in the opposite direction to that in which it is rotating. For squirrel-cage induction motors, the braking action can be cushioned so as to reduce the shock to the machine and power system by the use of resistance connected in series with the reversed connections to the supply. For wound-rotor induction motors, the plugging torque can be controlled by adjustments of the resistance in the motor secondary circuit. For synchronous motors, the d-c field circuit is de-energized during the plugging operation and the motor is plugged in the same manner as a squirrel-cage induction motor. For d-c motors, additional resistance must be used in series with the reversed power connections. When it is imperative that the motor come to a stop without reversal, a zero-speed switch or a timing relay must be used to open the motor circuit when the machine comes to a stop.

Advantages:
Simple arrangement and installation.
Fast operating performance.
Free to rotate after stopping in contrast to mechanically set brake.
No friction parts and freedom from maintenance.
Suitable for large motors and severe duty.

Disadvantages:
Requires reversing controller.
Requires zero-speed switch or consistent timing relay if reversing is to be prevented.
Power must be available. Cannot plug if power fails.
Power system must be capable of supplying the peak plugging current.
Motor windings may require special bracing.
If motor and its load must positively be held stationary when the motor is de-energized, then additional spring-set or other type of mechanical brake is necessary.

204. In dynamic braking, the armature of the motor is disconnected from the power supply and the load will drive the motor as generator. The generator action is loaded either through resistance banks or through a part of the motor winding. For d-c shunt or compound motors, the armature is disconnected from the line and connected to a resistor bank. The shunt field is left connected to the supply line. For d-c series motors, the machine is disconnected from the supply and the armature and series-field circuits are segregated from each other. The field winding is connected in series with the proper limiting resistance to the supply line. The armature is connected to a resistor bank load. Emergency dynamic braking of series motors can be accomplished by disconnecting the motor from the line, reversing the interconnection between the series field and armature, and then connecting the two in series to a resistor bank load.

For dynamic braking of squirrel-cage induction motors, a source of excitation must be provided. Three methods of providing this excitation are (1) from a separate source of direct current, (2) from the a-c supply through a rectifier, and (3) by means of capacitors. In the first method, dynamic braking is accomplished by disconnecting the motor from the supply and connecting one phase of the motor primary to a separate source of direct current. The motor will then be driven by the load as a generator and will load itself through the induced current in the motor secondary flowing through the squirrel-cage winding. The d-c excitation must be removed at the end of the braking period, or the windings will overheat. In the second method, dynamic braking is accomplished in the same manner as in the first method except that the d-c supply for the excitation is obtained from the a-c supply through a single-phase rectifier. The rectifier is usually of the contact, or barrier-layer, type. A diagram of the connections required is shown in Fig. 108. In the third method, a capacitor is permanently connected across the motor terminals. In braking, the motor is disconnected from the supply. The capacitor will supply the motor with excitation so that it will function as an induction generator. The braking action is produced by the power losses inside the machine. Improvement of the braking action can be obtained by connecting a loading resistor in parallel with the capacitor. The larger the capacitor, the greater will be the braking action. All braking action ceases with this method at about one-third of synchronous speed.

For wound-rotor induction motors, dynamic braking could be accomplished by all three of the methods just described for squirrel-cage motors. However, the first method, using a separate source of direct current for excitation, is usually the only one

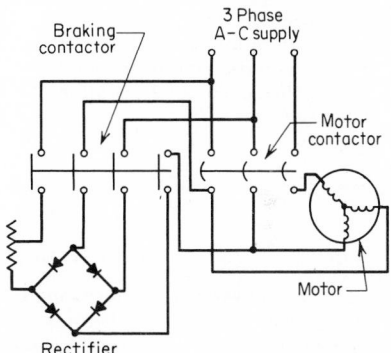

FIG. 108 *Dynamic braking of induction motor with rectified direct current.*

that is feasible. The amount of the braking action can be controlled through adjustment of the secondary resistance. For synchronous motors, dynamic braking is accomplished by disconnecting the motor armature from the a-c supply and connecting the armature to a resistor bank load. The field is left excited from direct current.

Advantages:

Cannot reverse the motor. No zero-speed switch or other antireversing device is required.

Smooth, positive retardation without the shock of mechanically set brake and less severe than plugging.

Braking torque easily adjustable by varying the d-c excitation or, as in wound-rotor induction-motor applications, by varying the motor secondary resistors.

In dynamic braking of small a-c motors by use of capacitors, the braking is independent of the power supply; furthermore, the capacitor furnishes power-factor correction while the motor is operating.

Disadvantages:

Requires source of d-c excitation during the braking period, except in capacitor braking.

Braking not available if exciting source fails.

More expensive and more complicated than plugging. If the source of excitation is not already available and it is necessary to install additional equipment, the extra cost may be prohibitive.

Control must provide means for disconnecting the excitation at the expiration of the braking period.

Useless as a holding force after motor has come to rest and is de-energized.

Capacitor dynamic braking is ineffective and ceases to exist below approximately one-third speed; therefore, it is of little value except on drives involving considerable friction. Cost of capacitor braking is prohibitive with large motors.

Rectifier-excited dynamic braking is impracticable and expensive for large motors.

205. Regenerative braking cannot be used for stopping a motor. It will produce braking action only when the load overhauls the motor and drives the motor at a speed above the speed-load characteristic of the motor. When a load overhauls its drive motor, except for series d-c motors, the voltage generated in the machine will be greater than the supply-line voltage. Consequently the motor will function as a generator and feed power back into the supply line. This is an inherent characteristic of the motor and does not require any changing of connections or control equipment.

If a series d-c motor is overhauled by its load, the motor loses its excitation and becomes incapable of regenerative braking unless the connections are changed. Therefore, to use regenerative braking on a series motor, the series field and armature must be segregated from each other and connected individually to the supply. Sufficient resistance must be connected in series with the series field so that the current will be held to normal value.

Advantages:

No extra equipment is required except for series-wound d-c motors. Can be made effective with d-c motors at reduced speeds by strengthening the motor field, i.e., by lowering the speed at which the motor will regenerate.

Disadvantages:

Effective only at overhauling speeds. Useless as a means of stopping.

Where d-c motors must be made to regenerate at low speeds, the control becomes involved and expensive. The motor may require special fields.

CONVERSION EQUIPMENT

206. The conversion of alternating current to direct current is usually effected with a motor generator set, a synchronous converter, an electronic rectifier, a contact (barrier-layer) rectifier, or solid-state semiconductor rectifiers. A discussion of rectifiers is given in Div. 6.

207. A motor generator set consists of a motor mechanically coupled to and driving one or more generators. The motor is usually alternating current and is mounted on the same bedplate and on the same shaft with the generator or generators which it drives. A motor generator set can be employed to convert electrical energy from one voltage or frequency to another voltage or frequency, to convert alternating current to direct current, or to convert direct current to alternating current. Where an a-c motor is used, it may be of either the induction or synchronous type. The induction type has the advantages of low first cost and rugged construction. It may also be wound for voltages as high as 13,500 volts. This will, in many cases, eliminate the necessity for transformers. It has, however, poorer speed regulation and lower power factor. A synchronous-motor drive is probably more frequently used for large-capacity installations than is the induction motor. The synchronous motor is inherently a constant-speed motor. Therefore by its use a more nearly constant voltage can be maintained at the generator terminals than by the use of an induction motor. The field of the synchronous motor may be overexcited. It then acts as a synchronous condenser, thus improving the power factor.

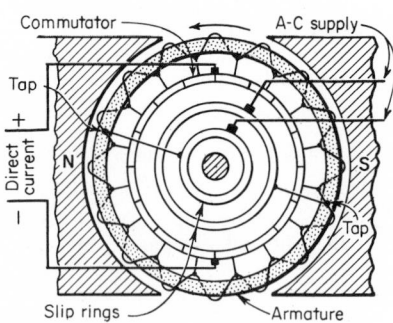

FIG. 109 *Diagram of two-pole single-phase synchronous converter.*

208. A synchronous converter (sometimes called a rotary converter) for converting alternating to direct current or vice versa consists (Fig. 109) of a d-c motor equipped with slip rings. Taps are brought out from equidistant points on the armature winding and connected to these slip rings. As ordinarily used the machine is then driven as a synchronous motor, by an alternating emf which is impressed on the armature through the slip rings. As the armature rotates, an alternating emf is induced in the armature winding, as in any d-c generator. This alternating induced emf is rectified by the commutator and leaves the brushes as a pulsating or direct current. If a synchronous converter is utilized for converting alternating current to direct current, it is called a **direct converter,** or merely a converter. If it converts direct current to alternating current, it is called an **inverted converter.** If the main-pole flux distribution is such that the induced emf has a sine-wave form, then (see Table **209** for values)

$$\frac{E_{ac}}{E_{dc}} = 0.707 \left(\sin \frac{180}{n} \right) \tag{6}$$

wherein E_{ac} = the effective alternating-current voltage, in volts between adjacent slip rings; E_{dc} = the direct-current voltage, in volts; and n = number of slip rings for a bipolar machine or the number of taps per pair of poles for a multipolar machine.

209. Ratio of the Effective A-C to D-C Voltage with Different Numbers of Taps

Number of taps per pair of poles	Number of phases	$\frac{E_{ac}}{E_{dc}}$ (between adjacent taps)	$\frac{E_{ac}}{E_{dc}}$ (line voltage)
2	1	0.707	0.707
3	3	0.612	0.612
4	4 or 2	0.500	0.707
6	6	0.354	{ 0.707 (diametrical) { 0.612 (double Δ)
12	12	0.183	0.682 (double chord)

NOTE. Synchronous converters are subject to hunting. The cause of hunting and the remedy are the same as for a synchronous motor.

210. The methods of starting a synchronous converter are (1) from its d-c side as a shunt motor, (2) by means of an auxiliary motor mounted on its shaft, and (3) if polyphase, from its a-c side as an induction motor. Whatever method is used, the armature must be brought up almost to synchronous speed before the load is applied to the generator.

211. Usual Relation among Number of Poles, Phases, Taps, and Slip Rings of a Synchronous Converter

Phases	2 pole		4 pole		6 pole		8 pole		12 pole	
	Slip rings	Taps	Slip rings	Taps	Slip rings	Taps	Slip rings	Taps	Slip rings	Taps
1	2	2	2	4	2	6	2	8	2	12
2	4	4	4	8	4	12	4	16	4	24
3	3	3	3	6	3	9	3	12	3	18
6	6	6	6	12	6	18	6	24	6	36

NOTE. The tendency of modern practice in large three-phase conversion installations is to use a six-phase converter. It is connected to the three-phase line through a set of transformers.

212. The relation between the values of direct and alternating current of any synchronous converter is

$$I_{dc} = 0.354 \times (I_{ac}) \times (n) \times (\text{power factor}) \times (\text{efficiency}) \tag{7}$$

where I_{dc} = direct current, in amperes; I_{ac} = effective alternating current, in amperes; and n is as given in Eq. (6).

213. A frequency-changer motor generator consists of an a-c generator or generators driven by an induction or a synchronous motor or motors. The frequency of the generator is different from that of the motor. Since the speed regulation of the induction motor is inherently poorer, a synchronous driving motor is usually applied. The output frequency of a set which is driven by a synchronous motor will vary only with the input frequency and not with the load. The synchronous motor can also be utilized for improving the power factor of the energy-supplying system. Since the motor and the generator are mounted on the same shaft and hence rotate at the same speed, the desired frequency change must be obtained by a proper ratio between the number of motor poles and the number of generator poles. The ratio between the frequency applied to the motor and the frequency which the generator will supply is exactly equal to the ratio between the number of poles on the motor and the number of poles on the generator. That is,

$$\frac{\text{No. of poles on motor}}{\text{No. of poles on generator}} = \frac{\text{frequency applied to motor}}{\text{frequency supplied by generator}} \tag{8}$$

For 60- to 25-cycle conversion this practically limits the speed to 300 rpm with 24 poles on the 60-cycle machine and 10 poles on the 25-cycle machine.

TROUBLES OF A-C MOTORS AND GENERATORS – THEIR LOCALIZATION AND CORRECTION

214. Troubles of A-C Machinery. Much of the material under this heading is based on that in the book "Motor Troubles," by E. B. Raymond.

215. Induction Motor Troubles (H. M. Nichols, "Power and the Engineer"). The author asserts that the unsatisfactory operation of an induction motor may be due to either external or internal conditions. The voltage or the frequency may be wrong, or there may be an overload on the machine. Low voltage is the most frequent cause of trouble. The starting current sometimes amounts to twice the running current, with the result that the voltage is particularly low at starting. The best remedy for this disorder is larger transformers and larger motor leads, one or both. The troubles that occur most frequently within the motor itself are caused by faulty insulation and by an uneven air gap due to the springing of the motor shaft or to excessive wear in the bearings. If a wound-rotor machine refuses to start, the trouble may be due to an open circuit in the rotor winding. Most wound-rotor motors designed to employ a starting resistance will not start at all if the resistance is left out of the secondary circuit with the secondary circuit open. A short-circuited coil in the motor will make its existence known by local heating in the latter.

216. Troubles of A-C Generators (Westinghouse Instruction Book). The following causes may prevent a-c generators from developing their normal emf:

The speed of the generator may be below normal.

The switchboard instruments may be incorrect, and the voltage may be higher than that indicated, or the current may be greater than is shown by the readings.

The voltage of the exciter may be low because its speed is below normal, its series field is reversed, or part of its shunt field is reversed or short-circuited.

The brushes of the exciter may be incorrectly set.

A part of the field rheostat or other unnecessary resistance may be in the field circuit.

The power factor of the load may be abnormally low.

217. Causes of Shutdowns of Induction Motors. Sometimes there is trouble from blowing fuses. Or possibly, and more serious, the fuses do not blow, and the motor, perhaps humming loudly, comes to a standstill. Under these conditions the current may be ten times normal, so that the heating effect, being increased as the square of the current or a hundredfold, causes the machine to burn out its insulation.

Since the torque or turning power of an induction motor is proportional to the square of the applied voltage (one-half voltage produces only one-quarter torque), it is evident that lowering the voltage has a decided effect upon the ability of the motor to carry load and may be the cause of its stopping. Another cause may be that the load on the motor is more than equal to its maximum output.

The bearings may have become worn, so that the air gap (which ordinarily is not much over 0.040 in. and on small motors may be as small as 0.015 in.) has been gradually reduced at the lower side of the rotor to practically zero. The rotor commences to rub on the stator. The friction soon becomes so great that it is more than the motor can carry. The result is that it shuts down.

A shutdown may be due to bearings introducing excessive friction. Hot bearings, in turn, may be due to excess of belt tension, dirt in the oil, oil rings not turning, or improper alignment of the motor to the machine that it drives. Hence, under such conditions, it should be ascertained whether the voltage has been normal, whether the air gap is such that the armature is free from the field, and whether the load imposed upon the motor is more than that for which it was designed. In any installation a system should be arranged whereby an inspector will examine the gap, bearings, etc., periodically.

Rarely, shutting down may be due to the working out of the starting switch, which may be located within the armature. Such a switch is operated by a lever engaging a collar which bears on contacts which, as they move inward, cut out the resistance which is in series with the rotor winding and is located within it.

If the short-circuiting brushes work back, introducing resistance into the armature circuit while the machine is trying to carry load, it will at once slow down in speed and probably stop, usually burning out the starting resistance. Of course, this can occur only from faulty construction. The remedy is to fit the brushes properly so that they will not work out. It is well to inspect them at the time of air-gap inspection.

218. Low Torque While Starting Induction Motors. Even when the circuit to the motor is closed, sometimes it does not start. The same general laws of voltage, etc., apply to the motor at starting as when running. Hence, the points mentioned in Sec. **217** should be investigated and if necessary corrected. The resistance, which is frequently inserted in the armature, may be short-circuited, thus giving a low starting torque. With a wound-rotor motor it is necessary, in order to obtain a proper starting torque with a reasonable current, that a resistance be inserted in the rotor circuit. The resistance not only limits the current, which would, with the motor standing still, be large, but causes the current of the armature to assume a more effective phase relation, so that with the same current a far larger torque is obtained. A partial or complete short-circuit of the resistance will reduce the starting torque.

219. Low Maximum Output of Induction Motors. The maximum load which a motor can carry may be less than desired or less than the name plate indicates. This may be due to improper interconnection of the motor windings or to low line voltage. If the line voltage is considerably below the rated voltage of the motor, the maximum torque that the motor can develop may be so reduced that the motor will stall on small overloads. Many motors are designed for operation at two voltages, for example, 110/220 or 220/440. This is accomplished by dividing the stator winding into two parts. For operation on the low-voltage rating, the two parts of the winding should be connected in parallel, while for operation on the high-voltage rating, the two parts should be connected in series. Sometimes, when a motor is put in service on a supply which has a voltage corresponding to the low-voltage rating of the motor, the windings are connected in series. With this connection the motor would be operating at half rated voltage. This wrong connection will be indicated by the motor's starting very slowly or failing to start or by stalling without overheating and without tripping the overcurrent devices.

220. Winding Faults of Induction Motors. When a new induction motor is received, it sometimes happens that, when an attempt is made to operate the machine, although it will start, the currents are excessive and unbalanced, undue heating appears, or a peculiar noise is emitted, accompanied possibly by dimming of the lights on the same circuit and the lowering of speed, with perhaps actual shutdown of other induction motors thereon. If, after examination, there is found to be no difficulty with the air gap, belt tension, starting resistance, or bearings, the probabilities are that the coils of the motor have been wrongly connected or that the winding has been damaged during transportation. Certain indications of these conditions are shown by instrument readings. The winding faults in a three-phase motor may be:

1. One coil of the rotor may be open-circuited. The armature or rotor may have a defective winding just as may the stator.

2. Two coils or phases of the armature may be open-circuited.

3. Armature may be connected properly, but stator coil or phase may be reversed.

4. Part of stator may be short-circuited.

5. One phase of stator may be open-circuited.

221. With an open circuit in field or stator in a three-phase motor, current would flow only in two legs. There would be no current in the other leg, and the motor would not start from rest with all switches closed. However, a three-phase motor or a two-phase motor will run and do work single-phase if it is assisted in starting. The starting torque is zero, but as the speed increases the torque increases.

With a small motor, giving a pull on the belt will introduce enough torque so that it will pick up its load. Therefore while an open circuit in the field winding should be found and repaired, if there is not time for repairs, the motor can be operated single-phase to about two-thirds of normal load. The power-factor conditions and effects on the rest of the circuit are practically no worse than when the motor is running three-phase. The torque of a 1-hp three-phase induction motor from rest to synchronism, when running single-phase, is indicated in Fig. 89.

222. Squirrel-cage Armature or Rotor Troubles. Unusual operation due to reversals of phase, phases open-circuited, and other causes occur with squirrel-cage armatures as well as with wound armatures. Poor soldering of the armature bars may be the cause. Sometimes a solder flux that will ensure proper operation for a while can be used, but time will develop poor electrical contacts due to chemical action at the joints. If the resistances of all the squirrel-cage joints are uniformly high, the effect is simply like that of an armature having a high resistance, which causes a lowering of the speed and local heating at the joints. If some of the joints are perfect but some bad, the motor may not have the ability to come up to speed, and there will be unbalanced currents.

223. Effects of Unbalanced Voltages on Induction Motors. The maximum output of a polyphase induction motor may be materially decreased if the voltages impressed on the different phases are unequal. On a three-phase system the three voltages between the legs 1–2, 2–3, and 1–3 should be approximately equal. Also on a two-phase system the voltage 1–2 should equal 3–4. If these voltages impressed on the induction motor are not equal, the maximum output of the motor as well as the current in the various legs is proportionately affected.

For example, with a two-phase motor, if the voltages in the two legs differ by 20 per cent, a condition sometimes met in normal practice, the output of the motor may be reduced 25 per cent. Then, instead of being able to give its maximum output of, say, 150 per cent for a few moments, it will give but 112 per cent. The varying loads which the motor may have to carry may shut it down. In cases of low maximum output, the relative voltages on the various legs should always be investigated. If they vary, the trouble may be due to this variation.

In addition to the effect on the maximum output, the unequal distribution of current in a two-phase motor under such conditions may be quite serious. Consider a specific case of a 15-hp six-pole 1,200-rpm 220-volt motor, with the voltage on one leg 220 and the voltage on the other leg 180; current in leg 1 was 60 amp and in leg 2 was 35 amp at full load. The normal current at full load was 35 amp. Thus the fuse might blow in the phase carrying the high current, causing the motor to run single-phase. If an attempt is made to start the motor, the blown fuse not being noticed, there would be no starting torque.

Where unbalanced voltages are detected, make a careful check for a blown fuse. Often a service or feeder fuse will open and go undetected, except for slight unbalanced line-to-line voltages. This occurs on installations, such as sewer treatment plants, where some large pump, vacuum, or blower motors run continuously. If a "main" fuse opens while one of these motors is running, the motor itself "generates" the "third" phase, and other motors will start and run at reduced efficiency. If three-phase motors are protected by three overload relays the large line current in one motor lead will cause the circuit to open. Accordingly, check for open fuses in the feeder or service switch if properly sized motor overload devices trip out frequently.

If only two overload protective devices are provided for three-phase motors, the excessive current could be in the "unprotected" leg and cause a motor-winding failure.

Where no fuses have been detected and unbalanced line-to-line voltages exist, check to see whether single-phase loads connected to the three-phase system are properly balanced.

After checking for open fuses and balanced single-phase loads, call the electric power company if unbalanced voltages appear on the line side of the main service switch.

224. Induction-motor Starting-compensator Troubles. Sometimes a mistake is made in the connections to the compensator, so that full voltage is used at starting and the lesser voltage after throwing over the switch. Then the motor at starting takes excessive current, and since the maximum output is in proportion to the square of the voltage, the motor capacity is much reduced when it is apparently running on the operating position. Such action, therefore, can usually be accounted for by a wrong connection in the compensator. Sometimes a motor connected to a compensator takes more current at starting than it should, under which condition a lower tap should be tried. Compensators are usually supplied with various taps, and the one should be selected which produces the least disturbance on the line, giving at the same time the desired starting torque on the motor.

When a motor, having been connected to a compensator, will not start, the cause may be entirely in the compensator. The compensator may have become open-circuited, owing to a flash within. The switch may have become deranged so that it will not close, or a connection within the compensator may have become loosened. Possibly, when a motor will not start when connected to a compensator just installed, one secondary coil of the compensator may be improperly interconnected.

225. Induction-motor Collector-ring Troubles. It is essential that the contact of the brushes on the collector rings be good, or the contact resistance will be so great as to slow the motor down and to cause heating of the collector itself. This effect is particularly noticeable when carbon brushes are used. The contact resistance of a carbon brush under normal operation pressure and carrying its usual density of current (40 amp per sq in.) is 0.04 ohm per sq in. Thus, under normal conditions, the drop is 0.04 × 40, which equals 1.6 volts. If the contact is only one-quarter the surface, this drop would be 6.4 volts and might materially affect the speed of the motor. Thus, if the speed is below synchronous speed more than it should be, an investigation of the fit of the brush upon the collector may show up the trouble.

If copper brushes are used, this trouble is much less liable to occur, since the drop of the voltage due to contact resistance when running at normal density (150 amp per sq in.) is only one-tenth that of carbon. The same trouble may occur owing to the pigtail, which is generally used with carbon brushes, making poor contact with the carbon, which gives the same effect as a poor contact with the collector itself.

226. Improper End Play in Induction Motors. Induction motors are so designed that the revolving parts will play endwise in the bearing, 1/16 in. or so. If in setting up the machine the bearings so limit this end action that the rotor does not lie exactly in the middle of the stator, there is a strong magnetic pull tending to center the rotor. If the bearings will not permit this centering, the thrust collars must take the extra thrust, which in an induction motor is considerable. If in addition to the magnetic thrust the belt pull is such as also to draw in the same direction, the trouble is increased. The end force may be such as to heat the bearing excessively and to cause cutting, soon rendering the motor inoperative.

In case of trouble with bearings, the end play should be tested by pushing against the shaft with a small piece of wood, placed on the shaft center. With the machine operating under normal conditions there should be no particular difficulty in pushing the shaft first one way from one side and then the other way from the other side. If it is found that the revolving part is hugging closely against one side, the trouble can be corrected by either pressing the spider along the shaft in a direction toward which the hugging is occurring or driving the tops of the lamination teeth in the same direction. With a wooden wedge the tops of the teeth can often be without any difficulty driven over 1/8 to 3/16 in. This movement will usually correct the trouble. Driving the teeth of the stator 1/8 in. or so in the opposite direction to that of the end thrust will usually accomplish the same result. It is best to choose the teeth (stator or rotor) which are most easily driven over. The thin long ones move more easily than do the short broad ones.

227. Oil Leakage of Induction Motors. Sometimes a bearing will permit oil to be drawn out, perhaps a very little at a time. Ultimately enough will accumulate to show on the outside or on the windings of the machine. Although a motor will run for a period with its windings wet with ordinary lubricating oil without being apparently injured, insulation soaked with oil will deteriorate and eventually fail.

One of the principal causes is a suction of the oil due to the drafts of air from the rotor, and one of the best methods of stopping the trouble, under ordinary conditions, is to cut grooves as shown in Fig. 110 at *B* and *D*. These grooves on a 50-hp motor may be 1/8 in. deep and 3/16 in. wide. Each groove has three holes drilled through the bearing shell to convey the oil collected by the grooves into the oilwell. These grooves are just as effective with a split as with a solid bearing. It is impossible here to go into the various causes of oil leakage. The grooves as suggested are a general remedy and cover many cases.

228. General Summary of Synchronous-motor Troubles. Failure of a synchronous motor to start is often due to faulty connections in the auxiliary apparatus. These should be carefully inspected for open circuits or poor connections. An open circuit in one phase of the motor itself or a short circuit will prevent the motor from starting. Most synchronous motors are provided with an ammeter in each phase so that the last two causes can be determined from their indications — no current in one phase in case of an open circuit and excessive current in case of a short circuit. Either condition will usually be accompanied by a decided buzzing noise, and a short-circuited coil will often be quickly burned out. The effect of a short circuit is sometimes caused by two grounds on the machine.

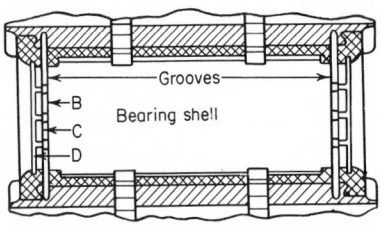

FIG. 110 *Grooves to prevent oil leakage.*

Starting troubles should never be assumed until a trial has been made to start the motor light, i.e., with no load except its own friction. It may be that the starting load is too great for the motor.

If the motor starts but fails to develop sufficient torque to carry its load when the field circuit has been closed, the trouble will usually be found in the field circuit. First, determine whether or not the exciter is giving its normal voltage. Assuming the exciter voltage to be correct, the trouble will probably be due to one of the following causes: (1) open circuit in the field winding or rheostat or (2) short circuit or reversal of one or more of the field spools. An open circuit can often be located by inspection or by use of a magneto.

The majority of field troubles are caused by excessive induced voltage at start or by the field circuit being broken. This excessive voltage may break down the insulation between field winding and frame or between turns on any one field spool, thus short-circuiting one or more turns, or it may even burn the field conductor off, causing an open circuit.

Causes of overheating in synchronous motors are about the same as those in a-c generators. Probably the most common cause of overheating is excessive armature current due to an attempt to make the motor carry its rated load and at the same time compensate for a power factor lower than that for which it was designed. If the motor is not correcting low power factor but doing mechanical work only, the field current should be adjusted so that the armature current is minimum for the average load that the motor carries.

229. Difficulties in Starting Synchronous Motors. A synchronous motor starts as an induction motor. The starting torque, as in an induction motor, is proportional to the square of the applied voltage. For example, if the voltage is halved, the starting effort is quartered. When a synchronous motor will not start, it may be because the voltage on the line has been pulled down below the value necessary for starting.

In general, at least half voltage is required to start a synchronous motor. Difficulty in starting may also be caused by an open circuit in one of the lines to the motor. Assume the motor to be three-phase. If one of the lines is open, the motor becomes single-phase, and no single-phase synchronous motor, as such, is self-starting. The motor will, therefore, not start and will soon get hot. The same condition is true of a two-phase motor if one of the phases is open-circuited.

Difficulty in starting may be due to a rather slight increase in static friction. It may be that the bearings are too tight, perhaps from cutting during the previous run. Excessive belt tension, in case the synchronous motor is belted to its load, or any cause which increases starting friction will probably give trouble. Difficulty in starting may be due to field excitation being on the motor. After excitation exceeds one-quarter normal value, the starting torque is influenced. With full field on, most synchronous motors will not start at all. The field should be short-circuited through a proper resistance during the starting period.

Usually compensators are used for starting synchronous motors. If there is a reversed phase in a compensator or if the windings of the armature of the synchronous motor are connected incorrectly, there will be little starting torque. Incorrect connection can be located by noting the unbalanced entering current. Readings to determine this unbalancing should be taken with the armature revolving slowly. The revolving can be effected by any mechanical means. While the motor is standing still, even with correct connections, the armature currents of the three phases usually differ somewhat. This is due to the position of the poles in relation to the armature, but when the armature is revolving slowly, the currents should average up. If the rotor cannot be revolved mechanically, similar points on each phase of the armature must be found. Then when the rotor is set successively at these points, the currents at each setting should be the same. Each phase, when located in a certain specific position as related to a pole, should, with right connections, take a certain specific current. With wrong connections the currents will not be the same.

230. Open Circuit in the Field of a Synchronous Motor. If in the operation of a synchronous motor the field current breaks for any reason, the armature current will appreciably increase, causing either a shutdown or excessive heat. It becomes important therefore in synchronous motors to have the field circuit permanently established.

231. Short Circuit in an Armature Coil of a Synchronous Motor. A short circuit in an armature coil of a synchronous motor burns it out completely, charring it down to the bare copper. When this occurs, the symptoms are so evident that there is no difficulty in identifying the trouble. Such a coil may under ordinary circumstances be cut out and operation continued. In an induction motor, the current in the short-circuited coil rises only to a certain value but heats it many times more than normal. It is not necessarily burned out immediately, and perhaps it may not be burned out at all.

232. Hunting of Synchronous Motors. Synchronous motors served by certain primary sources of energy tend to "hunt." The periodicity of the swinging is determined by properties of the armature and the circuit. It may reach a certain magnitude and there stick, or the swinging may increase until finally the motor breaks down altogether. This trouble usually occurs on long lines having considerable resistance between the source of energy and the synchronous motor. Sometimes it occurs under the most favorable conditions. Irregular rotation of a prime mover, such as a single-cylinder steam engine, is often responsible for the trouble. The usual remedy is to apply to the poles bridges of copper or brass in which currents are induced by the wavering of the armature. These currents tend to stop the motion. Different companies use different forms of bridges. When hunting or pulsating occurs and the motor is not already equipped with bridges, it is best to consult the manufacturer. In general, the weaker the field on a synchronous motor, the less the pulsation. Sometimes pulsation may be so reduced that no trouble results, simply by running with a somewhat weaker field current.

233. Improper Armature Connections in Synchronous Motors. This trouble usually manifests itself by unbalanced entering currents and by a negligible or very low starting torque. The circuits should be traced out and the connections remade until the three entering currents for three-phase or the two entering currents for two-phase are approximately equal. These currents will not be equal even with correct connection when the armature is standing still.

234. Bearing troubles of synchronous motors are similar to those of induction motors. A difference is that with a synchronous motor the air gap between the revolving element and the poles is relatively large, so that the wearing of the bearing, which throws the armature out of center, is not so serious as with an induction motor. End play should be treated the same as with an induction motor.

235. Collector Rings and Brushes. One of the most common sources of trouble with synchronous motors is sparking at the collector rings. Much of this trouble is due to the lack of proper care. The collector rings are one of the most important parts of the machine, and they should be frequently inspected.

Any black spots that appear on the surface of the collector should be removed by rubbing lightly with fine sandpaper the first time that the machine is shut down. It is very important that this be done because, although these spots are not serious in themselves, they will lead to pitting of the rings and the necessity of regrinding. However, no harm is done to the rings if the condition is corrected at once.

Sometimes an imprint of the brushes will be found on the surface of the collectors. This may occur on a machine which is subjected to moisture or acid fumes which will act on the surface of the ring. In case the machine is shut down for any length of time, the fumes will act upon the surface of the ring except where it is in contact with the brushes. The surface of the ring will be slightly high at this point. This causes the brush to jump slightly and arc and thus burn its imprint on the ring.

In such an installation it is good practice for the operator, when shutting down the machine, to apply a little paraffin to the rings as the motor comes to a stop and while they are still warm. In general, rings give better service when the motor is run continuously than when it is shut down part of the time.

Another cause of brush imprint on the rings is a slight unbalance in the rotor, which causes a jerk or movement in the rings once every revolution. This results in jumping of the brush, with a consequent small arc, which in time burns an imprint of the brush on the ring.

Brush imprints due to fumes will occur at any point where the motor happens to stop. Imprints due to a rotor unbalance will always occur at the same place on the ring relative to the rotor.

Since there is always an electrolytic action on the surface of an iron ring, the collector operation is improved by occasionally reversing the polarity of the rings. Sometimes trouble will occur on one ring only, and by reversing the polarity every day or so the trouble will entirely disappear.

Occasionally ring trouble will arise from a ring not being of uniform hardness, so that it wears unevenly. Such a ring should be replaced. Small pinholes in the surface of a cast-iron ring will not cause trouble.

236. Bearing Troubles of Motors and Generators. Modern generators and motors have self-oiling bearings. They should be filled to such a height that the rings will carry sufficient oil upon the shaft. If the bearings are too full, oil will be thrown out along the shaft. Watch the bearings carefully from the time the machine is first started until the bearings are warmed up; then note the oil level. The expansion of the oil due to heat and foaming raises the level considerably during that time. The oil should be renewed about once in 6 months or oftener if it becomes dirty or causes the bearings to heat.

The bearings must be kept clean and free from dirt. They should be examined frequently to see that the oil supply is properly maintained and that the oil rings do not stick. Use only the best quality of oil. New oil should be run through a strainer if it appears to contain any foreign substances. If the oil is used a second time, it should first be filtered and, if warm, allowed to cool. If a bearing becomes hot, first feed heavy lubricant copiously, loosen the nuts on the bearing cap, and then, if the machine is belt-connected, slacken the belt. If no relief is afforded by these means, shut down, keeping the machine running slowly until the shaft is cool, in order that the bearing may not "freeze." Renew the oil supply before starting again. A new machine should always be run at a slow speed for an hour or so in order to see that it operates properly. The bearings should be inspected at regular intervals to ensure that they always remain in good condition. The higher the speed, the more care should be taken in this regard.

A warm bearing or "hot box" is probably due to one of the following causes: (1) excessive belt tension, (2) failure of the oil rings to revolve with the shaft, (3) rough bearing surface, and (4) improper lining up of bearings or fitting of the journal boxes.

CARE OF MOTORS [1]

237. Modern methods of design and construction have made the electric motor one of the least complicated and most dependable forms of machinery in existence and have thereby made the matter of its maintenance one of comparative simplicity. This statement should not, however, be taken to mean that proper maintenance is not important; on the contrary, it must be given careful consideration if the best performance and longest life are to be expected from the motor. The two major features, from the standpoint of their effect upon the general performance of the motor, are those of

[1] Courtesy of General Electric Co.

proper lubrication and the care given to the insulation, because they concern the most vital, and probably the most vulnerable, parts of the machine.

238. Lubrication. The designs of bearings and bearing housings of motors have been wonderfully improved in the last few years. The point has now been reached where the bearings of modern motors, whether sleeve, ball, or roller, require only very infrequent attention.

This advance in the art is not yet fully appreciated, for, although there may have been some necessity for more frequent attention in the case of older designs with housings less tight than on modern machines, oiling and greasing of new motors are quite often entrusted to uninformed and careless attendants, with the result that oil or grease is copiously and frequently applied to the outside as well as the inside of bearing housings. Some of the excess lubricant is carried into the machine and lodges on the windings, where it catches dirt and thereby hastens the ultimate failure of the insulation.

The modern designs provide for a plentiful supply of oil or grease being held in dusttight and oiltight housings. If the proper amount of a suitable lubricant is applied before starting, there should be no need to refill the housings for several months, even in dusty places. Infrequent though periodic and reasonable attention to modern bearings of any type will tend toward longer life of both bearings and insulation.

239. Greasing Ball Bearings. Only a high grade of grease, having the following general characteristics, should be used for ball-bearing lubrication:

1. Consistency a little stiffer than that of Vaseline, maintained over the operating-temperature range.

2. Melting point preferably over 150°C.

3. Freedom from separation of oil and soap under operating and storage conditions.

4. Freedom from abrasive matter, acid, and alkali.

In greasing a motor, care must be taken not to add too large a quantity of grease, as this will cause too high an operating temperature with resulting expansion and leaking of the grease, especially with large bearings operated at slow speeds.

1. PRESSURE-RELIEF SYSTEMS. The following procedure is recommended for greasing ball-bearing motors equipped with a pressure-relief greasing system:

Make sure—by wiping clean the pressure-gun fitting, bearing housing, and relief plug—that no dirt gets into the bearing with the grease. Always remove the relief plug from the bottom of the bearing before using the grease gun. This prevents putting excessive pressure inside the bearing housing. Excessive pressure might rupture the bearing seals.

With a clean screwdriver or similar tool, free the relief hole of any hardened grease, so that any excess grease will run freely from the bearing. With the motor running, add grease with a hand-operated pressure gun until it begins to flow from the relief hole. This tends to purge the housing of old grease. If it might prove dangerous to lubricate the motor while it is running, follow the procedure with the motor at a standstill.

Allow the motor to run long enough after adding grease to permit the rotating parts of the bearing to expel all excess grease from the housing. This very important step prevents overgreasing the bearing. Stop the motor and replace the relief plug tightly with a wrench.

2. OTHER TYPES. A motor that is not equipped with the pressure-gun fitting and relief plug on the bearing housing cannot be greased by the procedures previously described.

Under average operating conditions, the grease with which the bearing housings of these motors were packed before leaving the factory is sufficient to last approximately one year. When the first year of service has elapsed and once a year thereafter (or oftener if conditions warrant), the old grease should be removed and the bearings supplied with new grease.

To do this, disassemble the bearing housings and clean the inside of the housings and housing plates or caps and the bearings with a suitable solvent. When thoroughly cleansed of old grease, reassemble all parts except the outer plates or caps.

Apply new grease, either by hand or from a tube, over and between the balls. The amount of grease to be used varies with the type and frame size of the particular motor. The instruction sheet that accompanied the motor should be consulted for this information.

Addition of the correct amount of grease fills the bearing housing one-third to one-half full. More than the amount specified must not be used. When the motor is re-assembled, any V grooves that are found in the housing lip should be refilled with grease—preferably a fibrous, high-temperature-sealing grease—which will act as an additional protective seal against the entrance of dirt or foreign particles.

240. The technique for greasing motors equipped with roller bearings is very similar to that used for ball bearings.

Specific instructions for the individual design should be followed, however, because more frequent greasing or slight changes in technique may sometimes be necessary.

241. Oiling Sleeve Bearings. The oil level in sleeve-bearing housings should be checked periodically with the motor stopped. If the motor is equipped with an oil filler gage, the gage should be approximately three-quarters full at all times.

If the oil is dirty, drain it off by removing the drain plug, which is usually located in the bottom or side of the bearing housing. Then flush the bearing with clean oil until the outcoming oil is clean.

In fractional-horsepower motors, there may be no means of checking oil level, as all the oil may be held in the waste packing. In such cases, a good general rule for normal motor service is to add 30 to 70 drops of oil at the end of the first year and to reoil at the end of each subsequent 1,000 hr of motor operation.

Most fractional-horsepower motors built today require lubrication about once a year. Small fan and agitator motors will often require more frequent lubrication, with 3-month intervals between oilings.

242. Cleaning Bearings.

1. SLEEVE BEARINGS. Sleeve-bearing housings are provided with liberal settling chambers into which dust, dirt, and oil sludge collect. The only cleaning necessary is to remove the drain plug and drain the oil, which will flush out most of the settled material with it.

Whenever the motor is disassembled for general cleaning, the bearing housing should be washed out with a solvent. Before being assembled, the bearing lining should be dried and the shaft covered with a film of oil.

2. BALL BEARINGS. The pressure-relief method of greasing motors, described above, tends to purge the bearing housing of used grease. Complete cleaning of bearings, therefore, is required at infrequent intervals only. For a thorough and convenient flushing when the bearings are not disassembled, the following method is recommended:

Wipe clean the housing, pressure-gun, and relief fittings, and then remove both fittings. Every care should be taken to keep dirt out of the bearings. A bit of abrasive once in a bearing may not be removed even with the most thorough cleaning. Afterwards, it may become dislodged and get between the bearing surfaces with serious results.

With a clean screwdriver or a similar tool, free the pressure-fitting hole in the top of the bearing housing of hardened grease. Also free the relief-plug hole in the bottom of the housing of old grease to permit easy expulsion of the old grease during the cleaning process after the solvent is added.

Fill a syringe with any suitable modern-type grease solvent and inject some of it into the bearing housing through the pressure-fitting hole, while the motor is running. As the grease becomes thinned by the solvent, it will drain out through the relief hole. Continue to add solvent until it drains out quite clear.

Replace the relief plug and inject solvent until it can be seen splashing in the filling hole. Allow the solvent to churn for a few minutes, and then remove the relief plug and drain off the solvent. Repeat the churning operation until the solvent runs clean.

When using any type of solvent for flushing, replace the relief plug and inject a small amount of light lubricating oil. Allow it to churn for a minute or two before draining off. This will flush out the solvent. To complete the job, grease the bearing, using the method previously described.

This method permits the cleaning of all standard motors operating at an angle not exceeding 15 deg from the horizontal (except totally enclosed, fan-cooled motors). For these motors, the bearing at the pulley end can be flushed as described. To clean the fan-end bearing, first remove the fan cover and fan in order to make the drain plug at the bottom of the housing accessible.

243. Care of Insulation. Motors should be stored in a dry, clean place until ready for installation. Heat should be supplied, especially for larger high-voltage machines, to protect against alternate freezing and thawing. This is equally applicable to spare coils.

Motors that have been long in transit in moist atmosphere or have been idle for an extended period without heat to prevent the accumulation of moisture should be thoroughly dried out before being placed in service. Machines may also become wet by accident, or they may "sweat" as a result of a difference in their temperature and that of the surrounding air, just as cold water pipes "sweat" in a warm, humid atmosphere. This condition is, of course, very injurious and should be prevented, particularly in the case of large or important motors, by keeping them slightly warm at all times. Current at a low voltage can be passed through the windings, electric heaters can be used, or even steam pipes can be utilized for protective purposes. During extended idle periods, tarpaulins can be stretched over the motor and a small heater put inside to maintain the proper temperature.

244. Drying Out. If a motor has become wet from any cause whatever, it should be dried out thoroughly before being operated again. The most effective method is to pass current through the windings, using a voltage low enough to be safe for the winding in its moist condition. For 2,200-volt motors, 220 volts is usually satisfactory for circulating this drying-out current. Thermometers should be placed on the windings to see that they are being heated uniformly. Temperatures should not exceed 90°C (Class A insulation). Applying the heat internally in this manner drives out all moisture and is particularly effective on high-voltage motors, where the insulation is comparatively thick.

Heat can be applied externally by placing heating units around or in the machine, covering the whole with canvas or other covering and leaving a vent at the top to permit the escape of moisture. In doing this it is essential that there be a circulation of warm air over all the surfaces to be dried. The air should be allowed to escape as soon as it has absorbed moisture. Therefore, the heaters should be so placed and baffles so arranged as to get a natural draft, or small fans can be used to force circulation. Twelve-inch fans set to blow air across the fronts of "glow heaters" and then into the lower part of a machine from opposite sides, and so on up around the windings and out the top, will produce excellent results. The temperature of the winding should not be allowed to exceed 100°C for Class A insulated motors. Smaller machines can conveniently be placed in ovens, the same temperature limits being observed.

245. Insulation-resistance Tests. The time required for complete drying out depends considerably on the size and voltage of the motor. Insulation-resistance measurements should be taken at intervals of 4 or 5 hr until a fairly constant value is reached. This value should at least equal the recommended Institute of Electrical and Electronic Engineers Standard, which is

$$\text{Megohms} = \frac{\text{voltage}}{\text{kva}/100 + 1,000} \tag{9}$$

The insulation resistance of dry motors in good condition is considerably higher than this value.

The more convenient way to measure this resistance is through the use of a megohmmeter, although if a 500-volt d-c source is available, readings can be taken with a voltmeter. The ungrounded side of the system should be connected to all the motor terminals through the voltmeter, the opposite or grounded side being connected directly to the motor frame. The insulation resistance is found by the method of Sec. **177** of Div. 1.

When the voltmeter method is used, the connection to the frame should always be made through a fuse of not more than 10 amp in size. The circuit should be tested, and the side showing a complete or partial ground then connected to the frame through the fuse.

Obviously, the insulation resistance varies over a wide range, depending upon moisture, temperature, cleanliness, etc., but it is a good indication of the general condition of the insulation and its ability to stand the operating voltage. Such readings should be taken before a high-potential test to determine whether the insulation is ready for such a test and afterwards to make sure that the high potential has not injured the insulation.

246. High-potential Tests. High-potential tests should be made after drying out or after repairs to determine the dielectric strength of the insulation. New windings should successfully stand a high-potential test of twice normal voltage plus 1,000. There is some disagreement as to the proper value to use for motors that have been in operation for some time, but it is reasonable to assume that, after thorough cleaning and drying, the winding of a used motor should stand 150 per cent of normal voltage for 1 min.

Small high-potential testing sets are available for such work and are of such capacity that very little damage will result from a breakdown during the test.

247. Periodic Inspection. A systematic and periodic inspection of motors is necessary to ensure best operation. Of course, some machines are installed where conditions are ideal, where dust, dirt, and moisture are not present to an appreciable degree, but most motors are located where some sort of dirt accumulates in the windings, lowering the insulation resistance and cutting down creepage distance. Steel-mill dusts are usually highly conductive, if not abrasive, and lessen creepage distances. Other dusts are highly abrasive and actually cut the insulation in being carried through by the ventilating air. Fine cast-iron dust quickly penetrates most insulating materials. Hence the desirability of cleaning the motors periodically. If conditions are extremely severe, open motors might require a certain amount of cleaning each day. For less severe conditions, weekly inspection and partial cleaning are desirable. Most machines require a complete overhauling and thorough cleaning about once a year.

For the weekly cleaning, the motor should be blown out, using moderate-pressure, dry, compressed air (of about 25 to 30 lb per sq in. pressure). Where conducting and abrasive dusts are present, even lower pressure may be necessary, and suction is to be preferred, as damage can easily be caused by blowing the dust and metal chips into the insulation. On most d-c motors and large a-c motors the windings are usually fairly accessible, and the air can be properly directed to prevent such damage.

On the larger a-c machines the air ducts should be blown out so that the ventilating air can pass through as intended.

On large machines, insulation-resistance readings should be taken in the manner heretofore indicated. As long as the readings are consistent, the condition of the insulation would ordinarily be considered good. Low readings would indicate increased current leakage to ground or to other conductors, owing to one of perhaps several causes, such as deteriorated insulation, moisture, dirty or corroded terminals, etc.

Inspection and servicing should be systematic. Frequency of inspection and degree of thoroughness may vary and will have to be determined by the maintenance engineer. They will be governed by (1) the importance of the motors in the production scheme (if the motor fails, will production be slowed seriously?), (2) percentage of day the motor operates, (3) nature of service, (4) environment.

An inspection schedule must, therefore, be elastic and adapted to the needs of each plant. The following schedule, covering both a-c and d-c motors, is based on average conditions in so far as duty and dirt are concerned.

EVERY WEEK

1. Examine commutator and brushes.
2. Check oil level in bearings.
3. See that oil rings turn with shaft.
4. See that shaft is free of oil and grease from bearings.
5. Examine starter, switch, fuses, and other controls.
6. Start motor and see that it is brought up to speed in normal time.

EVERY 6 MONTHS

1. Clean motor thoroughly, blowing out dirt from windings, and wipe commutator and brushes.
2. Inspect commutator clamping ring.
3. Check brushes and renew any that are more than half worn.

4. Examine brush holders and clean them if dirty. Make sure that brushes ride free in the holders.

5. Check brush pressure.

6. Check brush position.

7. Drain, wash out, and renew oil in sleeve bearings.

8. Check grease in ball or roller bearings.

9. Check operating speed or speeds.

10. See that end play of shaft is normal.

11. Inspect and tighten connections on motor and control.

12. Check current input and compare with normal.

13. Run motor and examine drive critically for smooth running, absence of vibration, worn gears, chains, or belts.

14. Check motor foot bolts, end-shield bolts, pulley, coupling, gear and journal set-screws, and keys.

15. See that all covers, belt and gear guards are in good order, in place, and securely fastened.

ONCE A YEAR

1. Clean out and renew grease in ball- or roller-bearing housings.

2. Test insulation by megger (megohmmeter).

3. Check air gap.

4. Clean out magnetic dirt that may be hanging on poles.

5. Check clearance between shaft and journal boxes of sleeve-bearing motors to prevent operation with worn bearings.

6. Clean out undercut slots in commutator.

7. Examine connections of commutator and armature coils.

8. Inspect armature bands.

Records. The maintenance man should have a record card for every motor in the plant. All repair work, with the cost, and every inspection can be entered on the record. In this way, excessive amounts of attention or expense will show up and the causes can be determined and corrected.

Inspection records will also serve as a guide to tell when motors should be replaced because of the high cost to keep them operating. Misapplications, poor drive engineering, and the like will also be disclosed.

248. Brush Inspection. The first essential for satisfactory operation of brushes is free movement of the brushes in their holders. Uniform brush pressure is necessary to assure equal current distribution. Adjustment of brush holders should be set so that the face of the holder is approximately ⅛ in. up from the commutator; any distance greater than this will cause brushes to wedge, resulting in chattering and excessive sparking.

Check the brushes to make sure that they will not wear down too far before the next inspection. Keep an extra set of brushes available so that replacement can be made when needed. Sand in new brushes, and run the motor without load as long as possible.

It is false economy to use brushes down to the absolute minimum length before replacement. Cases have been known where brushes had worn down until the metal, where the pigtail connects to the brush, touched the commutator. This, of course, caused severe damage to the commutator.

Make sure that each brush surface in contact with the commutator has the polished finish that indicates good contact and that the polish covers all this surface of the brush. Check the freedom of motion of each brush in the brush holder.

When replacing a brush, be sure to put it in the same brush holder and in its original position. It has been found helpful to scratch a mark on one side of the brush when removing it so that it will be replaced properly.

Check the springs that hold the brushes against the commutator. Improper spring pressure may lead to commutator wear and excessive sparking. Excessive heating may have annealed the springs, in which case they should be replaced and the cause of heating corrected. Larger motors have means for adjusting the spring pressure, which should be 2 to 2½ lb per sq in. of area of brush contact with the commutator.

249. Commutator Inspection. Inspect the commutator for color and condition. It should be clean, smooth, and a polished-brown color where the brushes ride on it. A bluish color indicates overheating of the commutator.

Roughness of the commutator should be removed by sandpapering or stoning. Never use emery cloth or an emery stone. For this operation, run the motor without load. If sandpaper is used, wrap it partly around a wood block.

The stone is essentially a piece of grindstone, known to the trade as a commutator stone. Press the stone or sandpaper against the commutator with moderate pressure with the motor running without load, and move it back and forth across the commutator surface.

Use care not to come in contact with live parts.

If the armature is very rough, it should be taken out and the commutator turned down in a lathe. When this is done, it is usually necessary to cut back the insulation between the commutator bars slightly. After the commutator has been turned down, the brushes should be sanded and run in as described previously. This is not necessary after light sandpapering or stoning.

250. Cleaning. About once a year, or oftener if conditions warrant, motors should be cleaned thoroughly. Smaller motors, the windings of which are not particularly accessible, should be taken apart.

First, the heavy dirt and grease should be removed with a heavy, stiff brush, wooden or fiber scrapers, and cloths. Rifle-cleaning bristle brushes can be used in the air ducts. Dry dust and dirt may be blown off, using dry compressed air at moderate pressure, for example, 25 to 50 lb pressure at the point of application, taking care to blow the dirt out from the winding. As stated before, if the dirt and dust are metallic, conducting, or abrasive, air pressure may drive the material into the insulation and damage it. Hence, for such conditions, pressure is not so satisfactory as a suction system. If compressed air at low pressure is used, care must be taken to direct it properly so that the dust will not cause damage and will not be pocketed in the various corners.

Grease, oil, and sticky dirt are easily removed by applying cleaning liquids specifically designed for the purpose. Any of these liquids evaporate quickly and, if not applied too generously, will not soak or injure the insulation.

In case one of the other liquids must be used, it should be applied out-of-doors or in a well-ventilated room. It must be remembered that gasoline or naphtha vapor is heavier than air and will flow into pits, basements, etc., and may remain there for hours or even days. The casual smoker or a spark from a hammer or chisel or even from a shoe nail may cause a serious explosion. Therefore, proper ventilation of the room is essential and may require specially piped ventilating fans. The use of carbon tetrachloride obviates the explosion hazard, but some ventilation is required to remove the vapor, which might affect the safety and comfort of the workmen.

There are several good methods of applying the cleansing liquid. A cloth, saturated in the liquid, can be used to wipe the coils. A paint brush, dipped in the liquid container, is handy to get into corners and crevices and between small coils. Care should be taken not to soak the insulation, as would be the case if coils or small machines were dipped into the liquid.

Probably the best method of applying the liquid is to spray it on. A spray gun, paint-spraying appliance, or an ordinary blowtorch is often used with good results, although the last device is likely to give a heavier spray than desirable.

An atomizer will give excellent results using a pressure of about 80 lb if the insulation is in good condition or 40 to 50 lb if the insulation is old. The atomizer should be held not more than 5 or 6 in. away from the coils.

Although the insulation will dry quickly at ordinary room temperature after such cleaning methods, it is highly desirable to heat it to drive off all moisture before applying varnish. This heating or drying-out process has already been discussed and therefore need only be mentioned here.

If the motor can be spared from service long enough, the insulation should be dried out by heating to from 90 to 100°C. While the motor is warm, a high-grade insulating varnish should be applied. For severe acid, alkali, or moisture conditions, a black plastic baking varnish or epoxy resin is best. Where oil or dusts are present a clear or yellow varnish or epoxy resin should be used.

The varnish may be sprayed or brushed on. For small stators or rotors, it is best to dip the windings into the varnish, cleaning off the adjacent metal parts afterward by using a solvent of the varnish. After applying the varnish, the best results are obtained by baking for 6 to 7 hr at about 100°C. Experience with particular conditions of operation or the condition of the insulation may indicate the desirability of applying a second coat of the same varnish, followed again by 6 to 7 hr of baking at 100°C.

If the machine must be put back in service quickly, or if facilities are not available for baking, fairly good results will be obtained by applying one of the quick-drying black or clear varnishes which dry in a few hours at ordinary room temperatures.

Insulation-resistance readings should be taken, as explained previously, to determine whether the winding is in satisfactory condition for applying a high-potential test. After this test, it is good practice to run the motor without load for a short time to make certain that everything has been connected, assembled, and adjusted properly.

Motors should generally be given an overhauling at intervals of five years or so normally or, if the service is more severe, more frequently. This practice is beneficial in avoiding breakdowns and in extending the useful life of the equipment. Where periodic overhauling is practiced, the following notes may be helpful.

Check the motor air gap, between stator and rotor, with feelers for uniformity. Too little clearance at the bottom may indicate worn bearings.

Take the motor apart and inspect it thoroughly. Measurement of the bearings and journals may disclose need for new bearing linings. Remove the waste from waste-packed bearings and rearrange or replace it, so that any glaze on the wool is removed from its point of contact with the shaft. Any gummy deposit on the wool should be replaced. All lubricant should be cleaned out of the bearings and a fresh supply put in when the motor is reassembled.

The rotors should be cleaned with a solvent to remove any accumulated dirt, after which any rust should be removed with fine sandpaper (not emery paper). When clean and dry, the rotors should be coated with a good grade of clear varnish or lacquer to protect them from moisture. To prevent injury to the bearings, they should be completely protected with a clean rag when the motor is disassembled.

The rotors of wound-rotor motors should be given the same treatment as the stators. In addition, soldered joints and binding cords should be inspected and any weakness remedied.

The stator bore should be cleaned of dirt with a solvent, and any rust should be removed with fine sandpaper (not emery paper). Care should be taken during this operation not to damage the top sticks or end turns of the stator winding. When the stator bore has dried, any remaining dirt in the bore should be wiped out with a cloth or brushed out with a soft brush. A hand bellows or dry compressed air at low pressure may also be used.

CONTROL EQUIPMENT FOR MOTORS

251. Electric Controller Terminology.   Acid-resistant Apparatus.   Apparatus so constructed that it will not be readily injured by acid fumes.

Constant-torque Resistor (Machine Duty).[1]   A resistor for use in the armature or rotor circuit of a motor in which the current remains practically constant throughout the entire speed range (USA Standard). This means that the horsepower output of the motor decreases directly with the speed, as in the case of a motor driving a plunger pump. Here, the work done by the motor at one-half speed is one-half that done at full speed. The term "machine duty" is not meant to imply that any motor driving a machine should have a machine-duty resistor.

Continuous Duty.   A requirement of service that demands operation at substantially constant load for an unlimited period (USA Standard).

Dripproof Apparatus.   Apparatus so constructed or protected that its successful operation is not interfered with when subjected to falling moisture or dirt (USA Standard).

---

[1] The two types of regulating resistors are laid out very differently in ohmic value and current-carrying capacity and cannot be used interchangeably. All orders for such resistors should specify whether they are for machine or fan duty.

Driptight Apparatus. Apparatus so protected as to exclude falling moisture or dirt. Driptight apparatus may be semienclosed apparatus if it is provided with suitable protection integral with the apparatus or so enclosed as to exclude effectively falling solid or liquid material (USA Standard).

Drum Controller. A drum controller is a controller that utilizes a drum switch as the main switching element (USA Standard).

Drum Switch. A drum switch is a switch having electric connecting parts in the form of fingers, held by spring pressure against contact segments or surfaces on the periphery of a rotating cylinder or sector (USA Standard).

Dustproof Apparatus. Apparatus so constructed or protected that the accumulation of dust will not interfere with its successful operation (USA Standard).

Dusttight Apparatus. Apparatus so constructed that dust will not enter the enclosing case (USA Standard).

Duty of a Controller. The specific function or functions that are designed to be accomplished with respect to the operation of the motor, such as starting, speed control, reversing, and stopping, and, in addition, the frequency and length of time of operation (USA Standard).

Electric Controller. A device, or group of devices, which serves to govern in some predetermined manner the electric power delivered to the apparatus to which it is connected (USA Standard).

NOTE. The term controller therefore is properly applied to dial-type starters, rheostats, contactor panels, etc. It is not limited to controllers of the drum type.

Fan-duty Resistor.[1] A resistor for use in the armature or rotor circuit of a motor in which the current is approximately proportional to the speed of the motor (USA Standard). For example, a fan driven at one-half its normal speed requires less than one-half as much torque as it would require running at its normal speed, and the work done by the motor will be less than one-quarter as much as that done at normal speed.

Full-magnetic Controller. A controller having all its basic functions[2] performed by electromagnets (USA Standard).

Example. One which performs all its operations after the closure of the master switch, such as a magnetic control panel with a "start-stop," push-button station.

Fume-resistant Apparatus. Apparatus so constructed that it will not be readily injured by the specified fumes (USA Standard).

Gasproof Apparatus. Apparatus so constructed or protected that the specified gas will not interfere with its successful operation (USA Standard).

Gastight Apparatus. Apparatus so constructed that the specified gas will not enter the enclosing case under specified conditions of pressure (USA Standard).

Isolating Switch. An isolating switch is a switch intended for isolating an electric circuit from the source of power. It is intended to be operated only when the circuit has been opened by some other means (USA Standard).

Machine Duty. See Constant-torque Resistor.

Magnetic Contactor. A contactor actuated by electromagnetic means (USA Standard).

Example. Shunt contactor.

Manual Controller. A controller having all its basic functions performed by hand (USA Standard).

Example. A hand-starting rheostat or drum-type controller.

Master Switch. A device which serves to govern the operation of contactors and auxiliary devices of an electric controller (USA Standard).

Example. A master switch may be automatic, such as a float switch or pressure regulator, or it may be manually operated, such as a drum, push-button, or knife switch.

---

[1] The two types of regulating resistors are laid out very differently in ohmic value and current-carrying capacity and cannot be used interchangeably. All orders for such resistors should specify whether they are for machine or fan duty.

[2] By "basic function" is usually meant acceleration, retardation, line closing, and reversing (USA Standard).

Moisture-resistant Apparatus. Apparatus so constructed or treated that it will not be readily injured by a moist atmosphere. (Such apparatus shall be capable of operating in a very humid atmosphere, such as found in mines, evaporating rooms, etc.) (USA Standard.)

Open-phase Relay. A relay that functions by reason of the opening of one phase of a polyphase circuit (USA Standard).

Overload Protection. The effect of a device operative on excessive current, but not necessarily on short circuit, to cause and maintain the interruption of current flow to the device governed. When it is a function of a controller for a motor, device employed shall provide for interrupting any operating overloads [1] but shall not be required to interrupt short circuits (USA Standard).

Overload Relay. An overcurrent relay in the circuit of a motor that functions at a predetermined value of the current to cause the disconnection of the motor from the line (USA Standard).

Periodic Duty. A requirement of service that demands operation for alternate periods of load and rest in which the load conditions are well defined and recurrent as to magnitude, duration, and character (USA Standard).

Phase-failure Protection. The effect of a device, operative on the failure of power in one wire of a polyphase circuit, to cause and maintain the interruption of power on the circuit (USA Standard).

Phase-reversal Protection. The effect of a device, operative on the reversal of the phase rotation on a polyphase circuit, to cause and maintain the interruption of power in all the circuit (USA Standard).

Relay. A device that is operative by a variation in the conditions of one electric circuit to effect the operation of other devices in the same or another electric circuit (USA Standard).

Semimagnetic Controller. A controller having part of its basic functions performed by electromagnets and part by other means (USA Standard).

Service of a Controller. The specific application in which the controller is to be used, as for example:
1. General purpose, which covers the occasional starting of motors.
2. Crane and hoist.
3. Elevator.
4. Machine tool, etc. (USA Standard.)

Sleetproof Apparatus. Apparatus so constructed or protected that the accumulation of sleet will not interfere with its successful operation (USA Standard).

Splashproof Apparatus. Apparatus so constructed and protected that external splashing will not interfere with its successful operation (USA Standard).

Submersible Apparatus. Apparatus so constructed that it will operate successfully when submerged in water under specified conditions of pressure and time (USA Standard).

Temperature Relay. A relay that functions at a predetermined temperature in the apparatus protected (USA Standard).

Undervoltage Protection. The effect of a device, operative on the reduction or failure of voltage, to cause and maintain the interruption of power to the main circuit (USA Standard).

Undervoltage Release. The effect of a device, operative on the reduction or failure of voltage, to cause the interruption of power to the main circuit, but not to prevent the reestablishment of the main circuit on return of voltage (USA Standard).

Watertight Apparatus. Apparatus so constructed that a stream of water from a hose (not less than 1 in. in diameter), under a head of about 35 ft and from a distance of about 10 ft, can be played on the apparatus for several minutes without leakage (USA Standard).

Weatherproof Apparatus. Apparatus so constructed or protected that exposure to the weather will not interfere with its successful operation (USA Standard).

252. Enclosure of Controllers. Except where the control equipment is mounted on

---

[1] By "operating loads" is meant a current not in excess of six times the rated full-load current for a-c motors or four times the full-load current for d-c motors (USA Standard).

switchboard panels under the control of experienced operators, the control equipment of motors should be enclosed in a metal case. Different types of enclosures, such as general purpose, dripproof, watertight, etc., are available to meet the requirements of any surrounding conditions. For definitions of these terms, refer to Sec. **251.** Most general-purpose controllers are enclosed in a sheet-metal case. If a controller must be placed in a hazardous location in explosive atmospheres, the advice of the experts of the control manufacturers should be consulted. The standard types of nonventilated enclosures are given in Sec. **253.** They are typical of the kinds available.

253. Classification of Standard Types of Nonventilated Enclosures for Electric Controllers (National Electrical Manufacturers Association) is as follows:

TYPE 1. GENERAL PURPOSE. A general-purpose enclosure is intended primarily to prevent accidental contact with the enclosed apparatus. It is suitable for general-purpose applications indoors where it is not exposed to unusual service conditions.

A Type 1 enclosure serves as a protection against dust and light indirect splashing but is not dusttight.

When a nonventilated enclosure is specified for equipment consisting in part of devices that require ventilation (electron tubes, resistors, etc.), such devices may be mounted in a ventilated portion of the enclosure, provided that they are capable of operating satisfactorily and without hazard when so mounted.

TYPE 2. DRIPTIGHT. A driptight enclosure is intended to prevent accidental contact with the enclosed apparatus and, in addition, is so constructed as to exclude falling moisture or dirt.

A Type 2 enclosure is suitable for application where condensation may be severe such as is encountered in cooling rooms and laundries. It meets the requirements of dripproof and driptight.

NOTE. Driptight apparatus may be semienclosed apparatus if it is provided with suitable protection integral with the apparatus, or so enclosed as to exclude effectively falling solid or liquid material.

TYPE 3. WEATHER-RESISTANT (WEATHERPROOF). A weather-resistant enclosure is intended to provide suitable protection against specified weather hazards. It is suitable for use outdoors.

A Type 3 enclosure is suitable for application outdoors on ship docks, canal locks, and construction work, and for application in subways and tunnels. It meets the requirements of splashproof, weatherproof, sleetproof, and moisture-resistant.

TYPE 4. WATERTIGHT. A watertight enclosure is designed to meet the hose test described in the following note.

A Type 4 enclosure is suitable for application outdoors on ship docks and in dairies, breweries, etc.

NOTE. Enclosures shall be tested by subjection to a stream of water. A hose with a 1-in. nozzle shall be used and shall deliver at least 65 gal per min. The water shall be directed on the enclosure from a distance of not less than 10 ft and for a period of 5 min. During this period it may be sprayed in any one or more directions as desired. There shall be no leakage of water into the enclosure under these conditions.

TYPE 5. DUSTTIGHT. A dusttight enclosure is provided with gaskets or their equivalent to exclude dust. It meets the requirements of dusttight.

When a nonventilated enclosure is specified for equipment consisting in part of devices that require ventilation (electron tubes, resistors, etc.), such devices may be mounted in a ventilated portion of the enclosure, provided that they are capable of operating satisfactorily and without hazard when so mounted. For enclosures suitable for Class II locations of the National Electrical Code, see Type 9.

A Type 5 enclosure is suitable for application in steel mills, cement mills, and other locations where it is desirable to exclude dust.

TYPE 6. SUBMERSIBLE. A Type 6 enclosure is suitable for application where the equipment may be subject to submersion, as in quarries, mines, and manholes. The design of the enclosure will depend upon the specified conditions of pressure and time.

TYPE 7 (A, B, C, OR D). HAZARDOUS LOCATIONS – CLASS I, AIR BREAK (*See Note in Paragraph on Type 8 Enclosures*). These enclosures are designed to meet the application requirements of the National Electrical Code for Class I hazardous locations which may be in effect from time to time. In this type of equipment, the circuit interruption occurs in air.

The letter or letters following the type number indicate the particular group or groups of hazardous locations (as defined in the National Electrical Code) for which the enclosure is designed. The designation is incomplete without a suffix letter or letters.

TYPE 8 (A, B, C, OR D). HAZARDOUS LOCATIONS – CLASS I, OIL-IMMERSED. These enclosures are designed to meet the application requirements of the National Electrical Code for Class I hazardous locations which may be in effect from time to time. The apparatus is immersed in oil.

The letter or letters following the type number indicate the particular group or groups of hazardous locations (as defined in the National Electrical Code) for which the enclosure is designed. The designation is incomplete without a suffix letter or letters.

NOTE. In order to avoid confusion in referring to equipment sometimes known as "explosion-proof" (Types 7 and 8), it is recommended that apparatus designed for use in Class I, Group A, B, C, or D locations be described in one of the following ways, whichever is applicable:

1. Control listed by Underwriters' Laboratories, Inc., for use in Class I, Group A, B, C, or D locations.

2. Control designed to conform with the manufacturer's interpretation of the requirements of Underwriters' Laboratories, Inc.

3. Control of a size and nature for which there are no existing Underwriters' Laboratories, Inc., standards or testing facilities.

TYPE 9 (E, F, OR G). HAZARDOUS LOCATIONS – CLASS II. These enclosures are designed to meet the application requirements of the National Electrical Code for Class II hazardous locations which may be in effect from time to time.

The letter or letters following the type number indicate the particular group or groups of hazardous locations (as defined in the National Electrical Code) for which the enclosure is designed. The designation is incomplete without a suffix letter or letters.

TYPE 10. BUREAU OF MINES – EXPLOSION-PROOF. A Type 10 enclosure is designed to meet the explosion-proof requirements of the U.S. Bureau of Mines which may be in effect from time to time. It is suitable for use in gassy coal mines.

TYPE 11. ACID- AND FUME-RESISTANT – OIL-IMMERSED. This enclosure provides for the immersion of the apparatus in oil such that it is suitable for application where the equipment is subject to acid or other corrosive fumes.

A Type 11 enclosure is suitable for application indoors where the equipment may be subject to corrosive acid or fumes as in chemical plants, plating rooms, sewage plants, etc. The apparatus is immersed in oil.

NOTE. When an enclosure is required to meet the requirements of acid-resistant or fume-resistant, the design will depend on the conditions of exposure.

TYPE 12. INDUSTRIAL USE. A Type 12 enclosure is designed for use in those industries where it is desired to exclude such materials as dust, lint, fibers and flyings, oil seepage, or coolant seepage.

When a nonventilated enclosure is specified for equipment consisting in part of devices that require ventilation (electron tubes, resistors, etc.), such devices may be mounted in a ventilated portion of the enclosure, provided that they are capable of operating satisfactorily and without hazard when so mounted.

254. Motor controllers are classified according to the method of performing the necessary operations, as follows:

1. Manual.
2. Magnetic.
   a. Full magnetic with automatic master switch.
   b. Full magnetic with manual master switch.
   c. Semimagnetic.

The following table lists the NEMA controller sizes for single- and three-phase motor controllers.

Controller Sizes —
NEMA Designations [a]

Motor voltage	Motor maximum horsepower	Starter size
Single-phase 115	$\frac{1}{3}$	00
	1	0
	2	1
	3	1P [a]
	3	2 [a]
230	1	00
	2	0
	3	1
	5	1P [a]
	7½	2 [a]
Three-phase 110	¾	00
	2	0
	3	1
	7½	2
	15	3
	25	4
208/220	1½	00
	3	0
	7½	1
	15	2
	30	3
	50	4
	100	5
	200	6
	300	7
	450	8
	800	9
440, 550	2	00
	5	0
	10	1
	25	2
	50	3
	100	4
	200	5
	400	6
	600	7
	900	8
	1,600	9

[a] Size 1P rated 36 amp continuous.
Size 2 rated 45 amp continuous.

In a manual controller all the basic operations, such as closing of switches and movement of rheostat handles, etc., are performed by hand.

In a magnetic controller the basic functions of closing of switches or movement of rheostat handles are performed by magnetic contactors (see Sec. **255**). A full-magnetic controller is one which automatically performs all its operations in the proper sequence after the closure of a master switch. The master switch for a full-magnetic controller, such as a float switch, a pressure switch or regulator, or a time switch, is frequently automatically operated. In other cases, the master switch, such as a push-button, drum, or knife switch, is manually operated. A semimagnetic controller operates with a combination of manual and magnetic performance. In some cases, part of the basic operations are performed by hand and the rest by means of magnetic contactors. In other types of semimagnetic controllers, all the basic operations are performed with magnetic contactors but the time and sequence of the operation of the contactors is controlled by hand.

255. A magnetic contactor is a switch operated by an electromagnet. One form of magnetic contactor is shown in Fig. 111, which illustrates the basic parts. It consists of a stationary electric magnet, as at *a* in Fig. 111, a movable iron armature *b*, on which are mounted an electrical contact *c* and a stationary electrical contact *d*. When there is no current flowing through the operating coil *e* of the electrical magnet *a*, the armature is held away from the magnet by means of gravitational force or a spring. Under this condition the contacts *c* and *d* are open. When the operating coil is energized, the magnet attracts the armature and closes the electrical contacts *c* and *d*.

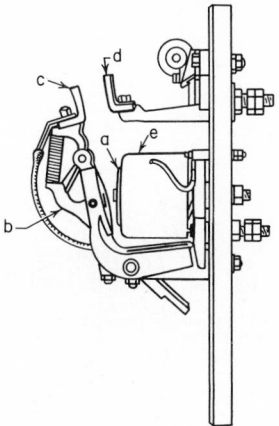

FIG. 111 *Magnetic contactor.* (*Square D Co.*)

Magnetic contactors may be of the shunt or series type, depending upon the connection of the operating coil. In the shunt contactor the operating coil is connected across the terminals of the circuit or portion of the circuit that the contactor is controlling. In some cases the operating coil of a shunt contactor might be connected to a separate source of supply from the circuit controlled by the contactor. A series contactor has its operating coil connected in series with the circuit which is controlled by the contactor.

256. Series contactors for motor-control application are constructed so that the contactor will not close until the current of the circuit has dropped below a definite value. They are made in two general forms: single-coil and two-coil. The single-coil type is referred to simply as a series contactor, while the two-coil type is called a series lockout contactor. Both of the types, however, possess the lockout feature of the contactor; i.e., they are held open until the current has dropped to some definite value.

The general principle of operation of the single-coil type can be understood from a study of Fig. 112. The current passing through the operating coil produces an mmf which acts upon two magnetic paths. One path is through the core of the coil, a section of restricted area *A*, the armature, and main air gap back to the core of the coil. The other path is through the core of the coil, adjustable air gap, tail of armature *B*, armature, and main air gap back to the core of the coil. When no current is passing through the coil, the armature is in the open position. When a large current is passing through the operating coil, the mmf is so strong that the part *A* of restricted area becomes saturated so that the flux through this part cannot exceed a certain amount. The magnetic flux through the adjustable air gap and part *B* will vary with the current through the operating coil, and this path will not become saturated. Any flux passing across the adjustable air gap produces an attracting force on the tail of the armature *B* which tends to hold the armature open against the closing force exerted between the core and the main part of the armature. As the current reduces in value, the flux across the adjustable air gap reduces and thus reduces the holding-out force on tail *B*. After the current has reduced to a certain value, which depends upon the adjustment of the adjustable air gap, the holding-out force on tail *B* is not sufficient to overcome the closing force exerted by the core upon the main part of the armature, and the contactor closes.

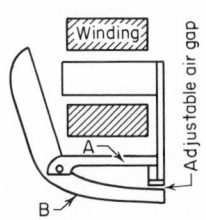

FIG. 112 *A series-contactor operating magnet.*

In the two-coil type of series contactor (Fig. 113), two coils are connected in series with each other and the circuit to be controlled. The armature is pivoted so that one coil, the larger of the two, acts upon one side of the armature, exerting a force tending to close the contactor. The smaller coil acts upon the other side of the armature and exerts a force tending to hold the contactor open. The areas of the magnetic circuits are so designed that the force tending to close the contactor remains practically constant regardless of the value of current while the force tending to hold the contactor open varies with the current. Therefore, after the current has decreased to a certain value, the holding-out force is not sufficient to overcome the closing force and the contactor closes. The air gap of the locking-out circuit can be adjusted so that the current above which the contactor holds open can be adjusted over a wide range.

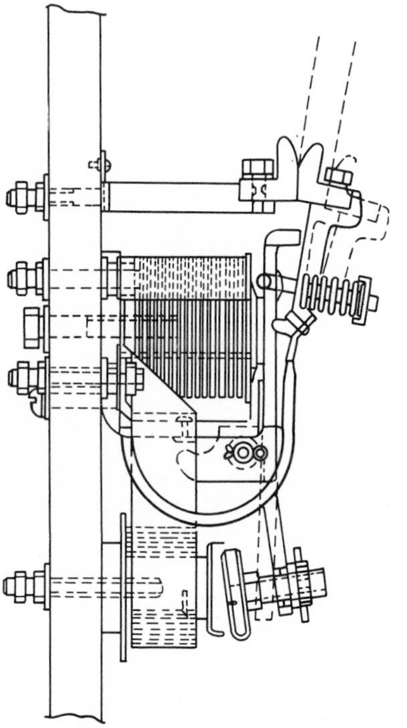

257. Overload Protective Devices. Most motor controllers have incorporated with them as an integral part of the controller some device for protecting the motor against overloads that will be harmful to the motor. These overload protective devices are made in many different types and forms of construction, depending upon the ideas of the different manufacturers of control equipment. Those made by reliable manufacturers are listed by the Underwriters' Laboratories, Inc. Before purchasing control equipment, care should be taken to make sure that the equipment has been listed by them. All the following types of overload protective devices are used in motor-control equipment.

1. Standard fuses.
2. Time-delay fuses.
3. Thermal cutouts.
4. Thermal release devices.
5. Thermal relays.
6. Magnetic overload relays.

For a description of these devices see Div. 4.

For selection of overload protective devices with respect to both size and type refer to Secs. **430, 431,** and **432.**

258. Undervoltage Devices. Many motor starters are provided with either an undervoltage protective device or an undervoltage release device.

FIG. 113 *Magnetic lockout contactor.*

An undervoltage protective device is one which opens the supply circuit to the motor upon failure or reduction of voltage and which maintains the circuit open until it is again closed by the operator.

An undervoltage release device is one which operates on a reduction or failure of voltage, thereby opening the main circuit, but it does not prevent the automatic reclosing of the main circuit upon the return of normal voltage. It is applied in conjunction with some automatic starters. In certain applications, such as fans, blowers, and pumps, an automatic starter provided with an undervoltage release may be advantageously used. Its operation on a reduction or failure of voltage will stop the motor. Then the reestablishment of voltage causes the automatic starter to restart the motor, thus minimizing the shutdown period. An undervoltage release should not be employed in applications where an unexpected return of power would endanger an operator.

259. The methods of controlling the acceleration of motors with the type of power system on which they may be used are given on page 7-131. The simplest method is no control, in which the motor is thrown directly across the line by means of a manual or magnetic switch. The speed of acceleration of the motor and the magnitude and duration of the starting current depend solely upon the characteristics of the motor and its connected load.

With manual control of the acceleration the speed of acceleration depends upon the judgment of the operator. Manual control of acceleration can be obtained through the use of manual controllers or semimagnetic controllers. In the semimagnetic controllers of this type the time and sequence of closing of the magnetic contactors are controlled by means of a manually operated master switch.

With automatic acceleration the only part of the starting operation that may be dependent upon the operator is the initiation of the sequence of events (such as pushing a start button). When this is done, the resulting sequence of operations is automatically performed and controlled by means of contactors alone or contactors controlled by relays.

Methods	Applicable to
A. No control (across-the-line starting)	A-c and small d-c motors
B. Manual	A-c and d-c
C. Automatic:	
1. Time:	
a. Solenoid with action retarded by an adjustable dashpot	D-c
b. Pneumatic timer	A-c and d-c
c. Timing relay	A-c and d-c
d. Inductive time limit	A-c and d-c
e. Condenser charge (neotime)	A-c or d-c
2. Current	A-c and d-c
3. Counter-emf	D-c
4. Time current:	
a. Magnetic relay	D-c
b. Condenser charge (neotime current)	A-c
5. Frequency	A-c

260. In time-limit acceleration the closing of the respective contactor contacts is controlled by a timing device so that the starting resistance is shorted out of the circuit or connections to the autotransformer are changed in a certain definite time. Most modern automatic starters are of the time-limit type. They are used for all general-purpose applications. The other types of automatic acceleration are used for special applications where they have advantages over the time-limit type. The timing of the closing of the respective contactors for time-limit acceleration can be accomplished in several ways as listed in Sec. **259.**

261. With time-limit acceleration provided by means of a solenoid with action retarded by an adjustable dashpot, the time of closing of the magnetic accelerating contactors is controlled by means of a fluid dashpot attached to the lower part of the operating rod of a solenoid. In some starters the dashpot-controlled solenoid is a timing relay (Sec. **265**) which controls the time of closing of the operating coil of a magnetic accelerating contactor (Sec. **262**). In others the dashpot-controlled solenoid provides the operating force for the closing of the contacts of a multifinger contactor (Sec. **263**).

262. A fluid-dashpot timing relay is illustrated in Fig. 114. The motion of the plunger of the solenoid is retarded by the adjustable fluid dashpot which is attached to the lower end of the solenoid plunger. The delayed time for the closing of the relay contacts can be adjusted from 2 to 30 sec. The dashpot is filled with a silicone fluid whose viscosity is affected only very slightly by changes in temperature. These relays will operate satisfactorily in ambient temperatures from +120 to −30°F.

263. Time-limit control of acceleration by means of a multifinger dashpot-controlled contactor is illustrated by the motor starter shown in Fig. 115. The four contact fingers are all connected by spring connections to the same arm, which is operated by the solenoid coil. Pushing the start button closes a circuit from the positive side of the line through the solenoid coil and back to the negative side of the line. The solenoid now being energized exerts a torque upon the multifinger contact arm and closes the main contact. This connects the armature of the motor to the line in series with the total starting resistance. The closing of the main-line contact also connects the shunt field of the motor directly across the line. As soon as the solenoid is energized and closes the main contact, the accelerating contactors also try to close, since all the contact fingers are connected to the same arm. The arm is prevented from moving far enough to close the accelerating contacts by means of the timing mechanism. The stationary contacts are so arranged that it requires a greater movement of the contact arm to close each consecutive contact. The movement of the contact arm is controlled by the retarding liquid dashpot. The time of the accelerating period may

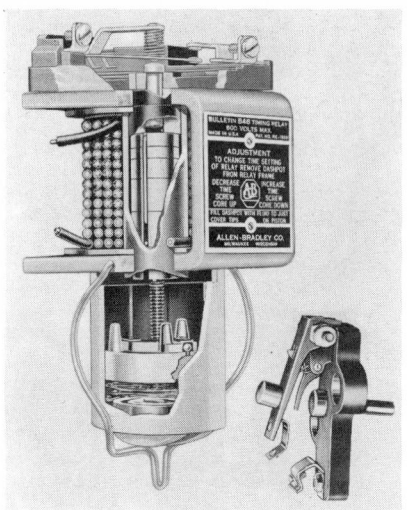

FIG. 114   *Fluid-dashpot timing relay.* (*Allen-Bradley Co.*)

FIG. 115   *Time-limit acceleration by means of multifinger liquid-dashpot starter.* (*Cutler-Hammer, Inc.*)

be adjusted by a screw on the outside of the dashpot which adjusts the fluid-escapement orifice.

264. Contactors equipped with pneumatic timers provide a means for time control of acceleration. The timer of Fig. 116 consists of an air chamber and an adjustable vent which controls the time delay of the operation of the contactors. The timer is actuated by means of a lever attached to the arm of a contactor.

The principle of controlling acceleration by means of a mercury timer is shown in Fig. 117. All contactors except the last acceleration contactor are equipped with a pneumatic timer. When the start button is pressed, current flows from $L1$, through

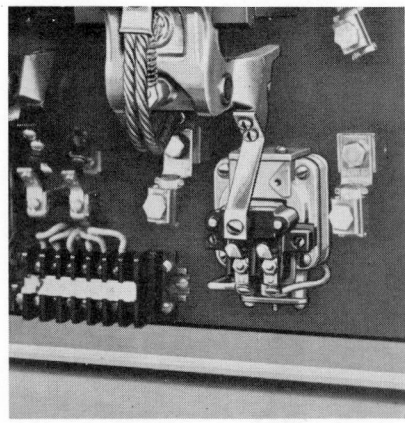

FIG. 116   *Pneumatic timer.* (*Square D Co.*)

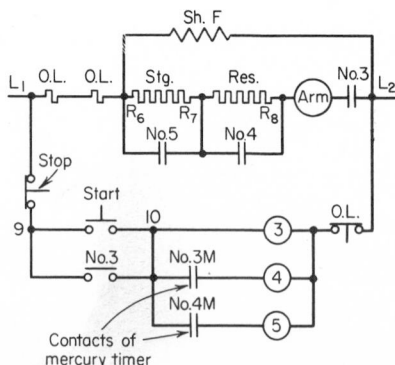

FIG. 117   *Schematic diagram showing principle of time-limit acceleration by means of pneumatic timers.*

stop and start buttons to 10, through the operating coil $\widehat{3}$, through contacts $\overset{\text{O.L.}}{\multimap\!\!\multimap}$ and back to $L2$. This energizes the operating coil $\widehat{3}$ of the mainline contactor $\overset{3}{\dashv\vdash}$. Contactor $\overset{3}{\dashv\vdash}$ closes, connecting the motor across the line in series with all the start-ing resistance. When contactor $\overset{3}{\dashv\vdash}$ closes, it closes its auxiliary contacts $\overset{3}{\multimap\,\multimap}$, which provides a means of energizing the operating coils of the contactors when the start button is released. The closing of contactor 3 causes the pneumatic timer $3M$ to start to function. After a certain definite time required for the air to pass through the orifice of the plunger, pneumatic timer $3M$ closes its contacts $\overset{3M}{\dashv\vdash}$. This energizes the operating coil $\widehat{4}$ of accelerating contactor 4, which closes its contacts $\overset{4}{\dashv\vdash}$. This shorts the resistance $R_7 - R_8$. The closing of contactor 4 causes the pneumatic timer $4M$, attached to it, to start to function. After a certain definite time this timer closes its contacts $\overset{4M}{\dashv\vdash}$, energizing the operating coil $\widehat{5}$ of accelerating contactor 5. Con-tactor 5 operates, closing its contacts $\overset{5}{\dashv\vdash}$ and shorting out resistance $R_6 - R_7$. The motor is now connected directly across the line.

265. Timing relays are the most commonly used device for obtaining automatic con-trol of motor acceleration. A timing relay is a device which, when energized, will oper-ate to close or open its contacts after a definite lapse of time from the instant that the relay was energized. Time-limit control of motor acceleration is accomplished with these relays through their time control of the closing or opening of the operating cir-cuits of the motor-accelerating contactors.

The more common types are pneumatic timing relays, fluid-dashpot timing relays, and synchronous-motor timing relays. The fluid-dashpot and pneumatic relays are operated by a magnetic coil which, when energized, exerts a pull upon the central movable member or plunger. The time taken for the movable member to close or open the contacts of the relay is governed by the retarding action of the dashpot or air bellows.

Dashpot timing relays (Fig. 114) are equipped with an adjustable fluid dashpot. The fluid used should be one whose viscosity is not affected by changes in ambient temperature. The timing range of these relays can be adjusted from about 2 to 30 sec.

Pneumatic relays (Fig. 118) are equipped with an air chamber and adjustable vent which controls the time delay in the operation of the relay. The timing range of these relays can be adjusted from about 0.2 to 200 sec.

Synchronous-motor timer relays (Fig. 119) consist of a set of contacts driven from the shaft of a very small synchronous motor, so that there is a definite time lag between the starting of the motor and the closing of the contacts. A controller utilizing such a relay is described in Sec. **312.**

266. Acceleration controlled by means of inductive time-limit contactors or relays makes use of the inductive time-lag effect of the decay of current in a heavily inductive circuit. This method of timing is often called magnetic timing. In controllers em-ploying this method, each accelerating contactor may be of the inductive time-limit type or of the ordinary shunt type with each controlled by means of an inductive time relay. Inductive time-limit contactors may be of the normally open-contact (holdout type) or of the normally closed type.

267. An inductive time-limit accelerating contactor of the normally open-contact type (Fig. 120) consists of a pivoted armature acted upon by two coils located on oppo-site sides of the pivot point. The main operating coil acts to close the contactor, while the auxiliary coil acts to hold the contactor open. In the diagram of the controller of Fig. 121 the coils marked $2R$, $3R$, $4R$, and $5R$ are the main operating coils of the respec-tive inductive time-limit contactors $2R$, $3R$, $4R$, and $5R$. The coils marked $HC2$, $HC3$, $HC4$, and $HC5$ are the holdout coils of the contactors $2R$, $3R$, $4R$, and $5R$, respectively.

268. The principle of controlling the acceleration by means of inductive time-limit accelerating contactors of the normally open-contact type is illustrated by the typical

FIG. 118 *Pneumatic timing relay.* (*Westinghouse Electric Corp.*)

FIG. 119 *Synchronous-motor timer relay.* (*General Electric Co.*)

control diagram of Fig. 121. In addition to the contactors, an iron-core inductive unit is required. This inductance consists of a set of coils $TC1$, $TC2$, $TC3$, $TC4$, and $TC5$ wound on a common iron core. In starting the motor from rest, if the operator moves the master switch to the running position for forward direction of rotation, the circuits of operating coils $1F$, $2F$, and M are closed. These coils operate their respective contactors, causing contacts $1F$, $2F$, and M to close. This connects the motor across the line in series with all the starting resistance. Voltage will be impressed upon coils $TC1$, $TC3$, $TC4$, and $TC5$, causing these coils to be energized and to hold out their respective contactors. But the coils are so connected that the mmfs of the coils just neutralize each other, so that no flux is produced in the core. There is therefore no current in the closed circuit of coils $HC2$ and $TC2$, and contactor $2R$ is free to close when its operating coil is energized. As soon as contactors $1F$ and M have closed, auxiliary contacts on these contactors close the circuits of the operating coils $2R$, $3R$, $4R$, and $5R$. Contactor $2R$ immediately closes, shorting out the section of resistance $R_1 - R_2$ and shorting coil $HC3$ through $TC3$. This unbalances the mmfs of the inductance, and a definite flux is produced in the core. This change in flux and the inductance of coils $HC3$ and $TC3$ oppose the decay of current in $HC3$ and $TC3$. After

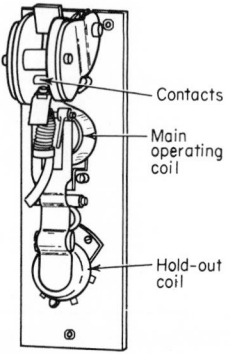

FIG. 120 *Inductive time-limit contactor of the normally open contact type.*

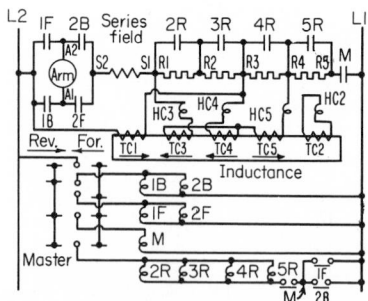

FIG. 121 *Schematic diagram of connections for inductive time-limit acceleration.* (*Cutler-Hammer, Inc.*)

a certain lapse of time the current in $HC3$ will drop to nearly zero. The holdout coil $HC3$ of the contactor $3R$, being now de-energized while its main coil $3R$ is energized, causes contactor $3R$ to close. The closing of contactor $3R$, shorting coils $HC4$ and $TC4$, again unbalances the flux. After a definite time lapse, the current in $HC4$ will drop to nearly zero and contactor $4R$ will close. Closing of $4R$ shorts coils $HC5$ and $TC5$ and once again unbalances the flux. After another definite time interval the current $HC5$ drops to nearly zero and contactor $5R$ is allowed to close. The motor is then connected directly to the line.

When plugging, i.e., throwing from full speed in one direction to full speed in the other, it is desired to have a time delay in the closing of contactor $2R$. Coil $TC1$ is connected across the armature and resistance R_1-R_2. The current through coil TC therefore depends upon the sum of the voltage across the armature and the resistor R_1-R_2. The voltage across the armature when starting from rest is very low, but when plugging, it is normal line voltage. In plugging, therefore, the current through $TC1$ is much higher than it is when starting from rest. This larger current through $TC1$ unbalances the mmfs of the inductance and produces a flux which induces a current in shorted coils $HC2$ and $TC2$. This induced current will hold out contactor $2R$ until the current has had time to reduce to nearly zero.

269. The principle of time-limit acceleration by means of inductive time-limit contactors of the normally closed-contact type is illustrated in Fig. 123. A contactor of this type is shown in Fig. 122. A copper tube encircles the magnetic core of the contactor, over which two operating coils are wound. These two coils act in opposition to each other. When the main winding is open-circuited after having been carrying current, the magnetic flux decreases. This decrease in flux induces a heavy current in the enclosed copper tube. The induced

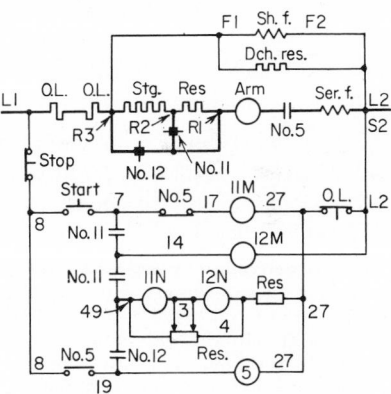

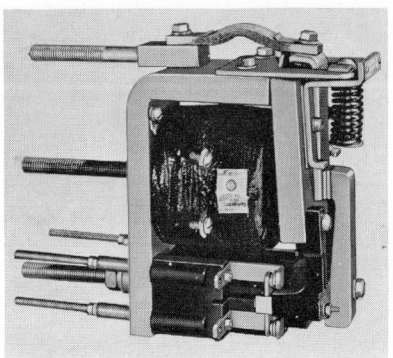

FIG. 122 *Inductive time contactor of the normally closed contact type. (Westinghouse Electric Corp.)*

FIG. 123 *Schematic diagram showing principle of time-limit acceleration by means of inductive time-limit contactors of normally closed contact type.*

current opposes the decay of the flux, so that there is a considerable lapse of time after the circuit of the main coil is opened before the flux decays sufficiently to allow the armature to be released. The length of time delay will depend upon the original value of the flux, which can be controlled by adjustment of the current in the neutralizing winding.

Acceleration is automatically performed in the following manner: When the start button is pressed, current flows from $L1$, through stop and start contacts to 7, through contacts, operating coil, contacts, and back to line $L2$. The armature of contactor 11 is therefore attracted, opening its main contacts ➧II and closing its auxiliary contacts ⊥II. The closing of the two sets of auxiliary contacts ⊥II ener-gizes main operating coil -⊛(12/M)- and neutralizing coils -(11/N)- and -(12/N)-. The arma-ture of contactor 12 is therefore attracted, opening its main contacts and closing its auxiliary contacts ⊥I2. This energizes the operating coil (5), which closes the main-line contactor 5. The motor is then connected to the line in series with all the starting resistance. When contactor 5 closes, it opens its auxiliary contacts ₒ⁵ₒ and closes its auxiliary contacts ⁵/₋ₒ ₒ . The closing of contacts ⁵/₋ₒ ₒ keeps the operating circuits of the contactors energized when the start button is released. Opening of contacts ₒ⁵ₒ opens the main operating coil circuit -(11/M)- , so that after a definite time, deter-mined by the adjustment of the resistances controlling -(11/N)- and -(12/N)-, contactor 11 drops out and thereby closes its main contacts, shorting out the resistance $R_1 - R_2$. At the same time, auxiliary contacts ⊥II are opened, which opens the circuit of the main operating coil -(12/M)-. After a definite time the flux of contactor 12 decreases a sufficient amount so that contactor 12 drops out, closing its main contacts and shorting out resistance $R_3 - R_2$. The motor is now connected directly across the line. As con-tactor 12 drops out, its auxiliary contact ⊥I2 opens, which disconnects all the operat-ing coils of the accelerating contactors. In case of an overload, the operating coils or bimetallic heater elements open the contacts ₒ.ₗ./₋ₒₜₒ, de-energizing the operating coil (5) of the main-line contactor so that the motor is disconnected from the line and will not start up again until pressing the start button again starts the above sequence of starting operations. To stop the motor, the stop button is pressed, which opens the circuit of the operating coil(5) of the main-line contactor.

270. Acceleration by means of inductive time relays requires the use, for each step of resistance, of an ordinary shunt contactor in conjunction with a magnetic time relay. A magnetic time (inductive-time) relay can be constructed in just the same manner as the inductive-time accelerating contactors of the normally closed-contact type de-scribed in Sec. **269.** The only differences are that it is smaller in size and that its main contacts are not capable of carrying as heavy currents. The principle of operation in obtaining acceleration by this means is shown in Fig. 124. The same general system of symbols is used as given in Sec. **269** and Fig. 123. The main contacts of the line contactor are ⁵/⊣⊢. The contacts of the regular shunt-coil accelerating contactors are ³/⊣⊢ and ⁴/⊣⊢. The main contacts of the inductive-time-limit relays are ➧II and ➧I2. When the start button is pressed, current flows from $L1$ through the stop and start buttons to 7, through contacts ₒ⁵ₒ, operating coil -(11/M)-, contacts ₒ.ₗ./₋ₒₜₒ, and back to line $L2$. The armature of relay 11 is therefore attracted, opening its main contacts ➧II , which opens the circuit of operating coil (3). At the same time auxiliary con-tacts ¹¹/⊣⊢ close, thus energizing operating coil -(12/M)- and neutralizing coils -(11/N)- and -(12/N)-. The armature of relay 12 is therefore attracted, opening its main contacts ➧I2 which open the circuit of operating coil (4). At the same time auxiliary contacts ¹²/⊣⊢ close, energizing operating coil(5), which closes the main-line contactor 5. The motor is then connected to the line in series with all the starting resistance. When contactor 5 closes, it closes its auxiliary contact $\frac{5}{\circ\ \circ}$ and opens its auxiliary contact $_\circ\overset{5}{\circ}_\circ$. The closing of $\overset{5}{\circ\circ}$ makes power available for the operating coils when the start button is released. Opening of contact $_\circ\overset{5}{\circ}_\circ$ opens the main operating-coil circuit $-(\overset{11}{M})-$ so that after a definite time determined by the adjustment of the resistances controlling the neutralizing coils $-(\overset{11}{N})-$ and $-(\overset{12}{N})-$ relay 11 drops out and thereby closes its main contacts $\blacktriangleright$11. Closing of contacts $\blacktriangleright$11 energizes the operating coil (3), which operates contactor 3, shorting out the resistance R_2-R_3. As relay 11 drops out, it opens its auxiliary contacts $\overset{11}{\dashv\vdash}$, which open the circuit of the main operating coil $-(\overset{12}{M})-$ of relay 12. After a definite time, the flux of relay 12 decreases a sufficient amount so that relay 12 drops out, closing its main contacts $\blacktriangleright$12 and energizing the operating coil (4). Operating coil (4) closes the contacts of contactor 4, which short out the resistance R_3-R_4. The motor is now connected directly across the line. As relay 12 drops out, its auxiliary contacts $\overset{12}{\dashv\vdash}$ open, which disconnects all the operating coils of the accelerating relays.

271. Time acceleration controlled by means of the time required to charge a capacitor is another effective method. The application of this method to a d-c motor is shown in Fig. 125. When the start button is pressed, current flows from $L1$ through the start and stop buttons, through the operating coil $-(M)-$ and back to $L2$. This energizes the operating coil $-(M)-$ of the main-line contactor, which closes its contacts $\overset{M}{\dashv\vdash}$ and connects the motor across the line in series with all the starting resistance. When contactor M closes, it also closes its auxiliary contacts $\overset{1}{\circ_M\circ}$, which provide a means of supplying power to the operating coils when the start button is released. Current

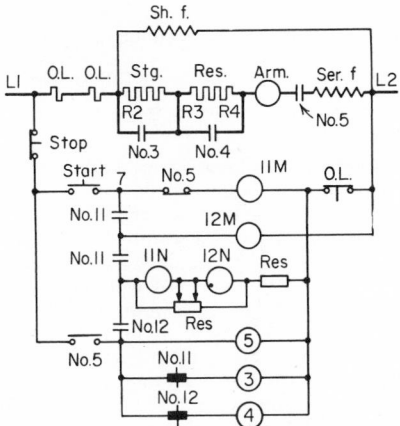

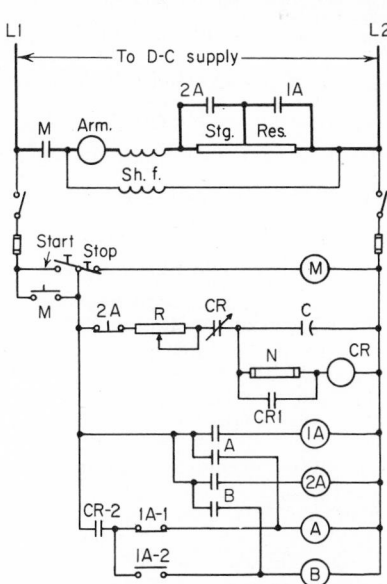

FIG. 124 *Schematic diagram showing principle of operation of time-limit acceleration by means of inductive time-limit relays.*

FIG. 125 *Schematic diagram showing principle of time-limit acceleration by means of capacitor-charge method applied to a d-c motor. (Square D Co.)*

will also flow through contacts $\underset{\text{2A}}{\multimap\!\!\multimap}$, resistance R, contacts $\underset{\text{CR}}{\Vdash}$, and capacitor C. After a certain time delay depending upon the value of resistance R and the capacity of the capacitor C, the voltage across the capacitor will reach the ignition voltage of the neon tube N. The gas of the tube will then break down and become conducting, so that current will pass through tube N and the operating coil $-\!(CR)\!-$ of relay CR. Relay CR then operates and closes the two sets of contacts $\underset{\text{CRI}}{\dashv\vdash}$ and $\underset{\text{CR2}}{\dashv\vdash}$ and opens contacts $\underset{\text{CR}}{\Vdash}$. Closing of contacts $\underset{\text{CR2}}{\dashv\vdash}$ allows current to flow through $\underset{\text{IAI}}{\multimap\!\!\multimap}$ and operating coil $-\!(A)\!-$ of relay A. Relay A operates, closing its two sets of contacts $\underset{\text{A}}{\dashv\vdash}$, which allow current to flow through operating coil $-\!(IA)\!-$ and also provide a permanent path for current through operating coil $-\!(A)\!-$ so that the relay will be held closed upon the opening of $\underset{\text{CR2}}{\dashv\vdash}$ contacts. Operating coil $-\!(IA)\!-$ causes contactor 1A to close its contacts $\underset{\text{IA}}{\dashv\vdash}$, thus shorting out a section of the starting resistance. The opening of $\underset{\text{CR}}{\Vdash}$ contacts and closing of $\underset{\text{CRI}}{\dashv\vdash}$ contacts disconnect the capacitor from the supply and provide a discharge path for the capacitor through the coil $-\!(CR)\!-$. It takes only about $1/20$ to $1/30$ sec for the capacitor to discharge, so that operating coil $-\!(CR)\!-$ is very rapidly de-energized, and contacts $\underset{\text{CRI}}{\dashv\vdash}$ and $\underset{\text{CR2}}{\dashv\vdash}$ open and contacts $\underset{\text{CR}}{\Vdash}$ close before contactor 1A closes. This starts the capacitor on another charging cycle. When contactor 1A closes, it opens its auxiliary contacts $\underset{\text{IAI}}{\multimap\!\!\multimap}$ and closes its auxiliary contacts $\underset{\text{IA2}}{\multimap\!\!\multimap}$. After a certain time the capacitor again is charged to a sufficient voltage so that the neon tube breaks down and again operates relay CR. Current will then flow through contacts $\underset{\text{CR2}}{\dashv\vdash}$, $\underset{\text{IA2}}{\multimap\!\!\multimap}$, and the operating coil $-\!(B)\!-$ of relay B. Relay B closes its two sets of contacts $\underset{\text{B}}{\dashv\vdash}$, which allow current to flow through the operating coil $-\!(2A)\!-$ and also provide a permanent path for current through operating coil $-\!(B)\!-$, so that the relay B will remain closed upon the opening of $\underset{\text{CR2}}{\dashv\vdash}$ contacts. Operating coil $-\!(2A)\!-$ causes contactor 2A to close its contacts $\underset{\text{2A}}{\dashv\vdash}$, thus shorting out the other section of resistance and connecting the motor directly across the line. When contact 2A closes, it also opens its auxiliary contacts $\underset{\text{2A}}{\multimap\!\!\multimap}$, which open the capacitor and tube timing circuit.

In the application of this method of acceleration to a-c motors (Fig. 126) it is necessary to use two auxiliary relays for each accelerating contactor except the last one. Alternating-current contactors close much more rapidly than d-c ones, and if the additional auxiliary relay were not employed, an accelerating contactor would close before the CR relay could drop out. The operating coil of the next accelerating contactor would be immediately energized, and thus two accelerating contactors would close at one operation of the capacitor timer with practically no time lag between the closing of the two accelerating contactors. In using this system on an a-c circuit it is necessary to provide a d-c source for charging the capacitor. This is done by means of a small radio potential transformer connected to a full-wave rectifier tube as shown in Fig. 126. The action of the timing circuit is exactly the same as for the d-c application previously described. When the motor is started, the first operation of relay CR allows current to flow through contacts $\underset{\text{CR2}}{\dashv\vdash}$, contacts $\underset{\text{IA3}}{\multimap\!\!\multimap}$, and the operating coil (C) of auxiliary relay C. Relay C closes its two sets of contacts $\underset{\text{CI}}{\dashv\vdash}$ and $\underset{\text{C2}}{\dashv\vdash}$. The closing of contacts $\overset{C1}{\dashv\vdash}$ causes relay A and contactor 1A to function in the same manner as previously described for d-c operation. The closing of contact $\overset{C2}{\dashv\vdash}$ and opening of contacts $\overset{C}{\nVdash}$ keep relay C closed and the circuit of operating coil --(B)-- open until relay CR has had time to open. The second functioning of the timing circuit and operation of

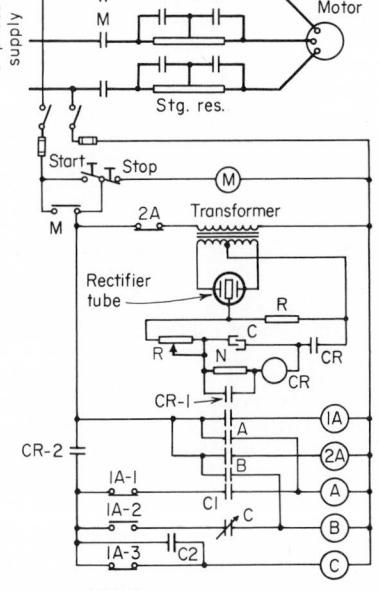

relay CR causes relay B and contactor 2A to function, thus connecting the motor directly to the line.

272. With current-limit acceleration the cutting out of the various steps of starting resistance or the changing of taps on an autotransformer is controlled by the decay of the starting current as the motor accelerates. The rapidity of the closing of the successive contactors depends upon the load of the motor. With light loads the motor will accelerate on each step more rapidly, so that the current decreases more rapidly and causes the successive contactors to function in a shorter length of time. The total length of time for the starting period therefore depends upon the load.

FIG. 126 *Schematic diagram showing principle of time-limit acceleration by means of capacitor-charge method applied to a polyphase squirrel-cage motor. (Square D Co.)*

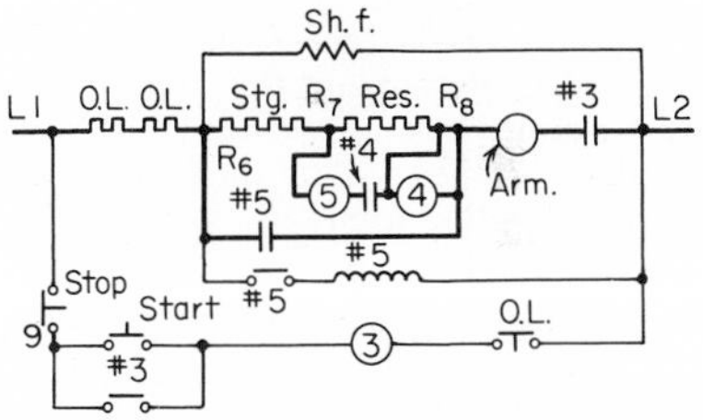

FIG. 127 *Schematic diagram showing principle of current-limit acceleration by means of series contactors of the single-coil type.*

Current-limit acceleration is performed by means of series contactors of the types described in Sec. **256.** Acceleration can be accomplished by using series contactors of the single-coil type as shown in Fig. 127. Pressing the start button energizes the operating coil (3) of the main-line contactor 3 so that line contacts $\overset{3}{\dashv\vdash}$ close, connecting the motor to the line in series with the starting resistance. When the starting current has decreased to the value for which the series contactor 4 is adjusted, operating coil (4) closes its contactor 4. The closing of contacts $\overset{4}{\dashv\vdash}$ shorts out the section of resistance $R_7 - R_8$ and allows the starting current to pass through operating coil (5) of the second series accelerating contactor. When the starting current has decreased to the value for which the series contactor 5 is adjusted, operating coil (5) closes its contactor 5. Closing of contacts $\overset{5}{\dashv\vdash}$ shorts out all the starting resistance and also the main operating coils of contactors 4 and 5, so that there will be no danger of these contactors dropping out under light loads. Contactor 5 has an auxiliary shunt holding coil $\overset{5}{\sim\!\!\sim\!\!\sim}$ which holds this contactor closed after it has once been closed by its main operating coil $\overset{5}{\textcircled{5}}$. When contactor 5 closes, it also closes its auxiliary contacts $\overset{5}{\underset{\circ\ \circ}{}}$, thus energizing the auxiliary holding-coil circuit for the contactor. The motor is now connected directly to the line.

The method of controlling acceleration by means of two-coil series lockout contactors (Sec. **256**) is shown in Fig. 128. Pressing the start button energizes the operating coil $\overset{3}{\textcircled{3}}$ of the main-line contactor 3 so that line contacts $\overset{3}{\dashv\vdash}$ close, connecting the motor to the line in series with the starting resistance. When the starting current has decreased to the value below that for which the lockout coil $\overset{}{\dashv\textcircled{4L}\vdash}$ of contactor 4 will hold this contactor open, contactor 4 closes its contacts $\overset{4}{\dashv\vdash}$. This shorts out the section of starting resistance $R_7 - R_8$ and the lockout coil $\overset{}{\dashv\textcircled{4L}\vdash}$ of contactor 4 so that the contactor will not drop out under light loads. The current now passes through the operating coil $\textcircled{5}$ and lock-out coil $\overset{}{\dashv\textcircled{5L}\vdash}$ of contactor 5 which locks open until the current has dropped in value to the amount for which the contactor is adjusted to operate. When the current has dropped to this value, contactor 5 closes its contacts $\overset{5}{\dashv\vdash}$, which short out the resistance $R_6 - R_7$ and the lockout coil $\overset{}{\dashv\textcircled{5L}\vdash}$ With the lockout coils shorted out, these contactors do not need any auxiliary shunt holding coil, since the series operating coils will hold the contactors closed with only about 5 per cent of their normal current. The motor is now connected directly across the line.

273. Counter-emf acceleration is really a special method of current-limit acceleration, since the current that flows through the motor depends upon the value of the counter-emf. It is applicable only to d-c motors. The time required for the starting period will depend upon the load on the motor just the same as for the other current-limit acceleration methods.

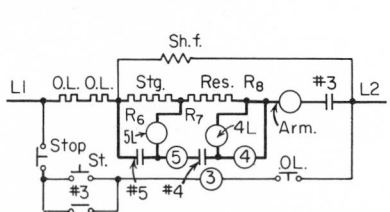

FIG. 128 *Schematic diagram showing principle of current-limit acceleration by means of series contactors of the two-coil type.*

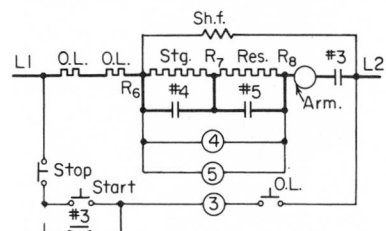

FIG. 129 *Schematic diagram showing principle of counter-emf acceleration.*

When acceleration is controlled by the counter-emf method, the operating coils of the magnetic contactors are connected across the armature winding (Fig. 129). At standstill no counter-emf is produced in the armature winding. As soon as the motor starts to revolve, a counter-emf is generated in the armature winding. The counter-emf is directly proportional to the speed so that, as the motor speeds up, the counter-emf increases. Since the operating coils of the magnetic contactors are connected across the armature, their operation depends upon the value of the counter-emf. The magnetic contactors are adjusted so that it requires a definite value of counter-emf to operate each one, a higher value of counter-emf being required to operate each successive contactor. When the speed has reached a value so that the counter-emf is sufficient to operate one of the contactors, the contactor closes and shorts out a section of the starting resistance.

274. Time-current control of acceleration, as the name implies, is a combination of time and current control of the accelerating period. With time control the time of acceleration is entirely independent of the load on the motor, while with current control the time of acceleration depends entirely upon the load on the motor. With time-current control, the time of acceleration is modified by the load on the motor but is not entirely dependent upon the load.

One method of obtaining time-current control of acceleration is through the use of the time-current acceleration relay of Fig. 130. This relay consists of a series operating coil A, an adjustable steel core C, an air gap F, a movable circular aluminum sleeve E, carrying the movable contacts G, and a set of stationary contacts H. When the circuit of the operating coil is closed, the current changes in a very short time from zero to some definite value, depending upon the circuit in series with which the coil is connected. A magnetic flux is built up rapidly in the iron core C and air gap F. This flux also links with the aluminum sleeve E, which forms a closed single-turn conductor. The rapid change of flux linked with the sleeve E causes considerable current to be induced in the sleeve. The current through the operating coil and the induced current in the aluminum sleeve are in such directions that they produce a repelling force between the coil

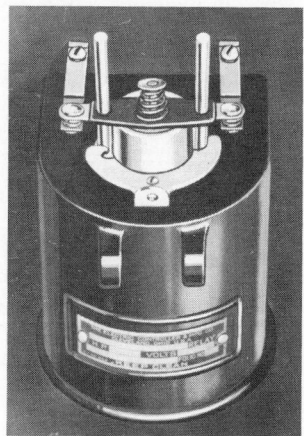

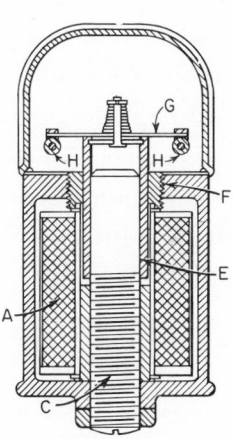

I. Complete relay.   *II. Cross-section view.*

FIG. 130   *Time-current relay. (Square D Co.)*

and the sleeve. The sleeve is therefore rapidly propelled upward upon the closing of the operating-coil circuit. The parts are so designed that considerable force is exerted upon the sleeve, and it would travel 1 ft or more if it were not for the fact that, as the tube starts to move, it passes through the field F, which now causes eddy currents to be set up in the sleeve. These eddy currents cause a retarding action, just the same as a wattmeter vane is retarded as it is forced through a magnetic field, and this, combined with the force of gravity, stops the sleeve, which then starts to fall under the force of gravity. Inasmuch as current still flows through A, causing flux in F, the sleeve is likewise retarded by eddy currents in the downward direction the same as it is retarded in the upward direction. This retarding action therefore provides a time delay, which may be as much as 2.75 sec, in the closing of contacts G and H. The length of time will be dependent upon the current in A and the adjustment of the steel core C. Since the current in A determines the strength of the flux in F, C, and E, it will be seen that a lower current in A will cause the sleeve to jump less distance, and the retarding action in the downward direction will be less, so the time also will be less. In practice, the current in A is the same as the motor current, so that when heavy current flows in the motor owing to a heavy load, the time will be longer, and when the motor current is less as on light loads, the time will be less. Hence we have time-current control, i.e., a system of control where the time is modified by the current or load on the motor.

The maximum time of operation can be adjusted by moving the adjustable steel core C. Moving the core changes the air gap F. Adjusting C so as to increase the air gap will shorten the maximum time of operation.

The principle of time-current control of acceleration with these time-current relays is illustrated by the elementary control circuit of Fig. 131. When the start button is pressed, the operating coil ③ of the main-line contactor 3 is energized. Contacts $\overset{3}{\dashv\vdash}$ close and connect the motor to the line in series with the starting resistance. Upon the closing of contactor 3 current passes through the operating coil ⑥ of time-current relay 6, and the auxiliary contacts $\overset{3}{\multimap\multimap}$ of contactor 3 close. Current will start to flow through operating coil ④, but before its contactor 4 has time to close its contacts $\overset{4}{\dashv\vdash}$, the aluminum sleeve of relay 6 has been raised and opens the contacts $\overset{6}{\multimap\multimap}$ of this relay, thereby opening the circuit of operating coil ④. After a time delay depending upon the setting of relay 6 and the load on the motor, the aluminum sleeve of relay 6 drops and recloses contacts $\overset{6}{\multimap\multimap}$. The operating coil ④ of contactor 4 is now energized and contactor 4 operates, closing its contacts $\overset{4}{\dashv\vdash}$. This shorts out the resistance $R_9 - R_{10}$, closes auxiliary contacts $\overset{4}{\multimap\multimap}$, and energizes the operating coil ⑦ of time-current relay 7. Current will start to flow through the operating coil ⑤ of contactors 5, but before the contactor can close, the aluminum sleeve of relay 7 has jumped up and opened the contacts $\overset{7}{\multimap\multimap}$. After a time delay, the aluminum sleeve of relay 7 drops, reclosing the contacts $\overset{7}{\multimap\multimap}$ of this relay and energizing the operating coil ⑤ of contactor 5. Contactor 5 now operates and closes its contacts $\overset{5}{\dashv\vdash}$. The motor is now connected directly to the line.

275. Time-current acceleration utilizing the principle of the time required to charge a capacitor is a development of the E C & M Division of the Square D Co. This method is similar to the time-limit acceleration method described in Sec. **271** with the addition of other capacitors, resistors, and a second rectifier so that the time of charging of capacitor C is modified by the motor current. The application of this method to a squirrel-cage motor is shown in Fig. 132. The d-c source of power for charging the capacitor C is obtained from the voltage across two load resistors supplied by two rectifiers connected in series. The recti-

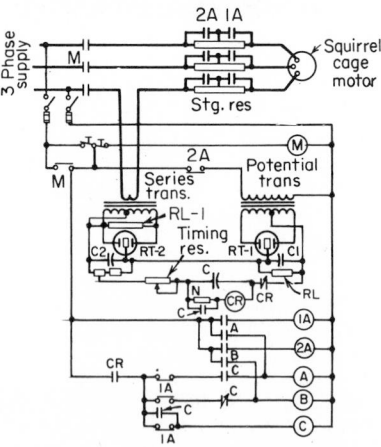

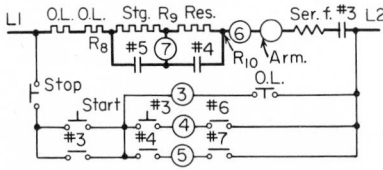

FIG. 131 *Schematic diagram showing principle of time-current acceleration by means of a magnetic time-current relay.*

FIG. 132 *Schematic diagram showing principle of time-current acceleration by means of capacitor-charge method. (Square D Co.)*

fiers are so connected that their voltages oppose each other. The voltage produced by one rectifier is controlled by the motor current through the series transformer which supplies rectifier tube *RT-2*. The combined voltage for operating the timer is thus modified by the motor current. The greater the motor current, the lower the combined voltage for charging capacitor *C*, and therefore the time for the capacitor to become charged will be increased.

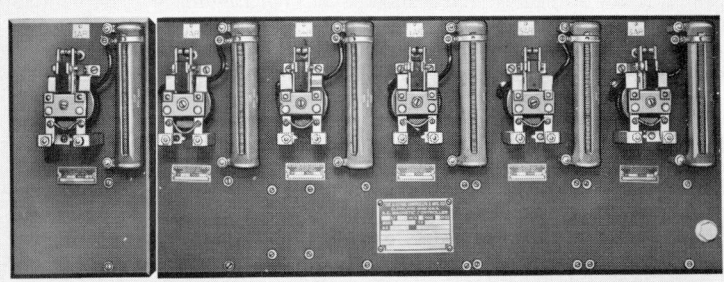

fig. 133 *Frequency relays for control of acceleration of a wound-rotor induction motor. (Square D Co.)*

276. Frequency control of acceleration is a development of the E C & M Division of the Square D Co. for application to wound-rotor induction motors. The operation of the frequency relays employed in this method depends upon the action of resonant circuits. An a-c circuit which contains both inductance and capacity will be resonant at some definite frequency, depending upon the value of the inductance and the capacity. At the resonant frequency, such a circuit will pass a very much higher value of current than at any other frequency. The current of such circuits will increase with frequency up to the resonant frequency. The operating coils of the frequency relays, which have a certain value of inductance, will produce a resonant circuit when connected in series with an external condenser. If condensers of different capacities are used with a set of relays, the respective relays will become resonant at different frequencies (Fig. 133). The higher the capacity, the lower is the resonant frequency.

The application of this method of acceleration to a wound-rotor induction motor is shown in Fig. 134. The relays *PR*, 1*AR*, 2*AR*, and 3*AR* are frequency relays. Each relay operating coil in series with its capacitor is connected to a potentiometer rheostat so that it can be adjusted to the proper current. The relays are supplied with power from the secondary resistor so as to receive a maximum voltage of 90 volts, on 60-cycle circuits, when the motor primary is first connected to the line. The relays have normally closed contacts. After a relay has attracted its armature, the armature will not

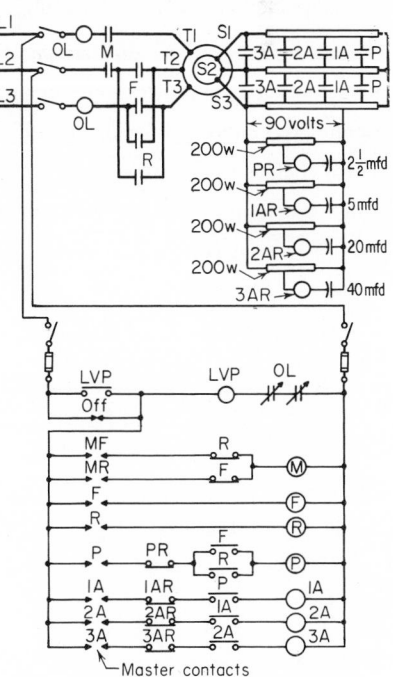

fig. 134 *Schematic diagram showing principal of frequency acceleration.*

drop out until the current of the operating coil has dropped to a certain value. The frequency at which the current reaches the drop-out value will vary with the resonant frequency of the circuit. The higher the resonant frequency, the higher the frequency at which the drop-out current will be reached. The relays are connected in series with progressively larger values of capacity, so that the resonant frequencies of the relays progressively decrease. The drop-out currents will occur at progressively lower frequencies. At standstill the frequency of the secondary circuit of an induction motor is the same as that of the primary supply circuit and decreases as the speed of the motor increases. It is approximately zero at full speed. The frequency relays will therefore drop out progressively as the motor accelerates. The operation of the motor illustrated can be controlled manually by moving the master controller to successive positions, or the acceleration can be made fully automatic by throwing the master to the last position. If the master is thrown to the last position forward, when the motor is at rest, the master contacts MF, F, P, $1A$, $2A$, and $3A$ will all be closed. The motor will then be automatically accelerated as follows: Operating coils $-(M)-$ and $-(F)-$ are first energized, which operate contactors F and M and close contacts $\overset{F}{\dashv\vdash}$ and $\overset{M}{\dashv\vdash}$. Closing of contactor F closes its auxiliary contacts $\overset{F}{\underset{\circ\ \circ}{}}$. The motor is now connected to the line with resistance in its rotor circuit. The starting current in the rotor circuit energizes the operating coils PR, $1AR$, $2AR$, and $3AR$ of all the frequency relays. The relay PR, which is the plugging relay and which has only $2\frac{1}{2}$ μf in series with its coil, will not pass enough current to operate. Since all the frequency relays have normally closed contacts, the contacts $\overset{P}{\underset{\circ\ \circ}{}}$ of relay PR will stay closed and operating coil $-(P)-$ of contactor P will be energized. Thus contactor P will close its contacts $\overset{P}{\dashv\vdash}$ immediately. The frequency relays $1AR$, $2AR$, and $3AR$ will operate immediately upon passage of current through the motor and therefore will open their contacts $\underset{\circ\ \circ}{1AR}$, $\underset{\circ\ \circ}{2AR}$, and $\underset{\circ\ \circ}{3AR}$. Closure of contactor P closes its auxiliary contacts $\underset{\circ\ \circ}{PR}$, but operating coil $-(1A)-$ will not be energized until relay $1AR$ drops out and closes its contacts $\underset{\circ\ \circ}{1AR}$. Relay $1AR$ will drop out after the motor has accelerated to a sufficient speed so that the frequency of the rotor is such as to cause the current of operating coil $-(1AR)-$ to decrease to the drop-out value. When relay $1AR$ drops out, it closes its contacts $\underset{\circ\ \circ}{1AR}$ and energizes the operating coil $-(1A)-$ of contactor $1A$. Contactor $1A$ then operates and closes its contacts $\overset{1A}{\dashv\vdash}$, shorting out some of the resistance. In a similar manner as the motor accelerates, frequency relays $2AR$ and $3AR$ drop out at progressively higher speeds and cause contactors $2A$ and $3A$ to close.

277. Methods of Starting D-C Motors. As discussed in Sec. **134**, d-c motors are almost always started with resistance in series with the armature winding. Both manual and automatic starters are used.

278. Available Types of Controllers for D-C Motors

Type	Remarks
1. Manual starters:	
a. Across the line..................................	Available in nonreversing and reversing types without dynamic braking
b. Starting rheostats (dial-type starters).	Suitable only for nonreversing service without dynamic braking
c. Drum...	Suitable for nonreversing and reversing service with or without dynamic braking
d. Multiple switch................................	Suitable only for nonreversing service without dynamic braking
2. Manual-starting and speed-regulating controllers:	
a. Starting and speed-regulating rheostats (dial-type controllers).	Suitable only for nonreversing service without dynamic braking
b. Drum...	Suitable for nonreversing and reversing service with or without dynamic braking
3. Magnetic starters:	
a. Time-limit acceleration.....................	
b. Current-limit acceleration	Available in nonreversing and reversing types with or without
c. Counter-emf-limit acceleration..........	dynamic braking
d. Time-current acceleration	

279. Across-the-line starters for d-c motors are made as standard equipment in sizes up to and including 2 hp. They consist of some form of safety-enclosed manually operated switch made in a rugged and compact manner. They can be obtained with or without thermal overload release devices. Those of the smaller types are sometimes called auxiliary or secondary breakers (see Div. 4). Most of the overload release devices are of the automatic self-resetting type, so that, after the occurrence of an overload, service is restored by simply throwing the handle to the extreme "off" and then to the "on" position. The release mechanism generally is constructed on the trip-free principle so that the switch cannot be held closed against a dangerous overload. These starters cannot be provided with undervoltage release or protective devices. Typical starters of these types are shown in Figs. 135, 136*A*, 136*B*, 136*C*, and 137.

280. Starting rheostats for d-c motors, sometimes called dial or face-plate starters, consist of a series of contacts mounted on an insulating panel and connected to different points in a resistance unit (see Fig. 138). An arm or dial bearing a contact is arranged so that it can be moved across the stationary row of contacts. A starting rheostat is shown in Fig. 139, and wiring diagrams of similar starters in Fig. 138. Moving the arm to the first contact closes the armature circuit in series with the starting resistance. As the arm is moved across the buttons, sections of the starting resistance are successively cut out of the circuit until the last contact is reached. Then all the resistance has been

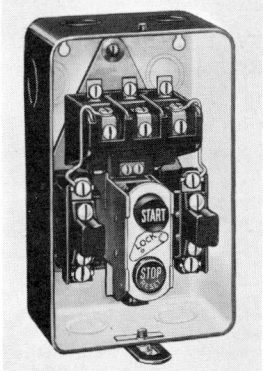

I. *Push-button type.*　　II. *Enclosed toggle-switch type for surface mounting.*　　III. *Open type for switch-box mounting.*

FIG. 135　*Manual across-the-line starters for d-c motors.*　(*Allen-Bradley Co.*)

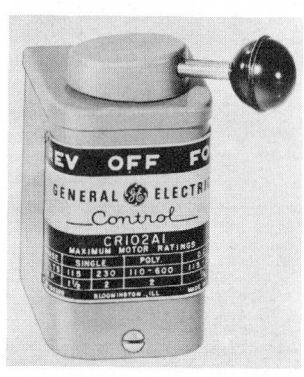

FIG. 136A *Toggle-switch manual across-the-line starter for d-c motor. (Westinghouse Electric Corp.)*

FIG. 136B *Drum-type manual across-the-line starting switch for d-c motor. (General Electric Co.)*

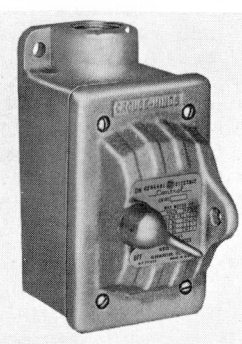

FIG. 136C *Toggle-switch types of manual across-the-line starters for d-c motors. Left, regular surface-mounting type. Center, dusttight and watertight type. Right, flush-mounting type. (General Electric Co.)*

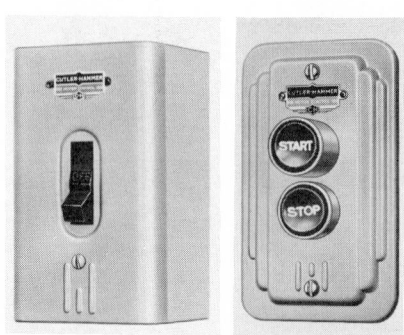

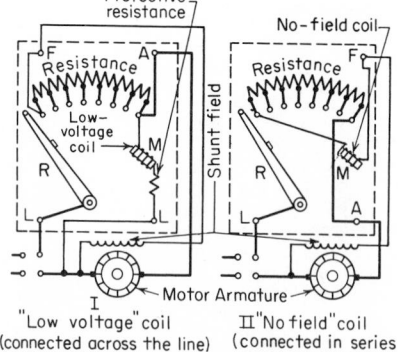

FIG. 137 *Manual across-the-line starters for d-c motors. Left, toggle-switch type. Right, push-button type. (Cutler-Hammer, Inc.)*

FIG. 138 *Diagram showing low-voltage protection provided by low-voltage coil and by a no-field coil.*

cut out of the circuit, and the armature is connected directly across the line. These starting rheostats are not suitable for reversing or dynamic braking service. They can be used for starting series, shunt, or compound-wound motors.

281. Undervoltage protective devices for starting rheostats can be operated by either a low-voltage coil or a no-field coil (Fig. 138). On a manually operated starter, each device usually consists of an electromagnet M, which under conditions of normal voltage holds the operating arm R in the running position, and a spring (not shown in the diagram) which returns the operating arm to the "off" position upon failure or decrease of voltage. Starters are sometimes so constructed that instead of the electromagnet being made strong enough to hold the arm in the running position against the force of the spring, a catch is provided which will engage and hold the arm after it has been manually moved to the running position. Then, if the voltage drops below a predetermined value, the electromagnet disengages the catch. This releases the arm, which is returned to the "off" position by the spring. The magnet coil may be connected directly across the line (Fig. 138, I) with a protective resistance in series, in which case it is called a low-voltage coil, or it may be connected in series with the shunt field (Fig. 138, II), in which case it is called a no-field coil. Both arrangements provide low-voltage protection. If the coil is connected

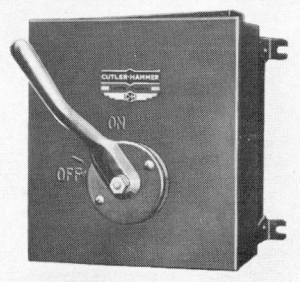

FIG. 139 *Starting rheostat of dial type for d-c motor. (Cutler-Hammer, Inc.)*

across the line, the current carried by the coil, and therefore the coil losses, will be less than if it is connected in series with the shunt field. The difference between the maximum and minimum field currents of wide-speed-range, adjustable-speed motors renders it impractical to design a series-connected holding coil which will operate satisfactorily throughout the range.

282. In starting a d-c motor (see Fig. 138), close the line switch and move the operating arm of the rheostat step by step over the contacts, waiting a few seconds on each contact for the motor speed to accelerate. If this process is performed too quickly, the motor may be injured by excessive current; if too slowly, the rheostat may be injured. If the motor fails to start on the first step, move promptly to the second step and if necessary to the third, but no farther. If no start is made when the third step is reached, open the line switch at once, allow the starter handle to return to the "off" position, and look for faulty connections, overload, etc. The time of starting a motor with full-load torque should not, as a general rule, exceed 15 sec for rheostats for motors of 5 hp and lesser output, and 30 sec for those of greater output.

283. In stopping a d-c motor, open the line switch. The arm will return automatically to the "off" position. Never force the operating arm of any starting rheostat back to the "off" position.

284. Overload protection is not generally provided in starting rheostats. Overload protection must be provided at some other point in the motor circuit by means of fuses, circuit breakers, safety switches with thermal overload protection, or magnetic contactors controlled by overload relays.

285. Drum-switch starters are made in a variety of types. They can be obtained for both reversing and nonreversing service and with or without contacts for dynamic braking. They are used for series, shunt, and compound motors. The essential features of a drum starter are a central movable drum upon which are mounted a set of contact segments and a set of stationary contact fingers. A typical drum starter is illustrated in Fig. 140. The movement of the drum is controlled by means of a handle on top of the starter case. As this handle is moved from the "off" position, the armature circuit is closed in series with the starting resistance by means of the first set of movable segments on the drum making contact with the first set of stationary fingers. As the handle is moved around, the resistance is short-circuited step by step by the contacts located farther around on the drum. Small starters of this type are self-contained with the starting resistance mounted in a ventilated box on the rear of the drum switch.

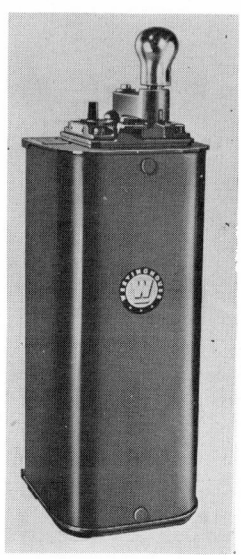

FIG. 140 *Drum controller for d-c motor. Left, with cover removed. Right, with enclosing cover in place. (Westinghouse Electric Corp.)*

In the larger sizes the resistance is mounted separately from the drum switch. Drum controllers do not provide any overload or undervoltage protection. Overload protection may be provided by fuses or a circuit breaker mounted separate from the controller. A magnetic contactor with an overload relay will provide both overload and undervoltage protection. Such a protective unit has the advantage that it may be electrically interlocked with the drum switch so that the line contactor cannot be closed unless the drum switch is in the "off" position. This safeguards against the possibility of the motor being thrown directly across the line. Connections for a typical magnetic-contactor protective panel are shown in Fig. 141.

286. The manually operated multiple-switch starter for d-c motors (Fig. 142) comprises a number of switches S, which are manually closed in sequence. Thereby the resistances R are shunted out of circuit as the armature accelerates. The switches are so mechanically interlocked that their being closed in any other than the proper sequence is prevented. When the last switch S_5 is closed, all the resistance is short-circuited. The switches, after being closed, are held in the closed position by a catch. This catch is in turn held by a low-voltage-protective magnet M.

FIG. 141 *Diagram of connections for magnetic overload protective unit for use with drum starter.*

Upon the failure of voltage, the catch is released and all the switches are thrown to the "off" position by gravity or by a spring. A switch of this type is especially adapted for starting large motors. A sufficient time period will elapse in the ordinary closing of the switches to provide a protection against too rapid acceleration. The arrangement of a number of switches in parallel tends to minimize heating of the contacts, particularly of the contact of the last switch S_5. One of the contact blocks of each switch is

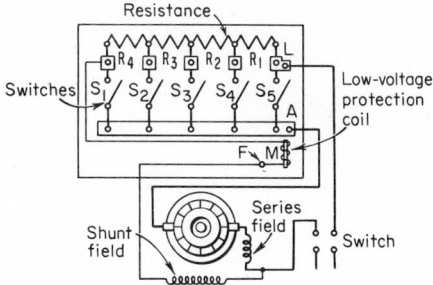

FIG. 142 *Diagram of connections for a multiple-switch starter.*

often made of laminated copper strips and the other of carbon. The laminated brushes and the copper-to-carbon arcing contacts render a switch of this type exceptionally adaptable for use with large motors. Overload protection must be provided outside the starter. These starters are suitable for series, shunt, or compound motors in nonreversing service without dynamic braking.

287. Apparatus for Field Control of Shunt or Compound Motors. The variable resistance in series with the shunt field, necessary for speed control of shunt or compound motors by the field-control method, may be provided by means of a field rheostat separate from the starting rheostat, or the starting rheostat and the field rheostat may be combined into a single piece of equipment forming a combined starting and speed-adjusting controller. Such combined starting and speed-adjustment controllers are available in both the dial and the drum types of construction.

288. Drum controllers for combined starting and speed adjustment (field control) are provided with two sets of contacts, one set for the control of the starting resistance and the other set for controlling the speed of the motor through the variation of the shunt-field resistance. Although controllers of this type (Fig. 143) find their most frequent applications on machine tools, they are very desirable for any service where the work is severe and where the expense of a controller is justified. Machine-tool work usually requires a combination starting and speed-regulating controller, i.e., one whereby the motor is started by cutting out armature resistance. After the motor is started, its speed is regulated by varying the amount of resistance in series with the shunt field. These controllers can be purchased for this service and for control or starting service of practically any type. The methods of construction and connection are so numerous that only one type of drum controller, one which is used for machine-tool service, will be described here.

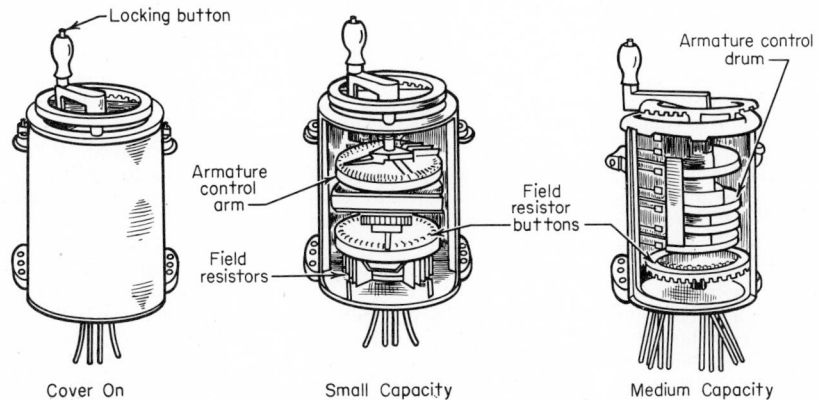

FIG. 143 *Machine-tool controllers.*

Advantages of controllers of this type are that the contacts and arm are entirely enclosed and that the movement of a single handle in one direction or the other starts the motor in a corresponding direction and brings it to the running speed desired. The operating arm remains securely locked at the proper notch until released by the operator by pressing a button in the handle.

There are two switching devices in the controllers shown in Fig. 143. One connects to the armature or starting resistor, and the other connects to the field-control resistor. Both switching devices are operated by the same handle. In drum controllers of small capacity the armature switching device consists of an arm passing over contact buttons, and all the resistors are mounted within the drum; i.e., the controller is self-contained. In controllers of large capacity, the armature resistance is cut in and out by a rotating drum similar to that used in street-railway service and all the resistors are mounted external to the controller. The field resistance is cut in and out by a rotating arm passing over contact buttons in all but the largest controllers, for which a drum is used. Arc shields between drum segments and blowout coils are provided where necessary. The controllers can be arranged to provide dynamic braking. Speed ranges of from 1:2 to possibly 1:6 are usually provided.

289. Operation of Drum-type Machine-tool Controllers (Fig. 143). Continuous movement of the operating handle in either direction first starts the motor in the corresponding direction of rotation, then cuts out the starting resistance, and finally cuts in the field resistance until the desired running speed is reached. The handle should be moved over the starting notches in not over 15 sec for motors of possibly 10 hp capacity and in not over 30 sec for larger motors. The starting resistance should not be used for speed control.

For a quick stop when operating with weakened field, move the handle quickly to the first running notch, hold it there momentarily, and then move it to the "off" position; the application of full field strength when the speed is high causes dynamic braking, thus checking the speed quickly and without shock. For a very quick emergency stop, the handle can be moved to the first reversing notch after checking the speed by dynamic braking, but this operation causes severe mechanical and electrical stresses; this reversing should never be carried beyond the first notch. When the motor is to be at rest for any length of time, open the line switch.

290. Apparatus for Armature Speed Control of D-C Motors. When armature speed control is employed, the same piece of equipment serves for both starting and speed control. An ordinary starting controller should not be used for armature speed control, however, as it is designed not for continuous duty but only for intermittent service as is required in starting. In employing a controller for armature speed control, one must make sure that it is designed for that type of service and not simply for starting duty. Controllers suitable for armature control are available in both the rheostat and the drum types.

291. Rheostat-type armature-control speed regulators (Fig. 144) are used for speed reduction with shunt, compound, or series motors in nonreversing service where the torque required decreases with the speed but remains constant at any given speed as with fans, blowers, and centrifugal pumps. They can also be used for applications where the torque is independent of the speed, as with job printing presses. However, this method of speed control is not suitable for such applications where there is operation for long periods at reduced speed, since such operation is not economical. It is not possible, where the torque varies, to obtain constant speed with these controllers.

In the regulator shown, the low-voltage release consists of an electromagnet enclosed in an iron shell, a sector on the pivot end of the operating arm, and a strong spring which tends to return the arm to the "off" position. The magnet is mounted directly below the pivot of the arm, and its coil is connected in shunt across the line in series with a protecting resistance. When the magnet is energized, its plunger rises and forces a steel ball into one of a series of depressions in the sector on the arm with sufficient force to hold the arm against the action of the spring; each depression corresponds to a contact. The arm can be easily moved by the operator, however, as the ball rolls when the arm is turned. When the voltage fails, the magnet plunger falls and the spring throws the operating arm to the "off" position. Standard commercial rheostats of this type are designed to give about 50 per cent speed reduction on the first notch. See the

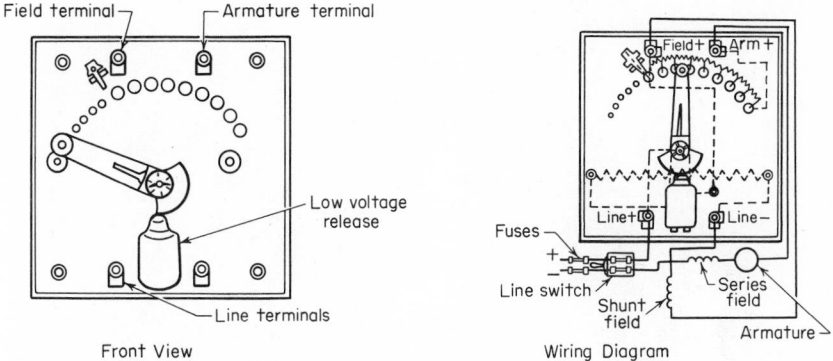

FIG. 144 *Armature-control speed regulator, removed from enclosing box.*

following paragraph on operation for further information.   An armature-control speed regulator mounted in a steel enclosure is shown in Fig. 145.

292. Operation of Armature-control Speed Regulators (Fig. 144).   Continuous motion of the operating arm starts the motor and brings it gradually to maximum speed. Moving the arm over the first few contact buttons increases the shunt-field strength if the motor is shunt or compound.   The movement over the succeeding buttons cuts out armature resistance and permits the motor to speed up.

293. Drum controllers suitable for armature speed control are widely used for crane and hoist motors and in railway applications.   Their general appearance and construction is the same as for the drum starter shown in Fig. 140.   Crane controllers are arranged for reversing service and usually for dynamic braking.

294. Magnetic starters for d-c motors are available in a large number of different types for reversing and nonreversing duty, with or without dynamic braking, and for inching and jogging service.   They can be used with constant-speed or adjustable-speed shunt or compound motors and with series motors.   When they are used with adjustable-speed motors, speed control is obtained by means of a field rheostat mounted separately from the magnetic controller.

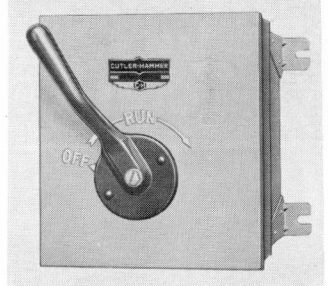

FIG. 145 *Armature-control speed regulator in steel enclosure.   (Cutler-Hammer, Inc.)*

Where armature speed control is required, it is obtained by controlling the functioning of the contactors by means of a master controller.   The operator adjusts the master controller to the position for the desired speed, and this initiates the functioning of the contactors, which adjusts the resistance to the corresponding value.

Magnetic starters consist of the necessary magnetic contactors and relays mounted on a panel and generally enclosed in a sheet-metal cabinet.   Practically all magnetic starters and controllers are equipped with some form of overload protective relay which opens the circuit of the operating coil of the line contactor upon the occurrence of an overload on the motor.   The master switch for initiating the operation of the controller may consist of an automatic float or pressure switch, a push-button switch, or a drum or rotary switch.   The automatic switches and the push-button masters are used for simple control such as starting and stopping or starting, stopping, and reversing, while the drum or rotary switch is employed where full speed control by the operator is required, as for the control of cranes, hoists, etc.   "No-voltage protection" or release is provided through the operating coil of the main-line contactors, since upon failure or abnormal reduction of the line voltage, the operating coil of the contactor will be de-energized

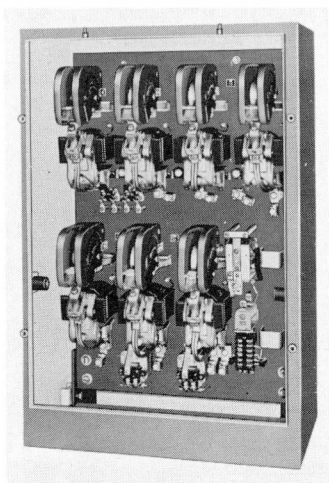

FIG. 146 *Liquid-dashpot controller for d-c motor. (Allen-Bradley Co.)*

FIG. 147 *Pneumatic-relay-type time-limit controller for d-c motor. (Square D Co.)*

and the contactor will open the motor circuit. The principles of the different methods of automatically controlling the acceleration are discussed in Secs. **259** to **275**. The appearance of typical magnetic controllers is shown in Figs. 146 to 151 inclusive.

295. Field relays must be used with magnetic starters when field speed control is employed. This is necessary in order to ensure that the motor will be started with full field. These relays are called vibrating or fluttering relays, since during the acceleration or deceleration of the motor their armatures flutter or vibrate between the open

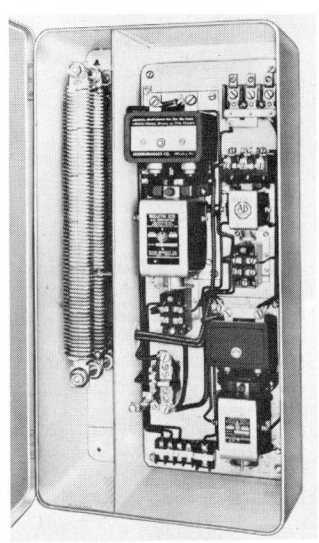

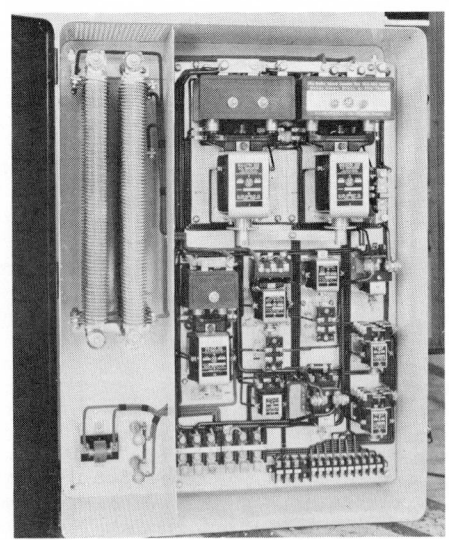

I. *Nonreversing type.*

II. *Reversing type.*

FIG. 148 *Pneumatic-relay-type time-limit controllers for d-c motors. (Allen-Bradley Co.)*

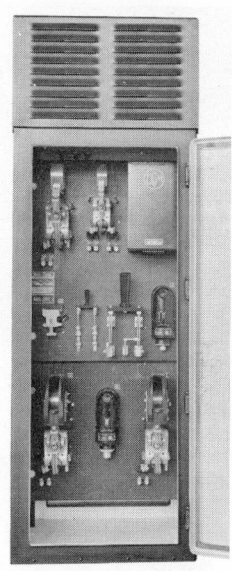

FIG. 149 *Inductive time-limit controller for d-c motor. (Westinghouse Electric Corp.)* FIG. 150 *Capacitor-charge-type time-limit controller for d-c motor. (Square D Co.)*

and closed position, alternately shorting and cutting in the field resistance. The operating coil of the relay is connected in series with the armature of the motor, and the contacts are connected across the shunt-field rheostat. During the starting period, whenever the armature current exceeds the value for which the relay is set, the relay will close, short-circuiting the field resistance so that the field strength is maximum. After the starting resistance in series with the armature has been cut out of the circuit, the field relay will hold in until the motor has accelerated sufficiently to reduce the armature current to the value which will allow the field relay to drop out. As it drops out, the field resistance will be cut into the field circuit, thus weakening the field strength. This weakening of the field reduces the counter-emf and therefore will cause the armature current to increase and further accelerate the motor. The increase in armature current causes the field relay to close again, short-circuiting the field resistance. This action is rapidly repeated, the relay vibrating between open and closed positions until the motor has been accelerated to the speed for which the field rheostat is adjusted. The armature current is then at its normal value and is not sufficient to operate the field relay, which remains open with the field resistance cut into the field circuit.

296. D-c protective panels are employed primarily for the protection of crane installations. The panel shown in Fig. 152 provides overload, undervoltage, and short-circuit protection.

297. D-c safety disconnect switches, as shown in Fig. 153, are specially designed to provide in a very satisfactory manner for the disconnect switch required by the National Electrical Code for crane installations. The switch in Fig. 153 is arranged for lever operation but is not difficult to close, as are most large-size manually operated disconnect switches. Pushing the operating handle up closes the double-pole control circuit contacts and energizes the magnetic coil to close the switch and connect power to the crane. Pulling the operating handle down breaks both sides of the control circuit. The operating handle will also force the main contacts open if the main contactor fails to open by breaking the control circuit.

I. *Current-limit type. (Ward-Leonard Electric Co.)*

II. *Counter-emf type. (Ward-Leonard Electric Co.)*

III. *Time-current type in NEMA Type IV (watertight) cabinet. (Square D Co.)*

FIG. 151 *Typical magnetic controllers for d-c motors.*

IV. *Time-current type.* (*Square D Co.*)

FIG. 151   (*Continued*)

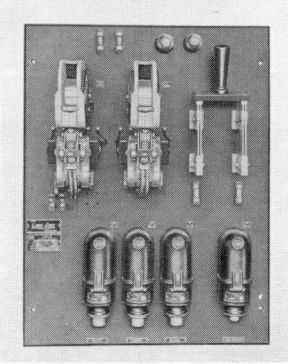

FIG. 152 *Direct-current protective panel.*
(*Square D Co.*)

FIG. 153   *Direct-current motor disconnect switch.* (*Square D Co.*)

298. Methods of Starting Polyphase Squirrel-cage Induction Motors.

1. Full-voltage (across the line).
2. Reduced voltage.
   a. By means of autotransformer (compensator).
   b. By means of series resistor.
   c. By means of series reactor.

Any polyphase induction motor can be safely started by applying full voltage at starting without harm to the motor, but as discussed in Sec. **130,** the heavy starting current
drawn from the line by this method may produce too great power and voltage fluctu-

ations in the power-supply system. When the starting current must be reduced, one of the methods listed in (2) above is employed for reducing the voltage impressed on the motor during starting. In method *a* the motor is connected at start to the secondary of an autotransformer. After the machine has accelerated sufficiently, the motor is switched over to full line voltage. With this method there are just two steps in the sequence of starting operations: reduced voltage of some definite value and then directly to full line voltage. Starters employing the transformer method of reducing the voltage are called compensators or autotransformer starters. In method *b*, resistance is connected in series with the motor leads from the supply. One or more steps of resistance can be employed. In most cases only one step is used, so that the motor is first connected to the line with some definite value of resistance in series, and then, after the machine has accelerated sufficiently, it is thrown over to full line voltage. Where the starting conditions are more severe or the starting current must be more closely regulated, additional steps are employed for cutting out the resistance. Method *c* is similar to the series-resistance method except that reactance is inserted in series with the motor during starting instead of resistance. With this method only one step of reactance is used.

For the same value of starting torque developed, the autotransformer method of starting will limit the first value of peak starting current to the lowest value. The amount of power consumed during the starting period will be considerably less than with resistance starting. A disadvantage of this method is that the motor is generally entirely disconnected from the supply during the transition period from reduced to full line voltage. This causes a second peak current to be drawn from the line at the instant that full voltage is applied. Some power companies will not allow the use of autotransformer starters for this reason.

With resistance starting, the motor is connected to the supply continuously throughout the starting period, the motor impressed voltage being increased by shorting out the starting resistance. Although there will be an increase in line current whenever some or all of the starting resistance is short-circuited, the magnitude of such peaks will not be nearly so great as the peak current involved at the instant when full voltage is applied with autotransformer starting. The resistance-starting method has the advantage that it produces very smooth starting conditions with respect both to strains imposed upon the motor and load and to the power and voltage fluctuations produced in the supply circuit during the starting period. Resistance starting is used in cases where the strains imposed upon the load with compensator starting would be detrimental or where this method is required by power-supply-company regulations. The resistance method is not generally satisfactory unless a starting torque of 50 per cent or less of full-load torque is sufficient.

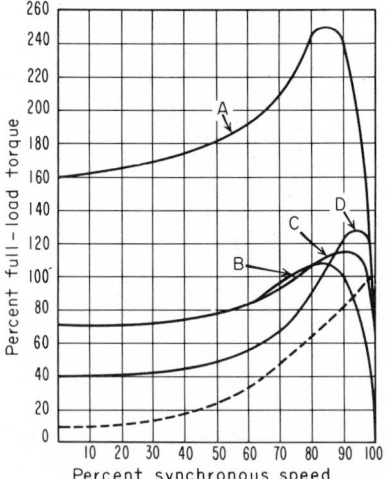

FIG. 155 *Accelerating torque characteristics of a squirrel-cage induction motor. (Allis-Chalmers.)*

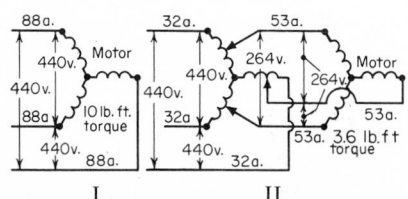

FIG. 154 *Starting with (I) and without (II) compensator.*

With series-reactance starting, the same as in resistance, the motor connections do not have to be broken during the starting period. The reactor is short-circuited when the motor attains its maximum speed on reduced voltage. For the same current drawn from the line, reactance starting will develop the same starting torque as resistance starting. Reactance starting has the advantages over resistance starting that less power is consumed during the starting period and that the transition peaks of current will be less, owing to the opposing effect of the inductance to sudden changes in the current. For the same number of steps reactance starting will produce the smoothest starting conditions of any of the three methods of starting. However, in the smaller sizes, control equipment of this type is more expensive than either of the other two and for all sizes is more expensive than resistance starting. It is not practicable to make reactance starters for more than two steps of starting control, so that, by using a greater number of steps, smoother starting can be obtained with resistance starting. For many large motors, a reactance starter will be cheaper than a transformer starter, since only two sets of switching contacts are required for a one-step starter as compared with three sets for a transformer starter. For these reasons, reactance starting is utilized only in the case of very large motors when one or two steps of starting will be satisfactory.

On account of the lower cost of across-the-line starters the general practice is to use this type of starting wherever it is possible to use motors whose starting currents are within the allowable limits.

Refer to Fig. 155 and Secs. **300, 301** and **302** for further comparison.

299. Starting with and without Compensators. The starting current taken by a squirrel-cage induction motor at the instant of starting is equal to the applied emf divided by the impedance of the motor. Only the duration of this current, and not its value, is affected by the torque against which the motor is required to start. The effect of starting without and with a compensator is illustrated by diagrams I and II in Fig. 154. In this diagram, motor I is thrown directly on a 440-volt line. The impedance of the motor is 5 ohms per phase; the starting torque, 10 lb at 1 ft radius; and the current taken, 88 amp. In diagram II a compensator is inserted, stepping down the line voltage from 440 to 60 per cent of 440, or 264 volts. This reduces the starting current of the motor to 60 per cent of 88, or 53 amp, and the starting torque becomes $(0.6)^2 \times 10$, or 3.6 lb at 1 ft radius. The current in the line is reduced to 60 per cent of 53, or 32 amp.

Thus when a compensator is used, the starting torque of the motor can be reduced to approximately the value required by the load and the current taken from the line correspondingly decreased.

300. General Comparison of Starting Conditions among Three Types of Reduced-voltage Starters
(Allis-Chalmers)

Characteristic	Autotransformer type	Primary resistor type	Reactor type
Starting line current at same motor terminal voltage	Least	More than autotransformer type	
Starting power factor	Low	High	Low
Quantity of power drawn from the line during starting	Less	More than autotransformer type	
Torque	Torque increases slightly with speed	Torque increases greatly with speed	
Torque efficiency	The autotransformer-type starter provides the highest motor starting torque of any reduced-voltage starter for each ampere drawn from the line during the starting period	Low	Low
Smoothness of acceleration	Motor is momentarily disconnected from the line during transfer from start to run	Smoother. As the motor gains speed, the current decreases. Voltage drop across resistor or reactor decreases and motor terminal voltage increases. Transfer is made with little change in motor terminal voltage	
Cost	Equal	Lower in small sizes, otherwise equal	Equal
Ease of control	Equal	Equal	Equal
Maintenance	Equal	Equal	Equal
Safety	Equal	Equal	Equal
Reliability	Equal	Equal	Equal
Line disturbance	Varies with line conditions and type of load		

301. Comparison of Current Torque Starting Characteristics for Squirrel-cage Motor
(Allis-Chalmers)
(Refer to Fig. 155)

Method of starting	Starting current drawn from the line as a percentage of full-load current	Starting torque as a percentage of full-load torque
Connecting motor directly to the line-full potential	470	160
Autotransformer 80 % tap.	335	105
Resistor or reactor starter to give 80 % applied voltage	375	105
Autotransformer 65 % tap.	225	67
Resistor or reactor starter to give 65 % applied voltage	305	67
Resistor or reactor starter to give 58 % applied voltage.	273	54
Autotransformer 50 % tap.	140	43
Resistor or reactor starter to give 50 % applied voltage.	233	43

302. Comparison of Autotransformer and Resistance for Decreasing Voltage for Starting Squirrel-cage Motors. The motor in Fig. 156 is supposed to require 100 amp to start it, i.e., to provide the energy needed to produce the necessary starting torque. At I, where an autotransformer is used to lower the voltage to 110, a current of 100 amp is produced in the motor primary with a current in the line of 50 amp. This condition is due to the transformer action of the autotransformer. At II the running connections are shown wherein the autotransformer is entirely disconnected from the circuit. At

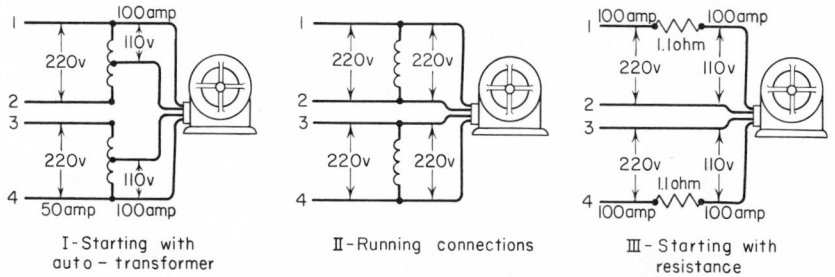

I-Starting with auto-transformer   II-Running connections   III-Starting with resistance

FIG. 156 *Starting with resistance and with compensator.*

III are illustrated the conditions that would obtain were the voltage lowered for start-ing by inserting resistance in series with the line. Obviously 100 amp must flow in all portions of the line even though the resistance of 1.1 ohms reduces the line voltage of 220 to a voltage of 110, which is impressed on the motor. There is a loss of energy in the resistance. For the same line starting current the starting torque available with the resistance method will be considerably less than that developed when a compen-sator is employed. As was stated in Sec. **298,** the resistance-starting method has the advantage that it produces very smooth starting conditions with respect to both the strains imposed upon the motor and load and the voltage fluctuations produced in the supply circuit during the starting period. A comparison of starting torques and currents when reducing the voltage in the two different ways is given in Table **301.**

303. Across-the-line starters are made in a variety of different types. Starters of the same general type differ from one another in details of construction, depending upon the ideas of the manufacturer. The most common types of across-the-line starters are given in the following list:

1. Plain motor-starting switch with no overload protection.
2. Single-throw switch with thermal overload protection.
3. Magnetic switch with thermal overload protection.

304. The plain motor-starting switch is simply a tumbler, rotary, lever, or drum switch constructed in an especially rugged manner. It does not provide any overload or under-voltage protection. It is used for nonreversing duty in small sizes up to 2 hp and for reversing duty up to 15 hp. Some representative types are illustrated in Figs. 157 and 158.

305. Single-throw across-the-line starting switches with thermal overload protection are shown in Figs. 159, 160, and 161. The thermal overload protection can be obtained by means of thermal cutouts, by means of time-lag fuses, or by means of a thermal over-load release device. When thermal cutouts or time-lag fuses are used, the cutouts or fuses must be replaced after their rupture by an overload. With thermal overload re-leases there is nothing to renew after the occurrence of an overload. For a more com-plete discussion of the principles of thermal overload protective devices refer to Div. 4. In the switches provided with a thermal overload release device, an overload trips the holding catch of the switch and allows the switch to open. These starters do not provide any undervoltage protection.

306. Magnetic across-the-line starting switches consist of a magnetically operated switch controlled from a push-button station. They are provided usually with thermal-relay overload and undervoltage protection. In the switch shown in Fig. 162 pressing the start button closes the circuit of the operating coil of the magnetic switch. This allows a current to flow from one side of the line, through the start button, through the

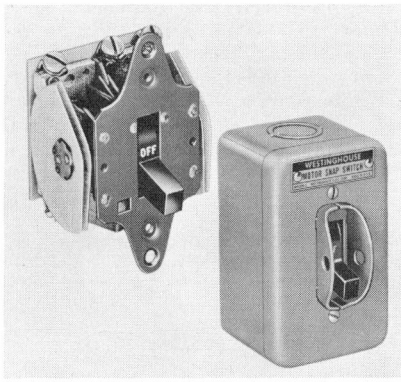

I. *Snap-switch type.*

II. *Drum-switch type.*

FIG. 157   *Plain motor-starting switches without overload protection for polyphase squirrel-cage motors.   (Westinghouse Electric Corp.)*

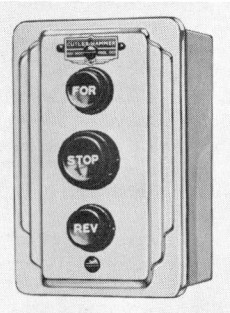
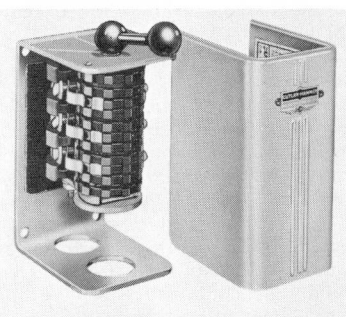

I. *Push-button-operated type.*   II. *Drum-switch type.*

FIG. 158   *Plain motor-starting switches without overload protection for polyphase squirrel-cage motors.   (Cutler-Hammer, Inc.)*

operating coil, and back to the other side of the line.   The operating coil, being energized, closes the magnetic switch.   The switch in closing also closes an auxiliary contact so that, when the start button is released, the operating coil is still energized. To stop the motor the stop button is pressed.   This opens the circuit of the operating coil, allowing the switch to open.   In case of an overload the thermal relays expand and open contact. This de-energizes the operating coil and allows the switch to open. If the voltage of the line fails or falls to a low value, the operating coil will not be energized sufficiently to hold the contacts of the switch closed. As the switch opens, the contacts are opened, so the motor will not start upon return of normal voltage until the start button is pressed.

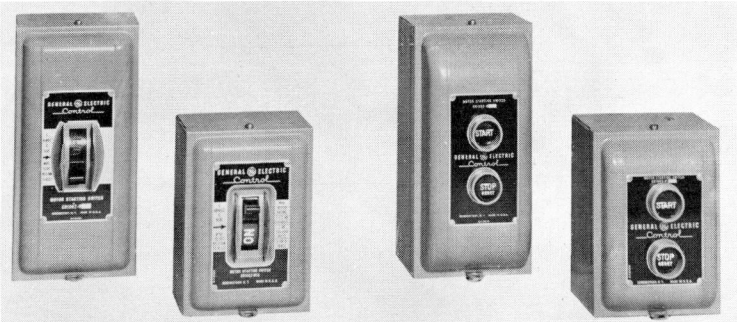

FIG. 159 *Manual across-the-line starters with thermal overload protection for polyphase squirrel-cage motors. (General Electric Co.)*

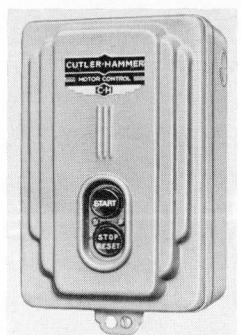  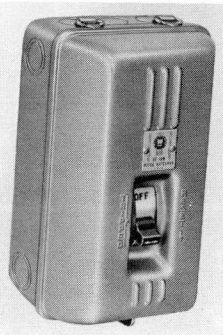

I. *Cutler-Hammer Inc.*   II. *Ward-Leonard Electric Co.*   III. *Ward-Leonard Electric Co.*

FIG. 160 *Typical manual across-the-line starters with thermal overload protection for polyphase squirrel-cage motors.*

FIG. 161 *Manual across-the-line starter with overload protection for polyphase squirrel-cage motor. (Allen-Bradley Co.)*

I. *With cover closed.*   II. *With cover removed.*

FIG. 162 *Magnetic across-the-line starter for polyphase squirrel-cage motor. (Westinghouse Electric Corp.)*

I. *With cover closed.*   II. *With cover removed.*

FIG. 163 *Reversing-type magnetic across-the-line starter for polyphase squirrel-cage motor. (Westinghouse Electric Corp.)*

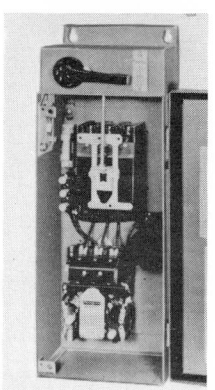

I   II   III   IV

FIG. 164 *Combination magnetic across-the-line starters for polyphase squirrel-cage motors. I. Appearance of all types with cover closed. II. With no-fuse motor-circuit switch. III. With fused motor-circuit switch. IV. With time-limit circuit breaker. (Westinghouse Electric Corp.)*

Magnetic across-the-line starting switches are made in a variety of types for both nonreversing and reversing duty. The reversing types consist of two magnetic switches electrically interlocked so as to prevent the closing of both switches at the same time (Fig. 163).

307. Combination Magnetic Across-the-line Starters. Magnetic across-the-line starters can be purchased which include in the same metal enclosure other branch-motor-circuit protective and switching equipment. The following different combinations are available as standard equipment:

1. Magnetic starter and no-fuse motor-circuit switch (Fig. 164, II).
2. Magnetic starter and fused motor-circuit switch (Fig. 164, III).
3. Magnetic starter and time-limit circuit breaker (Fig. 164, IV).

The National Electrical Code rules require the installation of a motor-circuit switch on the line side of each magnetic starter. These combinations make a very compact and neat installation for the fulfillment of these requirements. Almost any desired combination can be obtained for either nonreversing or reversing service. It is very often desirable to include in the enclosure a set of test jacks so that meters can be easily plugged into the motor circuit for analysis of voltage, current, and power conditions.

308. Safety-enclosed circuit breakers (see Div. 4) of the magnetic-overload-trip type can be employed for across-the-line starters for polyphase induction motors. Breakers used for this purpose should be equipped with overload protection of the inverse-time-lag type. Such breakers will fulfill the functions of starter, motor-overload protective device, and motor-circuit switch. Two circuit breakers mechanically interlocked so that both breakers could not be closed simultaneously could be employed for reversing service.

309. Commercial compensators or autostarters consist of an autotransformer, a double-throw switching device, and overload and undervoltage protective devices, all compactly mounted in a sheet-metal case. They can be obtained for either manual or magnetic operation. The manual type is provided with a lever outside the case which controls the double-throw-switch mechanism. When the handle is in the "off" position, the motor and autotransformer are both disconnected from the line. Throwing the lever to the "start" position connects the autotransformer to the line and the motor to the secondary taps of the autotransformer applying the reduced voltage for starting. When the handle is thrown to the "run" position, the motor is connected directly to the line and the autotransformer is entirely disconnected from the circuit. The switching mechanism is so designed that it cannot be left in the "start" position but will automatically return to the "off" position unless thrown to the "run" position after the start.

Most manual compensators are provided with a "stop" button so interconnected with the overload protective device that, if pressed, the button will actuate the device and open the compensator contacts.

In the automatic compensator the same sequence of operations as in the hand-operated type is performed automatically after the operator has pressed the starting button. The acceleration may be time-limit or current-limit controlled. Most automatic compensator starters employ the time-limit method. The closing of the start button closes the operating coil of a magnetic contactor which connects the motor to the line through the autotransformer. With time-limit control after a sufficient time has elapsed, a definite-time relay closes its contacts, completing the operating circuit of a second magnetic contactor. The closing of this second contactor disconnects the autotransformer from the circuit and throws the motor directly across the line. With current-limit control, a current-limit relay closes the operating-coil circuit of the second contactor after the current has been reduced to the proper value.

In order to stop the motor it is necessary simply to depress the stop button, which opens the operating coil of the magnetic contactor, allowing the contacts to open and disconnect the motor from the line.

Compensators are provided with two or more sets of secondary taps on the autotransformers so that the voltage best suited to the required starting conditons may be used. Typical compensators are shown in Figs. 165 to 168.

The standard compensator does not provide for reversing duty. For such service an additional reversing switch of either the manual or magnetic type would be required.

310. Overload protection on autotransformer starters is provided by means of ther-

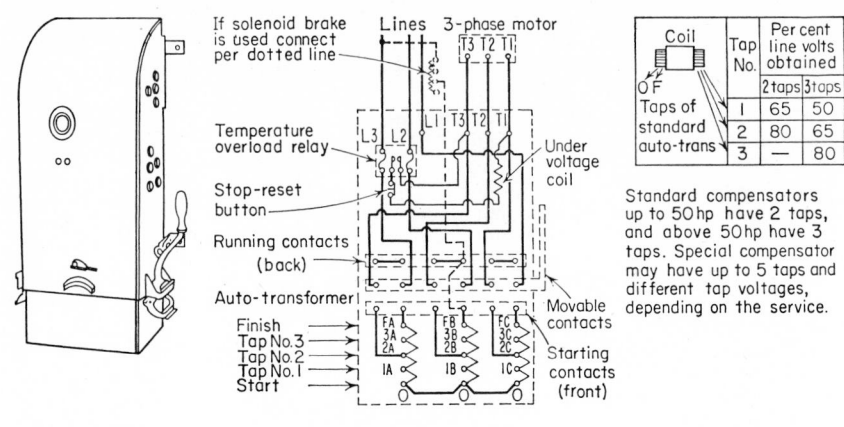

I—Compensator in enclosure

II—Diagram of connections

III—Auto-transformer taps

FIG. 165 *Manual compensator for squirrel-cage motor. (General Electric Co.)*

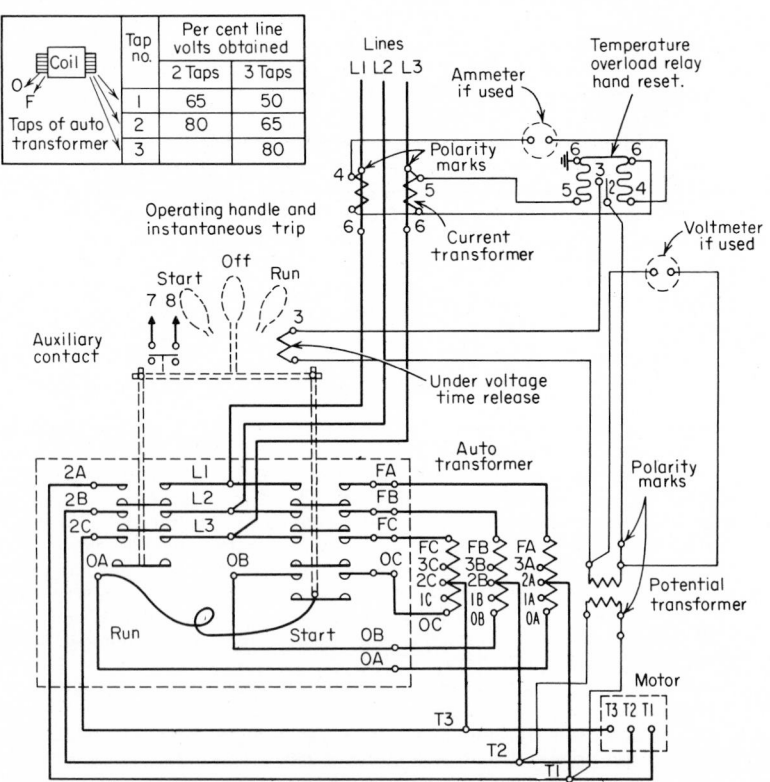

FIG. 166 *Manual-compensator diagram for high-voltage squirrel-cage motor. (General Electric Co.)*

mal or magnetic relays. In manual compensators the overload relay opens the holding-coil circuit, allowing the switch of the compensator to return to the "off" position. In magnetic compensators the overload relay breaks the circuit of the operating coil of the magnetic contactor so that the contactor opens. Typical connections for overload protection with thermal relays are shown in Fig. 165 and those for magnetic relays in Fig. 168. The relays generally are arranged so that they can be adjusted to operate at different currents. Thermal relays inherently have inverse-time characteristics. When magnetic relays are employed, they generally are equipped with devices to give the inverse-time feature. The overload relays of compensators used for high-voltage motors are isolated from the high-voltage circuit by means of current transformers, as shown in Fig. 166.

311. Undervoltage protection is almost always provided on autotransformer starters. For manual compensators the holding coil of the compensator switch acts as the under-voltage coil (see Figs. 165 and 166). The holding coil is connected across the line when the switch is in the running position. If the voltage of the line drops sufficiently, the coil is de-energized to such an extent that the switch is released and returned to its "off" position by its spring. For magnetic compensators the operating coil of the running contactor acts as the undervoltage coil (see Fig. 168). If the voltage of the line drops sufficiently, this operating coil is de-energized to such an extent that it cannot hold the running contactor closed. The holding or operating coils of compensators for high-voltage motors are energized from the secondary of a small-voltage transformer, as shown in Fig. 166. The secondary voltage of these transformers is generally 110 volts.

312. A magnetic compensator is shown in Fig. 167. It consists of a running contactor, a starting contactor, autotransformer, accelerating relay, and an overload relay. In the compensator illustrated, acceleration is time controlled. This is the more usual method of automatically controlling acceleration, but current control is also employed. The compensator of Fig. 168 functions as follows. When the start button is pressed, a circuit is closed from L_2, through the stop and start buttons, to 2, to 12, through accelerating relay contact to 6, through operating coil of starting contactor to 5, through overload relay contacts to 8, and back to L_1. The operating coil of the starting contactor is thus energized, and the starting contactor closes applying reduced voltage to the motor through the transformer. At the same time a circuit is closed from L_2, through stop and start buttons to 2, through the motor of the accelerating relay to 5, through overload relay to 8, and back to L_1. Current through coil D closes contact 1–2 and allows current to flow from L_2 through stop button to 1, through contact 1–2 to 12, through 12–6 to operating coil of starting contactor, and back to L_1, even though the start button is opened. After a certain definite time the timing motor opens contacts 12–6 and closes contacts 12–4. The opening of contacts 12–6 breaks the circuit of the operating coil of the starting contactor, allowing the contactor to open, and closes contact 5. The closing of contacts 12–4 and 5 allows current to flow from L_2

FIG. 167 *Magnetic compensator for squirrel-cage motor. (Westinghouse Electric Corp.)*

through the stop button to 1, through contact 1–2 to 12, through contact 12–4, through the operating coil of the run contactor, through contact 5, through the overload relay to 8, and back to L_1. The operating coil of the running contactor is thus energized, and this contactor closes, applying full voltage to the motor. Opening the overload relay or pressing the stop button will open the circuit of coil D. This de-energizing of D will allow contact 1–2 to open, which breaks the circuit to the operating coil of the running contactor, allowing this contactor to open and disconnect the motor from the line.

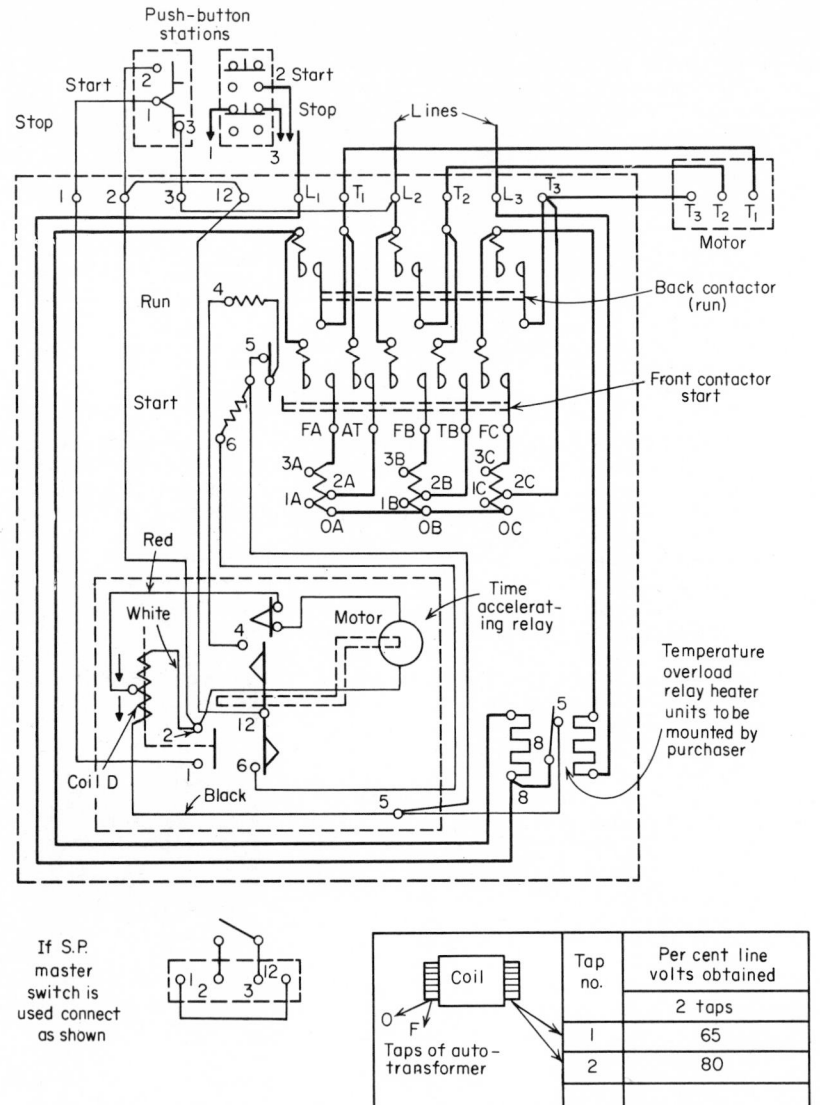

FIG. 168 *Diagram of connections for a magnetic compensator.* (*General Electric Co.*)

313. Commercial primary-resistance starters for squirrel-cage induction motors are made in both manual and magnetic types. The magnetic types generally provide time-limit acceleration. They are similar to the starters for d-c motors except that they are provided with resistors and switching equipment for each phase, all phases being switched simultaneously. In some types the resistance is all cut out in one step, while in others the starting resistance is cut out in several steps. The manual starters may be of the dial or drum type. With the manual starters, overload and undervoltage (if desired) protection must be provided separately from the starter in the same manner as discussed in Sec. **284**. A magnetic starter is shown in Fig. 169 and the wiring diagram for a typical magnetic primary-resistance starter in Fig. 170. Magnetic starters are provided with overload protection and either undervoltage protection or release as desired. Primary-resistance starters of the drum and magnetic types can be obtained for reversing or nonreversing service.

Resistance starters (Fig. 171) which feature the graphite compression disk resistors are used for manually starting polyphase squirrel-cage motors where it is desirable that the load be accelerated very smoothly or where the initial starting current must be kept down to prevent lamp flicker. These starters are suitable for use on any application where the time required to bring the motor to full speed does not exceed 15 sec. At least 4 min must elapse between repeated starts.

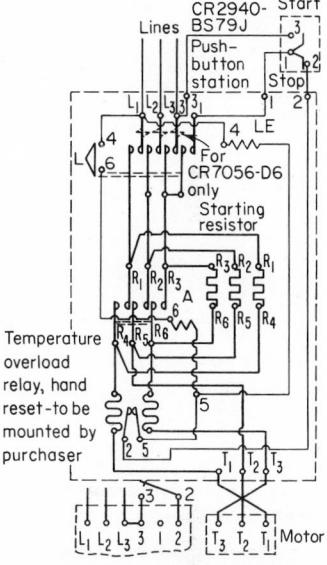

If S.P. Master switch is used in place of push button station connect as shown

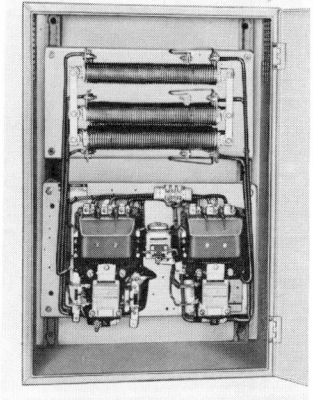

FIG. 169 *Magnetic primary-resistance starter for a squirrel-cage motor. (Westinghouse Electric Corp.)*

FIG. 170 *Diagram of connections for a magnetic primary-resistance starter for a squirrel-cage motor. (General Electric Co.)*

The hand lever mounted on the right side of these starters is used to control the compression of the graphite disk in the resistors and thus obtain stepless control of the starting current. As the handle is raised, the resistance in the line becomes less and less, until at the "on" position, the resistor units are shorted out by a magnetic contactor, two motor overload relays are introduced, and no-voltage protection is automatically provided. The starting lever is then returned to the "off" position. The motor is stopped by pushing the molded "stop" button mounted in the cover of the starter cabinet.

Stepless compression resistance starters (Fig. 172) are designed for automatically starting squirrel-cage motors at reduced voltage. They take care of two specific requirements, namely, to increase the starting current steplessly, thereby preventing lamp flicker on network systems used for both power and light, and to provide velvet-smooth acceleration for squirrel-cage motors used on applications where a starting shock to the driven machine is objectionable or might cause real trouble.

These starters utilize graphite disk resistors which vary in resistance smoothly and steplessly as pressure is applied to the column of disks. Pressure is applied by the d-c solenoid and the rate by which pressure is applied can be varied over a wide range. The motor starting current is gradually increased without any sudden inrush, so that lamp flicker on interconnected power and lighting circuits is eliminated. The load is accelerated smoothly without any sudden jerk.

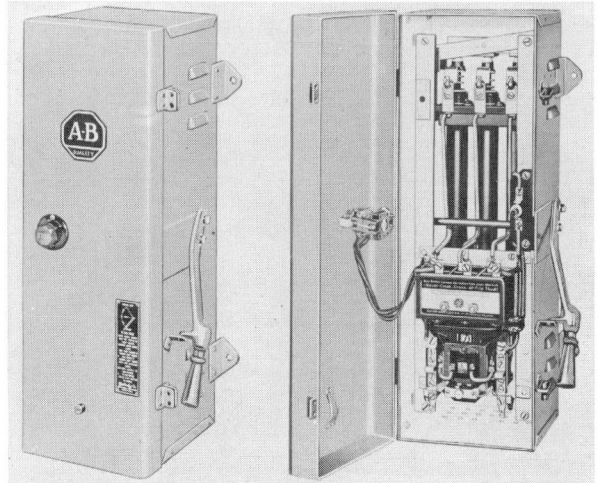

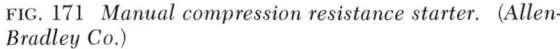

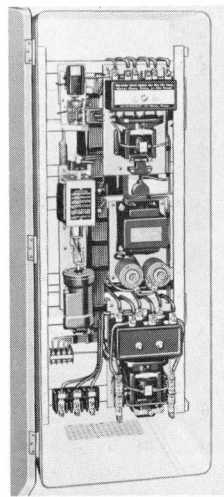

FIG. 171 *Manual compression resistance starter.* (*Allen-Bradley Co.*)

FIG. 172 *Automatic compression resistance starter.* (*Allen-Bradley Co.*)

314. Control apparatus for multispeed squirrel-cage induction motors is made in the following types:

1. Across-the-line starters.
    a. Mechanically interlocked manual switches or circuit breakers.
    b. Drum switches.
    c. Electrically interlocked magnetic contactors.
2. Primary-resistor reduced-voltage starters.
    a. Drum switches.
    b. Magnetic.

The fundamental principles and general construction of these starters are similar to starters of the corresponding types for single-speed, squirrel-cage motors, except that they must provide means for making the necessary changes in the connections of the stator winding for different speeds. Where separate switches are employed for the different connections, provision should be made for mechanically or electrically interlocking the switches. Otherwise the switches for different speeds might accidentally be closed at the same time and cause a short circuit.

315. Starters for Automatic-start Induction Motors. The starters for automatic-start induction motors of the normal-construction type may consist of any one of the types of across-the-line starters as described in preceding sections for single-speed polyphase squirrel-cage induction motors. Automatic-start induction motors of the special construction described in Sec. 170 are started with magnetic starters. These starters consist of a primary contactor, a secondary contactor, thermal overload relays, and a timing relay mounted in a common enclosure. When the push button or the automatic control is actuated, the primary magnetic contactor closes immediately, connecting the line to the motor. The secondary magnetic contactor is still open, the low-resistance winding is open-circuited, and the high-resistance short-circuited winding limits the starting current and produces a correspondingly high starting torque. The motor commences to turn and comes quickly up to speed, and after a certain time interval the secondary magnetic contactor closes, short-circuiting the low-resistance winding. The motor then operates with low slip and temperature rise and with good efficiency until it is shut down by the operation of the push button or automatic control, when the magnetic contactors open and the motor is ready for another start. The timing relay is adjustable over a wide range, and its operation is not affected by temperature or age.

316. Controllers for wound-rotor motors are manufactured in dial, drum, and magnetic types. The same piece of equipment is utilized for both starting and speed control when speed control is desired. The same precautions must be taken in using a controller for speed control, however, as are outlined in Sec. **290** for armature speed controllers for d-c motors.

317. Dial controllers for wound-rotor motors are similar to dial controllers for d-c motors, except that they have two or three sets of resistances controlled by means of two or three contact arms (Fig. 173). These controllers control the resistance in the

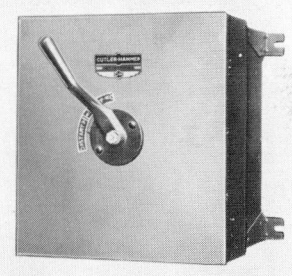

FIG. 173 *Dial-type starter or speed regulator for wound-rotor motor. (Cutler-Hammer Inc.)*

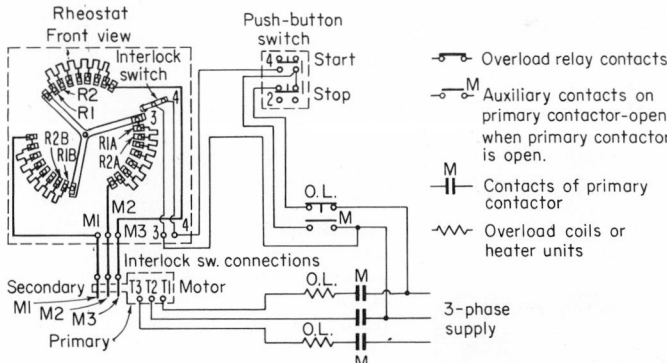

FIG. 174 *Diagram of connections for dial-type secondary controller with primary magnetic switch interlocked with secondary controller.*

rotor circuit only, so a separate switch and overload protection must be provided in the stator circuit. It is best to have this primary line switch of the magnetic type so that it can be electrically interlocked with the secondary controller. With such an arrangement the motor cannot be started unless the resistance is cut into the rotor circuit. The connections of a wound-rotor motor with such a controller are shown in Fig. 174. For reversing service a reversing switch is provided in the stator circuit.

318. Drum controllers for wound-rotor motors are similar in appearance and general construction to those employed for d-c motors (see Fig. 140), except that the movable contacts control two or three sets of resistances instead of only one set. In addition to those contacts for controlling the rotor resistance, some drum controllers are provided with contacts for opening and closing the stator circuit. If the drum is not so designed, it is best to have the line switch of the magnetic type so interlocked with the secondary

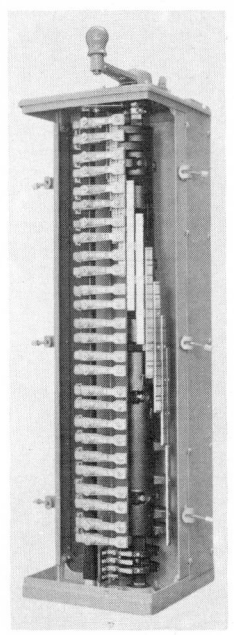

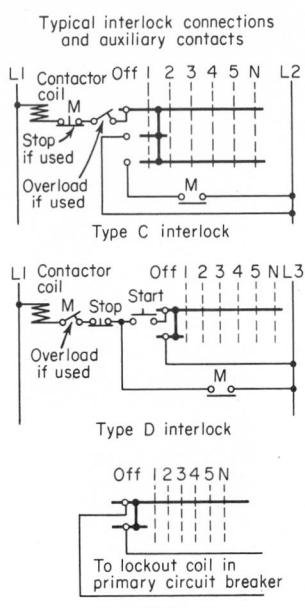

Typical interlock connections and auxiliary contacts

Type C interlock

Type D interlock

Type E interlock

FIG. 175 *Drum controller for secondary control of wound-rotor motors. (Cutler-Hammer Inc.)*

controller that the line switch cannot be closed unless the resistance is cut into the rotor circuit (Fig. 175).

Controllers of this type are suitable for nonreversing or reversing service. Overload protection and undervoltage protection, if desired, must be provided in the stator circuit.

319. Magnetic controllers for wound-rotor induction motors consist of a primary contactor and one or more secondary contactors, depending upon the number of steps of secondary resistance employed. They can be obtained for reversing or nonreversing duty. Reversing starters require two electrically interlocked primary contactors. Time acceleration is employed for most of these controllers, but current limit or frequency limit is used for some applications. A typical magnetic controller for a wound-rotor motor is shown in Fig. 176.

A multicircuit-escapement-type timing relay controls the sequence and time of operation of the successive contactors. A controller using frequency control of acceleration is shown in Fig. 177.

320. A-c protective panels (Fig. 178) are employed primarily for the protection of crane installations. They provide overload, undervoltage, and short-circuit protection.

321. A-c safety disconnect switches are designed especially for crane installations. They perform the same functions as the d-c safety disconnect switches discussed in Sec. **297.**

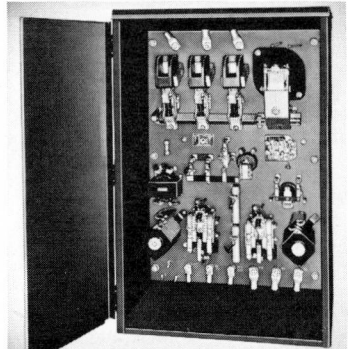

FIG. 176 *Magnetic controller for wound-rotor motor using time-limit control. (Westinghouse Electric Corp.)*

FIG. 177 *Magnetic controller for wound-rotor motor using frequency control of acceleration.* (*Square D Co.*)

322. The starting equipment for the commutator type of polyphase induction motor generally consists simply of some type of across-the-line starter, as described in Secs. **303** to **308**. In the special cases where resistance is connected in series with the secondary for starting, the control would be similar to that employed for wound-rotor motors. The speed control can be regulated by shifting the brushes in any one of the following three ways:

1. By means of a handwheel mounted on the motor.

2. By means of a handwheel located conveniently for the operator and connected to the brush-operating shaft by a chain drive.

3. By means of a pilot motor and reduction-gear mechanism which is mounted on the main motor frame and controlled by push buttons located at the most convenient point for the operator.

Typical connections for a magnetic controller used when motor speed is hand adjusted are shown in Fig. 179. The operating coil of the contactor is connected in series

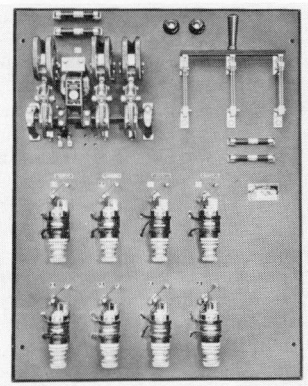

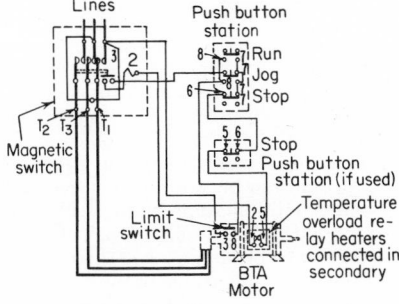

FIG. 178 *A-c protective panel.* (*Square D Co.*)

FIG. 179 *Diagram of connections for control of commutator-type polyphase induction motor when using hand adjustment of speed.* (*General Electric Co.*)

with a limit switch on the motor, so that the contactor will not operate unless the brushes are adjusted to the low-speed position. When a secondary resistor is employed for special starting conditions or for obtaining creeping speeds, a magnetic controller is always employed. This controller will consist of a primary contactor electrically interlocked with a secondary contactor.

323. The control equipment for synchronous motors of conventional design is the same as that for squirrel-cage induction motors with the addition of the necessary field-control equipment. The control equipment is usually of either a semiautomatic or full-automatic type. The semiautomatic type for reduced-voltage transformer starting consists of a standard manual compensator, a field-actuating relay and contactor, a field rheostat, and overload and undervoltage protective devices. When the starter is in the "off" position, the field circuit is short-circuited through a proper value of resistance. The throwing of the handle of the compensator to the "start" position connects the motor to the line through the low-voltage taps of the compensator, leaving the field short-circuited. When the handle is thrown to the "run" position, the motor is connected directly to the full line voltage, and the field-actuating relay is energized. When the motor has reached approximately synchronous speed or after a definite time, the relay operates and energizes the field contactor, which applies excitation to the motor field.

The essential parts of a full-automatic controller for reduced-voltage transformer starting are a line contactor, an accelerating contactor, a definite-time relay, a field-actuating relay and contactor, an autotransformer, a field rheostat, and overload and undervoltage protective devices. When the controller is in the "off" position, the field circuit is short-circuited through the proper value of resistance. Pushing the start button energizes the accelerating contactor, which connects the autotransformer to the line and the motor to the secondary taps of the autotransformer. At the same time the definite-time relay is energized. After the definite-time interval, which corresponds to the setting of the definite-time relay, the accelerating contactor opens and the line contactor closes. The opening of the accelerating contactor disconnects the autotransformer from the line and disconnects the motor from the autotransformer. The closing of the line contactor connects the motor directly to the line and energizes the field-actuating relay. When the motor reaches approximately synchronous speed, the field relay closes and energizes the field contactor, which closes and applies excitation to the field circuit.

An automatic starter for full-voltage starting of synchronous motors (Figs. 180 and 181) consists of a line contactor, a field-actuating relay and contactor, a field rheostat, and overload and undervoltage protective devices. Pushing the start button energizes the line contactor and connects the motor directly across the line with the field short-circuited through the proper value of resistance. When the motor reaches nearly synchronous speed, the contacts of the field-actuating relay automatically close. At a definite time after this the field contactor closes, applying excitation to the field circuit.

Resistance starters for synchronous motors of conventional design are generally fully automatic. They are similar to primary-resistance starters for squirrel-cage induction motors with, as mentioned above, the necessary relays and contactors for field control.

A saturable-reactor type of controller is employed sometimes for very large motors when a large number of starting steps are required. The principle of this method of acceleration is illustrated in Fig. 182. Each phase is supplied with a saturable reactor, which is built on a three-leg iron core. Coils on the outside legs of the reactors are connected in series with the motor, and coils on the middle leg are connected to a source of direct current in series with a rheostat. In starting the motor the d-c coils are at first disconnected from their supply. The reactor then has a high impedance to alternating current and limits the first inrush of current. The d-c coils are then energized with all the resistance of their control rheostat cut into the circuit. The current in the d-c coils decreases the impedance of the a-c coils. As the rheostat cuts resistance out of the d-c circuit, the direct current increases still further, reducing the impedance of the a-c coils until the reactor core is saturated and the impedance of the a-c coils is practically zero. A large number of steps is thus easily available for starting the motor. An actual controller would generally be automatically operated and would include field-control equipment for the motor.

324. The control equipment for synchronous motors with wound-rotor secondaries will generally consist of a fully automatic magnetic controller of the same general type as used for wound-rotor induction motors with the addition of relays and contactors for field control.

325. Control Equipment for Single-phase Motors. Single-phase motors are almost always started by throwing directly across the line. Some type of across-the-line starter similar to those discussed in Secs. **303** to **308** for polyphase motors is employed.

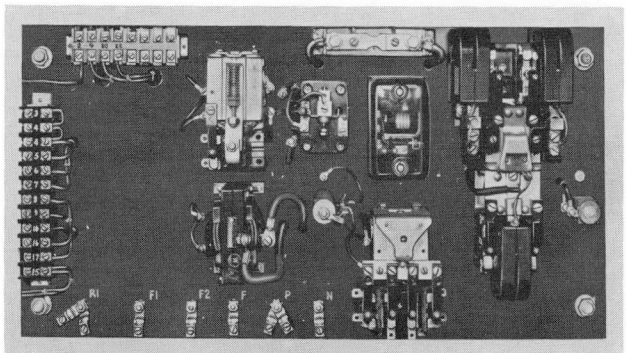

I. *Control panel removed from case.*

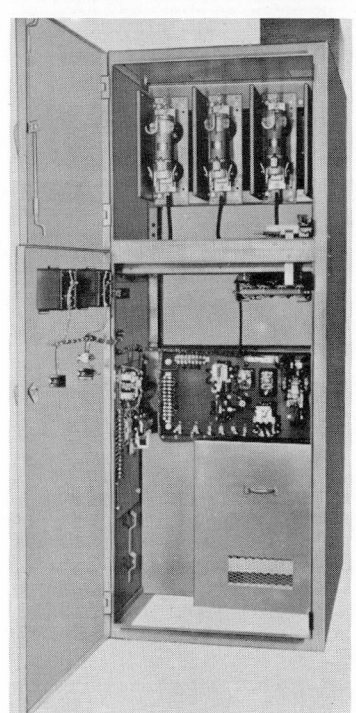

II. *Complete starter in case.*

FIG. 180 *Automatic synchronous-motor starter. (Westinghouse Electric Corp.)*

Some of the manual types with thermal overload protection are frequently called secondary breakers. They are not really circuit breakers, for they are not designed for interrupting short circuits. Typical manual across-the-line starters are shown in Fig. 183.

When the starting current of the larger sizes is greater than allowable, a dial or drum starting rheostat similar to those for d-c motors is generally employed.

MOTOR DRIVES AND APPLICATION

326. Design of Motor Drives. The proper design of motor drives for machines is a very important problem. It involves not only the selection of a type and rating of motor but also selection of a method of connecting the motor to the driven machine and selection of control equipment. It is affected by power supply, driven-machine requirements, space limitations, safety and working conditions for operators, initial cost and operating costs, production and quality of product, and surrounding conditions. The objective is to obtain a final installation which will be the best when all considerations are taken into account. The manner of attacking and the complexity of the solution of the problem depend upon the particular case. In some cases the limitations are so definitely fixed that they dictate only one answer. For instance, a machine requires a speed of 1,600 rpm and a full-load power of 24 hp with a very occasional peak of 28 hp and an average load of 20 hp. It is not necessary to maintain an absolutely fixed ratio of speed between driving and driven shaft. No speed control is required, but the speed should not vary more than 10 per cent with load

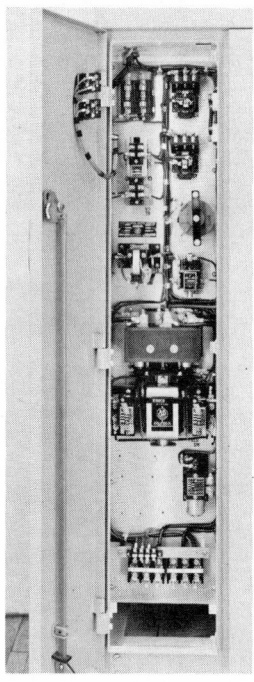

FIG. 181 *Automatic synchronous-motor starter. (Allen-Bradley Co.)*

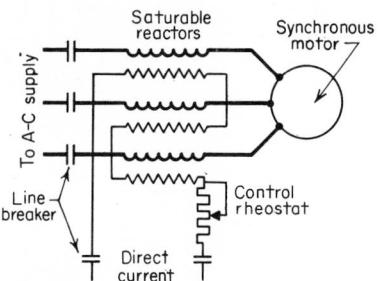

FIG. 182 *Connections for starting synchronous motor with saturable reactors.*

changes. The starting-torque requirements are very light, but the power company will allow only exceptionally low starting currents. The power supply is 60 cycles, 220 volts, three-phase. The machine is operated in a dry and clean location with normal temperatures. In this case there is no difficulty in making the proper selection. A normal-torque, normal-starting-current, or a normal-torque, low-starting-current 25-hp, four-pole, 220-volt, three-phase 1,800-rpm, open squirrel-cage induction motor with reduced-voltage starting equipment would be used. The motor would be belt-connected to the machine.

In many cases the problem is not so simple and it cannot be split up into several simple isolated problems that can be answered individually, such as selection of type and rating of motor, method of connection, etc. The selection of the type of motor and the method of connection are interdependent, so that the whole problem must be considered as a unit, carefully weighing all factors involved. Generally several different plans can be used. Each one should be worked out with respect to initial cost, operating costs, and maintenance; then the possible solutions should be weighed against each other, taking into account, in addition to the above costs, the effect of the proposed drives upon safety and working conditions of operators and upon production and quality of product.

It is evident that in order to design proper motor-drive installations it is necessary to have a knowledge of the different methods of mechanical connections and of their advantages and limitations and all the other important factors that will affect the correct selection of motors. In the following paragraphs the important points that must be considered in the selection of motors and mechanical connections are discussed, followed by tables which, it is believed, will be helpful guides to proper selection. In the latter part of this division (Secs. **377** to **420**) is given the procedure for the design of the different types of drives.

327. Methods of Driving Machines. There are two methods that can be employed for driving the individual machines of a shop. Each machine may be equipped with its own individual motor. This is called individual drive. In other cases a single motor may be employed to drive a group of machines by means of shafting and belts. This is called group drive. Group drive at one time was

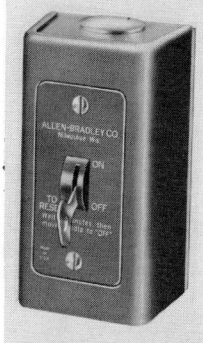

I. *Enclosed type.*   II. *Open type for mounting in wall switch box.*

FIG. 183 *Manual across-the-line starters for single-phase motors. (Allen-Bradley Co.)*

widely used. Individual drive, however, has proved to have so many advantages that it is used to drive practically all modern machines.

328. Motors can be mechanically connected to machines in several ways. When the speed of the motor is the same as the speed desired for the machine, direct coupling of the motor shaft to the machine shaft is used. When the speed of the motor is different from the speed of the machine shaft, a connection must be used which will give the proper speed ratio between the motor and the machine. A speed ratio may be secured by using a flat belt, V belts, a chain, or a set of gears. With belts the speed ratio is inversely proportional to the effective diameter of the two pulleys. With chain or gears the speed ratio is inversely proportional to the number of teeth on the two sprockets or gears. In some cases a variation in speed can be obtained by using variable-diameter pulleys or more than one set of gears, which can be shifted.

329. The factors to be considered in selecting the method of connection of the motor to the machine are the speed ratio desired, the peak loads to be transmitted, the positiveness of the drive, the space required, the noise, the maintenance, the appearance, and the first cost of the motor and the method of connection. Since the horsepower of a motor is given by the following formula,

$$\text{hp} = \frac{6.28 \times \text{rpm} \times T}{33,000} \text{ (see Sec. } \mathbf{68}, \text{ Div. 1)} \tag{10}$$

it follows that for a given horsepower, if the speed of the motor is increased, the torque needed is decreased. To produce torque in a motor costs money for windings to create the necessary magnetic flux and for steel to provide a path for the flux. Therefore, the smaller the torque and consequently the higher the speed, the cheaper will be the motor. For very high speeds, however, the extra strength which must be built into the rotor to enable it to withstand the high centrifugal force more than offsets the saving due to the lower torque required.

The 1,800-rpm motor is usually the cheapest motor, higher speed motors being more expensive on account of the higher centrifugal force and lower speed motors being more expensive on account of the greater flux and torque required. Therefore, one of the first factors to consider in the selection of the mechanical connection of the motor to the machine is to see if an 1,800-rpm motor can be used. The speed of the shaft on the machine to which the motor is to be connected varies with the type of machine and is frequently much lower than 1,800 rpm. For example, on forging machines using large flywheels the shaft speed may be as low as 50 to 60 rpm; on machine tools, such as lathes, drills, millers, etc., it may be between 200 and 300 rpm. Speeds as high as 1,000 to 2,000 rpm occur on grinders and woodworking machines. In most cases, therefore, some reduction in speed is required between the motor and the machine. Direct connection of the motor to the machine shaft with a flexible or rigid coupling can be used only where the speed of the shaft can be the same as the speed of the motor. Belts, gears, or chains must be used in all other cases to effect a change of speed between the motor and the shaft.

For a speed of 1,200 rpm, a 1,200-rpm motor directly coupled to the shaft will usually be more practical than an 1,800-rpm motor with a belt, gear, or chain connection to the 1,200-rpm shaft. For speeds between 600 and 13 rpm, gear motors can be used. These motors have a rotor speed of 1,800 rpm and gears built into the end frame of the motor to give the output shaft speed desired. These motors cost about twice as much as a high-speed motor with belt drive but are frequently used on account of the saving in space and elimination of troublesome belts. They are available in three classes of construction, according to the severity of service (see Sec. **122**).

330. Belt drive (refer to Secs. **377** to **403**) is the least expensive method of connection where speed ratio is required. The factors to be considered when applying a belt drive are speed ratio, pulley sizes, belt speeds, distance between pulley centers, type of belt, size of belt, number of belts, number of pulleys, use of idler pulleys, and slippage. The maximum speed ratio which can be obtained with belt drive is limited by the practical sizes of pulleys obtainable, the arc of contact of the belt on the smaller pulley, and the practical distance between the pulleys. The maximum practical speed ratio may be as high as 10:1 for fractional-horsepower motors but is about 6:1 for ordinary sizes and not more than 4:1 for motors of 50 hp and up. As the diameter of a motor pulley is reduced, the strains on the motor bearings and shaft are increased. A minimum size of pulley is therefore specified by NEMA, as given in Sec. **388**. The maximum diameter of a motor pulley is in nearly all cases limited by the belt speed, which should not exceed 5,000 ft per min. This will occur only for machines which operate at a higher speed than the motor. Flat belts are slightly cheaper than V belts but have a shorter life and are more noisy and more dangerous. Flat belts with a high speed ratio usually require idler pulleys, and space must be available for the idler pulley when required. There is always some slippage between the belt and the pulleys, and a belt drive should be used only where a positive drive is not required.

331. Maximum Horsepower Limits for Two-bearing Motors for Belt Drive
(General Electric Co.)

Motor speed, rpm	Flat-belt drive, max hp	V-belt drive, max hp	Motor speed, rpm	Flat-belt drive, max hp	V-belt drive, max hp
1,700–1,800	40	60; ball-brg, 75	680–720	200	300
1,440–1,500	40	60; ball-brg, 75	560–600	200	300
1,150–1,200	75	100; ball-brg, 125	500–514	150	300
850– 900	125	200	440–450	150	250

332. Chain drive (refer to Sec. **419**) is a more positive drive than belt drive, and although it is more expensive than belt drive, it is used where slippage under varying loads is not desired. The factors to be considered when applying a chain drive are speed ratio, the size of sprockets, width of chain, chain speed, and noise. The maximum speed ratio for a chain drive is about 8:1 with a maximum chain speed of 1,500 ft per min. For quietness and smoothness a speed of 600 ft per min or less is desirable. A chain drive is more noisy than belt drive.

333. Maximum Horsepower Limits for Two-bearing Motors for Chain Drive
(General Electric Co.)

Motor speed, rpm	Max hp	Motor speed, rpm	Max hp	Motor speed, rpm	Max hp
1,700–1,800	5	1,150–1,200	25	720–750	75
1,440–1,500	10	850– 900	50		

334. Gear drive (refer to Sec. **404**) is an absolutely positive drive but is the most expensive method of connection. The factors to be considered when applying a gear drive are speed ratio, gear sizes, pitch-line speed, space, and noise. The maximum speed ratio is about 10:1 for a single set of gears, but any speed ratio is obtainable by using several sets of gears. Where the pinion of ordinary spur gearing is mounted on the motor shaft, two-bearing motors should be limited to the maximum horsepower values given for chain drive in Sec. **333**. The maximum pitch-line speed with steel pinions is about 1,300 ft per min. Gear drive usually is compact and takes up only a small space but is more noisy than the other methods. It should be used on any application where slippage or breaking of the belt or chain would be seriously dangerous. It can also be used for much larger speed ratios than are practical with belts or gears.

335. Speed Limitations for Belt, Gear, and Chain Drives
(Allis-Chalmers)

This table, based on NEMA definitions, represents good practice (under normal operating conditions) for the use of these drives on motors and generators which are not provided with outboard bearings.

Full-load rpm of motor or generator		Max hp rating of motor	Max kw rating of generator
Above	Including		
Flat-belt drive[a]			
2,400	3,600	20	15
1,800	2,400	30	20
1,200	1,800	40	30
900	1,200	75	50
750	900	125	75
720	750	150	100
560	720	200	150
V-belt drive[b]			
2,400	3,600	20	15
1,800	2,400	40	30
1,200	1,800	75	50
900	1,200	125	75
750	900	200	100
720	750	250	150
560	720	300	200
Gear drive—[c,d]			
1,500	1,800	7½	5
1,200	1,500	15	10
900	1,200	25	15
750	900	50	30
560	750	75	50
Chain drive[e]			
2,400	3,600	20	15
1,800	2,400	40	30
1,200	1,800	75	40
900	1,200	125	75
750	900	200	125
720	750	250	150
560	720	300	200

[a] See NEMA MG1-3.14 and MG1-3.14a for dimensions of standard pulleys and for limiting dimensions of pulleys.

[b] Limiting dimensions of V-belt sheaves for general-purpose motors in frames 505 and smaller are given in NEMA MG1-3.16 and MG1-3.16a. Limiting dimensions for V-belt sheaves for motors in frames larger than 505 have not been standardized; they are specified by the motor manufacturer.

[c] These values are based on the use of steel pinions.

[d] In general, for quiet operation and freedom from severe vibration, the peripheral speed of cut-steel gearing at the pitch diameter should not exceed 1,400 ft per min. For further information, see American Standard Gear Tolerances and Inspection, Publication No. B6.6-1946, or latest revision thereof.

[e] Limiting dimensions of chain-drive sprockets for general-purpose motors in frames 505 and smaller are given in NEMA MG1-3.15 and MG1-3.15a. Limiting dimensions of chain-drive sprockets for motors in frames larger than 505 have not been standardized; they are specified by the motor manufacturer.

NOTES. The above limitations are based on the use of pulleys, etc., as standardized by NEMA. The limitations will be less than those given when motors are belted to low-speed drives, such as countershafts.

The above values are not intended to establish a definite dividing line below which the use of outboard bearings is not standard, but rather to establish a dividing line which will indicate to the motor user what the manufacturers consider to be good practice in general service.

The use of outboard bearings is approved and recommended for belted motors in frame sizes of 250 hp, 575 to 600 rpm and larger.

Where an outboard bearing is specified, it is assumed that the necessary three-bearing-type base plate and slide rails, if required, are included with the motor.

336. Comparison of Methods of Connection for Adjustable-speed Drive

Type of motor	Type of drive	Space required	Speed variation ratio	First cost
Constant speed..........	Variable pitch motor pulley	Same as V-belt connection	$1\frac{1}{4}:1$	Low
Constant speed..........	Separate unit with variable-diameter pulleys	Considerable	$3\frac{1}{2}:1$	Medium
Constant speed..........	Variable-diameter pulley unit built on motor housing	Moderate	$3\frac{1}{2}:1$	Medium
Constant speed..........	Variable-position rollers	Small	$10:1$	High
Adjustable speed........	Direct coupling	Small	$4:1$	High

337. Comparison of Methods of Connection for Constant-speed Drive

Type of drive	Relative noise	Space required	Speed ratio obtainable	Peak load transmitted	First cost
1. Direct coupling, standard motor	0	Small; motor must extend out from end of drive shaft	0	Limited only by motor	1 (considered as 100 per cent)
2. Direct coupling, general-purpose gear motor	Slight	Same as 1. Angle drive obtainable in small motors	Any	Full load	2 times the standard motor
3. Direct coupling, special-purpose gear motor	Slight	Same as 2	Any	150 per cent of full load	$2\frac{1}{2}$ times the standard motor
4. Direct coupling, heavy-duty gear motor	Slight	Same as 2	Any	200 per cent of full load	3 times the standard motor
5. V belt...........	0	Moderate	10:1 in fractional-horsepower sizes; down to 4:1 for 50 hp and up	Any by multiplying motor horsepower by a service factor[1]	$1\frac{1}{3}$ times the standard motor
6. Flat belt........	Considerable	Considerable	Same as 5	Same as 5	Slightly higher than for standard motor
7. Chain...........	Considerable	Moderate	8:1	Same as 5	$1\frac{1}{3}$ times the standard motor
8. Gear...........	High	Small	10:1, single reduction; 100:1, double reduction	Same as 5	$1\frac{1}{2}$ times the standard motor

[1] Refer to Sec. **382**.

338. The important factors to be considered in selecting a motor are:

1. Power supply.
   a. Type of system—d-c or a-c; frequency; number of phases.
   b. Voltage and frequency conditions.
   c. Effect of motors on power-supply system. d. Power rates.
2. Requirements of driven machine.
   a. Speed. b. Mechanical arrangement.
   c. Power and torque. d. Special conditions.
3. Surrounding conditions.
   a. Ambient temperature. b. Atmospheres.
   c. Water. d. Altitude. e. Quietness.
4. Codes, standards, and ordinances.

A summary of motor characteristics is given in Sec. **361**.

339. The type of power-supply system available in most cases answers the question of whether a-c or d-c motors will be used as well as the frequency of the motors if a-c. For most applications either a-c or d-c motors will be satisfactory. In some cases special requirements of extra-wide speed range, large number of adjustable-speed machines, or severe accelerating or reversing duty may justify the conversion of alternating to direct current.

If a new power plant is to be installed, the operating conditions may sometimes affect the choice of current. Even in this case the characteristics of the new plant generally should agree with those of the nearest central station in order to obtain breakdown service and to operate economically with central-station energy on reduced loads. For certain applications, d-c motors are preferable—for example, in adjustable-speed service, as in machine-tool operation, in service where frequent starts must be made with very high torque, or in reversing service, as in the operation of cranes, hoists, etc. The voltage of a-c circuits can be so readily transformed up or down that such energy is more economical for distribution over considerable areas. For plants extending over a considerable area or distributing energy to distances, say, of ¼ mile or more, alternating current is nearly always more economical.

For a-c motors, three-phase, 60 cycles is most desirable except for small fractional-horsepower motors. The demand for two-phase motors is small, and they are therefore not generally available in stock for quick shipment. If a multispeed motor is desired where the power supply is two-phase, it is best to transform to three-phase for this machine, as multispeed motors are difficult to wind for two-phase. Standard 60-cycle motors are usually suitable for operation on 50-cycle systems with some modification in their ratings and characteristics. The demand for 40- or 25-cycle motors is so small that they are not generally available in stock. For special high-speed applications in the woodworking industry and for portable tools, motors of higher frequencies than 60 cycles are available and are sometimes advantageous. The power supply can be obtained by means of an induction frequency changer.

340. The conditions of the supply voltage and frequency, if alternating current, with respect to value and regulation must be known in order to select the proper motors and control. With a-c systems the voltage can, of course, be changed through transformers wherever it is advisable. Table **341** gives a guide for good practice in the maximum and minimum horsepower limits for the different standard motor voltages.

Motors will operate successfully under some conditions of voltage and frequency variations but not necessarily in accordance with the standards established for operation at normal rating (see Sec. **128**).

Where the variations in voltage and frequency exceed those limits, special motors and control will probably be required.

The voltage regulation of the supply should be known in order to select motors which will deliver sufficient torque, even with the probable drop in voltage, to start and carry the load. All induction-motor torques and synchronous-motor starting torque and pull-in torque vary as the voltage squared.

The speed of a-c motors will be affected by the frequency of the supply voltage as discussed in previous sections for each type of motor.

341. Guide to Horsepower Limits of Individual Motors for Different Systems

Voltage	Min hp	Max hp	Voltage	Min hp	Max hp
D-c			A-c, two- and three-phase		
115	None	30	110–115–120	None	15
230	None	200	220–230–240	None	200
550–600	½	None	440–550	None	500
A-c, one-phase			2,200	40	None
110–115–120	None	1½	4,000	75	None
220–230–240	None	10	6,600	400	None
440–550	5	10			

342. The effects of motors and their control on the power-supply system will affect the selection of the proper type of motor.

The effect of motor-starting currents upon the supply and permissible limits for starting currents are discussed in Sec. **130**.

With fluctuating loads, care should be taken to see that the following limits are not exceeded:

1. Frequencies of current pulsation in the range of 250 to 600 per minute may cause objectionable light flicker even if the voltage variation is as small as ½ of 1 per cent.

2. The usual limit for current pulsation is 66 per cent of motor full-load current, although in some cases the system regulation may require a limit of 30 or 40 per cent to avoid light flicker.

343. Effect of Power Rates on Motor Selection. When speed adjustment is required, the energy charge in the power rates should be considered in the selection of the type of motor and in making selection between mechanical adjustable-speed drive and an adjustable-speed motor.

The power rates are generally based on the maximum demand of the consumers. The choice of motor and use of flywheels may smooth out the power demand. This will keep the maximum demand down and lower the rate.

A power-factor clause is incorporated in many rate schedules. These adjust the rate according to the power factor of the load or involve a penalty or bonus for power factors that are below or above certain values. In such cases, consideration should be given to the use of synchronous motors or power capacitors.

344. Effect of Speed Requirements on Motor Selection. Since there is a great difference in the speed characteristics of different types of motors, the maximum allowable speed regulation (variation in speed with load) on the driven machine is an important factor in the selection of the proper motor. The actual operating speed, number of speeds, and the speed range required are factors which must be considered in the joint selection of type of motor and mechanical connection. See Secs. **328** to **337** for description and comparison of different methods of mechanical connection. Where speed control of the driven machine is required, it can be obtained through speed control of a motor of the proper type or by means of a motor coupled to the machine through a mechanical speed-adjusting connection.

Close speed regulation is desirable for many applications such as machine tools, textile machinery, and similar work.

Where large peak loads occur, wide speed regulation is desirable. This will allow the motor to slow down under the peak loads and reduce the horsepower carried at these moments. If the motor has a small speed regulation, it may be greatly overloaded at the peak loads unless the machine is equipped with an exceptionally large motor.

For peak loads occurring periodically, where the peaks occur less than 25 times per minute, flywheels should be employed with motors having a wide speed regulation. This will allow the use of a smaller motor and will tend to even out the peaks of power drawn from the supply.

345. Mechanical-arrangement features of the driven machine should be taken into account in motor selection. The General Electric Co. makes the following recommendations:

1. HORIZONTAL OR VERTICAL SHAFT. Arrangement of the driven machine usually determines whether a horizontal or vertical motor is needed. Horizontal motors are more generally available and less expensive: most grease-lubricated, ball-bearing motors will operate in either position. Fractional-horsepower, waste-packed, sleeve-bearing motors are satisfactory for short periods of vertical operation where no thrust is involved.

2. TILTED SHAFT. If momentary, this will require special construction of bearing housings for oil-ring-lubricated, sleeve-bearing motors, to avoid loss of lubricant. In case of long periods of tilted operation, bearings suitable for end thrust may be necessary. Ball-bearing motors with grease lubrication are suitable for tilted operation.

3. INVERTED OPERATION AND ROLLING. *a.* Where the driven machine requires mounting the motor with the feet above or to one side of the shaft, rearrangement of the end shields of most motors makes them suitable.

b. If the driven machine requires operation of the motor at a changing angle from the horizontal (shaft remaining horizontal) of more than 10 or 12 deg, ball-bearing motors will usually be required. Within this angle, sleeve-bearing motors with modified oil gages are applicable.

4. PORTABLE MACHINES. A portable type of driven machine may require motors

and control of greater compactness and less weight than standard and may necessitate special bearing construction for ring-oiled, sleeve-bearing motors.

346. The horsepower and torque requirements of the driven machine are main factors in determining the proper motor rating, type of motor, and motor-control equipment. The greatest care should be exercised in determining as accurately as possible the horsepower required and both the starting- and running-torque requirements. The motor not only must have sufficient horsepower and torque capacity under running conditions but must be able to develop sufficient torque at starting in order to start the load satisfactorily under the most severe starting conditions that may be encountered in that particular application. Sometimes all these requirements will be known from past experience. In all cases, where it is possible, it is best to conduct tests so that the power and torque requirements can be accurately determined. Money spent in such determinations is wisely expended even if it requires the rental of a motor for conducting the tests. In performing tests it should be remembered that the test-motor losses must be subtracted from the power input to the motor, since the motor to be purchased is rated on horsepower output.

If the power and torque requirements cannot be determined from past experience or test, the information can generally be obtained from the manufacturer of the machine to be driven or from the motor experts of motor manufacturers. Wherever there seems to be any question with respect to the accuracy of such information, it should be carefully checked, since the machine-tool manufacturers often overestimate the horsepower required so as to be on the safe side. The result is that the motors run only partially loaded at considerably reduced efficiency. The electrical losses and interest and depreciation on the unnecessary extra investment may be a considerable amount in a large installation.

Whenever the frequency of the starting periods is great, more than four to six times per hour, it is best to consult the motor manufacturers. Such frequent starting may require special motors and controls.

Many machines work on a definite duty cycle that repeats at regular intervals.[1] Often this horsepower value occurs during the cycle when the values of power required and the length of their duration are known, and the rating of the motor required can be calculated by the rms method.

Multiply the square of the horsepower required for each part of the cycle by the time in seconds necessary to complete that part of the cycle. Divide the sum of these results by the effective time in seconds to complete the whole cycle. Extract the square root of this last result. This gives the rms horsepower. If the motor is stopped for part of the cycle, only one-third of the rest period should be used in determining the effective time for open motors (enclosed motors use one-half of the rest period). This is due to the reduction in cooling effect when the motor is at rest.

Example. Assume a machining operation where an open motor operates at 8-hp load for 4 min, 6-hp load for 50 sec, 10-hp load for 3 min and the motor is at rest for 6 min, after which the cycle is repeated.

$$\text{rms hp} = \sqrt{\frac{(8^2 \times 240) + (6^2 \times 50) + (10^2 \times 180)}{240 + 50 + 180 + \dfrac{360}{3}}} = \sqrt{59.5} = 7.7 \text{ hp}$$

Use 7.5-hp motor.

NOTE. For fast-repeating cycles involving reversals and deceleration by plugging, the additional heating due to reversing and external WR^2 loads must be taken into consideration, and a more elaborate duty-cycle analysis than shown above is required. It is necessary to know the torque, time, and motor speed for each portion of the duty cycle—such as acceleration, running with load, running without load, deceleration, and at rest.

For such detailed duty cycles it is sometimes more convenient to calculate on the basis of torque required rather than on the horsepower basis. The following formula may be helpful:

[1] Courtesy of Westinghouse Electric Corp.

Accelerating time for constant torque

$$\text{Time in sec} = \frac{wk^2 \times (\text{change in rpm})}{308 \times \text{torque (lb-ft) available from motor}} \tag{11}$$

The above formula can be used when the accelerating torque is substantially constant. If the accelerating torque varies considerably, the accelerating time should be calculated in increments; the average accelerating torque during the increment should be used. The size of the increment used depends on the accuracy required. Fair accuracy is obtained if the minimum accelerating torque is not less than 50 per cent of the maximum accelerating torque during the increment.

In addition to determining the horsepower rating with regard to heat capacity, a check should also be made to assure that the peak loads, even though of short duration, imposed by the driven machine do not exceed the maximum power the motor will develop without stalling. From tables of locked-rotor and maximum running torque values, determine the maximum torque in terms of full-load torque. This value should always exceed peak torque imposed by the duty cycle. Preferably, this should be at least 25 per cent greater in order to compensate for unusual conditions, such as low voltage, high friction, etc.

347. Horsepower Rating of Motor. After having determined the horsepower requirements of the load, select a motor with sufficient horsepower rating to take care of these requirements. See Sec. **128** for discussion of motor ratings.

348. Any special conditions of operation of the driven machine must be carefully considered. Some machines such as propeller-type fans and deep-well pumps impose an axial thrust on the motor bearings. In some cases standard ball-bearing motors will furnish sufficient thrust capacity. For extremely heavy thrusts, special plate-type, oil-lubricated bearings may be required.

For some tools such as precision grinders, in order to ensure high quality of the finished product, specially balanced motors are required in order to give very small amplitudes of vibration.

Sometimes the driven machine requires limited or even zero end play. This will necessitate the use of preloaded ball bearings or sleeve bearings with end-play-limiting devices.

349. The surrounding conditions of temperature, atmospheres, and water must be carefully determined in the application of motors. Refer to Sec. **126** for a discussion of the different standard types of enclosures available and a guide to the surrounding conditions under which their applications will be satisfactory. For a discussion of rating of motors and effect of room temperatures upon operation, refer to Sec. **128**. When the motor and control will be subjected to any unusual risk such as those listed below, the manufacturers should be consulted.

UNUSUAL RISKS

1. Exposed to chemical fumes.   2. Operated in damp places.
3. Operated at speeds in excess of specified overspeed.
4. Exposed to combustible or explosive dust.
5. Exposed to gritty or conducting dust.   6. Exposed to lint.
7. Exposed to steam.   8. Operated in poorly ventilated rooms.
9. Operated in pits or where entirely enclosed in boxes.
10. Exposed to inflammable or explosive gases.
11. Exposed to temperatures above 40°C or below 10°C.
12. Exposed to oil vapor.   13. Exposed to salt air.
14. Exposed to abnormal shock or vibration from external sources.

350. Water (General Electric Co.). Where operation for long periods under water is required, special enclosed equipment, with counter air pressure to prevent the entrance of water, is usually necessary.

For occasional flooding or submersion, extremely tight totally enclosed nonventilated motors equipped with stuffing boxes may suffice.

Where "hosing down" or splashing of water is involved, splashproof motors will usually meet all but extreme conditions, the latter requiring enclosed motors.

351. Altitude (General Electric Co.). No change in design is considered necessary for most electric machines for altitudes not exceeding 3,300 ft above sea level. For higher altitudes, the temperature rise of electric machinery generally will increase approximately 1 per cent for each 330-ft increase in altitude above 3,300 ft.

352. Quietness (General Electric Co.). Installations in residences and in public buildings, such as theaters, hospitals, and schools, may require the use of quiet motors and sound-isolating bases. In many cases, special building layout and construction may be needed to ensure the necessary degree of quietness.

353. Codes, Standards, Ordinances (General Electric Co.). Motors and control must conform to local and national standards such as shown below in order to (1) permit connection of power, (2) satisfy safety and fire requirements, and (3) permit lowest insurance rates.

1. NEMA standards, which specify mounting dimensions for induction motors and, in general, minimum performance characteristics for all types of motors and control.

2. IEEE standards, which specify temperature limits for insulation materials and prescribe the methods of rating and testing apparatus.

3. The National Electrical Code, which is the general guide of inspectors in determining acceptability of enclosures, protection, and installation of motors.

4. State laws, which stress safety and reduction of fire hazards.

5. City ordinances, which may specify particular construction considered necessary locally to avoid fires and accidents.

354. Standard Ratings of Motors. The standard horsepower ratings of motors are $\frac{1}{20}$, $\frac{1}{12}$, $\frac{1}{8}$, $\frac{1}{6}$, $\frac{1}{4}$, $\frac{1}{3}$, $\frac{1}{2}$, $\frac{3}{4}$, 1, $1\frac{1}{2}$, 2, 3, 5, $7\frac{1}{2}$, 10, 15, 20, 25, 30, 40, 50, 60, 75, 100, 125, 150, 200, 225, 250, 300, 350, 400, 450, 500, 600, 700, 800, 900, 1,000, 1,250, 1,500, 1,750, 2,000, 2,250, 2,500, 3,000, 3,500, 4,000, 4,500, and 5,000 hp.

The standard full-load speed ratings for constant-speed, integral-horsepower d-c motors are 3,500, 1,750, 1,150, 850, 690, 575, 500, 450, 400, 350, 300, 250, 200, 150, and 100 rpm.

The standard full-load speed ratings for constant-speed, fractional-horsepower d-c motors from $\frac{1}{20}$ to $\frac{1}{3}$ hp are 3,450, 1,725, 1,140, and 850 rpm. For motors of $\frac{1}{2}$ hp they are 3,450, 1,725, and 1,140. For motors of $\frac{3}{4}$ hp they are 3,450 and 1,725.

The standard speeds for 60-cycle synchronous motors are 3,600, 1,800, 1,200, 900, 720, 600, 514, 450, 400, 360, 327, 300, 277, 257, 240, 225, 200, 180, 164, 150, 138, 128, 120, 109, 100, 95, 90, 86, and 80 rpm.

The standard synchronous speeds for 60-cycle, polyphase induction motors are 3,600, 1,800, 1,200, 900, 720, 600, 514, and 450 rpm.

The standard synchronous speeds for 60-cycle, single-phase motors are 3,600, 1,800, 1,200, and 900 rpm.

The approximate full-load speeds of induction motors can be obtained from the synchronous speeds by means of the approximate full-load slips (see Sec. **361**).

The standard voltages are as follows:

1. Direct-current integral-horsepower motors and single-phase and universal motors .... 115 and 230 volts
2. Direct-current fractional-horsepower motors .... 32, 115, and 230 volts
3. Alternating-current polyphase motors.. 110, 208,[a] 220, 440, 550, 2,300, 4,000, 4,600, and 6,600 volts

[a] Applies to 60-cycle circuits only.

NOTE. It is not practical to build motors of all horsepower ratings for all of the standard voltages.

The standard frequencies are as follows:

1. ALTERNATING-CURRENT MOTORS. The standard frequency shall be 25, 50, and 60 cycles per second.

2. UNIVERSAL MOTORS. The standard frequency shall be 60 cycles a-c.

NOTE. Universal motors will operate successfully on all frequencies below 60 cycles and on direct current.

355. Service Factors. A general-purpose a-c motor, or, when applicable any a-c motor having a rated temperature rise of 40°C continuous duty, is suitable for continuous operation at rated load under normal conditions. When the voltage and frequency are maintained at the values specified on the nameplate, the motor may be overloaded up to the horsepower obtained by multiplying the rated horsepower by the service factor shown on the nameplate. When the motor is operated at any service factor greater than 1, it will have a higher temperature rise and may have different efficiency, power factor, and speed than at rated load, while the locked-rotor torque and current and breakdown torque will remain unchanged. Usual service factors are described in the accompanying table.

Service Factors

Horse-power	Synchronous speed, rpm						
	3,600	1,800	1,200	900	720	600	514
$\frac{1}{20}$	1.4	1.4	1.4	1.4			
$\frac{1}{12}$	1.4	1.4	1.4	1.4			
$\frac{1}{8}$	1.4	1.4	1.4	1.4			
$\frac{1}{6}$	1.35	1.35	1.35	1.35			
$\frac{1}{4}$	1.35	1.35	1.35	1.35			
$\frac{1}{3}$	1.35	1.35	1.35	1.35			
$\frac{1}{2}$	1.25	1.25	1.25	1.15[a]			
$\frac{3}{4}$	1.25	1.25	1.15[a]	1.15[a]			
1	1.25	1.15[a]	1.15[a]	1.15[a]			
$1\frac{1}{2}$–125[a]	1.15	1.15	1.15	1.15	1.15	1.15	1.15
150[a]	1.15	1.15	1.15	1.15	1.15	1.15	
200[a]	1.15	1.15	1.15	1.15	1.15		

[a] For polyphase squirrel-cage integral-horsepower motors these service factors apply only to designs A, B, and C motors.

356. Effects of Variation of Voltage and Frequency upon the Performance of Induction Motors (NEMA Standards).

1. Induction motors are at times operated on circuits of voltage or frequency other than those for which the motors are rated. Under such conditions, the performance of the motor will vary from the standard rating. The following is a brief statement of some operating results caused by small variations of voltage and frequency and is indicative of the general character of changes produced by such variations in operating conditions.

2. Voltage variations of 10 per cent on power circuits are allowed in most commission rules. However, changing the voltage applied to an induction motor has the effect of changing its proper rating as to power factor and efficiency in proportion to the square of the applied voltage. Thus a 5-hp motor operated at 10 per cent above the rated voltage would have characteristics proper for a 6-hp motor (6.05-hp to be exact) and operated at 10 per cent below the rated voltage, those of a 4-hp motor (more exactly, 4.05 hp). It is, of course, obvious that if the rating of a motor were greatly increased in this way, the safe heating would frequently be exceeded.

3. In a motor of normal characteristics at full-rated horsepower load, a 10 per cent increase of voltage above that given on the nameplate would usually result in a slight improvement in efficiency and a decided lowering in power factor. A 10 per cent decrease of voltage below that given on the nameplate would usually give a slight decrease of efficiency and an increase in power factor.

4. The locked-rotor and pull-out torque will be proportional to the square of the voltage applied. With a 10 per cent increase or decrease in voltage from that given on the nameplate, the heating at rated horsepower load will not exceed safe limits when operating in ambient temperatures of 40°C or less, although the rated temperature rise may be exceeded.

5. An increase of 10 per cent in voltage will result in a decrease of slip of about 17 per cent, while a reduction of 10 per cent will increase the slip about 21 per cent. Thus, if the slip at rated voltage were 5 per cent, it would be increased to 6.05 per cent if the voltage were reduced 10 per cent.

6. A frequency higher than the rated frequency usually improves the power factor but decreases locked-rotor torque and increases the speed, friction, and windage. At a frequency lower than the rated frequency, the speed is, of course, decreased, locked-rotor torque is increased, and power factor is slightly decreased. For certain kinds of motor load, such as in textile mills, close frequency regulation is essential.

7. If variations in both voltage and frequency occur simultaneously, the effects will be superimposed. Thus, if the voltage is high and the frequency low, the locked-rotor torque will be very greatly increased, but the power factor will be decreased and the temperature rise increased with normal load.

8. The foregoing facts apply particularly to general-purpose motors. They may not always be true in connection with special motors, built for a particular purpose, or as applied to very small motors.

357. Operation of 220-volt General-purpose Induction Motors on 208-volt Network Systems (NEMA Standard). A 220-volt general-purpose induction motor, when operated with 208 volts at the motor terminals, will deliver approximately 11 per cent less locked rotor and breakdown torques and draw from 0 to 4 per cent more line current at rated load as compared with operation with exactly 220 volts at the terminals. Network systems normally have less voltage variation than radial systems and are commonly held to about a minus 5 per cent variation as compared with the usually accepted minus 10 per cent variation for the radial systems. Hence, a 220-volt motor which delivers sufficient locked-rotor and breakdown torques for successful operation on the minimum voltage of a 220-volt radial system will have essentially equal torques on the minimum voltage of a 208-volt network system. Therefore, 220-volt general-purpose motors can be and often are used on 208-volt network systems.

NOTE. Some 208-volt systems are not network systems and may have more than a minus 5 per cent voltage variation.

358. Characteristics of Polyphase Two-, Four-, Six-, and Eight-pole 60-cycle Integral-horsepower Induction Motors Operated on 50 Cycles (NEMA Standard).

1. SPEEDS. The synchronous speeds of 60-cycle motors when operated on 50 cycles will be 5/6 of the 60-cycle synchronous speed. The full-load speeds of 60-cycle motors when operated on 50 cycles at the rated 60-cycle voltage will be approximately 5/6 of the 60-cycle full-load speed. When voltages less than the 60-cycle rated voltage are applied, the slip will be increased approximately inversely as the square of the ratios of voltages. For example, when a 60-cycle 440-volt motor is operated at 410 volts, 50 cycles, the slip will be increased approximately 15 per cent over the slip at 440 volts, 50 cycles. Also, when operated at 380 volts, 50 cycles, the slip will be increased approximately 35 per cent over the slip at 440 volts, 50 cycles.

2. TORQUES. The full-load torques in pound-feet of 60-cycle motors operated on 50 cycles will be approximately 6/5 of the 60-cycle full-load torques in pound-feet.

The breakdown torques in pound-feet of 60-cycle motors when operated on 50 cycles at the rated 60-cycle voltage will be approximately 135 per cent of the 60-cycle breakdown torque in pound-feet. Therefore, the 50-cycle breakdown torque expressed in percentage of the 50-cycle full-load torque will be approximately 112 per cent of the 60-cycle breakdown torque expressed in percentage of the 60-cycle full-load torque. When voltages less than the rated 60-cycle voltages are applied, the breakdown torques will be decreased as the square of the voltages. For example, when a 440-volt 60-cycle motor is operated at 410 volts, 50 cycles, the breakdown torque will be reduced approximately 13 per cent below the torque at 440 volts, 60 cycles; also when operated at 380 volts, 50 cycles, the breakdown torque will be reduced approximately 25 per cent below the torque at 440 volts, 50 cycles. From the above, it may be seen that a 60-cycle 440-volt motor having 200 per cent breakdown torque will also have a 200 per cent breakdown torque as a 50-cycle motor operated at approximately 415 volts, and when operated on 50 cycles at 380 volts, the breakdown torque will be approximately 167 per cent of the full-load 50-cycle torque.

The locked-rotor torques of 60-cycle motors operated on 50 cycles will vary in the same manner as the breakdown torques described above. For example, when a 440-volt 60-cycle motor having a 135 per cent locked-rotor torque expressed in percentage of 60-cycle full-load torque is operated on 50 cycles, 380 volts, it may have as low as

110 per cent locked-rotor torque expressed in percentage of 50-cycle full-load torque.

3. LOCKED-ROTOR CURRENT.   The locked-rotor current of 60-cycle motors, when operated on 50 cycles at the rated 60-cycle voltage, will be approximately 15 per cent higher in amperes than the 60-cycle values. The 50-cycle value of locked-rotor current will vary in direct proportion to any slight variation in voltage from the rated 60-cycle voltage.

For example, a 60-cycle 440-volt motor with a locked-rotor current of 290 amp will have approximately 334 amp on 50 cycles at 440 volts and approximately 315 amp at 415 volts and 50 cycles.

The code letter appearing on the motor nameplate to indicate locked-rotor kva per horsepower applies only to the 60-cycle rating of the motor.

4. TEMPERATURE RISE.   The temperature rises of 60-cycle motors when operated on 50 cycles will be higher than those attained on 60-cycle operation. When 60-cycle general-purpose open motors having a service factor of 1.15 and a full-load temperature rise of 40°C are suitable for operation on 50-cycle circuits and are operated on 50 cycles at the 60-cycle voltage and horsepower rating, they will have no service factor and will operate with a temperature rise not exceeding 50°C. In general, the temperature rise of 440-volt 60-cycle 40°C motors when operated on 50 cycles will be approximately the same for any voltage between 440 and 415 volts. When such motors are operated on 380 volts, 50 cycles, at rated load, they will have a temperature rise of approximately 60°C.

NOTE. 1. Sixty-cycle motors equipped with speed-responsive switching devices may require mechanical modification for satisfactory operation at 50 cycles.

NOTE. 2. The information given above is based on motors rated 60 cycles, 440 volts. The same relationship will apply to motors of other standard voltage ratings.

359. Operation of D-C Motors on Rectified Alternating Current (NEMA Standard). When a d-c motor is operated from a rectified a-c supply, its performance may differ materially from that of the same motor when operated from a d-c source of supply having the same effective value of voltage. At the same load, its temperature rise and noise level may be increased and the commutation is likely to be adversely affected. The degree of difference will depend upon the character of the rectified voltage.

Ordinarily, motors to be used on such rectified voltages are designed especially for such service. Direct-current motors should not be applied to such rectified circuits except after consulting the motor manufacturer regarding the performance characteristics that might be expected from the particular motor when so used.

360. Operation of D-C Motors by Reduced Armature Voltage (NEMA Standard). When a d-c motor is operated below base speed by reduced armature voltage, it may be necessary to reduce its torque load below rated full-load torque to avoid overheating of the motor.

7-188

361. Summary of Motor Characteristics

Type of motor	Standard hp ratings	Speed characteristics	Speed control	Locked-rotor starting currents with rated impressed voltage in percentage of full-load current	Starting torque in percentage of full load rated torque	Max. running torque in percentage of full-load rated torque	General application suited for
1. Direct current, shunt, constant speed	Up to 200	Constant; not more than 10 per cent change in speed from no load to full load	Speed may be increased 25 per cent above normal by field control; speed may be reduced any amount below normal by armature control but speed then varies widely with load	Very high; normally reduced to 150 per cent of rated full-load current by series starting resistance	Maximum with full voltage, 250 to 300; when started in normal manner, average, 150	Would occur at standstill but limited by commutation to 200	Constant- or slightly adjustable-speed service with light or medium starting duty
2. Direct current, shunt, adjustable speed	Up to 200	Nearly constant for any field adjustment, not more than 15 per cent change in speed from no load to full load	Speed range of 4:1 for all loads by field control. Speed may be reduced by armature control but speed then varies widely with load	Same as 1	Same as 1	Same as 1	Adjustable-speed service with close speed regulation and either light or medium starting duty. Motors available for either constant-torque or constant-horsepower service
3. Direct current, compound, 20 per cent series, 80 per cent shunt	Up to 200	Slightly varying speed, changes approximately 25 per cent from no load to full load	Same as 1	Same as 1	Maximum with full voltage; 300 to 350; when started in normal manner, —average 170	Would occur at standstill but limited by commutation to 300	Heavy starting duty or intermittent peak-load service or combination of the two duties
4. Direct current, compound, 50 per cent series, 50 per cent shunt	3 to 200	Varying	Same as 1	Same as 1	Maximum with full voltage, 400; when started in normal manner, average 200	Would occur at standstill but limited by commutation to 350	Heavy intermittent starting duty or heavy running loads for short periods with alternate light load periods; adjustable varying-speed service

	hp	Speed		Starting torque	Maximum momentary torque	Starting current	Service
5. Direct current series	3 to 200	Varying	Same as 1	Same as 1	Maximum with full voltage, 450; when started in normal manner, 225 to 300	Would occur at standstill but limited by commutation to 400	Heavy intermittent starting duty or heavy running loads for short periods of time; adjustable, varying-speed service. Motor should at all times be loaded or under control of operator
6. Polyphase, squirrel cage, normal torque, low starting current	$\frac{1}{10}$ to 400	Constant; speed changes approximately 3 to 5 per cent from no load to full load	None	500 to 1,000. May not meet power companies' limitations. Up to 5 hp, generally started with full voltage; above 5 hp, generally started with reduced voltage. Current drawn from line proportional to square of voltage for transformer starting and directly proportional to voltage for resistance starting	Varies with square of voltage applied to motor; 105 to 150 for full voltage	200 to 250	Constant-speed service with no speed control; light-starting-duty service unless it is permissible to start with full voltage
7. Polyphase, squirrel cage, normal torque, low starting current	$7\frac{1}{2}$ to 200	Same as 6	None	500 to 550. Within the limitations of most power companies up to and including 30-hp size. Above 30-hp size may not be within power companies' limitations. Current depends upon voltage same as for 6	Same as 6	200 to 225	Constant-speed service with no speed control; medium starting duty. Used in place of motor 6 when its use will eliminate employment of reduced-voltage starting
8. Polyphase, squirrel cage, high torque, low starting current	$1\frac{1}{2}$ to 150	Same as 6	None	Same as 7	Varies with square of voltage applied to motor; 220 to 275 for full voltage	200 to 250	Constant-speed service with no speed control; heavy starting duty if at not too frequent intervals and if starting period is of not too long duration
9. Polyphase, squirrel cage, low torque, low starting current	40 to 100	Same as 6	None	350 to 550. Within the limitations of most power companies, current depends upon voltage same as for 6	Varies with square of voltage applied to motor, 50 to 100 for full voltage	125 to 175	Constant-speed service with no speed control, light starting duty only

Summary of Motor Characteristics (*Continued*)

Type of motor	Standard hp ratings	Speed characteristics	Speed control	Locked-rotor starting currents with rated impressed voltage in percentage of full-load current	Starting torque in percentage of full load rated torque	Max. running torque in percentage of full-load rated torque	General application suited for
10. Polyphase, squirrel cage, high-resistance rotor, medium slip	½ to 150	Slightly varying speed; speed changes from 7 to 12 per cent from no load to full load	None	400 to 800. Within the limitations of most power companies. Reduced-voltage starting not satisfactory owing to nature of applications	300 to 400	300 to 400. Occurs at standstill	Service with intermittent peak loads, when peak loads occur less than 25 times per minute; heavy starting duty if at not too frequent intervals and if starting period is of not too long duration
11. Polyphase, squirrel cage, high resistance rotor, high slip	1 to 50	Medium varying speed; speed changes from 12 to 17 per cent from no load to full load	None	300 to 500. Within the limitations of most power companies. Reduced-voltage starting not satisfactory owing to nature of applications	225 to 250	225 to 400. Occurs at standstill	Frequent heavy starting duty, intermittent loads of not too long duration where varying speed is satisfactory
12. Polyphase, squirrel cage, multispeed	½ to 125	Multispeed 2, 3, or 4 definite speeds available; speed changes approximately 5 per cent from no load to full load at highest speed and approximately 25 per cent at lowest speed	Speed controlled by changing number of poles of stator winding; maximum of 4 definite speeds; no speed control between steps	These motors may be obtained in any one of the types of items 6, 7, 8, or 9			Adjustable-speed service where 2, 3, or 4 definite speeds will be satisfactory. Whether motor with characteristics of 6, 7, 8, or 9 is selected depends upon requirements of service as given under these types. Available in designs for constant-hp, constant-torque, variable-torque, variable-hp service
13. Polyphase, squirrel cage, automatic start	½ to 75	Constant; speed changes from 4 to 6 per cent from no load to full load	None	350 to 375. Within the limitations of practically all power companies	225 to 250. Pull-in torques of from 150 to 200	200 to 250	Constant-speed service with no speed control; heavy starting duty if at not too frequent intervals and if starting period is of not too long duration

Type							
14. Polyphase, wound rotor	½ to 1,000	Depends upon the resistance in the rotor circuit; constant (4 to 6 per cent change from no load to full load) with rotor short-circuited; varying with resistance in rotor circuit (greater resistance, greater variation in speed from no load to full load)	Speed can be reduced to 50 per cent below normal at full load by resistance in rotor circuit; only small reduction in speed can be obtained at light loads	250 to 300. Within limitations of all power companies	200 to 275	200 to 275	Constant-speed service with no speed control for very heavy or frequent starting duty or where starting period is of long duration (resistance in rotor circuit during starting period only); adjustable varying-speed service; service with peak loads for short periods; different types of service require resistors of different ratings
15. Polyphase, commutator type, brush shifting	5 to 50	Adjustable speed; changes from 5 to 25 per cent from no load to full load depending upon speed setting	Speed range of 3:1 by shifting brushes; very low speeds obtained by inserting resistance in secondary	125 to 175. Within limitations of all power companies	140 to 250	140 to 250 at low speeds; 300 to 400 at high speeds	Adjustable-speed service of the constant-torque type; heavy starting-duty service if at not too frequent intervals and if starting period is of not too long duration
16. Synchronous, general purpose, high speed unity power factor	20 to 5,000	Constant: no speed change from no load to full load	None	400 to 800. May not be within limitations of power company. Current depends upon voltage same as for item 6	100 to 125 for full voltage for sizes up to 500 hp; 80 to 100 for full voltage for sizes above 500 hp. Varies with square of voltage applied to motor	150 to 175	Constant-speed service with no speed control and light starting duty; fairly steady load; for power-factor correction

Summary of Motor Characteristics (*Continued*)

Type of motor	Standard hp ratings	Speed characteristics	Speed control	Locked-rotor starting currents with rated impressed voltage in percentage of full-load current	Starting torque in percentage of full load rated torque	Max. running torque in percentage of full-load rated torque	General application suited for
17. Synchronous, general purpose, high speed, 80 per cent power factor	20 to 5,000	Same as 16	None	Same as 16	125 to 200 for full voltage for sizes up to 500 hp; 100 to 150 for full voltage for sizes above 500 hp. Varies with square of voltage applied to motor	200 to 250	Constant-speed service with no speed control where greater power-factor correction is desired than item 16 will provide, or where starting duty is more severe or where peak loads occur. Heavy starting duty if started with full voltage; medium starting duty if started with reduced voltage
18. Synchronous, special purpose, high speed, low torque, low starting current, unity or 80 per cent power factor	20 to, 5,000	Same as 16	None	May be designed for starting currents with rated impressed voltage of from 300 to 500 per cent of full-load current	50 to 100 for full voltage depending upon design; lower values of starting torque correspond to lower values of starting currents. Varies with square of voltage applied to motor	150 to 300 depending upon design	Constant-speed service with no speed control, light starting duty, for power-factor correction. Used in place of 16 in order to limit starting current without reducing voltage
19. Synchronous, special purpose, high speed, high torque, low starting current	20 to 5,000	Same as 16	None	450 to 500 for single-phase wound rotor; 200 to 300 for polyphase wound rotor	150 to 200. Always started with rated voltage applied to motor and external resistance in rotor circuit	150 to 250	Constant-speed service with no speed control for heavy starting duty, for power-factor correction

20. Synchronous, low-speed, engine and compressor types, unity and 80 per cent power factor	20 to 5,000	Same as 16	None	225 to 350 for full voltage. Within limitations of most power companies. Varies with voltage same as 6	40 to 50 for full voltage. Varies with square of applied voltage	140 to 175 for compressor types; 150 to 200 for unity-power-factor-engine type; 200 to 250 for 80 per cent power-factor-engine type	Constant-speed service with no speed control for direct connection to slow-speed machines such as compressors; light starting duty, for power-factor correction
21. Synchronous, low speed special service conventional design, unity or 80 per cent power factor	20 to 5,000	Same as 16	None	325 to 700 for full voltage. May not be within limitations of power company. Varies with voltage same as 6	50 to 200 for full voltage depending upon design; lower values of starting torque correspond to lower values of starting current. Varies with square of applied voltage	150 to 250 depending upon design	Constant-speed service with no speed control, light or medium starting duty, for power-factor correction. Used in place of 20 for heavier starting duty
22. Synchronous, low speed, special service, wound rotor, unity or 80 per cent power factor	20 to 5,000	Same as 16	None	450 to 550 for single-phase wound rotor; 265 to 365 for polyphase wound rotor	150 to 200. Always started with rated voltage applied to motor and external resistance in rotor	175 to 250	Constant-speed service with no speed control, heavy starting duty, for power-factor correction
23. Single-phase shading-coil type	$\frac{1}{250}$ to $\frac{1}{4}$	Constant; speed changes approximately 6 per cent from no load to full load	None	High, but owing to small size always satisfactory for full-voltage starting	Very low	Approximately 150	Constant-speed service with no speed control; for very light starting duty
24. Single phase, split phase starting (inductive), general purpose	$\frac{1}{20}$ to $\frac{1}{2}$	Constant; speed changes approximately 6 per cent from no load to full load	None	High, but owing to small size will be within limitations of power companies if manufactured so as to meet NEMA specifications	75 to 175 for full voltage; varies with square of impressed voltage	175 to 225	Constant-speed service with no speed control; for light starting duty

Summary of Motor Characteristics (*Continued*)

Type of motor	Standard hp ratings	Speed characteristics	Speed control	Locked-rotor starting currents with rated impressed voltage in percentage of full-load current	Starting torque in percentage of full load rated torque	Max. running torque in percentage of full-load rated torque	General application suited for
25. Single phase, split-phase starting (inductive), high torque	$1/6$ to $1/3$	Same as 23	None	High; approximately 850; exceeds NEMA specifications	150 to 275 for full voltage; varies with square of impressed voltage	225 to 350	Constant-speed service with no speed control; for heavy starting duty
26. Single phase, capacitor start, induction run	$1/8$ to $3/4$	Same as 23	None	Lower than 24. Always satisfactory to start with full voltage	275 to 400	200 to 300	Constant-speed service with no speed control; for heavy starting duty
27. Single phase, capacitor start, capacitor run, two-value capacitor, high torque	$1/8$ to 10	Same as 23	None	Within the limitations of most power companies. Always satisfactory to start smaller sizes with full voltage	275 to 450	200 to 300	Constant-speed service with no speed control for heavy starting duty. Have better power factors than item 26
28. Single phase, capacitor start, capacitor run, single-value capacitor, low torque	$1/2$ to 10	Same as 23	None	Within the limitations of most power companies; lower than item 27; generally started with full voltage	40 to 60	150 to 200	Constant-speed service with no speed control for light starting duty
29. Single phase, multispeed capacitor	$1/20$ to $1/2$	Practically constant for high speed; varies considerably for lower speeds	Speed control by changing impressed voltage; 2 or 3 definite speeds, no speed control between steps	Always satisfactory to start with full voltage	Approximately 60–75 for highest voltage setting; varies with square of applied voltage	Approximately 175 for highest voltage and speed setting. Varies as square of voltage for other setting	Adjustable-speed service where 2 or 3 definite speeds are satisfactory; very light starting duty; may not be satisfactory for belt drives

30. Single phase, repulsion start, induction run	⅛ to 15	Same as 23	None	200 to 350; in the larger sizes may not be within limitation of power company	300 to 500 for full voltage; varies with square of impressed voltage	175 to 225	Constant-speed service with no speed control for light or heavy starting duty
31. Single phase, repulsion induction	½ to 10	Same as 23	None	Within limitations of most power companies	225 to 300 for full voltage	Occurs at standstill	Constant-speed service with no speed control for either light or heavy starting duty. Will not take care of as heavy starting duty as 30
32. Single phase, repulsion brush shifting	¼ to 3	Varying	Speed range 4:1 for full load. Very little speed control possible at light loads. 3:1 range for 75 per cent load	Within limitations of most power companies	125 to 300 for full voltage	Above 400 for max. speed; decreases with speed reduction	Adjustable varying speed service; heavy starting duty; service with peak loads for short periods
33. Single phase, series, universal for operation on a-c or d-c	1/50 to 1	Varying	Speed can be reduced any amount by resistance in series with motor	High, but owing to small size will be within limitations of most power companies. Sizes from ½ to 1 hp may require reduced voltage	275 to 400 for a-c full voltage; 300 to 500 for d-c full voltage	Would occur at standstill but maximum safe running limited by commutation	Service requiring speed control where large variation in speed with load is not objectionable; heavy starting duty. Must be directly connected to load

362. Guide to Selection of Type of Motor

Load requirements		Types of motors suitable		
Running	Starting	Direct current	Polyphase alternating current	Single-phase alternating current
All classes of loads requiring constant speed with no speed control.	Very light starting duty	Shunt, constant-speed type	1. Normal torque, normal starting current, squirrel-cage induction 2. Normal torque, low starting current, squirrel-cage induction 3. Low torque, low starting current, squirrel-cage induction 4. Synchronous, general purpose, high speed 5. Synchronous, special purpose, high speed, low torque 6. Synchronous, low speed, engine compressor, and special service conventional types	1. Split-phase (inductive) 2. Low-torque capacitor 3. Shading coil (only for extremely light starting duty)
	Light starting duty (starting torque not greater than 100 per cent of full-load torque)	Shunt, constant-speed type	1. Normal torque, normal starting current, squirrel-cage induction 2. Normal torque, low starting current, squirrel-cage induction 3. Synchronous general purpose, high speed 4. Synchronous, high speed, special service, low torque 5. Synchronous, low speed, special service, conventional type	1. Split-phase (inductive) 2. High-torque capacitor or capacitor start induction run
	Medium starting duty (starting torque from 100 to 150 per cent of full-load torque)	Shunt, constant-speed type	1. Normal torque, low starting current, squirrel-cage induction in sizes up to 30 hp inclusive 2. High torque, low starting current, squirrel-cage induction 3. Synchronous, general purpose, high speed 4. Synchronous, special purpose, high speed, high torque 5. Synchronous, low speed, special service, conventional or wound-rotor types	1. Repulsion induction 2. Repulsion start, induction run 3. High-torque capacitor or capacitor start, induction run

	Heavy starting duty if at not too frequent intervals and if starting period is of not too long duration (starting torque from 150 to 200 per cent of full-load torque)	Shunt, constant-speed type	1. High-torque, low starting-current, squirrel-cage induction in sizes up to 30 hp. incl. 2. Automatic-start induction 3. Wound-rotor induction with resistance in rotor only during starting period 4. Synchronous, general purpose, high speed 5. Synchronous, special purpose, high speed, high torque 6. Synchronous, low speed, special service, conventional or wound-rotor types	1. Repulsion induction 2. Repulsion start, induction run 3. High-torque capacitor or capacitor start, induction run
All classes of loads requiring adjustable speed with not much change in speed from no load to full load for any speed setting	Very heavy starting duty requiring starting torques above 200 per cent of full-load torque or very frequent starting or starting periods of long duration	Compound, with series field cut-out after starting	Wound rotor with resistance in rotor only during starting period	1. Repulsion induction 2. Repulsion start, induction run 3. High-torque capacitor or capacitor start, induction run
	Light starting duty (starting torque not greater than 100 per cent of full-load torque)	Shunt, adjustable-speed type for either constant-horsepower or constant-torque service	1. Multispeed squirrel-cage induction for either constant horsepower or constant-torque service 2. Commutator, brush-shifting type of induction motor for constant-torque service	Multispeed capacitor
	Medium starting duty (starting torque from 100 to 150 per cent of full-load torque)	Shunt, adjustable-speed type for either constant-horsepower or constant-torque service	1. Multispeed squirrel-cage induction if it is permissible to start directly across the line for either constant-horsepower or constant-torque service 2. High-torque, multispeed, squirrel-cage induction 3. Commutator, brush-shifting type of induction motor for constant-torque service	
	Heavy starting duty, if at not too frequent intervals and if starting periods are of not too long duration (starting torque from 150 to 200 per cent of full-load torque)	Shunt, adjustable-speed type for either constant-horsepower or constant-torque service	1. Special high-torque, multispeed, squirrel-cage induction for either constant-horsepower or constant-torque service 2. Commutator, brush-shifting type of induction motor for constant-torque service	

Guide to Selection of Type of Motor (Continued)

Load requirements		Types of motors suitable		
Running	Starting	Direct current	Polyphase alternating current	Single-phase alternating current
	Very heavy starting duty requiring starting torque above 200 per cent of full-load torque, very frequent starting or starting periods of long duration	Compound wound with series field cut out after starting	Commutator, brush-shifting type of induction with resistance in secondary during starting period	
Intermittent peak loads where it is desirable for motor to have slightly varying-speed characteristics in order to prevent excess motor overloads (flywheel machines); peak loads should occur less than 25 times per minute; any service where a slightly varying-speed characteristic is not objectionable or is desirable	Light or heavy starting duty if at not too frequent intervals and if starting periods are of not too long duration	Compound, 20 per cent series, 80 per cent shunt	High-resistance rotor, squirrel-cage induction (medium slip)	
	Very heavy starting duty or starting at very frequent intervals or starting periods of long duration	Compound, 20 per cent series, 80 per cent shunt	1. Wound-rotor induction with some resistance always in rotor circuit 2. High-resistance rotor, squirrel-cage induction (high slip)	
Varying or adjustable varying-speed service; any service where it is desirable or not objectionable to have speed decrease with increasing load; service requiring heavy torque for short periods with some speed control during light loads	Any type of starting duty	1. Compound, 50 per cent series, 50 per cent shunt 2. Series if motor is always under control of operator or if there is no danger of motor losing its load or if motor is protected by an overspeed device	Wound rotor	1. Series 2. Repulsion, brush-shifting type 3. Repulsion

363. Speed-control Application Chart—Adjustable-speed Motors and Drives
(Westinghouse Electric Corp.)

Primary power	Type of service	Speed range, Maximum			Standard speed ranges available	Speed control adjustable under load					Speed regulation			Hp range	Braking available	Type of motor or drive
		Constant hp	Constant torque	In combination		By remote operation	For preset jogging speed	For creeping	For presetting	For holding on overhauling load	At max speed	At base speed	At min speed			
Motors																
A-C	Constant hp or constant torque	4:1	4:1	4:1	4 fixed speeds	Standard	Optional[c]	Not available	Standard	Yes	3-5%	3-5%	3-5%	1-200	Regenerative or dynamic (special)	A-C multispeed induction motor
	Constant torque	.....	2:1[a]	......	2:1[a]	Special[b]	Optional	Special	Optional	No	3-5%	....	50%	1-200	Dynamic (special)	A-C wound-rotor induction motor
D-C	Constant hp	8:1	......	......	4:1 6:1 8:1	Special[b]	Optional	Optional	Optional	No	15-25%	5-15%	....	1-200	Dynamic (optional)	D-C standard adjustable-speed motor
Drives																
A-C	Combination constant hp and constant torque	4:1	8:1	16:1	8:1 12:1 16:1	Standard	Optional	Optional	Standard	Within 20%	20-30%	10-15%	20-40%	1-200	Regenerative (standard) or dynamic (optional)	Motor-generator set adjustable-voltage d-c drives
		4:1	50:1	200:1	5:1 20:1 50:1	Standard	Optional	Optional	Standard	No	2-8%[d]	2-8%[d]	2-8%[d]	⅛-30	Dynamic (standard)	Electronic adjustable-voltage drive
		20:1	1½:1	30:1	30:1 120:1 (available)	Not available	Standard	Not available	Standard	No	1%	1%	1%	10-100	Regenerative	Planer type variable voltage drive
D-C	Constant hp	4:1 6:1	......	......	4:1 6:1	Not available	Standard	Not available	Standard	No	15-25%	15%	....	5-100	Dynamic (standard) on inching, dynamic and plugging on automatic	Planer-type constant-voltage drive

[a] Speed ranges up to 4:1 can be obtained if the motor is oversize or if the torque load becomes smaller at reduced speeds (such as on fan, blower, centrifugal pump).
[b] Motor-operated drum or rheostat.
[c] Motor runs at full speed if jog button is held down.
[d] Speed can be set practically flat at minimum speed and will not exceed 2 at 8 per cent at any other speed.
[e] From any speed down to lowest synchronous speed.

364. Representative Applications of D-C Motors

Shunt	Compound	Series
Agitators	Balers	Bailing presses
Blowers	Bending rolls	Bridges
Conveyors	Bulldozers	Cranes
Fans	Metal drawers	Car retarders and pullers
Line shafts	Punch presses	Coke-oven machinery
Printing presses	Shears	Hoists
Pumps		Hydraulic gages
Mixers		Lorry cars
Most woodworking machines		Rotary car dumpers
Most machine tools		Yard locomotives

365. Representative Applications of Squirrel-cage Induction Motors

Normal-torque, normal-starting-current, and normal-torque, low-starting-current types	High-torque, low-starting current type	Low-torque, low-starting-current type	High-resistance rotor type	Multispeed type
Blowers	Agitators	Blowers	Balers	Centrifugal transformers
Boring mills	Baking machinery	Centrifugal pumps	Bulldozers	Dough mixers
Drilling machines	Candy machinery	Fans	Metal drawing machines	Elevators
Pumps	Conveyors	Motor generators	Punch presses	Feed mechanisms
Line-shaft drive	Crushers		Shears	Ironers
Most woodworking machines	Canning machines		Elevators	Some machine tools
Most machine tools	Elevators		Cranes	Oil-well pumping and pulling
	Grinders		Hoists	Printing presses
	Flour-mill machinery		Dumbwaiters	Pumps and fans
	Milling machines			Tumblers
	Mixers			Stokers
	Pulverizers			Conveyors
	Reciprocating pumps and compressors			
	Refrigerators			
	Revolving screens			

366. Representative Applications of Wound-rotor, Brush-shifting, and Synchronous Motors

Wound rotor	Polyphase brush-shifting, commutator motor	Synchronous motors
Bascule lift and swing bridges	Aluminum-foil machines	*High speed*
Cranes	Bakery machinery	Band saws
Coke pushers	Boilerhouse fans	Blowers
Hoists	Centrifugal compressors and pumps	Compressors
Hydraulic gates	Cable-stranding machines	Cotton gins
Lorry cars	Cloth-printing machines	Fans
Main roll drives in iron and steel mills	Cotton-mill calenders	Grinding and crushing machinery
Rotary car dumpers	Linoleum calendars	Jordans and beaters
Yard locomotives	Paper winders	Metal rolling mills
	Printing presses	Mill line shafts
	Reciprocating pumps	Pumps
	Oil-refinery machinery	*Low speed*
	Some machine tools	Air and gas compressors
	Some steel-mill main roll drivers	Band-saw mills
	Stokers	Jordans
	Table drive for plate-glass grinders	Pulp grinders
	Tandem drive for textile mills	Refrigerating machinery
	Tube machines and calenders in rubber-goods factories	

367. Typical Torque Requirements of Synchronous-motor Applications

(Allis-Chalmers)

The following, taken in the main from NEMA MG1-8.9, represent typical locked-rotor, pull-in and pull-out torque requirements of various synchronous motor applications.

In individual cases, lower values may be satisfactory or higher values may be necessary, depending upon the characteristics of the particular machine and the effect of locked-rotor kva on the line voltage.

Application	Typical torque requirements, per cent of full-load torque					Max "load Wk^2" ratio (approx)
	Locked-rotor (static)		Pull-in		Pull-out	
	Un-loaded	Loaded	Un-loaded	Loaded		

1. Centrifugal Machinery—Blowers, Compressors, Fans, and Pumps

Application	Un-loaded	Loaded	Un-loaded	Loaded	Pull-out	Max Wk²
Blowers[a,b]						10–15
Compressors[a,b]						15–25
Fans—(except sintering)[a]						20–50
Inlet or discharge valve closed[b]	40		60		150	
Inlet or discharge valve open[b]		40		100	150	
Sintering—inlet gates either open or closed[b]		40		100	150	25–60
Propeller-type—discharge open		40		100	150	25
Pumps—centrifugal (horizontal)						1
With discharge valve closed:[b]						
High- and medium-speed	40		50–60		150	
Low-speed	40		70–100		150	
With discharge valve open—centrifugal (vertical)		40		100	150	
With discharge valve closed:[b]						
High- and medium-speed	50		60–70		150	
Low-speed	50		75–100		150	
With discharge valve open		50		100	150	
Adjustable-blade—vertical[b]	50		40		150	1
Screw-type						1
Started dry	40		30		150	
Primed, discharge open		40		100	150	
Axial-flow type						1
With discharge open		40		100	150	
With discharge closed		40		200–300	Same	

2. Cement, Rock Products, and Mining Machinery

Application	Un-loaded	Loaded	Un-loaded	Loaded	Pull-out	Max Wk²
Grinding mills:						
Attrition[a]	100		60		175	12
Ball and *Compeb:*						
Rock and coal		150		110	150	2
Ore		175		110	175	2
Rod and tube mills—ore		175		110	175	3
Crushers						
B. and W	200		100		250	3
Bradley-Hercules	100	160	80–100	125	250	3
Cone	100		100		250	6
Gyratory	100		70–100		250	4
Jaw	100		70–100		250	2
Roll	100		70–100		250	3
Hammer mills[a]	120		100		250	15–40
Flotation machines		150–175		110	175	1
Fuller mills		125–150		110	175	

Typical Torque Requirements of Synchronous-motor Applications (*Continued*)

Application	Typical torque requirements, per cent of full-load torque					Max "load Wk^2" ratio (approx)
	Locked-rotor (static)		Pull-in		Pull-out	
	Unloaded	Loaded	Unloaded	Loaded		
3. Metal Rolling Mills						
Structural and rail:						
Roughing	40	......	30	......	300	
Finishing	40	......	30	......	250	
Plate	40	......	30	......	300	
Merchant trains	60	......	40	......	250	
Billet, skelp and sheet bar (continuous with lay-shaft drive)	60	......	40	......	250	1
Hot-strip, continuous, individual drive roughing stands	50	......	40	......	250–300	
Tube-piercing and expanding	60	......	40	......	300–350	
Tube-rolling (plug)	60	......	40	......	250	
Tube-reeling	60	......	40	......	250	
Sheet and tin (cold-rolling)	......	200	......	150	250	
Brass and copper:						
Roughing	50	......	40	......	250	
Finishing	......	150	......	125	250	
4. Pulp and Paper Machinery						
Beaters:						
Standard	......	125	......	100	150	5
Breaker	......	125	......	100	200	5
Chippers (empty)[a]	60	......	50	......	250	30–60
Hydraupulpers	......	125	......	125	150	
Jordans (plug out)	50	......	50	......	150	1
Pulp grinders:						
Magazine type	50	......	50	......	150	5
3 or 4 pocket type	40	......	30	......	150	4
Screens—centrifugal	......	50	......	100	150	1
Vacuum pumps—(Hytor)	......	60	......	100	200	4
Wood hogs[a]	60	......	60	100	225	30
5. Reciprocating Machinery						
Blowing engines	40	......	50	......	150	
Compressors						
Air and gas	40	......	30	......	150	10
Ammonia (discharge pressures 100 to 250 lb per sq in.)	40	......	30	......	150	7
Ammonia boosters:[a,e]						
Freon	40	......	50	......	150	4
Carbon dioxide (with piston-rod diameter of 30 to 60 % of piston diameter):						
Single-cylinder, double acting[a]	40–120	......	40	......	150	5–10
Two-cylinder, double acting	40–90	......	40	......	150	4–7
Pumps—positive displacement	......	......	......	......	......	1
Started dry	40	......	30	......	150	
Bypassed	40	......	40	......	150	
Not bypassed (3-cylinder)	......	150	......	100	150	
Vacuum pumps[a]	40	......	60	......	150	10

Typical Torque Requirements of Synchronous-motor Applications (*Continued*)

Application	Typical torque requirements, per cent of full-load torque					Max "load Wk^2" ratio (approx)
	Locked-rotor (static)		Pull-in		Pull-out	
	Un-loaded	Loaded	Un-loaded	Loaded		
6. Rubber Mills						
Banbury mixers....................	......	125	......	100	250	1
Line shafts.......................	......	125	......	110	225	1
Plasticators......................	......	125	......	100	250	1
Individual drive..................	......	125	......	100	250	1
7. Sawmills						
Saws:						
Band mill[a].....................	80	....	40	....	250	100
Edger.........................	40	....	30	....	250	1
Gang[a].........................	60	....	30	....	200	10
Trimmer.......................	40	....	30	....	200	1
Wood hogs[a]......................	60	....	60	100	225	30
8. Miscellaneous						
Blowers—positive displacement, rotating, cycloidal type[a].........	40	....	40	....	150	8
Bowl mills—(coal pulverizer) (with common motor for pulverizer and exhaust fan)[d].................	......	150	......	125	150	
Compressors—positive displacement, rotating, sliding-vane type:						
Bypass open...................	60	....	30	....	150	
Inlet open, bypass closed........	......	60	......	100	150	
Flour mill line shafts[a].............	......	175	......	110	150	5–15
Gas cleaners (Thiessen)[a]..........	40	....	60	....	150	25
Vacuum pumps (Hytor) in other than paper mill service[a]..	40	....	60	....	150	4

[a] These applications have high inertia, and the Wk^2 of the load may require a motor design which cannot be determined from the torque requirements alone. For these applications the motor manufacturer should always be provided with the actual values of the Wk^2 of the load.

[b] The torque requirements may vary for the individual machine. The manufacturer should be consulted.

[c] May require higher torques under certain conditions; such as starting with cold air when rating is based upon normally warm air.

[d] On some mills the exhaust fan may be separately driven and different torque values will apply; in either case the mill manufacturer should be consulted.

[e] Torque and flywheel effect requirements will vary widely with different pressure-differential operating conditions and starting method.

368. Synchronous-motor Application Data
(Westinghouse Electric Corp.)

Unusual operating conditions may modify the requirements. For type of motor to produce the required starting torque see Table **183.**

Application	Method of connecting motor to load	Starting conditions	Per cent			Remarks
			Starting torque	Pull-in torque	Pull-out torque	
Cement, Rock Products, and Metal Mining						
Ball mills, mining..........	Coupled to mill pinion	Mills loaded at start	175–200	110–120	175	Full-voltage starting or resistance control for wound-rotor types. Indicating wattmeter on control
Crushers, gyratory...........	Coupled or belted	Loaded	150–200	100–125	200	Full-voltage starter required. Continuous operation—varying load
Hammer mill................	Coupled	Loaded	150	115	250	Full-voltage starting recommended
Jaw........................	Coupled or belted	Loaded	150–225	100–125	250	Full-voltage starter required. Continuous load extremely irregular with high peaks
Roll........................	Coupled or belted	Loaded	225	100	225	Full-voltage starter
Bradley-Hercules...........	Coupled	Unloaded	80	100	175	Full-voltage starting. Continuous load
Hercules mills, cement......	Coupled to mill pinion shaft by resilient flexible coupling; good for severe misalignment and vibration	Loaded	150–200	100–110	175	Special full-voltage starting. Liners may be installed under pedestals to provide compensation for mill settling. Motors should be provided with dustproof bearings
Rod mills, mining..........	Coupled or belted (Lenix drive) to gear	Loaded	200	120	175	Special full-voltage starter required
Tube mills..................	Coupled by flexible coupling to reducing gear	Loaded	190	120	175	Special full-voltage starter required
Compressors and Blowers						
Blowers, cycloidal, positive...	Coupled or engine type	Unloaded	40–60	40–60	150	Standard Control. Full-voltage starting recommended. Two-speed motors sometimes used
Turbo, high-speed...........	Direct connected or step-up gear	Unloaded, discharge closed	40	60	150	Special reduced-voltage starting
Blowing engines reciprocating.	Engine type	Unloaded	40	40–60	150	Standard control. Full-voltage starting recommended

Compressors, air	Engine type	Unloaded	40	40	150	Standard control. Full-voltage starting recommended. Flywheel effect important
Ammonia and ammonia booster	High speed, belted; low speed, usually engine type, occasionally coupled	Unloaded by by-pass	40	40	150	Standard control. Full-voltage starting recommended. Flywheel effect important
Freon	High speed, belted; low speed, usually engine type, occasionally coupled	Unloaded by by-pass	45	60	150	Standard control. Full-voltage starting recommended. Flywheel effect important
Gas, reciprocating	High speed, belted; low speed, engine type	Unloaded by by-pass	40	40	150	Standard control except on magnetic control a gastight push button is recommended. Full-voltage starting usually used. Flywheel effect important. Control and exciting equipment usually installed in separate room
Fans						
Exhaust and ventilating	Coupled or belted	Usually loaded	50	60–125	150	Reduced- or full-voltage starting. WR^2 of fan must be considered
Flour Mills						
Line shaft	Coupled or belted	Loaded	175–225	100–125	175	Full-voltage starting required
Lumber						
Band saws and resaws	Coupled or belted	Unloaded. Torques depend on WR^2 of saw	80–125	75–115	200–250	Full-voltage starting. Accelerating time, 45 to 90 sec. Special motor for starting high inertia load
Pulp and Paper						
Jordans	Coupled with flexible coupling	Unloaded	50	50	150	Standard control. Full-voltage starting recommended
Beaters	Belted	Loaded	125	100	175	Full-voltage starting recommended
Pulp grinders	Coupled by flexible coupling	Unloaded	50	50	150	Standard control. Full-voltage type recommended
Wood hogs and chippers	Coupled or engine type	Unloaded. Torques depend on WR^2 of machine	83–125	80–110	225	Full-voltage starting recommended

Synchronous-motor Application Data (Continued)

Application	Method of connecting motor to load	Starting conditions	Per cent			Remarks
			Starting torque	Pull-in torque	Pull-out torque	
Pumps						
Centrifugal, water, oil, sewage.	Coupled by flexible coupling	Valves either open or closed. Usually closed	Valves open or closed, 35–20	Valves closed, 35–50 valves open, 100–120	150	Standard control, full or reduced voltage
Reciprocating..............	Coupled by flexible coupling to pump pinion shaft	Unloaded or by-passed	50–75	25–50	150	Use standard-price-book control. Full-voltage type recommended
Reciprocating, vacuum......	Belted or direct-connected engine type	Unloaded	30–50	60–85	150	Use standard-price-book control. Full-voltage type recommended. Horse-power should be based on peak-load conditions
Rotating vacuum..........	Belted or direct-connected engine type	Loaded	40	55–100	150	Standard control. Horsepower should be based on peak-load conditions
Rubber						
Banbury mixers and plastica-tors	Direct drive or through reduction gear	Usually unloaded. May reverse under load in emergency	125–150	100–110	250	Special reversing control required. Usually full-voltage starting. Occasionally two-speed motors
Mill lines, rubber..........	Low speed, direct coupled; high-speed, coupled to reducing gear	Usually loaded. May reverse under load in emergency	110–150	110–125	175–250	Full-voltage dynamic braking control with or without reversing recommended. Semimagnetic or magnetic reduced volt-age may be used in some cases

Steel

	Mechanical connection	Duty				Control	
Piercing mills..........	Direct-connected by flexible coupling; sometimes coupled to reducing gears	Unloaded. May be reversed under load in emergency	80–100	50–60	300–350	Special control required. type recommended	Full-voltage
Continuous mills; steel rolling, sheet, bar, billet, skelp, strip mills	Direct-connected by flexible coupling, usual practice. Sometimes coupled to reducing gear using higher speed motors	Unloaded. May be reversed under load in emergency	50–100	50–100	250–350	Special control required. type recommended	Full-voltage
Rod mills..........	Direct-connected by flexible coupling	Unloaded. May reverse under load in emergency	60–100	50–60	225–275	Special control required. type recommended	Full-voltage
Sizing and reducing mills......	Direct-connected by flexible coupling; sometimes coupled to reducing gears	Unloaded. May reverse under load in emergency	80–100	50–60	300–350	Special control required. type recommended	Full-voltage

369. Operating Speeds of Various Machine Tools

Saws, circular, wood	9,000 ft per min at rim
Band, wood	4,000 ft per min at rim
Band, hot iron and steel	200–300 ft per min at rim
Grindstones	800 ft per min at rim
Emery wheels	5,000 ft per min at rim
Drills, for wrought iron	12 ft per min outer edge
For cast iron	8 ft per min outer edge
Milling cutters, for brass	120 ft per min outer edge
For cast-iron	60 ft per min outer edge
For wrought iron	50 ft per min outer edge
Wrought steel	35 ft per min outer edge
Screw cutting, gun metal, etc.	30 ft per min at circum
Steel	8 ft per min at circum
Boring, cast-iron	10 ft per min at circum
Sawing	
Brass	70 ft per min at circum
Gun metal	30 ft per min at circum
Steel	25 ft per min at circum
Wrought iron	30 ft per min at circum
Cast iron	20 ft per min at circum

370. Motor-driven Pumps (Westinghouse Electric Corp.). Either d-c or a-c motors are satisfactory. For most cases, shunt-wound d-c or squirrel-cage a-c motors and synchronous motors in sizes above 25 hp are suitable, but when the starting conditions are severe, as when the pump must be started against a full discharge pipe, compound-wound d-c and wound-rotor a-c motors are preferable.

For small centrifugal pumps, squirrel-cage motors are suitable. On large size units, squirrel-cage or synchronous motors are used. On many government building specifications wound-rotor motors are specified due to their low starting currents.

$$\text{Water hp} = \frac{\text{gpm} \times \text{tdh (in ft)}}{3,960} = \frac{\text{gpm} \times \text{tdh (in lb)}}{1,720}$$

$$\text{bhp} = \frac{\text{gpm} \times \text{tdh (in ft)}}{3,960 \times \text{pump eff}}$$

$$\text{kw input} = \frac{\text{gpm} \times \text{tdh (in ft)}}{5,308 \times \text{pump eff} \times \text{motor eff}}$$

$$\text{kwhr per million gallons pumped} = \frac{\text{tdh (in ft)} \times 3.1456}{\text{pump eff} \times \text{motor eff}}$$

$$\text{Velocity} = \frac{\text{gpm}}{2.45 \times D^2} \qquad \text{Velocity head} = \frac{V^2}{64.4}$$

NOTE. When the head is expressed in feet, formulas are correct only for liquids of 1.0 specific gravity.

Abbreviations

gpm = gallons per minute   mgd = million gallons daily
bhp = brake horsepower   rpm = revolutions per minute
tdh = total dynamic head

On plunger pumps high-starting-torque squirrel-cage motors are recommended so as to take care of the full pump load plus the accelerating load. For boiler feed service and other applications requiring variable-speed motors, a wound-rotor motor with continuous-duty resistors should be used.

371. Motor-driven Fans and Blowers (Westinghouse Electric Corp.). The approximate horsepower required to drive fans and blowers may be obtained from the curve (in Fig. 184) when the cubic feet per minute and water gage pressure are known. Horsepower for pressures and quantities not shown on the curves may be figured from the following formula (the average ventilating fan has an efficiency of 60 per cent):

$$\text{hp} = \frac{\text{cfm} \times \text{pressure in inches water gage}}{6,346 \times \text{fan efficiency}} \tag{12}$$

cfm = cubic feet per minute

The horsepower required by a fan varies approximately as the cube of the speed, and the volume directly as the speed. The motor horsepower should exceed the rated horsepower of a forward curved fan by approximately 20 per cent but can be close to the rated horsepower of backward curved fans with nonoverload characteristics. If the fan speed will be increased by adjustable pitch sheaves or sheave changes, the motor rating should be based on the highest speed.

Standard shunt-wound direct-current or normal-torque a-c motors have sufficient starting torque. Synchronous motors are used where power-factor correction is desired.

Multispeed variable-torque squirrel-cage motors are recommended when the volume of air must be varied. Any combination of 1,800-, 1,200-, 900-, and 600-rpm speeds can be supplied. If the volume variation obtained with fixed motor speeds is not suitable, a wound-rotor induction motor with the proper control will allow speed adjustment between 100 and 50 per cent of the motor speed. Shunt-wound d-c motors with suitable control give variable speed adjustment over the same range as wound-rotor motors.

372. Motor-driven Compressors (Westinghouse Electric Corp.). Compressors equipped with unloaders can be started by normal-starting-torque a-c motors NEMA Design B. Compressors which start loaded require high-starting-torque a-c motors NEMA Design C.

Most air-conditioning compressors 50 tons and smaller start loaded and consequently require motor starting torques of 200 to 220 per cent of full-load torque. High-starting-torque Type A motors (Design C) will develop these torques when started across the line. With across-the-line starting, the total current inrush is the locked-rotor current of the motor. When a low-starting-current, high-starting-torque motor will not meet the inrush or torque requirements, a wound-rotor motor and Class 13-100 magnetic starter are recommended.

Compressors larger than 50 tons are usually equipped with unloaders which reduce the starting torque.

Large reciprocating compressors are generally driven by high-speed belted or low-speed direct-connected engine-type synchronous motors.

The horsepower required can be determined by using the following instructions applied to the curves in Fig. 185.

Air Compressors at Any Level. Curve A can be used when the discharge pressure and cubic feet per minute are known. The curves are lines of constant horsepower. Dotted lines are for two-stage water-cooled units.

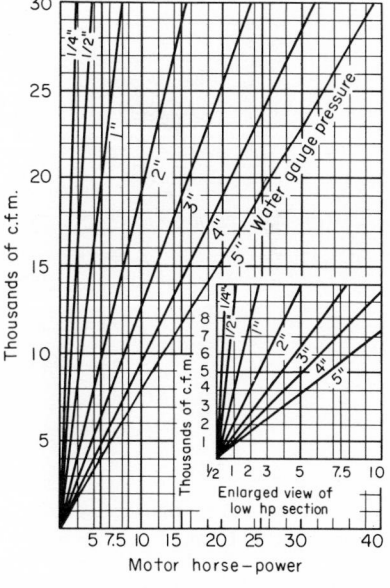

FIG. 184 *Curves for horsepower required to drive fans and blowers. (Westinghouse Electric Corp.)*

Air Compressors at Any Altitude. First select the equivalent sea level pressure from curve B. This will take care of the increase in compression ratio above the sea-level ratio. Then from curve A determine the total horsepower for the pressure corresponding to the equivalent sea-level pressure and free air capacity you desire. Multiply this horsepower by the correction factor from curve C.

Ice Making, Main Compressor. Multiply the number of tons of ice required per 24-hr day by:

3.5 hp per ton for compressors up to 50 tons capacity.

3.25 hp per ton for compressors of 50 to 200 tons capacity.

3.1 hp per ton for compressors over 200 tons capacity.

Air Conditioning, Main Compressor. Multiply the number of tons of refrigeration required by:

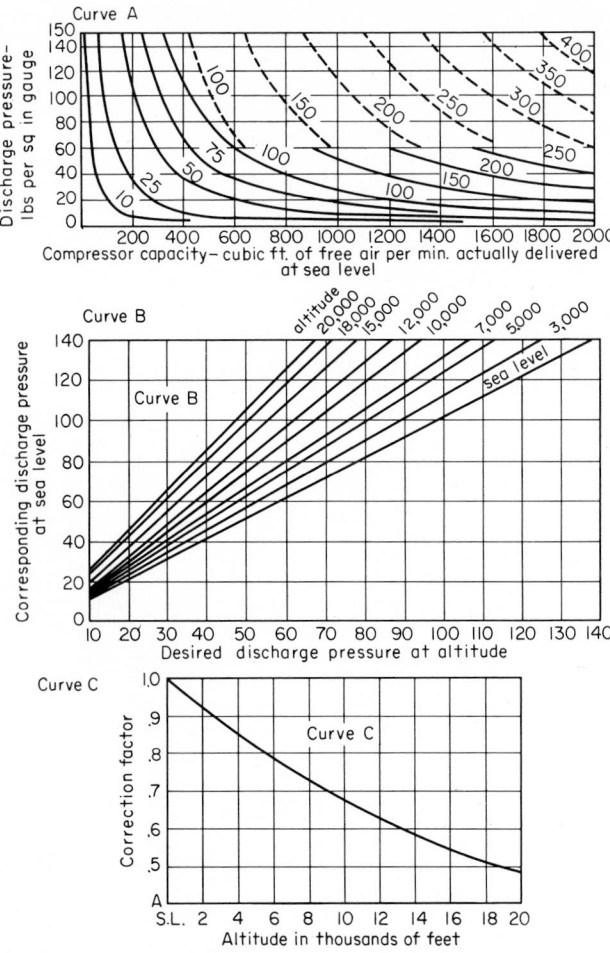

FIG. 185 *Curves for determining horsepower required to drive compressors.* (*Westinghouse Electric Corp.*)

1.25 hp per ton for compressors of ½ to 5 tons capacity.

1.1 hp per ton for compressors of 5 to 50 tons capacity.

1.0 hp per ton for compressors of above 50 tons capacity.

Commercial and Industrial Refrigeration without Ice Making, Main Compressor. Multiply the number of tons of refrigeration required by:

1.5 hp per ton for compressors of 1 to 5 tons capacity.

1.4 hp per ton for compressors of 5 to 50 tons capacity.

1.3 hp per ton for compressors above 50 tons capacity.

This information should be used for estimating purposes only. For any unusual condition or for more accurate information, the compressor manufacturer should be consulted.

Wound-rotor induction motors and special controls are used on centrifugal compressors when speed adjustment is required. On constant-speed applications high-speed synchronous motors are usually suitable, although wound-rotor motors may be required to meet extremely low current limitations.

373. Foundations are necessary to support and maintain in alignment generators and other electrical machines of any considerable size. Foundations are made of masonry. Brick or stone set in mortar (preferably cement mortar) will do, but concrete is almost universally used because it is usually the cheapest. A 1:3:6 (1 part cement, 3 parts sand, and 6 parts crushed stone or gravel by bulk) or even a 1:3:7 mixture of concrete will give excellent results. Brick or stone for foundations can be set in mortar consisting of 1 part cement and 3 parts sand.

374. The size of a foundation is determined by the size of the machine supported and by the stresses imposed by the machine. The area of base of any foundation must be great enough so that its weight and the weight of the machine supported will not cause it to sink into the soil. Where a machine is not subjected to any external forces, i.e., where it is self-contained, the only requirement of the foundation (provided the machine is not one that vibrates excessively) is to keep it from sinking into the ground and the lightest possible foundation that will do this will be satisfactory. Therefore motor generators and rotary converters do not require heavy foundations. Machines that are driven by or drive external apparatus require foundations heavy enough to resist the tendency of the external apparatus to tip or to displace the foundation. No rule can be given for determining the proper weight for a foundation in such a case. However, with a solid foundation, it is usually true that if the foundation is large enough to include all the foundation bolts of the machine and to extend to good bottom, it will be sufficiently heavy. Experience is required to enable one to design the lightest possible foundation that will do, so it is well for the beginner to be sure that his foundation is heavy enough.

375. Foundation for a Gear Motor (Westinghouse Electric Corp.). A foundation or mounting which provides rigidity and prevents "weaving" or "flexing," with resultant misalignment of the shafts, is essential to the successful operation of a gear drive.

A concrete foundation should be used whenever possible and should be carefully prepared to conform with data regarding bolt spacing and physical measurements contained in the identified dimension leaflet.

Gear motors are designed with a tolerance of $+0$ and $-\frac{1}{32}$ in. between the shaft center and the base. Therefore, shimming may be required. Shims of various thicknesses, slotted to slide around the foundation bolts, should be used. After alignment has been secured through shimming, the gear motor should be bolted down and grouted in. When the unit must be installed on structural foundations, a supporting base plate of steel should be provided to obtain proper rigidity. This plate should be of a thickness not less than the diameter of the holding-down bolts.

376. Alignment of Motors. After the motor is properly located and the right kind of mounting has been built, the next step is to align the motor properly with its drive. The following procedure is recommended by the General Electric Co.: Belt drive is the most common form of mechanical transmission, but the principles involved and the methods used in aligning apply, in general, equally well for chain drive. The tools usually used for aligning motors or line shafting are the square, plumb bob, and level. Tool manufacturers also build combination squares and levels and similar tools that are a material aid in quickly and accurately aligning machinery.

The first step to be taken when aligning two machines is to see if they are level. It is possible for a machine to be out of line in more than one plane. If, by placing a level or plumb on the machine, it is found to be out a certain amount, the motor must then be mounted so that it will also be out a like amount.

A simple and easy method of aligning a motor pulley with the driven pulley is shown in Fig. 186. First, the crown or

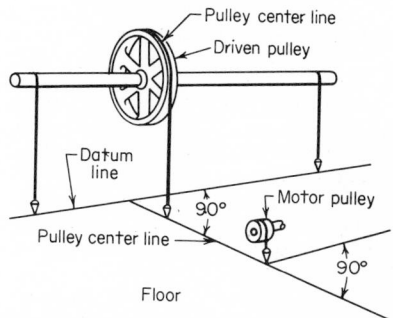

FIG. 186 *Method of aligning two pulleys.* (*General Electric Co.*)

center line of the pulleys must be on the same center line, and second, the motor shaft must be parallel to the driven shaft.

By using a plumb bob and drawing a datum line on the floor, a base of operation is established. Next, drop a plumb line from the center of the driven pulley to the floor. With a square, draw a line perpendicular to the datum line. Next, drop a plumb line from the center of the motor pulley and move the motor up or back until the plumb bob rests on the center line of the driven pulley. From the pulley center line, perpendiculars can be drawn through the centers of the holes in the motor feet. A level should be used to see that the line shafting is level. If it is not, then the motor feet must be shimmed up so that the motor shaft and the line shaft will be "out of level" the same amount. Chain drive can be aligned in a similar manner.

With belt drive, a sliding base is nearly always used to allow for belt adjustment. Another method, therefore, is to use the following procedure when aligning two pulleys:

1. Place the motor on the base so that there will be an equal amount of adjustment in either direction, and firmly fasten the motor to the base by means of the four holding-down bolts.

2. Mount the motor pulley on the motor shaft.

3. Locate the base and motor in approximately the final position, as determined by the length of belt.

4. Stretch a string from the face of the driven pulley toward the face of the motor pulley.

5. Parallel the face of the motor pulley with this string.

6. Using a scratch pin, mark the end positions of the sliding base.

7. Extend these lines.

8. Move the base and motor away from the string an amount equal to one-half the difference in face width of the two pulleys. Use the two extended lines as a guide to keep the base in its proper position.

9. The belt should now be placed on the pulleys to see if it operates satisfactorily. If it does not operate properly, the base can be shifted slightly until proper operation is obtained.

10. Finally, firmly fasten the base to the floor, ceiling, or side walls by means of lag screws or bolts.

377. In designing a V-belt drive the following factors should be considered: speed-reduction factor, pitch diameters of pulleys, belt speed, distance between pulley centers, cross-sectional size of belt, and number of belts to use.

378. The method of designing V-belt drives for satisfactory operation is outlined as follows through the courtesy of the Allis-Chalmers Manufacturing Co.

1. Determine the speed ratio = motor rpm/machine rpm.

2. From Table **379** determine the section of V belt to use, according to the horse-power and synchronous-speed rating of the motor. Where two sections are given, the design should be made for both and then a decision made at the end as to which should be used.

3. From Table **381** and the speed ratio determined in 1, select pitch diameters for the sheaves. Pitch diameter for the machine sheave should equal the pitch diameter for the motor sheave multiplied by the speed ratio. The motor sheave should not be too small, as the horsepower transmitted increases with the increase in size of the small sheave. The machine sheave must not be too large, however. Consideration must be given to the size of the machine and the available space for the sheave.

4. From Table **382** determine the service factor for the drive, according to the type of motor and type of machine.

5. From Table **383** determine the arc of contact of the V belt on the small sheave and the correction factor for belt horsepower.

6. Compute the horsepower required for the belts by multiplying the rated motor horsepower by the service factor obtained from 4.

7. Compute the velocity of the belt $= \pi dn/12$, where $d =$ diameter of motor sheave in inches and $n =$ approximate full-load speed of motor.

8. From Table **379** determine the horsepower rating of each belt, according to the belt velocity and the pitch diameter of the motor sheave.

9. Determine the number of belts required =

$$\frac{\text{horsepower required (from 6)}}{\text{horsepower rating of belt (from 8)} \times \text{service factor (from 4)}} \tag{13}$$

Use the next larger whole number. This should preferably be a small number, such as 4 or 5, although in the case of large horsepower ratings or low speeds a larger number may be necessary. In case of doubt try the next larger belt section and re-calculate.

379. V-belt Sections to Use

Hp rating of motor	Syn. speed of motor	V-belt section	Hp rating of motor	Syn. speed of motor	V-belt section
1½ and less	All	A	60	1,800	C
			60	1,200–900	C or D
2–7½	All	A or B	60	720 and less	D
7½	900 and less	B or C	75	1,800	C
			75	1,200–900	C or D
10	1,800	A or B	75	720 and less	D or E
10	1,200–900	B			
10	720 and less	B or C	100	1,800	C
			100	1,200 and less	D
15	1,800	B			
15	1,200–900	B or C	125	1,200–900	D
15	720 and less	C	125	720 and less	D or E
20	1,800	B or C	150	1,200–900	D
20	1,200 and less	C	150	720 and less	E
25–30	All	C	200	1,200–900	D
			200	720 and less	E
40	1,800	C			
40	1,200–900	C or D	250 and over	All	E
40	720 and less	D			
50	1,800–900	C or D			
50	720 and less	D			

380. Standard Sections of V Belts

Section	Greatest width, in.	Thickness, in.	Section	Greatest width, in.	Thickness, in.
A	½	11/32	D	1¼	¾
B	21/32	7/16	E	1½	1
C	⅞	17/32			

381. Standard Pitch Diameters for Sheaves for V-belt Drives
(Allis-Chalmers)

Section A	Section B	Section C	Section D	Section E	Section A	Section B	Section C	Section D	Section E
Pressed steel		Cast iron			Cast iron				
3.0	5.4	9.0	13	20	12	15	38	48	72
3.2	5.6	9.2	13.4	21	13	16	40	50	74
3.4	5.8	9.4	13.8	22	14	17	42	52	76
3.6	6.0	9.6	14	23	15	18	44	54	78
3.8	6.2	9.8	14.2	24	16	19	46	56	80
4.0	6.4	10.0	14.6	25	17	20	48	58	82
4.2	6.6	10.2	15	26	18	21	50	60	84
4.4	6.8	10.6	15.4	27	19	22	52	62	86
4.6	7.4	11	16	28	20	23	54	64	88
4.8	8.6	12	17	29	21	24	56	66	90
5.0	9.4	13	18	30	22	25	58	68	92
5.2	11.0	14	19	31	23	26	60	70	94
5.4	12.4	15	20	32	24	27	62	72	96
5.6	15.4	16	21	33	25	28	64	74	
5.8	18.4	17	22	34	26	29	66	76	
6.0	Cast iron	18	23	35	27	30	68	78	
6.2	5.4	19	24	36	28	31	70	80	
6.4	5.6	20	25	38	29	32	72	82	
7.0	5.8	21	26	40	30	33		84	
8.2	6.0	22	27	42	31	34		86	
9.0	6.2	23	28	44	32	35		88	
10.6	6.4	24	29	46	33	36		90	
12.0	6.6	25	30	48	34	38		92	
15.0	6.8	26	31	50	35	40		94	
18.0	7.0	27	32	52	36	42		96	
	8.0	28	33	54	38	44			
	8.6	29	34	56	40	46			
Cast iron	9.0	30	35	58		48			
4	10.0	31	36	60		50			
5	11.0	32	38	62		52			
6	12.0	33	40	64		54			
7	13.0	34	42	66		56			
8	13.6	35	44	68		58			
9	14	36	46	70		60			
10									
11									

382. Service Factors for Horsepower Loads on V-belt Drives
(Allis-Chalmers)

	Electric motors										Engines			
	A-C								D-C		Gas and diesel			
	Squirrel cage		High torque	Wound rotor (slip-ring)	Synchronous		Single phase							
Applications	Normal torque, line start	Normal torque, compensator start	High torque	Wound rotor (slip-ring)	Normal torque	High torque	Repulsion and split-phase	Capacitor	Shunt wound	Compound wound	4 or more cyl.; above 700 rpm	4 or more cyl.; below 700 rpm	Steam	Line shafts and clutch starting
Agitators, paddle-propeller:														
Liquid	1.0	1.0	1.2											
Semiliquid	1.2	1.0	1.4	1.2										
Brick and clay machinery:														
Auger machines	...	1.2	1.4	1.4	...	...	...	...		1.4	...	...	...	2.0
De-airing machines	...	1.2	1.4	1.4	...	...	...	...		1.4	...	...	...	2.0
Cutting table	...	1.2	1.4	1.4	...	...	...	...		...	...	...	...	2.0
Pug mill	1.5	1.3	1.8	1.5										
Mixer	...	1.2	1.6	1.4										
Granulator	...	1.2	1.4	1.4										
Dry press	...	1.2	1.6	1.4										
Rolls	...	1.2	1.4	1.4										
Bakery machinery:														
Dough mixer	1.2	...	...	...	...	...	1.2	1.0						
Compressors:														
Centrifugal	1.2	1.2	...	1.4	1.4	...	...	...	1.2	...	1.2			
Rotary	1.2	1.2	...	1.4	1.4	...	1.2	1.2	1.2	...	1.2			
Reciprocating:														
3 or more cylinders	1.2	1.2	...	1.4	1.4	...	...	...	1.2					
1 or 2 cylinders	1.4	1.4	...	1.5	1.5	...	...	...	1.2					
Conveyors:														
Apron	...	1.4	1.6	...	...	...	...	...	1.4	...	...	...	...	1.6
Belt (ore, coal, sand)	...	1.2	1.4	...	...	...	...	...	1.2	...	...	...	...	1.4
Belt (light package)	...	1.0	1.1	...	...	...	...	...	1.0	...	...	...	...	1.2
Oven	...	1.0	1.1	...	...	...	...	...	1.0	...	...	...	...	1.2
Screw	...	1.6	1.8	...	...	...	...	...	1.6	...	...	...	...	1.8
Bucket	...	1.4	1.6	...	...	...	...	...	1.4	...	...	...	...	1.6
Pan	...	1.4	1.6	...	...	...	...	...	1.4	...	...	...	...	1.6
Flight	...	1.6	1.8	...	...	...	...	...	1.6	...	...	...	...	1.8
Elevator	...	1.4	1.6	...	...	...	...	...	1.4	...	...	...	...	1.6
Crushing machinery:														
Jaw crushers	...	1.4	1.6	1.4	...	...	...	...		1.4	1.4	...	...	1.6
Gyratory crushers	...	1.4	1.6	1.4	1.4	1.6	...	...		1.4	1.4	...	...	1.6
Cone crushers	...	1.4	1.6	1.4	...	...	...	...		1.6	1.4	...	...	1.6
Crushing rolls	...	1.4	1.6	1.4	...	...	...	...		1.4	1.4	...	...	1.6
Ball, pebble and	...	1.4	1.6	1.4	1.4	1.6	...	...		1.4	1.6	...	...	1.6
tube mills	...	1.4	1.6	1.4	1.4	...	...	...		1.4	...	...	...	1.6
Fans and blowers:														
Centrifugal	1.2	1.2	...	1.4	...	...	...	...	1.2	...	1.2			
Propeller	1.4	1.4	2.0	1.6	...	2.0	...	...	1.4	...	1.4			
Induced draft	1.2	1.2	...	1.4	...	...	...	...	1.4	...	1.4			
Mine fans	1.6	1.4	2.0	...	...	2.0	...	...	...	...	1.6			
Positive blowers	1.6	1.6	...	2.0	2.0	2.0	...	...	...	...	1.6			
Exhausters	1.2	1.2	...	1.4	...	...	...	...	1.4	...	...	...	1.5	1.5
Flour-, feed-, cereal-mill machinery:														
Bolters and sifters	...	1.0												
Grinders and hammer mills	...	1.4	...	...	...	...	...	...		...	1.6			
Purifiers and reels	1.2	1.4												
Main-line shaft drive	1.4	1.4	1.6	1.4	1.4	...	...	...		...	1.8			
Separator	1.0	1.0												
Roller mills	...	1.4												
Generator and exciters	1.2	...	...	...	...	...	...	...	1.2	...	2.0	...	1.4	1.4

Service Factors for Horsepower Loads on V-belt Drives (Continued)

Applications	A-C Squirrel cage: Normal torque, line start	Squirrel cage: Normal torque, compensator start	Squirrel cage: High torque	Wound rotor (slip-ring)	Synchronous: Normal torque	Synchronous: High torque	Single phase: Repulsion and split-phase	Single phase: Capacitor	D-C Shunt wound	D-C Compound wound	Engines Gas and diesel: 4 or more cyl.; above 700 rpm	4 or more cyl.; below 700 rpm	Steam	Line shafts and clutch starting
Laundry machinery:														
Washers	1.2									1.2				
Extractors	1.2									1.2				
Tumblers	1.2									1.2				
Dampeners	1.2									1.2				
Flatwork ironers	1.2									1.2				
Line shafts	1.4	1.4		1.4	1.4	2.0	1.4	1.4	1.4	1.4	1.6		1.6	1.6
Machine tools:														
Grinders	1.2			1.4			1.2	1.0	1.2	1.2				
Boring mills	1.2			1.4					1.2	1.2				
Lathes	1.0			1.2			1.0	1.0	1.0	1.0				
Milling machines	1.2			1.4					1.2	1.2				
Screw machines	1.0			1.0			1.0	1.0	1.0	1.0				
Cam cutters	1.0			1.0					1.0	1.0				
Planers	1.2			1.4			1.2	1.0	1.2	1.2				
Shapers	1.0			1.0			1.0	1.0	1.0	1.0				
Drill press	1.0			1.0			1.0	1.0	1.0	1.0				
Drop hammers	1.0			1.0			1.0	1.0	1.0	1.0				
Shears	1.2			1.4			1.2	1.2	1.2	1.0				
Mills:														
Pebble		1.4	1.6	1.4						1.4				1.6
Rod		1.4	1.6	1.4						1.4				1.6
Ball		1.4	1.6	1.4						1.4				1.6
Roller mills		1.4	1.6	1.4						1.4				1.6
Flaking mills		1.6	1.6	1.4						1.4				1.6
Tumbling barrels		1.6	1.6	1.4						1.4				1.6
Oil-field machinery:[a]														
Slush pumps										1.4	1.4	1.6	1.4	1.4
Pumping units	1.2	1.2	1.4							1.4				1.6
Pipe-line pumps, centrifugal	1.2	1.2	1.4						1.4	1.4				
Draw works (intermittent)										1.3		1.0	1.0	
Paper machinery:														
Jordan engines	1.5	1.3	1.8	1.5	1.6	1.8			1.5	1.5				
Beaters	1.4	1.4		1.4					1.4	1.4				1.8
Calenders	1.2	1.2		1.2					1.2	1.2				
Agitators	1.2	1.0	1.4	1.2					1.2	1.2				1.6
Driers	1.2	1.2		1.2					1.2	1.2				
Paper machines	1.4	1.4		1.5					1.5	1.5				1.6
Printing machinery:														
Rotary press	1.2	1.2		1.2					1.2					
Embossing press	1.2	1.2		1.2					1.2	1.2				
Folders	1.2	1.2		1.2					1.2					
Paper cutters	1.2	1.2		1.2					1.2	1.2				
Linotype machines	1.2	1.2							1.2					
Flat-bed press	1.2	1.2		1.2					1.2					
Pumps:														
Centrifugal	1.2	1.2	1.4	1.4			1.2	1.2						
Gear	1.2	1.2	1.4	1.4			1.2	1.2						
Rotary	1.2	1.2	1.4	1.4			1.2	1.2	1.2		1.2			

[a] Hoisting service factor based on total engine horsepower (continuous rating). Electric drive factor based on continuous rating of motor.

Service Factors for Horsepower Loads on V-belt Drives (*Continued*)

Applications	Electric motors										Engines			
	A-C								D-C		Gas and diesel			
	Squirrel cage				Synchronous	Single phase								
	Normal torque, line start	Normal torque, compensator start	High torque	Wound rotor (slip-ring)	Normal torque	High torque	Repulsion and split-phase	Capacitor	Shunt wound	Compound wound	4 or more cyl.; above 700 rpm	4 or more cyl.; below 700 rpm	Steam	Line shafts and clutch starting
Pumps:—(*Continued*)														
Reciprocating:														
3 or more cylinders	1.2	1.2	...	1.4	1.4	1.6	...	...	...	...	1.8	...	1.8	
1 or 2 cylinders	1.4	1.4	...	1.6	1.6	1.8	...	...	...	...	2.0	...	2.0	
Dredge pumps	1.4	1.4	...	1.4	...	...	...	...	...	...	2.0	...	2.0	
Rubber-plant machinery:														
Calenders	1.4	1.4	1.4	1.4	...	1.8	...	...	...	...	...	...	2.0	
Banbury mills	1.4	1.4	1.4	1.4	...	1.8	...	...	...	...	...	...	2.0	
Mixers	1.4	1.4	1.4	1.4	...	1.8	...	...	...	...	...	...	2.0	
Screens:														
Vibrating	1.2	1.2	1.4											
Conical	1.2	1.2												
Revolving	1.2	1.2												
Textile machinery:														
Spinning frames	1.6	...		1.8										
Twisters	1.6	...		1.8										
Looms	1.2													
Warpers	1.2													
Reels	1.2													

383. Correction Factors for Horsepower Rating of V Belts According to Arc of Contact on Small Sheave

Arc of contact,[a] deg	V-belt sheaves on both shafts	V-belt sheave to flat pulley	Arc of contact,[a] deg	V-belt sheaves on both shafts	V-belt sheave to flat pulley
	Correction factor			Correction factor	
180	1.00	0.74	130	0.86	0.86
170	0.98	0.77	120	0.83	0.83
160	0.95	0.79	110	0.79	0.79
150	0.92	0.82	100	0.74	0.74
140	0.89	0.84	90	0.69	0.69

[a] Arc of contact $= 180 - (D - d)60/C$, where D = pitch diameter of large pulley (for flat pulleys add the thickness of belt to the pulley diameter); d = pitch diameter of small pulley; and C = center distance.

384. Horsepower Ratings for V Belts

"A" Section

Velocity, ft per min	Pitch diam, in.						
	2.6	3.0	3.4	3.8	4.2	4.6	5.0 and larger
1,000	0.5	0.7	0.8	0.9	0.9	1.0	1.0
1,100	0.6	0.7	0.9	1.0	1.0	1.1	1.1
1,200	0.6	0.8	1.0	1.0	1.1	1.2	1.2
1,300	0.7	0.9	1.0	1.1	1.2	1.3	1.3
1,400	0.7	0.9	1.1	1.2	1.3	1.4	1.4
1,500	0.8	1.0	1.1	1.3	1.4	1.4	1.5
1,600	0.8	1.0	1.2	1.3	1.4	1.5	1.6
1,700	0.9	1.1	1.3	1.4	1.5	1.6	1.7
1,800	0.9	1.2	1.4	1.5	1.6	1.7	1.8
1,900	0.9	1.2	1.4	1.6	1.7	1.8	1.9
2,000	1.0	1.3	1.5	1.6	1.8	1.9	2.0
2,100	1.0	1.3	1.5	1.7	1.9	2.0	2.1
2,200	1.1	1.4	1.6	1.8	1.9	2.0	2.2
2,300	1.1	1.4	1.6	1.8	2.0	2.1	2.3
2,400	1.1	1.4	1.7	1.9	2.0	2.2	2.3
2,500	1.1	1.5	1.7	2.0	2.1	2.3	2.4
2,600	...	1.6	1.8	2.0	2.2	2.3	2.5
2,700	...	1.6	1.8	2.1	2.3	2.4	2.6
2,800	...	1.6	1.9	2.1	2.3	2.5	2.6
2,900	...	1.6	1.9	2.2	2.4	2.6	2.7
3,000	...	...	2.0	2.2	2.4	2.6	2.7
3,100	...	...	2.0	2.3	2.5	2.6	2.8
3,200	...	...	2.0	2.3	2.5	2.7	2.9
3,300	...	...	2.1	2.4	2.6	2.7	2.9
3,400	...	...	...	2.4	2.7	2.8	3.0
3,500	...	...	...	2.5	2.7	2.8	3.0
3,600	...	...	...	2.5	2.7	2.9	3.1
3,700	...	...	...	2.5	2.8	2.9	3.1
3,800	...	...	...	...	2.8	3.0	3.2
3,900	...	...	...	...	2.8	3.0	3.2
4,000	...	...	...	...	2.8	3.0	3.3
4,100	...	...	...	...	2.9	3.1	3.3
4,200	...	...	...	...	...	3.1	3.3
4,300	...	...	...	...	...	3.1	3.3
4,400	...	...	...	...	...	3.2	3.4
4,500	...	...	...	...	...	3.2	3.4
4,600	...	...	...	...	...	...	3.4
4,700	...	...	...	...	...	...	3.4
4,800	...	...	...	...	...	...	3.4
4,900	...	...	...	...	...	...	3.4
5,000	...	...	...	...	...	...	3.4

Horsepower Ratings for V Belts (*Continued*)

"B" Section

Velocity, ft per min	Pitch diam, in.					
	5.0	5.4	5.8	6.2	6.6	7.0 and larger
1,000	1.3	1.4	1.5	1.6	1.7	1.8
1,100	1.4	1.5	1.6	1.7	1.8	1.9
1,200	1.5	1.6	1.7	1.8	1.9	2.0
1,300	1.6	1.8	1.9	2.0	2.1	2.2
1,400	1.7	1.9	2.0	2.1	2.2	2.3
1,500	1.8	2.0	2.1	2.3	2.4	2.5
1,600	1.9	2.1	2.3	2.4	2.5	2.6
1,700	2.0	2.2	2.4	2.5	2.7	2.8
1,800	2.2	2.4	2.5	2.7	2.8	2.9
1,900	2.3	2.5	2.6	2.8	3.0	3.1
2,000	2.4	2.6	2.8	2.9	3.1	3.2
2,100	2.4	2.7	2.9	3.1	3.2	3.4
2,200	2.5	2.8	3.0	3.2	3.4	3.5
2,300	2.6	2.9	3.1	3.3	3.5	3.6
2,400	2.7	3.0	3.2	3.4	3.6	3.7
2,500	2.8	3.1	3.3	3.5	3.7	3.9
2,600	2.9	3.2	3.4	3.6	3.8	4.0
2,700	3.0	3.3	3.5	3.7	3.9	4.1
2,800	3.0	3.3	3.6	3.8	4.1	4.3
2,900	3.1	3.4	3.7	3.9	4.2	4.4
3,000	3.2	3.5	3.8	4.0	4.3	4.5
3,100	3.2	3.6	3.9	4.1	4.4	4.6
3,200	3.3	3.6	4.0	4.2	4.5	4.7
3,300	3.3	3.7	4.0	4.3	4.6	4.8
3,400	3.4	3.7	4.1	4.4	4.7	4.9
3,500	3.4	3.8	4.1	4.4	4.7	4.9
3,600	3.4	3.8	4.2	4.5	4.8	5.0
3,700	3.5	3.9	4.3	4.5	4.8	5.1
3,800	3.5	3.9	4.3	4.6	4.9	5.2
3,900	3.5	3.9	4.3	4.6	4.9	5.2
4,000	3.5	4.0	4.4	4.7	5.0	5.3
4,100	3.5	4.0	4.4	4.7	5.0	5.3
4,200	3.5	4.0	4.4	4.7	5.1	5.4
4,300	3.5	4.0	4.4	4.7	5.1	5.4
4,400	3.5	4.0	4.4	4.8	5.1	5.4
4,500	3.5	4.0	4.4	4.8	5.1	5.4
4,600	3.4	4.0	4.4	4.8	5.1	5.5
4,700	3.4	3.9	4.4	4.8	5.2	5.5
4,800	3.4	3.9	4.4	4.8	5.2	5.5
4,900	3.3	3.9	4.3	4.8	5.1	5.5
5,000	3.3	3.8	4.3	4.7	5.1	5.5

Horsepower Ratings for V Belts (*Continued*)

"C" Section

Velocity, ft per min	Pitch diam, in.					
	7.0	8.0	9.0	10.0	11.0	12.0 and larger
1,000	2.0	2.5	2.8	3.1	3.4	3.6
1,100	2.2	2.7	3.1	3.5	3.7	3.9
1,200	2.4	2.9	3.4	3.8	4.0	4.3
1,300	2.6	3.2	3.7	4.1	4.4	4.6
1,400	2.7	3.4	3.9	4.4	4.7	5.0
1,500	2.9	3.6	4.2	4.6	5.0	5.3
1,600	3.1	3.9	4.5	4.9	5.3	5.7
1,700	3.3	4.1	4.7	5.3	5.6	6.0
1,800	3.4	4.3	5.0	5.5	5.9	6.3
1,900	3.6	4.5	5.2	5.8	6.2	6.6
2,000	3.7	4.7	5.5	6.1	6.5	7.0
2,100	3.9	4.9	5.7	6.3	6.8	7.3
2,200	4.0	5.1	5.9	6.6	7.1	7.6
2,300	4.2	5.3	6.2	6.8	7.4	7.9
2,400	4.3	5.5	6.4	7.1	7.7	8.2
2,500	4.5	5.7	6.6	7.3	8.0	8.5
2,600	4.6	5.8	6.8	7.6	8.2	8.8
2,700	4.7	6.0	7.0	7.8	8.4	9.0
2,800	4.8	6.2	7.2	8.0	8.7	9.3
2,900	4.9	6.3	7.4	8.3	9.0	9.6
3,000	5.0	6.5	7.6	8.5	9.2	9.8
3,100	5.1	6.6	7.8	8.7	9.5	10.1
3,200	5.2	6.7	7.9	8.9	9.7	10.3
3,300	5.3	6.9	8.1	9.1	9.9	10.6
3,400	...	7.0	8.3	9.3	10.1	10.8
3,500	...	7.1	8.4	9.4	10.3	11.0
3,600	...	7.2	8.5	9.6	10.5	11.2
3,700	...	7.3	8.7	9.8	10.7	11.4
3,800	...	7.4	8.8	9.9	10.9	11.6
3,900	...	...	8.9	10.1	11.0	11.8
4,000	...	...	9.0	10.2	11.2	12.0
4,100	...	...	9.1	10.3	11.3	12.2
4,200	...	...	9.2	10.4	11.5	12.3
4,300	...	...	9.3	10.5	11.6	12.5
4,400	...	...	...	10.6	11.7	12.6
4,500	...	...	...	10.7	11.8	12.7
4,600	...	...	...	10.8	11.9	12.9
4,700	...	...	...	10.8	12.0	13.0
4,800	...	...	...	10.9	12.1	13.3
4,900	...	...	...	....	12.1	13.2
5,000	...	...	...	....	12.2	13.2

Horsepower Ratings for V Belts (*Continued*)
"D" Section

Velocity, ft per min	Pitch diam, in.					
	12.0	13.0	14.0	15.0	16.0	17.0 and larger
1,000	4.5	5.1	5.6	6.1	6.5	6.8
1,100	4.9	5.8	6.2	6.7	7.2	7.5
1,200	5.3	6.1	6.7	7.3	7.7	8.2
1,300	5.7	6.5	7.2	7.8	8.4	8.8
1,400	6.1	7.0	7.8	8.4	9.0	9.4
1,500	6.5	7.5	8.2	9.0	9.6	10.1
1,600	6.9	7.9	8.8	9.5	10.2	10.7
1,700	7.3	8.4	9.3	10.1	10.8	11.4
1,800	7.7	8.8	9.8	10.6	11.3	12.0
1,900	8.0	9.2	10.2	11.1	11.9	12.6
2,000	8.4	9.7	10.7	11.7	12.5	13.2
2,100	8.8	10.1	11.2	12.2	13.0	13.8
2,200	9.1	10.5	11.7	12.7	13.6	14.4
2,300	9.5	10.9	12.1	13.2	14.1	14.9
2,400	9.8	11.3	12.6	13.7	14.6	15.5
2,500	10.1	11.6	12.9	14.1	15.1	16.0
2,600	10.4	12.0	13.4	14.6	15.6	16.6
2,700	10.6	12.3	13.8	15.0	16.1	17.1
2,800	10.9	12.7	14.1	15.5	16.6	17.6
2,900	11.2	13.0	14.5	15.9	17.0	18.1
3,000	11.4	13.3	14.9	16.3	17.5	18.6
3,100	11.7	13.6	15.2	16.7	17.9	19.0
3,200	11.9	13.9	15.6	17.1	18.4	19.5
3,300	12.1	14.1	15.9	17.4	18.9	19.9
3,400	12.2	14.4	16.2	17.7	19.1	20.3
3,500	12.4	14.6	16.5	18.1	19.5	20.7
3,600	12.6	14.8	16.7	18.4	19.8	21.1
3,700	12.7	15.0	17.0	18.7	20.2	21.5
3,800	12.8	15.2	17.2	18.9	20.4	22.2
3,900	....	15.3	17.4	19.2	20.7	22.3
4,000	....	15.5	17.6	19.4	21.0	22.5
4,100	....	15.6	17.8	19.6	21.3	22.8
4,200	....	....	17.9	19.8	21.5	23.0
4,300	....	....	18.0	20.0	21.8	23.0
4,400	....	....	18.1	20.1	21.9	23.3
4,500	....	....	....	20.3	22.1	23.5
4,600	....	....	....	20.4	22.3	23.9
4,700	....	....	....	20.5	22.4	24.1
4,800	....	....	....	....	22.5	24.2
4,900	....	....	....	....	22.6	24.3
5,000	....	....	....	....	22.6	24.4

Horsepower Ratings for V Belts (*Continued*)
"E" Section

Velocity, ft per min	Pitch diam, in.								
	20	21	22	23	24	25	26	27	28 and larger
1,000	8.0	8.5	9.0	9.4	9.8	10.2	10.5	10.9	11.1
1,100	8.7	9.3	9.8	10.3	10.8	11.2	11.6	11.9	12.2
1,200	9.5	10.1	10.7	11.2	11.7	12.2	12.6	13.0	13.3
1,300	10.2	10.9	11.6	12.1	12.7	13.1	13.6	14.0	14.4
1,400	11.0	11.7	12.4	13.0	13.6	14.1	14.6	15.0	15.4
1,500	11.7	12.5	13.2	13.9	14.5	15.1	15.6	16.1	16.5
1,600	12.4	13.3	14.1	14.8	15.4	16.0	16.6	17.1	17.5
1,700	13.1	14.0	14.9	15.6	16.3	16.9	17.5	18.1	18.6
1,800	13.8	14.8	15.7	16.5	17.2	17.9	18.5	19.0	19.6
1,900	14.5	15.5	16.4	17.3	18.0	18.8	19.4	20.0	20.6
2,000	15.2	16.2	17.2	18.1	18.9	19.6	20.3	21.0	21.6
2,100	15.8	17.0	18.0	18.9	19.7	20.5	21.2	21.9	22.5
2,200	16.5	17.6	18.7	19.7	20.6	21.4	22.1	22.8	23.5
2,300	17.1	18.3	19.4	20.4	21.4	22.2	23.0	23.7	24.4
2,400	17.7	18.9	20.1	21.2	22.2	23.1	23.9	24.6	25.3
2,500	18.3	19.6	20.8	21.9	23.0	23.9	24.7	25.5	26.3
2,600	18.9	20.2	21.5	22.6	23.7	24.7	25.5	26.4	27.1
2,700	19.4	20.8	22.1	23.3	24.4	25.4	26.4	27.2	28.0
2,800	19.9	21.4	22.8	24.0	25.1	26.2	27.1	28.0	28.9
2,900	20.4	22.0	23.4	24.7	25.8	26.9	27.9	28.8	29.7
3,000	20.9	22.7	24.0	25.3	26.5	27.6	28.6	29.6	30.5
3,100	21.4	23.0	24.5	26.0	27.2	28.3	29.4	30.4	31.3
3,200	21.8	23.5	25.1	26.5	27.8	29.0	30.1	31.1	32.0
3,300	22.3	24.0	25.6	27.1	28.4	29.6	30.7	31.8	32.8
3,400	22.6	24.5	26.1	27.6	29.0	30.2	31.4	32.5	33.5
3,500	23.0	24.9	26.6	28.1	29.5	30.8	32.0	33.1	34.2
3,600	23.4	25.3	27.0	28.6	30.0	31.4	32.6	33.8	34.8
3,700	23.7	25.6	27.4	29.1	30.6	31.9	33.2	34.4	35.5
3,800	24.0	26.0	27.8	29.5	31.0	32.4	33.7	34.9	36.1
3,900	24.2	26.3	28.2	29.9	31.5	32.9	34.3	35.5	36.6
4,000	24.5	26.6	28.5	30.3	31.9	33.4	34.7	36.0	37.2
4,100	....	26.8	28.8	30.6	32.3	33.8	35.2	36.5	37.7
4,200	....	27.1	29.1	30.9	32.6	34.2	35.6	37.0	38.2
4,300	....	....	29.3	31.2	33.0	34.6	36.0	37.4	38.7
4,400	....	....	29.5	31.5	33.3	34.9	36.4	37.8	39.1
4,500	....	....	....	31.7	33.5	35.2	36.7	38.2	39.5
4,600	....	....	....	31.9	33.7	35.5	37.0	38.5	39.9
4,700	....	....	....	....	33.9	35.7	37.3	38.8	40.2
4,800	....	....	....	....	34.1	35.9	37.5	39.1	40.5
4,900	....	....	....	....	....	36.0	37.7	39.3	40.7
5,000	....	....	....	....	....	36.2	37.9	39.5	40.9

385. Procedure in Planning a Flat-belt Drive (General Electric Co.).

1. Check reduction ratio of speed required against limits of Sec. **330**.

2. Determine pulley diameters from Secs. **388** and **390**.

3. Check available distances between centers of shafts against limits of Secs. **387** and **391**.

4. Determine belt speed from Secs. **389** and **392**.

5. Determine horsepower that will be transmitted per inch of width of belt from Secs. **393** and **394**.

6. Determine width of belt required from Sec. **395**.

7. Determine required width of pulleys from Sec. **396** and check against standard motor-pulley widths from Sec. **388**.

386. Belt Slip. The effect of creepage and slip is to reduce the speed of the driven pulley and, consequently, the power transmitted. For commercial applications it will be close enough to multiply the calculated speed of the driven shaft by 98 per cent, assuming 2 per cent slip. The diameter of the driven pulley should be slightly smaller than that calculated on the basis of no slip in order to get a certain speed at the driven shaft. In other words, the speed of the driven shaft is reduced by slip unless compensated for by reducing the driven-pulley diameter a proportionate amount.

A small amount of belt slip is not harmful, but excessive slip is. Severe slippage burns the belt, quickly destroying its usefulness, while, at best, the belt surface is polished so that the grip on the pulley is materially reduced. Belt slip can be detected by noting the condition of the pulley surface. When the belt is slipping, the pulley will have a very shiny appearance, as contrasted to the smooth but rather dull appearance it should have.

Excessive slip is caused by poorly designed drives, where the driving pulley is too small or the load too great; by running the belt too loose; or by not giving proper attention to the care of the belt.

387. Arc of Contact for Flat-belt Drives. One of the factors affecting the amount of power that can be transmitted by a belt of given width is the arc of contact (the distance the belt wraps around the pulley). As this arc of contact decreases, the belt width must be increased to transmit the same horsepower with 2 per cent slip; Table **394**, however, allows a factor of safety sufficient to take care of installations which are in accordance with the recommendations for belt ratios and center distances given in this subdivision. If it is necessary to exceed the limits given, it may be necessary to use a belt tightener.

388. Application of Flat-belt Pulley Dimensions and Belt Widths to General-purpose Motors (NEMA Standard).   General-purpose motors having continuous time rating with the frame sizes, horsepower, and speed ratings given in the following paragraphs are designed to operate with flat-belt pulleys and belts within the limiting dimensions listed.

A. Direct-current Integral-horsepower Motors

Frame number	Horsepower at, rpm						Standard pulley			Minimum pulley			
	1,750	1,150	850	690	575	500	Pulley diam, in.	Pulley width, in.	Belt width, in.	Min pulley diam, in.	Max pulley width, in.	Belt width, in.	Pulley bore, in.
203	1	....	....	.....	.....	....	3	3	2½	2½	3	2½	¾
204	1½	1	....	.....	.....	....	3	3	2½	2½	3	2½	¾
224	2	1½	¾	½	.....	....	4	3½	3	2½	3½	3	1
225	3	2	1	¾	½	....	4	3½	3	3	3½	3	1
254	5	3	2–1½	1½–1	1–¾	....	4½	4½	4	3½	4½	4	1½
284	7½	5	3	2	2–1½	1½–1¾	5	4½	4	4	5½	5	1¼
	10	7½	5	.....	.....	....	6	5½	5	5	6¾	6	
	15	10	7½	.....	.....	....	7	6¾	6	6	7¾	7	
	20	15	10	.....	.....	....	8	6¾	6	6	9¾	9	
	25	....	.....	.....	.....	....	9	7¾	7	6	9¾	9	
	30	20	15	.....	.....	....	9	7¾	7	7	11	10	
	40	25	20	.....	.....	....	10	7¾	7	7	11	10	
		30	25	.....	.....	....	10	7¾	7	9	12	11	
		40	30	.....	.....	....	11	11	10	9	13	12	
		50	.....	.....	.....	....	12	12	11	11	13	12	
		60	.....	.....	.....	....	12	12	11	11	17	16	
		....	40	.....	.....	....	12	12	11	11	13	12	
		75	.....	.....	.....	....	14	13	12	12	17	16	
			50	.....	.....	....	14	13	12	11	17	16	
			60	.....	.....	....	14	13	12	12	17	16	
			75	.....	.....	....	15	15	14				

B. Single-phase Integral-horsepower Motors

Frame number	Horsepower at, rpm				Standard pulley			Minimum pulley			Pulley bore, in.
	3,600	1,800	1,200	900	Pulley diam, in.	Pulley width, in.	Belt width, in.	Min pulley diam, in.	Max pulley width, in.	Belt width, in.	
203	1½	1	....	......	3	3	2½	2½	3	2½	¾
204	2	1½	¾	. ....	3	3	2½	2½	3	2½	¾
224	3	2	1	½	4	3½	3	2½	3½	3	1
225	5	3	1½	¾	4	3½	3	3	3½	3	1
254	7½	5	2	1½–1	4½	4½	4	3½	4½	4	1⅛
		....	3	2	5	4½	4	3½	4½	4	
		7½	5	3	5	4½	4	4	5½	5	
		10	7½	5	6	5½	5	5	6¾	6	
		15	10	7½	7	6¾	6	6	7¾	7	
		20	15	10	8	6¾	6	6	9¾	9	
		....	20	15	9	7¾	7	7	11	10	
		25	....	......	9	7¾	7	6	9¾	9	
			25	20	10	7¾	7	7	11	10	
				25	10	7¾	7	9	12	11	

C. Integral-horsepower Motors—Polyphase Induction

Frame number	Horsepower at, rpm								Standard pulley			Minimum pulley			Pulley bore, in.
	3,600	1,800	1,200	900	720	600	514	450	Pulley diam, in.	Pulley width, in.	Belt width, in.	Min pulley diam, in.	Max pulley width, in.	Belt width, in.	
110, 208, 220, 440 and 550 Volts															
203	1½	1	¾	....	....	....	....	....	3	3	2½	2½	3	2½	¾
204	2	1½	1	½	....	....	....	....	3	3	2½	2½	3	2½	¾
224	3	2	1½	¾	½	....	....	....	4	3½	3	2½	3½	3	1
225	5	3	2	1	¾	½	....	....	4	3½	3	3	3½	3	1
254	7½	5	3	2-1½	1½-1	1-¾	....	....	4½	4½	4	3½	4½	4	1⅛
284	10	7½	5	3	2	1½	1-¾	¾	5	4½	4	4	5½	5	1¼
324	15	....	....	....	....	....	....	....	5	6¾	6	5	6¾	6	1⅝
324	....	10	7½	5	3	2	1½	1	6	5½	5	5	6¾	6	1⅝
326	20	....	....	....	....	....	....	....	5	6¾	6	5	6¾	6	1⅝
326	....	15	10	7½	5	3	2	1½	8	6¾	6	6	7¾	7	1⅝
364	....	25-20	15	10	7½	5	....	....	9	7¾	7	6	9¾	9	1⅞
365	....	30	20	15	10	7½	3	2	9	7¾	7	7	11	10	1⅞
404	....	40	25	20	15	10	5	3	10	8¾	8	7	11	10	2⅛
405	....	....	30	25	20	15	7½	5	10	8¾	8	9	12	11	2⅛
444	....	....	40	30	25	20	10	7½	12	11	10	9	13	12	2⅜
445	....	....	50	40	30	25	15	10	12	11	10	11	13	12	2⅜
504U	....	....	60	50	40	30	20	15	15	13	12	11	17	16	2⅞
505	....	....	75	60	50	40	25	20	15	13	12	12	17	16	2⅞
2300 Volts, Three Phase															
445	....	....	40	....	....	....	....	....	12	11	10	11	13	12	2⅜
504U	....	....	50	40	....	....	....	....	15	13	12	11	17	16	2⅞
505	....	....	60	50	....	....	....	....	15	13	12	12	17	16	2⅞
	....	....	75	....	....	....	....	....	15	13	12	12	17	16	2⅞

389. Belt Speeds for Flat Belts

Full-load speed of motor, rpm	Pulley diam, in.										
	3½	4	4½	5	5½	6	7	8	9	10	11
	Belt speed, ft per min										
1,750	1,605	1,835	2,060	2,290	2,520	2,750	3,205	3,670	4,125	4,580	5,040
1,450	1,330	1,520	1,710	1,900	2,090	2,275	2,660	3,040	3,420	3,800	4,170
1,150	1,055	1,205	1,355	1,505	1,655	1,810	2,110	2,410	2,710	3,010	3,315
860	790	900	1,015	1,130	1,240	1,350	1,575	1,800	2,030	2,255	2,480
690	....	725	815	905	995	1,085	1,265	1,445	1,625	1,810	1,990
575	....	....	680	755	830	905	1,055	1,205	1,355	1,505	1,655

Full-load speed of motor, rpm	Pulley diam, in.										
	12	13	14	15	16	17	18	19	20	21	22
	Belt speed, ft per min										
1,450	4,560	4,930									
1,150	3,615	3,915	4,220	4,520	4,820	5,120					
860	2,705	2,930	3,160	3,380	3,610	3,835	4,060	4,280	4,510	4,740	4,960
690	2,170	2,350	2,530	2,710	2,890	3,075	3,250	3,435	3,615	3,800	3,980
575	1,805	1,955	2,105	2,260	2,410	2,560	2,710	2,860	3,010	3,160	3,310

Full-load speed of motor, rpm	Pulley diam, in.										
	23	24	25	26	27	28	29	30	31	32	33
	Belt speed, ft per min										
690	4,160	4,340	4,520	4,700	4,880	5,060					
575	3,460	3,610	3,760	3,915	4,060	4,210	4,360	4,515	4,665	4,815	4,965

The above table is based on the formula

$$\text{Belt speed in feet per minute} = \frac{3.1416 \times \text{pulley diameter in inches} \times \text{rpm}}{12} \quad (14)$$

390. Determining Pulley Diameters. The following rules are given for determining pulley diameters and speeds:

1. Diameter of driven pulley =

$$\frac{\text{diameter of motor pulley} \times \text{full-load motor speed in rpm}}{\text{rpm of driven pulley}}$$

2. Diameter of motor pulley =

$$\frac{\text{diameter of driven pulley} \times \text{rpm of driven pulley}}{\text{full-load motor speed in rpm}}$$

3. rpm of driven pulley =

$$\frac{\text{diameter of motor pulley} \times \text{full-load motor speed}}{\text{diameter of driven pulley}}$$

4. rpm of motor =

$$\frac{\text{diameter of driven pulley} \times \text{speed of driven pulley}}{\text{diameter of motor pulley}}$$

The above formulas can be applied to any belt drive by substituting the terms "driver" and "rpm of driver" for "motor pulley" and "motor speed."

CAUTION. The desired driven speed should be increased 2 per cent in above formulas to allow for belt slip.

It is desirable to utilize the standard pulleys furnished with the motors wherever possible. The use of special pulleys on electric motors is limited by mechanical dimensions and by the permissible bearing pressure, which, for the transmission of a certain horsepower, increases as the pulley diameter decreases. The maximum pulley diameter is determined by mechanical dimensions. These are in addition to the usual requirements of proper belt speed and width to transmit the power involved.

391. Center Distances for Flat-belt Drives. A short center distance is bad for two reasons: it means a shorter belt, so that flexure occurs at each cross section more frequently, and the arc of contact on the smaller pulley frequently becomes so small that power can no longer be effectively transmitted. Two and a half times the diameter of the larger pulley should be the minimum center distance, with from three to five a better figure.

392. Flat-belt Speed. Belts should not be run at speeds above 5,000 ft per min. Above this speed there is not sufficient friction contact between belt and pulley, because of the effect of centrifugal force tending to "throw" the belt.

Table **389** gives the belt speed in feet per minute corresponding to various motor speeds and pulley diameters.

393. Horsepower Transmitted by Flat Belts. The pulley must be large enough to transmit the horsepower, which ordinarily will not be the motor-horsepower rating but a figure somewhat larger, to take care of possible overloads and peak loads. In ordinary applications, 125 per cent of the motor rating may be allowed for a safety factor in the usual sizes of motors.

In general, the product of the diameter and belt width *of a special* pulley should at least equal the product of the corresponding dimensions of the *standard* pulley recommended for that size and speed of motor. Assuming that the diameters have been tentatively chosen as best for the desired purpose, the horsepower that can be transmitted will depend upon the pulley material, the belt width, its quality and number of plies, the distance between centers, and the relative angular location of the driving and driven pulley.

Table **394** shows the horsepower per inches of width transmitted by good leather belting running over paper pulleys with 180-deg arc of contact and no slip. For iron pulleys, multiply figures given by 0.62; for wood pulleys, multiply by 0.41 (for belt speeds, see Table **389**).

394. Horsepower Transmitted per Inch of Width of Flat Leather Belts

To obtain the horsepower transmitted by belts of any width, multiply the figure shown for the given belt speed by the width of the belt used.

Belt speed, ft per min	Hp per in. of width	Belt speed, ft per min	Hp per in. of width	Belt speed, ft per min	Hp per in. of width	Belt speed, ft per min	Hp per in. of width
Single Belting							
900	1.25	2,000	2.78	3,100	4.31	4,200	5.84
1,000	1.39	2,100	2.92	3,200	4.45	4,300	5.98
1,100	1.53	2,200	3.06	3,300	4.59	4,400	6.12
1,200	1.67	2,300	3.20	3,400	4.72	4,500	6.26
1,300	1.81	2,400	3.33	3,500	4.86	4,600	6.40
1,400	1.95	2,500	3.47	3,600	5.00	4,700	6.54
1,500	2.09	2,600	3.61	3,700	5.14	4,800	6.68
1,600	2.22	2,700	3.75	3,800	5.28	4,900	6.82
1,700	2.36	2,800	3.89	3,900	5.42	5,000	6.96
1,800	2.50	2,900	4.03	4,000	5.56		
1,900	2.64	3,000	4.17	4,100	5.70		
Double Belting							
900	1.79	2,000	3.97	3,100	6.16	4,200	8.34
1,000	1.99	2,100	4.17	3,200	6.36	4,300	8.54
1,100	2.19	2,200	4.37	3,300	6.55	4,400	8.74
1,200	2.39	2,300	4.57	3,400	6.75	4,500	8.94
1,300	2.58	2,400	4.77	3,500	6.95	4,600	9.13
1,400	2.78	2,500	4.97	3,600	7.15	4,700	9.33
1,500	2.98	2,600	5.16	3,700	7.35	4,800	9.53
1,600	3.18	2,700	5.36	3,800	7.55	4,900	9.73
1,700	3.38	2,800	5.56	3,900	7.74	5,000	9.93
1,800	3.58	2,900	5.76	4,000	7.94		
1,900	3.78	3,000	5.96	4,100	8.14		

The figures shown in Table **394** are for "regular" single-ply and double-ply belts. The values for horsepower transmitted by "light" belts will be 80 per cent of values shown; by "heavy" belts, 115 per cent of values shown.

395. Belt Width for Flat Belts. For a given diameter, the minimum belt width is determined by the horsepower to be transmitted; the maximum width is limited by the possible overhang and the safe strain which may be placed on the bearing.

To obtain the belt width necessary to transmit a given horsepower, divide the horsepower which is to be transmitted by the figures given in Table **394,** if paper pulleys are used. For iron pulleys, multiply the quotient thus obtained by 1.6; for wood pulleys, by 2.4.

Stock sizes of belts increase in width by the following increments:

Belt Width, In.	Increment, In.
½–1	⅛
1 –4	¼
4 –7	½
7 –30	1
30 –56	2
Above 56	4

The foregoing represents average practice; stock sizes of different manufacturers may vary slightly from the figures given.

NOTES. A good handy rule to remember is: A single-ply belt 1 in. wide and running at 1,000 ft per min will deliver approximately 1 hp (up to about 3,000 rpm).

Round belts of 0.25 and 0.5 in. diameter are fully equal to single belts of 1 and 3 in., respectively.

396. Pulley widths should exceed belt widths by the following amounts:

Pulley diam, in.	Iron pulley, in.	Paper pulley, in.
Under 2	¼	¼
2– 5	½	½
5–10	½	¾
10–20	½	1
20–24	¾	1
24–36	¾	1½
Above 36	¾	2

397. Arrangement of Belts and Pulleys. A typical belt-drive layout is shown in Fig. 187. The best arrangement of belts and pulleys is with the center line through the pulleys in a horizontal plane. This is called horizontal drive. The drive should be arranged so that the lower side of the belt is driving in order that the sag of the upper side of the belt will tend to increase the arc of contact. This is illustrated in Fig. 188. The sag should be about 1½ in. for every 10 ft of center distance between shafts. If it is too loose,

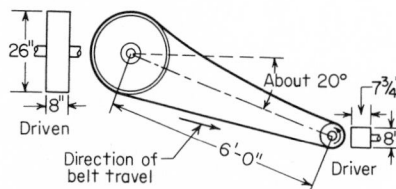

FIG. 187 *General sketch of belt layout.* (*General Electric Co.*)

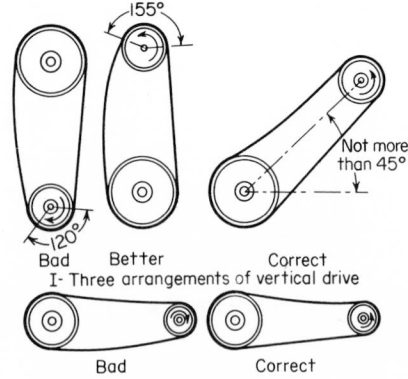

FIG. 188 *Arrangement of belts.* (*General Electric Co.*)

the belt will have an unsteady flapping motion which will injure both belt and machinery; if it is too tight, the bearings will be worn and the belt quickly destroyed.

Vertical drives, the mounting of one pulley above another, should be avoided. This is particularly true where the lower pulley is the smaller. The effective tension and arc of contact are reduced in vertical drives so that the normal load cannot be carried. It is better if the angle of the belt with the floor does not exceed 45 deg (see Fig. 188).

Where several belts transmit power from a line shaft, it is advantageous, where possible, to locate the line shaft so that the bearing pressures can be equalized and reduced by alternating the direction of drive, first on one side, then on the other.

398. Rule for Finding Length of Belts. When it is not feasible to measure with the tapeline the length required, the following rule, which gives an accurate result when the pulleys are of the same diameter and an approximately accurate result when the pulleys are of different diameters, can be used:

Add the diameters of the two pulleys (D and d, Fig. 189) together, divide the result by 2, and multiply the quotient by $3^{1}/_{7}$; add the product to twice the distance L between

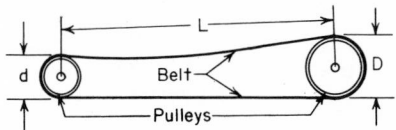

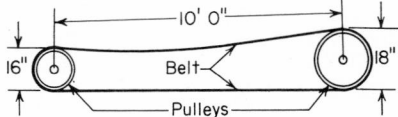

FIG. 189 *Notation for belt-length formula.*   FIG. 190 *Example of finding belt length.*

the centers of the shafts, and the result is the length required. All values should be expressed either in feet or in inches. Expressed as a formula, using the notation of Fig. 189, the rule becomes

$$\text{Length of belt} = [(D + d)1.57] + 2L \qquad (15)$$

Example. What is the length of the belt required for the two pulleys of Fig. 190? Diameters of pulleys are 16 and 18 in. Distance between centers is 10 ft or 120 in.

Solution. Substitute in the formula

$$\text{Length of belt} = [(18 + 16)1.57] + 2 \times 120 = (34 \times 1.57) + 240 = 293.4 \text{ in.} = \frac{293.4}{12} = 24.4 \text{ ft}$$

If one pulley is considerably larger than the other, a little extra allowance should be made, because the distance between the points of tangency of the belt on the two pulleys is somewhat greater than the exact distance between the centers of the shafts.

399. Rule for Measuring Belts in the Roll. Add to the diameter of the roll in inches the diameter of the hole in the center of the roll. Multiply this sum by the number of coils in the roll and multiply this product by 1.32. The three figures on the left indicate the number of feet in the roll.

Example. Roll of 5-in. single leather belt measures $37^{5}/_{8}$ in. outside diameter; hole is $4^{5}/_{8}$ in. in diameter; number of coils in roll is 84. How long is the belt?

Solution. Using the above rule

$$(37^{5}/_{8} + 4^{5}/_{8}) \times 84 = 42^{1}/_{4} \times 84 = 3,549 \times 1.32 = 4,684.68$$

The first three figures on the left indicate that the roll contains $468^{1}/_{2}$ ft. By actual measurement the roll is found to contain 469 ft (Page Belting Co.).

400. Splicing Belts (Page Belting Co.). Where possible, the ends of the belt should be fastened together by splicing and cementing. If belts are to be laced or fastened otherwise than with cement, cut off the ends perfectly true, using a try square. Punch the holes exactly opposite one another in the two ends as in Fig. 191. The grain side of the belt should be run next to the pulley, and the belt should be run off, not against, the laps. Undoubtedly, exclusive of cementing, lacing is the best method for fastening belt ends together, as the lacing is as flexible as the belt and runs noiselessly over the pulleys. The best lacing is in the end the cheapest. Cheap lacing is very expensive in the long run.

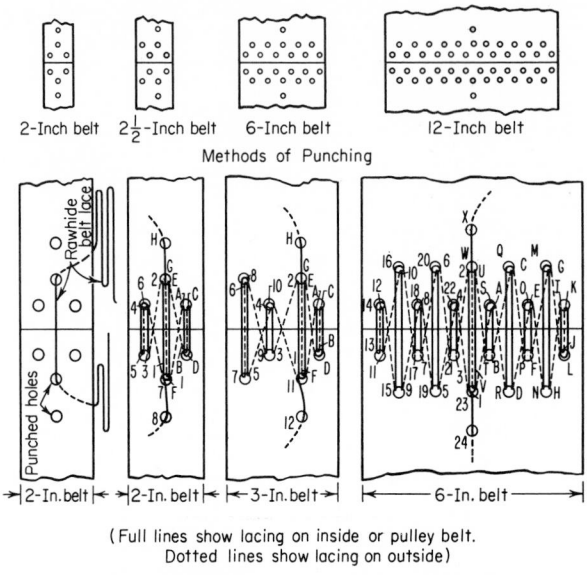

2-Inch belt　　2½-Inch belt　　6-Inch belt　　　12-Inch belt

Methods of Punching

→|2-In.belt|←　→|2-In. belt|←　|←—3-In.belt—→|　|←————— 6-In. belt —————→|

(Full lines show lacing on inside or pulley belt.
Dotted lines show lacing on outside)

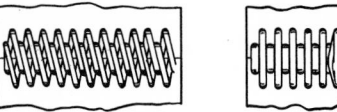

Outside 12-inch belt laced　　　Pulley side 12-inch belt laced

Finished Joint

FIG. 191 *Method of lacing belts.*

Use a small lace so that the holes will be small. For belts 1 to 2¼ in. wide, use ¼-in. lacing; 2½ to 4½ in., use 5/16-in. lacing; 5 to 12 in., use 3/8-in. lacing. For wider belts use wider lacing in proportion. Avoid thick lacing. Light, strong lacing is the best.

In punching a belt for lacing, it is desirable to use an oval punch, the longer diameter of the punch lying parallel with the length of the belt, so that a minimum amount of leather across the belt will be cut out. There should be in each end of the belt two rows of holes, placed zigzag. Make the holes the smallest possible that will admit the lace. In a 2-in. belt there should be 3 holes in each end; in a 2½-in. belt, 4 holes; in a 3-in. belt, 5 holes; in a 4-in. belt, 7 holes; in a 5-in. belt, 9 holes; in a 6-in. belt, 11 holes; in an 8-in. belt, 15 holes; in a 10-in. belt, 19 holes; in a 12-in. belt, 23 holes.

The center of no hole should come nearer to the side of the belt than 5/8 in. or nearer the end than 7/8 in. The second row should be at least 1¾ in. from the end. On wide belts these distances should be even a little greater.

Begin to lace in the center of the belt and take great care to keep the ends exactly in line and to lace both sides with equal tightness. The lacing positively must not be crossed on the side of the belt that runs next to the pulley.

401. In putting on new belts, a common rule is to draw them up and stretch them ⅛ in. for every foot in length of belt.

The strongest part of belt leather is near the flesh side, about one-third the way through from that side. It is, therefore, desirable to run the grain (hair) side on the pulley in order that the strongest part of the belt may be subject to the least wear. The flesh side is not so apt to crack as is the grain side when the belt is old; hence it is better to crimp the grain than to stretch it. Leather belts run with the grain side to the pulley will drive 30 per cent more than if run with the flesh side. The belt, as well as the pulley, adheres best when smooth, and the grain side adheres best because it is smoother.

402. A belt adheres much better and is less apt to slip when run at a high speed than at a low speed. Therefore, it is better to gear a mill with small pulleys and run them at high velocity than to have large pulleys and run them slower. A mill thus geared costs less and has a much neater appearance than with large, heavy pulleys.

403. Belt Troubles. The belt on any belt-connected machine should be tight enough to run without slipping, but the tension should not be too great, or the bearings will heat. The crowns of driving and driven pulleys should be alike, as "wobbling" of belts is sometimes caused by pulleys having unlike crowns. If this is caused by bad joints, they should be broken and cemented over again. A wave motion or flapping is usually caused by slippage between the belt and pulley, resulting from grease spots, etc. It may, however, be a warning of an excessive overload.

This fault may sometimes be corrected by increasing the tension, but a better remedy is to clean the belt. A back and forth movement on the pulley is caused by unequal stretching of the edges of the belt. If this does not cure itself shortly, examine the joints. If they are evenly made and remain so, the belt is bad and should be discarded.

404. Gear Drive. Gearing is the most positive form of power transmission and is frequently employed when the motor can be mounted directly on a machine. The points to be considered on a gear drive are the following: (1) speed reduction, (2) pitch of the gears, (3) number of teeth on the gears (pinion and gear), (4) face of the gear, (5) pitch-line speed, (6) distance between centers, (7) use of idler gears, and (8) mounting of the motor.

The speed reduction is the same as for the belt drive. Each motor rating has a minimum pinion to limit stresses to safe values. The pitch, number of teeth, and face for motor pinions have been standardized for back-geared motors, and the best practice when gearing a motor directly to machines is to use these motor pinions if possible. Table **415** gives the standard motor ratings and other valuable gearing information. (The information on gear drives given herein is largely from an article in the *American Machinist*, by A. G. Popcke.)

405. The method of gearing depends largely upon the distance between centers and the space available for the motors. In all cases the pinion must not be selected smaller than the minimum specified in Table **415**. The pitch-line speed must not exceed the limits given. There are two general cases covering the mounting of a motor to drive a machine through gears; these are:

1. Where the dimension of the motor or machine limits the distance between centers of the motor shaft and the driven shaft.

2. Where the limitation of (1) does not exist.

The first case occurs when a motor is mounted on top, side, or bottom of a machine, as shown in Fig. 192. The dimension causing limitations is indicated by A in these illustrations. The proper distance can be obtained by using large enough gears; the limit is pitch-line speed. An intermediate idler gear frequently overcomes the difficulties here experienced.

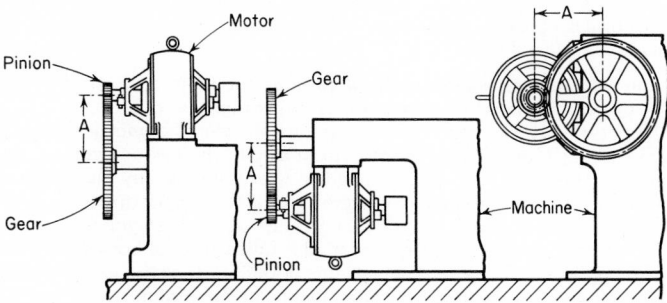

FIG. 192 *Motor mountings for gear drive (distances between gear centers limited).*

In the second case the relation of the motor and machine is shown in Fig. 193. In this case the motor can be mounted on a base, and the motor pinion can mesh with the gear on the machine in any convenient position.

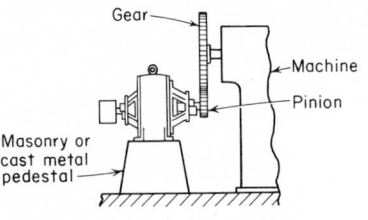

FIG. 193 *Motor mounting for gear drive (no limitation to center distance).*

If reductions greater than 7:1 are required, it is usually necessary to obtain the reduction by the use of two sets of gears. The back-geared motors discussed under Belt Drive can be used to furnish one set of gears in these cases. Thus if a reduction of 10:1 is desired, a back-geared motor with a standard 6:1 reduction, with a further reduction from the countershaft of the motor to the machine of $^{10}\!/_6$:1 or 1.66:1, will fulfill the requirements.

Example. The speed of the driven shaft of the machine is 210 rpm, the hp is 10, the motor is mounted on the machine, and the limiting distance between centers is 12 in. What are the sizes of gear and pinion to be used? The machine is a punch and shear.

Solution. In this case a pitch-line speed of approximately 1,000 ft per min will be employed. Table **415** shows that a 10-hp motor at 850 rpm is the highest speed motor that can be used for this pitch-line speed. The ratio of reduction is then

$$\frac{850}{210} = 4.05 \text{ (use 4:1)}$$

The distance between centers for any set of gears is determined by the formula

$$a = \frac{b}{2P} \quad \text{in.} \tag{16}$$

where a = the distance between centers in inches; b = the sum of the number of teeth in both gears; and P = the diametral pitch. In this case

$$a \text{ or } 12 = \frac{b}{2 \times 5} \qquad b = 120$$

The number of teeth in the pinion is

$$\frac{b}{\text{Ratio of reduction plus 1}} = \frac{120}{5} = 24 = \text{number of teeth}$$

The number of teeth in the gear is $4 \times 24 = 96$.

Table **415** shows that the pitch-line speed for the motor with 20 teeth is 890 ft per min. The pitch-line speed with 24 teeth is

$$\frac{24}{20} \times 890 = 1,068 \text{ ft per min}$$

If quiet operation is desired, a cloth or rawhide pinion should be used with a 3¾-in. face. Thus the gears are specified as follows:

Motor pinion — rawhide, $P = 5$, face 3¾ in., 24 teeth. Machine gear — steel, $P = 5$, face 3 in., 96 teeth.

The bore for each is determined by the diameter of the shaft to which it is connected. The pinion is wider than the gears, so that the rawhide engages only with the gear. If it were the same width, the brass endplates of the rawhide pinion would engage with the gear, causing noise.

406. In the selection or specification of pinions for motors (C. W. Drake, *Electric Journal*) for geared applications, three dimensions must be determined, namely, the face, the diameter, and the pitch. These dimensions vary symmetrically according to the strength required, or, in other words, according to the torque exerted in transmitting power. As the horsepower and speed of the motor in any case determine the torque, it is evident these are the factors determining the proper dimensions of a pinion for the motor. A line of pinions with dimensions increasing symmetrically with the torque will therefore answer the purpose for all combinations of horsepower and speed. Every geared application requires special consideration, since the nature of the service, the shaft diameter, etc., may affect the dimensions of the pinion.

In gear drive the pinion is subject to most rapid wear owing to its smaller diameter. It is as important to have a pinion of good wearing qualities as it is to have one of sufficient strength, and for a pinion of a given material, the ability to withstand wear depends mainly, if not wholly, on the width of the face. With a steel pinion and a cast-iron gear the former is usually the limiting factor of life and the latter the limiting factor of strength.

407. Cast-steel gears are about twice as strong as cast iron and should be used when the face of a corresponding cast-iron gear would be 4.5 in. or more, although the cost is approximately double that of cast iron. With continuous contact all along the length of the teeth, the strength of the gear is approximately proportional to the face and the square of the circular pitch, but gear teeth seldom make such contact until worn down in service. With new gears the whole pressure is brought to bear on the high spots, and stripping may occur before they are worn down; hence the necessity of using the stronger material.

408. Bronze and Rawhide Pinions. For equal strength the working face of rawhide pinions must be about 25 per cent wider than corresponding steel pinions. For quiet operation, only the rawhide should be in contact with the gear, although for high-torque motors and other severe service the gears may be widened to cover the entire pinion, thus making use of the metal flanges. Where steel pinions would make objectionable noise, rawhide pinions should be used if the stresses permit, since the pitch-line speed with a rawhide pinion is limited more by the rapid wear of the pinion than by noise. A pitch-line speed of 2,000 ft per min is considered a fair average limit for rawhide, but 2,500 to 3,000 ft per min can be used under especially favorable conditions regarding attendance, lubrication, absence of moisture, or high temperature and for intermittent service or where the life of the pinion is not important.

The wear and noise of bronze pinions are intermediate between those of rawhide and steel. Bronze pinions are particularly adapted to conditions where heat and moisture prohibit the use of rawhide. Their cost is about the same as rawhide.

409. Noise of Gears and Pitch-line Speed Limits. Spur gears ordinarily begin to make a noticeable noise at pitch-line speeds of about 600 ft per min but under average conditions may not become disagreeably noisy with pitch-line speeds under 1,200 ft per min. The amount of noise allowable depends on the noise made by surrounding machinery, on the character of the workmen, and on the nature of the work in the vicinity. A noise that would be unnoticeable in a boiler shop might be exceedingly disagreeable in a shop that was otherwise comparatively quiet. Where noise is not a limiting feature, there is no limit to allowable pitch-line speeds, except the increased wear and depreciation of the motor, gears, and driven machine, but depreciation may become a very important factor with high pitch-line speeds, say 2,500 ft per min or sometimes even less. Tests recently made to determine a design for gears that will give the least noise and yet have sufficient strength and wearing qualities indicate the following facts, other conditions being the:

1. Gears having large teeth give forth a relatively greater volume of noise at a low pitch that does not carry far, while gears having smaller teeth give forth a smaller volume of noise at a higher pitch that carries farther.

2. Most of the noise comes from the gear and not from the pinion or the motor.

3. A gear designed so that it will give a dead sound when struck a blow with the hammer will be the least noisy in operation.

410. Conditions for Noiseless Operation of Gears. Rigid and massive supports and close-fitting bearings for both the motor and the driven machine are conducive to a noiseless gear drive, and the pinion should always be placed close to the motor bearing. A gear application with motor mounted upon the ceiling might be twice as noisy as the same application with motor mounted on a concrete foundation.

411. Pinions for High-torque Motors. For series motors and those heavily compounded, as bending-roll motors, or for motors subject to very severe service of any kind, select a pinion suitable for a constant-speed motor of the same rated rpm but of about 50 per cent higher horsepower.

412. Selection of Ratio for Back-geared Motors. A ratio of about 6:1 is usually standard for back-geared motors and should be selected wherever possible, but smaller ratios down to 3:1 or maximum ratios up to 7:1 can be obtained in certain capacities of motors for service where the conditions of the application warrant the use of such ratios (see preceding paragraphs on this subject).

413. Outboard Bearings for Gear Drive. Outboard bearings should be used for motors of about 40 hp and above in heavy geared service requiring continuous operation with frequent reversing and overloads — also for all motors of about 100 hp and above in any geared service. The proper use of outboard bearings cannot be emphasized too strongly, since on account of increased expense there is a tendency to omit them even where good engineering demands their use.

414. How to Use the Chart for Determining Gear Dimensions (C. W. Drake, *Electric Journal*). The dimensions for pinions for average conditions of motor-drive service are given in Fig. 194. This chart is useful in making preliminary estimates or selections of pinions for geared motors. The chart applies without correction **to steel pinions only.** The diameters are considered about standard for the various ratings, although both smaller and larger pinions can generally be used, the limiting size for small pinions being the strength and number of teeth, and, for large pinions, the pitch-line speed.

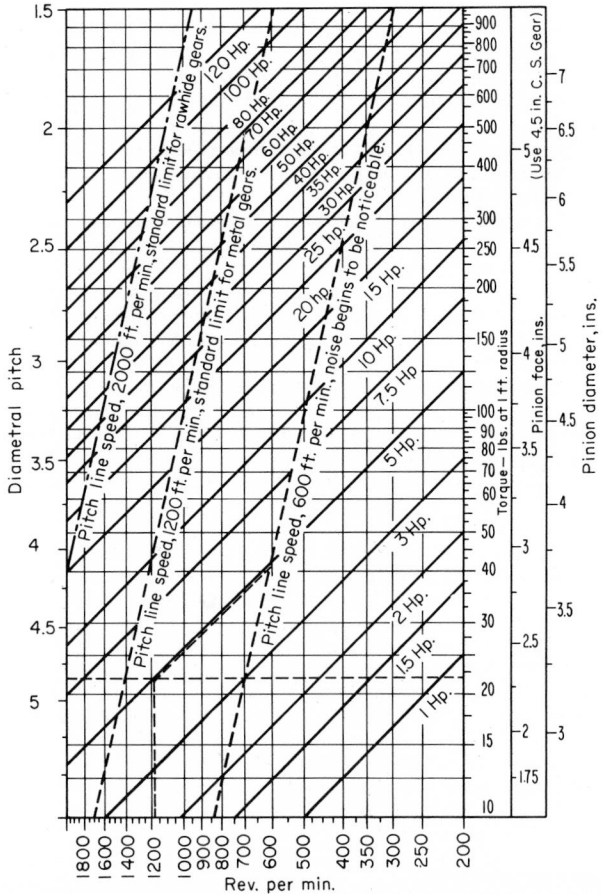

FIG. 194 *Chart for determining approximate commercial values of pinion diameter, pinion face, diametral pitch, pitch-line speed, and torque, with revolutions per minute and horsepower of motor given.*

Example. To determine the steel pinion for a 5-hp motor at 1,200 rpm, find the intersection of the oblique line marked 5 hp with the horizontal line through 1,200 rpm. On the vertical line through this intersection may be found 21.9-lb torque, 2.3-in. pinion face, 3.2-in. pitch diameter, and a diametral pitch of 4.85. A 2.25-in. pinion face is good practice here, since pinion-face dimensions with fractions smaller than 0.25 in. are not commonly used. The diametral pitch is also usually a whole number, except for very large pinions, where half pitches are sometimes used, so that a pitch of 5 would probably be used in the above case. Since the number of teeth is the product of the pitch diameter and the diametral pitch, the assumed pitch diameter, 3.2 in., is satisfactory with the 5 pitch, because it gives a whole number of teeth, i.e., 16.

415. Gear Data for Motor Applications

(A. G. Popcke, *American Machinist*)

Hp	Rpm	Diam. pitch	Number of teeth			Face		Standard pitch-line speed	Min diam	Max no. of teeth for pitch-line speed of	
			Standard pinion	Min rawhide pinion	Min steel pinion	Steel	Rawhide and cloth			1,000 ft per min	2,000 ft per min
1	1,700	8	17	15	13	1	1½	940	1.63	18	36
1	1,200	8	17	15	13	1½	2	665	1.63	25	50
2	1,700	8	17	15	13	1½	2	940	1.63	18	36
2	1,200	8	22	20	19	1¾	2¼	870	2.38	25	50
2	850	6	18	21	19	1¾	2¼	615	2 38	36	72
3	1,800	8	22	20	19	1¾	2¼	1,300	2.38	...	34
	1,150	8	22	21	19	1¾	2¼	830	2.38	26	52
	850	6	18	18	18	2¾	3⅜	670	3.0	27	54
5	1,800	8	22	21	19	1¾	2¼	1,300	2.38	...	34
	1,200	6	18	18	18	2¾	3⅜	940	3.0	19	38
	850	6	21	19	18	2¾	3⅜	990	3.0	27	54
7½	1,700	6	18	18	18	2¾	3⅜	1,400	3.0	...	26
	1,150	6	21	19	18	2¾	3⅜	1,050	3.0	20	40
	975	5	19	18	18	3	3¾	970	3.6	19	38
	850	5	19	18	18	3	3¾	850	3.6	22	44
	650	5	20	18	18	3	3¾	685	3.6	29	58
10	1,700	6	21	19	18	2¾	3⅜	1,420	3.0	...	27
	1,300	6	22	19	18	2¾	3⅜	1,250	3.0	...	35
	1,150	5	19	18	18	3	3¾	1,150	3.6	...	33
	850	5	20	18	18	3	3¾	890	3.6	22	44
	730	5	21	18	18	3½	4¼	805	3.6	26	52
	600	5	21	19	19	3½	4¼	665	3.8	31	62
15	1,700	5	19	18	18	3	3¾	1,700	3.6	...	22
	1,250	5	20	18	18	3	3¾	1,300	3.6	...	30
	1,150	5	21	18	18	3½	4¼	1,210	3.6	...	35
	825	5	21	19	19	3½	4¼	910	3.8	23	46
	675	4½	22	18	18	4	5	870	4.0	25	50
	600	4½	22	19	19	4	5	770	4.22	29	58
20	1,700	5	20	18	18	3	3¾	1,780	3.6	...	22
	1,100	5	21	19	19	3½	4¼	1,220	3.8	...	35
	900	4½	22	18	18	4	5	1,150	4.0	19	38
	750	4½	22	19	19	4	5	960	4.22	23	46
	650	4	21	18	18	4¼	5¼	890	4.5	23	46
25	1,400	5	21	19	19	3½	4¼	1,550	3.8	...	27
	1,100	4½	22	18	18	4	5	1,400	4.0	...	31
	950	4½	22	19	19	4	5	1,220	4.22	..	36
	825	4	21	18	18	4¼	5¼	1,130	4.5	18	36
	600	4	22	19	18	4¼	5¼	860	4.5	25	50
30	1,700	5	21	19	19	3½	4¼	1,880	3.8	...	22
	1,150	4½	22	19	19	4	5	1,470	4.22	...	30
	975	4	21	18	18	4¼	5¼	1,330	4.5	...	31
	725	4	22	19	18	4¼	5¼	1,050	4.5	21	42
	600	3¼	20	...	18	4½	...	970	5.53	20	40
35	1,700	4½	22	18	18	4	5	2,180	4.0	...	20
	1,150	4	21	18	18	4¼	5¼	1,580	4.5	...	27
	850	4	22	19	18	4¼	5¼	1,220	4.5	18	36
	675	3¼	20	...	18	4½	...	1,080	5.53	18	36
40	1,700	4½	22	19	19	4	5	2,180	4.22	...	20
	950	4	22	19	18	4¼	5¼	1,370	4.5	...	32
	775	3¼	20	...	18	4½	...	1,250	5.53	...	32
	600	3	18	...	15	4½	...	940	5.0	19	38
50	1,700	4	21	18	18	4¼	5¼	2,340	4.5	...	18
	975	3¼	20	...	18	4½	...	1,580	5.53	...	25
	750	3	18	...	15	4½	...	1,170	5.0	15	30
	565	3	20	...	18	4½	...	990	6.0	20	40

416. Adjustable-speed Motor Ratings and Pulley and Gear Data for Use When Connecting Adjustable-speed Motors to Drive Machinery

(A. G. Popcke, *American Machinist*)

Hp	Rpm		Smallest pulley		Gear data						Pitch-line speed at min diam		Max teeth not to exceed 2,000 ft per min at max speed
						Face							
	Min	Max	Diam	Face	Pitch	Steel	Raw-hide	Min teeth	Min diam		Min speed	Max speed	
1	740	2,200	3	3	8	1¾	2¼	19	2.38		460	1,380	27
	600	1,800	3	3	8	1¾	2¼	19	2.38		375	825	46
	450	1,800	3	4	8	1¾	2¼	19	2.38		280	1,120	34
2	1,100	2,200	3	3	8	1¾	2¼	19	2.38		690	1,380	27
	740	2,200	3	4	8	1¾	2¼	19	2.38		460	1,380	27
	450	1,800	4	4½	6	2¾	3⅜	18	3.0		355	1,420	25
3	1,000	2,000	3	4	8	1¾	2¼	19	2.38		625	1,250	30
	660	2,000	4	4½	6	2¾	3⅜	13	3.0		520	1,560	23
	450	1,800	4½	5	6	2¾	3⅜	18	3.0		355	1,422	25
	375	1,500	5	6	6	2¾	3⅜	18	3.0		294	1,176	30
5	1,000	2,000	4	4½	6	2¾	3⅜	18	3.0		790	1,580	23
	750	1,500	4½	5	6	2¾	3⅜	18	3.0		590	1,180	30
	600	1,800	5	6	6	2¾	3⅜	18	3.0		470	1,410	25
	450	1,800	6	7	5	3	3¾	18	3.6		425	1,700	21
	375	1,500	6	7½	5	3½	4¼	18	3.6		355	1,420	25
7½	900	1,800	5	6	6	2¾	3⅜	18	3.0		705	1,410	25
	800	1,600	5	6	5	3	3¾	18	3.6		755	1,510	24
	600	1,800	6	7	5	3	3¾	18	3.6		570	1,710	21
	500	1,500	6	7½	5	3½	4¼	18	3.6		475	1,425	25
	450	1,800	6½	9	5	3½	4¼	19	3.8		450	1,800	21
	350	1,400	6½	9	5	3½	4¼	19	3.8		350	1,400	27
10	850	1,700	6	7	5	3	3¾	18	3.6		800	1,600	22
	750	1,500	6	7	5	3	3¾	18	3.6		710	1,420	25
	600	1,800	6	7½	5	3½	4¼	18	3.6		570	1,710	21
	500	1,500	6½	9	5	3½	4¼	19	3.8		500	1,500	25
	450	1,800	6½	9	5	3½	4¼	19	3.8		450	1,800	21
	375	1,500	7	8	4½	4	5	18	4.0		390	1,560	23
15	780	1,560	6½	9	5	3½	4¼	19	3.8		780	1,560	24
	600	1,200	7	8	4½	4	5	18	4.0		630	1,260	28
	500	1,500	7½	9½	4½	4	5	19	4.22		555	1,665	23
	400	1,200	8	9½	4	4¼	5¼	18	4.5		470	1,410	25
	375	1,500	9	10½	4	4¼	5¼	18	4.5		440	1,760	20
20	650	1,300	7½	9½	4½	4	5	19	4.22		720	1,440	26
	550	1,100	8	9½	4	4¼	5¼	18	4.5		645	1,290	28
	500	1,500	9	10½	4	4¼	5¼	18	4.5		590	1,770	20
	400	1,200	10	11	3¼	4½	...	18	5.53		580	1,740	21
	300	1,200	12	13	3	4½	...	15	5.0		390	1,560	19
25	550	1,100	9	10½	4	4¼	5¼	18	4.5		645	1,290	28
	400	1,200	12	13	3	4½	...	15	5.0		525	1,575	19
	300	1,200	12½	15	3	4½	...	18	6.0		470	1,880	19
30	550	1,100	10	11	3¼	4½	...	18	5.53		800	1,600	23
	350	1,050	12½	15	3	4½	...	18	6.0		550	1,650	22
	250	1,000	14	18	3	4½	...	18	6.0		390	1,560	23
40	550	1,100	12	13	3	4½	...	15	5.0		720	1,440	21
	350	1,050	12½	15	3	4½	...	18	6.0		550	1,650	22
	250	1,000	16	21	3	4½	...	19	6.33		415	1,660	23
50	500	1,000	12½	15	3	4½	...	18	6.0		790	1,580	23
	325	975	16	21	3	4½	...	19	6.33		540	1,620	23

417. Gearing Definitions and Formulas. A circle whose circumference passes through the point of contact on each tooth of a gear or pinion when this point is on the line connecting the centers of the two wheels is called the **pitch circle.** The diameter of this circle is the **pitch diameter,** and its circumference is the **pitch line.**

Diameter, when applied to gears, is always understood to mean the pitch diameter.

Diametral pitch is the number of teeth to each inch of the pitch diameter. To illustrate: if a pinion has 18 teeth and the pitch diameter is 3 in., there are 6 teeth to each inch of the pitch diameter, and the diametral pitch is 6.

Circular pitch is the distance from the center of one tooth to the center of the next, measured along the pitch line.

In the following formulas, for use in gear problems:

d_1 = pitch diameter of pinion
d = outside diameter of pinion
p = circular pitch
p^1 = diametral pitch
S = distance between centers
　　 = $\frac{1}{2}(D^1 + d^1)$

D^1 = pitch diameter of gear
D = outside diameter of gear
n = number of teeth on pinion
N = number of teeth on gear

r = gear ratio = $\dfrac{N}{n} = \dfrac{D^1}{d^1} = \dfrac{D}{d}$

$$\pi = 3.1416$$

$$p = \frac{\pi}{p^1} = \frac{\pi d}{n+2} \qquad (17)$$

$$p^1 = \frac{\pi}{p} = \frac{n+2}{d} \qquad (18)$$

$$n = d^1 p^1 = \frac{\pi d^1}{p} = dp^1 - 2 \qquad (19)$$

$$p^1 = \frac{n}{d^1} \qquad (20)$$

$$S = \frac{N+n}{2p^1} \qquad (21)$$

$$d^1 = \frac{2S}{r+1} \qquad (22)$$

$$D^1 = \frac{2Sr}{r+1} \qquad (23)$$

$$n = \frac{2Sp^1}{r+1} \qquad (24)$$

$$N = \frac{3Sp^1 r}{r+1} \qquad (25)$$

$$S = \frac{d^1(r+1)}{2} \qquad (26)$$

418. Gear and Belt Drives for Adjustable-speed Motors. Table **415** deals with constant-speed motors. Adjustable-speed motor problems are solved similarly. The belt speeds and pitch-line speeds must be carefully considered at the maximum speeds of the motors. The minimum pulleys and pinions are determined by the minimum speeds of the motors. Table **416** gives the ratings commonly used and pulley and gear information.

419. The design of chains is more complicated than that of belts and gears, and it is, therefore, best to let the various chain manufacturers specify the chain, giving them the necessary information. The minimum sprocket to be used on a motor as specified by NEMA standards is given in Table **420**. Chain speed should not exceed 1,200 to 1,600 ft per min. The best practice does not exceed 1,000 ft per min. For factors that must be considered see Sec. **332**.

420. Application of Sprocket Dimensions to General-purpose Motors (NEMA Standard). General-purpose motors having continuous time rating with the frame sizes, horsepower, and speed ratings given in the following paragraphs are designed to operate with chain drives within the limiting sprocket dimensions listed. Selection of sprocket dimensions is made by the chain-drive vendor and the motor purchaser, but, to assure satisfactory motor operation, the selected pitch diameter shall not be smaller than the dimensions listed.

A. Direct-current Integral-horsepower Motors

Frame number	Horsepower at, rpm							Chain sprocket min pitch diam, in.
	3,500	1,750	1,150	850	690	575	500	
203	1½	1	¾	.....	.....	....	....	2.04
204	2	1½	1	½	.....	....	....	2.04
224	3	2	1½	¾	½	....	....	2.04
225	5	3	2	1	¾	½	....	2.04
254	7½	5	3	2–1½	1½–1	1–¾	....	2.16
284	10	7½	5	3	2	....	1–¾	2.28

B. Single-phase Integral-horsepower Motors

Frame number	Horsepower at, rpm				Chain sprocket min pitch diam, in.
	3,600	1,800	1,200	900	
203	1½	1	...	.....	2.04
204	2	1½	¾	.....	2.04
224	3	2	1	½	2.04
225	5	3	1½	¾	2.04
254	7½	5	2	1½–1	2.16

C. Integral-horsepower Motors—Polyphase Induction

Frame number	Horsepower at, rpm								Chain sprocket min pitch diam, in.
	3,600	1,800	1,200	900	720	600	514	450	
110, 208, 220, 440, and 550 Volts									
203	1½	1	¾	.....	.....	....	....	....	2.04
204	2	1½	1	½	.....	....	....	....	2.04
224	3	2	1½	¾	½	....	....	....	2.04
225	5	3	2	1	¾	½	....	....	2.04
254	7½	5	3	2–1½	1½–1	1–¾	....	....	2.16
284	10	7½	5	3	2	1½	1–¾	¾	2.28
324	15	10	7½	5	3	2	1½	1	2.75
326	20	15	10	7½	5	3	2	1½	3.11
364	....	20–25	15	10	7½	5	....	....	3.11
365	....	30	20	15	10	7½	3	2	3.67
404	....	40	25	20	15	10	5	3	3.67
405	....	50	30	25	20	15	7½	5	4.56
444	....	60	40	30	25	20	10	7½	4.56
445	....	75	50	40	30	25	15	10	5.51
504U	....	.....	60	50	40	30	20	15	5.51
505	....	.....	75	60	50	40	25	20	6.10
2,300 Volts, Three Phase									
445	....	50–60	40	.....	.....	....	....	....	5.51
504U	....	75	50	40	.....	....	....	....	5.51
505	....	.....	60	50	.....	....	....	....	6.10

MOTOR CIRCUITS

421. The National Electrical Code rules definitely specify certain requirements with respect to the size and location of the component parts of motor branch circuits. The following tables and rules are in accordance with the 1968 edition of the Code. Certain cities have adopted motor wiring tables and rules which may be more exacting than those required by the Code. In such communities these local requirements should be followed in preference to the tables presented herein.

In the following sections the terminology of the National Electrical Code with respect to **within sight** is adhered to. A distance of more than 50 ft is considered equivalent to being **out of sight,** even though there may be no obstructions between the two points.

Full-load Motor Currents. According to the National Electrical Code, whenever the current rating of a motor is used to determine the current-carrying capacity of conductors, switches, branch-circuit overcurrent devices, etc., the values given in Tables **7** to **10** of Div. 11, including footnotes, should be used in lieu of the actual current rating marked on a motor nameplate. Motor-running overcurrent protection should be based on the motor nameplate current rating. If a motor is marked in amperes but not in horsepower, the horsepower rating should be assumed to be that corresponding to the value given in Tables **7** to **10** of Div. 11, prorated if necessary.

422. Types of Motor Branch Circuits. Branch circuits supplying motors as required by the National Electrical Code may be divided into three types, as follows: (1) a branch circuit supplying only a single motor, (2) a branch circuit supplying several motors but no other equipment except that directly associated with the motors, and (3) a branch circuit supplying one or more motors and/or lamps and receptacles.

423. Rating or Setting for Individual Motor Circuit. The motor branch-circuit over-current device shall be capable of carrying the starting current of the motor. Short-circuit and ground-fault overcurrent protection shall be considered as being obtained when the overcurrent device has a rating or setting not exceeding the values given in Tables **40** and **41** of Div. 11. An instantaneous-trip circuit breaker (without time delay) shall be used only if it is adjustable and is part of a combination controller having overcurrent protection in each conductor and the combination is especially approved for the purpose.

Exception: Where the overcurrent protection specified in the tables is not sufficient for the starting current of the motor:

1. The rating or setting of a fuse or time-limit circuit breaker may be increased but shall in no case exceed 225 per cent of the full load current for sealed hermetic compressor motors of 400 kva locked rotor or less, nor more than 400 per cent for all other motors.

2. The setting of an instantaneous-trip circuit breaker (without time delay) may be increased over 700 per cent but shall in no case exceed 1,300 per cent of the motor full-load current.

3. Torque motor branch circuits shall be protected at the motor nameplate current rating.

For a multispeed motor, a single short-circuit and ground-fault protective device may be used for one or more windings of the motor provided the rating of the protective device does not exceed the above applicable percentage of the nameplate rating of the smallest winding protected.

Where maximum protective-device ratings shown on the manufacturer's heater table for use with a motor controller are less than 15 amp, the protective-device rating shall not exceed the manufacturer's values marked on the equipment.

424. Several Motors on One Branch Circuit. Two or more motors may be connected to the same branch circuit under any of the following conditions:

1. Several motors each not exceeding 1 hp in rating may be used on a branch circuit protected at not more than 20 amp at 125 volts or less, or 15 amp at 600 volts or less, provided that all of the following conditions are met:

a. The full-load rating of each motor shall not exceed 6 amp.

b. The rating of the branch-circuit protective device marked on any of the controllers shall not be exceeded.

c. Individual running overcurrent protection shall conform to Sec. **430**.

2. If the branch-circuit protective device is selected not to exceed that allowed by Sec. **423** for the motor of the smallest rating, two or more motors each having individual running overcurrent protection may be connected to a branch circuit when it can be determined that the branch-circuit protective device will not open under the most severe normal conditions of service that might be encountered.

3. Except as provided for in condition 4, two or more motors of any rating, each having individual running overcurrent protection, may be connected to one branch circuit provided all the following conditions are complied with:

a. Each motor-running overcurrent device must be approved for group installation with a specified maximum rating of fuse and/or circuit breaker.

b. Each motor controller must be approved for group installation with a specified maximum rating of fuse and/or circuit breaker.

c. Each circuit breaker must be of the time-limit type and approved for group installation.

d. The branch circuit shall be protected by fuses or time-limit circuit breakers having a rating not exceeding that specified in Sec. **423** for the largest motor connected to the branch circuit plus an amount equal to the sum of the full-load current ratings of all other motors connected to the circuit.

e. The branch-circuit fuses or time-limit circuit breakers must not be larger than allowed by condition 12 of Sec. **430** for the thermal cutout or relay protecting the smallest motor of the group.

f. The conductors of any tap supplying a single motor need not have individual branch-circuit protection provided they comply with either of the following: (1) no conductor to the motor shall have an ampacity lower than that of the branch-circuit conductors, or (2) no conductor to the motor shall have an ampacity lower than one-third that of the branch-circuit conductors, with a minimum in accordance with Sec. **437,** the conductors to the motor-running protective device being not more than 25 ft long and being protected from physical damage.

4. A room air conditioner shall be treated as a single motor unit in determining its branch-circuit requirements when all the following conditions are met:

a. The unit is cord-connected.

b. Its rating is not more than 40 amp full-load current and 250 volts single phase.

c. Total full-load current is shown on the unit nameplate rather than that of individual motor currents.

d. The rating of the branch-circuit protective device does not exceed the ampacity of the branch-circuit conductors or the rating of the receptacle, whichever is less.

425. Motors on General-purpose Branch Circuits. Overcurrent protection for motors used on general-purpose branch circuits shall be provided as follows:

1. One or more motors without individual running overcurrent protection may be connected to general-purpose branch circuits only where the limiting conditions specified for each of two or more motors in condition 1 of Sec. **424** are complied with.

2. Motors of larger ratings than specified in condition 1 of Sec. **424** may be connected to general-purpose branch circuits only in case each motor is equipped with running overcurrent protection selected to protect the motor as specified in Sec. **430.** Both the controller and the motor-running overcurrent device shall be approved for group installation with the protective device of the branch circuit to which the motor is connected (see Sec. **424**).

3. Where a motor is connected to a branch circuit by means of a plug and receptacle, and individual running overcurrent protection is omitted as provided in condition 1, a rating of the plug and receptacle shall not exceed 15 amp at 125 volts or 10 amp at 250 volts. Where individual overcurrent protection is required as provided in condition 2 for a motor or motor-operated appliance provided with an attachment plug for attaching to the branch circuit through a receptacle, the running overcurrent device shall be an integral part of the motor or of the appliance. The rating of the plug and receptacle shall be assumed to determine the rating of the circuit to which the motor may be connected.

4. The overcurrent device protecting a branch circuit to which a motor or motor-operated appliance is connected shall have sufficient time delay to permit the motor to start and accelerate its load.

426. Multimotor and Combination Load Equipment. The rating of the branch-circuit protective device for multimotor and combination load equipment shall not exceed the rating marked on the equipment.

427. The component parts of a motor branch circuit for an individual motor are shown in Fig. 195.

P_1—**Overload Protective Device in Feeder or Main.** May consist of fuses or circuit breaker. Refer to Sec. **440.**

S_B—**Branch-circuit Switch.** Not required by National Electrical Code rules. May consist of switch or circuit breaker. If switch is used, must have fuse clips large enough to accommodate fuses required at P_2. If circuit breaker is used for branch-circuit overload protective device, it will serve double purpose of branch-circuit switch and circuit protective device. Refer to Sec. **436.**

P_2—**Branch-circuit Overload Protective Device.** May consist of fuses or circuit breaker. If circuit breaker is used, it will serve the double purpose of branch-circuit switch and overload protective device. Refer to Sec. **435.**

S_M—**Motor Switch.** May consist of switch or circuit breaker. Must have a continuous-duty rating of at least 115 per cent of the motor full-load current. For motors of 50 hp and under and for all cases when switch is used for shutting down the motor, switch must be of the motor-circuit type. If the switch is fused, the fuse clips must be large enough to accommodate size of fuses required at P_3. Switch S_M must be either located within sight of the motor or arranged so that it can be locked in the open position. If switch S_M is of the two-throw or two-position type (Diagram II) for cutting the motor overload protective device out of the circuit during the starting period, the switch must be so arranged that it cannot be left in the starting position. S_M must be within sight from controller C (refer to Sec. **433**).

P₃—Motor Overload Protective Device. May consist of fuses, thermal cutouts, thermal relays or magnetic relays. Generally not required for intermittent-duty motors. This device shall be rated or selected to trip at not more than 125 per cent of the motor full-load current rating for sealed (hermetic-type) refrigeration compressor motors and motors marked to have a temperature rise not over 40°C, and at not more than 115 per cent for all other types of motors. This value may be modified as permitted by Sec. **430**, condition 6. The motor overload protective device is generally incorporated in the controller C and mounted inside the controller case. Refer to Secs. **430** to **432**.

C—Motor Controller. Refer to Sec. **429**.

W₁—Branch-circuit Tap Wires from Point of Connection to Feeder to Branch-circuit Overload Protective Device. If branch-circuit overload protective device is located at point of connection to feeder, the carrying capacity of tap wires must be at least 125 per cent of the motor full-load current. If the length L of the wires from the point of connection to the branch-circuit overload protective device is 25 ft or less, the carrying capacity of the tap wires must be at least one-third of the carrying capacity of the feeder. If the length L of the wires from the point of connection to the feeder to the branch-circuit overload protective device is greater than 25 ft, the tap wires must be of the same size as the feeder.

W₂—Branch-circuit Wires from Branch-circuit Overload Protective Device to Motor. Must have carrying capacity of at least 125 per cent of motor full-load current for continuous-duty motors. Refer to Sec. **437**.

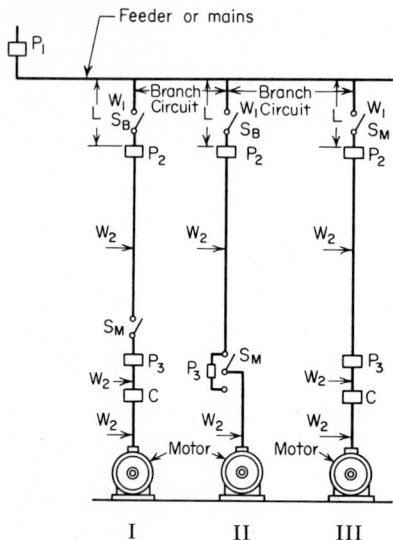

FIG. 195 *Single-line diagrams giving requirements for component parts of branch motor circuits with branch overload protection.*

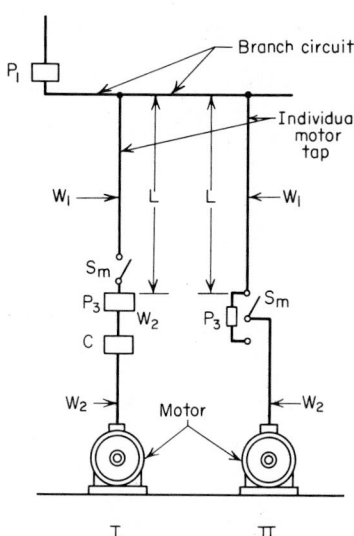

FIG. 196 *Single-line diagrams giving requirements for motor circuits when branch-circuit overload protective device is omitted.*

428. The component parts of a motor branch circuit supplying several motors are shown in Fig. 196.

P₁—Overload Protective Device in Branch Circuit. May consist of fuses or circuit breaker. If motor overload protective device consists of thermal cutouts or overload relays, the rating of the fuses or setting of the circuit breaker must not be greater than permitted in condition 12 of Sec. **430** unless the motor overload protective device is approved for group installation.

If the motor overload protective devices are cut out during the starting period, P_1 must consist of fuses rated or time-limit circuit breakers set at not more than 400 per cent of the full-load current of smallest motor so protected. Refer to Sec. **435**.

S_M — **Combined Motor and Branch-circuit Switch.** May consist of switch or circuit breaker. Must have a continuous-duty rating of at least 115 per cent of the motor full-load current. For motors of 50 hp and under and for all cases when switch is used for shutting down the motor, switch must be of the motor-circuit type. If switch is fused, the fuse clips must be large enough to accommodate the size of fuses required at P_3. If switch is used for shutting down motor, switch should be located as close as possible to motor and its driven machinery and in the most accessible location for operator. If switch is not used for shutting down motor, it may be located remote from motor, provided that it is either located within sight of motor or so arranged that it can be locked in the open position. If switch is of the two-position or double-throw type (Diagram II) for cutting the motor overload protective device out of the circuit during the starting period, the switch must be so arranged that it cannot be left in the starting position. If S_M is a fused switch or circuit breaker the supply from P_1 is a feeder. Refer to Sec. **436**.

P_3 — **Motor Overload Protective Device.** May consist of fuses, thermal cutouts, thermal relays, magnetic relays, or circuit breaker. This device shall be rated or selected to trip at not more than 125 per cent of the motor full-load current rating for sealed (hermetic-type) refrigeration compressor motors and motors marked to have a temperature rise not over 40°C, and at not more than 115 per cent for all other types of motors. This value may be modified as permitted by Sec. **430**, condition 6. The motor overload protective device is generally incorporated in the controller C and mounted inside the controller case. Refer to Secs. **430** to **432**.

C — **Motor Controller.** Refer to Sec. **429**.

W_1 — **Individual Motor Tap Wires from Point of Connection to Branch Circuit to Motor Overload Protective Device.** If motor overload protective device is located at point of connection to the branch circuit, the carrying capacity of wires must be at least 125 per cent of the motor full-load current. If the length L of the wires is 25 ft or less, the carrying capacity of the wires must be at least one-third of the carrying capacity of the branch-circuit wires. If the length L of the wires is greater than 25 ft, the wires must be of the same size as the branch-circuit wires.

W_2 — **Branch-circuit Wires from Motor Overload Protective Device to Motor.** Must have a carrying capacity of at least 125 per cent of motor full-load current for continuous-duty motors. Refer to Sec. **437**.

429. Motor Controllers. Each motor must be provided with a suitable controller that will be capable of starting and stopping the motor and of performing any other control functions that are required for the satisfactory operation of the motor, such as speed control. The different types of motor-control equipment are discussed in Secs. **251** to **325**. A controller for an a-c motor must be capable of interrupting the current of the motor under stalled-rotor conditions. Each motor must have its own individual controller except that, for motors of 600 volts or less, a single controller may serve a group of motors under any one of the following conditions:

1. If a number of motors drive several parts of a single machine or piece of apparatus such as metal and woodworking machines, cranes, hoists, and similar apparatus.

2. If a group of motors is under the protection of one overcurrent device as permitted in condition 1 for motor branch circuits as given in Secs. **424** and **425**.

3. If a group of motors is located in a single room within sight of the controller location. A distance of more than 50 ft is considered equivalent to being out of sight.

The controller must have a horsepower rating that is not less than that of the motor, except as follows:

1. STATIONARY MOTOR OF ⅛ HP OR LESS. For a stationary motor rated at ⅛ hp or less that is normally left running and is so constructed that it cannot be damaged by overload or failure to start, such as clock motors and the like, the branch-circuit overcurrent device may serve as the controller.

2. STATIONARY MOTOR OF 2 HP OR LESS. For a stationary motor rated at 2 hp or less and 300 volts or less, the controller may be a general-use switch having an ampere rating at least twice the full-load current rating of the motor. On a-c circuits, general-use snap switches suitable only for use on a-c (not general-use ac-dc snap switches) may be used to control a motor having a full-load current rating not exceeding 80 per cent of the ampere rating of the switch.

3. PORTABLE MOTOR OF ⅓ HP OR LESS. For a portable motor rated at ⅓ hp or less, the controller may be an attachment plug and receptacle.

4. CIRCUIT BREAKER AS CONTROLLER. A branch-circuit circuit breaker, rated in amperes only, may be used as a controller. When this circuit breaker is also used for overcurrent protection, it shall conform to the appropriate provisions of this section governing overcurrent protection.

5. Sealed (Hermetic-type) Refrigeration Compressor Motors. The motor controller shall have both a continuous-duty full-load current rating and a locked-rotor current rating not less than the nameplate full-load current and locked-rotor current, respectively, of the compressor. Motor controllers rated in horsepower or in full-load current shall be selected on the basis of the nameplate full-load current and locked-rotor current, respectively, of the compressor. For full-load current, the horsepower rating shall be selected from Tables 7 to 10, inclusive, of Div. 11 and for locked-rotor current, the horsepower rating shall be selected from Table 44 of Div. 11. If the nameplate full-load current and locked-rotor current do not correspond to the currents shown in Tables 7 to 10 and Table 44, respectively, the horsepower rating corresponding to the next higher value shall be selected. If two different horsepower ratings are obtained when applying Tables 7 to 10 and Table 44, a horsepower rating at least equal to the larger of the two values obtained shall be selected.

A controller need not open all conductors to the motor unless it serves as a disconnecting means or unless one pole of the controller is placed in a permanently grounded conductor.

Machines of the following types shall be provided with speed-limiting devices unless the inherent characteristics of the machines, the system, or the load and the mechanical connection thereto are such as to limit the speed safely or unless the machine is always under the manual control of a qualified operator.

1. Separately excited d-c motors.
2. Series motors.
3. Motor-generators and converters that can be driven at excessive speed from the d-c end, as by a reversal of current or decrease in load.

Adjustable-speed motors, if controlled by means of field regulation, shall be so equipped and connected that they cannot be started under weakened field unless the motor is designed for such starting.

The controller for a motor should be located as near as possible to the motor in order to make the length of the control wires between the controller and the motor as short as possible. The point from which the motor is controlled should be located as close as is feasible to the motor and its driven machinery and must at least be within sight of the motor and its driven machinery unless one of the following conditions is complied with:

1. The controller disconnecting means is capable of being locked in the open position.
2. A manually operable switch, which will disconnect the motor from its source of supply, is placed within sight of the motor location.

The control point should be located so that it will be in the most accessible location for the operator of the machine driven by the motor. In the case of manual controllers the location of the control point will be the same as the location of the controller. For magnetic controllers the location of the control point will be the point of location of the "start" and "stop" push buttons, which may or may not be the same as the location of the controller. A disconnecting means is required within sight from the controller location.

430. Overload Protection of Motors. Each continuous-duty motor must be protected against excessive overloads under running conditions by some approved protective device. This protective device, except for motors rated at more than 600 volts, may consist of thermal cutouts, thermal relays, thermal release devices, or magnetic relays in connection with the motor controller, fuses, or time-limit circuit breakers.

The National Electrical Code requires that the protection be as follows:

1. More than 1 Hp. Each continuous-duty motor rated more than 1 hp shall be protected against running overcurrent by one of the following means:

a. A separate overcurrent device that is responsive to motor current. This device shall be rated or selected to trip at no more than the following per cent of the motor full-load current rating:

Motors with a marked service factor not less than 1.15............... 125%
Motors with a marked temperature rise not over 40°C................ 125%
Sealed (hermetic-type) motor compressors:
    Overload relays 140%
    Other devices.. 125%
All other motors.. 115%

For a multispeed motor, each winding connection shall be considered separately. This value may be modified as permitted by paragraph 6.

When a separate motor-running overcurrent device is so connected that it does not carry the total current designated on the motor nameplate, such as for wye-delta starting, the proper percentage of nameplate current applying to the selection or setting of the overcurrent device shall be clearly designated on the equipment, or the manufacturer's selection table shall take this into account.

b. A thermal protector integral with the motor, approved for use with the motor which it protects on the basis that it will prevent dangerous overheating of the motor due to overload or failure to start. If the motor current-interrupting device is separate from the motor, and its control circuit is operated by a protective device integral with the motor, it shall be so arranged that the opening of the control circuit will result in interruption of current to the motor.

c. For motors larger than 1,500 hp, a protective device employing embedded temperature detectors which cause current to the motor to be interrupted when the motor attains a temperature rise greater than marked on the nameplate in an ambient of 40°C.

Standards for the application of embedded temperature detectors are given in the USA Standards for Rotating Electrical Machinery, USAS C50.2-1955 and C50.4-1965.

2. 1 HP OR LESS, MANUALLY STARTED.

a. Each continuous-duty motor rated at 1 hp or less that is not permanently installed, is manually started, and is within sight from the controller location shall be considered as protected against overcurrent by the overcurrent device protecting the conductors of the branch circuit. This branch-circuit overcurrent device shall not be larger than that specified in Table **42** of Div. 11, except that any such motor may be used at 125 volts or less on a branch circuit protected at 20 amp.

b. Any such motor that is not in sight from the controller location shall be protected as specified in paragraph 3. Any motor rated at 1 hp or less that is permanently installed shall be protected in accordance with paragraph 3.

3. 1 HP OR LESS, AUTOMATICALLY STARTED. Any motor of 1 hp or less that is started automatically shall be protected against overcurrent by the use of one of the following means:

a. A separate overcurrent device that is responsive to motor current. This device shall be rated or selected to trip at no more than the following percentage of the motor full-load current rating:

Motors with a marked service factor not less than 1.15	125%
Motors with a marked temperature rise not over 40°C	125%
Sealed (hermetic-type) motor compressors:	
Overload relays	140%
Other devices	125%
All other motors	115%

For a multispeed motor, each winding connection shall be considered separately. This value may be modified as permitted by paragraph 6.

b. A thermal protector integral with the motor, approved for use with the motor which it protects on the basis that it will prevent dangerous overheating of the motor due to overload or failure to start. Where the motor current-interrupting device is separate from the motor, and its control circuit is operated by a protective device integral with the motor, it shall be so arranged that the opening of the control circuit will result in interruption of current to the motor.

c. The motor shall be considered as being properly protected where it is part of an approved assembly that does not normally subject the motor to overloads and is also equipped with other safety controls (such as the safety combustion controls of a domestic oil burner) which protect the motor against damage due to stalled rotor current. Where such protective equipment is used, it shall be indicated on the nameplate of the assembly where it will be visible after installation.

d. In case the impedance of the motor windings is sufficient to prevent overheating due to failure to start, the motor may be protected as specified in paragraph 2*a* for manually started motors.

Many a-c motors of less than 1/20 hp, such as clock motors, series motors, etc., and also some larger motors such as torque motors, come within this classification. It does not include split-phase motors having automatic switches to disconnect the starting windings.

4. WOUND-ROTOR SECONDARIES.   The secondary circuits of wound-rotor a-c motors, including conductors, controllers, resistors, etc., shall be considered as protected against overcurrent by the motor-running overcurrent device.

5. INTERMITTENT AND SIMILAR DUTY.   A motor used for a condition of service which is inherently short-time, intermittent, periodic, or varying duty (as illustrated by Table 12 of Div. 11) is considered as protected against overcurrent by the branch-circuit overcurrent device, provided the overcurrent protection does not exceed that specified in Tables 40 and 41 of Div. 11.

Any motor is considered to be for continuous duty unless the nature of the apparatus which it drives is such that the motor cannot operate continuously with load under any condition of use.

6. SELECTION OF SETTING OF PROTECTION DEVICE.   Where the values specified for motor-running overcurrent protection do not correspond to the standard sizes or ratings of fuses, nonadjustable circuit breakers, thermal cutouts, thermal relays, the heating elements of thermal trip motor switches, or possible settings of adjustable circuit breakers adequate to carry the load, the next higher size, rating, or setting may be used, but not exceeding 140 per cent of the motor full-load current rating of motors marked with a service factor not less than 1.15, sealed (hermetic-type) refrigeration compressor motors and motors marked to have a temperature rise not over 40°C, and not higher than 130 per cent of the full-load current rating for all other motors.   If not shunted during the starting period of the motor, the protective device shall have sufficient time delay to permit the motor to start and accelerate its load.

7. SHUNTING DURING STARTING PERIOD.   If the motor is manually started (including starting with a magnetic starter having push-button control), the running overcurrent protection may be shunted or cut out of circuit during the starting period of the motor provided that the device by which the overcurrent protection is shunted or cut out cannot be left in the starting position, and the motor shall be considered as protected against overcurrent during the starting period if fuses or time-delay circuit breakers rated or set at not over 400 per cent of the full-load current of the motor are so located in the circuit as to be operative during the starting period of the motor.   The motor-running overcurrent protection shall not be shunted or cut out during the starting period if the motor is automatically started.

8. FUSES, IN WHICH CONDUCTOR.   If fuses are used for motor-running protection, a fuse shall be inserted in each ungrounded conductor, except that a fuse shall also be inserted in a grounded conductor under the circumstances set forth in the note following the next table.

9. DEVICES OTHER THAN FUSES, IN WHICH CONDUCTOR.   If devices other than fuses are used for motor-running protection, the following table shall govern the minimum allowable number and location of overcurrent units such as trip coils, relays, or thermal cutouts.

10. NUMBER OF CONDUCTORS DISCONNECTED BY OVERCURRENT DEVICE.   Motor-running protective devices, other than fuses, thermal cutouts or thermal protectors, shall simultaneously open a sufficient number of underground conductors to interrupt current flow to the motor.

11. MOTOR CONTROLLER AS RUNNING PROTECTION.   A motor controller may also serve as the running overcurrent device if the number of overcurrent units complies with paragraph 9 and if these overcurrent units are operative in both the starting and running position in the case of a d-c motor and in the running position in the case of an a-c motor.   When a nonautomatic motor controller serves as the running overcurrent device, it is recommended that all ungrounded conductors be opened.

12. THERMAL CUTOUTS AND RELAYS.   Thermal cutouts, overload relays, and other devices for motor-running protection which are not capable of opening short circuits shall be protected by fuses or circuit breakers with ratings or settings in accordance with Sec. 423 unless approved for group installation, and marked to indicate the maximum size of fuse or time-limit circuit breaker by which they must be protected.

13. AUTOMATIC RESTARTING.   A motor-running protective device that can restart a motor automatically after overcurrent tripping shall not be installed unless approved

Running Overcurrent Units

Kind of motor	Supply to system	Number and location of over-current units, such as trip coils, relays, or thermal cutouts
1-phase a-c or d-c	2-wire, 1-phase a-c or d-c ungrounded	1 in either conductor
1-phase a-c or d-c	2-wire, 1-phase a-c or d-c, one conductor grounded	1 in ungrounded conductor
1-phase a-c or d-c	3-wire, 1-phase a-c or d-c, grounded-neutral	1 in either ungrounded conductor
2-phase a-c	3-wire, 2-phase a-c, ungrounded	2, one in each phase
2-phase a-c	3-wire, 2-phase a-c, one conductor grounded	2 in ungrounded conductors
2-phase a-c	4-wire, 2-phase a-c grounded or ungrounded	2, one per phase in ungrounded conductors
2-phase a-c	5-wire 2-phase a-c, grounded neutral or ungrounded	2, one per phase in any ungrounded phase wire
3-phase a-c	3-wire, 3-phase a-c, ungrounded	2 in any 2 conductors[a]
3-phase a-c	3-wire, 3-phase a-c, one conductor grounded	2 in ungrounded conductors[a]
3-phase a-c	3-wire, 3-phase a-c grounded-neutral	2 in any 2 conductors[a]
3-phase a-c	4-wire, 3-phase a-c grounded-neutral or ungrounded	2 in any 2 conductors, except the neutral[a]

[a] Three running overcurrent units shall be used where three-phase motors are installed in isolated, inaccessible, or unattended locations, unless the motor is protected by other approved means.

UNATTENDED (definition): Lacking the presence of a person (not necessarily an electrician) capable of exercising responsible control of the motor under consideration. Such a person need not be in sight of the motor at all times but must be available for opening the motor circuit in the event of motor overheating.

for use with the motor it protects. A motor that can restart automatically after shutdown shall not be installed so that its automatic restarting can result in injury to persons.

431. Application of Fuses for Motor Overload Protection. If regular fuses are used for the overload protection of a motor, the fuses will have to be shunted during the starting period, since a regular fuse having a rating of 125 per cent of the motor full-load current would be blown by the starting current. Many cases of d-c motor and some wound-rotor-induction-motor installations will be an exception to this rule. Aside from these exceptions it is not common practice to use regular fuses for the overload protection of motors. Time-lag fuses can be satisfactorily employed for the overload protection of motors, since ones rated at 125 per cent of the motor full-load current will not be blown by the starting current for ordinary conditions of motor service. In fact the manufacturers of these fuses recommend that, for ordinary service, fuses of a smaller rating than 125 per cent of the motor full-load current be employed. Typical heavy service conditions are:

1. Motors slightly overloaded.
2. Motors with severe starting conditions, such as large fans, compressors, etc.
3. Motors which are started frequently or reversed quickly.
4. Motors which have the protective time-lag fuses located in places where high ambient temperatures prevail.

For extremely severe conditions the maximum values permitted in Tables **40** and **41** of Div. 11 may have to be used. They will meet the Code requirements for motor protection. For fractional-horsepower motors, time-lag fuses mounted directly on the motor will often be found advantageous.

Direct-current motors under ordinary conditions of service will not require a starting current of such value that it would blow regular fuses rated at 125 per cent of the motor full-load current. Standard manual starters for d-c motors are equipped with a starting resistance of a value which will limit the starting current on the first step to 150 per cent of the motor full-load current. This current for the normal duration of the starting period would not blow a fuse rated at 125 per cent of the full-load current. For ordinary conditions of service, therefore, regular fuses can be used for the protection of d-c motors. In many cases what has been said for d-c motors will hold true for wound-rotor induction motors.

432. Thermoguard and guardistor motors (Westinghouse Electric Corp.) are equipped with built-in protection mounted directly in the motor.

The built-in watchman in the thermoguard motor consists of a thermostat which when heated above a certain temperature opens two small contacts within the enclosing case of the thermostat. The thermostat is mounted on the windings or the stator iron of a motor. The contacts are provided with leads so that they may be connected in a control circuit in a manner that will cause the controller to disconnect the motor or give a warning signal when the thermostat operates because of overheating of the motor (see Fig. 197).

In the guardistor motor-protective system, the element is a ceramic disk about the size of an aspirin tablet. The faces have a metallic coating and are fitted with leads. The element is encapsulated in an epoxy resin with compatible thermal, electrical, and mechanical characteristics. In practice, three PTC thermistors, one in each phase and connected in series, are used for a three-phase motor (Fig. 198).

At normal winding temperatures, the resistance of the PTC thermistor is low and remains virtually constant up to its critical temperature. Beyond this point, a small increase in temperature greatly increases the resistance. When the temperature of any of the PTC thermistors transgresses the critical or switching temperature range, the circuit operates to give a warning or to disconnect the power. When cooling occurs, the circuit returns to normal resistance and the motor can be restarted. Either manual or automatic reset can be used. By varying the composition of the ceramic disks, the critical range can be changed.

On the guardistor motor designed for warning only, a type NE-51 neon glow lamp is mounted on the conduit box for visual warning (see Fig. 199, I). This lamp can also be supplied for remote mounting (if specified), for those installations where the motor conduit box would not be visible.

The guardistor motor used for control and warning has the necessary control mounted on a plate for open panel mounting. This control will take the motor off the line, operate a warning signal, or do both (see Fig. 199, II).

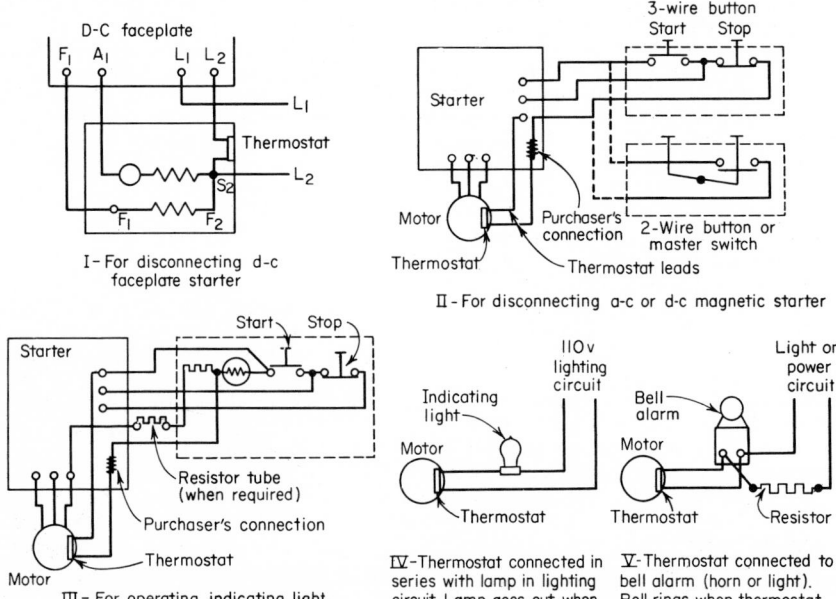

FIG. 197 *Connections for thermostats of thermoguard motors. (Westinghouse Electric Corp.)*

433. Motor Switches. Each motor with its controller must be provided with some form of approved manual disconnecting means, as at S_M in Figs. 195 and 196. This dis-

connecting means, when in the open position, must disconnect both the controller and the motor from all ungrounded supply wires. It must be of a type which will plainly indicate whether it is in the open or closed position. For motors rated at not more than 600 volts it may consist of a manually operated air-break switch, manually operated circuit breaker, or a manually operated oil switch. An oil switch used for this purpose must not, except with special permission, have a rating greater than 100 amp. The oil switch or circuit breaker may be equipped for electrical operation in addition to the hand mechanism. For motors rated at more than 600 volts, the equipment required for the branch-circuit protection will constitute the disconnecting means.

No additional switch is required with most types of manual across-the-line starters, since their switch acts as the

FIG. 198 *Method of locating PTC thermistors for protection of a three-phase motor. (Westinghouse Electric Corp.)*

disconnecting means. All magnetic types of starters and controllers must be provided with a switch ahead of the starter and within sight of it. All autotransformer starters require a separate disconnecting switch ahead of the starter.

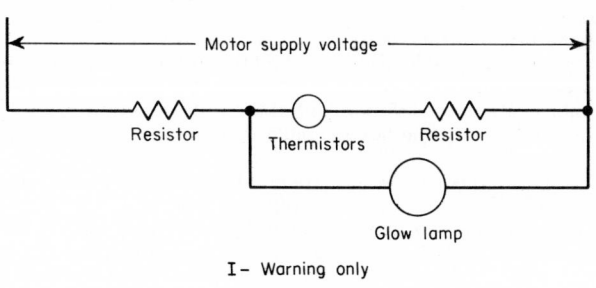

I- Warning only

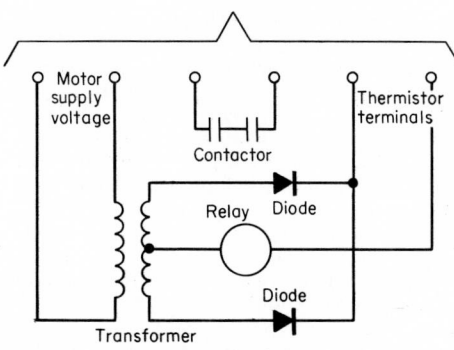

II - Control and warning

FIG. 199 *Basic circuits for guardistor-protected motors. (Westinghouse Electric Corp.)*

If fuses are used for the overload protection of the motor and the starting current of the motor is greater than the time delay of the fuses, a double-throw or a two-position switch will be required in order to short-circuit the running fuses during the starting period as at II in Figs. 195 and 196. This switch must be of such a type that it cannot be left in the starting position.

The motor switch must be a motor-circuit switch, rated in horsepower, or a circuit breaker except under the following conditions:

1. For stationary motors of 1/8 hp or less the branch-circuit overload device may serve as the disconnecting means.

2. For stationary motors of 2 hp or less operating at not more than 300 volts, a general-use switch having an ampere rating at least twice the full-load–motor-current rating may be used. On a-c circuits, general-use snap switches suitable only for use on a-c (not general-use ac-dc snap switches) may be used to disconnect a motor having a full-load current rating not exceeding 80 per cent of the ampere rating of the switch.

3. A general-use switch may be used for motors of a size over 2 hp but not larger than 50 hp which are equipped with a compensator starter, provided that all of the following provisions are complied with:

   a. The motor drives a generator provided with overcurrent protection.

   b. The controller is capable of interrupting the stalled-rotor current, is provided with a no-voltage release and with overload protection not exceeding 125 per cent of the motor full-load current rating.

   c. Separate fuses or a circuit breaker, rated or set at not more than 150 per cent of the motor rated current, are provided in the branch circuit.

4. For stationary motors that are rated at more than 50 hp, the disconnecting means may be a motor-circuit switch also rated in amperes, a general-use switch, or an isolating switch.

Isolating switches for motors exceeding 50 hp, not capable of interrupting stalled-rotor currents, shall be plainly marked "Do not open under load."

5. For portable motors an attachment plug and receptacle may serve as the disconnecting means.

A motor-circuit switch is intended for use in a motor branch circuit and is rated in horsepower. It must be capable of interrupting the maximum operating overload current of a motor of the same horsepower as the switch at the rated voltage. It must have a continuous rating of at least 115 per cent of the full-load current of the motor. If a fused switch is used, it must be large enough to accommodate the size of fuses employed.

The disconnecting means for sealed (hermetic-type) refrigeration compressors shall be selected on the basis of the nameplate full-load current and locked-rotor current, respectively, of the compressor motor. For full-load current, the horsepower rating shall be selected from Tables **7** to **10** of Div. 11 inclusive and for locked-rotor current, the horsepower rating shall be selected from Table **44** of Div. 11. If the nameplate full-load current and locked-rotor current do not correspond to the currents shown in Tables **7** to **10** and Table **44** of Div. 11, respectively, the horsepower rating corresponding to the next higher value shall be selected. If two different horsepower ratings are obtained when applying Tables **7** to **10** and Table **44,** a horsepower rating at least equal to the larger of the two values obtained shall be selected.

If the motor switch is used for shutting down the motor, it should be located as close as possible to the motor and its driven machinery and in the most accessible location for the operator. If the motor switch is not used for shutting down the motor but simply as a disconnecting means, it may be located at any convenient readily accessible point, provided it either is within sight of the motor or can be locked in the open position. Under these conditions one switch may be employed to serve the double purpose of motor- and branch-circuit switch as shown at S_M in III of Fig. 195. If an installation consists of a single motor, the service switch may serve as the disconnecting means, provided it meets all the above conditions.

434. Group Switching. Under any one of the following conditions the National Electrical Code rules will allow a single switch to be provided for a group of motors if the motors are rated at not more than 600 volts:

1. Where a number of motors drive several parts of a single machine or piece of apparatus, such as metal and woodworking machines, cranes, and hoists.

2. Where a group of motors is under the protection of one set of overcurrent devices as permitted by the Code (see Sec. **430**).

3. Where a group of motors is in a single room within sight of the location of the disconnecting means.

The disconnecting means shall have a rating not less than is required for a single motor the rating of which equals the sum of the horsepowers or currents of all the motors of the group.

435. Branch-circuit Protection. The wires of motor branch circuits must be protected against overload by means of some protective device located at the point where the branch-circuit wires are connected to the feeder or main, as at location P_2 in Fig. 195. The National Electrical Code rules, however, allow the size of these branch-circuit overload protective devices to be considerably greater than the allowable carrying capacity of the wires. This is for the purpose of allowing the passage of the starting current without the employment of excessively large conductors.

With this practice, the motor overload protective device will protect against overloads of moderate severity and the branch-circuit protective device will protect against short circuits. The recommended maximum rating of fuses and setting of circuit breakers for motor branch circuits supplying an **individual motor** are given in Tables **39** to **41** of Div. 11.

The National Electrical Manufacturers' Association (NEMA) has adopted a standard of identifying code letters that may be marked by the manufacturers on motor nameplates to indicate the motor kilovolt-ampere input with locked rotor. These code letters with their classification are given in Table **39** of Div. 11. In determining the starting current to employ for circuit calculations, use values from Table **40** of Div. 11 if the motor nameplate is marked with the NEMA identifying code letter; otherwise, use values from Table **41** of Div. 11.

Although the branch-circuit overload protective device must pass the starting current of the motor, it is not necessary that the rating of the overload protective device be as great as the maximum value of the starting current of the motor. Owing to the time-lag characteristics of fuses or time-limit circuit breakers, the starting current, which lasts for only a short time, will not rupture fuses or operate time-limit circuit breakers of a considerably smaller rating than the maximum value of the starting current. The percentage of the maximum starting current that fuses must be rated for or time-limit circuit breakers set for, in order that the starting current will not open the circuit, depends upon the frequency and duration of the starting periods. Under ordinary starting conditions, fuses rated or time-limit circuit breakers set at from 50 to 67 per cent of the maximum starting current will allow the passage of the starting current. Branch motor circuits protected according to the percentages of the full-load currents given in Tables **39, 40,** and **41** of Div. 11 will allow the passage of the starting current for ordinary starting service. If the values for branch-circuit protective devices given in these tables do not correspond to the standard sizes or ratings of fuses, nonadjustable circuit breakers, or thermal devices, or possible settings of adjustable circuit breakers adequate to carry the load, the next higher size, rating, or setting may be used. When it is found that the maximum rating or setting of the motor branch-circuit protective device recommended in these tables is not large enough to allow the motor to start, the authority enforcing the Code may permit a sufficient increase in the rating or setting of the protective device to allow the motor to start.

Either fuses or circuit breakers may be employed for the protection of motor branch circuits for motors rated at not more than 600 volts.

When circuit breakers are used, they must have a continuous current rating of not less than 115 per cent of the full-load current rating of the motor.

It is often not convenient or practicable to locate the branch-circuit overload protective device directly at the point where the branch-circuit wires are connected to the main. In such cases the size of the branch-circuit wires between the feeder and the branch-circuit protective device must be the same size as the mains, unless the length of these wires is not greater than 25 ft. When the length of the branch-circuit wires between the main and the branch-circuit protective device is not greater than 25 ft, the Code rules allow the size of these wires to be such that they have a carrying capacity of only one-third of the carrying capacity of the mains (see Fig. 196) if they are protected against physical damage.

If the motor overload protective device consists of thermal cutouts or overload relays, the main must be protected by fuses rated at or circuit breakers set for approximately four times the full-load current of the smallest motor fed from the circuit unless the motor overload protective device is approved for group installation. If the motor overload protective device is approved for group installation, the overload protection of the main must not exceed the maximum allowable value as stamped on the motor overload protective device. Some motor overload protective devices are approved for use with main or feeder fuses as large as 100 amp.

If the motor overcurrent running protection is shorted out during the starting period, the branch-circuit protection must be rated or set at not over 400 per cent of the full-load current of the motor.

Each motor branch circuit and feeder of more than 600 volts shall be protected against overcurrent by one of the following means:

1. A circuit breaker of suitable rating so arranged that it can be serviced without hazard.

2. Fuses of the oil-filled or other suitable type. Fuses shall be used with suitable disconnecting means, or they shall be of a type that can also serve as the disconnecting means. They shall be so arranged that they cannot be re-fused or replaced while they are energized. The voltage and current ratings of fuses shall be limited to the values permitted by the code.

3. Differential protection can be employed to protect an a-c motor, the motor control apparatus, and the branch-circuit conductors against overcurrent due to short circuits or grounds. When all these elements are included within the protected zone of a differential protective system, the ratings or settings specified previously in this section do not apply.

A differential protective system is a combination of two or more sets of current transformers and a relay or relays energized from their interconnected secondaries.

The primaries of the current transformers are connected on both sides of the equipment to be protected, both ends of the motor phase windings being brought out for this purpose. All the apparatus and circuits included between the sets of current transformer primaries constitute the protected zone. The current transformer secondaries and the relay elements are so interconnected that the relay elements respond only to a predetermined difference between the currents entering and leaving the protected zone. When actuated, the relay or relays serve to trip the branch-circuit circuit breaker, thus disconnecting the motor, control apparatus in the motor circuit, and the branch-circuit conductors from the source of power and, in the case of a synchronous motor, de-energizing its field circuit.

436. Branch-circuit Switches. The National Electrical Code rules do not require a switch to be located on the line side of the overload protective device, as at S_B in Fig. 195, unless there is no switch located as at S_M in Fig. 195, I. When there is no switch located at S_M, a switch must be located at S_B in order to serve as a motor switch (see Sec. **433**). If a circuit breaker is employed for the branch-circuit overload protection, it will serve as both a switch and an overload protective device. Although not required, a branch-circuit switch is very convenient. It provides a means of disconnecting the entire branch circuit from the supply. When such a switch is not provided, the fuses must be removed from the circuit when the circuit is live. For this reason it is recommended that a branch-circuit switch be provided on all circuits operating at a voltage greater than 220 volts unless a safety-fuse type of panel is used (see Sec. **86**, Div. 4). The branch-circuit switch must have fuse clips large enough to accommodate the branch-circuit fuses, as required by Sec. **435**, and Tables **40** and **41** of Div. 11.

If a branch-circuit switch is located within sight of the motor controller location, it must comply with the requirements for a motor switch. Refer to Sec. **433**.

437. Size of Wire for Motor Branch Circuits. The wires of a branch circuit supplying a single continuous-duty motor must have a carrying capacity of at least 125 per cent of the full-load rated current of the motor. The size of the wires of a motor branch circuit supplying a single motor in short-time duty service may be different from those for a continuous-duty motor. In most cases the carrying capacity of the wires need not be greater than the percentages of the full-load current of the motor given in Table **12** of Div. 11.

The wires between the slip rings and the controller of a wound-rotor induction motor must have a carrying capacity of at least 125 per cent of the full-load secondary current of the motor for continuous-duty motors. For other than continuous-duty motors the carrying capacity of the wires must be not less than the percentages of full-load secondary currents as given in Table **12** of Div. 11. Where the secondary resistor is separate from the controller, the wires between the secondary controller and the resistance of a wound-rotor induction motor must have a carrying capacity which is not less than the percentages of the full-load secondary current of the motor given in Table **13** of Div. 11.

The wires of a branch circuit supplying several motors but no other equipment except that directly associated with the motors must have a current-carrying capacity of not less than 125 per cent of the full-load current rating of the largest motor plus the sum of the full-load current ratings of the remainder of the motors.

For the size of the tap conductors, refer to Secs. **427** and **428**.

If the tap between the feeder or main and the branch-circuit protective devices is not over 10 ft long and is protected against mechanical injury by conduit, electrical metallic tubing, or metal gutters, the tap from the feeder or main to the protective devices may be of the same size as the branch-circuit conductors.

438. Remote-control Circuits. Control circuits shall be so arranged that they will be disconnected from all sources of supply when the disconnecting means is in the open position. The disconnecting means may consist of two separate devices, one of which disconnects the motor and the controller from the source of power supply for the motor, and the other, the control circuit from its power supply. Where the two separate devices are used, they should be located immediately adjacent to one another.

Where a transformer or other device is used to obtain a reduced voltage for the control circuit and is located in the controller, such transformer or other device shall be connected to the load side of the disconnecting means for the control circuit.

The conductors of these control circuits will be considered as properly protected by the motor branch-circuit overcurrent protective devices under any one of the following conditions:

1. If the rating or setting of the branch-circuit overcurrent device is not more than 500 per cent of the carrying capacity of the control-circuit conductors.

2. If the controlled device and the point of control (start and stop buttons, pressure switch, thermostatic switch, etc.) are both located on the same machine and the control circuit does not extend beyond the machine.

3. If the opening of the control circuit would create a hazard, as, for example, the control circuit of pump motors, etc.

439. Size of Motor Feeders or Mains. For the determination of the size of motor mains or feeders, refer to Div. 3.

440. Overload Protection of Motor Feeders or Mains. The size of the protective equipment for motor feeders or mains is determined from the so-called starting current of the circuit, as explained in Sec. **54** of Div. 3.

Fuses or circuit breakers can be used for the overload protection of motor feeders or mains.

441. Motor-wiring tables are given in Tables **42** to **46** of Div. 11. These tables give data on the size of the component parts of motor branch circuits in accordance with the 1968 edition of the National Electrical Code. Refer to Sec. **421**. If the wiring is to be done in a locality which has adopted local motor-wiring tables of its own, the tables of that particular district should be adhered to instead of the values given here. The values for the sizes of wires given in the tables are the minimum sizes allowed by the Code. They do not take into account voltage drop in the circuit. For long circuits the voltage drop should be computed in order to determine whether the size of wire should be increased so as to keep the voltage drop within an allowable amount (see Div. 3).

442. Protection of Live Parts. The National Electrical Code requires that live parts shall be protected in a manner judged adequate to the hazard involved. The rules state:

1. WHERE REQUIRED. Exposed live parts of motors and controllers operating at 50 volts or more between terminals, except for stationary motors having commutators, collectors, and brush rigging located inside of motor end brackets and not conductively connected to supply circuits operating at more than 150 volts to ground, shall be guarded against accidental contact by enclosure, or by location as follows:

a. By installation in a room or enclosure which is accessible only to qualified persons.

b. By installation on a suitable balcony, gallery, or platform, so elevated and arranged as to exclude unqualified persons.

c. By elevation 8 ft or more above the floor.

d. So that it will be protected by a guard rail when the motor operates at 600 volts or less.

2. GUARDS FOR ATTENDANTS. If the live parts of motors or controllers operating at more than 150 volts to ground are guarded against accidental contact only by location as specified in paragraph 1, and if adjustment or other attendance may be necessary during the operation of the apparatus, suitable insulating mats or platforms shall be provided so that the attendant cannot readily touch live parts unless standing on the mats or platforms. Where necessary, steps and handrails should be installed on or about large machines to afford safe access to parts which must be examined or adjusted during operation.

CONTROL CIRCUITS

443. Electric control circuits represent a broad subject, and the reader is urged to refer to special books devoted to this important phase of motor circuitry. Two such books are "Control of Electric Motors," by Paisley B. Harwood, published by John Wiley & Sons, Inc., and "Modern Electric Controls," by J. F. McPartland, published by *Electrical Construction and Maintenance* of McGraw-Hill, Inc.

These textbooks provide an excellent insight on how to understand, select, and design control circuits.

444. Arrangement of Control Wiring in Grounded Circuits. It is a requirement of the National Electrical Code that if one side of a control circuit is *intentionally*

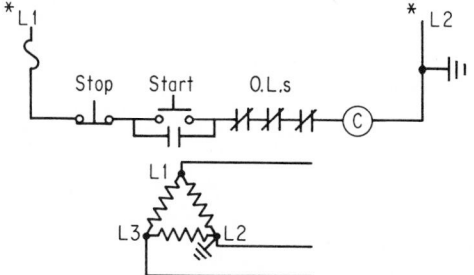

* L1 & L2 from end-grounded delta supply or;

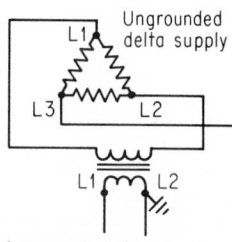

*L1&L2 from control trans.
where secondary L2 is grounded

When one side of the control circuit is grounded circuit shall be so arranged that an accidental gr. in remote-control devices will not <u>start</u> motor. Drawing shows acceptable arrangements

FIG. 200 *Arrangement of control wiring in grounded circuits. (Electrical Construction and Maintenance.)*

grounded, the control circuit shall be so arranged that an accidental ground in the remote-control devices will not *start* the motor. Figure 200 shows two methods that satisfy this Code rule. The elementary wiring diagram at the top of Fig. 200 shows the arrangement of a start-stop push button connected to the holding coil of a magnetic starter. Note that all control devices are connected to the L1 side of coil C, and the other side is connected to the grounded circuit conductor L2.

The L2 conductor could be the grounded conductor of an end-grounded three-phase delta supply, or the grounded conductor of the secondary winding of a control transformer.

445. Control Circuits from Ungrounded Systems. It is quite significant that the code rule described in Sec. **444** applies only to *grounded*-type control circuits and is concerned only about preventing a motor from being *accidentally* started.

In ungrounded three-phase 220- or 440-volt three-wire systems, there is always a possibility of one or more accidental grounds occurring in a control circuit connected to such systems. If *two* grounds occur in the same control circuit conductor at certain critical points, a motor could accidentally start, or, if a second ground develops after a motor has been started, it is possible that the motor will not *stop* after the "stop button" is pressed. There are two ways to prevent this. The first method is illustrated in Fig. 200, where a *control transformer* provides a *grounded* secondary, and the control circuit is wired as shown.

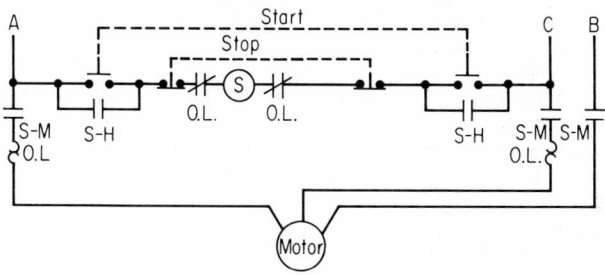

FIG. 201 *Ideal control circuit where the supply system or control circuit is ungrounded. (Electrical Construction and Maintenance.)*

The second method applies where the control circuit is taken directly from an *ungrounded* supply. The arrangement illustrated in Fig. 201 utilizes *double-pole* start and stop buttons wired with one pole of each button on opposite sides of coil S. With this arrangement one or more accidental grounds will not start the motor; nor will it *prevent the motor from being stopped* after the motor is in operation and a second ground occurs.

The arrangement shown in Fig. 201 is ideal where long control circuits are used, because pressing the "stop" button opens both lines to coil S, and line-to-line capacitive coupling will not keep the coil energized as it occasionally has done where standard start-stop control circuits were used.

ENGINE- AND GAS-TURBINE GENERATORS

446. Engine-driven generators (diesel, gasoline, or gas) are the most economical and practical source of *standby power* in a wide range of applications. They are sized from a few hundred watts to several hundred kilowatts. Control is obtained manually, remotely, or automatically. Units are designed either as stationary or mobile power stations. And cooling is obtained by natural convection fan-forced air or by circulating water.

Generator engines are generally four-cycle units having one to six cylinders, depending on size and capacity. In larger sets, ignition current is supplied by starting batteries. A typical arrangement is shown in Fig. 202.

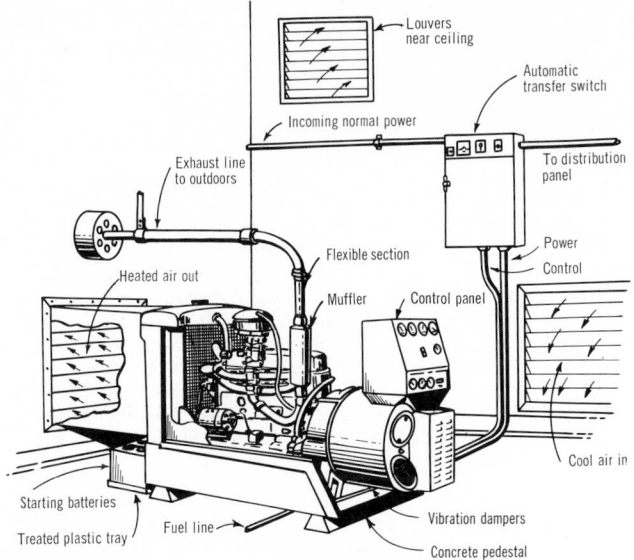

FIG. 202 *Typical installation of an engine-generator for a standby or emergency supply system. (Electrical Construction and Maintenance.)*

447. Location. In most instances, the power plant should be located close to the normal electric service and where it is warm enough to start easily. Locations where ambient temperatures may be unusually high should also be avoided because inefficient cooling may result. On the other hand, in locations where temperatures fall below 50°F, special accessories, such as an electric water jacket or manifold heater, may be needed to ensure dependable automatic starts.

448. Mounting. Smaller units, 10 kw and less, should be installed on a concrete foundation equipped with anchor bolts. In some cases, steel beam sections will make a satisfactory base. Such a base raises the plant off the floor for convenience in servicing and lessens the chance of accidental damage from loose objects, seepage, etc. For larger plants that are equipped with steel skids, a separate foundation may not be required.

Always allow at least 2 ft of unobstructed space around the power plant on all sides. This permits room for servicing the unit. If this space is not available, position the plant so that the carburetor, distributor, governor, fuel pump, oil fill, etc., are easily accessible.

449. Battery Mounting. Batteries should be mounted in a clean, dry location free from falling dirt or dust, and they should be installed on a wood base rather than on a concrete floor. Allow for easy maintenance of the battery.

450. Exhaust Piping. Exhaust pipes should be wrought iron, cast iron, or steel. Because exhaust fumes are dangerous, care should be taken to prevent leaks in the exhaust system. And the exhaust pipe should terminate outside away from doors, windows, or other openings.

451. Cooling. Ventilation openings must always be provided and located so that cool air can be brought in, forced through the engine cooling system and directly out without recirculating.

Other important installation considerations include fuel line and fuel tank installation, muffler requirements, heaters, battery charger, and automatic controls.

452. Load-transfer Switches. The two basic types of transfer switches are manual and automatic.

The manual control is a double-throw switch which is manually operated to transfer the load from normal to emergency power after the standby plant is running. An automatic transfer switch starts and stops the standby power plant and transfers the load by relays without any attention from an operator.

An installation of an automatic transfer switch should also include a trickle battery charger, voltage-sensitive relays, time-delay relays, clock-operated exerciser, testing facilities, and safety devices.

453. Gas-turbine Generators. In the larger sizes, from about 700 kw up, the turbine-driven generator offers a number of advantages as a source of power. These units are small in size and weight when compared to other types of power sources of the same capacity. They can provide much more power capability in the same space required for standby power using reciprocating engines.

Installation of gas-turbine generators is relatively simple because foundations are small and light, or not required at all for some skid-mounted units. Vibration is minimal. Cooling water is not required because the unit is normally air-cooled. However, soundproofing of the room or location in which the unit is installed may be required if the high-frequency vibrations emitted are objectionable. Effective equipment for soundproofing is available.

FIG. 203   *Cutaway view of a 200-kw gas-turbine generator.   (Caterpillar Tractor Co.)*

Other applications where the gas-turbine generator has been particularly successful include its use for total energy systems and for utility peak load service.

Figure 203 shows a cutaway view of a gas-turbine generator set which provides 200 kw at 60 cycles, 480Y/277 volts, along with heat energy for many commercial and industrial applications. Major components shown in cutaway are (left to right) the speed reducer and accessory drive section; the single-stage centrifugal air compressor; the combustion chamber and two axial-flow turbine wheels. Directly below these units in the engine base are the lube-oil sump and cooler.

DIVISION EIGHT

Outside Distribution

POLE LINES—GENERAL, CONSTRUCTION, AND EQUIPMENT

1. The reports of the committee on overhead line construction of the National Electric Light Association contain what are probably the best and most complete specifications for pole-line construction for lighting and power distribution that have ever been compiled. Some of the matter in this division regarding pole lines has been abstracted from those reports. The National Electric Light Association has been reorganized and succeeded by the Edison Electric Institute (EEI). As specifications and standards of the NELA organization are revised, they will be known as those of the EEI.

2. The National Electrical Safety Code, "U.S. Bureau of Standards Handbook," comprises an exhaustive collection of rules for proper installation, maintenance, and operation of electrical distribution systems. Companies are now, in general, endeavoring to follow these rules. Ultimately, it is believed, their adoption will be universal.

3. There are three principal types of overhead line construction:

1. Bare or weatherproof covered wire supported by insulators mounted on or hung from crossarms located on buildings or near the tops of poles.

2. Weatherproof covered wire supported by insulators mounted on racks on the side of buildings or poles.

3. Insulated aerial cable which is either self-supporting from clamps bolted to sides of poles or crossarms or supported by messenger cable from clamps bolted to the sides of poles or crossarms. (See Div. 2 for descriptions of the types of wire and cable.)

4. There are four main types of poles used for overhead line construction:

1. Wood poles.
2. Steel poles.
3. Reinforced-concrete poles.
4. Structural-steel fabricated towers.

5. The most common woods for poles are:

1. Western red cedar, found in the Rocky Mountain regions from southern Alaska to the central part of California.

2. Northern white cedar, found in Michigan, Wisconsin, Minnesota, and elsewhere throughout northeastern United States and southeastern Canada.

3. Southern yellow pine, found in Virginia, North and South Carolina, Tennessee, and south into Florida and west to Texas.

4. Chestnut, found in Virginia, West Virginia, and in some of the other southern states, virtually all blight-killed but in a good state of preservation.

5. Redwood, found on the Pacific Coast.

Of these, the yellow pine is most commonly used in the eastern states, red or white cedar in the central states, and redwood on the West Coast. According to the Standard Handbook, about two-thirds of all poles used are cedar.

6. Wood poles are classified into ten classes according to the circumference at the top of the pole and the circumference at a point 6 ft from the butt, as given in the following table:

Class	1	2	3	4	5	6	7	8	9	10
Min top circumference, in..	27	25	23	21	19	17	15	18	15	12
Length of pole, ft	Min circumference 6 ft from butt, in.									
Northern White Cedar Poles										
16	....	....	....	....	26.0	24.0	22.0	No butt requirement		
18	....	....	32.5	30.0	28.0	25.5	23.5			
20	39.5	37.0	34.0	31.5	29.0	27.0	25.0			
22	41.0	38.5	36.0	33.0	30.5	28.0	26.0			
25	43.5	41.0	38.0	35.5	32.5	30.0	28.0			
30	47.5	44.5	41.5	38.5	35.5	33.0	30.5			
35	50.5	47.5	44.0	41.0	38.0	35.0	32.5			
40	53.5	50.0	46.5	43.5	40.0	37.0				
45	56.0	52.5	49.0	45.5	42.0					
50	58.5	55.0	51.5	47.5	44.0					
55	61.0	57.5	53.5	49.5	46.0					
60	63.5	59.5	55.5	51.5						
Western Red Cedar Poles										
16	....	....	....	....	23.0	21.5	19.5	No butt requirement		
18	....	....	28.5	26.5	24.5	22.5	21.0			
20	34.5	32.0	30.0	28.0	25.5	23.5	22.0			
22	36.0	33.5	31.5	29.0	27.0	25.0	23.0			
25	38.0	35.5	33.0	30.5	28.5	26.0	24.5			
30	41.0	38.5	35.5	33.0	30.5	28.5	26.5			
35	43.5	41.0	38.0	35.5	32.5	30.5	28.0			
40	46.0	43.5	40.5	37.5	34.5	32.0				
45	48.5	45.5	42.5	39.5	36.5					
50	50.5	47.5	44.5	41.0	38.0					
55	52.5	49.5	46.0	42.5	39.5					
60	54.5	51.0	47.5	44.0						
65	56.0	52.5	49.0	45.5						
70	57.5	54.0	50.5	47.0						
75	59.5	55.5	52.0	48.5						
80	61.0	57.0	53.5	49.5						
85	62.5	58.5	54.5							
90	63.5	60.0	56.0							

Class	1	2	3	4	5	6	7	8	9	10
Min top circumference, in	27	25	23	21	19	17	15	18	15	12
Length of pole, ft	Min circumference 6 ft from butt, in.									
Creosoted Southern Pine Poles										
16	....	....	....	....	21.5	19.5	18.0	No butt requirement		
18	....	....	26.5	24.5	22.5	21.0	19.0			
20	31.5	29.5	27.5	25.5	23.5	22.0	20.0			
22	33.0	31.0	29.0	26.5	24.5	23.0	21.0			
25	34.5	32.5	30.0	28.0	26.0	24.0	22.0			
30	37.5	35.0	32.5	30.0	28.0	26.0	24.0			
35	40.0	37.5	35.0	32.0	30.0	27.5	25.5			
40	42.0	39.5	37.0	34.0	31.5	29.0	27.0			
45	44.0	41.5	38.5	36.0	33.0	30.5	28.5			
50	46.0	43.0	40.0	37.5	34.5	32.0	29.5			
55	47.5	44.5	41.5	39.0	36.0	33.5				
60	49.5	46.0	43.0	40.0	37.0	34.5				
65	51.0	47.5	44.5	41.5	38.5					
70	52.5	49.0	46.0	42.5	39.5					
75	54.0	50.5	47.0	44.0						
80	55.0	51.5	48.5	45.0						
85	56.5	53.0	49.5							
90	57.5	54.0	50.5							
Chestnut Poles										
16	....	....	....	....	22½	21	19½	No butt requirement		
18	....	....	28	26	24	22	20½			
20	33½	31½	29½	27	25	23	21½			
22	35	33	30½	28½	26½	24½	22½			
25	37	34½	32½	30	28	25½	24			
30	40	37½	35	32½	30	28	26			
35	42½	40	37½	34½	32	30	27½			
40	45	42½	39½	36½	34	31½	29½			
45	47½	44½	41½	38½	36	33	31			
50	49½	46½	43½	40	37½	34½	32			
55	51½	48½	45	42	39	36				
60	53½	50	46½	43½						
65	55	51½	48	45						
70	56½	53								

7. Approximate Weights of Wood Poles in Pounds
(The MacGilles and Gibbs Co.)

Northern white cedar

Length of pole, ft	Class 1	2	3	4	5	6	7	8	9	10
16	....	....	....	....	230	190	135	135	105	85
18	....	....	420	300	250	210	155	155	125	95
20	720	600	440	350	300	230	190	190	130	100
22	820	780	540	500	400	315	200	225	170	120
25	1,020	980	600	515	420	300	225	250	200	150
30	1,320	1,170	870	630	520	420	350	350	275	....
35	1,620	1,320	1,060	820	720	510	450	350	....	....
40	2,040	1,675	1,280	1,020	790	625	....	....	....	....
45	2,640	1,970	1,535	1,215	1,080	....	....	....	....	....
50	3,200	2,640	1,860	1,470	1,380	....	....	....	....	....
55	3,800	2,960	2,260	1,620	1,560	....	....	....	....	....
60	4,500	3,460	2,640	1,700	....	....	....	....	....	....
65	....	....	....	....	....	....	....	....	....	....
70	....	....	....	....	....	....	....	....	....	....
75	....	....	....	....	....	....	....	....	....	....
80	....	....	....	....	....	....	....	....	....	....
85	....	....	....	....	....	....	....	....	....	....
90	....	....	....	....	....	....	....	....	....	....

Western red cedar

Length of pole, ft	Class 1	2	3	4	5	6	7	8	9	10
16										
18										
20	700	600	500	400	300	225	200	180	135	100
22										
25	850	720	600	480	400	320	250	225	200	135
30	1,000	850	730	610	500	420	350	325	250	
35	1,200	1,000	850	750	650	560	470	450		
40	1,500	1,300	1,100	900	800	700				
45	1,800	1,550	1,300	1,150	1,000					
50	2,000	1,800	1,550	1,400	1,300					
55	2,300	2,000	1,750	1,600	1,600					
60	2,600	2,200	2,000	1,900						
65	3,200	2,500	2,300	2,200						
70	3,600	3,000	2,700	2,600						
75	4,200	3,600	3,100	3,000						
80	5,000	4,200	3,600	3,500						
85	5,500	4,500	4,000							
90	6,600	5,600	4,800							

8. Wood-pole Specifications.   The USA Standards Institute (USASI) has standardized the specifications and dimensions for wood poles.   The USA Standards Institute specifications provide that all poles shall be free from sap rot, cracks, bird holes, plugged holes, injurious checks, and damage by marine borers.   All poles shall be free from splits, shakes, hollow, and decay in the tops.   Nails, spikes, and other metal shall not be present unless specifically authorized by the purchaser.   There are further de-

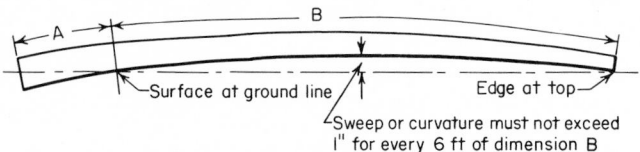

I– Sweep in one plane and one direction

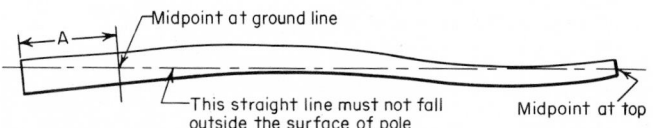

II–Sweep in two planes (Double Sweep) or in two directions in one plane (Reverse Sweep)
(Applies to western red cedar and southern pine poles only) For northern white cedar and chestnut poles the sweep in each plane must not exceed the value in I

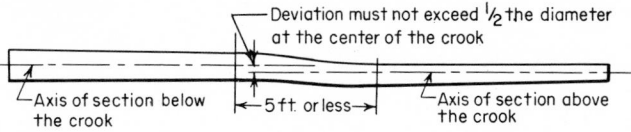

III–Short crook where the reference axes are approximately parallel

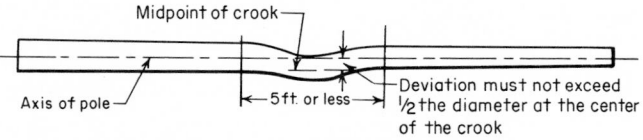

IV –Short crook where axes of sections above and below the crook coincide or are practically coincident

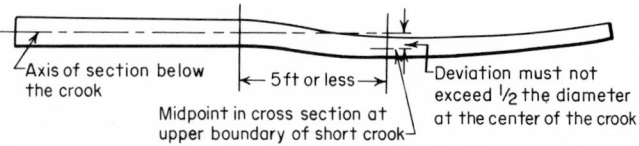

V–Short crook where axis of section above short crook is not parallel or coincident with axis below the crook

FIG. 1   *Allowable sweeps and crooks in wood poles.   (USA Standards Institute.)*

tailed restrictions regarding blue sap stain, hollow centers, shakes in the butt surface, splits, grain twist, insect damage, scars, etc., which vary with the different types of poles.   Anyone interested in such details is advised to consult the USASI.

Allowable deviations from straight poles are illustrated in Fig. 1.   Dimension *A* should be taken from the following table:

A, ft	3½	4	5	5½	6	6½	7	7½	8	8½	9	9½	10	10½	11
Total length of pole, ft...............	16–18	20–22	25	30	35–40	45	50	55	60	65	70	75	80	85	90

9. Preservation of Poles. Owing to the continually increasing scarcity of timber and the labor cost of replacing decayed poles, general practice is to impregnate poles with some substance which resists or retards decay. Southern pine poles generally are pressure-treated for their entire length. Common practice is to treat only the butt of poles of other woods, because, since these woods are naturally resistant to decay, practically all decay occurs within the portion 1½ ft above or below the ground line.

10. Methods of Butt Treating (Naugle Pole & Tie Co.). The specifications for each of the three methods of treating require: Poles shall be seasoned at least four **seasoning months** before the treatment (see Sec. 11). All fibrous inner bark and foreign substances must be thoroughly removed from that portion of the pole between the points 1½ ft above and 1½ ft below the ground line. In general, the methods of treatment are as follows: **Treatment A** provides for a continuous submersion in hot Carbolineum (a coal-tar derivative) for a minimum interval of 15 min. **Treatment AA** provides for a continuous submersion in hot creosote for a minimum interval of 15 min. **Treatment B** provides for a continuous submersion in hot creosote for a minimum interval of 4 hr, to be followed by a continuous submersion in cold creosote for a minimum interval of 2 hr. In each of these three treatments the poles are placed in upright tanks with the butts continuously submerged to a height of 1½ ft above the ground line.

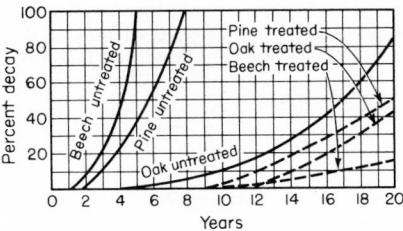

FIG. 2 *Life of treated and untreated poles.*

Figure 2 shows, as would be expected, that the softer and more porous woods that suffer most rapid decay are most benefited and have the longest life after treatment. Such woods can absorb the most oil. The cost of treatment varies with the amount of oil injected and with local conditions.

11. Calendar months are rated in equivalent seasoning months as follows:

Calendar month......	Jan.	Feb.	Mar.	Apr.	May	June	July	Aug.	Sept.	Oct.	Nov.	Dec.
Seasoning month.....	⅛	⅛	¼	½	¾	1	1	1	1	¾	⅜	⅛

Poles which have been properly piled for seasoning must be seasoned for a total of 4 seasoning months, counting the seasoning months as given in the above table. For example, poles which are cut in January or February must be seasoned to the end of August before the time will have equaled 4 "seasoning months."

12. Steel poles are made in three general types: (1) latticed, (2) expanded truss, and (3) tubular. The latticed type is made from structural-steel angles or channels joined and braced by latticed crossbars. The expanded truss is made from structural H sections, the web of which has been sheared by a rotary shear at fixed intervals so as to remove some of the metal. The pole is then heated to a cherry red and expanded by a special machine which grips the flanges and pulls them apart to the desired width (see Fig. 3). Latticed and expanded-truss steel poles are used for medium-voltage transmission lines with spans 250 to 350 ft in length. Their life is 25 to 50 years or more, depending on the adequacy of painting and upkeep. Tubular poles are built up from lengths of steel tubing, using a large-diameter tube for the base and successively smaller ones for the upper sections. They have been extensively used for street-railway and trolley-bus wiring in cities, where appearance is important. Their higher cost has prevented their use through open country.

13. Fabricated steel towers are made from four main structural angles as uprights, cross-braced with smaller structural angles. Steel towers are ordinarily used for high-voltage lines with spans over 350 ft.

14. The design of reinforced-concrete poles requires considerable skill. Where one who is unfamiliar with concrete-pole design must build them, he had best accept the proportions of poles that have been built and are giving good service. Figure 4 shows some of the major considerations. The pole is proportioned for a 150-ft span to withstand a gale successfully, with the wind at a velocity of 70 miles per hour and ½ in. of ice on the wires. The horizontal load thus imposed by the wind on all the 18 wires, tending to overturn the pole, is 2,100 lb. The sides of the reinforcing bars are 1¼ in. in from the faces of the pole. The concrete is a 1:2:4 mixture. It should be mixed wet,

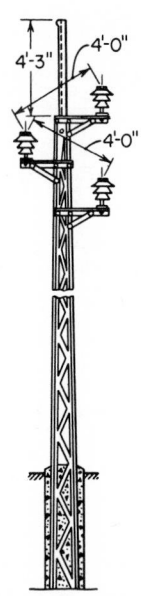

FIG. 3 *Bates expanded steel pole.*

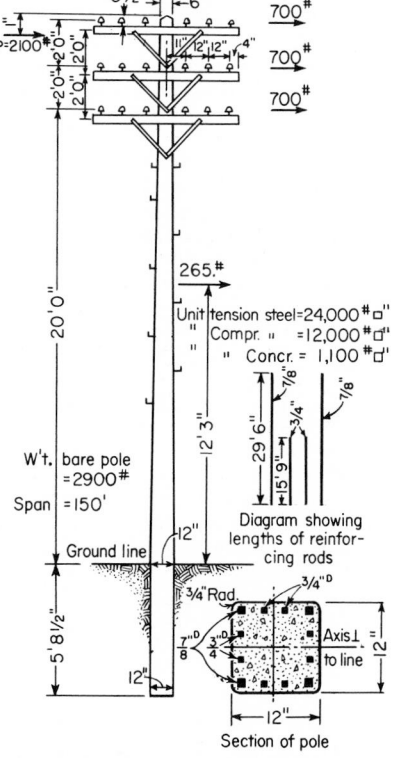

FIG. 4 *A 30-ft reinforced-concrete pole.*
(*Universal Portland Cement Co.*)

using carefully selected materials with the fine aggregate next to the forms. Air bubbles should be eliminated by careful tamping or churning. Corners of the pole should be chamfered off. The square reinforcing rods, which are of the mechanical-bond type, are bound together by a web system not shown in the illustration. The web system consists of a spiral of No. 12 steel wire wound outside the rods and securely bound to them. The rods are also secured together with horizontal ties 1 in. wide and ¼ in. thick, spaced 3 to 5 ft apart. The reinforcement thus forms an independent skeleton which can be assembled and lowered into the forms. It is likely that it is most economical to cast poles exceeding 35 ft in height in their final vertical positions. Shorter poles are erected with a derrick. Gains for crossarms and holes for bolts are cast in poles. Metal pole steps may be cast in solid also.

15. Reinforced-concrete poles (Standard Handbook) are the most permanent and usually the most expensive. The life of a properly designed concrete pole is practically unlimited. The facility with which special purposes can be served with reinforced concrete is also a great advantage. The exterior form can easily be modified to harmonize with any desired scheme of decoration. When it is desired to lead wires from the pole top to ground, the poles can be made hollow, and thus at a slight additional cost the wires are completely hidden from view and protected from the weather. Concrete poles may fail, but they will not fall to the ground. The principal drawback to this form of construction has been the cost and the difficulty of manufacture. They are heavy and cumbersome to transport, so that, where possible, it is well to make them in the neighborhood where they are to be used. Both concrete and steel poles can be transported in small packages over mountains and erected on the spot, but in this respect steel is much superior to concrete. Concrete poles are classified according to the horizontal load which can be applied to the pole 2 ft from the top:

Class	A	B	C	D	E
Horizontal load applied 2 ft from top, lb	4,000	3,000	2,000	1,500	1,000

16. Depth to Set Poles in the Ground. One rule is that they should, on straight lines, be set in the ground one-sixth of their lengths. The following table indicates good practice for normal soils:

Pole length, over all, ft	Depth to set in ground, ft		Pole length, over all, ft	Depth to set in ground, ft	
	Straight lines	Curves, corners, and points of extra strain		Straight lines	Curves, corners, and points of extra strain
30	5.5	6.0	55	7.0	7.5
35	6.0	6.5	60	7.5	8.0
40	6.0	6.5	65	8.0	8.5
45	6.5	7.0	70	8.0	8.5
50	7.0	7.5	75	8.5	9.0

17. The size of pole to use cannot be definitely specified without knowing local conditions. Municipal ordinances sometimes regulate the heights of poles and wires. Where there are trees along the line, the wires should be carried entirely above them or through the lower branches, which interfere less than do the higher ones where the foliage is thicker. (See Sec. **73** for required clearances of wires above the ground.) For lines on highways it is usually customary to place the lowest wire at least 18 ft above the highway, and 21 ft is better. Railway companies frequently specify 22 ft between the top of the rail and the lowest crossarm. Wires should be at least 15 ft above sidewalks. The height of the pole will depend upon the number of crossarms to be carried. It is desirable to avoid abrupt changes in the level of wire. Hence, where the line runs up hill and down dale, the longer poles should be used in the valleys.

Guy wires should, except where otherwise provided by ordinance, be at least 18 ft above a highway and 12 ft above a sidewalk.

Also in cities it is good practice to use 35-ft poles to carry either one or two crossarms, 40-ft poles to carry three or four crossarms, and 45-ft poles to carry over four crossarms. For suburban lines 30-ft poles are often used. For very light lines carrying only three or four wires, 6-in. poles 25 ft long are sometimes used, though so light a pole is inexpedient if the number of wires is likely to increase. The height of a pole is always considered as the total length over all.

18. Poles should be spaced, in straight portions of a line, about 125 ft apart. The usual maximum is 150 ft, and the minimum about 100 ft. In curves and at corners the spans

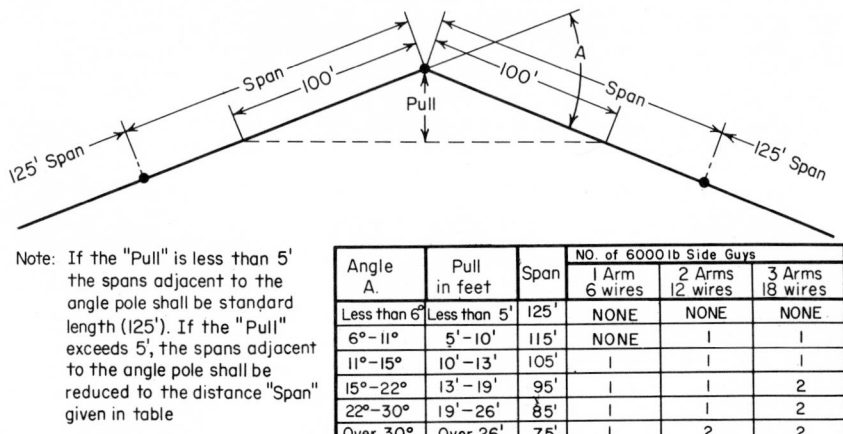

Note: If the "Pull" is less than 5' the spans adjacent to the angle pole shall be standard length (125'). If the "Pull" exceeds 5', the spans adjacent to the angle pole shall be reduced to the distance "Span" given in table

Angle A.	Pull in feet	Span	NO. of 6000 lb Side Guys		
			1 Arm 6 wires	2 Arms 12 wires	3 Arms 18 wires
Less than 6°	Less than 5'	125'	NONE	NONE	NONE
6°–11°	5'–10'	115'	NONE	1	1
11°–15°	10'–13'	105'	1	1	1
15°–22°	13'–19'	95'	1	1	2
22°–30°	19'–26'	85'	1	1	2
Over 30°	Over 26'	75'	1	2	2

FIG. 5 *Pole spacing and side guys on curves.* (*Edison Electric Institute.*)

should be about as indicated in Fig. 5. For rural lines the span may be lengthened to 200 or 250 ft. Spans up to 400 or 500 ft have been used for rural feeder lines employing aluminum cable, steel-reinforced.

19. Holes for poles should be large enough to admit the poles without any slicing or chopping and should be of the same diameter from top to bottom. The diameter of the hole should always be at least large enough so that a tamping bar can be worked on all sides between the pole and the sides of the hole.

20. Setting Poles. On straight lines poles should be set perpendicularly. On curves, poles should slant slightly so that the tension of the wires will tend to straighten them. In filling a hole after the pole is in it, only one shoveler should be employed and as many more men as can conveniently work around the pole should tamp in the earth as the shoveler throws it in. Some of the surplus earth should be piled around the butt of the pole so the water will drain away. Figure 6 illustrates the method of setting a pole with pikes.

21. Setting Poles with a Gin Pole. A few men can set a large pole with a gin pole as suggested in Fig. 7. The gin pole can be a short wooden pole or, where the poles to be raised are not too heavy, a length of wrought-iron pipe. The gin need be only one-half as long as the pole to be raised. In setting a pole the gin is first raised to an almost vertical position with its top over the pole hole. It is held in that position by fastening the guy lines. Then the hook of the tackle blocks is engaged in a sling around the pole and the pole is raised, by men or by a power unit, by pulling on the free end of the tackle block line. When high enough so that its lower end can be slipped into it,

FIG. 6 *Method of setting a pole with pikes.*

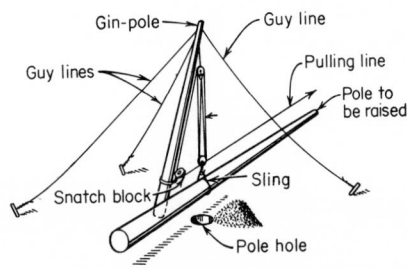

FIG. 7 *Gin pole for raising poles.*

the pole is dropped into the hole and adjusted to a vertical position with pikes, and the earth is tamped in. In modern practice gin poles are permanently mounted on trucks for transportation and are then called pole derricks. They are great savers of time and money. The methods illustrated in Figs. 6 and 7 are shown to assist those who install poles only occasionally.

22. Setting Poles in Loose and Weak Soils. On important lines it is customary to use a concrete setting for the pole (Fig. 8, I). A suitable mixture is 1 part cement, 3 parts sand, and 3 parts of broken stone or coarse gravel.

For somewhat less important lines where the soil is fairly firm the sand barrel (Fig. 8, II) is a valuable expedient. This consists of a strong barrel or barrels placed at the bottom of the hole into which the pole is set. The barrel is filled with a firm substantial soil. By this means the pole is given a larger bearing area. Sometimes a temporary sand barrel is used, consisting of a special iron cylinder that is placed around the pole, filled with firm dirt, and then hoisted away.

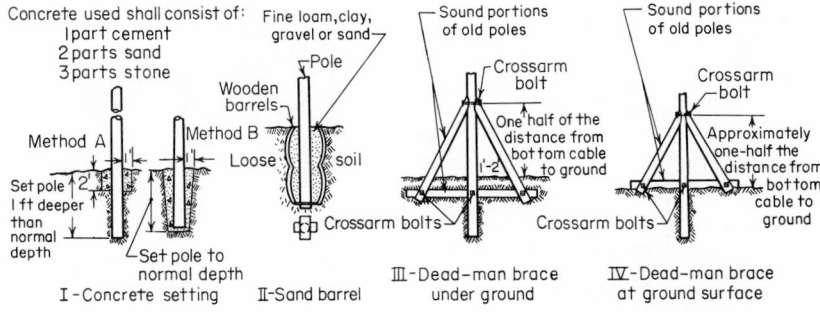

FIG. 8 *Methods of setting poles in poor soils.* *(General Electric Co.)*

In marshy ground another expedient for less important lines is to build a triangular brace from sound portions of old poles (Fig. 8, III and IV) bolted together. This provides a bearing area on or near the top of the soil which resists overturning of the pole. The method of Fig. 8, III, is preferable to the one in Fig. 8, IV, because the ground member will not rot so fast when it is completely underground. There is, however, somewhat more labor involved in digging the trench for the ground member. These methods are not so permanent as a concrete foundation and are recommended only where the expense of a concrete foundation does not seem warranted.

23. When poles are set in rock, the hole may be blasted or a hole 1½ in. in diameter may be drilled in the rock (Fig. 9) in which is placed an iron pin that extends about 6 in. above the surface. A similar hole is drilled in the butt of the pole, and the pole mounted on the pin. It must then be braced by three or four wood struts spiked to the pole 6 ft from the ground, running diagonally to the rock and formed thereto, or it can be braced by guy wires made fast to metal pins set in the rock.

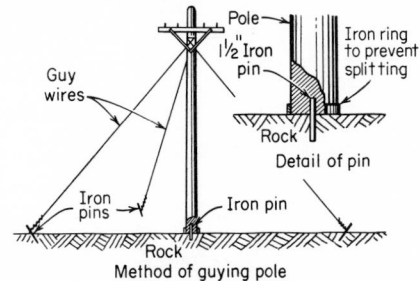

FIG. 9 *Method of setting pole on rock.*

24. Wooden poles which have rotted at the butt can be reinforced with a short stub pole set in the ground next to the regular pole and extending a few feet above the ground line. Various methods of stubbing are shown in Fig. 10, with the required materials in Fig. 11. In all cases two bands should be employed with spacings as given below. In Fig. 10 only the top band of the two is illustrated in several cases. Where a wire wrap is employed (Fig. 10C), four wraps should be made around the pole and six

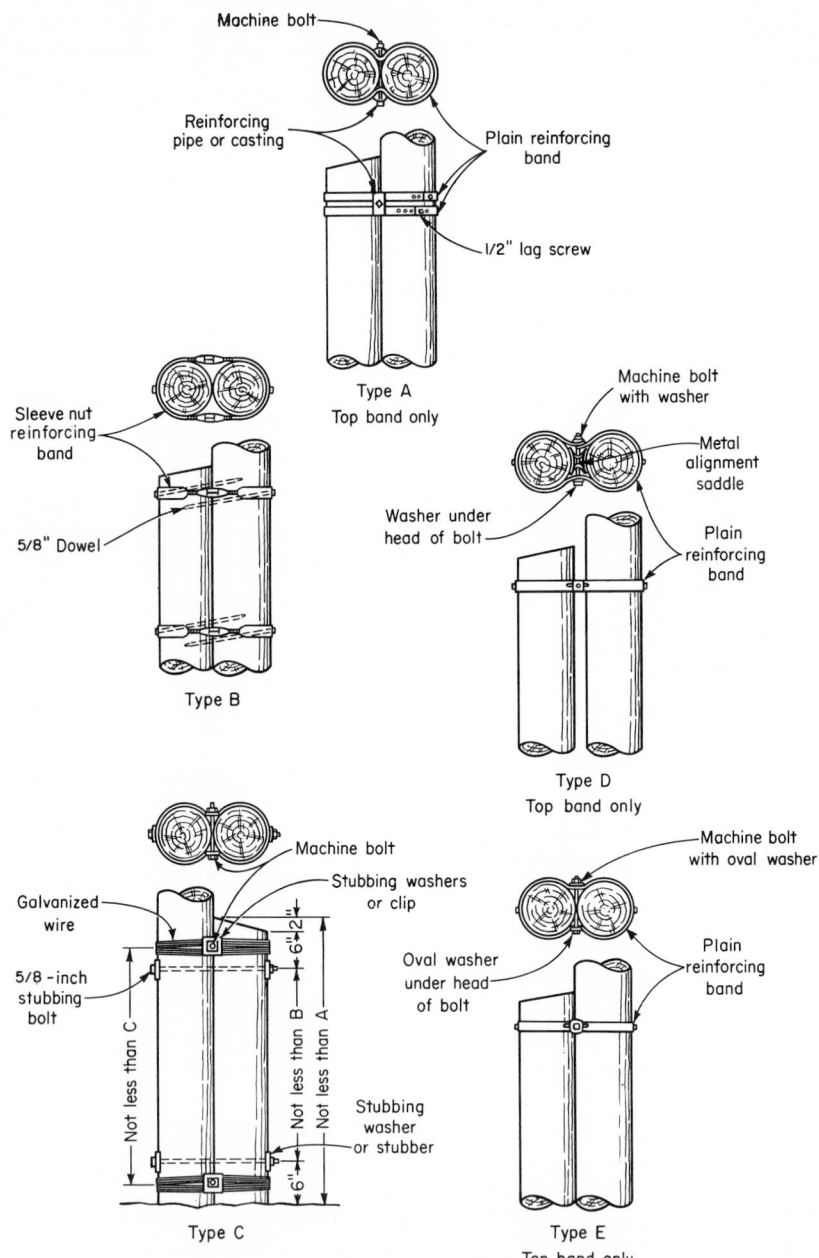

FIG. 10   *Methods of reinforcing with stubs.*   (*Hubbard & Co.*)

wraps around both the pole and stub for poles up to 40 ft long.   For poles longer than 40 ft 10 wraps should be used around both pole and stub.   In employing the method of Type C, Fig. 10, the following dimensions should be used: Dimension C should be not less than 30 in. for poles up to 45 ft long or 36 in. for poles from 45 to 50 ft long; dimension *A* should be not less than 38 in. for poles up to 45 ft long or 44 in. for poles from 45 to 50 ft long; dimension *B* should be not less than 24 in. for poles up to 45 ft long or 30 in. for poles from 45 to 50 ft long. Poles are generally stubbed so that the stub is across the line. Methods *D* and *E* will not be satisfactory if the stub is located along the line. The other methods can be used for either across-the-line or along-the-line stubbing. With method *B* the ⅝-in. dowels are not required if the poles are stubbed across the line.

25. Reinforcing Old Poles with Concrete and Steel. Wooden poles usually become unsafe because of butt rot at the ground line. Such poles can be repaired without moving the wires they support by reinforcing them with steel and concrete as shown in Fig. 12. For ordinary poles and conditions, 10 mild-steel rods ½ in. in diameter and 4 to 6 ft long are used for reinforcing. The lower end of each reinforcing rod is pointed and is driven into the portion of the butt that remains in the hole. The other end is bent at right angles, and pointed. It is driven into the pole above the ground line. A 1:2½:5 mixture of concrete is used for the main body, and a richer mixture is used for the portion above ground line and is molded in a cylindrical sheet-iron form. The concrete extends to about 1½ ft above the ground line. Poles 15 to 20 years old have been satisfactorily repaired by this method without moving the wires supported.

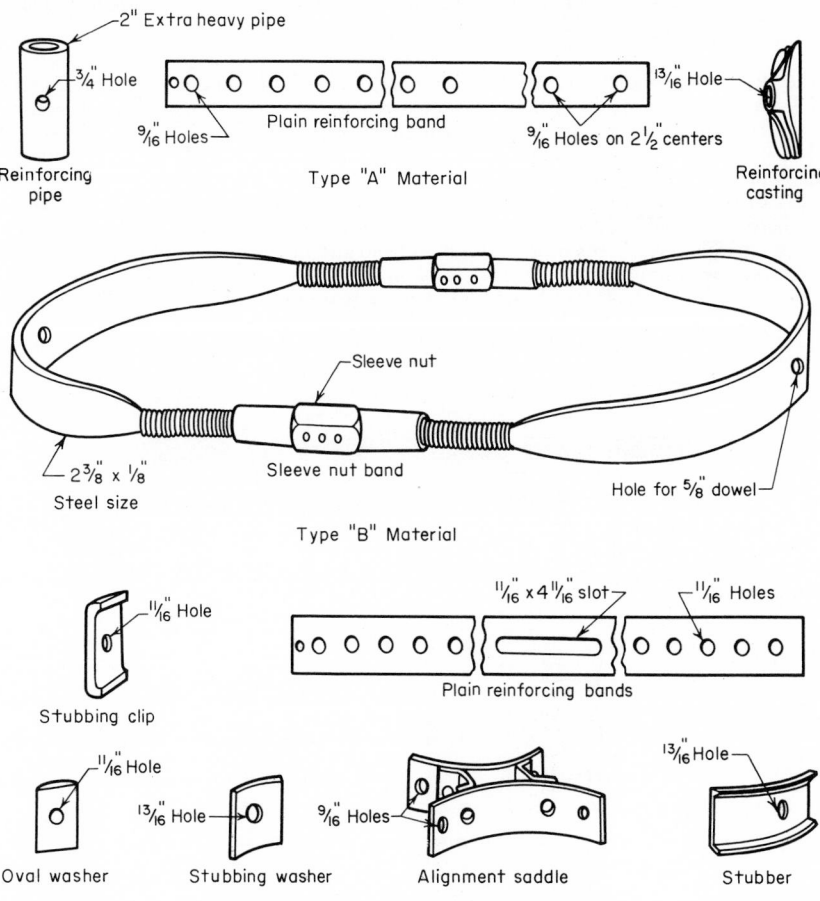

FIG. 11 *Materials for reinforcing with stubs.* (*Hubbard & Co.*)

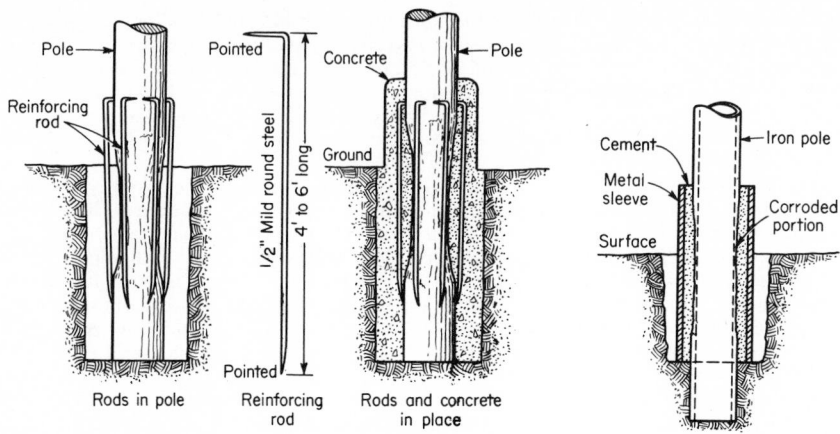

FIG. 12   *Reinforcing pole with concrete.*

FIG. 13   *Repairing metal pole.*

26. Repairing Steel Poles. Metal poles sometimes corrode very rapidly at the ground, and often when discovered the corrosion is too far advanced to make any preventive measures effective. A very satisfactory method (Fig. 13) of repairing steel poles is to place a loose-fitting metal sleeve around the butt of the pole and fill the space between the two with portland cement.

27. Crossarm bolts are used for fastening crossarms to the poles. These bolts are standard ⅝-in. galvanized machine bolts. See machine-bolt data in Div. 4 for dimensions. A square washer is used under both head and nut as shown in Figs. 47 and 70, I.

28. Double-arming bolts (Fig. 14) give a more rigid construction and greater economy than the old block-spacer method of tying two crossarms together. The double-arming bolts are furnished with a long rolled thread, galvanized and fitted with four square nuts. A square washer is used under each nut as shown in Figs. 48; and 70, II.

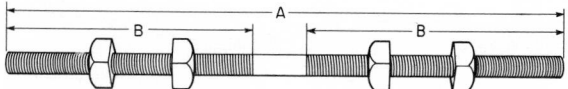

FIG. 14   *Double-arming bolts.   (Line Material Industries.)*

Diam of bolt, in.	A, in.[a]	B, in.[a]	Diam of bolt, in.	A, in.[a]	B, in.[a]
½	12	6	¾	12	5
	14	6		14	6
	16	8		16	8
	18	8		18	8
	20	8		20	8
	22	8		22	8
	24	8		24	8
⅝	12	6			
	14	6			
	16	6			
	18	8			
	20	8			
	22	8			
	24	8			

[a] Refer to Fig. 14.

29. Eyebolts (Fig. 15) are furnished with forged oval eye, rolled threads, and square nut, galvanized. Eyebolts are used for fastening guys, dead-ending insulators, and suspension insulators to crossarms, as shown in Figs. 41, I; 87; and 88. A square washer is used under nut and eye.

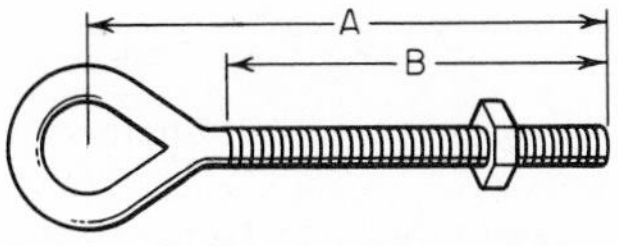

FIG. 15 *Standard eye bolt.* (*Line Material Industries.*)

Diam of bolt, in.	Opening in forged eye, in.	*A*, in.	*B*, in.	Diam of bolt, in.	Opening in forged eye, in.	*A*, in.	*B*, in.
½	1¼ × 1½	6	3	¾	1½ × 2	6	4
	1¼ × 1½	8	4		1½ × 2	8	4
	1¼ × 1½	10	4		1½ × 2	10	4
	1¼ × 1½	12	4		1½ × 2	12	4
	1¼ × 1½	14	6		1½ × 2	14	6
	1¼ × 1½	16	6		1½ × 2	16	6
	1¼ × 1½	18	6		1½ × 2	18	6
	1¼ × 1½	20	6		1½ × 2	20	6
⅝	1½ × 2	6	3				
	1½ × 2	8	4				
	1½ × 2	10	4				
	1½ × 2	12	4				
	1½ × 2	14	6				
	1½ × 2	16	6				
	1½ × 2	18	6				
	1½ × 2	20	6				
	1½ × 2	22	6				
	1½ × 2	24	6				

30. Double-arming eyebolts (Fig. 16) are furnished with forged oval eye and three square nuts, galvanized. Opening of eye is 1½ × 2 in. They are used for the same purposes as eyebolts in double-arm construction (see Figs. 41, IV; 48; and 86). Thimble-eye, double-arming bolts are also available which eliminate the use of a separate thimble in attaching guy wires to the eye of the bolt.

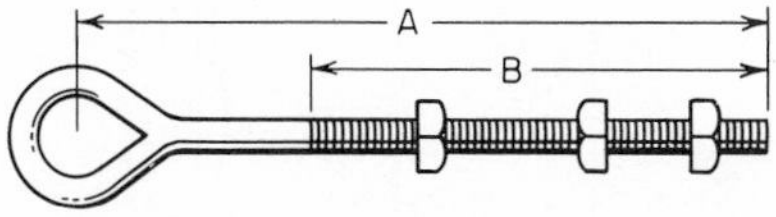

FIG. 16 *Double-arming eye bolt.* (*Line Material Industries.*)

Diam of bolt, in.	*A*, in.	*B*, in.	Diam of bolt, in.	*A*, in.	*B*, in.
⅝	16	12	¾	20	16
	18	14		22	18
	20	16		24	20
	22	18			
	24	20			

31. Eye nuts (Fig. 17) are used on through bolts, eyebolts, double-arming bolts, straight and angle thimble-eye bolts, crossarm bolts, anchor rods, and for other attachments where it is desired to convert a standard threaded bolt to a thimble-eye bolt.

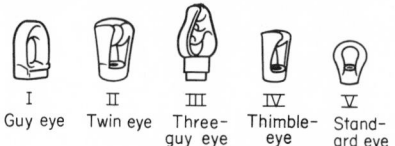

I Guy eye II Twin eye III Three-guy eye IV Thimble-eye V Standard eye

FIG. 17 *Eye nuts.* (Hubbard & Co.)

They are commonly used for dead-ending a messenger wire or span guy on the threaded end of an angle thimble-eye bolt on the opposite end of which is a down guy.

There are two types of eye nuts: (1) the standard eye (Fig. 17, V), which requires the use of a thimble, and (2) the thimble-eye, which has a thimble forged in it. The thimble-eye type is also made in a twin style (Fig. 17, II) to take two guy strands and in a three-guy style (Fig. 17, III) to take three guy strands. The guy eye (Fig. 17, I) serves the same purpose as the thimble-eye, merely being forged in a slightly different manner. Refer to Fig. 71, II, for application.

32. Common or buttonhead carriage bolts are used for attaching crossarm braces to crossarms. They are provided with a square shoulder under the head. A round washer is used under the head, as shown in Fig. 47.

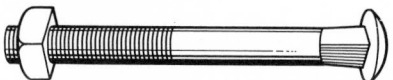

FIG. 18 *Carriage bolt.*

Diam, in.	Length, in.	Length of thread, in.	Approx shipping weight, lb per 100 pieces	Diam, in.	Length, in.	Length of thread, in.	Approx shipping weight, lb per 100 pieces
3/8	3	1 3/4	14.5	1/2	3	2 1/2	26.7
	3 1/2	1 3/4	16.5		3 1/2	3	29.2
	4	1 3/4	18.3		4	3	33.3
	4 1/2	1 3/4	20.0		4 1/2	3	36.7
	5	1 3/4	21.1		5	3	38.6
	5 1/2	1 3/4	22.5		5 1/2	3	41.2
	6	1 3/4	23.3		6	3	44.0
					7	3	50.0
					8	4	59.0
					10	4	72.0
					12	6	85.0
					14	6	99.0
					16	6	105.0

33. Lag screws are made in both the fetter-drive and gimlet-point types. The 1/4- and 5/16-in. screws are generally of the gimlet-point type, while all screws of larger diameter are generally of the fetter-drive type. Lag screws are used for attaching crossarm braces to poles, as shown in Figs. 47, 50, and 60.

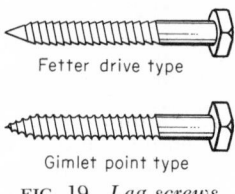

Fetter drive type

Gimlet point type

FIG. 19 *Lag screws.*

Diam, in.	Length, in.	Length of thread, in., and type	Approx shipping weight, lb per 100 pieces	Diam, in.	Length, in.	Length of thread, in., and type	Approx shipping weight, lb. per 100 pieces
¼	1½	1⅛ G.P.	2.0	½	2½	2 F.D.	18.4
	2	1⅝ G.P.	3.5		3	2½ F.D.	20.9
	2½	1¾ G.P.	5.0		3½	3 F.D.	23.4
	3	2 G.P.	6.5		4	2½ F.D.	26.0
	4	2½ G.P.	8.0		4½	2⅞ F.D.	27.8
5/16	2	1¾ G.P.	5.2		5	3¼ F.D.	32.1
	2½	2 G.P.	6.2		5½	3 F.D.	33.9
	3	2¼ G.P.	7.5		6	3 F.D.	38.3
	3½	2½ G.P.	9.7		6½	2⅞ F.D.	43.2
	4	2½ G.P.	11.9		7	3 F.D.	46.4
⅜	2¼	2 F.D.	8.8	⅝	4	3 F.D.	42.6
	2½	2 F.D.	9.7		4½	3 F.D.	46.0
	3	2 F.D.	11.0		5	3½ F.D.	50.6
	3½	2½ F.D.	12.8		5½	3 F.D.	55.2
	4	2⅞ F.D.	14.6		6	2⅞ F.D.	60.0
	4½	3 F.D.	16.4	¾	5	3 F.D.	74.5
	5	3 F.D.	16.9		6	3½ F.D.	84.9
	6	3 F.D.	19.9		7	4 F.D.	99.4
					8	4½ F.D.	112.2

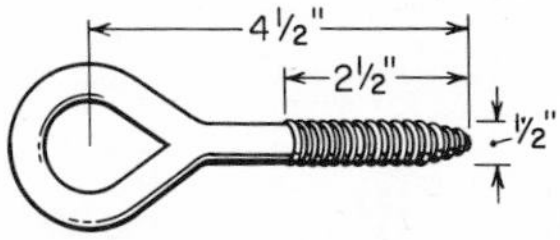

FIG. 20 *Lag-screw eye.* (*Line Material Industries.*)

34. Lag-screw eyes (Fig. 20) are galvanized and furnished with gimlet-point, lag-screw thread. The forged eye has a 1¼- by 1½-in. opening.

35. Washers used in overhead line construction are made of galvanized iron in both round and square types. Square washers are used under the heads and nuts of all crossarm bolts. Round washers are used under the heads of carriage bolts which fasten crossarm braces to crossarms.

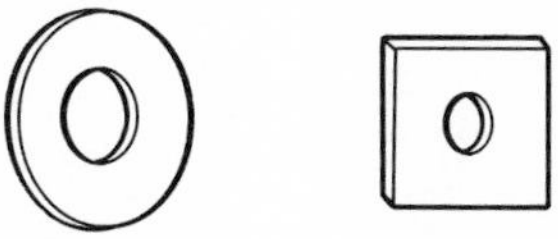

FIG. 21 *Washers.*

Outside diam, in.	Size of hole, in.	Thickness, in.	Size of bolt, in.		Dimensions, in.	Diam of hole, in.	Size of bolt, in.
			Mach	Carriage			
1	7/16	5/64	⅜		2 × 2 × ⅛	11/16	½ or ⅝
1¼	½	5/64	. . .	⅜	2¼ × 2¼ × 3/16	13/16	⅝ or ¾
1⅜	9/16	7/64	½	⅜	3 × 3 × 3/16	13/16	⅝ or ¾
1¾	11/16	⅛	⅝	½	3 × 3 × ¼	13/16	⅝ or ¾
2	13/16	⅛	¾	⅝	4 × 4 × 3/16	13/16	⅝ or ¾
					4 × 4 × ¼	15/16	¾ or ⅞
					4 × 4 × ½	1 3/16	1
					3½ × 3½ × ⅜	15/16	¾ or ⅞
					6 × 6 × ⅜	1 3/16	1

36. Standard Wooden Crossarms
(General Electric Supply Co.)

Pin holes Spacings, in. Center	Sides	Ends	Size, in.	Center bolt hole, in.	Brace length, in.	Size and length
			Electric Light Arms			$3\frac{1}{4} \times 4\frac{1}{4}$
28	....	4	$1\frac{17}{32}$	$\frac{5}{8}$	25	3 ft 2 pin
16	12	4	$1\frac{17}{32}$	$\frac{5}{8}$	28	4 ft 4 pin
18	17	4	$1\frac{17}{32}$	$\frac{5}{8}$	28	5 ft 4 pin
22	21	4	$1\frac{17}{32}$	$\frac{5}{8}$	32	6 ft 4 pin
16	12	4	$1\frac{17}{32}$	$\frac{5}{8}$	32	6 ft 6 pin
18	$17\frac{1}{2}$	4	$1\frac{17}{32}$	$\frac{5}{8}$	32	8 ft 6 pin
16	12	4	$1\frac{17}{32}$	$\frac{5}{8}$	32	8 ft 8 pin
16	$9\frac{3}{4}$	4	$1\frac{17}{32}$	$\frac{5}{8}$	32	$8\frac{1}{2}$ ft 10 pin
$17\frac{1}{2}$	$15\frac{3}{4}$	4	$1\frac{17}{32}$	$\frac{5}{8}$	42	10 ft 8 pin
16	12	4	$1\frac{17}{32}$	$\frac{5}{8}$	42	10 ft 10 pin
16	$9\frac{5}{8}$	$3\frac{7}{8}$	$1\frac{17}{32}$	$\frac{5}{8}$	42	10 ft 12 pin
			R.S.A. Arms			$3 \times 4\frac{1}{4}$
20	22	4	$\frac{9}{16}$	$1\frac{1}{16}$	...	6 ft 4 pin
19	$17\frac{1}{4}$	4	$\frac{9}{16}$	$1\frac{1}{16}$	...	8 ft 6 pin
19	$15\frac{1}{2}$	4	$\frac{9}{16}$	$1\frac{1}{16}$	...	10 ft 8 pin
16	$12\frac{3}{8}$	4	$\frac{9}{16}$	$1\frac{1}{16}$	...	10 ft 10 pin
			Western Union Arms			$3 \times 4\frac{1}{4}$
20	$11\frac{1}{2}$	3	$\frac{9}{16}$	$2\frac{1}{32}$	...	6 ft 6 pin
21	$11\frac{1}{2}$	3	$\frac{9}{16}$	$2\frac{1}{32}$	...	8 ft 8 pin
22	$11\frac{1}{2}$	3	$\frac{9}{16}$	$2\frac{1}{32}$	...	10 ft 10 pin
			Pony Telephone Arms			$2\frac{3}{4} \times 3\frac{3}{4}$
17	....	$3\frac{1}{2}$	$1\frac{9}{32}$	$\frac{5}{8}$	...	24 in. 2 pin
23	....	$3\frac{1}{2}$	$1\frac{9}{32}$	$\frac{5}{8}$	...	30 in. 2 pin
29	....	$3\frac{1}{2}$	$1\frac{9}{32}$	$\frac{5}{8}$	25	36 in. 2 pin
16	$9\frac{1}{2}$	$3\frac{1}{2}$	$1\frac{9}{32}$	$\frac{5}{8}$	28	42 in. 4 pin
16	$9\frac{3}{4}$	$3\frac{1}{2}$	$1\frac{9}{32}$	$\frac{5}{8}$	28	62 in. 6 pin
16	$9\frac{3}{4}$	$3\frac{3}{4}$	$1\frac{9}{32}$	$\frac{5}{8}$	28	82 in. 8 pin
16	$9\frac{3}{4}$	4	$1\frac{9}{32}$	$\frac{5}{8}$	28	102 in. 10 pin
16	$9\frac{5}{8}$	$3\frac{7}{8}$	$1\frac{9}{32}$	$\frac{5}{8}$	28	120 in. 12 pin
			N.E.L.A. Arms			$3\frac{1}{2} \times 4\frac{1}{2}$
30	....	4	$1\frac{17}{32}$	$1\frac{1}{16}$	28	3 ft 2 in. 2 pin
30	$14\frac{1}{2}$	4	$1\frac{17}{32}$	$1\frac{1}{16}$	38	5 ft 7 in. 4 pin
30	$14\frac{1}{2}$	4	$1\frac{17}{32}$	$1\frac{1}{16}$	38	8 ft 6 pin
30	12	4	$1\frac{17}{32}$	$1\frac{1}{16}$	38	9 ft 2 in. 8 pin
			N.E.L.A. (Light) Arms			$3\frac{1}{4} \times 4\frac{1}{4}$
30	....	4	$1\frac{17}{32}$	$1\frac{1}{16}$	28	3 ft 2 in. 2 pin
30	$14\frac{1}{2}$	4	$1\frac{17}{32}$	$1\frac{1}{16}$	38	5 ft 7 in. 4 pin
30	$14\frac{1}{2}$	4	$1\frac{17}{32}$	$1\frac{1}{16}$	38	8 ft 6 pin
30	12	4	$1\frac{17}{32}$	$1\frac{1}{16}$	38	9 ft 2 in. 8 pin
			New England Arms			$3\frac{1}{4} \times 4\frac{1}{4}$
30	....	3	$1\frac{17}{32}$	$1\frac{1}{16}$	33	3 ft 2 pin
30	$13\frac{1}{2}$	$4\frac{1}{2}$	$1\frac{17}{32}$	$1\frac{1}{16}$	36	5 ft 6 in. 4 pin
30	$13\frac{1}{2}$	$4\frac{1}{2}$	$1\frac{17}{32}$	$1\frac{1}{16}$	36	7 ft 9 in. 6 pin
30	$13\frac{1}{2}$	$4\frac{1}{2}$	$1\frac{17}{32}$	$1\frac{1}{16}$	36	10 ft 8 pin
			New England Power Arms			$3\frac{3}{4} \times 4\frac{3}{4}$
30	....	3	$1\frac{17}{32}$	$1\frac{1}{16}$	33	3 ft 2 pin
30	$13\frac{1}{2}$	$4\frac{1}{2}$	$1\frac{17}{32}$	$1\frac{1}{16}$	36	5 ft 6 in. 4 pin
30	$13\frac{1}{2}$	$4\frac{1}{2}$	$1\frac{17}{32}$	$1\frac{1}{16}$	36	7 ft 9 in. 6 pin
30	$13\frac{1}{2}$	$4\frac{1}{2}$	$1\frac{17}{32}$	$1\frac{1}{16}$	36	10 ft 8 pin
			Pacific Arms			$3\frac{1}{4} \times 4\frac{1}{4}$
28	....	4	$1\frac{17}{32}$	$\frac{5}{8}$	32	3 ft 2 pin
28	12	4	$1\frac{17}{32}$	$\frac{5}{8}$	32	5 ft 4 pin
28	12	4	$1\frac{17}{32}$	$\frac{5}{8}$	32	7 ft 6 pin
28	12	4	$1\frac{17}{32}$	$\frac{5}{8}$	42	9 ft 8 pin
28	12	4	$1\frac{17}{32}$	$\frac{5}{8}$	42	11 ft 10 pin

37. Wooden crossarms are generally made of Douglas fir, which, according to tests made by the U.S. Forest Service, is best suited for the purpose. Longleaf yellow pine and Norway pine also are used for cross-arms. Crossarm dimensions have not actually been standardized throughout the country. The dimensions of those carried as standard by one manufacturer are given in Sec. **36.** Great care should be exercised in ordering crossarms to give full specifications. It is generally best to furnish a sketch (Fig. 22) with accompanying dimensions for the required boring.

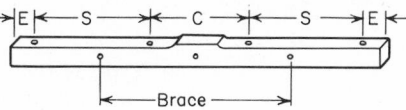

FIG. 22 *Sketch for boring of crossarm.*

Figure 23 shows the dimensions of crossarms recommended by the National Electric Light Association. These arms have a spacing between center pins of 30 in., which is believed to provide a safe climbing space. Arms of the NELA cross-sectional dimensions (Fig. 23) have not come into extensive use. It is modern practice not to paint crossarms as soon as they are made. They either are treated with a wood preservative or are permitted to season naturally for at least 3 months and are then painted with two coats of green white-lead paint before erection. Crossarms of Southern pine generally are pressure-treated against decay. It is not general practice to treat crossarms of other woods. No crossarm having a spacing of less than 20 in. between center pins or 12 in. between side pins should be used. The six-pin arm (Fig. 23) is recommended for general use.

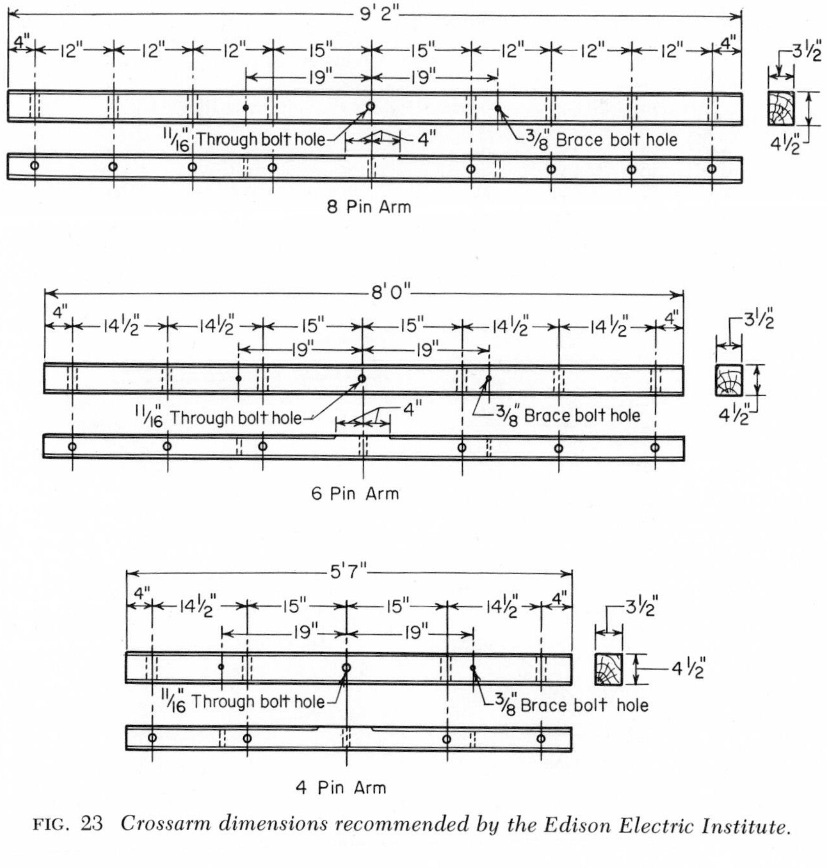

8 Pin Arm

6 Pin Arm

4 Pin Arm

FIG. 23 *Crossarm dimensions recommended by the Edison Electric Institute.*

38. Galvanized-steel crossarms are made from standard steel angles in three types, as given in Sec. **39.** They cost somewhat more than wooden crossarms but are more durable and will carry heavier loads. They are used for installations subjected to heavy strains and for higher voltage lines.

39. Types of Galvanized-steel Crossarms
(Hubbard & Co.)

Number of pins	Length, in.	Brace style	Pin spacing, in.		Size of angle, in.	Approximate shipping weight, lb per 100 pieces
			Pole pins	Side pins		
Telephone Arms—Pinholes, $1\frac{3}{16}$ In., Pole-mounting Hole, $1\frac{1}{16}$ In.						
2	20	Flat	16	....	$3 \times 2 \times \frac{3}{16}$	575
4	40	Flat	16	10	$3 \times 2 \times \frac{3}{16}$	1,125
6	60	Flat	16	10	$3 \times 3 \times \frac{1}{4}$	2,700
8	80	Flat	16	10	$3 \times 3 \times \frac{1}{4}$	3,600
10	100	Flat	16	10	$3 \times 3 \times \frac{1}{4}$	4,510
Electric-light Arms—Pinholes, $1\frac{3}{16}$ In., Pole-mounting Hole, $1\frac{1}{16}$ In.						
2	36	Flat	30	....	$3 \ \times 3 \ \times \frac{1}{4}$	1,625
4	65	Flat	30	$14\frac{1}{2}$	$3 \ \times 3 \ \times \frac{1}{4}$	2,915
6	94	Angle	30	$14\frac{1}{2}$	$3\frac{1}{2} \times 3\frac{1}{2} \times \frac{5}{16}$	6,215
8	$117\frac{3}{4}$	Angle	30	$13\frac{5}{8}$	$3\frac{1}{2} \times 3\frac{1}{2} \times \frac{5}{16}$	7,700
Power transmission Arms—Pinholes, $1\frac{3}{16}$ In., Pole-mounting Hole, $1\frac{1}{16}$ In.						
2	28	Flat	24	....	$3 \ \times 3 \ \times \frac{1}{4}$	1,290
2	40	Flat	36	....	$3 \ \times 3 \ \times \frac{1}{4}$	1,840
2	52	Flat	48	....	$3 \ \times 3 \ \times \frac{1}{4}$	2,410
4	76	Angle	24	24	$3 \ \times 3 \ \times \frac{1}{4}$	3,490
2	80	Angle	74	....	$3\frac{1}{2} \times 3\frac{1}{2} \times \frac{5}{16}$	5,280
4	116	Angle	38	36	$3\frac{1}{2} \times 3\frac{1}{2} \times \frac{5}{16}$	7,645

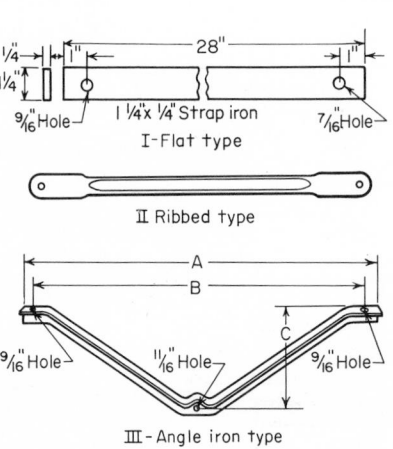

FIG. 24 *Standard crossarm braces.* (Hubbard & Co.)

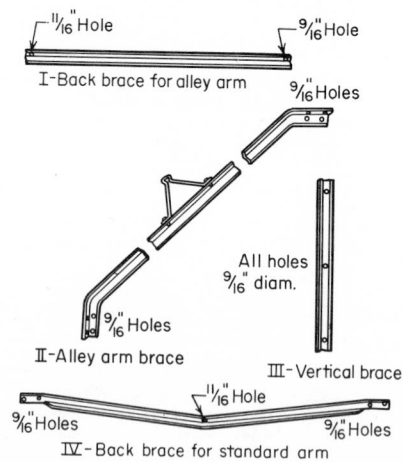

FIG. 25 *Special types of crossarm braces.* (Hubbard & Co.)

40. Crossarm braces are made from galvanized flat strap iron (Fig. 24, I), ribbed strap iron (Fig. 24, II), or angle iron (Fig. 24, III). Braces are attached to the back of each crossarm by a carriage bolt with the head of the bolt at the front with a round washer under it (Figs. 47 and 60). The braces are secured to the pole with a through bolt or a lag screw. The flat type is used for ordinary loads. It is made in lengths varying in 2-in. increments from 20 to 32 in., the 28-in. length being the most common. The ribbed type, being about 25 per cent stronger, is used for heavier loads. The angle-iron type is used for very heavy lines. The standard sizes are given in Table **41**, the first four being the Edison Electric Institute standard for power-company use. The alley-arm brace (Fig. 25, II) is used to support alley-type crossarms (see Sec. **62**). The vertical brace (Fig. 25, III) supports the upper crossarms from the lowest crossarm in alley-arm construction (Fig. 49). The back brace (Fig. 25, IV) is fastened at the back of the crossarm and on the back of the pole. It is used as an alternative to double-arm construction at crossings and at abrupt turns in the line. A back brace for alley arms is shown in Fig. 25, I.

41. Angle Crossarm Braces[a]
(Hubbard & Co.)

Dimensions, in.				Approx shipping weight, lb per 100 pieces
Angle size	A	B	C	
1½ × 1½ × 3⁄16	45	42	12	858
1½ × 1½ × 3⁄16	51	48	18	1,067
1½ × 1½ × 3⁄16	63	60	18	1,210
1¾ × 1¾ × 3⁄16	75	72	22	1,716
1½ × 1½ × 3⁄16	51	48	14	974
1½ × 1½ × 3⁄16	40	37	12	781
1½ × 1½ × 3⁄16	51	48	14¾	979
1¾ × 1¾ × 3⁄16	63	60	18	1,408
1¾ × 1¾ × 3⁄16	69	66	20	1,551
1¾ × 1¾ × 3⁄16	75	72	18	1,639
2 × 2 × 3⁄16	75	72	22	1,958

[a] Refer to Fig. 24, III.

42. Crossarm Back Braces (Fig. 25, IV)

Angle size, in.	Length over-all, in.	Approx shipping weight, lb per 100 pieces	Angle size, in.	Length over-all, in.	Approx shipping weight, lb per 100 pieces
1½ × 1½ × 3⁄16	48	550	1¾ × 1¾ × 3⁄16	94	1,540
1½ × 1½ × 3⁄16	60	825	1¾ × 1¾ × 3⁄16	109	2,204
1½ × 1½ × 3⁄16	72	1,200			

43. Insulators are used for insulating the electrical conduction wires and guy wires from the pole structure. The different types may be classified as pin, suspension, spool, strain, and wireholder insulators. Either pin-type (Fig. 26) or suspension-type insulators (Fig. 30) are used for supporting the wires of the main electrical circuits. Spool insulators (Fig. 32) are used principally in the assembly of insulator racks (Fig. 33) for supporting low-voltage distribution mains from the sides of poles or buildings. Combined with a clevis, they are sometimes used for dead-ending low-voltage main electrical circuits. Strain insulators are used principally for insulating guy wires from the pole structure so that contact with the lower portion of the guy will not be dangerous. One type of porcelain strain insulator is frequently used for dead-ending low-voltage main electrical circuits or distribution wires. Wire-holder-type insulators are used in various assemblies for supporting service wires on buildings and for supporting, on the pole structure, taps for certain street-lighting luminaires. Insulators are made of either glass or porcelain, the choice for any particular size and voltage being determined by weighing the electrical and mechanical characteristics against first cost. Glass has been most commonly used for pin insulators (Fig. 26, I) for voltages up to 5,000 volts. Porcelain has been most commonly used for pin insulators for higher voltages and for the other types of insulators.

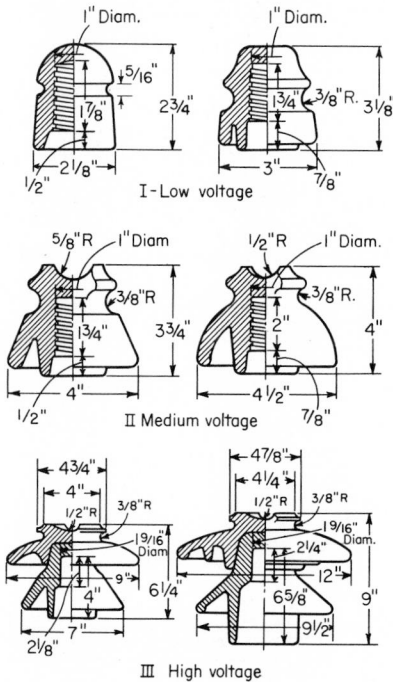

FIG. 26 *Typical pin-type insulators. (Locke Insulator Corp.)*

44. Pin-type insulators are molded with a central threaded hole so that the insulator is supported from threaded insulator pins mounted on the crossarms. These insulators are made in various shapes and with varying contours to meet the insulating requirements for different voltage classifications. For low-voltage work the insulators are generally grooved on the side for support of the wires. Medium-voltage insulators frequently have wire grooves on both top and sides and the higher voltage ones are made with only top grooves. Typical pin-type insulators are shown in Fig. 26.

45. Insulator Pins. Pin insulators of the type shown in Fig. 26 are fastened on crossarms with insulator pins which thread into the cast thread inside the insulator. Insulator pins may be wood, steel, steel and lead, or steel and wood (Fig. 27). The wood pins (Fig. 27, IV) are made from oak or locust, the locust being preferred as less apt to crack. Wood pins are used on communication circuits and low-voltage distribution circuits on account of their low cost. Steel pins (Fig. 27, I and II) are used on the higher voltage, longer span lines where the side loads on the pin are greater. Combination wood-cob-with-steel-bolt pins (Fig. 27, III) provide stronger construction than the plain wood at lower cost than all-steel pins. Lead adapters (Fig. 27, V) can be used with 1-in. steel pins to fit 1⅜-in. insulator threads.

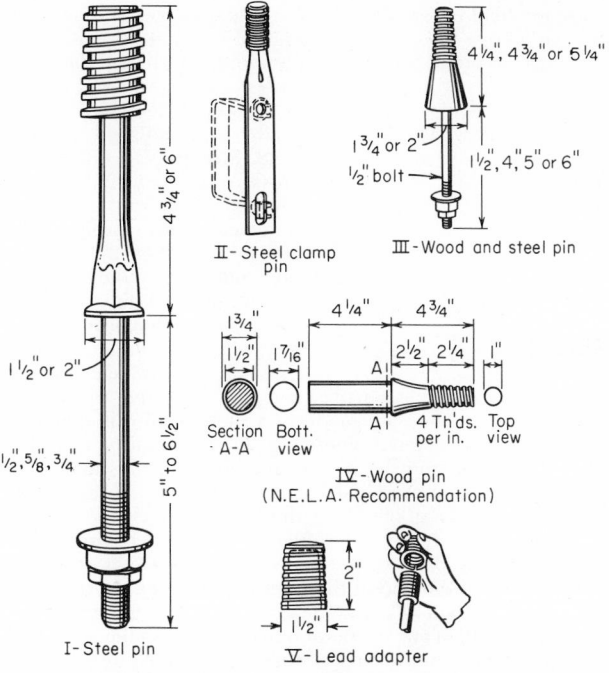

FIG. 27   *Insulator pins.*   (*Line Material Industries.*)

46. Wooden Insulator Pins.   All standard insulator pins of 1- and $1\frac{3}{8}$-in. top diameter have four threads to the inch and a tapering diameter of $\frac{1}{16}$-in. increase for each inch in length.

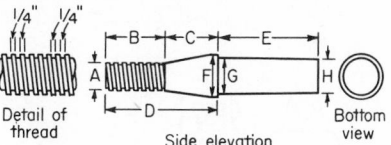

FIG. 28   *Wooden insulator pin.*

			Dimensions, In.					Shipping weight per 1,000, lb
A	*B*	*C*	*D*	*E*	*F*	*G*	*H*	
1	$2\frac{1}{2}$	$2\frac{1}{4}$	$4\frac{3}{4}$	$4\frac{1}{4}$	$1\frac{3}{4}$	$1\frac{1}{2}$	$1\frac{7}{16}$	400
1	$2\frac{1}{2}$	$4\frac{3}{4}$	$7\frac{1}{4}$	$4\frac{1}{4}$	2	$1\frac{1}{2}$	$1\frac{7}{16}$	510
1	$2\frac{1}{2}$	$4\frac{3}{4}$	$7\frac{1}{4}$	$4\frac{1}{4}$	$2\frac{1}{4}$	$1\frac{3}{4}$	$1\frac{11}{16}$	700
1	$2\frac{1}{2}$	4	$6\frac{1}{2}$	5	$2\frac{1}{2}$	2	$1\frac{15}{16}$	930
$1\frac{3}{8}$	$2\frac{1}{4}$	$2\frac{1}{2}$	$4\frac{3}{4}$	$4\frac{1}{4}$	$1\frac{7}{8}$	$1\frac{1}{2}$	$1\frac{7}{16}$	400
$1\frac{3}{8}$	$2\frac{1}{4}$	5	$7\frac{1}{4}$	$4\frac{1}{4}$	2	$1\frac{1}{2}$	$1\frac{7}{16}$	510
$1\frac{3}{8}$	$2\frac{1}{4}$	5	$7\frac{1}{4}$	$4\frac{1}{4}$	$2\frac{1}{4}$	$1\frac{3}{4}$	$1\frac{11}{16}$	700
$1\frac{3}{8}$	$2\frac{1}{4}$	$4\frac{1}{4}$	$6\frac{1}{2}$	5	$2\frac{1}{2}$	2	$1\frac{15}{16}$	930
$1\frac{3}{8}$	$2\frac{1}{4}$	$7\frac{1}{4}$	$9\frac{1}{2}$	5	3	2	$1\frac{15}{16}$	1,160
$1\frac{3}{8}$	$2\frac{1}{4}$	$8\frac{3}{4}$	11	5	$3\frac{1}{2}$	2	$1\frac{15}{16}$	1,280
$1\frac{3}{8}$	$2\frac{1}{4}$	$9\frac{3}{4}$	12	5	$3\frac{1}{2}$	2	$1\frac{15}{16}$	1,360

47. Wood pins are held in crossarms with a sixpenny nail as shown in Fig. 29. The nail should not be driven entirely in. Enough of its length should extend so that the cutting jaws of a pair of pliers can be forced under the head and the nail thereby withdrawn. If this suggestion is followed and it is necessary to remove a pin, it can be readily accomplished.

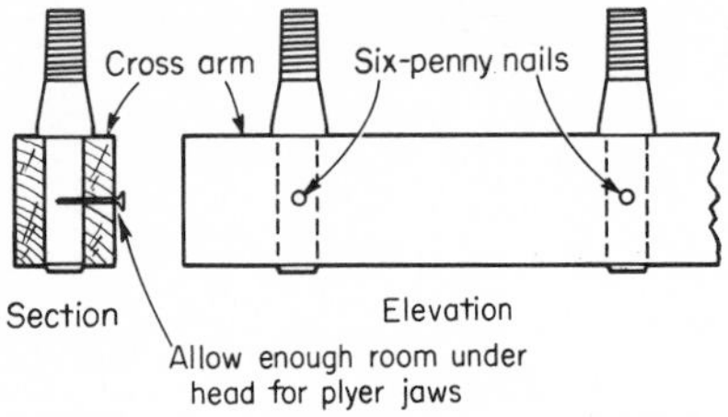

48. Steel pins are either clamped over the crossarm as in Fig. 27, II, or the rod projects through a hole in the crossarm and is held in place with a washer, square-head nut, and pal nut (Fig. 27, I). The clamp type does not weaken the crossarm by the drilling of the holes but is more expensive.

49. Suspension insulators are used to support wires from under crossarms. They are used on high-voltage lines where pin insulators would become large, expensive, and unwieldy and are sometimes used on lower voltage lines also. They are made in a number of different styles varying in hardware and petticoat diameters. There are three general types of hardware: hook and clevis, ball and socket, and the tongue and clevis as illustrated in Fig. 30. The hook type (Fig. 30, I) is used principally to support street-lighting units. Whether to use a ball-and-socket type (Fig. 30, II) or the tongue-and-clevis type (Fig. 30, III) on power circuits is mostly a matter of individual choice. With the tongue-and-clevis type a round pin is used to hold the tongue of one unit in the clevis of the other. A cotter pin slips through a hole in the end of the round pin to keep the pin from slipping out. With the ball-and-socket type the round pin is eliminated. The insulators are assembled by sliding the ball of one insulator into the socket of the next one from the side. A cotter pin is slipped in from the back of the socket, taking up sufficient space in the socket so that the ball cannot slide out. The socket clevis (Fig. 30, IV) is used where it is desired to support other hardware from the bottom of the insulator.

Suspension insulators are made up in strings as shown in Fig. 31. A clevis is used to support them from steel crossarms as shown in I. With wood crossarms a hook bolt through the crossarm can be used as in II or a clevis bolt as shown in III. The insulators are supported from each other with no additional hardware except the pins.

FIG. 29   *Fastening pin in crossarm.*

Cross arm   Six-penny nails

Section   Elevation

Allow enough room under head for plyer jaws

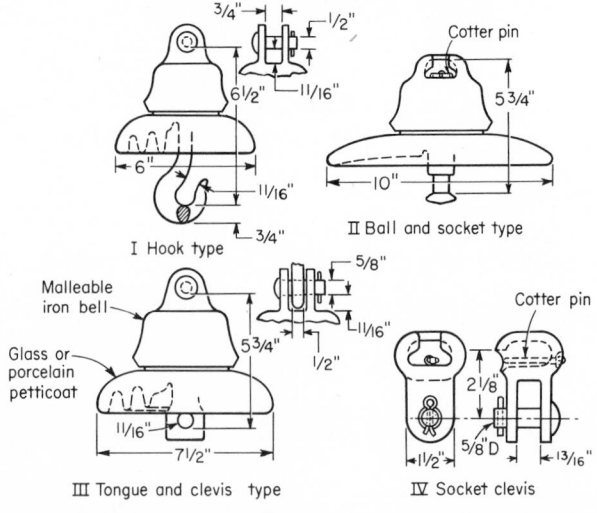

FIG. 30   *Suspension insulators.* (*Locke Insulator Corp.*)

I Hook type

II Ball and socket type

III Tongue and clevis type

IV Socket clevis

The wire is supported from the bottom insulator with a wire clamp which is made in various types depending on the size of the wire. The voltage rating of a complete assembly is determined by the manufacturer from flashover tests. The diameter and shape of the petticoat and the number of units in the string affect the voltage rating. Small diameter petticoats are preferred for locations where the insulators are subject to malicious damage from stones or bullets. The larger diameter units are ordinarily used on the longer strings on high-voltage lines, where the wires are at a greater height from the ground.

50. Spool- and wireholder-type insulators are used in single-wire or rack assemblies for supporting low-voltage circuits on the sides of poles and buildings and for dead-ending service wires on buildings, poles, and crossarms. In the rack assemblies (Fig. 33) the insulators are removable from the rack for easy replacement in case of breakage. The racks are made in two-, three-, and four-wire assemblies. Typical spool and wire-holder insulator assemblies are shown in Figs. 32 to 35.

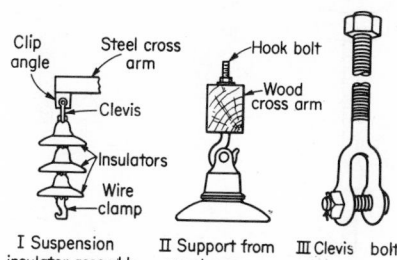

FIG. 31 *Details of suspension insulator supports.*

51. Strain insulators are used in guys and are also used in line wires at dead-ending points. Composition, porcelain, and wooden strain insulators are made. Wooden strain insulators (Fig. 36) were once popular with some companies and afford excellent insulation but have the objection that, if one burns, the wire that it supports falls. Composition and porcelain strain insulators can be made so that even if the insulating material fails, the supported wires will not fall. Figures 37

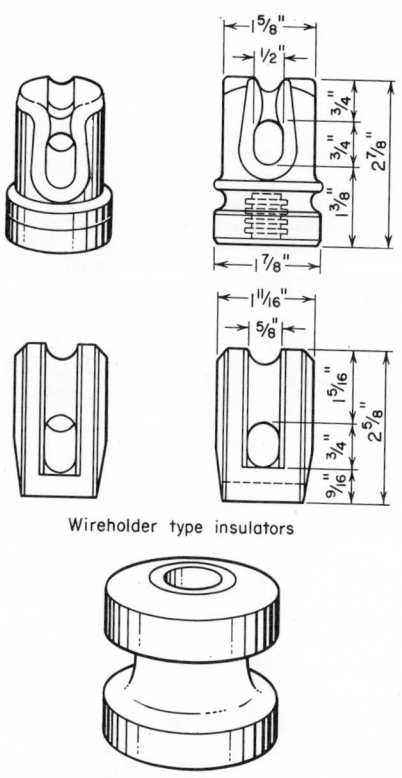

Wireholder type insulators

Spool type insulator

FIG. 32 *Typical spool- and wireholder-type insulators. (General Electric Co.)*

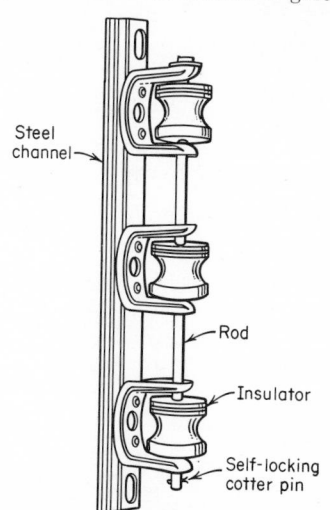

FIG. 33 *Low-voltage secondary rack. (Line Material Industries.)*

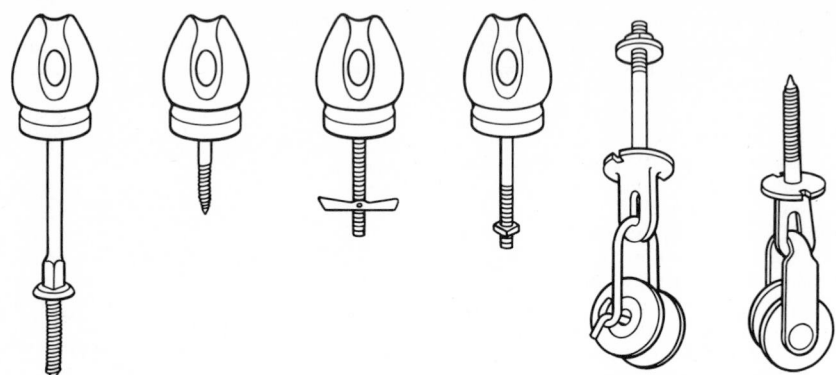

FIG. 34   *Typical single-wire insulator assemblies.   (General Electric Co.)*

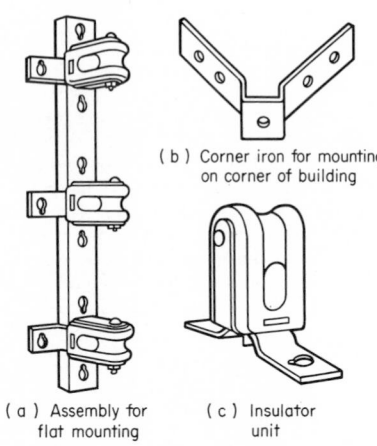

(b) Corner iron for mounting
on corner of building

(a) Assembly for
flat mounting

(c) Insulator
unit

FIG. 35   *Typical wireholder rack assembly.   (General Electric Co.)*

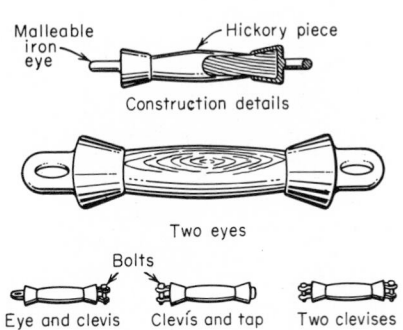

Malleable iron eye

Hickory piece

Construction details

Two eyes

Bolts

Eye and clevis   Clevis and tap   Two clevises

FIG. 36   *Wooden strain insulators.*

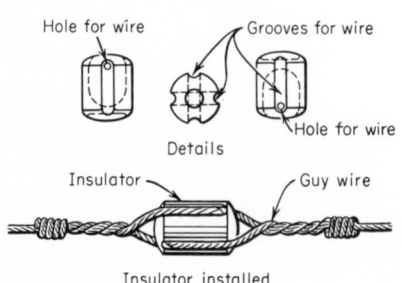

Hole for wire

Grooves for wire

Details

Hole for wire

Insulator

Guy wire

Insulator installed

FIG. 37.   *A porcelain strain insulator.*

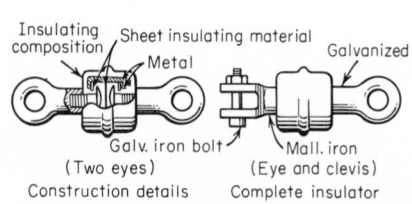

Insulating composition

Sheet insulating material

Metal

Galvanized

Galv. iron bolt
(Two eyes)
Construction details

Mall. iron
(Eye and clevis)
Complete insulator

FIG. 38   *Composition strain insulators.*

and 38 show types meeting these requirements. The strain insulator of Fig. 37 is inexpensive and satisfactory and has become very popular in electric-lighting-line construction.

52. Emergency strain insulators can be made by knocking the end out of common glass line-wire insulators as illustrated in Fig. 39. To break out the end, hold the insulator in one hand and strike the inside of the top a sharp blow with the handle of a pair of pliers or of a pair of connectors or with a screwdriver held in the other hand. Where one emergency insulator will not give sufficient insulation, two or more can be used in series. Emergency strain insulators thus made are not strong enough for heavy guy wires but are more suitable for insertion in line wires.

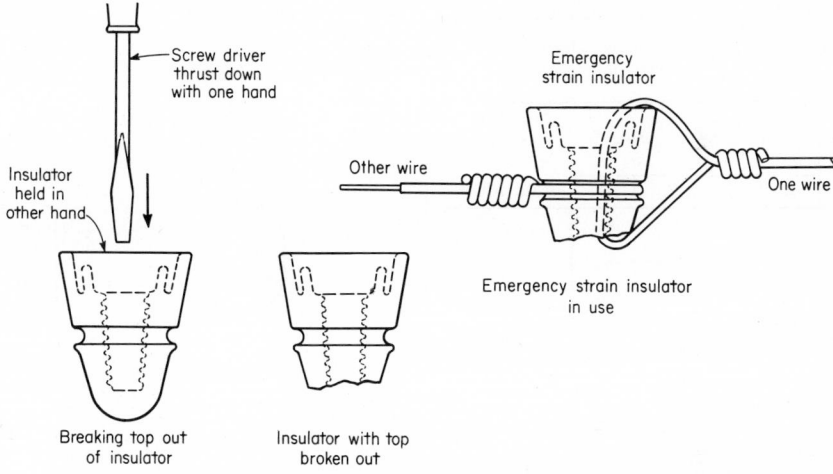

FIG. 39 *Emergency strain insulators.*

53. Clevises are used in making up assemblies connecting insulators, straps, strands, etc., together. Figure 40 illustrates some types of clevises. The forged clevises (Fig. 40, I) and bent strap clevises (Fig. 40, II) are used to connect dead-end insulators to crossarms (Fig. 41, I and II). The eye clevis (Fig. 40, III) will connect a dead-end insulator to another piece of hardware having a pin connection. The thimble clevis (Fig. 40, IV) will connect a stranded cable to an insulator assembly (Fig. 41, III). The strain-insulator clevis (Fig. 40, V) is used to connect a strain insulator of the type in Fig. 37 to an eyebolt or eye nut (Fig. 41, IV).

54. Guy anchor rods are used between the anchor in the ground and the guy strand. Figure 42, I, illustrates a roller type which allows the strand to turn on the rod and prevents twisting of the guy strand. Figure 42, II, is used to attach to a log anchor. Figure 42, III, is used when anchoring to solid rock or masonry. Guy anchor rods are made in $1/2$-, $5/8$-, $3/4$-, and 1-in. diameters.

55. In connecting a guy strand to the pole, the strand may be wrapped around the pole or may be connected to a special bolt. When the strand is wrapped around the pole, guy hooks (Fig. 43, I) are used to prevent the strand from slipping down the pole, and guy plates (Fig. 44, II) or shims (Fig. 44, I) are placed under the guy strand to prevent its cutting into the pole. The molding strain plate of Fig. 44, III, is used under the guy-wire wrap on poles where a ground wire runs down the pole. The plate will fit over NELA standard 1-in. ground-wire molding and prevent the guy strand from cutting or crushing the ground-wire molding.

An alternative to this method is to connect the guy to a thimble-eye bolt. The straight thimble-eye type (Fig. 43, II) is used when guying between a main pole and a stub pole. The angle thimble-eye type (Fig. 43, III) is used when guying into the ground. A J bolt (Fig. 43, IV) can also be used for attaching a guy wire to a pole, but this requires the use of a thimble (Fig. 43, V) in addition to the bolt. A stubbing washer should be used

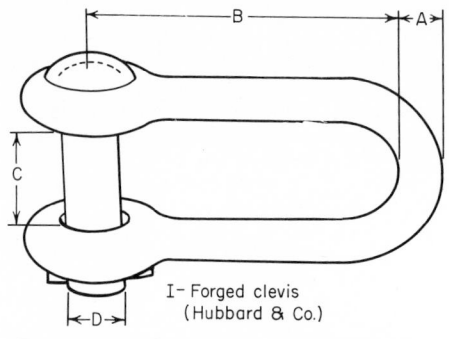

I– Forged clevis
(Hubbard & Co.)

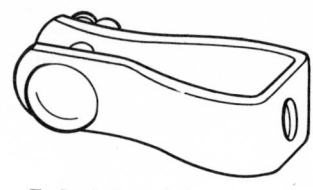

II– Bent strap clevis
(Line Material Industries)

Dimensions in inches				Approximate shipping weight
A	B	C	D	lbs,100 pcs.
1/2	2	11/16	5/8	66
9/16	3	1 3/8	3/4	146
9/16	4	1 3/8	3/4	160
1/2	3	3/4	5/8	85

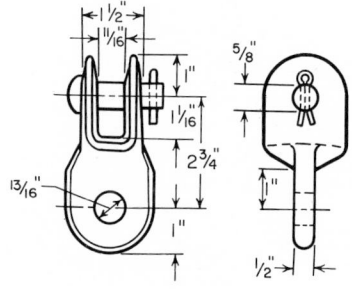

III–Clevis eye
(Corning Glass Co.)

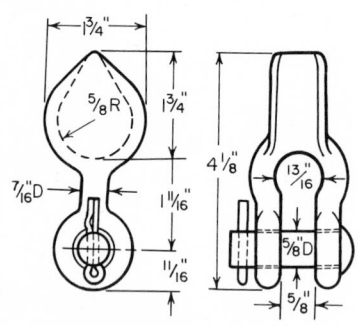

IV–Thimble clevis
(Ohio Brass Co.)

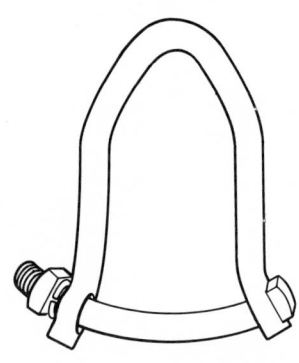

V– Strain insulator clevis
(Hubbard & Co.)

FIG. 40 *Clevises.*

under the nut of the thimble-eye or J bolt. Under the eye of the bolt a stubbing washer (Fig. 44, V) is used for a 90-deg guy and a guy plate of the type shown in Fig. 44, IV, for an angle guy. Guying construction is discussed in Sec. **100.**

56. When a guy strand is connected to a bolt or rod of small diameter, the strand should be wrapped around a thimble (Fig. 43, V) to prevent its being cut or broken from too sharp a bend.

57. Guy clamps (Fig. 45) are used for securing the ends of guy-wire strands. They are made in two-, three-, and four-bolt types.

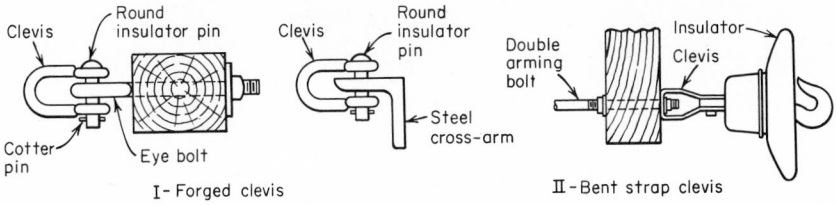

I– Forged clevis

II–Bent strap clevis

III– Thimble clevis connection
to dead end insulator

IV – Strain insulator clevis

FIG. 41 *Applications of clevises to crossarm connections. (Hubbard & Co.)*

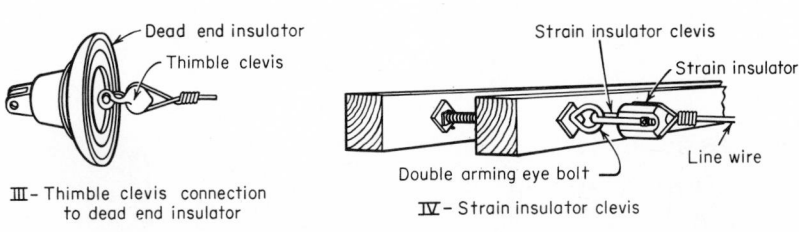

I–Roller type

II–Log type

III–Rock anchor

FIG. 42 *Guy anchor rods. (Line Material Industries.)*

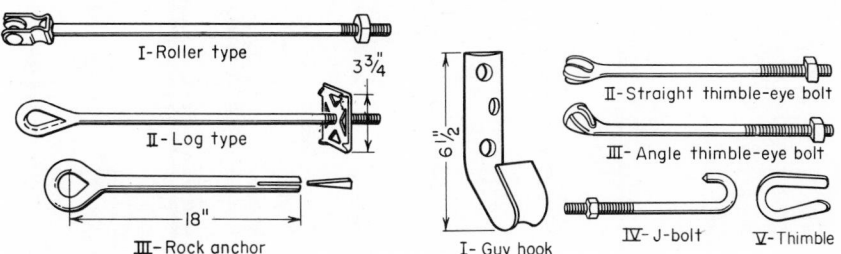

I– Guy hook

II–Straight thimble-eye bolt

III– Angle thimble-eye bolt

IV– J-bolt   V–Thimble

FIG. 43 *Guy hook, thimble-eye bolts, and J bolt. (Line Material Industries.)*

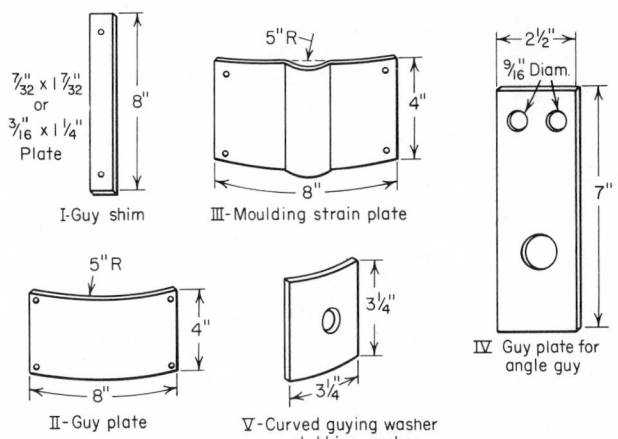

I–Guy shim

III–Moulding strain plate

II–Guy plate

V–Curved guying washer
or stubbing washer

IV Guy plate for
angle guy

FIG. 44 *Guy plates and shims. (Locke Insulator Corp. and Hubbard & Co.)*

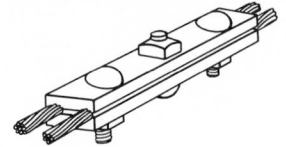

FIG. 45   *Guy clamp.*   (*Joslyn Mfg. Co.*)

Type	Length, In.
Two bolt, light...............	3
Two bolt, heavy..............	4
Three bolt, heavy............	4
Three bolt, heavy............	6
Three bolt, heavy............	6
Four bolt, heavy..............	8

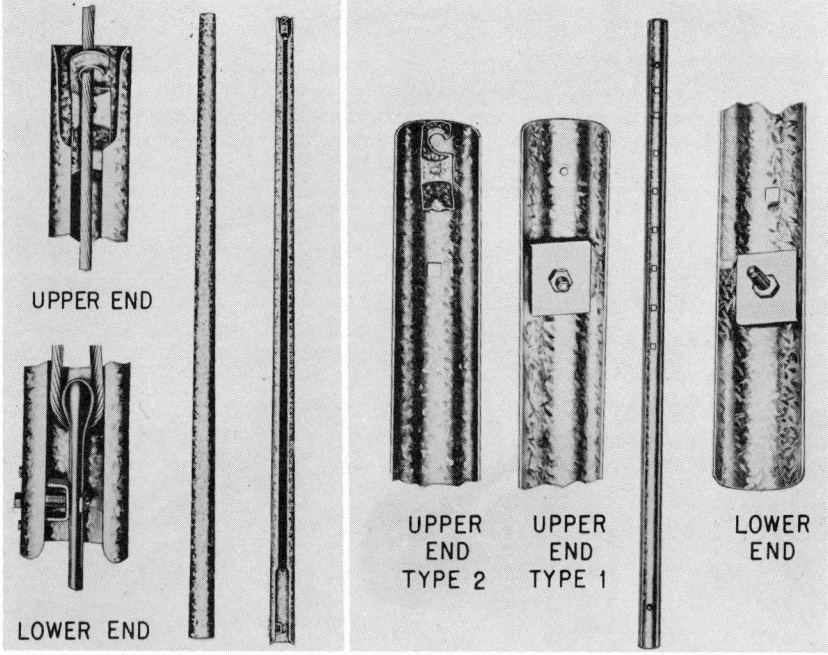

I. *Full-round type.*   II. *Half-round type.*

FIG. 46   *Guy-wire protectors.*   (*Line Material Industries.*)

58. Guy protector guards are installed over guy rods, at locations where the guy might be damaged by traffic, to conceal the connection of the guy strand to the eye of the guy rod, to make the guy more visible, and to minimize accidents. They may be made of a wood strip or of steel. One type of guard (Fig. 46) consists of a steel plate rolled into cylindrical form, leaving a split on one side. Special clamps are fastened to the strand, and the guard is slipped over the strand and held by the clamps. The split is turned down toward the ground so that it is not ordinarily noticeable.

59. For guy wire, seven-strand galvanized-steel cable is used. The National Electrical Safety Code recommends that for Grades A and B construction the maximum load in the guy should not exceed 50 per cent of the ultimate strength; for Grade C construction 75 per cent is allowable. The following table gives the strand sizes, weights, and ultimate strength of guy wire:

Diam, in	Approx weight, lb per 1,000 ft	Approx strength, lb	Diam, in.	Approx weight, lb per 1,000 ft	Approx strength, lb
¾	1,200	16,700	⅜	273	4,250
⅝	813	11,600	⁵⁄₁₆	205	3,200
⁹⁄₁₆	671	9,600	⁹⁄₃₂	164	2,570
½	517	7,400	¼	121	1,900
⁷⁄₁₆	399	5,700			

POLE-LINE CONSTRUCTION

60. A single crossarm assembly for a two-wire single-phase circuit is shown in Fig. 47. Additional insulators for three- or four-wire lines can be added to the arm 14½ in. closer to the pole from the insulators shown. This type of arm is used for normal spans and loads where there is a straight line with no obstructions.

61. Double arms are used wherever the stress on the arms is unusually severe or where every precaution is necessary to ensure safety. Double arms are often used on the poles at each side of a street intersection, at each side of railroad crossings, and at corners or other points where the direction of a line changes. Figures 48, 51, 52, 70, 86, 87, 89, and 90 show examples of double-armed poles. The two

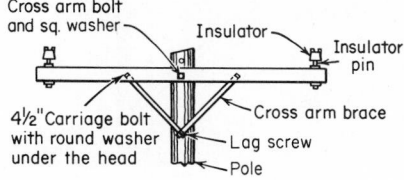

FIG. 47 *Single crossarm assembly.*

crossarms can be separated by wooden spacing blocks (Fig. 51), by spacing bolts or double-arming bolts (Fig. 48A), or by spacing nipples (Fig. 48B). The spacing blocks can be sawed from a crossarm. An ¹¹⁄₁₆-in. hole bored through the block and crossarm accommodates a ⅝-in. bolt. A washer is used under bolthead and nut. Spacing bolts or double-arming bolts can be used instead of spacing blocks (Fig. 48A); the bolts are threaded for most of their length. A galvanized-iron pipe nipple can also (Fig. 48B) be used to separate the crossarms. A ¾-in. spacing bolt probably provides the preferable and most economical method; spacing blocks rot readily, and the bolts through them corrode rapidly. Where an arm guy is to be attached to the crossarm, a double-arming eyebolt can be used as shown. Single-armed poles are now often used, particularly on junction poles, as shown in the accompanying

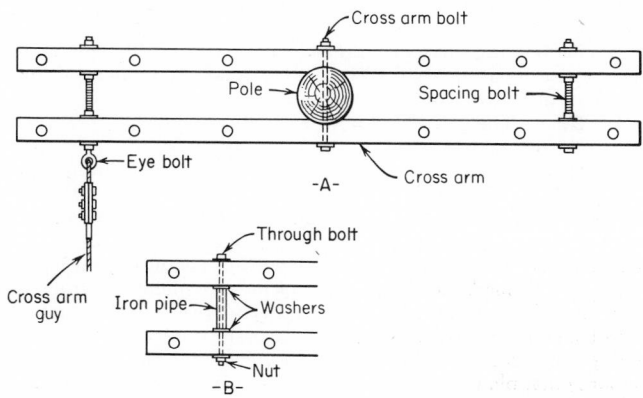

FIG. 48 *Method of arranging double arms.*

illustrations, in locations where double arms were formerly thought necessary. The single arms are preferable in that they allow greater climbing space for linemen.

62. Alley arms (Figs. 49 and 50) are used in alleys and other locations where it is necessary to clear obstructions by offsetting the crossarm toward one side of the pole. The crossarms will be special arms, but standard material can generally be used for the rest of the construction. Types of standard braces for side-arm construction are discussed in Sec. **40**. Side guys or crib braces (see Fig. 49) are used where the line wires are heavy to counteract the tendency of the pole to tip.

63. Reverse or buck arms are used at corners (see Figs. 51, 52, 86, and 87). In placing buck arms, ample room must be provided through which a lineman can reach the top of the pole. A 20-in. square space is the minimum. Crossarm braces on buck-arm poles should be attached to the arms at a point 23½ in. from the center of arm instead of at 19 in., the standard distance for ordinary framing. The ⅜-in. holes for the brace (carriage) bolts must be specially bored, at the above spacing, in buck arms. The 23-in. spacing is correct for 28-in. braces.

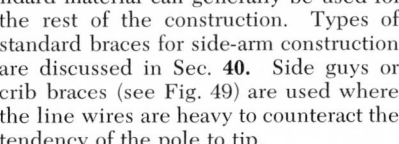

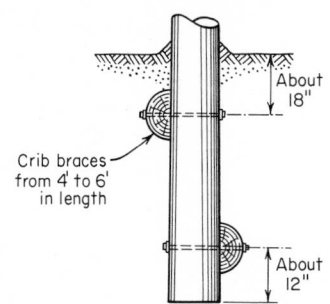

FIG. 49 *A side-arm pole.*

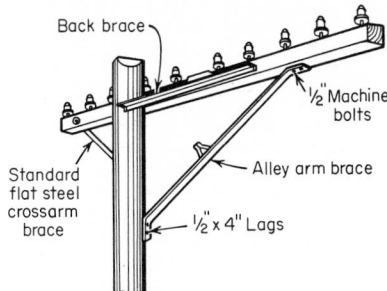

FIG. 50 *Bracing for alley arms.* (*Hubbard & Co.*)

64. A gain is a flat bearing surface on the pole at the point of attachment of the crossarm so that the crossarm will be rigid. The gain is usually formed by cutting a notch in the side of the pole, as shown in Fig. 53. The gaining template of Fig. 54 is convenient in laying out the gains. The gain should be exactly the width of the crossarm, ensuring a snug fit. In good work, gains should always be spaced on 24-in. centers and should be ½ in. deep. Nothing is accomplished by making them deeper. In using the gaining template (Fig. 53, II) the point of the "roof" of the template is placed exactly over the point of the roof of the pole and the template is shifted until its center line (which should be marked thereon) lies exactly under a cord stretched from the roof point to the center of the pole at the ground line. Then the positions of the crossarm gains are indicated by knife scratches made along the sides of the crosspieces on the template.

Where a gaining template is not available, a crossarm (Fig. 53, III) can be laid on the pole with a steel square held against its lower face, the outer edge of the short limb of the square lying at the center of the pole and the center of the crossarm. Rotate the crossarm in a horizontal plane until, by sighting, it is evident that the edge of the square coincides with an imaginary center line to a nail in the center of the butt at the ground line. Indicate the gain location by knife scratches along the crossarm sides.

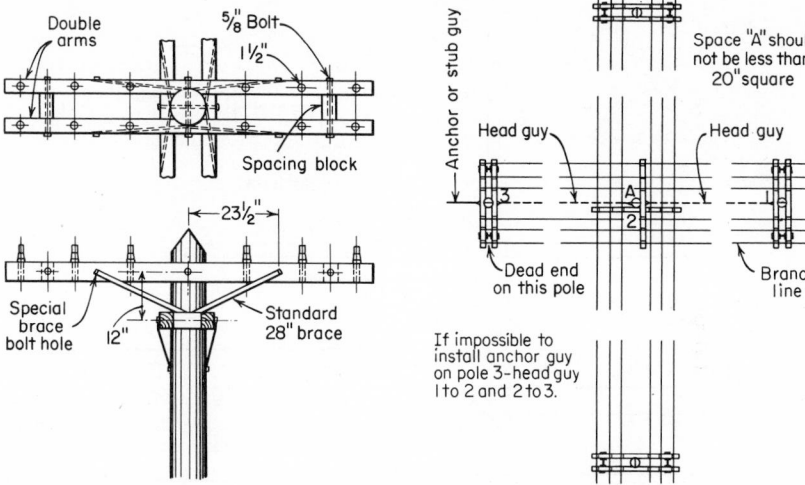

FIG. 51 *A buck-armed pole, double arms.*   FIG. 52 *Junction pole without double arms.*

65. Metal gains (Fig. 55, I) can be used in attaching the crossarm to the pole instead of notching the pole. By spacing the crossarm about ½ in. away from the pole they allow for complete drainage of water from the joint and prevent rotting of the pole and crossarm. Also, at double-arming locations, the use of metal gains spaces the crossarms about 2 in. farther apart, which allows more room between the pin insulators on the two arms and more room for tie wires, an important factor on the higher voltage lines. Metal gains are a great convenience when installing an additional crossarm to an existing pole

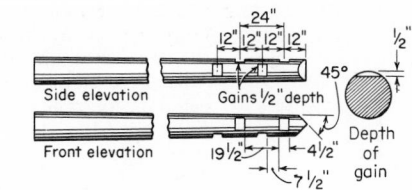

FIG. 53-I *Gains in pole.*

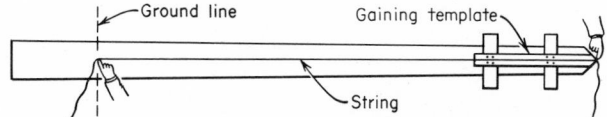

FIG. 53-II *Use of gaining template.*

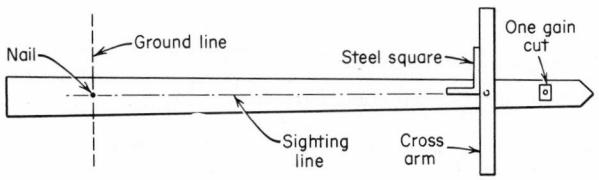

FIG. 53-III *Locating gain with steel square and crossarm.*

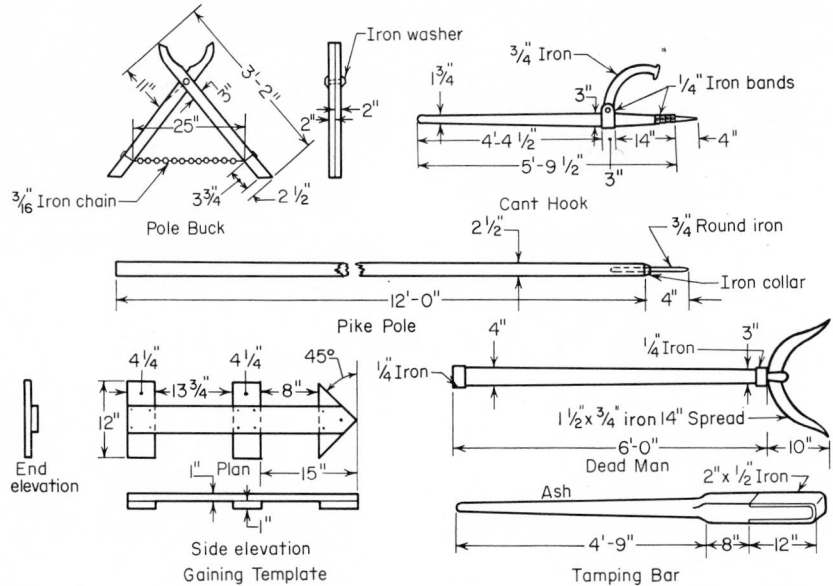

Note: The tool illustrated above as a Cant–Hook is properly termed a Peavie.
A peavie has a spike in the end of its handle, while a cant-hook has no spike.

FIG. 54   *Some line-construction tools.*

which did not have the gain cut in it.   In using metal gains a square washer can be used under the head of the through bolt (Fig. 55, III).   A better construction is to use a reinforcing plate (Fig. 55, II) located on the outside of the crossarm (Fig. 55, IV).   This makes for a more rigid construction and helps to prevent checking and splitting of the crossarm at the attachment point.

66. Pole steps (Fig. 56, I) can be located on the pole as shown in Fig. 57.   A $3/8$-in. hole 4 in. deep is bored for the iron step.   It is driven into the hole until it projects 6 in. from the pole and is then turned with a wrench until the hook end is vertical.   The wooden step is held to the pole with one 40-penny and one 20-penny nail or with cut spikes.   Often the wooden steps are omitted.   The lowest iron step should be at least $6\frac{1}{2}$ ft from the ground or other readily accessible place.   One wood block (or on private right of way more than one) may be placed on poles carrying communication cables or conductors below supply conductors, but the lowest block is not to be less than $3\frac{1}{2}$ ft from the ground or other readily accessi-

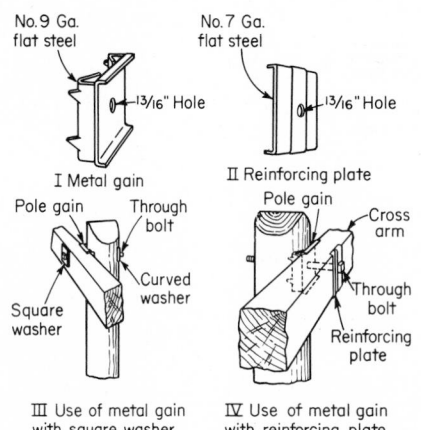

FIG. 55   *Metal gains.   (Hubbard & Co.)*

ble place.   On poles carrying only communication conductors, additional wood blocks may be used.

Detachable pole steps are available.   The one shown in Fig. 56, II, slips over the head of the special $9/16$- by 4-in. lag screw.   Turning is prevented by a punched projection.   The steps can be removed to prevent unauthorized climbing.

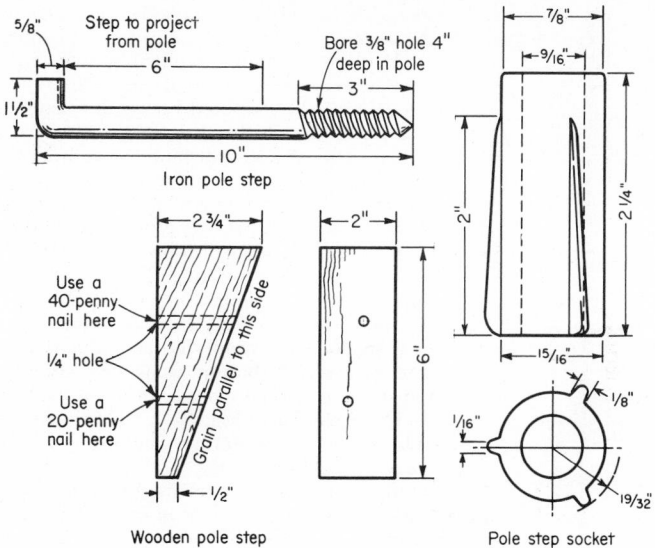

FIG. 56-I *Pole steps and socket.*

Pole-step sockets (Fig. 56, I) are sometimes substituted for the wooden steps. The sockets drive into a ⅞-in. hole. To climb the pole a lineman can temporarily insert bolts or similar pieces of metal into the sockets.

67. Secondary racks are mounted on the sides of poles or buildings to carry low-voltage mains, usually of 440 volts or less, to locations where building services are tapped off. Figure 58, II, illustrates the rack used as a dead end with a head guy to take the tension of the wires. The building service in this case is tapped with open wires. The higher voltage wires are shown mounted on the crossarm at the top of the pole. Figure 58, I, shows two secondary lines crossing; Fig. 58, III, shows a corner pole, Fig. 58, IV, shows the secondary wires supported on the side of the pole with an open-wire service tap; Fig. 58, V, shows a similar construction with taps to a service cable.

68. Distribution transformers reduce the primary line voltage to a low secondary voltage suitable for customers' use. They are mounted on the side of poles or on a platform between poles. Figure 59, I, shows such a transformer mounted on special crossarms in the space between the high-voltage wires at the top of the pole and the low-voltage wires on the secondary rack. Taps connect the primary

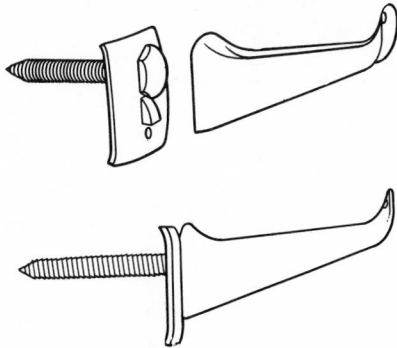

FIG. 56-II *Detachable pole step. (Joslyn Mfg. Co.)*

of the transformer, through fuses mounted on the extra crossarm, to the high-voltage wires. The secondary of the transformer is connected directly to the secondary wires at the secondary rack. Attention should be given to making these connections in a neat manner, using right-angle bends and running the several wires of a circuit parallel to each other. Wherever there is danger of a wire touching another wire or a crossarm or brace or coming too close to a pole, wire-holder insulators (Fig. 32) or pin insulators

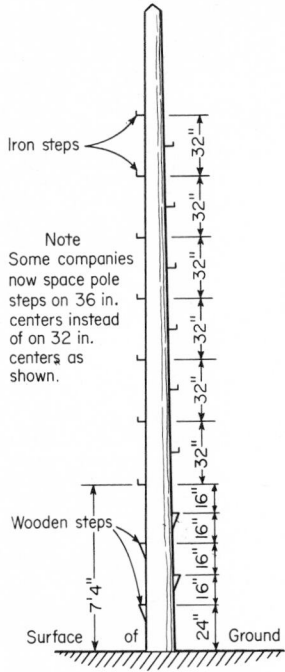

Iron steps

Note
Some companies
now space pole
steps on 36 in.
centers instead
of on 32 in.
centers as
shown.

Wooden steps

Surface of Ground

FIG. 57 *Location of pole steps on pole.*

should be installed on the sides of crossarms to keep the connecting wires in their proper position. Figure 59, II, shows a similar arrangement where the secondary wires are closer to the primary wires and the transformer must be mounted below the secondary wires. The insulators on the transformer crossarm keep the primary taps at a safe distance away from the secondary wires. A compact installation is shown in Fig. 59, III. Such an arrangement is quite satisfactory when there are only two primary wires spaced sufficiently far apart to give plenty of climbing and working space. A three-phase bank consisting of three single-phase transformers can be mounted on a platform supported from two poles located fairly close together. This is common practice for supplying an industrial plant. For three-phase distribution along city streets the three transformers can be mounted singly on adjacent poles, each one similar to Fig. 59, I. This practice is preferable where the transformer platform would be too conspicuous and unsightly. Additional details for the mounting of transformers are given in Div. 5.

69. In locating circuits on poles, the through wires or trunk lines should be carried on the upper crossarms and the local wires, those which are tapped frequently, should be carried on the lower crossarms. The two or three wires of a circuit should always be carried on adjacent pins. This is of particular importance with a-c circuits, as the inductance, and consequently the inductive voltage drop, is increased as the distance between the wires of a circuit is increased. Wires of a

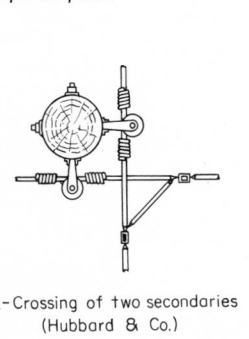

I–Crossing of two secondaries
(Hubbard & Co.)

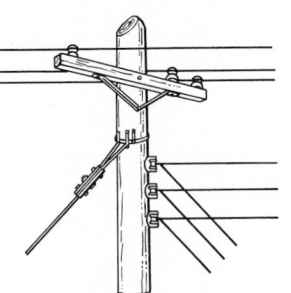

II–Dead end of secondary with
open wire service tap
(General Electric Co.)

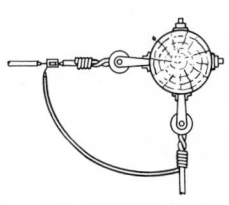

III– Corner construction
(Hubbard & Co.)

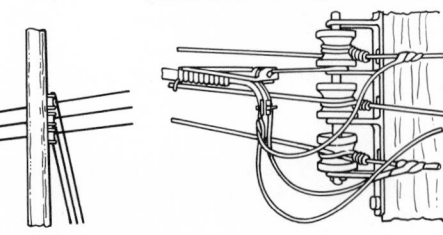

IV–Straight through
connection with
open wire service tap
(Hubbard & Co.)

V–Straight through
connection with
service cable tap
(James R. Kearney Co.)

FIG. 58 *Ways of using secondary racks.*

circuit should always take the same pin positions on all poles to facilitate trouble hunting. Series circuits which do not operate during the daytime may often be carried on the pole pins of a crossarm. High-tension multiple circuits that are "hot" continuously are well placed at the ends of the arms out of the way of linemen. The neutral wire should always be in the center of a three-wire circuit. Figure 60 shows one good arrangement on a two, four-pin-arm pole.

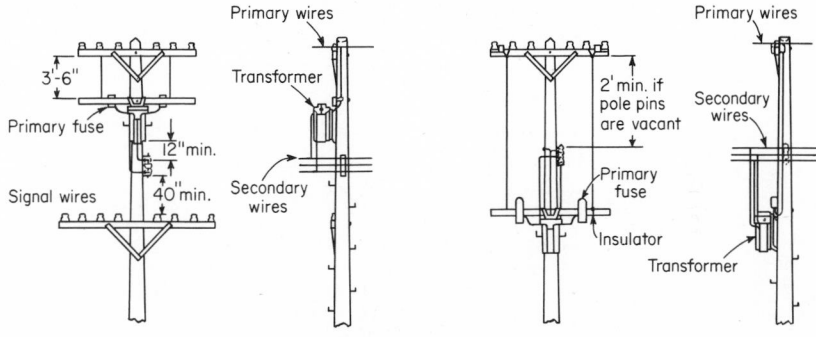

I Single phase transformer mounted in space between primary wires and secondary rack. (Line Material Industries)

II Single phase transformer mounted below secondary rack. (Line Material Industries)

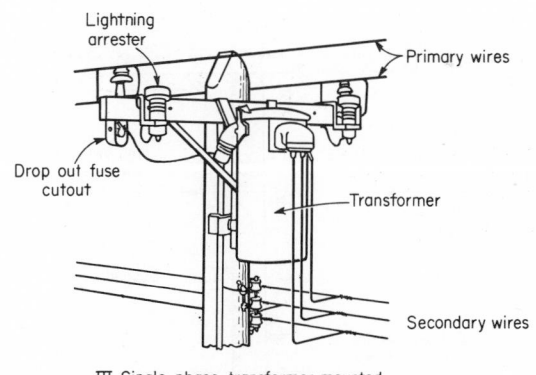

III Single phase transformer mounted on same cross arm with primary supply wires. (General Electric Co.)

FIG. 59 *Mounting and wiring of distribution transformers.*

70. Joint use of poles for circuits of different power companies or for circuits of a power company and a telephone or a telegraph company is frequently advantageous where the lines run along the same route (Fig. 61). In the rules for location of conductors and clearances, the power-company circuits are frequently called simply supply wires; the telephone and telegraph company circuits are called communication wires. The National Electrical Safety Code provides that when supply circuits of different companies are located on the same pole, the higher-voltage line should be carried at the higher level except that the lines of each company may be grouped together and always carried in the same relative position. For each company the lines of higher voltage should be located in the higher position. Whenever a lower-voltage line is carried above a higher-voltage one, it must be on the opposite side of the pole. A vertical clearance of at least 4 ft must be maintained between wires of different power companies, and a clearance of 6 ft must be used if required by the rules of Sec. **85.** Supply wires must be carried above communication wires except that minor extensions may be made to existing systems which were installed with the communication wires above.

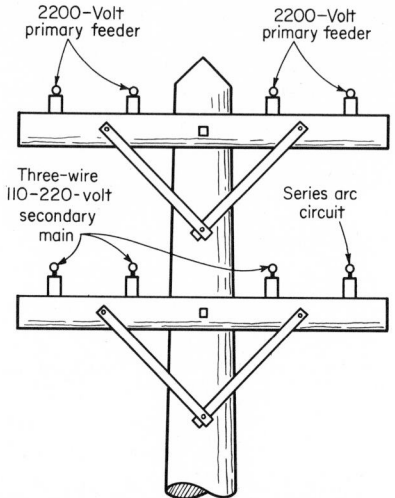

FIG. 60   *Location of circuits on a two-arm pole.*

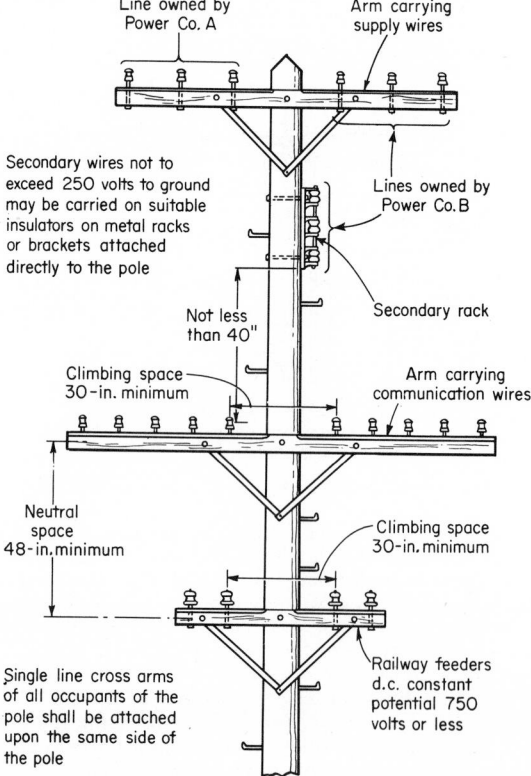

FIG. 61   *Construction of jointly used wood-pole lines carrying supply circuits and signal circuits, showing arrangement of attachments and clearances.   (Hubbard & Co.).*

Trolley feeder wires may be carried at the approximate level of the trolley wires irrespective of whether that location brings them above or below the communication wires. The climbing space (for a workman to climb the pole) between the wires nearest the pole on the lower level lines must be at least as great as given in the following table:

71. Minimum Horizontal Dimensions of Climbing Space
(National Electrical Safety Code)

Character of conductors adjacent to climbing space	Voltage of conductors	Horizontal dimensions of climbing space, in.			
		On poles used solely by		On jointly used poles	
		Communication conductors	Supply conductors	Supply conductors above communication conductors	Communication conductors above supply conductors[a]
Communication conductors	0–150	No requirement 24 recommended [c]	....	[b]	No requirement 24 recommended
	Exceeding 150		....	[b]	
Supply conductors........	Less than 300	....	24	24	30
	300–8,700	....	30	30	30
	8,700–15,000	....	36	36	36
	Exceeding 15,000	....	More than 36[c]	More than 36[c]	More than 36[c]

[a] This relation of levels is not, in general, desirable and should be avoided where practicable.

[b] Climbing space shall be the same as required for the supply conductors immediately above, with a maximum of 30 in., except that a climbing space of 16 in. across the line may be employed for communication cables or conductors where the only supply conductors at a higher level are secondaries (0 to 750 volts between conductors) supplying airport or airway marker lights or crossing over the communication line and attached to the pole top or to a pole-top extension fixture.

[c] Where practicable.

72. The basic vertical clearances above ground or rails given in Sec. **73** are the minimum clearances required by the National Electrical Safety Code under the following conditions:

1. Temperature of 60°F, no wind, with final unloaded sag or with initial unloaded sag in cases where wires are maintained approximately at initial unloaded sags.

2. With span lengths not greater than 175 ft for heavy loading districts, 250 ft for medium loading districts, or 350 ft for light loading districts. If any conductor consists of three strands, each strand of which is 0.09 in. or less in diameter, the maximum span length must be not greater than 150 ft for heavy loading districts or 225 ft for medium loading districts.

3. Voltages 0 to 50,000 volts between conductors.

4. Fixed supports for the conductors or wires.

When the above conditions are not fulfilled, the National Electrical Safety Code must be consulted for the increased clearances which are required.

73. Minimum Vertical Clearance of Wires above Ground or Rails in Feet
(National Electrical Safety Code)

[All voltages are between wires unless otherwise stated. Supply wires include trolley feeders.]

Nature of ground or rails underneath wires	Guys:[a] messengers; communication, span, and lightning protection wires; effectively grounded continuous-metal-sheath cables of all voltages	Open supply-line wires, arc wires, and service drops[h]			Trolley contact conductors and associated span or messenger wires[a]	
		0 to 750 volts	750 to 15,000 volts	15,000 to 50,000 volts	0 to 750 volts to ground	Exceeding 750 volts to ground
Where Wires Cross Over						
Track rails of railroads (except electrified railroads using overhead trolley conductors) handling freight cars on top of which men are permitted[b,p]	27[c,o]	27[c]	28[c]	30	22[d]	22[d]
Track rails of railroads (except electrified railroads using overhead trolley conductors) not included above[b]	18	18	20	22	18[e]	20[e]
Public streets, alleys or roads in urban or rural districts	18[f,m]	18	20	22	18[e]	20[e]
Driveways to residence garages	10	10	20	22	18[e]	20[e]
Spaces or ways accessible to pedestrians only	15[g]	15[h]	15	17	16[i]	18[i]
Where Wires Run along and within the Limits of Public Highways or Other Public Rights-of-way for Traffic						
Streets or alleys in urban districts	18[j,k,m]	18[j]	20	22	18[e]	20[e]
Roads in rural districts	14[j,k,l]	15[j]	18	20	18[e]	20[e]

NOTES TO TABLE 73

[a] Where subways, tunnels, or bridges require it, less clearances above ground or rails than required by above table may be used locally. The trolley contact conductor should be graded very gradually from the regular construction down to the reduced elevation.

[b] For wire crossings over railways handling only cars considerably lower than ordinary freight cars, the clearance may be reduced by an amount equal to the difference in height between the highest car handled and the highest ordinary freight car, but the clearance shall not be reduced below that required for street crossings.

[c] This clearance may be reduced to 25 ft where paralleled by trolley contact conductor on the same street or highway.

[d] In communities where 21 ft has been established, this clearance may be continued if carefully maintained. The elevation of the contact conductor should be the same in the crossing and next adjacent spans. (See rule 289, D, 2, for conditions which must be met where uniform height above rail is impracticable.)

[e] In communities where 16 ft has been established for trolley contact conductors 0 to 750 volts to ground or 18 ft for trolley contact conductors exceeding 750 volts or where local conditions make it impracticable to obtain the clearance given in the table, these reduced clearances may be used if carefully maintained.

[f] If a communication service drop, or a guy which is effectively insulated against the highest voltage to which it is exposed, up to 8,700 volts, crosses a street, alley or road, the clearance may be reduced to 16 ft at the side of the traveled way.

[g] This clearance may be reduced to the following values:

Feet

1. For communication conductors of circuits limited to 160 volts to ground and communication cables 8
2. For conductors of other communication circuits 10
3. For guys 8
4. For supply cable having effectively grounded continuous metal sheath, or insulated conductors supported on and cabled together with an effectively grounded messenger, all voltages 10

[h] This clearance may be reduced to the following values:

Feet

1. Supply wires (except trolley contact wires) limited to 300 volts to ground 12
2. Supply wires (except trolley contact wires) limited to 150 volts to ground and located at entrances to buildings 10
3. Where supply circuits of 550 volts or less, with transmitted power of 3,200 watts or less, are run along fenced (or otherwise guarded) private rights of way in accordance with the provisions specified in rule 220, B, 3 10

[i] Trolley contact conductors for industrial railways when not along or crossing over roadways may be placed at a lesser height if suitably guarded.

74. Supply Pole Wiring at Underground Risers (National Electrical Safety Code). Supply wires connecting to underground systems shall not be run open closer to the ground than is indicated by the following table:

Clearance above Ground for Open Supply Wiring

Location on pole	Voltage between conductors		
	0 to 750	750 to 15,000	More than 15,000
Side of pole adjacent to vehicular traffic..........	14	16	18
Side of pole not adjacent to vehicular traffic.......	8	11	13

75. The basic clearances between any two wires crossing each other and carried on different supports given in Sec. **76** are the minimum clearances required by the National Electrical Safety Code under the following conditions:

1. Temperature of 60°F, no wind, with the upper conductor or wire at its final unloaded sag and the lower conductor or wire at its initial unloaded sag.

2. Span lengths not greater than the following for the upper conductor or wire:

Loading district	Span lengths, ft
Heavy.............	175ᵃ
Medium..........	250ᵃ
Light.............	350

ᵃ 150 ft in heavy loading district and 225 ft in medium loading district for three-strand conductors, each wire of which is 0.09 in. or less in diameter.

3. Fixed supports for the upper conductor or wire. (For other conditions, see rule 233 B.)

When the above conditions are not fulfilled, the National Electrical Safety Code must be consulted for the increased clearances which are required.

Notes to Table 73 (*Continued*)

ʲ Where a pole line along a road is located relative to fences, ditches, embankments, etc., so that the ground under the line will never be traveled except by pedestrians, this clearance may be reduced to the following values:

	Feet
1. Communication conductors limited to 160 volts to ground and communication cables...............	8
2. Conductors of other communication circuits..	10
3. Supply conductors...	12
4. Guys..	8

ᵏ No clearance from ground is required for anchor guys not crossing streets, driveways, roads, or pathways, nor for anchor guys provided with traffic guards and paralleling sidewalk curbs.

ˡ This clearance may be reduced to 13 ft for communication conductors where no part of the line overhangs any part of the highway which is ordinarily traveled and where it is unlikely that loaded vehicles will be crossing under the line into a field.

ᵐ Where communication wires or cables cross over or run along alleys, this clearance may be reduced to 15 ft.

ⁿ A conductor which is effectively grounded throughout its length and is associated with a circuit of 0 to 22,000 volts may have the clearances specified for guys and messengers.

ᵒ This value may be reduced to 13 ft for conductors effectively grounded throughout their entire length and associated with supply circuits of 0 to 22,000 volts, only if such conductors are stranded, are of corrosion-resistant material, and conform to the strength and tension requirements for messengers given in rule 261 G.

ᵖ Adjacent to overhead bridges which restrict the practice of permitting men on top of cars, these clearances may be reduced, within the restricted area, by mutual agreement between the parties at interest, but in no case shall the wires or cables be at levels below the undersurface of the bridge.

ᵠ Also insulated conductors supported on and cabled together with an effectively grounded messenger, all voltages.

76. Wire-crossing Clearances in Feet
(National Electrical Safety Code)

(All voltages are between wires except for trolley contact conductors where voltages are to ground. The insertion of a given clearance in italics indicates that in general the lines operating at the voltage named above this clearance should not cross over the lines at the voltage to the left of the clearance in italics.)

Nature of wires crossed over	Communication wires, including cables and messengers	Open supply wires, 0 to 750 volts; supply cables, all voltages, having effectively grounded continuous metal sheaths or messengers; messengers associated with such cables		Open supply wires and service drops[f]		Guys, span wires, lightning-protection wires
		Line wires	Service drops	750 to 8,700 volts	8,700 to 50,000 volts	
Communication, including cables and messengers	2[b]	4[c,i]	2[i]	4[g]	6[j]	2[b]
Supply cables, all voltages, having effectively grounded continuous metal sheaths or messengers; messengers associated with such cables	4	2	2	2	4	2
Open supply wires:						
0–750 volts	4	2	2	2	4	2
750–8,700 volts	4	*2*	4	2	4	4
8,700–50,000 volts	6	*4*	6	4	4	4
Trolley contact conductors	4[d]	4[d,e]	4[d]	6	6	4[d]
Guys, span wires, lightning-protection wires, service drops 0–750 volts	2[b,h]	2	2	4	4	2[a,b]

[a] Completely insulated sections of guys attached to supporting structures having no conductor of more than 8,700 volts may have less than this clearance from each other.

[b] The clearance of communication conductors and their guy, span, and messenger wires from each other in locations where no other classes of conductors are involved may be reduced by mutual consent of the parties concerned, subject to the approval of the regulatory body having jurisdiction, except for fire-alarm wires and wires used in the operation of railroads or where one set of conductors is for public use and the other used in the operation of supply systems.

[c] A clearance of 2 ft may be permitted where the supply conductor is above the communication conductor, provided the crossing is not within 6 ft of any pole concerned in the crossing and the voltage to ground does not exceed 300 volts. (See note i.)

[d] Trolley-contact conductors of more than 750 volts should have at least 6-ft clearance. This clearance should also be provided over lower voltage trolley-contact conductors unless the cross-over conductors are beyond reach of a trolley pole leaving the trolley-contact conductor or are suitably protected against damage from trolley poles leaving the trolley-contact conductor.

[e] Trolley feeders are exempt from this clearance requirement for trolley-contact conductors if they are of the same nominal voltage and of the same system.

[f] A conductor which is effectively grounded throughout its length and is associated with a circuit of 0 to 22,000 volts may have the clearances specified for guys and messengers.

[g] This clearance shall be increased to 6 ft where the supply wires cross over a communication line within 6 ft horizontally of a communication pole.

[h] This clearance shall be increased to 4 ft where communication cables cross over open supply service wires.

[i] Where a 2-ft clearance is required at 60°F and where conditions are such that the sag in the upper conductor would increase more than 1.5 ft at the crossing point under the applicable loading of rule 251, the 2-ft clearance shall be increased by the amount of sag increase less 1.5 ft.

[j] Supply cable having effectively grounded continuous metal sheath, or insulated conductors supported on and cabled together with an effectively grounded messenger, of all voltages, and messengers associated with such cable, may have a clearance of 2 ft except where they cross under communication cables.

77. Clearances from Conductors of Another Line (National Electrical Safety Code). The clearance in any direction between any conductor of one line and any conductor of a second and conflicting line shall be not less than the largest value required by 1, 2, or 3 below at 60°F, no wind:

1. Four feet.

2. The values required by Sec. **79** or **80** for separation between conductors on the same support.

3. The apparent sag of the conductor having the greater sag, plus 0.2 in. per kilovolt of the highest voltage concerned.

78. The horizontal separations between line conductors attached to fixed supports shall be not less than the larger value required by either Sec. **79** or **80**.

79. Minimum Horizontal Separation at Supports between Line Conductors of the Same or Different Circuits

(National Electrical Safety Code)

(All voltages are between conductors except for railway feeders, which are to ground)

Class of circuit	Separa-tion, in.	Notes
Communication conductors......................	6	Preferable minimum. Does not apply at conductor transposition points
	3	Permitted where pin spacings less than 6 in. have been in regular use. Does not apply at conductor transposition points
Railway feeders:		
0–750 volts, No. 4/0 or larger..................	6	
0–750 volts, smaller than No. 4/0..............	12	Where 10- to 12-in. separation has already been established, by practice, it may be continued, subject to the provisions of rule 235, A, 2, (a), (2), for conductors having apparent sags not over 3 ft and for voltages not exceeding 8,700
750–8,700 volts............................	12	
Other supply conductors:		
0–8,700 volts..............................	12	
For all conductors of more than 8,700 volts add for each 1,000 volts in excess of 8,700 volts..........	0.4	

80. Minimum Horizontal Separation at Supports between Line Conductors According to Sags (National Electrical Safety Code). The separation at the supports of conductors of the same or different circuits of Grades B or C shall in no case be less than the values given by the following formulas, at 60°F, no wind. The requirements of rule 235, A, 2, (a), (1) apply if they give a greater separation than this rule.

For line conductors smaller than No. 2 AWG:

$$\text{Separation} = 0.3 \text{ in. per kv} + 7\sqrt{(S/3) - 8}$$

For line conductors of No. 2 AWG or larger:

$$\text{Separation} = 0.3 \text{ in. per kv} + 8\sqrt{S/12}$$

S is the apparent sag in inches of the conductor having the greater sag, and the separation is in inches.

81. Where suspension insulators are used and are not restrained from movement, the National Electrical Safety Code requires that the separation between conductors as required by Sec. **78** shall be increased so that one string of line insulators can swing transversely through an angle of 45 deg from a vertical position without reducing the values required by Sec. **78**.

82. Minimum Clearance, in Inches, in any Direction from Line Conductors to Supports and to Vertical or Lateral Conductors, Span or Guy Wires Attached to the Same Support (National Electrical Safety Code)

(All voltages are between conductors)

Clearance of line conductors from	Communication lines		Supply lines		
			0 to 8,700 volts		Exceeding 8,700 volts, add for each 1,000 volts of excess
	In general	On jointly used poles	In general	On jointly used poles	
Vertical and lateral conductors:					
Of same circuit...............................	3	3	3	3	0.25
Of other circuits..............................	3	3	6^f	6^f	0.4
Span and guy wires attached to same pole:					
General......................................	3^h	6^{a,h}	6	6	0 4
When parallel to line.........................	3^h	6^{a,h}	12^a	12^a	0.4
Lightning-protection wires parallel to line...........	^{b,e}	^{b,e}	^{b,e}	^{b,e}	0.4
Surfaces of crossarms..........................	3^c	3^c	3	3	0.2
Surfaces of poles..............................	3^c	5^c	3^{g,i}	5^{d,g}	0.2

^{a} For guy wires, if practicable. For clearances between span wires and communication conductors, see rule 238,E,3.

On jointly used poles, a guy that passes within 12 in. of supply conductors, and also within 12 in. of communication cables, shall be protected with a suitable insulating covering where it passes the supply conductors, unless it is effectively grounded or insulated with a strain insulator at a point below the lowest supply conductor and above the highest communication cable.

^{b} Clearance shall not be less than the separation required by Table 6 or rule 235,A,2,(a),(2) between two line conductors of the voltage concerned.

^{c} Communication conductors may be attached to supports on the sides or bottoms of crossarms or surfaces of poles with less clearances, if at least 40 in. from any supply line conductor of less than 8,700 volts to ground and at least 60 in. from any supply line conductor of more than 8,700 volts to ground carried on the same pole.

^{d} This clearance applies only to supply conductors carried on crossarms below communication conductors on joint poles.

Where supply conductors are above communication conductors, this clearance may be reduced to 3 in. except for supply conductors of 0 to 750 volts whose clearance may be reduced to 1 in.

^{e} For the purpose of applying the above table, the voltage of lightning-protection wires shall be considered as being the voltage to ground of the associated supply conductors.

^{f} For supply circuits of 0 to 750 volts, this clearance may be reduced to 3 in.

^{g} A neutral conductor that is effectively grounded throughout its length and is associated with a circuit of 0 to 22,000 volts may be attached directly to the pole surface.

^{h} Guys and messengers shall be attached to the same strain plates or to the same through bolts.

^{i} For supply circuits of 0 to 750 volts this clearance may be reduced to 1 in.

Where suspension insulators are used and are not restrained from movement, the conductor clearances from surfaces of supports, from span or guy wires, or from vertical or lateral conductors shall be such that the values of clearances required by a above will be maintained with an insulator swing of 45 deg from the vertical position on steel or concrete supports, or 30 deg if on wood poles.

83. Conductor Separation: Vertical Racks (National Electrical Safety Code). Conductors or cables may be carried on vertical racks or separate brackets other than wood placed vertically at one side of the pole and securely attached thereto if all the following conditions are met:

1. The voltage shall not be more than 750 volts, except that cable having effectively grounded continuous metal sheath, or insulated conductors supported on and cabled together with an effectively grounded messenger, may carry any voltage.

2. Conductors shall be of the same material or materials, except that different materials may be used if their sag-tension characteristics and arrangement are such that the separations specified in note c of Table **85** are maintained under all service conditions.

3. Vertical spacing between conductors shall be not less than the following:

Span Length, Ft	Vertical Clearance between Conductors, In.
0–150	4
150–200	6
200–250	8
250–300	12

84. The basic separations required by the National Electrical Safety Code for vertical separation between horizontal crossarms are given in Sec. **85.** For exceptions and requirements for special conditions consult the National Electrical Safety Code Handbook. Vertical separations between crossarms shall be measured from center to center.

85. Vertical Separation of Crossarms Carrying Conductors in Feet
(National Electrical Safety Code)
(All voltages are between conductors)

Conductors usually at lower levels	Supply conductors, preferably at higher levels[f]				
	Open wires,[g] 0 to 750 volts; cables, all voltages, having effectively grounded continuous metal sheath or messenger	750 to 8,700 volts	8,700 to 15,000 volts	15,000 to 50,000 volts	
				Same utility	Different utilities
Communication conductors:					
General................................	4[a,b]	4	6	...	6
Used in operation of supply lines...........	2	2[c]	4	4	6
Supply conductors:					
0 to 750 volts.........................	2	2[d]	4	4	6
750 volts to 8,700 volts..................	...	2[d]	4	4	6
8,700 volts to 15,000 volts:					
If worked on alive with long-handled tools, and adjacent circuits are neither killed nor covered with shields or protectors...	...	...	4	4	6
If not worked on alive except when adjacent circuits (either above or below) are killed or covered by shields or protectors, or by the use of long-handled tools not requiring linemen to go between live wires................................	...	...	2	4[e]	4[e]
Exceeding 15,000 volts, but not exceeding 50,000 volts............................	...	...	...	4[e]	4[e]

[a] Where supply circuits of 550 volts or less, with transmitted power of 3,200 watts or less, are run below communication circuits in accordance with rule 220, B, 3, the clearance may be reduced to 2 ft.

[b] In localities where the practice has been established of placing, on jointly used poles, crossarms carrying supply circuits of less than 300 volts to ground and crossarms carrying communication circuits at a vertical separation less than specified in the table, such existing construction may be continued until the said poles are replaced provided that—

The minimum separation between existing crossarms is not less than 2 ft— and that—

Extensions to the existing construction shall conform to the clearance requirements specified in this table.

When communication conductors are all in cable, a supply crossarm carrying only wires of not more than 300 volts to ground may be placed at not less than 2 ft above the point of attachment of the cable to the pole provided that—

The nearest supply wire on such crossarm shall be at least 30 in. horizontally from the center of the pole—and that

The cable should be placed so as not otherwise to obstruct the climbing space.

[c] This shall be increased to 4 ft when the communication conductors are carried above supply conductors unless the communication-line-conductor size is that required for Grade C supply lines.

[d] Where conductors are operated by different utilities, a minimum vertical spacing of 4 ft is recommended.

[e] These values do not apply to adjacent crossarms carrying phases of the same circuit or circuits.

[f] A conductor that is effectively grounded throughout its length and is associated with a supply circuit of 0 to 22,000 volts may have the clearance specified for cables having effective grounded continuous metal sheath or messenger.

[g] Also insulated conductors supported on and cabled together with an effectively grounded messenger, all voltages.

86. Outside Wiring as Specified by the National Electrical Code. Scope. This article applies to electrical equipment and wiring for the supply of utilization equipment located on or attached to the outside of public and private buildings; or run between buildings, structures or poles on other premises served; but shall not apply to equipment or wiring of an electric or communication utility used in the exercise of its function as a utility.

1. APPLICATION OF OTHER ARTICLES. Application of other Articles, including additional requirements to specific cases of equipment and conductors, are as follows:

ARTICLES

200 – Polarity Identification.
210 – Branch Circuits.
215 – Feeders.
230 – Services.
250 – Grounding.
500 – Hazardous Locations, General.
510 – Hazardous Locations, Specific.
600 – Signs and Outline Lighting.
710 – Circuits and Equipment Operating at More than 600 Volts.
725 – Remote Control and Signal Circuits.
800 – Communication Circuits.
810 – Radio and Television Circuits.

2. CALCULATION OF LOAD.

a. Branch Circuits. The load on every outdoor branch circuit is to be determined by the applicable provisions of article 220, as given in Div. 3 of this book.

b. Feeders. The load to be expected on every outdoor feeder is to be determined by the procedure specified in article 220, as given in Div. 3 of this book.

3. CONDUCTOR COVERING. Where within 10 ft of any building or structure, open conductors supported on insulators shall be insulated or covered. Conductors in cables or raceways, except Type MI cable, shall be of the rubber-covered or thermoplastic type and in wet locations shall comply with section 310-5. Conductors for festoon lighting shall be of the rubber-covered or thermoplastic type.

4. SIZE OF CONDUCTORS. The ampacity of outdoor branch circuits and feeder conductors shall be according to the rating in Tables **18** to **21** of Div. 11, in order to carry the loads determined under condition 2.

5. MINIMUM SIZE OF CONDUCTOR.

a. Overhead Spans. Overhead conductors shall not be smaller than No. 10 for spans up to 50 ft in length, and not smaller than No. 8 for longer spans.

b. Festoon Lighting. Overhead conductors for festoon lighting shall not be smaller than No. 12 unless supported by messenger wires (see section 730-25).

Definition: Festoon lighting is a string of outdoor lights suspended between two points more than 15 ft apart.

c. Over 600 Volts. Overhead conductors operating at more than 600 volts shall not be smaller than No. 6 when open individual conductors or smaller than No. 8 when in cable.

6. LIGHTING EQUIPMENT ON POLES OR OTHER STRUCTURES.

a. For the supply of lighting equipment installed on a single pole or structure, the branch circuits shall comply with the requirements of article 210 and paragraph *c* below.

b. A common neutral may be used for a multiwire branch circuit consisting of the neutral and not more than 8 ungrounded conductors. The ampacity of the neutral conductor shall be not less than the calculated sum of the currents in all ungrounded conductors connected to any one phase of the circuit.

c. Branch circuits supplying only ballasts for permanently installed electric discharge lighting fixtures for area illumination mounted on poles clear of buildings or on other structures may operate at not to exceed 500 volts between conductors, provided:

(1) Fixtures on poles are mounted at a height of 22 ft or more, and on other structures at a height of 18 ft or more.

(2) The wiring system is grounded wherever autotransformers supplied therefrom raise the voltage to a value greater than the supply circuit voltage.

7. DISCONNECTION.

a. For branch circuits as required in article 210 as given in Div. 9 of this book.

b. For feeders as required in article 215, as given in Div. 9 of this book. (At each building supplied by a feeder see section 230-76 and Div. 9 of this book.)

8. OVERCURRENT PROTECTION.

a. For branch circuits as required in article 210 as given in Div. 9 of this book.

b. For feeders as required in article 215 as given in Div. 9 of this book.

9. WIRING ON BUILDINGS. Outside wiring on surfaces of buildings may be installed for circuits when not in excess of 600 volts as open conductors on insulating supports, as multiple-conductor cable approved for the purpose, as aluminum-sheathed cable or MI cable, in rigid-metal conduit, in bus ways as provided in article 364, or in electrical metallic tubing. Circuits of more than 600 volts shall be installed as provided for services in section 230-101. Circuits for signs and outline lighting shall be installed as provided in article 600.

10. CIRCUIT EXITS AND ENTRANCES. Where outside branch and feeder circuits exit from or enter into buildings the installation shall comply with those requirements of article 230 which apply to service-entrance conductors.

11. OPEN-CONDUCTOR SUPPORTS. Open conductors shall be supported on glass or porcelain knobs, racks, brackets, or strain insulators approved for the purpose.

12. FESTOON SUPPORTS. In spans exceeding 40 ft the conductors shall be supported by messenger wire supported by approved strain insulators. Conductors or messenger wires shall not be attached to any fire escape, downspout, or plumbing equipment.

13. OPEN-CONDUCTOR SPACINGS. Conductors shall conform to the following spacings:

a. *Open Conductors Exposed to the Weather.* As provided in section 230-47.

b. *Open Conductors Not Exposed to Weather.* As provided in section 230-48.

c. *Over 600 Volts.* As provided in section 230-101(c).

d. *Separation from Other Circuits.* Open conductors shall be separated from open conductors of other circuits or systems by not less than 4 in.

e. *Conductors on Poles.* Conductors on poles shall have a separation of not less than 1 ft except when placed on racks or brackets. Conductors supported on poles shall provide a horizontal climbing space not less than the following:

Power conductors, below communication conductors.. 30 in.
Power conductors alone or above communication conductors: Less than 300 volts........ 24 in.
 Exceeding 300 volts.. 30 in.
Communication conductors below power conductors... Same as power conductors
Communication conductors alone or above power conductors................................... No requirement

14. SUPPORTS OVER BUILDINGS. See section 230-25.

15. POINT OF ATTACHMENT TO BUILDINGS. See section 230-26.

16. MEANS OF ATTACHMENT TO BUILDINGS. See section 230-27.

17. CLEARANCE FROM GROUND. Open conductors of not over 600 volts shall conform to the following:

10 ft—above finished grade, sidewalks or from any platform or projection from which they might be reached;
12 ft—over residential driveways and commercial areas such as parking lots and drive-in establishments not subject to truck traffic;
15 ft—over commercial areas, parking lots, agricultural or other areas subject to truck traffic;
18 ft—over public streets, alleys, roads, and driveways on other than residential property.

NOTE. For clearances of conductors of over 600 volts see National Electrical Safety Code.

18. CLEARANCES FROM BUILDINGS FOR CONDUCTORS NOT IN EXCESS OF 600 VOLTS.

a. *Clearance over Roof.* Open conductors shall have a clearance of not less than 8 ft from the highest point of roofs over which they pass with the following exceptions:

Exception No. 1. Where the voltage between conductors does not exceed 300 volts and the roof has a slope of not less than 4 in. in 12 in., the clearance may be not less than 3 ft.

Exception No. 2.   Open conductors of 300 volts or less which do not pass over other than a maximum of 4 ft of the overhang portion of the roof for the purpose of terminating at a through-the-roof raceway or approved support may be maintained at a minimum of 18 in. from any portion of the roof over which they pass.

For service drop conductors see section 230-22(a).

b. Horizontal Clearances.   Open conductors not attached to a building shall have a minimum horizontal clearance of 36 in.

c. Final Spans.   Final spans of feeders or branch circuits to buildings which they supply or from which they are fed may be attached to the building, but they shall be kept 3 ft from windows, doors, porches, fire escapes, or similar locations.

d. Zone for Fire Ladders.   Where buildings exceed three stories, or 50 ft in height, overhead lines shall be arranged where practicable so that a clear space (or zone) at least 6 ft wide will be left either adjacent to the buildings or beginning not over 8 ft from them, to facilitate the raising of ladders when necessary for fire fighting.

NOTE.   For clearance of conductors over 600 volts, consult National Electrical Safety Code.

19. MECHANICAL PROTECTION OF CONDUCTORS.   Mechanical protection of conductors on buildings, structures, or poles shall be as provided for services (section 230-46).

20. CONDUCTORS ENTERING BUILDINGS.   Conductors entering buildings shall be as provided for services (sections 230-44, 230-49, and 230-51).

21. MULTIPLE-CONDUCTOR CABLES ON EXTERIOR SURFACES OF BUILDINGS.   Multiple-conductor cables on exterior surfaces of buildings shall be as provided for service cable (section 230-50).

22. RACEWAYS ON EXTERIOR SURFACES OF BUILDINGS.   Raceways on exterior surfaces of buildings shall be made raintight and suitably drained.

23. UNDERGROUND CIRCUITS.   Underground circuits shall be as provided for services (sections 230-32 and 230-33).

24. OUTDOOR LIGHTING EQUIPMENT – LAMP HOLDERS.   Lamp holders shall be of molded composition, or other approved material of the weatherproof type, and where they are attached as pendants shall have the connections to the circuit wires staggered. Where lamp holders have terminals of a type that puncture the insulation and make contact with the conductors, they shall be attached only to conductors of the stranded type.

25. OUTDOOR LIGHTING EQUIPMENT – LOCATION OF LAMPS.   Location of lamps for outdoor lighting shall be below all live conductors, transformers, or other electric equipment, unless clearances or other safeguards are provided for relamping operations, or unless the installation is controlled by a disconnecting means which can be locked in the open position.

87. Tying in Wires.   Normally the wires should rest in the insulator grooves as shown in Fig. 62A, but where there is a side stress, the wires should be so arranged that the pull comes against the insulators rather than away from them (Fig. 62B).   A single tie for the smaller wires is shown in Fig. 63, I, and a back tie for the larger wires is shown in II.   The single tie wire is about 12 in. long, and the back tie about 18 in. long.   The back tie is made as follows: Bend the tie around the insulator under the line wire, with 4 in. on one side of the insulator and the balance on the other side. Wrap the short end three times around the line wire, leaving a space equal to the diameter of the tie wire between successive wraps.   Now wrap the long end of the tie

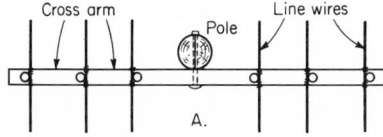

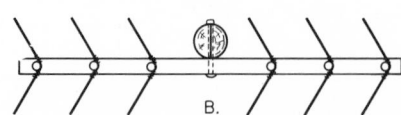

Arrangement on straight lines   Arrangement where there is a side strain

FIG. 62   *Positions of wires in insulator grooves.*

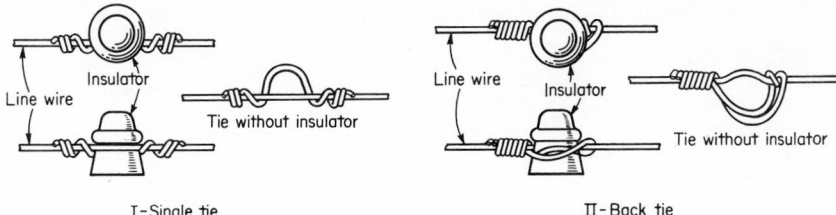

I–Single tie   II–Back tie

FIG. 63 *Methods of tying. Preferably the tie wires should not be cut off flush as shown above. Instead their ends should be permitted to stick out or to lie along the line wires. This is to facilitate their removal.*

wire three times completely around the line wire, then back around the insulator, and wrap it in the spaces left between the wraps of the other end of the tie wire. Refer to Fig. 63 for instructions regarding cutting of tie wires.

88. Different types of insulator ties which have been standardized by a western power company are shown in Fig. 64 and Table **89.** The company uses medium-hard-drawn line wire. Although good ties can be made with a medium-hard-drawn, weather-proof tie on a weatherproof line wire, medium-hard-drawn ties are not desirable on

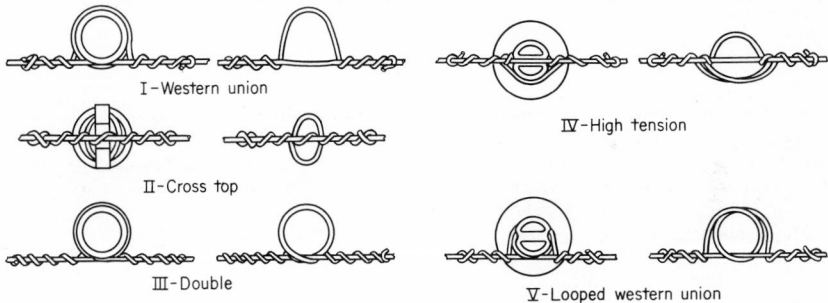

I–Western union

II–Cross top

III–Double

IV–High tension

V–Looped western union

FIG. 64 *Ties of the different types used in ordinary distribution systems (see Table* **89**).

bare wires, as the bending radius is too small for these stiff wires. Hence, annealed bare-wire ties are used for bare line wires. Annealed ties can be cut from purchased annealed copper. Do not use a tie wire twice, as, after once being bent and strained, it will be brittle. The following table of sizes has been recommended for ordinary stresses. For very heavy stresses heavier tie wires should be used.

Line wire, size	Tie wire, size	Kind of tie	Line wire, size	Tie wire, size	Kind of tie
6	6	Single	1	4	Back
4	6	Single	2/0 and larger	2	Back
2	4	Single			

Tie wire should usually have the same kind of insulation as the line wire which it confines. The National Electrical Code requires this on indoor work, and it is also good practice on outdoor work.

89. Table Showing Types of Insulator Ties for Different Services

Size of line wire, gage or in.	Insulator	Top or side	Tie material	Tie length, in.	Type of tie	Fig. 64
			Copper			
6 or 4 W P	D.G.D.P.	Side	6 W P m.h.d.	25	Western Union	I
2 W P	D.G.D.P.	Side	4 W P m.h.d.	27	Western Union	I
1/0 to 4/0 W P	Cable	Top	4 W P m.h.d.	36	Cross-top	II
1/0 to 4/0 W P	Cable	Side	4 W P m.h.d.	30	Western Union	I
6 or 4 bare	D.G.D.P.	Side	6 bare ann.	27	Double	III
6 or 4 bare	11 kv	Top	6 bare ann.	40	High-tension	IV
2 bare	11 kv	Top	4 bare ann.	40	High-tension	IV
1/0 to 4/0 bare	11 kv	Top	2 bare ann.	44	High-tension	IV
6 to 4 bare	11 kv	Side	6 bare ann.	40	Looped W.U.	V
2 bare	11 kv	Side	4 bare ann.	40	Looped W.U.	V
1/0 to 4/0 bare	11 kv	Side	2 bare ann.	48	Looped W.U.	V
			Steel			
$\frac{1}{4}$ and $\frac{5}{16}$	D.G.D.P.	Side	1 strand. $\frac{5}{16}$ in.	27	Double	III
$\frac{1}{4}$ and $\frac{5}{16}$	11 kv	Top	1 strand, $\frac{5}{16}$ in.	44	High-tension	IV
$\frac{3}{8}$	11 kv	Top	1 strand, $\frac{3}{8}$ in.	44	High-tension	IV
$\frac{1}{4}$ and $\frac{5}{16}$	11 kv	Side	1 strand, $\frac{5}{16}$ in.	48	Looped W.U.	V
$\frac{3}{8}$	11 kv	Side	1 strand, $\frac{3}{8}$ in.	48	Looped W.U.	V

90. The bare tie wires for uninsulated line wires should always be of the same metal as the line wire. If dissimilar metals are employed, electrolytic corrosion and a consequent weakening and possible breakage of the line wire at the tying point may result. That is, bare copper tie wires should always be used on bare copper line wires and galvanized-iron tie wires on galvanized-iron line wires.

91. In making up line-wire ties, the tie wire should not be drawn too tightly around the line wire. The tendency of the beginner is to do this, with the result that the line wire is weakened and will probably sever when it is first subjected to an unusual stress such as that which is likely to occur when a low temperature prevails.

92. In making ties on ACSR wire (see Div. 2) the conductor must first be reinforced by wrapping with armor rods twisted around the conductor with the aid of two special wrenches.

Armor rods are shipped in sets (bundles) with the ends taped and with the center marked. Remove the tape from one end of the set and thread the rods through the two armor-rod wrenches, making sure that both the wrenches open between the *same two rods*. Leaving the set taped at one end keeps the rods from sliding while the assembly is being sent aloft and keeps ends even while making the first twist.

Center the armor rods on the conductor over the point of support. Open the wrenches and then close them with the rods around the conductor (Fig. 65, I). Shift the wrenches on the rods to such a position that the middle third of the armor rods will be twisted with the first turn of the wrenches. Rotate the wrenches counterclockwise to make the lay of the rods in the *same* direction as the lay of the cable. Twist the rods to give them a permanent set, so that the wrenches do not tend to spring back. After twisting the middle third, cut the remaining tape and slide the wrenches half way to the ends. Turn the wrenches and twist the rods as before. Finally slide the wrenches as close as possible to the ends, twisting this last section the same as for previous settings.

The rods should be twisted snugly with a smooth lay. If they are twisted too tightly, there is a tendency to force one or more rods out of the layer, and the rods will stand away from the cable so that the assembly can be slipped along the conductor before the armor-rod clips are applied. There is a "stopping point," which can be felt after a little practice.

The armor-rod (V-bolt) clips should be applied about 1½ in. from the ends of the

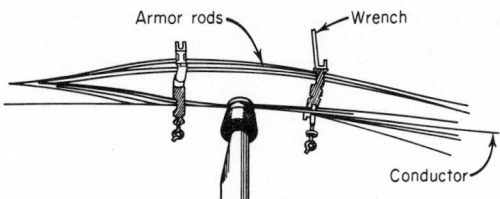

I – Initial step. Wrenches ready to be closed around conductor
leaving one end of rods taped.

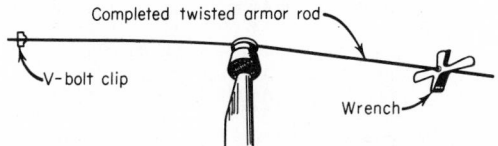

II – Final step. Wrench in final position ready for application
of second V-bolt clip.

FIG. 65 *Installing armor rods at insulator support for ACSR wire. (Aluminum Company of America.)*

assembly, which can best be accomplished by installing and tightening the V bolts while the armor-rod wrenches are still in their final twisting position (Fig. 65, II). This procedure leaves the ends of the rods slightly flared away from the conductor. If the wrenches are removed prior to tightening the armor-rod clips, the ends of the rods may have to be flared as a separate operation.

After installation of the armor rods the ties are made as shown in Fig. 66. Figure 66, I, shows a top tie with the conductor on top of the insulator, and Fig. 66, II, shows the conductor tied on the side groove of the insulator. Above each view is shown a sketch of the manner in which the tie wire is wrapped and looped.

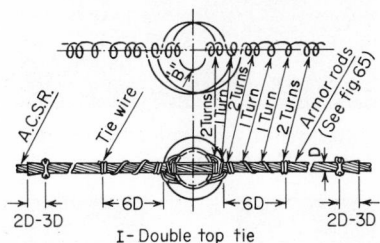

I – Double top tie

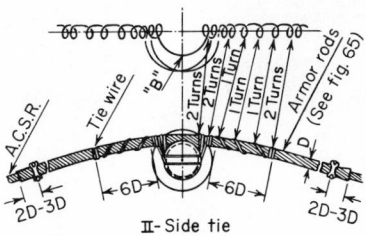

II – Side tie

FIG. 66 *Ties for ACSR wire. (Aluminum Company of America.)*

93. For ties on copperweld wire use annealed copper tie wires of the size given in the following table as recommended by the Copperweld Steel Co.:

Size of Conductor	Size of[1] Tie Wire	Length of Tie Wire[2]	
		Top Tie	Side Tie
3-Wire Stranded Conductors			
3 No. 6 AWG	6 AWG	54 in.	60 in.
3 No. 7 AWG	6 AWG	52 in.	58 in.
3 No. 8 AWG	6 AWG	50 in.	56 in.
3 No. 9 AWG	6 AWG	48 in.	54 in.
3 No. 10 AWG	8 AWG	44 in.	50 in.
3 No. 12 AWG	8 AWG	44 in.	50 in.
Type F Copperweld-copper Conductors			
1/0F	6 AWG	56 in.	62 in.
1F	6 AWG	54 in.	60 in.
2F	6 AWG	54 in.	60 in.
Copperweld-copper 3-wire Stranded Conductors			
2A	6 AWG	56 in.	62 in.
3A	6 AWG	54 in.	60 in.
4A	6 AWG	52 in.	58 in.
5A	6 AWG	50 in.	56 in.
6A	8 AWG	46 in.	52 in.
7A	8 AWG	44 in.	50 in.
8A	8 AWG	44 in.	50 in.
8C	8 AWG	44 in.	50 in.
8D	8 AWG	44 in.	50 in.
9½D	8 AWG	44 in.	50 in.

[1] Sizes listed apply to annealed copper tie wires. When using annealed copperweld for tie wire, size should be two gage sizes smaller than listed for annealed copper.
[2] Includes 4 in. additional length on each end for convenience in applying tie.

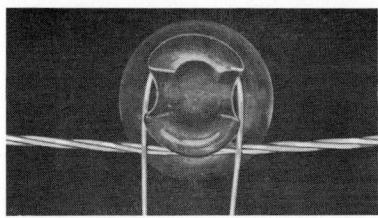

1. *Bend tie wire around insulator above conductor to form a U. Both legs of the tie wire should be of equal length after bending.*

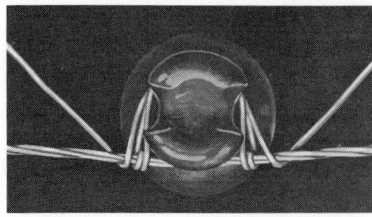

II. *Holding tie wire tightly against insulator, throw two tight close wraps around conductor on each side of the insulator; then cross legs of tie wire around insulator.*

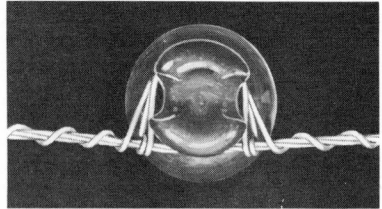

III. *Finish like top tie with six tight 45-deg spiral wraps on each side of the insulator. Bend back ends and cut off extra length of tie wire close to conductor.*

FIG. 67A   *Side tie for copperweld wire. (Copperweld Steel Co.)*

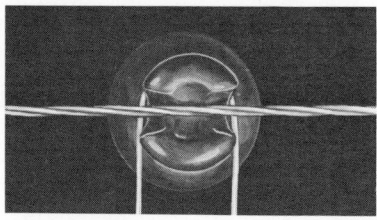

I. *Bend annealed tie wire of proper size and length around insulator under the conductor, forming a U. Both legs of tie wire should be of equal length after bending.*

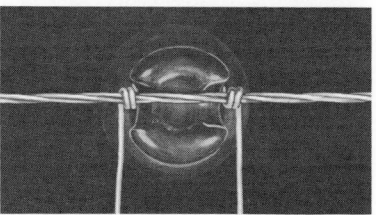

II. *Holding the tie wire tightly against the insulator throw two tight close wraps around the conductor on each side of the insulator, keeping these wraps snugly against the insulator.*

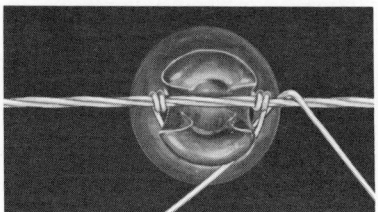

III. *Cross the legs of the tie wire around the insulator, right to left and left to right.*

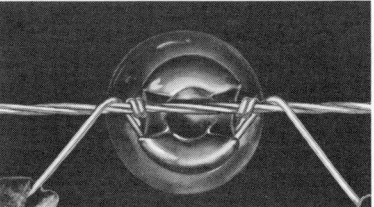

IV. *With both legs of the tie wire crossed, tightly wrap each leg spirally around the conductor at an angle of 45 deg.*

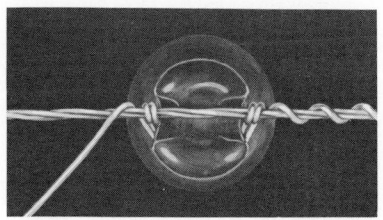

V. *Complete six spiral 45-deg wraps on each side of the insulator, bending back the ends and cutting them off short.*

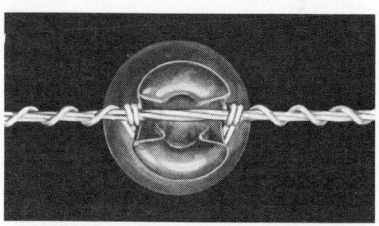

VI. *The finished top tie when made properly and tightly will greatly reduce any possibility of conductor chafing at the insulator.*

FIG. 67B   *Top tie for copperweld wire.   (Copperweld Steel Co.)*

For top ties on copperweld wire, the type shown in Fig. 67B is recommended.   For side ties, the one shown in Fig. 67A with three loops around the insulator is used.

NOTES ON TYING PRACTICE

1. Use only fully annealed tie wire.

2. Use a size of tie wire which can be readily handled, yet one which will provide adequate strength.

3. Use a length of tie wire sufficient for making the complete tie, including end allowance for gripping with the hands.   The extra length should be cut from each end after the tie is completed.

4. A good tie should:

a. Provide a secure binding between line wire, insulator, and tie wire.

b. Have positive contacts between the line wire and the tie wire to avoid any chafing contacts.

c. Reinforce line wire in the vicinity of insulator.

5. The ties illustrated can and should be applied without the use of pliers.

6. Avoid nicking the line wire.

7. Do not use a tie wire which has been previously used.

8. Do not use hard-drawn wires for tying or fire-burned wire, which is usually either only partially annealed or injured by overheating.

9. Careful workmanship is essential.

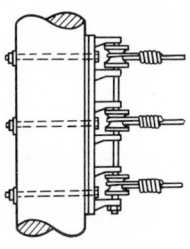

On secondary rack

FIG. 68 *Low-volt-age dead ends. (Hubbard & Co.)*

94. For dead-ending of line wires at the end of a run or at corners, various types of construction may be used. For low-voltage, secondary rack construction, a rack may be located on the front of the pole and the tension taken by bolts through the pole (Fig. 68). The wires are looped around the rack insulators, and the end of the wire is wrapped around the line conductor. Other low-voltage dead ends may be made up as in Fig. 69. In many current installations a single-wire bracket, similar to the one shown in Fig. 69, I, is used to attach triplex or fourplex cables, consisting of two or three insulated cables which are spiral-wrapped around a bare messenger wire (usually the neutral of the supply). For heavier loads a low-voltage dead end on a crossarm can be made by using a strain insulator as shown in Fig. 70, I. For higher voltages one or more suspension insulators with a clamp to grip the conductor, as shown in Fig. 70, II and III, can be used. Instead of the conductor clamp the conductor can be looped around a dead-end thimble (Fig. 71).

95. Where wires are carried through trees so that they would rub against branches, special tree wire (Fig. 72, I) should be used. However, wires through trees should be avoided if at all possible. This wire has a tougher insulation which will resist abrasion from the branches better than weather-proof wire. Where the tree branches are more or less continuous, the tree wire should be used exclusively. If there is a span or more of clearing, it will be economical to splice in weatherproof wire to run through the clear space. For especially severe conditions a length of tree-wire molding (Fig. 72, II, III, and IV) should be added to the wire where the wire passes close to heavy limbs or tree trunks. In some cases a tree insulator (Fig. 73) can be screwed to the limb or trunk of the tree. This insulator has a re-movable pin and roller (Fig. 73, II) so that the wire can be inserted without cutting and the pin replaced. The roller allows the wire to move freely without being cut. Wires should never be attached rigidly to trees because the swaying of the tree might break the wires.

96. Wire and Wire Sizes for Electric Light and Power Lines. No wire smaller than No. 6 is used in good construction for line wire. No. 8 is sometimes used for services not more than 75 ft long that do not cross a street. Solid wires are often used for sizes up to and including No. 2/0, and cable (stranded wire) is used for larger conductors. Triple-braid weather-

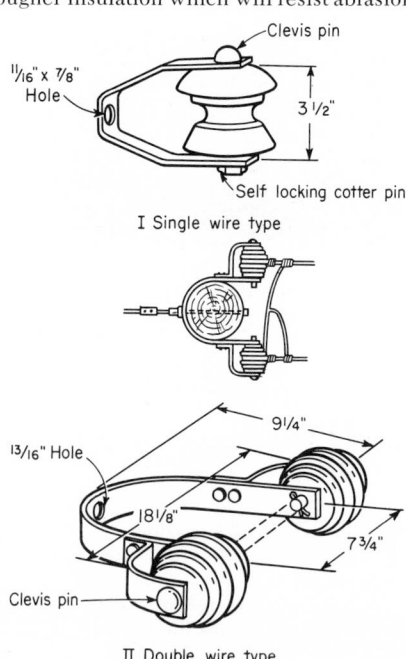

I Single wire type

II Double wire type

FIG. 69 *Dead-end insulators. (Line Material Industries.)*

proof is the standard insulation of aerial line wires. Annealed or soft-drawn wire is preferable to hard-drawn for services and secondary distribution lines because it is more readily handled and, in the sizes used, has ample tensile strength. Hard-drawn copper wire or steel-reinforced aluminum cable is preferable for transmission lines and feeders.

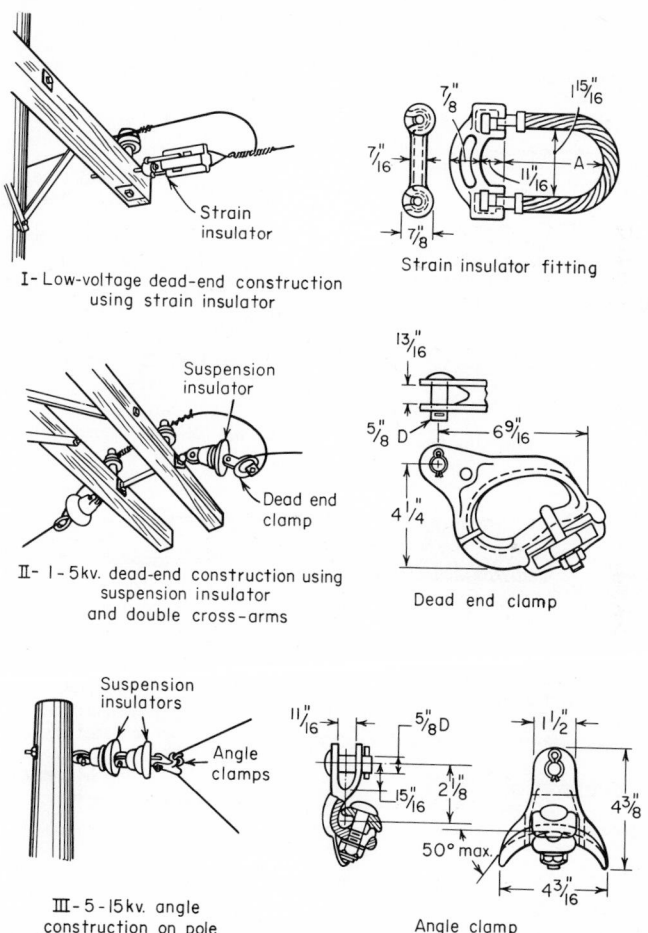

FIG. 70 *Types of clamps and dead-end construction.* (*Ohio Brass Co.*)

97. Stringing Wire. There are two methods, the choice depending on local conditions and the size and length of the circuit. By one method a reel of wire is set at one end of the line and a rope carried 1,500 or 2,000 ft over the crossarms and attached to the wire, which is then drawn over the arms. The other way is to place the reel on a cart, and after the end of the wire has been secured to the last pole, the cart is started and the wire paid out till the second pole is reached, and then the wire is hoisted up and laid on the arm. Wire should always be paid out from the coil, the coil revolving, so that the wire will not be twisted. Where wire is not received on reels, it should be placed on them before paying out.

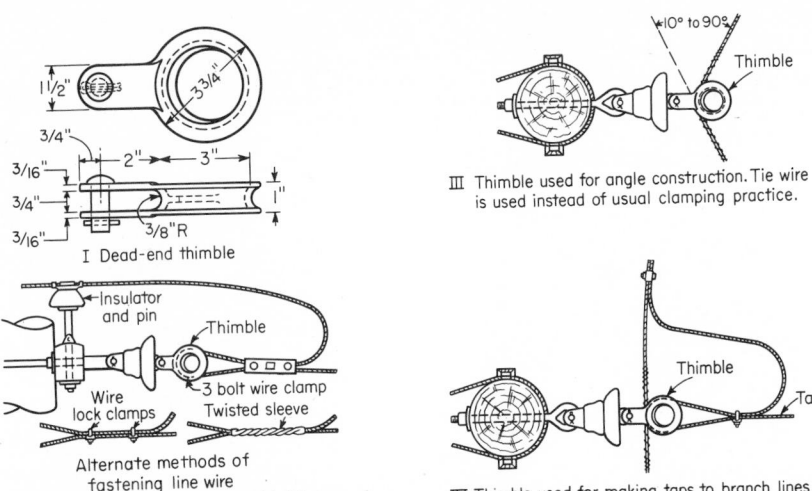

1 1/2"
3 3/4"
3/4"
2"
3"
3/16"
3/4"
1"
3/16"
3/8" R
I Dead-end thimble
10° to 90°
Thimble
III Thimble used for angle construction. Tie wire is used instead of usual clamping practice.
Insulator and pin
Thimble
3 bolt wire clamp
Wire lock clamps
Twisted sleeve
Alternate methods of fastening line wire
II Thimble used for dead-ending. With this type of construction the suspension insulator can be replaced without cutting the jumper and making a new dead-end.
Thimble
Tap
IV Thimble used for making taps to branch lines. The through conductor is tied in at the clevis

FIG. 71 *Dead-end construction with dead-end thimble.* (*Ohio Brass Co.*)

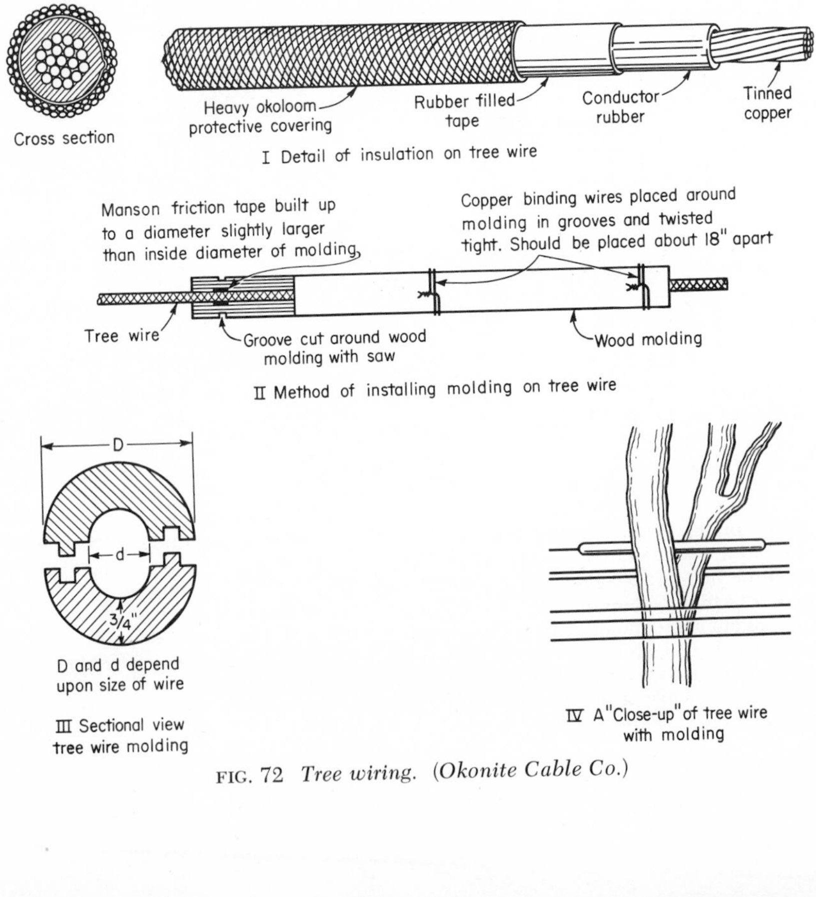

Cross section
Heavy okoloom protective covering
Rubber filled tape
Conductor rubber
Tinned copper
I Detail of insulation on tree wire
Manson friction tape built up to a diameter slightly larger than inside diameter of molding
Copper binding wires placed around molding in grooves and twisted tight. Should be placed about 18" apart
Tree wire
Groove cut around wood molding with saw
Wood molding
II Method of installing molding on tree wire
D
d
3/4"
D and d depend upon size of wire
III Sectional view tree wire molding
IV A "Close-up" of tree wire with molding

FIG. 72 *Tree wiring.* (*Okonite Cable Co.*)

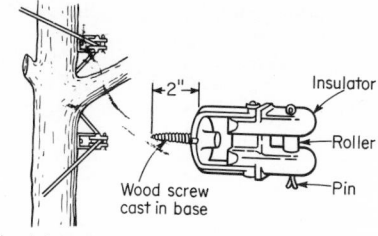

FIG. 73 *Tree insulator.* (*Line Material Industries.*)

I Insulator mounted on tree   II Detail of tree insulator

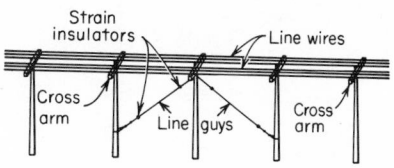

FIG. 74 *Line guys.*

POLE-LINE GUYING

98. Guying. Probably there are not so many guys on pole lines as there should be to ensure continuity of service and minimum maintenance expense. Lines should be guyed not for normal conditions but for the most severe conditions that are apt to obtain. The guys should be frequent and heavy enough to sustain the line after the heaviest snowstorm or during the worst possible windstorm. A guy should be used on every pole where the tension of the wires tends to pull the pole from its normal position.

Terminal poles should always be head-guyed, and on lines carrying three or more crossarms the two poles next to the terminal pole should also be head guyed to distribute the stress.

Line guys are installed on straight pole lines to reinforce them against the excess stresses introduced by storms. It is good practice to install head line guys, as shown in Fig. 74, at about every twentieth pole. This applies only to lines carrying more than one crossarm.

The installation of additional side guys, arranged at right angles to the line, to trees, stubs, or anchors is recommended. The side guys are attached to the same pole as the head guys.

Side guys should be installed at curves, the guys taking the direction of radii of the curves. Figure 5 shows a table that gives the number of side guys required for a given line with a given "pull." The pull is the distance from the pole to a line joining two points in the line 100 ft on either side of the pole (see Fig. 5).

Poles on either side of a long span should be head-guyed as shown in Fig. 75, I.

Lines on steep hills should be guyed as shown in Fig. 75, II, with head guys.

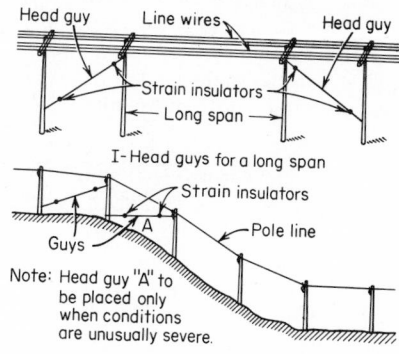

I–Head guys for a long span

Note: Head guy "A" to be placed only when conditions are unusually severe.

II–Head guys at a steep hill.

FIG. 75 *Head guy locations.*

Poles at each side of a railroad crossing, important highway crossing, or a crossing over another wire line should be head-guyed away from the crossing as in Fig. 75, I.

Guy wires should be kept more than 8 ft from the ground where possible to prevent persons from making accidental contact with them. A clearance of at least 3 ft should be maintained between guys and electric wires; otherwise changes in temperature may cause the wires to come in contact.

99. A guy assembly consists of the following parts:
1. Attachment to pole being guyed.
2. Guy wire containing one or two strain insulators.

3. Attachment to stub pole or to lower part of another pole or ground anchor, anchor rod, attachment of strand, and guard.

100. Some of the methods of making up a guy on a pole are shown in Fig. 76. The method of Fig. 76, I, is an easy one when some of the other materials are not at hand. The methods of Fig. 76, II and III, make a neater looking job when the hardware is

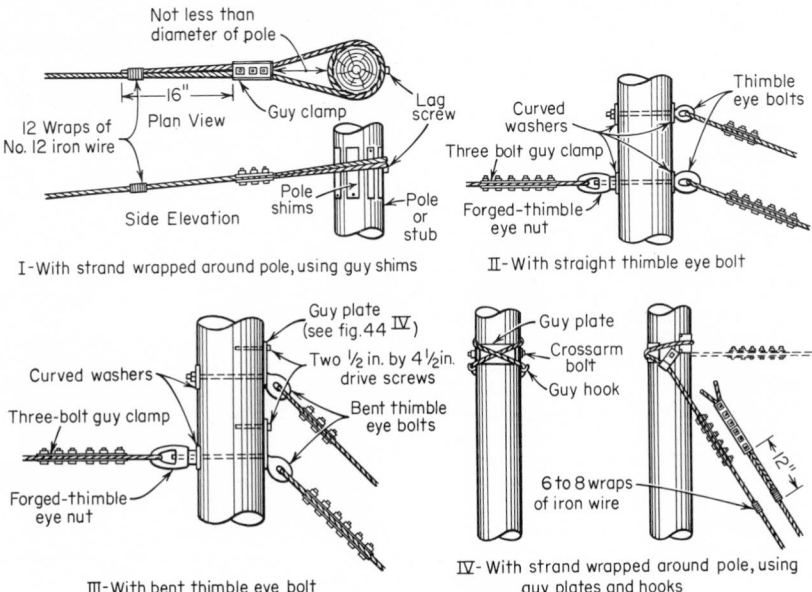

FIG. 76 *Methods of attaching guys to pole.* (*General Electric Co.*)

available. The method of Fig. 76, IV, is used at a stub pole. Refer to Sec. **55** for a discussion of the hardware required. Where there is but one guy per pole, it is made

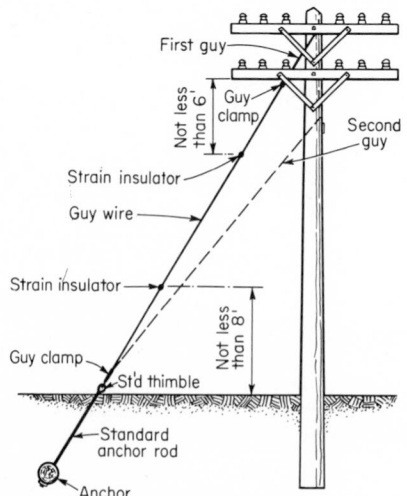

FIG. 77 *An anchor-guyed pole.*

around the pole just under the top crossarm as shown in Figs. 77 and 78. Where there are two guys to the pole, one is made up just under the top crossarm and one just under the bottom crossarm. Where more than two guys are used, the additional ones should be spaced as equally as possible between the top and the bottom guys that are made up under the top and bottom crossarms, respectively. Where there are two or more guys to a pole, each should be independent of the others. The different guy wires should not cross one another. Where two or more guys support a pole, a turnbuckle should be inserted in all but one to equalize the stresses.

101. Guy-wire Insulation. Strain insulators should be inserted in all guy wires to poles carrying electric-lighting or power wires. Two insulators should be inserted in each guy. One is located at least 6 ft from the pole itself or 6 ft below the lowest line wire. The other is located at least

6 ft from the lower end of the guy and at least 8 ft from the ground. The two strain insulators are sometimes coupled in series in short guys.

The assembly make-up of a strain insulator for a guy is shown in Fig. 79. The two ends of the guy strand are looped through the separate holes in the insulator. The guy-wire clamps hold the wire from slipping, and the No. 12 wrapping wire secures the end of the strand to the guy wire and provides a neat appearance for the assembly. Suitable clamps can be used in lieu of the No. 12 wrapping wire at guy-wire ends.

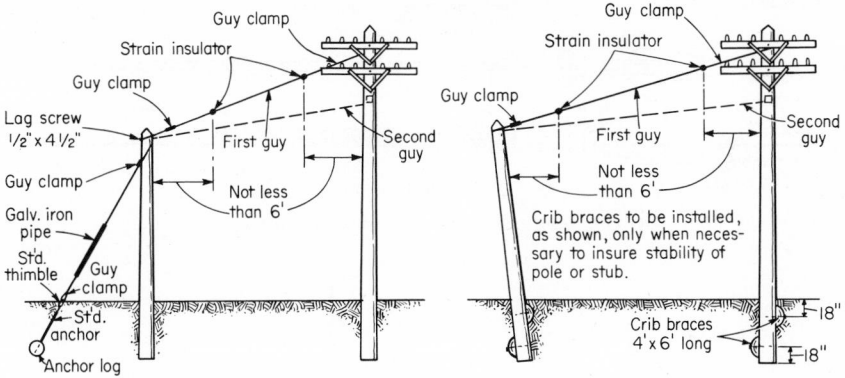

FIG. 78 *Poles guyed to stubs.*

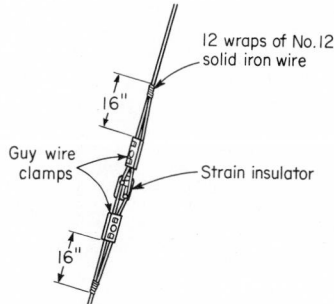

FIG. 79 *Method of making up a strain insulator in a guy strand. (Hubbard & Co.)*

101A. The number and size of clamps to use for each looped back connection on a guy strand are as follows:

Breaking strength of guy strand, lb	No. of clamps	Type of clamp	Breaking strength of guy strand, lb	No. of clamps	Type of clamp
4,000	1	Two bolt	10,000	2	Three bolt
6,000	1	Three bolt	16,000	3	Three bolt

102. The attachment of the guy strand to the anchor rod is shown in Fig. 80. Refer to Sec. **54** and Fig. 42 for description of anchor rods. The eye of the guy rod should extend about 3 ft above the surface of the earth. Guy rods should not be installed where they will interfere with traffic. A guy protector guard (see Sec. **58**) extending to about 8 ft above the ground should be placed over anchor guy wires near roadways, as shown in Fig. 78. The foot of an anchor guy should be as far away from the foot of the pole as possible—at least a distance equal to one-fourth the height of the pole.

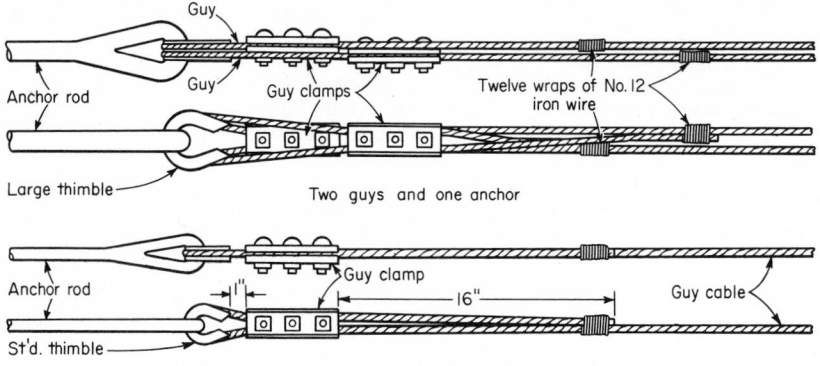

FIG. 80 *Methods of making up guys on guy rods.*

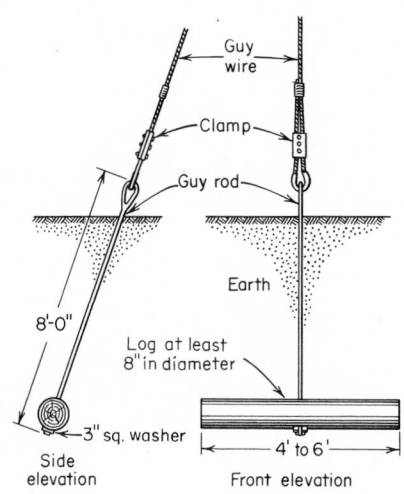

FIG. 81 *A guy rod and anchor.*

103. Anchors can be made from logs cut from the tops of old poles (Fig. 81), or patented metal or concrete anchors can be used. Figure 82 shows a variety of modern guy anchors which provide an effective support for guy rods. Table **104** gives the minimum size for anchor logs and rods and the depth of setting for anchors.

104. Size of Anchor Logs and Depth of Setting for Anchors

Size and number of guys	Min size of round logs for good soil	Length of rod below ground, ft	Size of guy rod
One No. 6 Wire or one 4,000 lb	3 ft × 6 in.	4	7 ft × ½ in.
One 6,000 lb	3 ft × 7 in.	4½	8 ft × ⅝ in.
One 10,000 lb	4 ft × 8 in.	5½	9 ft × ¾ in.
One 16,000 lb	5 ft × 10 in.	6½	10 ft × 1 in.
Two 6,000 lb	5 ft × 8 in.	5½	9 ft × 1 in.
Two 10,000 lb	5 ft × 10 in.	6 or 6½	10 ft × 1¼ in.
Two 16,000 lb	6 ft × 12 in.	6½ or 7	11 ft × 1½ in.

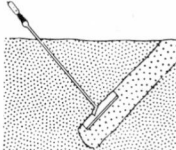

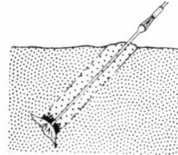

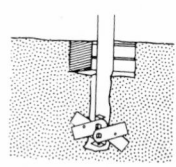

PLATE ANCHORS are used for general anchoring; are made of malleable iron or steel plates. They provide excellent holding power because pull is against undisturbed earth.

EXPANDING ANCHORS are used for general anchoring. Size of anchors in folded position ranges from 6 to 12 in. dia. Expanded sizes range from 50 to 300 sq. in.

KEY ANCHORS, sometimes called pole keys, are used where standard guying is impossible because of sidewalks, property restrictions, etc. Additional keying is necessary at ground level.

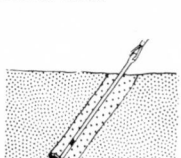

SCREW TYPE ANCHORS can be selected for general anchoring in gravel, sand, clay, fill, silt, and with extension, swamp soils. The corkscrew-like blade is made of drop-forged steel. No anchor hole is required; anchor is screwed into the ground with a wrench or bar.

ROCK ANCHORS are used for anchoring in rock, rocky soil or masonry. The expanding rock anchor is made of malleable iron, develops tremendous holding power through a wedging self-action.

CONE ANCHORS are made of steel and are used in bed rock, laminated rock, slate, sandstone, shale, hardpan, gravel, and medium-firm clay. Sizes range from 6 to 23 in. dia. It develops adequate holding power in class 2 soil through wedging action.

FIG. 82 *Various types of modern guy anchors.*

For the depth and holding strength of patented anchors the catalogs of the particular manufacturer must be consulted.

105. Patented guy anchors can be used in certain kinds of soil very effectively. Figure 83 shows one kind of anchor that is screwed into the earth with a wrench. The resistance of this sort of anchor to withdrawal from compact homogeneous soils is not determined by the weight of a column of earth the diameter of the anchor screw, but is determined by that of a cone with sides slanting at 45 deg and having the point of the anchor as an apex. Figure 84 illustrates this and shows the formula used for computing the withdrawal resistance. Figure 84 shows the anchor inserted perpendicularly, but an anchor should always be inserted at the same angle that the guy wire assumes so the rod of the anchor will be in a direct line with the guy wire. Section **106** gives the actual resistances to withdrawal of the anchors.

106. The actual holding power of patented guy anchors is an uncertain quantity, except in hard clays ("adobe," "hardpan," or "gumbo") for which Carpenter's formula (Fig. 84) can be used. The safest procedure is to test the anchor's resistance to withdraw in the soil in which it is to be used. A dynamometer can be employed for measuring the pull. Anchor manufacturers will gladly ship anchors on approval for tests and 30 days' trial. In general, the 5-in. Matthews Scrulix anchor (Fig. 84) should, in other than the hard clays, be used only for the lightest strains, say 1,100 to 2,500 lb, the 6-in. for 1,500 to 2,500 lb, the 7-in. for 2,500 to 5,000 lb, the 8-in. for 5,000 to 7,000 lb,

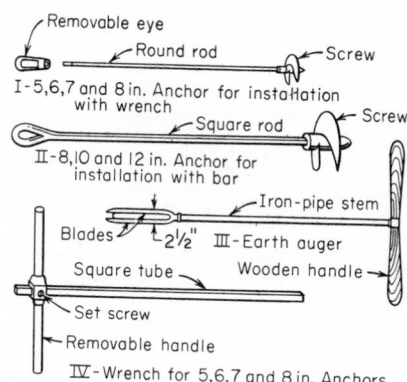

FIG. 83 *Matthews Scrulix anchors and wrenches.*

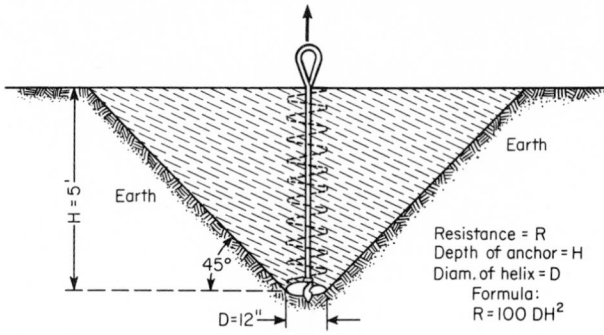

$H=5', D=12''.$ Then $R=100DH^2$ or $R=100 \times 12 \times 25$ or $R=30,000$ lbs.

FIG. 84   *Illustrating Carpenter's formula for resistance of Matthews anchor to withdrawal.*

the 10-in. for 7,000 to 10,000 lb, and the 12-in. for 10,000 to 12,000 lb. These holding powers are based on the anchor being screwed into the earth for a depth of at least 5 ft. For anchorages under shallow strands of water or in swampy or caving ground, the 8-, 10-, and 12-in. anchors having the square rods are very convenient.

107. Directions for Installing Matthews Guy Anchors. 5-, 6-, 7-, AND 8-IN. WITH RODS. Remove the eye of the anchor; pass the rod through the wrench and replace the eye, which will serve to hold the wrench rigidly to the anchor; then screw the anchor in, at the same angle as the guy wire is to run, as far as ground conditions will permit. When in as far as possible, remove the eye and pull out the wrench. Then replace the eye, thus making anchor ready for guy wires. The handle bars of the wrench are adjustable and held in place with a setscrew. They can be moved back as the anchor screws in.

8-, 10-, 12-IN. WITH RODS. Place bar or other lever in eye of anchor and screw it in as far as ground conditions will permit, always at the angle that the guy wire is to run. Time will be saved and the anchor will start easier if a few spadefuls of earth are removed before starting anchor. When the anchor is set, attach the guy strand to the eye. Always pull anchor back as far as possible before finally tying the guy wire.

IN DRY, HARD GROUND. In setting all anchors in hard ground, the work will be much easier if a small hole is first made with an earth auger (Fig. 83), a crowbar, or a wood auger with a long shank. This renders the insertion of the anchor easier. A little water poured down this hole before starting the anchor will help considerably where the ground is hard and dry. In installing 8-, 10-, and 12-in. anchors in very hard ground, clamp a lever to the rod by means of a chain a foot or so above the ground. As the anchor is screwed down, the lever can be moved up. The anchor will start more easily if a few spadefuls of earth are removed at the angle desired to set the guy. If a man stands on the helix of the anchor when starting until the point bites the ground, it will assist.

In localities where loose gravel or small flat rock occurs, drill a hole with an earth auger, a digging bar, or a crowbar, as suggested above. If a small rock is encountered, it can be broken by the bar. If a large rock is "discovered," the bar can be removed and the hole drilled in another place. This will allow the use of anchors in many places where otherwise it would seem impossible to install them.

108. The methods of installing stub guys are shown in Fig. 78. The stubs should be long enough so that the guy wires will clear roadways by at least 18 ft, sidewalks by 15 ft, and electric wires by 3 ft. Stubs are used only when a line cannot be guyed properly to trees or poles. Stubs should satisfy the specification for poles as given in Sec. 8.

109. In guying to a tree, tree blocks (Fig. 85) should be used, and the wire should pass but once around the tree. Tree guying is undesirable and should not be done unless absolutely necessary. Guys should preferably be attached to trunks or to limbs that

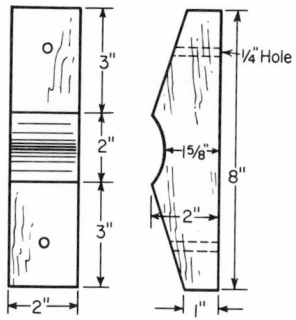

FIG. 85-I *Details of tree blocks.*

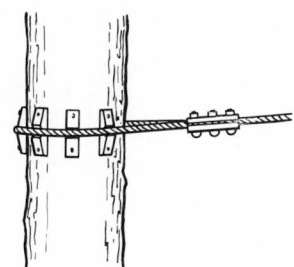

FIG. 85-II *Guy wire fastened to tree.*

are not less than 8 in. in diameter. Do not attach to a limb that will swing with the wind and sway the pole. Enough tree blocks should be used so that the guy wire cannot touch the tree.

110. Crossarm guys are used where the pull on a crossarm is unbalanced. Figures 48, 86, and 87 show examples. Crossarm guys usually extend from the arm to a pole or stub, but sometimes for light strains the Y or "bridle" guy (Fig. 88) is used.

111. A line must be thoroughly guyed where it crosses a road. Figures 89 and 90 show two methods of holding a line at such a point. The method involving the use of side guys is preferable, but the other one will give good service where side guys cannot be installed.

112. Where it is impossible to secure guying privileges along the desired route for a line, or where obstructions make guying difficult, the problem is generally solved by the use of self-supporting poles, a construction commonly referred to as "hog guying." This method of strengthening a pole is especially useful on corners, around curves, and at points where space is too limited for ordinary guying. The method of hog guying is illustrated in Fig. 91.

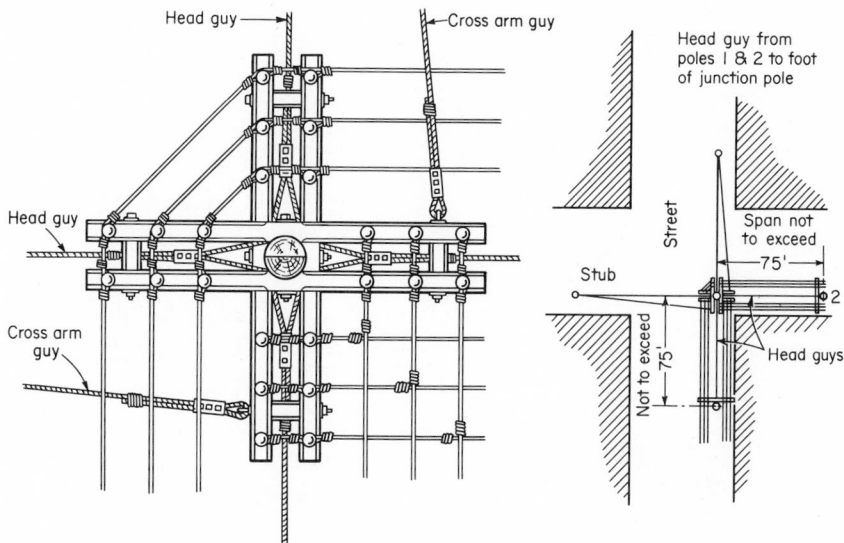

FIG. 86 *Method of turning corner with one pole.*

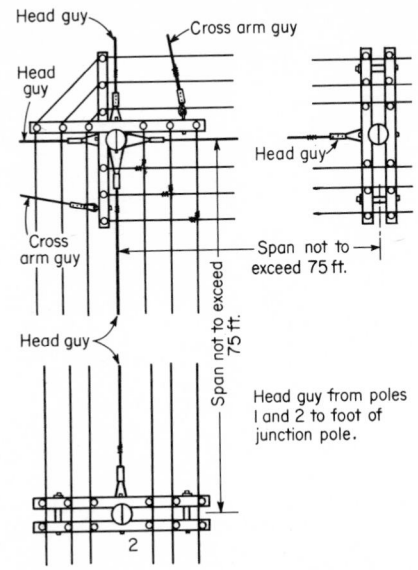

FIG. 87   *Corner pole without double arms.*

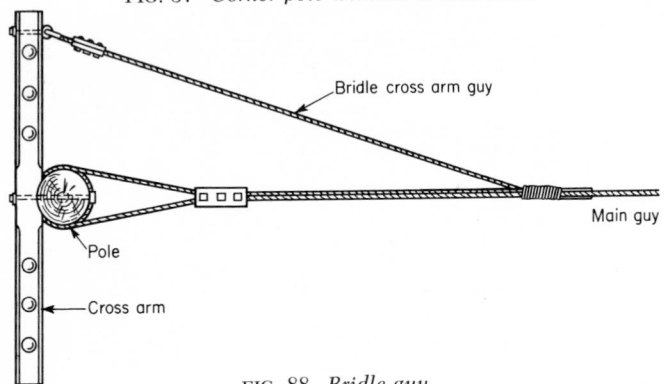

FIG. 88   *Bridle guy.*

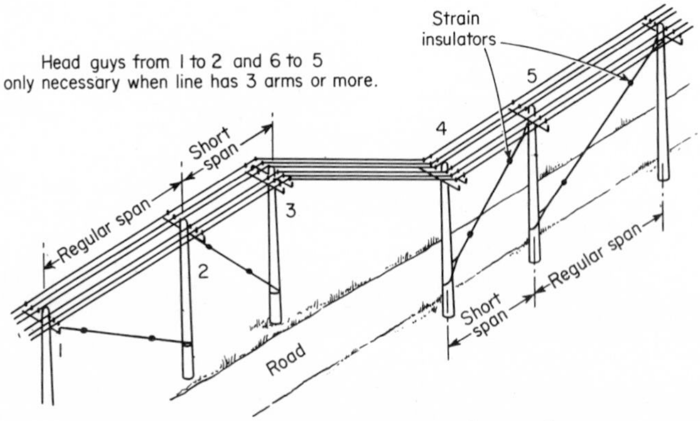

FIG. 89   *Guying at road crossing without side guys.*

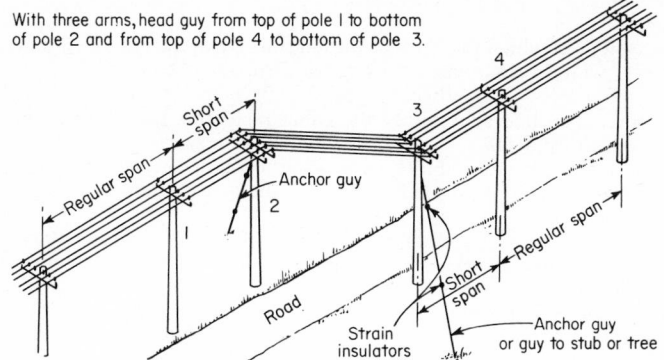

With three arms, head guy from top of pole 1 to bottom of pole 2 and from top of pole 4 to bottom of pole 3.

FIG. 90 *Guying at road crossing with side guys.*

113. Pole braces are used where guying is not feasible. They cost more than equivalent guys. Figure 92 shows methods of bracing poles. The upper end of each brace fits in a notch cut in the pole and is bolted thereto.

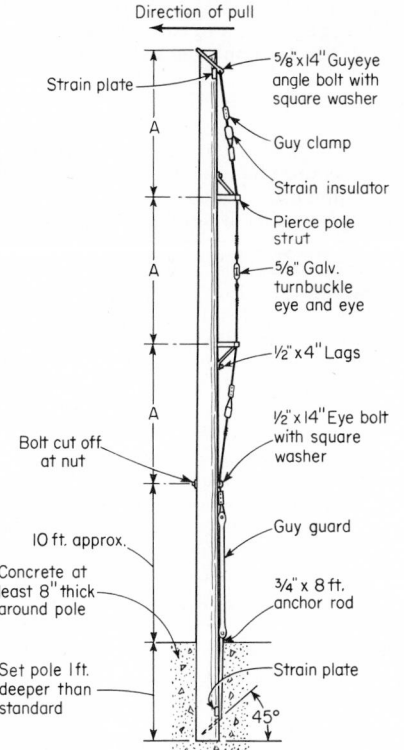

FIG. 91 *Details of self-supporting pole.*

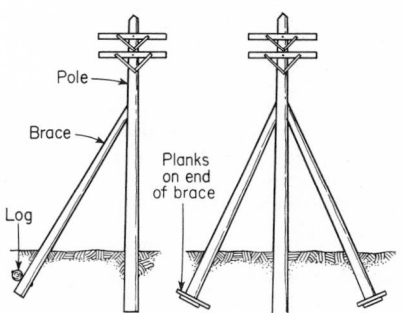

FIG. 92 *Bracing poles.*

UNDERGROUND WIRING

114. Underground systems are of three main types:
1. Duct line.
2. Cable buried directly in the ground.
3. Conduits located in tunnels.

A duct line consists of one or more conduits spaced close together with or without a concrete casing. The duct line is laid in a trench with the top at least 2 ft underground and covered over with earth; it should be covered with pavement if it is located under a street. The duct lines terminate in underground vaults, called manholes, where transformers and protective equipment are located and where cable splices are made. The cables are drawn into the ducts from one manhole to the next. This system is ordinarily used for general underground distribution work where there is more than one cable located in the same run or where the cable may have to be increased in size or replaced. Nonmetallic conduits must be encased in not less than 2 in. of concrete if contained conductors operate in excess of 600 volts.

With the system in which the cable is buried directly in the ground, a trench is dug, and the cable, which is of a type to resist the corrosive effects of the ground (called parkway or nonmetallic-armored cable; see Div. 2), is laid in the trench without any protection other than that afforded by the cable insulation and earth covering (refer to Sec. 154 for further details). This method is used for single-circuit runs where the load is apt to be steady and definite, as in street or parkway lighting systems. This method is also used for underwater lines, where the construction of a duct line would be difficult or impossible.

For groups of buildings in an industrial plant or institution, where tunnels between buildings must be constructed for steam and water lines, it is quite common to locate the electrical circuits in conduits or cable trays on the walls of the same tunnels.

115. Commercial conduit duct materials are fiber, vitrified tile, iron, asbestos composition, polyvinyl chloride (PVC), polyethylene (PE), styrene, and monolithic concrete.

116. Fiber conduit is widely used for ducts in underground construction. Fiber conduit is made of wood pulp which is treated and thoroughly saturated with a bituminous compound. The compound contains about 6 per cent of creosote to prevent rotting. The different sections of conduit are joined by means of self-aligning joints. They can be laid in the trench with great rapidity. The cost of laying fiber conduit is considerably less than for tile duct owing to its lightness and to the greater length of sections, which require fewer joints. Fiber conduit permits cables to be drawn into it readily because of its smooth oily interior. The ducts are laid in concrete with walls 3 in. thick on all sides. Generally, a spacing of 3 in. is employed between the different ducts of a run.

The standard sizes (nominal inside diameters) are 2, 3, 4, 4½, 5, and 6 in. Fiber conduit is made in standard lengths of 5 and 8 ft.

117. Plastic conduits, such as polyvinyl chloride (PVC), polyethylene (PE), and styrene, described in Divs. 4 and 9, are being widely used for underground installation because of low cost, ease of installation and minimum use of labor. Such conduits are available in lengths up to 30 ft, thereby reducing the number of couplings required in a given run.

118. Vitrified-clay single duct or hollow brick is the most popular for communication cables and is sometimes used for low-voltage power work. Figure 93 shows a typical length. The inside diameters of the round ducts are 3¼, 3½, 4¼, and 4½ in. A 3½-in.-square size is also available. The single duct is preferred because its walls are thick and, in laying, every joint is broken, eliminating the possibility of the arc of a short circuit on one cable affecting cables in other ducts in the same run. Single ducts can also be more readily laid around obstructions such as pipes,

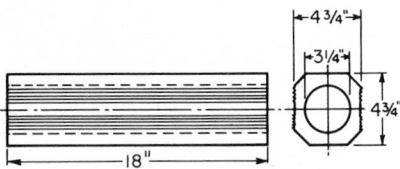

FIG. 93   *A piece of single duct.*

and furthermore, curves can be more readily formed with them than with multiple ducts.

119. Vitrified-clay multiple duct is frequently used for communication cables on account of the ease of assembly. The four-way multiple duct is the most popular size (Fig. 94), although the six-way duct is frequently used. Nine-, twelve-, and sixteenway multiple ducts can be manufactured, but they are seldom used because of their excessive weight and liability to breakage. The dimensions of the multiple ducts of a certain nominal size made by different manufacturers vary. Those shown in Fig. 94 for a four-way duct are typical. A 3¼-in.-square size is also available. Two- and three-duct sections are 24 in. long; the others, 36 in.

120. Iron conduit is sometimes used for duct lines, but since it costs more than other materials, it has not had general acceptance for this purpose. One important advantage is that it gives the cables better protection from damage during excavation. Wrought-iron is preferable to steel conduit, which is often sold for wrought iron, because the

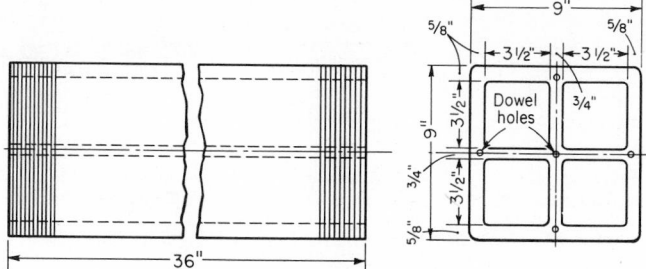

FIG. 94 *A piece of multiple duct.*

wrought iron resists corrosion much more effectively than does steel. See index for dimensions of wrought-iron conduit.

Wrought-iron conduit is frequently used to carry parkway lighting circuits if they are laid in filled ground which might be injurious to cable laid directly in the ground. The principal use for wrought-iron conduit in underground work is for laterals (see Sec. **137**).

121. Cable-in-Duct. A new popular system is cable-in-duct, which consists of a semi-rigid nonmetallic conduit and factory-installed conductors. Shipped in large reels, this system is easy to install, offset fittings and couplings are eliminated, and conductors can be withdrawn if necessary. Typical applications are for parkway, highway, and street lighting underground systems.

122. Asbestos composition conduit, called Transite, is made from asbestos fibers and cement rolled on steel mandrels under pressure. It is strong, light in weight, highly resistant to corrosion, incombustible, and noninductive and has low frictional resistance and high thermal conductivity for dissipating the heat from the cables. It is made in sizes from 2- to 6-in. iron-pipe size in 10-ft lengths, except that the 2-in. size comes in 5-ft lengths only. There are two grades, a light weight called Korduct, which should be used where concrete incasing construction is required owing to poor soil or where the duct is incorporated in building construction, and a standard weight called Transite Conduit. The standard weight can be used without concrete protection where the soil condition is reasonably good. It can also be used exposed to the weather on the sides of bridges or structures. Transite Conduit without concrete encasing will run 10 to 30 per cent cheaper than steel or fiber duct encased in concrete. Joints are made with a tapered Harrington coupling into which the two ends of the conduit make a sliding wedge fit. One tapered coupling is furnished with each length of Transite Conduit or Transite Korduct. Each coupling is machined on the inside to fit the standard taper of the corresponding duct end. Transite tapered couplings form silt-tight joints, assure rapid assembly, and correct duct alignment. They also permit slight changes in direction, enabling duct to be laid in large radius curves when necessary. When joints of a duct line using Transite tapered coupling must be guaranteed waterproof, a compound is used. Composed of asphalt and asbestos fibers, it sets slowly and yet adheres quickly and firmly to Transite. When it has set, a very solid waterproof bond is formed which resists all soil and atmospheric conditions. It is furnished in quart, 1-, 5-, and 30-gal containers and weighs about 10¼ lb per gal. Coverage in joints per gallon is 500 divided by the inside diameter of the duct in inches. For exposed installations, expansion couplings (Fig. 95, III) are used to take up vibrations, expansion and contraction due to temperature changes, and movement between the supporting structure and the duct. One-half of the expansion coupling has a larger diameter than the conduit. A durable rubber ring is installed between the conduit and the large-diameter half of the coupling which seals the joint and allows a movement of at least ¾ in. in either direction from the median. For severe weather conditions an expansion coupling should be used every 30 or 40 ft. Where the duct is protected from sun, rain, and freezing, as on the underside of bridges or within buildings, one expansion coupling every 50 to 100

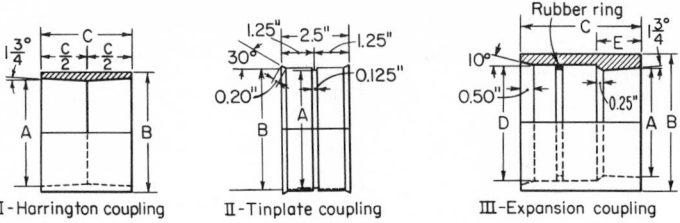

FIG. 95   *Couplings for Transite Conduit.*   (*Johns-Manville.*)

ft may be sufficient. Table **123** gives dimension and weights of Transite Conduit and Korduct and of the tapered couplings for use with each type.

123. Standard Dimensions and Weights of Transite Conduit and Korduct

Size, D	Transite Conduit						Transite Korduct						
	2	3	3½	4	5	6	2	3	3½	4	4½	5	6
D_1	2.58	3.62	4.12	4.62	5.68	6.68	2.36	3.39	3.89	4.39	4.89	5.45	6.46
D_5	2.49	3.53	4.03	4.52	5.58	6.58	2.31	3.34	3.84	4.33	4.83	5.38	6.38
D_4	2.48	3.52	4.02	4.50	5.56	6.56	2.30	3.33	3.83	4.32	4.82	5.37	6.37
D_3†	2.70	3.74	4.24	4.74	5.80	6.80	2.50	3.54	4.04	4.54	5.04	5.60	6.60
D_2	3.33	4.40	4.92	5.42	6.56	7.56	3.11	4.17	4.69	5.19	5.77	6.33	7.34
P	1.50	1.50	1.50	1.75	1.75	1.75	.75	.88	.88	1.00	1.00	1.13	1.25
E	1.75	1.75	1.75	2.00	2.00	2.00	1.00	1.13	1.13	1.25	1.25	1.38	1.50
T†	.35	.37	.37	.37	.40	.40	.25	.27	.27	.27	.27	.30	.30
L	3.50	3.50	3.50	4.00	4.00	4.00	2.00	2.25	2.25	2.50	2.50	2.75	3.00
Weight, lb. per ft[a]	2.3	3.3	3.9	4.4	6.0	7.0	2.0	2.5	3.0	3.5	4.0	5.0	6.0

† D_3 and T are nominals only.
[a] Weights are approximate and include one coupling per length.
Spacers or separators molded of plastic are available for use with Transite Korduct.

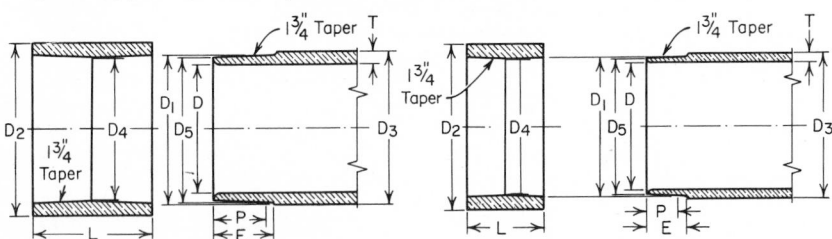

124. Monolithic concrete ducts can be built in two ways: (1) by using flexible Para rubber tubing as a core, (2) by using a duct-forming machine called a boat. In the rubber-tubing method, thick rubber tubes which are flexible but not readily collapsible are laid on a concrete base and separated with terra-cotta spacers. Concrete is then poured around them as in the other methods. When the concrete has set for a few hours, the tubings are withdrawn, leaving a very smooth concrete duct. In the boat method a track is built at the bottom of the trench. On this track runs the boat, which is really a die containing as many steel tubes as the number of ducts wanted. Concrete is fed into a hopper at the top and is tamped down around the tubes. The boat is moved slowly along the track either by hand or by power from an electric motor, leaving the finished duct extruding from the rear. The concrete is of a special mixture which is sufficiently solid to hold the form of the ducts as the boat moves along.

The rubber-tubing method is especially advantageous where the duct line must be threaded around other underground structures and pipes. It can be used to advantage in bringing duct lines into power stations and substations, as the duct can be formed in one continuous run from the street manhole to the switching-gallery floor. The main advantage of the boat method as well as the rubber-tubing method is that there is no material in the duct to decay. Both methods have proved more expensive than using fiber or asbestos conduit, so that for normal straight runs they cannot compete economically. For special irregularly shaped curves a section of the monolithic concrete duct, formed by the rubber-tubing method, may well be inserted even if the main run is made with one of the other materials.

125. In installing any kind of duct line a trench is excavated to such a depth that the top conduit will be 2 to 3 ft below the surface of the ground and so that the grade of the duct line will pitch toward the manholes about 1 ft in 100 ft so as to ensure effective drainage. For power cables the ducts should be arranged either two conduits wide or two conduits deep so that every conduit will have earth on at least one side of it. This is necessary for conduction into the cooler ground of the heat generated by the I^2R losses in the cables. For communication cables the heat loss is low, and the ducts can be arranged in any convenient way. There should be from 1 to 3 in. of earth or concrete between conduits for power systems to ensure that flame and heat from a short circuit in one conduit will not affect the adjacent cables. The 3-in. separation should be used on the higher-voltage lines. Conduits are held in position during construction of the duct line by plastic spacers (Fig. 96). The width of the trench will depend on the working space required and on whether concrete and concrete forms are used or not. With Transite Conduit concrete is not required unless the soil is not firm. If the soil is firm, the trench may be merely 1 or 2 in. wider than the space required by the conduits. With other conduits, where concrete is required, it should be about 3 in. thick outside the conduits. In good firm soils the trench can be dug to exactly this width and forms omitted, the concrete occupying all the space between the conduits and the earth wall. In ordinary and poor soils the trench should be made an additional 3 in. wider on each side to provide space for installing the forms.

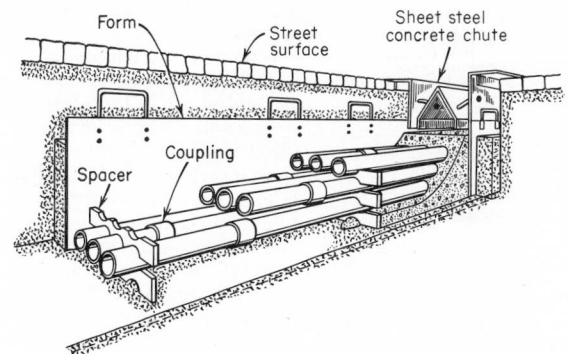

FIG. 96 *Construction of duct line.* (*Johns-Manville.*)

The bottom of the trench should be carefully rammed until solid so that undue stress will not be placed on the conduits. With concrete construction the 3-in. bed of concrete is then laid, over which the lower tier of conduits is placed with spacers to ensure the correct separation between conduits. Then the concrete is tamped around them, and thus each level is built up until the duct is completed with 3 in. of concrete on top. In laying Transite Conduit in firm soil, the process is similar except that earth takes the place of the concrete. Sometimes the spacers are removed after the conduits are held firmly in position by the backfill and before the spacers are completely covered over. At other times the spacers are left in to form a permanent part of the duct line.

126. Installing Single-duct Vitrified-tile Conduit. (See Fig. 97 for sections of duct runs.)

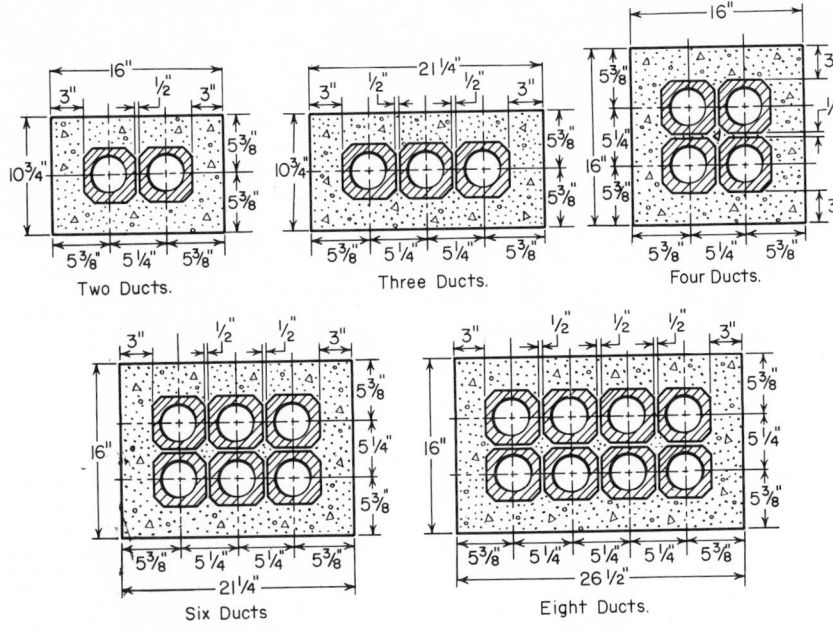

FIG. 97 *Arrangement of single-duct subway.*

Two Ducts.

Three Ducts.

Four Ducts.

Six Ducts

Eight Ducts.

After the bed is set, the duct is laid in cement mortar. A mandrel (Figs. 98 and 99) is used to keep the successive pieces in line. It is customary to enclose the conduit in a continuous concrete encasement 3 to 4 in. thick.

The mandrel is pulled through with a long hook as the conduit progresses to align the ducts. The leather washer scrapes away any mortar that has oozed through between joints and leaves the duct quite clean. The end of a No. 12 galvanized-iron wire is frequently attached to the inner end of the mandrel and is pulled into the conduit as its construction progresses. The wire is used to pull in the drawing-in rope which is used to pull in the cable.

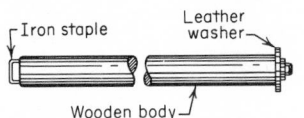

FIG. 98 *Mandrel for aligning conduit.*

The single ducts furnished by some manufacturers are provided with male and female ends, which assist in aligning the ducts.

127. Laying Multiple Duct. Multiple duct is laid in about the same way as single duct. Figure 100 shows sections of multiple-duct runs. The pieces are laid end to end, and the joints, if there is more than one tier in the subway, are broken. The pieces are maintained in alignment by iron dowel pins or keys (Fig. 101), which fit in holes in the pieces. All joints are wrapped with pieces of burlap or coarse muslin, 4 in. wide and 3 ft long for four-duct tile, which are moistened to make them stick. They are then coated with cement. The cloth prevents the entrance of cement or concrete into the ducts.

Sometimes a mandrel (Fig. 98) ¼ to ½ in. smaller than the hole is drawn through as the construction progresses, as suggested in Fig. 99, to ensure alignment of the pieces. The handle on the mandrel should be long enough to reach back two joints so that one can be sure that the last three pieces set align, as they may have become displaced in setting.

After the pieces are set, be careful that they are not displaced before the concrete jacket is deposited. The ducts should be cleaned out after the concrete jacket has been placed by drawing a wire brush or flue cleaner (Fig. 102) through them. The brush is somewhat bigger than the duct hole. Sometimes a metal scraper (Fig. 102) is also used.

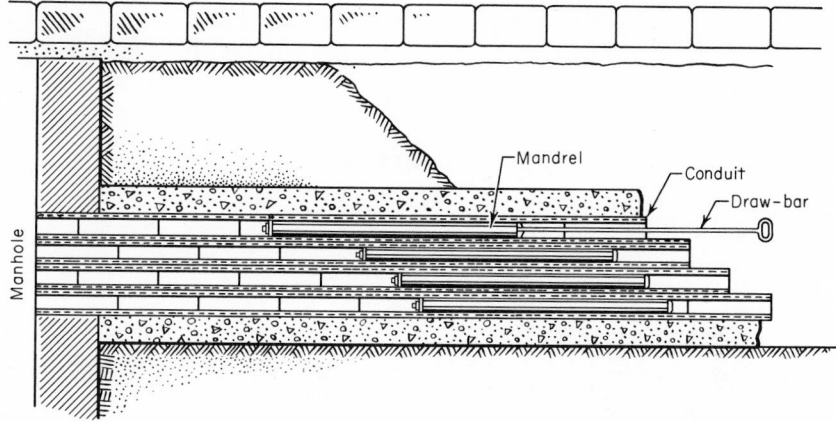

FIG. 99   *Showing use of mandrel.*

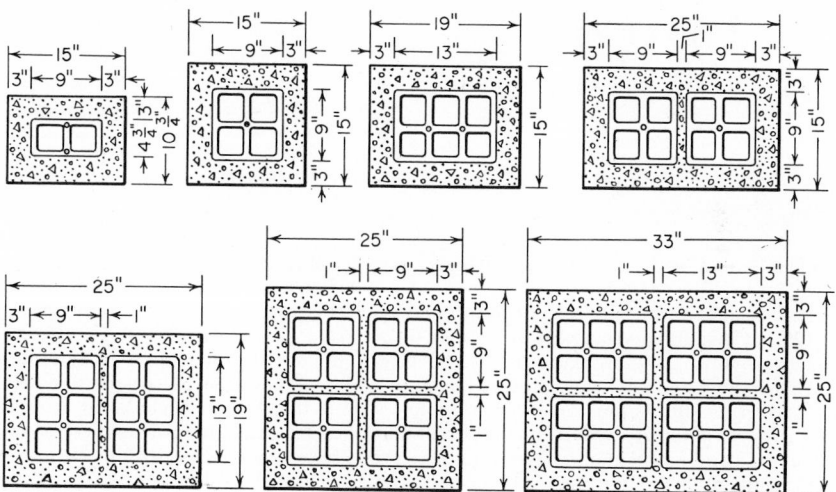

FIG. 100   *Sections of multiple duct.*

Multiple duct has been laid without any concrete casing, but with merely a concrete bed, as suggested in Fig. 103. This construction is economical in first cost but is apt to give trouble through settling of the earth or displacement due to future excavation.

Creosoted boards are sometimes laid on top of a conduit run to protect against laborers' picks. Experience has shown that the average laborer will stop when his pick strikes a board but that he will pick his way through concrete or duct material. Multiple-duct conduit can be carried around obstructions, as shown in Fig. 104, by beveling the ends of the pieces. If the turn is too short, it may be difficult or impossible to "rod" the duct and to pull the cable in.

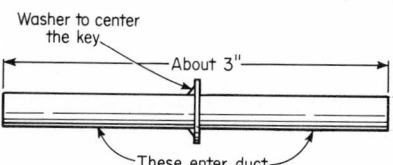

FIG. 101   *Steel key for multiple duct.*

128. To cut vitrified conduit a groove is chipped completely around the piece on the line at which it is desired to cut it. A hammer and cold chisel are used for chipping

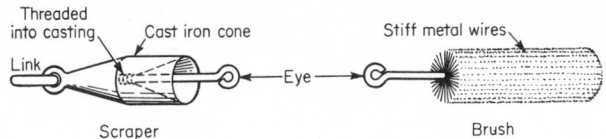

FIG. 102   *Scraper and brush for conduit.*

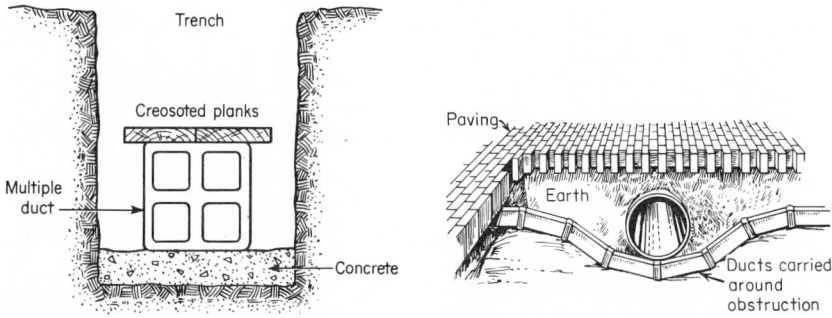

FIG. 103   *Protective planks over multiple duct.*

FIG. 104   *Breaking around an obstruction with vitrified duct. Where possible, the bend should pass over rather than under the obstruction. When it passes under the obstruction, water will collect in the pocket.*

the groove.   Usually it will break off on the chipped line after continued chipping, but it may not.   Some experience is required before one becomes skillful at this work.   Short lengths can be furnished by the conduit manufacturers, and their use is recommended.

129. In installing wrought-iron conduit no concrete casing is necessary if only one duct is involved.   Where there are several ducts in the run, the ducts are sometimes laid on a 3-in. foundation of concrete and concrete is tamped between and around the ducts as shown in Fig. 97 for single vitrified duct.   Where the ducts will not be exposed to the dangers of future excavation, the cost of the concrete is probably not justified.   Metal conduits can be obtained in 20-ft lengths.   Joints between adjacent lengths are made with conventional couplings.   The burrs at the ends of each conduit must be carefully removed to prevent damage to the cable.   Where it is inconvenient to use a coupling, a union can be used instead.   Metal conduit should be painted on the outside with asphalt or similar coating material to minimize corrosion.

130. Installing Fiber Conduit.   There are two methods of installing fiber conduit. In the "tier-by-tier" method, the lower tier of ducts is placed upon a concrete foundation in the trench and then covered with fresh concrete.   The second tier of ducts is then put in place on top of the concrete, covering the first tier of ducts.   This process is repeated with each tier of ducts until the required number of ducts have been installed.

In the "built-up" method, all the ducts are installed in a framework of spacers.   Then side forms are put in place and the concrete is poured over and around the ducts, thereby forming a monolithic concrete block.

When installing heavy-wall fiber conduit, it is recommended that after the line gradient is established, the trench surface be examined and all sharp or hard objects, such as stones, be eliminated.   The floor of the trench is then shaped to receive the lower one-quarter of the outside surface of the conduit.

Where the ground is too solid or rocky, 3 in. of selected backfill should be used under the conduit.   The conduit should then be covered with a 3-in. fine fill and tamped.

Care should be taken not to tamp the conduit directly. A power tamper may be used on the final fill. If more than one bank of ducts is being installed, there should be a 3-in. fill between banks and at least a 2-in. fill between duct rows.

Each length of conduit is provided with a taper sleeve joint coupling which provides a means of quick jointing. No cement or mastic is required to produce watertight joints. A block of wood and an ordinary hammer are all that is required to drive the taper sleeve joint on to the machined end of the conduit. The friction thus generated causes a bonding of the material which requires over 200 lb of straight-line pull to separate one from the other.

Many fittings are available to meet the varied needs of installation. These include:

1. Angle couplings to provide for offsets to avoid obstructions.
2. Adapters for connecting fiber conduit to threaded metal pipe of the same or different size.
3. 45- and 90-deg elbows and bends.
4. S bends.
5. Watertight caps for sealing duct ends.
6. Expansion joints for use where expansion and contraction are likely to occur.
7. Bell ends for use at conduit terminals in manholes.
8. Reducers for connecting one size of fiber conduit to another size of fiber conduit.

131. Installing Transite Conduit Directly in Earth without Concrete Encasement (Johns-Manville). **Trench Bottom.** The bottom should be graded smoothly, free of stones and soft spots. In rocky soil, a bedding of selected fill (fine granular soil) should be put down and tamped before laying conduit.

Supporting Duct. The primary requirement is to ensure full, even support throughout the duct length. The preferred method (shown at 1 in Fig. 105) is to make a cradle of earth by shaping the trench bottom to fit the duct and to dig recesses for couplings. An alternate method (shown at 2 and 3 in Fig. 105) is to provide support for each length of duct at two points. The supports can be provided by mounds of earth or wood blocks. The height of the support should be at least 1¾ in. to provide space for a

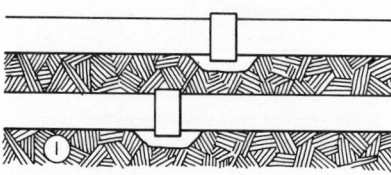

Preferred Method. Trench bottom shaped to fit duct, holes dug for couplings. Note that joints are staggered.

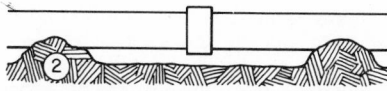

Alternate Method. Each length of duct supported by earth at two points before side filling. Minimum height of earth mounds must be 1 3/4".

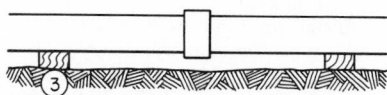

Alternate Method. Ducts supported by wood blocks at least 1 3/4" high. Remove blocks after duct line assembly, while placing fill under ducts.

FIG. 105 *Supporting Transite Conduit.* *(Johns-Manville.)*

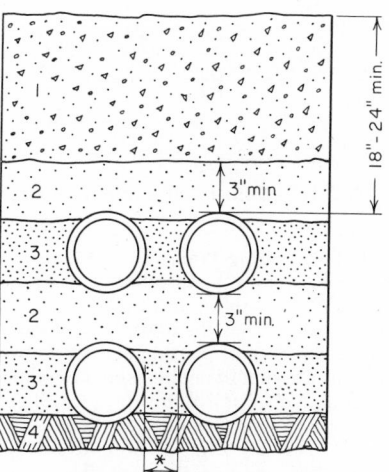

(1) Excavated material (2) Fine granular fill (3) Hand tamped (4) Undisturbed earth

*Horizontal spacing for power line minimum of 2" is recommended; for telephone lines no minimum is necessary

FIG. 106 *Two-tier Transite Conduit bank.* *(Johns-Manville.)*

uniform bed or selected backfill. CAUTION: Remove wood blocks after assembly and as side fill is placed under duct.

Side Filling. When ducts are installed, side-fill with soft dirt, sand, or other fine fill up to the top of the duct. Then tamp under and around the duct with hand tampers. Do not tamp on top of ducts. CAUTION: If combs are used for alignment when the duct tier is several ducts wide, make sure they are removed and vacant spaces filled and tamped.

Backfilling. When side filling is completed, cover the top tier with selected backfill for a minimum depth of 3 in. over the top of the duct. The remaining depth can then be filled with the excavated material provided all unusually large stones are removed. The entire backfill can now be tamped with power tampers if desired.

NOTE. When more than one tier is installed, side-fill, hand-tamp, and backfill with selected soil for a depth of 3 in. (see Fig. 106). Install the next tier of ducts, side-fill, hand-tamp under and around ducts, backfill with selected fill to depth of 3 in. over the top of the duct. Then continue backfill with regular excavated soil or install the next tier.

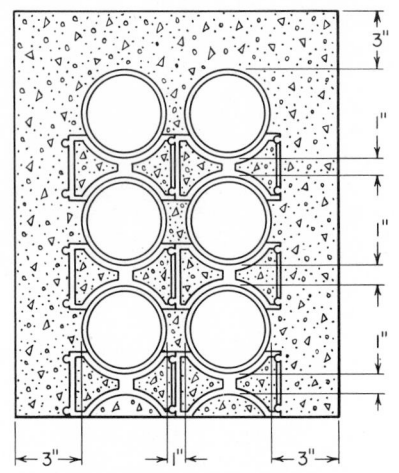

a. Cross-section of duct bank

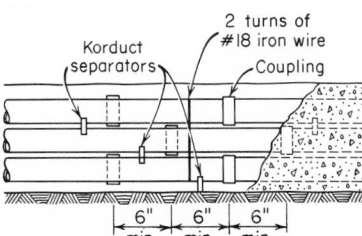

b. Elevation of duct bank – Note that both separators and joints are staggered. In so far as possible try to locate spacers about one-fifth of duct length from each end.

FIG. 107 *Built-up or monolithic method of installing Korduct. (Johns-Manville.)*

132. Installing Transite Korduct in Concrete (Johns-Manville). Two different methods are used for the installation of Transite Korduct in concrete. One is the built-up or monolithic method, and the other is the tier-by-tier method. The built-up or monolithic method has the advantage of speed of installation. It has the possible drawback that voids and air pockets may be formed through careless spading of the concrete envelope. It should not be used if the duct bank is narrow in width and four or more ducts high and duct separation is 1 in. The tier-by-tier method has the advantage of providing a concrete envelope which is solid and free from voids.

133. The Built-up or Monolithic Method of Installing Transite Korduct (Johns-Manville). **Trench Bottom.** The trench bottom should be smooth and graded. A foundation of continuous concrete, 3 in. thick, can be placed if desired. In unstable soil, a reinforced-concrete foundation is necessary. The concrete base should be mixed rather dry, then placed or rammed in the trench to form an evenly graded layer.

Assembly of Bank. Place separators on the trench bottom (Fig. 107) and then lay the first tier of ducts. If concrete base is used, lay bottom tier before the base has taken its initial set. Lay succeeding tiers on spacers placed on the top of the tier below. When the required number of ducts is built up, securely tie the entire assembly together. Unless concrete mix is to be very sloppy, it is not necessary to weight or brace. If weighting is desired, weights of 75 to 100 lb every 6 or 7 ft are sufficient.

Pouring Concrete. In pouring, avoid having a heavy mass of concrete fall directly on the duct. If unavoidable, protect with a plank. Direct the flow of concrete down the sides of the bank assembly to the bottom, compelling concrete to flow to the center of the bank and to rise up in the middle, thus filling all open spaces uniformly. To ensure absence of voids, work a long, flat slicing bar or spatula liberally and carefully up and down between the vertical rows of ducts.

Backfilling. After concrete has set, backfill with regular excavated soil.

134. The Tier-by-tier Method of Installing Transite Korduct (Johns-Manville). **Trench Bottom.** Grade the trench; place a foundation of concrete 3 in. thick on the bottom.

Assembly of Bank. Lay the bottom tier of ducts on the concrete base. Space ducts with wood combs (two per duct length). See Fig. 108. Cover the first tier with con-

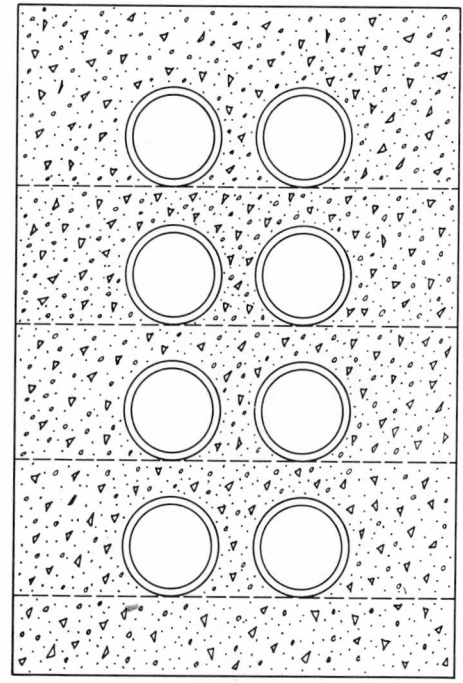

a. Cross-section

b. Type of wood comb used

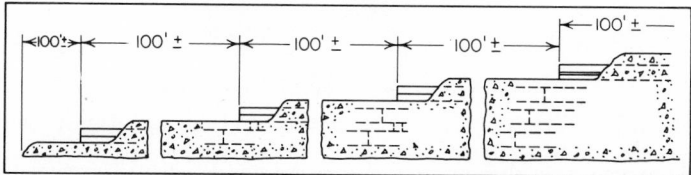

c. Elevation – If sufficient trench has been excavated, the laying of the ducts is usually done in 100 ft sections; thus concreting process can be continuous.

FIG. 108 *Tier-by-tier method of installing Korduct. (Johns-Manville.)*

crete to the level of the top of the comb. Remove combs and fill voids. Light tamping is advisable to ensure an even surface. Build up the desired bank by repeating successively the previous operation.

Concreting. If concrete is allowed to set before placing the next tier, it will be stronger and denser and ducts will have straighter alignment; it has the disadvantage that the bank will be a series of layers likely to leave and separate under heavy frost conditions. If successive tiers are laid before the concrete has a chance to set, a satisfactory bond will be obtained at the expense of tamping the rather dry concrete to ensure a satisfactory dense mass (see Fig. 108).

Backfilling. When the bank is complete, backfill with regular excavated soil.

135. Installation Hints and Aids for Transite (Johns-Manville):

1. GRADE. Minimum is usually about 3 in. per 100 ft of trench.

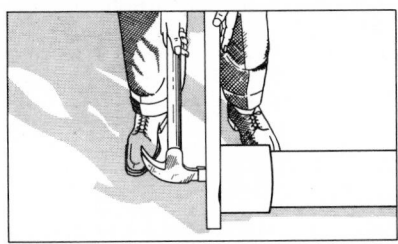

2. TO ATTACH COUPLING. Put the coupling on the duct end. Place a board against the coupling and tap the board lightly with a hammer until secure. Never force the coupling up to the shoulder of the duct. Never hit the coupling directly with hammer.

3. TO JOIN DUCT ENDS. Insert the next duct section in the coupling. Place another coupling on the free end. Then, use a board and hammer, as above, to secure the joint of duct and couplings.

4. TO MAKE WATERTIGHT JOINTS. Coat the duct end only with Transite joint-sealing compound. Apply coupling with twisting motion. Then tap lightly with a hammer, taking care to protect coupling with board, as in the above sketch. This method keeps excess compound out of the duct where it might adhere to cables.

Many fittings are available to meet the varied needs of installation. These include:

a. Angle couplings to provide for offsets to avoid obstructions.

b. Adapters for connecting Transite Conduit or Korduct to threaded metal pipe or fiber conduit of the same or different size.

c. 45- and 90-deg elbows and bends.

d. S and offset sweep bends.

e. Watertight caps for sealing duct ends.

f. Expansion joints for use where expansion and contraction is likely to occur.

g. Bell ends for use at conduit terminals in manholes.

h. Reducers for connecting one size of duct to another size of duct.

136. Concrete for conduit work should be clean; i.e., foreign substances should not be permitted to enter into its composition. If the surface on which it is to be mixed is not smooth and clean, mixing boards or pans should be used. Foreign material impairs the strength of concrete, and it becomes porous and leaky. The concrete should be mixed from portland cement, clean sand, and gravel or broken stone, in the proportions, by volume, of 1 part of cement to 3 parts of sand and 5 parts of gravel or stone. Just sufficient water should be used to wet the mixture thoroughly and to permit a small amount of water to come to the surface when the concrete is tamped into final position. The cement, sand, and stone should be "turned" on the mixing board at least three times dry and at least twice after wetting. The concrete should be placed immediately after mixing. When the concrete has been placed in the trench. several hours should be allowed for it to take its initial set before the trench is filled in. This is necessary to prevent throwing the ducts out of alignment or fracturing the "green" concrete.

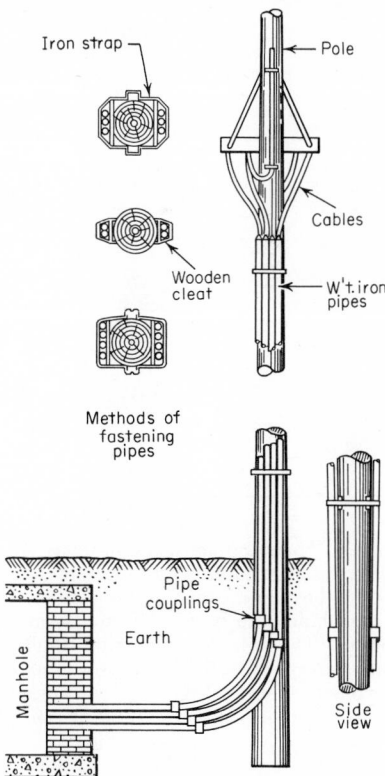

137. For laterals which carry the service cables from the duct lines to the buildings served. concrete construction is usually not justified. For this purpose Transite Conduit can be used. although iron conduit has been commonly employed for this purpose. Iron conduit can be bent at will, and it is often necessary to thread a network of underground structures with a lateral, especially if it has to cross the street. Usually wrought-iron conduit is used because this material resists the corrosive effect of the ground. An application of wrought-iron conduit from overhead to underground construction is illustrated in Fig. 109.

138. Manholes are necessary in a subway system to permit of the installation, removal, splicing, and rearrangement of the cables. A manhole is merely a subterranean vault or masonry chamber of sufficient size to permit proper manipulation of the cables. The conduits enter the vault, and on its sides devices are arranged whereby the cables within the manhole can be supported.

The location of manholes is determined largely by the layout of the district that is to be supplied with power. Wherever a branch or lateral extends from the main

FIG. 109 *Wrought-iron pipe laterals.*

subway, there must be a manhole, and there must be manholes at intersections of subways. In general, cables are not made in lengths exceeding 400 to 600 ft, and, as it is necessary to locate splices in manholes, the distance between manholes cannot exceed these values. Furthermore it is not advisable to pull in very long lengths of

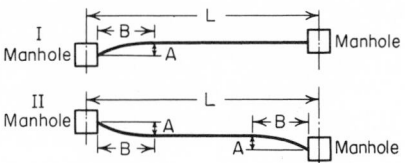

FIG. 110   *Offsets for main duct line.* (*I*) *Single curve.* (*II*) *Reverse curve.*

cable, because the mechanical strain on the conductors and sheath may then become too great during the pulling-in process. It is recommended that manholes be located not more than 500 ft apart. The lines should preferably be run straight between manholes. If curves are necessary, the offsets from a straight line and the distance between manholes should not exceed the values given in the following tables:

Single curve (see Fig. 110, I)				Reverse curve (see Fig. 110, II)			
A Curve offset	*B* Min length curve, ft	Max length *L* between manholes, ft		*A* Curve offset	*B* Min length curve, ft	Max length *L* between manholes, ft	
		4 ducts	6–16 ducts			4 ducts	6–16 ducts
0′ 1″	5	800	700	0′ 1″	5	800	700
0′ 3″	10	740	650	0′ 3″	15	740	650
0′ 6″	15	685	600	0′ 6″	25	655	575
0′ 10″	20	640	560	1′ 0″	35	570	500
1′ 3″	25	600	525	1′ 6″	40	515	450
1′ 9″	30	570	500	2′ 0″	45	485	425
2′ 4″	35	545	475	2′ 6″	50	455	400
3′ 0″	40	515	450	3′ 0″	55	435	380
3′ 9″	45	485	425	3′ 6″	60	420	365
4′ 7″	50	470	410	4′ 0″	65	400	350
5′ 6″	55	445	390	4′ 6″	70	385	335
6′ 6″	60	425	370	5′ 0″	75	365	320
7′ 6″	65	400	350	6′ 0″	80	345	300
8′ 9″	70	370	325	7′ 0″	85	320	280
10′ 0″	75	345	300	7′ 6″	90	310	270

139. Manholes are made in many shapes and sizes to meet the ideas of the designer and to satisfy local conditions. It is established, however, that the form shown in Fig. 111 is best for the average condition. Where there are obstacles about the point where a manhole is to be located, the form of the manhole must be modified so as to avoid them. The form approximating an ellipse (Fig. 113, I) is used so the cables will not be abruptly bent in training them around the manhole. When the rectangular type of manhole is used (Fig. 113, II), care must be taken not to bend the cables too sharply.

The size of manholes will vary with the number of cables to be accommodated, but in any case there must be sufficient room to work in the manhole. A 5- by 7-ft manhole (Fig. 111) is probably as large as will be required in isolated plant work, while a 3- by 4-ft manhole (Fig. 112) is about as small as should be used. When transformers are located in a manhole, the size should be increased to allow for working space around the transformer and for ventilation. About 2 or 3 cu ft of volume should be allowed per kilovolt-ampere of transformer rating.

Manholes are built of either brick or concrete or of both of these materials. Where many manholes are to be built of one size and there are no subterranean obstructions, concrete is usually the cheapest and best material. But where only a few are to be constructed or where there are many obstructions, a manhole with a concrete bottom, brick sides, and a concrete top is probably the best. Such a manhole can be constructed without having to wait for concrete to set before forms can be removed. There is a growing use of precast concrete manholes, shipped directly to the site.

140. A concrete manhole is built by first depositing the concrete floor (Fig. 111, II) and then erecting the form for the sides on this floor. In a self-supporting soil the sides of the hole constitute the form for the outside of the manhole. If the soil is not self-supporting, an outer form of rough planks must be made, which is usually left in the ground. Steel reinforcing—old rails are good—must be placed in the concrete top of a large manhole. In a small manhole the manhole head or cover will extend over the side walls, and no reinforcing or manhole roof, for that matter, is required. All reinforcing steel should be completely encased in concrete to prevent corrosion.

141. A manhole with brick walls is built (Fig. 111, I) by first depositing the concrete floor and then building up the brick walls thereon. Where the manhole is large, the roof can be of either steel-reinforced concrete or brick set between rails. Probably for installations where only a few manholes are to be built, the brick-between-rails method

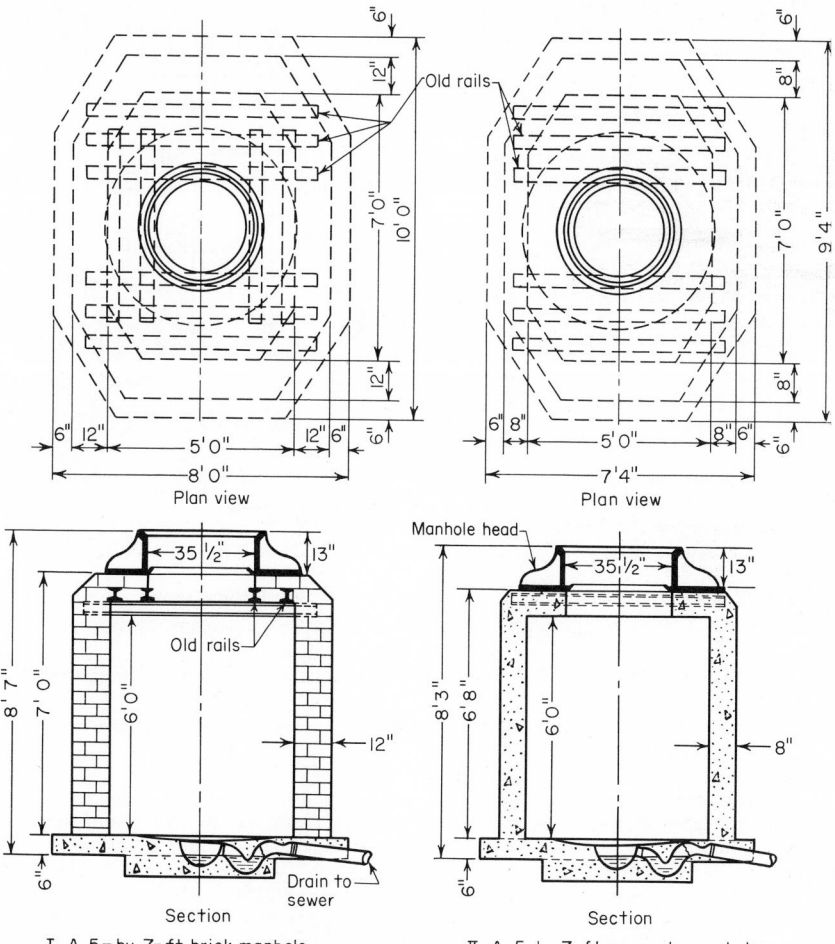

I-A. 5- by 7- ft. brick manhole. II-A. 5- by 7- ft. concrete manhole.

FIG. 111 *Typical manholes.*

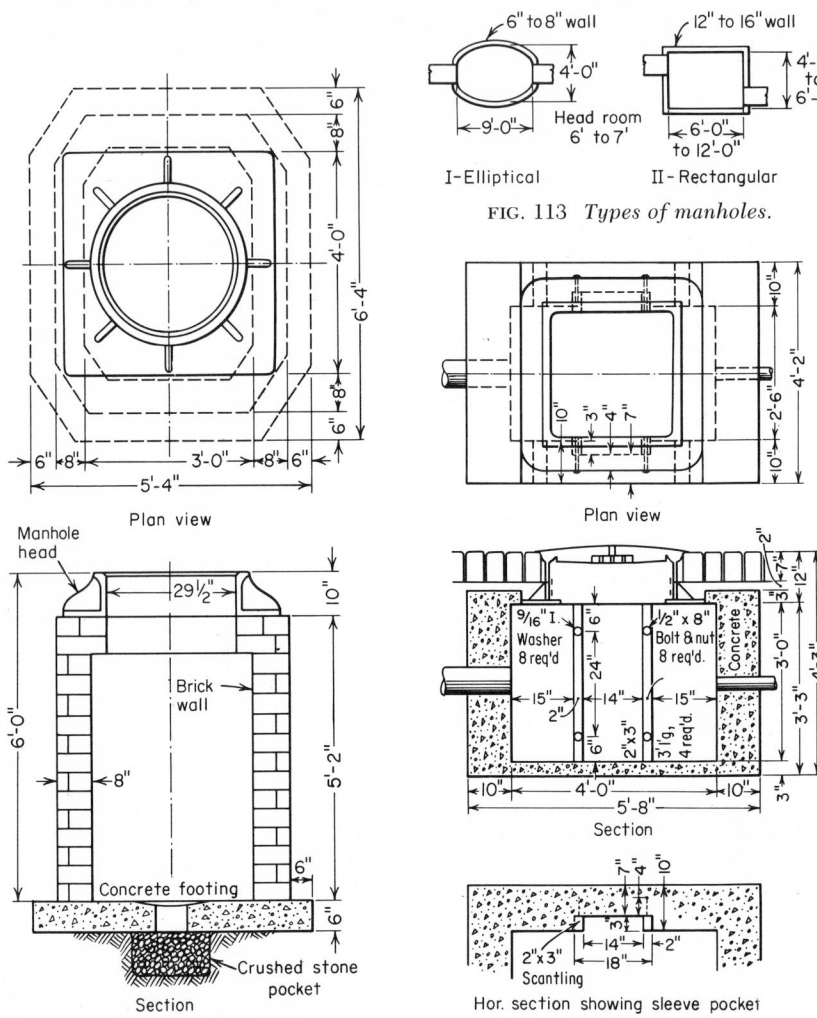

FIG. 113 *Types of manholes.*

FIG. 112 *A 3- by 4-ft manhole.*

FIG. 114 *A concrete service box.*

is the best. For a small manhole no masonry roof is necessary, as the cast-steel manhole head forms the roof.

Cement mortar for building brick manholes or for conduit construction can be made by mixing together 1 part of cement, 3 parts of sand, and about ⅓ part of water, all by volume.

142. Distribution or service boxes, so called, which are really small manholes, often serve the purpose of and can be used instead of larger vaults in industrial and isolated plant installations. A design for a concrete service box is shown in Fig. 114. A brick one would be of approximately the same dimensions. The depressions in the side walls are sleeve pockets. The splicing sleeves on the cables lie partially in these, after installation, and therefore less of the valuable working space of the box is occupied by them. In spite of the fact that a square manhole cover can fall into the hole, heads with square covers are often used for distribution boxes so as to provide an orifice giving maximum working room.

143. Manhole heads are frequently made of cast iron, but cast steel is better; the cover should always be of cast steel. Figure 115 shows a design for cast steel for a large manhole, and Fig. 116 one for a smaller manhole. Covers should be round so that they cannot drop into the hole accidentally.

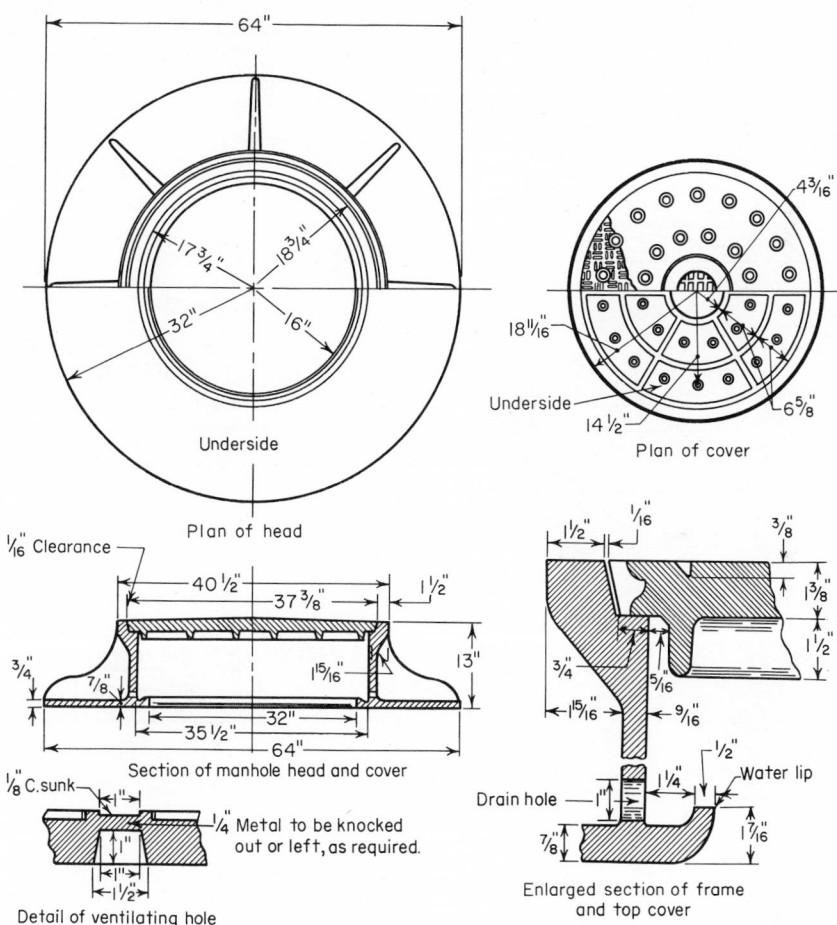

FIG. 115 *Head for large manholes.*

So-called watertight covers are now seldom used, as it is not feasible to make a satisfactory watertight cover at reasonable expense and water gets into the manholes in any event. Covers should not be fastened down because, if they are and accumulated gas in a manhole explodes, the vault and cover will be shattered. A ventilated cover should be used in order to allow the escape of gas. The newer types have ventilating slots over approximately 50 per cent of their area. Dirt and water will get into the hole, but the dirt can be cleaned out and the water will drain out and no harm will result. If ventilation is not provided, an explosion of gas may occur and do great damage.

144. Draining Manholes. Where feasible, a sewer connection should lead from the bottom of every manhole (see Fig. 111). The mouth of the trap should be protected by a strainer, made of noncorrodible wire, such as that used for leader pipes. Where a sewer connection cannot be made, there should be a hole in the manhole floor

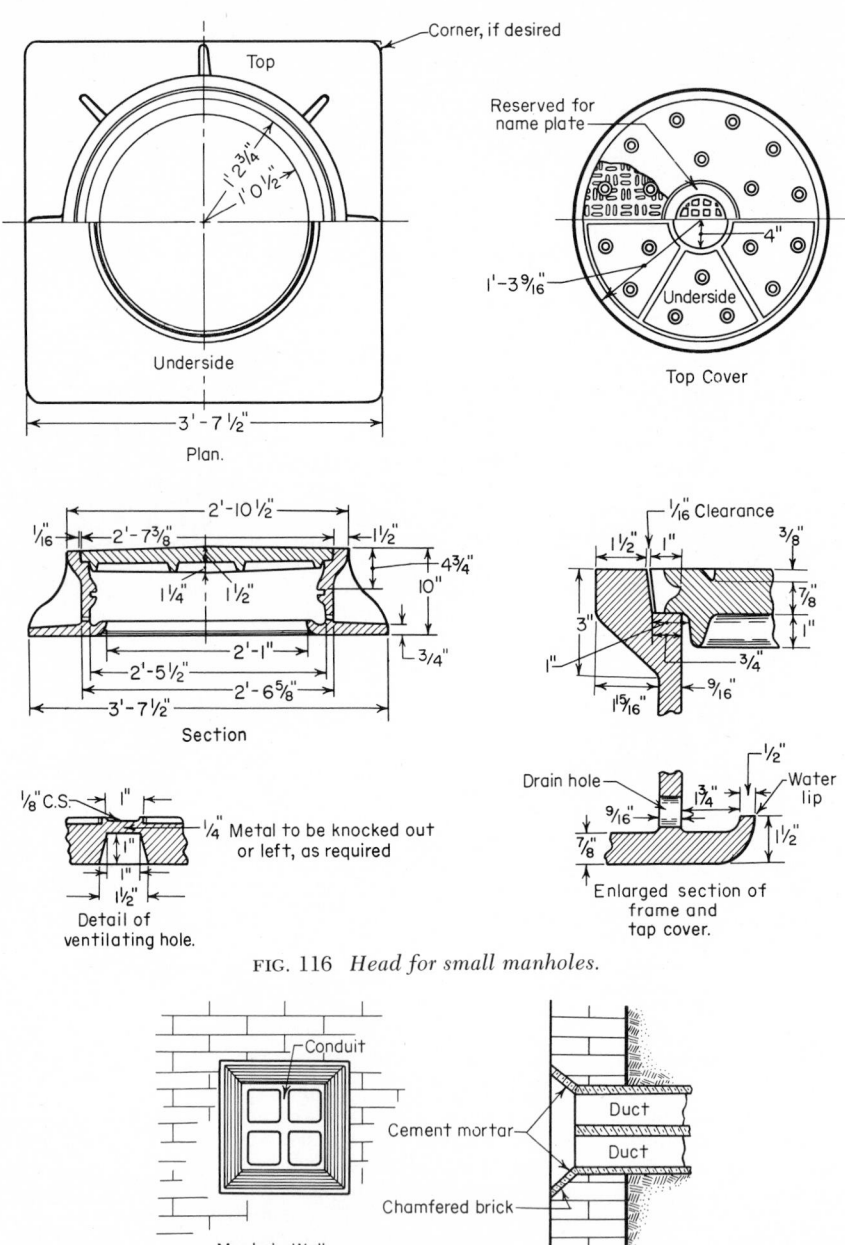

FIG. 116   *Head for small manholes.*

FIG. 117   *Chamfered wall at conduit entrance.*

so that water can drain out.   A pocket under the manhole filled with broken rock will promote effective drainage (see Fig. 112).

145. At the point where a conduit line enters a manhole, the walls should be chamfered off as shown in Fig. 117 to prevent the damage that might occur if a cable is bent over a sharp corner.

A precast conduit entrance can be made up on forms on the surface of the ground and then lowered into position in the side of the manhole. One type using porcelain duct bells is shown in Fig. 118. The smooth curved surface of the bell prevents the cable sheath from being cut where it starts to bend coming out of the duct line.

146. A manhole hook, a convenient tool for removing manhole heads, is shown in Fig. 119. A common pick can be used, but the tool shown is much more convenient.

147. In installing cables in conduit, if a pull-in wire was not installed at the time the ducts were placed, the conduit is rodded, a pull-in wire or the drawing-in cable is drawn through, cleaners are pulled through, and then the cable is drawn in.

148. Rodding. Rods are pieces of round hickory about ¾ in. diameter and 3 ft long (see Fig. 120). The ends of the rods are

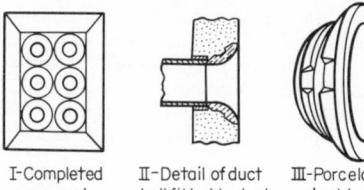

I–Completed precast entrance   II–Detail of duct bell fitted to duct   III–Porcelain duct bell

FIG. 118 *Manhole duct entrance using porcelain bells.* (*Line Material Industries.*)

equipped with brass knuckle-joint fittings so the rods can be readily joined together and disjoined. In rodding, a rod is pushed into the duct and a second rod is coupled to it. The two are pushed into the duct, a third rod joined on, and the process is repeated until the rods extend from manhole to manhole. A galvanized-iron wire is attached to the last rod, and the wire is drawn into the duct.

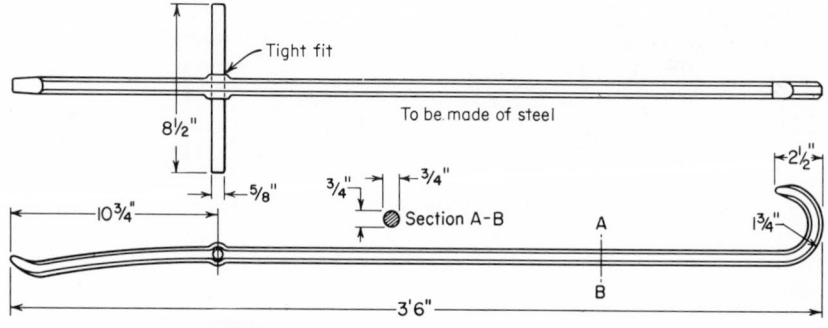

FIG. 119 *A manhole hook.*

FIG. 120 *Rods for conduit.*

A rope or flexible steel cable to which are attached a scraper and a brush (Fig. 102) is drawn through to ensure that the duct is clear and clean. To the end of this rope or cable another is attached which is used to pull in the electrical conductor cable.

Where the conduit is short, a steel fish wire or ribbon, like that used by electricians in wrought-iron conduit work, can be inserted instead of the rods.

149. Pulling in Cable. The cable can be attached to the pulling-in wire by any one of several methods. Figure 121C shows one that was formerly much used. Probably the best methods are those illustrated in Fig. 121 A and B. At A, a galvanized iron wire is laced around the cable in such a way that the harder it is pulled, the tighter it grips. At B is shown a "grip" spirally laced from flexible steel strands. It slips over the cable sheath readily, but when tension is applied, it effectively grips the cable. A swivel should always be inserted in any pulling-in line to prevent the untwisting of the drawing-in line under tension from twisting the cable.

After the cable is fastened to the pulling-in line, a "protector" is placed in the mouth of the duct to prevent abrasion of the cable. Metal protectors can be purchased, but a good one can be formed from a piece of sole leather.

The cable is bent, as shown in Fig. 122, from the cable reel to the mouth of the duct, and the pulling in commences. In the far manhole, sheaves are arranged over which the pulling-in line passes (see Fig. 122). If eyebolts were built in the manhole sides, the sheaves (snatch-blocks) can be fastened to them. Otherwise a guide-sheave rack (see Fig. 123 for detail and Fig. 122 for application) can be set up in the manhole.

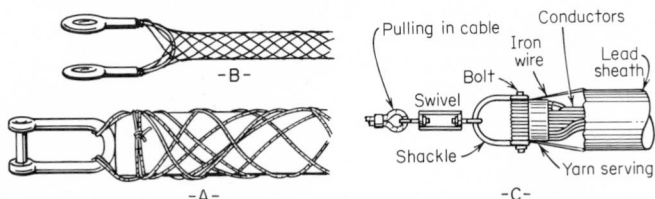

FIG. 121 *Methods of attaching cable to drawing-in line.*

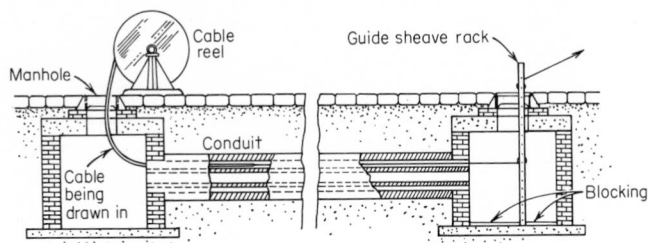

FIG. 122 *Drawing in cable with winch.*

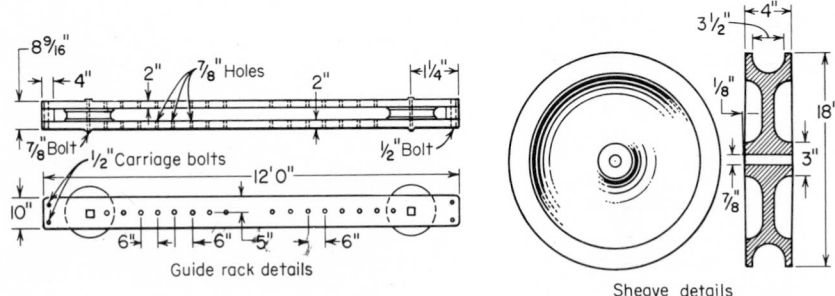

FIG. 123 *Guide sheave, rack, and sleeve.*

A winch, truck, or tractor can be used for the pulling. Men can pull a cable in if the run is not too long. The cable sheath should be greased as it is drawn in to ensure easy pulling. Where a length of cable longer than the distance between manholes is to be pulled through, it can pass over the sleeves on the guide-sleeve rack provided they are large enough in diameter. A manhole capstan (Fig. 124) is sometimes used instead of a winch on the surface of the ground. Enough cable should be pulled into the manhole to allow for forming it around the hole and splicing it. Do not permit a cable to hang over the sharp edge of a duct. Support it in the rack.

150. Supporting Cables in Manholes. Some provision must be made for supporting cables. Creosoted planks (Fig. 125) are sometimes bolted to the manhole sides, and the cables are held to the cleats with pipe straps. In other cases metal supports are used, several forms of which are on the market. One that can be readily made is shown in Fig. 126. A rack made of porcelain arms on a steel framework is shown in Fig. 127.

151. Eyebolts or stirrups should be set in manhole walls to provide means of attachment for the tackle used in pulling in cable (Fig. 125). An eyebolt or stirrup should be set opposite the point of entrance of each subway. Figure 128 shows the dimensions of a suitable stirrup.

152. Several cables should not be placed in one duct. Experience has shown that, although it is easy enough to install cables under such conditions and mechanically easy to withdraw them, the removal almost invariably ruins the cable, because after long lying in a duct the cables become so impacted with dust and grit that when one is drawn out, the sheath is stripped either from the cable itself or from one of its companions. Consequently, conduits are now almost exclusively built by arranging a sufficient number of ducts so that each cable can have its own exclusive compartment.

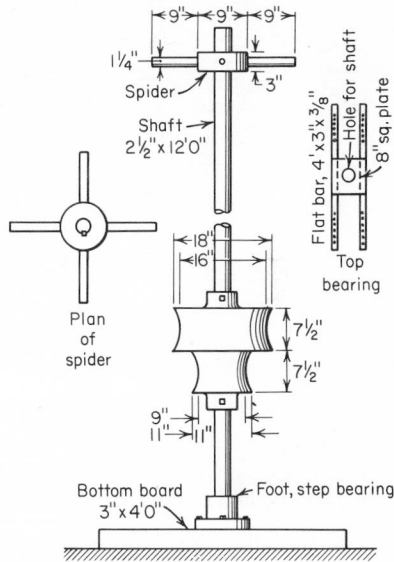

FIG. 124 *Manhole capstan.*

The maximum diameter of a cable that can be installed in a duct, as recommended by the Edison Electric Institute, is given in Sec. **33** of Div. 11.

153. In manholes and ducts cables should be so arranged that there will be a minimum of crossing and recrossing. An underground cable system should be carefully planned, and the duct should be so chosen for the cables that, as far as feasible, a cable will take the duct in the same relative position throughout the subway.

154. Installation of Cable Buried Directly in the Ground. Cable buried directly in the ground finds a wide field of application for installations of single circuits where the cost of duct construction would be prohibitive. Some of the more common applications are:

1. Street-lighting circuits, especially in cities whose outlying sections are without ducts.

2. Lighting and power circuits in parks, on estates, in industrial plants, parkways, etc.

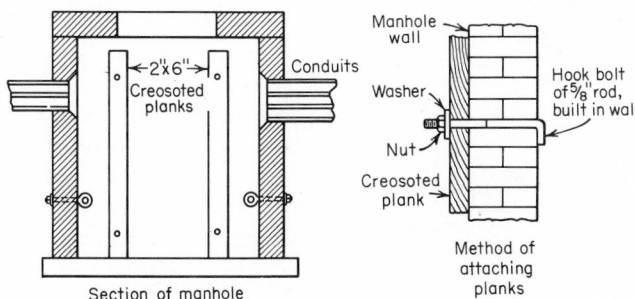

FIG. 125 *Creosoted plank cable supports.*

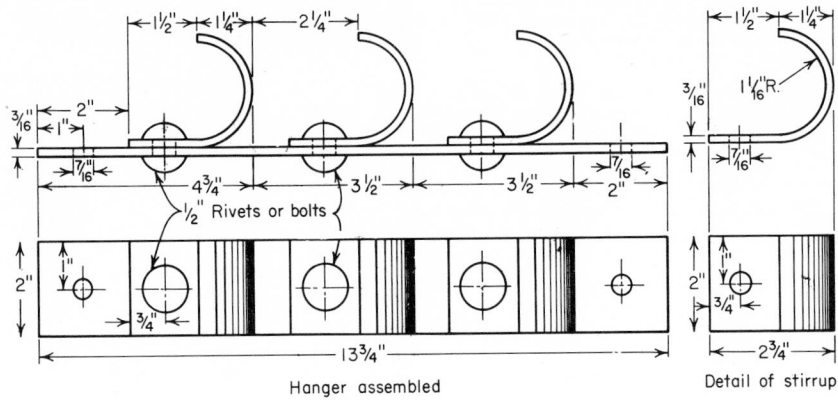

Hanger assembled   Detail of stirrup

FIG. 126 *Iron cable support.*

3. Connecting residences to mains, especially subdivisions and underground service in alleys.

4. Connecting houses, garages, and other buildings.

5. Railroad-yard and airport lighting.

6. Lighting and power circuits for amusement parks, baseball, football, and general sports.

7. High-wall power cable for strip mines.

8. Railway-signal circuits.

9. Crossings under small lakes and streams.

10. Horizontal runs in mines for power, lighting, and telephone circuits.

Both nonmetallic-armored cable and metallic-armored cable (parkway cable) are used for direct burial in the earth.   The nonmetallic-armored types are lighter in weight, more flexible, and easier to splice and are not subject to rust, crystallization, induced sheath power loss, or trouble from stray currents.   On the other hand, they do not give such good protection against mechanical injury.

The cables are installed either by digging a shallow open trench, laying in the cables, and refilling or by means of a gasoline-powered trencher-cable-layer.   When a trench is dug, it needs to be made only wide enough for convenient handling of the cable.   The cables (600 volts or less) need not be laid more than 18 in. under the surface except where subject to extreme mechanical hazard, such as at street intersections or under roadways.   At such points it is advisable to bury the cable at least 30 in. deep and to cover it with protective pads.

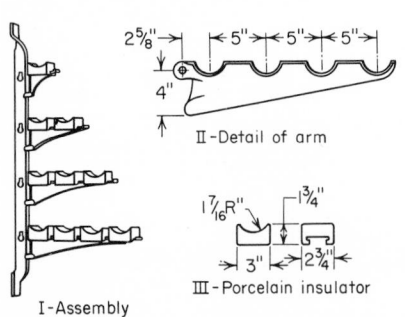

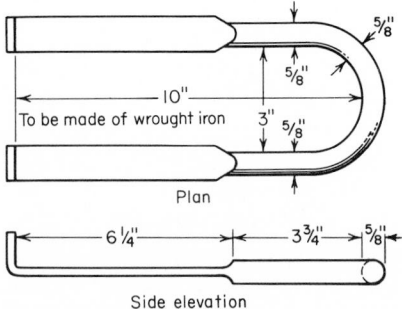

FIG. 127 *Cable rack.   (Line Material Industries.)*

FIG. 128 *Stirrup for manhole wall.*

155. Type UF and USE cables are code-designated single- or multiple-conductor cables suitable for direct burial in earth. These cables are described in Divs. 4 and 9 where typical applications at 600 volts or less are discussed.

156. Underground Conductors over 600 Volts. The National Electrical Code includes rules for the protection of underground conductors where the supply voltage exceeds 600 volts. These rules were introduced to minimize the hazards of "dig-ins," and the following table summarizes section 710-3(*b*) of the Code.

Summary Table of Earth Burial Depth Requirements for Raceways or Cables over 600 Volts — Underground Conductors

	Burial depth below grade, inches		
Wiring methods	General applications	Under streets or roadways	Under airport runways and defined adjacent areas
Rigid metal conduit...	30	24	No minimum depth
Direct-burial cable (if energized conductors are surrounded by effectively grounded multiple concentric conductors, closely and evenly spaced circumferentially)	30	30	18
Other wiring methods (such as rigid nonmetallic conduit encased in 2 in. of concrete or other types of direct-burial cables)	42	42	18 for cable — no minimum depth for conduit

NOTE. Above depths may be reduced 12 in. for each additional 2 in. of protective layer of concrete above the conductors.

GROUNDING OF SYSTEMS

157. Grounding of Distribution Circuits. The National Electrical Code requires that on systems supplying interior wiring circuits one wire of the circuit shall be grounded, provided that the voltage from any other conductor to ground will not exceed 300 volts on d-c systems or 150 volts on a-c systems. Grounding helps to prevent accidents to persons and damage by fire to property in case of lightning, breakdown between primary and secondary windings of the transformers, or accidental contact between high-voltage wires and low-voltage wires. If some point on the low-voltage circuit is grounded:

1. Lightning striking the wires will be conducted into the ground.

2. Breakdown of the transformer insulation between primary and secondary coils will reveal itself through blowing of the primary transformer fuses if one wire of the primary circuit comes in contact with one of the secondary wires.

3. See Sec. **170** for the importance of a low-impedance ground-path return.

158. The value of grounding is illustrated in Fig. 129. One of the primary circuit wires is grounded at the transformer. The secondary is grounded at the customer's water pipe. An accidental cross between ungrounded primary and secondary wires is shown by the dotted line. Current will flow through the cross connection, the secondary of the transformer, the customer's water-pipe ground, and up the ground connection to the other primary line. The voltage of the secondary wires to ground will be increased by the IZ drop through the water-pipe ground. A current of 100 amp times a ground resistance of 2 ohms (there is practically no reactance) giving 200 volts would represent very severe conditions. This means that the secondary voltage to ground would be the normal 110 volts plus the 200 volts, giving 310 volts, which would probably not do any damage before the primary protective devices would open and break the circuit. This type of accidental cross should open the substation-feeder circuit breaker. If the cross were in the transformer itself, the primary fuse would open. If, however, there were no ground connection, the primary 2,300 volts would be impressed on the secondary system, which is insulated for only 250 to 600 volts, and numerous insulation breakdowns and considerable damage to equipment would occur. Also, there would be danger to human life for anyone touching a fixture at such a time.

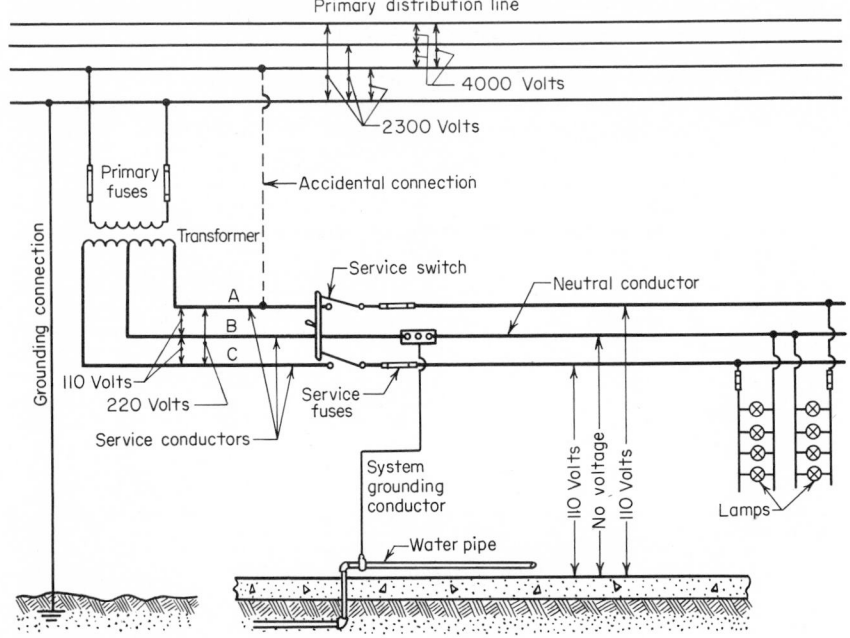

FIG. 129 *Ground connections for interior wiring systems.*

159. High-voltage transmission systems are also frequently grounded in order to reduce the voltage to ground and consequently the line insulation required. For example, if a 220-kv three-phase circuit has the windings of the supply transformer connected in Y, with the midpoint of the Y grounded, the voltage to ground will be $220 \div \sqrt{3} = 127$ kv. This reduction of the voltage to ground is of great value in insulating the transformer windings and in the number of insulators required for the line supports. At the same time, the advantage of the 220 kv in reducing the line current and line losses is retained.

160. Ground-wire connections to transformer secondaries should be made to the neutral point or wire if one is accessible. Where no neutral point is accessible, one side of the secondary circuit may be grounded. Figure 130 shows theoretical diagrams of ground connections to transformer secondaries, and Fig. 131 illustrates how some of

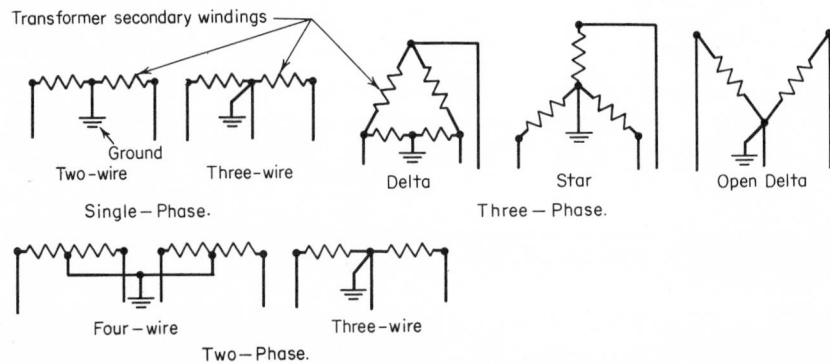

FIG. 130 *Theoretical diagrams of secondary ground connections.*

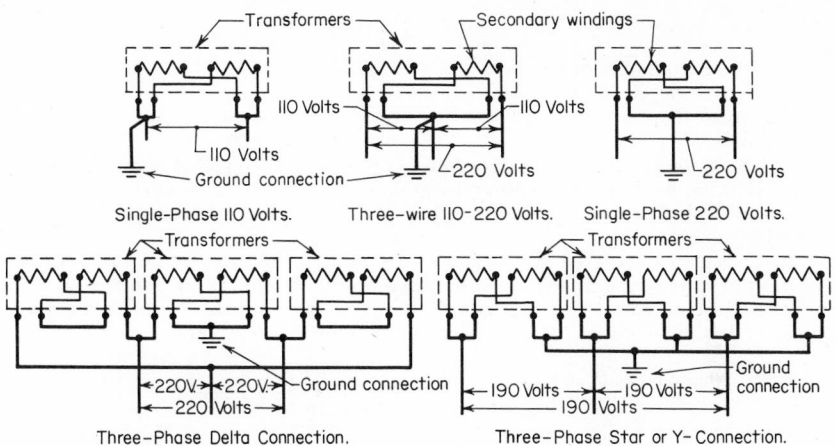

FIG. 131 *Ground connections to secondaries of commercial transformers.*

these connections are arranged with commercial transformers. The neutral point of each transformer feeding a two-phase, four-wire secondary should be grounded unless the motors taking energy from the secondary have interconnected windings. Where they are interconnected, the center or neutral point of only one transformer is grounded. No primary windings are shown in Figs. 130 and 131. In Fig. 131 the secondary winding of each transformer is shown divided into two sections, as it is in commercial transformers.

161. Ground rods made of steel pipe with copper-welded exterior surface (pointed at the bottom, Fig. 132) are extensively used. The rod is driven into the ground, and the ground wire fastened by a clamp near the top of the rod. The copper coating provides for a good electrical connection and affords resistance to corrosion from the weather and earth.

161A. Ground wires should be encased by wooden molding for a distance of at least 8 ft from the surface to protect against shocks to passers-by. Under certain conditions of soil moisture, a shock can be received from a ground wire by a person standing on the earth's surface. The ground pipe extends about 1 ft above ground and is not usually protected. Some companies encase the entire length of the ground wire in molding to protect the linemen.

No copper wire smaller than No. 8 should be used for a ground wire, and some companies use nothing smaller than No. 4. Copper wire is preferable. Bare wire is satisfactory and should be attached to the poles with cleats or straps. Staples, although used, should not be. The National Electrical Code requirements with respect

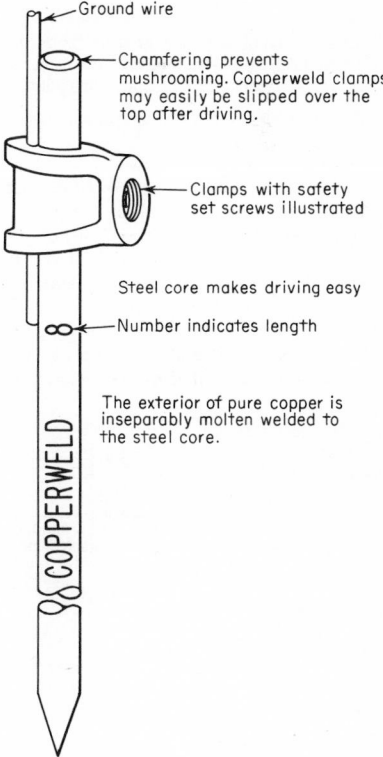

Ground wire

Chamfering prevents mushrooming. Copperweld clamps may easily be slipped over the top after driving.

Clamps with safety set screws illustrated

Steel core makes driving easy

Number indicates length

The exterior of pure copper is inseparably molten welded to the steel core.

COPPERWELD

FIG. 132 *Ground rod and clamp.* (*Copperweld Steel Co.*)

to size of ground wires are given in Div. 9. There should be a ground for each transformer or group of transformers, and when transformers feed a network with a neutral wire, there should, in addition, be a ground at least every 500 ft. The National Electrical Safety Code specifies that all ground pipes shall be galvanized and have a minimum nominal diameter of $\frac{1}{2}$ in. Steel or iron rods shall have a minimum cross-sectional dimension of $\frac{5}{8}$ in.

162. The National Electrical Safety Code implies that the ground resistance should be measured at the time of installing the ground, and that the ground resistance must not exceed 3 ohms for water-pipe grounds and 25 ohms for artificial (buried or driven) grounds.

163. To measure the ground resistance, two additional temporary grounds, consisting of short rods 2 or 3 ft long, must be driven in the ground at least 20 ft away from the ground being tested (Fig. 133, I). A direct-reading instrument called a ground-ohmer or groundometer can then be connected to the three grounds by means of insu-

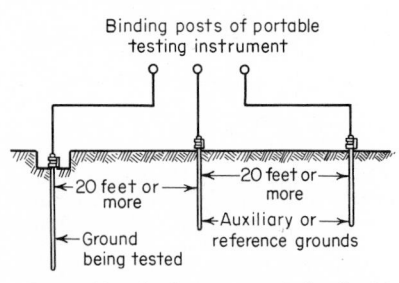 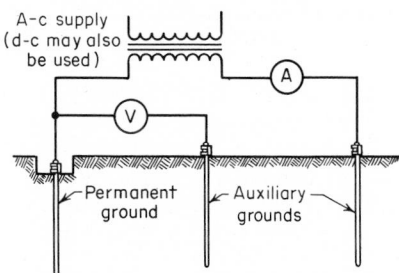

I – Location of reference grounds for direct reading, single-test method of measuring the resistance of a ground connection.

II – Connections for the fall of potential method of measuring ground resistance.

FIG. 133 *Circuits for measurement of ground resistance.* (*Copperweld Steel Co.*)

lated leads. A magneto or a battery in the instrument furnishes the necessary power. The instrument reads the ground resistance directly in ohms. If a source of direct or alternating current is available, the resistance can be measured by the fall-of-potential method with a voltmeter and ammeter, connections for which are shown in Fig. 133, II. The resistance is then calculated from $R_g = E/I$.

164. When testing ground resistance in city streets there may be no convenient place to drive the auxiliary grounds. In such a case a fire hydrant can be used for the auxiliary ground, or a pad made of several thicknesses of heavy cloth about 1 ft square and saturated with salt water can be placed on the sidewalk (Fig. 134).

165. Reduction of ground resistance in cases where it exceeds the allowable value of 25 ohms can be accomplished in several ways:

1. Use of a larger diameter ground rod.
2. Use of a longer ground rod.
3. Putting two, three, or more rods in parallel.
4. Chemical treatment of the soil.

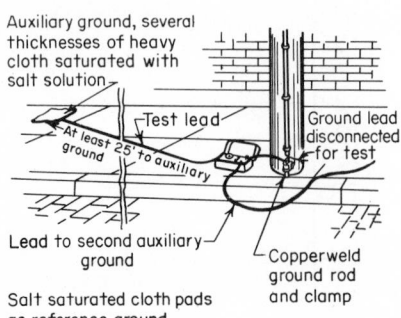

FIG. 134 *Testing ground resistances in paved streets.*

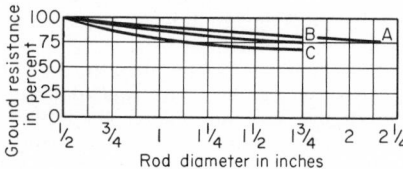

FIG. 135 *Effect of diameter of ground rod on ground resistance.* (*Copperweld Steel Co.*)

166. The effect of the use of a larger diameter rod is shown in Fig. 135. It will be noted that increasing the diameter of the ground rod does not effect much reduction in resistance, and use of ground rods larger than ¾ in. is not recommended. The diameter of the rod should be only large enough to permit it to be driven into the soil without bending.

167. Long ground rods made in sections coupled together are very effective where there is considerable depth of dry sand and good moist soil is many feet underground. Although the 8-ft minimum depth required by the National Electrical Code is sufficient for normal soil conditions, grounds as deep as 50 ft have been used in very poor soil. The calculated effect of the depth of rod on ground resistance is shown in Fig. 136. The curve is for uniform soil at all depths. In practice the soil is always firmer and more moist the

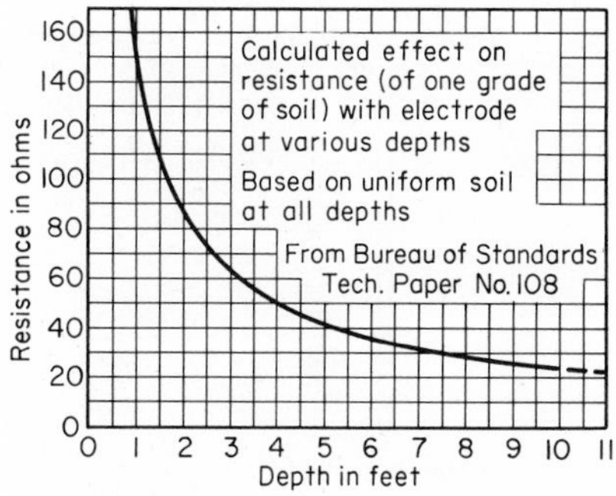

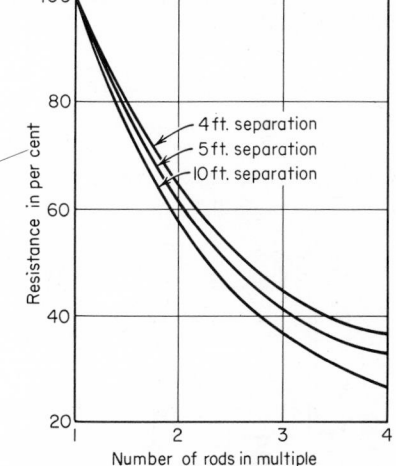

FIG. 136 *Effect of depth of ground rod on ground resistance. (Copperweld Steel Co.)*

FIG. 137 *Effect on ground resistance of placing ground rods in multiple. (Copperweld Steel Co.)*

deeper the ground, so that the decrease of resistance with increase of depth is usually greater than is shown by the curve.

168. Using several rods in multiple is a very effective means of lowering ground resistance as shown in Fig. 137. The recommended distance between rods is at least 6 ft, so that this method is more applicable to large steel-tower lines and substation structures than to wood-pole lines. Spacing rods as close together as the opposite sides of a wood pole is not recommended.

169. Chemical treatment of the soil is recommended for reducing ground resistance for those cases where the other methods of Secs. **166** to **168** are not practical.

There are two practical ways of accomplishing this result, as shown in Fig. 138. In the method of Fig. 138, I, a length of tile pipe is sunk in the ground a few inches from the ground rod and filled to within 1 ft or so of the ground level with magnesium sulfate, copper sulfate, or common rock salt. The magnesium sulfate is the most common, as it combines low cost with high electrical conductivity and low corrosive effect on the rod. This method is effective where there is limited space for soil treating, such as on city streets. The method of Fig. 138, II, is applicable where a circular or semicircular trench can be dug around the ground rod to hold the chemical. The chemical must be kept several inches away from direct contact with the ground rod to avoid corrosion of the rod. The first treatment requires 40 to 90 lb of chemical and will retain its effectiveness for 2 to 3 years. Each replenishment of the chemical extends the effectiveness for a longer period, so that future re-treating becomes less and less frequent. When the chemical is first installed, it is well to flood the treated area with water so that the chemical will diffuse through the soil. Thereafter normal rainfall will usually provide the necessary water for carrying the solution into the earth.

170. A low-impedance ground-path return is absolutely essential if line-to-ground faults in grounded systems are to open overcurrent devices in buildings. It is an important rule in the National Electrical Code (sec. 250-23b) which requires a grounded conductor of a grounded utility system to extend to every building served. Such grounded conductors are then bonded to the metallic enclosures of the service equipment, and the grounded conductor is connected to an electrode on the premises by a grounding electrode conductor which usually extends from a neutral bar in the service-equipment enclosure to the electrode. See Div. 9 for detailed Code rules to size grounded and grounding conductors.

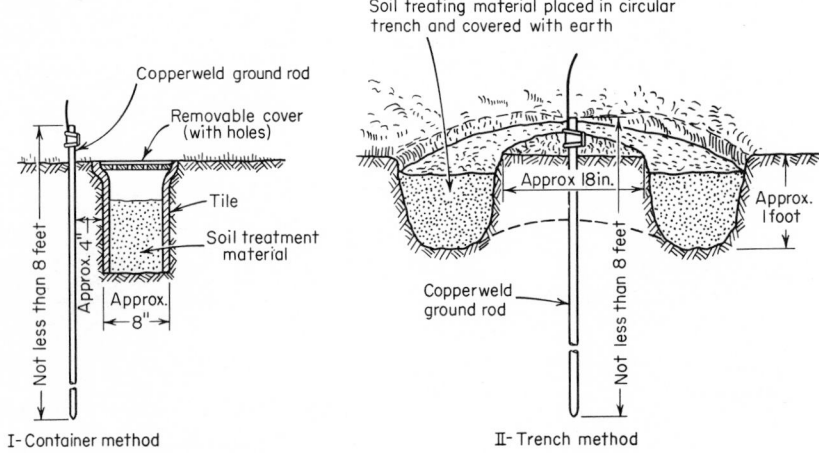

FIG. 138 *Methods of soil treatment for lowering of ground resistance. (Copperweld Steel Co.)*

Where a grounded conductor is properly bonded to the metallic service equipment, any line-to-ground fault from an ungrounded conductor to grounded equipment (raceways, cables, boxes, etc.) on the load side of overcurrent devices will be able to follow a low-impedance path to the grounded conductor at the supply transformer, thus permitting an overcurrent device to open quickly. All ground faults must be cleared as fast as possible to avoid extended exposure of energized metallic parts, which provides a serious shock hazard. It cannot be stressed too strongly that proper bonding of the grounded conductor of the supply system to the service-entrance equipment is essential for the proper operation of overcurrent devices in the event of line-to-ground faults. For low-magnitude ground faults, see information on ground-fault circuit interrupters in Div. 4.

DIVISION NINE

Interior Wiring

GENERAL

1. The National Electrical Code rules, which are the recommendations of the National Fire Protection Association (NFPA), should be followed in installing all interior wiring. These rules are revised every three years, and so it is inadvisable to include them in entirety in this book. A copy of the rules can be obtained from any local inspection bureau or purchased from the NFPA. All statements are made in accordance with the 1968 edition of the Code. The "NFPA Handbook of the National Electrical Code," published by the McGraw-Hill Book Company, Inc., gives the Code rules with illustrations and explanations of their application.

2. There are local regulations covering the installation of wiring, in force in many localities, which have been enacted by city or state governments. Sometimes these differ from the Code regulations, and so it is always well to be familiar with all the regulations in force before starting any work. The city and state rules are in reality laws and therefore take precedence over the National Electrical Code rules, which of themselves have no legal status.

3. Definitions (National Electrical Code). Definitions that duplicate those in USA Standard Definitions of Electrical Terms, C42, are marked with an asterisk (°). Those not so marked either differ from or are not found in the latest USA Standard or latest revision thereof.

°ACCESSIBLE (as applied to wiring methods). Not permanently closed in by the structure or finish of the building; capable of being removed without disturbing the building structure or finish. (See "Concealed" and "Exposed.")

°ACCESSIBLE (as applied to equipment). Admitting close approach because not guarded by locked doors, elevation or other effective means. (See "Readily Accessible.")

AMPACITY. Current-carrying capacity expressed in amperes.

APPLIANCE. An appliance is utilization equipment, generally other than industrial, normally built in standardized sizes or types, which is installed or connected as a unit to perform one or more functions such as clothes washing, air conditioning, food mixing, deep frying, etc.

APPLIANCE, FIXED. An appliance that is fastened or otherwise secured at a specific location.

APPLIANCE, PORTABLE. An appliance that is actually moved or can easily be moved from one place to another in normal use.

APPLIANCE, STATIONARY. An appliance that is not easily moved from one place to another in normal use.

APPROVED. Acceptable to the authority enforcing this Code.

°ASKAREL. A synthetic nonflammable insulating liquid which, when decomposed by the electric arc, evolves only nonflammable gaseous mixtures.

°ATTACHMENT PLUG (PLUG CAP) (CAP). An attachment plug is a device which, by insertion in a receptacle, establishes connection between the conductors of the attached flexible cord and the conductors connected permanently to the receptacle.

°AUTOMATIC. Automatic means self-acting, operating by its own mechanism when actuated by some impersonal influence, as, for example, a change in current strength, pressure, temperature, or mechanical configuration. (See "Nonautomatic.")

BONDING JUMPER. A reliable conductor to assure the required electric conductivity between metal parts required to be electrically connected.

BONDING JUMPER, CIRCUIT. The connection between portions of a conductor in a circuit to maintain required ampacity of the circuit.

BONDING JUMPER, EQUIPMENT. The connection between two or more portions of the equipment grounding conductor.

BONDING JUMPER, MAIN. The connection between the grounded circuit conductor and the equipment grounding conductor at the service.

°BRANCH CIRCUIT. A branch circuit is that portion of a wiring system extending beyond the final overcurrent device protecting the circuit.

A device not approved for branch-circuit protection such as a thermal cutout or motor overload protective device is not considered as the overcurrent device protecting the circuit.

°BRANCH CIRCUIT, APPLIANCE. An appliance branch circuit is a circuit supplying energy to one or more outlets to which appliances are to be connected; such circuits to have no permanently connected lighting fixtures not a part of an appliance.

BRANCH CIRCUIT, GENERAL PURPOSE. A branch circuit that supplies a number of outlets for lighting and appliances.

BRANCH CIRCUIT, INDIVIDUAL. A branch circuit that supplies only one utilization equipment.

BRANCH CIRCUIT, MULTIWIRE. A multiwire branch circuit is a circuit consisting of two or more ungrounded conductors having a potential difference between them, and an identified grounded conductor having equal potential difference between it and each ungrounded conductor of the circuit and which is connected to the neutral conductor of the system.

BUILDING. A structure that stands alone or is cut off from adjoining structures by fire walls with all openings therein protected by approved fire doors.

°CABINET. An enclosure designed either for surface or flush mounting and provided with a frame, mat, or trim in which swinging doors are hung.

CIRCUIT BREAKER. A device designed to open and close a circuit by nonautomatic means, and to open the circuit automatically on a predetermined overload of current, without injury to itself when properly applied within its rating.

°CONCEALED. Rendered inaccessible by the structure or finish of the building. Wires in concealed raceways are considered concealed, even though they may become accessible by withdrawing them.

CONDUCTOR.

Bare. A bare conductor is one having no covering or insulation whatsoever. (See "Conductor, Covered.")

Covered. A covered conductor is one having one or more layers of nonconducting materials that are not recognized as insulation under the Code. (See "Conductor, Bare.")

Insulated. An insulated conductor is one covered with material recognized as insulation.

°CONNECTOR, PRESSURE (SOLDERLESS). A pressure wire connector is a device that establishes the connection between two or more conductors or between one or more conductors and a terminal by means of mechanical pressure and without the use of solder.

CONTINUOUS LOAD. A load where the maximum current is expected to continue for 3 hr or more.

CONTROLLER. A device, or group of devices, which serves to govern, in some predetermined manner, the electric power delivered to the apparatus to which it is connected. See also section 430-81(*a*).

COOKING UNIT, COUNTER-MOUNTED. An assembly of one or more domestic surface heating elements for cooking purposes designed for flush mounting in, or supported by, a counter, and which assembly is complete with inherent or separately mountable controls and internal wiring. (See "Oven, Wall-mounted.")

°CUTOUT BOX. An enclosure designed for surface mounting and having swinging doors or covers secured directly to and telescoping with the walls of the box proper. (See "Cabinet.")

°DEMAND FACTOR. The demand factor of any system, or part of a system, is the ratio of the maximum demand of the system, or part of a system, to the total connected load of the system, or of the part of the system under consideration.

DEVICE. A unit of an electric system that is intended to carry but not utilize electric energy.

DISCONNECTING MEANS. A device, or group of devices, or other means whereby the conductors of a circuit can be disconnected from their source of supply.

DRY. See "Location—Dry."

°DUSTPROOF. So constructed or protected that dust will not interfere with its successful operation.

°DUSTTIGHT. So constructed that dust will not enter the enclosing case.

DUTY.

°*Continuous.* Continuous duty is a requirement of service that demands operation for alternate intervals of (1) load and no load; or (2) load and rest; or (3) load, no load, and rest.

°*Periodic.* Periodic duty is a type of intermittent duty in which the load conditions are regularly recurrent.

°*Short Time.* Short-time duty is a requirement of service that demands operation at a substantially constant load for a short and definitely specified time.

°*Varying.* Varying duty is a requirement of service that demands operations at loads, and for intervals of time, both of which may be subject to wide variation.

°ELECTRIC SIGN. A fixed, stationary or portable, self-contained, electrically illuminated utilization equipment with words or symbols designed to convey information or attract attention.

°ENCLOSED. Surrounded by a case that will prevent a person from accidentally contacting live parts.

EQUIPMENT. A general term including material, fittings, devices, appliances, fixtures, apparatus, and the like, used as a part of, or in connection with, an electrical installation.

°EXPLOSION-PROOF APPARATUS. Apparatus enclosed in a case which is capable of withstanding an explosion of a specified gas or vapor that may occur within it, and of preventing the ignition of a specified gas or vapor surrounding the enclosure by sparks, flashes, or explosion of the gas or vapor within, and which operates at such an external temperature that a surrounding flammable atmosphere will not be ignited thereby.

EXPOSED (as applied to live parts). Exposed means that a live part can be inadvertently touched or approached nearer than a safe distance by a person. It is applied to parts not suitably guarded, isolated, or insulated. (See "Accessible" and "Concealed.")

°EXPOSED (as applied to wiring method). Exposed means not concealed.

°EXTERNALLY OPERABLE. Externally operable means capable of being operated without exposing the operator to contact with live parts.

This term is applied to equipment, such as a switch, that is enclosed in a case or cabinet.

FEEDER. A feeder is the circuit conductors between the service equipment, or the generator switchboard of an isolated plant, and the branch-circuit overcurrent device.

FITTING. An accessory such as a lock nut, bushing, or other part of a wiring system that is intended primarily to perform a mechanical rather than an electrical function.

GARAGE. A building or portion of a building in which one or more self-propelled vehicles carrying volatile, flammable liquid for fuel or power are kept for use, sale, storage, rental, repair, exhibition, or demonstrating purposes, and all that portion of a building which is on or below the floor or floors in which such vehicles are kept and which is not separated therefrom by suitable cutoffs.

GROUND. A ground is a conducting connection, whether intentional or accidental, between an electric circuit or equipment and earth, or to some conducting body that serves in place of the earth.

GROUNDED. Grounded means connected to earth or to some conducting body which serves in place of the earth.

GROUNDED CONDUCTOR. A system or circuit conductor which is intentionally grounded.

GROUNDING CONDUCTOR. A conductor used to connect equipment or the grounded circuit of a wiring system to a grounding electrode or electrodes.

GROUNDING CONDUCTOR, MAIN (ungrounded system). The conductor connecting the equipment grounding conductor at the service to the grounding electrode.

GROUNDING CONDUCTOR, COMMON MAIN (grounded system). The conductor that connects both the circuit grounded conductor and the equipment grounding conductor to the grounding electrode.

The above definition does not apply to a conductor used as both the grounded and grounding conductor, as permitted in section 250-52 for services and section 250-60 for ranges and clothes driers.

GROUNDING CONDUCTOR, EQUIPMENT. A conductor used to connect the equipment being grounded to the service equipment enclosure.

GUARDED. Covered, shielded, fenced, enclosed, or otherwise protected, by means of suitable covers or casings, barriers, rails or screens, mats or platforms, to remove the liability of dangerous contact or approach by persons or objects to a point of danger.

HOISTWAY. Any shaftway, hatchway, well hole, or other vertical opening or space in which an elevator or dumbwaiter is designed to operate.

IDENTIFIED. Identified, as used in this Code in reference to a conductor or its terminal, means that such conductor or terminal is to be recognized as grounded.

°ISOLATED. Isolated means that an object is not readily accessible to persons unless special means for access are used.

°LIGHTING OUTLET. An outlet intended for the direct connection of a lamp holder, a lighting fixture, or a pendant cord terminating in a lamp holder.

LOCATION.

Damp. A location subject to a moderate degree of moisture, such as some basements, some barns, some cold storage warehouses, and the like.

Dry. A location not normally subject to dampness or wetness. A location classified as dry may be temporarily subject to dampness or wetness, as in the case of a building under construction.

Wet. A location subject to saturation with water or other liquids, such as locations exposed to weather, washrooms in garages, and like locations. Installations underground or in concrete slabs or masonry in direct contact with the earth shall be considered as wet locations.

LOW-ENERGY POWER CIRCUIT. A circuit that is not a remote-control or signal circuit but has the power supply limited in accordance with the requirements of Class 2 remote-control circuits.

Such circuits include electric door openers and circuits used in the operation of coin-operated phonographs.

MULTIOUTLET ASSEMBLY. A type of surface or flush raceway designed to hold conductors and attachment plug receptacles, assembled in the field or at the factory.

°NONAUTOMATIC. Nonautomatic means that the implied action requires personal intervention for its control. (See "Automatic.")

As applied to an electric controller, nonautomatic control does not necessarily imply a manual controller, but only that personal intervention is necessary.

°OUTLET. A point on the wiring system at which current is taken to supply utilization equipment.

°OUTLINE LIGHTING. An arrangement of incandescent lamps or gaseous tubes to outline and call attention to certain features such as the shape of a building or the decoration of a window.

OVEN, WALL-MOUNTED. A domestic oven for cooking purposes designed for mounting in or on a wall or other surface.

PANEL BOARD. A single panel or group of panel units designed for assembly in the form of a single panel; including buses, and with or without switches and/or automatic overcurrent protective devices for the control of light, heat, or power circuits of small individual as well as aggregate capacity; designed to be placed in a cabinet or cutout box placed in or against a wall or partition and accessible only from the front. (See "Switchboard.")

QUALIFIED PERSON. One familiar with the construction and operation of the apparatus and the hazards involved.

RACEWAY. Any channel for holding wires, cables, or bus bars which is designed expressly for, and used solely for, this purpose.

Raceways may be of metal or insulating material and the term includes rigid metal conduit, rigid nonmetallic conduit, flexible metal conduit, electrical metallic tubing, underfloor raceways, cellular concrete floor raceways, cellular metal floor raceways, surface raceways, structural raceways, wireways, and bus ways.

°RAINTIGHT. So constructed or protected that exposure to a beating rain will not result in the entrance of water.

°READILY ACCESSIBLE. Capable of being reached quickly, for operation, renewal, or inspections, without requiring those to whom ready access is requisite to climb over or remove obstacles or to resort to portable ladders, chairs, etc. (See "Accessible.")

RECEPTACLE (CONVENIENCE OUTLET). A receptacle is a contact device installed at an outlet for the connection of an attachment plug and flexible cord.

°RECEPTACLE OUTLET. An outlet where one or more receptacles are installed.

REMOTE-CONTROL CIRCUIT. Any electric circuit that controls any other circuit through a relay or an equivalent device.

SEALABLE EQUIPMENT. Equipment enclosed in a case or cabinet that is provided with means of sealing or locking so that live parts cannot be made accessible without opening the enclosure. The equipment may or may not be operable without opening the enclosure.

SEALED (HERMETIC TYPE) MOTOR COMPRESSOR. A mechanical compressor consisting of a compressor and a motor, both of which are enclosed in the same sealed housing, with no external shaft or shaft seals, the motor operating in the refrigerant atmosphere.

SERVICE. The conductors and equipment for delivering energy from the electricity supply system to the wiring system of the premises served.

°SERVICE CABLE. The service cable is the service conductors made up in the form of a cable.

SERVICE CONDUCTORS. The supply conductors that extend from the street main, or from transformers to the service equipment of the premises supplied.

SERVICE DROP. The overhead service conductors from the last pole or other aerial support to and including the splices, if any, connecting to the service-entrance conductors at the building or other structure.

SERVICE-ENTRANCE CONDUCTORS, OVERHEAD SYSTEM. The service conductors between the terminals of the service equipment and a point usually outside the building, clear of building walls, where joined by tap or splice to the service drop.

SERVICE-ENTRANCE CONDUCTORS, UNDERGROUND SYSTEM. The service conductors between the terminals of the service equipment and the point of connection to the service lateral.

Where service equipment is located outside the building walls, there may be no service-entrance conductors, or they may be entirely outside the building.

SERVICE EQUIPMENT. The necessary equipment, usually consisting of circuit breaker or switch and fuses, and their accessories, located near point of entrance of supply conductors to a building and intended to constitute the main control and means of cutoff for the supply to that building.

SERVICE LATERAL. The underground service conductors between the street main, including any risers at a pole or other structure or from transformers, and the first point of connection to the service-entrance conductors in a terminal box or meter or other enclosure with adequate space, inside or outside the building wall. Where there is no terminal box, or meter or other enclosure with adequate space, the point of connection shall be considered to be the point of entrance of the service conductors into the building.

SERVICE RACEWAY. The rigid metal conduit, electrical metallic tubing, or other raceway, that encloses the service-entrance conductors.

SETTING (OF CIRCUIT BREAKER). The value of the current at which it is set to trip.

SHOW WINDOW. A show window is any window used or designed to be used for the display of goods or advertising material, whether it is fully or partly enclosed or entirely open at the rear, and whether or not it has a platform raised higher than the street floor level.

SIGN. See "Electric Sign."

SIGNAL CIRCUIT. Any electric circuit that supplies energy to an appliance which gives a recognizable signal.

Such circuits include those for doorbells, buzzers, code-calling systems, signal lights, and the like.

SPECIAL PERMISSION. The written consent of the authority enforcing this Code.

SWITCHES.

°*General-use Switch.* A general use switch is a switch intended for use in general distribution and branch circuits. It is rated in amperes, and it is capable of interrupting its rated current at its rated voltage.

General-use Snap Switch. A form of general-use switch so constructed that it can be installed in flush device boxes, or on outlet box covers, or otherwise used in conjunction with wiring systems recognized by this Code.

A-C General-use Snap Switch. A form of general-use snap switch suitable only for use on a-c circuits for controlling the following:

1. Resistive and inductive loads (including electric discharge lamps) not exceeding the ampere rating at the voltage involved.

2. Tungsten-filament lamp loads not exceeding the amperes rating at 120 volts.

3. Motor loads not exceeding 80 per cent of the ampere rating of the switches at the rated voltage.

All a-c general-use snap switches are marked "A-C" in addition to their electrical rating.

A-C–D-C General-use Snap Switch. A form of general-use snap switch suitable for use on either d-c or a-c circuits for controlling the following:

1. Resistive loads not exceeding the ampere rating at the voltage involved.

2. Inductive loads not exceeding one-half the ampere rating at the voltage involved, except that switches having a marked horsepower rating are suitable for controlling motors not exceeding the horsepower rating of the switch at the voltage involved.

3. Tungsten-filament lamp loads not exceeding the ampere rating at 125 volts, when marked with the letter T.

A-C–D-C general-use snap switches are not generally marked A-C, D-C, but are always marked with their electrical rating.

°*Isolating Switch.* An isolating switch is a switch intended for isolating an electric circuit from the source of power. It has no interrupting rating, and it is intended to be operated only after the circuit has been opened by some other means.

Motor Circuit Switch. A switch, rated in horsepower, capable of interrupting the maximum operating overload current of a motor of the same horsepower rating as the switch at the rated voltage.

SWITCHBOARD. A large single panel, frame, or assembly of panels, on which are mounted, on the face or back or both, switches, overcurrent and other protective devices, buses, and usually instruments. Switchboards are generally accessible from the rear as well as from the front and are not intended to be installed in cabinets. (See "Panel Board.")

THERMAL CUTOUT. An overcurrent protective device which contains a heater element in addition to and affecting a renewable fusible member which opens the circuit. It is not designed to interrupt short-circuit currents.

THERMALLY PROTECTED (as applied to motors). The words "Thermally Protected" appearing on the nameplate of a motor or motor-compressor indicate that the motor is provided with a thermal protector.

THERMAL PROTECTOR (as applied to motors). A thermal protector is a protective device for assembly as an integral part of a motor or motor-compressor and which, when properly applied, protects the motor against dangerous overheating due to overload and failure to start.

The thermal protector may consist of one or more sensing elements integral with the motor or motor-compressor and an external control device.

°UTILIZATION EQUIPMENT. Utilization equipment is equipment that utilizes electric energy for mechanical, chemical, heating, lighting, or similar useful purposes.

°VENTILATED. Provided with a means to permit circulation of air sufficient to remove an excess of heat, fumes, or vapors.

VOLATILE FLAMMABLE LIQUID. A flammable liquid having a flash point below 100°F or whose temperature is above its flash point.

°VOLTAGE (OF A CIRCUIT). Voltage is the greatest root-mean-square (effective) difference of potential between any two conductors of the circuit concerned.

On various systems such as three-phase four-wire, single-phase three-wire, and three-wire d-c, there may be various circuits of various voltages.

VOLTAGE TO GROUND. In grounded circuits the voltage between the given conductor and that point or conductor of the circuit which is grounded; in ungrounded circuits, the greatest voltage between the given conductor and any other conductor of the circuit.

WATERTIGHT. So constructed that moisture will not enter the enclosing case.

°WEATHERPROOF. Weatherproof means so constructed or protected that exposure to the weather will not interfere with successful operation.

Raintight or watertight equipment may fulfill the requirements for "weatherproof." However, weather conditions vary, and consideration should be given to conditions resulting from snow, ice, dust, or temperature extremes.

4. Methods of Installing Interior Wiring.

1. Open wiring: on insulators.
2. Concealed knob and tube.
3. Rigid metal or nonmetallic conduit.
4. Flexible metal conduit.
5. Liquid-tight flexible metal conduit.
6. Metal-clad cable.
7. Surface raceways.
8. Electrical metallic tubing.
9. Nonmetallic-sheathed cable.
10. Mineral-insulated metal-sheathed cable.
11. Underground feeder and branch-circuit cable.
12. Service-entrance cable.
13. Nonmetallic extensions.
14. Structural raceways.
15. Underfloor raceways.
16. Underplaster extensions.
17. Wireways.
18. Bus ways.
19. Cellular-metal-floor raceways.
20. Cellular-concrete-floor raceways.
21. Bare-conductor feeders.
22. Multioutlet assemblies.
23. Continuous rigid cable supports.
24. Cablebus.

5. In the open-wiring method of installing interior wiring the wires are run either concealed or exposed on the ceiling, roof structure, or walls. They are supported on porcelain insulators of either the knob (Figs. 133, 134, and 135, Div. 4) or the cleat type (Figs. 137 and 138, Div. 4) so as to provide the necessary clearance between the wires and the surface wired over.

6. Concealed knob and tube wiring was one of the earliest methods of installing wiring. The wires were mounted on knobs and run through tubes where they pierced structural members of the building. They were then concealed by the wall and ceiling surface. This method is still allowed by the National Electrical Code, but is not used too often because of the large amount of labor required to install the wiring.

7. In the rigid-metal-conduit method of installing interior wiring the wires are supported and protected from mechanical injury by being installed in ferrous or nonferrous types of rigid metal conduits. Ferrous types are wrought iron or steel with coatings such as black enamel, electrogalvanizing, hot-dip galvanizing, or similar material. Nonferrous types include aluminum or brass (silicon-bronze). Various types of ferrous and nonferrous metal conduits are available with outer plastic coatings to provide optimum protection from corrosion.

Rigid conduit may be run exposed, supported directly on walls, ceilings, roof structures or on suitable hanger assemblies. It may also be concealed in partitions, ceilings, or floors. Provision for connection to the circuit at outlet and switch points is made by the insertion of sheet-steel, cast-metal boxes (steel or aluminum), or special conduit fittings in the conduit run. The special conduit fittings, LB, T, LL, LR, X, etc., are called by various trade names, such as Condulets or Unilets. Although rigid metal conduits are usually employed with threaded fittings and connections, there are many threadless fittings available for use without threading the conduit.

Conduit, fittings, and boxes are installed complete without wires. Then the wires are pulled into the conduit from fitting to fitting, box to box, or fitting to box. In hazardous locations only threaded connections (five full threads) are permitted.

8. Rigid nonmetallic conduit and fittings are constructed of a suitable nonmetallic material that is resistant to moisture and chemical atmospheres. For use above ground it must be flame-retardant and resistant to impact and crushing, to distortion due to heat under conditions likely to be encountered in service, and to low temperature or sunlight effects. The only type of nonmetallic conduit that is suitable for above-ground applications is the heavy-wall type constructed of polyvinyl chloride (PVC). Such conduits may be embedded in concrete in buildings or installed in wet locations such as laundries or dairies. It may also be buried directly in earth at potentials of 600 volts or less.

Other types of nonmetallic conduits, recognized solely for underground use, are those constructed of fiber, asbestos cement, soapstone, and high-density polyethylene. Depending upon construction and Underwriters' Laboratories listings, such conduits may or may not require concrete encasement. Complete lines of nonmetallic fittings and boxes are available. For underground application reference should be made to Div. 8.

9. The flexible metal-conduit method of installing wiring is used to a limited degree in frame buildings or similar applications where rigid raceways would be difficult to install and a pull-in, pull-out conduit system is desirable. Flexible metal conduit is often referred to as "Greenfield." The runs of conduit, boxes, and fittings are installed first as a complete system. Then the wires are installed in the same manner as in rigid metal conduit. The National Electrical Code states that flexible metal conduit may be used as a grounding means where both the conduit and fittings are approved for the purpose. Where not so approved, each run of flexible metal conduit must contain a bare or insulated grounding conductor, and this grounding conductor must be attached to each box or other equipment supplied by such conduit.

10. Liquid-tight flexible metal conduit has an outer liquid-tight jacket. It is not intended for general-use wiring. Wiring of this kind may be used only for the connection of motors or portable or stationary equipment where flexibility of connections is required. When used, it must be provided with suitable terminal connectors approved for the purpose. It cannot be used in sizes larger than 3 in., where subject to mechanical injury, where in contact with rapidly moving parts, where subject to temperatures above 60°C (140°F), or in any hazardous location except for motor connection in Division 2 areas. See Table 28 in Div. 11 for maximum sizes of conductors allowed.

11. Metal-clad cables includes types AC and MC. Type AC has a flexible metal armor and formerly was termed "armored cable." This cable is widely used for concealed and exposed wiring where flexibility and ease of installation are important factors. The factory-provided conductors are rubber, thermoplastic, varnished cambric, or similar types. Type AC cables (other than Type ACL, lead-covered) have an internal bonding strip of aluminum, in intimate contact with the armor. At outlets the bonding strip is merely folded back, and the connector or cable clamps are installed to secure the cable. Type MC cables are power cables: No. 4 copper and larger, or No. 2 aluminum and larger. The metal enclosure is either a covering of interlocking metal tape or an impervious, close-fitting, corrugated tube. Types MC and AC cables are suitable for exposed or concealed work in general applications.

12. Aluminum-sheathed cable, Type ALS, is a factory-assembled cable consisting of one or more insulated conductors enclosed in an impervious, continuous, closely fitting tube of aluminum. Special fittings are used for cable terminations and connections to boxes, outlets, and other locations. This cable is used in wet or damp locations or in all Division 2 hazardous locations and Class III, Division 1, hazardous locations. The cable may be run in both exposed and concealed work.

13. Surface raceways include both metallic and nonmetallic types. In the metallic type wires are inserted into a thin sheet-metal casing. The raceway is installed exposed on interior building surfaces. The metal molding is made with a flattened-oval or rectangular cross section. Numerous fittings, adapters, and boxes, specially designed for this system, are readily available from major manufacturers of this wiring system. Nonmetallic surface raceway has just been developed at this writing so that data and applications on this are presently unavailable. However, the National Electrical Code recognizes the nonmetallic type of raceway. Installations, boxes, and fittings are similar to those in the metallic system.

14. In the electrical-metallic-tubing method of installing wiring the wires are installed in a thin-walled metallic tube or thin-walled conduit, as it is sometimes called. Electrical metallic tubing is similar to rigid conduit except that it is constructed of much thinner material. Provisions for connecting outlets and switches to the circuit are made by means of special metallic-tubing fittings or by means of regular rigid-conduit fittings provided with an adapter. After the tubing and fittings have been installed as a complete system, the wires are pulled in from fitting to fitting as in the rigid-conduit method. Connectors and couplings are threadless types—such as set-screw, compression, indenter, or tap-on.

15. Nonmetallic-sheathed cable is made in two types, Type NM and Type NMC. The Type NM consists of two or three rubber- or thermoplastic-insulated wires bound together and protected by a plastic jacket, or a cotton-bound paper jacket with an outer heavy cotton braid, treated with a moisture- and heat-resisting compound. Type NMC cables are protected by an outer rubber sheath which contains no cotton or paper. Nonmetallic cable may be run exposed on walls and ceilings or concealed in the hollow spaces between partitions or between floors and ceilings. The cable is fastened directly to the surface of the walls, ceilings, or structural members with approved supports. Provision for outlets and switches is made by running the cable into outlet boxes. In most cases such cables contain an equipment grounding conductor.

16. Mineral-insulated metal-sheathed cable (Type MI) consists of one or more electrical conductors insulated and separated by a highly compressed refractory mineral insulation and protected from injury by enclosure in a liquid-tight and gas-tight metallic tube sheathing. The wires, insulation, and protective sheathing are manufactured as a unit. The method of installation is similar to that of metal-clad cable. Special approved fittings are used for terminating and connecting the cable to boxes and other equipment. At all points of termination of the cable an approved moisture seal must be provided.

17. Underground feeder and branch-circuit cable (Type UF) resembles Type USE service-entrance cable in general appearance. The insulation employed may consist of a special synthetic plastic compound. When single-conductor cables are used, all conductors of the circuit must be installed in the same trench or raceway. For multiple-conductor cable installations all conductors of the circuit together with the protective covering of the cable are installed as a unit, just as in metal-clad cable or nonmetallic-sheathed cable installations. Provision for outlets is made by running the cable into suitable outlet boxes. Underground feeder and branch-circuit cable wiring provides a convenient approved method for interior wiring in wet or corrosive locations. It may be installed underground either in ducts or buried directly in the earth. Multiple-conductor cables usually contain an equipment grounding conductor.

18. Service-entrance cable (see Div. 2) normally is used for the circuit from the point of attachment of the service conductors on the outside of the building to the service switch, load center, or meter cabinet just inside the building. It may, however, also be employed for the interior wiring on the load side of the service switch. It is not commonly used for general interior wiring but is used for certain special portions of the wiring such as to supply large appliances like an electric range, as a feeder to a distribution panel elsewhere in the building, or as a service cable to other buildings. For unrestricted use all the conductors must be rubber or thermoplastic insulated. If an uninsulated neutral is used, the cable must have a final nonmetallic outer covering, the voltage to ground must not exceed 150 volts, and it may be used only to supply a range, wall-mounted oven, or counter-mounted cooking equipment, or clothes drier, or, from a master service cabinet, to supply other buildings. The cable is fastened to the surface with straps spaced not over 4 ft 6 in. apart.

19. In the underfloor-raceway method of wiring the wires are installed in a sheet-metal or fiber casing which is embedded in the concrete or cement fill of the floor. Generally, the ducts or raceways are laid out in the floor to form a network. Provision is made at the intersections of the ducts for the pulling in and splicing of wires by means of special floor junction boxes. Sheet-metal-type raceways are provided with outlet openings spaced at regular intervals along the raceway. These outlet openings are either plugged or equipped with special floor-outlet fittings. With the fiber-duct type of raceway the raceway is first installed in the floor without any outlet openings. After the floor has been finished, outlets may be provided at any desired point along the duct runs by simply cutting a hole in the floor and duct and inserting a special floor-outlet fitting. In the underfloor-raceway systems the wires are pulled through the ducts in the same manner as for rigid-conduit work.

20. Underplaster extensions are wiring systems laid in a channel cut in the plaster surface of a wall, down to the face of masonry or other wall material. Rigid or flexible metal conduit, Type AC metal-clad cable, electrical metallic tubing, Type MI cable, or metal raceways approved for the purpose are laid in the channel and secured to the surface of the wall or ceiling structure. Provision for outlets is made by inserting shallow outlet boxes in the run of conduit, cable, tubing, or raceway. After the system has been secured in the channel, it is plastered over flush with the wall or ceiling surface.

21. A nonmetallic extension is an assembly of two insulated conductors within a nonmetallic jacket or an extruded thermoplastic covering. The classification includes both surface extensions, intended for mounting directly on the surface of walls or ceilings, and aerial cable, containing a supporting messenger cable as an integral part of the cable assembly. Nonmetallic extensions are permitted only where (1) the extension is from an existing outlet on a 15- or 20-amp branch circuit and (2) the extension is run exposed and in a dry location. Nonmetallic *surface* extensions are limited to residential or office buildings, and *aerial* cable is limited to industrial buildings where a highly flexible means for connecting equipment is required.

22. In the wireway method of wiring the wires are supported and protected in a sheet-metal trough. The sheet-metal trough is installed exposed, being mounted on the ceiling or walls, or supported from the roof structure. One side of the trough is fitted with a sheet-metal cover so that access can be had to the interior sections of the trough throughout its entire length. After the wireway has been installed as a complete system, the wires are laid in the trough and the cover is installed. Mains and feeders are run in the wireways with taps for branches taken off at the most convenient point through rigid or flexible metal conduit, connected to the wireway through knockouts provided on three sides of the trough. This system provides a flexible distribution system.

23. Bus-way systems of wiring consist of bare bus bars insulated from each other and supported and protected by a sheet-metal housing. The housing and bus bars are assembled as a unit in 10-ft or longer sections. The system is installed by supporting the housing from the ceiling, walls, or roof structure. Bus-way systems are extensively used for the feeder and main circuits in industrial plants. They are available in three general types: without provision for outlets, with provision for fixed outlets, and with provision for continuously movable outlets for portable tools and electric-welding work. With the type which has provision for fixed outlets, openings are provided every few inches for branch taps. The connection of a tap to the bus bars is accomplished through the insertion of a special power attachment plug in these openings. For the wiring of the branch circuit from the power plug to the apparatus to be supplied with power, flexible conduit, rigid conduit, or metal-clad cable may be employed. This method of wiring provides a very flexible system which meets in an economical manner the requirements of plants where production conditions necessitate the frequent shifting or replacement of machinery.

24. In the cellular-metal-floor-raceway wiring, the floor is constructed of special metal structural members containing hollow spaces or cells which form raceways for the wires. Provision for pulling in and splicing wires is made by means of locating special junction boxes in the floor between sections of the floor members. Outlet openings and fittings may be originally provided at regular intervals along the raceway formed by the cells, or outlets may be provided at any time after completion of the building construction by simply cutting a hole in the floor and cell wall and inserting a special floor-outlet fitting. After the complete floor structure has been erected and finished over, the wires are pulled through the raceway formed by the floor cell structure and the junction boxes.

25. In cellular-concrete-floor-raceways wiring, the floor is constructed of precast reinforced-concrete members. These precast members are provided with hollow voids which form smooth, round cells. These cells form raceways for the wires. Connections to the cells from a distribution center can be made by means of metal header ducts run horizontally across the precast slabs and embedded in the concrete fill over the slabs. Connection from these headers to the cells is made through handhole metal junction boxes. An outlet can be located at any point along a cell. An opening into the cell at the desired point is formed by drilling a hole through the concrete floor slab. The hole is then fitted with the proper outlet fitting, and the wires fished from a hand-hole junction box to the outlet.

26. Bare-conductor feeders are allowed only by special permission. When allowed, such a feeder installation consists of bare conductors supported on noncombustible, nonabsorptive insulating supports and enclosed in a chase, channel, or shaft of non-combustible material. This sytem is rarely used.

27. Multioutlet assemblies are a special form of surface raceway with built-in single receptacle outlets, every few inches. The assembly is supported on the surface of walls or in or on top of baseboards. It is used for convenience-outlet wiring in dwellings and commercial buildings for providing very convenient and adequate convenience outlets. The assembly is supplied with power through a cable or conduit run concealed in the walls and brought into the back or end of the assembly.

28. A cablebus system is an approved assembly of insulated conductors mounted in spaced relationship in a ventilated metal protective supporting structure, including fittings and conductor terminations. Cablebus may be used at any voltage up to 35 kv or current for which the spaced conductors are rated. Cablebus is ordinarily assembled at the point of installation from components specified by the manufacturer. First, the supporting structure is installed in the same manner as in a continuous rigid cable support system. Next the insulated conductors, not less than 1/0 with insulation ratings of 75°C or higher, are inserted. After this, insulating supports are installed so that the conductors are properly separated and supported at intervals not less than 3 ft for horizontal runs and 1½ ft for vertical runs. Conductor ampacity is based on the values for open conductors.

29. A continuous rigid cable support system is a unit or an assembly of units or sections, and associated fittings, made of steel, aluminum, or other noncombustible materials forming a continuous rigid structure used to support cables. The support system includes ladders, troughs, channels, and other similar support systems. It is also known as a "cable tray" system. A continuous rigid cable support system is not a wiring method and may be used only as the mechanical support for approved raceway or multiple-conductor cable wiring methods or specially approved multiple-conductor cables designed for use in cable trays. First, the support system is installed, and then the cables or raceways are installed and secured to the support. This system has particular merit in industrial applications or similar uses where many power, control, or signal cables are required and where flexibility is a major consideration.

30. Structural raceways are formed steel members approved for the installation of electric wires or cables within them, such as tubes or channels that are used as vertical members serving as studs or columns, or horizontal members used as beams or top plates with suitable covers, end closers, and fittings. Although this system is recognized by the National Electrical Code as an approved wiring method, no such systems are commercially available at this time, and only a few trial installations have been made.

31. Conductor Types and Applications

Trade name	Type letter[a]	Maximum operating temperature	Application provisions
Rubber-covered fixture wire, solid or 7-strand	RF-1	60°C 140°F	Fixture wiring. Limited to 300 volts
	RF-2	60°C 140°F	Fixture wiring, and as permitted in section 310-8
Rubber-covered fixture wire, flexible stranding	FF-1	60°C 140°F	Fixture wiring. Limited to 300 volts
	FF-2	60°C 140°F	Fixture wiring, and as permitted in section 310-8
Heat-resistant rubber-covered fixture wire, solid or 7-strand	RFH-1	75°C 167°F	Fixture wiring. Limited to 300 volts.
	RFH-2	75°C 167°F	Fixture wiring, and as permitted in section 310-8
Heat-resistant rubber-covered fixture wire, flexible stranding	FFH-1	75°C 167°F	Fixture wiring. Limited to 300 volts
	FFH-2	75°C 167°F	Fixture wiring, and as permitted in section 310-8
Thermoplastic-covered fixture wire, solid or stranded	TF	60°C 140°F	Fixture wiring, and as permitted in section 310-8, and for circuits as permitted in article 725
Thermoplastic-covered fixture wire, flexible stranding	TFF	60°C 140°F	Fixture wiring, and as permitted in section 310-8, and for circuits as permitted in article 725
Heat-resistant, thermoplastic-covered fixture wire, solid or stranded	TFN	90°C 194°F	Fixture wiring, and as permitted in section 310-8
Heat-resistant thermoplastic-covered fixture wire, flexible stranding	TFFN	90°C 194°F	Fixture wiring, and as permitted in section 310-8
Cotton-covered heat-resistant fixture wire	CF	90°C 194°F	Fixture wiring. Limited to 300 volts
Asbestos-covered heat-resistant fixture wire	AF	150°C 302°F	Fixture wiring. Limited to 300 volts and indoor dry locations
Fluorinated ethylene propylene fixture wire, solid or 7-strand	PF	150°C	Fixture wiring and as permitted in section 310-8
	PGF	302°F	
Fluorinated ethylene propylene fixture wire	PFF	150°C	Fixture wiring and as permitted in section 310-8
	PGFF	302°F	
Silicone rubber insulated fixture wire, solid or 7-strand	SF-1	200°C 392°F	Fixture wiring. Limited to 300 volts
	SF-2	200°C 392°F	Fixture wiring and as permitted in section 310-8

[a] Fixture wires are not intended for installation as branch-circuit conductors except as permitted in article 725.

Conductor Types and Applications (*Continued*)

Trade name	Type letter[a]	Maximum operating temperature	Application provisions
Silicone rubber insulated fixture wire,	SFF-1	150°C 302°F	Fixture wiring. Limited to 300 volts
flexible stranding	SFF-2	150°C 302°F	Fixture wiring and as permitted in section 310-8
Heat-resistant rubber	RH	75°C 167°F	Dry locations
Heat-resistant rubber	RHH	90°C 194°F	Dry locations
Moisture- and heat-resistant rubber	RHW	75°C 167°F	Dry and wet locations. For over 2,000 volts, insulation shall be ozone-resistant
Heat-resistant latex rubber	RUH	75°C 167°F	Dry locations
Moisture-resistant latex rubber	RUW	60°C 140°F	Dry and wet locations
Thermoplastic	T	60°C 140°F	Dry locations
Moisture-resistant thermoplastic	TW	60°C 140°F	Dry and wet locations
Heat-resistant thermoplastic	THHN	90°C 194°F	Dry locations
Moisture- and heat-resistant thermoplastic	THW	75°C 167°F	Dry and wet locations
Moisture- and heat-resistant thermoplastic	THWN	75°C 167°F	Dry and wet locations
Moisture- and heat-resistant cross-linked thermosetting polyethylene	XHHW	90°C 194°F / 75°C 167°F	Dry locations / Wet locations
Moisture-, heat-, and oil-resistant thermoplastic	MTW	60°C 140°F / 90°C 194°F	Wet locations, machine tool wiring (see article 670 and NFPA Standard No. 79) / Dry locations, machine tool wiring (see article 670 and NFPA Standard No. 79)
Moisture-, heat-, and oil-resistant thermoplastic	THW-MTW	75°C 167°F / 90°C 194°F	Dry and wet locations / Special applications *within* electric discharge lighting equipment. Limited to 1,000 open-circuit volts or less (size 14-8 only)
Thermoplastic and asbestos	TA	90°C 194°F	Switchboard wiring only
Thermoplastic and fibrous outer braid	TBS	90°C 194°F	Switchboard wiring only
Synthetic heat-resistant	SIS	90°C 194°F	Switchboard wiring only

[a] Fixture wires are not intended for installation as branch-circuit conductors except as permitted in article 725.

Conductor Types and Applications (*Continued*)

Trade name	Type letter *a*	Maximum operating temperature	Application provisions
Mineral insulation (metal-sheathed)	MI	85°C 185°F	Dry and wet locations with Type O termination fittings
		250°C 482°F	For special application
Silicone-asbestos	SA	90°C 194°F	Dry locations
		125°C 257°F	For special application
Fluorinated ethylene propylene	FEP or FEPB	90°C 194°F	Dry locations
		200°C 392°F	Dry locations—special applications
Varnished cambric	V	85°C 185°F	Dry locations only. Smaller than No. 6 by special permission
Asbestos and varnished cambric	AVA	110°C 230°F	Dry locations only
Asbestos and varnished cambric	AVL	110°C 230°F	Dry and wet locations
Asbestos and varnished cambric	AVB	90°C 194°F	Dry locations only
Asbestos	A	200°C 392°F	Dry locations only. Only for leads within apparatus or within raceways connected to apparatus. Limited to 300 volts
Asbestos	AA	200°C 392°F	Dry locations only. Only for leads within apparatus or within raceways connected to apparatus or as open wiring. Limited to 300 volts
Asbestos	AI	125°C 257°F	Dry locations only. Only for leads within apparatus or within raceways connected to apparatus. Limited to 300 volts
Asbestos	AIA	125°C 257°F	Dry locations only. Only for leads within apparatus or within raceways connected to apparatus or as open wiring
Paper		85°C 185°F	For underground service conductors, or by special permission

a Fixture wires are not intended for installation as branch-circuit conductors except as permitted in article 725.

OPEN WIRING ON INSULATORS

32. Open wiring on insulators is one of the cheapest methods of installing wiring. It finds application for temporary installations and in factories and mills for the installation of feeder circuits in some places where appearance is of little consequence. The wires may contain rubber or thermoplastic insulation. The wires must be supported at least every 4½ ft, except in mill buildings, where a support on each beam may be approved for wires No. 8 and larger if they are separated at least 6 in. Also, circuits using No. 8 or larger wire, where not likely to be disturbed, may be run across open spaces and supported at distances not greater than 15 ft if approved noncombustible, nonabsorptive insulating separators providing not less than 2½-in. separation between conductors are installed at intervals of not over 4½ ft. The wires must, in dry places, be separated ½ in. from the surface wired over and spaced 2½ in. apart for voltages up to 300. Above 300 volts and up to 600 volts, the wires must be separated from the surface wired over by at least 1 in. and must be spaced 4 in. apart. In wet places, wires must be at least 1 in. from surface wired over, for all voltages.

33. Knobs and Methods of Supporting Conductors on Them. Knobs for supporting conductors in interior work are of porcelain. Split knobs or cleats may be used for supporting conductors smaller than No. 8 American wire gage. Some methods of securing wires to knobs are shown in Fig. 1. The line tie of I is made by winding the conductor once around the knob, so both ends of the wire must be under tension to hold the wire in position. A tie wire is used as II. In making up the tie wire the slack can be drawn out of the conductor. A dead end or termination is shown at III.

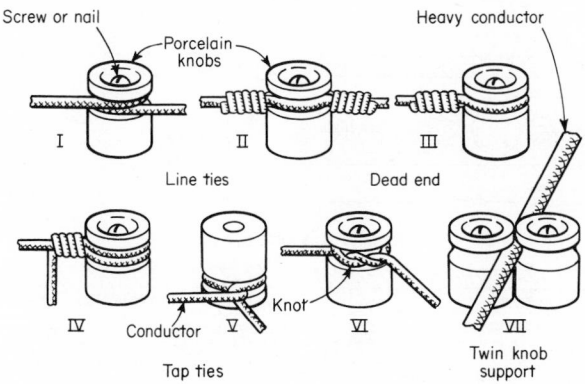

FIG. 1 *Methods of attaching to knobs.*

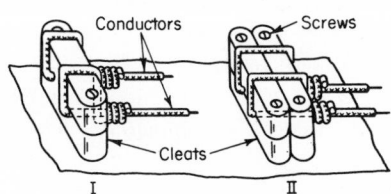

FIG. 2 *Dead-ending on cleats.*

Where it is necessary to change the direction of a run to get the conductor to an outlet or for any other reason, tap ties IV, V, and VI are used. It is not practicable to tie large conductors, so they may be supported as at VII.

For a discussion of types of knobs see Div. 4.

Nails used to support knobs must be not smaller than 10 penny and must be provided with cushion washers. When screws are used, they must penetrate the supporting wood to a depth equal to at least one-half the height of the knob or to at least the thickness of the cleat used.

34. Tie wires must have an insulation equal to that of the conductors they confine and may be used in connection with solid knobs for the support of wires of size No. 8 or larger.

35. The method of dead-ending on a cleat at the end of a run is illustrated in Fig. 2. After the wire is passed through the groove, the free end is given several short turns around the line. Where a long run is dead-ended, it is often advisable to fasten two sets of cleats in such a way that one bears against the other so that both will assume the strain as shown at II. For types and dimensions of cleats see Div. 4.

36. Methods of Terminating Heavy Conductors. At the ends of all important open-wire runs of wires larger than, say, No. 8, strain insulators engaging in some wire-tightening device should be used. Figure 3 illustrates some methods. Either tightening bolts or turnbuckles can be used. The insulator may be of the type extensively used in trolley-line construction as in I, II, and III, or it may be a heavy knob (IV) held to the tightening device with stout wire. Where a run changes direction, a cable clamp can often be used with economy, particularly with large conductors. Where a cable clamp is used, it is unnecessary to cut the conductor to change its direction and the necessity of making up turns about the line wire as in I and II is eliminated.

37. Different approved methods of exposed surface wiring are illustrated in Fig. 4. Which method should be used in any particular case is a matter that is largely determined by the size of the wire involved and other local conditions.

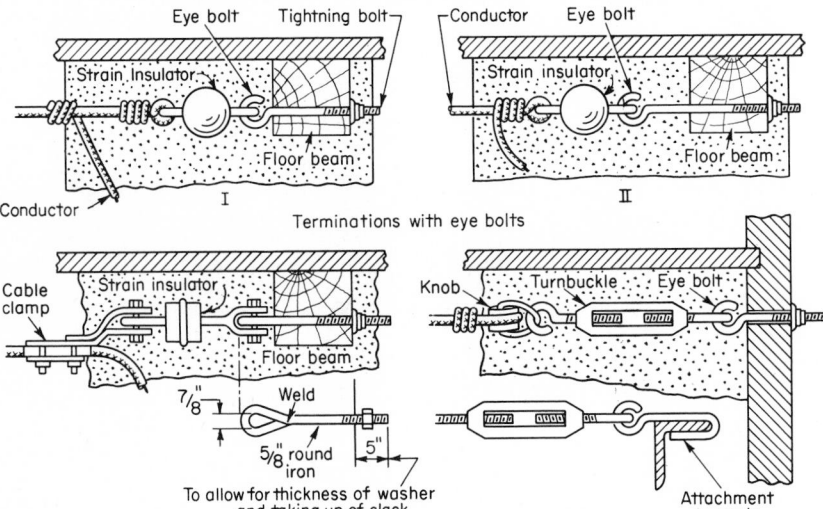

FIG. 3   *Methods of terminating conductors.*

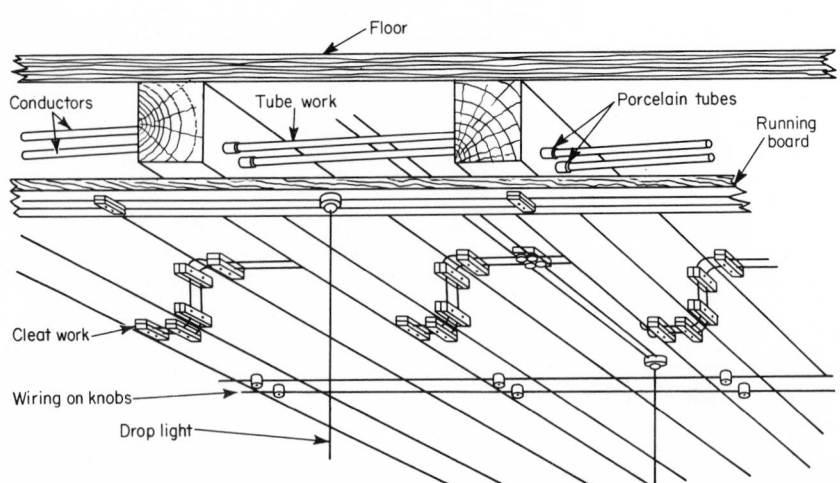

FIG. 4   *Open-work wiring in a mill building.*

38. Mechanical Protection of Exposed Surface Wiring. The wires must be protected on side walls from mechanical injury and, when crossing timbers where they might be disturbed, must be protected by guard strips or running board and guard strips as shown in Figs. 5 and 6. The guard strips must be at least ⅞ in. thick and at least as high as the insulators. Where a running board is used, it must be at least ½ in. thick and must extend at least 1 in. outside the conductors but not more than 2 in. The wires should also be protected by porcelain tubes when passing over pipes (Fig. 7) or any other members. Tie wires may be used in lieu of tape.

Conductors within 7 ft from the floor shall be considered exposed to mechanical injury. Suitable protection on side walls, therefore, should extend not less than 7 ft from the floor (Fig. 8). This may consist of substantial boxing, providing an air space

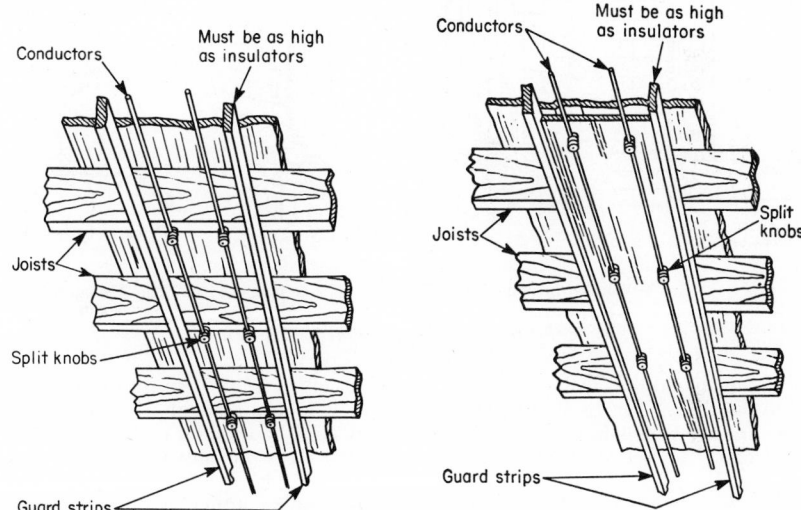

FIG. 5 *Guard strips to protect open wiring crossing ceiling joists.*

FIG. 6 *Running board with guard strips to protect open wiring crossing ceiling joists.*

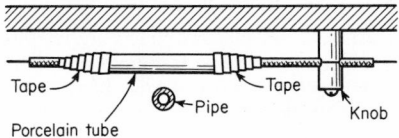

FIG. 7 *Protection of conductor passing over pipe.*

of 1 in. around the conductors, closed at the top (the wire passing through porcelain-bushed holes), or a conduit with fittings on each end providing individual bushed holes for each wire (Fig. 8, III).

39. Methods of carrying exposed wiring around and through beams are illustrated in Fig. 4, which shows the tube-and-cleat arrangements. In Fig. 9 are shown some methods that can be used when wires are supported on knobs.

40. In steel mill buildings heavy conductors may be carried on the lower chords of the roof trusses (Fig. 10). This is a good location as the conductors are out of the way and not apt to be disturbed. At each truss the conductors can be supported by one of the methods illustrated in Fig. 11. With the method of Fig. 11, I, the conductor merely rests in the insulator, and the entire longitudinal strain is taken by strain insulators attached to tightening bolts or turnbuckles at the ends of the run. This method has

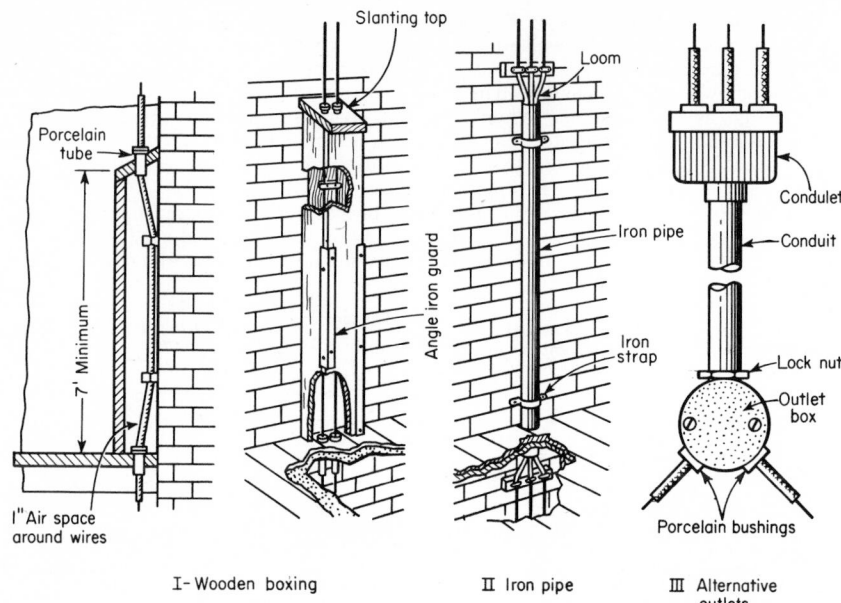

FIG. 8 *Protection of conductors on side walls.*

the disadvantage that if the conductor breaks at any point or is burnt in two, it will fall to the floor. The tie-wire method of II is seldom used, though it is satisfactory if cleats are not obtainable. (Split knobs or cleats must be used for conductors smaller than No. 8.) The cleat and through-bolt method of III is probably the best, all things considered. After the conductor has been drawn taut with the tightening bolts at the ends of the run, the cleat bolts are tightened and each cleat then assumes its share of the stress. Tie wires, which are unreliable and may cut into the insulation of the conductor, are unnecessary. Leather washers should be used between the insulator and bolt to prevent breakage.

41. For supporting conductors on steel angles the Universal Insulator Support (Figs. 12 and 13 and Table **42**) is a convenient fitting. It is of malleable iron and can be clamped on the flanges of steel beams, angles, channels, and Z bars and on round, square, and flat bars. It can also be attached to gas and water pipes and to the edges of plates and tanks. Two insulators can be fastened to each support when necessary. Cup-pointed, case-hardened setscrews are used. Leather washers should be used under the bolts that hold the insulators.

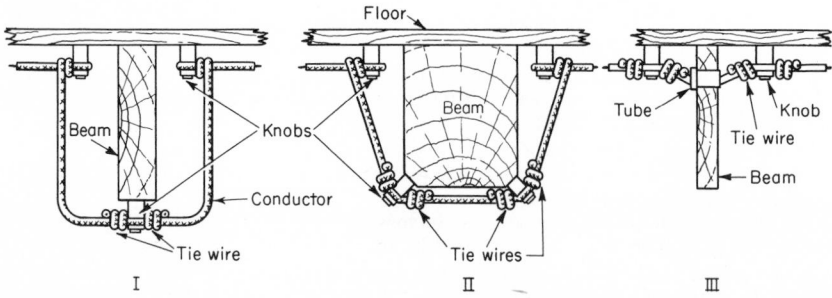

FIG. 9 *Open-work wiring with knobs.*

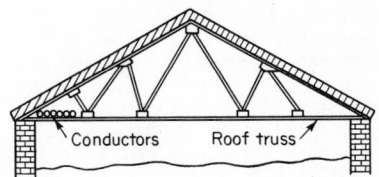

FIG. 10 *Conductors carried on roof truss.*

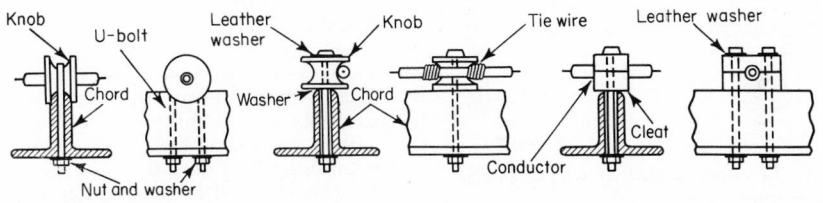

FIG. 11 *Attaching knobs to truss chords.*

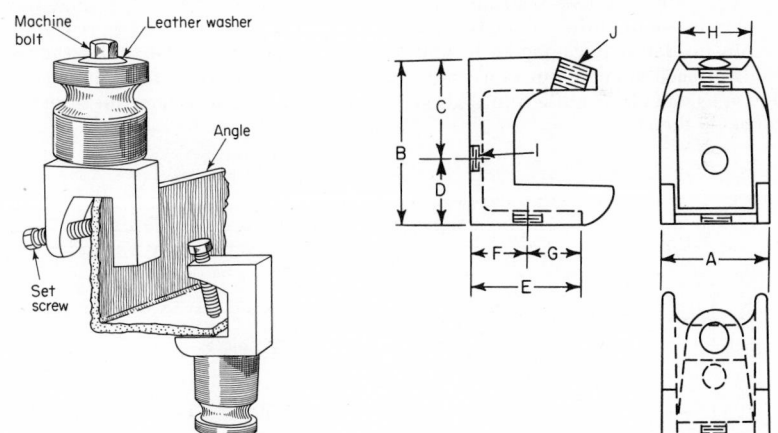

FIG. 12 *Universal Insulator Supports on an angle.*

FIG. 13 *The Universal Insulator Support.*

42. Dimensions of Universal Insulator Supports

(Steel City Div., Midland-Ross Corp., Pittsburgh, Pa.)

A, size, in.	For insulators, Nos.	B, in.	C, in.	D, in.	E, in.	F, in.	G, in.	H, in.	I, diam of tapped hole	J, diam of setscrew furnished
1	5, 5½	1½	⅞	⅝	1¹⁄₁₆	⁹⁄₁₆	½	¾	¼	⁵⁄₁₆
1½	10, 4, 4½	1¾	1¾	⅝	1½	⁹⁄₁₆	¾	¾	⁵⁄₁₆	⁷⁄₁₆
2	1, 3, 3 W.G., 3½, 24	2	1	1	2	1	1	¾	⅜	½
2½	25, 29, 34	2½	1¼	1¼	2½	1¼	1¼	¾	½	⅝

43. For supporting conductors on steel columns a wooden baseboard for the cleats clamped to the column with hook bolts (Fig. 14) is a good arrangement. The board must be cut out in back for the rivetheads in the column. Strap-iron cleats through which the hook bolts pass prevent warping and splitting.

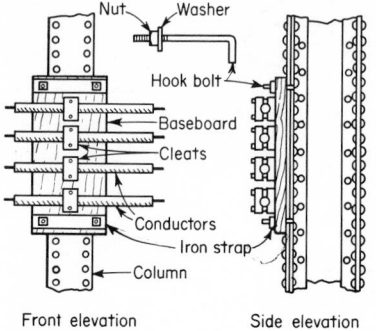

FIG. 14 *Attachment of wiring board to column.*

44. Wire racks are used to support conductors, principally heavy ones, where there are many conductors in the run. The conductors should have flameproof or slow-burning covering. A wire rack can be made of wood fashioned into a framework somewhat along the lines of the steel ones of Figs. 15 and 16. The cleats insulating the conductors are held to the frame with wood screws or, preferably, with machine or stove bolts. A commercial wire rack with a cast-iron base that can be bolted to any surface is shown in Fig. 17. Generally a steel-frame rack is preferable to a wooden one. The rack of steel angles of Fig. 15 was designed for installation in the top of a pipe tunnel. The insulators are held to the cross angles with bolts with a leather washer under the head of each. The structural-steel rack of Fig. 16, III is arranged for supporting from a ceiling. Angle crossarms can be used as at II, or the crossarms can each be formed of two iron straps as at I. With the two-strap method, drilling for the cleat bolts is unnecessary, and the cleats can be shifted along the arm into any desired position and there clamped fast. Strain insulators engaging in turnbuckles or tightening bolts should be used at the ends of each straight run to assume the strain and to provide for tightening, or else the arms and cleats at the run ends should be reinforced to assume the stress that will come on them.

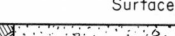

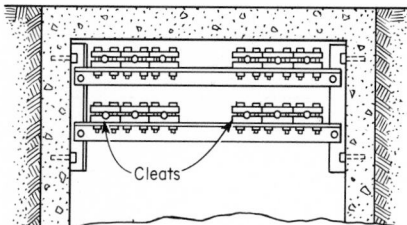

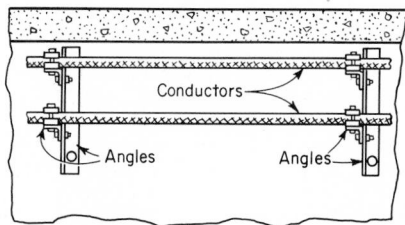

FIG. 15 *Angle-iron rack for conductors.*

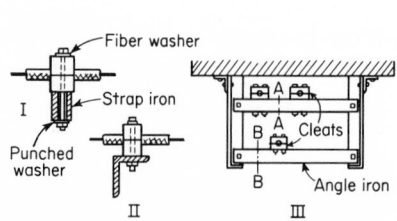

FIG. 16 *Rack composed of angles and strap iron. (I, section A-A; II, section B-B.)*

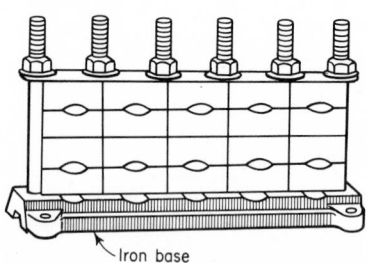

FIG. 17 *A commercial insulator rack.*

45. A method of supporting open wiring in concrete buildings is shown in Fig. 18. A round groove of ⅜-in. radius is cast in the faces of the beams, by having ¾-in. half-round molding nailed in the forms. Wrought-iron yokes are bent to fit the grooves as shown, and ½-in. bolts clamp them in position. Wooden blocks or sections of strap or angle iron can be bolted to the yokes for supporting the wire cleats.

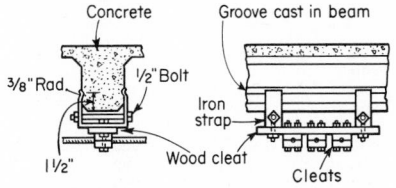

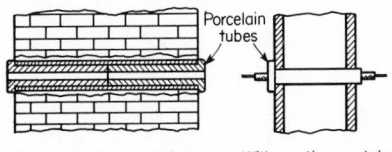

FIG. 18 *Supports for open wiring on a concrete beam.*

FIG. 19 *Protection through walls and partitions.*

46. Where conductors pass through floors, walls, or partitions, they must always be protected. Open-work wires can be protected with porcelain tubes (Fig. 19). The tube or bushing must be long enough to bush the entire length of the hole in one continuous piece, or else the hole must first be bushed by a continuous waterproof sleeve of noninductive material and the conductor must be so installed that it will be absolutely out of contact with the sleeve.

47. A tube for protecting a wire where it crosses another wire should always be so placed that the tube will not force the unprotected wire against the surface supporting the conductors.

48. Flexible tubing or "loom" (Fig. 20) is used mostly in connection with open wiring and concealed knob and tube wiring. When metal outlet boxes or switch boxes

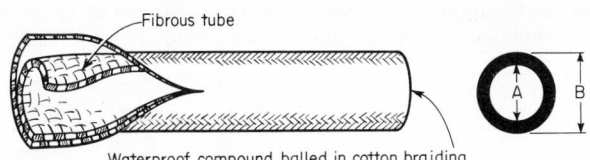

FIG. 20 *Flexible tubing.*

are used, flexible tubing is required from the last porcelain support, extending into the outlet box at least 1 in. and held in place by an approved fitting such as a universal bushing or a clamp.

Another application for flexible tubing is in buildings already completed where the wires are fished in between the walls and ceilings. The tubing is used as a covering on such wires separately encased. In concealed knob and tube work it is frequently impracticable to place wires 3 in. apart and 1 in. from the surface wired over as required by the National Electrical Code, and in such cases the wires must be separately encased in flexible tubing. In open wiring where the amount of separation required by the Code from the surface wired over cannot be maintained, the wires may also be encased in flexible tubing.

The following is a list of places where flexible tubing is applicable: in open work where wires are exposed nearer each other than 2½ in.; on wires crossing other wires; on wires crossing gas pipes, water pipes, iron beams, woodwork, brick, or stone; and at distributing centers or where space is limited and the 3-in. separation required cannot be maintained, each wire must be separately encased in a continuous length of flexible tubing.

Only continuous (unspliced) lengths of flexible tubing can be used for wire protection at outlets.

49. Properties of Flexible Tubing or Loom

A, inside diam, in.	B, outside diam, in.		Ft per coil	Largest wire, B&S or cir mils	Weight lb per 1,000 ft
	In decimals	To nearest 64 in.			
7/32	0.46	15/32	250	No. 14	50
1/4	0.50	1/2	250	No. 14	58
3/8	0.65	21/32	250	No. 12	75
1/2	0.78	25/32	200	No. 8	90
5/8	0.98	63/64	200	No. 4	120
3/4	1.06	1 1/16	150	No. 2	196
1	1.31	1 5/16	100	No. 2/0	250
1 1/4	1.63	1 41/64	100	200,000	400
1 1/2	1.88	1 57/64	Odd lengths	400,000	480
1 3/4	2.25	2 1/4	Odd lengths	600,000	590
2	2.63	2 41/64	Odd lengths	800,000	800
2 1/4	2.81	2 13/16	Odd lengths	1,100,000	810

50. Where conductors cross damp pipes, they should be carried over rather than under so that drippings will not strike the wires. Porcelain tubes, securely taped to the conductors, should be placed on the conductors over the point where they cross.

51. Rosettes for open surface wiring are used to connect the drop cords for the incandescent lamps to the branch circuits. A rosette with protected (concealed) contact lugs is preferable to one with exposed lugs. Figure 21 shows one good type. Another good method of supporting drop cords, particularly where there is vibration, is with the ceiling button illustrated in Fig. 22. The Code does not allow conductors to be dead-ended at a rosette.

52. Switches can be supported in exposed surface wiring as shown in Fig. 23. The switch can be mounted on a commercial porcelain switch block.

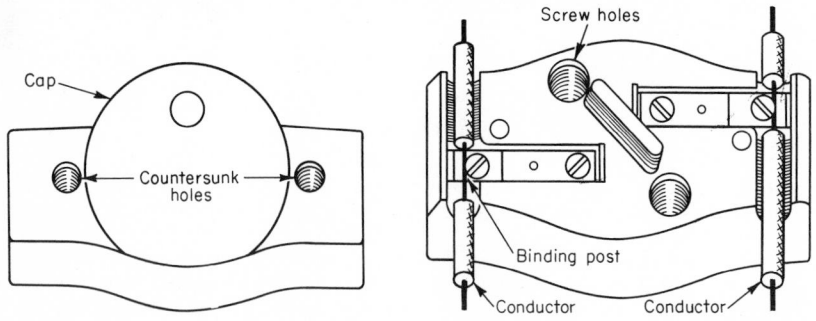

FIG. 21 *A cleat rosette.*

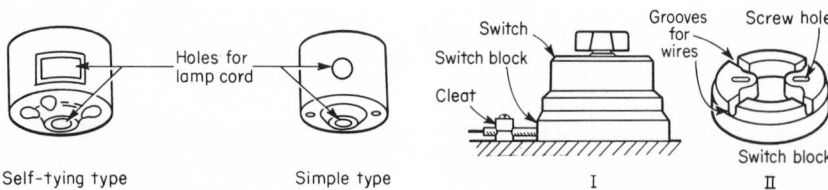

FIG. 22 *Ceiling buttons.*

FIG. 23 *Supporting switches in exposed-surface wiring.*

53. Entering Damp or Wet Locations (National Electrical Code). Conductors entering or leaving damp or wet locations shall have drip loops formed on them and shall then pass upward and inward from the outside of buildings or from the damp or wet location through noncombustible, nonabsorptive tubes.

CONCEALED KNOB AND TUBE WIRING

54. Concealed knob and tube wiring was used extensively at one time for the wiring of frame buildings where a low-cost installation was essential. It is still allowed by the National Electrical Code but is rarely used because more labor is required than with common cable systems. It has been superseded for low-cost installations by nonmetallic-sheathed cable.

55. When changing from open wiring or concealed knob and tube wiring to conduit, electrical-metallic-tubing, nonmetallic-sheathed-cable, metal-clad-cable, or surface-raceway wiring, a fitting or outlet box having a separately bushed hole for each conductor must be used.

RIGID-METAL-CONDUIT WIRING

56. Rigid-metal-conduit wiring is approved for both exposed and concealed work and for use in nearly all classes of buildings. For ordinary conditions, wiring in metal conduit is probably the best, although it is the most expensive. The advantages of metal conduit are (1) wires can be inserted and removed, (2) it provides a good ground path, (3) it is strong enough mechanically so that nails cannot be driven through it and so that it is not readily deformed by blows or by wheelbarrows being run over it, and (4) it successfully resists the normal action of cement when embedded in partitions or walls of concrete buildings.

57. When to Use Rigid-metal-conduit Wiring. In general, conduit wiring should be used whenever the job will stand the cost. Rigid conduit protects the conductors it contains and provides a smooth raceway permitting ready insertion or removal.

Conduits and fittings exposed to severe corrosive influences shall be of corrosion-resistant material suitable for the conditions. If practicable, the use of dissimilar metals in contact anywhere in the system shall be avoided to eliminate the possibility of galvanic action.

Meat-packing plants, tanneries, hide cellars, casing rooms, glue houses, fertilizer rooms, salt storage, some chemical works, metal refineries, pulp and paper mills, sugar mills, roundhouses, textile bleacheries, plants producing synthetic staples, some stables, and similar locations are judged to be occupancies where severe corrosive conditions are likely to be present.

Cinder Fill. Conduit, unless of corrosion-resistant material suitable for the purpose, shall not be used in or under cinder fill where subject to permanent moisture unless protected on all sides by a layer of noncinder concrete at least 2 in. thick or unless the conduit is at least 18 in. under the fill.

Wet Locations. In portions of dairies, laundries, canneries, and other wet locations and in locations where walls are frequently washed, the entire conduit system, including all boxes and fittings used therewith, shall be so installed and equipped as to prevent water from entering the conduit and the conduit shall be mounted so that there is at least 1/4-in. air space between the conduit and the wall or other supporting surface.

All supports, bolts, straps, screws, etc., shall be of corrosion-resistant materials or protected against corrosion by approved corrosion-resistant materials.

58. Corrosion-resistant rigid conduit is available in three general types: (1) aluminum, (2) silicon-bronze alloy, and (3) plastic coated.

Aluminum rigid conduit is useful in installations where certain chemical fumes or vapors are present which have little effect upon aluminum but have a severe corrosive effect upon steel. It is widely used because its light weight reduces installation labor costs. Uncoated or unprotected aluminum conduit should not be embedded in concrete or buried in earth, particularly where soluble chlorides are present.

A silicon-bronze-alloy conduit, known as Everdur electrical conduit, has special corrosive-resistance characteristics. Its use is advantageous for installations exposed to the weather as on bridges, piers, and dry docks and along the sea coast; in oil refineries and chemical plants; in sewage-disposal works; underground for water-supply works; and in wiring to underwater swimming pool lighting fixtures.

Plastic-coated rigid conduit consists of standard galvanized-steel conduit over the surface of which seamless coatings of polyvinyl chloride plastic have been extruded. Thus a uniform nonporous protective coating is formed over the entire length of the raceway. All couplings and fittings should be covered with plastic sleeves or carefully wrapped with three thicknesses of standard vinyl electric insulating tape. This plastic-coated conduit is flame resistant and highly resistant to action of oils, grease, acids, alkalies, and moisture; does not oxidize, deteriorate, or shrink when exposed to sunlight and weather; and provides excellent resistance to abrasion, impact, and other mechanical wear. Typical applications are meat-packing plants, malt-liquor industries, paper and allied industries, production plants for industrial organic and inorganic products, soap and related products industries, tanneries and leather-finishing plants, canneries, food-processing industries, dairies, fertilizer plants, and petroleum industries.

59. Dimensions of Corrosive-resistant Rigid Conduit. The internal and external diameters for aluminum conduit are the same as those for rigid-steel conduit. The internal diameter of plastic-coated rigid conduit, of course, is the same as that of standard rigid-steel conduit. The outside diameter of the plastic-coated is slightly greater as given in Table **61**. The external diameter of the silicon-bronze-alloy conduit is practically the same as for rigid steel conduit, but its internal diameter is slightly greater, as shown in the following table.

60. Everdur Rigid Conduit
(The Anaconda American Brass Co.)

| Nominal size, in. | Nominal dimensions, in. | | | Unit length without couplings, ft.-in. | Min weight of 10 unit lengths of conduit with couplings attached, lb |
| | Diameter | | Wall thickness | | |
	Outside	Inside			
¼	0.540	0.382	0.079	9-11½	40
⅜	0.675	0.503	0.086	9-11½	55
½	0.840	0.636	0.102	9-11¼	86
¾	1.050	0.834	0.108	9-11¼	115
1	1.315	1.075	0.120	9-11	164
1¼	1.660	1.382	0.139	9-11	242
1½	1.900	1.614	0.143	9-11	288
2	2.375	2.077	0.149	9-11	380
2½	2.875	2.519	0.178	9-10½	553
3	3.500	3.084	0.208	9-10½	790
3½	4.000	3.548	0.226	9-10¼	980
4	4.500	4.026	0.237	9-10¼	1,160

61. Plastic-coated Rigid Conduit
(General Electric Co.)

Size, in.	Weight, lb per 1,000 ft	Ft per bundle	External diameter, in.
½	855	100	0.900
¾	1,119	50	1.110
1	1,701	50	1.375
1¼	2,247	30	1.720
1½	2,688	10	1.960
2	3,601	10	2.435
2½	6,132	10	2.935
3	7,860	10	3.560
3½	9,433	10	4.060

62. Rigid-steel conduit is made in two types: white (galvanized) and black (enameled). The white conduit is galvanized and is the type which should be used where exposed to the weather, when embedded in concrete, or when installed in wet locations. The black conduit is coated with black enamel and is the type commonly used for general interior wiring. Except for special conditions no size smaller than ½ in. is allowed.

63. Standard Rigid Conduit and Couplings
(Wrought-iron or Steel)

Conduit

Couplings

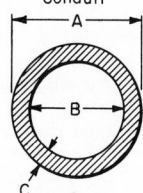

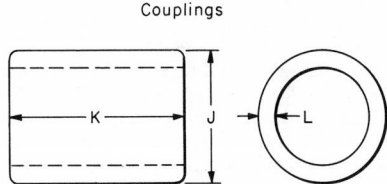

FIG. 24   *Section of conduit.*   FIG. 25   *Conduit couplings.*

Dimensions and Weights

Trade size, in.	Rigid steel conduit						Couplings		
	A, Approx. OD, in.	B, Approx. ID, in.	C, Approx. wall thickness, in.	Threads per in.	Approx wt per 1,000 ft, lb		J, OD, in.	K, Length, in.	Approx. wt per 100, lb
½	0.840	0.622	0.109	14	820		1.010	1⁹⁄₁₆	14
¾	1.050	0.824	0.113	14	1,120		1.250	1⅝	24
1	1.315	1.049	0.133	11½	1,600		1.525	2	39
1¼	1.660	1.380	0.140	11½	2,160		1.869	2¹⁄₁₆	47
1½	1.900	1.610	0.145	11½	2,680		2.155	2¹⁄₁₆	66
2	2.375	2.067	0.154	11½	3,500		2.730	2⅛	105
2½	2.875	2.469	0.203	8	5,600		3.250	3⅛	180
3	3.500	3.068	0.216	8	7,120		4.000	3¼	300
3½	4.000	3.548	0.226	8	8,520		4.500	3⅜	390
4	4.500	4.026	0.237	8	10,300		5.000	3½	400
5	5.563	5.047	0.258	8	13,910		6.296	3¾	760
6	6.625	6.065	0.280	8	18,500		7.390	4	1075

All tubes 10 ft long, threaded both ends, with coupling on one end.

64. Data on conduit couplings and elbows are given in Secs. **63, 66A,** and **71.** The weight columns are convenient for estimating transportation charges. The internal area is useful in determining the size of conduit for unusual combinations of conductors, as explained in Sec. **79.** Dimensions of elbows and couplings are often used in laying out work on the drawing board or in cases where clearances must be estimated in advance. Table **67** gives the dimensions of standard conduit threads.

Running threads are not allowed on conduit for connection at couplings.

65. Rigid Aluminum Conduit. The use of rigid aluminum conduit has gained wide acceptance because of its light weight; excellent grounding conductivity; ease of threading, bending, and installation; resistance to corrosion; and low losses for installed a-c circuits. Installations of rigid aluminum conduit require no maintenance, painting, or protective treatment in most applications. Because of its high resistance to corrosion this conduit should be used in many severely corrosive industrial environments such as sewerage plants, water treatment stations, filtration plants, many chemical plants, and installations around salt water.

When aluminum conduit is buried in concrete or mortar, a limited chemical reaction on the conduit surface forms a self-stopping coating. This prevents significant corrosion for the life of the structure. However, calcium chloride or similar soluble chlorides sometimes are used to speed concrete setting. In limiting the use of such speeding agents, the American Concrete Institute and most building codes recognize that embedded metals can be damaged by chlorides. As a result, if aluminum conduit is to be buried in concrete, the installer should be absolutely sure that the concrete will contain no chlorides. If there is any doubt, rigid steel conduit should be used, because, even though chlorides can damage steel conduit to some degree, this will not lead to cracking or spalling of concrete.

Although aluminum conduit can be buried safely in many soils, precautions are recommended because of unpredictable moisture, stray electric current, and chemical variations in almost every soil. To assure protection when buried directly in earth, aluminum *or steel conduit* should be coated with bituminous or asphalt paint, wrapped with plastic tape, or encased in a chloride-free concrete envelope.

Being a nonmagnetic metal, aluminum conduit reduces voltage drop in installed copper or aluminum wire up to 20 per cent of a corresponding steel conduit installation where a-c circuits are involved.

Tables **66** and **66A** list important data on rigid aluminum conduit.

66. Aluminum Rigid Conduit — Nominal 10-ft Lengths

Trade size	Lb per 100 ft [a]	No. per bundle	Lb per bundle[a]	Master shipping package			
				Bundles	Pieces	Feet	Lb[a]
$\frac{1}{2}$	29.8	10	29.80	20	200	2,000	596
$\frac{3}{4}$	39.8	10	39.80	20	200	2,000	796
1	58.9	10	58.90	10	100	1,000	589
$1\frac{1}{4}$	79.8	5	39.90	10	50	500	399
$1\frac{1}{2}$	95.6	5	47.80	10	50	500	478
2	128.8	5	64.40	9	45	450	580
$2\frac{1}{2}$	204.7	1	20.47	Loose	30	300	614
3	268.0	1	26.80	Loose	20	200	536
$3\frac{1}{2}$	321.3	1	32.13	Loose	20	200	642
4	382.1	1	38.21	Loose	20	200	764
5	521.5	1	52.15	Loose	8	80	417
6	677.5	1	67.75	Loose	6	60	406

[a] Nominal shipping weights.

66A. Aluminum Rigid Conduit Couplings

Trade size, inches	Outside diameter, inches	Length, inches	Nominal weight per 100 pieces, lb
$\frac{1}{2}$	$1^5/_{64}$	1.56	6.1
$\frac{3}{4}$	$1^{21}/_{64}$	1.62	9.1
1	$1^9/_{16}$	2.00	12.5
$1\frac{1}{4}$	$1^{o1}/_{64}$	2.06	18.9
$1\frac{1}{2}$	$2^7/_{32}$	2.06	23.3
2	$2^3/_4$	2.12	34.6
$2\frac{1}{2}$	$3^9/_{32}$	3.12	68.3
3	$3^{15}/_{16}$	3.25	91.4
$3\frac{1}{2}$	$4^7/_{16}$	3.37	108.0
4	5	3.50	142.0
5	$6^7/_{32}$	3.75	241.9
6	$7^5/_{16}$	4.00	321.0

67. Standard Conduit—Dimensions of Threads

Trade size of conduit, inches	Number of threads per inch	Total length L_4 of threads, inches[a]	Effective length L_2 of thread, inches	Pitch diameter E_0 at end of conduit, inches[b]
$\frac{1}{4}$	18	0.59	0.40	0.477
$\frac{3}{8}$	18	0.60	0.41	0.612
$\frac{1}{2}$	14	0.78	0.53	0.758
$\frac{3}{4}$	14	0.79	0.55	0.968
1	$11\frac{1}{2}$	0.98	0.68	1.214
$1\frac{1}{4}$	$11\frac{1}{2}$	1.01	0.71	1.557
$1\frac{1}{2}$	$11\frac{1}{2}$	1.03	0.72	1.796
2	$11\frac{1}{2}$	1.06	0.76	2.269
$2\frac{1}{2}$	8	1.57	1.14	2.720
3	8	1.63	1.20	3.341
$3\frac{1}{2}$	8	1.68	1.25	3.838
4	8	1.73	1.30	4.334
$4\frac{1}{2}$	8	1.78	1.35	4.831
5	8	1.84	1.41	5.391
6	8	1.95	1.51	6.446

[a] A minus tolerance of one thread applies to the total length of threads.
[b] A tolerance of ±0.005 in. applies to the pitch diameter.

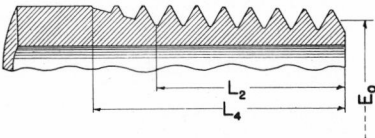

FIG. 26 *Conduit threads. The taper of threads shall be $\frac{3}{4}$ in. per ft; and the perfect thread shall be tapered for its entire length.*

68. Bushings are required to protect wires from abrasion where a conduit enters a box or other fitting unless the design of the box or fitting is such as to afford equivalent protection.

Connections of rigid conduit to enclosures can be made by a single lock nut (outside) and a single bushing (inside) if the bushing is tightly fitted against the wall of the enclosure. Double lock nuts (one inside and one outside) and a bushing always make a better connection than the single-lock-nut bushing method. The National Electrical

Code requires the double-lock-nut method if the circuit voltage exceeds 250 volts to ground or if wholly insulated bushings are utilized.

Where ungrounded conductors of No. 4 and larger size enter a raceway in a cabinet, pull box, junction box, or auxiliary gutter, the conductors shall be protected by a substantial bushing providing a smoothly rounded insulating surface. Figures 27 and 28 show two types of bushings that provide insulation protection. The bushing in Fig. 27 is wholly insulated and constructed of a tough phenolic with reinforced fibers. The

FIG. 27 *Wholly insulated conduit bushing. (Union Insulating Co.)*

FIG. 28 *Metal grounding bushing with insulated throat. (Union Insulating Co.)*

bushing in Fig. 28 is a metal grounding bushing with provisions for installing a bonding jumper from the bushing lug to a metal enclosure. The throat or collar is of insulating material to protect wires.

Tables **69** and **73** are useful when cutting knockouts into enclosures. The spacings listed in Table **69** allow enough room between adjacent knockouts for lock nuts and bushings to be attached.

69. Spacings for Conduit with Given Clearances and Punched-steel Conduit Lock Nuts

(All dimensions in inches)

The *clearance, C,* values are based on the *D* values given at the top of the next page.

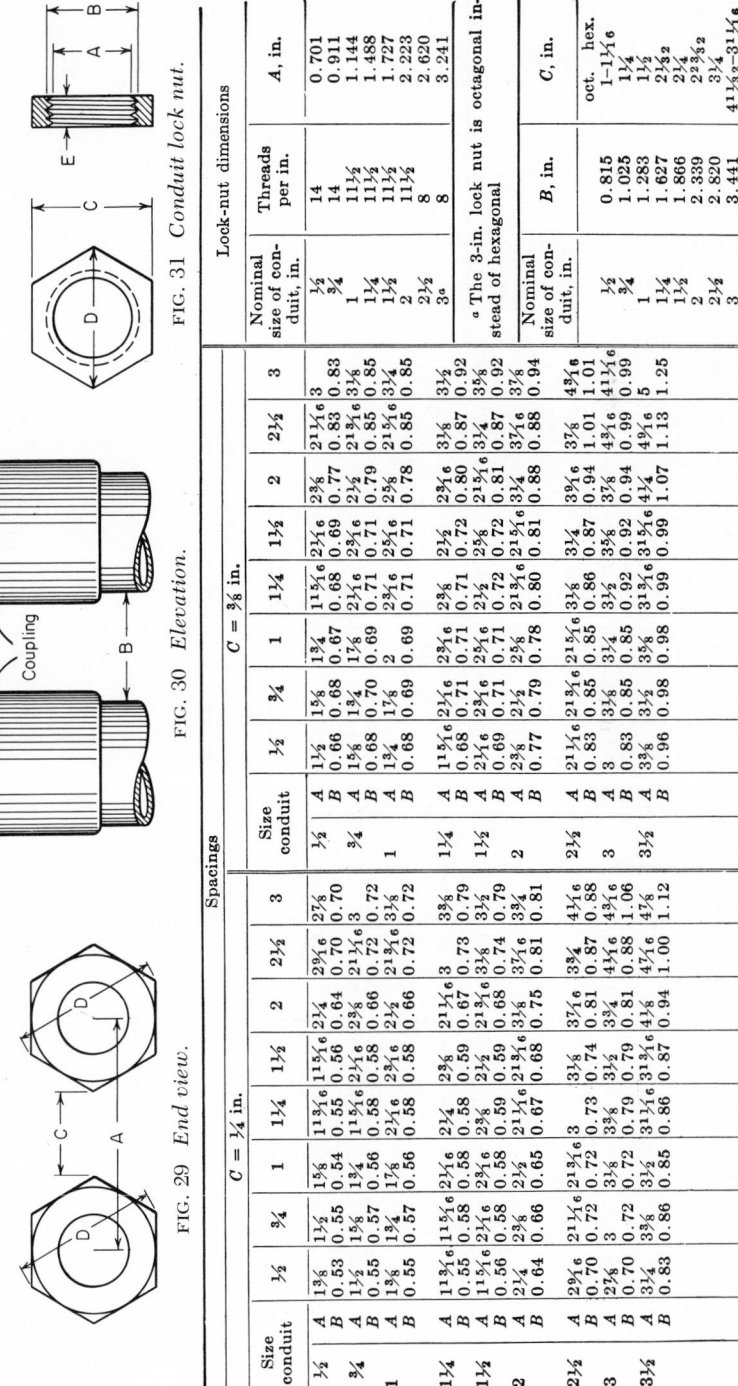

FIG. 29 *End view.*

FIG. 30 *Elevation.*

FIG. 31 *Conduit lock nut.*

Coupling

Spacings

C = 1/4 in.

Size conduit		1/2	3/4	1	1 1/4	1 1/2	2	2 1/2	3
1/2	A	1 3/8	1 1/2	1 5/8	1 13/16	1 15/16	2 1/4	2 9/16	2 7/8
	B	0.53	0.55	0.54	0.55	0.56	0.64	0.70	0.70
3/4	A	1 1/2	1 5/8	1 3/4	1 15/16	2 1/16	2 3/8	2 11/16	3
	B	0.55	0.57	0.56	0.58	0.58	0.66	0.72	0.72
1	A	1 3/8	1 3/4	1 7/8	2 1/16	2 3/16	2 1/2	2 13/16	3 1/8
	B	0.55	0.57	0.56	0.58	0.58	0.66	0.72	0.72
1 1/4	A	1 13/16	1 15/16	2 1/4	2 3/8	2 9/16	2 11/16	3	3 3/8
	B	0.55	0.58	0.58	0.58	0.59	0.67	0.73	0.79
1 1/2	A	1 15/16	2 1/16	2 3/8	2 3/8	2 1/2	2 13/16	3 1/8	3 1/2
	B	0.56	0.58	0.58	0.59	0.59	0.68	0.74	0.79
2	A	2 1/4	2 3/8	2 1/2	2 11/16	2 13/16	3 1/8	3 7/16	3 3/4
	B	0.64	0.66	0.65	0.67	0.68	0.75	0.81	0.81
2 1/2	A	2 9/16	2 11/16	2 13/16	3	3 1/8	3 7/16	3 3/4	4 1/16
	B	0.70	0.72	0.72	0.73	0.74	0.81	0.87	0.88
3	A	2 7/8	3	3 3/8	3 3/8	3 1/2	3 3/4	4 1/16	4 3/16
	B	0.70	0.72	0.72	0.79	0.79	0.81	0.88	1.06
3 1/2	A	3 1/4	3 3/8	3 1/2	3 11/16	3 11/16	4 7/8	4 7/16	4 7/8
	B	0.83	0.86	0.85	0.86	0.87	0.94	1.00	1.12

C = 3/8 in.

Size conduit		1/2	3/4	1	1 1/4	1 1/2	2	2 1/2	3
1/2	A	1 1/2	1 5/8	1 3/4	1 15/16	2 1/16	2 3/8	2 11/16	3
	B	0.66	0.68	0.67	0.68	0.69	0.77	0.83	0.83
3/4	A	1 5/8	1 3/4	1 7/8	2 1/16	2 3/16	2 1/2	2 13/16	3 1/8
	B	0.68	0.70	0.69	0.71	0.71	0.79	0.85	0.85
1	A	1 3/4	1 7/8	2	2 3/16	2 5/16	2 5/8	2 15/16	3 1/4
	B	0.68	0.69	0.69	0.71	0.71	0.78	0.85	0.85
1 1/4	A	1 15/16	2 1/16	2 3/8	2 3/8	2 1/2	2 13/16	3 1/8	3 3/8
	B	0.68	0.71	0.71	0.71	0.72	0.80	0.87	0.92
1 1/2	A	2 1/16	2 3/16	2 3/16	2 3/8	2 7/8	2 13/16	3 1/4	3 5/8
	B	0.69	0.71	0.71	0.72	0.72	0.81	0.87	0.92
2	A	2 3/8	2 1/2	2 5/8	2 13/16	2 15/16	3 1/4	3 7/16	3 7/8
	B	0.77	0.79	0.78	0.80	0.81	0.88	0.88	0.94
2 1/2	A	2 11/16	2 13/16	2 15/16	3 3/16	3 1/4	3 9/16	3 7/8	4 3/16
	B	0.83	0.85	0.85	0.86	0.87	0.94	1.01	1.01
3	A	3	3 3/16	3 1/4	3 1/2	3 5/8	3 7/8	4 3/16	4 11/16
	B	0.83	0.85	0.85	0.92	0.92	0.94	0.99	0.99
3 1/2	A	3 3/8	3 1/2	3 5/8	3 15/16	3 15/16	4 1/4	4 9/16	5
	B	0.96	0.98	0.98	0.99	0.99	1.07	1.13	1.25

Lock-nut dimensions

Nominal size of conduit, in.	Threads per in.	A, in.
1/2	14	0.701
3/4	14	0.911
1	11 1/2	1.144
1 1/4	11 1/2	1.488
1 1/2	11 1/2	1.727
2	11 1/2	2.223
2 1/2	8	2.620
3a	8	3.241

a The 3-in. lock nut is octagonal instead of hexagonal

Nominal size of conduit, in.	B, in.	C, in.
		oct. hex.
1/2	0.815	1–1 1/16
3/4	1.025	1 1/4
1	1.283	1 1/2
1 1/4	1.627	2 1/32
1 1/2	1.866	2 1/4
2	2.339	2 23/32
2 1/2	2.820	2 3/4
3	3.441	4 11/32–3 11/16

Spacings for Conduit with Given Clearances and Punched-steel Conduit Lock Nuts *(Continued)*

C = 1/2 in.									
Size conduit		1/2	3/4	1	1 1/4	1 1/2	2	2 1/2	3
1/2	*A*	1 5/8	1 3/4	1 7/8	2 1/16	2 3/16	2 1/2	2 13/16	3 1/8
	B	0.78	0.80	0.79	0.80	0.81	0.89	0.95	0.95
3/4	*A*	1 3/4	1 7/8	2	2 3/16	2 5/16	2 5/8	2 15/16	3 1/4
	B	0.80	0.82	0.81	0.83	0.83	0.91	0.97	0.97
1	*A*	1 7/8	2	2 1/8	2 5/16	2 7/16	2 3/4	3 1/16	3 3/8
	B	0.80	0.81	0.81	0.83	0.83	0.90	0.97	0.97
1 1/4	*A*	2 1/16	2 3/16	2 5/16	2 1/2	2 5/8	2 15/16	3 1/4	3 5/8
	B	0.80	0.83	0.83	0.83	0.84	0.92	0.99	1.04
1 1/2	*A*	2 3/16	2 5/16	2 7/16	2 5/8	2 3/4	3 1/16	3 3/8	3 3/4
	B	0.81	0.83	0.83	0.84	0.84	0.93	0.98	1.04
2	*A*	2 1/2	2 5/8	2 3/4	2 15/16	3 1/16	3 3/8	3 11/16	4
	B	0.89	0.91	0.90	0.92	0.93	1.00	1.00	1.06
2 1/2	*A*	2 13/16	2 15/16	3 1/16	3 1/4	3 3/8	3 11/16	4	4 5/16
	B	0.95	0.97	0.97	0.98	0.09	1.06	1.13	1.13
3	*A*	3 1/8	3 1/4	3 3/8	3 5/8	3 3/4	4	4 5/16	4 13/16
	B	0.95	0.97	0.97	1.04	1.04	1.06	1.14	1.14
3 1/2	*A*	3 1/2	3 5/8	3 3/4	3 15/16	4 1/16	4 1/8	4 11/16	5 5/16
	B	1.01	1.04	1.03	1.04	1.11	1.13	1.31	1.31

C = 5/8 in.									
Size conduit		1/2	3/4	1	1 1/4	1 1/2	2	2 1/2	3
1/2	*A*	1 3/4	1 7/8	2	2 3/16	2 5/16	2 5/8	2 15/16	3 1/4
	B	0.91	0.93	0.92	0.93	0.94	1.02	1.08	1.08
3/4	*A*	1 7/8	2	2 1/8	2 5/16	2 7/16	2 3/4	3 1/16	3 3/8
	B	0.93	0.95	0.94	0.96	0.96	1.04	1.10	1.10
1	*A*	2	2 1/8	2 1/4	2 7/16	2 9/16	2 7/8	3 3/16	3 1/2
	B	0.92	0.94	0.94	0.96	0.96	1.03	1.10	1.10
1 1/4	*A*	2 3/16	2 5/16	2 7/16	2 5/8	2 3/4	3 1/16	3 3/8	3 3/4
	B	0.93	0.96	0.96	0.96	0.97	1.05	1.12	1.17
1 1/2	*A*	2 5/16	2 7/16	2 9/16	2 3/4	2 7/8	3 3/16	3 1/2	4
	B	0.94	0.96	0.96	0.97	0.97	1.06	1.11	1.17
2	*A*	2 5/8	2 3/4	2 7/8	3 1/16	3 3/16	3 1/2	3 13/16	4 1/4
	B	1.02	1.04	1.03	1.05	1.05	1.13	1.13	1.19
2 1/2	*A*	2 15/16	3 1/16	3 3/16	3 3/8	3 1/2	3 13/16	4 1/8	4 1/2
	B	1.08	1.10	1.10	1.11	1.12	1.19	1.26	1.26
2	*A*	3 1/4	3 3/8	3 1/2	3 3/4	4	4 1/4	4 1/2	4 15/16
	B	1.08	1.10	1.10	1.17	1.17	1.19	1.24	1.24
3 1/2	*A*	3 5/8	3 3/4	3 7/8	4 1/16	4 3/16	4 1/2	4 13/16	5 1/4
	B	1.14	1.17	1.16	1.24	1.24	1.32	1.39	1.44

Nominal size of conduit, in.	*D*, in.	*E*, in.
	oct. hex.	oct. hex.
1/2	1 1/16–1 7/32	5/32–1/8
3/4	1 7/16	5/32
1	1 23/32	3/16
1 1/4	2 5/16	3/16
1 1/2	2 9/16	3/16
2	3 1/8	7/32
2 1/2	3 3/4	1/4
3	4 11/16–4	11/32–17/32

70. Conduit Chase Nipples

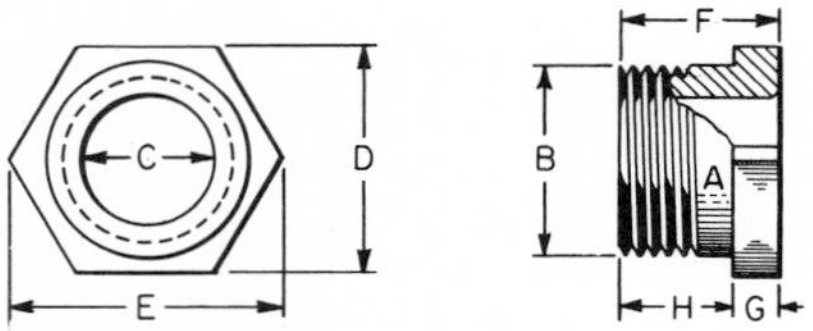

FIG. 32 *Conduit chase nipple.*

Size of conduit, in.	*A*, threads per in.	*B*, diam of threads, in.	*C*, in.	*D*, in.	*E*, in.	*F*, in.	*G*, in.	*H*, in.
1/2	14.0	0.82	0.62	1.00	1.15	0.62	0.12	0.50
3/4	14.0	1.02	0.82	1.25	1.44	0.81	0.19	0.62
1	11.5	1.28	1.04	1.37	1.59	0.94	0.25	0.69
1 1/4	11.5	1.63	1.38	1.75	2.02	1.06	0.25	0.81
1 1/2	11.5	1.87	1.61	2.00	2.31	1.12	0.31	0.81
2	11.5	2.34	2.06	2.50	2.89	1.31	0.31	1.00
2 1/2	8.0	2.82	2.46	3.00	3.46	1.44	0.37	1.06
3	8.0	3.44	3.06	3.75	4.33	1.50	0.37	1.12
3 1/2	8.0	3.94	3.54	4.25	4.91	1.62	0.44	1.19

71. Rigid-conduit Elbows

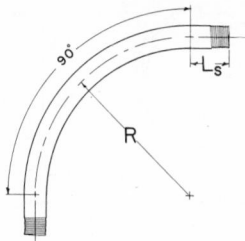

FIG. 33 *Conduit elbows, minimum radius for factory ells and ells made by a one-shot bender.*

Standard-radius Conduit Elbows

Trade size of conduit, inches	Minimum radius to center of tube, inches	Minimum straight length L_S at each end, inches
1/2	4	1½
3/4	4½	1½
1	5¾	1⅞
1¼	7¼	2
1½	8¼	2
2	9½	2
2½	10½	3
3	13	3⅛
3½	15	3¼
4	16	3⅜
4½	18	3½
5	24	3⅝
6	30	3¾

72. Conduit Nipples

 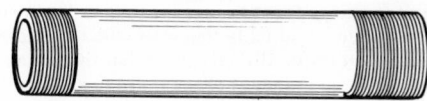 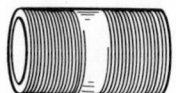

a. Close Nipples   b. Meter Service Nipples   c. Short Nipples

FIG. 34 *Conduit nipples.*

Size nipple, in.	Close Length	Close Wt, lb per 100 pieces	Short Length	Short Wt, lb per 100 pieces	2 in. long Wt, lb per 100 pieces	3 in. long Wt, lb per 100 pieces	4 in. long Wt, lb per 100 pieces	5 in. long Wt, lb per 100 pieces	6 in. long Wt, lb per 100 pieces	8 in. long Wt, lb per 100 pieces	10 in. long Wt, lb per 100 pieces	12 in. long Wt, lb per 100 pieces
½	1⅛	7	1½	9	12	19	25	32	38	51	64	77
¾	1⅜	11	2	17	. . .	25	34	43	51	68	85	103
1	1½	19	2	25	. . .	38	51	63	76	102	127	153
1¼	1⅝	28	2½	43	. . .	51	69	86	103	138	172	207
1½	1¾	36	2½	51	. . .	62	82	103	124	165	206	248
2	2	55	2½	69	. . .	83	111	139	167	228	278	334
2½	2½	110	3	132	. . .	. . .	176	220	264	353	441	529
3	2⅝	151	3	173	. . .	. . .	231	288	346	462	577	692
3½	. . .	. . .	. . .	. . .	. . .	. . .	. . .	. . .	418	558	697	837

73. Malleable-iron Conduit Bushings

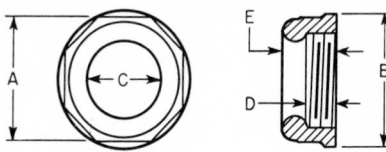

FIG. 35 *Conduit bushing.*

Nominal size of conduit, in.	A, in.	B, in.	C, in.	D, in.	E, in.
$\frac{3}{8}$	$\frac{25}{32}$	$\frac{27}{32}$	$\frac{15}{32}$	$\frac{3}{16}$	$\frac{11}{32}$
$\frac{1}{2}$	$1\frac{5}{16}$	$1\frac{1}{32}$	$\frac{19}{32}$	$\frac{1}{4}$	$\frac{13}{32}$
$\frac{3}{4}$	$1\frac{5}{32}$	$1\frac{1}{4}$	$\frac{3}{4}$	$\frac{1}{4}$	$\frac{15}{32}$
1	$1\frac{13}{32}$	$1\frac{17}{32}$	$\frac{31}{32}$	$\frac{5}{16}$	$\frac{17}{32}$
$1\frac{1}{4}$	$1\frac{11}{16}$	$1\frac{29}{32}$	$1\frac{5}{16}$	$\frac{3}{8}$	$\frac{19}{32}$
$1\frac{1}{2}$	$2\frac{1}{16}$	$2\frac{5}{32}$	$1\frac{17}{32}$	$\frac{13}{32}$	$\frac{5}{8}$
2	$2\frac{9}{16}$	$2\frac{11}{16}$	$1\frac{15}{16}$	$\frac{13}{32}$	$\frac{21}{32}$
$2\frac{1}{2}$	$3\frac{1}{16}$	$3\frac{5}{32}$	$2\frac{11}{32}$	$\frac{15}{32}$	$\frac{3}{4}$
3	$3\frac{11}{16}$	$3\frac{25}{32}$	$2\frac{27}{32}$	$\frac{17}{32}$	$\frac{7}{8}$

74. Table 70 of conduit chase nipple dimensions is, since the function of the chase nipple is about the same as that of the bushing, used for the same purposes as the bushing table. The chase nipple screws into a coupling (see Fig. 30), while the bushing screws onto the threaded end of a length of conduit. The chase nipple is more compact than the bushing and hence is preferable for some work.

75. Punched-steel lock nuts are shown in Table 69. Lock nuts are used on conduit on the outside of the box wherever the conduit enters an outlet box, and their dimensions must often be known in laying out panel or outlet boxes so that proper turning clearances can be provided for the nuts.

76. Table 69 of conduit spacings for different clearances between conduits and their lock nuts or nipples is exceedingly valuable to a man who is designing or erecting conduit work. From it he can determine directly just what the distance between centers of conduits should be for given clearances between nipples or conduit. These data are indispensable when laying out the centers of a row of holes through which conduit is to enter a panel box or in laying out the supports for a multiple-conduit run.

77. Bends. The National Electrical Code specifies that bends of rigid conduit shall be so made that the conduit will not be injured, and that the internal diameter of the conduit will not be effectively reduced. The radius of the curve of the inner edge of any field bend shall not be less than shown in Table **78**. See Table **71** for the minimum radius permitted for field bends made by "one-shot" benders.

The Code also specifies that a run of conduit between outlet and outlet, between fitting and fitting, or between outlet and fitting shall not contain more than the equivalent of four quarter bends (360 deg, total), including those bends located immediately at the outlet or fitting.

78. Radius of Conduit Field Bends, in Inches

Size of conduit, in.	Conductors without lead sheath	Conductors with lead sheath
1/2	4	6
3/4	5	8
1	6	11
1 1/4	8	14
1 1/2	10	16
2	12	21
2 1/2	15	25
3	18	31
3 1/2	21	36
4	24	40
4 1/2	27	45
5	30	50
6	36	61

79. The National Electrical Code specifies the size of conduit to use, depending upon the number, type, and size of conductors to be installed therein. The proper size of conduit can be determined from the following tables in Div. 11 (wiring at 600 volts or less):

1. For new work.. Table **25**
2. For rewiring existing conduits.. Table **25A**
3. For lead-covered cables... Table **26**
4. For combinations of conductors... Table **27**
5. Dimensions and areas of conduits.. Table **29**
6. Dimensions of rubber-covered and thermoplastic-covered conductors............ Table **30**
7. Special method of determining conductor fill in raceways .... Tables **47** to **51**

If bare conductors are to be installed in conduit, the dimensions of such conductors, as given in Table **64** of Div. 11, may be used in sizing a conduit.

80. Outlets for current-consuming equipment and wiring devices require the use of outlet boxes for concealed or exposed work, whereas conduit fittings (Fig. 38) are limited to exposed work.

81. Outlet boxes that are used for conduit wiring are of sheet steel, preferably coated with zinc. They not only hold the conduit ends firmly in position and form a pocket for enclosing wire joints but also constitute electrical connectors between the elements of the conduit system, all of which must be in good electrical contact. Each conduit run in an installation must terminate in an accessible outlet box. Outlet boxes are made in many different forms. For complete data and descriptions of outlet boxes see Div. 4. The required size of boxes is given in Sec. **320**.

82. All boxes should be installed so that the outer edge of the box or the cover mounted on the box will come flush with the surface of the plaster. The top of an outlet or junction box must never be concealed, as the wire splices inside must be accessible for inspection. The conduit must be fastened securely to the box by using a lock nut on the outside and a bushing on the inside of the box (see Sec. **68**).

83. Conduit junction boxes, which are in reality nothing more than pull boxes on a large scale, are often very convenient at points where several conduit lines intersect, as for instance over a switchboard (Fig. 36) from which conduit lines radiate. The junction box is usually supported from the ceiling and is best made of sheet iron on an angle-iron frame. The sides should be held on with machine screws turning into tapped holes in the frame so that they can be readily removed. Round holes can be cut in the sheet-iron sides for the conduits, or often preferably, slots can be provided instead. The conductors within the box can be carried from conduit outlet to conduit outlet in any direction desired, and the use of elbows and troublesome conduit crossings can thereby be avoided.

84. Pull boxes can often be advantageously substituted for elbows (Fig. 37). Large elbows are expensive. Where there are three or more right-angle turns in a run, a pull box should be inserted in any event. One pull box may be substituted for several

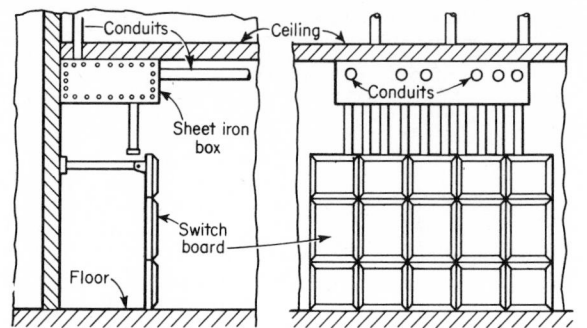

FIG. 36 *A sheet-iron conduit junction box.*

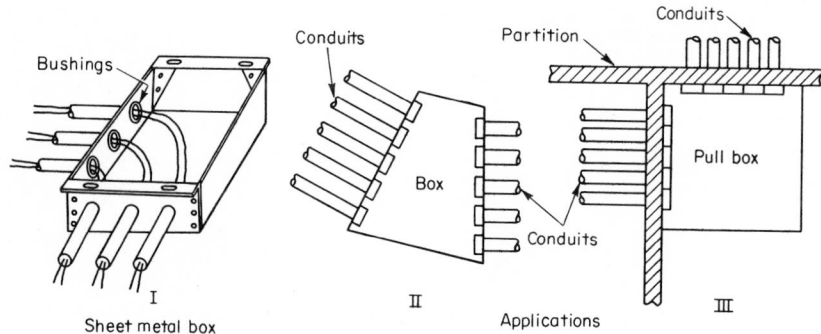

FIG. 37 *Conduit pull boxes.*

elbows. Wire can be pulled in more readily where there are pull boxes. Pull boxes are generally made of sheet steel (Fig. 37, I). Boxes should be made and drilled in the shop, where proper tools are available, rather than on the job. The required size of pull boxes is given in Sec. **324.**

85. Conduit fittings are appliances used to adapt conduit to different situations and conditions. Figure 38 shows some popular fittings, the applications of which are obvious. The National Electrical Code specifies that every conduit outlet must be equipped with an outlet box or approved fitting. A fitting like that of I or II placed on a conduit end fulfills this requirement. Elbows, crosses, and tees, as in III, V, and VI, respectively, can be obtained fitted with either metal or composition or porcelain wire-hole covers or with outlet or other devices. The fitting of IV is used on the end of an outdoor piece of conduit into which wires enter. Its shape is such that wires must enter upwardly, preventing the entrance of water. The wires can be pulled into the conduit and the fitting slipped over them and attached to the flange without it being necessary to turn the fitting. The fittings of VII and VIII can be used as pull boxes, to

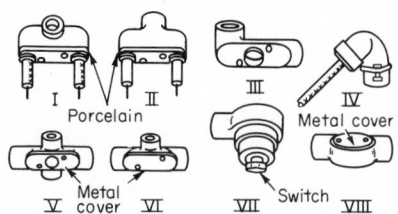

FIG. 38 *Some popular conduit fittings.*

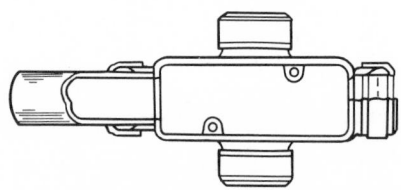

FIG. 39 *No-thread conduit fitting.* (*Appleton Electric Co.*)

support switches, or for a number of other purposes. Everyone interested in wiring should have the catalogues of the fitting manufacturers. These illustrate a great number of fitting combinations and applications.

Conduit fittings are made with their hubs for attachment to the conduit of either the threaded or threadless types.

86. Threadless fittings (Fig. 39) can be used with unthreaded conduit. Tightening glands or setscrews clamps the conduit within the fitting. Threadless fittings materially reduce the labor cost of conduit installation in many instances.

The National Electrical Code requires that threadless fittings be made tight and that, if installed in wet places or if buried in masonry, concrete, or fill, they be of a type to prevent water from entering the conduit.

87. Conduit should run as straight and direct as possible. There should never be more than the equivalent of four right-angle bends between outlets or fittings.

88. In installing exposed conduit runs where there are several conduits in the run, it is usually better to carry the erection of all of them along together rather than to complete one line before starting the others. If all are carried along together, it is easier to keep all the ducts parallel, particularly at turns, and the chances are that the job will therefore look better.

89. Galvanized-iron Pipe Straps of the Two-hole Type

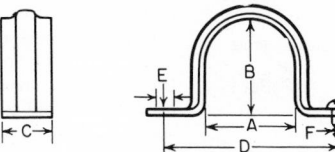

FIG. 40 *Pipe strap.*

Nominal size of conduit, in.	A, width of opening, in.	B, height of opening, in.	C, width of strap, in.	D, distance between centers of screw holes, in.	E, diam of screw hole, in.	F, size of wood screw to use		Approximate number per lb
						No.	in.	
1/4	9/16	1 7/32	5/8	1 1/16	0.20	8 ×	5/8	75
3/8	11/16	2 1/32	5/8	1 3/8	0.20	8 ×	3/4	72
1/2	7/8	2 5/32	5/8	1 5/8	0.20	8 ×	3/4	40
3/4	1 1/8	1	3/4	2 1/8	0.22	10 ×	3/4	29
1	1 3/8	1 11/32	3/4	2 3/8	0.22	10 ×	7/8	21
1 1/4	1 3/4	1 5/8	1 3/16	2 3/4	0.22	10 × 1		18
1 1/2	2	1 7/8	1 3/16	3	0.22	10 × 1		14
2	2 1/2	2 5/16	1	3 3/4	0.22	10 ×	1 1/4	12
2 1/2	2 3/4	2 15/16	7/8	4 3/8	0.25	11 ×	1 1/4	6

90. Conduit can be supported on surfaces with pipe straps which are made in two-hole (Fig. 40) and one-hole (Fig. 41) types. On wooden surfaces, wood screws secure the straps in position. On masonry surfaces, machine screws turning into lead expansion anchors can be used. (Refer to Div. 4 for types of expansion anchors.) Wooden plugs should never be used because no matter how well seasoned a plug appears to be, it will usually dry out some and loosen in the hole. The dimensions in Table **89** are valuable, when laying out multiple-conduit runs, to determine the spacings necessary between the conduits to allow

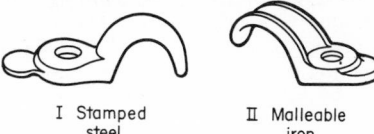

I Stamped steel   II Malleable iron

FIG. 41 *One-hole pipe straps. (General Electric Supply Corp.)*

for proper placing of the straps. The screw-hole dimensions enable one to order, in advance, screws of the proper diameters to support the straps.

91. Location of Conduit Supports. The National Electrical Code states that rigid-metal conduit shall be firmly secured within 3 ft of each outlet box, junction box, cabinet, or fitting. Such conduit shall be supported at least every 10 ft except that straight runs of conduit made up with approved threaded couplings may be secured as indicated in Table **92,** provided such fastening prevents transmission of stresses to terminations when conduit is deflected between supports.

92. Spacing of Rigid-metal-conduit Supports

Conduit Size Inches	Maximum Distance between Rigid-metal-conduit Supports, Feet
½ and ¾	10
1	12
1¼ and 1½	14
2 and 2½	16
3 and larger	20

93. Some commercial I-beam conduit hangers are shown in Figs. 42 and 43. The one at I is an I-beam clamp formed from wrought-iron strap. The hanger or clamp—the

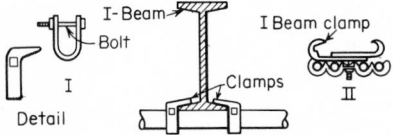

part that grips the beam—of that at II can be purchased of either stamped steel or malleable iron. The support—the yoke in which the conduits rest—is of malleable iron or spring steel and can be purchased to accommodate one or several conduits of different sizes.

FIG. 42 *Commercial conduit clamps.*

94. Conduit Hangers and Supports. A variety of conduit hangers and supports, and several applications, are shown in Fig. 43. U-channel supports are ideal for supporting several runs of conduits. In laying out these supports consideration should be given to future conduit runs as well as those to be installed initially. It is a simple matter to provide U channels or trapeze hangers with additional space for future conduits. Then this greatly reduces the cost of installing new conduit at a later date. With the U-channel system, as shown in Fig. 43, special clamps are slipped into the channel slot, and the top bolt of the clamp securely fastens the conduit to the U-channel.

The U channel can be directly fastened to a wall or ceiling, or it can be attached to bolted threaded rod hangers, suspended from ceilings, roof structures, or similar members.

Another excellent application for U-channel is in suspended ceilings which contain lift-out ceiling panels. In modern construction these lift-out panels provide ready access to mechanical and electrical equipment within the suspended ceiling area. Accordingly, it is important that conduits installed in these areas do not prevent the removal of panels or access to the suspended ceiling area. Rod-suspended U-channels provide the solution to conduit wiring in such areas.

Sections of U channel and associated fittings are available in aluminum or steel types.

Another type of material that can be used for supports is slotted-angle steel units. Numerous prepunched slots allow installers to bolt on rods, straps, and similar material without drilling holes. Slotted steel has unlimited applications in forming special structures, racks, braces, or similar items.

95. Conduit in concrete buildings—much of it at any rate—can be installed while the building is being erected. The outlets should be attached to the forms, and the conduits between outlets should be attached to reinforcing steel with metal tie wires so that the conduit can be poured around them (Fig. 44). Where several conduits pass through a wall, partition, or floor, a plugged sheet-metal tube (Fig. 45, I) should be set in the forms to provide a hole for them in the concrete. Where a single conduit is to pass through, a nipple (Fig. 45, II) or a plugged sheet-metal tube can be set in the forms.

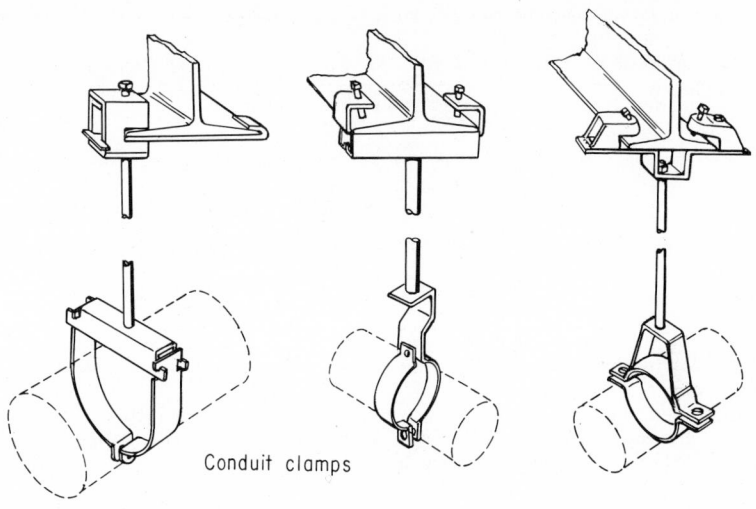

Conduit clamps

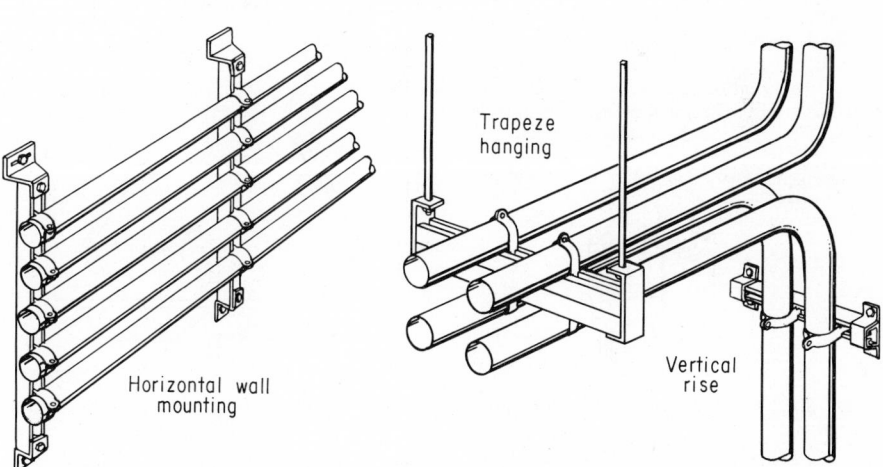

Trapeze hanging

Horizontal wall mounting

Vertical rise

FIG. 43 *Beam clamps, rod hangers and U-channel supports.*

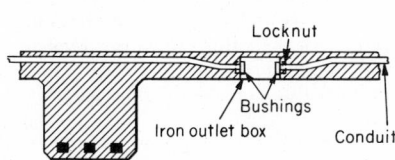

FIG. 44 *Conduit and outlet box in concrete.*

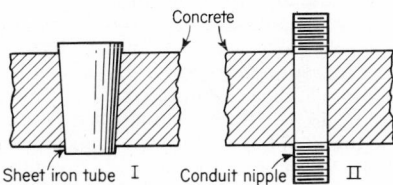

FIG. 45 *Methods of providing passage through concrete.*

96. Conductors in vertical conduits must be supported within the conduit system as indicated in the following table.

Conductor size	Conductors, ft	
	Aluminum	Copper
	Not greater than	
No. 18 to No. 8	100	100
No. 6 to No. 0	200	100
No. 00 to No. 0000	180	80
211,601–350,000 cir mils	135	60
350,001–500,000 cir mils	120	50
500,001–750,000 cir mils	95	40
Above 750,000 cir mils	85	35

The following methods of supporting cables will satisfy National Electrical Code requirements.

1. Approved clamping devices constructed of or employing insulated wedges inserted in the ends of the conduits (Fig. 46). With cables having varnished-cambric insulation, it may also be necessary to clamp the conductor.

2. Junction boxes may be inserted in the conduit system at the required intervals, in which insulating supports of approved type must be installed and secured in a satisfactory manner so as to withstand the weight of the conductors attached thereto, the boxes being provided with proper covers.

3. In junction boxes, by deflecting the cables (Fig. 47) not less than 90 deg and

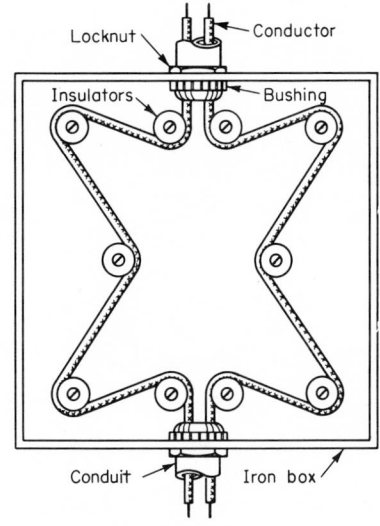

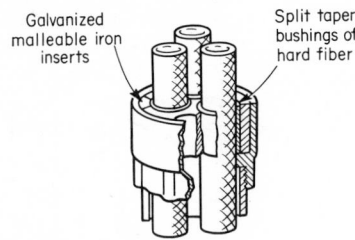

FIG. 46 *Cable support screwed on end of conduit.*

FIG. 47 *Supporting conductors in a vertical conductor run.*

carrying them horizontally to a distance not less than twice the diameter of the cable, the cables being carried on two or more insulating supports and additionally secured thereto by tie wires if desired. When this method is used cables shall be supported at intervals not greater than 20 per cent of those mentioned in the preceding tabulation.

97. Properly bent conduit turns look better than elbows and are therefore preferable for exposed work (see Fig. 48). If bends are formed to a chalk line, drawn as suggested in Sec. **98,** the conduits can be made to lie parallel at a turn in a multiple run as shown in Fig. 48, II. If standard elbows are used, it is impossible to make them lie parallel at the turns. They will have an appearance similar to that shown in I.

98. To Lay Out a Right-angle Conduit Bend. Draw a chalk-line diagram of the contour of the bend on the floor as follows (see Fig. 49): Draw a base line *CO* of any length. Lay off *AO* 4 units long. (The units may be any dimensions whatever.) With a cord and a piece of chalk with *O* as a center and a radius of 3 units describe the arc *IJ*.

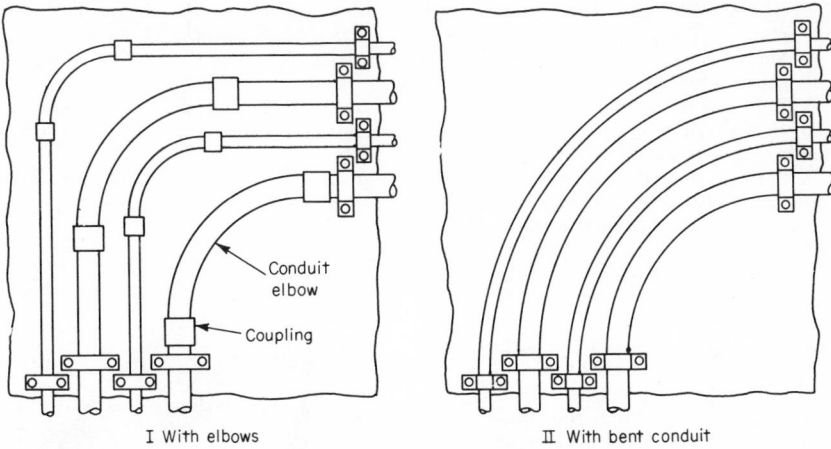

FIG. 48 *Right-angle turns with elbows and with bent conduit.*

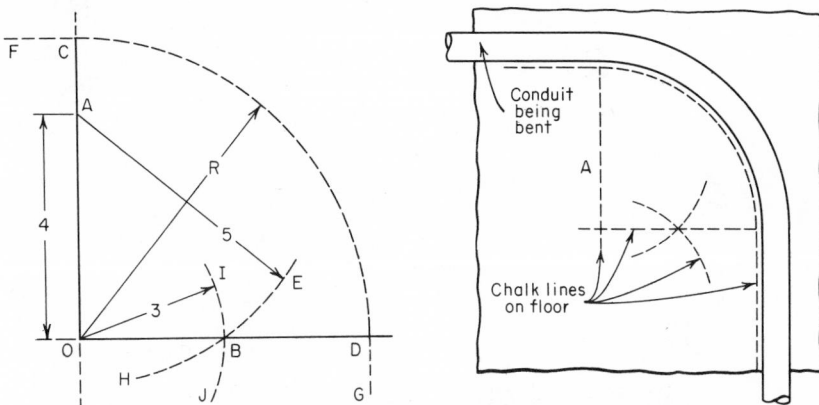

FIG. 49 *Laying out a right angle.*   FIG. 50 *Forming a conduit to chalk lines.*

With A as a center and a radius of 5 units describe the arc EH. The line OD drawn from O through B, the intersection of the two arcs, will be at right angles with CO.

CO and OD can now be prolonged for any desired distance. The arc CD is drawn with the cord and chalk with any required radius R. The conduit bend should lie parallel to this arc when the bend is laid on the floor for inspection as shown in Fig. 50. The radius of curvature of the inner edge of any field bend is required by the Code to be not less than shown in Tables **71** and **78.**

99. Conduit hickeys and benders are used to bend the smaller sizes of conduits. While the common "hickey" (Fig. 51) has been used successfully for many years for bending ½-, ¾-, and 1-in. conduit (1¼-, and 1½-, and 2-in. for small offsets), modern one-shot conduit *benders* and *hickeys,* as shown in Figs. 52, 52A, 52B, and 52C are being used by many electricians. These new benders and hickeys were invented by Jack Benfield, Detroit, Michigan. The specific features of value to the electrician are as follows:

1. An automatic malleable iron plumb bob, which swings free on a stainless steel pin, to give the operator a constant degree of bend indication from 0 to 90 deg.

2. The tools make short-, medium-, or long-radius bends. The patented flat back-

hook has a wide track-contoured rocking shoulder that maintains floor contact long enough to set the course of the bend in a plane vertical to the working surface.

3. Made from pearlitic alloy malleable iron, the tools have heavy sections with guard rails that protect the groove (shoe) and plumb-bob parts from damage.

4. Bold cast-in symbols are not only recessed but also paint-filled to serve as permanent bench marks or guide points for making accurate stub lengths and back-to-back bends.

5. For purposes of safety the socket for a handle has recessed threads and a stainless steel hex bolt that locks the hickey and handle together into one rigid assembly.

6. A straight-through-the-shaft hole serves as a straightener when conduit stubs get bent over in concrete deck work.

7. A patented inner hook contour prevents the tool from slipping. It will not chew into or nick galvanized surfaces or gouge into aluminum conduits.

8. The hook contour also features a back-pusher permitting the hickey to "grab-on" in reverse to remove an overbend, or shift the bend from side to side.

9. The tool and handle assembly stands upright on its own when not in use.

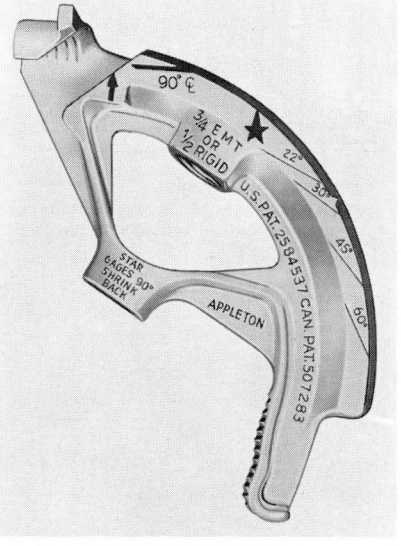

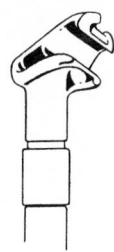

FIG. 51   *Standard conduit hickey.*

FIG. 52   *No. 2 Benfield bender for ½-in. rigid conduit or ¾-in. EMT. (Jack D. Benfield, patent holder.)*

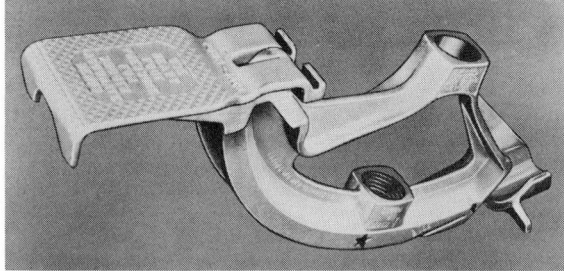

FIG. 52A   *No. 6 Benfield "Powr-Jack" bender for 1-in. rigid conduit or 1¼-in. EMT. (Jack D. Benfield, patent holder.)*

A Benfield model No. 2 bender is shown in Fig. 52. It is for ½-in. rigid conduit or ¾-in. EMT. A similar model No. 1 bender is for ½-in. EMT only, and a model No. 3 bender handles ¾-in. rigid conduit and 1-in. EMT.

The Benfield model No. 6 "Powr-Jack" bender, shown in Fig. 52A, has an extended two-position step to provide 200 per cent more leverage and simplify bending of 1-in. rigid conduit and 1¼-in. EMT. Outriggers on the hook steady the tool.

The Benfield model No. RH7 "one-shot" hickey (Fig. 52B) bends ½- and ¾-in. rigid conduit. The socket for the handle is open at the bottom to serve as a conduit "stub" straightener. A model No. RH8 hickey bends 1- or 1¼-in. rigid conduit.

Figure 52C shows a Benfield No. 9 "Uni-twin" bender during a bending operation. This tool contains two shoes, one for ½-in. EMT and the other for ½-in. rigid conduit or ¾-in. EMT. A special extra-high-strength steel handle has an expanded or flared end sleeve to serve as a stub straightener for ½-in. rigid conduit or ¾-in. EMT. A guide table provides instructions on how to measure up conduits for various types of bends (stubs, offsets, and saddles).

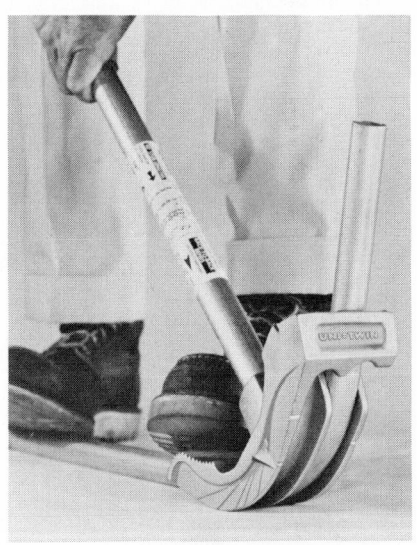

FIG. 52B   *No. RH7 Benfield hickey for ½- or ¾-in. rigid conduit. (Jack D. Benfield, patent holder.)*

FIG. 52C   *A No. 9 Benfield "Uni-twin" double-shoe bender for ½-in. EMT in one shoe and ½-in. rigid conduit or ¾-in. EMT in the other. (Jack D. Benfield, patent holder.)*

Figure 52D shows a comparison of the 90-deg bending radii of ½-in. rigid steel conduit made by a Benfield No. RH7 hickey (left) and a Benfield No. 2 bender. The hickey bend provides the shorter radius, but a longer radius can be made if several "bites" are taken during the bending operation. The radius of the bender is fixed.

These Benfield tools are available from wholesale electrical distributors throughout the United States and Canada. A computerized bending manual including instructions

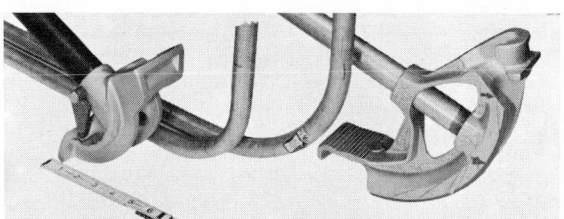

FIG. 52D   *Comparison of 90° bending radii made by a Benfield No. RH7 hickey (left) and a Benfield No. 2 bender. (Jack D. Benfield, patent holder.)*

for the use of these tools is now available. This 20-page manual is free on request from any of four franchised marketers:

1. Appleton Electric Co., Chicago, Ill. 60657
2. The Steelduct Co., Youngstown, Ohio 44501
3. Plastic Wire and Cable Corp., Jewett City, Conn. 06351
4. Irving Smith Ltd., Montreal, Quebec 28

100. Power Conduit Benders. For larger EMT or conduit sizes, hydraulic benders similar to the one shown in Fig. 53 are used in modern practice. Such benders are operated by a hand pump or a motor-driven pump. In general, two types are available. One type utilizes the "progression bend" method, where bends are laid out in marked spacings. Then every few degrees. the conduit is shifted to the next mark, and so on, until the bend is completed. The second type is called a "one-shot" bender, in which the bend can be made without shifting the conduit. A 90-deg bend made with a "one-shot bender" provides a radius about the size of a standard factory elbow. Various shoes are available for different EMT and

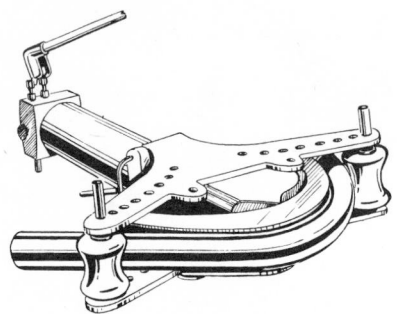

FIG. 53 *Hydraulic conduit bender.*

FIG. 54 *Condumatic power bender for* $^{1}/_{2}$-, $^{3}/_{4}$-, *and 1-in. rigid metal conduit.* (*The Ridge Tool Co.*)

conduit sizes and for different sweep sizes. Information on the proper use of hydraulic benders is available from manufacturers of such equipment, and their instruction books should be followed to obtain precision bends.

Figure 54 shows a "Condumatic" power bender for making precision bends with $^{1}/_{2}$-, $^{3}/_{4}$-, and 1-in. rigid conduit. This motor-operated tool is extremely useful on large construction jobs where many repetitive bends are required. The Greenlee power bender shown in Fig. 54A bends $^{1}/_{2}$- through 2-in. conduit or EMT. The photo shows four $^{3}/_{4}$-in. conduits being bent at one time.

101. A hydraulic pipe pusher is used for underground installations of rigid metal conduit. The "pusher" eliminates tedious trenching operations. The conduit, which must be equipped with a cap or point, is driven through the ground laterally. A common application is under streets or roadways.

Pipe pushers can be operated at different pressures, depending on the conduit size and the type of ground through which the conduit is driven. Standard pipe pushers permit pushes up to 7 ft without the pipe clamp being changed.

102. Cable pullers and wire reels (Fig. 55) are used for the installation of larger conductor sizes. Both are extremely useful on larger installations and save a great deal of time and labor. Multiple wire reels are also useful where a large number of small conductors are to be pulled into a single conduit. Figure 56 shows an electric-

FIG. 54A *Power bender provides 90-deg bends for four conduits at the same time.*
(Greenlee Tool Co., Div. of Greenlee Bros. & Co.)

motor-operated cable puller which is also helpful in pulling in conductors with minimum effort.

103. Threading Conduit. Dies for threading conduit are designed to produce a taper of ¾ in. per ft as described in Sec. **67.** It is usual practice when a lot of conduit is received to rethread all the ends which may have become filled with paint or dirt or distorted by blows. Rethreading will save more than its cost in that it ensures rapid erection. Always reream conduit after cutting a thread on it. Pipe-threading machines for threading conduit, preferably those operated by motors, should be used on big jobs, as they will soon pay for themselves in the time that they save.

104. Wrenches for Turning Conduit. The form of wrench shown in Fig. 57, I, appears to be the most popular for turning conduit. Chain wrenches (II) are not as yet much used for conduit work, but in instances where they have been tried, they have proved very satisfactory. Their advantages lie in the facts that they can be used with one hand after the chain is around the conduit and that they can be used in confined places and close to walls where a Stilson wrench could not be utilized.

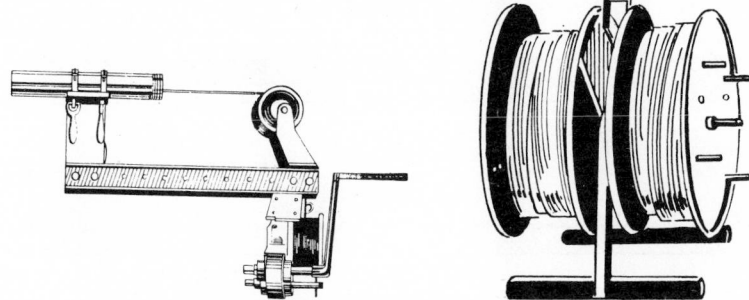

FIG. 55 *Hand-crank-operated cable puller and wire reel.*

105. Conduit ends should always be reamed. A reamer like that of Fig. 58 which can be turned by a bit brace is a good tool for small and medium-sized conduit. For conduit of the larger sizes, reamers which have long handles attached, giving the needed leverage, can be obtained. When conduit is received and after it is cut, the ends are frequently turned in (Fig. 59, I) and, when screwed together in a coupling, form a knifelike edge which will abrade insulation. When the ends are properly reamed, they appear as shown in Fig. 59, II, but if they are screwed together too tightly, they may turn up as at I, defeating the thing that reaming should accomplish. Where no other tool is available, conduit can be reamed by hand with a half-round file.

FIG. 56 *Motor-operated cable puller.*

106. The usual tool for cutting conduit is a hack saw. Pipe cutters should not be used because they leave a large burr on the inside of the conduit, which takes time to ream out. While cutting, the conduit should be held in a vise. On jobs where there is a great deal of conduit to cut, the installation of a motor-driven, cold-cutoff saw, such as is used for cutting structural steel and rails, will prove economical. A rapidly rotating steel disk without teeth cuts the pipe. Water must be sprayed on the disk to keep it cool. Other types of power saws are available.

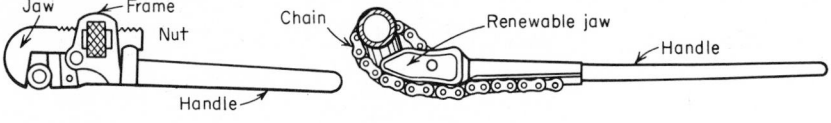

I Stilson wrench

II Chain wrench

FIG. 57 *Wrenches for conduit.*

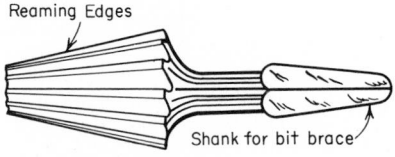

FIG. 58 *A bit-brace reamer.*

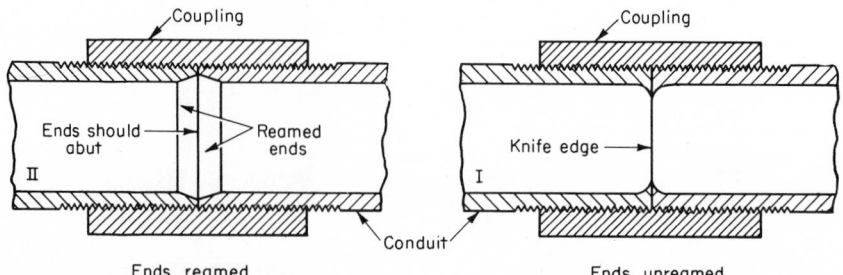

Ends reamed

Ends unreamed

FIG. 59 *Reamed and unreamed conduit ends.*

107. Fishing wire is tempered steel wire of rectangular cross section. It is a grade of wire that is used sometimes for corset steels and can be readily obtained at electrical supply houses. A fishing wire is termed a "snake" by some wiremen (see Table **111**). So that a fishing wire will slide readily past small obstructions, hooks should be bent in its ends as shown in Fig. 60. Before bending, the ends should be annealed by heating them to a red heat and allowing them to cool slowly. A small brass knob riveted to the end of a fishing wire (Fig. 61) is better than a hook as regards the ease with which

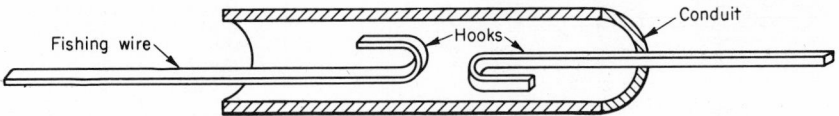

FIG. 60 *Hooks bent in fishing-wire ends.*

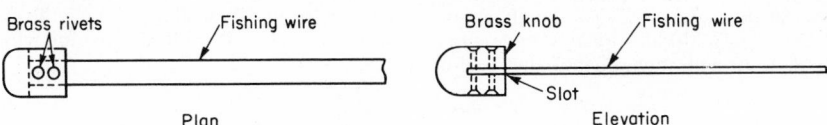

FIG. 61 *Knob on end of fishing wire.*

the wire can be pushed through conduit. Where fishing is difficult, it is sometimes necessary to push two "snakes" with hook ends into the wireway, one from each of the outlets, as shown in Fig. 60. The wires must be worked back and forth and twisted around until the two hooked ends engage. Then one wire can be pulled into the duct with the other.

108. When fishing from two ends, as in Fig. 60, it is often advisable to tie a loop of cord, possibly 1 ft long, in the hook of one wire and bend down the hook (Fig. 62). The other wire has an open hook which can be made to engage in the cord loop quite readily. It has been found that a fish wire will go through conduit more readily if prepared as in Fig. 63, by loosely winding the end with small wire or cord, so that the wire or cord cannot pull off.

109. Chain is used for vertical fishing. A small chain can be made to drop down a vertical wireway with little difficulty. With a partition, the noise made by the lower end of a chain that is jiggled up and down will disclose its location almost exactly.

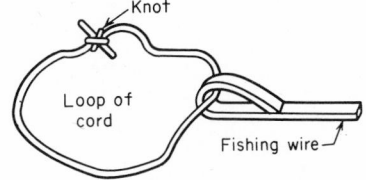

FIG. 62 *Cord loop on end of fishing wire.*

110. Galvanized-steel wire can be used for fishing. Any size from No. 14 up to, possibly, No. 6, as occasion demands, may be utilized, but in nearly every case the flat steel ribbon wire will be found preferable.

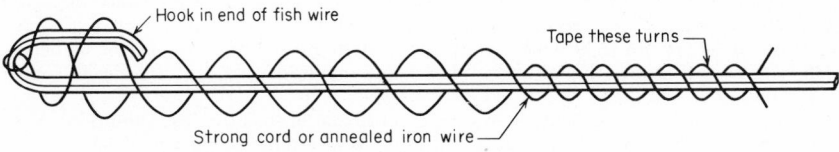

FIG. 63 *Fish-wire end prepared with cord.*

111. Dimensions of Steel Fish Wire

The ¼-in. width of wire is the size most frequently used. The wire is usually put up in coils of 50, 75, 100, 150, and 200 ft.

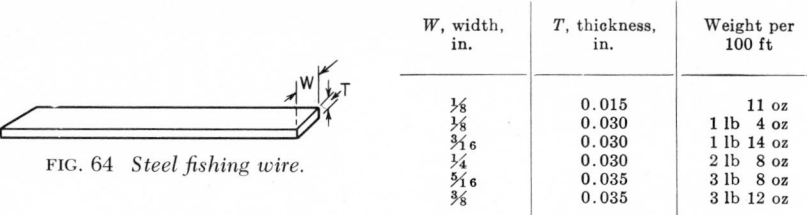

FIG. 64 *Steel fishing wire.*

W, width, in.	T, thickness, in.	Weight per 100 ft
⅛	0.015	11 oz
⅛	0.030	1 lb 4 oz
³⁄₁₆	0.030	1 lb 14 oz
¼	0.030	2 lb 8 oz
⁵⁄₁₆	0.035	3 lb 8 oz
⅜	0.035	3 lb 12 oz

112. In drawing wire into conduit it is a mistake to use so much force that the wire cannot be withdrawn. Conduits should be big enough so that excessive force is not necessary. Small conductors (Nos. 14 and 12) can be pulled in with the fish wire. Figure 65 shows how they can be attached to the fish wire, and Fig. 66 shows how the attachment should be served with tape to render pulling easy. It spoils any fishing wire to draw in with it conductors that pull hard.

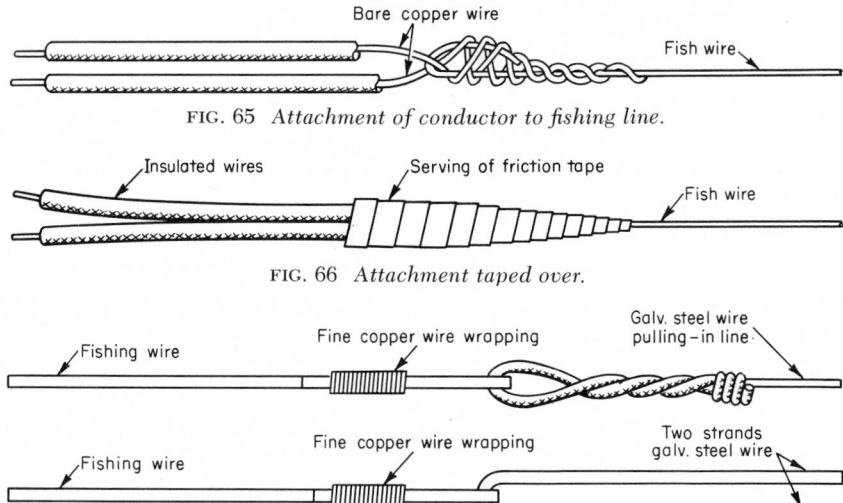

FIG. 65 *Attachment of conductor to fishing line.*

FIG. 66 *Attachment taped over.*

FIG. 67 *Attachment of pulling-in line to fish wire.*

For conductors larger than No. 12 and No. 14, unless the "pulls" are very easy, a pulling-in line which is drawn into the conduit with the fish wire should be used for hauling in the conductors. Number 10 or 12 Birmingham wire gage galvanized-steel wire makes a good pulling-in line and is probably better for heavy work than rope. Two strands can be used if necessary. Braided cord is better than twisted rope for a pulling-in line, because, when tension is applied, the rope tends to untwist. Sash cord is satisfactory for light work. Galvanized-steel pulling-in wire can be attached to fish wire as in Fig. 67. Nylon rope, blown into conduits by a "Jet-line" tool, is also recommended.

Three or four links from a chain of no greater diameter than the line should be made up in the end of a rope or cord pulling-in line. Wires to be drawn in or a fish line can be attached to the links (Fig. 68). One stranded conductor can be attached to a pulling-

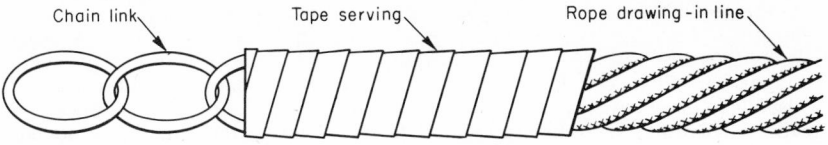

FIG. 68 *Chain links in end of pulling-in line.*

in line as in Fig. 69. The attachment should be taped over to make it smooth. If two conductors are to be pulled in, one of them is "made up" into a loop in the end of the pulling-in line, as shown in Fig. 69. The insulation is trimmed from this conductor for 6 in. or more, and the bared end of the other conductor is made up about the first one, forming a long tapering connection. If a hard pull is expected, it is advisable to solder the connection. The whole should be served with tape as in Fig. 66. If three wires are to be drawn in instead of two, the attachment is the same with the addition that the bared end of the third conductor is made up around the other two. The diameter at any section of the attachment must not exceed the over-all diameter of the wires, and the attachment should be in the form of a conical wedge. It is sometimes necessary to

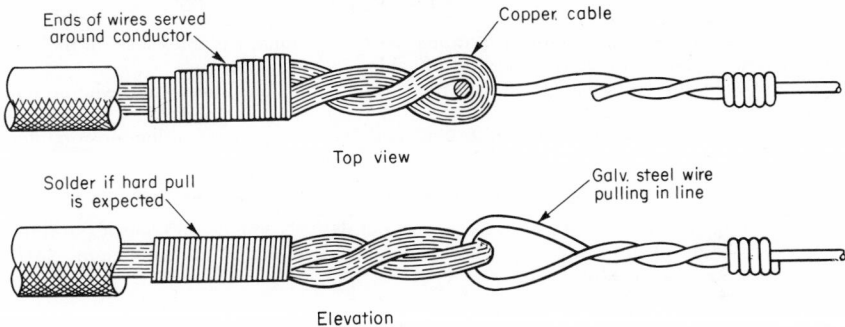

FIG. 69 *Attachment of stranded conductor to pull-in line.*

FIG. 70 *Metal basket grip.*

cut off possibly half of the strands of the bared ends and make up only the strands that remain to ensure that the attachment will be of sufficiently small diameter. A flexible metal basket grip (Fig. 70), available in many sizes, is also recommended. The web-like grip slips over the ends of cables, and when tension is applied, the grip tightens and the conductors are firmly secured.

113. Force for pulling-in wires is, in the case of easy pulls, supplied by men. Tackle blocks are permissible for heavy pulls. Cranes can often be used very effectively where they are available. Snatch blocks can be used to guide the pulling-in line to some point where it can be pulled either with the crane hook or by the crane in traveling along its runway. A lever can be used for hard pulls either by repeatedly fastening the pulling-in line to the lever or by gripping it with a pair of pliers and then prying against the pliers with the lever. Only a short pull is possible with each setting, and a succession of settings and pries is necessary to draw the conductors in.

114. In feeding conductors into conduit, care must be taken that they go in symmetrically and without lapping or twisting. If one conductor crosses another, it may make a hump that will wedge in the conduit. Soapstone blown into conduit renders pulling easier. One convenient way to get the powdered soapstone into the ducts is to place it in an elbow, place the elbow to the conduit, and then blow on the elbow. Powdered soapstone should be rubbed on the conductors as they are drawn into conduits, where the pulls are hard. Liquid paste, commonly known as "Wire Lube," is widely used in modern cable-pulling operations. Although in a paste form during cable pulls, the substance dries into a powder form, which aids in withdrawing conductors later on.

115. Calculations for Determining Tension. When conductors are installed with pulling eyes attached, maximum tension should not exceed 0.008 cir mil. Therefore

$$T = 0.008 \times N \times \text{cir mils}$$

where T (tension) is determined in pounds, N is the number of conductors being pulled in, and cir mils is the circular-mil area per conductor.

When cables are pulled with basket grips around sheaths, maximum strain on sheaths should not exceed 1,500 lb per sq in., if sheaths are of lead. Therefore

$$T = 4,712t(D - t)$$

where T (tension) is determined in pounds per square inch; t is thickness, in inches, of the sheath; and D is outside diameter of cable, also in inches.

When basket grips are used to pull in nonleaded cables maximum strain should not exceed 1,000 lb or the limitation determined by the pulling-eye method.

When cables are pulled into straight duct sections, pulling tension depends on total cable weight plus the coefficient of friction. Therefore

$$T = LWF$$

where T (tension) is total pulling tension in pounds; L is length, in feet, of the duct run; W is weight of the cable in pounds per square foot; and F, the coefficient, is 0.5 when ducts are well made.

INTERIOR OR ABOVEGROUND WIRING WITH RIGID NONMETALLIC CONDUIT

116. Rigid nonmetallic conduit of the heavy-wall polyvinyl chloride (PVC) type may be used for exposed wiring in:

1. Portions of dairies, laundries, canneries, or other wet locations.
2. Locations where walls are frequently washed.
3. Locations subject to severe corrosive influences.
4. Damp or dry locations not prohibited by Sec. **117.**
5. Locations subject to chemicals for which the PVC material is specifically approved.

It may also be embedded in concrete walls, floors, and ceilings of buildings.

117. Heavy-wall PVC conduit must not be used:

1. In hazardous locations, except as permitted in sections 514-8 and 515-5 of the National Electrical Code.
2. In the concealed spaces of combustible construction.
3. For the support of fixtures or other equipment.
4. Where subject to ambient temperatures exceeding those for which the conduit is approved.
5. In sunlight unless approved for the purpose. A PVC conduit which is sunlight-resistant is marked accordingly.

118. Underwriters' Laboratories lists rigid nonmetallic PVC conduit for aboveground applications with two different labels, as shown in Fig. 71. Label A is identified by a yellow background, and label B by a white background. The conduits are manufactured in sizes ½ to 6 in. The extra-heavy-wall-type conduit is utilized for special applications which require additional mechanical protection, such as pole risers or similar uses where conduit is subject to physical damage.

𝕬𝖓𝖉𝖊𝖗𝖜𝖗𝖎𝖙𝖊𝖗𝖘' 𝕷𝖆𝖇𝖔𝖗𝖆𝖙𝖔𝖗𝖎𝖊𝖘, 𝕵𝖓𝖈.
®
L I S T E D
RIGID NONMETALLIC CONDUIT
ABOVEGROUND AND UNDERGROUND
(A)

𝕬𝖓𝖉𝖊𝖗𝖜𝖗𝖎𝖙𝖊𝖗𝖘' 𝕷𝖆𝖇𝖔𝖗𝖆𝖙𝖔𝖗𝖎𝖊𝖘, 𝕵𝖓𝖈.
®
L I S T E D
RIGID NONMETALLIC CONDUIT
ABOVEGROUND AND UNDERGROUND
EXTRA HEAVY WALL
(B)

FIG. 71   *Identification of aboveground PVC conduits.*

119. Manufacturers' classifications for rigid nonmetallic PVC conduit are:

1. TYPE A. Thin wall for underground, encased in concrete.

2. TYPE 40. Heavy wall for direct burial in earth and limited aboveground installations.

3. TYPE 80. Extra-heavy wall for direct burial in earth and aboveground installations for general applications and where subject to physical damage as indicated in Sec. **118.**

From the classifications indicated in Secs. **117** and **118** it should be noted that only heavy-wall (Type 40) and extra-heavy-wall (Type 80) PVC conduits are suitable for aboveground applications. The Type A PVC conduit is limited to underground installations where encased in concrete, and such installations should be installed as indicated for underground work in Div. 8.

120. PVC conduit fittings are shown in Fig. 72. Also available are a wide variety of outlet boxes constructed of polyvinyl chloride or fiber-reinforced Bakelite.

121. Cutting PVC Conduit. This conduit can be easily cut with a fine-tooth handsaw. For sizes 2 through 6 in., a miter box or similar saw guide should be used to keep the material steady and assure a square cut. After cutting, deburr the conduit ends and

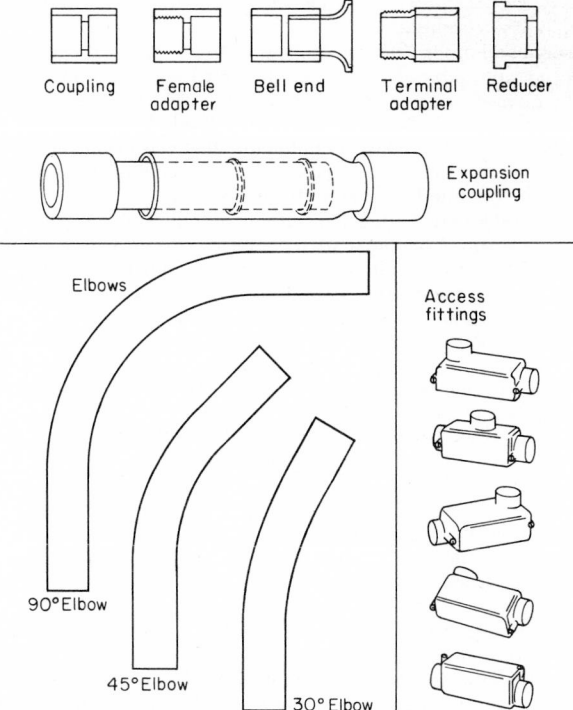

Coupling   Female adapter   Bell end   Terminal adapter   Reducer

Expansion coupling

Elbows

Access fittings

90° Elbow

45° Elbow

30° Elbow

FIG. 72   *Fittings and accessories for PVC conduit.*

wipe off dust, dirt, and plastic shavings. Deburring can be readily accomplished with a pocketknife.

122. Joining PVC Conduit. The conduit should be wiped clean and dry. After this, apply a coat of cement (use a natural bristle brush or aerosol spray cement) to the end of the conduit including the length of the fitting socket to be attached. Finally, push conduit and fittings firmly together, and then rotate the conduit in the fitting about a half-turn to distribute the cement evenly. The cementing and joining operation will not require more than one minute. Many manufacturers supply aersol spray cans or brush-top cans of PVC solvent cement, which may be used as a timesaving feature. In adapting PVC conduit to existing or metal equipment, a complete range of threaded adapters is available. Standard metallic lock nuts are used at these termination points, and bushings normally are not necessary.

123. Bending PVC Conduit. Although a complete line of factory elbows (90, 45, or 30 deg) are available (Fig. 72), heat bending of PVC conduit in the field can be easily accomplished. The most accepted method for sizes ½ through 2 in. is with an electric "hot box," which consists of a 115-volt 15-amp heating element and a 2-ft-long slot into which the section of conduit to be bent is placed.

Under normal conditions a complete bend can be made in less than one minute. When exact measurements are required, preheat a length of PVC conduit and then form it in place. This is possible because PVC conduit will remain pliable for at least 3 min after it has been heated.

Never use flame-type devices as a heat application to PVC conduit, because this excessive heat can ruin the conduit.

For installations of PVC larger than 2 in., factory elbows as shown in Fig. 72 should be obtained.

Other methods of bending PVC conduit include heater blankets and infrared heaters. The primary function of a heating device is to supply uniform heat over the entire area without scorching the conduit.

124. Expansion and Contraction. In applications where the conduit installation will be subject to constantly changing temperatures and the runs are long, consideration should be given to expansion and contraction of PVC conduit. In such instances an expansion coupling, such as shown in Fig. 72, should be installed near the fixed end of the run to take up any expansion or contraction that may occur. The coupling shown in Fig. 72 has a normal expansion range of 6 in. The coefficient of linear expansion of PVC conduit can be obtained from manufacturers' data.

Expansion couplings may be used in either underground or exposed applications. In underground or slab applications such couplings are seldom used, because expansion and contraction may generally be controlled by "bowing" the conduit slightly or immediate burial. After the conduit is buried, expansion and contraction ceases to be a factor. Care should be taken, however, to assure that contraction does not take place in a buried installation if the conduit should be left exposed for an extended period of time during widely variable temperature conditions.

125. Support of rigid nonmetallic conduit should be not less than specified in the following National Electrical Code table:

Conduit Size, Inches	Maximum Spacing between Supports, Feet
½ and ¾	4
1 and 2	5
2½ and 3	6
3½ to 5	7
6	8

In addition to this, rigid nonmetallic conduit shall be supported within 4 ft of each box, cabinet or other conduit termination.

126. Number of Conductors. The number of conductors permitted in a single nonmetallic conduit is determined in the same manner as described in Sec. **79.** In many instances nonmetallic conduits will contain equipment grounding conductors to ground metal-enclosed equipment or grounding-type receptacles supplied by such conduits.

If *bare* equipment conductors are used, the cross-sectional areas of these conductors, as listed in Table **64** of Div. 11, may be used in sizing the conduit. Accordingly, smaller conduit sizes may be permitted if bare instead of insulated grounding conductors are used.

It should be noted that extra-heavy-wall PVC conduit (Type 80) has a reduced cross-sectional area available for wiring space. The actual cross-sectional area is prominently marked on such conduits, and the conductor fill may be determined accordingly.

127. The number of bends in any run of conduit between outlet and outlet, fitting and fitting (LB, T, X) or between outlet and fitting shall not contain more than the equivalent of four quarter bends (360 deg), including those bends located immediately at the outlet or fitting.

128. Nonmetallic conduit lengths are normally available in 10-ft lengths. However, lengths up to 30 ft may be obtained for special applications. The longer lengths require fewer coupling connections and save time and labor.

129. Weight of Heavy-wall (Type 40) Rigid Nonmetallic PVC Conduit

Trade Size, Inches	Weight, Pounds per 100 Feet
$\frac{1}{2}$	16
$\frac{3}{4}$	21
1	31
$1\frac{1}{4}$	42
$1\frac{1}{2}$	50
2	67
$2\frac{1}{2}$	106
3	139
$3\frac{1}{2}$	168
4	197
5	268
6	348

130. PVC is a nonmagnetic conduit, and being nonmetallic, it provides less voltage drop and fewer reactance losses than is possible with metallic conduits with corresponding conductors used on a-c circuits.

131. Other types of rigid nonmetallic conduits, such as thin-wall PVC, fiber, concrete, asbestos cement, soapstone, and high-density polyethylene, are designed solely for use in underground work. They are not intended for interior and aboveground applications. These conduits and installation procedures are described in the underground wiring sections of Div. 8.

For systems 600 volts or less all types of rigid nonmetallic conduits must be 18 in. below the surface if buried directly in earth. Lesser depths are permitted if the conduit is encased in 2 in. of concrete. For circuits over 600 volts rigid nonmetallic conduits must be encased in 2 in. of concrete. Refer to Sec. **156** of Div. 8 for minimum burial depths for high voltages.

FLEXIBLE-METAL-CONDUIT WIRING

132. Flexible metal conduit can be used for many kinds of wiring, being in some cases preferable to rigid conduit. Its installation is much easier and quicker than the installation of rigid conduit, the latter coming in short pipe lengths, whereas the former may be had in lengths of 25 to 250 ft, depending on the size of the conduit. The rules governing the insulation on the wires are the same as for rigid conduit; outlet or switch boxes must be installed at all outlets or switches; the conduit must be continuous from outlet to outlet and must be securely fastened to the boxes.

Flexible metal conduit shall not be used (1) in wet locations, unless conductors are of the lead-covered type or of other type specially approved for the conditions; (2) in hoistways, except as provided in section 620-21 of the Code; (3) in storage-battery rooms; (4) in any hazardous location except as permitted by sections 501-4(*b*), 502-4, and 503-3 of the Code; or (5) where rubber-covered conductors are exposed to oil, gasoline, or other materials having a deteriorating effect on rubber.

Flexible metal conduit consists of a single strip of aluminum or galvanized steel, spirally wound on itself and interlocked in such a manner as to provide a round cross section of high mechanical strength and great flexibility.

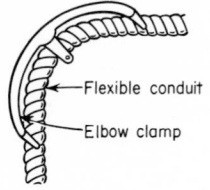

Its flexibility together with the continuous length procurable makes its use practicable when rigid conduit would be out of the question. For this reason it can be employed to advantage in finished frame buildings in place of the other forms of wiring so largely employed in these structures. The conduit is easily fished and requires no elbow fittings. These can be made with the conduit itself, but care should be exercised in properly fastening the conduit at elbows (Fig. 73). Fittings are on the market whereby changes from other forms of wiring can be easily made to flexible-conduit wiring. Iron plates should be used to protect the conduit from nails where it passes through slots in floor beams or studding.

FIG. 73 *Elbow clamp.*

133. Standard Sizes of Flexible Steel Conduit

FIG. 74 *Flexible steel conduit.*

B, nominal inside diam, in.	A, Min OD, in.	Bending radius, in.	Approx ft per coil	Min wt, lb per 1,000 ft
$\frac{5}{16}$	0.470	$1\frac{3}{4}$	250	150
$\frac{3}{8}$	0.560	2	250	255
$\frac{1}{2}$	0.860	3	100	470
$\frac{3}{4}$	1.045	4	50	595
1	1.300	5	50	1,020
$1\frac{1}{4}$	1.550	$6\frac{1}{4}$	50	1,250
$1\frac{1}{2}$	1.850	$7\frac{1}{2}$	25	1,625
2	2.350	10	25	2,125
$2\frac{1}{2}$	2.860	$12\frac{1}{2}$	25	2,630
3	3.360	15	25	3,130

134. Installation of Flexible Metal Conduit. Where exposed, it can be fastened to the surface with single-hole or two-hole straps (Figs. 40 and 41). The conduit must be secured at intervals not exceeding 4½ ft and within 12 in. from every outlet box or fitting. Where concealed, the conduit can be fished into place just as any concealed conductors are fished in.

Exposed runs of the conduit shall closely follow the finish of the building finish or of running boards to which the conduit is fastened, except:

1. Lengths of not more than 36 in. at terminals where flexibility is necessary.

2. In accessible attics and roof spaces.

3. On the underside of floor joists in basements where supported at each joist and so located as not to be subject to mechanical injury.

Where the conduit is used in accessible attics or roof spaces, the Code requires it to be installed as follows:

1. If run across the top floor joists or within 7 ft of floor or floor joist across the face of rafters or studding, the conduit shall be protected by substantial guard strips which are at least as high as the conduit. If the attic is not accessible by permanent stairs or ladders, protection will only be required within 6 ft of the nearest edge of scuttle hole or attic entrance.

2. If carried along the sides of rafters, studs, or floor joist, neither guard strips nor running boards shall be required.

Care must be exercised in making bends that the conduit is not injured.   The radius of the curve of the inner edge of any bend must be not less than permitted in Sec. **78**.

135. The number and size of conductors to install in flexible metal conduit is the same as for rigid metal conduit (refer to Sec. **79**).

136. The minimum size of flexible conduit that is allowed by the Code is ½ in. except as allowed by the Code for underplaster extensions, for motor wiring, or for a connection which is not over 72 in. in length, or longer on approved assemblies, to equipment where the use of ½ in. or larger size is not practicable.   In these exceptions ⅜-in. conduit may be used as follows:

Size, AWG	Max number of conductors in ⅜-in. flexible metal conduit		
	Types RF-32, RH	Type RHW	Types TF, T, TW, XHHW, RUH, RUW, THWN, THHN
18	4	–	8
16	3	–	6
14	3	2	5
12	2	2	4
10	–	–	3

137.   Flexible metal conduit is joined with couplings as illustrated in Fig. 75.   Short lengths can be coupled to longer pieces with the clamp of I and waste thereby prevented.   The clamp at II is used for coupling rigid to flexible conduit.

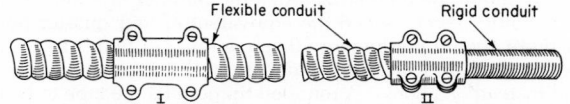

FIG. 75   *Couplings for flexible metal conduit.*

138.   Where elbows are formed in flexible conduit, some provision must be made to prevent the conduit from straightening out and thereby preventing the withdrawal of the conductors.   Pipe straps can be used in some cases, and in others an elbow clamp (Fig. 73) can be applied.

139. Flexible metal conduit can be connected into steel boxes with the connector illustrated in Fig. 76.   It is clamped to the armor with a bolt which provides a connection between armor and steel box. Figure 77 shows flexible metal conduit connected into an outlet box.

140. To cut flexible metal conduit a fine hack saw should be used.   Special vises can be purchased which have a slot across their jaws to guide the saw blade, the

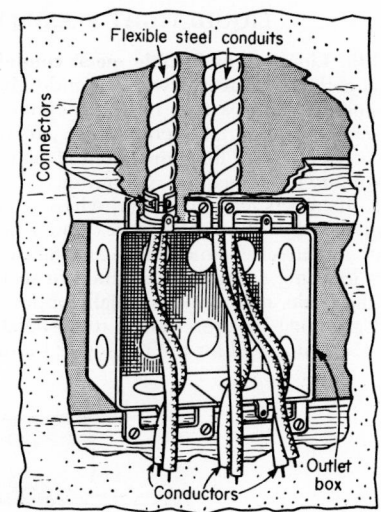

FIG.   77   *Flexible-metal-conduit   outlet box.*

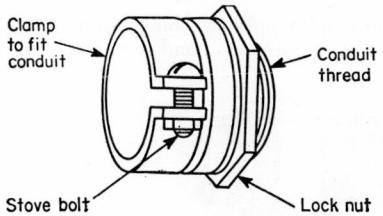

FIG. 76   *Connector for attaching flexible metal conduit to an outlet box.*

conduit being held between grooves in the jaws. Always cut flexible conduit straight across to ensure a proper fit into connectors.

141. For reaming flexible metal conduit a special reamer (Fig. 78) has been made, but inasmuch as the burr resulting from the hack-saw cut is very small, it can be readily removed with a three-cornered scraper made from a three-cornered file or it can be removed with an ordinary file. The reamer illustrated is for conduit of 1¼ in. or less diameter.

142. Fish plugs for pulling in flexible conduit (Fig. 79) are furnished by the conduit manufacturer for ⅜-, ½-, and ¾-in. flexible conduit. After the conduit has been cut off square in a vise with a hack saw, the fish plug is screwed into the tube and the fish or drawing-in wire attached to the plug for pulling in.

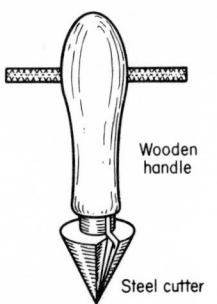

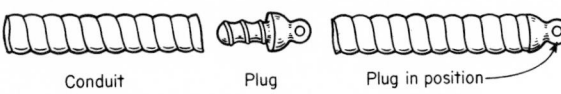

Conduit   Plug   Plug in position

FIG. 78   *Reamer for flexible conduit.*

FIG. 79   *Plug for pulling in flexible conduit.*

143. Pulling in Conductors. Conductors are pulled into flexible conduits in much the same manner as in rigid conduits (refer to Sec. **107**) with fish tapes or similar pulling means. It should be emphasized that the number of bends in any one run of flexible conduit should never exceed the equivalent of four quarter bends (360 deg), and preferably there should not be more than two quarter bends in a run. A fish tape, which is to be inserted into flexible conduit to pull in conductors, should contain a ball or oval end instead of a hook. A rounded tip permits the tape to be inserted without hanging onto convolutions of the flexible conduit.

144. Flexible metal conduit and fittings cannot be used as a grounding means unless they are specifically approved for the purpose. Where not so approved, the conduit must contain a bare or insulated equipment grounding conductor, which must be attached to all equipment supplied and connected to the flexible metal conduit.

LIQUID-TIGHT FLEXIBLE-METAL-CONDUIT WIRING

145. Liquid-tight flexible metal conduit is similar to regular flexible metal conduit except that it is covered with a liquid-tight plastic sheath (Fig. 80). It is not intended for general-purpose wiring but has definite advantages in many cases for the wiring of machines and portable equipment. Its use is restricted by the Code as follows:

1. It is allowed for connections of motors or portable and stationary equipment where flexibility of connection is required.

2. Its use is not allowed (*a*) where subject to physical damage; (*b*) where in contact with rapidly moving parts; (*c*) under conditions such that its temperature, with or without enclosed conductors carrying current, is above 60°C (140°F); (*d*) in any hazardous location, except as described in sections 501-4(*b*), 502-4, and 503-3 of article 500 of the Code, unless it is specially approved for such use.

Care must be exercised in its installation to employ only suitable terminal fittings that are approved for the purpose. Liquid-tight flexible metal conduit in sizes 1½ in.

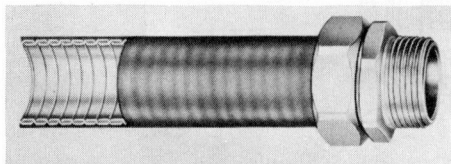

FIG. 80   *Liquid-tight flexible metal conduit.*   (*Electri-Flex Co.*)

and larger shall be bonded in accordance with section 250-79 of the Code, unless specifically approved for use without a separate bond.

The Code specifies that the maximum size used must not be larger than 3-in. electrical trade size.

146. Dimensions of Liquid-tight Flexible Metal Conduit

Nominal size electrical conduit, in.	Actual			
	ID, in.		OD, in.	
	Min	Max	Min	Max
⅜	0.484	0.504	0.690	0.710
½	0.622	0.642	0.820	0.840
¾	0.820	0.840	1.030	1.050
1	1.041	1.066	1.290	1.315
1¼	1.380	1.410	1.630	1.660
1½	1.560	1.590	1.870	1.900
2	2.005	2.045	2.335	2.375
2½	2.449	2.489	2.855	2.895
3	3.048	3.088	3.480	3.520

147. Conductor Size. The National Electrical Code specifies that the maximum size of conductor installed in liquid-tight flexible metal conduit shall not exceed the following values:

Trade Size of Conduit, Inches	Size of Conductor, AWG or Cir Mils
⅜	16
½	12
¾	8
1	6
1¼	2
1½	1
2	00
2½	0000
3	350,000 cir mils

METAL-CLAD-CABLE WIRING
(Types AC and MC)

148. A metal-clad cable is a fabricated assembly of insulated conductors in a flexible metallic enclosure.   Such a cable is designated as Type AC or Type MC.

149. Type AC cables (generally referred to as "armored cable") are branch-circuit and feeder cables with armor of flexible metal tape (Fig. 81).   Cables of the AC type, except ACL (lead-covered conductors), must have an internal bonding strip of copper or aluminum, in intimate contact with the armor for its entire length.   Most manufacturers use a flat aluminum ribbon as the bonding strip.   At terminations, the bond wire is simply folded back without connection to the enclosure or other such conductors.   Being in intimate contact with the

FIG. 81   *Type AC cable with bond wire.*

metal armor, the bond wire is intended to reduce the overall resistance of the cable. For cables of the AC type, insulated conductors must be one of the types listed in Sec. **123** of Div. 2.   In addition, the conductors must have an overall moisture-resistant and fire-retardant fibrous covering.   For ACT (thermoplastic conductors), a moisture-resistant fibrous covering is required only on the individual conductors.

Where not subject to physical damage, Type AC cable may be installed in both exposed and concealed work. Type AC cable may be used in dry locations; for under plaster extensions; and embedded in plaster finish on brick or other masonry, except in damp or wet locations. This cable may be run or fished in the air voids of masonry block or tile walls; where such walls are exposed or subject to excessive moisture or dampness or are below grade line, Type ACL cable must be used. Also, Type ACL must be used if the cable is exposed to the weather or to continuous moisture; run underground; embedded in masonry, concrete or fill in buildings in course of construction; or exposed to oil or other conditions having a deteriorating effect on the insulation.

Type AC cable must not be used where expressly prohibited in the Code, including (1) in theaters or assembly halls, except as provided in section 520-4 of the Code; (2) in motion picture studios; (3) in any hazardous location; (4) where exposed to corrosive fumes or vapors; (5) on cranes or hoists, except as provided in section 610-11, exception No. 3 of the Code; (6) in storage battery rooms; (7) in hoistways or on elevators, except as provided in section 620-21 of the Code; or (8) commercial garages where prohibited in article 511 of the Code.

150. Manipulating Type AC Cable. It must never be spliced except at outlets. Many methods of fastening cable in outlet boxes are in vogue. Clamps or box connectors can be used. Outlet and switch boxes specially adapted for flexible metal-clad cable should be used. Special cutters are available.

151. For cutting the cable to length, a shear, bolt cutter, or hack saw can be used. At each outlet or junction box the armor must also be cut back about 8 in. in order to leave

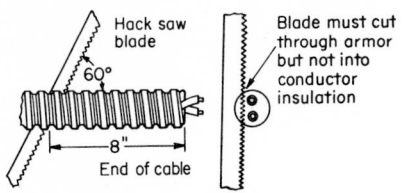

FIG. 82 *Method of cutting armor back from end of cable.*

sufficient free ends of wire for splicing. This cutting is done with a hack saw held so as to cut across the armor at an angle of about 60 deg with the axis of the cable (Fig. 82). Great care must be taken not to cut into the insulation on the conductors. As soon as the hack saw has cut through the armor on one side of the cable, the short piece of armor can be loosened from the main cable and slipped off the end.

152. The wires at the ends of Type AC cable should be protected by means of fiber bushings, although they are not required with lead-covered cable. The fiber bushings employed for this purpose are called antishort insulating bushings (Fig. 83). The split bushing is pinched together and slipped over the wires inside the armor, as illustrated in Fig. 84. It protects the insulation of the wires from the rough edges of the cut ends of the armor.

153. For fastening Type AC cable to outlet boxes a connector (Fig. 85) can be slipped over the end of the cable. The setscrew is tightened down against the armor. The threaded end of the connector slips into standard conduit knockouts, and the lock nut is then put on, holding the connector tight to the box. Another method is to use outlet boxes of the type shown in Fig. 86, which contain built-in cable clamps in which the clamp tightens down against the armor and holds it firmly in place.

154. Type AC Cable for Old Building Wiring. It can be used to great advantage in this work. An advantage possessed by it is that it can be run with almost utter disre-

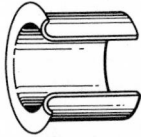

FIG. 83 *Antishort fiber bushing.*

FIG. 84 *Method of protecting wires with antishort bushings.*

gard of its contact with pipes or other materials and can be fished for long distances. Its own weight is sufficient to carry it down partitions, and it is stiff enough to fish between joists without the use of a fish wire. It or nonmetallic-sheathed cable can also be installed more quickly and with less cutting of walls, floors, etc., than can wires in flexible tubing.

155. The loop system of wiring is nearly always used for concealed work in order to avoid the use of junction boxes. The cables loop from one out-

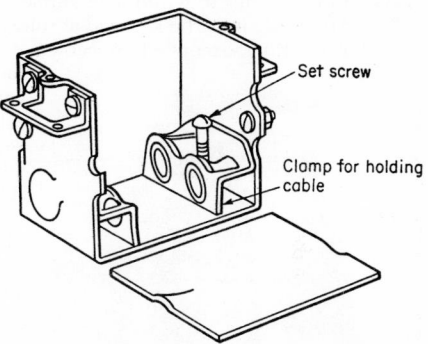

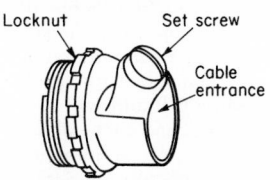

FIG. 85 *Box connector for Type AC metal-clad cable. (General Electric Supply Corp.)*

FIG. 86 *Outlet box with clamps for Type AC metal-clad cable. (General Electric Supply Corp.)*

let to the next outlet, and splices are made only at outlet boxes. All splices must be accessible for inspection, and if a junction box is used, the cover must be left accessible.

156. Type MC cables are power cables (Fig. 87) limited in size to conductors of No. 4 AWG and larger for copper and No. 2 AWG and larger for aluminum. The metal enclosures shall be either a covering of interlocking metal tape or an impervious close-fitting corrugated tube. Supplemental protection of an outer covering of corrosion-resistant material must be provided where such protection is required by section 300-5 of the Code. The cables must provide an adequate path for grounding purposes. For cables of the MC type, insulated conductors must be of a type listed in Sec. **123** of Div. 2 for rubber, thermoplastic, varnished cloth, asbestos–varnished cloth, or of a type especially approved for the purpose.

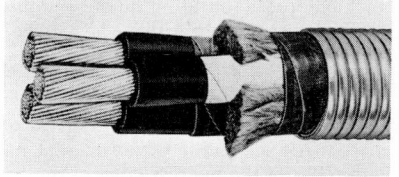

Except where otherwise specified in the Code, and where not subject to physical damage, Type MC cable may be installed for branch circuits or feeders in both concealed and exposed work as follows:

FIG. 87 *Type MC cable with aluminum sheath and aluminum conductors. (Kaiser Aluminum & Chemical Sales, Inc.)*

The cable may be used in partially protected areas, such as in continuous rigid cable supports and the like, in dry locations; and when any of the following conditions are met it may be used in wet locations.

a. The metallic covering is impervious to moisture.

b. A lead sheath or moisture-impervious jacket is provided under the metal covering.

c. The insulated conductors under the metallic covering are approved for use in wet locations.

At all points where Type MC cable terminates, suitable fittings designed for use with the particular wiring cable and the conditions of service must be used (see Fig. 88).

157. Bends. All bends shall be so made that the cable will not be injured, and the radius of the curve of the inner bend of any bend must be not less than seven times the diameter of Type MC cable or less than five times the diameter of Type AC cable.

158. Supports. Metal-clad cables must be secured by approved staples, straps, hangers, or similar fittings so designed and installed as not to injure the cable. The cable may be installed on the underside of floor joists in basements where supported at each joist and so located as not to be subject to physical damage.

Type AC cable must be secured at intervals not exceeding 4½ ft and within 12 in. from every outlet box or fitting, except where the cable is fished and except for lengths of not over 24 in. at terminals where flexibility is necessary. Staples or straps are used to support the cables to wired-over surfaces.

Type MC cable must be secured at intervals not exceeding 6 ft, and within 2 ft from every box or fitting, except where cable is fished. The cable may be installed on metal racks, trays, troughs, or continuous rigid cable supports, grounded as required in article 250 of the Code. The cables must be separated from each other by a distance of not less than one-quarter of a cable diameter. There must be no more than one layer of cables on a rack or other support member; each cable so installed must be supported at intervals not exceeding 6 ft and within 2 ft from every box or fitting, and each cable must be attached to the support at intervals of not more than 10 ft horizontally and 2 ft vertically.

159. Through Studs, Joists and Rafters. Metal-clad cable can be run through bored holes in studs, joists, or rafters. The holes must be bored at the approximate centers of the wood members or at least 2 in. from the nearest edge where practical. If there is no objection because of weakening of the structure, the Code will allow metal-clad cable to be laid in notches in the studding or joists provided that the cable is protected against

FIG. 88   *Connectors for Type MC cables.*

the driving of nails into it by having the notch covered with a steel plate at least ¹⁄₁₆ in. thick before the building finish is applied.

160. In Accessible Attics. Metal-clad cables in accessible attics shall be installed as follows:

1. If run across the top of floor joists, or within 7 ft of the floor or floor joists across the face of rafters or studs, in attics or roof spaces which are accessible, the cable shall be protected by substantial guard strips which are at least as high as the cable. If this space is not accessible by permanent stairs or ladders, protection will only be required within 6 ft of the nearest edge of the scuttle hole or attic entrance.

2. If cable is carried along the sides of rafters, studs, or floor joints, neither guard strips nor running boards shall be required.

SURFACE-RACEWAY WIRING

161. Wiring in surface metal raceway can be used for exposed work for branch-circuit or feeder conductors. It may be installed in dry locations. It shall not be used (1) where concealed, except that metal raceways approved for the purpose may be used for underplaster extensions; (2) where subject to severe physical damage unless approved for the purpose; (3) where the voltage is 300 volts or more between conductors unless the metal has a thickness of not less than 0.040 in.; (4) where subject to corrosive vapors; (5) in hoistways; or (6) in any hazardous location. The number of conductors installed in any raceway shall be no greater than the number for which the raceway is designed. Metal raceway must be continuous from outlet to outlet, junction box, or approved fittings designed especially for use with metal raceway. All outlets must be provided with approved terminal fittings which will protect the insulation of conductors from abrasion unless such protection is afforded by the construction of the boxes or fittings. Metal raceway should not be used in damp places.

Where combination raceways are used for the installation of signal, power, and lighting circuits, each system shall be run in a separate compartment of the raceway.

Raceways may be extended through dry walls, dry partitions, and dry floors if in unbroken lengths where passing through.

162. Surface Nonmetallic Raceway. There is a new line of surface nonmetallic raceways and fittings, manufactured by Johnson Plastic Corp., Chagrin Falls, Ohio, which has been listed by the Underwriters' Laboratories and conforms to National Electrical Code requirements.

Intended as a raceway for baseboard receptacles and other circuit supplies, it also serves a dual function as an attractive baseboard trim, and replaces conventional baseboards.

A feature of the "Johnsonite R-W" design is its simplicity and its ability to be tailored to any installation with only ten components.

Basically, the baseboard system contains a plastic back plate which is secured directly to the wall. Where receptacles are to be located, a metal bracket is attached through the back plate into the wall with wood screws or other fastening devices. Wires are then pulled in, and receptacles mounted in place and wired. The wires are held in place along the raceway by a retaining clip strip, which is fastened to the wall of the raceway about every 5 ft. This holds the wiring in place. Finally, the external baseboard cover and receptacle cover are snapped into place. Covers over receptacles are doubly anchored by means of a flange and a 6-32 screw into the outlet body.

The material used in this system is the same as is used with rigid PVC conduit. End caps and inside or outside corners are available. One side of each of these fittings is cemented to the baseboard cover.

National Electric Code rules state that surface nonmetallic raceway and fittings must be of suitable nonmetallic material which is resistant to moisture and chemical atmospheres. It must also be flame-retardant; and resistant to impact and crushing, distortion due to heat under conditions likely to be encountered in service, and to low-temperature effects.

Surface nonmetallic raceways may be installed in dry locations. They must not be used (1) where concealed, (2) where subject to severe physical damage unless approved for the purpose, (3) where the voltage is 300 volts or more between conductors, (4) in hoistways, (5) in any hazardous location, (6) where subject to ambient temperatures exceeding 50°C, or (7) for conductors whose insulation exceeds 75°C.

Other Code rules such as the number and size of conductors are the same as for surface metal raceways.

163. National metal raceway, called "Lay-in," is made by the National Electric Div., H. K. Porter Co., Inc. It consists of a channel capping that snaps over a channel base. The parts and assembly are illustrated in Fig. 89. Lay-in surface metal raceway is made in seven types:

1. 111 Xtensionduct.
2. 333 metal molding.
3. 888 metal molding.
4. 711-A metal Florduct.
5. 733-A metal Florduct.
6. 1700 Surfaceduct.
7. 3400 Twinduct.

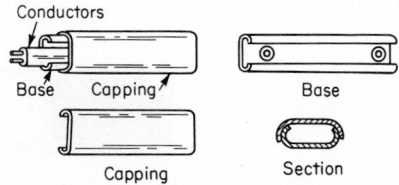

FIG. 89 *Parts and assembly of National metal raceway.*

The general installation procedure for all Lay-in raceway is the same. It consists of three basic steps:

1. Fasten the channel base to the supporting structure.
2. Lay in the wires. The wires are held in place by fiber retaining clips. Three clips are furnished with each length of raceway.
3. Snap the capping over the base at one end, and then press the capping into place by using the palm and shifting hands progressively toward other end.

These raceways are supported in place through holes in the back of the base by wood screws, toggle bolts, expansion plugs, or rawl drives.

A very complete line of fittings is available, including elbows, tees, crosses, terminations, junction boxes, receptacle and switch boxes, rosettes, etc. The application of

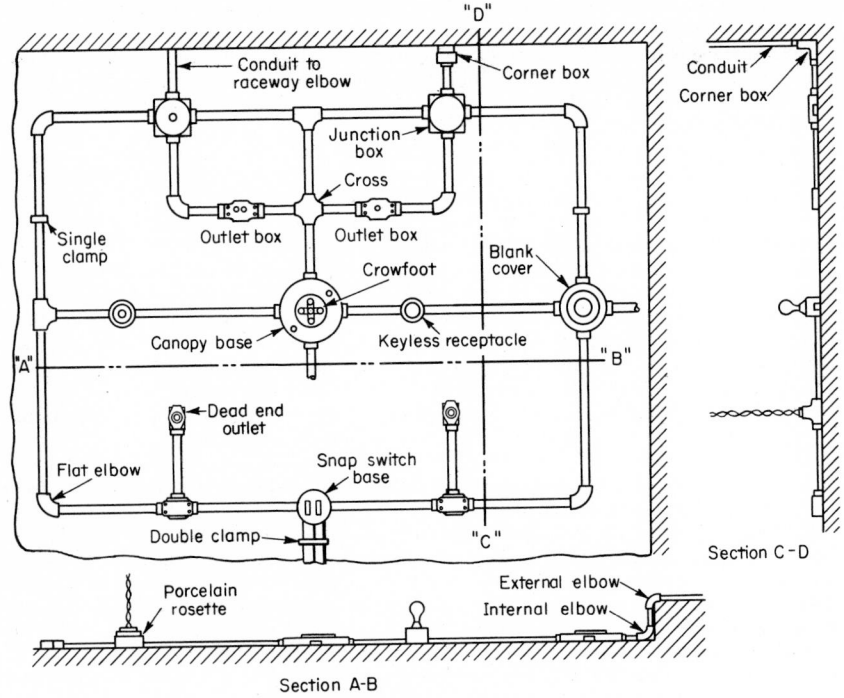

FIG. 90 *Application of metal raceway and fittings.*

raceway and fittings is illustrated in Fig. 90, which shows an imaginary layout to indicate how the material may be used.

164. Xtensionduct (Fig. 91) is the smallest size of Lay-in metal raceway. It is made in 5-ft lengths.

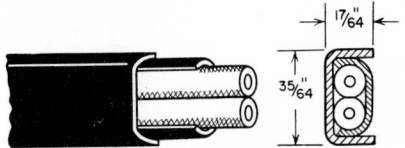

FIG. 91 *Xtensionduct. (National Electric Div., H. K. Porter Co., Inc.)*

Wire Capacity for Xtensionduct

	Single conductor					Annunciator	Telephone, twisted pair
	No. 6	No. 8	No. 10	No. 12	No. 14		
Type RH	..	..	..	2	3	10	4
Type TW or RUH	..	..	..	3	3		

165. Lay-in 333 metal molding (Fig. 92) is the smaller size of molding. It is made in lengths of 8 ft 4 in.

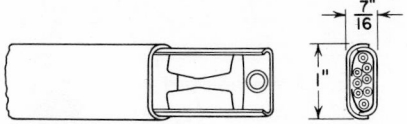

FIG. 92   *Lay-in 333 metal molding.   (National Electric Div., H. K. Porter Co., Inc.)*

Wire Capacity for 333 Metal Molding

	Single conductor					Annunciator	Telephone	
	No. 6	No. 8	No. 10	No. 12	No. 14		Twisted pair	Cable
Type RH	..	2.	3	6	7	25	8	Up to ¹¹/₃₂ diam
Type TW or RUH	2	3	6	8	9			

166. Lay-in 888 metal molding (Fig. 93) is the larger size of molding.   It is made in lengths of 8 ft 4 in.

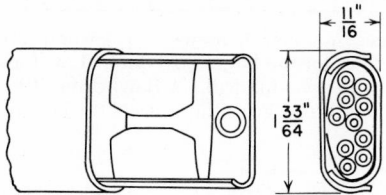

FIG. 93   *Lay-in 888 metal molding.   (National Electric Div., H. K. Porter Co., Inc.)*

Wire Capacity for 888 Metal Molding

	Single conductor					Annunciator	Telephone	
	No. 6	No. 8	No. 10	No. 12	No. 14		Twisted pair	Cable
Type RH	4	7	9	10	10	60	12	Up to two
Type TW or RUH	5	10	10	10	10			26 pair

167. Lay-in 711-A metal Florduct (Fig. 94) is the smaller size of Florduct.   It is made in 5-ft lengths.

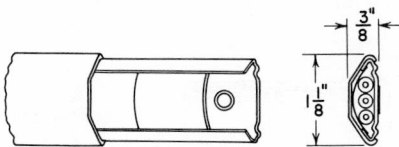

FIG. 94   *Lay-in 711-A Florduct.   (National Electric Div., H. K. Porter Co., Inc.)*

Wire Capacity for 711-A Florduct

	Single conductor					Annunciator	Telephone
	No. 6	No. 8	No. 10	No. 12	No. 14		
Type RH	..	2	2	4	7	20	4 twisted pair
Type TW or RUH	..	3	4	5	9		

168. Lay-in 733-A metal Florduct (Fig. 95) is the larger size of Florduct.   It is made in 5-ft lengths.

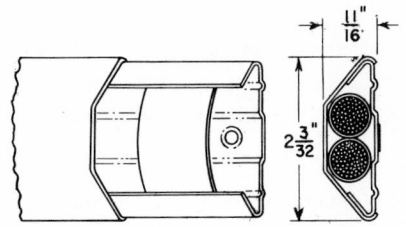

FIG. 95 *Lay-in 733-A Florduct.* *(National Electric Div., H. K. Porter Co., Inc.)*

Wire Capacity for 733-A Florduct

	Single conductor					Annunciator	Telephone	
	No. 6	No. 8	No. 10	No. 12	No. 14		Twisted pair	Cable
Type RH	4	7	10	10	10	50	8	Up to two
Type TW or RUH	6	10	10	10	10			26 pair

169. To install Florduct on wood floors use No. 4 wood screws for the smaller size duct and No. 8 wood screws for the larger size duct. For stone or concrete floors drill a hole about 1 in. deep with a $^3/_{16}$-in. drill. A Rawl-drive (Fig. 96) is then driven into the hole with a hammer and firmly grips the sides of the hole in the masonry. After the

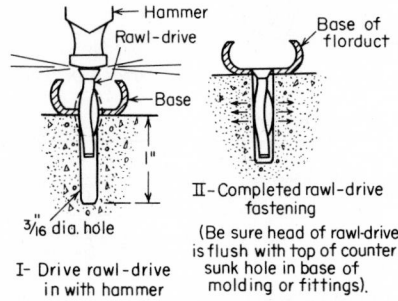

FIG. 96 *Method of fastening Florduct on masonry floor.* *(National Electric Div., H. K. Porter Co., Inc.)*

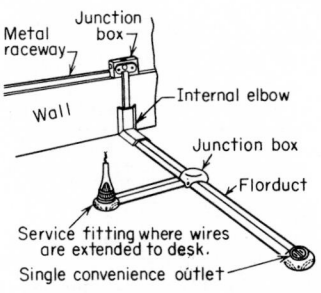

FIG. 97 *Installation of Florduct and outlets.* *(National Electric Div., H. K. Porter Co., Inc.)*

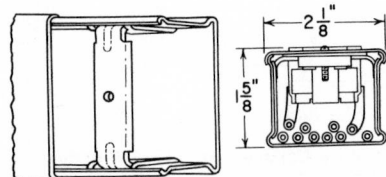

FIG. 98 *Lay-in Surfaceduct.* *(National Electric Div., H. K. Porter Co., Inc.)*

base of the duct is fastened in this way, the wires are laid in and the capping is snapped over the base the same as with the other raceways. Figure 97, representing a completed installation of Florduct, shows the method of attachment to wall-mounted raceway and also shows some of the fittings.

170. Surfaceduct (Fig. 98) is a Lay-in metal surface raceway designed for industrial and commercial use. All types of service can be supplied from it up to 60 amp. Device covers are available to adapt any manufacturer's approved outlet devices. A Surface-

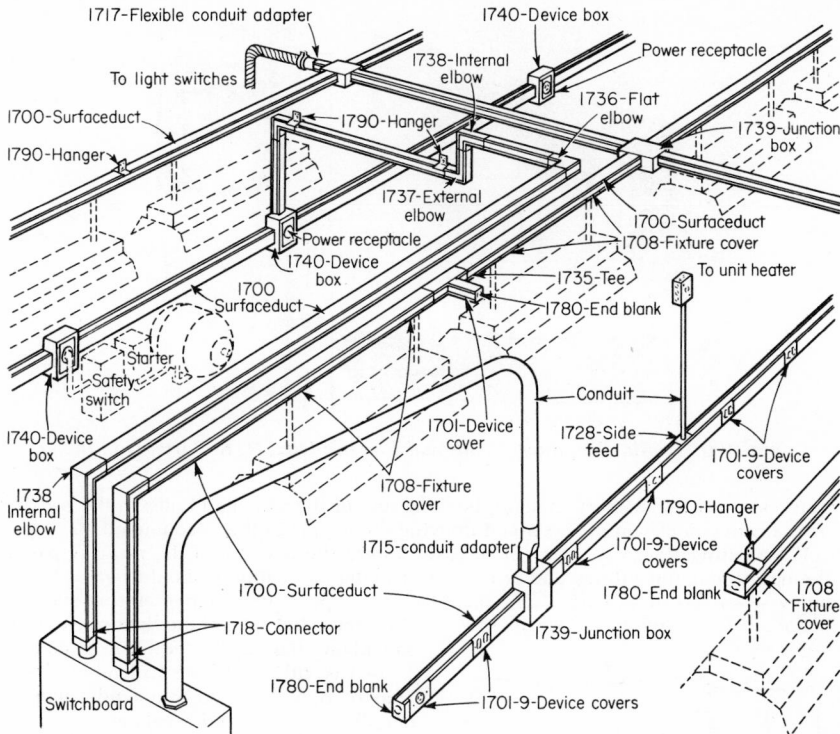

FIG. 99   *Illustration of Surfaceduct application.   (National Electric Div., H. K. Porter Co., Inc.)*

duct system is quickly accessible for future changes or relocation of service points.   One run of Surfaceduct can be used as a feeder duct for lighting, to furnish power to bench tools and other devices, as well as providing heavier service for motor-driven equipment.   The varied applications of Surfaceduct are illustrated in Fig. 99.   It is made in lengths of 10 ft.   The base is provided with ½- and ¾-in. knockouts.

Wire Capacity for 1700 Surfaceduct

Single conductor	No. 6	No. 8	No. 10	No. 12	No. 14
Capacity with devices:					
Types RH, RUH, T, TW.................	8	10	10	10	10
Capacity without devices:					
Type RH......................................	8	12	18	34	38
Types RUH, T, TW.......................	12	16	18	34	54

171. Twinduct (Fig. 100) is a Lay-in metal surface raceway which provides a combination high- and low-potential raceway.   Required devices and terminal blocks are mounted and wired prior to the mounting of the screw-supported cover.   Both raceways are readily accessible for maintenance, wiring changes, or addition to systems by removal of the single cover.   The low-potential raceway accommodates 50 twisted-pair telephone wires or several 26-pair cables.   Covers are available for telephone jacks.   Twinduct is available in 10-ft lengths.   The wire fill for the high-potential (upper) raceway is the same as given for No. 1700 Surfaceduct.

172. Installing National Metal Raceway. Separating.   Reasonable care should be exercised in separating the backing and capping preparatory to installation.   As the

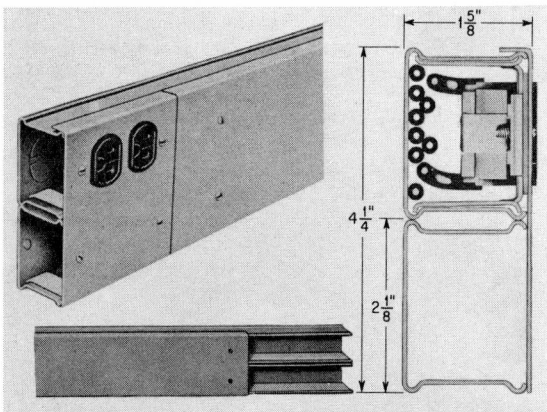

FIG. 100   *Lay-in Twinduct.*   (*National Electric Div., H. K. Porter Co., Inc.*)

quickest, most satisfactory method, hooking one of the punched holes in the backing over a convenient nail or screw and drawing the capping off is recommended.

173. Cutting Raceway.   Except in cases where the backing of the raceway passes through under the fittings and is not cut, backing and capping should be cut before being separated in all cases.   The manufacturer's specially designed cutting machine is the most effective tool.   A hack saw may be used.   Because of the light stock, hacksaw blades having fine teeth and commonly known as "tube saws" are preferable.   Some construction men recommend marking deeply with a file and breaking.

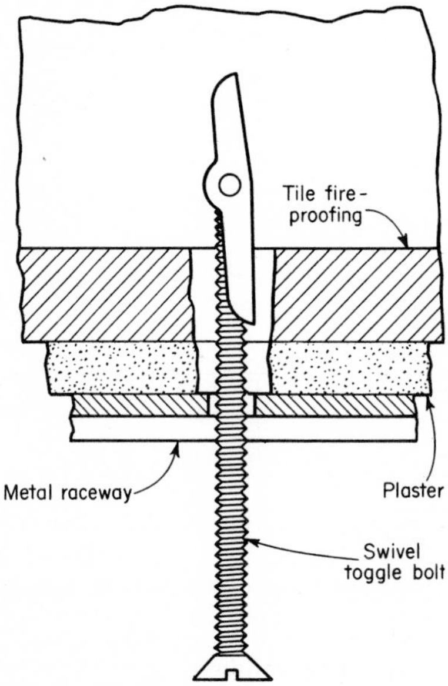

174. Bending Metal Raceway.   The raceway is readily bent and, with reasonable care, can be worked to any radius down to one of 4½ in.   Bends must be made in all cases before backing and capping are separated.

175. Supporting Raceway.   The backing is punched and countersunk every 2 ft for the supporting screws or bolts.   The support so afforded will usually be found more than ample, but further support can be secured through either additional punching, with a special punch, or use of a metal raceway clamp.   Figure 101 shows a toggle-bolt support for metal raceway.   When the metal raceway is installed on uneven surfaces, such as the ceilings of old buildings, the capping has a tendency to spring away from the backing.   This can be overcome by the use of two or three straps fastened over each length.

176. Loose Raceway Capping.   If the capping of the raceway is loose, it should be removed from the backing and tightened by tapping it with a mallet at points 8 in. apart on one edge only.

Tile fire-proofing

Metal raceway

Plaster

Swivel toggle bolt

FIG. 101   *Toggle bolt being inserted.*

177. Metal raceway can be mitered for elbows and bends by cutting it with a hack saw. Elbows and bends thus made have the advantage that they fit into corners more closely than do the purchased fittings.   Electrical conductivity is preserved by always leaving a

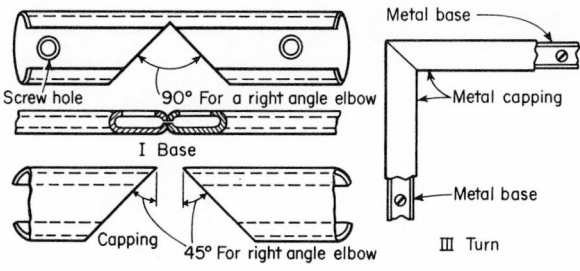

Screw hole   90° For a right angle elbow

I Base

Capping   45° For right angle elbow

II Miter cuts

Metal base

Metal capping

Metal base

III Turn

FIG. 102 *Mitered turn.*

portion of the backing intact.   Figure 102 shows how a turn can be made, and Fig. 103 shows the method for an elbow.

178. Wiremold metal raceways are made in three general types by the Wiremold Co. These types are designated as (1) Wiremold surface raceway used for general surface-raceway wiring systems, (2) Pancake overfloor raceway used for overfloor surface-raceway wiring, and (3) Plugmold raceway used primarily for multioutlet assemblies wiring (see Sec. **278**).   Plugmold can be used without receptacles as a general high-capacity surface wiring raceway.   The Wiremold surface raceway is a unit assembly, while the other two types consist of two separable parts, the base and the cover.

The appearance and dimensions of the different types and sizes are shown in Fig. 104. The wire capacities are given in Secs. **179** to **181A** inclusive.   Wiremold No. 200 and Plugmold Nos. 2000 and 2200 are made in 5-ft lengths.   The standard length for the other types is 10 ft, although some types are available also in 5-ft lengths.

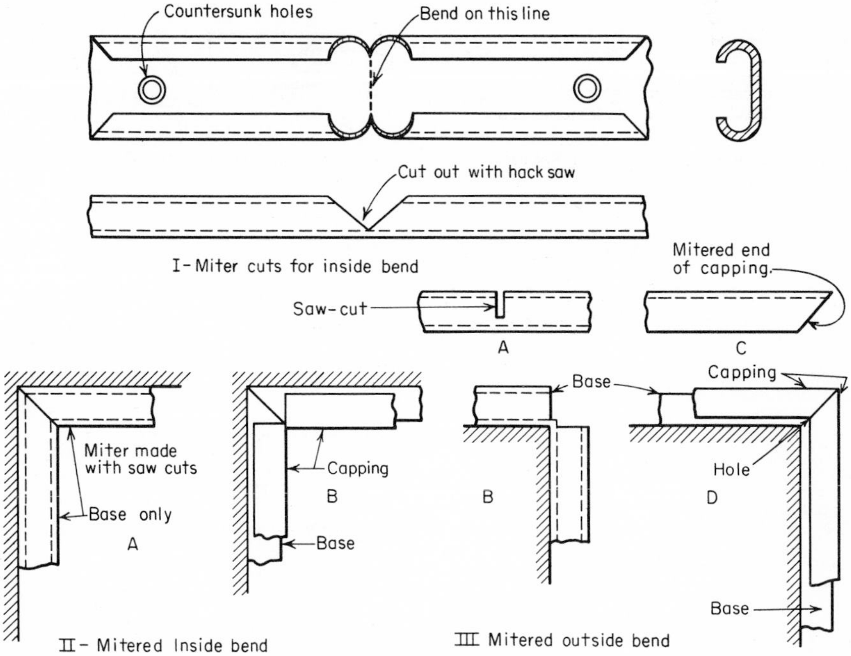

Countersunk holes   Bend on this line

Cut out with hack saw

I- Miter cuts for inside bend

Mitered end of capping.

Saw-cut

A

C

Miter made with saw cuts

Base only

A

Capping

B

Base

Base

B

Capping

Hole

D

Capping

Base

II- Mitered Inside bend

III Mitered outside bend

FIG. 103 *Mitered elbows.*

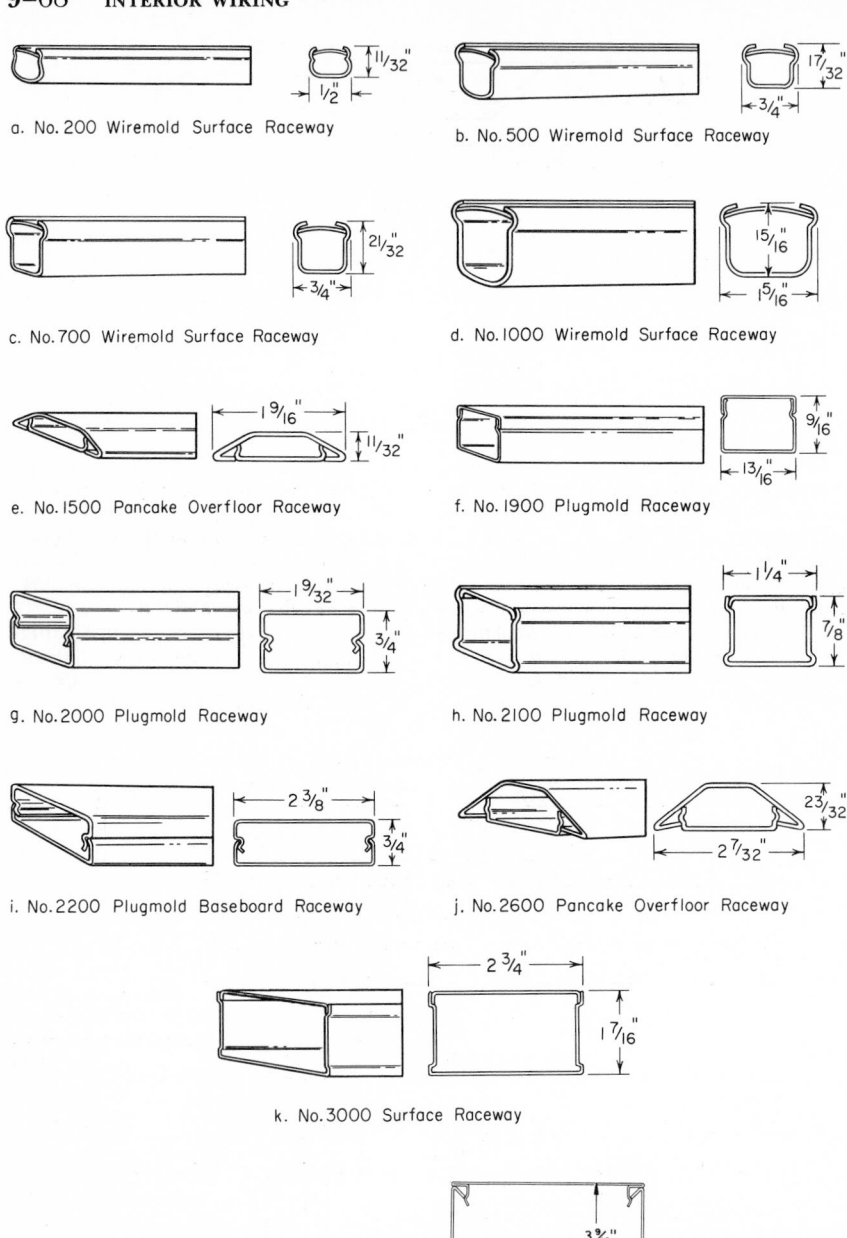

a. No. 200 Wiremold Surface Raceway

b. No. 500 Wiremold Surface Raceway

c. No. 700 Wiremold Surface Raceway

d. No. 1000 Wiremold Surface Raceway

e. No. 1500 Pancake Overfloor Raceway

f. No. 1900 Plugmold Raceway

g. No. 2000 Plugmold Raceway

h. No. 2100 Plugmold Raceway

i. No. 2200 Plugmold Baseboard Raceway

j. No. 2600 Pancake Overfloor Raceway

k. No. 3000 Surface Raceway

l. No. G 4000 Surface Raceway

m. No. G 6000 Surface Raceway

FIG. 104 *Types and dimensions of Wiremold raceways. (The Wiremold Co.)*

Wiremold surface metal raceway consists of a metal capping with its edges crimped over a slightly curved base. The capping is crimped on the base at the factory so that the capping and base are installed as a unit. The wires are pulled through the raceway from fitting to fitting in a manner similar to that employed in conduit work. The lengths are fastened together with a coupling (Fig. 105, I) which is fastened to the wall surface with a wood screw or toggle bolt. The base of the raceway is slipped under the end of the coupling before the screw or bolt is drawn up tight. A connection cover (Fig. 105, II) snaps over the ends of the raceway, closing the joint. Each section of raceway is secured at one or two intermediate points between the couplings by means of either one- or two-hole straps (Fig. 105, III and IV) screwed or bolted to the wall surface. The fittings and capping of Wiremold are finished in a neutral brown tint which blends well with most surroundings. The base of the raceway and the base plates of all fittings are given a special zinc treatment to prevent corrosion.

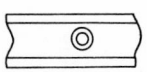  

I - Coupling   II-Connection cover   III-Two hole strap   IV _ One hole strap

FIG. 105 *Wiremold metal raceway and support details.*

Pancake overfloor raceway consists of two steel parts, a base and a cover. The parts have a natural galvanized finish. When this raceway is installed, the base is fastened to the floor by the appropriate means of wood screws, expansion shields, toggle bolts, etc. The conductors are then laid flat in the base of the raceway. After the connections have been completed, the cover is snapped in place over the base.

Plugmold raceway consists of two steel parts, a channel base and a snap-on cover. Both base and cover are available in the standard brown Wiremold finish or in a gray finish. When this raceway is installed, the channel base is fastened to the supporting structure with the appropriate means. The conductors are laid in the channel base, the necessary connections made, and the installation completed by snapping the cover over the base.

A very complete line of fittings, outlets, and receptacles is available for the different Wiremold raceways to meet the varied needs of installation.

179. Wire Capacities for Nos. 200 to 3000 Wiremold Raceways

For not more than the number of wires of sizes and types indicated in the following table, when no wiring devices are mounted on or in raceway:

Catalog Nos.	Wire size, AWG	Maximum number of wires		
		RH	T or RUH	THWN
200	14	3	3	3
	12	2	3	3
500	14	5	6	8
	12	4	6	7
	10	2	4	4
	8	....	2	2
700	14	7	8	11
	12	6	8	10
	10	3	6	6
	8	2	3	3
	6	....	....	2
1000	14	10	10	21
	12	10	10	18
	10	6	8	10
	8	5	8	10
	6	4	5	6
1900	14	3	3	3
	12	3	3	3
2000B, 2000C	14	3	3	3
	12	3	3	3
2100B, 2100C	14	17	17	23
	12	14	14	18
	10	10	10	12
	8	6	8	10
	6	4	5	6

For not more than number of wires of sizes and types indicated in following table, when no wiring devices are mounted on or in raceway:

Catalog No.	Wire size, AWG	Maximum number of wires					
		T, TW	THW	RUH, RUW	RH	RHH, RHW	THWN, THHN
3000	14	66	43	66	39	27	103
	12	52	35	52	32	23	77
	10	40	29	40	19	19	49
	8	22	17	22	11	11	28
	6	11	11	11	7	7	17
	4	8	8	8	5	5	10
	3	6	6	6	....	....	8
	2	5	5	5	....	....	7

180. Wire Capacities for Nos. 1500 and 2600 Overfloor Wiremold

For use on floors in dry locations where not subject to excessive mopping or scrubbing. Raceway to be used with not more than the number of wires of sizes and types indicated in following table:

Catalog Nos.	Wire size, AWG	Maximum number of wires		
		RH	T, TW, or RUH	THWN
1500	14	4	8	10
	12	4	6	8
	10	....	4	5
	8	....	4	4
	6	....	....	2
2600	14	10	10	16
	12	10	10	14
	10	6	8	10
	8	4	7	8
	6	2	4	6

181. Wire Capacities for Wiremold Nos. 1900 to 3000 Plugmold

For use with this manufacturer's attachment plug receptacles designed for mounting in raceway. Raceway to be used with not more than number of wires of sizes and types indicated in following table:

Catalog Nos.	Wire size, AWG	Maximum number of wires		
		RH	T, TW, or RUH	THWN
1900B, 1900C	14	3	3	
	12	3	3	
2000B, 2000C	14	3	3	
	12	3	3	
2100B, 2100C	14	6	10	
	12	6	10	
	10	....	8	
	8	....	6	
2200B, 2200C	14	10	10	14
	12	10	10	13
	10	6	10	12
	8	4	7	10
	6	....	3	7

NOTE. Catalog nos. 2100B and 2100C raceway may also be used with other wiring devices mounted in raceway. When so used, the suitable number of wires of given size and type is to be determined for the specific installation.

For use with fluorescent lamp fixture fittings, Catalog Nos. 20FL-1, 20FL-2, and 20FL-3. Raceway to be used with not more than the number of wires of sizes and types indicated in following table:

Catalog Nos.	Wire size, AWG	Maximum number of wires	
		RH	T or RU
2000B, 2000C	14	2	2
	12	2	2

For use with standard flush-mounted attachment plug receptacle of type not having pilot lights. Raceway to be used with not more than the number of wires of sizes and types indicated in following table:

Catalog No.	Wire size, AWG	Maximum number of wires	
		RH, RHH, RHW	T, THW, TW, RUH, RUW
3000	14	16	26
	12	14	18
	10	10	10
	8	6	8
	6	4	6

181A.   Wire Capacities for Nos. 4000 and 6000 Wiremold Raceways

For use with not more than the number of wires of sizes and types indicated in the following table:

Raceway with Barrier in Place and Using One Compartment as a Power Raceway

Cat-alog No.	Wire size, AWG	Maximum number of wires							
		With devices				Without devices			
		RH, RHW, RU, RUH, RUW, TW, T THW	THWN, THHN	T, TW	THW	RUH, RUW	RH	RHH, RHW	THWN, THHN
G-4000	14	17	32	68	44	68	40	28	106
	12	15	24	53	36	53	33	24	79
	10	11	15	41	29	41	20	20	50
	8	7	8	22	17	22	12	12	29
	6	4	7	11	11	11	7	7	17
	4	....	....	8	8	8	5	5	10
	3	....	....	7	7	7	....	....	9
	2	....	....	6	6	6	....	....	7

Raceway without Barrier in Place

Cat-alog No.	Wire size, AWG	Maximum number of wires								
		Without devices						With devices		
		T, TW	THW	RUH, RUW	RH	RHH, RHW	THWN, THHN	RH, RHW, RUH, THW	RU, RUW, T, TW	THHN, THWN
G-4000	14	138	91	138	81	57	215	21	17	34
	12	108	74	108	67	48	160	21	16	34
	10	83	60	83	40	40	101	15	12	18
	8	45	35	45	24	24	59	10	10	15
	6	22	22	22	15	15	36	....	....	10
	4	17	17	17	11	11	22			
	3	14	14	14	....	....	18			
	2	12	12	12	....	....	15			

Cat-alog No.	Wire size, AWG	Maximum number of wires								
		Without devices						With devices		
		T, TW	THW	RUH, RUW	RH	RHH, RHW	THWN, THHN	T, TW	THWN	RH, RHW, RHH, THW
G-6000	14	234	153	234	137	97	363	61	61	61
	12	184	126	184	114	82	270	54	54	54
	10	141	102	141	68	68	172	38	38	38
	8	77	60	77	41	41	99	27	27	27
	6	38	38	38	25	25	61	20	20	20
	4	29	29	29	19	19	37	8	10	5
	3	25	25	25	17	17	32			
	2	21	21	21	15	15	27	6	7	4
	1	15	15	......	11	11	20			
	1/0	13	13	......	10	10	16	4	5	3
	2/0	11	11	......	8	8	14	3	4	3

182. Cross-sectional Areas of Wiremold Raceways

Raceway No.	Area, Square Inches
200	0.11
500	0.20
700	0.25
1000	0.74
1500	0.22
1900	0.41
2000	0.80
2100	0.81
2200	1.50
2600	0.72
2800	0.95
3000	3.51
G-4000	7.22
G-6000	15.82

ELECTRICAL-METALLIC-TUBING WIRING

183. Wiring employing electrical metallic tubing (EMT) is widely used for commercial and industrial wiring systems. The National Electrical Code allows the installation of electrical metallic tubing, either concealed or exposed, where either during construction or afterward it will not be subject to severe physical damage. Electrical metallic tubing may be supported in buildings of fire-resistive construction on the face of masonry or other material of which walls or ceilings are composed. It may then be buried in concrete or plaster finish. Connections between lengths of tubing and between tubing and any fitting shall provide adequate mechanical strength and electrical continuity.

In installations having cinder concrete or fill, electrical metallic tubing must be protected on all sides by a layer of noncinder concrete at least 2 in. thick unless the tubing is at least 18 in. under the fill.

In installations where corrosive fumes or vapors may exist as in meat-packing plants, tanneries, hide cellars, casing rooms, glue houses, fertilizer rooms, salt storage, some chemical works, metal refineries, pulp mills, sugar mills, roundhouses, some stables, and similar locations, special tubing and fittings made of corrosion-resistant material approved for the purpose must be used (refer to Sec. **192**).

When installed in wet locations, such as dairies, laundries, and canneries, and in locations where the walls are frequently washed, the entire tubing system, including all its boxes and other fittings, shall be installed and equipped so as to prevent water from entering the tubing system and the tubing shall be mounted so that there is at least $1/4$-in. air space between it and the wall or other supporting surface. For these installations all the supporting materials, such as straps, bolts, and screws, must be of corrosion-resistant material or be protected against corrosion by approved materials.

The rules regarding bends, minimum size, and allowable number of conductors are the same as for rigid metal conduit. The maximum allowable size of tubing is 4 in.

184. Table 185 gives the sizes and weights of electrical metallic tubing. Since the inside diameters are the same as those for rigid metal conduit, the same tables of number of allowable wires in a conduit apply to the tubing. The wall is thinner, however, and the outside diameters of tubing are less than those for conduit. The regular metallic tubing has a round cross section and is made of galvanized steel. However, sizes over 2 in. have the same outside diameters as corresponding sizes of rigid metal conduit. Accordingly, the internal diameters of these larger sizes are slightly greater than those of other types of conduits.

185. Electrical Metallic Tubing

Size, inches	Approximate weight per 1,000 ft, lb	Diameter, inches		Wall thickness, inch
		Inside	Outside	
1/2	295	0.622	0.706	0.042
3/4	445	0.824	0.922	0.049
1	650	1.049	1.163	0.057
1 1/4	960	1.380	1.510	0.065
1 1/2	1,110	1.610	1.740	0.065
2	1,410	2.067	2.197	0.065
2 1/2	2,300	2.731	2.875	0.072
3	2,700	3.356	3.500	0.072
4	4,000	4.334	4.500	0.083

186. All outlet boxes and fittings for use with electrical metallic tubing must be of the threadless type, since owing to the thin wall it is not permissible to thread the tubing. Special threadless fittings similar to those employed for standard rigid conduit are manufactured for tubing. Standard rigid conduit fittings can be used with tubing if an adapter is employed. Sections of tubing can be joined by means of threadless couplings, which are available in steel and malleable-iron construction. Tubing is connected to outlet boxes by means of connectors. One end of the connector is made for threadless attachment to the tubing, and the other end is threaded and supplied with a lock nut for attachment to the box through a knockout. Raintight connections can be made to the tubing with some couplings and connectors. Standard 90-deg elbows (Fig. 106) are attached to the tubing by means of the above-described couplings. The dimensions of standard elbows are given in Sec. **187.** Raintight elbows and angle box connectors are available with the ends fitted with threadless fittings.

187. Standard 90-deg Elbows for EMT

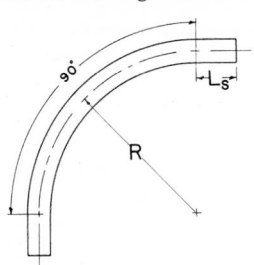

FIG. 106   *Standard radius, 90-deg elbow.*

(All dimensions in inches)

Trade size of tubing	Smallest acceptable radius R to center line of tubing	Shortest acceptable length Ls of each straight end portion of tubing
1/2	4	1 1/2
3/4	4 1/2	1 1/2
1	5 3/4	1 7/8
1 1/4	7 1/4	2
1 1/2	8 1/4	2
2	9 1/2	2
2 1/2	10 1/2	3
3	13	3 1/8
4	16	3 3/8

188. Threadless couplings and connectors for EMT are of the set-screw, compression, indenter, tap-on, two-piece, or squeeze types. Such fittings are classified as concrete-tight only, or raintight and concrete-tight. Accordingly, only fittings that are classified as being raintight can be used outdoors exposed to the weather or in wet locations. Except for the indenter-type fittings, EMT couplings and connectors can be installed with common hand tools. Indenter-type fittings require a special tool, and these fittings are made only up to 1 in. in size.

189. Supports for Electrical Metallic Tubing. The National Electrical Code requires electrical metallic tubing to be securely fastened in place at least every 10 ft and within 3 ft of each outlet box, junction box, cabinet, or fitting. Methods of support are similar to those described for rigid metal conduit. Figure 107 shows the use of spring clips to secure EMT to U-channel supports.

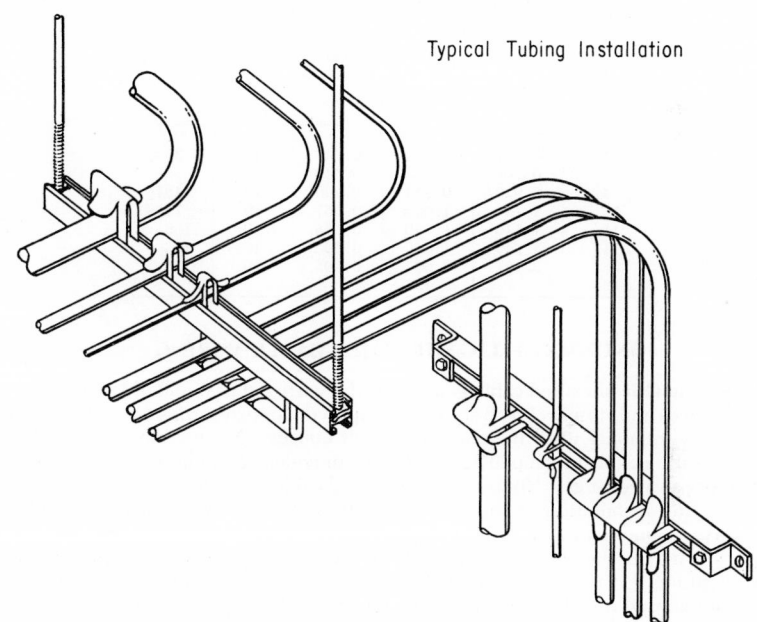

Typical Tubing Installation

FIG. 107   *Spring clips secure EMT to U-channel supports.*

190. Bending EMT. Bends in EMT must be so made that the tubing will not be injured and the internal diameter of the tubing will not be effectively reduced. The radius of the curve of the inner bend or any field bend shall not be less than shown in Secs. **71** and **78.** For ½-, ¾-, and 1-in. EMT a hand bender, as shown in Fig. 108, I, is used. The EMT hickey shown in Fig. 108, II, is only for making small offsets in 1¼-, 1½-, or 2-in. EMT. Almost all bends in sizes larger than 1 in. are made with hydraulic benders, and many rigid metal conduit hand *benders* are suitable for EMT. Refer to discussions in Secs. **99** and **100.**

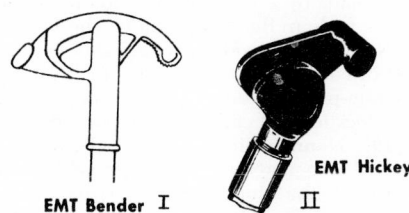

EMT Bender I   II   EMT Hickey

FIG. 108   *Typical EMT bender and hickey.*

191. Installation Methods. The techniques of installation described in the sections for rigid metal conduit will apply, in general, to electrical metallic tubing. Such items as junction or pull boxes, number of conductors permitted in a single raceway, and support hardware apply to both these wiring methods.

192. Corrosion-resistant metallic tubing is available in two types: (1) copper alloy and (2) plastic coated. The principles of construction and the characteristics of both these types are the same as for the corresponding types of corrosion-resistant rigid conduit as discussed in Sec. **58.**   The dimensions for silicon-bronze electrical metallic tubing, called Everdur electrical metallic tubing, are given in Sec. **193.**   They are practically the same as for steel electrical metallic tubing.

193. Data for Everdur Silicon-Bronze Electrical Metallic Tubing
(The Anaconda American Brass Co.)

Nominal size, in.	Nominal dimensions, in.			Unit length, ft	Min weight, lb per 100 ft
	Diameter		Wall thickness		
	Outside	Inside			
⅜	0.577	0.493	0.042	10	25½
½	0.706	0.622	0.042	10	32
¾	0.922	0.824	0.049	10	48½
1	1.163	1.049	0.057	10	71½
1¼	1.510	1.380	0.065	10	106
1½	1.740	1.610	0.065	10	123
2	2.197	2.067	0.065	10	156

NONMETALLIC-SHEATHED-CABLE WIRING

194. Nonmetallic-sheathed cable is used for the wiring of new and old residences and for small offices and stores.   It is frequently employed for extensions to existing installations and is commonly used in small apartment houses.   Nonmetallic-sheathed cable can be run either exposed on ceilings and walls or concealed in hollow partitions or between floors and ceilings.   Nonmetallic-sheathed cable provides a reasonably safe and reliable wiring installation of low first cost.   It is made in two types, Type NM and Type NMC.   Conductors are copper or aluminum.

Type NM may be used only in normally dry locations which are free from corrosive vapors or fumes.   It may be run or fished in air voids in masonry block or tile walls where not exposed or subject to excessive moisture or dampness.   Type NM must not be embedded in masonry, concrete, fill, or plaster or run in shallow chase in masonry or concrete and covered with plaster or similar finish.

Type NMC is moisture- and corrosion-resistant, so that its use is allowed in dry, moist, damp, or corrosive locations and in outside and inside walls of masonry block or tile.   If embedded in plaster or run in a shallow chase in masonry walls and covered with plaster within 2 in. of the finished surface, it shall be protected against damage from nails by a cover of corrosion-resistant coated steel at least ¹⁄₁₆ in. in thickness and ¾ in. wide in the case or under the final surface finish.

Neither Type NM nor Type NMC is allowed to be used as (1) service-entrance cable, (2) in commercial garages, (3) in theaters except as provided in section 520-4, (4) in motion-picture studios, (5) in storage-battery rooms, (6) in hoistways, (7) in any hazardous location, (8) embedded in poured cement, concrete, or aggregate.

195. Nonmetallic-sheathed cable, with or without grounding wires, is manufactured in both two- and three-conductor cables.   Each wire is insulated with rubber or thermoplastic of the same thickness as required on single wires, except that the cable may have an approved size of covered or bare conductor for grounding purposes only.   In Type NM cable the two or three conductors have an outer fibrous-braid covering or plastic jacket.   Type NMC cable is similar in construction to Type NM cable except that it is protected by an outer rubber or similar jacket.

196. When nonmetallic-sheathed cable is installed exposed, it is supported directly on the walls or ceiling with straps.   For three-wire cable, ordinary pipe straps are used. Standard ⅜-in. pipe straps fit Nos. 14(3), 12(3), and 10(3) sizes of sheathed cable; ½-in. pipe straps are required for No. 8(3); ¾-in. straps for No. 6(3); and 1-in. straps for No.

4(3). For two-wire cable, special flat straps are required, which are available from various manufacturers. The distance between supports must not be greater than 4½ ft, and there must be a support within 12 in. of each outlet box or fitting. The cable must follow the surface of the wall or ceiling and not break from beam to beam. Whenever nonmetallic-sheathed cable is run exposed within 7 ft of the floor, it must be suitably protected against mechanical injury. This protection may consist of a wooden or metal protecting strip or a piece of conduit or EMT. It is preferable to use either conduit or EMT, especially where the cable passes through floors.

197. When nonmetallic-sheathed cable is installed concealed in new buildings, the cable is fastened to the joists or beams by means of staples. The distance between supports should not be greater than 4½ ft. In wiring finished buildings, when it is impracticable to support the cable between outlets, it can be fished from outlet to outlet in the same manner as Type AC metal-clad cable. Where the cable is run through holes bored in studs, joists, etc., no protection is required. The holes should be bored as near to the center of the timber as possible and not less than 2 in. from the edge where practical. An approved method of installing nonmetallic-sheathed cable in a new building is shown in Fig. 109. Most inspection departments will allow nonmetallic-sheathed cable to be run concealed in furred walls or partitions, as shown in Fig. 110.

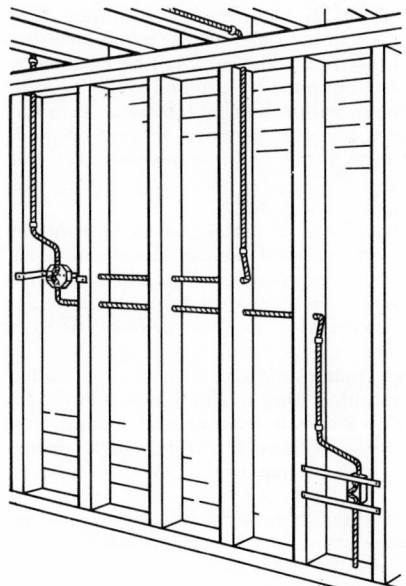

198. No joints or splices should be made in nonmetallic-sheathed-cable wiring ex-

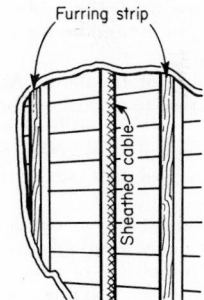

FIG. 109 *Method of installing nonmetallic-sheathed cable concealed in new buildings.*

FIG. 110 *Nonmetallic-sheathed cable installed concealed in a furred partition.*

cept in outlet or junction boxes. This rule applies to both exposed and concealed installation. The loop system is employed generally for concealed work. The cable is looped from outlet to outlet, and the use of junction boxes is avoided.

199. Bends in cable (National Electrical Code) shall be so made and other handling shall be such that the protective coverings of the cable will not be injured, and no bend shall have a radius less than five times the diameter of the cable.

200. An approved outlet box or fitting must be provided at all outlets or switch locations. The cable must be attached to the box with some form of approved device which will substantially close the opening in the box. This connection of the cable to the box can be accomplished by means of a box with a built-in clamp, or a clamp connector (Fig. 111) or a squeeze connector (Fig. 112) can be employed with a box having conduit knockouts. For data on metal boxes, see Sec. **113** of Div. 4.

201. Where the National Electrical Code rules require that outlet boxes be grounded, or where grounding-type receptacles are used, nonmetallic-sheathed cable can be obtained with a grounding wire built into the cable under the outer sheath. This grounding wire should be ripped back out of the cable for 6 or 8 in. before the cable is secured to the outlet box. If outlet boxes with built-in clamps are employed, the required contact between the box and the grounding wire is made by means of a small grounding clip. The connection is made by fastening the clip over the grounding wire and box (Fig. 113). These copper grounding clips are commonly called G clips.

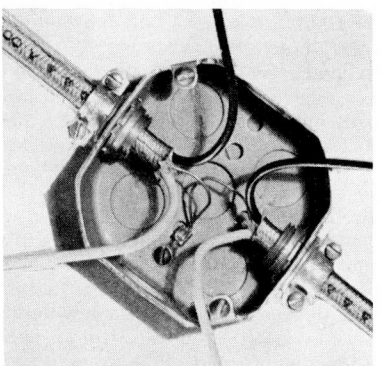

FIG. 111 *Nonmetallic-sheathed cable attached to outlet box by means of clamp connectors.*

202. Boxes of insulating material (Fig. 150 of Div. 4) can be used with nonmetallic-sheathed cable instead of metal boxes. With these boxes, grounding is limited, and it is not necessary to connect each box to a grounding conductor. The boxes shown in Fig. 150 of Div. 4 are made of Bakelite. They are used in the same way as metal boxes except that the cable need not be fastened to the box but must be fastened to the building structure within 8 in. of the box. Thin sections of phenolic are knocked out to provide openings to bring the cable into the box. Nonmetallic covers should be used with devices in these boxes.

203. A line of outlets for surface mounting with exposed nonmetallic-sheathed-cable wiring is available (Fig. 114). They are made of porcelain or plastic. A clamp inside the case holds the cable. There are terminal screws near each end so that cables can be brought in from both ends. The NEC requirements for these devices are given in Sec. **204.**

204. Devices of Insulating Material. Switch, outlet, and tap devices of insulating material may be used without boxes in exposed cable wiring and for concealed work for rewiring in existing buildings where the cable is concealed and fished. Openings in such devices shall form a close fit around the outer covering of the cable, and the device shall fully enclose that part of the cable from which any part of the covering has been removed.

Where connections to conductors are by binding screw terminals, there shall be available as many terminals as conductors, unless cables are clamped within the structure and terminals are of a type approved for multiple conductors.

205. Methods of installing nonmetallic-sheathed cable in accessible attics or roof spaces are shown in Fig. 115. When the cable is carried across the top of floor beams or across the face of rafters within 7 ft of the floor, the cable should be protected by guard strips, as shown at *B*. If the attic is accessible only through a scuttle hole without permanent stairs or ladders, the protection is required only within 6 ft of the edge of the scuttle hole. The cable may be supported along the sides of rafters, studs, or floor joists without any additional protection as at *D*.

FIG. 112 *Squeeze connector for attaching nonmetallic-sheathed cable to outlet box.*

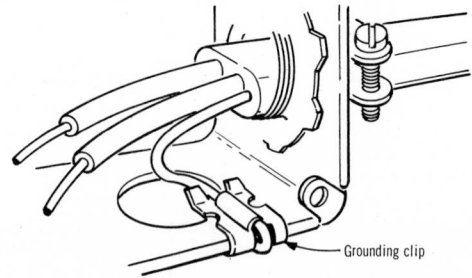

FIG. 113 *Grounding clip attached to metal box. (Electrical Construction and Maintenance.)*

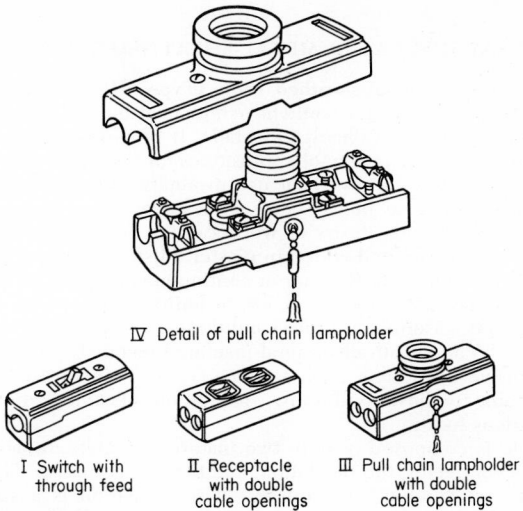

IV Detail of pull chain lampholder

I Switch with
through feed

II Receptacle
with double
cable openings

III Pull chain lampholder
with double
cable openings

FIG. 114   *Surface outlets for use with nonmetallic-sheathed cable. (Pass & Seymour, Inc.)*

206. Methods of installing nonmetallic-sheathed cable in unfinished cellars or basements are shown in Fig. 116.   The cable may be run through bored holes in the floor joists and along the sides or faces of joists without any additional protection such as running boards or guard strips, as shown at *A* and *B*.   When the cable is run at angles across the bottom faces of floor joists, the cable must be supported on the underside of running boards as shown at *C*.   Assemblies containing not smaller than two No. 6 or three No. 8 conductors may be secured directly on the bottom of the joists.

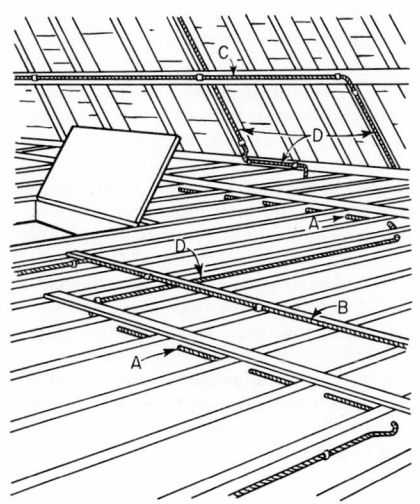

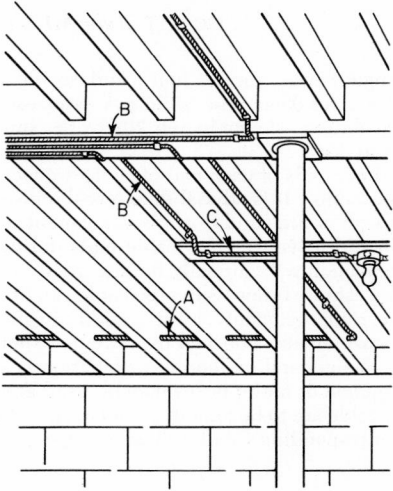

FIG. 115   *Methods of installing nonmetallic-sheathed cable in accessible attics or roof spaces.*

FIG. 116   *Methods of installing nonmetallic-sheathed cable in unfinished cellars or basements.*

MINERAL-INSULATED METAL-SHEATHED-CABLE WIRING

207. Mineral-insulated metal-sheathed cable (Type MI) was developed to fill the need for an electrical cable which would have high heat and water resistance and which would be not bulky and not difficult to install. It provides a general wiring system which is suitable for a great variety of applications for systems with voltages up to and including 600 volts. It is approved for use in almost any type of installation. The Code states that MI cable may be used for services, feeders, and branch circuits in both exposed and concealed work, in dry or wet locations; for under plaster extensions as provided in article 344; and embedded in plaster finish on brick or other masonry. It may be used where exposed to weather or continuous moisture, for underground runs and embedded in masonry, concrete or fill, in buildings in course of construction or where exposed to oil, gasoline, or other conditions not having a deteriorating effect on the metal sheath. The sheath of mineral-insulated metal-sheathed cable exposed to destructive corrosive conditions, such as some types of cinder fill, must be protected by materials suitable for those conditions. In addition MI cable is approved for installation in all hazardous locations.

Type MI cable is composed of only two materials, which are assembled as three components: the conductor, the insulation, and the outer sheath. The conductors are fabricated from high-conductivity copper. The insulation is a specially selected, highly compressed pure magnesium oxide which is processed to maintain permanently the excellent electrical characteristics inherent in this material. The sheath is a round, seamless copper tube which provides the requirements of heat and flame resistance, mechanical protection, and ductility. The wires, insulation, and protective copper sheath are manufactured as a unit, as shown in Fig. 117. MI cable is available in

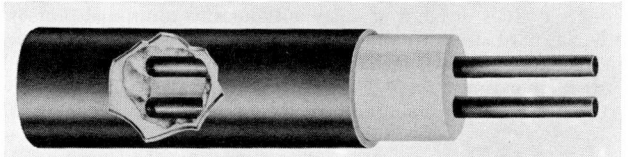

FIG. 117 *Type MI cable. (General Cable Corp.)*

single-, two-, three-, four-, and seven-conductor assemblies. Refer to Sec. **125** of Div. 2 for data. The cable possesses exceptional ability to withstand severe mechanical abuse as shown in Sec. **208** by the summary of mechanical properties as determined from tests.

Both ends of each coil of cable are factory-sealed to prevent ingress of moisture into the cable. It is advisable to reseal unused cable in coils that will stand around for any length of time and to apply permanent seals to each cable run as promptly as possible. Should moisture enter cable ends during field handling and installation, the affected insulation will normally be discarded in the process of stripping back and terminating the cable. If necessary, the cable can be further dried by careful application of a torch over approximately a 2-ft section of cable adjacent to the end. Insulation resistance measurements checked by a Megger should indicate adequate dryness.

The general method of installation is similar to that of metal-clad cable. Standard junction or outlet boxes may be used at each point of termination or when two lengths of cable are to be joined. The tap size of these units should be the same as listed under Corresponding Conduit Size as given in Sec. **125** of Div. 2.

208. Summary of Mechanical Tests on Mineral-insulated Cable

	Type MI	Metal-clad cable	EMT Type T	Rigid conduit Type T
Impact............	B	D	C	A
Crushing.........	A	D	C	B

NOTES. Performance is indicated by letter "grades"; A signifies best performance. EMT is electrical metallic tubing. Type T refers to Underwriters' Code Grade thermoplastic-insulated conductors. In the impact test, the cable was laid over an anvil hardy having a smoothly rounded edge with a ¼ in. radius. Weights of 50, 20, and 10 lb were dropped on the cable, and the length of drop determined which produced not more than two failures in 10 separate blows. In the crushing test the cable was crushed against the same anvil hardy used in the impact test by a flat steel plate in a compression-testing machine. The force required to crush the cable to 50 per cent of its original diameter was determined.

209. Installation of MI Cable. It is suggested that the MI be trained into position where the installation allows. The cable can also be snaked and fished into and through congested areas. In some cases, a simple rotating X frame has been used to advantage, facilitating paying off the cable as it is snaked through barriers. After training to position, the cable can be secured with one-hole clips, as offered by many manufacturers of conduit clips; multi-cable gang straps; channel and spring-set clip supporting arrangements; cable trays; conduit hangers; and spacing bars and straps.

The cable can be trained into final position by hand in most cases. True alignment can be ensured by tapping the cable lightly along its axis with a wooden mallet. True round sweeps can be made in the larger sized cable runs with a hand "hickey," but this usually is not necessary. NOTE. NEC requires that the radius of bends (at the inner edge of the bend) shall be not less than five cable diameters, and that cable (except where fished) be supported at intervals not exceeding 6 ft.

The copper itself being in an annealed condition, MI is easily worked. Keeping the cable straight when unwinding the coil facilitates final training. The cable is cut after measurement, allowing for conductor tails (stretching steel wire over the proposed run is an ideal method of measuring). MI can be terminated before or after it is laid in position.

If undue stressing and sharp bending are avoided during preliminary handling and roughing in, work hardening of the cable will be minimized, resulting in a more readily installed system.

In portions of dairies, laundries, canneries, and other wet locations and in locations where walls are frequently washed, the entire wiring system, including all boxes and

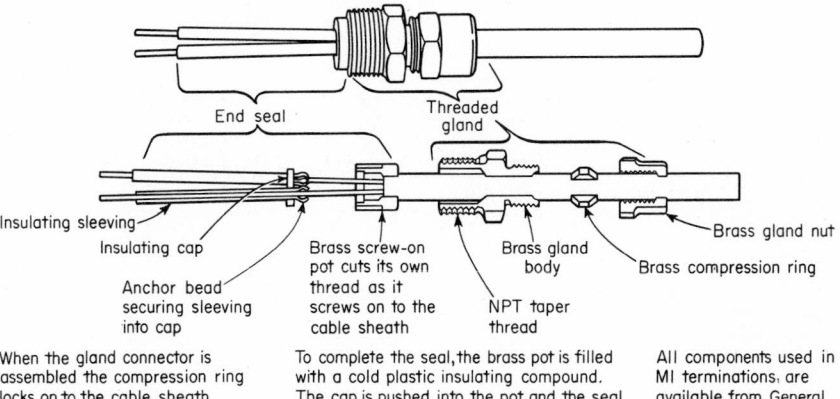

FIG. 118 *Standard termination for mineral-insulated cables suitable for use at temperatures up to 85°C. (General Cable Corp.)*

fittings used therewith, shall be made watertight and the cable shall be mounted so that there is at least ¼-in. air space between it and the wall or other supporting surface.

The Code states that at all points where mineral-insulated metal-sheathed cable terminates, an approved seal shall be provided immediately after stripping to prevent entrance of moisture into the mineral insulation and, in addition, the conductors extending beyond the sheath shall be insulated with an approved insulating material. Also, when Type MI cable is connected to boxes or equipment, the fittings shall be approved for the conditions of service. Safety MI cable terminal fittings (Fig. 118) are designed to seal the cable ends hermetically in order to prevent the entrance of moisture into the cable as well as mechanically secure the cable to the outlet box, motor, or other apparatus. The complete terminal consists of an end seal and a threaded gland.

210. Termination Dimensions

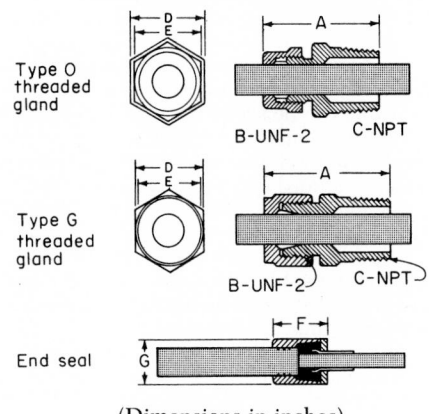

(Dimensions in inches)

Group size	Pot						
	A	B	C[a]	D	E	F	G
Type O Gland							
³⁄₈	1⁵⁄₁₆	¹⁄₂–20	³⁄₈–18	¹¹⁄₁₆	⁵⁄₈	⁹⁄₁₆	¹⁵⁄₃₂
¹⁄₂	1⁹⁄₁₆	⁵⁄₈–18	¹⁄₂–14	⁷⁄₈	³⁄₄	²⁷⁄₃₂	¹⁹⁄₃₂
³⁄₄	1³⁄₄	⁷⁄₈–14	³⁄₄–14	1¹⁄₁₆	1	1¹⁄₈	²⁵⁄₃₂
1	1¹⁵⁄₁₆[b]	1–14	1–11¹⁄₂	1⁵⁄₁₆	1¹⁄₈	1³⁄₈	³¹⁄₃₂
Type G Gland							
¹⁄₂	1³⁄₄	³⁄₄–16	¹⁄₂–14	⁷⁄₈	⁷⁄₈	²⁷⁄₃₂	¹⁹⁄₃₂
³⁄₄	2¹⁄₈	⁷⁄₈–14	³⁄₄–14	1¹⁄₁₆	1	1¹⁄₈	²⁵⁄₃₂
1	2¹⁄₂	1¹⁄₈–12	1–11¹⁄₂	1⁵⁄₁₆	1¹⁄₄	1³⁄₈	³¹⁄₃₂

[a] STD electrical conduit pipe thread.
[b] This dimension is 2⁵⁄₁₆ on sizes 637 and 684.

211. Termination Selection Chart

Application	Seals			Glands
	Designation	Sleeving	Sealant	
General use up to 85°C, wet and dry locations— UL listed	Type O	PVC	Type O plastic	Type O
Hazardous locations, wet and dry up to 85°C — UL listed	Type H	PVC	Type H epoxy	Type G
Low temperatures (below −10°C)	Low temperature	Silicone rubber (Fiberglas reinforced)	Type O plastic	Type O
High temperatures (up to 125°C)	High temperature	Silicone rubber (Fiberglas reinforced)	Type O epoxy	Type O

Ceramic-to-metal seals are available for temperatures in excess of 125°C.
NOTES.
1. Type G glands may be used as an alternative for Type O glands in any application.
2. Silicone rubber Fiberglas-reinforced sleeving may be used as an alternative for PVC sleeving in any general-use application.
3. Type H epoxy may be used as an alternative sealant in any application.
4. Type O plastic and Type O epoxy may be used as alternative sealants in Class I, Group B, and Class II, Groups E, F, and G hazardous locations.

212. Termination Procedure for MI Cable. Cable End Seal. Basic parts of the cable-seal termination and the complete seal are shown in Fig. 119. The following parts are required for making the seal.

1. "Screw-on-pot," a self-thread-brass cylinder.
2. Silicone-rubber or PVC tubing, for insulating the exposed conductor ends.
3. Insulating cap.
4. Sealing compound, a soft plastic material or two-part epoxy compound.
5. Crimping and stripping tools.

The cable-seal termination is made by removing the copper sheath with the stripping tool to expose the length of conductors needed for the connections, screwing the self-threading "screw-on pot" onto the end of the cable sheath, filling the pot with sealing compound, slipping the insulating tubing and cap assembly over the exposed conductors and pressing the cap down into the end of the "screw-on pot," and, finally, securing in place by crimping the edge of the pot down over the insulating cap. This insulates the end of each exposed conductor and provides a moisture seal over the insulation.

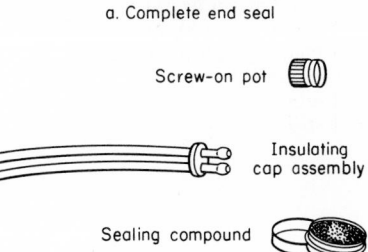

a. Complete end seal

Screw-on pot

Insulating cap assembly

Sealing compound

b. Components

FIG. 119 *End seal for MI cable. (General Cable Corp.)*

Threaded Gland. Figure 120 shows the parts of the threaded gland, with the gland in place before tightening and, finally, with the gland locked in the final position. The following parts are included:

1. Gland body.
2. Compression ring.
3. Gland nut.

These gland parts are slipped over the end of the cable before the termination is applied, in the order of first the gland nut, then the compression nut, and finally the gland body. When the gland nut is screwed into the gland body over the compression ring, the ring is compressed onto the cable sheath which anchors it into position.

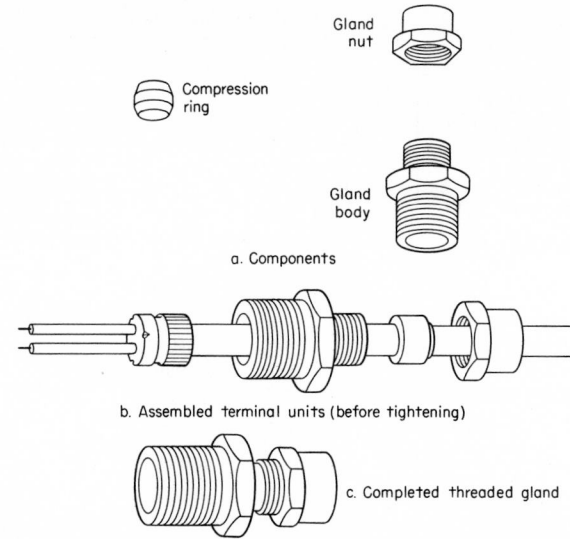

FIG. 120   *Threaded gland for MI cable.   (General Cable Corp.)*

This can be applied at any point on the cable, but usually it is brought clear up to the end with the cable-seal termination seated into the counterbored end of the gland body. The outer end of the gland body is threaded for lock nuts.

Assembly Tools.

1 hand vise.
1 screwdriver or nut driver.
1 copper tube cutter.
1 diagonal cutting pliers.
2 pipe wrenches.
1 crimping and compressing tool.
1 stripping tool.

213. Details of Termination Procedure for MI Cable
(General Cable Corp.)

1. Mark sheath only with a pencil at point which will expose desired conductor length

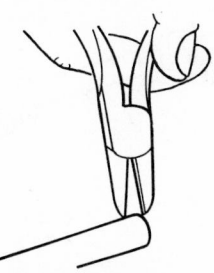

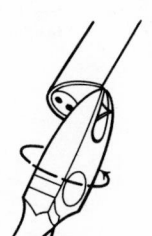

3. Use wrist motion to tear up "tag."

2. Use diagonal cutters to start the rip.

4. Engage the tag in the slot of the rod and twist it around the cable. Wrist motion is continued as rod revolves about cable axis.

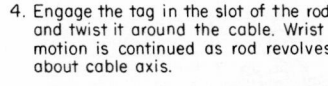

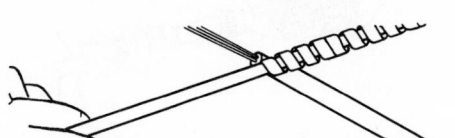

5. Keep rod at about 45° to the line of the cable. Keep bare rod against sheath and 45° will be regulated. Do not force tearing.

6. Bring stripping tool perpendicular to axis of cable. Then ring the cable sheath at the pencil mark using a copper tube cutter. The depth of the cut should be approximately one half the thickness of the cable sheath. Do not cut through sheath.

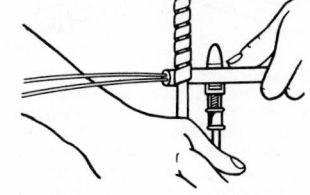

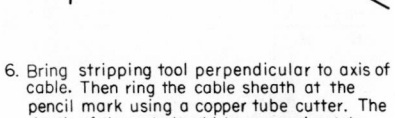

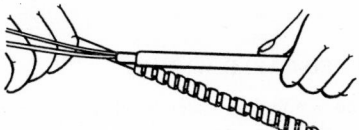

7. After ringing, continue stripping as shown in Fig. 5 and tear off squarely at the ring. Remove any burrs at the end of the cable sheath with diagonal cutters.

8. Slip the gland connector parts on to the cable in this order: gland nut, compression ring, gland body.

9. Engage the self-threading pot finger tight. See that pot is square. Then screw on with pipe wrench engaging all threads. Examine inside of pot for cleanliness and metallic slivers or dust. Test for alignment by bringing gland body up to enclose pot.

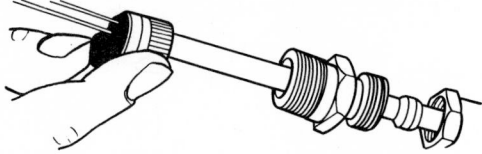

10. Press plastic compound into sealing pot until it is packed tightly. Important: Be sure the hands are free from metal dust or filings while feeding compound into pot.

11. Slip cap and sleeving sub assembly into position

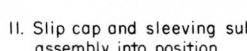

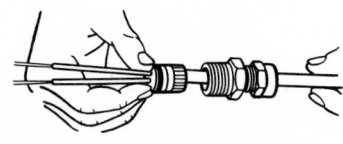

12. Force the insulating cap assembly into position on top of compound.

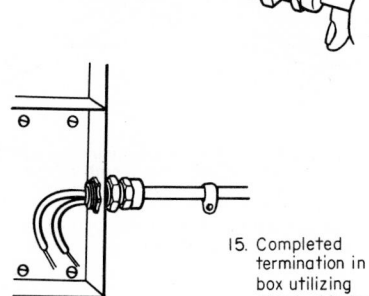

13. Slip the compression and crimping tool over the insulating leads

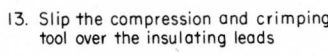

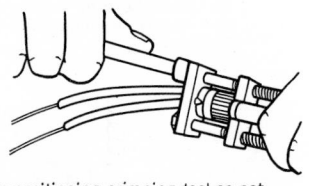

14. After positioning crimping tool on pot, compress the insulating washer into place flush with the top of the pot by tightening the two slotted cap screws. This operation compresses the compound in the pot and crimps the edge of the pot into the insulating cap, holding it in place. Remove compression tool.

15. Completed termination in box utilizing standard lock nut.

ALUMINUM-SHEATHED-CABLE WIRING

214. Aluminum-sheathed Type ALS cable is a factory-assembled cable consisting of one or more insulated conductors enclosed in an impervious, continuous, closely fitting tube of aluminum (Fig. 121). It must be used with approved fittings for terminating and connecting to boxes, outlets, and other equipment. Figure 122 shows the construction of a typical cast-aluminum connector with a screw-on pot in place. Such fittings and similar types are suitable for use in wet or dry locations, except that fittings suitable for use only in dry locations are so marked.

215. National Electrical Code rules state that aluminum-sheathed cable may be used in both concealed or exposed work, in dry or wet locations. If the sheath of aluminum-sheathed cable is exposed to destructive corrosive conditions, such as environments

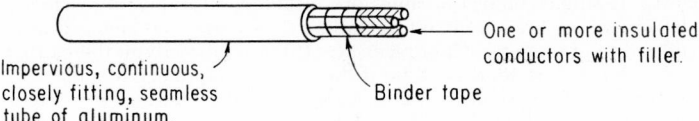

Impervious, continuous, closely fitting, seamless tube of aluminum.

Binder tape

One or more insulated conductors with filler.

FIG. 121   *Aluminum sheathed cable construction.*

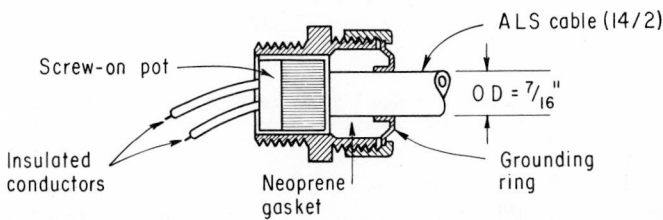

Screw-on pot

ALS cable (14/2)

$O D = \frac{7}{16}''$

Insulated conductors

Neoprene gasket

Grounding ring

FIG. 122   *Typical cast-aluminum connector.*

containing strong chlorides or caustic alkalis, or where vapors of chlorine or hydrochloric acid are present, it must be protected by materials suitable for those conditions.

Aluminum-sheathed cable should not be embedded in concrete or buried directly in earth. However, the cable is suitable for use in theaters, places of public assembly, Division 2 areas of Class I and II hazardous locations, Divisions 1 and 2 of Class III hazardous locations, and within ducts, plenum chambers, or similar spaces used for transporting high- or low-velocity environmental air.

216. Supports. Aluminum-sheathed cable shall be securely supported by staples, straps, hangers, or similar fittings so installed as not to injure the cable. Follow the general installation recommendations given in Sec. **209** for Type MI cable. Except where Type ALS cable is fished, it must be secured at intervals not exceeding 6 ft.

217. Bends in Type ALS cable must be so made that the cable will not be damaged and the radius of the curve on the inner edge of any bend must be less than shown in Fig. 123 for the various cable sizes.

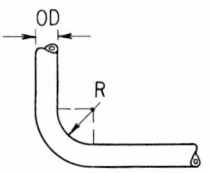

OD

R

Bends: Radius (R) shall not be less than:
(a) 10 times OD for cables with OD $\frac{3}{4}$ in. or less.
(b) 12 times OD for cables with OD over $\frac{3}{4}$ in. but not over $1\frac{1}{2}$ in.
(c) 15 times OD for cables with OD over $1\frac{1}{2}$ in.

FIG. 123   *Minimum bending radius.*

UNDERGROUND-FEEDER AND BRANCH-CIRCUIT-CABLE WIRING

218. Underground-feeder and branch-circuit cable provides an economical wiring system for wet and corrosive installations. Single-conductor Type UF cable resembles Type USE service-entrance cable in general appearance. The insulation employed consists of a plastic compound. The Code statements with respect to its use are: Underground-feeder and branch-circuit cable may be used underground, including direct burial in the earth, as feeder or branch-circuit cable when provided with overcurrent protection not in excess of the rated current-carrying capacity of the individual conductors. If single-conductor cables are installed, all cables of the feeder circuit, subfeeder circuit, or branch circuit, including the neutral conductor, if any, shall be run together in the same trench or raceway. If buried directly in the earth, the minimum burial depth permitted is 18 in. if the cable is unprotected, and 12 in. when a supplemental covering, such as a 2-in. concrete pad, metal raceway, pipe, or other suitable protection, is provided. Type UF cable may be used for interior wiring in wet, dry, or corrosive locations under the recognized wiring methods of this Code, and when installed as nonmetallic sheathed cable it shall conform with the provisions of article 336 and shall be of a multiple-conductor type. It must also be of a multiple-conductor type if installed in continuous rigid cable supports.

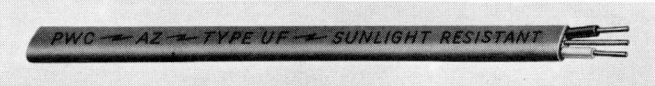

FIG. 123A   *Type UF cable, two-conductor with grounding wire, which is recognized as sunlight-resistant. (Plastic Wire & Cable Corp., Subsidiary of Triangle Industries, Inc.)*

This type of cable shall not be used (1) as service-entrance cable, (2) in commercial garages, (3) in theaters except as provided in section 520-4 of the Code, (4) in motion-picture studios, (5) in storage-battery rooms, (6) in hoistways, (7) in any hazardous location, (8) embedded in poured cement, concrete, or aggregate except where recognized in section 424-43(a) of the Code, (9) when exposed to direct sun rays, unless approved for the purpose (Fig. 123A).

Its general installation is similar to that for nonmetallic-sheathed cable.

INTERIOR WIRING WITH SERVICE-ENTRANCE CABLE

219. Service-entrance cable of Types SE or USE may be employed for interior wiring, installed either concealed or exposed. The construction of these cables is described in Sec. **221.** Cables with all the conductors insulated may be used for general interior wiring. Those without insulation on the grounded conductor may be used only on systems not exceeding 150 volts to ground, for range wall-mounted oven, counter-mounted cooking unit, and clothes-drier circuit, or as feeders to supply other buildings from the one containing the master service-entrance equipment. The cables with uninsulated grounding conductors must have a final nonmetallic outer covering. Cables which are used for interior wiring must be installed in accordance with the rules for nonmetallic-sheathed cable as discussed in Secs. **194** to **206.**

220. The principal use of service-entrance cable for interior wiring is for branch circuits supplying ranges or water heaters and in farm wiring as feeders from the master service to supply the other buildings that are wired for electricity. The cable is supported on the building structure by means of single-hole or two-hole cable straps made in different sizes to accommodate the size of cable. They are similar in appearance to those used for rigid conduit. Connection to switch or outlet boxes is made by means of a connector (Fig. 124), which is made in watertight and nonwatertight types. A typical range installation is shown in Fig. 125.

I Watertight Screw Connector.   II Nonwatertight Connector.

FIG. 124   *Box connectors for service-entrance cable. (General Electric Co.)*

221. Types of Cables. Two common types of cables are shown in Figs. 126 and 127. The three-conductor Type SE cable in Fig. 126 consists of two insulated conductors and one concentric-stranded, insulated conductor (generally used as the grounded-neutral conductor). This cable is limited to services that do not exceed 150 volts to ground, such as a 120/240-volt single-phase supply. If used as a three-wire 120/240-volt branch circuit to a range, wall-mounted oven, counter-mounted cooking unit, or clothes drier, this cable must originate at the service equipment. In such instances, the uninsulated neutral conductor may be used to ground the metal frame of the equipment supplied.

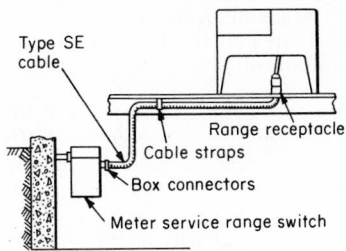

FIG. 125 *Installation of electric range wired with service-entrance cable.*

Figure 127 shows a single-conductor 4/0 aluminum Type USE cable, which is also suitable for use as a Type RHW (in wet locations) and a Type RHH (in dry locations). When used in direct burial applications, such a cable has a 75°C rating. The ampacity ratings of conductors are listed in Tables **18** to **21** of Div. **11**. For underground applications Type USE cable should be buried not less than the depths specified for Type UF cables in Sec. **218**. For over 600 volts refer to Sec. **156** of Div. **8**.

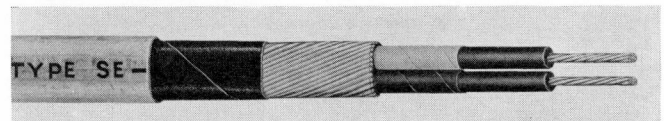

FIG. 126 *Type SE cable, three-conductor, with a concentric-stranded uninsulated conductor. (Kaiser Aluminum & Chemical Sales, Inc.)*

FIG. 127 *Single-conductor Type USE cable. (Kaiser Aluminum & Chemical Sales, Inc.)*

UNDERFLOOR RACEWAY WIRING

222. Underfloor raceway systems are used principally in office buildings for the installation of the wiring for telephone and signal systems and for convenience outlets for electrically operated office machinery. They provide a flexible system by means of which the location of outlets may be easily changed to accommodate the rearrangement of furniture and partitions. The National Electrical Code allows their use when embedded in the concrete or in concrete fill of floors. Their installation is allowed only in locations which are free from corrosive or hazardous conditions. No wires larger than the maximum size approved for the particular raceway shall be installed. The voltage of the system must not exceed 600 volts. The total cross-sectional area of all conductors in a duct must not be greater than 40 per cent of the interior cross-sectional area of the duct.

223. An underfloor raceway system consists of ducts laid below the surface of the floor and interconnected by means of special cast-iron floor junction boxes. The ducts for underfloor raceway systems are made of either fiber or steel. Fiber ducts are made in two types, the open-bottom type and the completely enclosing type. Steel ducts are always of the completely enclosing type, usually having a rectangular cross section. In the underfloor raceway system, provision is made for outlets by means of specially designed floor-outlet fittings which are screwed into the walls of the ducts. When fiber ducts are employed, the duct system is laid in the floor with or without openings or inserts for outlets. After the floor has been poured and finished as desired, the outlet fittings are installed into inserts or at any points along the ducts at which outlets are required. The method of installing outlet fittings is described in Sec. **237.** When steel ducts are employed, provision for the outlet fittings must be made at the time that the ducts are laid, before the floor or floor fill is poured. The steel ducts are manufactured with threaded openings for outlet connections at regularly spaced intervals along the

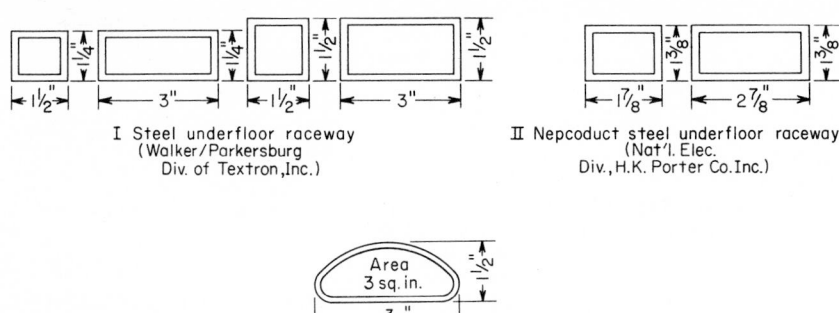

I Steel underfloor raceway
(Walker/Parkersburg
Div. of Textron,Inc.)

II Nepcoduct steel underfloor raceway
(Nat'l. Elec.
Div.,H.K. Porter Co.Inc.)

III Nonmetallic raceway
(The Flintkote Co.,Inc.
Pipe Products Group)

FIG. 128   *Dimensions of ducts for underfloor raceways.*

duct. During the installation of the raceway and the floor these outlet openings are closed with specially constructed plugs whose height can be adjusted to suit the floor level. The shapes and dimensions of the different types of ducts for underfloor raceways are shown in Fig. 128. For telephone and similar circuits, much wider ducts can be obtained.

224. General Rules for the Installation of Underfloor Raceways. In general, underfloor raceways should be installed so that there is at least ¾ in. of concrete or wood over the highest point of the ducts (see Figs. 129 and 130). However, in offices, approved raceways may be laid flush with the concrete if covered with linoleum or equivalent floor covering (see Fig. 131). When two or three raceways are installed flush with the concrete, they must either be contiguous with each other and joined to form

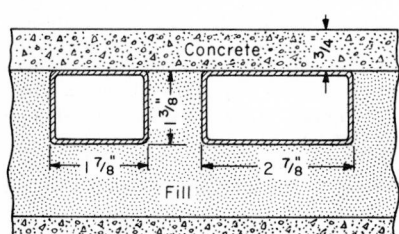

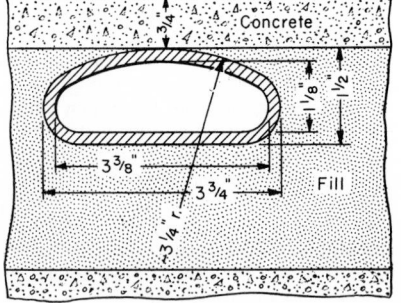

FIG. 129 *Any flat-top raceway 4 in. or less in width must be covered with wood or concrete at least ¾ in. in thickness except in office occupancies. (NFPA Handbook of the National Electrical Code.)*

FIG. 130 *Any fiber raceway 4 in. or less in width must be covered with wood or concrete at least ¾ in. in thickness. (NFPA Handbook of the National Electrical Code.)*

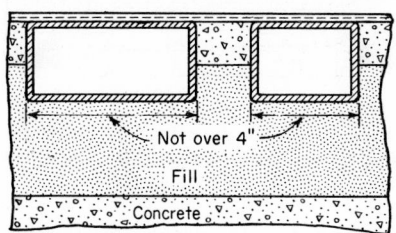

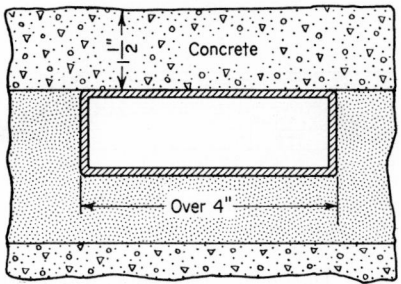

FIG. 131 *Approved raceways flush with concrete and covered with linoleum in an office occupancy. (NFPA Handbook of the National Electrical Code.)*

FIG. 132 *Any flat-top raceway over 4 in. wide must be covered with concrete at least 1½ in. in thickness if raceways are spaced less than 1 in. apart. (NFPA Handbook of the National Electrical Code.)*

a rigid assembly or be spaced at least ½ in. apart. Flat-top ducts over 4 in. wide but not over 8 in., spaced less than 1 in., must be covered with at least 1½ in. of concrete (see Fig. 132). It is standard practice to allow ¾-in. clearance between ducts run side by side. The center line of the ducts should form a straight line between junction boxes. If the spacing between raceways is 1 in. or more, the raceway may be covered with only 1 in. of concrete. All joints in the raceway between sections of ducts and at junction boxes should be made waterproof and with good electrical contact so that the raceways will be electrically continuous. Metal raceways must be properly grounded.

225. Wires of signal or telephone systems must not be run in the same duct as wires of lighting systems. Combination junction boxes accommodating the two or three ducts of multiple-duct systems may be employed, provided separate compartments are provided in the boxes for each system. It is best to keep the same relative location of compartments for the respective systems throughout the installation.

All joints in or taps to the conductors must be made in the junction boxes. No joints or taps should be made in the ducts of the raceway or at outlet insert points.

226. Junction boxes for use with underfloor raceways are specially constructed cast-iron boxes. They are available in single-compartment types and in combination boxes to accommodate multiple-duct systems having two or three raceways run side by side. The general construction of the junction boxes is similar for both fiber- and steel-duct systems. A typical single-compartment box is illustrated in Fig. 133, and a two-compartment box in Fig. 134. Most boxes are equipped with leveling screws so that the boxes can be leveled up with the duct

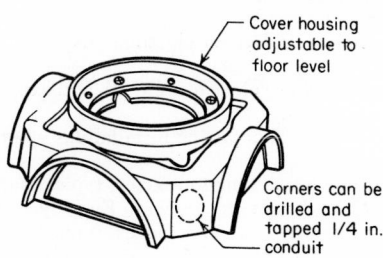

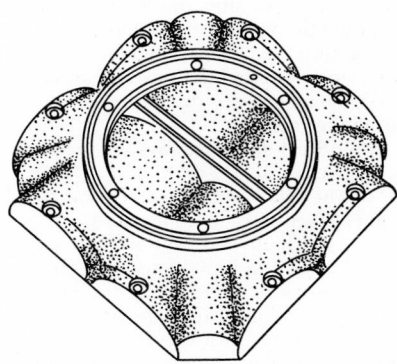

FIG. 133 *Single-compartment floor junction box.*

FIG. 134 *Two-compartment floor junction box for accommodating double-duct systems.*

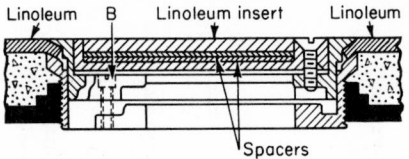

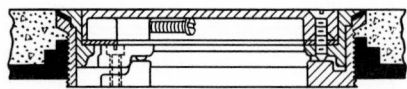

FIG. 135 *Floor junction-box cover for cement-finished floor.* (*National Electric Div., H. K. Porter Co., Inc.*)

FIG. 136 *Floor junction-box cover for linoleum-covered floors.* (*National Electric Div., H. K. Porter Co., Inc.*)

runs. The covers of the boxes also are adjustable with respect to height so that they can be accurately leveled to agree with the surface of the finished floor. Different types of covers are available that will be suitable for the different types of floor finishes. With plain cement-finished floors a plain brass cover set flush with the floor (Fig. 135) is

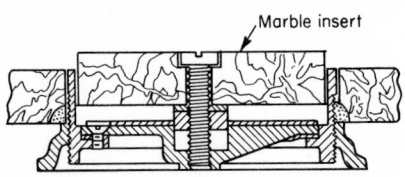

FIG. 137 *Floor junction-box cover for marble floors.* (*National Electric Div., H. K. Porter Co., Inc.*)

sometimes used. In other cases a recessed cover filled with cement is employed. For linoleum- or cork-covered floors a cover with a recess for a cork or linoleum insert is provided, as illustrated in Fig. 136. For marble or hardwood floors a recessed cover with a marble insert (Fig. 137) may be employed. With the recessed covers only a thin ring of brass shows in the finished floor, marking the location of the junction box.

227. Fittings must be installed at every end of a line of raceway with a marker extending through the floor to show the line of the duct. All dead ends of raceway must be closed with a suitable fitting.

228. In installing raceways every effort should be made to avoid low points which could form traps for water.

All connections to a raceway except those made through the inserts provided in the raceway shall be made by means of rigid conduit, EMT, or a special approved fitting (refer to Fig. 138).

229. Inserts (National Electrical Code) shall be leveled to the floor grade and sealed against the entrance of water. Inserts used with metal raceways shall be metal and shall be electrically continuous with the raceway. Inserts set in or on fiber raceways before the floor is laid shall be mechanically secured to the raceway. Inserts set in fiber raceways after the floor is laid shall be screwed into the raceway. In cutting through the raceway wall and setting inserts, chips and other dirt shall not be allowed to fall into the raceway, and tools shall be used which are so designed as to prevent the tool from entering the raceway and injuring conductors that may be in place.

When an outlet is discontinued, the conductors supplying the outlet shall be removed from the raceway.

230. Steel-duct raceways are made for two types of underfloor electrical distribution systems:

1. The two-level system—recommended for use where electrical growth and expansion of facilities are anticipated.

2. The single-level system—recommended for underfloor wiring installations where cost and design limitations are a factor.

The features of a two-level system showing raceways, junction boxes, typical supports, and other fittings are given in Fig. 138. Duct details are shown in Fig. 139.

The features of a one-level system showing raceways, junction boxes, typical supports, and other fittings are given in Fig. 140. Duct details for the raceway of one manufacturer are given in Fig. 141. For dimensions of ducts available by other manufacturers refer to Fig. 128 and the catalogs of such manufacturers.

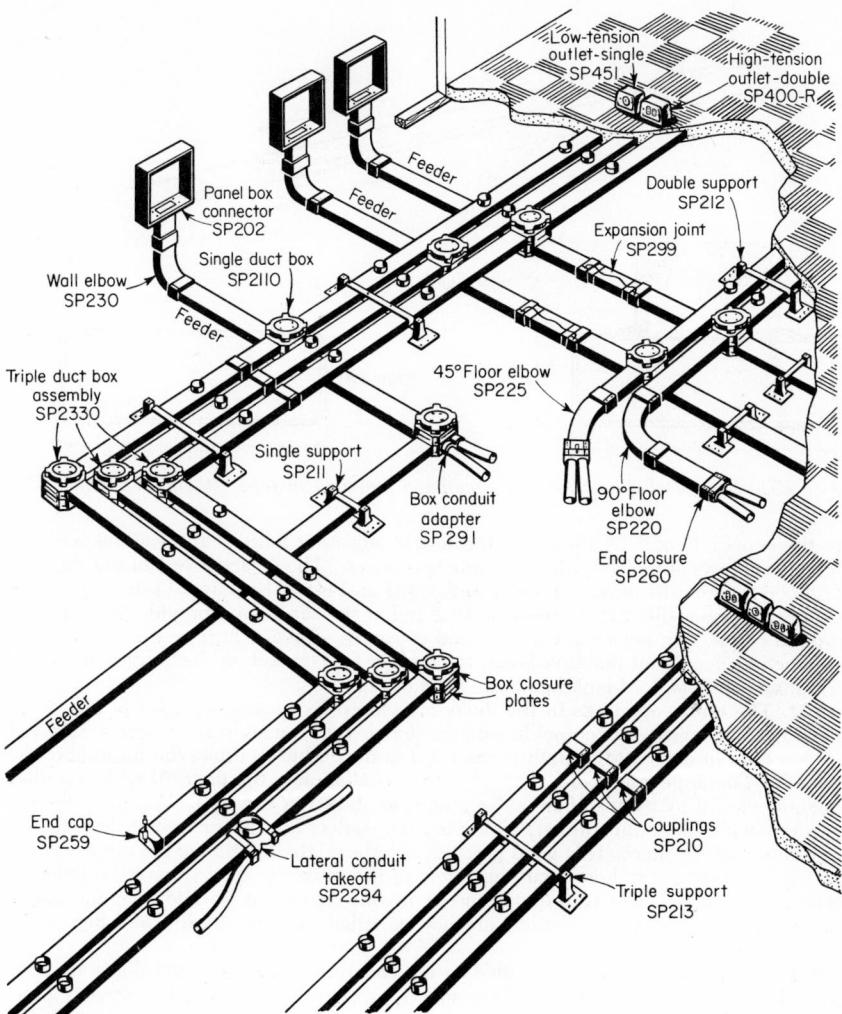

FIG. 138   *Component parts and method of installation for two-level steel underfloor raceways.   (General Electric Co.)*

231. Installation of Steel-duct Raceways.   The method of installing Nepcoduct, the steel-raceway system manufactured by the National Electric Div., H. K. Porter Co., Inc., in the concrete fill of floors is illustrated in Fig. 142.   The ducts are supported by means of saddle supports, which consist, as shown in Fig. 143, of two detachable parts, a base and saddle.   These supports are available for single-duct runs and in various combinations for supporting multiple-duct runs.   Supports should be located not more than 5 ft apart.   After the locations of junction boxes and duct runs have been marked out, the bases of the saddle supports are fastened to the floor by means of expansion bolts for concrete construction or by means of special toggle wires for hollow-tile work (see Fig. 142).   The saddle is then assembled to the base, and the ducts fastened to the saddle by means of the tie wires.   The complete raceway is then leveled and adjusted

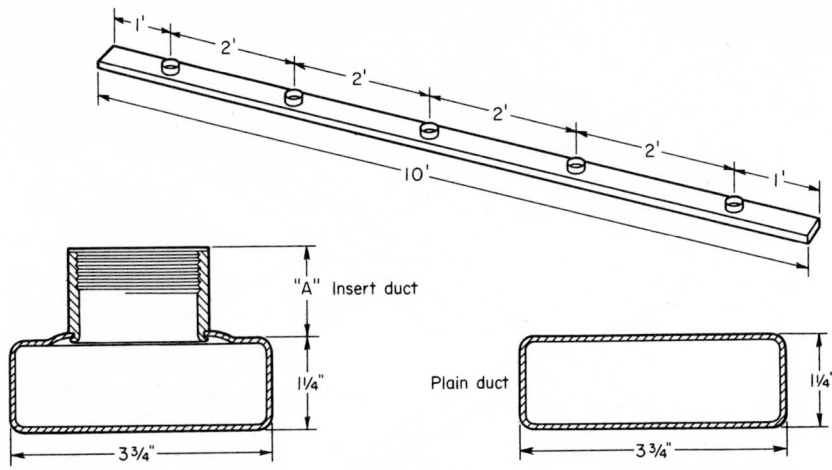

FIG. 139 *Duct and duct insert for two-level raceway system.* (*General Electric Co.*)

to the proper height by means of the height-adjusting bolts of the saddles and the leveling screws of the couplings and junction boxes. The adjacent sections of duct are fastened together by means of duct couplings (Fig. 144). The pointed setscrews of the couplings fasten the duct to the coupling and at the same time provide an electrical ground connection between the duct and coupling. Special fittings are available for connecting ducts and junction boxes to conduit, for connecting ducts directly to distribution cabinets, for blanking off the ends of ducts, etc.

232. The outlet openings in the ducts are closed by means of outlet plugs whose height can be adjusted to coincide with the floor level. A marker screw can be inserted in one plug of each 10-ft length of duct if it is desired to facilitate the location of the outlets. The appearance of a duct after the installation of the floor fill with an outlet opening closed by means of an outlet plug is as shown in Fig. 145. When the floor is covered with linoleum, rubber, cork, etc., the outlets are not extended through the covering until needed. It is good practice to indicate the location of the outlet inserts by means of an escutcheon marking screw in the plugs on each side of the junction boxes, as indicated in Fig. 146. Wood or marble floors can be laid over the outlet inserts (Fig. 147), and the outlets are not extended through the finished floor until actually needed.

233. When the raceway is installed in the concrete of the floor, the ducts are supported from the forms by means of the saddle supports, and the whole system is accurately leveled and adjusted for the proper height by means of the leveling screws and bolts on the fittings and saddle supports, before the floor is poured. In concrete-joist construction where the building codes will not allow the saddle support to be mounted directly on the concrete pans, a saddle bridge must be used to support the duct saddles. This method of installation is shown in Fig. 148.

234. Installation of Outlet Fittings in Steel-duct Raceway Systems. When a duct outlet is to be used for service, the small amount of concrete is removed from the top depression of the outlet plug. The plug is removed by unscrewing it from the duct with a plug-removal wrench. The removal of the plug forms a neat preformed passage through the concrete to the duct-outlet opening. The necessary wires are pulled in from the nearest junction box and threaded through the service fitting. The service fitting is then screwed into the duct outlet opening, and the floor flange adjusted.

When it is desired to locate an outlet at a point in a raceway where there is no preset insert plug, an afterset insert for the outlet can be made by the use of special tools available from the manufacturer. The method of making an afterinsert is illustrated in Fig. 149.

235. Trenchduct. Several makes of steel underfloor raceways are suitable for use with "Trenchduct." Figure 150 shows a section of Trenchduct supplying two runs of underfloor steel raceways. Trenchduct is available in standard 6 ft lengths at a depth of 2⅛ in. Other depths are available on special order. Ducts are shipped complete with three 18-in.-long cover sections. Cover plates are ¼-in.-thick roller-leveled steel. The Trenchduct is used to extend branch circuits from a panel board to the underfloor raceways, and the Trenchduct shown in Fig. 150 has a cross-sectional area of 22½ sq in. which allows many more conductors than a conduit feed.

Cover plates for Trenchducts are adjustable upward to ⅜ in. and downward to ⅜ in. from a standard position by means of leveling screws flush with the top surface cover. Adjustment to finished floor height is made by a screwdriver from the top.

Side-feed connectors provide bushed openings for feeds into the side of the Trenchduct. When specified, openings in Trenchduct are precut by the manufacturer. The

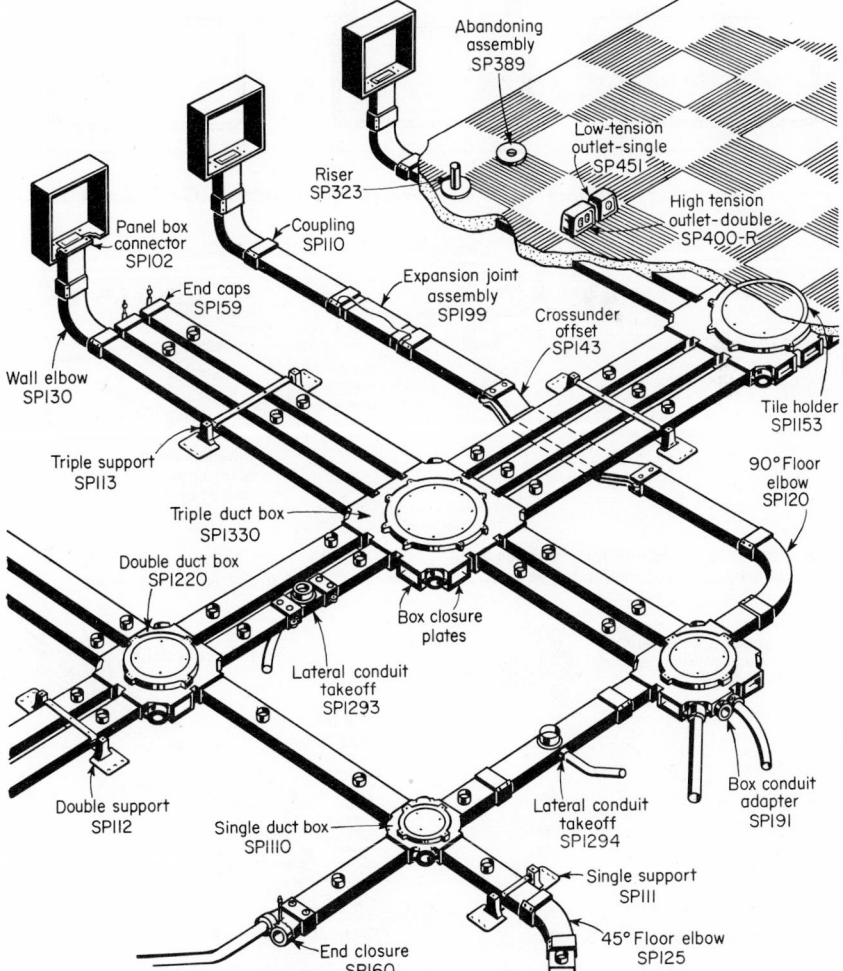

FIG. 140 *Component parts and method of installation for single-level steel underfloor raceway.* (General Electric Co.)

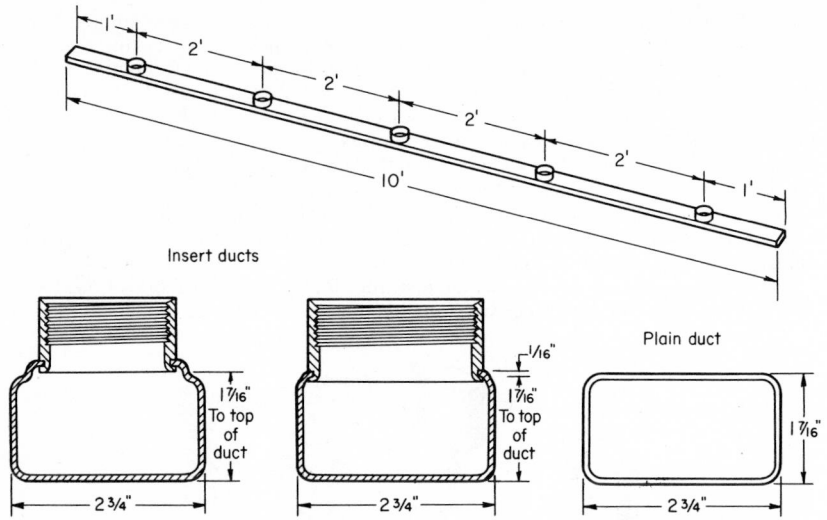

FIG. 141   *Duct and duct inserts for single-level raceway system.*   (*General Electric Co.*)

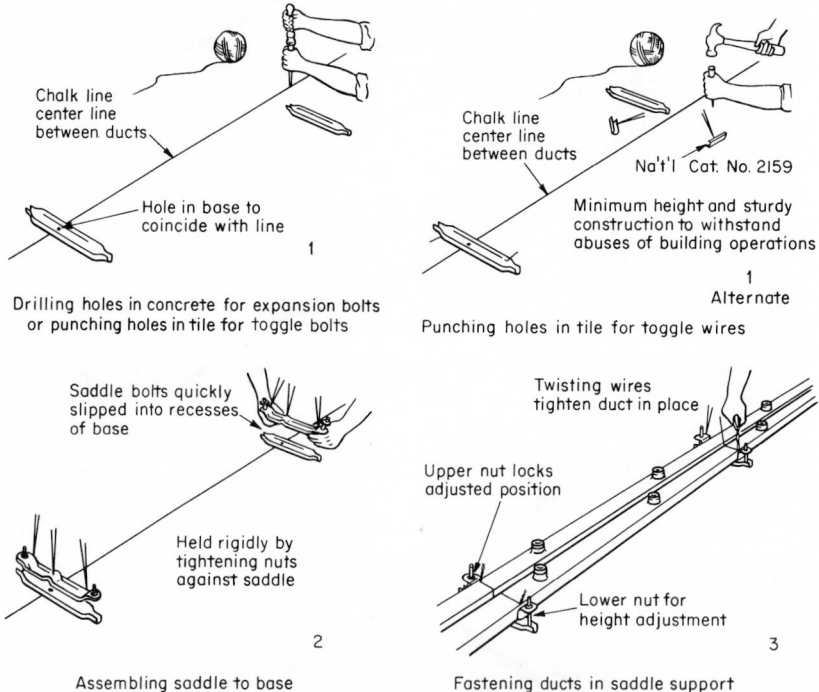

FIG. 142   *Method of installing steel underfloor raceway.*   (*National Electric Div., H. K. Porter Co., Inc.*)

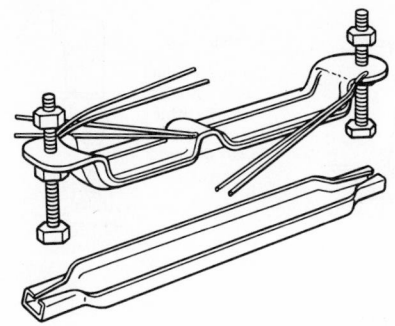

FIG. 143 *Saddle supports for one small and one large steel underfloor duct. (National Electric Div., H. K. Porter Co., Inc.)*

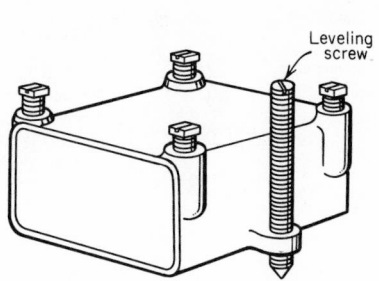

FIG. 144 *Coupling for steel underfloor raceway. (National Electric Div., H. K. Porter Co., Inc.)*

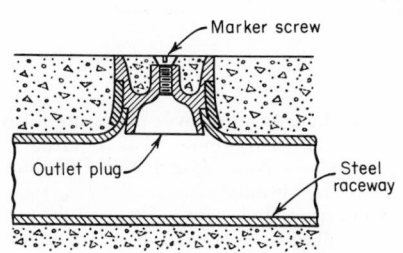

FIG. 145 *Appearance of outlet opening in steel underfloor raceway with opening closed by means of outlet plug.*

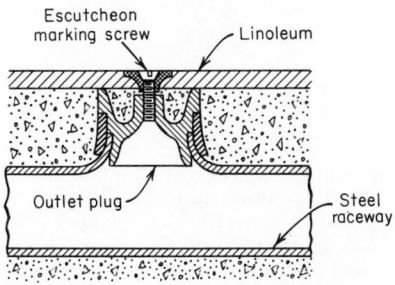

FIG. 146 *Outlet opening in steel underfloor raceway closed with outlet plug and concealed with linoleum floor covering.*

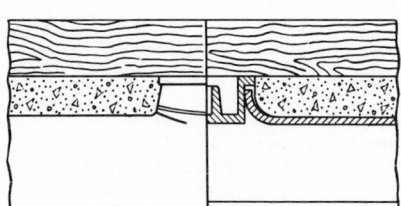

FIG. 147 *Outlet opening in steel underfloor raceway concealed by wood floor until outlet is needed. (National Electric Div., H. K. Porter Co., Inc.)*

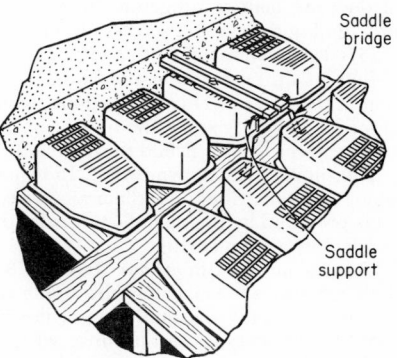

FIG. 148 *Method of supporting steel underfloor raceway in concrete-joist construction. (National Electric Div., H. K. Porter Co., Inc.)*

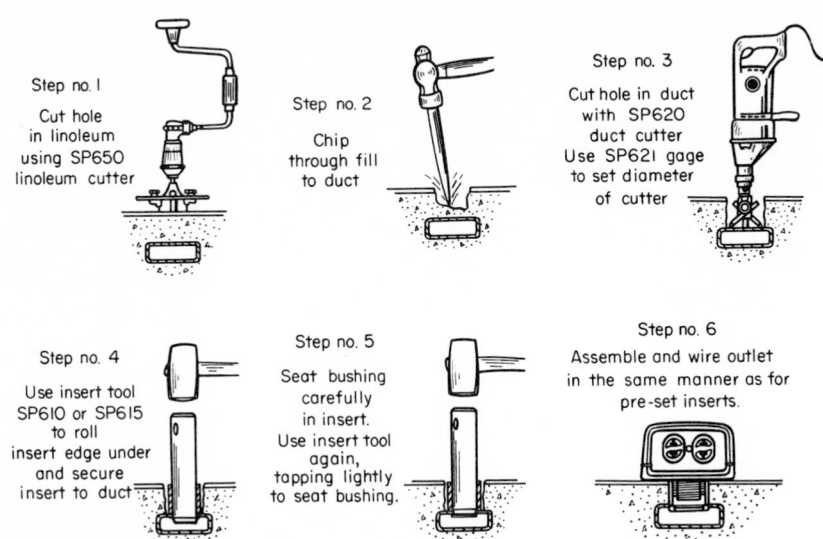

FIG. 149 *Method of making an outlet with an afterset insert.* (*General Electric Co.*)

Trenchduct is, in effect, a continuous junction box, because the cover plates are flush with the finished floor and one or more sections can be easily removed as required.

Vertical elbows turn the Trenchduct system up to a panel board with full duct capacity. Figure 150 shows typical components of the system.

236. Installation of Completely Enclosing Fiber-duct Raceways. Completely enclosing fiber-duct underfloor raceways may be installed in either the concrete or the concrete fill of floors in a manner similar to that described for steel-duct raceways in Sec. **231**. With the fiber-duct raceways there are preinserted provisions for outlets, or they can be provided without any openings for outlets. After the finished floor has been laid, an outlet may be provided at any preset insert, or at any point desired along the duct runs, as described in Sec. **237**. The main component parts of a fiber-duct underfloor raceway system are illustrated in Figs. 151 and 152. The different sections of duct are clamped together by means of a combination steel coupling and support provided with leveling screws for leveling the runs and adjusting to the proper height.

237. Installation of Outlet Fittings in Fiber-duct Raceway Systems. To establish outlets in a preset system after finish is in place, it is necessary to determine the location of the insert. This can be done by means of an insert finder. Then the flooring is chipped down to expose the insert cap. The cap is removed and a hole cut in the duct so that wires can be fished through and connected to the receptacle.

The procedures shown in Fig. 153 should be employed in installing an outlet fitting at any point in a fiber underfloor raceway of the completely enclosing type. The special tools provided by the manufacturers for this purpose should be used in order to ensure satisfactory workmanship.

238. Layout of Underfloor Raceway Systems. A very simple layout for an underfloor raceway system, called the single run-around, is shown in Fig. 154. Such a layout provides only the minimum of flexibility in the location of outlets. It is satisfactory for certain types of buildings when the installation cost must be limited and the desks will be located only around the side walls. This layout will provide outlets only for telephone and signal systems. A similar layout is shown in Fig. 155. This layout, having two separate raceways, provides outlets for electrically operated office machines from one raceway and outlets for telephones and signal systems from the other raceway.

239. In order to provide greater flexibility in the possible location of outlets over the entire area than is accomplished with the run-around layouts, grid layouts are

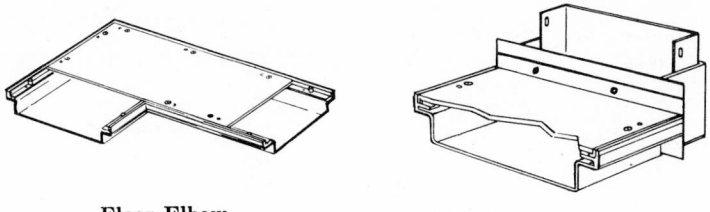

Floor Elbow

Vertical Elbow

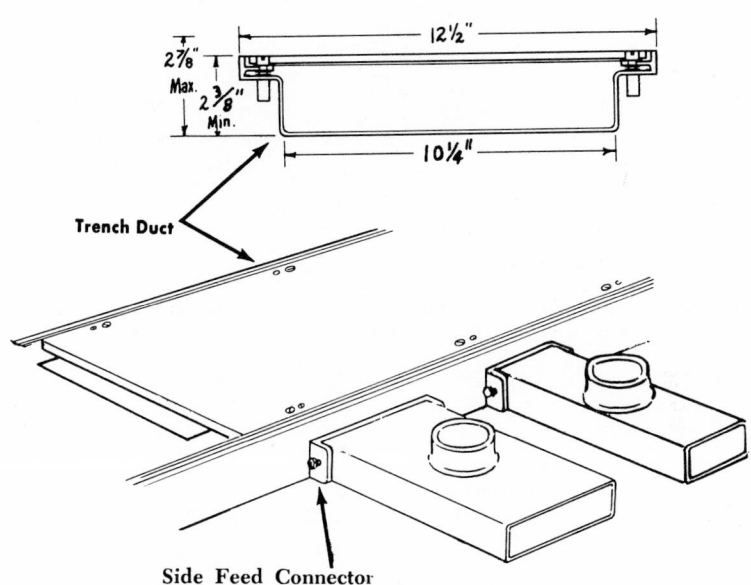

FIG. 150 *Typical components of a Trenchduct used in connection with underfloor steel raceway. (Triangle Conduit & Cable Co., Inc., Subsidiary of Triangle Industries, Inc.)*

employed. A typical single-grid layout is shown in Fig. 156, and a double grid in Fig. 157. The extent of the flexibility provided for the location of outlets depends upon the distance between parallel duct lines. For maximum flexibility the parallel lines of duct should be located approximately 5 ft apart with the outside runs located 3 ft from the outside walls. The distance between rows of junction boxes should be from 20 to 60 ft, depending upon the estimated number of outlets that will be required at any one time between junction boxes.

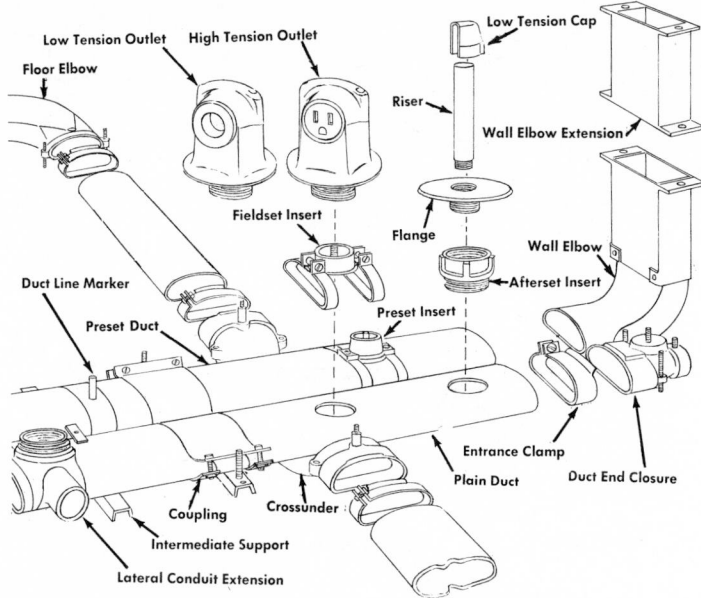

FIG. 151 *Component parts of a completely enclosed fiber underfloor raceway installa-tion. (The Flintkote Co., Inc., Pipe Products Group.)*

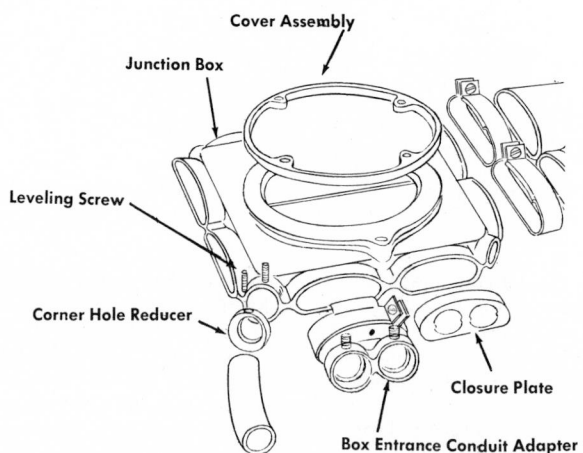

FIG. 152 *Junction box and associated fittings for a completely enclosed fiber underfloor raceway system. (The Flintkote Co., Inc., Pipe Products Group.)*

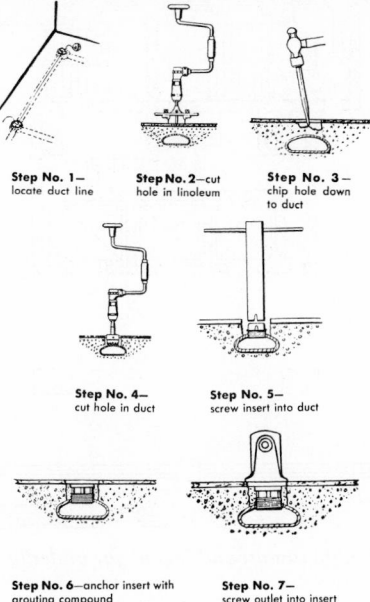

FIG. 153 *Method of installing afterset inserts into fiber underfloor raceways.* (*The Flintkote Co., Inc., Pipe Products Group.*)

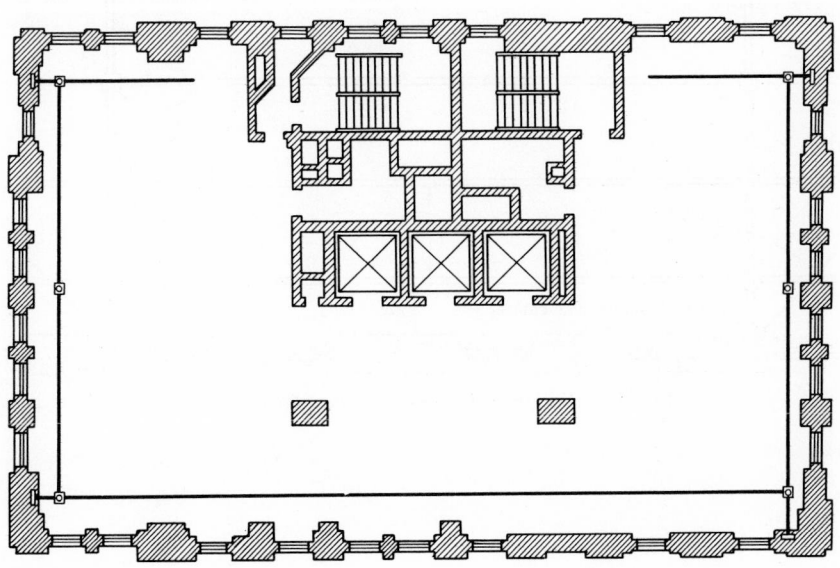

FIG. 154 *Single run-around layout for underfloor raceway.*

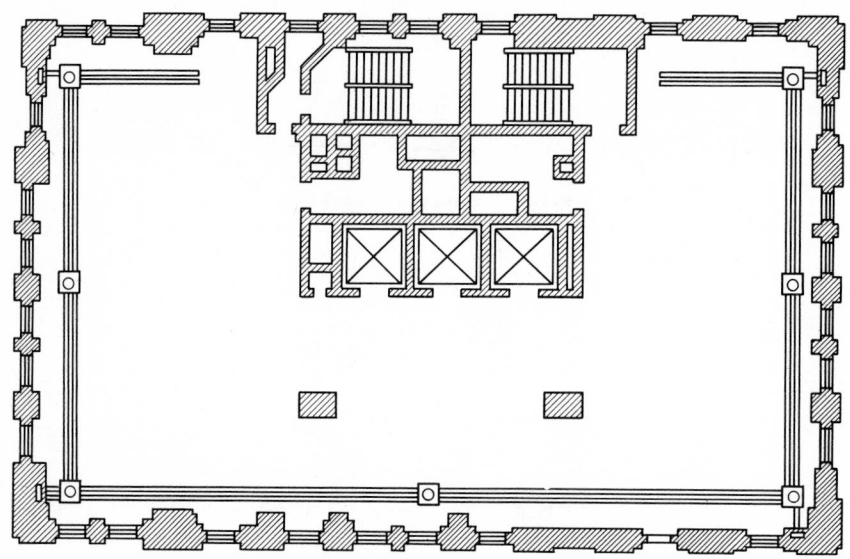

FIG. 155   *Double run-around layout for underfloor raceway.*

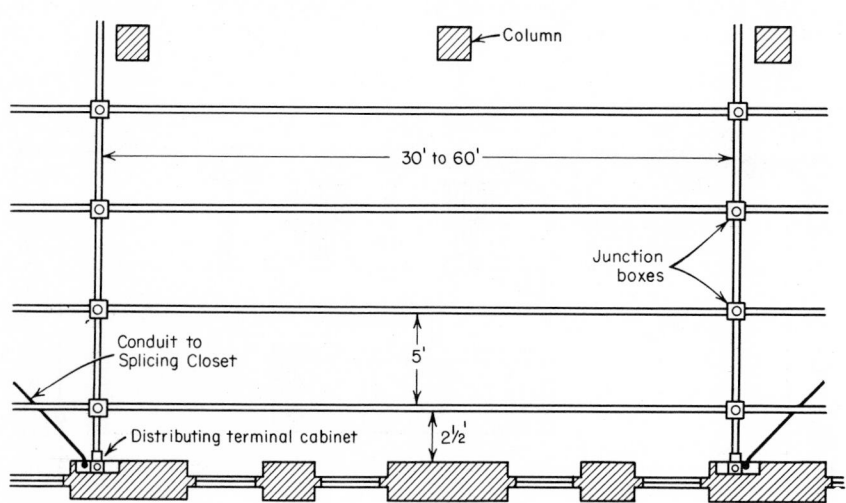

FIG. 156   *Single-grid layout for underfloor raceway.*

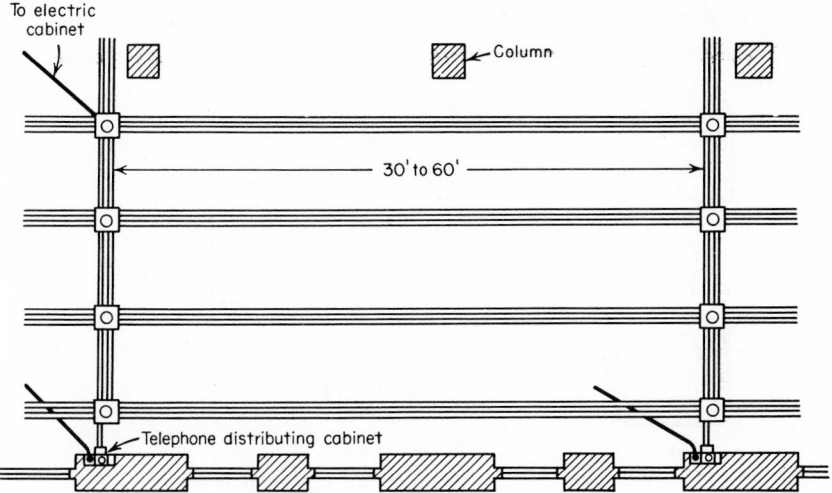

FIG. 157   *Double-grid layout for underfloor raceway.*

WIREWAY WIRING

240. Wireways may be installed only for exposed work. They must not be used where they will be subjected to severe physical damage or to corrosive vapors or in any hazardous location. Wireways intended for outdoor use shall be of approved raintight construction. Their principal application is for the installation of mains and feeders in industrial plants or other locations where a flexible means of supplying branch circuits is advantageous or where a large number of wires must be located in one run. They permit access to the wires and cables at all points throughout the system for tapping, splicing, rerouting, inspection, installation of additional wiring, or other changes, all without disturbing the existing work. A typical section of wireway is shown in Fig. 158. Three sides are provided with closely spaced knockouts for conduit or metal-clad cable attachment. The fourth side consists of a hinged cover which can be opened for installing wires and making splices. The lengths are coupled together with nuts and bolts which secure a sheet-metal hanger (Fig. 159, I) between the flanged ends of the duct sections for supporting the duct. Mains and feeders are run in the wireway with taps for branches taken off at the most convenient point through rigid or flexible conduit or metal-clad cable, connected to the wireway through the knockouts. Square plates are obtainable (Fig. 159, IV) for closing the ends of the duct. Junctions of wireways are formed by using a junction box or a tee (Fig. 159, II and III). Wireways are available in four sizes: 2½, 4, 6, and 8 in. square. No conductor larger than that for which the wireway is designed shall be installed in wireways, provided that the sum of the cross-sectional areas of all the conductors at any cross

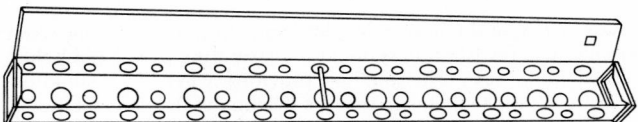

FIG. 158   *A length of wireway with hinged cover.*

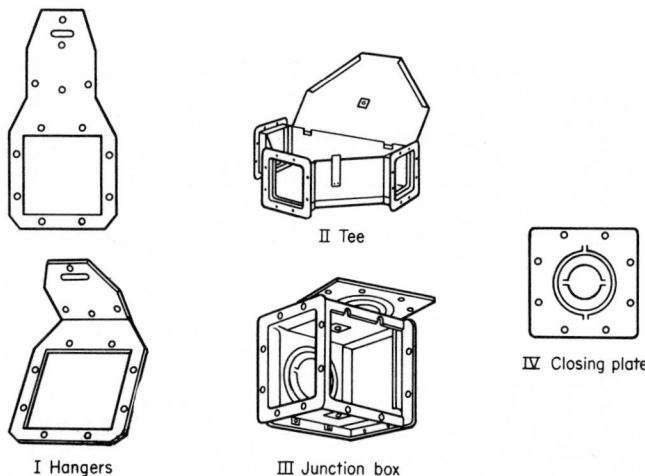

II Tee

IV Closing plate

I Hangers   III Junction box

FIG. 159 *Fittings for square duct.* (*Square D Co.*)

section does not exceed 20 per cent of the interior area of the wireway. Splices and taps may be located within the wireway, provided the cover is left accessible. The conductors including the splices must not fill the wireway to more than 75 per cent of its area. The wireway must not contain more than 30 conductors at any point except for signaling circuits or for control conductors between a motor and its starter, used only for starting duty. More than 30 *current-carrying* conductors may be installed in a wireway, at a 20 per cent maximum fill, if the reduction factors specified in Note 8 of Sec. **17**, Div. 11, are applied. Horizontal runs of wireways must be supported every 5 ft unless specifically approved for supports at greater intervals, but in no case shall the distance between supports exceed 10 ft. Vertical runs of wireway shall be securely supported at intervals not exceeding 15 ft and shall not have more than one joint between supports. Adjoining wireway sections shall be securely fastened together to provide a rigid joint. An unbroken length of wireway may extend transversely through a dry wall.

241. Cross-sectional Areas of Wireways

Wireway size, inches	Cross-sectional areas, sq in.		
	100%	75%	20%
2½ × 2½	6.25	4.68	1.25
4 × 4	16.00	12.00	3.20
6 × 6	36.00	27.00	7.20
8 × 8	64.00	48.00	12.80

242. In computing the proper size wireway, refer to Secs. **240** and **241**. Then determine the total cross-sectional area of the conductors to be installed from Tables **30** and **47** to **51** of Div. 11.

BUS-WAY WIRING

243. Bus way is one of the newer developments in interior wiring systems. It provides a flexible power-distribution system for distributing power and light in industrial and commercial buildings. This method provides a flexible method of connecting branch motor circuits to the mains so that the location of the branch taps can be readily and economically changed to suit the conditions of rearrangement of machines. This system finds a wide field of use in industrial plants where the layout of the machines must be continually changed in order to meet changing manufacturing conditions.

For installations of this type, although the first cost may be somewhat greater than for other methods of wiring, the saving derived from its flexibility in the relocation of machines without additional wiring expense soon overbalances the additional first cost. With the flexible bus-way method of wiring there is no ripping out and scrapping of old material and installing of new to meet the new layout conditions. Bus way may be installed in exposed dry locations for circuits of not more than 600 volts. It may also be used as risers and feeders in large apartments or commercial buildings. It must not be used where it will be subjected to severe physical damage or corrosive vapors, in hoistways, in any hazardous location, outdoors, or in wet or in damp locations unless specially approved for the purpose.

Bus ways may extend vertically through dry floors when totally enclosed (unventilated) where passing through and for a minimum distance of 6 ft above the floor to provide adequate protection from physical damage. Unbroken lengths of bus ways may extend transversely through dry walls.

A dead-end of a bus way shall be closed.

244. Overcurrent Protection of Feeders and Subfeeders (National Electrical Code). If the allowable current rating of the bus way does not correspond to a standard rating of the overcurrent device, the next higher rating may be used.

Overcurrent protection may be omitted at points where bus ways are reduced in size, provided that the smaller bus way does not extend more than 50 ft and has a current rating at least equal to one-third the rating or setting of the overcurrent device next back on the line and provided further that such bus way is free from contact with combustible material.

245. Branches (National Electrical Code). Branches from bus ways shall be made with bus ways or with rigid or flexible metal conduit, electrical metallic tubing, surface metal raceway, metal-clad cable, or suitable cord assemblies approved for hard usage for portable equipment or for the connection of stationary equipment to facilitate their interchange.

Where a bus way is used as a feeder, devices or plug-in connections for tapping off branch circuits from the bus way shall contain the overcurrent devices required for the protection of the branch circuits, except as permitted in section 240-15 of the Code and except for fixed or semifixed lighting fixtures, on which the branch-circuit overcurrent device may be a part of the fixture-cord plug on cord-connected fixtures and may be mounted on the fixture where fixtures without cords are plugged directly into the bus way.

246. Use of Bus Ways as Branch Circuits (National Electrical Code). A bus way may be used as a branch circuit of any one of the types described in article 210 of the Code. When so used, the rating or setting of the overcurrent device protecting the bus way shall determine the ampere rating of the branch circuit and the circuit shall in all respects conform with the requirements of article 210 applying to branch circuits of that rating. Bus ways which are used as branch circuits and which are so designed that loads can be connected at any point shall be limited to such lengths as will provide that in normal use the circuits will not be overloaded.

In general, the length of such run in feet should not exceed three times the ampere rating of the branch circuit.

247. Bus ways consist of busbars mounted in a sheet-metal enclosure or trough. They are available in several types which may be broadly classified as follows:

1. Current-limiting bus way.
2. Low-voltage-drop feeder bus way without plug-in provision.
3. Low-voltage-drop feeder bus way with plug-in provisions.
4. Plug-in bus way — power type.
5. Plug-in bus way — lighting type.
6. Trolley bus way.

Current-limiting bus way is used primarily in commercial, industrial, or institutional buildings for connection between the service entrance and the main switchboard or wherever it is desirable to reduce the available short-circuit current. Its use makes it possible to utilize standard switchboards, panel boards, and other electrical-distribution components throughout the building.

Low-voltage-drop feeder bus way without plug-in provision is used primarily in industrial buildings for connection between the service entrance and the main switch-

board or for high-capacity feeders to load centers. It is ideally suited for many other applications, such as risers and feeders to resistance welders and as feeders to high-frequency equipment.

Low-voltage-drop feeder bus way with plug-in provision is used primarily in industrial plants for feeders where the combination of high-capacity, low-voltage-drop char-

acteristics and numerous power tap-offs is required. Its use is also advantageous for risers in multistory buildings where frequent power tap-offs are required.

Plug-in bus way of the power type provides a low-cost flexible power-distribution system for industrial plants for supplying the individual power loads. In addition it

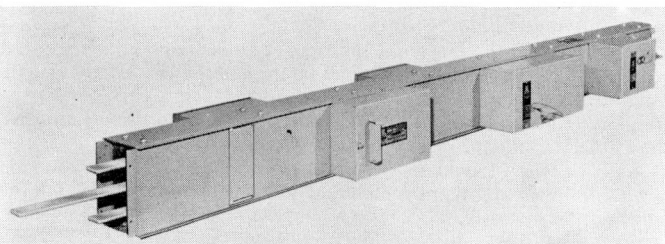

is often used in commercial buildings, manual training shops, laboratories, and garages when flexibility of power plug-in receptacles is necessary or desirable.

Plug-in bus way of the lighting type provides a low-cost, flexible power-distribution system for supplying low-capacity loads. It provides maximum flexibility for these low-capacity loads, since a power tap-off can be made at any point along the bus way. It is effectively used as the power-supply system for lighting fixtures, small power tools

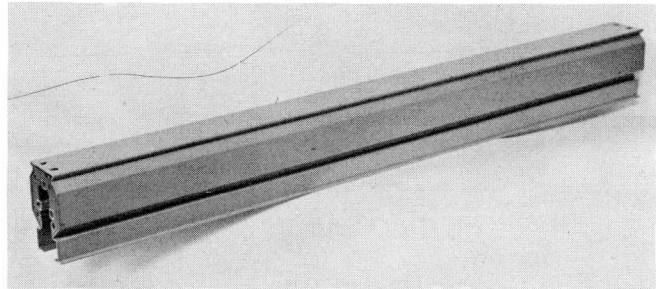

and machines in industrial plants, office buildings, department stores, garages, warehouses, truck terminals, shipping docks, and railway freight terminals.

Trolley bus way provides a completely flexible power-distribution system for supply-

ing individual loads wherever a mobile power take-off is required, such as for cranes and portable tools.

Most bus-way assemblies are available either with copper or aluminum bus bars.

248. Current-limiting bus way is designed so that it offers unusually high reactance so that it will limit the magnitude of short-circuit currents. It is available in ratings of 1,000, 1,350, 1,600, 2,000, 2,500, 3,000, and 4,000 amp for three- or four-wire three-phase systems. It can be obtained in any specified length of section up to 10 ft. Standard components are available to provide elbows, offsets, T connections, seal-off end boxes, switchboard stubs for connection in entering or leaving a switchboard, cable tap boxes to provide for junctions in main cable feeders or branches and for connection to transformers, and circuit-breaker or fuse adapters to provide for overcurrent protection of tap connections. A typical installation is illustrated in Fig. 160.

249. Methods of Mounting Current-limiting Bus Way. Current-limiting bus way can be installed in a variety of ways to suit any building or operating condition. It may be mounted flatwise horizontal (Fig. 161), edgewise horizontal, or as a vertical riser. Whenever possible, it is best to mount the bus way in the flat horizontal position, as this position of mounting will take the best advantage of the convection cooling permitted by the aerated housing design of the bus way. Some types of bus ways are marked to indicate mounting in a specific position.

In order to allow free circulation of air, a clear space of at least 2 in. should be provided between the bus way and a wall. Between the top surface of the bus way and a ceiling a clear space of at least 7 in. should be provided.

250. Procedure in Hanging and Joining Current-limiting Bus Way. The following procedure is recommended by the General Electric Co. for the installation of their Type CL current-limiting bus way (refer to Figs. 160 and 161).

STEP 1. Make up and install support rods or brackets on 5-ft centers which are to support standard hanger plates or channels.

STEP 2 (Fig. 161a). Raise Type CL bus way to the final level and put the hanger plates or channels in place to carry the weight.

STEP 3 (Fig. 161b). The standard sections butt together, and the housing is joined

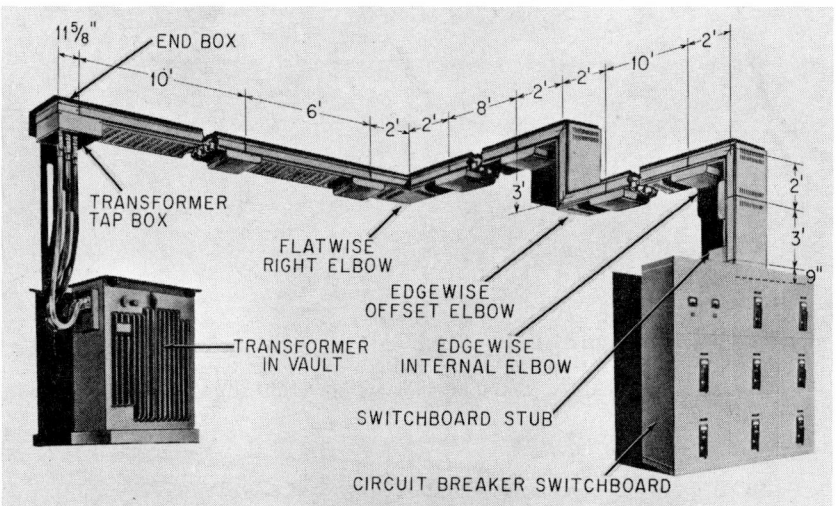

FIG. 160 *Typical installation of current-limiting bus way.* (*General Electric Co.*)

by fastening the splice plate, which is already attached to one end of the section of bus way. When the splice plate is fastened,ʹthe bus bars are ready to be joined.

STEP 4 (Fig. 161*c*). The bus bars are easily bolted together by the use of carriage bolts and lock washers.

Most bolts are accessible from one side of the housing. This is particularly advantageous where the run is mounted against the wall or other surface.

Generous spacings between bolts provide real "elbow room." Any type of flat, open-end wrench may be used. However, to assure proper tightness of connection, a torque wrench should be used.

The conductors are bare at the joints to facilitate initial installation and subsequent maintenance. Ample air clearances eliminate the need for taping. Solid covers provide protection from the entry of foreign material.

Two carriage bolts are used to join each pair of bus bars. Since the bolt holds itself from turning, only one wrench is required. The use of two bolts per joint assures large contact areas. Bolts have tapered shoulders so that they pull the bars into line as they are tightened. Lock washers prevent loosening after the bars have been pulled up tight. The joint cover is put into place and fastened to complete the joint.

STEP 5 (Fig. 161*d*). After the entire run is in final alignment, install the clip-type hangers, which fasten the Type CL securely to the hanger plates, or channels. For details of other hanging methods, refer to the manufacturer's instructions.

251. Low-voltage-drop feeder bus way without plug-in provision is used for feeders which require either no taps or only a few taps at definitely fixed points. It is available in ratings of 600, 800, 1,000, 1,350, 1,600, 2,000, 2,500, 3,000, 3,500, and 4,000 amp, and in two-pole and three-pole assemblies. The three-pole assemblies can be obtained for three- or four-wire systems. It can be obtained in any specified length of section up to 10 ft. Standard components of the same general types as discussed in Sec. **248** for current-limiting bus way are available for low-voltage-drop bus way. The methods of mounting and of installation are also similar to those for current-limiting bus way as discussed in Secs. **249** and **250**. A typical low-voltage-drop feeder bus way system without plug-in provision is shown in Fig. 162.

252. Low-voltage-drop feeder bus way with plug-in provision combines high-capacity and low-voltage-drop characteristics with plug-in flexibility. It is available in ratings of 600, 800, 1,000, 1,350, 1,600, 2,000, 2,500, 3,000, and 4,000 amp, and in two-pole and three-pole assemblies. The three-pole assemblies can be obtained for

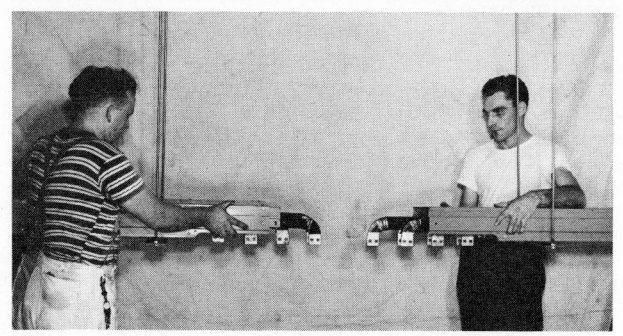

(*a*) *Step 2.*

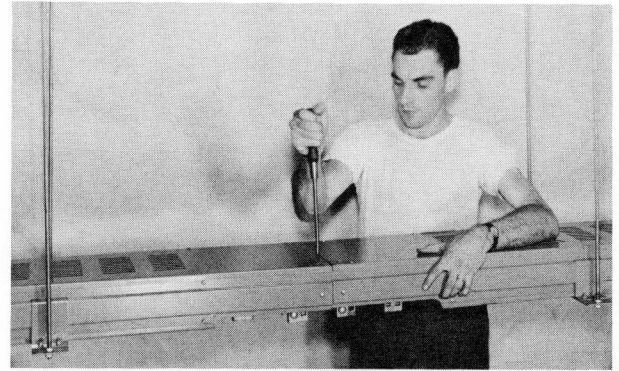

(*b*) *Step 3.*

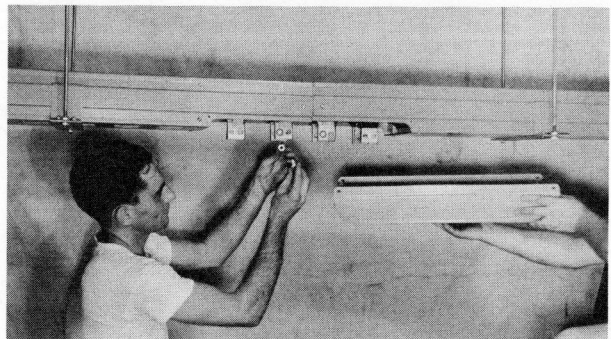

(*c*) *Step 4.*

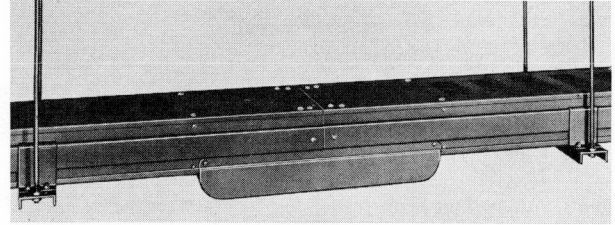

(*d*) *Step 5.*

FIG. 161 *Hanging procedure for current-limiting bus way.* (*General Electric Co.*)

three- or four-wire systems. The standard length of sections is 10 ft. Where shorter sections are required and for sections where no plug-in provisions are desired, sections of low-voltage-drop feeder bus way without plug-in provision can be used. The two types of low-voltage-drop feeder bus way made by the same manufacturer usually are interchangeable. Standard components are available to provide elbows, offsets, T connections, seal-off end boxes, and switchboard stubs for connection in entering or leaving a switchboard. The number of plug outlet provisions per 10-ft length varies with the manufacturer from 10 to 12. In all cases half of the outlets are on one side of the bus-way assembly and the other half on the opposite side of the assembly. The plug-in devices employed are the same as those used with plug-in bus way of the power type as discussed in Sec. **253**. The methods of mounting and of installation are similar to those for current-limiting bus way as discussed in Secs. **249** and **250**. A typical bus-

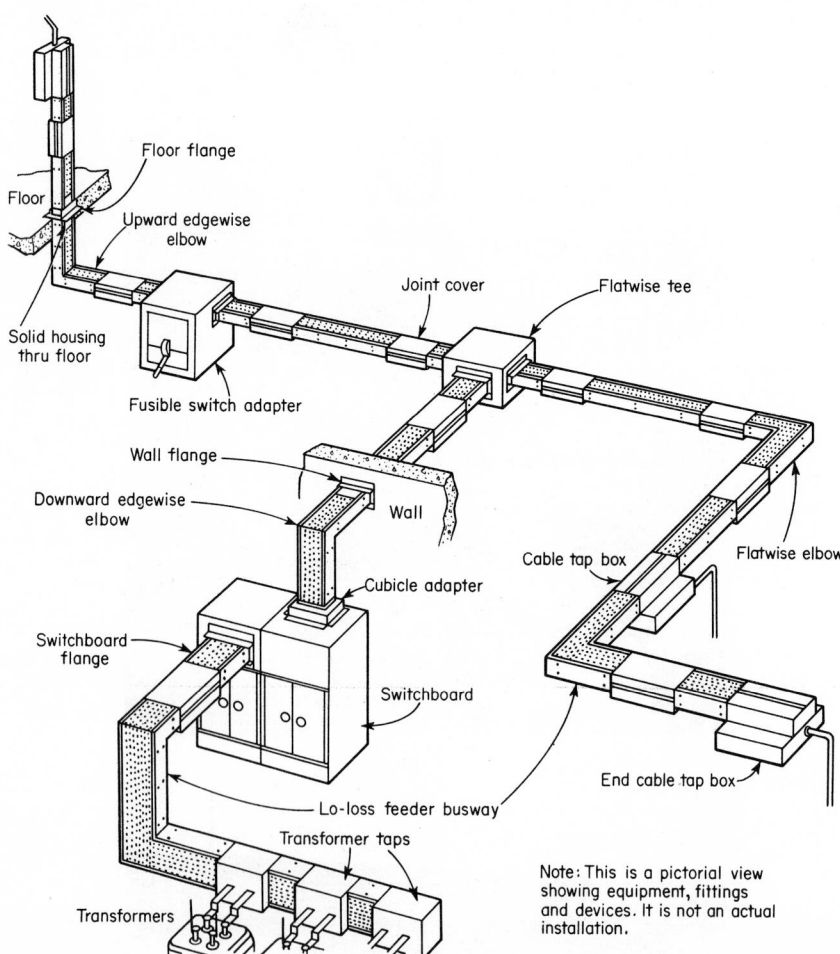

FIG. 162 *Typical low-voltage-drop feeder bus-way system.* (*National Electric Div., H. K. Porter Co., Inc.*)

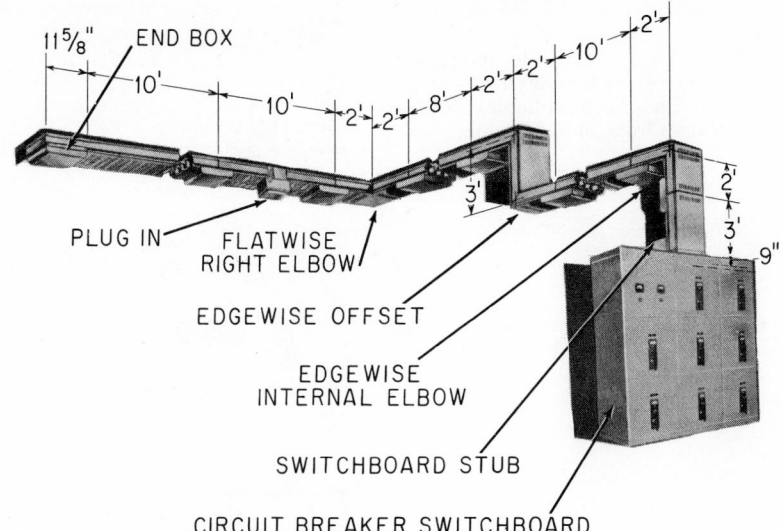

FIG. 163 *Bus-way system using combination of plug-in and non-plug-in low-voltage-drop feeder sections. (General Electric Co.)*

way system employing a combination of low-voltage-drop feeder units of both the plug-in and non-plug-in types is illustrated in Fig. 163.

253. Plug-in bus way of the power type is used for indoor systems where flexibility in the location of power outlets over a wide area is necessary or desirable. It is available in 100-, 225-, 400-, 800-, 1,000-, 1,250-, and 1,500-amp ratings and in two-pole and three-pole assemblies. The three-pole assemblies can be obtained for three- or four-wire systems. Sections are available in 10-, 5-, 3-, 2-, and 1-ft lengths. Provision for plug-in taps is made through outlets located on both sides of the assembly. The number of plug-in outlets that can be used simultaneously varies from 9 to 14 for the assemblies that are available from the different manufacturers. Most of the assemblies are provided with sliding cover plates or doors so that the holes for plug-in connections can be closed when not utilized. Standard components are available to provide elbows, offsets, T connections, crossovers, reducers for changing size of bus way, end closers, and expansion sections. Cable tap boxes are available for the purpose of providing for cable or conduit tap-offs or feed-ins. They are made in three types: (1) end-cable tap boxes for attachment at the ends of a plug-in bus-way run, (2) center-cable tap boxes for installation at any point in a bus-way run, and (3) plug-in-cable tap boxes for making a plug-in connection to a cable or conduit tap-off.

Plug-in devices are available in the following types:

1. Nonfusible plug-ins in 30-, 60-, 100-, and 200-amp sizes.
2. Fusible plug-ins in 30-, 60-, 100-, and 200-amp sizes.

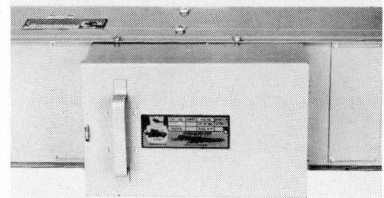

3. Safety switch nonfusible plug-ins in standard switch sizes from 30 to 600 amp.

4. Safety-switch fusible plug-ins in standard switch sizes from 30 to 600 amp.

5. Circuit-breaker plug-ins in sizes from 15 to 400 amp.

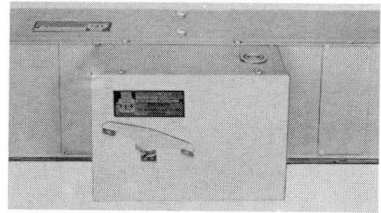

6. Capacitor plug-ins for power-factor improvement in sizes from 5 to 15 kvar.

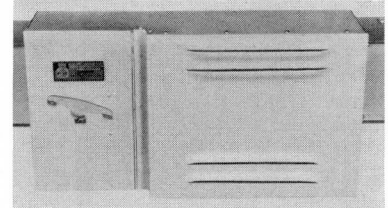

7. Single-phase transformer plug-ins rated up to 10 kva for supplying lights, small motors, or portable tools at 120 or 240 volts from 240- or 480-volt bus-way system.

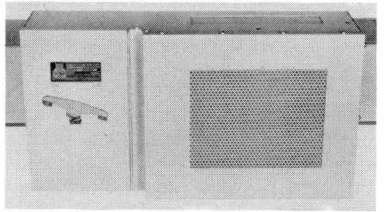

8. Ground detector and neutralizer plug-ins provided with neon glow lamps for detection and neutralizing resistors for dissipation of electric charge which may build up in long runs of bus way.

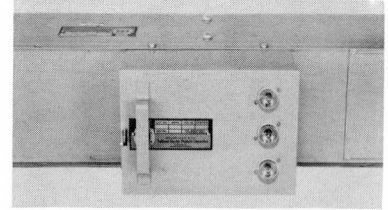

9. Temperature-indicator plug-ins which give visual warning by means of lighted lamp if temperature along bus way exceeds proper value.

(Photographs courtesy of National Electric Div., H. K. Porter Co., Inc.)

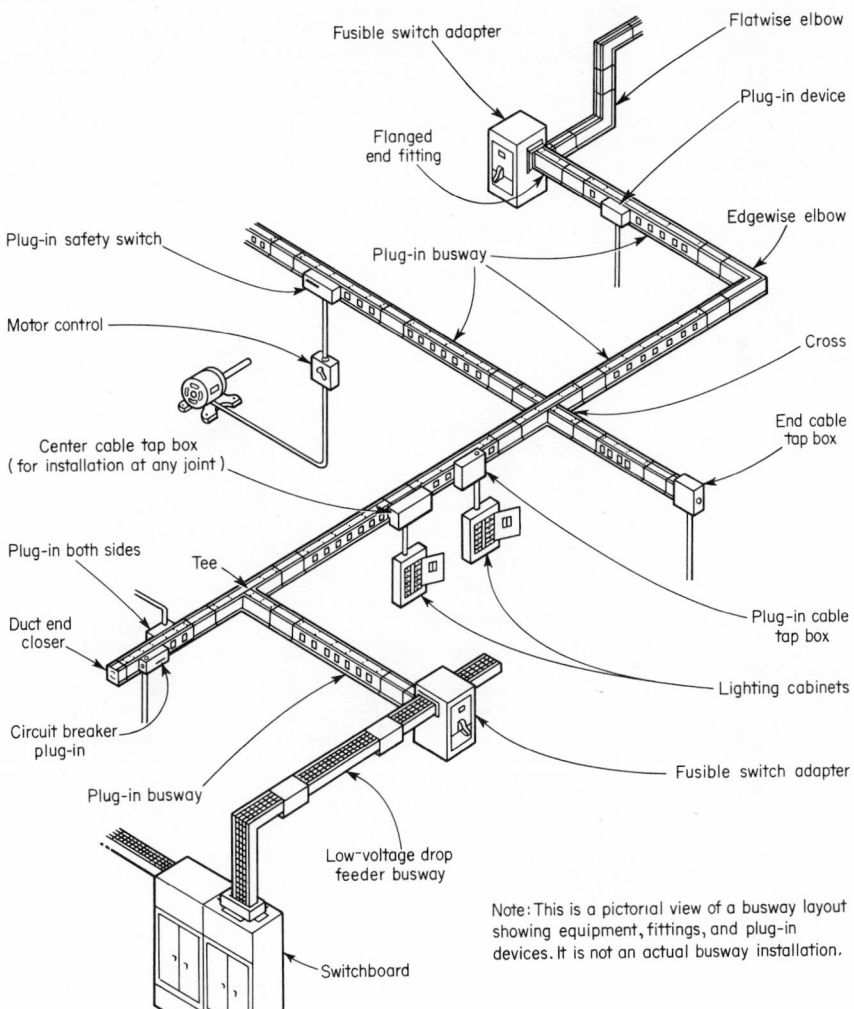

Fusible switch adapter

Flatwise elbow

Flanged
end fitting

Plug-in device

Plug-in safety switch

Plug-in busway

Edgewise elbow

Motor control

Cross

Center cable tap box
(for installation at any joint)

End cable
tap box

Plug-in both sides

Tee

Duct end
closer

Plug-in cable
tap box

Circuit breaker
plug-in

Lighting cabinets

Plug-in busway

Fusible switch adapter

Low-voltage drop
feeder busway

Note: This is a pictorial view of a busway layout
showing equipment, fittings, and plug-in
devices. It is not an actual busway installation.

Switchboard

FIG. 164 *Typical plug-in bus-way (power-type) system. (National Electric Div.,
H. K. Porter Co., Inc.)*

Branch circuits are taken out through the knockouts in the plug-in boxes, using
metal-clad cable, flexible conduit, or rigid conduit. If the vertical length of the branch
circuit is more than a few feet, it is desirable, when using cable or flexible conduit, to
attach the cable or conduit to a guy line in bringing it down. This puts the weight of
the cable on the guy line instead of on the connector to the box.

The application of the various components of plug-in bus ways is illustrated in the
typical bus-way-system layout shown in Fig. 164.

Typical methods of hanging plug-in bus way are shown in Fig. 165.

254. Plug-in bus way of the lighting type (Fig. 166) provides the greatest flexibility
in the location of outlets for low-current capacity loads. Only one rating, 50-amp, is
available for two-, three-, or four-wire systems. Standard sections may be obtained in

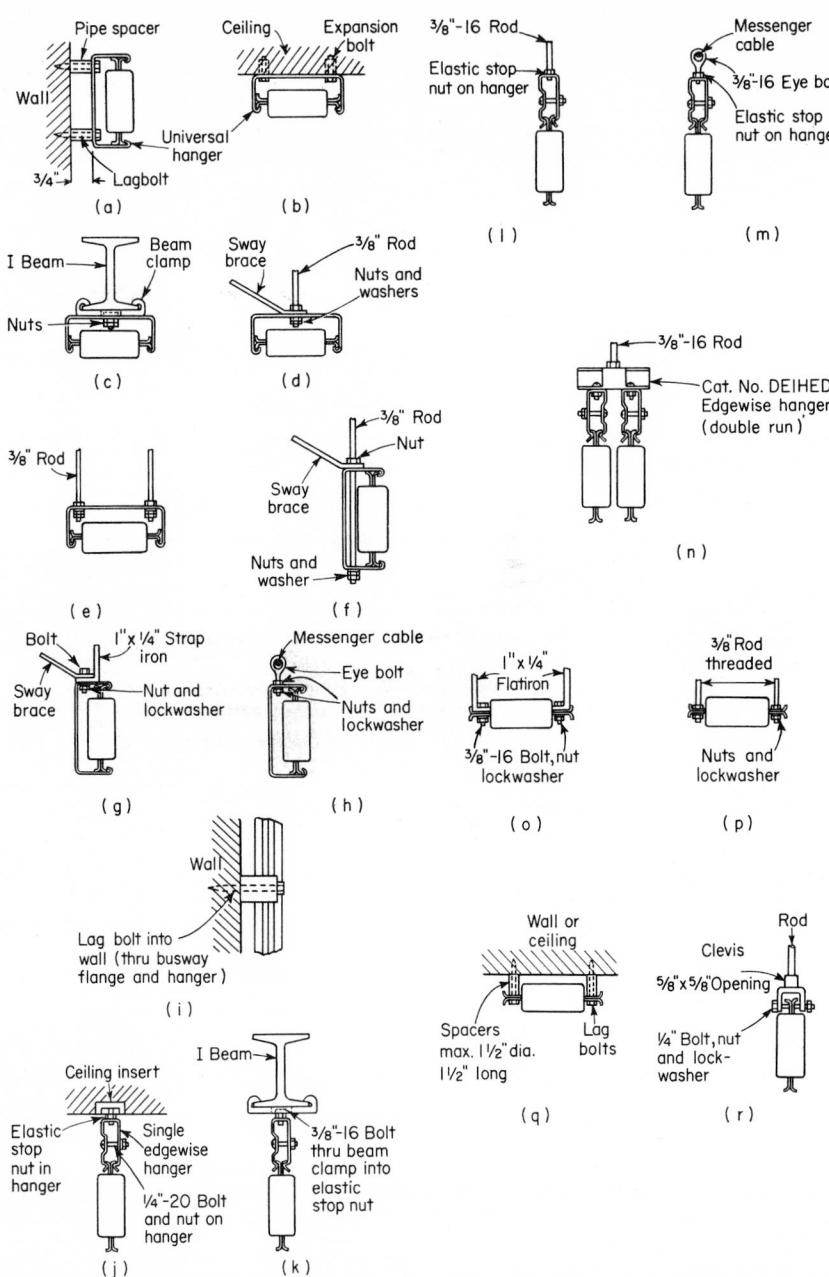

FIG. 165 *Methods of hanging plug-in bus way of power type.* (*General Electric Co.*)

lengths of 1, 2, 3, 4, 5, 6, 7, 8, 9, and 10 ft. In this type of bus way the steel housing does not completely enclose the bus assembly, but leaves a continuous ⅝-in. slot opening in the bottom. This provides a continuous overhead outlet so that power take-offs can be made by inserting plugs at any point along the entire length of the run of bus way. A slot closure is used to close the slot and prevent entrance of dust. It can easily be cut to required length with shears. Standard components are available as with the other types of bus way to provide for all the varying conditions of installation.

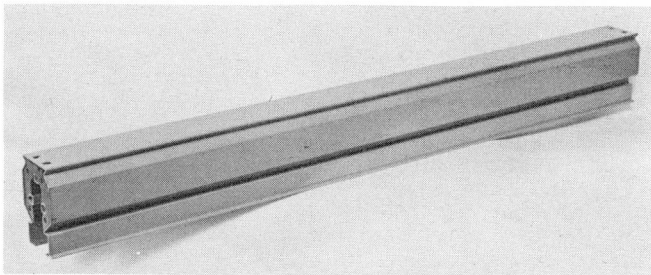

FIG. 166 *A section of plug-in bus way of the lighting type.* (*General Electric Co.*)

POWER TAKE-OFF DEVICES (Fig. 167) are available as follows:
Unfused Plugs. Unfused plugs are available for use with two-, three-, and four-pole systems as follows:
1. With terminals for wire connections.
2. With receptacles for convenience attachment caps or fusible convenience plugs.
3. With both terminal and receptacles incorporated in a single base.
4. Conduit box plugs similar to the terminal type except with the addition of the conduit box.
All unfused plugs, except those with conduit box, are provided with cable clamps suitable for multiconductor cable cords having ¹¹/₁₆ in. maximum diameter. A terminal screw with ground connection is mounted on the cable clamp.
To balance loads on three-pole systems or to obtain separate switching of circuits, polarity wedges are provided. These are inserted in a slot in either side of the two- and three-pole plugs. The cord clamp is then slipped over the plug ears to retain the wedges in position.
Since four-pole plugs are of fixed polarity, they are easily wired to agree with color-coded terminals. For easy identification, the polarizing wedge is also color coded. The plugs are inserted in the housing slot merely by compressing the cord clamps.
Terminal-type, two-pole plugs are rated 15 amp, 300 volts a-c; 20 amp, 250 volts a-c; and 15 amp, 125 volts a-c or d-c. Terminal-type, three- and four-pole plugs are rated 20 amp, 250 volts a-c.
Receptacle-type, two-pole plugs are available in ratings of 15 amp, 125 volts a-c or d-c, and 10 amp, 250 volts a-c.
Terminal- and receptacle-type, two-pole plugs are provided in ratings of 15 amp, 125 volts a-c or d-c, and 10 amp, 250 volts a-c, when an attachment plug is used. Without an attachment plug, these two-pole plugs are rated 15 amp, 300 volts a-c; 20 amp, 250 volts a-c; and 15 amp, 125 volts a-c or d-c.
Fusible Plugs. Fusible-type, two-pole plugs utilize a single cartridge fuse mounted in a fuse box and are rated 20 amp, 125 volts a-c or d-c. The three-pole and four-pole fusible plugs utilize three cartridge fuses and are rated 20 amp, 250 volts a-c. Fuses are not included with the units and should be procured separately.
Circuit-breaker Plugs. Circuit-breaker plugs are equipped with single-pole 15- or 20-amp circuit breakers enclosed in boxes. They are available for 120 volts a-c only.
Cross-sectional views of plug-in bus way of the lighting type are given in Fig. 168.

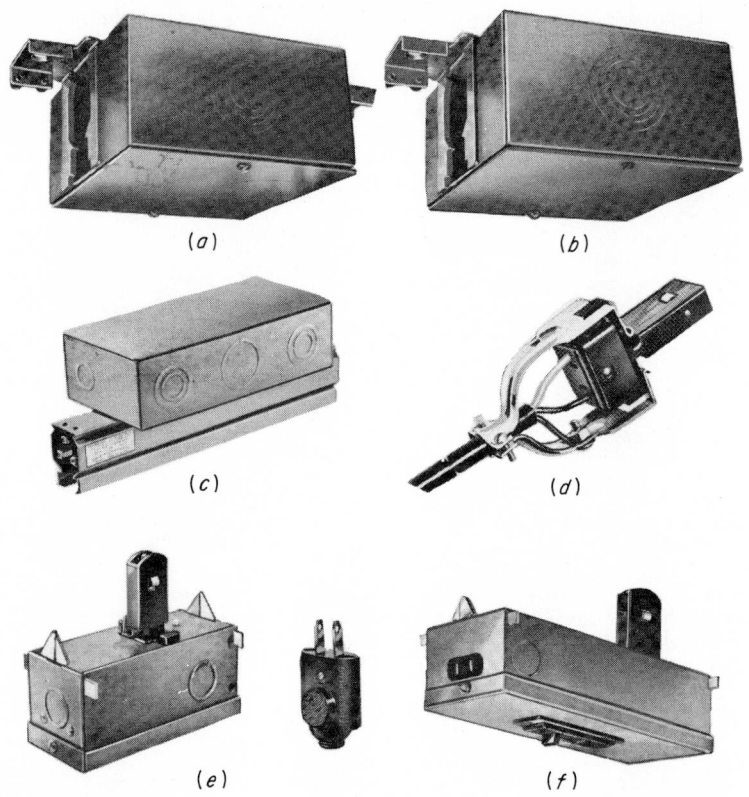

FIG. 167 *Feed-in boxes and power take-offs for plug-in bus way of the lighting type.*
(General Electric Co.) (a) Surface-type center feed-in box. (b) Surface-type end
feed-in box. (c) Suspended-type center feed-in box. (d) Terminal and receptacle-type
unfused plug with cable clamp. Note ground wire attached to cable clamp. (e) Fused
or unfused plug with conduit box (left); fusible convenience plug (right). (f) Circuit-
breaker plug.

Use this system only for the extension of 2-pole installations of this type	Use these systems for all other installations		
Two Pole 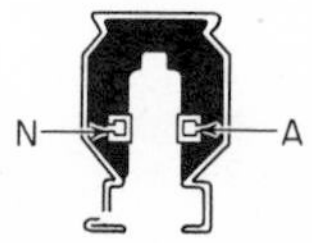	Two Pole LW 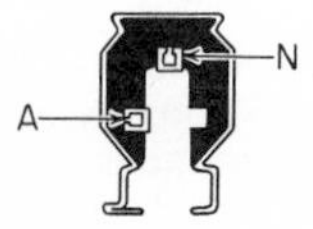	Three Pole LW 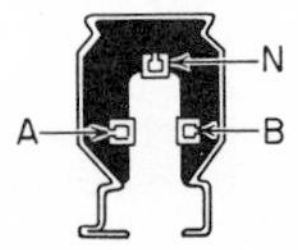	Four Pole LTG 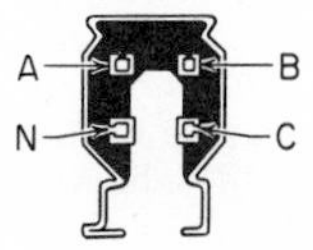

FIG. 168 *Cross-sectional views of plug-in bus way of the lighting type. (General*
Electric Co.)

255. Application data for plug-in bus way of the lighting type as given in the following paragraphs are taken from the statements of the General Electric Co. for their bus way types which are designated as **Types LW** and **LTG** bus ways. Type LW is two- or three-pole and Type LTG is four-pole.

The two-pole Type LW bus way is normally used only when two-wire circuits are involved and for low-initial-cost installations. It can be used for 120-, 240-, or 277-volt systems.

For most applications, the use of three- or four-pole Type LW or LTG bus way is recommended because of its greater load-carrying capacity. Where a two-pole system can carry 6 kva at 120 volts, a three-pole system can carry 12 kva and a four-pole system can carry 18 kva at the same voltage.

The three- and four-pole systems are operated at either 125/250 or 120/208 volts. They can also be connected to a 480Y/277-volt system provided the ungrounded legs are all connected to the same phase so that the maximum voltage between any two conductors is 277 volts, the maximum rating of the system. When this voltage is used, the individual circuits should not exceed 25 amp for the three-pole or $16\frac{2}{3}$ amp for the four-pole so the neutral bar will not be overloaded beyond its 50-amp rating.

In effect, three-pole Type LW bus way provides two independent circuits in the same housing while four-pole Type LTG bus way can be considered three independent circuits in one housing. Thus, the use of three- and four-pole systems provides greater switching flexibility, extra circuits at low cost, and greater service continuity.

Independently controlled circuits are desirable wherever it is necessary to control separate loads or separate portions of the same load. For example, a department store may require two or three different light circuits depending on the material displayed and an industrial plant may require one circuit for work periods and another for maintenance crews. By using single-pole breakers in each of the hot legs with a grounded neutral, it is easy to obtain maximum switching flexibility with three- and four-pole LW or LTG bus way.

In most distribution systems, normal day-lighting circuits are paralleled by other branch circuits. These additional circuits supply night-lighting, convenience outlets, small offices or washrooms, heaters, fans, portable tools, etc. If two-pole bus way is used, other loads must be supplied by other independent circuits which may be either Type LW bus way or wire and conduit. In many instances, a considerable saving can be effected by using three- or four-pole Type LW or LTG bus way to supply two or three of these circuits.

Where service continuity is essential, as in emergency lighting systems, it is desirable to split the loads among various circuits in a three- or four-pole housing. Then, if a temporary overload condition should occur on one phase, the single pole breaker in that circuit may trip but the other circuit will be left in operation. Thus, only a portion of the load will be shut down and production will not be lost.

256. Installation details as given by the General Electric Co. for their Type LTG bus way are as follows:

Adjacent sections or fittings of Type LTG bus way are joined quickly in six easy operations. No tools are needed to make the electrical connections, while only a screwdriver is required for the mechanical hookup. The wide bottom flange of the housing must be kept on the same side of the run throughout the installation to permit polarization of power take-off devices.

The plug design requires that the neutral conductors be located as shown in sketches in Fig. 168.

1. Simply insert the ends of the spring-loaded bus connectors (curved side facing the center of the housing) into the ends of the tubular conductors on one section.

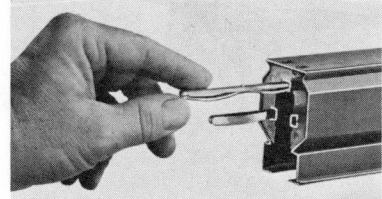

2. Insert alignment pins in loops on busway housing.

3. Slide the adjacent lengths together until they butt flush.

4. Back the setscrews off of the coupling plate.

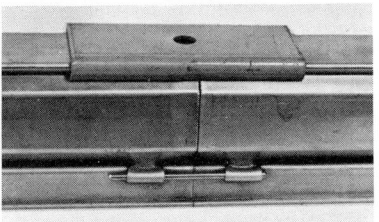

5. Place the coupling plate over the joint between sections or fittings and tighten the setscrews securely to assure a good bond and a continuous ground connection throughout the run. Slide alignment pin through adjacent loop.

6. Thoroughly test the system for grounds and short circuits before energizing.

Surface Hanging. Coupling plates (Fig. 169) and fixed plates (Fig. 170) lend themselves to surface hanging of Type LTG bus way. Holes are provided in the plates to receive screws or bolts for mounting the bus way.

FIG. 169 *Coupling plate.*

FIG. 170 *Fixed plate.*

Strap Hanging. When the strap-hanging method is used, coupling plates (Fig. 171), fixed plates (Fig. 172), and sliding plates (Fig. 173) are bolted to strap-iron supports hung from above.

FIG. 171 *Coupling plate bolted to strap iron support.*

FIG. 172 *Fixed plate bolted to strap iron support.*

FIG. 173 *Sliding plate bolted to strap iron support.*

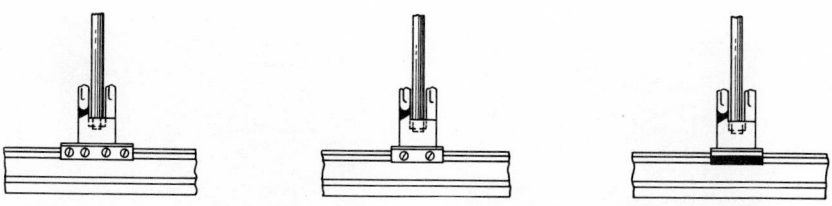

FIG. 174 *Messenger cable support hook. Left, with coupling plate; center, with fixed plate; right, with sliding plate.*

Rod Hanging. The rod-hanging method employs a messenger cable support hook in combination with a coupling plate, a fixed plate, or a sliding plate. Use of this type of hook and threaded hanger rods provides adjustment for leveling the run (Fig. 174).

Messenger Cable Suspension. Messenger cable suspension can be economically effected by the use of messenger cable support hooks with coupling plates, fixed plates, or sliding plates (Fig. 175). When suspended-type center feed-in boxes are required on messenger cable installations, a longer support hook should be used so flat messenger cables will clear the top of the feed-in box (Fig. 176).

257. Heavy-duty trolley bus way is available for power installations which require overhead trolley wires. In certain industries, as for example in automobile-body plants, overhead trolleys are required for supplying energy to portable tools. An example of heavy-duty trolley bus way is the TK Flex-A-Power system manufactured by the General Electric Co. The TK Flex-A-Power system consists of a steel housing containing bare channel-shaped copper conductors (Fig. 177). Power is tapped from the channel conductors by means of specially designed trolley collectors with or without provision for fuses in each branch wire. The housing may be obtained in curved (Fig. 178) as well as in standard straight sections. Typical installations are shown in Fig. 179. The trolley collectors can be inserted or removed at slide-out sections provided at intervals along the housing. This system provides an enclosed safety overhead trolley system.

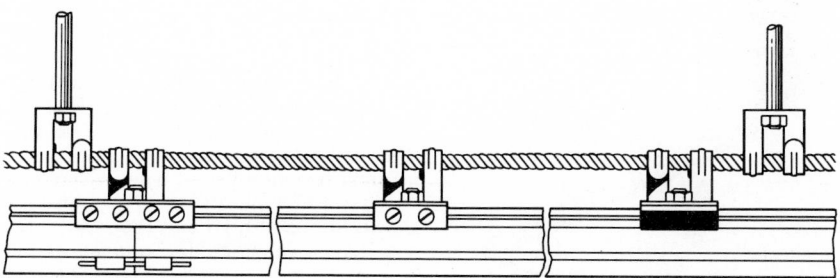

FIG. 175 *Messenger cable support. Left, with coupling plate; center, with fixed plate; right, with sliding plate. Note that the support is also used to support the cable.*

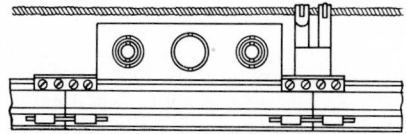

FIG. 176 *Messenger cable suspension of Type LTG bus way with suspended-type center feed-in box.*

 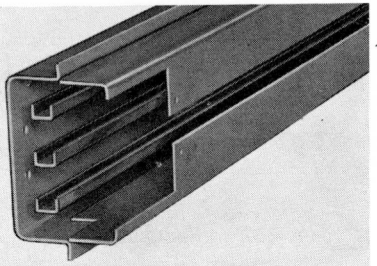

I. *Cross section.*   II. *Standard housing assembly.*

FIG. 177   *TK Flex-A-Power Housing. (General Electric Co.)*

There are three channel conductors which may be connected to any one of several different power-supply systems:

1. 110/220 volts, three wire, single phase.
2. 440 volts, two wire, single phase.
3. 220 volts, three wire, three phase.
4. 440 volts, three wire, three phase.
5. 550 volts, three wire, three phase.

The power-supply wires are brought to the channel conductors through feed-in boxes (Fig. 180), which may be located either at the end of a run or at any desired location along the top of a run. The capacity of the channel conductors is 100 amp, but the capacity of the trolley system may be made much greater than that by using several feed-in points.

The trolley runs on four or six wheels which bear on the flange on the sides of the overhead housing (Fig. 181, I and II). The current collectors are mounted on an insulating plate on the top of the trolley and are held against the underside of the copper buses by individual coil springs. There are two types of contacts which are made of copper and graphite impregnated with oil: (1) a double roller rated at 30 amp (Fig. 181, I) and (2) a contact shoe rated at 60 amp (Fig. 181, II). The trolley collectors are made in several different types to suit various types of applications. Two types are shown in Fig. 181, III and IV.

A lighter-weight trolley system rated at 50 amp made by the I-T-E/Imperial Corp., Bull Dog Electric Products Div., has an outlet-box-type trolley, which, in addition to supplying small tools, can be used to support lighting fixtures. The advantage claimed for this system is that the lights can be moved along with the tools. This is a

FIG. 178   *Curved sections of TK Flex-A-Power. (General Electric Co.)*

decided advantage in locations where normally only rough work requiring low values of illumination is performed. Then occasionally, when finer detailed work is set up, the lights can be moved closer together and the illumination built up to higher values for that section of the room. This is especially recommended for mercury-vapor lighting where the lamp wattage cannot be easily varied, since a given transformer will take only one size of lamp.

I. *Installation with unfused trolleys.*

II. *Installation with fused trolleys.*

FIG. 179   *Typical installations of TK Flex-A-Power.*   (*General Electric Co.*)

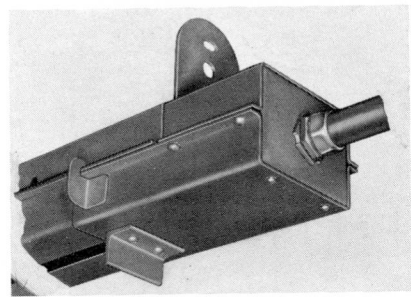 

I. *End feed-in box.*   II. *Center feed-in box.*

FIG. 180   *Feed-in boxes for TK Flex-A-Power.*   (*General Electric Co.*)

I. *Standard-duty roller-type trolley.*   II. *Heavy-duty shoe-type trolley.*

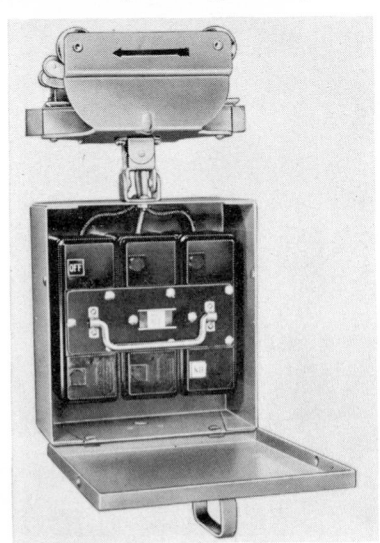 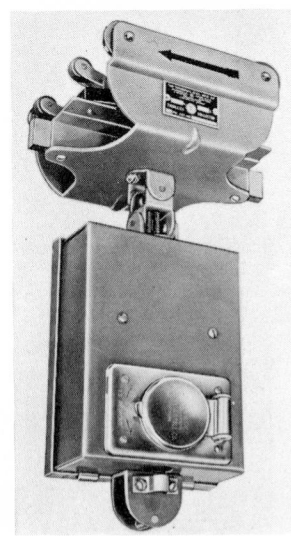

III. *Converti-Fuse trolley.*   IV. *Receptacle trolley.*

FIG. 181   *Trolleys for TK Flex-A-Power.*   (*General Electric Co.*)

CELLULAR-METAL-FLOOR-RACEWAY WIRING

258. Cellular-metal-floor raceways are formed by employing for the floor construction of the building structural members made of corrugated sheet steel. Seven types of cellular steel floor as made by the H. H. Robertson Co. of Pittsburgh, Pa., are shown in Fig. 182. Cross-sectional views of completed floors and their adaptation for the installation of the electric wiring system are given in Figs. 183 and 184.

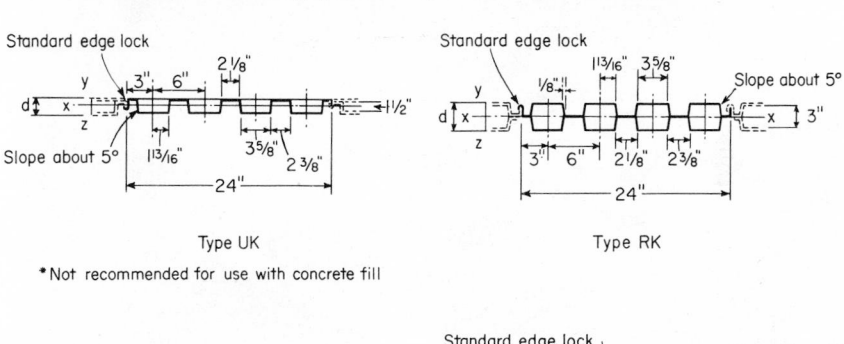

Type UK

*Not recommended for use with concrete fill

Type RK

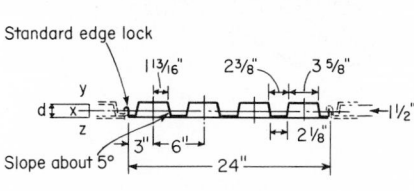

Type UKX

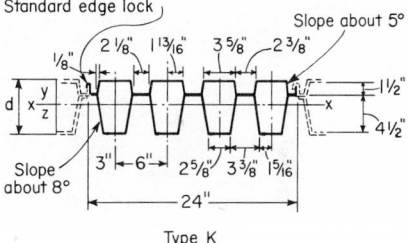

Type K

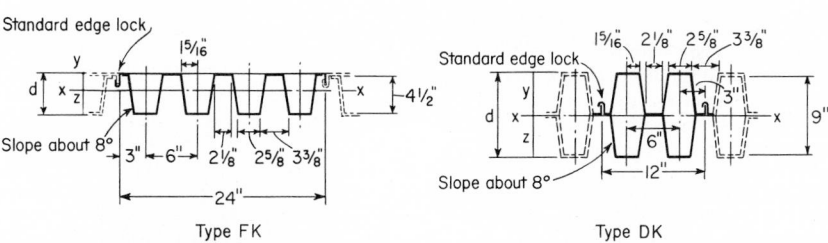

Type FK

*Not recommended for use with concrete fill

Type DK

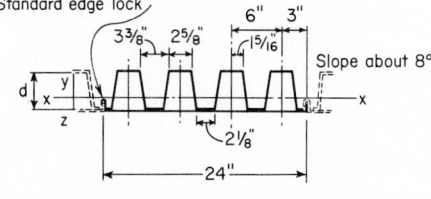

Type FKX

FIG. 182 *Types of cellular steel floors. (H. H. Robertson Co.)*

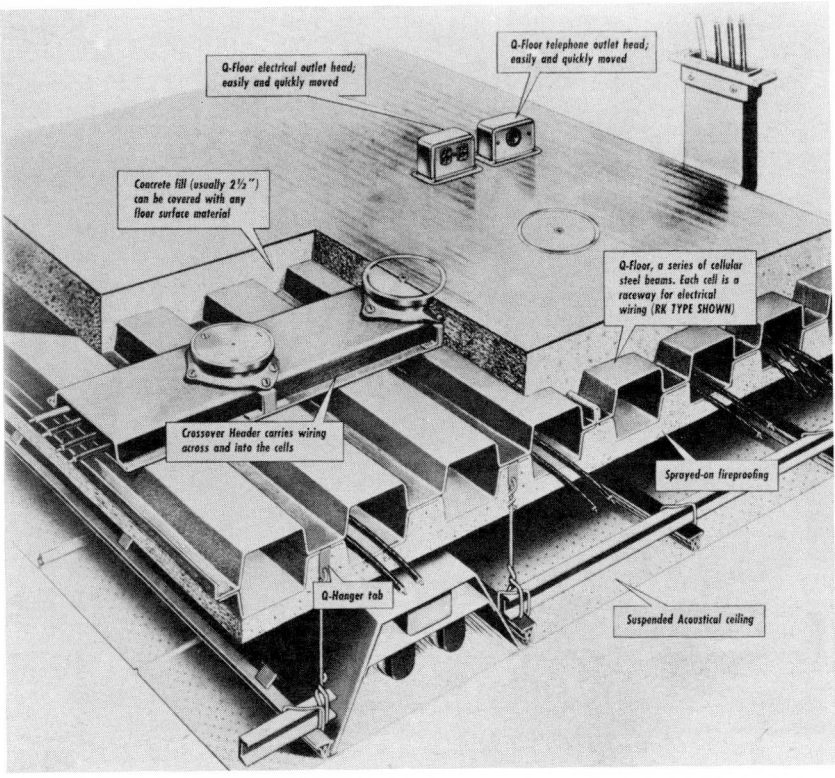

FIG. 183   *Model illustrating cellular-metal-floor raceway wiring.*   (*H. H. Robertson Co.*)

259. The cells which are not filled with concrete form the raceways for wiring and piping. In all the types the cells are 6 in. apart on centers, and the members are manufactured four cells wide with varying lengths to suit the span between beams. The cells are cross connected by headers formed over the beams in the space left between adjacent lengths of flooring. When headers connected to alternate cells are used, one raceway system can be formed for signal wires and another for power wires, with both systems kept entirely separate from each other. If any cells are used for piping, those cells must not be interconnected to the electrical raceway system.

260. In forming these floors, close cooperation is required between the structural and the electrical workmen. The structural men lay the floor members across the spans from beam to beam, fastening them to the beams and leaving about 4½ in. of space on top of the beams between the abutting ends of the floor members for formation of the header.

The raceway headers are formed by the electrical workmen in the space between members on top of the floor beams. A line of cells which is to form a raceway is interconnected at the ends of the sections by locating an access unit (Fig. 185) between the open ends of the aligning cells of adjacent sections.

The other cells are closed off with connecting units (Fig. 186) so as to form a continuous header across the beam to the raceway line of cells. Where one raceway system is to be built for power wiring and another for telephone wiring, the header for one system is built on one junction of floor beams and the header for the other system on another junction (Fig. 187). The wires for one system will pass through the lower portion of its cells under the header for the other system. The joints at the edges of the header units are sealed with a cold-flowing asphaltic compound.

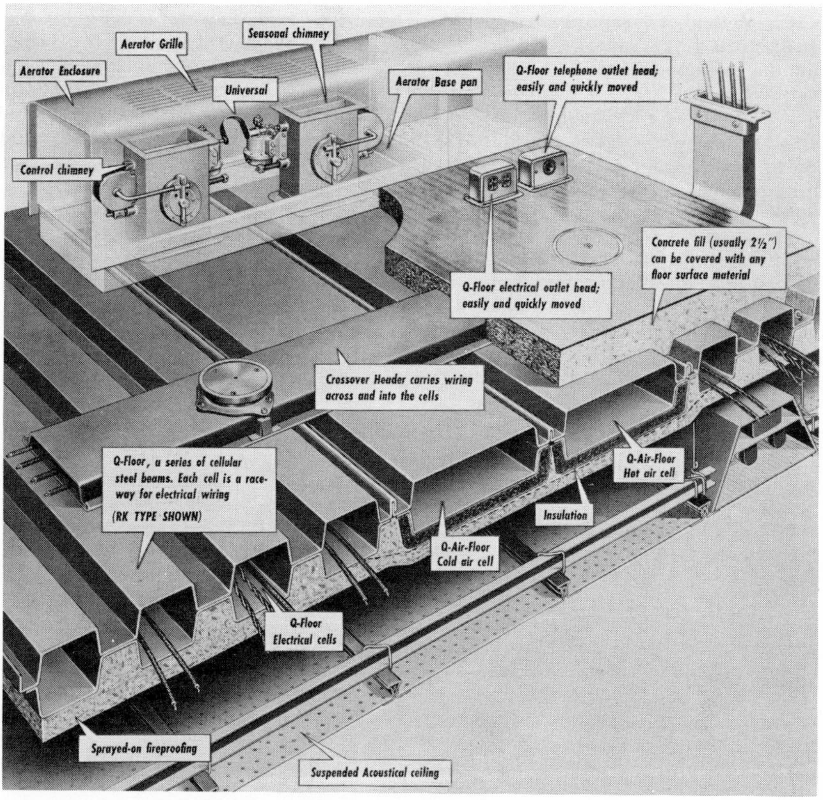

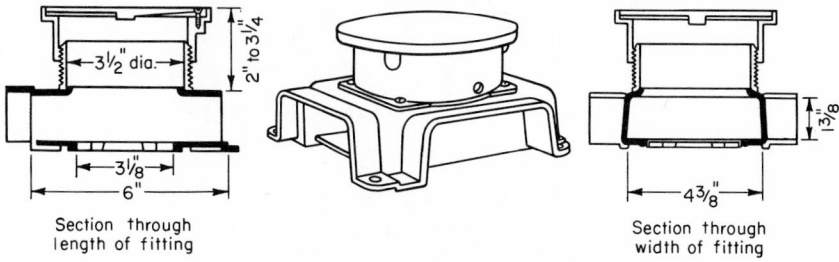

FIG. 184 *Model illustrating cellular metal floor with combination of electric, hot-air, and cold-air cells.* (H. H. Robertson Co.)

Section through
length of fitting

Section through
width of fitting

FIG. 185 *Access unit for cellular metal floors which have concrete fill.* (H. H. Robertson Co.)

261. The connection from a header to a panel board is made from special fittings as shown in Fig. 188. Connection to the header is made with an adapter (Fig. 189, II) to which is connected the vertical elbow (Fig. 189, I). Straight sections of duct 1 ft long (Fig. 189, IV) coupled together with couplings (Fig. 189, V) form the vertical run up the wall. The final section to the panel board is cut to length with a hack saw. The box connector (Fig. 189, III) holds the duct to the panel board. It requires an opening 1⅞ by 5¾ in. in the bottom of the panel-board box.

262. Method of Installing Floor Outlets. A hole of 1⅝ in. diameter is cut in the center of a cell with a saw-type drill (Fig. 190, I). A forming tool (Fig. 190, II) is turned into the hole to prepare the hole for reception of the outlet tap. For floors with a concrete fill of 2 to 3¼ in. a standard adjustable tap (Fig. 191, I) is then screwed into the hole. For fills of 1 to 2 in. a special tap is available. For fills of less than 1 in. a shallow tap (Fig. 191, IV) is set in the hole and held in place with three No. 12 self-tapping screws. Holes for the screws must be drilled in the cell with a No. 9 drill. The top of the standard tap can be adjusted in height to the floor level, and a blanking cover (Fig. 191, II) installed until after the floor is poured. When a floor outlet is installed, the blanking cover is removed, and an extension (Fig. 191, III) is screwed into the tap. The floor outlet is then screwed onto the extension, using a Warnock wrench

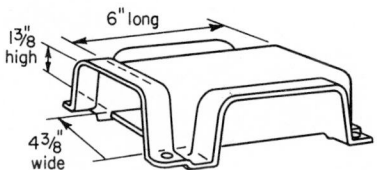

FIG. 186 *Connecting header unit.*

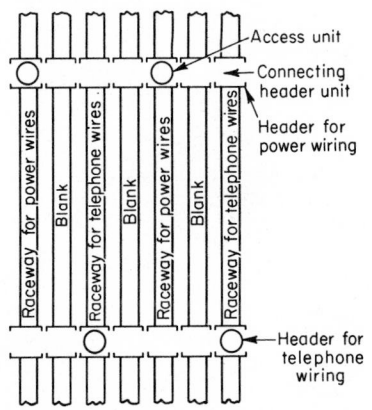

FIG. 187 *Method of forming separate headers for power and for telephone wiring.*

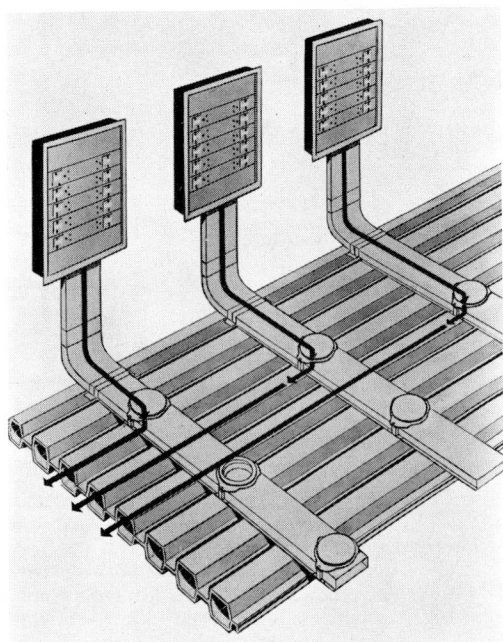

FIG. 188 *Connection of cellular-metal-floor headers to panel boards.* (*H. H. Robertson Co.*)

(Fig. 190, III) or other type of fabric wrench to avoid marring the fitting. With the shallow tap (Fig. 191, IV) the fitting screws onto the tap directly without the use of the extension. The complete outlet assembly is shown in Fig. 192. A duplex convenience outlet and an outlet for bringing out a telephone cord are shown in Fig. 193.

263. Cell markers should be located on the center of each cell near the opposite side of the room from the header for future location of cells, when outlets are not installed initially. The access units in the header will identify the cell locations at the header. A straight line between the center of an access unit and a cell marker will then identify the cell so that an outlet can be located accurately at any time in the future. Several types of cell markers are shown in Fig. 194. The double-slot screw (Fig. 194, I) can be used to identify power-wire cells, and the single-slot one (Fig. 194, II) to identify telephone-wire cells. In installing these markers (Fig. 195) a hole is drilled and tapped in the top of the cell for a 12-24 screw before the floor fill is laid. The brass marker with a headless screw is then fastened in place and adjusted in height to the level of the finished floor. The marker should then be grouted in place. After the floor has been poured and the finished floor covering laid, the headless screw is replaced with one of the grommeted brass screws (Fig. 194, I or II).

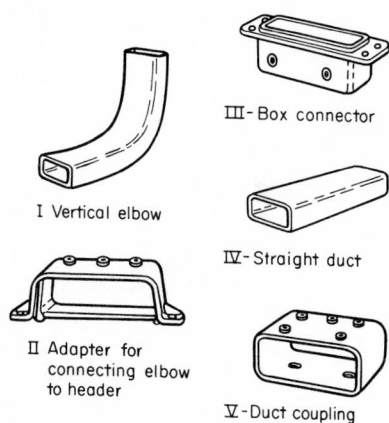

I Vertical elbow

II Adapter for connecting elbow to header

III- Box connector

IV- Straight duct

V- Duct coupling

FIG. 189   *Fittings for connecting cellular-metal-floor header to wall panel board.* (H. H. Robertson Co.)

264. Underside (ceiling) headers (Fig. 196) are generally used with Types FK inverted, UK inverted, RK, and UK floors of Fig. 182, because there is not sufficient room for the other headers in the shallow floor fill. Two sizes are available:

1. 2½ in. deep and 5 in. wide.
2. 4 in. deep and 6 in. wide.

A ceiling header mounted in the corner formed by the ceiling and wall so as to be as inconspicuous as possible is shown in Fig. 197. It is held in place with No. 12 self-

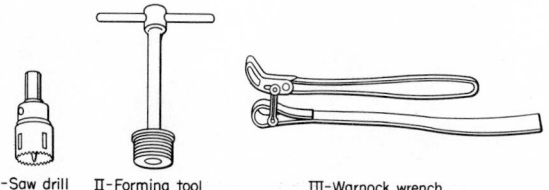

I-Saw drill   II-Forming tool   III-Warnock wrench

FIG. 190   *Tools for installing outlets in cellular-metal-floor raceways.* (H. H. Robertson Co.)

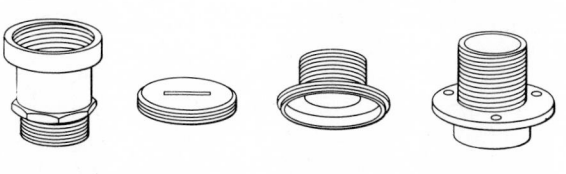

I-Adjustable top   II-Forming tool   III-Extension   IV-Shallow top

FIG. 191   *Fittings for cellular-metal-floor raceways.* (H. H. Robertson Co.)

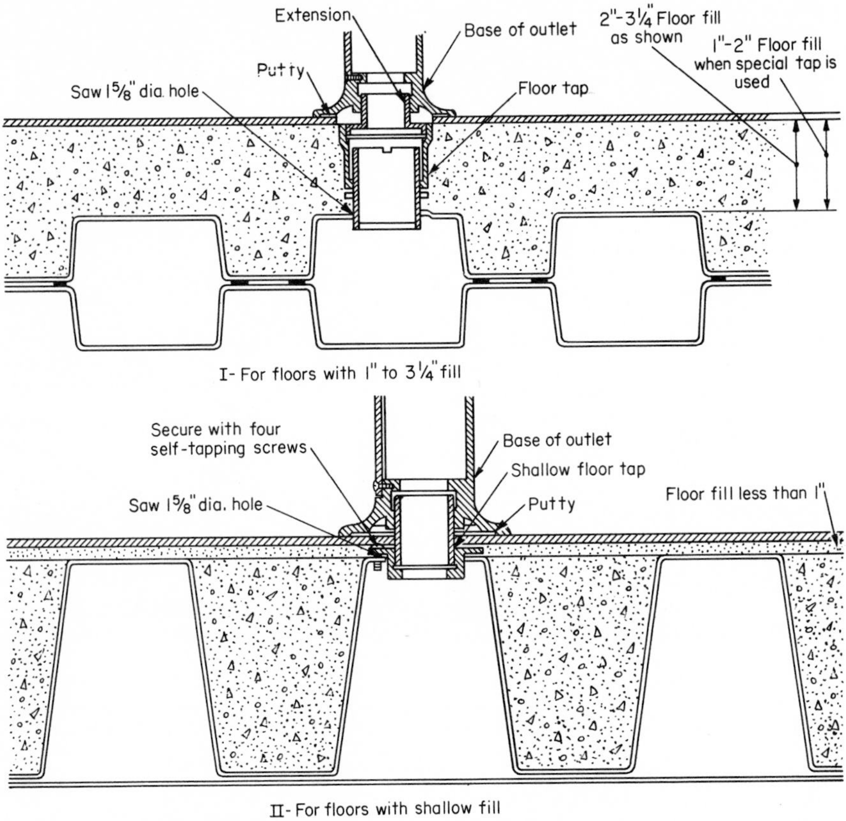

Extension

Base of outlet

2"-3¼" Floor fill as shown

1"-2" Floor fill when special tap is used

Saw 1⅝" dia. hole

Putty

Floor tap

I- For floors with 1" to 3¼" fill

Secure with four self-tapping screws

Base of outlet

Shallow floor tap

Saw 1⅝" dia. hole

Floor fill less than 1"

Putty

II- For floors with shallow fill

FIG. 192 *Assembly of floor outlets with cellular-metal-floor raceway. (H. H. Robertson Co.)*

I. *Duplex convenience outlet.*   II. *Telephone outlet.*

FIG. 193 *Outlets for use with cellular-metal-floor raceways. (H. H. Robertson Co.)*

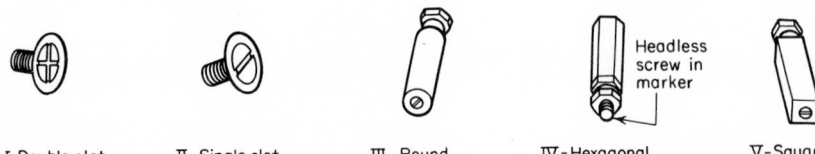

Headless screw in marker

I-Double slot marker screw

II- Single slot marker screw

III Round marker

IV-Hexagonal marker

V-Square marker

FIG. 194 *Markers for cellular-metal-floor raceways. (H. H. Robertson Co.)*

tapping screws which pass through holes drilled in the bottom of the raceways. Connection to a panel board is made with a special ell (Fig. 198, II) as shown in Fig. 199. Connection between the cells and the header is made by drilling a 2-in. hole in the cell to line up with the pilot opening in the header. A grommet (Fig. 198, I) with the lock nut removed is then inserted in the hole diagonally, as shown in Fig. 200. After the grommet has been adjusted to its proper position, the lock nut is screwed on and holds

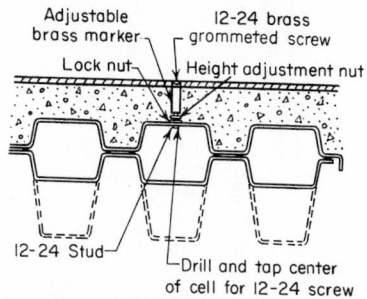

FIG. 195 *Detail showing cell marker.* (*H. H. Robertson Co.*)

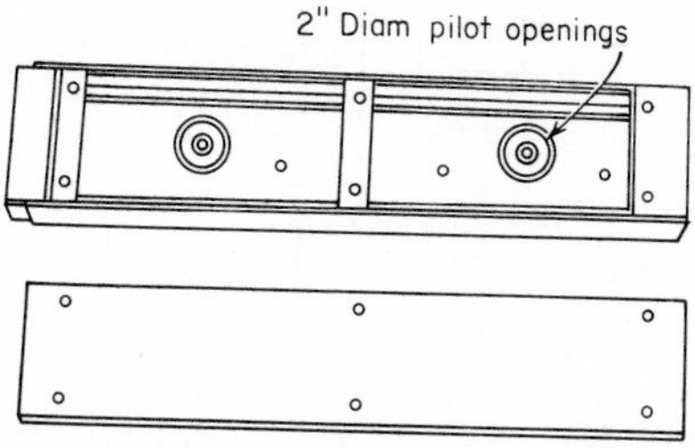

FIG. 196 *Underside header with cover removed.* (*H. H. Robertson Co.*)

the grommet firmly in place. At least two markers, as explained in Sec. **263,** should be located on top of the floor for each cell which does not have outlets installed initially.

265. Ceiling lighting fixtures can be hung and wired from cellular-metal-floor raceways as shown in Fig. 201. At I is shown a fixture-stud mounting using the stud illustrated in Fig. 202, I. The fixture stud is inserted through a 2-in. hole cut in the cell similar to the grommet assembly of Fig. 200. A mounting for fixtures which fasten on the cover of a 4-in. box is shown in Fig. 201, II. The box (Fig. 202, II) is held in place with a grommet. The knockouts in the box can be used for surface conduit wiring if desired. A conduit-hung fixture is supported from the cell by means of a hanger as shown in Fig. 201, III. The hanger (Fig. 202, III) is held in place with a lock nut in the same way as the grommet.

266. Trench Header Duct. A trench header duct can be used in lieu of the standard headers shown in Figs. 183 and 184. A typical trench header duct installation is shown in Fig. 203. It is run across the floor cells at right angles, and access to each cell is made through a grommet connection. The trench header duct shown in Fig. 203 contains barriers so that feeders, branch circuits, and telephone circuits are separated. The cover is flush with the floor, and flush screws secure the cover to the header duct. Each cover section is 3 to 6 ft long.

Trench header duct is made in widths of 9 to 36 in. and arranged to accept standard

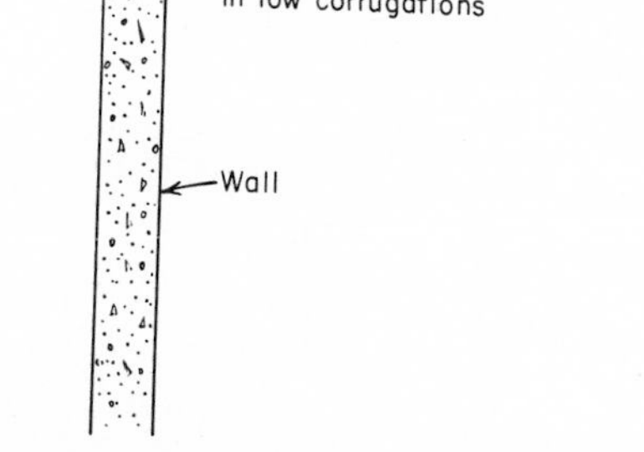

FIG. 197 *Section showing location and mounting of underside header.* (*H. H. Robertson Co.*)

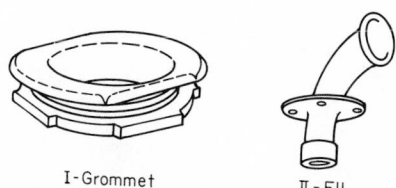

I - Grommet   II - Ell

FIG. 198 *Fittings for underside header.* (*H. H. Robertson Co.*)

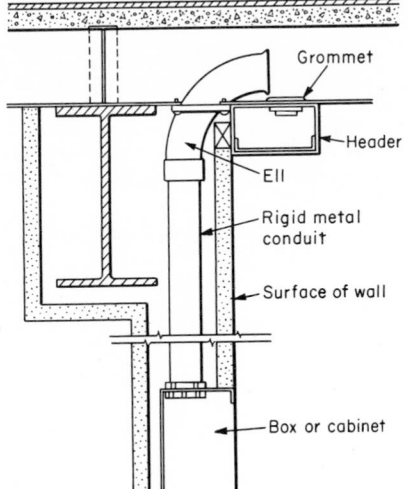

FIG. 199 *Section showing a method of connecting between underside header and panel.* (*H. H. Robertson Co.*)

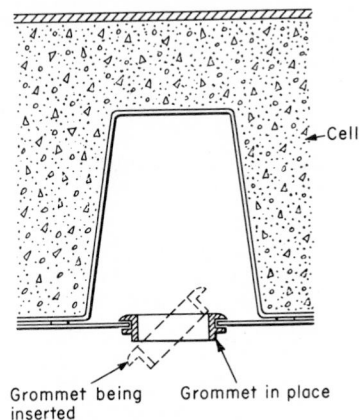

FIG. 200 *Showing method of inserting grommet into hole in cell.* (*H. H. Robertson Co.*)

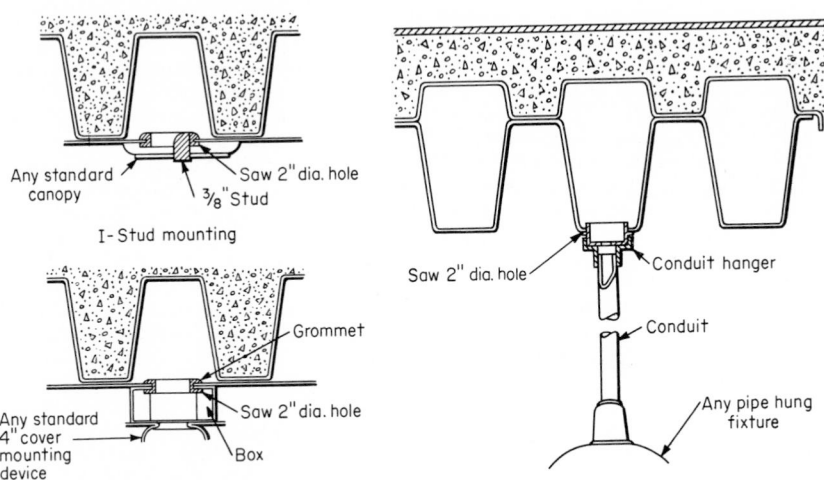

I- Stud mounting

II - Outlet box mounting

III - Conduit hung mounting

FIG. 201 *Methods of mounting ceiling fixtures from cellular-metal-floor raceways.* (*H. H. Robertson Co.*)

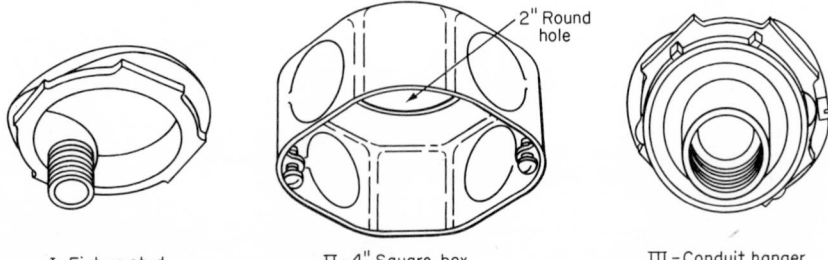

I - Fixture stud

II - 4" Square box

III - Conduit hanger

FIG. 202 *Fittings for ceiling fixtures.* (*H. H. Robertson Co.*)

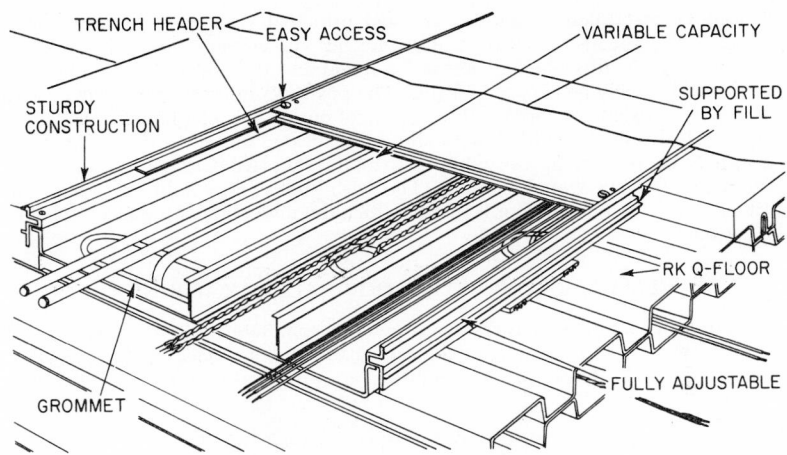

TRENCH HEADER — EASY ACCESS — VARIABLE CAPACITY

STURDY CONSTRUCTION

SUPPORTED BY FILL

RK Q-FLOOR

FULLY ADJUSTABLE

GROMMET

FIG. 203   *Trench header duct used for cellular-metal-floor raceway.*   (*H. H. Robertson Co.*)

floor tiles or similar floor coverings. This header system makes a neat installation, and access openings to the header duct are practically unnoticeable after the covers are installed. One or more cover sections can be easily removed when access to the trench duct or floor cells is necessary.

267. The cellular raceways are wired by fishing the wires from the access units to the outlets. No conductor larger than No. 1/0 may be installed except by special permission. The number of conductors in a cell is not limited as long as the total cross-sectional area of the conductors does not exceed 40 per cent of the internal area of the header or cell. All splices and taps must be made in the trench header duct or at junction boxes. The internal areas of the raceways are as follows:

	Entire area, sq in.	40 per cent
K cells.........................	20.25	8.10
RK cells.......................	11.25	4.50
FK, FK inverted cells..........	14.62	5.85
UK, UK inverted cells..........	5.62	2.24
DK cells.......................	29.24	11.70

All junction boxes and inserts must be leveled to the floor grade and sealed against the entrance of water. They must be made of metal and so installed that they will be electrically continuous with the raceway. In cutting a cell and in setting inserts great care must be exercised so that chips or other dirt will not fall into the raceway. Only tools which are specially designed so that they will not enter the cell and injure the conductors should be used.

The Code requires that when an outlet is discontinued, the conductors supplying it must be removed from the raceway, and that connections to cabinets and extensions from cells to outlets unless made by approved fittings must be made by means of rigid or flexible metal conduit.

268. Cellular-metal-floor-raceway wiring is not allowed in any hazardous location, or where subject to corrosive vapors. It is not allowed in commercial garages except for supplying ceiling outlets or extensions to the area below the floor but not above. Any cell or header that is used for electrical conductors may not be used for any other service, such as steam, water, air, gas, and drainage.

269. Cellular-metal-floor raceways are used principally for office buildings where the needs of the tenants for wiring outlets are not known very definitely in advance and where a high quality of adequacy and convenience of outlets and interior appearance is desired, having no exposed wiring. The position of the raceways may be varied in 6-in. increments, and a very flexible system of outlets for telephones, business machines, and desk lamps provided, with all outlets located under the desks out of sight. The cost may be lower than would be incurred if a standard floor with a large number of underfloor raceways were installed. The wiring for ceiling lighting outlets is also simplified where the type of floor is that in which the underside of the raceways serves as the ceiling.

CELLULAR-CONCRETE-FLOOR-RACEWAY WIRING

270. Cellular-concrete-floor raceways provide a complete underfloor electrical-distribution system. For this system the floor is constructed of precast reinforced-concrete members (Fig. 204). These precast members are provided with hollow voids which form smooth, round cells. These cells form raceways for the electrical wires. Con-

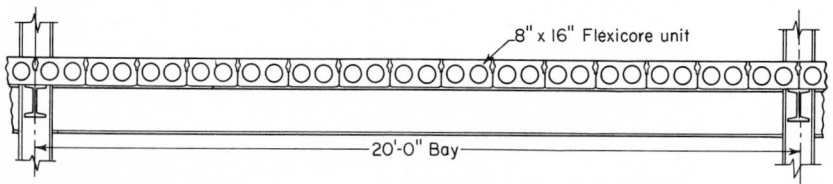

8" x 16" Flexicore unit

20'-0" Bay

FIG. 204 *Typical cross section of a cellular-concrete floor.* (*The Flexicore Co., Inc.*)

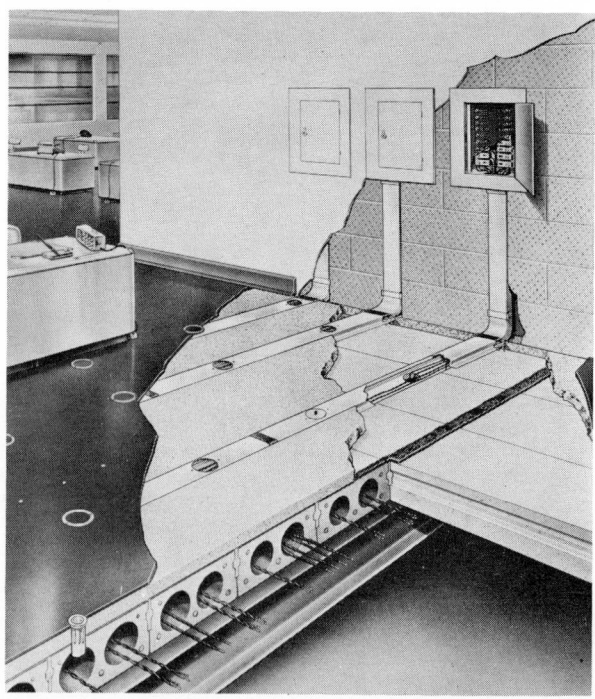

FIG. 205 *Electrical distribution with cellular-concrete-floor-raceway wiring.* (*The Flexicore Co., Inc.*)

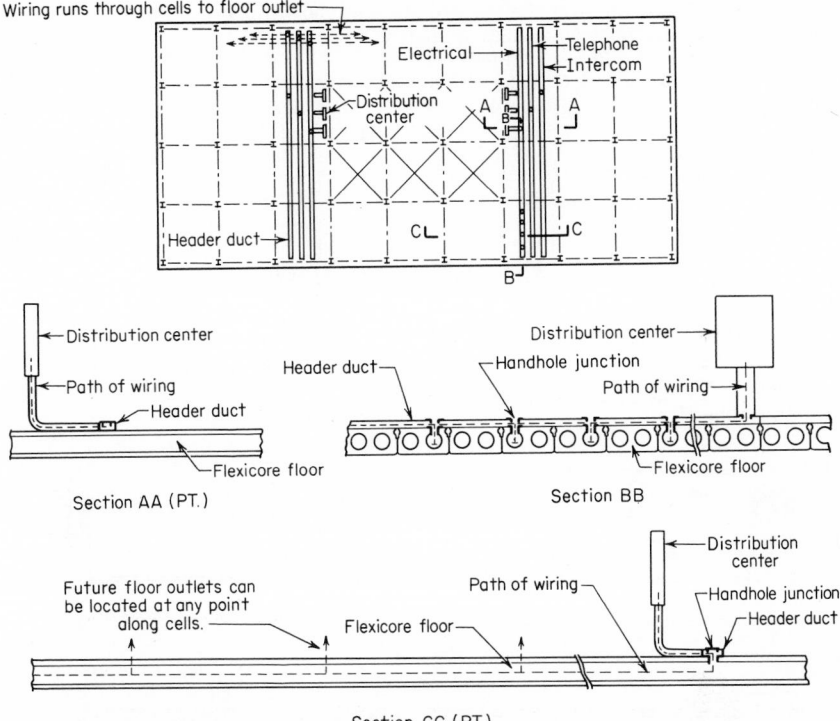

FIG. 206 *General principles of electrical distribution by means of cellular-concrete-floor raceways. (The Flexicore Co., Inc.)*

nections to the cells from a distribution center are made by means of metal header ducts which are run horizontally across the precast slabs and embedded in the concrete fill over the slabs. Connection from these headers to the cells is made through handhole metal junction boxes. An outlet can be located at any point along a cell. An opening into the cell at the desired point is formed by drilling a hole through the concrete floor slab. The hole is then fitted with the proper outlet fitting, and the wires fished from a handhole junction box to the outlet.

271. The National Electrical Code makes the following definitions: For the purpose of this article "precast cellular concrete floor raceways" shall be defined as the hollow spaces in floors constructed of precast cellular concrete slabs, together with suitable metal fittings designed to provide access to the floor cells in an approved manner. A "cell" shall be defined as a single, enclosed tubular space in a floor made of precast cellular concrete slabs, the direction of the cell being parallel to the direction of the floor member. Header ducts shall be defined as transverse metal raceways for electrical conductors, furnishing access to predetermined cells of a precast cellular concrete floor, thus providing for the installation of electrical conductors from a distribution center to the floor cells.

271A. Use of Cellular-concrete-floor-raceway Wiring (National Electrical Code). Conductors shall not be installed in precast cellular concrete floor raceways (1) where subject to corrosive vapor; (2) in hazardous locations; or (3) in commercial garages, except for supplying ceiling outlets or extensions to the area below the floor but not above. No electrical conductors shall be installed in any cell or header which contains a pipe for steam, water, air, gas, drainage, or any service other than electrical.

272. Electrical distribution by means of cellular-concrete-floor raceways is illustrated through Figs. 205, 206, and 207.

The precast slabs are available in two sizes as shown in Fig. 208. Flexicore Hi-stress Deck is available in five sizes as shown in Fig. 209.

Header ducts are available in different sizes.

The National Electrical Code makes the following specifications for header ducts: The header duct shall be installed in a straight line, at right angles to the cells. The header duct shall be mechanically secured to the top of the precast cellular concrete

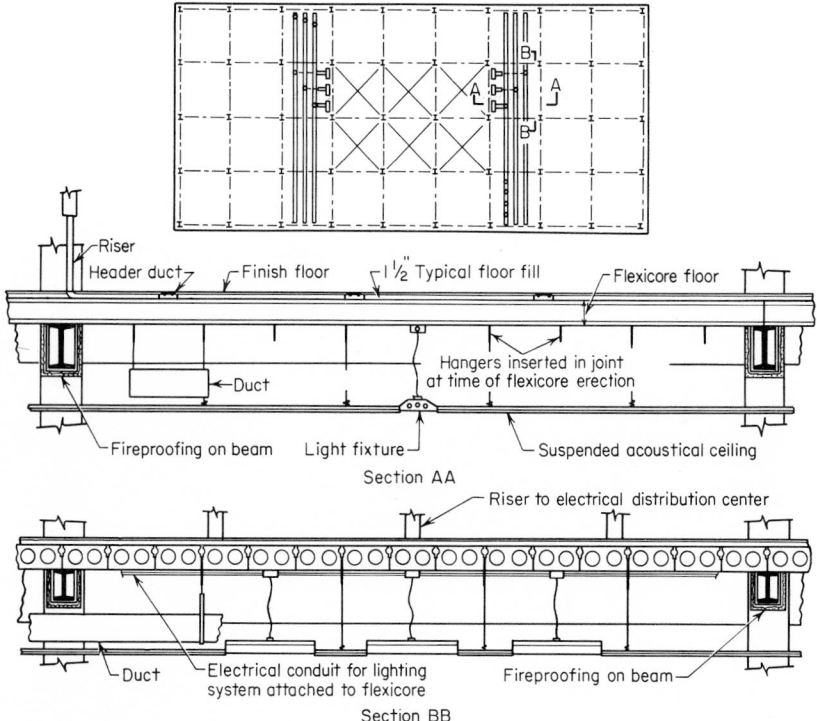

FIG. 207   *Some details of installation of cellular-concrete-floor-raceway wiring system.* (*The Flexicore Co., Inc.*)

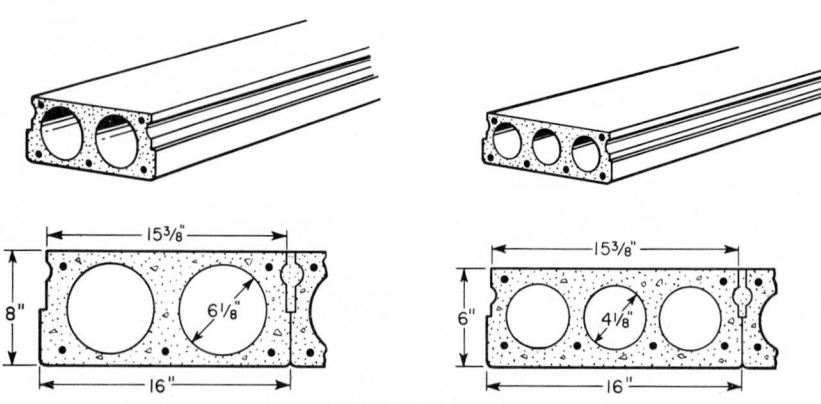

FIG. 208   *Cellular-concrete floor slabs.* (*The Flexicore Co., Inc.*)

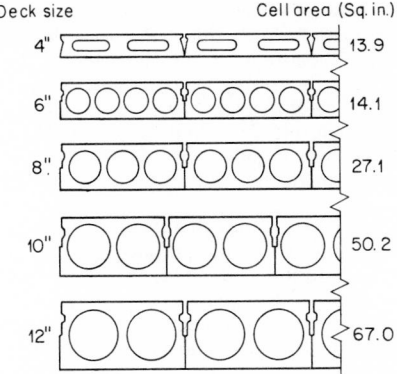

FIG. 209 *Flexicore Hi-stress Deck.* (*The Flexicore Co., Inc.*)

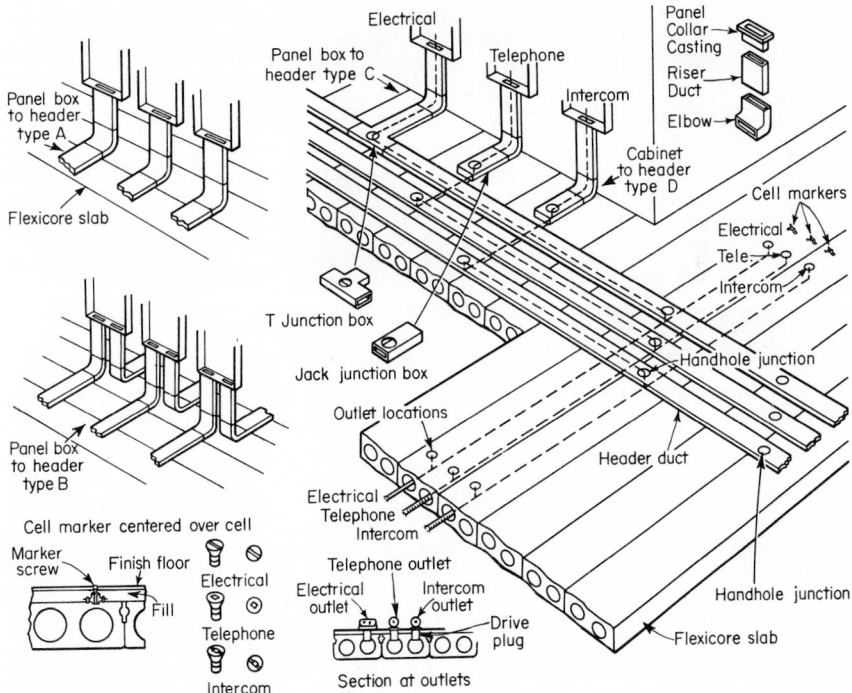

FIG. 210 *Details of installation of cellular-concrete-floor raceway.* (*The Flexicore Co., Inc.*)

floor and the top surface leveled to the floor finish. The end joints shall be closed by metallic closure fittings and sealed against the penetration of water. The header duct shall be electrically continuous throughout its entire length and shall be electrically bonded to the enclosure of the distribution center.

The method of making connection to cabinets or other enclosures is shown in Figs. 205, 206, and 210.

When the panel box or cabinet is located at right angles to the header (Types A and B, Fig. 210), the connection is made by an elbow and riser duct to the panel box. This is simply a continuation of the header up to the panel box.

When the panel box is parallel to the header (Type C), the connection is made with a T junction box, a short piece of header duct, an elbow, and a riser.

When parallel to the header, telephone and intercom cabinets are usually connected to the header as shown by Type D. The wire drops from the header through a handhole junction into a cell, through the cell, up through a jack junction box and then to the cabinet.

The National Electrical Code requires that these connections be made by means of metallic duct and fittings approved for the purpose.

Handhole junction boxes and their relation to the header duct and concrete cells are shown in Fig. 210. The National Electrical Code requires that junction boxes shall be leveled to the floor grade and sealed against the entrance of water. Junction boxes shall be of metal and shall be mechanically and electrically continuous with the header ducts.

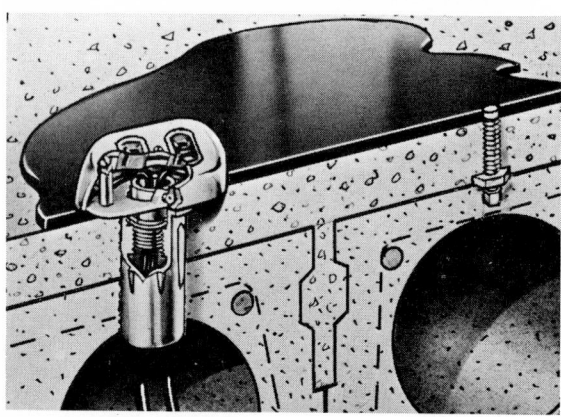

FIG. 211 *Installation of outlets and markers.* (*The Flexicore Co., Inc.*)

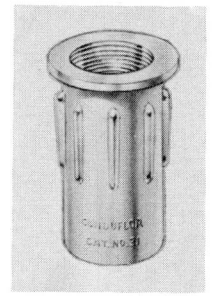

FIG. 212   *Outlet drive plug.* (*The Flexicore Co., Inc.*)

Markers (Figs. 210 and 211) are installed along each cell for the determination of its location and to mark the location of all hidden access points between a header and a cell which is intended for future use. These markers must extend through the floor covering, and a suitable number must be used for location of the cells and to provide for system identification.

273. High-capacity System. The system shown in Fig. 214 is designed to handle 82 100-pair plus 137 25-pair telephone cables, or the equivalent in other sizes. The cables feed from the panel through the channel slab, transversely through the 24-in. trench header duct, then down into the cells of the Flexicore deck. Wiring can run either direction to telephone floor outlets located at any point along the cells. Every second cell is assigned to telephones, providing lines of availability only 16 in. apart.

Electrical distribution is handled through the high-capacity trench header duct system shown. Many variations of both systems are possible.

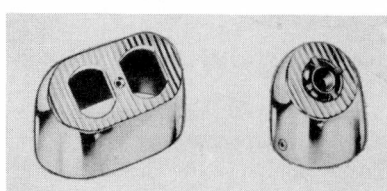

FIG. 213 *Outlet fittings. Left, electric-outlet fitting; right, telephone or intercom outlet.* (*The Flexicore Co., Inc.*)

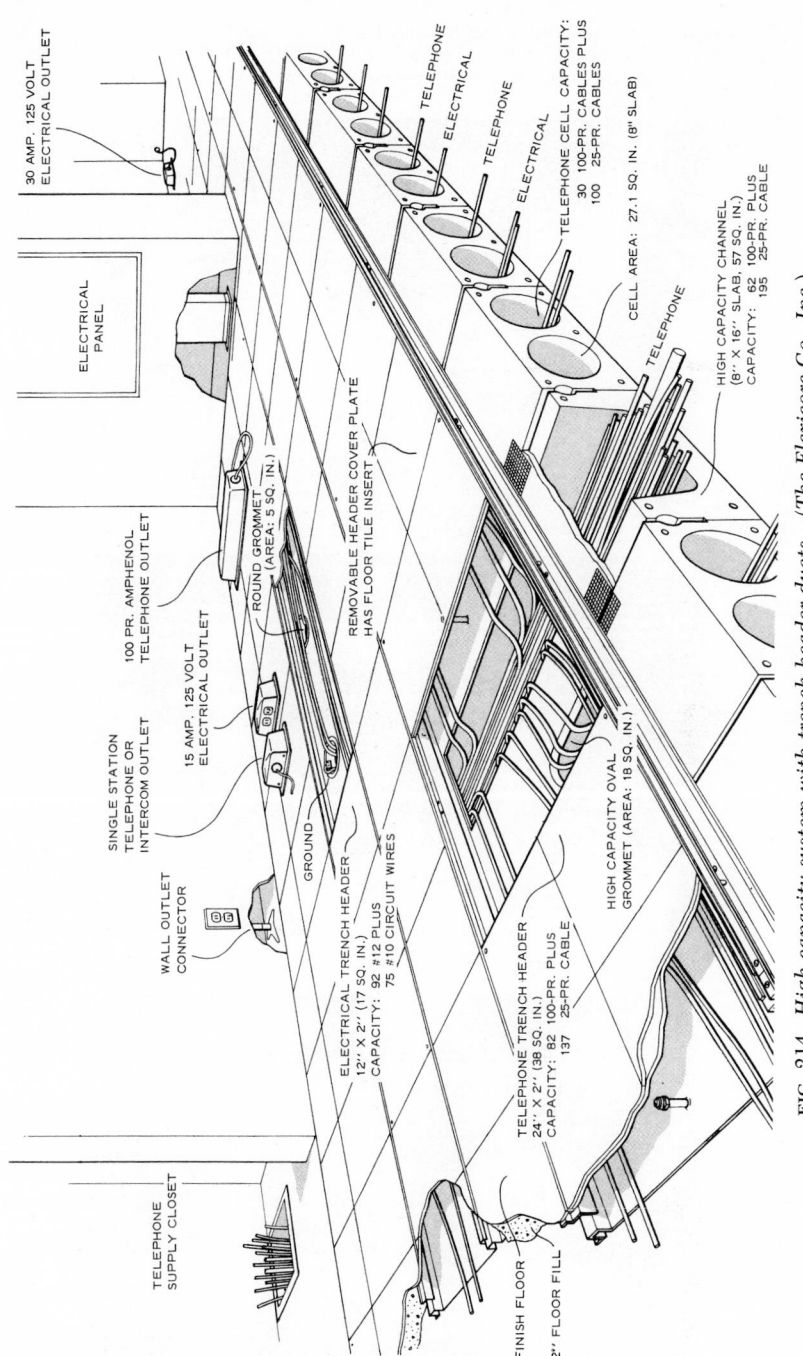

FIG. 214 *High-capacity system with trench header ducts.* (*The Flexicore Co., Inc.*)

30 AMP. 125 VOLT
ELECTRICAL OUTLET

ELECTRICAL
PANEL

TELEPHONE
ELECTRICAL
TELEPHONE
ELECTRICAL
TELEPHONE
ELECTRICAL

TELEPHONE CELL CAPACITY:
30 100-PR. CABLES PLUS
100 25-PR. CABLES

CELL AREA: 27.1 SQ. IN. (8" SLAB)

TELEPHONE

HIGH CAPACITY CHANNEL
(8" X 16" SLAB, 57 SQ. IN.)
CAPACITY: 62 100-PR. PLUS
195 25-PR. CABLE

ROUND GROMMET
(AREA: 5 SQ. IN.)

REMOVABLE HEADER COVER PLATE
HAS FLOOR TILE INSERT

SINGLE STATION
TELEPHONE OR
INTERCOM OUTLET

100 PR. AMPHENOL
TELEPHONE OUTLET

15 AMP. 125 VOLT
ELECTRICAL OUTLET

WALL OUTLET
CONNECTOR

GROUND

ELECTRICAL TRENCH HEADER
12" X 2" (17 SQ. IN.)
CAPACITY: 92 #12 PLUS
75 #10 CIRCUIT WIRES

TELEPHONE TRENCH HEADER
24" X 2" (38 SQ. IN.)
CAPACITY: 82 100-PR. PLUS
137 25-PR. CABLE

HIGH CAPACITY OVAL
GROMMET (AREA: 18 SQ. IN.)

FINISH FLOOR

2" FLOOR FILL

TELEPHONE
SUPPLY CLOSET

9–137

274. Inserts for the location of outlets can be located at any point along a cell. Typical outlets and their installation are shown in Figs. 210, 211, 212, and 213. The procedure in installing an outlet is as follows:

1. Mark location of outlet. Use cell markers to line up center of cell.

2. Drill hole for outlet using 1⅞-in. core bit.

3. Drive in outlet drive plug.

4. Screw in floor outlet nipple.

5. Fish wire to outlet location.

(*The Flexicore Co., Inc.*)

6. Install outlet box. Floor outlets can be installed at any time during the life of the building.

275. The National Electrical Code requirements for inserts are as follows: Inserts shall be leveled to the floor grade and sealed against the entrance of water. Inserts shall be of metal and shall be fitted with receptacles of the grounded type. A ground conductor shall connect the insert receptacles to a positive ground connection provided on the header duct. In cutting through the cell wall for setting inserts or other purposes (such as providing access openings between header duct and cells) chips and other dirt shall not be allowed to fall into the raceway, and the tool used shall be so designed as to prevent the tool from entering the cell and injuring the conductors.

276. Discontinued Outlets (National Electrical Code). When an outlet is discontinued, the conductors supplying the outlet shall be removed from the header and cell.

277. Conductors (National Electrical Code). No conductor larger than No. 0 shall be installed, except by special permission.

The total cross-sectional area of all conductors in a header or in an individual cell shall not exceed 40 per cent of the interior cross-sectional area of the header or cell, except that if the raceway contains only Type AC metal-clad cable or nonmetallic-sheathed cable or both, this limitation shall not apply.

Splices and taps shall be made only in header duct access units or junction boxes.

WIRING WITH MULTIOUTLET ASSEMBLIES

278. Multioutlet assemblies consist of a metallic or nonmetallic assembly with convenience outlets built in every few inches. In one type made by the Wiremold Co. (Fig. 215) the outlets may be spaced as desired along the raceway and connected by wires laid in the raceway. In another type (Fig. 216) the outlets are built in at fixed intervals and connected by copper strips which terminate in terminal screws at each end of each length of raceway. This type is made in three styles according to the position in which it is to be used: (1) the chair-rail style for flat-surface mounting, (2) the baseboard-cap style for mounting on the top of baseboards or in corners of mantels and cabinets, and (3) the baseboard-insert style for recessing in the baseboard or in a plastered wall. Blank sections through which standard-type wires may be run to join plug-in sections are available for use behind radiators or for other inaccessible places where the expensive plug-in strip is not needed. Multioutlet assemblies are used to provide adequate plug receptacles for the utmost convenience in the use of appliances, in dwelling-type use and for industrial and commercial applications.

The National Electrical Code specifications for the use of multioutlet assemblies are as follows: Multioutlet assembly may be used in dry locations. It shall not be used (1) where concealed, except that the back and sides of metal multioutlet assembly may be surrounded by the building finish and nonmetallic multioutlet assembly may be recessed in the baseboard; (2) where subject to severe physical damage unless approved for the purpose; (3) where the voltage is 300 volts or more between conductors unless assembly is of metal having a thickness of not less than 0.040 in.; (4) where subject to corrosive vapors; (5) in hoistways; or (6) in any hazardous locations. Metal multioutlet assembly may be extended through (not run within) dry partitions providing arrangements are made for removing the cap or cover on all exposed portions and no outlet falls within the partitions.

279. Various ways of mounting the chair-rail style on plastered walls are shown in Fig. 217. Toggle bolts are used except where a wood strip is available, as in III, when wood screws can be used. The chair-rail style is intended for mounting on flat surfaces at a considerable height above the baseboard. The curved surfaces on the top and bottom give the installation a neat appearance.

280. The baseboard-cap type has a flat surface on one edge and is curved on the other edge. It is used as illustrated in Fig. 218, where there is a corner against which the flat edge can be placed. The curved edge gives a finished appearance to the corner. In this type of mounting, there is usually a wood background so that wood screws can be used for fastening.

281. The baseboard type is set into the wall so that the surface of the strip is flush with the wall surface. When finished buildings are wired with this type, the molding on top of the baseboard is removed, the plug-in strip is placed on top of the baseboard,

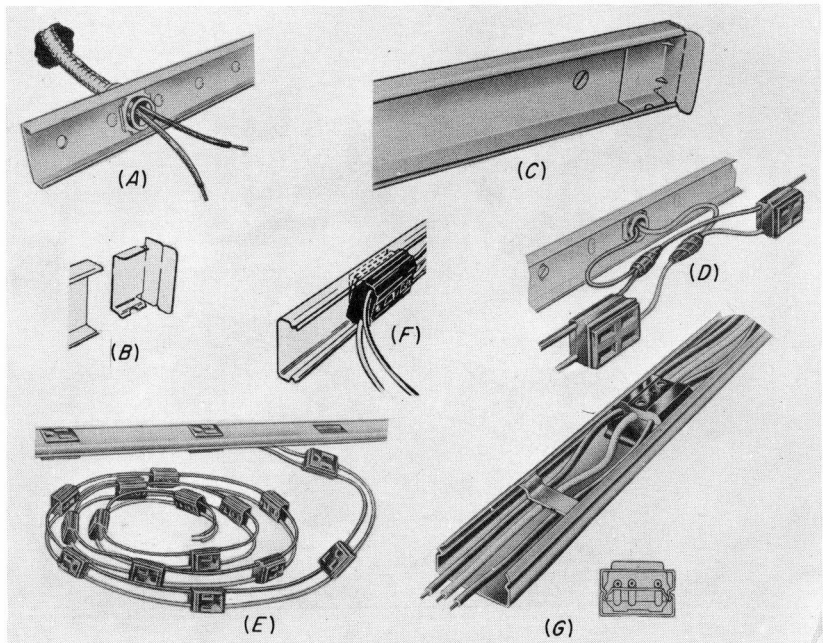

FIG. 215 *Installation of multioutlet assembly of the Plugmold-Snapicoil type. (1) Remove knockout (from inside out) for feed connection and fasten ½-in. connector into base with a lock nut A; no special fittings are needed; there is plenty of room to spin the lock nut. (2) At the end of run, install No. 2010B blank-end fitting in the base, B and C. (3) Mount base to surface through screw piercings or knockouts, using No. 6 flathead screws. (Some types of surfaces require other methods of fastening.) (4) Lay out Snapicoil, and cover sections to avoid having outlet directly in a corner or over a feed connection. (5) Splice feed wires onto Snapicoil conductors D. Note: In a three-wire harness, black wire with yellow lettering should be used for the switch leg. (6) Snap Snapicoil receptacles into 2000C Holecut cover, E and F; wire clip can be used in cover G or base to keep wires inside raceways. (7) Snap cover, complete with receptacles, into base. (The Wiremold Co.)*

and the molding is placed against the plug-in strip (Fig. 219, III). For new installations a channel can be left in tile, glass, or marble surfaces as shown in Fig. 219, I and II, or the plaster can be channeled as shown in Fig. 219, IV.

282. Plug-in strip is made in various lengths from 6 in. to 9 ft. The lengths are joined together as shown in Fig. 220. Copper links connect the terminal screws on two adjoining lengths of plug-in strip (Fig. 220, I). Then insulating plates are placed over the terminals (Fig. 220, II), and the joint is covered with a coupling of the same exterior finish as the plug-in strip.

283. The method of bringing in the supply circuit is shown in Fig. 221. Junction boxes are available for either metal-clad cable or rigid conduit. The junction box has a hub in the back with a setscrew for clamping metal-clad cable or threaded for ½-in. conduit connection (Fig. 221, I). The circuit wires are stripped as shown, and two short lengths of building wire are spliced to them so that the circuit will feed both ways from the junction box. The junction box is then placed against the wall, and the wires are connected to the terminal screws in the adjoining plug-in strips (Fig. 221, II). The middle section of the junction box is closed by means of a cover, held in place by

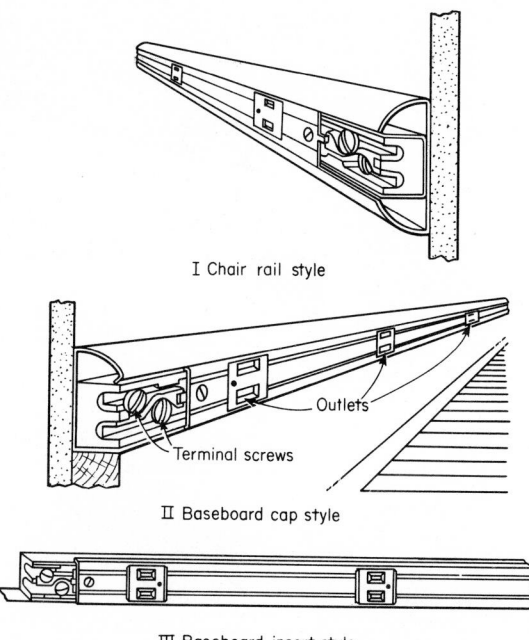

I Chair rail style

II Baseboard cap style

Outlets

Terminal screws

III Baseboard insert style

FIG. 216 *Plug-in strip.* (*National Electric Div., H. K. Porter Co., Inc.*)

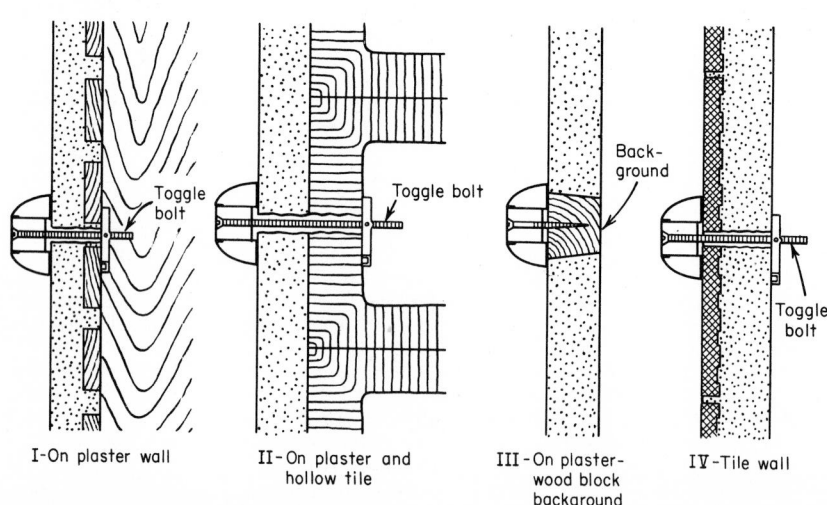

Toggle bolt

Toggle bolt

Back-ground

Toggle bolt

I-On plaster wall

II-On plaster and hollow tile

III-On plaster-wood block background

IV-Tile wall

FIG. 217 *Methods of mounting chair-rail style of plug-in strip.* (*National Electric Div., H. K. Porter Co., Inc.*)

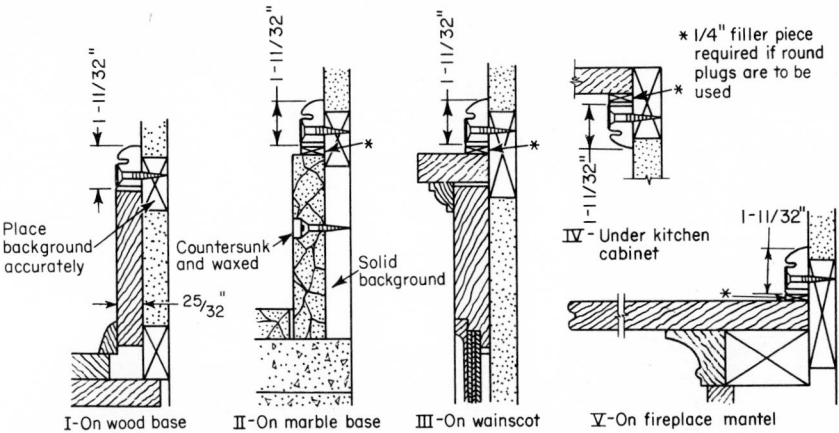

FIG. 218   *Methods of mounting baseboard-cap style of plug-in strip.* (*National Electric Div., H. K. Porter Co., Inc.*)

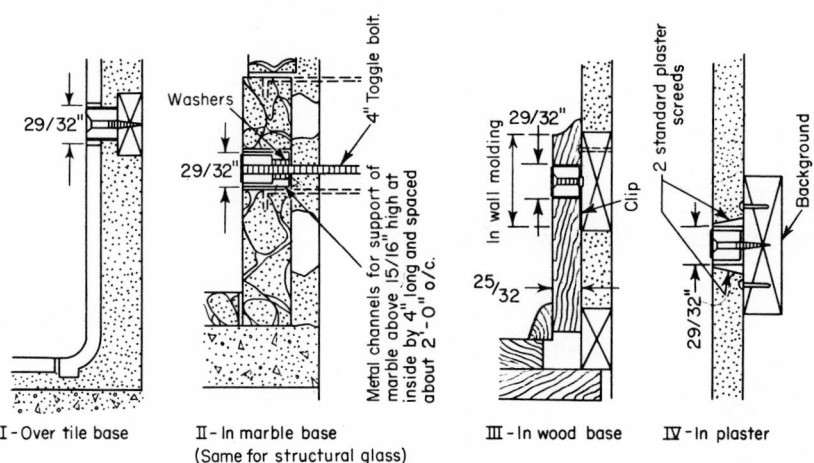

FIG. 219   *Methods of mounting baseboard-insert style of plug-in strip.* (*National Electric Div., H. K. Porter Co., Inc.*)

two screws.   Over each pair of terminals an insulating plate is placed and then covered with a coupling plate.

284. Heavier Duty Multioutlet Assemblies.   The types of multioutlet assemblies discussed in the previous sections are of the light-duty type.   Heavier duty multioutlet assemblies are available in the following types:

1. Two-wire with grounding strip for grounding of equipment.
2. 20-amp receptacle type.
3. 30-amp receptacle type.
4. 50-amp receptacle type.
5. Combination raceway and multioutlet assembly (Fig. 222).

Baseboard types of combination multioutlet assembly and surface raceway are available.   Two types are shown in Figs. 223 and 224.

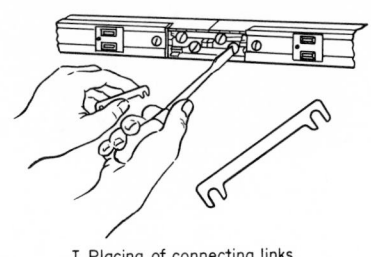

I Placing of connecting links

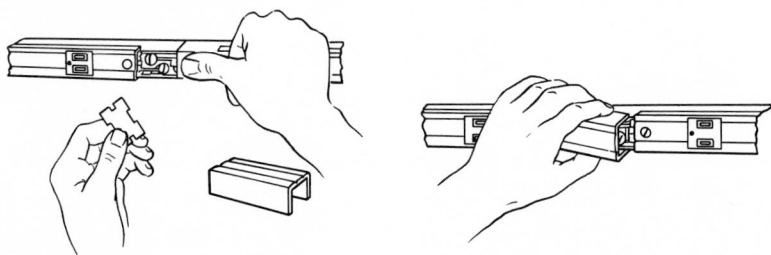

II Placing of insulating plates   III Covering joint with joiner coupling

FIG. 220   *Method of coupling plug-in strips together.* (*National Electric Div., H. K. Porter Co., Inc.*)

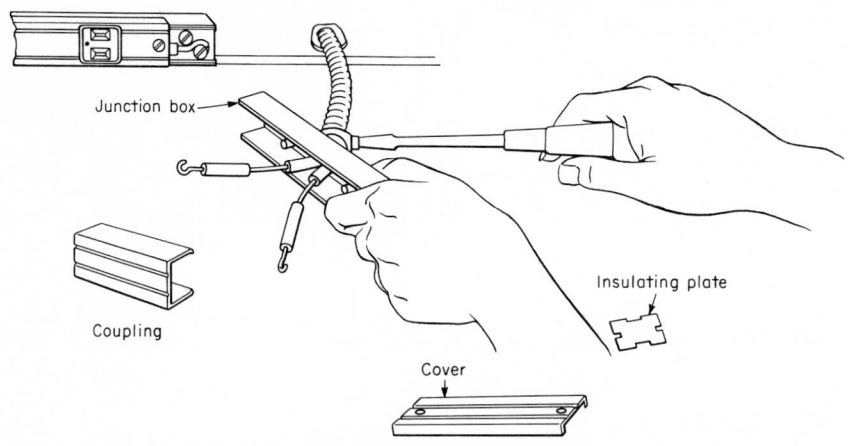

Junction box

Insulating plate

Coupling

Cover

I - Connecting cable to junction box

Splices

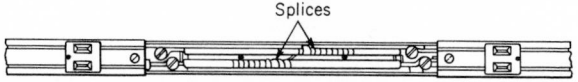

II - With splices and wiring completed

FIG. 221   *Method of bringing supply circuit into plug-in strip.* (*National Electric Div., H. K. Porter Co., Inc.*)

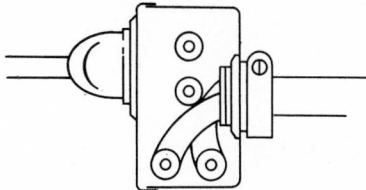

FIG. 222 *Combination raceway and multioutlet assembly. Up to three No. 12 Type TW electric conductors can be installed in the raceway space located beneath the standard plug-in strip assembly. The additional conductors may be wired either three-phase or single-phase. (National Electric Div., H. K. Porter Co., Inc.)*

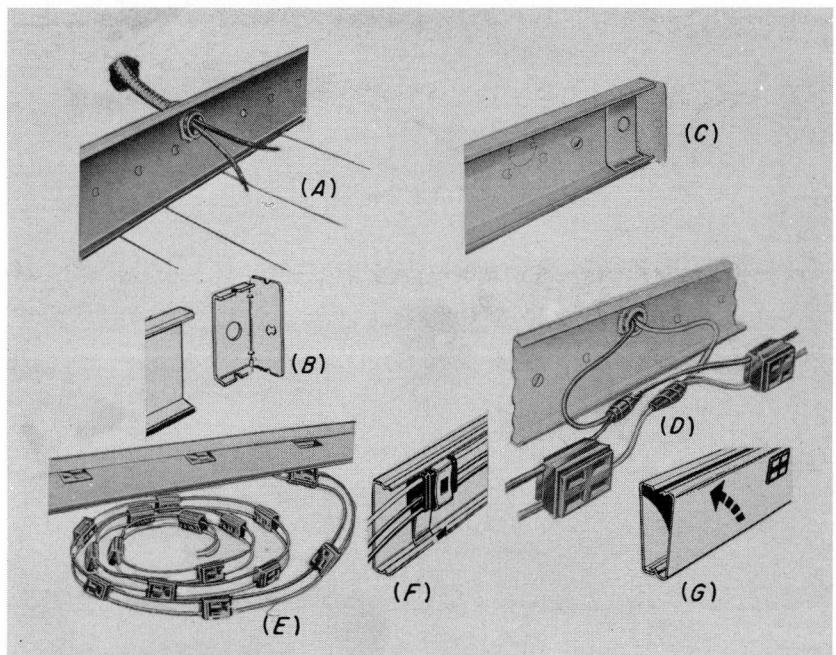

FIG. 223 *Installation of Plugmold baseboard. (1) Remove knockout (from inside out) for feed connection and fasten ½-in. connector into base with a lock nut A; no special fittings are needed. (2) At the end of run, install No. 2210B blank-end fitting in the base, B and C. (3) Mount base to surface through screw piercings or knockouts, using No. 6 flat-head screws. (Some types of surfaces require other methods of fastening.) (4) Lay out Snapicoil and cover sections to avoid having outlet directly in a corner or over a feed connection. (5) Splice feed wires onto Snapicoil conductors D. Note: In a three wire harness, black wire with yellow lettering should be used for the switch leg. (6) Insert Snapicoil receptacles into 2200C Holecut cover, and snap device clip in place, E and F. Clip can also be used in base to keep wires inside raceways. (7) Snap cover, complete with receptacles, into 2200B base G. (The Wiremold Co.)*

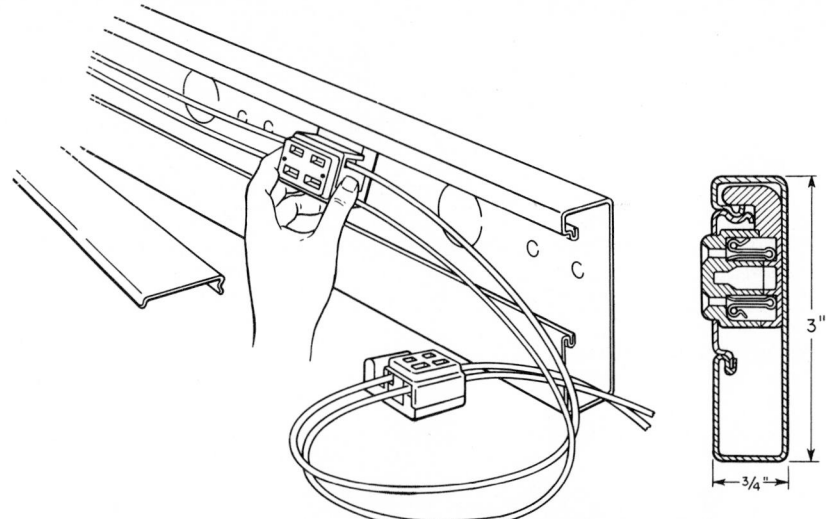

FIG. 224   *Baseduct.   (National Electric Div., H. K. Porter Co., Inc.)*

CABLEBUS WIRING

285. Cablebus is an approved assembly of insulated conductors mounted in "spaced" relationship in a ventilated metal protective supporting structure including fittings and conductors.   Typical components are shown in Fig. 225, which also includes some of the major National Electrical Code rules for cablebus.

The original manufacturer of the cablebus wiring system was Husky Products, Inc., subsidiary of Burndy Corp.   The system is highly desirable in industrial applications for larger feeders or branch circuits at 600 volts or less, and in higher distribution voltages of 5 or 15 kv.   It can also be used for primary feeders in high-rise buildings or commercial buildings where load-center unit substations are to be used.   Cablebus can be used indoors or outdoors in wet or dry locations.

The entire system is factory-fabricated with bottom support blocks (Fig. 225) in place.

The size of cablebus structures will vary according to the number of conductors. Figure 226 shows the four sizes of insulator blocks that are presently available—3-conductor, 6-conductor, 12-conductor, and 18-conductor.   Phase arrangements for three-phase circuits are also shown in Fig. 226 to provide a closely balanced impedance.   Because of carefully selected conductor spacing, transposition of conductors is not required.   Controlled spacing also assures low impedance and low voltage drop. The cablebus framework is an all-welded construction for maximum strength and 12-ft spacing of supports.   High-pressure splice joints between framework sections provide an excellent path or ground, and the installed framework serves a grounding conductor.

286. Types of Conductor.   The manufacturer of cablebus recommends that only thermoplastic or thermosetting conductors be used in cablebus.   At the present time, combining the insulation's electrical and physical qualities with the cost, the preferred insulation is cross-linked polyethylene.   Since cablebus is a ventilated enclosure, and conductors are separated by insulating blocks, conductor ampacities may be determined on the basis of single conductors in free air, as in Tables **18** and **20** of Div. 11. Generally, 90°C rated conductors are recommended.

287. Installation Procedures.   The basic installation of the cablebus framework is similar to that of a continuous rigid cable support system (Sec. **289**).   Typical arrangements are shown in Fig. 227 where cablebus is used for primary and secondary feeders and circuits.   The conductor pulling tools are the same as those shown in Fig. 233 for

Article 365 — Cablebus

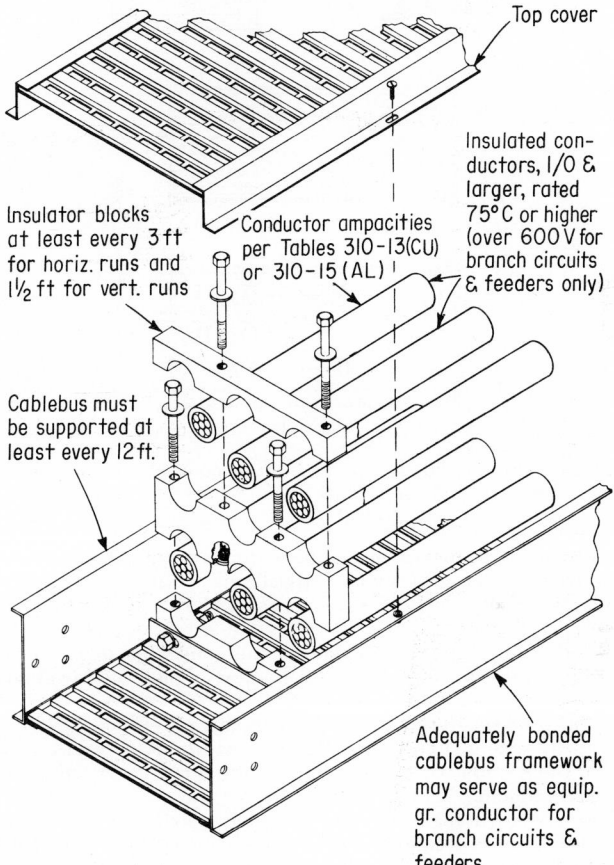

Top cover

Insulated con-
ductors, 1/0 &
larger, rated
75°C or higher
(over 600 V for
branch circuits
& feeders only)

Insulator blocks
at least every 3 ft
for horiz. runs and
1½ ft for vert. runs

Conductor ampacities
per Tables 310-13(CU)
or 310-15 (AL)

Cablebus must
be supported at
least every 12 ft.

Adequately bonded
cablebus framework
may serve as equip.
gr. conductor for
branch circuits &
feeders

FIG. 225 *Elements of a typical cablebus system and major Code requirements.* (*Electrical Construction and Maintenance.*)

continuous rigid cable supports. Conductors are pulled in after the basic framework has been completely installed. After conductors are pulled in and arranged in proper phase sequence, they are secured to the insulating blocks. The final step is the installation of top covers.

288. National Electrical Code Rules. The following Code rules apply to cablebus.

1. Cablebus shall be installed only for exposed work. It may be installed outdoors or in corrosive, wet, or damp locations if approved for the purpose.

2. If adequately bonded, cablebus framework may be used as the equipment grounding conductor for branch circuits and feeders.

3. The current-carrying conductors in cablebus shall have an insulation rating of at least 75°C and shall be of an approved type.

4. The size and number of conductors shall be that for which the cablebus is designed, and in no case less than 1/0.

5. Insulated conductors shall be supported on blocks or other mounting means designed for the purpose.

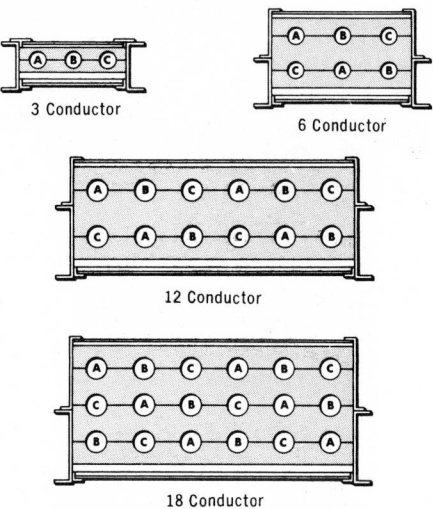

FIG. 226 *Sizes of insulating blocks and three-phase conductor arrangements.* (*Husky Products, Inc., Subsidiary of Burndy Corp.*)

6. The individual conductors in a cablebus shall be supported at intervals not greater than 3 ft for horizontal runs and 1½ ft for vertical runs. Vertical and horizontal spacing between conductors shall be not less than one conductor diameter at the points of support.

7. When the allowable current rating of cablebus conductors does not correspond to a standard rating of the overcurrent device, the next higher rated overcurrent device may be used.

8. Cablebus shall be securely supported at intervals not exceeding 12 ft.

9. Cablebus may extend transversely through partitions or walls, other than fire walls, provided the section within the wall is continuous, protected against physical damage, and unventilated.

10. Except where fire stops are required, cablebus may extend vertically through floors and platforms in wet locations where (*a*) there are curbs or other suitable means to prevent water flow through the floor or platform opening and (*b*) where the cablebus is totally enclosed at the point where it passes through the floor or platform and for a distance of 6 ft above the floor or platform.

11. Except where fire stops are required, cablebus may extend vertically through dry floors and platforms, provided the cablebus is totally enclosed at the point where it passes through the floor or platform and for a distance of 6 ft above the floor or platform.

12. Cablebus shall utilize approved fittings for changes in horizontal or vertical direction of the run, dead ends, terminations in or on connected apparatus or equipment or the enclosures for such equipment, and additional physical protection where required, such as guards for severe mechanical protection.

13. Approved terminating means shall be used for connections to cablebus connections.

14. Sections of cablebus shall be electrically bonded either by inherent design of the mechanical joints or by applied bonding means.

15. Each section of cablebus shall be marked with the manufacturer's name or trade designation and the maximum diameter, number, voltage rating, and ampacity of conductors to be installed. Markings shall be so located as to be visible after installation.

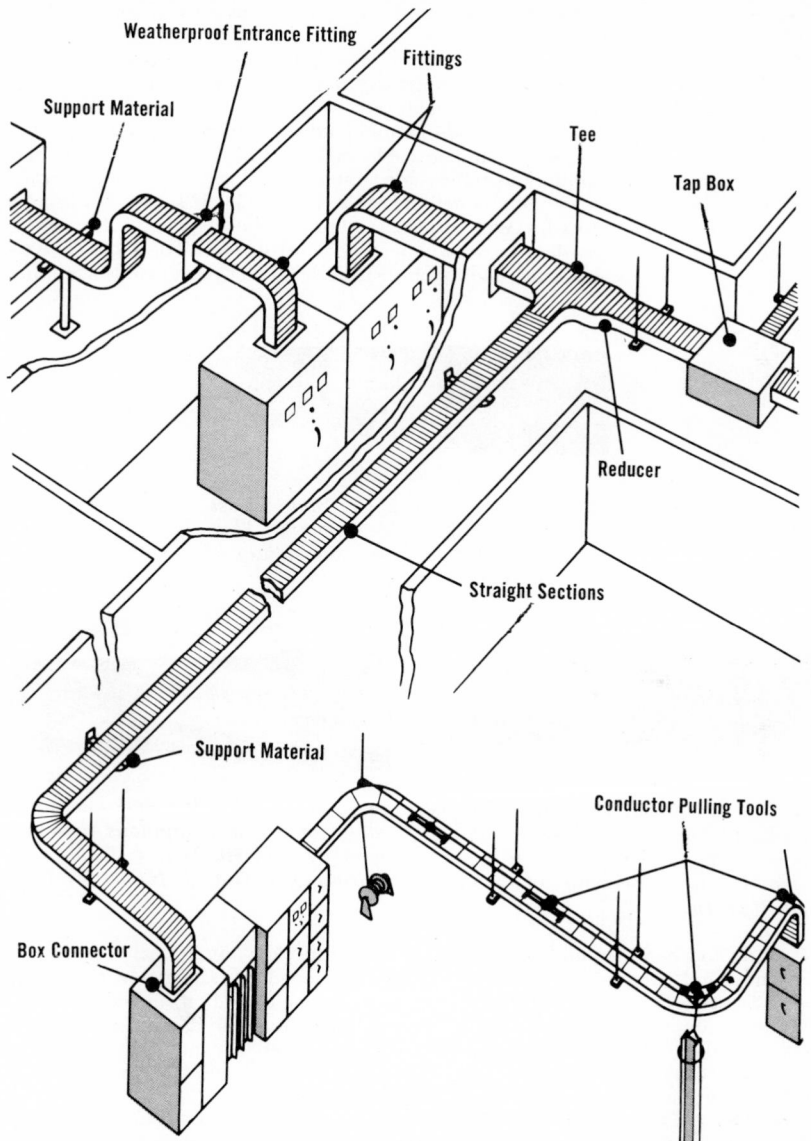

FIG. 227 *Typical cablebus runs for primary and secondary distribution.* (*Husky Products, Inc., Subsidiary of Burndy Corp.*)

CONTINUOUS RIGID CABLE SUPPORTS

289. A continuous rigid cable support is a unit or an assembly of units or sections, and associated fittings, made of metal or other noncombustible materials which form a continuous rigid structure to support cables. Continuous rigid cable supports include ladders, troughs, channels, trays, and similar structures. Continuous rigid cable supports are often called "cable trays" and such support systems are constructed of steel or aluminum.

The National Electrical Code allows continuous rigid cable supports to contain conduit or raceway with its contained conductors; mineral-insulated (MI) cable; aluminum-sheathed (ALS) cable; metal-clad cable (AC or MC); nonmetallic-sheathed cable (NM or NMC); multiple-conductor underground feeder and branch-circuit cable (UF); and multiple-conductor service-entrance cable (SE or USE). In practice the most common types used in continuous rigid cable supports are Type MC metal-clad cable (Fig. 87) and specially designed nonmetallic cables (Figs. 228, 229, and 230) listed by Underwriters' Laboratories for such support systems. These special cables are restricted for use in fire-resistant or noncombustible construction. The cable shown in Fig. 228 is a polyvinyl chloride- and nylon-insulated 600-volt power cable with three

FIG. 228　A 600-volt power cable for use in continuous rigid cable supports. (Plastic Wire & Cable Corp., Subsidiary of Triangle Industries, Inc.)

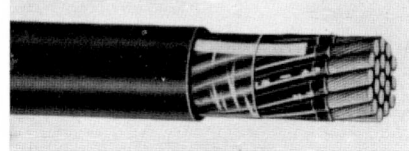

FIG. 229　A 600-volt 19-conductor cable suitable for power control circuits and for use in cable supports. (Plastic Wire & Cable Corp., Subsidiary of Triangle Industries, Inc.)

FIG. 230　A 600-volt power and control cable for use in continuous rigid cable supports. (Plastic Wire & Cable Corp., Subsidiary of Triangle Industries, Inc.)

2/0 conductors and a grounding conductor. The cable shown in Fig. 229 has the same insulation and contains nineteen No. 12 stranded conductors, suitable for 600-volt power or control circuits. Figure 230 also has the same insulation, and contains three 4/0 power conductors and four No. 12 control conductors, all suitable for 600 volts. Cables similar to these can be obtained with a wide variety of conductor sizes. These nonmetallic cables and Type MC metal-clad cables can be installed in continuous rigid cable supports much more easily than other types of cables.

290. Types of Continuous Rigid Cable Supports. There are several manufacturers of continuous rigid cable supports, and the types shown in Figs. 231 and 232 are manufactured by the Globe Div., United States Gypsum. These drawings show various types of continuous rigid cable supports (channel type, solid-cover type, louvered-cover type, ladder type, and solid-bottom type). Also illustrated are a variety of fittings used with the support system, such as elbows or offsets, blind ends, tees, crosses, reducers, dividers, and box connectors. As can be seen in Figs. 231 and 232, continuous rigid cable supports provide a highly flexible system in any application where a number of power and/or control cables are required. Cable supports are secured in a manner similar to that described in the sections on rigid metal conduit and busways.

An excellent feature of the cable support system is that cables can be added, revamped, or removed with minimum effort. When laying out such systems, it is well to plan for future needs by obtaining supports larger than necessary for the initially installed cables.   Manufacturers offer many different widths and lengths for each section of continuous support system, and it is recommended that representatives of these firms be contacted when such installations are contemplated.

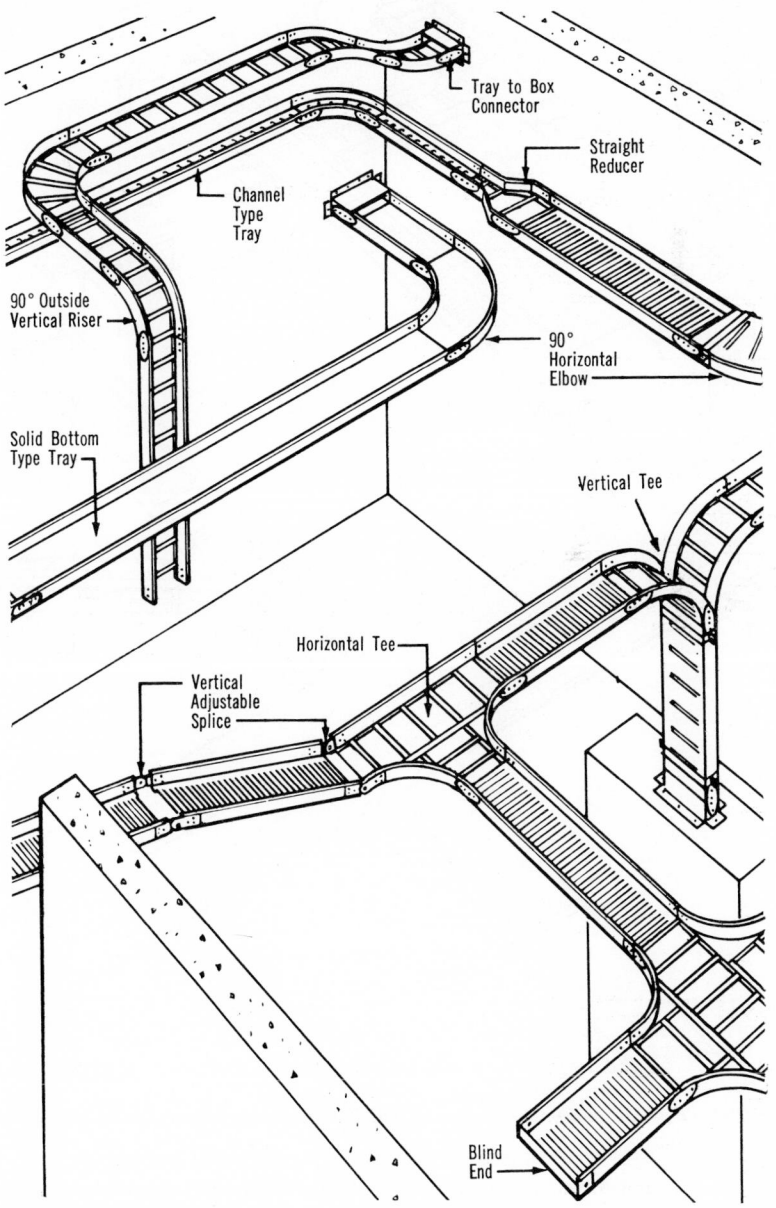

FIG. 231   *Typical components of a CABLE-STRUT System.   (Globe Div., United States Gypsum.)*

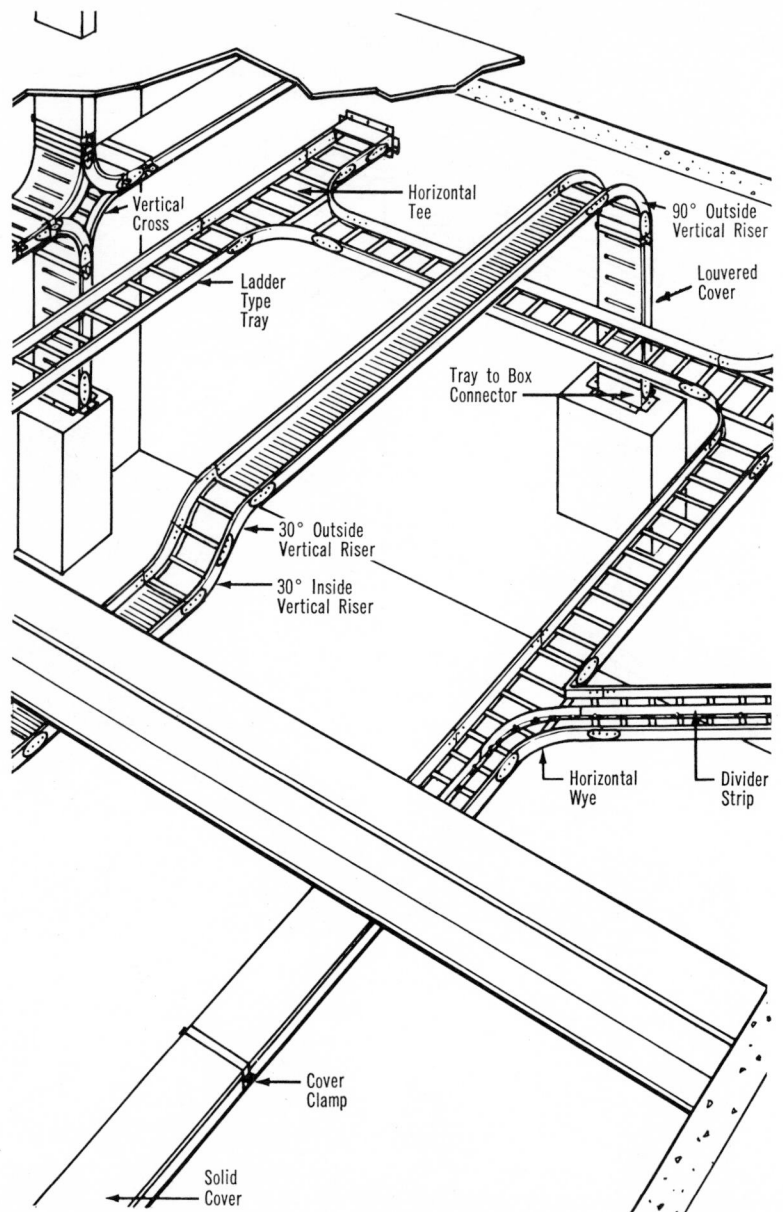

FIG. 232 *Typical components of a CABLE-STRUT system. (Globe Div., United States Gypsum.)*

291. Installation Aids. To simplify the pulling of cables into continuous rigid cable supports the tools shown in Fig. 233 are typical of those offered by manufacturers of these support systems. Locating rollers and pulleys at the proper locations in the support system speeds up the installation of cables and prevents damage to cables during

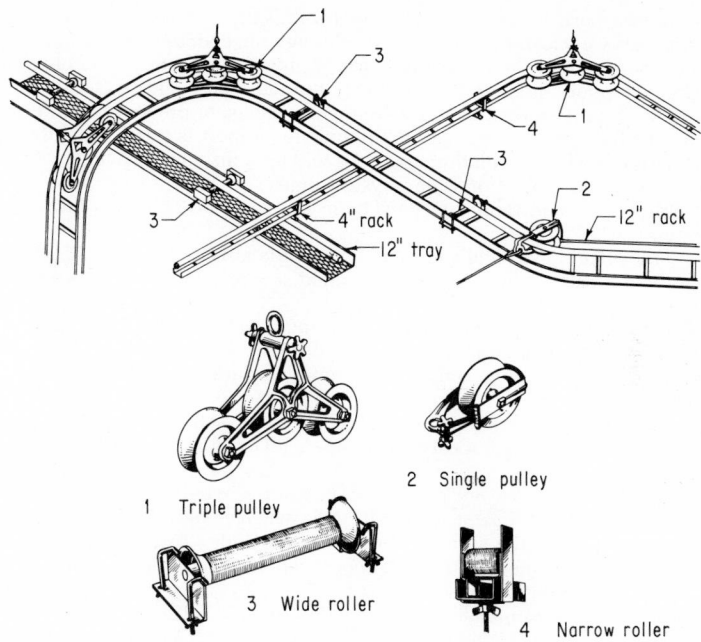

1   Triple pulley
2   Single pulley
3   Wide roller
4   Narrow roller

Installation aids available

FIG. 233 *Installation aids available to simplify cable pulling in continuous rigid cable supports. (Electrical Construction and Maintenance.)*

the process of installation. After cables are installed, they should be spaced and supported as indicated in Sec. **292.**

292. National Electrical Code rules for continuous rigid cable supports are as follows:

1. The cable support must have suitable strength and rigidity to provide adequate support for all contained wiring and shall not have sharp edges, burrs, or projections injurious to the insulation or jackets of the wiring.

2. Metal supports must be adequately protected against corrosion or shall be of corrosion-resistant material.

3. Side rails or equivalent structural members are required for the cable supports.

4. Suitable fittings must be used for changes in direction and elevation of runs of the cable supports.

5. The support system must be installed as a complete system.

6. Each run of cable support shall be complete before the installation of cables.

7. Cable supports must be mechanically connected to any enclosure or raceway into which the contained cables extend or terminate.

8. In portions of runs where additional physical protection is required, noncombustible covers or enclosures providing the required protection must be used.

9. Installations involving different systems which must be separated shall include a separation by means of a solid noncombustible partition or compartment in the cable support.

10. When cable supports are installed in tiers, the minimum clearance between tiers must be 12 in.

11. Cable supports may extend transversely through partitions or walls, other than fire walls, if the section of the support within the wall is continuous and unventilated. Where an opening in a partition or wall provides 2 in. minimum clearance above and on both sides, a ventilated type of support may be used.

12. Cable supports may extend vertically through dry floors and platforms if the cable support is totally enclosed where it passes through the floor or platform opening and for a distance of 6 ft above the floor or platform to provide protection from physical injury.

13. Cable supports may extend vertically through floors and platforms in wet locations where (a) there are curbs or other suitable means to prevent water flow through the floor or platform opening, and (b) the cable support is totally enclosed where it passes through the floor or platform opening and for a distance of 6 ft above the floor or platform to provide protection from physical injury.

14. Cable splices and cable taps must be made in junction boxes or fittings approved for the purpose.

15. In other than horizontal runs, and where side rails do not provide adequate containment of the cables, they must be fastened securely to tranverse members of the cable support.

16. Where cable supports are located adjacent to each other, a 24-in. minimum working space should be maintained on one side of each cable support, or where grouped in rows adjacent to each other, a 32-in. minimum working space should be maintained over each cable support.

17. Except as provided in paragraph 11 a minimum vertical clearance of 6 in. should be maintained from the top of cable supports to all ceilings, beams, and other obstructions.

18. Cable supports must not be used in hoistways; where the cables supported are subject to severe physical damage; and in areas which contain readily combustible contents as determined by the authority enforcing the Code.

19. Cable supports may be used to support cables in hazardous locations where the cables are approved for such use.

20. All metal sections of cable supports and fittings must be bonded and effectively grounded to provide a continuous circuit for fault current. A cable support must not be used as a grounded circuit conductor or as an equipment grounding conductor.

21. Where cables containing not more than three current-carrying conductors are installed in ventilated cable supports, and spacing is maintained at from one-quarter to one cable diameter, the factors in the following table must be to the ampacities of the cables used:

Factors for Cables with Maintained Spacing

Number of cables	Horizontally					
Vertically	1	2	3	4	5	6
1	1.00	0.93	0.87	0.84	0.83	0.82
2	0.89	0.83	0.79	0.76	0.75	0.74
3	0.80	0.76	0.72	0.70	0.69	0.68
4	0.77	0.72	0.68	0.67	0.66	0.65
5	0.75	0.70	0.66	0.65	0.64	0.63
6	0.74	0.69	0.64	0.63	0.62	0.61

22. Cable ampacities must be in accordance with Note 8 of Sec. **17**, Div. 11, where (a) cables are not spaced; (b) spacing is maintained between cables of more than three current-carrying conductors; or (c) unventilated cable supports are used.

GENERAL REQUIREMENTS FOR WIRING INSTALLATIONS

CONDUCTOR REQUIREMENTS

293. Size of Conductors. No wire smaller than No. 14 is allowed for general interior wiring work. Wires of No. 18 or No. 16 may be used for fixture wiring, flexible cords, and some other special applications as given in Sec. **32** of Div. 3. Although No. 14 wire is allowed for branch circuits, it is good practice not to use smaller than No. 12. Number 12 wire costs only about 20 per cent more than No. 14, can usually be placed in the same size conduit or raceway, will have greater mechanical strength, and will reduce the voltage drop and the I^2R heating loss in the wires by approximately 40 per cent. Solid conductors of larger size than No. 8 are not allowed to be used in conduit or raceways. For ease in handling, it is good practice to use stranded conductors in the larger sizes for open wiring also. The size of wire required, according to the amount of current to be carried by the circuit, is discussed in Sec. **31** of Div. 3, and the ampere current-carrying capacities are given in Tables **12** to **24** of Div. 11.

294. All ungrounded conductors must be protected by fuses or circuit breakers rated in accordance with the allowable carrying capacity of the conductors as given in Sec. **295** and located at the point where the conductor receives its supply, with the following exceptions:

1. For building-service conductors the overcurrent protection is located at the same point as the other service-entrance equipment, which may be at the load end of the service-entrance conductors, or it may be located at the outer end.

2. The overcurrent protection may be omitted provided the overcurrent unit farther back on the circuit is rated not greater than the carrying capacity of the smaller conductor.

3. Taps to individual outlets and circuit conductors supplying a single household electric range shall be considered as protected by the branch-circuit overcurrent devices when in accordance with the requirements of sections 210-19, 210-20, and 210-25 of the Code.

4. If a tap conductor is not over 10 ft long, does not extend beyond the switchboard, panel board, or control devices which it supplies; is enclosed in conduit, EMT, or metal gutters; and has a current-carrying capacity not less than the sum of the capacities of the circuits which it supplies, it need not be separately protected.

5. If the conductor is not over 25 ft long, is protected from mechanical injury, and has a current-carrying capacity not less than one-third that of the conductor from which it is supplied, a single circuit breaker or set of fuses may be located at the load end of the conductor.

6. For individual motor branch circuits, refer to Sec. **435**, Div. 7.

7. For feeders or main conductors supplying more than one motor, refer to Sec. **440**, Div. 7.

8. Fixture wires and cords. Fixture wire or flexible cord, size No. 16 or No. 18, and tinsel cord shall be considered as protected by 20-amp overcurrent devices except as provided in the Code for remote-control and signal circuits. Fixture wire of the sizes permitted by the Code for taps from branch circuits shall be considered as protected by the overcurrent protection of the 30-, 40-, and 50-amp branch circuits. Flexible cord approved for use with specific appliances shall be considered as protected by the overcurrent device of the branch circuit when conforming to the following:

20-amp circuits, No. 18 cord and larger.

30-amp circuits, cord of 10-amp capacity and over.

40- and 50-amp circuits, cord of 20-amp capacity and over.

295. Rating of the Overcurrent Protective Devices. The rating of the overcurrent protective device must be as given below except for the exceptions referred to in paragraphs 6 to 8 of Sec. **294.** Fuses or circuit breakers shall have ratings not greater than the allowable carrying capacity of the conductor which they protect, except as follows:

1. When the standard ampere ratings and settings of overcurrent devices do not correspond with the allowable current-carrying capacities of conductors, the next higher standard rating and setting may be used in ratings of 800 amp or less.

2. Adjustable-trip circuit breakers of the thermal-trip, magnetic-time-delay-trip or instantaneous-trip types shall be set to operate at not more than 125 per cent of the allowable current-carrying capacity of the conductor.

The effect of the temperature on the operation of thermally controlled circuit breakers should be taken into consideration in the application of such circuit breakers when they are subjected to extremely low or extremely high temperatures.

The allowable carrying capacity of wires is given in Tables **18** to **22** of Div. 11, and the common sizes of fuses and circuit breakers in Table **35** of Div. 11 and section 240-5(*b*) of the Code.

296. Grounded conductors must not be fused and must not have a circuit breaker in them unless the circuit breaker opens all the wires of the circuit at the same time. The size of the grounded conductor may be changed whenever the sizes of the other conductors are changed provided the other conductors are protected as outlined in Secs. **294** and **295** (see Div. 8, Sec. **157,** for an explanation of the reason for grounding one conductor of a wiring system).

297. Overcurrent Devices in Multiple. Except for circuit breakers which are assembled and approved as a single unit, overcurrent devices must not be arranged or installed in multiple.

298. Enclosures for Protective Devices (National Electrical Code). Overcurrent devices shall be enclosed in cutout boxes or cabinets unless a part of a specially approved assembly which affords equivalent protection or unless mounted on switchboards, panel boards, or controllers located in rooms or enclosures free from easily ignitible material and dampness. The operating handle of a circuit breaker may be accessible without opening a door or cover.

DAMP OR WET LOCATIONS. Enclosures for overcurrent devices in damp or wet locations shall be of a type approved for such locations and shall be mounted so there is at least ¼-in. air space between the enclosure and the wall or other supporting surface.

VERTICAL POSITION. Enclosures for overcurrent devices shall be mounted in a vertical position unless in individual instances this is shown to be impracticable.

ROSETTES. Fuses shall not be mounted in rosettes.

DISCONNECTION OF FUSES AND THERMAL CUTOUTS BEFORE HANDLING. Disconnecting means shall be provided on the supply side of all fuses or thermal cutouts in circuits of more than 150 volts to ground and cartridge fuses in circuits of any voltage, if accessible to other than qualified persons, so that each individual circuit containing fuses or thermal cutouts can be independently disconnected from the source of electrical energy, except as provided in section 230-73 of the Code and except that a single disconnecting means may be used to control a group of circuits each protected by fuses or thermal cutouts under the conditions described in section 430-112 of the Code.

ARCING OR SUDDENLY MOVING PARTS. Arcing or suddenly moving parts shall comply with the following:

a. Location. Fuses and circuit breakers shall be so located or shielded that persons will not be burned or otherwise injured by their operation.

b. Suddenly Moving Parts. Handles or levers of circuit breakers and similar parts which may move suddenly in such a way that persons in the vicinity are liable to be injured by being struck by them shall be guarded or isolated.

299. Flexible cords are used for wiring fixtures, for connection of portable lamps or appliances, for elevator cables, for wiring of cranes and hoists, or for the connection of approved stationary devices to facilitate their interchange or to prevent transmission of noise or vibration, or to facilitate the removal of fixed or stationary appliances for maintenance or repair. (See Div. 2 for a complete listing of flexible cords.) Flexible cords must be not smaller than No. 18 unless specially approved, and if the load connected to them is not greater than their carrying capacity, they are considered as sufficiently protected by the branch-circuit overcurrent device of the branch circuit from which they are tapped. For the carrying capacity of fixture wire see Table **22,** Div. 11. Cords must be connected to devices so that tension in the cord will not be taken by the terminal screws. This can be accomplished by knotting the cord inside the device (Fig. 234), by winding it with tape, or by using a clamp fitting. Where flexible cords pass through the cover of an outlet box, the hole must have a smooth, well-rounded surface; where they enter lamp holders, they must be protected by insulating bushings. Flexible cords must be used in continuous lengths without splice or tap. For voltages between 300 and 600, cords of No. 10 and smaller shall have at least ³/₆₄ in. of rubber or thermoplastic insulation on each conductor unless Type S, SO, STO, or ST cord is used.

In the wiring of fixtures, use conductors having insulation suitable for the current, voltage, and temperature to which they will be subjected. The splice between the fixture conductors and the circuit conductors must be easily accessible for inspection without requiring disconnection of the wiring. This is accomplished by making the canopy so that it will slide down the fixture stem (Fig. 236).

300. Splicing of Conductors. Conductors in conduit or raceway systems must be continuous from outlet to outlet and must not be spliced or tapped within the raceway or conduit itself, except in wireways or auxiliary gutters. Instructions for the proper splicing of conductors are given in Div. 2.

301. Conductors may be placed in multiple in sizes 1/0 and larger provided they are the same length and size and have the same type of insulation and conductor material.

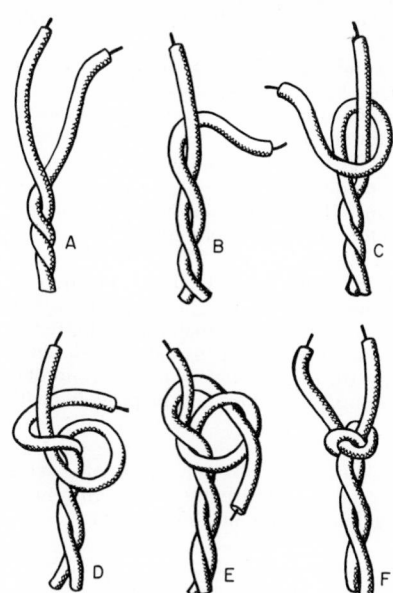

FIG. 234 *Method of tying supporting knot in flexible cord (see Sec. 299 for description).*

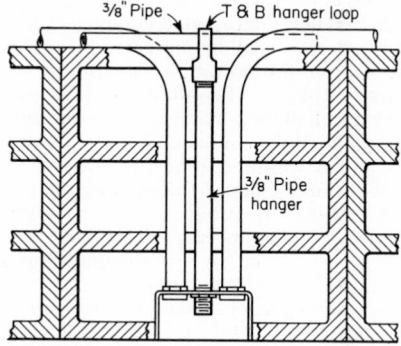

FIG. 235 *Support for outlet box in terra-cotta ceiling.*

The conductors shall be arranged and terminated at each end in such a manner as to ensure equal division of the total current between all the parallel conductors. If the parallel circuits should be carried in different conduits or raceways, at least one wire of each phase must be carried in each conduit or raceway.

302. Induced Currents in Metal Enclosures (National Electrical Code). In metal enclosures, the conductors of circuits operating on alternating current shall be so arranged as to avoid overheating of the metal by induction. When the capacity of a circuit is such that it is impracticable to run all conductors in one enclosure, the circuit may be divided and two or more enclosures may be used, provided each phase conductor of the circuit and the neutral conductor, where one is used, are installed in each enclosure. The conductors of such an installation must conform to the provisions of Sec. **301** for multiple conductors.

Induced currents in an enclosure can be avoided by so grouping the conductors in one enclosure that the current in one direction will be substantially equal to the current in the opposite direction.

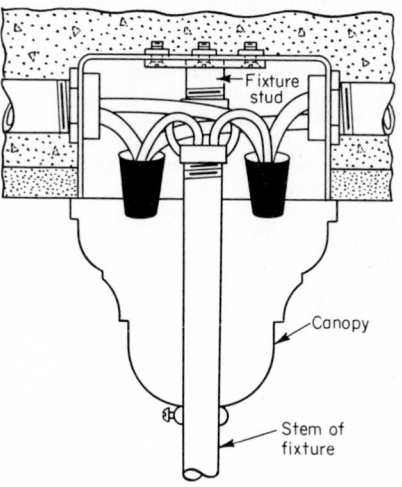

FIG. 236 *Method of supporting fixture from a fixture stud.*

In the case of circuits supplying vacuum or electric discharge lighting systems or signs or x-ray apparatus, and underplaster extensions permitted by sections 344-1 to 344-5 inclusive of the Code, the currents carried by the conductors are so small that a single conductor may be placed in a metal enclosure or pass through metal without causing trouble from induction.

Where the conductors of a circuit pass through individual holes in the wall of a metal cabinet, the effect of induction may be minimized by (1) cutting slots in the metal between the individual holes through which the conductors of the circuit pass, or (2) passing all the conductors in the circuit through an aluminum wall or insulating block used to cover a hole in the metal cabinet, sufficiently large for all the conductors of the circuit and providing individual holes for the separate conductors.

303. At outlets and switch locations at least 6 in. of free conductor must be left for the making of joints and connection of wiring devices, except where conductors are intended to loop without joints through boxes and fittings.

304. When ungrounded conductors of No. 4 and larger enter a cabinet, junction, or pull box, they shall be protected by a smoothly rounded insulating bushing unless they are separated from the raceway fitting by substantial insulating material securely fastened in place. If conduit bushings are constructed wholly of insulating material, a lock nut shall be provided both inside and outside the enclosure to which the conduit is attached. If the conductors enter the cabinet vertically, a gutter must be provided with a width as specified in Sec. 82, Div. 4.

305. Conductors of Different Systems.

1. Conductors of light and power systems of 600 volts or less may occupy the same enclosure, without regard to whether the individual circuits are alternating current or direct current, only where all conductors are insulated for the maximum voltage of any conductor within the enclosure.

2. Conductors of light and power systems of over 600 volts shall not occupy the same enclosure with conductors of light and power systems of 600 volts or less.

3. Secondary wiring to electric-discharge lamps of 1,000 volts or less may occupy the same enclosure as the branch circuit conductors.

4. Control, relay, and ammeter conductors used in connection with any motor or starter may occupy the same enclosure as the motor circuit conductors.

5. Conductors of signal or radio systems shall not occupy the same enclosure with conductors of light or power systems except as permitted for elevators in section 620-36; for sound recording in section 640-6; for remote-control low-energy power and signal circuits in sections 725-16 and 725-42; and for communication systems in sections 800-3 and 800-21 of the Code.

6. Primary leads of electric discharge lamp ballasts, insulated for the primary voltage of the ballast, when contained within the individual wiring enclosure may occupy the same fixture enclosure as the branch-circuit conductors.

306. When conductors or cables are run through bored holes in studs and joists, the holes should be bored at the approximate centers of wood members or at least 2 in. from the nearest edge where practical. Where there is no objection because of weakening the building structure, metal-clad or nonmetallic-sheathed cable may be laid in notches in the studding or joists if the cable at those points is protected against the driving of nails into it by having the notch covered with a steel plate at least $\frac{1}{16}$ in. thick before the building finish is applied.

307. Conductors in vertical raceways (any metallic enclosure for conductors) must be supported at intervals not greater than those given in Sec. 96 under Conduit Wiring.

308. Wiring in Ducts, Plenums, and Other Air-handling Spaces (National Electrical Code). No wiring systems of any type shall be installed in ducts used to transport dust, loose stock, or flammable vapors; nor shall any wiring system of any type be installed in any duct, or shaft containing only such ducts, used for vapor removal or ventilation of commercial-type cooking equipment.

Wiring systems of MI cable, ALS cable, electrical metallic tubing, or rigid metal conduit may be installed in ducts or plenum chambers used to transport higher-velocity environmental air. Flexible metal conduit may be used, in lengths not to exceed 4 ft, to connect physically adjustable equipment and devices permitted to be in these ducts and plenum chambers. The connectors used with flexible metal conduit shall effectively close any openings in the connection. Equipment and devices may only be installed within such ducts or plenum chambers if necessary for their direct action upon, or sensing of, the contained air. If equipment or devices are installed and illumination is necessary to facilitate maintenance and repair, enclosed gasketed-type fixtures may be installed.

Hollow spaces that are used as ducts or plenum chambers for lower-velocity environmental air, other than those described in the previous paragraph, may contain MI cable, ALS cable, electrical metallic tubing, rigid metal conduit, flexible metal conduit, and other electrical equipment that is permitted within the concealed spaces of such structures, provided:

1. The wiring materials, including fixtures, are suitable for the expected ambient temperature to which they will be subjected.

2. The wiring system, including fixtures, in no way reduces the fire-protective rating of the construction in which they are installed.

3. Flexible metal conduit shall be limited to the connection of devices, equipment, and fixtures in lengths not exceeding 4 ft. The connectors used with flexible metal conduit shall effectively close any openings in the connection.

Exception No. 1. The above provisions shall not apply to integral fan systems specifically approved for the purpose.

Exception No. 2. This section does not include habitable rooms or areas of buildings, the prime purpose of which is not air handling.

NFPA Standard for the Installation of Air Conditioning and Ventilating Systems, No. 90A, sets forth requirements of building used for ducts and plenums.

The wiring systems used for data-processing systems and located within air-handling areas created by raised floors shall conform to article 645.

309. The approved types of insulation of conductors for different installations are given in Sec. 31.

310. Insulation Resistance. To provide a reasonable factor of safety against short circuits and grounds, completed wiring systems should undergo an insulation resistance test. The proper instrument for making this test is a megohmmeter. The National Electrical Code formerly contained recommended values of resistance for various circuit sizes. However, these values were deleted from the Code because they were misleading. Cable and conductor installations provide a wide variation of conditions with respect to the resistance of insulation. These variations are due to the many types of insulating materials used, insulation thickness, voltage rating, and the length of the circuit. Long circuits may be subject to wide variations in temperature, and this can influence the insulation resistance values in a given test.

While insulation resistance readings are quantitative, they are also relative and comparable. Accordingly, such readings can be used to indicate the presence of moisture, dirt, and deterioration. Although the operation of a megohmmeter insulation tester is fairly simple, one must know how to interpret the results, and instructions provided for such instruments should be carefully followed.

Because a discussion of all the factors involved with these instruments and various test methods is beyond the scope of this book, anyone interested in this subject should review an instruction manual for insulation testers. Such a manual, "Instruction Manual for Megger Insulation Testers," can be purchased from the James G. Biddle Co., Plymouth Meeting, Pa. This manual includes instructions for connecting and operating Megger insulation testing instruments, directions for making insulation resistance tests on various types of electrical equipment, supplementary instructions and explanations to assist the person who makes the test, and valuable material on how to interpret insulation resistance readings.

311. Grounded Conductor. Every interior wiring system must have a grounded conductor except as allowed by the Code for certain specific conditions. The grounded conductor must be continuously identified throughout the system.

Where an identified grounded conductor is run to a lamp holder or any other screw-shell device, the identified grounded conductor must be connected to the screw shell. This does not apply to screw shells that serve as fuse holders.

GENERAL INSTALLATION REQUIREMENTS

312. Working Space about Electric Equipment (600 Volts or Less) (National Electrical Code). Sufficient access and working space shall be provided and maintained around all electric equipment to permit ready and safe operation and maintenance of such equipment.

1. WORKING CLEARANCES. Except as elsewhere required or permitted in this Code, the dimension of the working space in the direction of access to live parts, operating at not more than 600 volts, which are likely to require examination, adjustment, servicing, or maintenance while alive, shall not be less than indicated in the following table. Distances are to be measured from the live parts when such are exposed, or from the enclosure front or opening when such are enclosed.

Minimum Clear Working Space, in Feet

Voltage to ground	Conditions		
	1	2	3
0–150	2½	2½	3
151–600	2½	3½	4

1. Exposed live part on one side and no live or grounded part on the other side of the working space or exposed live parts on both sides effectively guarded by suitable wood or other insulating materials. Insulated wire or insulated bus bars operating at not more than 300 volts shall not be considered live parts.

2. Exposed live parts on one side and grounded parts on the other side. Concrete, brick, or tile walls shall be considered as grounded.

3. Exposed live parts on both sides of the work space (not guarded as provided in condition 1) with the operator between.

Exception No. 1. Working space is not required in back of assemblies such as deadfront switchboards or control centers when there are no renewable or adjustable parts such as fuses or switches on the back and when all connections are accessible from other locations than the back.

Exception No. 2. Smaller spaces may be permitted by the authority having jurisdiction where it is judged that the particular arrangement of the installation will provide adequate accessibility.

2. CLEAR SPACES. Working space required by this section shall not be used for storage. When normally enclosed live parts are exposed for inspection or servicing, the working space, if in a passageway or general open space, shall be suitably guarded.

3. ACCESS AND ENTRANCE TO WORKING SPACE. At least one entrance of sufficient area shall be provided to give access to the working space around electric equipment.

4. FRONT WORKING SPACE. In all cases where there are live parts normally exposed on the front of switchboards or control centers, the working space in front of such boards or panels shall be not less than 3 ft.

5. ILLUMINATION. Adequate illumination shall be provided for all working spaces about switchboards and control centers.

6. HEADROOM. The minimum headroom of working spaces around switchboards or control centers where there are live parts exposed at any time shall be 6¼ ft.

For higher voltages see article 710.

313. All cables and raceways must be continuous from outlet to outlet and from fitting to fitting and must be securely fastened in place. Fittings must be mechanically secured to conduits, raceways, and boxes; and the entire metallic-enclosure system must form an electrically continuous conductor. If different portions of a conduit or raceway system are exposed to widely different temperatures, as in refrigerating or cold-storage plants, provision must be made to prevent circulation of air through the raceway from a warmer to a colder section.

314. Protection against Corrosion. Metal raceways, cable armor, boxes, cable sheathing, cabinets, metallic elbows, couplings, fittings, supports, and support hardware shall be of materials suitable for the environment in which they are to be installed.

1. Ferrous raceways, cable armor, boxes, cable sheathing, cabinets, metallic elbows, couplings, fittings, supports, and support hardware shall be suitably protected against corrosion inside and outside (except threads at joints) by a coating of approved corrosion-resistant material, such as zinc, cadmium, or enamel. Where protected from corrosion solely by enamel, they shall not be used out of doors or in wet locations as described in paragraph 3. When boxes or cabinets have an approved system of organic coatings and are marked "Raintight" or "Outdoor Type," they may be used out of doors.

2. Unless made of materials judged suitable for the condition, or unless corrosion protection approved for the condition is provided, ferrous or nonferrous metallic raceways, cable armor, boxes, cable sheathing, cabinets, elbows, couplings, fittings, supports, and support hardware shall not be installed in concrete or in direct contact with the earth, or in areas subject to severe corrosive influences.

3. In portions of dairies, laundries, canneries, and in locations where walls are frequently washed or where there are surfaces of absorbent materials, such as damp paper or wood, the entire wiring system, including all boxes, fittings, conduits, and cable used therewith, shall be mounted so that there is at least one-quarter-inch air space between it and the wall or supporting surface.

Meat-packing plants, tanneries, hide cellars, casing rooms, glue houses, fertilizer rooms, salt storage, some chemical works, metal refineries, pulp mills, sugar mills, roundhouses, some stables, and similar locations are judged to be occupancies where severe corrosive conditions are likely to be present.

315. Outlet boxes (see Div. 4) must be provided at each outlet, switch, or junction point for all wiring systems except open wiring. The boxes must be made of metallic material, except that for open wiring on insulators, concealed knob and tube wiring, nonmetallic-sheathed cable, or nonmetallic raceways the boxes may be of nonmetallic construction. Wherever a change is made from open or concealed knob and tube wiring to one of the other types of wiring, a box or terminal fitting which has a separately bushed hole for each conductor must be used. In terminating conduit wiring at switchboards and control-apparatus locations an insulating bushing instead of a box may be used, and the conductors bunched, taped, and painted with insulating paint. If conductors are lead-covered, the bushing need not be an insulated one.

Care must be exercised in installing boxes and fittings in damp or wet locations so that they are either placed or equipped to prevent moisture or water from entering and accumulating within the box or fitting. In wet locations the boxes or fittings must be of the weatherproof type. The Code recommends that boxes of nonconductive material be used with nonmetallic-sheathed cable when such cable is used in locations where there is likely to be occasional moisture present, such as in dairy barns.

Round outlet boxes are not allowed where conduits or connectors requiring the use of lock nuts or bushings are to be connected to the side of the box.

316. Supports. Boxes shall be securely and rigidly fastened to the surface upon which they are mounted, or securely and rigidly embedded in concrete or masonry. Except as otherwise provided in this section, boxes shall be supported from a structural member of the building either directly or by using a substantial and approved metallic or wooden brace. If of wood, the brace shall not be less than nominal 1 in. thickness. If of metal, it shall be corrosion-resistant and shall be not less than 0.0239 in. thick (No. 24 MSG gage).

Where mounted in new walls in which no structural members are provided or in existing walls in previously occupied buildings, boxes less than 100 cu in. in size, specifically approved for the purpose, shall be affixed with approved anchors or clamps so as to provide a rigid and secure installation.

Threaded boxes or fittings less than 100 cu in. in size which do not contain devices or support fixtures may be considered adequately supported if two or more conduits are threaded into the box wrench-tight and are supported within 3 ft of the box on two or more sides as is required by this section.

Exception: Junction boxes for swimming pool underwater lighting fixtures may be supported by the connecting conduit where at least two connecting conduits are threaded into the box and rigidly supported within 18 in. of the junction box.

317. Ceiling outlet boxes may be supported with wood screws projecting through the holes in the bottom of the box, in frame construction when a wood background is available. Where boxes must be supported between wooden beams, bar hangers as shown in Sec. **119** of Div. 4 are used. The hangers are fastened with nails or wood screws to the beams. The box is fastened to the hanger by means of the fixture stud or with two bolts. With concealed conduit wiring in reinforced-concrete ceilings the conduits and the edges of the backing plate of the concrete boxes, bearing against the concrete, support the box. With terra-cotta ceilings a tee made of ⅜-in. pipe substantially bearing on the top of the terra cotta should be used (Fig. 235). The pipe projects through the fixture-stud knockout in the back of the box and forms the fixture stud. For exposed wiring on concrete ceilings, screws and lead expansion sleeves should be used. For exposed wiring on steelwork the box should be bolted or clamped to the steel.

For exposed wiring on plastered ceilings the box may be fastened on the surface with toggle bolts.

318. Wall outlet boxes in frame construction are fastened to the studs with side hangers which form part of the box (see Sec. **117,** Div. 4). With concealed wiring in concrete or brick walls the masonry, being built tight around the box, supports it. The conduit prevents the box from coming loose from the wall. If a pocket has been cut in a brick wall to receive an outlet box and the wall has been channeled for the conduit, the box should be fastened to the wall by means of two expansion sleeves. With concealed wiring in concrete construction, for the support of a fixture which is of too great weight to be safely hung on an ordinary ⅜-in. fixture stud, the outlet box should be supported by means of a pipe support similar to that of Fig. 235, embedded in the concrete. For exposed wiring on concrete and brick walls the box may be fastened with wood screws in lead expansion sleeves.

319. Lighting fixtures are usually supported from the fixture stud in the outlet box (Fig. 236). A hickey is screwed onto the fixture stud, and the fixture stem is screwed into the hickey. The fixture wires are brought out of the fixture stem through the holes in the hickey and spliced to the circuit wires. The canopy is then slipped up against the ceiling and fastened to the fixture stem with a setscrew. In many cases it is preferable to use outlet boxes which have the fixture stud made integral with the back of the box. In case that type of box is not available, a separate fixture stud (Fig. 237) may be installed. The no-bolt type (Fig. 237, I) is used for supporting the box from a bar hanger. The body of the stud is on the back of the hanger with the threaded portion projecting through the hanger and through a hole in the center of the box. The nut is screwed on the stud inside the box and holds the box to the hanger. The bolted type (Fig. 237, II) either is bolted to the back of the box or, when the box is supported from a wooden member, is held in place with wood screws. The National Electrical Code

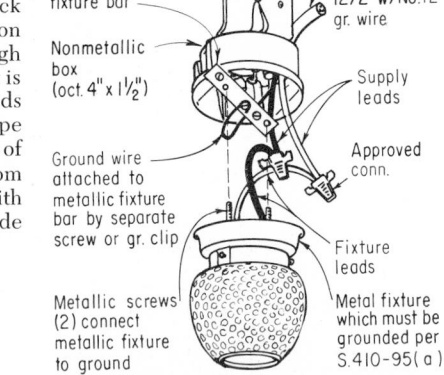

FIG. 238 *Method of securing and connecting a lightweight fixture to a nonmetallic box.*

Labels in figure: Metallic fixture bar — ; Nonmetallic box (oct. 4″ x 1½″); Ground wire attached to metallic fixture bar by separate screw or gr. clip; Metallic screws (2) connect metallic fixture to ground; NM cable 12/2 w/No.12 gr. wire; Supply leads; Approved conn.; Fixture leads; Metal fixture which must be grounded per S.410-95(a)

I-No bolt types   II-Bolted type

FIG. 237 *Fixture studs.*

requires that a fixture which weighs more than 6 lb or exceeds 16 in. in any dimension must not be supported by the screw shell of the lamp holder. Small lighting fixtures consisting of a lamp holder and a small shade may be supported from a pendant cord. In this case a box cover with a round hole in the center is used. A knot is tied in the cord inside the box (Fig. 234) so that the knot will bear against the cover and support the weight of the fixture. With exposed conduit wiring, elbow or tee conduit fittings are frequently used. The fixture is supported with a short length of conduit which threads into the fixture and into the hub which projects down from the fitting. Sometimes the upper part of the fixture is designed to be fastened as the cover on a 3¼- or 4-in. outlet box. A fixture which weighs more than 50 lb must be supported independently of the outlet box. Figure 238 shows a typical method of attaching a lightweight fixture to a nonmetallic box.

320. Number of Conductors in a Box (National Electrical Code). Boxes shall be of sufficient size to provide free space for all conductors enclosed in the box.

1. The maximum number of conductors, including grounding conductors but not counting fixture wires, permitted in outlet and junction boxes shall be as in the following tables with the exceptions noted.

Deep Boxes

Box dimensions, inches (trade size)	Cubic inch capacity	Maximum number of conductors			
		No. 14	No. 12	No. 10	No. 8
3¼ × 1½ octagonal	10.9	5	4	4	3
3½ × 1½ octagonal	11.9	5	5	4	3
4 × 1½ octagonal	17.1	8	7	6	5
4 × 2⅛ octagonal	23.6	11	10	9	7
4 × 1½ square	22.6	11	10	9	7
4 × 2⅛ square	31.9	15	14	12	10
4¹¹⁄₁₆ × 1½ square	32.2	16	14	12	10
4¹¹⁄₁₆ × 2⅛ square	46.4	23	20	18	15
3 × 2 × 1½ device	7.9	3	3	3	2
3 × 2 × 2 device	10.7	5	4	4	3
3 × 2 × 2¼ device	11.3	5	5	4	3
3 × 2 × 2½ device	13.0	6	5	5	4
3 × 2 × 2¾ device	14.6	7	6	5	4
3 × 2 × 3½ device	18.3	9	8	7	6
4 × 2⅛ × 1½ device	11.1	5	4	4	3
4 × 2⅛ × 1⅞ device	13.9	6	6	5	4
4 × 2⅛ × 2⅛ device	15.6	7	6	6	5

See section 370-18 of the Code where boxes are used as pull and junction boxes.

Shallow Boxes of Less than 1½-in. Depth

Box dimensions, inches (trade size)	Max. number of conductors		
	No. 14	No. 12	No. 10
3¼	4	4	3
4	6	6	4
4¹¹⁄₁₆	8	6	6
1¼ × 4 sq	9	7	5

The tables in paragraph 1 apply where no fittings or devices, such as fixture studs, cable clamps, hickeys, switches, or receptacles, are contained in the box. Where one or more fixture studs, cable clamps, or hickeys are contained in the box, the number of conductors shall be one less than shown in the tables, with a further deduction of one conductor for one or several flush devices mounted on the same strap. A conductor running through the box is counted as one conductor, and each conductor originating outside the box and terminating inside the box is counted as one conductor. Conductors of which no part leaves the box are not to be counted in the above computation. If single flush boxes are ganged and each section is occupied by a flush device or combination of flush devices on the same strap, the limitations will apply to each section individually. One or more grounding conductors are counted as one conductor.

2. For combinations not shown in the above tables the following table shall apply:

Size of Conductor	Free Space within Box for Each Conductor, Cu In.
No. 14	2
No. 12	2.25
No. 10	2.5
No. 8	3
No. 6	5

3. Boxes other than those described in the tables in paragraph 1 shall be durably and legibly marked with their cubic inch capacity by the manufacturer.

Paragraphs 1 and 2 of this section of the Code do not apply to conductors used for rewiring existing raceways, or to terminal housings supplied with motors (see section 430-12 of the Code).

321. Conductors Entering Boxes or Fittings (National Electrical Code). Conductors entering boxes or fittings shall be protected from abrasion, and shall conform to the following:

1. OPENINGS TO BE CLOSED. Openings through which conductors enter shall be adequately closed.

2. METAL BOXES AND FITTINGS. If metal outlet boxes or fittings are used with open wiring or concealed knob-and-tube work, conductors shall enter through insulating bushings or, in dry places, through flexible tubing extending from the last insulating support and firmly secured to the box or fitting. Where raceway or cable is used with metal outlet boxes or fittings, the raceway or cable shall be secured to such boxes and fittings.

3. NONMETALLIC BOXES. If nonmetallic boxes are used with open wiring or concealed knob-and-tube work, the conductors shall enter through individual holes. Where flexible tubing is used to encase the conductor, the tubing shall extend from the last insulating support and may be run into the box or terminate at the wall of the box. If nonmetallic-sheathed cable is used, the cable assembly shall enter the box through a knockout opening. Clamping of individual conductors or cables to the box is not required if supported within 8 in. of the box.

Unused openings in boxes and fittings shall be effectively closed to afford protection substantially equivalent to that of the wall of the box or fitting. Metal plugs or plates shall not be used with nonmetallic boxes or fittings unless recessed at least ¼ in. from the outer surface.

322. Location. All junction boxes must be installed so that the wiring contained in them is accessible without removing any part of the building, sidewalks, or paving.

In walls or ceilings of concrete, tile or other noncombustible material (National Electrical Code), boxes and fittings shall be so installed that the front edge of the box or fitting will not set back of the finished surface more than ¼ in. In walls and ceilings constructed of wood or other combustible material, outlet boxes and fittings shall be flush with the finished surface or project therefrom.

323. Covers and Canopies (National Electrical Code). In completed installations each outlet box shall be provided with a cover unless a fixture canopy is used.

1. Nonmetallic or metallic covers and plates may be used with nonmetallic outlet boxes. When metallic covers or plates are used, they are subject to the grounding requirements of the Code.

2. If a fixture canopy or pan is used, any combustible wall or ceiling finish exposed between the edge of the canopy or pan and the outlet box shall be covered with noncombustible material.

3. Covers of outlet boxes having holes through which flexible cord pendants pass shall be provided with bushings designed for the purpose or shall have smooth, well-rounded surfaces on which the cords may bear. So-called hard-rubber or composition bushings shall not be used.

324. Pull and Junction Boxes (National Electrical Code). Pull and junction boxes shall conform to the following:

1. MINIMUM SIZE. For raceways of 1 in. trade size and larger, containing conductors

of No. 6 or larger, and for cables [1] containing conductors of No. 6 or larger, the minimum dimensions of a pull or junction box installed in a raceway or cable run shall conform to the following:

a. Straight Pulls. In straight pulls the length of the box shall be not less than eight times the trade diameter of the largest raceway.

b. Angle or U Pulls. Where angle or U pulls are made, the distance between each raceway entry inside the box and the opposite wall of the box shall not be less than six times the trade diameter of the largest raceway. This distance shall be increased for additional entries by the amount of the sum of the diameters of all other raceway entries on the same wall of the box. The distance between raceway entries enclosing the same conductor shall not be less than six times the trade diameter of the larger raceway.

c. Boxes of lesser dimensions than those required in subparagraphs *a* and *b* of this section may be used for installations of combinations of conductors that are less than the maximum conduit fill (of conduits being used) permitted by Table **25** of Div. 11, provided that the box has been approved for and is permanently marked with the maximum number of conductors and the maximum AWG size permitted.

Exception: Terminal housings supplied with motors which shall comply with the provisions of section 430-12 of the Code.

2. CONDUCTORS IN PULL OR JUNCTION BOXES. In pull boxes or junction boxes having any dimension over 6 ft, all conductors shall be cabled or racked up in an approved manner.

3. COVERS. All pull boxes, junction boxes, and fittings shall be provided with covers approved for the purpose. Where metallic covers are used, they shall comply with the grounding requirements of section 250-42 of the Code.

325. Cabinets and Cutout Boxes. The requirements of the National Electrical Code with respect to cabinets and cutout boxes are as follows:

1. DAMP OR WET LOCATIONS. In damp or wet locations, cabinets and cutout boxes of the surface type shall be so placed or equipped as to prevent moisture or water from entering and accumulating within the cabinet or cutout box and shall be mounted so there is at least 1/4-in. air space between the enclosure and the wall or other supporting surface. Cabinets or cutout boxes installed in wet locations shall be weatherproof.

2. POSITION IN WALL. In walls of concrete, tile, or other noncombustible material, cabinets shall be so installed that the front edge of the cabinet will not set back of the finished surface more than 1/4 in. In walls constructed of wood or other combustible material, cabinets shall be flush with the finished surface or project therefrom.

3. UNUSED OPENINGS. Unused openings in cabinet or cutout boxes shall be effectively closed to afford protection substantially equivalent to that of the wall of the cabinet or cutout box. If metal plugs or plates are used with nonmetallic cabinets or cutout boxes, they shall be recessed at least 1/4 in. from the outer surface.

4. CONDUCTORS ENTERING CABINETS OR CUTOUT BOXES. Conductors entering cabinets or cutout boxes shall be protected from abrasion and shall conform to the following:

a. Openings to Be Closed. Openings through which conductors enter shall be adequately closed.

b. Metal Cabinets and Cutout Boxes. If metal cabinets or cutout boxes are used with open wiring or concealed knob-and-tube work, conductors shall enter through insulating bushings or, in dry places, through flexible tubing extending from the last insulating support and firmly secured to the cabinet or cutout box.

5. DEFLECTION OF CONDUCTORS. Conductors entering or leaving cabinets or cutout boxes and the like shall conform to the following:

a. Width of Gutters. Conductors shall not be deflected within a cabinet unless a gutter having a width in accordance with the following table is provided:

[1] When transposing cable size into raceway size in subparagraphs *a* and *b*, the minimum trade size raceway required for the number and size of conductors in the cable shall be used.

Minimum Bending Space in Inches

Size of wire, AWG or 1,000 cir mils	Wires per terminal				
	1	2	3	4	5
14–8	Not specified				
6	1½				
4–3	2				
2	2½				
1	3				
0–00	3½				
000–0000	4	6	8		
250 MCM	4½	6	8	10	
300–350 MCM	5	8	10	12	
400–500 MCM	6	8	10	12	14
600–700 MCM	8	10	12	14	16
750–900 MCM	8				
1,000–1,250 MCM	10				
1,500–2,000 MCM	12				

NOTE. The distance shall be measured in a straight line from the end of the lug or wire connector (in the direction that the wire leaves the terminal) to the wall or barrier.

b. Insulation at Bushings. Where ungrounded conductors of No. 4 or larger enter a raceway in a cabinet, pull box, junction box, or auxiliary gutter, the conductors shall be protected by a substantial bushing providing a smoothly rounded insulating surface unless the conductors are separated from the raceway fitting by substantial insulating material securely fastened in place. If conduit bushings are constructed wholly of insulating material, a lock nut shall be provided both inside and outside the enclosure to which the conduit is attached.

6. SPACE IN ENCLOSURES. Cabinets and cutout boxes shall conform to the following:

a. To Accommodate Conductors. Cabinets and cutout boxes shall be selected which have sufficient space to accommodate all conductors installed in them without crowding.

b. Used as Junction Boxes. Switch or overcurrent enclosures shall not be used as junction boxes, troughs, or raceways for conductors feeding through or tapping off to other switches or overcurrent devices unless special designs are employed to provide adequate space for this purpose.

7. SIDE OR BACK WIRING SPACES OR GUTTERS. Cabinets and cutout boxes shall be provided with back wiring spaces, gutters, or wiring compartments as required by paragraphs *c* and *d* of section 373-11 of the Code.

326. Auxiliary Gutters (National Electrical Code). Auxiliary gutters, used to supplement wiring spaces at meter centers, distribution centers, switchboards, and similar points of interior wiring systems, may enclose conductors or bus bars but shall not be used to enclose switches, overcurrent devices, or other appliances or apparatus.

1. EXTENSION BEYOND EQUIPMENT. An auxiliary gutter shall not extend a greater distance than 30 ft beyond the equipment which it supplements, except in elevator work. Any further extension shall comply with the rules for wireways or bus ways.

2. SUPPORTS. Gutters shall be supported throughout their entire length at intervals not exceeding 5 ft.

3. COVERS. Covers shall be securely fastened to the gutter.

4. NUMBER OF CONDUCTORS. Auxiliary gutters shall not contain more than 30 conductors at any cross section unless the conductors are for signaling circuits or are controller conductors between a motor and its starter and are used only for starting duty. The sum of the cross-sectional areas of all contained conductors at any cross section of an auxiliary gutter shall not exceed 20 per cent of the interior cross-sectional area of the gutter.

5. CARRYING CAPACITY OF COPPER BARS. The current carried continuously in bare conductors in auxiliary gutters shall not exceed 1,000 amp per sq in. of cross section of the conductor. Aluminum bare conductors are limited to 700 amp per sq in.

6. CLEARANCE OF BARE LIVE PARTS. Bare conductors shall be securely and rigidly supported so that the minimum clearance between bare current-carrying metal parts of

opposite polarities mounted on the same surface shall be not less than 2 in. or less than 1 in. for parts that are held free in the air. A spacing not less than 1 in. shall be secured between bare current-carrying metal parts and any metal surface. Adequate provision shall be made for expansion and contraction of copper or aluminum bars.

7. SPLICES AND TAPS. Splices and taps shall conform to the following:

a. Splices or taps, made and insulated by approved methods, may be located within gutters if they are accessible by means of removable covers or doors. The conductors, including splices and taps, shall not fill the gutter to more than 75 per cent of its area.

b. Taps from bare conductors shall leave the gutter opposite their terminal connections, and conductors shall not be brought in contact with uninsulated current-carrying parts of opposite polarity.

c. All taps shall be suitably identified at the gutter as to the circuit or equipment which they supply.

d. Tap connections from conductors in auxiliary gutters shall be provided with over-current protection in conformity with the provisions of Secs. **294** and **295.**

8. CONSTRUCTION. Auxiliary gutters shall be constructed in accordance with the following:

a. Gutters shall be so constructed and installed that adequate electrical and mechanical continuity of the complete raceway system will be secured.

b. Gutters shall be of substantial construction and shall provide a complete enclosure for the contained conductors. All surfaces, both interior and exterior, shall be suitably protected from corrosion. Corner joints shall be made tight, and, where the assembly is held together by rivets or bolts, these shall be spaced not more than 12 in. apart.

c. Suitable bushings, shields, or fittings having smooth rounded edges shall be provided where conductors pass between gutters, through partitions, around bends, between gutters and cabinets or junction boxes, and at other locations where necessary to prevent abrasion of the insulation of the conductors.

d. Gutters shall be constructed of sheet metal of thicknesses not less than in the following table:

Max width of the widest surface of gutters	U.S. Standard sheet steel gage	Thickness in.
Up to and including 6 in........................	No. 16	0.0598
Over 6 in. and not over 18 in....................	No. 14	0.0747
Over 18 in. and not over 30 in...................	No. 12	0.1046
Over 30 in.......................................	No. 10	0.1345

e. Where insulated conductors are deflected within the auxiliary gutter, either at the ends or where conduits, fittings, or other raceways enter or leave the gutter, or where the direction of the gutter is deflected more than 30 deg, dimensions correspond to those required for cabinets and cutout boxes as given in Sec. **325.**

f. Auxiliary gutters intended for outdoor use shall be of approved raintight construction.

GROUNDING

327. There are two types of grounds in interior wiring systems:

1. System grounds (common main grounding conductors).

2. Equipment and conductor-enclosure grounds.

A system ground refers to the condition of having one wire of a circuit connected to ground. The reason for doing this is explained in Secs. **157** and **158, Div. 8.**

An equipment or conductor-enclosure ground refers to connecting the non-current-carrying metal parts of the wiring system or equipment to ground. This is done so that the metal parts with which a person might come in contact are always at or near ground potential. With this condition there is less danger that a person touching the equipment or conductor enclosure will receive a shock. Also metal conduit, raceways, and boxes may be in contact with metal parts of the building at several points. If an accidental contact occurs between an ungrounded conductor and its metal enclosure, a current may flow to ground through a stray path made up of sections of metal lath, metal partitions, piping, or other similar conductors. If the equipment is grounded, the resistance of the path through the grounding conductor will usually be much less than the resistance through the stray path, and not much current will flow through the stray path. Sufficient current will usually flow through the grounded path to blow the circuit fuse or trip the circuit breaker and thus open the circuit until repairs can be made. On the other hand, if the equipment is not grounded, sufficient current may flow through the stray path to heat up some section to a sufficient temperature to ignite wood or other inflammable material with which it is in contact. The current may not be sufficient to operate the fuse or circuit breaker, especially if the contact occurs on large-sized feeders.

328. The following items of equipment and conductor enclosures must be grounded:

1. ALL METALLIC CONDUCTOR ENCLOSURES, except in runs of less than 25 ft, which are free from probable contact with ground, grounded metal, metal lath, or conductive thermal insulation and which, if within reach from grounded surfaces, are guarded against contact by persons.

2. FIXED EQUIPMENT – GENERAL. Under any of the following conditions, exposed non-current-carrying metal parts of fixed equipment, which are liable to become energized, shall be grounded.

   a. Where equipment is supplied by means of metal-clad wiring.

   b. Where equipment is located in a wet location and is not isolated.

   c. Where equipment is located within reach of a person who can make contact with any grounded surface or object.

   d. Where equipment is located within reach of a person standing on the ground.

   e. Where equipment is in a hazardous location.

   f. Where equipment is in electrical contact with metal or metal lath.

   g. Where equipment operates with any terminal at more than 150 volts to ground, except as follows:

   (1) Enclosures for switches or circuit breakers where accessible to qualified persons only.

   (2) Metal frames of electrically heated devices, exempted by special permission, in which case the frames shall be permanently and effectively insulated from ground.

   (3) Transformers mounted on wooden poles at a height of more than 8 ft from the ground.

3. FIXED EQUIPMENT – SPECIFIC. Exposed non-current-carrying metal parts of the following kinds of equipment, regardless of voltage, shall be grounded:

   a. Frames of motors as specified in section 430-142 of the Code.

   b. Controller cases for motors, except lined covers of snap switches.

   c. Electric equipment of elevators and cranes.

   d. Electric equipment in garages, theaters, and motion-picture studios, except pendant lamp holders on circuits of not more than 150 volts to ground.

   e. Motion-picture projection equipment.

   f. Electric signs and associated equipment, unless these are inaccessible to unauthorized persons and are also insulated from ground and from other conductive objects.

   g. Generator and motor frames in an electrically operated organ, unless the generator is effectively insulated both from ground and from the motor driving it.

   h. Switchboard frames and structures supporting switching equipment, except that frames of direct-current single-polarity switchboards need not be grounded where effectively insulated.

   i. Equipment supplied by Class 1 and Class 2 remote-control and signaling circuits where part B of article 250 of the Code requires those circuits to be grounded.

4. NONELECTRICAL EQUIPMENT. The following metal parts shall be grounded:

   a. Frames and tracks of electrically operated cranes.

   b. The metal frame of a nonelectrically driven elevator car to which electric conductors are attached.

   c. Hand-operated metal shifting ropes or cables of electric elevators.

d. Metal enclosures such as partitions and grill work around equipment carrying voltages in excess of 750 volts between conductors, unless in substations or vaults under the sole control of the supply company.

Where extensive metal in or on buildings may become energized and is subject to personal contact, adequate bonding and grounding will provide additional safety.

5. EQUIPMENT CONNECTED BY CORD AND PLUG. Under any of the following conditions, exposed non-current-carrying metal parts of cord- and plug-connected equipment which are liable to become energized shall be grounded:

a. In hazardous locations (see articles 500 to 517 of the Code).

b. When operated at more than 150 volts to ground, except:

(1) Motors, where guarded.

(2) Metal frames of electrically heated appliances exempted by section 422-16 of the Code.

c. In residential occupancies, (1) refrigerators, freezers, air conditioners, and (2) clothes-washing, clothes-drying, and dish-washing machines, sump pumps, and (3) portable, hand-held, motor-operated tools and appliances of the following types: drills, hedge clippers, lawn mowers, wet scrubbers, sanders and saws.

Exception: Portable tools and appliances covered by item (3) of paragraph c, protected by an approved system of double insulation, or its equivalent, need not be grounded. Where such an approved system is employed the equipment shall be distinctively marked.

Portable tools or appliances not provided with special insulating or grounding protection are not intended to be used in damp, wet, or conductive locations.

d. In other than residential occupancies, (1) refrigerators, freezers, air conditioners, and (2) clothes-washing, clothes-drying, and dish-washing machines, sump pumps, and (3) portable, hand-held, motor-operated tools and appliances of the following types: drills, hedge clippers, lawn mowers, wet scrubbers, sanders, and saws, and (4) cord- and plug-connected appliances used in damp or wet locations, or by persons standing on the ground or on metal floors or working inside metal tanks or boilers, and (5) portable tools that are likely to be used in wet and conductive locations.

Exception No. 1: Portable tools that are likely to be used in wet and conductive locations need not be grounded where supplied through an insulating transformer with ungrounded secondary of not over 50 volts.

Exception No. 2: Portable tools covered by items (3), (4) and (5) of paragraph d and appliances covered by item (3) of paragraph d, protected by an approved system of double insulation, or its equivalent, need not be grounded. Where such an approved system is employed, the equipment shall be distinctively marked. Where conditions of maintenance and supervision assure that proper grounding of tools or appliances will be maintained (as, for example, on some factory production lines), it is recommended that grounded-type tools and appliances be used.

It is recommended that the frames of all portable motors that operate at more than 50 volts to ground be grounded.

329. The types of wiring systems required to have a system ground are as follows:

1. Two-wire d-c systems of not more than 300 volts supplying interior wiring unless the system supplies industrial equipment in limited areas and is equipped with a ground detector as described in Div. 1.

It is recommended that two-wire, d-c systems operating at more than 300 volts between conductors be grounded if a neutral point can be established such that the maximum difference of potential between the neutral point and any other point on the system does not exceed 300 volts. It is recommended that two-wire, d-c systems be not grounded if the voltage to ground of either conductor would exceed 300 volts after grounding.

2. Three-wire d-c systems supplying interior wiring.

3. Alternating-current systems, provided the grounded conductor is so arranged that the maximum voltage to ground is between 50 and 150 volts. Grounding is also recommended where the voltage to ground will be between 150 and 300 volts and is allowable in some cases on higher voltages. Any uninsulated service conductor must be grounded.

4. Alternating-current systems of less than 50 volts if supplied by transformers from systems of more than 150 volts to ground or from ungrounded systems or if run overhead outside buildings.

5. Secondary circuits of current and potential instrument transformers, when primary winding is connected to a circuit of 300 volts or more to ground, and in all cases when mounted on switchboard.

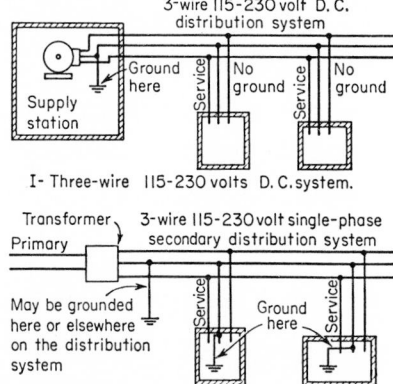

I- Three-wire 115-230 volts D.C. system.

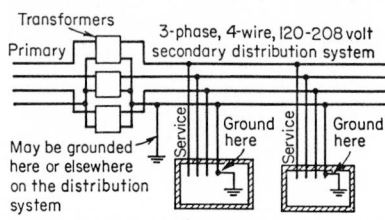

II-Three-wire 115-230 volts single phase A.C. system.

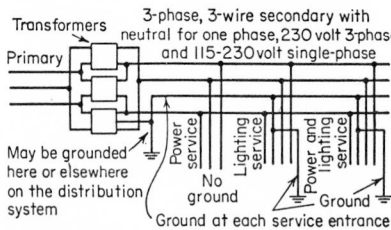

III-Four-wire 120-208 volts three-phase A.C. system.

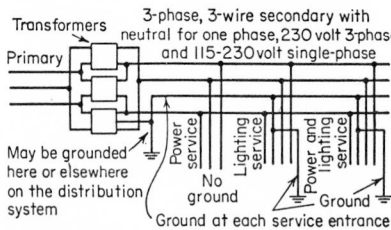

IV- Four wire 230 volts three-phase A.C. system, with one phase arranged three wire, 115-230 volts.

FIG. 239 *Location of system grounds.* (*NFPA Handbook of the National Electrical Code.*)

Electric-furnace circuits are not required to be grounded.

330. Circuits Which Must Not Be Grounded. Circuits for electric cranes operating over combustible fibers in Class III hazardous locations (refer to Sec. **383** for description of hazardous locations).

331. The Location of the System Ground (Fig. 239). 1. For d-c systems the ground must be at the supply station and nowhere else.

2. For a-c systems there must be a ground at the secondary of the transformer supplying the system. There must be another ground at each building service on the supply side of the service switch.

3. For two or more buildings served by a master service the ground must be located at each building utilizing two or more branch circuits, or if the building houses livestock, or if equipment is required to be grounded.

4. For a separately derived system which is not connected to an exterior distribution system the common main grounding conductor shall be made at the transformer, generator, or other source of supply or at the switchboard on the supply side of the first switch controlling the system.

332. The Conductor to Be Grounded. For alternating-current interior wiring systems the conductor to be grounded shall be as follows:

1. Single-phase two-wire: the identified conductor.

2. Single-phase three-wire: the identified neutral conductor.

3. Multiphase systems having one wire common to all phases: the identified common conductor.

4. Multiphase systems having one phase grounded: the identified conductor.

5. Multiphase systems in which one phase is used as in (2): the identified neutral conductor. One phase only can be grounded.

The identified conductor is commonly known as "the white wire."

333. The non-current-carrying metallic parts of fixed equipment are considered to be satisfactorily grounded under any one of the following conditions (fixed equipment includes boxes, cabinets, and fittings):

1. If metallically connected to grounded cable armor or the grounded metal enclosure of conductors. This is the common and preferable method.

2. By a grounding conductor run with circuit conductors, this conductor may be uninsulated, but if an individual covering is provided for this conductor, it shall be finished to show a green color.

3. Electric equipment secured to and in contact with the grounded structural metal frame of a building shall be deemed to be grounded.

4. Metal car frames supported by metal hoisting cables attached to or running over sheaves or drums of elevator machines shall be deemed to be grounded where the machine is grounded in accordance with the Code.

5. By special permission, other means for grounding fixed equipment may be used.

334. Portable and/or Cord and Plug-connected Equipment. The non-current-carrying metal parts of cord- and plug-connected equipment required to be grounded may be grounded in any one of the following ways:

1. By means of the metal enclosure of the conductors feeding such equipment, provided an approved grounding-type attachment plug is used, one fixed contacting member being for the purpose of grounding the metal enclosure, and provided, further, that the metal enclosure of the conductors is attached to the attachment plug and to the equipment by connectors approved for the purpose.

Exception: The grounding contacting member of grounding-type attachment plugs on the power supply cord of portable hand-held, hand-guided, or hand-supported tools or appliances may be of the movable self-restoring type.

Attachment plug caps are not intended to be used as terminations for metal-clad cable or flexible metal conduit.

2. By means of a grounding conductor run with the power supply conductors in a cable assembly or flexible cord that is properly terminated in an approved grounding-type attachment plug having a fixed grounding contacting member. The grounding conductor in a cable assembly may be uninsulated; but where an individual covering is provided for such conductors, it shall be finished a continuous green color or a continuous green color with one or more yellow stripes.

Exception: The grounding contacting member of grounding-type attachment plugs on the power supply cord of portable tools or portable appliances may be of the movable self-restoring type.

3. A separate flexible wire or strap, insulated or bare, protected as well as practicable against physical damage may be used only by special permission except where a part of an approved portable equipment.

335. Bonding at Service Equipment. The electrical continuity of the grounding circuit for the following equipment and enclosures shall be assured by one of the means given in Sec. **336.**

1. The service raceways or service cable armor or sheath, except as provided in sections 230-63(*b*) and 250-55 of the Code.

2. All service equipment enclosures containing service-entrance conductors, including meter fittings, boxes, or the like, interposed in the service raceways or armor.

3. Any conduit or armor that forms part of the grounding conductor to the service raceway.

336. Continuity at Service Equipment. Electrical continuity at service equipment shall be assured by one of the following means:

1. Bonding equipment to the grounded service conductor in a manner provided in section 250-113 of the Code.

2. Threaded couplings and threaded bosses on enclosures with joints shall be made up wrench-tight where rigid conduit is involved.

3. Threadless couplings made up tight for rigid metal conduit and electrical metallic tubing.

4. Bonding jumpers meeting the other requirements of this section. Bonding jumpers shall be used around concentric or eccentric knockouts which are punched or otherwise formed so as to impair the electric connection to ground.

5. Other devices (not lock nuts and bushings) approved for the purpose.

337. The equipment and conductor-enclosure ground should be located as close to the service entrance or source of supply as practicable. This ground must be so located that no conductor enclosure is grounded through a grounding conductor smaller than

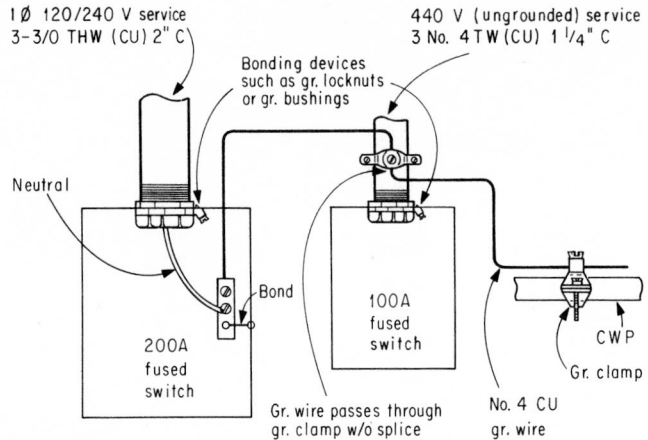

FIG. 240 *A single grounding conductor for grounded and ungrounded systems.*

required by the tables in paragraphs 2*a* and 2*b* of Sec. **338.** A common method is to run the equipment ground from the service-switch enclosure. As far as practicable, all other equipment is then connected to ground by electrically continuous conductor enclosures from the service switch. Bonding jumpers or ground wires are used to connect isolated equipment to grounded equipment. Figure 240 shows a single common grounding conductor which grounds a grounded system and the metallic equipment of both an ungrounded system and the grounded system.

338. Size of System Grounding Conductor.

1. For d-c systems: not smaller than the largest conductor supplied by the system and in no case smaller than No. 8. An exception to this rule is a system supplied by a balancer set. In such installations, if the grounded circuit conductor is a neutral derived from a balancer winding or a balancer set protected in an approved manner, the size of the grounding conductor shall not be less than that of the neutral conductor but in no case smaller than No. 8.

2. For a-c systems and service equipment as follows:

a. The size of the grounding conductor for an a-c system or for a common grounding conductor shall not be less than is given in the following table, except that where connected to made electrodes the conductor need not be larger than No. 6 copper wire or its equivalent in carrying capacity.

(Sizes are in AWG or 1,000 cir mils)

Largest service conductor or equivalent for multiple conductors		Grounding conductor	
Copper	Aluminum	Copper	Aluminum[a]
2 or smaller	0 or smaller	8	6
1 or 0	2/0 or 3/0	6	4
2/0 or 3/0	4/0 or 250 MCM	4	2
Over 3/0 to 350 MCM	Over 250 to 500 MCM	2	0
Over 350 to 600 MCM	Over 500 to 900 MCM	0	3/0
Over 600 to 1,100 MCM	Over 900 to 1,750 MCM	2/0	4/0
Over 1,100 MCM	Over 1,750 MCM	3/0	250 MCM

[a] See installation restrictions in section 250-92(*a*) of the Code. See section 250-23(*b*) of the Code.

b. If the wiring system is not grounded at the premises, the size of a grounding conductor for a service raceway, for the metal sheath or armor of a service cable, and for service equipment shall be not less than is given in the following table, except that where connected to made electrodes the conductor need not be larger than No. 6 copper or its equivalent in carrying capacity.

(Sizes are in AWG or 1,000 cir mils)

Largest service conductor or equivalent for multiple conductors		Grounding conductor			
Copper	Aluminum	Copper	Aluminum	Conduit or pipe	Electrical metallic tubing
2 or smaller	0 or smaller	8	6	$\frac{1}{2}$	$\frac{1}{2}$
1 or 0	2/0 or 3/0	6	4	$\frac{1}{2}$	1
2/0 or 3/0	4/0 or 250 MCM	4	2	$\frac{3}{4}$	$1\frac{1}{4}$
Over 3/0 to 350 MCM	Over 250 to 500 MCM	2	0	$\frac{3}{4}$	$1\frac{1}{4}$
Over 350 to 600 MCM	Over 500 to 900 MCM	0	3/0	1	2
Over 600 to 1,100 MCM	Over 900 to 1,750 MCM	2/0	4/0	1	2
Over 1,100 MCM	Over 1,750 MCM	3/0	250 MCM	1	2

339. Size of Equipment Grounding Conductors for Grounding Interior Raceway and Equipment

Rating or setting of automatic overcurrent device in circuit ahead of equipment, conduit, etc., (amp) not exceeding:	Size of wire, AWG or 1,000 cir mils	
	Copper	Aluminum[a]
15	14	12
20	12	10
30	10	8
40	10	8
60	10	8
100	8	6
200	6	4
400	3	1
600	1	2/0
800	0	3/0
1,000	2/0	4/0
1,200	3/0	250 MCM
1,600	4/0	350 MCM
2,000	250 MCM	400 MCM
2,500	350 MCM	500 MCM
3,000	400 MCM	600 MCM
4,000	500 MCM	800 MCM
5,000	700 MCM	1,000 MCM
6,000	800 MCM	1,200 MCM

[a] See installation restrictions in Sec. **340.**

340. The National Electrical Code specifications for the material and installation of grounding conductors are as follows:

1. MATERIAL.

a. For System or Common Grounding Conductor. The grounding conductor of a wiring system shall be of copper or other corrosion-resistant material. The conductor may be solid or stranded, insulated or bare. Except in cases of bus bars, the grounding conductor shall be without joint or splice throughout its length. If the grounding conductor is not of copper, its electrical resistance per linear foot shall not exceed and its tensile strength shall not be less than that of the allowable copper conductor for such a purpose.

b. For Conductor Enclosures and Equipment Only. The grounding conductor for equipment and for conduit and other metal raceways or enclosures for conductors may be a conductor of copper or other corrosion-resistant material, stranded or solid, insulated or bare, a bus bar, or a rigid metal conduit, electrical metallic tubing or flexible metal conduit and fittings both approved for grounding purposes, the armor of Type AC metal-clad cable, Type MI or ALS cable. Under conditions favorable to corrosion, a suitable corrosion-resistant material shall be used. All bolted and threaded connections at joints and fittings shall be made tight by the use of suitable tools.

2. INSTALLATION.

a. System or Common Grounding Conductor. A grounding conductor, No. 4 or larger, may be attached to the surface on which it is carried without the use of knobs, tubes, or insulators. It need not have protection unless exposed to severe physical damage. A No. 6 grounding conductor, which is free from exposure to physical damage, may be run along the surface of the building construction without metal covering or protection, where it is rigidly stapled to the construction; otherwise it shall be in conduit, electrical metallic tubing, or cable armor. Grounding conductors smaller than No. 6 shall be in conduit, electrical metallic tubing, or cable armor. Metallic enclosures for grounding conductors shall be electrically continuous from the point of attachment to cabinets or equipment to the grounding electrode, and shall be securely fastened to the ground clamp or fitting. Metallic enclosures which are not physically continuous from cabinet or equipment to the grounding electrode can be made electrically continuous by bonding each end to the grounding conductor. Where rigid metal conduit or steel pipe is used as protection for a grounding conductor, the installation shall comply with the requirement of article 346 of the Code; where electrical metallic tubing is used, the installation shall comply with the requirements of article 348 of the Code. Aluminum grounding conductors shall not be used where in direct contact with masonry or the earth or where subject to corrosive conditions. If used outside, aluminum grounding conductors shall not be installed within 18 in. of the earth.

b. Conductor Enclosures and Equipment Only. A grounding conductor for conductor enclosures and equipment only shall meet the requirements of the preceding paragraph *a* of this section, except that where smaller than No. 6, as permitted by Sec. **339,** it need not be armored or installed in a raceway if run through the hollow spaces of a wall or partition or otherwise run so as to be not subject to mechanical injury.

341. Cord-connected and Pendant Equipment (National Electrical Code). For grounding cord-connected or pendant equipment, the conductors of which are protected by fuses or circuit breakers rated or set at not exceeding 20 amp, No. 18 copper wire may be used. Conductors of No. 16 or 18 copper which are used for grounding cord-connected equipment shall be part of an approved flexible-cord assembly. For grounding cord-connected or pendant equipment protected at more than 20 amp, the table in Sec. **339** shall be followed.

342. The grounding electrodes may be:

1. WATER PIPE. A metallic underground water piping system, either local or supplying a community, shall always be used as the grounding electrode where such a piping system is available. If the buried portion of the metallic piping system is less than 10 ft (including well casings bonded to the piping system) or there is some likelihood of the piping system being disconnected, it shall be supplemented by one or more of the grounding electrodes given in items 2 to 5, inclusive. Also, where a water system is not available, one or more of the grounding electrodes given in 2 to 5 may be used.

2. THE METAL FRAME OF THE BUILDING, if effectively grounded.

3. A CONTINUOUS METALLIC UNDERGROUND PIPING SYSTEM. Connecting to a gas piping system is subject to local approval.

4. OTHER LOCAL METALLIC UNDERGROUND SYSTEMS, such as piping, tanks, and the like.

5. A MADE ELECTRODE consisting of a concrete-encased electrode driven pipe, driven rod, buried plate, or other approved device conforming to the following:

a. Concrete-encased Electrodes. Not less than 20 ft of bare copper conductor of a size specified in the table in paragraph 2*a* of Sec. **338,** and in no case smaller than No. 4 encased along the bottom of a concrete foundation footing which is in direct contact with the earth.

b. Plate Electrodes. Each plate electrode shall present not less than 2 sq ft of surface to exterior soil. Electrodes of iron or steel plates shall be at least ½ in. in thickness. Electrodes of nonferrous metal shall be at least 0.06 in. in thickness.

c. Pipe Electrodes. Electrodes of pipe or conduit shall be not smaller than the
3/4-in. trade size and, if of iron or steel, shall have the outer surface galvanized or otherwise metal-coated for corrosion protection.

d. Rod Electrodes. Electrodes of rods of steel or iron shall be at least 5/8 in. in diameter. Approved rods of nonferrous materials or their approved equivalent used for
electrodes shall be not less than 1/2 in. in diameter.

e. Installation. Electrodes should, as far as practicable, be embedded below permanent moisture level. Except where rock bottom is encountered, pipes or rods shall
be driven to a depth of at least 8 ft regardless of size or number of electrodes used.
Pipes or rods when less than standard commercial length shall preferably be of one
piece. Such pipes or rods shall have clean metal surfaces and shall not be covered
with paint, enamel, or other poorly conducting materials. Where rock bottom is encountered at a depth of less than 4 ft, electrodes shall be buried in a horizontal trench,
and if pipes or rods are used as the electrode, they shall comply with paragraphs *c* and *d*
of this section and shall not be less than 8 ft in length. Each electrode shall be separated at least 6 ft from any other electrode, including those used for signal circuits,
radio, lightning rods, or any other purpose.

f. Resistance. Made electrodes shall, if practicable, have a resistance to ground not
to exceed 25 ohms. If the resistance is not as low as 25 ohms, two or more electrodes
connected in parallel shall be used.

Continuous metallic underground water or gas piping systems in general have a
resistance to ground of less than 3 ohms. Metal frames of buildings and local metallic
underground piping systems, metal well casings, and the like have, in general, a resistance substantially below 25 ohms. It is recommended that in locations where it is
necessary to use made electrodes for grounding interior wiring systems, additional
grounds, such as connections to a system ground conductor, be placed on the distribution circuit. It is also recommended that single electrode grounds, when installed and
periodically afterward, be tested for resistance.

343. Location of Connection to Grounding Electrode (National Electric Code).

1. To WATER PIPES. System or common grounding conductors shall be attached to
a water piping system on the street side of the water meter or on a cold-water pipe of
adequate current-carrying capacity as near as practicable to the water service entrance
to the building. If the source of the water supply is from a driven well in the basement
of the premises, the connection shall be made as near as practicable to the well. Where
practicable, the point of attachment shall be accessible. If the point of attachment is
not on the street side of the water meter, the water piping system shall be made electrically continuous by bonding together all parts between the attachment and the
street side of the water meter or the pipe entrance which are liable to become disconnected, as at meters, valves, and service unions. Equipment may be grounded to a
cold-water pipe near the equipment.

2. To GAS PIPES. If permitted, the point of attachment of a grounding conductor to
gas piping shall always be on the street side of the gas meter, and shall be accessible
where practicable.

3. To OTHER ELECTRODES. The grounding conductor shall be attached to other
electrodes permitted in Sec. **342** at a point which will assure a permanent ground.
Where practicable the point of attachment shall be accessible.

344. Attachment of Grounding Conductor (National Electrical Code).

Attachment to Circuits and Equipment. The grounding conductor, bond, or bonding
jumper shall be attached to circuits, conduits, cabinets, equipment, and the like, which
are to be grounded, by means of suitable lugs, pressure connectors, clamps, or other
approved means, except that connections which depend upon solder shall not be used.

Attachment to Electrodes. The grounding conductor shall be attached to the grounding electrode by means of (1) an approved bolted clamp of cast bronze or brass or of
plain or malleable cast iron, (2) a pipe fitting, plug, or other approved device, screwed
into the pipe or into the fitting, or (3) other equally substantial approved means. The
grounding conductor shall be attached to the grounding fitting by means of suitable
lugs, pressure connectors, clamps, or other approved means, except that connections
which depend upon solder shall not be used. Not more than one conductor shall be

connected to the grounding electrode by a single clamp or fitting, unless the clamp or fitting is of a type approved for such use.

Ground Clamps.   For the grounding conductor of a wiring system the sheetmetal-strap type of ground clamp is not considered adequate unless the strap is attached to a rigid metal base which, when installed, is seated on the water pipe or other electrode and the strap is of such material and dimensions that it is not liable to stretch during or after installation.

Ground clamps for use on copper water tubing and copper, brass, or lead pipe should preferably be of copper, and those for use on galvanized or iron pipe should preferably be of galvanized iron and so designed as to avoid physical damage to pipe.   Ground clamps used with aluminum grounding conductors should be approved for the purpose.

Protection of Attachment.   Ground clamps or other fittings, unless approved for general use without protection, shall be protected from ordinary physical damage (1) by being placed where they are not liable to be damaged or (2) by being enclosed in metal, wood, or equivalent protective covering.

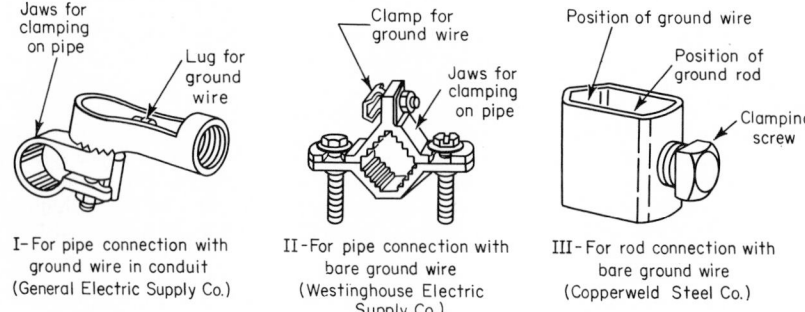

I–For pipe connection with ground wire in conduit (General Electric Supply Co.)

II–For pipe connection with bare ground wire (Westinghouse Electric Supply Co.)

III–For rod connection with bare ground wire (Copperweld Steel Co.)

FIG. 241   *Ground-wire clamps.*

Figure 241 shows some types of grounding clamps.   For the smaller ground wires, which must be enclosed in conduit, the type in Fig. 241, I, is used.   For bare ground wire connected to a water or gas pipe, use the type in Fig. 241, II.   The type in Fig. 241, III, is for a bare wire to be attached to a ground rod.

345. On grounded wiring systems the conductor which is connected to ground must be identified throughout the system.

a. Insulated conductors of No. 6 or smaller, except conductors of Type MI cable, shall have an outer identification of white or natural gray color.   The grounded conductors of Type MI cable shall be identified by distinctive marking at the terminals during the process of installation.

b. Insulated conductors larger than No. 6 shall have an outer identification of white or natural gray color, or shall be identified by distinctive white marking at terminals during process of installation.

c. Where, on a 4-wire delta-connected secondary, the midpoint of one phase is grounded to supply lighting and similar loads, that phase conductor having the higher voltage to ground shall be indicated by tagging or other effective means at any point where a connection is to be made if the neutral conductor is present.

All ungrounded conductors must be finished in black or red or any color contrasting to white.   At the terminals of wiring devices the grounded conductor must be connected to the nickel- or zinc-colored terminal.   On screw-shell lamp holders the grounded conductor must be connected to the screw shell itself.   No single-pole switch or circuit breaker and no fuse shall be used in a grounded conductor.

346. Service entrance for the electrical system of a building may be made by means of overhead or underground service conductors. A service consists of the service conductors and the service equipment. The service conductors are the conductors which supply a building with electrical energy from an electric power system outside the building. They consist of that portion of the supply conductors which extend from the street distribution main or distribution transformer to the service equipment of the building. The service conductors may be located overhead or underground. For overhead conductors the service conductors include the conductors from the last line pole to the service equipment. The service conductors of an overhead service are further classified into two parts: the service-drop conductors and the service-entrance conductors. The **service-drop conductors** are the overhead service conductors from the last line pole or other aerial support to and including the splices, if any, connecting to the service-entrance conductors at the building or other structure. The **service-entrance conductors** of an overhead service are that portion of the service conductors between the service equipment and a point outside the building, clear of the building walls, where they are joined by tap or splice to the service drop.

347. The service equipment must consist of an externally operated disconnecting device and overcurrent protective device.

The disconnecting device must provide a readily accessible means for disconnecting all the service conductors from the source of supply. It may consist of a single switch or manually operated circuit breaker or not more than six switches or six manually operated circuit breakers. In Fig. 242, if there had been only six occupants in the building, the master service switch would not have been required. In multiple-occupancy buildings each occupant must have access to his disconnecting means. Circuit breakers may be equipped with electrical remote control provided that the breaker has in addition a manually operable handle. The disconnecting means must be of a type which will plainly indicate whether it is in the open or closed position. The service switch or breaker must be located as close as is feasible to the point of entrance of the service conductors to the building. It may be located either outside or inside the building. If the switch or breaker does not open the grounded conductor, other means must be provided at the service entrance for disconnecting the grounded conductor of

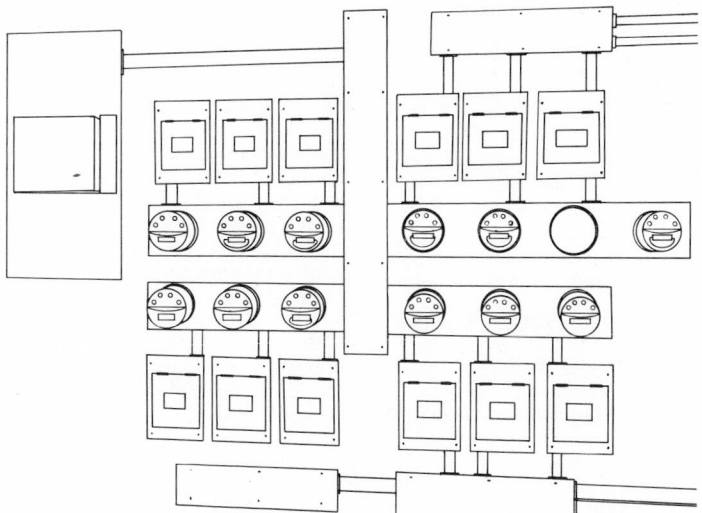

FIG. 242 *Arrangement of meters and service for a multitenant building.*

the supply from the interior wiring. The connection to a neutral terminal bar in the service switch will constitute a satisfactory disconnecting means.

A service switch must have a rating which is not less than the fuse holder in series with it, and the rating must be at least as great as the minimum allowable load (refer to Sec. 52 of Div. 3). Except in special cases of very small occupancies, it is not good practice to install a service switch or circuit breaker that has a rating less than 60 amp. A 30-amp switch should not be used for a two-wire service supplying more than two 15-amp branch circuits. For single-family residences with an initial load of 10 kw or more computed in accordance with Code regulations, or if the initial installation has more than five two-wire branch circuits (refer to Div. 3), the service equipment shall have a rating of not less than 100 amp.

Each ungrounded service conductor must be provided with overcurrent protection. The protection may consist of a single set of fuses or circuit breakers or not more than six sets of fuses or six circuit breakers. For rating of fuses or setting of circuit breakers, refer to Secs. 294 and 295. No overcurrent device shall be inserted in a grounded conductor except a circuit breaker which simultaneously opens all conductors of the service. The protective devices must be located at the same point as the disconnecting means unless located at the outer end of the service raceway.

In addition to the disconnecting means and the protective devices, when the building is supplied directly from public-utility mains, the service equipment will include the kilowatthour meter for the measurement of the power consumption. For small or multiple-occupancy buildings, the branch-circuit distribution equipment frequently is also grouped along with the service equipment (see Fig. 242). If the service overcurrent protective devices are locked or sealed or otherwise not readily accessible, the branch-circuit overcurrent devices must be installed as close as is practicable to the load side of the service equipment. They must be in an accessible location, and be of a lower rating than the service overcurrent device.

The construction and types of service equipment are discussed under switches in Div. 4.

348. There are six possible different arrangements or sequences for service equipment consisting of switch, fuses, and meter, as follows:

1. Switch-fuse-meter.
2. Switch-meter-fuses.
3. Fuses-switch-meter.
4. Fuses-meter-switch.
5. Meter-switch-fuses.
6. Meter-fuses-switch.

When circuit breakers are employed, there are, of course, only two possible sequences: meter-circuit breaker or circuit breaker-meter.

The proper order for placing the switch, fuses, and meter in the circuit has been the subject for much dispute and not enough standardization, each power company reserving for itself the decision on the proper method. Each method has its advantages, and it has been a matter for local decision as to which advantage seems most important to the individual power company.

349. A master service is a service which supplies more than one building under single management. If the buildings are supplied from a private distribution system, the services should be installed in accordance with the general requirements for services from a public utility. In those installations which include properties with their own generating plant, the conductors running from one building to another are not considered as service conductors.

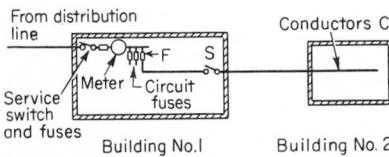

FIG. 243 *Two buildings under single management. No service fuses are required in building 2 if fuses F are of proper rating to protect conductors C. A switch S must be installed to control conductors C. Switch S may be in building 1 if accessible to persons using building 2; otherwise it must be in building 2. (NFPA Handbook of the National Electrical Code.)*

The supply to each building must be separately controlled and properly protected by overcurrent devices. The control should consist of an externally operable enclosed safety switch or a circuit breaker. The control may be located in the building served or in another building, provided that it is accessible to persons using the installation. Garages and outbuildings of residences and farms come under this class of installation. Methods of meeting these requirements are illustrated in Figs. 243 and 244. Although not required and not shown in the figures, it is best practice to equip each building with its own individual control and protection located inside the building itself. The pro-

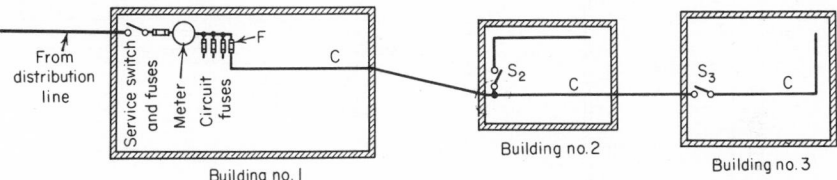

FIG. 244 *Three buildings under single management. If properly protected by fuses F, conductors C require no other fuse protection. A switch S_2 must be provided to control the wiring in building 2, and a switch S_3 to control the wiring in building 3. Switch S_3 may be in either building 1 or building 2 if readily accessible to persons using building 3. (NFPA Handbook of the National Electrical Code.)*

tection for each building should have a lower rating or setting than the protection at F in the figures, so that in case of trouble the protection of any one building will function without operating the device at F.

No service should supply one building from another unless they are under the same management.

350. No building should be supplied by more than one set of service conductors from the same secondary distribution system or from the same transformer except as follows:

1. FIRE PUMPS. If a separate service is required for fire pumps.

2. EMERGENCY LIGHTING. If a separate service is required for emergency lighting purposes.

3. CAPACITY REQUIREMENTS. If capacity requirements make multiple services desirable.

4. BUILDINGS OF LARGE AREA. By special permission, if more than one service drop is necessary owing to the area over which a single building extends.

5. MULTIPLE-OCCUPANCY BUILDINGS. By special permission, in multiple-occupancy buildings where there is no available space for service equipment accessible to all the occupants.

6. BUILDINGS OF MULTIPLE OCCUPANCY may have two or more separate sets of service-entrance conductors which are tapped from one service drop (Fig. 245), or two or more subsets of service-entrance conductors may be tapped from a single set of main service conductors (Fig. 246).

7. WHERE ADDITIONAL SERVICES ARE REQUIRED FOR DIFFERENT CLASSES OF USE, such as needs for different voltage, frequency, or phase, or different rate schedules for different types of use of electric power.

Separate services may be brought into a single building for power and light, respectively, when the lighting is supplied from a separate secondary distribution main as shown in Fig. 247.

Separate services may be brought into a single building for power and light, respectively, if each service is supplied through a separate transformer (Fig. 248) or if the lighting service is supplied from one transformer of a polyphase bank of transformers supplying the power.

351. Size of Service Conductors. Service conductors must have a current-carrying capacity sufficient to supply the load of the building (refer to Div. 3) and regardless of the actual load must have a current-carrying capacity not less than that required by the

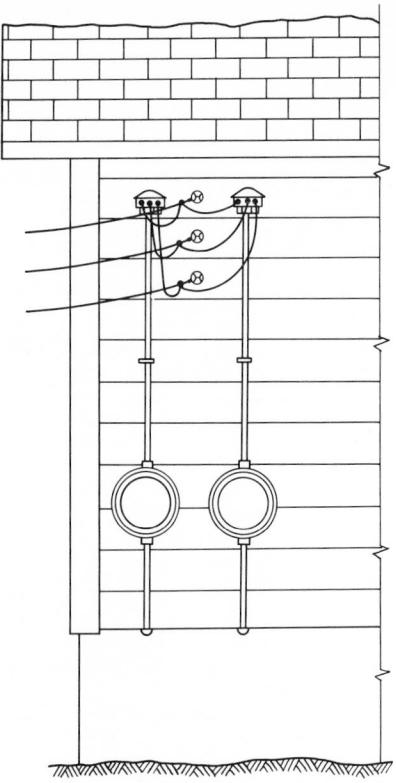

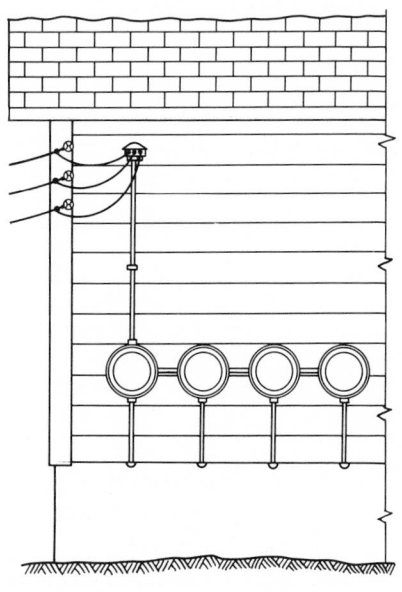

FIG. 245　*Two sets of service-entrance conductors tapped from one service drop.* (*NFPA Handbook of the National Electrical Code.*)

FIG. 246　*Four subsets of service-entrance conductors tapped from one set of main service conductors.* (*NFPA Handbook of the National Electrical Code.*)

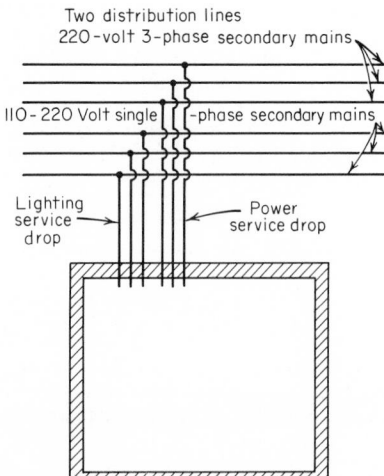

FIG. 247　*Separate services for power and light.*

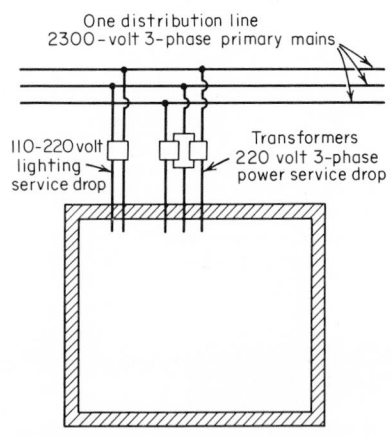

FIG. 248　*Separate services for power and light.*

minimum load requirements of Div. 3. Also, regardless of the load, no wire should be smaller than the following minimum sizes:

Conductors	Minimum Allowable Size
Service entrance for all installations, except ones supplying a single branch circuit	No. 6, except No. 8 by special permission or if supplying only two 2-wire branch circuits
Service entrance supplying a single branch circuit.......	No. 12 (but in no case smaller than size of branch circuit supplied)
Service drop...	No. 10 for soft-drawn copper; No. 12 for medium or hard-drawn copper
Service of over 600 volts..	No. 6, except that in multiconductor cables No. 8 may be used

For single-family residences with an initial load of 10 kw or more computed in accordance with the Code, or if the initial installation has more than five two-wire branch circuits, the service shall be a minimum of 100 amp, 3-wire.

It is recommended that a minimum of 100-amp 3-wire service be provided for all individual residences.

352. Splicing of Service Conductors. Service conductors shall be without splices except as follows:

1. At point of tap connection to distribution main.

2. At point of junction of service-drop and service-entrance conductors.

3. Clamped or bolted connections in a meter enclosure are permitted.

4. Taps to main service conductors are permitted as provided in subparagraph 6 of Sec. **350.**

5. A connection is permitted, if properly enclosed, where an underground service conductor enters a building and is to be extended to the service equipment or meter in another form of approved service raceway or service cable.

6. A connection is permitted where service conductors are extended from a service drop to an outside meter location and returned to connect to the service-entrance conductors of an existing installation.

353. Terminating Raceway at Service Equipment (National Electrical Code). If conduit, electrical metallic tubing, or service cable is used for service conductors, the inner end shall enter a terminal box or cabinet or be made up directly to an equivalent fitting, enclosing all live metal parts, except that if the service disconnecting means is mounted on a switchboard having exposed bus bars on the back, the raceway may be equipped with a bushing which shall be of the insulating type unless lead-covered conductors are used.

354. Typical service installations of proper and improper construction are shown in Fig. 249. Overhead services to occupancies having relatively small loads, such as residences and small stores, are generally made with one of the installations shown in Fig. 249, II and III. The installation in Fig. 249, I, violates Code rules because the service head is not located above the point of attachment of the service drop conductors to the building. The present trend is toward installations of the types shown in Figs. 249, II and III, and 250. A good service installation for a low-roof building is shown in Fig. 250. Occasionally the service switch is also mounted outside the building along with the meter.

In congested city residential districts an underground service using underground service-entrance cable is frequently run from overhead lines where a change to underground distribution is planned at a later date. This procedure facilitates the changeover, as the part of the cable which is above ground may in the future be taken down and placed underground and run directly into the underground distribution box. In cities where the distribution is all underground, direct-burial cable or rigid conduit is the most common method of running services. The advantage of the conduit system is that, in case the service needs to be replaced for any reason, the cable may be pulled out of the conduit and another one installed without having to dig up the pavement or sidewalk. For apartment-house service a meter trough is installed in which are mounted the meter sockets, one for each apartment, in one or more horizontal rows (Fig. 242). Directly under each meter is a branch-circuit distribution panel containing fuses or circuit breakers for the branch-circuit protection for the apartment. In some cases a service switch is provided for each apartment, and a feeder is run to the apartment with the branch-circuit distribution panel located in the apartment.

355. For commercial or industrial services the maximum demand is usually metered as well as the kilowatthours. Where the demand is of the order of a few kilowatts, this may be done with a single meter which has a demand-indicating pointer as well as the usual meter dials (Fig. 251). For larger installations a separate indicating-demand meter is installed (Fig. 252). A recording type of demand meter may also be employed for installations of more than about 150 amp; current transformers are usually required in order to reduce the current which the meter has to handle. For an underground service from an urban network system, the service equipment consists of a main fused switch or circuit breaker, a set of current transformers in a sheet-metal cabinet, and meters as outlined above. If the supply comes from a radial feeder system, a transformer bank with an oil circuit breaker and disconnect switches is installed at the building ahead of the above service equipment. For an overhead service a transformer bank is installed just outside the building, on a concrete foundation on the ground or on an elevated platform between two poles. The bank will contain high-voltage fuses and lightning arresters in addition to the transformers. The service conductors are then brought into the building in conduit or as individual wires to the

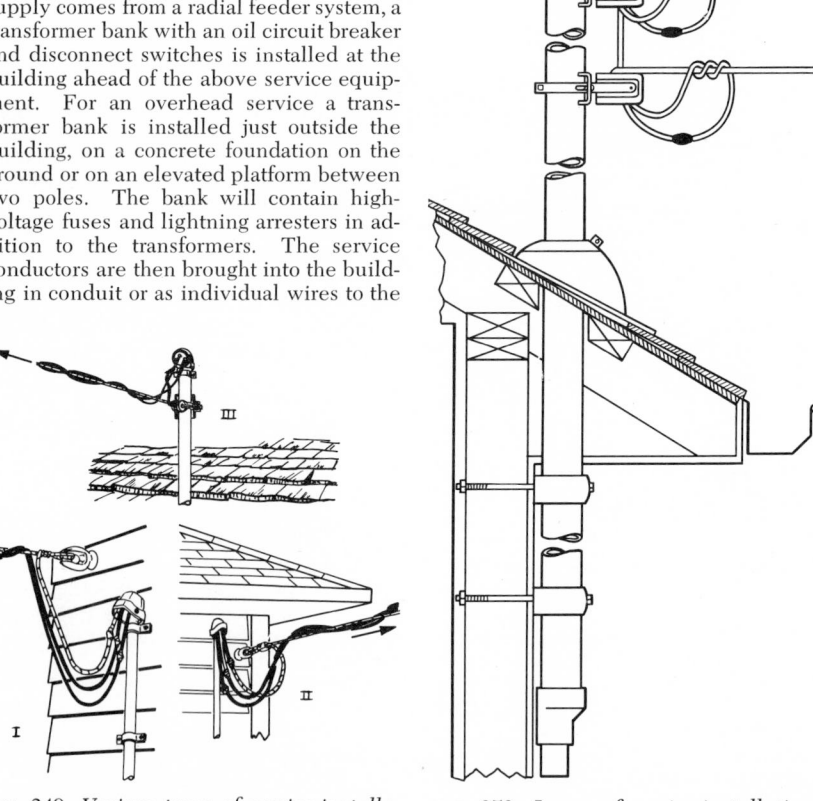

FIG. 249 *Various types of service installations. Drawing I violates the Code. (Electrical Construction and Maintenance.)*

FIG. 250 *Low-roof service installation. (Hubbard & Co.)*

service equipment. Sometimes the metering is installed so as to measure the input to the transformers so that the customer pays directly for the transformer losses. When this is done, high-voltage current and potential transformers are installed in the leads to the primary of the transformers. The meters may then be located in a weatherproof cabinet outside the building or located inside the building wall, as before, with a conduit to carry the secondary leads from the instrument transformers.

356. Connections Ahead of Disconnecting Means. The National Electrical Code allows service fuses, meters, high-impedance shunt circuits (such as potential coils of meters, etc.), supply conductors for time switches, surge protective capacitors, instrument transformers, lightning arresters and circuits for emergency sys-

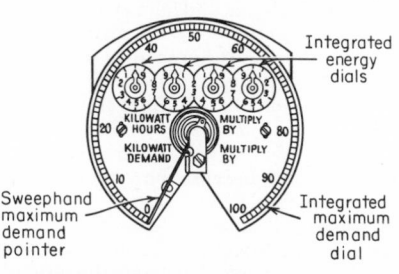

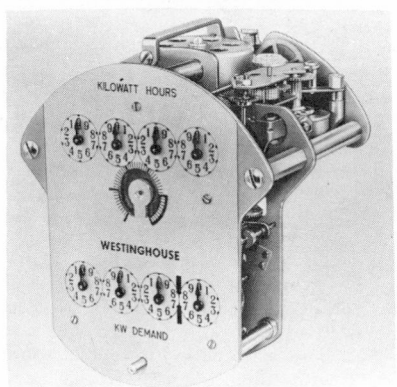

FIG. 251 *Dial for a watthour meter with demand-indicating pointer. (Westinghouse Electric Corp.)*

FIG. 252 *Indicating-demand meter. (Westinghouse Electric Corp.)*

tems, fire pump equipment, and fire and sprinkler alarms as provided in section 230-94 of the Code to be connected on the supply side of the disconnecting means.

CRANE WIRING

357. Wiring for cranes consists of the following elements:
1. Collector switch.
2. Main collector contact conductors.
3. Cab main-line switch.
4. Bridge collector contact conductors.
5. Motor-circuit wiring.

358. A collector switch or circuit breaker must be installed in every circuit feeding crane wires. A fused switch is most frequently used to provide overload protection, although in important installations, where reliability is essential — where equipment must be placed back in service after an accident, in minimum time — circuit breakers are used. From an electrical standpoint the best location for the switch is at the center of the run.

It must be readily operable from the ground, be within sight of the crane or hoist and the collector conductors, and be of a type which can be locked in the open position. It shall open all ungrounded conductors simultaneously.

359. The main collector contact conductors are bare copper trolley wires or structural-steel conductors that are erected parallel to the crane runway. The location of the conductors is determined by conditions. Sometimes the crane builder specifies that the conductors must be located in a certain position, and in other cases the purchaser selects and specifies the position of the conductors, and the crane manufacturer arranges the current collectors on the crane accordingly.

360. Trolley wire for cranes is hard-drawn copper, the same as used in electric traction. Hard-drawn wire must be used to prevent excessive stretching. Round wire is erected where the method of support adopted does not involve the use of trolley ears for holding it at intermediate points between the ends of the run. Where trolley ears are used figure-eight or, preferably, grooved trolley wire should be used, because it can be readily held in screw-clamp trolley ears. Round wire can be used with trolley ears, but the ear flanges of these must be hammered down around the wire, a time-consuming operation requiring some skill; also, a round-wire ear introduces a hump on the wire and makes the trolley wheel jump and draw an arc when the wheel passes over the raised place. Either 0, 2/0, 3/0, or 4/0 wire is usually required. The wire size required is ordinarily specified by the crane builder, but in any case it should be large enough so that the voltage drop in it will not much exceed 3 or 4 per cent of the line voltage with all the crane motors operating at full load. In no case should the wires be smaller than the minimum allowable sizes given in Sec. **371** for bridge collector conductors.

361. Trolley rails of structural steel are being used to some extent instead of copper trolley wire to supply current to cranes and other moving electrical machinery. The steel rails are made sufficiently heavy so that they cannot break and fall as copper wires occasionally do. Sometimes strap steel bars are used, but more frequently a section is adopted, such as an angle or a tee, which has considerable stiffness in all directions. Steel conductors should be painted, except on the contact edge or face, to prevent corrosion. Either a shoe or a trolley wheel can be used to collect current from a steel conductor rail. A shoe or spoon, which makes a rubbing contact, is probably preferable for the average application. Trolley-wheel collectors that travel at high speeds are not successful for current collection from steel conductors, because the wheel tends to bounce and jump from the rigid rail at joints and uneven places.

362. The main collector contact conductors must be isolated by elevation or provided with suitable guards so that persons cannot inadvertently touch the live parts while in contact with the ground or with conducting material connected to the ground. If the crane travels over easily ignitible combustible fibers and materials, the collector conductors must be protected by barriers so arranged as to prevent the escape of sparks or hot particles. Probably the best location for the collector conductors on a bridge-crane runway is between the flanges of and parallel to one of the crane girders. Here the conductors are out of the way and well protected and can be readily supported. It is not often that they are erected in any other position. Occasionally the trolley wires can be supported from the roof trusses above the crane runway and are installed similarly to the trolley wires for trolley cars. A pole collector with a wheel at its upper end, exactly like a trolley-car pole but much shorter, is used. Where the spacing between roof trusses is very great, this method may not give good results because of the wire swinging and the trolley coming off. The collector conductors, when carried along runways, should normally be supported on insulating supports at intervals not exceeding 20 ft and separated from each other at least 6 in. except that a spacing of not less than 3 in. may be used for monorail hoists. If wires are used, they should be secured at the ends with approved strain insulators and so mounted on intermediate insulators that the extreme displacement of the wires will not bring them closer than 1½ in. from the surface wired over. Where necessary the intervals between supports may be increased up to 40 ft provided that the separation between conductors is increased proportionately. All sections of the conductors must be so joined that a continuous electrical connection is provided. The collector conductors must not supply any equipment other than that of the crane or cranes which they are designed to serve.

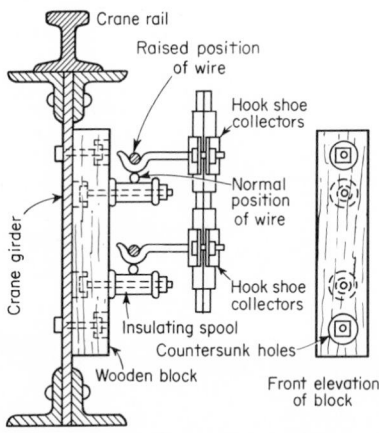

FIG. 253 *Intermediate bracket for trolley wire.*

363. Methods of supporting crane trolley wires differ with conditions. If the crane is provided with hook-shoe collectors (Fig. 253), which slide along under and carry the weight of the trolley wire, the wire is rigidly held only at the terminations at the ends of the run and is kept from sagging by intermediate, insulating brackets, like those shown in Fig. 253. If trolley-wheel current collectors are used, the tension in the wire is taken by the terminations, and the wire is also rigidly held by trolley ears at intermediate points.

364. Terminations are made as shown in Fig. 254. Strain insulators separate the trolley wire electrically from the building members, and either a turnbuckle or an eyebolt with a long thread can be used for pulling the slack from the wire and adjusting its tension. The terminations should be depended upon to assume the entire tension of the wire. The intermediate supports are placed merely to prevent excessive sagging. The members which take the stresses of the eyebolts at the terminations should

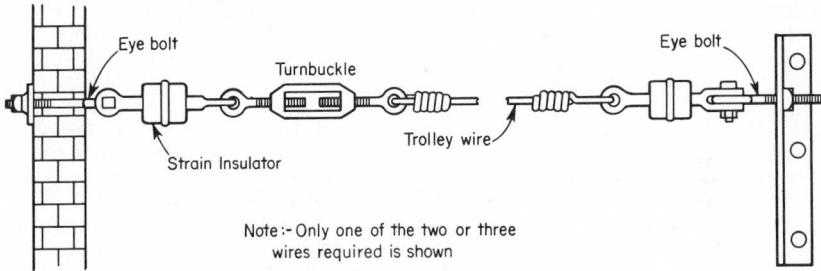

FIG. 254 *Trolley supports at ends of run.*

be very substantial or thoroughly braced, because on them depends the reliability of the entire installation. The eyebolts, turnbuckles, and strain insulators should be not smaller than the ⅝-in. size.

365. Intermediate supports for crane trolley wires, the supports installed between the terminations to prevent sagging, can be arranged as shown in Figs. 253, 255, and 256. The bracket of Fig. 253 is, as above outlined, applicable only where the crane has hook-shoe collectors. The block of wood that supports the insulating spools should be thoroughly dry and treated with an insulating paint. The bolt holes in it should be deeply countersunk to eliminate the possibility of grounds. The spools

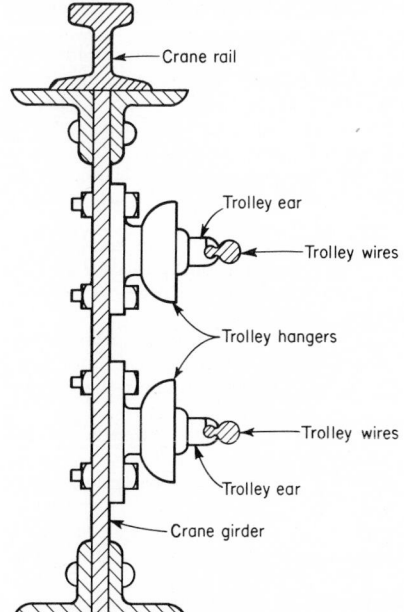

FIG. 255 *Trolley hanger support.*

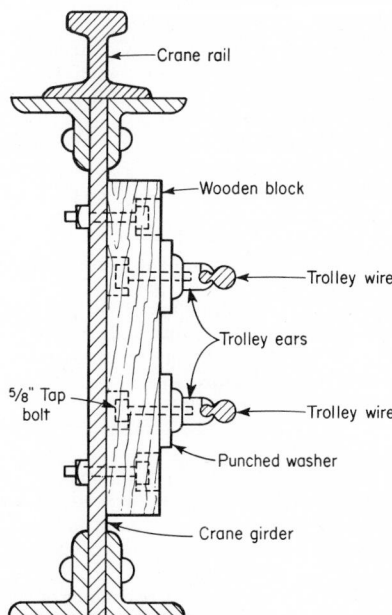

FIG. 256 *Trolley ear supports.*

should be of porcelain. Porcelain tubes with porcelain knobs at the ends to form flanges will do. The length of the insulator between flanges should be at least 4 in. Spools turned from fiber are sometimes used. The spools should be so arranged that there will be at least a ½-in. clearance between them and the hook shoe when it passes along.

In a fireproof building, where the crane has trolley-wheel collectors, the wires can be supported by trolley ears as in Fig. 256. The wooden supporting block must be thoroughly painted, and the bolt holes in it deeply countersunk to prevent the possibility of grounds. Tap bolts, screwing in from the rear, support the screw-clamp trolley ears which seat against washers. Figure-eight or, preferably, grooved trolley wire is used. The wire should be drawn tightly at the terminations, and the ears should be installed every 8 or 10 ft.

For an outdoor crane, as well as for indoor applications, the wires can be supported in some cases as shown in Fig. 255. Standard street-railway-type trolley hangers and ears are used, which provide excellent insulation. The hangers can, provided a proper location of the trolley wires results, be bolted directly to the crane girder.

366. There are almost numberless ways in which steel conductor rails can be arranged and supported. The arrangement of a structural-steel tee conductor or trolley rail is shown in Fig. 257. Although the arrangement illustrated was developed for serving monorail cranes, which travel on the lower flanges of I beams, only minor modifications in the supporting forging would be required to adapt it for serving bridge cranes or other similar traveling electrical machines. Note that a feature of the method is that no drilling or close fitting is required in the field. The only piece that is different for different jobs is the supporting forging, but this can be formed and drilled in the shop. The only tools required to erect the rail are a hack saw for cutting the tee, which is purchased in 30-ft lengths, and a wrench for setting the bolts. No bolt smaller than ⅝ in. diameter is used, because smaller ones than this can be twisted asunder too easily. A 1½- by 1½- by ³/₁₆-in. T bar was selected, because this is about the smallest size that is rigid enough to sustain itself effectively between supports. A T bar of this size has a conductivity equivalent to that of a 109,800-cir mil copper conductor, i.e., a copper conductor between Nos. 0 and 2/0 in size.

The insulating hanger (Fig. 257, II) is similar to a trolley hanger but smaller. A malleable-iron bell encloses the molded material that supports and insulates the hanger stud. The Johns-Manville Co. makes the insulator to special order, and its mold number is 4689-B. The splicing plate (IV) and the clamp (V) are castings, preferably malleable iron, and the only machine work on them is the drilling and tapping of the holes. The section insulator (VI) consists of two castings, a fiber dividing block, and two wrought-iron clamping plates. Directions for spacing the insulating supports when erecting the conductor are given on the illustration. The terminal lug (VIII) is forked instead of annular, so that it can be readily disconnected for isolating circuits for testing without taking out a bolt.

Rigid collector conductors must have insulating supports spaced at intervals of not more than eighty times the vertical dimension of the conductor, but in no case greater than 15 ft, and spaced apart sufficiently to give a clear electrical separation of conductors or adjacent collectors of not less than 1 in.

367. Track as Circuit Conductor (National Electrical Code). Monorail, tramrail, or crane-runway tracks may be used as a conductor of current for one phase of a three-phase a-c system furnishing power to the carrier, crane, or trolley, provided the following conditions are fulfilled:

1. The conductors for supplying the other two phases of the power supply shall be insulated.

2. The power for all phases shall be obtained from an insulating transformer.

3. The voltage shall not exceed 300 volts.

4. The rail serving as a conductor shall be effectively grounded at the transformer and may also be grounded by the fittings used for the suspension or attachment of the rail to a building or structure.

368. In computing the resistance of steel trolley rails, the area in square inches of the section involved can be taken from one of the steel companies' handbooks, such as are issued by the Cambria and Carnegie steel companies; the area in circular mils can then be obtained by using the rule given below. By dividing this area by 6.14, which is the approximate ratio of the resistance of mild steel to that of copper, the equivalent copper area of the steel conductor results. Then by using the standard formula for the resistance of a copper conductor, the actual resistance of the steel is obtained.

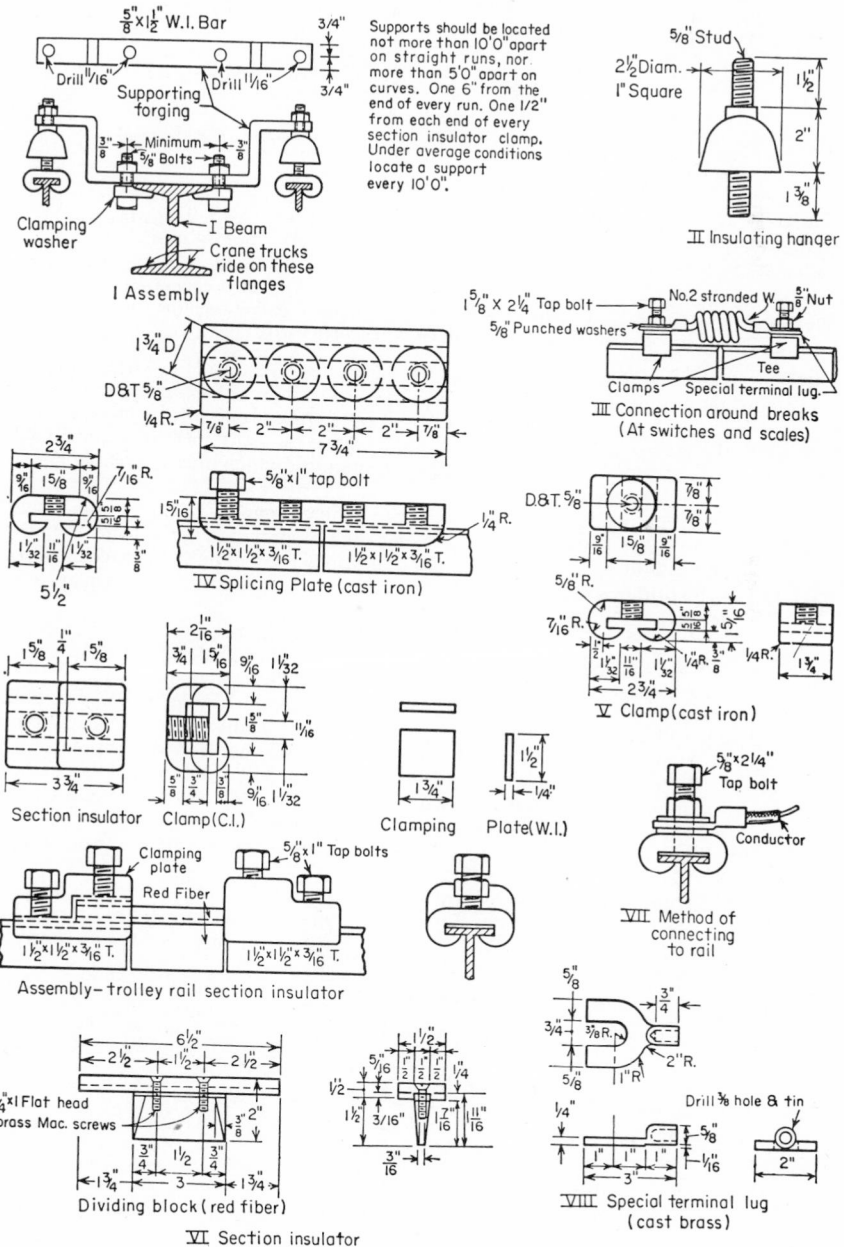

FIG. 257 *Steel trolley rail.*

Example. What is the resistance of 160 ft of 1½- by 1½- by ³/₁₆-in. steel angle? (See Fig. 258 for a picture of the section.)

Solution. By referring to a handbook, it will be noted that the area of 1½- by 1½- by ³/₁₆-in. steel angle is 0.53 sq in. Then, to find its area in circular mils,

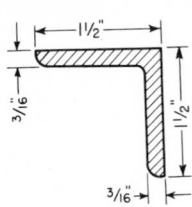

FIG. 258 *Section of 1½- by 1½- by ³/₁₆-in. steel angle.*

$$\text{Cir mils} = \frac{\text{area in sq in.}}{0.000,000,785,4} = \frac{0.53}{0.000,000,785,4}$$

$$= 674,800 \text{ cir mils.}$$

Then   Equivalent in copper $= \dfrac{\text{cir mils area of steel}}{6.14}$

$$= \frac{674,800}{6.14} = 109,800 \text{ cir mils}$$

Then the resistance of the 160-ft length will be

$$\text{Resistance (for copper)} = \frac{11 \times \text{ft}}{\text{cir mils}} = \frac{11 \times 160}{109,800} = 0.016 \text{ ohm}$$

The resistance, therefore, of 160 ft of 1½- by 1½- by ³/₁₆-in. steel angle is 0.016 ohm. It is evident from the equivalent copper area of the steel (109,800 cir mils) that the conductivity of the steel section will lie between the conductivities of No. 1/0 (105,500 cir mils) and No. 2/0 (133,100 cir mils) copper wire.

The equivalent copper area in circular mils can be used in any of the wiring formulas for computing drop in a steel conductor, just as the actual area of a copper conductor is used in the same formulas, and the result will be a correct one for the steel section. Obviously the above method is approximate, because the constants are approximate, but it is quite accurate enough for wiring computations, which always involve necessarily inaccurate assumptions.

369. Switch in Cab (National Electrical Code). Where a crane is operated from a cage or cab, a motor-circuit switch or circuit breaker shall be provided in the leads from the runway contact conductors. The switch or circuit breaker shall be in the cage or cab or mounted on the bridge and operable from the cage or cab when the trolley is at one end of the bridge.

On both a-c and d-c crane protective panels, the continuous ampere rating of the main-line switch or circuit breaker and main-line contactors shall be not less than 50 per cent of the combined short-time ampere ratings of the motors or less than 75 per cent of the short-time ampere rating of the motors required for any single crane motion.

370. Bridge collector conductors are required across the crane bridge for carrying the circuit to the carriage and hoist motors. They are usually made of bare copper wires supported in the same general way as described in Secs. **362** to **365** except that bridge collector conductors shall be kept at least 2½ in. apart and, if the span exceeds 80 ft, insulating saddles shall be placed at intervals not exceeding 50 ft.

It is recommended that the distance between wires be greater than 2½ in. where practicable.

371. Contact Conductors. The current-carrying capacity of contact conductors should be not less than 50 per cent of the combined short-time ampere ratings of the motors supplied by them, nor less than 75 per cent of the sum of the short-time ampere ratings of the motors required for any single crane motion.

The National Electrical Code requires that the size of contact wires shall be not less than the following:

Distance between Rigid Supports, Ft	Size of Wire
0–30	No. 6
31–60	No. 4
Over 60	No. 2

372. The motor-circuit wiring must be rubber or thermoplastic type, except that in dry locations it may be of varnished-cambric or asbestos-varnished-cambric type. Type MI cable is allowed both in dry and wet locations. Conductors exposed to external heat or connected to resistors shall have an insulation approved by the Code for the temperature and location. Where conductors not having a flame-resistant outer covering are grouped together, the group shall be covered with a flame-resistant tape.

The conductors must be of a size as given in Table **14** of Div. 11. The wiring must be enclosed in a raceway or be Type MI or Type ALS cable. Where flexible connections to motors or controllers are necessary, flexible metal raceways, metal-clad cable, multiple-conductor rubber-covered cable, or an approved nonmetallic enclosure may be used. Short runs for control equipment in the cab or on the bridge may be enclosed in auxiliary gutters. Short lengths of conductors at resistors and collectors may be left open. A common-return conductor may be used for the several motors of a single crane or hoist.

373. Motor Control and Protective Equipment. The hoist of cranes must be provided with a limit switch which will control the upper limit of travel. It is best practice to arrange the control levers of all traveling cranes, in any one installation, in the same relative position in all the cages of the different cranes. The National Electrical Code allows two motors with their leads, which operate a single hoist, carriage, truck, or bridge and are controlled as a unit by one controller, to be protected by a single over-load device. The device should be located in the cab if there is one.

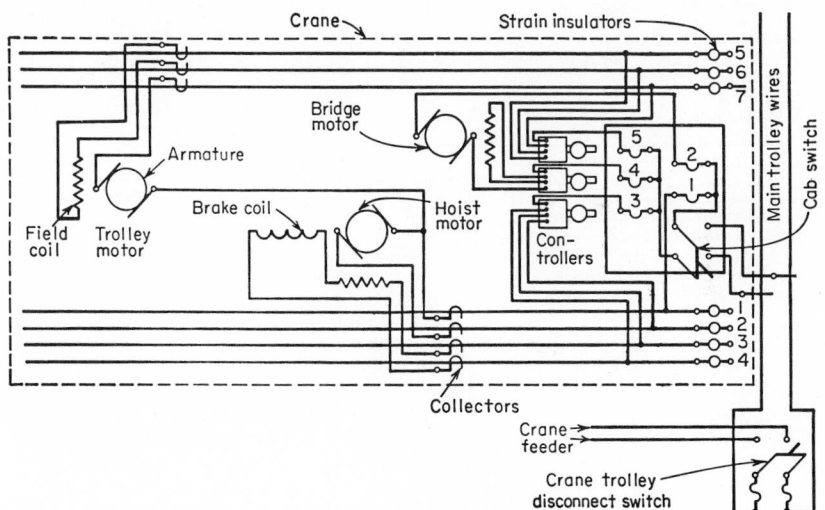

FIG. 259 *Direct-current crane wiring diagram.*

374. A crane-wiring diagram is given in Fig. 259, which is typical for a d-c, three-motor, traveling bridge crane. Variations in crane wiring and control schemes are practically numberless. For d-c cranes, series motors are almost invariably used, while for a-c cranes, wound-rotor motors are used.

WIRING FOR CIRCUITS OVER 600 VOLTS

375. For wiring circuits operating at more than 600 volts, the conductors must have an insulation sufficient for the particular voltage employed. The wires must be in-stalled in rigid conduit, raceways, or in open runs of metal-clad cable, except that in lo-cations accessible to qualified persons only, open runs of nonmetallic-sheathed cable, bare conductors, and bare bus bars may be used. Open runs of braid-covered insulated conductors must have flame-retardant braid, or the braid covering must be treated with a flame-retardant saturant after installation. The braid covering must be stripped back at conductor terminals a distance which, if practicable, is not less than 1 in. for each kilovolt of the conductor-to-ground voltage. Shielding is required on solid dielectric-insulated conductors used for voltages greater than:

	Voltage above which shielding is required, kv (L-L)			
	Neutral grounded		Neutral ungrounded	
Method of installation	Fibrous covered	Ozone-resistant jacket covering	Fibrous covered	Ozone-resistant jacket covering
In metallic conduit or trough above grade located indoors and in dry locations:				
Single conductor..............................	2	5*	2	3
Multiconductor................................	2	5	2	5
Underground ducts and conduits and other wet locations:				
Single conductor..............................	2	3†	2	3
Multiconductor................................	2	5	2	5
On insulators:				
Only multiconductor; not required under 5 kv.........	...	...	3	5
Directly in soil:				
Single conductor..............................	...	3	...	3
Multiconductor................................	...	5	...	5

    * It is presumed that installation conditions will be such as to maintain a high level of jacket surface resistivity and so minimize the possibility of destructive discharge. Pulling dry or the use of insulating-type pulling lubricants will help attain these conditions. Where surface contamination cannot be prevented and high-surface resistivity cannot be maintained, metallic shielding shall be used at over 3 kv.
    NOTE: Sheathed single or 3-conductor cables require no shielding for voltages of 5 kv and less. In the case of portable equipment cables it is good practice to specify shielding for all voltages above 2 kv.
    † For three single-conductor cables, cabled together without over-all outer covering, the value is 5 kv.

The metallic shielding or any other static voltage shields on shielded cable shall be stripped back to a safe distance according to the circuit voltage at all terminations of the shielding, as in potheads and joints. At such points, suitable methods such as the use of potheads, terminators, stress cones, or similar devices shall be employed for stress reduction, and the metallic-shielding tape shall be grounded.

376. Circuit Breakers (National Electrical Code). Indoor installations shall consist of metal-enclosed units or fire-resistant cell-mounted units except that open mounting of circuit breakers is permissible in locations accessible to qualified persons only.

Circuit breakers used to control oil-filled transformers should be located outside the transformer vault.

Circuit breakers shall have a means of indicating the open and closed position of the breaker at the point(s) from which they may be operated.

Circuit breakers shall be trip-free in all positions. In every installation the circuit breaker rating in respect to closing, carrying, or interrupting capabilities shall not be less than the short-circuit duty at the point of application.

Oil circuit breakers shall be so arranged or located that adjacent readily combustible structures or materials are safeguarded in an approved manner. Adequate space separation, fire-resistant barriers or enclosures, trenches containing sufficient coarse crushed stone, and properly drained oil enclosures such as dikes or basins are recognized as suitable for this purpose.

377. Fuse Holders and Fuses (National Electrical Code).

1. Fuses which expel flame in opening the circuit shall be so designed or arranged that they will function properly without hazard to persons or property.

2. Fuse holders shall be designed so that they can be deenergized while replacing a fuse unless the fuse and fuse holder are designed to permit fuse replacement by qualified persons using equipment designed for the purpose without deenergizing the fuse holder.

3. When high-voltage fused cutouts are installed in a building or a transformer vault,

they shall be of a type designed for use in buildings. Where such cutouts are not suitable to interrupt the circuit manually while carrying full load, an approved switch or contactor shall be provided which is capable of interrupting the entire load. In addition, the cutouts shall be interlocked with the approved interrupter or bear a conspicuous sign reading "Do Not Open Cutout Under Load."

The cutouts shall be so located that they may be readily and safely operated and refused. Fuses shall be accessible from a clear floor space.

4. Load-interrupter switches may be used providing suitable fuses or circuit breakers are applied in conjunction with these devices to interrupt fault currents. When these devices are used in combination, they shall be so coordinated electrically that they will safely withstand the effects of closing, carrying, or interrupting all possible currents up to the assigned maximum short-circuit rating.

378. Isolating Means (National Electrical Code). Means shall be provided to isolate an item of equipment completely. The use of isolating switches is not necessary if there are other ways of de-energizing the equipment for inspection and repairs. Isolating switches should be interlocked with the associated circuit interrupting device to prevent their being opened under load; otherwise signs warning against opening them under load shall be provided. Barriers should be provided on both sides of each pole of indoor open-type isolating switches. A fuse holder and fuse, designed for the purpose, may be used as an isolating switch.

379. Space Separation. The National Electrical Code requires that a minimum air separation in indoor installations (but not within apparatus) between bare live conductors and between such conductors and adjacent surfaces be maintained as follows:

Circuit voltage, kv	Minimum air separation indoors,[a] inches	
	Between bare live conductors	Between bare live conductors and adjacent surfaces
2.5	5	4
5.0	6	5
7.5	7	6
15.0	12	7
23.0	15	10
34.5	18	13
46.0	21	17
69.0	31	25

[a] The values given are the minimum permissible space separation under favorable service conditions. They should be increased under unfavorable service conditions or wherever space limitations permit.

380. Work Space and Guarding. The National Electrical Code requires the following protection:

1. WORKING SPACE. The minimum clear working space in front of electric equipment, such as switchboards, control panels, switches, circuit breakers, motor controllers, relays, and similar equipment shall not be less than set forth in the following table unless otherwise specified in this Code.

**Minimum Clear Working Space in Front
of Electric Equipment in Feet**

Voltage to ground	Conditions		
	1	2	3
601–2,500	3	4	5
2,501–7,500	4	5	6
Over 7,500	5	6	9

1. Exposed live parts on one side and no live or grounded parts on the other side of the working space or exposed live parts on both sides effectively guarded by suitable wood or other insulating materials. Insulated wire or insulated bus bars operating at not more than 300 volts shall not be considered live parts.

2. Exposed live parts on one side and grounded parts on the other side. Concrete, brick or tile walls will be considered as grounded surfaces.

3. Exposed live parts on both sides of the work space (not guarded as provided in condition 1) with the operator between.

Exception: Working space is not required in back of assemblies such as dead-front switchboards or control assemblies when there are no renewable or adjustable parts such as fuses or switches on the back and when all connections are accessible from other locations than the back.

2. SEPARATION FROM LOW-POTENTIAL EQUIPMENT. When switches, cutouts or other equipment operating at 600 volts or less are installed in a room or enclosure where there are exposed live parts or exposed wiring operating at more than 600 volts, the high-potential equipment shall be effectively separated from the space occupied by the low-potential equipment by a suitable partition, fence, or screen.

Exception: Switches or other equipment operating at 600 volts or less and serving only equipment within the high-voltage vault, room, or enclosure may be installed in the high-voltage enclosure, room, or vault if accessible to qualified persons only.

3. LOCKED ROOMS OR ENCLOSURES. The entrances to all buildings, rooms, or enclosures containing exposed live parts or exposed conductors operating in excess of 600 volts shall be kept locked, except where such entrances are at all times under the observation of a qualified attendant.

Where the voltage exceeds 600 volts, permanent and conspicuous warning signs shall be provided, reading substantially as follows: "Warning—High Voltage—Keep Out."

4. ILLUMINATION. Adequate illumination shall be provided for all working spaces around electric equipment. The light outlets shall be so arranged that persons changing lamps or making repairs on the lighting system will not be endangered by live parts or other equipment.

The points of control shall be so located that persons are not liable to come into contact with any live part or moving part of the equipment while turning on the lights.

5. HEADROOM. The minimum headroom above working spaces around switching equipment where there are live parts exposed at any time shall be not less than 6½ ft.

381. Isolation by Elevation. The National Electrical Code requires that the distance from working spaces to unguarded live parts be not less than:

Voltage between phases	Min vertical clearance of unguarded parts	
	Ft	In.
601– 6,600	8	0
6,601– 11,000	9	0
11,001– 22,000	9	3
22,001– 33,000	9	6
33,001– 44,000	9	10
44,001– 66,000	10	5
66,001– 88,000	11	0
88,001–110,000	11	7
110,001–132,000	12	2

WIRING FOR CIRCUITS LESS THAN 50 VOLTS

382. For wiring circuits of less than 50 volts, conductors not smaller than No. 12 must be used. If the conductors supply more than one appliance or appliance receptacle, they must not be smaller than No. 10. Not more than eight lamp holders or receptacles or a total load of more than 320 watts may be connected to a branch circuit. Motors or appliances rated at more than 320 watts must have individual branch circuits. Receptacles must be rated at not less than 15 amp; in kitchens, laundries, and other locations where portable appliances are likely to be used, the receptacles must be rated at not less than 20 amp.

WIRING FOR HAZARDOUS LOCATIONS

383. Hazardous locations are divided by the National Electrical Code into three classes. Each of these is further subdivided into Divisions 1 and 2. In Division 1 the hazardous material is more or less freely present in the air in connection with manufacture. In Division 2 the hazardous material is confined in containers; and explosive mixtures with air will occur only in case of accident or through failure of ventilating systems to operate properly.

CLASS I. Locations in which flammable gases or vapors are or may be present in the air in quantities sufficient to produce explosive or ignitible mixtures.

CLASS II. Locations which are hazardous because of the presence of combustible dust.

CLASS III. Locations which are hazardous because of the presence of easily ignitible fibers or flyings but in which such fibers or flyings are not likely to be in suspension in air in quantities sufficient to produce ignitible mixtures.

384. Equipment for installation in hazardous locations must be tested and approved for use, according to the following classification of the hazard involved.

Group A. Atmospheres containing acetylene.

Group B. Atmospheres containing hydrogen or gases or vapors of equivalent hazard such as manufactured gas.

Group C. Atmospheres containing ethyl-ether vapors, ethylene, or cyclopropane.

Group D. Atmospheres containing gasoline, hexane, naphtha, benzene, butane, propane, alcohol, acetone, benzol, lacquer solvent vapors, or natural gas.

Group E. Atmospheres containing metal dust, including aluminum, magnesium, and their commercial alloys and other metals of similarly hazardous characteristics.

Group F. Atmospheres containing carbon black, coal or coke dust.

Group G. Atmospheres containing flour, starch, or grain dusts.

385. In Class I, Division 1, hazardous locations all wiring must be in threaded rigid metal conduit with explosionproof fittings or Type MI cable. Division 2 locations may use flexible metal fittings, flexible metal raceway with approved fittings, or flexible cord approved for extra hard usage where necessary, as at motor terminals. All equipment such as circuit breakers, fuses, motors, generators, and controllers must be totally enclosed in explosionproof housings.

386. In Class II, Division 1, hazardous locations the wiring must be in threaded rigid conduit or Type MI cable, with flexible metal conduit or type S cord where necessary, as at motor terminals, and must have threaded fittings. All equipment must be in dustproof cabinets with motors and generators in totally enclosed fan-cooled housings. In Division 2 locations electrical metallic tubing, dusttight wireways, or Type ALS and MC cables with approved termination fittings may also be used.

387. In Class III, Division 1, hazardous locations the wiring must be of the same type as in Class II, and the use of approved Type MC or ALS cable is also permitted. In Division 2 locations open wiring is permitted under certain conditions. Motors or generators must be totally enclosed. For further special rules for hazardous locations in regard to receptacles, plugs, lighting fixtures, portable cords, cranes, control equipment, service equipment, panel boards, etc., consult the National Electrical Code.

INSTALLATION OF APPLIANCES

388. Connection to Circuit and Protection. A portable appliance may be connected only to a receptacle having a rating at least as great as the appliance.

The standard duplex convenience outlet receptacle is rated at 15 amp and may supply a single 15-amp fixed appliance or a 12-amp portable appliance if used on a 15-amp branch circuit. Heavy-duty receptacles rated at 20, 30, and 50 amp may be obtained for higher current appliances. On new installations all 15- and 20-amp receptacles must be of the grounding-type. Refer to Div. 4 for description of receptacles. Most household appliances, such as toasters, hot plates, percolators, flat irons, waffle irons, refrigerators, radiant heaters, roasters, portable ovens, etc., are rated at less than 12 amp, so that they may be used in the standard outlet on a 15-amp circuit.

Appliances other than motor-operated ones are not generally required to have individual overload protection.

389. In wiring appliances one of the approved types of cords listed in Division 2 should be used. If the appliance is rated at more than 50 watts and temperatures of more than 121°C (250°F) are produced on surfaces with which the cord is apt to be in contact, one of the types of heater cords must be used. Every heating appliance which is intended to be applied to combustible material, as a smoothing iron, must be equipped with a stand, which may be separate or a part of the appliance. Each heating appliance intended to be located in a fixed position must have ample protection provided between the appliance and adjacent combustible material.

390. Disconnecting Means (National Electrical Code). Each appliance shall be provided with a means for disconnection from all ungrounded conductors as follows:

1. PORTABLE APPLIANCES. For portable appliances (including household ranges and clothes driers) a separable connector or an attachment plug and receptacle may serve as the disconnecting means. The rating of a receptacle or of a separable connector shall not be less than the rating of any appliance connected thereto, except that demand factors authorized elsewhere in this Code may be applied. Attachment plug caps and connectors shall conform to the following:

a. Live Parts. They shall be so constructed and installed as to guard against inadvertent contact with live parts.

b. Interrupting Capacity. They shall be capable of interrupting their rated current without hazard to the operator.

c. Interchangeability. They shall be so designed that they will not fit into receptacles of lesser rating.

For household electric ranges, a plug and receptacle connection at the rear base of a range, if it is accessible from the front by removal of a drawer, is considered as meeting the intent of this rule.

2. STATIONARY APPLIANCES. For fixed or stationary appliances rated at not over 300 va or 1/8 hp, the branch-circuit overcurrent device may serve as the disconnecting means. For fixed or stationary appliances of greater rating the branch-circuit switch or circuit breaker may, if readily accessible to the user of the appliance, serve as the disconnecting means.

3. UNIT SWITCHES. Switches which are a part of an appliance shall not be considered as taking the place of the single disconnecting means required by this section unless there are other means for disconnection as follows:

a. Multifamily Dwellings. In multifamily (more than two) dwellings, the disconnecting means shall be within the apartment or on the same floor as the apartment in which the appliance is installed and may control lamps and other appliances.

b. Two-family Dwellings. In two-family dwellings, the disconnecting means may be outside the apartment in which the appliance is installed. This will permit an individual switch for the apartment to be used.

c. Single-family Dwellings. In single-family dwellings, the service disconnecting means may be used.

d. Other Occupancies. In other occupancies, the branch-circuit switch or circuit breaker, if readily accessible to the user of the appliance, may be used for this purpose.

4. SWITCH OR CIRCUIT BREAKER TO BE INDICATING. Switches or circuit breakers used as disconnecting means shall be of the indicating type.

5. MOTOR-DRIVEN APPLIANCES. A switch or circuit breaker which serves as the disconnecting means for a stationary motor-driven appliance of more than 1/8 hp shall be located within sight of the motor controller or shall be capable of being locked in the open position.

391. Portable appliances, except those specified in section 250-45 of the Code, need not be grounded unless they operate at a voltage of more than 150 to ground.

392. Signals and Temperature-limiting Devices for Heated Appliances. In other than residence occupancies, each electrically heated appliance or group of electrically heated appliances intended to be applied to combustible material shall be installed in connection with a signal unless the appliance is provided with an integral temperature-limiting device.

393. The electric range consists of a number of heater elements each rated at 1,000, 1,200, 1,500, or 2,000 watts, so that it must usually be supplied with an individual three-wire branch circuit. The heater elements usually contain two units controlled by connecting the units in various combinations of series and parallel between the two lines and the neutral. A range, hot plate, or similar appliance with surface heating elements, having a maximum demand of more than 60 amp, as calculated in accordance with Table 2 of Div. 11, shall have the main circuit subdivided into two or more circuits, each provided with overcurrent protection rated at not more than 50 amp. Infrared lamp heating appliances shall have overcurrent protection not exceeding 50 amp.

Many modern residential installations utilize counter-mounted cooking units and wall ovens.

ELECTRIC COMFORT CONDITIONING

394. Introduction. As a practical guide to electric comfort conditioning, these sections are designed to provide a general understanding of when to use electric heating and cooling systems, how to estimate heat loss, what type of equipment is available, and where comfort conditioning equipment should be located.

395. When to Use Electric Heating and Cooling. Electric heating and cooling systems are used in all types of buildings, and there are outdoor spot heating systems in addition to snow-melting and deicing systems.

396. Residential Buildings. Electric heating and cooling systems for single-family dwellings and many multifamily dwellings have become accepted throughout the United States. Whether it is most desirable economically, a personal preference, or a luxury depends upon its usage by the occupants, the construction of the building, and the local electric utility rates (cost per kilowatthour of electricity for heating).

1. THE ADVANTAGES OF ELECTRIC HEATING include individual room control, long life of the equipment, space-saving features, cleanliness, and safety. However, the user can abuse these advantages by leaving doors, windows, or fireplace chimney flues open; overheating; or improper building construction or insulation. Improper usage by the occupant is usually the reason for excessive utility bills.

2. INSULATION. If electric heat is to be operated economically, it is important to consider the value of insulation. A well-insulated residence requires less equipment and results in lower operating costs. Savings in equipment cost and annual operating costs generally pay for the increased cost of added insulation, storm windows, and storm doors.

3. IN SELECTING INSULATION, it is important to consider its effectiveness in terms of resistance to heat transfer and not just the thickness of the insulation. The effectiveness of the insulation (for ceilings, walls, and floors) is judged in terms of its R (resistance) value. The insulation manufacturer will indicate the R value for a given thickness. For buildings with electric comfort conditioning, the National Mineral Wool Insulation Association specifies a minimum resistance as follows: Ceilings $= R19$; walls $= R11$; floors $= R13$.

4. THE CONSTRUCTION OF THE WALL OR CEILING (roof) is not too significant if the minimum R value is provided. Storm windows (and doors), or double-glazed glass, more than double the R value of the glass area.

5. A HOUSE WITH A HEATED BASEMENT need not have insulation under the floor, but there should be insulation under a floor which is over an exposed crawl space. The most effective insulation for concrete slabs is around the exposed outside edge. Perimeter slab insulation can be extended down vertically about 24 in. or can be installed around the edge of the slab about the same distance.

6. TO PROTECT THE INSULATION FROM the negative effect of moisture from within the house, a vapor barrier on the inside face of the insulation is recommended. The vapor barrier must be protected from damage, and any tears or holes must be repaired.

7. A WELL-INSULATED BUILDING may become an excessively humid building. To avoid excessive humidity buildup, a *humidistat* should be used to control one or more exhaust fans or a fresh-air ventilator. The humidistat closes the circuit to the fans when the relative humidity exceeds the preselected humidistat setting.

The operation of a humidistat is similar to a thermostat except that the sensing element responds to humidity instead of heat. Also the element in a humidistat most commonly consists of a series of human hairs, which respond to changes in the relative humidity. In a home the relative humidity rises because of the use of dishwashers, driers, washing machines, showers, sinks, and similar sources where use of water or production of moisture occurs.

8. HEAT LOSS. A residential building, insulated to the previously indicated specifications, will have a heat loss of about *10 watts per sq ft or one watt per cu ft.*

9. HEAT LOSS SURVEY. Before the actual load requirements are determined, a heat loss survey of all exposed rooms should be made. If, for example, in the New York City area, with an outside design temperature of 0°F and an inside design temperature of 70°F, the heat loss is to be determined for a frame residence, the loss for each exposed room can be calculated in the same manner as in the following example for a 12- by 10- by 8-ft corner bedroom (Bedroom A).

	Sq ft		Factor		Heat loss, watts
Gross outside wall windows.....	176		–		–
(and doors)..........................	24	×	12	=	288
Net outside walls....................	152	×	1.6	=	243
Ceiling.................................	120	×	1.0	=	120
Floor....................................	120	×	2.0	=	240
Infiltration............................	960	×	0.4	=	384
Total heat loss.......................					1,275

10. STEPS IN CALCULATING HEAT LOSS.

a. Determine heat-loss factor in watts per sq ft by the *R* value. Refer to the "NEMA Electric Heating Guide," "The Electric Heating and Cooling Handbook" (published by Edison Electric Institute), or the ASHRAE Guide and Data Books.

b. Multiply the total sq ft area for all exposed areas by this factor. (Deduct exposed glass and door area from gross wall area to determine net wall area.)

c. Multiply the cu ft volume by the infiltration or air change factor.

d. Add all products for the total heat loss of the room.

e. Add the heat loss of all the rooms to determine the total heat loss of the house. See the following example:

Rooms	Heat Loss, Each Room, Watts
Living room...................................	2,350
Bedroom A....................................	1,275
Bedroom B....................................	980
Bathroom......................................	610
Kitchen–dining..............................	1,420
Hall	735
Total heat loss...............................	7,370

11. TO DETERMINE ANNUAL OPERATING COST, CHECK WITH THE LOCAL UTILITY for the conversion factor for kilowatthours. If the heat loss is 7,370 watts and the conversion factor is 1.4, multiply the heat loss of 7,370 watts by 1.4, which equals 10,318, the total number of kilowatthours required to provide a 70°F indoor temperature during the heating period. A similar "heat gain" study can be made to determine the cooling load. Once the kilowatthour consumption is estimated, multiply 10,318 kilowatthours by 0.012 (1.2 cents), the 1969 base rate for electric heating in New York City. This gives $123.82, which is the estimated annual operating cost for electric heating. On the basis of an eight-month heating season, the average operating cost per month is $15.45. Heat-loss calculations of this type may also be made for apartment buildings, small commercial buildings, and other small buildings. For large commercial or institutional buildings, other factors, particularly that of fresh air changes, must be considered.

397. Commercial or Industrial Buildings. Many factors are involved in considering the use of electric heating in a commercial, industrial, or institutional building. Usually, a consulting engineer or heating specialist will perform a feasibility study which compares electric heating with other types of heating systems. The study will compare not only the cost of fuel but also the annual capital costs and maintenance costs over a period of years. The selection of electric heating, however, will generally depend upon the cost of electricity.

398. Types of Equipment. There are many types of electric heaters, varieties of housings, heating elements, and methods of distributing the heat into the heated area.

1. ELECTRIC HEATERS are convector, fan-forced, or radiant types. The heater contains a resistance element which heats air or water. All such heaters provide both radiant and convection heat. The ratio depends upon the type of heater. Radiant heaters provide the highest radiation-to-convection ratios.

2. IN RESIDENTIAL BUILDINGS a centralized system may be an electric furnace, boiler, or heat-pump system. A decentralized system could include the use, entirely, or in combination, of baseboard heaters, wall heaters, floor-drop-in heaters, ceiling heaters, or ceiling panels or heating cables. The decentralized systems allow for individual room control. Central systems have central control but often have the advantage of combining heating and cooling in the same duct system. The conversion of a fossil-fuel-fired hot-air or hot-water system can be readily accomplished by replacing the existing furnace or boiler with an *electric* furnace or hot-water boiler.

3. IN COMMERCIAL BUILDINGS, central systems are available with large banks of electric duct heaters in conjunction with air handlers. Electric hot water or steam boilers are available in large kilowatt capacities. Central heating and cooling systems can be used in conjunction with perimeter baseboard-type heaters.

Perimeter heaters will counteract external-wall heat loss and allow control of the heaters in modular sections.

4. UNITARY SYSTEMS in commercial buildings permit combinations of heating and cooling with control of each room or area.

5. THROUGH-THE-WALL HEATING AND AIR-CONDITIONING UNITS, particularly in school buildings, help to reduce engineering and maintenance costs. Unitary equipment breakdown only affects a single room or area instead of the entire building or large section when a central system becomes defective.

6. ROOFTOP EQUIPMENT saves building space in low-ceiling commercial buildings, while providing large-capacity electric heat and cooling into a ceiling plenum or duct system.

7. MOST ELECTRICALLY HEATED BUILDINGS will use electricity for domestic hot water. All-electric kitchens complete the application of electricity in the *total-electric* concept.

8. PARTIAL BUILDING HEAT is another common application for unitary heaters.

9. INFRARED HEATERS provide spot heating for indoor or outdoor heating applications. Electric heating cables or mats for snow melting, deicing, or pipeline heating offer convenience and reduction of costs unavailable in other systems.

399. Equipment Capacities. The following equipment is described for various applications in Secs. **400** to **406.**

400. Electric furnaces (Fig. 260) are made in capacities of 4 to 35 kw at 240 volts, single phase or three phase.

FIG. 260 *Electric furnace.* (*Edwin L. Wiegand Co., Subsidiary of Emerson Electric Co.*)

This heating assembly is a compact package heating system for new buildings or conversion applications in homes, apartments, or small commercial buildings. The furnace can be positioned in the ducts so that it can be used for upflow, downflow, or horizontal discharge in basements, attics, utility rooms, or utility closets.

Heating elements can be internally wired to be energized in 5-kw stages, at 60-sec intervals, to prevent power surges. As part of the electric furnace system, summer air conditioning or an electronic air cleaner may be added at any time without changing the blower or duct system. Some units are designed to be used with a split-system air conditioner. Low-voltage, wall-mounted controls are usually installed in a central part of the building.

401. A hydronic boiler is shown in Fig. 261. Capacities are from 6 to 30 kw at 240 volts, single phase.

FIG. 261 *A hydronic electric boiler.* (*Edwin L. Wiegand Co., Subsidiary of Emerson Electric Co.*)

These wall-mounted hot-water boilers are compact in size (between two and eight cu ft) and weigh about 120 lbs. A typical boiler has incremental stages (5 kw or less), which sequence at 30- to 45-sec intervals to eliminate a large power surge. Centrally located low-voltage wall-mounted controls operate the boiler.

402. Heat Pump. Capacities range from 23,000 to 236,000 Btu for heating and 2 to 20 tons for cooling, single phase or three phase, at several voltage ratings.

The residential heat pump is a boxlike unit, which is installed inside or outside of the building, although it is usually outside with air-to-air heat transfer. The heat pump designed for outdoor installation is roof-mounted, through-the-wall, or remote-mounted. In cold climates (below 20°F outdoor design) supplementary space heating equipment is used in conjunction with the heat pump. An accessory kit is available for low-ambient operation.

The heat pump is regarded as a low-operating-cost heating and cooling system with a centrally mounted combination heating-cooling thermostat. Large-capacity heat pumps are sometimes used for commercial or industrial buildings.

403. Residential unitary systems include several types of electric heaters or combination units.

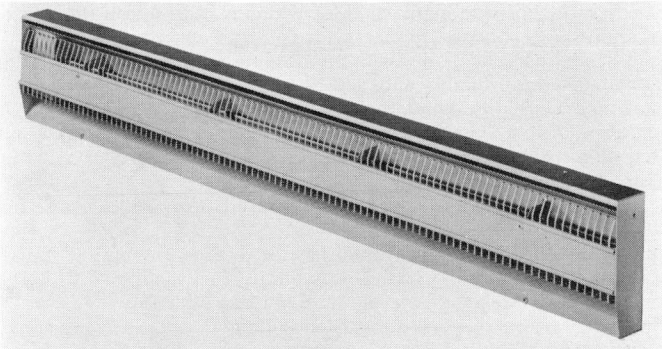

FIG. 262   *Baseboard heating section.   (Anchor Electric Div., Solar Basic Industries.)*

1. BASEBOARD HEATERS are commonly used, and Fig. 262 shows a typical unit. Capacities range from 375 to 3,500 watts at 120, 208, or 240 volts.

These heaters are usually surface-mounted convector units with finned-tubular or cast-aluminum (Fig. 263) heating elements.   Ratings are in terms of *watt density. Low-watt density* is about 175 watts per ft, *medium-watt density* is about 225 watts per ft, and *high-watt density* is about 275 watts per ft.

Heater lengths range from 2 to 12 ft and heights are usually 6 to 9 in.   The heaters are controlled by integral line-voltage thermostats, thermostat sections, line-voltage wall thermostats, or low-voltage wall thermostats.

These heaters are most commonly used to provide perimeter heating, particularly under the windows of outside walls.   They can be easily installed in both new or existing buildings.   Many baseboard heaters provide a full-length wireway.   They have knockouts in the bottom, side, and back for electrical supply connections.   A plastic seal can be provided on the back of the heater to maintain a neat appearance when installed against an uneven wall.   An air deflector directs heated air away from the wall. A "free-floating" element reduces expansion and contraction noises.

FIG. 263   *Cast-aluminum electric heating elements.   (Climate Control Div., The Singer Co.)*

Heater accessories include blank sections which can be cut on the job for wall-to-wall installations.

A thermostat section is available with or without duplex receptacles, although a receptacle section itself is available with some heaters. A control section, with or without a thermostat, may be used to switch the same source of power from an "off" position to a "heat" position or to a "cool" position. A room air conditioner is plugged into the top of this section. Also available is a section that contains a relay or transformer/relay for use with a low-voltage thermostat.

2. RADIANT WALL HEATERS are also widely used. Capacities range from 500 to 6,000 watts at 120, 208, or 240 volts.

Residential units of this type are for surface or recessed mounting. Small-capacity (500- to 1,500-watt) heaters are used in bathrooms or other small rooms. Large-capacity (2- to 6-kw) heaters are designed for add-on rooms, new construction, or existing room areas. The radiant heater may have a resistance element or glass panel with embedded resistance material. A typical glass unit, rated at 750 watts, is shown in Fig. 264.

FIG. 264 A 750-watt recessed heater with a glass heating panel. (Berko Electric Mfg. Corp., Div. of Weil-McLain.)

FIG. 265 Recessed forced-air wall heater with built-in thermostat and fan switch. (Climate Control Div., The Singer Co.)

This heater features a built-in thermostat and shallow depth for recessed applications (2 in. in some cases). For ease of installation, there are knockouts on the back, bottom, or side.

3. A FORCED-AIR WALL HEATER is shown in Fig. 265. Capacities range from 660 to 4,000 watts at 120, 208, 240, or 277 volts.

These residential units can be recessed, semirecessed, or surface-mounted. Most commonly, this type of heater has a built-in thermostat with a positive "off" position. The lower-capacity heaters (660 to 1,500 watts) are used in bathrooms and other small rooms. The higher-capacity heaters (2 to 4 kw) are commonly used in basements, recreation rooms, or add-on rooms. In the larger heaters there are several options. Some units have a fan-delay switch, built-in safety switch, a fuse-disconnect, or a low-voltage transformer. A self-lubricating motor is common in the larger heaters. Also, a permanent-type filter is available in large-capacity heaters.

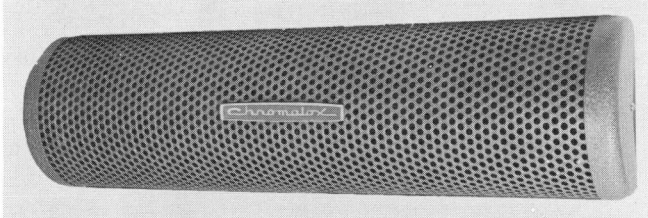

FIG. 266   *Convector wall heater.   (Edwin L. Wiegand Co., Subsidiary of Emerson Electric Co.)*

FIG. 267   *Fan-forced recessed kick-space heater.   (Edwin L. Wiegand Co., Subsidiary of Emerson Electric Co.)*

Some of these heaters utilize the counterflow principle of heat and air distribution. They may be controlled by a separate line- or low-voltage thermostat in conjunction with an integral or remote relay.   A fan switch permits summer operation.

4. A CONVECTOR WALL HEATER is shown in Fig. 266.   Capacities range from 500 to 5,000 watts at 120, 208, or 240 volts.

These convector units can be surface- or recess-mounted with integral or remote controls.   Low-wattage heaters can be used in shops, corridors, breezeways, and basements.   Larger-wattage convectors can be used to heat basements, attics, or any area where limited wall space prevents the use of baseboard heaters.

5. A FAN-FORCED KICK-SPACE OR BASE-BOARD HEATER is shown in Fig. 267.   Capacities range from 750 to 4,000 watts at 208 or 240 volts.

Such heaters can be surface- or recess-mounted.   They are well suited where baseboard radiation is desired but only limited space is available.   The kick-space heater has a quiet tangential blower and is particularly suitable for kitchens or bathrooms where adequate wall space is not available. It is recessed into the kick-space area under a cabinet or counter.   Control is by a separate wall-mounted line-voltage thermostat.

6. A WALL-MOUNTED ELECTRIC FIRE-PLACE is shown in Fig. 268.   Capacities range from 2,000 to 5,000 watts at 240 volts.

This unit is a forced-air surface-mounted heater designed to look like a fireplace.

FIG. 268   *Wall-mounted electric fireplace.   (Edwin L. Wiegand Co., Subsidiary of Emerson Electric Co.)*

It has a glowing grate with realistic logs in a steel cabinet which is finished in matte black or copper-tone enamel.   It is ideal for dens, beach and mountain cabins, offices, motels, restaurants, and lounges.   The electric fireplace can have a built-in thermostat and fan-delay control; it is also available with a remote wall-mounted low-voltage thermostat.

7. A COMBINATION HEAT, LIGHT, AND EXHAUST CEILING UNIT is shown in Fig. 269. Capacities of the heater range from 1,320 to 1,650 watts at 120 volts.   Lighting consists of two 60-watt incandescent lamps, and the small exhaust fan is rated at 60 cfm.

FIG. 269   *Combination heat, light and exhaust ceiling unit.   (Edwin L. Wiegand Co., Subsidiary of Emerson Electric Co.)*

This combination unit is recessed in the ceiling of bathrooms.   A wall-mounted switch panel and thermostat provides individual control of the heater, light, and an automatic damper-operated exhaust fan.   Some units have plug-in connections.

8. A RADIANT AND FORCED-AIR CEILING HEATER is available in capacities of 600 to 1,250 watts at 120 volts.

A typical unit is attached directly to a flush 3½- or 4-in. ceiling outlet box.   This heater is commonly used in small bathrooms, playrooms, and powder rooms.   A small fan is used to force heat away from the ceiling; the primary heat is radiant.   In some heaters, a center-mounted 100-watt incandescent lamp is available for lighting.

9. FORCED-AIR CEILING HEATERS range in capacities from 1,000 to 1,525 watts at 120, 208, or 240 volts.

Such forced-air units can be surface-mounted on a standard flush 3½- or 4-in. ceiling outlet box.   Commonly used in bathrooms or powder rooms, the fan-forced heater is approved for standard 60°C supply wires, such as Type TW.   It is available with adjustable mounting brackets and an automatic plug-in connection.   Control is by a wall-mounted thermostat.

10. RADIANT CEILING HEATERS range in capacities from 600 to 1,500 watts at 120, 208, or 240 volts.

The ceiling-mounted residential radiant heater can be recessed or surface-mounted on a standard flush 3½- or 4-in. ceiling outlet box.   Available with a center-located 100-watt incandescent lamp and plug-in connections, the heaters are approved for 60°C supply wires.   The radiant ceiling heater is commonly used in bathrooms, powder rooms, or other small rooms.   Control is by a wall-mounted thermostat.

11. RADIANT CEILING PANEL HEATERS range in capacities from 235 to 1,000 watts at 120, 208, or 240 volts.

The residential radiant ceiling panel is constructed of laminated glass, gypsum dry wall, or radiant metal.   It can be surface-mounted, recessed, or used in a T-bar con-

struction module, usually in panels 2 to 4 ft wide and 3 to 12 ft long. The depth of
the heater is ¾ to 1 in. The surface finish can be painted. A typical unit contains
a 4-in. terminal box and a 3-ft flexible metal conduit. Controlled by a separate wall-
mounted thermostat, the ceiling panel may be used for small rooms, spot heating, or
complete area heating.

12. A TYPICAL RUN OF CEILING HEATING CABLE is shown in Fig. 270. Capacities
range from 200 to 5,000 watts at 120, 208, or 240 volts, and lengths are from 75 to 1,800
ft.

Ceiling cable is embedded in plaster or laminated ceiling construction for individual
rooms or complete house heating. Color-coded cables are electrically insulated and resistant to high temperature, water absorption, aging effects, and chemical action. The
cables are usually rated at 2¾ watts per ft. They must not be cut in the field, and
identification labels must not be removed.

Nonheating lead wires, 7 ft or longer, extend to the thermostat or a junction box. For
installation (Fig. 271), the cable is stapled to a nonmetallic fire-resistant surface at
least every 16 in. After the first plaster coat has been applied, cables should be tested
for continuity and insulation resistance (at least 100,000 ohms measured to ground).
Minimum spacing between cable runs is 1½ in. on centers with the closest spacing
near the outside walls. Cables should clear lighting fixtures by at least 8 in. and other
metallic materials by 6 in. General electric wiring (for lights, etc.) should be run over
the thermal insulation and at least 2 in. over the heated ceiling surface.

13. FLOOR HEATING CABLE has unlimited heat capacities which vary with the conductor resistance, type of cable, and length of cable. Ratings are from 120 to 600 volts.
In residential occupancies ratings are 120, 208, or 240 volts.

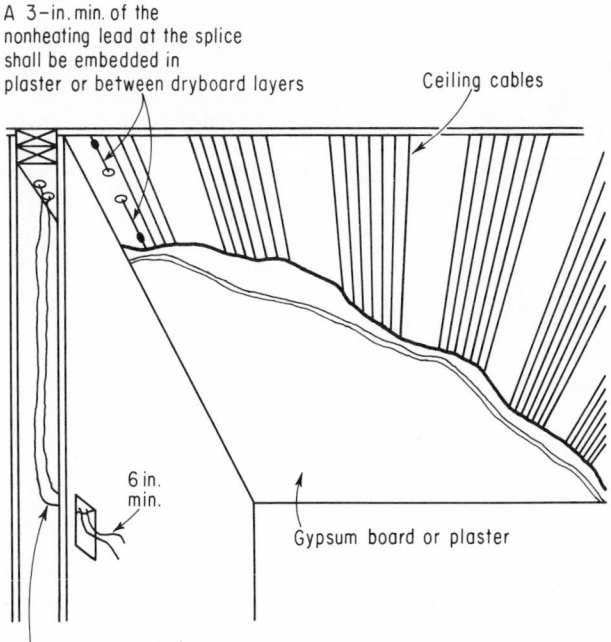

FIG. 270 *Installation of ceiling heating cable. Adjacent cable runs must be spaced not
less than 1½ in. on centers. (Electrical Construction and Maintenance.)*

Heating cables are used in floors to form radiant panel systems. Cables most commonly used are polyvinyl chloride–sheathed cables or mineral-insulated (MI) copper-sheathed cables. In concrete, cables must be of a material that is resistant to any chemical action in the concrete. Cables may be interwoven as part of a properly grounded prefabricated mat. They may be of predesigned lengths which are spaced to provide a desired radiant heat output. Cables such as Type MI are available at several different resistances. Single- or two-conductor cables at specified lengths will have varied heat capacities, depending upon the applied voltage. Heating cables may be installed in one or two pours with adjacent runs not less than 1 in. on centers and with a spacing of at least 1 in. between cable runs and metallic bodies embedded in the floor. Nonheating leads must be protected where they leave the floor by rigid metal conduit, EMT, or, with MI cable, by approved current-carrying nonheating cable sections. Control of floor heating systems is by a thermostat with a capillary and sensing element attached. The sensing bulb is embedded in the slab so that it will respond to typical temperature changes.

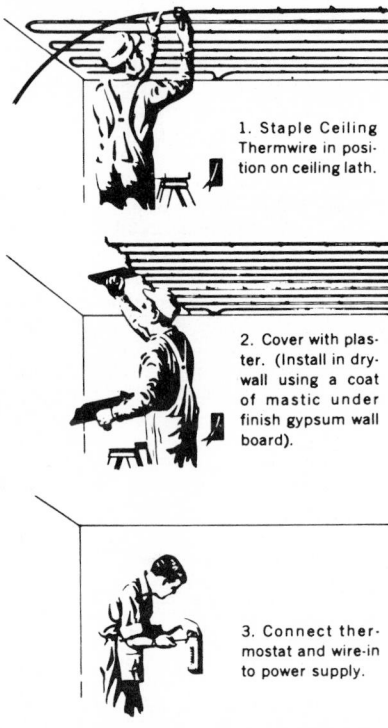

1. Staple Ceiling Thermwire in position on ceiling lath.

2. Cover with plaster. (Install in drywall using a coat of mastic under finish gypsum wall board).

3. Connect thermostat and wire-in to power supply.

FIG. 271 *Three steps in installing ceiling heating cable. (Edwin L. Wiegand Co., Subsidiary of Emerson Electric Co.)*

14. A FLOOR DROP-IN HEATER is shown in Fig. 272. Capacities range from 300 to 2,000 watts at 120, 208, 240, or 277 volts.

Residential floor drop-in heaters are resistance convector units, fan-forced units, or units that have a chamber with antifreeze water sealed in and heated electrically. They are best applied to counteract downdrafts from floor-to-ceiling windows or sliding glass doors. They can be installed in wood or concrete floors. The fan-forced heater may have an integral thermostat, but the control for most units is by a line- or low-voltage wall thermostat.

404. Central systems for commercial-type occupancies are of the types described in the following paragraphs.

1. AN OUTDOOR ROOF-MOUNT HEATING AND COOLING UNIT is shown in Fig. 273.

Electric heating capacities are custom designed for a particular installation. Cooling capacities range from 2 to 200 tons at 208 volts, single or three phase; 277 volts, single phase; and 480 volts, single or three phase.

All-electric heating and cooling machines are designed for roof-mount outdoor conditions. Custom fabrication provides machines with job-specified heating and cooling capacities. Multizone staging from a remote monitoring panel can establish the roof-mount machine as the heating and cooling plant for a one- or two-story building. Supermarkets, office buildings, laboratories, warehouses, machine shops, and aircraft plants are good applications for roof-mount equipment. Space-saving economy is a major feature of roof-mount equipment. Staged or step control for the heating section, with fresh-air damper control, provides a well-balanced automated system.

2. COMMERCIAL STEAM OR HOT-WATER BOILERS (Fig. 274) are available in capacities up to 3,000 kw at 208, 240, and 480 volts, single or three phase.

Commercial steam or hot-water boilers are designed for conversion of electric energy to heat in the form of steam or hot water. Hot-water boilers are used as a replacement for fuel-fired boilers; as the heating component for a chilled water-cooling system; as a

FIG. 272   *Floor drop-in heater.   (Edwin L. Wiegand Co., Subsidiary of Emerson Electric Co.)*

safe method of heating a hazardous area, or as a side-arm faucet water heater.   A typical boiler is provided with low-water cutoff, safety relief valve, temperature control, water gage, high-temperature limit switch, contactors, internal fusing, full insulation, and enameled steel jacket.   The electric boiler occupies much less floor area than other types of boilers and does not require retubing, flue cleaning, burner cleaning, damper adjusting, or chemical additives.

Steam boilers are available with ½ to 30 bhp, 1 to 250 lb per sq in., and are built to ASME and Underwriters' Laboratories standards.   Boilers include a safety valve, steam pressure gage, pressure regulator, low-water cutoff, automatic feed control, control switch, pilot light, outlet valves, and drain valves.   A condensate tank is recommended to reuse the condensed steam.

405. Commercial unitary systems are described in the following paragraphs.

1. AN INFRARED HEATER is shown in Fig. 275.   Capacities are 500 to 7,600 watts at 120, 208, 240, 277, 440, 480, and 600 volts.

The heating elements consist of metal-sheathed units, quartz tubes, or quartz lamps.

FIG. 273   *Large-capacity electric heating/cooling central system unit mounted on roof. (Miller-Picking Corp.)*

The following table describes the characteristics of these three infrared sources:

Characteristics of Three Infrared Sources

Characteristic	Quartz Lamp	Quartz Tube	Metal Sheath
Relative heat intensity.................	Very high	Low to medium high	Medium to high
Splash resistance..........................	Very good	Very good	Very good
Color blindness............................	Fair	Very good	Very good
Life expectancy............................	5,000 hr or more	5,000 hr or more	Consult manufacturers
Visible light................................	High	Low	Low
Heat-up and cool-down time..........	A few seconds	2 min or more	About 2 min
Relative cost per kw.....................	Medium high	Medium	Medium
Filament or source temperature	About 4,000°F	About 1,200 to 1,800°F	About 1,200 to 1,800°F
Vibration resistance.....................	Medium	Medium	Very good

Infrared heaters are used for complete indoor heating, spot heating, outdoor heating, and outdoor snow melting. For outdoor heating and snow melting it is preferable to use the quartz lamp and to shield the element and fixture from strong winds as much as possible. Rapid cooling of the element diminishes radiation effectiveness. For spot heating, use two fixtures aimed at the center of the target area, at about a 45-deg angle. Do not irradiate outside walls or surfaces over 6 ft above the floor. For complete comfort heating, install ½ watt for each degree of operational temperature desired above the minimum ambient "ever" reached in a specific area. For spot heating provide 1 watt per sq ft per degree of temperature difference. For outdoor heating provide 2 watts per sq ft per degree of temperature difference. If, for example, the area to be heated is a storefront sidewalk 100 ft long by 10 ft wide, in New York City, proceed as follows (assuming an outside design of 0°F and a desired temperature of 50°F):

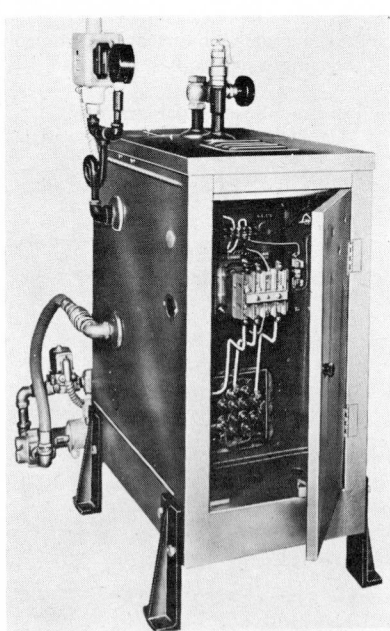

FIG. 274 *Commercial-type electric boiler. (Edwin L. Wiegand Co., Subsidiary of Emerson Electric Co.)*

$$100 \times 10 = 1,000 \text{ sq ft}$$
$$\underline{\times \quad 2} \text{ watts per sq ft}$$
$$2,000$$
$$\underline{\times \ 50}$$
$$100,000 \text{ watts or 100 kw}$$

Select fixtures in accordance with the manufacturers' recommendations. The radiation patterns are determined by the reflector design and the resulting beam pattern. Beam patterns range from a 30- to a 90-degree angle. They may be symmetrical or asymmetrical. Fixtures may have one, two, or three elements. Marquee-type heaters are recessed into an overhead masonry canopy. For snow melting applications, twice the suggested outdoor capacity is recommended. Provide 150 to 200 watts per sq ft of area for most applications. Control of infrared heaters is by switch, input control, ambient temperature thermostat, or any combination of these devices. A high-limit thermostat is recommended for most applications.

2. A HORIZONTAL UNIT HEATER is shown in Fig. 276. Capacities range from 1.5 to 50 kw at 120 or 208 volts, single and three phase; 240 volts, single and three phase; 277 volts, single phase; and 480 or 600 volts, single and three phase.

Horizontal unit heaters can be installed

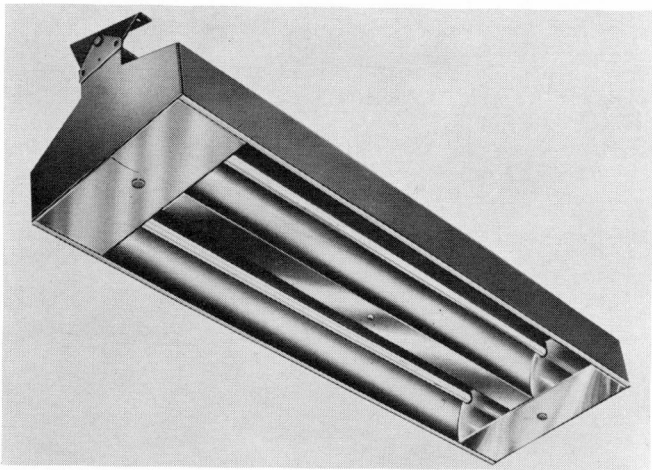

FIG. 275   *An infrared heater with two T-3 quartz lamps.   (Edwin L. Wiegand Co., Subsidiary of Emerson Electric Co.)*

on the wall or hung from the ceiling with bracket or swivel adjustments.   They are ideal for use in warehouses, factories, or entranceways.   Unit heaters are normally located along the outside wall with the direction of airflow in a circular fashion.   Large-capacity heaters can be provided with duct collars or deflectors.   Unit heaters are commonly controlled by a remote thermostat and may have remote or built-in contactors. A fan-delay switch can be provided to prevent the fan from operating until the heating elements have reached the desired temperature.   An explosion-proof model is available to conform with Class I, Group D, requirements.

3. SEVERAL TYPES OF VERTICAL UNIT HEATERS are shown in Fig. 277.   Capacities are 10 to 50 kw at 208 and 480 volts, single or three phase.   The ceiling-suspended vertical unit heater has integral relays and one- or two-stage remote control.   It can be surface-mounted or recessed with air discharge through four optional louver arrangements which permit virtually any desired air pattern at the floor level.   Diffusers are of the radial, cone, anemostat, or louver type.   Internally mounted automatic control relays and overheat and motor overload protection are usually provided.   These heavy-duty units can be used in factories, garages, and warehouses, with high-bay mounting up to 33 ft above the floor.

4. AN AUDITORIUM UNIT VENTILATOR is shown in Fig. 278.   Capacities are 12 to 400 kw; 1,200 to 15,000 cfm; and 208, 240, or 480 volts, three phase.

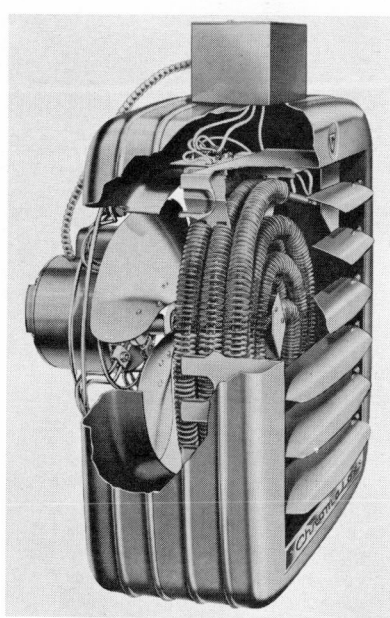

FIG. 276   *Cutaway view of a horizontal unit heater.   (Edwin L. Wiegand Co., Subsidiary of Emerson Electric Co.)*

FIG. 277   *Various types of vertical unit heaters.   (Edwin L. Wiegand Co., Subsidiary of Emerson Electric Co.)*

FIG. 278   *Auditorium unit ventilator.   (Edwin L. Wiegand Co., Subsidiary of Emerson Electric Co.)*

This unit ventilator provides the proper heating, ventilating, and natural cooling required in school auditoriums, gymnasiums, libraries, and other areas where large-capacity systems and quiet operation are essential.   It may be installed for horizontal, upright, or inverted operation on the ceiling, wall, or floor; directly in the area to be served; or in an adjacent location and connected by ductwork.   These units feature a special attenuator and enclosed motor and drive designed for quiet operation.   Step control is frequently used.

5. A TYPICAL WALL CONVECTOR UNIT is shown in Fig. 279.   Capacities are 750 to 4,000 watts at 208, 240, and 480 volts, single and three phase.   Commercial wall convectors can be surface-mounted or recessed with front or top discharge.   These units are

used in commercial, industrial, or institutional buildings in offices, corridors, and entrances. Cabinet convectors are available with integral or remote controls.

6. A COMMERCIAL FORCED-AIR WALL HEATER is similar to the heater shown in Fig. 265. Capacities are 1.5 to 4 kw at 120, 208, 240, or 277 volts, single phase. The commercial forced-air heater can be surface-mounted or recessed. Tamper-proof construction makes this unit ideal for entryways, lobbies, corridors, stairwells, and rest rooms in all types of commercial buildings. Fan and discharge louvers direct air downward, keeping the floor warm and dry.

7. A SILL-LINE CONVECTOR UNIT is shown in Fig. 280. Capacities are 120 to 750 watts per lin ft at 208, 240, 277, and 480 volts, three phase, in one- or two-stage control. Commercial sill-line heaters are available at different heights and many different wattage outputs. Lengths vary from 2 to 8 ft to provide modular or wall-to-wall design.

FIG. 279 *Wall convector unit for surface mounting. (Edwin L. Wiegand Co., Subsidiary of Emerson Electric Co.)*

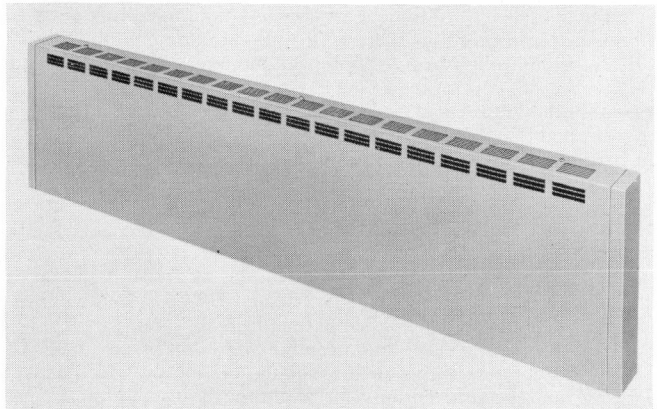

FIG. 280 *Sill line convector heater. (Edwin L. Wiegand Co., Subsidiary of Emerson Electric Co.)*

These units are available with blank sections, filler sections, matching sleeves, end caps, inside and outside corners, and conduit covers. Sill-line heaters are surface-mounted with front or top discharge where perimeter radiation is desired. They should be mounted at least 2 in. above the floor. Built-in controls may be integral to the unit, or they can be provided in a filler section. The filler section can contain a relay for a 120-volt remote-control circuit, a disconnect switch, or a circuit breaker.

8. A PEDESTAL CONVECTOR HEATER is shown in Fig. 281. Capacities from 500 to 3,500 watts at 208, 240, and 277 volts, single phase.

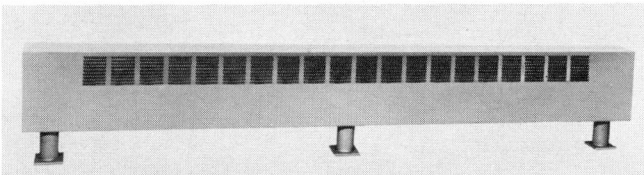

FIG. 281 *Pedestal convector heater.* (*Edwin L. Wiegand Co., Subsidiary of Emerson Electric Co.*)

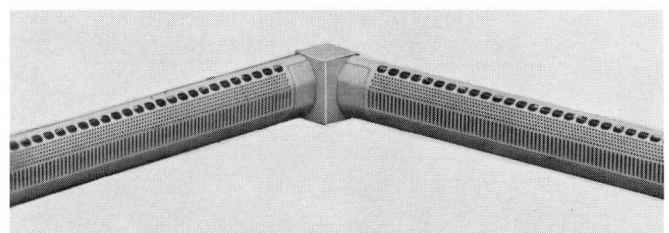

FIG. 282 *Low-silhouette draft barrier wall heater with corner connections.* (*Edwin L. Wiegand Co., Subsidiary of Emerson Electric Co.*)

This heater is a convector which is used to heat floor-to-ceiling glass areas. It can be mounted on a new concrete floor or bolted to the surface of an existing floor. Pedestal-type heaters can be installed individually or end to end in continuous runs. They provide a basic perimeter system designed especially for corridors, lobbies, foyers, and entryways — particularly for hard-to-heat areas where floor-to-ceiling glass creates cold downdraft problems and prohibits the use of wall-mounted equipment. This special downdraft heater is controlled by a separate wall-mounted thermostat with an optional integral relay for remote control by a time clock.

9. DRAFT-BARRIER WALL HEATERS are shown in Fig. 282. Capacities are 100 to 200 watts per lin ft at 120, 208, 240, and 277 volts, single phase.

The draft-barrier wall heaters are low silhouette units (3 to 6 in. high) designed to counteract downdraft at window areas. They are mounted under the sill, from wall to wall at floor level, or within modular confines in commercial office buildings. Electric connections can be made from either end on some units or through the back. Built-in thermal relays and thermostats are available.

10. COMMERCIAL BASEBOARD HEATERS are similar to the unit shown in Fig. 262. Capacities are 300 to 1,250 watts at 120, 208, 240, and 277 volts, single phase. Commercial-grade baseboard heaters are available in lengths of 2, 5, and 8 ft. They are surface-mounted 2 in. off the floor. These units can be controlled by an attached thermostat section or by a wall-mounted line- or low-voltage thermostat. End caps, blank sections, and inside and outside corners for wall-to-wall installation are available as required.

11. CABINET UNIT HEATER is shown in Fig. 283. Capacities are 1.5 to 30 kw at 208, 240, 277, and 480 volts, single phase or three phase.

FIG. 283 *Cabinet unit heater.* (*Edwin L. Wiegand Co., Subsidiary of Emerson Electric Co.*)

The commercial cabinet unit heater can be used free-standing, wall-mounted, or ceiling-mounted. Surface or recessed installation is applicable to wall- or ceiling-type heaters. An inverted model is available for unusual installations. The cabinet unit heater can be provided with tamper-proof integral or remote wall-mounted controls. A two- or three-speed fan motor, providing 200 to 1,250 cfm, may have a fan selector switch to provide quiet operation. A fan-delay thermostat is used to prevent circulation of unheated air. This type of heater is designed primarily for entranceways, corridors, and lobbies in offices, airport terminals, schools, and retail stores. There are some units which can provide a choice of 25 or 100 per cent outside air with dampers for ventilation cooling and air filters that can be cleaned.

12. A UNIT VENTILATOR AND AIR CONDITIONER is shown in Fig. 284. Heating capacities are 1.3 to 36 kw at 208, 240, 277, and 480 volts, single or three phase. Cooling capacities range from 8,000 to 27,000 Btu.

The packaged electric unit ventilator and its companion unit, the unitary air conditioner, are through-the-wall machines. The electric unit ventilator is installed under windows, has a wall sleeve and louvered opening in the wall, and is designed for use in school classrooms, auditoriums, gymnasiums, offices, libraries, or other high-occupancy areas. It heats, cools, and ventilates with outdoor air (600 to 1,500 cfm). Usually, there is internal wiring for step-control switching. An optional built-in electric demand limiter is available. Controls may be integral or remote; electric, electronic, or pneumatic. The controls of one unit ("master") may be used in the same area to control other units ("slaves"). The unit ventilator is usually installed against an outside wall, though it may also be ceiling-mounted. The through-the-wall heating and cooling unit may have an integral cooling (compressor) section, or it may be remote-mounted.

13. A TYPICAL DUCT HEATER is shown in Fig. 285. Wattage combinations are virtually unlimited with single- and three-phase connections and multistage control at 120 to 600 volts. Electric duct heaters are used in ducts, plenums, or air handlers, for primary heat, terminal booster heat, or air-conditioning reheat. Open-coil or metal-

FIG. 284   *Combination heating/cooling ventilator.   (Edwin L. Wiegand Co., Subsidiary of Emerson Electric Co.)*

FIG. 285   *Duct heater section with six elements.   (Edwin L. Wiegand Co., Subsidiary of Emerson Electric Co.)*

sheathed finned tubular heaters (Fig. 285) are available for insertion into an existing duct, or, with a flange, as part of a new duct.   In order to conform to duct sizes, heaters are manufactured at different horizontal and vertical dimensions for mounting on the side or bottom of the duct.   Integral controls may include automatic reset of thermal cutouts, built-in relays, transformer, fuses or circuit breakers, fan interlock relay, pilot switches, and pilot lights.   The National Electrical Code specifies a maximum 60-amp branch circuit for overcurrent protection with a maximum connected load of 48 amp, and zero clearance, automatic reset of thermal overload, and separate manual reset for a "backup" thermal overload system.   Duct heaters are controlled by duct stats or remote wall controls.   For large-capacity heaters a step controller is used.

406. Electric snow melting systems consist of resistance-type wire or cable embedded in concrete or asphalt.   The design of snow melting systems depends upon the area, geographical conditions, wind conditions, and the expectations of the user (see Table **52** of Div. 11).   Generally, for melting snow at temperatures between 32 and 0°F, the system will be designed at 40 to 60 watts per sq ft.   Depending on wind factor, temperature, and the rate of snowfall, the area will be kept free and clear of any snow formation if the system is energized about 30 minutes prior to a snowfall.

The heat-transfer environment may be asphalt or concrete, and the heating element may be in the form of a mat or a heating cable.   In asphalt, install the mats 12 in. from the edge with the largest mats on a straight run. Mats may be installed on an existing slab with a 2-in. blacktop surface cover. The surface asphalt should be fine-grain with no stones larger than ⅜ in. diameter.

In concrete, the mats or cable should be located within expansion joints generally no farther than 20 ft apart. The concrete slab should contain crushed-rock aggregate (not river gravel) and should be at least 4-in. thick. There should be a well-prepared base with adequate drainage and suitable reinforcement.

Junction boxes for connection of feeders to cables or mat lead wires should be located out of the area or in a nearby wall. They should not be installed flush with the snow-melting-surface area. Mats or cables should be installed 1½ to 2 in. below the surface. If they are installed in two pours of concrete, a binder or bonding agent should be used between pours. Cables should be tested before installation, during installation, and on completion of installation.

Snow melting mats, for walkways, driveways, or steps (Fig. 286) are made of resistance wires embedded in a polyvinyl chloride sheath, interwoven in chicken wire or plastic webbing. The wire may have a copper overbraid for positive grounding.

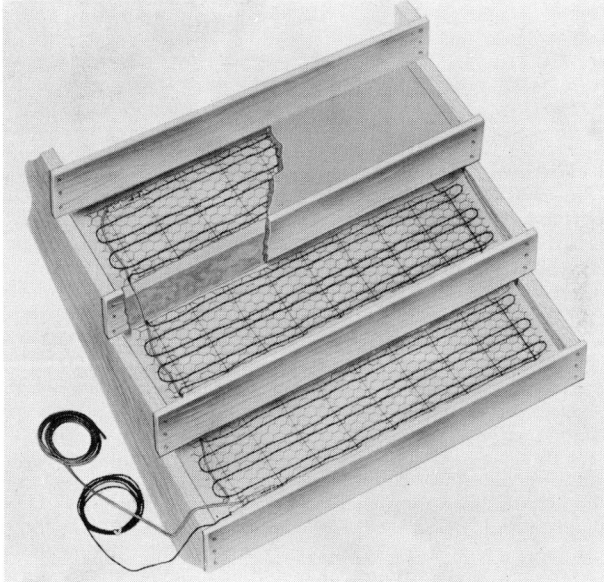

FIG. 286 *Snow-melting cable for steps. (Edwin L. Wiegand Co., Subsidiary of Emerson Electric Co.)*

Single- or two-conductor Type MI (mineral-insulated) cable with varied resistances is factory-fabricated at specified lengths of heating leads and nonheating leads. Hot-to-cold wire connectors and end caps are factory-brazed. Type MI cable is semirigid and can be hand-bent at the construction site to conform to desired spacing (usually 3 to 9 in.). It has the advantage of being durable in different asphalt or concrete environments.

Heating cables may be controlled by switch or by automatic snow control (Fig. 287). It is recommended that a high-limit thermostat be installed in the slab to prevent the system from operating at higher temperatures (50°F or more).

407. Electric Heating Controls. Electric space heating equipment may be specified with a built-in thermostat and relay or with a wall thermostat. Commercial installations often require the use of a contactor. Step controllers or solid-state controls may

FIG. 287 *Automatic snow control device. (Edwin L. Wiegand Co., Subsidiary of Emerson Electric Co.)*

be used with electric comfort heating equipment. For safety, most heaters are provided with spot or linear overheat protection.

408. Sizing Room Air Conditioners. As a general rule, room air conditioners can be sized on the basis of 30 Btu/hr/sq ft of space in a given room. Room air conditioners are rated in Btu (British thermal units) of cooling capacity. Units are available at 120-volt ratings up to 12,000 Btu in most cases. Current ratings range from 7½ to 12 amp for 120-volt units. In planning outlets, however, it is important to know whether the room air conditioner (window- or through-the-wall type) will be 120 or 240 volts, because some manufacturers provide 240-volt ratings for units of 9,000 Btu or more.

409. Code Rules for Fixed Space Heating Equipment. Article 424 of the National Electrical Code covers installations of fixed electric space heating equipment. The following paragraphs describe the major provisions of this Code article.

1. BRANCH CIRCUITS. All circuits for space-heating, snow-melting, and deicing equipment are considered as "continuous loads." As such, the load on any single or multioutlet branch circuit cannot exceed 80 per cent of the branch-circuit rating (12 amp on a 15-amp circuit, 16 amp on a 20-amp circuit, etc.). Generally, space heating equipment can be connected to 15-, 20-, or 30-amp multioutlet branch circuits. Infrared or snow melting systems can be connected to 15-, 20-, 30-, 40-, or 50-amp multioutlet branch circuits. Refer to Div. 3 for feeder or service calculations for a group of heaters.

2. CONTROLLERS AND DISCONNECTING MEANS.

a. Thermostats and thermostatically controlled switching devices which indicate an "off" position and which interrupt line current shall open all ungrounded conductors when the control device is in this "off" position.

b. Thermostats and thermostatically controlled switching devices which do not have an off position are not required to open all ungrounded conductors.

c. Remote-control thermostats do not need to meet the requirements of paragraphs *a* and *b*. These devices shall not serve as the disconnecting means.

d. Switching devices consisting of combined thermostats and manually controlled switches that serve both as controllers and disconnecting means shall open all ungrounded conductors when manually placed in the "off" position or be so designed that the circuit cannot be energized automatically after the device has been manually placed in the "off" position.

3. DUCT HEATERS.

a. Means shall be provided to assure uniform and adequate airflow over the heater.

b. Means should be provided to ensure that the fan circuit is energized when the first heater circuit is energized.

c. Each duct heater shall be provided with an integral approved automatic-reset temperature-limiting control or controllers to deenergize the circuit(s). In addition, an integral, independent, supplemental control or controllers shall be provided in each duct heater which will disconnect enough conductors to interrupt current flow. This control shall be manually resettable or replaceable.

d. Duct-heater controller equipment shall be accessible with the disconnecting means installed at or within sight of the controller.

410. Other Reference Material. With the fast development of the electric heating market, continuous references should be made to the latest NEMA standards and publications of the Electric Heating Association (EHA). An excellent series of articles, published in a continuing basis, is available through *Electrical Construction and Maintenance* magazine, McGraw-Hill, Inc. This publication provides an "Electric Heating Forum" which includes all up-to-date technical and practical information on electric heating.

WIRING FOR ELECTRIC SIGNS AND OUTLINE LIGHTING

411. Types of Signs. Electric signs or outline lighting may consist of incandescent lamps or gaseous-discharge tubing (commonly called neon signs). Refer to Div. 10 for discussion of lamps and tubing.

412. Methods of Wiring Incandescent Electric Signs (Data on Electric Signs, The National Electric Light Association). Lamps burning in multiple may be connected either two wire or three wire, as shown in Fig. 288. In series wiring, lamps may be connected in either straight series or multiple series, as shown. Where transformers (see Sec. **60** of Div. 5 for information on sign transformers) are used to obtain low voltage, lamps may be connected either two wire or three wire as in standard multiple wiring, the transformer reducing the voltage from the regular 110- or 220-volt circuits to the voltage required by the lamp. The ordinary multiple wiring can be changed to straight series wiring by merely clipping the alternate connections between lamps (Fig. 289).

In a large sign any combination of series or multiple series may be used. With straight series wiring, should one lamp in the series burn out, all the lamps in that series

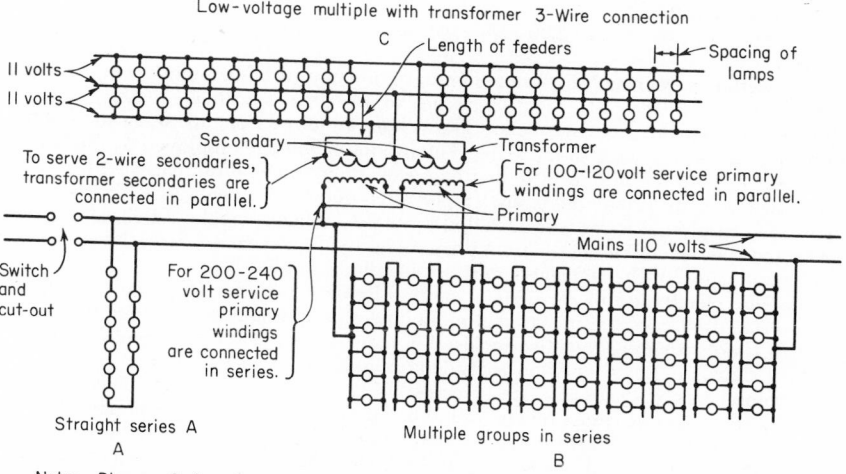

Note: Diagram C for alternating current only, others may be used on A.C. or D.C.

FIG. 288 *Methods of connecting sign lamps.*

will be out. If the lamps are connected in multiple series, the failure of one lamp does not cause any of the other lamps to go out. However, there should not be less than eight to ten lamps in each multiple group, or the failure of one lamp will cause too much current to flow through the other lamps of the same group, thus shortening their lives.

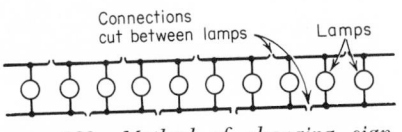

FIG. 289 *Method of changing sign wiring from multiple to series.*

413. Different effects of flashing or motion can be obtained with incandescent signs by the use of a sign flasher. Cams or a drum are mounted on a shaft that is rotated by a small electric motor (Fig. 290). The circumferences of the cams or of the drums are so cut that, in the brush-type flashers, the brushes will make contact only during certain predetermined portions of a revolution and thereby complete the electric circuit through the sign lamps only during that period. In the carbon-type flashers the cams, instead of carrying current and making and breaking the contacts directly, operate to open and close carbon-break contact switches which control the sign lamps. The possible variations in arrangement of cams and drums for producing different effects are almost numberless. Flashers are available for high- or low-voltage circuits.

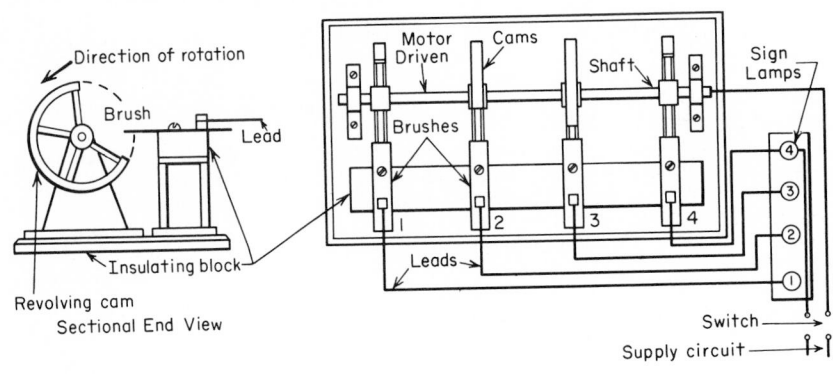

Plan and Wiring Diagram

FIG. 290 *The elementary sign flasher.*

414. Method of Wiring Neon-lamp Signs. Neon lamps used for signs are of the high-voltage type (see Div. 10). The lamps are supplied from ordinary lighting circuits through small step-up transformers. The voltage required depends upon the length of neon-lamp tubing used in the sign. The maximum voltage employed on the lamps is 15,000. When the length of tubing is greater than can be illuminated with 15,000 volts, two or more transformers are employed as required. Practically always neon signs are completely wired and installed by the manufacturers, the purchaser simply providing the necessary outlets from the general lighting system. Also, the servicing and maintenance of the signs generally are handled by specialists.

415. The installation of all signs or outline lighting, whether of the incandescent or gaseous-discharge type, must meet the following requirements: All equipment and devices used with signs must be enclosed in metal boxes. Except for portable incandescent signs, the boxes must be grounded unless they are insulated from ground and other conducting surfaces and are inaccessible to unauthorized persons. Each sign, except a portable one, must be controlled by an enclosed, externally operable switch or breaker located within sight of the sign or, if not so located, capable of being locked in the open position. All devices, such as switches, flashers, etc., unless of a specific type approved for this type of application, must have a current rating which is not less than twice the current rating of the transformer supplying the sign. The circuits should be so arranged that none will have a load of more than 15 amp.

416. The installation of signs (600 volts or less) must be in accordance with the following National Electrical Code requirements.

Conductors shall be installed as follows:

1. METHOD OF WIRING.   Conductors shall be installed as open conductors on insulators, or in rigid metal conduit, flexible metal conduit, electrical metallic tubing, metal-clad cable, metal troughing, Type ALS cable or Type MI cable.

2. INSULATION AND SIZE.   Conductors shall be of a type approved for general use and, except in portable signs and for short leads permanently attached to lampholders or ballasts, shall be not smaller than No. 14.

3. EXPOSED TO THE WEATHER.   Conductors in raceways, metal-clad cable, or enclosures exposed to the weather shall be of the lead-covered type or other type specially approved for the conditions.

4. NUMBER OF CONDUCTORS IN RACEWAY.   For sign flashers the number of conductors in conduit or tubing may be in accordance with Tables **25** to **27** of Div. **11**.

5. OPEN CONDUCTORS.   Open conductors on insulators shall comply with the provisions of *the Code as given in Secs.* **32** *to* **53** and, if outdoors, *with the requirements given in Div.* 8, except that the separation between conductors need be only 2 in., and that open conductors may be supported by lamp holders located not more than 1 ft apart.

6. CONDUCTORS SOLDERED TO TERMINALS.   Where the conductors are fastened to lamp holders other than of the pin type, they shall be soldered to the terminals, and the exposed parts of conductors and terminals shall be treated to prevent corrosion.   Where the conductors are fastened to pin-type lamp holders which protect the terminals from the entrance of water and which have been found acceptable for sign use, the conductors shall be of the stranded type but need not be soldered to the terminals.

7. LAMP HOLDERS.   Lamp holders shall be of the unswitched type with bodies made of suitable insulating material and shall be so constructed and installed as to prevent turning.   Miniature lamp holders shall not be employed for outdoor signs and outline lighting.

417. The installation of signs and outline lighting exceeding 600 volts must be in accordance with the following National Electrical Code requirements (Secs. **418** to **423**):

418. Installation of Conductors.   Conductors shall be installed as follows:

1. WIRING METHODS.   Conductors shall be installed as open work, as concealed conductors on insulators, or in rigid or flexible metal conduit or electrical metallic tubing. Conductors may be run from the ends of tubing to the grounded mid-point of transformers specifically designed for the purpose and provided with terminals at the mid-point.   Where such connections are made to the transformer-grounded mid-point, the connections between the high-voltage terminals of the transformer and the line ends of the tubing shall be as short as possible.

2. INSULATION AND SIZE.   Conductors shall be of a type approved for the purpose and for the voltage of the circuit, and shall not be smaller than No. 14.

3. BENDS IN CONDUCTORS.   Sharp bends in the conductors shall be avoided.

4. OPEN CONDUCTORS—INDOORS.   Open conductors indoors shall be mounted on noncombustible, nonabsorptive insulators.   Insulators of porcelain shall be glazed on all exposed surfaces.   A separation of at least 1½ in. shall be maintained between conductors and between conductors and other objects.   Conductors shall not be located where subject to mechanical injury.

5. CONCEALED CONDUCTORS ON INSULATORS—INDOORS.   Concealed conductors on insulators shall be separated from each other and from all objects other than the insulators on which they are mounted by a spacing of not less than 1½ in. for voltages above 10,000 volts, and not less than 1 in. for voltages of 10,000 or less.   They shall be installed in channels lined with noncombustible material and used for no other purpose, except that the primary circuit conductors may be in the same channel.   The insulators shall be of noncombustible, nonabsorptive material.

6. SHOW WINDOWS AND SIMILAR LOCATIONS.   If conductors hang freely in the air, away from combustible material, and if not subject to physical damage, as in some show-window displays, they need not be otherwise protected.

7. CONDUCTORS IN RACEWAYS.   If the conductors are covered with lead or other metal sheathing, the covering shall extend beyond the end of the raceway, and the sur-

face of the cable shall not be injured where the covering terminates. In damp or wet locations, the insulation on all conductors shall extend beyond the metal covering or raceway at least 4 in. for voltages over 10,000, 3 in. for voltages over 5,000 but not exceeding 10,000, and 2 in. for voltages of 5,000 or less. In dry locations, the insulation shall extend beyond the end of the metal covering or raceways not less than 2½ in. for voltages over 10,000, 2 in. for voltages over 5,000 but not exceeding 10,000, and 1½ in. for voltages of 5,000 or less. For conductors at grounded mid-point terminals, no spacing is required. Not more than 20 ft of cable from one secondary terminal shall be run in metal raceway.

8. OPEN CONDUCTORS—OUTDOORS. Open conductors outdoors shall be mounted on noncombustible, nonabsorptive insulators. Insulators of porcelain shall be glazed on all exposed surfaces. A separation of at least 2 in. shall be maintained between conductors and between conductors and other objects. Where subject to physical damage, or where within reach from ground, roof, or window, conductors shall be enclosed in raceways or suitably guarded. If guarded, a spacing of not less than 1½ in. shall be maintained between conductors and the enclosure unless the enclosure is nonconducting and noncombustible.

419. Transformers. Transformers shall comply with the following:

1. VOLTAGE. The transformer secondary open-circuit voltage shall not exceed 15,000 volts with an allowance on test of 1,000 volts additional. In end-grounded transformers the secondary, open-circuit voltage shall not exceed 7,500 volts with an allowance on test of 500 volts additional.

2. TYPE. Transformers shall be of a type approved for the purpose and shall be limited in rating to a maximum of 4,500 va. Open core-and-coil-type transformers shall be limited to 5,000 volts with an allowance on test of 500 volts and to indoor applications in small portable signs. Transformers for outline lighting installations shall have secondary current ratings not in excess of 30 ma unless they and all wiring connected to them are installed in accordance with the provisions of article 410 of the Code for electric discharge lighting of the same voltage.

3. EXPOSED TO WEATHER. Transformers used outdoors shall be of the weatherproof type or shall be protected from the weather by enclosure in the sign body or in a separate metal box.

4. TRANSFORMER SECONDARY CONNECTIONS. The high-voltage windings of transformers shall not be connected in parallel and shall not be connected in series, except that two transformers each having one end of its high-voltage winding connected to the metal enclosure may have their high-voltage windings connected in series to form the equivalent of a mid-point grounded transformer. The grounded ends shall be connected by insulated conductors not smaller than No. 14.

5. ACCESSIBILITY. Transformers shall be accessible.

420. Tubing. Electric discharge tubing shall conform to the following:

1. DESIGN. The tubing shall be of such length and design as not to cause a continuous overvoltage on the transformer.

2. SUPPORT. Tubing shall be adequately supported on noncombustible, nonabsorptive supports. Tubing supports should, if practicable, be adjustable.

3. CONTACT WITH FLAMMABLE MATERIAL AND OTHER SURFACES. The tubing shall be free from contact with flammable material and shall be located where not normally exposed to physical damage. If operating in excess of 7,500 volts, the tubing shall be supported on noncombustible, nonabsorptive, insulating supports which maintain a spacing of not less than ¼ in. between the tubing and the nearest surface.

421. Terminals and receptacles for electric discharge tubing shall comply with the following:

1. TERMINALS. The terminals of the tubing shall be inaccessible to unqualified persons and isolated from combustible material and grounded metal or shall be enclosed. If enclosed, they shall be separated from grounded metal and combustible material by nonabsorptive, noncombustible insulating material approved for the purpose or by 1½ in. of air. Terminals shall be relieved from stress by the independent support of the tubing.

2. TUBE CONNECTIONS OTHER THAN WITH RECEPTACLES. If tubes do not terminate

in receptacles designed for the purpose, all live parts of tube terminals and conductors shall be so supported as to maintain a separation of at least 1½ in. between conductors or between conductors and any grounded metal.

3. RECEPTACLES. Electrode receptacles for gas tubing shall be of noncombustible, nonabsorptive insulating material approved for the purpose.

4. BUSHINGS. Where electrodes enter the enclosure of outdoor signs or of an indoor sign operating at a voltage in excess of 7,500 volts, bushings shall be used unless receptacles are provided or the sign is wired with bare wire mounted on approved supports which maintain the tubing in proper position. Bushings shall be of noncombustible nonabsorptive material. Where bare wiring is used, the conductor shall be not less than No. 14 solid copper, shall be supported so as to prevent sagging and lessening of the spacing required elsewhere in this section, and electrode terminal assemblies shall be of an approved type and supported not more than 6 in. from the electrode terminals.

5. SHOW WINDOWS. In the exposed type of show-window signs, terminals shall be (1) enclosed by receptacles approved for the purpose or (2) where hanging in air, free from grounded surfaces, enclosed in sleeves of vulcanized fiber, phenolic composition, or other suitable material which overlaps all live parts by at least ½ in.

6. RECEPTACLES AND BUSHING SEALS. A flexible, nonconducting seal may be used to close the opening between the tubing and the receptacle or bushing against the entrance of dust or moisture. This seal shall not be in contact with grounded conductive material and shall not be depended upon for the insulation of the tubing.

7. ENCLOSURES OF METAL. Metal enclosures for electrodes shall be of not less than No. 24 MSG (.0239 in.) sheet metal.

8. ENCLOSURES OF INSULATING MATERIAL. Enclosures of insulating material shall be noncombustible, nonabsorptive and approved for the voltage of the circuit.

422. Switches on Doors. Doors or covers giving access to uninsulated parts of indoor signs or outline lighting exceeding 600 volts and accessible to the general public either shall be provided with interlock switches which on the opening of the doors or covers disconnect the primary circuit or shall be so fastened that the use of other than ordinary tools will be necessary to open them.

423. Enclosures. Enclosures for signs and outline lighting shall conform to the following:

1. CONDUCTORS AND TERMINALS. Sign boxes, cabinets, and outline troughs shall have conductors and terminals, except the supply leads, enclosed.

2. CUTOUTS, FLASHERS, ETC. Cutouts, flashers, and similar devices shall be enclosed in metal boxes, the doors of which shall be arranged so that they can be opened without removing obstructions or finished parts of the enclosure.

3. ENCLOSURES EXPOSED TO WEATHER. Enclosures for outside use shall be weatherproof and shall have an ample number of drain holes, each not larger than ½ or smaller than ¼ in. Wiring connections shall not be made through the bottoms of enclosures exposed to the weather unless the enclosures are of the raintight type.

4. MATERIAL. Except for portable signs of the indoor type, signs and outline lighting shall be constructed of metal or other noncombustible material. Wood may be used for external decoration if placed at least 2 in. from the nearest lamp holder or current-carrying part.

5. STRENGTH. Enclosures shall have ample strength and rigidity.

6. THICKNESS OF METAL. Sheet copper shall be at least 20 oz (0.028 in.). Sheet steel may be of No. 28 MSG (0.0149 in.) except that for outline lighting and for electric discharge signs sheet steel shall be of No. 24 MSG (0.0239 in.) unless ribbed, corrugated, or embossed over its entire surface, when it may be of No. 26 MSG (0.0179 in.).

7. PROTECTION OF METAL. All steel parts of enclosures shall be galvanized or otherwise protected from corrosion.

424. Current-carrying Capacities of Flashers. Double-pole flashers are made in four sizes that will carry respectively 15, 30, 45, or 60 amp per switch. Single-pole carbon flashers are made that will carry 5 amp per switch. Brush-type flashers are rated at from 2 to 5 amp on each brush and are not reliable for greater currents.

REMOTE-CONTROL, LOW-ENERGY POWER, LOW-VOLTAGE POWER, AND SIGNAL CIRCUITS

425. A remote-control circuit is any electrical circuit which controls any other circuit through a relay or an equivalent device.

426. A low-energy power circuit is a circuit which is not a remote-control or signal circuit but which has its power supply limited in accordance with the requirements of Class 2 remote-control circuits, as given in Sec. **432.** Examples of such circuits are electric door-opener circuits and circuits used in the operation of coin-operated phonographs. These circuits are considered as Class 2 remote-control circuits with respect to the National Electrical Code requirements for their installation.

427. Low-voltage Power Circuits. Circuits which are neither remote-control nor signal circuits but which operate at not more than 30 volts where the current is not limited in accordance with the requirements of Class 2 remote-control circuits and which are supplied from a source not exceeding 1,000 va are considered as Class 1 remote-control circuits with respect to the National Electrical Code requirements for their installation.

428. A signal circuit is any electrical circuit supplying energy to an appliance which gives a recognizable signal. Such circuits include circuits for doorbells, buzzers, code-calling systems, signal lights, and the like.

429. Safety-control Devices. Remote-control circuits to safety-control devices, the failure of operation of which would introduce a direct fire or life hazard, shall be considered as Class 1 circuits.

Room thermostats, service hot-water temperature-regulating devices, and similar controls used in conjunction with electrically-controlled domestic heating equipment are not considered to be safety-control devices.

430. Remote-control and Signal Circuits in Communication Cables. Remote-control and signal circuits, which use conductors in the same cable with communication circuits, shall, for the purpose of this discussion, be classified as communication circuits and meet the requirements of such circuits (refer to articles 800, 810, and 820 of the National Electrical Code).

431. Hazardous Locations. Any remote-control or signal circuit or any circuit considered as such by the Code which is installed in a hazardous location must meet the Code requirements for hazardous-location installation in addition to the requirements for remote-control circuits.

432. Remote-control and signal circuits are divided by the National Electrical Code into two classes as follows:

1. CLASS 1. Systems in which the power is not limited.

2. CLASS 2. Systems in which the power is limited in accordance with the following voltage and current limitations:

a. Maximum 15 Volts, 5 Amp. Circuits in which the open-circuit voltage does not exceed 15 volts and having overcurrent protection of not more than 5-amp rating. If the current supply is from a transformer or other device having energy-limiting characteristics and approved for the purpose or from primary batteries, the overcurrent protection may be omitted.

b. 15 to 30 Volts, 3.2 Amp. Circuits in which the open-circuit voltage exceeds 15 volts but does not exceed 30 volts and having overcurrent protection of not more than 3.2-amp rating. If the current supply is from a transformer or other device having energy-limiting characteristics and approved for the purpose or from primary batteries, the overcurrent protection may be omitted.

c. 30 to 60 Volts, 1.6 Amp. Circuits in which the open-circuit voltage exceeds 30 volts but does not exceed 60 volts and having overcurrent protection of not more than 1.6-amp rating. If the current supply is from a transformer or other device having energy-limiting characteristics and approved for the purpose, the overcurrent protection may be omitted.

d. 60 to 150 Volts, 1 Amp. Circuits in which the open-circuit voltage exceeds 60 volts but does not exceed 150 volts and having overcurrent protection of not more than

1-amp rating, provided that such circuits are equipped with current-limiting means other than overcurrent protection which will limit the current as a result of a fault to not exceeding 1 amp.

e. *Maximum* 150 *Volts*, 5 *Milliamp.* Circuits in which the open-circuit voltage does not exceed 150 volts provided that such circuits are equipped with current-limiting means, other than overcurrent protection, which are approved for the purpose and which will limit the current as a result of a fault to not exceeding 5 ma.

CLASS 1 SYSTEMS

433. The installation of Class 1 systems must be in accordance with the general National Electrical Code requirements for the installations of electrical circuits except as stated in the special Code specifications as given in the following sections (Secs. **434** to **443** inclusive).

434. Conductor Sizes. Numbers 18 and 16 gage conductors may be used if installed in a raceway or a cable approved for the purpose or in flexible cords in accordance with the provisions of article 400 of the Code.

435. Conductor Insulation. Conductors larger than No. 16 shall be thermoplastic-covered Type T, or other approved type. Fixed conductors Nos. 18 and 16 gage shall have an insulation at least equal to that of Type TF thermoplastic-covered fixture wire. Conductors approved for the purpose having insulation of a thickness less than specified above or having other kinds of insulation may be used.

436. Number of Conductors in Raceways. The number of conductors of remote-control or signal circuits in a raceway must be determined according to Table **25**, Div. 11; and note 8 of Sec. **17**, Div. 11, applies only to continuous loads (3 hr or more). Where there are four or more conductors in a raceway, some of which are remote-control, as permitted by section 300-3, the provisions of note 8 of Sec. **17**, Div. 11, shall apply, as determined by the number of power and lighting circuit conductors only, unless the remote-control conductors are classed as continuous loads.

437. Conductors of Different Systems. Conductors of two or more Class 1 remote-control and/or signal circuits may occupy the same enclosure or raceway without regard to whether the individual systems or circuits are alternating or direct current, provided all conductors are insulated for the maximum voltage of any conductor in the enclosure or raceway. Conductors of remote-control, low-energy power and signal circuits, in which the current is limited as for Class 2 systems, shall be considered as Class 1 system conductors for the purpose of this requirement if insulated and installed in accordance with the provisions for Class 1 system conductors. Power-supply conductors may occupy the same enclosure or raceway with Class 1 system conductors when supplying only equipment to which Class 1 system conductors are connected.

438. Mechanical Protection of Remote-control Circuits. Where damage to a remote-control circuit would introduce a hazard as covered in Sec. **429** all conductors of such remote-control circuits shall be installed in conduit, electrical metallic tubing, or Type MI cable, or be otherwise suitably protected from physical damage.

439. Overcurrent Protection. Conductors shall be protected against overcurrent in accordance with the general Code requirements except as follows:

1. CONDUCTORS OF NOS. 18 AND 16. Conductors of Nos. 18 and 16 shall be considered as protected by overcurrent devices of 20-amp rating or setting.

2. OMISSION OF OVERCURRENT PROTECTION. In remote-control and signal circuits having main and branch circuits, the branch circuits need not be individually protected against overcurrent, if the operating voltage does not exceed 30 volts.

3. TRANSFORMER DEVICES supplying low-voltage power circuits shall be provided with overcurrent protection in the secondary circuit rated or set at not more than 250 per cent of the rated secondary current of the transformer. Such protection and mounting shall be approved for the purpose. Overcurrent protection required shall not be interchangeable with protection of a higher voltage. The overcurrent protection may be an integral part of a transformer or other power-supply device approved for the purpose.

440. Location of Overcurrent Protection. Overcurrent devices shall be located at the point where the conductor to be protected receives its supply unless the overcurrent device protecting the larger conductor also protects the smaller conductor in accordance with the current-carrying-capacity tables of Div. 11.

441. Circuits Extending beyond One Building. Class 1 remote-control and signal circuits which extend aerially beyond one building shall also meet the requirements of article 730 of the Code.

442. Grounding. Class 1 remote-control and signal circuits shall be grounded in accordance with article 250 of the Code.

443. Transformer Rating. Transformer devices supplying low-voltage power circuits shall be approved for the purpose and be restricted in their rated output to not exceeding 1,000 va and to not exceeding 30 volts. They shall be marked where plainly visible to show their rated output and the voltage to be applied to the circuit.

A transformer is considered as meeting the 1,000-va requirement if the approximate temperature limit is reached at 1,000-va load.

CLASS 2 SYSTEMS

444. The National Electrical Code requirements for the installation of Class 2 systems are given in the following sections (Sec. **445** to **450,** inclusive):

445. Overcurrent Protection and Mounting. Where current is limited in Class 2 systems by means of overcurrent protection, such protection and its mounting shall be approved for the purpose.

Overcurrent protection required shall not be interchangeable with protection of a higher rating. The overcurrent protection may be an integral part of a transformer or other power-supply device approved for the purpose.

446. Transformer Rating. Transformer devices supplying Class 2 systems shall be approved for the purpose and be restricted in their rated output to not exceeding 100 va. Such devices shall not be paralleled or otherwise interconnected. They shall be marked where plainly visible to show the voltage to be applied to the circuit. A transformer is considered as meeting the 100-va requirement if the approximate temperature limit is reached at a 100-va load.

447. On Supply Side of Overcurrent Protection, Transformers or Current-limiting Devices. Conductors and equipment on supply side of overcurrent protection, transformers, or current-limiting devices shall be installed in accordance with the appropriate requirements of chapter 3 of the Code. Transformers or other devices supplied from electric light and power circuits shall be protected by an overcurrent device with a rating or setting not exceeding 20 amp.

448. On Load Side of Overcurrent Protection, Transformer or Current-limiting Devices. Conductors on load side of overcurrent protection, transformer, or current-limiting devices shall be insulated and shall comply with the following:

1. SEPARATION FROM OTHER CONDUCTORS. Conductors shall be separated from conductors of electric light and power circuits as follows:

a. Open Conductors. Conductors shall be separated at least 2 in. from any light or power conductors or Class 1 signal or control circuits not in a raceway nor in metal-sheathed, metal-clad, nonmetallic-sheathed, or Type UF cables unless permanently separated from the conductors of the other system by a continuous and firmly fixed nonconductor, such as porcelain tubes or flexible tubing, additional to the insulation on the wire.

b. In Raceways and Boxes. Conductors of Class 2 remote-control and signal circuits shall not be placed in any raceway, compartment, outlet box, or similar fitting with conductors for either light and power circuits or Class 1 signal and control circuits, unless the conductors of the different systems are separated by a partition; provided that this shall not apply to conductors in outlet boxes, junction boxes, or similar fittings or compartments where power supply conductors are introduced solely for supplying power to the remote-control or signal equipment to which the other conductors in the enclosure are connected (see Sec. **437**).

c. In Shafts. Open conductors may be run in the same shaft with conductors for light and power where the conductors of the two systems are separated at least 2 in. or where the conductors of either system are encased in noncombustible tubing. Where the lighting or power conductors are run in a raceway, or in metal-sheathed or metal-clad or nonmetallic-sheathed or Type UF cables, neither the 2-in. separation nor the noncombustible tubing is required. In hoistways conductors shall be installed in rigid conduit or electrical metallic tubing, except as provided for in section 620-21, Exception No. 1, of the Code.

2. VERTICAL RUNS. Conductors in a vertical run in a shaft or partition shall have fire-resistant covering capable of preventing the carrying of fire from floor to floor, except where conductors are encased in tubing or other outer covering of noncombustible material or are located in a fireproof shaft having fire stops at each floor. Where three or more conductors are used, it is recommended that such conductors be grouped under a common braid or covering.

449. Circuits Extending beyond One Building. Class 2 remote-control and signal circuits which extend beyond one building and are so run as to be subject to accidental contact with light or power conductors operating at a potential exceeding 300 volts shall also meet the requirements of sections 800-2, 800-11, and 800-12 of the Code.

450. Grounding. Class 2 remote-control and signal circuits and equipment shall be grounded in accordance with article 250 of the Code.

SIGNAL SYSTEMS

451. The suggestions for the installation of signal systems given in the following sections (Secs. **452** to **462A,** inclusive) are for the installation of Class 2 systems only.

452. Types of Conductors. Because the conductors for Class 2 systems are small (No. 18 or No. 16) it is suggested that only copper wire be used. Common Class 2 conductors are thermoplastic-insulated or covered with a cotton braid. Whenever possible such cables should be provided in a cable form with an outer jacket such as thermoplastic or similar material. In a multiple-conductor form the conductors will be protected much more than with single conductors or twisted pairs. Multiple-conductor cables with an outer sheath are readily available with any number of color-coded conductors.

453. Supports for Cables. Extreme care must be taken in securing cables to wood supports. Staple machines, specifically designed for the purpose, or square hand-driven staples can be used. If Class 2 cables are pulled through holes in wood members which also contain power cables, the Class 2 cables should be pulled in last to avoid damage to the signal cable. If installed in attics, basements, or other open areas, Class 2 cables should be attached to solid surfaces; and runs across open spans should be avoided to prevent physical damage from objects that may be placed in contact with such cables.

454. In fishing for vertical wires a piece of small chain 2 ft long is attached to a length of strong cord. The chain and cord are pushed through a hole bored for the wire at the top of the partition, and the noise made by the chain when the cord is pulled up and down will indicate the location of any obstruction. With the obstruction located, the baseboard or floor board can be taken out and a hole can be bored or some other means adopted to provide a pocket whereby the chain can be reached. Also, a long extension bit can be used.

455. The steel fish bit (Fig. 291) is a useful tool in installing signal wires. The bit has a hole in its end. After the bit has been bored through an orifice, the wire to be drawn through is made up through the hole and the wire and bit are together drawn back through the orifice. The use of a fish wire is thereby eliminated. In a floor or ceiling, the orifice having been bored, it may be more convenient to withdraw the bit first and then thread the wire through the hole at the end of the bit and push the bit back through the hole. Good bits of this type are so tempered that they will drill through wood, masonry, wrought iron, or structural steel.

456. Electric bell circuits are shown in Fig. 292. Many of these are quite simple but are included so that all will be together for the electrician's reference. Two ordinary vibrating bells will not work well together in series, so, when it is necessary to connect two or more in series, one should be a single-stroke bell, as in IV. A multiple arrangement (II) is preferable to a series arrangement, and the batteries for a multiple arrangement are more effective if connected in multiple. Try a series and a multiple arrange-

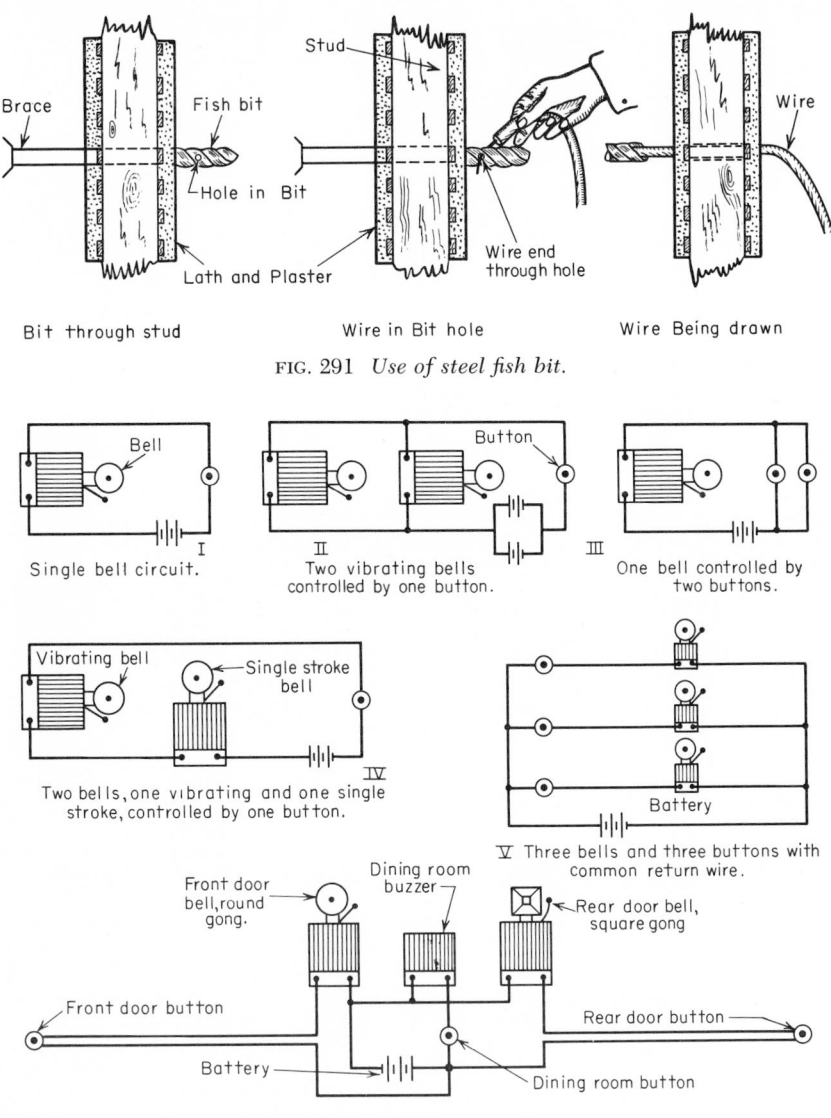

Bit through stud Wire in Bit hole Wire Being drawn

FIG. 291 *Use of steel fish bit.*

FIG. 292 *Elementary electric-bell circuits.*

ment of cells and ascertain which works best. Where several signal bells must be located together, gongs of different types (VI), each of which gives a different sound, can be used.

457. Power Supply for Bell Circuits. Although in the diagrams a battery has been shown as the power source, whenever an a-c supply is available a bell-ringing transformer stepping the voltage down to about 6 to 18 volts is usual (refer to Div. 5 for description of bell-ringing transformers). The transformer eliminates the trouble of having to replace batteries. It is of the high-reactance type, which has a no-load loss of only a few watts and which will deliver a maximum current of only a few amperes even when short-circuited. Types are available which can be mounted on the cover of a standard 3¼-in. outlet box, or where appearance is important, a flush type with a louvered cover which can be mounted inside a switch box is available (Fig. 293).

On important signaling systems where the a-c supply is not fully dependable, a storage battery is used and kept charged with a rectifier.

458. Return-call bell circuits for different services are shown in Fig. 294. With these, when a station is signaled, the party called can signal back by pressing his button. In general ground return circuits are undesirable, as one ground on one of the normally ungrounded wires may render the system inoperative; furthermore, there are often "stray" currents flowing in the earth, which may interfere with the operation of the bell circuits. With the arrangement of Fig. 294, VII, when the calling station is the one at the single-stroke bell, the caller may be sure that the called station is ringing, because it is the vibrating bell at that station that causes the single-stroke bell to ring.

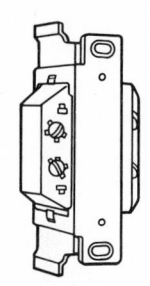

FIG. 293 *Bell-ringing transformer for switchbox mounting. (Edwards Co., Inc.)*

459. Apartment-house and speaking-tube bell-wiring circuits are shown in Fig. 295. One battery or transformer serves for all stations. Frequently a wire larger than the other wiring is used for the battery or transformer wire, which supplies all the stations.

460. Electric bells of different types are shown in Fig. 296. The vibrating bell is the one commonly used. The single-stroke bell can be used in series with a vibrating bell, which will open and close the circuit and thereby make the single-stroke bell also operate. Door chimes are used more today than bells. A door chime has a plunger which strikes against a bar or hollow tube to produce a pleasing musical note. The enclosed bars (Fig. 297, A and B) are made with either a single-note or a double-note type. With the double-note type a single note sounds for the bell push from one door and a double note for the bell push from another door. The cathedral chimes (Fig. 297,D, E, and F) play a series of musical notes.

461. A double-contact three-point or return-call push button (Fig. 298) is used in return-call bells and annunciator circuits. Applications of push buttons of this type are shown in the diagrams.

462. Bell-ringing or chime transformers should always, where there is alternating current, be used for operating signaling systems such as those for bell and annunciator service. A well-made bell-ringing or chime transformer will last indefinitely. The National Electrical Code rules specify that the transformers shall be of special design; that the primary wiring shall be installed in accordance with the rules for light, power, and heat wiring; and that the secondary wiring shall be installed in accordance with the rules for signal-system wiring. A well-designed bell-ringing transformer consumes very little energy.

462A.   Fire, Smoke, and Burglar Alarms. There are so many types of fire, smoke, and burglar alarm systems or combination systems available today that a detailed discussion here would not be practical. Deluxe transistorized intercom systems include provisions for fire detection; and closed-circuit television systems, infrared detection systems, photocells, and similar techniques are widely used for intrusion detection. All these systems are of a special nature, and it is recommended that manufacturers of these products be contacted when any of these systems are contemplated. Circuitry of these systems is relatively simple, and equipment is furnished complete with identified wiring terminals to simplify installation. Most of the modern protection equipment is transistorized, and servicing is done by specialists in this field. Figure 302 shows typical single- and multiple-zone home fire alarm systems. Division 6 covers some of the basic circuitry and components used in such equipment.

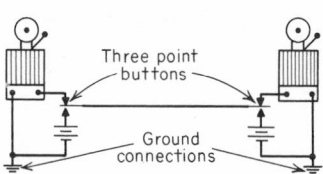

I Single line and ground return call. 2-batteries, special 3-point return call buttons.

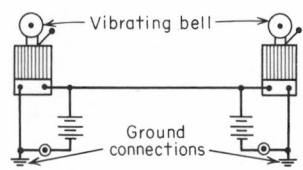

II Single line and ground return call. 2-batteries. 2 point buttons. Bells ring simultaneously.

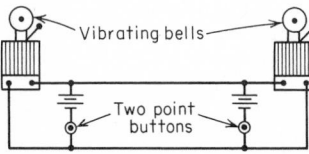

III 2-Line return call. 2-batteries. 2-point buttons. Bells ring simultaneously.

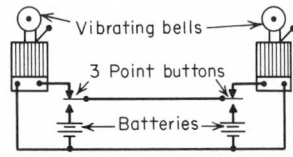

IV 2-Line Return call. 2-batteries. Special 3 Point or return call buttons.

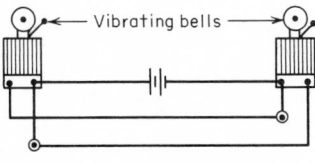

V 3-Line return call. 1-battery. Each bell controlled independently by one button.

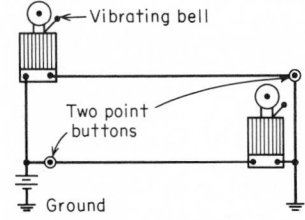

VI 2-Line and ground return call 1.-battery. 2-Point buttons.

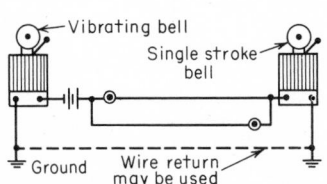

VII Return call. 1-vibrating and 1-single stroke bell.

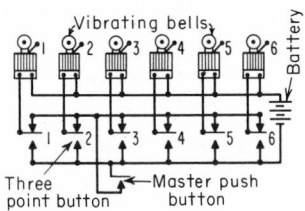

VIII Each Individual bell can be rung by its own button, and all bells can be rung simultaneously by master button.

FIG. 294   *Return call and master-button electric-bell circuits.*

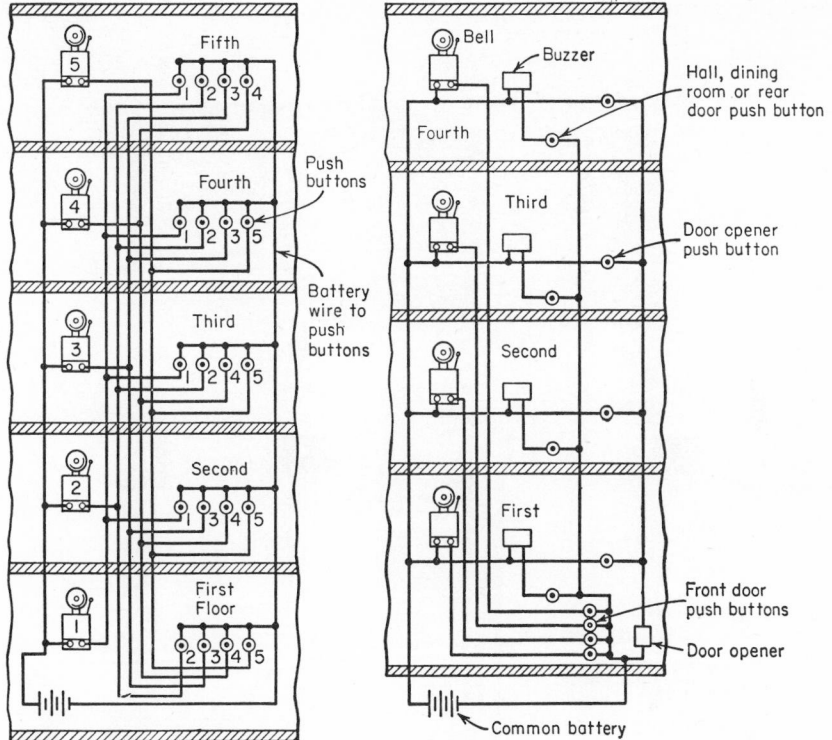

I—Speaking tube system operated from one battery. Each station can be signaled from any other station

II—Bell wiring in an apartment house using a single battery

FIG. 295 *Apartment-house bell circuits.*

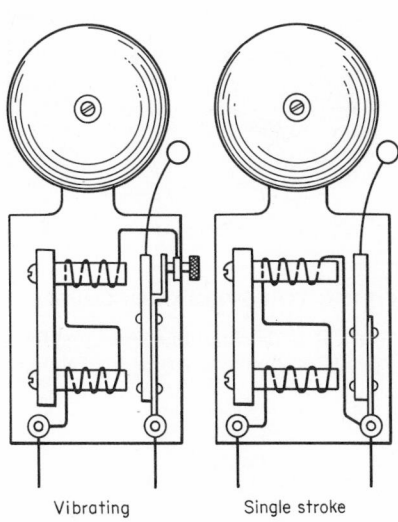

Vibrating   Single stroke

FIG. 296 *Electric bells of different types.*

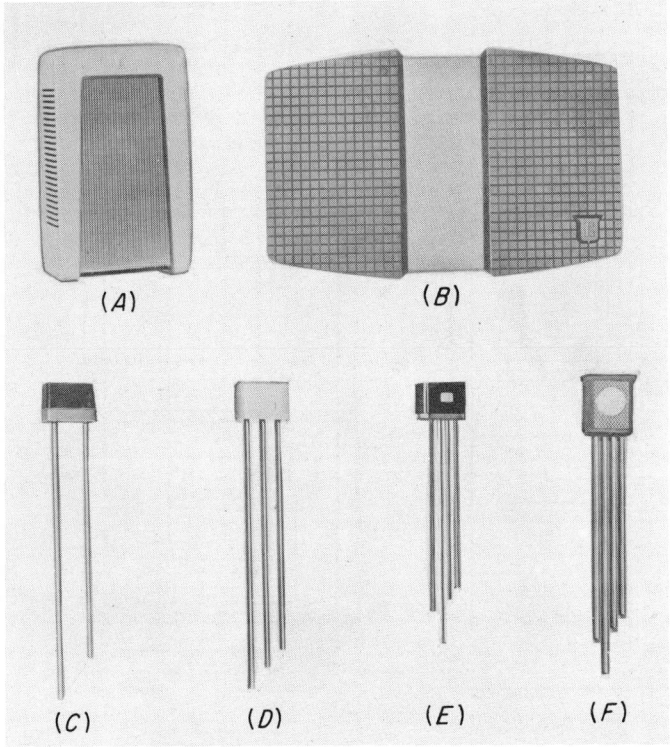

FIG. 297   *Door chimes.* (*Edwards Co., Inc.*)

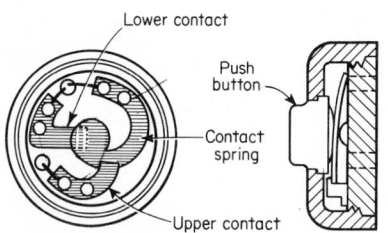

FIG. 298   *Three-point push button.*

WIRING FOR SPECIAL OCCUPANCIES

463. The National Electrical Code should be consulted for special rules on installations in the following special occupancies or for the following special equipment or conditions:

Garages.

Aircraft hangars.

Gasoline-dispensing and service stations.

Bulk storage plants.

Finishing processes.

Combustible anesthetics.

Theaters and assembly halls.
Motion picture studios and similar locations.
Motion picture projectors.
Elevators, dumbwaiters, and escalators.
Electric welders.
Sound-recording and similar equipment.
Organs.
X-ray equipment.
Induction and dielectric-heating equipment.
Metalworking machine tools.
Emergency systems.
Radio and television equipment.
Mobile homes.
Recreational vehicles.
Standby power generation systems.
Swimming pools.
Marina and boatyard wiring.
Data processing systems.

DESIGN OF INTERIOR WIRING INSTALLATIONS

GENERAL CONSIDERATIONS

464. Factors Affecting Wiring Layouts ("Standard Handbook"). In conduit work the space available often dictates that the feeders be split up into two or more feeder lines so as to guard against complete shutdown should anything happen to one feeder.

In reinforced-concrete floors a cross section of the floor must be studied to see that there will be sufficient space for the reinforcing rods, conduit or raceways, and necessary thickness of concrete. This is especially true where conduits cross. The local building code should be consulted to see what restrictions are placed on floor installations. A minimum thickness of 1 in. of concrete over conduits and raceways should be used to prevent cracking.

Example. The building code may allow floors 4 in. thick with ³⁄₄-in. reinforcing rods located with 1 in. of concrete covering the underside (Fig. 299). This would mean that there is a minimum space of 1¼ in. between the top of the reinforcing rods and the top of any conduit. For this installation, ³⁄₄-in. conduit, which has an outside diameter of 1.05 in. (Sec. **63**), would be the largest size allowable. There could be no crosses of conduit because even two ½-in. conduits would take up 2 × 0.84 = 1.68 in. of space, which is more than the 1¼ in. available.

In brick walls there must be two thicknesses of brick in order to conceal conduits, and the distance between them must be studied to determine the maximum size for vertical runs of conduit. These are only a few of the possible examples where space for wiring must be considered. Very often the mistake is made of installing feeders just large enough to carry the present load, and when additions are called for, the feeders are overloaded and additional feeders must be installed at great expense. Conduits for feeders and mains should be of sufficient size to permit the installation of feeders or mains of a carrying capacity of 150 per cent of the present connected load. Also, spare conduits can be installed.

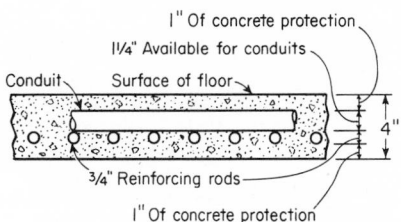

FIG. 299 *Study of space available for conduits in reinforced concrete floors.*

465. Wiring methods to be used are determined by a consideration of national and local code requirements, reliability, appearance, and cost. In planning a wiring installation, it should be decided which methods of wiring are allowable for the particular occupancy and electric system being considered. Then the cost of each allowable method should be weighed against the appearance, the degree of protection afforded, reliability, and probable years of service that will be realized. Both cost of material and cost of labor must be considered.

1. For RESIDENCES. Metal-clad cable concealed in the partitions is very practical, giving good reliability at moderate cost. Where a less expensive installation is desired, nonmetallic-sheathed cable may be used. Sometimes this is used for a few large-sized circuits such as to the electric range where the difference in cost is considerable, even if the rest of the wiring is metal-clad cable. The expense of metal raceways is usually not justified except in very large residences of the highest grade of construction. Where the highest degree of adequacy for convenience outlets is desired, multioutlet assemblies should be employed for this part of the wiring.

2. For REWIRING OF OLD BUILDINGS OF RESIDENTIAL OR COMMERCIAL OCCUPANCY, surface raceways, metal-clad cable, nonmetallic-sheathed cable, or electrical metallic tubing are the usual expedients. Surface raceways give the best appearance if the wiring must be exposed. Metal-clad cable or nonmetallic-sheathed cable is the most practical for that part of the wiring which can be fished through the partitions.

3. For SMALL COMMERCIAL BUILDINGS AND APARTMENT BUILDINGS of frame or brick and frame construction, metal-clad cable, nonmetallic-sheathed cable, or electrical metallic tubing concealed in the partitions is generally the most practical.

4. For OFFICE AND PUBLIC BUILDINGS of steel, concrete, terra-cotta or similar construction, the cost of wiring is only a small percentage of the total cost of the building. In order to keep the offices rented to business firms, the electric system should provide the very best in appearance and adequacy of service. Therefore the wiring should be concealed, employing rigid metal conduit or electrical metallic tubing for ceiling lights and feeders, and underfloor raceways or cellular-floor raceways for desk outlets for power and signaling circuits.

5. For INDUSTRIAL BUILDINGS metal raceways are generally used for branches, with busways, metal-clad cables, or conduits for feeders.

6. For LARGE-SIZED MAIN FEEDERS the method of wiring should be considered very carefully because the high unit costs may make a considerable difference in the total cost of the installation.

Very often, combinations of wiring methods are used in the same building, each method being used where its advantages make it desirable.

466. For rewiring of buildings using existing conduits, the National Electrical Code allows such conduits to have a larger number of conductors than for new work, depending on the type and size of conductors (see Tables **25A, 27,** and **47** to **51** of Div. 11).

467. The branch circuits used in interior wiring may be classified as follows:

TYPE 1. This is an individual branch circuit that supplies only one utilization equipment.

TYPE 2. This is a branch circuit that supplies two or more outlets. These branch circuits are further classified by the National Electrical Code according to the rating of the fuse or circuit breaker that protects the circuit. The Code recognizes five types of these multioutlet branch circuits. They are 15-, 20-, 30-, 40-, and 50-amp branch circuits, respectively. The Code provides certain restrictions on the rating of outlets, size of wire, and equipment to be supplied, as given in Sec. **470.**

468. Maximum Loads for Branch Circuits. Type 1 branch circuits may supply loads of any capacity. If the load consists of a motor-operated appliance, the load must not exceed 80 per cent of the branch-circuit wires. Also the load must not exceed 80 per cent of the rating of the branch circuit where any load will continue for 3 hr or more. For details of the requirements for motor branch circuits refer to Div. 7.

Branch circuits are required by the Code to have maximum loads which conform to the following:

1. APPLIANCES CONSISTING OF MOTORS AND OTHER LOADS. Where a circuit supplies only motor-operated appliance loads, article 430 shall apply (refer to Div. 7). For other than a portable appliance, the branch-circuit size shall be calculated on the basis of 125 per cent of motor load where the motor is larger than $\frac{1}{8}$ hp plus the sum of the other loads.

2. OTHER LOADS. The total load shall not exceed the branch-circuit rating and shall

not exceed 80 per cent of the rating where the load will continue for 3 hr or more, such as store lighting and similar loads. In computing the load of lighting units that employ ballasts, transformers, or autotransformers, the load shall be based on the total of the ampere rating of such units and not on the wattage of the lamps.

EXCEPTION: RANGE LOADS. See Note 5 of Table 2 in Div. 11.

469. Permissible loads for Type 2 branch circuits are specified by the Code as follows:

1. 15- AND 20-AMP BRANCH CIRCUITS. Lighting units and/or appliances. The rating of any one portable appliance shall not exceed 80 per cent of the branch-circuit rating. The total rating of fixed appliances shall not exceed 50 per cent of the branch-circuit rating if lighting units or portable appliances are also supplied.

2. 30-AMP BRANCH CIRCUITS. Fixed lighting units with heavy-duty lamp holders in other than dwelling occupancies or appliances in any occupancy. The rating of any one portable appliance shall not exceed 24 amp.

3. 40- AND 50-AMP BRANCH CIRCUITS. Fixed lighting units with heavy-duty lamp holders in other than dwelling occupancies, fixed cooking appliances, or infrared heating appliances.

The term "fixed" as used in this section recognizes cord connections where otherwise permitted.

470. Lighting and Appliance Branch Circuits
(Types FEP, FEPB, RUW, SA, T, TW, RH, RUH, RHW, RHH, THHN, THW, THWN, and XHHW conductors in raceway or cable)

Circuit rating, amp	15	20	30	40	50
Conductors (minimum size):					
Circuit wires[a]	14	12	10	8	6
Taps	14	14	14	12	12
Fixture wires and cords	Refer to section 240-5(a), Exception No. 3 of Code				
Overcurrent protection, amp	15	20	30	40	50
Outlet devices:					
Lamp holders permitted	Any type	Any type	Heavy duty	Heavy duty	Heavy duty
Receptacle rating, amp	15 max.	15 or 20	30	40 or 50	50
Maximum load, amp	15	20	30	40	50
Permissible load	b	b	c	d	e

[a]These ampacities are for copper conductors where derating is not required. See Sec. 17 of Div. 11 and Tables 18 to 21A of Div. 11.

[b]Refer to section 210-24(a) of the Code.

[c]Refer to section 210-24(b) of the Code.

[d]Refer to section 210-24(c) of the Code.

[e]Refer to section 210-24(d) of the Code.

471. The minimum required loads for which branch circuits and feeders must be supplied shall meet the Code requirements as determined from Table **5**, Div. 11. Where the maximum load of a branch circuit will continue for 3 hr or more, such as store lighting and similar loads, the minimum unit loads specified in Table **5** of Div. 11 shall be increased by 25 per cent in order that the wiring system may have sufficient branch-circuit and feeder capacity to ensure safe operation.

472. Branch Circuits Required. The National Electrical Code requires that branch circuits shall be installed as follows:

1. LIGHTING AND APPLIANCE CIRCUITS. For lighting, and for appliances, including motor-operated appliances, not specifically provided for in paragraph 2, branch circuits shall be provided for a computed load not less than that determined by section 220-2 of the Code. (Refer to Table **5**, Div. 11.)

The number of circuits shall be not less than that determined from the total computed load and the capacity of circuits to be used, but in every case the number shall be sufficient for the actual load to be served and the branch-circuit loads shall not exceed the maximum loads specified in Secs. **468** to **470.**

Where the load is computed on a "watts per square foot" basis, the total load, insofar as practical, shall be evenly proportioned among the branch circuits according to their capacity.

For general illumination in dwelling occupancies, it is recommended that not less than one branch circuit be installed for each 500 sq ft of floor area in addition to the receptacle circuits called for in paragraph 2.

2. SMALL APPLIANCE BRANCH CIRCUITS, DWELLING OCCUPANCIES. For the small appliance load in kitchen, pantry, family room, and breakfast room of dwelling occupancies, two or more 20-amp appliance branch circuits in addition to the branch circuits specified in paragraph 1 of this section shall be provided for all receptacle outlets in these rooms, and such circuits shall have no other outlets.

Receptacle outlets supplied by at least two appliance receptacle branch circuits shall be installed in the kitchen.

At least one 20-amp branch circuit shall be provided for laundry receptacle(s) required in section 210-22(b) of the Code.

Receptacle outlets installed solely for the support of and the power supply for electric clocks may be installed on lighting branch circuits.

A three-wire 115/230-volt branch circuit is the equivalent of two 115-volt receptacle branch circuits.

Where a grounding receptacle is required as in section 210-21(b) of the Code, the branch circuit or branch-circuit raceway shall include or provide a grounding conductor to which the grounding contacts of the grounding receptacle shall be connected. The metal armor of Type AC metal-clad cable, the sheath of Type MI or ALS cables, or a metallic raceway shall be acceptable as a grounding conductor.

3. OTHER CIRCUITS. For specific loads not otherwise provided for in paragraphs 1 or 2, branch circuits shall be as required by other sections of the code.

473. Feeder loads should be determined in accordance with instructions given in Div. 3. Instructions for determining the minimum allowable loads required by the National Electrical Code are given in Table **5**, Div. 11.

474. The size of conductors required with respect to both carrying capacity and voltage drop is discussed in Div. 3. For Type 2 branch circuits also refer to Sec. **470** of this division.

475. Overcurrent Protection of Circuits. Except for the branch circuit to an individual motor, the rating of the overcurrent protective devices of a circuit shall not be in excess of the carrying capacity of the circuit conductor. If a branch circuit supplies only a single appliance of 10-amp or more rating, the rating of the overcurrent devices must not exceed 150 per cent of the rating of the appliance. For branch circuits supplying two or more outlets refer to Sec. **469**. For motor branch circuits refer to Div. 7.

476. The voltage to ground on branch circuits supplying lamp holders, fixtures, or standard receptacles of 15-amp or less rating shall not exceed 150 volts, except: (1) In industrial establishments or in stores where the conditions of maintenance and supervision assure that only competent individuals will service the lighting fixtures, the voltage of branch circuits which supply only lighting fixtures that are equipped with mogulbase screw-shell lamp holders or with lamp holders of other types approved for the application, mounted not less than 8 ft from the floor, which do not have switch control as an integral part of the fixture, shall not exceed 300 volts to ground. (2) In industrial establishments, office buildings, schools, stores, and public and commercial areas of other buildings, such as hotels or transportation terminals, the voltage of branch circuits which supply only the ballasts for electric discharge lamps mounted in permanently installed fixtures, by other than screw-shell-type lamp holders, which do not have manual switch control as an integral part of the fixture, shall not exceed 300 volts to ground. Where screw-shell-type lamp holders are used for electric discharge lamps, the fixtures shall be installed not less than 8 ft from the floor. (3) For infrared industrial heating appliances as described in section 422-15 of the Code. (4) In railway properties as described in section 110-19 of the Code. (5) The branch circuits supplying the ballasts for electric discharge lamps mounted in permanently installed fixtures on poles for the illumination of areas such as highways, bridges, athletic fields, parking lots, at a height not less than 22 ft, or on other structures such as tunnels at a height not less than 18 ft, shall not exceed 500 volts between conductors when installed as provided in section 730-7(a) of the Code.

477. In dwelling occupancies, the voltage between conductors supplying lamp holders of the screw-shell type, receptacles, or appliances shall not exceed 150 volts, except that the voltage between conductors may exceed 150 volts when supplying only permanently connected appliances, portable appliances of more than 1,380 watts, and portable motor-operated appliances of ¼ hp or greater rating.

RESIDENTIAL WIRING

478. In planning the wiring for a residence secure the floor plans of the building and locate the outlets and switch circuits as shown in Fig. 301.   Consult the local utility company concerning their service-equipment requirements with respect to type and sequence of equipment, location of meter, etc.   Decide whether fuses or circuit breakers should be used for circuit protection.   If the power company uses an outdoor meter located outside the kitchen or back hall, a service panel located in the inside wall at that point will probably be the best.   Consideration should be given to running three-wire feeders to distribution centers on the first and second floors, at which points fuses or circuit breakers will control the branch circuits.

A very helpful guide for the design of residential wiring is given in the "Residential Wiring Design Guide" prepared by the Industry Committee on Interior Wiring Design.   A large portion of the content of this handbook is reproduced in the following Secs. **479** to **512** inclusive through the courtesy of the Industry Committee on Interior Wiring Design.   (The Guide is published by the Edison Electric Institute, 750 Third Ave., New York.)

479. Location of Lighting Outlets.   Proper illumination is an essential element of modern electrical living.   The amount and type of illumination required should be fitted to the various seeing tasks carried on in the home.   There must also be planned lighting for recreation and entertainment.   In many instances, best results are achieved by a blend of lighting from both fixed and portable luminaires.   Good home lighting, therefore, requires thoughtful planning and careful selection of fixtures, portable lamps, and the other lighting equipment to be used.   The "Recommended Practice of Residence Lighting," published by the Illuminating Engineering Society,[1] is suggested as a guide for this planning.

Where lighting outlets are mentioned in these standards, their types and locations should conform with the lighting fixtures or equipment to be used.   Unless a specified location is stated, lighting outlets may be located anywhere within the area under consideration to produce the desired lighting effects.

480. Location of Convenience Outlets.   Convenience outlets preferably should be located near the ends of wall space, rather than near the center, thus reducing the likelihood of being concealed behind large pieces of furniture.   Unless otherwise specified, outlets should be located approximately 12 in. above the floor line.

481. Location of Wall Switches.   Wall switches should normally be located at the latch side of doors or at the traffic side of arches and within the room or area to which the control is applicable.   Some exceptions to this practice are the control of exterior lights from indoors; the control of stairway lights from adjoining areas, when stairs are closed off by doors at head or foot; and the control of lights from the access space adjoining infrequently used areas, such as storage areas.   Wall switches are normally mounted at a height of approximately 48 in. above the floor line.

482. Multiple-switch Control.   All spaces for which wall-switch controls are required and which have more than one entrance shall be equipped with multiple-switch control at each principal entrance.   If this requirement would result in the placing of switches controlling the same light within 10 ft of each other, one of the switch locations may be eliminated.

Where rooms may be lighted from more than one source, as when both general and supplementary illumination are provided from fixed sources, multiple switching is required for one set of controls only.   Usually this is applied to the means of general illumination.

Principal entrances are those commonly used for entry to or exit from a room when going from a lighted to an unlighted condition or the reverse.   For instance, a door from a living room to a porch is a principal entrance to the porch.   However, it would not

[1] 345 E. 47th St., New York, N.Y. 10017.

necessarily be considered a principal entrance to the living room unless the front entrance to the house is through the porch.

483. Dual-purpose Rooms. Where a room is intended to serve more than one function, such as a combination living-dining room or a kitchen-laundry, convenience and special-purpose outlet provisions of these standards are separately applicable to the respective areas. Lighting-outlet provisions may be combined in any manner that will assure general over-all illumination as well as local illumination of work surfaces. When locations for wall switches are considered, the area is considered as a single room.

484. Dual Functions of Outlets. In any instance where an outlet is located so as to satisfy two different provisions of the standard of adequacy, only one outlet need be installed at that location. In such instances, particular attention should be paid to any required wall-switch control, as additional switching may be necessary.

For example, a lighting outlet in an upstairs hall may be located at the head of the stairway, thus satisfying both a hall lighting-outlet and a stairway lighting-outlet provision of the standards with a single outlet. Stairway provisions will necessitate multiple-switch control of this lighting outlet at head and foot of the stairway. In addition, the multiple-switch control rule, given above, when applied to the upstairs hall, may require a third point of control elsewhere in the hall because of its length.

485. Exterior Entrances.

Lighting Provisions. One or more lighting outlets, as architecture dictates, wall-switch controlled, at front and trade entrances. Where a single wall outlet is desired, location on the latch side of the door is preferable.

It is recommended that lighting outlets, wall-switch controlled, be installed at other entrances.

The principal lighting requirements at entrances are the illumination of steps leading to the entrance and of faces of people at the door. Outlets in addition to those at

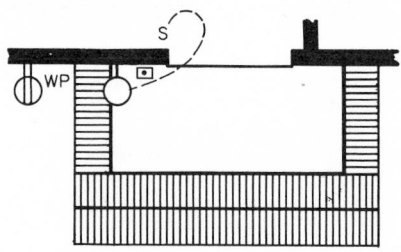

the door are often desirable for post lights to illuminate terraced or broken flights of steps or long approach walks. These outlets should be wall-switch controlled inside the house entrance.

Convenience Outlets. A weatherproof outlet, preferably near the front entrance, located at least 18 in. above grade.

It is recommended that this outlet be controlled by a wall switch inside the entrance for convenient operation of outdoor decorative lighting. Additional outlets along the exterior of the house are recommended to serve decorative garden treatments and for the use of appliances or electric garden tools, such as lawn mowers and hedge trimmers. Such outlets should also be wall-switch controlled.

486. Living Rooms.

Lighting Provisions. Some means of general illumination is essential. This lighting may be provided by ceiling or wall fixtures; by lighting in coves, valances, or cornices; or by portable lamps. Provide lighting outlets, wall-switch controlled, in locations appropriate to the lighting method selected.

These provisions also apply to sun rooms, enclosed porches, television rooms, libraries, dens, and similar areas.

The installation of outlets for decorative-lighting accent is recommended, such as picture illumination and bookcase lighting.

Convenience Outlets. Convenience outlets shall be placed so that no point along the floor line in any wall space is more than 6 ft from an outlet in that space. Where the installation of windows extending to the floor prevents meeting this requirement by the use of ordinary convenience outlets, equivalent facilities shall be installed using other appropriate means.

If, in lieu of fixed lighting, general illumination is provided from portable lamps, two convenience outlets or one plug position in two or more split-receptacle convenience outlets shall be wall-switch controlled.

In the case of switch-controlled convenience outlets, it is recommended that split-receptacle outlets be used in order not to limit the location of radios, television sets, clocks, etc.

It is recommended that one convenience outlet be installed flush in a mantel shelf, if construction permits.

It is recommended that, in addition, a single convenience outlet be installed in combination with the wall switch at one or more of the switch locations for the use of the vacuum cleaner of other portable appliances. Outlets for the use of clocks, radios, decorative lighting, etc., in bookcases and other suitable locations are recommended.

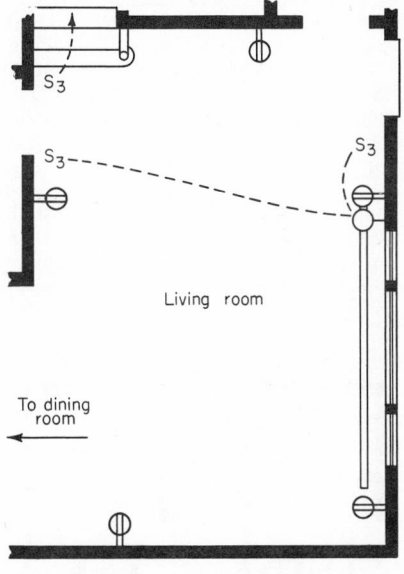

Special-purpose Outlets. It is recommended that one outlet for a room air conditioner be installed wherever a central air-conditioning system is not planned. See Sec. **408**.

487. Dining Areas.

Lighting Provisions. Each dining room, dining area combined with another room, or breakfast nook shall have at least one lighting outlet, wall-switch controlled.

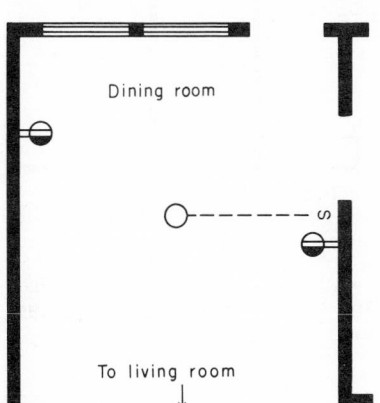

Such outlets are normally located over the probable location of the dining or breakfast table to provide direct illumination of the area.

Convenience Outlets. Convenience outlets placed so that no point along the floor line in any wall space is more than 6 ft from an outlet in that space. When dining or breakfast table is to be placed against a wall, one of these outlets shall be placed at the table location, just above table height.

Where open counter space is to be built in, an outlet shall be provided above counter height for the use of portable appliances.

Convenience outlets in dining areas should be of the split-receptacle type for connection to appliance circuits (see Sec. **503**).

488. Bedrooms.

Lighting Provisions. Good general illumination is particularly essential in the bedroom. This shall be provided from a ceiling fixture or from lighting in valances, coves, or cornices. Provide outlets, wall-switch controlled, in locations appropriate to the method selected.

Light fixtures over full-length mirrors or a light source at the ceiling located in the bedroom and directly in front of the clothes closets may serve as general illumination.

Master-switch control in the master bedroom, as well as at other strategic points in the home, is suggested for selected interior and exterior lights.

Convenience Outlets. Outlets shall be placed so that there is a convenience outlet on each side and within 6 ft of the center line of each probable individual bed location. Additional outlets shall be placed so that no point along the floor line in any other wall space is more than 6 ft from an outlet in that space.

It is recommended that convenience outlets be placed only 3 to 4 ft from the center line of the probable bed locations. The popularity of bedside radios and clocks, bed lamps, and electric blankets makes increased plug-in positions at bed locations essential.

It is recommended that, at one of the switch locations, a receptacle outlet be provided for the use of a vacuum cleaner, floor polisher, or other portable appliances.

Special-purpose Outlets. The installation of one heavy-duty, special-purpose outlet in each bedroom for the connection of room air conditioners is recommended. Such outlets may also be used for operating portable space heaters during cool weather in climates where a small amount of local heat is sufficient. See Sec. **408.**

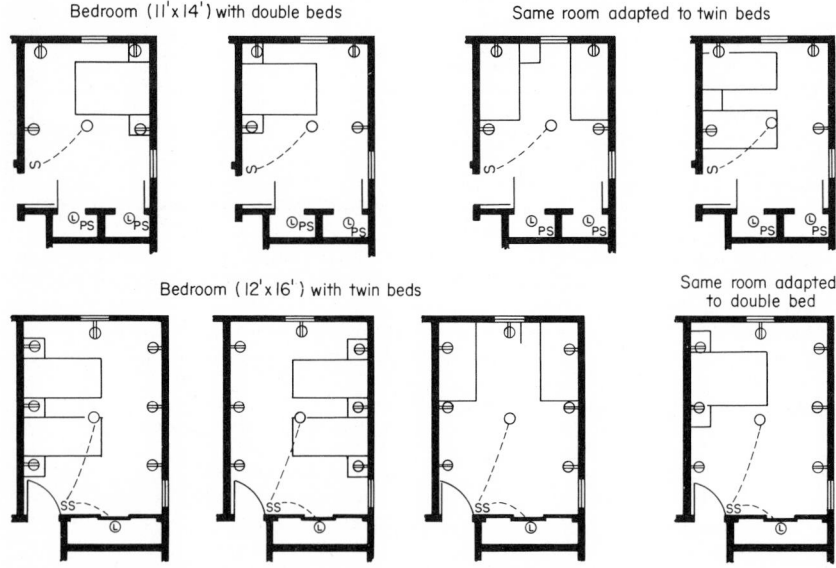

FIG. 300 *Outlet locations in typical bedrooms.* (*Residential Wiring Handbook.*)

NOTE. The illustrations in Fig. 300 show the application of these standards to both double- and twin-bed arrangements and also their application where more than one probable bed location is available within the room.

489. Bathrooms and Lavatories.

Lighting Provisions. Illumination of both sides of the face when at the mirror is essential. There are several methods that may be employed to achieve good lighting at this location and in the rest of the room. Lighting outlets shall be installed to provide for the method selected, bearing in mind that a single concentrated light source, on either the ceiling or the side wall, is not acceptable. All lighting outlets should be wall-switch controlled.

A ceiling outlet located in line with the front edge of the basin will provide improved

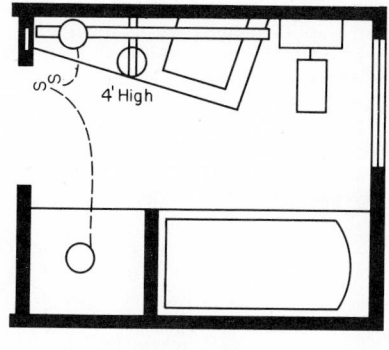

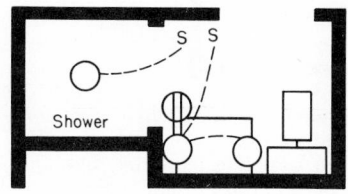

lighting at the mirror, general room lighting, and safety lighting for combination shower and tub.

When more than one mirror location is planned, equal consideration should be given to the lighting in each case.

It is recommended that a switch-controlled night light be installed.

Where an enclosed shower stall is planned, an outlet for a vaporproof luminaire should be installed, controlled by a wall switch outside the stall.

Convenience Outlets.   One outlet near the mirror, 3 to 5 ft above the floor.

It is recommended that an outlet be installed at each separate mirror or vanity space and also at any space that might accommodate an electric towel drier, electric razor, etc.

A receptacle which is a part of a bathroom lighting fixture should not be considered as satisfying this requirement.

Special-purpose Outlets.   It is recommended that each bathroom be equipped with an outlet for a built-in-type electric space heater.

Also recommended is an outlet for a built-in ventilating fan, wall-switch controlled.

490. Kitchen.

Lighting Provisions.   Provide outlets for general illumination and for lighting at the sink. These lighting outlets shall be wall-switch controlled. Lighting design should provide for illumination of the work areas, sink, range, counters, and tables.

Undercabinet lighting fixtures within easy reach may have local-switch control. Consideration should also be given to outlets to provide inside lighting of cabinets.

Convenience Outlets.   One outlet for the refrigerator and one outlet for each 4 lin ft of work-surface frontage, with at least one outlet to serve each work surface. Work-surface outlets to be located approximately 44 in. above floor line.

If a planning desk is to be installed, one outlet shall be located to serve this area.

Table space to have one outlet, preferably just above table level.

An outlet is recommended at any wall space that may be used for ironing or for an electric roaster.

Convenience outlets in the kitchen, other than that for the refrigerator, should be

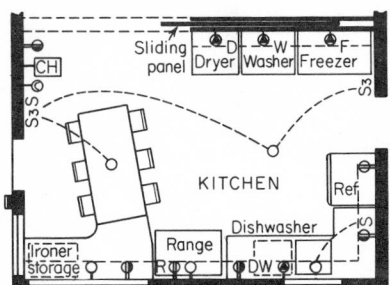

of the split-receptacle type for connection to two or more appliance circuits (see Sec. **503**).

Special-purpose Outlets. One outlet each for a range and ventilating fan and an outlet or outlets for a dishwasher or food waste disposer if necessary plumbing facilities are installed.

Provision shall be made for the use of an electric clock. The clock should be located so as to be easily visible from all parts of the kitchen. Recessed receptacle with clock hanger is recommended.

It is recommended that an outlet be provided for a food freezer either in the kitchen or in some other convenient location.

491. Laundry and Laundry Areas.

Lighting Provision. For complete laundries, lighting outlets shall be installed to provide proper illumination of work areas, such as laundry tubs, sorting table, and washing, ironing, and drying centers. At least one lighting outlet in the room shall be wall-switch controlled.

For laundry trays in unfinished basement, one ceiling outlet, centered over the trays.

It is recommended that all laundry lighting be wall-switch controlled.

Convenience Outlet. At least one convenience outlet.

In some instances, one of the special-purpose outlets, properly located, may satisfy this requirement. The convenience outlet is intended for such purposes as laundry hot plate, sewing machine, etc.

Convenience outlets in laundry area should be of the split-receptacle type for connection to two appliance circuits (see Sec. **503**).

Special-purpose Outlets. One outlet for each of the following pieces of equipment:

Automatic washer.

Hand iron or ironer.

Clothes dryer.

The installation of outlets for a ventilating fan and a clock is highly desirable. If an electric water heater is to be installed, the requirements can be obtained from the local utility.

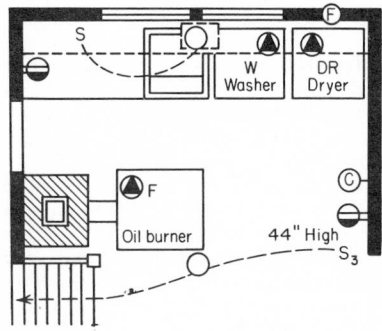

492. Closets.

Lighting Provision. One outlet for each closet. Where shelving or other conditions make the installation of lights within a closet ineffective, lighting outlets should be so located in the adjoining space as to provide light within the closet.

The installation of wall switches near the closet door or door-type switches is recommended.

493. Halls.

Lighting Provisions. Lighting outlets, wall-switch controlled, shall be installed for proper illumination of the entire area. Particular attention should be paid to irregularly shaped areas.

These provisions apply to passage halls, reception halls, vestibules, entries, foyers, and similar areas.

It is recommended that a switch-controlled night light be installed in any hall giving access to bedrooms.

Convenience Outlets. One outlet for each 15 lin ft of hallway, measured along center line. Each hall over 25 sq ft in floor area shall have at least one outlet.

In reception halls and foyers, convenience outlets shall be placed so that no point along the floor line in any wall space is more than 10 ft from an outlet in that space.

It is recommended that at one of the switch outlets a convenience receptacle be provided for connection of vacuum cleaner, floor polisher, etc.

494. Stairways.

Lighting Provisions. Wall or ceiling outlets shall be installed to provide adequate illumination of each stair flight. Outlets shall have multiple-switch control at the head and foot of the stairway, so arranged that full illumination can be turned on from either floor but that lights in halls furnishing access to bedrooms can be extinguished without interfering with ground-floor usage.

These provisions are intended to apply to any stairway at both ends of which are finished rooms. For stairways to unfinished basements or attics, see Secs. **497** and **498**, respectively.

Whenever possible, switches should be grouped together and never located so close to steps that a fall might result from a misstep while reaching for a switch.

Convenience Outlets. At intermediate landings of a large area, an outlet is recommended for decorative lamp, night light, vacuum cleaner, etc.

495. Recreation Room.

Lighting Provisions. Some means of general illumination is essential. This lighting may be provided by ceiling or wall fixtures or by lighting in coves, valances, or cornices. Provide lighting outlets, wall-switch controlled, in locations appropriate to the lighting method selected.

Selection of lighting method for use in the recreation room should take into account the type of major activities for which the room is planned.

Convenience Outlets. Convenience outlets shall be placed so that no point along the floor line in any wall space is more than 6 ft from an outlet in that space.

It is recommended that one convenience outlet be installed flush in the mantel shelf where construction permits. Outlets for the use of clock, radio, television, ventilat-

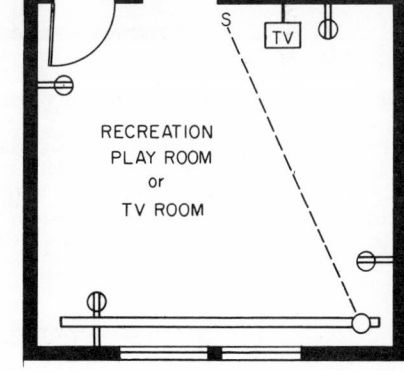

ing fan, motion-picture projector, and the like, should be located in relation to their intended use.

496. Utility Room or Space.

Lighting Provisions. Lighting outlets placed to illuminate furnace area and workbench, if planned. At least one lighting outlet to be wall-switch controlled.

Convenience Outlets. One convenience outlet, preferably near the furnace location or near any planned workbench location.

Special-purpose Outlet. One outlet for electrical equipment used in connection with furnace operation.

497. Basement.

Lighting Provisions. Lighting outlets shall be placed to illuminate designated work areas or equipment locations, such as at furnace, pump, workbench, etc. Additional outlets shall be installed near the foot of the stairway, in each enclosed space, and in

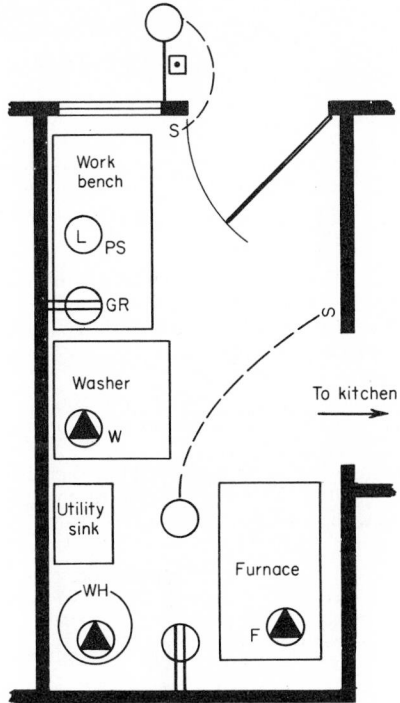

open spaces so that each 150 sq ft of open space is adequately served by a light in that area.

In unfinished basements the light at the foot of the stairs shall be wall-switch controlled near the head of the stairs. Other lights may be pull-chain controlled.

In basements with finished rooms, with garage space, or with other direct access to outdoors, the stairway lighting provisions apply.

It is recommended that for basements which will be infrequently visited a pilot light be installed in conjunction with the switch at the head of the stairs.

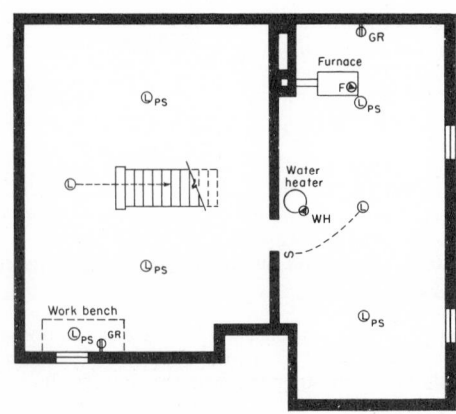

Convenience Outlets.   At least two convenience outlets shall be provided.   If a workbench is planned, one outlet shall be placed at this location.

Basement convenience outlets are useful near furnace; at play area; for basement laundries, darkrooms, and hobby areas; and for appliances, such as dehumidifier, portable space heater, etc.

Special-purpose Outlet.   One outlet for electrical equipment used in connection with furnace operation.

An outlet for a food freezer is recommended.

498. Accessible Attic.

Lighting Provisions.   One outlet for general illumination, wall-switch controlled from foot of stairs.   When no permanent stairs are installed, this lighting outlet may be pull-chain controlled if located over the access door.   Where an unfinished attic is planned for later development into rooms, the attic-lighting outlet shall be switch controlled at top and bottom of stairs.

One outlet for each enclosed space.

These provisions apply to unfinished attics.   For attics with finished rooms or spaces, see appropriate room classifications for requirements.

The installation of a pilot light in conjunction with the switch controlling the attic light is recommended.

Convenience Outlets.   One outlet for general use.

If open stairway leads to future attic rooms, provide a junction box with direct connection to the distribution panel for future extension to convenience outlets and lights when rooms are finished.

A convenience outlet in the attic is desirable for providing additional illumination in dark corners and also for the use of a vacuum cleaner and its accessories in cleaning.

Special-purpose Outlet.   The installation of an outlet, multiple-switch controlled from desirable points throughout the house, is recommended in connection with the use of a summer cooling fan.

499. Porches.

Lighting Provisions.   Each porch, breezeway, or other similar roofed area of more than 75 sq ft in floor area shall have a lighting outlet, wall-switch controlled.   Large or irregularly shaped areas may require two or more lighting outlets.

Multiple-switch control shall be installed at entrances when the porch is used as a passage between the house and garage.

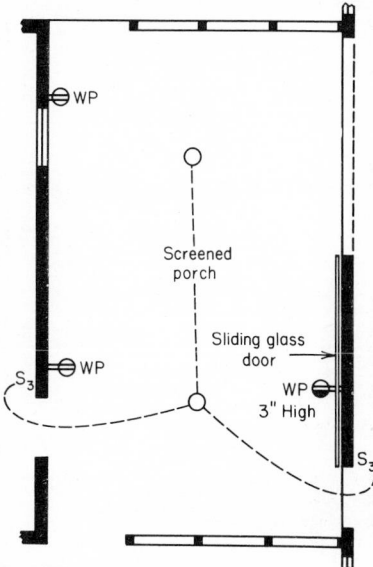

Convenience Outlets. One convenience outlet, weatherproof if exposed to moisture, for each 15 ft of wall bordering porch or breezeway.

It is recommended that all such outlets be controlled by a wall switch inside the door.

The split-receptacle convenience outlet shown in the illustration is intended to be connected to a three-wire appliance branch circuit. This area is considered an outdoor dining area.

500. Terraces and Patios.

Lighting Provisions. The installation of an outlet on the building wall or on a post centrally located in the area is recommended for the purpose of providing fixed general illumination. Such outlets should be wall-switch controlled just inside the house door opening onto the area.

Convenience Outlets. One weatherproof outlet located at least 18 in. above grade line for each 15 lin ft of house wall bordering terrace or patio.

It is recommended that these outlets be wall-switch controlled from inside the house.

501. Garage or Carport.

Lighting Provisions. At least one ceiling outlet, wall-switch controlled, for one- or two-car storage area.

If garage has no covered access from house, provide one exterior outlet, multiple-switch controlled from garage and residence.

If garage is to be used for purposes additional to car storage, such as to include work-bench, closets, laundry, attached porch, etc., rules appropriate to these uses should be employed.

An exterior outlet, wall-switch controlled, is recommended for all garages. Additional interior outlets are often desirable even if no specific additional use is planned for the garage. For long driveways, additional illumination, such as by post lighting, is recommended. These lights should be wall-switch controlled from the house.

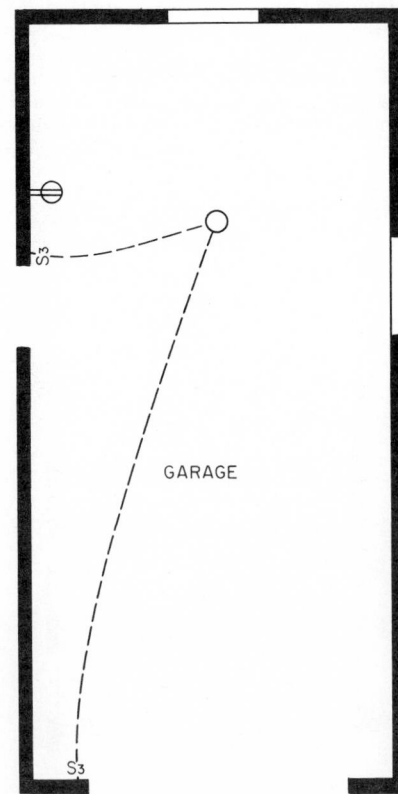

Convenience Outlets. At least one outlet for one- or two-car storage area.

Special-purpose Outlets. If food freezer, workbench, or automatic door opener is planned for installation in the garage, outlets appropriate to these uses should be provided.

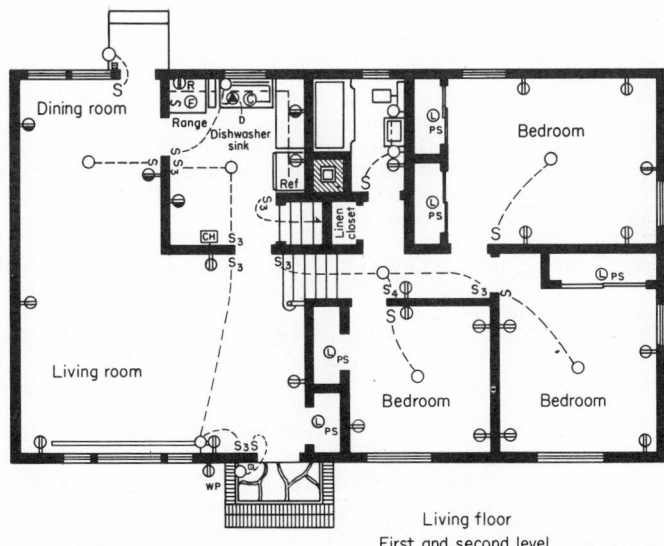

Living floor
First and second level

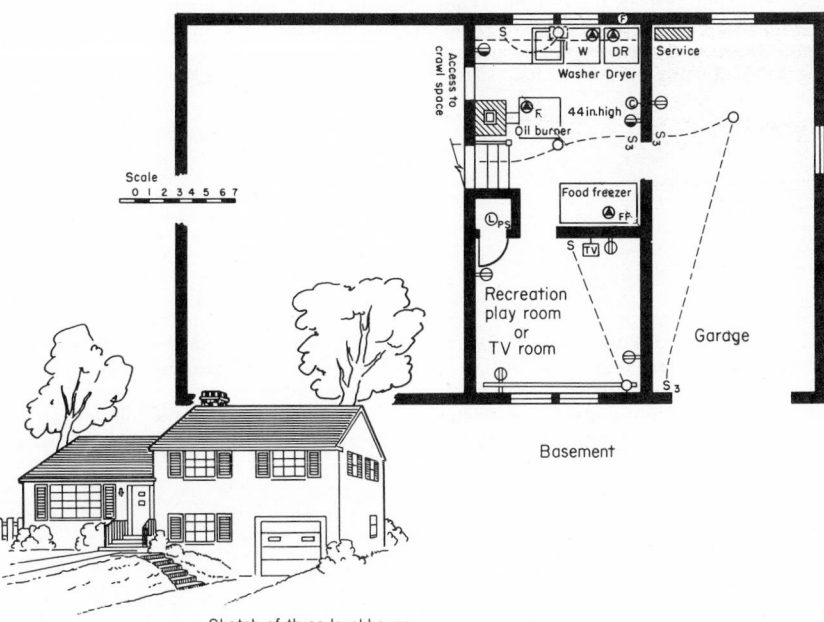

Sketch of three level house

FIG. 301 *Application of outlet requirements in typical home.* (*Residential Wiring Design Guide.*)

502. Exterior Grounds.

Lighting Provisions. Lighting outlets for floodlights are often desirable for illumination of surrounding grounds. These outlets may be located on the exterior of the house or garage or on posts or poles appropriately placed. All outlets should be switch controlled from within the house. Multiple- and master-switch control from strategic points is also desirable.

503. Branch Circuits.

General-purpose Circuits (15 or 20 Amp). General-purpose circuits shall supply all lighting outlets throughout the house and all convenience outlets except the convenience outlets in the kitchen, dining room or dining areas of other rooms, breakfast room or nook, and laundry or laundry area. These general-purpose circuits shall be provided on the basis of one 20-amp circuit for not more than each 500 sq ft or one 15-amp circuit for not more than each 375 sq ft of floor area. Outlets supplied by these circuits shall be divided equally among the circuits.

These requirements for general-purpose branch circuits take into consideration the provision in the current edition of the National Electrical Code for either 20- or 15-amp general-purpose circuits. The floor-area designations are in keeping with present-day usage of such circuits.

It is recommended that separate branch circuits be provided for lighting and for convenience outlets in living rooms and bedrooms and that the branch circuits serving convenience outlets in these rooms be of the three-wire type, equipped with split-wired receptacles.

Appliance Circuits (20 Amp, Three Wire, 115/230 Volts). At least one three-wire 115/230-volt 20-amp branch circuit, equipped with split-wired receptacles for all convenience outlets in the kitchen, family room, dining room or dining areas of other rooms, and breakfast room or nook. Another such circuit shall also be extended to the laundry or laundry area to serve any convenience outlets there.

The use of three-wire circuits for supplying convenience outlets in the locations mentioned is an economical means for dividing the load and offers practical operating advantages. Such circuits provide greater capacity at individual outlet locations and lessen voltage drop in the circuit. They also provide greater flexibility in the use of appliances. For maximum effectiveness in utilization the upper half of all receptacles should be connected to the same side of the circuit.

Individual-equipment Circuits. Circuits shall be provided for the following equipment:

Item	Conductor Capacity
Range (up to 21-kw rating)	50 amp, 3 wire, 115/230 volts
Combination washer-dryer	40 amp, 3 wire, 115/230 volts
Automatic washer	20 amp, 2 wire, 115 volts
Electric clothes dryer	30 amp, 3 wire, 115/230 volts
Fuel-fired heating equipment (if installed)	15 amp or 20 amp, 2 wire, 115 volts
Dishwasher and waste disposer (if necessary plumbing is installed)	20 amp-3 wire, 115/230 volts
Water heater (if installed)	Consult local utility

Spare circuit equipment shall be provided for at least two future 20-amp two-wire 115-volt circuits in addition to those initially installed. If the branch circuit or distribution panel is installed in a finished wall, raceways shall be extended from the panel cabinet to the nearest accessible unfinished space for future use.

Consideration should also be given to the provision of circuits for the following commonly used household appliances and items of equipment. The table does not list all the equipment available.

Item	Conductor Capacity
Attic fan	20 amp, 2 wire, 115 volts (switched)
Room air conditioners	20 amp, 2 wire, 230 volts or 20 amp, 3 wire, 115/230 volts
Central air-conditioning unit	40 amp, 2 wire, 230 volts
Food freezer	20 amp, 2 wire, 115 volts
Water pump (where used)	20 amp, 2 wire, 115 or 230 volts
Bathroom heater	20 amp, 2 wire, 115 or 230 volts
Workshop or bench	20 amp, 3 wire, 115/230 volts

In some instances, one of the circuits recommended may serve two devices which are not likely to be used at the same time, such as an attic fan and a bathroom heater. The majority of appliances for residential use are made for 110 to 120 volts. There is, however, a growing tendency to make fixed appliances for use on 220- to 240-volt circuits. It is recommended that the higher voltage be preferred in those cases where a choice exists.

Consideration should also be given to the provision of circuits for patios or "outdoor" living rooms and for exterior decorative or flood lighting.

A number of different systems of electrical house heating are now being used in some areas. These systems are presently a matter of individual engineering design for the house in question and local climatic conditions. Wiring and service capacity for such purposes are not, therefore, included in this Handbook.

504. Feeder Circuits. It is strongly recommended that consideration be given to the installation of branch-circuit protective equipment, served by appropriate-size feeders, at locations throughout the house rather than at a single location.

505. Service Entrance. All services shall be three wire.

For houses up to 3,000 sq ft in floor area, the size of the service-entrance conductors and the rating of the service equipment should not be less than 150 amp. These capacities are sufficient to provide for lighting, for portable appliances, and for the equipment for which individual-equipment circuits are required, as listed in Sec. 503.

For larger houses or for houses in which more than one additional unit selected from the second list in Sec. 503 is installed, a 200-amp service should be installed.

Experience indicates that the most serious obstacle to the use of items of electrical equipment and appliances, in addition to those initially provided for, has been inadequate service conductors and related equipment.

Because of the many major uses of electricity in the kitchen requiring individual-equipment circuits, it is recommended that the electric service equipment be located near or on a kitchen wall to minimize installation and wiring costs. Such locations will usually also be found to be convenient to laundries, thus minimizing circuit runs to laundry appliances as well.

506. Entrance Signals. Entrance push buttons shall be installed at each commonly used entrance door and connected to the door chime, giving a distinctive signal for front and rear entrance. Electrical supply for entrance signals is to be obtained from adequate bell-ringing or chime transformer installed at the fuse-box or circuit-breaker location.

In the smaller house the door chime is often installed in the kitchen, providing it will be heard throughout the house. If not, the door chime should be installed at a more central location, usually the entrance hall. In the larger house extension signals are often necessary to ensure being heard throughout the living quarters.

Entrance-signal conductors should be no smaller than the equivalent of No. 18 AWG copper wire.

507. Communication. For the residence with accommodations for a resident servant, additional signal and communication devices are recommended. These include a dining-room-to-kitchen signal operated from a push button attached to the underside of dining table or a foot-operated floor tread placed under the table; flush annunciator in the kitchen with push-button stations in each bedroom, the living room, recreation room, porch, etc.; flush intercommunicating telephone installed in the kitchen, with corresponding telephone stations in master bedroom, recreation room, and other desirable locations. Intercommunicating telephones should be operated from a power unit recommended and furnished by the manufacturer of the telephones, and connected to the a-c lighting service.

508. Home Fire Alarm. Automatic fire-alarm protection is recommended, with detectors in the basement oil-burner or furnace area and the storage space as a minimum. Alarm bell and test button should be installed in the master bedroom or other desirable location in the sleeping area. Operating supply should be from a separate bell-ringing transformer recommended and furnished by the manufacturer of the alarm equipment. Alarm system should operate from a separate and independent transformer rather than from the entrance-signal or other transformer, because of the in-

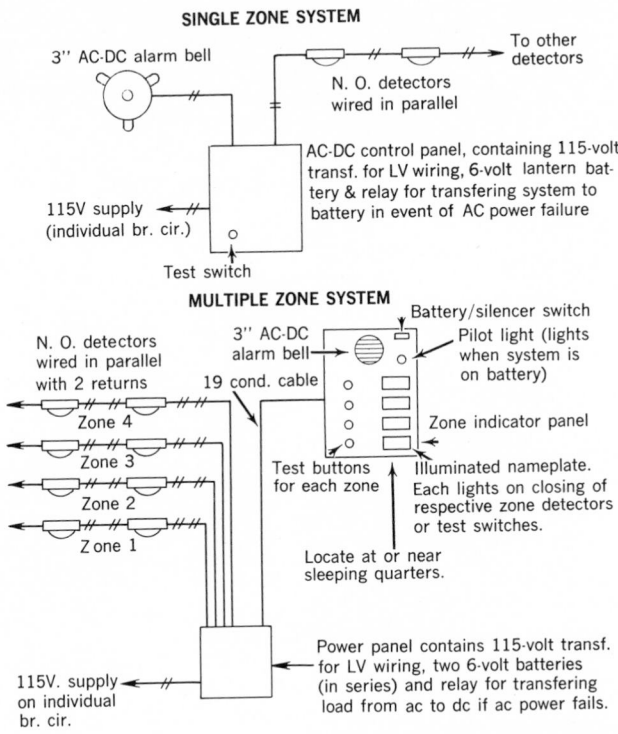

SINGLE ZONE SYSTEM

3" AC-DC alarm bell

To other detectors

N. O. detectors wired in parallel

AC-DC control panel, containing 115-volt transf. for LV wiring, 6-volt lantern battery & relay for transfering system to battery in event of AC power failure

115V supply (individual br. cir.)

Test switch

MULTIPLE ZONE SYSTEM

Battery/silencer switch

N. O. detectors wired in parallel with 2 returns

3" AC-DC alarm bell

19 cond. cable

Pilot light (lights when system is on battery)

Zone 4

Zone 3

Zone 2

Zone 1

Zone indicator panel

Test buttons for each zone

Illuminated nameplate. Each lights on closing of respective zone detectors or test switches.

Locate at or near sleeping quarters.

Power panel contains 115-volt transf. for LV wiring, two 6-volt batteries (in series) and relay for transfering load from ac to dc if ac power fails.

115V. supply on individual br. cir.

FIG. 302 *Typical single- and multiple-zone fire alarm systems.*

creased possibility of failure due to causes originating in the entrance-signal or other system. Figure 302 shows typical single- and multiple-zone systems.

509. Television. For television antenna connection, provide a nonmetallic outlet box of the standard type, connected to an accessible location in the attic or basement by a suitable 300-ohm transmission line (unshielded in a UHF service area). Sufficient slack of the transmission line should be provided in the attic to reach any reasonable location of the antenna. If the transmission line is shielded, the shield should be grounded. Where an unshielded transmission line is used, grounding should be in accordance with the National Electrical Code and the line kept away from pipes and other wires. A convenience outlet should be provided adjacent to the television outlet, which will be in addition to the convenience outlets provided for other purposes in the room. Television antennas should be of types suitable for the specific area, and they should be adequately supported and guyed. Antennas should not be attached to chimneys.

Plug-in TV outlets can be installed in all areas of the home where television sets will be used. This includes living rooms, dens, family rooms, and recreation rooms. Couplers should be used when two or more television sets are designated. The coupler can be located in the attic or basement at a central point. After the lead-in wires are connected to the line terminals of the coupler, branch runs are made to each area where a television set will be used.

510. Radio. In their modern form, radio receivers used purely for the reception of broadcast communication seldom require antenna and ground connections. If FM reception is desired, it is recommended that provisions similar to those for television be included.

511. Telephone. It is recommended that at least one outlet be installed, served by a raceway extending to unfinished portions of the basement or attic. The outlet should be centrally located and readily accessible from the living room, dining room, and kitchen. A desirable location for a second outlet is the master bedroom.

Where finished rooms are located on more than one floor, at least one telephone outlet should be provided on each such floor.

It is suggested that the local telephone company be consulted for details of service connection prior to construction, particularly in regard to the installation of protector cabinets and raceways leading to finished basements, where contemplated.

512. Radio/Intercom Systems. Major manufacturers offer a wide variety of home intercom systems—from simple intercom stations to radio/intercom systems with integral plug-in jacks for connection to record charger, hi-fi, or stereo equipment.

The basic system uses a master control station, located in the kitchen and interconnected to remote stations throughout the house and at entrance doors. Such systems permit "answering" the door; waking children in the morning; listening in on the nursery; piping radio programs or music to remote stations; and many other practical uses.

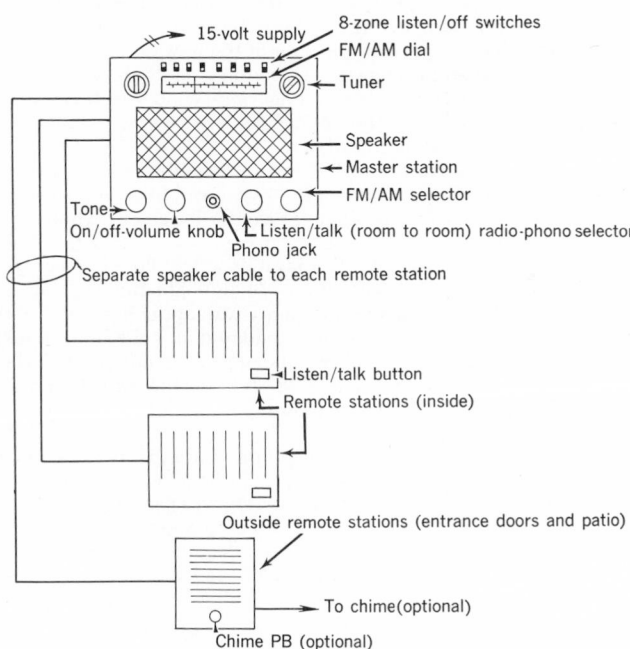

FIG. 303 *Basic eight-zone radio intercom system.*

A more complete system (Fig. 303) contains a built-in AM-FM radio, a phonojack; and inside remote stations permit room-to-room conversations. These units are transistorized and, as such, can be left on continuously because there is only a slight amount of current consumption even when the intercom system or radio is in use. Typical systems are supplied by a transformer with a secondary voltage of 16 volts. Many systems contain a built-in door chime which can be heard at any remote station. More elaborate systems include a fire or smoke detection system.

WIRING FOR RESIDENTIAL OUTDOOR LIGHTING

513. General Considerations. The following recommendations for wiring for residential outdoor lighting have been taken from a booklet of that name published by the Construction Materials Division of the General Electric Co.

Factors that must be considered before making any outdoor wiring installation are family habits and the facilities that the family wishes to enjoy, style and construction of house, size and topography of property, and, most important of all, whether the service entrance is large enough to handle the additional load, whether spare circuits are available at the panel board or new circuits must be added, and the length of the circuits required for the various outdoor lighting and outlet installations.

In general it will probably be found that the permanently installed outdoor wiring to be used beyond the house should be run underground from the point where it emerges from the house to the point where the equipment is to be used. There are, of course, exceptions. When the house is multistoried, overhead wiring may be used. In almost all other cases, from the viewpoint of both safety and aesthetics, underground circuits will be found preferable. Sometimes a combination of overhead and underground wiring will be most satisfactory.

Any circuit installed in an existing dwelling for out-of-door use should be a new circuit originating at the panel board rather than an extension of an existing circuit. In all cases circuits for outdoor use should be restricted to this purpose only.

In laying out new out-of-door wiring, it should be recognized that even though the homeowner considers that the primary purpose of the new circuits is to provide lighting only, this cannot be taken for granted. Once the circuits are installed and outdoor outlets are available, there will probably be a heavy demand from this source for power for appliances and tools. Not less, therefore, than two 20-amp circuits or one three-wire 120/240-volt circuit should be installed.

514. Running the Circuits from Panel Board to Outside. The style and construction of the house will determine how the circuits are run from the panel board to the outside. Most installations will be either (1) from a basement where the walls are concrete or cement block or (2) from above ground level when the panel board is located either in the garage or other interior location at first floor level of the house.

1. When Panel Board Is in Basement. In this situation, wiring is generally brought to the outside either through the masonry wall of the basement or through the sill on top of the foundation. Factors to be considered are whether the installation is to be underground or overhead. If underground, going directly through the basement wall and coming out below ground level (Fig. 304) on the outside is the least conspicuous. Where convenient shrubbery will hide the conduit, it may be easier to come out through the sill (Fig. 305).

Either of these methods may be chosen when the wiring is to be overhead. In this case, since a length of conduit will have to run up the side of the house, it is well to come out of the basement at a point where shrubbery will partially conceal the installation. Occasionally, in frame construction, the circuit for overhead wiring can be fished up through the walls to a point of departure at the desired elevation of the house.

2. When Panel Board Is in Garage or House. In many newer houses, especially those without basements, the panel board is installed in the attached garage or in some

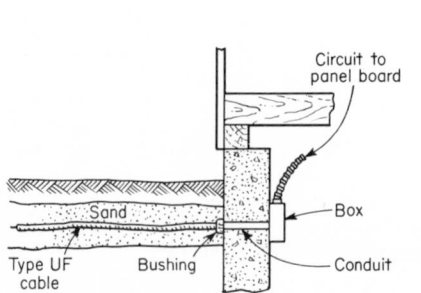

FIG. 304 *Running the circuit from panel board through masonry.*

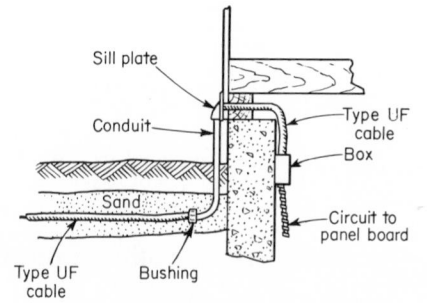

FIG. 305 *Running circuit from panel board through sill.*

other handy but inconspicuous part of the house. In such cases, the circuit is run from panel board through the wall of the garage or house (Fig. 306) at the most convenient point. Thought should be given to the point selected so that the installation is as unobtrusive as possible.

515. Underground Circuits. Circuits run underground offer a number of advantages to the homeowner. They are not subject to damage from storms, nor are they exposed to mechanical damage. Most important, such circuits are invisible and do not, therefore, mar the appearance of the grounds and gardens.

The most economical underground installation for both feeders and branch circuits is Type UF (underground feeder) cable. This cable is approved by the National Electrical Code for direct burial in the ground without additional protection.

Underground cable is laid in a trench at least 20 in. deep to prevent possible damage from normal spading. The bottom of the trench should be free from stones. This is easily accomplished by using a layer of sand or sifted dirt in the bottom of the trench (Fig. 307). Cable is laid directly on top of this layer. When cable enters building or leaves the ground, slack should be provided in the form of an S curve to permit expansion with extreme changes in temperature. Where cable enters a building, after cable has been installed, fill all openings through foundation with sealing compound so that water from rain or melting snow cannot follow the cable into the building.

The National Electrical Code requires that underground feeder cables must be installed in continuous lengths from outlet to outlet and from fitting to fitting. Splices can be made only within a proper enclosure.

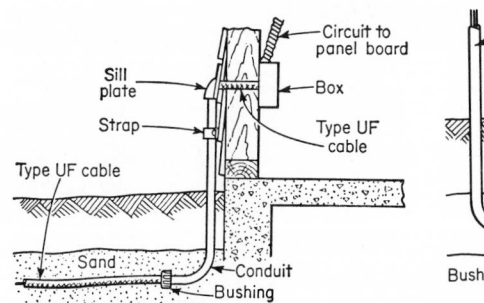

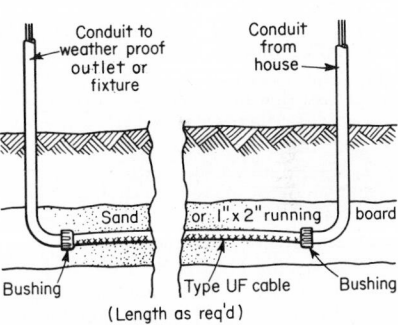

FIG. 306 *Running circuit from panel board through garage wall.*

FIG. 307 *Type UF cable used for underground circuits.*

In some areas of the yard, where it is felt that digging might accidentally occur to the depth of the cable, a concrete pad or a 1- by 2-in. running board can be laid over the cable before the trench is filled (Fig. 307). Under driveways or roadways or where heavy loading might occur, it is also desirable to use a board, concrete pad, or conduit.

For outdoor wiring in sections of the country that are known to be termite infested or subject to attack by rodents, or wherever extra protection to the Type UF underground circuits is required, galvanized rigid steel conduit may be used for mechanical protection. When rigid conduit for the complete circuit run is used, feeders and branch circuits may be of any approved type of moisture-resistant wire such as Types TW, RHW, or THWN.

516. Multiple-family Buildings or Apartments. The recommendations for residences can be applied to individual apartments for lighting, convenience, and switch outlets. Where central heating is supplied, it is unlikely that an electric heater will be used in the bathroom or that many heavy-duty appliances will be used at one time. Therefore two 20-amp branch circuits supplying convenience outlets in dining room and kitchen generally will be sufficient in addition to a 15-amp branch circuit for every 500 sq ft of floor area. It is recommended that a three-wire, 120/240-volt, No. 8 range circuit be installed for each apartment.

For nonrentable areas under the control of the building management the following rules from the "Handbook of Interior Wiring Design," prepared by the Industry Committee on Interior Wiring Design, represent good practice:

1. ENTRANCES.   *a.* Sufficient outlets shall be installed to provide electrical service consistent with the general architectural treatment, but in no case shall there be less than one outlet for an outside lantern or two for outside wall brackets.

b. At least one ceiling outlet shall be installed for each 150 sq ft of vestibule space.

c. At least one wall outlet shall be installed over each group of letter boxes covering a lineal distance of 8 ft or less.

2. LOBBY OR MAIN HALLWAY.   *a.* At least one ceiling outlet per 125 sq ft of floor area shall be installed provided that:

(1) No area has outlets spaced more than 15 ft apart.

(2) No elevator door or stair well is more than 6 ft from the nearest ceiling outlet.

b. At least one convenience outlet shall be installed for every 12 ft of wall space for portable lamps and general utility purposes (vacuum cleaners, floor polishers, etc.).

c. Provision shall be made for additional outlets to furnish such illumination as is demanded by the architectural treatment. This may be in the form of decorative wall brackets, urns, pedestals, built-in units, etc.

3. UPPER HALLWAYS.   *a.* At least one ceiling outlet shall be installed per 150 sq ft of floor area, provided that:

(1) No area has ceiling outlets spaced more than 15 ft apart if arranged on alternate circuits or 30 ft if adjacent outlets are on the same circuit.

(2) No elevator door or staircase is more than 6 ft from the nearest ceiling outlet.

(3) No section of a hallway not in a straight line from another shall be without at least one ceiling outlet.

b. At least one convenience outlet shall be installed per floor, with additional outlets spaced so that no point in a hallway is more than 25 ft from a convenience outlet.

4. HALL SWITCHES.   *a.* All ceiling outlets plus the outlets for entrance lighting shall be controlled by switches.

b. Where all ceiling outlets on any one floor are controlled by a single switch, this switch shall be of a type or shall be located so as to be inaccessible to the general public.

c. Where more than one switch controls the ceiling outlets on a particular floor, at least one switch shall be inaccessible to the general public. This switch shall control outlets installed under the following provisions.

(1) It must control the outlet nearest the stair well or the elevator door.

(2) It must control outlets so that the spacing between any two is not greater than 30 ft.

(3) It must control an outlet in every space not in direct line from the outlet near the stair well or the elevator door.

5. STAIR WELLS.   *a.* Where enclosed stair wells are installed (such as in masonry construction), there shall be an outlet for lighting on each landing.

b. Where exit lights are required, they shall be installed in accordance with all rules and regulations covering their use.

6. BASEMENT AREAS.   Lighting outlets shall be provided in basement areas on the basis of at least one ceiling outlet per 200 sq ft, plus additional outlets and necessary switch control if such basement areas are available to tenants for laundry, storage, or other purposes.

7. OIL BURNERS, AIR-CONDITIONING EQUIPMENT, ETC.   Circuits shall be individually provided for each such piece of equipment in accordance with the size and rating of each motor or heater.

8. ELEVATORS.   Power and light feeders for elevator service shall be of the size required by the elevator manufacturer.

517. The arrangement of the service and feeders will depend on the system of metering employed. Where each apartment is to be metered and billed for all its power, a meter service switch and meter should be provided for each apartment and one or two for the building management. These should be located in rows along the walls in the basement. Each apartment must be on an individual feeder from the meter service switch. The load on the feeder should be computed in accordance with the instructions given in Div. 3. If an electric range is not supplied by the feeder, a two-wire feeder is usually sufficient. Where the feeders can be grouped and the building is supplied by a three-phase four-wire a-c supply, three apartments can be supplied from a single neutral. If an electric range is supplied, three-wire feeders should be used. When the power company will bill the building management on a lower rate for power than they do for lighting, two meters with separate circuits for each should be provided. Where there are more than six meter service switches, the service must be brought in through a single circuit breaker or fused service switch, the size to be determined in accordance with the instructions of Div. 3. Where the power is to be billed to the building management and included in the rent, the circuit is brought in through a single circuit breaker or fused service switch as before.

Circuits for either one or two meters, depending on whether the power company bills the power on a separate rate from the lighting, should be provided. A distribution center with a safety-enclosed fused knife switch or circuit breaker for each feeder should be installed. The feeders can then supply distribution panel boards in the halls on each floor, or one feeder can be installed for each three apartments. The latter plan is preferred, as it facilitates a change to the other metering system in case a different policy should prove advisable in the future. Frequently a combination of these two systems is employed in which the management is billed for and provides certain definite services, such as the electric range, refrigerator, or air-conditioning equipment, the probable cost of which is relatively easy to determine and much cheaper when paid for on a wholesale rate taking advantage of the low demand factor which applies to a large number of customers. Then the customer has a separate service through his individual meter for lighting and small appliances. The method of wiring is with metal-clad cable or nonmetallic-sheathed cable for small buildings of frame construction. Conduit wiring is usually employed for the larger buildings of masonry construction.

518. With any of the above plans each apartment should have its own distribution panel board containing fuses or circuit breakers for the branch circuits. Fuse panels are cheaper, but circuit breakers will reduce labor in calls for service due to short circuits in portable cords and appliances. In either case the panel board should be located on the wall of the kitchen or hall.

WIRING FOR COMMERCIAL AND INDUSTRIAL OCCUPANCIES

519. Electrical Distribution Systems for Commercial and Industrial Use ("Electrical Systems Design" by Joseph F. McPartland). In any electrical system, the distribution system involves the methods and equipment used to carry power from the service equipment to the overcurrent devices protecting the branch circuits. The distribution system carries power to lighting panel boards, power panel boards, and motor control centers and to the branch-circuit protective devices for individual motor or power loads. Depending upon the type of building, the size and nature of the total load, various economic factors, and local conditions, a distribution system may operate at a single voltage level or may involve one or more transformations of voltage. A distribution system might also incorporate change in frequency of a-c power or rectification from a-c to d-c power.

Design of a distribution system, therefore, is a matter of selecting circuit layouts and equipment to accomplish electrical actions and operations necessary for the conditions of voltage, current, and frequency. This means relating such factors as service voltage, distribution voltage or voltages, conductors, transformers, converters, switches, protective devices, regulators, and power-factor corrective means to economy, load conditions, continuity of service, operating efficiency, and future power requirements. Of course, the factors of capacity, accessibility, flexibility, and safety must be carefully included in design considerations for distribution.

The basic classification of distribution systems is according to voltage level used to carry the power either directly to the branch circuits or to load-center transformers or substations at which feeders to branch circuits originate. The most common types of distribution systems based on voltage are discussed in Div. 3.

520. Types of Electrical Distribution Systems. The descriptions and discussions of the different types of electrical distribution systems given in this section and the following Secs. **521** to **532** inclusive are reproduced from "Westinghouse Architects' and Engineers' Electrical Data Book" through the courtesy of The Westinghouse Electric Corporation.

In the great majority of cases, power is supplied to a building at the utilization voltage. In practically all these cases, the distribution of power within the building is achieved through the use of a simple radial distribution system. This system is the first type described on the following pages from the low-voltage bus to the loads.

In those cases where service is available at the building at some voltage higher than the utilization voltage to be used, the system design engineer has a choice of a number of types of systems which he may use. This discussion covers seven major types of distribution systems and practical modifications of several of them.

Simple-radial.
Loop-primary radial.
Banked-secondary radial.
Primary-selective radial.
Secondary-selective radial.
Simple network.
Primary-selective network.

521. Simple-radial System. The conventional simple-radial system receives power at the utility supply voltage at a single substation and steps the voltage down to the utilization level.

Low-voltage feeder circuits run from the substation bus to switchgear assemblies and panel boards that are located with respect to the loads as shown in Fig. 308. Each feeder is connected to the substation bus through a circuit breaker. Relatively small circuits are used to distribute power to the loads from the switchgear assemblies and panel boards.

Since the entire load is served from a single source, full advantage can be taken of the diversity among the loads. This makes it possible to minimize the installed transformer capacity. However, the voltage regulation and efficiency of this system are poor because of the low-voltage feeders and single source. The costs of the low-voltage

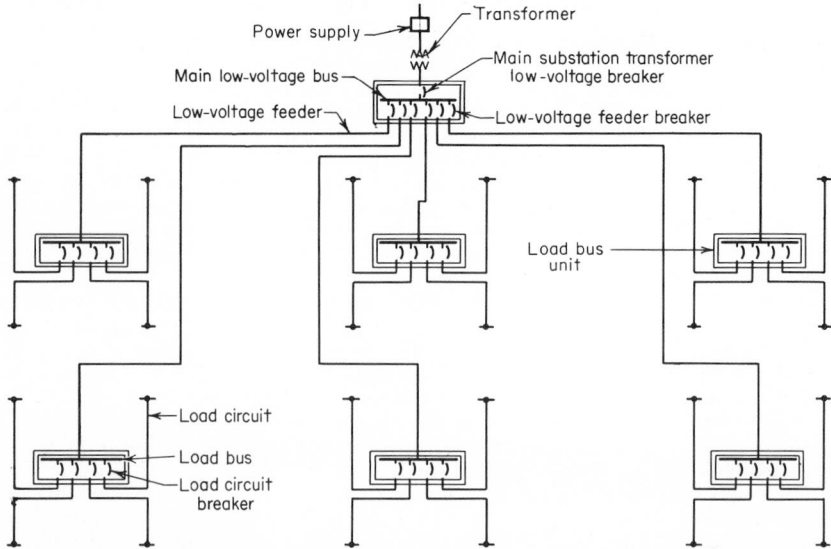

FIG. 308   *Conventional simple-radial system.*

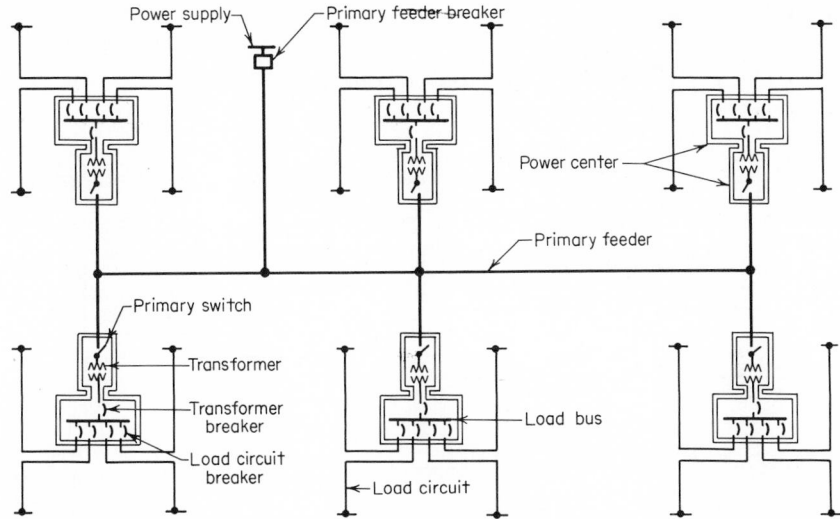

FIG. 309 *Modern simple-radial system.*

feeder circuits and their associated circuit breakers are high when the feeders are long and the peak demand is above 1,000 kva.

A fault on the substation bus or in the substation transformer will interrupt service to all loads. Service cannot be restored until the necessary repairs have been made. A low-voltage feeder circuit fault will interrupt service to all loads supplied over that feeder.

A modern and improved form of the conventional simple-radial system distributes power at a primary voltage. The voltage is stepped down to utilization level in the several load areas within the building through power center transformers. The transformers are usually connected to their associated load bus through a circuit breaker, as shown in Fig. 309. Each power center is a factory-assembled unit substation consisting of a three-phase liquid-filled or air-cooled transformer, an integrally mounted primary switch, and low-voltage metal-enclosed circuit breakers. Circuits are run to the loads from these circuit breakers.

Since each transformer is located within a specific load area, it must have sufficient capacity to carry the peak load of that area. Consequently, if any diversity exists among the load areas, this modified system requires more transformer capacity than the basic form of the simple radial system. However, because power is distributed to the load areas at a primary voltage, losses are reduced, voltage regulation is improved, feeder circuit costs are reduced substantially, and the large low-voltage feeder circuit breakers are eliminated. In many cases the interrupting duty imposed on the load circuit breakers is reduced.

This modern form of the simple radial system will usually be lower in initial investment than any other type of distribution system for buildings in which the peak load is above 1,000 kva. It is poor, however, from the standpoints of service continuity and flexibility. A fault on the primary feeder circuit or in one transformer will cause an outage to all loads. In the case of the feeder fault, service is interrupted to all loads until the trouble is eliminated. When a transformer fault occurs, service can be restored to all loads except those served by the faulty transformer by opening the transformer primary switch and reclosing the primary feeder breaker.

Reducing the number of transformers per feeder through adding more primary feeder circuits will improve the flexibility and service continuity of this system. This, of course, increases the investment in the system but minimizes the extent of an outage due to a transformer or feeder fault.

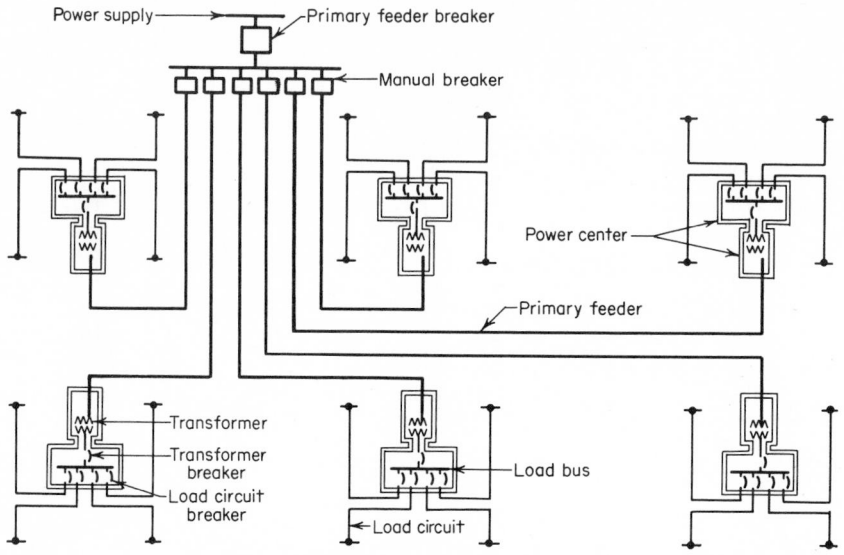

FIG. 310 *Modified modern simple radial system.*

If one primary feeder is used per transformer, as in Fig. 310, the system is comparable in service continuity to the single substation form of the simple radial system. This system arrangement will usually be very expensive. The cost can be materially reduced, however, by replacing the automatic feeder circuit breakers with manually operated breakers or load-break switches and backing up a number of these switches with one automatic circuit breaker.

In this modified form of the simple radial system, a primary feeder fault interrupts service to all loads. Service can be restored to all loads except those associated with the faulted system element by opening the load-break switch on the faulted circuit and closing the circuit breaker. Service can be restored to the remaining loads when the necessary repairs are made.

522. Loop-primary Radial System. This system is similar in principle to the modern form of simple radial system. It provides for quick restoration of service when a primary feeder or transformer fault occurs, as does the modified simple radial system of Fig. 310, and at a lower investment. A sectionalized primary loop controlled by a single primary feeder breaker is used as shown in Fig. 311 rather than a radial primary feeder.

Manually operated load-break switches are installed in the feeder for sectionalizing purposes. Two are located where the feeder branches to form the loop, and the others are located at the transformers. This makes it possible to disconnect any transformer and its associated section of loop from the rest of the system.

When a transformer or primary feeder fault occurs, the main feeder breaker opens and interrupts service to all loads. Increasing the number of primary loop feeders will reduce the extent of the outage from a fault but will also increase the system investment. The faulty section of loop and its associated transformer can be disconnected from the system by the load-break switches. Service can then be restored to all but the disconnected portion of the system by closing the primary feeder breaker. Service cannot, however, be restored to the loads in the area where the transformer or primary loop section is in trouble until the necessary repairs are made.

The cost of this system as illustrated is only slightly more than that of the modern simple radial system of Fig. 309. The primary cable cost is a little greater, and there are two additional load-break switches in the system. The load-break switches associ-

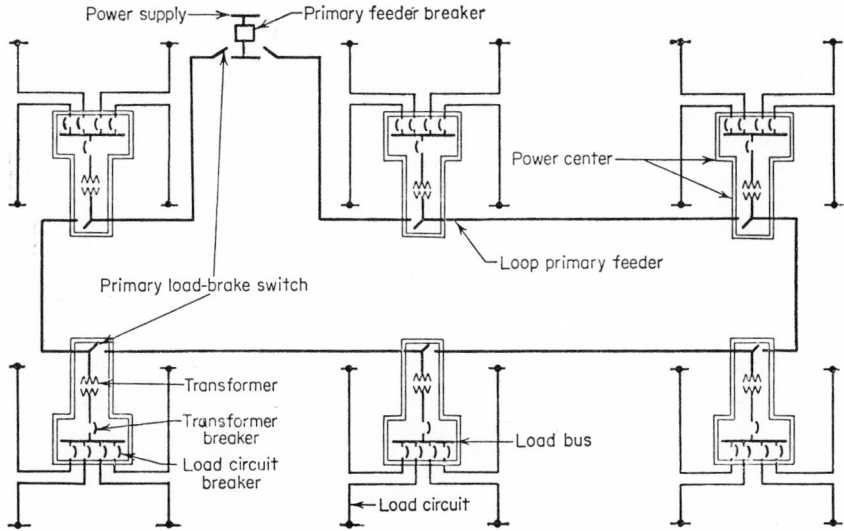

FIG. 311 *Loop-primary radial system.*

ated with the transformers will cost little more than the disconnecting switches in the primary leads of the transformers of the simple radial system.

523. Banked-secondary Radial System. This system permits quick restoration of service to all loads following a primary feeder or transformer fault. It uses a secondary loop, as shown in Fig. 312, to provide an emergency supply when a fault occurs in a transformer or a section of the primary loop. The primary circuit arrangement is the same as that in the loop-primary radial system of Fig. 311.

The primary feeder arrangement of the simple radial system of Fig. 310 can be used to give the same results, but it usually will be more costly.

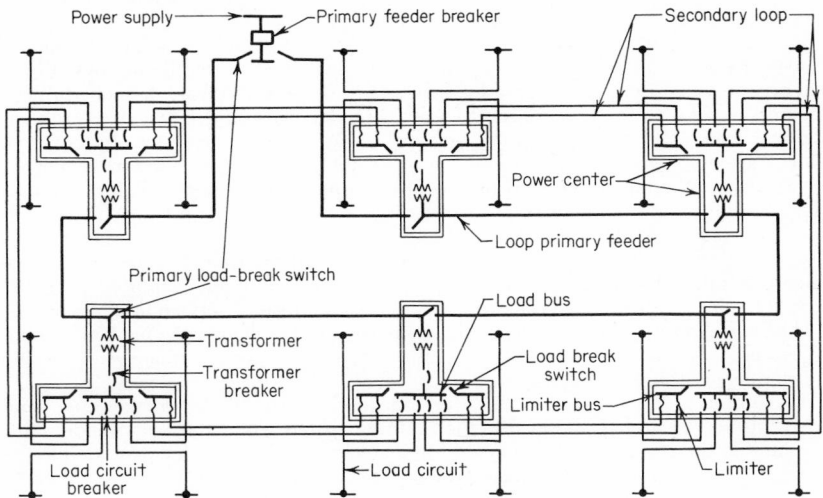

FIG. 312 *Banked-secondary radial system.*

A primary feeder or transformer fault causes the main breaker to operate and drop all load. Service can be restored by opening the two load-break switches and the low-voltage breaker of the transformer adjacent to the fault and closing the primary feeder breaker. When the primary feeder breaker is reclosed, service is restored to all loads. Those loads connected to the load bus associated with the disconnected transformer are supplied over the secondary loop from adjacent load buses.

The secondary loop gives a number of important advantages other than providing an emergency supply to restore service. It helps equalize the loads on all transformers and thus makes it unnecessary to match the transformer capacity at each load center to the load connected to each load bus.

Balancing transformer capacity and load in each load area may be a real problem on all other types of radial systems except the radial system of Fig. 308. The secondary loop permits one kva rating of transformer to be used throughout the system, and load circuits can be run directly from the nearest bus to the loads.

Advantage is taken of the diversity among the loads because all transformers are connected in parallel. As a result, there usually is a saving in transformer capacity over that required in any other form of radial system except the simple radial system of Fig. 308. Also, this system is better adapted for across-the-line starting of relatively large motors than is any other type of radial system because the starting current is supplied through several transformers in parallel rather than through a single transformer. Thus, if the starting of large motors is involved, the use of this system may result in a saving in the cost of motor-starting equipment. Likewise, it is the most satisfactory type of radial system for combined light and power secondary circuits.

In the banked-secondary radial system, fault current flows not only through the transformer associated with a faulted load bus or circuit but also through other transformers and over the secondary loop to the fault. The resulting increase in fault current may require the use of load circuit breakers having a higher interrupting rating than needed in other types of modern radial systems. This possible increase in cost may or may not be offset by savings in transformer capacity and secondary conductors.

It is difficult to make a general cost comparison between this system and the loop-primary radial system. In some buildings the additional cost of the secondary loop will be offset by the saving in transformer capacity and secondary conductors. In other buildings, because of lack of diversity and a relatively uniform distribution of load, these savings are very small and the system will cost more than the loop-primary radial system by about the cost of the secondary loop. However, the advantages of quick restoration of service to all loads, greater flexibility, higher efficiency, and better voltage conditions may justify the extra cost.

524. Primary-selective Radial System. The primary-selective radial system, as shown in Fig. 313, differs from those previously described in that it employs at least two primary feeder circuits in each load area. It is designed so that when one primary circuit is out of service, the remaining feeder or feeders have sufficient capacity to carry the total load. While three or more primary feeders may be used, usually only two feeders are employed. Half of the transformers are normally connected to each of the two feeders. When a fault occurs on one of the primary feeders, only half of the load in the building is dropped. In the systems discussed previously a primary feeder fault causes an outage to all loads in the building.

Double-throw or primary-selector switches are used with all transformers so that when a primary feeder fault occurs, the transformers normally supplied from the faulted feeder can be switched to the good feeder and restore service to all loads.

The short-circuit duty on the load circuit breakers is less than in the banked-secondary radial system and is about the same as for all other types of radial systems using transformers within the load areas.

If a fault occurs in one transformer, the associated primary feeder breaker opens and interrupts service to half the load in the building, just as when a primary feeder fails. The faulted transformer is disconnected by moving its primary-selector switch to the open position. Service is then restored to all loads except those normally supplied by the defective transformer by closing the primary feeder breaker.

Service cannot be restored to the loads normally served by the faulted transformer until the transformer is repaired or replaced.

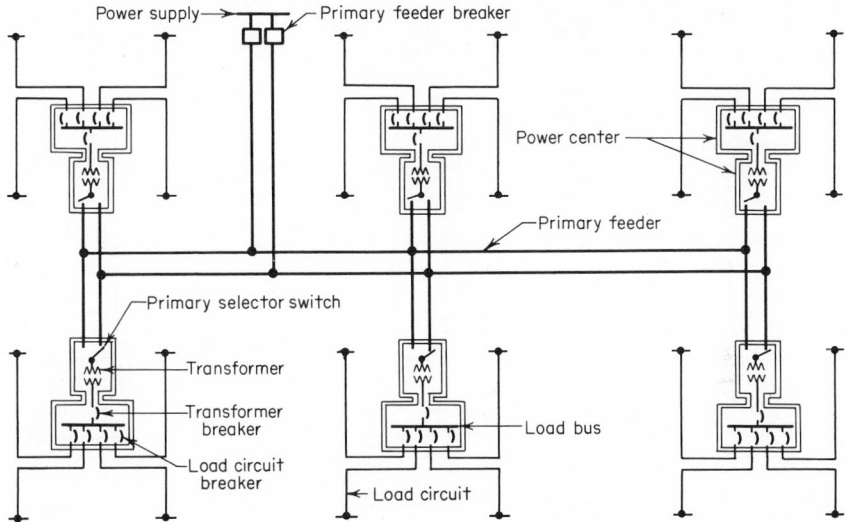

FIG. 313 *Primary-selective radial system.*

Cost of the primary-selective radial system is greater than that of the simple radial system of Fig. 309 because of the additional primary feeder breaker, the use of primary-selector switches, and the greater amount of primary feeder cable required. The benefits derived from the reduction in the amount of load dropped when a primary feeder or transformer fault occurs, plus the quick restoration of service to all or most of the loads, may more than offset the greater cost.

The primary-selective radial system, however, is not so good as the banked-secondary radial system from the standpoint of restoring service to the loads after a primary feeder or transformer fault. It is only a little better than the loop-primary radial system in this respect. In some cases, particularly in fairly large buildings with medium or light-load density, about the same quality of service can be rendered at less cost by using the loop-primary radial system employing two separate loops instead of one. In this case, half of the transformers are connected to each loop of the system.

525. Secondary-selective Radial System. This system uses the same principle of duplicate feed from the power-supply point as the primary-selective radial system. In this system, however, the duplication is carried all the way to each load bus on the secondary side of the transformers instead of just to the primary terminals of the transformers. This arrangement permits quick restoration of service to all loads when a primary feeder or transformer fault occurs, as does the banked-secondary radial system.

The usual form of secondary-selective radial system is shown in Fig. 314. Each load area in the building is supplied over two primary feeders and through two transformers. The capacity of each of these transformers must be such that it can safely carry the entire load in the area served by both transformers. Each transformer is connected through a transformer breaker to a secondary bus section to which half of the radial load circuits are connected.

A bus-tie breaker is provided for connecting the two secondary or load bus sections at each load center. Normally this bus-tie breaker is open and the system operates as two parallel systems entirely independent of each other beyond the power supply points. The bus-tie breaker is interlocked with the two transformer breakers so that it cannot be closed unless one of the transformer breakers is open. This is done to keep the interrupting duty imposed on the load circuit breakers to a minimum.

A primary feeder fault causes half of the load in the building to be dropped, as with the primary-selective radial system. Service can be restored by opening the transformer breakers associated with the faulted feeder and closing all bus-tie breakers.

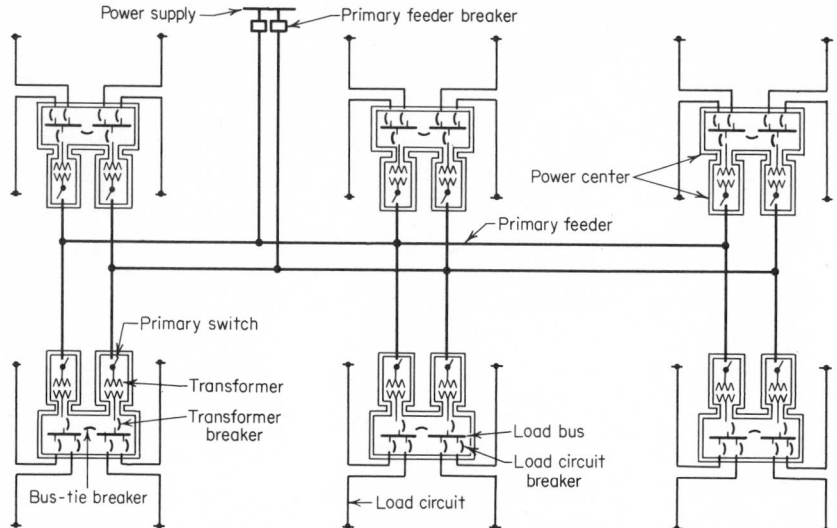

FIG. 314   *Secondary-selective radial system.*

When this is done, the entire load is fed over one primary feeder and through half of the transformers. Therefore, both primary feeders must be capable of carrying the entire load, as with the primary-selective radial system, and much more transformer capacity is required.

A fault in a transformer causes the associated primary feeder breaker to trip and interrupts service to half the building load. Service can be restored by opening the disconnecting switch on the primary and the circuit breaker on the secondary of the faulted transformer, closing the associated bus-tie breaker, and reclosing the primary feeder breaker. This manual switching restores the system to normal operating conditions except that the faulted transformer is de-energized and its load is being supplied through the adjacent transformer.

Cost of the secondary-selective radial system usually will be considerably more than that of the radial systems previously discussed with the exception of the system shown in Fig. 308, which uses one large substation and low-voltage feeders, and the banked-secondary radial system of Fig. 312. This is due chiefly to the large amount of transformer capacity required to provide complete duplicate power supply to the secondary load buses. Because of this spare transformer capacity, the regulation provided by the secondary-selective radial system under normal conditions is better than that of the systems previously discussed, with the possible exception of the banked-secondary radial system.

From the standpoint of voltage fluctuation when a load such as a relatively large motor is thrown on the system, this system is not so good as the banked-secondary radial system. The advantage that the secondary-selective radial system offers over the banked-secondary radial system is that a primary feeder or transformer fault causes only one-half the load to be dropped instead of all the load in the area. Both systems permit the quick restoration of service to all loads when a primary feeder or transformer fault occurs.

The banked-secondary radial system has more flexibility and can be more readily adapted to changing load conditions than can the secondary-selective radial system.

A modified form of secondary-selective radial system that will often be less costly than the common form previously described is shown in Fig. 315. In this system there is only one transformer at each load center, instead of two. Pairs of adjacent load buses are connected by secondary cables or bus and thus permit picking up the load of any bus when a primary feeder or transformer fault occurs.

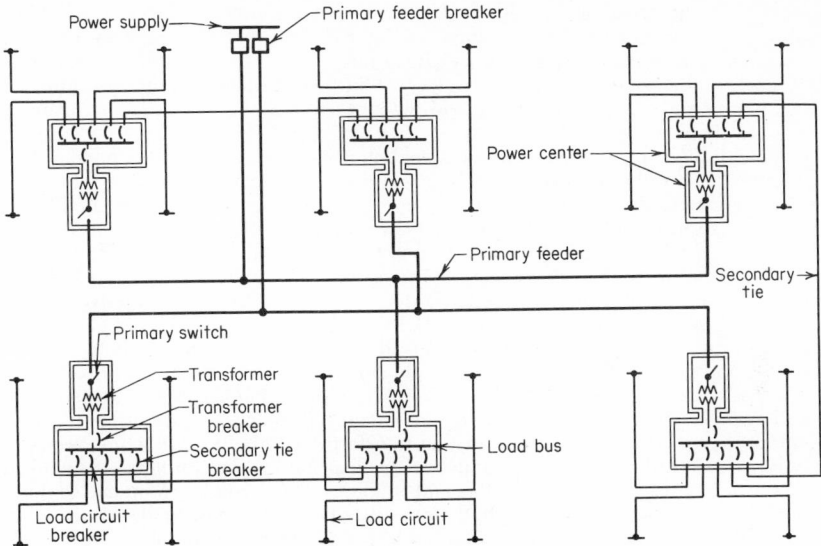

FIG. 315 *Modified secondary-selective radial system.*

Each tie circuit is connected to each of its two load buses through a secondary-tie circuit breaker. Each secondary-tie breaker is interlocked so that it cannot be closed unless one of the two transformer breakers is open.

There are two ways in which this single-transformer-substation form of secondary-selective radial system can be handled. One is to use the same number and rating of transformers as in the usual form of the system. Essentially, this results in twice as many load areas with half as much load in each area. This arrangement has the advantage of reducing the average length of the radial load circuits and thereby reduces the cost of the secondary conductors. When compared with the other types of distribution systems, both this and the usual form of secondary-selective radial system introduce the problem of balancing the loads on twice the usual number of load buses.

The other way in which the system can be handled is to use the same number of load areas as in Fig. 314. With one transformer of twice the kva rating at each load center, the result is half the number of transformers but the same total transformer capacity. Because of the smaller number of transformers of larger rating, this will often be the lowest cost form of secondary-selective radial system.

Basically, the single-transformer-substation form of secondary-selective radial system, regardless of the number and size of the transformers used, functions as described in connection with the more usual form of this system.

526. Simple Network System. The a-c secondary network system is the system that has been used for many years to distribute electric power in the high-density, downtown areas of cities. Modifications of this type of system make it applicable to serve loads within buildings.

The best-known advantage of the secondary network system is continuity of service. No single fault anywhere on the system will interrupt service to more than a small part of the system load. Most faults will be automatically cleared without interrupting service to any load. Another outstanding advantage that the network system offers is its flexibility to meet changing and growing load conditions at minimum cost and with minimum interruption of service to the other loads. In addition to flexibility and service reliability, the secondary network system provides exceptionally uniform and good voltage regulation, and its high efficiency materially reduces the cost of losses.

Three major differences between the network system and the simple radial system account for the outstanding advantages of the network. First, a network protector is connected in the secondary leads of each network transformer in place of the usual transformer secondary breaker as shown in Fig. 316. Second, the secondaries of all transformers are connected together by a ring bus or secondary loop from which the loads are supplied over short radial circuits. Third, the primary supply has sufficient capacity to carry the entire building load without overloading when any one primary feeder is out of service.

A network protector is a specially designed, motor-closed, and shunt-tripped air circuit breaker controlled by network relays. The network relays function to close the breaker automatically only when voltage conditions are such that its associated transformer will supply load to the secondary loop and to open the breaker automatically when power flows from the secondary loop to the network transformer. The purpose of the network protector is to protect the secondary loop and the loads served from it against transformer and primary feeder faults by disconnecting the defective feeder-transformer unit from the loop when a back-feed occurs.

The chief purpose of the secondary loop is to provide an alternate supply to any load bus when the primary feeder which normally supplies it is de-energized, so as to prevent any service interruption when a transformer or feeder fault occurs. The use of the loop, however, gives at least four other important advantages. First, it saves transformer capacity. It permits lightly loaded transformers to help those which are more heavily loaded and thus tends to equalize the load on all transformers. Second, it saves secondary load circuit conductors and conduit. The secondary loop makes it unnecessary to match the load supplied from any one load bus with the transformer capacity at that point. Loads can be served from the loop at load buses located between network transformers, and the load circuits can be run directly to the loads from the nearest load bus. This permits the use of very short radial circuits and results in a considerable saving in secondary cable and conduit when compared with the load circuits of a simple radial system. Third, it gives lower system losses and greatly improved voltage conditions. The voltage regulation on a network system is such that both lights and power can be fed from the same load bus. Much larger motors can be started across the line than on a simple radial system. This often results in greatly simplified motor control and permits the use of relatively large low-voltage motors with their less expensive control.

The fourth important advantage resulting from the use of the secondary loop is the much greater system flexibility it provides. New or relocated loads can be supplied

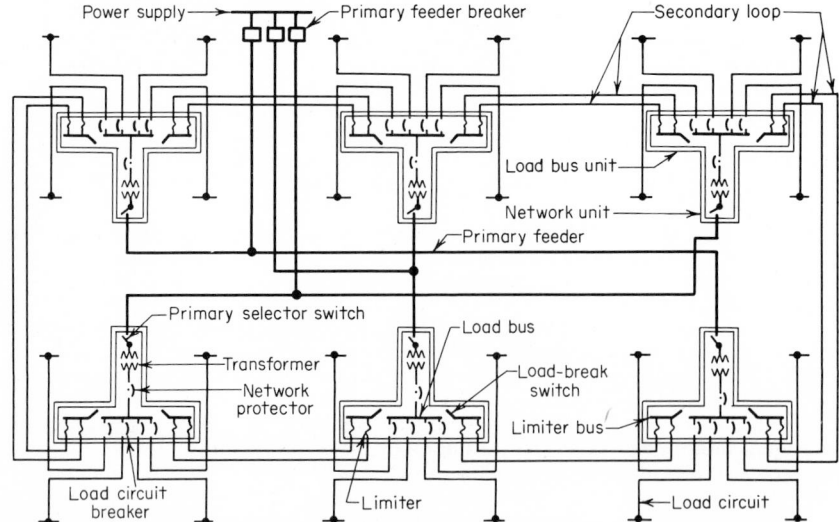

FIG. 316 *Simple network system.*

directly from the nearest load bus without the necessity of reconnecting other loads to keep within the transformer capacity of the secondary substation to which the load is to be added. Complete network power centers or load bus units can be relocated in the loop, or new units can be added to the loop to meet changing load conditions. The loop capacity requires no change when additional network power centers are connected to it if each new transformer is of no larger rating than those originally used. The loop permits these system changes to be made without interrupting service to existing loads. This greater flexibility of the network system permits the system to be changed more easily, more quickly, and at less cost to meet changing load conditions than can be done with a radial system.

Since the length of the secondary loop (which is in essence an extended bus) is considerably longer than the buses used with the usual radial systems, the probability of faults on it is greater. It therefore becomes necessary to protect the system against faults on this bus or loop so that a fault on it will be automatically disconnected without interrupting service. To accomplish this, the secondary loop should consist of a minimum of two three-phase circuits. These separate circuits should be bused at each point where power is supplied to the loop through a transformer and at each point where a radial load circuit is served from the loop. Each individual loop circuit should be connected to these bus points through limiters.

A limiter is a device for disconnecting a faulted cable from a distribution system and for protecting the unfaulted portions of that cable against serious thermal damage. This is accomplished by means of a circuit-opening member which is heated and destroyed by the current passing through it. The fusible circuit-opening member is completely enclosed so that there is no visible flame or smoke when the limiter operates. Limiters for building networks are suitable for use on circuits of 600 volts and below and have an interrupting rating of 50,000 amp. Limiters are designed for use with various sizes of cable and are rated in cable size. The largest limiter is rated 600,000 cir mils. The minimum fusing current of a limiter is about three to three and one-half times the National Electrical Code continuous-current rating of the cable with which it is designed to be used. This value of fusing current is necessary to ensure positive selectivity among the limiters in the secondary loop. If limiters having appreciably lower values of fusing current were used, those on both the good conductors and the faulted conductor would function on the minimum definite time portion of their time-current curves for high fault currents. This means that not only the limiters in the faulted loop conductor but a number of those in the good conductors would blow almost instantly and in some cases cause unnecessary interruptions of service. In addition to preventing unnecessary limiter blowings, the high fusing current value of limiters also has the advantage of keeping the normal temperature of the limiter terminals relatively low so that its associated cable can safely carry its rated current.

If loads are to be supplied from the secondary loop at points other than those at which the network transformers are connected to the loop, the current rating of the loop should be equal to the full-load current of one of the transformers supplying the loop. The current rating of the loop can be safely reduced to 67 per cent of the above value if loads are supplied from the loop only at transformer locations. If more than one kva rating of network transformer is used, the current rating of the loop should be based on the full-load current of the largest network transformer connected to the loop. When loads are served from the loop at points other than transformer locations, the maximum amount of load which should be supplied from the loop between any two adjacent transformers should not exceed the full-load rating of the larger of the two transformers.

To obtain satisfactory selectivity between limiters under all fault conditions, a minimum of two similar single-conductor cables per phase should be used in the secondary loop. The size and number of conductors used in any case should be selected to give the lowest installed loop cost. However, the conductors used should not be larger than about 600,000-cir-mil cable.

Loads are served from the secondary loop at conveniently located load buses over relatively short radial circuits. These load circuits are taken off the load buses through air circuit breakers. The breakers should provide adequate overload protection for their associated circuits and should be capable of interrupting the fault current available at that point on the system. The average interrupting duty on the load breakers in a network system will often be higher than the duty on the load breakers in a radial system having the same connected transformer capacity.

The optimum size and number of primary feeders can be used in the secondary network system because the loss of any primary feeder and its associated transformers does not result in the loss of any load. In spite of the spare capacity required in primary feeders, this will often result in a saving in primary feeder and switchgear cost when compared with a radial system. This is due to the fact that in many radial systems, more and smaller feeders are often used in order to keep down the extent of the outage when a primary feeder fault occurs.

When a fault occurs on a primary feeder or in a transformer, the fault is isolated from the system through the automatic tripping of the primary feeder circuit breaker and all the network protectors associated with that feeder circuit. This operation does not interrupt service to any loads. When the necessary repairs have been made, the system is restored to normal operating conditions by closing the feeder circuit breaker. All network protectors associated with that feeder will close automatically.

The simple network system sometimes takes a form commonly known as a spot-network system. With this system, emergency capacity to prevent a service interruption when a primary feeder or transformer fault occurs is provided by making a spare primary cable and transformer available at each load center instead of tying the load areas together by a secondary loop, as in the usual simple network.

The simple spot-network system resembles the secondary-selective radial system in that each load area is supplied over two or more primary feeders through two or more transformers. In this system, however, the transformers are connected through network protectors to a single load bus, as shown in Fig. 317. Since the transformers at each load bus operate in parallel, a primary feeder or transformer fault does not cause any service interruption. The transformers supplying each load bus will normally carry equal loads, whereas equal loading of the two transformers supplying a load center in the secondary-selective radial system is difficult to obtain. The interrupting duty imposed on the load circuit breakers will be greater with the simple spot-network system than with the secondary-selective radial system.

Simple spot-network systems are more economical than the other forms of network systems for buildings where there are heavy concentrations of load covering small areas, with considerable distances between these concentrations and very little load

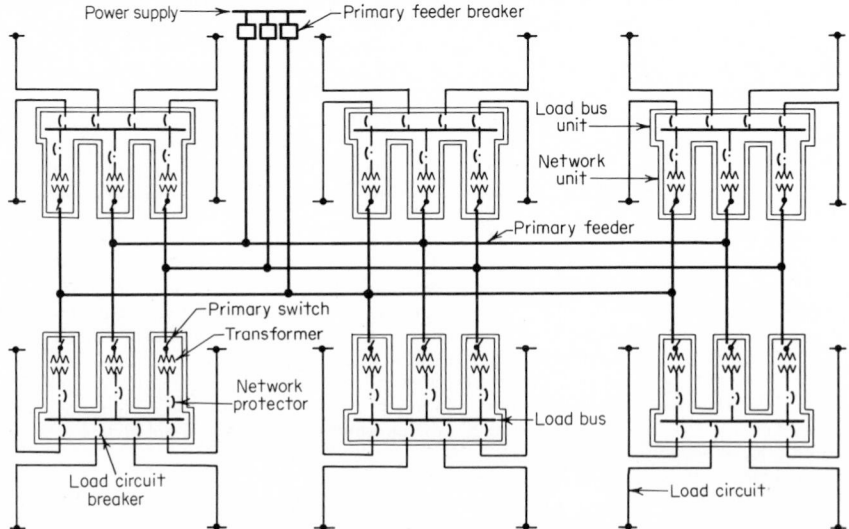

FIG. 317 *Simple spot-network system.*

in the areas between them. The chief disadvantage of spot-network systems is that they are not nearly so flexible for growing and shifting loads as are the other forms of network systems. Simple spot-network systems are used where a high degree of service continuity is required, flexibility is of minor importance, and their cost is less than the network systems using a secondary loop. The simple spot-network system is most economical where three or more primary feeders are required. This is because supplying each load bus through three or more transformers greatly reduces the spare cable and transformer capacity that is required.

527. Primary-selective Network. This is the most generally applicable and widely used form of industrial secondary network system. It is similar in principle to the simple network system, offers almost all of its advantages, and is the lowest cost network system for buildings or load areas requiring only two or three primary feeders. Saving in first cost when compared with the simple network system is accomplished by using the principle of duplicate or alternate feed to each transformer, as with the primary-selective radial system. This practically eliminates the necessity for spare transformer capacity and reduces the interrupting duty imposed on the load circuit breakers but does not reduce the amount of spare primary feeder capacity required.

Each transformer in the primary-selective network system is equipped with a primary selector switch. Two primary feeders are run to each transformer, as shown in Fig. 318. In a building requiring two primary feeders, each feeder must be capable of supplying the entire load in the building. Each transformer is connected to a load bus through a network protector. The radial circuits serving the loads are connected to the load bus through circuit breakers. A secondary loop, such as is used in the banked-secondary radial and the simple network systems, connects each load bus to the two adjacent load buses. One-half of the network transformers are normally connected to each primary feeder.

A primary feeder fault causes the faulty feeder and its transformers to be disconnected from the system by the automatic operation of the primary feeder breaker and associated network protectors. The entire building load is then carried over the remaining primary feeder and one-half of the network transformers. The transformers associated with the faulty feeder can be connected to the good feeder by manually operating their selector switches. This relieves the overload on the transformers normally associated with the good feeder.

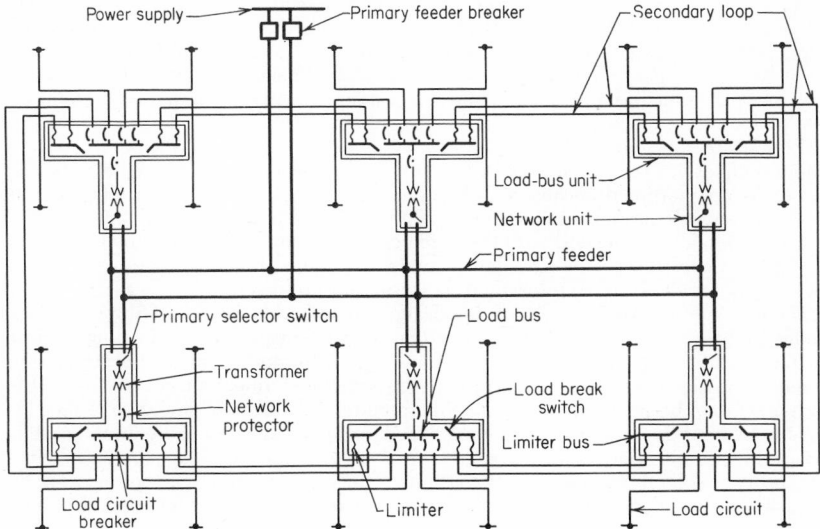

FIG. 318 *Primary-selective network system.*

A transformer fault is isolated from the system by the operation of the primary feeder breaker and the network protectors associated with the primary feeder. The defective transformer can be disconnected from the primary feeder by opening its selector switch. The feeder and its good transformers can be immediately returned to service. A primary feeder or transformer fault will not cause any interruption of service to the load.

Cost of the primary-selective network system compares very favorably with that of the secondary-selective radial system. In buildings where the load is quite uniform and there is little diversity among load centers, the secondary-selective radial system usually will be lower in initial investment than the network system. However, in buildings where the load is nonuniform and there is appreciable diversity among load centers, the primary-selective network system often will be lower in first cost than the secondary-selective radial system.

It is common practice to supply the radial circuits only from the load buses to which the network transformers are connected. At times a reduction in system cost can be made by serving loads from the loop at points between transformers. When this is done, the loop cables should preferably be paralleled and the loads taken off through load bus units. Each load bus unit should be similar to those used where network transformers connect to the loop and consists of a load bus, two limiter buses with load-break switches and limiters, and load circuit breakers. Connecting loads to the secondary loop in this manner reduces the average length of the secondary load circuits.

By tapping all loads from the secondary loop at the nearest point, the amount of secondary load circuit conductors can be reduced to a minimum. This cannot be done practically when using a cable secondary loop if limiters are installed in the loop conductors at each load take-off point. Such a form of network system is practical, however, if two or more parallel runs of plug-in bus duct are used for the secondary loop.

In this system, the transformers connect to a bus through network protectors, as in Fig. 318, except that there usually will be no load circuit breakers in the bus units. All loads usually are supplied through the load-break switches to the limiter buses and then through the limiters into the bus ducts that tie the adjacent bus units together.

This form of network system requires larger conductors in the secondary loop than those using the cable loop previously described. It also sacrifices something in service continuity when compared with network systems where the loads are fed from load bus units connected in a cable loop. This is because a fault in a section of the bus duct loop will cause an outage to the loads served from that section.

As with the simple network system, the primary-selective network may also take the form of a spot-network system. Each transformer in the primary-selective spot-network system is equipped with a primary-selector switch and arranged for connection to either of two primary feeders, as shown in Fig. 319. This largely eliminates the necessity for spare transformer capacity, and the system is ordinarily designed without providing for such capacity.

Primary feeder and transformer faults on this system are cleared without any interruption of service to the loads as in the simple spot-network system. When a primary feeder is de-energized because of a feeder fault, the transformers associated with the good feeder will carry as high as 160 to 200 per cent of their rated kva until the transformers normally associated with the defective feeder are switched to the good feeder by operation of their primary-selector switches. After this switching operation has been completed, all the overloads on the system are relieved.

When a spot-network system of this design is used, a transformer failure requires a reduction in the load served from its load bus to prevent serious overloading of the remaining transformer connected to that bus. A transformer failure will occur so infrequently, however, that the cost of providing spare transformer capacity throughout the system cannot be justified to eliminate the remote probability of having to reduce load on one bus. If the possibility of having to reduce load is objectionable, it will cost less to use the simple spot-network system than to provide the necessary spare capacity in the primary-selective spot-network system. The primary-selective spot-network system, when designed without spare transformer capacity, will cost less than the simple spot-network system if two primary feeders and two transformers per load bus are used. Where three or more primary feeders are required, the simple spot-network system will be lower in cost than the primary-selective spot-network system.

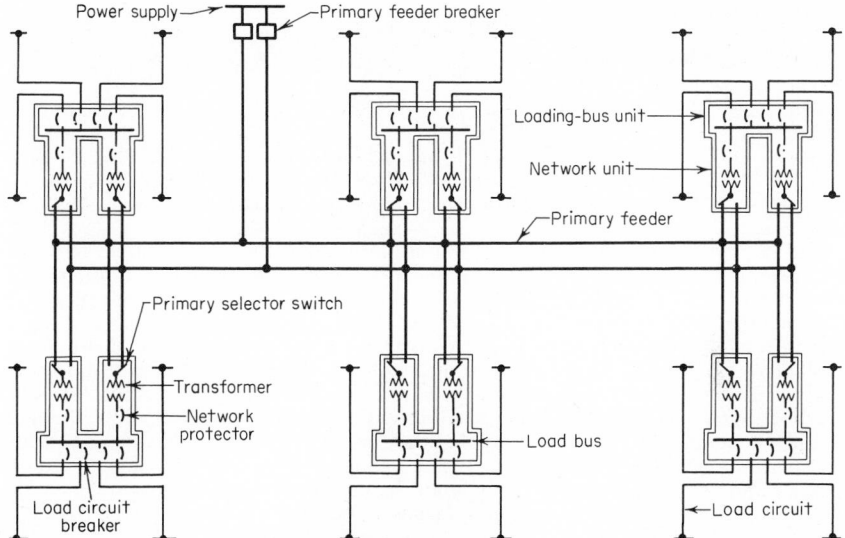

FIG. 319   *Primary-selective spot-network system.*

528. Influence of Buildings on Design.   Building distribution systems are too often selected on the basis of using the system having the lowest initial investment. This practice usually results in the installation of a system which is neither the best nor the most economical system for the building when all factors are considered and properly evaluated.

All the major characteristics of the different types of distribution systems should be evaluated in the light of the building load requirements in order to select the best system. The six major characteristics are initial investment, flexibility, service continuity, voltage regulation, efficiency, and cost of operation and maintenance.

The best system is that which gives the greatest value per dollar of investment and provides adequate electric service. This is rarely the system with the lowest initial investment.

Flexibility is the system's ability to be adapted to changing load conditions with the minimum of service interruptions and minimum cost of necessary changes.

Service continuity is measured in terms of the amount of load dropped with faults at different locations on the system, taking into account the likelihood of faults in the various locations.

Under voltage regulation, the change in voltage with load variations, the uniformity of this change at the various load points throughout the system, and the change in voltage resulting from suddenly applied loads should be considered.

The over-all efficiency of the system from the power-supply point or points to the utilization devices should be taken into account for both light-load and heavy-load conditions of operation.

Operating and maintenance costs are influenced by the nature and amount of equipment in the system and the ability to inspect, test, and maintain the equipment with minimum interruption of service.

The general arrangement and choice of the type of system depends upon type and purpose of the building. In this discussion buildings shall be considered as belonging to one of these five classifications:

Large vertical buildings (of less than about 12 stories high).

Tall (high-rise) commercial buildings.

Large horizontal buildings (such as shopping centers and large one-floor offices).

Groups of small buildings (such as hospitals and educational institutions).

Industrial plants.

The quality of service required by the loads varies somewhat within each of the five classifications, depending upon the purposes of the buildings and the activities carried on within them.

529. Large Vertical Buildings. Large vertical buildings, such as office buildings, stores, apartments, hospitals, and hotels, require a high quality of electric service because the operation of essential equipment in the buildings depends directly on a reliable supply of electric power. Network systems are recognized as the best means of assuring satisfactory electric service in large buildings. However, in some cases, such as warehouses, interruptions of service for inspection and maintenance or as a result of faults may not interfere with the function of the building or cause hazards. In these cases, simple radial, primary-selective radial, or secondary-selective radial systems are used depending upon the extent and duration of interruptions that can be tolerated and the importance of small savings in initial cost.

The network system is generally accepted as the most desirable form of distribution system for large buildings because it is the most economical method of providing reliability and good voltage characteristics. It is essential to have these characteristics in the distribution system for most large buildings because the activities in the buildings usually depend on a continuous supply of electric power with good voltage characteristics. Reliability is important because a failure of power that may stop elevators, pumps, and ventilating systems not only results in stopping the activities in the buildings but may result in danger to the occupants. Obviously, good voltage regulation is essential in order to obtain the most effective output from lamps and other utilization devices. Good voltage regulation becomes particularly important when the same system supplies both the lighting and the power loads.

The relatively high load demands in large buildings encourage the use of large undesirable concentrations of transformer capacity in secondary substations with the result that very high fault currents are available in many cases. This requires expensive switchgear equipment to give adequate protection to the system against all possible faults in low-voltage circuits within the system. The power supply in buildings should be carefully designed to limit the fault currents to reasonable values so that less expensive equipment can be used. Several small substations instead of a few big substations can be used to reduce interrupting duties.

The interrupting duty on the low-voltage breakers in the substations directly affects the cost of the distribution system. High-interrupting-capacity breakers are more expensive than low-interrupting-capacity breakers. In general, the cost of the distribution system will materially increase if the interrupting duty exceeds 50,000 amp. Therefore, it is desirable to plan the distribution system so that the interrupting duty does not exceed this value. In buildings where the total load is not more than a few hundred kva, it is not difficult to keep the interrupting duty below this value, and frequently it is possible to limit the interrupting duty to 25,000 amp. The difference in cost between a substation using 25,000-amp breakers and one using 50,000-amp breakers is a relatively small part of the total cost of the substation. Therefore, it is not economical to make extensive special arrangements to reduce the interrupting duty where it is between 25,000 and 50,000 amp. On the other hand, when it is necessary to install switchgear having an interrupting capacity higher than 50,000 amp, the switchgear may become a large part of the total cost, and considerable expenditures to reduce the interrupting duty to 50,000 amp may be justified. Relatively small substations distributed throughout the building generally mean that the low-voltage feeders will be short and that the voltage regulation will be better. Furthermore, the small substations can be installed in smaller spaces. Frequently, it will be easier to find several small spaces for substations than to find or provide one large space in the building for one substation. Another advantage of using a number of small substations is that it is easier to find space to carry the low-voltage feeder conduits away from the substation.

The form of the network system most frequently used in large buildings is the simple spot-network system. However, a simple network system having several interconnected secondary substations is used in some cases.

When the distribution system in a building is continuously supervised by capable operators, the total transformer capacity sometimes can be reduced by using high-voltage selector switches instead of disconnecting switches on the network transformers. When four or more primary feeders are available, it is generally as economical to use disconnect switches and provide the necessary reserve transformer capacity as to use the more expensive selector switches. Selector switches should not be used in any case where it is likely that the selector switches may not be operated promptly in an emergency.

The distributed type of simple network system is primarily applicable to very large buildings where the low-voltage feeders can be materially shorter with this type of network than if a spot network were used. In such applications, the extra cost of the secondary ties may be more than offset by savings in low-voltage feeder circuits because the substations are located closer to the load centers. This form of network system may also provide better voltage conditions at the load centers than could be provided by a spot network and relatively long, low-voltage feeder circuits.

The spot network is particularly applicable to medium-sized buildings having only a few floors. In these cases, the savings in low-voltage feeders that could be obtained by using two or more small substations in a distributed form of network usually do not justify the expense of the secondary ties and their protective equipment. The spot network, of course, gives the same degree of reliability as does the distributed form of the network. Obviously, two or more spot networks can be used in larger buildings with the same resulting savings in low-voltage feeder circuits. However, this means that there would be a greater number of smaller transformers and a correspondingly greater number of network protectors. The smaller units generally have a higher cost per kva than the larger units, so that a number of small spot networks may cost more than a distributed network in an extensive system.

530. Tall Buildings. Tall buildings are generally built in the densely loaded areas in cities. Almost without exception, the loads in these areas are served by secondary-network systems. This makes it practical and economical to use some form of network system in a tall building. The nature of such a building practically requires a network system. Access to the major part of the building is accomplished almost entirely by elevators. Hence, it is imperative that power be continuously available for operation of the elevators to avoid the hazard of panic or serious inconvenience resulting from a power outage. Furthermore, fire protection, water supply, heating, and ventilating depend for their operation on the availability, at all times, of electric power supply. These considerations practically limit the choice of a distribution system to some form of secondary network. Usually three or more primary feeders are available within the area to supply the building, so that either a simple spot-network system or a simple network system is feasible. Various arrangements of these two systems are used, depending on the height of the building, the location of the major loads within the building, and the total load demand.

In most modern tall commercial buildings there is likely to be a large air-conditioning load. When this load and the other power loads such as elevators, ventilating and heating equipment, fire pumps, water pumps, and related auxiliaries are taken into account, the power demand is likely to be more than the lighting load and may be as much as three or four times the lighting load. This proportion of power and lighting loads should be considered in the choice of utilization voltage. The power load will usually be the principal factor in the choice of locations for the distribution equipment.

Generally speaking, the practical maximum height that 208Y/120-volt circuits can be carried in a tall building is about 12 stories. This limitation depends to a considerable extent on the relative cost of space for the distribution equipment in various parts of the building. The limitation of about 12 stories is based on including in the cost of the distribution system a charge for all the space used above the basements equal to the value of the same amount of commercially usable space. On this basis there is a thumb rule that major distribution centers will occur about every 25 floors in a tall office building. This is a very general rule, and the locations of the elevator equipment and major air-conditioning loads and other power loads in the building may make other locations of the distribution equipment more economical. The locations of the secondary substations involved in the distribution system in the building should be very carefully considered. Some specific comparisons have indicated that a much closer spacing of the secondary substations than 25 stories is economical. A closer spacing of the units improves the voltage conditions within the building and reduces losses in the system.

The simplest form of network system for a tall building is the simple spot-network system. In this system, a spot-network substation comprising the necessary number of network transformers and the associated low-voltage switchgear equipment is located at or near the major loads in the building. Therefore, the spot-network substation in the basement is generally the biggest of the various secondary substations. The locations of the power loads in the basement area or a logical segregation of the load may make two or more spot-network substations feasible. In this form of the network system, several primary-feeder circuits are carried up through the building to the various spot-network substation locations where the corresponding network transformers are connected to the primary feeders.

In many of the locations where tall buildings are built, it is practical to operate the building distribution system as part of the low-voltage secondary network in the area around the building. This involves the use of a simple network system within the building with secondary-tie circuits between the various network substations and the secondary-main system in the area around the building. The ties between the secondary means of the utility network system and the building distribution system permit interchange of power between the two systems. This augments the reliability of the network system within the building and to some extent may improve the voltage conditions within the building. Since the same primary feeders that supply the building may also supply network units in the area around the building, there is some advantage in interconnecting the two systems to make sure that the network equipment all functions in the same manner. The desirability of interconnecting the building network system with a surrounding local network system may offset some of the advantages of a 460-volt system within the building. The network system in the area around the building will be a 208Y/120-volt system in most cases.

The simple network system involves some variations of the secondary ties between the network substations within the building. In their simplest form, these ties are purely tie circuits and do not supply loads at any time except by interchange of power from one substation to another. When this form of secondary tie is used, it generally will have only about two-thirds as much carrying capacity as the rated current of the largest of the associated network transformers. This provides enough capacity to make up for the outage of one transformer at one of the network substations. Generally, the carrying capacity of the tie circuits is practically independent of the number of network units at any load bus. The secondary ties between the building system and the surrounding network system usually have about the same capacity as the ties between network substations within the building.

The capacity of the secondary ties can be increased to provide·for tapping loads directly from the secondary ties between network substations. Basically, such a tie can be treated in two general ways. One way is to form load buses at every point along the tie where loads are tapped as indicated in Fig. 320. If this is done, the capacity of the tie circuit will depend on the amount of load tapped off the circuit and the size of the network units associated with the tie. The capacity should be enough to carry all the loads tapped from the circuit, from one end of the circuit, as well as a reasonable amount of power interchanged between the network substations. In a simple case where single-transformer network substations are interconnected by a tie circuit of this type, the total capacity of the circuit should be about equal to the rated current of one of the associated network transformers.

If load buses are not established in the tie circuit and the loads are tapped from one or another of the parallel branches of the tie circuit, the total carrying capacity of the tie circuit should be correspondingly increased. The reason for this is that it is unlikely that the load can be equally divided among the parallel branches of the tie circuit. Even if equal division of connected load were possible, the diversity among the loads would mean that the load on one branch would not always be the same as that on another. Therefore, in this type of circuit the total carrying capacity should be at least 1⅓ times the rated current of one of the associated transformers where there is only one transformer in each of the interconnected network substations.

The forms of the secondary-tie circuit illustrated in Fig. 320 consider only the use of paralleled three-phase circuits to form the tie circuit because practical and convenient sizes of conductors can be used and overcurrent protection for the circuits can be economically provided.   It is possible, of course, to use a single conductor per phase, such as a heavy bus, to form the tie circuit.   To get the necessary carrying capacity in this way is likely to be expensive, and providing overcurrent protection for such a circuit is expensive and requires heavy protective equipment.

Another form of tie circuit that has been used is a secondary bus running the full height of the building.   This form of tie circuit in effect is an extended spot network with the spot-network bus extending from the basement of the building to the uppermost network unit.   In this arrangement the load circuits at the various floors are connected directly to the riser bus through protective devices or through a switchboard connected to the riser bus through a suitable protective device.   The major disadvantage of this arrangement is the length of the spot-network bus.   It is necessary to install

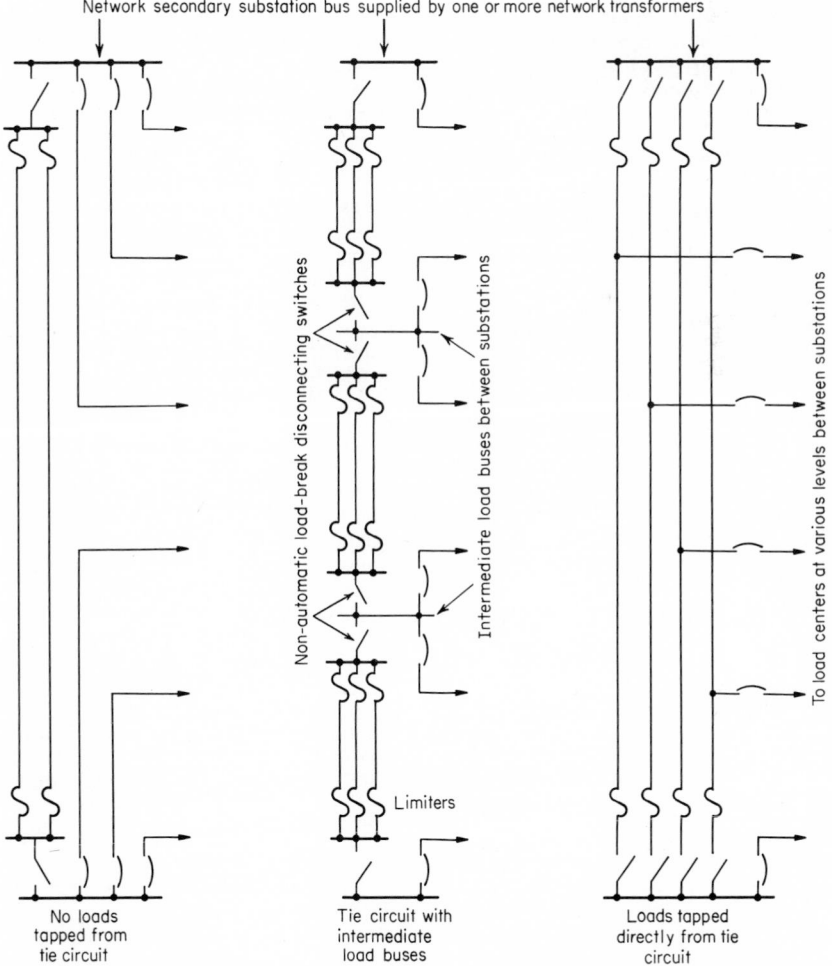

FIG. 320   *Three arrangements of secondary tie circuits between network substations in tall commercial buildings.*

this bus in such a way that there is practically no possibility of a fault on this bus. This can be accomplished by segregation of the phases by barriers between the buses. However, such an installation is expensive. The capacity of such a bus should be somewhat more than the total load connected to the bus between adjacent network transformers. Some excess above this total load value would be required for the interchange of power between network units when one of the primary feeder circuits is out of service.

The distribution of power within a tall building necessarily involves the use of transformers within the building. It is very important to choose transformers that minimize the possibility of fire or other damage to the building or injury to people in the building resulting from a transformer failure. For this reason, ventilated or sealed dry-type transformers are used in buildings. These types of transformers eliminate the hazard of fire and explosion damage resulting from a transformer failure.

531. Large Horizontal Buildings. Under the classification of large horizontal buildings, probably the most important with respect to numbers, size, and magnitude of load are shopping centers.

Shopping centers may be classified into three types with regard to size. They are the neighborhood shopping center that is designed to serve 5,000 to 20,000 people, the district shopping center that serves 20,000 to 100,000 people, and the regional shopping center that serves a market of over 100,000 people.

Shopping centers will usually take one of the five general physical arrangements. The simplest type, usually associated with the neighborhood shopping center, is the strip layout. A common variation of this simple layout is the L-shape layout.

The mall, the court, and the ring are three layouts that are used mostly in the district shopping center.

The fifth type, the group or cluster of buildings, is generally used for the large regional shopping centers.

The physical layout of a shopping center will have an influence on the design of the electric distribution system. For instance, a system utilizing a loop secondary circuit can be used to advantage in the mall-, ring-, or group-type shopping centers but may not be economical for the strip or court arrangement. The large loads in a shopping center will usually dictate where the power-center transformers must be located. If power centers must be located at these large loads, the loads in between them may be served over radial circuits from the power centers. However, if the distance between the power centers becomes great, using a system that permits the tapping of services off a secondary circuit running between power centers would be advantageous.

The selection of the utilization voltage or voltages to be used in shopping centers should not be limited to the choice of 120/240 volts single-phase, 440 volts three-phase, or 208Y/120 volts three-phase. The magnitude, locations, and characteristics of the loads in shopping centers make it appear that the use of a three-phase, four-wire, grounded-wye, 460Y/265-volt system would prove to be more economical in many cases.

Table **532** compares the distribution systems discussed previously for several magnitudes of load in each of the five types of shopping centers. The comparisons are made on a column basis, and it is not intended that the ratings in different columns should be compared.

The ratings take into account initial investment, service continuity, flexibility to handle new or changing loads, operation and maintenance costs, voltage regulation, and efficiency. Each of these factors has been weighted in proportion to its relative importance for each load magnitude and type of shopping center. The A ratings indicate that analysis of the system has shown it to rate as the top of the 12 systems compared in each column. The other quality ratings are given in terms of percentage of value of the A system.

Rating	Per Cent
B	81–90
C	71–80
D	61–70
E	51–60
F	41–50

532. Comparison of Distribution Systems for Several Types of Shopping Centers

(Type of shopping center, loads in kva)

	Strip or L			Mall			Court			Ring			Group or cluster		
	100–1,000	1,000–2,500	2,500 and up	100–1,000	1,000–2,500	2,500 and up	100–1,000	1,000–2,500	2,500 and up	100–1,000	1,000–2,500	2,500 and up	1,000–2,500	2,500–5,000	5,000 and up
Conv. simple-radial	D	D	E	E	E	F+	D	D	E	E	E	F+	E	F+	F
Modern simple-radial	A	A	B	A−	B−	C	A	A	B	A−	B−	C	B−	C	D
Modified modern simple-radial	C	C	C	B+	D	D−	C	C	C	C	D	D−	D	D−	E
Loop-primary radial	A	A	B+	B	B	C	A	A	B+	B+	B	C	B	C	D
Banked-secondary radial	C	C	B	B	B−	C	C	C	B	B	B−	C	B−	C	C
Primary-selective radial	B−	B	B	D	C	D+	B−	B	B	B	C	D+	C	D+	D
Secondary-selective radial	C−	C	C	D	D	D−	C−	C	C	D	D	D−	D	D−	E
Modified secondary-selective radial	D	C	C	D	D	D−	C	C	C	D	D	D−	D	D−	E
Simple network	C	B	A−	B+	A−	A	D	D	A−	B+	A−	A	A−	A	A
Simple spot-network	D	C−	A	A	A	B	B−	B−	A−	A	B	A	B	A	A
Primary-selective network	C	B	A	B	A	A	D	C−	A	A	B	A	B	A	A
Primary-selective spot-network	C	B	B	B	B	B	C	B	B	B	B	B	B	B	B

9–271

533. Methods of Supplying Power to Individual Motor Loads. The layout of the last stage of a motor distribution system will depend upon the type of building, construction characteristics of the building, motor size, types of motors to be served, and the flexibility desired in order to take care of changing location of loads. In one type of layout the branch circuit to each motor is run from a power panel. In another type of layout the branch circuits to individual motors are tapped from a feeder. The features of the different types of motor distribution layouts are shown in Fig. 321.

The following discussion of the application of these methods is reproduced from "Electrical Systems Design" by McPartland.

Miscellaneous motor loads in the majority of commercial and institutional buildings and in many industrial buildings are usually circuited from power panels to which feeders deliver power. This type of distribution is a standard method of motor circuiting, generally limited to handling a number of motors of small integral-horsepower or fractional-horsepower sizes, located in a relatively small area such as a fan room or pump room. The feeder to a power panel may be a riser in a multistory commercial or institutional building, run from a basement switchboard. In a one-level industrial area, the feeder to a power panel may be run from a main or load-center switchboard or from a load-center substation in a high-voltage distribution system. In commercial and industrial buildings, motor feeders may be run from a main switchboard or a load-center substation to a motor-control center serving a large group of motors in a machine room or in any compact area where the motors are relatively close together and close to the control center assembly. The motor-control center contains all the control, protection, and disconnecting means for the motor circuits supplied.

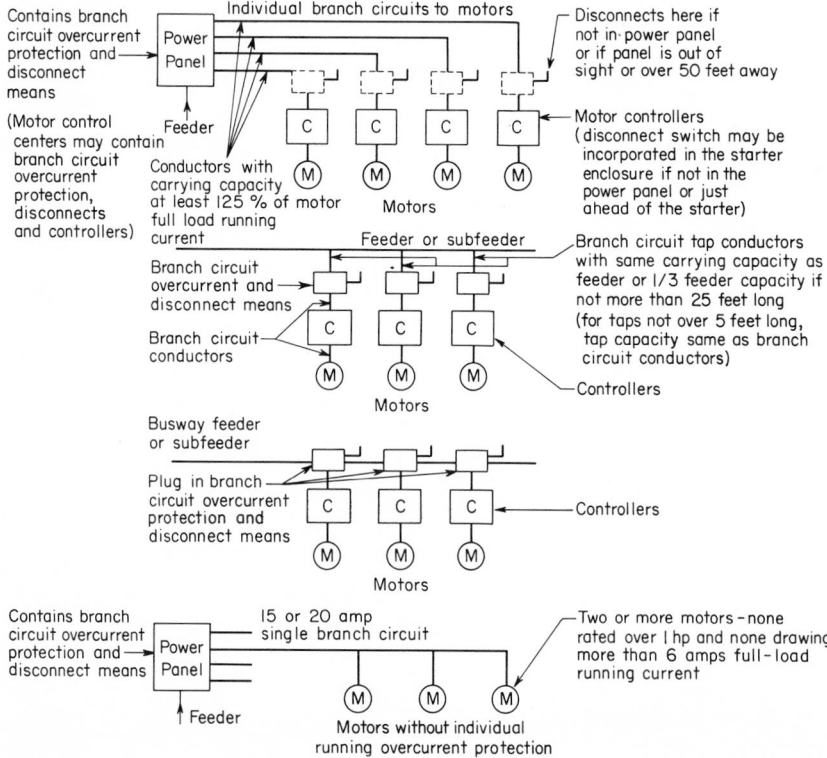

FIG. 321 *Methods of power distribution to individual motors.* (*Electrical Systems Design.*)

In industrial buildings, where a large number of motors are used over a large area, distribution of power to the individual motor loads generally follows the method of tapping motor branch circuits from the feeder. Such circuits may be tapped in several ways, with various combinations of branch-circuit overcurrent protection and motor control and disconnect means. The feeder in such an arrangement may originate from a main switchboard or from a load-center substation. In multistory buildings, such as office buildings or institutions, taps to motor branch circuits on a particular floor may be taken from a subfeeder originating in a load-center switchboard which is fed by a riser from the main switchboard in the basement. The feeder-tap method of supplying motor branch circuits is, of course, the basis for plug-in busway distribution to spread-out motor loads. In the system, the plug-in busway may be a feeder or subfeeder depending upon its origin. From a main switchboard, it would be a feeder. From a load-center switchboard, it would be a subfeeder. However, from a load-center substation, the plug-in busway would be a feeder—a secondary feeder derived from the transformation down from the primary feeder to the substation.

534. Adequate Wiring for Lighting and Convenience Outlets in Commercial, Public, and Industrial Structures. It is very important in designing the interior wiring for a building to make adequate provisions not only for the present demands but also for the probable future demands. The levels of illumination demanded by industry and commerce are being constantly increased. In order that a building may keep pace with this advancement without an excessive expense in the reconstruction of its wiring, it is necessary that the wiring be more than adequate to provide merely for the present needs. Double carrying capacity can be provided in the original wiring installation for less than 25 per cent additional cost. In order to provide a guide for adequate wiring, the following recommendations from the "Handbook of Interior Wiring Design" are given:

1. OUTLET LOCATION. COMMERCIAL AND PUBLIC OCCUPANCIES. *a. Ceiling Outlets for General Illumination.* Whenever possible, ceiling outlets should be uniformly spaced and located so that the spacing will be approximately the same in both directions. In **offices** and **schoolrooms,** the spacing between adjacent outlets shall not exceed the distance from floor to ceiling. In other interiors, the space may be extended to 1¼ times the ceiling height. The space between an outlet and a wall should not exceed one-half of the average distance between outlets. In **halls** and **corridors,** spacing should not exceed 20 ft.

In locating outlets on any floor plan, building construction features should be considered, especially ceiling beams. These are not always shown on the floor plans, yet they may seriously affect a lighting layout. This is particularly true for indirect lighting.

b. Stores — Convenience Outlets. There shall be installed at least one convenience outlet for each 400 sq ft of floor area or major part thereof, these outlets to be uniformly distributed over the entire area. Preference shall be given to the placing of these outlets in supporting columns and side walls, but no part of the floor area shall be more than 15 ft from an outlet.

c. Stores — Outlets for Window Illumination. Provision for show-window illumination shall be made by (1) a junction box on wall or column at suitable height above transom bar or possible false ceiling to which all circuits of show-window reflectors or spotlights can be connected or (2) individual outlets spaced as recommended below.

For medium screw lamp holders, outlets for show-window reflectors should be located 12 to 18 in. apart. For mogul screw lamp holders, outlets for show-window reflectors should be located 15 to 24 in. apart; for fluorescent lamps, as required by the lighting layout. The specific layout is to be governed by the standard loads of Sec. **535.** Whenever more than one circuit per window is necessary, adjacent outlets should be on different circuits.

For spot or floodlights, at least two outlets per window shall be symmetrically placed, with an additional outlet for every 8 ft (or major fraction) in excess of 16 ft.

d. Stores — Convenience Outlets in Show Windows. In or near the floor of each window, there shall be installed at least one convenience outlet for each 50 sq ft of platform or floor area used for window display, but in no case shall there be less than two convenience outlets per window.

e. Stores—Outlets for Case Lighting. Outlets shall be provided in the floor or wall for termination of the circuits for show-case and wall-case lighting. Such outlets shall be suitably located for connection to the lighting equipment and shall be governed by the standard loads as listed in Sec. **535** (Show Cases, Wall Cases).

f. Offices and Schools, Convenience Outlets. In each separate office room with 400 sq ft or less of floor area, there shall be installed at least one convenience outlet for each 20 lin ft of wall space. In each separate office with more than 400 sq ft of floor area, there shall be installed at least four convenience outlets for the first 400 sq ft of floor area and at least two outlets for each additional 400 sq ft or major fraction thereof. Outlets should be placed at suitable locations to serve all parts of the office space. Certain offices, as, for example, professional and display offices, require many more outlets than are specified above, and the wiring needs must be individually studied where such probable occupancy is known.

For typical schoolrooms at least one convenience outlet shall be placed along the front wall and at least one along the rear wall.

g. Offices and Stores—Fans. Unless made unnecessary by provision for complete air-conditioning, outlets for fans shall be installed on the basis of at least two for each 400 sq ft or major portion thereof. Such outlets shall be placed approximately 7 ft above the floor and shall be of a type from which the fan may be mechanically suspended.

h. Stores—Signs. Where no other equivalent provision is made for sign lighting, a rigid metal conduit or electrical metallic tubing, not smaller than 1 in., shall be run to the front face of the building for each intended or probable individual store occupancy. Such raceway shall terminate outside the building at a point suitable for connection to the sign and shall terminate inside the building at a cabinet. Feeder capacity to this cabinet and service capacity shall be based upon a sign load of not less than 50 watts per lineal foot of store frontage, only the frontage on the principal street being considered if the store faces more than one street. Space provision shall be allowed for the connection and placement of a time switch to the sign circuit.

2. OUTLET LOCATION. INDUSTRIAL OCCUPANCIES. *a. Ceiling Outlets for General Illumination.* The many special considerations of industrial lighting make it necessary to develop the outlet locations around the lighting layout. Local lighting units frequently supplement general illuminations; special directional overhead sources are often necessary. In planning outlet locations, these must be considered as part of the complete installation. In halls and corridors lighted from a single row of outlets, the spacing between outlets shall not exceed 20 ft.

b. Convenience Outlets. At least one convenience outlet in each bay in both manufacturing and storage spaces.

3. STANDARD LOADS FOR GENERAL ILLUMINATION. The number of branch circuits and the capacities of the feeders and service shall be based upon the loads specified in Secs. **535** and **536** as minimum. Where a known load is to be supplied that will exceed the loading here specified, the circuits, feeders, and service shall be based upon such known load.

The tabulated values represent the present acceptable standards of IES foot-candle values. From these, the watts per square foot for each occupancy were determined by considering average conditions found in such occupancy, together with the accepted methods and equipment used in providing such illumination levels. In certain cases the standard loads include allowance for convenience outlets as well as for general illumination. The calculated wattage standards were based on the use of fluorescent and mercury-vapor equipment for large areas and incandescent for local and supplementary lighting.

4. BRANCH CIRCUITS.[1] The minimum number of branch circuits shall be based on the present connected load as follows:

a. For two-wire 15-amp circuits, the load per circuit shall not exceed 1,000 watts.

b. For multiwire 15-amp circuits, the load shall not exceed 1,000 watts between each outside wire and the neutral.

---

[1] These standards are based upon 15-amp protection of branch circuits. If local regulations limit the load on branch circuits to less than these requirements, the wattage and area limits herein specified must be proportionately reduced.

c. For circuits designed for heavy-duty lamp holders, the load per circuit shall not exceed 1,500 watts for No. 10 wire, 2,500 watts for No. 8, and 3,000 watts for No. 6.

The following considerations of wire size and circuit runs shall apply:

d. No wire smaller than No. 12 shall be used for any circuit.

e. Where the run from a panel board to the first outlet of a lighting branch circuit exceeds 50 ft, the size of wire used shall be at least one size larger than that determined by any of the above considerations. The calculated size may be used between outlets.

f. Where the run from a panel board to the first outlet of a convenience-outlet circuit exceeds 100 ft, No. 10 wire or larger shall be used for such run.

g. No runs longer than 100 ft between panel board and the first outlet of a lighting branch circuit shall be made unless the intended load is so small that the voltage drop can be restricted to 2 per cent between panel board and any outlet on that circuit. To avoid this condition, panel boards should be relocated or additional panel boards installed.

The following considerations in regard to combinations of outlets shall apply:

h. No convenience outlet shall be supplied by the same branch circuit that supplies ceiling or show-window lighting outlets.

i. Outlets for show-window spotlights shall be on separate circuits from general show-window outlets.

j. The number of convenience outlets included on one circuit shall be based on the listing in the following table.

Outlets per Circuit

Location	Max
Barber shops, beauty parlors, etc.	2
Medical, dental, and similar offices	2
Store show windows (for spotlights)	3
Store show windows (at floor)	6
Display areas in retail stores	6
School classrooms	6
Manufacturing spaces	6
Office spaces	8
Storage spaces	10

5. CIRCUIT CONTROL. Suitable provision shall be made for the control of all circuits except those supplying convenience outlets only, and control of the latter circuits is recommended. Circuits may be controlled individually, in groups, or by a combination of both methods.

In a retail store, individual control at the panel boards by means of circuit switches or circuit breakers is usually preferable. In most other occupancies, control should be provided by means of local switches or circuit breakers. Frequently it is necessary to provide two or more switches for the local control of outlets supplied by a single branch circuit.

Provision shall be made for control of all circuits supplying a single sign by means of an external manually operable switch or circuit breaker, and in each case a suitable time switch shall also be provided to effect the same control.

In a retail store, each circuit supplying outlets in one or more show windows shall be individually controlled, and provision shall be made for the installation of a time switch for group control of all such circuits.

Group control of circuits for general illumination or for special decorative effects, by means of remote-control switches, is desirable in certain large spaces such as large offices, large reading rooms, museums, art galleries, and ballrooms.

6. PANEL BOARDS. The number and location of panel boards shall be based on the number of branch circuits and the distance or runs as specified in paragraph 4 of these adequacy standards.

On each panel board one spare circuit shall be provided for each five circuits utilized in the initial installation. Where flush-type cabinets are used, provision shall be made for bringing a corresponding number of circuit conductors to the ceiling of the story served, or to the ceiling of the story immediately below, or to both points. Such provision may consist of circuit conductors or empty raceways terminating in boxes suitably located for future extensions.

Provision shall be made for control of show-window lighting by such grouping of circuits to a panel board as to enable a time switch to be suitably installed.

7. FEEDERS. *a. Carrying Capacity.* The carrying capacity of each feeder or subfeeder shall be based on the number of separate circuits which it supplies, computed as follows:

(1) *Overhead Lighting Circuits.* Assumed as having 1,000 watts for each 15-amp circuit and 1,500 watts for each 20-amp circuit.

(2) *Convenience-outlet Circuits.* Assumed load of 1,000 watts per circuit.

(3) *Spare Panel-board Circuits.* Assumed load of 500 watts.

(4) *Nonitemized and Heavy-duty Additional Circuits.* Specific load for which designed.

To the total of these four, such demand factors as permitted by the National Electrical Code may be applied. (Refer to Div. 3 for additional information.)

b. Provision for Future. In all determinations of feeder size, consideration should be given to increasing the capacity of the initial system by 50 per cent to provide for future growth at a minimum of unwarranted expense. In cases where an ultimate feeder size does not exceed No. 4 wire, the excess capacity should be installed immediately. In other cases, one of the following methods should be made a part of the original layout.

(1) The installation of oversize raceways, so that the conductors installed can be withdrawn at any time and replaced by conductors of suitable larger size.

(2) The installation or arrangement of the installed equipment so that additional feeders can be installed later at a minimum of expense to furnish the ultimate capacity.

(3) The installation of feeders of excess size.

c. Voltage Drop. Feeders and subfeeders shall be of such size that the total voltage drop from any panel board to the point where connection is made to the lines of the utility supplying services shall not exceed 1 per cent (see Div. 3 for method of calculation). To compute such drop, the ultimate demand as calculated above shall be used wherever the wire size based on such demand is installed immediately. Where provision for the future is made in some other way (oversize raceways, etc.), the voltage drop shall be computed on the basis of the carrying capacity of the wire used.

8. FEEDER DISTRIBUTION CENTER. A feeder distribution center in the form of a panel board, switchboard, or group of enclosed switches or circuit breakers shall be provided for the control and protection of each feeder.

Except where oversize feeders are provided in the original installation as recommended in the preceding section, provision shall be made at the feeder distribution center for the connection and suitable protection of feeders of increased size or of supplemental feeders. This can be accomplished by providing additional protective devices as part of the original installation, or by so designing the original equipment that space, bus capacity, and facilities for making connections will be available.

9. SERVICE-ENTRANCE ADEQUACY STANDARDS (75°C RATED COPPER CONDUCTORS):

Initial load, amp	Service switch, amp	Conductor size, gage No. or cir mils	Initial load, amp	Service switch, amp	Conductor size, gage No. or cir mils
1– 23	60	8	118–133	200	4/0
24– 33	60	6	134–150	400	4/0
34– 47	100	4			
48– 60	100	2	151–167	400	250,000
61– 67	100	1	168–183	400	300,000
			184–200	400	350,000
68– 83	200	1/0	201–217	400	400,000
84–100	200	2/0	218–267	400	500,000
101–117	200	3/0			

10. SERVICE CONDUCTORS AND EQUIPMENT. The minimum capacity of the service required for the initial load depends on the total number of feeders supplied by it, whose individual loads are determined as specified in paragraph 7. Where applicable, demand factors as permitted by the National Electrical Code may be used (see Sec. **44** of Div. 3). To determine the probable required ultimate capacity of the service conductors and equipment, 50 per cent should be added to the calculated initial load.

Where the calculated initial load does not exceed 267 amp, service conductors and equipment having the capacity needed for the ultimate load should be included as part of the original installation. The recommended equipment for various initial loads is tabulated in paragraph 9.

Where the initial load exceeds 267 amp, a study should be made of each individual case to determine what provision should be made for a future increase in the load.

535. Standard Loads for Lighting in Commercial Buildings

Occupancy	Watts per sq ft	Occupancy	Watts per sq ft
Armories: drill sheds and exhibition halls. (This does not include lighting circuits for demonstration booths, special exhibit spaces, etc.)	5	Minor surgeries—1,500 watts per area This and the above figure include allowance for directional control. Special wiring for emergency systems must also be considered	
Art galleries:		Laboratories	5
General	3	Hotels:	
On paintings—50 watts per running foot of usable wall area		Lobby, not including provision for conventions, exhibits	5
Auditoriums	4	Dining room	4
Automobile showrooms	6	Kitchen	5
Banks:		Bedrooms, including allowance for convenience outlets	3
Lobby	4	Corridors—20 watts per running foot	
Counters—50 watts per running foot including service for signs and small motor applications, etc.		Writing room, including allowance for convenience outlets	5
Offices and cages	5	Library:	
Barber shop and beauty parlors. (This does not include circuits for special equipment)	5	Reading rooms. This includes allowance for convenience outlets	6
Billiards:		Stack room—12 watts per running foot of facing stacks	
General	3	Motion-picture houses and theaters:	
Tables—450 watts per table.		Auditoriums	2
Bowling:		Foyer	3
Alley runway and seats	5	Lobby	5
Pins—300 watts per set of pins		Museums:	
Churches:		General	3
Auditoriums	2	Special exhibits—supplementary lighting	5
Sunday-school rooms	5	Office buildings:	
Pulpit or rostrum	5	Private offices, no close work	5
Club rooms:		Private offices, with close work	7
Lounge	2	General offices, no close work	5
Reading rooms	5	General offices, with close work	7
The above two uses are so often combined that the higher figure is advisable. It includes provision for convenience outlets		File room, vault, etc.	3
		Reception room	2
Courtrooms	5	Post office:	
Dance halls. (No allowance has been included for spectacular lighting, spots, etc.)	2	Lobby	3
		Sorting, mailing, etc.	5
Drafting rooms	7	Storage, file room, etc.	3
Fire-engine houses	2	Professional offices:	
Gymnasiums:		Waiting rooms	3
Main floor	5	Consultation rooms	5
Shower rooms	2	Operating offices	7
Locker rooms	2	Dental chairs—600 watts per chair	
Fencing, boxing, etc.	5	Railway:	
Handball, squash, etc.	5	Depot—waiting room	3
Halls and interior passageways—20 watts per running foot		Ticket offices—general	5
Hospitals:		On counters 50 watts per running foot	
Lobby, reception room	3	Rest room, smoking room	3
Corridors—20 watts per running foot		Baggage, checking office	3
Wards, including allowance for convenience outlets for local illumination	3	Baggage storage	2
		Concourse	2
Private rooms, including allowance for convenience outlets for local illumination	5	Train platform	2
		Restaurants, lunchrooms, and cafeterias:	
Operating room	5	Dining areas	3
Operating tables or chairs:		Food displays—50 watts per running foot of counter (including service aisle)	
Major surgeries—3,000 watts per area		Schools:	
		Auditoriums	3
		If to be used as a study hall—5 watts per sq ft	

Standard Loads for Lighting in Commercial Buildings (*Continued*)

Occupancy	Watts per sq ft	Occupancy	Watts per sq ft
Schools (Continued):		Medium cities:[a]	
Class and study rooms..............	5	Brightly lighted district—500 watts per running foot of glass	
Drawing room.....................	7		
Laboratories......................	5	Neighborhood stores—250 watts per running foot of glass frontage	
Manual training...................	5		
Sewing room......................	7	Small cities and towns—300 watts per running foot of glass frontage[a]	
Sight-saving classes................	7		
Showcases—25 watts per running foot		Lighting to reduce daylight window reflections—1,000 watts per running foot of glass	
Show windows:			
Large cities:[a]		Stores, large department and specialty:	
Brightly lighted district—700 watts per running foot of glass		Main floor..........................	6
Secondary business locations—500 watts per running foot of glass		Other floors.........................	6
		Stores in outlying districts..............	5
Neighborhood stores—250 watts per running foot of glass		Wall cases—25 watts per running foot	

NOTE. Figures based on use of fluorescent equipment for large-area application, incandescent for local or supplementary lighting.

[a] Wattages shown are for white light with incandescent filament lamps. Where color is to be used, wattages should be doubled.

536. Standard Loads for General Lighting in Industrial Occupancies

Occupancy	Watts per sq ft	Occupancy	Watts per sq ft
Aisles, stairways, passageways 10 watts per running foot		Cloth products:	
Assembly:		Cutting, inspecting, sewing:	
Rough.........................	3.0	Light goods.....................	4.5
Medium.......................	4.5	Dark goods.....................	*4.5
Fine..........................	*4.5	Pressing, cloth treating (oil cloth, etc.):	
Extra fine.....................	*4.5	Light goods.....................	3.0
Automobile manufacturing:		Dark goods.....................	6.0
Assembly line..................	*4.5	Coal breaking, washing, screening.......	2.0
Frame assembly................	3.0	Dairy products........................	4.0
Body assembly.................	4.5	Engraving............................	*4.5
Body finishing and inspecting........	*4.5	Forge shops, welding..................	2.0
Bakeries............................	4.0	Foundries:	
Book binding:		Charging floor, tumbling, cleaning, pouring, shaking out..............	2.0
Folding, assembling, pasting.........	3.0		
Cutting, punching, stitching, embossing	4.0	Rough molding and core making......	2.0
Breweries:		Fine molding and core making........	4.0
Brewhouse.....................	3.0	Garages:	
Boiling, keg washing, etc............	3.0	Storage...........................	2.0
Bottling.......................	4.0	Repair and washing.................	*3.0
Candy making......................	4.0	Glassworks:	
Canning and preserving..............	4.0	Mixing and furnace rooms, pressing and Lehr glass-blowing machines....	3.0
Chemical works:			
Hand furnaces, stationary driers and crystallizers.....................	2.0	Grinding, cutting glass to size, silvering.	4.5
		Fine grinding, polishing, beveling, etching, inspecting, etc.................	*4.5
Mechanical driers and crystallizers, filtrations, evaporators, bleaching...	2.0		
		Glove manufacturing:	
Tanks for cooking, extractors, percolators, nitrators, electrolytic cells.....	3.0	Light goods:	
		Cutting, pressing, knitting, sorting..	4.5
Clay products and cements		Stitching, trimming, inspecting.....	4.5
Grinding, filter presses, kiln rooms.....	2.0	Dark goods:	
Moldings, pressing, cleaning, trimming.	2.0	Cutting, pressing, etc..............	*4.5
Enameling.........................	3.0	Stitching, trimming, etc...........	*4.5
Glazing............................	4.0	Hangars—aeroplane:	
		Storage—live......................	2.0

Standard Loads for General Lighting in Industrial Occupancies (*Continued*)

Occupancy	Watts per sq ft	Occupancy	Watts per sq ft
Hangars (Continued):		Fine hand painting and finishing......	*3.0
Repair department.................	*3.0	Extra-fine hand painting and finishing	
Hat manufacturing:		(automobile bodies, piano cases, etc.).	*3.0
Dyeing, stiffening, braiding, cleaning,		Paper-box manufacturing:	
and refining:		Light............................	3.0
Light...........................	2.0	Dark............................	4.0
Dark...........................	4.5	Storage of stock....................	2.0
Forming, sizing, pouncing, flanging,		Paper manufacturing:	
finishing, and ironing:		Beaters, grinding, calendering........	2.0
Light...........................	3.0	Finishing, cutting, trimming..........	4.5
Dark...........................	6.0	Plating.............................	2.0
Sewing:		Polishing and burnishing..............	3.0
Light...........................	4.5	Power plants, engine rooms, boilers:	
Dark...........................	*4.5	Boilers, coal and ash handling, storage-	
Ice making, engine and compressor room.	2.0	battery rooms....................	2.0
Inspection:		Auxiliary equipment, oil switches and	
Rough...........................	3.0	transformers.....................	2.0
Medium.........................	4.5	Switchboard, engines, generators, blow-	
Fine.............................	*4.5	ers, compressors..................	3.0
Extra fine........................	*4.5	Printing industries:	
Leather manufacturing:		Matrixing and casting...............	2.0
Vats.............................	2.0	Miscellaneous machines..............	3.0
Cleaning, tanning, and stretching.....	2.0	Presses and electrotyping............	4.5
Cutting, fleshing, and stuffing.........	3.0	Lithographing......................	*4.5
Finishing and scarfing...............	4.5	Linotype, monotype, typesetting, im-	
Leatherworking:		posing stone, engraving............	*4.5
Pressing, winding, and glazing:		Proof reading......................	*4.5
Light...........................	2.0	Receiving and shipping...............	2.0
Dark...........................	4.5	Rubber manufacturing and products:	
Grading, matching, cutting, scarfing,		Calendars, compounding mills, fabric	
sewing:		preparation, stock cutting, tubing	
Light...........................	4.5	machines, solid tire operations, me-	
Dark...........................	*4.5	chanical goods, building, vulcanizing.	3.0
Locker rooms.......................	2.0	Bead building, pneumatic-tire building	
Machine shops:		and finishing, inner-tube operation,	
Rough bench- and machine work......	3.0	mechanical-goods trimming, treading	4.5
Medium bench- and machine work,		Sheet-metal works:	
ordinary automatic machines, rough		Miscellaneous machines, ordinary	
grinding, medium buffing and polish-		bench work.....................	3.0
ing............................	4.5	Punches, presses, shears, stamps,	
Fine bench- and machine work, fine		welders, spinning, medium bench-	
automatic machines, medium grind-		work...........................	4.5
ing, fine buffing and polishing.......	*4.5	Tin-plate inspection.................	*4.5
Extra-fine bench- and machine work,		Shoe manufacturing:	
grinding, fine work................	*4.5	Hand turning, miscellaneous bench-	
Meat packing:		and machine work................	2.0
Slaughtering.......................	2.0	Inspecting and sorting raw material,	
Cleaning, cutting, cooking, grinding,		cutting, and stitching:	
canning, packing..................	4.5	Light............................	4.5
Milling—grain foods:		Dark............................	*4.5
Cleaning, grinding, and rolling........	2.0	Lasting and welting.................	4.5
Baking or roasting...................	4.5	Soap manufacturing:	
Flour grading......................	4.5	Kettle houses, cutting, soap chip and	
Offices:		powder.........................	3.0
Private and general:		Stamping, wrapping and packing, fill-	
No close work....................	5.0	ing, and packing soap powder.......	4.5
Close work......................	7.0	Steel and iron mills: bar, sheet and wire	
Drafting rooms.....................	7.0	products:	
Packing and boxing..................	3.0	Soaking pits and reheating furnaces...	2.0
Paint manufacturing.................	3.0	Charging and casting floors..........	2.0
Paint shops:		Muck and heavy rolling, shearing	
Dipping, spraying, firing, rubbing,		(rough by gage), pickling, and clean-	
ordinary hand painting and finishing.	3.0	ing.............................	2.0
		Plate inspection, chipping...........	*4.5

Standard Loads for General Lighting in Industrial Occupancies (*Continued*)

Occupancy	Watts per sq ft	Occupancy	Watts per sq ft
Steel and iron mills (Continued):		Silk:	
Automatic machines, light and cold rolling, wire drawing, shearing (fine by line)................	4.5	Winding, throwing, dyeing........	4.5
		Quilling, warping, weaving, finishing:	
Stone crushing and screening:		Light goods....................	4.5
Belt-conveyor tubes, main-line shafting spaces, chute rooms, inside of bins...........................	2.0	Dark goods....................	6.0
		Woolen:	
		Carding, picking, washing, combing..	3.0
Primary breaker room, auxiliary breakers under bins..................	2.0	Twisting, dyeing.................	3.0
Screens...........................	3.0	Drawing-in, warping:	
Storage-battery manufacturing, molding of grids...........................	3.0	Light goods....................	4.5
		Dark goods....................	6.0
Store- and stock rooms:		Weaving:	
Rough bulky material................	2.0	Light goods....................	4.5
Medium or fine material requiring care.	3.0	Dark goods....................	6.0
Structural-steel fabrication.............	3.0	Knitting machines................	4.5
Sugar grading......................	5.0	Tobacco products:	
Testing:		Drying, stripping, general...........	3.0
Rough...........................	3.0	Grading and sorting...............	*4.5
Fine.............................	4.5	Toilet and wash rooms................	2.0
Extra-fine instruments, scales, etc.....	*4.5	Upholstering, automobile, coach, furniture.........................	4.5
Textile mills:		Warehouse.........................	2.0
Cotton:		Woodworking:	
Opening and lapping, carding, drawing, roving, dyeing..............	3.0	Rough sawing and benchwork........	2.0
		Sizing, planing, rough sanding, medium machine and bench-work, gluing, veneering, cooperage..............	4.5
Spooling, spinning, drawing, warping, weaving, quilling, inspecting, knitting, slashing (over beam end).	4.5	Fine bench- and machine work, fine sanding and finishing............	6.0

The figures given in this table are average design loads for general lighting. In those cases marked with an asterisk (*), the load values provide only for large-area lighting applications. Local lighting must then be provided as an additional load.

The figures given are based on the use of fluorescent and mercury-vapor equipment of standard design. Adjustments can be made for use of higher or lower efficiency equipment. For equal lighting intensities from incandescent units, the figures must be at least doubled.

Use of these figures in computing number and loading of circuits and feeders should always be checked against the conditions and requirements of the particular area. The figures are not substitutes for lighting design.

In any case, need for particular color quality of light, special intensities, or control of light must be determined as part of the lighting design, and wattages and circuit requirements must be provided accordingly.

537. Allowance for growth in feeders ("Electrical Systems Design") should begin with the spare capacity designed into the branch circuits. For all circuits loaded to 50 per cent of capacity, it can be assumed that there is an allowance for growth of each circuit load by an amount equal to 30 per cent of the circuit capacity. This allowance is based on the Code limitation of 80 per cent load on circuits which are in operation for 3 hr or longer or on circuits which supply motor-operated appliances in addition to other appliances and/or lighting. The 30 per cent growth allowance in each circuit should be converted to total watts figure and added to the total load on the feeder as calculated above. This grand total then represents the required feeder capacity to handle the full circuit load on the panel board. The next step is to provide capacity in the feeder for anticipated load growth (plus some amount for possible unforeseen future requirements).

From experience, modern design practice dictates the sizing of feeders to allow increase of at least 50 per cent in load on a feeder where analysis reveals any load-growth possibilities. Such analysis depends upon the type of building, the work performed, the plans or expectations of management with respect to expansion of facilities or growth of business, the type of distribution system used, locations of centers of loads, permanence of various load conditions, and particular economic conditions. Depending upon thorough study of all these factors, the advisability of spare capacity can be determined for each feeder in a distribution system. But where study demands extra capacity in a feeder, substantial growth allowance—50 per cent—is generally essential to realize the sought-after economy of future electrical expansion. Skimpy upsizing of feeder conductors or raceways has proved a major shortcoming of past electrical design work. This is particularly true in tall office buildings, apartment houses, and other commercial buildings in which elimination of riser bottlenecks represents a large part of the total modernization cost.

Spare capacity in feeders may be provided in one or more of several ways. If the anticipated increase in feeder load is to be made in the near future, the extra capacity should usually be included in the conductor size and installed as part of the initial electrical system. In many small office or commercial buildings and apartment houses, extra capacity should automatically be included in the initial size of the feeder conductors, provided the size is not greater than No. 2 after adding the 50 per cent of extra capacity. Other methods of providing for growth in feeder load are as follows:

1. Selection of raceways larger than required by the initial size and number of feeder conductors. With this provision, the conductors can be replaced with larger sizes if required at a later date. The advisability of this step should be carefully determined in the case of risers or underground or concealed feeder raceway runs. In some cases, a compromise can be made between providing spare capacity in the feeder conductor size and up-sizing the feeder raceway.

2. Including spare raceways in which conductors can be installed at a later date to obtain capacity for load growth. Such arrangements of multiple raceways must be carefully laid out and related to the existing over-all system. The types of feeder distribution centers or main switchboards and the layouts of local branch-circuit panel boards must be able to accommodate future expansion of distribution capacity based on the use of spare raceways, with modification and regrouping of feeder loads.

538. Control of Groups of Receivers (Other than Hall or Night Lights) from the Main Switchboard. Where it is desirable to control a group of receivers from the main switchboard in the basement, a separate feeder must be carried from it to each group to be so controlled. Usually the feeder system can be laid out without regard to the control of the room lights, because, as a rule, they do not have to be controlled from the switchboard. It is usually advisable to have each of the lower floors, up to and including the ground floor, on a separate switch, as these floors often require light when the others do not. Special lighting appliances such as sign, clock-dial, and outside dome lights require separate feeders from the switchboard, because they are turned on and off at set times from the switchboard. Certain motors may require similar control. In hotels the feeder switches are never opened except in case of accident so, from a control standpoint only, it is not necessary to subdivide hotel feeders. Where tenants of portions of buildings pay for the light they use, it is often desirable to carry a separate feeder from the switchboard to each tenant's suite so that all meters can be located together at the switchboard. Suites can be metered separately by cutting meters in the mains at the suites, but this may be undesirable.

539. The control of hall lights from the main switchboard is an important consideration. In private dwellings it does not usually pay to install a separate feeder for the hall lights, and it may not be necessary in a hotel, where attendants are constantly passing in the halls. In a majority of public buildings, however, separate control of the hall lights is very desirable if not necessary. The usual problem is, then, whether there shall be one or two sets of hall-light feeders. With two sets of feeders for hall lights, local switches can be eliminated and control effected entirely from the main switchboard. Two sets of hall feeders increase the cost of installation, but the saving in energy usually justifies them. By arranging two sets of feeders, one set serving, say, one-third the hall lights and the other the remaining two-thirds, the smaller group can be used for dark days and for an all-night circuit, and a saving in energy will result. Where there are two sets of hall lights thus controlled, the wiring of outlets should be such that there will be a uniform distribution of light, whichever set is lighted. Where tenants pay for the energy used in their suites, a separate feeder for the hall lights is indispensable.

FARM WIRING

540. Farm Wiring. The use of electric power on the farm is continually increasing. In order that the farm electrical system may be adequate and give the best results in expenditure of money and satisfactory service, it is essential that the system be properly and wisely planned, that good materials and equipment be employed throughout, and that good workmanship be employed in its installation. In most cases the best installation will be achieved by the use of a power pole, as shown in Fig. 322. The power pole will be the central distribution point of the electrical system. The power company will run its supply lines from its main pole line to the power pole of the farm and down the pole to their meter. From the power pole, the consumer will distribute the electric power by overhead or underground lines to the different buildings. In rare instances, it may not be possible to erect a power pole. In this case, the power lines from the public utility will terminate at a building, probably the farmhouse. The meter will then be installed at this point. This method introduces some complications and is recommended only where the erection of the power pole is very difficult or impossible.

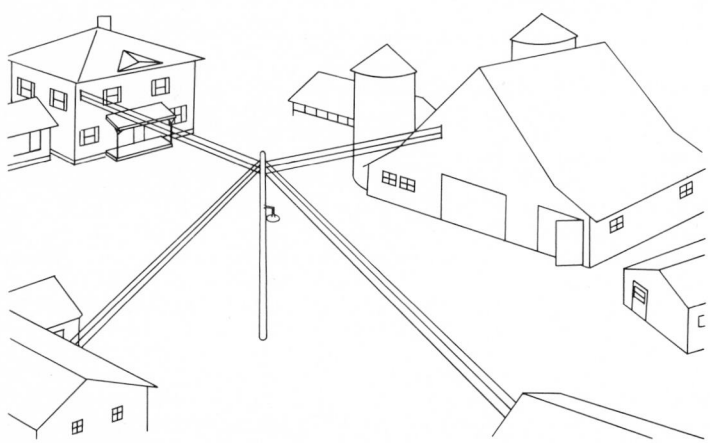

FIG. 322 *Power pole for farm-building distribution feeders.* (*General Electric Co.*)

The first step in planning the farm electric system is to determine the power demands for each building. The diversity of farm work makes it impossible to set down definite load requirements to fit all farms. Every kind of farming has its own needs in so far as power, machinery, and appliances are concerned. However, a number of wiring requirements are fundamental to the various farm buildings. No matter where the farm is located or how the buildings are constructed, certain minimum standards of wiring must be followed to obtain satisfactory electrical service. The following sections specify proper wiring for average conditions. They take into consideration the correct number of outlets, the proper switching, modern lighting, and adequate wire sizes for the machinery and appliances that are normally used in specific farm buildings. They are intended as a basic guide. If more equipment is to be installed than is included in these specifications or if the farming operations are of a special nature, the specifications must be varied to suit the special needs.

541. Typical Computed Loads and Probable Maximum Demands

Building	Computed load	Probable demand
Farm residence...............................	19 kw	13 kw
Dairy barn, medium size, including milkhouse and one 5-hp motor...........................	20 kw	12 kw
Dairy barn, large size, including milkhouse and one 7½-hp motor.........................	27 kw	15 kw
Same, two 7½-hp motors.....................	36 kw	24 kw
Milking barn with milkhouse..................	7.5 kw	5.8 kw
Milkhouse only..............................	6.0 kw	4.8 kw
Beef-cattle, horse, sheep, and hog barns, medium size, with 5-hp motor.......................	14 kw	10 kw
Same, large size, with 7½-hp motor............	20 kw	15 kw
Poultry laying house:		
1,000 sq ft...............................	1.8 kw	1.8 kw
4,000 sq ft...............................	8.7 kw	6.4 kw
8,000 sq ft...............................	15.2 kw	11.7 kw
Brooder house, per brooder:		
Infrared.................................	2.25 kw	2 kw
Standard brooder........................	1.25 kw	1 kw
Farm shop, with welder......................	17 kw	10 kw
Sweet-potato curing and storage...............	1.5 watts per cu ft or 4 watts per bu	1.5 watts per cu ft or 4 watts per bu
Machinery sheds, stock shelters, and miscellaneous buildings...........................	1 watt per sq ft floor area	1 watt per sq ft floor area

SOURCE: "Farmstead Wiring Handbook."

542. Other Loads ("Design Manual on Steel Electrical Raceways" published by American Iron and Steel Institute). Over and beyond the electrical requirements of individual buildings are a number of other loads for which provision must be made. These include such diverse items as water pumps (water system and irrigation), immersion heaters, water warmers, hay driers and hoists, forage handling, silo unloaders, and other miscellaneous equipment. Some idea of typical loads encountered is given by the following selected examples:

Forage handling:
Blower type...................... 20-hp motor
Inclined elevator............... 2- to 3-hp motor
Silo unloaders...................... 3- to 5-hp motor
Bulk-milk coolers................. Varies with size and type. 1 to 5 hp for one or more motors

Such additional loads should be kept in mind when surveying a farm operation for initial wiring or rewiring, and provisions made in the system design to handle such equipment.

543. Specifications for Dairy Barn.

Lights. In back of cows one lighting outlet every 12 ft, in front of cows a lighting outlet approximately every 20 ft. One or two lights on top of the silo, so installed that they will light silo and chute. Only general illumination is needed in the haymow. Floodlights above the hay line on opposite walls of the barn will therefore give the required lighting.

Convenience outlets should be placed approximately 15 ft apart in a row back of the cows. Where cows face in, outlets should be on the wall, up high enough so that cattle cannot come in contact with them. Where cows face out, outlets should be suspended from the ceiling on heavy-duty cords. They must be hung so that they can be reached easily yet high enough not to obstruct traffic.

In open spaces a convenience outlet should be installed for each 600-sq-ft area.

Switches. It is best to install separate switches for each row of lights in the barn. In small barns, however, all lights in back of the cows may be on one switch. When two or more entrances are used frequently, at least one row of lights should be controlled by three-way switches. The switch for the lights in the haymow should be mounted at a convenient location on the barn floor and should also be equipped with a pilot light. To have a visible indication when the light is burning in the silo, a switch with pilot light is recommended mounted at the entrance of the silo chute.

Circuits. The service-entrance panel for the barn must be adequate to take care of the load. Since some of the equipment needs special circuits, it is important to have an entrance panel of the proper capacity.

The following number of circuits is recommended as a minimum. However, additional equipment or change in barn layout may make it necessary to deviate from this recommendation.

Lights	2 circuits (depending on size of barn)
Milking machine	1 circuit (230 volts)
Feed grinder	1 circuit (230 volts)
Utility motor	1 circuit (230 volts)
Convenience outlets	1 circuit (depending on size of barn)
Fans	1 or more (depending on size of barn)
Hay drier	1 circuit (230 volts)

544. Specifications for Milkhouse.

Lights. In most cases a center light will be sufficient except where the milkhouse is unusually large. Then additional lights will be necessary over the work areas, especially where the utensils are washed.

Convenience Outlets. At least one convenience outlet for general use should be installed at a convenient location in the milkhouse. It is advisable to put this outlet on a heavy-duty 20-amp circuit.

Switches. All lights should be controlled by a switch at the entrance.

Circuits. Where it is connected to the barn, the circuits for the milkhouse may be included in the barn entrance panel.

When the milkhouse is separate, a special entrance panel must be installed.

The following circuits are recommended as a minimum:

Lights and outlets	1 circuit
Milk cooler	1 circuit
Water heater	1 circuit (230 volts)
Sterilizer	1 circuit (230 volts)
Ventilating fan	1 circuit (if fan is small, it may be connected to light and outlet circuit)

545. Specifications for Workshop, Garage, and Machine Shed.

Frequently the workshop, garage, and machine shed are one building, subdivided to serve all three purposes. The wiring for this building must therefore be arranged to suit this special condition.

Lights:

Workshop. A well-lighted workshop is absolutely necessary for doing good work. Two types of lighting are needed—general lighting for the entire workshop and localized lighting over the workbench and near permanently located equipment.

For this reason, a ceiling light must be installed for every 200 ft of floor area, at least one and possibly two lights over the workbench, and conveniently located lights over the stationary tools such as drill press, plane, forge, or saw.

Garage. One light over the front of the cars and another one at the rear will permit making minor repairs to the car and other equipment.

Machine Shed. One or two ceiling lights, depending on the size of the shed, give sufficient general illumination. Lights must be properly placed for best results.

Convenience Outlets:

Workshop. Convenience outlets in the workshop have to serve many different purposes. There must be a sufficient number, properly located, to facilitate the work. Install at least two convenience outlets over the workbench and other outlets throughout the workshop for the connection of the electric tools. A heavy-duty outlet must be installed for the portable welder.

Garage. A convenience outlet at the rear wall of the garage permits the use of portable tools, battery charger, and extension lights.

Machine Shed. Since the welder may frequently be used in the machine shed, a heavy-duty outlet should be provided. Other convenience outlets should be considered for the connection of portable tools such as drills and soldering irons.

Switches:

Workshop. The ceiling lights in the workshop should be controlled by a single-pole switch near the entrance. The lights over the workbench and fixed equipment can be controlled by pull-chain switches inside the fixture.

Garage. A single-pole switch near the entrance of the garage is needed for the control of the ceiling lights.

Machine Shed. The same type of switch control should be used here as in the garage.

Circuits. As in the barn and milkhouse, the service-entrance panel for the workshop must have the correct capacity for the load. Since all the equipment will never be used at one and the same time, a reasonable diversity factor may be taken into consideration.

The number of circuits depends, of course, on the equipment and machinery installed. However, the following minimum should be carefully considered:

```
Lights ..................................... 1 circuit
Convenience outlet.................. 1 circuit
Wood saw and planer............... 1 circuit (No. 12 wire)
Portable welder....................... 1 circuit (230 volts)
```

546. Specifications for Poultry House.

Lights. Lighting in the poultry house serves to increase egg production in addition to providing light for seeing. One light should be installed for each 200 sq ft of floor area, but if pens are smaller than 200 sq ft, at least one light per pen must be provided for.

The same general lighting arrangement should also be kept in the poultry-house workroom with additional local lighting for egg cleaning, grading, poultry scalding, waxing, etc.

Since ultraviolet light promotes healthier, stronger birds, sunlamps should be installed over feeding troughs.

It is also recommended that at least one germicidal fixture for each 100 sq ft of floor area of laying pens be installed. These lamps should be on a separate switch so that they can be turned off when someone is working in the pen.

Convenience Outlets. In the laying pens, to connect the water warmer, at least one convenience outlet should be installed for every 200 sq ft of floor area. The outlets are best located at the ceiling and should be equipped with the locking type of receptacle.

In the brooder house, the same arrangement of receptacles is recommended to serve brooders and water warmers. In the workroom, convenience outlets must be installed for the egg cleaner, candler, grader, poultry scalder, and waxer.

The feed-grinder and feed-mixer motors have to have special heavy-duty outlets on a 230-volt circuit.

Switches. Lights for all the laying pens should be connected to a regular switch as well as to an automatic time switch. The time switch will make morning lights to control egg production possible.

The ceiling lights in the workroom should be on a separate switch from the lights in the laying pens. The local lighting over the work areas can be controlled by wall switches or by pull-chain switches in the fixtures. Germicidal lamps, being on at all times, do not need a switch.

Circuits. The following circuits are recommended for the poultry house as a minimum:

```
Lights................................... 1 circuit (depending on size of poultry house)
Ultraviolet lamps ................... 1 circuit (depending on size of poultry house)
Germicidal lamps.................... 1 circuit (depending on size of poultry house)
Convenience outlets............... 1 circuit
Brooder outlets...................... 1 circuit each brooder
Feed mixer............................ 1 circuit (230 volts)
Feeder grinder ...................... 1 circuit (230 volts)
```

547. Specifications for Hog House or Sheep Shed. For general illumination, a lighting outlet every 20 ft along the passageways should be sufficient. These lights should be controlled by a single-pole switch near the entrance. Convenience outlets are needed in the farrowing pen for the connection of the pig brooders. This outlet should be about 3 ft above the floor and in a corner of the pen.

548. Specifications for Granary and Corncrib. Lights over the center of the drive spaced 20 ft apart are needed in the granary and corncrib. These lights should be controlled with a switch at the entrance. Upstairs, a light is needed for approximately every 200 sq ft of storage area with a switch and pilot light installed downstairs near the stairs. At least one power outlet is needed downstairs for the connection of the grain elevator.

549. Specifications for Farmyard. In the farmyard, electricity serves many important functions. Lights properly switched help in performing the evening chores. Outlets are needed throughout the yard for connection of the portable utility motor. Therefore, a plan for the wiring for a farm should include proper lighting and outlets outdoors. In general, the following simple rules will be sufficient:

Lights. Install at least three lights in the yard—one at the house, one at the barn, and one at the workshop or garage. They should be at least 15 ft above the ground to allow a wide spread of light.

Outlets. Heavy-duty, weatherproof outlets are needed for the connection of the utility motor. One should be mounted at the barn near the silo and others at all places where farm chores will employ the utility motor. If the pumphouse is located adjacent to the yard, a separate circuit to the pump motor should be provided.

Switches. To make it possible to turn the lights on or off from several different points, three- and four-way switches must be installed. A switch at the house, one at the barn, and a third one at another convenient place are recommended for maximum efficiency.

550. Planning the Farm Wiring System. After the required loads have been determined, the wiring system can be planned. The system will be considered in three parts: (1) the power pole, (2) distribution feeders, and (3) interior wiring of each building.

551. Power Pole. To be of best service, the power pole (Fig. 322) should be erected in a spot as central to the different electrical loads as possible. Often this is somewhere halfway between the house and the barn.

Normally a main switch and fuse or circuit breaker will not be required. However, it is good practice to install one on the power pole. A rain-tight main switch on the power pole will permit the power to be cut off from one centrally located point. A feeder of the required current-carrying capacity for the entire farm load must be run from the meter to the main switch if used and up to the top of the pole. The distribution feeders will be tapped off from this main feeder at the top of the pole. Regardless of the present load, the main feeder should not be less than No. 2 wire.

The entire wiring system must be grounded at the power pole. This is usually done with driven ground rods (refer to Sec. **342**). The grounding is a very important safety measure, and the advice of the power supplier or local inspection bureau should be obtained with respect to the proper method to employ.

552. Distribution Feeders. An individual feeder from the power pole to each building is best. However, the location of the buildings may make it necessary to connect one building from another. Similarly, to buildings with very small electrical loads, it may be equally good and less expensive to extend feeders from a nearby building. This feeder, when tapped on the outside of the building, without going through the service-entrance panel of the first building, permits additional load and future extensions in the second building. Additional wiring can be installed without affecting the load in the first building. No matter how small the load in any one building may be, this method is recommended.

The length of the feeder from pole to building and the electrical load inside determine the size of the feeder.

For mechanical strength, no feeder can be smaller than No. 10 wire when the span is 50 ft or less. A span longer than 50 ft needs wire No. 8 or larger.

The actual size of the feeder can be calculated by the methods given in Div. 3. The voltage drop for any feeder should not exceed 2 per cent.

If one or more buildings are connected from another, feeder sizes from the power pole to the first building must be increased. Use 100 per cent of the building having the largest load plus 50 per cent of the combined load of the other buildings. No one can foretell how quickly the use of electricity will be increased. It is therefore recommended that feeders at least one size larger than the load figures indicate should be used. Refer to Sec. **5,** Part B, of Div. 11 for National Electrical Code feeder demand factors on farm properties.

It is recommended that all feeders shall be three-wire 115/230 volts. However, for a small load in a particular building, a two-wire 115-volt feeder may be satisfactory. Feeders to buildings having a load of 3,450 watts or more or to buildings having a motor of 1/2 hp must be three-wire.

553. Wiring of Buildings. Normally the power-distribution feeder for the power pole to a building is secured to the building with an insulator bracket (see Div. 8). Brackets should be mounted high enough so that the power feeders are never suspended lower than 18 ft over driveways, for clearance of loaded wagons, and 10 ft over footwalks.

From the insulator bracket service-entrance conductors are run down the side of the building to a point where they enter the building and connect to the service-entrance panel. Service-entrance cable is recommended for this purpose. This cable with its tough nonmetallic outer covering protects cattle from coming in contact with metallic parts of the wiring system.

The table in Sec. **554** will give an idea of the size of service-entrance panels required (refer to Secs. **346** to **356** for information on service entrances).

It is recommended that metal-clad cable or nonmetallic-sheathed cable be employed for the interior wiring of the buildings (refer to preceding sections of this division for information on wiring, and refer to Secs. **543** to **549** of this division for information on requirements for lights, convenience outlets, switches, and circuits).

At each building the wiring system must be grounded. This is in addition to the ground at the power pole. Grounds must be established at each point of entrance to each building, and if possible, all these grounds should be tied together on driven grounds. Also, for added safety, the farm water system should be tied at each building to the driven ground for that building. This is important. A well-grounded wiring system adds to the safety of the entire installation.

554. Service-entrance Requirements

Type of building	Installation	Service-entrance conductors, amp (All services are 3-wire, 115/230-volt, unless otherwise specified)
Dairy barn (complete barn, including milk room) up to 2,500 sq ft	Normal amount of lighting, ventilation, milker, milk cooler, water pump, dairy water heater, milkhouse heater, gutter cleaner (3 hp), hay drier, or utility motor (5 hp)	100
Same, above 2,500 sq ft	Normal amount of lighting, ventilation, milker, milk cooler, water pump, dairy water heater, milkhouse heater, gutter cleaner (5 hp), hay drier, or utility motor (7 hp)	125
Same, above 2,500 sq ft	Same as above, but two 7½-hp motors	195
Milking barn or "milking parlor"—includes milk room—(cows not housed)	Normal amount of lighting, milker, milk cooler, dairy water heater, milkhouse heater, ventilation	55
Milkhouse (when separate from barn)	Normal amount of lighting, milk cooler, dairy water heater, milkhouse heater	55
Horse, beef-cattle, sheep, and hog barns up to 2,500 sq ft	Normal amount of lighting, ventilation, pig or lamb brooders, water pump, antifreezing protection on plumbing, utility motor (5 hp)	70
Same, above 2,500 sq ft	Normal amount of lighting, ventilation, pig or lamb brooders, water pump, antifreezing protection on plumbing, utility motor (7½ hp)	100
Poultry laying house (including feed room) up to 4,000 sq ft pen floor area	Normal amount of lighting, ventilation, water warmers, antifreezing protection on plumbing, automatic feeders, feed grinder (up to 1 hp)	55
Same, above 4,000 sq ft pen floor area	Normal amount of lighting, ventilation, water warmers, antifreezing protection on plumbing, automatic feeders, feed grinder (up to 2 hp)	70
Poultry brooder house, portable type	Light and outlet for single brooder and water warmer	20 (2-wire, 115-volt)
Poultry brooder house, permanent type, up to six pens	Normal amount of lighting, ventilation, brooders, water warmers, antifreezing protection on plumbing	55
Poultry brooder house, permanent type, above six pens	Normal amount of lighting, ventilation, brooders, water warmers, antifreezing protection on plumbing	70 minimum; estimate 2,000 watts per pen
Poultry-cleaning and -dressing house	Normal amount of lighting, poultry scalder, waxer, wax reclaimer, picker, and refrigeration	55
Farm shop	Normal amount of lighting, bench tools (tool grinder, drill, soldering iron, etc.), farm welder, air compressor, saw, and battery charger	70
General farm buildings	Minimum capacity where lighting, motors and miscellaneous 115- and 230-volt equipment will be used	50
Storage sheds, stock shelters	Lighting and small portable equipment—not over two 2-wire bench circuits	40[a] (2-wire, 115-volt)

[a] Ordinarily such buildings are supplied by a feeder or circuit from another building. In such cases, this is not a "service" as defined by the National Electrical Code. Where a brooder house or similar structure is supplied directly from power source, the minimum permissible size of service-entrance conductors would be No. 8 for two two-wire branch circuits.

If the building is served by a feeder from another building the minimum size of service-entrance conductors would be No. 10 for two two-wire branch circuits. For a single branch-circuit source, the minimum permissible size of service-entrance conductors would be No. 8 for two two-wire branch circuits.

NOTE. All the capacities listed above assume service for the individual building only. Where other buildings are supplied from any of these services, the capacity of the service would have to be increased accordingly.

WIRING FINISHED BUILDINGS

555. In laying out old-house wiring installations, the first things to be considered are the location of the meter and the panel board and the point where the wires are to enter.   The meter should generally be located at a readily accessible point outside the house.   In the smaller houses, the panel board should be located near the meter, and in the larger houses, where there are a number of branch circuits, at the central point of distribution, i.e., at some point on the second floor, preferably the hall.   The point of entry should be located with reference to the accessibility of the service connection.

556. Typical Wiring Plan of an Old Building.   Figure 323 shows the routes taken by the wires, to chandeliers and switches, within walls and under floors.   The point of entry for the mains in this case is the kitchen, on the outer wall of which are located the main switch, the fuse block, and the meter.   Double-pole switches are shown, as they were required in certain cities in installations where combination gas and electric fixtures are used.   Single-pole switches installed in accordance with National Electrical Code rules are practically

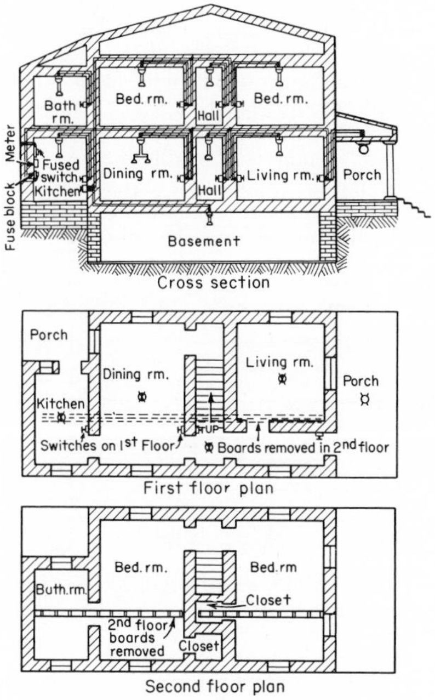

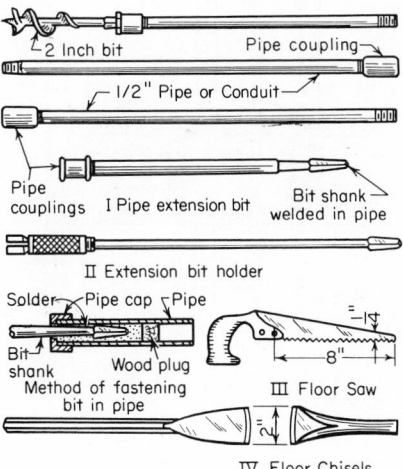

FIG. 323 *Wiring of a five-room house.*

FIG. 324   *Tools used in wiring old buildings.*

as good for the average installation.   The methods of carrying conductors to single-pole switches will be obvious from a study of the illustration.

The dotted lines show the flooring boards taken up on the second floor, and the fixture and switch locations on the first floor are indicated.   The switch locations are within easy fishing distance.

The flooring boards are removed on the second floor in such locations as to pass under one partition only and with regard to accessibility of the outlet and switch openings below.

In many houses of the type shown, the space between roof and second-floor ceiling is sealed, in which case a hole is cut in the ceiling of a closet and the opening is provided with a trap door.

557. Special Tools Used in Wiring Old Buildings (see Fig. 324).

1. PIPE EXTENSION BIT. Used to drill, up from the cellar or down from the third floor, through crosspieces or headers in a partition where it is impossible to get over or under them. A 1- or 2-in. bit is used, making a hole large enough to take several cables. Instances are known where boring has been done from the cellar to the third floor successfully, although the necessity for this is very rare. Figure 325 illustrates the application of this device. A bit brace or power drill can be used for turning it, or if the space is restricted a pipe wrench can be used.

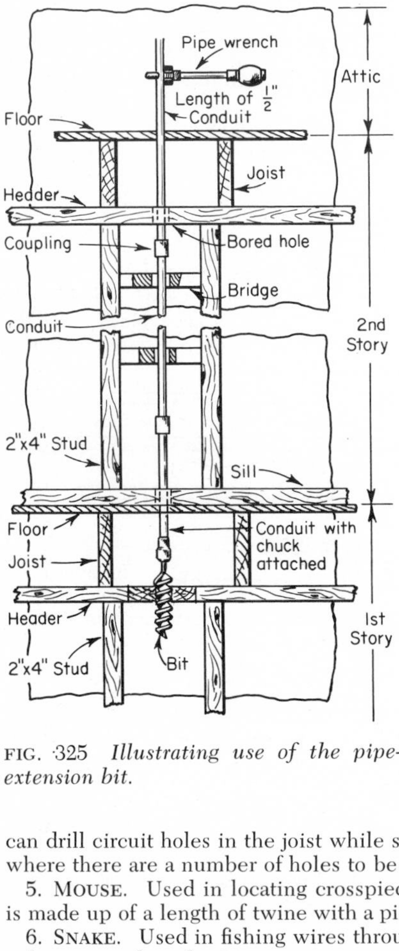

2. FLOOR SAW. Used in removing flooring boards, made short enough so that it cannot be pushed through the plaster of the ceiling below. The blade is ¼ in. wide at the point and approximately 8 in. long with a handle similar to that of a keyhole saw.

3. FLOOR CHISELS. Used in removing the flooring boards. The chisels are from 12 to 24 in. long and 2 in. wide at the point.

4. EXTENSION-BIT HOLDER. Used in a bit brace for drilling holes in joist. They are 2 to 3 ft long, and enable the wireman to drill holes in a recess or in places where a long bit would be needed. By coupling two of the holders together, the wireman

FIG. 325 *Illustrating use of the pipe-extension bit.*

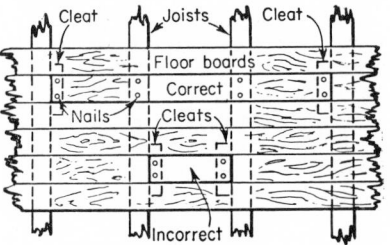

FIG. 326 *Methods of locating cleats to support floor boards that have been removed.*

can drill circuit holes in the joist while standing, which renders the work much easier where there are a number of holes to be drilled.

5. MOUSE. Used in locating crosspieces and finding clear spaces in partitions. It is made up of a length of twine with a piece of lead or other heavy material on its end.

6. SNAKE. Used in fishing wires through partitions or under floors; made of rectangular or round steel wire.

558. Removing Flooring Boards. First a slot must be made in the seam between flooring boards of sufficient size to enable the floor-saw blade (Fig. 324) to be inserted. This is best done with a sharp, narrow chisel having a ⅝-in. blade. Then the saw blade is inserted, and the tongue at the junction of the flooring boards is sawed off the full length of board to be removed. The wireman can tell when he reaches the joist at which he wishes to end his cut. At this point the chisel blade is placed with the flat part across the board at edge of the joist, and another small slot made. Then the board is sawed off even with the joist and can be easily removed with a floor chisel (Fig. 324). When the board is replaced, a cleat is nailed to the joist (Fig. 326) for the board to rest on, and then the board is nailed down, or better yet, screwed down, so that if it is necessary to get at the wires again it can be done with little trouble. When the flooring is fastened down, two nails or screws should be put in each joist. When only one nail is used, the board is apt to squeak when walked over. To ensure a substantial job, any floor board that is removed should be long enough to bridge at least two joists.

559. Fishing to Center Outlets. A great deal depends on the layout of the house. Let us assume that the joists run parallel to the street. If the house is one with a side or center hall on the second floor, the circuits can be run the length of the hall, necessitating the removal of two boards for that distance. Wires can then be fished from the center of the room by cutting a small hole at the chandelier location or by cutting a pocket in the floor directly above the location of the outlet. If it is necessary to take up the boards in the floor at some distance from the partitions, another pocket will have to be taken up close to the partition in order to drop the switch loops and to go through to the other side. This is necessary when the hall is in the center, with the rooms to be wired on each side.

If, as is the case with some of the smaller houses, there is no hall on the second floor and the rooms are directly in the rear of each other, the boards can be taken up through the doorways and the wires dropped to the switches, outlets, and the panel board in the kitchen very readily (see Fig. 323). Where there are hardwood floors, the wires must be fished from the center of the room to a closet or to a point where the baseboard can be removed so as to get into a partition going either up or down. In a great many cases it is necessary to drop to the cellar and then come up again in another location for the switch loop. Where this is necessary, the most convenient place for the panel board is in the cellar.

560. Wiring for Switch Loops. In a great many cases the bringing out of the switch loops at outlets at a proper distance from the floor is the most difficult part of wiring old houses, on account of the crosspieces or bridges sometimes found in partitions. The method to be used must be determined by the wireman on the job, according to the conditions found. Following are some of the methods used:

First, with his mouse, he finds if the runway is clear; if so, the rest is easy. But if he finds there are crosspieces, he locates their position by measurements with the mouse and marks the location on the wall. If the crosspieces are above the proper positions for the switch, he will probably use one of the following methods of getting around it:

1. Remove the doorstop strip from the frame of the doorway (Fig. 327), bore through on each side of the crosspiece, cut a recess in the inside of the frame, and then fish the wires around.

2. If on the second floor and there is no partition directly above, the wireman can use a pipe extension bit (Fig. 324, I), drilling one hole large enough to fish the switch loop through.

3. If the crosspiece is not too far above the proposed location of the switch, holes can be drilled on a slant from switch opening.

4. Remove the wallpaper directly over the crosspiece, which can easily be done, especially in an old house where there are several thicknesses of paper, either dry or by dampening it. This can be done by cutting an X through the paper at the point over which the opening is to be made and bending the paper back, but taking care not to bend it enough to crease it. Then cut a hole smaller then the paper removed and bore holes or cut away the crosspiece enough so that the wires will pass. If there

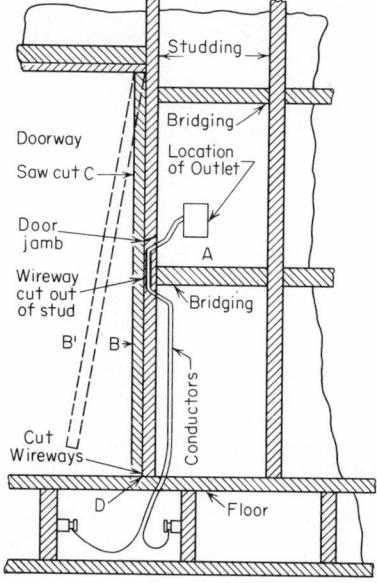

FIG. 327 *Carrying wires around a bridge.*

is a figure or flower where the crosspiece is located, it can be cut out with a sharp knife, and after the hole is plastered up with plaster of paris, the paper can be replaced very neatly. A careful man usually performs this operation very successfully.

5. Sometimes a wireman will attempt to remove these crosspieces, when he can get at them from above, by putting a piece of pipe down between the partition and hitting it with a heavy hammer. This method is apt to cause damage to the plaster by bulging or breaking it out and is not recommended.

561. Examining Partition Interiors. With a pocket flashlight and a little mirror the interior of a wall or partition which would ordinarily be inaccessible can be inspected (Fig. 328). The mirror is introduced in the outlet hole, and the flashlight and eye are held behind it as illustrated. The mirror reflects the light of the lamp onto the place to be illuminated, at the same time reflecting the image back to the eye.

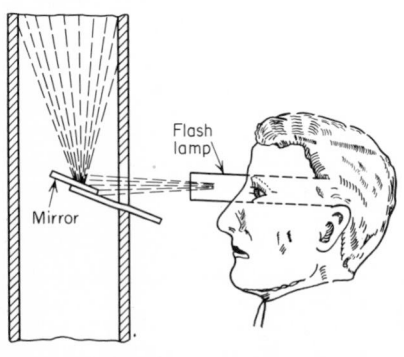

FIG. 328 *Examining partition interior.*

562. Cutting in Device Boxes. Openings for switch or receptacle boxes must be slightly larger than 2 by 3 in. (the front dimensions of standard device boxes). Such holes should be cut after it has been established that cables can be readily fished in, whenever possible. In wood lath and plaster walls measure off a 2-in.-wide mark at the approximate location of the switch. Carefully remove the plaster within the 2-in. mark until a full wood lath is exposed. The center of the wood lath now becomes the center of the 2- by 3-in. box. Invert the box and mark off the remainder of the rectangular box to establish a pattern. Then carefully remove the plaster within the marking. This will expose about one-half a lath above and below the fully exposed lath. Use a sharp keyhole saw to cut away the portions of laths to allow the box to be installed.

If a box with ears is used (see sketch 39, Sec. **113** of Div. 4) the ears can be secured to the top and bottom pieces of lath with ¾-in.-long No. 4 flathead wood screws. Enough plaster must be removed to allow the ears to seat against the lath. The ears can be adjusted so that the front edge of the box will be nearly flush with the surface. Before installing the devices and faceplates, it is a good practice to spackle all openings around the box and ears.

Since most modern homes use a dry-wall construction, such as plasterboard, a 2- by 3-in. hole can be readily cut with a plasterboard knife or a sharp keyhole saw. For such applications use a "cut-in" box similar to the one described in Sec. **120** and Fig. **152** of Div. 4.

563. Ceiling Boxes. There are 3- and 4-in. ceiling boxes similar in construction to the boxes described in Sec. **562.** However, they should be used for lightweight lighting fixtures only. A preferred method of many electricians is the use of 3- or 4-in. round "pan" boxes which are ½ or ¾ in. in depth (refer to sketches 22 to 25, Sec. **113** of Div. 4). They can be mounted to a ceiling joist with or without removing plaster or plasterboard. If a ½-in. pan fixture is used, the canopy of many fixtures will fit over the box and tight against the ceiling. Where this is not possible, a sufficient amount of ceiling material can be removed to allow the shallow box to be secured directly to a ceiling joist. The box should be fastened to the joist with two No. 8 wood screws. Then this arrangement will provide a much more rigid support for fixtures than most other methods. If the space above the ceiling is accessible, standard methods of mounting ceiling boxes should be employed.

DIVISION TEN

Electric Lighting

PRINCIPLES AND UNITS

1. Explanation of Light. Light ("Standard Handbook for Electrical Engineers") may be defined as radiant energy of those wave lengths to which the human eye is sensitive. Figure 1 shows the complete radiant energy spectrum of electromagnetic waves, which travel through space at the velocity of approximately 186,000 miles per second. The longer waves are the ones used in radio communication; the shortest ones are the X rays and cosmic rays. The waves to which the eye is sensitive are those near the middle of the spectrum, of a length of about 0.0004 to 0.0008 mm. An enlarged section of this part of the spectrum is shown in the figure.

The effect of light upon the eye gives us the sensation of sight. The impression of color depends upon the wave length of the light falling upon the eye. There are three primary colors of light—red, green, and violet. Violet light has the shortest wave length of the radiant energy to which the eye is sensitive, red the longest, and green an intermediate wave length between that of violet and red. These three colors are called the primary colors, because light of any one of them cannot be produced by combining light of any other colors. Light of any other color than these three can be produced by combining in the proper proportions light of two or all three of the primary colors.

2. Propagation of Light. Rays of light travel in straight lines unless interfered with by some medium that absorbs or deflects them. Whenever a light wave strikes a different medium from that through which it has been passing, there are three fundamental phenomena that may occur—absorption, reflection, or refraction. Whenever

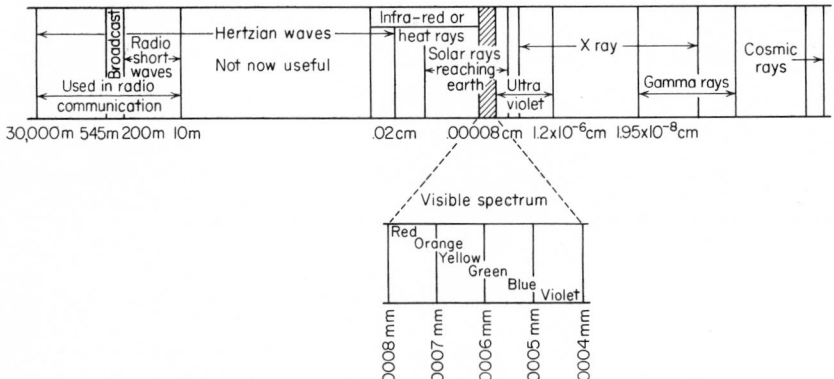

FIG. 1 *The radiant energy spectrum.*

light waves strike any object, a portion of their energy is absorbed, the amount depending upon the nature of the substance. This absorbed energy is dissipated in the form of heat. The remaining portion of the light may be all transmitted through the substance, all reflected back from the surface, or part transmitted and part reflected, depending upon the nature of the substance and the angle at which the light impinges upon the surface of the object. If the light strikes the object perpendicularly to the surface, it is either transmitted in a straight line through the substance or reflected back from its surface in the same direction in which it impinged upon the surface. If light strikes an object at an angle other than 90 deg to its surface, then either the light is transmitted through the object but in an altered direction (refraction) or the light is reflected back from the object but in a different direction from that in which it impinged

10-2

upon the object (reflection). With most objects all three of the phenomena occur, some of the light impinging upon them being absorbed, some transmitted through (refracted), and some reflected back from the surface.

3. Absorption. Although some of the energy of a ray of light is always absorbed whenever a light ray impinges upon an object, the amount absorbed varies over wide limits, depending upon the nature of the object, the molecular construction, the wave length or color of the incident light, and the angle at which the light strikes the surface. All objects do not absorb light of different wave lengths in the same proportion. It is this phenomenon which accounts for the characteristic color of objects (see Sec. **13**). Since objects do not absorb the same proportion of the incident light of different colors, the amount of light absorbed by an object depends upon the color or wave length of the light impinging upon the object. Tables **4** and **12** give the percentage of incident white light that is absorbed by various types of surfaces.

4. Coefficients (Per Cent) of Absorption of Globes and Shades

Material	Absorption, per cent	Material	Absorption, per cent
Clear glass globes...................	5–12	Medium opalescent globes...........	25–40
Light sandblasted globes.............	10–20	Amber glass.......................	40–60
Alabaster globes....................	10–20	Heavy opalescent globes............	30–60
Canary-colored globes...............	15–20	Flame-glass globes..................	30–60
Light-blue alabaster globes...........	15–25	Enameled glass.....................	60–70
Heavy blue alabaster globes..........	15–30	White diffuse plastic................	65–90
Ribbed glass globes.................	15–30	Signal-green globes.................	80–90
Clear plastic globes.................	20–40	Ruby-glass globes..................	85–90
Opaline glass globes................	15–40	Cobalt-blue globes.................	90–95
Ground-glass globes................	20–30		

5. Absorption is the loss of light flux which occurs when the flux is reflected by a reflecting surface or when it passes through a translucent or so-called transparent material.

Per cent absorption = 100 per cent − per cent reflection − per cent transmitted   (1)

6. Reflection of Light (Fig. 2) is the redirecting of light rays by a reflecting surface. Whenever light energy strikes an opaque object or surface, part is absorbed by the surface and part is reflected. Light-colored surfaces reflect (Table **9**) a larger part of

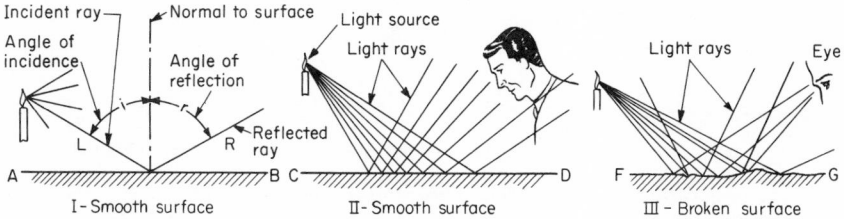

FIG. 2 *Illustrating the reflection of light. (Note that the angle of incidence i always equals the angle of reflection r.)*

the light thrown on them than do dark-colored surfaces, whereas dark surfaces absorb a larger part of the light and black surfaces absorb nearly all the light which reaches them.

NOTE. Consider first a smooth surface *AB* (Fig. 2, I), on which a ray of light *L* falls. This ray will be so reflected in the direction *R* that the angle *i* is exactly equal to the angle *r*. Consider now the effect of a number of rays falling on a smooth surface *CD* (Fig. 2, II). Each ray will be reflected in such a way that it leaves the surface at the same angle at which it strikes it. The eye if held as shown would perceive only the light reflected into it. Consider now a broken surface such as *FG* (Fig. 2, III). Each ray of light is reflected from that portion of the surface on which it falls, just as though that point were on a smooth surface. The result is that the light is scattered, and if the surface is irregular enough, the eye placed at any point will receive reflections from many points of the surface. All opaque surfaces except polished surfaces have innumerable minute irregularities like the surface in Fig. 2, III. This alone enables them to be seen.

7. The different kinds of reflection will now be considered. **Regular reflection** is that (Fig. 3, I and 3*A*, I) wherein the angle of incidence *i* is equal to the angle of reflection *r*. This kind of reflection is obtained from mirrored glass, prismatic glass, and polished metal surfaces. **Spread reflection** (Fig. 3, II and 3*A*, II) is that wherein the maximum intensity of the reflected light follows the law of regular reflection, except

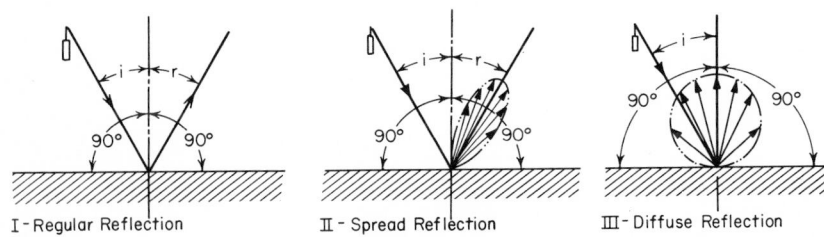

FIG. 3 *Illustrating classifications of reflection.*

that a part of the light is scattered slightly out of this line. Spread reflection is obtained from etched prismatic glass and from rough metallic surfaces. **Diffuse reflection** (Fig. 3, III) is that wherein the maximum intensity of the reflected light is normal to the reflecting surface. This holds over a large range of the angle of incidence. This kind of reflection is usually caused by reflection from particles beneath the surface (see Fig. 3*A*, III). Diffuse reflection may be obtained from opal glass, porcelain enamel, paint enamel, and paint finishes commonly used for interior decoration of walls and ceilings.

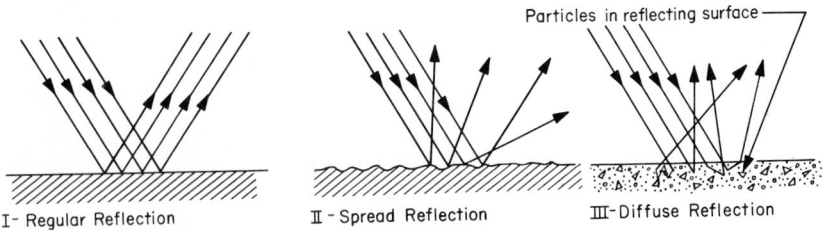

FIG. 3A *Magnified view of preceding illustration.*

8. Reflecting Power of Surfaces. Different surfaces reflect different percentages of the light falling upon them. The illumination of a small room having poorly reflecting walls may sometimes be improved by changing the wall coverings. If the room is large or if reflectors are used to throw the light downward so that not much light reaches the walls, a change in the wall covering will have little effect on the general illumination.

9. The following table of reflection coefficients (Bell, "Art of Illumination") is useful in showing the relative reflective value of wall coverings in rooms.

Material	Reflection, per cent	Material	Reflection, per cent
Highly polished silver................	92	Chrome-yellow paper................	62
Optical mirrors silvered on surface.....	70–85	Yellow wallpaper....................	40
Highly polished brass................	70–75	Light-pink paper....................	36
Highly polished copper...............	60–70	Blue wallpaper......................	25
Highly polished steel................	60	Dark-brown paper...................	13
Speculum metal.....................	60–80	Vermilion paper.....................	12
Polished gold.......................	50–55	Blue-green paper....................	12
Burnished copper....................	40–50	Cobalt blue.........................	12
White blotting paper.................	82	Glossy black paper..................	5
White cartridge paper...............	80	Deep chocolate paper...............	4
Porcelain enamel....................	70–80	Black cloth.........................	1.2
Ordinary foolscap.:.................	70	Black velvet........................	0.4
Polished aluminum..................	67	Black, theoretically perfect..........	0.0

10. Refraction. Whenever a light ray passes from one medium into another of greater or less density, the direction of the ray is altered. This is called refraction. Refraction may be one of three types: regular, irregular or spread, or diffuse, depending upon the nature of the construction of the substance and the character of its surfaces.

Regular refraction occurs with plain glass or glass prisms as shown in Fig. 4. Light in passing through a substance goes through two refractions, one upon entering the substance and one upon leaving the substance. If the surfaces of the object are parallel, as in a piece of glass (Fig. 4, I), the direction of the light leaving the object is parallel to the direction of the light impinging upon the object. If the surfaces of the object are not

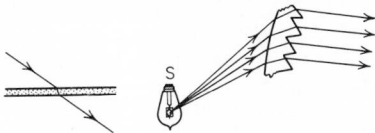

I. *Plain glass.*   II. *Prisms.*

FIG. 4 *Regular refraction.*

parallel, as in the prism of Fig. 4, II, the light leaving the object will not be in a direction parallel to the incident light. A prism can be constructed to refract the light from its different surfaces so that light is not transmitted through the prism but is reflected back as shown in Fig. 5.

Irregular or spread refraction occurs with light transmitted through glass with a rough surface such as etched or frosted glass, as shown in Fig. 6. Such a surface can

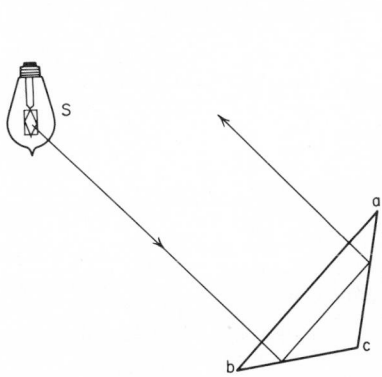

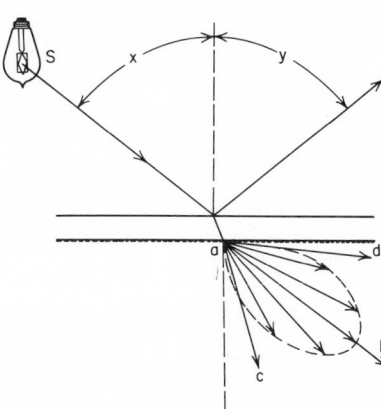

FIG. 5 *Total reflection with prism. (General Electric Co., Nela Park Engineering Dept.)*

FIG. 6 *Spread refraction with etched glass. (General Electric Co., Nela Park Engineering Dept.)*

be considered as consisting of a great number of very small smooth surfaces making slight angles with each other. The individual rays of light emitting from such a surface are refracted at slightly different angles but all in the same general direction. Thus the light transmitted through a substance with such a surface is refracted in the same general direction but with the beam spread somewhat from what it would be for regular refraction.

The composition of opal glass is such that it contains a number of minute opaque particles throughout its structure. Light striking such an object travels through the

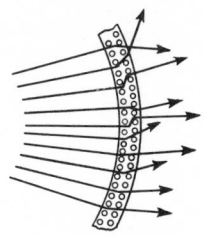

FIG. 7 *Diffuse refraction.*

glass until it strikes one of these opaque particles, from which it is either reflected back or transmitted through the glass to the other surface. The total beam of light striking the object is thus split up by the innumerable small opaque particles, part being reflected back in all directions, and part being refracted through the glass in all directions. The portion that is transmitted (refracted) through the glass is **diffusely refracted.**

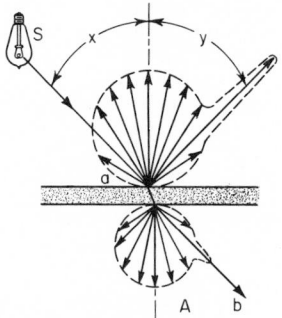

FIG. 8 *Diffuse reflection and refraction with opal glass.* (General Electric Co., Nela Park Engineering Dept.)

An idea of how diffuse refraction takes place can be gained from Fig. 7. In Fig. 8 the diffuse reflection and refraction of a ray of light impinging upon a piece of opal glass are indicated.

11. Most Frequently Used Lighting Units, Abbreviations, Symbols, and the Corresponding Hydraulic Analogies

Photometric quantity	Name of unit	Abbreviation	Symbol	Hydraulic analogy
Luminous flux	Lumen	lm	F	Gal per min
Luminous intensity........	Candela	cp	I	Pressure in lb per sq in.
Illumination..................	Foot-candle	ft-c	E	Incident gal per sq ft per min
Luminance	Lambert	Lambert	L	Issuing gal per sq ft per min

12. Reflection, Transmission, and Absorption Characteristics of Materials
(General Electric Co., Nela Park Engineering Department)

Material	Light reflected			Light transmitted			Light absorbed
	In concentrated beam	In spread beam	Diffused in all directions	In concentrated beam	In spread beam	Diffused in all directions	
Crystal glass:							
Clear	8-10[a]	....	....	80-85	....	....	5-10
Frosted or pebbled[b]	4-5	5-10	....	....	70-85	....	5-15
Frosted or pebbled[c]	....	8-12	....	....	72-87	....	5-15
White glass:							
Very light density[b]	4-5[a]	....	10-20	5-20	....	50-55	8-12
Very light density[c]	4-5[a]	3-4	10-20	....	5-20	50-55	10-15
Heavy density	....	....	40-70	....	....	10-45	10-20
Mirrored glass	82-88	....	....	....	....	....	12-18
Polished metal:							
Silver	92	....	....	....	....	....	8
Chromium	65	....	....	....	....	....	35
Aluminum	62	....	....	....	....	....	38
Alzak aluminum	75-85	70-80	....	....	....	....	15-30
Nickel	55	....	....	....	....	....	45
Tin	63	....	....	....	....	....	37
Steel	60	....	....	....	....	....	40
Porcelain enamel steel	4-5[a]	....	60-70	....	....	....	25-35
Mat-finished metal:							
Aluminum	....	62	....	....	....	....	38
White oxidized aluminum	....	70-75	....	....	....	....	25-30
Aluminum paint	....	60-65	....	....	....	....	35-40
Mat surfaces:							
White plaster	....	....	90-95	....	....	....	5-10
White blotting paper	....	....	80-85	....	....	....	15-20
White paper (calendered)	4-5[a]	....	75-80	....	....	....	15-20
White paint (dull)	....	....	75-80	....	....	....	20-25
White paint (semimat)	....	2-4	70-75	....	....	....	20-25
White paint (gloss)	4-5[a]	....	70-75	....	....	....	20-25
Black paint (gloss)	4-5[a]	....	3-5	....	....	....	85-92
Black paint (dull)	....	....	3-5	....	....	....	95-97
Magnesium carbonate	....	....	98-99	....	....	....	1-2
Plastic:							
Clear	....	....	....	....	60-80	....	40-20
White diffuse	....	....	....	....	....	5-35	65-95

[a] For angles up to 45 deg; for angles greater than 45 deg, this value rises considerably; angle of incidence as X, Fig. 6.

[b] Smooth side toward light source.

[c] Roughed on side toward light source.

13. Color of Objects. Our impression of the color of objects is due to the color of the light that the object reflects or transmits to our eyes. In Sec. 2 it was stated that all objects absorb a certain portion of the light that falls upon them but that all objects do not absorb the same proportion of light of the different wave lengths. It is through this different absorption that different objects have unlike colors. If all objects absorbed light in exactly the same manner, all objects would appear to have the same color. In order that things may appear in their true colors, they must be observed under white light, i.e., light containing all three primary colors in the right proportion. An article which absorbs no light or which absorbs light of the three primary colors in the same proportion as they are combined to produce white light will transmit from its surface light in a condition unchanged from that in which the light fell upon the object. Such an object would appear white in color. An object which absorbs all or nearly all the light which falls upon it will have no color or, in other words, will be black. An object which absorbs all the green and violet rays will be red in color, since it will transmit to our eyes only red light. In order that an object may appear in its true color, the light falling upon it must contain light of the wave length that the object reflects or transmits. Thus, light falling upon a red object must contain red light if the object is to appear in its true color. A red object viewed under a light which contains only green and violet rays will appear black, since the object is capable of reflecting only red rays.

14. Color temperature (Westinghouse Electric Corp.) is a term sometimes used to describe the color of the light from a source by comparing it with the color of a *black body,* a theoretical "complete radiator" which absorbs all radiation that falls on it and in turn radiates a maximum amount of energy in all parts of the spectrum. A black body, like any other incandescent body, changes color as its temperature is raised. The light from a white fluorescent lamp is similar in color to the light from a black body at a temperature of approximately 3500°K,[1] and the lamp is accordingly said to have a color temperature of 3500°K. The light from a daylight fluorescent lamp is bluer, and the black body must be raised to 6500°K to match it. Hence the daylight lamp has a color temperature of 6500°K.

Color temperature is not a measure of the *actual temperature* of an object. It defines *color only.* Some light sources, such as a sodium vapor lamp or a green or pink fluorescent lamp, will not match the color of a black body at any temperature, and therefore no color temperatures can be assigned to them.

Color Temperatures, °K
(Approximate values)

Blue sky	10,000–30,000
Overcast sky	7000
Noon sunlight	5250
Fluorescent lamps:	
Daylight	6500
Cool white	4500
White	3500
Warm white	3000
500-watt daylight incandescent lamp	4000
Photoflood lamp	3415
General-service incandescent lamps	2500–3050
Candle flame	1800

15. Luminous flux (which, as is explained later, is measured in lumens) is a flow of light, i.e., light energy or light waves. Luminous flux always originates from some source of light, such as the sun, a candle, or an incandescent lamp. But luminous flux can be redirected by reflecting surfaces. The luminous flux which emanates directly or is reflected from objects to the human eye is the medium whereby the objects are seen. Although there is no actual flow of anything material in a flux of light, there is a flow of light waves.

16. A true point source of light (Fig. 9) is a luminous mathematical point which emits luminous flux uniformly in all directions. It is a theoretical concept which cannot actually exist. It is, however, used—and is necessary—for the development of the quantities and units used in lighting computations.

---

[1] Kelvin is a temperature scale which has its zero point at −273°C.

NOTE. An actual light source may be considered as a point source, without prohibitive error if the distance between the source and the location at which the source is viewed or examined is at least ten times the greatest dimension of the source.

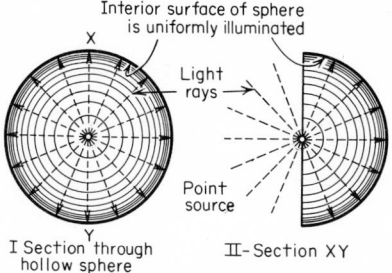

FIG. 9 *Diagrammatical illustration of light rays emitted by a point source of light.*

17. The luminous intensity of a given source of light in a certain specified direction is a measure of the ability of the source to project light in that direction. Luminous intensity is measured in a unit which is called either the candela or candlepower.

NOTE. The luminous intensity of actual light sources is generally greater in certain directions than in others. Thus, in Fig. 10, the luminous intensity of the lamp is greatest in the horizontal direction.

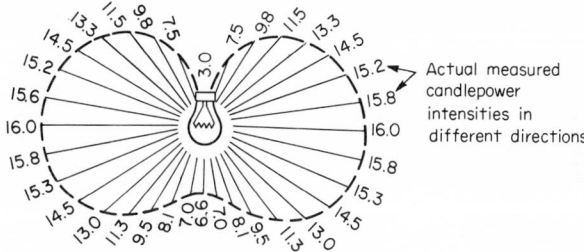

FIG. 10 *Luminous intensities in different directions around an incandescent lamp.*

18. The candela or candlepower is defined as the luminous intensity or light-producing power in the horizontal direction of a standard lamp which is made and used in accordance with U.S. Bureau of Standards specifications.

NOTE. The luminous intensity of an ordinary sperm candle (Fig. 11) in the horizontal direction is about 1 candle. Thus was derived the name of the unit, candela.

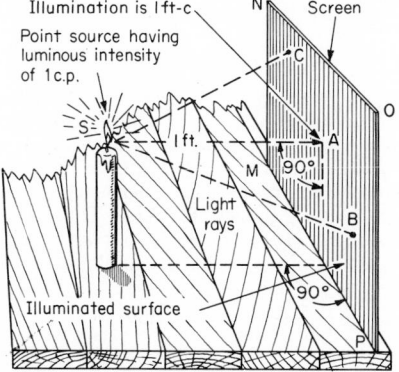

FIG. 11 *Illustrating an intensity of illumination of 1 ft-c.*

19. The true luminous intensity or candlepower of a light source can be obtained only when the source is a true point source (Sec. **16**). But a true point source does not exist. It is merely a mathematical concept. Now, the luminous intensity of an actual light source, in a certain direction, is (Fig. 12) due to the combined effects of a number of point sources in the surface of the actual light source. Hence, the luminous intensity of an actual light source, in a given direction, as determined with a photometer (Sec. **27**), is not the true candlepower (luminous intensity) but is the apparent luminous intensity (apparent candlepower) in that direction.

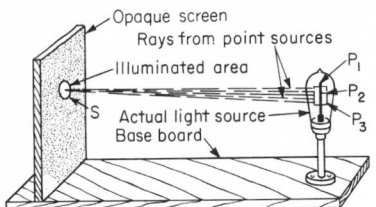

Opaque screen
Rays from point sources
Illuminated area
P_1
P_2
S Actual light source
P_3
Base board

FIG. 12 *Showing that the illumination at point S is due to the combined effects of an infinite number of point sources P_1, P_2, P_3, etc.*

20. "Illumination" is measured in "foot-candles." The foot-candle is defined as that illumination which is produced (Fig. 11) by a 1-cp point source (or its equivalent) on a surface which is exactly 1 ft distant from the point source.

EXPLANATION. If, in Fig. 11, the light source S is assumed to be a point source of luminous flux, then the illumination at point A, which is exactly 1 ft from S, is (by definition) 1 ft-c. Since the illuminated surface $MNOP$ is a plane, the point A is the only point on the surface which has an illumination of 1 ft-c. The illumination at any other point on the surface, such as B or C, is less than 1 ft-c because it is farther away from S than is A. If, however, the sphere of Fig. 9 has an internal radius of 1 ft and the true point source (Sec. **16**) has a luminous intensity of 1 candle, then every point on the interior surface of the sphere will have an illumination of 1 ft-c.

21. "Illumination" is really the density of the luminous flux which impinges on the surface of an illuminated object. The average density of anything on a surface may be numerically represented by the number of things on the whole surface divided by the number of unit areas in the surface. Thus, as will be further explained in Sec. **25,** if the luminous flux, in lumens, which impinges on a surface is divided by the area of that surface in square feet, the average illumination over the surface will be the result.

22. Luminous flux is measured in lumens. A lumen is defined as that quantity of incident luminous flux which will, when uniformly distributed over a surface having an area of 1 sq ft, produce an illumination of 1 ft-c on every point of the surface.

NOTE. When luminous flux impinges nonuniformly on a surface, then a lumen is the quantity of luminous flux which will, on 1 sq ft area of the surface, produce an average illumination of 1 ft-c.

23. A point source of light of 1 candle luminous intensity emits 12.57 lumens. It has been shown (Sec. **20** and Fig. 9) that a 1-cp point source of light located at the center of a hollow sphere of 1-ft radius will produce an illumination of 1 ft-c on every point of the interior surface of the sphere. Now the superficial area of a sphere = $4 \times 3.1416 \times r^2$. Hence, this 1-ft-radius sphere will have an area of

$$4 \times 3.1416 \times 1 \times 1 = 12.57 \text{ sq ft}$$

Since every point on the surface of this sphere has an illumination of 1 ft-c, there must, to satisfy the definition of the lumen (Sec. **22**), be as many lumens emitted by the 1-cp point source as there are square feet in the surface of the sphere. The sphere has an area of 12.57 sq ft. Therefore every 1-cp point source of light emits 12.57 lumens.

24. To obtain the output of a light source in lumens when its mean spherical candlepower is known, substitute in the following formula. This formula is strictly accurate only for a true point source (Sec. **16**) of light, but it gives results sufficiently accurate for all practical purposes if the mean spherical candlepower (Sec. **29**) is substituted for I.

$$F = 12.57 \times I \qquad \text{lumens} \qquad (2)$$

where F = total luminous flux emitted by the light source, in lumens; and I = luminous intensity or candlepower of a point source, in candles or, with sufficient accuracy for most practical purposes, the mean spherical candlepower of an actual light source.

Example. The mean spherical candlepower of a light source is 68.8. What quantity of luminous flux is emitted in lumens?

Solution. By For. (2), luminous flux $F = 12.57 \times I = 12.57 \times 68.8 = 865$ lumens.

25. "Illumination" in "foot-candles" is really "lumens per square foot." From the definition of the lumen in Sec. 22 1 lumen of flux spread out over an area of 1 sq ft produces 1 ft-c average illumination over that surface; 2 lumens would produce 2 ft-c, etc. Similarly, 10 lumens spread out over an area of 5 sq ft would produce an average illumination of $10 \div 5 = 2$ ft-c. Likewise, 1 lumen spread out over an area of 2 sq ft would produce an illumination of $1 \div 2 = 0.5$ ft-c. Thus, it is evident that lumens $\div$ sq ft area = average foot-candles illumination.

Example. A room which has an area of 600 sq ft has 3,300 lumens of luminous flux impinging on the working plane. What is the average illumination, in foot-candles, on the working plane?

Solution. By equation given above, average foot-candles illumination = lumens $\div$ sq ft area = $3,300 \div 600 = 5.5$ ft-c.

26. The illumination, in foot-candles, which, from a light source, impinges on a surface, varies inversely as the square of the distance from the source. This is true absolutely for a true point source (Sec. **16**). It is approximately true if the distance is at least ten times the largest dimension of the light source.

EXPLANATION. Assume (Fig. 13) that the 1-cp point source P is placed at the center of a hollow spherical shell which has an internal radius D of 1 ft. Then, a section A of the shell, having an area of 1 sq ft, will have on its inner surface an illumination of 1 ft-c. This follows from the preceding discussions. Furthermore, from the definition of the lumen (Sec. **22**), just 1 lumen of flux is lighting

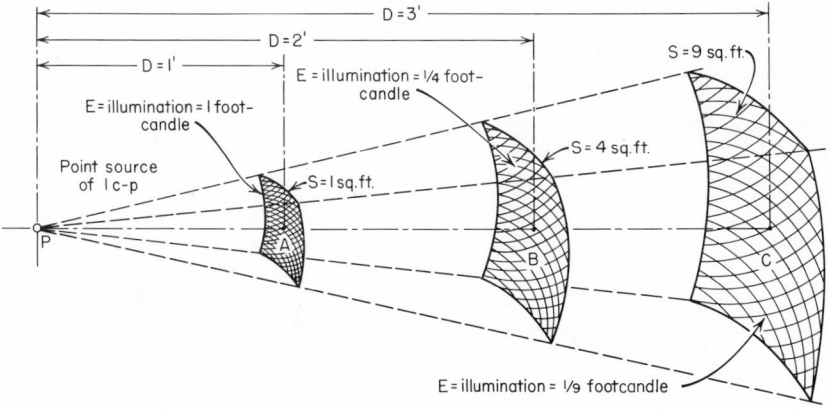

FIG. 13 *Illustrating the "inverse-square law."*

this surface. Now, if the 1-ft-radius sphere be removed and the 1-cp source be placed at the center of a 2-ft radius sphere, i.e., one of double the radius, then the same luminous flux will be spread out over an area B of 4 sq ft. (This follows because of the geometric fact that similar areas vary directly as the square of similar dimensions.) The illumination on B will be 1 lumen $\div$ 4 sq ft $= 0.25$ ft-c. Thus by doubling the distance from the source, the illumination has been quartered. Similarly, it can be shown for C that with the distance D increased three times the illumination provided by 1 lumen of flux is one-ninth of what it was with the distance of 1 ft. Thus, illumination varies inversely as the square of the distance from the source.

27. The photometer is an instrument which is used for determining the luminous intensity, in candles, of a light source. The understanding of the principle of a photometer can be obtained from a study of Fig. 14. Note that any determination made with a photometer gives apparent candlepower. However (Sec. **26**), if the location at which the intensity is measured is at a sufficient distance (d_2, Fig. 14) from the source, then the source may for all practical purposes be considered as a point source, and the value obtained for the unknown candlepower will be accurate well within the limits of error of experimental observation.

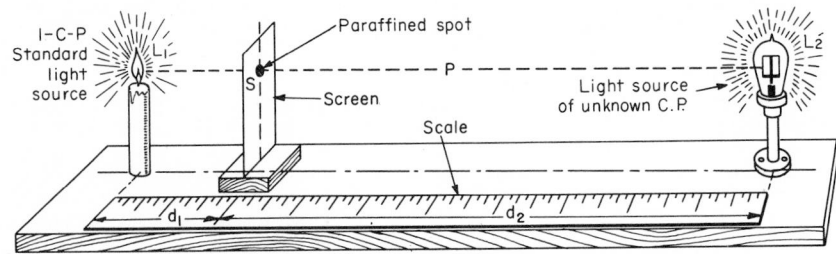

FIG. 14   *Illustrating the principle of the photometer.*

NOTE. The principle of the photometer is illustrated in Fig. 14. A semitransparent spot S is made on the white unglazed-paper screen with a drop of melted paraffin. Suppose a light source L_1, which has been standardized, indirectly, with the Standard Light Unit at Washington, D.C., and found to have an intensity of 1 candle in the horizontal direction L_1S, is placed at a distance d_1 from the screen on a line P, which is perpendicular to the plane of the screen and which passes through the centers of S and L_2. The light L_2 is then moved backward and forward along P until the spot S is either invisible, or the least visible. When this adjustment has been made, both of the lights will be producing the same illumination on S. That is, the spot S intercepts the same amount of luminous flux from L_1 as from L_2. It has been shown (Sec. **26**) that the density of luminous flux, or the illumination, varies inversely as the square of the distance from the source of light. Hence if both faces of S are equally illuminated, the apparent luminous intensity must vary as the squares of the distances. If $d_2 = 8$ ft and $d_1 = 2$ ft, then the candlepower of $L_2 = (64 \div 4) = 16$ times that of L_1. Or the luminous intensity of L_2 is 16 candles in the horizontal direction. It should be noted that the candlepower of a light source will usually be different in different directions (see Fig. 10).

28. Mean horizontal candlepower is the average of the candlepowers of a lamp in all directions in a horizontal plane. This term is now applied only to special lamps for laboratory test work.

29. Mean spherical candlepower is the average of the candlepowers of a lamp in all directions. It is measured by putting the lamp in the center of a sphere photometer (Fig. 15). The sphere has a small window of milk glass which is shielded from the direct rays of the lamp by a small opaque screen. The inner surface of the sphere is painted flat white for good reflection of the light. The candlepower of the window is compared with the horizontal candlepower of a standard lamp. This candlepower must

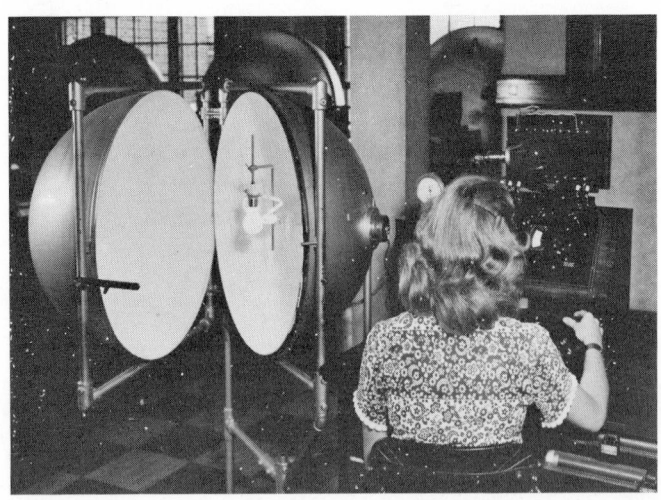

FIG. 15   *Sphere photometer.* (*General Electric Co.*)

be multiplied by a constant for the particular sphere to take account of the loss of light absorbed on the inner surface of the sphere and in the glass window. The mean spherical candlepower is used principally with the equation of Sec. **24** to obtain the lumen output in which the lamp is rated.

30. The efficiency of an electric-light source is stated in **lumens per watt.** This term is obtained by dividing the lumen output of the source by the watts input.

31. Candlepower Distribution Curves. Since the common light-giving sources either alone or in conjunction with the reflecting equipment used with them do not have the same light-giving power or candlepower in all directions, photometric graphs are employed in order to indicate the candlepower of the source in all directions. Curves giving this information for a light source are called candlepower distribution curves or simply distribution curves. Many lamps or lamps with their reflectors have the same candlepower in all directions in any one horizontal plane. This fact enables the candlepower in any direction from such a source to be determined from a single distribution curve which gives the candlepowers in all directions in a vertical plane through the center of the light source.

32. How to Read a Photometric Graph. In the photometric graph of Fig. 16, I, the candlepower directly downward is indicated by measuring it off on the vertical to a given scale. Thus, XA represents the candlepower directly below the light. Similarly the distances XB, XC, XD, XE, XF, and XG represent to scale candlepowers around the light at angles above the vertical of 15, 30, 45, 60, 75, and 90 deg. Similarly the candlepowers above 90 deg can be measured off to the given scale along lines at their respective angles. These points are then joined by a continuous line $GFED$, etc., and this line, completed for the 360 deg, is called the photometric distribution graph of the

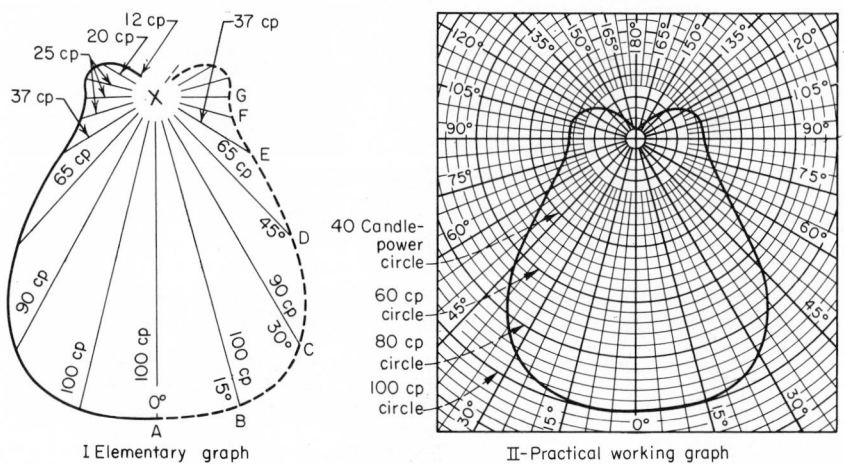

I Elementary graph   II-Practical working graph

FIG. 16   *Photometric graphs.*

light source. Figure 16, I, shows such a completed photometric curve, but in practice it is customary to use circular lines, as indicated on Fig. 16, II, to show the scale to which the candlepowers are plotted. The candlepower of the light unit can be measured at as few or as many angles as necessary, the accuracy of the resultant graph being largely determined by the number of angles taken.

33. The area of the distribution graph is not proportional to the amount of light given off. *B* (Fig. 71) represents a smaller total flux, by an amount equal to the absorption in the reflector, than does graph *A*, though it has a larger area. Such a graph as *B* is useful for determining the intensity of light at any given angle and for determining the total luminous output, as explained in Sec. **34.** These data may be required for any one of a number of practical operations.

34. The method of computing from its distribution graph the total flux, in lumens, emitted by a symmetrical light source is this: From the distribution graph of any light unit, as Fig. 16, take the candlepower at 5 deg and multiply it by the 0–10 factor as given in Table **36**. This gives the lumens in the 0–10-deg zone. Similarly, to obtain the lumens in the 10–20-deg zone, take the candlepower at 15 deg and multiply it by the 10–20-deg factor as given in Table **36**. The total lumens emitted in any large zone are obtained by adding the lumens of all the 10-deg zones contained in the large zone. If the sum total of the lumens is thus obtained for the 0–180-deg zone, the result is the total flux, in lumens, emitted by the source.

Example. What is the total flux emitted by a light source having a distribution graph as shown in Fig. 16?
Solution:

Deg	Candlepower	Zone factor	Lumens
(1)	(2)	(3)	(4)
5	100	0.095	9.50
15	98	0.283	27.45
25	94	0.463	43.50
35	84	0.628	52.75
45	66	0.774	51.10
55	46	0.897	41.25
65	33	0.992	32.71
75	27	1.058	28.55
85	26	1.091	28.37
95	26	1.091	28.37
105	25	1.058	26.48
115	24	0.992	23.80
125	20	0.897	17.94
135	15	0.774	11.60
145	12	0.628	7.54
155	8	0.463	3.70
165	4	0.283	1.13
175	4	0.095	0.38
		Total =	436.12

Total flux emitted = 436.12 lumens.
Column 2 is obtained from the graph (Fig. 16). Column 3 is obtained from Table **36**. Column 4 is obtained by multiplying the values in Column 2 by the corresponding values of Column 3.

NOTE. The total flux in lumens emitted by a light source can be computed graphically as follows: On the candlepower distribution graph (Fig. 16) measure the horizontal distance between the vertical axis (0–180-deg line) and the point where the candlepower graph crosses the 5-deg line. Then lay off this distance on the candlepower scale to which the distribution graph is plotted. Multiply the value thus obtained by 1.1, and the result is the quantity of luminous flux, in lumens, emitted by the light source in the 0–10-deg zone. To determine the flux in any 10-deg zone, it is only necessary to measure the horizontal distance between the vertical axis and the point where the candlepower graph crosses the center of the 10-deg zone under consideration and then proceed as above. To obtain the total lumens emitted in any large zone lay off the horizontal distances between the vertical axis and the point where the candlepower graph cuts the center of each 10-deg zone contained within the large zone successively along the edge of a strip of paper. Then lay off the total length on the candlepower scale and multiply the result by 1.1.

For the determination of the lumen output of nonsymmetric or asymmetric luminaires, such as conventional fluorescent units, readings of candlepower must be taken in a number of planes. From these readings a weighted average candlepower is obtained for each zone.

For fluorescent lighting units, candlepower readings often are taken in five planes, at 0, 22½, 45, 67½, and 90 deg from a plane through the luminaire axis. Candlepower values are measured in each of these planes at 10-deg intervals (5, 15, 25 deg, etc.). If the candlepower readings in the five planes (0, 22½, 45, 67½, and 90 deg) for any one zone are designated respectively as A, B, C, D, and E, then their weighted average for that zone is obtained by the formula

$$cp = \frac{A + 2B + 2C + 2D + E}{8}$$

In some laboratories for similar tests, candlepower readings are taken in three planes only (0, 45, and 90 deg), as in Fig. 17. The candlepower values in A (crosswise) and B (lengthwise) plus twice the values in C (45 deg) are added. The sum divided by 4 equals the average candlepower.

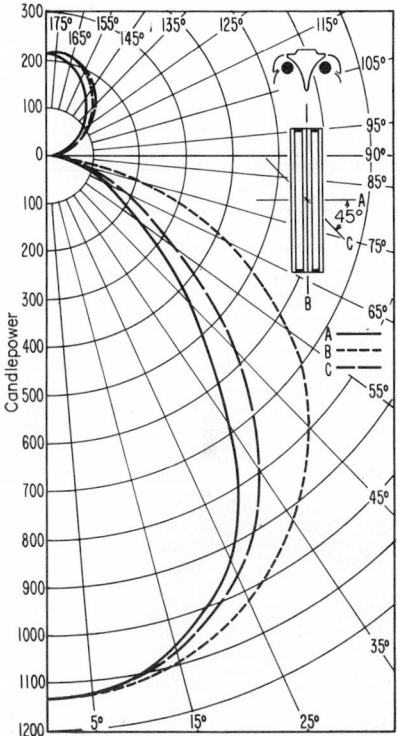

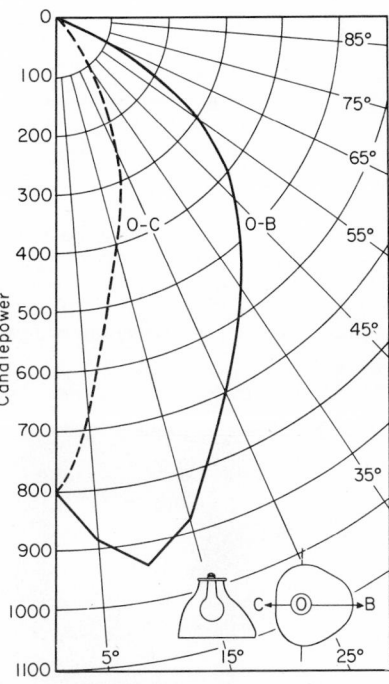

FIG. 17 *The average candlepower multiplied by the zone constant gives the zone lumens. Candlepower values at a given angle in curves A and B are added to twice the value in curve C at the same angle. This sum is divided by 4 to get the weighted average candlepower.*

FIG. 18 *Candlepower distribution curves of nonsymmetrical sources such as show window reflectors vary widely, and their interpretation depends on the specific planes in which they are taken.*

Similarly, nonsymmetric or asymmetric luminaires for filament lamps have such wide variations in candlepower at a given angle about the vertical that an average reading from which to compute zonal lumens cannot be obtained by rotating the unit. Candlepower distribution curves for such equipment are prepared from data obtained in specific planes, and in interpreting such curves one must be careful to observe the planes they represent (see Fig. 18).

35. The mean spherical candlepower (Sec. **29**) of a light source can be determined (1) directly, by means of the sphere photometer (Sec. **29** and Fig. 15), and (2) indirectly, by computing the total lumens from the distribution graph, as explained in the preceding paragraph, and dividing the result by 12.57.

Example. What is the mean spherical candlepower of the light source, the distribution graph of which is shown in Fig. 16.

Solution. By example under Sec. **34**, the total flux of the source = 436.12 lumens. The mean spherical candlepower = 436.12 ÷ 12.57 = 34.6.

36. Factors to Obtain the Lumens in the 10-deg Zones around a Light Source. To obtain the lumens in any zone, multiply the candlepower at the center of the zone by the factor for that zone.

Degree zones		Factor	Degree zones		Factor
0–10	170–180	0.095	50–60	120–130	0.897
10–20	160–170	0.283	60–70	110–120	0.992
20–30	150–160	0.463	70–80	100–110	1.058
30–40	140–150	0.628	80–90	90–100	1.091
40–50	130–140	0.774			

37. The foot-candle meter (commonly called **sight meter**) is an instrument for measuring illumination directly in foot-candles. It consists of one or two photronic cells connected to a microammeter. When light falls on the photronic cell, a voltage is generated and current flows through the meter approximately in proportion to the foot-candle illumination on the cell. The small pocket type of meter is usually called a sight meter (Fig. 19). It has a single photronic cell and a single scale, calibrated in foot-candles. The scale is also calibrated in visual tasks to be done so that the meter can be

FIG. 19 *The sight meter. (General Electric Co.)*

used readily by persons not familiar with technical terms. The meter is placed with the window of the photronic cell parallel to the plane on which it is desired to measure the illumination. Higher values of illumination (such as those of daylight intensity) can be measured by slipping a screen called a multiplier over the front of the cell. Thus, part of the light is absorbed by the screen, and the illumination will be the value read on the meter multiplied by the constant for the multiplier.

Larger and more accurate meters (Fig. 20) have two cells connected in parallel to increase the current output. They also have two or three different resistors which can be connected in series with the meter circuit by use of a toggle selector switch. The dial is provided with several different scales to correspond to the different resistors. The light output of the photronic cells decreases with age and use, so that they should be calibrated frequently for accurate results. Calibration can be checked by setting up in a dark room (Fig. 21) a laboratory standard lamp whose mean horizontal candlepower is known (Sec. **28**). The voltage applied to the lamp must be the exact value for which it is calibrated. The cell should be held in a vertical position about 2 or 3 ft horizontally from the lamp. Then, by definition,

$$\text{Foot-candles} = \frac{\text{cp}}{S^2} \qquad (3)$$

where cp = candlepower of lamp and S = distance from lamp to cell in feet.

Foot-candle meters are usually calibrated with incandescent lamps and therefore are strictly accurate only when used with light from incandescent lamps. They can be obtained calibrated for use with daylight fluorescent lamps, however. When they are used with any other quality or color of light, the results are good only for very rough comparisons, the accuracy decreasing as the color of the light is further removed from the color of the light for which the meter was calibrated.

FIG. 20 *The foot-candle meter. (Weston Instrument Div. of Daystrom, Inc.)*

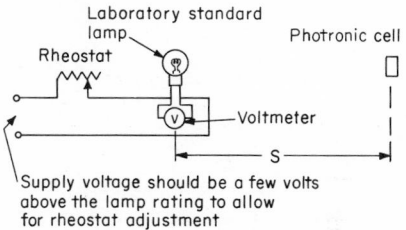

Supply voltage should be a few volts above the lamp rating to allow for rheostat adjustment

FIG. 21 *Diagram for calibration of foot-candle meter.*

The General Electric Co., for example, states that their pocket-size light meter is calibrated under a color temperature (refer to Sec. **14**) of 2700°K. They further state: This value was chosen because it is fairly representative of electric lighting in general, considering the effect of walls, etc., and the reading of the instrument applies directly for a fair range of color temperature. Color- and cosine-corrected meters are now available. For light from common illuminants the readings are multiplied by a factor, as indicated in the following table:

Approximate Multiplying Factors for GE Light-meter Scale Readings

Source	Correction Factor
Filament lamps (2700–3400°K)	1.0
High-intensity mercury (Type E-H1)	1.0
Sun at noon—4800°K	0.8
Average daylight—6500°K	0.7
Fluorescent standard warm white	1.1
Fluorescent de luxe warm white	1.0
Fluorescent soft white	0.9
Fluorescent white	None
Fluorescent standard cool white	1.0
Fluorescent de luxe cool white	0.9
Fluorescent daylight	0.9
Fluorescent red	0.7
Fluorescent pink	1.3
Fluorescent gold	1.3
Fluorescent blue	0.5
Fluorescent green	1.5

38. Glare (Fig. 22) is defined as any brightness within the field of vision of such a character as to cause discomfort, annoyance, interference with vision or eye fatigue.

NOTE. Glare may be subdivided into three different classes: (1) Direct glare (Fig. 22, II), which results when one looks directly at a brilliant light source. (2) Contrast glare, which is caused by brightness contrast. An example of this is the visual discomfort produced by a brilliant auto-mobile headlight shining in the eyes on a dark night. The same headlight would cause no discomfort in the daytime. The annoyance experienced at night is due solely to the contrast between the bright head-light and the dark surroundings. (3) Reflected glare (Fig. 22, I), which is produced by light being reflected directly into the eyes from a polished, a white, or a light-colored surface. Glass desk plates, highly polished furniture, glazed paper, and mirrors may occasion reflected glare.

FIG. 22 *Illustrating methods of causing glare.*

39. "Brightness" is the property of lighted objects which enables them to be seen by virtue of the light issuing from them. Technically, brightness is the density of luminous flux issuing or projected from a light source or from some illuminated surface.

NOTE. The relation between brightness and illumination. Illumination is the density of the luminous flux impinging on an illuminated surface. Just as illumination measures incident-luminous-flux density, so brightness measures issuing-luminous-flux density. It is due solely to the light issuing or reflected from things that we see. There might be great illumination (incident-luminous-flux density) on a dead-black object in a room with dead-black walls, and yet that object would be invisible, because the black would absorb (see Table 9) all the light which impinged on it and would reflect none to the eye.

40. The units of brightness are the **lambert**, the **millilambert**, the **foot-lambert**, and the **candela per unit of area.** The lambert is by definition the brightness of a perfectly diffusing surface which radiates or reflects 1 lumen per sq cm, while the millilambert is 0.001 of this value. The foot-lambert is the brightness of a surface which radiates or reflects 1 lumen per sq ft. As its name implies, the candela per square inch is the brightness of a surface which radiates 1 candlepower per sq in. The lambert and the candela per square inch are commonly used for high brightness such as light sources, while the millilambert and the foot-lambert are used for designating ordinary illuminated surfaces.

41. The working equations for brightness computations are

$$b = 2.05 \, L \qquad (4)$$

$$F = 6.45 \, SL \qquad (5)$$

where b = brightness in candles per square inch; L = brightness in lamberts; F = total luminous flux in lumens; and S = area of the surface in square inches.

Example. A light source has a brightness of 500 cp per sq in. What is its brightness expressed in lamberts?

Solution. By For. (4),

$$L = \frac{b}{2.05} = \frac{500}{2.05} = 243.5 \text{ lamberts}$$

Example. An incandescent-lamp filament has a surface area of 0.4 sq in. and emits 1,580 lumens. What is its brightness in lamberts?

Solution. By For. (5),

$$L = \frac{F}{6.45S} = \frac{1,580}{6.45 \times 0.4} = 612 \text{ lamberts}$$

42. The relation between the illumination incident on and the brightness reflected from an illuminated surface can be understood from a consideration of the following facts: No surface, however smooth, is a perfect reflector, since some of the luminous flux impinging on the surface will be absorbed thereby. Therefore, when the surface brightness resulting from the reflection of the impinging light rays or illumination is computed, the coefficient of reflection (Table **9**) of the material must be considered. The brightness equals the illumination times the coefficient of reflection.

$$\text{Milli-}L = 1.076 \times E \times m \qquad \text{millilamberts} \tag{6}$$

where Milli-L = average surface brightness over the surface under consideration in millilamberts; E = the incident illumination on the surface in foot-candles; and m = the absolute coefficient of reflection (Table **9**) of the surface material.

Example. A surface of ordinary foolscap paper has an illumination of 5 ft-c. What is its brightness?

Solution. The coefficient of reflection of ordinary foolscap is (Table **9**) 0.70. By For. (6),

Brightness = $1.076 \times E \times m = 1.076 \times 5 \times 0.70 = 3.77$ millilamberts

43. Conversion Factors for Various Units of Brightness

Values in units in this column × conversion factor = values in units at top of column	Candles per sq in.	Lamberts	Milli-lamberts	Foot-lamberts
Candles per sq in............................	1	0.487	487	452
Lamberts....................................	2.054	1	1,000	929
Millilambert...............................	0.00205	0.001	1	0.929
Foot-lambert...............................	0.00221	0.00108	1.076	1

44. The maximum brightness beyond which glare will result (see Sec. **38** for Glare) is specified by Ward Harrison in his "Electric Lighting." Ordinarily, the brightness of a lighting unit which is in the central portion of the visual field should not exceed from 1 to 1.5 lamberts (2 to 3 candles per sq in. of projected area). Higher values of brightness will produce a sensation of glare. If the eyes are not to be fatigued when the unit is viewed continually, the brightness should not exceed 0.25 lambert. It should be noted that the maximum permissible brightness is somewhat influenced by the darkness of the surroundings (see Contrast Glare under Sec. **38**).

44A. Brightness of Light Sources

Source	Approximate Lamberts		
Incandescent lamp with opal globe.....................	0.24	–	1.46
Incandescent lamp inside frosted globe...............	7	–	15
Fluorescent lamp, white and daylight.................	1.2	–	2.6
Fluorescent lamp, green.....................................	2.4	–	3.6
Fluorescent lamp, red.......................................	0.12	–	0.23
Fluorescent lamp, pink, blue, gold......................	0.83	–	1.8
Candle flame..	1.46	–	1.95
Cooper-Hewitt lamp..	4.9	–	9.8
Acetylene-burner flame	29	–	50
Vacuum-incandescent-lamp filament	460	–	700
Gas-filled-incandescent-lamp filament.................	3,000	–	4,000
Neon tube (red)...	0.24		
Neon-mercury tube (green or blue)......................	0.05	–	0.1
Mercury arc (quartz tube)	290	–	490
Sky..	0.7	–	2.0
Sun, on horizon	1,000		
Sun, 30 deg above horizon.................................	243,000		
Sun, at noon..	450,000		
Ceiling over indirect-lighting fixture...................	0.01	–	0.1
Walls when lighted by diffused daylight.............	0.001	–	0.05

45. Brightness (Westinghouse Electric Corp.) is usually measured visually, by matching a comparison field inside the meter to the test surface. The Macbeth illuminometer, calibrated in foot-lamberts or candles per square inch and sighted directly at the test surface, can be used for the measurement of brightness. Small, self-contained instruments designed specifically as brightness meters operate on the same general principle. The brightness of the comparison field in these meters is adjusted by various methods, such as changing the distance of the comparison lamp or varying the current through it, or the use of a graduated neutral filter. By means of a series of neutral filters the range is extended to include the brightnesses of most reflecting and translucent surfaces and some light sources.

Rough approximations of the brightness values of diffuse reflecting and transmitting surfaces can be obtained with some cell-type foot-candle meters. For a reflecting material, the cell is placed against the test surface and then drawn away slowly until a constant reading is obtained (a distance of 2 to 6 in.). The meter indication at that point, multiplied by a factor of 1.25 to correct for light striking the cell at oblique angles, is the approximate brightness in foot-lamberts. The foot-lambert brightness of a transmitting surface is similarly measured by placing the cell against the surface and multiplying the reading by 1.25.

Portable visual photometers, in which the brightness of a calibrated test plate placed at the point of measurement is compared visually with a standardized reference lamp, are also used for illumination measurements in the field. The Macbeth illuminometer (Fig. 23), the most commonly used instrument of this type, has a photometer head and viewing eyepiece at one end of a light-tight tube which contains a small lamp mounted on a movable rod. When the instrument is sighted at the white test plate, the optical system of the photometer head brings to the eye of the observer a circular central field illuminated by light reflected from the plate, surrounded by a wide ring illuminated by the reference lamp in the tube. Measurements are made by moving the reference lamp back and forth to find the point where the two fields are of equal brightness. A direct foot-candle reading is then taken from a scale on the outside of the tube. The scale is so arranged that the indications decrease inversely as the square of the distance between the reference lamp and the head, in accordance with the inverse square law. Calibrated filters, which can be inserted on either side of the head to reduce the brightness of either field, make it possible to read a wide range of illumination values. Visual photometers, although not so convenient as the cell-type meters, are less susceptible to certain types of error and when properly used by experienced observers are capable of producing more accurate results.

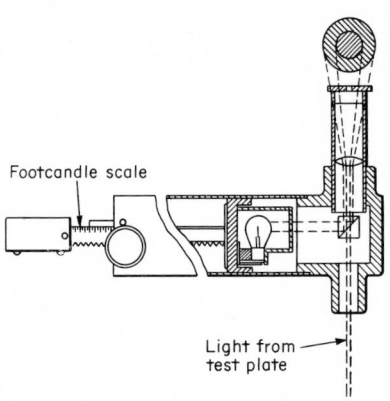

Footcandle scale

Light from test plate

FIG. 23 *Macbeth illuminometer.*

46. In the General Electric brightness meter (Fig. 24), the brightness of the comparison field is varied by a photographic film gradient; the lamp is stationary, and its light is transmitted through a white glass plate. In this instrument, the operator views the photometric field in the upper eyepiece shown at the right. The field contains two aluminized trapezoids which image the comparison field. The test field or surface to be measured is brought into focus by the lens tube at the left end of the meter. When the knurled wheel is rotated, the trapezoid field is adjusted to a brightness which matches the surrounding test field. When the balance is obtained, the operator reads the scale in range both upward and downward from the normal range of 2 to 50 foot-lamberts. The screens have multiplying factors of "×10" and "×100," which when used together become "×1,000." Thus the upper range of the meter is 1,000 times 50 or 50,000 foot-lamberts. The range can be extended downward by the

FIG. 24 *General Electric brightness meter.* (*General Electric Co.*)

reducing screens in the same manner, to 0.002 foot-lambert. The optical system which is used to focus on the object to be measured is of such magnification that it is possible to measure a surface 1 ft wide and several feet long at a distance of 500 ft.

ELECTRIC-LIGHT SOURCES

47. Electric-light sources may be classified as follows:

A. Visible-light sources.
    1. Incandescent (filament).
    2. Fluorescent.
    3. Gaseous discharge.
        a. High-intensity (mercury, metal halide and high-pressure sodium).
        b. Neon.
        c. Argon (glow).
B. Ultraviolet-light sources.
    1. Sunlight lamps.
    2. Black-light lamps.
    3. Germ-killing lamps.
    4. Photochemical lamps.
    5. Ozone lamps.
C. Infrared heating lamps.
D. Xenon flash tubes.

INCANDESCENT (FILAMENT) LAMPS

48. The incandescent lamp consists of a filament which is a highly refractory conductor mounted in a transparent or translucent glass bulb and provided with a suitable electrically connecting base. The filament is heated by the passage of an electric current through it to such a high temperature that it becomes incandescent and emits light. In incandescent lamps of the older types the air was, in so far as practicable, exhausted from the space within the bulb and surrounding the conductor (filament), forming a partial vacuum. But in many of the modern lamps this space is filled with an inert transparent gas—like nitrogen, for example. The conductor must have a high melting point or high vaporizing temperature and a high resistance; it must be hard and not become plastic when heated. In vacuum-type lamps the vacuum must be good, not only to prevent the oxidation of the filament but also to prevent the loss of heat, which would reduce the efficiency. In non-vacuum-type lamps (gas-filled lamps) the gas used must be inert so as not to combine chemically with the filament material. The bulb must be transparent or translucent to permit the passage of light, not porous, so that it will retain the vacuum or inert gas, and strong to withstand handling and use.

49. Classification of Incandescent Lamps. Incandescent lamps may be classified in six different ways, according to:

1. The class of lamp.
2. The shape of the bulb.
3. The finish of the bulb.

4. The type of the base.
5. The type of filament.
6. The type of service.

50. Class of Lamp. Incandescent lamps are classified as Type B or Type C. The Type B lamp is one in which the filament operates in a vacuum. The Type C lamp is one which is gas-filled.

51. Classification According to Shape of Bulb (Fig. 25). The standard-line shape is employed for general-lighting-service lamps up to and including the 100-watt size.

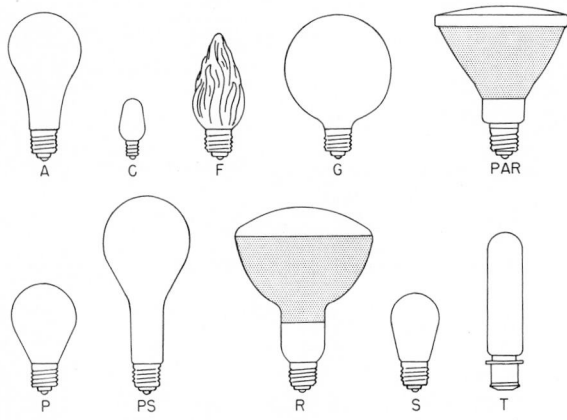

FIG. 25 *Bulb designations of incandescent lamps.* (*Westinghouse Electric Corp.*)

Lamps of 150 watts and larger for general lighting service are made in the pear shape. The other shapes are utilized for lamps designed for special classes of service. Lumi-line lamps are included in the tubular classification.

Shape of bulb	Designating letter	Shape of bulb	Designating letter
Standard line......	A	Pear shaped.......	P or PS
Cone shaped.......	C	Reflector..........	R
Flame shaped......	F	Straight side.......	S
Globular...........	G	Tubular...........	T
Parabolic..........	PAR		

Lamps are designated by a letter and figure, as PS-30. The letter indicates the shape of bulb and the figure the greatest diameter of the bulb in eighths of an inch. Thus, a PS-30 lamp is a lamp with a pear-shaped bulb with a diameter of $^{30}/_8$, or $3\frac{3}{4}$ in.

52. Classification According to Finish of Bulb.

1. Clear.
2. Inside frosted.
3. White bowl.
4. Silvered bowl.
5. De luxe white.

6. Daylight.
7. Inside colored.
8. Outside colored.
9. Colored glass.
10. Outside coating.

53. Finish of Bulbs. Incandescent lamps can be obtained with the bulbs finished in several different ways as listed in Sec. **52.** With the clear lamps the bulb is made of clear glass which leaves the filament exposed to view. Clear-bulb lamps are used with reflecting equipment which completely conceals the lamp from view. They are employed in some cases with open-bottom types of reflecting equipment, when the units are mounted so high that the lamps are not in the line of vision. Inside-frosted lamps have the entire inside surface of the bulb coated with a frosting which leaves the exterior surface perfectly smooth. This finish conceals the bright filament and diffuses the light emitted from the lamp. Inside-frosted lamps are used with open-bottom types of reflecting equipment and in places where no reflecting equipment is employed. White-bowl lamps have the lower inner portion of the bulb sprayed with a white washable enamel (Fig. 26). This increases the size of the visible light source when viewed from below, reducing the apparent brilliancy and diffusing the light rays so as to reduce the danger of glare. The white-bowl finish is the one employed generally for lamps of larger size than 100 watts when used with open-bottom types of reflectors. Silvered-bowl lamps have a coating of mirror silver on the lower half of the bowl, which shields the brilliant filament and forms a highly efficient reflecting surface for indirect lighting. The upper part of the bulb is inside frosted to eliminate streaks and shadows of fixture supports. Silvered-bowl lamps should be used only in fixtures designed for them, because the silvering directs the heat toward the socket assembly, which will therefore tend to operate at a higher temperature than with clear lamps. Semisilvered lamps are available in a restricted number of sizes. These semisilvered bowl lamps have a small open area in the silvering at the bottom of the bowl. This construction is employed primarily for store-lighting applications in order to provide direct down-lighting emphasis over counters or display areas. De luxe white lamps have the entire interior surface of the lamp covered with a fine coating of silica. This coating gives a high degree of diffusion which softens shadows and reduces shiny reflections. Since bulb blackening is not apparent through the diffusing coating, the lamps appear clean and white throughout their life.

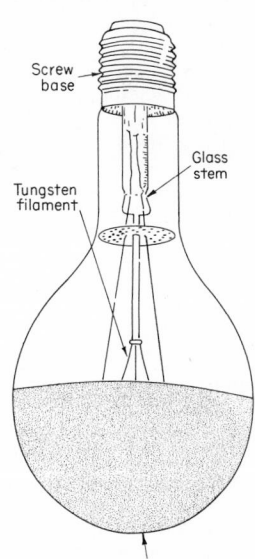

Screw base

Glass stem

Tungsten filament

Translucent coating of white material

FIG. 26 *White-bowl in-candescent lamp.*

54. Daylight lamps have a blue bulb made of a special blue-green glass. Noon sunlight, which is usually considered as the standard white light, consists of a combination of equal amounts of the three primary colors: red, green, and violet. The ordinary Mazda lamp produces light in which the red rays predominate. The blue-green glass of the bulb of daylight lamps absorbs part of the reddish rays emitted by the filament of the lamp, giving a resultant light which approaches the whiteness of noon sunlight. The glass absorbs about one-third of the total light emitted by the filament. Consequently, in order to obtain a given intensity of illumination of the daylight quality, it is necessary to use 50 per cent more wattage than would be required with clear lamps. These lamps are widely used for show-window and other lighting for which sunlight color is desirable. They are, however, being displaced by the more efficient and more economical daylight fluorescent lamp.

55. Colored Bulbs (Westinghouse Electric Corp.). Colored light is obtained from filament lamps by the subtractive method, that is, by means of a separate filter or a bulb so processed that light of colors other than that desired is largely absorbed. Colored bulbs used in lamp manufacture are of natural colored glass or of clear glass having a coating applied to either the inner or the outer surface of the bulb by one of several different processes. Natural-colored bulbs, wherein chemicals are added to the ingredients of the glass to produce the desired color, are regularly available in daylight blue, blue, amber, green, and ruby. Of these colors, daylight blue is the most widely used. The characteristics of the daylight blue bulb are such as to reduce the preponderance of red and yellow light common to incandescent lamps, with the result that the light produced more nearly approaches daylight in color. Since this is accomplished at the expense of increased lamp cost and of some 35 per cent absorption in light, daylight blue lamps should be used only where the lighting requirements make it necessary. Natural-colored bulbs produce light of purer colors than coated bulbs and are often used in preference to the latter for theatrical and photographic lighting.

Coated colored lamps are made by spraying either the inside or the outside of the bulb or by applying a fused enamel (*ceramic*) coating to the outside of the bulb. The colors in most common use are red, blue, green, yellow, orange, ivory, and white.

Where decorative or display lighting is involved, coated colored lamps are to be preferred to natural-colored lamps because of their lower cost. Enameled and inside sprayed bulbs are satisfactory for either indoor or outdoor use.

QUARTZ-HALOGEN LAMPS

55A. Quartz-halogen lamps (General Electric Co.) are incandescent filament lamps but are markedly different from conventional lamps in size and structure. They represent the first commercially successful application of the "iodine cycle" in filament lamps. In the iodine cycle, evaporated tungsten returns to the filament, with the result that the inside walls of the bulb (tube) do not blacken.

Basically, there are two types of quartz-halogen lamps available. One is a T3 quartz tube in which a coiled filament extends from one end of the tube to the other to double-ended lamp bases, and iodine or other halogens are used in the sealed tube. The other is the T3 tube located in a PAR reflector housing (Fig. 26A).

The average life of the double-ended T3 quartz lamp is about twice the life of a regular 500-watt general-service PS-35 lamp, or 2,000 hr. Although the initial light output of these lamps is about the same (22 lumens per watt), at the end of 1,000 hr

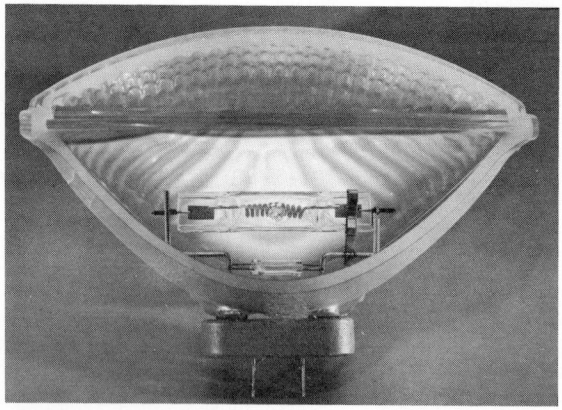

FIG. 26A *PAR-Q quartz-halogen lamp with a T-3 quartz lamp inside of a PAR-56 envelope.* (*General Electric Co.*)

the quartz-halogen lamp produces about 13 per cent more light than the standard general-service lamp. The average life of the PAR-Q (T3 tube in a PAR reflector housing) is double that of the T3 lamps, or 4,000 hr.

These lamps offer high light output from the compact equipment. For example, the reflector for the 1,500-watt T3 quartz-halogen lamp is only 1 ft long, and 6 or 7 in. wide.

The 500-watt PAR-Q lamp combines the excellent efficiency and long life characteristics of a T3 quartz-halogen lamp with the precise beam control of a PAR bulb. The lamp filament is sealed inside a quartz tube (Fig. 26A), which is enclosed in a PAR-56 bulb. Accurate beam control is gained by mounting the quartz tube at the focal point of the PAR bulb's reflector. Light output at the end of life (4,000 hr) for PAR-Q lamps is 40 per cent greater than for standard 500-watt PAR lamps.

For data on quartz-halogen lamps refer to Table 101A.

56. Classification According to Type of Base (Fig. 27).

1. Bayonet.
2. Candelabra.
3. Intermediate.
4. Medium.
5. Three-contact medium.
6. Admedium.
7. Mogul.
8. Three-contact mogul.
9. Disk.
10. Medium prefocus.
11. Mogul prefocus.
12. Medium bipin.
13. Medium bipost.
14. Mogul bipost.

57. Lamp Bases. There are in use a number of different types of bases for incandescent lamps (Fig. 27). Of these, the bayonet, candelabra, and intermediate base are used on the small-sized (miniature) lamps. The medium base, used on general-service lamps of 300 watts and less, is the most common type. The mogul base is used on sizes of 300 watts and up. The admedium is slightly larger in diameter than the medium and is used on some of the mercury Mazda lamps. The three-contact base is used with a three-lite type of lamp. The disk base is used on lumiline lamps.

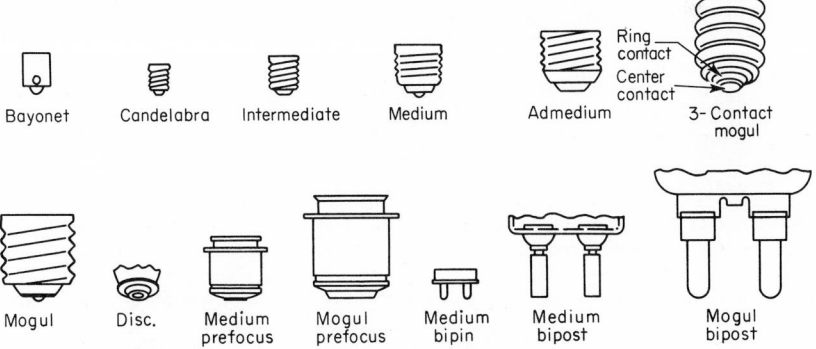

FIG. 27   *Bases for incandescent lamps.* (*Westinghouse Electric Corp.*)

The medium and mogul prefocused bases are used on certain types of concentrated-filament lamps, such as those for picture projection and aviation service, where it is desirable to have the light source accurately located. The medium bipin base is for fluorescent lamps. The medium bipost base is made in 500-, 750-, and 1,000-watt lamp sizes for use principally with indirect fixtures, where it allows a better design of fixture and better radiation of heat than is obtainable with the mogul-base type. For the very large size lamps of 1,500 watts and up for floodlighting service the mogul bipost is the standard.

58. Classification According to Type of Filament. Several different types of filament structure are used. The filament structure is designated by a letter or letters to indicate whether the wire is straight or coiled and by an arbitrary number sometimes followed by a letter to indicate the arrangement of the filament on the supports. Prefix letters include S (straight), wire is straight or slightly corrugated; C (coil), wire is wound into a helical coil or it may be deeply fluted; CC (coiled coil), wire is wound into a helical coil and this coiled wire again wound into a helical coil.

59. Classification of Incandescent Lamps According to Type of Service:

1. General lighting service.
    a. Clear bulb.
    b. Inside-frosted bulb.
    c. White bowl bulb.
    d. Silvered-bowl bulb.
    e. De luxe white bulb.
2. Special lighting service.
    a. Daylight lamps.
    b. Decorative lamps.
    c. Rough-service lamps.
    d. Three-lite lamps.
    e. Tubular lamps.
    f. Vibration lamps.
3. Miscellaneous lighting service.
    a. Appliance- and indicator-service lamps.
    b. Aviation-service lamps.
    c. Country-home-service lamps.
    d. High-voltage lamps.
    e. Low-voltage lamps.
    f. Marine-service lamps.
    g. Mine-service lamps.
    h. Optical-service lamps.
    i. Photographic lamps.
    j. Photo-service lamps.
    k. Picture-projection lamps.
    l. Projector and reflector lamps.
    m. Sign lamps.
    n. Spotlight- and floodlight-service lamps.
    o. Street-lighting-service lamps.
    p. Street-railway-service lamps.
    q. Traffic-signal lamps.
    r. Train- and locomotive-service lamps.

60. General-lighting-service lamps are those of 115-, 120-, or 125-volt rating for the ordinary uses in homes, stores, offices, schools, factories, etc.

61. Special-lighting-service lamps are for use in similar locations, but they have some special design feature, such as shape or color of bulb, or other special design features.

For explanation of daylight lamps refer to Sec. **54.**

Decorative lamps for general and special lighting are colored lamps that are available in a number of different types (see Sec. **55**). They can be used to provide special effects in homes, theaters, shops, restaurants, and lobbies and foyers of public buildings. In addition to the usually completely colored bowl lamps, lamps are available with only the bowl coated with colored enamel. They are called decorative enamel bowl lamps. The colors of the bowls are warm, pleasing tints of pink or ivory. They are intended for use in open-type single and cluster ceiling fixtures in homes, clubs, restaurants, and public buildings.

Special yellow enameled lamps are available which often are called insect-repellent lamps. Although these lamps are excellent for decorative lighting, they are designed primarily for outdoor lighting during the season of night-flying insects. They have less attraction for insects than lamps of other colors. They are used on open porches, outdoor recreation areas, filling stations, camps, roadside stands, and any other place where people enjoy outside activities under lights.

Rough-service lamps are specially constructed so that the filament can withstand sudden bumps and other forms of rough treatment. They are used principally in extension-cord service in garages, industrial plants, and similar applications where they will be subjected to excessive shock in service.

For explanation of three-lite lamps refer to Sec. **62.**

Tubular incandescent lamps for special general lighting service are available in the lumiline type and the showcase type.

The lumiline lamps with their long bulb, 1 in. in diameter, give a continuous line of light which is well suited where space limitation is a factor such as in displays, niches, small coves, signs, mirrors, paintings, and luminous panels. These lamps have contact caps at each end of the bulb of the disk-base type. Specially designed sockets or lamp holders are required. The lumiline lamps are available with clear, inside-frosted, white, or colored glass tubes.

Showcase lamps (Fig. 28) are tubular lamps with conventional screw bases, which are designed primarily for the lighting of showcases but which, also, are used for the lighting of shallow-depth displays and other special applications requiring small trough-type reflectors. These lamps are available in clear, inside-frosted, and the special

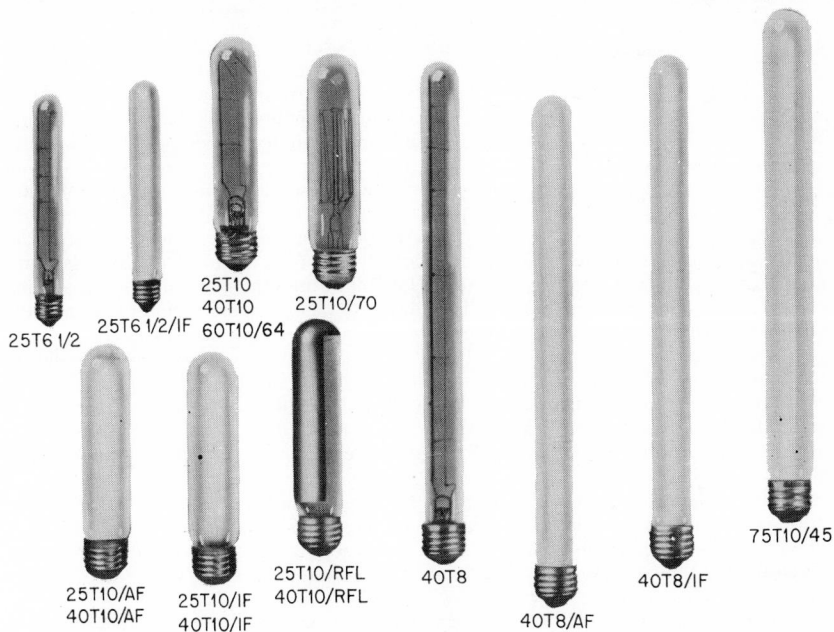

FIG. 28 *Showcase lamps. (General Electric Co.)*

showcase-reflector types. The showcase-reflector type is made with a tubular bulb with the upper half inside-aluminized so that it can be used in showcases, shelves, speakers' stands, etc., in an ordinary socket without any reflector. A spring contact on the base allows for adjustment of the lamp in the socket in order to throw the light rays in any desired direction.

Vibration lamps are particularly designed for use on or near rotating machinery and other places where relatively high-frequency vibration exists. Certain of these lamps are equipped with a special type of filament wire designed to operate suitably under vibration conditions.

62. The three-lite lamp has two separate filaments in the one bulb (Fig. 29). One filament consumes double the wattage of the other, and the filaments can be lighted separately or together to produce three different levels of illumination, namely, 50/100/150 watts or 100/200/300 watts. These lamps are particularly applicable to study lamps, reading lamps, and indirect floor lamps so that the user, with a single lamp, can adjust the illumination from that for decorative and casual use to full brilliancy for close seeing. They can also be used in stores so that daylight can be supplemented with an economical use of electric light and the illumination can be varied to suit different occasions.

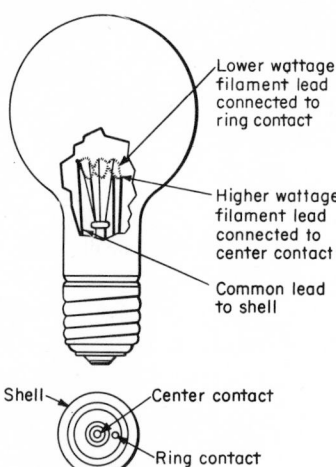

FIG. 29 *Three-lite lamp.* (*General Electric Co.*)

63. Appliance- and indicator-service lamps are specially designed for use with appliances and equipment for home and commercial use. These lamps, when properly used, provide effective illumination of equipment exteriors and interiors and also give clear indications of operations in progress.

64. Aviation-service (airport) lamps are specially designed to provide for the special conditions encountered in the vital lighting for safety at airport landing fields. Several types are required in order to provide for satisfactory approach, beacon, running, taxiway, etc., lighting.

65. Country-home-service lamps are rated for 30 volts and designed for operation on battery-generator sets as used on farms and in other places where central-station service is not available.

66. High-voltage-service lamps, rated at 230 and 250 volts, are available for use in locations where only the higher voltage is available. These lamps are less rugged and less efficient than the general-lighting-service type. The reason for this is that the filament has to be of longer and finer wire to have sufficient resistance to limit the current to approximately one-half the value for the same-wattage general-service lamp. For this reason their use in any new installation where the lower voltage could be made available is not encouraged.

67. Low-voltage-service lamps, rated at 6, 12, 30, 32, 60, and 64 volts, respectively, are available for use on electrical systems such as for automobiles, boats, garden lighting, miniature interior fixtures or desk lamps, underwater swimming-pool fixtures, and trains.

68. Marine lamps are specially designed to take care of the special maritime illumination requirements. These special lamps are used on shipboard to outline and identify vessels for seaway safety and to signal between ships. On land they provide a source for lighthouse beacons. Underwater, they illuminate areas where divers must work.

69. Mine lamps are specially designed to meet the special conditions encountered in the general illumination of mines and mine equipment.

70. Lamps for optical devices are available in a great variety of types to meet the special requirements of the devices which are used in the optical field of science, industry, and education.

71. Photographic lamps are spotlight lamps designed with concentrated filaments for maximum light output in the controlled beams of spotlights used in theaters, television studios, motion-picture and other photographic studios. For best lighting results, the filaments of these lamps must be accurately positioned, and the lamps should include mounting characteristics that will properly locate the filament in relation to the spotlight optical system.

72. Photo-service lamps are made in two types:
1. Photoflash lamps.
2. Photoflood lamps.

The **photoflash lamp** (Fig. 30) consists of a bulb containing magnesium foil in an atmosphere of oxygen. When the lamp is connected to a source of voltage, which may be either two flashlight cells or a 110- to 125-volt power circuit, the foil burns with a brilliant flash lasting about ⅟₅₀ sec.

The **photoflood lamp** is similar to the regular inside-frosted incandescent lamp except that the filament is designed to operate at a higher temperature. This lamp emits much more light than the general-service lamp for the same wattage, but its life is much shorter, for example, 2 hr for the smallest size to 10 hr for the largest size.

The **photoflash lamp** is used to illuminate scenes for the taking of photographs, whereas the photoflood lamp is used for continuous illumination in the taking of moving pictures. The photoflood lamp is also used by commercial photographers for studio portrait work and by amateur photographers for interior photographs.

FIG. 30 *Photoflash lamps. (General Electric Co.)*

73. Picture-projection lamps (Fig. 31) are for use in motion-picture and stereopticon projectors for throwing the picture on the screen. This lamp has a tubular bulb with a concentrated filament, which permits a high-wattage lamp to be encased in a small bulb. Owing to the high operating temperature of the filament the rated life is only from 25 to 50 hr.

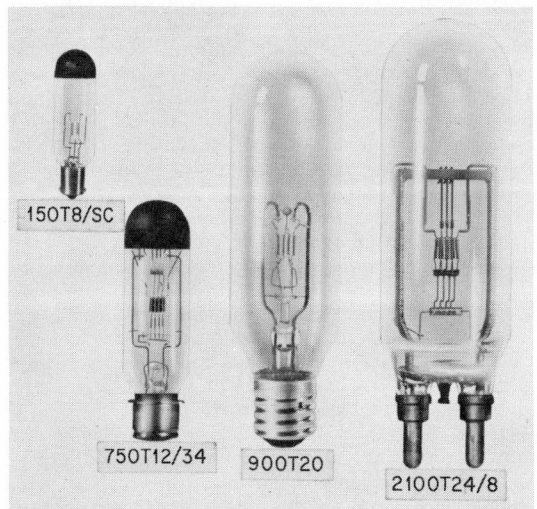

FIG. 31 *Picture-projection lamps. (General Electric Co.)*

74. Reflector and projector lamps (Fig. 32) are made with a parabolic-shaped bulb having a mirrored surface on the inside of the neck, and a fixed-focus filament. They can be used with a plain socket to form a highly efficient spotlight. The projector type has a lens built into the face of the lamp for better control of the light. This lamp is made of heat-resisting glass so that it can be used either indoors or where exposed to the weather. The reflector type has an inside-frosted glass bulb which is not weatherproof and does not provide so accurate control of the light but costs only about two-thirds as much as the projector type. Both types can be obtained in either a concentrating-spotlight or a wide-floodlight type. These bulbs are available with integral quartz-halogen lamps.

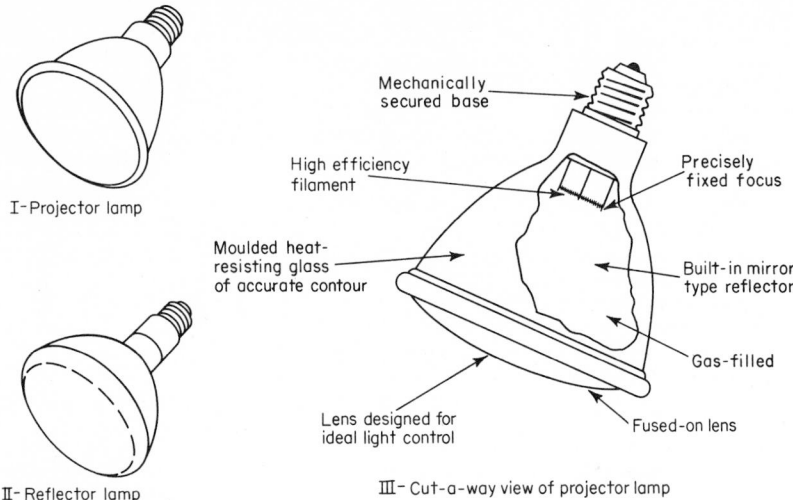

I–Projector lamp

II–Reflector lamp
(Westinghouse Co.)

Mechanically secured base

High efficiency filament

Precisely fixed focus

Moulded heat-resisting glass of accurate contour

Built-in mirror type reflector

Gas-filled

Lens designed for ideal light control

Fused-on lens

III–Cut-a-way view of projector lamp

FIG. 32 *Reflector and projector lamps.*

75. Sign and decorative lamps are ones designed especially for outdoor signs, Christmas and other decorations, carnivals, fairs, and festoon lighting. They are used also for many interior applications. While millions of ordinary gas-filled lamps are used in enclosed and other types of electric signs, those designated particularly as "sign" lamps are mostly of the vacuum type. Lamps of this type are best adapted for exposed sign and festoon service because the lower bulb temperature of vacuum lamps minimizes thermal cracks due to the contact of rain and snow. Some low-wattage sign lamps, however, are gas-filled for use in flashing signs. This causes more rapid cooling of the filament and reduces the trailing effect which slow-cooling vacuum lamps might produce. Bulb temperatures of these low-wattage gas-filled lamps are sufficiently low to permit exposed outdoor use.

76. Spotlight and floodlight lamps have concentrated filaments, accurately positioned with respect to the base. They are used in equipments which produce accurately controlled beams of light. There are several "companion listings" of spotlight and flood-light lamps having the same dimensions but differing in life design. Floodlight lamps are used where burning hours are long, such as in building floodlighting and show-window lighting. Spotlight lamps are used for those applications where burning hours are short and higher light output is needed—particularly in the blue and green portions of the visible spectrum. The T-12 and T-14 lamps are for use in ellipsoidal projectors where used for show windows and interior displays. The floodlight lamps are used also for underwater units. A typical lamp is shown in Fig. 33.

77. Street-lighting-service lamps are ones made specifically for use in street-lighting luminaires. They are made for series or multiple operation. A typical lamp is shown in Fig. 34. The series lamps are for operation on constant-current series circuits. They are made for 6.6-, 7.5-, 15-, and 20-amp circuits.

78. Street-railway-service lamps operate five-in-series of the trolley voltage of 550 or 600 volts, for general illumination, destination signs, etc., in streetcars. There are also 30- and 60-volt types which operate with automatic short-circuiting relays to short the lamp out of the circuit when the lamp burns out. These types operate with approximately 20-in-series or 10-in-series on 600 volts.

79. Traffic-signal lamps (Fig. 35) are clear lamps which are designed with a short light-center length for focusing the rays to give a signal indication of required brightness for traffic-signal use.

80. Train and locomotive lamps are specially designed to withstand the intense vibrations and shocks encountered in this service. They are available in different

 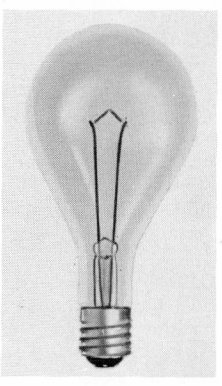 

FIG. 33 *Floodlight lamp. (General Electric Co.)*   FIG. 34 *Street-lighting-service lamp. (General Electric Co.)*   FIG. 35 *Traffic-signal lamp. (General Electric Co.)*

voltages from 30 to 75 volts for regular train-lighting service and for locomotive-cab and headlighting service.

81. Burning Position (Westinghouse Electric Corp.). With some few exceptions general-lighting-service lamps can be burned in any position. However, the lumen maintenance of Type C lamps is best when they are burned base up. This is because the tungsten blackening is conducted upward by the gas and is always deposited above the filament. When the lamp is burned base up, the blackening collects in the area of the bulb adjacent to the base, where the light is already partially intercepted by the base, socket, and luminaire husk. If the lamp is burned base down, the blackening collects in the bowl of the bulb, where it causes a much greater reduction in light output. Lamps burned in a horizontal position are affected similarly.

Certain types of lamps, particularly projection, spotlight, floodlight, and some street series lamps, are not designed for universal burning and should always be used in the position designated by the manufacturer's published data. The reason for this may be the construction of the filament, which would be likely to sag or short-circuit if burned in a position other than that for which it is designed. Operation in an incorrect position sometimes places the filament directly under a glass part which might be softened by the heat. If a lamp containing a collector grid is burned in any other position than with the grid directly above the filament, the special construction will not be effective in controlling blackening.

82. Lamp Temperatures (Westinghouse Electric Corp.). Operation of lamps under conditions which cause excessive bulb and base temperatures may result in melting of the bulb, softening of the base cement, and loosening of the base or in extreme cases damage to the socket and adjacent wiring. Most fixtures are properly designed to dissipate the heat generated by the lamps, but severe conditions such as might be induced by overvoltage operation or the use of lamps of higher wattage than the manufacturer's rating may give rise to difficulty. If metal parts of shades, reflectors, or fixtures are allowed to come in contact with the bulb of a gas-filled lamp, the local cooling effect may result in glass cracks which will cause lamp failure (sometimes violent). Maximum safe operating temperatures for best lamp performance are shown in the following table.

Maximum Safe Operating Temperatures
(Approximate Figures)

Soft glass bulb	300°C
Hard glass bulb	435–475°C
Cemented base:	
Regular	175°C
Special "Hi-Temp"	230°C
Mechanical base	225°C
Bipost base	285°C

Gas-filled lamps, because of the convection currents within the bulb, have higher bulb temperatures than vacuum lamps. Therefore vacuum lamps are preferable for use in exposed outdoor locations, where snow or rain may strike the hot bulb. Gas-filled lamps exposed to the elements should have hard or heat-resisting glass bulbs.

83. Vibration and Shock (Westinghouse Electric Corp.). Tungsten wire heated to incandescence becomes somewhat soft and pliable, and filament coils may be distorted or broken if the lamp is subjected to shock or vibration while burning. Vibration, especially of the low-amplitude high-frequency variety, is an insidious enemy of satisfactory lamp performance and should be guarded against wherever possible. There are available a number of commercial sockets and fixtures designed to protect the lamps by absorbing vibration.

Where vibration cannot be eliminated by these means, special *vibration-service* lamps, provided with extra filament supports, should be used. The construction of vibration-service lamps is such that they will give most satisfactory performance if burned in a vertical position, either base up or base down. They should never be used where they are likely to receive extreme shocks.

For use on extension cords and in any service where excessive shocks may be encountered, there are available *rough-service* lamps with a special type of shock-resisting filament construction. Rough-service lamps are designed to operate in any burning position and can be used in place of vibration-service lamps where it is necessary to burn lamps horizontally. Both vibration- and rough-service lamps sacrifice some efficiency to strength of construction and are more expensive than standard lamps; they should, therefore, be used only where required by service conditions.

84. The life of an incandescent lamp (i.e., the useful life) is always understood to mean the total hours of burning before the candle power drops to 80 per cent of the initial unless the lamp becomes useless because of broken filament or other cause prior to this. The total or burnout life of a lamp is the hours of burning before failure of the filament.

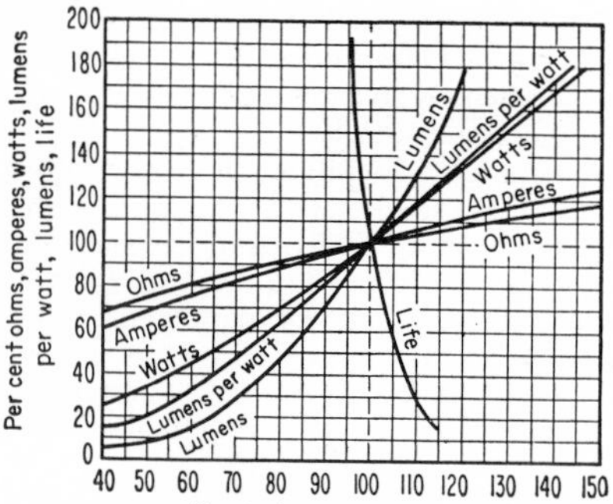

FIG. 36 *Variation in characteristics of incandescent lamps with voltage. (General Electric Co.)*

The average life of standard lamps for general lighting purposes varies from 750 hr for some lamps, 1,000 hr for others, to 2,500 hr for certain sizes and types. The approximate hours of life are specified by the manufacturer. The life of a lamp is materially affected by the voltage impressed upon it. Operating a lamp at less than its rated voltage will prolong the life of the lamp, while operating at higher than rated voltage will shorten its life. This does not mean that it is good practice to operate lamps at less than their rated voltage. Decreasing the voltage on a lamp decreases the light given out by the lamp, but the percentage of decrease in light is much greater than the percentage of decrease in voltage, so that the efficiency of operation is much poorer. Figure 36 shows percentage variation in characteristics of Mazda lamps with variation from normal voltage. Consider a 120-volt lamp operating at 114 volts. The voltage impressed on the lamp is 95 per cent of rated voltage. From Fig. 36 the lumens emitted by the lamp will be reduced to 84 per cent of the rated value. Thus a 5 per cent reduction in voltage results in a 16 per cent reduction in light output.

85. Clear-bulb Incandescent Lamps for General Lighting Service
(General Electric Co.)

Lamp ordering abbreviation	Watts	Bulb	Base	Volts	Std. pkg. qty.	Class	Filament	Approx life, hr	Approx initial lumens	Light center length, in.	Max over-all length, in.
10S14	10	S-14	Med.	120	120	B	C-9	1,500	80	2½	3½
15A15/CL	15	A-15	Med.	120	120	B	C-9	1,200	144	2⅜	3½
25A/CL	25	A-19	Med.	120	120	B	C-9	1,000	270	2½	3 15/16
40A/CL	40	A-19	Med.	120	120	C	C-9	1,000	465	2⅞	4¼
50A/CL	50	A-19	Med.	120	120	C	CC-6	1,000	665	3⅛	4 7/16
60A/CL	60	A-19	Med.	120	120	C	CC-6	1,000	840	3⅛	4 7/16
75A/CL	75	A-19	Med.	120	120	C	CC-6	750	1,150	3⅛	4 7/16
100A/CL	100	A-21	Med.	120	120	C	CC-6	750	1,640	3⅞	5 5/16
150A/CL	150	A-23	Med.	120	60	C	CC-6	750	2,700	4⅝	6 5/16
150/CL	150	PS-25	Med.	120	60	C	C-9	750	2,600	5¼	6 15/16
200A/CL	200	A-25	Med.	120	60	C	CC-6	750	3,800	5¼	6 15/16
200	200	PS-30	Med.	120	60	C	C-9	750	3,700	6	8 1/16
200PS30/12	200	PS-30	Mog.	120	60	C	C-9	750	3,650	6⅜	8 7/16
300M	300	PS-30	Med.	120	60	C	C-9	750	5,950	6	8 1/16
300	300	PS-35	Mog.	120	24	C	C-9	1,000	5,700	7	9⅜
500	500	PS-40	Mog.	120	24	C	C-9	1,000	9,900	7	9¾
750	750	PS-52	Mog.	120	6	C	CC-8	1,000	16,700	9½	13 1/16
1000	1,000	PS-52	Mog.	120	6	C	CC-8	1,000	23,000	9½	13 1/16
1500[a]	1,500	PS-52	Mog.	120	6	C	C-7A	1,000	33,000	9½	13 1/16
1M/PS52/44[b]	1,000	PS-52	Mog.	120	6	C	C-7A	1,000	21,500	9½	13 1/16
1500PS52/46[a,b]	1,500	PS-52	Mog.	120	6	C	C-7A	1,000	33,000	9½	13 1/16

[a] Recommended burning position any within 60 deg of vertically base up or base down, but lumen maintenance is best when burned vertically, base up.

[b] Special glass bulb—heat-resistant.

86. Inside-frosted-bulb Incandescent Lamps for General Lighting Service
(General Electric Co.)

Lamp ordering abbreviation	Watts	Bulb	Base	Volts	Std. pkg. qty.	Class	Filament	Approx life, hr	Lumens	Light center length, in.	Max over-all length, in.
10S14/IF	10	S-14	Med.	120	120	B	C-9	1,500	79	2½	3½
15A15	15	A-15	Med.	120	120	B	C-9	1,200	142	2⅜	3½
25A	25	A-19	Med.	120	120	B	C-9	1,000	265	2½	3 15/16
40A	40	A-19	Med.	120	120	C	C-9	1,000	465	2⅞	4¼
50A	50	A-19	Med.	120	120	C	CC-6	1,000	665	3⅛	4 7/16
60A	60	A-19	Med.	120	120	C	CC-6	1,000	840	3⅛	4 7/16
75A	75	A-19	Med.	120	120	C	CC-6	750	1,150	3⅛	4 7/16
100A	100	A-21	Med.	120	120	C	CC-6	750	1,640	3⅞	5 5/16
150A	150	A-23	Med.	120	60	C	CC-6	750	2,700	4⅝	6 5/16
150	150	PS-25	Med.	120	60	C	C-9	750	2,600	5¼	6 15/16
200A	200	A-25	Med.	120	60	C	CC-6	750	3,800	5¼	6 15/16
200/IF	200	PS-30	Med.	120	60	C	C-9	750	3,700	6	8 1/16
300M/IF	300	PS-30	Med.	120	60	C	C-9	750	5,950	6	8 1/16
300/IF	300	PS-35	Mog.	120	24	C	C-9	1,000	5,700	7	9⅜
500/IF	500	PS-40	Mog.	120	24	C	C-9	1,000	9,900	7	9¾
750/IF	750	PS-52	Mog.	120	6	C	CC-8	1,000	16,700	9½	13 1/16
750T24[a,b]	750	T-24	Md. Bip.	120	24	C	C-13	1,000	14,200	5½	9⅛
1M/T24[a,b]	1,000	T-24	Md. Bip.	120	24	C	C-13	1,000	20,000	5½	9⅛
1000/IF	1,000	PS-52	Mog.	120	6	C	CC-8	1,000	23,000	9½	13 1/16
1500/IF[c]	1,500	PS-52	Mog.	120	6	C	C-7A	1,000	33,000	9½	13 1/16

[a] Burn base up.

[b] Special glass bulb—heat-resistant.

[c] Recommended burning position any within 60 deg vertically base up or base down, but lumen maintenance is best when burned vertically base up.

87. White-bowl and Silvered-bowl Incandescent Lamps for General Lighting Service (General Electric Co.)

Lamp ordering abbreviation	Watts	Bulb	Base	Volts	Description	Std. pkg. qty.	Class	Filament	Approx life, hr	Light center length, in.	Max over-all length, in.
White-bowl Lamps											
150/WB	150	PS-25	Med.	120	Inside white	60	C	C-9	750	5¼	6¹⁵⁄₁₆
200/WB	200	PS-30	Med.	120	Inside white	60	C	C-9	750	6	8¹⁄₁₆
300/WB	300	PS-35	Mog.	120	Inside white	24	C	C-9	1,000	7	9⅜
Silvered-bowl Lamps											
60A/SB	60	A-19	Med.	120	I. F. silvered	120	C	CC-6	1,000	3⅛	4⁷⁄₁₆
100A/1SB[a]	100	A-21	Med.	120	I. F. silvered	120	C	CC-6	1,000	3⅞	5⁵⁄₁₆
100A/1SBIF[a]	100	A-21	Med.	120	I. F. silvered	120	C	CC-6	1,000	3⅞	5⁵⁄₁₆
150/SB	150	PS-25	Med.	120	I. F. silvered	60	C	C-9	1,000	5¼	6¹⁵⁄₁₆
200/SBIF	200	PS-30	Med.	120	I. F. silvered	60	C	C-9	1,000	6	8¹⁄₁₆
200 SBIF/1	200	PS-30	Med.	120	I. F. semisilv.	60	C	C-9	1,000	6	8¹⁄₁₆
300MS/SBIF	300	PS-35	Md. skt.	120	I. F. silvered	24	C	C-9	1,000	7½	9⅞
300/SBIF	300	PS-35	Mog.	120	I. F. silvered	24	C	C-9	1,000	7	9⅜
300/SBIF/1	300	PS-35	Mog.	120	I. F. semisilv.	24	C	C-9	1,000	7	9⅜
500/SBIF	500	PS-40	Mog.	120	I. F. silvered	24	C	C-9	1,000	7	9¾
500/SBIF/1	500	PS-40	Mog.	120	I. F. semisilv.	24	C	C-9	1,000	7	9¾
750/SBIF	750	PS-52	Mog.	120	I. F. silvered	6	C	C-7A	1,000	9½	13¹⁄₁₆
1000/SBIF	1,000	PS-52	Mog.	120	I. F. silvered	6	C	C-7A	1,000	9½	13¹⁄₁₆

[a] For use only in porcelain sockets and in fixtures so designed that the temperatures of the lamp and fixture do not exceed limits for satisfactory operation.

88. De Luxe White Incandescent Lamps for General Lighting Service (General Electric Co.)

Lamp ordering abbreviation	Watts	Bulb	Base	Volts	Description	Std. pkg. qty.	Class	Filament	Approx life, hr	Lumens	Light center length, in.	Max over-all length, in.
30/230M/1W	30-200-230	PS-25	3C.	120	High-low De Luxe white[a]	60	C	2C-2R	1,000	270 3,250 3,520	3⅞	5¹⁵⁄₁₆
60A/W	60	A-19	Med.	120	White	120	C	CC-6	1,000	835	...	4⁷⁄₁₆
100A/W	100	A-21	Med.	120	White	120	C	CC-6	750	1,640	3⅞	5⁵⁄₁₆
150R/W	150	R-40	Med.	120	White indirect[a]	24	C	C-9	1,000	2,200	...	6⅛
50/150R/W	50-100-150	R-40	3C. Med.	120	White indirect[a] Three lite	24	C	2C-2R	1,000	580 1,420 2,000	...	6⅛
50/150M/W	50-100-150	PS-25	3C. Med.	120	White indirect[a]	60	C	2C-2R	750	.....	3⅞	5¹⁵⁄₁₆
100/300	100-200-300	G-30	3C. Mog.	120	White indirect Three lite[a]	60	C	2C-2R	1,000	1,410 3,250 4,660	...	6¾

[a] Burn base down.

89. Daylight and Decorative-enamel-bowl Incandescent Lamps
(General Electric Co.)

Lamp ordering abbreviation	Watts	Bulb	Base	Volts	Description	Std. pkg. qty.	Class	Fila-ment	Approx life, hr	Lu-mens	Light center length, in.	Max over-all length, in.
					Daylight Lamps							
10S14/D	10	S-14	Med.	115–125	Clear	120	B	C-9	1,500	47	2½	3½
25A/D	25	A-19	Med.	115–125	Clear	120	B	C-9	1,000	169	2½	3¹⁵⁄₁₆
60A/D	60	A-19	Med.	115–125	Inside frosted	120	C	CC-6	1,000	490	3⅛	4⁷⁄₁₆
100A/D	100	A-23	Med.	115–125	Inside frosted	120	C	CC-6	750	980	4⅜	6⅛
150/D	150	PS-25	Med.	115–125	Inside frosted	60	C	C-9	1,000	1,320	5¼	6¹⁵⁄₁₆
150/DCL	150	PS-25	Med.	115–125	Clear	60	C	C-9	1,000	1,320	5¼	6¹⁵⁄₁₆
200/D	200	PS-30	Med.	115–125	Clear	60	C	C-9	1,000	2,000	6	8⅛
					Decorative-enamel-bowl Lamps							
50GA	50	GA-25	Med.	115–125	Semiindirect[a] I. F. decorated enamel bowl	60	C	C-9	1,000	600	...	4⁷⁄₁₆
50GA/DPK	50	GA-25	Med.	115–125	Dawn pink[a] enamel bowl	60	C	C-9	1,000	600	...	4⁷⁄₁₆
100GA	100	GA-30	Med.	115–125	Semiindirect[a] I. F. decorated enamel bowl	60	C	C-9	1,000	1,450	...	6³⁄₁₆

[a] Burn base up.

90. General Decorative Incandescent Lamps
(General Electric Co.)

Lamp ordering abbreviation	Watts	Bulb	Base	Volts	Description	Std. pkg. qty.	Class	Filament	Approx life, hr	Lumens	Light center length, in.	Max over-all length, in.
6S6/R	6	S-6	Cand.	115–125	Red	240	B	C-7A	1,500	...	...	1⅞
6S6/W	6	S-6	Cand.	115–125	White	240	B	C-7A	1,500	...	...	1⅞
7½S	7½	S-11	Med.	115–125	Clear	120	B	C-7A	1,400	52	...	2¼
7½S/CO	7½	S-11	Med.	115–125	Orange	120	B	C-7A	1,400	...	...	2¼
7½S/CB	7½	S-11	Med.	115–125	Blue	120	B	C-7A	1,400	...	...	2¼
7½S/CG	7½	S-11	Med.	115–125	Green	120	B	C-7A	1,400	...	...	2¼
7½S/CR	7½	S-11	Med.	115–125	Red	120	B	C-7A	1,400	...	...	2¼
7½S/CW	7½	S-11	Med.	115–125	White	120	B	C-7A	1,400	...	...	2¼
15FC	15	F-10	Cand.	115–125	Clear	60	B	C-7A	750	145	...	3¹⁄₁₆
15FC/FT	15	F-10	Cand.	115–125	OC-Flametint	60	B	C-7A	750	...	...	3¹⁄₁₆
15FC/V	15	F-10	Cand.	115–125	OC-Ivory	60	B	C-7A	750	...	...	3¹⁄₁₆
15FC/W	15	F-10	Cand.	115–125	OC-White	60	B	C-7A	750	...	...	3¹⁄₁₆
15FN	15	F-10	Inter.	115–125	Clear	60	B	C-7A	750	145	...	3⅛
15FN/W	15	F-10	Inter.	115–125	White	60	B	C-7A	750	...	...	3⅛
15S11/13	15	S-11	Cand.	115–125	Clear	120	B	C-7A	750	145	1⅝	2¼
15T8C	15	T-8	Cand.	115–125	Clear	60	B	C-7A	750	144	...	3¹⁄₁₆
15T8C/W	15	T-8	Cand.	115–125	OC-White	60	B	C-7A	750	...	...	3¹⁄₁₆
15T8/N	15	T-8	Inter.	115–125	Clear	60	B	C-7A	750	144	...	3⅛
15B9½	15	B-9½	Cand.	115–125	Clear	60	B	C-7A	750	147	...	3⁵⁄₁₆
15B9½/W	15	B-9½	Cand.	115–125	OC-White	60	B	C-7A	750	...	...	3⁵⁄₁₆
25F	25	F-15	Med.	115–125	Clear	120	B	C-9	750	275	...	4½
25F/FT	25	F-15	Med.	115–125	OC-Flametint	120	B	C-9	750	...	...	4½
25F/V	25	F-15	Med.	115–125	OC-Ivory	120	B	C-9	750	...	...	4½
25F/W	25	F-15	Med.	115–125	OC-White	120	B	C-9	750	...	...	4½
25G16½C	25	G-16½	Cand.	115–125	Clear	60	B	C-7A	750	260	...	3
25G16½C/W	25	G-16½	Cand.	115–125	White	60	B	C-7A	750	...	...	3
25G18½/FT	25	G-18½	Med.	115–125	OC-Flametint	120	B	C-9	750	...	...	3⁹⁄₁₆
25G18½/V	25	G-18½	Med.	115–125	OC-Ivory	120	B	C-9	750	...	...	3⁹⁄₁₆
25G18½/W	25	G-18½	Med.	115–125	OC-White	120	B	C-9	750	...	...	3⁹⁄₁₆
25G25/FT	25	G-25	Med.	120	OC-Flametint	60	B	C-9	750	...	...	4⁷⁄₁₆
25G25/V	25	G-25	Med.	120	OC-Ivory	60	B	C-9	750	...	...	4⁷⁄₁₆
25G25/W	25	G-25	Med.	120	OC-White	60	B	C-9	750	...	...	4⁷⁄₁₆
40F15	40	F-15	Med.	115–125	Clear	120	C	C-9	750	450	...	4½
40F15/W	40	F-15	Med.	115–125	White	120	C	C-9	750	...	...	4½
40G/FT	40	G-25	Med.	115–125	OC-Flametint	60	B	C-9	750	...	...	4⁷⁄₁₆
40G/V	40	G-25	Med.	115–125	OC-Ivory	60	B	C-9	750	...	...	4⁷⁄₁₆
40G/W	40	G-25	Med.	115–125	OC-White	60	B	C-9	750	...	...	4⁷⁄₁₆
60A21/AO	60	A-21	Med.	115–125	OC-Amber Orange	120	C	C-9	1,000	...	...	4¹⁵⁄₁₆
60A21/B	60	A-21	Med.	115–125	OC-Blue	120	C	C-9	1,000	...	3⅜	4¹⁵⁄₁₆
60A21/FT	60	A-21	Med.	115–125	OC-Flametint	120	C	C-9	1,000	...	3⅜	4¹⁵⁄₁₆
60A21/G	60	A-21	Med.	115–125	OC-Green	120	C	C-9	1,000	...	3⅜	4¹⁵⁄₁₆
60A21/V	60	A-21	Med.	115–125	OC-Ivory	120	C	C-9	1,000	...	3⅜	4¹⁵⁄₁₆
60A21/RO	60	A-21	Med.	115–125	OC-Old rose	120	C	C-9	1,000	...	3⅜	4¹⁵⁄₁₆
60A21/R	60	A-21	Med.	115–125	OC-Red	120	C	C-9	1,000	...	3⅜	4¹⁵⁄₁₆
60A21/Y	60	A-21	Med.	115–125	OC-Yellow	120	C	C-9	1,000	...	3⅜	4¹⁵⁄₁₆

91. Coloramic Decorative Incandescent Lamps
(General Electric Co.)

Lamp ordering abbreviation	Watts	Bulb	Base	Volts	Description	Std. pkg. qty.	Class	Fila-ment	Approx life, hr	Max over-all length, in.	Light center length, in.
25F/DPK	25	F15 Decorative	Med.	115–125	Coloramic dawn pink	120	B	C-9	750	4½	
50GA/DPK	50	GA-25	Med.	115–125	Coloramic enamel bowl dawn pink	60	C	C-9	1,000	4⁷⁄₁₆	
60A/DPK	60	A-19	Med.	115–125	Coloramic dawn pink	120	C	CC-6	1,000	4⁷⁄₁₆	3⅞
100/300/DPK	100 200 300	G-30	3C. Mog.	115–125	Three-lite indirect coloramic dawn pink	60	C	2C-2R	1,000	6¾	3⅞
50/150M/SKY	50 100 150	PS-25	3C. Med.	115–125	Coloramic three-lite sky blue	60	C	2C-2R	750	5¹⁵⁄₁₆	3⅞
50/150M/SPG	50 100 150	PS-25	3C. Med.	115–125	Coloramic three-lite spring green	60	C	2C-2R	750	5¹⁵⁄₁₆	3⅞
50/150M/SUN	50 100 150	PS-25	3C. Med.	115–125	Coloramic three-lite sun gold	60	C	2C-2R	750	5¹⁵⁄₁₆	3⅞
50/150M/DPK	50 100 150	PS-25	3C. Med.	115–125	Coloramic three-lite dawn pink	60	C	2C-2R	750	5¹⁵⁄₁₆	3⅞
75A/SKY	75	A-19	Med.	115–125	Coloramic sky blue	120	C	CC-6	1,000	4⁷⁄₁₆	3⅞
75A/SPG	75	A-19	Med.	115–125	Coloramic spring green	120	C	CC-6	1,000	4⁷⁄₁₆	3⅞
75A/SUN	75	A-19	Med.	115–125	Coloramic sun gold	120	C	CC-6	1,000	4⁷⁄₁₆	3⅞
75A/DPK	75	A-19	Med.	115–125	Coloramic dawn pink	120	C	CC-6	1,000	4⁷⁄₁₆	3⅞
100A/SKY	100	A-21	Med.	115–125	Coloramic sky blue	120	C	CC-6	1,000	5⁵⁄₁₆	3⁷⁄₁₆
100A/SPG	100	A-21	Med.	115–125	Coloramic spring green	120	C	CC-6	1,000	5⁵⁄₁₆	3⅞
100A/SUN	100	A-21	Med.	115–125	Coloramic sun gold	120	C	CC-6	1,000	5⁵⁄₁₆	3⅞
100A/DPK	100	A-21	Med.	115–125	Coloramic dawn pink	120	C	CC-6	1,000	5⁵⁄₁₆	3⅞
150A/SKY	150	A-23	Med.	115–125	Coloramic sky blue	60	C	CC-6	1,000	6⁵⁄₁₆	3⅞
150A/SPG	150	A-23	Med.	115–125	Coloramic spring green	60	C	CC-6	1,000	6⁵⁄₁₆	3⅞
150A/SUN	150	A-23	Med.	115–125	Coloramic sun gold	60	C	CC-6	1,000	6⁵⁄₁₆	3⅞
150A/DPK	150	A-23	Med.	115–125	Coloramic dawn pink	60	C	CC-6	1,000	6⁵⁄₁₆	3⅞

92. Yellow (Insect-repellent) Incandescent Lamps
(General Electric Co.)

Lamp ordering abbreviation	Watts	Bulb	Base	Volts	Std. pkg. qty.	Class	Filament	Approx life, hr	Max over-all length, in.
25A/Y	25	A-19	Med.	115–125	120	B	C-9	1,000	$3^{15}\!/_{16}$
40A/Y	40	A-21	Med.	115–125	120	B	C-9	1,000	$4^{7}\!/_{16}$
60A/Y	60	A-19	Med.	115–125	120	C	CC-6	1,000	$4^{7}\!/_{16}$
100A21/61Y	100	A-21	Med.	115–125	120	C	CC-6	1,000	$5^{5}\!/_{16}$
150PS25/Y	150	PS-25	Med.	115–125	60	C	C-9	1,000	$6^{15}\!/_{16}$

93. Rough-service and Vibration-service Incandescent Lamps
(General Electric Co.)

Lamp ordering abbreviation	Watts	Bulb	Base	Volts	Description	Std. pkg. qty.	Class	Fila-ment	Approx life, hr	Lu-mens	Light center length, in.	Max over-all length, in.
					Rough-service Lamps							
25A/RS	25	A-19	Med.	120	Inside frosted	120	B	C-17	1,000	225	$2\frac{1}{2}$	$3^{15}\!/_{16}$
50A/RS	50	A-19	Med.	120	Inside frosted	120	B	C-22	1,000	460	$2\frac{1}{2}$	$3^{15}\!/_{16}$
50A19/5	50	A-19	Med.	120	Clear	120	B	C-22	1,000	465	$2\frac{1}{2}$	$3^{15}\!/_{16}$
50A19/3	50	A-19	Med.	120	I. F. out. ctd. Cl. lacquer	120	B	C-22	1,000	460	$2\frac{1}{2}$	$3^{15}\!/_{16}$
75A21/RS	75	A-21	Med.	120	Inside frosted	120	B	C-22	1,000	710	$2\frac{7}{8}$	$4^{7}\!/_{16}$
100A/RS	100	A-21	Med.	120	Inside frosted	120	C	C-17	1,000	1,230	$3\frac{7}{8}$	$5^{5}\!/_{16}$
150/RS	150	PS-25	Med.	120	Inside frosted	60	C	C-17	1,000	2,100	$5\frac{1}{4}$	$6^{15}\!/_{16}$
200PS30/23	200	PS-30	Med.	120	Inside frosted	60	C	C-9	1,000	3,380	6	$8\frac{1}{16}$
200PS30/24	200	PS-30	Med.	120	Clear	60	C	C-9	1,000	3,380	6	$8\frac{1}{16}$
300/RS	300	PS-35	Mog.	120	Clear	24	C	C-9	1,000	5,250	7	$9\frac{3}{8}$
500/RS	500	PS-40	Mog.	120	Clear	24	C	C-9	1,000	9,400	7	$9\frac{3}{4}$
					Vibration-service Lamps							
25A/VS	25	A-19	Med.	120	Inside frosted	120	B	C-9	1,000	250	$2\frac{1}{2}$	$3^{15}\!/_{16}$
25A/CL/VS	25	A-19	Med.	120	Clear	120	B	C-9	1,000	255	$2\frac{1}{2}$	$3^{15}\!/_{16}$
50A/VS	50	A-19	Med.	120	Inside frosted	120	B	C-9	1,000	550	$2\frac{1}{2}$	$3^{15}\!/_{16}$
50A/CL/VS	50	A-19	Med.	120	Clear	120	B	C-9	1,000	555	$2\frac{1}{2}$	$3^{15}\!/_{16}$
100A23/28	100	A-23	Med.	120	Inside frosted	120	C	C-9	1,000	1,350	$4\frac{3}{8}$	$6\frac{1}{16}$
150/VS	150	PS-25	Med.	120	Inside frosted	60	C	C-9	1,000	2,250	$5\frac{1}{4}$	$6^{15}\!/_{16}$

94. Three-lite Incandescent Lamps
(General Electric Co.)

Lamp ordering abbreviation	Watts	Bulb	Base	Volts	Std. pkg. qty.	Class	Filament	Approx life, hr	Light center length, in.	Max over-all length, in.	Approx initial lumens
30/100	{ 30 / 70 / 100 }	A-21	3c med.	120	120	C	2C-9	750	3¾	5⁵⁄₁₆	300, 980, 1,280
30/230M/1W	{ 30 / 200 / 230 }	A-25	3c med.	120	120	C	2C-2R	1,000	3⅞	5¹⁵⁄₁₆	270, 3,250, 3,520
50/150M	{ 50 / 100 / 150 }	PS-25	3c med.	120	60	C	2C-2R	750	3⅞	5¹⁵⁄₁₆	610, 1,520, 2,130
50/150	{ 50 / 100 / 150 }	PS-25	3c mog.	120	60	C	2C-2R	1,000	5	6¹³⁄₁₆	590, 1,450, 2,040
50/150M/W	{ 50 / 100 / 150 }	PS-25	3c med.	120	60	C	2C-2R	750	3⅞	5¹⁵⁄₁₆	
50/150R/W	{ 50 / 100 / 150 }	R-40ᵃ	3c med.	120	24	C	2C-2R	1,000	...	6⅛	580, 1,420, 2,000
100/300	{ 100 / 200 / 300 }	G-30ᵃ	3c mog.	120	60	C	2C-2R	1,000	3¾	6¾	1,410, 3,250, 4,660

ᵃ Burn base down.

95. Lumiline Incandescent Lamps
(General Electric Co.)

Lamp ordering abbreviation	Watts	Bulb	Base	Volts	Description	Std. pkg. qty.	Class	Filament	Approx life, hr	Lumens	Max over-all length, in.
L30/IF	30	T-8	Disk	115–125	Inside frosted	24	B	C-8	1,500	255	17¾
L30/W	30	T-8	Disk	115–125	White	24	B	C-8	1,500	210	17¾
L40	40	T-8	Disk	115–125	Clear	24	B	C-8	1,500	370	11¾
L40/IF	40	T-8	Disk	115–125	Inside frosted	24	B	C-8	1,500	365	11¾
L40/MB	40	T-8	Disk	115–125	Moonlight blue	24	B	C-8	1,500	...	11¾
L40/EM	40	T-8	Disk	115–125	Emerald	24	B	C-8	1,500	...	11¾
L40/O	40	T-8	Disk	115–125	Orange	24	B	C-8	1,500	...	11¾
L40/SPK	40	T-8	Disk	115–125	Surprise pink	24	B	C-8	1,500	...	11¾
L40/ST	40	T-8	Disk	115–125	Straw	24	B	C-8	1,500	...	11¾
L40/W	40	T-8	Disk	115–125	White	24	B	C-8	1,500	...	11¾
L40/R	40	T-8	Disk	115–125	Red	24	B	C-8	1,500	...	11¾
L60	60	T-8	Disk	115–125	Clear	24	B	C-8	1,500	565	17¾
L60/IF	60	T-8	Disk	115–125	Inside frosted	24	B	C-8	1,500	560	17¾
L60/MB	60	T-8	Disk	115–125	Moonlight blue	24	B	C-8	1,500	...	17¾
L60/EM	60	T-8	Disk	115–125	Emerald	24	B	C-8	1,500	...	17¾
L60/O	60	T-8	Disk	115–125	Orange	24	B	C-8	1,500	...	17¾
L60/SPK	60	T-8	Disk	115–125	Surprise pink	24	B	C-8	1,500	...	17¾
L60/ST	60	T-8	Disk	115–125	Straw	24	B	C-8	1,500	...	17¾
L60/W	60	T-8	Disk	115–125	White	24	B	C-8	1,500	470	17¾

96. Showcase Incandescent Lamps
(General Electric Co.)

Lamp ordering abbreviation	Watts	Bulb	Base	Volts	Description	Std. pkg. qty.	Class	Fila-ment	Approx life, hr	Lumens	Max over-all length, in.
25T6½	25	T-6½	Inter.	120	Clear	60	B	C-8	1,000	240	5½
25T6½/IF	25	T-6½	Inter.	120	I. F. showcase	60	B	C-8	1,000	240	5½
40T8	40	T-8	Med.	120	Clear	24	B	C-23	1,000	410	11⅞
40T8/IF	40	T-8	Med.	120	I. F. showcase	24	B	C-23	1,000	405	11⅞
25T10	25	T-10	Med.	120	Clear	60	B	C-8	1,000	260	5⅝
25T10/IF	25	T-10	Med.	120	I. F. showcase	60	B	C-8	1,000	255	5⅝
25T10/RFL	25	T-10	Med.	120	Refl. showcase	60	C	CC-8	1,000	215	5⅝
40T10	40	T-10	Med.	120	Clear	60	B	C-8	1,000	430	5⅝
40T10/IF	40	T-10	Med.	120	Inside frosted	60	B	C-8	1,000	425	5⅝
40T10/RFL	40	T-10	Med.	120	Reflector showcase	60	C	CC-8	1,000	430	5⅝
60T10/64	60	T-10	Med.	120	Showcase	60	C	C-8	1,000	710	5⅝
75T10/45	75	T-10	Med.	120	Showcase	24	B	C-23	1,000	800	11⅞

97. Higher-voltage [a] Incandescent Lamps for General Lighting Service
(General Electric Co.)

Lamp ordering abbreviation	Watts	Bulb	Base	Description	Std. pkg. qty.	Class	Fila-ment	Approx life, hr	Lumens	Light center length, in.	Max over-all length, in.
15A	15	A-17	Med.	Inside frosted	120	B	C-9	1,000	120	2⅜	3⅝
25A	25	A-19	Med.	Inside frosted	120	B	C-17A	1,000	225	2½	3¹⁵⁄₁₆
50A	50	A-19	Med.	Inside frosted	120	B	C-17A	1,000	485	2½	3¹⁵⁄₁₆
50A/RS	50	A-19	Med.	Rough service	120	B	C-17A	1,000	450	2½	3¹⁵⁄₁₆
50A19/37	50	A-19	Med.	Clear	120	B	C-17A	1,000	480	2½	3¹⁵⁄₁₆
60A21	60	A-21	Med.	Inside frosted	120	B	C-17A	1,000	580	2⅞	4⁷⁄₁₆
100A	100	A-21	Med.	Inside frosted	120	C	C-7A	1,000	1,280	3⅞	5⁵⁄₁₆
100A/CL	100	A-21	Med.	Clear	120	C	C-7A	1,000	1,280	3⅞	5⁵⁄₁₆
100A/RS	100	A-21	Med.	Rough service	120	C	C-17	1,000	900	3⅞	5⁵⁄₁₆
150PS25	150	PS-25	Med.	Clear	60	C	C-7A	1,000	2,050	5¼	6¹⁵⁄₁₆
200	200	PS-30	Med.	Clear	60	C	C-9	1,000	3,040	6	8¹⁄₁₆
200/IF	200	PS-30	Med.	Inside frosted	60	C	C-9	1,000	3,040	6	8¹⁄₁₆
300MS	300	PS-35	Med. skt.	Clear	24	C	C-7A	1,000	4,800	7½	9⅞
300	300	PS-35	Mog.	Clear	24	C	C-7A	1,000	4,800	7	9⅜
300/IF	300	PS-35	Mog.	Inside frosted	24	C	C-7A	1,000	4,800	7	9⅜
500	500	PS-40	Mog.	Clear	24	C	C-7A	1,000	8,950	7	9¾
500/IF	500	PS-40	Mog.	Inside frosted	24	C	C-7A	1,000	8,950	7	9¾
750	750	PS-52	Mog.	Clear	6	C	C-7A	2,000	13,300	9½	13¹⁄₁₆
750/IF	750	PS-52	Mog.	Inside frosted	6	C	C-7A	2,000	13,300	9½	13¹⁄₁₆
1000	1,000	PS-52	Mog.	Clear	6	C	C-7A	2,000	18,600	9½	13¹⁄₁₆
1500	1,500	PS-52	Mog.	Clear	6	C	C-7A	2,000	27,000	9½	13¹⁄₁₆

[a] 230, 250, 277 or 300 volts.

98. Projector Incandescent Lamps
(General Electric Co.)
Clear-glass Lamps

Lamp ordering abbreviation	Watts and bulb	Base type	Beam type	Std. pkg. qty.	Approx beam spread, deg[a]	Approx initial beam, lumens	Approx total lumens	Approx initial cp avg in 10 deg cone[b]	Max over-all length, in.
75PAR/SP[c]	75-watt	Med. skt.	Spot	12	......	......	770	......	5⁵⁄₁₆
75PAR/FL[c]	PAR 38	Med. skt.	Flood	12	......	......	770	......	5⁵⁄₁₆
150PAR/SP[c]	150-watt	Med. skt.	Spot	12	30 × 30	1,100	1,730	10,500	5⁵⁄₁₆
150PAR/3SP[c]	PAR 38	Med. side-prong	Spot	12	30 × 30	1,100	1,730	10,500	4⁵⁄₁₆
150PAR/FL[c]	....	Med. skt.	Flood	12	60 × 60	1,350	1,730	3,400	5⁵⁄₁₆
150PAR/3FL[c]	....	Med. side-prong	Flood	12	60 × 60	1,350	1,730	3,400	4⁵⁄₁₆
200PAR46/3NSP	200-watt	Med. side-prong	Narrow spot	8	17 × 23	1,200	2,350	30,000	4
200PAR46/3MFL	PAR 46	Med. side-prong	Med. flood	8	20 × 40	1,300	2,350	11,000	4
300PAR56/NSP	300-watt	Mog. end prong	Narrow spot	8	15 × 20	1,800	3,650	70,000	5
300PAR56/MFL	PAR 56	Mog. end prong	Med. flood	8	20 × 35	2,000	3,650	22,000	5
300PAR56/WFL	....	Mog. end prong	Wide flood	8	30 × 60	2,100	3,650	10,000	5
500PAR64/NSP	500-watt	Ext. mog. end prong	Narrow spot	8	13 × 20	3,000	6,000	110,000	6
500PAR64/MFL	PAR 64	Ext. mog. end prong	Med. flood	8	20 × 35	3,400	6,000	35,000	6
500PAR64/WFL	....	Ext. mog. end prong	Wide flood	8	35 × 65	3,500	6,000	12,000	6

The rated average life of projector (PAR) lamps is 2,000 hr. The average lumens and candlepower is 85 per cent of initial.
[a] To 10 per cent of maximum candlepower.
[b] Candlepower average in the central 5-deg cone for SP and NSP, in 10-deg cone for MFL and WFL.
[c] Heat resistant glass.

Colored-glass Lamps

Lamp ordering abbreviation	Description	Watts	Bulb	Base	Std. pkg. qty.	Class	Filament	Max over all length, in.	Approx life, hr
150PAR/B	Blue	150	PAR-38	Med. skt.	12	C	CC-6	5⁵⁄₁₆	2,000
150PAR/BW	Blue white	150	PAR-38	Med. skt.	12	C	CC-6	5⁵⁄₁₆	2,000
150PAR/G	Green	150	PAR-38	Med skt.	12	C	CC-6	5⁵⁄₁₆	2,000
150PAR/PK	Pink	150	PAR-38	Med. skt.	12	C	CC-6	5⁵⁄₁₆	2,000
150PAR/R	Red	150	PAR-38	Med. skt.	12	C	CC-6	5⁵⁄₁₆	2,000
150PAR/Y	Yellow	150	PAR-38	Med. skt.	12	C	CC-6	5⁵⁄₁₆	2,000

99. Reflector Incandescent Lamps
(General Electric Co.)
Reflector Lamps (Clear Glass)

Lamp ordering abbreviation	Watts and bulb	Base type	Beam type	Std. pkg. qty.	Approx beam spread, deg[a]	Approx initial beam, lumens[a]	Approx total lumens	Approx initial cp avg in 10-deg cone	Max over-all length, in.
30R20	30-watt R-20	Medium	Flood	60	85	144	200	290	$3^{15}/_{16}$
75R30/SP	75-watt	Medium	Spot	60	50	400	770	1,800	$5\frac{3}{8}$
75R30/FL	R-30	Medium	Flood	60	130	610	770	430	$5\frac{3}{8}$
150R/SP	150-watt	Medium	Spot	24	40	810	1,780	6,000	$6\frac{1}{2}$
150R/FL	R-40	Medium	Flood	24	110	1,500	1,780	1,250	$6\frac{1}{2}$
300R/SP	300-watt	Medium	Spot	24	35	1,800	3,700	13,500	$6\frac{1}{2}$
300R/SP/1[b]	R-40	Medium	Spot	24	35	1,600	3,700	13,500	$6\frac{7}{8}$
300R/3SP[b]		Mogul	Spot	24	35	.....	3,700	.....	$7\frac{1}{4}$
300R/FL		Medium	Flood	24	115	2,800	3,700	2,700	$6\frac{1}{2}$
300R/FL/1[b]		Medium	Flood	24	115	2,700	3,700	2,700	$6\frac{7}{8}$
300R/3FL[b]		Mogul	Flood	24	115	2,700	3,700	2,700	$7\frac{1}{4}$
500R/3SP[b]	500-watt	Mogul	Spot	24	35	3,100	6,400	22,000	$7\frac{1}{4}$
500R/3FL[b]	R-40	Mogul	Flood	24	115	5,400	6,400	5,200	$7\frac{1}{4}$
500R52	500R-52	Mogul	Refl. Fl.	6	......	......	7,550	.....	$11\frac{3}{4}$
750R52	750R-52	Mogul	Refl. Fl.	6	......	......	12,700	.....	$11\frac{3}{4}$
1M/RB52	1000-RB-52	Mogul	Refl. Fl.	6	......	......	16,300	.....	$12\frac{3}{4}$

The rated average life of reflector (R) lamps is 2,000 hr.   The average lumens and candlepower are 85 per cent of initial.
[a] To 10 per cent of maximum candlepower.
[b] Heat-resistant glass.

Reflector Color Lamps

Lamp ordering abbreviation	Description	Watts	Bulb	Base	Volts	Std. pkg. qty.	Class	Filament	Max over-all length, in.	Approx life, hr
150R/R	Red	150	R-40	Medium	115–125	12	C	C-11	$6\frac{7}{8}$	2,000
150R/PK	Pink	150	R-40	Medium	115–125	12	C	C-11	$6\frac{7}{8}$	2,000
150R/G	Green	150	R-40	Medium	115–125	12	C	C-11	$6\frac{7}{8}$	2,000
150R/Y	Yellow	150	R-40	Medium	115–125	12	C	C-11	$6\frac{7}{8}$	2,000
150R/BW	Blue white	150	R-40	Medium	115–125	12	C	C-11	$6\frac{7}{8}$	2,000
150R/B	Blue	150	R-40	Medium	115–125	12	C	C-11	$6\frac{7}{8}$	2,000

100. Sign and Decorative Incandescent Lamps
(General Electric Co.)

Lamp ordering abbreviation	Watts	Bulb	Base	Volts	Description	Std. pkg. qty.	Class	Fila-ment	Approx life, hr	Lu-mens	Light center length, in.	Max over-all length, in.
6S14	6	S-14	Med.	115–125	Clear	120	B	C-9	1,500	41	2½	3½
6S14/IF	6	S-14	Med.	115–125	Inside frosted	120	B	C-9	1,500	41	2½	3½
10S11N	10	S-11	Inter.	115–125	Clear	120	B	C-7A	1,500	80	1⅝	2⁵⁄₁₆
10S11N/CB	10	S-11	Inter.	115–125	Blue	120	B	C-7A	1,500	...	...	2⁵⁄₁₆
10S11N/CG	10	S-11	Inter.	115–125	Green	120	B	C-7A	1,500	...	...	2⁵⁄₁₆
10S11N/CR	10	S-11	Inter.	115–125	Red	120	B	C-7A	1,500	...	...	2⁵⁄₁₆
10S11N/CO	10	S-11	Inter.	115–125	Orange	120	B	C-7A	1,500	...	...	2⁵⁄₁₆
10S11N/CFT	10	S-11	Inter.	115–125	Flametint	120	B	C-7A	1,500	...	...	2⁵⁄₁₆
10S11N/CY	10	S-11	Inter.	115–125	Yellow	120	B	C-7A	1,500	...	...	2⁵⁄₁₆
10S11N/CW	10	S-11	Inter.	115–125	White	120	B	C-7A	1,500	...	...	2⁵⁄₁₆
11S14	11	S-14	Med.	120	Clear	120	B	C-9	3,000	80	3½	2½
11S14IF	11	S-14	Med.	120	Inside frosted	120	B	C-9	3,000	79	3½	2½
11S14/B	11	S-14	Med.	115–125	Blue	120	B	C-9	3,000	...	3½	2½
11S14/G	11	S-14	Med.	115–125	Green	120	B	C-9	3,000	...	3½	2½
11S14/O	11	S-14	Med.	115–125	Orange	120	B	C-9	3,000	...	3½	2½
11S14/R	11	S-14	Med.	115–125	Red	120	B	C-9	3,000	...	3½	2½
11S14/W	11	S-14	Med.	115–125	White	120	B	C-9	3,000	...	3½	2½
11S14/Y	11	S-14	Med.	115–125	Yellow	120	B	C-9	3,000	...	3½	2½
10S14/CB	10	S-14	Med.	115–125	Blue	120	B	C-9	1,500	...	...	3½
10S14/CG	10	S-14	Med.	115–125	Green	120	B	C-9	1,500	...	...	3½
10S14/CR	10	S-14	Med.	115–125	Red	120	B	C-9	1,500	...	...	3½
10S14/CO	10	S-14	Med.	115–125	Orange	120	B	C-9	1,500	...	...	3½
10S14/CY	10	S-14	Med.	115–125	Yellow	120	B	C-9	1,500	...	...	3½
10S14/CW	10	S-14	Med.	115–125	White	120	B	C-9	1,500	...	...	3½
10S14/CFT	10	S-14	Med.	115–125	Flametint	120	B	C-9	1,500	...	...	3½
10S14/CV	10	S-14	Med.	115–125	Ivory	120	B	C-9	1,500	...	...	3½
10S14/CR2	10	S-14	Med.	115–125	Rose	120	B	C-9	1,500	...	...	3½
15A17/AO	15	A-17	Med.	115–125	Amber-orange	120	B	C-9	1,200	...	...	3⅝
15A17/B	15	A-17	Med.	115–125	Blue	120	B	C-9	1,200	...	...	3⅝
15A17/FT	15	A-17	Med.	115–125	Flametint	120	B	C-9	1,200	...	...	3⅝
15A17/G	15	A-17	Med.	115–125	Green	120	B	C-9	1,200	...	...	3⅝
15A17/V	15	A-17	Med.	115–125	Ivory	120	B	C-9	1,200	...	...	3⅝
15A17/RO	15	A-17	Med.	115–125	Old rose	120	B	C-9	1,200	...	...	3⅝
15A17/R	15	A-17	Med.	115–125	Red	120	B	C-9	1,200	...	...	3⅝
15A17/W	15	A-17	Med.	115–125	White	120	B	C-9	1,200	...	...	3⅝
15A17/Y	15	A-17	Med.	115–125	Yellow	120	B	C-9	1,200	...	...	3⅝
20A17/5	20	A-17	Med.	115–125	Clear Flashing sign	120	C	C-9	1,000	150	2⅜	3⅝
25A/O	25	A-19	Med.	115–125	Orange	120	B	C-9	1,000	...	...	3¹⁵⁄₁₆
25A/FT	25	A-19	Med.	115–125	Flametint	120	B	C-9	1,000	...	...	3¹⁵⁄₁₆
25A/Y	25	A-19	Med.	115–125	Yellow	120	B	C-9	1,000	...	...	3¹⁵⁄₁₆
25A/R2	25	A-19	Med.	115–125	Old rose	120	B	C-9	1,000	...	...	3¹⁵⁄₁₆
25A/B	25	A-19	Med.	115–125	Blue	120	B	C-9	1,000	...	...	3¹⁵⁄₁₆
25A/G	25	A-19	Med.	115–125	Green	120	B	C-9	1,000	...	...	3¹⁵⁄₁₆
25A/R	25	A-19	Med.	115–125	Red	120	B	C-9	1,000	...	...	3¹⁵⁄₁₆
25A/W	25	A-19	Med.	115–125	White	120	B	C-9	1,000	220	...	3¹⁵⁄₁₆
25A/V	25	A-19	Med.	115–125	Ivory	120	B	C-9	1,000	...	...	3¹⁵⁄₁₆
40A/O	40	A-21	Med.	115–125	Orange	120	B	C-9	1,000	...	...	4⁷⁄₁₆
40A/B	40	A-21	Med.	115–125	Blue	120	B	C-9	1,000	...	...	4⁷⁄₁₆
40A/FT	40	A-21	Med.	115–125	Flametint	120	B	C-9	1,000	...	...	4⁷⁄₁₆
40A/G	40	A-21	Med.	115–125	Green	120	B	C-9	1,000	...	...	4⁷⁄₁₆
40A/V	40	A-21	Med.	115–125	Ivory	120	B	C-9	1,000	...	...	4⁷⁄₁₆
40A/R	40	A-21	Med.	115–125	Red	120	B	C-9	1,000	...	...	4⁷⁄₁₆
40A/R2	40	A-21	Med.	115–125	Rose	120	B	C-9	1,000	...	...	4⁷⁄₁₆
40A/Y	40	A-21	Med.	115–125	Yellow	120	B	C-9	1,000	...	...	4⁷⁄₁₆

101. Spotlight and Floodlight Incandescent Lamps
(General Electric Co.)

Lamp ordering abbreviation	Watts	Bulb	Base	Volts	Burning position	Std. pkg. qty.	Class	Fila-ment	Approx life, hr	Lumens	Light center length, in.	Max over-all length, in.
Floodlight Lamps												
250G/FL	250	G-30	Med.	120	Base	60	C	C-5	800	3,850	3	5⅛
400G/FL	400	G-30	Med.	120	down	60	C	C-5	800	6,700	3	5⅛
500G/FL	500	G-40	Mog.	120	to	24	C	C-5	800	8,800	4¼	7 5/16
1M/G40FL	1,000	G-40[a]	Mog.	120	hori-	24	C	C-5	800	19,000	5¼	8
1500G48/6	1,500	G-48	Mog.	120	zontal	6	C	C-5	800	31,000	5¼	8⅝
Spotlight Lamps												
500T12/8	500	T-12	Med. pf.	120	Base up	24	C	C-13	800	......	3½	6⅛
500T14/7	500	T-14	Med.bip.	120	Base up	24	C	C-13	800	......	4	6⅜
500T20/45	500	T-20	Med.	120		24	C	C-13	500	......	3	5½
500T20/64	500	T-20	Med. pf.	120	Base	24	C	C-13	500	......	2 3/16	5¾
400G/SP	400	G-30	Med.	120	down to	60	C	C-5	200	7,800	3	5⅛
500G/SP	500	G-40	Mog.	120	hori-	24	C	C-5	200	10,100	4¼	7 1/16
1M/G40SP4¼	1,000	G-40[a]	Mog.	120	zontal	24	C	C-5	200	22,500	4¼	7 1/16
1M/G40PSP	1,000	G-40[a]	Mog. pf.	120	[b]	24	C	C-5	200	22,500	3 15/16	8 7/16

[a] Heat-resistant glass.
[b] Not recommended for burning between horizontal and base up.

101A. Quartz-Halogen Lamps for General Lighting
(Catalogs of lamp manufacturers)

Watts	Bulb	Volts	Approximate lumens		Rated life, hours
			Initial	Mean	
Clear Tubular Lamps[a]					
45	T-2½	7	630	625	1,000
75	T-3	28	1,600	–	2,000
250	T-4	120	4,400	4,260	2,000
300	T-3	120	6,000	5,800	2,000
300	T-4	120	5,550	–	2,000
400	T-4	120	7,400	7,200	2,000
500	T-3	120	10,500	10,200	2,000
500	T-4	120	10,250	9,950	2,000
1,000	T-3	240	21,000	20,400	2,000
1,250	T-3	208	27,500	26,600	2,000
1,500	T-3	240[b]	33,800	32,800	2,000
PAR and R Lamps[c]					
250	PAR-38	120	3,120	2,930	3,000
500	PAR-56	120	7,000	6,550	4,000
500	R-40	120	7,000	6,550	4,000
1,000	PAR-64	120	17,000	15,980	4,000
1,000	E-37	120	20,500	19,500	3,000
1,000	R-60	120	17,000	15,980	3,000
1,500	R-60	120	31,200	29,600	3,000

[a] Clear tubular lamps only are listed. Most of these lamps are also supplied frosted, as well as with other specifications.
[b] Also available for 208, 220, and 227 volts.
[c] These lamps are available for both spot and floodlight distributions.
NOTE: Lamps listed here are for general lighting purposes. For complete listings, see lamp manufacturers' catalogs.

101B. Low-voltage Lamps for Swimming Pools
(Catalogs of lamp manufacturers)

Watts	Volts	Bulb	Rated life, hours	Initial lumens	Peak beam candlepower
100	12	PAR-38	1,000	–	7,000
200	12	PAR-56	500	–	24,000
250	12	R-40	1,000	4,000	24,000
300	12	R-40	1,000	5,000	24,000
300	12	PAR-56	1,000	6,000	13,500
500	12	PAR-64	1,000	10,000	20,000

101C. Low-voltage High-intensity Narrow-beam Lamps
(Catalogs of lamp manufacturers)

Watts	Volts	Bulb	Beam spread, degrees	Maximum initial beam candlepower	Rated life, hours
25	5.5	PAR-36	4.5 × 5.5	30,000	1,000
25	5.5	PAR-46	4.5 × 5.5	55,000	1,000
120	6.0	PAR-64	5 × 9	180,000	3,000
120	6.0	PAR-64	5 × 9	220,000	1,000
120	6.0	PAR-64	4.5 × 7	210,000	2,000
15	12.0	R-14	9	1,335	2,000
25	12.0	R-14	11	1,835	2,000

101D. Lamps with Dichroic Reflectors[a]
(Catalogs of lamp manufacturers)

Watts	Bulb	Base	Beam pattern
75	PAR-38	Medium socket	Flood
150	PAR-36	Medium socket	Spot
150	PAR-38	Medium socket	Flood
300	PAR-56	EMEP[d]	Narrow spot
300	PAR-56	EMEP	Medium flood
300	PAR-56	EMEP	Wide flood

Lamps with Dichroic Color Filters[b]

Watts	Bulb	Beam	Beam spread, degrees	Colors
150	PAR-38	Spot	30 × 30	A, B, G, R, Y, BW[c]

[a] Multilayer metallic coating forming reflector reflects light, transmits heat, thus providing a cooler beam of light.

[b] Dichroic interference film coatings on inside surface of cover lens selectively transmit the wavelength of a specific color through the lens, reflecting all other wavelengths.

[c] Colors: Amber, Blue, Green, Red, Yellow, Blue-White.

[d] Extended mogul end prongs.

102. Street-lighting Incandescent Lamps
(General Electric Co.)

Lamp ordering abbreviation	Lumens	Watts	Bulb	Base	Volts	Burning position	Std. pkg. qty.	Class	Filament	Approx life, hr	Light center length, in.	Max over-all length, in.
Multiple Street-lighting Lamps—Regular												
85A23/48	1,000	85	A-23	Med.	120	Any	120	C	C-9	1,500	4⅜	6¹⁄₁₆
175PS25/63	2,500	175	PS-25	Med.	120	Any	60	C	C-9	1,500	5¼	6¹⁵⁄₁₆
268PS35/55	4,000	268	PS-35	Mog.	120	Any	24	C	C-9	1,500	7	9⅜
370PS40/50	6,000	370	PS-40	Mog.	120	Any	24	C	C-9	1,500	7	9¾
575PS40/51	10,000	575	PS-40	Mog.	120	Any	24	C	C-7A	1,500	7	9¾
800PS52/79	15,000	800	PS-52	Mog.	120	Any	6	C	C-7A	1,500	9½	13¹⁄₁₆
Multiple Street-lighting Lamps—Group Replacement												
58A19/62	600	58	A-19	Med.	120	Any	120	C	C 9	3,000	2⅞	4¼
92A23/49	1,000	92	A-23	Med.	120	Any	120	C	C-9	3,000	4⅜	6¹⁄₁₆
189PS25/64	2,500	189	PS-25	Med.	120	Any	60	C	C-9	3,000	5¼	6¹⁵⁄₁₆
295PS35/58	4,000	295	PS-35	Mog.	120	Any	24	C	C-9	3,000	7	9⅜
405PS40/54	6,000	405	PS-40	Mog.	120	Any	24	C	C-9	3,000	7	9¾
620PS40/53	10,000	620	PS-40	Mog.	120	Any	24	C	C-7A	3,000	7	9¾
860PS52/80	15,000	860	PS-52	Mog.	120	Any	6	C	C-7A	3,000	9½	13¹⁄₁₆

Lamp ordering abbreviation	Rated initial lumens	Clear bulb	Base	Volts	Amp	Burning position	Std. pkg. qty.	Class	Filament	Avg life, hr	Avg light center length, in.	Max over-all length, in.
Series Street-lighting Lamps—Regular												
600/66	600	PS-25	Mog.	6.4	6.6	Any	60	C	C-8	2,000	5⅜	7⅛
1M/66	1,000	PS-25	Mog.	9.5	6.6	Any	60	C	C-8	2,000	5⅜	7⅛
1M/75	1,000	PS-25	Mog.	8.3	7.5	Any	60	C	C-8	2,000	5⅜	7⅛
2500/66PS25	2,500	PS-25	Mog.	21.5	6.6	Base up	60	C	C-2V	2,000	5⅜	7⅛
2500/66	2,500	PS-35	Mog.	21.6	6.6	Any	24	C	C-2V	2,000	7	9⅜
2500/75	2,500	PS-35	Mog.	19.2	7.5	Any	24	C	C-2V	2,000	7	9⅜
4M/66	4,000	PS-35	Mog.	32.8	6.6	Any	24	C	C-2V	2,000	7	9⅜
4M/75	4,000	PS-35	Mog.	29.1	7.5	Any	24	C	C-2V	2,000	7	9⅜
4M/15BU	4,000	PS-35	Mog.	13.8	15	Base up	24	C	C-2V	2,000	7	9⅜
4M/15BD	4,000	PS-35	Mog.	13.8	15	Base down	24	C	C-2V	2,000	6¼	9⅜
6M/66	6,000	PS-40	Mog.	48.4	6.6	Any	24	C	C-2V	2,000	7	9¾
6M/20BU	6,000	PS-40	Mog.	14.9	20	Base up	24	C	C-2V	2,000	7	9¾
6M/20BD	6,000	PS-40	Mog.	14.9	20	Base down	24	C	C-2V	2,000	6¼	9¾
10M/20BU	10,000	PS-40	Mog.	24.4	20	Base up	24	C	C-7	2,000	7	9¾
10M/20BD	10,000	PS-40	Mog.	24.4	20	Base down	24	C	C-7	2,000	6¼	9¾
10M/66	10,000	PS-40	Mog.	79.7	6.6	Any	24	C	C-7A	2,000	7	9¾
15M/20BU	15,000	PS-40	Mog.	35.9	20	Base up	24	C	C-7	2,000	7	9¾
Series Street-lighting Lamps—Group Replacement												
600/66R	600	PS-25	Mog.	6.7	6.6	Any	60	C	C-8	3,000	5⅜	7⅛
1M/66R	1,000	PS-25	Mog.	9.8	6.6	Any	60	C	C-8	3,000	5⅜	7⅛
1M/75R	1,000	PS-25	Mog.	8.7	7.5	Any	60	C	C-8	3,000	5⅜	7⅛
2500/66R/PS25	2,500	PS-25	Mog.	22.3	6.6	Base up	60	C	C-2V	3,000	5⅜	7⅛
2500/66R	2,500	PS-35	Mog.	22.4	6.6	Any	24	C	C-2V	3,000	7	9⅜
2500/75R	2,500	PS-35	Mog.	19.8	7.5	Any	24	C	C-2V	3,000	7	9⅜
4M/66R	4,000	PS-35	Mog.	34.2	6.6	Any	24	C	C-2V	3,000	7	9⅜
4M/75R	4,000	PS-35	Mog.	30.0	7.5	Any	24	C	C-2V	3,000	7	9⅜
4M/15R/BU	4,000	PS-35	Mog.	14.6	15	Base up	24	C	C-2V	3,000	7	9⅜
4M/15R/BD	4,000	PS-35	Mog.	14.6	15	Base down	24	C	C-2V	3,000	6¼	9⅜
6M/66R	6,000	PS-40	Mog.	50.0	6.6	Any	24	C	C-2V	3,000	7	9¾
6M/20R/BU	6,000	PS-40	Mog.	15.7	20	Base up	24	C	C-2V	3,000	7	9¾
6M/20R/BD	6,000	PS-40	Mog.	15.7	20	Base down	24	C	C-2V	3,000	6¼	9¾
10M/66R	10,000	PS-40	Mog.	86.6	6.6	Any	24	C	C-7A	3,000	7	9¾
10M/20R/BU	10,000	PS-40	Mog.	25.3	20	Base up	24	C	C-7	3,000	7	9¾
10M/20R/BD	10,000	PS-40	Mog.	25.3	20	Base down	24	C	C-7	3,000	6¼	9¾

FLUORESCENT LAMPS

103. The fluorescent lamp (Fig. 37) is an electronic device (see Sec. **1** of Div. 6). It functions through conduction in a gas. It consists of a long straight or circular tube containing a drop of mercury and a small amount of argon gas with electrodes sealed into each end. Both electrodes are so constructed that they can function as cathodes (emitters of electrons into the enclosure). The lamp will therefore conduct in either direction and pass alternating current. The inside surface of the tube is coated with a fluorescent chemical (Sec. **106**). Fluorescent lamps can be constructed with hot or

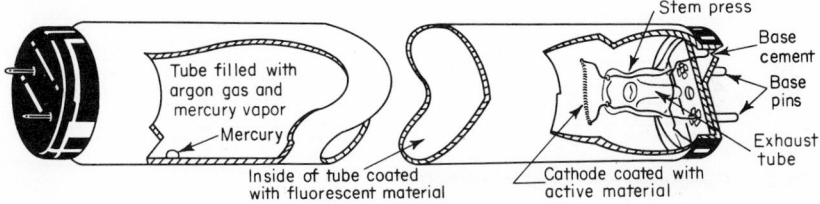

FIG. 37 *Fluorescent-lamp construction.* (*General Electric Co.*)

cold cathodes (see Fig. 38 and Sec. **11** of Div. 6). Hot cathodes are constructed of coated tungsten filaments wound in coil form. Cold cathodes are made of iron, shaped in thimblelike form in order to give a large emitting area. Cold cathodes require a higher voltage drop across the lamp for the production of the emission. Lamps with cold cathodes will consequently not have such high efficiency, i.e., lumens per watt. However, because of their inherently long life, cold-cathode lamps are advantageous for special custom-built shapes and patterns and for applications where it is difficult to replace the lamp. Most general-purpose lamps are operated with hot cathodes. Some of the general-purpose lamps are started with cold cathodes by applying a sufficiently high voltage to produce electric-field emission. However, after the lamp has conducted for only a fraction of a second, the impinging arc will heat a few of the segments of the cathode filament wire to a red-hot temperature. The cathode then produces thermionic emission, and the lamp continues to function under hot-cathode operation.

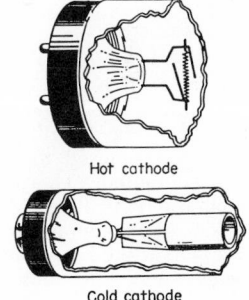

Hot cathode

Cold cathode

FIG. 38 *Cathodes for fluorescent lamps.*

104. Operation of Fluorescent Lamps. Although all general-purpose fluorescent lamps operate with hot cathodes, they are started with either hot-cathode or cold-cathode action. Hot-cathode starting is called preheat starting, and cold-cathode starting is called instant starting, since the lamps light almost instantaneously upon the closing of the lamp circuit. The preheat-start lamps are constructed with bipin bases at each end, as shown in Fig. 37. The instant-start lamps are constructed with either bipin or single-pin bases at each end. In either construction the filament of instant-start lamps is short-circuited in the base. The only purpose in making some of the instant-start lamps with bipin bases is so that these lamps can be used in the conventional type of bipin lamp holder which is employed for preheat-start lamps. However, the bipin instant-start lamps will not operate on the same ballast circuits as those employed for preheat lamps.

The principles of operation of a preheat-start fluorescent lamp can be understood from a study of the schematic diagram of Fig. 39. This figure shows the simplest connections that it is possible to employ for operation of these lamps. A reactor, connected in series with the lamp, is always required for starting and stabilizing the operation. Switch S is an automatic starting switch, or starter as it is called. This switch is in its closed position when no current is passing through the circuit. When the circuit switch is closed, the two filaments are connected in series through switch S to the supply voltage. No current will flow through the lamp between the filaments, since this path is short-circuited by switch S and also the argon gas is not in a conducting state when the filaments are cold. Current will flow through the filaments, heating them to the proper temperature and vaporizing the mercury. After a few seconds, switch S automatically opens, breaking the circuit and causing the reactor to produce a high voltage between the two filaments. This strikes an arc through the argon gas and the mercury vapor, the purpose of the argon being to facilitate the starting of the arc. Refer to Sec. **126** for the operating characteristics of various types of starters.

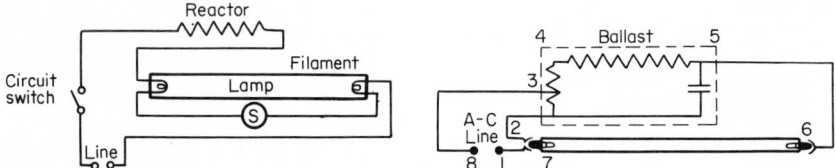

FIG. 39   *Circuit for fluorescent lamp and simple reactor.*   FIG. 40   *Circuit for instant-start fluorescent lamp.*

The mercury-vapor arc produces a large amount of ultraviolet-light radiation, which impinges on the fluorescent chemicals on the inside of the tube, causing them to fluoresce and emit a brilliant light, the color of which may be pink, gold, green, or blue depending upon the chemical used (see Table **106**). By combining chemicals, a white light or a blue daylight can be obtained.

The simplest circuit that it is possible to employ for an instant-start lamp is shown in Fig. 40. A ballast reactor is always required, as with the preheat-start lamp. Since the lamp starts with cold cathodes, no starter switch is required. However, the circuit must be so arranged that (1) a high voltage will be impressed across the lamp when the lamp circuit is closed and (2) the voltage across the lamp is reduced to its normal operating value as soon as conduction takes place and the lamp is started. The simple circuit of Fig. 40 will perform these two functions. At the instant that the circuit to the lamp is closed, there is no conduction through the lamp and terminals 6 and 7 are open-circuited. The reactor 2-3-4 will act as a step-up autotransformer and produce from 6 to 7 a voltage of a magnitude considerably greater than the line voltage from 1 to 8. This high voltage will strike an arc through the argon gas and start conduction. As soon as the lamp conducts, the self-inductance of the ballast reactor 4-5 reduces the voltage across the lamp to normal operating voltage. A fraction of a second after the arc is struck, the filaments are heated sufficiently by the arc to produce thermionic emission. The production of visible light in the instant-start lamp is the same as that described in the preceding paragraph for the preheat-start lamp.

105. There are five principal methods of operation (General Electric Co.). Some lamps may be operated by only one method; some lamps may be operated by more than one. The following describes these five operating methods.

1. PREHEAT OR SWITCH STARTING (WITH STARTERS OR MANUAL STARTING SWITCHES). If fluorescent-lamp cathodes are preheated before the lamp is started, relatively inexpensive ballasts can be used. Such preheating is readily accomplished by means of manual switches (used in desk lamps and portable lamps) or by automatic starters (where fixtures are controlled from a wall switch). Starters are available in either standard or no-blink types. The latter are obtainable in either the manual reset (Watch Dog) or automatic reset designs and in the range of sizes needed for the different lamps. The Watch Dog is recommended in most instances because it eliminates "flashing" or "blinking" at the end of lamp life, saves ballast wear, and lasts much longer.

2. TRIGGER START (NO STARTERS). This method permits operation of some smaller preheat-start fluorescent lamps without starters, yet gives practically instant starting.

Although lamp life is a little shorter and thus lamp cost a little higher, maintenance is greatly simplified and convenience of use much improved. No special lamp is required, but the lighting fixture must be equipped with the proper size of trigger-start ballast. This automatically provides cathode preheat without starters. Trigger-start ballasts are currently available for 14-, 15-, 20-, and 30-watt general-line fluorescent lamps and for 8- and 12-in. Circline lamps.

3. RAPID START (NO STARTERS). This system used with rapid-start, high-output, very-high-output, or power-groove lamps combines the simplicity of trigger start with the low cost of conventional switch starting. It requires the use of special low-loss triple-coiled cathodes to reduce cathode heating losses and is coated with Dri-Film to assure rapid starting even under adverse conditions. Rapid-start lamps will give good performance in fixtures employing glow-type starters. The lamps should be used with rapid-start ballasts designed to provide adequate preheat automatically with low losses. Lamps glow as soon as turned on and come up to uniform full brightness in approximately 2 sec.

While lamp and ballast prices are slightly higher, these are offset by elimination of the starter and starter maintenance costs. Rapid-start lamps are available in the 40-watt T-12 size, all Circline sizes, and in high-output, very-high-output, and power-groove lamps designed for greater current to secure higher light output.

4. INSTANT START (NO STARTERS). Through the use of higher-voltage ballasts, these lamps can be started without preheat. They are equipped with triple-coiled cathodes that afford in general the same long life obtained from the popular sizes of general-line switch-start lamps. While they look just like switch-start lamps of the same wattage, instant-start lamps are not electrically interchangeable with them, for the cathode leads are short-circuited inside the lamp base to ensure safety in use. Therefore instant-start lamps cannot be preheated in starter-type circuits. Furthermore, general-line lamps should not be used on instant-start ballasts or much shorter lamp life will result.

Instant-start lamps are available in 40-watt T-12 and 40-watt T-17 sizes. They are also available, on special order, in the 30-watt T-8 size.

5. SLIMLINE (INSTANT START WITHOUT STARTERS). Slimline lamps combine all the advantages of the instant-start lamp with much greater convenience in handling and easier maintenance. The lamps are equipped with extra-strong single-pin bases that fit easily and solidly in rugged push-pull sockets. This combination makes lamp installation fast and easy.

In the 8-ft sizes, slimlines are among the most efficient lamps made. In addition to increased efficiency, the longer length reduces the number of lamps and fixtures required in a given installation. This, together with the elimination of starters, reduces the amount of maintenance required in a fluorescent lighting system.

These advantages, together with the long trouble-free life offered by GE slimline lamps, assure continuing growth in popularity.

Slimline fluorescent lamps are available in 42- and 64-in. lengths in the T-6 bulb size, in 72- and 96-in. lengths in T-8, and in 48-, 72-, and 96-in. lengths in the most popular T-12 diameter.

106. Data on Fluorescent Chemicals
(In addition to the phosphor, manganese is usually present as an activator)

Phosphor	Lamp color	Exciting range[a]	Sensitivity peak	Emitted range	Emitted peak
Calcium tungstate............	Blue	2,200–3,000[b]	2,720	3,100–7,000	4,400
Calcium silicate..............	Orange	2,200–3,000	2,537	5,000–7,200	6,100
Magnesium tungstate.........	Blue-white	2,200–3,200	2,850	3,600–7,200	4,800
Zinc silicate.................	Green	2,200–2,960	2,537	4,600–6,400	5,250
Calcium halo phosphate.......	White	1,800–3,200	2,500	3,500–7,500	5,800
Cadmium silicate.............	Yellow-pink	2,200–3,200	2,400	4,800–7,400	5,950
Cadmium borate.............	Pink	2,200–3,600	2,500	5,200–7,500	6,150
Calcium phosphate...........	Deep-red	2,200–3,600	3,130	5,600–8,300	6,500
Calcium phosphate...........	Blue ultra	2,200–3,200	2,500–2,800	3,200–4,500	3,600
Calcium phosphate...........	Blue ultra	2,200–2,650	2,475	2,700–4,000	3,250

[a] 2,200 A is lower limit of measurements.
[b] All values are given in angstroms. The angstrom, used to measure wave length of radiation, is 1/100,000,000 cm in length.

107. Fluorescent-lamp Colors. Fluorescent lamps are available in a range of strong colors and in several different "whites." The saturated colors — red, pink, gold, green, and blue — are used for decorative effects, while the whites serve for both decorative and general lighting purposes. All fluorescent lamps except gold and red are white when unlighted. Different phosphors produce the different colors when lamps are lighted.

White fluorescent lamps are designed to combine three elements important in lighting effects: (1) efficiency — most light per dollar, (2) color-rendering properties — the ability to bring out the beauty of colored materials and objects, and (3) "whiteness" — their appearance in relation to either natural outdoor daylight or the traditional artificial illumination such as filament lamps.

The choice among fluorescent "whites" always involves compromise among these three elements. Obtaining best color-rendering properties necessitates reduction in efficiency. Choice of whiteness affects both efficiency and color-rendering properties. The descriptions below outline the effects obtained from the most popular whites.

Cool white combines high efficiency with reasonably good color rendition. It is the most widely used fluorescent-lamp color in factories, offices, and schools. It blends well with natural daylight.

Warm white provides the highest efficiency in white fluorescent lamps. It emphasizes orange, yellow and yellow-green at the expense of other colors. It is generally used where highest efficiency is more important than color rendition.

De luxe cool white most closely simulates the appearance and color-rendering properties of natural daylight. It is widely used in stores such as supermarkets, florists, men's wear shops, and other places where excellent color rendition of natural daylight is needed. Also used in factory and office installations where best appearance of colors is important.

Home-lite (formerly de luxe warm white) simulates the warm friendly effects of filament lighting in both "whiteness" and color rendering. It is usually first choice in residence, restaurants, beauty parlors, department stores, bakeries, and other places where "homelike" lighting effects are wanted.

Daylight, soft white, and white are still available for replacement purposes in existing installations and for new installations where their appearance or color-rendering properties are particularly suitable.

108. Bases for Fluorescent Lamps (see Fig. 41). Lamps incorporating preheat or rapid-start cathodes require four electrical contacts, which in the standard line of lamps take the form of a bipin base at either end. There are three standard types of bipin bases: miniature bipin, medium bipin, and mogul bipin. In Circline lamps the contacts are brought together in a four-pin base located between the two cathodes where

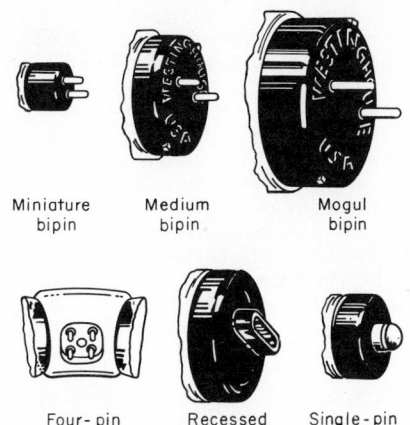

Miniature   Medium   Mogul
bipin   bipin   bipin

Four- pin   Recessed   Single- pin
double contact

FIG. 41 *Bases for fluorescent lamps. (Westinghouse Electric Corp.)*

the ends of the lamp adjoin. The high-output rapid-start lamps have recessed double-contact-type bases.

Lamps of the instant-start type require only two contacts, slimline lamps having single-pin bases. The 40-watt instant-start hot-cathode lamp has the medium bipin base but contains an electrical bridging member between the pair of contacts at each end, producing in effect a single contact for each cathode. Because of this construction, these lamps cannot be operated in circuits containing starters. Cold-cathode lamps are also instant-start lamps and have a single contact at each end, usually in the form of a cap base.

109. Types of Visible-light Fluorescent Lamps.

1. General line.
    a. T-5 lamps (for use with starters).
    b. T-8 lamps (for use with starters).
    c. T-12 lamps (for use with starters).
    d. T-12 lamp—instant start (no starter used).
    e. T-17 lamps (for use with starters).
    f. T-17 lamp—instant start (no starter used).
2. Rapid start (no starter used).
3. High output—rapid start (no starter used).
4. Slimline—instant start.
5. Circline—rapid start (no starter used).

110. General-line Lamps. The 4-, 6-, 8-, and 13-watt T-5 fluorescent lamps are generally used where space for lamps is limited and where the inherent cool light and color quality of fluorescent lamps are desired. In stores they are applied in niches, showcases, and shelving to enhance the function and appearance of miniature displays, signs, and models. In industrial plants they supply light locally for machine work, fine assembly, inspection, and other supplementary lighting applications. In offices they are built into business machines and similar devices for increased visibility of dials, scales, and keyboards.

The 15-watt T-8 lamp is used extensively in homes for kitchen, bathroom, and mirror lighting. In stores it lights showcases, niches, and signs. In industry it is used for local lighting at machines and workbenches—also in portable desk lamps. When it is used with the trigger-start ballast, starting is nearly instantaneous.

The 30-watt T-8 lamp is applied in stores for showcase, wallcase, and perimeter lighting and in homes for valances over narrow windows. It is used in polished parabolic reflectors where the diameter is advantageous for good control.

The 14-watt T-12 lamp is used for supplementary lighting in stores and industry. It is applied where space does not permit use of the longer 15-watt lamp. It has been employed in portable lamps using a low-wattage filament lamp for a ballast.

The 15-watt T-12 lamp has a lower bulb brightness than the 15-watt T-8 lamp for about the same amount of light. It is preferred over the T-8 lamp if used without shielding as is sometimes done for bathroom mirror lighting and some other applications. Its many uses parallel those of the 15-watt T-8.

The 20-watt T-12 lamp is one of the most widely used fluorescent lamps. It is employed in home fixtures for lighting in kitchens, bathrooms, basements, and recreation rooms. It is used in window valances and under shelving and cupboards for decorative and utilitarian lighting. It can be used to light closets, washrooms, and small areas. It is also employed for supplementary lighting in offices and factories. In stores it lights fitting mirrors, niches, and wallcase displays. It can be operated by trigger-start ballasts.

The 25-watt T-12 33-in. lamp is the longest T-12 lamp which can be operated from 120 volts a-c with a simple choke ballast. It is principally used in homes, either in general lighting fixtures or built into window valances and kitchen work spaces.

The 40-watt T-12 preheat lamp is used extensively for general lighting in every field of application. It is employed in strips or channels for lighting valances in homes and stores, for display fixtures, show windows, and hundreds of other services. The 90-watt T-17 lamps produce more light per foot than any other preheat lamps. The 90-watt lamp is used in industry for general lighting and also in offices, stores and show windows. Specially designed low-temperature lamps are recommended for use in temperatures from 50 to 0°F.

Instant-start types reduce maintenance and ensure more reliable starting when used outdoors in cold weather.

The 40-watt T-17 lamp has a comparatively low surface brightness. It is used for high-quality lighting installations in schools and offices and for special industry applications where it is important to minimize direct and reflected glare.

111. Rapid start 40-watt T-12 fluorescent lamps simplify lighting maintenance for the user and give, in effect, instant starting at costs comparable to those of the 40-watt preheat lamp. Starters are eliminated from the electrical circuit. This is accomplished with a cathode design in the lamp somewhat different from that of the preheat lamp and with a ballast having low-voltage windings which apply heating to the cathodes at starting and during operation. Rated lamp life and light output are the same as for the preheat.

Dimming. Forty-watt T-12 rapid-start lamps can be dimmed from full brightness to nearly full blackout by means of special ballasts and dimmers especially designed for this service.

Flashing. Special ballasts similar to the dimming ballasts, but providing somewhat higher cathode-heating current, have been designed for flashing rapid-start and high-output lamps. Lamp life in flashing service is not yet established but is expected to reach normal rated values.

112. High-output Rapid-start Lamps. The high-output line of T-12 lamps (24- to 96-in.) operates at 800 to 1,000 ma. Since the lamps are of rapid-start design, two electrical contacts are required at each base. The recessed double-contact base was developed to meet this requirement and, at the same time, to eliminate any hazard from electrical shock.

The high-output rapid-start lamp gives about 40 per cent more light than the 96-in. T-12 slimline or 40-watt lamp. Because of the higher current load and thus higher bulb wall temperature, this lamp performs best in ventilated fixtures. Typical open-top fixtures that allow substantial amounts of upward light provide excellent ventilation. Efficient surface-mounted and recessed fixtures have also been developed.

Because of the higher bulb wall temperature, the high-output lamps perform better in low-temperature applications than 430-ma lamps.

Another step in higher output fluorescent lamps is the power-groove lamp (Fig. 41A).

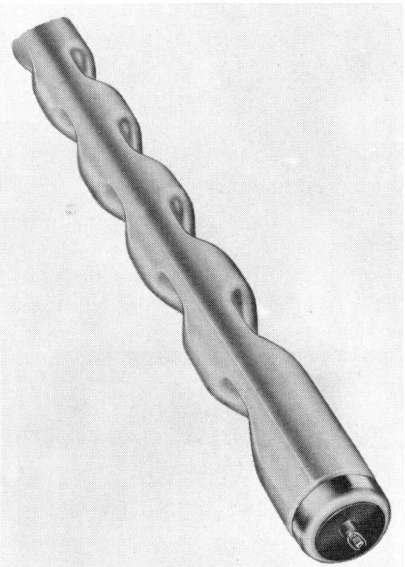

FIG. 41A *Power-groove lamp. (General Electric Co.)*

This lamp has a U- or crescent-shaped cross section. The exciting ultraviolet radiation produced within the bulb has a shorter distance to travel before striking the fluorescent material or phosphor than it would have from the center of a corresponding bulb of circular cross section. The full benefit of the greater amount of ultraviolet radiation generated is obtained with the power-groove construction. Less opportunity is provided for reabsorption of this radiation by the mercury vapor before it strikes the phosphor. The "rails" along the grooves serve to keep the mercury pressure inside the bulb near the optimum value, by providing cool spots, which condense out excessive mercury vapor. The bridges between the grooves assure adequate bulb strength.

The distribution of light from this lamp differs from that of conventional sources. The total light in the 0 to 90-deg zone is equal to the total in the 90- to 180-deg zone, but in the 0- to 30- and 150- to 180-deg zones, the relative light output is approximately 12 per cent more than that from a tubular cross section of equal total light output. In most fixture designs this directional effect can be used to advantage. Like the high-output lamp, the power-groove lamp maintains its light output well at low temperatures. Again, enclosed fixtures will provide maximum output in most low-temperature applications.

113. Slimline lamps are a family of fluorescent lamps which are instant-starting, with single-pin bases. In general, they have advantages in wiring installation and maintenance over other fluorescent lamps. The rugged single-pin base combined with "push-pull" insertion in sockets has become very popular. Slimline lamps are available in a range of lengths and diameters to fit general and supplementary lighting needs in nearly all fields of application.

The 96T12 is the most prominent slimline lamp for general lighting service. The maintenance advantages of the 8-ft lamp result from fewer parts in the lighting systems than preheat types require for the same amount of light—lamps, sockets, ballasts, starters etc., being considered.

The 72T12 and 48T12 are 6- and 4-ft companions, respectively, of the 96T12 which permit finishing out the ends of continuous rows where the 8-ft lamp is used. These lamps are also used for general lighting where shorter fixture lengths are desired for scale or to fit an architectural module.

The 96T8 and 72T8 are appropriate for use in fixtures of thin, unobtrusive design. They can be conveniently concealed in coves, coffers, or other restricted areas. Their operation at one of three current ratings, determined by the rating of the ballast used, gives considerable range in choice of lighting level and fixture brightness.

The 42T6 and 64T6 are designed to fit the standard 4- and 6-ft store showcases. Their ³/₄-in. diameter means minimum visual obstruction for all types of displays. The small diameter also permits accurate control with polished, concentrating reflectors for wallcase, show window, cove, wall or mural lighting, and many other specialized applications.

Slimline lamps of all lengths are popular for use in illuminating outdoor plastic signs.

114. Circline Lamps. Fluorescent lamps are also made in the form of a half circle and a circle. These are known as Circlarc and Circline lamps, respectively, and have the preheat type of cathode. Circline fluorescent lamps (Fig. 42) are now available

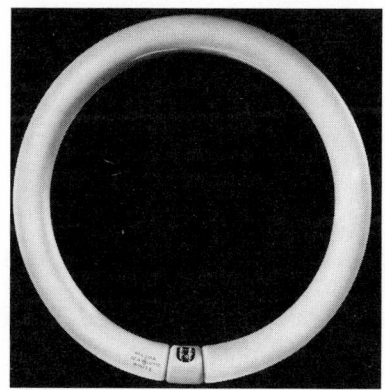

FIG. 42 *Circline fluorescent lamp.* (*General Electric Co.*)

in three diameters, 8-, 12-, and 16-in. They are widely used in home lighting fixtures and portable lamps. They are also used for decorative lighting in restaurants, theaters, lobbies, lounges, and other commercial areas. They are adapted for some inspection processes in industry. The 8- and 12-in.-diameter lamps can be operated on trigger-start ballasts. See Table **122** for lamp data.

115. T-5 Fluorescent Lamps
(General Electric Co.)
(For use with starters)

Lamp ordering abbreviation	Nominal lamp watts	Bulb	Length, in.	Base	Description	Standard package quantity	Approx life, hr[a]	Approx initial lumens[b]	Approx lumens at 40% rated avg life
F4T5/CW	4	T-5	6	Min. bip.	Cool white	24	4,000	113	86
F6T5/CW	6	T-5	9	Min. bip.	Cool white	24	6,000	260	195
F6T5/W	6	T-5	9	Min. bip.	White	24	6,000	260	187
F8T5/CW	8	T-5	12	Min. bip.	Cool white	24	6,000	420	330
F8T5/W	8	T-5	12	Min. bip.	White	24	6,000	420	320
F13T5/CW	13	T-5	21	Min. bip.	Cool white	24	7,500	820	640

[a] Life under specified test conditions with lamps turned off and restarted no oftener than once every 3 burning hours.

[b] Approximate initial lumens after 100 hr operation.

116. T-8 Fluorescent Lamps
(General Electric Co.)
(For use with starters)

Lamp ordering abbreviation	Nominal lamp watts	Bulb	Length, in.	Base	Description	Standard package quantity	Approx life, hr[a]	Approx initial lumens[b]	Approx lumens at 40% rated avg life
F15T8/CW	15	T-8	18	Med. bip.	Cool white	24	7,500	870	720
F15T8/CWX	15	T-8	18	Med. bip.	De luxe cool white	24	7,500	612	475
F15T8/WWX	15	T-8	18	Med. bip.	Home-line	24	7,500	600	470
F15T8/D	15	T-8	18	Med. bip.	Daylight	24	7,500	710	590
F15T8/W	15	T-8	18	Med. bip.	White	24	7,500	850	705
F15T8/WW	15	T-8	18	Med. bip.	Warm white	24	7,500	850	705
F15T8/SW	15	T-8	18	Med. bip.	Soft white/N	24	7,500	590	460
F15T8-B	15	T-8	18	Med. bip.	Blue	24	7,500		
F15T8/G	15	T-8	18	Med. bip.	Green	24	7,500		
F15T8/GO	15	T-8	18	Med. bip.	Gold	24	7,500		
F15T8/PK	15	T-8	18	Med. bip.	Pink	24	7,500		
F15T8/R	15	T-8	18	Med. bip.	Red	24	7,500		
F30T8/CW	30	T-8	36	Med. bip.	Cool white	24	7,500	2,100	1,760
F30T8/CWX	30	T-8	36	Med. bip.	De luxe cool white	24	7,500	1,580	1,250
F30T8/WWX	30	T-8	36	Med. bip.	Home-line	24	7,500	1,520	1,200
F30T8/D	30	T-8	36	Med. bip.	Daylight	24	7,500	1,820	1,530
F30T8/W	30	T-8	36	Med. bip.	White	24	7,500	2,180	1,830
F30T8/WW	30	T-8	36	Med. bip.	Warm white	24	7,500	2,180	1,830
F30T8/SW	30	T-8	36	Med. bip.	Soft white/N	24	7,500	1,500	1,200
F30T8/B	30	T-8	36	Med. bip.	Blue	24	7,500		
F30T8/G	30	T-8	36	Med. bip.	Green	24	7,500		
F30T8/GO	30	T-8	36	Med. bip.	Gold	24	7,500		
F30T8/PK	30	T-8	36	Med. bip.	Pink	24	7,500		
F30T8/R	30	T-8	36	Med. bip.	Red	24	7,500		

[a] Life under specified test conditions with lamps turned off and restarted no oftener than once every 3 burning hous.

[b] Approximate initial lumens after 100 hr operation.

117. T-12 (14- to 25-watt) Fluorescent Lamps
(General Electric Co.)
(For use with starters)

Lamp ordering abbreviation	Nominal lamp watts	Bulb	Length, in.	Base	Description	Standard package quantity	Approx life, hr[a]	Approx initial lumens[b]	Approx lumens at 40% rated avg life
F14T12/CW	14	T-12	15	Med. bip.	Cool white	24	6,000	710	640
F14T12/CWX	14	T-12	15	Med. bip.	De luxe cool white	24	6,000	470	366
F14T12/WWX	14	T-12	15	Med. bip.	Home-line	24	6,000	460	360
F14T12/D	14	T-12	14	Med. bip.	Daylight	24	6,000	585	525
F14T12/W	14	T-12	15	Med. bip.	White	24	6,000	720	648
F14T12/WW	14	T-12	15	Med. bip.	Warm white	24	6,000	720	645
F14T12/W/1	14	T-12	15	Med. bip.	White[c]	24	7,500	610	
F15T12/CW	15	T-12	18	Med. bip.	Cool white	24	7,500	770	675
F15T12/CWX	15	T-12	18	Med. bip.	De luxe cool white	24	7,500	520	405
F15T12/WWX	15	T-12	18	Med. bip.	Home-line	24	7,500	505	394
F15T12/D	15	T-12	18	Med. bip.	Daylight	24	7,500	650	540
F15T12/W	15	T-12	18	Med. bip.	White	24	7,500	770	640
F15T12/WW	15	T-12	18	Med. bip.	Warm white	24	7,500	770	640
F20T12/CW	20	T-12	24	Med. bip.	Cool white	24	7,500	1,220	1,100
F20T12/CWX	20	T-12	24	Med. bip.	De luxe cool white	24	7,500	850	690
F20T12/WWX	20	T-12	24	Med. bip.	Home-line	24	7,500	820	665
F20T12/D	20	T-12	24	Med. bip.	Daylight	24	7,500	875	820
F20T12/W	20	T-12	24	Med. bip.	White	24	7,500	1,250	1,060
F20T12/WW	20	T-12	24	Med. bip.	Warm white	24	7,500	1,250	1,060
F20T12/SW	20	T-12	24	Med. bip.	Soft white	24	7,500	810	690
F20T12/B	20	T-12	24	Med. bip.	Blue	24	7,500		
F20T12/G	20	T-12	24	Med. bip.	Green	24	7,500		
F20T12/GO	20	T-12	24	Med. bip.	Gold	24	7,500		
F20T12/PK	20	T-12	24	Med. bip.	Pink	24	7,500		
F20T12/R	20	T-12	24	Med. bip.	Red	24	7,500		
F20T12/CW/1	20	T-12	24	Med. bip.	Cool white[c]	24			
F20T12/D/1	20	T-12	24	Med. bip.	Daylight[c]	24			
F25T12/CW/33	25	T-12	33	Med. bip.	Cool white	24	7,500	1,815	1,540
F25T12/WWX/33	25	T-12	33	Med. bip.	Home-line	24	7,500	1,850	1,570
F25T12/D/33	25	T-12	33	Med. bip.	Daylight	24	7,500	1,520	1,290

[a] Life under specified test conditions with lamps turned off and restarted no oftener than once every 3 burning hours.

[b] Approximate initial lumens after 100 hr operation.

[c] Direct-current operation.

118. T-17 (40- and 90-watt) Fluorescent Lamps
(General Electric Co.)

Lamp ordering abbreviation	Nominal lamp watts	Bulb	Length, in.	Base	Description	Standard package quantity	Approx life, hr[a]	Approx initial lumens[b]	Approx lumens at 40% rated avg life
Fluorescent Lamps (for Use with Starters)									
F90T17/CW	90	T-17	60	Mog. bip.	Cool white	12	9,000	6,000	5,350
F90T17/D	90	T-17	60	Mog. bip.	Daylight	12	9,000	5,200	4,350
F90T17/W	90	T-17	60	Mog. bip.	White	12	9,000	6,300	5,650
Instant-start Fluorescent Lamps (No Starters Used)[c]									
F40T17/CW/IS	40	T-17	60	Mog. bip.	Cool white	12	7,500	2,800	2,520

[a] Life under specified test conditions with lamps turned off and restarted no oftener than once every 3 burning hours.

[b] Approximate initial lumens after 100 hr operation.

[c] The pins of these lamps are short-circuited inside the end caps, and lamp will not operate on preheat ballast circuits.

119. Preheat/Rapid-start Fluorescent Lamps
(General Electric Co.)

Lamp ordering abbreviation	Nominal lamp watts	Bulb	Length, in.	Base	Description	Std. package qty.	Approx life, hr	Approx initial lumens	Approx lumens at 40% rated avg life
F40T12/CW	40	T-12	48	Med. bipin	Cool white	24	15,000	3,120	2,840
F40T12/CWX	40	T-12	48	Med. bipin	De luxe cool white	24	15,000	2,130	1,780
F40T12/WWX	40	T-12	48	Med. bipin	De luxe warm white	24	15,000	2,080	1,740
F40T12/D	40	T-12	48	Med. bipin	Daylight	24	15,000	2,600	2,370
F40T12/W	40	T-12	48	Med. bipin	White	24	15,000	3,170	2,880
F40T12/WW	40	T-12	48	Med. bipin	Warm white	24	15,000	3,170	2,880
F40T11/SW	40	T-12	48	Med. bipin	Soft white	24	15,000	1,940	1,650
F40T12/B	40	T-12	48	Med. bipin	Blue (deep)	24	15,000	450	
F40T12/G	40	T-12	48	Med. bipin	Green	24	15,000	4,500	
F40T12/GO	40	T-12	48	Med. bipin	Gold	24	15,000	2,400	
F40T12/PK	40	T-12	48	Med. bipin	Pink	24	15,000	1,160	
F40T12/R	40	T-12	48	Med. bipin	Red	24	15,000	200	
F40T12/CW/S	40	T-12	48	Med. bipin	Cool white	24	12,000	3,200	2,980

120. High-output and Power-groove Fluorescent Lamps
(General Electric Co.)

Lamp ordering abbreviation	Nominal lamp watts	Bulb	Length, in.	Base	Description[a]	Standard package quantity	Approx life, hr[b]	Approx initial lumens[c]
					High-output Fluorescent Lamps (No Starters Used)			
F48T12/CW/HO	60	T-12	48	Recessed Double cont.	Cool white	24	12,000	4,000
F48T12/WW/HO	60	T-12	48		Warm white	24	12,000	4,000
F72T12/CW/HO	85	T-12	72		Cool white	12	12,000	6,450
F72T12/WW/HO	85	T-12	72		Warm white	12	12,000	6,300
F100T12/CW/HO	100	T-12	72	Mog. bipin	Cool white street lt. lp.	12	12,000[d]	6,900
F96T12/CW/HO	110	T-12	96	Recessed Double cont.	Cool white	12	12,000	9,000
F96T12/WW/HO	110	T-12	96		Warm white	12	12,000	8,900
F96T12/CWX/HO	110	T-12	96		De luxe cool white	12	12,000	6,100
F96T12/WWX/HO	110	T-12	96		Home-line	12	12,000	5,950
					Power-groove Fluorescent Lamps (No Starters Used)			
F48PG17/CW	110	PG-17	48	Recessed D. C.	Cool white	12	9,000	6,900
F72PG17/CW	165	PG-17	72	Recessed D. C.	Cool white	8	9,000	10,900
F96PG17/CW	200	PG-17	96	Recessed D. C.	Cool white	8	9,000	15,500

[a] This lamp is designed and rated for operation in supplementary cathode preheat circuits, for which specifications are available from the lamp manufacturer.

[b] Life under specified test conditions with lamps turned off and restarted no oftener than once every 3 burning hours.

[c] Approximate initial lumens after 100 hr operation.

[d] Life under specified test conditions with lamps turned off and restarted no oftener than once every 10 burning hours.

121. Slimline Fluorescent Lamps
(General Electric Co.)
(Instant start—no starters used)

Lamp ordering abbreviation	Nominal lamp watts	Bulb	Length, in.	Base	Description	Standard package quantity	Approx life, hr[a]	Approx initial lumens[b,c]	Approx lumens at 40% rated avg life
				T-6 Approx ¾ In. Diameter					
F42T6/CW	25	T-6	42	Single pin	Cool white	24	7,500	1,750	1,450
F42T6/CWX	25	T-6	42	Single pin	De luxe cool white	24	7,500	1,300	1,020
F42T6/WWX	25	T-6	42	Single pin	Home-line	24	7,500	1,280	1,000
F42T6/W	25	T-6	42	Single pin	White	24	7,500	1,820	1,510
F42T6/WW	25	T-6	42	Single pin	Warm white	24	7,500	1,820	1,510
F64T6/CW	40	T-6	64	Single pin	Cool white	24	7,500	2,800	2,350
F64T6/CWX	40	T-6	64	Single pin	De luxe cool white	24	7,500	2,550	1,620
F64T6/W	40	T-6	64	Single pin	White	24	7,500	2,850	2,390
F64T6/WW	40	T-6	64	Single pin	Warm white	24	7,500	2,850	2,390
F64T6/SW	40	T-6	64	Single pin	Soft white/N	24	7,500	1,880	1,330
				T-8 Approx 1 In. Diameter					
F72T8/CW	35	T-8	72	Single pin	Cool white	24	7,500	3,000	2,600
F72T8/CWX	35	T-8	72	Single pin	De luxe cool white	24	7,500	2,070	1,740
F72T8/W	35	T-8	72	Single pin	White	24	7,500	2,950	2,600
F72T8/WW	35	T-8	72	Single pin	Warm white	24	7,500	2,950	2,600
F96T8/CW	50	T-8	96	Single pin	Cool white	24	7,500	4,100	3,750
F96T8/CWX	50	T-8	96	Single pin	De luxe cool white	24	7,500	2,870	2,460
F96T8/WWX	50	T-8	96	Single pin	Home-line	24	7,500	2,840	2,440
F96T8/W	50	T-8	96	Single pin	White	24	7,500	3,900	3,600
F96T8/WW	50	T-8	96	Single pin	Warm white	24	7,500	3,900	3,600
F96T8/D	50	T-8	96	Single pin	Daylight	24	7,500	3,500	3,220
				T-12 Approx 1½ In. Diameter					
F48T12/CW	40	T-12	48	Single pin	Cool white	24	9,000	2,800	2,580
F48T12/CWX	40	T-12	48	Single pin	De luxe cool white	24	9,000	2,020	1,660
F48T12/WWX	40	T-12	48	Single pin	Home-line	24	9,000	1,970	1,620
F48T12/W	40	T-12	48	Single pin	White	24	9,000	3,000	2,600
F48T12/WW	40	T-12	48	Single pin	Warm white	24	9,000	3,000	2,600
F48T12/D	40	T-12	48	Single pin	Daylight	24	9,000	2,500	2,160
F72T12/CW	55	T-12	72	Single pin	Cool white	12	15,000	4,400	4,110
F72T12/CWX	55	T-12	72	Single pin	De luxe cool white	12	15,000	3,080	2,510
F72T12/WWX	55	T-12	72	Single pin	Home-line	12	15,000	3,000	2,450
F72T12/W	55	T-12	72	Single pin	White	12	15,000	4,450	3,960
F72T12/WW	55	T-12	72	Single pin	Warm white	12	15,000	4,450	3,960
F96T12/CW	75	T-12	96	Single pin	Cool white	12	15,000	6,200	5,800
F96T12/CWX	75	T-12	96	Single pin	De luxe cool white	12	15,000	4,300	3,830
F96T12/WWX	75	T-12	96	Single pin	Home-line	12	15,000	4,100	3,650
F96T12/W	75	T-12	96	Single pin	White	12	15,000	6,250	5,840
F96T12/WW	75	T-12	96	Single pin	Warm white	12	15,000	6,250	5,840
F96T12/SW	75	T-12	96	Single pin	Soft white/N	12	15,000	4,250	3,700
F96T12/D	75	T-12	96	Single pin	Daylight	12	15,000	5,400	5,050

[a] Life under specified test conditions with lamps turned off and restarted no oftener than once every 3 burning hours.

[b] Approximate initial lumens after 100 hr operation.

[c] Approximate initial lumens for F42T6 and F72T8 lamps are for operation at 200 ma.

122. Circline Fluorescent Lamps[a]
(General Electric Co.)
(Rapid start—no starters used)

Lamp ordering abbreviation	Nominal lamp watts	Bulb	Outside diam, in.	Base	Description	Standard package quantity	Approx life, hr[b]	Approx initial lumens[c]	Approx lumens at 40% rated avg life
FC8T9/CW	22	T-9	8¼	4-pin	Cool white	12	7,500	950	720
FC8T9/WWX	22	T-9		4-pin	Home-line	12	7,500	745	515
FC12T10/CW	32	T-10	12	4-pin	Cool white	12	7,500	1,750	1,550
FC12T10/WWX	32	T-10		4-pin	Home-line	12	7,500	1,240	990
FC16T10/CW	40	T-10	16	4-pin	Cool white	12	7,500	2,300	1,930
FC16T10/WWX	40	T-10		4-pin	Home-line	12	7,500	1,660	1,390

[a] In addition to rapid-start operation these lamps will give fully as good performance in any present circuit as the previous lamps did.
[b] Life under specified test conditions with lamps turned off and restarted no oftener than once every 3 burning hours.
[c] Approximate initial lumens after 100 hr operation.

123. Auxiliary Equipment. The operation of fluorescent lamps requires certain auxiliary equipment. Each fluorescent lamp requires a ballast assembly, generally called a ballast (Fig. 43). The characteristic of the mercury arc in the tube is that of a varying unstable resistance, which requires a high voltage to start the arc. Each lamp must therefore be equipped with a ballast reactor, which performs a twofold purpose. It provides a high induced starting voltage for striking the arc and, after conduction has

FIG. 43 *Cases for fluorescent-lamp ballasts. (General Electric Co.)*

started, stabilizes the operating impedance of the circuit in order to maintain the operating current at a steady value. Figure 44 shows the wiring diagrams for the more common ballasts.

Since the ballast reactor used with the lamps gives an over-all lagging power factor of only 0.45 to 0.50, the installation of any considerable number of fluorescent lamps with simply a ballast reactor would require uneconomical size of wire and distribution transformer ratings in the circuits supplying the lamps. The power factor of the lamp circuit can be raised to a high value by connecting a capacitor of the proper rating across the lamp circuit. The use of power-factor-correcting capacitors is recommended. Many power companies have adopted rules and several states have passed laws limiting the minimum power factor permissible in fluorescent-lamp installations. The power-factor correcting capacitor may be included as an integral part of the ballast assembly, or a large capacitor may be connected across the circuit supplying several lamps.

For lamps started by the preheat-start method a starting switch is required. The different types of starting switches are explained in Sec. **126.**

Trigger-, rapid-, and instant-start lamps require only a ballast; no starting switch is used. The ballasts, however, must be ones that are properly designed for the particular type of starting employed.

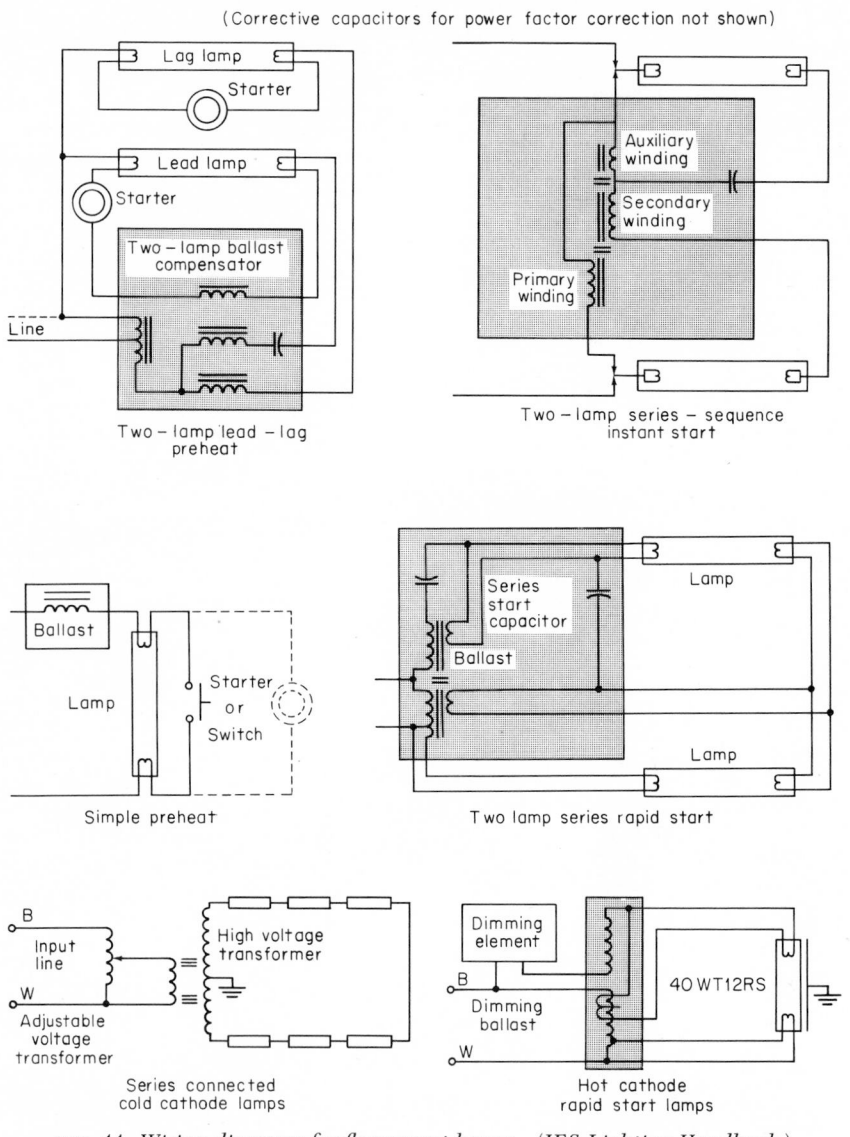

FIG. 44 *Wiring diagrams for fluorescent lamps.* (*IES Lighting Handbook.*)

124. Ballast Assemblies. Certain parts of the auxiliary equipment required for fluorescent lamps are made up as a unit by the manufacturers and assembled inside a single metal case (Fig. 43). The complete assembly is generally termed the ballast. Single-ballast assemblies are available for single-lamp, two-lamp (tulamp), three-lamp, and four-lamp luminaire installations. The automatic starting switch required for the preheat-start lamps is not combined with the ballast unit but is made as a separate unit.

125. Representative Ballasts for Fluorescent Lamps. Data for any fluorescent ballast may be obtained from manufacturers of these devices. Such manufacturers offer catalogs which include tables describing the various characteristics of each type of ballast. This information includes nominal lamp watts, circuit voltage, sound rating, dimensions, weight, watts loss, power factor, line current, and type of case. Since ballast designs are frequently revised, or new ones are added, only the latest catalogs should be used to assure proper information.

126. The starting switches required for preheat-start lamps must perform at least the following functions:

1. Close the circuit between the two filaments when the lamp circuit is energized.

2. Open the circuit between the two filaments after a sufficient lapse of time for the filaments to be heated to the proper temperature.

Starting switches are available in four types: (1) manual starting switches, (2) automatic glow-switch starter, (3) automatic Watch-Dog or No-Blink starters, and (4) automatic thermal-switch starters.

The manual starting switch is the simplest concept of a starter switch. It consists of a single push-button type of switch,

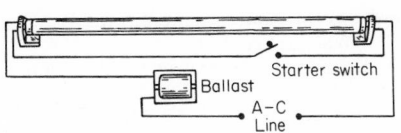

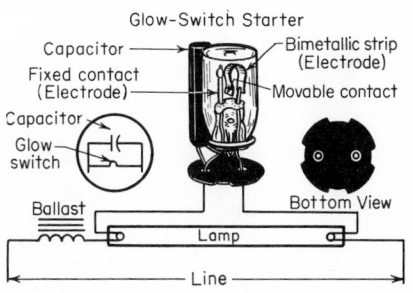

FIG. 45 *Fluorescent-lamp circuit with push-button starting switch.*

FIG. 46 *Fluorescent-lamp circuit with glow-switch starter.*

as indicated in Fig. 45. When the lamp is started, the push button is held down for a second or two and then released. Manual starting switches of this type are often used for desk-type fluorescent lamps.

The automatic **glow-switch starter** (Fig. 46) consists of a glass bulb containing neon or argon gas and two electrodes. One electrode is a U-shaped bimetallic strip, and the other electrode is a fixed rod. On starting, when there is practically no voltage drop at the ballast, the voltage at the starter is sufficient to produce a glow discharge between the U-shaped bimetallic strip and the fixed-contact or center electrode (see Fig. 47A). The heat from the glow actuates the bimetallic strip, the contacts close, and cathode preheating begins (see Fig. 47B). This shorts out the glow discharge so the bimetal cools, and in a very short time the contacts open (see Fig. 47C). The induc-

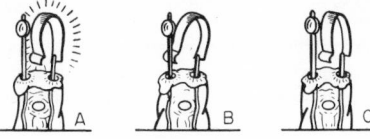

FIG. 47 *Glow-switch starter, showing operating positions of contacts.*

tive voltage kick from the ballast is then sufficient to start the lamp. During normal operation, there is not enough voltage across the lamp to produce further starter glow; the contacts therefore remain open, and the starter consumes no energy.

The Watch-Dog starter (one manufacturer's trade name) (Fig. 48) contains a glow switch, and, during normal starting, the switch functions in the manner described. This starter has an added feature, which consists of a wire-coil heater element actuating a bimetallic arm that serves as a latch to hold a second switch in a normal closed position. When a lamp is deactivated or will not start for some reason after repeated attempts have been made by blinking on and off, enough heat is developed by the intermittent flow of cathode-preheating current so that the latch pulls away and releases a spring-operated switch in the starter circuit. This occurs after 15 to 20 sec at rated line voltage, thus removing the annoyance of blinking and conserving the life of the starter. At the time the lamp is replaced, the starter is reset to operating position by pushing down on the reset button at the top of the starter. The No-Blink starter is another

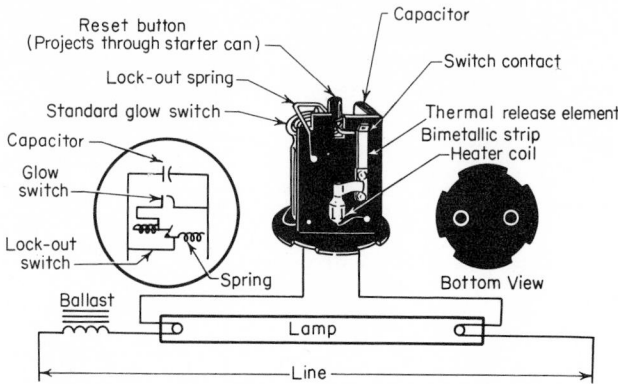

FIG. 48   *Fluorescent-lamp circuit with Watch-Dog starter.*

manufacturer's trade name for a starter that performs the same function as the Watch-Dog starter. Its operation is similar to that of the Watch-Dog starter.

The thermal-switch starter consists of a bimetallic switch element heated by a separate heater element. The arrangement and connections for such a starter are shown in Fig. 49. When the lamp is cold, the bimetallic switch element is closed. When the lamp circuit is energized, the bimetallic switch element connects the ballast, starter heating element, and lamp cathodes in series across the supply line. The cathode-preheating current, in passing through the starter heating element, heats the bimetallic switch element. After the proper lapse of time, the heating of the bimetallic switch element opens the contacts of the bimetallic switch element and breaks the circuit through the lamp filaments. The inductive kick then starts the lamp. The normal operating current passes through the starter heating element. The bimetallic switch element is therefore held open as long as the lamp continues to conduct. The thermal-switch starter consumes some energy during operation, $\frac{1}{2}$ watt for the smaller size and $1\frac{1}{2}$ watts for the larger size. The thermal-switch starters probably give the best all-around performance. They provide an adequate preheating period, a high induced starting voltage, and characteristics that are inherently less susceptible to line-voltage variations.

A small capacitor is connected across the switch contacts in many types of automatic starting switches. It aids in the starting but is primarily useful to shunt out line-lead harmonics that may cause radio interference.

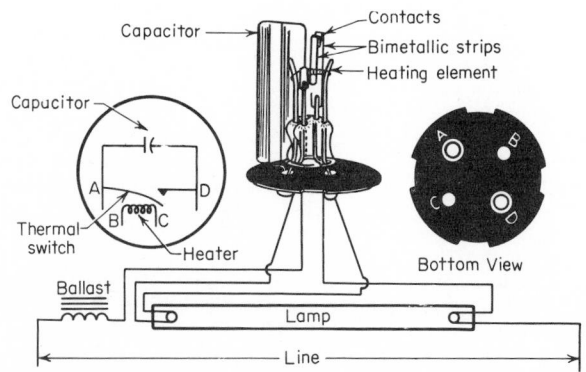

FIG. 49   *Circuit for fluorescent lamp with thermal-switch starter.*

The general appearance of automatic starting switches is shown in Fig. 50.

Automatic starting switches are mounted in special starter sockets that are available as a separate unit or as a unit combined with a fluorescent lamp holder.

127. Wiring Arrangement. A typical wiring arrangement for a fluorescent lamp and its auxiliaries is shown in Fig. 51. The sockets, or lamp holders as they are called for fluorescent lamps, of course are entirely different from those for incandescent lamps. Care must be exercised to obtain the proper lamp holder for the particular lamp which is being used.

128. Ballast Life and Temperatures. The conventional ballast is enclosed in a container filled with a heavy impregnating compound which congeals around the choke coils and condenser. This serves to radiate heat and, by its compactness, to eliminate or minimize noise or hum. The wattage loss in the ballast creates heat, and suitable ventilation must be provided in fixture design or in places where ballasts are installed so that the temperature is kept within safe limits. If the temperature rises too high, the capacitor will fail and cause excessive heating and eventual failure of the internal windings.

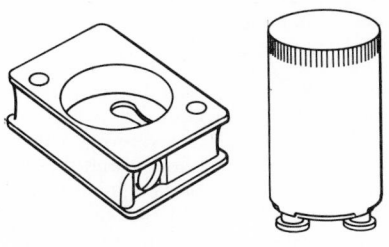

I Starter socket   II Switch

FIG. 50 *Fluorescent-lamp starter switch and socket.*

Excessive ballast temperatures may be the result of one of the following:

1. Shorted starter in preheat circuits.
2. Burned-out lamp.
3. Rectifying lamp (near end of lamp life).
4. Line-voltage fluctuation. (Certain types of ballasts are sensitive to line-voltage fluctuation, and, therefore, overheat at higher line voltages.)
5. Improper design of fixture so that ballast heat cannot be dissipated efficiently.
6. Improper location of fixture which prevents proper heat dissipation.
7. Improper selection of ballast for type of lamps used.

At a maximum temperature of 105°C (221°F) *within the winding*, or 90°C (194°F) *measured on the case*, and a maximum capacitor temperature of 70°C (158°F), the expected ballast life is about 12 years. An increase of 10°C (18°F) beyond these limits will cut ballast life by as much as 50 per cent.

The National Electrical Code requires that all fluorescent fixtures used indoors must incorporate ballast protection other than for simple reactor ballasts as shown in Figs. 45 and 46. In response to this Code rule Underwriters' Laboratories now has a standard that requires the use of Class P (Protected) ballasts for indoor fixtures. Class P

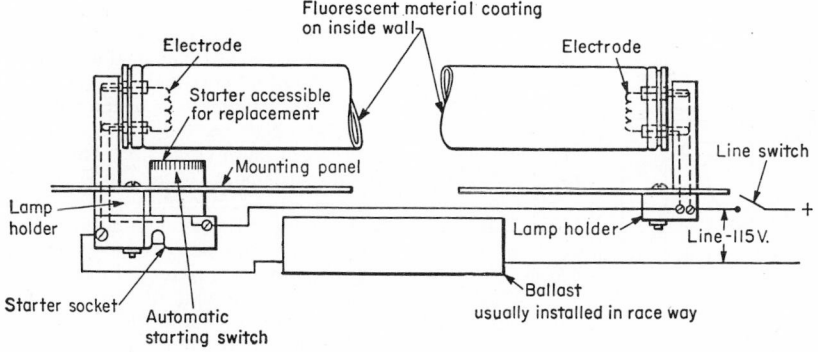

FIG. 51 *Assembly of fluorescent lamp, starter, and reactor.*

ballasts contain inherent *thermal* devices and/or *thermal* fuses, which will automatically open if the maximum temperature of the ballast is exceeded. Only Class P ballasts should be used as replacements in fixtures designed for the use of such ballasts. On the other hand, non–Class P ballasts should be used as replacements in fixtures designed before the Class P program. Otherwise, nuisance tripping or early ballast failures may result.

Although external fusing of ballast (consisting of small quick-blow glass-tube fuses rated close to the normal ballast current rating) provides some degree of ballast protection, such fuses respond only to line current and do not respond to temperatures inside of ballasts. Since some internal ballast faults will cause excessive temperatures without an increase in line current, the fuse will not sense such faults. Accordingly, all present Class P ballasts contain *internal* thermal devices or fuses which respond to internal temperatures. External fusing will, however, provide a backup protection for Class P ballasts, and they will afford a high degree of protection for other types of ballasts if sized according to the recommendations of fuse and ballast manufacturers.

129. Noise Ratings of Ballasts. Ballasts are noise-rated according to laboratory standards. Such a rating is indicative only as a guide for installation practice but does in no way attempt to specify one ballast type over another as far as specific installations of fluorescent lamps are concerned.

Noise ratings are designated by letter, starting with A—the quietest—up through F. The A rating is best for home applications, for example, where the surrounding and competitive noise level may be at a minimum. In an industrial plant with attendant operation noises, ballast hum may be of no importance. Not all individual ballasts, regardless of their general noise rating, produce annoyable hum or noise. Chances are that noise potential of different ballast designs is significant only in exceptionally quiet places. Individual ballasts of any noise rating may by some chance become offensive. Likewise, the ballast hum or noise vibration may be induced into the wiring channel or fixture and may be minimized or emphasized by the method used in mounting and clamping the ballast within the fixture.

130. The life of a fluorescent lamp is affected not only by the voltage and current supplied to it but also by the number of times it is started. Electron emission material is "sputtered off" from the electrodes continuously during the operation of the lamp and in larger quantities each time the lamp starts. Since the normal end of life is reached when the emission material is completely consumed from one of the electrodes, the greater the number of burning hours per start, the longer the life of the lamp. When the emission material is exhausted, lamps on a preheat type of circuit will blink on and off as the electrodes heat but the arc fails to strike. Lamps designed for instant start or rapid start will simply fail to operate. Blinking lamps should be removed from the circuit promptly to protect both the starter and the ballast from overheating.

The rated average life of a fluorescent lamp in burning hours is based upon the average life of large representative groups of lamps measured in the laboratory under specified test conditions. Many fluorescent lamps have a rated average life up to 15,000 hr at three burning hours per start.

Ordinarily, with suitable auxiliaries, line voltage, and frequency the rated average life will be obtained in service.

131. The temperature of the bulb has a decided effect on the efficiency of the fluorescent lamp (Fig. 52). The best efficiency occurs at 100 to 120°F, which is the operating temperature corresponding to an ambient room temperature of 70 to 80°F. The efficiency decreases slowly as the temperature is increased above normal but decreases very rapidly as the temperature is decreased below normal. For this reason the fluorescent lamp is not satisfactory for locations where it will be

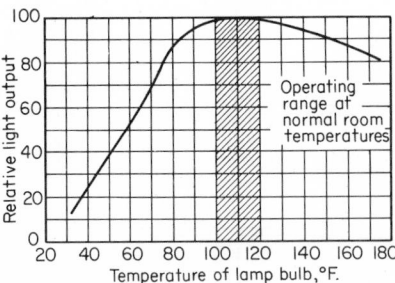

FIG. 52 *Effect of bulb-wall temperature on the efficiency of the fluorescent lamp.*

subject to wide variations in temperature. This reduction in efficiency with low surrounding air temperature can be minimized by enclosing the lamp within a clear glass tube so that the lamp will operate at more nearly its desirable temperature (Fig. 53).

132. Variations in line voltage produce less effect on fluorescent lamps than on incandescent lamps, the phase relationship among line voltage, lamp voltage, and auxiliary voltage being such that the lamp voltage varies inversely as the square root of the line voltage (Fig. 54). For this

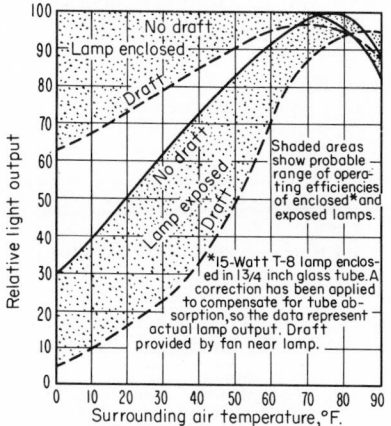

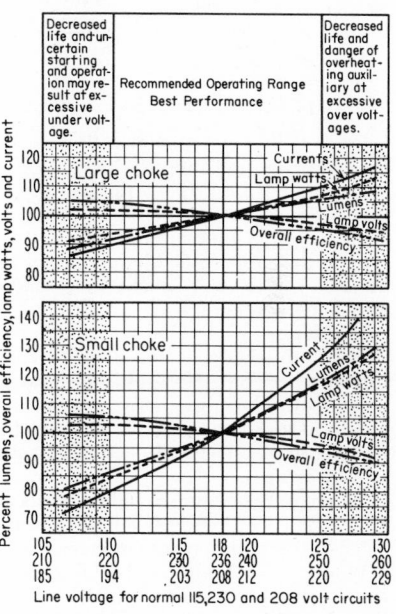

FIG. 53 *Effect of surrounding air temperature on the efficiency of the fluorescent lamp.*

FIG. 54 *Effect of variation of line voltage on the operating characteristics of fluorescent lamps.*

reason, fluorescent lamps are rated for a nominal circuit voltage of 110 to 125, and the auxiliary is designed for 118 volts, instead of 110, 115, or 120 volts as in the case of incandescent lamps. Line voltage less than 110 may make the starting of the arc uncertain; over 125 volts may overheat the auxiliary. Line voltages less than 110 or greater than 125 will decrease the life of the lamp. Although auxiliaries are available for operating the lamps on 220- to 250-volt and 199- to 216-volt systems, there is no advantage in using these voltages, and it is expected that 110- to 125-volt or 265- to 277-volt operation will become practically standard.

133. Radio Interference. The performance of the mercury arc of a fluorescent lamp at the electrodes is associated with an electrical instability that sets up a continuous series of radio waves. There are three ways in which these waves may reach the radio and interfere with reception:

1. Direct radiation from the bulb to the radio aerial circuit.
2. Direct radiation from the electric supply line to the aerial circuit.
3. Line feedback from the lamp through the power line to the radio.

The direct radiation from the bulb diminishes rapidly as the radio is separated from a lamp, and this effect can be controlled by proper positioning of the radio and its aerial. The table shows the extent and comparative amount of bulb radiation for various sizes of fluorescent lamps. It will be seen that, if the aerial is at least 9 ft from the lamp, interference by bulb radiation is negligible.

Extent of Bulb Radiation

(Values are relative)

Lamp	Aerial 2 ft from lamp	Aerial 4 ft from lamp	Aerial 6 ft from lamp	Aerial 8 ft from lamp	Aerial 10 ft from lamp
40- or 100-watt........	100	47	9	4	0
30-watt..............	90	43	8	1	0
20-watt..............	75	35	7	0	0
15-watt..............	55	26	5	0	0

If the radio must remain within the bulb-radiation range, it will be necessary to take the following precautions:

1. Connect the aerial to the radio by means of a shielded lead-in wire with the shield grounded, or install a "doublet" type of aerial with twisted pair leads.

2. Provide a good ground for the radio.

3. Aerial proper must be out of bulb- and line-radiation range. The use of a correct antenna system will usually help reduce radio interference by providing a better station signal strength.

Interference from line radiation and line feedback can best be minimized by the proper application of line filters at each lamp or fixture. A simple form of filter is a three-section capacitor unit. One such unit per fixture (or for each 8 ft of lamps in a cove) will reduce line noise approximately 75 per cent. Where it is desirable to eliminate line noise completely, the inductive-capacitor type is recommended. This filter has a current-carrying capacity of 2 amp, which is, for example, about the load of four 40-watt lamps.

Where only one or two radios are located near a fluorescent installation and the aerial circuit has been properly shielded from bulb and line radiation, a single line filter located at the radio power outlet will suffice.

Where radios located in buildings adjoining the fluorescent installation are receiving line-feedback type of interference, it is practical to install a single filter such as the three-section capacitor unit at each panel box feeding fluorescent lamp circuits.

Where it is necessary to filter each lamp or fixture, the filter should be located as close to the lamps as possible. This precaution should be taken because of line radiation between lamp and filter.

Lamp holders improperly spaced resulting in poor contact with lamp base pins can also generate interference, as can fluorescent fixtures improperly grounded. Failure to ground the neutral of branch circuits (as required in the National Electrical Code) is an additional cause. If the service lines are not properly grounded, filters will be much less effective.

Fluorescent equipments destined for home or other use where radios are likely to be present should have the proper radio-interference filter in each fixture.

134. Direct-current Operation. If fluorescent lamps are used on d-c circuits, special auxiliaries and proper series resistance must be employed. However, d-c operation is inferior to that of normal a-c operation in several respects: (1) the over-all efficiency of light production is much less on d-c circuits because the series resistance consumes about as much wattage as the lamp itself; (2) rated average life is only 80 per cent of the a-c value; (3) suitable line reversing switches to change polarity with each lamp start should be provided for 30-, 40-, and 100-watt lamps; and (4) lumen maintenance may be somewhat less favorable. On the other hand, the color of the light and the total light output compare favorably with normal a-c operation, and problems of power factor and stroboscopic effect are, of course, eliminated.

135. High-frequency Operation (General Electric Co.). While 60 cycles is the standard frequency for a-c distribution, higher frequencies have a number of advantages in fluorescent lamp operation. Frequencies in the range of 300 to 600 cycles permit the use of small, lightweight ballasts of the inductive type which need be only half of the size and weight of equivalent 60-cycle ballasts. The higher frequencies also make it feasible to use a small simple capacitance-type ballast, not practical on 60 cycles. With either type there is a gain in over-all efficiency. Instant starting of lamps can be accomplished with simple circuits containing fewer and lighter weight components.

High-frequency operation has been used on airplanes because of the weight saving by using 208-volt, 400-cycle generators and small capacitor ballasts. In bus service lamps are operated at variable frequency from 80 cycles with motor idling to 500 cycles at full speed. Voltage regulators are used to hold the voltage fairly constant.

The lamp efficiency in lumens per watt versus frequency is shown in the graph for sine-wave operation. The efficiency increases slightly as frequency is increased from 60 to 360 cycles per second. Another gain of approximately 10 per cent is indicated by laboratory tests if frequency is increased to 7,000 cycles per second. However, frequencies above 1,000 cycles per second present problems in the distribution systems and switch gear so that the practical range of frequencies appears to be from 300 to 900 cycles per second.

With higher frequency operation the bulk of the ballast weight and wattage loss is removed from the lighting fixture and placed in the power supply, which serves both as a frequency changer and as a transformer. Thus it is practical to increase lamp loading to obtain greater light output per lamp and to reduce the ballast size and weight.

136. Swirling and Spiraling (General Electric Co.). This refers to all conditions where the lighted lamp appears to fluctuate in brightness from end to end. The cause is attributed principally to particles of materials loosened from the cathode and floating in the arc stream. Such particles usually settle to the bulb when the current is turned off for a few minutes. This temporary swirling may occur in new lamps and is not serious. Where swirling persists, some operating condition may be the cause of the particles being cast into the arc stream. High-impact starting voltage may jar loose such material, and this high-voltage starting of preheat-type circuits may be due to (1) a starter that is not working properly to give adequate preheat, (2) a ballast of inadequate design, (3) lack of proper starting aids in the case of trigger-start and rapid-start ballasts, (4) lack of a compensator in the starting circuit of the lead lamp in a lead-lag ballast, or (5) any other circuit condition such as low supply voltage where neither starter nor ballast functions normally, yet where lamps may occasionally start by high-voltage impact alone without preheat.

Instant-start lamps have cathodes designed to withstand high-voltage starting. Where new lamps of this type swirl persistently, the lamp may be at fault and should be replaced. At the end of normal lamp life, when no electron-emissive material remains on the cathode, the high starting voltage disintegrates even the metallic parts of the cathode, which then invade the arc stream. This is the cause of excessive swirling that characterizes the "end of life" period of instant-start lamps.

137. Operating Suggestions (General Electric Co.). To secure the best performance of fluorescent lamps, it is important that the user understand how to maintain his fluorescent installation properly. Many factors that affect the performance of these lamps were never encountered with incandescent filament lamps, and the user must realize that some of these new elements of satisfactory service are within his control.

For example, if a filament lamp does not light when current is applied, the one single, positive conclusion is that the lamp is burned out or defective. No such conclusion should be made in the case of the fluorescent lamp. This lamp, though perfect in all respects, may not start or operate properly through no fault of its design or manufacture.

Average Life. Since mortality laws apply to fluorescent as well as to filament lamps, it is not unusual for some fluorescent lamps to fail after a few hundred hours while others will last longer than their rated average life to balance out the normal early failures.

Normal Failure. The electroemissive material on fluorescent-lamp electrodes is used up during the life of the lamp, the "sputtering off" being more rapid during starting. Therefore, a longer life will be obtained if lamps are allowed to operate continuously instead of being turned on and off frequently. Rated life should be obtained on the average if lamps are operated for normal periods of 3 or 4 hr.

When the active material on the electrodes is used up, the lamp will simply blink on and off, sometimes with a shimmering effect during the period that the lamp remains lighted. Most fluorescent lamps fail in this manner.

Normal Depreciation. The light output at 100 hr is used for rating purposes, because the loss during this period may amount to as much as 10 per cent. The average light output during life is approximately 90 per cent of the 100-hr rating value.

Blackening. Fluorescent lamps blacken rather uniformly throughout the length of the tube during life, though this is not noticed unless an old lamp is compared with a new one in front of a light source. At the end of life, the lamps usually show a dense blackening at either one end or both. Also, there may be dark rings, slightly brownish in color, at one end or both. On the average, there should be little indication of either blackening or rings during the first 500 hr of operation. If the lamp has not given a proper length of service when this occurs, it may be due to improper starting, frequent starting with short operating periods, improper ballast equipment, unusually high or low voltage, improper wiring, or a defective lamp.

End blackening should not be confused with a mercury deposit which sometimes condenses around the bulb at the ends. This mercury condensation appears to be more common with the 1-in.-diameter lamps than with the 1½-in. sizes. It is occasionally visible on new lamps but should evaporate after the lamp has been in operation for some time. However, it may reappear later when the lamps cool. Frequently, dark streaks appear lengthwise of the tube owing to small globules of mercury cooling on the lower (or cooler) part of the lamp. Mercury condensation is quite common on lamps in louvered units owing to the cooling effects of air circulation around the louvers.

Mercury may condense at any place on the tube if a cold object is allowed to lie against it for a short period. Such spots near the center section may not again evaporate. When condensation occurs in this manner, rotating the lamp 180 deg in the lamp holders may give a more favorable position for evaporation or may place the spot in a less conspicuous place from an appearance standpoint.

Near the end of life, some lamps may develop a very dense spot about ½ in. wide and extending almost halfway around the bulb, centering about 1 in. from the base. This is quite normal, but should a spot develop early in life, it is an indication of excessive starting or operating current. This may be due to a ballast off-rating or to an unusually high circuit voltage.

Occasionally a lamp may develop a ring or gray band at one end or both. Such rings are usually located about 2 in. from either base. These rings have no effect on the lamp performance and are no indication that a lamp is near failure.

Circuit Voltage. The circuit voltage should be within the ballast rating, although 110- to 125-volt ballasts *may in some cases* give satisfactory lamp performance on circuits as low as 105 or as high as 130 volts. Ballasts designed for 265 to 277 volts *may sometimes* give satisfactory results on line voltages as low as 260 and as high as 285 volts. Excessive under- or overvoltage is injurious to the lamp.

Transformer Hum. Characteristic "transformer hum" is inherent in lamp ballast equipment, although the noise may "come and go," varying considerably with individual ballasts. If ballasts are mounted on soft rubber, neoprene, or similar nonrigid mountings, the vibrations due to the magnetic action in the chokes will not be transferred to supporting members and disconcerting auxiliary hum will be reduced to a minimum. Such vibration insulation, however, will inhibit heat radiation and transfer to such a point that ballast ambient-temperature limits will be exceeded.

Low-temperature Operation. In most cases, satisfactory starting and performance can be expected at temperatures considerably below 50°F by (1) keeping the voltage in the upper half of the ballast rating, (2) conserving lamp heat by enclosure or by some other suitable means, and (3) using thermal starting switches.

Starting Difficulty. Starting difficulties may be due to a number of causes other than the starter itself. In general, any difficulty in starting may result in premature end blackening and short lamp life.

If a Lamp Makes No Effort to Start. First the lamp should be checked to make sure that it is properly seated in the sockets. If so, the starter should be checked; it may have reached the end of life and should be replaced. If this fails to correct the trouble, the lamp should be checked in another circuit, and, if necessary, the voltage can be checked at the sockets. If no indication of power is found at the sockets, the circuit connections are incorrect or the ballast is defective.

If a Lamp Is Slow in Starting. A sluggish starter is usually the cause of such trouble, and the starter should be replaced.   Low line voltage, low ballast rating, and omission of starting compensator in the leading circuit of two-lamp ballasts can also result in slow starting.

If the Ends of a Lamp Remain Lighted.   This indicates a short circuit in the starter, and it should be replaced.   Starters that have been in service for some time frequently fail in this manner.   If the ends of a lamp in a new installation remain lighted, it is possible that the wiring is incorrect.   Of course, where short-circuiting types of No-Blink or Watch-Dog starters are used, the lamp ends will remain lighted in a normally failed lamp; this automatically corrects itself when the lamp is replaced.

If a Lamp Blinks On and Off.   This is the usual indication of a normal failure of a lamp.   It will usually be found more convenient to put in a new starter first and then, if blinking continues, renew the lamp.   Low circuit voltage, low ballast rating, low temperature, and cold drafts may individually cause difficulties of this nature, or several may be contributing factors.   It is also possible for improper circuit connections to cause such blinking.   The annoyance of blinking lamps can be avoided by using No-Blink starters in installations employing lamps for which such types of starters are available.

CAUTION.   If the ends of a lamp remain lighted or the lamp blinks on and off, the trouble should immediately be corrected or the lamp or starter removed from the circuit.   A blinking lamp can shortly ruin both lamp and starter.   Ordinary starters can be replaced with No-Blink starters (where available) which remove the starter element from the circuit if lamps fail to light after a reasonable number of attempts.

Early end blackening indicates improper operating conditions.   Heavy end blackening early in life indicates that the active material on the electrodes is being sputtered off too rapidly.   It may be due to:

1. High or low voltage.   For best results, the circuit voltage should be within ballast rating.

2. Loose contacts (most likely at lamp holder) causing lamp to blink on and off. Remedy: Lamp holders should be rigidly mounted and properly spaced.   See that lamps are securely seated in lamp holders.

3. Improperly designed ballasts or ballast outside specification limits.   Remedy: The use of ballasts approved by the Electrical Testing Laboratories will usually eliminate trouble of this nature.

4. Defective or worn-out starter, causing lamp to blink "on" and "off" or prolonged flashing of the lamp at each start or ends of the lamp to remain lighted over a period of time.   Remedy: Replace with new starter.

5. Omission of starting compensator in leading circuit of a two-lamp ballast. Remedy: Install a compensator.

6. Improper wiring of units.

Damaged Lamps.   Fluorescent lamps are of rugged construction and will withstand a considerable amount of rough handling.   However, a severe side blow may jar the cathode loose or break the stem.   If a lamp or package of lamps is dropped or severely bumped on the end, the shock may break the base insulation and, more important, the concealed exhaust tube may be broken; this will admit air into the bulb.   The latter may not be revealed by casual inspection.

Cathodes can be examined by viewing the end of the bulb against a pinhole of light which casts a shadow of the cathode on the bulb wall.   If cathodes appear to be intact but in a lamp that has leaked air, no end glow will take place and the lamp will not start; if only a minute quantity of air has seeped in, the end glow may appear deep violet or pinkish in color.   Where large numbers of lamps are to be tested, a spark-coil tester brushed over the base pins is the quickest way to test for glow, the lack of which identifies defective or broken lamps.

With preheat, bipin lamps a simple test will show whether or not cathodes are intact. The filament cathodes are designed for preheating at relative low voltage, and if 115 volts is applied directly to the base pins, the cathode filament will instantly burn off, generally at both leads with little fusing of the metal.   The stem may also crack, resulting in an air leak.   To test the cathode circuit, test each end separately by connecting the two base pins in series with an ordinary 115- or 120-volt incandescent lamp on a 115- or 120-volt circuit.   Use a 25-watt lamp for miniature bipin based lamps, a 60-watt lamp for 14- to 40-watt lamps, and a 200-watt size for testing 90- and 100-watt fluorescent-lamp cathodes.

GASEOUS-DISCHARGE LAMPS—GENERAL

138. Light is produced by gaseous-conduction methods (General Electric Co.) when proper energy transitions result from electron displacement within the atomic structure of the gas involved. Applied voltage at the electrodes gives acceleration to free electrons which, in the course of their travel, strike atoms and displace electrons from their normal atomic positions. Radiations of a particular wave length result as the displaced electrons return to their normal position in the atomic structure; this wave length depends on the gas used and the degree of electron displacement.

Once the discharge begins, the enclosed arc becomes a light source with one electrode acting as a cathode and the other as an anode. The electrodes will exchange functions as the supply changes polarity. This principle is employed in high-intensity-discharge and neon lamps.

HIGH-INTENSITY DISCHARGE LAMPS FOR GENERAL ILLUMINATION

139. Classification of High-intensity-discharge Lamps.

1. Mercury lamps.
   a. Reflector types.
   b. Clear-glass types.
   c. Phosphor-coated (fluorescent mercury) types.
2. Metal halide lamps.
3. High-pressure sodium.
4. Special types.

140. Relatively high-pressure electric-discharge lamps are photochemical types which consist of a glass or quartz arc tube sealed within an outer glass jacket or bulb. They have main electrodes at each end of the arc tube, with a third starting electrode adjacent to the upper main electrode. This starting electrode is in series with a ballasting resistance capsule and is connected to the lower main electrode. The outer bulb serves to regulate and maintain the high operating temperature of the inner arc tube. The arc tube contains a small quantity of pure argon gas for starting and a small amount of mercury (in the mercury-vapor lamp) which gradually vaporizes during the starting interval. Lamp design and manufacture are matters of extraordinary care and skill because of the high-temperature operation and its effect on stability of lamp parts under variable service conditions.

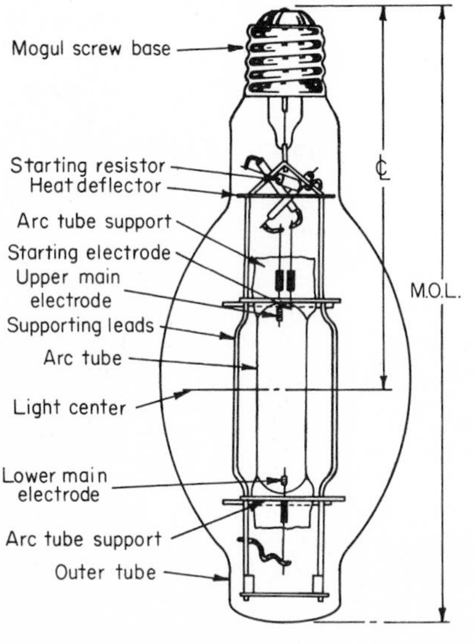

Mogul screw base

Starting resistor
Heat deflector
Arc tube support
Starting electrode
Upper main electrode
Supporting leads
Arc tube
Light center
Lower main electrode
Arc tube support
Outer tube

M.O.L.

FIG. 55 *Mercury lamp of outer-bulb type of construction.*

141. Lamps with an outer bulb have the construction features and essential parts of a mercury-vapor lamp as shown in Fig. 55.

The lamp consists essentially of an inner arc tube made of quartz to withstand the high temperatures resulting when the lamp builds up to normal wattage. Two main electron-emissive electrodes are located at opposite ends of the tube; these are made of coiled tungsten wire. Near the upper main electrode is a third or starting electrode in series with a ballasting resistor and connected to the lower main-electrode lead wire.

The arc tube in the mercury lamp contains a small amount of pure argon gas which is used as a conducting medium to facilitate the starting of the arc before the mercury is vaporized. When voltage is applied, an electric field is set up between the starting electrode and the adjacent main electrode. This ionizing potential causes current to flow, and as the main arc strikes, the heat generated gradually vaporizes the mercury. When the arc tube is filled with mercury vapor, it creates a low-resistance path for current to flow between the main electrodes. When this takes place, the starting electrode and its high-resistance path become automatically inactive.

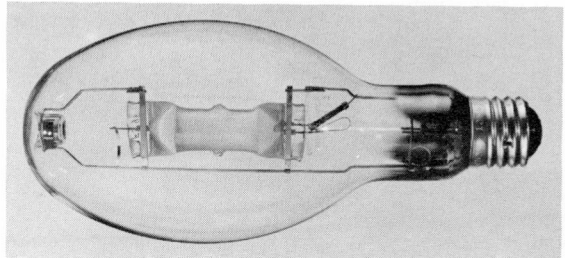

FIG. 56   *Metal halide lamp.* (*General Electric Co.*)

Once the discharge begins, the enclosed arc becomes a light source with one electrode acting as a cathode and the other as an anode. The electrodes will exchange functions as the a-c supply changes polarity.

The quantity of mercury in the arc tube is very carefully measured to maintain quite an exact vapor pressure under design conditions of operation. This pressure differs with wattage sizes, depending on arc-tube dimensions, voltage-current relationships, and various other design factors.

Efficient operation requires the maintenance of a high temperature of the arc tube. For this reason the arc tube is enclosed in an outer bulb, which makes the arc tube less subject to surrounding temperature or cooling by air circulation. About half an atmosphere of nitrogen is introduced in the space between the arc tube and the outer bulb.

142. Metal halide lamps are similar to mercury lamps, except that they use other metals or combinations of metals which provide radiation characteristics similar to those of mercury. Research resulted in a practical system of introducing these metals into an arc chamber in such a way that they could be easily vaporized without being electrically or chemically unstable. Starting with an arc tube containing mercury, the desired metals are added in the form of their halide salts, usually iodides. The currently available lamps nominally employ iodides of sodium, thallium, and indium, in addition to mercury. The result is a lamp design which generates light with a 50 per cent higher efficiency than the mercury arc, and with considerably better color quality. A typical lamp is shown in Fig. 56, and Table **150E** shows typical ratings.

143. The high-pressure sodium lamp (Fig. 56A) has the highest light-producing efficiency of any commercial source of white light. It was made possible by the invention of a means of effectively sealing metal ends and electrodes to a tube of special ceramic material in a combination that can withstand high temperatures and corrosive

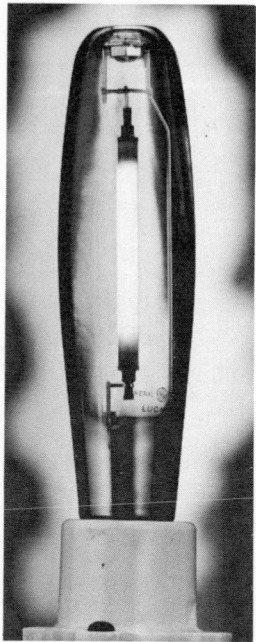

FIG. 56A   *High-pressure sodium lamp.* (*General Electric Co.*)

effects produced by intensely hot vapors of the alkaline metals used in the tube. The arc in the present high-pressure sodium lamp is principally of metallic sodium. Sodium had been used at lower temperatures and pressures for many years (and still is in some countries) as a light source for applications where its characteristic monochromatic yellow light would not be a drawback, such as in street lighting near dangerous intersections. The modern high-pressure lamp is the result of the temperature-pressure combination in a sodium arc which yields much better color quality and compactness, and with substantially higher luminous efficacy than has been available previously for white light. Because of its compactness and great light output, this lamp is expected to be a key factor in the future growth of lighting. Table **150F** shows typical ratings.

144. Efficiency and Spectral Control (General Electric Co.). The mercury-vapor pressure at which a lamp operates accounts in a large measure for the difference in luminous efficiency and spectral distribution of energy among the various types of lamps. In general, higher operating vapor pressure tends to shift a larger proportion of the radiated energy to longer wave lengths. At extremely high pressures there is the tendency to broaden the line spectral into wider bands. Present lamp designs have a range of vapor pressure from one-thousandth of normal atmospheric pressure in fluorescent-type lamps to 110 times atmospheric pressure in the tiny 1,000-watt capillary lamp. For the general-service lamps the vapor pressure is within the range of one-tenth to ten times atmospheric pressure.

Within the visible region the mercury spectrum, or energy radiated, consists of four principal wavelengths. The lack of radiation in the red end results in a greenish-blue light. Looking at a lighted mercury lamp the source itself appears to emit a daylight-white. The absence of red radiation causes most colored objects to appear distorted in color value. Blue, green, and yellow colors of objects are emphasized, while orange and red objects appear brownish or black. Where more normal appearance of people or objects is of importance, the practice has been to combine mercury lamps with filament lamps which are rich in red radiation to achieve a good color balance.

Color correction has now been incorporated in the design of mercury lamps by the use of fluorescent materials coated on the inside of the outer bulb. Refer to Sec. **147.** Tables **150A, 150B, 150C,** and **150D** list several of the more popular mercury lamps with the latest USASI code designations.

145. Reflector-type Lamps (Fig. 57). The light distribution from the elongated arc tube of the mercury lamp is mostly in a horizontal pattern. Suitable reflectors intercept and control about 80 per cent of the light — only 20 per cent downward being uncontrolled by usual reflector design.

This large percentage of the light output subjected to reflector control puts a premium on keeping reflecting surfaces bright and clean, since any depreciation of reflecting surfaces due to dust and dirt means just that much waste of light paid for but not utilized. The advantage of reflector-type lamps is that the sealed-in silvered reflecting surfaces do not deteriorate throughout the life of the lamp. The expense and nuisance of cleaning fixtures have always been bothersome problems to the point of actual neglect, which means not only a waste of both lamp and current but, more significant in over-all effect, the loss of illumination for production efficiency.

The H400-R1(H33-1FY)[1] is the unmodified mercury lamp in an internally silvered R-52 reflector bulb. Its maintenance cost is low, and it gives up to 54 per cent more light than the H400 A1(H33-1AR) lamp and up to 36 per cent more than the H400 E1(H33-1CD/E) lamp.

The H400-RC1(H33-1DN/C) combines top color improvement with high efficiency. In this color-improved lamp a phosphor coating is used instead of the metallic reflector. This white powder acts as a diffuse reflector but allows approximately one-third of the light to be transmitted through the coating. This upward light can be used to illuminate the ceiling and upper side walls or can be redirected by an external reflector which also acts as a shield against high lamp brightness and as a protection to the lamp from thermal or mechanical shock. The white mercury RW-1 (H33-1DN/W) is recommended for most 400-watt mercury applications. It provides more light than other 400-watt

---

[1] Figures in parentheses are USASI code designations.

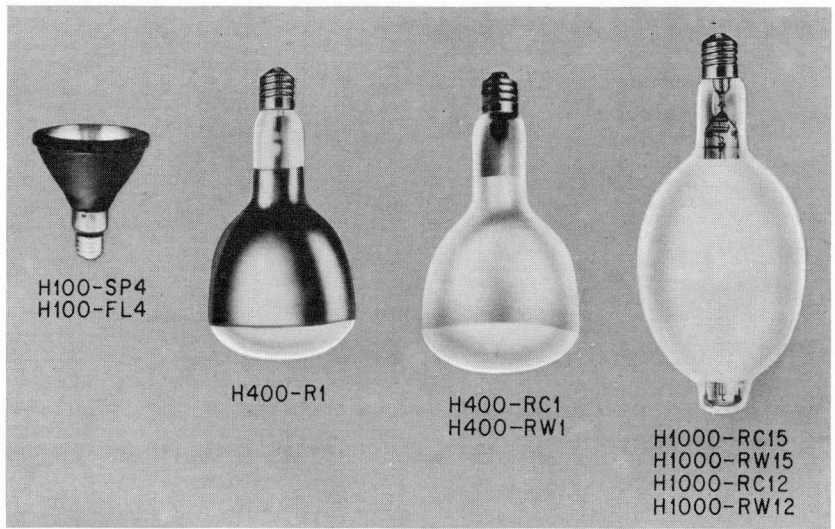

FIG. 57 *Reflector-type mercury lamps.* (*General Electric Co.*)

mercury lamps and low maintenance cost, and the specially designed phosphor produces a desirable white light, but not so much color improvement as the RC-1(H33-1DN/C).

"Semireflector" lamps in the 1,000-watt size have been added to the expanding line of mercury lamps. In these lamps the base half inside the outer jacket is coated with phosphor (either "color-improved" or "white"). Light distribution from these lamps is similar to that from the 400-watt phosphor-coated reflector lamps. These lamps are the "color-improved" H1000-RC15 (H36-15KY/C) and the "white" H1000-RW15 (H36-15KY/W).

146. Clear-glass mercury lamps have an outer bulb of clear glass. Representative clear glass lamps are shown in Fig. 58.

147. Phosphor-coated (Fluorescent Mercury) Lamps. Refer to Fig. 59. Much effort has been expended in recent years in improving the color of the light produced by mercury lamps. The development of special phosphors has been the result. The

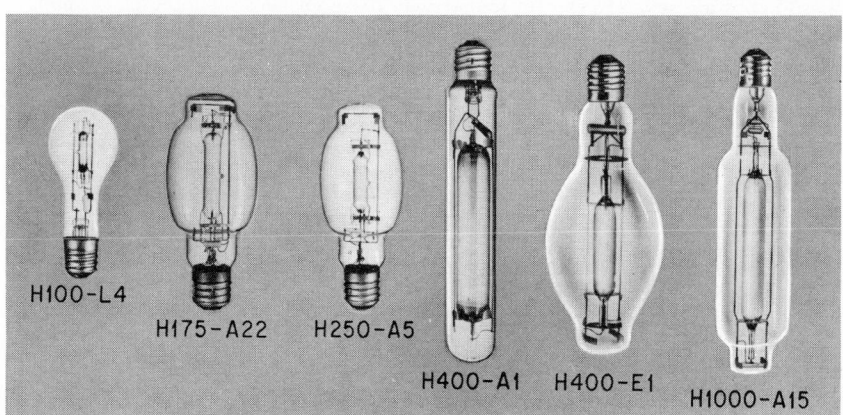

FIG. 58 *Clear-glass mercury lamps.* (*General Electric Co.*)

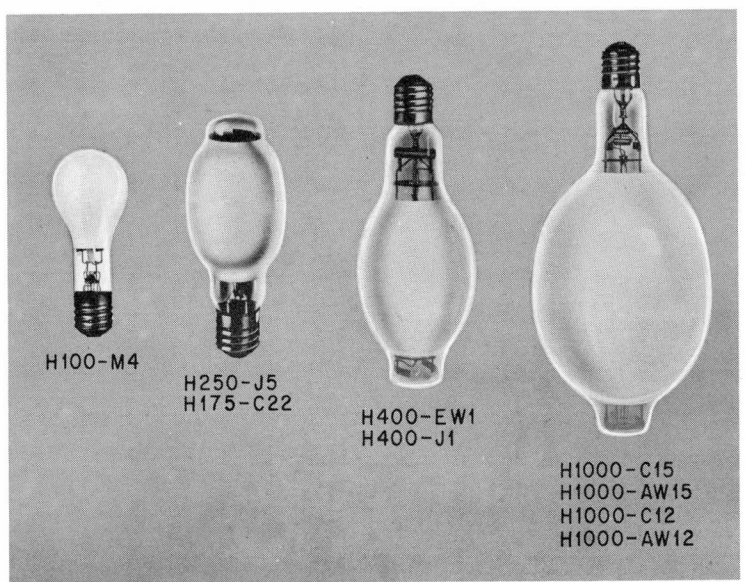

FIG. 59 *Phosphor-coated mercury lamps.* (*General Electric Co.*)

function of the phosphors is to convert the invisible, and formerly unused, ultraviolet energy into visible light. In all of these lamps the phosphor is applied to the inner surface of the jacket or bulb surrounding the arc tube.

The first practical phosphor coatings used with mercury lamps produced a "color-improved" light. These phosphors belong to the germanate family and produce primarily red light. Mercury lamps coated with this color-improved type of phosphor are made in 100-, 175-, 250-, 400-, and 1,000-watt sizes. The resulting color of light is approximately the same as that produced with a combination of equal wattages of unmodified mercury and filament lamps.

Another color development in phosphor-coated mercury lamps is the "white" mercury lamp. This lamp uses a special phosphor (strontium magnesium orthophosphate) which converts ultraviolet energy to a broad band of visible energy. Efficiencies of these lamps are several per cent higher than those for corresponding clear lamps—higher, too, than the efficiencies of color-improved lamps. Along with increased efficiency, the white lamps offer a small but worthwhile bonus of color improvement over the clear lamps—about equivalent, for example, to adding 150 watts of filament light to the H400-E1 (H33-1CD/E). These lamps are available in the same types as the 400- and 1,000-watt color-improved lamps.

Among both the color-improved and the white mercury lamps are several lamps that have the desirable feature of having a reflector incorporated in their design. These reflector-type lamps not only control light but also reduce the need for maintenance because their output is relatively unaffected by dirt and dust.

The 400-watt reflector lamps (R-52 shape) are available with either the color-improved phosphor (H400-RC1) (H33-1DN/C) or the white phosphor (H400-RW1) (H33-1DN/W). In both cases the phosphor serves as an excellent reflector as well as a producer of visible light. Also in the R-52 shape is the silvered-reflector H400-R1 (H33-1FY). This lamp has no phosphor. It is well suited to some applications where dirt and dust collection is severe and where color rendition is not important.

148. Special types of mercury lamps include lamps which generally are used as black-light sources and other lamps of special construction or application. Some special lamps are shown in Fig. 60.

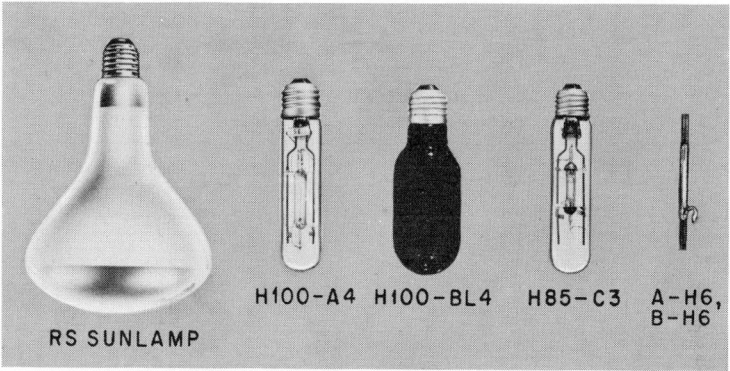

H100-A4   H100-BL4   H85-C3   A-H6, B-H6

RS SUNLAMP

FIG. 60 *Special types of mercury lamps. (General Electric Co.)*

For description of the RS sunlamp refer to Sec. **175.**

The 1,000-watt B-H6 is an air-blast-cooled lamp used in such special applications as searchlighting. The water-cooled version is the A-H6.

149. The transmission characteristics of the different types of glass used for the outer bulb of mercury lamps are given by the curves of Fig. 61. The letter designation of the different types of glass correspond to the designation of bulb-glass type for the different mercury lamps listed in Tables **150A, 150B,** and **150C.**

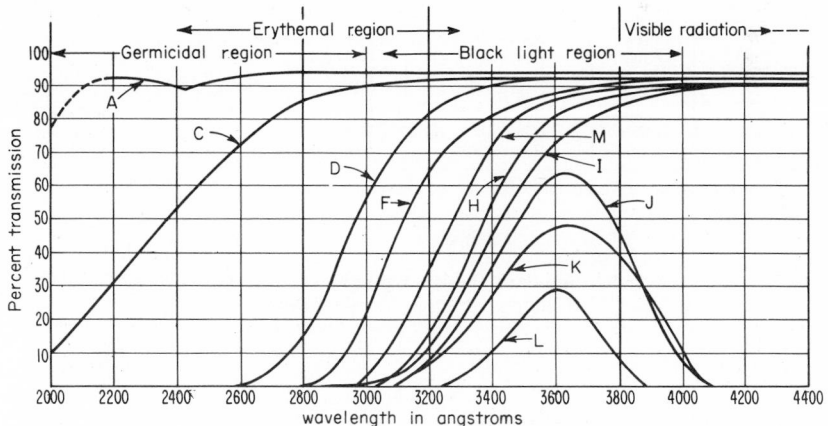

FIG. 61 *Transmission characteristics of glass used in outer bulbs.*

150. Ratings of popular high-intensity discharge lamps are listed in Tables **150A, 150B, 150C, 150D, 150E,** and **150F.**

150A. Standard Clear Mercury Lamps[a]
(Catalogs of lamp manufacturers)

Fig. 61 reference letter	Watts	USASI code	Bulb shape	Initial lumens	
				Vertical[b]	Horizontal[b]
M	175	H39-22KB	BT-28	7,300	6,900
M	250	H37-5KB	BT-28	11,000	10,500
M	400	H33-1CD	BT-37	20,500	19,500
M	400	H33-1BA[c]	BT-37	20,500	19,500
H	400	H33-1AR	T-16	19,500	18,500
H	700	H35-18NA	BT-46	37,000	34,600
H	1,000	H34-12GV	BT-56	55,000	52,000

[a] Some of the more popular types of mercury lamps used for general lighting purposes. These lamps are also available in color improved, white, deluxe white, as well as clear. See manufacturers' bulletins for full listings and comprehensive technical data.
[b] Light output varies with burning position.
[c] Designed for "base down to horizontal" burning, for use in series street lighting circuits.

150B. Standard Mercury Reflector Lamps
(Catalogs of lamp manufacturers)

Fig. 61 reference letter	Watts	USASI code	Bulb[a]	Initial vertical lumens	Rated life, hours
D	100	H44-4GS	PAR-38	2,400	12,000
D	100	H44-4JM	PAR-38	2,400	12,000
M	175	H39-22BM	R-40	5,600	24,000
M	400	H33-1FY	R-52	18,000	24,000
M	400	H33-1LN	R-60	15,000	24,000
M	1,000	H36-15FP	R-80	57,500	24,000
H	1,000	H36-15KY/W	BT-56	58,000	24,000

[a] Data shown above are for clear or inside frost lenses. See manufacturers' listings for data on other bulb finishes or colors.

150C. Standard Deluxe White Mercury Lamps
(Catalogs of lamp manufacturers)

Fig. 61 reference letter	Watts	USASI code	Bulb shape	Initial vertical lumens	Rated life, hours
	40	H45-AY/DX	B-21	1,200	16,000
	50	H46-DL/DX	E-17	1,550	10,000
	75	H43-A7/DX	E-17	2,700	16,000
	100	H38-AY/DX	B-21	4,300	16,000
	100	H38-4MP/DX	A-23	3,700	10,000
	100	H38-4JA/DX/E	E-23½	3,850	24,000
	100	H38-4JA/DX	BT-25	4,400	24,000
	175	H39-22KC/DX/E	E-28	7,800	24,000
	250	H37-5KC/DX/E	E-28	11,000	24,000
M	400	H33-1GL/DX/E	E-37	21,500	24,000
M	400	H33-1GL/DX	BT-37	21,500	24,000
H	700	H35-18ND/DX	BT-46	39,000	24,000
H	1,000	H36-15GW/DX	BT-56	58,500	24,000
H	1,000	H34-12GW/DX	BT-56	57,500	16,000

NOTE: Each manufacturer uses his own color description, and lumen outputs for the same type lamps vary slightly from one manufacturer to another. Manufacturers' literature should be checked for specific data and for other details not shown here.

150D. Self-ballasted Mercury Lamps[a]
(Catalogs of lamp manufacturers)

Watts	Bulb	Description	Rated life, hours	Initial lumens
160	PS30	Phosphor-coated	8,000	3,125–3,520
250	PS35	Phosphor-coated	10,000	5,750–6,250
500	PS40	Phosphor-coated	14,000	14,750
500	E37	Phosphor-coated	14,000	11,550
700	R57	Silver white flood	16,000	16,800
750	R60	Flood or spot	16,000	40,000–65,000

[a] Incandescent-filament ballast and high-pressure mercury-vapor-quartz discharge tube combined in same glass-bulb envelope.

NOTE: All lamps designed for specific voltage ratings, from 115 volts to 250 volts, and should be ordered for specific voltage which will apply. Light output varies according to designed voltage ratings.

150E. Metal Halide Lamps
(Catalogs of lamp manufacturers)

Watts	Bulb[a]	Manufacturers code	Initial lumens	Rated life, hours
400	E-37	MV-400[b]	31,500	7,500
400	BT-37	M-400[c]	32,000	10,500
1,000	BT-56	MV-1000[b]	90,000	6,000
1,000	BT-56	M-1000[c]	90,000	7,500

[a] Clear bulbs, designed for "base-up" or "base-down" burning.
[b] "MV" lamps are "Multi-Vapor" trademarked lamps by General Electric Co., Large Lamp Dept.
[c] "M" lamps are "Metalarc" trademarked lamps by Sylvania Electric Products, Inc.
NOTE: Metal halide lamps are for use only with auxiliary equipment designed to produce proper electrical values.

150F. High-pressure Sodium Lamps
(Catalogs of lamp manufacturers)

Watts	Bulb[a]	Manu-facturers' code[b]	Initial lumens	Rated life, hours
275	E-18	LU-275[b]	27,500	6,000
400	E-18	LU-400[b]	42,000	6,000

[a] Clear bulbs, designed for "base-up" or "base-down" burning.
[b] "LU" lamps are "Lucalox" trademarked lamps by General Electric Co., Large Lamp Dept.

151. Weather-resistant Mercury Lamps. Modern mercury lamps have an outer bulb made of borosilicate glass, which will withstand high temperatures and will resist thermal shocks such as those imposed by cold raindrops striking a hot bulb. This construction provides a wide variety of weather-resistant mercury lamps in sizes from 50 to 3,000 watts.

152. Auxiliary Equipment (General Electric Co.). The mercury lamp, like any gaseous-discharge source, has a "negative" resistance characteristic. This means that, unless some current-limiting device is used, the current in the lamp will rise indefinitely or until the parts are destroyed. Ballasts, usually called transformers, are therefore used to limit current.

Ballasts are designed to deliver the specific voltages required by the lamp under the variety of line conditions that may be encountered. Typical wiring diagrams are shown in Fig. 62. Typical transformers are shown in Fig. 62A.

The transformers are designed for operation at 77°F ambient temperatures. They can be operated in temperatures up to 105°F for 10 per cent of the time with little loss in transformer life. Care should be taken in the installation of transformers to permit free circulation of air to prevent overheating.

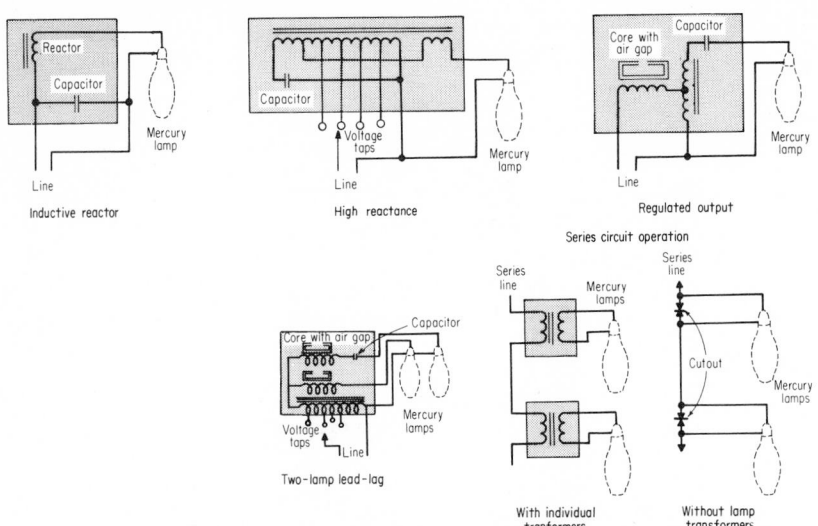

FIG. 62 *Wiring diagrams for mercury lamp ballasts.* (*IES Lighting Handbook.*)

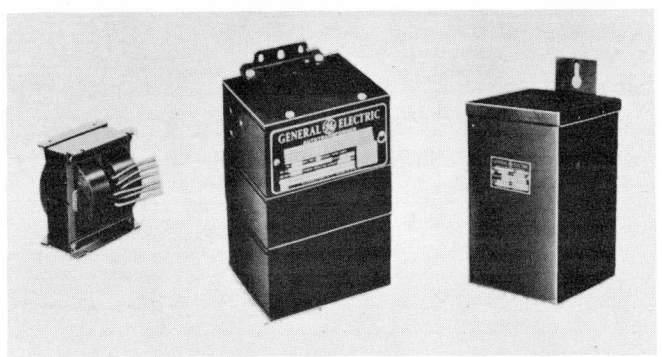

FIG. 62A *Transformers for mercury lamps.* (*General Electric Co.*)

Unless otherwise specified, these transformers are not recommended for operation of lamps in ambient temperatures below 32°F.

Weatherproof transformers are available for operation down to −20°F. Moistureproof units provide the same weather protection but are not recommended where temperatures fall below 10°F.

Outdoor lighting applications, such as street lighting and floodlighting, require ballasts that provide reliable lamp starting at low temperatures. Such requirements are met by ballasts especially designed for low-temperature operations.

A modern concept is the installation of the ballast or transformer integral with the reflector housing for the high-intensity-discharge lamp used in the reflector. This simplifies wiring and reduces labor costs.

153. Data for typical high-intensity-discharge lamp ballasts may be obtained from manufacturers of such equipment.

154. Starting and Restarting High-intensity-discharge Lamps (General Electric Co.). Mercury at normal room temperatures is a liquid and must be vaporized before it becomes a conducting vapor. At low lamp voltages the mercury is slow to vaporize and come up to full light output. In outdoor winter temperatures such as street-lighting and flood-lighting applications, specially designed transformers to supply higher open-circuit voltages are necessary to start mercury lamps.

Lead-lag two-lamp transformers should *not* be used under low-temperature operating conditions, since the lamp on the lead circuit either will fail to light or will not come up to full brightness.

To vaporize all the mercury and for the lamp to come up to full brilliancy requires a few minutes — usually 4 to 8 min, depending on the design. In practice the time may be longer or shorter depending upon the conditions of ambient temperature and applied voltage.

High-intensity-discharge lamps will go out in case of current interruption or of excessively low voltage. They will not restart until the lamps have cooled down and the internal vapor pressure becomes reduced to the point of restarting the arc with the voltage available. This time interval is again variable between 4 and 8 min, but this again will depend on in-service conditions.

155. Voltage Requirements (General Electric Co.). Lamps are designed for one specific terminal voltage, and all provisions for the supply of this required voltage are governed by proper selection of transformers designed for operation on line voltage conditions encountered in service.

Lamps must be operated within rather close limits of the desired voltage — not more than 5 per cent above or below rating. Current and wattage vary about 2 per cent for each 1 per cent variation in volts to the lamp. Undervoltage reduces starting reliability; excessive overvoltage with increased wattage is likely to raise both lamp and transformer temperatures beyond safe limits. Light output varies about 3 to 1 in per cent of voltage variation.

156. Economic Life (General Electric Co.). High-intensity-discharge lamps, like any other lamps, gradually decline in light output throughout life. Some high-intensity-discharge lamps having inherent long-life characteristics may decline as much as 50 per cent in light output during life. For this reason, it has been found to be more economical to replace lamps before burnout than to continue operating them at their reduced output. By replacing lamps at an "economic life," rather than actual life, it is possible to increase the maintained lighting level with a given number of lamps and thus reduce lighting costs. For most operating conditions this economic life will range from 6,000 to 20,000 hr for some types.

157. Lamp Temperature (Westinghouse Electric Corp.). Because mercury-vapor lamps are long-lived, operating temperatures are particularly important. The effect of heat is partly a function of time, and the longer the life of the lamp, the greater the possibility of damage from high temperatures. Excessive bulb and base temperatures may cause lamp failure or unsatisfactory performance due to softening of the glass, damage to the quartz arc tube by moisture driven out of the outer bulb, softening of the basing cement or solder, or corrosion of the base, socket, or lead-in wires. The use of any reflecting equipment that might concentrate heat and light rays on either the inner arc tube or the outer bulb must be avoided.

The temperatures listed in the following table do not represent maximum safe operating temperatures in actual service. They are the temperatures which should not be exceeded in a laboratory test, with a new luminaire and a new lamp, operating at rated watts, and an ambient temperature of 25°C. Allowance is made for higher temperatures in service due to bulb blackening, overvoltage operation, high ambient temperatures, etc. If a lamp in a given luminaire does not exceed the rated base and bulb temperatures under laboratory conditions, it should be safe in service under all ordinary circumstances.

Luminaire Test Temperature Limits for Mercury Lamps
(Measured at 25°C ambient)

Lamp, watts	Outer bulb, °C	Base, °C[a]
100	400	170
	370	210
175	370	210
250	370	210
400	400	210
	370	210
	370	210
	400	210
700	370	210
1,000	370	210
	370	210
	400	210
	400	210
3,000	375 min to 550 max	
	375 min to 650 max	

[a] A 10°C higher test temperature is considered acceptable in street-lighting and outdoor floodlighting fixtures because the ambient temperatures during operation are generally lower than in other types of service.

158. Application of High-intensity-discharge Lamps for General Lighting (Westinghouse Electric Corp.). Mercury lamps are most commonly used for street and highway lighting and in high bay installations covering large areas, as in steel mills, aircraft plants, and foundries. The development of fluorescent mercury lamps has made possible a greater use of mercury lamps for industrial lighting and floodlighting. In addition to the color improvement, the source brightness is much lower than that of conventional mercury lamps or tungsten filaments, which is a favorable characteristic for the design of comfortable lighting installations.

The latest metal halide and high-pressure sodium lamps are being used wherever a better color rendering quality of light is desired, such as in supermarkets, parking areas, street lighting, building floodlighting, sports lighting where the games are to be televised in color, and similar applications. Deluxe white mercury lamps and metal halide lamps are frequently used for lighting interior areas where color rendition is important, such as in food stores, supermarkets, and banking interiors.

159. Spectral Distribution (General Electric Co.). For general lighting, mercury lamps are usually selected on the basis of lumen output, although thought is naturally given to such other factors as color rendition, cost, and wattage. But for applications of invisible ultraviolet radiation, the selection is based on an examination of the spectral data of the lamp. Ultraviolet radiation is reflected and controlled by the same means and with practically the same efficiency as visible light.

The average watts radiated in various wave-length bands is given in Table **160**. Individual lamps may vary considerably from these values because of differences in glass thickness and absorption characteristics and bulb-operating temperature.

Mercury lamps produce some radiation in the near-infrared region. The bulk of this wattage, however, heats the bulb and is dissipated by conduction through the socket and fixture parts or by convection. Hence, equipment design must adequately provide for controlling lamp operating temperatures and for dissipating heat.

By the use of Sec. **160,** a comparison of energy output in the various spectral regions can be obtained for a variety of mercury lamps.

The effectiveness of energy for black-light applications is represented by the energy in the near-ultraviolet region. Such applications usually require absorption of visible light by special filters, which also absorb some of the black-light energy, as indicated by curves *J*, *K* and *L* of Fig. 61.

Subtraction of the total watts radiated from the watts input to the lamp will give, roughly, the watts dissipated as heat. The mercury spectrum does produce some radiation lines or bands in the near infrared region, about 40 watts in the H400-A1.

E-Viton values indicate the relative erythemal (skin-reddening) output. An E-Viton corresponds to the quantity of radiant energy that produces as much reddening of the skin as 10 μw (0.00001 watts) of energy at a wave length of 2,967 A. The RS sunlamp is particularly effective because its reflector directs energy in a concentrated beam delivering 6 E-Vitons per sq cm at a distance of 30 in. from the lamp axis. This amount of energy is sufficient to produce a mild sunburn on untanned skin in 5 to 10 min and is equivalent to 15 to 18 min exposure to the midsummer sun.

160. Spectral Data
(General

Lamp-ordering abbreviation	. . . .	RS	H85-C-3	H100-BL4	H100-SP4-FL4	H100-A4	H100-L4	H100-M4	H175-A22	H250-A5	H250-J5
Wave-length band, angstroms	Principal lines										
Far ultraviolet:											
2,200–2,300	. . . . .	. . . . .	0.02								
2,300–2,400	. . . . .	. . . . .	. . . .		Not transmitted by lamp bulb						
2,400–2,500	. . . . .	. . . . .	. . . .								
2,500–2,600	2,537	. . . . .	0.07								
2,600–2,700	2,652	0.004	0.35								
2,700–2,800	. . . . .	. . . . .	0.05								
Middle ultraviolet:											
2,800–2,900	2,804–2,894	0.05	0.70	. . . . .	. . . .	. . . .	. . . .	. . . . .	0.01	. . . .	. . . . .
2,900–3,000	2,967	0.13	0.65	. . . . .	. . . .	0.02	0.02	. . . . .	0.10	0.04	. . . . .
3,000–3,100	3,022	0.34	0.76	. . . . .	0.01	0.19	0.19	0.004	0.32	0.24	0.006
3,100–3,200	3,131	0.88	1.65	. . . . .	0.05	0.83	0.83	0.02	1.51	1.26	0.043
Near ultraviolet:											
3,200–3,300	. . . . .	0.07	0.33	. . . . .	0.02	0.22	0.22	0.01	0.38	0.38	0.02
3,300–3,400	3,341	0.16	0.45	0.005	0.06	0.42	0.42	0.03	0.77	0.72	0.06
3,400–3,500	. . . . .	0.05	0.21	0.006	0.03	0.15	0.15	0.01	0.38	0.35	0.02
3,500–3,600	. . . . .	0.09	0.22	0.018	0.07	0.16	0.16	0.04	0.30	0.40	0.11
3,600–3,700	3,654	2.51	3.29	0.623	1.06	3.82	3.82	1.16	7.79	6.22	2.93
3,700–3,800	. . . . .	0.09	0.25	0.024	0.11	0.22	0.22	0.10	0.27	0.37	0.18
3,800–4,000	. . . . .	0.13	0.40	0.009	0.09	0.34	0.34	0.18	0.40	0.56	0.31
Visible:											
4,000–4,100	4,047	0.72	1.09	0.004	0.50	1.10	1.10	0.50	2.11	3.25	1.46
4,100–4,300	. . . . .	0.09	0.42	. . . . .	0.13	0.48	0.48	0.20	0.28	0.55	0.25
4,300–4,400	4,358	1.48	1.96	. . . . .	1.23	2.22	2.22	0.88	3.99	6.77	2.78
4,400–5,400	4,916	0.30	0.84	. . . . .	0.31	0.57	0.57	0.43	0 94	1.28	1.00
5,400–5,500	5,461	1.73	2.28	. . . . .	1.56	2.59	2.59	2.06	4.92	7.83	6.54
5,500–5,700	. . . . .	0.15	0.29	. . . . .	0.14	0.21	0.21	0.18	0.36	0.52	0.44
5,700–5,800	5,780	2.06	1.20	. . . . .	1.62	2.16	2.16	1.90	4.88	7.71	7.15
5,800–7,600	6,938	0.99	1.00	. . . . .	0.51	0.76	0.76	4.54	1.58	2.28	12.20
SUMMARY: Region	Units										
Far ultraviolet	Watts	0.004	0.49	0	0	0	0	0	0	0	0
	E-Vitons	110	13,795	0	0	0	0	0	0	0	0
Middle ultraviolet	Watts	1.40	3.76	0	0.06	1.04	1.04	0.024	1.94	1.54	0.049
	E-Vitons	34,670	115,000	0	475	13,780	13,780	315	56,200	19,675	480
Near ultraviolet	Watts	3.10	5.15	0.69	1.44	5.33	5.33	1.53	10.29	9.00	3.63
	E-Vitons	230	779	5.50	80	640	640	40	2,225	1,100	75
Visible	Watts	7.52	9.08	0.004	6.00	10.09	10.09	10.69	21.06	30.19	38.86
	Lumens	2,500	2,850	0.01	2,300	3,500	3,500	3,300	7,000	11,000	10,500

for Mercury Lamps
Electric Co.).

B-H6	H400-A1	H400-E1	H400-EW1	H400-J1	H400-R1	H400-RC1	H400-RW1	H1000-C12	H1000-A15	H1000-C15	H1000-RC15	H3000-A9
0.55												
2.38												
8.64			Not transmitted by lamp bulb									
3.03												
7.26												
7.14												
14.33	.....	0.05										
17.62	.....	0.24	0.10	.....	.....	0.02	0.07	.....	0.19	.....	0.10	
15.49	.. ..	0.91	0.15	0.03	0.03	0.19	1.17	0.07	0.91	0.03	0.29	
20.18	.....	2.92	0.74	0.17	0.12	0.47	1.54	0.46	5.13	0.40	2.19	0.12
9.38	.....	0.82	0.48	0.08	0.15	0.35	0.67	0.18	2.41	0.21	1.08	
16.90	0.03	2.02	1.05	0.24	0.41	0.61	1.48	0.65	5.62	0.72	1.97	0.28
6.00	.....	0.67	0.69	0.13	0.30	0.32	0.89	0.40	2.77	0.50	1.30	0.09
10.96	0.16	0.78	0.66	0.31	0.46	0.40	0.73	0.55	2.37	0.62	1.26	1.60
34.91	3.20	16.05	15.84	5.39	9.79	7.92	16.25	21.55	44.72	17.79	29.90	40.91
14.63	0.23	0.73	0.64	0.35	0.53	0.42	0.62	0.93	4.53	0.91	1.62	1.84
16.53	0.22	1.18	1.00	0.59	0.81	0.65	0.97	1.62	6.57	1.61	3.42	3.11
25.48	3.41	6.08	4.73	2.96	4.30	3.39	4.34	6.89	14.22	8.46	10.26	41.37
17.53	0.37	1.09	0.84	0.62	0.73	0.66	0.88	0.75	2.55	1.36	2.14	2.95
40.79	8.30	12.22	9.65	5.54	8.96	6.77	8.94	13.49	27.25	16.23	21.19	87.22
47.54	1.26	3.06	4.26	4.04	2.18	2.53	3.87	4.04	7.92	7.05	7.51	6.95
31.21	11.33	13.87	13.20	11.76	11.89	11.42	13.36	26.32	36.29	23.05	31.90	93.65
16.86	0.47	1.08	1.89	1.01	1.18	0.98	2.15	3.18	2.97	4.04	3.71	3.66
22.53	11.20	15.59	15.27	13.80	13.93	14.36	13.80	40.09	38.61	40.83	36.20	100.52
44.06	2.52	4.27	12.51	23.41	4.32	21.59	11.76	57.01	14.64	61.92	43.31	13.90
29.00	0	0	0	0	0	0	0	0	0	0	0	0
993,600	0	0	0	0	0	0	0	0	0	0	0	0
67.62	0	4.12	0.99	0.20	0.15	0.68	2.78	0.53	6.23	0.43	2.58	0.12
2,552,000	0	78,700	18,860	2,355	2,280	11,720	24,300	4,820	75,200	2,900	30,500	370
109.31	3.84	22.25	20.36	7.09	12.45	10.67	21.61	25.88	68.99	22.36	40.55	47.83
26,200	30.00	2,830	1,520	325	555	950	2,150	830	8,020	930	3,050	280
246,000	38.86	57.27	62.35	63.14	47.49	61.70	59.10	151.77	144.45	162.94	156.22	350.22
65,000	15,500	21,000	23,000	20,000	18,500	20,500	22,000	51,500	54,000	51,500	53,000	132,000

NEON LAMPS

161. Neon lamps may be classified into two types: (1) high voltage and (2) low voltage.

162. High-voltage neon lamps (Fig. 63) consist of two terminals or electrodes set into the opposite ends of a glass tube which contains neon, helium, or argon gas, with or without mercury, at low vapor pressure.

Like all gaseous-discharge lamps a higher voltage is required to start the arc than is required for continuous operation. These lamps are supplied from a high-reactance transformer in which the secondary voltage falls rapidly as the current drain is increased. This feature provides the higher voltage required to start the lamp and tends to make the arc circuit stable. Even if the secondary terminals should become short-circuited, no more than full-load current will flow, so that the transformer will not be

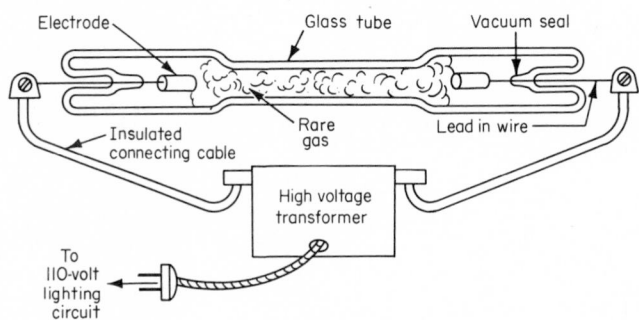

FIG. 63 *Schematic diagram of gas-filled tube and transformer.* (*Miller and Fink, "Neon Signs."*)

damaged. A high voltage, 2,000 to 15,000 volts depending on the length and diameter of the tubing and the gas used, is applied to the electrodes at the ends of the tubing by means of this transformer.

The tubing can be made to produce a number of different colors, depending on the gas used, the color of the glass tubing, and whether or not mercury is added. Table **163** gives the colors available.

163. Colors Obtainable from Neon Tubes
(From Miller and Fink, "Neon Signs")

Color produced	Gas used	Mercury used	Color of glass tubing used	Gas pressure, mm of mercury
Standard Colors				
Red..........................	Neon	No	Clear	10 and over
Dark red.......................	Neon	No	Soft red	10 and over
Gold..........................	Helium	No	Soft yellow (noviol)	3
White.........................	Helium	No	Clear	3
Light green...................	Argon	Yes	Soft canary (Uranium oxide)	8
Medium green..................	Argon	Yes	Soft yellow (noviol)	8
Light blue....................	Argon	Yes	Clear	8
Dark blue.....................	Argon	Yes	Soft blue	8
Colors Available but Not Widely Used				
Soft red.	Neon	No	Soft opal	10 and over
Orange........................	Neon	No	Soft yellow (noviol)	10 and over
Soft white....................	Helium	No	Soft opal	3
Dark green....................	Argon	Yes	Soft medium amber	8
Red lavender..................	Neon	No	Soft dark purple	10 and over

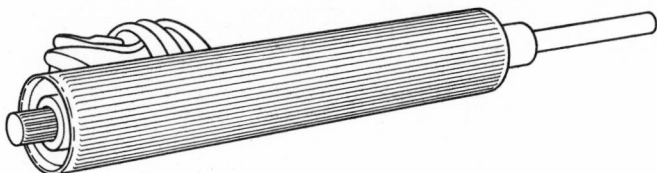

FIG. 64 *A high-tension spark coil for testing the vacuum system. The knob at the end is used to control the intensity of the spark which appears at the metal tip of the device. (Miller and Fink, "Neon Signs.")*

164. The gas pressure as given in Table **165** must be determined quite accurately during manufacture. If the pressure is too low, the resistance of the tubing and the cathode voltage drop will be high and the tendency to sputter will be great. Sputtering means that the metal of the electrode evaporates and deposits on the tube, causing the ends of the tube to blacken. This process lowers the gas pressure still further until the tube flickers and finally fails to light. If the pressure is too high, the light will not be brilliant. The gas pressure can be tested by holding a special type of spark coil (Fig. 64) against either the glass or the electrode wire.

165. Gas Pressure Determined by Color, Using Spark-coil Tester
(Miller and Fink, "Neon Signs")

Coil held against	Color observed	Gas pressure, mm. of mercury	Remarks
Electrode wire........	Purple	200	Color visible only at edge of electrode shell
Electrode wire........	Purple	150	Faint glow in tube
Electrode wire........	Purple	50	Fair glow in tube
Electrode wire........	Blue purple	15	Dark glow
Electrode wire........	Red purple	4	
Electrode wire........	Lavender	2	
Electrode wire........	Light lavender	1	
Glass...............	Dark blue	0.25	
Glass...............	Light blue	0.10	
Glass...............	Very light blue	0.01	
Glass...............	Blue disappears	0.005	No glow in tube, blue haze near glass wall

166. The principal application of neon lamps is for sign lighting. They are particularly adapted for this class of illumination owing to their bright colors and the fact that the tubes lend themselves readily to the forming of letters and figures. The brilliant single-color red, blue, or green light has an eye appeal in outdoor advertising which white light cannot offer. The orange-red light of the neon tube penetrates great distances, making neon signs stand out with a brilliance and sparkle even on rainy nights. The flexibility of these thin glass tubes in the forming of trade-marks, special figures, and animated designs also adds to their desirability to the advertiser. Finally, the relatively low wattage (about 4 to 6 watts per foot of tubing) makes the operating cost relatively low.

167. The diameter of tubing used is from 7 to 15 mm ($\frac{1}{4}$ to $\frac{5}{8}$ in.). These sizes are convenient to work with and thoroughly practical for almost all applications. The voltage required per foot of tubing varies with the diameter of the tubing as given in Fig. 65. The smaller sized tubes give the more brilliant light but require the greatest voltage per foot of tube.

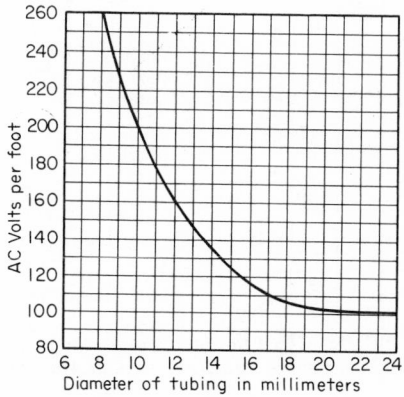

FIG. 65 *The voltage per foot required to operate tubing of various diameters filled with neon gas. (Miller and Fink, "Neon Signs.")*

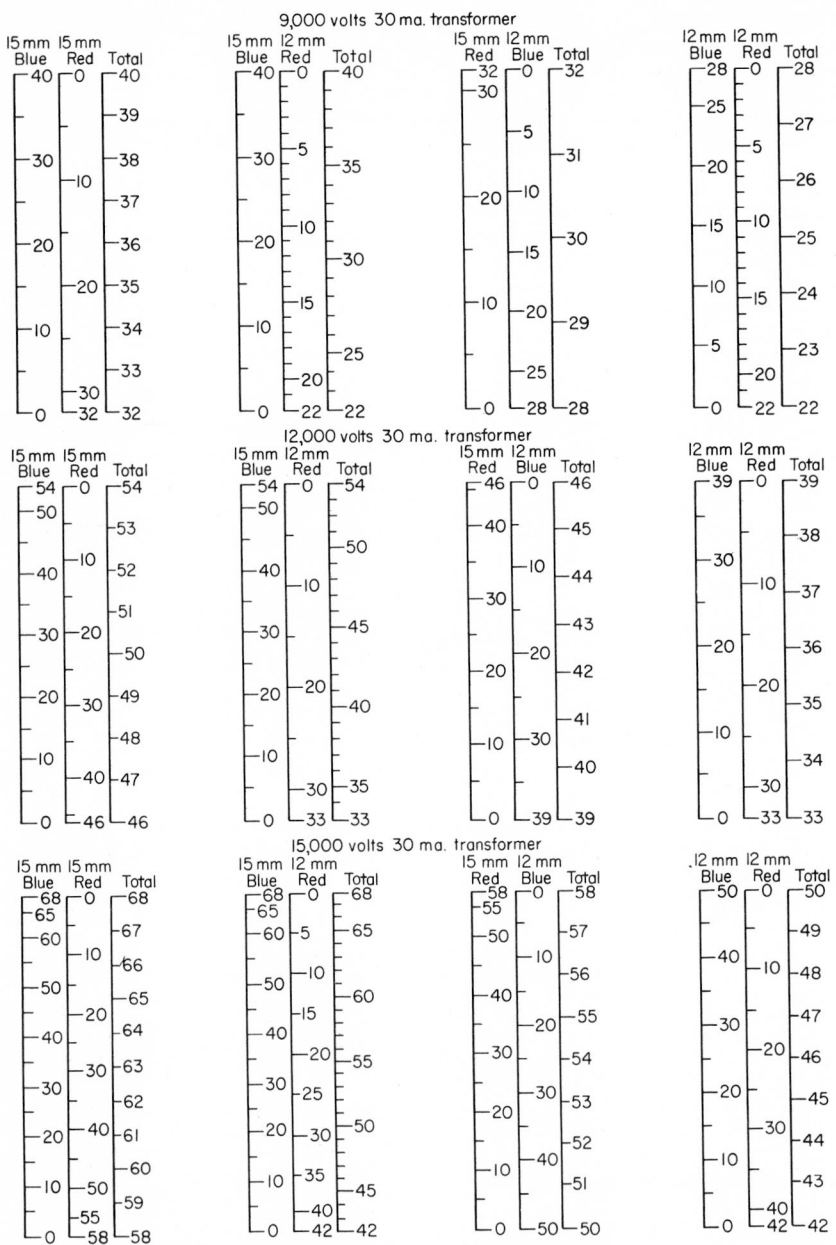

FIG. 66   *Chart for determining the footage of combinations of red and mercury tubing which may be run from a single transformer.*   (Miller and Fink, "Neon Signs.")

168. The transformers are rated according to secondary voltage and short-circuit current in milliamperes. Table **170** gives a list of standard transformers with the length of tubing in feet which can be supplied by each. This length varies with the diameter of the tubing and the gas used. Where it is desired to combine two different sizes and colors of tubing in series on one transformer, the chart of Fig. 66 can be used. Any combination of lengths which are side by side in one column in the chart can be used on the transformer whose rating is given above the chart.

For example, a 9,000-volt, 30-ma transformer may supply (in the first column of the chart) 20 ft of 15-mm blue tubing and 16 ft of 15-mm red or (in the third column) 20 ft of 15-mm red and 11 ft of 12-mm blue, making a total of 36 ft in the first case of the larger tubing and 31 ft in the second case of the combination of the larger and the medium-sized tubing. Note that, as the diameter of the tubing is decreased, the number of feet which can be supplied decreases on account of the rise in the voltage per foot, as shown in Fig. 65.

169. In the make-up of signs one section of tubing usually forms two or three letters. The different sections of tubes are then connected in series with wire jumpers until as many feet of tubing have been assembled as can be handled by the transformer to be used, as determined from Table **170**. In large signs several transformers can be used, each connected to its own section of tubing. The crossovers of tubing between letters can be blocked out by winding the tubing with tape and covering it with a waterproof varnish, or the tubes can be painted with a nonmetallic opaque paint. The glass should be made perfectly clean before painting by rubbing with a wet cloth and drying. Metallic paint (with lead or copper base) should never be used on the tubing, as it will conduct electricity and may cause a corona discharge between the tube and the housing which will attack the glass.

170. Transformer Chart, Showing Maximum Number of Feet of Tubing a Given Transformer Will Carry

(Miller and Fink, "Neon Signs")

Transformer specifications					Color of tubing															
					Red						Blue						White or gold			
Secondary volts	Secondary milliamperes short-circuited	Volt-amperes	Operating primary watts	Primary amperes, open	Diameter of tubing, mm															
					7	9	10	11	12	15	7	9	10	11	12	15	9	10	11	12
15,000	60	875	400	8.0	...	28	32	36	43	60	...	34	38	44	54	70	..	13	18	23
15,000	30	450	210	4.0	...	27	31	34	42	58	...	32	36	42	50	68	9	12	16	22
12,000	30	350	175	3.2	...	21	24	28	33	46	...	26	29	34	39	54	7	9	12	17
12,000	25	280	145	2.5	...	18	23	25	30	40	...	22	27	31	36	49	..	7	10	15
9,000	30	280	130	2.5	...	14	17	19	22	32	...	18	20	23	28	40	..	6	9	12
9,000	18	200	80	1.8	9	12	15	17	20	28	11	15	18	20	24	34				
7,500	30	245	100	2.2	..	9	12	15	17	21	...	12	15	18	21	26				
7,500	20	150	72	1.3	7	9	12	15	17	..	8	12	15	18	21					
7,500	18	140	70	1.2	7	9	12	15	17	..	8	12	15	18	21					
6,000	30	170	88	1.5	...	...	9	11	13	17	...	...	11	13	15	22				
6,000	20	130	60	1.1	6	7	9	11	13	17	7	9	11	13	15	22				
5,000	30	160	70	1.4	...	...	8	9	11	15	...	...	9	11	13	18				
5,000	20	100	50	0.9	...	6	8	9	11	15	...	...	9	11	13	18				
5,000	18	95	48	0.8	5	6	8	9	11	15	6	8	9	11	13	17				
4,000	30	130	60	1.1	...	5	6	7	8	12	...	...	8	9	10	14				
4,000	20	75	38	0.6	...	5	6	7	8	..	...	6	8	9	10					
4,000	18	70	36	0.6	...	5	6	7	8	..	...	6	8	9	10					
3,500	18	70	35	0.6	2	3	4	5	6	..	3	4	5	6	7					
3,000	20	55	30	0.5	1.5	2	3	4	5	..	2	3	4	5	6					
2,000	20	45	22	0.4	1	1.5	2	3	4	..	1.5	2.5	3	4	5					

This chart compiled from an average taken from various charts listed by leading transformer companies in the United States. Values given are conservative, to allow for variations in glass diameters.

171. Low-voltage, neon-glow lamps (Fig. 67) are operated on 105- to 125-volt d-c or a-c systems. They contain two plates to form electrodes spaced with their abutting edges about $1/16$ to $1/8$ in. apart. The bulb is filled with neon gas in some types and argon in others, as indicated in Table **172**. A high-resistance coil in the base or external is connected in series with the electrodes and serves to limit the current, no auxiliary devices being necessary. When the circuit is closed, the 110 to 125 volts causes the small air space between the plates to become ionized. A glow discharge takes place between the plates and then spreads so as virtually to cover the surface of the plates. The plates are very rugged and long-lived, failure usually being due to the burning out of the

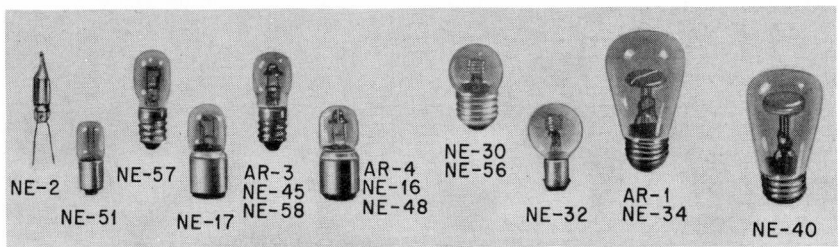

FIG. 67 *Low-voltage neon-glow lamps.* (*General Electric Co.*)

series resistance. When these lamps are used on direct current, only one electrode glows, whereas on alternating current both electrodes glow. They can therefore be used as an a-c–d-c detector device. They may be used as pilot and indicator lamps in industry, for stroboscopic lamps in the laboratory, and as all-night lights in homes. Their low wattage, long life, and dependability make them ideal for such uses. The characteristics of neon-glow lamps are given in Table **172**.

172. Glow Lamps—105–125 Volts
(General Electric Co.)

Order designation	Watts (nominal)	Bulb	Base	Max over-all length, in.	Approximate		Series resistance, ohms[a]
					Starting voltage		
					A-C	D-C	
NE-2	1/25	T-2	Unbased (wire term.)	$1\frac{1}{16}$	65	90	200000 EX
NE-51	1/25	T-3¼	S. C. bay. min	$1\frac{3}{16}$	65	90	200000 EX
NE-48	1/4	T-4½	D. C. bay. cand.	1½	65	90	30000 EX
NE-45	1/4	T-4½	Cand. screw	1⅝	65	90	30000 IN
NE-30	1	S-11	Medium screw	2½	60	85	7500 IN
NE-32	1	G-10	D. C. bay. cand.	$2\frac{3}{16}$	60	85	7500 EX
NE-34	2	S-14	Medium screw	3½	60	85	3500 IN
NE-36	2	S-14	SK. D. C. bay. cand.	$3^{15}/_{16}$	60	85	3500 EX
NE-40	3	S-14	Medium screw	3½	60	85	2200 IN
NE-42	3	S-14	Sk. D. C. bay. cand.	$3^{15}/_{16}$	60	85	2200 EX
AR-3	1/4	T-4½	Cand. screw	1⅝	80	115	15000 IN
AR-4	1/4	T-4½	D. C. bay. cand.	1½	80	115	15000 EX
AR-1	2	S-11	Med. screw	3½	65	90	3500 IN

[a] EX—external; IN—internal.
NE-56 is similar to NE-30 but designed for 210- to 250-volt circuits.

173. Argon-glow lamps, which consist of a mixture of gases, radiate mainly blue, violet, and in the near-ultraviolet region. The negative glow appears blue-violet. The fact that there is strong radiation in the near-ultraviolet region can be demonstrated by the fluorescent effects produced on uranium glass and many phosphorescent and fluorescent substances. Commercially, therefore, the argon-glow lamps are used to some extent as convenient ultraviolet sources.

ULTRAVIOLET-LIGHT SOURCES

174. Ultraviolet-light sources are lamps which are designed primarily to produce light of wave lengths in the ultraviolet part of the spectrum (see Fig. 1). It should be understood that not all ultraviolet light is the same. There are at present four recognized bands of ultraviolet light. The band in which the light from any source falls depends upon the wave length of the light emitted. Each of the recognized bands differs widely from the others in its characteristics, usefulness, and field of application. The four bands are as follows: the near-ultraviolet or fluorescent region, erythemic region, abiotic or bactericidal region, and the Shuman region. They are listed above in the order of decreasing wave length of the light, the wave length of the near ultraviolet being closest to that of visible light. The light from the ordinary fluorescent lamp originates at its source as light in the near-ultraviolet band. This nonvisible light is transformed into visible light by the fluorescence of the coating on the lamp tube under the influence of the near-ultraviolet light. The light output from the lamp, therefore, becomes visible light, so that the ordinary fluorescent lamp is not an ultraviolet-light source. However, by the use of special phosphors for the coating of fluorescent lamps, fluorescent lamps can be made to be sources of ultraviolet light.

The common methods of producing ultraviolet radiations are (1) by carbon and tungsten arcs, (2) by tungsten filaments operated at higher temperatures than in ordinary lamps, and (3) by gaseous-discharge lamps of proper design. Ultraviolet light can be used for healthful radiation as in the case of the sunlight lamps, for photographic printing, for illuminating fluorescent materials for analysis or for theatrical effects, or for the killing of germs as in the case of the germicidal or sterilamps.

175. Sunlight Lamps (General Electric Co.). All mercury-vapor lamps generate ultraviolet rays which cause sunburn or suntan. These rays are transmitted only when special glass bulbs are used. The middle ultraviolet radiation between 2,800 and 3,300 A is effective, but the peak of effectiveness comes at 2,967 A, which is one of the important mercury lines. Shorter wave lengths in the germicidal region cause quick sunburn or skin reddening (erythema), but they do not penetrate deeply into the skin to cause tanning. The longer wave lengths in the above range penetrate deeper and cause tanning.

Various types of sunlamps, including fluorescent, have been developed. The S-1 sunlamp, introduced in 1929, was the first popular artificial sunlamp source, and many thousands were bought in the past by individuals for home use. Few new S-1 equipments are being sold today largely because of the weight and bulk of the transformer and auxiliary reflector required. The self-contained RS reflector sunlamp with built-in starting switch and filament ballast has largely displaced other types because of its simplicity in use.

The RS sunlamp (Fig. 68) is a self-contained unit with a 100-watt mercury discharge element and a 175-watt tungsten-filament resistance ballast incorporated within an ultraviolet-transmitting, reflector-type bulb. The internal bimetallic starting switch first allows current to pass through the filament ballast and an auxiliary starting electrode which brings the latter up to emitting temperature. The switch is so placed that in several seconds the heat from the filament ballast causes the bimetallic switch to open and the full line voltage starts the mercury element. The temperature of the filament and the resultant light output is then reduced because the filament is in series with the mercury arc, and this change is noticeable both in light intensity and color quality as a starting characteristic. During operation the heat from the filament ballast is sufficient to hold the starting switch open. The starting switch is similar in operating characteristics to thermal-type starters used for fluorescent lamps.

As presently designed, the lamp will operate satisfactorily only on either 50- or 60-cycle current on 110- to 125-volt a-c circuits. Design voltage is 118 volts, and the ultraviolet output rated at 35,000 E-Vitons varies about 1 per cent for each percent variation from this median line voltage.

The RS lamp takes around 3 min to reach full ultraviolet output on starting and approximately 5 min for restarting. Part of this time is required for the bimetallic switch to cool down and close, and no light is produced in this interval. Direct-current operation is not recommended because arcing at the contacts of the built-in thermal switch results in short life. The life of the RS lamp on normal a-c circuits in household use has been estimated at approximately 600 applications, or 1,000 hr when operated 5 hr per start.

Since the sun's rays reaching the earth contain no rays shorter than 2,800 A, the bulbs of sunlamps are made of special glass which, like the atmosphere, absorbs the shorter rays. Quartz bulb lamps generate and transmit much erythemal energy in the far ultraviolet region not encountered in natural sunshine and therefore are not well adapted for popular sunlamp uses.

Type R S Sunlamp

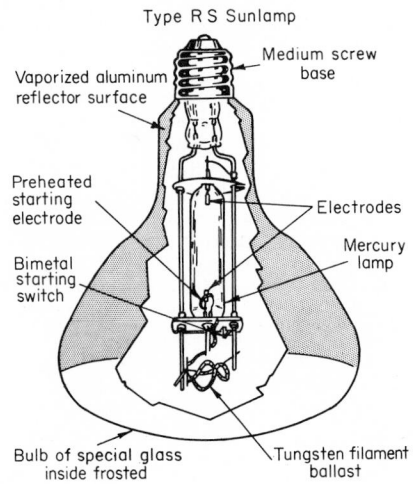

FIG. 68   *RS mercury-vapor sun lamp.*   (*General Electric Co.*)

176. Black light (General Electric Co.) is the popular name for near-ultraviolet radiant energy. The label is not a very precise one. Whether or not this energy *looks* black is debatable. Certainly it *isn't* light, because the human eye is insensitive to it.

The interesting thing about black light is that when it falls on certain materials it makes them fluoresce, i.e., emit visible light. What actually occurs is a conversion of energy: the black light that falls upon the fluorescent surface is absorbed and then re-radiated at longer wave lengths — wave lengths to which the eye is sensitive. So surfaces that contain or are treated with fluorescent chemicals glow, white or in color, when irradiated by black light. If the surroundings are kept dark, as they often are, the effect is that of self-luminous elements floating in space.

The weirdly beautiful and dramatic effects that black light makes possible account for its popularity in the fields of decoration, display, and advertising. In its many and rapidly expanding workaday uses, black light makes it possible to see things that otherwise could not be seen.

The most important man-made sources of black light are black-light fluorescent and mercury lamps. Filament lamps are weak and inefficient sources of black light, and argon-glow lamps produce it in only very small quantities. Carbon arcs produce useful amounts of black light. Radiant energy from the sun and sky contains a strong black-light component.

Data for black light lamps are given in Table **177.**

177. Black Light Lamps
(General Electric Co.)

Nom lamp watts	Ordering abbrev.	Bulb	Nom length, in.	Base	Std. pkg. quan.	Approx fluorens	Lumens from same size std. cool white lamp
				Fluorescent Lamps General Line			
2	MF2T6/BL	T-6	2⅜	D.C. indexing	120	110	
3	MF3RP12/BL	RP-12	2⁹⁄₁₆	D.C. indexing	120	200	
4	MF5000	RP-12	2⁹⁄₁₆	D.C. indexing	120	220	
4	F4T4/BL	T-4	5⅜	Oval small 4-pin	24	270	
4	F4T5/BL	T-5	6	Min bipin	24	270	
4	F4T5/BLB	T-5	6	Min bipin	24	225	100
4	MF5001	T-5	6	Min pinless	24	85	
6	F6T5/BL	T-5	9	Min bipin	24	570	
6	F6T5/BLB	T-5	9	Min bipin	24	480	210
8	F8T5/BL	T-5	12	Min bipin	24	890	
8	F8T5/BLB	T-5	12	Min bipin	24	760	330
15	F15T8/BL	T-8	18	Med. bipin	24	1,950	
15	F15T8/BLB	T-8	18	Med. bipin	24	1,650	730
20	F20T12/BL	T-12	24	Med. bipin	24	3,500	
20	F20T12/BLB	T-12	24	Med. bipin	24	3,000	1,000
30	F30T8/BL	T-8	36	Med. bipin	24	5,100	
30	F30T8/BLB	T-8	36	Med. bipin	24	4,300	1,890
40	F40T12/BL	T-12	48	Med. bipin	24	8,100	
40	F40T12/BLB	T-12	48	Med. bipin	24	6,900	2,500
40	F40T12/BL/IS	T-12	48	Med. bipin	24	8,100	
90	F90T17/BL	T-17	60	Mog. bipin	12	16,500	5,150
				Rapid Start			
40	F40T12/BL/RS	T-12	48	Med. bipin	24	8,100	
40	F40T12/BLB/RS	T-12	48	Med. bipin	24	6,900	2,500
60	F48T12/BL/RS	T-12	48	Recessed D.C.	24	10,000	3,250
				Circline			
32	FC12T10/BL	T-10	12 (diam)	4-pin	12	5,000	1,550

Black Light Lamps (*Continued*)

Slimline—Single-pin Bases

Bulb	Ordering abbrev.	Nom length, in.	Std. pkg. qty.	Nom lamp current, ma	Approx fluorens	Lumens from same size std. cool white lamp
T-6	F42T6/BL	42	24	200	4,500	1,480
				300	5,400	1,850
	F64T6/BL	64	24	200	7,500	2,450
				300	9,100	3,050
T-8	F96T8/BL	96	24	200	11,000	3,550
				300	14,300	4,450

Mercury Lamps

Nom lamp watts	Ordering abbrev.	Bulb	Base	Max over-all length, in.	Rated life, hr	Std. pkg. qty.	Approx fluorens	Approx lumens
100	H85-C3	T-10	Med.	5⅝	500	12	5,070	2,800
	H100-A4	T-10	Admed.	5⅝	6,000	12	5,030	3,500
	H100-BL4	T-16	Admed.	5½	1,000	12	690	0.01
	H100-SP4	PAR-38	Admed. Skt.	5⁷⁄₁₆	2,000	12	1,440	2,300
	H100-FL4	PAR-38	Admed. Skt.	5⁷⁄₁₆	2,000	12	1,440	2,300
250	H250-A5	BT-28	Mog.	8¼	6,000	12	9,000	11,000
400	H400-E1	BT-37	Mog.	11½	6,000	6	22,250	21,000
	H400-E1T	T-20	Mog.	11	6,000	12	19,000	20,000

Argon Lamps

Nom lamp watts	Lamp number	Bulb	Base	Max over-all length, in.	Starting volts		Useful life, hr	Std. pkg. qty.	Approx fluorens
					A-C	D-C			
¼	AR-3	T-4½	Cand.	1⅝	80	115	150	100	1
2	AR-1	S-14	Med.	3½	65	90	1,000	100	7

Filament Lamps

Nom lamp watts	Ordering abbrev.	Bulb	Base	Volts	Max over-all length, in.	Approx life, hr	Std. pkg. qty.	Approx fluorens	Approx lumens
250	250A21/60	A-21	Med.	105–125	4¹⁵⁄₁₆	50	120	470	0.7

178. Filters (General Electric Co.). Most sources of black light produce visible light along with the ultraviolet. In the great majority of applications this visible light is undesirable. If it is not screened out by means of filters, it illuminates not only the luminous areas but also their surroundings. This, of course, reduces brightness contrasts and robs the display (or whatever the application may be) of its effectiveness. So almost always some sort of light-absorbing filter is placed between the black light source and the irradiated surface. In the case of the BLB fluorescent lamps, the H100-BL4 mercury lamps, and the Purple X filament lamp, the filter is an integral part of the lamp.

Filters having a wide range of characteristics are used for black-light applications. At one extreme there are filters that pass virtually no visible light and not very much ultraviolet; at the other extreme are deep-blue sheet glasses that transmit appreciable visible light and a great deal of near ultraviolet. Scientifically designed black-light filters are regularly supplied in molded squares or roundels or in sheet glass. They are used in all black-light applications that require a high degree of absorption of the visible light. Some of the deep-blue sheet glasses being used as black-light filters were not originally intended for this service. But since their near-ultraviolet transmission is high, their cost low, and they are easily cut to any desired size, they are used in many applications in which some visible light can be tolerated.

179. Applications of Black Light.
1. Inspection of foods.
2. Sorting of laundry where invisible laundry marks are used.
3. Inspection of cast and machined parts.
4. Detection of leaks in hydraulic systems.
5. Inspection of textiles.
6. Photoproductive processes.
7. Location of mineral deposits.
8. In advertising for producing different effects in the illumination of outdoor sign boards.
9. Lighting of show-window displays.
10. Decorative purposes in the lighting of murals.
11. Diagnostic purposes in the medical and biological fields.
12. Checking of cleanliness in restaurants, public rest rooms, dairies, etc.

180. Germ-killing or bactericidal lamps, which are called sterilamps by the Westinghouse Electric Corp. (Fig. 69) and germicidal lamps by the General Electric Co., have

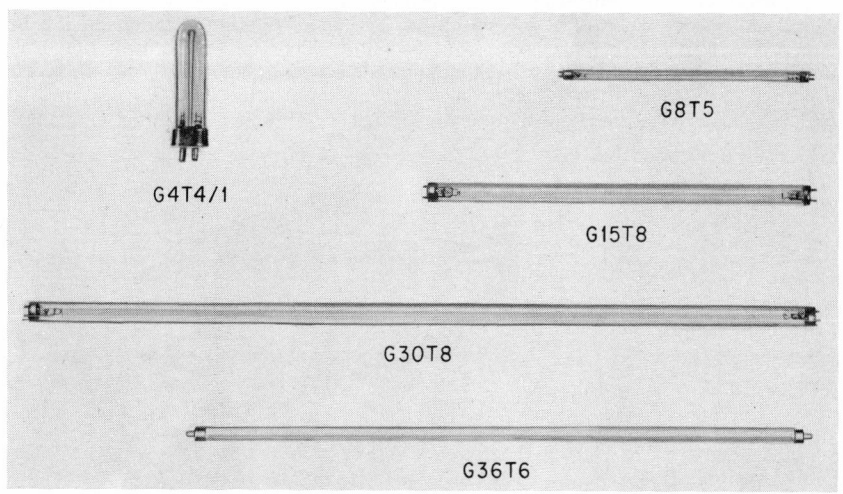

G8T5

G4T4/1

G15T8

G30T8

G36T6

FIG. 69 *Sterilamps.* (*Westinghouse Electric Corp.*)

been developed for use in many places for sterilizing and prevention of mold. The germ-killing lamp is a gaseous-discharge lamp consisting of a long tube containing mercury vapor and inert gases. It gives out ultraviolet radiation in the bactericidal band which kills bacteria of many kinds. The General Electric 5-watt size can be operated in an ordinary socket, but all the others require auxiliary control equipment, such as a reactor, transformer, relays, etc.

181. The principal uses for germicidal and sterilamps are:

1. For storage and aging of meat. The meat when exposed to ultraviolet radiation can be kept in a warm, high-humidity atmosphere where it will age and become tender much more rapidly with no formation of mold or slime and with no loss of weight due to drying out.

2. For irradiation of bread dough to prevent the formation of mold.

3. For sterilizing drinking glasses, hospital instruments, toilet seats, etc., to prevent the spread of disease.

4. For use over the hospital operating table to prevent wound infections after major operations.

182. Photochemical lamps (General Electric Co.) designate a family of mercury lamps designed for specialized applications of ultraviolet radiation. The lamps with tubular quartz bulbs transmit the full range of generated radiation. Since these emit short-wave germicidal radiation, they must be used with utmost caution. Bare tubes must not be exposed to the eyes or skin. Where lamps are used exposed, short-wave-absorbing glass filters should surround the lamp.

Ultraviolet radiation from quartz lamps is extremely useful as a catalyst in many industrial chemical processes such as polymerization, halogenation, chlorination, and oxidization. Similarly the lamps are highly effective for ultraviolet therapy.

Quartz lamps are used by manufacturers for weathering tests on paints, dyes, and other finishes. Since high concentration of energy from lamps is possible, a few hours' exposure may be equivalent to many days' exposure to natural sunlight. These lamps have also found widespread use in the sterilization of water. This method is particularly desirable when the taste and odor from chemical sterilization are objectionable.

Photochemical lamps are used for black-and-white printing, blueprinting, copyboard lighting, diazo printing, and vacuum-frame printing. Some lamps use an ultraviolet-transmitting glass which does not transmit far ultraviolet. These are excellent photographic lamps, since many of their strongest emission lines lie close to the maximum sensitivity of most photosensitive materials.

183. Ozone Lamp (Fig. 70). The ozone-producing lamp (General Electric Co.) is a small low-voltage mercury-vapor lamp in an S-11 bulb. It consumes only 4 watts. The arc forms between the two segments of a V-shaped coiled tungsten filament in an atmosphere of mercury vapor at very low pressure. The lamp operates at 10½ volts with a normal current of 350 ma. Although the lamp generates the full mercury spectrum, the low vapor pressure favors efficient generation in the short-wave ultraviolet region. This is also true of the operating pressures of germicidal and fluorescent lamps.

I. *Lamp.*   II. *Ballast.*

FIG. 70 *Ozone lamp.* (*General Electric Co.*)

The ozone lamp uses a bulb that transmits the 1849A radiation, which produces ozone. It is used in plug-in types of equipments, which shield the lamp from exposure to the eyes but allow free circulation of air close to the bulb.

Ozone is concentrated oxygen and is produced by sparking electrical machinery or by electrical storms in nature. It is unstable, and the extra oxygen atom created is free to combine with odorous vapors in the air and change their chemical composition. Ozone itself has a tangy, invigorating smell. It is always present in some degree in the air, but high concentrations are poisonous.

Only minute quantities of 1849A radiation are produced by the ozone lamp, but only minute quantities are needed or desirable. Of the 4,000 mw (4 watts) input to the lamp, only 1 mw is emitted at 1849A. It emits 100 mw of 2537A germicidal radiation, but is a relatively weak source compared with the output of standard germicidal lamps.

Ozone lamps will operate on either alternating or direct current and on any circuit voltage above 28 volts. Standard inductive ballasts are available for 120-volt circuits. Several lamps can be operated in series from one ballast, but the operation of more than one lamp reduces the current slightly to each lamp, which in turn reduces the ultraviolet output. Resistance ballasting can also be used. On 110–125-volt circuits, a 40-watt filament lamp in series with the ozone lamp will provide proper operation. Ballasting for any line voltage is simply a matter of figuring the proper resistance or inductance to supply the lamp with its nominal 10½ volts and 350-ma current.

The 40A15/1 40-watt appliance lamp is frequently used as a ballast for the ozone lamps in driers. In any application where this ballast lamp might be splashed with water while hot, a special 35A/A15 110-volt 35-amp resistance ballast lamp is available. Since this ballast lamp is a vacuum lamp, its bulb remains at relatively low temperature during operation.

INFRARED HEATING LAMPS

184. Heating or drying lamps are incandescent lamps with filaments which operate at a lower color temperature (2500 instead of about 3000°K) so that most of the radiation occurs in the infrared part of the spectrum with wave lengths longer than those of visible light.

Infrared lamps have many uses in commercial and industrial applications for heating and drying and on the farm for brooding of poultry and animals. Important features of these lamps include rapid heat transfer, efficient operation, simple oven construction, low oven first cost, adaptability to conveyor-line production, cleanliness, and low maintenance cost. The several wattages in each bulb size permit a wide range of temperatures.

The 250 PS30/33 brooder lamp is a specially designed, low-cost lamp, particularly effective for brooding older chicks and larger animals. It is interchangeable with R-40 lamps in existing brooder equipment. It eliminates "hot spots" and provides a wider distribution of heat.

The T-3 infrared quartz lamps are capable of delivering over three times the energy concentration provided by the 375-watt R-40 lamps. They can be used in compact trough reflectors for concentrated radiation.

185. Data on Infrared Heating Lamps
(General Electric Co.)

Lamp watts	Ordering abbrev.	Bulb	Base	Voltage range	Design volts[a]	Light center length, in.	Max overall length, in.
			Reflector Lamps				
125	125R40	R-40	Med. skirted	115–125	115	—	$7\frac{1}{4}$
250	250R40/1	R-40	Med. screw[b]	115–120	115	—	$6\frac{1}{2}$
250	250R40/10[e]	R-40	Med. screw[b]	115–125	115	—	$6\frac{7}{8}$
250	250PS30/33[c]	PS-30	Med. screw[b]	115–125	115	—	$8\frac{1}{16}$
250	250R40/4	R-40	Med. skirted	115–125	115	—	$7\frac{1}{4}$
250	250R40/5[d]	R-40	Med. skirted	115–125	115	—	$7\frac{5}{8}$
375	375R40	R-40	Med. skirted	115–125	115	—	$7\frac{1}{4}$
375	375R40/1[d]	R-40	Med. skirted	115–125	115	—	$7\frac{5}{8}$
375	375R40/10[e]	R-40	Med. skirted	115–125	115	—	$7\frac{5}{8}$
			Lamps Requiring Auxiliary Reflectors				
125	125G30	G-30	Med. skirted	115–125	115	5	$7\frac{1}{8}$
250	250G30	G-30	Med. skirted	115–125	115	5	$7\frac{1}{8}$
375	375G30	G-30	Med. skirted	115–125	115	5	$7\frac{1}{8}$
500	500G30/1	G-30	Med. skirted	115–125	115	5	$7\frac{1}{8}$
500	500T40/3[d]	T-40	Med. bipost	115–125	115	$3\frac{1}{16}$	$7\frac{1}{4}$
1,000	1M/T40/3[d]	T-40	Med. bipost	115–125	115	$3\frac{1}{16}$	$7\frac{1}{4}$
			Tubular Quartz Lamps			*Lighted length, in.*	
375	375T3	T-3 trans.	Sleeve	115–125	120	5	$8\frac{13}{16}$
500	500T3	T-3 trans.	Sleeve	115–125	120	5	$8\frac{13}{16}$
500	500T3/CL	T-3 clear	Sleeve	115–125	120	5	$8\frac{13}{16}$
1,000	1000T3	T-3 trans.	Sleeve	230–250	240	10	$13\frac{13}{16}$
1,000	1000T3/CL[f]	T-3 clear	Sleeve	230–250	240	10	$11\frac{15}{16}$
1,600	1600T3	T-3 trans.	Sleeve	230–250	240	16	$19\frac{13}{16}$
2,500	2500T3	T-3 trans.	Sleeve	460–500	480	25	$28\frac{13}{16}$
2,500	2500T3	T-3 trans.	Sleeve	575–625	600	25	$28\frac{13}{16}$
2,500	2500T3/CL	T-3 clear	Sleeve	460–500	480	25	$28\frac{13}{16}$
3,800	3800T3	T-3 trans.	Sleeve	550–600	575	38	$41\frac{13}{16}$
5,000	5000T3	T-3 trans.	Sleeve	920–1000	930	50	$53\frac{13}{16}$
5,000	5000T3/CL	T-3 clear	Sleeve	920–1000	960	50	$53\frac{13}{16}$

[a] Life in excess of 5,000 hr; each 1 per cent departure from design center will change wattage by approximately $1\frac{1}{2}$ per cent.

[b] Bases not designed to withstand oven temperatures.

[c] Brooder lamp with reflectorized pear-shaped bulb.

[d] Bulb of special heat-resistant glass.

[e] Bulb of special heat-resistant glass with red end.

[f] For intermittent burning only.

LUMINAIRES

186. Purpose of Luminaires. A luminaire is a device which directs, diffuses, or modifies the light given out by the illuminating source in such a manner as to make its use more economical, effective, and safe to the eye. The luminaire includes the fixture stem and canopy, the reflector, and lamp socket, and the enclosing materials. Since the light from a bare lamp is given off approximately equally in all directions, in order to use the light economically some accessory is required to direct the light to the desired areas. As most lamps have a high brilliancy, it is desirable in producing satisfactory illumination that the eye be shielded from the source in order to eliminate direct glare.

It would not be possible to illuminate an area with bare lamps, unless an excessively large number of closely spaced units were employed, without the production of dense deep shadows. In many cases the artistic appearance of the illuminating system is of great importance, so that the luminaire must possess decorative features as well as those necessary for satisfactory illumination.

187. Distribution Graphs of Luminaires. The effect of a luminaire in changing the direction and distribution of the light given out by a light source is best expressed by a distribution graph. Figure 71 shows such a graph for a bare lamp and for the same lamp with a reflector. The graph represents the light in a single vertical plane through the center of the light unit, and it is assumed that the light in all similar vertical planes is similarly distributed. See Sec. **32,** How to Read a Photometric Graph.

Figure 72 shows a sample photometric test report for a 500-watt luminous-bowl indirect luminaire. A report of

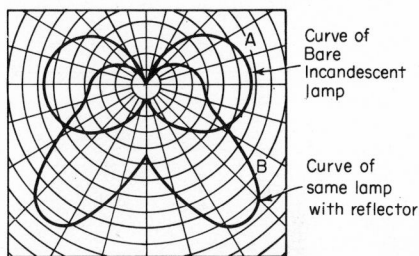

Curve of
Bare
Incandescent
lamp

Curve of
same lamp
with reflector

FIG. 71 *Comparison between distribution curve of a bare incandescent lamp and that of the same lamp equipped with a suitable reflector.*

this type is used in comparing luminaires with one another as to relative distribution of light, type of illumination, lumen-output efficiency, and brightness.

188. Classification of Luminaires.

1. According to system of illumination produced.
    a. Direct.
    b. Semidirect.
    c. General diffuse or direct-indirect.
    d. Semiindirect.
    e. Indirect.
2. According to the amount that the luminaire encloses the lamp.
    a. Open.
    b. Enclosed.
3. According to class of service.
    a. Industrial.
    b. Commercial and institutional.
    c. Residential.
    d. Street lighting.
    e. Floodlighting.
4. According to the material used for reflection or transmission of the light.
    a. Steel.
    b. Aluminum.
    c. Opal glass.
    d. Prismatic glass.
    e. Glass and metal.
    f. Plastic.
    g. Plastic and metal.
5. According to method of mounting.
    a. Suspended.
    b. Surface mounted.
    c. Recessed or built in.
6. According to light source.
    a. Incandescent lamp.
    b. High-intensity-discharge lamp.
    c. Fluorescent lamp.

Westinghouse Lamp Division
Westinghouse Electric and Manufacturing Company
Commercial Engineering Laboratory
Photometric Test Report
Luminous bowl indirect lighting unit

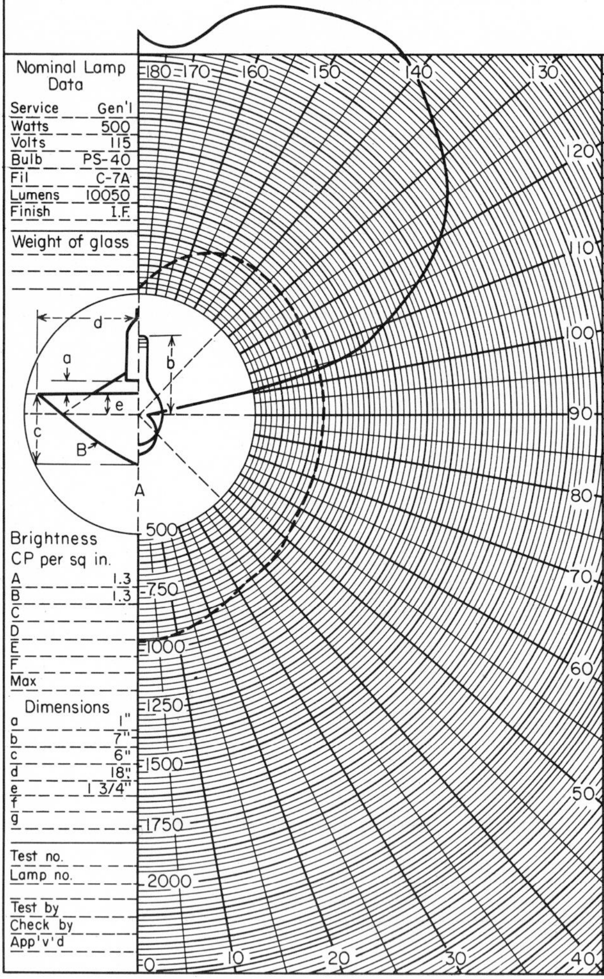

Nominal Lamp Data
Service Gen'l
Watts 500
Volts 115
Bulb PS-40
Fil C-7A
Lumens 10050
Finish I.F.
Weight of glass
d
a
b
e
c
B
A
Brightness CP per sq in.
A 1.3
B 1.3
C
D
E
F
Max
Dimensions
a 1"
b 7"
c 6"
d 18"
e 1 3/4"
f
g
Test no.
Lamp no.
Test by
Check by
App'v'd
180 170 160 150 140 130 120 110 100 90 80 70 60 50 40 30 20 10 0
500 750 1000 1250 1500 1750 2000

Apparent candlepower		
Angle	Bare lamp	Luminaire
0	971	159
5	957	159
15	930	156
25	885	145
35	844	128
45	836	109
55	813	86
65	799	70
75	794	53
85	787	47
90	780	59
MLHCP	822	86
95	789	127
105	795	930
115	804	1315
125	793	1623
135	782	1777
145	772	1931
155	744	1890
165	661	1767
175	568	1592
180	537	1633
MUHCP	778	1274
MSCP	800	680

Zonal Lumens		
Zone	Bare lamp	Luminaire
0-10	91	15
10-20	263	44
20-30	410	67
30-40	530	80
40-50	641	84
50-60	730	77
60-70	793	69
70-80	840	56
80-90	859	51
90-100	861	139
100-110	841	984
110-120	798	1305
120-130	712	1455
130-140	605	1375
140-150	485	1213
150-160	344	876
160-170	187	502
170-180	54	151
Total	10050	8543

Zone	Lumens	Total bare % Clear lamp
0-60	367	3.7
0-90	543	5.4
90-180	8000	79.6
0-180	8543	85

FIG. 72 *Photometric test report.* (*Westinghouse Electric Corp.*)

189. Direct lighting can be defined as a lighting system in which practically all (90 to 100 per cent) the light of the luminaires is directed in angles below the horizontal directly toward the usual working areas (Fig. 73, I). This type of lighting is produced by luminaires, which range from industrial-type steel or aluminum reflectors to fixtures mounted above large light-source areas such as glass panels and skylights. Although, in general, such a system provides illumination on the working surfaces most efficiently, this may be at the expense of other factors such as excessive contrasts of the light source with the surroundings, troublesome shadows, or direct and reflected glare.

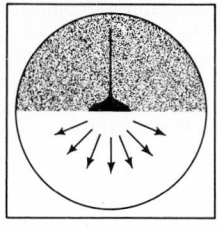

I. *Direct.*

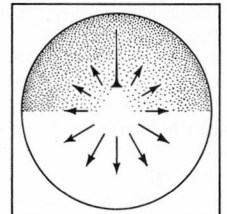

II. *Semidirect.*

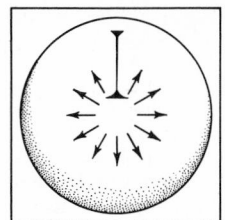

III. *General diffuse.*

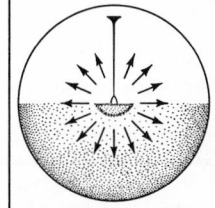

IV. *Semiindirect.*

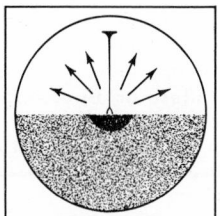

V. *Indirect.*

FIG. 73 *Systems of illumination. (General Electric Co.)*

190. Indirect Lighting (Westinghouse Electric Corp.). Ninety to 100 per cent of the light output of the luminaire is directed toward the ceiling at angles above the horizontal (Figs. 73, V and 74, 1). Practically all the light effective at the working plane is redirected downward by the ceiling and to a lesser extent by the side walls. Since the ceiling is in effect the light source, the illumination produced is quite diffuse in character. While indirect lighting is not so efficient as some of the other systems on a purely quantitative basis, the even distribution and absence of shadows and reflected glare frequently make it the most desirable type of installation for offices, schools, and other similar applications. Because room finishes play such an important part in redirecting the light, it is particularly important that they be as light in color as possible and carefully maintained in good condition. The ceilings should always have a matte finish if reflected images of the light source are to be avoided.

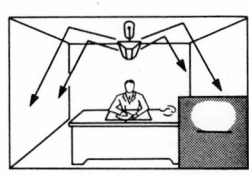

l. Indirect

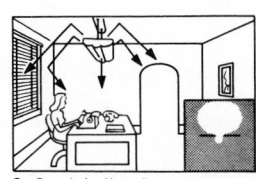

2. Semi-indirect

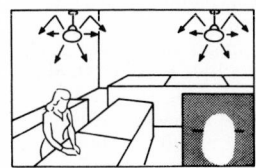

3. General diffuse

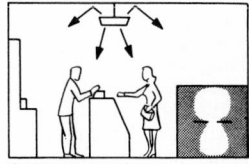

4. Direct-indirect

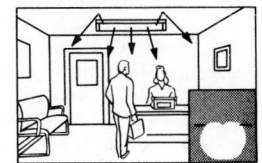

5. Semi-direct

FIG. 74 *Systems of illumination. (Westinghouse Electric Corp.)*

Glass or plastic luminaires in this classification are known as "luminous indirect," while metal luminaires which transmit no light are totally indirect. The translucent type is sometimes more desirable than the totally indirect because a luminous fixture is less sharply silhouetted against the relatively bright ceiling. Indirect illumination may also be provided by means of architectural coves. Luminaire suspension length, or cove proportions, must be carefully selected to provide uniform ceiling coverage, where desired, and to prevent excessive ceiling brightness.

191. Semiindirect Lighting (Westinghouse Electric Corp.). Sixty to 90 per cent of the light output of the luminaire is directed toward the ceiling at angles above the horizontal (Figs. 73, IV, and 74, 2), while the balance is directed downward. Semiindirect lighting has most of the advantages of the indirect system, but is slightly more efficient and is sometimes preferred to achieve a desirable brightness ratio between the ceiling and luminaire in high-level installations. The diffusing medium employed in these luminaires is glass or plastic of a lower density than that employed in indirect equipment.

192. General Diffuse or Direct-Indirect Lighting (Westinghouse Electric Corp.). Forty to 60 per cent of the light is directed downward at angles below the horizontal. The major portion of the illumination produced on ordinary working planes is a result of the light coming directly from the luminaire. There is, however, a substantial portion of the light directed to the ceiling and side walls. Where these are light in color, the upward light provides a brighter background against which to view the luminaire, in addition to supplying a substantial indirect component which adds materially to the diffuse character of the illumination. The difference between the *general diffuse* (Figs. 73, III, and 74, 3) and *direct-indirect* (Fig. 74, 4) classifications is in the amount of light produced in a horizontal direction. The general diffuse type is exemplified by the enclosing globe which distributes light nearly uniformly in all directions, while the direct-indirect luminaire produces very little light in a horizontal direction, owing to the density of its side panels. Glass, plastic, or louvered bottoms are commonly used with the latter type of luminaire to provide lamp shielding.

193. Semidirect Lighting (Westinghouse Electric Corp.). Sixty to 90 per cent of the light is directed downward at angles below the horizontal (Figs. 73, II, and 74, 5). The footcandles effective under this system at normal working planes are primarily a result of the light coming directly from the luminaire. The portion of the light directed to the ceiling results in a relatively small indirect component, the greatest value of which is that it brightens the ceiling area around the luminaire, with a resultant lowering of brightness contrasts. Equipment of this type is exemplified by the cylindrical glass-enclosed fluorescent luminaire or the open-bottom glass shade for incandescent lamps.

194. An open luminaire is one which only partially encloses the lamp. Open direct-lighting luminaires have the lamp exposed to view from at least one direction. The luminaires of Figs. 77, 78, 80, I, and 81, I, III, and IV are open-type, direct-lighting units.

195. An enclosed luminaire completely encloses the lamp from view from any direction. The one shown in Fig. 81, II is an enclosed direct-lighting luminaire.

196. Classification of Luminaires According to Class of Service. Industrial service refers to use in factories and manufacturing establishments. Commercial service refers to use in offices, stores, and public buildings. Residential use means use in houses and apartments; street lighting means the illumination of streets, roads, and highways; and floodlighting means the illumination of outdoor areas such as painted signs, recreational grounds, automobile parking spaces, and building exteriors.

197. Steel reflectors have a sheet-steel base coated with porcelain enamel, paint enamel, or aluminum paint to form the reflecting surface. The best types of steel reflectors are those coated with porcelain enamel, since their reflecting surface is very efficient, permanent, durable, and easily cleaned. Paint-enamel reflectors when new are quite efficient, but the reflecting surface deteriorates very rapidly. Aluminum-painted reflectors are slightly better than paint-enamel ones but not so permanent as the porcelain-enamel ones.

Steel reflectors are used in the manufacture of many luminaires of the direct and indirect types.

198. Aluminum reflectors are used in many different types of luminaires. The reflecting surface is usually given an electrochemical treatment called Alzak which removes the impurities from the aluminum and gives it a hard durable surface which has a high reflection efficiency of approximately 90 per cent. Like the steel reflectors, they are used in luminaires for both direct and indirect lighting.

199. Opal glass is a white diffusing glass (Sec. 10) which transmits light with a loss of only about 15 to 35 per cent, the amount depending on the density of the glass. It breaks up the light rays so that the lamp is not visible and glare is kept at a minimum. Opal glass is used for enclosed diffusing luminaires for incandescent lamps and for side-panel shields in some commercial fluorescent luminaires.

200. Prismatic glass consists of clear glass which is molded into scientifically designed prisms. Each prism is designed with reference to the position of the light source. By proper design, distribution curves of the extensive, intensive, or focusing types are obtained. The extensive reflector or globe refractor distributes the light over a wide angle below the horizontal (Fig. 75, I), the maximum intensity being at an angle of about 45 deg with the vertical.

Intensive reflectors, globes, and lenses (Fig. 75, II) throw the light more directly downward, the maximum intensity occurring between 0 and 25 deg with the vertical.

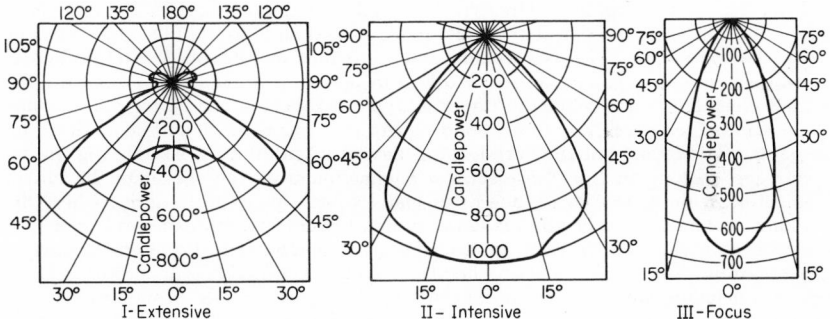

FIG. 75   *Distribution characteristic curves for direct prismatic glass luminaires. (Holophane Co., Inc.)*

Focusing globes, lenses, and reflectors (Fig. 75, III) concentrate the light to a small area, producing greatest intensity of illumination along the axis of the reflector. Focusing units give an end-on candlepower approximately 3½ times as great as the rated horizontal candlepower of the lamp. The area intensely illuminated is a circle, the diameter of which should be one-half the height of the lamp above the plane of illumination; outside this limit the intensity falls rapidly but not so abruptly as to give the effect of a spot of light. Holophane "focusing" units give their maximum candlepowers at about 10 deg from the vertical.

Prismatic-glass units are used in many direct, semidirect, and semiindirect luminaires. The different types of prismatic units employed are reflectors, globes, and lenses. Some luminaires employ only a single type of unit, and others employ a combination of types of units. Luminaires employing prismatic-glass units are available for incandescent, fluorescent, and mercury lamps.

201. Combination glass and metal luminaires are used principally for enclosed direct-lighting units. The metal part of the unit usually directs the light, while the glass is used for diffusing purposes or simply for the enclosure of the unit so that it will be dust- or vaportight.

202. Plastics are used to some extent in luminaires for incandescent lamps and to quite a great extent for fluorescent lamps. The incandescent luminaires employing plastics are of the semiindirect type (very close to indirect). For fluorescent units plastic is used in many direct and direct-indirect luminaires for side-panel shielding. It is also used quite extensively for bottom and side enclosures for direct and semidirect fluorescent units.

203. A combination of plastic and metal is used for some fluorescent luminaires. In some units the plastic is used for side-panel shielding. In others it is used to enclose the bottom of the unit for diffusing purposes or for making the unit dust- and vaportight.

204. Method of Mounting. Suspended mounting refers to hanging the luminaire from the ceiling with a chain, tube, conduit, or cord pendant suspension. Surface mounting refers to placing the body of the luminaire directly against the ceiling. Built-in mounting refers to placing the luminaire in recesses in the ceiling or on the walls or structural members, so that it forms a part of the architectural treatment of the building interior.

205. Luminaires for use with incandescent lamps are available for all classes of service. For discussion of street-lighting and floodlighting equipment refer to Secs. **261** and **269.** Incandescent luminaires for residential use are available in a great variety of types, which are too numerous to be discussed here.

206. The industrial luminaires for incandescent lamps are of either the metal or glass-metal type. The more common types are discussed in the following sections.

207. Enameled-steel reflector luminaires for incandescent lamps are made in several different types of assemblies. One type has a reflector and hood pressed in one piece. When the nut is loosened at the top, the reflector will slide up on the stem, exposing the socket for wiring. This is a weatherproof type for use outdoors and for indoor installation where interchangeability of reflectors and ease of cleaning are not the important considerations. With the turn-lock type of reflector, the entire reflector and socket can be removed from the supporting cap by a quarter turn and taken down for cleaning. The prongs of the turn-locking device, in addition to supporting the reflector and socket, provide the electrical connection from the socket to the circuit terminated in the cap. This type is especially advantageous in locations where the cleaning of reflectors in position is going to be difficult. The threaded-reflector type has a reflector which can be removed from the socket and hood by unscrewing. Several shapes of reflectors will fit the same hoods. Hoods are available with a threaded connection for fixture-stem suspension or with a flange having holes for mounting as the cover of a 4-in. outlet box. With the threaded type the reflectors can be taken down for cleaning, and different reflectors inserted in the same hood, depending on the distribution curve of light desired. The snap-on type is designed so that it can be fastened on pendant sockets. The reflector holder snaps on the reflector, and then the whole assembly screws onto the threads on the outside of an ordinary brass socket. The vaportight type (Fig. 76) is for interior use in wet atmospheres. It requires a cast outlet box with a threaded opening. The reflector is bolted to a ring which threads on the outside of the box opening. A threaded glass globe screws into the inside of the box opening against a gasket, which seals the box against entrance of moisture. A metal guard is used for low mounting heights or other locations where it is necessary to protect the globe from mechanical injury. The guard screws on the outside of the box opening.

These enameled-steel reflector assemblies are all available in several shapes for specific purposes as shown in Figs. 77 and 78. The flat cone (Fig. 77, I) and the shallow bowl (Fig. 77, II) are used for yard and aisle lighting for wide distribution of light, where the quality of the light is unimportant and glare from the partially exposed lamp not objectionable. The RLM dome (Fig. 77, III) is a standard dome reflector which must comply with standard specifications of the Reflector and Lamp Manufacturers as regards contour and quality of the porcelain reflecting surface. This type of reflector is the one commonly used for general interior industrial lighting. The deep-bowl type (Fig. 77, IV) is used frequently where the units must be hung very low, as over workbenches. Angle reflectors (Fig. 78) are used in industrial lighting to supplement the overhead units in very high interiors and for special types of service which require

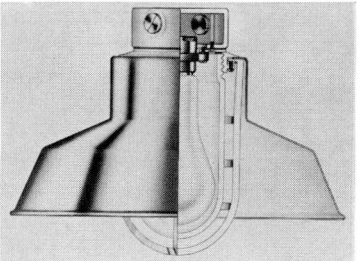

I. *With junction box.*

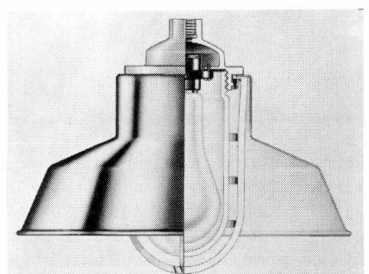

II. *For pendant mounting.*   III. *For outlet box mounting.*

FIG. 76 *Vaportight units.* (*The Miller Co.*)

very good illumination on vertical planes. They are used also for the lighting of bill-boards and painted signs.

Specially designed deep-bowl type of units also are available for high bay mounting.

The use of silvered-bowl lamps in steel reflectors will provide well-diffused illumination.

Glass covers are available for enclosing the bottom of steel reflectors in order to make them dusttight.

208. The glassteel diffuser luminaire for incandescent lighting is a combination glass-and-steel direct-lighting unit which is employed for high-quality industrial lighting. It

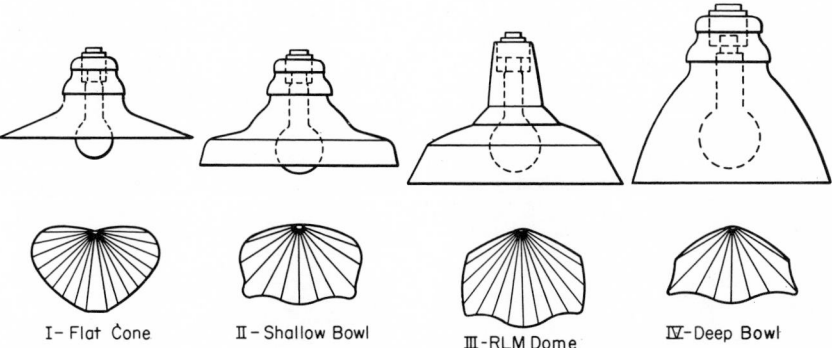

I- Flat Cone   II - Shallow Bowl   III-RLM Dome   IV-Deep Bowl

FIG. 77 *Contour outlines of typical enameled-steel reflectors with their characteristic distribution curves.*

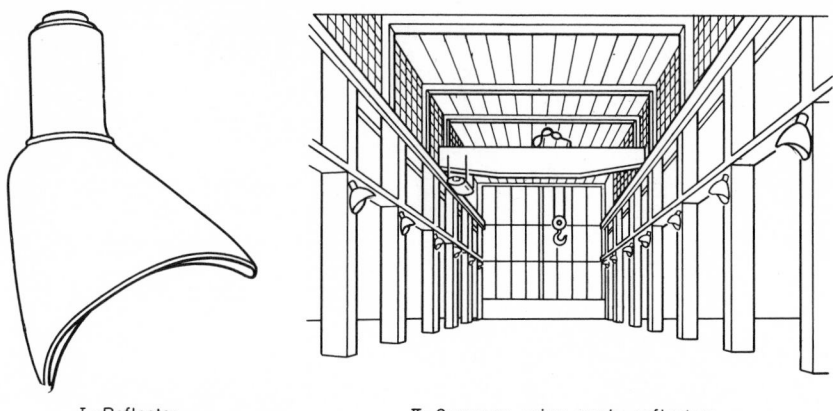

I -Reflector   II- Craneway using angle reflectors

FIG. 78 *Elliptical-angle steel reflector. (Benjamin Div., Thomas Industries, Inc.)*

consists of a completely enclosing opal-glass globe (Fig. 79) mounted inside a dome-shaped, porcelain-enameled reflector. The porcelain reflector has the same general construction as the standard RLM dome reflector. Small openings in the top of the dome allow a small portion of the light to be directed to the ceiling. This illumination

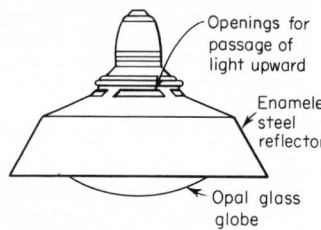

FIG. 79 *Glassteel diffuser.*

of the ceiling produces natural and cheerful working conditions, whereas with the RLM dome reflectors the ceiling is left in darkness. The enclosing globe of the glassteel diffuser shields the lamp from view and diffuses the light, reducing the glare effect. The glassteel diffuser is made in all the types of assemblies explained under enameled-steel luminaires.

209. Aluminum luminaires for incandescent lamps are chiefly of the high-bay type (Fig. 80). They provide more accurate control of light than is obtainable with the enameled-steel reflectors and are recommended where the mounting height is high compared with the width of the area to be lighted. A concentrating type is used where the units are sufficiently high so that it is best to locate the units closer together than the mounting height and for high-mounted units in narrow interiors. A spread type gives better illumination on vertical surfaces and can be used where the spacing is up to 1½ times the mounting height. These

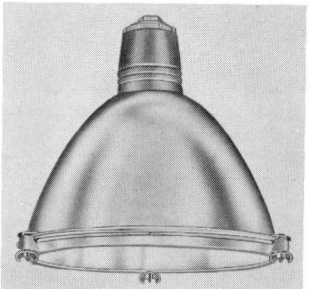

I. *Open type.*   II. *Vaportight type.*

FIG. 80 *Aluminum high-bay luminaires. (The Miller Co.)*

luminaires are made in the one-piece and in the turn-lock types as described in Sec. **207.**

Steel-clad units, which consist of an Alzak aluminum reflector protected by a porcelain-enamel steel housing, are available for severe service conditions. These units may be provided with glass covers for protection against moisture and noncombustible dust.

210. Prismatic-glass luminaires for industrial use with incandescent and mercury vapor lamps are available in low-bay (Fig. 81, I and IV) and high-bay (Fig. 81, III) types. The basic unit is provided with an open-bottom, prismatic-glass reflector which produces semidirect illumination. In cases where upward light is not required but where protection against moisture (condensate, leakage, etc.) from the ceiling is desirable, an aluminum cover can be used over the prismatic reflector without

I. *Incandescent lamp unit, low-bay mounting.*

II. *Vapor- and dusttight incandescent unit.*

III. *High-bay mercury-vapor lamp unit (protective drip-shield type).*

IV. *Low-bay mercury-vapor lamp unit (open-yoke type).*

FIG. 81 *Industrial-type prismatic-glass luminaires. (Holophane Co., Inc.)*

materially affecting the downward distribution of light. Guards of either wire- or louver-type construction are available for protection of the lamp. These units, in addition to their industrial applications, are also widely used in certain commercial types of buildings, such as gymnasiums and supermarkets.

Another prismatic-glass luminaire for industrial use with incandescent lamps is an all-purpose vapor- and dusttight unit. This luminaire consists of a prismatic-glass reflector-refractor and a cast-metal fitter with stainless-steel supporting bails assembled to normally closed type cam latches. This unit is shown in Fig. 81, II. It is used in chemical, petroleum, ordnance, generating-station, textile, woodworking, food-processing, and similar industries.

211. Luminaires for high-intensity-discharge lamps are generally intended for high-bay mounting in industrial interiors. Luminaires are available in enameled steel, Alzak aluminum, and prismatic-glass types. The metal units are of the same general type of construction as similar luminaires used for lighting with incandescent lamps. Refer to Secs. **207** and **209.**

Prismatic-glass units are available for both high-bay and low-bay mounting. Refer to Fig. 81. Both the high-bay and the low-bay units consist of a prismatic-glass reflector with the outside of the reflector protected by a sealed and permanently spun-on metal cover.

212. Industrial luminaires for fluorescent lamps generally employ porcelain-enameled steel reflectors. They provide direct illumination. Both open and enclosed units are available for two to four lamp assemblies. The open units may be of the open- or closed-end type of construction. The tops of the reflectors may be solid or provided with apertures (refer to Figs. 82, 83, and 84). These open units may have

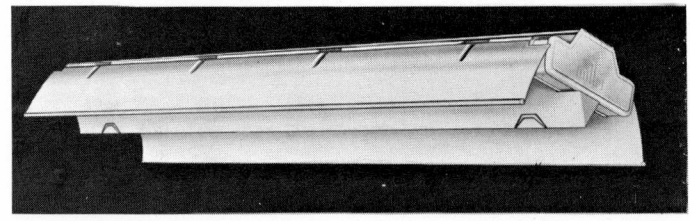

FIG. 82 *Partially open-end type of steel fluorescent luminaire.* (*The Miller Co.*)

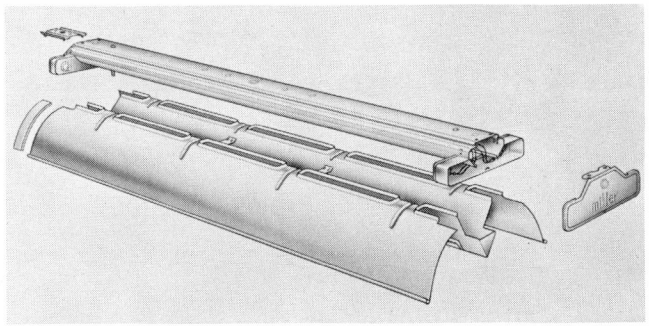

FIG. 83 *Construction of open-type fluorescent luminaire, showing longitudinal shield.* (*The Miller Co.*)

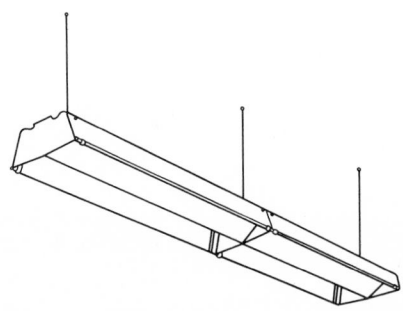

FIG. 84 *Closed-end type of steel fluorescent luminaire.* (*The Wakefield Div., ITT Corp.*)

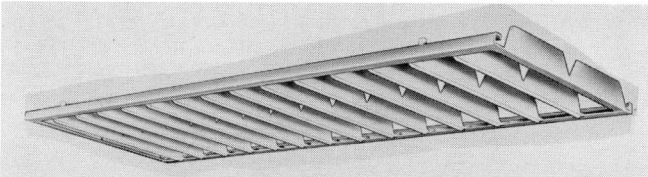

FIG. 85   *Louver for use with open-type fluorescent luminaire.   (The Miller Co.)*

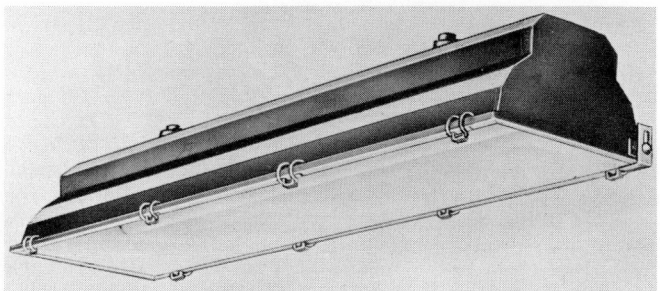

FIG. 86   *Closed-type fluorescent luminaire for hazardous locations.   (Benjamin Div., Thomas Industries, Inc.)*

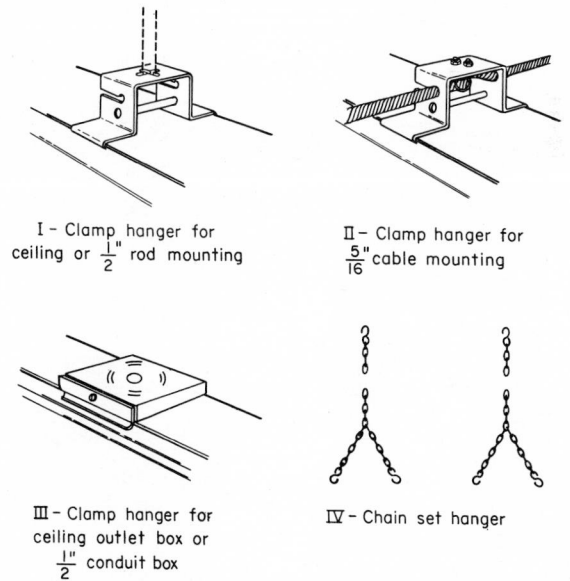

I – Clamp hanger for ceiling or $\frac{1}{2}$" rod mounting

II – Clamp hanger for $\frac{5}{16}$" cable mounting

III – Clamp hanger for ceiling outlet box or $\frac{1}{2}$" conduit box

IV – Chain set hanger

FIG. 87   *Methods of suspension for industrial fluorescent luminaires.   (The Miller Co.)*

just a plain reflector, or the reflector may be fitted with a longitudinal shield or with louvers (refer to Fig. 85).   The shield is positioned between the lamps and provides a crosswise shielding angle of approximately 27 deg from the horizontal.   Closed units are provided with glass or plastic covers across the bottom of the luminaire.   Closed units with sealed covers are available for hazardous locations (see Fig. 86).

Different mounting methods are shown in Figs. 87 and 88.

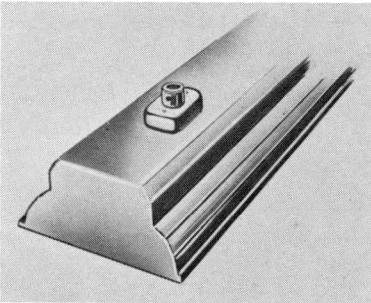

FIG. 88 *Fluorescent luminaire with boss for rod suspension from ceiling.* (*Benjamin Div., Thomas Industries, Inc.*)

213. The ballast for fluorescent lamps is mounted in the supporting channel or base of the luminaire. The construction to accommodate the ballast for one type of industrial unit is shown in Fig. 89.

214. Fluorescent luminaires for commercial lighting are made in a great variety of types. They can be obtained to produce illumination of any one of the different systems of illumination listed in Sec. **188,** item 1. All the various materials listed in Sec. **188,** item 4, are employed for the reflection and diffusion of the light in fluorescent luminaires of the different constructions available. Probably the best method of obtaining an appreciation of all the various types available is through a study of the latest catalogs of fixture manufacturers.

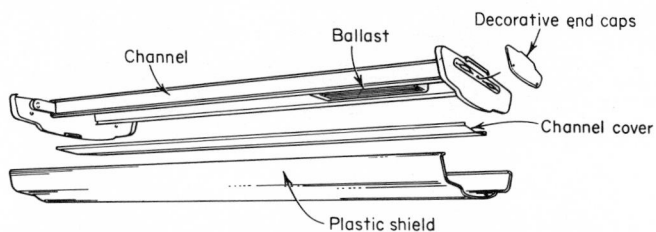

FIG. 89 *Construction of semiindirect fluorescent luminaire.* (*Westinghouse Electric Corp.*)

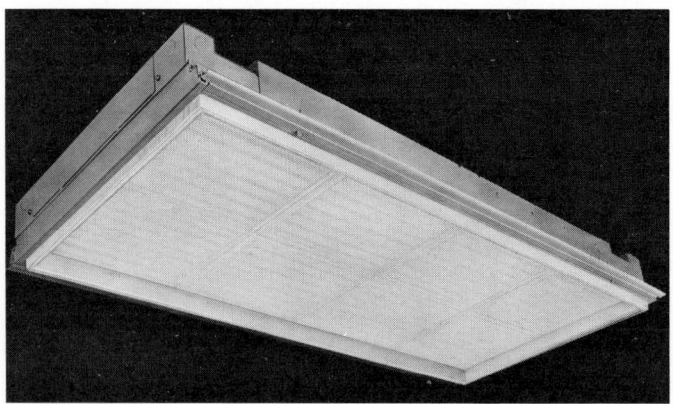

FIG. 90 *Large-area fluorescent ceiling unit.* (*Holophane Co., Inc.*)

Commercial fluorescent luminaires may be classified as follows:
1. Large-area ceiling units.
2. Troffers.
3. Conventional suspended or surface units.

Large-area ceiling units (refer to Figs. 90, 90A, and 91) are available in 2- by 2-, 2- by 4-, and 4- by 4-ft panels which can be mounted to achieve almost any geometrical design. The luminous surface of the panels may be made of glass or plastic. Units are available for surface or recess mounting.

FIG. 90A   *Illumination with large-area fluorescent ceiling units.   (Westinghouse Electric Corp.)*

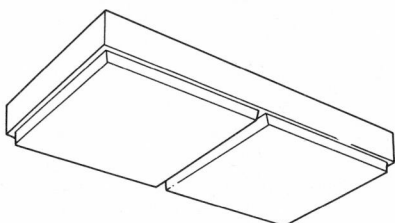

FIG. 91   *Large-area surface-mounted fluorescent lighting.   (Benjamin Div., Thomas Industries, Inc.)*

Translucent wall-to-wall lighting (Fig. 92) is illumination by means of one large luminous area. It does not employ luminaires unless the whole luminous ceiling is considered one large luminaire. The diffusing panels for wall-to-wall lighting may be of plastic or louver construction.

Troffers are fluorescent luminaires which are mounted in recesses in the ceiling so that the surface of the unit is practically flush with the ceiling. A typical troffer luminaire is shown in Fig. 93, and the method of installing troffers in a suspended plaster ceiling in Fig. 94. Troffers are available for installation in almost any type of ceiling. Troffers (Fig. 95) may be of the open type, louvered, or covered with a glass, prismatic-glass, or plastic cover.

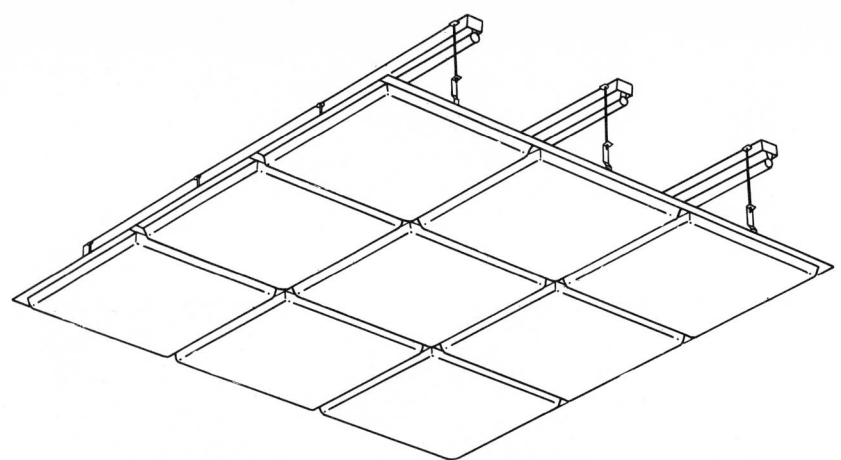

FIG. 92 *Wall-to-wall fluorescent lighting.* (*The Wakefield Div., ITT Corp.*)

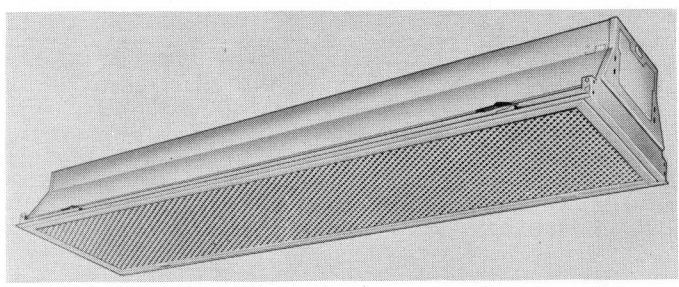

FIG. 93 *Troffer fluorescent luminaire.* (*The Miller Co.*)

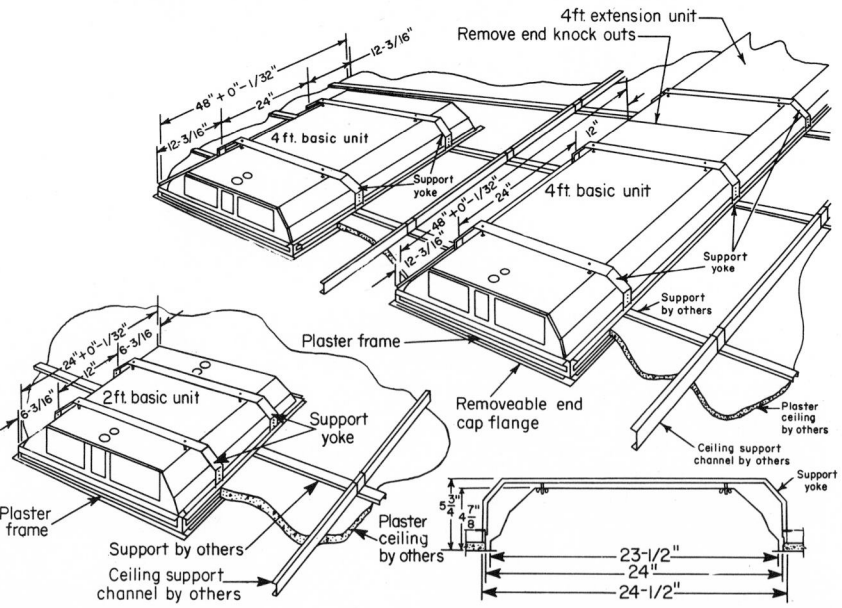

FIG. 94 *Installation of flanged troffers in a suspended plaster ceiling.* (*The Wakefield Div., ITT Corp.*)

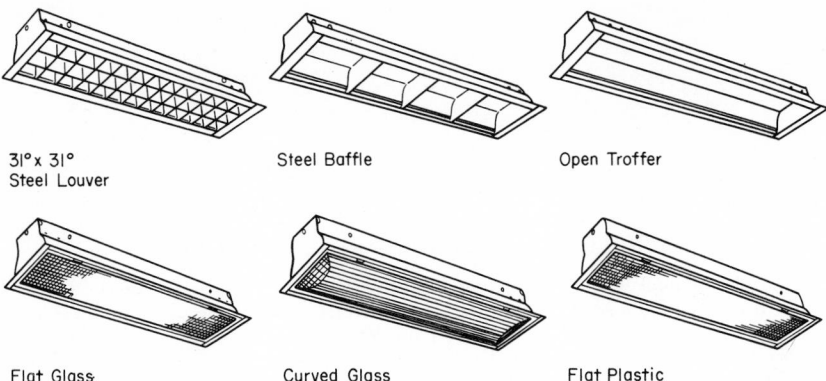

31° x 31°
Steel Louver

Steel Baffle

Open Troffer

Flat Glass

Curved Glass

Flat Plastic

FIG. 95 *Covers for troffer luminaires.* (*Benjamin Div., Thomas Industries, Inc.*)

Conventional suspended or surface luminaires (Figs. 96 and 97) are available in units for producing illumination of any one of the different systems.

215. The size of luminaire for incandescent lamps should be such that the wattage rating of the lamp to be used with it will correspond to the wattage rating of the luminaire. This is necessary for the proper distribution of light, for adequate dissipation of the heat produced by the lamp, and for preventing excessive brightness of the unit. An exception to this is that a smaller-sized lamp can be used if an adapter is used in the socket to bring the lamp bowl into the proper position in the luminaire. When replacing lamps, always use the same size as was used previously unless careful investigation is made as to whether a different size will be satisfactory.

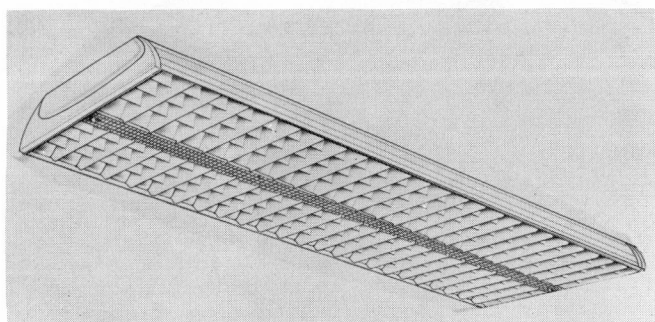

I. *The Miller Co.*

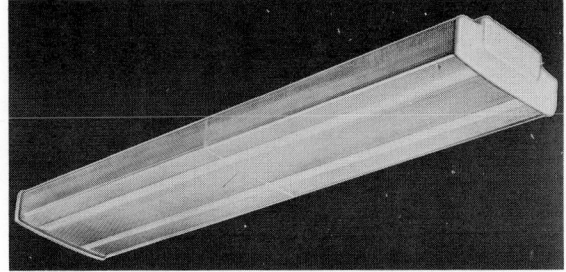

II. *Holophane Co., Inc.*

FIG. 96 *Direct-indirect fluorescent luminaires.*

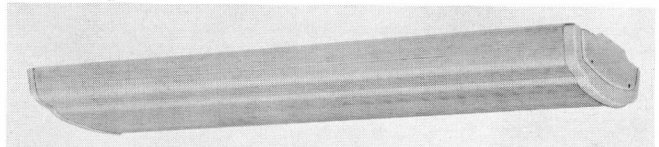

FIG. 97 *Semiindirect fluorescent luminaire. (Westinghouse Electric Corp.)*

PRINCIPLES OF LIGHTING-INSTALLATION DESIGN

216. The general purpose of artificial lighting is to enable things to be seen readily. Since things are seen by the light which is reflected from them (see Brightness, Sec. **39**) into the eye, it is necessary, in an effective lighting installation, that the lighting units be of such number and so arranged as to render most easily seen those things which it is desired to see. To accomplish this, recognition must be made of the effect of light on the human eye.

217. Physiological Features of Artificial Lighting. To appreciate properly the principles of scientific lighting, it is necessary to understand the mechanism of the eye. Figure 98 (from "Primer of Illumination," copyright by Illuminating Engineering Society) shows the parts of the eye as they would appear if it were cut through from back to front vertically. In the process of seeing, the light passes through the cornea, pupil, and lens of the eye to the retina, just as in a camera light passes through the lens to the sensitized film. The picture is formed on the retina, which is a layer made up of the ends of nerve fibers which gather into the optic nerve and go directly to the brain.

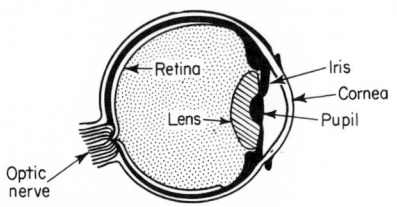

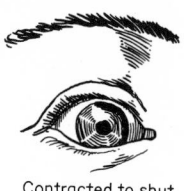

Expanded when illumination is dim   Contracted to shut out excessive light

FIG. 98 *Essential parts of the eye shown in section.*

FIG. 99 *Expansion and contraction of the pupil of the eye.*

218. The optic nerve sends along the picture to the brain. The lens of the eye, unlike that of the camera, automatically changes in thickness to focus or make a clear image on the retina for seeing at different distances. This focusing action is called the accommodation of the eye, and when the light is dim or bad, the focusing muscle vainly hunts for some focus which may make objects look clear and gets tired in trying to do it. The muscles which move the eye about also get tired in the same way, and the result is eyestrain, which stirs up pain and headache just as any other overtired muscles of the body may set up an ache.

219. The iris (which gives the eye its color) serves to regulate the amount of light which reaches the eye. In very dim light it opens out making the pupil big, as shown in Fig. 99, and in very bright light it shuts up as shown and thus keeps out a flood of brilliant light which might hurt the retina. The protective action of the pupil is fairly good but by no means complete, for it seldom becomes smaller than shown in the illustration, however bright the light. From a study of Fig. 99 we may deduce:

1. When trying to see any object, do not allow a light to shine into the eyes, and do not face a brightly lighted area. In addition to tiring the retina, the superfluous light causes the pupil to contract, so that less light from the lighted object reaches the retina. An object which would seem well lighted in a room with dark walls and with no light shining in the eyes will appear poorly lighted in a bright room with light walls or when

a light is shining in the eyes, simply because the pupil is smaller. This also explains why a higher light intensity is necessary in the daytime than at night. It is generally easier to read with the same light source in a room having dark walls than if the walls are light in color—though the total illumination on the page will probably be less. Reflected light from glossy paper produces the same effect as light surroundings. The effect produced by a light shining directly into the eyes is termed *glare* (see Sec. 38).

2. A fluctuating light causes the pupil to be constantly changing. This is very tiring to the muscles which control the iris and if long continued may even work a permanent injury.

3. The lens of the eye is not corrected, as is a photographic lens, for color variations. It cannot focus sharply red and blue light from the same object simultaneously, although this is ordinarily not noticed. As white light is composed of all colors, it follows that we can see more clearly, i.e., objects appear sharper and more distinct, by a monochromatic light (light of only one color) than even by daylight. The light from the mercury-vapor lamps closely approximates this condition.

4. Illumination should be uniform; otherwise the eye, in continually attempting to adapt itself to the unequal conditions, becomes tired in the same way as with a fluctuating light.

Correct lighting enables one to see clearly with minimum tiring of the eyes. To secure this, all the above conditions must be satisfied.

220. The requirements of a satisfactory lighting installation (Ward Harrison, "Electric Lighting") are (1) sufficient light of unvarying intensity on all principal surfaces, whether horizontal, vertical, or oblique planes; (2) a comparable intensity of light on adjacent areas and on the walls; (3) light of a color and spectral character suited to the purpose for which it is employed; (4) freedom from glare and from glaring reflections; (5) light so directed and diffused as to prevent objectionable shadows or contrasts of intensity; (6) a lighting effect appropriate for the location and lighting units which are in harmony with their surroundings, whether lighted or unlighted; (7) a system which is simple, reliable, easy of maintenance, and in initial and operating cost not out of proportion to the results attained. The neglect of any one of these requirements may result in an unsatisfactory installation.

221. Intensity of Illumination. Although the eye is capable of adjusting itself to perceive objects over a wide range of intensities, the speed of this perception and the ability to distinguish fineness of detail is improved as the intensity increases, until the intensity becomes so great that a blinding effect is produced. An intensity of illumination that will be so high as to produce a blinding effect is, however, far above the range of intensities utilized in artificial illumination. The effect of the intensity of illumination upon the length of time required for the perception of objects is shown in Fig. 100. The effect of the intensity of illumination upon the length of time required for the discrimination of detail is shown in Fig. 101. From a study of the curve of

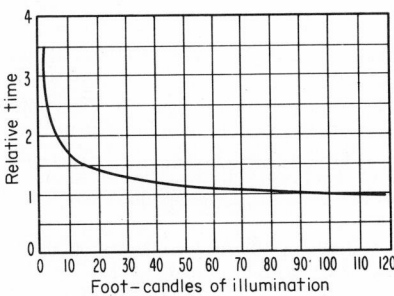

FIG. 100 *Effect of intensity of illumination upon time required for perception.* (*General Electric Co., Nela Park Engineering Dept.*)

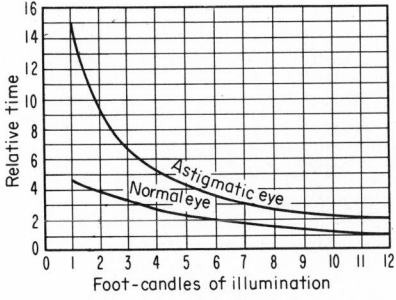

FIG. 101 *Effect of intensity of illumination upon time required for discrimination of detail.* (*General Electric Co., Nela Park Engineering Dept.*)

Fig. 100 it is seen that the speed of perception increases approximately proportionally to the intensity of illumination, until an illumination of 5 ft-c is reached. Above this point the increase in speed of perception for a given increase in intensity gradually decreases. From these facts it was at one time erroneously considered that intensities of illumination above 5 ft-c were of little practical value in making things more clearly seen. That this is not true has been definitely proved not only by laboratory tests but also by practical tests in actual working areas. High levels of illumination have been found to result in an actual saving in dollars and cents owing to the increased production and decrease in spoilage produced by their use. Recommended values of intensities are given in Table **243.**

222. Blink Test. In order to have some definite and scientific way of measuring eyestrain and fatigue, the General Electric Co. devised the "blink" test. In this test the number of blinks per minute which the eye makes involuntarily are counted. This is done when the eyes are in a rested condition and then again after an hour of work at the various usual tasks of the individual under different levels of illumination. The rate of increase in blinking is taken as a measure of eye and nerve fatigue. The rate of blinking always increases some with working or reading, but the higher the illumination intensity, up to at least 75 or 100 ft-c, the lower is the rate of blinking, especially where attention to fine detail is required. The results of these tests have been considered in making up the values for Table **243.**

223. Elimination of Glare. The greatest care should be exercised in designing a lighting installation to avoid the presence of any one of the three types of glare described in Sec. **38.** In order that a lighting unit which is in the central portion of the visual field may not produce glare, its brightness should not exceed from 2 to 3 candles per sq in. of apparent area. If the eyes are not to be fatigued when the unit is viewed continually, the brightness should not exceed $1/2$ candle per sq in. of apparent area. The maximum permissible brightness is, of course, influenced by the darkness of the surroundings.

No less important than the elimination of direct glare is the avoidance of reflected glare or specular reflection. Its effects are often more harmful than those due to direct glare. The use of highly polished furniture, plate-glass desk tops, and glossy finishes on walls should be avoided. A large expanse of too-light-finished wall surface will be a cause of harmful glare in offices, schoolrooms, and other locations where the occupants of the room must sit facing the wall for long periods of time. Although it is always desirable to have walls finished in light colors such as cream or buff in order to utilize as effectively as possible the light emitted by the source, the reflection factor of the lower walls should not be so high as to cause eye fatigue to the occupants. For rooms where the occupants must face the walls for long periods of time, the reflection factor of the part of the wall below eye level should not be greater than 50 per cent.

224. Production of Shadows. The character of the shadow cast by an object depends upon the uniformity of the illumination in the area and upon the direction of the light falling upon the object. If the light falling upon an object is coming from one direction only, a sharp dense shadow will be cast. As the number of the directions in which light is impinging upon an object is increased, the sharpness and denseness of the shadow cast will be reduced. A shadow will still be cast even if the object is illuminated from all directions unless the intensity of the illumination is the same in all directions. In order, therefore, completely to eliminate shadows, the illumination must be uniform and completely diffused, i.e., so the illumination of any point will be produced by light from all directions. The less uniform the illumination is or the fewer the directions of light falling upon an object, the more dense and sharp will be the shadows cast.

The desirability of shadows in an illuminated area depends upon the nature of the installation. In no installation is it desirable to have complete uniformity of illumination, i.e., illumination with no shadows or contrast in the intensity of illumination. Such illumination would produce a cold and flat effect that would be tiresome to the eye. Nor could the shape and contour of objects be discerned. On the other hand, it is equally bad to have illumination which results in very dark, dense shadows and excessive contrasts in the intensity of illumination of different areas. Such illumination would be very hard on the eyes, owing to the continual change in the size of the pupil as the field of vision is varied. When shadows are too dark, an object cannot be distinguished from its shadow, the shape of the object is not clearly seen, and objects in the shadows are not discernible. These conditions are frequent causes of accidents in poorly illuminated areas.

Shadows of the proper quality are of great value in observing objects in their three dimensions, in determining the shape of an object, and in determining irregularities in surfaces. They are of no value in the observation of plane surfaces. Shadows should never be dark and dense. Where shadows are essential, they should be soft and luminous so that the object is clearly discernible from its shadow and so that there is no great marked contrast in intensity of illumination.

225. Uniformity of illumination is usually expressed as a maximum deviation from the average or mean intensity of illumination. It is not necessary to have the illumination of an area exactly uniform in order that the contrasts in the illumination of different portions will be unobservable by the eye or so that the shadows will be too dense or sharp. The degree of uniformity of illumination obtained depends upon the ratio of the spacing distance of the lighting units to their mounting heights. For any reflector there is a maximum spacing of the units for a given mounting height that should not be exceeded if satisfactory uniformity of illumination is to be obtained. The effect of the spacing of the units upon the uniformity of illumination is illustrated in Fig. 102. Although this maximum spacing distance varies somewhat for reflectors giving different distribution of the light emitted by them, it is a good general rule to make the spacing distance equal to the mounting height. A greater spacing distance is likely to result in sharp and too dense shadows. One need not hesitate to use a closer spacing distance than that equal to the mounting height if desired, since the closer the spacing, the more uniform will be the illumination of the area. For the

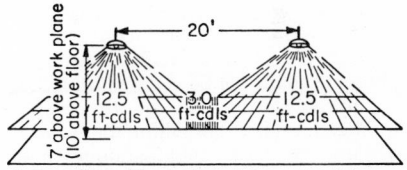

I- Nonuniform illumination, too great spacing between units. (Foot candle values based on 200-watt units.)

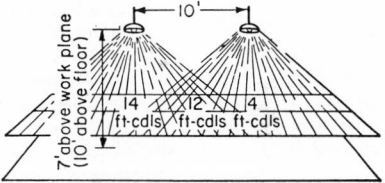

II- Uniform illumination, proper spacing of units. (Foot candle values based on 200-watt units.)

FIG. 102 *Effect of spacing of outlets on uniformity of illumination.*

average installation it is best to keep the spacing distance of the units within the values recommended for specific luminaires. If the ceiling is unusually high, closer spacing distances may be advisable in order to reduce the density of the shadows. In the illumination of certain areas such as storage spaces, it is permissible to space the units slightly farther apart.

226. Methods of Illumination. With respect to the arrangement of the light sources the methods of illumination may be divided into four classes as follows:

1. Localized.
2. General.
3. Group or localized general.
4. Combination of general and localized.

In the **localized method** an individual lighting unit of small wattage is supplied for each worker, machine, or workbench; the units are supported at a low level so as to bring the light close to the work. There is no attempt to produce uniform illumination over the total area.

With the **general illumination method** the lighting units are supported fairly close to the ceiling or at least a considerable distance above the working plane. They are spaced uniformly throughout the area without special regard to the location of machinery, furniture, etc., and at such a distance from one another as to give nearly uniform illumination.

The **group method** is somewhat of a compromise between the localized and general methods. The lighting units are mounted close to the ceiling or at a considerable distance above the working plane. The units are not spaced uniformly but are located with respect to the machinery, position of operators, etc., so as to give sufficient illumination for work at each machine. The illumination of the area is not uniform.

In the **combination of general and localized methods** uniform illumination is supplied over the complete area by means of units located according to the general method. This illumination is supplemented with local lights for certain operations that require a higher intensity than that required for the main area.

227. Comparison of Methods of Illumination. The localized arrangement of lighting units in industrial and most commercial applications should be a thing of the past and should never be tolerated. It produces very dense shadows and such low intensities in the general area that it is likely to be the cause of very serious accidents. Such a method will prove to be very harmful to the occupants of the room, owing to direct glare from the low-hung lamps, and may so blind the operators of machines that they will be severely injured.

For the great majority of installations the general method of arranging the light sources is the most satisfactory. It is the method most commonly employed. For some classes of work which require a very high intensity of illumination at the working point, it would not be economical to light the whole area to this high intensity. These conditions can be satisfactorily met by means of the combination of the general and localized methods, provided the local lamps are well shielded to prevent the possibility of glare. With the combination method the ratio of local to general illumination intensity should not be greater than 10:1. In other words, if some operations require 75 ft-c the general illumination should be not less than 7½ ft-c.

In some places where there are machines with large overhanging parts and in rooms with high obstructions, the group method will direct the light upon the working parts better than the general arrangement. The group method is frequently a good arrangement for rooms containing a number of similar machines arranged in rows.

228. Effect of Proportions of Room. Of the light which strikes the walls of a room, only part is reflected back into the room to become useful upon the working plane. Consequently, the greater the proportion of the total light that is directed to the walls, the lower is the intensity of illumination on the working plane, or stated in another way, the greater the proportion of the total light that is directed to the walls, the larger must the lamps be to produce a given intensity on the working plane. The proportion of the light that strikes the walls depends upon the size of the room and the height at which the units are mounted. In a large room the ratio between the wall area and the floor area is less than for a small room. Thus, for the same mounting height a smaller proportion of the total light will strike the walls than in a small room. In large rooms, therefore, less light is absorbed by the walls than in small rooms.

In a room of given dimensions, if the mounting height of the units is increased, more light will fall upon the walls. One should be careful not to get the impression that it is best to mount the units as low as possible. Although less light is absorbed by the walls with low-hung units, there are other more important factors that are affected by the mounting height. As the mounting height of the units is reduced, the spacing between them must also be reduced in order to produce uniform illumination and so that the shadows will not be too dense. The cost of installing a large number of small units is greater than that of installing a smaller number of larger units. Also, the larger-sized lamps are much more efficient with respect to the number of lumens produced per watt. As a result, the saving from the use of large units mounted high more than offsets the increased absorption of light by the walls. For practically all installations it is best to mount the units as high as possible. There is less probability of glare with high-mounted units than with low-hung ones, since the units are not so likely to be in the field of view.

228A. Room Cavity Ratios. A room cavity ratio is used as the measure of the effect of room proportions upon the useful utilization of the light given out by the luminaire. Values of room cavity ratios are given in Table A of Sec. **238**. The room cavity ratio serves as a reference index for use with Tables **240, 241,** and **242** in determining the coefficient of utilization.

229. Effect of Character of Finish of Walls. Of the light that falls upon the walls or ceiling of a room, the percentage that is reflected back into the room depends upon the color of the wall and ceilings and the type of paint employed. The lighter the color, the greater will be the coefficient of reflection. The reflection factor of two freshly painted walls of practically the same color may differ, however, by several per cent, depending upon the grade of paint employed. The reflection factor of a surface decreases as time elapses after the painting. The amount of this depreciation in reflecting power varies widely with different grades of paint. It is important to have the walls and ceiling light in color and to employ a good grade of paint which will have a high initial reflection factor that does not depreciate an excessive amount with age. The walls, however, should not be made so bright as to be a source of glare (see Sec. 223).

230. Location of Lighting Equipment. The lighting units for general illumination should be located symmetrically throughout the area to be illuminated. When the room is divided into bays by means of columns, roof trusses, or girders, or when the ceiling is divided into panels, the units should be arranged symmetrically, for the sake of appearance, with respect to such architectural divisions, provided it will not interfere with the uniformity of illumination. Fluorescent luminaires generally are arranged in rows or in some other symmetrical pattern which will fit in with the architectural arrangement of the area and the utilization of the space. Incandescent and mercury-vapor units generally are arranged in the form of squares or rectangles. Typical layouts are shown in Fig. 103.

It is important that the units be placed at the centers of squares and not at the corners. Figure 104 shows a method of locating outlets which is undesirable because it gives a very low intensity of illumination near the walls compared with that at the center of the room. Figure 105 shows the correct method of locating outlets in the centers of the squares. In certain cases, notably in office lighting and in rooms with benches located along the walls, it may, to minimize shadows, be desirable to place the outer rows of outlets somewhat nearer the side walls of the room than they would be if symmetrically arranged as shown in Fig. 105.

In laying out a lighting installation the maximum permissible spacing distance for the production of uniform illumination and satisfactory density of shadows should be determined first. The maximum permissible spacing for direct, semidirect, or general diffusing luminaires depends upon the candlepower-distribution characteristics of the luminaire.

When the maximum spacing has been determined, then locate the units on a plan of the area so that they will be located symmetrically with respect to architectural conditions and at the same time will not exceed the maximum permissible spacing distance.

When the outlets are located above traveling cranes, the staggered system (Fig. 103e) is preferable so that, as the crane moves along, it cuts off the light from only one unit at a time. If it is not desired to use the staggered system, additional lighting outlets, with special shock-absorbing sockets, should be located on the underside of the crane truss so that, as the crane moves along, the light from those units replaces the light from the regular outlets which are cut off by the crane.

In buildings of mill-type construction the units are usually supported on the lower chord of the roof truss or suspended from the roof purlins. When the units are mounted on the lower chord of the roof truss, the illumination near the walls at each end of the building is low. When work must be carried on in these areas, it is better to support the units from the purlins or to locate a row of angle units along each end wall.

High mounting is desirable because then the lamps are out of the way of cranes and are less apt to be broken, the glare is reduced to a minimum, and in the case of a light ceiling there is more reflection and better diffusion of light. The lamps should be lowered in locations where there is horizontal overhead belting, to the level of the bottom of the belting; otherwise a portion of the light is ineffective. It may be necessary, for the same reason, to install two or three units in an area where the conditions would otherwise warrant only one unit.

231. Reflection factor is the percentage of light reflected from a surface, such as a

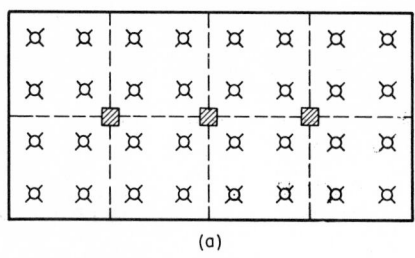

(a)

Four units per bay— This is the most common system for the square bay of usual dimensions.

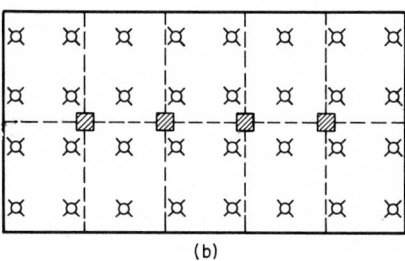

(b)

Four-two system — This is equivalent to three units per bay and is an alternative to four per bay where spacing allows.

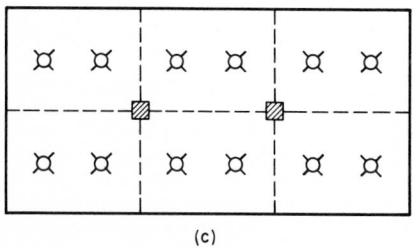

(c)

Two units per bay— Usually applicable only in narrow bays where the width is less than two-thirds the length.

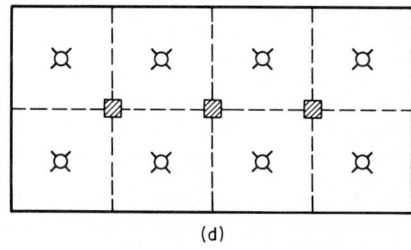

(d)

One unit per bay — A very common practice, but satisfactory only where bay size is no greater than the maximum permissible spacing— an unusual condition.

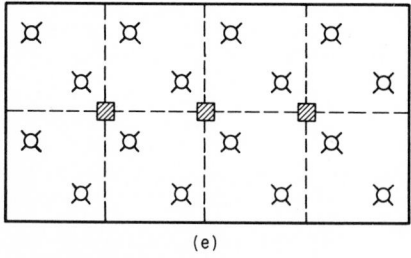

(e)

Staggered system— A recourse where one unit per bay is unsatisfactory and where four per bay is unnecessary. Less favorable appearance, and certain areas near walls may be inadequately lighted. Often expensive to wire.

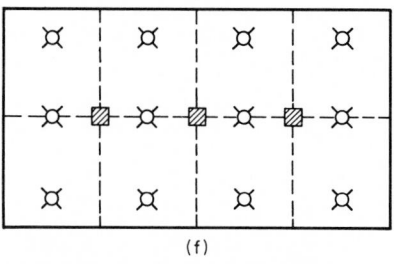

(f)

Interspaced system — Applicable in rectangular bays where one unit per bay would exceed the permissible spacing in one direction, and where center row will not interfere with future structural arrangements, such as added office partitions.

FIG. 103 *Layouts of lighting units for symmetrical spacing.* (*General Electric Co., Nela Park Engineering Dept.*)

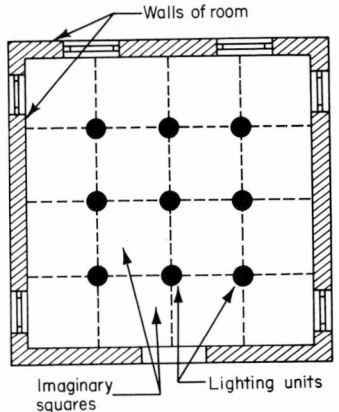

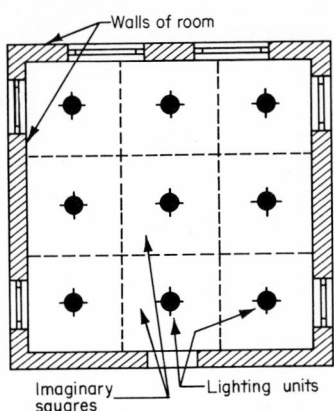

FIG. 104 *Incorrect arrangement of light-ing units.*   FIG. 105 *Correct arrangement of lighting units.*

wall or ceiling, to the total light falling on the surface. The difference between the reflection factor and 100 per cent represents the percentage of light which is absorbed by the surface and lost. Reflection factors for some of the common colors are given in Table **239A.** The reflection factor varies with the roughness of the surface as well as with the darkness of the color.

232. The coefficient of utilization is the over-all efficiency of the lighting installation: the ratio of the useful lumens which get down to the working plane to the total lumens generated by the lamp. Tables **240, 241,** and **242** give values for the coefficient of utilization for different types of luminaires, subdivided according to room cavity ratios and reflection factors for walls and for the ceiling. For more complete data refer to the "IES Lighting Handbook."

233. Maintenance of Lighting Equipment. The intensity of illumination produced by a lighting installation will be somewhat less, after the system has been in use for some time, than the intensity was when the system was first installed. This depreciation in the lighting system is due to the decrease in efficiency of the filament of the lamp and use and to the decrease in reflecting efficiency of the reflecting equipment, walls, and ceiling, which is the result of the natural deterioration of the surface with age, and of the collection of dust and dirt.

In the design of lighting installations, a maintenance factor is used to take into account this depreciation. It has values less than unity, so that when the initial illumination is multiplied by the maintenance factor, the actual illumination after a period of several months' use will be obtained.

The amount of depreciation will vary from 25 to 45 per cent, corresponding to a maintenance factor of 0.75 to 0.55, depending upon the type and material of the reflecting equipment, the system of illumination employed, the local conditions of dust and dirt, and the frequency of cleaning of equipment and repainting of walls. All lighting units should be adequately cleaned at regular intervals in order to prevent a waste of energy and low intensity of illumination. The frequency for the cleaning periods depends upon the degree of prevalence of dust and dirt and upon the type of luminaire.

234. There are four principal methods used in calculating illumination:
1. Point-by-point method.
2. Lumen-per-foot method.
3. Zonal cavity method (general lighting).
4. Beam-lumens method (floodlighting).

235. The point-by-point method is based on the inverse-square law that the intensity of light flux varies inversely as the square of the distance from the light source to the point of measurement (see Sec. **26** and Fig. 106). The illumination on any plane perpendicular to the light rays is given by the following formula:

$$\text{Foot-candles (on perpendicular plane)} = \frac{cp}{D^2} \tag{7}$$

where cp = the candlepower of the light source in the direction in which the distance D is taken; and D = the perpendicular distance from the light source to the illuminated plane in feet.

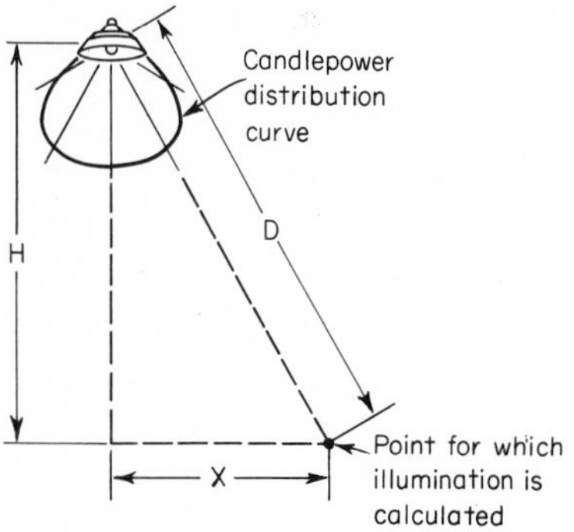

FIG. 106 *Point-by-point method of lighting calculations.*

Since the illumination of the horizontal plane is the value usually desired, the formula must be multiplied by the ratio H/D (see Fig. 106) or

$$\text{Foot-candles (on horizontal plane)} = \frac{cp \times H}{D^3} \tag{8}$$

If the illumination on a vertical plane is desired, the basic formula (7) must be multiplied by the ratio X/D (see Fig. 106) or

$$\text{Foot-candles (on vertical plane)} = \frac{cp \times X}{D^3} \tag{8a}$$

The illumination at any point is obtained by adding the foot-candles due to each light source which is sending rays of light to the point.

It is obvious that the point-by-point method is practical for use only with the direct type of lighting, for with any other system of illumination the number of light sources which would have to be considered would make the calculations prohibitively tedious. Even with the direct system it is usually necessary to calculate the foot-candles from several different light sources. This method is especially applicable to calculating localized lighting where only a single light source needs to be considered.

236. Lumen-per-foot Method (General Electric Co.). The predetermining of lighting levels for supplementary lighting systems in which continuous linear sources are used can be accomplished from empirical data based on the lumens per foot of the source. These data are adaptable for relatively short distances between the light source and the work or display where the inverse-square law obviously does not apply. The lumen-per-foot method employs the following formulas:

Where the lamp and reflector have been selected,

$$\text{Foot-candles} = K \times \text{lumens per foot of source}$$

Where a foot-candle level is desired,

$$\text{Necessary lumens per foot} = \frac{\text{foot-candles desired}}{K}$$

In the formulas the constant K refers, respectively, to either one of two constants K_H or K_V as given in Tables A, B, C, and D for horizontal and vertical illumination.

Two types of luminaires are specified: broad distribution as from a unit with a mat-finish reflector and narrow distribution as from a polished metal reflector. The beam in both cases is presumed to be aimed at a plane 4 ft from the source through point A.

The importance of the reflector is evident from a comparison of Tables C and D. The average K value at 4 ft in C is 0.009; in D, 0.021. This difference is 133 per cent.

The actual values from which the tables were compiled are readings taken at the mid-point of luminaires 12 ft in length. For conventional lighting systems, the foot-candle levels would normally drop at the ends of rows unless additional lamps or lamps of higher output are provided.

Table A. Horizontal Illumination

Horizontal ft-c $= K_H \times$ lamp—lumens per foot

Broad distribution—white enamel reflector

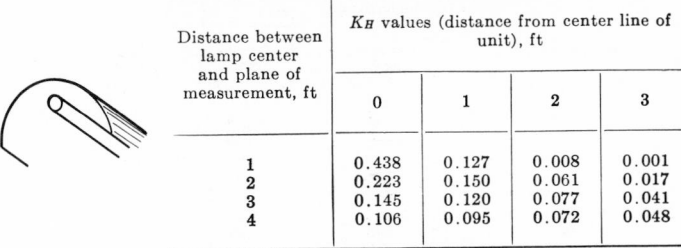

Distance between lamp center and plane of measurement, ft	K_H values (distance from center line of unit), ft			
	0	1	2	3
1	0.438	0.127	0.008	0.001
2	0.223	0.150	0.061	0.017
3	0.145	0.120	0.077	0.041
4	0.106	0.095	0.072	0.048

Table B. Horizontal Illumination

Horizontal ft-c $= K_H \times$ lamp—lumens per foot

Narrow distribution—polished aluminum reflector

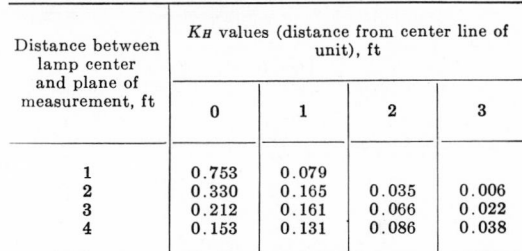

Distance between lamp center and plane of measurement, ft	K_H values (distance from center line of unit), ft			
	0	1	2	3
1	0.753	0.079		
2	0.330	0.165	0.035	0.006
3	0.212	0.161	0.066	0.022
4	0.153	0.131	0.086	0.038

Table C. Vertical Illumination

Vertical ft-c $= K_V \times$ lamp—lumens per foot

Broad distribution—white painted cornice, no reflector

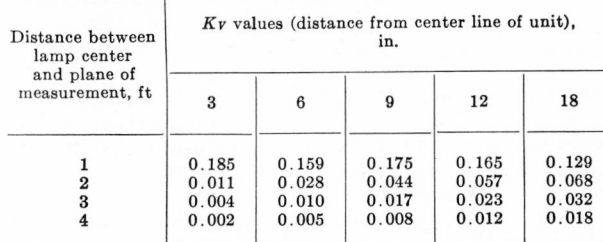

Distance between lamp center and plane of measurement, ft	K_V values (distance from center line of unit), in.				
	3	6	9	12	18
1	0.185	0.159	0.175	0.165	0.129
2	0.011	0.028	0.044	0.057	0.068
3	0.004	0.010	0.017	0.023	0.032
4	0.002	0.005	0.008	0.012	0.018

Table D. Vertical Illumination

Vertical ft-c $= K_V \times$ lamp—lumens per foot

Narrow distribution—polished aluminum reflector

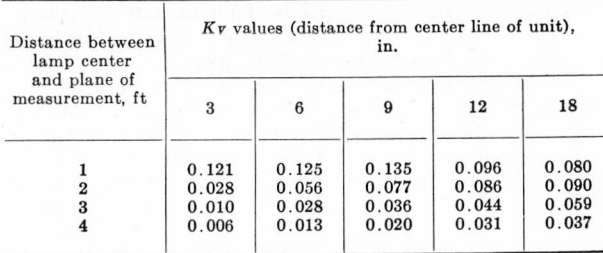

Distance between lamp center and plane of measurement, ft	K_V values (distance from center line of unit), in.				
	3	6	9	12	18
1	0.121	0.125	0.135	0.096	0.080
2	0.028	0.056	0.077	0.086	0.090
3	0.010	0.028	0.036	0.044	0.059
4	0.006	0.013	0.020	0.031	0.037

237. Lumens per Foot (Initial Lumens per Nominal Length) for Fluorescent Lamps
(Standard Cool White)[a]
(General Electric Co.)

General Line Lamps

Lamp designation	Lumens per ft	Lumens (initial)	Nominal length, in.
4WT-5	226	113	6
6WT-5	346	260	9
8WT-5	420	420	12
13WT-5	468	820	21
14WT-12	568	710	15
15WT-8	580	870	18
15WT-12	481	770	18
20WT-12	610	1,220	24
25WT-12	660	1,850	33
30WT-8	770	2,100	36
40WT-12	780	3,120	48
40WT-17	560	2,800	60
90WT-17	1,180	5,900	60
100WT-17	1,160	5,800	60

Slimline Lamps

Lamp designation	Lumens per ft	Lumens (initial)	Nominal length, in.	Watts
42″ T-6	500	1,750	42	25.0
64″ T-6	525	2,800	64	40.0
72″ T-8	500	3,000	72	35.0
96″ T-8	513	4,100	96	50.0
48″ T-12	725	2,900	48	40.0
72″ T-12	733	4,400	72	55.0
96″ T-12	775	6,200	96	75.0

Rapid-start Lamps

48″ T-12	1,000	4,000	48	60.0
72″ T-12	1,075	6,450	72	85.0
96″ T-17	1,125	9,000	96	110.0

[a] For lumens per foot of other colors use the following multiplying factors: de luxe cool white 0.71; de luxe warm white 0.71; daylight 0.93, soft white 0.68, green 1.2, gold 0.6, blue 0.45, pink 0.45.

238. The Zonal-cavity Method. The lumen method of calculating illumination has been in use for many years, and is based on the theory that average illumination is equal to lumens divided by the work area over which they are distributed. Newer methods of analysis of lighting distributions, taking into account the concept of inter-reflection of light, have led to more accurate coefficient of utilization data, and have been adopted in the new Illuminating Engineering Society (IES) approved method of lighting calculations called the *zonal-cavity method*. This method provides increased flexibility in lighting calculations, including greater accuracy, but still adheres to the basic concept that foot-candles are equal to light flux over an area (the lumen method).

The zonal-cavity method assumes that an area to be lighted will be made up of a series of cavities which have effective reflectances with respect to one another and to the work plane. Basically, the area is divided into three spaces, or cavities, a "ceiling cavity," a "room cavity," and a "floor cavity." These are shown graphically in Fig. 107.

In using the zonal-cavity method, there are four basic steps to be followed in making a calculation: (1) determine cavity ratios; (2) determine effective cavity reflectances; (3) select coefficient of utilization; (4) compute average foot-candle level.

STEP 1. DETERMINE CAVITY RATIOS. Cavity ratios may be determined by calculation, using formulas (13), (14) and (15) in Sec. **239,** which is the basic and most accurate method; or the values may be found in Table A, Cavity Ratios, in this section for typical sized cavities which cover a wide range of room dimensions. For a more complete table of cavity ratios, see Fig. 9-2 in the "IES Lighting Handbook," 4th edition.

Step 2. Determine Effective Cavity Reflectances. Table B in this section provides a means of converting the combination of actual wall and ceiling or actual wall and floor reflectances into a single effective ceiling cavity reflectance, ρcc, and a single effective floor cavity reflectance, ρfc. Note that if the luminaire is recessed or surface-mounted, or if the floor is the work plane, the ceiling cavity ratio or floor cavity ratio will be 0, and then the actual reflectance of the ceiling or floor will also be the effective reflectance. When using reflectance values of room surfaces, the expected maintained values should be used for calculation of maintained foot-candles, or if initial foot-candle values are desired, the initial reflectance values should be used.

Step 3. Select Coefficient of Utilization (CU). Using the ρcc, ρfc, and ρW (wall reflectance) determined in step 2, and knowing the room cavity ratio previously calculated in step 1, formula (14) in Sec. **239,** refer to the coefficient of utilization in the CU table for the luminaire under consideration. Tables showing CU values for currently typical popular types of luminaires are given in Tables **240, 241,** and **242.** For more complete data, see the "IES Lighting Handbook." Manufacturers of lighting equipment will also supply CU data for their own luminaires upon request. Note that since the CU tables are linear, linear interpolations can be made for exact cavity ratios or reflectance combinations.

Step 4. Compute Average Foot-Candle Level. Use the standard lumen method [formula (11) in Sec. **239**] to compute the foot-candle level that will be obtained. When maintained illumination levels are to be calculated, the maintenance factor (MF) should include lamp lumen depreciation (LLD), and luminaire dirt depreciation

Table A. Cavity Ratios
(From "IES Lighting Handbook," 4th ed.)

Room dimensions, feet		Cavity depth										
Width	Length	1.0	1.5	2.0	2.5	3.0	4.0	6	8	10	12	16
8	10	1.1	1.7	2.2	2.8	3.4	4.5	6.7	9.0	11.3		
	14	1.0	1.5	2.0	2.5	3.0	3.9	5.9	7.8	9.7	11.7	
	20	0.9	1.3	1.7	2.2	2.6	3.5	5.2	7.0	8.8	10.5	
10	10	1.0	1.5	2.0	2.5	3.0	4.0	6.0	8.0	10.0	12.0	
	14	0.9	1.3	1.7	2.1	2.6	3.4	5.1	6.9	8.6	10.4	
	20	0.7	1.1	1.5	1.9	2.3	3.0	4.5	6.0	7.5	9.0	12.0
	40	0.6	0.9	1.2	1.6	1.9	2.5	3.7	5.0	6.2	7.5	10.0
12	12	0.8	1.2	1.7	2.1	2.5	3.3	5.0	6.7	8.4	10.0	
	16	0.7	1.1	1.5	1.8	2.2	2.9	4.4	5.8	7.2	8.7	11.6
	36	0.6	0.8	1.1	1.4	1.7	2.2	3.3	4.4	5.5	6.6	8.8
	50	0.5	0.8	1.0	1.3	1.5	2.1	3.1	4.1	5.1	6.2	8.2
14	14	0.7	1.1	1.4	1.8	2.1	2.9	4.3	5.7	7.1	8.5	11.4
	20	0.6	0.9	1.2	1.5	1.8	2.4	3.6	4.9	6.1	7.3	9.8
	42	0.5	0.7	1.0	1.2	1.4	1.9	2.9	3.8	4.7	5.7	7.6
20	20	0.5	0.7	1.0	1.2	1.5	2.0	3.0	4.0	5.0	6.0	8.0
	45	0.4	0.5	0.7	0.9	1.1	1.4	2.2	2.9	3.6	4.3	5.8
	90	0.3	0.5	0.6	0.8	0.9	1.2	1.8	2.4	3.0	3.6	4.8
30	30	0.3	0.5	0.7	0.8	1.0	1.3	2.0	2.7	3.3	4.0	3.4
	60	0.3	0.4	0.5	0.6	0.7	1.0	1.5	2.0	2.5	3.0	4.0
	90	0.2	0.3	0.4	0.6	0.7	0.9	1.3	1.8	2.2	2.7	3.6
42	42	0.2	0.4	0.5	0.6	0.7	1.0	1.4	1.9	2.4	2.8	3.8
	90	0.2	0.3	0.3	0.4	0.5	0.7	1.0	1.4	1.7	2.1	2.8
	200	0.1	0.2	0.3	0.4	0.4	0.6	0.9	1.1	1.4	1.7	2.3
60	60	0.2	0.2	0.3	0.4	0.5	0.7	1.0	1.3	1.7	2.0	2.7
	100	0.1	0.2	0.3	0.3	0.4	0.5	0.8	1.1	1.3	1.6	2.1
	300	0.1	0.1	0.2	0.2	0.3	0.4	0.6	0.8	1.0	1.2	1.6
100	100	0.1	0.1	0.2	0.2	0.3	0.4	0.6	0.8	1.0	1.2	1.6
	300	0.1	0.1	0.1	0.2	0.2	0.3	0.4	0.5	0.7	0.8	1.1

(LDD). Light source manufacturers can supply the LLD factor for any type of lamps, and the LDD factor should be based upon the luminaire's dirt attraction or dirt retention characteristics, and the degree of dirtiness of the areas where it is to be used. Procedures for making these calculations are given in the "IES Lighting Handbook," 4th edition.

In making lighting calculations for a proposed project, the lighting designer should have all the facts required for use in his calculations. Included would be the end-use application of the space; the physical dimensions; the color and reflectance values of the ceiling, walls, and floor; the layout of furniture or machinery, including colors of the various furnishings, etc.; and a knowledge of the degree of cleanliness (or dirtiness) of the area which will affect maintenance of the lighting levels. The degree of accuracy of the lighting calculations is influenced directly by the degree of accuracy involved in these various factors. The zonal-cavity method of making lighting calculations offers a high degree of accuracy in the calculated results. But the results cannot be any more accurate than the data used to make the calculations, including estimates of maintenance factors.

Table B. Per Cent Effective Ceiling or Floor Cavity Reflectance for Various Reflectance Combinations
(From "IES Lighting Handbook," 4th ed.)

Ceiling or floor cavity ratio	% ceiling or floor reflectance														
	80			70			50			30			10		
	% wall reflectance														
	70	50	30	70	50	30	70	50	30	50	30	10	50	30	10
0	80	80	80	70	70	70	50	50	50	30	30	30	10	10	10
0.1	79	78	78	69	69	68	49	49	48	30	29	29	10	10	10
0.3	77	75	74	68	66	64	49	47	46	29	28	27	10	10	9
0.5	75	73	70	66	64	61	48	46	44	28	27	25	11	10	9
0.6	75	71	68	65	62	59	47	45	43	28	26	25	11	10	9
0.8	73	69	65	64	60	56	47	43	41	27	25	23	11	10	8
1.0	71	66	61	63	58	53	46	42	39	27	24	22	11	9	8
1.2	70	64	58	61	56	50	45	41	37	26	23	20	12	9	7
1.4	68	62	55	60	54	48	45	40	35	26	22	19	12	9	7
1.6	67	60	53	59	52	45	44	39	33	25	21	18	12	9	7
1.8	65	58	50	57	50	43	43	37	32	25	21	17	12	9	6
2.0	64	56	48	56	48	41	43	37	30	24	20	16	12	9	6
2.2	63	54	45	55	46	39	42	36	29	24	19	15	13	9	6
2.4	61	52	43	54	45	37	42	35	27	24	19	14	13	9	6
2.6	60	50	41	53	43	35	41	34	26	23	18	13	13	9	5
2.8	59	48	39	52	42	33	41	33	25	23	18	13	13	9	5
3.0	58	47	38	51	40	32	40	32	24	22	17	12	13	8	5
3.3	56	44	35	49	39	30	39	31	23	22	16	11	13	8	5
3.6	54	42	33	48	37	28	39	30	21	21	15	10	13	8	5
3.9	53	40	30	47	36	26	38	29	20	21	15	10	13	8	4
4.2	51	39	29	46	34	25	37	28	19	20	14	9	13	8	4
4.5	50	37	27	45	33	24	37	27	19	20	14	8	14	8	4
4.8	49	36	25	44	32	23	36	26	18	19	13	8	14	8	4
5.0	48	35	25	43	32	22	36	26	17	19	13	7	14	8	4

Table C. Factors for Effective Floor Cavity Reflectance Other than 20 Per Cent[a]
(From "IES Lighting Handbook," 4th ed.)

Factor	% effective ceiling cavity reflectance, ρcc							
	80		70		50		10	
	% wall reflectance, ρW							
	50	30	50	30	50	30	50	30
1	1.08	1.08	1.07	1.06	1.05	1.04	1.01	1.01
3	1.05	1.04	1.05	1.04	1.03	1.03	1.01	1.01
5	1.04	1.03	1.03	1.02	1.02	1.02	1.01	1.01
6	1.03	1.02	1.03	1.02	1.02	1.02	1.01	1.01
8	1.03	1.02	1.02	1.02	1.02	1.01	1.01	1.01
10	1.02	1.01	1.02	1.01	1.02	1.01	1.01	1.01

[a]For 30% effective floor cavity reflectance, multiply by appropriate factor above.
For 10% effective floor cavity reflectance, divide by appropriate factor above.

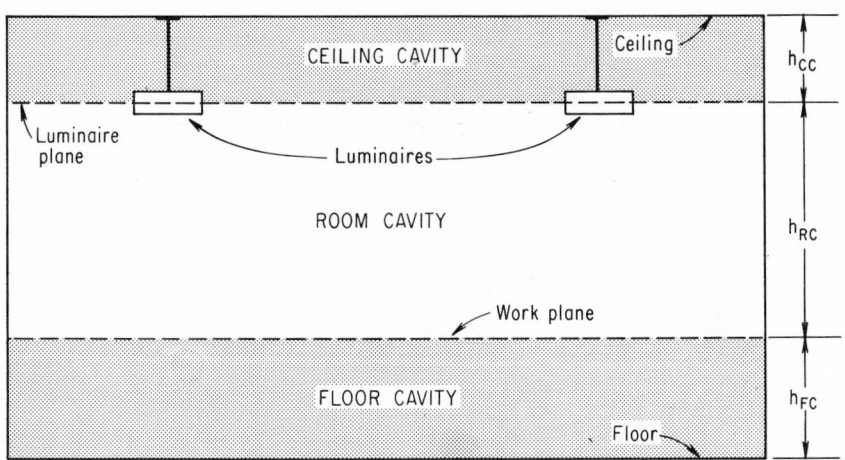

FIG. 107 *Basic cavity dimensions of space.*

239. Lighting Design Formulas.[1]
THE LUMEN METHOD.

$$\text{Foot-candles} = \frac{\text{lumens}}{\text{area in sq ft}} \tag{9}$$

$$\text{Initial FC} = \frac{\text{lamp lumens} \times \text{CU}}{\text{area in sq ft}} \tag{10}$$

$$\text{Maintained FC} = \frac{\text{LL} \times \text{CU} \times \text{MF}}{\text{area in sq ft}} \tag{11}$$

$$\text{MF} = \text{LLD} \times \text{LDD} \tag{12}$$

where FC = foot-candles
LL = lamp lumens
CU = coefficient of utilization
MF = maintenance factor
LLD = lamp lumen depreciation factor
LDD = luminaire dirt depreciation factor

[1] From "IES Lighting Handbook," 4th ed.

IES ZONAL CAVITY METHOD.
Ceiling cavity ratio:

$$CCR = \frac{5h_{cc}(L+W)}{L \times W}$$ (13)

Room cavity ratio:

$$RCR = \frac{5h_{rc}(L+W)}{L \times W}$$ (14)

Floor cavity ratio:

$$FCR = \frac{5h_{fc}(L+W)}{L \times W}$$ (15)

where h_{cc} = distance in ft from luminaire to ceiling
h_{rc} = distance in ft from luminaire to work plane
h_{fc} = distance in ft from work plane to floor
L = length of room in ft
W = width of room in ft

TABLES FOR INTERIOR ILLUMINATION DESIGN

239A. Reflection Factors of Colored Surfaces

Color	Reflection factor, per cent	Color	Reflection factor, per cent
Flat white............	75–85	Light green..........	40–50
Ivory...............	70–75	Gray...............	30–50
Buff.................	60–70	Blue...............	25–35
Yellow.............	55–65	Red................	15–20
Light tan............	45–55	Dark brown........	10–15

240. Incandescent Lighting
Coefficients of Utilization for Typical Luminaires ($\times$ 0.01)
Effective Floor Cavity Reflectance 20 Per Cent (ρfc = 0.20)
(Gotham Lighting Corp. and Sylvania Lighting Div.)

Room cavity ratio, RCR	Effective ceiling cavity reflectance, ρcc						Typical luminaires, description
	80		70		50		
	Wall reflectance, ρW						
	50	30	50	30	50	30	
							PAR-38 open unit
1	89	88	88	87	85	84	
2	83	81	82	80	81	79	
5	79	77	79	76	78	75	
6	78	75	77	75	77	75	
8	74	71	73	71	73	71	
10	71	69	71	69	71	69	
							PS-25 Fresnelens
1	69	68	69	68	66	65	
3	60	57	59	56	57	55	
5	52	48	51	47	50	47	
6	49	44	48	44	47	44	
8	42	38	41	37	40	37	
10	36	32	36	32	35	32	
							A-23 low brightness
1	59	58	58	57	56	55	
3	52	50	52	50	50	49	
5	47	44	46	44	46	43	
6	45	42	44	42	43	41	
8	39	37	39	36	39	36	
10	35	32	35	32	34	32	
							PAR-38 microgroove
1	72	72	70	70	68	68	
3	67	65	66	64	65	63	
5	63	60	62	60	61	59	
6	61	59	61	59	60	58	
8	58	56	58	56	57	56	
10	56	54	56	54	55	53	
							PAR-38 ellipsoidal unit
1	49	48	48	48	47	46	
3	45	44	45	43	44	42	
5	42	40	41	40	41	39	
6	40	38	40	38	39	38	
8	37	35	37	35	37	35	
10	35	33	35	33	34	33	

241. High-intensity Discharge Lighting
Coefficients of Utilization for Typical Luminaires ($\times$ 0.01)
Effective Floor Cavity Reflectance 20 Per Cent ($\rho fc = 0.20$)
("IES Lighting Handbook," 4th ed., and lighting manufacturers' published reference material)

Room cavity ratio, RCR	Coefficients of utilization						Typical luminaires, description

Effective ceiling cavity reflectance, ρcc / Wall reflectance, ρW

400W aluminum

ρcc	80		50		10	
ρW	50	30	50	30	50	30
1	89	87	81	79	72	71
3	77	72	71	68	65	63
5	65	60	62	58	57	54
6	61	56	57	53	54	50
8	52	46	49	45	46	43
10	42	36	39	35	37	37

400W H.P. sodium

ρcc	80		70		50	
ρW	50	30	50	30	50	30
1	88	86	86	84	82	81
3	77	73	76	72	73	70
5	67	63	66	62	65	61
6	63	58	62	58	61	57
8	56	51	54	51	54	50
10	48	44	46	44	47	43

400W R-60 mercury

ρcc	70		50		30	
ρW	50	30	50	30	50	30
1	103	100	99	96	93	91
3	82	75	79	73	72	68
5	64	56	62	56	54	50
6	54	49	53	48	47	43
8	40	36	39	36	35	33
10	27	25	27	25	24	23

400W prismatic reflector

RCR						
1	77	76	73	71	68	67
3	66	63	63	60	59	57
5	56	51	53	49	51	47
6	52	47	49	45	47	43
8	43	38	41	37	40	36
10	35	30	33	29	32	28

Coefficients of Utilization for Typical Luminaires ($\times$ 0.01)
Effective Floor Cavity Reflectance 20 Per Cent ($\rho fc = 0.20$)
("IES Lighting Handbook." and manufacturers' catalogs)

Room cavity ratio, RCR	Effective ceiling cavity reflectance, ρcc						Typical luminaires, description
	80		70		50		
	Wall reflectance, ρW						
	50	30	50	30	50	30	
							12″-wide troffer
1	73	70	70	68	66	64	
3	59	54	57	53	54	50	
5	47	42	46	41	44	39	
6	43	38	42	37	40	35	
8	35	30	34	29	32	28	
10	29	23	28	23	27	22	
							2′ × 4′ white troffer
1	69	66	67	65	65	63	
3	53	49	52	48	50	47	
5	42	36	41	36	40	34	
6	38	31	37	31	36	30	
8	30	25	30	25	29	24	
10	25	19	24	19	24	18	
							2′ × 2′ troffer (U-tubes)
1	71	69	69	67	67	65	
3	57	53	56	52	54	51	
5	46	41	46	41	44	40	
6	42	36	41	36	40	36	
8	34	29	33	28	33	28	
10	28	23	27	22	27	22	
							4-lamp 2′ × 4′ troffer
1	58	56	57	55	55	53	
3	47	43	46	43	45	42	
5	38	34	37	33	37	33	
6	34	30	34	30	33	29	
8	27	23	27	23	26	23	
10	23	19	23	19	22	19	
							Prismatic wrap-around
1	70	68	67	65	63	61	
3	56	51	54	50	51	47	
5	45	40	44	39	41	37	
6	41	35	39	34	37	33	
8	33	27	32	27	30	26	
10	26	21	26	21	24	20	
							2-lamp porcelain
1	86	83	82	79	75	72	
3	68	62	65	60	60	56	
5	54	47	52	46	48	43	
6	49	42	47	40	43	38	
8	39	32	38	31	35	30	
10	32	26	31	25	29	23	
							4-lamp Alzak unit
1	83	80	—	—	74	72	
3	67	61	—	—	60	56	
5	53	47	—	—	48	44	
6	48	42	—	—	43	39	
8	37	32	—	—	34	30	
10	29	24	—	—	26	22	
							2/40W-3′ × 3′ unit
1	66	64	—	—	62	60	
3	53	48	—	—	50	46	
5	42	37	—	—	40	36	
6	38	33	—	—	37	32	
8	31	26	—	—	30	25	
10	25	20	—	—	24	20	

243. Levels of Illumination—Currently Recommended
("IES Lighting Handbook")

While for convenience of use this table sometimes lists locations rather than tasks, the recommended footcandle values have been arrived at for specific visual tasks. The tasks selected for this purpose have been the more difficult ones which commonly occur in the various areas.

In order to assure these values at all times, higher initial levels should be provided as required by the maintenance conditions.

Where tasks are located near the perimeter of a room, special consideration should be given to the arrangement of the luminaires in order to provide the recommended level of illumination on the task.

The illumination levels shown in the table are intended to be minimum on the task irrespective of the plane in which it is located. The commonly used lumen method of illumination calculation gives results only for a horizontal work plane. The ratio of vertical to horizontal illumination will generally vary from ⅛ for luminaires having narrow distribution to ½ for luminaires of wide distribution. Where the levels thus achieved are inadequate, special luminaire arrangements must be used or supplemental lighting equipment employed.

Supplementary luminaires may be used in combination with general lighting to achieve these levels. The general lighting should not be less than 20 ft-c and should contribute at least one-tenth the total illumination level.

Many of the following values have appeared, or in the future will appear, in other reports of the Society, some of which are jointly sponsored with other agencies and organizations.

Area	Foot-candles on tasks*	Area	Foot-candles on tasks*
		Interior Lighting	
Airplane manufacturing:		Rough, difficult seeing.............	50
Stock parts:		Medium.......................	100
Production....................	100	Fine...........................	500
Inspection....................	200a	Extra fine.....................,.......	1,000
Parts manufacturing:			
Drilling, riveting, and screw fastening....................	70	Auditoriums:	
Spray booths.................	100	Assembly only..................	15
Sheet aluminum layout and template work, shaping and smoothing of small parts for fuselage. wing sections, cowling, etc........................	100	Exhibitions....................	30
		Social activities................	5
Welding:			
General illumination...........	50	Automobile showrooms (see Stores)	
Supplementary illumination......	1,000		
Subassembly:		Automobile manufacturing:	
Landing gear, fuselage, wing sections, cowling and other large units....................	100	Frame assembly.................	50
		Chassis assembly line............	100
		Final assembly and inspection line..	200a
Final assembly:		Body manufacturing:	
Placing of motors, propellers, wing sections and landing gear.	100	Parts.......................	70
		Assembly....................	100
Inspection of assembled ship and its equipment....................	100	Finishing and inspecting........	200a
Machine-tool repairs.............	100		
		Bakeries:	
Airplane hangars—repair service only	100	Mixing room...................	50
		Face of shelves (vertical illumination)......................	30
Armories:		Inside of mixing bowl (vertical mixers)......................	50
Drill.........................	20	Fermentation room..............	30
Exhibitions....................	30	Make-up room:	
		Bread.......................	30
Art galleries:		Sweet yeast raised products......	50
General.......................	30	Proofing room...................	30
On paintings (supplementary)......	30b	Oven room.....................	30
On statuary and other displays.....	100c	Fillings and other ingredients......	50
		Decorating and icing:	
Assembly:		Mechanical..................	50
Rough, easy seeing..............	30	Hand.......................	100
		Scales and thermometers.........	50
		Wrapping room.........	30

* Minimum on the task at any time. For general notes see beginning of tabulation. For other notes see end of tabulation.

Levels of Illumination – Currently Recommended (*Continued*)

Area	Foot-candles on tasks*	Area	Foot-candles on tasks*
Banks:		Auxiliaries, battery rooms, boiler feed pumps, tanks, compressors, and gage area..................	20
Lobby:			
General......................	50	Boiler platforms.................	10
Writing areas.................	70	Burner platforms................	20
Tellers' stations................	150	Cable room, circulator or pump bay.	10
Posting and keypunch............	150	Coal conveyor, crusher, feeder, scale areas, pulverizer, fan area, transfer tower.....................	10
Barbershops and beauty parlors......	100	Condensers, deaerator floor, evaporator floor and heater floors......	10
		Control rooms:	
Bookbinding:		Vertical face of switchboards:	
Folding, assembling, pasting, etc...	70	Simplex or section of duplex facing operator:	
Cutting, punching, and stitching...	70	Type A—Large centralized control room 66 in. above floor....................	50
Embossing and inspection.........	200ᵃ	Type B—Ordinary control room 66 in. above floor...	30
		Section of duplex facing away from operator.............	30
Breweries:		Bench boards (horizontal level)..	50
Brewhouse......................	30	Area inside duplex switchboards.	10
Boiling and keg washing..........	30	Rear of all switchboard panels (vertical)...................	10
Filling (bottles, cans, kegs).......	50	Emergency lighting, all areas....	3
		Dispatch boards:	
Candymaking:		Horizontal plane (desk level)....	50
Box department.................	50	Vertical face of board (48 in. above floor, facing operator):	
Chocolate department:		System load dispatch room....	50
Husking, winnowing, fat extraction, crushing and refining, feeding.....................	50	Secondary dispatch room....	30
Bean cleaning, sorting, dipping, packing, and wrapping........	50	Hydrogen and carbon dioxide manifold area.....................	20
Milling......................	100	Chemical laboratory.............	50
Cream making—mixing, cooking and molding................	50	Precipitators....................	10
Gumdrops and jellied forms........	50	Screen house....................	20
Hand decorating.................	100	Soot or slag blower platform......	10
Hard candy:		Steam headers and throttles......	10
Mixing, cooking and molding....	50	Switchgear, power...............	20
Die cutting and sorting..........	100	Telephone-equipment room........	20
Kiss making and wrapping........	100	Tunnels or galleries, piping........	10
		Turbine bay subbasement.........	20
Canning and preserving:		Turbine room....................	30
Initial grading raw material samples.	50	Visitors' gallery.................	20
Tomatoes.....................	100	Water-treating area..............	20
Color grading (cutting rooms)...	200ᵃ		
Preparation:		**Chemical works:**	
Preliminary sorting:		Hand furnaces, boiling tanks, stationary driers, stationary and gravity crystallizers...........	30
Apricots and peaches.........	50		
Tomatoes....................	100	Mechanical furnaces, generators and stills, mechanical driers, evaporators, filtration, mechanical crystallizers, bleaching............	30
Olives......................	150		
Cutting and pitting.............	100		
Final sorting..................	100	Tanks for cooking, extractors, percolators, nitrators, electrolytic cells.........................	30
Canning:			
Continuous-belt canning........	100		
Sink canning..................	100		
Hand packing.................	50		
Olives.......................	100		
Examination of canned samples.:..	200ᵃ		
Container handling:			
Inspection....................	200ᵃ		
Can unscramblers..............	70		
Labeling and cartoning.........	30		
		Churches and synagogues:	
Central station:		Altar, ark, reredos...............	100ᵉ
Air-conditioning equipment, air preheater and fan floor, ash sluicing..	10	Chairᵈ and chancel..............	30ᵉ

* Minimum on the task at any time. For general notes see beginning of tabulation. For other notes see end of tabulation.

Levels of Illumination — Currently Recommended (*Continued*)

Area	Foot-candles on tasks*	Area	Foot-candles on tasks*
Classrooms.......................	30	Tanks, vats:	
Pulpit, rostrum (supplementary		Light interiors.................	20
illumination)..................	50*e*	Dark interiors.................	100
Main worship area*d*:		Thermometer (on face)...........	50
Light and medium interior finishes	15*e*	Weighing room..................	30
For churches with special zeal...	30*d*	Scales........................	70
Art glass windows (test recommended):			
Light color....................	50	Dance halls......................	5
Medium color..................	100		
Dark color....................	500	Depots, terminals, and stations:	
Especially dense windows........	1,000	Waiting room..................	30
		Ticket offices:	
Clay products and cements:		General.......................	100
Grinding, filter presses, kiln rooms..	30	Ticket rack and counters........	100
Molding, pressing, cleaning and		Rest rooms and smoking room.....	30
trimming....................	30	Baggage checking................	50
Enameling.....................	100	Concourse.....................	10
Color and glazing—rough work....	100	Platforms......................	20
Color and glazing—fine work......	300*a*	Toilets and washrooms...........	30
Cleaning and pressing industry:		Dispatch boards (see Central station)	
Checking and sorting............	50		
Dry and wet cleaning and steaming.	50	Drafting rooms (see Offices)	
Inspection and spotting..........	500*a*		
Pressing:		Electrical equipment manufacturing:	
Machine.....................	150	Impregnating..................	50
Hand.......................	150	Insulating: coil winding..........	100
Repair and alteration............	200*a*	Testing.......................	100
Cloth products:		Elevators, freight and passenger.....	20
Cloth inspection.................	2,000*a*		
Cutting........................	300*a*	Engraving (wax)..................	200*a*
Sewing........................	500*a*		
Pressing.......................	300*a*	Explosives:	
		Hand furnaces, boiling tanks, stationary driers, stationary and	
Club and lodge rooms:		gravity crystallizers.............	30
Lounge and reading rooms........	30	Mechanical furnace, generators and	
Auditoriums (see Auditoriums)		stills, mechanical driers, evaporators, filtration mechanical crystallizers......................	30
Coal tipples and cleaning plants:		Tanks for cooking, extractors, percolators, nitrators..............	30
Breaking, screening and cleaning...	10		
Picking........................	300*a*	Farms—milkhouse.................	10
Control rooms (see Central station)		Fire hall (see Municipal buildings)	
Courtrooms		Flour mills:	
Seating area....................	30	Rolling, sifting, purifying.........	50
Court activity area..............	70	Packing.......................	30
		Product control.................	100
Dairy products:		Cleaning, screens, man lifts, aisleways and walkways, bin checking.	30
Fluid-milk industry:			
Boiler room...................	30	Forge shops......................	50
Bottle storage.................	30		
Bottle sorting.................	50	Foundries:	
Bottle washers................	*f*	Annealing (furnaces)..............	30
Can washers..................	30	Cleaning......................	30
Cooling equipment.............	30	Core making:	
Filling: inspection..............	100	Fine........................	100
Gages (on face)................	50	Medium.....................	50
Laboratories..................	100	Grinding and chipping...........	100*a*
Meter panels (on face)..........	50		
Pasteurizers...................	30		
Separators....................	30		
Storage refrigerator............	30		

* Minimum on the task at any time.   For general notes see beginning of tabulation.   For other notes see end of tabulation.

Levels of Illumination—Currently Recommended (*Continued*)

Area	Foot-candles on tasks*	Area	Foot-candles on tasks*
Inspection:		Dental suite:	
Fine........................	500[a]	Waiting room:	
Medium.....................	100	General.....................	15
Molding:		Reading....................	30
Medium.....................		Operatory, general..............	70
Large......................	100	Instrument cabinet.............	150
Pouring.....................	50	Dental chair..................	1,000
Sorting.....................	50	Laboratory, bench.............	100
Cupola.....................	50	Recovery room..............	5
Shakeout...................	20	Electroencephalographic suite:	
	30	Office.....................	100
Garages—automobile and truck:		Workroom....................	30
Service garages:		Patients' room................	30
Repairs....................		Emergency room:	
Active traffic areas..............	100	General.....................	100
Parking garages:	20	Local.......................	2,000
Entrance....................		EKG, BMR, and specimen room:	
Traffic lanes..................	50	General.....................	20
Storage.....................	10	Specimen table (supplementary)	50
	5	Examination and treatment room:	
Gasoline station (see Service station)		General....................	50
		Examining table..............	100
Glassworks:		Eye, ear, nose, and throat suite:	
Mix and furnace rooms, pressing		Dark room...................	10
and lehr, glass-blowing machines.	30	Eye examination and treatment	
Grinding, cutting glass to size, sil-		room......................	50
vering.......................	50	Ear, nose, and throat room......	50
Fine grinding, beveling, polishing..	100	Exits, at floor.................	5
Inspection, etching, and decorating.	200[a]	Flower room...................	10
		Formula room..................	30
Glove manufacturing:		Fracture room:	
Pressing....................	300[a]	General.....................	50
Knitting....................	100	Fracture table................	200
Sorting.....................	100	Laboratories:	
Cutting.....................	300[a]	Assay rooms.................	30
Sewing and inspection...........	500[a]	Worktables...................	50
		Close work...................	100
Hangars (see Airplane hangars)		Linen closet.....................	10
		Lobby......................	30
Hat manufacturing:		Lounge rooms..................	30
Dyeing, stiffening, braiding, clean-		Medical-records room............	100
ing, and refining..............	100	Nurses' station:	
Forming, sizing, pouncing, flanging,		General.....................	20
finishing, and ironing...........	200[a]	Desk and charts..............	50
Sewing......................	500[a]	Medicine room counter..........	100
		Nurses' workroom..............	30
Homes (see Residences)		Nurseries:	
		General.....................	10
Hospitals:		Examination table.............	70
Anesthetizing and preparation room	30	Playroom, pediatric.............	30
Autopsy and morgue:		Obstetrical:	
Autopsy room..............	100	Clean-up room.................	30
Autopsy table.................	2,500	Scrub-up room.................	30
Morgue, general.............	20	Labor room...................	20
Central sterile supply:		Delivery room, general..........	100
General.....................	30	Delivery table.................	2,500
Needle sharpening..............	150	Pharmacy:	
Corridor:		General.....................	30
General....................	10	Worktable....................	100
Operating and delivery suites and		Active storage.................	30
laboratories..................	20	Alcohol vault..................	10
Cystoscopic room:		Private rooms and wards:	
General.....................	100	General.....................	10
Cystoscopic table..............	2,500	Reading.....................	30

* Minimum on the task at any time. For general notes see beginning of tabulation. For other notes see end of tabulation.

Levels of Illumination – Currently Recommended (*Continued*)

Area	Foot-candles on tasks*	Area	Foot-candles on tasks*
Psychiatric disturbed patients' areas	10	Difficult........................	100
Radioisotope facilities:		Highly difficult.................	200a
Radiochemical laboratory.......	30	Very difficult...................	500a
Up-take measuring room........	20	Most difficult...................	1,000a
Examination table..............	50		
Retiring room...................	10	Iron and steel manufacturing:	
Sewing room:		Open hearth:	
General......................	20	Stock yard....................	10
Work area...................	100	Charging floor................	20
Solariums......................	20	Pouring slide:	
Stairways......................	20	Slag pits....................	20
Surgery:		Control platforms...........	30
Instrument and sterile supply		Mold yard....................	5
room.......................	30	Hot top......................	30
Clean-up room (instruments)....	100	Hot top storage..............	10
Scrub-up room................	30	Checker cellar................	10
Operating room, general........	100	Buggy and door repair........	30
Operating table................	2,500	Stripping yard................	20
Recovery room................	30	Scrap stock yard.............	10
Therapy:		Mixer building...............	30
Physical......................	20	Calcining building...........	10
Occupational..................	30	Skull cracker.................	10
Toilets.........................	10	Rolling mills:	
Utility room....................	20	Blooming, slabbing, hot strip, hot	
Waiting room:		sheet.......................	30
General......................	15	Cold strip, plate..............	30
Reading......................	30	Pipe, rod, tub, wire drawing.....	50
X-ray room and facilities:		Merchant and sheared plate....	30
Radiography and fluoroscopy....	10	Tin plate mills:	
Deep and superficial therapy....	10	Tinning and galvanizing........	50
Darkroom.....................	10	Cold-strip rolling..............	50
Waiting room, general..........	15	Motor room, machine room.......	30
Waiting room, reading..........	30	Inspection:	
Viewing room.................	30	Black, plate, bloom, and billet	
Filing room, developed films.....	30	chipping....................	100
		Tin plate, other bright surfaces..	100i
Hotels:			
Bathrooms:		Jewelry and watch manufacturing....	500a
Mirror......................	30g		
General.....................	10	Kitchens (see Restaurants or Residences)	
Bedrooms:			
Reading (books, magazines, newspapers)	30	Laundries:	
Ink writing..................	30h	Washing......................	30
Make-up.....................	30i	Flatwork ironing, weighing, listing,	
General.....................	10	marking..................	50
Corridors, elevators, and stairs....	20	Machine and press finishing, sorting	70
Entrance foyer.................	30	Fine hand ironing..............	100
Front office....................	50		
Linen room:		Leather manufacturing:	
Sewing......................	100	Cleaning, tanning and stretching,	
General.....................	20	vats......................	30
Lobby:		Cutting, fleshing, and stuffing......	50
General lighting...............	10	Finishing and scarfing............	100
Reading and working areas......	30		
Marquee:		Leatherworking:	
Dark surroundings............	30	Pressing, winding, and glazing.....	200
Bright surroundings...........	50	Grading, matching, cutting, scarfing, and sewing..............	300
Ice making—engine and compressor			
room.........................	20	Library:	
		Reading room:	
Inspection:		Study and notes...............	70
Ordinary......................	50	Ordinary reading..............	30

* Minimum on the task at any time.   For general notes see beginning of tabulation.   For other notes see end of tabulation.

Levels of Illumination — Currently Recommended (Continued)

Area	Foot-candles on tasks*	Area	Foot-candles on tasks*
Stacks............................	30	Corridors, elevators, escalators, stairways.....................	20[k]
Book repair and binding..........	50		
Cataloguing.....................	70	Packing and boxing (see Materials handling)	
Card files......................	70		
Check-in and check-out desks......	70		
		Paint manufacturing:	
Locker rooms....................	20	General......................	30
		Comparing mix with standard.....	200[i]
Machine shops:			
Rough bench and machine work...	50	Paint shops:	
Medium bench and machine work, ordinary automatic machines, rough grinding, medium buffing and polishing.................	100	Dipping, simple spraying, firing....	50
		Rubbing, ordinary hand painting and finishing art, stencil and special spraying................	50
Fine bench and machine work, fine automatic machines, medium grinding, fine buffing and polishing...........................	500[a]	Fine hand painting and finishing...	100
		Extra-fine hand painting and finishing (automobile bodies, piano cases, etc.)....................	300[a]
Extra-fine bench and machine work, grinding, fine work	1,000[a]		
		Paper-box manufacturing—general manufacturing area...............	50
Materials handling:			
Wrapping, packing, labeling.......	50	Paper manufacturing:	
Picking stock, classifying.........	30	Beaters, grinding, calendering.....	30
Loading, trucking...............	20	Finishing, cutting, trimming, paper-making machines...............	50
Inside truck bodies and freight cars......................	10	Hand counting, wet end of paper machine....................	70
		Paper machine reel, paper inspection and laboratories...........	100
Meat packing:		Rewinder......................	150
Slaughtering....................	30		
Cleaning, cutting, cooking, grinding, canning, packing..........	100	Plating...........................	30
		Polishing and burnishing...........	100
Municipal buildings—fire and police: Police:		Power plants (see Central station)	
Identification records..........	150	Post offices:	
Jail cells and interrogation rooms	30	Lobby, on tables................	30
Fire hall:		Sorting, mailing, etc.............	100
Dormitory...................	20		
Recreation room..............	30	Printing industries:	
Wagon room.................	30	Type foundries:	
		Matrix making, dressing type....	100
Museums (see Art galleries)		Font assembly—sorting........	50
		Hand casting.................	50
Offices:		Machine casting...............	50
Cartography, designing, detailed drafting.....................	200	Printing plants:	
		Color inspection and appraisal...	200[a]
Accounting, auditing, tabulating, bookkeeping, business-machine operation, reading poor reproductions, rough layout drafting.....	150	Machine composition...........	100
		Composing room................	100
		Presses.......................	70
		Imposing stones...............	150
Regular office work, reading good reproductions, reading or transcribing handwriting in hard pencil or on poor paper, active filing, index references, mail sorting....	100	Proof reading.................	150
		Electrotyping:	
		Molding, routing, finishing, leveling molds, trimming.........	100
		Blocking, tinning..............	50
Reading or transcribing handwriting in ink or medium pencil on good-quality paper, intermittent filing	70	Electroplating, washing, backing.	50
		Photoengraving:	
Reading high contrast or well-printed material, tasks and areas not involving critical or prolonged seeing such as conferring, interviewing, inactive files and washrooms......................	30	Etching, staging...............	50
		Blocking......................	50

* Minimum on the task at any time. For general notes see beginning of tabulation. For other notes see end of tabulation.

Levels of Illumination—Currently Recommended (*Continued*)

Area	Foot-candles on tasks*	Area	Foot-candles on tasks*
Routing, finishing, proofing	100	Food displays—twice the general levels but not under	50
Tint laying	100	Kitchen, commercial:	
Masking	100	Inspection, checking and pricing	70
Professional offices (see Hospitals)		Other areas	30
Receiving and shipping (see Materials handling)		Rubber goods—mechanical:	
		Stock preparation:	
Residences:		Plasticating, milling, and Banbury	30
Specific visual tasks[j]:		Calendering	50
Table games	30	Fabric preparation—stock cutting and hose looms	50
Kitchen activities:		Extruded products	50
Sink	70	Molded products and curing	50
Range and work surfaces	50	Inspection	200[a]
Laundry, trays, ironing board, ironer	50	Rubber tire and tube manufacturing:	
Reading and writing, including studying:		Stock preparation:	
Books, magazines, newspapers	30	Plasticating, milling, and Banbury	30
Handwriting, reproduction and poor copies	70	Calendering	50
Desks, study	70	Fabric preparation—stock cutting and bead building	50
Reading music scores:		Tube and tread tubing machines	50
Simple scores	30	Tire building:	
Advanced scores	70	Solid tires	30
(When score is substandard size, and notations are printed on the lines, 150 ft-c or more are needed.)		Pneumatic tires	50
		Curing department—tube and casing	70
Sewing:		Final inspection—tube, casing	200[a]
Dark fabrics (fine detail, low contrast)	200	Wrapping	50
Prolonged periods (light to medium fabrics)	100	Sawmills—grading redwood lumber	300
Occasional periods (light fabrics)	50	Schools:[s]	
Occasional periods (coarse thread, large stitches, high contrast thread to fabric)	30	Reading printed material	30
		Reading pencil writing	70
Shaving, make-up, grooming; on the face at mirror locations	50	Spirit duplicated material:	
General lighting:		Good	30
Entrances, hallways, stairways, stair landings	10[m]	Poor	100
Living room, dining room, bedroom, family room, sunroom, library, game or recreation room	10[m]	Drafting, benchwork	100[a]
		Lip reading, chalkboards, sewing	150[a]
Kitchen, laundry, bathroom	30	Service space:	
		Stairways	20
Restaurants, lunchrooms, cafeterias:		Elevators, freight and passenger	20
Dining areas:		Corridors	20
Cashier	50	Storage (see Storage rooms)	
Intimate type:		Toilets and washrooms	30
Light environment	10		
Subdued environment	3	Service stations:	
For cleaning	20	Service bays	30
Leisure type:		Salesroom	50
Light environment	30	Shelving and displays	100
Subdued environment	15	Rest rooms	15
Quick-service type:		Storage	5
Bright surroundings[n]	100	Sheet-metal works:	
Normal surroundings[n]	50	Miscellaneous machines, ordinary benchwork	50
		Presses, shears, stamps, spinning, medium benchwork	50
		Punches	50
		Tin-plate inspection, galvanized	200[i]
		Scribing	200[i]

* Minimum on the task at any time.   For general notes see beginning of tabulation.   For other notes see end of tabulation.

Levels of Illumination—Currently Recommended (*Continued*)

Area	Foot-candles on tasks*	Area	Foot-candles on tasks*
Shoe manufacturing—leather:		Stores:º	
Cutting and stitching:		Circulation areas................	30
Cutting tables................	300ª	Merchandising areas:	
Marking, buttonholing, skiving,		Service.....................	100
sorting, vamping and counting.	300ª	Self-service...................	200
Stitching—dark materials........	300ª	Showcases and wall cases:	
Making and finishing—nailers, sole		Service.....................	200
layers, welt beaters and scarfers,		Self-service...................	500
trimmers, welters, lasters, edge		Feature displays:	
setters, sluggers, randers, wheel-		Service.....................	500
ers, treers, cleaning, spraying,		Self-service...................	1,000
buffing, polishing, embossing.....	200	Stockrooms.....................	30
Shoe manufacturing—rubber:		Structural steel fabrication..........	50
Washing, coating, mill run com-			
pounding.....................	30	Sugar refining:	
Varnishing, vulcanizing, calender-		Grading.........................	50
ing, upper and sole cutting......	50	Color inspection.................	200
Sole rolling, lining, making and			
finishing processes..............	100	Testing:	
		General.......................	50
Show windows:º		Extra-fine instruments, scales, etc..	200ª
Daytime lighting:			
General.......................	200	Textile mills—cotton:	
Feature.......................	1,000	Opening, mixing, picking.........	30
Nighttime lighting:		Carding and drawing............	50
Main business districts—highly		Slubbing, roving, spinning and	
competitive:		spooling....................	50
General....................	200	Beaming and splashing on comb:	
Feature....................	1,000	Gray goods...................	50
Secondary business districts or		Denims......................	150
small towns:		Inspection:	
General....................	100	Gray goods (hand turning)......	100
Feature....................	500	Denims (rapidly moving)........	500ª
Open-front stores (see display		Automatic tying-in...............	150ª
lighting under Stores)		Weaving.......................	100
		Drawing-in by hand.............	200ª
Soap manufacturing:			
Kettle houses, cutting, soap chip		Textile mills—silk and synthetics:	
and powder...................	30	Manufacturing—soaking, fugitive	
Stamping, wrapping and packing,		tinting, and conditioning or set-	
filling and packing soap powder	50	ting of twist...................	30
		Winding, twisting, rewinding and	
Stairways (see Service space)		coning, quilling, slashing:	
		Light thread..................	50
Steel (see Iron and steel)		Dark thread..................	200
		Warping (silk or cotton system)—	
Stone crushing and screening:		on creel, on running ends, on reel,	
Belt conveyor tubes, main-line		on beam, on warp at beaming...	100
shafting spaces, chute rooms, in-		Drawing-in on heddles and reed....	200ª
side of bins...................	10	Weaving.......................	100
Primary breaker room, auxiliary			
breakers under bins............	10	Textile mills—woolen and worsted:	
Screens........................	20	Opening, blending, picking........	30
		Grading.........................	100ª
Storage-battery manufacturing—		Carding, combing, recombing, and	
molding of grids.................	50	gilling......................	50
		Drawing:	
Storage rooms or warehouses:		White.......................	50
Inactive.......................	5	Colored.....................	100
Active:		Spinning (frame):	
Rough bulky..................	10	White.......................	50
Medium......................	20	Colored.....................	100
Fine.........................	50		

* Minimum on the task at any time.   For general notes see beginning of tabulation.   For other notes see end of tabulation.

Levels of Illumination—Currently Recommended (*Continued*)

Area	Foot-candles on tasks*	Area	Foot-candles on tasks*
Spinning (mule):		Folding.........................	70
White.........................	50		
Colored.......................	100	Theatres and motion-picture houses	
Twisting—white.................	50	Auditoriums:	
Winding:		During intermission............	5
White.........................	30	During picture.................	0.1
Colored.......................	50	Foyer..........................	5
Warping:		Lobby.........................	20
White.........................	50		
White (at reed)................	100	Tobacco products:	
Colored.......................	100	Drying, stripping, general........	30
Colored (at reed)..............	300ᵃ	Grading and sorting............	200ᵃ
Weaving:			
White.........................	100	Toilets and washrooms..............	30
Colored.......................	200		
Gray goods room:		Upholstering—automobile, coach,	
Burling.......................	150ᵃ	furniture.....................	100
Sewing........................	300ᵃ		
Folding.......................	70	Warehouse (see Storage rooms)	
Wet finishing:			
Fulling.......................	50	Welding:	
Scouring......................	50	General illumination............	50
Crabbing......................	50	Precision manual arc welding......	1,000ᵃ
Drying........................	50		
Dyeing........................	100ᵃ	Woodworking:	
Dry finishing:		Rough sawing and benchwork.....	30
Napping.......................	70	Sizing, planing, rough sanding, medium quality machine and benchwork, gluing, veneering, cooperage	50
Shearing......................	100		
Conditioning..................	70		
Pressing......................	70	Fine bench- and machine work, fine sanding and finishing...........	100
Inspecting (perching)..........	2,000ᵃ		

Exterior Lighting

Area	Foot-candles	Area	Foot-candles
Building:		Coal unloading:	
General construction.............	10	Dock (loading or unloading zone).	5
Excavation work................	2	Barge storage area.............	0.5
		Car dumper...................	0.5ᵃ
Building exteriors and monuments—		Tipple........................	5
floodlighted:		Coal-storage area................	0.1
Bright surroundings:		Conveyors.....................	2
Light surfaces.................	15	Entrances:	
Medium-light surfaces..........	20	Generating or service building:	
Medium-dark surfaces..........	30	Main.......................	10
Dark surfaces.................	50	Secondary..................	2
Dark surroundings:		Gatehouse:	
Light surfaces.................	5	Pedestrian entrance..........	10
Medium-light surfaces..........	10	Conveyor entrance...........	5
Medium-dark surfaces..........	15	Fence.........................	0.2
Dark surfaces.................	20	Fuel-oil delivery headers.........	5
		Oil storage tanks................	1
Bulletin and poster boards:		Open yard......................	0.2
Bright surroundings:		Platforms—boiler, turbine deck....	5
Light surfaces.................	50	Roadway:	
Dark surfaces.................	100	Between or along buildings......	1
Dark surroundings:		Not bordered by buildings.......	0.5
Light surfaces.................	20	Substation:	
Dark surfaces.................	50	General horizontal.............	2
		Specific vertical (on disconnects).	2
Central station:			
Catwalks......................	2	Coal yards (protective)............	0.2
Cinder dumps..................	0.1	Dredging......................	2

* Minimum on the task at any time.   For general notes see beginning of tabulation.   For other notes see end of tabulation.

Levels of Illumination—Currently Recommended (*Continued*)

Area	Foot-candles on tasks*
Flags, floodlighted (see Bulletin and poster boards)	
Gardens:[p]	
General lighting	0.5
Path, steps, away from house	1
Backgrounds—fences, walls, trees, shrubbery	2
Flower beds, rock gardens	5
Trees, shrubbery, when emphasized	5
Focal points, large	10
Focal points, small	20
Gasoline station (see Service stations)	
Highways	[q]
Loading and unloading platforms	20
Freight-car interiors	10
Lumberyards	1
Parking lots	5
Piers:	
Freight	20
Passenger	20
Prison yards	5
Protective lighting:	
Boundaries:	
Glare projection technique (isolated)	0.15
General lighting technique (nonisolated)	0.20
Entrances:	
Active (pedestrian and/or conveyance)	5
Inactive (normally locked, infrequently used)	1
Vital locations or structures	5
Building surrounds	1

Area	Foot candles on tasks*
Active shipping area surrounds	5
Storage areas—active	20
Storage areas—inactive	1
Loading and unloading platforms	20
General inactive areas	0.20
Quarries	5
Railroad yards:	
Receiving	0.2
Classification	0.3
Roadways	[q]
Service station (at grade)	

Service station (at grade)	Dark surrounding	Light surrounding
Approach	1.5	3
Driveway	1.5	5
Pump island area	20	30
Building faces (exclusive of glass)	10[r]	30[r]
Service areas	3	7

Area	Foot candles on tasks*
Shipyards:	
General	5
Ways	10
Fabrication areas	30
Smokestacks with advertising messages (see Bulletin and poster boards)	
Storage yards (active)	20
Streets	[q]
Water tanks with advertising messages (see Bulletin and poster boards)	

Sports Lighting

	Target	Shooting line
Archery:		
Tournament	10[r]	10
Recreational	5[r]	5

Badminton:	
Tournament	30
Club	20
Recreational	10

	Infield	Outfield
Baseball:		
Major league	150	100
AA and AAA league	75	50
A and B league	50	30
C and D league	30	20
Semipro and municipal league	20	15
Junior league (Class I and Class II)	40	30
On seats during game		2
On seats before and after game		5

Basketball:	
College and professional	50
College intramural and high school with spectators	30
College intramural and high school without spectators	20
Recreational (outdoor)	10

	On land	150 ft from shore
Bathing beaches	1	3[r]

* Minimum on the task at any time. For general notes see beginning of tabulation. For other notes see end of tabulation.

Levels of Illumination—Currently Recommended (*Continued*)

Area	Foot-candles on tasks*	Area	Foot-candles on tasks*
Billiards (on table):		Assemblies....................	10
Tournament...................	50	Dances.......................	5
Recreational..................	30	Lockers and shower rooms........	10
General area.................	10		
		Handball:	
	Lanes **Pins**	Tournament...................	30
Bowling:		Club........................	20
Tournament.............. 20	50ʳ	Recreational..................	10
Recreational.............. 10	30ʳ		
		Horseshoes:	
Bowling on the green:		Tournament...................	10
Tournament..................	10	Recreational..................	5
Recreational..................	5		
		Ice hockey:	
Boxing or wrestling (ring):		College or professional...........	50
Championship..................	500	Amateur league.................	20
Professional..................	200	Recreational..................	10
Amateur......................	100		
Seats during bout..............	2	Lacrosse.......................	20
Seats before and after bout.......	5		
		Quoits.........................	5
	Pier or dock **Target**	**Racing:**	
Casting:		Bicycle........................	20
Bait.................. 10	5ʳ	Motor (midget auto or motorcycle).	20
Dry fly............... 10	5ʳ	Horse.........................	20
Wet fly............... 10	5ʳ	Dog...........................	30
Croquet:		**Rifle range:**	
Tournament..................	10	On target......................	50ʳ
Recreational..................	5	Firing point....................	10
		Range.........................	5
	Tees **Rink**	**Roque:**	
Curling—indoor.............. 20	10	Tournament...................	20
		Recreational..................	10
Football:			
(Index: Distance from nearest sideline to the farthest row of spectators.)		**Shuffleboard:**	
		Tournament...................	10
		Recreational..................	5
Class I: Over 100 ft............	100		
Class II: 50 to 100 ft............	50	**Skating:**	
Class III: 30 to 50 ft............	30	Roller rink....................	5
Class IV: Under 30 ft...........	20	Ice rink (indoor or outdoor).......	5
Class V: No fixed seating facilities..	10	Lagoon, pond, or flooded area......	1
It is generally conceded that the distance between the spectators and the play is the first consideration in determining the class and lighting requirements. However, the potential seating capacity of the stands should also be considered and the following ratio is suggested: Class I for over 30,000 spectators; Class II for 10,000 to 30,000; Class III for 5,000 to 10,000 and Class IV for under 5,000 spectators		**Skeet shoot:**	
		Target, surface at 60 ft..........	30ʳ
		Firing point, general............	10
		Ski-slope practice..................	0.5
		Soccer:	
		Professional and college..........	30
		High school....................	20
Golf driving:		Athletic field..................	10
General on the tees..............	10		
At 200 yd.....................	5ʳ		**Infield** **Outfield**
Practice and putting green........	10	**Softball:**	
		Professional and championship..................... 50	30
Gymnasiums (refer to individual sports listed separately):		Semipro.................... 30	20
Exhibitions, matches.............	30	Industrial league............ 20	15
General exercising and recreation...	20	Recreational................ 10	7.5

* Minimum on the task at any time.   For general notes see beginning of tabulation.   For other notes see end of tabulation.

Levels of Illumination — Currently Recommended (*Continued*)

Area	Foot-candles on tasks*	Area		Foot-candles on tasks*
			Lawn	Table
Squash:	30	Tennis:		
Tournament....................	20	Tournament..................	30	50
Club............................	10	Club........................	20	30
Recreational....................		Recreational.................	10	20
Swimming pools:	10	Trapshoot:		
General, overhead...............		Target, at 150 ft.............		30ʳ
Underwater:		Firing point, general.............		10
Outdoors.....................	s			
Indoors......................	t	Volleyball:		
		Tournament....................		20
		Recreational....................		10

Transportation Lighting

Area	Foot-candles on tasks*	Area	Foot-candles on tasks*
Airplanes—passenger compartment:		Stairs:	
General........................	5	Passenger..................	10
Reading (at seat)...............	20	Crew......................	5
		Entrance, passenger...........	10ᵛ
Airports:		Lounges, passenger and officers..	10ˣ
Hangar apron...................	1	Recreation rooms, crew.........	20
Terminal-building apron:		On tables...................	30
Parking area.................	0.5	Dining room, passengers........	10ʷ
Loading area.................	2	Mess room, officers and crew....	10
		On tables...................	15
Automobiles—license plates........	0.5	Libraries....................	10
		For reading.................	30
Motor coaches:		Smoking rooms...............	5ˣ
City driving....................	30	Enclosed promenades, along in-	
Country driving.................	15	board bulkhead for reading....	10
		Barbershop and beauty parlor...	20
Trolley coaches and streetcars.......	30	On subject..................	50
		Cocktail lounges..............	5ʷ
Rapid-transit cars.................	30	Bars.......................	5ʷ
		Ballrooms...................	5ʷ
Railway passenger cars:		Swimming pools, indoor beaches..	10ᵛ
Reading and writing:		Shopping areas...............	20ᵘ
General.....................	20	Theaters:	
Detail......................	50	During show...............	0.1
Washroom section:		Intermission...............	5
General.....................	15	Gymnasiums..................	20
Mirror......................	30	Hospital:	
Toilet section.................	5	Operating room.............	50ᵘ
Dining car....................	15	Dental room................	30ᵘ
Taverns.....................	10	Dispensary.................	30ᵘ
Social areas..................	20	Wards.....................	5ᵘ
Steps and vestibules...........	10	Doctor's office..............	20ᵘ
		Waiting room...............	10ˣ
Railway mail cars:		Radio room, passenger foyer.....	10ᶻ
Mail-bag racks and letter cases....	30	Passenger counter, purser's office	20
Mail storage...................	15	Navigating areas:	
		Wheelhouse (not used underway)	5
Ships:		Chartroom..................	10
Living areas:		On chart table..............	50
Staterooms:		Radar room.................	5
Crew......................	5ᵘ	Gyro room..................	5
Officers....................	5ᵘ	Radio room.................	10ᵘ
Passengers..................	5ᵘ	Ship's offices................	20
Berth, on reading plane.......	15	On desks and worktables......	50
Mirrors, at face..............	50	For bookkeeping and auditing.	50
Baths:		Log room...................	10
Crew......................	5	On desk...................	50
Public.....................	5	Service areas:	
Officers....................	5	Galley.....................	20ᵘ
Passengers..................	5	Laundry...................	15ᵘ
Mirrors, at face..............	50	Pantry....................	15ᵘ
Passageways..................	5	Sculleries..................	15ᵘ
Stair foyers, passenger.........	10		

* Minimum on the task at any time. For general notes see beginning of tabulation. For other notes see end of tabulation.

Levels of Illumination — Currently Recommended (*Continued*)

Area	Foot-candles on tasks*	Area	Foot-candles on tasks*
Food preparation...............	20ᵘ	Switchboards, vertical illumination:	
Food storage (nonrefrigeration)..	5	At top.....................	30
Refrigerated spaces (ship's stores).	5	3 ft above deck..............	10
Butchershop..................	15ᵘ	Steering-gear room.............	5
Print shop....................	30ᵘ	Pump room...................	1
Tailor shop...................	50ᵘ	Gage and control boards (vertical	
Post offices..................	20ᵘ	illumination) on gages........	30
Lockers.....................	3	Shaft alley...................	3
Telephone exchange............	10ᵘ	Dry cargo holds (permanent fix-	
Storerooms..................	5	ture)......................	1ᵘ
Operating areas:		Refrigerated cargo loading and	
Engine rooms (working areas)...	10ᵘ	unloading..................	3ᵘ
Boiler rooms (working areas)....	10ᵘ	Workshops...................	20
Fan rooms....................	5	On work...................	50
Motor-generator rooms (cargo		Cargo hatches:	
handling)..................	5	Over hatch area.............	5
Generator and switchboard rooms	10	Adjacent deck area..........	3
Windlass rooms...............	5		

* Minimum on the task at any time.   For general notes see beginning of tabulation.

ᵃ Obtained with a combination of general lighting plus specialized supplementary lighting. Care should be taken to keep within the recommended brightness ratios. These seeing tasks generally involve the discrimination of fine detail for long periods of time and under conditions of poor contrast. To provide the required illumination, a combination of the general lighting indicated plus specialized supplementary lighting is necessary. The design and installation of the combination system must provide not only a sufficient amount of light but also the proper direction of light, diffusion, and eye protection. As far as possible it should eliminate direct and reflected glare as well as objectionable shadows.

ᵇ Dark paintings with fine detail should have two to three times higher illumination.

ᶜ In some cases, much more than 100 ft-c is necessary to bring out the beauty of the statuary.

ᵈ Reduced or dimmed during sermon, prelude, or meditation.

ᵉ Two-thirds this value if interior finishes are dark (less than 10 per cent reflectance) to avoid high brightness ratios, such as between hymnbook pages and the surroundings. Careful brightness planning is essential for good design.

ᶠ Special lighting such that (1) the luminous area shall be large enough to cover the surface which is being inspected and (2) the brightness be within the limits necessary to obtain comfortable contrast conditions. This involves the use of sources of large area and relatively low brightness in which the source brightness is the principal factor rather than the footcandles produced at a given point.

ᵍ For close inspection, 50 ft-c.

ʰ Pencil handwriting, reading of reproductions, and poor copies require 70 ft-c.

ⁱ For close inspection, 50 ft-c.   This may be done in the bathroom, but if a dressing table is provided, local lighting should provide the level recommended.

ʲ The specular surface of the material may necessitate special consideration in selection and placement of lighting equipment, or orientation of the work.

ᵏ Or not less than one-fifth the level in adjacent areas.

ˡ Brightness of visual task must be related to background brightness.

ᵐ General lighting for these areas need not be uniform in character.

ⁿ Including street and nearby establishments.

ᵒ (1) Values are illumination on the merchandise on display or being appraised.   The plane in which lighting is important may vary from horizontal to vertical. (2) Specific appraisal areas involving difficult seeing may be lighted to substantially higher levels. (3) Color rendition of fluorescent lamps is important.   Incandescent and fluorescent usually are combined for best appearance of merchandise. (4) Illumination may often be made nonuniform to tie in with merchandising layout.

ᵖ Values based on a 25 per cent reflectance, which is average for vegetation and typical outdoor surfaces.   These figures must be adjusted to specific reflectances of materials lighted for equivalent brightnesses.   Levels give satisfactory brightness patterns when viewed from dimly lighted terraces or interiors.   When viewed from dark areas they may be reduced by at least one-half; or they may be doubled when a high key is desired.

ᵠ See Sec. 260.

ʳ Vertical.

ˢ 60 lamp lumens per square foot of surface.

ᵗ 100 lamp lumens per square foot of surface.

ᵘ Supplementary lighting should be provided in this space to produce the higher levels of lighting required for specific seeing tasks involved.

ᵛ The installation should be such that the level of illumination can be increased to at least 40 ft-c for daytime embarkation.

ʷ In public areas such as lounges, ballrooms, bars, smoking rooms, and dining rooms, the footcandle values may vary widely, depending upon the atmosphere desired, the decorative scheme and the use made of the room.

ˣ See footnotes u and w.

ʸ Also underwater lights and sunlamps.

ᶻ Tasks are listed here rather than areas, as previously published.

INTERIOR-LIGHTING SUGGESTIONS

244. Residence Lighting. In the lighting of the home, the decorative element should predominate. The lighting must, however, comply with the general rules of lighting (Sec. **220**) concerning color, shadows, glare, and illumination. A room in which yellow or red is the predominant color gives a warm cheerful impression, whereas a room furnished in blue tends to produce the opposite sensation. Shade and softened shadows are preferable to sharp shadows or to no shadows. It is especially important that glare be minimized. Luminous ceilings can be installed in kitchens, dining rooms and bathrooms.

Detailed recommendations for residence lighting are given in a booklet prepared by the Committee on Residence Lighting of the Illuminating Engineering Society and titled "Recommended Practice for Residence Lighting."

Kitchen. The kitchen requires plenty of well-diffused light. Except for very large rooms one 100-watt or one 150-watt lamp in a diffusing-glass enclosed unit will furnish satisfactory general illumination. For exceptionally large rectangular rooms two units may be required. Circline units are also recommended. Unless the room is very small with light-colored walls and ceilings, the general illumination should be augmented by additional localized ceiling or bracket units. A single light in the center of the kitchen usually compels the cook to work entirely in her own shadow, whether at the range, the sink, or the kitchen cabinet or table. A single fluorescent ceiling unit over the center of the sink or a bracket at each side of the sink is nearly always necessary to eliminate shadows and provide adequate illumination at the sink. Often it is advisable to locate similar units at the range and counter work areas.

Bedroom. The illumination requirements of the bedroom are somewhat similar to those for the kitchen. General illumination should be provided by means of a centrally located ceiling unit of low brightness so that it will not be uncomfortable to the eyes of one lying in bed. Additional illumination should be provided at the dresser or bureau by means of either brackets or a portable lamp on each side of the mirror. A bracket or wall-mounted fluorescent unit should be provided at the head of each bed unless localized table luminaires are used for providing illumination for reading at these locations. Better illumination for this purpose is generally obtained by the wall-mounted bracket or fluorescent units.

Living Room. Although there is a general tendency at the present time to eliminate the ceiling fixture, it is the opinion of experts that there will be a reaction to this practice. The central ceiling fixture if of a properly shaded type is the most desirable means of obtaining the general level of illumination required for festive occasions. For a quiet evening at home a lower level of general illumination can be obtained by means of the indirect type of floor and table lamps. The chief function of bracket lamps is for ornamentation, and they should not be relied upon for providing the necessary light for useful purposes.

Dining Room. There are several satisfactory methods of illuminating the dining room, the selection depending upon personal taste. General illumination may be provided by means of a centrally located dome or indirect-lighting unit. Where a dome is employed, it should be hung just high enough above the table so that it will not obstruct the view of persons seated on opposite sides of the table and low enough to hide the lamps from view entirely. The correct mounting height will usually be with the bottom of the dome 24 in. above the table top. Cove lighting by means of fluorescent lamps concealed in a trough a few inches down from the ceiling may be used. Wall brackets for decorative effects are also common.

Bathroom. In the bathroom the illumination of the mirror requires the greatest consideration. For the best illumination of the mirror three luminaries are needed, (1) one at each side of the mirror and (2) one mounted overhead. Fairly good results can be obtained with the use of only two units located one at each side of the mirror. If only one unit is used, it should be mounted overhead and centered with respect to the mirror. For small bathrooms the mirror wall brackets will supply sufficient general illumination for the rest of the room. In rooms of any appreciable size a central enclosing unit should be used in addition to the bracket lamps. A ceiling-mounted heat or sun lamp will provide healthful ultraviolet light for the winter months.

245. Store Lighting. The object of the lighting in a store is twofold. Primarily, sufficient illumination must be provided to enable articles for sale to be seen plainly. But of almost equal importance is the advertising value. The lighting units should be so selected as to give a pleasing and cheerful appearance to the store as a whole, without glare. Stores may be divided into three classes: (1) the small store, in which efficiency is of first importance; (2) the large store, such as a department store, in which efficiency is necessary on account of the large areas to be lighted but in which it must be balanced by artistic appearance, the result being a compromise between the two; (3) shops, large or small, in which the articles for sale are of a special type and the profits large enough so that even the most inefficient system can be afforded if it is sufficiently attractive to appeal to customers. The general requirements which must be satisfied are outlined in the following sections.

General Features of Store Lighting. General lighting best meets the requirements for the lighting of stores. The lamps should be arranged symmetrically with respect to bays or pillars. Direct glare must be very carefully avoided. The position of the counters need not be considered in spacing the lamps. Local accurate-color-matching units are advisable at certain points, such as ribbon and piece-goods counters.

The intensity of illumination must be varied with the articles which are to be sold. Furniture requires well-diffused lighting of relatively low intensity. Colored dress goods, men's clothing, rugs and carpets, etc., require a high intensity. In many installations, side light is necessary and should be given special attention in selecting types of units and reflectors. Cut glass and jewelry should be so lighted as to sparkle and glitter. Bare lamps and mirrored reflectors may be used in ornamental-type luminaires for this purpose. Glare is to a certain extent, in this case, unavoidable, but the light units can usually be so located as to be out of the customer's range of vision when he is inspecting the ware. Pictures require a high intensity with the light units at such an angle that light will not be reflected from the surface of the painting or from the glass directly into the observer's eyes. Individual units or mirrored-trough reflectors, with fluorescent or tubular tungsten lamps, are ordinarily used.

Deluxe cool-white fluorescent lighting units should be used to illuminate all items in which color is important, such as women's dresses, coats, and furs; men's suits and coats; draperies and curtains; tapestries; and neckties. Concealed fluorescent units may also be used in wall valances or coves for decorative effects.

Showcases ("Lighting Handbook," Westinghouse Electric Corp.). A showcase interior should have more illumination than the top of the case, but not more than about twice as much. Where the illumination on top is in the 30- to 75-ft-c range, T-6 or T-8 slimlines inside the case, operated at 200 ma, provide sufficient light; for higher foot-candles on the top, an operating current of 300 ma is sometimes recommended. Too great a differential between the illumination inside the case and that on the top, where the merchandise is normally inspected more closely prior to purchase, is not advisable. Many products examined under an illumination level significantly lower than that under which they were displayed lose some of their attraction. This is not a consideration with feature displays, since they are seldom removed for inspection.

The plot in Fig. 108 indicates the approximate initial foot-candles perpendicular to the source at various angles for each 100 rated lamp lumens per foot of case length. The figures above the arcs represent foot-candles obtained with a fluores-

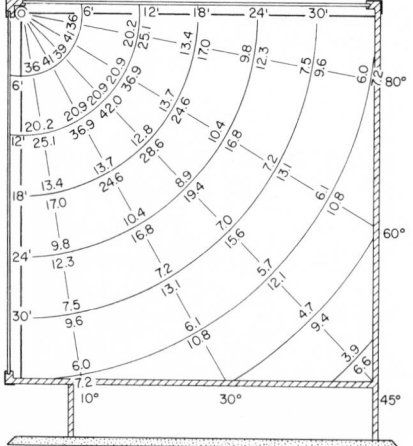

FIG. 108 *Initial foot-candles for each 100 rated lamp lumens per foot of showcase length.*

cent lamp in a specular showcase reflector. The figures below the arcs represent foot-candles obtained with standard filament reflector showcase lamps and differ from the fluorescent values because of beam control.

Wall Cases ("Lighting Handbook," Westinghouse Electric Corp.). Wall cases generally should be illuminated to approximately the same level as counter display areas. However, higher levels are desirable where the brightness of the wall case and the adjoining sales space is to be used partly to pull traffic into the area. One of the most important features of the lighting of wall cases for wearing apparel is that it be designed to light the entire case from top to bottom rather than just the shoulders of the garments. The illumination at the bottom should be at least one-tenth of that at the top.

	Horizontal distance—H, in.							
Vertical distance— V, in.	Values with symmetrical reflector, ft-c				Values without reflector, ft-c			
	6	12	18	24	6	12	18	24
6	21.4	15.7	12.1	9.8	30.6	22.8	16.5	13.5
12	12.0	12.8	12.1	10.2	11.3	14.7	13.6	12.2
18	7.4	9.6	10.0	9.1	5.2	8.8	10.2	9.6
24	4.4	6.9	8.8	7.7	2.6	5.0	6.6	7.2
30	2.6	4.8	6.9	6.8	1.4	3.3	4.4	5.2
36	2.0	3.8	5.2	6.1	1.0	2.2	3.2	4.1
42	1.4	2.8	4.1	5.0	0.6	1.4	2.2	3.0
48	0.8	1.9	2.8	4.1	0.4	1.0	1.6	2.2
54	0.8	1.6	2.4	3.4	0.4	0.8	1.4	1.6
60	0.6	1.2	1.9	2.6	0.3	0.8	1.0	1.4

The above table lists the approximate illumination in foot-candles produced by fluorescent lamps on a vertical surface for each 100 rated lamp lumens per foot of case length. The specular symmetrical reflector was so adjusted that its maximum candlepower was directed at a point 42 in. below the lamp. Where no reflector was used the entire inner surface of the valance was painted white.

246. Show-window Lighting. Since the primary object of a show window is to attract attention, it should be illuminated to a sufficient intensity so that it will stand out from its surroundings. Table **248** gives a guide to the proper spacing and size of lamps for show windows in different locations. Great care should be exercised in designing show-window lighting so that the lamps will be concealed from view. The lighting equipment should be concealed from view either by recessing in the ceiling or by means of a valance between the reflector and the front glass of the window. A good way to blind your prospective customer so he cannot see the goods on display in your window is to put exposed lamps around the window borders, suspend them from chandeliers, or so install them in the top of the window that his eye cannot escape them (see Fig. 109).

Shadows are necessary in window lighting in order to produce the desired effects, but they should not be too sharply defined. The light should come from in front of the goods. If the lamps are placed in the middle of the show-window ceiling, the front of the goods displayed in the front of the window will be in darkness because of the shadows cast by them.

If the back of the display window is not boxed in, or if the window back is of glass, a valance or curtain should be provided to screen the window lamps from the store and to prevent back reflection to an observer on the sidewalk.

Customers' attention should be attracted by illuminating selected articles with spotlights. Where decorative effects are desired, colored spotlights may be used, and motor-operated dimmers can add motion and dramatic effects. Fluorescent units bring out the beauty of floral displays and give out very little heat. Daylight lamps bring out the beauty of polished aluminum and chromium-plated articles.

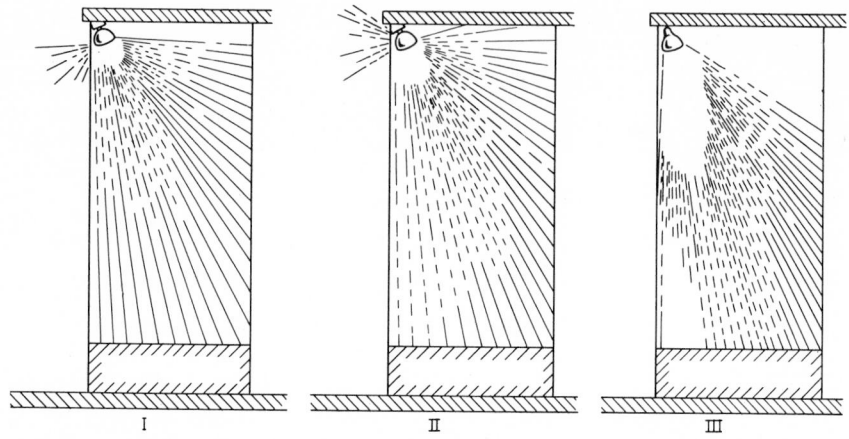

I   II   III

Effect with improperly selected reflectors   Effect with proper reflectors

FIG. 109   *Illustrating good and bad window lighting.*

247. Show-window Lighting Equipment.   Angle-type prismatic or mirrored reflectors installed in a vertical position along the front upper edge of the window are employed for show-window lighting.   These special angle reflectors for show-window lighting are manufactured in many shapes in order to meet the varied requirements for the different types and sizes of windows.   More than one row of reflectors with the lamps on several circuits is employed in many modern show windows so that a variety of lighting effects with respect to both intensities and color can be obtained.   Beautiful artistic effects can be produced by the use of colored light obtained by placing a gelatin screen or glass roundel of the desired color over the mouth of the reflector.   Spotlights are often used in addition to the regular lighting units in order to illuminate special parts of a display to a high intensity.   Spotlights will greatly enhance the effects produced.   No general rules can be given concerning the shadows and color of light to be used.   Innumerable effects can be obtained.   By experiment, the display manager should determine the proper effect for each display to be lighted.

248. Spacing of Reflectors and Sizes of Lamps for Show-window Illumination
(Westinghouse Lamp Co.)

Population of city or town	Location of store	Spacing of reflectors, in.	Size of Mazda lamps, watts
5,000 or less	Main streets	15	150
	Side streets	18	150
5,000–50,000	Main streets	12	150–200
	Side streets	15	150
Above 50,000	Super white way	15	500
	Metropolitan district	12	200
	Main streets	12	150–200
	Side streets	15	150

249. Method of Computing Show-window Illumination.   The average intensity of illumination produced on the floor or back wall of a show window can be obtained from the following formula.

$$\text{Intensity of illumination in foot-candles} = \frac{A}{B} \qquad (16)$$

wherein A = a factor depending upon the size and spacing of lamps (Table **250**) and B = a factor depending upon the dimensions of the window and the type of reflecting equipment (Tables **251** and **252**).

Example. Determine the foot-candles of illumination produced on the walls and floor of a window 8 ft high and 6 ft deep lighted with 150-watt distributing units spaced 18 in. apart.

Solution. From Table **250,** factor A for 150-watt lamps spaced 18 in. apart is 1,470. From Table **252** for distributing reflectors, a depth of window of 6 ft and a height of window of 8 ft give a value of 26 for factor B for the wall and a value of 13 for factor B for the floor.

$$\text{Average intensity on wall in foot-candles} = \frac{A}{B} = \frac{1,470}{26}$$

$$= 56.5 \text{ ft-c}$$

$$\text{Average intensity on floor in foot-candles} = \frac{A}{B} = \frac{1,470}{13}$$

$$= 113 \text{ ft-c}$$

250. A Factors
(Curtis Lighting, Inc.)

Reflector spacing, in.	Size of lamps, watts				
	100	150	200	300	500
	A factors				
12	1,350	2,200	3,200		
15	1,080	1,760	2,560	4,000	7,520
18	900	1,470	2,130	3,330	6,270
24	675	1,100	1,600	2,500	4,700
30	540	880	1,280		
36	450	730			

251. B Factors for Concentrating Reflectors
(Curtis Lighting, Inc.)

Height of window, ft		Depth of window, ft							
		2	3	4	5	6	8	10	12
		B factors for concentrating reflectors							
4	Wall	18	26	35	60	125	165	250	400
	Floor	5	6	7	8	9	12	15	18
6	Wall	18	27	38	41	55	80	165	250
	Floor	6	7	8	10	11	14	16	20
8	Wall	18	27	38	40	50	70	125	200
	Floor	11	9	9	11	12	15	18	20
10	Wall	20	29	38	45	50	70	100	140
	Floor	13	10	10	11	13	15	18	20
12	Wall	24	30	38	45	55	75	85	110
	Floor	13	12	12	13	13	16	19	21
14	Wall	28	31	38	45	55	75	80	105
	Floor	13	13	14	14	15	17	20	22

252. B Factors for Distributing Reflectors
(Curtis Lighting, Inc.)

Height of window, ft		Depth of window, ft							
		2	3	4	5	6	8	10	12
		B factors for distributing reflectors							
4	Wall	10	13	17	21	25	33	45	55
	Floor	6	7	8	9	10	12	15	17
6	Wall	11	15	19	22	26	35	38	55
	Floor	8	8	9	10	11	13	16	18
8	Wall	13	16	18	19	26	33	41	50
	Floor	11	11	12	12	13	15	18	20
10	Wall	16	18	21	23	27	35	41	50
	Floor	14	14	14	15	15	17	20	21
12	Wall	18	20	22	25	29	33	41	50
	Floor	19	18	17	17	17	18	20	22
14	Wall	21	23	25	28	31	41	43	50
	Floor	20	20	20	20	20	20	23	25

253. School and Office Lighting. As school and office work are usually performed during the daylight hours, any artificial illumination is usually in conjunction with the available daylight. Since practically all the work done in an office or school is on plane surfaces such as papers and books, shadows not only are unnecessary but are objectionable. Also, since the persons must use artificial illumination for long periods of time, the glare should be minimum. The above requirements render indirect and semi-indirect units especially suitable for office and school illumination. The units should, as a general rule, be given a closer spacing than for other classes of service. This will produce a more gradual shading of any shadows and will also afford a greater flexibility in desk and partition arrangement.

Choice of Light Source ("Lighting Handbook," Westinghouse Electric Corp.). Either fluorescent or incandescent lamps can be used to achieve good-quality office and school lighting. However, at levels in excess of 70 ft-c the attainment of satisfactory quality becomes difficult with incandescent systems. To determine the most economical type of source for a particular installation a cost analysis should be made.

254. Lighting Codes and Legislation. A few states, including California, Oklahoma, Idaho, Ohio, Kentucky, Oregon, Maryland, Washington, Massachusetts, Wisconsin, Pennsylvania, New Jersey, and New York, have enacted statutes or lighting codes regulating lighting in industrial plants. Since it is the intention of the states only to protect the welfare of the citizens against undue accident hazard, the illuminations required by the statutes are usually much too low for the best efficiency. Any lighting installation planned according to the principles set forth in this division will in all probability satisfy any state code. However, before a lighting installation is made in a factory or industrial plant, the designer should fully acquaint himself with any pertinent legislation.

HEAT-WITH-LIGHT FOR BUILDING SPACES

255. Luminaires for Environmental Control. Not too many years ago architects designed buildings primarily as space enclosures. The end use for which the space enclosures were designed usually dictated the type and design of the buildings, and how the space was divided and arranged. Comfort conditioning of the space for people normally consisted of a heating system for use in cold weather, and a ventilating system for warm weather, which more recently is an air-conditioning system.

Progress in building design and construction, and in technological developments in space conditioning, has changed the architects' objective in the design of buildings. Presently, the emphasis is not only on space enclosure tailored to the needs of the occupants, but also on environment and environmental control of lighting, heating, cooling, acoustics, space flexibility, and esthetic appearance (pleasing colors, etc.).

Visual and thermal conditions have become two of the most important considerations in planned interior environment. Visual comfort is controlled primarily by quality and quantity of illumination. And adequate illumination of proper quality for high visual performance and high visual comfort increases electric energy loads, which also means higher heat gain. Thus, lighting systems that provide adequate quality illumination may have considerable effect on the thermal conditions within the buildings. Thermal comfort is controlled through a proper balance in temperature, relative humidity, and air motion. Accordingly, light- and heat-producing characteristics of the lighting system have become dominant factors in the thermal equation.

This expanded use of lighting heat heralds a new era in environmental design. It provides the opportunity to supply all or a substantial part of a building's heating requirements from lighting systems with accompanying benefits, and control of lighting heat is necessary for the most effective utilization of this energy.

256. Integrated Lighting-Heating-Cooling Systems. There has been a growing coordinated activity between electrical and mechanical engineers since 1958, when the Illuminating Engineering Society adopted new and higher recommended levels of illumination for most seeing tasks. This activity has resulted in many new techniques for handling lighting heat loads, which are based on the integration and correlation of lighting, heating, and cooling systems. Although many approaches to this problem are possible, the basic one is to divert all possible lighting heat gain from the occupied spaces in buildings to keep the capacity of the *cooling* system as low as possible. Another objective is to recapture some or all of this lighting heat gain, to keep the capacity of the *heating* system as low as possible. This heat may be removed from interior areas of the building which need cooling, for example, and redirected to perimeter areas which need heating at the same time.

257. Air-handling Troffers. In the typical integrated system, heat from the lighting system is removed by passing return air from the air-conditioned space through vents integral with the luminaires over the warm surfaces of lamps, ballasts, and luminaires, into the plenum or return air duct, and back through the return side of the air-conditioning system. After tempering, the supply air is redistributed, entering the conditioned spaces through a different set of vents, which are also integral with the luminaires. Luminaires designed for this purpose are called "air-handling" troffers. There is also available an "air-water" luminaire, in which circulating water through the luminaires removes the lighting heat.

By combining lighting, heating, and cooling services in a single outlet element (the luminaire), the conflict for space both above and on the ceiling is reduced. This integration forces coordinated design and produces as its visual result an architecturally clean, uncluttered ceiling.

Many lighting manufacturers now have available air-handling troffers, in a range of sizes and for a variety of air-handling requirements: (1) static (non-air-handling); (2) air supply; (3) air return; and (4) combination air supply, air return. These luminaires may be integrated with either cooling systems or heating systems, or both. Installation methods conform generally to those for standard fluorescent troffers.

There are also available several complete ceiling systems combining both air-supply and air-return provisions, some of which use conventional fluorescent luminaires, and some of which incorporate special air-handling luminaires which are an integral part of the ceiling system. Typical examples are shown in Figs. 110, 111, and 112. The air-handling troffer in Fig. 110 supplies cool air to the occupied space below the ceiling, and returns warm air from the occupied space through the troffer to the open plenum above. Heat from lamps and ballasts is also removed. Warm plenum air may be discarded or mixed with fresh air and recirculated for heating specific occupied spaces.

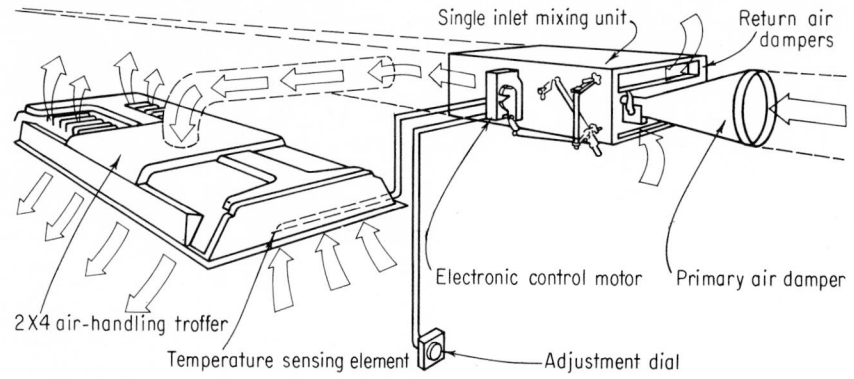

FIG. 110 *Air-handling troffer by Day-Brite. (Div. of Emerson Electric Co.)*

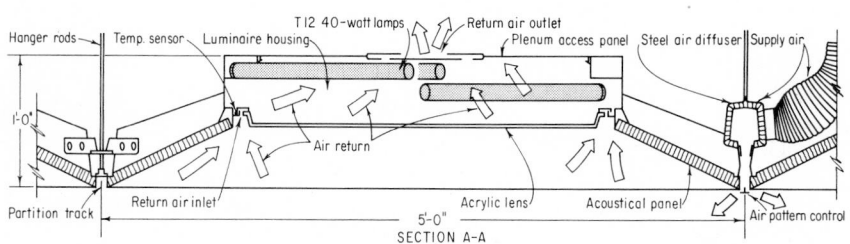

FIG. 111 *Unified ceiling system by Day-Brite. (Div. of Emerson Electric Co.)*

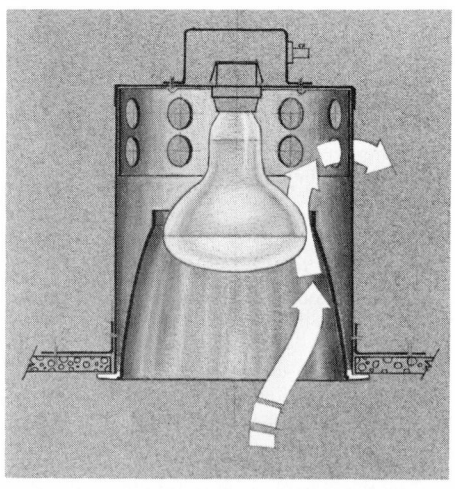

FIG. 112 *Recessed incandescent downlights integrated with heating and cooling systems. (Prescolite Mfg. Corp.)*

The unified ceiling system in Fig. 111 provides complete environmental control through a modular-size integrated package. Each module combines lighting, heating, cooling, sound control, partition tracks for flexibility, shielding of the lighted portion of a luminaire in "line of vision," and good appearance.

The recessed incandescent downlight (Fig. 112) is integrated with heating and cooling systems to the extent that lighting heat may be exhausted to the plenum space and discharged as waste or reused.

STREET LIGHTING

The following material is reproduced from "Lighting Handbook" through the courtesy of the Westinghouse Electric Corp.

258. General Requirements for Street Lighting. Good street and highway lighting, often termed "traffic safety lighting," not only promotes safer conditions for drivers but provides greater safety for pedestrians as well. It enhances the community value of a street by its attractive appearance, which is usually reflected in higher property values. Well-lighted streets also act as a deterrent to criminal activity.

In order to achieve truly effective street lighting it is essential that the installation be well planned. Planned street lighting should follow the American Standard Practice for Roadway Lighting of the Illuminating Engineering Society and will involve the following considerations:

1. Traffic classification of the street.
2. Determination of the proper lighting intensity for the street classification.
3. Selection of luminaires according to the light distribution needed for the street.
4. Determination of the mounting height of the luminaire above the road surface and the proper linear spacing between luminaires.

Each step follows the preceding one in logical order, and the following tables and charts will assist in the accurate planning of an installation.

259. Street Classification. A traffic classification should be made of all streets so that the lighting system design will be in keeping with the particular needs of each street or highway. The table shows the vehicular traffic volume classification recommended by the Street Lighting Committee of the Institute of Traffic Engineers.

It is recommended that all streets be further classified by the volume of pedestrian traffic during the night hours of maximum usage:

Classification of Traffic	Vehicles per Hour[a]
Very light traffic	Under 150
Light traffic	150– 500
Medium traffic	500–1,200
Heavy traffic	1,200–2,400
Very heavy traffic	2,400–4,000
Heaviest traffic	Over 4,000

[a] Maximum night hour in both directions.

Light or no pedestrian traffic, as on streets in residential or in most warehouse areas, on express, elevated or depressed roadways or on open highways.

Medium pedestrian traffic, as on secondary business streets and on some industrial streets.

Heavy pedestrian traffic, as on business streets.

260. Lighting Intensity. The proper lighting intensity for each roadway classification may be determined from the following table.

Recommendation for Average Horizontal Foot-candles[a] in Lumens per Square Foot
("IES Lighting Handbook")

Roadways (other than expressways or freeways)				Expressways and freeways	
Roadway classification	Area classification			Classification	Expressways
	Downtown	Inter-mediate	Outlying and rural		
Major	2.0	1.2	0.9	Continuous urban	1.4[b]
Collector	1.2	0.9	0.6	Continuous rural	1.0
Local or minor	0.9	0.6	0.2[c]	Interchange urban	2.0
				Interchange rural	1.4

[a] The average horizontal foot-candles recommended represent average illumination on the roadway pavement when the illuminating source is at its lowest output and when the luminaire is in its dirtiest condition.

[b] 2.0 foot-candles in downtown area.

[c] Residential.

NOTE. In using the table the following factors should be considered:

1. Intersecting converging and diverging roadway areas at grade require higher illumination than that recommended herein. The illumination in these areas should be at least equal to the sum of the illumination values provided on the roadways that form the intersection.

2. The lowest foot-candle value at any point on the pavement should not be less than *one-third* the average value. The only exception to this requirement applies to residential roadways where the lowest foot-candle value at any point may be as low as one-sixth the average value.

These recommended foot-candle levels are the average values on the roadway between curbs. The lowest intensity at any point should not be less than one-fourth of these values. The figures given above are based on favorable pavement reflectance of the order of 10 per cent. When the reflectance is low (3 per cent or less), the illumination recommended should be increased 50 per cent. When the reflectance is unusually high (20 per cent or more), the recommended values may be decreased 25 per cent.

261. Selection of Luminaire. Luminaires should be selected according to their pattern of light distribution, so as to conform not only to the light intensity required but to the physical characteristics of the street to be lighted. Typical lateral candlepower distribution curves for several types of luminaires are shown. Lateral beam width is measured to half maximum candlepower.

Type I Luminaire. Type I is a two-way lateral distribution having a preferred lateral width of 15 deg on each side of the reference line (total 30 deg), with an acceptable range of 10 to less than 20 deg. It projects two beams in opposite directions along

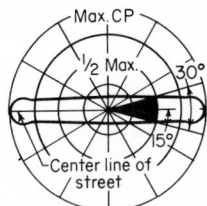

the roadway, parallel to the curb line. The candlepower distribution is similar on both sides of the vertical plane of maximum candlepower. Luminaires with this type of distribution are generally applicable to locations near the center of a roadway, where the mounting height is approximately equal to the roadway width.

Four-way Type I Luminaire. Four-way Type I is a distribution having four principal concentrations at lateral angles of approximately 90 deg to one another, each with

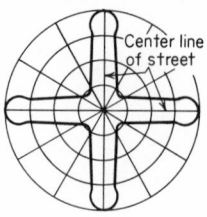

a width of 20 to less than 40 deg as in Type I. This distribution is generally applicable to luminaires located over or near the center of a right-angle intersection.

TYPE II LUMINAIRE. Type II distributions have a preferred lateral width of 25 deg with an acceptable range of 20 to less than 30 deg. This distribution is generally ap-

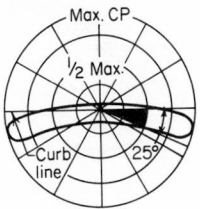

plicable to luminaires located at or near the side of relatively narrow roadways, where the width of the roadway does not exceed 1.6 times the mounting height.

FOUR-WAY TYPE II LUMINAIRE. Four-way Type II distributions have four principal light concentrations, each with a width of 20 to less than 30 deg as in Type II. This

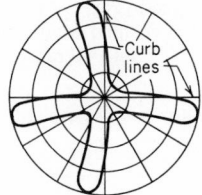

distribution is generally applicable to luminaire locations near one corner of a right-angle intersection.

TYPE III LUMINAIRE. Type III distributions have a preferred lateral width of 40 deg with an acceptable range of 30 to less than 50 deg. This type of distribution is intended

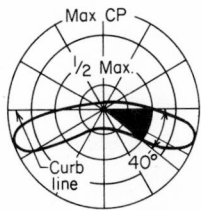

for luminaires mounted at or near the side of medium-width roadways, where the width of the roadway does not exceed 2.7 times the mounting height.

TYPE IV LUMINAIRE. Type IV distributions have a preferred lateral width of 60 deg with an acceptable width of 50 deg or more. This type of distribution is intended for

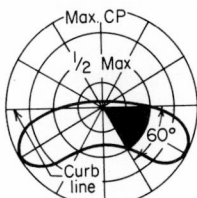

side-of-road mounting and is generally used on wide roadways (width up to 3.7 times the mounting height).

TYPE V LUMINAIRE. Type V distribution is essentially circular, with equal candle-power at all lateral angles. This type of distribution is intended for luminaire mount-

ing at or near the center of a roadway, in the center islands of parkways, and at inter-sections.

262. Mounting Height and Spacing of Luminaires. Two considerations are of para-mount importance in determining optimum mounting height: the desirability of mini-mizing direct glare from the luminaire and the need for a reasonably uniform distribu-tion of illumination on the street surface. The higher the luminaire is mounted, the farther it is above the normal line of vision and the less glare it creates. However, the attainment of uniform illumination requires a certain relationship between mounting height, luminaire spacing, and the vertical angle of maximum candlepower for the specific luminaire (usually between 70 and 80 deg).

Relationship between spacing and mounting height

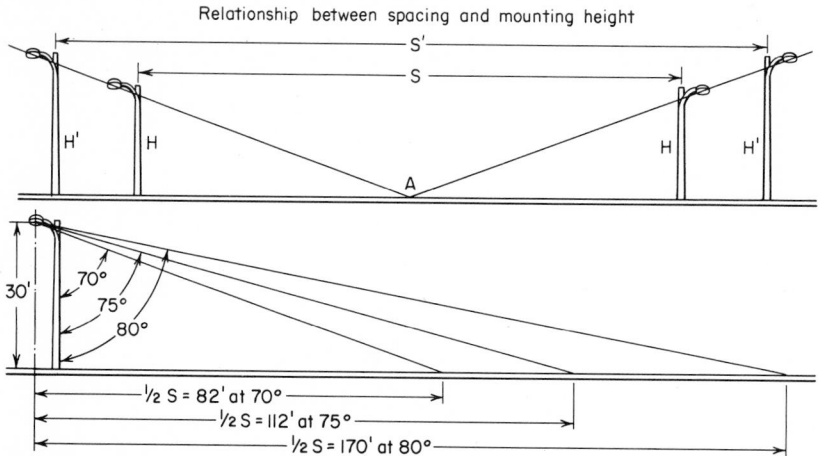

For a given luminaire the ratio of pole spacing to mounting height should be low enough so that the light at the angle of maximum vertical candlepower will strike the street at least halfway to the adjacent pole. To provide greater uniformity on busy streets the spacing is often reduced as much as 50 per cent, which provides 100 per cent overlap of vertical beams.

The mounting heights recommended by the Illuminating Engineering Society's Committee on Street and Highway Lighting take into account both the objective of minimum glare and that of maximum uniformity. Greater mounting heights may often be preferable, but heights less than those recommended cannot be considered good practice.

Minimum Luminaire Mounting Heights
("IES Lighting Handbook")

Maximum luminaire candlepower	Minimum mounting height, ft		
	Cutoff	Semicutoff	Noncutoff
Under 5000	20	20	25
Under 10,000	20	25	30
Under 15,000	25	30	35
Over 15,000	30	35	40

FLOODLIGHTING

263. Modern floodlighting (General Electric Co.) meets many utilitarian requirements as well as many applications concerned with decoration, esthetics, or advertising value. Protecting property after nightfall, completing a construction job within the time allotted, illuminating a dangerous traffic intersection, and prolonging the hours of play on recreational areas are only a few of the almost infinite applications of utilitarian floodlighting.

As an advertising medium that compels attention without detracting from the beauty or dignity of a building, floodlighting offers its best proof by the many excellent examples to be found in almost every city. The natural beauty of churches, civic buildings, monuments, and gardens is often enhanced by skillfully applied floodlighting.

264. Floodlighting Design. The following material on floodlighting design including sports floodlighting (Table **267**) is reproduced from "Lighting Handbook" through the courtesy of the Westinghouse Electric Corp. Consult manufacturers of floodlighting equipment for more detailed information.

The type of area to be lighted, the possible location of equipment, and the variation in surrounding conditions impose problems in design which tend to make standardization difficult. There are, however, certain basic rules which may be followed in installation design.

DESIGN PROCEDURE

265. Step 1. Determine the Level of Illumination. In Table **243** are listed the illumination levels for many floodlighting applications. These levels are designated as "foot-candles in service," and allowances must be made for reasonable depreciation in the original design.

In lighting buildings, monuments, etc., the reflection factor of the object and the brightness of the surroundings must be considered in order to determine the amount of light necessary (Table **266**).

266. Recommended Illumination Levels for Floodlighting
("IES Lighting Handbook")

Surface material	Reflectance, per cent	Surround	
		Bright	Dark
		Recommended level, foot-candles	
Light marble, white or cream terra-cotta, white plaster	70–85	15	5
Concrete, tinted stucco, light gray and buff limestone, buff face brick	45–70	20	10
Medium gray limestone, common tan brick, sandstone	20–45	30	15
Common red brick, brownstone, stained wood shingles, dark gray brick	10–20[a]	50	20

[a] Buildings or areas of materials having a reflectance of less than 20 per cent usually cannot be floodlighted economically, unless they carry a large amount of high-reflectance trim.

267. Recommended Illumination Levels for Sports Lighting

Application	Foot-candles maintained in service	Application	Foot-candles maintained in service
Sports lighting			
Badminton:		Club	20
Tournament	30	Recreational	10
Club	20		
Recreational	10	Horseshoe pitching:	
		Tournament	10
Baseball:		Recreational	5
Seats:			
During game	2	Playgrounds	5
Before and after game	5		

Application	In-field	Out-field	Application	Foot-candles
Major League	150	100	Race tracks:	
AAA and AA League	75	50	Seats	2
A and B League	50	30	Track	20
C and D League	30	20		
Semipro and municipal	20	15	Rifle range:	

				Out-door	In-door
Basketball:			On target	30ᵃ	50ᵃ
College and Professional	50		Firing point	10	10
High school	30		Range	...	5
Recreational	10				

Application	Foot-candles	Application	Foot-candles
Bathing beaches (surf)	3ᵃ	Shuffleboard:	
		Tournament	10
		Recreational	5

Billiards:	General	On Table	Skating:		
Tournament	10	50	Rink (indoor or outdoor)	5	
Recreational	10	30	Pond or flooded area	1	

			Skeet shooting, target surface at 60 ft	30ᵃ

Bowling:	General	On Pins	Ski slope, practice	0.5
Tournament	20	50ᵃ	Soccer:	
Recreational	10	30ᵃ	College and professional	30
			High school	20
Boxing or wrestling:			Recreational	10
Seats:				
During bout	2		Softball:	
Before and after bout	5			

Ring:			In-field	Out-field
Championship	500	Pro and championship	50	30
Professional	200	Semipro	30	20
Amateur	100	Industrial league	20	10
		Recreational	10	5

Croquet:		Squash:	
Tournament	10	Tournament	30
Recreational	5	Club	20
		Recreational	10
Football:			
Class I	100	Swimming pools	10
Class II	50		
Class III	30	Tennis:	

			Table	Lawn
Class IV	20	Tournament	50	30
Class V	10	Club	30	20
		Recreational	20	10

Gymnasium:		Trapshooting:	
Locker and shower rooms	10	Target surface at 150 ft	30ᵃ
Exercise rooms, fencing, boxing, wrestling, basketball, volleyball, softball, and general exercise	20	Firing point—general	10
Exhibition games and matches	30	Volleyball:	
		Tournament	20
Handball:		Recreational	10
Tournament	30		

ᵃ Vertical.
See Table **243** for more complete data.

268. Step 2.   Determine the Type and Location of Floodlights.   Light for floodlighting applications can be supplied by either open or enclosed equipment.   The enclosed floodlight provides a higher maintained efficiency and more accurate beam control, as well as protecting the lamp and reflector from the weather.   Open floodlights sometimes require the use of hard glass lamps to prevent breakage caused by rain, snow, or insects striking the hot bulb.   Hard glass lamps are necessary where the floodlight does not provide adequate shielding for the lamp or where the equipment is to be used under adverse weather conditions.   Although the initial cost of an enclosed floodlight is higher than that of an open floodlight, an installation of enclosed equipment is often more economical ultimately because of the higher maintained efficiency and the fact that standard soft glass lamps can be used under all weather conditions.

Enclosed floodlighting equipment may be of either the "general-purpose" or the "heavy-duty" class.   The general-purpose floodlight is one in which the inner surface of the housing serves as the reflecting surface.   The heavy-duty floodlight is more rugged, since its aluminum or glass reflector is protected by a metal housing.   Units designed especially for lighting the ground are called "ground-area" floodlights.

269. Data on Typical Floodlight Equipment

Floodlight	Advantages	Lamp	Beam spread[a]	Typical beam lumens		
				500-watt	1,000-watt	1,500-watt
Heavy duty or general purpose	Good light control, weathertight, adaptable to wide variety of applications, easy to maintain	Floodlight service	Type 1	3,000	6,600	10,500
		Floodlight or clear general service	Type 2	3,200	8,000	13,500
			Type 3	3,800	8,500	15,000
			Type 4	4,200	10,000	16,000
		Clear general service	Type 5	5,200	11,000	18,000
					1,000-watt	1,500-watt
Ground area enclosed	Good light control; weathertight; easily serviced, good lamp burning position; high efficiency	Clear general service	Type 2		9,000	14,000
			Type 3		10,000	16,000
			Type 4		11,500	19,000
			Type 5		12,000	19,000
			Type 6		12,000	19,000
					1,000-watt	1,500-watt
Ground area open	Light weight, good lamp burning position, low initial cost	Clear general service	Type 4		8,500	13,000
			Type 5		12,000	19,000
			Type 6		15,000	23,000
				75-watt	150-watt	300-watt
Projector or reflector lamp	Low cost, small size, low maintenance cost	PAR-38 spot PAR-38 flood R-40 spot[b] R-40 flood[b]	Type 3	450	1,200	
			Type 4	550	1,500	
			Type 5			3,200
			Type 6			3,200

[a] For classification of beam spreads by Type, see the following table.
[b] Hard glass lamp.

The finish of the reflector has an important influence on beam spread. Most enclosed units are available with either a narrow-beam (specular finish) or a wide-beam (diffuse finish) reflector. The beam spread can be further controlled by the cover glass, three general types of which are available:

Stippled lens — diffuses the light, increasing the beam spread in both the horizontal and vertical planes.

Spread lens — spreads the light in one plane only, either horizontal or vertical.

Plain lens — does not alter the beam spread appreciably.

In heavy-duty equipment the choice of lamp also influences the beam spread. The floodlighting service lamp, by virtue of its more concentrated filament, produces a narrower beam spread than the general-service lamp.

Approximate Beam Spreads of Typical Floodlights

Lamp type	Enclosed floodlights						Open floodlights
	Narrow-beam			Wide-beam			
	Plain lens	Stippled lens	Med.-spread lens	Plain lens	Stippled lens	Wide-spread lens	
General-purpose Floodlights							
General service...	30 × 30° Type 3	60 × 60° Type 4	35 × 60° Type 3	80 × 80° Type 5	100 × 100° Type 6	85 × 130° Type 5	45 × 45° to 150 × 150° Types 3–6
Heavy-duty Floodlights							
General service....	25 × 25° Type 2	55 × 55° Type 4	25 × 50° Type 2	85 × 85° Type 5	95 × 95° Type 5	85 × 130° Type 5	
Floodlight service	15 × 15° Type 1	45 × 45° Type 3	20 × 45° Type 1				

Although the open floodlight is not well adapted to producing accurate beam control or a narrow beam spread, many units are available with an auxiliary reflector which produces a concentration of light at a specific angle, usually in the center of the beam. Most auxiliary reflectors are semidiffuse and must be kept clean to function properly.

To simplify the specification of equipment the National Electrical Manufacturers' Association has introduced a series of type numbers specifying beam spread and group letters specifying floodlight construction. In order to meet NEMA standards a floodlight must conform to certain construction requirements as well as have a certain minimum efficiency for a given beam spread.

Although the choice of beam spread for a particular application depends upon individual circumstances, the following general principles apply:

1. The greater the distance from the floodlight to the area to be lighted, the narrower the beam spread desired.

2. Since by definition the candlepower at the edge of a floodlight beam is 10 per cent of the candlepower near the center of the beam, the illumination level at the edge of the beam is one-tenth or less of that at the center. To obtain reasonable uniformity of illumination the beams of individual floodlights must overlap each other as well as the edge of the surface to be lighted.

3. The percentage of beam lumens falling outside the area to be lighted is usually lower with narrow-beam units than with wide-beam units. Thus narrow-beam floodlights are preferable where they will provide the necessary degree of uniformity of illumination and the proper foot-candle level.

NEMA Floodlight Classification System

Type	Beam spread, average of vertical and horizontal spread for approximately symmetrical units, deg	Enclosed general purpose		Open porcelain enameled	
		Group A, diam less than 17 in.	Group B, diam 17 in. and over	Group C, without auxiliary reflector	Group D, with auxiliary reflector
		Minimum beam efficiency, per cent			
1	10 to less than 18	34	35		
2	18 to less than 29	36	36		
3	29 to less than 46	39	45		
4	46 to less than 70	42	50	. . .	35
5	70 to less than 100	46	50	. . .	40
6	100 and over	. . .	. . .	55	60

For a floodlight with an elliptical-spread lens, the type is determined by the spread of the minor axis. The lens is designated as medium-spread if it increases the spread in one plane 20 to 40 deg and wide-spread if it increases it 40 deg or more.

270. Typical Floodlighting Applications

Application	Location of equipment	Class of equipment
	At edge of area and mounted as high as possible. Spacing not to exceed four times mounting height	Preferred: ground area enclosed Alternate: ground area open General purpose enclosed Heavy duty Type 4, 5, or 6
	Immediately inside and below concealing parapet—maximum distance from face of building to be lighted	Preferred: heavy duty Alternate: general purpose enclosed Projector lamps (if vertical throw is short) Type 3, 4, or 5
	In banks at suitable location. One bank normally should cover an area whose height and length is not greater than the distance from the units to the face of the building	Preferred: heavy duty Alternate: general purpose enclosed Type 1, 2, 3, or 4
	At edge of area where they will not hinder traffic. Minimum mounting height—20 ft	Preferred: ground area enclosed Projector lamps Alternate: ground area open Type 5 or 6
	On ground 5 to 25 ft from vertical surface, concealed by hedge, low structure, or natural elevation	Preferred: heavy duty Alternate: general purpose enclosed Projector lamps Type 3, 4, 5, or 6

The location of floodlighting equipment is usually dictated by the type of application and the physical surroundings. If the area is large, individual towers or poles spaced at regular intervals may be required to light it evenly; smaller areas may require only one tower with all equipment concentrated on it, or adjacent buildings may be utilized as floodlight locations. The accompanying chart will aid in the selection of the right equipment and its proper location for a number of typical floodlighting applications.

In planning any floodlighting system it is important that the light be properly controlled. Strong light directed parallel to a highway or railroad track can be a dangerous source of glare to oncoming traffic, and light thrown indiscriminately on adjacent property may be a serious nuisance.

271. Step 3. Determine the Coefficient of Beam Utilization. To determine the number of floodlights that will be required to produce a specified level of illumination in a given situation, it is necessary to know the number of lumens in the beam of the floodlight and the percentage of the beam lumens striking the area to be lighted. The beam lumens can be obtained from the manufacturer's catalogue, or for rough calculations may be estimated from the table in Sec. **269.** The ratio of the lumens striking the floodlighted surface to the beam lumens is called the *coefficient of beam utilization* (CBU). Where an area is uniformly lighted the average CBU of the floodlights in the installation is always less than 1.0.

The coefficient of beam utilization for any individual floodlight will depend on its location, the point at which it is aimed, and the distribution of light within its beam. In general it may be said that the average CBU of all the floodlights in an installation should fall within the range of 0.60 to 0.90. If less than 60 per cent of the beam lumens are utilized, it is a definite indication that a more economical lighting plan should be possible by using different locations or narrower beam floodlights. On the other hand, if the CBU is over 0.90 it is probable that the beam spread selected is too narrow and the resultant illumination will be spotty. Accurate determination of the CBU is possible only after the aiming points have been selected. However, an estimated CBU can be determined by experience, or by making calculations for several potential aiming points and using the average figure thus obtained.

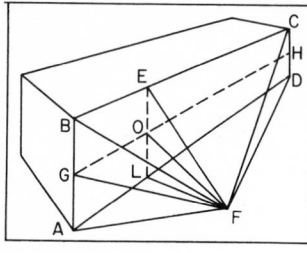

If   EO = OL = 25
      AL = FL = 40
      LD = 80

Then: angle LFO = 32°
            EFO = 19°
            BFE = 32°
            GFO = 41°
            AFL = 45°
            CFE = 51°
            HFO = 60°
            DFL = 64°

The CBU of the floodlight at F is about .81

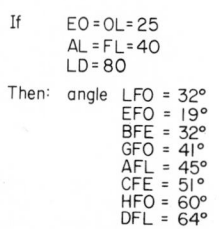

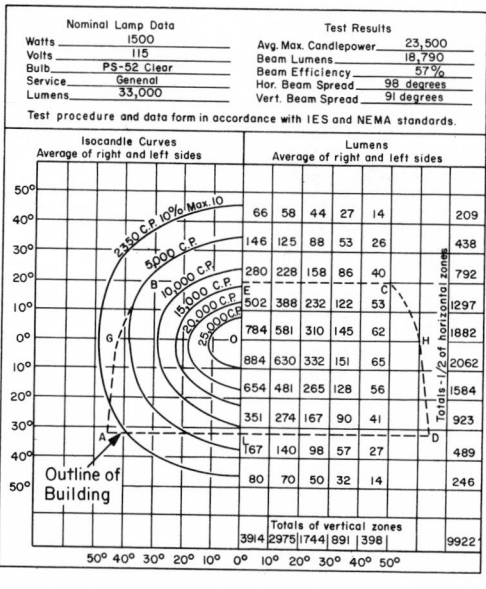

To make such calculations the floodlighted area is superimposed on the photometric grid and the ratio of the lumens inside this area to the total beam lumens is determined. All horizontal lines on a building (or straight lines on a ground area which are parallel to a line perpendicular to the beam axis) appear as straight horizontal lines on the grid if the floodlight is so aimed that its beam axis is perpendicular to a horizontal line on the face of the building. All vertical lines except the one through the beam axis appear slightly curved.

272. Step 4. Estimate the Maintenance Factor. Lighting efficiency is seriously impaired by blackened lamps and by dirt on the reflecting and transmitting surfaces of the equipment. To compensate for the gradual depreciation of illumination on the floodlighted area, a maintenance factor must be applied in the calculations to make allowance for the following:

1. Loss of light output due to dirt on the lamp, reflector, and cover glass. Under comparable conditions, enclosed floodlights have a higher maintained efficiency than open units because the cover glass protects both the reflector and the lamp from the accumulation of dirt.

2. Loss in light output of the lamp with life. Because some of the light must pass through the bulb more than once before finally leaving the floodlight, bulb blackening also lowers floodlight efficiency, the reduction in beam lumens being about double the reduction in bare lamp output.

The following maintenance factors have been widely used:
Enclosed floodlights, 0.75.   Open floodlights, 0.65.

However, where the atmosphere is not clean, where the floodlights are cleaned infrequently, or where lamps are replaced only on burnout, a realistic appraisal of in-service conditions will require the use of considerably lower maintenance factors. Differences

Average Bare Lamp Lumens throughout Life (Approximate) at Rated Voltage

Incandescent lamps	Per cent of initial	Mercury lamps	Per cent of initial
500-watt PS-40	89	400-watt A-H1	87
750-watt PS-52	87	400-watt E-H1	81
1,000-watt PS-52	83	400-Watt J-H1	79
1,500-watt PS-52	80	1,000-watt A-H15	77

in lumen maintenance among lamp types and sizes should also be considered. The higher the wattage for a given bulb size or the smaller the bulb for a given wattage, the more dense the bulb blackening and the greater the depreciation in light output. For this reason the lumen maintenance of general-service PS-bulb lamps is better than that of floodlight-service G-bulb lamps. The maintenance factors given above are based on PS-bulb lamps; they should be lowered about five to ten points when G-bulb lamps are used.

With narrow-beam floodlights, dirt on the reflector and cover glass tends to widen the beam spread, reducing the maximum candlepower more than the total light output. Thus for a small lighted area utilizing only the central part of a beam (e.g., a 4-ft archery target at 100 yd), a smaller percentage of the beam lumens will strike the target after the floodlight has become dirty. Therefore the depreciation in foot-candle intensity will be greater than the depreciation in total light output, and it will be necessary to consider this in selecting a maintenance factor.

273. Step 5.   Determine the Number of Floodlights Required.

$$\text{Number of floodlights} = \frac{\text{area} \times \text{foot-candles}}{\text{beam lumens} \times \text{CBU} \times \text{MF}}$$

Area—Surface area to be lighted in square feet.

Foot-candles—As selected from table under step 1.

Beam lumens—Refer to manufacturer's catalogue for equipment under consideration. Where the lamps are to be burned at other than rated voltage the beam lumens, and hence the number of floodlights required, is altered. The increase in lumen output for 5 and 10 per cent overvoltage operation is indicated in Sec. **276.**

CBU—Coefficient of beam utilization. Refer to step 3.

MF—Maintenance factor. Refer to step 4.

274. Step 6.   Check for Coverage and Uniformity. After a tentative layout has been made (steps 1 to 5), the uniformity can be checked by calculating the intensity of illumination at a few points on the floodlighted surface. This may be done by the point-by-point method described in Sec. **235,** using either a candlepower-distribution curve or an isocandle diagram. If the uniformity is found to be unsatisfactory, a larger number of units may have to be used.

APPLICATIONS

275. Application Notes. Buildings and Monuments. The floodlighting of a building or a monument is primarily a problem in esthetics, and each installation must be studied individually. Under some circumstances, particularly with small, utilitarian buildings or larger buildings which have no special architectural features, uniform illumination is desirable. To create an appearance of uniform brightness over the entire facade of a building, it is usually necessary to increase the actual brightness appreciably toward the top. Higher brightness at the top of a building also increases its apparent height.

With buildings of classical design or special architectural character uniform illumination often defeats the purpose of the lighting, which should aim to preserve and emphasize the architectural form. Buildings are designed primarily for daytime appearance, when the light comes from above. This effect is almost impossible to duplicate with floodlights, which must be mounted in nearby locations and usually at a height no greater than the elevation of the building. However, it is often possible to achieve a result that is interesting and pleasing, although quite different from the daytime appearance. Shadows are essential to relief, and contrasts in brightness levels or sometimes in color can be used advantageously to bring out important details and to suppress others. Sculpture or architectural detail requires particularly careful treatment to avoid flatness or grotesque shadows that may entirely distort the appearance as conceived by the artist or architect.

Excavation and Construction. Approximately one 1,500-watt, two 1,000-watt, or three 500-watt units will be required for each 5,000 sq ft of excavation area or for each 1,000 to 2,000 sq ft of construction area. It is usually most satisfactory to mount floodlights in groups of two or more on wood poles or towers 40 to 70 ft above ground. A minimum of two poles should be used, with enough poles on larger jobs to provide coverage at any working point from two or three floodlight banks. Fixed-pole spacing may be from 1½ to 3 times mounting height and as much as 5 times mounting height on large projects. Occasionally it is practical to provide one or two portable poles mounted on timber sled bases. Where a mechanical shovel or crane is used, it is advisable to mount an automatic leveling floodlight on the boom.

Railway Yards and Freight Terminals. There are two general types of railway-yard lighting, the unidirectional system and the parallel opposing system. The first is applicable only to tracks on which the traffic is all in one direction, the light being directed with the traffic flow. Glare is entirely eliminated, but seeing is entirely by direct light without the advantages of silhouette effect. The parallel opposing system

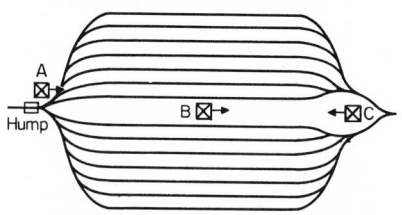

Unidirectional lighting—Use towers A and B
Parallel opposed lighting—Use towers A and C

is used where the traffic flows in both directions. Here seeing is accomplished by direct light from the tower behind the observer and by silhouette of cars and glint from the rails produced by light from the tower ahead of the observer.

Tower locations are determined by track layouts and operating methods, but in general the spacings should not exceed 1,000 to 2,000 ft for the parallel opposing system or 800 to 1,000 ft for the unidirectional system. The first tower in the classification yard should be near the ladder tracks but on the approach side of the hump, so that spill light, or a separate floodlight if necessary, illuminates the hump area. Narrow yards can be lighted by single towers located in the center. Wide yards should have pairs of towers opposite each other, each about one-fourth the yard width from the edge. Except for spacings well below the values noted above, 90 ft should be considered a minimum mounting height.

The lighting of outdoor freight terminals without covered platforms is similar to that of railroad yards except that the intensities must be much higher. Poles must be placed at the ends of the platforms to prevent interference with vehicular traffic and in line with the platforms to avoid shadows thrown by cars standing on the tracks. Mounting heights of from 60 to 80 ft, depending on the average length of throw, are required. Heavy-duty floodlights are recommended for all railroad service.

Color. Color can be provided in floodlighting installations in any one of several ways. Amber, blue, and red cover glasses are generally available for standard enclosed floodlights to replace the regular lens. Or the floodlight can be recessed in a niche, the opening of which is covered with a filter. Where smaller amounts of colored light are needed, the 75- or 150-watt PAR-38 or the hard glass 300-watt R-40 lamp may be used with a colored lens. Any color filter absorbs a large amount of light, and this loss must be considered in designing the installation. The following approximate transmission values are found in typical commercial color filters: amber, 40 to 60 per cent; red, 10 to 20 per cent; green, 5 to 20 per cent; and blue, 3 to 10 per cent. Although less colored light than white light is usually required for equal advertising or decorative effectiveness, it is desirable to determine by experiment the exact amount of colored light necessary for any particular application.

Mercury Floodlighting. Mercury floodlighting finds its greatest application in roadway, parking-area, and certain types of decorative lighting, being particularly effective on many building exteriors, lawns and shrubbery because of its distinctive colors. Its high efficiency and long life are the chief advantages of mercury lighting.

The color-corrected fluorescent mercury-vapor lamp retains the advantages of high efficiency and long life while providing a complete spectrum for good color rendition. It has found wide use in many interior and sports lighting installations.

276. Sports Lighting (Westinghouse Electric Corp.). Either enclosed or open floodlights can be used for sports lighting. However, enclosed units are strongly recommended. A given level of illumination can be produced with fewer enclosed floodlights than are required if wide-beam open units are used.

The level of illumination required depends upon several factors, among which are the speed of the game, the skill of the players, and the number of spectators and their distance from the field of play. Economic considerations are also important. High intensities of illumination are desirable for almost all sports, but since lower levels are acceptable in some cases, a variety of layouts are suggested.

Approximate Performance 1,000- and 1,500-watt Lamps

Voltage	Light	Watts	Lamp life
Rated................	100 %	100 %	100 %
5 % over rated.........	117 %	108 %	50 %
10 % over rated........	135 %	116 %	30 %

In certain sports installations where the lighting is operated less than about 500 hr per year, it is economical to use short-life lamps or to burn standard lamps at higher than rated voltage. This reduces the power cost and the required number of floodlights. For less than 200 hr per season general-service lamps at 10 per cent overvoltage are recommended. Where the lights are used between 200 and 500 hr per year, operation of general-service lamps at 5 per cent overvoltage is preferable.

The layouts that follow will produce the recommended levels of illumination if high-quality floodlights are mounted and operated as indicated. Some latitude in beam-spread requirements is acceptable where several floodlights are mounted on a single pole, provided the resulting average beam spread is approximately the same as that specified.

NOTE. Standards for sports lighting are being revised by the IES and the NEMA as this edition is going to press. Accordingly, the revised standards, which include data for high-intensity discharge lighting equipment, should be used when they become available.

277. Archery

The floodlight provides visibility of the arrow throughout flight.

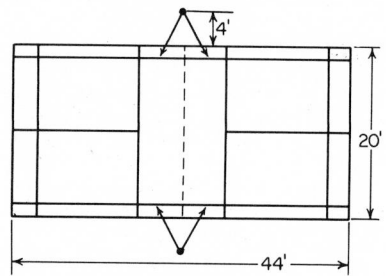

Floodlights .... Per target
          1 Type 1, Group A
          1 PAR-38 projector flood
          2 PAR-38 projector spots (optional)
Lamps .... For enclosed floodlight
          Distance up to 30 yd— 250-watt G-30 bulb
                   30 to 50 yd— 500-watt G-40 bulb
                 50 to 100 yd—1,000-watt G-40 bulb
Mounting height.................. Enclosed floodlight 10 ft above ground
          PAR-38 flood on same pole 8 ft above ground
          PAR-38 spots on ground about 10 feet in front of and on either side of target (optional)
Poles .... One per target

278. Badminton (NEMA Recommendation)

Indoor courts may be lighted with industrial diffusing units along the sidelines.

Class	Floodlights				Lamp watts	Total load, kw
	Type	Group	No. per pole	Total No.		
Recreational.........	5 or 6	A C	2 2	4 4	750 1,000	3 4

Lamps .... General-service PS-52 bulb
Mounting height.................. 20 to 25 ft above court
Poles .... 2 per court

279. Baseball (NEMA Recommendations)

More open floodlights than enclosed
units are required to produce a given
level of illumination.

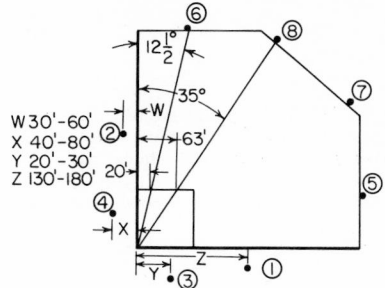

| Class | Floodlights | | | Total load, kw | Min. mtg. height, ft |
	Type	Group	Total No.		
Major League..................	3, 4 or 5	B	1,000	1,740	120
AAA and AA..................	3, 4 or 5	B	500	870	110
A and B......................	3, 4 or 5	B	320	560	90
	or 4, 5 or 6	C or D	440	765	
C and D......................	3, 4 or 5	B	240	420	70
	or 4, 5 or 6	C or D	320	560	
Semipro and municipal..........	3, 4 or 5	B	160	280	70
	or 4, 5 or 6	C or D	220	380	

Lamps.......................... 1,500-watt general-service PS-52 clear-bulb lamp at 10% overvoltage
Distribution.................. Approximately 10% of total floodlights on each of poles 3 through 8 and 20% on each of
poles 1 and 2

280. Basketball — Indoor

If ceiling is lower than 20 ft, more
units on closer spacing should be
used and recessed in the ceiling if
possible. Luminaires should be
rigidly mounted, and lamps should
be protected from the ball.

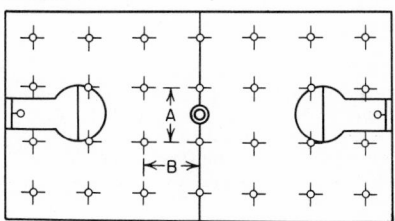

| Class | Fixture | Lamp watts | Spacing, ft | |
			A	B
Fluorescent				
College or pro.........	2-lamp direct[a]	90	8½	[b]
High school...........	2-lamp direct[a]	90	14	[b]
Recreational..........	2-lamp direct	40	12	11
Incandescent				
College or pro.........	Deep bowl reflector	1,000 PS-52 I.F.	12	12
High school...........	Deep bowl reflector	750 PS-52 I.F.	13	13
Recreational..........	Deep bowl reflector	300 PS-35 I.F.	13	13

[a] Three-lamp 40-watt fixtures (continuous rows) may be substituted for two-lamp 90-watt fixtures.
[b] Continuous rows.

Mounting height................. On ceiling

281. Basketball — Outdoor (NEMA Recommendation)

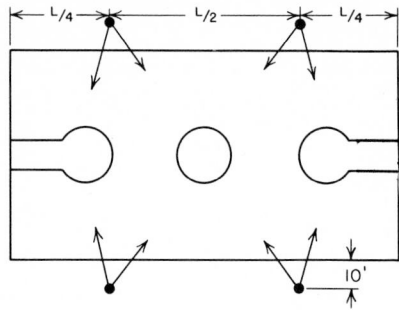

Wide-beam floodlights are required to illuminate the ball when it is a considerable distance above the court.

Class	Floodlights				Total load, kw
	Type	Group	No. per pole	Total No.	
Recreational.........	5 or 6	B C	2 3	8 12	12 18

Lamps................................. 1,500-watt general-service PS-52 bulb
Mounting height.................. 30 ft above court
Poles................................. 4 per court

282. Billiards

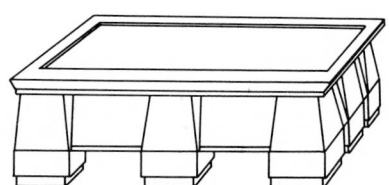

In large commercial parlors where a number of tables are installed, general illumination of high intensity proves more satisfactory than individual luminaires over each table.

Equipment.......................... Tournament: 2 two-lamp fluorescent fixtures with louvers
                                             Recreational: 1 two-lamp fluorescent fixture with louvers
Lamps............................... 40-watt T-12 fluorescent
Load .... 200 or 100 watts
Mounting height.................. 7 ft above floor

283. Bowling

Luminaires should be shielded by false ceiling beams or baffles unless they are of the asymmetric type. They should be positioned so as to provide even illumination along the alley with higher intensity on the pins. Behind the foul line any type of general-area-lighting equipment may be employed.

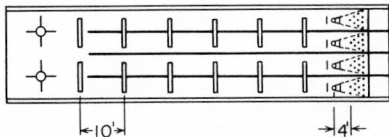

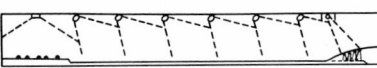

Equipment...........................	6 two-lamp direct fluorescent fixtures per pair of alleys
	2 150-watt PAR-38 projector floods per alley over pins
Lamps...............................	40-watt T-12 fluorescent
	150-watt PAR-38 flood
Load.................................	1,200 watts per pair of alleys
Mounting height...................	9 ft minimum

284. Boxing (NEMA Recommendation)

The class of bout will determine the level of illumination.

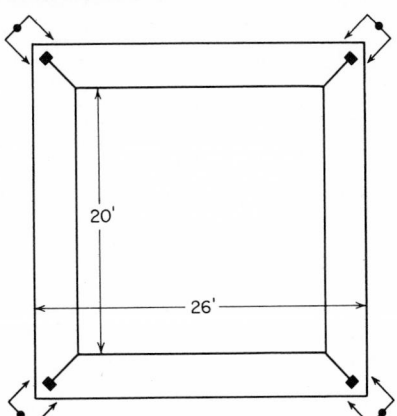

Class	Floodlights				Lamp watts	Total load, kw
	Type	Group	No. per pole	Total No.		
Championship..........	3	B	4	16	1,740ᵃ	28
	or 4	D	8	32	1,740ᵃ	56
Professional...........	4	B	2	8	1,740ᵃ	14
	or 4	D	3	12	1,740ᵃ	21
Amateur...............	4	B	2	8	1,000	8
	or 4	D	2	8	1,500	12

ᵃ 1,500-watt PS-52 bulb lamp operated at 10 per cent overvoltage.

Lamps................................	General-service PS-52 clear bulb
Mounting height..................	15 to 20 ft above ring

285. Croquet (NEMA Recommendation)

To provide comparable levels of illumination higher wattage lamps are required for open floodlights than for enclosed units.

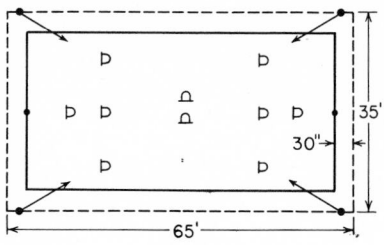

Class	Floodlights				Lamp watts	Total load, kw
	Type	Group	No. per pole	Total No.		
Tournament.............	5	B	1	4	1,000	4
	or 6	C	1	4	1,500	6
Recreational.............	5	A	1	4	500	2
	or 6	C	1	4	750	3

Lamps................................. General-service PS bulb
Mounting height.................. 20 to 25 ft above court
Poles.................................. 4 per court

286. Football (NEMA Recommendation)

The distance between the farthest row of spectators and the nearest sideline (see table) determines the lighting requirements, but the seating capacity should also be considered. Either of the pole plans shown or any intermediate longitudinal spacing is considered good practice. Local conditions determine the exact pole locations.

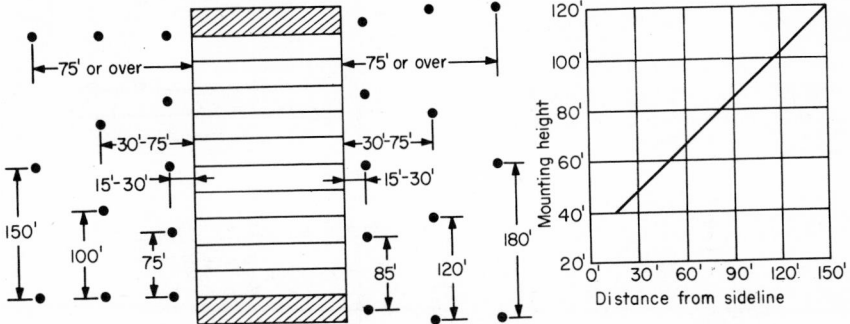

Class	Distance—poles to sideline, ft	No. of poles	Floodlights				Total load, kw
			Type	Group	No. per pole	Total No.	
I	Over 140	6	1 or 2	B	90	540	940
	100–140	6	2 or 3	B	80	480	835
II	75–100	6	3	B	36	216	380
	50–75	8	3	B	24	192	335
III	30–50	8	4	B	16	128	225
IV	15–30	10	5	B	8	80	140
	15–30	10	6	D	12	120	210
	15–30	10	6	C	18	180	315
V	15–30	10	5	B	4	40	70
	15–30	10	6	D	6	60	105
	15–30	10	6	C	8	80	140

Class	Distance farthest spectators to field, ft	Seating capacity
I	Over 100	Over 30,000
II	50–100	10,000–30,000
III	30–50	5,000–10,000
IV	Under 30	5,000
V	No fixed seating facilities	

Lamps............ 1,500-watt general-service PS-52 clear-bulb lamp at 10% overvoltage.

287. Golf Driving Range (NEMA Recommendation)

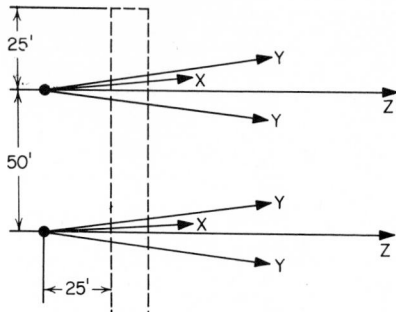

The floodlights should be directed so as to provide illumination on the ball throughout its flight.

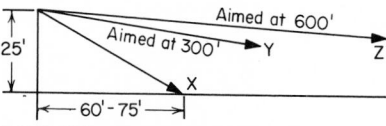

Floodlights				Lamp	Load per pole, kw
Aiming point	Type	Group	No. per pole		
X	5	B	1	1,500-watt PS-52 clear general service	
Y	3	B	2	1,500-watt PS-52 clear general service	7.5
Z	1	A	3	1,000-watt G-40 clear floodlight service	

Mounting height................ 25 to 30 ft above tees
Poles................................. One for every 50 ft of range width; minimum — 2 poles

288. Handball — Outdoor (NEMA Recommendation)

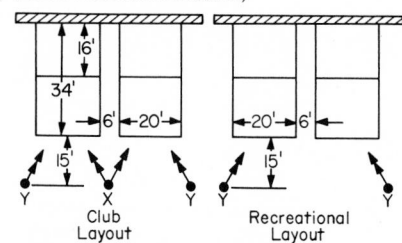

Glare is largely eliminated by locating the floodlights behind the players.

Class	Floodlights					Lamp watts	Total load, kw
	Type	Group	No. per pole		Total No.		
			X	Y			
Club.................	5	B	4	2	8	1,000	8
	or 6	C	4	2	8	1,500	12
Recreational...........	5	B	...	2	4	1,000	4
	or 6	C	...	2	4	1,500	6

Lamps................................. General-service PS-52 bulb
Mounting height.................. At least 25 ft above court
Poles................................. For club play, 3 per pair of courts
For recreational play, 2 per pair of courts

289. Horseshoe Pitching (NEMA Recommendation)

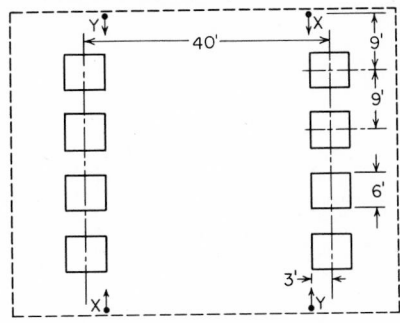

Floodlights should be directed across courts to prevent direct glare.

Class	No. of courts	Floodlights					Lamp watts	Total load, kw
		Type	Group	No. per pole		Total No.		
				X	Y			
Tournament.........	4–6	5	B	1	1	4	1,500	6
	or 6		C	2	2	8	1,000	8
	1–3	5	B	1	a	2	1,500	3
	or 6		C	2	a	4	1,000	4
Recreational.........	4–6	5	B	1	1	4	750	3
	or 6		C	1	1	4	1,000	4
	1–3	5	B	1	a	2	750	1.5
	or 6		C	1	a	2	1,000	2

a For one to three courts no Y poles are required.

Lamps............................... General-service PS-52 bulb
Mounting height.................. At least 20 ft above court
Poles................................. 4 for 4–6 court layout, 2 for 1–3 court layout

290. Ice Skating — Outdoor (NEMA Recommendation)

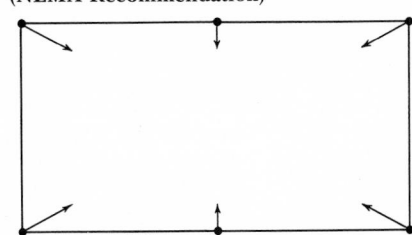

The design suggested produces satisfactory illumination for recreational skating.

Area	Floodlights		Watts per sq ft
	Type	Group	
Rink.........	5	A or B	0.85
	or 6	C	1.25
Pond.........	5	A or B	0.17
	or 6	C	0.25

The size of the area determines the number and wattage of the floodlights.

Lamps............................... 500- to 1,500-watt general service PS bulb
Mounting height.................. At least 20 ft above ice
Pole spacing........................ Not to exceed 4 times mounting height

291. Race Tracks

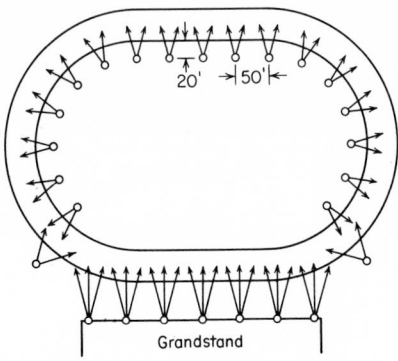

The lighting equipment should be so positioned and directed as to keep glare and shadows at a minimum.

Floodlights .... Type 2 or 3, Group B with medium elliptical-spread cover glass
Lamps............................. 1,500-watt general-service PS-52 clear bulb
Load............................... Varies with track size
Mounting data.................. 40 ft high and 20 ft inside inner edge of track

292. Shuffleboard (NEMA Recommendation)

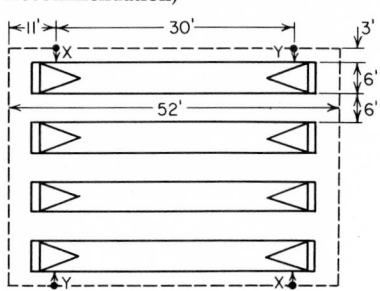

Floodlights should be directed across the court to prevent glare.

Class	No. of courts	Floodlights					Lamp watts	Total load, kw
		Type	Group	No. per pole		Total No.		
				X	Y			
Tournament..........	4–6	5	B	1	1	4	1,500	6
	or 6	C	2	2	8	1,000	8
	1–3	5	B	1	*a*	2	1,500	3
	or 6	C	2	*a*	4	1,000	4
Recreational..........	4–6	5	B	1	1	4	750	3
	or 6	C	1	1	4	1,000	4
	1–3	5	B	1	*a*	2	750	1.5
	or 6	C	1	*a*	2	1,000	2

a For one to three courts no Y poles are required.

Lamps................................. General-service PS-52 bulb
Mounting height.................. At least 20 ft above court
Poles................................... 4 for 4–6 court layout, 2 for 1–3 court layout

293. Skeet Shooting

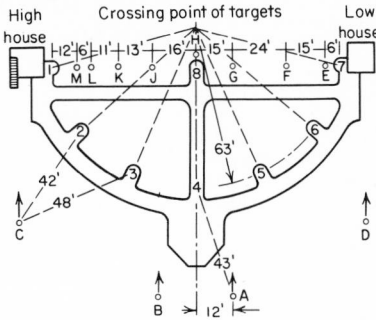

Visor shields should be provided for the sides of floodlights *C* and *D* next to the firing positions. Floodlights *E* to *M* may be shielded by shrubbery.

			Floodlights			
			Aiming, deg		Mounting height, ft	Lamp watts
Location	Group	Type	Direction	Elevation		
A and *B*	B	4, 5, or 6	a	a	24	1,000
C and *D*	B	4, 5, or 6	b	b	24	1,000
E	A	5 or 6	10 left	18 up	On ground	500
F	A	5 or 6	5 left	29 up	On ground	500
G	A	5 or 6	30 right	43 up	On ground	500
HJKL	A	5 or 6	Straight	45 up	On ground	500
M	A	5 or 6	30 left	55 up	On ground	500

a *A* and *B* floodlights aimed at point 6 ft to right and left respectively of No. 8 position and slightly below horizontal.
b *C* and *D* floodlights aimed toward front and above high house and low house respectively.

Lamps.................. General-service PS clear bulb
Operate at 10% overvoltage
Load.................... 9.3 kw at 10% overvoltage

294. Soccer (NEMA Recommendation)

For larger or smaller fields, the number of floodlights and the pole spacings should be altered in proportion to the area of the field.

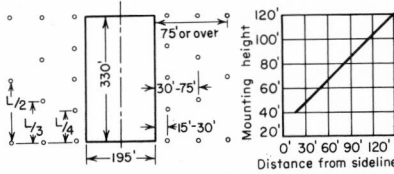

	Distance poles to sideline, ft	No. of poles	Floodlights				Total load, kw
Class			Type	Group	No. per pole	Total No.	
Professional and college.........	Over 140	6	1 or 2	B	30	180	315
	100–140	6	2 or 3	B	28	168	290
	75–100	6	3	B	24	144	250
	50–75	8	3	B	16	128	220
High school..................	30–50	8	4	B	12	96	165
	15–30	10	5	B	10	100	175
	15–30	10	5 or 6	D	14	140	245
	15–30	10	6	C	20	200	350
Recreational..................	15–30	10	5	B	6	60	105
	15–30	10	5 or 6	D	8	80	140
	15–30	10	6	C	10	100	175

Lamps.................. 1,500-watt general-service PS-52 clear-bulb lamp at 10% overvoltage

295. Softball — Professional and Industrial League (Drawn from NEMA Recommendation)

The distance to the poles in the outfield is determined by the size of the field.

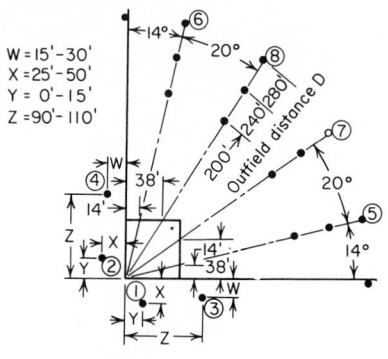

W = 15'-30'
X = 25'-50'
Y = 0'-15'
Z = 90'-110'

Class	Out-field distance *D*, ft	Layout for Type 3, 4, or 5 Group B floodlights				Layout for Type 6 Group D floodlights				Min mtg. height, ft	
		No. per pole			Total No.	No. per pole			Total No.	Poles	
		Poles				Poles					
		1–2	3–4	5–8		1–2	3–4	5–8		1–4	5–8
Pro and championship..........	280	14	30	18	160	18	38	27	220	50	60
	240	14	20	13	120	18	30	16	160	50	55
Semipro......................	280	8	18	14	108	10	28	18	148	40	55
	240	8	14	10	84	10	22	12	112	40	50
Industrial League..............	280	5	10	7	58	7	14	9	78	35	50
	240	5	7	5	44	7	10	6	58	35	45
	200	5	5	3	32	7	7	4	44	35	40

Lamps................ 1,500-watt general-service PS-52 clear-bulb lamp at 10% overvoltage

296. Softball—Recreational (Drawn from NEMA Recommendation)

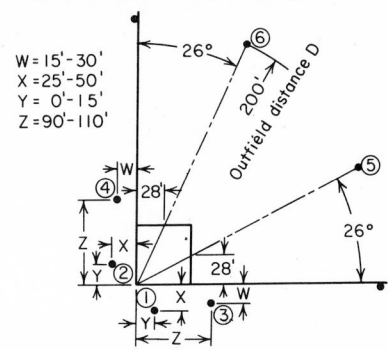

Open floodlights without auxiliary reflectors may also be used for soft-ball lighting installations, but a larger number are required to provide equal illumination.

W = 15'-30'
X = 25'-50'
Y = 0'-15'
Z = 90'-110'

Class	Out-field distance D, ft	Layout for Type 3, 4, or 5 Group B floodlights				Layout for Type 6 Group D floodlights				Min mtg. height, ft	
		No. per pole			Total No.	No. per pole			Total No.	Poles	
		Poles				Poles					
		1–2	3–4	5–6		1–2	3–4	5–6		1–4	5–6
Recreational........	200	2	3	3	16	3	4	4	22	35	40

Lamps.................. 1,500-watt general-service PS-52 clear-bulb lamp at 10% overvoltage

297. Swimming Pool—Underwater Floodlights (NEMA Recommendation)

Especially designed equipment is mounted in niches in the walls of the pool.

Location of pool	Watts per sq ft	
	Good practice	Mini-mum
Outdoors..............	3	1.5
Indoors................	5	3.0

Lamp watts	B max, ft, where D is over 5 ft	B' max, ft, where D is less than 5 ft	E, in. below water line
250– 400 500–1,500	4 6	5 7½	18–24

Lamps.................. Floodlight-service clear G-bulb. Consult fixture manufacturer if 12-volt units are to be used.

298. Swimming Pool — Overhead Floodlights (NEMA Recommendation)

The number of floodlights and the lamp size is determined by the size of the area and the type of equipment.

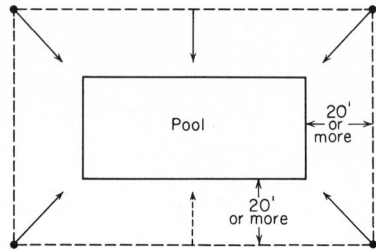

Floodlights .... Type 5, Group A or B, or Type 6, Group C
Lamps .... 500- to 1,500-watt general-service PS bulb
Load .... For Group A or B floodlights, 1.7 watts per sq ft
For Group C floodlights, 2.5 watts per sq ft
(both pool and surrounding area to be lighted)
Mounting height .... At least 20 ft above water
Pole spacing .... Not to exceed 4 times mounting height

299. Tennis — Single Court (NEMA Recommendation)

Floodlights must be directed sufficiently high to provide even illumination on the ball during flight.

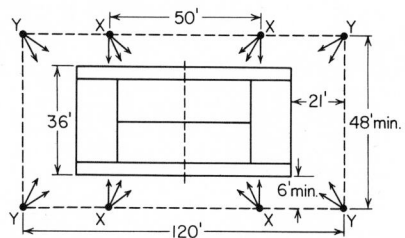

Class	No. of poles	Floodlights					Lamp watts	Total load, kw
		Type	Group	No. per pole		Total No.		
				X	Y			
Tournament............	8	5	B	3	2	20	1,500	30
		or 6	C	4	3	28	1,500	42
Club.................	8	5	B	2	1	12	1,500	18
		or 6	C	3	2	20	1,500	30
Recreational............	4	5	B	2	a	8	1,000	8
		or 6	C	2	a	8	1,500	12

[a] For recreational play the Y poles are eliminated and the X poles are located 60 instead of 50 ft apart.

Lamps .... General-service PS-52 bulb
Mounting height .... 30 ft above court

300. Tennis—Two Courts (NEMA Recommendation)

Floodlights must be directed sufficiently high to provide even illumination on the ball during flight.

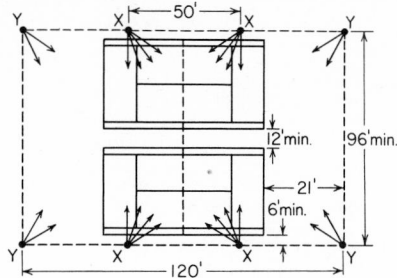

Class	No. of poles	Floodlights						Total load, kw
		Type	Group	No. per pole			Total No.	
				X	Y			
Club...................	8	5	B	4	2		24	36
		or 6	C	5	3		32	48
Recreational............	8	5	B	2	1		12	18
	or	or 6	C	3	1		16	24
	4	5	B	3	a		12	18
		or 6	C	4	a		16	24

a In the four-pole layout the Y poles are eliminated and the X poles are located 60 instead of 50 ft apart.

Lamps............................... 1,500-watt general-service PS-52 bulb
Mounting height.................. 30 ft above court

301. Table Tennis

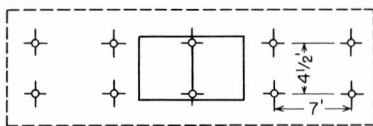

Club and tournament

Where louvered fluorescent luminaires are used, they may be
mounted either lengthwise or crosswise of the table.

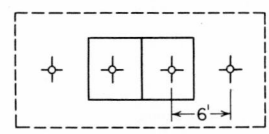

Recreational

Class	Fixtures		Lamp watts	Total load, kw	Mtg. height above table, ft
	No.	Type			
Tournament..........	10	Deep bowl	200	2.3	6
Club................	10	Deep bowl*b*	150	1.6	6
Recreational.........	2 or 4*a*	Deep bowl*b*	150	0.3 or 0.6	4½

a For skilled play four luminaires mounted 4½ to 6 ft above the table should be used.
b Louvered fluorescent luminaires for two 40-watt lamps may also be used.

Lamps.................. General-service inside-frosted PS bulb
Operate at 10% overvoltage for tournament and 5% overvoltage for club play

302. Trapshooting (NEMA Recommendation)

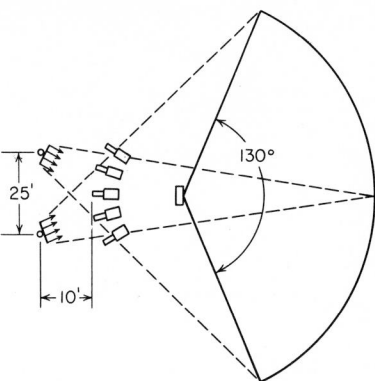

Uniform illumination will prevent apparent variation in bird speed.

Floodlights .... 8 Type 2, Group B
Lamps .... 1,500-watt general-service PS-52 clear-bulb lamp at 10% overvoltage
Load .... 12 kw
Mounting height.................. 20 ft above ground
Poles................................... 2

303. Volleyball — Outdoor (NEMA Recommendation)

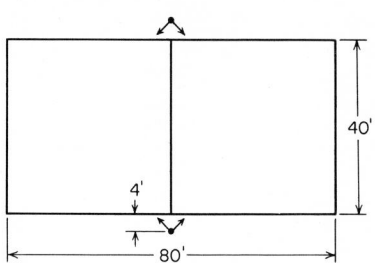

Wide-beam floodlights are necessary to provide uniform illumination.

Class	Floodlights				Total load, kw
	Type	Group	No. per pole	Total No.	
Tournament...........	5	B	3	6	9
	or 6	C	5	10	15
Recreational..........	5	B	2	4	6
	or 6	C	3	6	9

Lamps................................. 1,500-watt general-service PS-52 bulb
Mounting height.................. 20 to 25 ft above court
Poles................................... 2 per court

DIVISION ELEVEN

Wiring and Design Tables

1. Standard Sizes of Lamps for General Illumination, in Watts

Incandescent (filament)	Fluorescent (preheat)	Fluorescent (circular)	Fluorescent (rapid-start, standard)	Fluorescent (rapid-start, HO)	Fluorescent (rapid-start, VHO, or Power Groove)	Mercury vapor	Metal halide	Quartz halogen
10	4	22	30	35	100	100	175	250
15	6	32	40	50	110*	175	400	400
25	8	40	....	55	135*	250	1,000	500
40	13	....	....	75	150	400	.....	1,000
50	14	....	....	80	160*	700		1,250
60	15	....	....	85	200	1,000		1,500
75	20	....	....	95	215*	1,500		
100	25			100	....	3,000		
150	30			110				
200	40							
300	90							
500	100							
750								
1,000								
1,500								

* Power Groove type.
For more complete data on lamps refer to Div. 10.

2. Demand Loads for Household Electric Ranges, Wall-mounted Ovens, Counter-mounted Cooking Units, and Other Household Cooking Appliances Over 1¾-kw Rating

Column *A* to be used in all cases except as otherwise permitted in Note 4 below

Number of appliances	Maximum demand, kw (see Notes)	Demand factors (see Note 4), per cent	
	Column *A* (not over 12-kw rating)	Column *B* (less than 3½-kw rating)	Column *C* (3½- to 8¾-kw rating)
1	8	80	80
2	11	75	65
3	14	70	55
4	17	66	50
5	20	62	45
6	21	59	43
7	22	56	40
8	23	53	36
9	24	51	35
10	25	49	34
11	26	47	32
12	27	45	32
13	28	43	32
14	29	41	32
15	30	40	32
16	31	39	28
17	32	38	28
18	33	37	28
19	34	36	28
20	35	35	28
21	36	34	26
22	37	33	26
23	38	32	26
24	39	31	26
25	40	30	26
26–30	15 kw plus 1 kw for each range	30	24
31–40		30	22
41–50	25 kw plus ¾ kw for each range	30	20
51–60		30	18
61 and over		30	16

NOTE 1. **Over-12- to 27-kw ranges all of the same rating.** For ranges individually rated more than 12 kw but not more than 27 kw, the maximum demand in Column A shall be increased 5 per cent for each additional kilowatt of rating or major fraction thereof by which the rating of individual ranges exceeds 12 kw.

NOTE 2. **Over-12- to 27-kw ranges of unequal ratings.** For ranges individually rated more than 12 kw and of different ratings but none exceeding 27 kw, an average value of rating shall be calculated by adding together the ratings of all ranges to obtain the total connected load (using 12 kw for any range rated less than 12 kw) and dividing by the total number of ranges; and then the maximum demand in Column A shall be increased 5 per cent for each kilowatt or major fraction thereof by which this average value exceeds 12 kw.

NOTE 3. This table does not apply to commercial ranges. See Table **3A** for demand factors for commercial cooking equipment.

NOTE 4. **Over 1¾ to 8¾ kw.** In lieu of the method provided in Column A, loads rated more than 1¾ kw but not more than 8¾ kw may be considered as the sum of the nameplate ratings of all the loads, multiplied by the demand factors specified in Column B or C for the given number of loads.

NOTE 5. **Branch-circuit load.** Branch-circuit load for one range may be computed in accordance with Table **2.** The branch-circuit load for one wall-mounted oven or one counter-mounted cooking unit shall be the nameplate rating of the appliance. The branch-circuit load for a counter-mounted cooking unit and not more than two wall-mounted ovens, all supplied from a single branch circuit and located in the same room, shall be computed by adding the nameplate ratings of the individual appliances and treating this total as equivalent to one range.

3. Demand Factors for Household Electric Clothes Driers

Number of Driers	Demand Factor, Per Cent
1	100
2	100
3	100
4	100
5	80
6	70
7	65
8	60
9	55
10	50
11–13	45
14–19	40
20–24	35
25–29	32.5
30–34	30
35–39	27.5
40 up	25

The demand factor permitted in Sec. 5, Paragraph 10 will not apply when this table is used.

3A. Feeder Demand Factors for Commercial Electric Cooking Equipment, Including Dishwasher Booster Heaters, Water Heaters, and Other Kitchen Equipment

Number of Units of Equipment	Demand Factors (per cent)
1	100
2	100
3	90
4	80
5	70
6 and over	65

4. Demand Factors for Lighting Loads

Type of Occupancy	Unit Load per Sq Ft, Watts
Armories and auditoriums	1
Banks	2
Barber shops and beauty parlors	3
Churches	1
Clubs	2
Court rooms	2
Dwellings (other than hotels)°	3
Garages – commercial (storage)	1/2
Hospitals	2
Hotels and motels, including apartment houses without provisions for cooking by tenants°	2
Industrial commercial (loft) buildings	2
Lodge rooms	1½
Office buildings	5
Restaurants	2
Schools	3
Stores	3
Warehouses (storage)	1/4
In any of the above occupancies except single-family dwellings and individual apartments of multi-family dwellings:	
Assembly halls and auditoriums	1
Halls, corridors, closets	1/2
Storage spaces	1/4

° All receptacle outlets of 15-amp or less rating in single-family and multifamily dwellings and in guest rooms of hotels and motels (except those connected to the receptacle appliance circuits) may be considered as outlets for general illumination, and no additional load need be included for such outlets.

5. Data for Determining National Electrical Code Minimum Allowable Lighting and Appliance Loads

Calculation of Feeder Loads

The computed load of a feeder shall be not less than the sum of all branch-circuit loads supplied by the feeder, subject to the following provisions:

1. GENERAL LIGHTING. The demand factors listed in Table **A** may be applied to that portion of the total branch-circuit load computed for general illumination. These demand factors shall not be applied in determining the number of branch circuits for general illumination supplied by the feeders. See paragraphs 7 and 8.

The demand factors herein are based on minimum load conditions and 100 per cent power factor, and in specific instances may not provide sufficient capacity for the installation contemplated. In view of the trend toward higher intensity lighting systems and increased loads due to more general use of fixed and portable appliances, each installation should be considered as to the load likely to be imposed and the capacity increased to insure safe operation. Where electric discharge lighting systems are to be installed, high-power-factor type should be used or the conductor capacity may need to be increased.

A. Calculation of Feeder Loads by Occupancies

Type of occupancy	Portion of lighting load to which demand factor applies, watts	Demand factor, per cent
Dwellings—other than hotels..........................	First 3,000 or less at	100
	Next 3,001 to 120,000 at	35
	Remainder over 120,000 at	25
Hospitals*..	First 50,000 or less at	40
	Remainder over 50,000 at	20
Hotels and motels—including apartment houses without provision for cooking by tenants*	First 20,000 or less at	50
	Next 20,001 to 100,000 at	40
	Remainder over 100,000 at	30
Warehouses (storage).................................	First 12,500 or less at	100
	Remainder over 12,500 at	50
All others..	Total wattage	100

* The demand factors shall not apply to the computed load of subfeeders to areas in hospitals, hotels, and motels where entire lighting is likely to be used at one time, as in operating rooms, ballrooms, or dining rooms.

2. SHOW-WINDOW LIGHTING. For show-window lighting a load of not less than 200 watts shall be included for each linear foot of show window, measured horizontally along its base.

3. MOTORS. For motors, a load computed according to the provisions of Secs. **6 to 14** shall be included.

4. NEUTRAL FEEDER LOAD. The neutral feeder load shall be the maximum unbalance of the load determined by Sec. **4**. The maximum unbalanced load shall be the maximum connected load between the neutral and any one ungrounded conductor, except that the load thus obtained shall be multiplied by 140 per cent for five-wire two-phase systems. For a feeder supplying household electric ranges, wall-mounted ovens, and counter-mounted cooking units, the maximum unbalanced load shall be considered as 70 per cent of the load on the ungrounded conductors, as determined in accordance with Sec. **2**. For 3-wire d-c or single-phase a-c, 4-wire 3-phase, and 5-wire 2-phase systems, a further demand factor of 70 per cent may be applied to that portion of the unbalanced load in excess of 200 amp. There shall be no reduction of the neutral capacity for that portion of the load which consists of electric discharge lighting.

5. FIXED ELECTRICAL SPACE HEATING. The computed load of a feeder supplying fixed electrical space heating equipment shall be the total connected load on all branch circuits.

Exception No. 1. Where reduced loading of the conductors results from units operating on duty cycle, intermittently, or from all units not operating at one time, the authority enforcing the code may grant permission for feeder conductors to be of a capacity less than 100 per cent, provided the conductors are of sufficient capacity for the load so determined.

*Exception No. 2. Paragraph 5 does not apply when feeder capacity is calculated in accordance with the optional method in Sec. **46** of Div. 3 for single-family dwellings.*

6. NONCOINCIDENT LOAD. In adding the branch-circuit loads to determine the feeder load, the smaller of two dissimilar loads may be omitted from the total where it is unlikely that both of the loads will be served simultaneously.

7. SMALL APPLIANCES. The computed branch-circuit load for receptacle outlets in other than dwelling occupancies, for which the allowance is not more than 1½ amp per outlet, may be included with the general lighting load and subject to the demand factors in paragraph 1.

DWELLING OCCUPANCIES

The requirements in the following paragraphs 8 to 11 apply to dwelling-type occupancies and are supplemental to the preceding paragraphs 1 to 7.

8. SMALL APPLIANCES.

a. Dwelling Occupancies. In single-family dwellings, in individual apartments of multifamily dwellings having provisions for cooking by tenants, and in each hotel suite having a serving pantry, a feeder load of not less than 1,500 watts for each two-wire circuit shall be included for small appliances (portable appliances supplied from receptacles of 15- or 20-amp rating) in pantry and breakfast room, dining room, kitchen, and family room. Where the load is subdivided through two or more feeders, the computed load for each shall include not less than 1,500 watts for each two-wire circuit for small appliances. These loads may be included with the general lighting load and subject to the demand factors in paragraph 1.

b. Laundry Circuit. A feeder load of not less than 1,500 watts shall be included for each two-wire laundry circuit. This load may be included with the general lighting load and subject to the demand factors in paragraph 1.

9. ELECTRIC RANGES. The feeder load for household electric ranges and other cooking appliances, individually rated more than 1¾ kw, may be calculated in accordance with Table **2**.

In order to provide for possible future installation of ranges or higher ratings, it is recommended that where ranges of less than 8¾-kw ratings or wall-mounted ovens and counter-mounted cooking units are to be installed, the feeder capacity be not less than the maximum demand value specified in Column A of Table **2**.

Where a number of single-phase ranges are supplied by a three-phase four-wire feeder, the current shall be computed on the basis of the demand of twice the maximum number of ranges connected between any two-phase wires. See example in Sec. **50** of Div. 3.

10. FIXED ELECTRICAL APPLIANCES (OTHER THAN RANGES, CLOTHES DRIERS, AIR-CONDITIONING EQUIPMENT, OR SPACE-HEATING EQUIPMENT). Where four or more fixed electrical appliances other than electric ranges, clothes driers, air-conditioning equipment, or space-heating equipment are connected to the same feeder in a single or multifamily dwelling, a demand factor of 75 per cent may be applied to the fixed-appliance load.

11. SPACE HEATING AND AIR COOLING. In adding branch-circuit loads for space heating and air cooling in dwelling occupancies, the smaller of the two loads may be omitted from the total where it is unlikely that both of the loads will be served simultaneously.

12. FARM BUILDINGS. Feeders supplying farm buildings (excluding dwellings) or loads consisting of two or more branch circuits shall have minimum capacity computed in accordance with the following table:

B. Demand Computation for Farm Buildings or Loads

Load in Amperes at 230 Volts	Per Cent of Connected Load
Loads expected to operate without diversity, but not less than 125% full-load current of the largest motor and not less than first 60 amp	100
Next 60 amp of all other loads..	50
Remainder of other load..	25

NOTE 1. For services to farm dwellings, see paragraphs 8 to 11.
NOTE 2. For service at main point of delivery to farmstead, see paragraph 13.

13. FARM SERVICES.

a. Service equipment and service-entrance conductors for individual farm buildings (excluding dwellings) shall have minimum capacity computed in accordance with paragraph 12.

b. Minimum capacity of service conductors and service equipment, if any, at the main point of delivery to farms (including dwellings) shall be determined in accordance with the following formula:

100 per cent of the largest demand computed in accordance with paragraph 12.

75 per cent of the second largest demand computed in accordance with paragraph 12.

65 per cent of the third largest demand computed in accordance with paragraph 12.

50 per cent of the demands of remaining loads computed in accordance with paragraph 12.

NOTE 1. Consider as a single computed demand the total of the computed demands of all buildings or loads having the same function.
NOTE 2. The demand of the farm dwelling, if included in the demands of this formula, should be computed in accordance with Note 1 of Table **B.**

6. Average Demand Factors for Motor Loads[a]

Number of motors	Character of load	Demand factor
1– 5	Individual drives—tools, etc.	1.00
6– 10	Individual drives—tools, etc.	0.75
10– 15	Individual drives—tools, etc.	0.70
15– 20	Individual drives—tools, etc.	0.65
20– 30	Individual drives—tools, etc.	0.60
30– 50	Individual drives—tools, etc.	0.50
50– 75	Individual drives—tools, etc.	0.45
75–100	Individual drives—tools, etc.	0.40
Above 100	Individual drives—tools, etc.	0.40
6– 10	Group drives	0.85
Above 10	Group drives	0.70–0.45
	Fans, compressors, pumps, etc.	1.00–0.85

[a] Permission for the use of a demand factor should be obtained from the authority enforcing the National Electrical Code.

7. Average Full-load Currents of D-C Motors[a]

Hp	120 volts	240 volts
¼	2.9	1.5
⅓	3.6	1.8
½	5.2	2.6
¾	7.4	3.7
1	9.4	4.7
1½	13.2	6.6
2	17	8.5
3	25	12.2
5	40	20
7½	58	29
10	76	38
15	....	55
20	....	72
25	....	89
30	....	106
40	....	140
50	....	173
60	....	206
75	....	255
100	....	341
125	....	425
150	....	506
200	....	675

[a] These values of full-load currents are for motors running at base speed.

8. Average Full-load Currents of Single-phase Motors[a]

Hp	115 volts	230 volts
⅙	4.4	2.2
¼	5.8	2.9
⅓	7.2	3.6
½	9.8	4.9
¾	13.8	6.9
1	16	8
1½	20	10
2	24	12
3	34	17
5	56	28
7½	80	40
10	100	50

[a] These values of full-load currents are for motors running at usual speeds and motors with normal torque characteristics. Motors built for especially low speeds or high torques may have higher full-load currents, and multispeed motors will have full-load current varying with speed, in which case the nameplate current ratings shall be used.

To obtain full-load currents of 208- and 200-volt motors, increase corresponding 230-volt motor full-load currents by 10 and 15 per cent, respectively.

The voltages listed are rated motor voltages. Corresponding nominal system voltages are 110 to 120, 220 to 240, and 440 to 480.

9. Average Full-load Currents of Two-phase Motors (Four-wire)[a]
(1968 National Electrical Code)

Hp	Induction-type squirrel-cage and wound-rotor, amperes					Synchronous-type unity-power factor,[b] amperes			
	115 volts	230 volts	460 volts	575 volts	2,300 volts	220 volts	440 volts	550 volts	2,300 volts
1/2	4	2	1	0.8					
3/4	4.8	2.4	1.2	1.0					
1	6.4	3.2	1.6	1.3					
1 1/2	9	4.5	2.3	1.8					
2	11.8	5.9	3	2.4					
3	....	8.3	4.2	3.3					
5	....	13.2	6.6	5.3					
7 1/2	....	19	9	8					
10	....	24	12	10					
15	....	36	18	14					
20	....	47	23	19					
25	....	59	29	24	....	47	24	19	
30	....	69	35	28	....	56	29	23	
40	....	90	45	36	....	75	37	31	
50	....	113	56	45	....	94	47	38	
60	....	133	67	53	14	111	56	44	11
75	....	166	83	66	18	140	70	57	13
100	....	218	109	87	23	182	93	74	17
125	....	270	135	108	28	228	114	93	22
150	....	312	156	125	32	......	137	110	26
200	....	416	208	167	43	......	182	145	35

[a] These values of full-load current are for motors running at speeds usual for belted motors and motors with normal torque characteristics. Motors built for especially low speeds or high torques may require more running current, and multispeed motors will have full-load current varying with speed, in which case the nameplate current rating shall be used. Current in common conductor of two-phase three-wire system will be 1.41 times value given.

[b] For 90 and 80 per cent power factor these figures should be multiplied by 1.1 and 1.25, respectively.

The voltages listed are rated motor voltages. Corresponding nominal system voltages are 110 to 120, 220 to 240, 440 to 480, and 550 to 600 volts.

10. Average Full-load Currents of Three-phase Motors[a]
(1968 National Electrical Code)

Hp	Induction-type squirrel-cage and wound-rotor, amperes					Synchronous-type unity-power factor,[b] amperes			
	115 volts	230 volts	460 volts	575 volts	2,300 volts	220 volts	440 volts	550 volts	2,300 volts
1/2	4	2	1	0.8					
3/4	5.6	2.8	1.4	1.1					
1	7.2	3.6	1.8	1.4					
1½	10.4	5.2	2.6	2.1					
2	13.6	6.8	3.4	2.7					
3	....	9.6	4.8	3.9					
5	....	15.2	7.6	6.1					
7½	....	22	11	9					
10	....	28	14	11					
15	....	42	21	17					
20	....	54	27	22					
25	....	68	34	27	....	54	27	22	
30	....	80	40	32	....	65	33	26	
40	....	104	52	41	....	86	43	35	
50	....	130	65	52	....	108	54	44	
60	....	154	77	62	16	128	64	51	12
75	....	192	96	77	20	161	81	65	15
100	....	248	124	99	26	211	106	85	20
125	....	312	156	125	31	264	132	106	25
150	....	360	180	144	37	......	158	127	30
200	....	480	240	192	49	......	210	168	40

For full-load currents of 208- and 200-volt motors, increase the corresponding 220-volt motor full-load current by 6 and 10 per cent, respectively.

[a] These values of full-load current are for motors running at speeds usual for belted motors and motors with normal torque characteristics. Motors built for especially low speeds or high torques may require more running current, and multispeed motors will have full-load current varying with speed, in which case the nameplate current rating shall be used.

[b] For 90 and 80 per cent pf the above figures shall be multiplied by 1.1 and 1.25, respectively.

The voltages listed are rated motor voltages. Corresponding nominal system voltages are 110 to 120, 220 to 240, 440 to 480, and 550 to 600 volts.

11. Capacitor Ratings for Use with Three-phase 60-cycle Motors[a]

Induction motor horsepower rating	Nominal motor speed, rpm											
	3,600		1,800		1,200		900		720		600	
	Capacitor rating, kvar	Line current reduction, %	Capacitor rating, kvar	Line current reduction, %	Capacitor rating, kvar	Line current reduction, %	Capacitor rating, kvar	Line current reduction, %	Capacitor rating, kvar	Line current reduction, %	Capacitor rating, kvar	Line current reduction, %
3	1.5	14	1.5	15	1.5	20	2	27	2.5	35	3.5	41
5	2	12	2	13	2	17	3	25	4	32	4.5	37
7½	2.5	11	2.5	12	3	15	4	22	5.5	30	6	34
10	3	10	3	11	3.5	14	5	21	6.5	27	7.5	31
15	4	9	4	10	5	13	6.5	18	8	23	9.5	27
20	5	9	5	10	6.5	12	7.5	16	9	21	12	25
25	6	9	6	10	7.5	11	9	15	11	20	14	23
30	7	8	7	9	9	11	10	14	12	18	16	22
40	9	8	9	9	11	10	12	13	15	16	20	20
50	12	8	11	9	13	10	15	12	19	15	24	19
60	14	8	14	8	15	10	18	11	22	15	27	19
75	17	8	16	8	18	10	21	10	26	14	32.5	18
100	22	8	21	8	25	9	27	10	32.5	13	40	17
125	27	8	26	8	30	9	32.5	10	40	13	47.5	16
150	32.5	8	30	8	35	9	37.5	10	47.5	12	52.5	15
200	40	8	37.5	8	42.5	9	47.5	10	60	12	65	14
250	50	8	45	7	52.5	8	57.5	9	70	11	77.5	13
300	57.5	8	52.5	7	60	8	65	9	80	11	87.5	12
350	65	8	60	7	67.5	8	75	9	87.5	10	95	11
400	70	8	65	6	75	8	85	9	95	10	105	11
450	75	8	67.5	6	80	8	92.5	...	100	9	110	11
500	77.5	8	72.5	6	82.5	8	97.5	9	107.5	9	115	10

[a] For use with three-phase 60-cycle NEMA Classification B motors to raise full-load power factor to approximately 95 per cent.

12. Minimum Ampacities for Conductors Supplying Motors Used for Short-time, Intermittent, Periodic, or Varying Duty

Classification of service	Percentages of nameplate current rating			
	5-min rating	15-min rating	30- and 60-min rating	Continuous rating
Short-time duty: operating valves, raising or lowering rolls, etc.	110	120	150	
Intermittent duty: freight and passenger elevators, tool heads, pumps, drawbridges, turntables, single-operator arc welders for manual welding, etc.	85	85	90[a]	140
Periodic duty: rolls, ore, and coal-handling machines, etc.	85	90	95	140
Varying duty	110	120	150	200

[a] This figure also applies for conductors which supply a motor-generator single-operator arc welder which has a 60 per cent duty cycle rating.

13. Ampacities of Wires between Secondary Controller of Wound-rotor Induction Motors and Resistors

Resistor Duty Classification (NEMA Apparatus Division)	Ampacity of Wire, Per Cent of Full-load Secondary Current
Light starting duty	35
Heavy starting duty	45
Extra-heavy starting duty	55
Light intermittent duty	65
Medium intermittent duty	75
Heavy intermittent duty	85
Continuous duty	110

14. Ampacities of Insulated Conductors in Raceway or Cable Used with Short-time-rated Crane and Hoist Motors

Max operating temp	60°C		75°C		90°C		110°C	
Size, AWG or 1,000 cir mils	Type T, TW		Type RH, RHW, THW, THWN, XHHW		Type TA, AVB, RHH, SA, FEP, FEPB, THHN, XHHW[a]		Type AVA	
	60 min	30 min	60 min	30 min	60 min	30 min	60 min	30 min
16 AWG	10	10	10	12				
14	20	20	25	26	31	32	38	40
12	25	25	30	33	36	40	45	50
10	35	35	40	43	49	52	60	65
8	45	50	55	60	63	69	73	80
6	57	70	76	86	83	94	93	105
5	65	80	85	95	95	106	109	121
4	77	95	100	117	111	130	126	147
3	90	115	120	141	131	153	145	168
2	107	130	137	160	148	173	163	190
1	130	150	143	175	158	192	177	215
0	160	180	190	233	211	259	239	295
00	195	225	222	267	245	294	275	331
000	245	280	280	341	305	372	339	413
0000	295	350	300	369	319	399	352	440
250 MCM	350	375	364	420	400	461	447	516
300	410	475	455	582	497	636	554	707
350	460	550	486	646	542	716	616	809
400	515	580	538	688	593	760	666	856
450	565	640	600	765	660	836	740	930
500	620	700	660	847	726	914	815	1,004

Other insulations approved for the temperatures and location may be substituted for those shown in this table. The allowable ampacities of conductors used with 15-min motors shall be the 30-min ratings increased by 12 per cent. Conductors shall not be smaller than No. 14.

Exception: No. 16 may be used for crane and hoist motor and control circuits only when the application meets the ampacities of table above and provided the conductors are protected against physical damage.

[a] Dry locations only.

Contact Conductors. The size of contact wires shall be not less than the following:

Distance between End Strain Insulators, Ft	Size of Wire
0–30	No. 6
31–60	No. 4
Over 60	No. 2

15. Curve for Determining Ampacities at 60 Cycles of Bare Concentric Stranded Copper Conductors for 30°C Rise over 40°C Ambient

For outdoor service, 25 per cent increase in ampacities is permissible.

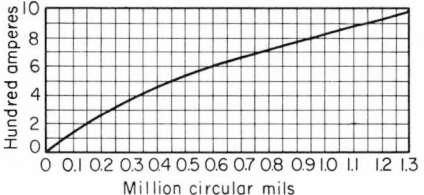

16. Curve for Determining Ampacities for Weatherproof Covered Concentric Stranded Copper Conductors Installed Outside Buildings

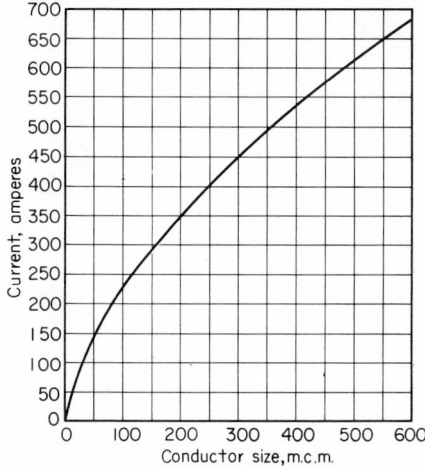

17. National Electrical Code Allowable Ampacities of Conductors for All Interior Wiring (Tables **18** to **22,** inclusive).

NOTES TO TABLES 18 THROUGH 21

AMPACITY. The maximum continuous ampacities of copper conductors are given in Tables **18** and **19.** The ampacities of aluminum conductors are given in Tables **20** and **21.**

1. EXPLANATION OF TABLES. For explanation of Type Letters, and for recognized size of conductors for the various conductor insulations see Sec. **123** of Div. 2. For flexible cords see Sec. **126** of Div. 2.

2. APPLICATION OF TABLES. For open wiring, cablebus, and for concealed knob-and-tube work, the allowable ampacities of Tables **18** and **20** shall be used. For all other recognized wiring methods, the allowable ampacities of Tables **19** and **21** shall be used, unless otherwise provided in this Code.

3. ALUMINUM CONDUCTORS. For aluminum conductors, the allowable ampacities shall be in accordance with Tables **20** and **21.**

4. BARE CONDUCTORS. Where bare conductors are used with insulated conductors, their allowable ampacities shall be limited to those permitted for the insulated conductors of the same size.

5. TYPE MI CABLE. The temperature limitation on which the ampacities of Type MI cable are based is determined by the insulating materials used in the end seal. Termination fittings incorporating unimpregnated organic insulating materials are limited to 85°C operation.

6. ULTIMATE INSULATION TEMPERATURE. In no case shall conductors be associated together in such a way with respect to the kind of circuit, the wiring method employed, or the number of conductors, that the limiting temperature of the conductors will be exceeded.

7. USE OF CONDUCTORS WITH HIGHER OPERATING TEMPERATURES. Where the room temperature is within 10°C of the maximum allowable operating temperature of the insulation, it is desirable to use an insulation with a higher maximum allowable operating temperature, although insulation can be used in a room temperature approaching its maximum allowable operating-temperature limit if the current is reduced in accordance with the correction factors for different room temperatures as shown in the Correction Factor Table, Note 15.

8. MORE THAN THREE CONDUCTORS IN A RACEWAY OR CABLE. Tables **19** and **21** give the allowable ampacities for not more than three conductors in a raceway or cable. Where the number of conductors in a raceway or cable exceeds three, the allowable ampacity of each conductor shall be reduced as shown in the following table:

Number of Conductors	Per Cent of Values in Tables **19** and **21**
4 to 6	80
7 to 24	70
25 to 42	60
43 and above	50

Exception No. 1. When conductors of different systems are installed in a common raceway or cable the derating factors shown above apply to the number of power and lighting conductors only.

Exception No. 2. If any of the above deratings are applied and limit the branch-circuit load to 80 per cent or less no additional derating is required for continuous-load branch circuits.

Where the number of conductors in a raceway or cable exceeds three, or where single conductors or multiconductor cables are stacked or bundled without maintaining spacing and are not installed in raceways, the individual ampacity of each conductor shall be reduced as shown in the above table.

9. WHERE TYPE XHHW cross-linked thermosetting polyethylene insulated wire is used in wet locations, the allowable ampacities shall be those of column 3 in Tables **18, 19, 20,** and **21**. Where used in dry locations, the allowable ampacities shall be those of column 4 in Tables **18, 19, 20,** and **21**.

10. OVERCURRENT PROTECTION. Where the standard ratings and settings of overcurrent devices do not correspond with the ratings and settings allowed for conductors, the next higher standard rating and setting may be used.

11. NEUTRAL CONDUCTOR.

a. A neutral conductor which carries only the unbalanced current from other conductors, as in the case of normally balanced circuits of three or more conductors, shall not be counted in determining ampacities as provided for in Note 8.

b. In a three-wire circuit consisting of two-phase wires and the neutral of a four-wire three-phase Y-connected system, a common conductor carries approximately the same current as the other conductors and shall be counted in determining ampacities as provided in Note 8.

Where the major portion of the load consists of electric discharge lighting, there may be harmonic currents present in the neutral conductor which may be equal to the phase currents; thus the neutral could be considered to be a current-carrying conductor.

12. VOLTAGE DROP. The allowable ampacities in Tables **18** through **21** are based on temperature alone and do not take voltage drop into consideration.

13. DETERIORATION OF INSULATION. It should be noted that even the best grades of rubber insulation will deteriorate in time, and so eventually will need to be replaced.

14. ALUMINUM SHEATHED CABLE. The ampacities of Type ALS cable are determined by the temperature limitation of the insulated conductors incorporated within the cable. Hence the ampacities of aluminum sheathed cable may be determined from the columns in Tables **19** and **21** applicable to the type of insulated conductors employed within the cable. See Note 9.

15. CORRECTION FACTORS.

Ambient Temperatures over 30°C (86°F)

Ambient		Conductor rating						
°C		60	75	85	90	110	125	220
	°F	140	167	185	194	230	257	392
40	104	0.82	0.88	0.90	0.90	0.94	0.95	
45	113	0.71	0.82	0.85	0.85	0.90	0.92	
50	122	0.58	0.75	0.80	0.80	0.87	0.89	
55	131	0.41	0.67	0.74	0.74	0.83	0.86	
60	140	....	0.58	0.67	0.67	0.79	0.83	0.91
70	158	....	0.35	0.52	0.52	0.71	0.76	0.87
75	167	....	....	0.43	0.43	0.66	0.72	0.86
80	176	....	....	0.30	0.30	0.61	0.69	0.84
90	194	....	....	....	....	0.50	0.61	0.80
100	212	....	....	....	....	....	0.51	0.77
120	248	....	....	....	....	....	....	0.69
140	284	....	....	....	....	....	....	0.59

18. Allowable Ampacities of Insulated Copper Conductors
Single Conductor in Free Air
Based on Room Temperature of 30°C (86°F)
(1968 National Electrical Code)

	Temperature rating of conductor							
°C	60	75	85	90	110	125	200	
°F	140	167	185	194	230	257	392	
Size, AWG or 1,000 cir mils	RUW (14-2), T, TW	RH, RHW, RUH (14-2), THW, THWN, XHHW	V, MI	TA, TBS, SA, AVB, SIS, FEP, FEPB, RHH, THHN, XHHW[a]	AVA, AVL	AI (14-8), AIA	A (14–8), AA, FEP,[b] FEPB[b]	Bare and covered conductors
14 AWG	20	20	30	30[c]	40	40	45	30
12	25	25	40	40[c]	50	50	55	40
10	40	40	55	55[c]	65	70	75	55
8	55	65	70	70	85	90	100	70
6	80	95	100	100	120	125	135	100
4	105	125	135	135	160	170	180	130
3	120	145	155	155	180	195	210	150
2	140	170	180	180	210	225	240	175
1	165	195	210	210	245	265	280	205
0	195	230	245	245	285	305	325	235
00	225	265	285	285	330	355	370	275
000	260	310	330	330	385	410	430	320
0000	300	360	385	385	445	475	510	370
250 MCM	340	405	425	425	495	530	......	410
300	375	445	480	480	555	590	......	460
350	420	505	530	530	610	655	......	510
400	455	545	575	575	665	710	......	555
500	515	620	660	660	765	815	......	630
600	575	690	740	740	855	910	......	710
700	630	755	815	815	940	1,005	......	780
750	655	785	845	845	980	1,045	......	810
800	680	815	880	880	1,020	1,085	......	845
900	730	870	940	940	....	....	......	905
1,000	780	935	1,000	1,000	1,165	1,240	......	965
1,250	890	1,065	1,130	1,130	....	....	......	....
1,500	980	1,175	1,260	1,260	1,450	....	......	1,215
1,750	1,070	1,280	1,370	1,370	....	....	......	....
2,000	1,155	1,385	1,470	1,470	1,715	....	......	1,405

[a] For dry locations only. See Sec. 31, Div. 9.

[b] Special use only. See Sec. 31, Div. 9.

These ampacities relate only to conductors described in Sec. 31, Div. 9.

[c] The ampacities for Types FEP, FEPB, RHH, THHN, and XHHW conductors for sizes AWG 14, 12, and 10 shall be the same as designated for 75°C conductors in this table.

For ambient temperatures over 30°C see Correction Factors, Note 15 in Sec. 17.

19. Allowable Ampacities of Insulated Copper Conductors
Not More than Three Conductors in Raceway or Cable, or Direct Burial
Based on Room Temperature of 30°C, 86°F
(1968 National Electrical Code)

				Temperature Rating of Conductor			
°C °F	60 140	75 167	85 185	90 194	110 230	125 257	200 392
Size, AWG or 1,000 cir mils	RUW (14-2), T, TW	RH, RHW, RUH (14-2), THW, THWN, XHHW, THW-MTW	V, MI	TA, TBS, SA, AVB, SIS, FEP, FEPB, RHH, THHN, XHHW[a]	AVA, AVL	AI (14-8), AIA	A (14-8), AA, FEP[b] FEPB[b]
14 AWG	15	15	25	25[c]	30	30	30
12	20	20	30	30[c]	35	40	40
10	30	30	40	40[c]	45	50	55
8	40	45	50	50	60	65	70
6	55	65	70	70	80	85	95
4	70	85	90	90	105	115	120
3	80	100	105	105	120	130	145
2	95	115	120	120	135	145	165
1	110	130	140	140	160	170	190
0	125	150	155	155	190	200	225
00	145	175	185	185	215	230	250
000	165	200	210	210	245	265	285
0000	195	230	235	235	275	310	340
250 MCM	215	255	270	270	315	335	
300	240	285	300	300	345	380	
350	260	310	325	325	390	420	
400	280	335	360	360	420	450	
500	320	380	405	405	470	500	
600	355	420	455	455	525	545	
700	385	460	490	490	560	600	
750	400	475	500	500	580	620	
800	410	490	515	515	600	640	
900	435	520	555	555			
1,000	455	545	585	585	680	730	
1,250	495	590	645	645			
1,500	520	625	700	700	785		
1,750	545	650	735	735			
2,000	560	665	775	775	840		

[a] For dry locations only. See Sec. **31**, Div. 9.
[b] Special use only. See Sec. **31**, Div. 9.
These ampacities relate only to conductors described in Sec. **31**, Div. 9.
[c] The ampacities for Types FEP, FEPB, RHH, THHN, and XHHW conductors for sizes AWG 14, 12, and 10 shall be the same as designated for 75°C conductors in this table.
For ambient temperatures over 30°C see Correction Factors, Note 15 in Sec. **17**.

19A. Ampacities of Insulated Copper Conductors at Various Deratings
In Raceways or Cables at Room Temperatures Not over 30°C (86°F)

Size, AWG or 1,000 cir mils	Ampacity														
	100%			80%			70%			60%			50%		
	60°C	75°C	90°C	60°C	75°C	90°C	60°C	75°C	90°C	60°C	75°C	90°C	60°C	75°C	90°C
14 AWG	15	15	15	12	12	12	10	10	10	9	9	9	7	7	7
12	20	20	20	16	16	16	14	14	14	12	12	12	10	10	10
10	30	30	30	24	24	24	21	21	21	18	18	18	15	15	15
8	40	45	50	32	36	40	28	31	35	24	27	30	20	22	25
6	55	65	70	44	52	56	38	45	49	33	39	42	27	32	35
4	70	85	90	56	68	72	49	59	63	42	51	54	35	42	45
3	80	100	105	64	80	84	56	70	73	48	60	63	40	50	52
2	95	115	120	76	92	96	66	80	84	57	69	72	47	57	60
1	110	130	140	88	104	112	77	91	98	66	78	84	55	65	70
0	125	150	155	100	120	124	87	105	108	75	90	93	62	75	77
00	145	175	185	116	140	148	101	122	129	87	105	111	72	87	92
000	165	200	210	132	160	168	115	140	147	99	120	126	82	100	105
0000	195	230	235	156	184	188	136	161	164	117	138	141	97	115	117
250 MCM	215	255	270	172	204	216	150	178	189	129	153	162	107	127	135
300	240	285	300	192	228	240	168	199	210	144	171	180	120	142	150
350	260	310	325	208	248	260	182	217	227	156	186	195	130	155	162
400	280	335	360	224	268	288	196	234	252	168	201	216	140	167	180
500	320	380	405	256	304	324	224	266	283	192	228	243	160	190	202

60°C conductors – RUW, T, TW.
75°C conductors – RH, THW, THWN, RUH, XHHW (wet locations); RHW.
90°C conductors – THHN, RHH, FEP, FEPB, XHHW (dry locations).

20. Allowable Ampacities of Insulated Aluminum Conductors
Single Conductor in Free Air
Based on Room Temperature of 30°C (86°F)
(1968 National Electrical Code)

	Temperature rating of conductor							
°C °F	60 140	75 167	85 185	90 194	110 230	125 257	200 392	
Size, AWG or 1,000 cir mils	RUW (12-2), T, TW	RH RHW, RUH (12-2), THW, THWN, XHHW	V, MI	TA, TBS, SA, AVB, SIS, RHH, THHN, XHHW[a]	AVA, AVL	AI (12-8), AIA	A (12-8), AA	Bare and covered conductors
12 AWG	20	20	30	30[b]	40	40	45	30
10	30	30	45	45[b]	50	55	60	45
8	45	55	55	55	65	70	80	55
6	60	75	80	80	95	100	105	80
4	80	100	105	105	125	135	140	100
3	95	115	120	120	140	150	165	115
2	110	135	140	140	165	175	185	135
1	130	155	165	165	190	205	220	160
0	150	180	190	190	220	240	255	185
00	175	210	220	220	255	275	290	215
000	200	240	255	255	300	320	335	250
0000	230	280	300	300	345	370	400	290
250 MCM	265	315	330	330	385	415	......	320
300	290	350	375	375	435	460	......	360
350	330	395	415	415	475	510	......	400
400	355	425	450	450	520	555	......	435
500	405	485	515	515	595	635	......	490
600	455	545	585	585	675	720	......	560
700	500	595	645	645	745	795	......	615
750	515	620	670	670	775	825	......	640
800	535	645	695	695	805	855	......	670
900	580	700	750	750	......	......	......	725
1,000	625	750	800	800	930	990	......	770
1,250	710	855	905	905				
1,500	795	950	1,020	1,020	1,175	......	......	985
1,750	875	1,050	1,125	1,125				
2,000	960	1,150	1,220	1,220	1,425	......	......	1,165

These ampacities relate only to conductors described in Sec. **31**, Div. 9.

[a] For dry locations only. See Sec. **31**, Div. 9.

[b] The ampacities for Types RHH, THHN, and XHHW conductors for sizes AWG 12 and 10 shall be the same as designated for 75°C conductors in this table.

For ambient temperatures over 30°C see Correction Factors, Note 15 in Sec. **17**.

21. Allowable Ampacities of Insulated Aluminum Conductors
Not More than Three Conductors in Raceway or Cable, or Direct Burial
Based on Room Temperature of 30°C (86°F)
(1968 National Electrical Code)

	Temperature Rating of Conductor						
°C	60	75	85	90	110	125	200
°F	140	167	185	194	230	257	392
Size, AWG or 1,000 cir mils	RUW (12-2), T, TW	RH, RHW, RUH (12-2), THW, THWN, XHHW	V, MI	TA, TBS, SA, AVB, SIS, RHH, THHN, XHHW[a]	AVA, AVL	AI (12-8), AIA	A (12-8), AA
12 AWG	15	15	25	25[b]	25	30	30
10	25	25	30	30[b]	35	40	45
8	30	40	40	40	45	50	55
6	40	50	55	55	60	65	75
4	55	65	70	70	80	90	95
3	65	75	80	80	95	100	115
2[c]	75	90	95	95	105	115	130
1[c]	85	100	110	110	125	135	150
0[c]	100	120	125	125	150	160	180
00[c]	115	135	145	145	170	180	200
000[c]	130	155	165	165	195	210	225
0000	155	180	185	185	215	245	270
250 MCM	170	205	215	215	250	270	
300	190	230	240	240	275	305	
350	210	250	260	260	310	335	
400	225	270	290	290	335	360	
500	260	310	330	330	380	405	
600	285	340	370	370	425	440	
700	310	375	395	395	455	485	
750	320	385	405	405	470	500	
800	330	395	415	415	485	520	
900	355	425	455	455			
1,000	375	445	480	480	560	600	
1,250	405	485	530	530			
1,500	435	520	580	580	650		
1,750	455	545	615	615			
2,000	470	560	650	650	705		

These ampacities relate only to conductors described in Sec. 31, Div. 9.

[a] For dry locations only. See Sec. 31, Div. 9.

[b] The ampacities for Types RHH, THHN, and XHHW conductors for sizes AWG 12 and 10 shall be the same as designated for 75°C conductors in this table.

[c] For three-wire single-phase service the allowable ampacity of RH, RHH, RHW, and THW aluminum conductors is: No. 2 – 100 amp, No. 1 – 110 amp, No. 1/0 – 125 amp, No. 2/0 – 150 amp, No. 3/0 – 170 amp, No. 4/0 – 200 amp.
For ambient temperatures over 30°C see Correction Factors, Note 15 in Sec. 17.

21A. Ampacities of Insulated Aluminum Conductors at Various Deratings
In Raceways or Cables at Room Temperatures Not over 30°C (86°F)

Size, AWG or 1,000 cir mils	Ampacity														
	100%			80%			70%			60%			50%		
	60°C	75°C	90°C	60°C	75°C	90°C	60°C	75°C	90°C	60°C	75°C	90°C	60°C	75°C	90°C
12 AWG	15	15	15	12	12	12	10	10	10	9	9	9	7	7	7
10	25	25	25	20	20	20	17	17	17	15	15	15	12	12	12
8	30	40	40	24	32	32	21	28	28	18	24	24	15	20	20
6	40	50	55	32	40	44	28	35	38	24	30	33	20	25	27
4	55	65	70	44	52	56	38	45	49	33	39	42	27	32	35
3	65	75	80	52	60	64	45	52	56	39	45	48	32	37	40
2[a]	75	90	95	60	72	76	52	63	66	45	54	57	37	45	47
1[a]	85	100	110	68	80	88	59	70	77	51	60	66	42	50	55
0[a]	100	120	125	80	96	100	70	84	87	60	72	75	50	60	62
00[a]	115	135	145	92	108	116	80	94	101	69	81	87	57	67	72
000[a]	130	155	165	104	124	132	91	108	115	78	93	99	65	77	82
0000[a]	155	180	185	124	144	148	108	126	129	93	108	111	77	90	92
250 MCM	170	205	215	136	164	172	119	143	150	102	123	129	85	102	107
300	190	230	240	152	184	192	133	161	168	114	138	144	95	115	120
350	210	250	260	168	200	208	147	175	182	126	150	156	105	125	130
400	225	270	290	180	216	232	157	189	203	135	162	174	112	135	145
500	260	310	330	208	248	264	182	217	231	156	186	198	130	155	165

60°C conductors—RUW, T, TW.

75°C conductors—RH, THW, THWN, RUH, XHHW (wet locations); RHW.

90°C conductors—THHN, RHH, FEP, FEPB, XHHW (dry locations).

[a] For three-wire single-phase service or subservice circuits the allowable ampacity of RH, RHH, RHW, and THW aluminum conductors is: No. 2—100 amp, No. 1—110 amp, No. 1/0—125 amp, No. 2/0—150 amp, No. 3/0—170 amp, No. 4/0—200 amp.

22. Allowable Ampacities of Flexible Cord
Based on Room Temperature of 30°C (86°F)
(1968 National Electrical Code)

This table gives the allowable ampacity for not more than three current-carrying conductors in a cord. If the number of current-carrying conductors in a cord is four to six, the allowable ampacity of each conductor shall be reduced to 80 per cent of the values for not more than three current-carrying conductors in the table. A conductor used for equipment grounding, and a neutral conductor that carries only the unbalanced current from other conductors, as in the case of normally balanced circuits of three or more conductors, are not considered to be current-carrying conductors. Where a single conductor is used for both equipment grounding and to carry unbalanced current from other conductors, it shall not be considered to be a current-carrying conductor.

Size, AWG	Rubber Types TP, TS / Thermoplastic Types TPT, TSP	Rubber Types PO, C, PD, E, EO, EN, S, SO, SRD, SJ, SJO, SV, SVO, SP / Thermoplastic Types ET, ETP, ST, STO, SRDT, SJT, SJTO, SVT, SVTO, SPT		Types AFS, AFSJ, HC, HPD, HSJ, HSJO, HS, HSO, HPN, SVHT	Types AVPO, AVPD	Cotton Types CFPD[a] / Asbestos Types AFC[a], AFPD[a]
		A[b]	B[b]			
27[c]	0.5					
18	.....	7	10	10	17	6
17	.....	....	....	12		
16	.....	10	13	15	22	8
15	.....	....	....	17		
14	.....	15	18	20	28	17
12	.....	20	25	30	36	23
10	.....	25	30	35	47	28
8	.....	35	40			
6	.....	45	55			
4	.....	60	70			
2	.....	80	95			

[a] These types are used almost exclusively in fixtures where they are exposed to high temperatures and ampere ratings are assigned accordingly.

[b] The ampacities under subheading A in column 3 are applicable to three-conductor cords and four-conductor cords connected to utilization equipment, with three conductors carrying current. The ampacities under subheading B in column 3 are applicable to two-conductor cords and three-conductor cords connected to the utilization equipment, with two conductors carrying current.

[c] Tinsel cord.

NOTE 1. Ultimate insulation temperature: In no case shall conductors be associated together in such a way with respect to the kind of circuit, the wiring method employed, or the number of conductors, that the limiting temperature of the conductors will be exceeded.

NOTE 2. SVHT made only in No. 18 and 17 AWG sizes.

22A. Allowable Ampacities of Fixture Wire
Based on Ambient Temperature of 30°C (86°F)
(1968 National Electrical Code)

Fixture wire	Size, AWG		
	18	16	14
Thermoplastic Types:			
TF, TFF, TFN, TFFN	6	8	17
Cotton Type CF[a]	6	8	17
Asbestos Type AF[a]	6	8	17
Silicone rubber Types:[a]			
SF-1, SF-2, SFF-1, SFF-2	6	8	17
Fluorinated ethylene propylene Types:[a]			
PF, PGF, PFF, PGFF	6	8	17
Rubber Types:			
RF-1, RF-2, FF-1, FF-2, RFH-1, RFH-2, FFH-1, FFH-2	5	7	

[a] These types are used almost exclusively in fixtures where they are exposed to high temperatures and ampere ratings are assigned accordingly.

NOTE. Ultimate insulation temperature: In no case shall conductors be associated together in such a way with respect to the kind of circuit, the wiring method employed, or the number of conductors, that the limiting temperature of the conductors will be exceeded.

23. Curves for Determining Ampacity of Aluminum Cable, Steel-reinforced
(Aluminum Company of America)

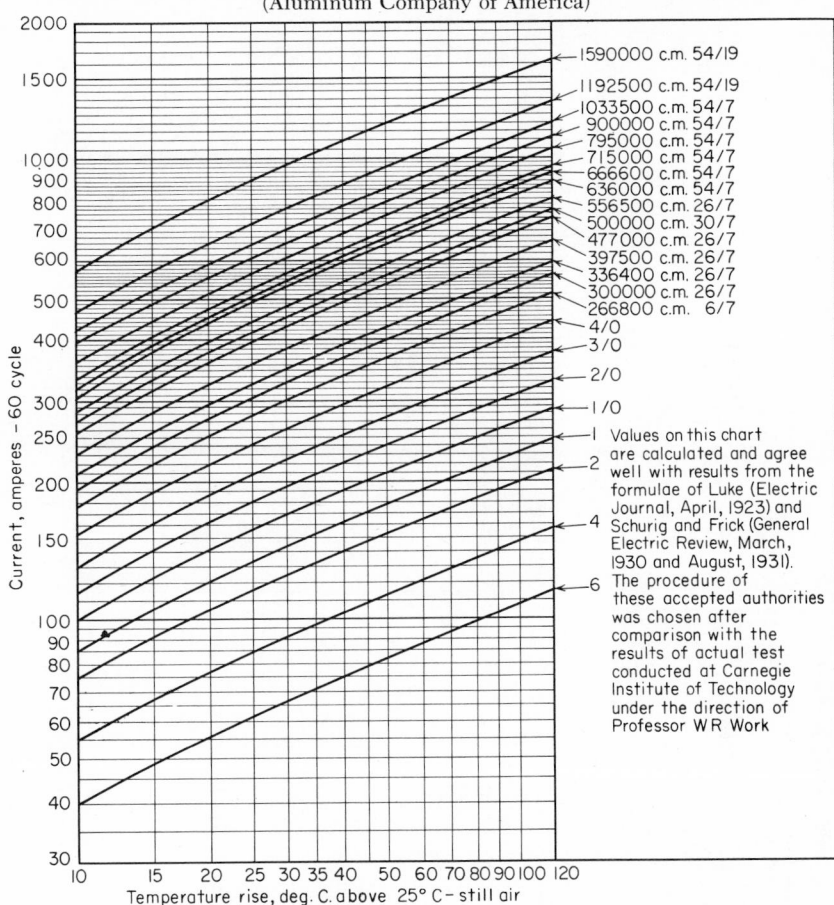

Values on this chart are calculated and agree well with results from the formulae of Luke (Electric Journal, April, 1923) and Schurig and Frick (General Electric Review, March, 1930 and August, 1931). The procedure of these accepted authorities was chosen after comparison with the results of actual test conducted at Carnegie Institute of Technology under the direction of Professor W R Work

24. Ampacities of Parkway Cables Buried Directly in Ground[a]

Conductor size, AWG or 1,000 cir mils	Max allowable ampacity per conductor (copper)		Conductor size, AWG or 1,000 cir mils	Max allowable ampacity per conductor (copper)	
	Single-conductor cable, amp	Three-conductor cable, amp		Single-conductor cable, amp	Three-conductor cable, amp
8 AWG	85	60	3/0 AWG	335	225
6	115	80	4/0	385	255
4	150	100	250 MCM	445	285
2	195	130	300	470	315
1	220	150	350	515	345
1/0	255	170	400	555	375
2/0	295	195	500	635	425

[a] Table based on earth temperature of 20°C (68°F). Rubber-insulated conductors in accordance with IPCEA specification. Average soil condition, sandy loam, 10 per cent moisture. Average depth of burial 18 in. Other cables sufficiently far away to prevent mutual heating. Rated voltages up to 5 kv, grounded neutral.

Tables **25** to **27** apply only to complete conduit systems, and not to short sections of conduit used for the protection of exposed wiring from physical damage.

Where conduit nipples having a maximum length not to exceed 6 in. are installed between boxes, cabinets, gutters, switch cases, and similar enclosures, the conductor fill in such nipples may be increased to not more than 60 per cent of the internal cross-sectional area of the conduit, and Note 8 of Sec. **17** does not apply to this condition.

25. Maximum Number of Conductors in Trade Sizes of Conduit or Tubing—New Work

Based on Per Cent Conductor Fill, Table 27, for New Work
(1968 National Electrical Code)

Col. A = Types RF-2, RFH-2, RH, RHH, RHW, RUH, RUW, T, TF, THW, TW, XHHW (AWG 14 to 6), FEPB (AWG 6 to 2)
Col. B = FEP, THHN, THWN, TFN, PF, PGF, XHHW (AWG 4 to 2,000 MCM), FEPB (AWG 14 to 8)

Derating factors for more than three conductors in raceway: see Note 8 of Sec. 17.

Size, AWG or 1,000 cir mil	½" A	½" B	¾" A	¾" B	1" A	1" B	1¼" A	1¼" B	1½" A	1½" B	2" A	2" B	2½" A	2½" B	3" A	3" B	3½" A	3½" B	4" A	4" B	4½" A	4½" B	5" A	5" B	6" A	6" B
18 AWG	7	11	12	20	20	33	35	58	49	80	80	131	115	187	176											
16	6	9	10	16	17	27	30	47	41	64	68	106	98	151	150											
14	4	8	6	15	10	24	18	43	25	58	41	96	58	137	90		121		155		197					
12	3	6	5	11	8	18	15	32	21	43	34	71	50	102	76	158	103		132		168					
10	1	4	4	7	7	11	13	20	17	27	29	45	41	65	64	100	86	134	110	172	140		173			
8	1	2	3	4	4	6	7	11	10	16	17	26	25	37	38	58	52	78	67	100	85	127	105	157	152	
6	1	1	1	2	3	4	4	7	6	9	10	16	15	23	23	35	32	47	41	61	52	78	64	96	93	139
4	1	1	1	1	1	2	3	4	5	6	8	9	12	14	18	21	24	29	31	37	40	48	49	59	72	85
3			1	1	1	2	3	3	4	5	7	8	10	12	16	18	21	24	28	31	35	40	44	50	63	72
2			1	1	1	1	3	3	3	4	6	7	9	10	14	15	19	20	24	26	31	34	38	42	55	61
1					1	1	1	2	3	3	4	5	7	7	10	11	14	15	18	20	23	25	29	31	42	45
0					1	1	1	2	2	2	4	4	6	6	9	9	12	13	16	16	20	21	25	25	37	38
2/0					1	1	1	1	1	2	3	3	5	5	8	8	11	11	14	14	18	18	22	22	32	32
3/0						1	1	1	1	1	3	3	4	4	7	7	9	9	12	12	15	15	19	19	27	27
4/0							1	1	1	1	2	2	3	3	6	6	8	8	10	10	13	13	16	16	23	23
250 MCM							1		1	1	2	2	3	3	5	5	6	6	8	8	11	11	13	13	19	19
300									1	1	1	1	3	3	4	4	5	5	8	7	9	9	11	11	16	16
350									1	1	1	1	1	2	3	3	5	5	6	6	8	8	10	10	15	15
400									1		1	1	1	1	3	3	4	4	6	6	7	7	9	9	13	13
500									1		1	1	1	1	3	3	4	4	5	5	6	6	8	8	11	11
600											1		1	1	1	2	3	3	4	4	5	5	6	6	9	9
700											1				1	1	3	3	3	3	4	4	6	6	8	8
750											1				1	1	3	3	3	3	4	4	5	5	8	8
800											1				1	1	2	2	3	3	4	4	5	5	7	7
900											1				1	1	1	2	3	3	4	4	4	4	7	7
1,000															1	1	1	1	3	3	3	3	4	4	6	6
1,250															1	1	1		1	2	3	3	3	3	5	5
1,500																			1	1	2	2	3	3	4	4
1,750																			1	1	2	2	2	2	4	4
2,000																			1	1	1	1	1	1	3	3

25A. Maximum Number of Conductors in Trade Sizes of Conduit or Tubing—Rewiring[a]

Based on Per Cent Conductor Fill, Table 27, for Rewiring
(1968 National Electrical Code)

Col. A = THW, TW, T, TF, RUH, RUW, (RHH and RHW without outer covering), XHHW (AWG 14 to 6), FEPB (AWG 6 to 2)

Col. B = THWN, THHN, FEP, TFN, PF, PGF, XHHW (AWG 4 to 2,000 MCM), FEPB (AWG 14 to 8)

Derating factors for more than three conductors in raceway: see Note 8 of Sec. 17.

Size, AWG or 1,000 cir mils	½ in A	½ in B	¾ in A	¾ in B	1 in A	1 in B	1¼ in A	1¼ in B	1½ in A	1½ in B	2 in A	2 in B	2½ in A	2½ in B	3 in A	3 in B	3½ in A	3½ in B	4 in A	4 in B	4½ in A	4½ in B	5 in A	5 in B	6 in A	6 in B
18 AWG	13	19	24	33	38	53	68	93	93	127	152	170	176													
16	11	15	19	27	31	43	55	76	75	103	123	154	176													
14	5	13	10	24	16	39	29	69	40	94	65	114	93	164	143		192									
12	4	10	8	18	13	29	24	51	32	70	53		76	104	117		157									
10	4	6	6	11	11	18	19	32	26	44	43	72	61	60	95	160	127		163							
8	1	3	4	6	6	10	11	19	15	26	25	42	36	37	56	93	75	125	96	160	123		152			
6	1	1	2	4	4	6	7	11	10	15	16	25	23	22	36	56	48	76	62	98	79	125	97	154	141	
4	1	1	1	2	3	4	5	7	7	9	12	16	17	19	27	35	36	47	46	60	60	76	73	94	106	136
3	1	1	1	1	2	3	4	6	6	8	10	13	15	16	23	29	31	39	40	51	51	65	63	80	91	116
2	1	1	1	1	1	3	4	5	5	7	9	11	13	12	20	25	27	33	34	43	44	54	54	67	78	97
1			1	1	1	1	2	3	4	5	6	8	9	10	14	18	19	25	25	32	32	40	39	50	57	72
0			1	1	1	1	2	3	3	4	5	7	8	8	12	15	16	21	21	27	27	34	33	42	48	61
2/0			1		1	1	1	2	3	3	4	6	7	7	10	13	14	17	18	22	23	28	28	35	41	51
3/0					1	1	1	1	2	3	4	5	5	6	9	11	12	14	15	18	19	24	24	29	35	42
4/0					1	1	1	1	1	2	3	4	5	4	7	9	10	12	13	15	16	20	20	24	29	35
250 MCM			1		1		1	1	1	1	2	3	4	4	6	7	8	9	10	12	13	16	16	20	23	28
300							1	1	1	1	2	3	3	4	5	6	7	8	9	11	11	14	14	17	20	24
350							1	1	1	1	1	2	3	3	4	5	6	7	8	9	10	12	12	15	18	21
400									1	1	1	1	2	2	4	5	5	6	7	8	9	11	11	13	16	19
500									1	1	1	1	1	1	3	4	4	6	6	7	7	9	9	11	14	16
600									1		1	1	1	1	3	3	4	4	5	5	6	7	7	8	11	12
700											1	1	1	1	2	2	3	3	4	4	5	6	7	7	10	11
750											1	1	1	1	2	2	3	3	4	4	5	6	6	7	9	10
800											1	1	1	1	2	1	3	3	4	4	5	5	6	6	9	10
900											1	1	1		1	1	2	3	3	3	4	5	5	6	8	9
1,000											1	1	1		1	1	2	2	3	3	4	4	5	5	7	8
1,250															1	1	1	1	2	2	3	3	4	4	6	6
1,500															1	1	1	1	1	1	3	3	3	3	5	5
1,750															1	1	1	1	1	1	2	2	3	3	4	4
2,000															1	1	1	1	1	1	2	2	2	3	4	4

[a] For Types RF-2, RFH-2, RH, RHH, see columns A, Table 25.

26. Trade Sizes in Inches of Conduit or Tubing for Number of Conductors
Lead-covered Types RL and RHL – 600 volts
(1968 National Electrical Code)

Size, AWG or 1,000 cir mils	Number of conductors in one conduit or tubing											
	Single-conductor cables				2-conductor cables				3-conductor cables			
	1	2	3	4	1	2	3	4	1	2	3	4
14 AWG	½	¾	¾	1	¾	1	1	1¼	¾	1¼	1½	1½
12	½	¾	¾	1	¾	1	1¼	1¼	1	1¼	1½	2
10	½	¾	1	1	¾	1¼	1¼	1½	1	1½	2	2
8	½	1	1¼	1½	1	1¼	1½	2	1	2	2	2½
6	¾	1¼	1½	1½	1¼	1½	2	2½	1¼	2½	3	3
4	¾	1¼	1½	1½	1¼	2	2½	2½	1½	3	3	3½
3	¾	1¼	1½	2	1¼	2	2½	3	1½	3	3	3½
2	1	1¼	1½	2	1¼	2	2½	3	1½	3	3½	4
1	1	1½	2	2	1½	2½	3	3½	2	3½	4	4½
0	1	2	2	2½	2	2½	3	3½	2	4	4½	5
00	1	2	2	2½	2	3	3½	4	2½	4	4½	5
000	1¼	2	2½	2½	2	3	3½	4	2½	4½	4½	6
0000	1¼	2½	2½	3	2½	3	3½	4½	3	5	6	6
250 MCM	1¼	2½	3	3	.....	.....	.....	.....	3	6	6	
300	1½	3	3	3½	.....	.....	.....	.....	3½	6	6	
350	1½	3	3	3½	.....	.....	.....	.....	3½	6	6	
400	1½	3	3	3½	.....	.....	.....	.....	3½	6	6	
500	1½	3	3½	4	.....	.....	.....	.....	4	6		
600	2	3½	4	4½								
700	2	4	4	5								
750	2	4	4	5								
800	2	4	4½	5								
900	2½	4	4½	5								
1,000	2½	4½	4½	6								
1,250	3	5	5	6								
1,500	3	5	6	6								
1,750	3	6	6									
2,000	3½	6	6									

The above sizes apply to straight runs or with nominal offsets equivalent to not more than two quarter-bends.

27. Combination of Conductors in Conduit or Tubing
(National Electrical Code)

For groups or combinations of conductors not included in Table 25 for new work, Table 25A for rewiring, or Table 26, the conduit or tubing shall be of such size that the sum of the cross-sectional areas of the individual conductors will not be more than the percentage of the interior cross-sectional area of the conduit or tubing shown in the table below.

Percentages of Area of Conduit or Tubing to Be Occupied by Conductors

Types of conductors	Number of conductors				
	1	2	3	4	Over 4
1. New work Types FEP, FEPB, T, TW, TF, THW, RUH, RUW, XHHW, THWN, THHN, TFN, PF, PFG.........	35	25^a	25^a	25^a	25^a
2. New work Types RF-2, RFH-2, RH, RHH, RHW................................	53	31	40	40	40
3. All types—rewiring..........................	53	31	40	40	40
4. Lead-covered..................................	55	30	40	38	35

For ampacity of more than three conductors in a conduit or tubing, see Note 8 of Sec. 17.

See Tables 29 to 32 for dimensions of conductors, conduit and tubing, and raceway.

When, in new work, conductors limited to 25 per cent fill are to be in the same conduit or tubing as conductors limited to 40 per cent fill, the combined fill shall not be greater than 40 per cent nor shall any conductor size or type, when used with conductors of other size or type, occupy more than its allowable fill when used alone.

^{a} The percentage fill for these conductors may be increased to those given in category 2 where the total conductor fill is based on the dimensions for Type RHW conductors as given in column 3 of Table 30.

28. Maximum Size of Conductor for Installation in Liquid-tight Flexible Metal Conduit

Trade Size of Conduit, in.	Maximum Size of Conductor, AWG or 1,000 cir mils
3/8	16 AWG
1/2	12
3/4	8
1	6
1 1/4	2
1 1/2	1
2	00
2 1/2	0000
3	350 MCM

Tables 29 to 32. Tables 29 to 32 give the nominal size of conductors and conduit or tubing designated by the National Electrical Code for use in computing size of conduit or tubing for various combinations of conductors. The dimensions represent average conditions only, and although variations will be found in dimensions of conductors and conduits of different manufacture, these variations will not affect the computation.

29. Dimensions and Per Cent Area of Conduit and of Tubing

Areas of Conduit or Tubing for the Combinations of Wires Permitted in Table 27

(1968 National Electrical Code)

Trade size, inches	Internal diameter, inches	Total, 100%	Non-lead-covered					Lead-covered				
			25%	31%	35%	40%	53%	1 conductor, 55%	2 conductors, 30%	3 conductors, 40%	4 conductors, 38%	Over 4 conductors, 35%
½	0.622	0.30	0.08	0.09	0.11	0.12	0.16	0.17	0.09	0.12	0.11	0.11
¾	0.824	0.53	0.13	0.16	0.19	0.21	0.28	0.29	0.16	0.21	0.20	0.19
1	1.049	0.86	0.22	0.27	0.30	0.34	0.46	0.47	0.26	0.34	0.33	0.30
1¼	1.380	1.50	0.38	0.47	0.53	0.60	0.80	0.83	0.45	0.60	0.57	0.53
1½	1.610	2.04	0.51	0.63	0.71	0.82	1.08	1.12	0.61	0.82	0.78	0.71
2	2.067	3.36	0.84	1.04	1.18	1.34	1.78	1.85	1.01	1.34	1.28	1.18
2½	2.469	4.79	1.20	1.48	1.68	1.92	2.54	2.63	1.44	1.92	1.82	1.68
3	3.068	7.38	1.85	2.29	2.58	2.95	3.91	4.06	2.21	2.95	2.80	2.58
3½	3.548	9.90	2.48	3.07	3.47	3.96	5.25	5.44	2.97	3.96	3.76	3.47
4	4.026	12.72	3.18	3.94	4.45	5.09	6.74	7.00	3.82	5.09	4.83	4.45
4½	4.506	15.94	3.99	4.94	5.56	6.38	8.45	8.77	4.78	6.38	6.06	5.56
5	5.047	20.00	5.00	6.20	7.00	8.00	10.60	11.00	6.00	8.00	7.60	7.00
6	6.065	28.89	7.22	8.96	10.11	11.56	15.31	15.89	8.67	11.56	10.98	10.11

Area, square inches

30. Dimensions of Rubber-covered and Thermoplastic-covered Conductors

(No. 18 to No. 8 solid; No. 6 and larger, stranded)
(1968 National Electrical Code)

Size, AWG or 1,000 cir mils (1)	Types RF-2, RFH-2, RH, RHH,[a] RHW,[a] SF-2		Types TF, T, THW, TW, RUH,[c] RUW[c]		Types TFN, THHN, THWN		Types FEP, FEPB, PF, PGF		Type XHHW	
	Approx. diam., inches (2)	Approx. area, sq in. (3)	Approx. diam., inches (4)	Approx. area, sq in. (5)	Approx. diam., inches (6)	Approx. area, sq in. (7)	Approx. diam., inches (8)[e]	Approx. area, sq in. (9)[e]	Approx. diam., inches (10)	Approx. area, sq in. (11)
18AWG	0.146	0.0167	0.106	0.0088	0.089	0.0064	0.081	0.0052		
16	0.158	0.0196	0.118	0.0109	0.100	0.0079	0.092	0.0066		
14	³⁄₆₄ in. 0.171	0.0230	0.131	0.0135	0.105	0.0087	0.105 0.105	0.0087 0.0087	0.129	0.0131
14	³⁄₆₄ in. 0.204[d]	0.0327[d]	0.162[b]	0.0206[b]						
12	³⁄₆₄ in. 0.188[d]	0.0278[d]	0.148	0.0172	0.122	0.0117	0.121 0.121	0.0115 0.0115	0.146	0.0167
12	³⁄₆₄ in. 0.221[d]	0.0384[d]	0.179[b]	0.0251[b]						
10	0.242	0.0460	0.168	0.0224	0.153	0.0184	0.142 0.142	0.0159 0.0159	0.166	0.0216
10			0.199[b]	0.0311[b]						
8	0.311	0.0760	0.228	0.0408	0.201	0.0317	0.189 0.169	0.0280 0.0225	0.224	0.0394
8			0.259[b]	0.0526[b]						
6	0.397	0.1238	0.323	0.0819	0.257	0.0519	0.244 0.302	0.0467 0.0716	0.282	0.0625
4	0.452	0.1605	0.372	0.1087	0.328	0.0845	0.292 0.350	0.0669 0.0962	0.328	0.0845
3	0.481	0.1817	0.401	0.1263	0.356	0.0995	0.320 0.378	0.0803 0.1122	0.356	0.0995
2	0.513	0.2067	0.433	0.1473	0.388	0.1182	0.352 0.410	0.0973 0.1316	0.388	0.1182
1	0.588	0.2715	0.508	0.2027	0.450	0.1590			0.450	0.1590
0	0.629	0.3107	0.549	0.2367	0.491	0.1893			0.491	0.1893
00	0.675	0.3578	0.595	0.2781	0.537	0.2265			0.537	0.2265
000	0.727	0.4151	0.647	0.3288	0.588	0.2715			0.588	0.2715
0000	0.785	0.4840	0.705	0.3904	0.646	0.3278			0.646	0.3278
250MCM	0.868	0.5917	0.788	0.4877	0.716	0.4026			0.716	0.4026
300	0.933	0.6637	0.843	0.5581	0.771	0.4669			0.771	0.4669
350	0.985	0.7620	0.895	0.6291	0.822	0.5307			0.822	0.5307
400	1.032	0.8365	0.942	0.6969	0.869	0.5931			0.869	0.5931
500	1.119	0.9834	1.029	0.8316	0.955	0.7163			0.955	0.7163
600	1.233	1.1940	1.143	1.0261					1.073	0.9043
700	1.304	1.3355	1.214	1.1575					1.145	1.0297
750	1.339	1.4082	1.249	1.2252					1.180	1.0936
800	1.372	1.4784	1.282	1.2908					1.210	1.1499
900	1.435	1.6173	1.345	1.4208					1.270	1.2668
1,000	1.494	1.7531	1.404	1.5482					1.330	1.3893
1,250	1.676	2.2062	1.577	1.9532					1.500	1.7672
1,500	1.801	2.5475	1.702	2.2748					1.620	2.0612
1,750	1.916	2.8895	1.817	2.5930					1.740	2.3779
2,000	2.021	3.2079	1.922	2.9013					1.840	2.6590

[a] Dimensions of RHH and RHW without outer covering are the same as those of THW.
[b] Dimensions of THW in sizes 14 to 8. No. 6 THW and larger have the same dimensions as T.
[c] No. 14 to No. 2.
[d] The dimensions of Types RHH and RHW.
[e] Values in left side of column are for Type FEP, and values in right side of column are for Type FEPB.

11-29

31. Dimensions of Lead-covered Conductors
Types RL, RHL, and RUL
(National Electrical Code)

Size, AWG or 1,000 cir mils	Single conductor		Two conductor		Three conductor	
	Diam., in.	Area, sq in.	Diam., in.	Area, sq in.	Diam., in.	Area, sq in.
14 AWG	0.28	0.062	0.28 × 0.47	0.115	0.59	0.273
12	0.29	0.066	0.31 × 0.54	0.146	0.62	0.301
10	0.35	0.096	0.35 × 0.59	0.180	0.68	0.363
8	0.41	0.132	0.41 × 0.71	0.255	0.82	0.528
6	0.49	0.188	0.49 × 0.86	0.369	0.97	0.738
4	0.55	0.237	0.54 × 0.96	0.457	1.08	0.916
2	0.60	0.283	0.61 × 1.08	0.578	1.21	1.146
1	0.67	0.352	0.70 × 1.23	0.756	1.38	1.49
0	0.71	0.396	0.74 × 1.32	0.859	1.47	1.70
00	0.76	0.454	0.79 × 1.41	0.980	1.57	1.94
000	0.81	0.515	0.84 × 1.52	1.123	1.69	2.24
0000	0.87	0.593	0.90 × 1.64	1.302	1.85	2.68
250 MCM	0.98	0.754	....	.....	2.02	3.20
300	1.04	0.85	....	.....	2.15	3.62
350	1.10	0.95	....	.....	2.26	4.02
400	1.14	1.02	....	.....	2.40	4.52
500	1.23	1.18	....	.....	2.59	5.28

NOTE.   No. 14 to No. 8, solid conductors; No. 6 and larger, stranded conductors.   Data for $\frac{3}{64}$-in. insulation not yet compiled.

32. Dimensions of Asbestos-varnished-cambric-insulated Conductors
Types AVA, AVB, and AVL
(National Electrical Code)

Size, AWG or 1,000 cir mils	Type AVA		Type AVB		Type AVL	
	Approx. diam., in.	Approx. area, sq in.	Approx. diam., in.	Approx. area, sq in.	Approx. diam., in.	Approx. area, sq in.
14 AWG	0.245	0.047	0.205	0.033	0.320	0.080
12	0.265	0.055	0.225	0.040	0.340	0.091
10	0.285	0.064	0.245	0.047	0.360	0.102
8	0.310	0.075	0.270	0.057	0.390	0.119
6	0.395	0.122	0.345	0.094	0.430	0.145
4	0.445	0.155	0.395	0.123	0.480	0.181
2	0.505	0.200	0.460	0.166	0.570	0.255
1	0.585	0.268	0.540	0.229	0.620	0.300
0	0.625	0.307	0.580	0.264	0.660	0.341
00	0.670	0.353	0.625	0.307	0.705	0.390
000	0.720	0.406	0.675	0.358	0.755	0.447
0000	0.780	0.478	0.735	0.425	0.815	0.521
250 MCM	0.885	0.616	0.855	0.572	0.955	0.715
300	0.940	0.692	0.910	0.649	1.010	0.800
350	0.995	0.778	0.965	0.731	1.060	0.885
400	1.040	0.850	1.010	0.800	1.105	0.960
500	1.125	0.995	1.095	0.945	1.190	1.118
550	1.165	1.065	1.135	1.01	1.265	1.26
600	1.205	1.140	1.175	1.09	1.305	1.34
650	1.240	1.21	1.210	1.15	1.340	1.41
700	1.275	1.28	1.245	1.22	1.375	1.49
750	1.310	1.35	1.280	1.29	1.410	1.57
800	1.345	1.42	1.315	1.36	1.440	1.63
850	1.375	1.49	1.345	1.43	1.470	1.70
990	1.405	1.55	1.375	1.49	1.505	1.78
950	1.435	1.62	1.405	1.55	1.535	1.85
1,000	1.465	1.69	1.435	1.62	1.565	1.93

NOTE. No. 14 to No. 8, solid; No. 6 and larger, stranded; except AVL, where all sizes are stranded.

Varnished-cambric-insulated Conductors, Type V. The insulation thickness for varnished-cambric conductors, Type V, is the same as for rubber-covered conductors, Type RH, except for Nos. 14 and 12, which have 3/64-in. insulation for varnished-cambric and 2/64-in. insulation for rubber-covered conductors, and for No. 8, which has 3/64-in. insulation for varnished-cambric and 4/64-in. insulation for rubber-covered conductors. Tables **25** (columns A) and **26** may, therefore, be used for the number of varnished-cambric-insulated conductors in a conduit or tubing.

33. Maximum Diameter of Cable to Be Installed in Various Sizes and Types of Ducts for Underground Duct Installation

(All dimensions are in inches)

Nominal diam of duct	Condition (see notes below)		Monolithic concrete		Single-camp. tile		Multiple tile		Fiber duct		Iron or steel conduit[d]		"Stone" duct	
			Actual diam of duct	Diam of cable	Actual diam of duct	Diam of cable	Actual diam of duct	Diam of cable	Actual diam of duct	Diam of cable	Actual diam of duct	Diam of cable	Actual diam of duct	Diam of cable
3	(1)	a	3⅜	2¾	3⅜	2⅞	3⅜	2⅞	3	2½	3	2⅜		
		b	3⅜	2⅝	3⅜	2¾	3⅜	2¾	3	2⅜	3	2¼		
		c	3⅜	2½	3⅜	2⅝	3⅜	2⅝	3	2¼	3	2⅛		
	(2)	a	3⅜	3	3⅜	3⅛	3⅜	3⅛	3	2¾	3	2⅝		
		b	3⅜	2⅞	3⅜	3	3⅜	3	3	2⅝	3	2½		
		c	3⅜	2¾	3⅜	2⅞	3⅜	2⅞	3	2½	3	2⅜		
3½	(1)	a	3⅞	3¼	3⅝	3⅛	3⅝	3⅛	3½	3	3½	2⅞	3½	3
		b	3⅞	3⅛	3⅝	3	3⅝	3	3½	2⅞	3½	3¾	3½	2⅞
		c	3⅞	3	3⅝	2⅞	3⅝	2⅞	3½	2¾	3½	2⅝	3½	2¾
	(2)	a	3⅞	3½	3⅝	3⅜	3⅝	3⅜	3½	3¼	3½	3⅛	3½	3⅛
		b	3⅞	3⅜	3⅝	3¼	3⅝	3¼	3½	3⅛	3½	3	3½	3
		c	3⅞	3¼	3⅝	3⅛	3⅝	3⅛	3½	3	3½	2⅞	3½	2⅞
4	(1)	a	4⅛	3⅜	4⅜	3¾	...	...	4	3⅜	4	3¼	4	3⅜
		b	4⅛	3¼	4⅜	3⅝	...	...	4	3¼	4	3⅛	4	3¼
		c	4⅛	3⅛	4⅜	3½	...	...	4	3⅛	4	3	4	3⅛
	(2)	a	4⅛	3⅝	4⅜	4	...	...	4	3⅝	4	3½	4	3½
		b	4⅛	3½	4⅜	3⅞	...	...	4	3½	4	3⅜	4	3⅜
		c	4⅛	3⅜	4⅜	3¾	...	...	4	3⅜	4	3¼	4	3¼
5	(1)	a	4⅞	4⅛	...	...	...	...	5	4¼	5	4⅛		
		b	4⅞	4	...	...	...	...	5	4⅛	5	4		
		c	4⅞	3⅞	...	...	...	...	5	4	5	3⅞		
	(2)	a	4⅞	4⅜	...	...	...	...	5	4½	5	4⅜		
		b	4⅞	4¼	...	...	...	...	5	4⅜	5	4¼		
		c	4⅞	4⅛	...	...	...	...	5	4¼	5	4⅛		

For more than one cable, the diameter is that of the circumscribing circle.
NOTE. For dimensions of cable refer to Div. 2.
(1) Conservative maximum size.
(2) Exceptional maximum size.
[a] Straight section less than 300 ft long.
[b] Straight section from 300 to 600 ft long.
[c] Curved section less than 300 ft long, one or two bends of 50- to 250-ft radius.
[d] Also includes polyvinyl-chloride (PVC) conduit, polyethylene (PE) conduit and styrene conduit.

34. Isolation by Elevation and Clear Working Space
(National Electrical Code)

Voltage between phases	Minimum vertical clearance of unguarded parts	
	Ft	In.
601–6,600	8	0
6,601–11,000	9	0
11,001–22,000	9	3
22,001–33,000	9	6
33,001–44,000	9	10
44,001–66,000	10	5
66,001–88,000	11	0
88,001–110,000	11	7
110,001–132,000	12	2

35. Ordinary Ratings of Overload Protective Devices in Amperes

Plug fuses	Cartridge fuses[b]	Large-sized magnetic breakers		Small magnetic breakers made by Heinemann Elec. Co.	Thermal breakers[a]	Time-lag fuses		Overload relays and releases for use with manual or magnetic switches
		Rating	Range of setting			Screw-base type	Cartridge type	
	1	3	3– 6	Any ampere	10	1.0	1	½
3	3	6	6– 12	or frac-	15	1.25	1.25	¾
6	6	10	10– 20	tional-am-	20	1.6	1.6	1
10	10	15	15– 30	pere rating	25	2.0	2.0	1½
15	15	20	20– 40	from 50 ma	35	2.5	2.5	2
20	20	25	25– 50	to 35 amp				
25	25	35	35– 70		50	3.2	3.2	2½
30	30	50	50– 100		70	4.0	4.0	3
...	35	70	70– 140		90	5.0	5.0	3½
...	40	90	90– 180		100	6.25	6.25	4
...	45	100	100– 200		125	8.0	8	4½
...	50	125	125– 250		150	10.0	10	5
...	60	150	150– 300		175	12.0	12	6
...	70	175	175– 350		200	14.0	15	7
...	80	200	200– 400		225	15.0	20	8
...	90	225	225– 450		250	20.0	25	9
...	100	250	250– 500		275	25.0	30	10
...	110	275	275– 550		300	30.0	35	12
...	125	300	300– 600		325	.....	40	14
...	150	325	325– 650		350	.....	45	16
...	175	350	350– 700		400	.....	50	18
...	200	400	400– 800		450	.....	60	20
...	225	500	500– 1,000		500	.....	70	22
...	250	600	600– 1,200		550	.....	80	24
...	300	800	800– 1,600		600	.....	90	28
...	350	1,000	1,000– 2,000		...	.....	100	32
...	400	1,200	1,200– 2,400		...	.....	110	36
...	450	1,600	1,600– 3,200		...	.....	125	40
...	500	2,000	2,000– 4,000		...	.....	150	45
...	600	2,500	2,500– 5,000		...	.....	175	50
...	...	3,000	3,000– 6,000		...	.....	200	55
...	...	4,000	4,000– 8,000		...	.....	225	60
...	...	5,000	5,000–10,000		...	.....	250	65
...	...	6,000	6,000–12,000		...	.....	300	70
...	...	8,000	8,000–16,000		...	.....	350	75
...	...	10,000	10,000–20,000		...	.....	400	80
...	...	.....	....		...	.....	450	
...	...	.....	....		...	.....	500	
...	...	.....	....		...	.....	600	

[a] Nonadjustable thermal magnetic.
[b] Class H, J, or K fuses. Class G fuses are 15, 20, 25, 30, 40, 45, 50, and 60 amp.

36. Ratings of High-capacity and Current-limiting (Class L) Fuses in Amperes

Over 600	1,500	2,500	4,500
	1,600	3,000	5,000
800			6,000
1,000	1,800	3,500	
1,200	2,000	4,000	

37. Number of Overcurrent Units, Such as Trip Coils or Relays, for Protection of Circuits
(Refer to Sec. 294 of Div. 9 and Fig. 1 of this division)

Systems	Number and Location of Overcurrent Units[a]
2-wire single-phase a-c or d-c, ungrounded	Two (one in each conductor. Diagram 1 of Fig. 1).
2-wire single-phase a-c or d-c, one wire grounded	One (in ungrounded conductor. Diagram 2 of Fig. 1).
2-wire single-phase a-c or d-c, mid-point grounded	Two (one in each conductor. Diagram 3 of Fig. 1).
2-wire single-phase a-c derived from 3-phase, with ungrounded neutral	Two (one in each conductor. Diagram 4 of Fig. 1).
2-wire single-phase derived from 3-phase, grounded neutral system by using outside wires of 3-phase circuit	Two (one in each conductor. Diagram 5 of Fig. 1).
3-wire single-phase a-c or d-c, ungrounded neutral	Three (one in each conductor. Diagram 6 of Fig. 1).
3-wire single-phase a-c or d-c, grounded neutral	Two (one in each conductor except neutral conductor. Diagram 7 of Fig. 1).
3-wire 2-phase, a-c, common wire ungrounded	Three (one in each conductor. Diagram 8 of Fig. 1).
3-wire 2-phase, a-c, common wire grounded	Two (one in each conductor except common conductor. Diagram 9 of Fig. 1).
4-wire 2-phase, ungrounded, phases separate	Four (one in each conductor. Diagram 10 of Fig. 1).
4-wire 2-phase, grounded neutral or 5-wire 2-phase, grounded neutral	Four (one in each conductor except neutral conductor. Diagrams 11 and 12 of Fig. 1).
3-wire 3-phase, ungrounded	Three (one in each conductor. Diagram 13 of Fig. 1[b]).
3-wire 3-phase, 1 wire grounded	Two (one in each ungrounded conductor. Diagram 14 of Fig. 1).
3-wire 3-phase, grounded neutral	Three (one in each conductor. Diagram 15 of Fig. 1[b]).
3-wire 3-phase, mid-point of one phase grounded	Three (one in each conductor. Diagram 17 of Fig. 1[b]).
4-wire 3-phase, grounded neutral	Three (one in each ungrounded conductor. Diagram 18 of Fig. 1[b]).
4-wire 3-phase, ungrounded neutral	Four (one in each conductor. Diagram 19 of Fig. 1).

[a] An overcurrent unit may consist of a series overcurrent tripping device or the combination of a current transformer and a secondary overcurrent tripping device. Either two or three secondary overcurrent tripping devices may be used with three current transformers on a three-phase system similar to those shown in Diagrams 15 and 18 in Fig. 1.

[b] When three current transformers are used instead of three series overcurrent tripping devices shown in Diagrams 13, 15, 17, and 18 in Fig. 1, the secondary tripping devices may consist of three secondary overcurrent tripping devices or two secondary overcurrent tripping devices with a residual current tripping device of a lower range. See Diagram 16 of Fig. 1.

Where standard devices are not available with three or four overcurrent units as required in the table, it is permissible to substitute two overcurrent units and one fuse where three overcurrent units are called for, two overcurrent units and two fuses where four overcurrent units are called for. The fuse or fuses are to be placed in the conductors not containing an overcurrent unit. This practice, however, of substituting fuses for overcurrent units is to be discouraged for obvious reasons.

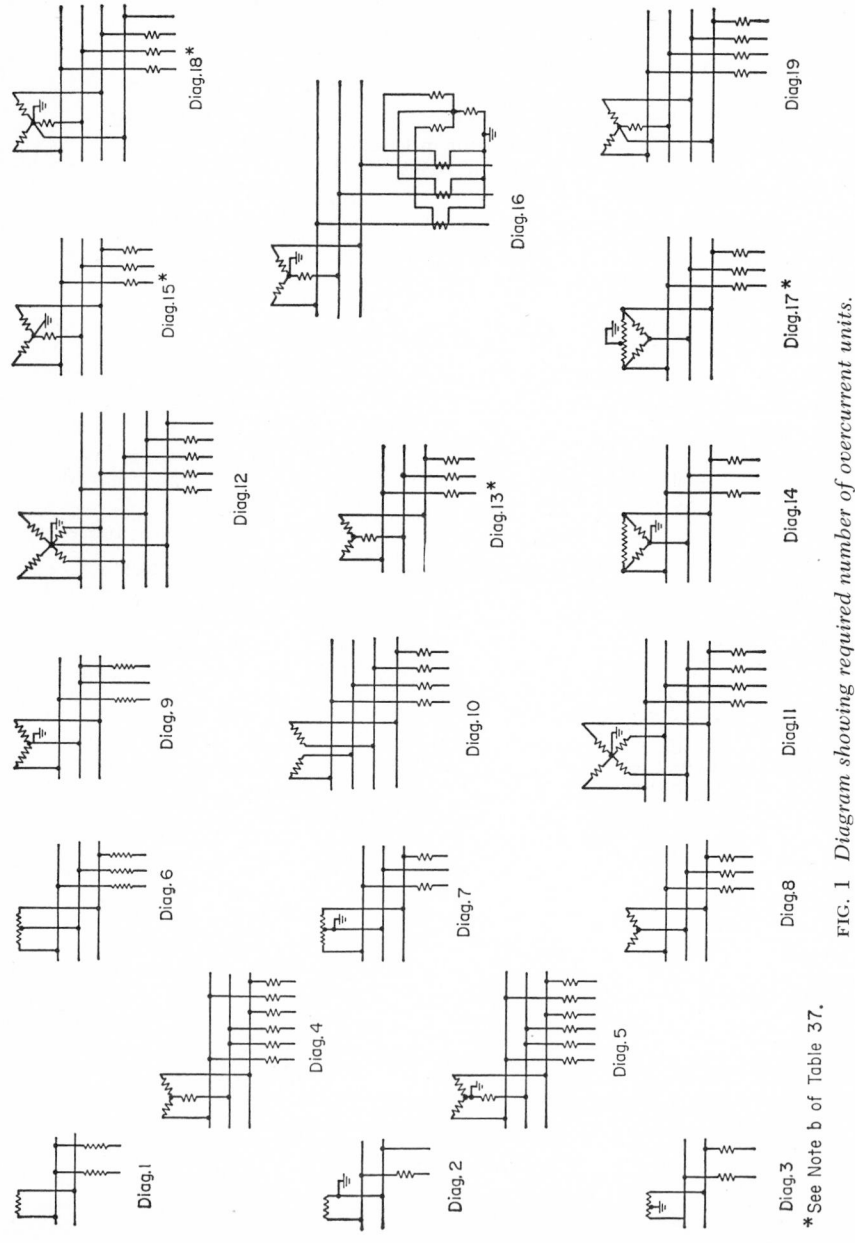

FIG. 1 *Diagram showing required number of overcurrent units.*

* See Note b of Table 37.

38. Number and Location of Running Overcurrent Units Other than Fuses for Protection of Motors

Kind of motor	Supply to system	Number and location of overcurrent units, such as trip coils, relays, or thermal cutouts
1-phase a-c or d-c	2-wire 1-phase a-c or d-c, ungrounded	1 in either conductor
1-phase a-c or d-c	2-wire 1-phase a-c or d-c, one conductor grounded	1 in ungrounded conductor
1-phase a-c or d-c	3-wire 1-phase a-c or d-c, grounded-neutral	1 in either ungrounded conductor
2-phase a-c	3-wire 2-phase a-c, ungrounded	2, one in each phase
2-phase a-c	3-wire 2-phase a-c, one conductor grounded	2 in ungrounded conductors
2-phase a-c	4-wire 2-phase a-c, grounded or ungrounded	2, one per phase in ungrounded conductors
2-phase a-c	5-wire 2-phase a-c, grounded neutral or ungrounded	2, one per phase in any ungrounded phase wire
3-phase a-c	3-wire 3-phase a-c, ungrounded	2 in any 2 conductors[a]
3-phase a-c	3-wire 3-phase a-c, one conductor grounded	2 in ungrounded conductors[a]
3-phase a-c	3-wire 3-phase a-c, grounded-neutral	2 in any 2 conductors[a]
3-phase a-c	4-wire 3-phase a-c, grounded-neutral or ungrounded	2 in any 2 conductors, except the neutral[a]

[a] NOTE. Three running overcurrent units shall be used where three-phase motors are installed in isolated, inaccessible, or unattended locations, unless the motor is protected by other approved means.

UNATTENDED (Definition): Lacking the presence of a person (not necessarily an electrician) capable of exercising responsible control of the motor under consideration. Such a person need not be in sight of the motor at all times but must be available for opening the motor circuit in the event of motor overheating.

39. The National Electrical Manufacturers' Association has adopted a standard of identifying code letters that may be marked by the manufacturer on motor nameplates to show the motor kilovolt-ampere input with locked rotor. The meaning of the code letters is as follows:

Letter designation	Kva per hp with locked rotor	Letter designation	Kva per hp with locked rotor
A	0–3.14	K	8.0–8.99
B	3.15–3.54	L	9.0– 9.99
C	3.55–3.99	M	10.0–11.19
D	4.0 –4.49	N	11.2–12.49
E	4.5 –4.99	P	12.5–13.99
F	5.0 –5.59	R	14.0–15.99
G	5.6 –6.29	S	16.0–17.99
H	6.3 –7.09	T	18.0–19.99
J	7.1 –7.99	U	20.0–22.39
		V	22.4 and up

40. Maximum Rating or Setting of Motor-branch-circuit Protective Devices for Motors Marked with a Code Letter Indicating Locked-rotor Kilovolt-amperes
(Average starting currents)

Type of motor	Fuse rating	Circuit-breaker setting	
		Instantane-ous type	Time-limit type
	Per cent of full-load current		
All a-c, single-phase and polyphase, squirrel-cage, and synchronous motors with full-voltage, resistor or reactor starting:			
Code letter A...	150	700	150
Code letters B to E	250	700	200
Code letters F to V..	300	700	250
All a-c, squirrel-cage, and synchronous motors with autotransformer starting:			
Code letter A...	150	700	150
Code letters B to E	200	700	200
Code letters F to V..	250	700	200

For certain exceptions to the values specified see Sec. **435,** Div. 7. The values given in the last column also cover the ratings of nonadjustable, time-limit types of circuit breaker.

Synchronous motors of the low-torque, low-speed type (usually 450 rpm or lower), such as are used to drive reciprocating compressors, pumps, etc., which start up unloaded, do not require a fuse rating or circuit-breaker setting in excess of 200 per cent of full-load current.

For motors not marked with a code letter, see Table **41.**

41. Maximum Rating or Setting of Motor-branch-circuit Protective Devices for Motors Not Marked with a Code Letter Indicating Locked-rotor KVA

Type of motor	Per cent of full-load current		
	Fuse rating (see also Table **42**, Columns 4, 5, 6, 7)	Circuit-breaker setting	
		Instantaneous type	Time-limit type
Single-phase, all types	300	700	250
Squirrel-cage and synchronous (full-voltage, resistor and reactor starting)	300	700	250
Squirrel-cage and synchronous (autotransformer starting):			
Not more than 30 amp...	250	700	200
More than 30 amp..	200	700	200
High-reactance squirrel-cage:			
Not more than 30 amp...	250	700	250
More than 30 amp..	200	700	200
Wound-rotor...	150	700	150
Direct-current:			
Not more than 50 hp...	150	250	150
More than 50 hp..	150	175	150
Sealed (hermetic-type) refrigeration compressor[a] 400 kva locked-rotor or less	175[b]	.....	175[b]

For certain exceptions to the values specified see Sec. **435** of Div. 7. The values given in the last column also cover the ratings of nonadjustable, time-limit types of circuit breakers which may also be modified as in Sec. **435** of Div. 7.

Synchronous motors of the low-torque low-speed type (usually 450 rpm or lower) such as are used to drive reciprocating compressors, pumps, etc., which start up unloaded, do not require a fuse rating or circuit-breaker setting in excess of 200 per cent of full-load current.

For motors marked with a code letter, see Table **40**.

[a] The locked-rotor kva is the product of the motor voltage and the motor locked-rotor current (LRA) given on the motor nameplate divided by 1,000 for single-phase motors, or divided by 580 for 3-phase motors.

[b] This value may be increased to 225 per cent if necessary to permit starting.

42. Overcurrent Protection for Motors

(See Tables **40** and **41**)

The current values in column 1 are to be taken from Tables 7 to 10, including footnotes, but the values shown for running protection in columns 2 and 3 must be modified if nameplate full-load-current values are different, as provided in section 430-6 of the Code (refer to Sec. 435, Div. 7). The current values shown in columns 5 and 6 must be reduced by 8 per cent for all motors other than open-type motors marked to have a temperature rise not over 40°C. For certain exceptions to the values in columns 4, 5, 6, and 7, see Sec. **435** of Div. 7. See Sec. **435** of Div. 7 for values to be used for several motors on one branch circuit.

Full-load-current rating of motor, amp	For running protection of motors[a]		Maximum allowable rating or setting of branch-circuit protective devices							
	Max rating of nonadjustable protective devices, amp	Max setting of adjustable protective devices, amp	With code letters: Single-phase, squirrel-cage, and synchronous. Full voltage, resistor or reactor starting, Code letters F to V inclusive. Without code letters: same as above		With code letters: Single-phase, squirrel-cage, and synchronous. Full voltage, resistor or reactor start, Code letters B to E inclusive, Code letters F to V inclusive. Without code letters (not more than 30 amp): Squirrel-cage and synchronous, autotransformer start, high-reactance squirrel-cage[b]		With code letters: Squirrel-cage and synchronous autotransformer start, Code letters B to E inclusive. Without code letters (more than 30 amp): Squirrel-cage and synchronous, autotransformer start, high-reactance squirrel-cage[b]		With code letters: All motors Code letter A. Without code letters: D-c and wound-rotor motors	
			Fuses	Circuit breakers (nonadjustable overload trip)	Fuses	Circuit breakers (nonadjustable overload trip)	Fuses	Circuit breakers (nonadjustable overload trip)	Fuses	Circuit breakers (nonadjustable overload trip)
(1)	(2)	(3)	(4)		(5)		(6)		(7)	
1[c]	2[d]	1.25[d]	15	15	15	15	15	15	15	15
2[c]	3[d]	2.50[d]	15	15	15	15	15	15	15	15
3[c]	4[d]	3.75[d]	15	15	15	15	15	15	15	15
4[c]	6[d]	5.0[d]	15	15	15	15	15	15	15	15
5[c]	8[d]	6.25[d]	15	15	15	15	15	15	15	15
6[d]	8[d]	7.50[d]	20	15	15	15	15	15	15	15
7[d]	10[d]	8.75[d]	25	20	20	15	20	15	15	15
8	10[d]	10.0[d]	25	20	20	20	20	20	15	15
9	12[d]	11.25[d]	30	30	25	20	20	20	15	15
10	15[d]	12.50[d]	30	30	25	20	20	20	15	15
11[d]	15[d]	13.75	35	30	30	30	25	30	20	20
12	15	15.00	40	30	30	30	25	30	20	20
13	20	16.25	40	40	35	30	30	30	25	20
14	20	17.50	45	40	35	30	30	30	25	20
15	20	18.75	45	40	40	30	30	30	25	30

C1	C2	C3	C4	C5	C6	C7	C8	C9	C10	Index
30	25	40	35	40	40	40	50	20.00	20	16
30	30	40	35	40	45	50	60	21.25	25	17
30	30	40	40	40	45	50	60	22.50	25	18
30	30	40	40	40	50	50	60	23.75	25	19
40	35	50	45	50	50	50	60	25.00	25	20
40	40	50	50	50	60	70	70	27.50	30	22
50	45	70	60	70	60	70	80	30.00	30	24
50	45	70	60	70	70	70	80	32.50	35	26
50	50	70	70	70	70	70	90	35.00	35	28
70	60	70	70	70	80	100	90	37.50	40	30
70	60	100	80	100	80	100	100	40.00	40	32
70	60	100	80	100	90	100	110	42.50	45	34
70	70	100	90	100	100	100	110	45.00	45	36
70	70	100	90	100	100	100	125	47.50	50	38
100	80	100	100	100	100	100	125	50.00	50	40
100	80	100	100	100	110	125	125	52.50	50	42
100	80	125	110	125	110	125	125	55.00	60	44
100	90	125	110	125	125	125	150	57.50	60	46
100	90	125	125	125	125	125	150	60.00	60	48
100	90	125	125	125	125	125	150	62.50	60	50
100	90	125	125	125	150	150	175	65.00	70	52
100	100	150	150	150	150	150	175	67.00	70	54
125	100	150	150	150	150	150	175	70.00	70	56
125	110	150	150	150	150	150	175	72.50	70	58
125	110	150	150	150	150	150	200	75.00	80	60
125	110	150	150	150	175	175	200	77.50	80	62
125	125	175	175	175	175	175	200	80.00	80	64
125	125	175	175	175	175	175	200	82.50	80	66
150	125	175	175	175	175	175	225	85.00	90	68
150	125	175	175	175	175	175	225	87.50	90	70
150	150	200	200	200	200	200	225	90.00	90	72
150	150	200	200	200	200	200	225	92.50	90	74
150	150	200	200	200	200	200	250	95.00	100	76
150	150	200	200	200	200	200	250	97.50	100	78
150	150	200	200	200	200	200	250	100.00	100	80
150	150	200	200	200	225	225	250	102.50	110	82
150	150	200	200	200	225	225	300	105.00	110	84
150	150	200	200	200	225	225	300	107.50	110	86
150	150	200	200	200	225	225	300	110.00	110	88
150	150	200	200	200	225	225	300	112.50	110	90
150	150	200	200	200	250	250	300	115.00	125	92
150	150	200	200	200	250	250	300	117.50	125	94
150	150	200	200	200	250	250	300	120.00	125	96
150	150	200	200	200	250	250	300	122.50	125	98
150	150	200	200	200	250	250	300	125.00	125	100

Overcurrent Protection for Motors (*Continued*)

Full-load-current rating of motor, amp	For running protection of motors[a]		With code letters: Single-phase, squirrel-cage, and synchronous. Full voltage, resistor or reactor starting, Code letters F to V inclusive. Without code letters: same as above		With code letters: Single-phase, squirrel-cage, and synchronous. Full voltage, resistor or reactor start, Code letters B to E inclusive. Autotransformer start, Code letters F to V inclusive. Without code letters (not more than 30 amp): Squirrel-cage and synchronous, autotransformer start, high-reactance squirrel-cage[b]		With code letters: Squirrel-cage and synchronous autotransformer start, Code letters B to E inclusive. Without code letters (more than 30 amp): Squirrel-cage and synchronous, autotransformer start, high-reactance squirrel-cage[b]		With code letters: All motors Code letter A. Without code letters: D-c and wound-rotor motors	
	Max rating of nonadjustable protective devices, amp	Max setting of adjustable protective devices, amp	Fuses	Circuit breakers (nonadjustable overload trip)	Fuses	Circuit breakers (nonadjustable overload trip)	Fuses	Circuit breakers (nonadjustable overload trip)	Fuses	Circuit breakers (nonadjustable overload trip)
(1)	(2)	(3)	(4)		(5)		(6)		(7)	
105	150	131.50	350	300	300	225	225	225	175	175
110	150	137.50	350	300	300	225	225	225	175	175
115	150	144.00	350	300	300	250	250	250	175	175
120	150	150.00	400	300	300	250	250	250	200	200
125	175	156.50	400	350	350	250	250	250	200	200
130	175	162.50	400	350	350	300	300	300	200	200
135	175	169.00	450	350	350	300	300	300	225	225
140	175	175.00	450	350	350	300	300	300	225	225
145	200	181.50	450	400	400	300	300	300	225	225
150	200	187.50	450	400	400	300	300	300	225	225
155	200	194.00	500	400	400	350	350	350	250	250
160	200	200.00	500	400	400	350	350	350	250	250
165	225	206.00	500	500	450	350	350	350	250	250
170	225	213.00	500	500	450	350	350	350	300	300
175	225	219.00	600	500	450	350	350	350	300	300

Maximum allowable rating or setting of branch-circuit protective devices

180	225	225.00	600	500	450	400	400	400	300	300
185	250	231.00	600	500	500	400	400	400	300	300
190	250	238.00	600	500	500	400	400	400	300	300
195	250	244.00	600	500	500	400	400	400	300	300
200	250	250.00	600	500	500	400	400	400	300	300
210	250	263.00	800	600	600	500	450	500	350	350
220	300	275.00	800	600	600	500	450	500	350	350
230	300	288.00	800	600	600	500	500	500	350	350
240	300	300.00	800	600	600	500	500	500	400	400
250	300	313.00	800	700	800	500	500	500	400	400
260	350	325.00	800	700	800	600	600	600	400	400
270	350	338.00	1000	700	800	600	600	600	450	500
280	350	350.00	1000	700	800	600	600	600	450	500
290	350	363.00	1000	800	800	600	600	600	450	500
300	400	375.00	1000	800	800	600	600	600	450	500
320	400	400.00	1000	800	800	700	800	700	500	500
340	450	425.00	1200		1000	700	800	700	600	600
360	450	450.00	1200		1000	800	800	800	600	600
380	500	475.00	1200		1000	800	800	800	600	600
400	500	500.00	1200		1000	800	800	800	600	600
420	600	525.00	1600		1200		1,000		800	700
440	600	550.00	1600		1200		1,000		800	700
460	600	575.00	1600		1200		1,000		800	700
480	600	600.00	1600		1200		1,000		800	800
500		625.00	1600		1600		1,000		800	800

a For the running protection of motors, see Sec. **430** of Div. 7.

b High-reactance squirrel-cage motors are those designed to limit the starting current by means of deep-slot secondaries or double-wound secondaries and are generally started on full voltage.

c For the grouping of small motors under the protection of a single set of fuses, see Sec. **435** of Div. 7.

d For running protection of motors of 1 hp or less, see Sec. **430** of Div. 7.   For setting of branch circuit breakers, see Tables **40** and **41**.

42A. Condensed Three-phase Motor Table
(Induction-type, full-voltage starting, 220/440 volts)
Code Letters F to V, and No Code Letters

Horse-power	Full-load current, amperes	Min AWG/MCM Wire / Conduit sizes		Running protection		Branch-circuit protection	
		CU[a]	AL[b]	Nonadjustable types	Adjustable types	Switch-fuse (max size for standard fuses)	CB (max size)
½	2/1	$\frac{14}{1/2} \big/ \frac{14}{1/2}$	$\frac{12}{1/2} \big/ \frac{12}{1/2}$	3/2	2.5/1.25	30–15/30–15	15/15
¾	2.8/1.4	$\frac{14}{1/2} \big/ \frac{14}{1/2}$	$\frac{12}{1/2} \big/ \frac{12}{1/2}$	4/3	3.5/1.75	30–15/30–15	15/15
1	3.5/1.8	$\frac{14}{1/2} \big/ \frac{14}{1/2}$	$\frac{12}{1/2} \big/ \frac{12}{1/2}$	5/3	4.37/2.25	30–15/30–15	15/15
1½	5/2.5	$\frac{14}{1/2} \big/ \frac{14}{1/2}$	$\frac{12}{1/2} \big/ \frac{12}{1/2}$	8/4	6.25/3.12	30–15/30–15	15/15
2	6.5/3.3	$\frac{14}{1/2} \big/ \frac{14}{1/2}$	$\frac{12}{1/2} \big/ \frac{12}{1/2}$	10/6	8.12/4.12	30–20/30–15	20/15
3	9/4.5	$\frac{14}{1/2} \big/ \frac{14}{1/2}$	$\frac{12}{1/2} \big/ \frac{12}{1/2}$	12/8	11.25/5.62	30–30/30–15	30/15
5	15/7.5	$\frac{12}{1/2} \big/ \frac{14}{1/2}$	$\frac{10}{3/4} \big/ \frac{12}{1/2}$	20/10	18.75/9.37	60–45/30–25	40/20
7½	22/11	$\frac{10}{3/4} \big/ \frac{14}{1/2}$	$\frac{8}{3/4} \big/ \frac{12}{1/2}$	30/15	27.5/13.75	100–70/60–35	70/30
10	27/14	$\frac{8}{3/4} \big/ \frac{12}{1/2}$	$\frac{8}{3/4} \big/ \frac{10}{3/4}$	35/20	33.75/17.5	100–90/60–45	70/40
15	40/20	$\frac{6}{1} \big/ \frac{10}{3/4}$	$\frac{6}{1} \big/ \frac{10}{3/4}$	50/25	50/25	200–125/60–60	100/50
20	52/26	$\frac{6}{1} \big/ \frac{8}{3/4}$	$\frac{4}{1\frac{1}{4}} \big/ \frac{8}{3/4}$	70/35	65/32.5	200–175/100–80	150/70
25	64/32	$\frac{4}{1\frac{1}{4}} \big/ \frac{8}{3/4}$	$\frac{2}{1\frac{1}{4}} \big/ \frac{8}{3/4}$	80/40	80/40	200–200/100–100	175/100
30	78/39	$\frac{3}{1\frac{1}{4}} \big/ \frac{6}{1}$	$\frac{1}{1\frac{1}{2}} \big/ \frac{6}{1}$	100/50	97.5/48.75	400–250/200–125	200/100
40	104/52	$\frac{1}{1\frac{1}{2}} \big/ \frac{6}{1}$	$\frac{00}{2} \big/ \frac{4}{1\frac{1}{4}}$	150/70	130/65	400–350/200–175	300/150
50	125/63	$\frac{00}{2} \big/ \frac{4}{1\frac{1}{4}}$	$\frac{0000}{2\frac{1}{2}} \big/ \frac{2}{1\frac{1}{4}}$	175/80	156.5/78.7	400–400/200–200	350/175
60	150/75	$\frac{000}{2} \big/ \frac{2}{1\frac{1}{4}}$	$\frac{250}{2\frac{1}{2}} \big/ \frac{1}{1\frac{1}{2}}$	200/100	187.5/93.7	600–450/400–225	400/200
75	185/93	$\frac{250}{2\frac{1}{2}} \big/ \frac{1}{1\frac{1}{2}}$	$\frac{350}{3} \big/ \frac{0}{2}$	250/125	231/116.25	600–600/400–300	500/250
100	246/123	$\frac{350}{3} \big/ \frac{00}{2}$	$\frac{500}{3} \big/ \frac{000}{2}$	350/175	307.5/153.7	800–800/400–400	700/350

[a] 60°C wire—No. 14 to No. 8; 75°C wire—No. 6 and larger.
[b] 60°C wire—No. 12 to No. 10; 75°C wire—No. 8 and larger.
NOTE 1. In the dual values shown, the figures to the left in each column are for motors connected at 220 volts; the figures to the right are for 440-volt motors.
NOTE 2. Conduit sizes are based on Columns A of Table 25.

43. Standard General-purpose-switch Sizes

(All sizes in amperes)

Regular open knife blade	Open Klamp-tite	Open toggle	Enclosed safety	Regular open knife blade	Open Klamp-tite	Open toggle	Enclosed safety
30	400	300	30	1,200	4,000	2,500	1,200
60	600	500	60	.....	5,000	3,000	1,600
100	800	600	100	.....	.....	4,000	2,000
200	1,000	800	200	.....	.....	5,000	2,500
400	1,200	1,000	400	.....	.....	6,000	3,000
600	1,600	1,200	600	.....	.....	8,000	4,000
800	2,000	1,600	800	.....	.....	10,000	5,000
	3,000	2,000					6,000

44. Locked-rotor Current Conversion Table
As Determined from Horsepower and Voltage Rating
For Use Only with Sealed (Hermetic-type)
Refrigeration Compressor Motors
(Refer to Sec. **429** of Div. 7)
Conversion Table

Max hp rating	Motor locked-rotor, amp					
	Single-phase		Two- or three-phase			
	115 volts	230 volts	110 volts	220 volts	440 volts	550 volts
½	58.8	29.4	24	12	6	4.8
¾	82.8	41.4	33.6	16.8	8.4	6.6
1	96	48	42	21	10.8	8.4
1½	120	60	60	30	15	12
2	144	72	78	39	19.8	15.6
3	204	102	....	54	27	24
5	336	168	....	90	45	36
7½	480	240	....	132	66	54
10	600	300	....	162	84	66
15	.....	.....	....	240	120	96
20	.....	.....	....	312	156	126
25	.....	.....	....	384	192	156
30	.....	.....	....	468	234	186
40	.....	.....	....	624	312	246
50	.....	.....	....	750	378	300
60	.....	.....	....	900	450	360
75	.....	.....	....	1,110	558	444
100	.....	.....	....	1,476	738	588
125	.....	.....	....	1,860	930	744
150	.....	.....	....	2,160	1,080	864
200	.....	.....	....	2,880	1,440	1,152

45. Horsepower Ratings of Fused Switches
(Underwriters' Laboratories, Inc.)

Rating of fuse-holders, amperes	Switch rating, volts	"Standard" and "maximum" horsepower ratings			
		Two-pole single-phase	Two-pole d-c	Three-pole three-phase	Four-pole two-phase
30	120 a-c	½ 2°		1½ 3°	2 3°
60		1½ 3°		3 7½°	3 10°
30	125 d-c		2 3°		
60			5		
30	240 a-c	1½ 3°		3 7½°	3 10°
60		3 10°		7½ 15°	7½ 20°
100		7½ 15°		15 30°	15 30°
200		15		25 60°	30 50°
400				50 100°	50
600				75 100°	
800				100	
30	250 d-c		5		
60			10		
100			20		
200			40		
400			50		
30	480 a-c	3 7½°		5 15°	7½ 20°
60		5 20°		15 30°	15 40°
100		10 30°		25 60°	25 50°
200		25 50°		50 100°	50
400				100	
30	600 a-c	3 10°		7½ 20°	10 25°
60		10 25°		15 50°	20 50°
100		15 40°		30 75°	30 50°
200		30 50°		60 100°	50
400				100	
30	600 d-c		10 15°		
60			25 30°		
100			40 50°		
200			50		

° The ratings in this table are "standard" ratings except for the "maximum" ratings, which are indicated by the asterisks. "Maximum" horsepower ratings are achieved with the use of time-delay fuses.

46. Minimum Branch-circuit Sizes for Motors
Based on Conductor Ampacities Where Not More than Three
Conductors Are Installed in Raceway or Cable

Full-load current rating of motor, amperes	Wire size, AWG or 1,000 cir mils			
	60°C		75°C	
	Cu	Al	Cu	Al
12 or less	14 AWG	12 AWG	14 AWG	12 AWG
to 16	12	10	12	10
to 20	10	10	10	10
to 24	10	8	10	8
to 32	8	6	8	8
to 36	6	4	8	6
to 40	6	4	6	6
to 44	6	4	6	4
to 52	4	3	6	4
to 56	4	2	4	3
to 60	3	2	4	3
to 64	3	1	4	2
to 68	2	1	4	2
to 72	2	1/0	3	2
to 76	2	1/0	3	1
to 80	1	1/0	3	1
to 88	1	2/0	2	1/0
to 92	1/0	2/0	2	1/0
to 96	1/0	3/0	1	1/0
to 100	1/0	3/0	1	2/0
to 104	2/0	3/0	1	2/0
to 108	2/0	4/0	1/0	2/0
to 116	2/0	4/0	1/0	3/0
to 120	3/0	4/0	1/0	3/0
to 124	3/0	4/0	2/0	3/0
to 132	3/0	250 MCM	2/0	4/0
to 136	4/0	250	2/0	4/0
to 140	4/0	300	2/0	4/0
to 144	4/0	300	3/0	4/0
to 152	4/0	300	3/0	250 MCM
to 156	4/0	350	3/0	250
to 160	250 MCM	350	3/0	250
to 164	250	350	4/0	250
to 168	250	350	4/0	300
to 172	250	400	4/0	300
to 180	300	400	4/0	300
to 184	300	500	4/0	300
to 200	350	500	250 MCM	350
to 204	350	500	250	400

Tables **47** to **51** show the aggregate cross-sectional areas of Types RHW, RHH, RH, T, TW, THW, THWN, THHN, FEP, FEPB, and XHHW conductors in sizes No. 14 up to 500 MCM. Although each table lists up to only nine wires for each wire size, multiples of ten can be obtained by moving the decimal point for any figure one place to the right for each multiple of 10. As an example, in Table **48** one No. 14 TW is 0.0135 sq in.; thus ten No. 14 TW would be 0.135 sq in., and ninety No. 14 TW would be 1.215 sq in. Accordingly, these tables eliminate complex multiplication, and raceway sizes can be easily calculated by simply adding the cross-sectional areas of various wire combinations and then comparing this total to the allowable percentage fill for the type of raceway involved.

Example: A conduit for new work will contain three No. 10, three No. 12, and three No. 14 TW conductors. From Table **48** three No. 10 TW = 0.0672 sq in.; three No. 12 TW = 0.0516 sq in.; and three No. 14 TW = 0.0405 sq in. This combination totals 0.1593 sq in. Referring to Tables **27** and **29** (under 25 per cent fill column), a 1-in. conduit would be the minimum size for these nine wires. In rewiring, by using the 40 per cent column in Table **29**, an existing ¾-in. conduit could contain this same combination of conductors.

It should be noted that Table **27** determines the maximum conductor fill for new or existing conduits according to conductor types where wire sizes are mixed, and Table **29** lists the permissible fills in square inches (usually 25 or 40 per cent for each conduit size).

Tables **47** to **51** can also be used where different types of conductors are installed in the same conduit. After obtaining the total cross-sectional area of any combination, refer to Table **27** for permissible fills, and then examine Table **29** for the correct conduit size.

Significantly, the only raceways that provide different methods of determining sizes are conduits (rigid, EMT, or flexible). All other types of raceways are sized according to the dimensions of the conductor types selected by the designer or installer. A 40 per cent conductor fill is permitted in underfloor raceways, cellular metal concrete floor raceways.

A wireway can be filled to 20 per cent of the interior cross-sectional area of a given size wireway, using the dimensions of the conductor selected. The same procedure may be followed in sizing auxiliary gutters.

47. Conductor Areas in Square Inches
For Combinations of Conductors for New Work Where Not Included in
Table **25**, Columns A

Size, AWG or 1,000 cir mils	Number of conductors								
	1	2	3	4	5	6	7	8	9
14 AWG	0.0327	0.0654	0.0981	0.1308	0.1635	0.1962	0.2289	0.2616	0.2943
12	0.0384	0.0768	0.1152	0.1536	0.1920	0.2304	0.2688	0.3072	0.3456
10	0.0460	0.0920	0.1380	0.1840	0.2300	0.2760	0.3220	0.3680	0.4140
8	0.0760	0.1520	0.2280	0.3040	0.3800	0.4560	0.5320	0.6080	0.6840
6	0.1238	0.2476	0.3714	0.4952	0.6190	0.7428	0.8666	0.9904	1.1142
4	0.1605	0.3210	0.4815	0.6420	0.8025	0.9630	1.1235	1.2840	1.4445
3	0.1817	0.3634	0.5451	0.7268	0.9085	1.0902	1.2719	1.4536	1.6353
2	0.2067	0.4134	0.6201	0.8268	1.0335	1.2402	1.4469	1.6536	1.8603
1	0.2715	0.5430	0.8145	1.0860	1.3575	1.6290	1.9005	2.1720	2.4435
0	0.3107	0.6214	0.9321	1.2428	1.5535	1.8642	2.1749	2.4856	2.7963
00	0.3578	0.7156	1.0734	1.4312	1.7890	2.1468	2.5046	2.8624	3.2202
000	0.4151	0.8302	1.2453	1.6604	2.0755	2.4906	2.9057	3.3208	3.7359
0000	0.4840	0.9680	1.4520	1.9360	2.4200	2.9040	3.3880	3.8720	·4.3560
250 MCM	0.5917	1.1834	1.7751	2.3668	2.9585	3.5502	4.1419	4.7336	5.3253
300	0.6837	1.3674	2.0511	2.7348	3.4185	4.1022	4.7859	5.4696	6.1533
350	0.7620	1.5240	2.2860	3.0480	3.8100	4.5720	5.3340	6.0960	6.8580
400	0.8365	1.6730	2.5095	3.3460	4.1825	5.0190	5.8555	6.6920	7.5285
500	0.9834	1.9668	2.9502	3.9336	4.9170	5.9004	6.8838	7.8672	8.8506

NOTE. Where conductors of several sizes are to be installed in the same conduit and the combination includes one or more bare conductors, the dimensions listed in Table **64** may be used for the bare conductors, even in new work. These dimensions are based on the dimensions of Type RHW or RHH wire as shown in column 3, Table **30**. See Tables **27** and **29** for permissible conductor fill in conduits.

48. Area in Square Inches of Types T, TW, THW,[a] RH,[b] RHH,[c] and RHW[c]
For Combinations of Such Conductors Where Not Shown in Table 25 or 25A

Size, AWG or 1,000 cir mils	Number of conductors								
	1	2	3	4	5	6	7	8	9
14 AWG	0.0135	0.0270	0.0405	0.0540	0.0675	0.0810	0.0945	0.1080	0.1215
12	0.0172	0.0344	0.0516	0.0688	0.0860	0.1032	0.1204	0.1376	0.1548
10	0.0224	0.0448	0.0672	0.0896	0.1120	0.1344	0.1568	0.1792	0.2016
8	0.0408	0.0816	0.1224	0.1632	0.2040	0.2448	0.2856	0.3264	0.3672
6	0.0819	0.1638	0.2457	0.3276	0.4095	0.4914	0.5733	0.6552	0.7371
4	0.1087	0.2174	0.3261	0.4348	0.5435	0.6522	0.7609	0.8696	0.9783
3	0.1263	0.2526	0.3789	0.5052	0.6315	0.7578	0.8841	1.0104	1.1367
2	0.1473	0.2946	0.4419	0.5892	0.7365	0.8838	1.0311	1.1784	1.3257
1	0.2027	0.4054	0.6081	0.8108	1.0135	1.2162	1.4189	1.6216	1.8243
0	0.2367	0.4734	0.7101	0.9468	1.1835	1.4202	1.6569	1.8936	2.1303
00	0.2781	0.5562	0.8343	1.1124	1.3905	1.6686	1.9467	2.2248	2.5029
000	0.3288	0.6576	0.9864	1.3152	1.6440	1.9728	2.3016	2.6304	2.9592
0000	0.3904	0.7808	1.1712	1.5616	1.9520	2.3424	2.7328	3.1232	3.5136
250 MCM	0.4877	0.9754	1.4631	1.9508	2.4385	2.9262	3.4139	3.9016	4.3893
300	0.5581	1.1162	1.6743	2.2324	2.7905	3.3486	3.9067	4.4648	5.0229
350	0.6291	1.2582	1.8873	2.5164	3.1455	3.7746	4.4037	5.0328	5.6619
400	0.6969	1.3938	2.0907	2.7876	3.4845	4.1814	4.8783	5.5752	6.2721
500	0.8316	1.6632	2.4948	3.3264	4.1580	4.9896	5.8212	6.6528	7.4844
14[a]	0.0206	0.0412	0.0618	0.0824	0.1030	0.1236	0.1442	0.1648	0.1854
12[a]	0.0251	0.0502	0.0753	0.1004	0.1255	0.1506	0.1757	0.2008	0.2259
10[a]	0.0311	0.0622	0.0933	0.1244	0.1555	0.1866	0.2177	0.2488	0.2799
8[a]	0.0526	0.1052	0.1578	0.2104	0.2630	0.3156	0.3682	0.4208	0.4734
14[b]	0.0230	0.0460	0.0690	0.0920	0.1150	0.1380	0.1610	0.1840	0.2070
12[b]	0.0278	0.0556	0.0834	0.1112	0.1390	0.1668	0.1946	0.2224	0.2502

[a] THW dimensions only. In all other sizes THW dimensions are the same as those for TW.
[b] Dimensions of No. 14 and No. 12 Type RH conductors with 2/64-in. insulation. These dimensions apply where such conductors are used for new work or rewiring with all types of raceways.
[c] Types RHH and RHW without outer covering have same dimensions as THW. See Tables 27 and 29 for permissible conductor fill in conduits.

49. Conductor Area in Square Inches
For Combinations of Types FEP and FEPB Conductors Not Shown in Table 25 or 25A

Size, AWG	Number of conductors								
	1	2	3	4	5	6	7	8	9
14	0.0087	0.0174	0.0261	0.0348	0.0435	0.0522	0.0609	0.0696	0.0783
12	0.0115	0.0230	0.0345	0.0460	0.0575	0.0690	0.0805	0.0920	0.1035
10	0.0159	0.0318	0.0477	0.0636	0.0795	0.0954	0.1113	0.1272	0.1431
8[a]	0.0280	0.0560	0.0840	0.1120	0.1400	0.1680	0.1960	0.2240	0.2520
8[b]	0.0225	0.0450	0.0675	0.0900	0.1125	0.1350	0.1575	0.1800	0.2025
6[a]	0.0467	0.0934	0.1401	0.1868	0.2335	0.2802	0.3269	0.3736	0.4203
6[b]	0.0716	0.1432	0.2148	0.2864	0.3580	0.4296	0.5012	0.5728	0.6444
4[a]	0.0669	0.1338	0.2007	0.2676	0.3345	0.4014	0.4683	0.5352	0.6021
4[b]	0.0962	0.1924	0.2886	0.3848	0.4810	0.5772	0.6734	0.7696	0.8658
3[a]	0.0803	0.1606	0.2409	0.3212	0.4015	0.4818	0.5621	0.6424	0.7227
3[b]	0.1122	0.2244	0.3366	0.4488	0.5610	0.6732	0.7854	0.8976	1.0098
2[a]	0.0973	0.1946	0.2919	0.3892	0.4865	0.5838	0.6811	0.7784	0.8757
2[b]	0.1316	0.2632	0.3948	0.5264	0.6580	0.7896	0.9212	1.0528	1.1844

[a] FEP only.
[b] FEPB only.
See Tables 27 and 29 for permissible conductor fill in conduits.

50. Conductor Area in Square Inches
For Combinations of Type THWN or THHN Conductors Not Shown in Table
25 or 25A

Size, AWG or 1,000 cir mils	Number of conductors								
	1	2	3	4	5	6	7	8	9
14 AWG	0.0087	0.0174	0.0261	0.0348	0.0435	0.0522	0.0609	0.0696	0.0783
12	0.0117	0.0234	0.0351	0.0468	0.0585	0.0702	0.0819	0.0936	0.1053
10	0.0184	0.0368	0.0552	0.0736	0.0920	0.1104	0.1288	0.1472	0.1656
8	0.0317	0.0634	0.0951	0.1268	0.1585	0.1902	0.2219	0.2536	0.2853
6	0.0519	0.1038	0.1557	0.2076	0.2595	0.3114	0.3633	0.4152	0.4671
4	0.0845	0.1690	0.2535	0.3380	0.4225	0.5070	0.5915	0.6760	0.7605
3	0.0995	0.1990	0.2985	0.3980	0.4975	0.5970	0.6965	0.7960	0.8955
2	0.1182	0.2364	0.3546	0.4728	0.5910	0.7092	0.8274	0.9456	1.0638
1	0.1590	0.3180	0.4770	0.6360	0.7950	0.9540	1.1130	1.2720	1.4310
0	0.1893	0.3786	0.5679	0.7572	0.9465	1.1358	1.3251	1.5144	1.7037
00	0.2265	0.4530	0.6795	0.9060	1.1325	1.3590	1.5855	1.8120	2.0385
000	0.2715	0.5430	0.8145	1.0860	1.3575	1.6290	1.9005	2.1720	2.4435
0000	0.3278	0.6556	0.9834	1.3112	1.6390	1.9668	2.2946	2.6224	2.9502
250 MCM	0.4026	0.8052	1.2078	1.6104	2.0130	2.4156	2.8182	3.2208	3.6234
300	0.4669	0.9338	1.4007	1.8676	2.3345	2.8014	3.2683	3.7352	4.2021
350	0.5307	1.0614	1.5921	2.1228	2.6535	3.1842	3.7149	4.2456	4.7763
400	0.5931	1.1862	1.7793	2.3724	2.9655	3.5586	4.1517	4.7448	5.3379
500	0.7163	1.4326	2.1489	2.8652	3.5815	4.2978	5.0141	5.7304	6.4467

See Tables 27 and 29 for permissible conductor fill in conduits.

51. Conductor Area in Square Inches
For Combinations of Type XHHW Conductors Not Shown in Table 25 or 25A

Size, AWG or 1,000 cir mils	Number of conductors								
	1	2	3	4	5	6	7	8	9
14 AWG	0.0131	0.0262	0.0393	0.0524	0.0655	0.0786	0.0917	0.1048	0.1179
12	0.0167	0.0334	0.0501	0.0668	0.0835	0.1002	0.1169	0.1336	0.1503
10	0.0216	0.0432	0.0648	0.0864	0.1080	0.1296	0.1512	0.1728	0.1944
8	0.0394	0.0788	0.1182	0.1576	0.1970	0.2364	0.2758	0.3152	0.3546
6	0.0625	0.1250	0.1875	0.2500	0.3125	0.3750	0.4375	0.5000	0.5625
4	0.0845	0.1690	0.2535	0.3380	0.4225	0.5070	0.5915	0.6760	0.7605
3	0.0995	0.1990	0.2985	0.3980	0.4975	0.5970	0.6965	0.7960	0.8955
2	0.1182	0.2364	0.3546	0.4728	0.5910	0.7092	0.8274	0.9456	1.0638
1	0.1590	0.3180	0.4770	0.6360	0.7950	0.9540	1.1130	1.2720	1.4310
0	0.1893	0.3786	0.5679	0.7572	0.9465	1.1358	1.3251	1.5144	1.7037
00	0.2265	0.4530	0.6795	0.9060	1.1325	1.3590	1.5855	1.8120	2.0385
000	0.2715	0.5430	0.8145	1.0860	1.3575	1.6290	1.9005	2.1720	2.4435
0000	0.3278	0.6556	0.9834	1.3112	1.6390	1.9668	2.2946	2.6224	2.9502
250 MCM	0.4026	0.8052	1.2078	1.6104	2.0130	2.4156	2.8182	3.2208	3.6234
300	0.4669	0.9338	1.4007	1.8676	2.3355	2.8024	3.2693	3.7362	4.2031
350	0.5307	1.0614	1.5921	2.1228	2.6535	3.1842	3.7149	4.2456	4.7763
400	0.5931	1.1862	1.7793	2.3724	2.9655	3.5586	4.1517	4.7448	5.3379
500	0.7163	1.4326	2.1489	2.8652	3.5815	4.2978	5.0141	5.7304	6.4467

See Tables 27 and 29 for permissible conductor fill in conduits.

52. Electric Snow Melting System Design Data
Design Heat Density Installed in Slab, Watts per Square Foot of Heated Area

Location	Residential,[a] Class I		Commercial-Industrial,[b] Class II		Critical,[c] Class III	
	Theoretical[d]	Common densities actually installed[e]	Theoretical[d]	Common densities actually installed[e]	Theoretical[d]	Common densities actually installed[e]
Arkansas						
Ft. Smith	....	20	....	40	......	45
Little Rock	....	20	....	30	......	50
Colorado						
Colorado Springs	20	....	26	....	120	....
Denver	....	42	....	50	......	60
Pueblo	....	....	....	45	......	60
Connecticut						
Hartford	47	30	104	50	107	70
Middletown	....	40–60	....	40–60	......	60–70
New Haven	....	40	....	40	......	60
Delaware						
Wilmington	....	30	....	40	......	50
District of Columbia						
Washington	48	30–40	50	40–55	59	55–60
Idaho						
Mt. Home	21	....	37	....	57	....
Illinois						
Chicago	37	40	68	50	144	60
Peoria	....	40	....	45–50	......	55–60
Rockford	....	42	....	40–60	......	....
Springfield	....	40	....	45–50	......	55–60
Indiana						
Elkhart	....	....	....	42	......	....
Hartford City	....	....	....	35	......	....
Indianapolis	....	40	....	40	......	40–60
South Bend	....	....	....	52	......	50–55
Iowa						
Dubuque	....	40	....	40–60	......	....
Kansas						
Kansas City	....	40	....	50	......	60
Salina	35	....	49	....	94	....
Topeka	....	40	....	40	......	60
Wichita	....	50	....	50	......	50
Kentucky						
Ashland	....	....	....	42	......	....
Maine						
Caribou-Limestone	37	....	57	....	126	....
Bangor	....	40	....	40	......	60
Portland	....	40	....	40	......	60
Maryland						
Baltimore	44	30–45	95	45–55	105	50–70
Massachusetts						
Boston	44	40–45	95	50–60	105	60–75
Falmouth	38	....	59	....	68	....
Fall River	....	40	....	40	......	60
Springfield	....	40	....	40	......	80

Electric Snow Melting System Design Data (*Continued*)

Location	Residential,[a] Class I		Commercial-Industrial,[b] Class II		Critical,[c] Class III	
	Theoretical[d]	Common densities actually installed[e]	Theoretical[d]	Common densities actually installed[e]	Theoretical[d]	Common densities actually installed[e]
Michigan						
Detroit	28	40–60	57	60	105	60
Sault Ste. Marie	21	....	59	....	87	....
Jackson	....	40	....	60	......	80
Minnesota						
Duluth	34	....	85	....	153	....
Minneapolis–St. Paul	26	42–75	64	60–75	104	70–75
Missouri						
Kansas City	....	42	....	40–50	......	60–70
St. Joseph	....	42	....	42	......	....
St. Louis	50	40–60	62	40–60	81	60
Montana						
Great Falls	34	....	57	....	153	....
Nebraska						
Lincoln	26	40–50	83	40–50	101	60
Omaha	....	40–45	....	60	......	60
Nevada						
Reno	40	....	63	....	64	....
New Hampshire						
Concord–Manchester	....	50	....	50	......	75
New Jersey						
Atlantic City	....	30	....	40	......	60
Morristown	....	40	....	50	......	60
New Mexico						
Albuquerque	29	....	34	....	69	....
New York						
Buffalo–Niagara Falls	33	....	79	60	126	....
New York City	50	35–50	122	40–50	140	50–60
Poughkeepsie	....	40	....	60–70	......	50–80
Syracuse	....	40–60	....	60	......	60
North Carolina						
Charlotte	....	42	....	30–42	......	42
Ohio						
Canton	....	30	....	36	......	....
Cincinnati	....	40	....	50	......	60
Cleveland	...	40	....	....	......	45–55
Columbus	21	30	30	40	104	50
Findlay	....	....	....	40	......	60
Ironton	....	30	....	40	......	....
Lima	....	40	....	40	......	70
Portsmouth	....	30–40	....	40	......	....
Steubenville	....	40	....	45	......	....
Oklahoma						
Oklahoma City	27	25	33	40	144	45
Tulsa	....	20	....	30	......	40
Oregon						
Portland	35	42	40	42	46	60

Electric Snow Melting System Design Data (*Continued*)

Location	Residential,[a] Class I		Commercial-Industrial,[b] Class II		Critical,[c] Class III	
	Theoret- ical[d]	Common densities actually installed[e]	Theoret- ical[d]	Common densities actually installed[e]	Theoret- ical[d]	Common densities actually installed[e]
Pennsylvania						
Allentown..............................	....	40	....	44–55	......	60
Johnstown..............................	....	30	....	40	......	70
Philadelphia...........................	40	40	94	40–60	108	40–100
Pittsburgh..............................	37	30–40	65	30–60	113	60
Rhode Island						
Providence.............................	....	45	....	65	......	....
So. Dakota						
Rapid City	24	....	42		183	....
Tennessee						
Memphis................................	55	....	59	....	87	....
Kingsport..............................	....	....	....	42	......	....
Nashville	....	40	....	40	......	60
Texas						
Amarillo................................	40	....	59	....	99	....
Utah						
Ogden	40	....	89	....	89	....
Vermont						
Bennington	....	50	....	50	......	75
Burlington.............................	37	50	58	50	100	75
Virginia						
Richmond..............................	....	30	....	40	......	....
Abingdon...............................	....	30	....	30	......	....
Washington						
Seattle...................................	38	....	53	....	55	....
Spokane.................................	36	30–40	52	30–45	78	....
West Virginia						
Wheeling...............................	....	35	....	35–50	......	....
Bluefield................................	....	....	....	40	......	80
Parkersburg...........................	....	30	....	45	......	60
Beckley	....	40	....	40	......	....
Charleston	....	40	....	45	......	50
Morgantown...........................	....	30	....	45	......	60
Wisconsin						
Milwaukee.............................	....	45	....	50–65	......	65
Wyoming						
Cheyenne...............................	34	....	53	....	174	....

[a] *Residential:* Residential walks or driveways and interplant areaways – will allow snow to completely cover area temporarily, but will not accumulate for worse conditions of 93 per cent of snow frequency. Minimum recommended installed intensity: 30 watts per sq ft.

[b] *Commercial-Industrial:* Commercial sidewalks, steps, and driveways – will allow snow to completely cover area temporarily, but will not accumulate for worse conditions of 100 per cent of snow frequency. Minimum recommended installed intensity: 40 watts per sq ft.

[c] *Critical:* Toll plazas of highways and bridges, and aprons and loading areas of airports – will melt snow immediately for 98 per cent of snow frequency. Minimum recommended intensity: 60 watts per sq ft. Per section 424-75(b) of the National Electrical Code, installed heating intensity of embedded cable or wire systems shall not exceed 120 watts per sq ft.

[d] Based on adjustment for assumed 40 per cent heat loss through edge and bottom of slab. Figures from ASHRAE.

[e] Based on survey of actual practice as reported by 66 electric utilities. Survey made during spring, 1966.

53. Outside Design Temperatures and Yearly Degree-Days

The outside design temperatures given in this table are design dry-bulb temperatures in common use. These temperatures and the yearly degree-days are taken from ASHRAE, "Heating, Ventilating, Air Conditioning Guide." Outside temperatures are based on an occurrence of once in 13 years.

State and city	Outside design temperature, °F	Yearly degree-days	State and city	Outside design temperature, °F	Yearly degree-days
Alabama			Dubuque	−15	7,271 (A)
Anniston	12	2,820 (A)	Keokuk	−13	5,663
Birmingham	12	2,780 (A)	Sioux City	−15	7,012 (A)
Mobile	22	1,612 (A)	Kansas		
Montgomery	18	2,137 (A)	Concordia	−11	5,323
Arizona			Dodge City	−9	5,058 (A)
Flagstaff	−4	7.525 (A)	Topeka	−8	5,209 (A)
Phoenix	36	1,698 (A)	Wichita	−6	4,571 (A)
Yuma	38	951 (A)	Kentucky		
Arkansas			Lexington	−2	4,979 (A)
Fort Smith	6	3,188 (A)	Louisville	−2	4,439 (A)
Little Rock	8	2,982 (A)	Louisiana		
California			New Orleans	26	1,317 (A)
Eureka	32	4,632	Shreveport	14	2,117 (A)
Fresno	32	2,532 (A)	Maine		
Los Angeles	41	2,015 (A)	Eastport	−9	8,246
Red Bluff	......	2,546 (A)	Greenville	......	9,439
Sacramento	30	2,822 (A)	Portland	−9	7,681 (A)
San Diego	43	1,574 (A)	Maryland		
San Francisco	37	3,421 (A)	Baltimore	8	4,787 (A)
San Jose	38	2,410	Massachusetts		
Colorado			Boston	0	5,791 (A)
Denver	−12	6,132 (A)	Fitchburg	......	6,743
Durango	−6	7,143	Nantucket	......	6,102 (A)
Grand Junction	−3	5,796 (A)	Michigan		
Pueblo	−14	5,709 (A)	Detroit	−4	6,404 (A)
Connecticut			Grand Rapids	−4	7,075 (A)
Hartford	−2	6,139 (A)	Lansing	−8	6,982 (A)
New Haven	0	6,026 (A)	Sault Ste. Marie	−19	9,475 (A)
District of Columbia			Minnesota		
Washington	10	4,333 (A)	Duluth	−27	9,937 (A)
Florida			Minneapolis	−23	7,853 (A)
Apalachicola	25	1,307	St. Paul	−23	7,804 (A)
Jacksonville	28	1,243 (A)	Mississippi		
Key West	53	89 (A)	Meridian	14	2,333 (A)
Miami	35	178 (A)	Vicksburg	15	2,000
Pensacola	24	1,435	Missouri		
Tampa	36	674 (A)	Columbia	−9	5,113 (A)
Georgia			Kansas City	−8	4,888 (A)
Atlanta	11	2,826 (A)	St. Louis	−5	4,699 (A)
Augusta	20	2,138 (A)	Springfield	−5	4,693 (A)
Macon	20	2,049 (A)	Montana		
Savannah	24	1,710 (A)	Billings	−31	7,106
Idaho			Havre	−39	8,213
Boise	−10	5,890 (A)	Helena	−39	8,250 (A)
Lewiston	−12	5,483 (A)	Kalispell	......	8,055 (A)
Pocatello	−17	6,976 (A)	Miles City	−35	7,850 (A)
Illinois			Missoula	......	7,873 (A)
Cairo	0	3,756	Nebraska		
Chicago	−11	6,310 (A)	Lincoln	−15	6,104 (A)
Peoria	−13	6,087 (A)	North Platte	−15	6,546 (A)
Springfield	−10	5,693 (A)	Omaha	−17	6,160 (A)
Indiana			Valentine	−21	7,075
Evansville	−4	4,360 (A)	Nevada		
Fort Wayne	−7	6,287 (A)	Reno	3	6,036 (A)
Indianapolis	−8	5,611 (A)	Winnemucca	−9	6,369 (A)
Terre Haute	−6	5,366 (A)	New Hampshire		
Iowa			Concord	−11	7,612 (A)
Charles City	−21	7,504	New Jersey		
Davenport	−12	6,091	Atlantic City	8	4,741
Des Moines	−13	6,446 (A)	Cape May	......	4,870

(A) Temperatures recorded at airport stations.   Other temperatures recorded at city stations.

Outside Design Temperatures and Yearly Degree-Days (Continued)

State and city	Outside design temperature, °F	Yearly degree-days	State and city	Outside design temperature, °F	Yearly degree-days
Newark	0	5,252 (A)	Greenville	10	3,060 (A)
Sandy Hook	0	5,369	South Dakota		
Trenton	2	5,068	Huron	−21	7,902 (A)
New Mexico			Rapid City	−22	7,535 (A)
Albuquerque	8	4,389 (A)	Tennessee		
Roswell	4	3,424 (A)	Chattanooga	8	3,384 (A)
Sante Fe	3	6,123	Knoxville	5	3,590 (A)
New York			Memphis	6	3,137 (A)
Albany	−9	6,962 (A)	Nashville	3	3,513 (A)
Binghamton	−7	7,537 (A)	Texas		
Buffalo	−5	6,838 (A)	Abilene	7	2,657 (A)
Canton	−22	8,305	Amarillo	−2	4,345 (A)
Ithaca	−4	6,914	Austin	......	1,713 (A)
New York–LaGuardia	5	4,989 (A)	Brownsville	30	617 (A)
Oswego	−7	6,975	Corpus Christi	23	1,011 (A)
Rochester	−4	6,863 (A)	Dallas	8	2,272 (A)
Syracuse	−10	6,520 (A)	Del Rio	......	1,407 (A)
North Carolina			El Paso	20	2,641 (A)
Asheville	5	4,072	Fort Worth	8	2,361 (A)
Charlotte	14	3,205 (A)	Galveston	23	1,233 (A)
Raleigh	14	3,369 (A)	Houston	19	1,388 (A)
Wilmington	20	2,323 (A)	Palestine	11	1,980
North Dakota			Port Arthur	20	1,340 (A)
Bismarck	−31	9,033 (A)	San Antonio	19	1,579 (A)
Devils Lake	−32	9,940	Utah		
Williston	−35	9,068	Modena	−15	6,598
Ohio			Salt Lake City	−1	5,866 (A)
Cincinnati	−3	5,195 (A)	Vermont		
Cleveland	−5	6,006 (A)	Burlington	−17	7,865 (A)
Columbus	−3	5,615 (A)	Virginia		
Dayton	−4	5,597 (A)	Cape Henry	17	3,307
Sandusky	−4	5,859	Lynchburg	11	4,153 (A)
Toledo	−5	6,394 (A)	Norfolk	15	3,454 (A)
Oklahoma			Richmond	11	3,955 (A)
Oklahoma City	−1	644 (A)	Washington		
Oregon			North Head	20	5,211
Baker	−14	7,087	Seattle	15	4,438
Medford	5	4,547 (A)	Seattle–Tacoma	......	5,275 (A)
Portland	10	4,632 (A)	Spokane	−16	6,852 (A)
Roseburg	19	4,122	Tacoma	15	4,866
Pennsylvania			Walla Walla	−12	4,848
Erie	−3	6,116	Yakima	......	5,845 (A)
Harrisburg	4	5,258 (A)	West Virginia		
Philadelphia	6	4,866 (A)	Elkins	−4	5,773 (A)
Pittsburgh	−3	5,905 (A)	Parkersburg	−1	4,750
Reading	3	5,060	Wisconsin		
Scranton	−2	6,047	Green Bay	−20	8,259 (A)
Rhode Island			La Crosse	−20	7,650 (A)
Block Island	7	5,843 (A)	Madison	−19	7,417 (A)
Providence	1	6,125 (A)	Milwaukee	−17	7,205 (A)
South Carolina			Wyoming		
Charleston	22	1,973 (A)	Cheyenne	−19	7,562 (A)
Columbia	19	2,435 (A)	Lander	−30	8,303 (A)

(A) Temperatures recorded at airport stations.   Other temperatures recorded at city stations.

54. Maximum Allowable Voltage Drop
(In accordance with good practice; refer to Sec. 35 of Div. 3)

Circuits	Voltage drop, per cent	System voltages						Remarks
		110	115	220	230	440	550	
		Voltage drop						
For Total Drop of 5 Per Cent								
Lighting: Branches.......	3	3.3	3.4	6.6	6.9			In accordance with recommendations of the National Electrical Code
Mains and feeders combined..	2	2.2	2.3	4.4	4.6			
Total..........	5	5.5	5.8	11.0	11.5			
For Total Drop of 4 Per Cent								
Lighting: Branches.......	2	2.2	2.3	4.4	4.6			In accordance with recommendations prepared by Industry Committee on Interior Wiring Design
Mains and feeders combined..	2	2.2	2.3	4.4	4.6			
Total..........	4	4.4	4.6	8.8	9.2			
For Total Drop of 5 Per Cent								
Power: Branches.......	2	2.2	2.3					In accordance with recommendations prepared by Industry Committee on Interior Wiring Design
Mains and feeders combined..	3	3.3	3.5					
Total..........	5	5.5	5.8					
For Total Drop of 5 Per Cent								
Power: Branches.......	1	...	...	2.2	2.3	4.4	5.5	In accordance with recommendations prepared by Industry Committee on Interior Wiring Design
Mains and feeders combined..	4	...	...	8.8	9.2	17.6	22.0	
Total..........	5	...	...	11.0	11.5	22.0	27.5	
For Total Drop of 5 Per Cent								
Power: Branches.......	3	...	...	6.6	6.9	13.2	16.5	In accordance with recommendations of the National Electrical Code
Mains and feeders combined..	2	...	...	4.4	4.6	8.8	11.0	
Total..........	5	...	...	11.0	11.5	22.0	27.5	

55. Graph for Computing Conductor Sizes for Circuits According to Voltage Drop
(See Sec. 59 of Div. 3)

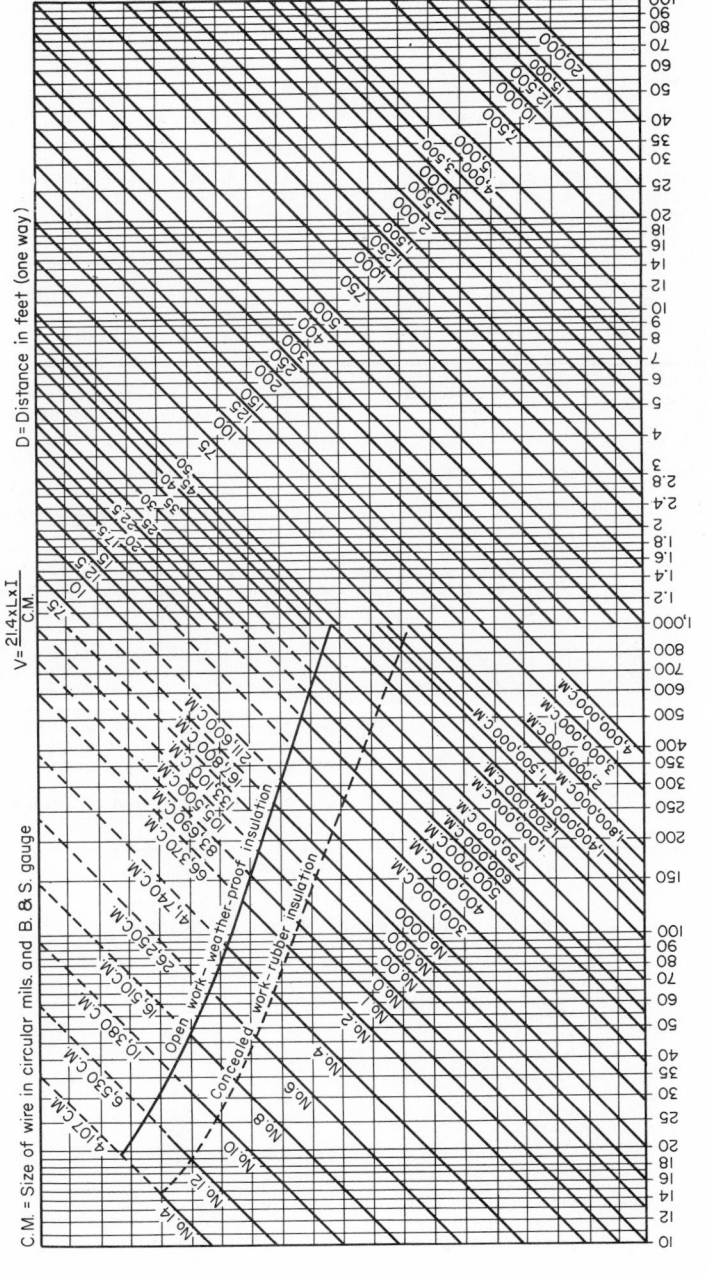

$V = \dfrac{21.4 \times L \times I}{C.M.}$

D = Distance in feet (one way)

V = Drop in volts

C.M. = Size of wire in circular mils, and B. & S. gauge

I = Current in amperes

56. Effect of inductance can be neglected unless the size of wire exceeds the following values:

Type of load	Size of wire with following spacings											
	In conduit	2½ in.	4 in.	5 in.	6 in.	8 in.	12 in.	18 in.	24 in.	36 in.	48 in.
Incandescent lamps—60 cycles	4/0	2/0	1/0	1/0	1	1	2	2	2	3	3
Incandescent lamps—25 cycles	600,000	400,000	300,000	4/0	4/0	4/0	3/0	3/0	3/0	3/0	2/0
Motors—60 cycles.............	1	3	4	4	5	5	5				
Motors—25 cycles.............	4/0	00	0	0	0	1	1	2	2	2	3

57. Effective Spacings of Wires to Use for Different Systems

System	Arrangement of wires	Effective spacing that should be used with Mershon diagram or table of ratio of reactance to resistance
Single-phase three-wire	Any	Use spacing between outside wires
Two-phase, any number of wires	Any	Use a spacing equal to average distance between centers of wires of the same phase
Three-phase		Effective spacing = $\sqrt[3]{ABC}$ when wires are transposed so that each wire occupies each position for approximately one-third of the length of the line
		Effective spacing = $\sqrt[3]{ABC}$ when wires are transposed so that each wire occupies each position for approximately one-third of the length of the line
		Effective spacing = $1.26A$ when wires are transposed so that each wire occupies each position for approximately one-third of the length of the line The position of the neutral in a four-wire system does not affect the spacing

58. Approximate Power Factors of Apparatus

Type of Apparatus	Power Factor
Incandescent lamps and heaters......................................	1.0
Fluorescent lamps and mercury-vapor lamps[a]..................	0.5–0.95
Induction motors:[b]	
1 hp	0.67
2 hp	0.73
3 hp	0.80
5 hp	0.83
7½–25 hp...	0.86
30–50 hp..	0.89
60–125 hp..	0.92
150–200 hp...	0.93
Synchronous motors	0.8 to 1.0 leading

NOTE. All power factors less than unity are lagging except for synchronous motors.

[a] For more accurate information refer to Div. 10.

[b] The values of power factor for induction motors are average values when the motors are operating at 75 per cent of rated load.

59. 60-cycle Ratios – Reactance to Resistance

Ratios for distance between wires (see Sec. 5T)

Type	Size, AWG	Area, cir mils	In conduit	2½ in.	3 in.	4 in.	5 in.	6 in.	8 in.	12 in.	18 in.	2 ft	3 ft	4 ft	5 ft	6 ft	7 ft	8 ft
	....	2,000,000	....	....	7.07	8.23	9.16	9.90	11.10	12.80	14.40	15.70	17.30	18.50	19.20	20.10	20.80	21.40
	....	1,800,000	....	....	6.52	7.58	8.46	9.15	10.20	11.70	13.20	14.30	15.80	17.00	17.70	18.40	19.00	19.40
	....	1,700,000	....	....	6.30	7.30	8.05	8.72	9.70	11.20	12.60	13.60	15.00	16.10	16.90	17.40	18.00	18.50
	....	1,600,000	....	....	5.97	6.96	7.67	8.30	9.22	10.60	11.90	12.90	14.20	15.20	16.00	16.40	17.00	17.50
	....	1,500,000	....	....	5.70	6.62	7.25	7.90	8.75	9.95	11.30	12.10	13.40	14.30	15.00	15.60	16.00	16.40
	....	1,400,000	....	....	5.40	6.26	6.90	7.40	8.28	9.43	10.60	11.50	12.60	13.50	14.10	14.70	15.20	15.50
	....	1,200,000	....	....	4.84	5.52	6.10	6.55	7.28	8.26	9.20	10.00	11.00	11.70	12.20	12.80	13.10	13.40
	....	1,100,000	....	....	4.51	5.20	5.70	6.11	6.75	7.70	8.60	9.25	10.20	10.80	11.40	11.80	12.10	12.40
	....	1,000,000	2.89	3.66	4.22	4.81	5.29	5.65	6.25	7.10	7.92	8.52	9.37	9.96	10.40	10.80	11.10	11.40
	..	950,000	....	....	4.05	4.60	5.05	5.42	6.00	6.80	7.55	8.12	8.95	9.50	9.95	10.30	10.60	10.90
	..	900,000	2.69	3.39	3.92	4.43	4.87	5.20	5.75	6.50	7.24	7.82	8.50	9.10	9.52	9.82	10.10	10.40
	..	850,000	....	....	3.76	4.24	4.65	4.97	5.46	6.20	6.90	7.40	8.15	8.65	9.03	9.33	9.65	9.85
	..	800,000	2.49	3.12	3.55	4.03	4.42	4.70	5.17	5.83	6.55	7.00	7.65	8.15	8.50	8.80	9.10	9.30
	..	750,000	....	....	3.39	3.84	4.18	4.48	4.91	5.55	6.18	6.63	7.25	7.70	8.05	8.35	8.60	8.78
	..	700,000	2.06	2.84	3.21	3.66	3.98	4.25	4.65	5.23	5.82	6.25	6.83	7.25	7.60	7.85	8.10	8.27
Stranded	..	650,000	....	....	3.06	3.42	3.73	3.98	4.35	4.90	5.46	5.85	6.40	6.77	7.10	7.32	7.55	7.73
	..	600,000	1.85	2.52	2.85	3.21	3.47	3.70	4.07	4.55	5.05	5.42	5.93	6.30	6.55	6.80	6.98	7.15
	..	550,000	....	....	2.66	2.98	3.22	3.44	3.76	4.22	4.68	5.00	5.45	5.80	6.05	6.27	6.45	6.60
	..	500,000	1.75	2.30	2.48	2.78	2.99	3.20	3.51	3.92	4.35	4.63	5.05	5.35	5.60	5.78	5.90	6.08
	..	450,000	....	....	2.26	2.52	2.74	2.90	3.16	3.54	3.90	4.18	4.55	4.84	5.04	5.20	5.32	5.47
	..	400,000	1.49	1.93	2.07	2.30	2.48	2.64	2.88	3.21	3.54	3.77	4.12	4.35	4.55	4.68	4.82	4.91
	..	350,000	1.01	1.54	1.87	2.08	2.23	2.37	2.58	2.87	3.17	3.38	3.68	3.88	4.05	4.17	4.30	4.39
	..	300,000	....	....	1.63	1.81	1.95	2.06	2.23	2.49	2.74	2.92	3.16	3.34	3.48	3.60	3.70	3.77
	..	250,000	....	....	1.41	1.56	1.67	1.76	1.91	2.13	2.34	2.50	2.70	2.85	2.97	3.06	3.13	3.20
	4/0	211,600	0.76	1.17	1.23	1.36	1.46	1.54	1.66	1.84	2.02	2.15	2.33	2.46	2.55	2.63	2.69	2.76
	3/0	167,772	0.64	0.97	1.02	1.11	1.20	1.26	1.36	1.50	1.64	1.74	1.88	1.98	2.06	2.12	2.16	2.22
	2/0	133,079	0.54	0.80	0.84	0.91	0.98	1.03	1.11	1.22	1.33	1.41	1.52	1.60	1.66	1.71	1.75	1.79
	1/0	105,560	0.38	0.66	0.69	0.75	0.80	0.84	0.90	1.00	1.08	1.15	1.23	1.30	1.35	1.39	1.42	1.45
	1	83,694	0.32	0.54	0.57	0.62	0.66	0.70	0.74	0.81	0.88	0.94	1.00	1.06	1.10	1.13	1.15	1.17
	2	66,358	0.26	0.45	0.47	0.50	0.53	0.56	0.60	0.65	0.71	0.75	0.81	0.85	0.88	0.90	0.92	0.95

60-cycle Ratios – Reactance to Resistance (*Continued*)

Ratios for distance between wires (see Sec. **57**)

Type	Size, AWG	Area, cir mils	In conduit	2½ in.	3 in.	4 in.	5 in.	6 in.	8 in.	12 in.	18 in.	2 ft	3 ft	4 ft	5 ft	6 ft	7 ft	8 ft
Stranded	3	52,624	0.22	0.37	0.38	0.41	0.44	0.45	0.48	0.53	0.58	0.60	0.65	0.68	0.70	0.72	0.74	0.75
	4	41,738	0.15	0.30	0.31	0.34	0.35	0.37	0.40	0.43	0.47	0.49	0.53	0.55	0.57	0.59	0.60	0.61
	5	33,088	0.14	0.25	0.25	0.27	0.29	0.30	0.32	0.35	0.37	0.40	0.42	0.44	0.46	0.47	0.48	0.49
Solid	4/0	211,600	0.77	1.18	1.25	1.38	1.48	1.56	1.69	1.87	2.06	2.18	2.37	2.50	2.60	2.68	2.72	2.81
	3/0	167,772	0.65	0.98	1.04	1.14	1.22	1.29	1.39	1.53	1.68	1.78	1.92	2.04	2.10	2.17	2.20	2.27
	2/0	133,079	0.55	0.81	0.85	0.94	1.00	1.05	1.13	1.25	1.36	1.44	1.55	1.64	1.70	1.75	1.79	1.84
	1/0	105,560	0.39	0.67	0.70	0.77	0.82	0.86	0.92	1.01	1.11	1.17	1.26	1.32	1.37	1.41	1.45	1.48
	1	83,694	0.33	0.55	0.59	0.63	0.67	0.71	0.76	0.83	0.90	0.95	1.03	1.08	1.12	1.15	1.17	1.20
Solid	2	66,358	0.27	0.46	0.48	0.52	0.55	0.57	0.61	0.67	0.73	0.77	0.83	0.87	0.89	0.92	0.94	0.96
	3	52,624	0.23	0.38	0.39	0.42	0.44	0.46	0.49	0.54	0.58	0.61	0.66	0.69	0.71	0.74	0.75	0.77
	4	41,738	0.16	0.31	0.32	0.34	0.36	0.38	0.40	0.44	0.48	0.50	0.53	0.56	0.58	0.60	0.61	0.62
	5	33,088	0.15	0.25	0.26	0.28	0.30	0.31	0.33	0.36	0.39	0.40	0.43	0.45	0.47	0.48	0.50	0.50

60. 25-cycle Ratios – Reactance to Resistance

Distance between wires (see Sec. **57**)

Ratio

Type	Size, AWG	Area, cir mils	In conduit	2½ in.	3 in.	4 in.	5 in.	6 in.	8 in.	12 in.	18 in.	2 ft	3 ft	4 ft	5 ft	6 ft	7 ft	8 ft
		2,000,000			2.93	3.42	3.82	4.12	4.60	5.32	5.98	6.52	7.20	7.68	8.00	8.35	8.67	8.92
		1,800,000			2.74	3.17	3.50	3.79	4.25	4.86	5.47	5.95	6.60	7.02	7.40	7.64	7.88	8.06
		1,700,000			2.62	3.02	3.34	3.64	4.04	4.65	5.24	5.67	6.25	6.70	7.02	7.27	7.50	7.70
		1,600,000			2.48	2.89	3.19	3.46	3.84	4.38	4.93	5.35	5.90	6.30	6.65	6.85	7.10	7.25
		1,500,000			2.38	2.76	3.04	3.27	3.63	4.15	4.68	5.05	5.60	5.96	6.24	6.48	6.68	6.83
		1,400,000			2.27	2.60	2.87	3.08	3.44	3.92	4.42	4.77	5.25	5.60	5.88	6.10	6.30	6.43
		1,200,000			2.02	2.31	2.54	2.72	3.02	3.44	3.85	4.18	4.58	4.87	5.12	5.32	5.45	5.60
		1,100,000			1.87	2.15	2.38	2.55	2.81	3.20	3.56	3.85	4.24	4.50	4.75	4.90	5.03	5.17
		1,000,000	1.20	1.53	1.78	2.00	2.20	2.36	2.60	2.95	3.31	3.55	3.91	4.16	4.35	4.48	4.63	4.76
		950,000			1.70	1.91	2.10	2.25	2.49	2.83	3.16	3.38	3.70	3.96	4.14	4.27	4.40	4.53
Stranded		900,000	1.12	1.42	1.63	1.85	2.03	2.17	2.38	2.71	3.02	3.25	3.54	3.79	3.97	4.08	4.20	4.32
		850,000			1.57	1.77	1.95	2.08	2.28	2.57	2.86	3.08	3.39	3.60	3.75	3.89	4.01	4.10
		800,000	1.03	1.30	1.48	1.69	1.84	1.96	2.15	2.42	2.72	2.91	3.17	3.38	3.54	3.65	3.77	3.87
		750,000			1.41	1.60	1.74	1.87	2.05	2.32	2.57	2.77	3.02	3.21	3.36	3.47	3.57	3.66
		700,000	0.86	1.18	1.34	1.52	1.65	1.77	1.93	2.18	2.42	2.60	2.85	3.02	3.16	3.27	3.36	3.44
		650,000	0.77	1.05	1.27	1.43	1.56	1.66	1.81	2.04	2.28	2.42	2.66	2.83	2.96	3.04	3.14	3.22
		600,000			1.19	1.34	1.44	1.55	1.70	1.90	2.11	2.25	2.47	2.62	2.72	2.82	2.90	2.98
		550,000	0.73	0.96	1.10	1.24	1.34	1.43	1.56	1.76	1.94	2.08	2.27	2.41	2.51	2.62	2.68	2.74
		500,000			1.03	1.15	1.25	1.33	1.46	1.63	1.81	1.93	2.12	2.23	2.33	2.42	2.46	2.53
		450,000			0.95	1.05	1.14	1.21	1.32	1.47	1.63	1.75	1.90	2.01	2.09	2.16	2.22	2.28
		400,000	0.62	0.81	0.86	0.96	1.03	1.10	1.20	1.33	1.47	1.57	1.72	1.81	1.89	1.95	2.01	2.05
		350,000			0.78	0.86	0.93	0.99	1.07	1.20	1.32	1.41	1.53	1.62	1.68	1.75	1.80	1.83
		300,000	0.42	0.64	0.68	0.76	0.81	0.86	0.93	1.04	1.15	1.22	1.32	1.40	1.45	1.50	1.54	1.57
		250,000			0.59	0.65	0.69	0.74	0.80	0.89	0.97	1.04	1.12	1.19	1.23	1.27	1.30	1.34
	4/0	211,600	0.32	0.49	0.51	0.57	0.61	0.64	0.69	0.77	0.84	0.90	0.97	1.02	1.06	1.09	1.12	1.15

25-cycle Ratios—Reactance to Resistance (*Continued*)

				Distance between wires (see Sec. 57)														
				Ratio														
Type	Size, AWG	Area, cir mils	In conduit	2½ in.	3 in.	4 in.	5 in.	6 in.	8 in.	12 in.	18 in.	2 ft	3 ft	4 ft	5 ft	6 ft	7 ft	8 ft
Stranded	3/0	167,772	0.27	0.40	0.42	0.46	0.50	0.52	0.56	0.62	0.68	0.73	0.79	0.83	0.86	0.88	0.90	0.93
	2/0	133,079	0.23	0.33	0.35	0.38	0.41	0.43	0.46	0.51	0.55	0.59	0.63	0.66	0.69	0.71	0.73	0.75
	1/0	105,560	0.16	0.28	0.29	0.31	0.33	0.35	0.38	0.41	0.45	0.48	0.51	0.54	0.56	0.58	0.59	0.60
	1	83,694	0.13	0.23	0.24	0.26	0.28	0.29	0.31	0.34	0.37	0.39	0.42	0.44	0.46	0.47	0.48	0.49
	2	66,358	0.11	0.19	0.19	0.21	0.22	0.24	0.25	0.27	0.30	0.31	0.34	0.35	0.36	0.38	0.38	0.39
	3	52,624	0.09	0.15	0.16	0.17	0.18	0.19	0.20	0.22	0.24	0.25	0.27	0.28	0.29	0.30	0.31	0.31
	4	41,738	0.06	0.12	0.13	0.14	0.15	0.15	0.16	0.18	0.19	0.20	0.22	0.23	0.24	0.24	0.25	0.25
	5	33,088	0.06	0.10	0.10	0.11	0.12	0.12	0.13	0.14	0.16	0.16	0.18	0.18	0.19	0.19	0.20	0.20
Solid	4/0	211,600	0.33	0.50	0.52	0.58	0.62	0.65	0.71	0.78	0.86	0.91	0.99	1.04	1.08	1.12	1.14	1.17
	3/0	167,772	0.28	0.41	0.43	0.48	0.51	0.54	0.58	0.64	0.70	0.74	0.80	0.84	0.88	0.90	0.92	0.95
	2/0	133,079	0.24	0.34	0.36	0.39	0.42	0.44	0.47	0.52	0.57	0.60	0.65	0.68	0.71	0.73	0.74	0.76
	1/0	105,560	0.17	0.29	0.29	0.32	0.34	0.36	0.38	0.42	0.46	0.49	0.52	0.55	0.57	0.59	0.60	0.72
	1	83,694	0.14	0.24	0.24	0.26	0.28	0.29	0.31	0.35	0.38	0.40	0.43	0.45	0.47	0.48	0.49	0.50
	2	66,358	0.12	0.20	0.20	0.22	0.23	0.24	0.25	0.28	0.30	0.32	0.35	0.36	0.37	0.39	0.39	0.40
	3	52,624	0.10	0.16	0.16	0.17	0.18	0.19	0.20	0.22	0.24	0.25	0.27	0.29	0.30	0.31	0.31	0.32
	4	41,738	0.07	0.13	0.13	0.14	0.15	0.16	0.17	0.18	0.20	0.21	0.22	0.23	0.24	0.25	0.25	0.26
	5	33,088	0.07	0.11	0.11	0.13	0.12	0.13	0.14	0.15	0.16	0.17	0.18	0.19	0.20	0.20	0.21	0.21

61. Alternating-current Drop Factors

Ratio of reactance to resistance	Power factor							
	1.00	0.95	0.90	0.85	0.80	0.70	0.60	0.40
	Drop factor							
0.1	1.00	1.00	1.00	0.94	0.88	0.80	0.70	0.60
0.2	1.00	1.01	1.01	0.98	0.92	0.86	0.82	0.67
0.3	1.00	1.05	1.05	1.02	0.99	0.93	0.89	0.74
0.4	1.00	1.08	1.10	1.08	1.04	1.00	0.93	0.82
0.5	1.00	1.11	1.14	1.13	1.10	1.07	1.01	0.92
0.6	1.01	1.15	1.18	1.19	1.15	1.14	1.09	1.01
0.7	1.02	1.18	1.23	1.24	1.21	1.20	1.17	1.11
0.8	1.02	1.21	1.28	1.29	1.28	1.27	1.24	1.20
0.9	1.03	1.25	1.33	1.34	1.34	1.35	1.32	1.29
1.0	1.04	1.28	1.37	1.39	1.40	1.41	1.39	1.38
1.1	1.05	1.32	1.41	1.44	1.45	1.48	1.47	1.46
1.2	1.06	1.35	1.46	1.30	1.51	1.55	1.54	1.55
1.3	1.07	1.39	1.51	1.55	1.57	1.62	1.63	1.64
1.4	1.08	1.43	1.55	1.61	1.64	1.70	1.71	1.72
1.5	1.10	1.47	1.60	1.67	1.70	1.77	1.80	1.81
1.6	1.10	1.51	1.65	1.74	1.77	1.85	1.87	1.90
1.7	1.13	1.55	1.70	1.79	1.84	1.92	1.95	1.99
1.8	1.15	1.59	1.76	1.85	1.91	1.99	2.04	2.08
1.9	1.17	1.63	1.82	1.91	1.98	2.06	2.11	2.16
2.0	1.18	1.68	1.87	1.96	2.04	2.14	2.19	2.25
2.1	1.20	1.72	1.92	2.03	2.10	2.21	2.28	2.35
2.2	1.22	1.77	1.98	2.09	2.17	2.29	2.37	2.45
2.3	1.23	1.82	2.03	2.15	2.23	2.37	2.45	2.53
2.4	1.25	1.87	2.09	2.22	2.30	2.44	2.53	2.62
2.5	1.27	1.91	2.14	2.28	2.37	2.52	2.60	2.71
2.6	1.30	1.95	2.20	2.34	2.44	2.60	2.67	2.80
2.7	1.32	1.99	2.26	2.41	2.51	2.68	2.74	2.98
2.8	1.35	2.05	2.32	2.47	2.57	2.76	2.82	3.07
2.9	1.37	2.10	2.39	2.54	2.64	2.83	2.91	3.15
3.0	1.40	2.15	2.45	2.60	2.72	2.90	3.00	3.23
3.1	1.42	2.20	2.51	2.66	2.80	2.97	3.10	3.31
3.2	1.45	2.26	2.57	2.73	2.87	3.05	3.20	3.39
3.3	1.48	2.31	2.63	2.80	2.93	3.12	3.30	3.47
3.4	1.51	2.36	2.69	2.87	3.00	3.20	3.39	3.56
3.5	1.53	2.42	2.74	2.94	3.08	3.27	3.48	3.65
3.6	1.57	2.47	2.80	3.00	3.15	3.35	3.56	3.75
3.7	1.60	2.52	2.86	3.07	3.23	3.43	3.65	3.85

62. The Mershon Diagram

See Sec. **72** of Div. 3 for directions as to its use and application. (The side of each small square equals 1 per cent; percentage of resistance is measured horizontally and percentage of reactance vertically.)

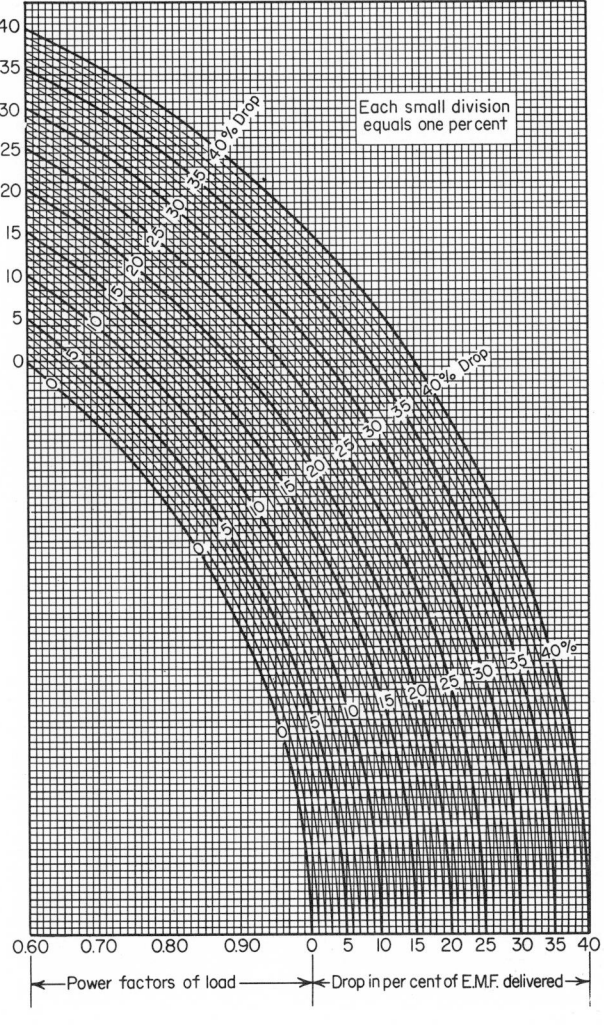

63. Average D-C Resistances and Correction Factors for A-C Resistances and Reactances for Copper Conductors

Size, AWG or cir mils	D-c resistance, ohms per 1,000 ft			60-cycle correction factors[b]			
				Single conductor, a-c resistance[c]		Three conductors	
	At 50°C[a]	At 60°C[a]	At 70°C[a]	Standard strand	Annular	A-c resistance	Reactance (for cable with magnetic binder)
8	0.705	0.735	0.765	1.00	....	1.00	1.26
6	0.445	0.464	0.482	1.00	....	1.00	1.26
4	0.279	0.292	0.303	1.00	....	1.00	1.26
2	0.176	0.184	0.191	1.00	....	1.01	1.26
1	0.140	0.146	0.152	1.00	....	1.01	1.26
1/0	0.117	0.115	0.120	1.00	....	1.02	1.26
2/0	0.0877	0.0915	0.0952	1.00	....	1.03	1.26
3/0	0.0696	0.0725	0.0755	1.00	....	1.04	1.26
4/0	0.0552	0.0575	0.0598	1.00	....	1.05	1.26
250,000	0.0467	0.0486	0.0506	1.01	....	1.06	1.26
300,000	0.0390	0.0406	0.0423	1.01	....	1.07	1.26
350,000	0.0336	0.0348	0.0362	1.01	....	1.08	1.26
400,000	0.0292	0.0304	0.0317	1.02	....	1.10	1.25
500,000	0.0234	0.0244	0.0254	1.02	....	1.13	1.25
600,000	0.0195	0.0203	0.0211	1.03	....	1.16	1.24
700,000	0.0167	0.0174	0.0181	1.03	....	1.19	1.24
750,000	0.0156	0.0162	0.0169	1.04	1.02	1.21	1.23
800,000	0.0147	0.0153	0.0159	1.05	1.02		
1,000,000	0.0117	0.0122	0.0127	1.07	1.03		
1,250,000	0.0093	0.0097	0.0101	1.11	1.03		
1,500,000	0.0078	0.0081	0.00842	1.15	1.04		
1,750,000	0.00667	0.00695	0.00724	1.19	1.05		
2,000,000	0.00583	0.00607	0.00632	1.24	1.06		

[a] Temperature correction is 0.39 per cent per degree centigrade (positive for higher temperatures, negative for lower temperatures).

[b] These are multiplying factors.

[c] Allows for skin effect only.

64. Properties of Conductors

Size, AWG or 1,000 cir mils	Area, cir mils	Concentric-lay stranded conductors		Bare conductors		D-c resistance, ohms per 1,000 ft at 25°C (77°F)		
						Copper		Alumi-num
		No. of wires	Diam. each wire, in.	Diam., in.	Area,[a] sq in.	Bare conductor	Tinned conductor	
18 AWG	1,620	Solid	0.0403	0.0403	0.0013	6.51	6.79	10.7
16	2,580	Solid	0.0508	0.0508	0.0020	4.10	4.26	6.72
14	4,110	Solid	0.0641	0.0641	0.0032	2.57	2.68	4.22
12	6,530	Solid	0.0808	0.0808	0.0051	1.62	1.68	2.66
10	10,380	Solid	0.1019	0.1019	0.0081	1.018	1.06	1.67
8	16,510	Solid	0.1285	0.1285	0.013	0.6404	0.659	1.05
6	26,240	7	0.0612	0.184	0.027	0.410	0.427	0.674
4	41,740	7	0.0772	0.232	0.042	0.259	0.269	0.424
3	52,620	7	0.0867	0.260	0.053	0.205	0.213	0.336
2	66,360	7	0.0974	0.292	0.067	0.162	0.169	0.266
1	83,690	19	0.0664	0.332	0.087	0.129	0.134	0.211
0	105,600	19	0.0745	0.372	0.109	0.102	0.106	0.168
00	133,100	19	0.0837	0.418	0.137	0.0811	0.0843	0.133
000	167,800	19	0.0940	0.470	0.173	0.0642	0.0668	0.105
0000	211,600	19	0.1055	0.528	0.219	0.0509	0.0525	0.0836
250 MCM	250,000	37	0.0822	0.575	0.260	0.0431	0.0449	0.0708
300	300,000	37	0.0900	0.630	0.312	0.0360	0.0374	0.0590
350	350,000	37	0.0973	0.681	0.364	0.0308	0.0320	0.0505
400	400,000	37	0.1040	0.728	0.416	0.0270	0.0278	0.0442
500	500,000	37	0.1162	0.813	0.519	0.0216	0.0222	0.0354
600	600,000	61	0.0992	0.893	0.626	0.0180	0.0187	0.0295
700	700,000	61	0.1071	0.964	0.730	0.0154	0.0159	0.0253
750	750,000	61	0.1109	0.998	0.782	0.0144	0.0148	0.0236
800	800,000	61	0.1145	1.030	0.833	0.0135	0.0139	0.0221
900	900,000	61	0.1215	1.090	0.933	0.0120	0.0123	0.0197
1,000	1,000,000	61	0.1280	1.150	1.039	0.0108	0.0111	0.0177
1,250	1,250,000	91	0.1172	1.289	1.305	0.00863	0.00888	0.0142
1,500	1,500,000	91	0.1284	1.410	1.561	0.00719	0.00740	0.0118
1,750	1,750,000	127	0.1174	1.526	1.829	0.00616	0.00634	0.0101
2,000	2,000,000	127	0.1255	1.630	2.087	0.00539	0.00555	0.00885

[a] Area given is that of a circle having a diameter equal to the over-all diameter of a stranded conductor.

The values given in the table are from Handbook 100 of the National Bureau of Standards, except that those in the 8th column are from Specification B33 of the American Society for Testing and Materials, and those in the 9th column from Standard No. S-19-81 of the Insulated Power Cable Engineers Association and Standard No. WC3-1964 of the National Electrical Manufacturers' Association.

The resistance values in the last three columns are applicable only to direct current. When conductors larger than No. 4/0 are used with alternating current, the multiplying factors in Table **65** should be used to compensate for skin effect.

65. Multiplying Factors for Converting D-C Resistance to 60-cycle A-C Resistance

Size, AWG or 1,000 cir mils	Multiplying factor			
	For nonmetallic-sheathed cables in air or nonmetallic conduit		For metallic-sheathed cables or all cables in metallic raceways	
	Copper	Aluminum	Copper	Aluminum
Up to 3 AWG	1	1	1	1
2	1	1	1.01	1.00
1	1	1	1.01	1.00
0	1.001	1.000	1.02	1.00
00	1.001	1.001	1.03	1.00
000	1.002	1.001	1.04	1.01
0,000	1.004	1.002	1.05	1.01
250 MCM	1.005	1.002	1.06	1.02
300	1.006	1.003	1.07	1.02
350	1.009	1.004	1.08	1.03
400	1.011	1.005	1.10	1.04
500	1.018	1.007	1.13	1.06
600	1.025	1.010	1.16	1.08
700	1.034	1.013	1.19	1.11
750	1.039	1.015	1.21	1.12
800	1.044	1.017	1.22	1.14
1,000	1.067	1.026	1.30	1.19
1,250	1.102	1.040	1.41	1.27
1,500	1.142	1.058	1.53	1.36
1,750	1.185	1.079	1.67	1.46
2,000	1.233	1.100	1.82	1.56

66. Direct-current Resistance of Solid Copper Wire

Size, AWG	Max resistance, ohms per 1,000 ft at 68°F			
	Soft or annealed	Medium hard	Hard drawn	Tinned, soft drawn
4/0	0.04993	0.05019	0.05045	
3/0	0.06296	0.06329	0.06361	
2/0	0.07939	0.07980	0.08021	
1/0	0.1001	0.1006	0.1011	
1	0.1262	0.1282	0.1287	0.1275
2	0.1592	0.1617	0.1625	0.1608
3	0.2007	0.2038	0.2049	0.2028
4	0.2531	0.2570	0.2584	0.2557
5	0.3192	0.3241	0.3258	0.3225
6	0.4025	0.4087	0.4108	0.4066
7	0.5075	0.5154	0.5181	0.5127
8	0.6400	0.6499	0.6533	0.6465
9	0.8070	0.8195	0.8238	0.8153
10	1.018	1.033	1.039	1.039
11	1.283	1.303	1.310	1.310
12	1.618	1.643	1.652	1.652
13	2.040	2.072	2.083	2.083
14	2.573	2.613	2.626	2.626
15	3.244	3.295	3.312	3.312
16	4.091	4.154	4.176	4.176
17	5.158	5.239	5.266	5.266
18	6.505	6.606	6.640	6.640
19	8.202	8.330	8.373	8.373
20	10.34	10.50	10.56	10.56
21	13.04	13.24	13.31	13.31
22	16.45	16.70	16.79	16.79
23	20.74	21.06	21.17	21.17
24	26.15	26.56	26.69	27.26
25	32.97	33.49	33.66	34.37
26	41.58	42.23	42.44	43.34
27	52.43	53.25	53.52	54.66
28	66.11	67.14	67.49	68.92
29	83.37	84.66	85.10	87.85
30	105.1	106.8	107.3	110.8
31	132.6	134.6	135.3	139.7
32	167.2	169.8	170.6	176.1
33	210.8	214.1	215.2	222.1
34	265.8	269.9	271.3	280.1
35	335.2	340.4	342.1	353.2
36	422.6	429.2	431.4	445.4
37	532.9	541.2	544.0	561.6
38	672.0	682.4	686	708.1
39	847.4	860.5	865	893
40	1069	1085	1091	1126
41	1347	1368	1375	
42	1699	1725	1734	
43	2142	2176	2187	
44	2702	2743	2758	
45	3406	3459	3477	

The above resistances are maximum values for nominal diameters based upon ASTM specification resistivities, as follows:

Conductor	Lb per mile-ohm	Equivalent IACS per cent conductivity
Soft or annealed (ASTM Spec. B 3)..................................	891.58	98.16
Medium hard (ASTM Spec. B 2):		
Diameter 0.460 in.—0.325 in. (No. 4/0—No. 1/0 AWG)..............	896.15	97.66
Diameter 0.324 in.—0.040 in. (No. 1—No. 18 AWG........	905.44	96.66
Hard drawn (ASTM Spec. B 1):		
Diameter 0.460 in.—0.325 in. (No. 4/0—No. 1/0 AWG)..............	900.77	97.16
Diameter 0.324 in.—0.040 in. (No. 1—No. 18 AWG)................	910.15	96.16

For wire sizes smaller than No. 18 AWG in medium-hard and hard-drawn tempers:
No ASTM requirements; resistances for these sizes in above table based on 905.44 lb per mile-ohm (96.66 per cent conductivity) for medium-hard wire, and 910.15 lb per mile-ohm (96.16 per cent conductivity) for hard-drawn wire.
The above data are approximate and subject to normal manufacturing tolerances.

67. Direct-current Resistance of Stranded Copper Wire

	Size	Resistance, ohms per 1,000 ft at 68°F			
AWG	Circular mils	Soft or annealed	Medium hard	Hard drawn	Tinned, soft drawn
...	5,000,000	0.002219			
...	4,500,000	0.002465			
...	4,000,000	0.002747			
...	3,500,000	0.003139			
...	3,000,000	0.003628			
...	2,500,000	0.004353			
...	2,000,000	0.005388	....	....	0.005444
...	1,750,000	0.006158	....	....	0.006221
...	1,500,000	0.007185	....	....	0.007258
...	1,250,000	0.008622	....	....	0.008710
...	1,000,000	0.01078	0.01094	0.01100	0.01089
...	900,000	0.01197	0.01216	0.01222	0.01210
...	800,000	0.01347	0.01368	0.01375	0.01361
...	750,000	0.01438	0.01459	0.01467	0.01452
...	700,000	0.01540	0.01563	0.01572	0.01555
...	600,000	0.01796	0.01824	0.01834	0.01833
...	500,000	0.02155	0.02189	0.02200	0.02178
...	450,000	0.02395	0.02432	0.02445	0.02419
...	400,000	0.02684	0.02736	0.02750	0.02722
...	350,000	0.03079	0.03127	0.03143	0.03143
...	300,000	0.03592	0.03648	0.03667	0.03667
...	250,000	0.04311	0.04378	0.04400	0.04400
4/0	211,600	0.05093	0.05172	0.05199	0.05145
3/0	167,800	0.06422	0.06522	0.06556	0.06556
2/0	133,100	0.08097	0.08223	0.08256	0.08266
1/0	105,500	0.1021	0.1037	0.1043	0.1042
1	83,690	0.1288	0.1308	0.1315	0.1314
2	66,370	0.1624	0.1649	0.1658	0.1657
3	52,630	0.2047	0.2059	0.2070	0.2090
4	41,740	0.2582	0.2596	0.2610	0.2635
5	33,100	0.3256	0.3274	0.3291	0.3323
6	26,250	0.4105	0.4128	0.4149	0.4191
7	20,820	0.5176	....	....	0.5284
8	16,510	0.6528	....	....	0.6663
9	13,090	0.8233	....	....	0.8402
10	10,380	1.038	....	....	1.060
12	6,530	1.650	....	....	1.685
14	4,107	2.624	....	....	2.679
16	2,583	4.172	....	....	4.350
18	1,624	6.636	....	....	6.917
20	1,022	10.54	....	....	11.00

Resistances: Maximum values for nominal diameters based upon ASTM Spec. B 3 resistivity of 891.58 lb per mile-ohm (equivalent to 98.16 per cent IACS conductivity), increased as follows for stranding.

Size, Cir Mils or AWG	Per Cent of Increase of Resistance
5,000,000–4,500,000..................	5
4,000,000–3,500,000..................	4
3,000,000–2,500,000..................	3
2,000,000– 250,000..................	2
4/0– 20..................	2

68. Data on D-C and A-C Resistance for Copper Conductors
(Anaconda Wire & Cable Co.)

Conductor size, AWG or MCM	D-c resistance at 25°C, ohms per 1,000 ft				A-c/D-c resistance ratio (including skin effect and proximity effect)						Multiconductor or 2 or 3 single-conductor cables in same metallic conduit
	Solid	Stranded			Single-conductor cable in air or in separate nonmetallic duct						
		Concentric and sector	Annular	Segmental	Concentric strand at 65°C (149°F)		Annular strand at 65°C (149°F)		Segmental strand 60 cps		Concentric and sector strand at 60 cps and 25°C (77°F)
					25 cps	60 cps	25 cps	60 cps	25°C	65°C	
14	2.58	......	......	......	1.000	1.000	.....	.....	.....	.....	1.000
12	1.62	......	......	......	1.000	1.000	.....	.....	.....	.....	1.000
10	1.02	......	......	......	1.000	1.000	.....	.....	.....	.....	1.000
8	0.641	0.654	......	......	1.000	1.000	.....	.....	.....	.....	1.000
6	0.403	0.410	......	......	1.000	1.000	.....	.....	.....	.....	1.000
4	0.253	0.259	......	......	1.000	1.000	.....	.....	.....	.....	1.000
2	0.159	0.162	......	......	1.000	1.000	.....	.....	.....	.....	1.010
1	0.126	0.129	......	......	1.000	1.000	.....	.....	.....	.....	1.010
1/0	0.100	0.102	......	......	1.000	1.000	.....	.....	.....	.....	1.020
2/0	0.0795	0.0811	......	......	1.000	1.000	.....	.....	.....	.....	1.030
3/0	0.0630	0.0642	......	......	1.000	1.000	.....	.....	.....	.....	1.040
4/0	0.0500	0.0509	......	......	1.000	1.000	.....	.....	.....	.....	1.050
250	......	0.0431	......	......	1.000	1.005	.....	.....	.....	.....	1.060
300	......	0.0360	......	......	1.000	1.006	.....	.....	.....	.....	1.070
350	......	0.0308	......	......	1.000	1.009	.....	.....	.....	.....	1.080
400	......	0.0270	......	......	1.000	1.011	.....	.....	.....	.....	1.100
450	......	0.0240	......	......	1.000	1.014	.....	.....	.....	.....	1.115
500	......	0.0216	......	......	1.000	1.018	.....	.....	.....	.....	1.130
550	......	0.0196	......	......	1.000	1.021	.....	.....	.....	.....	1.145
600	......	0.0180	......	......	1.005	1.025	.....	.....	.....	.....	1.160
650	......	0.0166	......	......	1.005	1.029	.....	.....	.....	.....	1.175
700	......	0.0154	......	......	1.006	1.034	.....	.....	.....	.....	1.190
750	......	0.0144	0.0147	......	1.007	1.039	1.004	1.021	.....	.....	1.210
800	......	0.0135	0.0136	......	1.008	1.044	1.004	1.021			
850	......	0.0127	0.0128	......	1.009	1.049	1.005	1.023			
900	......	0.0120	0.0120	......	1.010	1.055	1.005	1.025			
950	......	0.0114	0.0115	......	1.011	1.061	1.006	1.028			
1,000	......	0.0108	0.0106	0.0108	1.012	1.067	1.006	1.031	1.018	1.013	
1,250	......	0.00863	0.00864	0.00867	1.019	1.102	1.007	1.034	1.028	1.021	
1,500	......	0.00719	0.00720	0.00723	1.027	1.142	1.007	1.037	1.039	1.030	
1,750	......	0.00616	0.00621	0.00619	1.037	1.185	1.008	1.043	1.053	1.040	
2,000	......	0.00539	0.00550	0.00542	1.048	1.233	1.009	1.045	1.068	1.052	
2,250	......	0.00484	0.00484	0.00484	1.059	1.276	1.011	1.056	1.085	1.065	
2,500	......	0.00436	0.00438	0.00434	1.071	1.326	1.012	1.066	1.102	1.078	
3,000	......	0.00363	0.00358	0.00361	1.100	1.424	1.019	1.105	1.141	1.109	
3,500	......	0.00314	0.00306	0.00310	1.130	1.513	1.020	1.110	1.182	1.141	
4,000	......	0.00275	0.00274	0.00271	1.165	1.605	1.021	1.116	1.225	1.178	
4,500	......	0.00247	0.00252	......	1.200	1.685	1.022	1.118			
5,000	......	0.00222	0.00224	......	1.237	1.765	1.023	1.121			

National Bureau of Standards Circular 31

IPCEA V-C Specs. 5th ed., 1946

Direct-current resistance based on 100 per cent conductivity including allowance made for stranding.
Temperature conversion:

$$R_2 = R_{25}[1 + 0.00385(T_2 - 25)]$$

where R_2 = resistance at operating temperature, °C; R_{25} = resistance at 25°C; T_2 = operating temperature, °C.

Example. Determine a-c resistance of three-conductor, 350,000-cir-mil sector, 0.375-in. paper, 0.125-in. lead-shielded cable at 70°C operating temperature.

Solution. A-c resistance = 0.0308 × [1 + .00385(70 − 25)] × 1.080 = 0.0390 ohms per conductor per 1,000 ft.

69. Skin-effect Ratio for Tubular Copper Conductors

This table gives the conductor diameter in inches d, and the 60-cycle, skin-effect ratio or ratio of a-c to d-c resistance, both for the ordinary form of stranding (inside diameter = 0) and for tubular conductors.

| Size, 1,000 cir mils | Inside diam of tubular conductor, in. | | | | | | | |
| | 0 | | 0.25 | | 0.50 | | 0.75 | |
	d	Ratio	d	Ratio	d	Ratio	d	Ratio
3,000	1.998	1.439	2.02	1.39	2.08	1.36	2.15	1.29
2,500	1.825	1.336	1.87	1.28	1.91	1.24	2.00	1.20
2,000	1.631	1.239	1.67	1.20	1.72	1.17	1.80	1.12
1,500	1.412	1.145	1.45	1.12	1.52	1.09	1 63	1.06
1,000	1.152	1.068	1.19	1.05	1.25	1.03	1.39	1.02
800	1.031	1.046	1.07	1.04	1.16	1.02	1.28	1.01
600	.893	1.026	.94	1.02	1.04	1.01		
500	.814	1.018	.86	1.01	.97	1.01		
400	.728	1.012	.78	1.01				
300	.630	1.006						

| Size, 1,000 cir mils | Inside diam of tubular conductor, in. | | | | | | | |
| | 1.00 | | 1.25 | | 1.50 | | 2.00 | |
	d	Ratio	d	Ratio	d	Ratio	d	Ratio
3,000	2.27	1.23	2.39	1.19	2.54	1.15	2.87	1.08
2,500	2.12	1.16	2.25	1.12	2.40	1.09	2.75	1.05
2,000	1.94	1.09	2.09	1.06	2.25	1.05	2.61	1.02
1,500	1.75	1.04	1.91	1.03	2.07	1.02	2.47	1.01
1,000	1.53	1.01	1.72	1.01				
800	1.45	1.01						

70. Average Resistance for All-steel Conductors

Size and type of conductor	D-c resistance ohms per 1,000 ft at 68°F	A-c, 60-cycle resistance at various loadings, ohms per 1,000 ft at 68°F				
		1 amp	5 amp	10 amp	15 amp	20 amp
Type S:						
4 BWG, solid............	1.5	1.6	1.7	1.9	2.1	2.4
6 BWG, solid............	2.1	2.2	2.2	2.3	2.6	
8 BWG, solid............	3.2	3.3	3.4	3.7		
Type S-3:						
4 BWG, three-wire......	1.5	1.6	1.6	1.6	1.7	1.7
6 BWG, three-wire......	2.1	2.2	2.2	2.2	2.3	
8 BWG, three-wire......	3.2	3.3	3.3	3.4		

71. Average Resistance for Copper-Steel Conductors

Size, AWG	D-c resistance, ohms	A-c resistance, ohms
2	0.160	0.17
4	0.256	0.27
6	0.406	0.41
8	0.646	0.66
10	1.050	1.06
12	1.660	1.68

72. Average D-C Resistance for Copperweld Conductors

SOLID CONDUCTORS:

30 per cent conductivity—multiply resistance of solid copper wire of same size by 3.33

40 per cent conductivity—multiply resistance of solid copper wire of same size by 2.5

STRANDED CONDUCTORS:

30 per cent conductivity—multiply resistance of solid copper wire of same size as each strand by the product of number of strands times 3.4

40 per cent conductivity—multiply resistance of solid copper wire of same size as each strand by the product of number of strands times 2.55

See Tables **73** and **74.**

73. Data for Copperweld Conductors
(Anaconda Wire & Cable Co.)

Conductor			D-c resistance at 20°C (68°F) Conductivity, ohms per 1,000 ft		Resistance per conductor, ohms per mile								Reactance per conductor per mile at 60 cps 1-ft spacing		
					At 25°C (77°F)				At 75°C (167°F)				Inductive x_L		Capacitive x_C
					Conductivity				Conductivity						
					40%		30%		40%		30%		40%	30%	30% and 40%
Nominal size, AWG or cir mils or in.	Number and size of wires, AWG	Over-all diam, in.	40%	30%	D-c	60 cps	D-c	60 cps	D-c	60 cps	D-c	60 cps	Ohms	Ohms	Megohms
								Solid							
4	1	0.2043	0.6337	0.8447											
5	1	0.1819	0.7990	1.065											
165	1	0.1650	0.9715	1.295											
6	1	0.1620	1.008	1.343											
7	1	0.1443	1.270	1.694											
8	1	0.1285	1.602	2.136											
128	1	0.1280	1.614	2.152											
9	1	0.1144	2.020	2.693											
104	1	0.1040	2.445	3.260											
10	1	0.1019	2.547	3.396											
12	1	0.0808	4.051												
080	1	0.0800	4.133												

Concentric Strand

Size	Stranding														
7/8	19 X X #5	0.910	0.04264	0.05685	0.229	0.254	0.306	0.331	0.272	0.391	0.363	0.499	0.539	0.592	0.0971
13/16	19 X X #6	0.810	0.05377	0.07168	0.289	0.314	0.386	0.411	0.343	0.472	0.458	0.605	0.553	0.606	0.1005
23/32	19 X X #7	0.721	0.06780	0.09039	0.365	0.390	0.486	0.511	0.433	0.573	0.577	0.737	0.567	0.621	0.1040
21/32	19 X X #8	0.642	0.08550	0.1140	0.460	0.485	0.613	0.638	0.546	0.698	0.728	0.902	0.582	0.635	0.1074
9/16	19 X X #9	0.572	0.1078	0.1437	0.580	0.605	0.773	0.798	0.688	0.753	0.917	1.106	0.595	0.649	0.1109
5/8	7 X X X #4	0.613	0.09143	0.1219	0.492	0.512	0.656	0.676	0.584	0.680	0.788	0.887	0.587	0.640	0.1088
9/16	7 X X X #5	0.546	0.1153	0.1537	0.620	0.640	0.827	0.847	0.736	0.840	0.981	1.099	0.601	0.654	0.1122
1/2	7 X X X #6	0.486	0.1454	0.1938	0.782	0.802	1.042	1.062	0.928	1.040	1.237	1.364	0.615	0.668	0.1157
7/16	7 X X X #7	0.433	0.1833	0.2444	0.986	1.006	1.315	1.335	1.170	1.291	1.560	1.697	0.629	0.683	0.1191
3/8	7 X X X #8	0.385	0.2312	0.3081	1.244	1.264	1.658	1.678	1.476	1.606	1.967	2.12	0.644	0.697	0.1226
1 1/32	7 X X X #9	0.343	0.2915	0.3886	1.568	1.588	2.09	2.11	1.861	2.00	2.48	2.64	0.658	0.711	0.1260
9/16	7 X X X #10	0.306	0.3676	0.4900	1.978	1.998	2.64	2.66	2.35	2.50	3.13	3.30	0.671	0.725	0.1294
	3 X X #5	0.392	0.2685	0.3579	1.445	1.457	1.926	1.938	1.714	1.772	2.29	2.35	0.617	0.654	0.1221
	3 X X #6	0.349	0.3385	0.4513	1.821	1.833	2.43	2.44	2.16	2.22	2.88	2.95	0.631	0.668	0.1255
	3 X X #7	0.311	0.4269	0.5691	2.30	2.31	3.06	3.07	2.73	2.79	3.63	3.71	0.645	0.682	0.1289
	3 X X #8	0.277	0.5383	0.7176	2.90	2.91	3.86	3.87	3.44	3.51	4.58	4.66	0.659	0.696	0.1324
	3 X X #9	0.247	0.6788	0.9049	3.65	3.66	4.87	4.88	4.33	4.41	5.78	5.86	0.673	0.710	0.1358
	3 X X #10	0.220	0.8559	1.141	4.61	4.62	6.14	6.15	5.46	5.55	7.28	7.38	0.687	0.724	0.1392
	3 X X #12	0.174	1.361	.....	7.32	7.34	.....	.....	8.69	8.78	.....	.....	0.715	.....	0.1462

Temperature coefficient of resistance is 0.0021 per degree Fahrenheit.

74. Data for Copperweld Composite Cables
(Anaconda Wire & Cable Co.)

Hard-drawn copper equivalent area, 1,000 cir mils or AWG	Type	D-c resistance at 20°C (68°F), ohms per 1,000 ft	Approximate current rating at 60 cps, amp	Resistance per conductor, ohms per mile				Reactance per conductor per mile at 60 cps 1-ft spacing	
				At 25°C (77°F)		At 50°C (122°F)		Inductive x_L, ohms	Capacitive x_c, megohms
				D-c	60 cps	D-c	60 cps		
350	E	0.03143	660	0.1658	0.1812	0.1812	0.204	0.463	0.1014
350	EK	0.03143	680	0.1658	0.1705	0.1812	0.1882	0.450	0.1034
350	V	0.03143	650	0.1655	0.1828	0.1809	0.206	0.460	0.1027
300	E	0.03667	600	0.1934	0.209	0.211	0.235	0.473	0.1037
300	EK	0.03667	610	0.1934	0.1981	0.211	0.219	0.460	0.1057
300	V	0.03667	590	0.1930	0.210	0.211	0.237	0.469	0.1050
250	E	0.04400	540	0.232	0.248	0.254	0.279	0.484	0.1064
250	EK	0.04400	540	0.232	0.237	0.254	0.261	0.471	0.1084
250	V	0.04400	530	0.232	0.249	0.253	0.281	0.480	0.1077
4/0	E	0.05199	480	0.274	0.290	0.300	0.326	0.493	0.1088
4/0	G	0.05199	460	0.273	0.298	0.299	0.342	0.517	0.1103
4/0	EK	0.05199	490	0.274	0.279	0.300	0.308	0.481	0.1109
4/0	V	0.05199	470	0.274	0.291	0.299	0.328	0.490	0.1101
4/0	F	0.05199	470	0.273	0.287	0.299	0.322	0.505	0.1120
3/0	E	0.06556	420	0.346	0.361	0.378	0.407	0.508	0.1123
3/0	J	0.06556	410	0.344	0.372	0.377	0.428	0.541	0.1118
3/0	G	0.06556	400	0.344	0.369	0.377	0.423	0.531	0.1137
3/0	EK	0.06556	420	0.346	0.351	0.378	0.386	0.495	0.1143
3/0	V	0.06556	410	0.345	0.362	0.377	0.408	0.504	0.1136
3/0	F	0.06556	410	0.344	0.358	0.377	0.401	0.519	0.1155
2/0	K	0.08265	360	0.434	0.466	0.475	0.535	0.570	0.1129
2/0	J	0.08265	350	0.434	0.462	0.475	0.530	0.555	0.1152
2/0	G	0.08265	350	0.434	0.459	0.475	0.525	0.545	0.1171
2/0	V	0.08265	360	0.435	0.452	0.476	0.509	0.518	0.1170
2/0	F	0.08265	350	0.434	0.448	0.475	0.501	0.533	0.1189
1/0	K	0.1043	310	0.548	0.579	0.599	0.664	0.584	0.1164
1/0	J	0.1043	310	0.548	0.576	0.599	0.659	0.569	0.1186
1/0	G	0.1043	310	0.548	0.573	0.599	0.654	0.559	0.1206
1/0	F	0.1043	310	0.548	0.562	0.599	0.627	0.547	0.1224
1	N	0.1315	280	0.691	0.726	0.755	0.832	0.614	0.1171
1	K	0.1315	270	0.691	0.722	0.755	0.825	0.598	0.1198
1	J	0.1315	270	0.691	0.719	0.755	0.820	0.583	0.1221
1	G	0.1315	260	0.691	0.716	0.755	0.815	0.573	0.1240
1	F	0.1315	270	0.691	0.705	0.755	0.786	0.561	0.1258
2	P	0.1658	250	0.871	0.909	0.952	1.040	0.643	0.1172
2	N	0.1658	240	0.871	0.906	0.952	1.035	0.627	0.1205
2	K	0.1658	240	0.871	0.902	0.952	1.028	0.612	0.1232
2	J	0.1658	230	0.871	0.899	0.952	1.022	0.598	0.1255
2	A	0.1658	240	0.869	0.882	0.950	0.979	0.592	0.1241
2	G	0.1658	230	0.871	0.896	0.952	1.016	0.587	0.1275
2	F	0.1658	230	0.871	0.885	0.952	0.985	0.575	0.1292
3	P	0.2090	220	1.098	1.136	1.200	1.296	0.657	0.1207
3	N	0.2090	210	1.098	1.133	1.200	1.289	0.641	0.1239
3	K	0.2090	210	1.098	1.129	1.200	1.281	0.626	0.1266
3	J	0.2090	200	1.098	1.126	1.200	1.275	0.611	0.1289
3	A	0.2090	210	1.096	1.109	1.198	1.229	0.606	0.1275
4	P	0.2636	190	1.385	1.423	1.514	1.616	0.671	0.1241
4	N	0.2636	180	1.385	1.420	1.514	1.610	0.655	0.1274
4	D	0.2636	190	1.382	1.399	1.511	1.542	0.628	0.1256
4	A	0.2636	180	1.382	1.395	1.511	1.545	0.620	0.1310

Data for Copperweld Composite Cables (*Continued*)

Hard-drawn copper equivalent area, AWG or MCM	Type	D-c resistance at 20°C (68°F), ohms per 1,000 ft	Approxi-mate current rating at 60 cps amp	Resistance per conductor, ohms per mile				Reactance per conductor per mile at 60 cps 1-ft spacing	
				At 25°C (77°F)		At 50°C (122°F)		Inductive x_L, ohms	Capacitive x_C, megohms
				D-c	60 cps	D-c	60 cps		
5	P	0.3291	160	1.747	1.785	1.909	2.02	0.685	0.1275
5	D	0.3291	160	1.742	1.759	1.905	1.939	0.642	0.1290
5	A	0.3291	160	1.742	1.755	1.905	1.941	0.634	0.1345
6	D	0.4150	140	2.20	2.22	2.40	2.44	0.656	0.1325
6	A	0.4150	140	2.20	2.21	2.40	2.44	0.648	0.1379
6	C	0.4150	130	2.20	2.21	2.40	2.44	0.651	0.1386
7	D	0.5232	120	2.77	2.79	3.03	3.07	0.670	0.1359
7	A	0.5232	120	2.77	2.78	3.03	3.07	0.658	0.1388
8	D	0.6598	110	3.49	3.51	3.82	3.86	0.684	0.1393
8	A	0.6598	100	3.49	3.51	3.82	3.87	0.672	0.1422
8	C	0.6598	100	3.49	3.51	3.82	3.86	0.679	0.1453
9½	D	0.9170	85	4.91	4.93	5.37	5.42	0.712	0.1462

75. Resistance of Aluminum Cable, Steel-reinforced

A-c resistance, ohms per mile of single conductor at 25°C

Size, 1,000 cir mils or AWG (B&S) aluminum	No. of layers of alum. over steel core	No. of wires Alum.	No. of wires Steel	Copper equiv., cir. mils or AWG based on copper 97%, alum. 61%	D-c resistance, ohms per mile at 0 amp and 25°C	200 amp per sq in. 25 cycles	200 amp per sq in. 50 cycles	200 amp per sq in. 60 cycles	400 amp per sq in. 25 cycles	400 amp per sq in. 50 cycles	400 amp per sq in. 60 cycles	800 amp per sq in. 25 cycles	800 amp per sq in. 50 cycles	800 amp per sq in. 60 cycles	1,000 amp per sq in. 25 cycles	1,000 amp per sq in. 50 cycles	1,000 amp per sq in. 60 cycles	1,400 amp per sq in. 25 cycles	1,400 amp per sq in. 50 cycles	1,400 amp per sq in. 60 cycles
1,590 MCM	3	54	19	1,000,000	0.0587	0.0589	0.0592	0.0594	0.0590	0.0595	0.0598	0.0595	0.0611	0.0619	0.0600	0.0625	0.0638	0.0615	0.0670	0.0698
1,510.5	3	54	19	950,000	0.0618	0.0620	0.0623	0.0625	0.0621	0.0626	0.0629	0.0626	0.0642	0.0650	0.0630	0.0655	0.0668	0.0545	0.0698	0.0726
1,431	3	54	19	900,000	0.0652	0.0654	0.0658	0.0659	0.0655	0.0661	0.0663	0.0660	0.0676	0.0684	0.0665	0.0690	0.0703	0.0678	0.0730	0.0756
1,351.5	3	54	19	850,000	0.0691	0.0693	0.0696	0.0698	0.0694	0.0699	0.0702	0.0698	0.0713	0.0721	0.0703	0.0728	0.0740	0.0715	0.0765	0.0790
1,272	3	54	19	800,000	0.0734	0.0736	0.0740	0.0742	0.0737	0.0743	0.0746	0.0741	0.0756	0.0764	0.0746	0.0770	0.0782	0.0757	0.0805	0.0829
1,192.5	3	54	19	750,000	0.0783	0.0785	0.0789	0.0791	0.0786	0.0792	0.0795	0.0790	0.0804	0.0812	0.0794	0.0818	0.0830	0.0805	0.0851	0.0874
1,113	3	54	19	700,000	0.0839	0.0841	0.0845	0.0848	0.0842	0.0849	0.0852	0.0846	0.0860	0.0867	0.0850	0.0873	0.0885	0.0860	0.0904	0.0927
1,033.5	3	54	7	650,000	0.0903	0.0906	0.0910	0.0913	0.0907	0.0913	0.0917	0.0910	0.0924	0.0931	0.0914	0.0935	0.0945	0.0924	0.0967	0.0988
954	3	54	7	600,000	0.0979	0.0980	0.0983	0.0985	0.0981	0.0986	0.0989	0.0986	0.100	0.101	0.0990	0.101	0.102	0.0998	0.104	0.106
900	3	54	7	566,000	0.104	0.104	0.104	0.105	0.104	0.105	0.105	0.104	0.106	0.107	0.105	0.107	0.108	0.106	0.110	0.112
874.5	3	54	7	550,000	0.107	0.107	0.107	0.108	0.107	0.108	0.109	0.107	0.109	0.110	0.108	0.110	0.111	0.109	0.113	0.115
795	3	54	7	500,000	0.117	0.118	0.119	0.119	0.118	0.119	0.119	0.118	0.119	0.120	0.118	0.120	0.121	0.119	0.123	0.125
795	2	26	7	500,000	0.117	0.117	0.117	0.117	0.117	0.117	0.117	0.117	0.117	0.117	0.117	0.117	0.117	0.117	0.117	0.117
795	2	30	19	500,000	0.117	0.117	0.117	0.117	0.117	0.117	0.117	0.117	0.117	0.117	0.117	0.117	0.117	0.117	0.117	0.117
715.5	3	54	7	450,000	0.131	0.131	0.132	0.133	0.131	0.132	0.133	0.131	0.133	0.133	0.131	0.133	0.134	0.133	0.137	0.139
715.5	2	26	7	450,000	0.131	0.131	0.131	0.131	0.131	0.131	0.131	0.131	0.131	0.131	0.131	0.131	0.131	0.131	0.131	0.131
715.5	2	30	19	450,000	0.131	0.131	0.131	0.131	0.131	0.131	0.131	0.131	0.131	0.131	0.131	0.131	0.131	0.131	0.131	0.131
666.6	3	54	7	419,000	0.140	0.140	0.141	0.142	0.140	0.141	0.142	0.141	0.143	0.143	0.141	0.143	0.144	0.142	0.146	0.148
636	3	54	7	400,000	0.147	0.147	0.148	0.149	0.147	0.148	0.149	0.148	0.149	0.150	0.148	0.151	0.152	0.149	0.153	0.156
636	2	26	7	400,000	0.147	0.147	0.147	0.147	0.147	0.147	0.147	0.147	0.147	0.147	0.147	0.147	0.147	0.147	0.147	0.147
636	2	30	19	400,000	0.147	0.147	0.147	0.147	0.147	0.147	0.147	0.147	0.147	0.147	0.147	0.147	0.147	0.147	0.147	0.147
605	3	54	7	380,500	0.154	0.155	0.155	0.156	0.155	0.156	0.156	0.155	0.157	0.158	0.156	0.159	0.160	0.157	0.161	0.163
605	2	26	7	380,500	0.154	0.154	0.154	0.154	0.154	0.154	0.154	0.154	0.154	0.154	0.154	0.154	0.154	0.154	0.154	0.154
556.5	2	26	7	350,000	0.168	0.168	0.168	0.168	0.168	0.168	0.168	0.168	0.168	0.168	0.168	0.168	0.168	0.168	0.168	0.168
556.5	2	30	7	350,000	0.168	0.168	0.168	0.168	0.168	0.168	0.168	0.168	0.168	0.168	0.168	0.168	0.168	0.168	0.168	0.168

Size						1	2	3	4	5	6	7	8	9	10	11	12	13	14	15
500 MCM	2	30	7	314,500		0.187	0.187	0.187	0.187	0.187	0.187	0.187	0.187	0.187	0.187	0.187	0.187	0.187	0.187	0.187
477	2	26	7	300,000		0.196	0.196	0.196	0.196	0.196	0.196	0.196	0.196	0.196	0.196	0.196	0.196	0.196	0.196	0.196
477	2	30	7	300,000		0.196	0.196	0.196	0.196	0.196	0.196	0.196	0.196	0.196	0.196	0.196	0.196	0.196	0.196	0.196
397.5	2	26	7	250,000		0.235	0.235	0.235	0.235	0.235	0.235	0.235	0.235	0.235	0.235	0.235	0.235	0.235	0.235	0.235
397.5	2	30	7	250,000		0.235	0.235	0.235	0.235	0.235	0.235	0.235	0.235	0.235	0.235	0.235	0.235	0.235	0.235	0.235
336.4	2	26	7	4/0		0.278	0.278	0.278	0.278	0.278	0.278	0.278	0.278	0.278	0.278	0.278	0.278	0.278	0.278	0.278
336.4	2	30	7	4/0		0.278	0.278	0.278	0.278	0.278	0.278	0.278	0.278	0.278	0.278	0.278	0.278	0.278	0.278	0.278
300	2	26	7	188,700		0.311	0.311	0.311	0.311	0.311	0.311	0.311	0.311	0.311	0.311	0.311	0.311	0.311	0.311	0.311
300	2	30	7	188,700		0.311	0.311	0.311	0.311	0.311	0.311	0.311	0.311	0.311	0.311	0.311	0.311	0.311	0.311	0.311
266.8	2	26	7	3/0		0.350	0.350	0.350	0.350	0.350	0.350	0.350	0.350	0.350	0.350	0.350	0.350	0.350	0.350	0.350
266.8 AWG	1	6	7	3/0		0.489	0.454	0.384	0.425	0.406	0.368	0.388	0.378	0.359	0.355	0.353	0.351	0.352	0.351	0.350
4/0	1	6	1	2/0		0.548	0.521	0.468	0.510	0.493	0.458	0.485	0.474	0.452	0.453	0.450	0.444	0.446	0.445	0.443
3/0	1	6	1	1/0		0.647	0.624	0.579	0.611	0.597	0.570	0.594	0.584	0.566	0.569	0.566	0.560	0.561	0.560	0.556
2/0	1	6	1	1		0.777	0.758	0.720	0.739	0.730	0.711	0.727	0.721	0.708	0.712	0.709	0.704	0.707	0.705	0.703
1/0	1	6	1	2		0.941	0.927	0.898	0.907	0.901	0.890	0.899	0.895	0.888	0.892	0.890	0.886	0.889	0.888	0.885
1	1	6	1	3		1.17	1.16	1.13	1.13	1.13	1.12	1.12	1.12	1.12	1.12	1.12	1.12	1.12	1.12	1.12
2	1	6	1	4		1.45	1.44	1.42	1.42	1.42	1.41	1.41	1.41	1.41	1.41	1.41	1.41	1.41	1.41	1.41
3	1	6	1	5		1.80	1.80	1.78	1.78	1.78	1.78	1.78	1.78	1.78	1.78	1.78	1.78	1.78	1.78	1.78
4	1	6	1	6		2.24	2.24	2.24	2.24	2.24	2.24	2.24	2.24	2.24	2.24	2.24	2.24	2.24	2.24	2.24
5	1	6	1	7		2.82	2.82	2.82	2.82	2.82	2.82	2.82	2.82	2.82	2.82	2.82	2.82	2.82	2.82	2.82
6	1	6	1	8		3.56	3.56	3.56	3.56	3.56	3.56	3.56	3.56	3.56	3.56	3.56	3.56	3.56	3.56	3.56
203 MCM	1	8	7	127,700		0.524	0.509	0.477	0.483	0.477	0.466	0.472	0.469	0.463	0.463	0.462	0.461	0.461	0.461	0.460
203.2	1	16	19	127,800		0.524	0.509	0.477	0.483	0.477	0.466	0.472	0.469	0.463	0.463	0.462	0.461	0.461	0.461	0.460
211.3	1	12	7	132,900		0.503	0.487	0.458	0.464	0.459	0.448	0.453	0.451	0.445	0.445	0.444	0.443	0.443	0.443	0.442
190.8	1	12	7	120,000		0.558	0.542	0.508	0.515	0.509	0.497	0.502	0.499	0.493	0.493	0.492	0.491	0.491	0.491	0.490
176.9	1	12	7	111,200		0.601	0.584	0.548	0.555	0.548	0.535	0.541	0.538	0.532	0.531	0.530	0.529	0.529	0.529	0.528
159	1	12	7	100,000		0.669	0.649	0.609	0.617	0.610	0.595	0.602	0.598	0.591	0.590	0.589	0.588	0.588	0.588	0.587
134.6	1	12	7	84,600		0.790	0.767	0.720	0.729	0.721	0.703	0.711	0.707	0.699	0.699	0.698	0.695	0.695	0.695	0.694
110.8	1	12	7	69,600		0.960	0.932	0.874	0.886	0.876	0.855	0.864	0.859	0.849	0.850	0.848	0.845	0.845	0.845	0.843
101.8	1	12	7	64,160		1.044	1.008	0.951	0.963	0.952	0.929	0.940	0.934	0.923	0.923	0.922	0.919	0.919	0.919	0.918
80	1	8	1	50,310		1.223	1.214	1.184	1.181	1.178	1.176	1.172	1.172	1.171	1.170	1.170	1.170	1.170	1.170	1.170

See notes following Table 76.

76. Direct-current Resistance for All-aluminum Wire

Size, cir mils	Ohms per mile at 25°C for 61% conductivity	Size, AWG	Size, cir mils	Ohms per mile at 25°C for 61% conductivity
1,590,000	0.0587	...	500,000	0.187
1,150,000	0.0618	...	477,000	0.196
1,431,000	0.0652	...	397,500	0.235
1,351,500	0.0691	...	3:6,400	0.278
1,272,000	0.0734	...	300,000	0.311
1,192,500	0.0783	...	266,800	0.350
1,113,000	0.0839	4/0	211,600	0.441
1,033,500	0.0903	3/0	167,806	0.556
954,000	0.0979	2/0	133,077	0.702
874,500	0.107	1/0	105,535	0.885
795,000	0.117	1	83,693	1.12
750,000	0.124	2	66,371	1.41
715,500	0.131	3	52,635	1.78
636,000	0.147	4	41,741	2.24
556,500	0.168			

NOTES:

1. The d-c resistances are based on aluminum of 61 per cent conductivity. For stranded conductors, the resistances are 2 per cent greater than the equivalent solid conductor. This allows for increase of length due to an average length of lay as recommended by the Institute of Electrical and Electronic Engineers.

2. In computing the resistances of aluminum cable, steel-reinforced, no deduction is made for the conductance of the steel core.

3. The a-c resistances are based on calculations developed from actual tests.

4. No allowance has been made for increased length because of sag when the conductors are suspended.

77. Reactance of Single-conductor, Standard-strand, and Three-conductor Cables without Magnetic Binder (for Small Spacings)

Ohms per 1,000 ft to Neutral—at 60 cycles. (General Electric Co.)

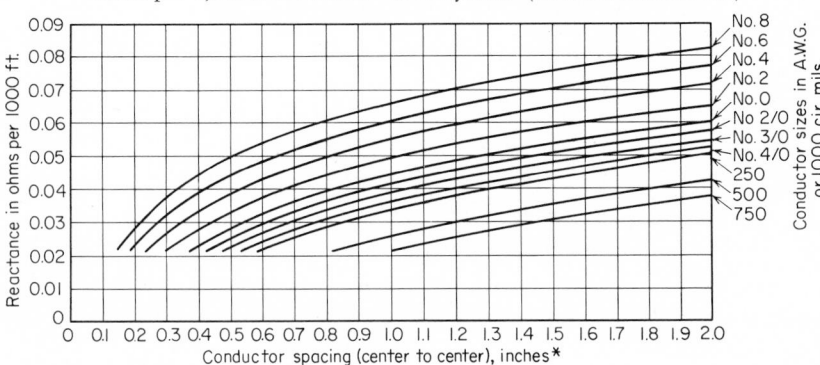

*See table 57

78. Reactance of Single-conductor, Standard-strand, and Three-conductor Cables without Magnetic Binder (for Large Spacings)

Ohms per 1,000 ft to Neutral — at 60 cycles.   (General Electric Co.)

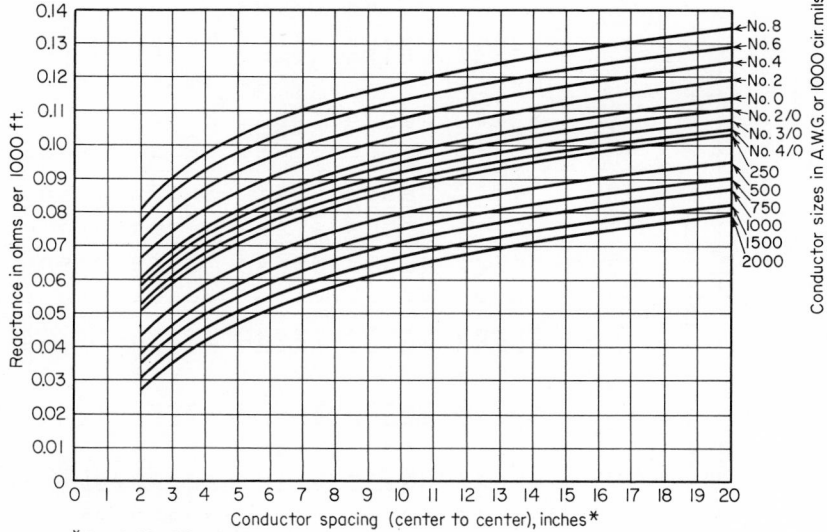

*See table 57

79. Reactance of Single-conductor, Annular Cables

Ohms per 1,000 ft to Neutral — at 60 cycles.   (General Electric Co.)

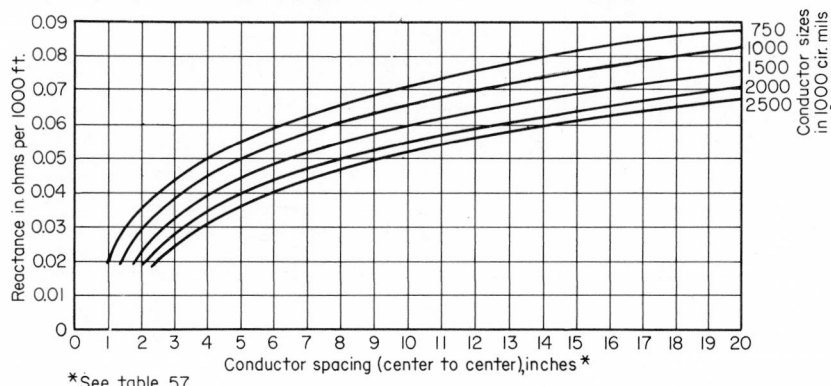

*See table 57

80. Twenty-five-cycle Reactance per Mile Stranded-copper Conductors Overhead Transmission Lines

(From Nesbit, "Electrical Characteristics of Transmission Circuits")

25-cycle reactance x, ohms per mile, of each conductor of a single-phase, two-phase, or three-phase circuit. (See footnotes)

Circular mils	American wire gage (B&S)	Number of wires	Outside diam, in.	2 in. (5.1 cm)	4 in. (10.2 cm)	6 in. (15.2 cm)	8 in. (20.3 cm)	10 in. (25.4 cm)	12 in. (30.5 cm)	15 in. (38.1 cm)	18 in. (45.7 cm)	21 in. (53.3 cm)	24 in. (61.0 cm)	27 in. (68.6 cm)	30 in. (76.2 cm)	33 in. (83.8 cm)	36 in. (91.4 cm)
2,000,000	...	127	1.631	0.0582	0.0932	0.114	0.128	0.140	0.149	0.160	0.169	0.177	0.184	0.190	0.195	0.200	0.204
1,900,000	...	127	1.590	0.0595	0.0945	0.115	0.130	0.141	0.150	0.161	0.171	0.178	0.185	0.191	0.196	0.201	0.206
1,800,000	...	127	1.548	0.0609	0.0959	0.116	0.131	0.142	0.151	0.163	0.172	0.180	0.186	0.192	0.198	0.203	0.207
1,700,000	...	127	1.504	0.0623	0.0973	0.118	0.132	0.144	0.153	0.164	0.173	0.181	0.188	0.194	0.199	0.204	0.208
1,600,000	...	127	1.459	0.0638	0.0989	0.119	0.134	0.145	0.154	0.166	0.175	0.183	0.189	0.195	0.201	0.206	0.210
1,500,000	...	91	1.412	0.0656	0.100	0.121	0.136	0.147	0.156	0.167	0.177	0.184	0.191	0.197	0.202	0.207	0.212
1,400,000	...	91	1.364	0.0673	0.102	0.123	0.137	0.149	0.158	0.169	0.178	0.186	0.193	0.199	0.204	0.209	0.213
1,300,000	...	91	1.315	0.0692	0.104	0.125	0.139	0.151	0.160	0.171	0.180	0.188	0.195	0.201	0.206	0.211	0.215
1,200,000	...	91	1.263	0.0712	0.106	0.127	0.141	0.153	0.162	0.173	0.182	0.190	0.197	0.203	0.208	0.213	0.217
1,100,000	...	91	1.209	0.0734	0.108	0.129	0.144	0.155	0.164	0.175	0.185	0.192	0.199	0.205	0.210	0.215	0.220
1,000,000	...	61	1.152	0.0760	0.111	0.132	0.146	0.157	0.167	0.178	0.187	0.195	0.202	0.208	0.213	0.218	0.222
950,000	...	61	1.123	0.0773	0.112	0.133	0.147	0.159	0.168	0.179	0.188	0.196	0.203	0.209	0.214	0.219	0.223
900,000	...	61	1.093	0.0787	0.114	0.134	0.149	0.160	0.169	0.181	0.190	0.198	0.204	0.210	0.216	0.220	0.225
850,000	...	61	1.062	0.0801	0.115	0.136	0.150	0.161	0.171	0.182	0.191	0.199	0.206	0.212	0.217	0.222	0.226
800,000	...	61	1.031	0.0816	0.117	0.137	0.152	0.163	0.172	0.184	0.193	0.201	0.207	0.213	0.219	0.223	0.228
750,000	...	61	0.998	0.0833	0.118	0.139	0.153	0.165	0.174	0.185	0.194	0.202	0.209	0.215	0.220	0.225	0.229
700,000	...	61	0.964	0.0850	0.120	0.141	0.155	0.166	0.176	0.187	0.196	0.204	0.211	0.217	0.222	0.227	0.231
650,000	...	61	0.929	0.0869	0.122	0.142	0.157	0.168	0.177	0.189	0.198	0.206	0.213	0.218	0.224	0.229	0.233
600,000	...	37	0.891	0.0893	0.124	0.145	0.159	0.171	0.180	0.191	0.200	0.208	0.215	0.221	0.226	0.231	0.235
550,000	...	37	0.853	0.0915	0.127	0.147	0.162	0.173	0.182	0.193	0.203	0.210	0.217	0.223	0.228	0.233	0.238
500,000	...	37	0.814	0.0939	0.129	0.149	0.164	0.175	0.184	0.196	0.205	0.213	0.220	0.225	0.231	0.236	0.240
450,000	...	37	0.772	0.0965	0.132	0.152	0.167	0.178	0.187	0.198	0.208	0.215	0.222	0.228	0.233	0.238	0.243
400,000	...	19	0.725	0.100	0.135	0.156	0.170	0.182	0.191	0.202	0.211	0.219	0.226	0.232	0.237	0.242	0.246
350,000	...	19	0.679	0.104	0.139	0.159	0.174	0.185	0.194	0.206	0.215	0.223	0.229	0.235	0.241	0.245	0.250
300,000	...	19	0.628	0.108	0.143	0.163	0.178	0.189	0.198	0.209	0.219	0.227	0.233	0.239	0.245	0.249	0.254

Distance D between centers of conductors[a]

Size of conductor

Twenty-five-cycle Reactance per Mile Stranded-copper Conductors Overhead Transmission Lines (Continued)

25-cycle reactance x, ohms per mile, of each conductor of a single-phase, two-phase, or three-phase circuit. (See footnotes)

| Size of conductor | | Number of wires | Outside diam, in. | Distance D between centers of conductors[a] | | | | | | | | | | | | | |
Circular mils	American wire gage (B&S)			2 in. (5.1 cm)	4 in. (10.2 cm)	6 in. (15.2 cm)	8 in. (20.3 cm)	10 in. (25.4 cm)	12 in. (30.5 cm)	15 in. (38.1 cm)	18 in. (45.7 cm)	21 in. (53.3 cm)	24 in. (61.0 cm)	27 in. (68.6 cm)	30 in. (76.2 cm)	33 in. (83.8 cm)	36 in. (91.4 cm)
250,000	....	19	0.574	0.112	0.147	0.168	0.182	0.194	0.203	0.214	0.223	0.231	0.238	0.244	0.249	0.254	0.258
211,600	0000	7	0.522	0.119	0.154	0.175	0.189	0.201	0.210	0.221	0.230	0.238	0.245	0.251	0.256	0.261	0.265
167,806	000	7	0.464	0.125	0.160	0.181	0.195	0.206	0.216	0.227	0.236	0.244	0.251	0.257	0.262	0.267	0.271
133,077	00	7	0.414	0.131	0.166	0.186	0.201	0.212	0.222	0.233	0.242	0.250	0.257	0.263	0.268	0.273	0.277
105,535	0	7	0.368	0.137	0.172	0.192	0.207	0.218	0.227	0.239	0.248	0.256	0.262	0.268	0.274	0.279	0.283
83,693	1	7	0.328	0.143	0.178	0.198	0.213	0.224	0.233	0.245	0.254	0.262	0.268	0.274	0.280	0.284	0.289
66,371	2	7	0.292	0.149	0.184	0.204	0.219	0.230	0.239	0.250	0.260	0.267	0.274	0.280	0.285	0.290	0.295
52,635	3	7	0.260	0.154	0.189	0.210	0.224	0.236	0.245	0.256	0.265	0.273	0.280	0.286	0.291	0.296	0.301
41,741	4	7	0.232	0.160	0.195	0.216	0.230	0.242	0.251	0.262	0.271	0.279	0.286	0.292	0.297	0.302	0.306
33,102	5	7	0.206	0.166	0.201	0.222	0.236	0.247	0.257	0.268	0.277	0.285	0.292	0.298	0.303	0.308	0.312
26,251	6	7	0.184	0.172	0.207	0.228	0.242	0.253	0.263	0.274	0.283	0.291	0.298	0.304	0.309	0.314	0.318

The table values were derived from the equation $x = 2\pi f L$, in which x is the reactance in ohms; L is the inductance in henrys per mile of single conductor; and f is the frequency. The reactance at any other frequency than 25 cycles is $f/25$ times the table values.

The reactance x' at any spacing D' not given in the table is equal to the reactance x at the *next smaller* spacing D given in the table plus the quantity $0.1164 \log_{10} D'/D$. Thus $x' = x + 0.1164 \log_{10} D'/D$. Or the reactance in ohms to be added to that at the next smaller spacing may be taken from table below.

D'/D	1.05	1.10	1.15	1.20	1.25	1.30	1.35	1.40	1.45	1.50	1.55	1.60	1.65	1.70	1.75	1.80	1.85	1.90	1.95	2.00
$x+$	0.002	0.005	0.007	0.009	0.011	0.013	0.015	0.017	0.019	0.020	0.022	0.024	0.025	0.027	0.028	0.030	0.031	0.032	0.034	0.035

[a] For any three-phase arrangement of conductors $D = \sqrt[3]{ABC}$. This resolves itself into $D = A$, B or C for symmetrical triangular spacing and into $D = 1.26\ A$ or B for regular flat spacing, it being immaterial whether the conductors are in a horizontal or vertical plane.

Unsymmetrical triangular spacing

Symmetrical triangular spacing

Irregular flat spacing

Regular flat spacing

Twenty-five-cycle Reactance per Mile Stranded-copper Conductors Overhead Transmission Lines (*Continued*)

25-cycle reactance x, ohms per mile, of each conductor of a single-phase, two-phase or three-phase circuit.   (See footnotes)

Circular mils	American wire gage (B&S)	3.5 ft (1.07 m)	4 ft (1.22 m)	5 ft (1.52 m)	6 ft (1.83 m)	7 ft (2.13 m)	8 ft (2.44 m)	9 ft (2.74 m)	11 ft (3.35 m)	13 ft (3.96 m)	15 ft (4.57 m)	17 ft (5.18 m)	19 ft (5.79 m)	21 ft (6.40 m)	23 ft (7.01 m)	25 ft (7.62 m)	30 ft (9.14 m)	35 ft (10.67 m)
																	Distance D between centers of conductors^a	
2,000,000	....	0.212	0.219	0.230	0.239	0.247	0.254	0.260	0.270	0.278	0.286	0.292	0.298	0.303	0.307	0.312	0.321	0.329
1,900,000	....	0.213	0.220	0.231	0.241	0.248	0.255	0.261	0.271	0.280	0.287	0.293	0.299	0.304	0.309	0.313	0.322	0.330
1,800,000	....	0.215	0.222	0.233	0.242	0.250	0.257	0.263	0.273	0.281	0.288	0.295	0.300	0.305	0.310	0.314	0.323	0.331
1,700,000	....	0.216	0.223	0.234	0.243	0.251	0.258	0.264	0.274	0.283	0.290	0.296	0.302	0.307	0.311	0.316	0.325	0.333
1,600,000	....	0.218	0.225	0.236	0.245	0.253	0.260	0.266	0.276	0.284	0.291	0.298	0.303	0.308	0.313	0.317	0.326	0.334
1,500,000	....	0.219	0.226	0.238	0.247	0.255	0.261	0.267	0.277	0.286	0.293	0.299	0.305	0.310	0.315	0.319	0.328	0.336
1,400,000	....	0.221	0.228	0.239	0.248	0.256	0.263	0.269	0.279	0.288	0.295	0.301	0.307	0.312	0.316	0.321	0.330	0.338
1,300,000	....	0.223	0.230	0.241	0.250	0.258	0.265	0.271	0.281	0.289	0.297	0.303	0.309	0.314	0.318	0.323	0.332	0.340
1,200,000	....	0.225	0.232	0.243	0.252	0.260	0.267	0.273	0.283	0.291	0.299	0.305	0.311	0.316	0.320	0.325	0.334	0.342
1,100,000	....	0.227	0.234	0.245	0.255	0.262	0.269	0.275	0.285	0.294	0.301	0.307	0.313	0.318	0.323	0.327	0.336	0.344
1,000,000	....	0.230	0.237	0.248	0.257	0.265	0.272	0.278	0.288	0.296	0.304	0.310	0.315	0.321	0.325	0.329	0.339	0.346
950,000	....	0.231	0.238	0.249	0.258	0.266	0.273	0.279	0.289	0.298	0.305	0.311	0.317	0.322	0.326	0.331	0.340	0.348
900,000	....	0.233	0.239	0.251	0.260	0.268	0.274	0.280	0.290	0.299	0.306	0.313	0.318	0.323	0.328	0.332	0.341	0.349
850,000	....	0.234	0.241	0.252	0.261	0.269	0.276	0.282	0.292	0.300	0.308	0.314	0.320	0.325	0.329	0.333	0.343	0.350
800,000	....	0.236	0.242	0.254	0.263	0.271	0.277	0.283	0.293	0.302	0.309	0.315	0.321	0.326	0.331	0.335	0.344	0.352
750,000	....	0.237	0.244	0.255	0.264	0.272	0.279	0.285	0.295	0.304	0.311	0.317	0.323	0.328	0.332	0.337	0.346	0.354
700,000	....	0.239	0.246	0.257	0.266	0.274	0.281	0.287	0.297	0.305	0.313	0.319	0.324	0.330	0.334	0.338	0.348	0.355
650,000	....	0.241	0.248	0.259	0.268	0.276	0.283	0.289	0.299	0.307	0.314	0.321	0.326	0.331	0.336	0.340	0.349	0.357
600,000	....	0.243	0.250	0.261	0.270	0.278	0.285	0.291	0.301	0.310	0.317	0.323	0.329	0.334	0.338	0.343	0.352	0.360
550,000	....	0.245	0.252	0.263	0.273	0.280	0.287	0.293	0.303	0.312	0.319	0.325	0.331	0.336	0.341	0.345	0.354	0.362
500,000	....	0.248	0.255	0.266	0.275	0.283	0.290	0.296	0.306	0.314	0.321	0.328	0.333	0.338	0.343	0.347	0.356	0.364
450,000	....	0.250	0.257	0.269	0.278	0.286	0.292	0.298	0.308	0.317	0.324	0.330	0.336	0.341	0.346	0.350	0.359	0.367
400,000	....	0.254	0.261	0.272	0.282	0.289	0.296	0.302	0.312	0.321	0.328	0.334	0.340	0.345	0.349	0.354	0.363	0.371
350,000	....	0.258	0.264	0.276	0.285	0.293	0.299	0.305	0.316	0.324	0.331	0.338	0.343	0.348	0.353	0.357	0.366	0.374
300,000	....	0.262	0.268	0.280	0.289	0.297	0.303	0.309	0.319	0.328	0.335	0.341	0.347	0.352	0.357	0.361	0.370	0.378

Twenty-five-cycle Reactance per Mile Stranded-copper Conductors Overhead Transmission Lines (*Continued*)

25-cycle reactance x, ohms per mile, of each conductor of a single-phase, two-phase or three-phase circuit. (See footnotes)

Size of conductor		Distance D between centers of conductors[a]																
Circular mils	American wire gage (B&S)	3.5 ft (1.07 m)	4 ft (1.22 m)	5 ft (1.52 m)	6 ft (1.83 m)	7 ft (2.13 m)	8 ft (2.44 m)	9 ft (2.74 m)	11 ft (3.35 m)	13 ft (3.96 m)	15 ft (4.57 m)	17 ft (5.18 m)	19 ft (5.79 m)	21 ft (6.40 m)	23 ft (7.01 m)	25 ft (7.62 m)	30 ft (9.14 m)	35 ft (10.67 m)
250,000	....	0.266	0.273	0.284	0.293	0.301	0.308	0.314	0.324	0.333	0.340	0.346	0.352	0.357	0.361	0.366	0.375	0.383
211,600	0000	0.273	0.280	0.291	0.300	0.308	0.315	0.321	0.331	0.340	0.347	0.353	0.359	0.364	0.368	0.373	0.382	0.390
167,806	000	0.279	0.286	0.297	0.306	0.314	0.321	0.327	0.337	0.345	0.353	0.359	0.365	0.370	0.374	0.378	0.388	0.395
133,077	00	0.285	0.292	0.303	0.312	0.320	0.327	0.333	0.343	0.351	0.358	0.365	0.370	0.375	0.380	0.384	0.394	0.401
105,535	0	0.291	0.297	0.309	0.318	0.326	0.333	0.338	0.349	0.357	0.364	0.371	0.376	0.381	0.386	0.390	0.399	0.407
83,693	1	0.297	0.303	0.315	0.324	0.332	0.338	0.344	0.354	0.363	0.370	0.377	0.382	0.387	0.392	0.396	0.405	0.413
66,371	2	0.302	0.309	0.321	0.330	0.338	0.344	0.350	0.360	0.369	0.376	0.382	0.388	0.393	0.398	0.402	0.411	0.419
52,635	3	0.308	0.315	0.326	0.336	0.343	0.350	0.356	0.366	0.375	0.382	0.388	0.394	0.399	0.404	0.408	0.417	0.425
41,741	4	0.314	0.321	0.332	0.341	0.349	0.356	0.362	0.372	0.381	0.388	0.394	0.400	0.405	0.409	0.414	0.423	0.431
33,102	5	0.320	0.327	0.338	0.347	0.355	0.362	0.368	0.378	0.386	0.394	0.400	0.406	0.411	0.415	0.419	0.429	0.436
26,251	6	0.326	0.333	0.344	0.353	0.361	0.368	0.374	0.384	0.392	0.399	0.406	0.411	0.417	0.421	0.425	0.435	0.442

The table values were derived from the equation $x = 2\pi f L$, in which x is the reactance in ohms; L is the inductance in henrys per mile of single conductor; and f is the frequency. The reactance at any other frequency than 25 cycles is $f/25$ times the table values.

The reactance x' at any spacing D' not given in the table is equal to the reactance x at the *next smaller* spacing D given in the table plus the quantity $0.1164 \log_{10} D'/D$. Thus $x' = x + 0.1164 \log_{10} D'/D$. Or the reactance in ohms to be added to that at the next smaller spacing may be taken from table below.

D'/D	1.05	1.10	1.15	1.20	1.25	1.30	1.35	1.40	1.45	1.50	1.55	1.60	1.65	1.70	1.75	1.80	1.85	1.90	1.95	2.00
$x+$	0.002	0.005	0.007	0.009	0.011	0.013	0.015	0.017	0.019	0.020	0.022	0.024	0.025	0.027	0.028	0.030	0.031	0.032	0.034	0.035

[a] For any three-phase arrangement of conductors $D = \sqrt[3]{ABC}$. This resolves itself into $D = A$, B or C for symmetrical triangular spacing and into $D = 1.26\,A$ or B for regular flat spacing, it being immaterial whether the conductors are in a horizontal or vertical plane.

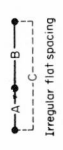

Unsymmetrical triangular spacing

Symmetrical triangular spacing

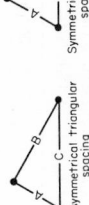

Irregular flat spacing

Regular flat spacing

81. Sixty-cycle Reactance per Mile Stranded-copper Conductors Overhead Transmission Lines
(From Nesbit, "Electrical Characteristics of Transmission Circuits")

60-cycle reactance x, ohms per mile, of each conductor of a single-phase, two-phase, or three-phase circuit. (See footnotes)

Distance D between centers of conductors[a]

Circular mils	American wire gage (B&S)	Number of wires	Outside diameter, in.	2 in. (5.1 cm)	4 in. (10.2 cm)	6 in. (15.2 cm)	8 in. (20.3 cm)	10 in. (25.4 cm)	12 in. (30.5 cm)	15 in. (38.1 cm)	18 in. (45.7 cm)	21 in. (53.3 cm)	24 in. (61.0 cm)	27 in. (68.6 cm)	30 in. (76.2 cm)	33 in. (83.8 cm)	36 in. (91.4 cm)
2,000,000	....	127	1.631	0.140	0.224	0.273	0.308	0.335	0.357	0.384	0.406	0.425	0.441	0.455	0.468	0.480	0.490
1,900,000	....	127	1.590	0.143	0.227	0.276	0.311	0.338	0.360	0.387	0.409	0.428	0.444	0.459	0.471	0.483	0.494
1,800,000	....	127	1.548	0.146	0.230	0.279	0.314	0.341	0.363	0.391	0.413	0.431	0.448	0.462	0.475	0.486	0.497
1,700,000	....	127	1.504	0.150	0.234	0.283	0.318	0.345	0.367	0.394	0.416	0.435	0.451	0.465	0.478	0.490	0.500
1,600,000	....	127	1.459	0.153	0.237	0.287	0.321	0.349	0.371	0.398	0.420	0.439	0.455	0.469	0.482	0.493	0.504
1,500,000	....	91	1.412	0.157	0.241	0.291	0.326	0.353	0.375	0.402	0.424	0.443	0.459	0.473	0.486	0.498	0.508
1,400,000	....	91	1.364	0.162	0.246	0.295	0.330	0.357	0.379	0.406	0.428	0.447	0.463	0.477	0.490	0.502	0.512
1,300,000	....	91	1.315	0.166	0.250	0.299	0.334	0.361	0.383	0.411	0.433	0.451	0.468	0.482	0.495	0.506	0.517
1,200,000	....	91	1.263	0.171	0.255	0.304	0.339	0.366	0.388	0.415	0.438	0.456	0.472	0.487	0.500	0.511	0.522
1,100,000	....	91	1.209	0.176	0.260	0.309	0.344	0.371	0.394	0.421	0.443	0.461	0.478	0.492	0.505	0.516	0.527
1,000,000	....	61	1.152	0.182	0.267	0.316	0.351	0.378	0.400	0.427	0.449	0.468	0.484	0.498	0.511	0.523	0.533
950,000	....	61	1.123	0.186	0.270	0.319	0.354	0.381	0.403	0.430	0.452	0.471	0.487	0.501	0.514	0.526	0.536
900,000	....	61	1.093	0.189	0.273	0.322	0.357	0.384	0.406	0.433	0.455	0.474	0.490	0.505	0.517	0.529	0.540
850,000	....	61	1.062	0.192	0.276	0.326	0.360	0.388	0.410	0.437	0.459	0.478	0.494	0.508	0.521	0.532	0.543
800,000	....	61	1.031	0.196	0.280	0.329	0.364	0.391	0.413	0.440	0.463	0.481	0.497	0.512	0.525	0.536	0.547
750,000	....	61	0.998	0.200	0.284	0.333	0.368	0.395	0.417	0.444	0.466	0.485	0.501	0.516	0.528	0.540	0.551
700,000	....	61	0.964	0.204	0.288	0.337	0.372	0.399	0.421	0.449	0.471	0.489	0.506	0.520	0.533	0.544	0.555
650,000	....	61	0.929	0.209	0.293	0.342	0.377	0.404	0.426	0.453	0.475	0.494	0.510	0.524	0.537	0.549	0.559
600,000	....	37	0.891	0.214	0.298	0.348	0.382	0.410	0.432	0.459	0.481	0.500	0.516	0.530	0.543	0.554	0.565
550,000	....	37	0.853	0.220	0.304	0.353	0.388	0.415	0.437	0.464	0.486	0.505	0.521	0.535	0.548	0.560	0.570
500,000	....	37	0.814	0.225	0.309	0.359	0.394	0.421	0.443	0.470	0.492	0.511	0.527	0.541	0.554	0.565	0.576
450,000	....	37	0.772	0.232	0.316	0.365	0.400	0.427	0.449	0.476	0.498	0.517	0.533	0.548	0.560	0.572	0.582
400,000	....	19	0.725	0.241	0.325	0.374	0.409	0.436	0.458	0.485	0.507	0.526	0.542	0.557	0.569	0.581	0.592
350,000	....	19	0.679	0.249	0.333	0.382	0.417	0.444	0.466	0.493	0.516	0.534	0.550	0.565	0.578	0.589	0.600
300,000	....	19	0.628	0.258	0.342	0.392	0.426	0.454	0.476	0.503	0.525	0.544	0.560	0.574	0.587	0.598	0.609

Sixty-cycle Reactance per Mile Stranded-copper Conductors Overhead Transmission Lines (*Continued*)

Size of conductor — Circular mils	American wire gage (B&S)	Number of wires	Outside diam, in.	2 in. (5.1 cm)	4 in. (10.2 cm)	6 in. (15.2 cm)	8 in. (20.3 cm)	10 in. (25.4 cm)	12 in. (30.5 cm)	15 in. (38.1 cm)	18 in. (45.7 cm)	21 in. (53.3 cm)	24 in. (61.0 cm)	27 in. (68.6 cm)	30 in. (76.2 cm)	33 in. (83.8 cm)	36 in. (91.4 cm)
									Distance *D* between centers of conductors[a]								
250,000	.....	19	0.574	0.269	0.353	0.403	0.438	0.465	0.487	0.514	0.536	0.555	0.571	0.585	0.598	0.610	0.620
211,600	0000	7	0.522	0.286	0.370	0.419	0.454	0.481	0.504	0.531	0.553	0.571	0.588	0.602	0.615	0.626	0.637
167,806	000	7	0.464	0.300	0.384	0.434	0.468	0.495	0.518	0.545	0.567	0.586	0.602	0.616	0.629	0.640	0.651
133,077	00	7	0.414	0.314	0.398	0.448	0.482	0.510	0.532	0.559	0.581	0.600	0.616	0.630	0.643	0.654	0.665
105,535	0	7	0.368	0.328	0.412	0.462	0.497	0.524	0.546	0.573	0.595	0.614	0.630	0.644	0.657	0.668	0.679
83,693	1	7	0.328	0.342	0.427	0.476	0.511	0.538	0.560	0.587	0.609	0.628	0.644	0.658	0.671	0.683	0.693
66,371	2	7	0.292	0.356	0.441	0.490	0.525	0.552	0.574	0.601	0.623	0.642	0.658	0.672	0.685	0.697	0.707
52,635	3	7	0.260	0.371	0.455	0.504	0.539	0.566	0.588	0.615	0.637	0.656	0.672	0.686	0.699	0.711	0.721
41,741	4	7	0.232	0.385	0.469	0.518	0.553	0.580	0.602	0.629	0.651	0.670	0.686	0.700	0.713	0.725	0.735
33,102	5	7	0.206	0.399	0.483	0.532	0.567	0.594	0.616	0.643	0.665	0.684	0.700	0.714	0.727	0.739	0.749
26,251	6	7	0.184	0.413	0.497	0.546	0.581	0.608	0.630	0.657	0.679	0.698	0.714	0.729	0.741	0.753	0.763

The table values were derived from the equation $x = 2\pi fL$, in which x is the reactance in ohms. L is the inductance in henrys per mile of single conductor and f is the frequency. The reactance at any other frequency than 60 cycles is $f/60$ times the table values.

The reactance x at any spacing D' not given in the table is equal to the reactance x at the *next smaller* spacing D given in the table plus the quantity $0.2794 \log_{10} D'/D$. Thus $x' = x + 0.2794 \log_{10} D'/D$. Or the reactance in ohms to be added to that at the next smaller spacing may be taken from table below.

D'/D	1.05	1.10	1.15	1.20	1.25	1.30	1.35	1.40	1.45	1.50	1.55	1.60	1.65	1.70	1.75	1.80	1.85	1.90	1.95	2.00
$x+$	0.006	0.012	0.017	0.022	0.027	0.032	0.036	0.041	0.045	0.049	0.053	0.057	0.061	0.064	0.068	0.071	0.075	0.078	0.081	0.084

[a] For any three-phase arrangement of conductors $D = \sqrt[3]{ABC}$. This resolves itself into $D = A$, B or C for symmetrical triangular spacing and into $D = 1.26\,A$ or B for regular flat spacing, it being immaterial whether the conductors are in a horizontal or vertical plane.

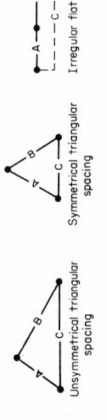

Unsymmetrical triangular spacing

Symmetrical triangular spacing

Irregular flat spacing

Regular flat spacing

Sixty-cycle Reactance per Mile Stranded-copper Conductors Overhead Transmission Lines (Continued)

60-cycle reactance x, ohms per mile, of each conductor of a single-phase, two-phase, or three-phase circuit. (See footnotes)

Distance D between centers of conductors[a]

Circular mils	American wire gage (B&S)	3.5 ft (1.07 m)	4 ft (1.22 m)	5 ft (1.52 m)	6 ft (1.83 m)	7 ft (2.13 m)	8 ft (2.44 m)	9 ft (2.74 m)	11 ft (3.35 m)	13 ft (3.96 m)	15 ft (4.57 m)	17 ft (5.16 m)	18 ft (5.79 m)	21 ft (6.40 m)	23 ft (7.01 m)	25 ft (7.62 m)	30 ft (9.14 m)	35 ft (10.67 m)
2,000,000		0.509	0.525	0.552	0.574	0.593	0.609	0.624	0.648	0.668	0.686	0.701	0.714	0.727	0.738	0.748	0.770	0.788
1,900,000		0.512	0.528	0.555	0.578	0.596	0.613	0.627	0.651	0.671	0.689	0.704	0.717	0.730	0.741	0.751	0.773	0.792
1,800,000		0.515	0.532	0.559	0.581	0.600	0.616	0.630	0.654	0.675	0.692	0.707	0.721	0.733	0.744	0.754	0.776	0.795
1,700,000		0.519	0.535	0.562	0.584	0.603	0.619	0.634	0.658	0.678	0.696	0.711	0.724	0.736	0.747	0.758	0.780	0.798
1,600,000		0.523	0.539	0.566	0.588	0.607	0.623	0.637	0.662	0.682	0.699	0.714	0.728	0.740	0.751	0.761	0.783	0.802
1,500,000		0.527	0.543	0.570	0.592	0.611	0.627	0.641	0.666	0.686	0.703	0.719	0.732	0.744	0.755	0.765	0.787	0.806
1,400,000		0.531	0.547	0.574	0.596	0.615	0.631	0.646	0.670	0.690	0.708	0.723	0.736	0.748	0.759	0.770	0.792	0.810
1,300,000		0.535	0.552	0.579	0.601	0.620	0.636	0.650	0.674	0.695	0.712	0.727	0.741	0.753	0.764	0.774	0.796	0.815
1,200,000		0.540	0.557	0.584	0.606	0.624	0.641	0.655	0.679	0.700	0.717	0.732	0.746	0.758	0.769	0.779	0.801	0.820
1,100,000		0.546	0.562	0.589	0.611	0.630	0.646	0.660	0.685	0.705	0.722	0.737	0.751	0.763	0.774	0.784	0.806	0.825
1,000,000		0.552	0.568	0.595	0.617	0.636	0.652	0.666	0.691	0.711	0.728	0.744	0.757	0.769	0.780	0.790	0.813	0.831
950,000		0.555	0.571	0.598	0.620	0.639	0.655	0.670	0.694	0.714	0.732	0.747	0.760	0.772	0.783	0.794	0.816	0.834
900,000		0.558	0.574	0.601	0.624	0.642	0.659	0.673	0.697	0.717	0.735	0.750	0.763	0.776	0.787	0.797	0.819	0.838
850,000		0.562	0.578	0.605	0.627	0.646	0.662	0.676	0.701	0.721	0.738	0.753	0.767	0.779	0.790	0.800	0.822	0.841
800,000		0.565	0.582	0.609	0.631	0.649	0.666	0.680	0.704	0.725	0.742	0.757	0.771	0.783	0.794	0.804	0.826	0.845
750,000		0.569	0.585	0.613	0.635	0.653	0.670	0.684	0.708	0.729	0.746	0.761	0.775	0.787	0.798	0.808	0.830	0.849
700,000		0.573	0.590	0.617	0.639	0.658	0.674	0.688	0.712	0.733	0.750	0.765	0.779	0.791	0.802	0.812	0.834	0.853
650,000		0.578	0.594	0.621	0.643	0.662	0.678	0.693	0.717	0.737	0.755	0.770	0.783	0.795	0.806	0.817	0.839	0.857
600,000		0.584	0.600	0.627	0.649	0.668	0.684	0.698	0.723	0.743	0.760	0.775	0.789	0.801	0.812	0.822	0.844	0.863
550,000		0.589	0.605	0.632	0.654	0.673	0.689	0.704	0.728	0.748	0.766	0.781	0.794	0.806	0.817	0.828	0.850	0.868
500,000		0.595	0.611	0.638	0.660	0.679	0.695	0.709	0.734	0.754	0.771	0.786	0.800	0.812	0.823	0.833	0.855	0.874
450,000		0.601	0.617	0.644	0.667	0.685	0.701	0.716	0.740	0.760	0.778	0.793	0.806	0.819	0.830	0.840	0.862	0.881
400,000		0.610	0.626	0.654	0.676	0.694	0.711	0.725	0.749	0.769	0.787	0.802	0.816	0.828	0.839	0.849	0.871	0.890
350,000		0.618	0.635	0.662	0.684	0.702	0.719	0.733	0.757	0.778	0.795	0.810	0.824	0.836	0.847	0.857	0.879	0.898
300,000		0.628	0.644	0.671	0.693	0.712	0.728	0.742	0.767	0.787	0.804	0.819	0.833	0.845	0.856	0.866	0.888	0.907
250,000		0.639	0.655	0.682	0.704	0.723	0.739	0.753	0.778	0.798	0.815	0.831	0.844	0.856	0.867	0.877	0.899	0.918

Sixty-cycle Reactance per Mile Stranded-copper Conductors Overhead Transmission Lines (*Continued*)

60-cycle reactance x, ohms per mile, of each conductor of a single-phase, two-phase or three-phase circuit. (See footnotes)

Size of conductor		Distance D between centers of conductors[a]																
Circular mils	American wire gage (B&S)	3.5 ft (1.07 m)	4 ft (1.22 m)	5 ft (1.52 m)	6 ft (1.83 m)	7 ft (2.13 m)	8 ft (2.44 m)	9 ft (2.74 m)	11 ft (3.35 m)	13 ft (3.96 m)	15 ft (4.57 m)	17 ft (5.16 m)	18 ft (5.79 m)	21 ft (6.40 m)	23 ft (7.01 m)	25 ft (7.62 m)	30 ft (9.14 m)	35 ft (10.67 m)
211,600	0000	0.656	0.672	0.699	0.721	0.740	0.756	0.770	0.795	0.815	0.832	0.847	0.861	0.873	0.884	0.894	0.916	0.935
167,806	000	0.670	0.686	0.713	0.735	0.754	0.770	0.784	0.809	0.829	0.846	0.861	0.875	0.887	0.898	0.908	0.930	0.949
133,077	00	0.684	0.700	0.727	0.749	0.768	0.784	0.798	0.823	0.843	0.860	0.875	0.889	0.901	0.912	0.922	0.944	0.963
105,535	0	0.698	0.714	0.741	0.763	0.782	0.798	0.812	0.837	0.857	0.874	0.890	0.903	0.915	0.926	0.936	0.958	0.977
83,693	1	0.712	0.728	0.755	0.777	0.796	0.812	0.826	0.851	0.871	0.888	0.904	0.917	0.929	0.940	0.950	0.973	0.991
66,371	2	0.726	0.742	0.769	0.791	0.810	0.826	0.841	0.865	0.885	0.902	0.918	0.931	0.943	0.954	0.964	0.987	1.005
52,635	3	0.740	0.756	0.783	0.805	0.824	0.840	0.855	0.879	0.899	0.917	0.932	0.945	0.957	0.968	0.979	1.001	1.019
41,741	4	0.754	0.770	0.797	0.819	0.838	0.854	0.869	0.893	0.913	0.931	0.946	0.959	0.971	0.982	0.993	1.015	1.033
33,102	5	0.768	0.784	0.811	0.833	0.852	0.868	0.883	0.907	0.927	0.945	0.960	0.973	0.986	0.997	1.007	1.029	1.048
26,251	6	0.782	0.798	0.825	0.848	0.866	0.882	0.897	0.921	0.941	0.959	0.974	0.987	1.000	1.011	1.021	1.043	1.062

The table values were derived from the equation $x = 2\pi fL$, in which x is the reactance in ohms, L is the inductance in henrys per mile of single conductor and f is the frequency. The reactance at any other frequency than 60 cycles is $f/60$ times the table values.

The reactance x' at any spacing D' not given in the table is equal to the reactance x at the *next smaller* spacing D given in the table plus the quantity $0.2794 \log_{10} D'/D$. Thus $x' = x + 0.2794 \log_{10} D'/D$. Or the reactance in ohms to be added to that at the next smaller spacing may be taken from table below.

D'/D	1.05	1.10	1.15	1.20	1.25	1.30	1.35	1.40	1.45	1.50	1.55	1.60	1.65	1.70	1.75	1.80	1.85	1.90	1.95	2.00
$x+$	0.006	0.012	0.017	0.022	0.027	0.032	0.036	0.041	0.045	0.049	0.053	0.057	0.061	0.064	0.068	0.071	0.075	0.078	0.081	0.084

[a] For any three-phase arrangement of conductors $D = \sqrt[3]{ABC}$. This resolves itself into $D = A$, B or C for symmetrical triangular spacing and into $D = 1.26\,A$ or B for regular flat spacing, it being immaterial whether the conductors are in a horizontal or vertical plane.

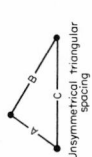

Unsymmetrical triangular spacing

Symmetrical triangular spacing

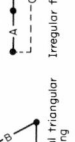

Irregular flat spacing

Regular flat spacing

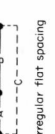

11-89

82. Average 60-cycle Reactance of All-steel Amerductors, in Ohms per 1,000 Ft of Conductor at 68°F

Size, BWG	Spacing[a] between conductors, in.	Reactance, ohms per 1,000 ft for various loadings									
		Three-wire strand, Type S-3					Solid wire, Type S				
		1 amp	5 amp	10 amp	15 amp	20 amp	1 amp	5 amp	10 amp	15 amp	20 amp
	12	0.22	0.24	0.28	0.31	0.35	0.35	0.50	0.69	0.84	1.07
	24	0.24	0.26	0.29	0.33	0.37	0.37	0.52	0.71	0.86	1.09
4	36	0.25	0.26	0.30	0.34	0.38	0.38	0.53	0.72	0.87	1.10
	48	0.25	0.27	0.31	0.35	0.39	0.38	0.53	0.72	0.88	1.10
	60	0.26	0.28	0.32	0.36	0.39	0.39	0.54	0.73	0.88	1.11
	120	0.27	0.29	0.33	0.37	0.41	0.40	0.56	0.75	0.90	1.13
	12	0.24	0.28	0.32	0.36	....	0.45	0.62	0.83	1.06	
	24	0.26	0.30	0.34	0.37	....	0.46	0.64	0.84	1.07	
6	36	0.27	0.31	0.34	0.38	....	0.47	0.65	0.85	1.08	
	48	0.27	0.31	0.35	0.39	....	0.48	0.65	0.86	1.09	
	60	0.28	0.32	0.36	0.39	....	0.49	0.66	0.86	1.09	
	120	0.30	0.33	0.37	0.41	....	0.50	0.67	0.88	1.11	
	12	0.27	0.30	0.34	....	....	0.47	0.70	0.97		
	24	0.28	0.32	0.36	....	....	0.49	0.72	0.98		
8	36	0.29	0.33	0.37	....	....	0.50	0.73	0.99		
	48	0.30	0.33	0.37	....	....	0.51	0.74	1.00		
	60	0.31	0.34	0.38	....	....	0.51	0.74	1.01		
	120	0.32	0.36	0.39	....	....	0.53	0.76	1.02		

[a] See Table 57.

83. Average 60-cycle Reactance of Steel-copper Amerductors, in Ohms per 1,000 Ft of Conductor at 68°F

Size, AWG	Reactance, ohms per 1,000 ft, for various spacings[a] between conductors					
	12 in.	24 in.	36 in.	48 in.	60 in.	120 in.
2	0.13	0.15	0.16	0.17	0.17	0.19
4	0.13	0.14	0.15	0.16	0.16	0.18
6	0.13	0.14	0.15	0.16	0.16	0.18
8	0.13	0.14	0.15	0.16	0.17	0.18
10	0.15	0.17	0.17	0.18	0.19	0.20
12	0.17	0.18	0.19	0.20	0.20	0.22

[a] See Table 57.

84. 60-cycle Reactances of Copperweld-copper and Copperweld Conductors, in Ohms per 1,000 Ft of Each Conductor

Conductor	Distance between centers of conductors, in.[a]								
	12	24	36	48	60	72	84	96	108
Composite Cables Copperweld—Copper Conductors									
2A	0.121	0.137	0.146	0.153	0.158	0.162	0.166	0.169	0.172
3A	0.124	0.140	0.149	0.156	0.161	0.165	0.169	0.172	0.175
4A	0.127	0.143	0.152	0.159	0.164	0.168	0.172	0.175	0.178
5A	0.129	0.145	0.154	0.161	0.166	0.170	0.174	0.177	0.180
6A	0.132	0.148	0.157	0.164	0.169	0.173	0.177	0.180	0.183
7A	0.135	0.151	0.160	0.167	0.172	0.176	0.180	0.183	0.186
8A	0.138	0.154	0.163	0.170	0.175	0.179	0.183	0.186	0.189
8C	0.138	0.154	0.163	0.170	0.175	0.179	0.183	0.186	0.188
8D	0.138	0.154	0.164	0.170	0.175	0.180	0.183	0.186	0.189
9½D	0.144	0.160	0.169	0.175	0.181	0.185	0.188	0.191	0.194
Copperweld Conductors—3-wire Strands									
3 No. 8 AWG	0.137	0.153	0.162	0.169	0.174	0.178	0.182	0.185	0.188
3 No. 9 AWG	0.139	0.155	0.164	0.171	0.176	0.180	0.184	0.187	0.190
3 No. 10 AWG	0.142	0.158	0.167	0.174	0.179	0.183	0.187	0.190	0.193
3 No. 11 AWG	0.145	0.161	0.170	0.177	0.182	0.186	0.190	0.193	0.196
3 No. 12 AWG	0.147	0.163	0.172	0.179	0.184	0.188	0.192	0.195	0.198
Copperweld Conductors—Solid Wires									
No. 6 AWG	0.144	0.160	0.169	0.176	0.181	0.185	0.189	0.192	0.195
No. 7 AWG	0.146	0.162	0.171	0.178	0.183	0.187	0.191	0.194	0.197
No. 8 AWG	0.149	0.165	0.174	0.181	0.186	0.190	0.194	0.197	0.200

NOTE.   For description of composite cables refer to Div. 2.
[a] See Table 57.

60-cycle reactances for other spacing can be determined from the following formula:

$$X_d = X_{12} + 0.05293 \log_{10} \left(\frac{d}{12}\right)$$

where X_d = 60-cycle reactance, in ohms per 1,000 ft for a spacing of d inches; X_{12} = 60-cycle reactance, in ohms per 1,000 ft for a spacing of 12 in.; and d = spacing between centers of conductors, in inches.

85. 25-cycle Reactance^a per Mile of Single-conductor Aluminum Cable, Steel-reinforced

25-cycle reactance x, ohms per mile, of each conductor of a single-phase, two-phase, or three-phase circuit

Multiple-layer Conductors^b—All Current Densities

Cir mils or AWG (B&S) Alum.	No. of wires Alum.	Steel	Distance d between centers of conductors, ft^e																	
			2	2.5	3	3.5	4	5	6	7	8	9	11	13	15	17	19	21	23	25
1,590,000	54	19	0.185	0.196	0.205	0.213	0.220	0.231	0.240	0.248	0.255	0.261	0.271	0.279	0.286	0.292	0.298	0.303	0.308	0.312
1,510,500	54	19	0.186	0.197	0.206	0.214	0.221	0.232	0.241	0.249	0.256	0.262	0.272	0.281	0.288	0.294	0.300	0.305	0.309	0.314
1,431,000	54	19	0.187	0.198	0.208	0.216	0.222	0.234	0.243	0.251	0.257	0.263	0.274	0.282	0.289	0.296	0.301	0.306	0.311	0.315
1,351,500	54	19	0.189	0.200	0.209	0.217	0.224	0.235	0.244	0.252	0.259	0.265	0.275	0.283	0.291	0.297	0.303	0.308	0.312	0.316
1,272,000	54	19	0.190	0.202	0.211	0.219	0.225	0.237	0.246	0.254	0.260	0.266	0.276	0.285	0.292	0.298	0.304	0.309	0.314	0.318
1,192,500	54	19	0.192	0.203	0.212	0.220	0.227	0.238	0.247	0.255	0.262	0.268	0.278	0.287	0.294	0.300	0.306	0.311	0.315	0.320
1,113,000	54	19	0.194	0.205	0.214	0.222	0.229	0.240	0.249	0.257	0.264	0.270	0.280	0.288	0.296	0.302	0.307	0.312	0.317	0.321
1,033,500	54	7	0.195	0.207	0.216	0.224	0.230	0.242	0.251	0.259	0.265	0.271	0.282	0.290	0.297	0.304	0.309	0.314	0.319	0.323
954,000	54	7	0.198	0.209	0.218	0.226	0.233	0.244	0.253	0.261	0.268	0.274	0.284	0.292	0.299	0.306	0.311	0.316	0.321	0.325
900,000	54	7	0.199	0.210	0.219	0.227	0.234	0.245	0.255	0.262	0.269	0.275	0.285	0.294	0.301	0.307	0.313	0.318	0.323	0.327
874,000	54	7	0.200	0.211	0.220	0.228	0.235	0.246	0.256	0.263	0.270	0.276	0.286	0.295	0.302	0.308	0.314	0.319	0.324	0.328
795,000	54	7	0.202	0.213	0.223	0.230	0.237	0.248	0.258	0.265	0.272	0.278	0.288	0.297	0.304	0.310	0.316	0.321	0.326	0.330
795,000	26	7	0.201	0.212	0.222	0.229	0.236	0.247	0.257	0.264	0.271	0.277	0.287	0.296	0.303	0.309	0.315	0.320	0.324	0.329
795,000	30	19	0.199	0.210	0.219	0.227	0.234	0.245	0.255	0.262	0.269	0.275	0.285	0.293	0.301	0.307	0.313	0.318	0.322	0.326
715,500	54	7	0.205	0.216	0.225	0.233	0.240	0.251	0.260	0.268	0.275	0.281	0.291	0.299	0.307	0.313	0.319	0.324	0.328	0.332
715,500	26	7	0.204	0.215	0.224	0.232	0.239	0.250	0.259	0.267	0.274	0.280	0.290	0.298	0.306	0.312	0.317	0.323	0.327	0.331
715,500	30	19	0.201	0.212	0.222	0.230	0.237	0.248	0.257	0.265	0.272	0.278	0.288	0.296	0.304	0.310	0.315	0.320	0.325	0.329
666,600	54	7	0.207	0.218	0.227	0.235	0.242	0.253	0.262	0.270	0.277	0.283	0.293	0.301	0.308	0.315	0.320	0.325	0.330	0.334
636,000	54	7	0.208	0.219	0.228	0.236	0.243	0.254	0.263	0.271	0.278	0.284	0.294	0.302	0.310	0.316	0.322	0.327	0.331	0.335
636,000	26	7	0.207	0.218	0.227	0.235	0.242	0.253	0.262	0.270	0.277	0.283	0.293	0.301	0.309	0.315	0.320	0.326	0.330	0.334
636,000	30	19	0.205	0.216	0.225	0.233	0.240	0.251	0.260	0.268	0.275	0.281	0.291	0.299	0.306	0.313	0.318	0.323	0.328	0.332
605,000	54	7	0.209	0.220	0.230	0.237	0.244	0.255	0.265	0.272	0.279	0.285	0.295	0.304	0.311	0.317	0.323	0.328	0.332	0.337
605,000	26	7	0.208	0.219	0.228	0.236	0.243	0.254	0.264	0.271	0.278	0.284	0.294	0.303	0.310	0.316	0.322	0.327	0.331	0.336
556,500	26	7	0.210	0.221	0.230	0.238	0.245	0.256	0.266	0.273	0.280	0.286	0.296	0.305	0.312	0.318	0.324	0.329	0.334	0.338
556,500	30	7	0.208	0.219	0.228	0.236	0.243	0.254	0.263	0.271	0.278	0.284	0.294	0.302	0.310	0.316	0.322	0.327	0.331	0.336

Single-layer Conductors[a]—Current Density 0 Amp per Sq In.

Size			1.15	1.20	1.25	1.30	1.35	1.40	1.45	1.50	1.55	1.60	1.65	1.70	1.75	1.80	1.85	1.90	1.95	2.00
500,000	30	7	0.210	0.222	0.231	0.239	0.245	0.257	0.266	0.274	0.280	0.286	0.297	0.305	0.312	0.319	0.324	0.329	0.334	0.338
477,000	26	7	0.214	0.225	0.235	0.242	0.249	0.260	0.270	0.277	0.284	0.290	0.300	0.309	0.316	0.322	0.328	0.333	0.337	0.342
477,000	30	7	0.212	0.223	0.232	0.240	0.247	0.258	0.267	0.275	0.282	0.288	0.298	0.306	0.316	0.320	0.325	0.331	0.335	0.339
397,500	26	7	0.219	0.230	0.239	0.247	0.254	0.265	0.274	0.282	0.289	0.295	0.305	0.313	0.320	0.325	0.332	0.337	0.342	0.346
397,500	30	7	0.216	0.227	0.237	0.244	0.251	0.263	0.272	0.279	0.286	0.292	0.302	0.311	0.318	0.324	0.330	0.335	0.340	0.344
336,400	26	7	0.223	0.234	0.243	0.251	0.258	0.269	0.278	0.286	0.293	0.299	0.309	0.317	0.325	0.331	0.337	0.342	0.346	0.350
336,400	30	7	0.220	0.232	0.241	0.249	0.256	0.267	0.276	0.284	0.291	0.297	0.307	0.315	0.322	0.329	0.334	0.339	0.344	0.348
300,000	26	7	0.226	0.237	0.246	0.254	0.261	0.272	0.281	0.289	0.296	0.302	0.312	0.320	0.328	0.334	0.340	0.345	0.349	0.353
300,000	30	7	0.223	0.235	0.244	0.252	0.258	0.270	0.279	0.287	0.293	0.299	0.310	0.318	0.325	0.332	0.337	0.342	0.347	0.351
266,800	26	7	0.229	0.240	0.249	0.257	0.264	0.275	0.284	0.293	0.299	0.305	0.315	0.323	0.330	0.337	0.342	0.348	0.352	0.356
266,800	6	7	0.229	0.241	0.250	0.258	0.264	0.276	0.285	0.293	0.299	0.305	0.316	0.324	0.331	0.338	0.343	0.348	0.353	0.357
4/0	6	1	0.253	0.265	0.274	0.282	0.288	0.300	0.309	0.317	0.323	0.329	0.339	0.348	0.355	0.362	0.367	0.372	0.377	0.381
3/0	6	1	0.260	0.271	0.281	0.288	0.295	0.306	0.316	0.323	0.330	0.336	0.346	0.355	0.362	0.368	0.374	0.379	0.384	0.388
2/0	6	1	0.266	0.277	0.287	0.294	0.301	0.312	0.322	0.329	0.336	0.342	0.352	0.361	0.368	0.374	0.380	0.385	0.390	0.394
1/0	6	1	0.272	0.283	0.292	0.300	0.307	0.318	0.327	0.335	0.342	0.348	0.358	0.366	0.374	0.380	0.386	0.391	0.395	0.399
1	6	1	0.277	0.288	0.297	0.305	0.312	0.323	0.332	0.340	0.347	0.353	0.363	0.372	0.379	0.385	0.391	0.396	0.400	0.405
2	6	1	0.282	0.293	0.302	0.310	0.317	0.328	0.338	0.345	0.352	0.358	0.368	0.377	0.384	0.390	0.396	0.401	0.405	0.410
3	6	1	0.287	0.298	0.307	0.315	0.322	0.333	0.343	0.350	0.357	0.363	0.373	0.382	0.389	0.395	0.401	0.406	0.410	0.415
4	6	1	0.292	0.304	0.313	0.321	0.327	0.339	0.348	0.356	0.362	0.368	0.379	0.387	0.394	0.400	0.406	0.411	0.416	0.420
5	6	1	0.297	0.309	0.318	0.326	0.332	0.344	0.353	0.361	0.368	0.373	0.384	0.392	0.399	0.406	0.411	0.416	0.421	0.425
6	6	1	0.303	0.314	0.324	0.331	0.338	0.349	0.359	0.366	0.373	0.379	0.389	0.398	0.405	0.411	0.417	0.422	0.427	0.431
203,000	8	7	0.237	0.248	0.257	0.265	0.272	0.283	0.292	0.300	0.307	0.313	0.323	0.331	0.338	0.345	0.350	0.356	0.360	0.364
203,200	16	19	0.226	0.238	0.247	0.255	0.262	0.273	0.282	0.290	0.297	0.302	0.313	0.321	0.328	0.335	0.340	0.345	0.350	0.354
211,300	12	7	0.230	0.241	0.251	0.258	0.265	0.276	0.286	0.293	0.300	0.306	0.316	0.325	0.332	0.338	0.344	0.349	0.353	0.358
190,800	12	7	0.233	0.244	0.253	0.261	0.267	0.279	0.288	0.296	0.303	0.309	0.319	0.327	0.335	0.341	0.347	0.352	0.356	0.360
176,900	12	7	0.235	0.246	0.255	0.263	0.270	0.281	0.290	0.298	0.305	0.311	0.321	0.329	0.337	0.343	0.348	0.353	0.358	0.362

D'/D	1.05	1.10	1.15	1.20	1.25	1.30	1.35	1.40	1.45	1.50	1.55	1.60	1.65	1.70	1.75	1.80	1.85	1.90	1.95	2.00
x+	0.002	0.005	0.007	0.009	0.011	0.013	0.15	0.017	0.019	0.020	0.022	0.024	0.025	0.027	0.028	0.030	0.031	0.032	0.034	0.035

a The table values were derived from the equation $x = 2\pi f L$, in which x = the reactance in ohms; L = the inductance in henrys per mile of single conductor; and f = the frequency. The reactance at any other frequency than 25 cycles is $f/25$ times the table values. The reactance x' at any spacing D' not given in the table is equal to the reactance x at the next smaller spacing D given in the table plus the quantity $0.1164 \log_{10} D'/D$. Thus $x' = x + 0.1164 \log_{10} D'/D$. Or the reactance, in ohms, to be added to that at the next smaller spacing may be taken from table below:

b By multiple-layer conductors is meant conductors with two or more layers of aluminum over the steel core.
c See Table **57**.
d By single-layer conductors is meant conductors with one layer of aluminum over the steel core.

11–93

25-cycle Reactance^a per Mile of Single-conductor Aluminum Cable, Steel-reinforced (Continued)

Cir mils or AWG (B&S) Alum.	No. of wires Alum.	No. of wires Steel	Distance d between centers of conductors, ft^c																	
			2	2.5	3	3.5	4	5	6	7	8	9	11	13	15	17	19	21	23	25

25-cycle reactance x, ohms per mile, of each conductor of a single-phase, two-phase, or three-phase circuit

Single-layer Conductors^d—Current Density 0 Amp per Sq In. (Continued)

Cir mils or AWG	Alum.	Steel	2	2.5	3	3.5	4	5	6	7	8	9	11	13	15	17	19	21	23	25
159,000	12	7	0.237	0.249	0.258	0.266	0.272	0.284	0.293	0.301	0.307	0.313	0.323	0.332	0.339	0.345	0.351	0.356	0.361	0.365
134,600	12	7	0.241	0.253	0.262	0.270	0.276	0.288	0.297	0.305	0.312	0.317	0.328	0.336	0.343	0.350	0.355	0.360	0.365	0.369
110,800	12	7	0.246	0.258	0.267	0.275	0.282	0.293	0.302	0.310	0.317	0.323	0.333	0.341	0.348	0.355	0.360	0.365	0.370	0.374
101,800	12	7	0.249	0.260	0.269	0.277	0.284	0.295	0.304	0.312	0.319	0.325	0.335	0.343	0.350	0.357	0.362	0.367	0.372	0.376
80,000	8	1	0.276	0.288	0.297	0.305	0.311	0.323	0.332	0.339	0.346	0.352	0.362	0.371	0.378	0.384	0.390	0.395	0.400	0.404

Single-layer Conductors^d—Current Density 600 Amp per Sq In.

Cir mils or AWG	Alum.	Steel	2	2.5	3	3.5	4	5	6	7	8	9	11	13	15	17	19	21	23	25
266,800	6	7	0.237	0.248	0.257	0.265	0.272	0.283	0.292	0.300	0.307	0.313	0.323	0.332	0.339	0.345	0.351	0.356	0.360	0.365
4/0	6	1	0.262	0.273	0.282	0.290	0.297	0.308	0.317	0.325	0.332	0.338	0.348	0.356	0.364	0.370	0.376	0.381	0.385	0.389
3/0	6	1	0.266	0.277	0.286	0.294	0.301	0.312	0.321	0.329	0.336	0.342	0.352	0.361	0.368	0.374	0.380	0.385	0.389	0.394
2/0	6	1	0.270	0.282	0.291	0.299	0.305	0.317	0.326	0.334	0.340	0.346	0.357	0.365	0.372	0.379	0.384	0.389	0.394	0.398
0	6	1	0.275	0.286	0.295	0.303	0.310	0.321	0.330	0.338	0.345	0.351	0.361	0.369	0.377	0.383	0.389	0.394	0.398	0.402
1	6	1	0.279	0.291	0.300	0.308	0.314	0.326	0.335	0.343	0.349	0.355	0.366	0.374	0.381	0.388	0.393	0.398	0.403	0.407
2	6	1	0.284	0.295	0.304	0.312	0.319	0.330	0.339	0.347	0.354	0.360	0.370	0.379	0.386	0.392	0.398	0.403	0.407	0.411
3	6	1	0.288	0.299	0.309	0.316	0.323	0.335	0.344	0.351	0.358	0.364	0.374	0.383	0.390	0.396	0.402	0.407	0.412	0.416
4	6	1	0.293	0.304	0.313	0.321	0.328	0.339	0.348	0.356	0.363	0.369	0.379	0.387	0.395	0.401	0.407	0.412	0.416	0.420
5	6	1	0.298	0.310	0.319	0.327	0.333	0.345	0.354	0.362	0.368	0.374	0.384	0.393	0.400	0.406	0.412	0.417	0.422	0.426
6	6	1	0.304	0.316	0.325	0.332	0.339	0.351	0.360	0.368	0.374	0.380	0.390	0.399	0.406	0.412	0.418	0.423	0.428	0.432
203,000	8	7	0.243	0.253	0.262	0.270	0.277	0.288	0.297	0.305	0.312	0.318	0.328	0.337	0.344	0.350	0.355	0.361	0.366	0.370
203,200	16	19	0.232	0.243	0.252	0.260	0.267	0.278	0.287	0.295	0.302	0.308	0.318	0.326	0.334	0.340	0.346	0.351	0.355	0.360
211,300	12	7	0.235	0.247	0.256	0.264	0.271	0.282	0.291	0.299	0.306	0.312	0.322	0.330	0.337	0.344	0.349	0.354	0.359	0.363
190,800	12	7	0.238	0.249	0.259	0.266	0.273	0.284	0.294	0.301	0.308	0.314	0.324	0.333	0.340	0.346	0.352	0.357	0.361	0.366
176,900	12	7	0.240	0.251	0.260	0.268	0.275	0.286	0.296	0.303	0.310	0.316	0.326	0.335	0.342	0.348	0.354	0.360	0.364	0.368
159,000	12	7	0.243	0.254	0.263	0.271	0.278	0.289	0.298	0.306	0.313	0.319	0.329	0.337	0.344	0.351	0.356	0.361	0.366	0.370
134,600	12	7	0.247	0.258	0.267	0.275	0.282	0.293	0.302	0.310	0.317	0.323	0.330	0.342	0.349	0.355	0.361	0.366	0.370	0.375
110,800	12	7	0.252	0.263	0.272	0.280	0.287	0.298	0.307	0.315	0.322	0.328	0.338	0.346	0.354	0.360	0.366	0.371	0.377	0.380
101,800	12	7	0.254	0.265	0.274	0.282	0.289	0.300	0.309	0.317	0.324	0.330	0.340	0.349	0.356	0.362	0.368	0.373	0.377	0.382
80,000	8	1	0.281	0.292	0.301	0.309	0.316	0.327	0.336	0.344	0.351	0.357	0.367	0.376	0.383	0.389	0.395	0.400	0.404	0.409

Single-layer Conductors[d]—Current Density 1,200 Amp per Sq In.

			1.15	1.20	1.25	1.30	1.35	1.40	1.45	1.50	1.55	1.60	1.65	1.70	1.75	1.80	1.85	1.90	1.95	2.00
266,800	6	7	0.270	0.281	0.291	0.298	0.305	0.316	0.326	0.333	0.340	0.346	0.356	0.365	0.372	0.378	0.384	0.389	0.393	0.398
4/0	6	1	0.273	0.284	0.294	0.301	0.308	0.319	0.329	0.336	0.343	0.349	0.359	0.368	0.375	0.381	0.387	0.392	0.397	0.401
3/0	6	1	0.278	0.290	0.299	0.307	0.313	0.325	0.334	0.342	0.348	0.354	0.365	0.373	0.380	0.387	0.392	0.397	0.402	0.406
2/0	6	1	0.282	0.294	0.303	0.311	0.317	0.329	0.338	0.346	0.352	0.358	0.369	0.377	0.384	0.391	0.396	0.401	0.406	0.410
1/0	6	1	0.285	0.296	0.306	0.313	0.320	0.332	0.341	0.348	0.355	0.361	0.371	0.380	0.387	0.393	0.399	0.404	0.409	0.413
1	6	1	0.288	0.299	0.308	0.314	0.323	0.334	0.343	0.351	0.358	0.364	0.374	0.382	0.390	0.396	0.402	0.407	0.411	0.415
2	6	1	0.290	0.301	0.310	0.316	0.325	0.336	0.345	0.353	0.360	0.366	0.376	0.384	0.392	0.398	0.403	0.409	0.413	0.417
3	6	1	0.292	0.303	0.312	0.320	0.327	0.338	0.347	0.355	0.362	0.368	0.378	0.386	0.394	0.400	0.406	0.411	0.415	0.419
4	6	1	0.294	0.305	0.315	0.322	0.329	0.340	0.350	0.357	0.364	0.370	0.380	0.389	0.396	0.402	0.408	0.413	0.418	0.422
5	6	1	0.301	0.312	0.321	0.329	0.336	0.347	0.357	0.364	0.371	0.377	0.387	0.396	0.403	0.409	0.415	0.420	0.424	0.429
6	6	1	0.306	0.318	0.327	0.335	0.341	0.353	0.362	0.370	0.376	0.382	0.393	0.401	0.408	0.415	0.420	0.425	0.430	0.434
203,000	8	7	0.268	0.280	0.289	0.297	0.304	0.315	0.324	0.332	0.339	0.344	0.355	0.363	0.370	0.377	0.382	0.387	0.392	0.396
203,200	16	19	0.258	0.270	0.279	0.287	0.293	0.305	0.314	0.322	0.328	0.334	0.344	0.353	0.360	0.366	0.372	0.377	0.382	0.386
211,300	12	7	0.262	0.273	0.283	0.290	0.297	0.308	0.318	0.325	0.332	0.338	0.348	0.357	0.364	0.370	0.376	0.381	0.385	0.390
190,800	12	7	0.265	0.276	0.285	0.293	0.300	0.311	0.320	0.328	0.335	0.341	0.351	0.359	0.366	0.373	0.378	0.383	0.388	0.392
176,900	12	7	0.267	0.278	0.287	0.295	0.302	0.313	0.322	0.330	0.337	0.343	0.353	0.361	0.368	0.375	0.380	0.385	0.390	0.394
159,000	12	7	0.269	0.280	0.290	0.298	0.304	0.315	0.325	0.333	0.339	0.345	0.355	0.364	0.371	0.377	0.383	0.388	0.393	0.397
134,600	12	7	0.273	0.285	0.294	0.302	0.308	0.320	0.329	0.337	0.343	0.349	0.360	0.368	0.375	0.382	0.387	0.392	0.397	0.401
110,800	12	7	0.278	0.290	0.299	0.307	0.313	0.325	0.334	0.342	0.348	0.354	0.364	0.373	0.380	0.386	0.392	0.397	0.402	0.406
101,800	12	7	0.280	0.292	0.301	0.309	0.315	0.327	0.336	0.344	0.350	0.356	0.367	0.375	0.382	0.389	0.394	0.399	0.404	0.408
80,000	8	1	0.294	0.305	0.314	0.322	0.329	0.340	0.349	0.357	0.364	0.370	0.380	0.389	0.396	0.402	0.408	0.413	0.417	0.422

[a] The table values were derived from the equation $x = 2\pi fL$, in which x = the reactance in ohms; L = the inductance in henrys per mile of single conductor; and f = the frequency. The reactance at any other frequency than 25 cycles is $f/25$ times the table values. The reactance x' at any spacing D' not given in the table is equal to the reactance x at the next smaller spacing D given in the table plus the quantity $0.1164 \log_{10} D'/D$. Thus $x' = x + 0.1164 \log_{10} D'/D$. Or the reactance, in ohms, to be added to that at the next smaller spacing may be taken from table below:

D'/D	1.05	1.10	1.15	1.20	1.25	1.30	1.35	1.40	1.45	1.50	1.55	1.60	1.65	1.70	1.75	1.80	1.85	1.90	1.95	2.00
$x+$	0.002	0.005	0.007	0.009	0.011	0.013	0.015	0.017	0.019	0.020	0.022	0.024	0.025	0.027	0.028	0.030	0.031	0.032	0.034	0.035

[c] See Table 57.

[d] By single-layer conductors is meant conductors with one layer of aluminum over the steel core.

86. 60-cycle Reactance[a] per Mile of Single-conductor Aluminum Cable, Steel-reinforced

Distance d between centers of conductors, ft[c]

60-cycle reactance x, ohms per mile, of each conductor of a single-phase, two-phase, or three-phase circuit

Multiple-layer Conductors[b]—All Current Densities

Cir mils or AWG (B&S) alum.	No. of wires		2	2.5	3	3.5	4	5	6	7	8	9	11	13	15	17	19	21	23	25
	Alum.	Steel																		
1,590,000	54	19	0.443	0.470	0.492	0.511	0.527	0.554	0.576	0.595	0.611	0.625	0.650	0.670	0.686	0.701	0.716	0.728	0.739	0.749
1,510,500	54	19	0.446	0.473	0.495	0.514	0.530	0.557	0.579	0.598	0.614	0.628	0.653	0.673	0.690	0.706	0.719	0.731	0.742	0.752
1,431,000	54	19	0.449	0.476	0.499	0.517	0.533	0.561	0.583	0.601	0.618	0.632	0.656	0.676	0.694	0.709	0.722	0.734	0.746	0.756
1,351,500	54	19	0.453	0.480	0.502	0.521	0.537	0.564	0.586	0.605	0.621	0.635	0.660	0.680	0.697	0.713	0.727	0.738	0.749	0.759
1,272,000	54	19	0.456	0.484	0.506	0.524	0.541	0.568	0.590	0.608	0.625	0.639	0.663	0.684	0.701	0.716	0.730	0.742	0.752	0.763
1,192,500	54	19	0.460	0.487	0.510	0.528	0.544	0.572	0.594	0.612	0.628	0.643	0.667	0.688	0.705	0.720	0.734	0.746	0.757	0.767
1,113,000	54	19	0.464	0.492	0.514	0.532	0.549	0.576	0.598	0.616	0.633	0.647	0.671	0.692	0.709	0.724	0.737	0.750	0.761	0.771
1,033,500	54	7	0.469	0.496	0.518	0.537	0.553	0.580	0.602	0.621	0.637	0.654	0.676	0.696	0.714	0.729	0.742	0.754	0.765	0.775
954,000	54	7	0.474	0.501	0.523	0.542	0.559	0.585	0.607	0.626	0.642	0.656	0.681	0.701	0.719	0.734	0.747	0.759	0.770	0.780
900,000	54	7	0.477	0.504	0.527	0.546	0.561	0.588	0.611	0.630	0.646	0.660	0.684	0.705	0.722	0.737	0.751	0.763	0.774	0.784
874,000	54	7	0.479	0.506	0.518	0.547	0.563	0.590	0.612	0.631	0.647	0.662	0.686	0.706	0.723	0.739	0.752	0.764	0.775	0.785
795,000	54	7	0.485	0.512	0.534	0.553	0.569	0.596	0.618	0.637	0.653	0.667	0.692	0.712	0.729	0.745	0.758	0.770	0.781	0.791
795,000	26	7	0.483	0.510	0.532	0.550	0.567	0.594	0.616	0.635	0.651	0.665	0.689	0.710	0.727	0.742	0.756	0.768	0.779	0.789
795,000	30	19	0.477	0.504	0.526	0.545	0.561	0.588	0.611	0.629	0.645	0.660	0.684	0.704	0.722	0.737	0.750	0.762	0.774	0.783
715,500	54	7	0.491	0.518	0.541	0.559	0.576	0.602	0.625	0.644	0.660	0.674	0.698	0.719	0.736	0.751	0.765	0.777	0.788	0.798
715,500	26	7	0.489	0.516	0.538	0.557	0.573	0.600	0.622	0.641	0.657	0.671	0.696	0.716	0.733	0.748	0.762	0.774	0.785	0.795
715,500	30	19	0.483	0.510	0.533	0.552	0.568	0.595	0.617	0.636	0.652	0.666	0.691	0.711	0.728	0.743	0.757	0.769	0.780	0.790
666,600	54	7	0.496	0.523	0.545	0.564	0.580	0.607	0.629	0.648	0.664	0.678	0.703	0.723	0.740	0.756	0.769	0.781	0.792	0.802
636,000	54	7	0.498	0.526	0.547	0.566	0.582	0.610	0.631	0.650	0.667	0.681	0.705	0.725	0.743	0.758	0.772	0.784	0.795	0.805
636,000	26	7	0.496	0.523	0.546	0.564	0.580	0.607	0.630	0.648	0.664	0.679	0.703	0.723	0.741	0.756	0.769	0.782	0.792	0.803
636,000	30	19	0.491	0.518	0.540	0.559	0.575	0.602	0.624	0.643	0.659	0.673	0.697	0.718	0.735	0.751	0.746	0.774	0.787	0.797
605,000	54	7	0.501	0.529	0.551	0.569	0.585	0.613	0.635	0.653	0.670	0.684	0.708	0.729	0.746	0.761	0.775	0.787	0.798	0.808
605,000	26	7	0.499	0.526	0.548	0.567	0.583	0.610	0.632	0.651	0.667	0.682	0.706	0.726	0.744	0.759	0.773	0.784	0.796	0.806
556,500	26	7	0.504	0.531	0.553	0.572	0.588	0.615	0.638	0.656	0.672	0.687	0.711	0.731	0.748	0.764	0.777	0.789	0.800	0.811
556,500	30	7	0.498	0.526	0.548	0.566	0.582	0.610	0.632	0.650	0.667	0.681	0.705	0.726	0.743	0.758	0.772	0.784	0.795	0.805
500,000	30	7	0.505	0.532	0.554	0.573	0.589	0.616	0.638	0.657	0.673	0.687	0.712	0.732	0.749	0.765	0.778	0.790	0.801	0.811
477,000	26	7	0.514	0.541	0.563	0.581	0.598	0.625	0.647	0.665	0.682	0.696	0.720	0.741	0.758	0.773	0.787	0.799	0.810	0.820

Single-layer Conductors[d]—Current Density 0 Amp per Sq In.

Size	Al	St																			
477,000	30	7	0.508	0.535	0.557	0.576	0.592	0.619	0.641	0.660	0.676	0.690	0.715	0.735	0.752	0.768	0.781	0.794	0.804	0.814
397,500	26	7	0.525	0.552	0.574	0.593	0.609	0.636	0.658	0.677	0.693	0.707	0.723	0.752	0.769	0.780	0.798	0.810	0.821	0.831
397,500	30	7	0.519	0.546	0.568	0.587	0.603	0.630	0.652	0.671	0.685	0.701	0.726	0.746	0.763	0.779	0.792	0.804	0.813	0.826
336,400	26	7	0.534	0.562	0.584	0.602	0.619	0.646	0.668	0.687	0.703	0.717	0.742	0.762	0.779	0.794	0.808	0.820	0.831	0.841
336,400	30	7	0.529	0.556	0.578	0.597	0.613	0.640	0.662	0.681	0.697	0.712	0.736	0.756	0.774	0.789	0.802	0.814	0.825	0.835
300,000	26	7	0.542	0.569	0.591	0.610	0.626	0.653	0.675	0.694	0.710	0.724	0.748	0.769	0.786	0.801	0.813	0.827	0.838	0.848
300,000	30	7	0.536	0.563	0.585	0.604	0.620	0.647	0.669	0.688	0.704	0.718	0.743	0.763	0.780	0.796	0.809	0.821	0.832	0.842
266,800	26	7	0.549	0.576	0.598	0.617	0.633	0.660	0.682	0.701	0.717	0.731	0.756	0.776	0.793	0.802	0.822	0.834	0.845	0.855
266,800	6	7	0.550	0.578	0.600	0.618	0.635	0.662	0.684	0.702	0.719	0.733	0.757	0.778	0.795	0.810	0.824	0.836	0.847	0.857
4/0	6	1	0.608	0.635	0.657	0.676	0.692	0.719	0.741	0.760	0.776	0.790	0.815	0.835	0.852	0.868	0.881	0.893	0.904	0.914
3/0	6	1	0.624	0.651	0.673	0.692	0.708	0.735	0.757	0.776	0.792	0.806	0.831	0.851	0.869	0.884	0.897	0.909	0.920	0.930
2/0	6	1	0.638	0.665	0.688	0.706	0.722	0.750	0.772	0.790	0.806	0.821	0.845	0.866	0.883	0.898	0.912	0.924	0.935	0.945
1/0	6	1	0.652	0.679	0.701	0.720	0.736	0.763	0.785	0.804	0.820	0.834	0.859	0.879	0.897	0.912	0.925	0.937	0.948	0.958
1	6	1	0.664	0.691	0.714	0.732	0.748	0.776	0.798	0.816	0.832	0.847	0.871	0.892	0.909	0.924	0.938	0.950	0.961	0.971
2	6	1	0.676	0.704	0.726	0.744	0.760	0.788	0.810	0.828	0.845	0.859	0.883	0.904	0.921	0.936	0.950	0.962	0.973	0.983
3	6	1	0.688	0.716	0.738	0.756	0.773	0.800	0.822	0.840	0.857	0.871	0.895	0.916	0.933	0.948	0.962	0.974	0.985	0.995
4	6	1	0.701	0.728	0.751	0.769	0.785	0.812	0.835	0.853	0.869	0.884	0.908	0.929	0.946	0.961	0.974	0.985	0.998	1.01
5	6	1	0.714	0.741	0.763	0.782	0.798	0.825	0.847	0.866	0.882	0.896	0.921	0.941	0.958	0.973	0.987	0.998	1.01	1.02
6	6	1	0.727	0.754	0.777	0.795	0.811	0.838	0.861	0.879	0.895	0.910	0.934	0.955	0.972	0.987	1.00	1.01	1.02	1.03
203,000	8	7	0.567	0.593	0.616	0.634	0.651	0.678	0.700	0.719	0.735	0.749	0.774	0.794	0.811	0.826	0.840	0.852	0.863	0.873
203,200	16	19	0.542	0.569	0.592	0.610	0.627	0.653	0.676	0.694	0.711	0.725	0.749	0.769	0.787	0.802	0.815	0.828	0.838	0.849
211,300	12	7	0.551	0.578	0.601	0.619	0.635	0.662	0.685	0.703	0.719	0.734	0.758	0.779	0.796	0.811	0.824	0.837	0.847	0.858
190,800	12	7	0.557	0.584	0.607	0.625	0.641	0.668	0.691	0.709	0.725	0.740	0.764	0.785	0.802	0.817	0.831	0.843	0.854	0.864
176,000	12	7	0.562	0.589	0.611	0.630	0.646	0.673	0.695	0.714	0.730	0.745	0.769	0.789	0.806	0.821	0.835	0.847	0.858	0.868

D/D	1.05	1.10	1.15	1.20	1.25	1.30	1.35	1.40	1.45	1.50	1.55	1.60	1.65	1.70	1.75	1.80	1.85	1.90	1.95	2.00
x+	0.006	0.012	0.017	0.022	0.027	0.032	0.036	0.041	0.045	0.049	0.053	0.057	0.061	0.064	0.068	0.071	0.075	0.078	0.081	0.084

a The table values were derived from the equation $x = 2\pi f L$, in which x = the reactance in ohms; L = the inductance in henrys per mile of single conductor; and f = the frequency. The reactance at any frequency other than 60 cycles is $f/60$ times the table values. The reactance x' at any spacing D' not given in the table is equal to the reactance x at the next smaller spacing D given in the table plus the quantity $0.2794 \log_{10} D'/D$. Thus $x' = x + 0.2794 \log_{10} D'/D$. Or the reactance in ohms to be added to that at the next smaller spacing may be taken from table below.

b By multiple-layer conductors is meant conductors with two or more layers of aluminum over the steel core.
c See Table 57.
d By single-layer conductors is meant conductors with one layer of aluminum over the steel core.

60-cycle Reactance[a] per Mile of Single-conductor Aluminum Cable, Steel-reinforced (Continued)

60-cycle reactance x, ohms per mile, of each conductor of a single-phase, two-phase, or three-phase circuit

Cir mils or AWG (B&S) alum.	Alum.	Steel	Distance d between centers of conductors, ft[e]																	
	No. of wires		2	2.5	3	3.5	4	5	6	7	8	9	11	13	15	17	19	21	23	25
Single-layer Conductors[d]—Current Density 0 Amp per Sq In.—(Continued)																				
159,000	12	7	0.568	0.595	0.618	0.636	0.653	0.679	0.702	0.720	0.737	0.751	0.775	0.795	0.813	0.828	0.841	0.854	0.865	0.875
134,600	12	7	0.578	0.605	0.628	0.646	0.662	0.690	0.712	0.730	0.748	0.761	0.785	0.806	0.823	0.838	0.852	0.864	0.875	0.885
110,800	12	7	0.590	0.617	0.639	0.658	0.674	0.701	0.723	0.742	0.759	0.773	0.797	0.817	0.835	0.850	0.863	0.875	0.887	0.897
101,800	12	7	0.595	0.622	0.645	0.663	0.690	0.706	0.729	0.747	0.763	0.778	0.802	0.823	0.840	0.855	0.869	0.881	0.892	0.902
80,000	8	1	0.663	0.690	0.712	0.731	0.747	0.774	0.796	0.815	0.831	0.845	0.870	0.890	0.907	0.923	0.936	0.948	0.959	0.969
Single-layer Conductors[d]—Current Density 600 Amp per Sq In.																				
266,800	6	7	0.568	0.595	0.618	0.636	0.652	0.679	0.702	0.720	0.736	0.751	0.775	0.796	0.813	0.828	0.842	0.854	0.865	0.875
4/0	6	1	0.628	0.655	0.677	0.696	0.712	0.739	0.761	0.780	0.796	0.810	0.835	0.855	0.872	0.888	0.901	0.913	0.924	0.934
3/0	6	1	0.638	0.665	0.687	0.706	0.722	0.749	0.771	0.790	0.806	0.820	0.845	0.865	0.883	0.898	0.911	0.923	0.934	0.944
2/0	6	1	0.648	0.676	0.698	0.716	0.733	0.760	0.782	0.800	0.817	0.831	0.855	0.876	0.893	0.908	0.922	0.934	0.945	0.955
1/0	6	1	0.659	0.686	0.708	0.727	0.743	0.770	0.793	0.811	0.827	0.842	0.866	0.886	0.904	0.919	0.932	0.944	0.955	0.966
1	6	1	0.670	0.698	0.720	0.738	0.754	0.782	0.804	0.822	0.838	0.853	0.877	0.898	0.915	0.930	0.944	0.956	0.967	0.977
2	6	1	0.681	0.708	0.730	0.749	0.765	0.792	0.814	0.833	0.849	0.863	0.888	0.908	0.926	0.941	0.954	0.966	0.977	0.987
3	6	1	0.691	0.719	0.741	0.759	0.776	0.803	0.825	0.843	0.860	0.874	0.898	0.919	0.936	0.951	0.965	0.977	0.988	0.998
4	6	1	0.702	0.730	0.752	0.770	0.786	0.814	0.836	0.854	0.871	0.885	0.909	0.930	0.947	0.962	0.976	0.988	0.999	1.01
5	6	1	0.716	0.743	0.765	0.783	0.800	0.827	0.849	0.868	0.884	0.898	0.923	0.943	0.960	0.975	0.989	1.00	1.01	1.02
6	6	1	0.730	0.757	0.779	0.798	0.814	0.841	0.863	0.882	0.898	0.912	0.937	0.957	0.975	0.990	1.00	1.02	1.03	1.04
203,000	8	7	0.580	0.604	0.627	0.645	0.662	0.689	0.711	0.729	0.746	0.760	0.785	0.805	0.822	0.837	0.848	0.863	0.874	0.884
203,200	16	19	0.553	0.580	0.602	0.621	0.638	0.664	0.687	0.705	0.722	0.736	0.760	0.780	0.798	0.813	0.826	0.838	0.849	0.860
211,300	12	7	0.562	0.589	0.611	0.630	0.646	0.673	0.696	0.714	0.730	0.745	0.770	0.789	0.807	0.822	0.835	0.847	0.858	0.869
190,800	12	7	0.568	0.595	0.618	0.636	0.652	0.679	0.702	0.720	0.736	0.751	0.775	0.795	0.813	0.827	0.841	0.854	0.864	0.875
176,900	12	7	0.573	0.600	0.622	0.641	0.657	0.684	0.706	0.725	0.741	0.756	0.780	0.800	0.817	0.832	0.846	0.858	0.869	0.880
159,000	12	7	0.579	0.606	0.628	0.647	0.664	0.690	0.713	0.731	0.748	0.762	0.786	0.806	0.824	0.839	0.852	0.864	0.876	0.886
134,600	12	7	0.589	0.616	0.639	0.657	0.673	0.700	0.723	0.741	0.757	0.772	0.796	0.817	0.834	0.849	0.863	0.875	0.886	0.896
110,800	12	7	0.601	0.628	0.650	0.669	0.685	0.712	0.734	0.753	0.769	0.784	0.808	0.828	0.846	0.861	0.874	0.886	0.898	0.908
101,800	12	7	0.606	0.633	0.656	0.674	0.690	0.717	0.740	0.758	0.774	0.789	0.813	0.834	0.851	0.866	0.880	0.892	0.903	0.913
80,000	8	1	0.674	0.701	0.724	0.742	0.758	0.785	0.808	0.826	0.843	0.857	0.881	0.901	0.919	0.934	0.947	0.960	0.970	0.981

Single-layer Conductors[d]—Current Density 1,200 Amp per Sq In.

266,800	6	7	0.648	0.675	0.697	0.716	0.732	0.759	0.781	0.800	0.816	0.830	0.855	0.875	0.892	0.907	0.921	0.933	0.944	0.954
4/0	6	1	0.655	0.682	0.705	0.723	0.739	0.766	0.789	0.807	0.823	0.838	0.862	0.883	0.900	0.915	0.929	0.941	0.952	0.962
3/0	6	1	0.668	0.695	0.717	0.736	0.752	0.779	0.802	0.820	0.836	0.851	0.875	0.895	0.913	0.928	0.941	0.953	0.964	0.975
2/0	6	1	0.677	0.705	0.727	0.745	0.762	0.789	0.811	0.829	0.846	0.860	0.884	0.905	0.922	0.937	0.951	0.963	0.974	0.984
1/0	6	1	0.684	0.711	0.734	0.752	0.768	0.796	0.818	0.836	0.852	0.867	0.891	0.912	0.929	0.944	0.958	0.970	0.981	0.991
1	6	1	0.690	0.717	0.740	0.754	0.774	0.802	0.824	0.842	0.858	0.873	0.897	0.918	0.935	0.950	0.964	0.976	0.987	0.997
2	6	1	0.695	0.722	0.744	0.758	0.779	0.806	0.828	0.847	0.863	0.877	0.902	0.922	0.940	0.955	0.968	0.980	0.991	1.00
3	6	1	0.700	0.727	0.749	0.768	0.784	0.811	0.833	0.852	0.868	0.882	0.907	0.927	0.944	0.960	0.973	0.985	0.996	1.01
4	6	1	0.706	0.733	0.755	0.774	0.790	0.817	0.839	0.858	0.874	0.888	0.913	0.933	0.950	0.966	0.979	0.991	1.00	1.01
5	6	1	0.722	0.749	0.771	0.790	0.806	0.833	0.855	0.874	0.890	0.904	0.929	0.949	0.967	0.982	0.995	1.01	1.02	1.03
6	6	1	0.735	0.762	0.785	0.803	0.819	0.846	0.869	0.887	0.903	0.918	0.942	0.963	0.980	0.995	1.01	1.02	1.03	1.04
203,000	8	7	0.625	0.651	0.674	0.693	0.709	0.736	0.758	0.777	0.793	0.807	0.831	0.852	0.869	0.884	0.898	0.910	0.921	0.931
203,200	16	19	0.600	0.627	0.650	0.668	0.685	0.711	0.734	0.752	0.769	0.783	0.807	0.828	0.845	0.860	0.874	0.886	0.897	0.907
211,300	12	7	0.609	0.636	0.659	0.677	0.693	0.720	0.743	0.761	0.777	0.792	0.816	0.837	0.854	0.869	0.883	0.895	0.906	0.916
190,800	12	7	0.615	0.642	0.665	0.683	0.699	0.726	0.749	0.767	0.783	0.798	0.822	0.843	0.860	0.875	0.889	0.901	0.912	0.922
176,900	12	7	0.620	0.647	0.669	0.688	0.704	0.731	0.753	0.772	0.788	0.803	0.827	0.847	0.864	0.880	0.893	0.905	0.916	0.926
159,000	12	7	0.626	0.653	0.676	0.694	0.711	0.737	0.760	0.779	0.795	0.809	0.833	0.854	0.871	0.886	0.900	0.912	0.923	0.933
134,600	12	7	0.636	0.664	0.686	0.704	0.720	0.748	0.770	0.788	0.805	0.819	0.843	0.864	0.881	0.896	0.910	0.922	0.933	0.943
110,800	12	7	0.648	0.675	0.697	0.716	0.733	0.759	0.782	0.800	0.817	0.831	0.855	0.875	0.893	0.908	0.921	0.933	0.945	0.955
101,800	12	7	0.653	0.680	0.703	0.721	0.737	0.765	0.787	0.805	0.821	0.836	0.860	0.881	0.898	0.913	0.927	0.939	0.950	0.960
80,000	8	1	0.704	0.732	0.754	0.772	0.789	0.816	0.838	0.856	0.873	0.887	0.911	0.932	0.949	0.964	0.978	0.990	1.001	1.011

D'/D	1.05	1.10	1.15	1.20	1.25	1.30	1.35	1.40	1.45	1.50	1.55	1.60	1.65	1.70	1.75	1.80	1.85	1.90	1.95	2.00
$x+$	0.006	0.012	0.017	0.022	0.027	0.032	0.036	0.041	0.045	0.049	0.053	0.057	0.061	0.064	0.068	0.071	0.075	0.078	0.081	0.084

a The table values were derived from the equation $x = 2\pi fL$, in which x = the reactance in ohms; L = the inductance in henrys per mile of single conductor; and f = the frequency. The reactance at any other frequency than 60 cycles is $f/60$ times the table values. The reactance x' at any spacing D' not given in the table is equal to the reactance x at the next smaller spacing D given in the table plus the quantity $0.2794 \log_{10} D'/D$. Thus $x' = x + 0.2794 \log_{10} D'/D$. Or the reactance, in ohms, to be added to that at the next smaller spacing may be taken from table below:

c See Table **57.**

d By single-layer conductors is meant conductors with one layer of aluminum over the steel core.

87. Electrical Symbols for Architectural Plans[a]

Ceiling Wall

GENERAL OUTLETS

◯	⊸◯	Outlet
Ⓑ	⊸Ⓑ	Blanked Outlet
Ⓓ		Drop Cord
Ⓔ	⊸Ⓔ	Electric Outlet For use only when circle used alone might be confused with columns, plumbing symbols, etc.
Ⓕ	⊸Ⓕ	Fan Outlet
Ⓙ	⊸Ⓙ	Junction Box
Ⓛ	⊸Ⓛ	Lamp Holder
Ⓛ$_{PS}$	⊸Ⓛ$_{PS}$	Lamp Holder with Pull Switch
Ⓢ	⊸Ⓢ	Pull Switch
Ⓥ	⊸Ⓥ	Outlet for Vapor Discharge Lamp
Ⓧ	⊸Ⓧ	Exit-light Outlet
Ⓒ	⊸Ⓒ	Clock Outlet (Specify Voltage)

CONVENIENCE OUTLETS

⊜	Duplex Convenience Outlet
⊜$_{1,3}$	Convenience Outlet other than Duplex 1=Single, 3=Triplex, etc.
⊜$_{WP}$	Weatherproof Convenience Outlet
⊜$_R$	Range Outlet
⊜$_S$	Switch and Convenience Outlet
⊜Ⓡ	Radio and Convenience Outlet
◭	Special Purpose Outlet (Des. in Spec.)
⦿	Floor Outlet

SWITCH OUTLETS

S	Single-pole Switch
S$_2$	Double-pole Switch
S$_3$	Three-way Switch
S$_4$	Four-way Switch
S$_D$	Automatic Door Switch
S$_E$	Electrolier Switch
S$_K$	Key-operated Switch
S$_P$	Switch and Pilot Lamp
S$_{CB}$	Circuit Breaker
S$_{WCB}$	Weatherproof Circuit Breaker
S$_{MC}$	Momentary Contact Switch
S$_{RC}$	Remote-control Switch
S$_{WP}$	Weatherproof Switch
S$_F$	Fused Switch
S$_{WF}$	Weatherproof Fused Switch

SPECIAL OUTLETS

⊖$_{a,b,c,etc.}$ S$_{a,b,c,etc.}$

Any standard symbol as given above
with the addition of a lower-case subscript
letter may be used to designate some
special variation of standard equipment
of particular interest in a specific set of
architectural plans.

When used they must be listed in the
Key of Symbols on each drawing and if
necessary further described in the
specifications.

AUXILIARY SYSTEMS

▣	Pushbutton
▱	Buzzer
▭ₒ	Bell
◇	Annunciator
◀	Outside Telephone
◁	Interconnecting Telephone
◁◁	Telephone Switchboard
Ⓣ	Bell-ringing Transformer
Ⓓ	Electric Door Opener
Ⓕₒ	Fire-alarm Bell
Ⓕ	Fire-alarm Station
▨	City Fire-alarm Station
FA	Fire-Alarm Central Station
FS	Automatic Fire-alarm Device
W	Watchman's Station
⟦W⟧	Watchman's Central Station
H	Horn
N	Nurse's Signal Plug
M	Maid's Signal Plug
R	Radio Outlet
⟦SC⟧	Signal Central Station
▢	Interconnection Box
⊣ᴵⵑᴵⵑᴵ	Battery
—·—·	Auxiliary System Circuits

Note: Any line without further designation
indicates a 2-wire system. For a
greater number of wires designate with
numerals in manner similar to —·—
12-No. 18W-3/4"C., or designate by
number corresponding to listing in
Schedule.

▢$_{a,b,c}$ Special Auxiliary Outlets
Subscript letters refer to notes on plans
or detailed description in specifications.

Electrical Symbols for Architectural Plans[a] (*Continued*)

PANELS, CIRCUITS, AND MISCELLANEOUS

■ Lighting Panel

▨ Power Panel

—— Branch Circuit; Concealed in Ceiling or Wall

—·— Branch Circuit; Concealed in Floor

———— Branch Circuit; Exposed

➤—— Home Run to Panel Board. Indicate number of circuits by number of arrows.
Note: Any circuit without further designation indicates a two-wire circuit. For a greater number of wires indicate as follows: ⫫ (3 wires) ⫫⫫ (4 wires), etc.

—— Feeders. Note: Use heavy lines and designate by number corresponding to listing in Feeder Schedule.

⊒▭⊑ Underfloor Duct and Junction Box—Triple System
Note: For a double or single system eliminate one or two lines. This symbol is equally adaptable to auxiliary system layouts.

Ⓖ Generator

Ⓜ Motor

Ⓘ Instrument

Ⓣ Power Transformer (Or draw to scale.)

⊠ Controller

▭ Isolating Switch

[a] Abstracted from USA Standard (USA) Z32.9-1943, approved by American Institute of Architects Committee 32 under sponsorship of IEEE and ASME.

It is not the intention of this standard to set the size of the particular conventions as used on the drawing. The size of wire or conduit is not to be designated or implied by the symbol.

The symbols can be modified by upper-case letters and other distinguishing marks placed in the center and by subscript letters or numbers placed at the lower right. Upper-case letters as subscripts refer to standard types, numerals to standard numerical variations; lower-case letters should be explained in the key of symbols accompanying the drawing(s).

INDEX

The numbers referenced in the index represent the **Division** and **Section** number — not the page number. For example, an index reference to **10-57** means Division **10,** Section **57.** Within each Division all Section numbers are placed in numerical order so there should be no difficulty in locating any Section number.

A table of contents appears at the beginning of each Division which describes the various topics within the Division. These are listed by page numbers and so indicated in the Division table of contents.

1